CONGRESSIONAL VOTING GUIDE

A TEN YEAR COMPILATION

FOURTH EDITION

Compiled by

Victor W. Bosnich

The H. W. Wilson Company

1992

The author wishes to thank Congressional Quarterly, Inc. for their kind permission to reprint the descriptions of measures and the presidential support scores from *Congressional Quarterly Weekly Reports*.

Printed in the United States of America

First edition 1987
Third edition 1991

Library of Congress Cataloging-in-Publication Data

Bosnich, Victor W.
    Congressional voting guide : a ten year compilation / compiled by
Victor W. Bosnich. -- 4th Ed.
      p. cm.
    Includes indexes.
    ISBN 0-8242-0833-1
    1. United States. Congress--Voting. 2. United States--Politics
and government--1981-1989. 3. United States--Politics and
government--1989-   I. Title
JK1051.B67 1992
328.73'0775--dc20   92-12140
                                                CIP

Contents

Introduction

Congressional Voting Guide is a ten-year compilation of the voting records of members of the 102nd Congress on selected important measures. It covers 144 major bills, including nominations, amendments and veto overrides, from both the U.S. House of Representatives and the U.S. Senate. *CVG* is designed to be a handy and affordable reference tool for libraries and individuals interested in how House and Senate members have voted in the past and, therefore, how they might vote in the future. With regard to the issues, *CVG* is completely unbiased and contains no recommendations or editorials.

The measures chosen were those that have created wide public interest and debate, and consequently received a close vote when put to the floor. The measures were chosen after a careful analysis of every bill, voted on each year, taking into account coverage provided by newspapers and periodicals. In order to give the reader a true picture of where each member stands, the measures chosen are those which address a single, specific issue. Many measures encompass so many issues that a representative or senator is forced to take an all-or-nothing position; this does not provide any insight into whether he or she supports specific items within the bill. *CVG* allows the reader to see precisely how each member voted on individual issues as they came for a floor vote.

Although *CVG* covers the period from 1982 to 1992, the majority of the bills are from 1988 to 1992 in order to document more thoroughly the positions of recently elected members. Some issues have been included more than once because of their importance or because voting positions changed. Thus, the reader can determine which members cast "swing votes" on tax bills, gun control, foreign aid, abortion, and others.

The guide is organized in two main parts: **House Voting Records** and **Senate Voting Records**. Each part is arranged alphabetically by state and presents for every member of Congress a brief biography followed by a list of measures (in abbreviated form) with an indication of how the member voted on each issue.

For a fuller understanding of the bills, two other sections, **House Measures** and **Senate Measures**, give a description of every bill, together with the date and result of the vote and a breakdown of the vote by political party. The Democratic vote is further analyzed between Northern Democrats and Southern Democrats because of the disparity in their voting patterns. (Southern Democrats are members from Alabama, Arkansas, Florida, Georgia, Kentucky, Louisiana, Mississippi, North Carolina, Oklahoma, South Carolina, Tennessee, Texas, and Virginia.) A key to abbreviations and symbols used in this book is located on page vii.

Further access to the data is provided by two indexes: a **Name Index** refers users not only to a member's voting record but also to any bills in the Lists of Measures of which he or she is a sponsor; and a **Subject Index** refers users to the descriptions of bills in the House Measures and Senate Measures.

An added feature is presidential support scores for the years 1990 and 1991, which appear at the end of each member's voting record. These scores, which are derived from a member's votes on all the years' measures before Congress, not just on those selected for this book, indicate how often he or she has voted with the stated position of the president. The president's position, when it was made known, is stated within the description of the bills in the House Measures and Senate Measures sections. For a condensed analysis of President Bush's announced positions on the issues, see page 425. Also included are positions taken by the Reagan administration when Bush was vice president.

Readers who want to contact the president or a member of Congress may do so by writing or calling:

> The President of the United States
> The White House
> Washington, DC 20500
> (202) 456-1414
>
> Honorable [representative's name]
> U.S. House of Representatives
> Washington, DC 20515
> (202) 224-3121
>
> Honorable [senator's name]
> U.S. Senate
> Washington, DC 20510
> (202) 224-3121

> Victor W. Bosnich
> April 1992

Key to Abbreviations and Symbols

Y	=	Voted "for" (yea)
N	=	Voted "against" (nay)
#	=	Paired "for" (agreement with an opposing member not to vote)
X	=	Paired "against" (agreement with an opposing member not to vote)
+	=	Announced "for" after the vote was taken
--	=	Announced "against" after the vote was taken
P	=	Voted "present"
C	=	Voted "present" to avoid possible conflict of interest
?	=	Did not vote or otherwise make a position known
R	=	Republican
D	=	Democrat
I	=	Independent (refers to Bernard Sanders of Vermont)
ND	=	Northern Democrats
SD	=	Southern Democrats (Alabama, Arkansas, Florida, Georgia, Kentucky, Louisiana, Mississippi, North Carolina, Oklahoma, South Carolina, Tennessee, Texas, and Virginia)
HR	=	House of Representatives Bill
H Con Res	=	House Concurrent Resolution
H J Res	=	House Joint Resolution
S	=	Senate Bill
S Con Res	=	Senate Concurrent Resolution
S J Res	=	Senate Joint Resolution

SAMPLE HOUSE AND SENATE MEASURES

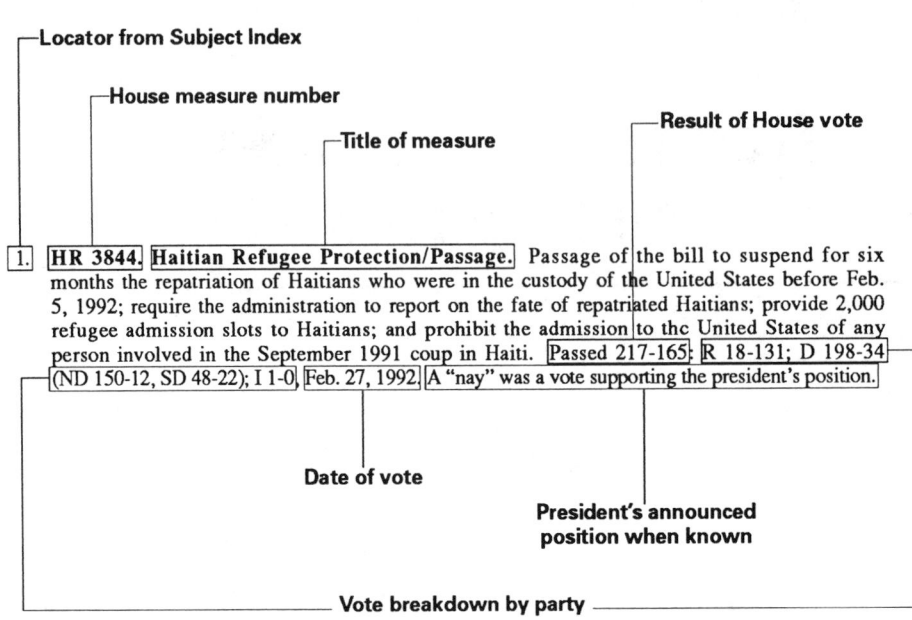

Locator from Subject Index

House measure number

Title of measure

Result of House vote

1. **HR 3844. Haitian Refugee Protection/Passage.** Passage of the bill to suspend for six months the repatriation of Haitians who were in the custody of the United States before Feb. 5, 1992; require the administration to report on the fate of repatriated Haitians; provide 2,000 refugee admission slots to Haitians; and prohibit the admission to the United States of any person involved in the September 1991 coup in Haiti. Passed 217-165; R 18-131; D 198-34 (ND 150-12, SD 48-22); I 1-0, Feb. 27, 1992. A "nay" was a vote supporting the president's position.

Date of vote

President's announced position when known

Vote breakdown by party

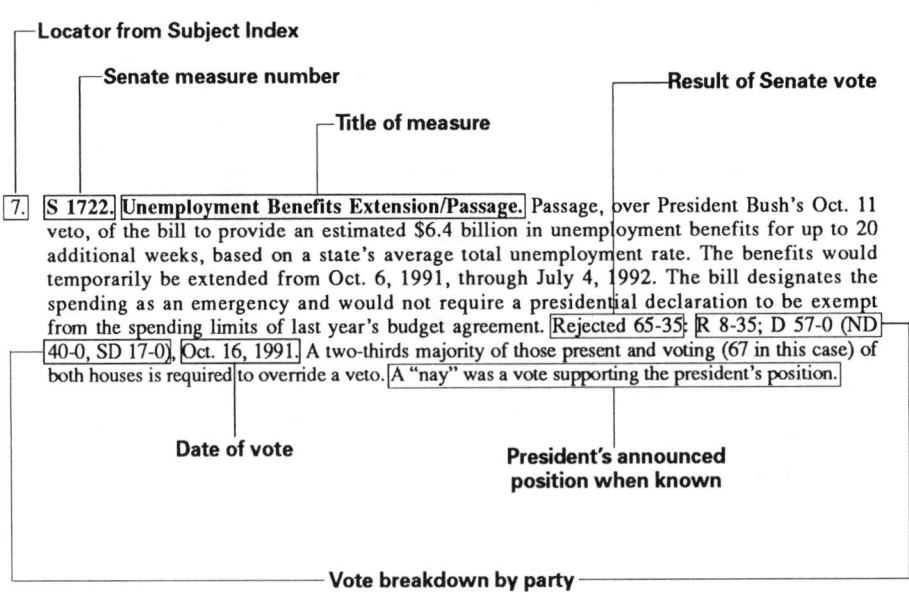

Locator from Subject Index

Senate measure number

Title of measure

Result of Senate vote

7. **S 1722. Unemployment Benefits Extension/Passage.** Passage, over President Bush's Oct. 11 veto, of the bill to provide an estimated $6.4 billion in unemployment benefits for up to 20 additional weeks, based on a state's average total unemployment rate. The benefits would temporarily be extended from Oct. 6, 1991, through July 4, 1992. The bill designates the spending as an emergency and would not require a presidential declaration to be exempt from the spending limits of last year's budget agreement. Rejected 65-35; R 8-35; D 57-0 (ND 40-0, SD 17-0), Oct. 16, 1991. A two-thirds majority of those present and voting (67 in this case) of both houses is required to override a veto. A "nay" was a vote supporting the president's position.

Date of vote

President's announced position when known

Vote breakdown by party

House Measures

In this section House Measures are listed in reverse chronological order, i.e., starting with the most recent. The number in the lefthand margin of each entry is a locator from the Subject Index.

1. **HR 3844. Haitian Refugee Protection/Passage.** Passage of the bill to suspend for six months the repatriation of Haitians who were in the custody of the United States before Feb. 5, 1992; require the administration to report on the fate of repatriated Haitians; provide 2,000 refugee admission slots to Haitians; and prohibit the admission to the United States of any person involved in the September 1991 coup in Haiti. Passed 217-165: R 18-131; D 198-34 [ND 150-12, SD 48-22]; I 1-0, Feb. 27, 1992. A "nay" was a vote supporting the president's position.

2. **HR 4210. 1992 Tax Bill/Passage.** Passage of the bill to give workers a temporary tax credit worth up to $400 for couples and $200 for individuals a year to be paid for with a 10 percent surtax on millionaires and a new top income tax rate of 35 percent on individuals with taxable income higher than $85,000 and couples above $145,000. The package includes indexing of capital gains, passive loss deductions for real estate developers, permanent extension of certain tax breaks, penalty-free withdrawals from Individual Retirement Accounts for first homes and medical and educational expenses, and other provisions designed to spur economic growth. Passed 221-209: R 1-163; D 219-46 [ND 156-27, SD 63-19]; I 1-0, Feb. 27, 1992. A "nay" was a vote supporting the president's position.

3. **H Res 258. "October Surprise" Investigation.** Adoption of the resolution to authorize the Speaker to appoint 13 House members to a task force to investigate allegations that the 1980 Reagan campaign conspired to delay the release of 52 American hostages in Iran until after the 1980 election. Adopted 217-192: R 0-158; D 216-34 [ND 156-13, SD 60-21]; I 1-0, Feb. 5, 1992.

4. **HR 3750. Campaign Finance/Passage.** Passage of the bill to provide lower mail costs and up to $200,000 in public matching funds for the first $200 of individual contributions for House candidates who have raised more than $60,000 in individual contributions of less than $200 and agreed to a voluntary spending limit of $600,000. All House candidates would be limited to $200,000 in contributions from political action committees. Passed 273-156: R 21-144; D 251-12 [ND 176-4, SD 75-8]; I 1-0, Nov. 25, 1991. A "nay" was a vote supporting the president's position.

5. **HR 2. Family and Medical Leave Act/Passage.** Passage of the bill to require employers with 50 or more employees to provide up to 12 weeks of unpaid leave a year for a serious illness, the birth or adoption of a child, or to care for a seriously ill child, spouse or parent. Passed 253-177: R 35-129; D 217-48 [ND 169-12, SD 48-36]; I 1-0, Nov. 13, 1991. A "nay" was a vote supporting the president's position.

6. **HR 2686. Fiscal 1992 Interior Appropriations/Recommittal Motion.** Lowery, R-Calif., motion to recommit the conference report with instruction to accept the Senate provision that would prohibit the use of funds by the National Endowment for the Arts to promote,

disseminate or produce materials that depict or describe, in a patently offensive way, sexual or excretory activities or organs. Motion rejected 205-214: R 128-32; D 77-181 [ND 30-147, SD 47-34]; I 0-1, Oct. 24, 1991.

7. **HR 3371. Omnibus Crime Bill/Race-Based Sentencing.** Hyde, R-Ill., amendment to strike the provisions that allow death row prisoners to raise certain race-bias claims in habeas corpus appeals. Adopted 238-180: R 151-8; D 87-171 [ND 33-144, SD 54-27]; I 0-1, Oct. 22, 1991. A "yea" was a vote supporting the president's position.

8. **HR 3371. Omnibus Crime Bill/Fairness in Death Sentencing Act.** McCollum, R-Fla., amendment to replace the Fairness in Death Sentencing Act, which allows minorities to challenge a death sentence as discriminatory if statistics show a disproportionate number of their race being condemned to die, with the Equal Justice Act, which prohibits the consideration of race in determining a defendant's sentence and the use of statistics to invalidate a sentence. Adopted 223-191: R 150-6; D 73-184 [ND 26-149, SD 47-35]; I 0-1, Oct. 22, 1991. A "yea" was a vote supporting the president's position.

9. **HR 3371. Omnibus Crime Bill/Search and Seizure.** McCollum, R-Fla., amendment to codify the "good faith" exception to the exclusionary rule that allows evidence seized without a warrant but under an objectively reasonable belief that the search was in conformity with the Fourth Amendment to be used against a defendant. Adopted 247-165: R 156-3; D 91-161 [ND 38-132, SD 53-29]; I 0-1, Oct. 17, 1991. A "yea" was a vote supporting the president's position.

10. **HR 3371. Omnibus Crime Bill/Assault Weapons.** Volkmer, D-Mo., amendment to strike the provisions that prohibit the ownership or sale of 13 types of semi-automatic assault weapons. The amendment would also delete provisions that make it illegal to own or sell ammunition clips of more than seven rounds. Adopted 247-177: R 133-29; D 114-147 [ND 53-124, SD 61-23]; I 0-1, Oct. 17, 1991.

11. **HR 3371. Omnibus Crime Bill/Death Penalty Replacement.** Staggers, D-W.Va., en bloc amendment to provide mandatory life imprisonment without parole in all places where the bill imposes the death penalty and to require restitution of no less than half of offender's earnings to the victim's family. Rejected 101-322: R 5-156; D 95-166 [ND 89-88, SD 6-78]; I-1-0, Oct. 16 1991.

12. **HR 1470. Vertical Price Fixing/Conspiracy Factor.** Fish, R-N.Y., amendment to require a plaintiff to show evidence that a conspiracy to fix prices was the major rather than a substantial contributing factor in the termination of a contract in order to receive a jury trial. Rejected 196-218: R 148-13; D 48-204 [ND 13-162, SD 35-42]; I 0-1, Oct. 10, 1991.

13. **HR 3040. Unemployment Benefits Extension/Passage.** Passage of the bill to permanently extend unemployment benefits to long-term unemployed workers for up to 20 additional weeks at an estimated cost of $6.3 billion through fiscal 1996. The bill automatically declares the benefits to be emergency spending and would not require a presidential declaration to be exempt from the spending requirements of last year's budget agreement. Passed 283-125: R 48-107; D 234-18 [ND 172-2, SD 62-16]; I 1-0, Sept. 17, 1991. A "nay" was a vote supporting the president's position. (An unemployment benefits extension bill was later passed by both houses with the president's approval.)

14. **HR 2507. National Institutes of Health Reauthorization/Passage.** Passage of the bill to reauthorize the National Cancer Institute and the National Heart, Lung and Blood Institute and other programs of the National Institutes of Health. The bill would also overturn the administration's ban on research using tissue from aborted fetuses. Passed 274-144: R 40-119; D 233-25 [ND 159-16, SD 74-9]; I 1-0, July 25, 1991. A "nay" was a vote supporting the president's position.

15. **HR 5. Striker Replacement/Passage.** Passage of the bill to prohibit employers from hiring permanent replacements for workers striking over economic issues, if the strike was by union-represented employees. Passed 247-182: R 16-149; D 230-33 [ND 178-0, SD 52-33]; I 1-0, July 17, 1991. A "nay" was a vote supporting the president's position.

16. **HR 2621. Fiscal 1992 Foreign Operations Appropriations/Passage.** Passage of the bill to provide $15,196,532,000 in new budget authority for foreign military and economic assistance and export financing in fiscal 1992. The administration requested $27,626,542,022. Passed 301-102: R 103-52; D 197-50 [ND 142-25, SD 55-25]; I 1-0, June 19, 1991.

17. **HR 2519. Fiscal 1992 VA and HUD Appropriations/Restore Space Station Funding.** Chapman, D-Texas, en bloc amendments to provide $1.9 billion for the space station *Freedom*, restoring its funding to the fiscal 1991 level, and to offset the increase by holding all NASA programs to fiscal 1991 levels -- a decrease of $1.7 billion -- and by cutting $217 million from Housing and Urban Development public housing operating subsidies that would not be available until the last 10 days of fiscal 1992. Adopted 240-173: R 133-27; D 107-145 [ND 55-114, SD 52-31]; I 0-1, June 6, 1991. A "yea" was a vote supporting the president's position.

18. **HR 1. Civil Rights Act of 1991/Passage.** Passage of the bill to reverse or modify a series of Supreme Court rulings that narrowed the reach and remedies of job discrimination laws and to authorize compensatory and punitive damages for victims of discrimination based on sex, religion or disability. Passed 273-158: R 22-143; D 250-15 [ND 177-4, SD 73-11]; I 1-0; June 5, 1991. A "nay" was a vote supporting the president's position.

19. **HR 1. Civil Rights Act of 1991/Unlimited Punitive Damages.** Towns, D-N.Y., substitute amendment to provide for unlimited punitive damages for discrimination based on sex, religion or disability as opposed to the $150,000 cap provided for in the Brooks, D-Texas, substitute; ban sex discrimination in private contracts; define "business necessity" as a practice that bears a substantial and demonstrable relationship to job performance; and for other purposes. The substitute generally follows the committee bill and does not contain the compromise language contained in the Brooks substitute, including language explicitly prohibiting the use of quotas and banning the use of race-based adjustments to hiring-test scores. Rejected 152-277: R 6-159; D 145-118 [ND 122-58, SD 23-60]; I 1-0, June 4, 1991. A "nay" was a vote supporting the president's position.

20. **HR 2427. Fiscal 1992 Energy and Water Appropriations/Superconducting Super Collider.** Slattery, D-Kan., amendment to eliminate all funding for the superconducting super collider, $434 million, by reducing the bill's funding level for general science and research activities by $390 million and transferring $43.5 million to the construction of an injector for the "Tevatron" particle accelerator at the Fermi National Accelerator Laboratory in Illinois. Rejected 165-251: R 58-101; D 106-150 [ND 86-87, SD 20-63]; I 1-0, May 29, 1991. A "nay" was a vote supporting the president's position.

21. **HR 2100. Fiscal 1992 Defense Authorization/SDI.** Dellums, D-Calif., amendment to terminate the Strategic Defense Initiative Organization and permit only a basic SDI research program funded at $1.1 billion. Rejected 118-266: R 2-149; D 115-117 [ND 104-55, SD 11-62]; I 1-0, May 20, 1991. A "nay" was a vote supporting the president's position.

22. **HR 7. Handgun Waiting Period/Passage.** Passage of the bill to require a seven-day waiting period for handgun purchases, allowing local law enforcement authorities to check the background of prospective buyers to determine whether they have a criminal record. The waiting period requirement would end when a national computer system for instant checks became operational. Passed 239-186: R 60-102; D 179-83 [ND 138-41, SD 41-42]; I 0-1, May 8, 1991.

23. **S 419. RTC Financing/Conference Report.** Adoption of the conference report (thus clearing the measure for the president) to provide $30 billion to the Resolution Trust Corporation (RTC) to cover losses of failed thrifts in fiscal 1991; require that future requests for additional funding be accompanied by a spending plan; expand the RTC's affordable housing program; and require the RTC to report on steps taken to award contracts to companies owned and controlled by minorities. Adopted 225-188: R 119-40; D 106-147 [ND 63-110, SD 43-37]; I 0-1, March 21, 1991. A "yea" was a vote supporting the president's position.

24. **HJ Res 77. Use of Force Against Iraq/Passage.** Passage of the joint resolution to authorize the use of military force if Iraq has not withdrawn from Kuwait and complied with U.N. Security Council resolutions by Jan. 15. The resolution authorizes the use of force and

the expenditure of funds under the War Powers Act. Passed 250-183: R 164-3; D 86-179 [ND 33-147, SD 53-32]; I 0-1, Jan. 12, 1991. A "yea" was a vote supporting the president's position.

25. **HR 5114. Fiscal 1991 Foreign Operations Appropriations/Conference Report.** Adoption of the conference report on the bill to appropriate $15,389,400,887 in fiscal 1991 for foreign military and economic assistance and export financing. The president requested $15,518,826,537. Adopted 188-162: R 63-82; D 125-80 [ND 92-46, SD 33-34], Oct. 27, 1990.

26. **S 358. Legal Immigration Revision/Conference Report.** Adoption of the conference report (thus clearing the measure for the president on the bill to increase the number of visas for those coming to the United States to work, establish a new category of diversity visas for immigrants from countries that have accounted for very few immigrants under the current system, impose an overall cap on immigration at 675,000 starting in fiscal 1996, suspend deportation of certain spouses and children of newly legalized aliens, and temporarily suspend deportation of Salvadorans. Adopted 264-118: R 93-64; D 171-54 [ND 137-15, SD 34-39], Oct. 27, 1990. A "yea" was a vote supporting the president's position.

27. **HR 5422. Fiscal 1991 Intelligence Appropriations/Aid to UNITA.** Separate vote at the request of Hyde, R-Ill., on the Solarz, D-N.Y., amendment to suspend military aid to the National Union for the Total Independence of Angola (UNITA) -- a rebel group fighting the Angolan government -- if the government of Angola agrees to accept a cease-fire and a political settlement for the conflict in Angola; receives no military aid from the Soviet Union; and offers free and fair multiparty elections in which UNITA is free to participate. Adopted 207-206: R 12-156; D 195-50 [ND 158-10, SD 37-40], Oct. 17, 1990. A "nay" was a vote supporting the president's position.

28. **HR 5835. Fiscal 1991 Omnibus Reconciliation Act/Democratic Alternative.** Rostenkowski, D-Ill., en bloc amendment to provide smaller increases in the Medicare premium and deductible; delete revenue provisions, including the gas tax, the petroleum fuels tax, the extension of the Medicare tax to additional state and local employees, and the limit on itemized deductions; eliminate the "bubble" and lift the top marginal tax rate to 33 percent; create a 10 percent surtax on income above $1 million; increase the minimum tax rate; delay indexing for one year; provide a limited tax break for capital gains; and for other purposes. Adopted 238-192: R 10-164; D 228-28 [ND 157-16, SD 71-12], Oct. 16, 1990. A "nay" was a vote supporting the president's position.

29. **HR 5803. Fiscal 1991 Defense Appropriations/Across-the-Board Cut.** Traficant, D-Ohio, amendment to cut defense spending in the bill by 5 percent across the board, resulting in a cut of about $14 billion. Rejected 97-319: R 11-158; D 86-161 [ND 77-91, SD 9-70], Oct. 12, 1990. A "nay" was a vote supporting the president's position.

30. **HR 4328. Textile Trade Act/Veto Override.** Passage, over President Bush's Oct. 5 veto, of the bill to limit the growth of imports of textiles and apparel to 1 percent annually, establish permanent quotas for most non-rubber footwear imports at 1989 levels, authorize the special allocation of textile quotas for countries increasing their purchases of U.S. agricultural goods, and for other purposes. Rejected 275-152: R 70-103; D 205-49 [ND 131-41, SD 74-8], Oct. 10, 1990. A two-thirds majority of those present and voting (285 in this case) of both houses is required to override a veto. A "nay" was a vote supporting the president's position.

31. **HR 4739. Fiscal 1991 Defense Authorization/Abortion Services.** Fazio, D-Calif., amendment to provide military personnel and their dependents stationed overseas with reproductive health services, including privately paid abortions, at military hospitals. Rejected 200-216: R 35-139; D 165-77 [ND 113-50, SD 52-27], Sept. 18, 1990. A "nay" was a vote supporting the president's position.

32. **HR 3950. Farm Programs Reauthorization/High-Income Farmers.** Schumer, D-N.Y., amendment to prohibit all payments, purchases and loans under the wheat, feed grains, cotton, honey, rice, oil seeds, and wool and mohair programs for any person with an adjusted gross income of $100,000 or more. Rejected 159-263: R 66-109; D 93-154 [ND 85-82, SD 8-72], July 25, 1990.

33. **HR 770. Family and Medical Leave Act/Veto Override.** Passage, over President Bush's June 29 veto, of the bill to require public and private employers to give unpaid leave to care for a newborn child or a seriously ill child, parent or spouse, or to use as medical leave due to a serious health condition. Rejected 232-195: R 38-138; D 194-57 [ND 156-14, SD 38-43], July 25, 1990. A two-thirds majority of those present and voting (285 in this case) of both houses is required to override a veto. A "nay" was a vote supporting the president's position.

34. **HR 5258. Balanced Budget Statute/Passage.** Passage of the bill to require that the president submit a balanced budget, that the Budget committee's report balanced budgets and that both houses consider a balanced budget each year. Passed 282-144: R 42-131; D 240-13 [ND 161-10, SD 79-3], July 18, 1990.

35. **HJ Res 268. Balanced Budget Constitutional Amendment/Passage.** Passage of the joint resolution to propose an amendment to the Constitution to require a balanced budget, mandating that federal outlays not exceed estimated receipts in any fiscal year unless Congress approved a specific excess expenditure by a three-fifths vote. Rejected 279-150: R 169-5; D 110-145 [ND 44-129, SD 66-16], July 17, 1990. A two-thirds majority of those present and voting (286 in this case) of both houses is required for passage of a joint resolution proposing an amendment to the Constitution. A "yea" was a vote supporting the president's position.

36. **H J Res 350. Constitutional Amendment on the Flag/Passage.** Brooks, D-Texas, motion to suspend the rules and pass the joint resolution to propose an amendment to the Constitution to prohibit the physical desecration of the U.S. flag. Rejected 254-177: R 159-17; D 95-160 [ND 43-130, SD 52-30], June 21, 1990. A two-thirds majority of those present and voting (288 in this case) of both houses is required for passage of a joint resolution proposing an amendment to the Constitution. A "yea" was a vote supporting the president's position.

37. **HR 2364. Amtrak Reauthorization/Veto Override.** Passage, over President Bush's May 24 veto, of the bill to reauthorize the National Railroad Passenger Corporation (Amtrak) for fiscal years 1989-92. Passed 294-123: R 58-116; D 236-7 [ND 166-0, SD 70-7], June 7, 1990. A two-thirds majority of those present and voting (278 in this case) of both houses is required to override a veto. A "nay" was a vote supporting the president's position.

38. **HR 3030. Clean Air Act Reauthorization/Transition Aid.** Wise, D-W.Va., amendment to authorize $250 million over a five-year period for a Clean Air Employment Transition Assistance program to provide workers who lose their jobs or have their wages reduced as a result of the bill with retraining assistance and up to six months of additional unemployment benefits. Adopted 274-146: R 43-126; D 231-20 [ND 169-2, SD 62-18], May 23, 1990. A "nay" was a vote supporting the president's position.

39. **HR 4636. Fiscal 1990 Foreign Aid Supplemental Authorizations/Military Aid.** Moakley, D-Mass., amendment to suspend 50 percent of El Salvador's military aid planned for fiscal years 1990 and 1991, depending on actions by the Salvadoran government or by the leftist guerrillas. Adopted 250-163: R 31-135; D 119-28 [ND 166-4, SD 53-24], May 22, 1990. A "nay" was a vote supporting the president's position.

40. **HR 3. Child Care/Passage.** Passage of the bill to expand programs providing federal aid for child care and increase the earned income tax credit for poor working families with children. Passed 265-145: R 47-119; D 218-26 [ND 154-13, SD 64-13], March 29, 1990. A "nay" was a vote supporting the president's position.

41. **HR 3660. Government Pay and Ethics Package/Passage.** Passage of the bill to phase out honoraria, revise ethics rules and raise salaries for members of the House of Representatives and high officials of the executive and judicial branches. Passed 252-174: R 84-89; D 168-85 [ND 121-52, SD 47-33], Nov. 16, 1989.

42. **HR 1465. Oil-Spill Liability/Liability Standards.** Miller, D-Calif., amendment to toughen the liability standards in the bill so that unlimited liability would be triggered by spills occurring due to "negligence," as opposed to "gross negligence and willful misconduct." Rejected 185-197: R 35-126; D 150-71 [ND 121-31, SD 29-40], Nov. 9, 1989. A "nay" was a vote supporting the president's position.

43. **HR 2991. Fiscal 1990 Commerce, Justice, State Appropriations/Japanese-American Reparations.** Smith, D-Iowa, motion that the House recede from its disagreement and concur in a Senate amendment with an amendment to set up a $1.25 billion entitlement to begin after Oct. 1, 1990, for reparations for Japanese-Americans who were forced into U.S. camps during World War II. Motion agreed to 249-166: R 58-113; D 191-53 [ND 152-13, SD 39-40], Oct. 26, 1989.

44. **HR 45. Chinese and Central American Stability/Passage.** Passage of the bill to grant "temporary protected status" to nationals of the People's Republic of China, Nicaragua and El Salvador residing in the United States, and to allow the attorney general to grant the special protective status to other foreign nationals who need safe haven because of turmoil in their home countries. Passed 258-162: R 49-124; D 209-38 [ND 157-10, SD 52-28], Oct. 25, 1989. A "nay" was a vote supporting the president's position.

45. **HR 2990. Fiscal 1990 Labor, HHS and Education Appropriations/Abortion Funding.** Boxer, D-Calif., motion that the House recede from its disagreement to the Senate amendment to permit the use of federal funds to pay for abortions in cases of "promptly reported" rape or incest. Motion agreed to 216-206: R 41-134; D 175-72 [ND 124-44, SD 51-28], Oct. 11, 1989. A "nay" was a vote supporting the president's position.

46. **Fiscal 1990 District of Columbia Appropriations/Religious Liberty and Academic Freedom.** Dannemeyer, R-Calif., amendment to the Green, R-N.Y., motion to instruct the House conferees on the bill to recede from their disagreement and concur in the Senate amendment to amend the D.C. Code to exempt religious educational institutions from laws prohibiting discrimination based on sexual orientation. Adopted 262-154: R 153-20; D 109-134 [ND 51-113, SD 58-21], Oct. 3, 1989.

47. **HR 3299. Fiscal 1990 Budget Reconciliation/Fairness Doctrine.** Oxley, R-Ohio, amendment to delete provisions in the bill that would enact the "fairness doctrine" requiring broadcasters to air both sides of political issues and permit the Federal Communications Commission to fine broadcasters for violation of the doctrine. Rejected 162-261: R 119-54; D 43-207 [ND 18-153, SD 25-54], Oct. 3, 1989. A "yea" was a vote supporting the president's position.

48. **HR 3299. Fiscal 1990 Budget Reconciliation/Alternative Revenue Package.** Rostenkowski, D-Ill., amendment to strike the Jenkins-Archer capital gains tax cut included in the reconciliation bill and substitute restored deductibility for Individual Retirement Accounts, a deficit-reduction trust fund and an increase from 28 percent to 33 percent in the marginal tax rates for the highest incomes. Rejected 190-239: R 1-175; D 189-64 [ND 152-20, SD 37-44], Sept. 28, 1989. A "nay" was a vote supporting the president's position.

49. **HR 3299. Fiscal 1990 Budget Reconciliation/Pension Boards.** Roukema, R-N.J., amendment to delete provisions in the bill that would require trustee boards that administer single-employer pension plans to consist of equal representation of employees and employers, effectively giving labor unions equal voice in pension plan decisions. Adopted 250-173: R 165-9; D 85-164 [ND 23-148, SD 62-16], Sept. 27, 1989.

50. **HR 2461. Fiscal 1990-91 Defense Department Authorization/Chemical Weapons Funding Cut.** Owens, D-Utah, amendment to eliminate $47 million from Army funds intended for the production of binary chemical munition projectiles and to prohibit the production of such munitions. Adopted 240-179: R 40-130; D 200-49 [ND 159-10, SD 41-39], July 27, 1989.

51. **HR 2461. Fiscal 1990-91 Defense Department Authorization/Plutonium and Uranium Ban.** Wyden, D-Ore., amendment to urge the president to seek a mutual U.S.-Soviet ban on the production of plutonium and highly enriched uranium for weapons purposes and to express the sense of the Congress that the United States and the Soviet Union should establish verification arrangements to monitor such a ban including mutual on-site inspections as necessary. Adopted 284-138: R 48-125; D 236-13 [ND 167-3, SD 69-10], July 27, 1989.

52. **HR 2461. Fiscal 1990-91 Defense Department Authorization/MX Deployment Cap.** Mavroules, D-Mass., amendment to cap at 50 the number of MX missiles to be deployed at any time. Adopted 259-160: R 31-140; D 228-20 [ND 167-2, SD 61-18], July 26, 1989.

53. **HR 2461. Fiscal 1990-91 Defense Department Authorization/"Stealth" Production.** Skelton, D-Mo., amendment to the Synar, D-Okla., amendment, to authorize $3.3 billion to purchase two B-2 "stealth" bombers. Rejected 176-244: R 123-50; D 53-194 [ND 18-149, SD 35-45], July 26, 1989.

54. **HR 2461. Fiscal 1990-91 Defense Department Authorization/BiologicalDefense Research Program.** Owens, D-Utah, amendment to require annual publication in the Federal Register of the location and nature of biological-warfare experiments. Adopted 274-151: R 48-125; D 226-26 [ND 163-7, SD 63-19], July 25, 1989.

55. **HR 2. Minimum-Wage Increase/Veto Override.** Passage, over President Bush's June 13 veto, of the bill to raise the minimum wage from $3.35 an hour to $4.55 over three years, and to provide for a 60-day training wage -- equal to 85 percent of the minimum -- for workers who have not worked a total of 60 days. Rejected 247-178: R 20-150; D 227-28 [ND 171-3, SD 56-25], June 14, 1989. A two-thirds majority of those present and voting (284 in this case) of both houses is required to override a veto. A "nay" was a vote supporting the president's position. (A bill was later passed by both houses, with the president's approval, that raised the minimum wage to $4.25 an hour.)

56. **S J Res 113, FS-X Plane Development/Passage.** Passage of the joint resolution to require that a subsequent U.S.-Japan agreement governing joint production of the FS-X bar transfer to Japanese firms of certain jet-engine technologies and prohibit the sale or transfer by Japan to any other country of the FS-X or any technologies developed in the FS-X project. Passed 241-168: R 36-131; D 205-37 [ND 141-21, SD 64-16], June 7, 1989. A "nay" was a vote supporting the president's position.

57. **H Con Res 106. Fiscal 1990 Budget Resolution/Black Caucus Substitute.** Dellums, D-Calif., substitute amendment (on behalf of the Congressional Black Caucus) to reduce the fiscal 1990 defense budget by $35.4 billion and raise $20.1 billion in additional revenue for domestic spending by raising the top marginal tax rates for individuals and corporations. Rejected 81-343: R 0-173; D 81-170 [ND 73-99, SD 8-71], May 4, 1989.

58. **HR 18. Uniform Poll Closing/Passage.** Passage of the bill to establish a single poll-closing time of 9 p.m. EST for presidential general elections in the 48 contiguous states and the District of Columbia and to extend daylight-saving time in the Pacific time zone for two weeks in presidential election years. Passed 238-154: R 55-107; D 183-47 [ND 134-21, SD 49-26], April 5, 1989.

59. **HR 5410. Foreign Investment Disclosure/Passage.** Passage of the bill to require foreign citizens who acquire a significant or controlling interest in a U.S. business or real estate to disclose certain facts about the acquisition. Passed 250-170: R 40-131; D 210-39 [ND 143-26, SD 67-13], Oct. 5, 1988. A "nay" was a vote supporting the president's position.

60. **HR 1154. Textile and Apparel Trade Act/Veto Override.** Passage, over President Reagan's Sept. 28 veto, of the bill to limit imports of textiles, apparel and footwear. Rejected 272-152: R 69-105; D 203-47 [ND 130-39, SD 73-8], Oct. 4, 1988. A two-thirds majority of those present and voting (283 in this case) of both houses is required to override a veto. A "nay" was a vote supporting the president's position.

61. **HR 4776. Fiscal 1989 District of Columbia Appropriations/Recommital Motion.** Dornan, R-Calif., motion to recommit to the conference committee the bill to appropriate fiscal 1989 funding for the District of Columbia, with instructions to insist on House language banning use of all funds, federal or local, for abortions or to agree to an amendment to that language to permit use of such funds in cases where the life of the mother would be endangered. Motion agreed to 228-188: R 140-32; D 88-156 [ND 52-114, SD 36-42], Sept. 28, 1988.

62. **HR 5142. AIDS Federal Policy/Recommital Motion.** McCollum, R-Fla., motion to recommit to the Energy and Commerce Committee the bill to authorize $1.2 billion over three years for voluntary AIDS blood testing, to create federal guarantees of confidentiality of test results, to expedite federal AIDS research efforts and to establish a national AIDS commission, with instructions to add language requiring physicians to notify spouses of those

who test positive for the AIDS virus. Motion rejected 105-279: R 95-59; D 10-220 [ND 4-155, SD 6-65], Sept. 23, 1988.

63. **HR 5210. Omnibus Drug Bill/Seized Conveyances.** Shaw, R-Fla., amendment to delete the bill's provisions that revise existing rules under which the government can seize conveyances used in drug trafficking. The amendment also would remove all "innocent owner" provisions in the bill, under which a vessel could not be confiscated if the drug violation occurred without the owner's knowledge. Rejected 169-229: R 124-45; D 45-184 [ND 17-139, SD 28-45], Sept. 15, 1988. A "yea" was a vote supporting the president's position.

64. **HR 1580. South Africa Sanctions/Passage.** Passage of the bill to prohibit nearly all U.S. trade with South Africa, except for imports of "strategic minerals"; to prohibit U.S. investment in South Africa, except in businesses owned by persons disadvantaged by apartheid; to require the president to retaliate against foreign companies that take advantage of U.S. sanctions; and to authorize $40 million in U.S. aid to blacks and other non-whites in South Africa. Passed 244-132: R 24-122; D 220-10 [ND 154-3, SD 66-7], Aug. 11, 1988. A "nay" was a vote supporting the president's position.

65. **S 2527. Plant Closings/Passage.** Passage of the bill to require larger employers to give 60 days' advance notice of plant closings or mass layoffs. Passed 286-136: R 54-120; D 232-16 [ND 167-0, SD 65-16], July 13, 1988. A "nay" was a vote supporting the president's position.

66. **HR 4481. Military Base Closings/Armey Substitute.** Armey, R-Texas, substitute to provide that military bases recommended by the commission on base realignment and closure be closed, unless both houses of Congress disapprove the report; that the list include only domestic bases; and that certain environmental-review requirements be waived. Adopted 223-186: R 152-18; D 71-168 [ND 45-115, SD 26-53], July 12, 1988. A "yea" was a vote supporting the president's position. (The bill, as amended by the Armey substitute, subsequently was passed by voice vote.)

67. **HR 1720. Welfare Reform/Instruction of Conferees.** Brown, R-Colo., motion to instruct the House conferees on the bill to keep the cost of the final bill at or under $2.8 billion and to "permit no impediments to work [for welfare recipients] beyond those contained in the Senate" bill. Motion agreed to 227-168: R 162-4; D 65-164 [ND 24-130, SD 41-34], July 7, 1988.

68. **HR 1158. Fair Housing/Discrimination Against Families.** Shaw, R-Fla., amendments to delete the provision barring discrimination in housing because a family has young children. Rejected en bloc 116-289: R 95-73; D 21-216 [ND 11-150, SD 10-66], June 23, 1988. A "yea" was a vote supporting the president's position.

69. **HR 4800. Fiscal 1989 HUD Appropriations/NASA Funding and Housing Assistance.** Schumer, D-N.Y., amendments to shift $400 million from funding for NASA research and development to various programs for the homeless, Urban Development Action Grants, other housing programs and the Environmental Protection Agency. Rejected en bloc 166-256: R 40-133; D 126-123 [ND 111-58, SD 15-65], June 22, 1988.

70. **HR 2470. Catastrophic Health Insurance/Conference Report.** Adoption of the conference report on the bill to cap the amounts for which Medicare beneficiaries will be financially liable for Medicare-covered services and to make other changes in the program. Adopted 328-72: R 98-63; D 230-9 [ND 159-5, SD 71-4], June 2, 1988.

71. **HR 1212. Polygraph Protection/Conference Report.** Adoption of the conference report on the bill to ban use of lie-detector tests for job applicants or workers. Exempted would be all federal, state and local governments; contractors or consultants to government agencies engaged in intelligence or national security activities; companies providing security services for specified purposes; companies engaged in the manufacture and distribution of controlled drugs; and employers with reasonable cause to suspect a worker of involvement in criminal wrongdoing that resulted in economic loss to the company. Adopted 251-120: R 58-91; D 193-29 [ND 148-2, SD 45-27), June 1, 1988.

72. **HR 4387. Fiscal 1989 Intelligence Authorization/Contra Aid.** Hyde, R-Ill., amendment to delete a provision that bars the CIA from spending any money -- including its contingency fund -- to aid the Nicaraguan contras. In effect, the amendment would have allowed the administration to resume covert aid to the guerrillas as of Oct. 1, the effective date of the bill. Rejected 190-214: R 149-17; D 41-197 [ND 8-153, SD 33-44], May 26, 1988. (The intelligence authorization bill was subsequently passed by voice vote.)

73. **HR 3. Omnibus Trade Bill/Veto Override.** Passage, over President Reagan's May 24 veto, of the bill to revise statutory procedures for dealing with unfair foreign trade practices and import damage to U.S. industries, to clarify the law against business-related bribes abroad by U.S. businesses, to streamline controls on militarily sensitive exports, to revise agriculture and education programs, to repeal the windfall-profits tax on oil and to require certain employers to provide workers with 60 days' notice of plant closings or layoffs. Passed 308-113: R 60-112; D 248-1 [ND 167-1, SD 81-0], May 24, 1988. A two-thirds majority of those present and voting (281 in this case) of both houses is required to override a veto. A "nay" was a vote supporting the president's position.

74. **HR 4264. Fiscal 1989 Defense Authorization/Accidental Launch Protection.** Spratt, D-S.C., amendment to express the sense of Congress that development efforts for the first phase of the strategic defense initiative (SDI) should focus on an accidental launch protection system in compliance with the traditional interpretation of the 1972 anti-ballistic missile (ABM) treaty, which would allow only one ground-based anti-missile site. The secretary of defense would be required to report to Congress on the status of such a system by March 1, 1989. Adopted 239-176: R 22-150; D 217-26 [ND 145-18, SD 72-8], May 11, 1988.

75. **HR 4264. Fiscal 1989 Defense Authorization/Air Force and MX Funding.** Hertel, D-Mich., amendment, as modified, to reduce Air Force funding by $500 million and prohibit use of Air Force funds for the MX intercontinental ballistic missile (ICBM). Rejected 143-265: R 11-159; D 132-106 [ND 118-42, SD 14-64], May 5, 1988. A "nay" was a vote supporting the president's position.

76. **HR 4264. Fiscal 1989 Defense Authorization/Budget Financing.** Kyl, R-Ariz., amendment to express the sense of Congress that, starting with fiscal year 1990, the defense budget for each fiscal year should provide for a modest but sustained real increase compared with the preceding year. Rejected 167-219: R 119-44; D 48-175 [ND 12-143, SD 36-32], May 2, 1988.

77. **HR 4264. Fiscal 1989 Defense Authorization/Burdensharing.** Bryant, D-Texas, amendment to reduce the number of U.S. troops in Europe by 30,000 in fiscal years 1991-93 and reduce the number in Japan by 7,000, unless other NATO nations and Japan increase their defense spending at a rate 1 percent higher than their economic growth rate and take other specified steps to assume a greater share of their defense. Rejected 120-240: R 17-134; D 103-106 [ND 72-71, SD 31-35], April 29, 1988. A "nay" was a vote supporting the president's position.

78. **HR 4264. Fiscal 1989 Defense Authorization/Nuclear Testing Ban.** Gephardt, D-Mo., amendment to ban nuclear tests with an explosive power greater than one kiloton and tests conducted outside of designated test areas, as long as the Soviet Union observes the same ban. Adopted 214-186: R 18-148; D 196-38 [ND 151-9, SD 45-29], April 28, 1988. A "nay" was a vote supporting the president's position.

79. **HR 4264. Fiscal 1989 Defense Authorization/ASAT Test Ban.** Brown, D-Calif., amendment to ban anti-satellite (ASAT) weapons tests against targets in space unless the president certified to Congress that the Soviet Union had conducted such a test. Rejected 197-205: R 11-155; D 186-50 [ND 152-10, SD 34-40], April 28, 1988. A "nay" was a vote supporting the president's position.

80. **HR 4264. Fiscal 1989 Defense Authorization/SALT II Treaty Compliance.** Dicks, D-Wash., amendment to limit the number of U.S. multiple-warhead ballistic missiles and cruise-missile-carrying bombers to the numbers specified in the unratified 1979 strategic arms limitation (SALT II) treaty, unless the president certifies that the Soviet Union has exceeded those limits after enactment of this bill. Adopted 240-174: R 23-148; D 217-26 [ND 160-7, SD 57-19], April 27, 1988. A "nay" was a vote supporting the president's position.

81. **S 557. Civil Rights Restoration Act/Passage.** Passage, over President Reagan's March 16 veto, of the bill to provide broad coverage of four civil rights laws -- Title IX of the 1972 Education Act Amendments; Title VI of the 1964 Civil Rights Act; Section 504 of the 1973 Rehabilitation Act; and the 1975 Age Discrimination Act -- by making clear that, if one entity of an institution receives federal funds, the entire institution must abide by the anti-discrimination laws. Passed (thus enacted into law) 292-133: R 52-123; D 240-10 [ND 167-1, SD 73-9], March 22, 1988. A two-thirds majority of those present and voting (284 in this case) of both houses is required to override a veto. A "nay" was a vote supporting the president's position.

82. **HR 285. Non-immigrant Crewmember Status/Passage.** Clay, D-Mo., motion to suspend the rules and pass the bill to prohibit non-immigrant aliens from working as strikebreakers during labor disputes involving U.S. international air carriers or ships. Motion agreed to 302-114: R 74-99; D 228-15 [ND 164-0, SD 64-15], March 22, 1988. A two-thirds majority of those present and voting (278 in this case) is required for passage under suspension of the rules.

83. **HR 1054. Military Medical Malpractice Suits/Passage.** Passage of a bill to allow active-duty members of the armed forces to file suit against the federal government for medical and dental malpractice occurring in military hospitals within the United States. Passed 312-61: R 100-44; D 212-17 [ND 151-4, SD 61-13], Feb. 17, 1988. A "nay" was a vote supporting the president's position.

84. **H J Res 444. Contra Aid/Passage.** Passage of the joint resolution to approve President Reagan's request of $36.25 million for continued military and non-military aid to the Nicaraguan contra guerrillas. Rejected 211-219: R 164-12; D 47-207 [ND 6-166, SD 41-41], Feb. 3, 1988. A "yea" was a vote supporting the president's position.

85. **HR 3545. Fiscal 1988 Budget Reconciliation/Conference Report.** Adoption of the conference report on the bill to meet deficit-reduction targets set by the fiscal 1988 budget resolution (H Con Res 93) and the November "budget summit" agreement between the White House and Congress. The bill provided for $9.1 billion in new taxes in fiscal 1988 and $14.1 billion in 1989, plus sales of government assets, user fees, savings from the Medicare and health program for the elderly, savings from farm subsidy and other programs, and savings from reduced interest payments on the federal debt to yield $17.6 billion in deficit reduction in fiscal 1988 and $22 billion in fiscal 1989. Adopted 237-181: R 44-130; D 193-51 [ND 134-34, SD 59-17], Dec. 21, 1987.

86. **HR 1720. Welfare Reform/Passage.** Passage of the bill, estimated to cost $5.7 billion over five years, to change the Aid to Families with Dependent Children program to a Family Support Program emphasizing education, training and work for welfare recipients, with the federal government paying 65 percent of the cost. Passed 230-194: R 13-163; D 217-31 [ND 157-12, SD 60-19], Dec. 16, 1987. A "nay" was a vote supporting the president's position.

87. **HR 3545. Fiscal 1988 Budget Reconciliation/Passage.** Passage of the bill to raise $11.9 billion in revenues and make spending cuts in accordance with the fiscal 1988 budget resolution (H Con Res 93). Passed 206-205; R 1-164; D 205-41 [ND 143-21, SD 62-20], Oct. 29, 1987. A "nay" was a vote supporting the president's position. (The bill included $2.6 billion in spending cuts.)

88. **HR 162. High-Risk Occupational-Disease Notification/Passage.** Passage of the bill to create a Risk Assessment Board to identify workers at risk of developing occupational diseases, require notification of such workers, provide for employer-paid monitoring and testing, and allow workers with symptoms of disease to be transferred to other jobs without loss of earnings or benefits. Passed 225-186: R 22-147; D 203-39 [ND 160-7, SD 43-32], Oct. 15, 1987. A "nay" was a vote supporting the president's position.

89. **H J Res 324. Permanent Debt-Limit Extension -- Gramm-Rudman Revision/ Conference Agreement.** Adoption of the conference report on the joint resolution to raise the permanent ceiling on the federal debt to $2.8 trillion, from $2.1 trillion; to establish an automatic spending-cut procedure; to set maximum allowable budget deficit targets: for fiscal 1988, $144 billion (or another, undetermined figure because the legislation limited 1988 mandatory spending cuts under the automatic procedure to $23 billion, regardless of the difference between the estimated deficit and the target); for fiscal 1989, $136 billion (or another,

undetermined figure because of a $36 billion limit on the mandated spending cuts); for fiscal 1990, $100 billion; for fiscal 1991, $64 billion; for fiscal 1992, $28 billion; for fiscal 1993, zero; to provide that the automatic spending-cut procedure would be triggered in most years if the estimated deficit exceeded the target by more than $10 billion; and to revise certain other budget rules. Adopted 230-176: R 105-65; D 125-111 [ND 74-88, SD 51-23], Sept. 22, 1987.

90. **HR 1315. Nuclear Regulatory Commission Authorization/Plant Licensing.** Markey, D-Mass., amendment to prohibit the Nuclear Regulatory Commission (NRC) from licensing for full-power operation the nuclear power plants at Seabrook, N.H., and Shoreham, N.Y., unless their emergency evacuation plans meet NRC rules as of June 1, 1987, which, in part, require state and local participation in planning. Rejected 160-261: R 12-160; D 148-101 [ND 130-40, SD 18-61], Aug. 5, 1987.

91. **HR 1414. Price-Anderson Amendments/Liability Limits.** Eckart, D-Ohio, amendments to remove the $63 million limit in the bill on deferred premiums paid by nuclear utilities after an accident and to substitute a limit of $10 million per year. The effect would be to remove the cap on how much compensation could be paid to accident victims. Rejected en bloc 119-300; R 14-158; D 105-142 [ND 101-66, SD 4-76], July 29, 1987. A "nay" was a vote supporting the president's position.

92. **HR 2470. Catastrophic Health Insurance Bill/Passage.** Passage of the bill to protect Medicare beneficiaries from catastrophic health-care costs and to otherwise expand the program. Passed 302-127: R 61-113; D 241-14 [ND 166-5, SD 75-9], July 22, 1987. A "nay" was a vote supporting the president's position. (This bill was later repealed by both houses.)

93. **HR 2890. Transportation Appropriations, Fiscal 1988/In-Flight Smoking.** Durbin, D-Ill., amendment to deny federal grants to any airport that permits any airline to provide service between its facilities and any other airport with an aircraft scheduled to be in the air for two hours or less on which smoking is permitted. Adopted 198-193: R 74-91; D 124-102 [ND 102-48, SD 22-54], July 13, 1987.

94. **HR 558. Urgent Relief for the Homeless.** Adoption of the conference report on the bill to authorize $443 million in fiscal 1987 and $616 million in fiscal 1988 to provide housing, health, food, job training and other assistance for the nation's homeless, and to set up an interagency homeless council to oversee federal homeless-aid programs. Adopted (thus cleared for the president) 301-115: R 62-108; D 239-7 [ND 163-4, SD 76-3], June 30, 1987. A "nay" was a vote supporting the president's position.

95. **HR 281. Construction Labor Law Amendments.** Passage of the bill to restrict the right of unionized companies to establish non-union subsidiaries that do the same work, a practice known as "double-breasting." Passed 227-197: R 27-148; D 200-49 [ND 165-3, SD 35-46], June 17, 1987. A "nay" was a vote supporting the president's position.

96. **HR 27. FSLIC Rescue/$15 Billion Plan.** St. Germain, D-R.I., amendment to increase the bill's $5 billion, two-year recapitalization borrowing authority to $15 billion over five years. Rejected 153-258: R 72-98; D 81-160 [ND 62-99, SD 19-61], May 5, 1987. A "yea" was a vote supporting the president's position.

97. **HR 3. Omnibus Trade Bill/Excess Trade Surplus Countries.** Gephardt, D-Mo., amendment to require identification of countries with excess trade surpluses with the United States and quantify the extent to which unfair trade practices contribute to that surplus, to mandate negotiations to eliminate those unfair trade practices, and, if negotiations fail or an agreement is not fully implemented, to mandate imposition of tariffs or quotas to yield annual 10 percent reductions in that country's trade surplus. Adopted 218-214: R 17-159; D 201-55 [ND 137-34, SD 64-21], April 29, 1987. A "nay" was a vote supporting the president's position.

98. **HR 1827. Fiscal 1987 Supplemental Appropriations/Budget Authority.** MacKay, D-Fla., amendment to reduce discretionary budget authority by an across-the-board cut of 21 percent in order to keep total appropriations within the ceiling set by the 1987 budget resolution. Adopted 263-123: R 121-39; D 142-84 [ND 82-69, SD 60-15], April 23, 1987. (The amendment would reduce spending $2.2 billion.)

99. **HR 3810. Immigration Reform.** Passage of the bill to overhaul the nation's immigration laws by creating a new system of penalties against employers who knowingly hire illegal aliens, providing legal status to millions of illegal aliens already in the United States, and creating a special program for foreigners to gain legal status if they have a history of working in U.S. agriculture. Passed 230-166: R 62-105; D 168-61 [ND 126-29; SD 42-321], Oct. 9, 1986. (The House subsequently moved to strike the provisions of S 1200, the Senate-passed version of the bill, and insert the provisions of HR 3810. The House then passed S 1200 by voice vote.)

100. **HR 4868. South African Sanctions.** Passage, over President Reagan's Sept. 26 veto, of the bill to impose economic sanctions against South Africa. Passed 313-83: R 81-79; D 232-4 [ND 163-0; SD 69-4], Sept. 29, 1986. A two-thirds majority of those present and voting (264 in this case) of both houses is required to override a veto. A "nay" was a vote supporting the president's position.

101. **HR 3838. Tax Overhaul.** Adoption of the conference report on the bill to revise the federal income tax system by reducing individual and corporate tax rates, eliminating or curtailing many deductions, credits and exclusions, repealing the investment tax credit, taxing capital gains as regular income and making other changes. Adopted 292-136: R 116-62; D 176-74 [ND 132-36; SD 44-38], Sept. 25, 1986. A "yea" was a vote supporting the president's position.

102. **HR 5484. Omnibus Drug Bill.** Hunter, R-Calif., amendment to the Bennett, D-Fla., amendment, to require that the president deploy the armed forces to halt substantially, within 45 days, the unlawful entry of aircraft and vessels carrying narcotics. Adopted 237-177: R 145-29; D 92-148 [ND 55-108; SD 37-40], Sept. 11, 1986. (The Bennett amendment, to allow the use of members of the armed services to assist drug enforcement officials outside the United States, as amended by the Hunter amendment, subsequently was adopted.) A "nay" was a vote supporting the president's position.

103. **HR 4428. Defense Authorization, Fiscal 1987.** Bennett, D-Fla., amendment to delete $1.1 billion for 12 MX missiles and add $250 million for various conventional weapons. Rejected 178-210: R 23-144; D 155-66 [ND 129-18; SD 26-48], Aug. 11, 1986.

104. **HR 3129. Omnibus Highway Bill.** McCurdy, D-Okla., amendment to establish a five-year test program permitting states to raise the speed limit from 55 mph to 65 mph on rural sections of the Interstate system. Rejected 198-218: R 117-57; D 81-161 [ND 45-120; SD 36-41], Aug. 6, 1986.

105. **HR 4428. Department of Defense Authorization, Fiscal 1987.** Traficant, D-Ohio, amendment to the Mavroules, D-Mass., amendment, to require the Pentagon to buy U.S.-built goods rather than competing foreign-built goods if the price of the U.S. items is not more than 5 percent higher than the foreign items. Adopted 241-163: R 74-100; D 167-63 [ND 115-39; SD 52-24], Aug. 5, 1986. (The Mavroules amendment later was adopted.)

106. **HR 5175. District of Columbia Appropriations, Fiscal 1987.** Dixon, D-Calif., motion that the Committee of the Whole rise and report the bill back to the House. Motion agreed to 241-173: R 23-152; D 218-21 [ND 156-7, SD 62-14], July 24, 1986. (The effect of the vote was to prevent consideration of amendments limiting spending on the appropriations bill, in this case the Dannemeyer, R-Calif., amendment to kill a District law barring insurers from refusing coverage to persons who test positive for acquired immune deficiency syndrome (AIDS). Such amendments are in order only following a defeated motion to rise and report.)

107. **H J Res 589. Saudi Arms Sale.** Passage of the joint resolution to prohibit the administration's proposed $354 million sale of missiles to Saudi Arabia. Passed 356-62: R 131-45; D 225-17 [ND 155-8; SD 70-9], May 7, 1986. A "nay" was a vote supporting the president's position.

108. **HR 4332. Firearms Law Reform.** Passage of the bill to revise the 1968 Gun Control Act to allow the interstate sales of rifles and shotguns and the interstate transportation of all types of firearms, to ease record-keeping requirements for firearms transactions and to limit federal agents to one unannounced inspection per year of a gun dealer's premises. Passed 292-130: R 161-15; D 131-115 [ND 62-103, SD 69-12], April 10, 1986. (The House subsequently

moved to strike the language of S 49, the Senate-passed version of the bill, and insert instead the language of HR 4332.) A "yea" was a vote supporting the president's position.

109. **HR 4332. Firearms Law Reform.** Hughes, D-N.J., amendment to the Volkmer, D-Mo., substitute for the Judiciary Committee substitute, to bar the interstate transportation of handguns. Rejected 177-242: R 40-136; D 137-106 [ND 115-48; SD 22-58], April 9, 1986.

110. **HR 2817. Superfund Reauthorization, Fiscal 1986-90.** Edgar, D-Pa., amendment to require companies to make public an inventory of their emissions of chemicals known to cause or suspected of causing cancer, birth defects or other chronic diseases. Adopted 212-211: R 34-143; D 178-68 [ND 146-22, SD 32-46], Dec. 10, 1985. (The Edgar amendment previously had been adopted in the Committee of the Whole.)

111. **HR 2817. Superfund Reauthorization, Fiscal 1986-90.** Frank, D-Mass., amendment to permit persons injured by the release of toxic substances to sue responsible parties in federal court, except for damages incurred and discovered before enactment. Rejected 162-261: R 20-157; D 142-104 [ND 117-50; SD 25-54], Dec. 10, 1985.

112. **HR 2817. Superfund Reauthorization, Fiscal 1986-90.** Downey, D-N.Y., amendment to strike provisions for a broad-based or "value-added" tax and to provide $10 billion over five years for the "superfund" hazardous-waste cleanup program through increased taxes on chemical feedstocks, petroleum and hazardous-waste disposal and through general revenues. Adopted 220-206: R 73-105; D 147-101 [ND 127-42; SD 20-59], Dec. 10, 1985.

113. **HR 1616. Plant Closing Notification.** Passage of the bill to require employers of at least 50 full-time employees to give workers 90 days' notice of any plant shutdown or layoff involving at least 100 employees or 30 percent of the work force. Rejected 203-208: R 20-154; D 183-54 [ND 153-5; SD 30-49], Nov. 21, 1985.

114. **HR 3128. Deficit-Reduction Amendments.** Passage of the bill to reduce the deficit $19.5 billion over fiscal 1986-88 through spending reductions in the Medicare program; tax increases on tobacco products, imports, coal manufacturers and employers participating in a federal pension plan; and user fees for Customs inspections. The bill would also make changes in the Aid to Families with Dependent Children program and reauthorize the Trade Adjustment Assistance program and related trade agencies. Passed 245-174: R 24-150; D 221-24 [ND 151-15; SD 70-9], Oct. 31, 1985. A "nay" was a vote supporting the president's position.

115. **HR 3500. Omnibus Budget Reconciliation, Fiscal 1986.** Passage of the bill to make changes in law to reduce spending by $60.9 billion over fiscal years 1986-88, to conform with the fiscal 1986 budget resolution (S Con Res 32) that called for $276 billion in spending cuts and higher revenues over three years. Passed 228-199: R 15-166; D 213-33 [ND 141-24, SD 72-9], Oct. 24, 1985. A "nay" was a vote supporting the president's position.

116. **HR 7. School Lunch and Child Nutrition Act.** Armey, R-Texas, substitute for the Bartlett, R-Texas, amendment, to eliminate the cash and commodity subsidy for lunches for children from families with incomes above 250 percent of the poverty line. Rejected 146-279: R 133-48; D 13-231 [ND 1-165, SD 12-66], Sept. 18, 1985. (The Bartlett amendment was subsequently rejected by voice vote.)

117. **HR 99. American Conservation Corps.** Passage of the bill to authorize such sums as Congress considers necessary in fiscal 1986-88 to establish an American Conservation Corps to put unemployed youths to work on conservation projects. Passed 193-191: R 18-148; D 175-43 [ND 137-13; SD 38-30], July 11, 1985. A "nay" was a vote supporting the president's position. (The cost of the bill was $75 million per year.)

118. **HR 1555. Foreign Assistance Authorization, Fiscal 1986.** Stratton, D-N.Y., amendment to repeal the so-called "Clark amendment" to the International Security and Development Cooperation Act of 1980, prohibiting assistance for military or paramilitary operations in Angola. Adopted 236-185: R 176-6; D 60-179 [ND 14-150; SD 46-29], July 10, 1985. A "yea" was a vote supporting the president's position.

119. **HR 1872. Department of Defense Authorization, Fiscal 1986.** Hertel, D-Mich., amendment to empower the inspector general of the Defense Department to suspend payments to a contractor or debar a contractor if he finds waste, fraud and abuse in connection with the contract. Rejected 176-240: R 24-153; D 152-87 [ND 134-27; SD 18-60], June 25, 1985.

120. **H Con Res 152. First Budget Resolution, Fiscal 1986.** Leath, D-Texas, amendment to reduce the deficit by $75 billion in fiscal 1986, and by $350 billion over fiscal 1986-88, by eliminating increases in cost-of-living adjustments for recipients of Social Security and other federal retirement programs and by raising $12 billion in new taxes, in combination with spending cuts outlined in the concurrent resolution. Rejected 56-372: R 15-165; D 41-207 [ND 18-150; SD 23-57], May 23, 1985.

121. **S J Res 71. MX Missile Authorization.** Passage of the joint resolution to approve authorization of $1.5 billion to procure 21 MX missiles in fiscal 1985. Passed 219-213: R 158-24; D 61-189 [ND 15-154; SD 46-35], March 26, 1985. A "yea" was a vote supporting the president's position.

122. **HR 1035. Emergency Farm Credit.** Passage of the bill to authorize advance Commodity Credit Corporation crop loans to farmers, to authorize $3 billion in Farmers Home Administration (FmHA) loan guarantees for restructured private loans to farmers, to revise rules for the FmHA loan guarantees and to authorize low-interest federal disaster loans to farmers in certain circumstances. Passed 318-103: R 84-93; D 234-10 [ND 158-6; SD 76-4], Feb. 27, 1985. A "nay" was a vote supporting the president's position.

123. **HR 6023. Generalized System of Preferences Renewal Act.** Gephardt, D-Mo., amendment to remove Taiwan, Hong Kong and South Korea from the list of countries eligible for duty-free treatment under the generalized system of preferences. Rejected 174-233: R 14-142; D 160-91 [ND 128-38; SD 32-53], Oct. 3, 1984. A "nay" was a vote supporting the president's position. (The bill subsequently was passed by voice vote.)

124. **HR 6301. Steel Import Stabilization.** Passage of the bill to request that the president negotiate a voluntary agreement with steel-producing nations to limit shipments to the United States to 17 percent of the U.S. market. The agreement would be contingent on domestic steel producers' willingness to modernize plants and aid unemployed or laid-off workers. The bill also would extend for two years the Trade Adjustment Assistance Program, which provides government help to workers whose jobs are eliminated because of foreign competition. Passed 285-134: R 63-98; D 222-36 [ND 156-16; SD 66-20], Oct. 3, 1984.

125. **HR 11. Education Amendments/School Prayer.** Walker, R-Pa., amendment to the Coats, R-Ind., amendment, to cut off federal education assistance to states and school districts with policies that prohibit silent or vocal prayer in public schools. Rejected 194-215: R 121-33; D 73-182 [ND 18-153; SD 55-29], July 26, 1984.

126. **HR 4170. Deficit Reduction.** Adoption of the conference report on the bill to raise $50 billion in new taxes and to cut Medicare and other spending by about $13 billion through fiscal year 1987. Adopted 268-155: R 76-86; D 192-69 [ND 126-46; SD 66-23], June 27, 1984. A "yea" was a vote supporting the president's position.

127. **HR 5167. Department of Defense Authorization.** Dellums, D-Calif., amendment to prohibit, during fiscal 1985, further deployment in Europe of Pershing II or ground-launched cruise missiles unless the North Atlantic Treaty Organization (NATO) notified the United States that there was a NATO consensus that further deployments should be made. Rejected 104-291: R 2-154; D 102-137 [ND 98-66; SD 4-71], May 31, 1984. A "nay" was a vote supporting the president's position.

128. **HR 5167. Department of Defense Authorization.** Dellums, D-Calif., amendment to delete $7.1 billion for procurement of 34 B-1 bombers. Rejected 163-254: R 19-142; D 144-112 [ND 130-40; SD 14-72], May 23, 1984. A "nay" was a vote supporting the president's position.

129. **HR 5167. Department of Defense Authorization.** Smith, D-Fla., amendment to bar the use of funds to purchase Sergeant York anti-aircraft guns (also called DIVADs) until certain

test results have been reported to Congress. Rejected 157-229: R 32-123; D 125-106 [ND 112-40; SD 13-66], May 17, 1984. A "nay" was a vote supporting the president's position.

130. **HR 5119. Foreign Assistance Authorization.** Broomfield, R-Mich., amendment to authorize President Reagan's requests for military, economic and development aid for Central American countries in fiscal 1984-1985, and to allow military aid for El Salvador in fiscal 1985 if the president certified to Congress that the government had made "demonstrated progress" on human rights and other issues. Adopted 212-208: R 156-8; D 56-200 [ND 7-167; SD 49-33], May 10, 1984. A "yea" was a vote supporting the president's position.

131. **H Con Res 290. Mining of Nicaraguan Waters.** Adoption of the concurrent resolution stating the sense of Congress that no appropriated funds should be used for planning, directing, executing or supporting the mining of ports or territorial waters of Nicaragua. Adopted 281-111: R 57-96; D 224-15 [ND 158-3; SD 66-12], April 12, 1984.

132. **HR 5394. Omnibus Budget Reconciliation Act.** Moore, R-La., motion to recommit the bill to the House Ways and Means Committee with instructions to include provisions imposing a one-year physician fee freeze for Medicare services and to strike provisions in the measure that increased spending. Motion rejected 172-242: R 157-2; D 15-240 [ND 3-170; SD 12-70], April 12, 1984.

133. **HR 4170. Deficit Reduction.** Passage of the bill to raise $49.2 billion in new taxes through fiscal 1987 by closing a wide range of tax loopholes; increasing taxes on distilled liquor, cigarettes and telephones; revamping taxation of the life insurance industry; and making other changes. Passed 318-97: R 95-66; D 223-31 [ND 155-14; SD 68-17], April 11, 1984. A "yea" was a vote supporting the president's position.

134. **HR 3648. Amtrak Improvement Act.** Broyhill, R-N.C., amendment to permit the Department of Transportation to sell Conrail unless Congress passes a law disapproving the sale. The bill would require Congress to approve any sale for it to take effect. Rejected 147-254: R 129-26; D 18-228 [ND 3-158; SD 15-70], March 6, 1984. A "yea" was a vote supporting the president's position.

135. **H J Res 1. Equal Rights Amendment.** Rodino, D-N.J., motion to suspend the rules and pass the joint resolution to propose an amendment to the Constitution declaring, "Equality of rights under the law shall not be denied or abridged by the United States or by any state on account of sex." Motion rejected 278-147: R 53-109; D 225-38 [ND 164-13; SD 61-25], Nov. 15, 1983. A two-thirds majority of those present and voting (284 in this case) is required for passage under suspension of the rules. A "nay" was a vote supporting the president's position.

136. **H J Res 364. Multinational Force in Lebanon.** Passage of the joint resolution to provide statutory authorization under the War Powers Resolution for continued U.S. participation in the multinational peacekeeping force in Lebanon for up to 18 months after the enactment of the resolution. Passed 270-161: R 140-27; D 130-134 [ND 70-105; SD 60-29], Sept. 28, 1983. A "yea" was a vote supporting the president's position.

137. **HR 1010. Coal Pipeline Act.** Passage of the bill to grant federal power of eminent domain to certified coal slurry pipeline companies. Rejected 182-235: R 85-75; D 97-160 [ND 52-120; SD 45-40], Sept. 27, 1983.

138. **HR 3133. Department of Housing and Urban Development Appropriations, Fiscal 1984.** Dannemeyer, R-Calif., amendment to prohibit the Environmental Protection Agency from using any funds provided by the bill to impose sanctions during fiscal 1984 on any area for failing to attain any national ambient air quality standard established under the Clean Air Act. Adopted 227-136: R 89-50; D 138-86 [ND 88-58; SD 50-28], June 2, 1983.

139. **HR 1900. Social Security Act Amendments.** Pickle, D-Texas, amendment to gradually raise the normal Social Security retirement age from 65 to 67 after the year 2000, and to delete provisions of the Ways and Means Committee bill that would reduce initial benefit levels beginning in the year 2000 and raise payroll taxes beginning in the year 2015. Adopted 228-202: R 152-14; D 76-188 [ND 23-152; SD 53-36], March 9, 1983. A "yea" was a vote supporting the president's position.

140. **HR 5133. Automobile Domestic Content Requirements.** Passage of the bill to require automakers to use set percentages of U.S. labor and parts in automobiles they sell in the United States. Passed 215-188: R 44-130; D 171-58 [ND 132-20; SD 39-38], Dec. 15, 1982. A "nay" was a vote supporting the president's position.

141. **H J Res 631. Continuing Appropriations, Fiscal 1983/Jobs.** Conte, R-Mass., motion to recommit the joint resolution to the Appropriations Committee with instructions to delete jobs program funding (Title II) and add $44 million in funding for Radio Liberty. Motion rejected 191-215: R 171-7; D 20-208 [ND 2-150; SD 18-58], Dec. 14, 1982. A "yea" was a vote supporting the president's position.

142. **HR 6211. Transportation Assistance Act of 1982.** Adoption of the rule (H Res 620) providing for House floor consideration of the bill to authorize funds for highway and mass transit programs for fiscal 1983-1986 and to increase gasoline and other highway taxes. Adopted 197-194: R 59-114; D 138-80 [ND 112-34; SD 26-46], Dec. 6, 1982. The bill increased the gasoline tax by a nickel and taxes on heavy trucks.

143. **H Con Res 345. First Budget Resolution, Fiscal 1983.** Oakar, D-Ohio, amendment, to the Latta, R-Ohio, substitute, to increase budget authority by $400 million and outlays by $4.85 billion for health programs in fiscal 1983 to accommodate Medicare funding at current services levels, and to make corresponding reductions in defense programs. Adopted 228-196: R 64-125; D 164-71 [ND 136-20; SD 28-51], May 27, 1982.

144. **HR 5922. Urgent Supplemental Appropriations, Fiscal 1982.** Boland, D-Mass., amendment to provide $1 billion to the Department of Housing and Urban Development for mortgage interest subsidy payments to home buyers with family income not exceeding 130 percent of the median income for their area. Adopted 343-67: R 128-52; D 215-15 [ND 149-6; SD 66-9], May 12, 1982. (The aid was increased to $3 billion in conference with the Senate, but later vetoed.)

House Voting Records

ALABAMA

CALLAHAN, H.L. (Sonny) -- Alabama 1st District [Republican]. Counties of Baldwin, Clarke, Escambia, Mobile, Monroe, Washington and Wilcox. Prior Terms: 1985-92. Born: September 11, 1932; Mobile, AL. Military Service: U.S. Navy, 1952-54. Occupation: Businessman; Alabama legislator (1970-78); Alabama senator.

1.	Protection to Haitian refugees	N	34.	Req submission of balanced budget	N
2.	Raise tax on wealthy; lower others	N	35.	Balanced budget amendment	Y
3.	Investigate Reagan hostage delay	N	36.	Amendment to ban flag desecration	Y
4.	Campaign finance revisions	N	37.	Reauthorize Amtrak-veto override	Y
5.	Unpaid leave to care for children	N	38.	Retraining aid for coal miners	N
6.	Restrict NEA use of funds	Y	39.	Suspend El Salvador military aid	Y
7.	Bar race-bias claim/habeas corpus	?	40.	Expand child care aid/tax credit	N
8.	Ban race as death sentence factor	?	41.	Raise House salary/omit honoraria	N
9.	Exceptions to exclusionary rule	?	42.	Toughen oil-spill liability	N
10.	Allow sale of assault weapons	?	43.	Restitution to Japanese interned	N
11.	Life in prison/abolish death penalty	?	44.	Protect Chinese & C.A. nationals	N
12.	Req conspiracy-price fixing cases	Y	45.	Abortion $ for rape/incest cases	N
13.	Unemployment benefits extension	N	46.	Allow religious schools to bar gays	Y
14.	Tissue use of aborted fetuses	N	47.	Bar broadcaster fairness doctrine	Y
15.	Bar replacement of union strikers	N	48.	Bar cap gains cut/reinstate IRA	N
16.	Hold foreign aid at $15b for '92	Y	49.	Bar unions equal voice in pension	Y
17.	Restore space station funding	Y	50.	Bar assembly of chemical weapons	N
18.	Civil Rights Act of 1991	N	51.	Ban plutonium/uranium production	N
19.	Unlimited damages-discrimination	N	52.	Cap MX missile deployment at 50	N
20.	Eliminate funds for supercollider	N	53.	Allow $3b for 2 stealth bombers	Y
21.	Terminate SDI except for research	N	54.	Publish bio-warfare experiments	N
22.	Req 7-day handgun waiting period	N	55.	Raise minimum wage-veto override	N
23.	Provide $30b for failed S&Ls	N	56.	Bar transfer of FS-X technology	?
24.	Allow use of force against Iraq	Y	57.	Cut defense and raise domestic $	N
25.	Allow $15b in foreign aid for '91	?	58.	Uniform poll closing in 48 states	N
26.	Revise & extend legal immigration	?	59.	Req foreign investment disclosure	Y
27.	Suspend aid to Angolan rebels	N	60.	Textile import quotas-veto override	Y
28.	Democratic tax plan proposals	N	61.	Bar abortion funding in Wash, DC	+
29.	Cut defense 5% across the board	N	62.	Notify spouses of AIDS+ carriers	Y
30.	Textile import quotas-veto override	Y	63.	Seize conveyance-drug trafficking	Y
31.	Abortion service for military abroad	N	64.	South Africa sanctions	N
32.	Limits on high income farmers	N	65.	60 days' notice of plant closings	N
33.	Family medical leave-veto override	N	66.	Close unneeded military bases	Y

CALLAHAN, H.L. (continued)

67. Keep welfare reform within $2.8b	Y	
68. Allow children housing exclusion	Y	
69. Shift $400m of NASA to homeless	N	
70. Cap Medicare patients' liability	Y	
71. Prohibit employee polygraph testing	N	
72. Allow CIA to fund Contras	Y	
73. Revise unfair trade practices	N	
74. Focus SDI on accidental launch	N	
75. Bar Air Force $ for MX missile	N	
76. Allow "real" increase in defense	Y	
77. Troop reduction in Europe of 50%	N	
78. Ban nuclear tests above 1 kiloton	N	
79. Ban anti-satellite missile tests	N	
80. Observe certain limits of SALT II	N	
81. Restore four Civil Rights laws	N	
82. Prohibit aliens as strikebreakers	Y	
83. Allow military malpractice suits	N	
84. Approval of $36m in Contra aid	Y	
85. $18b deficit reduction compromise	N	
86. Welfare reform of $5.7b for 5 years	N	
87. Raise taxes $12b/cut spending $3b	N	
88. Board to assess occupational risk	N	
89. Balanced budget by '93-via targets	Y	
90. Bar licensing of two nuclear plants	N	
91. Remove victims compensation cap	N	
92. Catastrophic health insurance	Y	
93. Ban airline smoking-2 hours or less	N	
94. $1b/two year aid for the homeless	N	

95. Bar non-unions in union companies	N
96. Increase FSLIC rescue to $15b	N
97. Impose quotas to lower trade deficit	N
98. Reduce discretionary budget 21%	N
99. Immigration reform/alien amnesty	N
100. South Africa sanctions-veto override	N
101. Tax overhaul to revise income tax	Y
102. Use of military in drug war	Y
103. Delete 12 MX/add conventional wpn	N
104. Raise speed limit to 65 mph	N
105. Require Pentagon to buy US goods	Y
106. AIDS insurance non-discrimination	N
107. Prohibit Saudi arms sales	Y
108. Ease Gun Control Act of 1968	Y
109. Bar interstate handgun transport	N
110. Make company emissions known	N
111. Allow toxic victims to sue in fed ct	N
112. Superfund waste cleanup of $10b	N
113. 90 days notice of plant closings	N
114. $20b in Medicare cuts/tax increases	N
115. Spending cuts and tax increases	N
116. Set school lunch lmt-250% poverty	Y
117. $75m for youth work projects	N
118. Allow Angolan military assistance	Y
119. Suspend defense payments for abuse	N
120. Drop SS COLAs/$12b tax increase	N
121. Approve $1.5b for 21 MX missiles	Y
122. Emergency farm credit/revisions	N

Presidential Support Score: 1991 - 65% 1990 - 63%

DICKINSON, WILLIAM L. -- Alabama 2nd District [Republican]. Counties of Barbour, Bullock, Butler, Coffee, Conecuh, Covington, Crenshaw, Dale, Geneva, Henry, Houston, Montgomery and Pike. Prior Terms: 1965-92. Born: June 5, 1925; Opelika, AL. Education: University of Alabama Law School. Military Service: U.S. Navy, WW II. Occupation: Judge.

1. Protection to Haitian refugees	?
2. Raise tax on wealthy; lower others	X
3. Investigate Reagan hostage delay	N
4. Campaign finance revisions	N
5. Unpaid leave to care for children	N
6. Restrict NEA use of funds	?
7. Bar race-bias claim/habeas corpus	Y
8. Ban race as death sentence factor	Y
9. Exceptions to exclusionary rule	Y
10. Allow sale of assault weapons	Y
11. Life in prison/abolish death penalty	N
12. Req conspiracy-price fixing cases	Y
13. Unemployment benefits extension	N
14. Tissue use of aborted fetuses	N
15. Bar replacement of union strikers	N
16. Hold foreign aid at $15b for '92	N
17. Restore space station funding	Y
18. Civil Rights Act of 1991	N
19. Unlimited damages-discrimination	N
20. Eliminate funds for supercollider	Y
21. Terminate SDI except for research	N
22. Req 7-day handgun waiting period	N
23. Provide $30b for failed S&Ls	?
24. Allow use of force against Iraq	Y
25. Allow $15b in foreign aid for '91	N
26. Revise & extend legal immigration	Y

27. Suspend aid to Angolan rebels	N
28. Democratic tax plan proposals	N
29. Cut defense 5% across the board	N
30. Textile import quotas-veto override	Y
31. Abortion service for military abroad	N
32. Limits on high income farmers	Y
33. Family medical leave-veto override	N
34. Req submission of balanced budget	N
35. Balanced budget amendment	Y
36. Amendment to ban flag desecration	Y
37. Reauthorize Amtrak-veto override	N
38. Retraining aid for coal miners	N
39. Suspend El Salvador military aid	N
40. Expand child care aid/tax credit	X
41. Raise House salary/omit honoraria	N
42. Toughen oil-spill liability	?
43. Restitution to Japanese interned	N
44. Protect Chinese & C.A. nationals	N
45. Abortion $ for rape/incest cases	Y
46. Allow religious schools to bar gays	Y
47. Bar broadcaster fairness doctrine	Y
48. Bar cap gains cut/reinstate IRA	N
49. Bar unions equal voice in pension	Y
50. Bar assembly of chemical weapons	N
51. Ban plutonium/uranium production	N
52. Cap MX missile deployment at 50	?

DICKINSON, WILLIAM L. (continued)

53. Allow $3b for 2 stealth bombers	Y	99. Immigration reform/alien amnesty	N
54. Publish bio-warfare experiments	N	100. South Africa sanctions-veto override	N
55. Raise minimum wage-veto override	N	101. Tax overhaul to revise income tax	Y
56. Bar transfer of FS-X technology	X	102. Use of military in drug war	N
57. Cut defense and raise domestic $	N	103. Delete 12 MX/add conventional wpn	N
58. Uniform poll closing in 48 states	N	104. Raise speed limit to 65 mph	Y
59. Req foreign investment disclosure	N	105. Require Pentagon to buy US goods	N
60. Textile import quotas-veto override	Y	106. AIDS insurance non-discrimination	N
61. Bar abortion funding in Wash, DC	N	107. Prohibit Saudi arms sales	N
62. Notify spouses of AIDS+ carriers	Y	108. Ease Gun Control Act of 1968	Y
63. Seize conveyance-drug trafficking	Y	109. Bar interstate handgun transport	N
64. South Africa sanctions	?	110. Make company emissions known	N
65. 60 days' notice of plant closings	N	111. Allow toxic victims to sue in fed ct	N
66. Close unneeded military bases	Y	112. Superfund waste cleanup of $10b	N
67. Keep welfare reform within $2.8b	Y	113. 90 days notice of plant closings	N
68. Allow children housing exclusion	Y	114. $20b in Medicare cuts/tax increases	N
69. Shift $400m of NASA to homeless	N	115. Spending cuts and tax increases	N
70. Cap Medicare patients' liability	Y	116. Set school lunch lmt-250% poverty	Y
71. Prohibit employee polygraph testing	Y	117. $75m for youth work projects	N
72. Allow CIA to fund Contras	Y	118. Allow Angolan military assistance	Y
73. Revise unfair trade practices	N	119. Suspend defense payments for abuse	N
74. Focus SDI on accidental launch	N	120. Drop SS COLAs/$12b tax increase	Y
75. Bar Air Force $ for MX missile	N	121. Approve $1.5b for 21 MX missiles	Y
76. Allow "real" increase in defense	Y	122. Emergency farm credit/revisions	Y
77. Troop reduction in Europe of 50%	N	123. Duty on Taiwan/Hong Kong/S Korea	N
78. Ban nuclear tests above 1 kiloton	N	124. Limit steel imports to 17%	N
79. Ban anti-satellite missile tests	N	125. Cut $ to schools that bar prayer	Y
80. Observe certain limits of SALT II	N	126. $50b-taxes; cut Medicare/spending	N
81. Restore four Civil Rights laws	N	127. Limit Pershing II/cruise in Europe	N
82. Prohibit aliens as strikebreakers	N	128. Delete $7.1b for 34 B-1 bombers	N
83. Allow military malpractice suits	N	129. Bar purchase of Sergeant York guns	N
84. Approval of $36m in Contra aid	Y	130. El Salvador military/economic aid	Y
85. $18b deficit reduction compromise	?	131. Bar mining of Nicaraguan waters	X
86. Welfare reform of $5.7b for 5 years	N	132. Physician fee freeze for Medicare	#
87. Raise taxes $12b/cut spending $3b	N	133. $49b in "sin"/phone/insurance taxes	N
88. Board to assess occupational risk	N	134. Allow sale of Conrail	N
89. Balanced budget by '93-via targets	N	135. Equal Rights Amendment	N
90. Bar licensing of two nuclear plants	?	136. Authorize Marines in Lebanon	Y
91. Remove victims compensation cap	?	137. Eminent domain for coal companies	N
92. Catastrophic health insurance	Y	138. Prohibit EPA clean air sanctions	?
93. Ban airline smoking-2 hours or less	N	139. SS retirement age increase/reforms	Y
94. $1b/two year aid for the homeless	N	140. Auto domestic content requirement	N
95. Bar non-unions in union companies	N	141. Delete jobs program funding	Y
96. Increase FSLIC rescue to $15b	Y	142. Highway-gas tax bill	N
97. Impose quotas to lower trade deficit	N	143. Cut $5b from defense for Medicare	N
98. Reduce discretionary budget 21%	N	144. Emergency housing aid of $1b	Y

Presidential Support Score: 1991 - 72%   1990 - 66%

BROWDER, GLEN -- Alabama 3rd District [Democrat]. Counties of Autauga, Calhoun, Chambers, Clay, Cleburne, Coosa, Elmore, Lee, Macon, Randolph, Russell, Talladega and Tallapoosa. Prior Terms: 1989 (Special Election)-1992. Born: January 15, 1943; Sumter, SC. Education: Presbyterian College (B.A.); Emory University (M.A., Ph.D.). Occupation: College public relations and alumni affairs assistant; newspaper sportswriter; U.S. Civil Service Commission investigator (1966-68); university professor (1971-89); state representative (1982-86) and Secretary of State (1987-89).

1. Protection to Haitian refugees	N	7. Bar race-bias claim/habeas corpus	Y
2. Raise tax on wealthy; lower others	Y	8. Ban race as death sentence factor	Y
3. Investigate Reagan hostage delay	Y	9. Exceptions to exclusionary rule	Y
4. Campaign finance revisions	Y	10. Allow sale of assault weapons	Y
5. Unpaid leave to care for children	N	11. Life in prison/abolish death penalty	N
6. Restrict NEA use of funds	N	12. Req conspiracy-price fixing cases	Y

BROWDER, GLEN (continued)

13. Unemployment benefits extension	Y	
14. Tissue use of aborted fetuses	Y	
15. Bar replacement of union strikers	Y	
16. Hold foreign aid at $15b for '92	Y	
17. Restore space station funding	Y	
18. Civil Rights Act of 1991	Y	
19. Unlimited damages-discrimination	N	
20. Eliminate funds for supercollider	N	
21. Terminate SDI except for research	N	
22. Req 7-day handgun waiting period	N	
23. Provide $30b for failed S&Ls	N	
24. Allow use of force against Iraq	Y	
25. Allow $15b in foreign aid for '91	Y	
26. Revise & extend legal immigration	N	
27. Suspend aid to Angolan rebels	N	
28. Democratic tax plan proposals	Y	
29. Cut defense 5% across the board	N	
30. Textile import quotas-veto override	Y	
31. Abortion service for military abroad	N	
32. Limits on high income farmers	N	
33. Family medical leave-veto override	N	
34. Req submission of balanced budget	Y	
35. Balanced budget amendment	Y	
36. Amendment to ban flag desecration	Y
37. Reauthorize Amtrak-veto override	Y
38. Retraining aid for coal miners	Y
39. Suspend El Salvador military aid	Y
40. Expand child care aid/tax credit	Y
41. Raise House salary/omit honoraria	N
42. Toughen oil-spill liability	Y
43. Restitution to Japanese interned	N
44. Protect Chinese & C.A. nationals	Y
45. Abortion $ for rape/incest cases	Y
46. Allow religious schools to bar gays	Y
47. Bar broadcaster fairness doctrine	N
48. Bar cap gains cut/reinstate IRA	N
49. Bar unions equal voice in pension	Y
50. Bar assembly of chemical weapons	N
51. Ban plutonium/uranium production	Y
52. Cap MX missile deployment at 50	Y
53. Allow $3b for 2 stealth bombers	N
54. Publish bio-warfare experiments	Y
55. Raise minimum wage-veto override	Y
56. Bar transfer of FS-X technology	Y
57. Cut defense and raise domestic $	N

Presidential Support Score: 1991 - 41% 1990 - 41%

BEVILL, TOM -- Alabama 4th District [Democrat] Counties of Blount, Cherokee, Cullman, De Kalb, Etowah, Fayette, Franklin, Lamar, Marion, Marshall, Pickens, St. Clair (pt.), Walker and Winston. Prior Terms: 1967-92. Born: March 27, 1921; Townley, AL. Education: University of Alabama (B.S. LL.B.). Military Service: U.S. Army, 1943-46. Occupation: Attorney; Alabama representative (1958-66).

1. Protection to Haitian refugees	N	
2. Raise tax on wealthy; lower others	Y	
3. Investigate Reagan hostage delay	Y	
4. Campaign finance revisions	Y	
5. Unpaid leave to care for children	Y	
6. Restrict NEA use of funds	N	
7. Bar race-bias claim/habeas corpus	Y	
8. Ban race as death sentence factor	Y	
9. Exceptions to exclusionary rule	Y	
10. Allow sale of assault weapons	Y	
11. Life in prison/abolish death penalty	N	
12. Req conspiracy-price fixing cases	Y	
13. Unemployment benefits extension	Y	
14. Tissue use of aborted fetuses	Y	
15. Bar replacement of union strikers	Y	
16. Hold foreign aid at $15b for '92	Y	
17. Restore space station funding	Y	
18. Civil Rights Act of 1991	Y	
19. Unlimited damages-discrimination	N	
20. Eliminate funds for supercollider	N	
21. Terminate SDI except for research	N	
22. Req 7-day handgun waiting period	N	
23. Provide $30b for failed S&Ls	N	
24. Allow use of force against Iraq	Y	
25. Allow $15b in foreign aid for '91	N	
26. Revise & extend legal immigration	N	
27. Suspend aid to Angolan rebels	N	
28. Democratic tax plan proposals	Y	
29. Cut defense 5% across the board	N	
30. Textile import quotas-veto override	Y	
31. Abortion service for military abroad	N	
32. Limits on high income farmers	N
33. Family medical leave-veto override	N
34. Req submission of balanced budget	Y
35. Balanced budget amendment	Y
36. Amendment to ban flag desecration	Y
37. Reauthorize Amtrak-veto override	Y
38. Retraining aid for coal miners	Y
39. Suspend El Salvador military aid	Y
40. Expand child care aid/tax credit	Y
41. Raise House salary/omit honoraria	N
42. Toughen oil-spill liability	Y
43. Restitution to Japanese interned	N
44. Protect Chinese & C.A. nationals	N
45. Abortion $ for rape/incest cases	N
46. Allow religious schools to bar gays	Y
47. Bar broadcaster fairness doctrine	Y
48. Bar cap gains cut/reinstate IRA	Y
49. Bar unions equal voice in pension	Y
50. Bar assembly of chemical weapons	N
51. Ban plutonium/uranium production	Y
52. Cap MX missile deployment at 50	N
53. Allow $3b for 2 stealth bombers	Y
54. Publish bio-warfare experiments	Y
55. Raise minimum wage-veto override	Y
56. Bar transfer of FS-X technology	Y
57. Cut defense and raise domestic $	N
58. Uniform poll closing in 48 states	N
59. Req foreign investment disclosure	Y
60. Textile import quotas-veto override	Y
61. Bar abortion funding in Wash, DC	Y
62. Notify spouses of AIDS+ carriers	N

BEVILL, TOM (continued)

63.	Seize conveyance-drug trafficking	Y	104.	Raise speed limit to 65 mph	Y
64.	South Africa sanctions	?	105.	Require Pentagon to buy US goods	Y
65.	60 days' notice of plant closings	Y	106.	AIDS insurance non-discrimination	Y
66.	Close unneeded military bases	N	107.	Prohibit Saudi arms sales	Y
67.	Keep welfare reform within $2.8b	Y	108.	Ease Gun Control Act of 1968	Y
68.	Allow children housing exclusion	N	109.	Bar interstate handgun transport	N
69.	Shift $400m of NASA to homeless	N	110.	Make company emissions known	N
70.	Cap Medicare patients' liability	Y	111.	Allow toxic victims to sue in fed ct	N
71.	Prohibit employee polygraph testing	Y	112.	Superfund waste cleanup of $10b	N
72.	Allow CIA to fund Contras	Y	113.	90 days notice of plant closings	Y
73.	Revise unfair trade practices	Y	114.	$20b in Medicare cuts/tax increases	N
74.	Focus SDI on accidental launch	Y	115.	Spending cuts and tax increases	Y
75.	Bar Air Force $ for MX missile	N	116.	Set school lunch lmt-250% poverty	?
76.	Allow "real" increase in defense	?	117.	$75m for youth work projects	N
77.	Troop reduction in Europe of 50%	?	118.	Allow Angolan military assistance	Y
78.	Ban nuclear tests above 1 kiloton	?	119.	Suspend defense payments for abuse	N
79.	Ban anti-satellite missile tests	?	120.	Drop SS COLAs/$12b tax increase	N
80.	Observe certain limits of SALT II	Y	121.	Approve $1.5b for 21 MX missiles	Y
81.	Restore four Civil Rights laws	Y	122.	Emergency farm credit/revisions	Y
82.	Prohibit aliens as strikebreakers	Y	123.	Duty on Taiwan/Hong Kong/S Korea	N
83.	Allow military malpractice suits	Y	124.	Limit steel imports to 17%	Y
84.	Approval of $36m in Contra aid	Y	125.	Cut $ to schools that bar prayer	Y
85.	$18b deficit reduction compromise	Y	126.	$50b-taxes; cut Medicare/spending	N
86.	Welfare reform of $5.7b for 5 years	Y	127.	Limit Pershing II/cruise in Europe	N
87.	Raise taxes $12b/cut spending $3b	N	128.	Delete $7.1b for 34 B-1 bombers	N
88.	Board to assess occupational risk	N	129.	Bar purchase of Sergeant York guns	N
89.	Balanced budget by '93-via targets	N	130.	El Salvador military/economic aid	?
90.	Bar licensing of two nuclear plants	N	131.	Bar mining of Nicaraguan waters	Y
91.	Remove victims compensation cap	N	132.	Physician fee freeze for Medicare	N
92.	Catastrophic health insurance	Y	133.	$49b in "sin"/phone/insurance taxes	Y
93.	Ban airline smoking-2 hours or less	N	134.	Allow sale of Conrail	N
94.	$1b/two year aid for the homeless	Y	135.	Equal Rights Amendment	Y
95.	Bar non-unions in union companies	Y	136.	Authorize Marines in Lebanon	Y
96.	Increase FSLIC rescue to $15b	N	137.	Eminent domain for coal companies	N
97.	Impose quotas to lower trade deficit	Y	138.	Prohibit EPA clean air sanctions	Y
98.	Reduce discretionary budget 21%	Y	139.	SS retirement age increase/reforms	N
99.	Immigration reform/alien amnesty	N	140.	Auto domestic content requirement	Y
100.	South Africa sanctions-veto override	Y	141.	Delete jobs program funding	Y
101.	Tax overhaul to revise income tax	Y	142.	Highway-gas tax bill	?
102.	Use of military in drug war	N	143.	Cut $5b from defense for Medicare	Y
103.	Delete 12 MX/add conventional wpn	N	144.	Emergency housing aid of $1b	Y

Presidential Support Score: 1991 - 42% 1990 - 42%

CRAMER, ROBERT E. (Bud) -- Alabama 5th District [Democrat]. Counties of Colbert, Jackson, Lauderdale, Lawrence, Limestone, Madison and Morgan. Prior Term: 1991-92. Born: August 22, 1947; Huntsville, AL. Education: Rhodes College; University of Alabama (B.A., J.D.). Occupation: Lawyer; law school instructor; Madison County assistant district attorney (1973-75) and district attorney (1981-90); Children's Advocacy Center founder-board president.

1.	Protection to Haitian refugees	N	12.	Req conspiracy-price fixing cases	Y
2.	Raise tax on wealthy; lower others	Y	13.	Unemployment benefits extension	Y
3.	Investigate Reagan hostage delay	N	14.	Tissue use of aborted fetuses	Y
4.	Campaign finance revisions	Y	15.	Bar replacement of union strikers	Y
5.	Unpaid leave to care for children	N	16.	Hold foreign aid at $15b for '92	Y
6.	Restrict NEA use of funds	N	17.	Restore space station funding	Y
7.	Bar race-bias claim/habeas corpus	Y	18.	Civil Rights Act of 1991	Y
8.	Ban race as death sentence factor	Y	19.	Unlimited damages-discrimination	N
9.	Exceptions to exclusionary rule	Y	20.	Eliminate funds for supercollider	N
10.	Allow sale of assault weapons	Y	21.	Terminate SDI except for research	N
11.	Life in prison/abolish death penalty	N	22.	Req 7-day handgun waiting period	N

CRAMER, ROBERT E. (continued)

23. Provide $30b for failed S&Ls	N	24. Allow use of force against Iraq Y

Presidential Support Score: 1991 - 38%

ERDREICH, BEN -- Alabama 6th District [Democrat]. County of Jefferson (pt.). Prior Terms: 1983-92. Born: December 9, 1938; Birmingham, AL. Education: Yale University (B.A.); University of Alabama School of Law (J.D.). Military Service: U.S. Army, 1963-65. Occupation: Attorney; Alabama representative (1970); county commissioner (1974-82).

1. Protection to Haitian refugees	N	55. Raise minimum wage-veto override	Y
2. Raise tax on wealthy; lower others	Y	56. Bar transfer of FS-X technology	Y
3. Investigate Reagan hostage delay	N	57. Cut defense and raise domestic $	N
4. Campaign finance revisions	Y	58. Uniform poll closing in 48 states	N
5. Unpaid leave to care for children	Y	59. Req foreign investment disclosure	Y
6. Restrict NEA use of funds	N	60. Textile import quotas-veto override	Y
7. Bar race-bias claim/habeas corpus	Y	61. Bar abortion funding in Wash, DC	Y
8. Ban race as death sentence factor	Y	62. Notify spouses of AIDS+ carriers	N
9. Exceptions to exclusionary rule	Y	63. Seize conveyance-drug trafficking	Y
10. Allow sale of assault weapons	Y	64. South Africa sanctions	Y
11. Life in prison/abolish death penalty	N	65. 60 days' notice of plant closings	Y
12. Req conspiracy-price fixing cases	Y	66. Close unneeded military bases	Y
13. Unemployment benefits extension	Y	67. Keep welfare reform within $2.8b	Y
14. Tissue use of aborted fetuses	Y	68. Allow children housing exclusion	N
15. Bar replacement of union strikers	Y	69. Shift $400m of NASA to homeless	Y
16. Hold foreign aid at $15b for '92	Y	70. Cap Medicare patients' liability	Y
17. Restore space station funding	Y	71. Prohibit employee polygraph testing	Y
18. Civil Rights Act of 1991	Y	72. Allow CIA to fund Contras	Y
19. Unlimited damages-discrimination	N	73. Revise unfair trade practices	Y
20. Eliminate funds for supercollider	N	74. Focus SDI on accidental launch	Y
21. Terminate SDI except for research	N	75. Bar Air Force $ for MX missile	N
22. Req 7-day handgun waiting period	N	76. Allow "real" increase in defense	Y
23. Provide $30b for failed S&Ls	N	77. Troop reduction in Europe of 50%	Y
24. Allow use of force against Iraq	Y	78. Ban nuclear tests above 1 kiloton	N
25. Allow $15b in foreign aid for '91	Y	79. Ban anti-satellite missile tests	N
26. Revise & extend legal immigration	N	80. Observe certain limits of SALT II	Y
27. Suspend aid to Angolan rebels	N	81. Restore four Civil Rights laws	Y
28. Democratic tax plan proposals	Y	82. Prohibit aliens as strikebreakers	Y
29. Cut defense 5% across the board	N	83. Allow military malpractice suits	Y
30. Textile import quotas-veto override	Y	84. Approval of $36m in Contra aid	Y
31. Abortion service for military abroad	Y	85. $18b deficit reduction compromise	N
32. Limits on high income farmers	N	86. Welfare reform of $5.7b for 5 years	Y
33. Family medical leave-veto override	Y	87. Raise taxes $12b/cut spending $3b	N
34. Req submission of balanced budget	Y	88. Board to assess occupational risk	Y
35. Balanced budget amendment	Y	89. Balanced budget by '93-via targets	Y
36. Amendment to ban flag desecration	Y	90. Bar licensing of two nuclear plants	N
37. Reauthorize Amtrak-veto override	Y	91. Remove victims compensation cap	N
38. Retraining aid for coal miners	Y	92. Catastrophic health insurance	Y
39. Suspend El Salvador military aid	Y	93. Ban airline smoking-2 hours or less	Y
40. Expand child care aid/tax credit	Y	94. $1b/two year aid for the homeless	Y
41. Raise House salary/omit honoraria	N	95. Bar non-unions in union companies	N
42. Toughen oil-spill liability	Y	96. Increase FSLIC rescue to $15b	N
43. Restitution to Japanese interned	N	97. Impose quotas to lower trade deficit	Y
44. Protect Chinese & C.A. nationals	Y	98. Reduce discretionary budget 21%	Y
45. Abortion $ for rape/incest cases	Y	99. Immigration reform/alien amnesty	N
46. Allow religious schools to bar gays	Y	100. South Africa sanctions-veto override	Y
47. Bar broadcaster fairness doctrine	N	101. Tax overhaul to revise income tax	Y
48. Bar cap gains cut/reinstate IRA	N	102. Use of military in drug war	Y
49. Bar unions equal voice in pension	Y	103. Delete 12 MX/add conventional wpn	N
50. Bar assembly of chemical weapons	N	104. Raise speed limit to 65 mph	Y
51. Ban plutonium/uranium production	Y	105. Require Pentagon to buy US goods	Y
52. Cap MX missile deployment at 50	Y	106. AIDS insurance non-discrimination	N
53. Allow $3b for 2 stealth bombers	N	107. Prohibit Saudi arms sales	Y
54. Publish bio-warfare experiments	Y	108. Ease Gun Control Act of 1968	Y

ERDREICH, BEN (continued)

109. Bar interstate handgun transport	N	
110. Make company emissions known	Y	
111. Allow toxic victims to sue in fed ct	N	
112. Superfund waste cleanup of $10b	N	
113. 90 days notice of plant closings	N	
114. $20b in Medicare cuts/tax increases	N	
115. Spending cuts and tax increases	Y	
116. Set school lunch lmt-250% poverty	N	
117. $75m for youth work projects	Y	
118. Allow Angolan military assistance	Y	
119. Suspend defense payments for abuse	N	
120. Drop SS COLAs/$12b tax increase	N	
121. Approve $1.5b for 21 MX missiles	Y	
122. Emergency farm credit/revisions	Y	
123. Duty on Taiwan/Hong Kong/S Korea	Y	
124. Limit steel imports to 17%	Y	
125. Cut $ to schools that bar prayer	Y
126. $50b-taxes; cut Medicare/spending	N
127. Limit Pershing II/cruise in Europe	--
128. Delete $7.1b for 34 B-1 bombers	N
129. Bar purchase of Sergeant York guns	N
130. El Salvador military/economic aid	Y
131. Bar mining of Nicaraguan waters	Y
132. Physician fee freeze for Medicare	N
133. $49b in "sin"/phone/insurance taxes	Y
134. Allow sale of Conrail	N
135. Equal Rights Amendment	Y
136. Authorize Marines in Lebanon	Y
137. Eminent domain for coal companies	N
138. Prohibit EPA clean air sanctions	Y
139. SS retirement age increase/reforms	N

Presidential Support Score: 1991 - 40%   1990 - 37%

HARRIS, CLAUDE -- Alabama 7th District [Democrat]. Counties of Bibb, Chilton, Choctaw, Dallas, Greene, Hale, Jefferson (pt.), Lowndes, Marengo, Perry, St. Clair (pt.), Shelby, Sumter and Tuscaloosa. Prior Terms: 1987-92. Born: June 29, 1940; Bessemer, AL. Education: University of Alabama (B.S., LL.B.). Military Service: Alabama Army National Guard. Occupation: Assistant district attorney (1966-1976); state circuit court judge (1977-1985).

1. Protection to Haitian refugees	N	38. Retraining aid for coal miners	Y
2. Raise tax on wealthy; lower others	Y	39. Suspend El Salvador military aid	Y
3. Investigate Reagan hostage delay	N	40. Expand child care aid/tax credit	Y
4. Campaign finance revisions	Y	41. Raise House salary/omit honoraria	N
5. Unpaid leave to care for children	N	42. Toughen oil-spill liability	Y
6. Restrict NEA use of funds	N	43. Restitution to Japanese interned	N
7. Bar race-bias claim/habeas corpus	Y	44. Protect Chinese & C.A. nationals	Y
8. Ban race as death sentence factor	Y	45. Abortion $ for rape/incest cases	Y
9. Exceptions to exclusionary rule	Y	46. Allow religious schools to bar gays	Y
10. Allow sale of assault weapons	Y	47. Bar broadcaster fairness doctrine	N
11. Life in prison/abolish death penalty	N	48. Bar cap gains cut/reinstate IRA	N
12. Req conspiracy-price fixing cases	Y	49. Bar unions equal voice in pension	Y
13. Unemployment benefits extension	Y	50. Bar assembly of chemical weapons	N
14. Tissue use of aborted fetuses	Y	51. Ban plutonium/uranium production	Y
15. Bar replacement of union strikers	Y	52. Cap MX missile deployment at 50	Y
16. Hold foreign aid at $15b for '92	Y	53. Allow $3b for 2 stealth bombers	N
17. Restore space station funding	Y	54. Publish bio-warfare experiments	Y
18. Civil Rights Act of 1991	Y	55. Raise minimum wage-veto override	Y
19. Unlimited damages-discrimination	N	56. Bar transfer of FS-X technology	Y
20. Eliminate funds for supercollider	N	57. Cut defense and raise domestic $	N
21. Terminate SDI except for research	N	58. Uniform poll closing in 48 states	N
22. Req 7-day handgun waiting period	N	59. Req foreign investment disclosure	Y
23. Provide $30b for failed S&Ls	N	60. Textile import quotas-veto override	Y
24. Allow use of force against Iraq	Y	61. Bar abortion funding in Wash, DC	Y
25. Allow $15b in foreign aid for '91	Y	62. Notify spouses of AIDS+ carriers	N
26. Revise & extend legal immigration	N	63. Seize conveyance-drug trafficking	Y
27. Suspend aid to Angolan rebels	N	64. South Africa sanctions	Y
28. Democratic tax plan proposals	Y	65. 60 days' notice of plant closings	N
29. Cut defense 5% across the board	N	66. Close unneeded military bases	Y
30. Textile import quotas-veto override	Y	67. Keep welfare reform within $2.8b	Y
31. Abortion service for military abroad	N	68. Allow children housing exclusion	N
32. Limits on high income farmers	N	69. Shift $400m of NASA to homeless	N
33. Family medical leave-veto override	N	70. Cap Medicare patients' liability	Y
34. Req submission of balanced budget	Y	71. Prohibit employee polygraph testing	Y
35. Balanced budget amendment	Y	72. Allow CIA to fund Contras	Y
36. Amendment to ban flag desecration	Y	73. Revise unfair trade practices	Y
37. Reauthorize Amtrak-veto override	Y	74. Focus SDI on accidental launch	Y

HARRIS, CLAUDE (continued)

75.	Bar Air Force $ for MX missile	N	87.	Raise taxes $12b/cut spending $3b	N
76.	Allow "real" increase in defense	Y	88.	Board to assess occupational risk	N
77.	Troop reduction in Europe of 50%	Y	89.	Balanced budget by '93-via targets	Y
78.	Ban nuclear tests above 1 kiloton	N	90.	Bar licensing of two nuclear plants	N
79.	Ban anti-satellite missile tests	N	91.	Remove victims compensation cap	N
80.	Observe certain limits of SALT II	N	92.	Catastrophic health insurance	Y
81.	Restore four Civil Rights laws	Y	93.	Ban airline smoking-2 hours or less	N
82.	Prohibit aliens as strikebreakers	Y	94.	$1b/two year aid for the homeless	Y
83.	Allow military malpractice suits	Y	95.	Bar non-unions in union companies	Y
84.	Approval of $36m in Contra aid	Y	96.	Increase FSLIC rescue to $15b	N
85.	$18b deficit reduction compromise	N	97.	Impose quotas to lower trade deficit	Y
86.	Welfare reform of $5.7b for 5 years	Y	98.	Reduce discretionary budget 21%	Y

Presidential Support Score: 1991 - 41%   1990 - 39%

ALASKA

YOUNG, DON -- Representative at Large [Republican]. Prior Terms: 1973 (Special Election)-1992. Born: June 9, 1933; Meridian, CA. Education: Chico State College. Occupation: River boat captain; educator, city councilman; mayor; Alaska representative (1966-70); Alaska senator (1970-73).

1.	Protection to Haitian refugees	N	37.	Reauthorize Amtrak-veto override	N
2.	Raise tax on wealthy; lower others	N	38.	Retraining aid for coal miners	N
3.	Investigate Reagan hostage delay	N	39.	Suspend El Salvador military aid	N
4.	Campaign finance revisions	N	40.	Expand child care aid/tax credit	N
5.	Unpaid leave to care for children	?	41.	Raise House salary/omit honoraria	Y
6.	Restrict NEA use of funds	N	42.	Toughen oil-spill liability	N
7.	Bar race-bias claim/habeas corpus	Y	43.	Restitution to Japanese interned	Y
8.	Ban race as death sentence factor	Y	44.	Protect Chinese & C.A. nationals	N
9.	Exceptions to exclusionary rule	Y	45.	Abortion $ for rape/incest cases	N
10.	Allow sale of assault weapons	Y	46.	Allow religious schools to bar gays	Y
11.	Life in prison/abolish death penalty	N	47.	Bar broadcaster fairness doctrine	N
12.	Req conspiracy-price fixing cases	Y	48.	Bar cap gains cut/reinstate IRA	N
13.	Unemployment benefits extension	Y	49.	Bar unions equal voice in pension	N
14.	Tissue use of aborted fetuses	N	50.	Bar assembly of chemical weapons	N
15.	Bar replacement of union strikers	Y	51.	Ban plutonium/uranium production	N
16.	Hold foreign aid at $15b for '92	Y	52.	Cap MX missile deployment at 50	N
17.	Restore space station funding	Y	53.	Allow $3b for 2 stealth bombers	Y
18.	Civil Rights Act of 1991	N	54.	Publish bio-warfare experiments	N
19.	Unlimited damages-discrimination	N	55.	Raise minimum wage-veto override	N
20.	Eliminate funds for supercollider	N	56.	Bar transfer of FS-X technology	N
21.	Terminate SDI except for research	N	57.	Cut defense and raise domestic $	N
22.	Req 7-day handgun waiting period	N	58.	Uniform poll closing in 48 states	Y
23.	Provide $30b for failed S&Ls	N	59.	Req foreign investment disclosure	N
24.	Allow use of force against Iraq	Y	60.	Textile import quotas-veto override	Y
25.	Allow $15b in foreign aid for '91	Y	61.	Bar abortion funding in Wash, DC	Y
26.	Revise & extend legal immigration	N	62.	Notify spouses of AIDS+ carriers	N
27.	Suspend aid to Angolan rebels	N	63.	Seize conveyance-drug trafficking	N
28.	Democratic tax plan proposals	N	64.	South Africa sanctions	?
29.	Cut defense 5% across the board	N	65.	60 days' notice of plant closings	Y
30.	Textile import quotas-veto override	Y	66.	Close unneeded military bases	N
31.	Abortion service for military abroad	N	67.	Keep welfare reform within $2.8b	Y
32.	Limits on high income farmers	N	68.	Allow children housing exclusion	N
33.	Family medical leave-veto override	Y	69.	Shift $400m of NASA to homeless	N
34.	Req submission of balanced budget	N	70.	Cap Medicare patients' liability	?
35.	Balanced budget amendment	Y	71.	Prohibit employee polygraph testing	?
36.	Amendment to ban flag desecration	Y	72.	Allow CIA to fund Contras	Y

YOUNG, DON (continued)

73.	Revise unfair trade practices	N		
74.	Focus SDI on accidental launch	N		
75.	Bar Air Force $ for MX missile	N		
76.	Allow "real" increase in defense	?		
77.	Troop reduction in Europe of 50%	N		
78.	Ban nuclear tests above 1 kiloton	N		
79.	Ban anti-satellite missile tests	N		
80.	Observe certain limits of SALT II	N		
81.	Restore four Civil Rights laws	Y		
82.	Prohibit aliens as strikebreakers	Y		
83.	Allow military malpractice suits	?		
84.	Approval of $36m in Contra aid	Y		
85.	$18b deficit reduction compromise	N		
86.	Welfare reform of $5.7b for 5 years	N		
87.	Raise taxes $12b/cut spending $3b	X		
88.	Board to assess occupational risk	Y		
89.	Balanced budget by '93-via targets	N		
90.	Bar licensing of two nuclear plants	N		
91.	Remove victims compensation cap	N		
92.	Catastrophic health insurance	Y		
93.	Ban airline smoking-2 hours or less	N		
94.	$1b/two year aid for the homeless	Y		
95.	Bar non-unions in union companies	N		
96.	Increase FSLIC rescue to $15b	Y		
97.	Impose quotas to lower trade deficit	N		
98.	Reduce discretionary budget 21%	Y		
99.	Immigration reform/alien amnesty	N		
100.	South Africa sanctions-veto override	Y		
101.	Tax overhaul to revise income tax	N		
102.	Use of military in drug war	?		
103.	Delete 12 MX/add conventional wpn	N		
104.	Raise speed limit to 65 mph	Y		
105.	Require Pentagon to buy US goods	Y		
106.	AIDS insurance non-discrimination	N		
107.	Prohibit Saudi arms sales	N		
108.	Ease Gun Control Act of 1968	Y		
109.	Bar interstate handgun transport	N		
110.	Make company emissions known	N		
111.	Allow toxic victims to sue in fed ct	N		
112.	Superfund waste cleanup of $10b	N		
113.	90 days notice of plant closings	Y		
114.	$20b in Medicare cuts/tax increases	N		
115.	Spending cuts and tax increases	Y		
116.	Set school lunch lmt-250% poverty	Y		
117.	$75m for youth work projects	Y		
118.	Allow Angolan military assistance	Y		
119.	Suspend defense payments for abuse	N		
120.	Drop SS COLAs/$12b tax increase	N		
121.	Approve $1.5b for 21 MX missiles	Y		
122.	Emergency farm credit/revisions	N		
123.	Duty on Taiwan/Hong Kong/S Korea	?		
124.	Limit steel imports to 17%	N		
125.	Cut $ to schools that bar prayer	Y		
126.	$50b-taxes; cut Medicare/spending	Y		
127.	Limit Pershing II/cruise in Europe	N		
128.	Delete $7.1b for 34 B-1 bombers	N		
129.	Bar purchase of Sergeant York guns	N		
130.	El Salvador military/economic aid	Y		
131.	Bar mining of Nicaraguan waters	Y		
132.	Physician fee freeze for Medicare	Y		
133.	$49b in "sin"/phone/insurance taxes	N		
134.	Allow sale of Conrail	N		
135.	Equal Rights Amendment	Y		
136.	Authorize Marines in Lebanon	Y		
137.	Eminent domain for coal companies	Y		
138.	Prohibit EPA clean air sanctions	?		
139.	SS retirement age increase/reforms	Y		
140.	Auto domestic content requirement	?		
141.	Delete jobs program funding	Y		
142.	Highway-gas tax bill	N		
143.	Cut $5b from defense for Medicare	N		
144.	Emergency housing aid of $1b	N		

Presidential Support Score: 1991 - 66%   1990 - 56%

ARIZONA

RHODES, JOHN J., III -- Arizona 1st District [Republican].   County of Maricopa (pt.).   Prior Terms: 1987-92.   Born: September 8, 1943; Mesa, AZ.   Education: Yale University (B.A.); University of Arizona (J.D.).   Military Service: U.S. Army, 1968-1970.   Occupation: Attorney; member, Mesa Board of Education (1973-1976) and Central Arizona Water Conservation District (1983-1986).

1.	Protection to Haitian refugees	?		
2.	Raise tax on wealthy; lower others	N		
3.	Investigate Reagan hostage delay	N		
4.	Campaign finance revisions	N		
5.	Unpaid leave to care for children	N		
6.	Restrict NEA use of funds	N		
7.	Bar race-bias claim/habeas corpus	Y		
8.	Ban race as death sentence factor	Y		
9.	Exceptions to exclusionary rule	Y		
10.	Allow sale of assault weapons	Y		
11.	Life in prison/abolish death penalty	N		
12.	Req conspiracy-price fixing cases	Y		
13.	Unemployment benefits extension	N		
14.	Tissue use of aborted fetuses	N		
15.	Bar replacement of union strikers	N		
16.	Hold foreign aid at $15b for '92	Y		
17.	Restore space station funding	Y		
18.	Civil Rights Act of 1991	N		
19.	Unlimited damages-discrimination	N		
20.	Eliminate funds for supercollider	N		
21.	Terminate SDI except for research	N		
22.	Req 7-day handgun waiting period	N		

RHODES, JOHN J., III (continued)

23.	Provide $30b for failed S&Ls	Y	61.	Bar abortion funding in Wash, DC	Y
24.	Allow use of force against Iraq	Y	62.	Notify spouses of AIDS+ carriers	Y
25.	Allow $15b in foreign aid for '91	N	63.	Seize conveyance-drug trafficking	Y
26.	Revise & extend legal immigration	Y	64.	South Africa sanctions	N
27.	Suspend aid to Angolan rebels	N	65.	60 days' notice of plant closings	N
28.	Democratic tax plan proposals	N	66.	Close unneeded military bases	Y
29.	Cut defense 5% across the board	N	67.	Keep welfare reform within $2.8b	Y
30.	Textile import quotas-veto override	N	68.	Allow children housing exclusion	Y
31.	Abortion service for military abroad	N	69.	Shift $400m of NASA to homeless	N
32.	Limits on high income farmers	N	70.	Cap Medicare patients' liability	N
33.	Family medical leave-veto override	N	71.	Prohibit employee polygraph testing	N
34.	Req submission of balanced budget	N	72.	Allow CIA to fund Contras	Y
35.	Balanced budget amendment	N	73.	Revise unfair trade practices	N
36.	Amendment to ban flag desecration	Y	74.	Focus SDI on accidental launch	N
37.	Reauthorize Amtrak-veto override	N	75.	Bar Air Force $ for MX missile	N
38.	Retraining aid for coal miners	N	76.	Allow "real" increase in defense	Y
39.	Suspend El Salvador military aid	N	77.	Troop reduction in Europe of 50%	N
40.	Expand child care aid/tax credit	N	78.	Ban nuclear tests above 1 kiloton	N
41.	Raise House salary/omit honoraria	Y	79.	Ban anti-satellite missile tests	N
42.	Toughen oil-spill liability	N	80.	Observe certain limits of SALT II	N
43.	Restitution to Japanese interned	N	81.	Restore four Civil Rights laws	N
44.	Protect Chinese & C.A. nationals	N	82.	Prohibit aliens as strikebreakers	N
45.	Abortion $ for rape/incest cases	N	83.	Allow military malpractice suits	Y
46.	Allow religious schools to bar gays	Y	84.	Approval of $36m in Contra aid	Y
47.	Bar broadcaster fairness doctrine	Y	85.	$18b deficit reduction compromise	Y
48.	Bar cap gains cut/reinstate IRA	N	86.	Welfare reform of $5.7b for 5 years	N
49.	Bar unions equal voice in pension	Y	87.	Raise taxes $12b/cut spending $3b	N
50.	Bar assembly of chemical weapons	N	88.	Board to assess occupational risk	N
51.	Ban plutonium/uranium production	N	89.	Balanced budget by '93-via targets	Y
52.	Cap MX missile deployment at 50	N	90.	Bar licensing of two nuclear plants	N
53.	Allow $3b for 2 stealth bombers	Y	91.	Remove victims compensation cap	N
54.	Publish bio-warfare experiments	N	92.	Catastrophic health insurance	N
55.	Raise minimum wage-veto override	N	93.	Ban airline smoking-2 hours or less	N
56.	Bar transfer of FS-X technology	N	94.	$1b/two year aid for the homeless	N
57.	Cut defense and raise domestic $	N	95.	Bar non-unions in union companies	N
58.	Uniform poll closing in 48 states	Y	96.	Increase FSLIC rescue to $15b	Y
59.	Req foreign investment disclosure	N	97.	Impose quotas to lower trade deficit	N
60.	Textile import quotas-veto override	N	98.	Reduce discretionary budget 21%	N

Presidential Support Score: 1991 - 82%   1990 - 77%

PASTOR, ED -- Arizona 2nd District [Democrat]. Counties of Maricopa (pt.), Pima (pt.), Pinal (pt.), Santa Cruz (pt.) and Yuma (pt.). Prior Term: 1991 (Special Election)-1992. Born: June 28, 1943; Claypool, AZ. Education: Arizona State University (B.A., J.D.). Occupation: High school chemistry teacher; Guadalupe Organization Inc. deputy director; staff member to Governor Castro; Maricopa County supervisor (1977-91).

1.	Protection to Haitian refugees	Y	7.	Bar race-bias claim/habeas corpus	N
2.	Raise tax on wealthy; lower others	Y	8.	Ban race as death sentence factor	N
3.	Investigate Reagan hostage delay	Y	9.	Exceptions to exclusionary rule	N
4.	Campaign finance revisions	Y	10.	Allow sale of assault weapons	N
5.	Unpaid leave to care for children	Y	11.	Life in prison/abolish death penalty	N
6.	Restrict NEA use of funds	N	12.	Req conspiracy-price fixing cases	N

Rep. Pastor was sworn in October 3, 1991 to succeed Morris K. Udall.

Presidential Support Score: 1991 - 33%

STUMP, BOB -- Arizona 3rd District [Republican]. Counties of Coconino, La Paz, Maricopa (pt.), Mohave, Yavapai and Yuma (pt.). Prior Terms: 1977-92. Born: April 4, 1927; Phoenix, AZ. Education: Arizona State University (B.A.). Military Service: WW II. Occupation: Arizona representative (1959-1967); Arizona senator (1967-76).

STUMP, BOB (continued)

1. Protection to Haitian refugees	N
2. Raise tax on wealthy; lower others	N
3. Investigate Reagan hostage delay	N
4. Campaign finance revisions	N
5. Unpaid leave to care for children	N
6. Restrict NEA use of funds	Y
7. Bar race-bias claim/habeas corpus	Y
8. Ban race as death sentence factor	Y
9. Exceptions to exclusionary rule	Y
10. Allow sale of assault weapons	Y
11. Life in prison/abolish death penalty	N
12. Req conspiracy-price fixing cases	Y
13. Unemployment benefits extension	N
14. Tissue use of aborted fetuses	N
15. Bar replacement of union strikers	N
16. Hold foreign aid at $15b for '92	N
17. Restore space station funding	Y
18. Civil Rights Act of 1991	N
19. Unlimited damages-discrimination	N
20. Eliminate funds for supercollider	N
21. Terminate SDI except for research	N
22. Req 7-day handgun waiting period	N
23. Provide $30b for failed S&Ls	N
24. Allow use of force against Iraq	Y
25. Allow $15b in foreign aid for '91	N
26. Revise & extend legal immigration	N
27. Suspend aid to Angolan rebels	N
28. Democratic tax plan proposals	N
29. Cut defense 5% across the board	N
30. Textile import quotas-veto override	N
31. Abortion service for military abroad	N
32. Limits on high income farmers	C
33. Family medical leave-veto override	N
34. Req submission of balanced budget	X
35. Balanced budget amendment	+
36. Amendment to ban flag desecration	Y
37. Reauthorize Amtrak-veto override	N
38. Retraining aid for coal miners	N
39. Suspend El Salvador military aid	N
40. Expand child care aid/tax credit	?
41. Raise House salary/omit honoraria	N
42. Toughen oil-spill liability	N
43. Restitution to Japanese interned	N
44. Protect Chinese & C.A. nationals	N
45. Abortion $ for rape/incest cases	N
46. Allow religious schools to bar gays	Y
47. Bar broadcaster fairness doctrine	Y
48. Bar cap gains cut/reinstate IRA	N
49. Bar unions equal voice in pension	Y
50. Bar assembly of chemical weapons	N
51. Ban plutonium/uranium production	N
52. Cap MX missile deployment at 50	N
53. Allow $3b for 2 stealth bombers	Y
54. Publish bio-warfare experiments	N
55. Raise minimum wage-veto override	N
56. Bar transfer of FS-X technology	N
57. Cut defense and raise domestic $	N
58. Uniform poll closing in 48 states	N
59. Req foreign investment disclosure	N
60. Textile import quotas-veto override	N
61. Bar abortion funding in Wash, DC	Y
62. Notify spouses of AIDS+ carriers	Y
63. Seize conveyance-drug trafficking	Y
64. South Africa sanctions	N

65. 60 days' notice of plant closings	N
66. Close unneeded military bases	Y
67. Keep welfare reform within $2.8b	Y
68. Allow children housing exclusion	Y
69. Shift $400m of NASA to homeless	N
70. Cap Medicare patients' liability	N
71. Prohibit employee polygraph testing	N
72. Allow CIA to fund Contras	Y
73. Revise unfair trade practices	N
74. Focus SDI on accidental launch	N
75. Bar Air Force $ for MX missile	N
76. Allow "real" increase in defense	Y
77. Troop reduction in Europe of 50%	N
78. Ban nuclear tests above 1 kiloton	N
79. Ban anti-satellite missile tests	N
80. Observe certain limits of SALT II	N
81. Restore four Civil Rights laws	N
82. Prohibit aliens as strikebreakers	N
83. Allow military malpractice suits	N
84. Approval of $36m in Contra aid	Y
85. $18b deficit reduction compromise	N
86. Welfare reform of $5.7b for 5 years	N
87. Raise taxes $12b/cut spending $3b	N
88. Board to assess occupational risk	N
89. Balanced budget by '93-via targets	Y
90. Bar licensing of two nuclear plants	N
91. Remove victims compensation cap	N
92. Catastrophic health insurance	N
93. Ban airline smoking-2 hours or less	N
94. $1b/two year aid for the homeless	N
95. Bar non-unions in union companies	N
96. Increase FSLIC rescue to $15b	N
97. Impose quotas to lower trade deficit	N
98. Reduce discretionary budget 21%	Y
99. Immigration reform/alien amnesty	N
100. South Africa sanctions-veto override	N
101. Tax overhaul to revise income tax	Y
102. Use of military in drug war	Y
103. Delete 12 MX/add conventional wpn	N
104. Raise speed limit to 65 mph	Y
105. Require Pentagon to buy US goods	N
106. AIDS insurance non-discrimination	N
107. Prohibit Saudi arms sales	Y
108. Ease Gun Control Act of 1968	Y
109. Bar interstate handgun transport	N
110. Make company emissions known	N
111. Allow toxic victims to sue in fed ct	N
112. Superfund waste cleanup of $10b	N
113. 90 days notice of plant closings	N
114. $20b in Medicare cuts/tax increases	N
115. Spending cuts and tax increases	N
116. Set school lunch lmt-250% poverty	Y
117. $75m for youth work projects	N
118. Allow Angolan military assistance	Y
119. Suspend defense payments for abuse	N
120. Drop SS COLAs/$12b tax increase	Y
121. Approve $1.5b for 21 MX missiles	Y
122. Emergency farm credit/revisions	N
123. Duty on Taiwan/Hong Kong/S Korea	N
124. Limit steel imports to 17%	N
125. Cut $ to schools that bar prayer	?
126. $50b-taxes; cut Medicare/spending	N
127. Limit Pershing II/cruise in Europe	N
128. Delete $7.1b for 34 B-1 bombers	N

STUMP, BOB (continued)

129.	Bar purchase of Sergeant York guns	?		
130.	El Salvador military/economic aid	Y		
131.	Bar mining of Nicaraguan waters	N		
132.	Physician fee freeze for Medicare	Y		
133.	$49b in "sin"/phone/insurance taxes	N		
134.	Allow sale of Conrail	Y		
135.	Equal Rights Amendment	N		
136.	Authorize Marines in Lebanon	Y		
137.	Eminent domain for coal companies	N		
138.	Prohibit EPA clean air sanctions	Y		
139.	SS retirement age increase/reforms	Y		
140.	Auto domestic content requirement	N		
141.	Delete jobs program funding	Y		
142.	Highway-gas tax bill	N		
143.	Cut $5b from defense for Medicare	N		
144.	Emergency housing aid of $1b	N		

Presidential Support Score: 1991 - 78% 1990 - 73%

KYL, JON -- Arizona 4th District [Republican]. Counties of Apache (pt.), Gila, Graham (pt.), Maricopa (pt.), Navajo and Pinal (pt.). Prior Terms: 1987-92. Born: April 25, 1942; Oakland, NE. Education: University of Arizona (B.A., LL.B.). Occupation: Phoenix Metro Chamber of Commerce chairman (1984-1985); attorney, Jennings, Strouss and Salmon.

1.	Protection to Haitian refugees	N	47.	Bar broadcaster fairness doctrine	Y
2.	Raise tax on wealthy; lower others	N	48.	Bar cap gains cut/reinstate IRA	N
3.	Investigate Reagan hostage delay	N	49.	Bar unions equal voice in pension	Y
4.	Campaign finance revisions	N	50.	Bar assembly of chemical weapons	N
5.	Unpaid leave to care for children	N	51.	Ban plutonium/uranium production	N
6.	Restrict NEA use of funds	N	52.	Cap MX missile deployment at 50	N
7.	Bar race-bias claim/habeas corpus	Y	53.	Allow $3b for 2 stealth bombers	Y
8.	Ban race as death sentence factor	Y	54.	Publish bio-warfare experiments	N
9.	Exceptions to exclusionary rule	Y	55.	Raise minimum wage-veto override	N
10.	Allow sale of assault weapons	Y	56.	Bar transfer of FS-X technology	N
11.	Life in prison/abolish death penalty	N	57.	Cut defense and raise domestic $	N
12.	Req conspiracy-price fixing cases	Y	58.	Uniform poll closing in 48 states	N
13.	Unemployment benefits extension	N	59.	Req foreign investment disclosure	N
14.	Tissue use of aborted fetuses	N	60.	Textile import quotas-veto override	N
15.	Bar replacement of union strikers	N	61.	Bar abortion funding in Wash, DC	Y
16.	Hold foreign aid at $15b for '92	Y	62.	Notify spouses of AIDS+ carriers	Y
17.	Restore space station funding	Y	63.	Seize conveyance-drug trafficking	Y
18.	Civil Rights Act of 1991	N	64.	South Africa sanctions	N
19.	Unlimited damages-discrimination	N	65.	60 days' notice of plant closings	N
20.	Eliminate funds for supercollider	N	66.	Close unneeded military bases	Y
21.	Terminate SDI except for research	N	67.	Keep welfare reform within $2.8b	Y
22.	Req 7-day handgun waiting period	N	68.	Allow children housing exclusion	Y
23.	Provide $30b for failed S&Ls	Y	69.	Shift $400m of NASA to homeless	N
24.	Allow use of force against Iraq	Y	70.	Cap Medicare patients' liability	N
25.	Allow $15b in foreign aid for '91	N	71.	Prohibit employee polygraph testing	N
26.	Revise & extend legal immigration	Y	72.	Allow CIA to fund Contras	Y
27.	Suspend aid to Angolan rebels	N	73.	Revise unfair trade practices	N
28.	Democratic tax plan proposals	N	74.	Focus SDI on accidental launch	N
29.	Cut defense 5% across the board	N	75.	Bar Air Force $ for MX missile	N
30.	Textile import quotas-veto override	N	76.	Allow "real" increase in defense	Y
31.	Abortion service for military abroad	N	77.	Troop reduction in Europe of 50%	N
32.	Limits on high income farmers	N	78.	Ban nuclear tests above 1 kiloton	N
33.	Family medical leave-veto override	N	79.	Ban anti-satellite missile tests	N
34.	Req submission of balanced budget	N	80.	Observe certain limits of SALT II	N
35.	Balanced budget amendment	Y	81.	Restore four Civil Rights laws	N
36.	Amendment to ban flag desecration	Y	82.	Prohibit aliens as strikebreakers	N
37.	Reauthorize Amtrak-veto override	N	83.	Allow military malpractice suits	N
38.	Retraining aid for coal miners	N	84.	Approval of $36m in Contra aid	Y
39.	Suspend El Salvador military aid	N	85.	$18b deficit reduction compromise	N
40.	Expand child care aid/tax credit	N	86.	Welfare reform of $5.7b for 5 years	N
41.	Raise House salary/omit honoraria	Y	87.	Raise taxes $12b/cut spending $3b	N
42.	Toughen oil-spill liability	N	88.	Board to assess occupational risk	N
43.	Restitution to Japanese interned	N	89.	Balanced budget by '93-via targets	Y
44.	Protect Chinese & C.A. nationals	N	90.	Bar licensing of two nuclear plants	N
45.	Abortion $ for rape/incest cases	N	91.	Remove victims compensation cap	N
46.	Allow religious schools to bar gays	Y	92.	Catastrophic health insurance	N

KYL, JON (continued)
93. Ban airline smoking-2 hours or less N
94. $1b/two year aid for the homeless N
95. Bar non-unions in union companies N

96. Increase FSLIC rescue to $15b N
97. Impose quotas to lower trade deficit N
98. Reduce discretionary budget 21% N

Presidential Support Score: 1991 - 81% 1990 - 79%

KOLBE, JIM -- Arizona 5th District [Republican]. Counties of Apache (pt.), Cochise, Graham (pt.), Greenlee, Pima (pt.), Pinal (pt.) and Santa Cruz (pt.). Prior Terms: 1985-92. Education: Northwestern University; Stanford University (M.B.A.). Occupation: Professional consultant; Arizona senator.

1. Protection to Haitian refugees	N	53. Allow $3b for 2 stealth bombers	N
2. Raise tax on wealthy; lower others	N	54. Publish bio-warfare experiments	Y
3. Investigate Reagan hostage delay	N	55. Raise minimum wage-veto override	N
4. Campaign finance revisions	N	56. Bar transfer of FS-X technology	N
5. Unpaid leave to care for children	N	57. Cut defense and raise domestic $	N
6. Restrict NEA use of funds	N	58. Uniform poll closing in 48 states	N
7. Bar race-bias claim/habeas corpus	Y	59. Req foreign investment disclosure	N
8. Ban race as death sentence factor	Y	60. Textile import quotas-veto override	N
9. Exceptions to exclusionary rule	Y	61. Bar abortion funding in Wash, DC	Y
10. Allow sale of assault weapons	Y	62. Notify spouses of AIDS+ carriers	N
11. Life in prison/abolish death penalty	N	63. Seize conveyance-drug trafficking	Y
12. Req conspiracy-price fixing cases	Y	64. South Africa sanctions	N
13. Unemployment benefits extension	N	65. 60 days' notice of plant closings	N
14. Tissue use of aborted fetuses	Y	66. Close unneeded military bases	Y
15. Bar replacement of union strikers	N	67. Keep welfare reform within $2.8b	Y
16. Hold foreign aid at $15b for '92	Y	68. Allow children housing exclusion	Y
17. Restore space station funding	N	69. Shift $400m of NASA to homeless	N
18. Civil Rights Act of 1991	N	70. Cap Medicare patients' liability	N
19. Unlimited damages-discrimination	N	71. Prohibit employee polygraph testing	N
20. Eliminate funds for supercollider	Y	72. Allow CIA to fund Contras	Y
21. Terminate SDI except for research	N	73. Revise unfair trade practices	N
22. Req 7-day handgun waiting period	N	74. Focus SDI on accidental launch	N
23. Provide $30b for failed S&Ls	Y	75. Bar Air Force $ for MX missile	N
24. Allow use of force against Iraq	Y	76. Allow "real" increase in defense	Y
25. Allow $15b in foreign aid for '91	Y	77. Troop reduction in Europe of 50%	Y
26. Revise & extend legal immigration	Y	78. Ban nuclear tests above 1 kiloton	N
27. Suspend aid to Angolan rebels	N	79. Ban anti-satellite missile tests	N
28. Democratic tax plan proposals	N	80. Observe certain limits of SALT II	N
29. Cut defense 5% across the board	N	81. Restore four Civil Rights laws	Y
30. Textile import quotas-veto override	N	82. Prohibit aliens as strikebreakers	N
31. Abortion service for military abroad	Y	83. Allow military malpractice suits	?
32. Limits on high income farmers	N	84. Approval of $36m in Contra aid	Y
33. Family medical leave-veto override	N	85. $18b deficit reduction compromise	N
34. Req submission of balanced budget	N	86. Welfare reform of $5.7b for 5 years	N
35. Balanced budget amendment	Y	87. Raise taxes $12b/cut spending $3b	N
36. Amendment to ban flag desecration	N	88. Board to assess occupational risk	N
37. Reauthorize Amtrak-veto override	N	89. Balanced budget by '93-via targets	Y
38. Retraining aid for coal miners	N	90. Bar licensing of two nuclear plants	N
39. Suspend El Salvador military aid	X	91. Remove victims compensation cap	N
40. Expand child care aid/tax credit	N	92. Catastrophic health insurance	N
41. Raise House salary/omit honoraria	Y	93. Ban airline smoking-2 hours or less	Y
42. Toughen oil-spill liability	N	94. $1b/two year aid for the homeless	N
43. Restitution to Japanese interned	Y	95. Bar non-unions in union companies	N
44. Protect Chinese & C.A. nationals	N	96. Increase FSLIC rescue to $15b	N
45. Abortion $ for rape/incest cases	Y	97. Impose quotas to lower trade deficit	N
46. Allow religious schools to bar gays	Y	98. Reduce discretionary budget 21%	Y
47. Bar broadcaster fairness doctrine	Y	99. Immigration reform/alien amnesty	N
48. Bar cap gains cut/reinstate IRA	N	100. South Africa sanctions-veto override	Y
49. Bar unions equal voice in pension	Y	101. Tax overhaul to revise income tax	Y
50. Bar assembly of chemical weapons	N	102. Use of military in drug war	Y
51. Ban plutonium/uranium production	Y	103. Delete 12 MX/add conventional wpn	N
52. Cap MX missile deployment at 50	N	104. Raise speed limit to 65 mph	Y

KOLBE, JIM (continued)

105. Require Pentagon to buy US goods	N	114. $20b in Medicare cuts/tax increases	N
106. AIDS insurance non-discrimination	Y	115. Spending cuts and tax increases	N
107. Prohibit Saudi arms sales	Y	116. Set school lunch lmt-250% poverty	Y
108. Ease Gun Control Act of 1968	Y	117. $75m for youth work projects	N
109. Bar interstate handgun transport	N	118. Allow Angolan military assistance	Y
110. Make company emissions known	Y	119. Suspend defense payments for abuse	N
111. Allow toxic victims to sue in fed ct	N	120. Drop SS COLAs/$12b tax increase	N
112. Superfund waste cleanup of $10b	N	121. Approve $1.5b for 21 MX missiles	Y
113. 90 days notice of plant closings	N	122. Emergency farm credit/revisions	N

Presidential Support Score: 1991 - 76%   1990 - 64%

ARKANSAS

ALEXANDER, BILL -- Arkansas 1st District [Democrat]. Counties of Arkansas, Clay, Cleburne, Craighead, Critenden, Cross, Fulton, Greene, Independence, Izard, Jackson, Lawrence, Lee, Mississippi, Monroe, Phillips, Poinsett, Prairie, Randolph, St. Francis, Sharp, Stone, Van Buren and Woodruff. Prior Terms: 1971-92. Born: January 16, 1934; Memphis, TN. Education: University of Arkansas; Southwestern University (B.A.); Vanderbilt University (LL.B.). Military Service: U.S. Army, 1951-53. Occupation: Legal research assistant; attorney; Arkansas Waterways commissioner; Port Authority secretary; attorney, Mississippi County Urban Renewal Agency.

1. Protection to Haitian refugees	?	35. Balanced budget amendment	N
2. Raise tax on wealthy; lower others	Y	36. Amendment to ban flag desecration	Y
3. Investigate Reagan hostage delay	Y	37. Reauthorize Amtrak-veto override	Y
4. Campaign finance revisions	N	38. Retraining aid for coal miners	?
5. Unpaid leave to care for children	Y	39. Suspend El Salvador military aid	?
6. Restrict NEA use of funds	N	40. Expand child care aid/tax credit	Y
7. Bar race-bias claim/habeas corpus	N	41. Raise House salary/omit honoraria	Y
8. Ban race as death sentence factor	N	42. Toughen oil-spill liability	N
9. Exceptions to exclusionary rule	Y	43. Restitution to Japanese interned	Y
10. Allow sale of assault weapons	Y	44. Protect Chinese & C.A. nationals	Y
11. Life in prison/abolish death penalty	N	45. Abortion $ for rape/incest cases	Y
12. Req conspiracy-price fixing cases	N	46. Allow religious schools to bar gays	Y
13. Unemployment benefits extension	?	47. Bar broadcaster fairness doctrine	N
14. Tissue use of aborted fetuses	Y	48. Bar cap gains cut/reinstate IRA	N
15. Bar replacement of union strikers	Y	49. Bar unions equal voice in pension	N
16. Hold foreign aid at $15b for '92	Y	50. Bar assembly of chemical weapons	N
17. Restore space station funding	N	51. Ban plutonium/uranium production	Y
18. Civil Rights Act of 1991	Y	52. Cap MX missile deployment at 50	N
19. Unlimited damages-discrimination	N	53. Allow $3b for 2 stealth bombers	Y
20. Eliminate funds for supercollider	N	54. Publish bio-warfare experiments	N
21. Terminate SDI except for research	?	55. Raise minimum wage-veto override	Y
22. Req 7-day handgun waiting period	N	56. Bar transfer of FS-X technology	Y
23. Provide $30b for failed S&Ls	Y	57. Cut defense and raise domestic $	Y
24. Allow use of force against Iraq	N	58. Uniform poll closing in 48 states	Y
25. Allow $15b in foreign aid for '91	N	59. Req foreign investment disclosure	Y
26. Revise & extend legal immigration	Y	60. Textile import quotas-veto override	Y
27. Suspend aid to Angolan rebels	Y	61. Bar abortion funding in Wash, DC	Y
28. Democratic tax plan proposals	Y	62. Notify spouses of AIDS+ carriers	N
29. Cut defense 5% across the board	N	63. Seize conveyance-drug trafficking	?
30. Textile import quotas-veto override	Y	64. South Africa sanctions	Y
31. Abortion service for military abroad	Y	65. 60 days' notice of plant closings	Y
32. Limits on high income farmers	N	66. Close unneeded military bases	N
33. Family medical leave-veto override	Y	67. Keep welfare reform within $2.8b	N
34. Req submission of balanced budget	Y	68. Allow children housing exclusion	N

ALEXANDER, BILL (continued)

69. Shift $400m of NASA to homeless	N
70. Cap Medicare patients' liability	Y
71. Prohibit employee polygraph testing	Y
72. Allow CIA to fund Contras	N
73. Revise unfair trade practices	Y
74. Focus SDI on accidental launch	Y
75. Bar Air Force $ for MX missile	N
76. Allow "real" increase in defense	N
77. Troop reduction in Europe of 50%	N
78. Ban nuclear tests above 1 kiloton	Y
79. Ban anti-satellite missile tests	Y
80. Observe certain limits of SALT II	Y
81. Restore four Civil Rights laws	Y
82. Prohibit aliens as strikebreakers	Y
83. Allow military malpractice suits	Y
84. Approval of $36m in Contra aid	N
85. $18b deficit reduction compromise	?
86. Welfare reform of $5.7b for 5 years	Y
87. Raise taxes $12b/cut spending $3b	Y
88. Board to assess occupational risk	Y
89. Balanced budget by '93-via targets	Y
90. Bar licensing of two nuclear plants	N
91. Remove victims compensation cap	?
92. Catastrophic health insurance	Y
93. Ban airline smoking-2 hours or less	Y
94. $1b/two year aid for the homeless	Y
95. Bar non-unions in union companies	Y
96. Increase FSLIC rescue to $15b	N
97. Impose quotas to lower trade deficit	Y
98. Reduce discretionary budget 21%	N
99. Immigration reform/alien amnesty	Y
100. South Africa sanctions-veto override	Y
101. Tax overhaul to revise income tax	Y
102. Use of military in drug war	N
103. Delete 12 MX/add conventional wpn	?
104. Raise speed limit to 65 mph	N
105. Require Pentagon to buy US goods	Y
106. AIDS insurance non-discrimination	Y

107. Prohibit Saudi arms sales	Y
108. Ease Gun Control Act of 1968	Y
109. Bar interstate handgun transport	N
110. Make company emissions known	Y
111. Allow toxic victims to sue in fed ct	Y
112. Superfund waste cleanup of $10b	N
113. 90 days notice of plant closings	Y
114. $20b in Medicare cuts/tax increases	Y
115. Spending cuts and tax increases	Y
116. Set school lunch lmt-250% poverty	N
117. $75m for youth work projects	Y
118. Allow Angolan military assistance	N
119. Suspend defense payments for abuse	N
120. Drop SS COLAs/$12b tax increase	N
121. Approve $1.5b for 21 MX missiles	N
122. Emergency farm credit/revisions	Y
123. Duty on Taiwan/Hong Kong/S Korea	Y
124. Limit steel imports to 17%	Y
125. Cut $ to schools that bar prayer	?
126. $50b-taxes; cut Medicare/spending	Y
127. Limit Pershing II/cruise in Europe	?
128. Delete $7.1b for 34 B-1 bombers	N
129. Bar purchase of Sergeant York guns	N
130. El Salvador military/economic aid	N
131. Bar mining of Nicaraguan waters	Y
132. Physician fee freeze for Medicare	Y
133. $49b in "sin"/phone/insurance taxes	Y
134. Allow sale of Conrail	N
135. Equal Rights Amendment	Y
136. Authorize Marines in Lebanon	Y
137. Eminent domain for coal companies	Y
138. Prohibit EPA clean air sanctions	?
139. SS retirement age increase/reforms	Y
140. Auto domestic content requirement	#
141. Delete jobs program funding	N
142. Highway-gas tax bill	?
143. Cut $5b from defense for Medicare	N
144. Emergency housing aid of $1b	Y

Presidential Support Score: 1991 - 37%   1990 - 27%

THORNTON, RAY -- Arkansas 2nd District [Democrat]. Counties of Conway, Faulkner, Lonoke, Perry, Pulaski, Saline, White and Yell. Prior Terms: 1973-78; 1991-92. Born: July 16, 1928; Conway, AR. Education: Yale University (B.A.); University of Arkansas (J.D.). Military Service: U.S. Navy, 1951-54. Occupation: Lawyer; university professor; state attorney general (1971-73); Lower Mississippi Valley Flood Control Assn. president (1977-78); university joint educational consortium executive director (1979-80); president, Arkansas State University (1980-84) and University of Arkansas (1984-89).

1. Protection to Haitian refugees	Y
2. Raise tax on wealthy; lower others	Y
3. Investigate Reagan hostage delay	Y
4. Campaign finance revisions	Y
5. Unpaid leave to care for children	Y
6. Restrict NEA use of funds	Y
7. Bar race-bias claim/habeas corpus	N
8. Ban race as death sentence factor	N
9. Exceptions to exclusionary rule	Y
10. Allow sale of assault weapons	Y
11. Life in prison/abolish death penalty	N
12. Req conspiracy-price fixing cases	Y

13. Unemployment benefits extension	Y
14. Tissue use of aborted fetuses	Y
15. Bar replacement of union strikers	Y
16. Hold foreign aid at $15b for '92	Y
17. Restore space station funding	Y
18. Civil Rights Act of 1991	Y
19. Unlimited damages-discrimination	Y
20. Eliminate funds for supercollider	N
21. Terminate SDI except for research	N
22. Req 7-day handgun waiting period	N
23. Provide $30b for failed S&Ls	N
24. Allow use of force against Iraq	Y

Presidential Support Score: 1991 - 35%

HAMMERSCHMIDT, JOHN PAUL -- Arkansas 3rd District [Republican]. Counties of Baxter, Benton, Boone, Carroll, Crawford, Franklin, Howard, Johnson, Logan, Madison, Marion, Montgomery, Newton, Polk, Pope, Scott, Searcy, Sebastion, Sevier and Washington. Prior Terms: 1967-92. Born: May 4, 1922; Harrison, AR. Education: The Citadel; Oklahoma A & M College; University of Arkansas. Military Service: U.S. Army Air Corps, WW II; Air Force Reserve. Occupation: Board chairman, Hammerschmidt Lumber Co.; board member, Harrison Federal Savings and Loan Assn.; boardmember, National Lumber and Building Material Dealers; president, Boone County Industrial Development Corp.; chairman, City Planning Commission; Harrison city councilman.

1.	Protection to Haitian refugees	N	55.	Raise minimum wage-veto override	N
2.	Raise tax on wealthy; lower others	N	56.	Bar transfer of FS-X technology	N
3.	Investigate Reagan hostage delay	N	57.	Cut defense and raise domestic $	N
4.	Campaign finance revisions	N	58.	Uniform poll closing in 48 states	N
5.	Unpaid leave to care for children	N	59.	Req foreign investment disclosure	N
6.	Restrict NEA use of funds	Y	60.	Textile import quotas-veto override	Y
7.	Bar race-bias claim/habeas corpus	Y	61.	Bar abortion funding in Wash, DC	Y
8.	Ban race as death sentence factor	Y	62.	Notify spouses of AIDS+ carriers	?
9.	Exceptions to exclusionary rule	Y	63.	Seize conveyance-drug trafficking	N
10.	Allow sale of assault weapons	Y	64.	South Africa sanctions	N
11.	Life in prison/abolish death penalty	N	65.	60 days' notice of plant closings	N
12.	Req conspiracy-price fixing cases	Y	66.	Close unneeded military bases	Y
13.	Unemployment benefits extension	N	67.	Keep welfare reform within $2.8b	Y
14.	Tissue use of aborted fetuses	Y	68.	Allow children housing exclusion	Y
15.	Bar replacement of union strikers	N	69.	Shift $400m of NASA to homeless	N
16.	Hold foreign aid at $15b for '92	?	70.	Cap Medicare patients' liability	Y
17.	Restore space station funding	Y	71.	Prohibit employee polygraph testing	N
18.	Civil Rights Act of 1991	N	72.	Allow CIA to fund Contras	Y
19.	Unlimited damages-discrimination	N	73.	Revise unfair trade practices	N
20.	Eliminate funds for supercollider	N	74.	Focus SDI on accidental launch	N
21.	Terminate SDI except for research	N	75.	Bar Air Force $ for MX missile	N
22.	Req 7-day handgun waiting period	N	76.	Allow "real" increase in defense	Y
23.	Provide $30b for failed S&Ls	Y	77.	Troop reduction in Europe of 50%	N
24.	Allow use of force against Iraq	Y	78.	Ban nuclear tests above 1 kiloton	N
25.	Allow $15b in foreign aid for '91	N	79.	Ban anti-satellite missile tests	N
26.	Revise & extend legal immigration	N	80.	Observe certain limits of SALT II	N
27.	Suspend aid to Angolan rebels	N	81.	Restore four Civil Rights laws	N
28.	Democratic tax plan proposals	N	82.	Prohibit aliens as strikebreakers	Y
29.	Cut defense 5% across the board	N	83.	Allow military malpractice suits	N
30.	Textile import quotas-veto override	Y	84.	Approval of $36m in Contra aid	Y
31.	Abortion service for military abroad	N	85.	$18b deficit reduction compromise	N
32.	Limits on high income farmers	N	86.	Welfare reform of $5.7b for 5 years	N
33.	Family medical leave-veto override	N	87.	Raise taxes $12b/cut spending $3b	N
34.	Req submission of balanced budget	N	88.	Board to assess occupational risk	N
35.	Balanced budget amendment	Y	89.	Balanced budget by '93-via targets	Y
36.	Amendment to ban flag desecration	Y	90.	Bar licensing of two nuclear plants	N
37.	Reauthorize Amtrak-veto override	N	91.	Remove victims compensation cap	N
38.	Retraining aid for coal miners	N	92.	Catastrophic health insurance	Y
39.	Suspend El Salvador military aid	?	93.	Ban airline smoking-2 hours or less	N
40.	Expand child care aid/tax credit	N	94.	$1b/two year aid for the homeless	?
41.	Raise House salary/omit honoraria	Y	95.	Bar non-unions in union companies	N
42.	Toughen oil-spill liability	N	96.	Increase FSLIC rescue to $15b	N
43.	Restitution to Japanese interned	N	97.	Impose quotas to lower trade deficit	N
44.	Protect Chinese & C.A. nationals	N	98.	Reduce discretionary budget 21%	Y
45.	Abortion $ for rape/incest cases	N	99.	Immigration reform/alien amnesty	N
46.	Allow religious schools to bar gays	Y	100.	South Africa sanctions-veto override	N
47.	Bar broadcaster fairness doctrine	Y	101.	Tax overhaul to revise income tax	N
48.	Bar cap gains cut/reinstate IRA	N	102.	Use of military in drug war	Y
49.	Bar unions equal voice in pension	Y	103.	Delete 12 MX/add conventional wpn	N
50.	Bar assembly of chemical weapons	N	104.	Raise speed limit to 65 mph	N
51.	Ban plutonium/uranium production	N	105.	Require Pentagon to buy US goods	N
52.	Cap MX missile deployment at 50	N	106.	AIDS insurance non-discrimination	N
53.	Allow $3b for 2 stealth bombers	Y	107.	Prohibit Saudi arms sales	Y
54.	Publish bio-warfare experiments	Y	108.	Ease Gun Control Act of 1968	Y

HAMMERSCHMIDT, JOHN P. (continued)

109. Bar interstate handgun transport	N	
110. Make company emissions known	N	
111. Allow toxic victims to sue in fed ct	N	
112. Superfund waste cleanup of $10b	N	
113. 90 days notice of plant closings	N	
114. $20b in Medicare cuts/tax increases	Y	
115. Spending cuts and tax increases	N	
116. Set school lunch lmt-250% poverty	N	
117. $75m for youth work projects	N	
118. Allow Angolan military assistance	Y	
119. Suspend defense payments for abuse	N	
120. Drop SS COLAs/$12b tax increase	N	
121. Approve $1.5b for 21 MX missiles	Y	
122. Emergency farm credit/revisions	Y	
123. Duty on Taiwan/Hong Kong/S Korea	N	
124. Limit steel imports to 17%	N	
125. Cut $ to schools that bar prayer	Y	
126. $50b-taxes; cut Medicare/spending	N	
127. Limit Pershing II/cruise in Europe	N
128. Delete $7.1b for 34 B-1 bombers	N
129. Bar purchase of Sergeant York guns	N
130. El Salvador military/economic aid	Y
131. Bar mining of Nicaraguan waters	N
132. Physician fee freeze for Medicare	Y
133. $49b in "sin"/phone/insurance taxes	N
134. Allow sale of Conrail	Y
135. Equal Rights Amendment	N
136. Authorize Marines in Lebanon	Y
137. Eminent domain for coal companies	N
138. Prohibit EPA clean air sanctions	Y
139. SS retirement age increase/reforms	Y
140. Auto domestic content requirement	N
141. Delete jobs program funding	Y
142. Highway-gas tax bill	N
143. Cut $5b from defense for Medicare	N
144. Emergency housing aid of $1b	Y

Presidential Support Score: 1991 - 71%   1990 - 59%

ANTHONY, BERYL, Jr. -- Arkansas 4th District [Democrat]. Counties of Ashley, Bradley, Calhoun, Chicot, Clark, Cleveland, Columbia, Dallas, Desha, Drew, Garland, Grant, Hempstead, Hot Spring, Jefferson, Lafayette, Lincoln, Little River, Miller, Nevada, Ouachita, Pike and Union. Prior Terms: 1979-92. Born: February 21, 1938; El Dorado, AR. Education: University of Arkansas(B.S., B.A., J.D.). Occupation: Attorney; assistant attorney general (1964-65); deputy prosecuting attorney (1966-70); prosecuting attorney (1971-76); legal counsel, Anthony Forest Products Co. (1977).

1. Protection to Haitian refugees	Y	
2. Raise tax on wealthy; lower others	Y	
3. Investigate Reagan hostage delay	N	
4. Campaign finance revisions	N	
5. Unpaid leave to care for children	Y	
6. Restrict NEA use of funds	N	
7. Bar race-bias claim/habeas corpus	N	
8. Ban race as death sentence factor	Y	
9. Exceptions to exclusionary rule	Y	
10. Allow sale of assault weapons	N	
11. Life in prison/abolish death penalty	N	
12. Req conspiracy-price fixing cases	Y	
13. Unemployment benefits extension	Y	
14. Tissue use of aborted fetuses	Y	
15. Bar replacement of union strikers	N	
16. Hold foreign aid at $15b for '92	N	
17. Restore space station funding	N	
18. Civil Rights Act of 1991	Y	
19. Unlimited damages-discrimination	N	
20. Eliminate funds for supercollider	N	
21. Terminate SDI except for research	?	
22. Req 7-day handgun waiting period	Y	
23. Provide $30b for failed S&Ls	Y	
24. Allow use of force against Iraq	N	
25. Allow $15b in foreign aid for '91	Y	
26. Revise & extend legal immigration	Y	
27. Suspend aid to Angolan rebels	Y	
28. Democratic tax plan proposals	Y	
29. Cut defense 5% across the board	N	
30. Textile import quotas-veto override	Y	
31. Abortion service for military abroad	Y	
32. Limits on high income farmers	N	
33. Family medical leave-veto override	Y	
34. Req submission of balanced budget	Y	
35. Balanced budget amendment	Y
36. Amendment to ban flag desecration	N
37. Reauthorize Amtrak-veto override	Y
38. Retraining aid for coal miners	Y
39. Suspend El Salvador military aid	Y
40. Expand child care aid/tax credit	Y
41. Raise House salary/omit honoraria	Y
42. Toughen oil-spill liability	N
43. Restitution to Japanese interned	Y
44. Protect Chinese & C.A. nationals	Y
45. Abortion $ for rape/incest cases	Y
46. Allow religious schools to bar gays	Y
47. Bar broadcaster fairness doctrine	N
48. Bar cap gains cut/reinstate IRA	N
49. Bar unions equal voice in pension	?
50. Bar assembly of chemical weapons	N
51. Ban plutonium/uranium production	?
52. Cap MX missile deployment at 50	Y
53. Allow $3b for 2 stealth bombers	Y
54. Publish bio-warfare experiments	N
55. Raise minimum wage-veto override	Y
56. Bar transfer of FS-X technology	Y
57. Cut defense and raise domestic $	N
58. Uniform poll closing in 48 states	N
59. Req foreign investment disclosure	Y
60. Textile import quotas-veto override	Y
61. Bar abortion funding in Wash, DC	N
62. Notify spouses of AIDS+ carriers	X
63. Seize conveyance-drug trafficking	Y
64. South Africa sanctions	Y
65. 60 days' notice of plant closings	Y
66. Close unneeded military bases	N
67. Keep welfare reform within $2.8b	N
68. Allow children housing exclusion	N

ANTHONY, BERYL, Jr. (continued)

69. Shift $400m of NASA to homeless	N
70. Cap Medicare patients' liability	Y
71. Prohibit employee polygraph testing	?
72. Allow CIA to fund Contras	N
73. Revise unfair trade practices	Y
74. Focus SDI on accidental launch	Y
75. Bar Air Force $ for MX missile	Y
76. Allow "real" increase in defense	N
77. Troop reduction in Europe of 50%	Y
78. Ban nuclear tests above 1 kiloton	Y
79. Ban anti-satellite missile tests	Y
80. Observe certain limits of SALT II	Y
81. Restore four Civil Rights laws	Y
82. Prohibit aliens as strikebreakers	Y
83. Allow military malpractice suits	Y
84. Approval of $36m in Contra aid	N
85. $18b deficit reduction compromise	Y
86. Welfare reform of $5.7b for 5 years	Y
87. Raise taxes $12b/cut spending $3b	Y
88. Board to assess occupational risk	Y
89. Balanced budget by '93-via targets	#
90. Bar licensing of two nuclear plants	N
91. Remove victims compensation cap	N
92. Catastrophic health insurance	Y
93. Ban airline smoking-2 hours or less	N
94. $1b/two year aid for the homeless	Y
95. Bar non-unions in union companies	N
96. Increase FSLIC rescue to $15b	N
97. Impose quotas to lower trade deficit	Y
98. Reduce discretionary budget 21%	Y
99. Immigration reform/alien amnesty	Y
100. South Africa sanctions-veto override	#
101. Tax overhaul to revise income tax	Y
102. Use of military in drug war	N
103. Delete 12 MX/add conventional wpn	Y
104. Raise speed limit to 65 mph	N
105. Require Pentagon to buy US goods	N
106. AIDS insurance non-discrimination	Y

107. Prohibit Saudi arms sales	Y
108. Ease Gun Control Act of 1968	Y
109. Bar interstate handgun transport	Y
110. Make company emissions known	N
111. Allow toxic victims to sue in fed ct	N
112. Superfund waste cleanup of $10b	N
113. 90 days notice of plant closings	N
114. $20b in Medicare cuts/tax increases	Y
115. Spending cuts and tax increases	Y
116. Set school lunch lmt-250% poverty	N
117. $75m for youth work projects	Y
118. Allow Angolan military assistance	Y
119. Suspend defense payments for abuse	N
120. Drop SS COLAs/$12b tax increase	Y
121. Approve $1.5b for 21 MX missiles	N
122. Emergency farm credit/revisions	Y
123. Duty on Taiwan/Hong Kong/S Korea	N
124. Limit steel imports to 17%	N
125. Cut $ to schools that bar prayer	N
126. $50b-taxes; cut Medicare/spending	Y
127. Limit Pershing II/cruise in Europe	X
128. Delete $7.1b for 34 B-1 bombers	N
129. Bar purchase of Sergeant York guns	?
130. El Salvador military/economic aid	N
131. Bar mining of Nicaraguan waters	Y
132. Physician fee freeze for Medicare	N
133. $49b in "sin"/phone/insurance taxes	Y
134. Allow sale of Conrail	N
135. Equal Rights Amendment	+
136. Authorize Marines in Lebanon	Y
137. Eminent domain for coal companies	N
138. Prohibit EPA clean air sanctions	N
139. SS retirement age increase/reforms	Y
140. Auto domestic content requirement	N
141. Delete jobs program funding	N
142. Highway-gas tax bill	Y
143. Cut $5b from defense for Medicare	Y
144. Emergency housing aid of $1b	Y

Presidential Support Score: 1991 - 44% 1990 - 27%

CALIFORNIA

RIGGS, FRANK D. -- California 1st District [Republican]. Counties of Del Norte, Glenn, Humboldt, Mendocino, Sonoma and Trinity. Prior Term: 1991-92. Born: September 5, 1950; Louisville, KY. Education: St. Mary's College; University of Maryland; Golden Gate University (B.A.). Military Service: U.S. Army. Occupation: Police officer; Sonoma County deputy sheriff; military police investigator; owner-president, property development and home building company; independent community bank founder.

1. Protection to Haitian refugees	Y
2. Raise tax on wealthy; lower others	N
3. Investigate Reagan hostage delay	N
4. Campaign finance revisions	N
5. Unpaid leave to care for children	N
6. Restrict NEA use of funds	Y
7. Bar race-bias claim/habeas corpus	Y
8. Ban race as death sentence factor	Y
9. Exceptions to exclusionary rule	Y

10. Allow sale of assault weapons	Y
11. Life in prison/abolish death penalty	N
12. Req conspiracy-price fixing cases	Y
13. Unemployment benefits extension	N
14. Tissue use of aborted fetuses	Y
15. Bar replacement of union strikers	N
16. Hold foreign aid at $15b for '92	Y
17. Restore space station funding	Y
18. Civil Rights Act of 1991	N

RIGGS, FRANK D. (continued)

19.	Unlimited damages-discrimination	N	22.	Req 7-day handgun waiting period	Y
20.	Eliminate funds for supercollider	N	23.	Provide $30b for failed S&Ls	Y
21.	Terminate SDI except for research	N	24.	Allow use of force against Iraq	N

Presidential Support Score: 1991 - 72%

HERGER, WALLY -- California 2nd District [Republican]. Counties of Butte, Colusa, Glenn, Lake (pt.), Napa (pt.), Nevada (pt.), Shasta, Siskiyou, Sutter, Tehoma, Trinity and Yuba. Prior Terms: 1987-92. Born: May 20, 1945; Sutter County, CA. Education: California State University. Occupation: Cattle rancher; propane gas company president and owner; state assemblyman (1980-1986).

1.	Protection to Haitian refugees	?	50.	Bar assembly of chemical weapons	N
2.	Raise tax on wealthy; lower others	N	51.	Ban plutonium/uranium production	N
3.	Investigate Reagan hostage delay	N	52.	Cap MX missile deployment at 50	N
4.	Campaign finance revisions	N	53.	Allow $3b for 2 stealth bombers	Y
5.	Unpaid leave to care for children	N	54.	Publish bio-warfare experiments	N
6.	Restrict NEA use of funds	Y	55.	Raise minimum wage-veto override	N
7.	Bar race-bias claim/habeas corpus	Y	56.	Bar transfer of FS-X technology	Y
8.	Ban race as death sentence factor	Y	57.	Cut defense and raise domestic $	N
9.	Exceptions to exclusionary rule	Y	58.	Uniform poll closing in 48 states	Y
10.	Allow sale of assault weapons	Y	59.	Req foreign investment disclosure	Y
11.	Life in prison/abolish death penalty	N	60.	Textile import quotas-veto override	N
12.	Req conspiracy-price fixing cases	Y	61.	Bar abortion funding in Wash, DC	Y
13.	Unemployment benefits extension	?	62.	Notify spouses of AIDS+ carriers	Y
14.	Tissue use of aborted fetuses	N	63.	Seize conveyance-drug trafficking	Y
15.	Bar replacement of union strikers	N	64.	South Africa sanctions	N
16.	Hold foreign aid at $15b for '92	N	65.	60 days' notice of plant closings	N
17.	Restore space station funding	Y	66.	Close unneeded military bases	Y
18.	Civil Rights Act of 1991	N	67.	Keep welfare reform within $2.8b	Y
19.	Unlimited damages-discrimination	N	68.	Allow children housing exclusion	Y
20.	Eliminate funds for supercollider	Y	69.	Shift $400m of NASA to homeless	N
21.	Terminate SDI except for research	N	70.	Cap Medicare patients' liability	N
22.	Req 7-day handgun waiting period	N	71.	Prohibit employee polygraph testing	N
23.	Provide $30b for failed S&Ls	N	72.	Allow CIA to fund Contras	Y
24.	Allow use of force against Iraq	Y	73.	Revise unfair trade practices	Y
25.	Allow $15b in foreign aid for '91	N	74.	Focus SDI on accidental launch	Y
26.	Revise & extend legal immigration	N	75.	Bar Air Force $ for MX missile	N
27.	Suspend aid to Angolan rebels	N	76.	Allow "real" increase in defense	Y
28.	Democratic tax plan proposals	N	77.	Troop reduction in Europe of 50%	N
29.	Cut defense 5% across the board	Y	78.	Ban nuclear tests above 1 kiloton	N
30.	Textile import quotas-veto override	N	79.	Ban anti-satellite missile tests	N
31.	Abortion service for military abroad	N	80.	Observe certain limits of SALT II	N
32.	Limits on high income farmers	N	81.	Restore four Civil Rights laws	N
33.	Family medical leave-veto override	N	82.	Prohibit aliens as strikebreakers	N
34.	Req submission of balanced budget	N	83.	Allow military malpractice suits	N
35.	Balanced budget amendment	Y	84.	Approval of $36m in Contra aid	Y
36.	Amendment to ban flag desecration	Y	85.	$18b deficit reduction compromise	N
37.	Reauthorize Amtrak-veto override	N	86.	Welfare reform of $5.7b for 5 years	N
38.	Retraining aid for coal miners	Y	87.	Raise taxes $12b/cut spending $3b	N
39.	Suspend El Salvador military aid	N	88.	Board to assess occupational risk	N
40.	Expand child care aid/tax credit	N	89.	Balanced budget by '93-via targets	N
41.	Raise House salary/omit honoraria	N	90.	Bar licensing of two nuclear plants	N
42.	Toughen oil-spill liability	N	91.	Remove victims compensation cap	N
43.	Restitution to Japanese interned	Y	92.	Catastrophic health insurance	N
44.	Protect Chinese & C.A. nationals	N	93.	Ban airline smoking-2 hours or less	N
45.	Abortion $ for rape/incest cases	N	94.	$1b/two year aid for the homeless	N
46.	Allow religious schools to bar gays	Y	95.	Bar non-unions in union companies	N
47.	Bar broadcaster fairness doctrine	N	96.	Increase FSLIC rescue to $15b	N
48.	Bar cap gains cut/reinstate IRA	N	97.	Impose quotas to lower trade deficit	N
49.	Bar unions equal voice in pension	Y	98.	Reduce discretionary budget 21%	Y

Presidential Support Score: 1991 - 68%   1990 - 69%

MATSUI, ROBERT T. -- California 3rd District [Democrat]. County of Sacramento (pt.) Prior Terms: 1979-92. Born: September 17, 1941; Sacramento, CA. Education: University of California (A.B.); Hastings College of Law (J.D.). Occupation: Attorney; city councilman (1971-78); vice mayor (1977).

1. Protection to Haitian refugees	Y		60. Textile import quotas-veto override	N
2. Raise tax on wealthy; lower others	Y		61. Bar abortion funding in Wash, DC	N
3. Investigate Reagan hostage delay	Y		62. Notify spouses of AIDS+ carriers	?
4. Campaign finance revisions	Y		63. Seize conveyance-drug trafficking	N
5. Unpaid leave to care for children	Y		64. South Africa sanctions	Y
6. Restrict NEA use of funds	?		65. 60 days' notice of plant closings	Y
7. Bar race-bias claim/habeas corpus	N		66. Close unneeded military bases	N
8. Ban race as death sentence factor	N		67. Keep welfare reform within $2.8b	N
9. Exceptions to exclusionary rule	?		68. Allow children housing exclusion	N
10. Allow sale of assault weapons	N		69. Shift $400m of NASA to homeless	Y
11. Life in prison/abolish death penalty	N		70. Cap Medicare patients' liability	Y
12. Req conspiracy-price fixing cases	N		71. Prohibit employee polygraph testing	Y
13. Unemployment benefits extension	Y		72. Allow CIA to fund Contras	N
14. Tissue use of aborted fetuses	Y		73. Revise unfair trade practices	Y
15. Bar replacement of union strikers	?		74. Focus SDI on accidental launch	Y
16. Hold foreign aid at $15b for '92	Y		75. Bar Air Force $ for MX missile	Y
17. Restore space station funding	Y		76. Allow "real" increase in defense	N
18. Civil Rights Act of 1991	Y		77. Troop reduction in Europe of 50%	N
19. Unlimited damages-discrimination	Y		78. Ban nuclear tests above 1 kiloton	Y
20. Eliminate funds for supercollider	N		79. Ban anti-satellite missile tests	Y
21. Terminate SDI except for research	Y		80. Observe certain limits of SALT II	Y
22. Req 7-day handgun waiting period	Y		81. Restore four Civil Rights laws	Y
23. Provide $30b for failed S&Ls	N		82. Prohibit aliens as strikebreakers	Y
24. Allow use of force against Iraq	N		83. Allow military malpractice suits	Y
25. Allow $15b in foreign aid for '91	Y		84. Approval of $36m in Contra aid	N
26. Revise & extend legal immigration	Y		85. $18b deficit reduction compromise	Y
27. Suspend aid to Angolan rebels	Y		86. Welfare reform of $5.7b for 5 years	Y
28. Democratic tax plan proposals	Y		87. Raise taxes $12b/cut spending $3b	Y
29. Cut defense 5% across the board	N		88. Board to assess occupational risk	Y
30. Textile import quotas-veto override	Y		89. Balanced budget by '93-via targets	Y
31. Abortion service for military abroad	Y		90. Bar licensing of two nuclear plants	N
32. Limits on high income farmers	N		91. Remove victims compensation cap	Y
33. Family medical leave-veto override	Y		92. Catastrophic health insurance	Y
34. Req submission of balanced budget	Y		93. Ban airline smoking-2 hours or less	Y
35. Balanced budget amendment	N		94. $1b/two year aid for the homeless	Y
36. Amendment to ban flag desecration	N		95. Bar non-unions in union companies	Y
37. Reauthorize Amtrak-veto override	Y		96. Increase FSLIC rescue to $15b	Y
38. Retraining aid for coal miners	Y		97. Impose quotas to lower trade deficit	N
39. Suspend El Salvador military aid	Y		98. Reduce discretionary budget 21%	N
40. Expand child care aid/tax credit	Y		99. Immigration reform/alien amnesty	Y
41. Raise House salary/omit honoraria	Y		100. South Africa sanctions-veto override	Y
42. Toughen oil-spill liability	Y		101. Tax overhaul to revise income tax	Y
43. Restitution to Japanese interned	Y		102. Use of military in drug war	N
44. Protect Chinese & C.A. nationals	Y		103. Delete 12 MX/add conventional wpn	Y
45. Abortion $ for rape/incest cases	Y		104. Raise speed limit to 65 mph	N
46. Allow religious schools to bar gays	N		105. Require Pentagon to buy US goods	N
47. Bar broadcaster fairness doctrine	N		106. AIDS insurance non-discrimination	Y
48. Bar cap gains cut/reinstate IRA	Y		107. Prohibit Saudi arms sales	Y
49. Bar unions equal voice in pension	N		108. Ease Gun Control Act of 1968	N
50. Bar assembly of chemical weapons	Y		109. Bar interstate handgun transport	Y
51. Ban plutonium/uranium production	Y		110. Make company emissions known	Y
52. Cap MX missile deployment at 50	Y		111. Allow toxic victims to sue in fed ct	Y
53. Allow $3b for 2 stealth bombers	N		112. Superfund waste cleanup of $10b	Y
54. Publish bio-warfare experiments	Y		113. 90 days notice of plant closings	Y
55. Raise minimum wage-veto override	Y		114. $20b in Medicare cuts/tax increases	Y
56. Bar transfer of FS-X technology	N		115. Spending cuts and tax increases	Y
57. Cut defense and raise domestic $	Y		116. Set school lunch lmt-250% poverty	N
58. Uniform poll closing in 48 states	Y		117. $75m for youth work projects	Y
59. Req foreign investment disclosure	N		118. Allow Angolan military assistance	N

MATSUI, ROBERT T. (continued)

119. Suspend defense payments for abuse	Y	
120. Drop SS COLAs/$12b tax increase	N	
121. Approve $1.5b for 21 MX missiles	N	
122. Emergency farm credit/revisions	Y	
123. Duty on Taiwan/Hong Kong/S Korea	Y	
124. Limit steel imports to 17%	Y	
125. Cut $ to schools that bar prayer	N	
126. $50b-taxes; cut Medicare/spending	Y	
127. Limit Pershing II/cruise in Europe	Y	
128. Delete $7.1b for 34 B-1 bombers	N	
129. Bar purchase of Sergeant York guns	N	
130. El Salvador military/economic aid	N	
131. Bar mining of Nicaraguan waters	Y	

132. Physician fee freeze for Medicare	N
133. $49b in "sin"/phone/insurance taxes	Y
134. Allow sale of Conrail	N
135. Equal Rights Amendment	Y
136. Authorize Marines in Lebanon	Y
137. Eminent domain for coal companies	N
138. Prohibit EPA clean air sanctions	Y
139. SS retirement age increase/reforms	Y
140. Auto domestic content requirement	Y
141. Delete jobs program funding	N
142. Highway-gas tax bill	Y
143. Cut $5b from defense for Medicare	Y
144. Emergency housing aid of $1b	Y

Presidential Support Score: 1991 - 28% 1990 - 21%

FAZIO, VIC -- California 4th District [Democrat]. Counties of Sacramento (pt), Solano (pt.) and Yolo. Prior Terms: 1979-92. Born: October 11, 1942; Winchester, MA. Education: Union College; California State University. Occupation: Cofounder, *California Journal* magazine; congressional and legislative consultant (1966-75); California assemblyman (1975-78).

1. Protection to Haitian refugees	Y	
2. Raise tax on wealthy; lower others	Y	
3. Investigate Reagan hostage delay	Y	
4. Campaign finance revisions	Y	
5. Unpaid leave to care for children	Y	
6. Restrict NEA use of funds	N	
7. Bar race-bias claim/habeas corpus	N	
8. Ban race as death sentence factor	N	
9. Exceptions to exclusionary rule	N	
10. Allow sale of assault weapons	N	
11. Life in prison/abolish death penalty	Y	
12. Req conspiracy-price fixing cases	N	
13. Unemployment benefits extension	Y	
14. Tissue use of aborted fetuses	Y	
15. Bar replacement of union strikers	Y	
16. Hold foreign aid at $15b for '92	Y	
17. Restore space station funding	Y	
18. Civil Rights Act of 1991	Y	
19. Unlimited damages-discrimination	Y	
20. Eliminate funds for supercollider	N	
21. Terminate SDI except for research	N	
22. Req 7-day handgun waiting period	Y	
23. Provide $30b for failed S&Ls	Y	
24. Allow use of force against Iraq	N	
25. Allow $15b in foreign aid for '91	Y	
26. Revise & extend legal immigration	Y	
27. Suspend aid to Angolan rebels	Y	
28. Democratic tax plan proposals	Y	
29. Cut defense 5% across the board	N	
30. Textile import quotas-veto override	Y	
31. Abortion service for military abroad	Y	
32. Limits on high income farmers	N	
33. Family medical leave-veto override	Y	
34. Req submission of balanced budget	Y	
35. Balanced budget amendment	N	
36. Amendment to ban flag desecration	N	
37. Reauthorize Amtrak-veto override	N	
38. Retraining aid for coal miners	Y	
39. Suspend El Salvador military aid	Y	
40. Expand child care aid/tax credit	Y	
41. Raise House salary/omit honoraria	Y	
42. Toughen oil-spill liability	Y	

43. Restitution to Japanese interned	Y
44. Protect Chinese & C.A. nationals	Y
45. Abortion $ for rape/incest cases	Y
46. Allow religious schools to bar gays	N
47. Bar broadcaster fairness doctrine	N
48. Bar cap gains cut/reinstate IRA	Y
49. Bar unions equal voice in pension	N
50. Bar assembly of chemical weapons	N
51. Ban plutonium/uranium production	Y
52. Cap MX missile deployment at 50	Y
53. Allow $3b for 2 stealth bombers	N
54. Publish bio-warfare experiments	Y
55. Raise minimum wage-veto override	Y
56. Bar transfer of FS-X technology	Y
57. Cut defense and raise domestic $	N
58. Uniform poll closing in 48 states	Y
59. Req foreign investment disclosure	Y
60. Textile import quotas-veto override	Y
61. Bar abortion funding in Wash, DC	N
62. Notify spouses of AIDS+ carriers	N
63. Seize conveyance-drug trafficking	N
64. South Africa sanctions	Y
65. 60 days' notice of plant closings	Y
66. Close unneeded military bases	N
67. Keep welfare reform within $2.8b	N
68. Allow children housing exclusion	N
69. Shift $400m of NASA to homeless	N
70. Cap Medicare patients' liability	Y
71. Prohibit employee polygraph testing	Y
72. Allow CIA to fund Contras	N
73. Revise unfair trade practices	Y
74. Focus SDI on accidental launch	Y
75. Bar Air Force $ for MX missile	N
76. Allow "real" increase in defense	Y
77. Troop reduction in Europe of 50%	?
78. Ban nuclear tests above 1 kiloton	Y
79. Ban anti-satellite missile tests	Y
80. Observe certain limits of SALT II	Y
81. Restore four Civil Rights laws	Y
82. Prohibit aliens as strikebreakers	Y
83. Allow military malpractice suits	?
84. Approval of $36m in Contra aid	N

FAZIO, VIC (continued)

85. $18b deficit reduction compromise	Y	
86. Welfare reform of $5.7b for 5 years	Y	
87. Raise taxes $12b/cut spending $3b	#	
88. Board to assess occupational risk	Y	
89. Balanced budget by '93-via targets	N	
90. Bar licensing of two nuclear plants	N	
91. Remove victims compensation cap	N	
92. Catastrophic health insurance	Y	
93. Ban airline smoking-2 hours or less	Y	
94. $1b/two year aid for the homeless	Y	
95. Bar non-unions in union companies	Y	
96. Increase FSLIC rescue to $15b	N	
97. Impose quotas to lower trade deficit	Y	
98. Reduce discretionary budget 21%	N	
99. Immigration reform/alien amnesty	Y	
100. South Africa sanctions-veto override	Y	
101. Tax overhaul to revise income tax	N	
102. Use of military in drug war	N	
103. Delete 12 MX/add conventional wpn	N	
104. Raise speed limit to 65 mph	Y	
105. Require Pentagon to buy US goods	N	
106. AIDS insurance non-discrimination	Y	
107. Prohibit Saudi arms sales	Y	
108. Ease Gun Control Act of 1968	N	
109. Bar interstate handgun transport	Y	
110. Make company emissions known	Y	
111. Allow toxic victims to sue in fed ct	N	
112. Superfund waste cleanup of $10b	N	
113. 90 days notice of plant closings	Y	
114. $20b in Medicare cuts/tax increases	Y	

115. Spending cuts and tax increases	Y	
116. Set school lunch lmt-250% poverty	N	
117. $75m for youth work projects	#	
118. Allow Angolan military assistance	N	
119. Suspend defense payments for abuse	N	
120. Drop SS COLAs/$12b tax increase	Y	
121. Approve $1.5b for 21 MX missiles	Y	
122. Emergency farm credit/revisions	Y	
123. Duty on Taiwan/Hong Kong/S Korea	Y	
124. Limit steel imports to 17%	Y	
125. Cut $ to schools that bar prayer	N	
126. $50b-taxes; cut Medicare/spending	Y	
127. Limit Pershing II/cruise in Europe	N	
128. Delete $7.1b for 34 B-1 bombers	Y	
129. Bar purchase of Sergeant York guns	Y	
130. El Salvador military/economic aid	N	
131. Bar mining of Nicaraguan waters	Y	
132. Physician fee freeze for Medicare	N	
133. $49b in "sin"/phone/insurance taxes	Y	
134. Allow sale of Conrail	N	
135. Equal Rights Amendment	Y	
136. Authorize Marines in Lebanon	Y	
137. Eminent domain for coal companies	N	
138. Prohibit EPA clean air sanctions	Y	
139. SS retirement age increase/reforms	N	
140. Auto domestic content requirement	Y	
141. Delete jobs program funding	N	
142. Highway-gas tax bill	Y	
143. Cut $5b from defense for Medicare	Y	
144. Emergency housing aid of $1b	Y	

Presidential Support Score: 1991 - 34%   1990 - 19%

PELOSI, NANCY P. -- California 5th District [Democrat]. City and County of San Francisco (pt.). Prior Terms: 1987 (Special Election)-1992. Birthplace: Baltimore, MD. Education: Trinity College. Occupation: Member, Democratic National Committee; Chair, California Democratic Party and 1984 Democratic National Convention Host Committee; Finance Chair, Democratic Senatorial Campaign Committee.

1. Protection to Haitian refugees	Y	
2. Raise tax on wealthy; lower others	Y	
3. Investigate Reagan hostage delay	Y	
4. Campaign finance revisions	Y	
5. Unpaid leave to care for children	Y	
6. Restrict NEA use of funds	N	
7. Bar race-bias claim/habeas corpus	N	
8. Ban race as death sentence factor	N	
9. Exceptions to exclusionary rule	N	
10. Allow sale of assault weapons	N	
11. Life in prison/abolish death penalty	Y	
12. Req conspiracy-price fixing cases	N	
13. Unemployment benefits extension	Y	
14. Tissue use of aborted fetuses	Y	
15. Bar replacement of union strikers	Y	
16. Hold foreign aid at $15b for '92	Y	
17. Restore space station funding	N	
18. Civil Rights Act of 1991	Y	
19. Unlimited damages-discrimination	Y	
20. Eliminate funds for supercollider	N	
21. Terminate SDI except for research	Y	
22. Req 7-day handgun waiting period	Y	
23. Provide $30b for failed S&Ls	Y	
24. Allow use of force against Iraq	N	

25. Allow $15b in foreign aid for '91	Y	
26. Revise & extend legal immigration	Y	
27. Suspend aid to Angolan rebels	Y	
28. Democratic tax plan proposals	Y	
29. Cut defense 5% across the board	Y	
30. Textile import quotas-veto override	N	
31. Abortion service for military abroad	Y	
32. Limits on high income farmers	Y	
33. Family medical leave-veto override	Y	
34. Req submission of balanced budget	Y	
35. Balanced budget amendment	N	
36. Amendment to ban flag desecration	N	
37. Reauthorize Amtrak-veto override	Y	
38. Retraining aid for coal miners	Y	
39. Suspend El Salvador military aid	Y	
40. Expand child care aid/tax credit	Y	
41. Raise House salary/omit honoraria	Y	
42. Toughen oil-spill liability	Y	
43. Restitution to Japanese interned	Y	
44. Protect Chinese & C.A. nationals	Y	
45. Abortion $ for rape/incest cases	Y	
46. Allow religious schools to bar gays	N	
47. Bar broadcaster fairness doctrine	N	
48. Bar cap gains cut/reinstate IRA	Y	

PELOSI, NANCY P. (continued)

49. Bar unions equal voice in pension	N	
50. Bar assembly of chemical weapons	Y	
51. Ban plutonium/uranium production	Y	
52. Cap MX missile deployment at 50	Y	
53. Allow $3b for 2 stealth bombers	N	
54. Publish bio-warfare experiments	Y	
55. Raise minimum wage-veto override	Y	
56. Bar transfer of FS-X technology	Y	
57. Cut defense and raise domestic $	Y	
58. Uniform poll closing in 48 states	Y	
59. Req foreign investment disclosure	Y	
60. Textile import quotas-veto override	N	
61. Bar abortion funding in Wash, DC	N	
62. Notify spouses of AIDS+ carriers	N	
63. Seize conveyance-drug trafficking	N	
64. South Africa sanctions	Y	
65. 60 days' notice of plant closings	Y	
66. Close unneeded military bases	N	
67. Keep welfare reform within $2.8b	N	
68. Allow children housing exclusion	N	
69. Shift $400m of NASA to homeless	Y	
70. Cap Medicare patients' liability	Y	
71. Prohibit employee polygraph testing	Y	
72. Allow CIA to fund Contras	N	

73. Revise unfair trade practices	Y	
74. Focus SDI on accidental launch	Y	
75. Bar Air Force $ for MX missile	Y	
76. Allow "real" increase in defense	N	
77. Troop reduction in Europe of 50%	Y	
78. Ban nuclear tests above 1 kiloton	Y	
79. Ban anti-satellite missile tests	Y	
80. Observe certain limits of SALT II	Y	
81. Restore four Civil Rights laws	Y	
82. Prohibit aliens as strikebreakers	Y	
83. Allow military malpractice suits	Y	
84. Approval of $36m in Contra aid	N	
85. $18b deficit reduction compromise	Y	
86. Welfare reform of $5.7b for 5 years	Y	
87. Raise taxes $12b/cut spending $3b	Y	
88. Board to assess occupational risk	Y	
89. Balanced budget by '93-via targets	N	
90. Bar licensing of two nuclear plants	Y	
91. Remove victims compensation cap	Y	
92. Catastrophic health insurance	Y	
93. Ban airline smoking-2 hours or less	Y	
94. $1b/two year aid for the homeless	Y	
95. Bar non-unions in union companies	Y	

Presidential Support Score: 1991 - 24%   1990 - 15%

BOXER, BARBARA -- California 6th District [Democrat]. Counties of Marin, San Francisco (pt.), San Mateo (pt.) and Solano (pt.). Prior Terms: 1983-92. Born: November 11, 1940; Brooklyn, NY. Education: Brooklyn College (B.A.). Occupation: Stockbroker and economic researcher (1962-65); journalist and associate editor (1972-74); congressional aid (1974-76); member, Marin County Board of Supervisors (1976-82).

1. Protection to Haitian refugees	Y	
2. Raise tax on wealthy; lower others	Y	
3. Investigate Reagan hostage delay	Y	
4. Campaign finance revisions	Y	
5. Unpaid leave to care for children	Y	
6. Restrict NEA use of funds	X	
7. Bar race-bias claim/habeas corpus	N	
8. Ban race as death sentence factor	N	
9. Exceptions to exclusionary rule	?	
10. Allow sale of assault weapons	N	
11. Life in prison/abolish death penalty	N	
12. Req conspiracy-price fixing cases	?	
13. Unemployment benefits extension	Y	
14. Tissue use of aborted fetuses	Y	
15. Bar replacement of union strikers	Y	
16. Hold foreign aid at $15b for '92	Y	
17. Restore space station funding	N	
18. Civil Rights Act of 1991	Y	
19. Unlimited damages-discrimination	Y	
20. Eliminate funds for supercollider	Y	
21. Terminate SDI except for research	Y	
22. Req 7-day handgun waiting period	Y	
23. Provide $30b for failed S&Ls	N	
24. Allow use of force against Iraq	N	
25. Allow $15b in foreign aid for '91	#	
26. Revise & extend legal immigration	?	
27. Suspend aid to Angolan rebels	Y	
28. Democratic tax plan proposals	Y	
29. Cut defense 5% across the board	Y	
30. Textile import quotas-veto override	N	

31. Abortion service for military abroad	Y	
32. Limits on high income farmers	N	
33. Family medical leave-veto override	Y	
34. Req submission of balanced budget	N	
35. Balanced budget amendment	N	
36. Amendment to ban flag desecration	N	
37. Reauthorize Amtrak-veto override	?	
38. Retraining aid for coal miners	Y	
39. Suspend El Salvador military aid	Y	
40. Expand child care aid/tax credit	Y	
41. Raise House salary/omit honoraria	Y	
42. Toughen oil-spill liability	Y	
43. Restitution to Japanese interned	Y	
44. Protect Chinese & C.A. nationals	Y	
45. Abortion $ for rape/incest cases	Y	
46. Allow religious schools to bar gays	N	
47. Bar broadcaster fairness doctrine	N	
48. Bar cap gains cut/reinstate IRA	Y	
49. Bar unions equal voice in pension	N	
50. Bar assembly of chemical weapons	Y	
51. Ban plutonium/uranium production	Y	
52. Cap MX missile deployment at 50	Y	
53. Allow $3b for 2 stealth bombers	N	
54. Publish bio-warfare experiments	Y	
55. Raise minimum wage-veto override	Y	
56. Bar transfer of FS-X technology	Y	
57. Cut defense and raise domestic $	Y	
58. Uniform poll closing in 48 states	Y	
59. Req foreign investment disclosure	Y	
60. Textile import quotas-veto override	N	

BOXER, BARBARA (continued)

61. Bar abortion funding in Wash, DC	N	
62. Notify spouses of AIDS+ carriers	N	
63. Seize conveyance-drug trafficking	N	
64. South Africa sanctions	#	
65. 60 days' notice of plant closings	Y	
66. Close unneeded military bases	?	
67. Keep welfare reform within $2.8b	N	
68. Allow children housing exclusion	N	
69. Shift $400m of NASA to homeless	Y	
70. Cap Medicare patients' liability	Y	
71. Prohibit employee polygraph testing	Y	
72. Allow CIA to fund Contras	N	
73. Revise unfair trade practices	Y	
74. Focus SDI on accidental launch	Y	
75. Bar Air Force $ for MX missile	Y	
76. Allow "real" increase in defense	N	
77. Troop reduction in Europe of 50%	Y	
78. Ban nuclear tests above 1 kiloton	Y	
79. Ban anti-satellite missile tests	Y	
80. Observe certain limits of SALT II	Y	
81. Restore four Civil Rights laws	Y	
82. Prohibit aliens as strikebreakers	Y	
83. Allow military malpractice suits	Y	
84. Approval of $36m in Contra aid	N	
85. $18b deficit reduction compromise	Y	
86. Welfare reform of $5.7b for 5 years	Y	
87. Raise taxes $12b/cut spending $3b	Y	
88. Board to assess occupational risk	Y	
89. Balanced budget by '93-via targets	?	
90. Bar licensing of two nuclear plants	Y	
91. Remove victims compensation cap	Y	
92. Catastrophic health insurance	Y	
93. Ban airline smoking-2 hours or less	Y	
94. $1b/two year aid for the homeless	Y	
95. Bar non-unions in union companies	Y	
96. Increase FSLIC rescue to $15b	N	
97. Impose quotas to lower trade deficit	Y	
98. Reduce discretionary budget 21%	Y	
99. Immigration reform/alien amnesty	Y	
100. South Africa sanctions-veto override	Y	

101. Tax overhaul to revise income tax	Y
102. Use of military in drug war	N
103. Delete 12 MX/add conventional wpn	Y
104. Raise speed limit to 65 mph	N
105. Require Pentagon to buy US goods	Y
106. AIDS insurance non-discrimination	Y
107. Prohibit Saudi arms sales	Y
108. Ease Gun Control Act of 1968	N
109. Bar interstate handgun transport	Y
110. Make company emissions known	Y
111. Allow toxic victims to sue in fed ct	Y
112. Superfund waste cleanup of $10b	Y
113. 90 days notice of plant closings	Y
114. $20b in Medicare cuts/tax increases	Y
115. Spending cuts and tax increases	Y
116. Set school lunch lmt-250% poverty	N
117. $75m for youth work projects	?
118. Allow Angolan military assistance	N
119. Suspend defense payments for abuse	Y
120. Drop SS COLAs/$12b tax increase	N
121. Approve $1.5b for 21 MX missiles	N
122. Emergency farm credit/revisions	Y
123. Duty on Taiwan/Hong Kong/S Korea	Y
124. Limit steel imports to 17%	Y
125. Cut $ to schools that bar prayer	N
126. $50b-taxes; cut Medicare/spending	Y
127. Limit Pershing II/cruise in Europe	Y
128. Delete $7.1b for 34 B-1 bombers	Y
129. Bar purchase of Sergeant York guns	?
130. El Salvador military/economic aid	N
131. Bar mining of Nicaraguan waters	Y
132. Physician fee freeze for Medicare	N
133. $49b in "sin"/phone/insurance taxes	Y
134. Allow sale of Conrail	N
135. Equal Rights Amendment	Y
136. Authorize Marines in Lebanon	N
137. Eminent domain for coal companies	N
138. Prohibit EPA clean air sanctions	Y
139. SS retirement age increase/reforms	N

Presidential Support Score: 1991 - 21%   1990 - 14%

MILLER, GEORGE -- California 7th District [Democrat]. County of Contra Costa (pt.). **Prior** Terms: 1975-92. Born: May 17, 1945; Richmond, CA. Education: Diablo Valley College; San Francisco State College; University of California Law School (J.D.). Occupation: Attorney; senator's legislative assistant.

1. Protection to Haitian refugees	Y	
2. Raise tax on wealthy; lower others	Y	
3. Investigate Reagan hostage delay	Y	
4. Campaign finance revisions	Y	
5. Unpaid leave to care for children	Y	
6. Restrict NEA use of funds	N	
7. Bar race-bias claim/habeas corpus	N	
8. Ban race as death sentence factor	N	
9. Exceptions to exclusionary rule	N	
10. Allow sale of assault weapons	N	
11. Life in prison/abolish death penalty	Y	
12. Req conspiracy-price fixing cases	N	
13. Unemployment benefits extension	Y	
14. Tissue use of aborted fetuses	Y	
15. Bar replacement of union strikers	Y	

16. Hold foreign aid at $15b for '92	Y
17. Restore space station funding	N
18. Civil Rights Act of 1991	Y
19. Unlimited damages-discrimination	Y
20. Eliminate funds for supercollider	Y
21. Terminate SDI except for research	Y
22. Req 7-day handgun waiting period	Y
23. Provide $30b for failed S&Ls	N
24. Allow use of force against Iraq	N
25. Allow $15b in foreign aid for '91	N
26. Revise & extend legal immigration	Y
27. Suspend aid to Angolan rebels	Y
28. Democratic tax plan proposals	Y
29. Cut defense 5% across the board	Y
30. Textile import quotas-veto override	N

MILLER, GEORGE (continued)

31. Abortion service for military abroad	Y	
32. Limits on high income farmers	Y	
33. Family medical leave-veto override	Y	
34. Req submission of balanced budget	Y	
35. Balanced budget amendment	N	
36. Amendment to ban flag desecration	N	
37. Reauthorize Amtrak-veto override	Y	
38. Retraining aid for coal miners	Y	
39. Suspend El Salvador military aid	Y	
40. Expand child care aid/tax credit	Y	
41. Raise House salary/omit honoraria	Y	
42. Toughen oil-spill liability	Y	
43. Restitution to Japanese interned	Y	
44. Protect Chinese & C.A. nationals	Y	
45. Abortion $ for rape/incest cases	Y	
46. Allow religious schools to bar gays	N	
47. Bar broadcaster fairness doctrine	N	
48. Bar cap gains cut/reinstate IRA	Y	
49. Bar unions equal voice in pension	N	
50. Bar assembly of chemical weapons	Y	
51. Ban plutonium/uranium production	Y	
52. Cap MX missile deployment at 50	Y	
53. Allow $3b for 2 stealth bombers	N	
54. Publish bio-warfare experiments	?	
55. Raise minimum wage-veto override	Y	
56. Bar transfer of FS-X technology	Y	
57. Cut defense and raise domestic $	Y	
58. Uniform poll closing in 48 states	#	
59. Req foreign investment disclosure	Y	
60. Textile import quotas-veto override	N	
61. Bar abortion funding in Wash, DC	N	
62. Notify spouses of AIDS+ carriers	N	
63. Seize conveyance-drug trafficking	N	
64. South Africa sanctions	Y	
65. 60 days' notice of plant closings	Y	
66. Close unneeded military bases	Y	
67. Keep welfare reform within $2.8b	N	
68. Allow children housing exclusion	N	
69. Shift $400m of NASA to homeless	Y	
70. Cap Medicare patients' liability	Y	
71. Prohibit employee polygraph testing	Y	
72. Allow CIA to fund Contras	N	
73. Revise unfair trade practices	Y	
74. Focus SDI on accidental launch	Y	
75. Bar Air Force $ for MX missile	Y	
76. Allow "real" increase in defense	N	
77. Troop reduction in Europe of 50%	?	
78. Ban nuclear tests above 1 kiloton	Y	
79. Ban anti-satellite missile tests	Y	
80. Observe certain limits of SALT II	Y	
81. Restore four Civil Rights laws	Y	
82. Prohibit aliens as strikebreakers	Y	
83. Allow military malpractice suits	Y	
84. Approval of $36m in Contra aid	N	
85. $18b deficit reduction compromise	Y	
86. Welfare reform of $5.7b for 5 years	Y	
87. Raise taxes $12b/cut spending $3b	N	

88. Board to assess occupational risk	Y	
89. Balanced budget by '93-via targets	N	
90. Bar licensing of two nuclear plants	Y	
91. Remove victims compensation cap	Y	
92. Catastrophic health insurance	Y	
93. Ban airline smoking-2 hours or less	Y	
94. $1b/two year aid for the homeless	Y	
95. Bar non-unions in union companies	Y	
96. Increase FSLIC rescue to $15b	N	
97. Impose quotas to lower trade deficit	N	
98. Reduce discretionary budget 21%	Y	
99. Immigration reform/alien amnesty	Y	
100. South Africa sanctions-veto override	?	
101. Tax overhaul to revise income tax	Y	
102. Use of military in drug war	N	
103. Delete 12 MX/add conventional wpn	#	
104. Raise speed limit to 65 mph	Y	
105. Require Pentagon to buy US goods	Y	
106. AIDS insurance non-discrimination	Y	
107. Prohibit Saudi arms sales	Y	
108. Ease Gun Control Act of 1968	N	
109. Bar interstate handgun transport	Y	
110. Make company emissions known	Y	
111. Allow toxic victims to sue in fed ct	Y	
112. Superfund waste cleanup of $10b	N	
113. 90 days notice of plant closings	Y	
114. $20b in Medicare cuts/tax increases	Y	
115. Spending cuts and tax increases	Y	
116. Set school lunch lmt-250% poverty	N	
117. $75m for youth work projects	?	
118. Allow Angolan military assistance	N	
119. Suspend defense payments for abuse	Y	
120. Drop SS COLAs/$12b tax increase	N	
121. Approve $1.5b for 21 MX missiles	N	
122. Emergency farm credit/revisions	Y	
123. Duty on Taiwan/Hong Kong/S Korea	Y	
124. Limit steel imports to 17%	N	
125. Cut $ to schools that bar prayer	N	
126. $50b-taxes; cut Medicare/spending	N	
127. Limit Pershing II/cruise in Europe	Y	
128. Delete $7.1b for 34 B-1 bombers	Y	
129. Bar purchase of Sergeant York guns	Y	
130. El Salvador military/economic aid	N	
131. Bar mining of Nicaraguan waters	Y	
132. Physician fee freeze for Medicare	N	
133. $49b in "sin"/phone/insurance taxes	Y	
134. Allow sale of Conrail	N	
135. Equal Rights Amendment	Y	
136. Authorize Marines in Lebanon	N	
137. Eminent domain for coal companies	N	
138. Prohibit EPA clean air sanctions	Y	
139. SS retirement age increase/reforms	N	
140. Auto domestic content requirement	Y	
141. Delete jobs program funding	N	
142. Highway-gas tax bill	Y	
143. Cut $5b from defense for Medicare	Y	
144. Emergency housing aid of $1b	Y	

Presidential Support Score: 1991 - 23%   1990 - 16%

DELLUMS, RONALD V. -- California 8th District [Democrat]. Counties of Alameda (pt.) and Contra Costa (pt.).   Prior Terms: 1971-92.   Born: November 24, 1935; Oakland, CA. Education: San Francisco State College (B.S.); University of California (M.S.W.).   Military

DELLUMS, RONALD V. (continued)

Service: U.S. Marine Corps. Occupation: Senior consultant, Social Dynamics, Inc.; city councilman (1967-71); psychiatric social worker (1962-64); associate director and director, Hunter's Point Youth Opportunities Center (1965-66); planning consultant (1966-67); director, Concentrated Employment Program (1967-68); lecturer.

1. Protection to Haitian refugees	Y	
2. Raise tax on wealthy; lower others	N	
3. Investigate Reagan hostage delay	Y	
4. Campaign finance revisions	Y	
5. Unpaid leave to care for children	Y	
6. Restrict NEA use of funds	N	
7. Bar race-bias claim/habeas corpus	X	
8. Ban race as death sentence factor	X	
9. Exceptions to exclusionary rule	N	
10. Allow sale of assault weapons	N	
11. Life in prison/abolish death penalty	Y	
12. Req conspiracy-price fixing cases	N	
13. Unemployment benefits extension	Y	
14. Tissue use of aborted fetuses	Y	
15. Bar replacement of union strikers	Y	
16. Hold foreign aid at $15b for '92	Y	
17. Restore space station funding	N	
18. Civil Rights Act of 1991	Y	
19. Unlimited damages-discrimination	Y	
20. Eliminate funds for supercollider	N	
21. Terminate SDI except for research	Y	
22. Req 7-day handgun waiting period	Y	
23. Provide $30b for failed S&Ls	N	
24. Allow use of force against Iraq	N	
25. Allow $15b in foreign aid for '91	N	
26. Revise & extend legal immigration	Y	
27. Suspend aid to Angolan rebels	Y	
28. Democratic tax plan proposals	Y	
29. Cut defense 5% across the board	Y	
30. Textile import quotas-veto override	Y	
31. Abortion service for military abroad	Y	
32. Limits on high income farmers	Y	
33. Family medical leave-veto override	Y	
34. Req submission of balanced budget	N	
35. Balanced budget amendment	N	
36. Amendment to ban flag desecration	N	
37. Reauthorize Amtrak-veto override	Y	
38. Retraining aid for coal miners	Y	
39. Suspend El Salvador military aid	Y	
40. Expand child care aid/tax credit	N	
41. Raise House salary/omit honoraria	Y	
42. Toughen oil-spill liability	Y	
43. Restitution to Japanese interned	Y	
44. Protect Chinese & C.A. nationals	Y	
45. Abortion $ for rape/incest cases	Y	
46. Allow religious schools to bar gays	N	
47. Bar broadcaster fairness doctrine	N	
48. Bar cap gains cut/reinstate IRA	Y	
49. Bar unions equal voice in pension	N	
50. Bar assembly of chemical weapons	Y	
51. Ban plutonium/uranium production	Y	
52. Cap MX missile deployment at 50	Y	
53. Allow $3b for 2 stealth bombers	N	
54. Publish bio-warfare experiments	Y	
55. Raise minimum wage-veto override	Y	
56. Bar transfer of FS-X technology	Y	
57. Cut defense and raise domestic $	Y	
58. Uniform poll closing in 48 states	Y	
59. Req foreign investment disclosure	Y	
60. Textile import quotas-veto override	Y	
61. Bar abortion funding in Wash, DC	N	
62. Notify spouses of AIDS+ carriers	N	
63. Seize conveyance-drug trafficking	N	
64. South Africa sanctions	Y	
65. 60 days' notice of plant closings	Y	
66. Close unneeded military bases	Y	
67. Keep welfare reform within $2.8b	N	
68. Allow children housing exclusion	?	
69. Shift $400m of NASA to homeless	Y	
70. Cap Medicare patients' liability	Y	
71. Prohibit employee polygraph testing	Y	
72. Allow CIA to fund Contras	N	
73. Revise unfair trade practices	Y	
74. Focus SDI on accidental launch	N	
75. Bar Air Force $ for MX missile	Y	
76. Allow "real" increase in defense	N	
77. Troop reduction in Europe of 50%	Y	
78. Ban nuclear tests above 1 kiloton	Y	
79. Ban anti-satellite missile tests	Y	
80. Observe certain limits of SALT II	Y	
81. Restore four Civil Rights laws	Y	
82. Prohibit aliens as strikebreakers	Y	
83. Allow military malpractice suits	Y	
84. Approval of $36m in Contra aid	N	
85. $18b deficit reduction compromise	Y	
86. Welfare reform of $5.7b for 5 years	Y	
87. Raise taxes $12b/cut spending $3b	Y	
88. Board to assess occupational risk	Y	
89. Balanced budget by '93-via targets	N	
90. Bar licensing of two nuclear plants	Y	
91. Remove victims compensation cap	Y	
92. Catastrophic health insurance	Y	
93. Ban airline smoking-2 hours or less	Y	
94. $1b/two year aid for the homeless	Y	
95. Bar non-unions in union companies	Y	
96. Increase FSLIC rescue to $15b	Y	
97. Impose quotas to lower trade deficit	Y	
98. Reduce discretionary budget 21%	N	
99. Immigration reform/alien amnesty	N	
100. South Africa sanctions-veto override	Y	
101. Tax overhaul to revise income tax	Y	
102. Use of military in drug war	N	
103. Delete 12 MX/add conventional wpn	Y	
104. Raise speed limit to 65 mph	N	
105. Require Pentagon to buy US goods	N	
106. AIDS insurance non-discrimination	Y	
107. Prohibit Saudi arms sales	Y	
108. Ease Gun Control Act of 1968	N	
109. Bar interstate handgun transport	Y	
110. Make company emissions known	Y	
111. Allow toxic victims to sue in fed ct	Y	
112. Superfund waste cleanup of $10b	Y	
113. 90 days notice of plant closings	Y	
114. $20b in Medicare cuts/tax increases	Y	
115. Spending cuts and tax increases	Y	
116. Set school lunch lmt-250% poverty	N	
117. $75m for youth work projects	Y	
118. Allow Angolan military assistance	N	

DELLUMS, RONALD V. (continued)

119.	Suspend defense payments for abuse	Y	132.	Physician fee freeze for Medicare	N
120.	Drop SS COLAs/$12b tax increase	N	133.	$49b in "sin"/phone/insurance taxes	Y
121.	Approve $1.5b for 21 MX missiles	N	134.	Allow sale of Conrail	N
122.	Emergency farm credit/revisions	Y	135.	Equal Rights Amendment	Y
123.	Duty on Taiwan/Hong Kong/S Korea	Y	136.	Authorize Marines in Lebanon	N
124.	Limit steel imports to 17%	Y	137.	Eminent domain for coal companies	N
125.	Cut $ to schools that bar prayer	N	138.	Prohibit EPA clean air sanctions	Y
126.	$50b-taxes; cut Medicare/spending	N	139.	SS retirement age increase/reforms	N
127.	Limit Pershing II/cruise in Europe	Y	140.	Auto domestic content requirement	Y
128.	Delete $7.1b for 34 B-1 bombers	Y	141.	Delete jobs program funding	N
129.	Bar purchase of Sergeant York guns	Y	142.	Highway-gas tax bill	Y
130.	El Salvador military/economic aid	N	143.	Cut $5b from defense for Medicare	Y
131.	Bar mining of Nicaraguan waters	Y	144.	Emergency housing aid of $1b	Y

Presidential Support Score: 1991 - 25%   1990 - 15%

STARK, FORTNEY H. (PETE) -- California 9th District [Democrat]. County of Alameda (pt.). Prior Terms: 1973-92. Born: November 11, 1940; Parkersburg, WV. Education: Massachusetts Institute of Technology (B.S.); University of California (M.B.A.). Military Service: U.S. Air Force, 1955-57. Occupation: Principal, Skaife and Co. Securities; founder, Beacon S & L Assn. (1961-63); founder and president, Security National Bank of California (1963-72).

1.	Protection to Haitian refugees	Y	41.	Raise House salary/omit honoraria	Y
2.	Raise tax on wealthy; lower others	Y	42.	Toughen oil-spill liability	Y
3.	Investigate Reagan hostage delay	?	43.	Restitution to Japanese interned	Y
4.	Campaign finance revisions	Y	44.	Protect Chinese & C.A. nationals	Y
5.	Unpaid leave to care for children	Y	45.	Abortion $ for rape/incest cases	Y
6.	Restrict NEA use of funds	N	46.	Allow religious schools to bar gays	N
7.	Bar race-bias claim/habeas corpus	N	47.	Bar broadcaster fairness doctrine	N
8.	Ban race as death sentence factor	N	48.	Bar cap gains cut/reinstate IRA	Y
9.	Exceptions to exclusionary rule	?	49.	Bar unions equal voice in pension	N
10.	Allow sale of assault weapons	N	50.	Bar assembly of chemical weapons	Y
11.	Life in prison/abolish death penalty	Y	51.	Ban plutonium/uranium production	Y
12.	Req conspiracy-price fixing cases	N	52.	Cap MX missile deployment at 50	Y
13.	Unemployment benefits extension	Y	53.	Allow $3b for 2 stealth bombers	N
14.	Tissue use of aborted fetuses	Y	54.	Publish bio-warfare experiments	Y
15.	Bar replacement of union strikers	Y	55.	Raise minimum wage-veto override	Y
16.	Hold foreign aid at $15b for '92	Y	56.	Bar transfer of FS-X technology	Y
17.	Restore space station funding	N	57.	Cut defense and raise domestic $	Y
18.	Civil Rights Act of 1991	Y	58.	Uniform poll closing in 48 states	Y
19.	Unlimited damages-discrimination	Y	59.	Req foreign investment disclosure	N
20.	Eliminate funds for supercollider	Y	60.	Textile import quotas-veto override	N
21.	Terminate SDI except for research	Y	61.	Bar abortion funding in Wash, DC	N
22.	Req 7-day handgun waiting period	Y	62.	Notify spouses of AIDS+ carriers	N
23.	Provide $30b for failed S&Ls	N	63.	Seize conveyance-drug trafficking	?
24.	Allow use of force against Iraq	N	64.	South Africa sanctions	Y
25.	Allow $15b in foreign aid for '91	?	65.	60 days' notice of plant closings	Y
26.	Revise & extend legal immigration	Y	66.	Close unneeded military bases	N
27.	Suspend aid to Angolan rebels	Y	67.	Keep welfare reform within $2.8b	N
28.	Democratic tax plan proposals	Y	68.	Allow children housing exclusion	N
29.	Cut defense 5% across the board	Y	69.	Shift $400m of NASA to homeless	Y
30.	Textile import quotas-veto override	N	70.	Cap Medicare patients' liability	Y
31.	Abortion service for military abroad	Y	71.	Prohibit employee polygraph testing	Y
32.	Limits on high income farmers	Y	72.	Allow CIA to fund Contras	N
33.	Family medical leave-veto override	Y	73.	Revise unfair trade practices	Y
34.	Req submission of balanced budget	Y	74.	Focus SDI on accidental launch	N
35.	Balanced budget amendment	N	75.	Bar Air Force $ for MX missile	Y
36.	Amendment to ban flag desecration	N	76.	Allow "real" increase in defense	N
37.	Reauthorize Amtrak-veto override	Y	77.	Troop reduction in Europe of 50%	Y
38.	Retraining aid for coal miners	Y	78.	Ban nuclear tests above 1 kiloton	Y
39.	Suspend El Salvador military aid	Y	79.	Ban anti-satellite missile tests	Y
40.	Expand child care aid/tax credit	Y	80.	Observe certain limits of SALT II	Y

STARK, FORTNEY H. (continued)

81. Restore four Civil Rights laws	Y	
82. Prohibit aliens as strikebreakers	Y	
83. Allow military malpractice suits	?	
84. Approval of $36m in Contra aid	N	
85. $18b deficit reduction compromise	Y	
86. Welfare reform of $5.7b for 5 years	Y	
87. Raise taxes $12b/cut spending $3b	N	
88. Board to assess occupational risk	Y	
89. Balanced budget by '93-via targets	N	
90. Bar licensing of two nuclear plants	Y	
91. Remove victims compensation cap	Y	
92. Catastrophic health insurance	Y	
93. Ban airline smoking-2 hours or less	Y	
94. $1b/two year aid for the homeless	Y	
95. Bar non-unions in union companies	Y	
96. Increase FSLIC rescue to $15b	Y	
97. Impose quotas to lower trade deficit	N	
98. Reduce discretionary budget 21%	Y	
99. Immigration reform/alien amnesty	Y	
100. South Africa sanctions-veto override	Y	
101. Tax overhaul to revise income tax	Y	
102. Use of military in drug war	N	
103. Delete 12 MX/add conventional wpn	Y	
104. Raise speed limit to 65 mph	N	
105. Require Pentagon to buy US goods	N	
106. AIDS insurance non-discrimination	Y	
107. Prohibit Saudi arms sales	Y	
108. Ease Gun Control Act of 1968	N	
109. Bar interstate handgun transport	Y	
110. Make company emissions known	Y	
111. Allow toxic victims to sue in fed ct	Y	
112. Superfund waste cleanup of $10b	Y	

113. 90 days notice of plant closings	Y
114. $20b in Medicare cuts/tax increases	Y
115. Spending cuts and tax increases	N
116. Set school lunch lmt-250% poverty	N
117. $75m for youth work projects	Y
118. Allow Angolan military assistance	?
119. Suspend defense payments for abuse	Y
120. Drop SS COLAs/$12b tax increase	?
121. Approve $1.5b for 21 MX missiles	N
122. Emergency farm credit/revisions	Y
123. Duty on Taiwan/Hong Kong/S Korea	Y
124. Limit steel imports to 17%	Y
125. Cut $ to schools that bar prayer	N
126. $50b-taxes; cut Medicare/spending	Y
127. Limit Pershing II/cruise in Europe	?
128. Delete $7.1b for 34 B-1 bombers	Y
129. Bar purchase of Sergeant York guns	?
130. El Salvador military/economic aid	N
131. Bar mining of Nicaraguan waters	Y
132. Physician fee freeze for Medicare	N
133. $49b in "sin"/phone/insurance taxes	Y
134. Allow sale of Conrail	?
135. Equal Rights Amendment	Y
136. Authorize Marines in Lebanon	N
137. Eminent domain for coal companies	N
138. Prohibit EPA clean air sanctions	N
139. SS retirement age increase/reforms	Y
140. Auto domestic content requirement	Y
141. Delete jobs program funding	N
142. Highway-gas tax bill	Y
143. Cut $5b from defense for Medicare	Y
144. Emergency housing aid of $1b	Y

Presidential Support Score: 1991 - 24%   1990 - 16%

EDWARDS, DON -- California 10th District [Democrat]. Counties of Alameda (pt.) and Santa Clara (pt.). Prior Terms: 1963-92. Born: January 6, 1915; San Jose, CA. Education: Stanford University; Stanford Law School. Military Service: U.S. Navy, 1942-45. Occupation: Agent, F.B.I. (1940-41); president, Valley Title Co.

1. Protection to Haitian refugees	Y	
2. Raise tax on wealthy; lower others	Y	
3. Investigate Reagan hostage delay	?	
4. Campaign finance revisions	Y	
5. Unpaid leave to care for children	Y	
6. Restrict NEA use of funds	N	
7. Bar race-bias claim/habeas corpus	N	
8. Ban race as death sentence factor	N	
9. Exceptions to exclusionary rule	N	
10. Allow sale of assault weapons	N	
11. Life in prison/abolish death penalty	Y	
12. Req conspiracy-price fixing cases	N	
13. Unemployment benefits extension	Y	
14. Tissue use of aborted fetuses	Y	
15. Bar replacement of union strikers	Y	
16. Hold foreign aid at $15b for '92	Y	
17. Restore space station funding	Y	
18. Civil Rights Act of 1991	Y	
19. Unlimited damages-discrimination	Y	
20. Eliminate funds for supercollider	N	
21. Terminate SDI except for research	Y	
22. Req 7-day handgun waiting period	Y	
23. Provide $30b for failed S&Ls	Y	

24. Allow use of force against Iraq	N
25. Allow $15b in foreign aid for '91	?
26. Revise & extend legal immigration	Y
27. Suspend aid to Angolan rebels	Y
28. Democratic tax plan proposals	Y
29. Cut defense 5% across the board	Y
30. Textile import quotas-veto override	Y
31. Abortion service for military abroad	Y
32. Limits on high income farmers	N
33. Family medical leave-veto override	Y
34. Req submission of balanced budget	Y
35. Balanced budget amendment	N
36. Amendment to ban flag desecration	N
37. Reauthorize Amtrak-veto override	Y
38. Retraining aid for coal miners	Y
39. Suspend El Salvador military aid	Y
40. Expand child care aid/tax credit	?
41. Raise House salary/omit honoraria	Y
42. Toughen oil-spill liability	?
43. Restitution to Japanese interned	Y
44. Protect Chinese & C.A. nationals	Y
45. Abortion $ for rape/incest cases	Y
46. Allow religious schools to bar gays	N

EDWARDS, DON (continued)

47. Bar broadcaster fairness doctrine	N	96. Increase FSLIC rescue to $15b	N
48. Bar cap gains cut/reinstate IRA	Y	97. Impose quotas to lower trade deficit	Y
49. Bar unions equal voice in pension	N	98. Reduce discretionary budget 21%	N
50. Bar assembly of chemical weapons	Y	99. Immigration reform/alien amnesty	N
51. Ban plutonium/uranium production	Y	100. South Africa sanctions-veto override	Y
52. Cap MX missile deployment at 50	Y	101. Tax overhaul to revise income tax	Y
53. Allow $3b for 2 stealth bombers	N	102. Use of military in drug war	N
54. Publish bio-warfare experiments	Y	103. Delete 12 MX/add conventional wpn	Y
55. Raise minimum wage-veto override	Y	104. Raise speed limit to 65 mph	N
56. Bar transfer of FS-X technology	Y	105. Require Pentagon to buy US goods	Y
57. Cut defense and raise domestic $	Y	106. AIDS insurance non-discrimination	Y
58. Uniform poll closing in 48 states	Y	107. Prohibit Saudi arms sales	Y
59. Req foreign investment disclosure	Y	108. Ease Gun Control Act of 1968	N
60. Textile import quotas-veto override	Y	109. Bar interstate handgun transport	Y
61. Bar abortion funding in Wash, DC	N	110. Make company emissions known	Y
62. Notify spouses of AIDS+ carriers	N	111. Allow toxic victims to sue in fed ct	Y
63. Seize conveyance-drug trafficking	N	112. Superfund waste cleanup of $10b	Y
64. South Africa sanctions	Y	113. 90 days notice of plant closings	Y
65. 60 days' notice of plant closings	Y	114. $20b in Medicare cuts/tax increases	Y
66. Close unneeded military bases	Y	115. Spending cuts and tax increases	Y
67. Keep welfare reform within $2.8b	N	116. Set school lunch lmt-250% poverty	N
68. Allow children housing exclusion	N	117. $75m for youth work projects	Y
69. Shift $400m of NASA to homeless	Y	118. Allow Angolan military assistance	N
70. Cap Medicare patients' liability	Y	119. Suspend defense payments for abuse	Y
71. Prohibit employee polygraph testing	Y	120. Drop SS COLAs/$12b tax increase	N
72. Allow CIA to fund Contras	N	121. Approve $1.5b for 21 MX missiles	N
73. Revise unfair trade practices	Y	122. Emergency farm credit/revisions	Y
74. Focus SDI on accidental launch	N	123. Duty on Taiwan/Hong Kong/S Korea	Y
75. Bar Air Force $ for MX missile	Y	124. Limit steel imports to 17%	Y
76. Allow "real" increase in defense	N	125. Cut $ to schools that bar prayer	N
77. Troop reduction in Europe of 50%	N	126. $50b-taxes; cut Medicare/spending	Y
78. Ban nuclear tests above 1 kiloton	Y	127. Limit Pershing II/cruise in Europe	Y
79. Ban anti-satellite missile tests	Y	128. Delete $7.1b for 34 B-1 bombers	Y
80. Observe certain limits of SALT II	Y	129. Bar purchase of Sergeant York guns	Y
81. Restore four Civil Rights laws	Y	130. El Salvador military/economic aid	N
82. Prohibit aliens as strikebreakers	Y	131. Bar mining of Nicaraguan waters	Y
83. Allow military malpractice suits	Y	132. Physician fee freeze for Medicare	N
84. Approval of $36m in Contra aid	N	133. $49b in "sin"/phone/insurance taxes	Y
85. $18b deficit reduction compromise	Y	134. Allow sale of Conrail	N
86. Welfare reform of $5.7b for 5 years	Y	135. Equal Rights Amendment	Y
87. Raise taxes $12b/cut spending $3b	Y	136. Authorize Marines in Lebanon	N
88. Board to assess occupational risk	Y	137. Eminent domain for coal companies	N
89. Balanced budget by '93-via targets	N	138. Prohibit EPA clean air sanctions	Y
90. Bar licensing of two nuclear plants	Y	139. SS retirement age increase/reforms	N
91. Remove victims compensation cap	Y	140. Auto domestic content requirement	Y
92. Catastrophic health insurance	Y	141. Delete jobs program funding	N
93. Ban airline smoking-2 hours or less	Y	142. Highway-gas tax bill	Y
94. $1b/two year aid for the homeless	Y	143. Cut $5b from defense for Medicare	Y
95. Bar non-unions in union companies	Y	144. Emergency housing aid of $1b	Y

Presidential Support Score: 1991 - 26%   1990 - 17%

LANTOS, TOM -- California 11th District [Democrat]. Counties of San Mateo (pt.) and Santa Clara (pt.). Prior Terms: 1981-92. Born: Feb. 1, 1928; Budapest. Education: University of Washington (B.A., M.A.); University of California. Occupation: Teacher; senior economic and foreign policy advisor; Presidential task force member, defense and foreign policy.

1. Protection to Haitian refugees	Y	6. Restrict NEA use of funds	N
2. Raise tax on wealthy; lower others	Y	7. Bar race-bias claim/habeas corpus	N
3. Investigate Reagan hostage delay	?	8. Ban race as death sentence factor	N
4. Campaign finance revisions	Y	9. Exceptions to exclusionary rule	N
5. Unpaid leave to care for children	Y	10. Allow sale of assault weapons	N

LANTOS, TOM (continued)

11. Life in prison/abolish death penalty	N	
12. Req conspiracy-price fixing cases	N	
13. Unemployment benefits extension	#	
14. Tissue use of aborted fetuses	Y	
15. Bar replacement of union strikers	Y	
16. Hold foreign aid at $15b for '92	Y	
17. Restore space station funding	Y	
18. Civil Rights Act of 1991	Y	
19. Unlimited damages-discrimination	Y	
20. Eliminate funds for supercollider	Y	
21. Terminate SDI except for research	N	
22. Req 7-day handgun waiting period	Y	
23. Provide $30b for failed S&Ls	Y	
24. Allow use of force against Iraq	Y	
25. Allow $15b in foreign aid for '91	Y	
26. Revise & extend legal immigration	Y	
27. Suspend aid to Angolan rebels	N	
28. Democratic tax plan proposals	Y	
29. Cut defense 5% across the board	Y	
30. Textile import quotas-veto override	Y	
31. Abortion service for military abroad	Y	
32. Limits on high income farmers	Y	
33. Family medical leave-veto override	Y	
34. Req submission of balanced budget	Y	
35. Balanced budget amendment	Y	
36. Amendment to ban flag desecration	N	
37. Reauthorize Amtrak-veto override	Y	
38. Retraining aid for coal miners	Y	
39. Suspend El Salvador military aid	Y	
40. Expand child care aid/tax credit	Y	
41. Raise House salary/omit honoraria	Y	
42. Toughen oil-spill liability	Y	
43. Restitution to Japanese interned	Y	
44. Protect Chinese & C.A. nationals	Y	
45. Abortion $ for rape/incest cases	Y	
46. Allow religious schools to bar gays	N	
47. Bar broadcaster fairness doctrine	N	
48. Bar cap gains cut/reinstate IRA	Y	
49. Bar unions equal voice in pension	N	
50. Bar assembly of chemical weapons	Y	
51. Ban plutonium/uranium production	Y	
52. Cap MX missile deployment at 50	Y	
53. Allow $3b for 2 stealth bombers	N	
54. Publish bio-warfare experiments	Y	
55. Raise minimum wage-veto override	Y	
56. Bar transfer of FS-X technology	N	
57. Cut defense and raise domestic $	N	
58. Uniform poll closing in 48 states	?	
59. Req foreign investment disclosure	Y	
60. Textile import quotas-veto override	Y	
61. Bar abortion funding in Wash, DC	N	
62. Notify spouses of AIDS+ carriers	N	
63. Seize conveyance-drug trafficking	N	
64. South Africa sanctions	Y	
65. 60 days' notice of plant closings	Y	
66. Close unneeded military bases	N	
67. Keep welfare reform within $2.8b	N	
68. Allow children housing exclusion	N	
69. Shift $400m of NASA to homeless	N	
70. Cap Medicare patients' liability	Y	
71. Prohibit employee polygraph testing	Y	
72. Allow CIA to fund Contras	N	
73. Revise unfair trade practices	Y	
74. Focus SDI on accidental launch	Y	

75. Bar Air Force $ for MX missile	N	
76. Allow "real" increase in defense	N	
77. Troop reduction in Europe of 50%	Y	
78. Ban nuclear tests above 1 kiloton	Y	
79. Ban anti-satellite missile tests	Y	
80. Observe certain limits of SALT II	Y	
81. Restore four Civil Rights laws	Y	
82. Prohibit aliens as strikebreakers	Y	
83. Allow military malpractice suits	?	
84. Approval of $36m in Contra aid	N	
85. $18b deficit reduction compromise	Y	
86. Welfare reform of $5.7b for 5 years	Y	
87. Raise taxes $12b/cut spending $3b	Y	
88. Board to assess occupational risk	Y	
89. Balanced budget by '93-via targets	Y	
90. Bar licensing of two nuclear plants	Y	
91. Remove victims compensation cap	Y	
92. Catastrophic health insurance	Y	
93. Ban airline smoking-2 hours or less	Y	
94. $1b/two year aid for the homeless	?	
95. Bar non-unions in union companies	Y	
96. Increase FSLIC rescue to $15b	N	
97. Impose quotas to lower trade deficit	Y	
98. Reduce discretionary budget 21%	Y	
99. Immigration reform/alien amnesty	Y	
100. South Africa sanctions-veto override	Y	
101. Tax overhaul to revise income tax	Y	
102. Use of military in drug war	Y	
103. Delete 12 MX/add conventional wpn	Y	
104. Raise speed limit to 65 mph	N	
105. Require Pentagon to buy US goods	Y	
106. AIDS insurance non-discrimination	Y	
107. Prohibit Saudi arms sales	Y	
108. Ease Gun Control Act of 1968	Y	
109. Bar interstate handgun transport	Y	
110. Make company emissions known	Y	
111. Allow toxic victims to sue in fed ct	Y	
112. Superfund waste cleanup of $10b	Y	
113. 90 days notice of plant closings	Y	
114. $20b in Medicare cuts/tax increases	Y	
115. Spending cuts and tax increases	Y	
116. Set school lunch lmt-250% poverty	N	
117. $75m for youth work projects	Y	
118. Allow Angolan military assistance	N	
119. Suspend SS defense payments for abuse	Y	
120. Drop SS COLAs/$12b tax increase	N	
121. Approve $1.5b for 21 MX missiles	N	
122. Emergency farm credit/revisions	Y	
123. Duty on Taiwan/Hong Kong/S Korea	Y	
124. Limit steel imports to 17%	Y	
125. Cut $ to schools that bar prayer	N	
126. $50b-taxes; cut Medicare/spending	Y	
127. Limit Pershing II/cruise in Europe	N	
128. Delete $7.1b for 34 B-1 bombers	Y	
129. Bar purchase of Sergeant York guns	N	
130. El Salvador military/economic aid	N	
131. Bar mining of Nicaraguan waters	?	
132. Physician fee freeze for Medicare	X	
133. $49b in "sin"/phone/insurance taxes	?	
134. Allow sale of Conrail	N	
135. Equal Rights Amendment	Y	
136. Authorize Marines in Lebanon	Y	
137. Eminent domain for coal companies	N	
138. Prohibit EPA clean air sanctions	Y	

LANTOS, TOM (continued)

139. SS retirement age increase/reforms	N	142. Highway-gas tax bill	?
140. Auto domestic content requirement	Y	143. Cut $5b from defense for Medicare	Y
141. Delete jobs program funding	N	144. Emergency housing aid of $1b	Y

Presidential Support Score: 1991 - 30%   1990 - 26%

CAMPBELL, TOM J. -- California 12th District [Republican]. Counties of San Mateo (pt.), Santa Clara (pt.) and Santa Cruz (pt.). Prior Terms: 1989-92. Born: August 14, 1952; Chicago, IL. Education: University of Chicago (B.A., M.A., Ph.D.); Harvard Law School (J.D.). Occupation: U.S. Court of Appeals and Supreme Court law clerk; lawyer; White House Fellow, Office of the Chief of Staff and White House Counsel (1980-1981); executive assistant to Deputy Attorney General William French Smith (1981); FTC Bureau of Competition director (1981-1983); law school professor.

1. Protection to Haitian refugees	N	30. Textile import quotas-veto override	N
2. Raise tax on wealthy; lower others	N	31. Abortion service for military abroad	Y
3. Investigate Reagan hostage delay	N	32. Limits on high income farmers	Y
4. Campaign finance revisions	N	33. Family medical leave-veto override	Y
5. Unpaid leave to care for children	Y	34. Req submission of balanced budget	N
6. Restrict NEA use of funds	N	35. Balanced budget amendment	Y
7. Bar race-bias claim/habeas corpus	Y	36. Amendment to ban flag desecration	Y
8. Ban race as death sentence factor	Y	37. Reauthorize Amtrak-veto override	N
9. Exceptions to exclusionary rule	Y	38. Retraining aid for coal miners	N
10. Allow sale of assault weapons	N	39. Suspend El Salvador military aid	Y
11. Life in prison/abolish death penalty	N	40. Expand child care aid/tax credit	Y
12. Req conspiracy-price fixing cases	Y	41. Raise House salary/omit honoraria	Y
13. Unemployment benefits extension	N	42. Toughen oil-spill liability	Y
14. Tissue use of aborted fetuses	?	43. Restitution to Japanese interned	Y
15. Bar replacement of union strikers	N	44. Protect Chinese & C.A. nationals	Y
16. Hold foreign aid at $15b for '92	?	45. Abortion $ for rape/incest cases	Y
17. Restore space station funding	Y	46. Allow religious schools to bar gays	N
18. Civil Rights Act of 1991	Y	47. Bar broadcaster fairness doctrine	Y
19. Unlimited damages-discrimination	Y	48. Bar cap gains cut/reinstate IRA	N
20. Eliminate funds for supercollider	Y	49. Bar unions equal voice in pension	Y
21. Terminate SDI except for research	+	50. Bar assembly of chemical weapons	Y
22. Req 7-day handgun waiting period	Y	51. Ban plutonium/uranium production	Y
23. Provide $30b for failed S&Ls	Y	52. Cap MX missile deployment at 50	N
24. Allow use of force against Iraq	Y	53. Allow $3b for 2 stealth bombers	Y
25. Allow $15b in foreign aid for '91	Y	54. Publish bio-warfare experiments	Y
26. Revise & extend legal immigration	N	55. Raise minimum wage-veto override	N
27. Suspend aid to Angolan rebels	N	56. Bar transfer of FS-X technology	N
28. Democratic tax plan proposals	N	57. Cut defense and raise domestic $	N
29. Cut defense 5% across the board	Y	58. Uniform poll closing in 48 states	Y

Presidential Support Score: 1991 - 61%   1990 - 50%

MINETA, NORMAN Y. -- California 13th District [Democrat]. County of Santa Clara (pt.). Prior Terms: 1975-92. Born: November 12, 1931; San Jose, CA. Education: University of California (B.S.). Military Service: U.S. Army, 1953-56. Occupation: Owner/agent, Mineta Insurance Agency; commissioner, Human Relations Committee (1962-64); commissioner, Housing Authority (1966-67); city councilman (1967-72); mayor (1971-74).

1. Protection to Haitian refugees	Y	11. Life in prison/abolish death penalty	Y
2. Raise tax on wealthy; lower others	Y	12. Req conspiracy-price fixing cases	N
3. Investigate Reagan hostage delay	Y	13. Unemployment benefits extension	Y
4. Campaign finance revisions	Y	14. Tissue use of aborted fetuses	Y
5. Unpaid leave to care for children	Y	15. Bar replacement of union strikers	Y
6. Restrict NEA use of funds	N	16. Hold foreign aid at $15b for '92	Y
7. Bar race-bias claim/habeas corpus	N	17. Restore space station funding	Y
8. Ban race as death sentence factor	N	18. Civil Rights Act of 1991	Y
9. Exceptions to exclusionary rule	N	19. Unlimited damages-discrimination	Y
10. Allow sale of assault weapons	N	20. Eliminate funds for supercollider	N

MINETA, NORMAN Y. (continued)

21.	Terminate SDI except for research	Y	83.	Allow military malpractice suits	Y
22.	Req 7-day handgun waiting period	Y	84.	Approval of $36m in Contra aid	N
23.	Provide $30b for failed S&Ls	Y	85.	$18b deficit reduction compromise	Y
24.	Allow use of force against Iraq	N	86.	Welfare reform of $5.7b for 5 years	Y
25.	Allow $15b in foreign aid for '91	Y	87.	Raise taxes $12b/cut spending $3b	Y
26.	Revise & extend legal immigration	Y	88.	Board to assess occupational risk	Y
27.	Suspend aid to Angolan rebels	Y	89.	Balanced budget by '93-via targets	N
28.	Democratic tax plan proposals	Y	90.	Bar licensing of two nuclear plants	Y
29.	Cut defense 5% across the board	N	91.	Remove victims compensation cap	Y
30.	Textile import quotas-veto override	Y	92.	Catastrophic health insurance	Y
31.	Abortion service for military abroad	Y	93.	Ban airline smoking-2 hours or less	N
32.	Limits on high income farmers	N	94.	$1b/two year aid for the homeless	Y
33.	Family medical leave-veto override	Y	95.	Bar non-unions in union companies	N
34.	Req submission of balanced budget	+	96.	Increase FSLIC rescue to $15b	N
35.	Balanced budget amendment	N	97.	Impose quotas to lower trade deficit	Y
36.	Amendment to ban flag desecration	N	98.	Reduce discretionary budget 21%	N
37.	Reauthorize Amtrak-veto override	Y	99.	Immigration reform/alien amnesty	Y
38.	Retraining aid for coal miners	Y	100.	South Africa sanctions-veto override	Y
39.	Suspend El Salvador military aid	Y	101.	Tax overhaul to revise income tax	Y
40.	Expand child care aid/tax credit	Y	102.	Use of military in drug war	N
41.	Raise House salary/omit honoraria	Y	103.	Delete 12 MX/add conventional wpn	Y
42.	Toughen oil-spill liability	Y	104.	Raise speed limit to 65 mph	N
43.	Restitution to Japanese interned	Y	105.	Require Pentagon to buy US goods	N
44.	Protect Chinese & C.A. nationals	Y	106.	AIDS insurance non-discrimination	Y
45.	Abortion $ for rape/incest cases	Y	107.	Prohibit Saudi arms sales	Y
46.	Allow religious schools to bar gays	N	108.	Ease Gun Control Act of 1968	N
47.	Bar broadcaster fairness doctrine	N	109.	Bar interstate handgun transport	Y
48.	Bar cap gains cut/reinstate IRA	N	110.	Make company emissions known	Y
49.	Bar unions equal voice in pension	N	111.	Allow toxic victims to sue in fed ct	Y
50.	Bar assembly of chemical weapons	Y	112.	Superfund waste cleanup of $10b	Y
51.	Ban plutonium/uranium production	Y	113.	90 days notice of plant closings	Y
52.	Cap MX missile deployment at 50	Y	114.	$20b in Medicare cuts/tax increases	Y
53.	Allow $3b for 2 stealth bombers	?	115.	Spending cuts and tax increases	N
54.	Publish bio-warfare experiments	Y	116.	Set school lunch lmt-250% poverty	N
55.	Raise minimum wage-veto override	Y	117.	$75m for youth work projects	Y
56.	Bar transfer of FS-X technology	Y	118.	Allow Angolan military assistance	N
57.	Cut defense and raise domestic $	Y	119.	Suspend defense payments for abuse	Y
58.	Uniform poll closing in 48 states	Y	120.	Drop SS COLAs/$12b tax increase	N
59.	Req foreign investment disclosure	Y	121.	Approve $1.5b for 21 MX missiles	N
60.	Textile import quotas-veto override	Y	122.	Emergency farm credit/revisions	Y
61.	Bar abortion funding in Wash, DC	N	123.	Duty on Taiwan/Hong Kong/S Korea	Y
62.	Notify spouses of AIDS+ carriers	N	124.	Limit steel imports to 17%	Y
63.	Seize conveyance-drug trafficking	N	125.	Cut $ to schools that bar prayer	N
64.	South Africa sanctions	#	126.	$50b-taxes; cut Medicare/spending	Y
65.	60 days' notice of plant closings	Y	127.	Limit Pershing II/cruise in Europe	Y
66.	Close unneeded military bases	N	128.	Delete $7.1b for 34 B-1 bombers	Y
67.	Keep welfare reform within $2.8b	N	129.	Bar purchase of Sergeant York guns	Y
68.	Allow children housing exclusion	N	130.	El Salvador military/economic aid	N
69.	Shift $400m of NASA to homeless	N	131.	Bar mining of Nicaraguan waters	Y
70.	Cap Medicare patients' liability	Y	132.	Physician fee freeze for Medicare	N
71.	Prohibit employee polygraph testing	Y	133.	$49b in "sin"/phone/insurance taxes	Y
72.	Allow CIA to fund Contras	N	134.	Allow sale of Conrail	N
73.	Revise unfair trade practices	Y	135.	Equal Rights Amendment	Y
74.	Focus SDI on accidental launch	Y	136.	Authorize Marines in Lebanon	N
75.	Bar Air Force $ for MX missile	Y	137.	Eminent domain for coal companies	Y
76.	Allow "real" increase in defense	N	138.	Prohibit EPA clean air sanctions	N
77.	Troop reduction in Europe of 50%	N	139.	SS retirement age increase/reforms	N
78.	Ban nuclear tests above 1 kiloton	Y	140.	Auto domestic content requirement	Y
79.	Ban anti-satellite missile tests	Y	141.	Delete jobs program funding	N
80.	Observe certain limits of SALT II	Y	142.	Highway-gas tax bill	Y
81.	Restore four Civil Rights laws	Y	143.	Cut $5b from defense for Medicare	N
82.	Prohibit aliens as strikebreakers	Y	144.	Emergency housing aid of $1b	Y

Presidential Support Score: 1991 - 30%   1990 - 16%

DOOLITTLE, JOHN T. -- California 14th District [Republican]. Counties of Alpine, Amador, El Dorado, Lassen, Modoc, Nevada, Placer, Plumas, San Joaquin (pt.), Shasta (pt.), Sierra and Siskiyou. Prior Term: 1991-92. Born: October 30, 1950; Glendale, CA. Education: University of California-Santa Cruz (B.A.); University of the Pacific (J.D.). Occupation: Lawyer; state senator (1981-90).

1. Protection to Haitian refugees	N		13. Unemployment benefits extension	X
2. Raise tax on wealthy; lower others	N		14. Tissue use of aborted fetuses	N
3. Investigate Reagan hostage delay	N		15. Bar replacement of union strikers	N
4. Campaign finance revisions	N		16. Hold foreign aid at $15b for '92	Y
5. Unpaid leave to care for children	N		17. Restore space station funding	Y
6. Restrict NEA use of funds	Y		18. Civil Rights Act of 1991	N
7. Bar race-bias claim/habeas corpus	Y		19. Unlimited damages-discrimination	N
8. Ban race as death sentence factor	Y		20. Eliminate funds for supercollider	N
9. Exceptions to exclusionary rule	Y		21. Terminate SDI except for research	X
10. Allow sale of assault weapons	Y		22. Req 7-day handgun waiting period	N
11. Life in prison/abolish death penalty	N		23. Provide $30b for failed S&Ls	Y
12. Req conspiracy-price fixing cases	Y		24. Allow use of force against Iraq	Y

Presidential Support Score: 1991 - 73%

CONDIT, GARY A. -- California 15th District [Democrat]. Counties of Fresno (pt.),Mariposa, Merced and Stanislaus. Prior Terms: 1989 (Special Election)-1992. Born: April 21, 1948; Salina, OK. Education: Modesto Junior College (A.A.); California State College (B.A.). Occupation: Ceres city councilman (1972-74) and mayor (1974-76); Stanislaus County supervisor (1976-82); state assemblyman (1982-89).

1. Protection to Haitian refugees	Y		26. Revise & extend legal immigration	Y
2. Raise tax on wealthy; lower others	N		27. Suspend aid to Angolan rebels	Y
3. Investigate Reagan hostage delay	N		28. Democratic tax plan proposals	N
4. Campaign finance revisions	Y		29. Cut defense 5% across the board	?
5. Unpaid leave to care for children	Y		30. Textile import quotas-veto override	Y
6. Restrict NEA use of funds	Y		31. Abortion service for military abroad	Y
7. Bar race-bias claim/habeas corpus	Y		32. Limits on high income farmers	N
8. Ban race as death sentence factor	Y		33. Family medical leave-veto override	Y
9. Exceptions to exclusionary rule	Y		34. Req submission of balanced budget	Y
10. Allow sale of assault weapons	Y		35. Balanced budget amendment	Y
11. Life in prison/abolish death penalty	N		36. Amendment to ban flag desecration	Y
12. Req conspiracy-price fixing cases	Y		37. Reauthorize Amtrak-veto override	Y
13. Unemployment benefits extension	Y		38. Retraining aid for coal miners	Y
14. Tissue use of aborted fetuses	Y		39. Suspend El Salvador military aid	Y
15. Bar replacement of union strikers	Y		40. Expand child care aid/tax credit	Y
16. Hold foreign aid at $15b for '92	N		41. Raise House salary/omit honoraria	N
17. Restore space station funding	N		42. Toughen oil-spill liability	Y
18. Civil Rights Act of 1991	Y		43. Restitution to Japanese interned	Y
19. Unlimited damages-discrimination	Y		44. Protect Chinese & C.A. nationals	Y
20. Eliminate funds for supercollider	N		45. Abortion $ for rape/incest cases	Y
21. Terminate SDI except for research	Y		46. Allow religious schools to bar gays	N
22. Req 7-day handgun waiting period	N		47. Bar broadcaster fairness doctrine	Y
23. Provide $30b for failed S&Ls	N		48. Bar cap gains cut/reinstate IRA	Y
24. Allow use of force against Iraq	Y		49. Bar unions equal voice in pension	N
25. Allow $15b in foreign aid for '91	N			

Presidential Support Score: 1991 - 36%   1990 - 25%

PANETTA, LEON E. -- California 16th District [Democrat]. Counties of Monterey, San Benito, San Luis Obispo (pt.) and Santa Cruz. Prior Terms: 1977-92. Born: June 28, 1938; Monterey, CA. Education: University of Santa Clara (B.A., J.D.). Military Service: U.S. Army, 1963-65. Occupation: Law Review editor; legislative assistant, U.S. Senate (1966-69); director, Office of Civil Rights, HEW; executive assistant, New York mayor (1970-71).

1. Protection to Haitian refugees	Y		3. Investigate Reagan hostage delay	Y
2. Raise tax on wealthy; lower others	Y		4. Campaign finance revisions	Y

PANETTA, LEON E. (continued)

5. Unpaid leave to care for children	Y	
6. Restrict NEA use of funds	N	
7. Bar race-bias claim/habeas corpus	Y	
8. Ban race as death sentence factor	N	
9. Exceptions to exclusionary rule	N	
10. Allow sale of assault weapons	N	
11. Life in prison/abolish death penalty	N	
12. Req conspiracy-price fixing cases	N	
13. Unemployment benefits extension	Y	
14. Tissue use of aborted fetuses	Y	
15. Bar replacement of union strikers	Y	
16. Hold foreign aid at $15b for '92	Y	
17. Restore space station funding	N	
18. Civil Rights Act of 1991	Y	
19. Unlimited damages-discrimination	Y	
20. Eliminate funds for supercollider	N	
21. Terminate SDI except for research	Y	
22. Req 7-day handgun waiting period	Y	
23. Provide $30b for failed S&Ls	Y	
24. Allow use of force against Iraq	N	
25. Allow $15b in foreign aid for '91	Y	
26. Revise & extend legal immigration	Y	
27. Suspend aid to Angolan rebels	Y	
28. Democratic tax plan proposals	Y	
29. Cut defense 5% across the board	N	
30. Textile import quotas-veto override	N	
31. Abortion service for military abroad	Y	
32. Limits on high income farmers	Y	
33. Family medical leave-veto override	Y	
34. Req submission of balanced budget	Y	
35. Balanced budget amendment	N	
36. Amendment to ban flag desecration	N	
37. Reauthorize Amtrak-veto override	Y	
38. Retraining aid for coal miners	Y	
39. Suspend El Salvador military aid	Y	
40. Expand child care aid/tax credit	Y	
41. Raise House salary/omit honoraria	Y	
42. Toughen oil-spill liability	Y	
43. Restitution to Japanese interned	Y	
44. Protect Chinese & C.A. nationals	Y	
45. Abortion $ for rape/incest cases	Y	
46. Allow religious schools to bar gays	N	
47. Bar broadcaster fairness doctrine	N	
48. Bar cap gains cut/reinstate IRA	Y	
49. Bar unions equal voice in pension	N	
50. Bar assembly of chemical weapons	Y	
51. Ban plutonium/uranium production	Y	
52. Cap MX missile deployment at 50	Y	
53. Allow $3b for 2 stealth bombers	N	
54. Publish bio-warfare experiments	Y	
55. Raise minimum wage-veto override	Y	
56. Bar transfer of FS-X technology	Y	
57. Cut defense and raise domestic $	N	
58. Uniform poll closing in 48 states	Y	
59. Req foreign investment disclosure	Y	
60. Textile import quotas-veto override	N	
61. Bar abortion funding in Wash, DC	N	
62. Notify spouses of AIDS+ carriers	N	
63. Seize conveyance-drug trafficking	N	
64. South Africa sanctions	Y	
65. 60 days' notice of plant closings	Y	
66. Close unneeded military bases	Y	
67. Keep welfare reform within $2.8b	N	
68. Allow children housing exclusion	N	

69. Shift $400m of NASA to homeless	Y	
70. Cap Medicare patients' liability	Y	
71. Prohibit employee polygraph testing	Y	
72. Allow CIA to fund Contras	N	
73. Revise unfair trade practices	Y	
74. Focus SDI on accidental launch	Y	
75. Bar Air Force $ for MX missile	Y	
76. Allow "real" increase in defense	N	
77. Troop reduction in Europe of 50%	Y	
78. Ban nuclear tests above 1 kiloton	Y	
79. Ban anti-satellite missile tests	Y	
80. Observe certain limits of SALT II	Y	
81. Restore four Civil Rights laws	Y	
82. Prohibit aliens as strikebreakers	Y	
83. Allow military malpractice suits	Y	
84. Approval of $36m in Contra aid	N	
85. $18b deficit reduction compromise	Y	
86. Welfare reform of $5.7b for 5 years	Y	
87. Raise taxes $12b/cut spending $3b	Y	
88. Board to assess occupational risk	N	
89. Balanced budget by '93-via targets	Y	
90. Bar licensing of two nuclear plants	Y	
91. Remove victims compensation cap	Y	
92. Catastrophic health insurance	Y	
93. Ban airline smoking-2 hours or less	Y	
94. $1b/two year aid for the homeless	Y	
95. Bar non-unions in union companies	Y	
96. Increase FSLIC rescue to $15b	N	
97. Impose quotas to lower trade deficit	Y	
98. Reduce discretionary budget 21%	Y	
99. Immigration reform/alien amnesty	Y	
100. South Africa sanctions-veto override	#	
101. Tax overhaul to revise income tax	Y	
102. Use of military in drug war	N	
103. Delete 12 MX/add conventional wpn	Y	
104. Raise speed limit to 65 mph	Y	
105. Require Pentagon to buy US goods	N	
106. AIDS insurance non-discrimination	Y	
107. Prohibit Saudi arms sales	Y	
108. Ease Gun Control Act of 1968	N	
109. Bar interstate handgun transport	Y	
110. Make company emissions known	Y	
111. Allow toxic victims to sue in fed ct	N	
112. Superfund waste cleanup of $10b	Y	
113. 90 days notice of plant closings	Y	
114. $20b in Medicare cuts/tax increases	Y	
115. Spending cuts and tax increases	Y	
116. Set school lunch lmt-250% poverty	N	
117. $75m for youth work projects	Y	
118. Allow Angolan military assistance	N	
119. Suspend defense payments for abuse	Y	
120. Drop SS COLAs/$12b tax increase	Y	
121. Approve $1.5b for 21 MX missiles	N	
122. Emergency farm credit/revisions	Y	
123. Duty on Taiwan/Hong Kong/S Korea	Y	
124. Limit steel imports to 17%	N	
125. Cut $ to schools that bar prayer	N	
126. $50b-taxes; cut Medicare/spending	Y	
127. Limit Pershing II/cruise in Europe	Y	
128. Delete $7.1b for 34 B-1 bombers	Y	
129. Bar purchase of Sergeant York guns	Y	
130. El Salvador military/economic aid	N	
131. Bar mining of Nicaraguan waters	Y	
132. Physician fee freeze for Medicare	N	

PANETTA, LEON E. (continued)

133.	$49b in "sin"/phone/insurance taxes	Y	139.	SS retirement age increase/reforms	N
134.	Allow sale of Conrail	N	140.	Auto domestic content requirement	N
135.	Equal Rights Amendment	Y	141.	Delete jobs program funding	N
136.	Authorize Marines in Lebanon	Y	142.	Highway-gas tax bill	Y
137.	Eminent domain for coal companies	Y	143.	Cut $5b from defense for Medicare	N
138.	Prohibit EPA clean air sanctions	+	144.	Emergency housing aid of $1b	Y

Presidential Support Score: 1991 - 35%   1990 - 20%

DOOLEY, CALVIN -- California 17th District [Democrat]. Counties of Fresno (pt.), Kern (pt.), Kings and Tulare. Prior Term: 1991-92. Born: January 11, 1954; Hanford, CA. Education: University of California-Davis (B.S.); Stanford University (M.S.). Occupation: Farmer; administrative assistant to state senator.

1.	Protection to Haitian refugees	Y	13.	Unemployment benefits extension	Y
2.	Raise tax on wealthy; lower others	Y	14.	Tissue use of aborted fetuses	Y
3.	Investigate Reagan hostage delay	Y	15.	Bar replacement of union strikers	Y
4.	Campaign finance revisions	Y	16.	Hold foreign aid at $15b for '92	Y
5.	Unpaid leave to care for children	Y	17.	Restore space station funding	Y
6.	Restrict NEA use of funds	N	18.	Civil Rights Act of 1991	Y
7.	Bar race-bias claim/habeas corpus	Y	19.	Unlimited damages-discrimination	N
8.	Ban race as death sentence factor	Y	20.	Eliminate funds for supercollider	Y
9.	Exceptions to exclusionary rule	Y	21.	Terminate SDI except for research	N
10.	Allow sale of assault weapons	N	22.	Req 7-day handgun waiting period	Y
11.	Life in prison/abolish death penalty	N	23.	Provide $30b for failed S&Ls	N
12.	Req conspiracy-price fixing cases	N	24.	Allow use of force against Iraq	N

Presidential Support Score: 1991 - 38%

LEHMAN, RICHARD H. -- California 18th District [Democrat]. Counties of Calaveras, Fresno (pt.), Mono, San Joaquin (pt.) and Tuolumne. Prior Terms: 1983-92. Born: July 20, 1948; Sanger, CA. Education: Fresno City College; California State University; University of California. Military Service: U.S. Army National Guard, 1970-76. Occupation: Administrative aide (1969-76); California assemblyman (1976-82).

1.	Protection to Haitian refugees	Y	28.	Democratic tax plan proposals	Y
2.	Raise tax on wealthy; lower others	N	29.	Cut defense 5% across the board	N
3.	Investigate Reagan hostage delay	N	30.	Textile import quotas-veto override	Y
4.	Campaign finance revisions	Y	31.	Abortion service for military abroad	Y
5.	Unpaid leave to care for children	Y	32.	Limits on high income farmers	N
6.	Restrict NEA use of funds	N	33.	Family medical leave-veto override	Y
7.	Bar race-bias claim/habeas corpus	Y	34.	Req submission of balanced budget	Y
8.	Ban race as death sentence factor	Y	35.	Balanced budget amendment	N
9.	Exceptions to exclusionary rule	N	36.	Amendment to ban flag desecration	N
10.	Allow sale of assault weapons	N	37.	Reauthorize Amtrak-veto override	?
11.	Life in prison/abolish death penalty	N	38.	Retraining aid for coal miners	Y
12.	Req conspiracy-price fixing cases	N	39.	Suspend El Salvador military aid	Y
13.	Unemployment benefits extension	Y	40.	Expand child care aid/tax credit	Y
14.	Tissue use of aborted fetuses	Y	41.	Raise House salary/omit honoraria	Y
15.	Bar replacement of union strikers	Y	42.	Toughen oil-spill liability	?
16.	Hold foreign aid at $15b for '92	Y	43.	Restitution to Japanese interned	Y
17.	Restore space station funding	Y	44.	Protect Chinese & C.A. nationals	Y
18.	Civil Rights Act of 1991	Y	45.	Abortion $ for rape/incest cases	Y
19.	Unlimited damages-discrimination	N	46.	Allow religious schools to bar gays	N
20.	Eliminate funds for supercollider	N	47.	Bar broadcaster fairness doctrine	Y
21.	Terminate SDI except for research	?	48.	Bar cap gains cut/reinstate IRA	Y
22.	Req 7-day handgun waiting period	Y	49.	Bar unions equal voice in pension	N
23.	Provide $30b for failed S&Ls	Y	50.	Bar assembly of chemical weapons	Y
24.	Allow use of force against Iraq	Y	51.	Ban plutonium/uranium production	Y
25.	Allow $15b in foreign aid for '91	N	52.	Cap MX missile deployment at 50	Y
26.	Revise & extend legal immigration	Y	53.	Allow $3b for 2 stealth bombers	N
27.	Suspend aid to Angolan rebels	Y	54.	Publish bio-warfare experiments	Y

LEHMAN, RICHARD H. (continued)

55. Raise minimum wage-veto override	Y
56. Bar transfer of FS-X technology	Y
57. Cut defense and raise domestic $	N
58. Uniform poll closing in 48 states	Y
59. Req foreign investment disclosure	Y
60. Textile import quotas-veto override	Y
61. Bar abortion funding in Wash, DC	N
62. Notify spouses of AIDS+ carriers	N
63. Seize conveyance-drug trafficking	N
64. South Africa sanctions	#
65. 60 days' notice of plant closings	Y
66. Close unneeded military bases	N
67. Keep welfare reform within $2.8b	?
68. Allow children housing exclusion	N
69. Shift $400m of NASA to homeless	Y
70. Cap Medicare patients' liability	Y
71. Prohibit employee polygraph testing	Y
72. Allow CIA to fund Contras	N
73. Revise unfair trade practices	Y
74. Focus SDI on accidental launch	Y
75. Bar Air Force $ for MX missile	Y
76. Allow "real" increase in defense	N
77. Troop reduction in Europe of 50%	?
78. Ban nuclear tests above 1 kiloton	Y
79. Ban anti-satellite missile tests	Y
80. Observe certain limits of SALT II	Y
81. Restore four Civil Rights laws	Y
82. Prohibit aliens as strikebreakers	Y
83. Allow military malpractice suits	Y
84. Approval of $36m in Contra aid	N
85. $18b deficit reduction compromise	N
86. Welfare reform of $5.7b for 5 years	Y
87. Raise taxes $12b/cut spending $3b	Y
88. Board to assess occupational risk	Y
89. Balanced budget by '93-via targets	N
90. Bar licensing of two nuclear plants	Y
91. Remove victims compensation cap	N
92. Catastrophic health insurance	Y
93. Ban airline smoking-2 hours or less	Y
94. $1b/two year aid for the homeless	Y
95. Bar non-unions in union companies	Y
96. Increase FSLIC rescue to $15b	N
97. Impose quotas to lower trade deficit	Y

98. Reduce discretionary budget 21%	N
99. Immigration reform/alien amnesty	Y
100. South Africa sanctions-veto override	Y
101. Tax overhaul to revise income tax	N
102. Use of military in drug war	Y
103. Delete 12 MX/add conventional wpn	Y
104. Raise speed limit to 65 mph	Y
105. Require Pentagon to buy US goods	Y
106. AIDS insurance non-discrimination	Y
107. Prohibit Saudi arms sales	+
108. Ease Gun Control Act of 1968	Y
109. Bar interstate handgun transport	Y
110. Make company emissions known	N
111. Allow toxic victims to sue in fed ct	Y
112. Superfund waste cleanup of $10b	Y
113. 90 days notice of plant closings	Y
114. $20b in Medicare cuts/tax increases	Y
115. Spending cuts and tax increases	Y
116. Set school lunch lmt-250% poverty	?
117. $75m for youth work projects	?
118. Allow Angolan military assistance	N
119. Suspend defense payments for abuse	Y
120. Drop SS COLAs/$12b tax increase	N
121. Approve $1.5b for 21 MX missiles	N
122. Emergency farm credit/revisions	Y
123. Duty on Taiwan/Hong Kong/S Korea	Y
124. Limit steel imports to 17%	Y
125. Cut $ to schools that bar prayer	N
126. $50b-taxes; cut Medicare/spending	Y
127. Limit Pershing II/cruise in Europe	Y
128. Delete $7.1b for 34 B-1 bombers	Y
129. Bar purchase of Sergeant York guns	?
130. El Salvador military/economic aid	N
131. Bar mining of Nicaraguan waters	Y
132. Physician fee freeze for Medicare	N
133. $49b in "sin"/phone/insurance taxes	Y
134. Allow sale of Conrail	N
135. Equal Rights Amendment	Y
136. Authorize Marines in Lebanon	Y
137. Eminent domain for coal companies	N
138. Prohibit EPA clean air sanctions	Y
139. SS retirement age increase/reforms	N

Presidential Support Score: 1991 - 38% 1990 - 19%

LAGOMARSINO, ROBERT J. -- California 19th District [Republican]. Counties of Santa Barbara and Ventura (pt.). Prior Terms: 1974 (Special Election)-1992. Born: September 4, 1926; Ventura, CA. Education: University of California; University of Santa Clara Law School (LL.B.). Military Service: U.S. Navy, WW II. Occupation: Attorney; Ojai city councilman (1958); mayor (1959-60); California senator (1961, 1964, 1966, 1970).

1. Protection to Haitian refugees	N
2. Raise tax on wealthy; lower others	N
3. Investigate Reagan hostage delay	N
4. Campaign finance revisions	N
5. Unpaid leave to care for children	N
6. Restrict NEA use of funds	Y
7. Bar race-bias claim/habeas corpus	Y
8. Ban race as death sentence factor	Y
9. Exceptions to exclusionary rule	Y
10. Allow sale of assault weapons	Y
11. Life in prison/abolish death penalty	N

12. Req conspiracy-price fixing cases	Y
13. Unemployment benefits extension	N
14. Tissue use of aborted fetuses	N
15. Bar replacement of union strikers	N
16. Hold foreign aid at $15b for '92	N
17. Restore space station funding	Y
18. Civil Rights Act of 1991	N
19. Unlimited damages-discrimination	N
20. Eliminate funds for supercollider	N
21. Terminate SDI except for research	N
22. Req 7-day handgun waiting period	Y

LAGOMARSINO, ROBERT J. (continued)

23. Provide $30b for failed S&Ls	Y	
24. Allow use of force against Iraq	Y	
25. Allow $15b in foreign aid for '91	Y	
26. Revise & extend legal immigration	N	
27. Suspend aid to Angolan rebels	N	
28. Democratic tax plan proposals	N	
29. Cut defense 5% across the board	N	
30. Textile import quotas-veto override	N	
31. Abortion service for military abroad	N	
32. Limits on high income farmers	Y	
33. Family medical leave-veto override	N	
34. Req submission of balanced budget	N	
35. Balanced budget amendment	Y	
36. Amendment to ban flag desecration	Y	
37. Reauthorize Amtrak-veto override	Y	
38. Retraining aid for coal miners	N	
39. Suspend El Salvador military aid	N	
40. Expand child care aid/tax credit	Y	
41. Raise House salary/omit honoraria	N	
42. Toughen oil-spill liability	Y	
43. Restitution to Japanese interned	Y	
44. Protect Chinese & C.A. nationals	N	
45. Abortion $ for rape/incest cases	N	
46. Allow religious schools to bar gays	Y	
47. Bar broadcaster fairness doctrine	Y	
48. Bar cap gains cut/reinstate IRA	N	
49. Bar unions equal voice in pension	Y	
50. Bar assembly of chemical weapons	N	
51. Ban plutonium/uranium production	N	
52. Cap MX missile deployment at 50	N	
53. Allow $3b for 2 stealth bombers	Y	
54. Publish bio-warfare experiments	N	
55. Raise minimum wage-veto override	N	
56. Bar transfer of FS-X technology	N	
57. Cut defense and raise domestic $	N	
58. Uniform poll closing in 48 states	Y	
59. Req foreign investment disclosure	N	
60. Textile import quotas-veto override	N	
61. Bar abortion funding in Wash, DC	Y	
62. Notify spouses of AIDS+ carriers	Y	
63. Seize conveyance-drug trafficking	Y	
64. South Africa sanctions	N	
65. 60 days' notice of plant closings	Y	
66. Close unneeded military bases	Y	
67. Keep welfare reform within $2.8b	Y	
68. Allow children housing exclusion	N	
69. Shift $400m of NASA to homeless	N	
70. Cap Medicare patients' liability	Y	
71. Prohibit employee polygraph testing	Y	
72. Allow CIA to fund Contras	Y	
73. Revise unfair trade practices	N	
74. Focus SDI on accidental launch	N	
75. Bar Air Force $ for MX missile	N	
76. Allow "real" increase in defense	Y	
77. Troop reduction in Europe of 50%	N	
78. Ban nuclear tests above 1 kiloton	N	
79. Ban anti-satellite missile tests	N	
80. Observe certain limits of SALT II	N	
81. Restore four Civil Rights laws	N	
82. Prohibit aliens as strikebreakers	N	
83. Allow military malpractice suits	Y	

84. Approval of $36m in Contra aid	Y	
85. $18b deficit reduction compromise	N	
86. Welfare reform of $5.7b for 5 years	N	
87. Raise taxes $12b/cut spending $3b	N	
88. Board to assess occupational risk	N	
89. Balanced budget by '93-via targets	Y	
90. Bar licensing of two nuclear plants	N	
91. Remove victims compensation cap	N	
92. Catastrophic health insurance	N	
93. Ban airline smoking-2 hours or less	Y	
94. $1b/two year aid for the homeless	N	
95. Bar non-unions in union companies	N	
96. Increase FSLIC rescue to $15b	Y	
97. Impose quotas to lower trade deficit	N	
98. Reduce discretionary budget 21%	Y	
99. Immigration reform/alien amnesty	Y	
100. South Africa sanctions-veto override	Y	
101. Tax overhaul to revise income tax	Y	
102. Use of military in drug war	Y	
103. Delete 12 MX/add conventional wpn	N	
104. Raise speed limit to 65 mph	Y	
105. Require Pentagon to buy US goods	N	
106. AIDS insurance non-discrimination	N	
107. Prohibit Saudi arms sales	N	
108. Ease Gun Control Act of 1968	Y	
109. Bar interstate handgun transport	N	
110. Make company emissions known	N	
111. Allow toxic victims to sue in fed ct	N	
112. Superfund waste cleanup of $10b	N	
113. 90 days notice of plant closings	N	
114. $20b in Medicare cuts/tax increases	N	
115. Spending cuts and tax increases	N	
116. Set school lunch lmt-250% poverty	Y	
117. $75m for youth work projects	Y	
118. Allow Angolan military assistance	N	
119. Suspend defense payments for abuse	N	
120. Drop SS COLAs/$12b tax increase	N	
121. Approve $1.5b for 21 MX missiles	Y	
122. Emergency farm credit/revisions	N	
123. Duty on Taiwan/Hong Kong/S Korea	N	
124. Limit steel imports to 17%	N	
125. Cut $ to schools that bar prayer	Y	
126. $50b-taxes; cut Medicare/spending	N	
127. Limit Pershing II/cruise in Europe	N	
128. Delete $7.1b for 34 B-1 bombers	N	
129. Bar purchase of Sergeant York guns	N	
130. El Salvador military/economic aid	Y	
131. Bar mining of Nicaraguan waters	Y	
132. Physician fee freeze for Medicare	Y	
133. $49b in "sin"/phone/insurance taxes	N	
134. Allow sale of Conrail	Y	
135. Equal Rights Amendment	N	
136. Authorize Marines in Lebanon	Y	
137. Eminent domain for coal companies	Y	
138. Prohibit EPA clean air sanctions	Y	
139. SS retirement age increase/reforms	Y	
140. Auto domestic content requirement	N	
141. Delete jobs program funding	Y	
142. Highway-gas tax bill	Y	
143. Cut $5b from defense for Medicare	N	
144. Emergency housing aid of $1b	Y	

Presidential Support Score: 1991 - 85% 1990 - 70%

THOMAS, WILLIAM M. -- California 20th District [Republican]. Counties of Kern (pt.), Los Angeles (pt.) and San Luis Obispo (pt.). Prior Terms: 1979-92. Born: December 6, 1941; Wallace, ID. Education: San Francisco State University (M.A.). Occupation: Professor (1965-74); California state legislator (1974-78).

1.	Protection to Haitian refugees	X	61.	Bar abortion funding in Wash, DC	N
2.	Raise tax on wealthy; lower others	N	62.	Notify spouses of AIDS+ carriers	Y
3.	Investigate Reagan hostage delay	?	63.	Seize conveyance-drug trafficking	Y
4.	Campaign finance revisions	N	64.	South Africa sanctions	N
5.	Unpaid leave to care for children	N	65.	60 days' notice of plant closings	Y
6.	Restrict NEA use of funds	Y	66.	Close unneeded military bases	Y
7.	Bar race-bias claim/habeas corpus	Y	67.	Keep welfare reform within $2.8b	Y
8.	Ban race as death sentence factor	Y	68.	Allow children housing exclusion	N
9.	Exceptions to exclusionary rule	Y	69.	Shift $400m of NASA to homeless	N
10.	Allow sale of assault weapons	Y	70.	Cap Medicare patients' liability	N
11.	Life in prison/abolish death penalty	N	71.	Prohibit employee polygraph testing	Y
12.	Req conspiracy-price fixing cases	Y	72.	Allow CIA to fund Contras	Y
13.	Unemployment benefits extension	X	73.	Revise unfair trade practices	#
14.	Tissue use of aborted fetuses	Y	74.	Focus SDI on accidental launch	N
15.	Bar replacement of union strikers	N	75.	Bar Air Force $ for MX missile	N
16.	Hold foreign aid at $15b for '92	Y	76.	Allow "real" increase in defense	Y
17.	Restore space station funding	Y	77.	Troop reduction in Europe of 50%	?
18.	Civil Rights Act of 1991	N	78.	Ban nuclear tests above 1 kiloton	X
19.	Unlimited damages-discrimination	N	79.	Ban anti-satellite missile tests	N
20.	Eliminate funds for supercollider	N	80.	Observe certain limits of SALT II	N
21.	Terminate SDI except for research	N	81.	Restore four Civil Rights laws	N
22.	Req 7-day handgun waiting period	Y	82.	Prohibit aliens as strikebreakers	N
23.	Provide $30b for failed S&Ls	Y	83.	Allow military malpractice suits	Y
24.	Allow use of force against Iraq	Y	84.	Approval of $36m in Contra aid	Y
25.	Allow $15b in foreign aid for '91	N	85.	$18b deficit reduction compromise	N
26.	Revise & extend legal immigration	N	86.	Welfare reform of $5.7b for 5 years	N
27.	Suspend aid to Angolan rebels	N	87.	Raise taxes $12b/cut spending $3b	X
28.	Democratic tax plan proposals	?	88.	Board to assess occupational risk	N
29.	Cut defense 5% across the board	N	89.	Balanced budget by '93-via targets	Y
30.	Textile import quotas-veto override	Y	90.	Bar licensing of two nuclear plants	N
31.	Abortion service for military abroad	Y	91.	Remove victims compensation cap	N
32.	Limits on high income farmers	N	92.	Catastrophic health insurance	N
33.	Family medical leave-veto override	N	93.	Ban airline smoking-2 hours or less	Y
34.	Req submission of balanced budget	N	94.	$1b/two year aid for the homeless	N
35.	Balanced budget amendment	Y	95.	Bar non-unions in union companies	N
36.	Amendment to ban flag desecration	Y	96.	Increase FSLIC rescue to $15b	Y
37.	Reauthorize Amtrak-veto override	Y	97.	Impose quotas to lower trade deficit	N
38.	Retraining aid for coal miners	X	98.	Reduce discretionary budget 21%	Y
39.	Suspend El Salvador military aid	X	99.	Immigration reform/alien amnesty	N
40.	Expand child care aid/tax credit	N	100.	South Africa sanctions-veto override	?
41.	Raise House salary/omit honoraria	Y	101.	Tax overhaul to revise income tax	N
42.	Toughen oil-spill liability	N	102.	Use of military in drug war	Y
43.	Restitution to Japanese interned	Y	103.	Delete 12 MX/add conventional wpn	N
44.	Protect Chinese & C.A. nationals	N	104.	Raise speed limit to 65 mph	Y
45.	Abortion $ for rape/incest cases	Y	105.	Require Pentagon to buy US goods	N
46.	Allow religious schools to bar gays	Y	106.	AIDS insurance non-discrimination	N
47.	Bar broadcaster fairness doctrine	Y	107.	Prohibit Saudi arms sales	N
48.	Bar cap gains cut/reinstate IRA	N	108.	Ease Gun Control Act of 1968	Y
49.	Bar unions equal voice in pension	Y	109.	Bar interstate handgun transport	N
50.	Bar assembly of chemical weapons	N	110.	Make company emissions known	N
51.	Ban plutonium/uranium production	N	111.	Allow toxic victims to sue in fed ct	N
52.	Cap MX missile deployment at 50	N	112.	Superfund waste cleanup of $10b	N
53.	Allow $3b for 2 stealth bombers	Y	113.	90 days notice of plant closings	N
54.	Publish bio-warfare experiments	N	114.	$20b in Medicare cuts/tax increases	N
55.	Raise minimum wage-veto override	N	115.	Spending cuts and tax increases	N
56.	Bar transfer of FS-X technology	N	116.	Set school lunch lmt-250% poverty	Y
57.	Cut defense and raise domestic $	N	117.	$75m for youth work projects	N
58.	Uniform poll closing in 48 states	Y	118.	Allow Angolan military assistance	Y
59.	Req foreign investment disclosure	N	119.	Suspend defense payments for abuse	N
60.	Textile import quotas-veto override	Y	120.	Drop SS COLAs/$12b tax increase	N

THOMAS, WILLIAM M. (continued)

121. Approve $1.5b for 21 MX missiles	Y	
122. Emergency farm credit/revisions	Y	
123. Duty on Taiwan/Hong Kong/S Korea	N	
124. Limit steel imports to 17%	N	
125. Cut $ to schools that bar prayer	N	
126. $50b-taxes; cut Medicare/spending	Y	
127. Limit Pershing II/cruise in Europe	N	
128. Delete $7.1b for 34 B-1 bombers	N	
129. Bar purchase of Sergeant York guns	Y	
130. El Salvador military/economic aid	Y	
131. Bar mining of Nicaraguan waters	Y	
132. Physician fee freeze for Medicare	Y	

133. $49b in "sin"/phone/insurance taxes	Y
134. Allow sale of Conrail	Y
135. Equal Rights Amendment	Y
136. Authorize Marines in Lebanon	Y
137. Eminent domain for coal companies	Y
138. Prohibit EPA clean air sanctions	Y
139. SS retirement age increase/reforms	Y
140. Auto domestic content requirement	N
141. Delete jobs program funding	#
142. Highway-gas tax bill	Y
143. Cut $5b from defense for Medicare	N
144. Emergency housing aid of $1b	Y

Presidential Support Score: 1991 - 72% 1990 - 54%

GALLEGLY, ELTON -- California 21st District [Republican]. Counties of Los Angeles (pt.) and Ventura (pt.). Prior Terms: 1987-92. Born: March 7, 1944; Huntington Park, CA. Occupation: Real estate businessman; Simi Valley city councilman (1979) and mayor (1980-1984).

1. Protection to Haitian refugees	N	
2. Raise tax on wealthy; lower others	N	
3. Investigate Reagan hostage delay	N	
4. Campaign finance revisions	N	
5. Unpaid leave to care for children	N	
6. Restrict NEA use of funds	Y	
7. Bar race-bias claim/habeas corpus	Y	
8. Ban race as death sentence factor	Y	
9. Exceptions to exclusionary rule	Y	
10. Allow sale of assault weapons	Y	
11. Life in prison/abolish death penalty	N	
12. Req conspiracy-price fixing cases	Y	
13. Unemployment benefits extension	N	
14. Tissue use of aborted fetuses	N	
15. Bar replacement of union strikers	N	
16. Hold foreign aid at $15b for '92	N	
17. Restore space station funding	Y	
18. Civil Rights Act of 1991	N	
19. Unlimited damages-discrimination	N	
20. Eliminate funds for supercollider	N	
21. Terminate SDI except for research	N	
22. Req 7-day handgun waiting period	Y	
23. Provide $30b for failed S&Ls	Y	
24. Allow use of force against Iraq	Y	
25. Allow $15b in foreign aid for '91	N	
26. Revise & extend legal immigration	N	
27. Suspend aid to Angolan rebels	N	
28. Democratic tax plan proposals	N	
29. Cut defense 5% across the board	N	
30. Textile import quotas-veto override	N	
31. Abortion service for military abroad	N	
32. Limits on high income farmers	N	
33. Family medical leave-veto override	N	
34. Req submission of balanced budget	N	
35. Balanced budget amendment	Y	
36. Amendment to ban flag desecration	Y	
37. Reauthorize Amtrak-veto override	N	
38. Retraining aid for coal miners	N	
39. Suspend El Salvador military aid	N	
40. Expand child care aid/tax credit	Y	
41. Raise House salary/omit honoraria	Y	
42. Toughen oil-spill liability	N	
43. Restitution to Japanese interned	N	

44. Protect Chinese & C.A. nationals	N
45. Abortion $ for rape/incest cases	N
46. Allow religious schools to bar gays	Y
47. Bar broadcaster fairness doctrine	Y
48. Bar cap gains cut/reinstate IRA	N
49. Bar unions equal voice in pension	Y
50. Bar assembly of chemical weapons	N
51. Ban plutonium/uranium production	N
52. Cap MX missile deployment at 50	N
53. Allow $3b for 2 stealth bombers	Y
54. Publish bio-warfare experiments	N
55. Raise minimum wage-veto override	N
56. Bar transfer of FS-X technology	N
57. Cut defense and raise domestic $	N
58. Uniform poll closing in 48 states	Y
59. Req foreign investment disclosure	N
60. Textile import quotas-veto override	N
61. Bar abortion funding in Wash, DC	Y
62. Notify spouses of AIDS+ carriers	Y
63. Seize conveyance-drug trafficking	Y
64. South Africa sanctions	N
65. 60 days' notice of plant closings	N
66. Close unneeded military bases	Y
67. Keep welfare reform within $2.8b	Y
68. Allow children housing exclusion	Y
69. Shift $400m of NASA to homeless	N
70. Cap Medicare patients' liability	Y
71. Prohibit employee polygraph testing	Y
72. Allow CIA to fund Contras	Y
73. Revise unfair trade practices	N
74. Focus SDI on accidental launch	N
75. Bar Air Force $ for MX missile	N
76. Allow "real" increase in defense	Y
77. Troop reduction in Europe of 50%	N
78. Ban nuclear tests above 1 kiloton	N
79. Ban anti-satellite missile tests	N
80. Observe certain limits of SALT II	N
81. Restore four Civil Rights laws	N
82. Prohibit aliens as strikebreakers	N
83. Allow military malpractice suits	N
84. Approval of $36m in Contra aid	Y
85. $18b deficit reduction compromise	N
86. Welfare reform of $5.7b for 5 years	N

GALLEGLY, ELTON (continued)

87. Raise taxes $12b/cut spending $3b	N		93. Ban airline smoking-2 hours or less	Y	
88. Board to assess occupational risk	N		94. $1b/two year aid for the homeless	N	
89. Balanced budget by '93-via targets	N		95. Bar non-unions in union companies	N	
90. Bar licensing of two nuclear plants	N		96. Increase FSLIC rescue to $15b	N	
91. Remove victims compensation cap	N		97. Impose quotas to lower trade deficit	N	
92. Catastrophic health insurance	N		98. Reduce discretionary budget 21%	Y	

Presidential Support Score: 1991 - 81%   1990 - 70%

MOORHEAD, CARLOS J.

MOORHEAD, CARLOS J. -- California 22nd District [Republican]. County of Los Angeles (pt.). Prior Terms: 1973-92. Born: May 6, 1922; Long Beach, CA. Education: University of California (B.A.); University of Southern California(J.D.). Military Service: U.S. Army WW II. Occupation: Attorney; director, Lawyer's Reference Service, Glendale Bar Assn.; president, Glendale Bar Assn.; California assemblyman.

1. Protection to Haitian refugees	N	49. Bar unions equal voice in pension	Y
2. Raise tax on wealthy; lower others	N	50. Bar assembly of chemical weapons	N
3. Investigate Reagan hostage delay	N	51. Ban plutonium/uranium production	N
4. Campaign finance revisions	N	52. Cap MX missile deployment at 50	N
5. Unpaid leave to care for children	N	53. Allow $3b for 2 stealth bombers	Y
6. Restrict NEA use of funds	Y	54. Publish bio-warfare experiments	N
7. Bar race-bias claim/habeas corpus	?	55. Raise minimum wage-veto override	N
8. Ban race as death sentence factor	?	56. Bar transfer of FS-X technology	Y
9. Exceptions to exclusionary rule	Y	57. Cut defense and raise domestic $	N
10. Allow sale of assault weapons	Y	58. Uniform poll closing in 48 states	Y
11. Life in prison/abolish death penalty	N	59. Req foreign investment disclosure	N
12. Req conspiracy-price fixing cases	Y	60. Textile import quotas-veto override	N
13. Unemployment benefits extension	N	61. Bar abortion funding in Wash, DC	Y
14. Tissue use of aborted fetuses	N	62. Notify spouses of AIDS+ carriers	Y
15. Bar replacement of union strikers	N	63. Seize conveyance-drug trafficking	Y
16. Hold foreign aid at $15b for '92	N	64. South Africa sanctions	N
17. Restore space station funding	Y	65. 60 days' notice of plant closings	N
18. Civil Rights Act of 1991	N	66. Close unneeded military bases	Y
19. Unlimited damages-discrimination	N	67. Keep welfare reform within $2.8b	Y
20. Eliminate funds for supercollider	Y	68. Allow children housing exclusion	Y
21. Terminate SDI except for research	N	69. Shift $400m of NASA to homeless	N
22. Req 7-day handgun waiting period	N	70. Cap Medicare patients' liability	N
23. Provide $30b for failed S&Ls	Y	71. Prohibit employee polygraph testing	N
24. Allow use of force against Iraq	Y	72. Allow CIA to fund Contras	Y
25. Allow $15b in foreign aid for '91	N	73. Revise unfair trade practices	N
26. Revise & extend legal immigration	N	74. Focus SDI on accidental launch	N
27. Suspend aid to Angolan rebels	N	75. Bar Air Force $ for MX missile	N
28. Democratic tax plan proposals	N	76. Allow "real" increase in defense	Y
29. Cut defense 5% across the board	N	77. Troop reduction in Europe of 50%	N
30. Textile import quotas-veto override	N	78. Ban nuclear tests above 1 kiloton	N
31. Abortion service for military abroad	N	79. Ban anti-satellite missile tests	N
32. Limits on high income farmers	N	80. Observe certain limits of SALT II	N
33. Family medical leave-veto override	N	81. Restore four Civil Rights laws	N
34. Req submission of balanced budget	N	82. Prohibit aliens as strikebreakers	N
35. Balanced budget amendment	Y	83. Allow military malpractice suits	Y
36. Amendment to ban flag desecration	Y	84. Approval of $36m in Contra aid	Y
37. Reauthorize Amtrak-veto override	N	85. $18b deficit reduction compromise	N
38. Retraining aid for coal miners	N	86. Welfare reform of $5.7b for 5 years	N
39. Suspend El Salvador military aid	N	87. Raise taxes $12b/cut spending $3b	N
40. Expand child care aid/tax credit	N	88. Board to assess occupational risk	N
41. Raise House salary/omit honoraria	Y	89. Balanced budget by '93-via targets	N
42. Toughen oil-spill liability	N	90. Bar licensing of two nuclear plants	N
43. Restitution to Japanese interned	N	91. Remove victims compensation cap	N
44. Protect Chinese & C.A. nationals	N	92. Catastrophic health insurance	N
45. Abortion $ for rape/incest cases	N	93. Ban airline smoking-2 hours or less	Y
46. Allow religious schools to bar gays	Y	94. $1b/two year aid for the homeless	N
47. Bar broadcaster fairness doctrine	Y	95. Bar non-unions in union companies	N
48. Bar cap gains cut/reinstate IRA	N	96. Increase FSLIC rescue to $15b	N

MOORHEAD, CARLOS J. (continued)

97. Impose quotas to lower trade deficit	N	
98. Reduce discretionary budget 21%	Y	
99. Immigration reform/alien amnesty	Y	
100. South Africa sanctions-veto override	N	
101. Tax overhaul to revise income tax	N	
102. Use of military in drug war	Y	
103. Delete 12 MX/add conventional wpn	N	
104. Raise speed limit to 65 mph	Y	
105. Require Pentagon to buy US goods	N	
106. AIDS insurance non-discrimination	N	
107. Prohibit Saudi arms sales	Y	
108. Ease Gun Control Act of 1968	Y	
109. Bar interstate handgun transport	N	
110. Make company emissions known	N	
111. Allow toxic victims to sue in fed ct	N	
112. Superfund waste cleanup of $10b	N	
113. 90 days notice of plant closings	N	
114. $20b in Medicare cuts/tax increases	N	
115. Spending cuts and tax increases	N	
116. Set school lunch lmt-250% poverty	Y	
117. $75m for youth work projects	N	
118. Allow Angolan military assistance	Y	
119. Suspend defense payments for abuse	N	
120. Drop SS COLAs/$12b tax increase	N	
121. Approve $1.5b for 21 MX missiles	Y
122. Emergency farm credit/revisions	N
123. Duty on Taiwan/Hong Kong/S Korea	N
124. Limit steel imports to 17%	N
125. Cut $ to schools that bar prayer	Y
126. $50b-taxes; cut Medicare/spending	N
127. Limit Pershing II/cruise in Europe	N
128. Delete $7.1b for 34 B-1 bombers	N
129. Bar purchase of Sergeant York guns	N
130. El Salvador military/economic aid	Y
131. Bar mining of Nicaraguan waters	N
132. Physician fee freeze for Medicare	Y
133. $49b in "sin"/phone/insurance taxes	N
134. Allow sale of Conrail	Y
135. Equal Rights Amendment	N
136. Authorize Marines in Lebanon	Y
137. Eminent domain for coal companies	Y
138. Prohibit EPA clean air sanctions	Y
139. SS retirement age increase/reforms	Y
140. Auto domestic content requirement	N
141. Delete jobs program funding	Y
142. Highway-gas tax bill	N
143. Cut $5b from defense for Medicare	N
144. Emergency housing aid of $1b	N

Presidential Support Score: 1991 - 82% 1990 - 74%

BEILENSON, ANTHONY C. -- California 23rd District [Democrat]. County of Los Angeles (pt.). Prior Terms: 1977-92. Born: October 26, 1932; New Rochelle, NY. Education: Harvard University (A.B., LL.B.). Occupation: California assemblyman (1963-66); California senator (1967-77).

1. Protection to Haitian refugees	N	
2. Raise tax on wealthy; lower others	N	
3. Investigate Reagan hostage delay	Y	
4. Campaign finance revisions	Y	
5. Unpaid leave to care for children	Y	
6. Restrict NEA use of funds	N	
7. Bar race-bias claim/habeas corpus	N	
8. Ban race as death sentence factor	N	
9. Exceptions to exclusionary rule	N	
10. Allow sale of assault weapons	N	
11. Life in prison/abolish death penalty	N	
12. Req conspiracy-price fixing cases	N	
13. Unemployment benefits extension	Y	
14. Tissue use of aborted fetuses	Y	
15. Bar replacement of union strikers	Y	
16. Hold foreign aid at $15b for '92	+	
17. Restore space station funding	N	
18. Civil Rights Act of 1991	Y	
19. Unlimited damages-discrimination	N	
20. Eliminate funds for supercollider	Y	
21. Terminate SDI except for research	Y	
22. Req 7-day handgun waiting period	Y	
23. Provide $30b for failed S&Ls	Y	
24. Allow use of force against Iraq	N	
25. Allow $15b in foreign aid for '91	Y	
26. Revise & extend legal immigration	N	
27. Suspend aid to Angolan rebels	Y	
28. Democratic tax plan proposals	Y	
29. Cut defense 5% across the board	N	
30. Textile import quotas-veto override	N	
31. Abortion service for military abroad	Y	
32. Limits on high income farmers	Y
33. Family medical leave-veto override	Y
34. Req submission of balanced budget	Y
35. Balanced budget amendment	N
36. Amendment to ban flag desecration	N
37. Reauthorize Amtrak-veto override	Y
38. Retraining aid for coal miners	N
39. Suspend El Salvador military aid	Y
40. Expand child care aid/tax credit	N
41. Raise House salary/omit honoraria	Y
42. Toughen oil-spill liability	Y
43. Restitution to Japanese interned	Y
44. Protect Chinese & C.A. nationals	N
45. Abortion $ for rape/incest cases	Y
46. Allow religious schools to bar gays	N
47. Bar broadcaster fairness doctrine	N
48. Bar cap gains cut/reinstate IRA	Y
49. Bar unions equal voice in pension	N
50. Bar assembly of chemical weapons	Y
51. Ban plutonium/uranium production	Y
52. Cap MX missile deployment at 50	Y
53. Allow $3b for 2 stealth bombers	N
54. Publish bio-warfare experiments	Y
55. Raise minimum wage-veto override	Y
56. Bar transfer of FS-X technology	N
57. Cut defense and raise domestic $	Y
58. Uniform poll closing in 48 states	Y
59. Req foreign investment disclosure	Y
60. Textile import quotas-veto override	N
61. Bar abortion funding in Wash, DC	N
62. Notify spouses of AIDS+ carriers	N

BEILENSON, ANTHONY C. (continued)

63. Seize conveyance-drug trafficking	N	
64. South Africa sanctions	?	
65. 60 days' notice of plant closings	Y	
66. Close unneeded military bases	Y	
67. Keep welfare reform within $2.8b	N	
68. Allow children housing exclusion	N	
69. Shift $400m of NASA to homeless	Y	
70. Cap Medicare patients' liability	N	
71. Prohibit employee polygraph testing	Y	
72. Allow CIA to fund Contras	N	
73. Revise unfair trade practices	Y	
74. Focus SDI on accidental launch	Y	
75. Bar Air Force $ for MX missile	Y	
76. Allow "real" increase in defense	N	
77. Troop reduction in Europe of 50%	N	
78. Ban nuclear tests above 1 kiloton	Y	
79. Ban anti-satellite missile tests	Y	
80. Observe certain limits of SALT II	Y	
81. Restore four Civil Rights laws	Y	
82. Prohibit aliens as strikebreakers	Y	
83. Allow military malpractice suits	Y	
84. Approval of $36m in Contra aid	N	
85. $18b deficit reduction compromise	Y	
86. Welfare reform of $5.7b for 5 years	Y	
87. Raise taxes $12b/cut spending $3b	Y	
88. Board to assess occupational risk	N	
89. Balanced budget by '93-via targets	N	
90. Bar licensing of two nuclear plants	Y	
91. Remove victims compensation cap	Y	
92. Catastrophic health insurance	N	
93. Ban airline smoking-2 hours or less	Y	
94. $1b/two year aid for the homeless	Y	
95. Bar non-unions in union companies	Y	
96. Increase FSLIC rescue to $15b	Y	
97. Impose quotas to lower trade deficit	N	
98. Reduce discretionary budget 21%	N	
99. Immigration reform/alien amnesty	Y	
100. South Africa sanctions-veto override	Y	
101. Tax overhaul to revise income tax	Y	
102. Use of military in drug war	N	
103. Delete 12 MX/add conventional wpn	Y	
104. Raise speed limit to 65 mph	N
105. Require Pentagon to buy US goods	N
106. AIDS insurance non-discrimination	Y
107. Prohibit Saudi arms sales	Y
108. Ease Gun Control Act of 1968	N
109. Bar interstate handgun transport	Y
110. Make company emissions known	Y
111. Allow toxic victims to sue in fed ct	Y
112. Superfund waste cleanup of $10b	Y
113. 90 days notice of plant closings	Y
114. $20b in Medicare cuts/tax increases	Y
115. Spending cuts and tax increases	Y
116. Set school lunch lmt-250% poverty	N
117. $75m for youth work projects	Y
118. Allow Angolan military assistance	N
119. Suspend defense payments for abuse	Y
120. Drop SS COLAs/$12b tax increase	N
121. Approve $1.5b for 21 MX missiles	N
122. Emergency farm credit/revisions	Y
123. Duty on Taiwan/Hong Kong/S Korea	Y
124. Limit steel imports to 17%	N
125. Cut $ to schools that bar prayer	N
126. $50b-taxes; cut Medicare/spending	Y
127. Limit Pershing II/cruise in Europe	Y
128. Delete $7.1b for 34 B-1 bombers	Y
129. Bar purchase of Sergeant York guns	Y
130. El Salvador military/economic aid	N
131. Bar mining of Nicaraguan waters	Y
132. Physician fee freeze for Medicare	N
133. $49b in "sin"/phone/insurance taxes	Y
134. Allow sale of Conrail	N
135. Equal Rights Amendment	Y
136. Authorize Marines in Lebanon	Y
137. Eminent domain for coal companies	Y
138. Prohibit EPA clean air sanctions	N
139. SS retirement age increase/reforms	Y
140. Auto domestic content requirement	N
141. Delete jobs program funding	?
142. Highway-gas tax bill	Y
143. Cut $5b from defense for Medicare	N
144. Emergency housing aid of $1b	N

Presidential Support Score: 1991 - 32% 1990 - 26%

WAXMAN, HENRY A. -- California 24th District [Democrat]. County of Los Angeles (pt.). Prior Terms: 1975-92. Born: September 12, 1939; Los Angeles, CA. Education: University of California (B.A., LL.B.). Occupation: Attorney; California assemblyman.

1. Protection to Haitian refugees	Y	
2. Raise tax on wealthy; lower others	Y	
3. Investigate Reagan hostage delay	Y	
4. Campaign finance revisions	Y	
5. Unpaid leave to care for children	Y	
6. Restrict NEA use of funds	N	
7. Bar race-bias claim/habeas corpus	N	
8. Ban race as death sentence factor	N	
9. Exceptions to exclusionary rule	?	
10. Allow sale of assault weapons	X	
11. Life in prison/abolish death penalty	#	
12. Req conspiracy-price fixing cases	N	
13. Unemployment benefits extension	Y	
14. Tissue use of aborted fetuses	Y	
15. Bar replacement of union strikers	Y	
16. Hold foreign aid at $15b for '92	Y
17. Restore space station funding	N
18. Civil Rights Act of 1991	Y
19. Unlimited damages-discrimination	Y
20. Eliminate funds for supercollider	N
21. Terminate SDI except for research	Y
22. Req 7-day handgun waiting period	Y
23. Provide $30b for failed S&Ls	Y
24. Allow use of force against Iraq	N
25. Allow $15b in foreign aid for '91	Y
26. Revise & extend legal immigration	Y
27. Suspend aid to Angolan rebels	Y
28. Democratic tax plan proposals	Y
29. Cut defense 5% across the board	N
30. Textile import quotas-veto override	N

WAXMAN, HENRY A. (continued)

31. Abortion service for military abroad	Y	
32. Limits on high income farmers	Y	
33. Family medical leave-veto override	Y	
34. Req submission of balanced budget	N	
35. Balanced budget amendment	N	
36. Amendment to ban flag desecration	N	
37. Reauthorize Amtrak-veto override	Y	
38. Retraining aid for coal miners	Y	
39. Suspend El Salvador military aid	Y	
40. Expand child care aid/tax credit	Y	
41. Raise House salary/omit honoraria	Y	
42. Toughen oil-spill liability	Y	
43. Restitution to Japanese interned	Y	
44. Protect Chinese & C.A. nationals	Y	
45. Abortion $ for rape/incest cases	Y	
46. Allow religious schools to bar gays	N	
47. Bar broadcaster fairness doctrine	N	
48. Bar cap gains cut/reinstate IRA	Y	
49. Bar unions equal voice in pension	N	
50. Bar assembly of chemical weapons	Y	
51. Ban plutonium/uranium production	Y	
52. Cap MX missile deployment at 50	Y	
53. Allow $3b for 2 stealth bombers	N	
54. Publish bio-warfare experiments	Y	
55. Raise minimum wage-veto override	Y	
56. Bar transfer of FS-X technology	Y	
57. Cut defense and raise domestic $	N	
58. Uniform poll closing in 48 states	N	
59. Req foreign investment disclosure	Y	
60. Textile import quotas-veto override	N	
61. Bar abortion funding in Wash, DC	N	
62. Notify spouses of AIDS+ carriers	N	
63. Seize conveyance-drug trafficking	?	
64. South Africa sanctions	Y	
65. 60 days' notice of plant closings	Y	
66. Close unneeded military bases	N	
67. Keep welfare reform within $2.8b	N	
68. Allow children housing exclusion	N	
69. Shift $400m of NASA to homeless	N	
70. Cap Medicare patients' liability	Y	
71. Prohibit employee polygraph testing	Y	
72. Allow CIA to fund Contras	N	
73. Revise unfair trade practices	Y	
74. Focus SDI on accidental launch	Y	
75. Bar Air Force $ for MX missile	Y	
76. Allow "real" increase in defense	N	
77. Troop reduction in Europe of 50%	N	
78. Ban nuclear tests above 1 kiloton	Y	
79. Ban anti-satellite missile tests	Y	
80. Observe certain limits of SALT II	Y	
81. Restore four Civil Rights laws	Y	
82. Prohibit aliens as strikebreakers	Y	
83. Allow military malpractice suits	Y	
84. Approval of $36m in Contra aid	N	
85. $18b deficit reduction compromise	Y	
86. Welfare reform of $5.7b for 5 years	Y	
87. Raise taxes $12b/cut spending $3b	#	

88. Board to assess occupational risk	Y	
89. Balanced budget by '93-via targets	N	
90. Bar licensing of two nuclear plants	Y	
91. Remove victims compensation cap	Y	
92. Catastrophic health insurance	Y	
93. Ban airline smoking-2 hours or less	Y	
94. $1b/two year aid for the homeless	Y	
95. Bar non-unions in union companies	Y	
96. Increase FSLIC rescue to $15b	Y	
97. Impose quotas to lower trade deficit	N	
98. Reduce discretionary budget 21%	?	
99. Immigration reform/alien amnesty	Y	
100. South Africa sanctions-veto override	Y	
101. Tax overhaul to revise income tax	Y	
102. Use of military in drug war	Y	
103. Delete 12 MX/add conventional wpn	Y	
104. Raise speed limit to 65 mph	N	
105. Require Pentagon to buy US goods	?	
106. AIDS insurance non-discrimination	Y	
107. Prohibit Saudi arms sales	Y	
108. Ease Gun Control Act of 1968	N	
109. Bar interstate handgun transport	Y	
110. Make company emissions known	Y	
111. Allow toxic victims to sue in fed ct	Y	
112. Superfund waste cleanup of $10b	Y	
113. 90 days notice of plant closings	Y	
114. $20b in Medicare cuts/tax increases	Y	
115. Spending cuts and tax increases	Y	
116. Set school lunch lmt-250% poverty	N	
117. $75m for youth work projects	Y	
118. Allow Angolan military assistance	?	
119. Suspend defense payments for abuse	Y	
120. Drop SS COLAs/$12b tax increase	N	
121. Approve $1.5b for 21 MX missiles	N	
122. Emergency farm credit/revisions	Y	
123. Duty on Taiwan/Hong Kong/S Korea	N	
124. Limit steel imports to 17%	N	
125. Cut $ to schools that bar prayer	N	
126. $50b-taxes; cut Medicare/spending	Y	
127. Limit Pershing II/cruise in Europe	Y	
128. Delete $7.1b for 34 B-1 bombers	Y	
129. Bar purchase of Sergeant York guns	Y	
130. El Salvador military/economic aid	N	
131. Bar mining of Nicaraguan waters	Y	
132. Physician fee freeze for Medicare	N	
133. $49b in "sin"/phone/insurance taxes	Y	
134. Allow sale of Conrail	N	
135. Equal Rights Amendment	Y	
136. Authorize Marines in Lebanon	N	
137. Eminent domain for coal companies	N	
138. Prohibit EPA clean air sanctions	Y	
139. SS retirement age increase/reforms	N	
140. Auto domestic content requirement	N	
141. Delete jobs program funding	N	
142. Highway-gas tax bill	Y	
143. Cut $5b from defense for Medicare	Y	
144. Emergency housing aid of $1b	Y	

Presidential Support Score: 1991 - 27%   1990 - 20%

ROYBAL, EDWARD R. -- California 25th District [Democrat].   County of Los Angeles (pt.).
Prior Terms: 1963-92. Born: February 10, 1916; Albuquerque, NM. Education: University
of California; Southwestern University. Military Service: U.S. Army, 1944-45. Occupation:

ROYBAL, EDWARD R. (continued)

Member, Civilian Conservation Corps (1934-35); social worker, public health educator, California Tuberculosis Assn.; director, health education, Los Angeles County Tuberculosis and Health Assn. (1942-49); Los Angeles City councilman (1949-62).

1. Protection to Haitian refugees	Y		61. Bar abortion funding in Wash, DC	N
2. Raise tax on wealthy; lower others	Y		62. Notify spouses of AIDS+ carriers	N
3. Investigate Reagan hostage delay	Y		63. Seize conveyance-drug trafficking	N
4. Campaign finance revisions	Y		64. South Africa sanctions	#
5. Unpaid leave to care for children	Y		65. 60 days' notice of plant closings	Y
6. Restrict NEA use of funds	N		66. Close unneeded military bases	N
7. Bar race-bias claim/habeas corpus	N		67. Keep welfare reform within $2.8b	N
8. Ban race as death sentence factor	N		68. Allow children housing exclusion	N
9. Exceptions to exclusionary rule	N		69. Shift $400m of NASA to homeless	Y
10. Allow sale of assault weapons	N		70. Cap Medicare patients' liability	Y
11. Life in prison/abolish death penalty	Y		71. Prohibit employee polygraph testing	Y
12. Req conspiracy-price fixing cases	N		72. Allow CIA to fund Contras	N
13. Unemployment benefits extension	Y		73. Revise unfair trade practices	Y
14. Tissue use of aborted fetuses	Y		74. Focus SDI on accidental launch	Y
15. Bar replacement of union strikers	Y		75. Bar Air Force $ for MX missile	Y
16. Hold foreign aid at $15b for '92	Y		76. Allow "real" increase in defense	N
17. Restore space station funding	N		77. Troop reduction in Europe of 50%	Y
18. Civil Rights Act of 1991	Y		78. Ban nuclear tests above 1 kiloton	Y
19. Unlimited damages-discrimination	Y		79. Ban anti-satellite missile tests	Y
20. Eliminate funds for supercollider	N		80. Observe certain limits of SALT II	Y
21. Terminate SDI except for research	?		81. Restore four Civil Rights laws	Y
22. Req 7-day handgun waiting period	?		82. Prohibit aliens as strikebreakers	Y
23. Provide $30b for failed S&Ls	Y		83. Allow military malpractice suits	Y
24. Allow use of force against Iraq	N		84. Approval of $36m in Contra aid	N
25. Allow $15b in foreign aid for '91	Y		85. $18b deficit reduction compromise	Y
26. Revise & extend legal immigration	Y		86. Welfare reform of $5.7b for 5 years	Y
27. Suspend aid to Angolan rebels	Y		87. Raise taxes $12b/cut spending $3b	Y
28. Democratic tax plan proposals	Y		88. Board to assess occupational risk	Y
29. Cut defense 5% across the board	Y		89. Balanced budget by '93-via targets	N
30. Textile import quotas-veto override	Y		90. Bar licensing of two nuclear plants	Y
31. Abortion service for military abroad	Y		91. Remove victims compensation cap	Y
32. Limits on high income farmers	N		92. Catastrophic health insurance	Y
33. Family medical leave-veto override	Y		93. Ban airline smoking-2 hours or less	Y
34. Req submission of balanced budget	Y		94. $1b/two year aid for the homeless	Y
35. Balanced budget amendment	N		95. Bar non-unions in union companies	Y
36. Amendment to ban flag desecration	N		96. Increase FSLIC rescue to $15b	N
37. Reauthorize Amtrak-veto override	Y		97. Impose quotas to lower trade deficit	N
38. Retraining aid for coal miners	Y		98. Reduce discretionary budget 21%	N
39. Suspend El Salvador military aid	Y		99. Immigration reform/alien amnesty	N
40. Expand child care aid/tax credit	Y		100. South Africa sanctions-veto override	Y
41. Raise House salary/omit honoraria	Y		101. Tax overhaul to revise income tax	Y
42. Toughen oil-spill liability	Y		102. Use of military in drug war	N
43. Restitution to Japanese interned	Y		103. Delete 12 MX/add conventional wpn	?
44. Protect Chinese & C.A. nationals	Y		104. Raise speed limit to 65 mph	Y
45. Abortion $ for rape/incest cases	Y		105. Require Pentagon to buy US goods	N
46. Allow religious schools to bar gays	N		106. AIDS insurance non-discrimination	Y
47. Bar broadcaster fairness doctrine	N		107. Prohibit Saudi arms sales	Y
48. Bar cap gains cut/reinstate IRA	Y		108. Ease Gun Control Act of 1968	N
49. Bar unions equal voice in pension	N		109. Bar interstate handgun transport	Y
50. Bar assembly of chemical weapons	Y		110. Make company emissions known	Y
51. Ban plutonium/uranium production	Y		111. Allow toxic victims to sue in fed ct	Y
52. Cap MX missile deployment at 50	Y		112. Superfund waste cleanup of $10b	Y
53. Allow $3b for 2 stealth bombers	N		113. 90 days notice of plant closings	Y
54. Publish bio-warfare experiments	Y		114. $20b in Medicare cuts/tax increases	Y
55. Raise minimum wage-veto override	Y		115. Spending cuts and tax increases	Y
56. Bar transfer of FS-X technology	Y		116. Set school lunch lmt-250% poverty	N
57. Cut defense and raise domestic $	#		117. $75m for youth work projects	?
58. Uniform poll closing in 48 states	N		118. Allow Angolan military assistance	N
59. Req foreign investment disclosure	Y		119. Suspend defense payments for abuse	Y
60. Textile import quotas-veto override	Y		120. Drop SS COLAs/$12b tax increase	N

ROYBAL, EDWARD R. (continued)

121. Approve $1.5b for 21 MX missiles	N	133. $49b in "sin"/phone/insurance taxes	Y
122. Emergency farm credit/revisions	Y	134. Allow sale of Conrail	?
123. Duty on Taiwan/Hong Kong/S Korea	Y	135. Equal Rights Amendment	Y
124. Limit steel imports to 17%	Y	136. Authorize Marines in Lebanon	N
125. Cut $ to schools that bar prayer	N	137. Eminent domain for coal companies	N
126. $50b-taxes; cut Medicare/spending	N	138. Prohibit EPA clean air sanctions	N
127. Limit Pershing II/cruise in Europe	Y	139. SS retirement age increase/reforms	N
128. Delete $7.1b for 34 B-1 bombers	Y	140. Auto domestic content requirement	Y
129. Bar purchase of Sergeant York guns	Y	141. Delete jobs program funding	N
130. El Salvador military/economic aid	N	142. Highway-gas tax bill	Y
131. Bar mining of Nicaraguan waters	Y	143. Cut $5b from defense for Medicare	Y
132. Physician fee freeze for Medicare	N	144. Emergency housing aid of $1b	Y

Presidential Support Score: 1991 - 29%   1990 - 16%

BERMAN, HOWARD L. -- California 26th District [Democrat]. County of Los Angeles (pt.). Prior Terms: 1983-92. Born: April 15, 1941; Los Angeles, CA. Education: University of California (B.A., LL.B.). Occupation: Attorney (1966-72); California assemblyman (1972).

1. Protection to Haitian refugees	Y	45. Abortion $ for rape/incest cases	Y
2. Raise tax on wealthy; lower others	Y	46. Allow religious schools to bar gays	N
3. Investigate Reagan hostage delay	Y	47. Bar broadcaster fairness doctrine	N
4. Campaign finance revisions	Y	48. Bar cap gains cut/reinstate IRA	Y
5. Unpaid leave to care for children	Y	49. Bar unions equal voice in pension	N
6. Restrict NEA use of funds	N	50. Bar assembly of chemical weapons	Y
7. Bar race-bias claim/habeas corpus	N	51. Ban plutonium/uranium production	Y
8. Ban race as death sentence factor	N	52. Cap MX missile deployment at 50	Y
9. Exceptions to exclusionary rule	N	53. Allow $3b for 2 stealth bombers	N
10. Allow sale of assault weapons	N	54. Publish bio-warfare experiments	Y
11. Life in prison/abolish death penalty	Y	55. Raise minimum wage-veto override	Y
12. Req conspiracy-price fixing cases	N	56. Bar transfer of FS-X technology	Y
13. Unemployment benefits extension	?	57. Cut defense and raise domestic $	Y
14. Tissue use of aborted fetuses	Y	58. Uniform poll closing in 48 states	?
15. Bar replacement of union strikers	Y	59. Req foreign investment disclosure	N
16. Hold foreign aid at $15b for '92	Y	60. Textile import quotas-veto override	N
17. Restore space station funding	N	61. Bar abortion funding in Wash, DC	N
18. Civil Rights Act of 1991	Y	62. Notify spouses of AIDS+ carriers	N
19. Unlimited damages-discrimination	Y	63. Seize conveyance-drug trafficking	N
20. Eliminate funds for supercollider	N	64. South Africa sanctions	Y
21. Terminate SDI except for research	Y	65. 60 days' notice of plant closings	Y
22. Req 7-day handgun waiting period	Y	66. Close unneeded military bases	Y
23. Provide $30b for failed S&Ls	Y	67. Keep welfare reform within $2.8b	N
24. Allow use of force against Iraq	Y	68. Allow children housing exclusion	N
25. Allow $15b in foreign aid for '91	Y	69. Shift $400m of NASA to homeless	Y
26. Revise & extend legal immigration	Y	70. Cap Medicare patients' liability	Y
27. Suspend aid to Angolan rebels	Y	71. Prohibit employee polygraph testing	?
28. Democratic tax plan proposals	Y	72. Allow CIA to fund Contras	N
29. Cut defense 5% across the board	Y	73. Revise unfair trade practices	Y
30. Textile import quotas-veto override	N	74. Focus SDI on accidental launch	Y
31. Abortion service for military abroad	Y	75. Bar Air Force $ for MX missile	Y
32. Limits on high income farmers	Y	76. Allow "real" increase in defense	N
33. Family medical leave-veto override	Y	77. Troop reduction in Europe of 50%	?
34. Req submission of balanced budget	Y	78. Ban nuclear tests above 1 kiloton	Y
35. Balanced budget amendment	N	79. Ban anti-satellite missile tests	Y
36. Amendment to ban flag desecration	N	80. Observe certain limits of SALT II	Y
37. Reauthorize Amtrak-veto override	Y	81. Restore four Civil Rights laws	Y
38. Retraining aid for coal miners	Y	82. Prohibit aliens as strikebreakers	Y
39. Suspend El Salvador military aid	Y	83. Allow military malpractice suits	Y
40. Expand child care aid/tax credit	Y	84. Approval of $36m in Contra aid	N
41. Raise House salary/omit honoraria	#	85. $18b deficit reduction compromise	Y
42. Toughen oil-spill liability	Y	86. Welfare reform of $5.7b for 5 years	Y
43. Restitution to Japanese interned	Y	87. Raise taxes $12b/cut spending $3b	Y
44. Protect Chinese & C.A. nationals	Y	88. Board to assess occupational risk	Y

BERMAN, HOWARD L. (continued)

89. Balanced budget by '93-via targets	N	
90. Bar licensing of two nuclear plants	Y	
91. Remove victims compensation cap	Y	
92. Catastrophic health insurance	Y	
93. Ban airline smoking-2 hours or less	Y	
94. $1b/two year aid for the homeless	Y	
95. Bar non-unions in union companies	Y	
96. Increase FSLIC rescue to $15b	Y	
97. Impose quotas to lower trade deficit	Y	
98. Reduce discretionary budget 21%	Y	
99. Immigration reform/alien amnesty	Y	
100. South Africa sanctions-veto override	Y	
101. Tax overhaul to revise income tax	Y	
102. Use of military in drug war	N	
103. Delete 12 MX/add conventional wpn	Y	
104. Raise speed limit to 65 mph	N	
105. Require Pentagon to buy US goods	?	
106. AIDS insurance non-discrimination	Y	
107. Prohibit Saudi arms sales	Y	
108. Ease Gun Control Act of 1968	N	
109. Bar interstate handgun transport	Y	
110. Make company emissions known	Y	
111. Allow toxic victims to sue in fed ct	Y	
112. Superfund waste cleanup of $10b	Y	
113. 90 days notice of plant closings	Y	
114. $20b in Medicare cuts/tax increases	Y	
115. Spending cuts and tax increases	Y
116. Set school lunch lmt-250% poverty	N
117. $75m for youth work projects	Y
118. Allow Angolan military assistance	N
119. Suspend defense payments for abuse	Y
120. Drop SS COLAs/$12b tax increase	N
121. Approve $1.5b for 21 MX missiles	N
122. Emergency farm credit/revisions	Y
123. Duty on Taiwan/Hong Kong/S Korea	N
124. Limit steel imports to 17%	N
125. Cut $ to schools that bar prayer	N
126. $50b-taxes; cut Medicare/spending	Y
127. Limit Pershing II/cruise in Europe	Y
128. Delete $7.1b for 34 B-1 bombers	Y
129. Bar purchase of Sergeant York guns	Y
130. El Salvador military/economic aid	N
131. Bar mining of Nicaraguan waters	Y
132. Physician fee freeze for Medicare	N
133. $49b in "sin"/phone/insurance taxes	Y
134. Allow sale of Conrail	?
135. Equal Rights Amendment	Y
136. Authorize Marines in Lebanon	Y
137. Eminent domain for coal companies	N
138. Prohibit EPA clean air sanctions	?
139. SS retirement age increase/reforms	N

Presidential Support Score: 1991 - 32%   1990 - 20%

LEVINE, MEL -- California 27th District [Democrat].   County of Los Angeles (pt.). Prior Terms: 1983-92.   Born: June 7, 1943; Los Angeles, CA.   Education: University of California; Princeton University (M.S.); Harvard Law School (J.D.).   Occupation: Attorney; Senate legislative assistant; California assemblyman.

1. Protection to Haitian refugees	?	
2. Raise tax on wealthy; lower others	Y	
3. Investigate Reagan hostage delay	?	
4. Campaign finance revisions	Y	
5. Unpaid leave to care for children	Y	
6. Restrict NEA use of funds	N	
7. Bar race-bias claim/habeas corpus	N	
8. Ban race as death sentence factor	N	
9. Exceptions to exclusionary rule	?	
10. Allow sale of assault weapons	X	
11. Life in prison/abolish death penalty	N	
12. Req conspiracy-price fixing cases	N	
13. Unemployment benefits extension	?	
14. Tissue use of aborted fetuses	Y	
15. Bar replacement of union strikers	Y	
16. Hold foreign aid at $15b for '92	?	
17. Restore space station funding	Y	
18. Civil Rights Act of 1991	Y	
19. Unlimited damages-discrimination	Y	
20. Eliminate funds for supercollider	N	
21. Terminate SDI except for research	Y	
22. Req 7-day handgun waiting period	Y	
23. Provide $30b for failed S&Ls	?	
24. Allow use of force against Iraq	Y	
25. Allow $15b in foreign aid for '91	Y	
26. Revise & extend legal immigration	Y	
27. Suspend aid to Angolan rebels	Y	
28. Democratic tax plan proposals	Y	
29. Cut defense 5% across the board	N	
30. Textile import quotas-veto override	N
31. Abortion service for military abroad	Y
32. Limits on high income farmers	Y
33. Family medical leave-veto override	Y
34. Req submission of balanced budget	Y
35. Balanced budget amendment	N
36. Amendment to ban flag desecration	N
37. Reauthorize Amtrak-veto override	Y
38. Retraining aid for coal miners	Y
39. Suspend El Salvador military aid	Y
40. Expand child care aid/tax credit	Y
41. Raise House salary/omit honoraria	Y
42. Toughen oil-spill liability	Y
43. Restitution to Japanese interned	Y
44. Protect Chinese & C.A. nationals	Y
45. Abortion $ for rape/incest cases	Y
46. Allow religious schools to bar gays	N
47. Bar broadcaster fairness doctrine	N
48. Bar cap gains cut/reinstate IRA	Y
49. Bar unions equal voice in pension	N
50. Bar assembly of chemical weapons	Y
51. Ban plutonium/uranium production	Y
52. Cap MX missile deployment at 50	Y
53. Allow $3b for 2 stealth bombers	N
54. Publish bio-warfare experiments	Y
55. Raise minimum wage-veto override	Y
56. Bar transfer of FS-X technology	Y
57. Cut defense and raise domestic $	N
58. Uniform poll closing in 48 states	N

LEVINE, MEL (continued)

59. Req foreign investment disclosure	N
60. Textile import quotas-veto override	N
61. Bar abortion funding in Wash, DC	N
62. Notify spouses of AIDS+ carriers	N
63. Seize conveyance-drug trafficking	?
64. South Africa sanctions	Y
65. 60 days' notice of plant closings	Y
66. Close unneeded military bases	Y
67. Keep welfare reform within $2.8b	N
68. Allow children housing exclusion	N
69. Shift $400m of NASA to homeless	N
70. Cap Medicare patients' liability	Y
71. Prohibit employee polygraph testing	Y
72. Allow CIA to fund Contras	N
73. Revise unfair trade practices	Y
74. Focus SDI on accidental launch	Y
75. Bar Air Force $ for MX missile	Y
76. Allow "real" increase in defense	N
77. Troop reduction in Europe of 50%	N
78. Ban nuclear tests above 1 kiloton	Y
79. Ban anti-satellite missile tests	Y
80. Observe certain limits of SALT II	Y
81. Restore four Civil Rights laws	Y
82. Prohibit aliens as strikebreakers	?
83. Allow military malpractice suits	Y
84. Approval of $36m in Contra aid	N
85. $18b deficit reduction compromise	Y
86. Welfare reform of $5.7b for 5 years	Y
87. Raise taxes $12b/cut spending $3b	Y
88. Board to assess occupational risk	Y
89. Balanced budget by '93-via targets	N
90. Bar licensing of two nuclear plants	Y
91. Remove victims compensation cap	Y
92. Catastrophic health insurance	Y
93. Ban airline smoking-2 hours or less	Y
94. $1b/two year aid for the homeless	Y
95. Bar non-unions in union companies	Y
96. Increase FSLIC rescue to $15b	?
97. Impose quotas to lower trade deficit	N
98. Reduce discretionary budget 21%	Y
99. Immigration reform/alien amnesty	Y

100. South Africa sanctions-veto override	Y
101. Tax overhaul to revise income tax	Y
102. Use of military in drug war	N
103. Delete 12 MX/add conventional wpn	Y
104. Raise speed limit to 65 mph	N
105. Require Pentagon to buy US goods	N
106. AIDS insurance non-discrimination	Y
107. Prohibit Saudi arms sales	Y
108. Ease Gun Control Act of 1968	N
109. Bar interstate handgun transport	Y
110. Make company emissions known	Y
111. Allow toxic victims to sue in fed ct	Y
112. Superfund waste cleanup of $10b	Y
113. 90 days notice of plant closings	Y
114. $20b in Medicare cuts/tax increases	Y
115. Spending cuts and tax increases	Y
116. Set school lunch lmt-250% poverty	N
117. $75m for youth work projects	Y
118. Allow Angolan military assistance	N
119. Suspend defense payments for abuse	Y
120. Drop SS COLAs/$12b tax increase	N
121. Approve $1.5b for 21 MX missiles	N
122. Emergency farm credit/revisions	Y
123. Duty on Taiwan/Hong Kong/S Korea	Y
124. Limit steel imports to 17%	N
125. Cut $ to schools that bar prayer	X
126. $50b-taxes; cut Medicare/spending	Y
127. Limit Pershing II/cruise in Europe	Y
128. Delete $7.1b for 34 B-1 bombers	N
129. Bar purchase of Sergeant York guns	Y
130. El Salvador military/economic aid	N
131. Bar mining of Nicaraguan waters	Y
132. Physician fee freeze for Medicare	N
133. $49b in "sin"/phone/insurance taxes	Y
134. Allow sale of Conrail	N
135. Equal Rights Amendment	Y
136. Authorize Marines in Lebanon	N
137. Eminent domain for coal companies	Y
138. Prohibit EPA clean air sanctions	+
139. SS retirement age increase/reforms	N

Presidential Support Score: 1991 - 18%   1990 - 19%

DIXON, JULIAN C. -- California 28th District [Democrat]. County of Los Angeles (pt.). Prior Terms: 1979-92. Born: August 8, 1934; Washington, DC. Education: Los Angeles State College (B.S.); Southwestern University (LL.B.). Military Service: U.S. Army 1957-60. Occupation: California state assemblyman (1972-78).

1. Protection to Haitian refugees	Y
2. Raise tax on wealthy; lower others	Y
3. Investigate Reagan hostage delay	Y
4. Campaign finance revisions	Y
5. Unpaid leave to care for children	Y
6. Restrict NEA use of funds	N
7. Bar race-bias claim/habeas corpus	N
8. Ban race as death sentence factor	N
9. Exceptions to exclusionary rule	N
10. Allow sale of assault weapons	N
11. Life in prison/abolish death penalty	Y
12. Req conspiracy-price fixing cases	N
13. Unemployment benefits extension	Y
14. Tissue use of aborted fetuses	Y

15. Bar replacement of union strikers	Y
16. Hold foreign aid at $15b for '92	Y
17. Restore space station funding	Y
18. Civil Rights Act of 1991	Y
19. Unlimited damages-discrimination	Y
20. Eliminate funds for supercollider	N
21. Terminate SDI except for research	?
22. Req 7-day handgun waiting period	Y
23. Provide $30b for failed S&Ls	N
24. Allow use of force against Iraq	N
25. Allow $15b in foreign aid for '91	Y
26. Revise & extend legal immigration	Y
27. Suspend aid to Angolan rebels	Y
28. Democratic tax plan proposals	Y

DIXON, JULIAN C. (continued)

29. Cut defense 5% across the board	N	
30. Textile import quotas-veto override	Y	
31. Abortion service for military abroad	Y	
32. Limits on high income farmers	N	
33. Family medical leave-veto override	Y	
34. Req submission of balanced budget	Y	
35. Balanced budget amendment	N	
36. Amendment to ban flag desecration	N	
37. Reauthorize Amtrak-veto override	Y	
38. Retraining aid for coal miners	Y	
39. Suspend El Salvador military aid	Y	
40. Expand child care aid/tax credit	Y	
41. Raise House salary/omit honoraria	Y	
42. Toughen oil-spill liability	Y	
43. Restitution to Japanese interned	Y	
44. Protect Chinese & C.A. nationals	Y	
45. Abortion $ for rape/incest cases	Y	
46. Allow religious schools to bar gays	N	
47. Bar broadcaster fairness doctrine	N	
48. Bar cap gains cut/reinstate IRA	Y	
49. Bar unions equal voice in pension	N	
50. Bar assembly of chemical weapons	Y	
51. Ban plutonium/uranium production	Y	
52. Cap MX missile deployment at 50	?	
53. Allow $3b for 2 stealth bombers	N	
54. Publish bio-warfare experiments	Y	
55. Raise minimum wage-veto override	Y	
56. Bar transfer of FS-X technology	Y	
57. Cut defense and raise domestic $	Y	
58. Uniform poll closing in 48 states	N	
59. Req foreign investment disclosure	Y	
60. Textile import quotas-veto override	Y	
61. Bar abortion funding in Wash, DC	N	
62. Notify spouses of AIDS+ carriers	N	
63. Seize conveyance-drug trafficking	N	
64. South Africa sanctions	Y	
65. 60 days' notice of plant closings	Y	
66. Close unneeded military bases	N	
67. Keep welfare reform within $2.8b	?	
68. Allow children housing exclusion	N	
69. Shift $400m of NASA to homeless	N	
70. Cap Medicare patients' liability	Y	
71. Prohibit employee polygraph testing	Y	
72. Allow CIA to fund Contras	N	
73. Revise unfair trade practices	Y	
74. Focus SDI on accidental launch	Y	
75. Bar Air Force $ for MX missile	Y	
76. Allow "real" increase in defense	N	
77. Troop reduction in Europe of 50%	Y	
78. Ban nuclear tests above 1 kiloton	Y	
79. Ban anti-satellite missile tests	Y	
80. Observe certain limits of SALT II	Y	
81. Restore four Civil Rights laws	Y	
82. Prohibit aliens as strikebreakers	Y	
83. Allow military malpractice suits	Y	
84. Approval of $36m in Contra aid	N	
85. $18b deficit reduction compromise	Y	
86. Welfare reform of $5.7b for 5 years	Y	

87. Raise taxes $12b/cut spending $3b	Y	
88. Board to assess occupational risk	Y	
89. Balanced budget by '93-via targets	N	
90. Bar licensing of two nuclear plants	Y	
91. Remove victims compensation cap	N	
92. Catastrophic health insurance	Y	
93. Ban airline smoking-2 hours or less	N	
94. $1b/two year aid for the homeless	Y	
95. Bar non-unions in union companies	Y	
96. Increase FSLIC rescue to $15b	N	
97. Impose quotas to lower trade deficit	Y	
98. Reduce discretionary budget 21%	N	
99. Immigration reform/alien amnesty	Y	
100. South Africa sanctions-veto override	Y	
101. Tax overhaul to revise income tax	N	
102. Use of military in drug war	N	
103. Delete 12 MX/add conventional wpn	?	
104. Raise speed limit to 65 mph	N	
105. Require Pentagon to buy US goods	Y	
106. AIDS insurance non-discrimination	Y	
107. Prohibit Saudi arms sales	Y	
108. Ease Gun Control Act of 1968	N	
109. Bar interstate handgun transport	Y	
110. Make company emissions known	Y	
111. Allow toxic victims to sue in fed ct	Y	
112. Superfund waste cleanup of $10b	Y	
113. 90 days notice of plant closings	Y	
114. $20b in Medicare cuts/tax increases	Y	
115. Spending cuts and tax increases	Y	
116. Set school lunch lmt-250% poverty	N	
117. $75m for youth work projects	Y	
118. Allow Angolan military assistance	N	
119. Suspend defense payments for abuse	Y	
120. Drop SS COLAs/$12b tax increase	N	
121. Approve $1.5b for 21 MX missiles	N	
122. Emergency farm credit/revisions	Y	
123. Duty on Taiwan/Hong Kong/S Korea	N	
124. Limit steel imports to 17%	Y	
125. Cut $ to schools that bar prayer	N	
126. $50b-taxes; cut Medicare/spending	Y	
127. Limit Pershing II/cruise in Europe	#	
128. Delete $7.1b for 34 B-1 bombers	N	
129. Bar purchase of Sergeant York guns	Y	
130. El Salvador military/economic aid	N	
131. Bar mining of Nicaraguan waters	Y	
132. Physician fee freeze for Medicare	N	
133. $49b in "sin"/phone/insurance taxes	Y	
134. Allow sale of Conrail	?	
135. Equal Rights Amendment	Y	
136. Authorize Marines in Lebanon	N	
137. Eminent domain for coal companies	N	
138. Prohibit EPA clean air sanctions	?	
139. SS retirement age increase/reforms	N	
140. Auto domestic content requirement	Y	
141. Delete jobs program funding	N	
142. Highway-gas tax bill	Y	
143. Cut $5b from defense for Medicare	Y	
144. Emergency housing aid of $1b	Y	

Presidential Support Score: 1991 - 26%   1990 - 20%

WATERS, MAXINE -- California 29th District [Democrat]. County of Los Angeles (pt.). Prior Term: 1991-92. Born: August 31, 1938; St. Louis, MO. Education: University of California-Los Angeles (B.A.). Occupation: State assemblywoman (1977-90).

1. Protection to Haitian refugees	Y	13. Unemployment benefits extension	Y
2. Raise tax on wealthy; lower others	Y	14. Tissue use of aborted fetuses	Y
3. Investigate Reagan hostage delay	Y	15. Bar replacement of union strikers	Y
4. Campaign finance revisions	Y	16. Hold foreign aid at $15b for '92	Y
5. Unpaid leave to care for children	Y	17. Restore space station funding	N
6. Restrict NEA use of funds	N	18. Civil Rights Act of 1991	Y
7. Bar race-bias claim/habeas corpus	X	19. Unlimited damages-discrimination	Y
8. Ban race as death sentence factor	X	20. Eliminate funds for supercollider	Y
9. Exceptions to exclusionary rule	N	21. Terminate SDI except for research	Y
10. Allow sale of assault weapons	N	22. Req 7-day handgun waiting period	Y
11. Life in prison/abolish death penalty	Y	23. Provide $30b for failed S&Ls	N
12. Req conspiracy-price fixing cases	N	24. Allow use of force against Iraq	N

Presidential Support Score: 1991 - 23%

MARTINEZ, MATTHEW G. -- California 30th District [Democrat]. County of Los Angeles (pt.). Prior Terms: 1982 (Special Election)-1992. Born: February 14, 1929; Walsenburg, CO. Military Service: U.S. Marine Corps. Occupation: Small businessman; member, Monterey Park Planning Commission; city councilman (1974-80); mayor; California assemblyman (1980-82).

1. Protection to Haitian refugees	Y	40. Expand child care aid/tax credit	Y
2. Raise tax on wealthy; lower others	Y	41. Raise House salary/omit honoraria	Y
3. Investigate Reagan hostage delay	Y	42. Toughen oil-spill liability	N
4. Campaign finance revisions	Y	43. Restitution to Japanese interned	Y
5. Unpaid leave to care for children	Y	44. Protect Chinese & C.A. nationals	Y
6. Restrict NEA use of funds	N	45. Abortion $ for rape/incest cases	Y
7. Bar race-bias claim/habeas corpus	N	46. Allow religious schools to bar gays	N
8. Ban race as death sentence factor	N	47. Bar broadcaster fairness doctrine	N
9. Exceptions to exclusionary rule	?	48. Bar cap gains cut/reinstate IRA	N
10. Allow sale of assault weapons	?	49. Bar unions equal voice in pension	N
11. Life in prison/abolish death penalty	N	50. Bar assembly of chemical weapons	Y
12. Req conspiracy-price fixing cases	N	51. Ban plutonium/uranium production	Y
13. Unemployment benefits extension	Y	52. Cap MX missile deployment at 50	Y
14. Tissue use of aborted fetuses	Y	53. Allow $3b for 2 stealth bombers	Y
15. Bar replacement of union strikers	Y	54. Publish bio-warfare experiments	Y
16. Hold foreign aid at $15b for '92	?	55. Raise minimum wage-veto override	Y
17. Restore space station funding	?	56. Bar transfer of FS-X technology	N
18. Civil Rights Act of 1991	Y	57. Cut defense and raise domestic $	N
19. Unlimited damages-discrimination	Y	58. Uniform poll closing in 48 states	Y
20. Eliminate funds for supercollider	N	59. Req foreign investment disclosure	Y
21. Terminate SDI except for research	?	60. Textile import quotas-veto override	Y
22. Req 7-day handgun waiting period	Y	61. Bar abortion funding in Wash, DC	N
23. Provide $30b for failed S&Ls	Y	62. Notify spouses of AIDS+ carriers	N
24. Allow use of force against Iraq	N	63. Seize conveyance-drug trafficking	N
25. Allow $15b in foreign aid for '91	Y	64. South Africa sanctions	Y
26. Revise & extend legal immigration	Y	65. 60 days' notice of plant closings	Y
27. Suspend aid to Angolan rebels	Y	66. Close unneeded military bases	N
28. Democratic tax plan proposals	Y	67. Keep welfare reform within $2.8b	N
29. Cut defense 5% across the board	Y	68. Allow children housing exclusion	N
30. Textile import quotas-veto override	Y	69. Shift $400m of NASA to homeless	Y
31. Abortion service for military abroad	Y	70. Cap Medicare patients' liability	Y
32. Limits on high income farmers	?	71. Prohibit employee polygraph testing	Y
33. Family medical leave-veto override	Y	72. Allow CIA to fund Contras	N
34. Req submission of balanced budget	Y	73. Revise unfair trade practices	N
35. Balanced budget amendment	N	74. Focus SDI on accidental launch	Y
36. Amendment to ban flag desecration	Y	75. Bar Air Force $ for MX missile	Y
37. Reauthorize Amtrak-veto override	Y	76. Allow "real" increase in defense	N
38. Retraining aid for coal miners	Y	77. Troop reduction in Europe of 50%	X
39. Suspend El Salvador military aid	Y	78. Ban nuclear tests above 1 kiloton	Y

MARTINEZ, MATTHEW G. (continued)

79. Ban anti-satellite missile tests	Y	
80. Observe certain limits of SALT II	Y	
81. Restore four Civil Rights laws	?	
82. Prohibit aliens as strikebreakers	?	
83. Allow military malpractice suits	Y	
84. Approval of $36m in Contra aid	N	
85. $18b deficit reduction compromise	N	
86. Welfare reform of $5.7b for 5 years	Y	
87. Raise taxes $12b/cut spending $3b	Y	
88. Board to assess occupational risk	Y	
89. Balanced budget by '93-via targets	?	
90. Bar licensing of two nuclear plants	N	
91. Remove victims compensation cap	N	
92. Catastrophic health insurance	Y	
93. Ban airline smoking-2 hours or less	Y	
94. $1b/two year aid for the homeless	Y	
95. Bar non-unions in union companies	Y	
96. Increase FSLIC rescue to $15b	N	
97. Impose quotas to lower trade deficit	Y	
98. Reduce discretionary budget 21%	?	
99. Immigration reform/alien amnesty	N	
100. South Africa sanctions-veto override	Y	
101. Tax overhaul to revise income tax	Y	
102. Use of military in drug war	N	
103. Delete 12 MX/add conventional wpn	?	
104. Raise speed limit to 65 mph	N	
105. Require Pentagon to buy US goods	Y	
106. AIDS insurance non-discrimination	Y	
107. Prohibit Saudi arms sales	Y	
108. Ease Gun Control Act of 1968	N	
109. Bar interstate handgun transport	?	
110. Make company emissions known	Y	
111. Allow toxic victims to sue in fed ct	Y
112. Superfund waste cleanup of $10b	Y
113. 90 days notice of plant closings	Y
114. $20b in Medicare cuts/tax increases	Y
115. Spending cuts and tax increases	Y
116. Set school lunch lmt-250% poverty	N
117. $75m for youth work projects	Y
118. Allow Angolan military assistance	N
119. Suspend defense payments for abuse	Y
120. Drop SS COLAs/$12b tax increase	N
121. Approve $1.5b for 21 MX missiles	N
122. Emergency farm credit/revisions	Y
123. Duty on Taiwan/Hong Kong/S Korea	N
124. Limit steel imports to 17%	Y
125. Cut $ to schools that bar prayer	N
126. $50b-taxes; cut Medicare/spending	Y
127. Limit Pershing II/cruise in Europe	Y
128. Delete $7.1b for 34 B-1 bombers	Y
129. Bar purchase of Sergeant York guns	Y
130. El Salvador military/economic aid	N
131. Bar mining of Nicaraguan waters	Y
132. Physician fee freeze for Medicare	N
133. $49b in "sin"/phone/insurance taxes	N
134. Allow sale of Conrail	N
135. Equal Rights Amendment	Y
136. Authorize Marines in Lebanon	N
137. Eminent domain for coal companies	Y
138. Prohibit EPA clean air sanctions	?
139. SS retirement age increase/reforms	N
140. Auto domestic content requirement	Y
141. Delete jobs program funding	N
142. Highway-gas tax bill	Y

Presidential Support Score: 1991 - 31%   1990 - 18%

DYMALLY, MERVYN M. -- California 31st District [Democrat]. County of Los Angeles (pt.).
Prior Terms: 1981-92. Born: May 12, 1926; Cedron, Trinidad, WI. Education: California State University (B.A., M.A.); United States International University (Ph.D.). Occupation: Teacher; California state assemblyman; California senator (1966-75); lieutenant governor (1975-79); goodwill ambassador in Africa and West Indies.

1. Protection to Haitian refugees	?	
2. Raise tax on wealthy; lower others	Y	
3. Investigate Reagan hostage delay	?	
4. Campaign finance revisions	Y	
5. Unpaid leave to care for children	Y	
6. Restrict NEA use of funds	N	
7. Bar race-bias claim/habeas corpus	N	
8. Ban race as death sentence factor	N	
9. Exceptions to exclusionary rule	N	
10. Allow sale of assault weapons	N	
11. Life in prison/abolish death penalty	?	
12. Req conspiracy-price fixing cases	N	
13. Unemployment benefits extension	?	
14. Tissue use of aborted fetuses	Y	
15. Bar replacement of union strikers	Y	
16. Hold foreign aid at $15b for '92	Y	
17. Restore space station funding	#	
18. Civil Rights Act of 1991	Y	
19. Unlimited damages-discrimination	Y	
20. Eliminate funds for supercollider	N	
21. Terminate SDI except for research	Y	
22. Req 7-day handgun waiting period	Y	
23. Provide $30b for failed S&Ls	N
24. Allow use of force against Iraq	--
25. Allow $15b in foreign aid for '91	Y
26. Revise & extend legal immigration	Y
27. Suspend aid to Angolan rebels	Y
28. Democratic tax plan proposals	Y
29. Cut defense 5% across the board	Y
30. Textile import quotas-veto override	Y
31. Abortion service for military abroad	Y
32. Limits on high income farmers	N
33. Family medical leave-veto override	Y
34. Req submission of balanced budget	Y
35. Balanced budget amendment	N
36. Amendment to ban flag desecration	N
37. Reauthorize Amtrak-veto override	Y
38. Retraining aid for coal miners	Y
39. Suspend El Salvador military aid	Y
40. Expand child care aid/tax credit	Y
41. Raise House salary/omit honoraria	Y
42. Toughen oil-spill liability	#
43. Restitution to Japanese interned	Y
44. Protect Chinese & C.A. nationals	Y

DYMALLY, MERVYN M. (continued)

45. Abortion $ for rape/incest cases	Y	95. Bar non-unions in union companies	Y
46. Allow religious schools to bar gays	N	96. Increase FSLIC rescue to $15b	N
47. Bar broadcaster fairness doctrine	N	97. Impose quotas to lower trade deficit	Y
48. Bar cap gains cut/reinstate IRA	Y	98. Reduce discretionary budget 21%	?
49. Bar unions equal voice in pension	N	99. Immigration reform/alien amnesty	N
50. Bar assembly of chemical weapons	Y	100. South Africa sanctions-veto override	Y
51. Ban plutonium/uranium production	Y	101. Tax overhaul to revise income tax	N
52. Cap MX missile deployment at 50	Y	102. Use of military in drug war	N
53. Allow $3b for 2 stealth bombers	N	103. Delete 12 MX/add conventional wpn	Y
54. Publish bio-warfare experiments	Y	104. Raise speed limit to 65 mph	N
55. Raise minimum wage-veto override	Y	105. Require Pentagon to buy US goods	Y
56. Bar transfer of FS-X technology	N	106. AIDS insurance non-discrimination	Y
57. Cut defense and raise domestic $	Y	107. Prohibit Saudi arms sales	Y
58. Uniform poll closing in 48 states	Y	108. Ease Gun Control Act of 1968	N
59. Req foreign investment disclosure	Y	109. Bar interstate handgun transport	Y
60. Textile import quotas-veto override	Y	110. Make company emissions known	N
61. Bar abortion funding in Wash, DC	N	111. Allow toxic victims to sue in fed ct	N
62. Notify spouses of AIDS+ carriers	N	112. Superfund waste cleanup of $10b	Y
63. Seize conveyance-drug trafficking	N	113. 90 days notice of plant closings	?
64. South Africa sanctions	Y	114. $20b in Medicare cuts/tax increases	Y
65. 60 days' notice of plant closings	Y	115. Spending cuts and tax increases	Y
66. Close unneeded military bases	N	116. Set school lunch lmt-250% poverty	N
67. Keep welfare reform within $2.8b	N	117. $75m for youth work projects	Y
68. Allow children housing exclusion	N	118. Allow Angolan military assistance	N
69. Shift $400m of NASA to homeless	Y	119. Suspend defense payments for abuse	Y
70. Cap Medicare patients' liability	Y	120. Drop SS COLAs/$12b tax increase	N
71. Prohibit employee polygraph testing	Y	121. Approve $1.5b for 21 MX missiles	N
72. Allow CIA to fund Contras	N	122. Emergency farm credit/revisions	Y
73. Revise unfair trade practices	Y	123. Duty on Taiwan/Hong Kong/S Korea	N
74. Focus SDI on accidental launch	Y	124. Limit steel imports to 17%	Y
75. Bar Air Force $ for MX missile	Y	125. Cut $ to schools that bar prayer	N
76. Allow "real" increase in defense	N	126. $50b-taxes; cut Medicare/spending	X
77. Troop reduction in Europe of 50%	#	127. Limit Pershing II/cruise in Europe	?
78. Ban nuclear tests above 1 kiloton	Y	128. Delete $7.1b for 34 B-1 bombers	N
79. Ban anti-satellite missile tests	Y	129. Bar purchase of Sergeant York guns	Y
80. Observe certain limits of SALT II	Y	130. El Salvador military/economic aid	N
81. Restore four Civil Rights laws	Y	131. Bar mining of Nicaraguan waters	?
82. Prohibit aliens as strikebreakers	Y	132. Physician fee freeze for Medicare	N
83. Allow military malpractice suits	?	133. $49b in "sin"/phone/insurance taxes	Y
84. Approval of $36m in Contra aid	N	134. Allow sale of Conrail	N
85. $18b deficit reduction compromise	N	135. Equal Rights Amendment	Y
86. Welfare reform of $5.7b for 5 years	Y	136. Authorize Marines in Lebanon	N
87. Raise taxes $12b/cut spending $3b	Y	137. Eminent domain for coal companies	Y
88. Board to assess occupational risk	Y	138. Prohibit EPA clean air sanctions	Y
89. Balanced budget by '93-via targets	Y	139. SS retirement age increase/reforms	N
90. Bar licensing of two nuclear plants	Y	140. Auto domestic content requirement	Y
91. Remove victims compensation cap	?	141. Delete jobs program funding	N
92. Catastrophic health insurance	Y	142. Highway-gas tax bill	Y
93. Ban airline smoking-2 hours or less	N	143. Cut $5b from defense for Medicare	Y
94. $1b/two year aid for the homeless	Y	144. Emergency housing aid of $1b	?

Presidential Support Score: 1991 - 21%   1990 - 11%

ANDERSON, GLENN M. -- California 32rd District [Democrat]. County of Los Angeles (pt.). Prior Terms: 1969-92. Born: February 21, 1913; Hawthorne, CA. Education: University of California (B.A.). Military Service: U.S. Army. Occupation: Mayor (1940); California state assemblyman (1943-51); lieutenant governor (1958, 1962); regent, University of California (1959-67); trustee, California State Colleges (1961-67); State Lands commissioner (1959-67).

1. Protection to Haitian refugees	Y	4. Campaign finance revisions	Y
2. Raise tax on wealthy; lower others	Y	5. Unpaid leave to care for children	Y
3. Investigate Reagan hostage delay	Y	6. Restrict NEA use of funds	N

ANDERSON, GLENN M. (continued)

7. Bar race-bias claim/habeas corpus	N	
8. Ban race as death sentence factor	N	
9. Exceptions to exclusionary rule	N	
10. Allow sale of assault weapons	N	
11. Life in prison/abolish death penalty	N	
12. Req conspiracy-price fixing cases	N	
13. Unemployment benefits extension	Y	
14. Tissue use of aborted fetuses	Y	
15. Bar replacement of union strikers	Y	
16. Hold foreign aid at $15b for '92	Y	
17. Restore space station funding	Y	
18. Civil Rights Act of 1991	Y	
19. Unlimited damages-discrimination	Y	
20. Eliminate funds for supercollider	N	
21. Terminate SDI except for research	?	
22. Req 7-day handgun waiting period	Y	
23. Provide $30b for failed S&Ls	Y	
24. Allow use of force against Iraq	Y	
25. Allow $15b in foreign aid for '91	N	
26. Revise & extend legal immigration	Y	
27. Suspend aid to Angolan rebels	Y	
28. Democratic tax plan proposals	Y	
29. Cut defense 5% across the board	N	
30. Textile import quotas-veto override	N	
31. Abortion service for military abroad	Y	
32. Limits on high income farmers	N	
33. Family medical leave-veto override	Y	
34. Req submission of balanced budget	Y	
35. Balanced budget amendment	N	
36. Amendment to ban flag desecration	N	
37. Reauthorize Amtrak-veto override	Y	
38. Retraining aid for coal miners	Y	
39. Suspend El Salvador military aid	Y	
40. Expand child care aid/tax credit	Y	
41. Raise House salary/omit honoraria	N	
42. Toughen oil-spill liability	N	
43. Restitution to Japanese interned	Y	
44. Protect Chinese & C.A. nationals	Y	
45. Abortion $ for rape/incest cases	Y	
46. Allow religious schools to bar gays	N	
47. Bar broadcaster fairness doctrine	N	
48. Bar cap gains cut/reinstate IRA	N	
49. Bar unions equal voice in pension	N	
50. Bar assembly of chemical weapons	Y	
51. Ban plutonium/uranium production	Y	
52. Cap MX missile deployment at 50	Y	
53. Allow $3b for 2 stealth bombers	Y	
54. Publish bio-warfare experiments	N	
55. Raise minimum wage-veto override	Y	
56. Bar transfer of FS-X technology	Y	
57. Cut defense and raise domestic $	N	
58. Uniform poll closing in 48 states	Y	
59. Req foreign investment disclosure	Y	
60. Textile import quotas-veto override	N	
61. Bar abortion funding in Wash, DC	N	
62. Notify spouses of AIDS+ carriers	N	
63. Seize conveyance-drug trafficking	?	
64. South Africa sanctions	Y	
65. 60 days' notice of plant closings	?	
66. Close unneeded military bases	?	
67. Keep welfare reform within $2.8b	?	
68. Allow children housing exclusion	N	
69. Shift $400m of NASA to homeless	N	
70. Cap Medicare patients' liability	Y	

71. Prohibit employee polygraph testing	Y	
72. Allow CIA to fund Contras	N	
73. Revise unfair trade practices	Y	
74. Focus SDI on accidental launch	Y	
75. Bar Air Force $ for MX missile	N	
76. Allow "real" increase in defense	N	
77. Troop reduction in Europe of 50%	N	
78. Ban nuclear tests above 1 kiloton	Y	
79. Ban anti-satellite missile tests	Y	
80. Observe certain limits of SALT II	Y	
81. Restore four Civil Rights laws	Y	
82. Prohibit aliens as strikebreakers	Y	
83. Allow military malpractice suits	Y	
84. Approval of $36m in Contra aid	N	
85. $18b deficit reduction compromise	N	
86. Welfare reform of $5.7b for 5 years	Y	
87. Raise taxes $12b/cut spending $3b	Y	
88. Board to assess occupational risk	Y	
89. Balanced budget by '93-via targets	N	
90. Bar licensing of two nuclear plants	N	
91. Remove victims compensation cap	N	
92. Catastrophic health insurance	Y	
93. Ban airline smoking-2 hours or less	Y	
94. $1b/two year aid for the homeless	Y	
95. Bar non-unions in union companies	Y	
96. Increase FSLIC rescue to $15b	N	
97. Impose quotas to lower trade deficit	N	
98. Reduce discretionary budget 21%	N	
99. Immigration reform/alien amnesty	Y	
100. South Africa sanctions-veto override	Y	
101. Tax overhaul to revise income tax	Y	
102. Use of military in drug war	Y	
103. Delete 12 MX/add conventional wpn	N	
104. Raise speed limit to 65 mph	N	
105. Require Pentagon to buy US goods	Y	
106. AIDS insurance non-discrimination	Y	
107. Prohibit Saudi arms sales	Y	
108. Ease Gun Control Act of 1968	Y	
109. Bar interstate handgun transport	Y	
110. Make company emissions known	Y	
111. Allow toxic victims to sue in fed ct	Y	
112. Superfund waste cleanup of $10b	N	
113. 90 days notice of plant closings	Y	
114. $20b in Medicare cuts/tax increases	Y	
115. Spending cuts and tax increases	N	
116. Set school lunch lmt-250% poverty	N	
117. $75m for youth work projects	Y	
118. Allow Angolan military assistance	Y	
119. Suspend defense payments for abuse	Y	
120. Drop SS COLAs/$12b tax increase	N	
121. Approve $1.5b for 21 MX missiles	Y	
122. Emergency farm credit/revisions	Y	
123. Duty on Taiwan/Hong Kong/S Korea	N	
124. Limit steel imports to 17%	Y	
125. Cut $ to schools that bar prayer	N	
126. $50b-taxes; cut Medicare/spending	N	
127. Limit Pershing II/cruise in Europe	N	
128. Delete $7.1b for 34 B-1 bombers	N	
129. Bar purchase of Sergeant York guns	N	
130. El Salvador military/economic aid	N	
131. Bar mining of Nicaraguan waters	Y	
132. Physician fee freeze for Medicare	N	
133. $49b in "sin"/phone/insurance taxes	N	
134. Allow sale of Conrail	N	

ANDERSON, GLENN M. (continued)

135.	Equal Rights Amendment	Y	140.	Auto domestic content requirement	N
136.	Authorize Marines in Lebanon	Y	141.	Delete jobs program funding	N
137.	Eminent domain for coal companies	Y	142.	Highway-gas tax bill	Y
138.	Prohibit EPA clean air sanctions	Y	143.	Cut $5b from defense for Medicare	Y
139.	SS retirement age increase/reforms	N	144.	Emergency housing aid of $1b	Y

Presidential Support Score: 1991 - 41%   1990 - 18%

DREIER, DAVID -- California 33rd District [Republican]. County of Los Angeles (pt.). Prior Terms: 1981-92. Born: July 5, 1952; Kansas City, MO. Education: Claremont Men's College (B.A., M.A.). Occupation: Director,corporate relations and assistant director, college relations, Claremont Men's College (1975-79).

1.	Protection to Haitian refugees	N	51.	Ban plutonium/uranium production	N
2.	Raise tax on wealthy; lower others	N	52.	Cap MX missile deployment at 50	N
3.	Investigate Reagan hostage delay	N	53.	Allow $3b for 2 stealth bombers	Y
4.	Campaign finance revisions	N	54.	Publish bio-warfare experiments	N
5.	Unpaid leave to care for children	N	55.	Raise minimum wage-veto override	N
6.	Restrict NEA use of funds	Y	56.	Bar transfer of FS-X technology	N
7.	Bar race-bias claim/habeas corpus	Y	57.	Cut defense and raise domestic $	N
8.	Ban race as death sentence factor	Y	58.	Uniform poll closing in 48 states	Y
9.	Exceptions to exclusionary rule	Y	59.	Req foreign investment disclosure	N
10.	Allow sale of assault weapons	Y	60.	Textile import quotas-veto override	N
11.	Life in prison/abolish death penalty	N	61.	Bar abortion funding in Wash, DC	Y
12.	Req conspiracy-price fixing cases	Y	62.	Notify spouses of AIDS+ carriers	#
13.	Unemployment benefits extension	N	63.	Seize conveyance-drug trafficking	Y
14.	Tissue use of aborted fetuses	N	64.	South Africa sanctions	N
15.	Bar replacement of union strikers	N	65.	60 days' notice of plant closings	N
16.	Hold foreign aid at $15b for '92	N	66.	Close unneeded military bases	Y
17.	Restore space station funding	Y	67.	Keep welfare reform within $2.8b	Y
18.	Civil Rights Act of 1991	N	68.	Allow children housing exclusion	Y
19.	Unlimited damages-discrimination	N	69.	Shift $400m of NASA to homeless	N
20.	Eliminate funds for supercollider	N	70.	Cap Medicare patients' liability	N
21.	Terminate SDI except for research	N	71.	Prohibit employee polygraph testing	N
22.	Req 7-day handgun waiting period	N	72.	Allow CIA to fund Contras	Y
23.	Provide $30b for failed S&Ls	Y	73.	Revise unfair trade practices	N
24.	Allow use of force against Iraq	Y	74.	Focus SDI on accidental launch	N
25.	Allow $15b in foreign aid for '91	N	75.	Bar Air Force $ for MX missile	N
26.	Revise & extend legal immigration	N	76.	Allow "real" increase in defense	Y
27.	Suspend aid to Angolan rebels	N	77.	Troop reduction in Europe of 50%	N
28.	Democratic tax plan proposals	N	78.	Ban nuclear tests above 1 kiloton	N
29.	Cut defense 5% across the board	N	79.	Ban anti-satellite missile tests	N
30.	Textile import quotas-veto override	N	80.	Observe certain limits of SALT II	N
31.	Abortion service for military abroad	N	81.	Restore four Civil Rights laws	N
32.	Limits on high income farmers	Y	82.	Prohibit aliens as strikebreakers	N
33.	Family medical leave-veto override	N	83.	Allow military malpractice suits	?
34.	Req submission of balanced budget	N	84.	Approval of $36m in Contra aid	Y
35.	Balanced budget amendment	Y	85.	$18b deficit reduction compromise	N
36.	Amendment to ban flag desecration	Y	86.	Welfare reform of $5.7b for 5 years	N
37.	Reauthorize Amtrak-veto override	N	87.	Raise taxes $12b/cut spending $3b	N
38.	Retraining aid for coal miners	N	88.	Board to assess occupational risk	N
39.	Suspend El Salvador military aid	N	89.	Balanced budget by '93-via targets	N
40.	Expand child care aid/tax credit	N	90.	Bar licensing of two nuclear plants	N
41.	Raise House salary/omit honoraria	N	91.	Remove victims compensation cap	N
42.	Toughen oil-spill liability	Y	92.	Catastrophic health insurance	N
43.	Restitution to Japanese interned	Y	93.	Ban airline smoking-2 hours or less	Y
44.	Protect Chinese & C.A. nationals	N	94.	$1b/two year aid for the homeless	N
45.	Abortion $ for rape/incest cases	N	95.	Bar non-unions in union companies	N
46.	Allow religious schools to bar gays	Y	96.	Increase FSLIC rescue to $15b	N
47.	Bar broadcaster fairness doctrine	Y	97.	Impose quotas to lower trade deficit	N
48.	Bar cap gains cut/reinstate IRA	N	98.	Reduce discretionary budget 21%	Y
49.	Bar unions equal voice in pension	Y	99.	Immigration reform/alien amnesty	N
50.	Bar assembly of chemical weapons	N	100.	South Africa sanctions-veto override	N

DREIER, DAVID (continued)

101. Tax overhaul to revise income tax	N	123. Duty on Taiwan/Hong Kong/S Korea	N
102. Use of military in drug war	Y	124. Limit steel imports to 17%	N
103. Delete 12 MX/add conventional wpn	N	125. Cut $ to schools that bar prayer	Y
104. Raise speed limit to 65 mph	Y	126. $50b-taxes; cut Medicare/spending	N
105. Require Pentagon to buy US goods	N	127. Limit Pershing II/cruise in Europe	N
106. AIDS insurance non-discrimination	N	128. Delete $7.1b for 34 B-1 bombers	N
107. Prohibit Saudi arms sales	Y	129. Bar purchase of Sergeant York guns	N
108. Ease Gun Control Act of 1968	Y	130. El Salvador military/economic aid	Y
109. Bar interstate handgun transport	N	131. Bar mining of Nicaraguan waters	N
110. Make company emissions known	N	132. Physician fee freeze for Medicare	Y
111. Allow toxic victims to sue in fed ct	N	133. $49b in "sin"/phone/insurance taxes	N
112. Superfund waste cleanup of $10b	N	134. Allow sale of Conrail	Y
113. 90 days notice of plant closings	N	135. Equal Rights Amendment	N
114. $20b in Medicare cuts/tax increases	N	136. Authorize Marines in Lebanon	Y
115. Spending cuts and tax increases	N	137. Eminent domain for coal companies	Y
116. Set school lunch lmt-250% poverty	Y	138. Prohibit EPA clean air sanctions	Y
117. $75m for youth work projects	N	139. SS retirement age increase/reforms	Y
118. Allow Angolan military assistance	Y	140. Auto domestic content requirement	N
119. Suspend defense payments for abuse	N	141. Delete jobs program funding	Y
120. Drop SS COLAs/$12b tax increase	N	142. Highway-gas tax bill	N
121. Approve $1.5b for 21 MX missiles	Y	143. Cut $5b from defense for Medicare	N
122. Emergency farm credit/revisions	N	144. Emergency housing aid of $1b	?

Presidential Support Score: 1991 - 84%   1990 - 73%

TORRES, ESTEBAN EDWARD -- California 34th District [Democrat]. County of Los Angeles (pt.). Prior Terms: 1983-92. Born: January 27, 1930; Miami, AZ. Military Service: U.S. Army. Occupation: Chief Steward, Local 230, United Auto Workers (1961); International Representative, Region 6, UAW (1963-64); Inter-American Representative in Washington, D.C. for UAW (1965-68); assistant director, International Affairs Department, UAW (1974-77); Ambassador to UNESCO (1977-79); White House aide.

1. Protection to Haitian refugees	?	32. Limits on high income farmers	N
2. Raise tax on wealthy; lower others	Y	33. Family medical leave-veto override	Y
3. Investigate Reagan hostage delay	Y	34. Req submission of balanced budget	Y
4. Campaign finance revisions	Y	35. Balanced budget amendment	N
5. Unpaid leave to care for children	Y	36. Amendment to ban flag desecration	N
6. Restrict NEA use of funds	N	37. Reauthorize Amtrak-veto override	Y
7. Bar race-bias claim/habeas corpus	N	38. Retraining aid for coal miners	Y
8. Ban race as death sentence factor	N	39. Suspend El Salvador military aid	Y
9. Exceptions to exclusionary rule	N	40. Expand child care aid/tax credit	Y
10. Allow sale of assault weapons	N	41. Raise House salary/omit honoraria	Y
11. Life in prison/abolish death penalty	N	42. Toughen oil-spill liability	Y
12. Req conspiracy-price fixing cases	N	43. Restitution to Japanese interned	Y
13. Unemployment benefits extension	Y	44. Protect Chinese & C.A. nationals	Y
14. Tissue use of aborted fetuses	Y	45. Abortion $ for rape/incest cases	Y
15. Bar replacement of union strikers	Y	46. Allow religious schools to bar gays	N
16. Hold foreign aid at $15b for '92	Y	47. Bar broadcaster fairness doctrine	N
17. Restore space station funding	Y	48. Bar cap gains cut/reinstate IRA	Y
18. Civil Rights Act of 1991	Y	49. Bar unions equal voice in pension	N
19. Unlimited damages-discrimination	Y	50. Bar assembly of chemical weapons	Y
20. Eliminate funds for supercollider	N	51. Ban plutonium/uranium production	Y
21. Terminate SDI except for research	+	52. Cap MX missile deployment at 50	Y
22. Req 7-day handgun waiting period	Y	53. Allow $3b for 2 stealth bombers	Y
23. Provide $30b for failed S&Ls	Y	54. Publish bio-warfare experiments	Y
24. Allow use of force against Iraq	N	55. Raise minimum wage-veto override	Y
25. Allow $15b in foreign aid for '91	Y	56. Bar transfer of FS-X technology	Y
26. Revise & extend legal immigration	Y	57. Cut defense and raise domestic $	Y
27. Suspend aid to Angolan rebels	Y	58. Uniform poll closing in 48 states	Y
28. Democratic tax plan proposals	Y	59. Req foreign investment disclosure	Y
29. Cut defense 5% across the board	Y	60. Textile import quotas-veto override	Y
30. Textile import quotas-veto override	Y	61. Bar abortion funding in Wash, DC	N
31. Abortion service for military abroad	Y	62. Notify spouses of AIDS+ carriers	N

TORRES, ESTEBAN EDWARD (continued)

63. Seize conveyance-drug trafficking	N	
64. South Africa sanctions	Y	
65. 60 days' notice of plant closings	Y	
66. Close unneeded military bases	?	
67. Keep welfare reform within $2.8b	N	
68. Allow children housing exclusion	N	
69. Shift $400m of NASA to homeless	Y	
70. Cap Medicare patients' liability	Y	
71. Prohibit employee polygraph testing	?	
72. Allow CIA to fund Contras	N	
73. Revise unfair trade practices	Y	
74. Focus SDI on accidental launch	Y	
75. Bar Air Force $ for MX missile	Y	
76. Allow "real" increase in defense	--	
77. Troop reduction in Europe of 50%	Y	
78. Ban nuclear tests above 1 kiloton	Y	
79. Ban anti-satellite missile tests	Y	
80. Observe certain limits of SALT II	Y	
81. Restore four Civil Rights laws	Y	
82. Prohibit aliens as strikebreakers	Y	
83. Allow military malpractice suits	Y	
84. Approval of $36m in Contra aid	N	
85. $18b deficit reduction compromise	Y	
86. Welfare reform of $5.7b for 5 years	Y	
87. Raise taxes $12b/cut spending $3b	Y	
88. Board to assess occupational risk	Y	
89. Balanced budget by '93-via targets	N	
90. Bar licensing of two nuclear plants	Y	
91. Remove victims compensation cap	Y	
92. Catastrophic health insurance	Y	
93. Ban airline smoking-2 hours or less	Y	
94. $1b/two year aid for the homeless	Y	
95. Bar non-unions in union companies	Y	
96. Increase FSLIC rescue to $15b	N	
97. Impose quotas to lower trade deficit	Y	
98. Reduce discretionary budget 21%	N	
99. Immigration reform/alien amnesty	Y	
100. South Africa sanctions-veto override	Y	
101. Tax overhaul to revise income tax	Y	

102. Use of military in drug war	N	
103. Delete 12 MX/add conventional wpn	Y	
104. Raise speed limit to 65 mph	N	
105. Require Pentagon to buy US goods	Y	
106. AIDS insurance non-discrimination	Y	
107. Prohibit Saudi arms sales	Y	
108. Ease Gun Control Act of 1968	N	
109. Bar interstate handgun transport	+	
110. Make company emissions known	Y	
111. Allow toxic victims to sue in fed ct	Y	
112. Superfund waste cleanup of $10b	Y	
113. 90 days notice of plant closings	Y	
114. $20b in Medicare cuts/tax increases	Y	
115. Spending cuts and tax increases	Y	
116. Set school lunch lmt-250% poverty	N	
117. $75m for youth work projects	Y	
118. Allow Angolan military assistance	N	
119. Suspend defense payments for abuse	Y	
120. Drop SS COLAs/$12b tax increase	N	
121. Approve $1.5b for 21 MX missiles	N	
122. Emergency farm credit/revisions	Y	
123. Duty on Taiwan/Hong Kong/S Korea	Y	
124. Limit steel imports to 17%	Y	
125. Cut $ to schools that bar prayer	N	
126. $50b-taxes; cut Medicare/spending	Y	
127. Limit Pershing II/cruise in Europe	Y	
128. Delete $7.1b for 34 B-1 bombers	N	
129. Bar purchase of Sergeant York guns	Y	
130. El Salvador military/economic aid	N	
131. Bar mining of Nicaraguan waters	Y	
132. Physician fee freeze for Medicare	N	
133. $49b in "sin"/phone/insurance taxes	Y	
134. Allow sale of Conrail	N	
135. Equal Rights Amendment	Y	
136. Authorize Marines in Lebanon	Y	
137. Eminent domain for coal companies	N	
138. Prohibit EPA clean air sanctions	+	
139. SS retirement age increase/reforms	N	

Presidential Support Score: 1991 - 25%   1990 - 17%

LEWIS, JERRY -- California 35th District [Republican]. Counties of Inyo, Los Angeles (pt.) and San Bernardino (pt.). Prior Terms: 1979-92. Born: October 21, 1934; Seattle, WA. Education: University of California (B.A.). Occupation: Life underwriter; California assemblyman (1968-78).

1. Protection to Haitian refugees	N	
2. Raise tax on wealthy; lower others	N	
3. Investigate Reagan hostage delay	N	
4. Campaign finance revisions	N	
5. Unpaid leave to care for children	N	
6. Restrict NEA use of funds	N	
7. Bar race-bias claim/habeas corpus	Y	
8. Ban race as death sentence factor	Y	
9. Exceptions to exclusionary rule	Y	
10. Allow sale of assault weapons	Y	
11. Life in prison/abolish death penalty	X	
12. Req conspiracy-price fixing cases	Y	
13. Unemployment benefits extension	X	
14. Tissue use of aborted fetuses	N	
15. Bar replacement of union strikers	N	
16. Hold foreign aid at $15b for '92	Y	

17. Restore space station funding	Y	
18. Civil Rights Act of 1991	N	
19. Unlimited damages-discrimination	N	
20. Eliminate funds for supercollider	N	
21. Terminate SDI except for research	N	
22. Req 7-day handgun waiting period	N	
23. Provide $30b for failed S&Ls	Y	
24. Allow use of force against Iraq	Y	
25. Allow $15b in foreign aid for '91	Y	
26. Revise & extend legal immigration	N	
27. Suspend aid to Angolan rebels	N	
28. Democratic tax plan proposals	N	
29. Cut defense 5% across the board	N	
30. Textile import quotas-veto override	N	
31. Abortion service for military abroad	N	
32. Limits on high income farmers	N	

LEWIS, JERRY (continued)

33. Family medical leave-veto override	N
34. Req submission of balanced budget	N
35. Balanced budget amendment	Y
36. Amendment to ban flag desecration	Y
37. Reauthorize Amtrak-veto override	N
38. Retraining aid for coal miners	N
39. Suspend El Salvador military aid	N
40. Expand child care aid/tax credit	N
41. Raise House salary/omit honoraria	Y
42. Toughen oil-spill liability	Y
43. Restitution to Japanese interned	Y
44. Protect Chinese & C.A. nationals	N
45. Abortion $ for rape/incest cases	N
46. Allow religious schools to bar gays	Y
47. Bar broadcaster fairness doctrine	Y
48. Bar cap gains cut/reinstate IRA	N
49. Bar unions equal voice in pension	Y
50. Bar assembly of chemical weapons	N
51. Ban plutonium/uranium production	N
52. Cap MX missile deployment at 50	N
53. Allow $3b for 2 stealth bombers	Y
54. Publish bio-warfare experiments	N
55. Raise minimum wage-veto override	N
56. Bar transfer of FS-X technology	N
57. Cut defense and raise domestic $	N
58. Uniform poll closing in 48 states	Y
59. Req foreign investment disclosure	X
60. Textile import quotas-veto override	?
61. Bar abortion funding in Wash, DC	Y
62. Notify spouses of AIDS+ carriers	N
63. Seize conveyance-drug trafficking	Y
64. South Africa sanctions	?
65. 60 days' notice of plant closings	N
66. Close unneeded military bases	Y
67. Keep welfare reform within $2.8b	Y
68. Allow children housing exclusion	N
69. Shift $400m of NASA to homeless	N
70. Cap Medicare patients' liability	#
71. Prohibit employee polygraph testing	?
72. Allow CIA to fund Contras	?
73. Revise unfair trade practices	N
74. Focus SDI on accidental launch	N
75. Bar Air Force $ for MX missile	N
76. Allow "real" increase in defense	?
77. Troop reduction in Europe of 50%	?
78. Ban nuclear tests above 1 kiloton	?
79. Ban anti-satellite missile tests	?
80. Observe certain limits of SALT II	N
81. Restore four Civil Rights laws	N
82. Prohibit aliens as strikebreakers	N
83. Allow military malpractice suits	?
84. Approval of $36m in Contra aid	Y
85. $18b deficit reduction compromise	N
86. Welfare reform of $5.7b for 5 years	N
87. Raise taxes $12b/cut spending $3b	N
88. Board to assess occupational risk	N

89. Balanced budget by '93-via targets	Y
90. Bar licensing of two nuclear plants	N
91. Remove victims compensation cap	N
92. Catastrophic health insurance	N
93. Ban airline smoking-2 hours or less	N
94. $1b/two year aid for the homeless	N
95. Bar non-unions in union companies	N
96. Increase FSLIC rescue to $15b	Y
97. Impose quotas to lower trade deficit	N
98. Reduce discretionary budget 21%	Y
99. Immigration reform/alien amnesty	Y
100. South Africa sanctions-veto override	N
101. Tax overhaul to revise income tax	Y
102. Use of military in drug war	Y
103. Delete 12 MX/add conventional wpn	X
104. Raise speed limit to 65 mph	Y
105. Require Pentagon to buy US goods	N
106. AIDS insurance non-discrimination	N
107. Prohibit Saudi arms sales	Y
108. Ease Gun Control Act of 1968	Y
109. Bar interstate handgun transport	N
110. Make company emissions known	N
111. Allow toxic victims to sue in fed ct	N
112. Superfund waste cleanup of $10b	N
113. 90 days notice of plant closings	N
114. $20b in Medicare cuts/tax increases	N
115. Spending cuts and tax increases	N
116. Set school lunch lmt-250% poverty	Y
117. $75m for youth work projects	N
118. Allow Angolan military assistance	Y
119. Suspend defense payments for abuse	N
120. Drop SS COLAs/$12b tax increase	N
121. Approve $1.5b for 21 MX missiles	Y
122. Emergency farm credit/revisions	N
123. Duty on Taiwan/Hong Kong/S Korea	N
124. Limit steel imports to 17%	N
125. Cut $ to schools that bar prayer	Y
126. $50b-taxes; cut Medicare/spending	N
127. Limit Pershing II/cruise in Europe	N
128. Delete $7.1b for 34 B-1 bombers	N
129. Bar purchase of Sergeant York guns	N
130. El Salvador military/economic aid	Y
131. Bar mining of Nicaraguan waters	N
132. Physician fee freeze for Medicare	Y
133. $49b in "sin"/phone/insurance taxes	N
134. Allow sale of Conrail	Y
135. Equal Rights Amendment	?
136. Authorize Marines in Lebanon	Y
137. Eminent domain for coal companies	N
138. Prohibit EPA clean air sanctions	Y
139. SS retirement age increase/reforms	Y
140. Auto domestic content requirement	N
141. Delete jobs program funding	Y
142. Highway-gas tax bill	Y
143. Cut $5b from defense for Medicare	N
144. Emergency housing aid of $1b	Y

Presidential Support Score: 1991 - 81% 1990 - 65%

BROWN, GEORGE E., Jr. -- California 36th District [Democrat]. Counties of Riverside (pt.) and San Bernardino (pt.). Prior Terms: 1963-70; 1973-92. Born: March 6, 1920; Holtville, CA. Education: University of California (B.A.). Military Service: U.S. Army, WW II.

BROWN, GEORGE E., Jr. (continued)

Occupation: Management consultant in engineering and personnel (1957-61); city councilman and mayor (1954-58); California assemblyman (1959-62).

1.	Protection to Haitian refugees	Y	62.	Notify spouses of AIDS+ carriers	?
2.	Raise tax on wealthy; lower others	Y	63.	Seize conveyance-drug trafficking	?
3.	Investigate Reagan hostage delay	Y	64.	South Africa sanctions	Y
4.	Campaign finance revisions	Y	65.	60 days' notice of plant closings	Y
5.	Unpaid leave to care for children	Y	66.	Close unneeded military bases	Y
6.	Restrict NEA use of funds	N	67.	Keep welfare reform within $2.8b	N
7.	Bar race-bias claim/habeas corpus	Y	68.	Allow children housing exclusion	?
8.	Ban race as death sentence factor	Y	69.	Shift $400m of NASA to homeless	N
9.	Exceptions to exclusionary rule	N	70.	Cap Medicare patients' liability	Y
10.	Allow sale of assault weapons	N	71.	Prohibit employee polygraph testing	Y
11.	Life in prison/abolish death penalty	Y	72.	Allow CIA to fund Contras	X
12.	Req conspiracy-price fixing cases	N	73.	Revise unfair trade practices	Y
13.	Unemployment benefits extension	Y	74.	Focus SDI on accidental launch	Y
14.	Tissue use of aborted fetuses	Y	75.	Bar Air Force $ for MX missile	N
15.	Bar replacement of union strikers	Y	76.	Allow "real" increase in defense	N
16.	Hold foreign aid at $15b for '92	?	77.	Troop reduction in Europe of 50%	Y
17.	Restore space station funding	Y	78.	Ban nuclear tests above 1 kiloton	Y
18.	Civil Rights Act of 1991	Y	79.	Ban anti-satellite missile tests	Y
19.	Unlimited damages-discrimination	Y	80.	Observe certain limits of SALT II	Y
20.	Eliminate funds for supercollider	N	81.	Restore four Civil Rights laws	Y
21.	Terminate SDI except for research	N	82.	Prohibit aliens as strikebreakers	Y
22.	Req 7-day handgun waiting period	Y	83.	Allow military malpractice suits	?
23.	Provide $30b for failed S&Ls	Y	84.	Approval of $36m in Contra aid	N
24.	Allow use of force against Iraq	N	85.	$18b deficit reduction compromise	Y
25.	Allow $15b in foreign aid for '91	Y	86.	Welfare reform of $5.7b for 5 years	Y
26.	Revise & extend legal immigration	Y	87.	Raise taxes $12b/cut spending $3b	Y
27.	Suspend aid to Angolan rebels	Y	88.	Board to assess occupational risk	Y
28.	Democratic tax plan proposals	Y	89.	Balanced budget by '93-via targets	?
29.	Cut defense 5% across the board	N	90.	Bar licensing of two nuclear plants	N
30.	Textile import quotas-veto override	Y	91.	Remove victims compensation cap	N
31.	Abortion service for military abroad	Y	92.	Catastrophic health insurance	Y
32.	Limits on high income farmers	N	93.	Ban airline smoking-2 hours or less	?
33.	Family medical leave-veto override	Y	94.	$1b/two year aid for the homeless	Y
34.	Req submission of balanced budget	Y	95.	Bar non-unions in union companies	Y
35.	Balanced budget amendment	N	96.	Increase FSLIC rescue to $15b	N
36.	Amendment to ban flag desecration	N	97.	Impose quotas to lower trade deficit	N
37.	Reauthorize Amtrak-veto override	Y	98.	Reduce discretionary budget 21%	N
38.	Retraining aid for coal miners	Y	99.	Immigration reform/alien amnesty	Y
39.	Suspend El Salvador military aid	?	100.	South Africa sanctions-veto override	Y
40.	Expand child care aid/tax credit	Y	101.	Tax overhaul to revise income tax	Y
41.	Raise House salary/omit honoraria	Y	102.	Use of military in drug war	N
42.	Toughen oil-spill liability	?	103.	Delete 12 MX/add conventional wpn	Y
43.	Restitution to Japanese interned	Y	104.	Raise speed limit to 65 mph	N
44.	Protect Chinese & C.A. nationals	Y	105.	Require Pentagon to buy US goods	?
45.	Abortion $ for rape/incest cases	Y	106.	AIDS insurance non-discrimination	Y
46.	Allow religious schools to bar gays	N	107.	Prohibit Saudi arms sales	Y
47.	Bar broadcaster fairness doctrine	N	108.	Ease Gun Control Act of 1968	N
48.	Bar cap gains cut/reinstate IRA	Y	109.	Bar interstate handgun transport	Y
49.	Bar unions equal voice in pension	N	110.	Make company emissions known	Y
50.	Bar assembly of chemical weapons	Y	111.	Allow toxic victims to sue in fed ct	Y
51.	Ban plutonium/uranium production	Y	112.	Superfund waste cleanup of $10b	Y
52.	Cap MX missile deployment at 50	Y	113.	90 days notice of plant closings	?
53.	Allow $3b for 2 stealth bombers	N	114.	$20b in Medicare cuts/tax increases	Y
54.	Publish bio-warfare experiments	Y	115.	Spending cuts and tax increases	?
55.	Raise minimum wage-veto override	Y	116.	Set school lunch lmt-250% poverty	N
56.	Bar transfer of FS-X technology	?	117.	$75m for youth work projects	?
57.	Cut defense and raise domestic $	Y	118.	Allow Angolan military assistance	N
58.	Uniform poll closing in 48 states	?	119.	Suspend defense payments for abuse	Y
59.	Req foreign investment disclosure	Y	120.	Drop SS COLAs/$12b tax increase	N
60.	Textile import quotas-veto override	Y	121.	Approve $1.5b for 21 MX missiles	N
61.	Bar abortion funding in Wash, DC	N	122.	Emergency farm credit/revisions	Y

BROWN, GEORGE E. (continued)

123. Duty on Taiwan/Hong Kong/S Korea	?		134. Allow sale of Conrail	N
124. Limit steel imports to 17%	Y		135. Equal Rights Amendment	Y
125. Cut $ to schools that bar prayer	N		136. Authorize Marines in Lebanon	Y
126. $50b-taxes; cut Medicare/spending	Y		137. Eminent domain for coal companies	Y
127. Limit Pershing II/cruise in Europe	Y		138. Prohibit EPA clean air sanctions	Y
128. Delete $7.1b for 34 B-1 bombers	N		139. SS retirement age increase/reforms	N
129. Bar purchase of Sergeant York guns	N		140. Auto domestic content requirement	?
130. El Salvador military/economic aid	N		141. Delete jobs program funding	N
131. Bar mining of Nicaraguan waters	Y		142. Highway-gas tax bill	Y
132. Physician fee freeze for Medicare	N		143. Cut $5b from defense for Medicare	Y
133. $49b in "sin"/phone/insurance taxes	Y		144. Emergency housing aid of $1b	Y

Presidential Support Score: 1991 - 38% 1990 - 19%

McCANDLESS, ALFRED A. (AL) -- California 37th District [Republican]. County of Riverside (pt.). Prior Terms: 1983-92. Born: July 23, 1927; Brawley, CA. Education: University of California (B.A.). Military Service: U.S. Marine Corps, 1945-46. Occupation: Business executive, General Motors, auto-truck dealership (1953-75); county supervisor (1971-82); member, county housing authority; founding member, Sunline Transit Agency.

1. Protection to Haitian refugees	N		44. Protect Chinese & C.A. nationals	N
2. Raise tax on wealthy; lower others	N		45. Abortion $ for rape/incest cases	Y
3. Investigate Reagan hostage delay	N		46. Allow religious schools to bar gays	Y
4. Campaign finance revisions	N		47. Bar broadcaster fairness doctrine	Y
5. Unpaid leave to care for children	N		48. Bar cap gains cut/reinstate IRA	N
6. Restrict NEA use of funds	Y		49. Bar unions equal voice in pension	+
7. Bar race-bias claim/habeas corpus	Y		50. Bar assembly of chemical weapons	N
8. Ban race as death sentence factor	Y		51. Ban plutonium/uranium production	N
9. Exceptions to exclusionary rule	Y		52. Cap MX missile deployment at 50	N
10. Allow sale of assault weapons	Y		53. Allow $3b for 2 stealth bombers	Y
11. Life in prison/abolish death penalty	N		54. Publish bio-warfare experiments	N
12. Req conspiracy-price fixing cases	Y		55. Raise minimum wage-veto override	N
13. Unemployment benefits extension	N		56. Bar transfer of FS-X technology	N
14. Tissue use of aborted fetuses	N		57. Cut defense and raise domestic $	N
15. Bar replacement of union strikers	N		58. Uniform poll closing in 48 states	Y
16. Hold foreign aid at $15b for '92	N		59. Req foreign investment disclosure	N
17. Restore space station funding	Y		60. Textile import quotas-veto override	N
18. Civil Rights Act of 1991	N		61. Bar abortion funding in Wash, DC	?
19. Unlimited damages-discrimination	N		62. Notify spouses of AIDS+ carriers	Y
20. Eliminate funds for supercollider	N		63. Seize conveyance-drug trafficking	Y
21. Terminate SDI except for research	N		64. South Africa sanctions	X
22. Req 7-day handgun waiting period	N		65. 60 days' notice of plant closings	N
23. Provide $30b for failed S&Ls	Y		66. Close unneeded military bases	Y
24. Allow use of force against Iraq	Y		67. Keep welfare reform within $2.8b	Y
25. Allow $15b in foreign aid for '91	N		68. Allow children housing exclusion	Y
26. Revise & extend legal immigration	N		69. Shift $400m of NASA to homeless	N
27. Suspend aid to Angolan rebels	N		70. Cap Medicare patients' liability	N
28. Democratic tax plan proposals	N		71. Prohibit employee polygraph testing	N
29. Cut defense 5% across the board	N		72. Allow CIA to fund Contras	Y
30. Textile import quotas-veto override	N		73. Revise unfair trade practices	N
31. Abortion service for military abroad	Y		74. Focus SDI on accidental launch	N
32. Limits on high income farmers	N		75. Bar Air Force $ for MX missile	N
33. Family medical leave-veto override	N		76. Allow "real" increase in defense	Y
34. Req submission of balanced budget	N		77. Troop reduction in Europe of 50%	N
35. Balanced budget amendment	Y		78. Ban nuclear tests above 1 kiloton	N
36. Amendment to ban flag desecration	Y		79. Ban anti-satellite missile tests	N
37. Reauthorize Amtrak-veto override	N		80. Observe certain limits of SALT II	N
38. Retraining aid for coal miners	N		81. Restore four Civil Rights laws	N
39. Suspend El Salvador military aid	N		82. Prohibit aliens as strikebreakers	N
40. Expand child care aid/tax credit	N		83. Allow military malpractice suits	N
41. Raise House salary/omit honoraria	N		84. Approval of $36m in Contra aid	Y
42. Toughen oil-spill liability	N		85. $18b deficit reduction compromise	N
43. Restitution to Japanese interned	N		86. Welfare reform of $5.7b for 5 years	N

McCANDLESS, ALFRED A. (continued)

87. Raise taxes $12b/cut spending $3b	N	
88. Board to assess occupational risk	N	
89. Balanced budget by '93-via targets	N	
90. Bar licensing of two nuclear plants	N	
91. Remove victims compensation cap	N	
92. Catastrophic health insurance	N	
93. Ban airline smoking-2 hours or less	?	
94. $1b/two year aid for the homeless	N	
95. Bar non-unions in union companies	N	
96. Increase FSLIC rescue to $15b	Y	
97. Impose quotas to lower trade deficit	N	
98. Reduce discretionary budget 21%	Y	
99. Immigration reform/alien amnesty	Y	
100. South Africa sanctions-veto override	N	
101. Tax overhaul to revise income tax	N	
102. Use of military in drug war	Y	
103. Delete 12 MX/add conventional wpn	N	
104. Raise speed limit to 65 mph	Y	
105. Require Pentagon to buy US goods	N	
106. AIDS insurance non-discrimination	N	
107. Prohibit Saudi arms sales	N	
108. Ease Gun Control Act of 1968	Y	
109. Bar interstate handgun transport	N	
110. Make company emissions known	N	
111. Allow toxic victims to sue in fed ct	N	
112. Superfund waste cleanup of $10b	N	
113. 90 days notice of plant closings	N	
114. $20b in Medicare cuts/tax increases	N	
115. Spending cuts and tax increases	N	
116. Set school lunch lmt-250% poverty	Y	
117. $75m for youth work projects	N	
118. Allow Angolan military assistance	Y	
119. Suspend defense payments for abuse	N	
120. Drop SS COLAs/$12b tax increase	N	
121. Approve $1.5b for 21 MX missiles	Y	
122. Emergency farm credit/revisions	N	
123. Duty on Taiwan/Hong Kong/S Korea	N	
124. Limit steel imports to 17%	N	
125. Cut $ to schools that bar prayer	Y	
126. $50b-taxes; cut Medicare/spending	N	
127. Limit Pershing II/cruise in Europe	N	
128. Delete $7.1b for 34 B-1 bombers	N	
129. Bar purchase of Sergeant York guns	N	
130. El Salvador military/economic aid	Y	
131. Bar mining of Nicaraguan waters	Y	
132. Physician fee freeze for Medicare	Y	
133. $49b in "sin"/phone/insurance taxes	N	
134. Allow sale of Conrail	Y	
135. Equal Rights Amendment	N	
136. Authorize Marines in Lebanon	Y	
137. Eminent domain for coal companies	Y	
138. Prohibit EPA clean air sanctions	Y	
139. SS retirement age increase/reforms	Y	

Presidential Support Score: 1991 - 85%   1990 - 71%

DORNAN, ROBERT K. -- California 38th District [Republican]. Counties of Los Angeles (pt.) and Orange (pt.). Prior Terms: 1977-82, 1985-92. Born: April 3, 1933; New York, NY. Education: Loyola University, Los Angeles. Military Service: U.S. Air Force, 1953-1958. Occupation: Broadcast journalist; combat photographer; professional pilot; television producer and talk show host.

1. Protection to Haitian refugees	Y	
2. Raise tax on wealthy; lower others	N	
3. Investigate Reagan hostage delay	N	
4. Campaign finance revisions	N	
5. Unpaid leave to care for children	N	
6. Restrict NEA use of funds	Y	
7. Bar race-bias claim/habeas corpus	Y	
8. Ban race as death sentence factor	Y	
9. Exceptions to exclusionary rule	Y	
10. Allow sale of assault weapons	Y	
11. Life in prison/abolish death penalty	N	
12. Req conspiracy-price fixing cases	Y	
13. Unemployment benefits extension	N	
14. Tissue use of aborted fetuses	N	
15. Bar replacement of union strikers	N	
16. Hold foreign aid at $15b for '92	Y	
17. Restore space station funding	Y	
18. Civil Rights Act of 1991	N	
19. Unlimited damages-discrimination	N	
20. Eliminate funds for supercollider	N	
21. Terminate SDI except for research	N	
22. Req 7-day handgun waiting period	Y	
23. Provide $30b for failed S&Ls	Y	
24. Allow use of force against Iraq	Y	
25. Allow $15b in foreign aid for '91	Y	
26. Revise & extend legal immigration	N	
27. Suspend aid to Angolan rebels	N	
28. Democratic tax plan proposals	N	
29. Cut defense 5% across the board	N	
30. Textile import quotas-veto override	Y	
31. Abortion service for military abroad	N	
32. Limits on high income farmers	N	
33. Family medical leave-veto override	N	
34. Req submission of balanced budget	N	
35. Balanced budget amendment	Y	
36. Amendment to ban flag desecration	Y	
37. Reauthorize Amtrak-veto override	N	
38. Retraining aid for coal miners	N	
39. Suspend El Salvador military aid	N	
40. Expand child care aid/tax credit	N	
41. Raise House salary/omit honoraria	N	
42. Toughen oil-spill liability	N	
43. Restitution to Japanese interned	Y	
44. Protect Chinese & C.A. nationals	N	
45. Abortion $ for rape/incest cases	N	
46. Allow religious schools to bar gays	Y	
47. Bar broadcaster fairness doctrine	N	
48. Bar cap gains cut/reinstate IRA	N	
49. Bar unions equal voice in pension	Y	
50. Bar assembly of chemical weapons	N	
51. Ban plutonium/uranium production	N	
52. Cap MX missile deployment at 50	N	
53. Allow $3b for 2 stealth bombers	Y	
54. Publish bio-warfare experiments	N	

DORNAN, ROBERT K. (continued)

55. Raise minimum wage-veto override	?
56. Bar transfer of FS-X technology	N
57. Cut defense and raise domestic $	N
58. Uniform poll closing in 48 states	Y
59. Req foreign investment disclosure	N
60. Textile import quotas-veto override	N
61. Bar abortion funding in Wash, DC	Y
62. Notify spouses of AIDS+ carriers	Y
63. Seize conveyance-drug trafficking	Y
64. South Africa sanctions	N
65. 60 days' notice of plant closings	N
66. Close unneeded military bases	Y
67. Keep welfare reform within $2.8b	Y
68. Allow children housing exclusion	Y
69. Shift $400m of NASA to homeless	N
70. Cap Medicare patients' liability	N
71. Prohibit employee polygraph testing	N
72. Allow CIA to fund Contras	Y
73. Revise unfair trade practices	N
74. Focus SDI on accidental launch	N
75. Bar Air Force $ for MX missile	N
76. Allow "real" increase in defense	Y
77. Troop reduction in Europe of 50%	N
78. Ban nuclear tests above 1 kiloton	N
79. Ban anti-satellite missile tests	N
80. Observe certain limits of SALT II	N
81. Restore four Civil Rights laws	N
82. Prohibit aliens as strikebreakers	Y
83. Allow military malpractice suits	N
84. Approval of $36m in Contra aid	Y
85. $18b deficit reduction compromise	N
86. Welfare reform of $5.7b for 5 years	N
87. Raise taxes $12b/cut spending $3b	N
88. Board to assess occupational risk	N
89. Balanced budget by '93-via targets	?
90. Bar licensing of two nuclear plants	N
91. Remove victims compensation cap	N

92. Catastrophic health insurance	N
93. Ban airline smoking-2 hours or less	Y
94. $1b/two year aid for the homeless	N
95. Bar non-unions in union companies	N
96. Increase FSLIC rescue to $15b	N
97. Impose quotas to lower trade deficit	N
98. Reduce discretionary budget 21%	Y
99. Immigration reform/alien amnesty	Y
100. South Africa sanctions-veto override	N
101. Tax overhaul to revise income tax	Y
102. Use of military in drug war	Y
103. Delete 12 MX/add conventional wpn	N
104. Raise speed limit to 65 mph	Y
105. Require Pentagon to buy US goods	N
106. AIDS insurance non-discrimination	N
107. Prohibit Saudi arms sales	Y
108. Ease Gun Control Act of 1968	Y
109. Bar interstate handgun transport	N
110. Make company emissions known	N
111. Allow toxic victims to sue in fed ct	N
112. Superfund waste cleanup of $10b	N
113. 90 days notice of plant closings	N
114. $20b in Medicare cuts/tax increases	N
115. Spending cuts and tax increases	N
116. Set school lunch lmt-250% poverty	Y
117. $75m for youth work projects	N
118. Allow Angolan military assistance	Y
119. Suspend defense payments for abuse	N
120. Drop SS COLAs/$12b tax increase	N
121. Approve $1.5b for 21 MX missiles	Y
122. Emergency farm credit/revisions	N
140. Auto domestic content requirement	N
141. Delete jobs program funding	Y
142. Highway-gas tax bill	Y
143. Cut $5b from defense for Medicare	N
144. Emergency housing aid of $1b	N

Rep. Dornan was not in office for votes 123-139.

Presidential Support Score: 1991 - 76%   1990 - 68%

DANNEMEYER, WILLIAM E. -- California 39th District [Republican]. County of Orange (pt.). Prior Terms: 1979-92. Born: September 22, 1929; Los Angeles,CA. Education: Santa Maria Junior College; Valparaiso University (B.A.); Hastings Law School (J.D.). Military Service: U.S. Army. Occupation: Deputy district attorney; assistant district attorney; Municipal Court judge pro tem; Superior Court judge pro tem; member, Orange County Criminal Justice Council; California legislator (1963-66); California general assemblyman (1976).

1. Protection to Haitian refugees	?
2. Raise tax on wealthy; lower others	N
3. Investigate Reagan hostage delay	?
4. Campaign finance revisions	N
5. Unpaid leave to care for children	N
6. Restrict NEA use of funds	+
7. Bar race-bias claim/habeas corpus	Y
8. Ban race as death sentence factor	Y
9. Exceptions to exclusionary rule	+
10. Allow sale of assault weapons	Y
11. Life in prison/abolish death penalty	N
12. Req conspiracy-price fixing cases	Y
13. Unemployment benefits extension	N

14. Tissue use of aborted fetuses	N
15. Bar replacement of union strikers	N
16. Hold foreign aid at $15b for '92	N
17. Restore space station funding	Y
18. Civil Rights Act of 1991	N
19. Unlimited damages-discrimination	N
20. Eliminate funds for supercollider	N
21. Terminate SDI except for research	N
22. Req 7-day handgun waiting period	N
23. Provide $30b for failed S&Ls	Y
24. Allow use of force against Iraq	Y
25. Allow $15b in foreign aid for '91	N
26. Revise & extend legal immigration	N

DANNEMEYER, WILLIAM E. (continued)

27.	Suspend aid to Angolan rebels	N	86. Welfare reform of $5.7b for 5 years	N
28.	Democratic tax plan proposals	N	87. Raise taxes $12b/cut spending $3b	N
29.	Cut defense 5% across the board	N	88. Board to assess occupational risk	N
30.	Textile import quotas-veto override	N	89. Balanced budget by '93-via targets	N
31.	Abortion service for military abroad	N	90. Bar licensing of two nuclear plants	N
32.	Limits on high income farmers	Y	91. Remove victims compensation cap	N
33.	Family medical leave-veto override	N	92. Catastrophic health insurance	N
34.	Req submission of balanced budget	N	93. Ban airline smoking-2 hours or less	Y
35.	Balanced budget amendment	Y	94. $1b/two year aid for the homeless	N
36.	Amendment to ban flag desecration	Y	95. Bar non-unions in union companies	N
37.	Reauthorize Amtrak-veto override	N	96. Increase FSLIC rescue to $15b	N
38.	Retraining aid for coal miners	N	97. Impose quotas to lower trade deficit	N
39.	Suspend El Salvador military aid	N	98. Reduce discretionary budget 21%	Y
40.	Expand child care aid/tax credit	N	99. Immigration reform/alien amnesty	Y
41.	Raise House salary/omit honoraria	N	100. South Africa sanctions-veto override	N
42.	Toughen oil-spill liability	N	101. Tax overhaul to revise income tax	N
43.	Restitution to Japanese interned	N	102. Use of military in drug war	Y
44.	Protect Chinese & C.A. nationals	N	103. Delete 12 MX/add conventional wpn	N
45.	Abortion $ for rape/incest cases	N	104. Raise speed limit to 65 mph	Y
46.	Allow religious schools to bar gays	Y	105. Require Pentagon to buy US goods	N
47.	Bar broadcaster fairness doctrine	N	106. AIDS insurance non-discrimination	N
48.	Bar cap gains cut/reinstate IRA	N	107. Prohibit Saudi arms sales	N
49.	Bar unions equal voice in pension	Y	108. Ease Gun Control Act of 1968	Y
50.	Bar assembly of chemical weapons	X	109. Bar interstate handgun transport	N
51.	Ban plutonium/uranium production	+	110. Make company emissions known	N
52.	Cap MX missile deployment at 50	--	111. Allow toxic victims to sue in fed ct	N
53.	Allow $3b for 2 stealth bombers	Y	112. Superfund waste cleanup of $10b	N
54.	Publish bio-warfare experiments	N	113. 90 days notice of plant closings	N
55.	Raise minimum wage-veto override	N	114. $20b in Medicare cuts/tax increases	N
56.	Bar transfer of FS-X technology	N	115. Spending cuts and tax increases	N
57.	Cut defense and raise domestic $	N	116. Set school lunch lmt-250% poverty	Y
58.	Uniform poll closing in 48 states	Y	117. $75m for youth work projects	N
59.	Req foreign investment disclosure	N	118. Allow Angolan military assistance	Y
60.	Textile import quotas-veto override	N	119. Suspend defense payments for abuse	N
61.	Bar abortion funding in Wash, DC	Y	120. Drop SS COLAs/$12b tax increase	N
62.	Notify spouses of AIDS+ carriers	Y	121. Approve $1.5b for 21 MX missiles	Y
63.	Seize conveyance-drug trafficking	Y	122. Emergency farm credit/revisions	N
64.	South Africa sanctions	N	123. Duty on Taiwan/Hong Kong/S Korea	N
65.	60 days' notice of plant closings	N	124. Limit steel imports to 17%	N
66.	Close unneeded military bases	Y	125. Cut $ to schools that bar prayer	+
67.	Keep welfare reform within $2.8b	Y	126. $50b-taxes; cut Medicare/spending	N
68.	Allow children housing exclusion	?	127. Limit Pershing II/cruise in Europe	N
69.	Shift $400m of NASA to homeless	N	128. Delete $7.1b for 34 B-1 bombers	N
70.	Cap Medicare patients' liability	N	129. Bar purchase of Sergeant York guns	Y
71.	Prohibit employee polygraph testing	N	130. El Salvador military/economic aid	N
72.	Allow CIA to fund Contras	Y	131. Bar mining of Nicaraguan waters	N
73.	Revise unfair trade practices	N	132. Physician fee freeze for Medicare	N
74.	Focus SDI on accidental launch	N	133. $49b in "sin"/phone/insurance taxes	N
75.	Bar Air Force $ for MX missile	N	134. Allow sale of Conrail	Y
76.	Allow "real" increase in defense	Y	135. Equal Rights Amendment	N
77.	Troop reduction in Europe of 50%	Y	136. Authorize Marines in Lebanon	N
78.	Ban nuclear tests above 1 kiloton	N	137. Eminent domain for coal companies	Y
79.	Ban anti-satellite missile tests	N	138. Prohibit EPA clean air sanctions	Y
80.	Observe certain limits of SALT II	N	139. SS retirement age increase/reforms	Y
81.	Restore four Civil Rights laws	N	140. Auto domestic content requirement	N
82.	Prohibit aliens as strikebreakers	N	141. Delete jobs program funding	Y
83.	Allow military malpractice suits	Y	142. Highway-gas tax bill	N
84.	Approval of $36m in Contra aid	Y	143. Cut $5b from defense for Medicare	N
85.	$18b deficit reduction compromise	N	144. Emergency housing aid of $1b	N

Presidential Support Score: 1991 - 71%   1990 - 75%

COX, CHRISTOPHER -- California 40th District [Republican]. County of Orange (pt.). Prior Terms: 1989-92. Born: October 26, 1952; St. Paul, MN. Education: University of Southern California (B.A.); Harvard Business School (M.B.A.); Harvard Law School (J.D.). Occupation: U.S. Circuit Court of Appeals law clerk; attorney, Latham & Watkins (1978-86); college professor; foreign daily newspaper translation service cofounder; Senior Associate Counsel to President Reagan (1986-88).

1.	Protection to Haitian refugees	N	30.	Textile import quotas-veto override	N
2.	Raise tax on wealthy; lower others	N	31.	Abortion service for military abroad	N
3.	Investigate Reagan hostage delay	N	32.	Limits on high income farmers	Y
4.	Campaign finance revisions	N	33.	Family medical leave-veto override	N
5.	Unpaid leave to care for children	N	34.	Req submission of balanced budget	N
6.	Restrict NEA use of funds	#	35.	Balanced budget amendment	Y
7.	Bar race-bias claim/habeas corpus	Y	36.	Amendment to ban flag desecration	Y
8.	Ban race as death sentence factor	Y	37.	Reauthorize Amtrak-veto override	N
9.	Exceptions to exclusionary rule	Y	38.	Retraining aid for coal miners	N
10.	Allow sale of assault weapons	Y	39.	Suspend El Salvador military aid	N
11.	Life in prison/abolish death penalty	N	40.	Expand child care aid/tax credit	N
12.	Req conspiracy-price fixing cases	Y	41.	Raise House salary/omit honoraria	Y
13.	Unemployment benefits extension	N	42.	Toughen oil-spill liability	N
14.	Tissue use of aborted fetuses	N	43.	Restitution to Japanese interned	N
15.	Bar replacement of union strikers	N	44.	Protect Chinese & C.A. nationals	N
16.	Hold foreign aid at $15b for '92	Y	45.	Abortion $ for rape/incest cases	N
17.	Restore space station funding	Y	46.	Allow religious schools to bar gays	Y
18.	Civil Rights Act of 1991	N	47.	Bar broadcaster fairness doctrine	Y
19.	Unlimited damages-discrimination	N	48.	Bar cap gains cut/reinstate IRA	N
20.	Eliminate funds for supercollider	N	49.	Bar unions equal voice in pension	Y
21.	Terminate SDI except for research	N	50.	Bar assembly of chemical weapons	N
22.	Req 7-day handgun waiting period	N	51.	Ban plutonium/uranium production	N
23.	Provide $30b for failed S&Ls	N	52.	Cap MX missile deployment at 50	N
24.	Allow use of force against Iraq	Y	53.	Allow $3b for 2 stealth bombers	Y
25.	Allow $15b in foreign aid for '91	Y	54.	Publish bio-warfare experiments	N
26.	Revise & extend legal immigration	N	55.	Raise minimum wage-veto override	N
27.	Suspend aid to Angolan rebels	N	56.	Bar transfer of FS-X technology	N
28.	Democratic tax plan proposals	N	57.	Cut defense and raise domestic $	N
29.	Cut defense 5% across the board	N	58.	Uniform poll closing in 48 states	Y

Presidential Support Score: 1991 - 77%   1990 - 75%

LOWERY, BILL -- California 41st District [Republican]. County of San Diego (pt.). Prior Terms: 1981-92. Born: May 2, 1947; San Diego, CA. Education: San Diego State College. Occupation: San Diego city councilman (1977); council liaison, San Diego Unified Port District; deputy mayor (1979).

1.	Protection to Haitian refugees	N	21.	Terminate SDI except for research	N
2.	Raise tax on wealthy; lower others	N	22.	Req 7-day handgun waiting period	Y
3.	Investigate Reagan hostage delay	N	23.	Provide $30b for failed S&Ls	Y
4.	Campaign finance revisions	N	24.	Allow use of force against Iraq	Y
5.	Unpaid leave to care for children	N	25.	Allow $15b in foreign aid for '91	Y
6.	Restrict NEA use of funds	Y	26.	Revise & extend legal immigration	N
7.	Bar race-bias claim/habeas corpus	Y	27.	Suspend aid to Angolan rebels	N
8.	Ban race as death sentence factor	Y	28.	Democratic tax plan proposals	N
9.	Exceptions to exclusionary rule	Y	29.	Cut defense 5% across the board	N
10.	Allow sale of assault weapons	Y	30.	Textile import quotas-veto override	N
11.	Life in prison/abolish death penalty	N	31.	Abortion service for military abroad	N
12.	Req conspiracy-price fixing cases	Y	32.	Limits on high income farmers	N
13.	Unemployment benefits extension	N	33.	Family medical leave-veto override	N
14.	Tissue use of aborted fetuses	N	34.	Req submission of balanced budget	N
15.	Bar replacement of union strikers	N	35.	Balanced budget amendment	Y
16.	Hold foreign aid at $15b for '92	Y	36.	Amendment to ban flag desecration	Y
17.	Restore space station funding	Y	37.	Reauthorize Amtrak-veto override	N
18.	Civil Rights Act of 1991	N	38.	Retraining aid for coal miners	N
19.	Unlimited damages-discrimination	N	39.	Suspend El Salvador military aid	N
20.	Eliminate funds for supercollider	N	40.	Expand child care aid/tax credit	N

LOWERY, BILL (continued)

41.	Raise House salary/omit honoraria	Y		93.	Ban airline smoking-2 hours or less	Y
42.	Toughen oil-spill liability	Y		94.	$1b/two year aid for the homeless	N
43.	Restitution to Japanese interned	Y		95.	Bar non-unions in union companies	N
44.	Protect Chinese & C.A. nationals	N		96.	Increase FSLIC rescue to $15b	N
45.	Abortion $ for rape/incest cases	N		97.	Impose quotas to lower trade deficit	N
46.	Allow religious schools to bar gays	Y		98.	Reduce discretionary budget 21%	Y
47.	Bar broadcaster fairness doctrine	Y		99.	Immigration reform/alien amnesty	Y
48.	Bar cap gains cut/reinstate IRA	N		100.	South Africa sanctions-veto override	Y
49.	Bar unions equal voice in pension	Y		101.	Tax overhaul to revise income tax	Y
50.	Bar assembly of chemical weapons	N		102.	Use of military in drug war	Y
51.	Ban plutonium/uranium production	N		103.	Delete 12 MX/add conventional wpn	N
52.	Cap MX missile deployment at 50	N		104.	Raise speed limit to 65 mph	Y
53.	Allow $3b for 2 stealth bombers	Y		105.	Require Pentagon to buy US goods	N
54.	Publish bio-warfare experiments	N		106.	AIDS insurance non-discrimination	N
55.	Raise minimum wage-veto override	N		107.	Prohibit Saudi arms sales	Y
56.	Bar transfer of FS-X technology	N		108.	Ease Gun Control Act of 1968	Y
57.	Cut defense and raise domestic $	N		109.	Bar interstate handgun transport	N
58.	Uniform poll closing in 48 states	Y		110.	Make company emissions known	N
59.	Req foreign investment disclosure	N		111.	Allow toxic victims to sue in fed ct	N
60.	Textile import quotas-veto override	N		112.	Superfund waste cleanup of $10b	N
61.	Bar abortion funding in Wash, DC	Y		113.	90 days notice of plant closings	N
62.	Notify spouses of AIDS+ carriers	Y		114.	$20b in Medicare cuts/tax increases	N
63.	Seize conveyance-drug trafficking	Y		115.	Spending cuts and tax increases	N
64.	South Africa sanctions	N		116.	Set school lunch lmt-250% poverty	Y
65.	60 days' notice of plant closings	N		117.	$75m for youth work projects	N
66.	Close unneeded military bases	Y		118.	Allow Angolan military assistance	Y
67.	Keep welfare reform within $2.8b	Y		119.	Suspend defense payments for abuse	N
68.	Allow children housing exclusion	N		120.	Drop SS COLAs/$12b tax increase	N
69.	Shift $400m of NASA to homeless	N		121.	Approve $1.5b for 21 MX missiles	Y
70.	Cap Medicare patients' liability	Y		122.	Emergency farm credit/revisions	N
71.	Prohibit employee polygraph testing	X		123.	Duty on Taiwan/Hong Kong/S Korea	N
72.	Allow CIA to fund Contras	Y		124.	Limit steel imports to 17%	N
73.	Revise unfair trade practices	N		125.	Cut $ to schools that bar prayer	Y
74.	Focus SDI on accidental launch	N		126.	$50b-taxes; cut Medicare/spending	Y
75.	Bar Air Force $ for MX missile	N		127.	Limit Pershing II/cruise in Europe	N
76.	Allow "real" increase in defense	Y		128.	Delete $7.1b for 34 B-1 bombers	N
77.	Troop reduction in Europe of 50%	?		129.	Bar purchase of Sergeant York guns	N
78.	Ban nuclear tests above 1 kiloton	N		130.	El Salvador military/economic aid	Y
79.	Ban anti-satellite missile tests	N		131.	Bar mining of Nicaraguan waters	N
80.	Observe certain limits of SALT II	N		132.	Physician fee freeze for Medicare	Y
81.	Restore four Civil Rights laws	N		133.	$49b in "sin"/phone/insurance taxes	N
82.	Prohibit aliens as strikebreakers	N		134.	Allow sale of Conrail	Y
83.	Allow military malpractice suits	Y		135.	Equal Rights Amendment	N
84.	Approval of $36m in Contra aid	Y		136.	Authorize Marines in Lebanon	Y
85.	$18b deficit reduction compromise	N		137.	Eminent domain for coal companies	Y
86.	Welfare reform of $5.7b for 5 years	N		138.	Prohibit EPA clean air sanctions	Y
87.	Raise taxes $12b/cut spending $3b	N		139.	SS retirement age increase/reforms	Y
88.	Board to assess occupational risk	N		140.	Auto domestic content requirement	N
89.	Balanced budget by '93-via targets	Y		141.	Delete jobs program funding	Y
90.	Bar licensing of two nuclear plants	N		142.	Highway-gas tax bill	Y
91.	Remove victims compensation cap	X		143.	Cut $5b from defense for Medicare	N
92.	Catastrophic health insurance	N		144.	Emergency housing aid of $1b	Y

Presidential Support Score: 1991 - 83%   1990 - 67%

ROHRABACHER, DANA -- California 42nd District [Republican]. Counties of Los Angeles (pt.) and Orange (pt.). Prior Terms: 1989-92. Born: June 21, 1947; Coronado, CA. Education: Los Angeles Harbor College; Long Beach State College (B.A.); University of Southern California (M.A.). Occupation: Reporter, City News Service/Radio News West; editorial writer, *Orange County Register*; special assistant and principal speechwriter to President Reagan.

1.	Protection to Haitian refugees	Y	2.	Raise tax on wealthy; lower others	N

ROHRABACHER, DANA (continued)

3. Investigate Reagan hostage delay	N	31. Abortion service for military abroad	N
4. Campaign finance revisions	N	32. Limits on high income farmers	Y
5. Unpaid leave to care for children	N	33. Family medical leave-veto override	N
6. Restrict NEA use of funds	Y	34. Req submission of balanced budget	N
7. Bar race-bias claim/habeas corpus	Y	35. Balanced budget amendment	Y
8. Ban race as death sentence factor	Y	36. Amendment to ban flag desecration	Y
9. Exceptions to exclusionary rule	Y	37. Reauthorize Amtrak-veto override	N
10. Allow sale of assault weapons	Y	38. Retraining aid for coal miners	N
11. Life in prison/abolish death penalty	N	39. Suspend El Salvador military aid	N
12. Req conspiracy-price fixing cases	Y	40. Expand child care aid/tax credit	N
13. Unemployment benefits extension	N	41. Raise House salary/omit honoraria	N
14. Tissue use of aborted fetuses	N	42. Toughen oil-spill liability	N
15. Bar replacement of union strikers	N	43. Restitution to Japanese interned	N
16. Hold foreign aid at $15b for '92	Y	44. Protect Chinese & C.A. nationals	Y
17. Restore space station funding	Y	45. Abortion $ for rape/incest cases	N
18. Civil Rights Act of 1991	N	46. Allow religious schools to bar gays	Y
19. Unlimited damages-discrimination	N	47. Bar broadcaster fairness doctrine	Y
20. Eliminate funds for supercollider	Y	48. Bar cap gains cut/reinstate IRA	N
21. Terminate SDI except for research	N	49. Bar unions equal voice in pension	Y
22. Req 7-day handgun waiting period	N	50. Bar assembly of chemical weapons	N
23. Provide $30b for failed S&Ls	N	51. Ban plutonium/uranium production	N
24. Allow use of force against Iraq	Y	52. Cap MX missile deployment at 50	N
25. Allow $15b in foreign aid for '91	Y	53. Allow $3b for 2 stealth bombers	N
26. Revise & extend legal immigration	Y	54. Publish bio-warfare experiments	N
27. Suspend aid to Angolan rebels	N	55. Raise minimum wage-veto override	N
28. Democratic tax plan proposals	N	56. Bar transfer of FS-X technology	N
29. Cut defense 5% across the board	N	57. Cut defense and raise domestic $	N
30. Textile import quotas-veto override	N	58. Uniform poll closing in 48 states	N

Presidential Support Score: 1991 - 70%   1990 - 74%

PACKARD, RONALD C. -- California 43rd District [Republican]. Counties of Orange (pt.) and San Diego (pt.). Prior Terms: 1983-92. Born: January 19, 1931; Meridian, ID. Education: Brigham Young University; Portland State University; University of Oregon Dental School. Military Service: U.S. Navy. Occupation: Dentist, U.S. Navy Dental Corps (1957-59); Board of Trustees, Carlsbad Unified School District (1962-74); member, Carlsbad city council; director, North County Transit District; mayor (1978-82); dentist, Packard Dental Clinic (since 1959); officer, Packard Development Corp. (since 1965); vice chairman, board of directors, First National Bank of North County (since 1981).

1. Protection to Haitian refugees	N	24. Allow use of force against Iraq	Y
2. Raise tax on wealthy; lower others	N	25. Allow $15b in foreign aid for '91	N
3. Investigate Reagan hostage delay	N	26. Revise & extend legal immigration	N
4. Campaign finance revisions	N	27. Suspend aid to Angolan rebels	N
5. Unpaid leave to care for children	N	28. Democratic tax plan proposals	N
6. Restrict NEA use of funds	Y	29. Cut defense 5% across the board	N
7. Bar race-bias claim/habeas corpus	Y	30. Textile import quotas-veto override	N
8. Ban race as death sentence factor	Y	31. Abortion service for military abroad	N
9. Exceptions to exclusionary rule	Y	32. Limits on high income farmers	N
10. Allow sale of assault weapons	Y	33. Family medical leave-veto override	N
11. Life in prison/abolish death penalty	N	34. Req submission of balanced budget	N
12. Req conspiracy-price fixing cases	Y	35. Balanced budget amendment	Y
13. Unemployment benefits extension	N	36. Amendment to ban flag desecration	Y
14. Tissue use of aborted fetuses	N	37. Reauthorize Amtrak-veto override	N
15. Bar replacement of union strikers	N	38. Retraining aid for coal miners	N
16. Hold foreign aid at $15b for '92	N	39. Suspend El Salvador military aid	N
17. Restore space station funding	Y	40. Expand child care aid/tax credit	N
18. Civil Rights Act of 1991	N	41. Raise House salary/omit honoraria	Y
19. Unlimited damages-discrimination	N	42. Toughen oil-spill liability	N
20. Eliminate funds for supercollider	N	43. Restitution to Japanese interned	N
21. Terminate SDI except for research	N	44. Protect Chinese & C.A. nationals	N
22. Req 7-day handgun waiting period	Y	45. Abortion $ for rape/incest cases	N
23. Provide $30b for failed S&Ls	N	46. Allow religious schools to bar gays	Y

PACKARD, RONALD C. (continued)

47. Bar broadcaster fairness doctrine	Y
48. Bar cap gains cut/reinstate IRA	N
49. Bar unions equal voice in pension	Y
50. Bar assembly of chemical weapons	N
51. Ban plutonium/uranium production	N
52. Cap MX missile deployment at 50	N
53. Allow $3b for 2 stealth bombers	Y
54. Publish bio-warfare experiments	N
55. Raise minimum wage-veto override	N
56. Bar transfer of FS-X technology	N
57. Cut defense and raise domestic $	N
58. Uniform poll closing in 48 states	Y
59. Req foreign investment disclosure	N
60. Textile import quotas-veto override	N
61. Bar abortion funding in Wash, DC	Y
62. Notify spouses of AIDS+ carriers	+
63. Seize conveyance-drug trafficking	Y
64. South Africa sanctions	N
65. 60 days' notice of plant closings	N
66. Close unneeded military bases	Y
67. Keep welfare reform within $2.8b	Y
68. Allow children housing exclusion	Y
69. Shift $400m of NASA to homeless	N
70. Cap Medicare patients' liability	Y
71. Prohibit employee polygraph testing	N
72. Allow CIA to fund Contras	Y
73. Revise unfair trade practices	N
74. Focus SDI on accidental launch	N
75. Bar Air Force $ for MX missile	N
76. Allow "real" increase in defense	Y
77. Troop reduction in Europe of 50%	N
78. Ban nuclear tests above 1 kiloton	N
79. Ban anti-satellite missile tests	N
80. Observe certain limits of SALT II	N
81. Restore four Civil Rights laws	N
82. Prohibit aliens as strikebreakers	N
83. Allow military malpractice suits	N
84. Approval of $36m in Contra aid	Y
85. $18b deficit reduction compromise	N
86. Welfare reform of $5.7b for 5 years	N
87. Raise taxes $12b/cut spending $3b	N
88. Board to assess occupational risk	N
89. Balanced budget by '93-via targets	N
90. Bar licensing of two nuclear plants	N
91. Remove victims compensation cap	N
92. Catastrophic health insurance	N
93. Ban airline smoking-2 hours or less	Y

94. $1b/two year aid for the homeless	N
95. Bar non-unions in union companies	N
96. Increase FSLIC rescue to $15b	N
97. Impose quotas to lower trade deficit	N
98. Reduce discretionary budget 21%	Y
99. Immigration reform/alien amnesty	Y
100. South Africa sanctions-veto override	N
101. Tax overhaul to revise income tax	Y
102. Use of military in drug war	Y
103. Delete 12 MX/add conventional wpn	N
104. Raise speed limit to 65 mph	Y
105. Require Pentagon to buy US goods	N
106. AIDS insurance non-discrimination	N
107. Prohibit Saudi arms sales	N
108. Ease Gun Control Act of 1968	Y
109. Bar interstate handgun transport	N
110. Make company emissions known	N
111. Allow toxic victims to sue in fed ct	N
112. Superfund waste cleanup of $10b	N
113. 90 days notice of plant closings	N
114. $20b in Medicare cuts/tax increases	N
115. Spending cuts and tax increases	N
116. Set school lunch lmt-250% poverty	Y
117. $75m for youth work projects	N
118. Allow Angolan military assistance	Y
119. Suspend defense payments for abuse	N
120. Drop SS COLAs/$12b tax increase	N
121. Approve $1.5b for 21 MX missiles	Y
122. Emergency farm credit/revisions	Y
123. Duty on Taiwan/Hong Kong/S Korea	N
124. Limit steel imports to 17%	N
125. Cut $ to schools that bar prayer	Y
126. $50b-taxes; cut Medicare/spending	Y
127. Limit Pershing II/cruise in Europe	N
128. Delete $7.1b for 34 B-1 bombers	N
129. Bar purchase of Sergeant York guns	N
130. El Salvador military/economic aid	Y
131. Bar mining of Nicaraguan waters	N
132. Physician fee freeze for Medicare	Y
133. $49b in "sin"/phone/insurance taxes	Y
134. Allow sale of Conrail	Y
135. Equal Rights Amendment	N
136. Authorize Marines in Lebanon	Y
137. Eminent domain for coal companies	Y
138. Prohibit EPA clean air sanctions	Y
139. SS retirement age increase/reforms	Y

Presidential Support Score: 1991 - 83%   1990 - 71%

CUNNINGHAM, RANDY -- California 44th District [Republican]. County of San Diego (pt.). Prior Term: 1991-92. Born: December 8, 1941; Los Angeles, CA. Education: University of Missouri (B.S., M.S., M.B.A.). Military Service: U.S. Navy (retired commander 1987). Occupation: Businessman.

1. Protection to Haitian refugees	N
2. Raise tax on wealthy; lower others	N
3. Investigate Reagan hostage delay	N
4. Campaign finance revisions	N
5. Unpaid leave to care for children	N
6. Restrict NEA use of funds	Y
7. Bar race-bias claim/habeas corpus	Y
8. Ban race as death sentence factor	Y

9. Exceptions to exclusionary rule	Y
10. Allow sale of assault weapons	Y
11. Life in prison/abolish death penalty	N
12. Req conspiracy-price fixing cases	Y
13. Unemployment benefits extension	Y
14. Tissue use of aborted fetuses	N
15. Bar replacement of union strikers	N
16. Hold foreign aid at $15b for '92	Y

CUNNINGHAM, RANDY (continued)

17. Restore space station funding	Y	21. Terminate SDI except for research	N
18. Civil Rights Act of 1991	N	22. Req 7-day handgun waiting period	N
19. Unlimited damages-discrimination	N	23. Provide $30b for failed S&Ls	Y
20. Eliminate funds for supercollider	N	24. Allow use of force against Iraq	Y

Presidential Support Score: 1991 - 78%

HUNTER, DUNCAN -- California 45th District [Republican]. Counties of Imperial and San Diego (pt.). Prior Terms: 1981-92. Born: May 31, 1948; Riverside, CA. Education: University of Montana; University of California; Western State University's College of Law (J.D.). Military Service: U.S. Army, 1969-71. Occupation: Attorney.

1. Protection to Haitian refugees	Y	52. Cap MX missile deployment at 50	N
2. Raise tax on wealthy; lower others	N	53. Allow $3b for 2 stealth bombers	Y
3. Investigate Reagan hostage delay	N	54. Publish bio-warfare experiments	N
4. Campaign finance revisions	N	55. Raise minimum wage-veto override	N
5. Unpaid leave to care for children	N	56. Bar transfer of FS-X technology	Y
6. Restrict NEA use of funds	Y	57. Cut defense and raise domestic $	N
7. Bar race-bias claim/habeas corpus	Y	58. Uniform poll closing in 48 states	Y
8. Ban race as death sentence factor	Y	59. Req foreign investment disclosure	Y
9. Exceptions to exclusionary rule	Y	60. Textile import quotas-veto override	Y
10. Allow sale of assault weapons	Y	61. Bar abortion funding in Wash, DC	Y
11. Life in prison/abolish death penalty	N	62. Notify spouses of AIDS+ carriers	Y
12. Req conspiracy-price fixing cases	Y	63. Seize conveyance-drug trafficking	Y
13. Unemployment benefits extension	?	64. South Africa sanctions	?
14. Tissue use of aborted fetuses	N	65. 60 days' notice of plant closings	N
15. Bar replacement of union strikers	N	66. Close unneeded military bases	Y
16. Hold foreign aid at $15b for '92	Y	67. Keep welfare reform within $2.8b	Y
17. Restore space station funding	Y	68. Allow children housing exclusion	Y
18. Civil Rights Act of 1991	N	69. Shift $400m of NASA to homeless	N
19. Unlimited damages-discrimination	N	70. Cap Medicare patients' liability	N
20. Eliminate funds for supercollider	N	71. Prohibit employee polygraph testing	N
21. Terminate SDI except for research	N	72. Allow CIA to fund Contras	Y
22. Req 7-day handgun waiting period	N	73. Revise unfair trade practices	N
23. Provide $30b for failed S&Ls	Y	74. Focus SDI on accidental launch	N
24. Allow use of force against Iraq	Y	75. Bar Air Force $ for MX missile	N
25. Allow $15b in foreign aid for '91	Y	76. Allow "real" increase in defense	Y
26. Revise & extend legal immigration	Y	77. Troop reduction in Europe of 50%	N
27. Suspend aid to Angolan rebels	N	78. Ban nuclear tests above 1 kiloton	N
28. Democratic tax plan proposals	N	79. Ban anti-satellite missile tests	N
29. Cut defense 5% across the board	N	80. Observe certain limits of SALT II	N
30. Textile import quotas-veto override	Y	81. Restore four Civil Rights laws	N
31. Abortion service for military abroad	N	82. Prohibit aliens as strikebreakers	N
32. Limits on high income farmers	N	83. Allow military malpractice suits	N
33. Family medical leave-veto override	N	84. Approval of $36m in Contra aid	Y
34. Req submission of balanced budget	N	85. $18b deficit reduction compromise	N
35. Balanced budget amendment	Y	86. Welfare reform of $5.7b for 5 years	N
36. Amendment to ban flag desecration	Y	87. Raise taxes $12b/cut spending $3b	N
37. Reauthorize Amtrak-veto override	N	88. Board to assess occupational risk	N
38. Retraining aid for coal miners	N	89. Balanced budget by '93-via targets	N
39. Suspend El Salvador military aid	N	90. Bar licensing of two nuclear plants	?
40. Expand child care aid/tax credit	N	91. Remove victims compensation cap	N
41. Raise House salary/omit honoraria	Y	92. Catastrophic health insurance	N
42. Toughen oil-spill liability	N	93. Ban airline smoking-2 hours or less	N
43. Restitution to Japanese interned	N	94. $1b/two year aid for the homeless	N
44. Protect Chinese & C.A. nationals	Y	95. Bar non-unions in union companies	N
45. Abortion $ for rape/incest cases	N	96. Increase FSLIC rescue to $15b	Y
46. Allow religious schools to bar gays	Y	97. Impose quotas to lower trade deficit	N
47. Bar broadcaster fairness doctrine	Y	98. Reduce discretionary budget 21%	N
48. Bar cap gains cut/reinstate IRA	N	99. Immigration reform/alien amnesty	N
49. Bar unions equal voice in pension	Y	100. South Africa sanctions-veto override	N
50. Bar assembly of chemical weapons	N	101. Tax overhaul to revise income tax	Y
51. Ban plutonium/uranium production	N	102. Use of military in drug war	Y

HUNTER, DUNCAN (continued)

103. Delete 12 MX/add conventional wpn	N	
104. Raise speed limit to 65 mph	N	
105. Require Pentagon to buy US goods	Y	
106. AIDS insurance non-discrimination	N	
107. Prohibit Saudi arms sales	Y	
108. Ease Gun Control Act of 1968	Y	
109. Bar interstate handgun transport	N	
110. Make company emissions known	N	
111. Allow toxic victims to sue in fed ct	N	
112. Superfund waste cleanup of $10b	N	
113. 90 days notice of plant closings	N	
114. $20b in Medicare cuts/tax increases	N	
115. Spending cuts and tax increases	N	
116. Set school lunch lmt-250% poverty	Y	
117. $75m for youth work projects	N	
118. Allow Angolan military assistance	Y	
119. Suspend defense payments for abuse	N	
120. Drop SS COLAs/$12b tax increase	N	
121. Approve $1.5b for 21 MX missiles	Y	
122. Emergency farm credit/revisions	?	
123. Duty on Taiwan/Hong Kong/S Korea	N	

124. Limit steel imports to 17%	Y	
125. Cut $ to schools that bar prayer	Y	
126. $50b-taxes; cut Medicare/spending	N	
127. Limit Pershing II/cruise in Europe	N	
128. Delete $7.1b for 34 B-1 bombers	N	
129. Bar purchase of Sergeant York guns	N	
130. El Salvador military/economic aid	Y	
131. Bar mining of Nicaraguan waters	N	
132. Physician fee freeze for Medicare	Y	
133. $49b in "sin"/phone/insurance taxes	N	
134. Allow sale of Conrail	Y	
135. Equal Rights Amendment	N	
136. Authorize Marines in Lebanon	Y	
137. Eminent domain for coal companies	Y	
138. Prohibit EPA clean air sanctions	Y	
139. SS retirement age increase/reforms	Y	
140. Auto domestic content requirement	Y	
141. Delete jobs program funding	Y	
142. Highway-gas tax bill	Y	
143. Cut $5b from defense for Medicare	N	
144. Emergency housing aid of $1b	N	

Presidential Support Score: 1991 - 80%   1990 - 69%

COLORADO

SCHROEDER, PATRICIA -- Colorado 1st District [Democrat]. Counties of Adams (pt.), Arapahoe (pt.) and Denver (pt.). Prior Terms: 1973-92. Born: July 30, 1940; Portland, OR. Education: University of Minnesota (B.A.); Harvard University (J.D.). Occupation: Field attorney, National Labor Relations Board (1964-66); law instructor, Community College of Denver (1969-70), University of Colorado (1969), and Regis College (1970-72); legal counsel, Planned Parenthood; hearing officer, Colorado State Department of Personnel (1971-72).

1. Protection to Haitian refugees	Y	
2. Raise tax on wealthy; lower others	N	
3. Investigate Reagan hostage delay	Y	
4. Campaign finance revisions	Y	
5. Unpaid leave to care for children	Y	
6. Restrict NEA use of funds	N	
7. Bar race-bias claim/habeas corpus	N	
8. Ban race as death sentence factor	N	
9. Exceptions to exclusionary rule	N	
10. Allow sale of assault weapons	N	
11. Life in prison/abolish death penalty	N	
12. Req conspiracy-price fixing cases	N	
13. Unemployment benefits extension	Y	
14. Tissue use of aborted fetuses	Y	
15. Bar replacement of union strikers	Y	
16. Hold foreign aid at $15b for '92	Y	
17. Restore space station funding	N	
18. Civil Rights Act of 1991	Y	
19. Unlimited damages-discrimination	Y	
20. Eliminate funds for supercollider	Y	
21. Terminate SDI except for research	Y	
22. Req 7-day handgun waiting period	Y	
23. Provide $30b for failed S&Ls	N	
24. Allow use of force against Iraq	N	

25. Allow $15b in foreign aid for '91	N	
26. Revise & extend legal immigration	Y	
27. Suspend aid to Angolan rebels	Y	
28. Democratic tax plan proposals	Y	
29. Cut defense 5% across the board	Y	
30. Textile import quotas-veto override	N	
31. Abortion service for military abroad	Y	
32. Limits on high income farmers	Y	
33. Family medical leave-veto override	Y	
34. Req submission of balanced budget	Y	
35. Balanced budget amendment	N	
36. Amendment to ban flag desecration	N	
37. Reauthorize Amtrak-veto override	Y	
38. Retraining aid for coal miners	Y	
39. Suspend El Salvador military aid	Y	
40. Expand child care aid/tax credit	Y	
41. Raise House salary/omit honoraria	N	
42. Toughen oil-spill liability	+	
43. Restitution to Japanese interned	Y	
44. Protect Chinese & C.A. nationals	Y	
45. Abortion $ for rape/incest cases	Y	
46. Allow religious schools to bar gays	N	
47. Bar broadcaster fairness doctrine	N	
48. Bar cap gains cut/reinstate IRA	Y	

SCHROEDER, PATRICIA (continued)

49. Bar unions equal voice in pension	N	
50. Bar assembly of chemical weapons	Y	
51. Ban plutonium/uranium production	Y	
52. Cap MX missile deployment at 50	Y	
53. Allow $3b for 2 stealth bombers	N	
54. Publish bio-warfare experiments	Y	
55. Raise minimum wage-veto override	Y	
56. Bar transfer of FS-X technology	Y	
57. Cut defense and raise domestic $	Y	
58. Uniform poll closing in 48 states	Y	
59. Req foreign investment disclosure	Y	
60. Textile import quotas-veto override	Y	
61. Bar abortion funding in Wash, DC	N	
62. Notify spouses of AIDS+ carriers	N	
63. Seize conveyance-drug trafficking	N	
64. South Africa sanctions	Y	
65. 60 days' notice of plant closings	Y	
66. Close unneeded military bases	N	
67. Keep welfare reform within $2.8b	Y	
68. Allow children housing exclusion	N	
69. Shift $400m of NASA to homeless	Y	
70. Cap Medicare patients' liability	Y	
71. Prohibit employee polygraph testing	Y	
72. Allow CIA to fund Contras	N	
73. Revise unfair trade practices	Y	
74. Focus SDI on accidental launch	Y	
75. Bar Air Force $ for MX missile	Y	
76. Allow "real" increase in defense	N	
77. Troop reduction in Europe of 50%	N	
78. Ban nuclear tests above 1 kiloton	Y	
79. Ban anti-satellite missile tests	Y	
80. Observe certain limits of SALT II	Y	
81. Restore four Civil Rights laws	Y	
82. Prohibit aliens as strikebreakers	Y	
83. Allow military malpractice suits	Y	
84. Approval of $36m in Contra aid	N	
85. $18b deficit reduction compromise	N	
86. Welfare reform of $5.7b for 5 years	Y	
87. Raise taxes $12b/cut spending $3b	Y	
88. Board to assess occupational risk	Y	
89. Balanced budget by '93-via targets	N	
90. Bar licensing of two nuclear plants	Y	
91. Remove victims compensation cap	+	
92. Catastrophic health insurance	Y	
93. Ban airline smoking-2 hours or less	Y	
94. $1b/two year aid for the homeless	+	
95. Bar non-unions in union companies	Y	
96. Increase FSLIC rescue to $15b	N	
97. Impose quotas to lower trade deficit	N
98. Reduce discretionary budget 21%	Y
99. Immigration reform/alien amnesty	N
100. South Africa sanctions-veto override	Y
101. Tax overhaul to revise income tax	N
102. Use of military in drug war	N
103. Delete 12 MX/add conventional wpn	Y
104. Raise speed limit to 65 mph	Y
105. Require Pentagon to buy US goods	N
106. AIDS insurance non-discrimination	Y
107. Prohibit Saudi arms sales	Y
108. Ease Gun Control Act of 1968	N
109. Bar interstate handgun transport	Y
110. Make company emissions known	Y
111. Allow toxic victims to sue in fed ct	Y
112. Superfund waste cleanup of $10b	Y
113. 90 days notice of plant closings	Y
114. $20b in Medicare cuts/tax increases	Y
115. Spending cuts and tax increases	Y
116. Set school lunch lmt-250% poverty	N
117. $75m for youth work projects	Y
118. Allow Angolan military assistance	N
119. Suspend defense payments for abuse	Y
120. Drop SS COLAs/$12b tax increase	N
121. Approve $1.5b for 21 MX missiles	N
122. Emergency farm credit/revisions	N
123. Duty on Taiwan/Hong Kong/S Korea	N
124. Limit steel imports to 17%	N
125. Cut $ to schools that bar prayer	N
126. $50b-taxes; cut Medicare/spending	N
127. Limit Pershing II/cruise in Europe	Y
128. Delete $7.1b for 34 B-1 bombers	Y
129. Bar purchase of Sergeant York guns	Y
130. El Salvador military/economic aid	N
131. Bar mining of Nicaraguan waters	Y
132. Physician fee freeze for Medicare	N
133. $49b in "sin"/phone/insurance taxes	N
134. Allow sale of Conrail	N
135. Equal Rights Amendment	Y
136. Authorize Marines in Lebanon	N
137. Eminent domain for coal companies	N
138. Prohibit EPA clean air sanctions	Y
139. SS retirement age increase/reforms	N
140. Auto domestic content requirement	?
141. Delete jobs program funding	?
142. Highway-gas tax bill	N
143. Cut $5b from defense for Medicare	Y
144. Emergency housing aid of $1b	Y

Presidential Support Score: 1991 - 18%   1990 - 18%

SKAGGS, DAVID -- Colorado 2nd District [Democrat]. Counties of Adams (pt.), Boulder, Clear Creek, Gilpin and Jefferson (pt.). Prior Terms: 1987-92. Born: January 22, 1943; Cincinnati, OH. Education: Wesleyan University (B.A.); Yale Law School (LL.B.). Military Service: U.S. Marine Corps, 1963-1965; Reserves, 1965-1968. Occupation: Attorney; partner, Skaggs, Stone & Sheehy; public member, state Board of Architects; attorney; Boulder County Board of Health; Democratic Party district chairman (1973) and vice-chairman (1977-1979); administrative assistant to Representative Wirth (1975-1977); state representative (1980-1986).

1. Protection to Haitian refugees	Y	4. Campaign finance revisions	Y
2. Raise tax on wealthy; lower others	Y	5. Unpaid leave to care for children	Y
3. Investigate Reagan hostage delay	Y	6. Restrict NEA use of funds	N

SKAGGS, DAVID (continued)

7. Bar race-bias claim/habeas corpus	N	
8. Ban race as death sentence factor	N	
9. Exceptions to exclusionary rule	N	
10. Allow sale of assault weapons	N	
11. Life in prison/abolish death penalty	Y	
12. Req conspiracy-price fixing cases	N	
13. Unemployment benefits extension	Y	
14. Tissue use of aborted fetuses	Y	
15. Bar replacement of union strikers	Y	
16. Hold foreign aid at $15b for '92	Y	
17. Restore space station funding	N	
18. Civil Rights Act of 1991	Y	
19. Unlimited damages-discrimination	N	
20. Eliminate funds for supercollider	N	
21. Terminate SDI except for research	Y	
22. Req 7-day handgun waiting period	Y	
23. Provide $30b for failed S&Ls	Y	
24. Allow use of force against Iraq	N	
25. Allow $15b in foreign aid for '91	Y	
26. Revise & extend legal immigration	Y	
27. Suspend aid to Angolan rebels	Y	
28. Democratic tax plan proposals	Y	
29. Cut defense 5% across the board	N	
30. Textile import quotas-veto override	N	
31. Abortion service for military abroad	Y	
32. Limits on high income farmers	N	
33. Family medical leave-veto override	Y	
34. Req submission of balanced budget	Y	
35. Balanced budget amendment	N	
36. Amendment to ban flag desecration	N	
37. Reauthorize Amtrak-veto override	Y	
38. Retraining aid for coal miners	Y	
39. Suspend El Salvador military aid	Y	
40. Expand child care aid/tax credit	Y	
41. Raise House salary/omit honoraria	Y	
42. Toughen oil-spill liability	Y	
43. Restitution to Japanese interned	Y	
44. Protect Chinese & C.A. nationals	Y	
45. Abortion $ for rape/incest cases	Y	
46. Allow religious schools to bar gays	N	
47. Bar broadcaster fairness doctrine	Y	
48. Bar cap gains cut/reinstate IRA	Y	
49. Bar unions equal voice in pension	Y	
50. Bar assembly of chemical weapons	Y	
51. Ban plutonium/uranium production	Y	
52. Cap MX missile deployment at 50	Y	

53. Allow $3b for 2 stealth bombers	N	
54. Publish bio-warfare experiments	Y	
55. Raise minimum wage-veto override	Y	
56. Bar transfer of FS-X technology	Y	
57. Cut defense and raise domestic $	N	
58. Uniform poll closing in 48 states	Y	
59. Req foreign investment disclosure	Y	
60. Textile import quotas-veto override	N	
61. Bar abortion funding in Wash, DC	N	
62. Notify spouses of AIDS+ carriers	N	
63. Seize conveyance-drug trafficking	N	
64. South Africa sanctions	Y	
65. 60 days' notice of plant closings	Y	
66. Close unneeded military bases	Y	
67. Keep welfare reform within $2.8b	Y	
68. Allow children housing exclusion	N	
69. Shift $400m of NASA to homeless	N	
70. Cap Medicare patients' liability	Y	
71. Prohibit employee polygraph testing	Y	
72. Allow CIA to fund Contras	N	
73. Revise unfair trade practices	Y	
74. Focus SDI on accidental launch	Y	
75. Bar Air Force $ for MX missile	Y	
76. Allow "real" increase in defense	N	
77. Troop reduction in Europe of 50%	N	
78. Ban nuclear tests above 1 kiloton	Y	
79. Ban anti-satellite missile tests	Y	
80. Observe certain limits of SALT II	Y	
81. Restore four Civil Rights laws	Y	
82. Prohibit aliens as strikebreakers	Y	
83. Allow military malpractice suits	Y	
84. Approval of $36m in Contra aid	N	
85. $18b deficit reduction compromise	Y	
86. Welfare reform of $5.7b for 5 years	Y	
87. Raise taxes $12b/cut spending $3b	Y	
88. Board to assess occupational risk	Y	
89. Balanced budget by '93-via targets	Y	
90. Bar licensing of two nuclear plants	Y	
91. Remove victims compensation cap	N	
92. Catastrophic health insurance	Y	
93. Ban airline smoking-2 hours or less	N	
94. $1b/two year aid for the homeless	Y	
95. Bar non-unions in union companies	Y	
96. Increase FSLIC rescue to $15b	Y	
97. Impose quotas to lower trade deficit	N	
98. Reduce discretionary budget 21%	Y	

Presidential Support Score: 1991 - 36% 1990 - 21%

CAMPBELL, BEN NIGHTHORSE -- Colorado 3rd District [Democrat]. Counties of Alamosa, Archuleta, Conejos, Costilla, Custer, Delta, Dolores, Eagle, Fremont (pt.), Garfield, Grand, Gunnison, Hinsdale, Huerfano, Jackson, La Plata, Mesa, Mineral, Moffat, Montezuma, Montrose, Ouray, Pitkin, Pueblo, Rio Blanco, Rio Grande, Routt, Saguache, San Juan, San Miguel and Summit. Prior Terms: 1987-92. Born: April 13, 1933; Auburn, CA. Education: University of California, San Jose (B.A.); Meiji University. Military Service: U.S. Air Force (1952-1954). Occupation: Truck driver; teacher; horse breeder and trainer; jewelry designer and manufacturer; state representative (1982-1986).

1. Protection to Haitian refugees	N	
2. Raise tax on wealthy; lower others	Y	
3. Investigate Reagan hostage delay	N	
4. Campaign finance revisions	N	
5. Unpaid leave to care for children	Y	

6. Restrict NEA use of funds	N	
7. Bar race-bias claim/habeas corpus	Y	
8. Ban race as death sentence factor	N	
9. Exceptions to exclusionary rule	Y	
10. Allow sale of assault weapons	Y	

CAMPBELL, BEN (continued)

11. Life in prison/abolish death penalty	N		55. Raise minimum wage-veto override	N
12. Req conspiracy-price fixing cases	Y		56. Bar transfer of FS-X technology	Y
13. Unemployment benefits extension	Y		57. Cut defense and raise domestic $	N
14. Tissue use of aborted fetuses	Y		58. Uniform poll closing in 48 states	Y
15. Bar replacement of union strikers	Y		59. Req foreign investment disclosure	Y
16. Hold foreign aid at $15b for '92	Y		60. Textile import quotas-veto override	Y
17. Restore space station funding	?		61. Bar abortion funding in Wash, DC	N
18. Civil Rights Act of 1991	Y		62. Notify spouses of AIDS+ carriers	N
19. Unlimited damages-discrimination	Y		63. Seize conveyance-drug trafficking	Y
20. Eliminate funds for supercollider	Y		64. South Africa sanctions	Y
21. Terminate SDI except for research	?		65. 60 days' notice of plant closings	Y
22. Req 7-day handgun waiting period	N		66. Close unneeded military bases	N
23. Provide $30b for failed S&Ls	N		67. Keep welfare reform within $2.8b	Y
24. Allow use of force against Iraq	Y		68. Allow children housing exclusion	N
25. Allow $15b in foreign aid for '91	N		69. Shift $400m of NASA to homeless	N
26. Revise & extend legal immigration	Y		70. Cap Medicare patients' liability	?
27. Suspend aid to Angolan rebels	N		71. Prohibit employee polygraph testing	Y
28. Democratic tax plan proposals	N		72. Allow CIA to fund Contras	N
29. Cut defense 5% across the board	N		73. Revise unfair trade practices	Y
30. Textile import quotas-veto override	Y		74. Focus SDI on accidental launch	Y
31. Abortion service for military abroad	Y		75. Bar Air Force $ for MX missile	N
32. Limits on high income farmers	N		76. Allow "real" increase in defense	N
33. Family medical leave-veto override	Y		77. Troop reduction in Europe of 50%	?
34. Req submission of balanced budget	Y		78. Ban nuclear tests above 1 kiloton	Y
35. Balanced budget amendment	Y		79. Ban anti-satellite missile tests	Y
36. Amendment to ban flag desecration	Y		80. Observe certain limits of SALT II	Y
37. Reauthorize Amtrak-veto override	Y		81. Restore four Civil Rights laws	Y
38. Retraining aid for coal miners	Y		82. Prohibit aliens as strikebreakers	Y
39. Suspend El Salvador military aid	Y		83. Allow military malpractice suits	Y
40. Expand child care aid/tax credit	Y		84. Approval of $36m in Contra aid	N
41. Raise House salary/omit honoraria	N		85. $18b deficit reduction compromise	Y
42. Toughen oil-spill liability	N		86. Welfare reform of $5.7b for 5 years	N
43. Restitution to Japanese interned	Y		87. Raise taxes $12b/cut spending $3b	Y
44. Protect Chinese & C.A. nationals	Y		88. Board to assess occupational risk	Y
45. Abortion $ for rape/incest cases	Y		89. Balanced budget by '93-via targets	Y
46. Allow religious schools to bar gays	Y		90. Bar licensing of two nuclear plants	Y
47. Bar broadcaster fairness doctrine	N		91. Remove victims compensation cap	N
48. Bar cap gains cut/reinstate IRA	N		92. Catastrophic health insurance	Y
49. Bar unions equal voice in pension	N		93. Ban airline smoking-2 hours or less	Y
50. Bar assembly of chemical weapons	Y		94. $1b/two year aid for the homeless	Y
51. Ban plutonium/uranium production	Y		95. Bar non-unions in union companies	Y
52. Cap MX missile deployment at 50	Y		96. Increase FSLIC rescue to $15b	N
53. Allow $3b for 2 stealth bombers	Y		97. Impose quotas to lower trade deficit	Y
54. Publish bio-warfare experiments	Y		98. Reduce discretionary budget 21%	N

Presidential Support Score: 1991 - 34%   1990 - 35%

ALLARD, WAYNE -- Colorado 4th District [Republican]. Counties of Adams (pt.), Arapahoe (pt.), Baca, Bent, Cheyenne, Crowley, Kiowa, Kit Carson, Larimer, Las Animas, Lincoln, Logan, Morgan, Otero, Phillips, Prowers, Sedgwick, Washington, Weld and Yuma. Prior Term: 1991-92. Born: December 2, 1943; Fort Collins, CO. Education: Colorado State University (D.V.M.). Occupation: Veterinarian; Loveland City health officer and Board of Health chairman; state senator.

1. Protection to Haitian refugees	N		10. Allow sale of assault weapons	Y
2. Raise tax on wealthy; lower others	N		11. Life in prison/abolish death penalty	N
3. Investigate Reagan hostage delay	N		12. Req conspiracy-price fixing cases	Y
4. Campaign finance revisions	N		13. Unemployment benefits extension	N
5. Unpaid leave to care for children	N		14. Tissue use of aborted fetuses	N
6. Restrict NEA use of funds	Y		15. Bar replacement of union strikers	N
7. Bar race-bias claim/habeas corpus	Y		16. Hold foreign aid at $15b for '92	Y
8. Ban race as death sentence factor	Y		17. Restore space station funding	Y
9. Exceptions to exclusionary rule	Y		18. Civil Rights Act of 1991	N

ALLARD, WAYNE (continued)

19.	Unlimited damages-discrimination	N	22.	Req 7-day handgun waiting period	N
20.	Eliminate funds for supercollider	N	23.	Provide $30b for failed S&Ls	N
21.	Terminate SDI except for research	N	24.	Allow use of force against Iraq	Y

Presidential Support Score: 1991 - 80%

HEFLEY, JOEL -- Colorado 5th District [Republican]. Counties of Arapahoe (pt.), Chaffee, Douglas, Elbert, El Paso, Fremont (pt.), Jefferson (pt.), Lake, Park and Teller. Prior Terms: 1987-92. Born: April 18, 1935; Ardmore, OK. Education: Oklahoma Baptist University (B.A.), Oklahoma State University (M.A.). Occupation: Director, non-profit community development organization, state representative (1977-78) and senator (1979-86).

1.	Protection to Haitian refugees	N	50.	Bar assembly of chemical weapons	N
2.	Raise tax on wealthy; lower others	N	51.	Ban plutonium/uranium production	N
3.	Investigate Reagan hostage delay	N	52.	Cap MX missile deployment at 50	N
4.	Campaign finance revisions	N	53.	Allow $3b for 2 stealth bombers	N
5.	Unpaid leave to care for children	N	54.	Publish bio-warfare experiments	N
6.	Restrict NEA use of funds	Y	55.	Raise minimum wage-veto override	N
7.	Bar race-bias claim/habeas corpus	Y	56.	Bar transfer of FS-X technology	N
8.	Ban race as death sentence factor	Y	57.	Cut defense and raise domestic $	N
9.	Exceptions to exclusionary rule	Y	58.	Uniform poll closing in 48 states	N
10.	Allow sale of assault weapons	Y	59.	Req foreign investment disclosure	N
11.	Life in prison/abolish death penalty	N	60.	Textile import quotas-veto override	N
12.	Req conspiracy-price fixing cases	Y	61.	Bar abortion funding in Wash, DC	Y
13.	Unemployment benefits extension	N	62.	Notify spouses of AIDS+ carriers	Y
14.	Tissue use of aborted fetuses	N	63.	Seize conveyance-drug trafficking	Y
15.	Bar replacement of union strikers	N	64.	South Africa sanctions	N
16.	Hold foreign aid at $15b for '92	N	65.	60 days' notice of plant closings	N
17.	Restore space station funding	Y	66.	Close unneeded military bases	Y
18.	Civil Rights Act of 1991	N	67.	Keep welfare reform within $2.8b	Y
19.	Unlimited damages-discrimination	N	68.	Allow children housing exclusion	Y
20.	Eliminate funds for supercollider	Y	69.	Shift $400m of NASA to homeless	N
21.	Terminate SDI except for research	N	70.	Cap Medicare patients' liability	N
22.	Req 7-day handgun waiting period	N	71.	Prohibit employee polygraph testing	N
23.	Provide $30b for failed S&Ls	N	72.	Allow CIA to fund Contras	Y
24.	Allow use of force against Iraq	Y	73.	Revise unfair trade practices	N
25.	Allow $15b in foreign aid for '91	N	74.	Focus SDI on accidental launch	N
26.	Revise & extend legal immigration	N	75.	Bar Air Force $ for MX missile	N
27.	Suspend aid to Angolan rebels	N	76.	Allow "real" increase in defense	Y
28.	Democratic tax plan proposals	N	77.	Troop reduction in Europe of 50%	N
29.	Cut defense 5% across the board	N	78.	Ban nuclear tests above 1 kiloton	N
30.	Textile import quotas-veto override	N	79.	Ban anti-satellite missile tests	N
31.	Abortion service for military abroad	N	80.	Observe certain limits of SALT II	N
32.	Limits on high income farmers	N	81.	Restore four Civil Rights laws	N
33.	Family medical leave-veto override	N	82.	Prohibit aliens as strikebreakers	N
34.	Req submission of balanced budget	Y	83.	Allow military malpractice suits	Y
35.	Balanced budget amendment	Y	84.	Approval of $36m in Contra aid	Y
36.	Amendment to ban flag desecration	Y	85.	$18b deficit reduction compromise	N
37.	Reauthorize Amtrak-veto override	N	86.	Welfare reform of $5.7b for 5 years	N
38.	Retraining aid for coal miners	N	87.	Raise taxes $12b/cut spending $3b	N
39.	Suspend El Salvador military aid	N	88.	Board to assess occupational risk	N
40.	Expand child care aid/tax credit	N	89.	Balanced budget by '93-via targets	N
41.	Raise House salary/omit honoraria	N	90.	Bar licensing of two nuclear plants	N
42.	Toughen oil-spill liability	N	91.	Remove victims compensation cap	N
43.	Restitution to Japanese interned	N	92.	Catastrophic health insurance	N
44.	Protect Chinese & C.A. nationals	N	93.	Ban airline smoking-2 hours or less	Y
45.	Abortion $ for rape/incest cases	N	94.	$1b/two year aid for the homeless	N
46.	Allow religious schools to bar gays	Y	95.	Bar non-unions in union companies	N
47.	Bar broadcaster fairness doctrine	Y	96.	Increase FSLIC rescue to $15b	N
48.	Bar cap gains cut/reinstate IRA	N	97.	Impose quotas to lower trade deficit	N
49.	Bar unions equal voice in pension	Y	98.	Reduce discretionary budget 21%	Y

Presidential Support Score: 1991 - 71%   1990 - 71%

SCHAEFER, DAN -- Colorado 6th District [Republican]. Counties of Adams (pt.), Arapahoe (pt.) and Jefferson (pt.). Prior Terms: 1983 (Special Election)-1992. Born: January 25, 1936; Gutenberg, IA. Education: Niagara University (B.A.). Occupation: Public relations consultant (1967-83); Colorado assemblyman (1977-78); Colorado senator (1979-83).

1. Protection to Haitian refugees	N	
2. Raise tax on wealthy; lower others	N	
3. Investigate Reagan hostage delay	N	
4. Campaign finance revisions	N	
5. Unpaid leave to care for children	N	
6. Restrict NEA use of funds	Y	
7. Bar race-bias claim/habeas corpus	Y	
8. Ban race as death sentence factor	Y	
9. Exceptions to exclusionary rule	Y	
10. Allow sale of assault weapons	Y	
11. Life in prison/abolish death penalty	N	
12. Req conspiracy-price fixing cases	Y	
13. Unemployment benefits extension	N	
14. Tissue use of aborted fetuses	N	
15. Bar replacement of union strikers	N	
16. Hold foreign aid at $15b for '92	Y	
17. Restore space station funding	Y	
18. Civil Rights Act of 1991	N	
19. Unlimited damages-discrimination	N	
20. Eliminate funds for supercollider	Y	
21. Terminate SDI except for research	N	
22. Req 7-day handgun waiting period	N	
23. Provide $30b for failed S&Ls	N	
24. Allow use of force against Iraq	Y	
25. Allow $15b in foreign aid for '91	Y	
26. Revise & extend legal immigration	N	
27. Suspend aid to Angolan rebels	N	
28. Democratic tax plan proposals	N	
29. Cut defense 5% across the board	N	
30. Textile import quotas-veto override	Y	
31. Abortion service for military abroad	N	
32. Limits on high income farmers	N	
33. Family medical leave-veto override	N	
34. Req submission of balanced budget	Y	
35. Balanced budget amendment	Y	
36. Amendment to ban flag desecration	Y	
37. Reauthorize Amtrak-veto override	Y	
38. Retraining aid for coal miners	Y	
39. Suspend El Salvador military aid	N	
40. Expand child care aid/tax credit	N	
41. Raise House salary/omit honoraria	N	
42. Toughen oil-spill liability	?	
43. Restitution to Japanese interned	N	
44. Protect Chinese & C.A. nationals	N	
45. Abortion $ for rape/incest cases	N	
46. Allow religious schools to bar gays	Y	
47. Bar broadcaster fairness doctrine	N	
48. Bar cap gains cut/reinstate IRA	N	
49. Bar unions equal voice in pension	Y	
50. Bar assembly of chemical weapons	N	
51. Ban plutonium/uranium production	Y	
52. Cap MX missile deployment at 50	N	
53. Allow $3b for 2 stealth bombers	Y	
54. Publish bio-warfare experiments	N	
55. Raise minimum wage-veto override	N	
56. Bar transfer of FS-X technology	N	
57. Cut defense and raise domestic $	N	
58. Uniform poll closing in 48 states	N	
59. Req foreign investment disclosure	N	
60. Textile import quotas-veto override	N	
61. Bar abortion funding in Wash, DC	Y
62. Notify spouses of AIDS+ carriers	Y
63. Seize conveyance-drug trafficking	Y
64. South Africa sanctions	N
65. 60 days' notice of plant closings	Y
66. Close unneeded military bases	Y
67. Keep welfare reform within $2.8b	Y
68. Allow children housing exclusion	Y
69. Shift $400m of NASA to homeless	N
70. Cap Medicare patients' liability	N
71. Prohibit employee polygraph testing	N
72. Allow CIA to fund Contras	Y
73. Revise unfair trade practices	Y
74. Focus SDI on accidental launch	N
75. Bar Air Force $ for MX missile	N
76. Allow "real" increase in defense	N
77. Troop reduction in Europe of 50%	N
78. Ban nuclear tests above 1 kiloton	N
79. Ban anti-satellite missile tests	N
80. Observe certain limits of SALT II	N
81. Restore four Civil Rights laws	N
82. Prohibit aliens as strikebreakers	N
83. Allow military malpractice suits	Y
84. Approval of $36m in Contra aid	Y
85. $18b deficit reduction compromise	N
86. Welfare reform of $5.7b for 5 years	N
87. Raise taxes $12b/cut spending $3b	N
88. Board to assess occupational risk	N
89. Balanced budget by '93-via targets	Y
90. Bar licensing of two nuclear plants	N
91. Remove victims compensation cap	N
92. Catastrophic health insurance	N
93. Ban airline smoking-2 hours or less	Y
94. $1b/two year aid for the homeless	N
95. Bar non-unions in union companies	N
96. Increase FSLIC rescue to $15b	N
97. Impose quotas to lower trade deficit	N
98. Reduce discretionary budget 21%	?
99. Immigration reform/alien amnesty	Y
100. South Africa sanctions-veto override	N
101. Tax overhaul to revise income tax	N
102. Use of military in drug war	Y
103. Delete 12 MX/add conventional wpn	N
104. Raise speed limit to 65 mph	Y
105. Require Pentagon to buy US goods	Y
106. AIDS insurance non-discrimination	N
107. Prohibit Saudi arms sales	Y
108. Ease Gun Control Act of 1968	Y
109. Bar interstate handgun transport	N
110. Make company emissions known	N
111. Allow toxic victims to sue in fed ct	N
112. Superfund waste cleanup of $10b	N
113. 90 days notice of plant closings	N
114. $20b in Medicare cuts/tax increases	N
115. Spending cuts and tax increases	N
116. Set school lunch lmt-250% poverty	Y
117. $75m for youth work projects	N
118. Allow Angolan military assistance	Y
119. Suspend defense payments for abuse	N
120. Drop SS COLAs/$12b tax increase	N

SCHAEFER, DAN (continued)

121. Approve $1.5b for 21 MX missiles	Y	
122. Emergency farm credit/revisions	N	
123. Duty on Taiwan/Hong Kong/S Korea	N	
124. Limit steel imports to 17%	N	
125. Cut $ to schools that bar prayer	Y	
126. $50b-taxes; cut Medicare/spending	N	
127. Limit Pershing II/cruise in Europe	N	
128. Delete $7.1b for 34 B-1 bombers	N	
129. Bar purchase of Sergeant York guns	Y	
130. El Salvador military/economic aid	Y	
131. Bar mining of Nicaraguan waters	N	
132. Physician fee freeze for Medicare	Y	
133. $49b in "sin"/phone/insurance taxes	N	
134. Allow sale of Conrail	Y	
135. Equal Rights Amendment	N	
136. Authorize Marines in Lebanon	Y	
137. Eminent domain for coal companies	Y	
138. Prohibit EPA clean air sanctions	Y	

Presidential Support Score: 1991 - 71%   1990 - 64%

CONNECTICUT

KENNELLY, BARBARA B. -- Connecticut 1st District [Democrat]. Counties of Hartford (pt.), Middlesex (pt.) and Tolland (pt.). Prior Terms: 1982 (Special Election)-1992. Born: July 10, 1936; Hartford, CT. Education: Trinity College (B.A., M.A.). Occupation: Vice chairwoman, Hartford Commission on Aging (1971-75); member, Hartford Court of Common Council (1975-79); secretary, State of Connecticut (1979-82); member, Boards of Trustees, Trinity College and Hartford College for Women; director, Hartford Architecture Conservation and Riverfront Recapture, Inc.

1. Protection to Haitian refugees	Y	
2. Raise tax on wealthy; lower others	Y	
3. Investigate Reagan hostage delay	Y	
4. Campaign finance revisions	Y	
5. Unpaid leave to care for children	Y	
6. Restrict NEA use of funds	N	
7. Bar race-bias claim/habeas corpus	N	
8. Ban race as death sentence factor	N	
9. Exceptions to exclusionary rule	N	
10. Allow sale of assault weapons	N	
11. Life in prison/abolish death penalty	N	
12. Req conspiracy-price fixing cases	N	
13. Unemployment benefits extension	Y	
14. Tissue use of aborted fetuses	Y	
15. Bar replacement of union strikers	Y	
16. Hold foreign aid at $15b for '92	Y	
17. Restore space station funding	Y	
18. Civil Rights Act of 1991	Y	
19. Unlimited damages-discrimination	Y	
20. Eliminate funds for supercollider	N	
21. Terminate SDI except for research	N	
22. Req 7-day handgun waiting period	Y	
23. Provide $30b for failed S&Ls	N	
24. Allow use of force against Iraq	N	
25. Allow $15b in foreign aid for '91	Y	
26. Revise & extend legal immigration	Y	
27. Suspend aid to Angolan rebels	Y	
28. Democratic tax plan proposals	Y	
29. Cut defense 5% across the board	N	
30. Textile import quotas-veto override	N	
31. Abortion service for military abroad	Y	
32. Limits on high income farmers	Y	
33. Family medical leave-veto override	Y	
34. Req submission of balanced budget	Y	
35. Balanced budget amendment	N	
36. Amendment to ban flag desecration	N	
37. Reauthorize Amtrak-veto override	Y	
38. Retraining aid for coal miners	Y	
39. Suspend El Salvador military aid	Y	
40. Expand child care aid/tax credit	Y	
41. Raise House salary/omit honoraria	Y	
42. Toughen oil-spill liability	?	
43. Restitution to Japanese interned	Y	
44. Protect Chinese & C.A. nationals	Y	
45. Abortion $ for rape/incest cases	Y	
46. Allow religious schools to bar gays	N	
47. Bar broadcaster fairness doctrine	N	
48. Bar cap gains cut/reinstate IRA	Y	
49. Bar unions equal voice in pension	Y	
50. Bar assembly of chemical weapons	Y	
51. Ban plutonium/uranium production	Y	
52. Cap MX missile deployment at 50	Y	
53. Allow $3b for 2 stealth bombers	N	
54. Publish bio-warfare experiments	Y	
55. Raise minimum wage-veto override	Y	
56. Bar transfer of FS-X technology	Y	
57. Cut defense and raise domestic $	N	
58. Uniform poll closing in 48 states	Y	
59. Req foreign investment disclosure	Y	
60. Textile import quotas-veto override	Y	
61. Bar abortion funding in Wash, DC	N	
62. Notify spouses of AIDS+ carriers	N	
63. Seize conveyance-drug trafficking	N	
64. South Africa sanctions	Y	
65. 60 days' notice of plant closings	Y	
66. Close unneeded military bases	Y	
67. Keep welfare reform within $2.8b	N	
68. Allow children housing exclusion	N	
69. Shift $400m of NASA to homeless	Y	
70. Cap Medicare patients' liability	Y	
71. Prohibit employee polygraph testing	Y	
72. Allow CIA to fund Contras	N	

KENNELLY, BARBARA B. (continued)

73.	Revise unfair trade practices	Y	109. Bar interstate handgun transport	Y
74.	Focus SDI on accidental launch	Y	110. Make company emissions known	Y
75.	Bar Air Force $ for MX missile	Y	111. Allow toxic victims to sue in fed ct	Y
76.	Allow "real" increase in defense	N	112. Superfund waste cleanup of $10b	Y
77.	Troop reduction in Europe of 50%	N	113. 90 days notice of plant closings	Y
78.	Ban nuclear tests above 1 kiloton	Y	114. $20b in Medicare cuts/tax increases	Y
79.	Ban anti-satellite missile tests	Y	115. Spending cuts and tax increases	Y
80.	Observe certain limits of SALT II	Y	116. Set school lunch lmt-250% poverty	N
81.	Restore four Civil Rights laws	Y	117. $75m for youth work projects	Y
82.	Prohibit aliens as strikebreakers	Y	118. Allow Angolan military assistance	N
83.	Allow military malpractice suits	Y	119. Suspend defense payments for abuse	N
84.	Approval of $36m in Contra aid	N	120. Drop SS COLAs/$12b tax increase	N
85.	$18b deficit reduction compromise	Y	121. Approve $1.5b for 21 MX missiles	N
86.	Welfare reform of $5.7b for 5 years	Y	122. Emergency farm credit/revisions	Y
87.	Raise taxes $12b/cut spending $3b	Y	123. Duty on Taiwan/Hong Kong/S Korea	Y
88.	Board to assess occupational risk	Y	124. Limit steel imports to 17%	Y
89.	Balanced budget by '93-via targets	N	125. Cut $ to schools that bar prayer	N
90.	Bar licensing of two nuclear plants	N	126. $50b-taxes; cut Medicare/spending	Y
91.	Remove victims compensation cap	N	127. Limit Pershing II/cruise in Europe	Y
92.	Catastrophic health insurance	Y	128. Delete $7.1b for 34 B-1 bombers	Y
93.	Ban airline smoking-2 hours or less	Y	129. Bar purchase of Sergeant York guns	N
94.	$1b/two year aid for the homeless	Y	130. El Salvador military/economic aid	N
95.	Bar non-unions in union companies	Y	131. Bar mining of Nicaraguan waters	Y
96.	Increase FSLIC rescue to $15b	N	132. Physician fee freeze for Medicare	N
97.	Impose quotas to lower trade deficit	Y	133. $49b in "sin"/phone/insurance taxes	Y
98.	Reduce discretionary budget 21%	Y	134. Allow sale of Conrail	N
99.	Immigration reform/alien amnesty	Y	135. Equal Rights Amendment	Y
100.	South Africa sanctions-veto override	Y	136. Authorize Marines in Lebanon	N
101.	Tax overhaul to revise income tax	Y	137. Eminent domain for coal companies	N
102.	Use of military in drug war	N	138. Prohibit EPA clean air sanctions	N
103.	Delete 12 MX/add conventional wpn	Y	139. SS retirement age increase/reforms	N
104.	Raise speed limit to 65 mph	N	140. Auto domestic content requirement	Y
105.	Require Pentagon to buy US goods	Y	141. Delete jobs program funding	N
106.	AIDS insurance non-discrimination	Y	142. Highway-gas tax bill	Y
107.	Prohibit Saudi arms sales	Y	143. Cut $5b from defense for Medicare	Y
108.	Ease Gun Control Act of 1968	N	144. Emergency housing aid of $1b	Y

Presidential Support Score: 1991 - 30%   1990 - 22%

GEJDENSON, SAM -- Connecticut 2nd District [Democrat]. Counties of Middlesex (pt.), New London, Tolland (pt.) and Windham. Prior Terms: 1981-92. Born: May 20, 1948; Eschwege, Germany. Education: Mitchell College (A.S.); University of Connecticut (B.A.). Occupation: Farmer; broker; town chairman; deputy sheriff; Connecticut representative (1974-78).

1.	Protection to Haitian refugees	Y	19. Unlimited damages-discrimination	Y
2.	Raise tax on wealthy; lower others	Y	20. Eliminate funds for supercollider	Y
3.	Investigate Reagan hostage delay	Y	21. Terminate SDI except for research	Y
4.	Campaign finance revisions	Y	22. Req 7-day handgun waiting period	Y
5.	Unpaid leave to care for children	Y	23. Provide $30b for failed S&Ls	N
6.	Restrict NEA use of funds	N	24. Allow use of force against Iraq	N
7.	Bar race-bias claim/habeas corpus	N	25. Allow $15b in foreign aid for '91	Y
8.	Ban race as death sentence factor	N	26. Revise & extend legal immigration	Y
9.	Exceptions to exclusionary rule	N	27. Suspend aid to Angolan rebels	Y
10.	Allow sale of assault weapons	N	28. Democratic tax plan proposals	Y
11.	Life in prison/abolish death penalty	Y	29. Cut defense 5% across the board	N
12.	Req conspiracy-price fixing cases	N	30. Textile import quotas-veto override	Y
13.	Unemployment benefits extension	Y	31. Abortion service for military abroad	Y
14.	Tissue use of aborted fetuses	Y	32. Limits on high income farmers	Y
15.	Bar replacement of union strikers	Y	33. Family medical leave-veto override	Y
16.	Hold foreign aid at $15b for '92	Y	34. Req submission of balanced budget	Y
17.	Restore space station funding	Y	35. Balanced budget amendment	N
18.	Civil Rights Act of 1991	Y	36. Amendment to ban flag desecration	N

GEJDENSON, SAM (continued)

37. Reauthorize Amtrak-veto override	Y	91. Remove victims compensation cap	N
38. Retraining aid for coal miners	Y	92. Catastrophic health insurance	Y
39. Suspend El Salvador military aid	Y	93. Ban airline smoking-2 hours or less	Y
40. Expand child care aid/tax credit	Y	94. $1b/two year aid for the homeless	Y
41. Raise House salary/omit honoraria	Y	95. Bar non-unions in union companies	Y
42. Toughen oil-spill liability	Y	96. Increase FSLIC rescue to $15b	N
43. Restitution to Japanese interned	Y	97. Impose quotas to lower trade deficit	Y
44. Protect Chinese & C.A. nationals	Y	98. Reduce discretionary budget 21%	Y
45. Abortion $ for rape/incest cases	Y	99. Immigration reform/alien amnesty	Y
46. Allow religious schools to bar gays	N	100. South Africa sanctions-veto override	Y
47. Bar broadcaster fairness doctrine	N	101. Tax overhaul to revise income tax	N
48. Bar cap gains cut/reinstate IRA	Y	102. Use of military in drug war	N
49. Bar unions equal voice in pension	N	103. Delete 12 MX/add conventional wpn	Y
50. Bar assembly of chemical weapons	Y	104. Raise speed limit to 65 mph	N
51. Ban plutonium/uranium production	Y	105. Require Pentagon to buy US goods	Y
52. Cap MX missile deployment at 50	Y	106. AIDS insurance non-discrimination	Y
53. Allow $3b for 2 stealth bombers	N	107. Prohibit Saudi arms sales	Y
54. Publish bio-warfare experiments	Y	108. Ease Gun Control Act of 1968	N
55. Raise minimum wage-veto override	Y	109. Bar interstate handgun transport	Y
56. Bar transfer of FS-X technology	Y	110. Make company emissions known	Y
57. Cut defense and raise domestic $	N	111. Allow toxic victims to sue in fed ct	Y
58. Uniform poll closing in 48 states	Y	112. Superfund waste cleanup of $10b	Y
59. Req foreign investment disclosure	N	113. 90 days notice of plant closings	Y
60. Textile import quotas-veto override	Y	114. $20b in Medicare cuts/tax increases	Y
61. Bar abortion funding in Wash, DC	N	115. Spending cuts and tax increases	Y
62. Notify spouses of AIDS+ carriers	N	116. Set school lunch lmt-250% poverty	N
63. Seize conveyance-drug trafficking	N	117. $75m for youth work projects	Y
64. South Africa sanctions	Y	118. Allow Angolan military assistance	N
65. 60 days' notice of plant closings	Y	119. Suspend defense payments for abuse	Y
66. Close unneeded military bases	N	120. Drop SS COLAs/$12b tax increase	N
67. Keep welfare reform within $2.8b	N	121. Approve $1.5b for 21 MX missiles	N
68. Allow children housing exclusion	N	122. Emergency farm credit/revisions	Y
69. Shift $400m of NASA to homeless	Y	123. Duty on Taiwan/Hong Kong/S Korea	Y
70. Cap Medicare patients' liability	Y	124. Limit steel imports to 17%	Y
71. Prohibit employee polygraph testing	Y	125. Cut $ to schools that bar prayer	N
72. Allow CIA to fund Contras	?	126. $50b-taxes; cut Medicare/spending	N
73. Revise unfair trade practices	Y	127. Limit Pershing II/cruise in Europe	Y
74. Focus SDI on accidental launch	Y	128. Delete $7.1b for 34 B-1 bombers	Y
75. Bar Air Force $ for MX missile	Y	129. Bar purchase of Sergeant York guns	Y
76. Allow "real" increase in defense	N	130. El Salvador military/economic aid	N
77. Troop reduction in Europe of 50%	N	131. Bar mining of Nicaraguan waters	Y
78. Ban nuclear tests above 1 kiloton	Y	132. Physician fee freeze for Medicare	N
79. Ban anti-satellite missile tests	Y	133. $49b in "sin"/phone/insurance taxes	Y
80. Observe certain limits of SALT II	Y	134. Allow sale of Conrail	N
81. Restore four Civil Rights laws	Y	135. Equal Rights Amendment	Y
82. Prohibit aliens as strikebreakers	Y	136. Authorize Marines in Lebanon	Y
83. Allow military malpractice suits	Y	137. Eminent domain for coal companies	N
84. Approval of $36m in Contra aid	N	138. Prohibit EPA clean air sanctions	N
85. $18b deficit reduction compromise	N	139. SS retirement age increase/reforms	N
86. Welfare reform of $5.7b for 5 years	Y	140. Auto domestic content requirement	Y
87. Raise taxes $12b/cut spending $3b	Y	141. Delete jobs program funding	N
88. Board to assess occupational risk	Y	142. Highway-gas tax bill	N
89. Balanced budget by '93-via targets	Y	143. Cut $5b from defense for Medicare	Y
90. Bar licensing of two nuclear plants	N	144. Emergency housing aid of $1b	Y

Presidential Support Score: 1991 - 23% 1990 - 19%

DeLAURO, ROSA -- Connecticut 3rd District [Democrat]. Counties of Fairfield (pt.), Middlesex (pt.) and New Haven (pt.). Prior Term: 1991-92. Born: March 2, 1943; New Haven, CT. Education: Marymount College (B.A.); Columbia University (M.A.); London School of Economics. Occupation: Executive assistant to New Haven mayor and city development administrator; chief of staff to Sen. Dodd; Countdown '87 and Emily's List executive director; Pax Americas co-chairperson.

DeLAURO, ROSA (continued)

1. Protection to Haitian refugees	Y	
2. Raise tax on wealthy; lower others	Y	
3. Investigate Reagan hostage delay	Y	
4. Campaign finance revisions	Y	
5. Unpaid leave to care for children	Y	
6. Restrict NEA use of funds	N	
7. Bar race-bias claim/habeas corpus	N	
8. Ban race as death sentence factor	N	
9. Exceptions to exclusionary rule	N	
10. Allow sale of assault weapons	N	
11. Life in prison/abolish death penalty	N	
12. Req conspiracy-price fixing cases	N	
13. Unemployment benefits extension	Y	
14. Tissue use of aborted fetuses	Y	
15. Bar replacement of union strikers	Y	
16. Hold foreign aid at $15b for '92	Y	
17. Restore space station funding	N	
18. Civil Rights Act of 1991	Y	
19. Unlimited damages-discrimination	Y	
20. Eliminate funds for supercollider	N	
21. Terminate SDI except for research	Y	
22. Req 7-day handgun waiting period	Y	
23. Provide $30b for failed S&Ls	N	
24. Allow use of force against Iraq	N	

Presidential Support Score: 1991 - 26%

SHAYS, CHRISTOPHER -- Connecticut 4th District [Republican]. County of Fairfield (pt.). Prior Terms: 1987 (Special Election)-1992. Born: October 18, 1945. Education: Principia College (B.A.); New York University (M.B.A., M.P.A.). Occupation: Peace Corps volunteer (1968-1970); state representative (1974-1987).

1. Protection to Haitian refugees	N	44. Protect Chinese & C.A. nationals	Y
2. Raise tax on wealthy; lower others	N	45. Abortion $ for rape/incest cases	Y
3. Investigate Reagan hostage delay	N	46. Allow religious schools to bar gays	N
4. Campaign finance revisions	Y	47. Bar broadcaster fairness doctrine	N
5. Unpaid leave to care for children	Y	48. Bar cap gains cut/reinstate IRA	N
6. Restrict NEA use of funds	Y	49. Bar unions equal voice in pension	Y
7. Bar race-bias claim/habeas corpus	N	50. Bar assembly of chemical weapons	Y
8. Ban race as death sentence factor	N	51. Ban plutonium/uranium production	Y
9. Exceptions to exclusionary rule	Y	52. Cap MX missile deployment at 50	Y
10. Allow sale of assault weapons	N	53. Allow $3b for 2 stealth bombers	N
11. Life in prison/abolish death penalty	Y	54. Publish bio-warfare experiments	Y
12. Req conspiracy-price fixing cases	Y	55. Raise minimum wage-veto override	Y
13. Unemployment benefits extension	N	56. Bar transfer of FS-X technology	Y
14. Tissue use of aborted fetuses	Y	57. Cut defense and raise domestic $	N
15. Bar replacement of union strikers	N	58. Uniform poll closing in 48 states	Y
16. Hold foreign aid at $15b for '92	Y	59. Req foreign investment disclosure	N
17. Restore space station funding	N	60. Textile import quotas-veto override	Y
18. Civil Rights Act of 1991	Y	61. Bar abortion funding in Wash, DC	N
19. Unlimited damages-discrimination	N	62. Notify spouses of AIDS+ carriers	N
20. Eliminate funds for supercollider	Y	63. Seize conveyance-drug trafficking	N
21. Terminate SDI except for research	Y	64. South Africa sanctions	Y
22. Req 7-day handgun waiting period	Y	65. 60 days' notice of plant closings	N
23. Provide $30b for failed S&Ls	Y	66. Close unneeded military bases	Y
24. Allow use of force against Iraq	Y	67. Keep welfare reform within $2.8b	N
25. Allow $15b in foreign aid for '91	Y	68. Allow children housing exclusion	N
26. Revise & extend legal immigration	Y	69. Shift $400m of NASA to homeless	Y
27. Suspend aid to Angolan rebels	Y	70. Cap Medicare patients' liability	Y
28. Democratic tax plan proposals	N	71. Prohibit employee polygraph testing	Y
29. Cut defense 5% across the board	Y	72. Allow CIA to fund Contras	N
30. Textile import quotas-veto override	Y	73. Revise unfair trade practices	N
31. Abortion service for military abroad	Y	74. Focus SDI on accidental launch	Y
32. Limits on high income farmers	Y	75. Bar Air Force $ for MX missile	Y
33. Family medical leave-veto override	Y	76. Allow "real" increase in defense	N
34. Req submission of balanced budget	Y	77. Troop reduction in Europe of 50%	N
35. Balanced budget amendment	Y	78. Ban nuclear tests above 1 kiloton	N
36. Amendment to ban flag desecration	N	79. Ban anti-satellite missile tests	N
37. Reauthorize Amtrak-veto override	Y	80. Observe certain limits of SALT II	Y
38. Retraining aid for coal miners	N	81. Restore four Civil Rights laws	Y
39. Suspend El Salvador military aid	Y	82. Prohibit aliens as strikebreakers	N
40. Expand child care aid/tax credit	Y	83. Allow military malpractice suits	Y
41. Raise House salary/omit honoraria	Y	84. Approval of $36m in Contra aid	N
42. Toughen oil-spill liability	Y	85. $18b deficit reduction compromise	N
43. Restitution to Japanese interned	Y	86. Welfare reform of $5.7b for 5 years	Y

SHAYS, CHRISTOPHER (continued)

87.	Raise taxes $12b/cut spending $3b	N	89. Balanced budget by '93-via targets	N
88.	Board to assess occupational risk	Y		

Presidential Support Score: 1991 - 58%   1990 - 34%

FRANKS, GARY A. -- Connecticut 5th District [Republican]. Counties of Fairfield (pt.) and New Haven (pt.). Prior Term: 1991-92. Born: February 9, 1953; Waterbury, CT. Education: Yale University (B.A.). Occupation: Real estate entrepreneur; Waterbury alderman (1985-1990).

1.	Protection to Haitian refugees	N	13.	Unemployment benefits extension	Y
2.	Raise tax on wealthy; lower others	N	14.	Tissue use of aborted fetuses	Y
3.	Investigate Reagan hostage delay	N	15.	Bar replacement of union strikers	N
4.	Campaign finance revisions	N	16.	Hold foreign aid at $15b for '92	Y
5.	Unpaid leave to care for children	N	17.	Restore space station funding	Y
6.	Restrict NEA use of funds	Y	18.	Civil Rights Act of 1991	N
7.	Bar race-bias claim/habeas corpus	Y	19.	Unlimited damages-discrimination	N
8.	Ban race as death sentence factor	Y	20.	Eliminate funds for supercollider	N
9.	Exceptions to exclusionary rule	Y	21.	Terminate SDI except for research	N
10.	Allow sale of assault weapons	Y	22.	Req 7-day handgun waiting period	N
11.	Life in prison/abolish death penalty	N	23.	Provide $30b for failed S&Ls	Y
12.	Req conspiracy-price fixing cases	Y	24.	Allow use of force against Iraq	Y

Presidential Support Score: 1991 - 74%

JOHNSON, NANCY L. -- Connecticut 6th District [Republican]. Counties of Fairfield (pt.), Hartford (pt.), Litchfield, New Haven (pt.) and Tolland (pt.). Prior Terms: 1983-92. Born: January 5, 1935; Chicago, IL. Education: University of Chicago; Radcliffe College; University of London on an English Speaking Union Scholarship. Occupation: President, Sheldon Community Guidance Clinic; member, board of directors, New Britain Bank and Trust; professor; Connecticut senator (1976-82).

1.	Protection to Haitian refugees	Y	31.	Abortion service for military abroad	Y
2.	Raise tax on wealthy; lower others	N	32.	Limits on high income farmers	Y
3.	Investigate Reagan hostage delay	N	33.	Family medical leave-veto override	Y
4.	Campaign finance revisions	N	34.	Req submission of balanced budget	Y
5.	Unpaid leave to care for children	Y	35.	Balanced budget amendment	Y
6.	Restrict NEA use of funds	N	36.	Amendment to ban flag desecration	N
7.	Bar race-bias claim/habeas corpus	Y	37.	Reauthorize Amtrak-veto override	Y
8.	Ban race as death sentence factor	Y	38.	Retraining aid for coal miners	Y
9.	Exceptions to exclusionary rule	Y	39.	Suspend El Salvador military aid	N
10.	Allow sale of assault weapons	N	40.	Expand child care aid/tax credit	Y
11.	Life in prison/abolish death penalty	N	41.	Raise House salary/omit honoraria	Y
12.	Req conspiracy-price fixing cases	Y	42.	Toughen oil-spill liability	Y
13.	Unemployment benefits extension	Y	43.	Restitution to Japanese interned	Y
14.	Tissue use of aborted fetuses	Y	44.	Protect Chinese & C.A. nationals	N
15.	Bar replacement of union strikers	N	45.	Abortion $ for rape/incest cases	Y
16.	Hold foreign aid at $15b for '92	Y	46.	Allow religious schools to bar gays	N
17.	Restore space station funding	Y	47.	Bar broadcaster fairness doctrine	N
18.	Civil Rights Act of 1991	N	48.	Bar cap gains cut/reinstate IRA	N
19.	Unlimited damages-discrimination	N	49.	Bar unions equal voice in pension	Y
20.	Eliminate funds for supercollider	Y	50.	Bar assembly of chemical weapons	N
21.	Terminate SDI except for research	N	51.	Ban plutonium/uranium production	Y
22.	Req 7-day handgun waiting period	Y	52.	Cap MX missile deployment at 50	Y
23.	Provide $30b for failed S&Ls	Y	53.	Allow $3b for 2 stealth bombers	N
24.	Allow use of force against Iraq	Y	54.	Publish bio-warfare experiments	Y
25.	Allow $15b in foreign aid for '91	Y	55.	Raise minimum wage-veto override	Y
26.	Revise & extend legal immigration	Y	56.	Bar transfer of FS-X technology	N
27.	Suspend aid to Angolan rebels	N	57.	Cut defense and raise domestic $	N
28.	Democratic tax plan proposals	N	58.	Uniform poll closing in 48 states	Y
29.	Cut defense 5% across the board	N	59.	Req foreign investment disclosure	N
30.	Textile import quotas-veto override	N	60.	Textile import quotas-veto override	N

JOHNSON, NANCY L. (continued)

61. Bar abortion funding in Wash, DC	N	101. Tax overhaul to revise income tax	Y
62. Notify spouses of AIDS+ carriers	N	102. Use of military in drug war	N
63. Seize conveyance-drug trafficking	N	103. Delete 12 MX/add conventional wpn	Y
64. South Africa sanctions	N	104. Raise speed limit to 65 mph	N
65. 60 days' notice of plant closings	Y	105. Require Pentagon to buy US goods	Y
66. Close unneeded military bases	Y	106. AIDS insurance non-discrimination	Y
67. Keep welfare reform within $2.8b	Y	107. Prohibit Saudi arms sales	Y
68. Allow children housing exclusion	N	108. Ease Gun Control Act of 1968	Y
69. Shift $400m of NASA to homeless	N	109. Bar interstate handgun transport	Y
70. Cap Medicare patients' liability	Y	110. Make company emissions known	N
71. Prohibit employee polygraph testing	Y	111. Allow toxic victims to sue in fed ct	N
72. Allow CIA to fund Contras	Y	112. Superfund waste cleanup of $10b	Y
73. Revise unfair trade practices	Y	113. 90 days notice of plant closings	Y
74. Focus SDI on accidental launch	N	114. $20b in Medicare cuts/tax increases	Y
75. Bar Air Force $ for MX missile	N	115. Spending cuts and tax increases	N
76. Allow "real" increase in defense	N	116. Set school lunch lmt-250% poverty	Y
77. Troop reduction in Europe of 50%	?	117. $75m for youth work projects	N
78. Ban nuclear tests above 1 kiloton	N	118. Allow Angolan military assistance	Y
79. Ban anti-satellite missile tests	N	119. Suspend defense payments for abuse	N
80. Observe certain limits of SALT II	Y	120. Drop SS COLAs/$12b tax increase	N
81. Restore four Civil Rights laws	Y	121. Approve $1.5b for 21 MX missiles	N
82. Prohibit aliens as strikebreakers	Y	122. Emergency farm credit/revisions	N
83. Allow military malpractice suits	?	123. Duty on Taiwan/Hong Kong/S Korea	N
84. Approval of $36m in Contra aid	Y	124. Limit steel imports to 17%	Y
85. $18b deficit reduction compromise	Y	125. Cut $ to schools that bar prayer	N
86. Welfare reform of $5.7b for 5 years	N	126. $50b-taxes; cut Medicare/spending	Y
87. Raise taxes $12b/cut spending $3b	N	127. Limit Pershing II/cruise in Europe	N
88. Board to assess occupational risk	N	128. Delete $7.1b for 34 B-1 bombers	N
89. Balanced budget by '93-via targets	Y	129. Bar purchase of Sergeant York guns	N
90. Bar licensing of two nuclear plants	N	130. El Salvador military/economic aid	Y
91. Remove victims compensation cap	N	131. Bar mining of Nicaraguan waters	Y
92. Catastrophic health insurance	N	132. Physician fee freeze for Medicare	Y
93. Ban airline smoking-2 hours or less	Y	133. $49b in "sin"/phone/insurance taxes	Y
94. $1b/two year aid for the homeless	Y	134. Allow sale of Conrail	Y
95. Bar non-unions in union companies	N	135. Equal Rights Amendment	Y
96. Increase FSLIC rescue to $15b	N	136. Authorize Marines in Lebanon	Y
97. Impose quotas to lower trade deficit	N	137. Eminent domain for coal companies	Y
98. Reduce discretionary budget 21%	Y	138. Prohibit EPA clean air sanctions	N
99. Immigration reform/alien amnesty	Y	139. SS retirement age increase/reforms	N
100. South Africa sanctions-veto override	Y		

Presidential Support Score: 1991 - 63% 1990 - 52%

DELAWARE

CARPER, THOMAS R. -- Representative at Large [Democrat]. Prior Terms: 1983-92. Born: January 23, 1947; Beckley, WV. Education: Ohio State University (B.A.); University of Delaware (M.A.). Military Service: U.S. Navy; Naval Reserves. Occupation: Industrial development specialist for the state division of Economic Development (1975-76): Delaware state treasurer (1976-82).

1. Protection to Haitian refugees	Y	9. Exceptions to exclusionary rule	Y
2. Raise tax on wealthy; lower others	N	10. Allow sale of assault weapons	N
3. Investigate Reagan hostage delay	N	11. Life in prison/abolish death penalty	N
4. Campaign finance revisions	Y	12. Req conspiracy-price fixing cases	N
5. Unpaid leave to care for children	Y	13. Unemployment benefits extension	Y
6. Restrict NEA use of funds	?	14. Tissue use of aborted fetuses	Y
7. Bar race-bias claim/habeas corpus	Y	15. Bar replacement of union strikers	Y
8. Ban race as death sentence factor	N	16. Hold foreign aid at $15b for '92	Y

CARPER, THOMAS R. (continued)

17. Restore space station funding	N	79. Ban anti-satellite missile tests	Y
18. Civil Rights Act of 1991	Y	80. Observe certain limits of SALT II	Y
19. Unlimited damages-discrimination	N	81. Restore four Civil Rights laws	Y
20. Eliminate funds for supercollider	N	82. Prohibit aliens as strikebreakers	Y
21. Terminate SDI except for research	Y	83. Allow military malpractice suits	Y
22. Req 7-day handgun waiting period	Y	84. Approval of $36m in Contra aid	N
23. Provide $30b for failed S&Ls	Y	85. $18b deficit reduction compromise	Y
24. Allow use of force against Iraq	Y	86. Welfare reform of $5.7b for 5 years	Y
25. Allow $15b in foreign aid for '91	Y	87. Raise taxes $12b/cut spending $3b	N
26. Revise & extend legal immigration	Y	88. Board to assess occupational risk	Y
27. Suspend aid to Angolan rebels	Y	89. Balanced budget by '93-via targets	Y
28. Democratic tax plan proposals	Y	90. Bar licensing of two nuclear plants	N
29. Cut defense 5% across the board	N	91. Remove victims compensation cap	Y
30. Textile import quotas-veto override	Y	92. Catastrophic health insurance	Y
31. Abortion service for military abroad	Y	93. Ban airline smoking-2 hours or less	Y
32. Limits on high income farmers	Y	94. $1b/two year aid for the homeless	Y
33. Family medical leave-veto override	Y	95. Bar non-unions in union companies	Y
34. Req submission of balanced budget	N	96. Increase FSLIC rescue to $15b	Y
35. Balanced budget amendment	Y	97. Impose quotas to lower trade deficit	Y
36. Amendment to ban flag desecration	N	98. Reduce discretionary budget 21%	Y
37. Reauthorize Amtrak-veto override	Y	99. Immigration reform/alien amnesty	Y
38. Retraining aid for coal miners	Y	100. South Africa sanctions-veto override	Y
39. Suspend El Salvador military aid	Y	101. Tax overhaul to revise income tax	Y
40. Expand child care aid/tax credit	Y	102. Use of military in drug war	Y
41. Raise House salary/omit honoraria	Y	103. Delete 12 MX/add conventional wpn	Y
42. Toughen oil-spill liability	N	104. Raise speed limit to 65 mph	Y
43. Restitution to Japanese interned	N	105. Require Pentagon to buy US goods	Y
44. Protect Chinese & C.A. nationals	Y	106. AIDS insurance non-discrimination	Y
45. Abortion $ for rape/incest cases	Y	107. Prohibit Saudi arms sales	Y
46. Allow religious schools to bar gays	Y	108. Ease Gun Control Act of 1968	N
47. Bar broadcaster fairness doctrine	N	109. Bar interstate handgun transport	Y
48. Bar cap gains cut/reinstate IRA	Y	110. Make company emissions known	Y
49. Bar unions equal voice in pension	N	111. Allow toxic victims to sue in fed ct	N
50. Bar assembly of chemical weapons	Y	112. Superfund waste cleanup of $10b	N
51. Ban plutonium/uranium production	Y	113. 90 days notice of plant closings	Y
52. Cap MX missile deployment at 50	Y	114. $20b in Medicare cuts/tax increases	Y
53. Allow $3b for 2 stealth bombers	N	115. Spending cuts and tax increases	N
54. Publish bio-warfare experiments	Y	116. Set school lunch lmt-250% poverty	N
55. Raise minimum wage-veto override	Y	117. $75m for youth work projects	N
56. Bar transfer of FS-X technology	Y	118. Allow Angolan military assistance	Y
57. Cut defense and raise domestic $	N	119. Suspend defense payments for abuse	N
58. Uniform poll closing in 48 states	Y	120. Drop SS COLAs/$12b tax increase	N
59. Req foreign investment disclosure	N	121. Approve $1.5b for 21 MX missiles	N
60. Textile import quotas-veto override	Y	122. Emergency farm credit/revisions	N
61. Bar abortion funding in Wash, DC	N	123. Duty on Taiwan/Hong Kong/S Korea	Y
62. Notify spouses of AIDS+ carriers	N	124. Limit steel imports to 17%	Y
63. Seize conveyance-drug trafficking	N	125. Cut $ to schools that bar prayer	N
64. South Africa sanctions	Y	126. $50b-taxes; cut Medicare/spending	Y
65. 60 days' notice of plant closings	Y	127. Limit Pershing II/cruise in Europe	N
66. Close unneeded military bases	Y	128. Delete $7.1b for 34 B-1 bombers	Y
67. Keep welfare reform within $2.8b	Y	129. Bar purchase of Sergeant York guns	N
68. Allow children housing exclusion	N	130. El Salvador military/economic aid	N
69. Shift $400m of NASA to homeless	Y	131. Bar mining of Nicaraguan waters	N
70. Cap Medicare patients' liability	N	132. Physician fee freeze for Medicare	N
71. Prohibit employee polygraph testing	?	133. $49b in "sin"/phone/insurance taxes	Y
72. Allow CIA to fund Contras	N	134. Allow sale of Conrail	N
73. Revise unfair trade practices	Y	135. Equal Rights Amendment	Y
74. Focus SDI on accidental launch	Y	136. Authorize Marines in Lebanon	N
75. Bar Air Force $ for MX missile	N	137. Eminent domain for coal companies	N
76. Allow "real" increase in defense	N	138. Prohibit EPA clean air sanctions	N
77. Troop reduction in Europe of 50%	N	139. SS retirement age increase/reforms	Y
78. Ban nuclear tests above 1 kiloton	Y		

Presidential Support Score: 1991 - 37%   1990 - 23%

FLORIDA

HUTTO, EARL -- Florida 1st District [Democrat]. Counties of Bay (pt.), Escombia, Okaloosa, Santa Rosa and Walton. Prior Terms: 1979-92. Born: May 12, 1926; Midland City, AL. Education: Troy State University (B.S.); Northwestern University. Military Service: U.S. Navy, 1944-46. Occupation: Owner and president, Earl Hutto Advertising Agency; founder, WPEX-FM; sports director, WEAR-TV, WSFA-TV, WJHG-TV; Florida representative (1972-78).

1. Protection to Haitian refugees	N	
2. Raise tax on wealthy; lower others	N	
3. Investigate Reagan hostage delay	?	
4. Campaign finance revisions	Y	
5. Unpaid leave to care for children	N	
6. Restrict NEA use of funds	Y	
7. Bar race-bias claim/habeas corpus	Y	
8. Ban race as death sentence factor	Y	
9. Exceptions to exclusionary rule	Y	
10. Allow sale of assault weapons	Y	
11. Life in prison/abolish death penalty	N	
12. Req conspiracy-price fixing cases	Y	
13. Unemployment benefits extension	N	
14. Tissue use of aborted fetuses	N	
15. Bar replacement of union strikers	N	
16. Hold foreign aid at $15b for '92	N	
17. Restore space station funding	Y	
18. Civil Rights Act of 1991	N	
19. Unlimited damages-discrimination	N	
20. Eliminate funds for supercollider	N	
21. Terminate SDI except for research	N	
22. Req 7-day handgun waiting period	Y	
23. Provide $30b for failed S&Ls	N	
24. Allow use of force against Iraq	Y	
25. Allow $15b in foreign aid for '91	N	
26. Revise & extend legal immigration	N	
27. Suspend aid to Angolan rebels	N	
28. Democratic tax plan proposals	Y	
29. Cut defense 5% across the board	N	
30. Textile import quotas-veto override	Y	
31. Abortion service for military abroad	N	
32. Limits on high income farmers	N	
33. Family medical leave-veto override	N	
34. Req submission of balanced budget	Y	
35. Balanced budget amendment	Y	
36. Amendment to ban flag desecration	Y	
37. Reauthorize Amtrak-veto override	?	
38. Retraining aid for coal miners	N	
39. Suspend El Salvador military aid	N	
40. Expand child care aid/tax credit	N	
41. Raise House salary/omit honoraria	N	
42. Toughen oil-spill liability	N	
43. Restitution to Japanese interned	N	
44. Protect Chinese & C.A. nationals	N	
45. Abortion $ for rape/incest cases	N	
46. Allow religious schools to bar gays	Y	
47. Bar broadcaster fairness doctrine	N	
48. Bar cap gains cut/reinstate IRA	N	
49. Bar unions equal voice in pension	Y	
50. Bar assembly of chemical weapons	N	

51. Ban plutonium/uranium production	N	
52. Cap MX missile deployment at 50	N	
53. Allow $3b for 2 stealth bombers	Y	
54. Publish bio-warfare experiments	Y	
55. Raise minimum wage-veto override	N	
56. Bar transfer of FS-X technology	Y	
57. Cut defense and raise domestic $	N	
58. Uniform poll closing in 48 states	Y	
59. Req foreign investment disclosure	Y	
60. Textile import quotas-veto override	Y	
61. Bar abortion funding in Wash, DC	Y	
62. Notify spouses of AIDS+ carriers	Y	
63. Seize conveyance-drug trafficking	Y	
64. South Africa sanctions	N	
65. 60 days' notice of plant closings	Y	
66. Close unneeded military bases	N	
67. Keep welfare reform within $2.8b	Y	
68. Allow children housing exclusion	N	
69. Shift $400m of NASA to homeless	N	
70. Cap Medicare patients' liability	Y	
71. Prohibit employee polygraph testing	N	
72. Allow CIA to fund Contras	Y	
73. Revise unfair trade practices	Y	
74. Focus SDI on accidental launch	N	
75. Bar Air Force $ for MX missile	N	
76. Allow "real" increase in defense	Y	
77. Troop reduction in Europe of 50%	N	
78. Ban nuclear tests above 1 kiloton	N	
79. Ban anti-satellite missile tests	N	
80. Observe certain limits of SALT II	N	
81. Restore four Civil Rights laws	N	
82. Prohibit aliens as strikebreakers	N	
83. Allow military malpractice suits	N	
84. Approval of $36m in Contra aid	Y	
85. $18b deficit reduction compromise	Y	
86. Welfare reform of $5.7b for 5 years	N	
87. Raise taxes $12b/cut spending $3b	Y	
88. Board to assess occupational risk	N	
89. Balanced budget by '93-via targets	Y	
90. Bar licensing of two nuclear plants	N	
91. Remove victims compensation cap	N	
92. Catastrophic health insurance	Y	
93. Ban airline smoking-2 hours or less	Y	
94. $1b/two year aid for the homeless	Y	
95. Bar non-unions in union companies	N	
96. Increase FSLIC rescue to $15b	N	
97. Impose quotas to lower trade deficit	N	
98. Reduce discretionary budget 21%	?	
99. Immigration reform/alien amnesty	Y	
100. South Africa sanctions-veto override	N	

HUTTO, EARL (continued)

101. Tax overhaul to revise income tax	N		123. Duty on Taiwan/Hong Kong/S Korea	N	
102. Use of military in drug war	N		124. Limit steel imports to 17%		N
103. Delete 12 MX/add conventional wpn	N		125. Cut $ to schools that bar prayer	Y	
104. Raise speed limit to 65 mph	N		126. $50b-taxes; cut Medicare/spending	Y	
105. Require Pentagon to buy US goods	N		127. Limit Pershing II/cruise in Europe		N
106. AIDS insurance non-discrimination	N		128. Delete $7.1b for 34 B-1 bombers		N
107. Prohibit Saudi arms sales	Y		129. Bar purchase of Sergeant York guns		?
108. Ease Gun Control Act of 1968	Y		130. El Salvador military/economic aid	Y	
109. Bar interstate handgun transport	Y		131. Bar mining of Nicaraguan waters		N
110. Make company emissions known	N		132. Physician fee freeze for Medicare	Y	
111. Allow toxic victims to sue in fed ct	N		133. $49b in "sin"/phone/insurance taxes	Y	
112. Superfund waste cleanup of $10b	N		134. Allow sale of Conrail		N
113. 90 days notice of plant closings	N		135. Equal Rights Amendment		N
114. $20b in Medicare cuts/tax increases	Y		136. Authorize Marines in Lebanon	Y	
115. Spending cuts and tax increases	Y		137. Eminent domain for coal companies	Y	
116. Set school lunch lmt-250% poverty	N		138. Prohibit EPA clean air sanctions	Y	
117. $75m for youth work projects	?		139. SS retirement age increase/reforms	Y	
118. Allow Angolan military assistance	Y		140. Auto domestic content requirement		N
119. Suspend defense payments for abuse	N		141. Delete jobs program funding		N
120. Drop SS COLAs/$12b tax increase	Y		142. Highway-gas tax bill		N
121. Approve $1.5b for 21 MX missiles	Y		143. Cut $5b from defense for Medicare		N
122. Emergency farm credit/revisions	Y		144. Emergency housing aid of $1b	Y	

Presidential Support Score: 1991 - 59%   1990 - 54%

PETERSON, DOUGLAS (PETE) -- Florida 2nd District [Democrat]. Counties of Baker, Bay (pt.), Bradford, Calhoun, Clay (pt.), Columbia, Dixie, Franklin, Gadsden, Gilchrist, Gulf, Hamilton, Holmes, Jackson, Jefferson, Lafayette, Leon, Levy, Liberty, Madison, Suwannee, Taylor, Union, Wakulla, and Washington. Prior Term: 1991-92. Born: June 26, 1935; Omaha, NE. Education: National War College; University of Tampa (B.S.); University of Michigan. Military Service: U.S. Air Force (ret. Col.). Occupation: Computer software equipment company co-founder; state boys' school headmaster.

1. Protection to Haitian refugees	Y	13. Unemployment benefits extension	Y	
2. Raise tax on wealthy; lower others	Y	14. Tissue use of aborted fetuses	Y	
3. Investigate Reagan hostage delay	Y	15. Bar replacement of union strikers	Y	
4. Campaign finance revisions	Y	16. Hold foreign aid at $15b for '92	Y	
5. Unpaid leave to care for children	Y	17. Restore space station funding	Y	
6. Restrict NEA use of funds	Y	18. Civil Rights Act of 1991	Y	
7. Bar race-bias claim/habeas corpus	Y	19. Unlimited damages-discrimination	Y	
8. Ban race as death sentence factor	N	20. Eliminate funds for supercollider	Y	
9. Exceptions to exclusionary rule	Y	21. Terminate SDI except for research	N	
10. Allow sale of assault weapons	Y	22. Req 7-day handgun waiting period	N	
11. Life in prison/abolish death penalty	N	23. Provide $30b for failed S&Ls	N	
12. Req conspiracy-price fixing cases	Y	24. Allow use of force against Iraq	N	

Presidential Support Score: 1991 - 37%

BENNETT, CHARLES E. -- Florida 3rd District [Democrat]. Counties of Duval (pt.) and Nassau. Prior Terms: 1949-92. Born: December 2, 1910; Jacksonville, FL. Education: University of Florida (B.A., J.D.). Military Service: U.S. Army, 1942. Occupation: Attorney; Florida representative (1941); author.

1. Protection to Haitian refugees	Y	8. Ban race as death sentence factor	Y	
2. Raise tax on wealthy; lower others	Y	9. Exceptions to exclusionary rule	Y	
3. Investigate Reagan hostage delay	Y	10. Allow sale of assault weapons	N	
4. Campaign finance revisions	N	11. Life in prison/abolish death penalty	N	
5. Unpaid leave to care for children	Y	12. Req conspiracy-price fixing cases	N	
6. Restrict NEA use of funds	Y	13. Unemployment benefits extension	Y	
7. Bar race-bias claim/habeas corpus	N	14. Tissue use of aborted fetuses	Y	

BENNETT, CHARLES E. (continued)

No.	Issue	Vote
15.	Bar replacement of union strikers	Y
16.	Hold foreign aid at $15b for '92	N
17.	Restore space station funding	Y
18.	Civil Rights Act of 1991	Y
19.	Unlimited damages-discrimination	N
20.	Eliminate funds for supercollider	Y
21.	Terminate SDI except for research	N
22.	Req 7-day handgun waiting period	Y
23.	Provide $30b for failed S&Ls	N
24.	Allow use of force against Iraq	N
25.	Allow $15b in foreign aid for '91	N
26.	Revise & extend legal immigration	N
27.	Suspend aid to Angolan rebels	Y
28.	Democratic tax plan proposals	Y
29.	Cut defense 5% across the board	N
30.	Textile import quotas-veto override	Y
31.	Abortion service for military abroad	Y
32.	Limits on high income farmers	Y
33.	Family medical leave-veto override	Y
34.	Req submission of balanced budget	Y
35.	Balanced budget amendment	Y
36.	Amendment to ban flag desecration	Y
37.	Reauthorize Amtrak-veto override	Y
38.	Retraining aid for coal miners	Y
39.	Suspend El Salvador military aid	Y
40.	Expand child care aid/tax credit	Y
41.	Raise House salary/omit honoraria	N
42.	Toughen oil-spill liability	Y
43.	Restitution to Japanese interned	Y
44.	Protect Chinese & C.A. nationals	N
45.	Abortion $ for rape/incest cases	Y
46.	Allow religious schools to bar gays	Y
47.	Bar broadcaster fairness doctrine	N
48.	Bar cap gains cut/reinstate IRA	Y
49.	Bar unions equal voice in pension	N
50.	Bar assembly of chemical weapons	N
51.	Ban plutonium/uranium production	Y
52.	Cap MX missile deployment at 50	Y
53.	Allow $3b for 2 stealth bombers	N
54.	Publish bio-warfare experiments	Y
55.	Raise minimum wage-veto override	Y
56.	Bar transfer of FS-X technology	Y
57.	Cut defense and raise domestic $	N
58.	Uniform poll closing in 48 states	Y
59.	Req foreign investment disclosure	Y
60.	Textile import quotas-veto override	N
61.	Bar abortion funding in Wash, DC	Y
62.	Notify spouses of AIDS+ carriers	N
63.	Seize conveyance-drug trafficking	Y
64.	South Africa sanctions	Y
65.	60 days' notice of plant closings	Y
66.	Close unneeded military bases	Y
67.	Keep welfare reform within $2.8b	Y
68.	Allow children housing exclusion	N
69.	Shift $400m of NASA to homeless	N
70.	Cap Medicare patients' liability	Y
71.	Prohibit employee polygraph testing	N
72.	Allow CIA to fund Contras	N
73.	Revise unfair trade practices	Y
74.	Focus SDI on accidental launch	Y
75.	Bar Air Force $ for MX missile	N
76.	Allow "real" increase in defense	Y
77.	Troop reduction in Europe of 50%	N
78.	Ban nuclear tests above 1 kiloton	Y
79.	Ban anti-satellite missile tests	Y
80.	Observe certain limits of SALT II	Y
81.	Restore four Civil Rights laws	Y
82.	Prohibit aliens as strikebreakers	Y
83.	Allow military malpractice suits	Y
84.	Approval of $36m in Contra aid	Y
85.	$18b deficit reduction compromise	Y
86.	Welfare reform of $5.7b for 5 years	Y
87.	Raise taxes $12b/cut spending $3b	Y
88.	Board to assess occupational risk	Y
89.	Balanced budget by '93-via targets	N
90.	Bar licensing of two nuclear plants	Y
91.	Remove victims compensation cap	N
92.	Catastrophic health insurance	Y
93.	Ban airline smoking-2 hours or less	Y
94.	$1b/two year aid for the homeless	Y
95.	Bar non-unions in union companies	Y
96.	Increase FSLIC rescue to $15b	N
97.	Impose quotas to lower trade deficit	N
98.	Reduce discretionary budget 21%	Y
99.	Immigration reform/alien amnesty	Y
100.	South Africa sanctions-veto override	Y
101.	Tax overhaul to revise income tax	Y
102.	Use of military in drug war	Y
103.	Delete 12 MX/add conventional wpn	Y
104.	Raise speed limit to 65 mph	N
105.	Require Pentagon to buy US goods	Y
106.	AIDS insurance non-discrimination	Y
107.	Prohibit Saudi arms sales	Y
108.	Ease Gun Control Act of 1968	N
109.	Bar interstate handgun transport	Y
110.	Make company emissions known	Y
111.	Allow toxic victims to sue in fed ct	Y
112.	Superfund waste cleanup of $10b	Y
113.	90 days notice of plant closings	Y
114.	$20b in Medicare cuts/tax increases	Y
115.	Spending cuts and tax increases	Y
116.	Set school lunch lmt-250% poverty	Y
117.	$75m for youth work projects	Y
118.	Allow Angolan military assistance	N
119.	Suspend defense payments for abuse	N
120.	Drop SS COLAs/$12b tax increase	N
121.	Approve $1.5b for 21 MX missiles	N
122.	Emergency farm credit/revisions	Y
123.	Duty on Taiwan/Hong Kong/S Korea	N
124.	Limit steel imports to 17%	N
125.	Cut $ to schools that bar prayer	Y
126.	$50b-taxes; cut Medicare/spending	Y
127.	Limit Pershing II/cruise in Europe	N
128.	Delete $7.1b for 34 B-1 bombers	N
129.	Bar purchase of Sergeant York guns	N
130.	El Salvador military/economic aid	Y
131.	Bar mining of Nicaraguan waters	Y
132.	Physician fee freeze for Medicare	Y
133.	$49b in "sin"/phone/insurance taxes	Y
134.	Allow sale of Conrail	N
135.	Equal Rights Amendment	N
136.	Authorize Marines in Lebanon	N
137.	Eminent domain for coal companies	N
138.	Prohibit EPA clean air sanctions	N
139.	SS retirement age increase/reforms	Y
140.	Auto domestic content requirement	N
141.	Delete jobs program funding	N
142.	Highway-gas tax bill	Y

BENNETT, CHARLES E. (continued)
143. Cut $5b from defense for Medicare N   144. Emergency housing aid of $1b Y

Presidential Support Score: 1991 - 33%   1990 - 33%

JAMES, CRAIG -- Florida 4th District [Republican]. Counties of Clay (pt.), Duval (pt.), Flagler, Putnam (pt.), St. Johns and Volusia. Prior Terms: 1989-92. Born: May 5, 1941; Augusta, GA. Education: Stetson University (B.S., J.D.). Military Service: U.S. Army National Guard and Army Reserves. Occupation: Lawyer; senior partner, James, Zimmerman and Paul.

1. Protection to Haitian refugees	N	30. Textile import quotas-veto override	N
2. Raise tax on wealthy; lower others	N	31. Abortion service for military abroad	N
3. Investigate Reagan hostage delay	N	32. Limits on high income farmers	N
4. Campaign finance revisions	Y	33. Family medical leave-veto override	N
5. Unpaid leave to care for children	Y	34. Req submission of balanced budget	N
6. Restrict NEA use of funds	Y	35. Balanced budget amendment	Y
7. Bar race-bias claim/habeas corpus	N	36. Amendment to ban flag desecration	Y
8. Ban race as death sentence factor	Y	37. Reauthorize Amtrak-veto override	N
9. Exceptions to exclusionary rule	Y	38. Retraining aid for coal miners	N
10. Allow sale of assault weapons	Y	39. Suspend El Salvador military aid	N
11. Life in prison/abolish death penalty	N	40. Expand child care aid/tax credit	Y
12. Req conspiracy-price fixing cases	Y	41. Raise House salary/omit honoraria	N
13. Unemployment benefits extension	N	42. Toughen oil-spill liability	Y
14. Tissue use of aborted fetuses	N	43. Restitution to Japanese interned	N
15. Bar replacement of union strikers	N	44. Protect Chinese & C.A. nationals	N
16. Hold foreign aid at $15b for '92	N	45. Abortion $ for rape/incest cases	N
17. Restore space station funding	Y	46. Allow religious schools to bar gays	Y
18. Civil Rights Act of 1991	N	47. Bar broadcaster fairness doctrine	Y
19. Unlimited damages-discrimination	N	48. Bar cap gains cut/reinstate IRA	N
20. Eliminate funds for supercollider	Y	49. Bar unions equal voice in pension	Y
21. Terminate SDI except for research	N	50. Bar assembly of chemical weapons	N
22. Req 7-day handgun waiting period	Y	51. Ban plutonium/uranium production	N
23. Provide $30b for failed S&Ls	N	52. Cap MX missile deployment at 50	N
24. Allow use of force against Iraq	Y	53. Allow $3b for 2 stealth bombers	Y
25. Allow $15b in foreign aid for '91	N	54. Publish bio-warfare experiments	N
26. Revise & extend legal immigration	N	55. Raise minimum wage-veto override	N
27. Suspend aid to Angolan rebels	N	56. Bar transfer of FS-X technology	N
28. Democratic tax plan proposals	N	57. Cut defense and raise domestic $	N
29. Cut defense 5% across the board	N	58. Uniform poll closing in 48 states	N

Presidential Support Score: 1991 - 66%   1990 - 58%

McCOLLUM, BILL -- Florida 5th District [Republican]. Counties of Lake (pt.), Orange (pt.) and Seminole. Prior Terms: 1981-92. Born: July 12, 1944; Brooksville, FL. Education: University of Florida (B.A., J.D.). Military Service: U.S. Navy, 1969. Occupation: Attorney, Pitts, Eubanks and Ross, P.A.

1. Protection to Haitian refugees	N	16. Hold foreign aid at $15b for '92	Y
2. Raise tax on wealthy; lower others	N	17. Restore space station funding	Y
3. Investigate Reagan hostage delay	N	18. Civil Rights Act of 1991	N
4. Campaign finance revisions	N	19. Unlimited damages-discrimination	N
5. Unpaid leave to care for children	N	20. Eliminate funds for supercollider	N
6. Restrict NEA use of funds	Y	21. Terminate SDI except for research	N
7. Bar race-bias claim/habeas corpus	Y	22. Req 7-day handgun waiting period	N
8. Ban race as death sentence factor	Y	23. Provide $30b for failed S&Ls	Y
9. Exceptions to exclusionary rule	Y	24. Allow use of force against Iraq	Y
10. Allow sale of assault weapons	Y	25. Allow $15b in foreign aid for '91	N
11. Life in prison/abolish death penalty	N	26. Revise & extend legal immigration	Y
12. Req conspiracy-price fixing cases	Y	27. Suspend aid to Angolan rebels	N
13. Unemployment benefits extension	N	28. Democratic tax plan proposals	N
14. Tissue use of aborted fetuses	N	29. Cut defense 5% across the board	N
15. Bar replacement of union strikers	N	30. Textile import quotas-veto override	N

McCOLLUM, BILL (continued)

31. Abortion service for military abroad	N
32. Limits on high income farmers	Y
33. Family medical leave-veto override	N
34. Req submission of balanced budget	N
35. Balanced budget amendment	Y
36. Amendment to ban flag desecration	Y
37. Reauthorize Amtrak-veto override	N
38. Retraining aid for coal miners	N
39. Suspend El Salvador military aid	N
40. Expand child care aid/tax credit	N
41. Raise House salary/omit honoraria	Y
42. Toughen oil-spill liability	N
43. Restitution to Japanese interned	N
44. Protect Chinese & C.A. nationals	N
45. Abortion $ for rape/incest cases	N
46. Allow religious schools to bar gays	Y
47. Bar broadcaster fairness doctrine	N
48. Bar cap gains cut/reinstate IRA	N
49. Bar unions equal voice in pension	Y
50. Bar assembly of chemical weapons	N
51. Ban plutonium/uranium production	N
52. Cap MX missile deployment at 50	N
53. Allow $3b for 2 stealth bombers	Y
54. Publish bio-warfare experiments	N
55. Raise minimum wage-veto override	N
56. Bar transfer of FS-X technology	N
57. Cut defense and raise domestic $	N
58. Uniform poll closing in 48 states	N
59. Req foreign investment disclosure	Y
60. Textile import quotas-veto override	N
61. Bar abortion funding in Wash, DC	Y
62. Notify spouses of AIDS+ carriers	Y
63. Seize conveyance-drug trafficking	N
64. South Africa sanctions	?
65. 60 days' notice of plant closings	N
66. Close unneeded military bases	Y
67. Keep welfare reform within $2.8b	N
68. Allow children housing exclusion	Y
69. Shift $400m of NASA to homeless	N
70. Cap Medicare patients' liability	Y
71. Prohibit employee polygraph testing	N
72. Allow CIA to fund Contras	Y
73. Revise unfair trade practices	N
74. Focus SDI on accidental launch	N
75. Bar Air Force $ for MX missile	N
76. Allow "real" increase in defense	Y
77. Troop reduction in Europe of 50%	N
78. Ban nuclear tests above 1 kiloton	N
79. Ban anti-satellite missile tests	N
80. Observe certain limits of SALT II	N
81. Restore four Civil Rights laws	N
82. Prohibit aliens as strikebreakers	N
83. Allow military malpractice suits	Y
84. Approval of $36m in Contra aid	Y
85. $18b deficit reduction compromise	N
86. Welfare reform of $5.7b for 5 years	N
87. Raise taxes $12b/cut spending $3b	N

88. Board to assess occupational risk	N
89. Balanced budget by '93-via targets	Y
90. Bar licensing of two nuclear plants	N
91. Remove victims compensation cap	N
92. Catastrophic health insurance	Y
93. Ban airline smoking-2 hours or less	Y
94. $1b/two year aid for the homeless	N
95. Bar non-unions in union companies	N
96. Increase FSLIC rescue to $15b	N
97. Impose quotas to lower trade deficit	N
98. Reduce discretionary budget 21%	Y
99. Immigration reform/alien amnesty	N
100. South Africa sanctions-veto override	N
101. Tax overhaul to revise income tax	Y
102. Use of military in drug war	N
103. Delete 12 MX/add conventional wpn	N
104. Raise speed limit to 65 mph	Y
105. Require Pentagon to buy US goods	N
106. AIDS insurance non-discrimination	N
107. Prohibit Saudi arms sales	Y
108. Ease Gun Control Act of 1968	Y
109. Bar interstate handgun transport	N
110. Make company emissions known	N
111. Allow toxic victims to sue in fed ct	N
112. Superfund waste cleanup of $10b	N
113. 90 days notice of plant closings	N
114. $20b in Medicare cuts/tax increases	X
115. Spending cuts and tax increases	N
116. Set school lunch lmt-250% poverty	Y
117. $75m for youth work projects	N
118. Allow Angolan military assistance	Y
119. Suspend defense payments for abuse	N
120. Drop SS COLAs/$12b tax increase	N
121. Approve $1.5b for 21 MX missiles	Y
122. Emergency farm credit/revisions	N
123. Duty on Taiwan/Hong Kong/S Korea	N
124. Limit steel imports to 17%	N
125. Cut $ to schools that bar prayer	Y
126. $50b-taxes; cut Medicare/spending	N
127. Limit Pershing II/cruise in Europe	N
128. Delete $7.1b for 34 B-1 bombers	N
129. Bar purchase of Sergeant York guns	N
130. El Salvador military/economic aid	Y
131. Bar mining of Nicaraguan waters	N
132. Physician fee freeze for Medicare	Y
133. $49b in "sin"/phone/insurance taxes	N
134. Allow sale of Conrail	Y
135. Equal Rights Amendment	N
136. Authorize Marines in Lebanon	Y
137. Eminent domain for coal companies	Y
138. Prohibit EPA clean air sanctions	Y
139. SS retirement age increase/reforms	Y
140. Auto domestic content requirement	N
141. Delete jobs program funding	Y
142. Highway-gas tax bill	N
143. Cut $5b from defense for Medicare	N
144. Emergency housing aid of $1b	Y

Presidential Support Score: 1991 - 76% 1990 - 74%

STEARNS, CLIFFORD B. -- Florida 6th District [Republican]. Counties of Alachua, Citrus, Hernando, Lake (pt.), Marion, Pasco (pt.), Putnam (pt.) and Sumter. Prior Terms: 1989-92. Born: April 16, 1941; Washington, DC. Education: George Washington University (B.S.).

STEARNS, CLIFFORD B. (continued)
Military Service: U.S. Air Force. Occupation: Senior negotiator, Columbia Broadcasting System; advertising firm account executive; motel management company president.

1.	Protection to Haitian refugees	N	30.	Textile import quotas-veto override	N
2.	Raise tax on wealthy; lower others	N	31.	Abortion service for military abroad	N
3.	Investigate Reagan hostage delay	N	32.	Limits on high income farmers	Y
4.	Campaign finance revisions	N	33.	Family medical leave-veto override	N
5.	Unpaid leave to care for children	N	34.	Req submission of balanced budget	Y
6.	Restrict NEA use of funds	Y	35.	Balanced budget amendment	Y
7.	Bar race-bias claim/habeas corpus	Y	36.	Amendment to ban flag desecration	Y
8.	Ban race as death sentence factor	Y	37.	Reauthorize Amtrak-veto override	N
9.	Exceptions to exclusionary rule	Y	38.	Retraining aid for coal miners	N
10.	Allow sale of assault weapons	Y	39.	Suspend El Salvador military aid	N
11.	Life in prison/abolish death penalty	N	40.	Expand child care aid/tax credit	N
12.	Req conspiracy-price fixing cases	Y	41.	Raise House salary/omit honoraria	N
13.	Unemployment benefits extension	Y	42.	Toughen oil-spill liability	N
14.	Tissue use of aborted fetuses	N	43.	Restitution to Japanese interned	N
15.	Bar replacement of union strikers	N	44.	Protect Chinese & C.A. nationals	N
16.	Hold foreign aid at $15b for '92	N	45.	Abortion $ for rape/incest cases	N
17.	Restore space station funding	Y	46.	Allow religious schools to bar gays	Y
18.	Civil Rights Act of 1991	N	47.	Bar broadcaster fairness doctrine	Y
19.	Unlimited damages-discrimination	N	48.	Bar cap gains cut/reinstate IRA	N
20.	Eliminate funds for supercollider	N	49.	Bar unions equal voice in pension	Y
21.	Terminate SDI except for research	N	50.	Bar assembly of chemical weapons	N
22.	Req 7-day handgun waiting period	Y	51.	Ban plutonium/uranium production	N
23.	Provide $30b for failed S&Ls	N	52.	Cap MX missile deployment at 50	N
24.	Allow use of force against Iraq	Y	53.	Allow $3b for 2 stealth bombers	N
25.	Allow $15b in foreign aid for '91	Y	54.	Publish bio-warfare experiments	N
26.	Revise & extend legal immigration	N	55.	Raise minimum wage-veto override	N
27.	Suspend aid to Angolan rebels	N	56.	Bar transfer of FS-X technology	N
28.	Democratic tax plan proposals	N	57.	Cut defense and raise domestic $	N
29.	Cut defense 5% across the board	N	58.	Uniform poll closing in 48 states	N

Presidential Support Score: 1991 - 71%   1990 - 71%

GIBBONS, SAM -- Florida 7th District [Democrat]. County of Hillsborough (pt.). Prior Terms: 1963-92. Born: January 20, 1920; Tampa, FL. Education: University of Florida (J.D.). Military Service: U.S. Army, WW II. Occupation: Attorney; Florida representative (1952-58); Florida senator (1958-62).

1.	Protection to Haitian refugees	Y	25.	Allow $15b in foreign aid for '91	N
2.	Raise tax on wealthy; lower others	Y	26.	Revise & extend legal immigration	Y
3.	Investigate Reagan hostage delay	Y	27.	Suspend aid to Angolan rebels	Y
4.	Campaign finance revisions	Y	28.	Democratic tax plan proposals	Y
5.	Unpaid leave to care for children	Y	29.	Cut defense 5% across the board	N
6.	Restrict NEA use of funds	Y	30.	Textile import quotas-veto override	N
7.	Bar race-bias claim/habeas corpus	N	31.	Abortion service for military abroad	Y
8.	Ban race as death sentence factor	N	32.	Limits on high income farmers	Y
9.	Exceptions to exclusionary rule	N	33.	Family medical leave-veto override	Y
10.	Allow sale of assault weapons	N	34.	Req submission of balanced budget	Y
11.	Life in prison/abolish death penalty	N	35.	Balanced budget amendment	Y
12.	Req conspiracy-price fixing cases	N	36.	Amendment to ban flag desecration	N
13.	Unemployment benefits extension	Y	37.	Reauthorize Amtrak-veto override	Y
14.	Tissue use of aborted fetuses	Y	38.	Retraining aid for coal miners	Y
15.	Bar replacement of union strikers	N	39.	Suspend El Salvador military aid	Y
16.	Hold foreign aid at $15b for '92	Y	40.	Expand child care aid/tax credit	Y
17.	Restore space station funding	Y	41.	Raise House salary/omit honoraria	Y
18.	Civil Rights Act of 1991	Y	42.	Toughen oil-spill liability	Y
19.	Unlimited damages-discrimination	Y	43.	Restitution to Japanese interned	Y
20.	Eliminate funds for supercollider	N	44.	Protect Chinese & C.A. nationals	Y
21.	Terminate SDI except for research	N	45.	Abortion $ for rape/incest cases	N
22.	Req 7-day handgun waiting period	Y	46.	Allow religious schools to bar gays	Y
23.	Provide $30b for failed S&Ls	Y	47.	Bar broadcaster fairness doctrine	N
24.	Allow use of force against Iraq	N	48.	Bar cap gains cut/reinstate IRA	Y

GIBBONS, SAM (continued)

49. Bar unions equal voice in pension	Y	97. Impose quotas to lower trade deficit	N
50. Bar assembly of chemical weapons	Y	98. Reduce discretionary budget 21%	Y
51. Ban plutonium/uranium production	Y	99. Immigration reform/alien amnesty	Y
52. Cap MX missile deployment at 50	Y	100. South Africa sanctions-veto override	Y
53. Allow $3b for 2 stealth bombers	N	101. Tax overhaul to revise income tax	Y
54. Publish bio-warfare experiments	Y	102. Use of military in drug war	N
55. Raise minimum wage-veto override	Y	103. Delete 12 MX/add conventional wpn	Y
56. Bar transfer of FS-X technology	?	104. Raise speed limit to 65 mph	N
57. Cut defense and raise domestic $	N	105. Require Pentagon to buy US goods	N
58. Uniform poll closing in 48 states	Y	106. AIDS insurance non-discrimination	Y
59. Req foreign investment disclosure	N	107. Prohibit Saudi arms sales	Y
60. Textile import quotas-veto override	N	108. Ease Gun Control Act of 1968	N
61. Bar abortion funding in Wash, DC	Y	109. Bar interstate handgun transport	Y
62. Notify spouses of AIDS+ carriers	Y	110. Make company emissions known	Y
63. Seize conveyance-drug trafficking	Y	111. Allow toxic victims to sue in fed ct	Y
64. South Africa sanctions	Y	112. Superfund waste cleanup of $10b	N
65. 60 days' notice of plant closings	Y	113. 90 days notice of plant closings	N
66. Close unneeded military bases	Y	114. $20b in Medicare cuts/tax increases	Y
67. Keep welfare reform within $2.8b	N	115. Spending cuts and tax increases	N
68. Allow children housing exclusion	N	116. Set school lunch lmt-250% poverty	Y
69. Shift $400m of NASA to homeless	N	117. $75m for youth work projects	Y
70. Cap Medicare patients' liability	Y	118. Allow Angolan military assistance	N
71. Prohibit employee polygraph testing	Y	119. Suspend defense payments for abuse	Y
72. Allow CIA to fund Contras	N	120. Drop SS COLAs/$12b tax increase	Y
73. Revise unfair trade practices	Y	121. Approve $1.5b for 21 MX missiles	N
74. Focus SDI on accidental launch	Y	122. Emergency farm credit/revisions	N
75. Bar Air Force $ for MX missile	N	123. Duty on Taiwan/Hong Kong/S Korea	N
76. Allow "real" increase in defense	?	124. Limit steel imports to 17%	?
77. Troop reduction in Europe of 50%	N	125. Cut $ to schools that bar prayer	Y
78. Ban nuclear tests above 1 kiloton	Y	126. $50b-taxes; cut Medicare/spending	Y
79. Ban anti-satellite missile tests	Y	127. Limit Pershing II/cruise in Europe	?
80. Observe certain limits of SALT II	?	128. Delete $7.1b for 34 B-1 bombers	Y
81. Restore four Civil Rights laws	Y	129. Bar purchase of Sergeant York guns	N
82. Prohibit aliens as strikebreakers	Y	130. El Salvador military/economic aid	N
83. Allow military malpractice suits	Y	131. Bar mining of Nicaraguan waters	Y
84. Approval of $36m in Contra aid	Y	132. Physician fee freeze for Medicare	N
85. $18b deficit reduction compromise	Y	133. $49b in "sin"/phone/insurance taxes	Y
86. Welfare reform of $5.7b for 5 years	Y	134. Allow sale of Conrail	N
87. Raise taxes $12b/cut spending $3b	Y	135. Equal Rights Amendment	Y
88. Board to assess occupational risk	Y	136. Authorize Marines in Lebanon	N
89. Balanced budget by '93-via targets	Y	137. Eminent domain for coal companies	?
90. Bar licensing of two nuclear plants	Y	138. Prohibit EPA clean air sanctions	Y
91. Remove victims compensation cap	N	139. SS retirement age increase/reforms	Y
92. Catastrophic health insurance	Y	140. Auto domestic content requirement	N
93. Ban airline smoking-2 hours or less	Y	141. Delete jobs program funding	N
94. $1b/two year aid for the homeless	Y	142. Highway-gas tax bill	Y
95. Bar non-unions in union companies	N	143. Cut $5b from defense for Medicare	N
96. Increase FSLIC rescue to $15b	N	144. Emergency housing aid of $1b	N

Presidential Support Score: 1991 - 41%   1990 - 32%

YOUNG, C. W. (BILL) -- Florida 8th District [Republican]. County of Pinellas (pt.). Prior Terms: 1971-92. Born: December 16, 1930; Harmarville, PA. Military Service: National Guard, 1948-57. Occupation: Florida senator (1960, 1964-70).

1. Protection to Haitian refugees	N	9. Exceptions to exclusionary rule	Y
2. Raise tax on wealthy; lower others	N	10. Allow sale of assault weapons	N
3. Investigate Reagan hostage delay	N	11. Life in prison/abolish death penalty	N
4. Campaign finance revisions	Y	12. Req conspiracy-price fixing cases	Y
5. Unpaid leave to care for children	N	13. Unemployment benefits extension	Y
6. Restrict NEA use of funds	Y	14. Tissue use of aborted fetuses	N
7. Bar race-bias claim/habeas corpus	N	15. Bar replacement of union strikers	N
8. Ban race as death sentence factor	Y	16. Hold foreign aid at $15b for '92	N

YOUNG, C. W. (continued)

17. Restore space station funding	Y	80. Observe certain limits of SALT II	N
18. Civil Rights Act of 1991	N	81. Restore four Civil Rights laws	N
19. Unlimited damages-discrimination	Y	82. Prohibit aliens as strikebreakers	N
20. Eliminate funds for supercollider	N	83. Allow military malpractice suits	Y
21. Terminate SDI except for research	N	84. Approval of $36m in Contra aid	Y
22. Req 7-day handgun waiting period	Y	85. $18b deficit reduction compromise	N
23. Provide $30b for failed S&Ls	N	86. Welfare reform of $5.7b for 5 years	N
24. Allow use of force against Iraq	Y	87. Raise taxes $12b/cut spending $3b	N
25. Allow $15b in foreign aid for '91	N	88. Board to assess occupational risk	N
26. Revise & extend legal immigration	N	89. Balanced budget by '93-via targets	N
27. Suspend aid to Angolan rebels	N	90. Bar licensing of two nuclear plants	N
28. Democratic tax plan proposals	N	91. Remove victims compensation cap	N
29. Cut defense 5% across the board	N	92. Catastrophic health insurance	Y
30. Textile import quotas-veto override	N	93. Ban airline smoking-2 hours or less	Y
31. Abortion service for military abroad	N	94. $1b/two year aid for the homeless	Y
32. Limits on high income farmers	Y	95. Bar non-unions in union companies	N
33. Family medical leave-veto override	N	96. Increase FSLIC rescue to $15b	Y
34. Req submission of balanced budget	N	97. Impose quotas to lower trade deficit	N
35. Balanced budget amendment	Y	98. Reduce discretionary budget 21%	Y
36. Amendment to ban flag desecration	Y	99. Immigration reform/alien amnesty	N
37. Reauthorize Amtrak-veto override	N	100. South Africa sanctions-veto override	N
38. Retraining aid for coal miners	N	101. Tax overhaul to revise income tax	Y
39. Suspend El Salvador military aid	N	102. Use of military in drug war	N
40. Expand child care aid/tax credit	Y	103. Delete 12 MX/add conventional wpn	N
41. Raise House salary/omit honoraria	Y	104. Raise speed limit to 65 mph	Y
42. Toughen oil-spill liability	N	105. Require Pentagon to buy US goods	N
43. Restitution to Japanese interned	N	106. AIDS insurance non-discrimination	N
44. Protect Chinese & C.A. nationals	N	107. Prohibit Saudi arms sales	Y
45. Abortion $ for rape/incest cases	N	108. Ease Gun Control Act of 1968	Y
46. Allow religious schools to bar gays	Y	109. Bar interstate handgun transport	Y
47. Bar broadcaster fairness doctrine	Y	110. Make company emissions known	N
48. Bar cap gains cut/reinstate IRA	N	111. Allow toxic victims to sue in fed ct	N
49. Bar unions equal voice in pension	Y	112. Superfund waste cleanup of $10b	Y
50. Bar assembly of chemical weapons	N	113. 90 days notice of plant closings	N
51. Ban plutonium/uranium production	N	114. $20b in Medicare cuts/tax increases	N
52. Cap MX missile deployment at 50	N	115. Spending cuts and tax increases	N
53. Allow $3b for 2 stealth bombers	Y	116. Set school lunch lmt-250% poverty	N
54. Publish bio-warfare experiments	N	117. $75m for youth work projects	N
55. Raise minimum wage-veto override	N	118. Allow Angolan military assistance	Y
56. Bar transfer of FS-X technology	N	119. Suspend defense payments for abuse	N
57. Cut defense and raise domestic $	N	120. Drop SS COLAs/$12b tax increase	N
58. Uniform poll closing in 48 states	?	121. Approve $1.5b for 21 MX missiles	Y
59. Req foreign investment disclosure	Y	122. Emergency farm credit/revisions	N
60. Textile import quotas-veto override	N	123. Duty on Taiwan/Hong Kong/S Korea	N
61. Bar abortion funding in Wash, DC	Y	124. Limit steel imports to 17%	Y
62. Notify spouses of AIDS+ carriers	Y	125. Cut $ to schools that bar prayer	Y
63. Seize conveyance-drug trafficking	Y	126. $50b-taxes; cut Medicare/spending	N
64. South Africa sanctions	N	127. Limit Pershing II/cruise in Europe	N
65. 60 days' notice of plant closings	N	128. Delete $7.1b for 34 B-1 bombers	N
66. Close unneeded military bases	N	129. Bar purchase of Sergeant York guns	N
67. Keep welfare reform within $2.8b	Y	130. El Salvador military/economic aid	Y
68. Allow children housing exclusion	Y	131. Bar mining of Nicaraguan waters	N
69. Shift $400m of NASA to homeless	N	132. Physician fee freeze for Medicare	N
70. Cap Medicare patients' liability	Y	133. $49b in "sin"/phone/insurance taxes	N
71. Prohibit employee polygraph testing	X	134. Allow sale of Conrail	N
72. Allow CIA to fund Contras	Y	135. Equal Rights Amendment	N
73. Revise unfair trade practices	Y	136. Authorize Marines in Lebanon	N
74. Focus SDI on accidental launch	N	137. Eminent domain for coal companies	Y
75. Bar Air Force $ for MX missile	N	138. Prohibit EPA clean air sanctions	Y
76. Allow "real" increase in defense	Y	139. SS retirement age increase/reforms	Y
77. Troop reduction in Europe of 50%	N	140. Auto domestic content requirement	N
78. Ban nuclear tests above 1 kiloton	N	141. Delete jobs program funding	Y
79. Ban anti-satellite missile tests	N	142. Highway-gas tax bill	N

YOUNG, C. W. (continued)

143. Cut $5b from defense for Medicare N   144. Emergency housing aid of $1b   Y

Presidential Support Score: 1991 - 73%   1990 - 68%

BILIRAKIS, MICHAEL -- Florida 9th District [Republican]. Counties of Hillsborough (pt.), Pasco (pt.) and Pinellas (pt.). Prior Terms: 1983-92. Born: July 16, 1930; Tarpon Springs, FL. Education: University of Pittsburgh (B.S.); University of Florida (J.D.). Military Service: U.S. Air Force, 1951-55. Occupation: Attorney; petroleum engineer; geophysical engineer; government contract negotiator; steel worker; county and municipal judge.

1. Protection to Haitian refugees	N	54. Publish bio-warfare experiments	N
2. Raise tax on wealthy; lower others	N	55. Raise minimum wage-veto override	N
3. Investigate Reagan hostage delay	N	56. Bar transfer of FS-X technology	N
4. Campaign finance revisions	Y	57. Cut defense and raise domestic $	N
5. Unpaid leave to care for children	N	58. Uniform poll closing in 48 states	N
6. Restrict NEA use of funds	Y	59. Req foreign investment disclosure	N
7. Bar race-bias claim/habeas corpus	#	60. Textile import quotas-veto override	N
8. Ban race as death sentence factor	#	61. Bar abortion funding in Wash, DC	Y
9. Exceptions to exclusionary rule	Y	62. Notify spouses of AIDS+ carriers	Y
10. Allow sale of assault weapons	Y	63. Seize conveyance-drug trafficking	Y
11. Life in prison/abolish death penalty	N	64. South Africa sanctions	N
12. Req conspiracy-price fixing cases	Y	65. 60 days' notice of plant closings	N
13. Unemployment benefits extension	N	66. Close unneeded military bases	Y
14. Tissue use of aborted fetuses	N	67. Keep welfare reform within $2.8b	Y
15. Bar replacement of union strikers	N	68. Allow children housing exclusion	Y
16. Hold foreign aid at $15b for '92	Y	69. Shift $400m of NASA to homeless	N
17. Restore space station funding	Y	70. Cap Medicare patients' liability	Y
18. Civil Rights Act of 1991	N	71. Prohibit employee polygraph testing	N
19. Unlimited damages-discrimination	N	72. Allow CIA to fund Contras	Y
20. Eliminate funds for supercollider	Y	73. Revise unfair trade practices	N
21. Terminate SDI except for research	N	74. Focus SDI on accidental launch	N
22. Req 7-day handgun waiting period	Y	75. Bar Air Force $ for MX missile	N
23. Provide $30b for failed S&Ls	Y	76. Allow "real" increase in defense	Y
24. Allow use of force against Iraq	Y	77. Troop reduction in Europe of 50%	N
25. Allow $15b in foreign aid for '91	N	78. Ban nuclear tests above 1 kiloton	N
26. Revise & extend legal immigration	N	79. Ban anti-satellite missile tests	N
27. Suspend aid to Angolan rebels	N	80. Observe certain limits of SALT II	N
28. Democratic tax plan proposals	N	81. Restore four Civil Rights laws	N
29. Cut defense 5% across the board	N	82. Prohibit aliens as strikebreakers	N
30. Textile import quotas-veto override	N	83. Allow military malpractice suits	?
31. Abortion service for military abroad	?	84. Approval of $36m in Contra aid	Y
32. Limits on high income farmers	N	85. $18b deficit reduction compromise	Y
33. Family medical leave-veto override	N	86. Welfare reform of $5.7b for 5 years	N
34. Req submission of balanced budget	N	87. Raise taxes $12b/cut spending $3b	N
35. Balanced budget amendment	Y	88. Board to assess occupational risk	N
36. Amendment to ban flag desecration	Y	89. Balanced budget by '93-via targets	N
37. Reauthorize Amtrak-veto override	N	90. Bar licensing of two nuclear plants	N
38. Retraining aid for coal miners	N	91. Remove victims compensation cap	N
39. Suspend El Salvador military aid	N	92. Catastrophic health insurance	N
40. Expand child care aid/tax credit	Y	93. Ban airline smoking-2 hours or less	N
41. Raise House salary/omit honoraria	Y	94. $1b/two year aid for the homeless	N
42. Toughen oil-spill liability	Y	95. Bar non-unions in union companies	N
43. Restitution to Japanese interned	N	96. Increase FSLIC rescue to $15b	Y
44. Protect Chinese & C.A. nationals	N	97. Impose quotas to lower trade deficit	N
45. Abortion $ for rape/incest cases	N	98. Reduce discretionary budget 21%	Y
46. Allow religious schools to bar gays	Y	99. Immigration reform/alien amnesty	N
47. Bar broadcaster fairness doctrine	N	100. South Africa sanctions-veto override	N
48. Bar cap gains cut/reinstate IRA	N	101. Tax overhaul to revise income tax	Y
49. Bar unions equal voice in pension	Y	102. Use of military in drug war	Y
50. Bar assembly of chemical weapons	N	103. Delete 12 MX/add conventional wpn	N
51. Ban plutonium/uranium production	N	104. Raise speed limit to 65 mph	Y
52. Cap MX missile deployment at 50	N	105. Require Pentagon to buy US goods	N
53. Allow $3b for 2 stealth bombers	Y	106. AIDS insurance non-discrimination	N

BILIRAKIS, MICHAEL (continued)

107. Prohibit Saudi arms sales	Y	
108. Ease Gun Control Act of 1968	Y	
109. Bar interstate handgun transport	N	
110. Make company emissions known	N	
111. Allow toxic victims to sue in fed ct	N	
112. Superfund waste cleanup of $10b	Y	
113. 90 days notice of plant closings	N	
114. $20b in Medicare cuts/tax increases	N	
115. Spending cuts and tax increases	N	
116. Set school lunch lmt-250% poverty	Y	
117. $75m for youth work projects	N	
118. Allow Angolan military assistance	Y	
119. Suspend defense payments for abuse	N	
120. Drop SS COLAs/$12b tax increase	N	
121. Approve $1.5b for 21 MX missiles	Y	
122. Emergency farm credit/revisions	N	
123. Duty on Taiwan/Hong Kong/S Korea	N	

124. Limit steel imports to 17%	Y
125. Cut $ to schools that bar prayer	Y
126. $50b-taxes; cut Medicare/spending	N
127. Limit Pershing II/cruise in Europe	N
128. Delete $7.1b for 34 B-1 bombers	N
129. Bar purchase of Sergeant York guns	Y
130. El Salvador military/economic aid	Y
131. Bar mining of Nicaraguan waters	Y
132. Physician fee freeze for Medicare	Y
133. $49b in "sin"/phone/insurance taxes	N
134. Allow sale of Conrail	Y
135. Equal Rights Amendment	N
136. Authorize Marines in Lebanon	Y
137. Eminent domain for coal companies	Y
138. Prohibit EPA clean air sanctions	Y
139. SS retirement age increase/reforms	Y

Presidential Support Score: 1991 - 78%   1990 - 51%

IRELAND, ANDY -- Florida 10th District [Republican]. Counties of DeSoto, Hardee, Manatee, Osceola (pt.) and Polk. Prior Terms: 1977-92. Born: August 23, 1930; Cincinnati, OH. Education: Yale University (B.S.); Columbia University; Louisiana State University. Occupation: City commissioner

1. Protection to Haitian refugees	N	
2. Raise tax on wealthy; lower others	N	
3. Investigate Reagan hostage delay	?	
4. Campaign finance revisions	N	
5. Unpaid leave to care for children	N	
6. Restrict NEA use of funds	Y	
7. Bar race-bias claim/habeas corpus	Y	
8. Ban race as death sentence factor	Y	
9. Exceptions to exclusionary rule	Y	
10. Allow sale of assault weapons	Y	
11. Life in prison/abolish death penalty	N	
12. Req conspiracy-price fixing cases	Y	
13. Unemployment benefits extension	N	
14. Tissue use of aborted fetuses	N	
15. Bar replacement of union strikers	N	
16. Hold foreign aid at $15b for '92	N	
17. Restore space station funding	Y	
18. Civil Rights Act of 1991	N	
19. Unlimited damages-discrimination	N	
20. Eliminate funds for supercollider	N	
21. Terminate SDI except for research	N	
22. Req 7-day handgun waiting period	N	
23. Provide $30b for failed S&Ls	Y	
24. Allow use of force against Iraq	Y	
25. Allow $15b in foreign aid for '91	N	
26. Revise & extend legal immigration	Y	
27. Suspend aid to Angolan rebels	N	
28. Democratic tax plan proposals	N	
29. Cut defense 5% across the board	N	
30. Textile import quotas-veto override	N	
31. Abortion service for military abroad	N	
32. Limits on high income farmers	N	
33. Family medical leave-veto override	N	
34. Req submission of balanced budget	N	
35. Balanced budget amendment	Y	
36. Amendment to ban flag desecration	Y	
37. Reauthorize Amtrak-veto override	N	
38. Retraining aid for coal miners	N	

39. Suspend El Salvador military aid	N
40. Expand child care aid/tax credit	N
41. Raise House salary/omit honoraria	Y
42. Toughen oil-spill liability	N
43. Restitution to Japanese interned	N
44. Protect Chinese & C.A. nationals	N
45. Abortion $ for rape/incest cases	N
46. Allow religious schools to bar gays	Y
47. Bar broadcaster fairness doctrine	N
48. Bar cap gains cut/reinstate IRA	N
49. Bar unions equal voice in pension	Y
50. Bar assembly of chemical weapons	N
51. Ban plutonium/uranium production	N
52. Cap MX missile deployment at 50	N
53. Allow $3b for 2 stealth bombers	N
54. Publish bio-warfare experiments	N
55. Raise minimum wage-veto override	N
56. Bar transfer of FS-X technology	N
57. Cut defense and raise domestic $	N
58. Uniform poll closing in 48 states	N
59. Req foreign investment disclosure	N
60. Textile import quotas-veto override	N
61. Bar abortion funding in Wash, DC	Y
62. Notify spouses of AIDS+ carriers	Y
63. Seize conveyance-drug trafficking	Y
64. South Africa sanctions	N
65. 60 days' notice of plant closings	N
66. Close unneeded military bases	Y
67. Keep welfare reform within $2.8b	Y
68. Allow children housing exclusion	Y
69. Shift $400m of NASA to homeless	N
70. Cap Medicare patients' liability	Y
71. Prohibit employee polygraph testing	N
72. Allow CIA to fund Contras	Y
73. Revise unfair trade practices	N
74. Focus SDI on accidental launch	N
75. Bar Air Force $ for MX missile	N
76. Allow "real" increase in defense	Y

IRELAND, ANDY (continued)

77. Troop reduction in Europe of 50%	N
78. Ban nuclear tests above 1 kiloton	N
79. Ban anti-satellite missile tests	N
80. Observe certain limits of SALT II	N
81. Restore four Civil Rights laws	N
82. Prohibit aliens as strikebreakers	N
83. Allow military malpractice suits	N
84. Approval of $36m in Contra aid	Y
85. $18b deficit reduction compromise	N
86. Welfare reform of $5.7b for 5 years	N
87. Raise taxes $12b/cut spending $3b	N
88. Board to assess occupational risk	N
89. Balanced budget by '93-via targets	Y
90. Bar licensing of two nuclear plants	N
91. Remove victims compensation cap	N
92. Catastrophic health insurance	N
93. Ban airline smoking-2 hours or less	Y
94. $1b/two year aid for the homeless	N
95. Bar non-unions in union companies	N
96. Increase FSLIC rescue to $15b	N
97. Impose quotas to lower trade deficit	N
98. Reduce discretionary budget 21%	Y
99. Immigration reform/alien amnesty	N
100. South Africa sanctions-veto override	Y
101. Tax overhaul to revise income tax	Y
102. Use of military in drug war	Y
103. Delete 12 MX/add conventional wpn	N
104. Raise speed limit to 65 mph	Y
105. Require Pentagon to buy US goods	?
106. AIDS insurance non-discrimination	N
107. Prohibit Saudi arms sales	Y
108. Ease Gun Control Act of 1968	#
109. Bar interstate handgun transport	N
110. Make company emissions known	N

111. Allow toxic victims to sue in fed ct	N
112. Superfund waste cleanup of $10b	Y
113. 90 days notice of plant closings	N
114. $20b in Medicare cuts/tax increases	N
115. Spending cuts and tax increases	N
116. Set school lunch lmt-250% poverty	Y
117. $75m for youth work projects	N
118. Allow Angolan military assistance	Y
119. Suspend defense payments for abuse	N
120. Drop SS COLAs/$12b tax increase	N
121. Approve $1.5b for 21 MX missiles	Y
122. Emergency farm credit/revisions	N
123. Duty on Taiwan/Hong Kong/S Korea	N
124. Limit steel imports to 17%	Y
125. Cut $ to schools that bar prayer	Y
126. $50b-taxes; cut Medicare/spending	Y
127. Limit Pershing II/cruise in Europe	N
128. Delete $7.1b for 34 B-1 bombers	N
129. Bar purchase of Sergeant York guns	N
130. El Salvador military/economic aid	Y
131. Bar mining of Nicaraguan waters	?
132. Physician fee freeze for Medicare	Y
133. $49b in "sin"/phone/insurance taxes	Y
134. Allow sale of Conrail	Y
135. Equal Rights Amendment	N
136. Authorize Marines in Lebanon	Y
137. Eminent domain for coal companies	Y
138. Prohibit EPA clean air sanctions	Y
139. SS retirement age increase/reforms	Y
140. Auto domestic content requirement	N
141. Delete jobs program funding	Y
142. Highway-gas tax bill	N
143. Cut $5b from defense for Medicare	N
144. Emergency housing aid of $1b	Y

Presidential Support Score: 1991 - 81%   1990 - 75%

BACCHUS, JIM -- Florida 11th District [Democrat]. Counties of Brevard, Indian River (pt.), Orange (pt.) and Osceola (pt.). Prior Term: 1991-92. Born: June 21, 1949; Nashville, TN. Education: Vanderbilt University (B.A.); Yale University (M.A.); Florida State University College of Law (J.D.). Military Service: U.S. Army Reserve and National Guard. Occupation: Newspaper reporter; lawyer; aide and advisor to state Governor and special assistant to Chief U.S. International Trade Negotiator Reuben Askew; Vice President, Greater Orlando Chamber of Commerce; volunteer civic action program chairman; state hotel/motel association and Comprehensive Plan Committee general counsel.

1. Protection to Haitian refugees	Y
2. Raise tax on wealthy; lower others	Y
3. Investigate Reagan hostage delay	Y
4. Campaign finance revisions	Y
5. Unpaid leave to care for children	Y
6. Restrict NEA use of funds	N
7. Bar race-bias claim/habeas corpus	Y
8. Ban race as death sentence factor	Y
9. Exceptions to exclusionary rule	Y
10. Allow sale of assault weapons	N
11. Life in prison/abolish death penalty	N
12. Req conspiracy-price fixing cases	?

13. Unemployment benefits extension	Y
14. Tissue use of aborted fetuses	Y
15. Bar replacement of union strikers	Y
16. Hold foreign aid at $15b for '92	Y
17. Restore space station funding	Y
18. Civil Rights Act of 1991	Y
19. Unlimited damages-discrimination	N
20. Eliminate funds for supercollider	?
21. Terminate SDI except for research	N
22. Req 7-day handgun waiting period	Y
23. Provide $30b for failed S&Ls	N
24. Allow use of force against Iraq	Y

Presidential Support Score: 1991 - 35%

LEWIS, TOM -- Florida 12th District [Republican]. Counties of Collier (pt.), Glades, Hendry, Highlands, Indian River (pt.), Martin, Okeechobee, Palm Beach (pt.) and St. Lucie. Prior Terms: 1983-92. Born: October 26, 1924; Philadelphia, PA. Education: University of Florida. Military Service: U.S. Air Force, WW II, Korean Conflict. Occupation: Corporate executive (1957-73); mayor and councilman (1964-71); realtor (1972-82); Florida representative (1972-80); Florida senator (1980-82).

1. Protection to Haitian refugees	N	
2. Raise tax on wealthy; lower others	N	
3. Investigate Reagan hostage delay	N	
4. Campaign finance revisions	N	
5. Unpaid leave to care for children	N	
6. Restrict NEA use of funds	Y	
7. Bar race-bias claim/habeas corpus	Y	
8. Ban race as death sentence factor	Y	
9. Exceptions to exclusionary rule	Y	
10. Allow sale of assault weapons	Y	
11. Life in prison/abolish death penalty	N	
12. Req conspiracy-price fixing cases	Y	
13. Unemployment benefits extension	Y	
14. Tissue use of aborted fetuses	N	
15. Bar replacement of union strikers	N	
16. Hold foreign aid at $15b for '92	N	
17. Restore space station funding	Y	
18. Civil Rights Act of 1991	N	
19. Unlimited damages-discrimination	N	
20. Eliminate funds for supercollider	N	
21. Terminate SDI except for research	N	
22. Req 7-day handgun waiting period	N	
23. Provide $30b for failed S&Ls	--	
24. Allow use of force against Iraq	Y	
25. Allow $15b in foreign aid for '91	N	
26. Revise & extend legal immigration	N	
27. Suspend aid to Angolan rebels	N	
28. Democratic tax plan proposals	N	
29. Cut defense 5% across the board	N	
30. Textile import quotas-veto override	N	
31. Abortion service for military abroad	N	
32. Limits on high income farmers	N	
33. Family medical leave-veto override	N	
34. Req submission of balanced budget	N	
35. Balanced budget amendment	Y	
36. Amendment to ban flag desecration	Y	
37. Reauthorize Amtrak-veto override	N	
38. Retraining aid for coal miners	N	
39. Suspend El Salvador military aid	N	
40. Expand child care aid/tax credit	N	
41. Raise House salary/omit honoraria	N	
42. Toughen oil-spill liability	N	
43. Restitution to Japanese interned	N	
44. Protect Chinese & C.A. nationals	N	
45. Abortion $ for rape/incest cases	N	
46. Allow religious schools to bar gays	Y	
47. Bar broadcaster fairness doctrine	Y	
48. Bar cap gains cut/reinstate IRA	N	
49. Bar unions equal voice in pension	Y	
50. Bar assembly of chemical weapons	Y	
51. Ban plutonium/uranium production	N	
52. Cap MX missile deployment at 50	N	
53. Allow $3b for 2 stealth bombers	Y	
54. Publish bio-warfare experiments	N	
55. Raise minimum wage-veto override	N	
56. Bar transfer of FS-X technology	N	
57. Cut defense and raise domestic $	N	
58. Uniform poll closing in 48 states	N	
59. Req foreign investment disclosure	N	
60. Textile import quotas-veto override	N	
61. Bar abortion funding in Wash, DC	N	
62. Notify spouses of AIDS+ carriers	Y	
63. Seize conveyance-drug trafficking	Y	
64. South Africa sanctions	N	
65. 60 days' notice of plant closings	N	
66. Close unneeded military bases	Y	
67. Keep welfare reform within $2.8b	Y	
68. Allow children housing exclusion	Y	
69. Shift $400m of NASA to homeless	N	
70. Cap Medicare patients' liability	Y	
71. Prohibit employee polygraph testing	N	
72. Allow CIA to fund Contras	Y	
73. Revise unfair trade practices	N	
74. Focus SDI on accidental launch	N	
75. Bar Air Force $ for MX missile	N	
76. Allow "real" increase in defense	Y	
77. Troop reduction in Europe of 50%	N	
78. Ban nuclear tests above 1 kiloton	N	
79. Ban anti-satellite missile tests	N	
80. Observe certain limits of SALT II	N	
81. Restore four Civil Rights laws	N	
82. Prohibit aliens as strikebreakers	N	
83. Allow military malpractice suits	Y	
84. Approval of $36m in Contra aid	Y	
85. $18b deficit reduction compromise	N	
86. Welfare reform of $5.7b for 5 years	N	
87. Raise taxes $12b/cut spending $3b	N	
88. Board to assess occupational risk	N	
89. Balanced budget by '93-via targets	N	
90. Bar licensing of two nuclear plants	N	
91. Remove victims compensation cap	N	
92. Catastrophic health insurance	Y	
93. Ban airline smoking-2 hours or less	Y	
94. $1b/two year aid for the homeless	N	
95. Bar non-unions in union companies	N	
96. Increase FSLIC rescue to $15b	N	
97. Impose quotas to lower trade deficit	N	
98. Reduce discretionary budget 21%	Y	
99. Immigration reform/alien amnesty	N	
100. South Africa sanctions-veto override	Y	
101. Tax overhaul to revise income tax	N	
102. Use of military in drug war	Y	
103. Delete 12 MX/add conventional wpn	N	
104. Raise speed limit to 65 mph	Y	
105. Require Pentagon to buy US goods	N	
106. AIDS insurance non-discrimination	N	
107. Prohibit Saudi arms sales	Y	
108. Ease Gun Control Act of 1968	Y	
109. Bar interstate handgun transport	N	
110. Make company emissions known	N	
111. Allow toxic victims to sue in fed ct	N	
112. Superfund waste cleanup of $10b	N	
113. 90 days notice of plant closings	N	
114. $20b in Medicare cuts/tax increases	N	
115. Spending cuts and tax increases	N	
116. Set school lunch lmt-250% poverty	Y	

LEWIS, TOM (continued)

117. $75m for youth work projects	N	
118. Allow Angolan military assistance	Y	
119. Suspend defense payments for abuse	N	
120. Drop SS COLAs/$12b tax increase	N	
121. Approve $1.5b for 21 MX missiles	Y	
122. Emergency farm credit/revisions	Y	
123. Duty on Taiwan/Hong Kong/S Korea	N	
124. Limit steel imports to 17%	N	
125. Cut $ to schools that bar prayer	Y	
126. $50b-taxes; cut Medicare/spending	N	
127. Limit Pershing II/cruise in Europe	N	
128. Delete $7.1b for 34 B-1 bombers	N	

129. Bar purchase of Sergeant York guns	N
130. El Salvador military/economic aid	Y
131. Bar mining of Nicaraguan waters	N
132. Physician fee freeze for Medicare	Y
133. $49b in "sin"/phone/insurance taxes	Y
134. Allow sale of Conrail	Y
135. Equal Rights Amendment	Y
136. Authorize Marines in Lebanon	Y
137. Eminent domain for coal companies	Y
138. Prohibit EPA clean air sanctions	Y
139. SS retirement age increase/reforms	N

Presidential Support Score: 1991 - 73% 1990 - 68%

GOSS, PORTER J. -- Florida 13th District [Republican]. Counties of Charlotte, Collier (pt.), Lee and Sarasota. Prior Terms: 1989-92. Born: November 26,1938; Waterbury, CT. Education: Yale University. Military Service: U.S. Army. Occupation: CIA clandestine services officer; newspaper cofounder; Sanibel city councilman and mayor; Lee county commissioner (1982-88); trust and financial services company director.

1. Protection to Haitian refugees	N
2. Raise tax on wealthy; lower others	N
3. Investigate Reagan hostage delay	N
4. Campaign finance revisions	N
5. Unpaid leave to care for children	N
6. Restrict NEA use of funds	Y
7. Bar race-bias claim/habeas corpus	Y
8. Ban race as death sentence factor	Y
9. Exceptions to exclusionary rule	Y
10. Allow sale of assault weapons	Y
11. Life in prison/abolish death penalty	N
12. Req conspiracy-price fixing cases	Y
13. Unemployment benefits extension	N
14. Tissue use of aborted fetuses	N
15. Bar replacement of union strikers	N
16. Hold foreign aid at $15b for '92	N
17. Restore space station funding	Y
18. Civil Rights Act of 1991	N
19. Unlimited damages-discrimination	N
20. Eliminate funds for supercollider	N
21. Terminate SDI except for research	N
22. Req 7-day handgun waiting period	Y
23. Provide $30b for failed S&Ls	Y
24. Allow use of force against Iraq	Y
25. Allow $15b in foreign aid for '91	Y
26. Revise & extend legal immigration	N
27. Suspend aid to Angolan rebels	N
28. Democratic tax plan proposals	N
29. Cut defense 5% across the board	N

30. Textile import quotas-veto override	N
31. Abortion service for military abroad	N
32. Limits on high income farmers	Y
33. Family medical leave-veto override	N
34. Req submission of balanced budget	N
35. Balanced budget amendment	Y
36. Amendment to ban flag desecration	Y
37. Reauthorize Amtrak-veto override	N
38. Retraining aid for coal miners	N
39. Suspend El Salvador military aid	N
40. Expand child care aid/tax credit	N
41. Raise House salary/omit honoraria	N
42. Toughen oil-spill liability	N
43. Restitution to Japanese interned	N
44. Protect Chinese & C.A. nationals	N
45. Abortion $ for rape/incest cases	Y
46. Allow religious schools to bar gays	Y
47. Bar broadcaster fairness doctrine	Y
48. Bar cap gains cut/reinstate IRA	N
49. Bar unions equal voice in pension	Y
50. Bar assembly of chemical weapons	N
51. Ban plutonium/uranium production	N
52. Cap MX missile deployment at 50	N
53. Allow $3b for 2 stealth bombers	Y
54. Publish bio-warfare experiments	N
55. Raise minimum wage-veto override	N
56. Bar transfer of FS-X technology	N
57. Cut defense and raise domestic $	N
58. Uniform poll closing in 48 states	N

Presidential Support Score: 1991 - 86% 1990 - 72%

JOHNSTON, HARRY A., II -- Florida 14th District [Democrat]. Counties of Broward (pt.) and Palm Beach (pt.). Prior Terms: 1989-92. Born: December 2, 1931; West Palm Beach, FL. Education: Virginia Military Institute; University of Florida Law School. Military Service: U.S. Army. Occupation: Lawyer; state senator (1975-86).

1. Protection to Haitian refugees	?
2. Raise tax on wealthy; lower others	Y
3. Investigate Reagan hostage delay	Y
4. Campaign finance revisions	Y

5. Unpaid leave to care for children	Y
6. Restrict NEA use of funds	N
7. Bar race-bias claim/habeas corpus	N
8. Ban race as death sentence factor	N

JOHNSTON, HARRY A., II (continued)

9. Exceptions to exclusionary rule	N	34. Req submission of balanced budget	Y
10. Allow sale of assault weapons	N	35. Balanced budget amendment	Y
11. Life in prison/abolish death penalty	N	36. Amendment to ban flag desecration	N
12. Req conspiracy-price fixing cases	N	37. Reauthorize Amtrak-veto override	?
13. Unemployment benefits extension	?	38. Retraining aid for coal miners	Y
14. Tissue use of aborted fetuses	Y	39. Suspend El Salvador military aid	Y
15. Bar replacement of union strikers	Y	40. Expand child care aid/tax credit	Y
16. Hold foreign aid at $15b for '92	Y	41. Raise House salary/omit honoraria	N
17. Restore space station funding	N	42. Toughen oil-spill liability	?
18. Civil Rights Act of 1991	Y	43. Restitution to Japanese interned	Y
19. Unlimited damages-discrimination	Y	44. Protect Chinese & C.A. nationals	N
20. Eliminate funds for supercollider	Y	45. Abortion $ for rape/incest cases	Y
21. Terminate SDI except for research	Y	46. Allow religious schools to bar gays	N
22. Req 7-day handgun waiting period	Y	47. Bar broadcaster fairness doctrine	N
23. Provide $30b for failed S&Ls	Y	48. Bar cap gains cut/reinstate IRA	Y
24. Allow use of force against Iraq	N	49. Bar unions equal voice in pension	Y
25. Allow $15b in foreign aid for '91	?	50. Bar assembly of chemical weapons	Y
26. Revise & extend legal immigration	?	51. Ban plutonium/uranium production	Y
27. Suspend aid to Angolan rebels	Y	52. Cap MX missile deployment at 50	Y
28. Democratic tax plan proposals	Y	53. Allow $3b for 2 stealth bombers	N
29. Cut defense 5% across the board	N	54. Publish bio-warfare experiments	Y
30. Textile import quotas-veto override	Y	55. Raise minimum wage-veto override	Y
31. Abortion service for military abroad	Y	56. Bar transfer of FS-X technology	Y
32. Limits on high income farmers	Y	57. Cut defense and raise domestic $	N
33. Family medical leave-veto override	Y	58. Uniform poll closing in 48 states	Y

Presidential Support Score: 1991 - 32%   1990 - 23%

SHAW, E. CLAY, Jr. -- Florida 15th District [Republican]. County of Broward (pt). Prior Terms: 1981-92. Born: April 19, 1939; Miami, FL. Education: Stetson University (B.A., J.D.); University of Alabama (M.A.). Occupation: Owner, wholesale nursery; assistant city attorney (1968); mayor, Fort Lauderdale (1975-81); city prosecutor (1968-69); judge (1969-71); city commissioner (1971-73); vice-mayor (1973-75); ambassador, Papua, New Guinea.

1. Protection to Haitian refugees	N	30. Textile import quotas-veto override	N
2. Raise tax on wealthy; lower others	N	31. Abortion service for military abroad	N
3. Investigate Reagan hostage delay	N	32. Limits on high income farmers	Y
4. Campaign finance revisions	N	33. Family medical leave-veto override	N
5. Unpaid leave to care for children	N	34. Req submission of balanced budget	N
6. Restrict NEA use of funds	Y	35. Balanced budget amendment	Y
7. Bar race-bias claim/habeas corpus	Y	36. Amendment to ban flag desecration	Y
8. Ban race as death sentence factor	Y	37. Reauthorize Amtrak-veto override	N
9. Exceptions to exclusionary rule	Y	38. Retraining aid for coal miners	N
10. Allow sale of assault weapons	Y	39. Suspend El Salvador military aid	N
11. Life in prison/abolish death penalty	N	40. Expand child care aid/tax credit	X
12. Req conspiracy-price fixing cases	Y	41. Raise House salary/omit honoraria	Y
13. Unemployment benefits extension	N	42. Toughen oil-spill liability	N
14. Tissue use of aborted fetuses	N	43. Restitution to Japanese interned	N
15. Bar replacement of union strikers	N	44. Protect Chinese & C.A. nationals	N
16. Hold foreign aid at $15b for '92	Y	45. Abortion $ for rape/incest cases	N
17. Restore space station funding	Y	46. Allow religious schools to bar gays	Y
18. Civil Rights Act of 1991	N	47. Bar broadcaster fairness doctrine	Y
19. Unlimited damages-discrimination	N	48. Bar cap gains cut/reinstate IRA	N
20. Eliminate funds for supercollider	N	49. Bar unions equal voice in pension	Y
21. Terminate SDI except for research	N	50. Bar assembly of chemical weapons	N
22. Req 7-day handgun waiting period	N	51. Ban plutonium/uranium production	N
23. Provide $30b for failed S&Ls	Y	52. Cap MX missile deployment at 50	N
24. Allow use of force against Iraq	Y	53. Allow $3b for 2 stealth bombers	N
25. Allow $15b in foreign aid for '91	?	54. Publish bio-warfare experiments	N
26. Revise & extend legal immigration	N	55. Raise minimum wage-veto override	N
27. Suspend aid to Angolan rebels	N	56. Bar transfer of FS-X technology	N
28. Democratic tax plan proposals	N	57. Cut defense and raise domestic $	N
29. Cut defense 5% across the board	N	58. Uniform poll closing in 48 states	N

SHAW, E. CLAY, Jr. (continued)

59. Req foreign investment disclosure	N		102. Use of military in drug war	Y
60. Textile import quotas-veto override	N		103. Delete 12 MX/add conventional wpn	N
61. Bar abortion funding in Wash, DC	Y		104. Raise speed limit to 65 mph	Y
62. Notify spouses of AIDS+ carriers	Y		105. Require Pentagon to buy US goods	N
63. Seize conveyance-drug trafficking	Y		106. AIDS insurance non-discrimination	N
64. South Africa sanctions	N		107. Prohibit Saudi arms sales	Y
65. 60 days' notice of plant closings	N		108. Ease Gun Control Act of 1968	Y
66. Close unneeded military bases	Y		109. Bar interstate handgun transport	N
67. Keep welfare reform within $2.8b	Y		110. Make company emissions known	N
68. Allow children housing exclusion	Y		111. Allow toxic victims to sue in fed ct	N
69. Shift $400m of NASA to homeless	N		112. Superfund waste cleanup of $10b	Y
70. Cap Medicare patients' liability	Y		113. 90 days notice of plant closings	N
71. Prohibit employee polygraph testing	N		114. $20b in Medicare cuts/tax increases	N
72. Allow CIA to fund Contras	Y		115. Spending cuts and tax increases	N
73. Revise unfair trade practices	Y		116. Set school lunch lmt-250% poverty	Y
74. Focus SDI on accidental launch	N		117. $75m for youth work projects	N
75. Bar Air Force $ for MX missile	N		118. Allow Angolan military assistance	Y
76. Allow "real" increase in defense	Y		119. Suspend defense payments for abuse	N
77. Troop reduction in Europe of 50%	N		120. Drop SS COLAs/$12b tax increase	N
78. Ban nuclear tests above 1 kiloton	N		121. Approve $1.5b for 21 MX missiles	Y
79. Ban anti-satellite missile tests	N		122. Emergency farm credit/revisions	Y
80. Observe certain limits of SALT II	N		123. Duty on Taiwan/Hong Kong/S Korea	N
81. Restore four Civil Rights laws	N		124. Limit steel imports to 17%	N
82. Prohibit aliens as strikebreakers	Y		125. Cut $ to schools that bar prayer	?
83. Allow military malpractice suits	Y		126. $50b-taxes; cut Medicare/spending	Y
84. Approval of $36m in Contra aid	Y		127. Limit Pershing II/cruise in Europe	N
85. $18b deficit reduction compromise	N		128. Delete $7.1b for 34 B-1 bombers	N
86. Welfare reform of $5.7b for 5 years	N		129. Bar purchase of Sergeant York guns	?
87. Raise taxes $12b/cut spending $3b	N		130. El Salvador military/economic aid	Y
88. Board to assess occupational risk	N		131. Bar mining of Nicaraguan waters	N
89. Balanced budget by '93-via targets	Y		132. Physician fee freeze for Medicare	Y
90. Bar licensing of two nuclear plants	N		133. $49b in "sin"/phone/insurance taxes	Y
91. Remove victims compensation cap	N		134. Allow sale of Conrail	Y
92. Catastrophic health insurance	Y		135. Equal Rights Amendment	N
93. Ban airline smoking-2 hours or less	N		136. Authorize Marines in Lebanon	Y
94. $1b/two year aid for the homeless	N		137. Eminent domain for coal companies	Y
95. Bar non-unions in union companies	N		138. Prohibit EPA clean air sanctions	Y
96. Increase FSLIC rescue to $15b	N		139. SS retirement age increase/reforms	Y
97. Impose quotas to lower trade deficit	N		140. Auto domestic content requirement	N
98. Reduce discretionary budget 21%	Y		141. Delete jobs program funding	Y
99. Immigration reform/alien amnesty	Y		142. Highway-gas tax bill	Y
100. South Africa sanctions-veto override	N		143. Cut $5b from defense for Medicare	N
101. Tax overhaul to revise income tax	Y		144. Emergency housing aid of $1b	N

Presidential Support Score: 1991 - 80%   1990 - 75%

SMITH, LAWRENCE J. -- Florida 16th District [Democrat]. Counties of Broward (pt.) and Dade (pt.). Prior Terms: 1983-92. Born: April 25, 1941; Brooklyn, NY. Education: New York University; Brooklyn Law School (LL.B., J.D.). Occupation: Member, Hollywood Planning and Zoning Board (1974-77); county advisory board (1978); Florida representative (1978-82); Governors Task Force on Criminal Justice Systems (1980-1981).

1. Protection to Haitian refugees	Y		12. Req conspiracy-price fixing cases	?
2. Raise tax on wealthy; lower others	Y		13. Unemployment benefits extension	Y
3. Investigate Reagan hostage delay	Y		14. Tissue use of aborted fetuses	Y
4. Campaign finance revisions	Y		15. Bar replacement of union strikers	Y
5. Unpaid leave to care for children	Y		16. Hold foreign aid at $15b for '92	Y
6. Restrict NEA use of funds	N		17. Restore space station funding	N
7. Bar race-bias claim/habeas corpus	Y		18. Civil Rights Act of 1991	Y
8. Ban race as death sentence factor	N		19. Unlimited damages-discrimination	Y
9. Exceptions to exclusionary rule	Y		20. Eliminate funds for supercollider	N
10. Allow sale of assault weapons	N		21. Terminate SDI except for research	Y
11. Life in prison/abolish death penalty	N		22. Req 7-day handgun waiting period	Y

SMITH, LAWRENCE J. (continued)

23. Provide $30b for failed S&Ls	+	
24. Allow use of force against Iraq	N	
25. Allow $15b in foreign aid for '91	Y	
26. Revise & extend legal immigration	Y	
27. Suspend aid to Angolan rebels	N	
28. Democratic tax plan proposals	Y	
29. Cut defense 5% across the board	N	
30. Textile import quotas-veto override	Y	
31. Abortion service for military abroad	Y	
32. Limits on high income farmers	N	
33. Family medical leave-veto override	Y	
34. Req submission of balanced budget	Y	
35. Balanced budget amendment	N	
36. Amendment to ban flag desecration	N	
37. Reauthorize Amtrak-veto override	Y	
38. Retraining aid for coal miners	Y	
39. Suspend El Salvador military aid	Y	
40. Expand child care aid/tax credit	Y	
41. Raise House salary/omit honoraria	Y	
42. Toughen oil-spill liability	Y	
43. Restitution to Japanese interned	Y	
44. Protect Chinese & C.A. nationals	Y	
45. Abortion $ for rape/incest cases	Y	
46. Allow religious schools to bar gays	N	
47. Bar broadcaster fairness doctrine	N	
48. Bar cap gains cut/reinstate IRA	Y	
49. Bar unions equal voice in pension	N	
50. Bar assembly of chemical weapons	Y	
51. Ban plutonium/uranium production	Y	
52. Cap MX missile deployment at 50	Y	
53. Allow $3b for 2 stealth bombers	N	
54. Publish bio-warfare experiments	Y	
55. Raise minimum wage-veto override	Y	
56. Bar transfer of FS-X technology	Y	
57. Cut defense and raise domestic $	N	
58. Uniform poll closing in 48 states	N	
59. Req foreign investment disclosure	Y	
60. Textile import quotas-veto override	Y	
61. Bar abortion funding in Wash, DC	N	
62. Notify spouses of AIDS+ carriers	N	
63. Seize conveyance-drug trafficking	N	
64. South Africa sanctions	Y	
65. 60 days' notice of plant closings	Y	
66. Close unneeded military bases	N	
67. Keep welfare reform within $2.8b	N	
68. Allow children housing exclusion	Y	
69. Shift $400m of NASA to homeless	N	
70. Cap Medicare patients' liability	Y	
71. Prohibit employee polygraph testing	Y	
72. Allow CIA to fund Contras	N	
73. Revise unfair trade practices	Y	
74. Focus SDI on accidental launch	Y	
75. Bar Air Force $ for MX missile	Y	
76. Allow "real" increase in defense	N	
77. Troop reduction in Europe of 50%	Y	
78. Ban nuclear tests above 1 kiloton	Y	
79. Ban anti-satellite missile tests	Y	
80. Observe certain limits of SALT II	Y	
81. Restore four Civil Rights laws	Y	
82. Prohibit aliens as strikebreakers	Y
83. Allow military malpractice suits	Y
84. Approval of $36m in Contra aid	Y
85. $18b deficit reduction compromise	Y
86. Welfare reform of $5.7b for 5 years	Y
87. Raise taxes $12b/cut spending $3b	Y
88. Board to assess occupational risk	Y
89. Balanced budget by '93-via targets	Y
90. Bar licensing of two nuclear plants	N
91. Remove victims compensation cap	N
92. Catastrophic health insurance	Y
93. Ban airline smoking-2 hours or less	Y
94. $1b/two year aid for the homeless	Y
95. Bar non-unions in union companies	Y
96. Increase FSLIC rescue to $15b	N
97. Impose quotas to lower trade deficit	Y
98. Reduce discretionary budget 21%	Y
99. Immigration reform/alien amnesty	Y
100. South Africa sanctions-veto override	Y
101. Tax overhaul to revise income tax	Y
102. Use of military in drug war	Y
103. Delete 12 MX/add conventional wpn	Y
104. Raise speed limit to 65 mph	N
105. Require Pentagon to buy US goods	Y
106. AIDS insurance non-discrimination	Y
107. Prohibit Saudi arms sales	Y
108. Ease Gun Control Act of 1968	N
109. Bar interstate handgun transport	Y
110. Make company emissions known	Y
111. Allow toxic victims to sue in fed ct	Y
112. Superfund waste cleanup of $10b	Y
113. 90 days notice of plant closings	Y
114. $20b in Medicare cuts/tax increases	Y
115. Spending cuts and tax increases	Y
116. Set school lunch lmt-250% poverty	N
117. $75m for youth work projects	?
118. Allow Angolan military assistance	N
119. Suspend defense payments for abuse	N
120. Drop SS COLAs/$12b tax increase	N
121. Approve $1.5b for 21 MX missiles	N
122. Emergency farm credit/revisions	N
123. Duty on Taiwan/Hong Kong/S Korea	N
124. Limit steel imports to 17%	N
125. Cut $ to schools that bar prayer	N
126. $50b-taxes; cut Medicare/spending	N
127. Limit Pershing II/cruise in Europe	N
128. Delete $7.1b for 34 B-1 bombers	N
129. Bar purchase of Sergeant York guns	N
130. El Salvador military/economic aid	N
131. Bar mining of Nicaraguan waters	N
132. Physician fee freeze for Medicare	N
133. $49b in "sin"/phone/insurance taxes	N
134. Allow sale of Conrail	N
135. Equal Rights Amendment	N
136. Authorize Marines in Lebanon	N
137. Eminent domain for coal companies	N
138. Prohibit EPA clean air sanctions	?
139. SS retirement age increase/reforms	N

Presidential Support Score: 1991 - 29%   1990 - 18%

LEHMAN, WILLIAM -- Florida 17th District [Democrat]. County of Dade (pt.). Prior Terms: 1973-92. Born: October 5, 1913; Selma, AL. Education: University of Alabama (B.S.). Occupation: Member, Dade County school board (1966-72).

1. Protection to Haitian refugees	Y	
2. Raise tax on wealthy; lower others	Y	
3. Investigate Reagan hostage delay	Y	
4. Campaign finance revisions	Y	
5. Unpaid leave to care for children	Y	
6. Restrict NEA use of funds	N	
7. Bar race-bias claim/habeas corpus	N	
8. Ban race as death sentence factor	N	
9. Exceptions to exclusionary rule	N	
10. Allow sale of assault weapons	N	
11. Life in prison/abolish death penalty	Y	
12. Req conspiracy-price fixing cases	N	
13. Unemployment benefits extension	?	
14. Tissue use of aborted fetuses	Y	
15. Bar replacement of union strikers	Y	
16. Hold foreign aid at $15b for '92	?	
17. Restore space station funding	N	
18. Civil Rights Act of 1991	Y	
19. Unlimited damages-discrimination	?	
20. Eliminate funds for supercollider	N	
21. Terminate SDI except for research	#	
22. Req 7-day handgun waiting period	?	
23. Provide $30b for failed S&Ls	Y	
24. Allow use of force against Iraq	N	
25. Allow $15b in foreign aid for '91	Y	
26. Revise & extend legal immigration	Y	
27. Suspend aid to Angolan rebels	Y	
28. Democratic tax plan proposals	Y	
29. Cut defense 5% across the board	N	
30. Textile import quotas-veto override	Y	
31. Abortion service for military abroad	Y	
32. Limits on high income farmers	Y	
33. Family medical leave-veto override	Y	
34. Req submission of balanced budget	Y	
35. Balanced budget amendment	N	
36. Amendment to ban flag desecration	N	
37. Reauthorize Amtrak-veto override	Y	
38. Retraining aid for coal miners	Y	
39. Suspend El Salvador military aid	Y	
40. Expand child care aid/tax credit	Y	
41. Raise House salary/omit honoraria	Y	
42. Toughen oil-spill liability	Y	
43. Restitution to Japanese interned	Y	
44. Protect Chinese & C.A. nationals	Y	
45. Abortion $ for rape/incest cases	Y	
46. Allow religious schools to bar gays	N	
47. Bar broadcaster fairness doctrine	N	
48. Bar cap gains cut/reinstate IRA	Y	
49. Bar unions equal voice in pension	N	
50. Bar assembly of chemical weapons	Y	
51. Ban plutonium/uranium production	Y	
52. Cap MX missile deployment at 50	Y	
53. Allow $3b for 2 stealth bombers	N	
54. Publish bio-warfare experiments	Y	
55. Raise minimum wage-veto override	Y	
56. Bar transfer of FS-X technology	Y	
57. Cut defense and raise domestic $	Y	
58. Uniform poll closing in 48 states	Y	
59. Req foreign investment disclosure	Y	
60. Textile import quotas-veto override	Y	
61. Bar abortion funding in Wash, DC	N	

62. Notify spouses of AIDS+ carriers	N	
63. Seize conveyance-drug trafficking	N	
64. South Africa sanctions	Y	
65. 60 days' notice of plant closings	Y	
66. Close unneeded military bases	Y	
67. Keep welfare reform within $2.8b	N	
68. Allow children housing exclusion	N	
69. Shift $400m of NASA to homeless	N	
70. Cap Medicare patients' liability	Y	
71. Prohibit employee polygraph testing	Y	
72. Allow CIA to fund Contras	N	
73. Revise unfair trade practices	Y	
74. Focus SDI on accidental launch	Y	
75. Bar Air Force $ for MX missile	Y	
76. Allow "real" increase in defense	N	
77. Troop reduction in Europe of 50%	N	
78. Ban nuclear tests above 1 kiloton	Y	
79. Ban anti-satellite missile tests	Y	
80. Observe certain limits of SALT II	Y	
81. Restore four Civil Rights laws	Y	
82. Prohibit aliens as strikebreakers	Y	
83. Allow military malpractice suits	Y	
84. Approval of $36m in Contra aid	N	
85. $18b deficit reduction compromise	Y	
86. Welfare reform of $5.7b for 5 years	Y	
87. Raise taxes $12b/cut spending $3b	Y	
88. Board to assess occupational risk	Y	
89. Balanced budget by '93-via targets	Y	
90. Bar licensing of two nuclear plants	N	
91. Remove victims compensation cap	Y	
92. Catastrophic health insurance	Y	
93. Ban airline smoking-2 hours or less	N	
94. $1b/two year aid for the homeless	Y	
95. Bar non-unions in union companies	Y	
96. Increase FSLIC rescue to $15b	N	
97. Impose quotas to lower trade deficit	N	
98. Reduce discretionary budget 21%	N	
99. Immigration reform/alien amnesty	Y	
100. South Africa sanctions-veto override	Y	
101. Tax overhaul to revise income tax	Y	
102. Use of military in drug war	N	
103. Delete 12 MX/add conventional wpn	Y	
104. Raise speed limit to 65 mph	N	
105. Require Pentagon to buy US goods	N	
106. AIDS insurance non-discrimination	Y	
107. Prohibit Saudi arms sales	Y	
108. Ease Gun Control Act of 1968	N	
109. Bar interstate handgun transport	Y	
110. Make company emissions known	Y	
111. Allow toxic victims to sue in fed ct	Y	
112. Superfund waste cleanup of $10b	Y	
113. 90 days notice of plant closings	Y	
114. $20b in Medicare cuts/tax increases	Y	
115. Spending cuts and tax increases	Y	
116. Set school lunch lmt-250% poverty	N	
117. $75m for youth work projects	Y	
118. Allow Angolan military assistance	N	
119. Suspend defense payments for abuse	Y	
120. Drop SS COLAs/$12b tax increase	N	
121. Approve $1.5b for 21 MX missiles	N	
122. Emergency farm credit/revisions	Y	

LEHMAN, WILLIAM (continued)

123. Duty on Taiwan/Hong Kong/S Korea	Y	
124. Limit steel imports to 17%	Y	
125. Cut $ to schools that bar prayer	N	
126. $50b-taxes; cut Medicare/spending	Y	
127. Limit Pershing II/cruise in Europe	Y	
128. Delete $7.1b for 34 B-1 bombers	Y	
129. Bar purchase of Sergeant York guns	?	
130. El Salvador military/economic aid	N	
131. Bar mining of Nicaraguan waters	Y	
132. Physician fee freeze for Medicare	N	
133. $49b in "sin"/phone/insurance taxes	Y	
134. Allow sale of Conrail	N	
135. Equal Rights Amendment	Y	
136. Authorize Marines in Lebanon	Y	
137. Eminent domain for coal companies	Y	
138. Prohibit EPA clean air sanctions	?	
139. SS retirement age increase/reforms	N	
140. Auto domestic content requirement	?	
141. Delete jobs program funding	?	
142. Highway-gas tax bill	?	
143. Cut $5b from defense for Medicare	Y	
144. Emergency housing aid of $1b	Y	

Presidential Support Score: 1991 - 26% 1990 - 19%

ROS-LEHTINEN, ILEANA -- Florida 18th District [Republican]. County of Dade (pt.). Prior Terms: 1989 (Special Election)-1992. Education: Miami Dade Community College (A.A.); Florida International University (B.A., M.S.); University of Miami (Ph.D. candidate). Occupation: Private elementary school founder; state representative (1982-86) and senator (1986-89).

1. Protection to Haitian refugees	Y	26. Revise & extend legal immigration	Y
2. Raise tax on wealthy; lower others	N	27. Suspend aid to Angolan rebels	N
3. Investigate Reagan hostage delay	N	28. Democratic tax plan proposals	N
4. Campaign finance revisions	N	29. Cut defense 5% across the board	N
5. Unpaid leave to care for children	Y	30. Textile import quotas-veto override	N
6. Restrict NEA use of funds	Y	31. Abortion service for military abroad	N
7. Bar race-bias claim/habeas corpus	Y	32. Limits on high income farmers	Y
8. Ban race as death sentence factor	Y	33. Family medical leave-veto override	Y
9. Exceptions to exclusionary rule	Y	34. Req submission of balanced budget	Y
10. Allow sale of assault weapons	N	35. Balanced budget amendment	Y
11. Life in prison/abolish death penalty	N	36. Amendment to ban flag desecration	Y
12. Req conspiracy-price fixing cases	Y	37. Reauthorize Amtrak-veto override	N
13. Unemployment benefits extension	Y	38. Retraining aid for coal miners	N
14. Tissue use of aborted fetuses	N	39. Suspend El Salvador military aid	N
15. Bar replacement of union strikers	N	40. Expand child care aid/tax credit	Y
16. Hold foreign aid at $15b for '92	Y	41. Raise House salary/omit honoraria	N
17. Restore space station funding	N	42. Toughen oil-spill liability	Y
18. Civil Rights Act of 1991	Y	43. Restitution to Japanese interned	Y
19. Unlimited damages-discrimination	N	44. Protect Chinese & C.A. nationals	Y
20. Eliminate funds for supercollider	Y	45. Abortion $ for rape/incest cases	N
21. Terminate SDI except for research	N	46. Allow religious schools to bar gays	Y
22. Req 7-day handgun waiting period	Y	47. Bar broadcaster fairness doctrine	Y
23. Provide $30b for failed S&Ls	Y	48. Bar cap gains cut/reinstate IRA	N
24. Allow use of force against Iraq	Y	49. Bar unions equal voice in pension	Y
25. Allow $15b in foreign aid for '91	Y		

Presidential Support Score: 1991 - 67% 1990 - 50%

FASCELL, DANTE B. -- Florida 19th District [Democrat]. Counties of Dade (pt.) and Monroe. Prior Terms: 1955-92. Born: March 9, 1917; Bridgehampton, Long Island, NY. Education: University of Miami (J.D.). Military Service: Florida National Guard, 1941-46; U.S. Armed Forces. Occupation: Florida representative (1950-54).

1. Protection to Haitian refugees	Y	11. Life in prison/abolish death penalty	N
2. Raise tax on wealthy; lower others	Y	12. Req conspiracy-price fixing cases	N
3. Investigate Reagan hostage delay	Y	13. Unemployment benefits extension	Y
4. Campaign finance revisions	Y	14. Tissue use of aborted fetuses	Y
5. Unpaid leave to care for children	Y	15. Bar replacement of union strikers	Y
6. Restrict NEA use of funds	N	16. Hold foreign aid at $15b for '92	Y
7. Bar race-bias claim/habeas corpus	N	17. Restore space station funding	Y
8. Ban race as death sentence factor	N	18. Civil Rights Act of 1991	Y
9. Exceptions to exclusionary rule	N	19. Unlimited damages-discrimination	Y
10. Allow sale of assault weapons	N	20. Eliminate funds for supercollider	N

FASCELL, DANTE B. (continued)

21. Terminate SDI except for research	N	
22. Req 7-day handgun waiting period	Y	
23. Provide $30b for failed S&Ls	Y	
24. Allow use of force against Iraq	Y	
25. Allow $15b in foreign aid for '91	Y	
26. Revise & extend legal immigration	Y	
27. Suspend aid to Angolan rebels	N	
28. Democratic tax plan proposals	Y	
29. Cut defense 5% across the board	N	
30. Textile import quotas-veto override	Y	
31. Abortion service for military abroad	Y	
32. Limits on high income farmers	N	
33. Family medical leave-veto override	Y	
34. Req submission of balanced budget	Y	
35. Balanced budget amendment	N	
36. Amendment to ban flag desecration	N	
37. Reauthorize Amtrak-veto override	Y	
38. Retraining aid for coal miners	Y	
39. Suspend El Salvador military aid	Y	
40. Expand child care aid/tax credit	Y	
41. Raise House salary/omit honoraria	Y	
42. Toughen oil-spill liability	Y	
43. Restitution to Japanese interned	Y	
44. Protect Chinese & C.A. nationals	Y	
45. Abortion $ for rape/incest cases	Y	
46. Allow religious schools to bar gays	N	
47. Bar broadcaster fairness doctrine	N	
48. Bar cap gains cut/reinstate IRA	Y	
49. Bar unions equal voice in pension	N	
50. Bar assembly of chemical weapons	Y	
51. Ban plutonium/uranium production	Y	
52. Cap MX missile deployment at 50	Y	
53. Allow $3b for 2 stealth bombers	N	
54. Publish bio-warfare experiments	Y	
55. Raise minimum wage-veto override	Y	
56. Bar transfer of FS-X technology	N	
57. Cut defense and raise domestic $	N	
58. Uniform poll closing in 48 states	Y	
59. Req foreign investment disclosure	N	
60. Textile import quotas-veto override	Y	
61. Bar abortion funding in Wash, DC	N	
62. Notify spouses of AIDS+ carriers	N	
63. Seize conveyance-drug trafficking	N	
64. South Africa sanctions	Y	
65. 60 days' notice of plant closings	Y	
66. Close unneeded military bases	N	
67. Keep welfare reform within $2.8b	N	
68. Allow children housing exclusion	N	
69. Shift $400m of NASA to homeless	N	
70. Cap Medicare patients' liability	Y	
71. Prohibit employee polygraph testing	Y	
72. Allow CIA to fund Contras	Y	
73. Revise unfair trade practices	Y	
74. Focus SDI on accidental launch	Y	
75. Bar Air Force $ for MX missile	N	
76. Allow "real" increase in defense	N	
77. Troop reduction in Europe of 50%	N	
78. Ban nuclear tests above 1 kiloton	Y	
79. Ban anti-satellite missile tests	Y	
80. Observe certain limits of SALT II	Y	
81. Restore four Civil Rights laws	Y	
82. Prohibit aliens as strikebreakers	Y	

83. Allow military malpractice suits	Y	
84. Approval of $36m in Contra aid	Y	
85. $18b deficit reduction compromise	Y	
86. Welfare reform of $5.7b for 5 years	Y	
87. Raise taxes $12b/cut spending $3b	Y	
88. Board to assess occupational risk	Y	
89. Balanced budget by '93-via targets	Y	
90. Bar licensing of two nuclear plants	N	
91. Remove victims compensation cap	N	
92. Catastrophic health insurance	Y	
93. Ban airline smoking-2 hours or less	Y	
94. $1b/two year aid for the homeless	Y	
95. Bar non-unions in union companies	Y	
96. Increase FSLIC rescue to $15b	N	
97. Impose quotas to lower trade deficit	Y	
98. Reduce discretionary budget 21%	Y	
99. Immigration reform/alien amnesty	Y	
100. South Africa sanctions-veto override	Y	
101. Tax overhaul to revise income tax	Y	
102. Use of military in drug war	N	
103. Delete 12 MX/add conventional wpn	Y	
104. Raise speed limit to 65 mph	N	
105. Require Pentagon to buy US goods	N	
106. AIDS insurance non-discrimination	Y	
107. Prohibit Saudi arms sales	Y	
108. Ease Gun Control Act of 1968	N	
109. Bar interstate handgun transport	Y	
110. Make company emissions known	Y	
111. Allow toxic victims to sue in fed ct	Y	
112. Superfund waste cleanup of $10b	Y	
113. 90 days notice of plant closings	Y	
114. $20b in Medicare cuts/tax increases	Y	
115. Spending cuts and tax increases	Y	
116. Set school lunch lmt-250% poverty	Y	
117. $75m for youth work projects	Y	
118. Allow Angolan military assistance	Y	
119. Suspend defense payments for abuse	N	
120. Drop SS COLAs/$12b tax increase	N	
121. Approve $1.5b for 21 MX missiles	N	
122. Emergency farm credit/revisions	Y	
123. Duty on Taiwan/Hong Kong/S Korea	Y	
124. Limit steel imports to 17%	Y	
125. Cut $ to schools that bar prayer	N	
126. $50b-taxes; cut Medicare/spending	Y	
127. Limit Pershing II/cruise in Europe	Y	
128. Delete $7.1b for 34 B-1 bombers	Y	
129. Bar purchase of Sergeant York guns	Y	
130. El Salvador military/economic aid	N	
131. Bar mining of Nicaraguan waters	Y	
132. Physician fee freeze for Medicare	Y	
133. $49b in "sin"/phone/insurance taxes	Y	
134. Allow sale of Conrail	N	
135. Equal Rights Amendment	Y	
136. Authorize Marines in Lebanon	Y	
137. Eminent domain for coal companies	Y	
138. Prohibit EPA clean air sanctions	Y	
139. SS retirement age increase/reforms	N	
140. Auto domestic content requirement	Y	
141. Delete jobs program funding	N	
142. Highway-gas tax bill	?	
143. Cut $5b from defense for Medicare	Y	
144. Emergency housing aid of $1b	N	

Presidential Support Score: 1991 - 37% 1990 - 24%

GEORGIA

THOMAS, ROBERT LINDSAY -- Georgia 1st District [Democrat]. Counties of Brantley, Bryan, Bulloch, Burke, Camden, Candler, Chatham, Effingham, Emanuel, Evans, Glynn, Jenkins, Liberty, Long, McIntosh, Montgomery, Screven, Tattnall, Toombs and Wayne. Prior Terms: 1983-92. Born: November 20, 1943; Patterson, GA. Education: University of Georgia. Military Service: Georgia Air National Guard. Occupation: Banker (1965-73); farmer; vice president and member, Wayne County Farm Bureau.

1. Protection to Haitian refugees	N	
2. Raise tax on wealthy; lower others	N	
3. Investigate Reagan hostage delay	?	
4. Campaign finance revisions	Y	
5. Unpaid leave to care for children	N	
6. Restrict NEA use of funds	N	
7. Bar race-bias claim/habeas corpus	Y	
8. Ban race as death sentence factor	Y	
9. Exceptions to exclusionary rule	Y	
10. Allow sale of assault weapons	Y	
11. Life in prison/abolish death penalty	N	
12. Req conspiracy-price fixing cases	N	
13. Unemployment benefits extension	Y	
14. Tissue use of aborted fetuses	Y	
15. Bar replacement of union strikers	N	
16. Hold foreign aid at $15b for '92	?	
17. Restore space station funding	Y	
18. Civil Rights Act of 1991	Y	
19. Unlimited damages-discrimination	N	
20. Eliminate funds for supercollider	N	
21. Terminate SDI except for research	N	
22. Req 7-day handgun waiting period	N	
23. Provide $30b for failed S&Ls	Y	
24. Allow use of force against Iraq	Y	
25. Allow $15b in foreign aid for '91	?	
26. Revise & extend legal immigration	?	
27. Suspend aid to Angolan rebels	N	
28. Democratic tax plan proposals	Y	
29. Cut defense 5% across the board	N	
30. Textile import quotas-veto override	Y	
31. Abortion service for military abroad	Y	
32. Limits on high income farmers	N	
33. Family medical leave-veto override	N	
34. Req submission of balanced budget	Y	
35. Balanced budget amendment	Y	
36. Amendment to ban flag desecration	Y	
37. Reauthorize Amtrak-veto override	Y	
38. Retraining aid for coal miners	Y	
39. Suspend El Salvador military aid	N	
40. Expand child care aid/tax credit	Y	
41. Raise House salary/omit honoraria	Y	
42. Toughen oil-spill liability	N	
43. Restitution to Japanese interned	N	
44. Protect Chinese & C.A. nationals	N	
45. Abortion $ for rape/incest cases	Y	
46. Allow religious schools to bar gays	Y	
47. Bar broadcaster fairness doctrine	N	
48. Bar cap gains cut/reinstate IRA	N	
49. Bar unions equal voice in pension	Y	
50. Bar assembly of chemical weapons	N	

51. Ban plutonium/uranium production	N	
52. Cap MX missile deployment at 50	N	
53. Allow $3b for 2 stealth bombers	Y	
54. Publish bio-warfare experiments	Y	
55. Raise minimum wage-veto override	N	
56. Bar transfer of FS-X technology	Y	
57. Cut defense and raise domestic $	N	
58. Uniform poll closing in 48 states	N	
59. Req foreign investment disclosure	Y	
60. Textile import quotas-veto override	N	
61. Bar abortion funding in Wash, DC	N	
62. Notify spouses of AIDS+ carriers	N	
63. Seize conveyance-drug trafficking	N	
64. South Africa sanctions	Y	
65. 60 days' notice of plant closings	N	
66. Close unneeded military bases	N	
67. Keep welfare reform within $2.8b	Y	
68. Allow children housing exclusion	Y	
69. Shift $400m of NASA to homeless	N	
70. Cap Medicare patients' liability	Y	
71. Prohibit employee polygraph testing	N	
72. Allow CIA to fund Contras	Y	
73. Revise unfair trade practices	Y	
74. Focus SDI on accidental launch	Y	
75. Bar Air Force $ for MX missile	N	
76. Allow "real" increase in defense	Y	
77. Troop reduction in Europe of 50%	N	
78. Ban nuclear tests above 1 kiloton	Y	
79. Ban anti-satellite missile tests	N	
80. Observe certain limits of SALT II	Y	
81. Restore four Civil Rights laws	Y	
82. Prohibit aliens as strikebreakers	Y	
83. Allow military malpractice suits	N	
84. Approval of $36m in Contra aid	Y	
85. $18b deficit reduction compromise	Y	
86. Welfare reform of $5.7b for 5 years	N	
87. Raise taxes $12b/cut spending $3b	Y	
88. Board to assess occupational risk	N	
89. Balanced budget by '93-via targets	Y	
90. Bar licensing of two nuclear plants	N	
91. Remove victims compensation cap	N	
92. Catastrophic health insurance	Y	
93. Ban airline smoking-2 hours or less	N	
94. $1b/two year aid for the homeless	Y	
95. Bar non-unions in union companies	N	
96. Increase FSLIC rescue to $15b	N	
97. Impose quotas to lower trade deficit	N	
98. Reduce discretionary budget 21%	Y	
99. Immigration reform/alien amnesty	Y	
100. South Africa sanctions-veto override	Y	

THOMAS, ROBERT LINDSAY (continued)

101. Tax overhaul to revise income tax	N	121. Approve $1.5b for 21 MX missiles	Y
102. Use of military in drug war	Y	122. Emergency farm credit/revisions	Y
103. Delete 12 MX/add conventional wpn	N	123. Duty on Taiwan/Hong Kong/S Korea	N
104. Raise speed limit to 65 mph	N	124. Limit steel imports to 17%	Y
105. Require Pentagon to buy US goods	N	125. Cut $ to schools that bar prayer	Y
106. AIDS insurance non-discrimination	Y	126. $50b-taxes; cut Medicare/spending	Y
107. Prohibit Saudi arms sales	Y	127. Limit Pershing II/cruise in Europe	N
108. Ease Gun Control Act of 1968	Y	128. Delete $7.1b for 34 B-1 bombers	N
109. Bar interstate handgun transport	N	129. Bar purchase of Sergeant York guns	N
110. Make company emissions known	Y	130. El Salvador military/economic aid	Y
111. Allow toxic victims to sue in fed ct	N	131. Bar mining of Nicaraguan waters	Y
112. Superfund waste cleanup of $10b	N	132. Physician fee freeze for Medicare	N
113. 90 days notice of plant closings	N	133. $49b in "sin"/phone/insurance taxes	Y
114. $20b in Medicare cuts/tax increases	Y	134. Allow sale of Conrail	N
115. Spending cuts and tax increases	Y	135. Equal Rights Amendment	N
116. Set school lunch lmt-250% poverty	N	136. Authorize Marines in Lebanon	Y
117. $75m for youth work projects	N	137. Eminent domain for coal companies	N
118. Allow Angola military assistance	Y	138. Prohibit EPA clean air sanctions	N
119. Suspend defense payments for abuse	N	139. SS retirement age increase/reforms	Y
120. Drop SS COLAs/$12b tax increase	Y		

Presidential Support Score: 1991 - 51%   1990 - 43%

HATCHER, CHARLES -- Georgia 2nd District [Democrat]. Counties of Baker, Ben Hill, Berrien, Brooks, Calhoun, Clay, Colquitt, Cook, Criso, Daugherty, Decatur, Early, Echols, Grady, Irwin, Lanier, Lee, Lowndes, Miller, Mitcheil, Quitman, Randolph, Seminole, Stewart, Terrell, Thomas, Tift, Turner, Webster and Worth. Prior Terms: 1981-92. Born: July 1, 1939; Doerun, GA. Education: Georgia Southern College (B.S.); University of Georgia (J.D.). Military Service: U.S. Air Force, 1958-62. Occupation: Attorney; teacher; Georgia representative (1973-80); governor's assistant.

1. Protection to Haitian refugees	?	33. Family medical leave-veto override	N
2. Raise tax on wealthy; lower others	Y	34. Req submission of balanced budget	Y
3. Investigate Reagan hostage delay	Y	35. Balanced budget amendment	Y
4. Campaign finance revisions	Y	36. Amendment to ban flag desecration	Y
5. Unpaid leave to care for children	?	37. Reauthorize Amtrak-veto override	Y
6. Restrict NEA use of funds	N	38. Retraining aid for coal miners	Y
7. Bar race-bias claim/habeas corpus	Y	39. Suspend El Salvador military aid	N
8. Ban race as death sentence factor	Y	40. Expand child care aid/tax credit	?
9. Exceptions to exclusionary rule	Y	41. Raise House salary/omit honoraria	Y
10. Allow sale of assault weapons	Y	42. Toughen oil-spill liability	N
11. Life in prison/abolish death penalty	N	43. Restitution to Japanese interned	N
12. Req conspiracy-price fixing cases	N	44. Protect Chinese & C.A. nationals	N
13. Unemployment benefits extension	Y	45. Abortion $ for rape/incest cases	Y
14. Tissue use of aborted fetuses	Y	46. Allow religious schools to bar gays	N
15. Bar replacement of union strikers	N	47. Bar broadcaster fairness doctrine	Y
16. Hold foreign aid at $15b for '92	Y	48. Bar cap gains cut/reinstate IRA	N
17. Restore space station funding	N	49. Bar unions equal voice in pension	Y
18. Civil Rights Act of 1991	Y	50. Bar assembly of chemical weapons	Y
19. Unlimited damages-discrimination	N	51. Ban plutonium/uranium production	Y
20. Eliminate funds for supercollider	N	52. Cap MX missile deployment at 50	N
21. Terminate SDI except for research	N	53. Allow $3b for 2 stealth bombers	N
22. Req 7-day handgun waiting period	Y	54. Publish bio-warfare experiments	N
23. Provide $30b for failed S&Ls	Y	55. Raise minimum wage-veto override	Y
24. Allow use of force against Iraq	Y	56. Bar transfer of FS-X technology	Y
25. Allow $15b in foreign aid for '91	Y	57. Cut defense and raise domestic $	N
26. Revise & extend legal immigration	Y	58. Uniform poll closing in 48 states	Y
27. Suspend aid to Angolan rebels	N	59. Req foreign investment disclosure	Y
28. Democratic tax plan proposals	Y	60. Textile import quotas-veto override	Y
29. Cut defense 5% across the board	N	61. Bar abortion funding in Wash, DC	N
30. Textile import quotas-veto override	Y	62. Notify spouses of AIDS+ carriers	N
31. Abortion service for military abroad	Y	63. Seize conveyance-drug trafficking	N
32. Limits on high income farmers	N	64. South Africa sanctions	?

HATCHER, CHARLES (continued)

65. 60 days' notice of plant closings	N	
66. Close unneeded military bases	N	
67. Keep welfare reform within $2.8b	?	
68. Allow children housing exclusion	N	
69. Shift $400m of NASA to homeless	N	
70. Cap Medicare patients' liability	Y	
71. Prohibit employee polygraph testing	N	
72. Allow CIA to fund Contras	Y	
73. Revise unfair trade practices	Y	
74. Focus SDI on accidental launch	Y	
75. Bar Air Force $ for MX missile	N	
76. Allow "real" increase in defense	Y	
77. Troop reduction in Europe of 50%	?	
78. Ban nuclear tests above 1 kiloton	Y	
79. Ban anti-satellite missile tests	N	
80. Observe certain limits of SALT II	Y	
81. Restore four Civil Rights laws	Y	
82. Prohibit aliens as strikebreakers	Y	
83. Allow military malpractice suits	Y	
84. Approval of $36m in Contra aid	Y	
85. $18b deficit reduction compromise	Y	
86. Welfare reform of $5.7b for 5 years	Y	
87. Raise taxes $12b/cut spending $3b	Y	
88. Board to assess occupational risk	?	
89. Balanced budget by '93-via targets	Y	
90. Bar licensing of two nuclear plants	N	
91. Remove victims compensation cap	N	
92. Catastrophic health insurance	Y	
93. Ban airline smoking-2 hours or less	N	
94. $1b/two year aid for the homeless	Y	
95. Bar non-unions in union companies	N	
96. Increase FSLIC rescue to $15b	N	
97. Impose quotas to lower trade deficit	N	
98. Reduce discretionary budget 21%	?	
99. Immigration reform/alien amnesty	Y	
100. South Africa sanctions-veto override	?	
101. Tax overhaul to revise income tax	Y	
102. Use of military in drug war	Y	
103. Delete 12 MX/add conventional wpn	N	
104. Raise speed limit to 65 mph	Y	

105. Require Pentagon to buy US goods	N
106. AIDS insurance non-discrimination	Y
107. Prohibit Saudi arms sales	Y
108. Ease Gun Control Act of 1968	Y
109. Bar interstate handgun transport	Y
110. Make company emissions known	N
111. Allow toxic victims to sue in fed ct	N
112. Superfund waste cleanup of $10b	N
113. 90 days notice of plant closings	N
114. $20b in Medicare cuts/tax increases	Y
115. Spending cuts and tax increases	Y
116. Set school lunch lmt-250% poverty	N
117. $75m for youth work projects	?
118. Allow Angolan military assistance	Y
119. Suspend defense payments for abuse	N
120. Drop SS COLAs/$12b tax increase	N
121. Approve $1.5b for 21 MX missiles	Y
122. Emergency farm credit/revisions	N
123. Duty on Taiwan/Hong Kong/S Korea	Y
124. Limit steel imports to 17%	Y
125. Cut $ to schools that bar prayer	?
126. $50b-taxes; cut Medicare/spending	Y
127. Limit Pershing II/cruise in Europe	?
128. Delete $7.1b for 34 B-1 bombers	N
129. Bar purchase of Sergeant York guns	N
130. El Salvador military/economic aid	Y
131. Bar mining of Nicaraguan waters	Y
132. Physician fee freeze for Medicare	N
133. $49b in "sin"/phone/insurance taxes	Y
134. Allow sale of Conrail	N
135. Equal Rights Amendment	Y
136. Authorize Marines in Lebanon	Y
137. Eminent domain for coal companies	N
138. Prohibit EPA clean air sanctions	N
139. SS retirement age increase/reforms	Y
140. Auto domestic content requirement	Y
141. Delete jobs program funding	N
142. Highway-gas tax bill	N
143. Cut $5b from defense for Medicare	N
144. Emergency housing aid of $1b	Y

Presidential Support Score: 1991 - 43% 1990 - 37%

RAY, RICHARD -- Georgia 3rd District [Democrat]. Counties of Bleckley, Butts, Chattahoochee, Crawford, Dooly, Harris, Houston, Lamar, Macon, Marion, Meriwether, Muscogee, Peach, Pike, Pulaski, Schley, Sumter, Talbot, Taylor, Troup and Upson. Prior Terms: 1983-92. Born: February 27, 1927; Fort Valley, GA. Military Service: U.S. Navy. Occupation: Worked family farm; established painting, pest control, and professional consulting service; councilman (1962); mayor (1964, 1966 and 1968); Senate administrative assistant 1972-82).

1. Protection to Haitian refugees	?
2. Raise tax on wealthy; lower others	?
3. Investigate Reagan hostage delay	N
4. Campaign finance revisions	?
5. Unpaid leave to care for children	N
6. Restrict NEA use of funds	Y
7. Bar race-bias claim/habeas corpus	Y
8. Ban race as death sentence factor	N
9. Exceptions to exclusionary rule	Y
10. Allow sale of assault weapons	Y
11. Life in prison/abolish death penalty	N
12. Req conspiracy-price fixing cases	Y

13. Unemployment benefits extension	N
14. Tissue use of aborted fetuses	N
15. Bar replacement of union strikers	N
16. Hold foreign aid at $15b for '92	N
17. Restore space station funding	N
18. Civil Rights Act of 1991	Y
19. Unlimited damages-discrimination	N
20. Eliminate funds for supercollider	N
21. Terminate SDI except for research	N
22. Req 7-day handgun waiting period	N
23. Provide $30b for failed S&Ls	Y
24. Allow use of force against Iraq	Y

RAY, RICHARD (continued)

25. Allow $15b in foreign aid for '91	N	
26. Revise & extend legal immigration	N	
27. Suspend aid to Angolan rebels	N	
28. Democratic tax plan proposals	Y	
29. Cut defense 5% across the board	N	
30. Textile import quotas-veto override	Y	
31. Abortion service for military abroad	N	
32. Limits on high income farmers	N	
33. Family medical leave-veto override	N	
34. Req submission of balanced budget	Y	
35. Balanced budget amendment	Y	
36. Amendment to ban flag desecration	Y	
37. Reauthorize Amtrak-veto override	Y	
38. Retraining aid for coal miners	N	
39. Suspend El Salvador military aid	N	
40. Expand child care aid/tax credit	N	
41. Raise House salary/omit honoraria	Y	
42. Toughen oil-spill liability	X	
43. Restitution to Japanese interned	N	
44. Protect Chinese & C.A. nationals	N	
45. Abortion $ for rape/incest cases	N	
46. Allow religious schools to bar gays	Y	
47. Bar broadcaster fairness doctrine	Y	
48. Bar cap gains cut/reinstate IRA	N	
49. Bar unions equal voice in pension	Y	
50. Bar assembly of chemical weapons	Y	
51. Ban plutonium/uranium production	N	
52. Cap MX missile deployment at 50	N	
53. Allow $3b for 2 stealth bombers	Y	
54. Publish bio-warfare experiments	N	
55. Raise minimum wage-veto override	N	
56. Bar transfer of FS-X technology	Y	
57. Cut defense and raise domestic $	N	
58. Uniform poll closing in 48 states	N	
59. Req foreign investment disclosure	Y	
60. Textile import quotas-veto override	Y	
61. Bar abortion funding in Wash, DC	Y	
62. Notify spouses of AIDS+ carriers	N	
63. Seize conveyance-drug trafficking	Y	
64. South Africa sanctions	Y	
65. 60 days' notice of plant closings	N	
66. Close unneeded military bases	N	
67. Keep welfare reform within $2.8b	?	
68. Allow children housing exclusion	?	
69. Shift $400m of NASA to homeless	?	
70. Cap Medicare patients' liability	X	
71. Prohibit employee polygraph testing	?	
72. Allow CIA to fund Contras	Y	
73. Revise unfair trade practices	Y	
74. Focus SDI on accidental launch	Y	
75. Bar Air Force $ for MX missile	?	
76. Allow "real" increase in defense	?	
77. Troop reduction in Europe of 50%	?	
78. Ban nuclear tests above 1 kiloton	?	
79. Ban anti-satellite missile tests	?	
80. Observe certain limits of SALT II	?	
81. Restore four Civil Rights laws	N	
82. Prohibit aliens as strikebreakers	N	

83. Allow military malpractice suits	N	
84. Approval of $36m in Contra aid	Y	
85. $18b deficit reduction compromise	Y	
86. Welfare reform of $5.7b for 5 years	N	
87. Raise taxes $12b/cut spending $3b	N	
88. Board to assess occupational risk	N	
89. Balanced budget by '93-via targets	N	
90. Bar licensing of two nuclear plants	N	
91. Remove victims compensation cap	N	
92. Catastrophic health insurance	N	
93. Ban airline smoking-2 hours or less	?	
94. $1b/two year aid for the homeless	?	
95. Bar non-unions in union companies	X	
96. Increase FSLIC rescue to $15b	N	
97. Impose quotas to lower trade deficit	N	
98. Reduce discretionary budget 21%	#	
99. Immigration reform/alien amnesty	N	
100. South Africa sanctions-veto override	Y	
101. Tax overhaul to revise income tax	N	
102. Use of military in drug war	N	
103. Delete 12 MX/add conventional wpn	N	
104. Raise speed limit to 65 mph	N	
105. Require Pentagon to buy US goods	N	
106. AIDS insurance non-discrimination	N	
107. Prohibit Saudi arms sales	N	
108. Ease Gun Control Act of 1968	Y	
109. Bar interstate handgun transport	N	
110. Make company emissions known	N	
111. Allow toxic victims to sue in fed ct	N	
112. Superfund waste cleanup of $10b	N	
113. 90 days notice of plant closings	N	
114. $20b in Medicare cuts/tax increases	Y	
115. Spending cuts and tax increases	Y	
116. Set school lunch lmt-250% poverty	Y	
117. $75m for youth work projects	N	
118. Allow Angolan military assistance	Y	
119. Suspend defense payments for abuse	N	
120. Drop SS COLAs/$12b tax increase	Y	
121. Approve $1.5b for 21 MX missiles	Y	
122. Emergency farm credit/revisions	Y	
123. Duty on Taiwan/Hong Kong/S Korea	N	
124. Limit steel imports to 17%	N	
125. Cut $ to schools that bar prayer	Y	
126. $50b-taxes; cut Medicare/spending	Y	
127. Limit Pershing II/cruise in Europe	N	
128. Delete $7.1b for 34 B-1 bombers	N	
129. Bar purchase of Sergeant York guns	N	
130. El Salvador military/economic aid	Y	
131. Bar mining of Nicaraguan waters	N	
132. Physician fee freeze for Medicare	N	
133. $49b in "sin"/phone/insurance taxes	Y	
134. Allow sale of Conrail	N	
135. Equal Rights Amendment	N	
136. Authorize Marines in Lebanon	N	
137. Eminent domain for coal companies	N	
138. Prohibit EPA clean air sanctions	Y	
139. SS retirement age increase/reforms	Y	

Presidential Support Score: 1991 - 60%   1990 - 53%

JONES, BEN -- Georgia 4th District [Democrat]. Counties of De Kalb (pt.), Fulton (pt.), Newton and Rockdale. Prior Terms: 1989-92. Born: 1941; Tarboro, NC. Education:

JONES, BEN (continued)
University of North Carolina-Chapel Hill. Occupation: Motion picture, stage and television entertainer; state film board chairman, Screen Actors' Guild president and state senate music industry committee member.

1. Protection to Haitian refugees	Y	30. Textile import quotas-veto override	Y
2. Raise tax on wealthy; lower others	Y	31. Abortion service for military abroad	Y
3. Investigate Reagan hostage delay	Y	32. Limits on high income farmers	N
4. Campaign finance revisions	Y	33. Family medical leave-veto override	N
5. Unpaid leave to care for children	N	34. Req submission of balanced budget	Y
6. Restrict NEA use of funds	N	35. Balanced budget amendment	Y
7. Bar race-bias claim/habeas corpus	N	36. Amendment to ban flag desecration	N
8. Ban race as death sentence factor	N	37. Reauthorize Amtrak-veto override	Y
9. Exceptions to exclusionary rule	N	38. Retraining aid for coal miners	Y
10. Allow sale of assault weapons	Y	39. Suspend El Salvador military aid	Y
11. Life in prison/abolish death penalty	N	40. Expand child care aid/tax credit	Y
12. Req conspiracy-price fixing cases	N	41. Raise House salary/omit honoraria	Y
13. Unemployment benefits extension	Y	42. Toughen oil-spill liability	Y
14. Tissue use of aborted fetuses	Y	43. Restitution to Japanese interned	Y
15. Bar replacement of union strikers	Y	44. Protect Chinese & C.A. nationals	Y
16. Hold foreign aid at $15b for '92	Y	45. Abortion $ for rape/incest cases	Y
17. Restore space station funding	N	46. Allow religious schools to bar gays	N
18. Civil Rights Act of 1991	Y	47. Bar broadcaster fairness doctrine	N
19. Unlimited damages-discrimination	N	48. Bar cap gains cut/reinstate IRA	N
20. Eliminate funds for supercollider	Y	49. Bar unions equal voice in pension	Y
21. Terminate SDI except for research	N	50. Bar assembly of chemical weapons	Y
22. Req 7-day handgun waiting period	Y	51. Ban plutonium/uranium production	Y
23. Provide $30b for failed S&Ls	N	52. Cap MX missile deployment at 50	Y
24. Allow use of force against Iraq	Y	53. Allow $3b for 2 stealth bombers	N
25. Allow $15b in foreign aid for '91	N	54. Publish bio-warfare experiments	Y
26. Revise & extend legal immigration	Y	55. Raise minimum wage-veto override	Y
27. Suspend aid to Angolan rebels	N	56. Bar transfer of FS-X technology	Y
28. Democratic tax plan proposals	N	57. Cut defense and raise domestic $	N
29. Cut defense 5% across the board	N	58. Uniform poll closing in 48 states	N

Presidential Support Score: 1991 - 27%   1990 - 34%

LEWIS, JOHN -- Georgia 5th District [Democrat]. Counties of DeKalb (pt.) and Fulton (pt.). Prior Terms: 1987-92. Born: February 21, 1940; Pike County AL. Education: American Baptist Theological Seminary (B.A.); Fisk University (B.A.). Occupation: Civil rights organizer; Southern Regional Council Voter Education Project director; associate director for Domestic and Anti-Poverty Operations, ACTION; Atlanta city councilman (1982-1986).

1. Protection to Haitian refugees	Y	22. Req 7-day handgun waiting period	Y
2. Raise tax on wealthy; lower others	Y	23. Provide $30b for failed S&Ls	N
3. Investigate Reagan hostage delay	Y	24. Allow use of force against Iraq	N
4. Campaign finance revisions	Y	25. Allow $15b in foreign aid for '91	N
5. Unpaid leave to care for children	Y	26. Revise & extend legal immigration	Y
6. Restrict NEA use of funds	N	27. Suspend aid to Angolan rebels	Y
7. Bar race-bias claim/habeas corpus	?	28. Democratic tax plan proposals	Y
8. Ban race as death sentence factor	N	29. Cut defense 5% across the board	Y
9. Exceptions to exclusionary rule	N	30. Textile import quotas-veto override	Y
10. Allow sale of assault weapons	N	31. Abortion service for military abroad	Y
11. Life in prison/abolish death penalty	Y	32. Limits on high income farmers	N
12. Req conspiracy-price fixing cases	N	33. Family medical leave-veto override	Y
13. Unemployment benefits extension	Y	34. Req submission of balanced budget	Y
14. Tissue use of aborted fetuses	Y	35. Balanced budget amendment	N
15. Bar replacement of union strikers	Y	36. Amendment to ban flag desecration	N
16. Hold foreign aid at $15b for '92	Y	37. Reauthorize Amtrak-veto override	Y
17. Restore space station funding	N	38. Retraining aid for coal miners	Y
18. Civil Rights Act of 1991	Y	39. Suspend El Salvador military aid	Y
19. Unlimited damages-discrimination	Y	40. Expand child care aid/tax credit	Y
20. Eliminate funds for supercollider	Y	41. Raise House salary/omit honoraria	Y
21. Terminate SDI except for research	?	42. Toughen oil-spill liability	Y

LEWIS, JOHN (continued)

43. Restitution to Japanese interned	Y	71. Prohibit employee polygraph testing	Y
44. Protect Chinese & C.A. nationals	Y	72. Allow CIA to fund Contras	N
45. Abortion $ for rape/incest cases	Y	73. Revise unfair trade practices	Y
46. Allow religious schools to bar gays	N	74. Focus SDI on accidental launch	Y
47. Bar broadcaster fairness doctrine	N	75. Bar Air Force $ for MX missile	Y
48. Bar cap gains cut/reinstate IRA	Y	76. Allow "real" increase in defense	N
49. Bar unions equal voice in pension	N	77. Troop reduction in Europe of 50%	Y
50. Bar assembly of chemical weapons	Y	78. Ban nuclear tests above 1 kiloton	Y
51. Ban plutonium/uranium production	Y	79. Ban anti-satellite missile tests	Y
52. Cap MX missile deployment at 50	Y	80. Observe certain limits of SALT II	Y
53. Allow $3b for 2 stealth bombers	N	81. Restore four Civil Rights laws	Y
54. Publish bio-warfare experiments	Y	82. Prohibit aliens as strikebreakers	Y
55. Raise minimum wage-veto override	Y	83. Allow military malpractice suits	Y
56. Bar transfer of FS-X technology	Y	84. Approval of $36m in Contra aid	N
57. Cut defense and raise domestic $	Y	85. $18b deficit reduction compromise	N
58. Uniform poll closing in 48 states	Y	86. Welfare reform of $5.7b for 5 years	Y
59. Req foreign investment disclosure	Y	87. Raise taxes $12b/cut spending $3b	Y
60. Textile import quotas-veto override	Y	88. Board to assess occupational risk	Y
61. Bar abortion funding in Wash, DC	N	89. Balanced budget by '93-via targets	N
62. Notify spouses of AIDS+ carriers	N	90. Bar licensing of two nuclear plants	N
63. Seize conveyance-drug trafficking	N	91. Remove victims compensation cap	N
64. South Africa sanctions	Y	92. Catastrophic health insurance	Y
65. 60 days' notice of plant closings	Y	93. Ban airline smoking-2 hours or less	N
66. Close unneeded military bases	N	94. $1b/two year aid for the homeless	Y
67. Keep welfare reform within $2.8b	N	95. Bar non-unions in union companies	Y
68. Allow children housing exclusion	N	96. Increase FSLIC rescue to $15b	N
69. Shift $400m of NASA to homeless	Y	97. Impose quotas to lower trade deficit	Y
70. Cap Medicare patients' liability	Y	98. Reduce discretionary budget 21%	Y

Presidential Support Score: 1991 - 22%   1990 - 16%

GINGRICH, NEWT -- Georgia 6th District [Republican]. Counties of Carroll, Clayton, Coweta, Douglas, Fayette, Fulton (pt.), Haralson, Heard, Henry, Paulding, Polk and Spalding. Prior Terms: 1979-92. Born: June 7, 1943; Harrisburg, PA. Education: Emory University (B.A.); Tulane University (M.A., Ph.D.). Occupation: Assistant professor, West Georgia College.

1. Protection to Haitian refugees	?	27. Suspend aid to Angolan rebels	N
2. Raise tax on wealthy; lower others	N	28. Democratic tax plan proposals	N
3. Investigate Reagan hostage delay	N	29. Cut defense 5% across the board	N
4. Campaign finance revisions	N	30. Textile import quotas-veto override	Y
5. Unpaid leave to care for children	N	31. Abortion service for military abroad	N
6. Restrict NEA use of funds	Y	32. Limits on high income farmers	N
7. Bar race-bias claim/habeas corpus	Y	33. Family medical leave-veto override	N
8. Ban race as death sentence factor	Y	34. Req submission of balanced budget	N
9. Exceptions to exclusionary rule	Y	35. Balanced budget amendment	Y
10. Allow sale of assault weapons	Y	36. Amendment to ban flag desecration	Y
11. Life in prison/abolish death penalty	N	37. Reauthorize Amtrak-veto override	N
12. Req conspiracy-price fixing cases	Y	38. Retraining aid for coal miners	N
13. Unemployment benefits extension	N	39. Suspend El Salvador military aid	N
14. Tissue use of aborted fetuses	N	40. Expand child care aid/tax credit	N
15. Bar replacement of union strikers	N	41. Raise House salary/omit honoraria	Y
16. Hold foreign aid at $15b for '92	Y	42. Toughen oil-spill liability	N
17. Restore space station funding	Y	43. Restitution to Japanese interned	Y
18. Civil Rights Act of 1991	N	44. Protect Chinese & C.A. nationals	N
19. Unlimited damages-discrimination	N	45. Abortion $ for rape/incest cases	N
20. Eliminate funds for supercollider	N	46. Allow religious schools to bar gays	Y
21. Terminate SDI except for research	N	47. Bar broadcaster fairness doctrine	Y
22. Req 7-day handgun waiting period	N	48. Bar cap gains cut/reinstate IRA	N
23. Provide $30b for failed S&Ls	Y	49. Bar unions equal voice in pension	Y
24. Allow use of force against Iraq	Y	50. Bar assembly of chemical weapons	N
25. Allow $15b in foreign aid for '91	?	51. Ban plutonium/uranium production	N
26. Revise & extend legal immigration	?	52. Cap MX missile deployment at 50	N

GINGRICH, NEWT (continued)

53. Allow $3b for 2 stealth bombers	Y		99. Immigration reform/alien amnesty	Y
54. Publish bio-warfare experiments	N		100. South Africa sanctions-veto override	Y
55. Raise minimum wage-veto override	N		101. Tax overhaul to revise income tax	Y
56. Bar transfer of FS-X technology	N		102. Use of military in drug war	Y
57. Cut defense and raise domestic $	N		103. Delete 12 MX/add conventional wpn	N
58. Uniform poll closing in 48 states	N		104. Raise speed limit to 65 mph	Y
59. Req foreign investment disclosure	N		105. Require Pentagon to buy US goods	N
60. Textile import quotas-veto override	Y		106. AIDS insurance non-discrimination	N
61. Bar abortion funding in Wash, DC	Y		107. Prohibit Saudi arms sales	Y
62. Notify spouses of AIDS+ carriers	Y		108. Ease Gun Control Act of 1968	Y
63. Seize conveyance-drug trafficking	Y		109. Bar interstate handgun transport	N
64. South Africa sanctions	?		110. Make company emissions known	N
65. 60 days' notice of plant closings	N		111. Allow toxic victims to sue in fed ct	N
66. Close unneeded military bases	Y		112. Superfund waste cleanup of $10b	N
67. Keep welfare reform within $2.8b	Y		113. 90 days notice of plant closings	N
68. Allow children housing exclusion	N		114. $20b in Medicare cuts/tax increases	N
69. Shift $400m of NASA to homeless	N		115. Spending cuts and tax increases	N
70. Cap Medicare patients' liability	N		116. Set school lunch lmt-250% poverty	Y
71. Prohibit employee polygraph testing	N		117. $75m for youth work projects	N
72. Allow CIA to fund Contras	Y		118. Allow Angolan military assistance	Y
73. Revise unfair trade practices	N		119. Suspend defense payments for abuse	N
74. Focus SDI on accidental launch	N		120. Drop SS COLAs/$12b tax increase	N
75. Bar Air Force $ for MX missile	N		121. Approve $1.5b for 21 MX missiles	Y
76. Allow "real" increase in defense	Y		122. Emergency farm credit/revisions	Y
77. Troop reduction in Europe of 50%	N		123. Duty on Taiwan/Hong Kong/S Korea	N
78. Ban nuclear tests above 1 kiloton	N		124. Limit steel imports to 17%	N
79. Ban anti-satellite missile tests	N		125. Cut $ to schools that bar prayer	Y
80. Observe certain limits of SALT II	N		126. $50b-taxes; cut Medicare/spending	?
81. Restore four Civil Rights laws	N		127. Limit Pershing II/cruise in Europe	N
82. Prohibit aliens as strikebreakers	N		128. Delete $7.1b for 34 B-1 bombers	N
83. Allow military malpractice suits	Y		129. Bar purchase of Sergeant York guns	Y
84. Approval of $36m in Contra aid	Y		130. El Salvador military/economic aid	Y
85. $18b deficit reduction compromise	N		131. Bar mining of Nicaraguan waters	N
86. Welfare reform of $5.7b for 5 years	N		132. Physician fee freeze for Medicare	Y
87. Raise taxes $12b/cut spending $3b	N		133. $49b in "sin"/phone/insurance taxes	Y
88. Board to assess occupational risk	N		134. Allow sale of Conrail	Y
89. Balanced budget by '93-via targets	Y		135. Equal Rights Amendment	N
90. Bar licensing of two nuclear plants	N		136. Authorize Marines in Lebanon	Y
91. Remove victims compensation cap	N		137. Eminent domain for coal companies	Y
92. Catastrophic health insurance	N		138. Prohibit EPA clean air sanctions	Y
93. Ban airline smoking-2 hours or less	N		139. SS retirement age increase/reforms	Y
94. $1b/two year aid for the homeless	N		140. Auto domestic content requirement	Y
95. Bar non-unions in union companies	N		141. Delete jobs program funding	Y
96. Increase FSLIC rescue to $15b	N		142. Highway-gas tax bill	N
97. Impose quotas to lower trade deficit	N		143. Cut $5b from defense for Medicare	N
98. Reduce discretionary budget 21%	N		144. Emergency housing aid of $1b	Y

Presidential Support Score: 1991 - 78%   1990 - 66%

DARDEN, GEORGE (Buddy) -- Georgia 7th District [Democrat]. Counties of Bartow, Catoosa, Chatooga, Cobb, Dade, Floyd and Walker. Prior Terms: 1983-92. Born: November 22, 1943. Education: University of Georgia. Occupation: Attorney; congressional aide; district attorney; Georgia representative.

1. Protection to Haitian refugees	N		10. Allow sale of assault weapons	Y
2. Raise tax on wealthy; lower others	Y		11. Life in prison/abolish death penalty	N
3. Investigate Reagan hostage delay	Y		12. Req conspiracy-price fixing cases	Y
4. Campaign finance revisions	Y		13. Unemployment benefits extension	Y
5. Unpaid leave to care for children	N		14. Tissue use of aborted fetuses	Y
6. Restrict NEA use of funds	Y		15. Bar replacement of union strikers	Y
7. Bar race-bias claim/habeas corpus	Y		16. Hold foreign aid at $15b for '92	Y
8. Ban race as death sentence factor	Y		17. Restore space station funding	Y
9. Exceptions to exclusionary rule	Y		18. Civil Rights Act of 1991	N

DARDEN, GEORGE (continued)

19. Unlimited damages-discrimination	N	
20. Eliminate funds for supercollider	N	
21. Terminate SDI except for research	N	
22. Req 7-day handgun waiting period	Y	
23. Provide $30b for failed S&Ls	Y	
24. Allow use of force against Iraq	Y	
25. Allow $15b in foreign aid for '91	N	
26. Revise & extend legal immigration	Y	
27. Suspend aid to Angolan rebels	N	
28. Democratic tax plan proposals	Y	
29. Cut defense 5% across the board	N	
30. Textile import quotas-veto override	Y	
31. Abortion service for military abroad	Y	
32. Limits on high income farmers	N	
33. Family medical leave-veto override	N	
34. Req submission of balanced budget	Y	
35. Balanced budget amendment	Y	
36. Amendment to ban flag desecration	Y	
37. Reauthorize Amtrak-veto override	Y	
38. Retraining aid for coal miners	Y	
39. Suspend El Salvador military aid	N	
40. Expand child care aid/tax credit	Y	
41. Raise House salary/omit honoraria	Y	
42. Toughen oil-spill liability	N	
43. Restitution to Japanese interned	N	
44. Protect Chinese & C.A. nationals	Y	
45. Abortion $ for rape/incest cases	N	
46. Allow religious schools to bar gays	Y	
47. Bar broadcaster fairness doctrine	N	
48. Bar cap gains cut/reinstate IRA	N	
49. Bar unions equal voice in pension	Y	
50. Bar assembly of chemical weapons	Y	
51. Ban plutonium/uranium production	Y	
52. Cap MX missile deployment at 50	N	
53. Allow $3b for 2 stealth bombers	N	
54. Publish bio-warfare experiments	Y	
55. Raise minimum wage-veto override	Y	
56. Bar transfer of FS-X technology	Y	
57. Cut defense and raise domestic $	N	
58. Uniform poll closing in 48 states	N	
59. Req foreign investment disclosure	Y	
60. Textile import quotas-veto override	Y	
61. Bar abortion funding in Wash, DC	Y	
62. Notify spouses of AIDS+ carriers	N	
63. Seize conveyance-drug trafficking	Y	
64. South Africa sanctions	Y	
65. 60 days' notice of plant closings	N	
66. Close unneeded military bases	N	
67. Keep welfare reform within $2.8b	Y	
68. Allow children housing exclusion	Y	
69. Shift $400m of NASA to homeless	N	
70. Cap Medicare patients' liability	Y	
71. Prohibit employee polygraph testing	N	
72. Allow CIA to fund Contras	Y	
73. Revise unfair trade practices	Y	
74. Focus SDI on accidental launch	Y	
75. Bar Air Force $ for MX missile	N	
76. Allow "real" increase in defense	Y	
77. Troop reduction in Europe of 50%	Y	

78. Ban nuclear tests above 1 kiloton	N	
79. Ban anti-satellite missile tests	N	
80. Observe certain limits of SALT II	Y	
81. Restore four Civil Rights laws	Y	
82. Prohibit aliens as strikebreakers	Y	
83. Allow military malpractice suits	N	
84. Approval of $36m in Contra aid	Y	
85. $18b deficit reduction compromise	Y	
86. Welfare reform of $5.7b for 5 years	N	
87. Raise taxes $12b/cut spending $3b	Y	
88. Board to assess occupational risk	N	
89. Balanced budget by '93-via targets	Y	
90. Bar licensing of two nuclear plants	N	
91. Remove victims compensation cap	N	
92. Catastrophic health insurance	Y	
93. Ban airline smoking-2 hours or less	N	
94. $1b/two year aid for the homeless	Y	
95. Bar non-unions in union companies	N	
96. Increase FSLIC rescue to $15b	Y	
97. Impose quotas to lower trade deficit	Y	
98. Reduce discretionary budget 21%	Y	
99. Immigration reform/alien amnesty	Y	
100. South Africa sanctions-veto override	Y	
101. Tax overhaul to revise income tax	N	
102. Use of military in drug war	Y	
103. Delete 12 MX/add conventional wpn	X	
104. Raise speed limit to 65 mph	Y	
105. Require Pentagon to buy US goods	N	
106. AIDS insurance non-discrimination	Y	
107. Prohibit Saudi arms sales	Y	
108. Ease Gun Control Act of 1968	Y	
109. Bar interstate handgun transport	N	
110. Make company emissions known	N	
111. Allow toxic victims to sue in fed ct	N	
112. Superfund waste cleanup of $10b	Y	
113. 90 days notice of plant closings	N	
114. $20b in Medicare cuts/tax increases	Y	
115. Spending cuts and tax increases	Y	
116. Set school lunch lmt-250% poverty	N	
117. $75m for youth work projects	Y	
118. Allow Angolan military assistance	Y	
119. Suspend defense payments for abuse	N	
120. Drop SS COLAs/$12b tax increase	N	
121. Approve $1.5b for 21 MX missiles	Y	
122. Emergency farm credit/revisions	Y	
123. Duty on Taiwan/Hong Kong/S Korea	N	
124. Limit steel imports to 17%	Y	
125. Cut $ to schools that bar prayer	Y	
126. $50b-taxes; cut Medicare/spending	N	
127. Limit Pershing II/cruise in Europe	N	
128. Delete $7.1b for 34 B-1 bombers	N	
129. Bar purchase of Sergeant York guns	N	
130. El Salvador military/economic aid	Y	
131. Bar mining of Nicaraguan waters	N	
132. Physician fee freeze for Medicare	N	
133. $49b in "sin"/phone/insurance taxes	Y	
134. Allow sale of Conrail	N	
135. Equal Rights Amendment	Y	

Presidential Support Score: 1991 - 49%   1990 - 43%

ROWLAND, J. ROY -- Georgia 8th District [Democrat]. Counties of Appling, Atkinson, Bacon, Baldwin, Bibb, Charlton, Clinch, Coffee, Dodge, Glascock, Greene, Hancock, Jasper, Jeff Davis, Jefferson, Johnson, Jones, Laurens, Monroe, Pierce, Putnam, Taliaferro, Telfair, Treutlen, Twiggs, Ware, Washington, Wheeler, Wilcox and Wilkinson. Prior Terms: 1983-92. Born: February 3, 1926; Wrightville, GA. Education: Emory University; South Georgia College; University of Georgia; Medical College of Georgia. Military Service: U.S. Army. Occupation: Family physician; Georgia representative (1976-82).

1. Protection to Haitian refugees	X	58. Uniform poll closing in 48 states	N
2. Raise tax on wealthy; lower others	N	59. Req foreign investment disclosure	Y
3. Investigate Reagan hostage delay	Y	60. Textile import quotas-veto override	Y
4. Campaign finance revisions	Y	61. Bar abortion funding in Wash, DC	N
5. Unpaid leave to care for children	N	62. Notify spouses of AIDS+ carriers	N
6. Restrict NEA use of funds	Y	63. Seize conveyance-drug trafficking	N
7. Bar race-bias claim/habeas corpus	Y	64. South Africa sanctions	Y
8. Ban race as death sentence factor	Y	65. 60 days' notice of plant closings	N
9. Exceptions to exclusionary rule	Y	66. Close unneeded military bases	Y
10. Allow sale of assault weapons	Y	67. Keep welfare reform within $2.8b	Y
11. Life in prison/abolish death penalty	N	68. Allow children housing exclusion	N
12. Req conspiracy-price fixing cases	Y	69. Shift $400m of NASA to homeless	Y
13. Unemployment benefits extension	#	70. Cap Medicare patients' liability	Y
14. Tissue use of aborted fetuses	Y	71. Prohibit employee polygraph testing	N
15. Bar replacement of union strikers	N	72. Allow CIA to fund Contras	N
16. Hold foreign aid at $15b for '92	Y	73. Revise unfair trade practices	Y
17. Restore space station funding	N	74. Focus SDI on accidental launch	Y
18. Civil Rights Act of 1991	Y	75. Bar Air Force $ for MX missile	N
19. Unlimited damages-discrimination	N	76. Allow "real" increase in defense	#
20. Eliminate funds for supercollider	N	77. Troop reduction in Europe of 50%	Y
21. Terminate SDI except for research	N	78. Ban nuclear tests above 1 kiloton	Y
22. Req 7-day handgun waiting period	Y	79. Ban anti-satellite missile tests	N
23. Provide $30b for failed S&Ls	Y	80. Observe certain limits of SALT II	Y
24. Allow use of force against Iraq	Y	81. Restore four Civil Rights laws	N
25. Allow $15b in foreign aid for '91	N	82. Prohibit aliens as strikebreakers	Y
26. Revise & extend legal immigration	N	83. Allow military malpractice suits	N
27. Suspend aid to Angolan rebels	N	84. Approval of $36m in Contra aid	N
28. Democratic tax plan proposals	Y	85. $18b deficit reduction compromise	Y
29. Cut defense 5% across the board	N	86. Welfare reform of $5.7b for 5 years	N
30. Textile import quotas-veto override	Y	87. Raise taxes $12b/cut spending $3b	Y
31. Abortion service for military abroad	Y	88. Board to assess occupational risk	N
32. Limits on high income farmers	N	89. Balanced budget by '93-via targets	Y
33. Family medical leave-veto override	N	90. Bar licensing of two nuclear plants	N
34. Req submission of balanced budget	Y	91. Remove victims compensation cap	N
35. Balanced budget amendment	Y	92. Catastrophic health insurance	Y
36. Amendment to ban flag desecration	Y	93. Ban airline smoking-2 hours or less	N
37. Reauthorize Amtrak-veto override	Y	94. $1b/two year aid for the homeless	Y
38. Retraining aid for coal miners	Y	95. Bar non-unions in union companies	N
39. Suspend El Salvador military aid	Y	96. Increase FSLIC rescue to $15b	N
40. Expand child care aid/tax credit	Y	97. Impose quotas to lower trade deficit	N
41. Raise House salary/omit honoraria	Y	98. Reduce discretionary budget 21%	Y
42. Toughen oil-spill liability	N	99. Immigration reform/alien amnesty	Y
43. Restitution to Japanese interned	N	100. South Africa sanctions-veto override	Y
44. Protect Chinese & C.A. nationals	Y	101. Tax overhaul to revise income tax	N
45. Abortion $ for rape/incest cases	Y	102. Use of military in drug war	Y
46. Allow religious schools to bar gays	Y	103. Delete 12 MX/add conventional wpn	N
47. Bar broadcaster fairness doctrine	N	104. Raise speed limit to 65 mph	N
48. Bar cap gains cut/reinstate IRA	N	105. Require Pentagon to buy US goods	N
49. Bar unions equal voice in pension	Y	106. AIDS insurance non-discrimination	Y
50. Bar assembly of chemical weapons	N	107. Prohibit Saudi arms sales	Y
51. Ban plutonium/uranium production	Y	108. Ease Gun Control Act of 1968	Y
52. Cap MX missile deployment at 50	Y	109. Bar interstate handgun transport	N
53. Allow $3b for 2 stealth bombers	N	110. Make company emissions known	N
54. Publish bio-warfare experiments	Y	111. Allow toxic victims to sue in fed ct	N
55. Raise minimum wage-veto override	N	112. Superfund waste cleanup of $10b	N
56. Bar transfer of FS-X technology	Y	113. 90 days notice of plant closings	N
57. Cut defense and raise domestic $	N	114. $20b in Medicare cuts/tax increases	Y

ROWLAND, J. ROY (continued)

115. Spending cuts and tax increases	Y	128. Delete $7.1b for 34 B-1 bombers	N
116. Set school lunch lmt-250% poverty	N	129. Bar purchase of Sergeant York guns	N
117. $75m for youth work projects	N	130. El Salvador military/economic aid	Y
118. Allow Angolan military assistance	Y	131. Bar mining of Nicaraguan waters	Y
119. Suspend defense payments for abuse	N	132. Physician fee freeze for Medicare	N
120. Drop SS COLAs/$12b tax increase	Y	133. $49b in "sin"/phone/insurance taxes	Y
121. Approve $1.5b for 21 MX missiles	Y	134. Allow sale of Conrail	N
122. Emergency farm credit/revisions	Y	135. Equal Rights Amendment	N
123. Duty on Taiwan/Hong Kong/S Korea	N	136. Authorize Marines in Lebanon	Y
124. Limit steel imports to 17%	Y	137. Eminent domain for coal companies	N
125. Cut $ to schools that bar prayer	Y	138. Prohibit EPA clean air sanctions	?
126. $50b-taxes; cut Medicare/spending	Y	139. SS retirement age increase/reforms	Y
127. Limit Pershing II/cruise in Europe	N		

Presidential Support Score: 1991 - 50%   1990 - 42%

JENKINS, ED -- Georgia 9th District [Democrat].   Counties of Banks, Cherokee, Dawson, Fannin, Forsyth, Franklin, Gilmer, Gordon, Gwinnett (pt.), Habersham, Hall, Hart, Jackson, Lumpkin, Murray, Pickens, Rabun, Stephens, Towns, Union, White and Whitfield.   Prior Terms: 1977-92.   Born: January 4, 1933; Young Harris, GA.   Education: Young Harris College (A.A.); University of Georgia (LL.B.).   Occupation: Attorney, assistant U.S. attorney; county and city attorney.

1. Protection to Haitian refugees	Y	41. Raise House salary/omit honoraria	Y
2. Raise tax on wealthy; lower others	Y	42. Toughen oil-spill liability	?
3. Investigate Reagan hostage delay	Y	43. Restitution to Japanese interned	N
4. Campaign finance revisions	Y	44. Protect Chinese & C.A. nationals	Y
5. Unpaid leave to care for children	Y	45. Abortion $ for rape/incest cases	N
6. Restrict NEA use of funds	?	46. Allow religious schools to bar gays	Y
7. Bar race-bias claim/habeas corpus	Y	47. Bar broadcaster fairness doctrine	N
8. Ban race as death sentence factor	Y	48. Bar cap gains cut/reinstate IRA	N
9. Exceptions to exclusionary rule	Y	49. Bar unions equal voice in pension	Y
10. Allow sale of assault weapons	Y	50. Bar assembly of chemical weapons	Y
11. Life in prison/abolish death penalty	N	51. Ban plutonium/uranium production	Y
12. Req conspiracy-price fixing cases	N	52. Cap MX missile deployment at 50	Y
13. Unemployment benefits extension	Y	53. Allow $3b for 2 stealth bombers	Y
14. Tissue use of aborted fetuses	Y	54. Publish bio-warfare experiments	Y
15. Bar replacement of union strikers	N	55. Raise minimum wage-veto override	Y
16. Hold foreign aid at $15b for '92	N	56. Bar transfer of FS-X technology	Y
17. Restore space station funding	Y	57. Cut defense and raise domestic $	N
18. Civil Rights Act of 1991	N	58. Uniform poll closing in 48 states	N
19. Unlimited damages-discrimination	N	59. Req foreign investment disclosure	Y
20. Eliminate funds for supercollider	N	60. Textile import quotas-veto override	Y
21. Terminate SDI except for research	N	61. Bar abortion funding in Wash, DC	Y
22. Req 7-day handgun waiting period	N	62. Notify spouses of AIDS+ carriers	N
23. Provide $30b for failed S&Ls	Y	63. Seize conveyance-drug trafficking	Y
24. Allow use of force against Iraq	N	64. South Africa sanctions	Y
25. Allow $15b in foreign aid for '91	?	65. 60 days' notice of plant closings	N
26. Revise & extend legal immigration	?	66. Close unneeded military bases	Y
27. Suspend aid to Angolan rebels	N	67. Keep welfare reform within $2.8b	Y
28. Democratic tax plan proposals	Y	68. Allow children housing exclusion	N
29. Cut defense 5% across the board	N	69. Shift $400m of NASA to homeless	N
30. Textile import quotas-veto override	Y	70. Cap Medicare patients' liability	Y
31. Abortion service for military abroad	N	71. Prohibit employee polygraph testing	N
32. Limits on high income farmers	N	72. Allow CIA to fund Contras	N
33. Family medical leave-veto override	Y	73. Revise unfair trade practices	Y
34. Req submission of balanced budget	Y	74. Focus SDI on accidental launch	Y
35. Balanced budget amendment	Y	75. Bar Air Force $ for MX missile	N
36. Amendment to ban flag desecration	Y	76. Allow "real" increase in defense	N
37. Reauthorize Amtrak-veto override	Y	77. Troop reduction in Europe of 50%	Y
38. Retraining aid for coal miners	N	78. Ban nuclear tests above 1 kiloton	Y
39. Suspend El Salvador military aid	N	79. Ban anti-satellite missile tests	N
40. Expand child care aid/tax credit	Y	80. Observe certain limits of SALT II	Y

JENKINS, ED (continued)

81.	Restore four Civil Rights laws	Y	113.	90 days notice of plant closings	N
82.	Prohibit aliens as strikebreakers	Y	114.	$20b in Medicare cuts/tax increases	Y
83.	Allow military malpractice suits	N	115.	Spending cuts and tax increases	Y
84.	Approval of $36m in Contra aid	Y	116.	Set school lunch lmt-250% poverty	N
85.	$18b deficit reduction compromise	Y	117.	$75m for youth work projects	Y
86.	Welfare reform of $5.7b for 5 years	Y	118.	Allow Angolan military assistance	Y
87.	Raise taxes $12b/cut spending $3b	Y	119.	Suspend defense payments for abuse	N
88.	Board to assess occupational risk	N	120.	Drop SS COLAs/$12b tax increase	N
89.	Balanced budget by '93-via targets	Y	121.	Approve $1.5b for 21 MX missiles	N
90.	Bar licensing of two nuclear plants	N	122.	Emergency farm credit/revisions	Y
91.	Remove victims compensation cap	N	123.	Duty on Taiwan/Hong Kong/S Korea	Y
92.	Catastrophic health insurance	Y	124.	Limit steel imports to 17%	Y
93.	Ban airline smoking-2 hours or less	N	125.	Cut $ to schools that bar prayer	Y
94.	$1b/two year aid for the homeless	Y	126.	$50b-taxes; cut Medicare/spending	Y
95.	Bar non-unions in union companies	N	127.	Limit Pershing II/cruise in Europe	?
96.	Increase FSLIC rescue to $15b	N	128.	Delete $7.1b for 34 B-1 bombers	?
97.	Impose quotas to lower trade deficit	Y	129.	Bar purchase of Sergeant York guns	N
98.	Reduce discretionary budget 21%	Y	130.	El Salvador military/economic aid	Y
99.	Immigration reform/alien amnesty	Y	131.	Bar mining of Nicaraguan waters	Y
100.	South Africa sanctions-veto override	Y	132.	Physician fee freeze for Medicare	N
101.	Tax overhaul to revise income tax	Y	133.	$49b in "sin"/phone/insurance taxes	Y
102.	Use of military in drug war	Y	134.	Allow sale of Conrail	Y
103.	Delete 12 MX/add conventional wpn	?	135.	Equal Rights Amendment	?
104.	Raise speed limit to 65 mph	Y	136.	Authorize Marines in Lebanon	Y
105.	Require Pentagon to buy US goods	Y	137.	Eminent domain for coal companies	N
106.	AIDS insurance non-discrimination	Y	138.	Prohibit EPA clean air sanctions	N
107.	Prohibit Saudi arms sales	Y	139.	SS retirement age increase/reforms	Y
108.	Ease Gun Control Act of 1968	Y	140.	Auto domestic content requirement	Y
109.	Bar interstate handgun transport	N	141.	Delete jobs program funding	Y
110.	Make company emissions known	Y	142.	Highway-gas tax bill	Y
111.	Allow toxic victims to sue in fed ct	N	143.	Cut $5b from defense for Medicare	N
112.	Superfund waste cleanup of $10b	N	144.	Emergency housing aid of $1b	Y

Presidential Support Score: 1991 - 45%   1990 - 44%

BARNARD, DOUG, Jr. -- Georgia 10th District [Democrat]. Counties of Barrow, Clarke, Columbia, Elbert, Gwinnett (pt.), Lincoln, McDuffie, Madison, Morgan, Oconee, Oglethorpe, Richmond, Walton, Warren and Wilkes. Prior Terms: 1977-92. Born: March 20, 1922; Augusta, GA. Education: Mercer University (B.A., LL.B.). Military Service: U.S. Army. Occupation: Executive secretary to the governor (1963-66); employee, Georgia Railroad Bank and Trust Co. (1948-49, 1950-62, 1966-76); employee, Federal Reserve Bank of America (1949-50); board member, Georgia Department of Transportation (1966-76); member, Augusta Transportation Authority (1973-76).

1.	Protection to Haitian refugees	?	20.	Eliminate funds for supercollider	N
2.	Raise tax on wealthy; lower others	N	21.	Terminate SDI except for research	N
3.	Investigate Reagan hostage delay	Y	22.	Req 7-day handgun waiting period	N
4.	Campaign finance revisions	Y	23.	Provide $30b for failed S&Ls	Y
5.	Unpaid leave to care for children	N	24.	Allow use of force against Iraq	Y
6.	Restrict NEA use of funds	Y	25.	Allow $15b in foreign aid for '91	N
7.	Bar race-bias claim/habeas corpus	Y	26.	Revise & extend legal immigration	N
8.	Ban race as death sentence factor	Y	27.	Suspend aid to Angolan rebels	N
9.	Exceptions to exclusionary rule	Y	28.	Democratic tax plan proposals	N
10.	Allow sale of assault weapons	Y	29.	Cut defense 5% across the board	X
11.	Life in prison/abolish death penalty	N	30.	Textile import quotas-veto override	Y
12.	Req conspiracy-price fixing cases	?	31.	Abortion service for military abroad	N
13.	Unemployment benefits extension	N	32.	Limits on high income farmers	N
14.	Tissue use of aborted fetuses	Y	33.	Family medical leave-veto override	N
15.	Bar replacement of union strikers	N	34.	Req submission of balanced budget	Y
16.	Hold foreign aid at $15b for '92	N	35.	Balanced budget amendment	Y
17.	Restore space station funding	Y	36.	Amendment to ban flag desecration	Y
18.	Civil Rights Act of 1991	N	37.	Reauthorize Amtrak-veto override	Y
19.	Unlimited damages-discrimination	N	38.	Retraining aid for coal miners	Y

BARNARD, DOUG, Jr. (continued)

39. Suspend El Salvador military aid	#	92. Catastrophic health insurance	N
40. Expand child care aid/tax credit	N	93. Ban airline smoking-2 hours or less	Y
41. Raise House salary/omit honoraria	Y	94. $1b/two year aid for the homeless	Y
42. Toughen oil-spill liability	X	95. Bar non-unions in union companies	N
43. Restitution to Japanese interned	Y	96. Increase FSLIC rescue to $15b	Y
44. Protect Chinese & C.A. nationals	N	97. Impose quotas to lower trade deficit	N
45. Abortion $ for rape/incest cases	N	98. Reduce discretionary budget 21%	Y
46. Allow religious schools to bar gays	?	99. Immigration reform/alien amnesty	X
47. Bar broadcaster fairness doctrine	?	100. South Africa sanctions-veto override	Y
48. Bar cap gains cut/reinstate IRA	N	101. Tax overhaul to revise income tax	Y
49. Bar unions equal voice in pension	Y	102. Use of military in drug war	Y
50. Bar assembly of chemical weapons	?	103. Delete 12 MX/add conventional wpn	N
51. Ban plutonium/uranium production	Y	104. Raise speed limit to 65 mph	Y
52. Cap MX missile deployment at 50	N	105. Require Pentagon to buy US goods	N
53. Allow $3b for 2 stealth bombers	Y	106. AIDS insurance non-discrimination	Y
54. Publish bio-warfare experiments	Y	107. Prohibit Saudi arms sales	Y
55. Raise minimum wage-veto override	N	108. Ease Gun Control Act of 1968	Y
56. Bar transfer of FS-X technology	Y	109. Bar interstate handgun transport	N
57. Cut defense and raise domestic $	N	110. Make company emissions known	N
58. Uniform poll closing in 48 states	N	111. Allow toxic victims to sue in fed ct	N
59. Req foreign investment disclosure	Y	112. Superfund waste cleanup of $10b	Y
60. Textile import quotas-veto override	Y	113. 90 days notice of plant closings	N
61. Bar abortion funding in Wash, DC	Y	114. $20b in Medicare cuts/tax increases	N
62. Notify spouses of AIDS+ carriers	X	115. Spending cuts and tax increases	Y
63. Seize conveyance-drug trafficking	?	116. Set school lunch lmt-250% poverty	N
64. South Africa sanctions	Y	117. $75m for youth work projects	N
65. 60 days' notice of plant closings	N	118. Allow Angolan military assistance	Y
66. Close unneeded military bases	N	119. Suspend defense payments for abuse	N
67. Keep welfare reform within $2.8b	Y	120. Drop SS COLAs/$12b tax increase	Y
68. Allow children housing exclusion	Y	121. Approve $1.5b for 21 MX missiles	Y
69. Shift $400m of NASA to homeless	N	122. Emergency farm credit/revisions	Y
70. Cap Medicare patients' liability	N	123. Duty on Taiwan/Hong Kong/S Korea	?
71. Prohibit employee polygraph testing	N	124. Limit steel imports to 17%	Y
72. Allow CIA to fund Contras	N	125. Cut $ to schools that bar prayer	Y
73. Revise unfair trade practices	Y	126. $50b-taxes; cut Medicare/spending	N
74. Focus SDI on accidental launch	Y	127. Limit Pershing II/cruise in Europe	?
75. Bar Air Force $ for MX missile	N	128. Delete $7.1b for 34 B-1 bombers	?
76. Allow "real" increase in defense	Y	129. Bar purchase of Sergeant York guns	?
77. Troop reduction in Europe of 50%	X	130. El Salvador military/economic aid	Y
78. Ban nuclear tests above 1 kiloton	N	131. Bar mining of Nicaraguan waters	?
79. Ban anti-satellite missile tests	N	132. Physician fee freeze for Medicare	N
80. Observe certain limits of SALT II	Y	133. $49b in "sin"/phone/insurance taxes	Y
81. Restore four Civil Rights laws	N	134. Allow sale of Conrail	N
82. Prohibit aliens as strikebreakers	N	135. Equal Rights Amendment	N
83. Allow military malpractice suits	Y	136. Authorize Marines in Lebanon	Y
84. Approval of $36m in Contra aid	Y	137. Eminent domain for coal companies	N
85. $18b deficit reduction compromise	N	138. Prohibit EPA clean air sanctions	N
86. Welfare reform of $5.7b for 5 years	N	139. SS retirement age increase/reforms	Y
87. Raise taxes $12b/cut spending $3b	N	140. Auto domestic content requirement	N
88. Board to assess occupational risk	N	141. Delete jobs program funding	N
89. Balanced budget by '93-via targets	Y	142. Highway-gas tax bill	N
90. Bar licensing of two nuclear plants	N	143. Cut $5b from defense for Medicare	N
91. Remove victims compensation cap	N	144. Emergency housing aid of $1b	Y

Presidential Support Score: 1991 - 60% 1990 - 49%

HAWAII

ABERCROMBIE, NEIL -- Hawaii 1st District [Democrat]. County of Honolulu (pt.). Prior Terms: 1986 (Special Election)-1986; 1991-92. Born: June 26, 1938; Buffalo, NY.

ABERCROMBIE, NEIL (continued)
Education: Union College (B.A.); University of Hawaii (M.A., Ph.D.). Occupation: Graduate university sociology teaching and research assistant, lecturer, and visiting professor; Marin County probation department senior deputy; Special Assistant to Hawaii Superintendent of Education; state representative (1975-78) and senator (1979-86); Honolulu city councilman (1989-90).

1. Protection to Haitian refugees	Y	15. Bar replacement of union strikers	Y
2. Raise tax on wealthy; lower others	Y	16. Hold foreign aid at $15b for '92	Y
3. Investigate Reagan hostage delay	Y	17. Restore space station funding	N
4. Campaign finance revisions	Y	18. Civil Rights Act of 1991	Y
5. Unpaid leave to care for children	Y	19. Unlimited damages-discrimination	Y
6. Restrict NEA use of funds	N	20. Eliminate funds for supercollider	N
7. Bar race-bias claim/habeas corpus	N	21. Terminate SDI except for research	Y
8. Ban race as death sentence factor	N	22. Req 7-day handgun waiting period	Y
9. Exceptions to exclusionary rule	N	23. Provide $30b for failed S&Ls	N
10. Allow sale of assault weapons	N	24. Allow use of force against Iraq	N
11. Life in prison/abolish death penalty	Y	99. Immigration reform/alien amnesty	Y
12. Req conspiracy-price fixing cases	N	100. South Africa sanctions-veto override	Y
13. Unemployment benefits extension	Y	101. Tax overhaul to revise income tax	Y
14. Tissue use of aborted fetuses	Y		

Rep. Abercrombie was not in office for votes 25-98.

Presidential Support Score: 1991 - 21%

MINK, PATSY -- Hawaii 2nd District [Democrat]. Counties of Hawaii, Honolulu (pt.), Kalawao, Kauai and Maui. Prior Terms: 1965-77; 1990 (Special Appointment)-1992. Born: December 26, 1927; Paia, Maui, HI. Education: University of Hawaii; Univ. of Chicago Law School. Occupation: College professor; lawyer; president, *The Public Reporter*; territorial House staff attorney, representative (1957-59) and senator (1959, 1963-64); Assistant Secretary of State for Oceans and International Environmental and Scientific Affairs (1977); Americans for Democratic Action president (1978-80); Honolulu city councilwoman (1983-87).

1. Protection to Haitian refugees	Y	16. Hold foreign aid at $15b for '92	Y
2. Raise tax on wealthy; lower others	Y	17. Restore space station funding	N
3. Investigate Reagan hostage delay	Y	18. Civil Rights Act of 1991	Y
4. Campaign finance revisions	Y	19. Unlimited damages-discrimination	Y
5. Unpaid leave to care for children	Y	20. Eliminate funds for supercollider	N
6. Restrict NEA use of funds	N	21. Terminate SDI except for research	Y
7. Bar race-bias claim/habeas corpus	N	22. Req 7-day handgun waiting period	Y
8. Ban race as death sentence factor	N	23. Provide $30b for failed S&Ls	N
9. Exceptions to exclusionary rule	N	24. Allow use of force against Iraq	N
10. Allow sale of assault weapons	N	25. Allow $15b in foreign aid for '91	?
11. Life in prison/abolish death penalty	Y	26. Revise & extend legal immigration	Y
12. Req conspiracy-price fixing cases	N	27. Suspend aid to Angolan rebels	Y
13. Unemployment benefits extension	Y	28. Democratic tax plan proposals	Y
14. Tissue use of aborted fetuses	Y	29. Cut defense 5% across the board	N
15. Bar replacement of union strikers	Y	30. Textile import quotas-veto override	Y

Presidential Support Score: 1991 - 19%   1990 - 22%

IDAHO

LaROCCO, LARRY -- Idaho 1st District [Democrat]. Counties of Ada (pt.), Adams, Benewah, Boise, Bonner, Boundary, Canyon, Clearwater, Gem, Idaho, Kootenai, Latah, Lewis, Nez Perce, Owyhee, Payette, Shoshone, Valley and Washington. Prior Term: 1991-92. Born: August 25, 1946; Van Nuys, CA. Education: University of Portland (B.A.); Boston University (M.A.). Military Service: U.S. Army, 1969-1972. Occupation: Brokerage firm vice president (1983-90).

LaROCCO, LARRY (continued)

1. Protection to Haitian refugees	Y		13. Unemployment benefits extension	Y
2. Raise tax on wealthy; lower others	Y		14. Tissue use of aborted fetuses	Y
3. Investigate Reagan hostage delay	Y		15. Bar replacement of union strikers	Y
4. Campaign finance revisions	Y		16. Hold foreign aid at $15b for '92	Y
5. Unpaid leave to care for children	N		17. Restore space station funding	Y
6. Restrict NEA use of funds	N		18. Civil Rights Act of 1991	Y
7. Bar race-bias claim/habeas corpus	Y		19. Unlimited damages-discrimination	N
8. Ban race as death sentence factor	N		20. Eliminate funds for supercollider	N
9. Exceptions to exclusionary rule	Y		21. Terminate SDI except for research	?
10. Allow sale of assault weapons	Y		22. Req 7-day handgun waiting period	N
11. Life in prison/abolish death penalty	N		23. Provide $30b for failed S&Ls	Y
12. Req conspiracy-price fixing cases	N		24. Allow use of force against Iraq	N

Presidential Support Score: 1991 - 41%

STALLINGS, RICHARD -- Idaho 2nd District [Democrat]. Counties of Ada (pt.), Bannock, Bear Lake, Bingham, Blaune, Booneville, Butte, Camas, Caribou, Cassia, Clark, Custer, Elmore, Franklin, Fremont, Gooding, Jefferson, Jerome, Lemhi, Lincoln, Madison, Minidoka, Oneida, Power, Teton and Twin Falls. Prior Terms: 1985-92. Born: October 7, 1940. Education: Weber State University (B.S.); Utah State University (M.A.). Occupation: Professor.

1. Protection to Haitian refugees	?		42. Toughen oil-spill liability	Y
2. Raise tax on wealthy; lower others	N		43. Restitution to Japanese interned	Y
3. Investigate Reagan hostage delay	Y		44. Protect Chinese & C.A. nationals	Y
4. Campaign finance revisions	Y		45. Abortion $ for rape/incest cases	N
5. Unpaid leave to care for children	N		46. Allow religious schools to bar gays	Y
6. Restrict NEA use of funds	N		47. Bar broadcaster fairness doctrine	N
7. Bar race-bias claim/habeas corpus	Y		48. Bar cap gains cut/reinstate IRA	N
8. Ban race as death sentence factor	N		49. Bar unions equal voice in pension	Y
9. Exceptions to exclusionary rule	Y		50. Bar assembly of chemical weapons	Y
10. Allow sale of assault weapons	Y		51. Ban plutonium/uranium production	Y
11. Life in prison/abolish death penalty	N		52. Cap MX missile deployment at 50	Y
12. Req conspiracy-price fixing cases	Y		53. Allow $3b for 2 stealth bombers	N
13. Unemployment benefits extension	Y		54. Publish bio-warfare experiments	Y
14. Tissue use of aborted fetuses	N		55. Raise minimum wage-veto override	Y
15. Bar replacement of union strikers	Y		56. Bar transfer of FS-X technology	?
16. Hold foreign aid at $15b for '92	Y		57. Cut defense and raise domestic $	N
17. Restore space station funding	Y		58. Uniform poll closing in 48 states	Y
18. Civil Rights Act of 1991	Y		59. Req foreign investment disclosure	N
19. Unlimited damages-discrimination	N		60. Textile import quotas-veto override	N
20. Eliminate funds for supercollider	N		61. Bar abortion funding in Wash, DC	Y
21. Terminate SDI except for research	N		62. Notify spouses of AIDS+ carriers	?
22. Req 7-day handgun waiting period	N		63. Seize conveyance-drug trafficking	Y
23. Provide $30b for failed S&Ls	#		64. South Africa sanctions	N
24. Allow use of force against Iraq	N		65. 60 days' notice of plant closings	Y
25. Allow $15b in foreign aid for '91	N		66. Close unneeded military bases	Y
26. Revise & extend legal immigration	N		67. Keep welfare reform within $2.8b	Y
27. Suspend aid to Angolan rebels	N		68. Allow children housing exclusion	N
28. Democratic tax plan proposals	N		69. Shift $400m of NASA to homeless	N
29. Cut defense 5% across the board	N		70. Cap Medicare patients' liability	N
30. Textile import quotas-veto override	N		71. Prohibit employee polygraph testing	Y
31. Abortion service for military abroad	N		72. Allow CIA to fund Contras	N
32. Limits on high income farmers	N		73. Revise unfair trade practices	Y
33. Family medical leave-veto override	N		74. Focus SDI on accidental launch	N
34. Req submission of balanced budget	Y		75. Bar Air Force $ for MX missile	N
35. Balanced budget amendment	Y		76. Allow "real" increase in defense	N
36. Amendment to ban flag desecration	Y		77. Troop reduction in Europe of 50%	?
37. Reauthorize Amtrak-veto override	Y		78. Ban nuclear tests above 1 kiloton	?
38. Retraining aid for coal miners	?		79. Ban anti-satellite missile tests	?
39. Suspend El Salvador military aid	Y		80. Observe certain limits of SALT II	Y
40. Expand child care aid/tax credit	N		81. Restore four Civil Rights laws	Y
41. Raise House salary/omit honoraria	N		82. Prohibit aliens as strikebreakers	Y

STALLINGS, RICHARD (continued)

83. Allow military malpractice suits	Y	
84. Approval of $36m in Contra aid	N	
85. $18b deficit reduction compromise	Y	
86. Welfare reform of $5.7b for 5 years	N	
87. Raise taxes $12b/cut spending $3b	N	
88. Board to assess occupational risk	Y	
89. Balanced budget by '93-via targets	Y	
90. Bar licensing of two nuclear plants	N	
91. Remove victims compensation cap	N	
92. Catastrophic health insurance	Y	
93. Ban airline smoking-2 hours or less	Y	
94. $1b/two year aid for the homeless	N	
95. Bar non-unions in union companies	N	
96. Increase FSLIC rescue to $15b	N	
97. Impose quotas to lower trade deficit	N	
98. Reduce discretionary budget 21%	Y	
99. Immigration reform/alien amnesty	Y	
100. South Africa sanctions-veto override	Y	
101. Tax overhaul to revise income tax	Y	
102. Use of military in drug war	Y	
103. Delete 12 MX/add conventional wpn	Y
104. Raise speed limit to 65 mph	Y
105. Require Pentagon to buy US goods	Y
106. AIDS insurance non-discrimination	Y
107. Prohibit Saudi arms sales	Y
108. Ease Gun Control Act of 1968	Y
109. Bar interstate handgun transport	N
110. Make company emissions known	Y
111. Allow toxic victims to sue in fed ct	N
112. Superfund waste cleanup of $10b	Y
113. 90 days notice of plant closings	#
114. $20b in Medicare cuts/tax increases	Y
115. Spending cuts and tax increases	Y
116. Set school lunch lmt-250% poverty	N
117. $75m for youth work projects	N
118. Allow Angolan military assistance	N
119. Suspend defense payments for abuse	Y
120. Drop SS COLAs/$12b tax increase	N
121. Approve $1.5b for 21 MX missiles	N
122. Emergency farm credit/revisions	Y

Presidential Support Score: 1991 - 50%   1990 - 42%

ILLINOIS

HAYES, CHARLES A. -- Illinois 1st District [Democrat]. County of Cook (pt.). Prior Terms: 1983 (Special Election)-1992. Born: February 17, 1918; Cairo, IL. Occupation: Civilian Conservation Corps worker; woodworker; International Vice President and Director of the United Food and Commercial Workers Union.

1. Protection to Haitian refugees	Y	
2. Raise tax on wealthy; lower others	Y	
3. Investigate Reagan hostage delay	Y	
4. Campaign finance revisions	Y	
5. Unpaid leave to care for children	Y	
6. Restrict NEA use of funds	N	
7. Bar race-bias claim/habeas corpus	N	
8. Ban race as death sentence factor	N	
9. Exceptions to exclusionary rule	N	
10. Allow sale of assault weapons	N	
11. Life in prison/abolish death penalty	Y	
12. Req conspiracy-price fixing cases	N	
13. Unemployment benefits extension	Y	
14. Tissue use of aborted fetuses	Y	
15. Bar replacement of union strikers	Y	
16. Hold foreign aid at $15b for '92	Y	
17. Restore space station funding	N	
18. Civil Rights Act of 1991	Y	
19. Unlimited damages-discrimination	Y	
20. Eliminate funds for supercollider	Y	
21. Terminate SDI except for research	Y	
22. Req 7-day handgun waiting period	Y	
23. Provide $30b for failed S&Ls	N	
24. Allow use of force against Iraq	N	
25. Allow $15b in foreign aid for '91	N	
26. Revise & extend legal immigration	N	
27. Suspend aid to Angolan rebels	Y	
28. Democratic tax plan proposals	Y	
29. Cut defense 5% across the board	#
30. Textile import quotas-veto override	Y
31. Abortion service for military abroad	Y
32. Limits on high income farmers	N
33. Family medical leave-veto override	Y
34. Req submission of balanced budget	Y
35. Balanced budget amendment	N
36. Amendment to ban flag desecration	N
37. Reauthorize Amtrak-veto override	Y
38. Retraining aid for coal miners	Y
39. Suspend El Salvador military aid	Y
40. Expand child care aid/tax credit	Y
41. Raise House salary/omit honoraria	Y
42. Toughen oil-spill liability	Y
43. Restitution to Japanese interned	Y
44. Protect Chinese & C.A. nationals	Y
45. Abortion $ for rape/incest cases	Y
46. Allow religious schools to bar gays	N
47. Bar broadcaster fairness doctrine	N
48. Bar cap gains cut/reinstate IRA	Y
49. Bar unions equal voice in pension	N
50. Bar assembly of chemical weapons	Y
51. Ban plutonium/uranium production	Y
52. Cap MX missile deployment at 50	Y
53. Allow $3b for 2 stealth bombers	N
54. Publish bio-warfare experiments	Y
55. Raise minimum wage-veto override	Y
56. Bar transfer of FS-X technology	Y

HAYES, CHARLES A. (continued)

57. Cut defense and raise domestic $	Y	98. Reduce discretionary budget 21%	N
58. Uniform poll closing in 48 states	Y	99. Immigration reform/alien amnesty	N
59. Req foreign investment disclosure	Y	100. South Africa sanctions-veto override	Y
60. Textile import quotas-veto override	Y	101. Tax overhaul to revise income tax	Y
61. Bar abortion funding in Wash, DC	N	102. Use of military in drug war	N
62. Notify spouses of AIDS+ carriers	N	103. Delete 12 MX/add conventional wpn	Y
63. Seize conveyance-drug trafficking	N	104. Raise speed limit to 65 mph	Y
64. South Africa sanctions	Y	105. Require Pentagon to buy US goods	Y
65. 60 days' notice of plant closings	Y	106. AIDS insurance non-discrimination	Y
66. Close unneeded military bases	N	107. Prohibit Saudi arms sales	Y
67. Keep welfare reform within $2.8b	N	108. Ease Gun Control Act of 1968	N
68. Allow children housing exclusion	N	109. Bar interstate handgun transport	Y
69. Shift $400m of NASA to homeless	Y	110. Make company emissions known	Y
70. Cap Medicare patients' liability	Y	111. Allow toxic victims to sue in fed ct	Y
71. Prohibit employee polygraph testing	Y	112. Superfund waste cleanup of $10b	Y
72. Allow CIA to fund Contras	N	113. 90 days notice of plant closings	Y
73. Revise unfair trade practices	Y	114. $20b in Medicare cuts/tax increases	Y
74. Focus SDI on accidental launch	Y	115. Spending cuts and tax increases	Y
75. Bar Air Force $ for MX missile	Y	116. Set school lunch lmt-250% poverty	N
76. Allow "real" increase in defense	N	117. $75m for youth work projects	Y
77. Troop reduction in Europe of 50%	Y	118. Allow Angolan military assistance	N
78. Ban nuclear tests above 1 kiloton	Y	119. Suspend defense payments for abuse	Y
79. Ban anti-satellite missile tests	Y	120. Drop SS COLAs/$12b tax increase	N
80. Observe certain limits of SALT II	Y	121. Approve $1.5b for 21 MX missiles	N
81. Restore four Civil Rights laws	Y	122. Emergency farm credit/revisions	Y
82. Prohibit aliens as strikebreakers	Y	123. Duty on Taiwan/Hong Kong/S Korea	Y
83. Allow military malpractice suits	Y	124. Limit steel imports to 17%	Y
84. Approval of $36m in Contra aid	N	125. Cut $ to schools that bar prayer	N
85. $18b deficit reduction compromise	N	126. $50b-taxes; cut Medicare/spending	N
86. Welfare reform of $5.7b for 5 years	Y	127. Limit Pershing II/cruise in Europe	Y
87. Raise taxes $12b/cut spending $3b	Y	128. Delete $7.1b for 34 B-1 bombers	Y
88. Board to assess occupational risk	Y	129. Bar purchase of Sergeant York guns	Y
89. Balanced budget by '93-via targets	N	130. El Salvador military/economic aid	N
90. Bar licensing of two nuclear plants	Y	131. Bar mining of Nicaraguan waters	?
91. Remove victims compensation cap	Y	132. Physician fee freeze for Medicare	N
92. Catastrophic health insurance	Y	133. $49b in "sin"/phone/insurance taxes	Y
93. Ban airline smoking-2 hours or less	Y	134. Allow sale of Conrail	N
94. $1b/two year aid for the homeless	Y	135. Equal Rights Amendment	Y
95. Bar non-unions in union companies	Y	136. Authorize Marines in Lebanon	N
96. Increase FSLIC rescue to $15b	N	137. Eminent domain for coal companies	Y
97. Impose quotas to lower trade deficit	Y		

Presidential Support Score: 1991 - 23%   1990 - 13%

SAVAGE, GUS -- Illinois 2nd District [Democrat]. County of Cook (pt.). Prior Terms: 1981-92. Born: October 30, 1925; Detroit, MI. Education: Roosevelt University (B.A.); Chicago-Kent College of Law. Military Service: World War II, 1943-46. Occupation: Editor.

1. Protection to Haitian refugees	Y	15. Bar replacement of union strikers	Y
2. Raise tax on wealthy; lower others	Y	16. Hold foreign aid at $15b for '92	N
3. Investigate Reagan hostage delay	Y	17. Restore space station funding	N
4. Campaign finance revisions	Y	18. Civil Rights Act of 1991	Y
5. Unpaid leave to care for children	Y	19. Unlimited damages-discrimination	Y
6. Restrict NEA use of funds	?	20. Eliminate funds for supercollider	N
7. Bar race-bias claim/habeas corpus	N	21. Terminate SDI except for research	Y
8. Ban race as death sentence factor	N	22. Req 7-day handgun waiting period	Y
9. Exceptions to exclusionary rule	N	23. Provide $30b for failed S&Ls	N
10. Allow sale of assault weapons	N	24. Allow use of force against Iraq	N
11. Life in prison/abolish death penalty	?	25. Allow $15b in foreign aid for '91	N
12. Req conspiracy-price fixing cases	?	26. Revise & extend legal immigration	N
13. Unemployment benefits extension	Y	27. Suspend aid to Angolan rebels	Y
14. Tissue use of aborted fetuses	Y	28. Democratic tax plan proposals	N

SAVAGE, GUS (continued)

29. Cut defense 5% across the board	Y	
30. Textile import quotas-veto override	Y	
31. Abortion service for military abroad	Y	
32. Limits on high income farmers	Y	
33. Family medical leave-veto override	Y	
34. Req submission of balanced budget	N	
35. Balanced budget amendment	N	
36. Amendment to ban flag desecration	N	
37. Reauthorize Amtrak-veto override	Y	
38. Retraining aid for coal miners	Y	
39. Suspend El Salvador military aid	Y	
40. Expand child care aid/tax credit	Y	
41. Raise House salary/omit honoraria	Y	
42. Toughen oil-spill liability	Y	
43. Restitution to Japanese interned	Y	
44. Protect Chinese & C.A. nationals	Y	
45. Abortion $ for rape/incest cases	Y	
46. Allow religious schools to bar gays	?	
47. Bar broadcaster fairness doctrine	N	
48. Bar cap gains cut/reinstate IRA	Y	
49. Bar unions equal voice in pension	N	
50. Bar assembly of chemical weapons	Y	
51. Ban plutonium/uranium production	Y	
52. Cap MX missile deployment at 50	Y	
53. Allow $3b for 2 stealth bombers	N	
54. Publish bio-warfare experiments	Y	
55. Raise minimum wage-veto override	Y	
56. Bar transfer of FS-X technology	Y	
57. Cut defense and raise domestic $	Y	
58. Uniform poll closing in 48 states	Y	
59. Req foreign investment disclosure	Y	
60. Textile import quotas-veto override	Y	
61. Bar abortion funding in Wash, DC	N	
62. Notify spouses of AIDS+ carriers	N	
63. Seize conveyance-drug trafficking	N	
64. South Africa sanctions	Y	
65. 60 days' notice of plant closings	Y	
66. Close unneeded military bases	N	
67. Keep welfare reform within $2.8b	N	
68. Allow children housing exclusion	N	
69. Shift $400m of NASA to homeless	Y	
70. Cap Medicare patients' liability	Y	
71. Prohibit employee polygraph testing	Y	
72. Allow CIA to fund Contras	N	
73. Revise unfair trade practices	Y	
74. Focus SDI on accidental launch	Y	
75. Bar Air Force $ for MX missile	Y	
76. Allow "real" increase in defense	N	
77. Troop reduction in Europe of 50%	Y	
78. Ban nuclear tests above 1 kiloton	Y	
79. Ban anti-satellite missile tests	Y	
80. Observe certain limits of SALT II	Y	
81. Restore four Civil Rights laws	Y	
82. Prohibit aliens as strikebreakers	Y	
83. Allow military malpractice suits	Y	
84. Approval of $36m in Contra aid	N	
85. $18b deficit reduction compromise	N	
86. Welfare reform of $5.7b for 5 years	Y	

87. Raise taxes $12b/cut spending $3b	Y	
88. Board to assess occupational risk	Y	
89. Balanced budget by '93-via targets	N	
90. Bar licensing of two nuclear plants	Y	
91. Remove victims compensation cap	Y	
92. Catastrophic health insurance	Y	
93. Ban airline smoking-2 hours or less	Y	
94. $1b/two year aid for the homeless	Y	
95. Bar non-unions in union companies	Y	
96. Increase FSLIC rescue to $15b	N	
97. Impose quotas to lower trade deficit	Y	
98. Reduce discretionary budget 21%	N	
99. Immigration reform/alien amnesty	N	
100. South Africa sanctions-veto override	Y	
101. Tax overhaul to revise income tax	Y	
102. Use of military in drug war	N	
103. Delete 12 MX/add conventional wpn	?	
104. Raise speed limit to 65 mph	N	
105. Require Pentagon to buy US goods	Y	
106. AIDS insurance non-discrimination	Y	
107. Prohibit Saudi arms sales	Y	
108. Ease Gun Control Act of 1968	N	
109. Bar interstate handgun transport	Y	
110. Make company emissions known	Y	
111. Allow toxic victims to sue in fed ct	Y	
112. Superfund waste cleanup of $10b	Y	
113. 90 days notice of plant closings	Y	
114. $20b in Medicare cuts/tax increases	Y	
115. Spending cuts and tax increases	Y	
116. Set school lunch lmt-250% poverty	N	
117. $75m for youth work projects	Y	
118. Allow Angolan military assistance	N	
119. Suspend defense payments for abuse	Y	
120. Drop SS COLAs/$12b tax increase	N	
121. Approve $1.5b for 21 MX missiles	N	
122. Emergency farm credit/revisions	Y	
123. Duty on Taiwan/Hong Kong/S Korea	Y	
124. Limit steel imports to 17%	Y	
125. Cut $ to schools that bar prayer	N	
126. $50b-taxes; cut Medicare/spending	N	
127. Limit Pershing II/cruise in Europe	Y	
128. Delete $7.1b for 34 B-1 bombers	Y	
129. Bar purchase of Sergeant York guns	Y	
130. El Salvador military/economic aid	N	
131. Bar mining of Nicaraguan waters	Y	
132. Physician fee freeze for Medicare	N	
133. $49b in "sin"/phone/insurance taxes	Y	
134. Allow sale of Conrail	N	
135. Equal Rights Amendment	Y	
136. Authorize Marines in Lebanon	N	
137. Eminent domain for coal companies	N	
138. Prohibit EPA clean air sanctions	Y	
139. SS retirement age increase/reforms	N	
140. Auto domestic content requirement	Y	
141. Delete jobs program funding	N	
142. Highway-gas tax bill	?	
143. Cut $5b from defense for Medicare	Y	
144. Emergency housing aid of $1b	Y	

Presidential Support Score: 1991 - 25%   1990 - 19%

RUSSO, MARTY -- Illinois 3rd District [Democrat]. County of Cook (pt.). Prior Terms: 1975-92. Born: January 23, 1944; Chicago, IL. Education: De Paul University (B.A., J.D.).

RUSSO, MARTY (continued)

Occupation: Law clerk, Illinois Appellate Court (1967-68); assistant state's attorney (1971-73).

1. Protection to Haitian refugees	?	62. Notify spouses of AIDS+ carriers	?
2. Raise tax on wealthy; lower others	N	63. Seize conveyance-drug trafficking	N
3. Investigate Reagan hostage delay	Y	64. South Africa sanctions	Y
4. Campaign finance revisions	Y	65. 60 days' notice of plant closings	Y
5. Unpaid leave to care for children	Y	66. Close unneeded military bases	Y
6. Restrict NEA use of funds	Y	67. Keep welfare reform within $2.8b	N
7. Bar race-bias claim/habeas corpus	Y	68. Allow children housing exclusion	Y
8. Ban race as death sentence factor	Y	69. Shift $400m of NASA to homeless	Y
9. Exceptions to exclusionary rule	N	70. Cap Medicare patients' liability	Y
10. Allow sale of assault weapons	N	71. Prohibit employee polygraph testing	Y
11. Life in prison/abolish death penalty	N	72. Allow CIA to fund Contras	N
12. Req conspiracy-price fixing cases	N	73. Revise unfair trade practices	Y
13. Unemployment benefits extension	Y	74. Focus SDI on accidental launch	N
14. Tissue use of aborted fetuses	Y	75. Bar Air Force $ for MX missile	Y
15. Bar replacement of union strikers	Y	76. Allow "real" increase in defense	N
16. Hold foreign aid at $15b for '92	N	77. Troop reduction in Europe of 50%	N
17. Restore space station funding	N	78. Ban nuclear tests above 1 kiloton	Y
18. Civil Rights Act of 1991	N	79. Ban anti-satellite missile tests	Y
19. Unlimited damages-discrimination	N	80. Observe certain limits of SALT II	Y
20. Eliminate funds for supercollider	Y	81. Restore four Civil Rights laws	N
21. Terminate SDI except for research	Y	82. Prohibit aliens as strikebreakers	Y
22. Req 7-day handgun waiting period	Y	83. Allow military malpractice suits	N
23. Provide $30b for failed S&Ls	N	84. Approval of $36m in Contra aid	N
24. Allow use of force against Iraq	N	85. $18b deficit reduction compromise	N
25. Allow $15b in foreign aid for '91	?	86. Welfare reform of $5.7b for 5 years	Y
26. Revise & extend legal immigration	?	87. Raise taxes $12b/cut spending $3b	N
27. Suspend aid to Angolan rebels	Y	88. Board to assess occupational risk	Y
28. Democratic tax plan proposals	Y	89. Balanced budget by '93-via targets	N
29. Cut defense 5% across the board	Y	90. Bar licensing of two nuclear plants	Y
30. Textile import quotas-veto override	Y	91. Remove victims compensation cap	N
31. Abortion service for military abroad	N	92. Catastrophic health insurance	Y
32. Limits on high income farmers	Y	93. Ban airline smoking-2 hours or less	Y
33. Family medical leave-veto override	Y	94. $1b/two year aid for the homeless	Y
34. Req submission of balanced budget	Y	95. Bar non-unions in union companies	Y
35. Balanced budget amendment	N	96. Increase FSLIC rescue to $15b	N
36. Amendment to ban flag desecration	N	97. Impose quotas to lower trade deficit	Y
37. Reauthorize Amtrak-veto override	Y	98. Reduce discretionary budget 21%	Y
38. Retraining aid for coal miners	Y	99. Immigration reform/alien amnesty	?
39. Suspend El Salvador military aid	Y	100. South Africa sanctions-veto override	Y
40. Expand child care aid/tax credit	Y	101. Tax overhaul to revise income tax	Y
41. Raise House salary/omit honoraria	Y	102. Use of military in drug war	Y
42. Toughen oil-spill liability	Y	103. Delete 12 MX/add conventional wpn	Y
43. Restitution to Japanese interned	?	104. Raise speed limit to 65 mph	N
44. Protect Chinese & C.A. nationals	N	105. Require Pentagon to buy US goods	Y
45. Abortion $ for rape/incest cases	N	106. AIDS insurance non-discrimination	N
46. Allow religious schools to bar gays	Y	107. Prohibit Saudi arms sales	Y
47. Bar broadcaster fairness doctrine	N	108. Ease Gun Control Act of 1968	N
48. Bar cap gains cut/reinstate IRA	Y	109. Bar interstate handgun transport	Y
49. Bar unions equal voice in pension	Y	110. Make company emissions known	Y
50. Bar assembly of chemical weapons	Y	111. Allow toxic victims to sue in fed ct	N
51. Ban plutonium/uranium production	Y	112. Superfund waste cleanup of $10b	N
52. Cap MX missile deployment at 50	Y	113. 90 days notice of plant closings	Y
53. Allow $3b for 2 stealth bombers	N	114. $20b in Medicare cuts/tax increases	Y
54. Publish bio-warfare experiments	Y	115. Spending cuts and tax increases	Y
55. Raise minimum wage-veto override	Y	116. Set school lunch lmt-250% poverty	N
56. Bar transfer of FS-X technology	Y	117. $75m for youth work projects	Y
57. Cut defense and raise domestic $	N	118. Allow Angolan military assistance	N
58. Uniform poll closing in 48 states	Y	119. Suspend defense payments for abuse	Y
59. Req foreign investment disclosure	Y	120. Drop SS COLAs/$12b tax increase	N
60. Textile import quotas-veto override	Y	121. Approve $1.5b for 21 MX missiles	N
61. Bar abortion funding in Wash, DC	Y	122. Emergency farm credit/revisions	Y

RUSSO, MARTY (continued)

123. Duty on Taiwan/Hong Kong/S Korea	Y
124. Limit steel imports to 17%	Y
125. Cut $ to schools that bar prayer	N
126. $50b-taxes; cut Medicare/spending	Y
127. Limit Pershing II/cruise in Europe	Y
128. Delete $7.1b for 34 B-1 bombers	?
129. Bar purchase of Sergeant York guns	Y
130. El Salvador military/economic aid	N
131. Bar mining of Nicaraguan waters	#
132. Physician fee freeze for Medicare	N
133. $49b in "sin"/phone/insurance taxes	Y

134. Allow sale of Conrail	N
135. Equal Rights Amendment	N
136. Authorize Marines in Lebanon	N
137. Eminent domain for coal companies	N
138. Prohibit EPA clean air sanctions	N
139. SS retirement age increase/reforms	N
140. Auto domestic content requirement	Y
141. Delete jobs program funding	N
142. Highway-gas tax bill	Y
143. Cut $5b from defense for Medicare	Y
144. Emergency housing aid of $1b	Y

Presidential Support Score: 1991 - 31%   1990 - 29%

SANGMEISTER, GEORGE -- Illinois 4th District [Democrat]. Counties of Cook (pt.), Kane (pt.), Kendall (pt.) and Will (pt). Prior Terms: 1989-92. Born: February 16, 1931; Joliet, IL. Education: Joliet Junior College; Elmhurst College (B.A.); John Marshall Law School (LL.B., J.D.). Military Service: U.S. Army. Occupation: Lawyer; circuit court officer; Will County state's attorney (1964-68); state representative (1972-76) and senator (1977-87).

1. Protection to Haitian refugees	N
2. Raise tax on wealthy; lower others	Y
3. Investigate Reagan hostage delay	N
4. Campaign finance revisions	Y
5. Unpaid leave to care for children	Y
6. Restrict NEA use of funds	Y
7. Bar race-bias claim/habeas corpus	Y
8. Ban race as death sentence factor	Y
9. Exceptions to exclusionary rule	N
10. Allow sale of assault weapons	N
11. Life in prison/abolish death penalty	N
12. Req conspiracy-price fixing cases	N
13. Unemployment benefits extension	Y
14. Tissue use of aborted fetuses	Y
15. Bar replacement of union strikers	Y
16. Hold foreign aid at $15b for '92	N
17. Restore space station funding	N
18. Civil Rights Act of 1991	Y
19. Unlimited damages-discrimination	N
20. Eliminate funds for supercollider	Y
21. Terminate SDI except for research	Y
22. Req 7-day handgun waiting period	Y
23. Provide $30b for failed S&Ls	N
24. Allow use of force against Iraq	N
25. Allow $15b in foreign aid for '91	?
26. Revise & extend legal immigration	?
27. Suspend aid to Angolan rebels	Y
28. Democratic tax plan proposals	N
29. Cut defense 5% across the board	N

30. Textile import quotas-veto override	N
31. Abortion service for military abroad	N
32. Limits on high income farmers	N
33. Family medical leave-veto override	Y
34. Req submission of balanced budget	Y
35. Balanced budget amendment	Y
36. Amendment to ban flag desecration	Y
37. Reauthorize Amtrak-veto override	Y
38. Retraining aid for coal miners	Y
39. Suspend El Salvador military aid	Y
40. Expand child care aid/tax credit	Y
41. Raise House salary/omit honoraria	N
42. Toughen oil-spill liability	N
43. Restitution to Japanese interned	?
44. Protect Chinese & C.A. nationals	Y
45. Abortion $ for rape/incest cases	Y
46. Allow religious schools to bar gays	Y
47. Bar broadcaster fairness doctrine	N
48. Bar cap gains cut/reinstate IRA	Y
49. Bar unions equal voice in pension	Y
50. Bar assembly of chemical weapons	Y
51. Ban plutonium/uranium production	Y
52. Cap MX missile deployment at 50	Y
53. Allow $3b for 2 stealth bombers	N
54. Publish bio-warfare experiments	Y
55. Raise minimum wage-veto override	Y
56. Bar transfer of FS-X technology	Y
57. Cut defense and raise domestic $	N
58. Uniform poll closing in 48 states	Y

Presidential Support Score: 1991 - 24%   1990 - 32%

LIPINSKI, WILLIAM O. -- Illinois 5th District [Democrat]. County of Cook (pt.). Prior Terms: 1983-92. Born: December 22, 1937; Chicago, IL. Education: Loras College. Occupation: Precinct captain; alderman (1975-83); president, Greater Midway Economic and Community Development Committee.

1. Protection to Haitian refugees	N
2. Raise tax on wealthy; lower others	Y
3. Investigate Reagan hostage delay	N
4. Campaign finance revisions	Y

5. Unpaid leave to care for children	Y
6. Restrict NEA use of funds	Y
7. Bar race-bias claim/habeas corpus	Y
8. Ban race as death sentence factor	Y

LIPINSKI, WILLIAM O. (continued)

9. Exceptions to exclusionary rule	N
10. Allow sale of assault weapons	N
11. Life in prison/abolish death penalty	N
12. Req conspiracy-price fixing cases	N
13. Unemployment benefits extension	Y
14. Tissue use of aborted fetuses	Y
15. Bar replacement of union strikers	Y
16. Hold foreign aid at $15b for '92	Y
17. Restore space station funding	Y
18. Civil Rights Act of 1991	N
19. Unlimited damages-discrimination	N
20. Eliminate funds for supercollider	Y
21. Terminate SDI except for research	N
22. Req 7-day handgun waiting period	Y
23. Provide $30b for failed S&Ls	N
24. Allow use of force against Iraq	N
25. Allow $15b in foreign aid for '91	?
26. Revise & extend legal immigration	?
27. Suspend aid to Angolan rebels	Y
28. Democratic tax plan proposals	Y
29. Cut defense 5% across the board	N
30. Textile import quotas-veto override	Y
31. Abortion service for military abroad	N
32. Limits on high income farmers	Y
33. Family medical leave-veto override	Y
34. Req submission of balanced budget	Y
35. Balanced budget amendment	Y
36. Amendment to ban flag desecration	Y
37. Reauthorize Amtrak-veto override	Y
38. Retraining aid for coal miners	Y
39. Suspend El Salvador military aid	N
40. Expand child care aid/tax credit	?
41. Raise House salary/omit honoraria	Y
42. Toughen oil-spill liability	?
43. Restitution to Japanese interned	Y
44. Protect Chinese & C.A. nationals	Y
45. Abortion $ for rape/incest cases	N
46. Allow religious schools to bar gays	Y
47. Bar broadcaster fairness doctrine	N
48. Bar cap gains cut/reinstate IRA	Y
49. Bar unions equal voice in pension	N
50. Bar assembly of chemical weapons	?
51. Ban plutonium/uranium production	Y
52. Cap MX missile deployment at 50	Y
53. Allow $3b for 2 stealth bombers	N
54. Publish bio-warfare experiments	?
55. Raise minimum wage-veto override	Y
56. Bar transfer of FS-X technology	Y
57. Cut defense and raise domestic $	N
58. Uniform poll closing in 48 states	?
59. Req foreign investment disclosure	Y
60. Textile import quotas-veto override	Y
61. Bar abortion funding in Wash, DC	Y
62. Notify spouses of AIDS+ carriers	?
63. Seize conveyance-drug trafficking	N
64. South Africa sanctions	?
65. 60 days' notice of plant closings	Y
66. Close unneeded military bases	N
67. Keep welfare reform within $2.8b	N
68. Allow children housing exclusion	Y
69. Shift $400m of NASA to homeless	N
70. Cap Medicare patients' liability	Y
71. Prohibit employee polygraph testing	Y
72. Allow CIA to fund Contras	Y

73. Revise unfair trade practices	Y
74. Focus SDI on accidental launch	Y
75. Bar Air Force $ for MX missile	N
76. Allow "real" increase in defense	Y
77. Troop reduction in Europe of 50%	Y
78. Ban nuclear tests above 1 kiloton	N
79. Ban anti-satellite missile tests	N
80. Observe certain limits of SALT II	N
81. Restore four Civil Rights laws	Y
82. Prohibit aliens as strikebreakers	Y
83. Allow military malpractice suits	Y
84. Approval of $36m in Contra aid	Y
85. $18b deficit reduction compromise	?
86. Welfare reform of $5.7b for 5 years	Y
87. Raise taxes $12b/cut spending $3b	?
88. Board to assess occupational risk	Y
89. Balanced budget by '93-via targets	Y
90. Bar licensing of two nuclear plants	N
91. Remove victims compensation cap	Y
92. Catastrophic health insurance	Y
93. Ban airline smoking-2 hours or less	Y
94. $1b/two year aid for the homeless	Y
95. Bar non-unions in union companies	Y
96. Increase FSLIC rescue to $15b	N
97. Impose quotas to lower trade deficit	Y
98. Reduce discretionary budget 21%	Y
99. Immigration reform/alien amnesty	Y
100. South Africa sanctions-veto override	Y
101. Tax overhaul to revise income tax	Y
102. Use of military in drug war	Y
103. Delete 12 MX/add conventional wpn	N
104. Raise speed limit to 65 mph	N
105. Require Pentagon to buy US goods	Y
106. AIDS insurance non-discrimination	Y
107. Prohibit Saudi arms sales	N
108. Ease Gun Control Act of 1968	N
109. Bar interstate handgun transport	Y
110. Make company emissions known	Y
111. Allow toxic victims to sue in fed ct	Y
112. Superfund waste cleanup of $10b	Y
113. 90 days notice of plant closings	Y
114. $20b in Medicare cuts/tax increases	Y
115. Spending cuts and tax increases	Y
116. Set school lunch lmt-250% poverty	N
117. $75m for youth work projects	Y
118. Allow Angolan military assistance	N
119. Suspend defense payments for abuse	Y
120. Drop SS COLAs/$12b tax increase	N
121. Approve $1.5b for 21 MX missiles	Y
122. Emergency farm credit/revisions	Y
123. Duty on Taiwan/Hong Kong/S Korea	Y
124. Limit steel imports to 17%	Y
125. Cut $ to schools that bar prayer	Y
126. $50b-taxes; cut Medicare/spending	Y
127. Limit Pershing II/cruise in Europe	N
128. Delete $7.1b for 34 B-1 bombers	N
129. Bar purchase of Sergeant York guns	Y
130. El Salvador military/economic aid	N
131. Bar mining of Nicaraguan waters	?
132. Physician fee freeze for Medicare	N
133. $49b in "sin"/phone/insurance taxes	Y
134. Allow sale of Conrail	N
135. Equal Rights Amendment	N
136. Authorize Marines in Lebanon	N

LIPINSKI, WILLIAM O. (continued)
137. Eminent domain for coal companies N
138. Prohibit EPA clean air sanctions N
139. SS retirement age increase/reforms Y

Presidential Support Score: 1991 - 38% 1990 - 41%

HYDE, HENRY J. -- Illinois 6th District [Republican]. Counties of Cook (pt.) and Du Page (pt.). Prior Terms: 1975-92. Born: April 18, 1924; Chicago, IL. Education: Georgetown University (B.S.S.); Loyola University (J.D.). Military Service: U.S. Navy, WW II. Occupation: Attorney; Illinois legislator (1967-74).

1. Protection to Haitian refugees Y	54. Publish bio-warfare experiments ?
2. Raise tax on wealthy; lower others N	55. Raise minimum wage-veto override N
3. Investigate Reagan hostage delay N	56. Bar transfer of FS-X technology N
4. Campaign finance revisions N	57. Cut defense and raise domestic $?
5. Unpaid leave to care for children Y	58. Uniform poll closing in 48 states ?
6. Restrict NEA use of funds Y	59. Req foreign investment disclosure N
7. Bar race-bias claim/habeas corpus Y	60. Textile import quotas-veto override N
8. Ban race as death sentence factor Y	61. Bar abortion funding in Wash, DC Y
9. Exceptions to exclusionary rule Y	62. Notify spouses of AIDS+ carriers N
10. Allow sale of assault weapons Y	63. Seize conveyance-drug trafficking Y
11. Life in prison/abolish death penalty N	64. South Africa sanctions N
12. Req conspiracy-price fixing cases N	65. 60 days' notice of plant closings N
13. Unemployment benefits extension N	66. Close unneeded military bases Y
14. Tissue use of aborted fetuses N	67. Keep welfare reform within $2.8b Y
15. Bar replacement of union strikers N	68. Allow children housing exclusion ?
16. Hold foreign aid at $15b for '92 N	69. Shift $400m of NASA to homeless N
17. Restore space station funding Y	70. Cap Medicare patients' liability Y
18. Civil Rights Act of 1991 N	71. Prohibit employee polygraph testing N
19. Unlimited damages-discrimination N	72. Allow CIA to fund Contras Y
20. Eliminate funds for supercollider N	73. Revise unfair trade practices N
21. Terminate SDI except for research N	74. Focus SDI on accidental launch N
22. Req 7-day handgun waiting period Y	75. Bar Air Force $ for MX missile N
23. Provide $30b for failed S&Ls Y	76. Allow "real" increase in defense Y
24. Allow use of force against Iraq Y	77. Troop reduction in Europe of 50% N
25. Allow $15b in foreign aid for '91 Y	78. Ban nuclear tests above 1 kiloton N
26. Revise & extend legal immigration Y	79. Ban anti-satellite missile tests N
27. Suspend aid to Angolan rebels N	80. Observe certain limits of SALT II N
28. Democratic tax plan proposals N	81. Restore four Civil Rights laws N
29. Cut defense 5% across the board N	82. Prohibit aliens as strikebreakers N
30. Textile import quotas-veto override N	83. Allow military malpractice suits ?
31. Abortion service for military abroad N	84. Approval of $36m in Contra aid Y
32. Limits on high income farmers N	85. $18b deficit reduction compromise Y
33. Family medical leave-veto override Y	86. Welfare reform of $5.7b for 5 years N
34. Req submission of balanced budget N	87. Raise taxes $12b/cut spending $3b N
35. Balanced budget amendment Y	88. Board to assess occupational risk N
36. Amendment to ban flag desecration Y	89. Balanced budget by '93-via targets N
37. Reauthorize Amtrak-veto override N	90. Bar licensing of two nuclear plants N
38. Retraining aid for coal miners N	91. Remove victims compensation cap N
39. Suspend El Salvador military aid N	92. Catastrophic health insurance N
40. Expand child care aid/tax credit N	93. Ban airline smoking-2 hours or less Y
41. Raise House salary/omit honoraria N	94. $1b/two year aid for the homeless Y
42. Toughen oil-spill liability N	95. Bar non-unions in union companies N
43. Restitution to Japanese interned Y	96. Increase FSLIC rescue to $15b N
44. Protect Chinese & C.A. nationals Y	97. Impose quotas to lower trade deficit N
45. Abortion $ for rape/incest cases N	98. Reduce discretionary budget 21% Y
46. Allow religious schools to bar gays Y	99. Immigration reform/alien amnesty N
47. Bar broadcaster fairness doctrine N	100. South Africa sanctions-veto override N
48. Bar cap gains cut/reinstate IRA N	101. Tax overhaul to revise income tax Y
49. Bar unions equal voice in pension Y	102. Use of military in drug war Y
50. Bar assembly of chemical weapons ?	103. Delete 12 MX/add conventional wpn N
51. Ban plutonium/uranium production ?	104. Raise speed limit to 65 mph Y
52. Cap MX missile deployment at 50 ?	105. Require Pentagon to buy US goods N
53. Allow $3b for 2 stealth bombers ?	106. AIDS insurance non-discrimination N

HYDE, HENRY J. (continued)

107. Prohibit Saudi arms sales	N	126. $50b-taxes; cut Medicare/spending N
108. Ease Gun Control Act of 1968	Y	127. Limit Pershing II/cruise in Europe N
109. Bar interstate handgun transport	N	128. Delete $7.1b for 34 B-1 bombers N
110. Make company emissions known	N	129. Bar purchase of Sergeant York guns N
111. Allow toxic victims to sue in fed ct	?	130. El Salvador military/economic aid Y
112. Superfund waste cleanup of $10b	Y	131. Bar mining of Nicaraguan waters N
113. 90 days notice of plant closings	N	132. Physician fee freeze for Medicare Y
114. $20b in Medicare cuts/tax increases	N	133. $49b in "sin"/phone/insurance taxes Y
115. Spending cuts and tax increases	N	134. Allow sale of Conrail Y
116. Set school lunch lmt-250% poverty	Y	135. Equal Rights Amendment N
117. $75m for youth work projects	N	136. Authorize Marines in Lebanon Y
118. Allow Angolan military assistance	Y	137. Eminent domain for coal companies N
119. Suspend defense payments for abuse	N	138. Prohibit EPA clean air sanctions Y
120. Drop SS COLAs/$12b tax increase	N	139. SS retirement age increase/reforms Y
121. Approve $1.5b for 21 MX missiles	Y	140. Auto domestic content requirement N
122. Emergency farm credit/revisions	N	141. Delete jobs program funding Y
123. Duty on Taiwan/Hong Kong/S Korea	N	142. Highway-gas tax bill N
124. Limit steel imports to 17%	N	143. Cut $5b from defense for Medicare N
125. Cut $ to schools that bar prayer	Y	144. Emergency housing aid of $1b Y

Presidential Support Score: 1991 - 85%   1990 - 68%

COLLINS, CARDISS -- Illinois 7th District [Democrat].   County of Cook (pt.).   Prior Terms: 1973 (Special Election)-1992.   Born: September 24, 1931; St. Louis, MO.   Education: Northwestern University.   Occupation: Stenographer; secretary; accountant; revenue auditor.

1. Protection to Haitian refugees	Y	38. Retraining aid for coal miners Y
2. Raise tax on wealthy; lower others	Y	39. Suspend El Salvador military aid Y
3. Investigate Reagan hostage delay	Y	40. Expand child care aid/tax credit Y
4. Campaign finance revisions	Y	41. Raise House salary/omit honoraria Y
5. Unpaid leave to care for children	Y	42. Toughen oil-spill liability Y
6. Restrict NEA use of funds	N	43. Restitution to Japanese interned Y
7. Bar race-bias claim/habeas corpus	?	44. Protect Chinese & C.A. nationals Y
8. Ban race as death sentence factor	?	45. Abortion $ for rape/incest cases ?
9. Exceptions to exclusionary rule	N	46. Allow religious schools to bar gays N
10. Allow sale of assault weapons	N	47. Bar broadcaster fairness doctrine N
11. Life in prison/abolish death penalty	Y	48. Bar cap gains cut/reinstate IRA Y
12. Req conspiracy-price fixing cases	N	49. Bar unions equal voice in pension N
13. Unemployment benefits extension	Y	50. Bar assembly of chemical weapons ?
14. Tissue use of aborted fetuses	Y	51. Ban plutonium/uranium production ?
15. Bar replacement of union strikers	Y	52. Cap MX missile deployment at 50 ?
16. Hold foreign aid at $15b for '92	Y	53. Allow $3b for 2 stealth bombers ?
17. Restore space station funding	N	54. Publish bio-warfare experiments ?
18. Civil Rights Act of 1991	Y	55. Raise minimum wage-veto override ?
19. Unlimited damages-discrimination	Y	56. Bar transfer of FS-X technology #
20. Eliminate funds for supercollider	Y	57. Cut defense and raise domestic $ Y
21. Terminate SDI except for research	Y	58. Uniform poll closing in 48 states Y
22. Req 7-day handgun waiting period	Y	59. Req foreign investment disclosure Y
23. Provide $30b for failed S&Ls	N	60. Textile import quotas-veto override Y
24. Allow use of force against Iraq	N	61. Bar abortion funding in Wash, DC N
25. Allow $15b in foreign aid for '91	Y	62. Notify spouses of AIDS+ carriers N
26. Revise & extend legal immigration	Y	63. Seize conveyance-drug trafficking ?
27. Suspend aid to Angolan rebels	Y	64. South Africa sanctions Y
28. Democratic tax plan proposals	Y	65. 60 days' notice of plant closings Y
29. Cut defense 5% across the board	Y	66. Close unneeded military bases Y
30. Textile import quotas-veto override	Y	67. Keep welfare reform within $2.8b N
31. Abortion service for military abroad	Y	68. Allow children housing exclusion N
32. Limits on high income farmers	N	69. Shift $400m of NASA to homeless Y
33. Family medical leave-veto override	Y	70. Cap Medicare patients' liability Y
34. Req submission of balanced budget	Y	71. Prohibit employee polygraph testing Y
35. Balanced budget amendment	N	72. Allow CIA to fund Contras N
36. Amendment to ban flag desecration	N	73. Revise unfair trade practices Y
37. Reauthorize Amtrak-veto override	Y	74. Focus SDI on accidental launch Y

COLLINS, CARDISS (continued)

75. Bar Air Force $ for MX missile	Y	
76. Allow "real" increase in defense	N	
77. Troop reduction in Europe of 50%	#	
78. Ban nuclear tests above 1 kiloton	Y	
79. Ban anti-satellite missile tests	Y	
80. Observe certain limits of SALT II	Y	
81. Restore four Civil Rights laws	Y	
82. Prohibit aliens as strikebreakers	Y	
83. Allow military malpractice suits	Y	
84. Approval of $36m in Contra aid	N	
85. $18b deficit reduction compromise	N	
86. Welfare reform of $5.7b for 5 years	Y	
87. Raise taxes $12b/cut spending $3b	Y	
88. Board to assess occupational risk	Y	
89. Balanced budget by '93-via targets	+	
90. Bar licensing of two nuclear plants	Y	
91. Remove victims compensation cap	Y	
92. Catastrophic health insurance	Y	
93. Ban airline smoking-2 hours or less	Y	
94. $1b/two year aid for the homeless	Y	
95. Bar non-unions in union companies	Y	
96. Increase FSLIC rescue to $15b	N	
97. Impose quotas to lower trade deficit	Y	
98. Reduce discretionary budget 21%	?	
99. Immigration reform/alien amnesty	Y	
100. South Africa sanctions-veto override	Y	
101. Tax overhaul to revise income tax	Y	
102. Use of military in drug war	N	
103. Delete 12 MX/add conventional wpn	Y	
104. Raise speed limit to 65 mph	Y	
105. Require Pentagon to buy US goods	Y	
106. AIDS insurance non-discrimination	Y	
107. Prohibit Saudi arms sales	Y	
108. Ease Gun Control Act of 1968	N	
109. Bar interstate handgun transport	Y	

110. Make company emissions known	Y
111. Allow toxic victims to sue in fed ct	Y
112. Superfund waste cleanup of $10b	Y
113. 90 days notice of plant closings	Y
114. $20b in Medicare cuts/tax increases	Y
115. Spending cuts and tax increases	Y
116. Set school lunch lmt-250% poverty	N
117. $75m for youth work projects	?
118. Allow Angolan military assistance	N
119. Suspend defense payments for abuse	Y
120. Drop SS COLAs/$12b tax increase	N
121. Approve $1.5b for 21 MX missiles	N
122. Emergency farm credit/revisions	Y
123. Duty on Taiwan/Hong Kong/S Korea	Y
124. Limit steel imports to 17%	Y
125. Cut $ to schools that bar prayer	N
126. $50b-taxes; cut Medicare/spending	N
127. Limit Pershing II/cruise in Europe	Y
128. Delete $7.1b for 34 B-1 bombers	Y
129. Bar purchase of Sergeant York guns	Y
130. El Salvador military/economic aid	N
131. Bar mining of Nicaraguan waters	Y
132. Physician fee freeze for Medicare	N
133. $49b in "sin"/phone/insurance taxes	Y
134. Allow sale of Conrail	?
135. Equal Rights Amendment	Y
136. Authorize Marines in Lebanon	N
137. Eminent domain for coal companies	N
138. Prohibit EPA clean air sanctions	?
139. SS retirement age increase/reforms	N
140. Auto domestic content requirement	Y
141. Delete jobs program funding	N
142. Highway-gas tax bill	Y
143. Cut $5b from defense for Medicare	Y
144. Emergency housing aid of $1b	Y

Presidential Support Score: 1991 - 23%   1990 - 10%

ROSTENKOWSKI, DAN -- Illinois 8th District [Democrat]. County of Cook (pt.). Prior Terms: 1959-92. Born: January 2, 1928; Chicago, IL. Education: St. John's Military Academy; Loyola University. Military Service: U.S. Army, Korean War. Occupation: Illinois representative; Illinois senator.

1. Protection to Haitian refugees	?	
2. Raise tax on wealthy; lower others	Y	
3. Investigate Reagan hostage delay	Y	
4. Campaign finance revisions	Y	
5. Unpaid leave to care for children	Y	
6. Restrict NEA use of funds	N	
7. Bar race-bias claim/habeas corpus	N	
8. Ban race as death sentence factor	Y	
9. Exceptions to exclusionary rule	N	
10. Allow sale of assault weapons	N	
11. Life in prison/abolish death penalty	N	
12. Req conspiracy-price fixing cases	N	
13. Unemployment benefits extension	Y	
14. Tissue use of aborted fetuses	Y	
15. Bar replacement of union strikers	Y	
16. Hold foreign aid at $15b for '92	Y	
17. Restore space station funding	N	
18. Civil Rights Act of 1991	Y	
19. Unlimited damages-discrimination	N	
20. Eliminate funds for supercollider	Y	

21. Terminate SDI except for research	N
22. Req 7-day handgun waiting period	Y
23. Provide $30b for failed S&Ls	Y
24. Allow use of force against Iraq	Y
25. Allow $15b in foreign aid for '91	?
26. Revise & extend legal immigration	?
27. Suspend aid to Angolan rebels	Y
28. Democratic tax plan proposals	Y
29. Cut defense 5% across the board	N
30. Textile import quotas-veto override	N
31. Abortion service for military abroad	N
32. Limits on high income farmers	Y
33. Family medical leave-veto override	Y
34. Req submission of balanced budget	Y
35. Balanced budget amendment	N
36. Amendment to ban flag desecration	N
37. Reauthorize Amtrak-veto override	Y
38. Retraining aid for coal miners	Y
39. Suspend El Salvador military aid	Y
40. Expand child care aid/tax credit	Y

ROSTENKOWSKI, DAN (continued)

41. Raise House salary/omit honoraria	Y	
42. Toughen oil-spill liability	Y	
43. Restitution to Japanese interned	Y	
44. Protect Chinese & C.A. nationals	Y	
45. Abortion $ for rape/incest cases	N	
46. Allow religious schools to bar gays	Y	
47. Bar broadcaster fairness doctrine	N	
48. Bar cap gains cut/reinstate IRA	Y	
49. Bar unions equal voice in pension	N	
50. Bar assembly of chemical weapons	Y	
51. Ban plutonium/uranium production	Y	
52. Cap MX missile deployment at 50	Y	
53. Allow $3b for 2 stealth bombers	N	
54. Publish bio-warfare experiments	Y	
55. Raise minimum wage-veto override	Y	
56. Bar transfer of FS-X technology	Y	
57. Cut defense and raise domestic $	?	
58. Uniform poll closing in 48 states	Y	
59. Req foreign investment disclosure	N	
60. Textile import quotas-veto override	N	
61. Bar abortion funding in Wash, DC	Y	
62. Notify spouses of AIDS+ carriers	N	
63. Seize conveyance-drug trafficking	?	
64. South Africa sanctions	Y	
65. 60 days' notice of plant closings	Y	
66. Close unneeded military bases	Y	
67. Keep welfare reform within $2.8b	N	
68. Allow children housing exclusion	N	
69. Shift $400m of NASA to homeless	Y	
70. Cap Medicare patients' liability	Y	
71. Prohibit employee polygraph testing	Y	
72. Allow CIA to fund Contras	N	
73. Revise unfair trade practices	Y	
74. Focus SDI on accidental launch	Y	
75. Bar Air Force $ for MX missile	N	
76. Allow "real" increase in defense	N	
77. Troop reduction in Europe of 50%	?	
78. Ban nuclear tests above 1 kiloton	?	
79. Ban anti-satellite missile tests	Y	
80. Observe certain limits of SALT II	Y	
81. Restore four Civil Rights laws	Y	
82. Prohibit aliens as strikebreakers	Y	
83. Allow military malpractice suits	?	
84. Approval of $36m in Contra aid	N	
85. $18b deficit reduction compromise	Y	
86. Welfare reform of $5.7b for 5 years	Y	
87. Raise taxes $12b/cut spending $3b	Y	
88. Board to assess occupational risk	Y	
89. Balanced budget by '93-via targets	Y	
90. Bar licensing of two nuclear plants	N	
91. Remove victims compensation cap	N	
92. Catastrophic health insurance	Y	

93. Ban airline smoking-2 hours or less	?
94. $1b/two year aid for the homeless	Y
95. Bar non-unions in union companies	?
96. Increase FSLIC rescue to $15b	N
97. Impose quotas to lower trade deficit	N
98. Reduce discretionary budget 21%	?
99. Immigration reform/alien amnesty	Y
100. South Africa sanctions-veto override	?
101. Tax overhaul to revise income tax	Y
102. Use of military in drug war	?
103. Delete 12 MX/add conventional wpn	Y
104. Raise speed limit to 65 mph	N
105. Require Pentagon to buy US goods	Y
106. AIDS insurance non-discrimination	Y
107. Prohibit Saudi arms sales	Y
108. Ease Gun Control Act of 1968	N
109. Bar interstate handgun transport	Y
110. Make company emissions known	Y
111. Allow toxic victims to sue in fed ct	N
112. Superfund waste cleanup of $10b	Y
113. 90 days notice of plant closings	Y
114. $20b in Medicare cuts/tax increases	?
115. Spending cuts and tax increases	Y
116. Set school lunch lmt-250% poverty	N
117. $75m for youth work projects	?
118. Allow Angolan military assistance	N
119. Suspend defense payments for abuse	Y
120. Drop SS COLAs/$12b tax increase	N
121. Approve $1.5b for 21 MX missiles	N
122. Emergency farm credit/revisions	Y
123. Duty on Taiwan/Hong Kong/S Korea	Y
124. Limit steel imports to 17%	Y
125. Cut $ to schools that bar prayer	?
126. $50b-taxes; cut Medicare/spending	Y
127. Limit Pershing II/cruise in Europe	N
128. Delete $7.1b for 34 B-1 bombers	N
129. Bar purchase of Sergeant York guns	N
130. El Salvador military/economic aid	?
131. Bar mining of Nicaraguan waters	Y
132. Physician fee freeze for Medicare	N
133. $49b in "sin"/phone/insurance taxes	Y
134. Allow sale of Conrail	N
135. Equal Rights Amendment	Y
136. Authorize Marines in Lebanon	Y
137. Eminent domain for coal companies	N
138. Prohibit EPA clean air sanctions	N
139. SS retirement age increase/reforms	Y
140. Auto domestic content requirement	N
141. Delete jobs program funding	N
142. Highway-gas tax bill	Y
143. Cut $5b from defense for Medicare	Y
144. Emergency housing aid of $1b	Y

Presidential Support Score: 1991 - 36%   1990 - 33%

YATES, SIDNEY R. -- Illinois 9th District [Democrat]. County of Cook (pt.). Prior Terms: 1949-62; 1965-92. Born: August 27, 1909; Chicago, IL. Education: University of Chicago (Ph.D., J.D.). Military Service: U.S. Navy. Occupation: Assistant attorney, Illinois state bank receiver (1935-37); assistant attorney general (1937-40); editor, law bulletin (1947); U.S. representative, Trusteeship Council, U.N. (1963-64).

1. Protection to Haitian refugees	Y	3. Investigate Reagan hostage delay	Y
2. Raise tax on wealthy; lower others	Y	4. Campaign finance revisions	Y

YATES, SIDNEY R. (continued)

5. Unpaid leave to care for children	Y	69. Shift $400m of NASA to homeless	Y
6. Restrict NEA use of funds	N	70. Cap Medicare patients' liability	Y
7. Bar race-bias claim/habeas corpus	N	71. Prohibit employee polygraph testing	?
8. Ban race as death sentence factor	N	72. Allow CIA to fund Contras	N
9. Exceptions to exclusionary rule	N	73. Revise unfair trade practices	Y
10. Allow sale of assault weapons	N	74. Focus SDI on accidental launch	?
11. Life in prison/abolish death penalty	Y	75. Bar Air Force $ for MX missile	#
12. Req conspiracy-price fixing cases	N	76. Allow "real" increase in defense	N
13. Unemployment benefits extension	Y	77. Troop reduction in Europe of 50%	?
14. Tissue use of aborted fetuses	Y	78. Ban nuclear tests above 1 kiloton	?
15. Bar replacement of union strikers	Y	79. Ban anti-satellite missile tests	?
16. Hold foreign aid at $15b for '92	#	80. Observe certain limits of SALT II	Y
17. Restore space station funding	N	81. Restore four Civil Rights laws	Y
18. Civil Rights Act of 1991	Y	82. Prohibit aliens as strikebreakers	Y
19. Unlimited damages-discrimination	Y	83. Allow military malpractice suits	Y
20. Eliminate funds for supercollider	N	84. Approval of $36m in Contra aid	N
21. Terminate SDI except for research	Y	85. $18b deficit reduction compromise	Y
22. Req 7-day handgun waiting period	Y	86. Welfare reform of $5.7b for 5 years	Y
23. Provide $30b for failed S&Ls	N	87. Raise taxes $12b/cut spending $3b	Y
24. Allow use of force against Iraq	N	88. Board to assess occupational risk	Y
25. Allow $15b in foreign aid for '91	Y	89. Balanced budget by '93-via targets	N
26. Revise & extend legal immigration	Y	90. Bar licensing of two nuclear plants	Y
27. Suspend aid to Angolan rebels	Y	91. Remove victims compensation cap	Y
28. Democratic tax plan proposals	Y	92. Catastrophic health insurance	Y
29. Cut defense 5% across the board	N	93. Ban airline smoking-2 hours or less	Y
30. Textile import quotas-veto override	Y	94. $1b/two year aid for the homeless	Y
31. Abortion service for military abroad	Y	95. Bar non-unions in union companies	Y
32. Limits on high income farmers	Y	96. Increase FSLIC rescue to $15b	Y
33. Family medical leave-veto override	Y	97. Impose quotas to lower trade deficit	N
34. Req submission of balanced budget	Y	98. Reduce discretionary budget 21%	?
35. Balanced budget amendment	N	99. Immigration reform/alien amnesty	?
36. Amendment to ban flag desecration	N	100. South Africa sanctions-veto override	Y
37. Reauthorize Amtrak-veto override	Y	101. Tax overhaul to revise income tax	Y
38. Retraining aid for coal miners	Y	102. Use of military in drug war	N
39. Suspend El Salvador military aid	Y	103. Delete 12 MX/add conventional wpn	+
40. Expand child care aid/tax credit	Y	104. Raise speed limit to 65 mph	N
41. Raise House salary/omit honoraria	N	105. Require Pentagon to buy US goods	N
42. Toughen oil-spill liability	Y	106. AIDS insurance non-discrimination	Y
43. Restitution to Japanese interned	Y	107. Prohibit Saudi arms sales	Y
44. Protect Chinese & C.A. nationals	Y	108. Ease Gun Control Act of 1968	N
45. Abortion $ for rape/incest cases	Y	109. Bar interstate handgun transport	Y
46. Allow religious schools to bar gays	N	110. Make company emissions known	Y
47. Bar broadcaster fairness doctrine	N	111. Allow toxic victims to sue in fed ct	Y
48. Bar cap gains cut/reinstate IRA	Y	112. Superfund waste cleanup of $10b	Y
49. Bar unions equal voice in pension	N	113. 90 days notice of plant closings	Y
50. Bar assembly of chemical weapons	Y	114. $20b in Medicare cuts/tax increases	Y
51. Ban plutonium/uranium production	Y	115. Spending cuts and tax increases	Y
52. Cap MX missile deployment at 50	Y	116. Set school lunch lmt-250% poverty	N
53. Allow $3b for 2 stealth bombers	N	117. $75m for youth work projects	Y
54. Publish bio-warfare experiments	Y	118. Allow Angolan military assistance	N
55. Raise minimum wage-veto override	Y	119. Suspend defense payments for abuse	Y
56. Bar transfer of FS-X technology	Y	120. Drop SS COLAs/$12b tax increase	N
57. Cut defense and raise domestic $	Y	121. Approve $1.5b for 21 MX missiles	N
58. Uniform poll closing in 48 states	Y	122. Emergency farm credit/revisions	Y
59. Req foreign investment disclosure	Y	123. Duty on Taiwan/Hong Kong/S Korea	Y
60. Textile import quotas-veto override	Y	124. Limit steel imports to 17%	N
61. Bar abortion funding in Wash, DC	N	125. Cut $ to schools that bar prayer	Y
62. Notify spouses of AIDS+ carriers	N	126. $50b-taxes; cut Medicare/spending	Y
63. Seize conveyance-drug trafficking	N	127. Limit Pershing II/cruise in Europe	Y
64. South Africa sanctions	Y	128. Delete $7.1b for 34 B-1 bombers	Y
65. 60 days' notice of plant closings	Y	129. Bar purchase of Sergeant York guns	Y
66. Close unneeded military bases	Y	130. El Salvador military/economic aid	N
67. Keep welfare reform within $2.8b	N	131. Bar mining of Nicaraguan waters	Y
68. Allow children housing exclusion	N	132. Physician fee freeze for Medicare	N

YATES, SIDNEY R. (continued)

133. $49b in "sin"/phone/insurance taxes	Y	
134. Allow sale of Conrail	N	
135. Equal Rights Amendment	Y	
136. Authorize Marines in Lebanon	N	
137. Eminent domain for coal companies	N	
138. Prohibit EPA clean air sanctions	Y	
139. SS retirement age increase/reforms	N	
140. Auto domestic content requirement	?	
141. Delete jobs program funding	N	
142. Highway-gas tax bill	Y	
143. Cut $5b from defense for Medicare	Y	
144. Emergency housing aid of $1b	Y	

Presidential Support Score: 1991 - 23%   1990 - 17%

PORTER, JOHN EDWARD -- Illinois 10th District [Republican]. Counties of Cook (pt.) and Lake (pt.). Prior Terms: 1980 (Special Election)-1992. Born: June 1, 1935; Evanston, Ill. Education: Massachusetts Institute of Technology; Northwestern University (B.S., B.A.); University of Michigan (J.D.). Military Service: U.S. Army Reserves, 1958-64. Occupation: Illinois representative (1973-79); attorney.

1. Protection to Haitian refugees	N		49. Bar unions equal voice in pension	Y	
2. Raise tax on wealthy; lower others	N		50. Bar assembly of chemical weapons	Y	
3. Investigate Reagan hostage delay	N		51. Ban plutonium/uranium production	Y	
4. Campaign finance revisions	N		52. Cap MX missile deployment at 50	Y	
5. Unpaid leave to care for children	N		53. Allow $3b for 2 stealth bombers	N	
6. Restrict NEA use of funds	Y		54. Publish bio-warfare experiments	Y	
7. Bar race-bias claim/habeas corpus	Y		55. Raise minimum wage-veto override	N	
8. Ban race as death sentence factor	Y		56. Bar transfer of FS-X technology	N	
9. Exceptions to exclusionary rule	Y		57. Cut defense and raise domestic $	N	
10. Allow sale of assault weapons	N		58. Uniform poll closing in 48 states	Y	
11. Life in prison/abolish death penalty	N		59. Req foreign investment disclosure	N	
12. Req conspiracy-price fixing cases	N		60. Textile import quotas-veto override	N	
13. Unemployment benefits extension	N		61. Bar abortion funding in Wash, DC	Y	
14. Tissue use of aborted fetuses	Y		62. Notify spouses of AIDS+ carriers	N	
15. Bar replacement of union strikers	N		63. Seize conveyance-drug trafficking	Y	
16. Hold foreign aid at $15b for '92	Y		64. South Africa sanctions	N	
17. Restore space station funding	Y		65. 60 days' notice of plant closings	N	
18. Civil Rights Act of 1991	N		66. Close unneeded military bases	Y	
19. Unlimited damages-discrimination	N		67. Keep welfare reform within $2.8b	Y	
20. Eliminate funds for supercollider	Y		68. Allow children housing exclusion	N	
21. Terminate SDI except for research	N		69. Shift $400m of NASA to homeless	N	
22. Req 7-day handgun waiting period	Y		70. Cap Medicare patients' liability	N	
23. Provide $30b for failed S&Ls	Y		71. Prohibit employee polygraph testing	--	
24. Allow use of force against Iraq	Y		72. Allow CIA to fund Contras	Y	
25. Allow $15b in foreign aid for '91	Y		73. Revise unfair trade practices	N	
26. Revise & extend legal immigration	Y		74. Focus SDI on accidental launch	Y	
27. Suspend aid to Angolan rebels	N		75. Bar Air Force $ for MX missile	Y	
28. Democratic tax plan proposals	N		76. Allow "real" increase in defense	N	
29. Cut defense 5% across the board	Y		77. Troop reduction in Europe of 50%	N	
30. Textile import quotas-veto override	N		78. Ban nuclear tests above 1 kiloton	Y	
31. Abortion service for military abroad	Y		79. Ban anti-satellite missile tests	Y	
32. Limits on high income farmers	Y		80. Observe certain limits of SALT II	N	
33. Family medical leave-veto override	N		81. Restore four Civil Rights laws	Y	
34. Req submission of balanced budget	N		82. Prohibit aliens as strikebreakers	N	
35. Balanced budget amendment	Y		83. Allow military malpractice suits	Y	
36. Amendment to ban flag desecration	N		84. Approval of $36m in Contra aid	Y	
37. Reauthorize Amtrak-veto override	N		85. $18b deficit reduction compromise	N	
38. Retraining aid for coal miners	N		86. Welfare reform of $5.7b for 5 years	N	
39. Suspend El Salvador military aid	N		87. Raise taxes $12b/cut spending $3b	N	
40. Expand child care aid/tax credit	N		88. Board to assess occupational risk	N	
41. Raise House salary/omit honoraria	Y		89. Balanced budget by '93-via targets	Y	
42. Toughen oil-spill liability	N		90. Bar licensing of two nuclear plants	N	
43. Restitution to Japanese interned	Y		91. Remove victims compensation cap	N	
44. Protect Chinese & C.A. nationals	Y		92. Catastrophic health insurance	Y	
45. Abortion $ for rape/incest cases	N		93. Ban airline smoking-2 hours or less	N	
46. Allow religious schools to bar gays	Y		94. $1b/two year aid for the homeless	N	
47. Bar broadcaster fairness doctrine	Y		95. Bar non-unions in union companies	N	
48. Bar cap gains cut/reinstate IRA	N		96. Increase FSLIC rescue to $15b	N	

PORTER, JOHN EDWARD (continued)

97. Impose quotas to lower trade deficit	N	
98. Reduce discretionary budget 21%	Y	
99. Immigration reform/alien amnesty	Y	
100. South Africa sanctions-veto override	N	
101. Tax overhaul to revise income tax	Y	
102. Use of military in drug war	Y	
103. Delete 12 MX/add conventional wpn	N	
104. Raise speed limit to 65 mph	Y	
105. Require Pentagon to buy US goods	N	
106. AIDS insurance non-discrimination	N	
107. Prohibit Saudi arms sales	Y	
108. Ease Gun Control Act of 1968	N	
109. Bar interstate handgun transport	Y	
110. Make company emissions known	N	
111. Allow toxic victims to sue in fed ct	N	
112. Superfund waste cleanup of $10b	Y	
113. 90 days notice of plant closings	N	
114. $20b in Medicare cuts/tax increases	Y	
115. Spending cuts and tax increases	Y	
116. Set school lunch lmt-250% poverty	Y	
117. $75m for youth work projects	N	
118. Allow Angolan military assistance	Y	
119. Suspend defense payments for abuse	N	
120. Drop SS COLAs/$12b tax increase	Y	

121. Approve $1.5b for 21 MX missiles	Y
122. Emergency farm credit/revisions	N
123. Duty on Taiwan/Hong Kong/S Korea	N
124. Limit steel imports to 17%	N
125. Cut $ to schools that bar prayer	N
126. $50b-taxes; cut Medicare/spending	Y
127. Limit Pershing II/cruise in Europe	N
128. Delete $7.1b for 34 B-1 bombers	N
129. Bar purchase of Sergeant York guns	Y
130. El Salvador military/economic aid	Y
131. Bar mining of Nicaraguan waters	N
132. Physician fee freeze for Medicare	Y
133. $49b in "sin"/phone/insurance taxes	Y
134. Allow sale of Conrail	Y
135. Equal Rights Amendment	Y
136. Authorize Marines in Lebanon	Y
137. Eminent domain for coal companies	Y
138. Prohibit EPA clean air sanctions	N
139. SS retirement age increase/reforms	Y
140. Auto domestic content requirement	N
141. Delete jobs program funding	Y
142. Highway-gas tax bill	N
143. Cut $5b from defense for Medicare	Y
144. Emergency housing aid of $1b	Y

Presidential Support Score: 1991 - 67%   1990 - 65%

ANNUNZIO, FRANK -- Illinois 11th District [Democrat]. County of Cook (pt.). Prior Terms: 1965-92. Born: January 12, 1915; Chicago, IL. Education: DePaul University (B.S., M.S.). Occupation: Teacher (1936-42); assistant supervisor, National Defense Program (1942-43); educational and legislative representative, United States Steelworkers of America (1943-48); Illinois director of labor (1948-52).

1. Protection to Haitian refugees	Y	
2. Raise tax on wealthy; lower others	Y	
3. Investigate Reagan hostage delay	Y	
4. Campaign finance revisions	Y	
5. Unpaid leave to care for children	Y	
6. Restrict NEA use of funds	N	
7. Bar race-bias claim/habeas corpus	Y	
8. Ban race as death sentence factor	N	
9. Exceptions to exclusionary rule	N	
10. Allow sale of assault weapons	N	
11. Life in prison/abolish death penalty	N	
12. Req conspiracy-price fixing cases	N	
13. Unemployment benefits extension	Y	
14. Tissue use of aborted fetuses	Y	
15. Bar replacement of union strikers	Y	
16. Hold foreign aid at $15b for '92	Y	
17. Restore space station funding	Y	
18. Civil Rights Act of 1991	N	
19. Unlimited damages-discrimination	N	
20. Eliminate funds for supercollider	N	
21. Terminate SDI except for research	N	
22. Req 7-day handgun waiting period	Y	
23. Provide $30b for failed S&Ls	N	
24. Allow use of force against Iraq	N	
25. Allow $15b in foreign aid for '91	Y	
26. Revise & extend legal immigration	Y	
27. Suspend aid to Angolan rebels	Y	
28. Democratic tax plan proposals	N	
29. Cut defense 5% across the board	N	
30. Textile import quotas-veto override	Y	

31. Abortion service for military abroad	N
32. Limits on high income farmers	Y
33. Family medical leave-veto override	Y
34. Req submission of balanced budget	Y
35. Balanced budget amendment	Y
36. Amendment to ban flag desecration	Y
37. Reauthorize Amtrak-veto override	Y
38. Retraining aid for coal miners	Y
39. Suspend El Salvador military aid	Y
40. Expand child care aid/tax credit	Y
41. Raise House salary/omit honoraria	Y
42. Toughen oil-spill liability	Y
43. Restitution to Japanese interned	Y
44. Protect Chinese & C.A. nationals	Y
45. Abortion $ for rape/incest cases	N
46. Allow religious schools to bar gays	Y
47. Bar broadcaster fairness doctrine	N
48. Bar cap gains cut/reinstate IRA	Y
49. Bar unions equal voice in pension	N
50. Bar assembly of chemical weapons	Y
51. Ban plutonium/uranium production	Y
52. Cap MX missile deployment at 50	Y
53. Allow $3b for 2 stealth bombers	N
54. Publish bio-warfare experiments	Y
55. Raise minimum wage-veto override	Y
56. Bar transfer of FS-X technology	Y
57. Cut defense and raise domestic $	N
58. Uniform poll closing in 48 states	Y
59. Req foreign investment disclosure	Y
60. Textile import quotas-veto override	Y

ANNUNZIO, FRANK (continued)

61.	Bar abortion funding in Wash, DC	Y		103.	Delete 12 MX/add conventional wpn	Y
62.	Notify spouses of AIDS+ carriers	N		104.	Raise speed limit to 65 mph	N
63.	Seize conveyance-drug trafficking	N		105.	Require Pentagon to buy US goods	Y
64.	South Africa sanctions	Y		106.	AIDS insurance non-discrimination	Y
65.	60 days' notice of plant closings	Y		107.	Prohibit Saudi arms sales	Y
66.	Close unneeded military bases	N		108.	Ease Gun Control Act of 1968	N
67.	Keep welfare reform within $2.8b	X		109.	Bar interstate handgun transport	Y
68.	Allow children housing exclusion	N		110.	Make company emissions known	Y
69.	Shift $400m of NASA to homeless	N		111.	Allow toxic victims to sue in fed ct	Y
70.	Cap Medicare patients' liability	Y		112.	Superfund waste cleanup of $10b	Y
71.	Prohibit employee polygraph testing	Y		113.	90 days notice of plant closings	Y
72.	Allow CIA to fund Contras	N		114.	$20b in Medicare cuts/tax increases	Y
73.	Revise unfair trade practices	Y		115.	Spending cuts and tax increases	Y
74.	Focus SDI on accidental launch	Y		116.	Set school lunch lmt-250% poverty	N
75.	Bar Air Force $ for MX missile	Y		117.	$75m for youth work projects	Y
76.	Allow "real" increase in defense	N		118.	Allow Angolan military assistance	N
77.	Troop reduction in Europe of 50%	N		119.	Suspend defense payments for abuse	N
78.	Ban nuclear tests above 1 kiloton	Y		120.	Drop SS COLAs/$12b tax increase	N
79.	Ban anti-satellite missile tests	Y		121.	Approve $1.5b for 21 MX missiles	N
80.	Observe certain limits of SALT II	Y		122.	Emergency farm credit/revisions	Y
81.	Restore four Civil Rights laws	Y		123.	Duty on Taiwan/Hong Kong/S Korea	Y
82.	Prohibit aliens as strikebreakers	Y		124.	Limit steel imports to 17%	Y
83.	Allow military malpractice suits	Y		125.	Cut $ to schools that bar prayer	N
84.	Approval of $36m in Contra aid	N		126.	$50b-taxes; cut Medicare/spending	Y
85.	$18b deficit reduction compromise	Y		127.	Limit Pershing II/cruise in Europe	Y
86.	Welfare reform of $5.7b for 5 years	Y		128.	Delete $7.1b for 34 B-1 bombers	N
87.	Raise taxes $12b/cut spending $3b	Y		129.	Bar purchase of Sergeant York guns	N
88.	Board to assess occupational risk	Y		130.	El Salvador military/economic aid	N
89.	Balanced budget by '93-via targets	Y		131.	Bar mining of Nicaraguan waters	Y
90.	Bar licensing of two nuclear plants	N		132.	Physician fee freeze for Medicare	N
91.	Remove victims compensation cap	N		133.	$49b in "sin"/phone/insurance taxes	Y
92.	Catastrophic health insurance	Y		134.	Allow sale of Conrail	N
93.	Ban airline smoking-2 hours or less	?		135.	Equal Rights Amendment	Y
94.	$1b/two year aid for the homeless	?		136.	Authorize Marines in Lebanon	Y
95.	Bar non-unions in union companies	?		137.	Eminent domain for coal companies	Y
96.	Increase FSLIC rescue to $15b	?		138.	Prohibit EPA clean air sanctions	N
97.	Impose quotas to lower trade deficit	?		139.	SS retirement age increase/reforms	Y
98.	Reduce discretionary budget 21%	?		140.	Auto domestic content requirement	Y
99.	Immigration reform/alien amnesty	Y		141.	Delete jobs program funding	N
100.	South Africa sanctions-veto override	Y		142.	Highway-gas tax bill	Y
101.	Tax overhaul to revise income tax	Y		143.	Cut $5b from defense for Medicare	Y
102.	Use of military in drug war	Y		144.	Emergency housing aid of $1b	Y

Presidential Support Score: 1991 - 39%   1990 - 35%

CRANE, PHILIP M. -- Illinois 12th District [Republican].   Counties of Cook (pt.), Lake (pt.) and McHenry (pt.).   Prior Terms: 1969 (Special Election)-1992.   Born: November 3, 1930; Chicago, IL.   Education: DePauw University; Hillsdale College; University of Michigan; University of Vienna; Indiana University (M.A., Ph.D.).   Occupation: Teacher; director of schools; trustee; director, Intercollegiate Studies Institute; chairman, American Conservative Union; author.

1.	Protection to Haitian refugees	N		12.	Req conspiracy-price fixing cases	Y
2.	Raise tax on wealthy; lower others	N		13.	Unemployment benefits extension	N
3.	Investigate Reagan hostage delay	N		14.	Tissue use of aborted fetuses	N
4.	Campaign finance revisions	N		15.	Bar replacement of union strikers	N
5.	Unpaid leave to care for children	N		16.	Hold foreign aid at $15b for '92	N
6.	Restrict NEA use of funds	Y		17.	Restore space station funding	Y
7.	Bar race-bias claim/habeas corpus	Y		18.	Civil Rights Act of 1991	N
8.	Ban race as death sentence factor	Y		19.	Unlimited damages-discrimination	N
9.	Exceptions to exclusionary rule	Y		20.	Eliminate funds for supercollider	?
10.	Allow sale of assault weapons	Y		21.	Terminate SDI except for research	?
11.	Life in prison/abolish death penalty	N		22.	Req 7-day handgun waiting period	N

CRANE, PHILIP M. (continued)

23.	Provide $30b for failed S&Ls	N	84. Approval of $36m in Contra aid	Y
24.	Allow use of force against Iraq	Y	85. $18b deficit reduction compromise	N
25.	Allow $15b in foreign aid for '91	?	86. Welfare reform of $5.7b for 5 years	N
26.	Revise & extend legal immigration	N	87. Raise taxes $12b/cut spending $3b	N
27.	Suspend aid to Angolan rebels	N	88. Board to assess occupational risk	N
28.	Democratic tax plan proposals	N	89. Balanced budget by '93-via targets	N
29.	Cut defense 5% across the board	N	90. Bar licensing of two nuclear plants	N
30.	Textile import quotas-veto override	N	91. Remove victims compensation cap	N
31.	Abortion service for military abroad	N	92. Catastrophic health insurance	N
32.	Limits on high income farmers	Y	93. Ban airline smoking-2 hours or less	N
33.	Family medical leave-veto override	N	94. $1b/two year aid for the homeless	N
34.	Req submission of balanced budget	N	95. Bar non-unions in union companies	N
35.	Balanced budget amendment	Y	96. Increase FSLIC rescue to $15b	N
36.	Amendment to ban flag desecration	Y	97. Impose quotas to lower trade deficit	N
37.	Reauthorize Amtrak-veto override	N	98. Reduce discretionary budget 21%	?
38.	Retraining aid for coal miners	N	99. Immigration reform/alien amnesty	N
39.	Suspend El Salvador military aid	N	100. South Africa sanctions-veto override	N
40.	Expand child care aid/tax credit	N	101. Tax overhaul to revise income tax	N
41.	Raise House salary/omit honoraria	N	102. Use of military in drug war	Y
42.	Toughen oil-spill liability	N	103. Delete 12 MX/add conventional wpn	N
43.	Restitution to Japanese interned	N	104. Raise speed limit to 65 mph	Y
44.	Protect Chinese & C.A. nationals	Y	105. Require Pentagon to buy US goods	N
45.	Abortion $ for rape/incest cases	N	106. AIDS insurance non-discrimination	N
46.	Allow religious schools to bar gays	N	107. Prohibit Saudi arms sales	Y
47.	Bar broadcaster fairness doctrine	Y	108. Ease Gun Control Act of 1968	Y
48.	Bar cap gains cut/reinstate IRA	N	109. Bar interstate handgun transport	N
49.	Bar unions equal voice in pension	Y	110. Make company emissions known	N
50.	Bar assembly of chemical weapons	N	111. Allow toxic victims to sue in fed ct	N
51.	Ban plutonium/uranium production	N	112. Superfund waste cleanup of $10b	N
52.	Cap MX missile deployment at 50	N	113. 90 days notice of plant closings	X
53.	Allow $3b for 2 stealth bombers	Y	114. $20b in Medicare cuts/tax increases	N
54.	Publish bio-warfare experiments	N	115. Spending cuts and tax increases	N
55.	Raise minimum wage-veto override	N	116. Set school lunch lmt-250% poverty	Y
56.	Bar transfer of FS-X technology	N	117. $75m for youth work projects	N
57.	Cut defense and raise domestic $	N	118. Allow Angolan military assistance	Y
58.	Uniform poll closing in 48 states	Y	119. Suspend defense payments for abuse	N
59.	Req foreign investment disclosure	N	120. Drop SS COLAs/$12b tax increase	N
60.	Textile import quotas-veto override	N	121. Approve $1.5b for 21 MX missiles	Y
61.	Bar abortion funding in Wash, DC	Y	122. Emergency farm credit/revisions	N
62.	Notify spouses of AIDS+ carriers	Y	123. Duty on Taiwan/Hong Kong/S Korea	N
63.	Seize conveyance-drug trafficking	Y	124. Limit steel imports to 17%	N
64.	South Africa sanctions	N	125. Cut $ to schools that bar prayer	Y
65.	60 days' notice of plant closings	N	126. $50b-taxes; cut Medicare/spending	N
66.	Close unneeded military bases	Y	127. Limit Pershing II/cruise in Europe	N
67.	Keep welfare reform within $2.8b	Y	128. Delete $7.1b for 34 B-1 bombers	N
68.	Allow children housing exclusion	Y	129. Bar purchase of Sergeant York guns	N
69.	Shift $400m of NASA to homeless	N	130. El Salvador military/economic aid	Y
70.	Cap Medicare patients' liability	N	131. Bar mining of Nicaraguan waters	N
71.	Prohibit employee polygraph testing	?	132. Physician fee freeze for Medicare	Y
72.	Allow CIA to fund Contras	Y	133. $49b in "sin"/phone/insurance taxes	N
73.	Revise unfair trade practices	N	134. Allow sale of Conrail	Y
74.	Focus SDI on accidental launch	N	135. Equal Rights Amendment	N
75.	Bar Air Force $ for MX missile	N	136. Authorize Marines in Lebanon	N
76.	Allow "real" increase in defense	Y	137. Eminent domain for coal companies	Y
77.	Troop reduction in Europe of 50%	N	138. Prohibit EPA clean air sanctions	Y
78.	Ban nuclear tests above 1 kiloton	N	139. SS retirement age increase/reforms	Y
79.	Ban anti-satellite missile tests	N	140. Auto domestic content requirement	N
80.	Observe certain limits of SALT II	N	141. Delete jobs program funding	Y
81.	Restore four Civil Rights laws	N	142. Highway-gas tax bill	N
82.	Prohibit aliens as strikebreakers	N	143. Cut $5b from defense for Medicare	N
83.	Allow military malpractice suits	?	144. Emergency housing aid of $1b	N

Presidential Support Score: 1991 - 71%   1990 - 84%

FAWELL, HARRIS W. -- Illinois 13th District [Republican]. Counties of Cook (pt.), Du Page (pt.) and Will (pt.). Prior Terms: 1985-92. Born: March 25, 1929; West Chicago, IL. Education: North Central College; Chicago-Kent College of Law (LL.D.). Occupation: Attorney, Fawell, James and Brooks; assistant state's attorney; state senator (1963-1977); member, state Commission on Children (1967-1977); general counsel, state Park Districts Association (1977-1984).

1. Protection to Haitian refugees	Y	
2. Raise tax on wealthy; lower others	N	
3. Investigate Reagan hostage delay	N	
4. Campaign finance revisions	N	
5. Unpaid leave to care for children	N	
6. Restrict NEA use of funds	Y	
7. Bar race-bias claim/habeas corpus	Y	
8. Ban race as death sentence factor	Y	
9. Exceptions to exclusionary rule	Y	
10. Allow sale of assault weapons	N	
11. Life in prison/abolish death penalty	N	
12. Req conspiracy-price fixing cases	Y	
13. Unemployment benefits extension	N	
14. Tissue use of aborted fetuses	Y	
15. Bar replacement of union strikers	N	
16. Hold foreign aid at $15b for '92	?	
17. Restore space station funding	Y	
18. Civil Rights Act of 1991	N	
19. Unlimited damages-discrimination	N	
20. Eliminate funds for supercollider	N	
21. Terminate SDI except for research	N	
22. Req 7-day handgun waiting period	Y	
23. Provide $30b for failed S&Ls	Y	
24. Allow use of force against Iraq	Y	
25. Allow $15b in foreign aid for '91	N	
26. Revise & extend legal immigration	Y	
27. Suspend aid to Angolan rebels	N	
28. Democratic tax plan proposals	N	
29. Cut defense 5% across the board	N	
30. Textile import quotas-veto override	N	
31. Abortion service for military abroad	Y	
32. Limits on high income farmers	Y	
33. Family medical leave-veto override	N	
34. Req submission of balanced budget	N	
35. Balanced budget amendment	Y	
36. Amendment to ban flag desecration	Y	
37. Reauthorize Amtrak-veto override	N	
38. Retraining aid for coal miners	N	
39. Suspend El Salvador military aid	N	
40. Expand child care aid/tax credit	N	
41. Raise House salary/omit honoraria	N	
42. Toughen oil-spill liability	Y	
43. Restitution to Japanese interned	N	
44. Protect Chinese & C.A. nationals	Y	
45. Abortion $ for rape/incest cases	Y	
46. Allow religious schools to bar gays	Y	
47. Bar broadcaster fairness doctrine	Y	
48. Bar cap gains cut/reinstate IRA	N	
49. Bar unions equal voice in pension	Y	
50. Bar assembly of chemical weapons	Y	
51. Ban plutonium/uranium production	Y	
52. Cap MX missile deployment at 50	N	
53. Allow $3b for 2 stealth bombers	Y	
54. Publish bio-warfare experiments	Y	
55. Raise minimum wage-veto override	N	
56. Bar transfer of FS-X technology	N	
57. Cut defense and raise domestic $	N	
58. Uniform poll closing in 48 states	Y	
59. Req foreign investment disclosure	N	
60. Textile import quotas-veto override	N	
61. Bar abortion funding in Wash, DC	N	
62. Notify spouses of AIDS+ carriers	+	
63. Seize conveyance-drug trafficking	Y	
64. South Africa sanctions	N	
65. 60 days' notice of plant closings	N	
66. Close unneeded military bases	Y	
67. Keep welfare reform within $2.8b	Y	
68. Allow children housing exclusion	Y	
69. Shift $400m of NASA to homeless	N	
70. Cap Medicare patients' liability	N	
71. Prohibit employee polygraph testing	N	
72. Allow CIA to fund Contras	Y	
73. Revise unfair trade practices	N	
74. Focus SDI on accidental launch	N	
75. Bar Air Force $ for MX missile	N	
76. Allow "real" increase in defense	Y	
77. Troop reduction in Europe of 50%	N	
78. Ban nuclear tests above 1 kiloton	Y	
79. Ban anti-satellite missile tests	N	
80. Observe certain limits of SALT II	Y	
81. Restore four Civil Rights laws	N	
82. Prohibit aliens as strikebreakers	N	
83. Allow military malpractice suits	Y	
84. Approval of $36m in Contra aid	Y	
85. $18b deficit reduction compromise	N	
86. Welfare reform of $5.7b for 5 years	N	
87. Raise taxes $12b/cut spending $3b	N	
88. Board to assess occupational risk	N	
89. Balanced budget by '93-via targets	N	
90. Bar licensing of two nuclear plants	N	
91. Remove victims compensation cap	N	
92. Catastrophic health insurance	N	
93. Ban airline smoking-2 hours or less	Y	
94. $1b/two year aid for the homeless	N	
95. Bar non-unions in union companies	Y	
96. Increase FSLIC rescue to $15b	N	
97. Impose quotas to lower trade deficit	N	
98. Reduce discretionary budget 21%	Y	
99. Immigration reform/alien amnesty	N	
100. South Africa sanctions-veto override	Y	
101. Tax overhaul to revise income tax	Y	
102. Use of military in drug war	Y	
103. Delete 12 MX/add conventional wpn	N	
104. Raise speed limit to 65 mph	N	
105. Require Pentagon to buy US goods	N	
106. AIDS insurance non-discrimination	N	
107. Prohibit Saudi arms sales	N	
108. Ease Gun Control Act of 1968	N	
109. Bar interstate handgun transport	Y	
110. Make company emissions known	Y	
111. Allow toxic victims to sue in fed ct	N	
112. Superfund waste cleanup of $10b	Y	
113. 90 days notice of plant closings	N	
114. $20b in Medicare cuts/tax increases	N	
115. Spending cuts and tax increases	N	
116. Set school lunch lmt-250% poverty	Y	

FAWELL, HARRIS W. (continued)

117. $75m for youth work projects	N	120. Drop SS COLAs/$12b tax increase N
118. Allow Angolan military assistance	Y	121. Approve $1.5b for 21 MX missiles Y
119. Suspend defense payments for abuse	Y	122. Emergency farm credit/revisions N

Presidential Support Score: 1991 - 75% 1990 - 70%

HASTERT, J. DENNIS -- Illinois 14th District [Republican]. Counties of Boone (pt.), Cook (pt.), De Kalb, Du Page (pt.), Kane (pt.), Kendall (pt.), La Salle (pt.), McHenry (pt.) and Marshall (pt.). Prior Terms: 1987-92. Born: January 2, 1942; Aurora, IL. Education: Wheaton College (B.A.); Northern Illinois University (M.S.). Occupation: Partner, family restaurant business; high school teacher/coach; state assemblyman (1980-1986).

1. Protection to Haitian refugees	N	50. Bar assembly of chemical weapons	X
2. Raise tax on wealthy; lower others	N	51. Ban plutonium/uranium production	N
3. Investigate Reagan hostage delay	N	52. Cap MX missile deployment at 50	N
4. Campaign finance revisions	N	53. Allow $3b for 2 stealth bombers	N
5. Unpaid leave to care for children	N	54. Publish bio-warfare experiments	N
6. Restrict NEA use of funds	Y	55. Raise minimum wage-veto override	N
7. Bar race-bias claim/habeas corpus	Y	56. Bar transfer of FS-X technology	N
8. Ban race as death sentence factor	Y	57. Cut defense and raise domestic $	N
9. Exceptions to exclusionary rule	Y	58. Uniform poll closing in 48 states	N
10. Allow sale of assault weapons	Y	59. Req foreign investment disclosure	Y
11. Life in prison/abolish death penalty	N	60. Textile import quotas-veto override	N
12. Req conspiracy-price fixing cases	Y	61. Bar abortion funding in Wash, DC	Y
13. Unemployment benefits extension	N	62. Notify spouses of AIDS+ carriers	Y
14. Tissue use of aborted fetuses	N	63. Seize conveyance-drug trafficking	Y
15. Bar replacement of union strikers	N	64. South Africa sanctions	N
16. Hold foreign aid at $15b for '92	Y	65. 60 days' notice of plant closings	N
17. Restore space station funding	Y	66. Close unneeded military bases	Y
18. Civil Rights Act of 1991	N	67. Keep welfare reform within $2.8b	Y
19. Unlimited damages-discrimination	N	68. Allow children housing exclusion	N
20. Eliminate funds for supercollider	N	69. Shift $400m of NASA to homeless	N
21. Terminate SDI except for research	N	70. Cap Medicare patients' liability	N
22. Req 7-day handgun waiting period	N	71. Prohibit employee polygraph testing	N
23. Provide $30b for failed S&Ls	Y	72. Allow CIA to fund Contras	Y
24. Allow use of force against Iraq	Y	73. Revise unfair trade practices	N
25. Allow $15b in foreign aid for '91	Y	74. Focus SDI on accidental launch	N
26. Revise & extend legal immigration	N	75. Bar Air Force $ for MX missile	N
27. Suspend aid to Angolan rebels	N	76. Allow "real" increase in defense	Y
28. Democratic tax plan proposals	N	77. Troop reduction in Europe of 50%	N
29. Cut defense 5% across the board	N	78. Ban nuclear tests above 1 kiloton	N
30. Textile import quotas-veto override	N	79. Ban anti-satellite missile tests	N
31. Abortion service for military abroad	N	80. Observe certain limits of SALT II	N
32. Limits on high income farmers	N	81. Restore four Civil Rights laws	N
33. Family medical leave-veto override	N	82. Prohibit aliens as strikebreakers	N
34. Req submission of balanced budget	Y	83. Allow military malpractice suits	Y
35. Balanced budget amendment	Y	84. Approval of $36m in Contra aid	Y
36. Amendment to ban flag desecration	Y	85. $18b deficit reduction compromise	N
37. Reauthorize Amtrak-veto override	N	86. Welfare reform of $5.7b for 5 years	N
38. Retraining aid for coal miners	N	87. Raise taxes $12b/cut spending $3b	N
39. Suspend El Salvador military aid	N	88. Board to assess occupational risk	N
40. Expand child care aid/tax credit	N	89. Balanced budget by '93-via targets	N
41. Raise House salary/omit honoraria	N	90. Bar licensing of two nuclear plants	N
42. Toughen oil-spill liability	N	91. Remove victims compensation cap	N
43. Restitution to Japanese interned	N	92. Catastrophic health insurance	N
44. Protect Chinese & C.A. nationals	N	93. Ban airline smoking-2 hours or less	N
45. Abortion $ for rape/incest cases	N	94. $1b/two year aid for the homeless	N
46. Allow religious schools to bar gays	Y	95. Bar non-unions in union companies	N
47. Bar broadcaster fairness doctrine	Y	96. Increase FSLIC rescue to $15b	N
48. Bar cap gains cut/reinstate IRA	N	97. Impose quotas to lower trade deficit	N
49. Bar unions equal voice in pension	Y	98. Reduce discretionary budget 21%	Y

Presidential Support Score: 1991 - 84% 1990 - 67%

EWING, THOMAS W. -- Illinois 15th District [Republican]. Counties of Champaign (pt.), De Witt, Ford, Grundy, Iroquois, Kankakee, La Salle (pt.), Livingston, Logan (pt.), McLean, Platt, Will (pt.) and Woodford (pt.). Prior Term: 1991 (Special Election)-1992. Born: September, 1935; Atlanta, IL. Education: Millikin University (B.S.); John Marshall Law School (J.D.). Military Service: U.S. Army and Army Reserves. Occupation: Attorney; farm owner-manager; Livingston County assistant state's attorney (1968-73); state representative (1975-91).

1. Protection to Haitian refugees	N	9. Exceptions to exclusionary rule	Y
2. Raise tax on wealthy; lower others	N	10. Allow sale of assault weapons	Y
3. Investigate Reagan hostage delay	N	11. Life in prison/abolish death penalty	N
4. Campaign finance revisions	N	12. Req conspiracy-price fixing cases	?
5. Unpaid leave to care for children	N	13. Unemployment benefits extension	N
6. Restrict NEA use of funds	Y	14. Tissue use of aborted fetuses	N
7. Bar race-bias claim/habeas corpus	Y	15. Bar replacement of union strikers	N
8. Ban race as death sentence factor	Y		

Rep. Ewing was sworn in July 10, 1991, to succeed Edward Madigan.

Presidential Support Score: 1991 - 86%

COX, JOHN W., Jr. -- Illinois 16th District [Democrat]. Counties of Boone (pt.), Carroll, Jo Daviess, Lee, Ogle, Stephenson, Whiteside and Winnebago. Prior Term: 1991-92. Born: July 10, 1947; Galena, IL. Education: University of Wisconsin-Platteville (B.S.); John Marshall Law School (J.D.). Military Service: U.S. Army. Occupation: Lawyer; Jo Daviess County state's attorney (1976-84); special state assistant attorney general (1984-87); college professor (1985-86); Galena city attorney (1989-90).

1. Protection to Haitian refugees	Y	13. Unemployment benefits extension	Y
2. Raise tax on wealthy; lower others	Y	14. Tissue use of aborted fetuses	Y
3. Investigate Reagan hostage delay	Y	15. Bar replacement of union strikers	Y
4. Campaign finance revisions	Y	16. Hold foreign aid at $15b for '92	Y
5. Unpaid leave to care for children	Y	17. Restore space station funding	N
6. Restrict NEA use of funds	N	18. Civil Rights Act of 1991	Y
7. Bar race-bias claim/habeas corpus	N	19. Unlimited damages-discrimination	N
8. Ban race as death sentence factor	N	20. Eliminate funds for supercollider	Y
9. Exceptions to exclusionary rule	N	21. Terminate SDI except for research	Y
10. Allow sale of assault weapons	N	22. Req 7-day handgun waiting period	Y
11. Life in prison/abolish death penalty	Y	23. Provide $30b for failed S&Ls	Y
12. Req conspiracy-price fixing cases	N	24. Allow use of force against Iraq	N

Presidential Support Score: 1991 - 28%

EVANS, LANE -- Illinois 17th District [Democrat]. Counties of Bureau, Fulton (pt.), Henderson, Henry, Knox, La Salle (pt.), McDonough (pt.), Marshall(pt.), Mercer, Peoria (pt.), Putnam, Rock Island, Stark and Warren. Prior Terms: 1983-92. Born: August 4, 1951; Rock Island, IL. Education: Augustana College (B.A.); Georgetown University Law Center. Military Service: U.S. Marine Corps. Occupation: Partner, Community Legal Clinic; legal counsel, National Association for the Advancement of Colored People and American Civil Liberties Union.

1. Protection to Haitian refugees	Y	12. Req conspiracy-price fixing cases	N
2. Raise tax on wealthy; lower others	Y	13. Unemployment benefits extension	Y
3. Investigate Reagan hostage delay	Y	14. Tissue use of aborted fetuses	Y
4. Campaign finance revisions	Y	15. Bar replacement of union strikers	Y
5. Unpaid leave to care for children	Y	16. Hold foreign aid at $15b for '92	Y
6. Restrict NEA use of funds	N	17. Restore space station funding	N
7. Bar race-bias claim/habeas corpus	N	18. Civil Rights Act of 1991	Y
8. Ban race as death sentence factor	N	19. Unlimited damages-discrimination	Y
9. Exceptions to exclusionary rule	N	20. Eliminate funds for supercollider	Y
10. Allow sale of assault weapons	N	21. Terminate SDI except for research	Y
11. Life in prison/abolish death penalty	Y	22. Req 7-day handgun waiting period	Y

EVANS, LANE (continued)

23.	Provide $30b for failed S&Ls	N
24.	Allow use of force against Iraq	N
25.	Allow $15b in foreign aid for '91	N
26.	Revise & extend legal immigration	Y
27.	Suspend aid to Angolan rebels	Y
28.	Democratic tax plan proposals	Y
29.	Cut defense 5% across the board	N
30.	Textile import quotas-veto override	Y
31.	Abortion service for military abroad	Y
32.	Limits on high income farmers	N
33.	Family medical leave-veto override	Y
34.	Req submission of balanced budget	Y
35.	Balanced budget amendment	N
36.	Amendment to ban flag desecration	N
37.	Reauthorize Amtrak-veto override	Y
38.	Retraining aid for coal miners	Y
39.	Suspend El Salvador military aid	Y
40.	Expand child care aid/tax credit	Y
41.	Raise House salary/omit honoraria	N
42.	Toughen oil-spill liability	Y
43.	Restitution to Japanese interned	Y
44.	Protect Chinese & C.A. nationals	Y
45.	Abortion $ for rape/incest cases	Y
46.	Allow religious schools to bar gays	N
47.	Bar broadcaster fairness doctrine	N
48.	Bar cap gains cut/reinstate IRA	Y
49.	Bar unions equal voice in pension	N
50.	Bar assembly of chemical weapons	Y
51.	Ban plutonium/uranium production	Y
52.	Cap MX missile deployment at 50	Y
53.	Allow $3b for 2 stealth bombers	N
54.	Publish bio-warfare experiments	Y
55.	Raise minimum wage-veto override	Y
56.	Bar transfer of FS-X technology	Y
57.	Cut defense and raise domestic $	Y
58.	Uniform poll closing in 48 states	Y
59.	Req foreign investment disclosure	Y
60.	Textile import quotas-veto override	Y
61.	Bar abortion funding in Wash, DC	N
62.	Notify spouses of AIDS+ carriers	N
63.	Seize conveyance-drug trafficking	N
64.	South Africa sanctions	Y
65.	60 days' notice of plant closings	Y
66.	Close unneeded military bases	N
67.	Keep welfare reform within $2.8b	N
68.	Allow children housing exclusion	N
69.	Shift $400m of NASA to homeless	Y
70.	Cap Medicare patients' liability	Y
71.	Prohibit employee polygraph testing	Y
72.	Allow CIA to fund Contras	N
73.	Revise unfair trade practices	Y
74.	Focus SDI on accidental launch	Y
75.	Bar Air Force $ for MX missile	Y
76.	Allow "real" increase in defense	N
77.	Troop reduction in Europe of 50%	Y
78.	Ban nuclear tests above 1 kiloton	Y
79.	Ban anti-satellite missile tests	Y
80.	Observe certain limits of SALT II	Y
81.	Restore four Civil Rights laws	Y

82.	Prohibit aliens as strikebreakers	Y
83.	Allow military malpractice suits	Y
84.	Approval of $36m in Contra aid	N
85.	$18b deficit reduction compromise	Y
86.	Welfare reform of $5.7b for 5 years	Y
87.	Raise taxes $12b/cut spending $3b	Y
88.	Board to assess occupational risk	Y
89.	Balanced budget by '93-via targets	N
90.	Bar licensing of two nuclear plants	Y
91.	Remove victims compensation cap	Y
92.	Catastrophic health insurance	Y
93.	Ban airline smoking-2 hours or less	Y
94.	$1b/two year aid for the homeless	Y
95.	Bar non-unions in union companies	Y
96.	Increase FSLIC rescue to $15b	N
97.	Impose quotas to lower trade deficit	Y
98.	Reduce discretionary budget 21%	N
99.	Immigration reform/alien amnesty	N
100.	South Africa sanctions-veto override	Y
101.	Tax overhaul to revise income tax	Y
102.	Use of military in drug war	N
103.	Delete 12 MX/add conventional wpn	?
104.	Raise speed limit to 65 mph	N
105.	Require Pentagon to buy US goods	Y
106.	AIDS insurance non-discrimination	Y
107.	Prohibit Saudi arms sales	Y
108.	Ease Gun Control Act of 1968	N
109.	Bar interstate handgun transport	Y
110.	Make company emissions known	Y
111.	Allow toxic victims to sue in fed ct	Y
112.	Superfund waste cleanup of $10b	Y
113.	90 days notice of plant closings	Y
114.	$20b in Medicare cuts/tax increases	Y
115.	Spending cuts and tax increases	Y
116.	Set school lunch lmt-250% poverty	N
117.	$75m for youth work projects	Y
118.	Allow Angolan military assistance	N
119.	Suspend defense payments for abuse	Y
120.	Drop SS COLAs/$12b tax increase	N
121.	Approve $1.5b for 21 MX missiles	N
122.	Emergency farm credit/revisions	Y
123.	Duty on Taiwan/Hong Kong/S Korea	Y
124.	Limit steel imports to 17%	Y
125.	Cut $ to schools that bar prayer	N
126.	$50b-taxes; cut Medicare/spending	Y
127.	Limit Pershing II/cruise in Europe	Y
128.	Delete $7.1b for 34 B-1 bombers	Y
129.	Bar purchase of Sergeant York guns	Y
130.	El Salvador military/economic aid	N
131.	Bar mining of Nicaraguan waters	Y
132.	Physician fee freeze for Medicare	N
133.	$49b in "sin"/phone/insurance taxes	Y
134.	Allow sale of Conrail	N
135.	Equal Rights Amendment	Y
136.	Authorize Marines in Lebanon	N
137.	Eminent domain for coal companies	N
138.	Prohibit EPA clean air sanctions	Y
139.	SS retirement age increase/reforms	N

Presidential Support Score: 1991 - 15%   1990 - 16%

MICHEL, ROBERT H. -- Illinois 18th District [Republican]. Counties of Brown, Cass, Fulton (pt.), Hancock, Logan (pt.), McDonough (pt.), Macon (pt.), Mason, Menard, Morgan, Peoria (pt.), Sangamon (pt.), Schuyler (pt.), Scott, Tazewell and Woodford (pt.). Prior Terms: 1957-92. Born: March 2, 1923; Peoria, IL. Education: Bradley University (B.S.). Military Service: U.S. Army. Occupation: Congressional administrative assistant (1949-56).

1. Protection to Haitian refugees	N	60. Textile import quotas-veto override	N
2. Raise tax on wealthy; lower others	N	61. Bar abortion funding in Wash, DC	Y
3. Investigate Reagan hostage delay	N	62. Notify spouses of AIDS+ carriers	?
4. Campaign finance revisions	N	63. Seize conveyance-drug trafficking	Y
5. Unpaid leave to care for children	N	64. South Africa sanctions	?
6. Restrict NEA use of funds	Y	65. 60 days' notice of plant closings	N
7. Bar race-bias claim/habeas corpus	Y	66. Close unneeded military bases	Y
8. Ban race as death sentence factor	Y	67. Keep welfare reform within $2.8b	Y
9. Exceptions to exclusionary rule	Y	68. Allow children housing exclusion	Y
10. Allow sale of assault weapons	Y	69. Shift $400m of NASA to homeless	Y
11. Life in prison/abolish death penalty	N	70. Cap Medicare patients' liability	Y
12. Req conspiracy-price fixing cases	Y	71. Prohibit employee polygraph testing	N
13. Unemployment benefits extension	N	72. Allow CIA to fund Contras	Y
14. Tissue use of aborted fetuses	N	73. Revise unfair trade practices	N
15. Bar replacement of union strikers	?	74. Focus SDI on accidental launch	N
16. Hold foreign aid at $15b for '92	Y	75. Bar Air Force $ for MX missile	N
17. Restore space station funding	Y	76. Allow "real" increase in defense	Y
18. Civil Rights Act of 1991	N	77. Troop reduction in Europe of 50%	N
19. Unlimited damages-discrimination	N	78. Ban nuclear tests above 1 kiloton	N
20. Eliminate funds for supercollider	N	79. Ban anti-satellite missile tests	N
21. Terminate SDI except for research	N	80. Observe certain limits of SALT II	N
22. Req 7-day handgun waiting period	?	81. Restore four Civil Rights laws	N
23. Provide $30b for failed S&Ls	Y	82. Prohibit aliens as strikebreakers	?
24. Allow use of force against Iraq	Y	83. Allow military malpractice suits	Y
25. Allow $15b in foreign aid for '91	Y	84. Approval of $36m in Contra aid	Y
26. Revise & extend legal immigration	Y	85. $18b deficit reduction compromise	Y
27. Suspend aid to Angolan rebels	N	86. Welfare reform of $5.7b for 5 years	N
28. Democratic tax plan proposals	N	87. Raise taxes $12b/cut spending $3b	N
29. Cut defense 5% across the board	?	88. Board to assess occupational risk	N
30. Textile import quotas-veto override	N	89. Balanced budget by '93-via targets	Y
31. Abortion service for military abroad	N	90. Bar licensing of two nuclear plants	N
32. Limits on high income farmers	N	91. Remove victims compensation cap	N
33. Family medical leave-veto override	N	92. Catastrophic health insurance	N
34. Req submission of balanced budget	N	93. Ban airline smoking-2 hours or less	N
35. Balanced budget amendment	Y	94. $1b/two year aid for the homeless	N
36. Amendment to ban flag desecration	Y	95. Bar non-unions in union companies	N
37. Reauthorize Amtrak-veto override	N	96. Increase FSLIC rescue to $15b	Y
38. Retraining aid for coal miners	N	97. Impose quotas to lower trade deficit	N
39. Suspend El Salvador military aid	N	98. Reduce discretionary budget 21%	N
40. Expand child care aid/tax credit	N	99. Immigration reform/alien amnesty	Y
41. Raise House salary/omit honoraria	Y	100. South Africa sanctions-veto override	N
42. Toughen oil-spill liability	N	101. Tax overhaul to revise income tax	Y
43. Restitution to Japanese interned	N	102. Use of military in drug war	Y
44. Protect Chinese & C.A. nationals	N	103. Delete 12 MX/add conventional wpn	N
45. Abortion $ for rape/incest cases	N	104. Raise speed limit to 65 mph	Y
46. Allow religious schools to bar gays	Y	105. Require Pentagon to buy US goods	N
47. Bar broadcaster fairness doctrine	Y	106. AIDS insurance non-discrimination	N
48. Bar cap gains cut/reinstate IRA	N	107. Prohibit Saudi arms sales	N
49. Bar unions equal voice in pension	Y	108. Ease Gun Control Act of 1968	Y
50. Bar assembly of chemical weapons	N	109. Bar interstate handgun transport	N
51. Ban plutonium/uranium production	N	110. Make company emissions known	N
52. Cap MX missile deployment at 50	N	111. Allow toxic victims to sue in fed ct	N
53. Allow $3b for 2 stealth bombers	Y	112. Superfund waste cleanup of $10b	Y
54. Publish bio-warfare experiments	N	113. 90 days notice of plant closings	N
55. Raise minimum wage-veto override	N	114. $20b in Medicare cuts/tax increases	N
56. Bar transfer of FS-X technology	N	115. Spending cuts and tax increases	N
57. Cut defense and raise domestic $	N	116. Set school lunch lmt-250% poverty	?
58. Uniform poll closing in 48 states	N	117. $75m for youth work projects	N
59. Req foreign investment disclosure	N	118. Allow Angolan military assistance	Y

MICHEL, ROBERT H. (continued)

119. Suspend defense payments for abuse	N	132. Physician fee freeze for Medicare	Y
120. Drop SS COLAs/$12b tax increase	N	133. $49b in "sin"/phone/insurance taxes	Y
121. Approve $1.5b for 21 MX missiles	Y	134. Allow sale of Conrail	Y
122. Emergency farm credit/revisions	N	135. Equal Rights Amendment	N
123. Duty on Taiwan/Hong Kong/S Korea	N	136. Authorize Marines in Lebanon	Y
124. Limit steel imports to 17%	N	137. Eminent domain for coal companies	Y
125. Cut $ to schools that bar prayer	Y	138. Prohibit EPA clean air sanctions	Y
126. $50b-taxes; cut Medicare/spending	Y	139. SS retirement age increase/reforms	Y
127. Limit Pershing II/cruise in Europe	N	140. Auto domestic content requirement	N
128. Delete $7.1b for 34 B-1 bombers	N	141. Delete jobs program funding	Y
129. Bar purchase of Sergeant York guns	N	142. Highway-gas tax bill	Y
130. El Salvador military/economic aid	Y	143. Cut $5b from defense for Medicare	N
131. Bar mining of Nicaraguan waters	N	144. Emergency housing aid of $1b	N

Presidential Support Score: 1991 - 81%   1990 - 75%

BRUCE, TERRY L. -- Illinois 19th District [Democrat]. Counties of Champaign (pt.), Clark, Clay, Coles, Crawford, Cumberland, Douglas, Edgar, Edwards, Effingham, Hamilton, Jasper, Lawrence, Richland, Vermilion, Wabash, Wayne and White. Prior Terms: 1985-92. Born: March 25, 1944. Education: University of Illinois (B.S., J.D.). Occupation: Attorney; Illinois senator.

1. Protection to Haitian refugees	Y	42. Toughen oil-spill liability	Y
2. Raise tax on wealthy; lower others	Y	43. Restitution to Japanese interned	Y
3. Investigate Reagan hostage delay	Y	44. Protect Chinese & C.A. nationals	Y
4. Campaign finance revisions	Y	45. Abortion $ for rape/incest cases	N
5. Unpaid leave to care for children	Y	46. Allow religious schools to bar gays	Y
6. Restrict NEA use of funds	Y	47. Bar broadcaster fairness doctrine	N
7. Bar race-bias claim/habeas corpus	N	48. Bar cap gains cut/reinstate IRA	Y
8. Ban race as death sentence factor	N	49. Bar unions equal voice in pension	N
9. Exceptions to exclusionary rule	N	50. Bar assembly of chemical weapons	Y
10. Allow sale of assault weapons	Y	51. Ban plutonium/uranium production	Y
11. Life in prison/abolish death penalty	N	52. Cap MX missile deployment at 50	Y
12. Req conspiracy-price fixing cases	N	53. Allow $3b for 2 stealth bombers	N
13. Unemployment benefits extension	Y	54. Publish bio-warfare experiments	Y
14. Tissue use of aborted fetuses	Y	55. Raise minimum wage-veto override	Y
15. Bar replacement of union strikers	Y	56. Bar transfer of FS-X technology	Y
16. Hold foreign aid at $15b for '92	Y	57. Cut defense and raise domestic $	N
17. Restore space station funding	N	58. Uniform poll closing in 48 states	N
18. Civil Rights Act of 1991	Y	59. Req foreign investment disclosure	Y
19. Unlimited damages-discrimination	Y	60. Textile import quotas-veto override	Y
20. Eliminate funds for supercollider	N	61. Bar abortion funding in Wash, DC	Y
21. Terminate SDI except for research	Y	62. Notify spouses of AIDS+ carriers	N
22. Req 7-day handgun waiting period	N	63. Seize conveyance-drug trafficking	Y
23. Provide $30b for failed S&Ls	N	64. South Africa sanctions	Y
24. Allow use of force against Iraq	N	65. 60 days' notice of plant closings	Y
25. Allow $15b in foreign aid for '91	N	66. Close unneeded military bases	N
26. Revise & extend legal immigration	Y	67. Keep welfare reform within $2.8b	Y
27. Suspend aid to Angolan rebels	Y	68. Allow children housing exclusion	N
28. Democratic tax plan proposals	Y	69. Shift $400m of NASA to homeless	N
29. Cut defense 5% across the board	N	70. Cap Medicare patients' liability	Y
30. Textile import quotas-veto override	Y	71. Prohibit employee polygraph testing	Y
31. Abortion service for military abroad	N	72. Allow CIA to fund Contras	N
32. Limits on high income farmers	N	73. Revise unfair trade practices	Y
33. Family medical leave-veto override	Y	74. Focus SDI on accidental launch	Y
34. Req submission of balanced budget	Y	75. Bar Air Force $ for MX missile	Y
35. Balanced budget amendment	N	76. Allow "real" increase in defense	N
36. Amendment to ban flag desecration	N	77. Troop reduction in Europe of 50%	Y
37. Reauthorize Amtrak-veto override	Y	78. Ban nuclear tests above 1 kiloton	Y
38. Retraining aid for coal miners	Y	79. Ban anti-satellite missile tests	Y
39. Suspend El Salvador military aid	Y	80. Observe certain limits of SALT II	Y
40. Expand child care aid/tax credit	Y	81. Restore four Civil Rights laws	Y
41. Raise House salary/omit honoraria	N	82. Prohibit aliens as strikebreakers	Y

BRUCE, TERRY L. (continued)

83. Allow military malpractice suits	Y	
84. Approval of $36m in Contra aid	N	
85. $18b deficit reduction compromise	Y	
86. Welfare reform of $5.7b for 5 years	N	
87. Raise taxes $12b/cut spending $3b	Y	
88. Board to assess occupational risk	Y	
89. Balanced budget by '93-via targets	Y	
90. Bar licensing of two nuclear plants	Y	
91. Remove victims compensation cap	N	
92. Catastrophic health insurance	Y	
93. Ban airline smoking-2 hours or less	N	
94. $1b/two year aid for the homeless	Y	
95. Bar non-unions in union companies	Y	
96. Increase FSLIC rescue to $15b	N	
97. Impose quotas to lower trade deficit	Y	
98. Reduce discretionary budget 21%	Y	
99. Immigration reform/alien amnesty	Y	
100. South Africa sanctions-veto override	Y	
101. Tax overhaul to revise income tax	N	
102. Use of military in drug war	N	
103. Delete 12 MX/add conventional wpn	Y
104. Raise speed limit to 65 mph	N
105. Require Pentagon to buy US goods	Y
106. AIDS insurance non-discrimination	Y
107. Prohibit Saudi arms sales	Y
108. Ease Gun Control Act of 1968	Y
109. Bar interstate handgun transport	N
110. Make company emissions known	Y
111. Allow toxic victims to sue in fed ct	Y
112. Superfund waste cleanup of $10b	N
113. 90 days notice of plant closings	Y
114. $20b in Medicare cuts/tax increases	Y
115. Spending cuts and tax increases	Y
116. Set school lunch lmt-250% poverty	N
117. $75m for youth work projects	Y
118. Allow Angolan military assistance	N
119. Suspend defense payments for abuse	Y
120. Drop SS COLAs/$12b tax increase	N
121. Approve $1.5b for 21 MX missiles	N
122. Emergency farm credit/revisions	Y

Presidential Support Score: 1991 - 30%   1990 - 20%

DURBIN, RICHARD J. -- Illinois 20th District [Democrat]. Counties of Adams, Calhoun, Christian, Fayette (pt.), Green, Jersey, Macon (pt.), Macoupin, Montgomery (pt.), Moultrie, Pike, Sangamon (pt.), Schuyler (pt.) and Shelby. Prior Terms: 1983-92. Born: November 21, 1944; East St. Louis, IL. Education: Georgetown University (B.A., J.D.). Occupation: U.S. Senate staff member; attorney; Illinois senator (1969-72, 1977-78); associate professor of Medical Humanities at Southern Illinois University.

1. Protection to Haitian refugees	Y	34. Req submission of balanced budget	Y
2. Raise tax on wealthy; lower others	Y	35. Balanced budget amendment	N
3. Investigate Reagan hostage delay	Y	36. Amendment to ban flag desecration	N
4. Campaign finance revisions	Y	37. Reauthorize Amtrak-veto override	Y
5. Unpaid leave to care for children	Y	38. Retraining aid for coal miners	Y
6. Restrict NEA use of funds	N	39. Suspend El Salvador military aid	Y
7. Bar race-bias claim/habeas corpus	N	40. Expand child care aid/tax credit	Y
8. Ban race as death sentence factor	N	41. Raise House salary/omit honoraria	Y
9. Exceptions to exclusionary rule	N	42. Toughen oil-spill liability	Y
10. Allow sale of assault weapons	N	43. Restitution to Japanese interned	Y
11. Life in prison/abolish death penalty	N	44. Protect Chinese & C.A. nationals	Y
12. Req conspiracy-price fixing cases	N	45. Abortion $ for rape/incest cases	Y
13. Unemployment benefits extension	Y	46. Allow religious schools to bar gays	N
14. Tissue use of aborted fetuses	Y	47. Bar broadcaster fairness doctrine	Y
15. Bar replacement of union strikers	Y	48. Bar cap gains cut/reinstate IRA	Y
16. Hold foreign aid at $15b for '92	Y	49. Bar unions equal voice in pension	N
17. Restore space station funding	N	50. Bar assembly of chemical weapons	Y
18. Civil Rights Act of 1991	Y	51. Ban plutonium/uranium production	Y
19. Unlimited damages-discrimination	Y	52. Cap MX missile deployment at 50	Y
20. Eliminate funds for supercollider	Y	53. Allow $3b for 2 stealth bombers	N
21. Terminate SDI except for research	Y	54. Publish bio-warfare experiments	Y
22. Req 7-day handgun waiting period	Y	55. Raise minimum wage-veto override	Y
23. Provide $30b for failed S&Ls	Y	56. Bar transfer of FS-X technology	N
24. Allow use of force against Iraq	N	57. Cut defense and raise domestic $	Y
25. Allow $15b in foreign aid for '91	N	58. Uniform poll closing in 48 states	Y
26. Revise & extend legal immigration	Y	59. Req foreign investment disclosure	Y
27. Suspend aid to Angolan rebels	Y	60. Textile import quotas-veto override	Y
28. Democratic tax plan proposals	Y	61. Bar abortion funding in Wash, DC	Y
29. Cut defense 5% across the board	Y	62. Notify spouses of AIDS+ carriers	N
30. Textile import quotas-veto override	Y	63. Seize conveyance-drug trafficking	Y
31. Abortion service for military abroad	N	64. South Africa sanctions	Y
32. Limits on high income farmers	N	65. 60 days' notice of plant closings	Y
33. Family medical leave-veto override	Y	66. Close unneeded military bases	Y

DURBIN, RICHARD J. (continued)

67. Keep welfare reform within $2.8b	N
68. Allow children housing exclusion	N
69. Shift $400m of NASA to homeless	Y
70. Cap Medicare patients' liability	Y
71. Prohibit employee polygraph testing	Y
72. Allow CIA to fund Contras	N
73. Revise unfair trade practices	Y
74. Focus SDI on accidental launch	Y
75. Bar Air Force $ for MX missile	Y
76. Allow "real" increase in defense	N
77. Troop reduction in Europe of 50%	Y
78. Ban nuclear tests above 1 kiloton	Y
79. Ban anti-satellite missile tests	Y
80. Observe certain limits of SALT II	Y
81. Restore four Civil Rights laws	Y
82. Prohibit aliens as strikebreakers	Y
83. Allow military malpractice suits	Y
84. Approval of $36m in Contra aid	N
85. $18b deficit reduction compromise	Y
86. Welfare reform of $5.7b for 5 years	Y
87. Raise taxes $12b/cut spending $3b	Y
88. Board to assess occupational risk	Y
89. Balanced budget by '93-via targets	Y
90. Bar licensing of two nuclear plants	Y
91. Remove victims compensation cap	Y
92. Catastrophic health insurance	Y
93. Ban airline smoking-2 hours or less	Y
94. $1b/two year aid for the homeless	Y
95. Bar non-unions in union companies	Y
96. Increase FSLIC rescue to $15b	Y
97. Impose quotas to lower trade deficit	Y
98. Reduce discretionary budget 21%	N
99. Immigration reform/alien amnesty	Y
100. South Africa sanctions-veto override	Y
101. Tax overhaul to revise income tax	Y
102. Use of military in drug war	N
103. Delete 12 MX/add conventional wpn	Y

104. Raise speed limit to 65 mph	Y
105. Require Pentagon to buy US goods	Y
106. AIDS insurance non-discrimination	Y
107. Prohibit Saudi arms sales	Y
108. Ease Gun Control Act of 1968	N
109. Bar interstate handgun transport	N
110. Make company emissions known	Y
111. Allow toxic victims to sue in fed ct	Y
112. Superfund waste cleanup of $10b	Y
113. 90 days notice of plant closings	Y
114. $20b in Medicare cuts/tax increases	Y
115. Spending cuts and tax increases	Y
116. Set school lunch lmt-250% poverty	N
117. $75m for youth work projects	Y
118. Allow Angolan military assistance	N
119. Suspend defense payments for abuse	Y
120. Drop SS COLAs/$12b tax increase	N
121. Approve $1.5b for 21 MX missiles	N
122. Emergency farm credit/revisions	Y
123. Duty on Taiwan/Hong Kong/S Korea	Y
124. Limit steel imports to 17%	Y
125. Cut $ to schools that bar prayer	N
126. $50b-taxes; cut Medicare/spending	Y
127. Limit Pershing II/cruise in Europe	N
128. Delete $7.1b for 34 B-1 bombers	Y
129. Bar purchase of Sergeant York guns	Y
130. El Salvador military/economic aid	N
131. Bar mining of Nicaraguan waters	Y
132. Physician fee freeze for Medicare	N
133. $49b in "sin"/phone/insurance taxes	Y
134. Allow sale of Conrail	N
135. Equal Rights Amendment	Y
136. Authorize Marines in Lebanon	N
137. Eminent domain for coal companies	N
138. Prohibit EPA clean air sanctions	Y
139. SS retirement age increase/reforms	N

Presidential Support Score: 1991 - 25%   1990 - 16%

COSTELLO, JERRY F. -- Illinois 21st District [Democrat]. Counties of Bond, Clinton (pt.), Madison, Montgomery (pt.) and St. Clair (pt.). Prior Terms: 1988 (Special Election)-1992. Born: September 25, 1949; East St. Louis, IL. Education: Belleville Area College (A.D.); Maryville College of the Sacred Heart (B.A.). Occupation: State judicial circuit court bailiff, deputy sheriff and court services director (1976-80); St. Clair county chief investigator for state's attorney office; St. Clair county board chairman (1981-88).

1. Protection to Haitian refugees	Y
2. Raise tax on wealthy; lower others	Y
3. Investigate Reagan hostage delay	N
4. Campaign finance revisions	Y
5. Unpaid leave to care for children	Y
6. Restrict NEA use of funds	Y
7. Bar race-bias claim/habeas corpus	N
8. Ban race as death sentence factor	N
9. Exceptions to exclusionary rule	N
10. Allow sale of assault weapons	Y
11. Life in prison/abolish death penalty	N
12. Req conspiracy-price fixing cases	N
13. Unemployment benefits extension	Y
14. Tissue use of aborted fetuses	Y
15. Bar replacement of union strikers	Y
16. Hold foreign aid at $15b for '92	N

17. Restore space station funding	N
18. Civil Rights Act of 1991	Y
19. Unlimited damages-discrimination	N
20. Eliminate funds for supercollider	N
21. Terminate SDI except for research	N
22. Req 7-day handgun waiting period	N
23. Provide $30b for failed S&Ls	N
24. Allow use of force against Iraq	N
25. Allow $15b in foreign aid for '91	N
26. Revise & extend legal immigration	Y
27. Suspend aid to Angolan rebels	Y
28. Democratic tax plan proposals	Y
29. Cut defense 5% across the board	N
30. Textile import quotas-veto override	Y
31. Abortion service for military abroad	N
32. Limits on high income farmers	N

COSTELLO, JERRY F. (continued)

33. Family medical leave-veto override	Y		49. Bar unions equal voice in pension	N
34. Req submission of balanced budget	Y		50. Bar assembly of chemical weapons	Y
35. Balanced budget amendment	Y		51. Ban plutonium/uranium production	Y
36. Amendment to ban flag desecration	Y		52. Cap MX missile deployment at 50	Y
37. Reauthorize Amtrak-veto override	Y		53. Allow $3b for 2 stealth bombers	N
38. Retraining aid for coal miners	Y		54. Publish bio-warfare experiments	Y
39. Suspend El Salvador military aid	Y		55. Raise minimum wage-veto override	Y
40. Expand child care aid/tax credit	Y		56. Bar transfer of FS-X technology	Y
41. Raise House salary/omit honoraria	N		57. Cut defense and raise domestic $	N
42. Toughen oil-spill liability	N		58. Uniform poll closing in 48 states	Y
43. Restitution to Japanese interned	Y		59. Req foreign investment disclosure	Y
44. Protect Chinese & C.A. nationals	Y		60. Textile import quotas-veto override	Y
45. Abortion $ for rape/incest cases	N		61. Bar abortion funding in Wash, DC	Y
46. Allow religious schools to bar gays	Y		62. Notify spouses of AIDS+ carriers	N
47. Bar broadcaster fairness doctrine	Y		63. Seize conveyance-drug trafficking	N
48. Bar cap gains cut/reinstate IRA	Y		64. South Africa sanctions	Y

Presidential Support Score: 1991 - 34%   1990 - 26%

POSHARD, GLENN -- Illinois 22nd District [Democrat]. Counties of Alexander, Clinton (pt.), Fayette (pt.), Franklin, Gallatin, Hardin, Jackson, Jefferson, Johnson, Marion, Massac, Monroe, Perry, Pope, Pulaski, Randolph, St. Clair (pt.), Saline, Union, Washington and Williamson. Prior Terms: 1989-92. Born: October 31, 1945; Herald, IL. Education: Southern Illinois University-Carbondale (B.S., M.S., Ph.D.). Military Service: U.S. Army. Occupation: High school teacher; state regional education service center assistant director and director; state senator (1984-88).

1. Protection to Haitian refugees	Y		30. Textile import quotas-veto override	Y
2. Raise tax on wealthy; lower others	Y		31. Abortion service for military abroad	N
3. Investigate Reagan hostage delay	Y		32. Limits on high income farmers	N
4. Campaign finance revisions	Y		33. Family medical leave-veto override	Y
5. Unpaid leave to care for children	Y		34. Req submission of balanced budget	Y
6. Restrict NEA use of funds	Y		35. Balanced budget amendment	Y
7. Bar race-bias claim/habeas corpus	N		36. Amendment to ban flag desecration	N
8. Ban race as death sentence factor	N		37. Reauthorize Amtrak-veto override	Y
9. Exceptions to exclusionary rule	N		38. Retraining aid for coal miners	Y
10. Allow sale of assault weapons	Y		39. Suspend El Salvador military aid	Y
11. Life in prison/abolish death penalty	N		40. Expand child care aid/tax credit	Y
12. Req conspiracy-price fixing cases	N		41. Raise House salary/omit honoraria	N
13. Unemployment benefits extension	Y		42. Toughen oil-spill liability	N
14. Tissue use of aborted fetuses	Y		43. Restitution to Japanese interned	Y
15. Bar replacement of union strikers	Y		44. Protect Chinese & C.A. nationals	Y
16. Hold foreign aid at $15b for '92	N		45. Abortion $ for rape/incest cases	N
17. Restore space station funding	N		46. Allow religious schools to bar gays	Y
18. Civil Rights Act of 1991	Y		47. Bar broadcaster fairness doctrine	N
19. Unlimited damages-discrimination	N		48. Bar cap gains cut/reinstate IRA	Y
20. Eliminate funds for supercollider	Y		49. Bar unions equal voice in pension	N
21. Terminate SDI except for research	Y		50. Bar assembly of chemical weapons	Y
22. Req 7-day handgun waiting period	N		51. Ban plutonium/uranium production	Y
23. Provide $30b for failed S&Ls	N		52. Cap MX missile deployment at 50	Y
24. Allow use of force against Iraq	N		53. Allow $3b for 2 stealth bombers	N
25. Allow $15b in foreign aid for '91	N		54. Publish bio-warfare experiments	Y
26. Revise & extend legal immigration	Y		55. Raise minimum wage-veto override	Y
27. Suspend aid to Angolan rebels	Y		56. Bar transfer of FS-X technology	Y
28. Democratic tax plan proposals	Y		57. Cut defense and raise domestic $	Y
29. Cut defense 5% across the board	Y		58. Uniform poll closing in 48 states	Y

Presidential Support Score: 1991 - 30%   1990 - 23%

INDIANA

VISCLOSKY, PETER J. -- Indiana 1st District [Democrat]. Counties of Lake (pt.), La Porte (pt.) and Porter (pt.). Prior Terms: 1985-92. Born: August 13, 1949. Education: Indiana University (B.S.); University of Notre Dame (J.D.); Georgetown University (LL.M.). Occupation: Attorney; congressional aide.

1. Protection to Haitian refugees	Y	
2. Raise tax on wealthy; lower others	Y	
3. Investigate Reagan hostage delay	Y	
4. Campaign finance revisions	Y	
5. Unpaid leave to care for children	Y	
6. Restrict NEA use of funds	N	
7. Bar race-bias claim/habeas corpus	N	
8. Ban race as death sentence factor	N	
9. Exceptions to exclusionary rule	N	
10. Allow sale of assault weapons	N	
11. Life in prison/abolish death penalty	Y	
12. Req conspiracy-price fixing cases	N	
13. Unemployment benefits extension	Y	
14. Tissue use of aborted fetuses	Y	
15. Bar replacement of union strikers	Y	
16. Hold foreign aid at $15b for '92	Y	
17. Restore space station funding	N	
18. Civil Rights Act of 1991	Y	
19. Unlimited damages-discrimination	N	
20. Eliminate funds for supercollider	Y	
21. Terminate SDI except for research	N	
22. Req 7-day handgun waiting period	Y	
23. Provide $30b for failed S&Ls	N	
24. Allow use of force against Iraq	N	
25. Allow $15b in foreign aid for '91	N	
26. Revise & extend legal immigration	Y	
27. Suspend aid to Angolan rebels	Y	
28. Democratic tax plan proposals	Y	
29. Cut defense 5% across the board	N	
30. Textile import quotas-veto override	Y	
31. Abortion service for military abroad	Y	
32. Limits on high income farmers	Y	
33. Family medical leave-veto override	Y	
34. Req submission of balanced budget	Y	
35. Balanced budget amendment	N	
36. Amendment to ban flag desecration	N	
37. Reauthorize Amtrak-veto override	Y	
38. Retraining aid for coal miners	Y	
39. Suspend El Salvador military aid	Y	
40. Expand child care aid/tax credit	Y	
41. Raise House salary/omit honoraria	N	
42. Toughen oil-spill liability	N	
43. Restitution to Japanese interned	Y	
44. Protect Chinese & C.A. nationals	Y	
45. Abortion $ for rape/incest cases	Y	
46. Allow religious schools to bar gays	N	
47. Bar broadcaster fairness doctrine	N	
48. Bar cap gains cut/reinstate IRA	Y	
49. Bar unions equal voice in pension	N	
50. Bar assembly of chemical weapons	Y	
51. Ban plutonium/uranium production	Y	
52. Cap MX missile deployment at 50	Y	
53. Allow $3b for 2 stealth bombers	N
54. Publish bio-warfare experiments	Y
55. Raise minimum wage-veto override	Y
56. Bar transfer of FS-X technology	Y
57. Cut defense and raise domestic $	N
58. Uniform poll closing in 48 states	Y
59. Req foreign investment disclosure	Y
60. Textile import quotas-veto override	Y
61. Bar abortion funding in Wash, DC	N
62. Notify spouses of AIDS+ carriers	N
63. Seize conveyance-drug trafficking	N
64. South Africa sanctions	Y
65. 60 days' notice of plant closings	Y
66. Close unneeded military bases	N
67. Keep welfare reform within $2.8b	N
68. Allow children housing exclusion	N
69. Shift $400m of NASA to homeless	Y
70. Cap Medicare patients' liability	Y
71. Prohibit employee polygraph testing	Y
72. Allow CIA to fund Contras	N
73. Revise unfair trade practices	Y
74. Focus SDI on accidental launch	Y
75. Bar Air Force $ for MX missile	Y
76. Allow "real" increase in defense	N
77. Troop reduction in Europe of 50%	N
78. Ban nuclear tests above 1 kiloton	Y
79. Ban anti-satellite missile tests	Y
80. Observe certain limits of SALT II	Y
81. Restore four Civil Rights laws	Y
82. Prohibit aliens as strikebreakers	Y
83. Allow military malpractice suits	Y
84. Approval of $36m in Contra aid	N
85. $18b deficit reduction compromise	Y
86. Welfare reform of $5.7b for 5 years	Y
87. Raise taxes $12b/cut spending $3b	Y
88. Board to assess occupational risk	Y
89. Balanced budget by '93-via targets	N
90. Bar licensing of two nuclear plants	Y
91. Remove victims compensation cap	N
92. Catastrophic health insurance	Y
93. Ban airline smoking-2 hours or less	Y
94. $1b/two year aid for the homeless	Y
95. Bar non-unions in union companies	Y
96. Increase FSLIC rescue to $15b	N
97. Impose quotas to lower trade deficit	Y
98. Reduce discretionary budget 21%	Y
99. Immigration reform/alien amnesty	Y
100. South Africa sanctions-veto override	Y
101. Tax overhaul to revise income tax	Y
102. Use of military in drug war	N
103. Delete 12 MX/add conventional wpn	Y
104. Raise speed limit to 65 mph	N

VISCLOSKY, PETER J. (continued)

105. Require Pentagon to buy US goods	Y	114. $20b in Medicare cuts/tax increases	Y
106. AIDS insurance non-discrimination	Y	115. Spending cuts and tax increases	Y
107. Prohibit Saudi arms sales	Y	116. Set school lunch lmt-250% poverty	N
108. Ease Gun Control Act of 1968	N	117. $75m for youth work projects	Y
109. Bar interstate handgun transport	Y	118. Allow Angolan military assistance	N
110. Make company emissions known	Y	119. Suspend defense payments for abuse	N
111. Allow toxic victims to sue in fed ct	N	120. Drop SS COLAs/$12b tax increase	N
112. Superfund waste cleanup of $10b	N	121. Approve $1.5b for 21 MX missiles	N
113. 90 days notice of plant closings	Y	122. Emergency farm credit/revisions	Y

Presidential Support Score: 1991 - 29%   1990 - 22%

SHARP, PHILIP R. -- Indiana 2nd District [Democrat]. Counties of Bartholomew (pt.), Decatur, Delaware (pt.), Fayette (pt.), Henry (pt.), Johnson, Marion (pt.), Randolph, Rush (pt.), Shelby and Wayne. Prior Terms: 1975-92. Born: July 15, 1942; Baltimore, MD. Education: Georgetown University (B.S., Ph.D.); Oxford University. Occupation: Associate professor, Ball State University; legislative assistant (1964-69).

1. Protection to Haitian refugees	Y	46. Allow religious schools to bar gays	Y
2. Raise tax on wealthy; lower others	Y	47. Bar broadcaster fairness doctrine	N
3. Investigate Reagan hostage delay	Y	48. Bar cap gains cut/reinstate IRA	Y
4. Campaign finance revisions	Y	49. Bar unions equal voice in pension	N
5. Unpaid leave to care for children	Y	50. Bar assembly of chemical weapons	Y
6. Restrict NEA use of funds	N	51. Ban plutonium/uranium production	Y
7. Bar race-bias claim/habeas corpus	N	52. Cap MX missile deployment at 50	Y
8. Ban race as death sentence factor	N	53. Allow $3b for 2 stealth bombers	N
9. Exceptions to exclusionary rule	Y	54. Publish bio-warfare experiments	Y
10. Allow sale of assault weapons	Y	55. Raise minimum wage-veto override	Y
11. Life in prison/abolish death penalty	Y	56. Bar transfer of FS-X technology	?
12. Req conspiracy-price fixing cases	N	57. Cut defense and raise domestic $	N
13. Unemployment benefits extension	Y	58. Uniform poll closing in 48 states	Y
14. Tissue use of aborted fetuses	Y	59. Req foreign investment disclosure	Y
15. Bar replacement of union strikers	Y	60. Textile import quotas-veto override	Y
16. Hold foreign aid at $15b for '92	Y	61. Bar abortion funding in Wash, DC	N
17. Restore space station funding	N	62. Notify spouses of AIDS+ carriers	N
18. Civil Rights Act of 1991	Y	63. Seize conveyance-drug trafficking	N
19. Unlimited damages-discrimination	Y	64. South Africa sanctions	Y
20. Eliminate funds for supercollider	Y	65. 60 days' notice of plant closings	Y
21. Terminate SDI except for research	--	66. Close unneeded military bases	Y
22. Req 7-day handgun waiting period	Y	67. Keep welfare reform within $2.8b	Y
23. Provide $30b for failed S&Ls	N	68. Allow children housing exclusion	N
24. Allow use of force against Iraq	N	69. Shift $400m of NASA to homeless	N
25. Allow $15b in foreign aid for '91	?	70. Cap Medicare patients' liability	Y
26. Revise & extend legal immigration	?	71. Prohibit employee polygraph testing	Y
27. Suspend aid to Angolan rebels	Y	72. Allow CIA to fund Contras	N
28. Democratic tax plan proposals	Y	73. Revise unfair trade practices	Y
29. Cut defense 5% across the board	Y	74. Focus SDI on accidental launch	Y
30. Textile import quotas-veto override	Y	75. Bar Air Force $ for MX missile	N
31. Abortion service for military abroad	Y	76. Allow "real" increase in defense	N
32. Limits on high income farmers	N	77. Troop reduction in Europe of 50%	Y
33. Family medical leave-veto override	Y	78. Ban nuclear tests above 1 kiloton	Y
34. Req submission of balanced budget	Y	79. Ban anti-satellite missile tests	Y
35. Balanced budget amendment	Y	80. Observe certain limits of SALT II	Y
36. Amendment to ban flag desecration	Y	81. Restore four Civil Rights laws	Y
37. Reauthorize Amtrak-veto override	Y	82. Prohibit aliens as strikebreakers	Y
38. Retraining aid for coal miners	Y	83. Allow military malpractice suits	?
39. Suspend El Salvador military aid	Y	84. Approval of $36m in Contra aid	N
40. Expand child care aid/tax credit	Y	85. $18b deficit reduction compromise	Y
41. Raise House salary/omit honoraria	N	86. Welfare reform of $5.7b for 5 years	Y
42. Toughen oil-spill liability	Y	87. Raise taxes $12b/cut spending $3b	Y
43. Restitution to Japanese interned	Y	88. Board to assess occupational risk	Y
44. Protect Chinese & C.A. nationals	Y	89. Balanced budget by '93-via targets	Y
45. Abortion $ for rape/incest cases	Y	90. Bar licensing of two nuclear plants	Y

SHARP, PHILIP R. (continued)

91.	Remove victims compensation cap	N	118.	Allow Angolan military assistance	Y
92.	Catastrophic health insurance	Y	119.	Suspend defense payments for abuse	Y
93.	Ban airline smoking-2 hours or less	N	120.	Drop SS COLAs/$12b tax increase	N
94.	$1b/two year aid for the homeless	Y	121.	Approve $1.5b for 21 MX missiles	N
95.	Bar non-unions in union companies	Y	122.	Emergency farm credit/revisions	Y
96.	Increase FSLIC rescue to $15b	N	123.	Duty on Taiwan/Hong Kong/S Korea	N
97.	Impose quotas to lower trade deficit	Y	124.	Limit steel imports to 17%	Y
98.	Reduce discretionary budget 21%	Y	125.	Cut $ to schools that bar prayer	Y
99.	Immigration reform/alien amnesty	Y	126.	$50b-taxes; cut Medicare/spending	Y
100.	South Africa sanctions-veto override	Y	127.	Limit Pershing II/cruise in Europe	N
101.	Tax overhaul to revise income tax	Y	128.	Delete $7.1b for 34 B-1 bombers	+
102.	Use of military in drug war	N	129.	Bar purchase of Sergeant York guns	--
103.	Delete 12 MX/add conventional wpn	Y	130.	El Salvador military/economic aid	N
104.	Raise speed limit to 65 mph	Y	131.	Bar mining of Nicaraguan waters	Y
105.	Require Pentagon to buy US goods	Y	132.	Physician fee freeze for Medicare	N
106.	AIDS insurance non-discrimination	N	133.	$49b in "sin"/phone/insurance taxes	Y
107.	Prohibit Saudi arms sales	Y	134.	Allow sale of Conrail	N
108.	Ease Gun Control Act of 1968	Y	135.	Equal Rights Amendment	Y
109.	Bar interstate handgun transport	N	136.	Authorize Marines in Lebanon	N
110.	Make company emissions known	Y	137.	Eminent domain for coal companies	Y
111.	Allow toxic victims to sue in fed ct	Y	138.	Prohibit EPA clean air sanctions	Y
112.	Superfund waste cleanup of $10b	Y	139.	SS retirement age increase/reforms	N
113.	90 days notice of plant closings	Y	140.	Auto domestic content requirement	Y
114.	$20b in Medicare cuts/tax increases	Y	141.	Delete jobs program funding	N
115.	Spending cuts and tax increases	N	142.	Highway-gas tax bill	N
116.	Set school lunch lmt-250% poverty	N	143.	Cut $5b from defense for Medicare	Y
117.	$75m for youth work projects	N	144.	Emergency housing aid of $1b	Y

Presidential Support Score: 1991 - 28%   1990 - 20%

ROEMER, TIMOTHY J. -- Indiana 3rd District [Democrat]. Counties of Elkhart, Kosciusko (pt.), La Porte (pt.), Marshall, St. Joseph and Starke. Prior Term: 1991-92. Born: October 30, 1956; South Bend, IN. Education: University of California-San Diego (B.A.); Notre Dame University (M.A., Ph.D.). Occupation: Aide to Rep. Brademas and Sen. DeConcini; university political science professor.

1.	Protection to Haitian refugees	Y	13.	Unemployment benefits extension	Y
2.	Raise tax on wealthy; lower others	N	14.	Tissue use of aborted fetuses	N
3.	Investigate Reagan hostage delay	Y	15.	Bar replacement of union strikers	Y
4.	Campaign finance revisions	Y	16.	Hold foreign aid at $15b for '92	N
5.	Unpaid leave to care for children	Y	17.	Restore space station funding	N
6.	Restrict NEA use of funds	N	18.	Civil Rights Act of 1991	Y
7.	Bar race-bias claim/habeas corpus	Y	19.	Unlimited damages-discrimination	N
8.	Ban race as death sentence factor	Y	20.	Eliminate funds for supercollider	N
9.	Exceptions to exclusionary rule	Y	21.	Terminate SDI except for research	N
10.	Allow sale of assault weapons	Y	22.	Req 7-day handgun waiting period	Y
11.	Life in prison/abolish death penalty	N	23.	Provide $30b for failed S&Ls	N
12.	Req conspiracy-price fixing cases	Y	24.	Allow use of force against Iraq	N

Presidential Support Score: 1991 - 43%

LONG, JILL -- Indiana 4th District [Democrat]. Counties of Adams, Allen, De Kalb, Huntington, Jay, Lagrange, Noble, Steuben, Wells and Whitley. Prior Terms: 1989 (Special Election)-1992. Born: July 15, 1952; Warsaw, IN. Education: Valparaiso University (B.S.); Indiana University (M.B.A., Ph.D.). Occupation: College and university professor; family farm owner and co-manager; Valparaiso city councilwoman; small business management consultant.

1.	Protection to Haitian refugees	Y	5.	Unpaid leave to care for children	Y
2.	Raise tax on wealthy; lower others	N	6.	Restrict NEA use of funds	Y
3.	Investigate Reagan hostage delay	Y	7.	Bar race-bias claim/habeas corpus	N
4.	Campaign finance revisions	Y	8.	Ban race as death sentence factor	N

LONG, JILL (continued)

9. Exceptions to exclusionary rule	Y	34. Req submission of balanced budget	Y
10. Allow sale of assault weapons	Y	35. Balanced budget amendment	Y
11. Life in prison/abolish death penalty	N	36. Amendment to ban flag desecration	Y
12. Req conspiracy-price fixing cases	Y	37. Reauthorize Amtrak-veto override	Y
13. Unemployment benefits extension	Y	38. Retraining aid for coal miners	Y
14. Tissue use of aborted fetuses	Y	39. Suspend El Salvador military aid	Y
15. Bar replacement of union strikers	Y	40. Expand child care aid/tax credit	N
16. Hold foreign aid at $15b for '92	N	41. Raise House salary/omit honoraria	N
17. Restore space station funding	Y	42. Toughen oil-spill liability	Y
18. Civil Rights Act of 1991	Y	43. Restitution to Japanese interned	Y
19. Unlimited damages-discrimination	N	44. Protect Chinese & C.A. nationals	N
20. Eliminate funds for supercollider	Y	45. Abortion $ for rape/incest cases	Y
21. Terminate SDI except for research	Y	46. Allow religious schools to bar gays	N
22. Req 7-day handgun waiting period	N	47. Bar broadcaster fairness doctrine	N
23. Provide $30b for failed S&Ls	N	48. Bar cap gains cut/reinstate IRA	N
24. Allow use of force against Iraq	N	49. Bar unions equal voice in pension	N
25. Allow $15b in foreign aid for '91	N	50. Bar assembly of chemical weapons	Y
26. Revise & extend legal immigration	N	51. Ban plutonium/uranium production	Y
27. Suspend aid to Angolan rebels	Y	52. Cap MX missile deployment at 50	Y
28. Democratic tax plan proposals	N	53. Allow $3b for 2 stealth bombers	N
29. Cut defense 5% across the board	N	54. Publish bio-warfare experiments	Y
30. Textile import quotas-veto override	Y	55. Raise minimum wage-veto override	Y
31. Abortion service for military abroad	Y	56. Bar transfer of FS-X technology	Y
32. Limits on high income farmers	N	57. Cut defense and raise domestic $	N
33. Family medical leave-veto override	Y	58. Uniform poll closing in 48 states	Y

Presidential Support Score: 1991 - 32%   1990 - 29%

JONTZ, JAMES -- Indiana 5th District [Democrat]. Counties of Carroll, Cass, Fulton, Grant, Howard, Jasper, Kosciusko (pt.), Lake (pt.), Miami, Newton, Porter (pt.), Pulaski, Wabash and White.   Prior Terms: 1987-92.   Born: December 18, 1951; Indianapolis, Ind. Education: Indiana University (A.B.); Purdue University; Butler University.   Occupation: Indiana Conservation Council excecutive director; Lake Michigan Federation program director; Indiana State Park system naturalist; state representative (1974-1984) and senator (1984-1986).

1. Protection to Haitian refugees	Y	28. Democratic tax plan proposals	Y
2. Raise tax on wealthy; lower others	Y	29. Cut defense 5% across the board	Y
3. Investigate Reagan hostage delay	Y	30. Textile import quotas-veto override	Y
4. Campaign finance revisions	Y	31. Abortion service for military abroad	Y
5. Unpaid leave to care for children	Y	32. Limits on high income farmers	N
6. Restrict NEA use of funds	N	33. Family medical leave-veto override	Y
7. Bar race-bias claim/habeas corpus	N	34. Req submission of balanced budget	Y
8. Ban race as death sentence factor	N	35. Balanced budget amendment	Y
9. Exceptions to exclusionary rule	N	36. Amendment to ban flag desecration	N
10. Allow sale of assault weapons	Y	37. Reauthorize Amtrak-veto override	Y
11. Life in prison/abolish death penalty	Y	38. Retraining aid for coal miners	Y
12. Req conspiracy-price fixing cases	N	39. Suspend El Salvador military aid	Y
13. Unemployment benefits extension	Y	40. Expand child care aid/tax credit	Y
14. Tissue use of aborted fetuses	Y	41. Raise House salary/omit honoraria	N
15. Bar replacement of union strikers	Y	42. Toughen oil-spill liability	Y
16. Hold foreign aid at $15b for '92	N	43. Restitution to Japanese interned	Y
17. Restore space station funding	N	44. Protect Chinese & C.A. nationals	Y
18. Civil Rights Act of 1991	Y	45. Abortion $ for rape/incest cases	Y
19. Unlimited damages-discrimination	Y	46. Allow religious schools to bar gays	N
20. Eliminate funds for supercollider	Y	47. Bar broadcaster fairness doctrine	N
21. Terminate SDI except for research	Y	48. Bar cap gains cut/reinstate IRA	Y
22. Req 7-day handgun waiting period	N	49. Bar unions equal voice in pension	N
23. Provide $30b for failed S&Ls	N	50. Bar assembly of chemical weapons	Y
24. Allow use of force against Iraq	N	51. Ban plutonium/uranium production	Y
25. Allow $15b in foreign aid for '91	N	52. Cap MX missile deployment at 50	Y
26. Revise & extend legal immigration	Y	53. Allow $3b for 2 stealth bombers	N
27. Suspend aid to Angolan rebels	Y	54. Publish bio-warfare experiments	Y

JONTZ, JAMES (continued)

55.	Raise minimum wage-veto override	Y	77.	Troop reduction in Europe of 50%	Y
56.	Bar transfer of FS-X technology	Y	78.	Ban nuclear tests above 1 kiloton	Y
57.	Cut defense and raise domestic $	N	79.	Ban anti-satellite missile tests	Y
58.	Uniform poll closing in 48 states	Y	80.	Observe certain limits of SALT II	Y
59.	Req foreign investment disclosure	Y	81.	Restore four Civil Rights laws	Y
60.	Textile import quotas-veto override	Y	82.	Prohibit aliens as strikebreakers	Y
61.	Bar abortion funding in Wash, DC	N	83.	Allow military malpractice suits	Y
62.	Notify spouses of AIDS+ carriers	N	84.	Approval of $36m in Contra aid	N
63.	Seize conveyance-drug trafficking	N	85.	$18b deficit reduction compromise	N
64.	South Africa sanctions	Y	86.	Welfare reform of $5.7b for 5 years	Y
65.	60 days' notice of plant closings	Y	87.	Raise taxes $12b/cut spending $3b	Y
66.	Close unneeded military bases	N	88.	Board to assess occupational risk	Y
67.	Keep welfare reform within $2.8b	N	89.	Balanced budget by '93-via targets	N
68.	Allow children housing exclusion	N	90.	Bar licensing of two nuclear plants	Y
69.	Shift $400m of NASA to homeless	Y	91.	Remove victims compensation cap	Y
70.	Cap Medicare patients' liability	Y	92.	Catastrophic health insurance	Y
71.	Prohibit employee polygraph testing	Y	93.	Ban airline smoking-2 hours or less	Y
72.	Allow CIA to fund Contras	N	94.	$1b/two year aid for the homeless	Y
73.	Revise unfair trade practices	Y	95.	Bar non-unions in union companies	Y
74.	Focus SDI on accidental launch	Y	96.	Increase FSLIC rescue to $15b	N
75.	Bar Air Force $ for MX missile	Y	97.	Impose quotas to lower trade deficit	Y
76.	Allow "real" increase in defense	N	98.	Reduce discretionary budget 21%	Y

Presidential Support Score: 1991 - 23%   1990 - 14%

BURTON, DAN -- Indiana 6th District [Republican]. Counties of Blackford, Boone, Clinton, Delaware (pt.), Hamilton, Hancock, Henry (pt.), Madison, Marion (pt.), Rush (pt.) and Tipton. Prior Terms: 1983-92. Born: June 21, 1938; Indianapolis, IN. Education: Indiana University. Military Service: U.S. Army, 1956-57. Occupation: Indiana representative (1967, 1977-79); Indiana senator (1968-76, 1980-82).

1.	Protection to Haitian refugees	?	33.	Family medical leave-veto override	N
2.	Raise tax on wealthy; lower others	N	34.	Req submission of balanced budget	N
3.	Investigate Reagan hostage delay	N	35.	Balanced budget amendment	Y
4.	Campaign finance revisions	N	36.	Amendment to ban flag desecration	Y
5.	Unpaid leave to care for children	N	37.	Reauthorize Amtrak-veto override	N
6.	Restrict NEA use of funds	Y	38.	Retraining aid for coal miners	N
7.	Bar race-bias claim/habeas corpus	Y	39.	Suspend El Salvador military aid	N
8.	Ban race as death sentence factor	Y	40.	Expand child care aid/tax credit	N
9.	Exceptions to exclusionary rule	Y	41.	Raise House salary/omit honoraria	Y
10.	Allow sale of assault weapons	Y	42.	Toughen oil-spill liability	X
11.	Life in prison/abolish death penalty	N	43.	Restitution to Japanese interned	N
12.	Req conspiracy-price fixing cases	Y	44.	Protect Chinese & C.A. nationals	N
13.	Unemployment benefits extension	N	45.	Abortion $ for rape/incest cases	N
14.	Tissue use of aborted fetuses	N	46.	Allow religious schools to bar gays	Y
15.	Bar replacement of union strikers	N	47.	Bar broadcaster fairness doctrine	N
16.	Hold foreign aid at $15b for '92	Y	48.	Bar cap gains cut/reinstate IRA	N
17.	Restore space station funding	Y	49.	Bar unions equal voice in pension	Y
18.	Civil Rights Act of 1991	N	50.	Bar assembly of chemical weapons	N
19.	Unlimited damages-discrimination	N	51.	Ban plutonium/uranium production	N
20.	Eliminate funds for supercollider	Y	52.	Cap MX missile deployment at 50	N
21.	Terminate SDI except for research	N	53.	Allow $3b for 2 stealth bombers	Y
22.	Req 7-day handgun waiting period	N	54.	Publish bio-warfare experiments	N
23.	Provide $30b for failed S&Ls	Y	55.	Raise minimum wage-veto override	N
24.	Allow use of force against Iraq	Y	56.	Bar transfer of FS-X technology	N
25.	Allow $15b in foreign aid for '91	?	57.	Cut defense and raise domestic $	N
26.	Revise & extend legal immigration	?	58.	Uniform poll closing in 48 states	Y
27.	Suspend aid to Angolan rebels	N	59.	Req foreign investment disclosure	N
28.	Democratic tax plan proposals	N	60.	Textile import quotas-veto override	N
29.	Cut defense 5% across the board	N	61.	Bar abortion funding in Wash, DC	Y
30.	Textile import quotas-veto override	Y	62.	Notify spouses of AIDS+ carriers	Y
31.	Abortion service for military abroad	N	63.	Seize conveyance-drug trafficking	Y
32.	Limits on high income farmers	N	64.	South Africa sanctions	N

BURTON, DAN (continued)

65.	60 days' notice of plant closings	N	103.	Delete 12 MX/add conventional wpn N
66.	Close unneeded military bases	Y	104.	Raise speed limit to 65 mph	Y
67.	Keep welfare reform within $2.8b	Y	105.	Require Pentagon to buy US goods	N
68.	Allow children housing exclusion	Y	106.	AIDS insurance non-discrimination	N
69.	Shift $400m of NASA to homeless	N	107.	Prohibit Saudi arms sales	Y
70.	Cap Medicare patients' liability	N	108.	Ease Gun Control Act of 1968	Y
71.	Prohibit employee polygraph testing	N	109.	Bar interstate handgun transport	N
72.	Allow CIA to fund Contras	Y	110.	Make company emissions known	N
73.	Revise unfair trade practices	N	111.	Allow toxic victims to sue in fed ct	N
74.	Focus SDI on accidental launch	N	112.	Superfund waste cleanup of $10b	N
75.	Bar Air Force $ for MX missile	N	113.	90 days notice of plant closings	N
76.	Allow "real" increase in defense	?	114.	$20b in Medicare cuts/tax increases	N
77.	Troop reduction in Europe of 50%	N	115.	Spending cuts and tax increases	N
78.	Ban nuclear tests above 1 kiloton	N	116.	Set school lunch lmt-250% poverty	Y
79.	Ban anti-satellite missile tests	N	117.	$75m for youth work projects	?
80.	Observe certain limits of SALT II	N	118.	Allow Angolan military assistance	Y
81.	Restore four Civil Rights laws	N	119.	Suspend defense payments for abuse	N
82.	Prohibit aliens as strikebreakers	N	120.	Drop SS COLAs/$12b tax increase	N
83.	Allow military malpractice suits	Y	121.	Approve $1.5b for 21 MX missiles	Y
84.	Approval of $36m in Contra aid	Y	122.	Emergency farm credit/revisions	N
85.	$18b deficit reduction compromise	N	123.	Duty on Taiwan/Hong Kong/S Korea N
86.	Welfare reform of $5.7b for 5 years	N	124.	Limit steel imports to 17%	Y
87.	Raise taxes $12b/cut spending $3b	N	125.	Cut $ to schools that bar prayer	Y
88.	Board to assess occupational risk	N	126.	$50b-taxes; cut Medicare/spending	N
89.	Balanced budget by '93-via targets	N	127.	Limit Pershing II/cruise in Europe	N
90.	Bar licensing of two nuclear plants	N	128.	Delete $7.1b for 34 B-1 bombers	N
91.	Remove victims compensation cap	N	129.	Bar purchase of Sergeant York guns	N
92.	Catastrophic health insurance	N	130.	El Salvador military/economic aid	Y
93.	Ban airline smoking-2 hours or less	Y	131.	Bar mining of Nicaraguan waters	N
94.	$1b/two year aid for the homeless	N	132.	Physician fee freeze for Medicare	Y
95.	Bar non-unions in union companies	N	133.	$49b in "sin"/phone/insurance taxes	Y
96.	Increase FSLIC rescue to $15b	?	134.	Allow sale of Conrail	Y
97.	Impose quotas to lower trade deficit	N	135.	Equal Rights Amendment	N
98.	Reduce discretionary budget 21%	N	136.	Authorize Marines in Lebanon	Y
99.	Immigration reform/alien amnesty	N	137.	Eminent domain for coal companies	Y
100.	South Africa sanctions-veto override	N	138.	Prohibit EPA clean air sanctions	Y
101.	Tax overhaul to revise income tax	N	139.	SS retirement age increase/reforms	Y
102.	Use of military in drug war	Y			

Presidential Support Score: 1991 - 75%   1990 - 77%

MYERS, JOHN T. -- Indiana 7th District [Republican]. Counties of Benton, Clay, Fountain, Hendricks, Montgomery, Morgan, Owen, Parke, Putnam, Sullivan, Tippecanoe, Vermillion, Vigo and Warren. Prior Terms: House: 1967-92. Born: February 8, 1927; Covington, IN. Education: Indiana State University (B.S.). Military Service: U.S. Army. Occupation: Cashier and trust officer, The Fountain Trust Co.

1.	Protection to Haitian refugees	N	17.	Restore space station funding	Y
2.	Raise tax on wealthy; lower others	N	18.	Civil Rights Act of 1991	N
3.	Investigate Reagan hostage delay	N	19.	Unlimited damages-discrimination	N
4.	Campaign finance revisions	N	20.	Eliminate funds for supercollider	N
5.	Unpaid leave to care for children	N	21.	Terminate SDI except for research	N
6.	Restrict NEA use of funds	Y	22.	Req 7-day handgun waiting period	N
7.	Bar race-bias claim/habeas corpus	Y	23.	Provide $30b for failed S&Ls	Y
8.	Ban race as death sentence factor	Y	24.	Allow use of force against Iraq	Y
9.	Exceptions to exclusionary rule	Y	25.	Allow $15b in foreign aid for '91	N
10.	Allow sale of assault weapons	Y	26.	Revise & extend legal immigration	N
11.	Life in prison/abolish death penalty	N	27.	Suspend aid to Angolan rebels	N
12.	Req conspiracy-price fixing cases	Y	28.	Democratic tax plan proposals	N
13.	Unemployment benefits extension	N	29.	Cut defense 5% across the board	N
14.	Tissue use of aborted fetuses	N	30.	Textile import quotas-veto override	N
15.	Bar replacement of union strikers	N	31.	Abortion service for military abroad	N
16.	Hold foreign aid at $15b for '92	N	32.	Limits on high income farmers	N

MYERS, JOHN T. (continued)

33. Family medical leave-veto override	N	89. Balanced budget by '93-via targets	N
34. Req submission of balanced budget	N	90. Bar licensing of two nuclear plants	N
35. Balanced budget amendment	Y	91. Remove victims compensation cap	N
36. Amendment to ban flag desecration	Y	92. Catastrophic health insurance	N
37. Reauthorize Amtrak-veto override	Y	93. Ban airline smoking-2 hours or less	N
38. Retraining aid for coal miners	N	94. $1b/two year aid for the homeless	N
39. Suspend El Salvador military aid	N	95. Bar non-unions in union companies	N
40. Expand child care aid/tax credit	N	96. Increase FSLIC rescue to $15b	N
41. Raise House salary/omit honoraria	Y	97. Impose quotas to lower trade deficit	N
42. Toughen oil-spill liability	N	98. Reduce discretionary budget 21%	N
43. Restitution to Japanese interned	N	99. Immigration reform/alien amnesty	N
44. Protect Chinese & C.A. nationals	Y	100. South Africa sanctions-veto override	N
45. Abortion $ for rape/incest cases	N	101. Tax overhaul to revise income tax	N
46. Allow religious schools to bar gays	Y	102. Use of military in drug war	N
47. Bar broadcaster fairness doctrine	Y	103. Delete 12 MX/add conventional wpn	N
48. Bar cap gains cut/reinstate IRA	N	104. Raise speed limit to 65 mph	Y
49. Bar unions equal voice in pension	Y	105. Require Pentagon to buy US goods	Y
50. Bar assembly of chemical weapons	N	106. AIDS insurance non-discrimination	Y
51. Ban plutonium/uranium production	N	107. Prohibit Saudi arms sales	N
52. Cap MX missile deployment at 50	N	108. Ease Gun Control Act of 1968	Y
53. Allow $3b for 2 stealth bombers	Y	109. Bar interstate handgun transport	N
54. Publish bio-warfare experiments	N	110. Make company emissions known	N
55. Raise minimum wage-veto override	N	111. Allow toxic victims to sue in fed ct	N
56. Bar transfer of FS-X technology	Y	112. Superfund waste cleanup of $10b	N
57. Cut defense and raise domestic $	N	113. 90 days notice of plant closings	N
58. Uniform poll closing in 48 states	N	114. $20b in Medicare cuts/tax increases	N
59. Req foreign investment disclosure	N	115. Spending cuts and tax increases	N
60. Textile import quotas-veto override	N	116. Set school lunch lmt-250% poverty	Y
61. Bar abortion funding in Wash, DC	Y	117. $75m for youth work projects	N
62. Notify spouses of AIDS+ carriers	Y	118. Allow Angolan military assistance	Y
63. Seize conveyance-drug trafficking	N	119. Suspend defense payments for abuse	N
64. South Africa sanctions	N	120. Drop SS COLAs/$12b tax increase	N
65. 60 days' notice of plant closings	N	121. Approve $1.5b for 21 MX missiles	Y
66. Close unneeded military bases	N	122. Emergency farm credit/revisions	Y
67. Keep welfare reform within $2.8b	?	123. Duty on Taiwan/Hong Kong/S Korea	N
68. Allow children housing exclusion	N	124. Limit steel imports to 17%	Y
69. Shift $400m of NASA to homeless	N	125. Cut $ to schools that bar prayer	N
70. Cap Medicare patients' liability	Y	126. $50b-taxes; cut Medicare/spending	N
71. Prohibit employee polygraph testing	N	127. Limit Pershing II/cruise in Europe	N
72. Allow CIA to fund Contras	Y	128. Delete $7.1b for 34 B-1 bombers	N
73. Revise unfair trade practices	N	129. Bar purchase of Sergeant York guns	N
74. Focus SDI on accidental launch	N	130. El Salvador military/economic aid	Y
75. Bar Air Force $ for MX missile	?	131. Bar mining of Nicaraguan waters	N
76. Allow "real" increase in defense	Y	132. Physician fee freeze for Medicare	Y
77. Troop reduction in Europe of 50%	N	133. $49b in "sin"/phone/insurance taxes	N
78. Ban nuclear tests above 1 kiloton	N	134. Allow sale of Conrail	Y
79. Ban anti-satellite missile tests	N	135. Equal Rights Amendment	N
80. Observe certain limits of SALT II	N	136. Authorize Marines in Lebanon	N
81. Restore four Civil Rights laws	N	137. Eminent domain for coal companies	?
82. Prohibit aliens as strikebreakers	Y	138. Prohibit EPA clean air sanctions	N
83. Allow military malpractice suits	N	139. SS retirement age increase/reforms	Y
84. Approval of $36m in Contra aid	Y	140. Auto domestic content requirement	N
85. $18b deficit reduction compromise	N	141. Delete jobs program funding	Y
86. Welfare reform of $5.7b for 5 years	N	142. Highway-gas tax bill	N
87. Raise taxes $12b/cut spending $3b	N	143. Cut $5b from defense for Medicare	N
88. Board to assess occupational risk	N	144. Emergency housing aid of $1b	Y

Presidential Support Score: 1991 - 75%   1990 - 69%

McCLOSKEY, FRANK -- Indiana 8th District [Democrat].   Counties of Crawford (pt.), Daviess, Gibson, Greene, Knox, Lawrence, Martin, Monroe (pt.), Orange, Pike, Posey, Spencer, Vanderburgh, Warrick and Washington (pt.).   Prior Terms: 1982 (Special Election)- 1992.   Born: June 12, 1939; Philadelphia, PA.   Education: Indiana University (A.B., J.D.).

McCLOSKEY, FRANK (continued)

Military Service: U.S. Air Force, 4 years.   Occupation: Newspaperman; mayor of Bloomington, Indiana (1971-82).

1.	Protection to Haitian refugees	Y	62.	Notify spouses of AIDS+ carriers	N
2.	Raise tax on wealthy; lower others	Y	63.	Seize conveyance-drug trafficking	N
3.	Investigate Reagan hostage delay	Y	64.	South Africa sanctions	Y
4.	Campaign finance revisions	Y	65.	60 days' notice of plant closings	Y
5.	Unpaid leave to care for children	Y	66.	Close unneeded military bases	N
6.	Restrict NEA use of funds	N	67.	Keep welfare reform within $2.8b	N
7.	Bar race-bias claim/habeas corpus	N	68.	Allow children housing exclusion	N
8.	Ban race as death sentence factor	N	69.	Shift $400m of NASA to homeless	N
9.	Exceptions to exclusionary rule	N	70.	Cap Medicare patients' liability	Y
10.	Allow sale of assault weapons	N	71.	Prohibit employee polygraph testing	Y
11.	Life in prison/abolish death penalty	Y	72.	Allow CIA to fund Contras	N
12.	Req conspiracy-price fixing cases	N	73.	Revise unfair trade practices	Y
13.	Unemployment benefits extension	Y	74.	Focus SDI on accidental launch	Y
14.	Tissue use of aborted fetuses	Y	75.	Bar Air Force $ for MX missile	Y
15.	Bar replacement of union strikers	Y	76.	Allow "real" increase in defense	N
16.	Hold foreign aid at $15b for '92	Y	77.	Troop reduction in Europe of 50%	Y
17.	Restore space station funding	N	78.	Ban nuclear tests above 1 kiloton	Y
18.	Civil Rights Act of 1991	Y	79.	Ban anti-satellite missile tests	Y
19.	Unlimited damages-discrimination	Y	80.	Observe certain limits of SALT II	Y
20.	Eliminate funds for supercollider	N	81.	Restore four Civil Rights laws	Y
21.	Terminate SDI except for research	N	82.	Prohibit aliens as strikebreakers	Y
22.	Req 7-day handgun waiting period	Y	83.	Allow military malpractice suits	Y
23.	Provide $30b for failed S&Ls	N	84.	Approval of $36m in Contra aid	N
24.	Allow use of force against Iraq	N	85.	$18b deficit reduction compromise	Y
25.	Allow $15b in foreign aid for '91	N	86.	Welfare reform of $5.7b for 5 years	Y
26.	Revise & extend legal immigration	Y	87.	Raise taxes $12b/cut spending $3b	Y
27.	Suspend aid to Angolan rebels	Y	88.	Board to assess occupational risk	Y
28.	Democratic tax plan proposals	Y	89.	Balanced budget by '93-via targets	Y
29.	Cut defense 5% across the board	N	90.	Bar licensing of two nuclear plants	Y
30.	Textile import quotas-veto override	Y	91.	Remove victims compensation cap	Y
31.	Abortion service for military abroad	Y	92.	Catastrophic health insurance	Y
32.	Limits on high income farmers	N	93.	Ban airline smoking-2 hours or less	Y
33.	Family medical leave-veto override	Y	94.	$1b/two year aid for the homeless	Y
34.	Req submission of balanced budget	Y	95.	Bar non-unions in union companies	Y
35.	Balanced budget amendment	N	96.	Increase FSLIC rescue to $15b	N
36.	Amendment to ban flag desecration	N	97.	Impose quotas to lower trade deficit	Y
37.	Reauthorize Amtrak-veto override	Y	98.	Reduce discretionary budget 21%	Y
38.	Retraining aid for coal miners	Y	99.	Immigration reform/alien amnesty	Y
39.	Suspend El Salvador military aid	Y	100.	South Africa sanctions-veto override	Y
40.	Expand child care aid/tax credit	Y	101.	Tax overhaul to revise income tax	Y
41.	Raise House salary/omit honoraria	Y	102.	Use of military in drug war	Y
42.	Toughen oil-spill liability	Y	103.	Delete 12 MX/add conventional wpn	Y
43.	Restitution to Japanese interned	Y	104.	Raise speed limit to 65 mph	Y
44.	Protect Chinese & C.A. nationals	Y	105.	Require Pentagon to buy US goods	Y
45.	Abortion $ for rape/incest cases	Y	106.	AIDS insurance non-discrimination	N
46.	Allow religious schools to bar gays	N	107.	Prohibit Saudi arms sales	Y
47.	Bar broadcaster fairness doctrine	N	108.	Ease Gun Control Act of 1968	Y
48.	Bar cap gains cut/reinstate IRA	Y	109.	Bar interstate handgun transport	N
49.	Bar unions equal voice in pension	N	110.	Make company emissions known	Y
50.	Bar assembly of chemical weapons	Y	111.	Allow toxic victims to sue in fed ct	Y
51.	Ban plutonium/uranium production	Y	112.	Superfund waste cleanup of $10b	Y
52.	Cap MX missile deployment at 50	Y	113.	90 days notice of plant closings	Y
53.	Allow $3b for 2 stealth bombers	N	114.	$20b in Medicare cuts/tax increases	Y
54.	Publish bio-warfare experiments	Y	115.	Spending cuts and tax increases	Y
55.	Raise minimum wage-veto override	Y	116.	Set school lunch lmt-250% poverty	N
56.	Bar transfer of FS-X technology	Y	117.	$75m for youth work projects	Y
57.	Cut defense and raise domestic $	N	118.	Allow Angolan military assistance	Y
58.	Uniform poll closing in 48 states	Y	119.	Suspend defense payments for abuse	Y
59.	Req foreign investment disclosure	Y	120.	Drop SS COLAs/$12b tax increase	N
60.	Textile import quotas-veto override	Y	123.	Duty on Taiwan/Hong Kong/S Korea	Y
61.	Bar abortion funding in Wash, DC	Y	124.	Limit steel imports to 17%	Y

McCLOSKEY, FRANK (continued)

125. Cut $ to schools that bar prayer	N	133. $49b in "sin"/phone/insurance taxes	Y
126. $50b-taxes; cut Medicare/spending	Y	134. Allow sale of Conrail	N
127. Limit Pershing II/cruise in Europe	N	135. Equal Rights Amendment	Y
128. Delete $7.1b for 34 B-1 bombers	Y	136. Authorize Marines in Lebanon	N
129. Bar purchase of Sergeant York guns	N	137. Eminent domain for coal companies	N
130. El Salvador military/economic aid	N	138. Prohibit EPA clean air sanctions	N
131. Bar mining of Nicaraguan waters	Y	139. SS retirement age increase/reforms	N
132. Physician fee freeze for Medicare	N		

Rep. McCloskey missed votes 121-122 because of an election dispute.

Presidential Support Score: 1991 - 29%   1990 - 20%

HAMILTON, LEE H. -- Indiana 9th District [Democrat]. Counties of Bartholomew (pt.), Brown, Clark, Crawford (pt.), Dearborn, Dubois, Fayette (pt.), Floyd, Franklin, Harrison, Jackson, Jefferson, Jennings, Monroe (pt.), Ohio, Perry, Ripley, Scott, Switzerland, Union and Washington (pt.). Prior Terms: 1965-92. Born: April 20, 1931; Daytona Beach, FL. Education: DePauw University (A.B.); Goethe University, Indiana University (J.D.). Occupation: Attorney; instructor, American Banking Institute.

1. Protection to Haitian refugees	Y	44. Protect Chinese & C.A. nationals	Y
2. Raise tax on wealthy; lower others	N	45. Abortion $ for rape/incest cases	N
3. Investigate Reagan hostage delay	Y	46. Allow religious schools to bar gays	Y
4. Campaign finance revisions	Y	47. Bar broadcaster fairness doctrine	Y
5. Unpaid leave to care for children	N	48. Bar cap gains cut/reinstate IRA	Y
6. Restrict NEA use of funds	Y	49. Bar unions equal voice in pension	Y
7. Bar race-bias claim/habeas corpus	N	50. Bar assembly of chemical weapons	N
8. Ban race as death sentence factor	N	51. Ban plutonium/uranium production	Y
9. Exceptions to exclusionary rule	Y	52. Cap MX missile deployment at 50	Y
10. Allow sale of assault weapons	Y	53. Allow $3b for 2 stealth bombers	N
11. Life in prison/abolish death penalty	Y	54. Publish bio-warfare experiments	Y
12. Req conspiracy-price fixing cases	N	55. Raise minimum wage-veto override	Y
13. Unemployment benefits extension	Y	56. Bar transfer of FS-X technology	Y
14. Tissue use of aborted fetuses	Y	57. Cut defense and raise domestic $	N
15. Bar replacement of union strikers	Y	58. Uniform poll closing in 48 states	Y
16. Hold foreign aid at $15b for '92	Y	59. Req foreign investment disclosure	Y
17. Restore space station funding	N	60. Textile import quotas-veto override	Y
18. Civil Rights Act of 1991	Y	61. Bar abortion funding in Wash, DC	Y
19. Unlimited damages-discrimination	N	62. Notify spouses of AIDS+ carriers	N
20. Eliminate funds for supercollider	Y	63. Seize conveyance-drug trafficking	N
21. Terminate SDI except for research	N	64. South Africa sanctions	Y
22. Req 7-day handgun waiting period	Y	65. 60 days' notice of plant closings	Y
23. Provide $30b for failed S&Ls	Y	66. Close unneeded military bases	Y
24. Allow use of force against Iraq	N	67. Keep welfare reform within $2.8b	N
25. Allow $15b in foreign aid for '91	Y	68. Allow children housing exclusion	N
26. Revise & extend legal immigration	Y	69. Shift $400m of NASA to homeless	N
27. Suspend aid to Angolan rebels	Y	70. Cap Medicare patients' liability	Y
28. Democratic tax plan proposals	Y	71. Prohibit employee polygraph testing	Y
29. Cut defense 5% across the board	Y	72. Allow CIA to fund Contras	N
30. Textile import quotas-veto override	N	73. Revise unfair trade practices	Y
31. Abortion service for military abroad	Y	74. Focus SDI on accidental launch	Y
32. Limits on high income farmers	N	75. Bar Air Force $ for MX missile	Y
33. Family medical leave-veto override	Y	76. Allow "real" increase in defense	N
34. Req submission of balanced budget	Y	77. Troop reduction in Europe of 50%	N
35. Balanced budget amendment	N	78. Ban nuclear tests above 1 kiloton	Y
36. Amendment to ban flag desecration	N	79. Ban anti-satellite missile tests	Y
37. Reauthorize Amtrak-veto override	Y	80. Observe certain limits of SALT II	Y
38. Retraining aid for coal miners	Y	81. Restore four Civil Rights laws	Y
39. Suspend El Salvador military aid	Y	82. Prohibit aliens as strikebreakers	Y
40. Expand child care aid/tax credit	Y	83. Allow military malpractice suits	Y
41. Raise House salary/omit honoraria	N	84. Approval of $36m in Contra aid	N
42. Toughen oil-spill liability	Y	85. $18b deficit reduction compromise	Y
43. Restitution to Japanese interned	Y	86. Welfare reform of $5.7b for 5 years	Y

HAMILTON, LEE H. (continued)

87. Raise taxes $12b/cut spending $3b	N	
88. Board to assess occupational risk	Y	
89. Balanced budget by '93-via targets	Y	
90. Bar licensing of two nuclear plants	Y	
91. Remove victims compensation cap	N	
92. Catastrophic health insurance	Y	
93. Ban airline smoking-2 hours or less	N	
94. $1b/two year aid for the homeless	Y	
95. Bar non-unions in union companies	N	
96. Increase FSLIC rescue to $15b	N	
97. Impose quotas to lower trade deficit	Y	
98. Reduce discretionary budget 21%	Y	
99. Immigration reform/alien amnesty	Y	
100. South Africa sanctions-veto override	Y	
101. Tax overhaul to revise income tax	Y	
102. Use of military in drug war	N	
103. Delete 12 MX/add conventional wpn	Y	
104. Raise speed limit to 65 mph	Y	
105. Require Pentagon to buy US goods	Y	
106. AIDS insurance non-discrimination	Y	
107. Prohibit Saudi arms sales	N	
108. Ease Gun Control Act of 1968	Y	
109. Bar interstate handgun transport	N	
110. Make company emissions known	Y	
111. Allow toxic victims to sue in fed ct	?	
112. Superfund waste cleanup of $10b	Y	
113. 90 days notice of plant closings	Y	
114. $20b in Medicare cuts/tax increases	Y	
115. Spending cuts and tax increases	N	

116. Set school lunch lmt-250% poverty	N	
117. $75m for youth work projects	N	
118. Allow Angolan military assistance	Y	
119. Suspend defense payments for abuse	N	
120. Drop SS COLAs/$12b tax increase	N	
121. Approve $1.5b for 21 MX missiles	N	
122. Emergency farm credit/revisions	Y	
123. Duty on Taiwan/Hong Kong/S Korea	N	
124. Limit steel imports to 17%	Y	
125. Cut $ to schools that bar prayer	Y	
126. $50b-taxes; cut Medicare/spending	Y	
127. Limit Pershing II/cruise in Europe	N	
128. Delete $7.1b for 34 B-1 bombers	Y	
129. Bar purchase of Sergeant York guns	N	
130. El Salvador military/economic aid	N	
131. Bar mining of Nicaraguan waters	Y	
132. Physician fee freeze for Medicare	N	
133. $49b in "sin"/phone/insurance taxes	Y	
134. Allow sale of Conrail	N	
135. Equal Rights Amendment	Y	
136. Authorize Marines in Lebanon	Y	
137. Eminent domain for coal companies	N	
138. Prohibit EPA clean air sanctions	N	
139. SS retirement age increase/reforms	Y	
140. Auto domestic content requirement	Y	
141. Delete jobs program funding	N	
142. Highway-gas tax bill	N	
143. Cut $5b from defense for Medicare	Y	
144. Emergency housing aid of $1b	Y	

Presidential Support Score: 1991 - 43% 1990 - 27%

JACOBS, ANDREW, Jr. -- Indiana 10th District [Democrat]. County of Marion (pt.). Prior Terms: 1965-72; 1975-92. Born: February 24, 1932; Indianapolis, IN. Education: Indiana University (B.S., LL.B.). Military Service: U.S. Marine Corps, 1950-52. Occupation: Attorney; Indiana representative (1959-60).

1. Protection to Haitian refugees	Y	
2. Raise tax on wealthy; lower others	N	
3. Investigate Reagan hostage delay	Y	
4. Campaign finance revisions	Y	
5. Unpaid leave to care for children	Y	
6. Restrict NEA use of funds	Y	
7. Bar race-bias claim/habeas corpus	N	
8. Ban race as death sentence factor	N	
9. Exceptions to exclusionary rule	Y	
10. Allow sale of assault weapons	Y	
11. Life in prison/abolish death penalty	Y	
12. Req conspiracy-price fixing cases	N	
13. Unemployment benefits extension	Y	
14. Tissue use of aborted fetuses	Y	
15. Bar replacement of union strikers	Y	
16. Hold foreign aid at $15b for '92	N	
17. Restore space station funding	N	
18. Civil Rights Act of 1991	Y	
19. Unlimited damages-discrimination	N	
20. Eliminate funds for supercollider	Y	
21. Terminate SDI except for research	Y	
22. Req 7-day handgun waiting period	Y	
23. Provide $30b for failed S&Ls	?	
24. Allow use of force against Iraq	N	
25. Allow $15b in foreign aid for '91	N	
26. Revise & extend legal immigration	Y	

27. Suspend aid to Angolan rebels	Y	
28. Democratic tax plan proposals	Y	
29. Cut defense 5% across the board	Y	
30. Textile import quotas-veto override	Y	
31. Abortion service for military abroad	Y	
32. Limits on high income farmers	Y	
33. Family medical leave-veto override	Y	
34. Req submission of balanced budget	Y	
35. Balanced budget amendment	Y	
36. Amendment to ban flag desecration	Y	
37. Reauthorize Amtrak-veto override	Y	
38. Retraining aid for coal miners	Y	
39. Suspend El Salvador military aid	Y	
40. Expand child care aid/tax credit	Y	
41. Raise House salary/omit honoraria	N	
42. Toughen oil-spill liability	N	
43. Restitution to Japanese interned	Y	
44. Protect Chinese & C.A. nationals	Y	
45. Abortion $ for rape/incest cases	Y	
46. Allow religious schools to bar gays	N	
47. Bar broadcaster fairness doctrine	Y	
48. Bar cap gains cut/reinstate IRA	N	
49. Bar unions equal voice in pension	N	
50. Bar assembly of chemical weapons	Y	
51. Ban plutonium/uranium production	Y	
52. Cap MX missile deployment at 50	Y	

JACOBS, ANDREW, Jr. (continued)

53. Allow $3b for 2 stealth bombers	N	99. Immigration reform/alien amnesty	N
54. Publish bio-warfare experiments	Y	100. South Africa sanctions-veto override	Y
55. Raise minimum wage-veto override	Y	101. Tax overhaul to revise income tax	N
56. Bar transfer of FS-X technology	Y	102. Use of military in drug war	Y
57. Cut defense and raise domestic $	N	103. Delete 12 MX/add conventional wpn	Y
58. Uniform poll closing in 48 states	Y	104. Raise speed limit to 65 mph	N
59. Req foreign investment disclosure	Y	105. Require Pentagon to buy US goods	Y
60. Textile import quotas-veto override	Y	106. AIDS insurance non-discrimination	Y
61. Bar abortion funding in Wash, DC	N	107. Prohibit Saudi arms sales	Y
62. Notify spouses of AIDS+ carriers	N	108. Ease Gun Control Act of 1968	N
63. Seize conveyance-drug trafficking	N	109. Bar interstate handgun transport	Y
64. South Africa sanctions	Y	110. Make company emissions known	Y
65. 60 days' notice of plant closings	Y	111. Allow toxic victims to sue in fed ct	Y
66. Close unneeded military bases	Y	112. Superfund waste cleanup of $10b	N
67. Keep welfare reform within $2.8b	N	113. 90 days notice of plant closings	Y
68. Allow children housing exclusion	N	114. $20b in Medicare cuts/tax increases	Y
69. Shift $400m of NASA to homeless	Y	115. Spending cuts and tax increases	N
70. Cap Medicare patients' liability	Y	116. Set school lunch lmt-250% poverty	N
71. Prohibit employee polygraph testing	Y	117. $75m for youth work projects	N
72. Allow CIA to fund Contras	N	118. Allow Angolan military assistance	N
73. Revise unfair trade practices	Y	119. Suspend defense payments for abuse	Y
74. Focus SDI on accidental launch	Y	120. Drop SS COLAs/$12b tax increase	N
75. Bar Air Force $ for MX missile	Y	121. Approve $1.5b for 21 MX missiles	N
76. Allow "real" increase in defense	N	122. Emergency farm credit/revisions	Y
77. Troop reduction in Europe of 50%	Y	123. Duty on Taiwan/Hong Kong/S Korea	Y
78. Ban nuclear tests above 1 kiloton	Y	124. Limit steel imports to 17%	Y
79. Ban anti-satellite missile tests	Y	125. Cut $ to schools that bar prayer	Y
80. Observe certain limits of SALT II	Y	126. $50b-taxes; cut Medicare/spending	Y
81. Restore four Civil Rights laws	Y	127. Limit Pershing II/cruise in Europe	Y
82. Prohibit aliens as strikebreakers	Y	128. Delete $7.1b for 34 B-1 bombers	Y
83. Allow military malpractice suits	Y	129. Bar purchase of Sergeant York guns	Y
84. Approval of $36m in Contra aid	N	130. El Salvador military/economic aid	N
85. $18b deficit reduction compromise	Y	131. Bar mining of Nicaraguan waters	Y
86. Welfare reform of $5.7b for 5 years	Y	132. Physician fee freeze for Medicare	N
87. Raise taxes $12b/cut spending $3b	Y	133. $49b in "sin"/phone/insurance taxes	Y
88. Board to assess occupational risk	Y	134. Allow sale of Conrail	N
89. Balanced budget by '93-via targets	N	135. Equal Rights Amendment	Y
90. Bar licensing of two nuclear plants	Y	136. Authorize Marines in Lebanon	N
91. Remove victims compensation cap	Y	137. Eminent domain for coal companies	N
92. Catastrophic health insurance	Y	138. Prohibit EPA clean air sanctions	Y
93. Ban airline smoking-2 hours or less	Y	139. SS retirement age increase/reforms	N
94. $1b/two year aid for the homeless	Y	140. Auto domestic content requirement	Y
95. Bar non-unions in union companies	Y	141. Delete jobs program funding	N
96. Increase FSLIC rescue to $15b	N	142. Highway-gas tax bill	N
97. Impose quotas to lower trade deficit	Y	143. Cut $5b from defense for Medicare	Y
98. Reduce discretionary budget 21%	Y	144. Emergency housing aid of $1b	Y

Presidential Support Score: 1991 - 27%   1990 - 23%

IOWA

LEACH, JIM -- Iowa 1st District [Republican]. Counties of Appanoose, Davis, Des Moines, Henry, Jefferson, Keokuk, Lee, Louisa, Lucas, Mahaska, Monroe, Muscatine, Scott, Van Buren, Wapello and Washington. Prior Terms: 1977-92. Born: October 15, 1942; Davenport, IA. Education: Princeton University (B.A.); Johns Hopkins University (M.A.); London School of Economics. Occupation: President, Flamegas Co. Inc.; administrative assistant to the director, Office of Economic Opportunity; Foreign Service Officer; director, Federal Home Loan Bank Board.

LEACH, JIM (continued)

1. Protection to Haitian refugees	N	
2. Raise tax on wealthy; lower others	N	
3. Investigate Reagan hostage delay	N	
4. Campaign finance revisions	Y	
5. Unpaid leave to care for children	Y	
6. Restrict NEA use of funds	N	
7. Bar race-bias claim/habeas corpus	Y	
8. Ban race as death sentence factor	Y	
9. Exceptions to exclusionary rule	Y	
10. Allow sale of assault weapons	N	
11. Life in prison/abolish death penalty	N	
12. Req conspiracy-price fixing cases	Y	
13. Unemployment benefits extension	Y	
14. Tissue use of aborted fetuses	Y	
15. Bar replacement of union strikers	N	
16. Hold foreign aid at $15b for '92	Y	
17. Restore space station funding	N	
18. Civil Rights Act of 1991	Y	
19. Unlimited damages-discrimination	N	
20. Eliminate funds for supercollider	Y	
21. Terminate SDI except for research	Y	
22. Req 7-day handgun waiting period	Y	
23. Provide $30b for failed S&Ls	Y	
24. Allow use of force against Iraq	Y	
25. Allow $15b in foreign aid for '91	Y	
26. Revise & extend legal immigration	Y	
27. Suspend aid to Angolan rebels	Y	
28. Democratic tax plan proposals	Y	
29. Cut defense 5% across the board	N	
30. Textile import quotas-veto override	N	
31. Abortion service for military abroad	Y	
32. Limits on high income farmers	N	
33. Family medical leave-veto override	N	
34. Req submission of balanced budget	Y	
35. Balanced budget amendment	Y	
36. Amendment to ban flag desecration	N	
37. Reauthorize Amtrak-veto override	Y	
38. Retraining aid for coal miners	N	
39. Suspend El Salvador military aid	Y	
40. Expand child care aid/tax credit	Y	
41. Raise House salary/omit honoraria	N	
42. Toughen oil-spill liability	Y	
43. Restitution to Japanese interned	Y	
44. Protect Chinese & C.A. nationals	Y	
45. Abortion $ for rape/incest cases	Y	
46. Allow religious schools to bar gays	Y	
47. Bar broadcaster fairness doctrine	N	
48. Bar cap gains cut/reinstate IRA	N	
49. Bar unions equal voice in pension	Y	
50. Bar assembly of chemical weapons	?	
51. Ban plutonium/uranium production	Y	
52. Cap MX missile deployment at 50	Y	
53. Allow $3b for 2 stealth bombers	N	
54. Publish bio-warfare experiments	Y	
55. Raise minimum wage-veto override	Y	
56. Bar transfer of FS-X technology	N	
57. Cut defense and raise domestic $	N	
58. Uniform poll closing in 48 states	Y	
59. Req foreign investment disclosure	Y	
60. Textile import quotas-veto override	N	
61. Bar abortion funding in Wash, DC	Y	
62. Notify spouses of AIDS+ carriers	N	
63. Seize conveyance-drug trafficking	N	
64. South Africa sanctions	Y	

65. 60 days' notice of plant closings	Y	
66. Close unneeded military bases	Y	
67. Keep welfare reform within $2.8b	Y	
68. Allow children housing exclusion	N	
69. Shift $400m of NASA to homeless	N	
70. Cap Medicare patients' liability	Y	
71. Prohibit employee polygraph testing	Y	
72. Allow CIA to fund Contras	N	
73. Revise unfair trade practices	Y	
74. Focus SDI on accidental launch	Y	
75. Bar Air Force $ for MX missile	Y	
76. Allow "real" increase in defense	N	
77. Troop reduction in Europe of 50%	Y	
78. Ban nuclear tests above 1 kiloton	Y	
79. Ban anti-satellite missile tests	Y	
80. Observe certain limits of SALT II	Y	
81. Restore four Civil Rights laws	Y	
82. Prohibit aliens as strikebreakers	Y	
83. Allow military malpractice suits	Y	
84. Approval of $36m in Contra aid	N	
85. $18b deficit reduction compromise	N	
86. Welfare reform of $5.7b for 5 years	N	
87. Raise taxes $12b/cut spending $3b	N	
88. Board to assess occupational risk	N	
89. Balanced budget by '93-via targets	N	
90. Bar licensing of two nuclear plants	N	
91. Remove victims compensation cap	N	
92. Catastrophic health insurance	Y	
93. Ban airline smoking-2 hours or less	Y	
94. $1b/two year aid for the homeless	Y	
95. Bar non-unions in union companies	N	
96. Increase FSLIC rescue to $15b	Y	
97. Impose quotas to lower trade deficit	N	
98. Reduce discretionary budget 21%	?	
99. Immigration reform/alien amnesty	Y	
100. South Africa sanctions-veto override	Y	
101. Tax overhaul to revise income tax	Y	
102. Use of military in drug war	N	
103. Delete 12 MX/add conventional wpn	Y	
104. Raise speed limit to 65 mph	N	
105. Require Pentagon to buy US goods	N	
106. AIDS insurance non-discrimination	Y	
107. Prohibit Saudi arms sales	Y	
108. Ease Gun Control Act of 1968	Y	
109. Bar interstate handgun transport	Y	
110. Make company emissions known	Y	
111. Allow toxic victims to sue in fed ct	Y	
112. Superfund waste cleanup of $10b	Y	
113. 90 days notice of plant closings	Y	
114. $20b in Medicare cuts/tax increases	Y	
115. Spending cuts and tax increases	N	
116. Set school lunch lmt-250% poverty	N	
117. $75m for youth work projects	Y	
118. Allow Angolan military assistance	N	
119. Suspend defense payments for abuse	Y	
120. Drop SS COLAs/$12b tax increase	N	
121. Approve $1.5b for 21 MX missiles	N	
122. Emergency farm credit/revisions	Y	
123. Duty on Taiwan/Hong Kong/S Korea	N	
124. Limit steel imports to 17%	N	
125. Cut $ to schools that bar prayer	N	
126. $50b-taxes; cut Medicare/spending	Y	
127. Limit Pershing II/cruise in Europe	Y	
128. Delete $7.1b for 34 B-1 bombers	Y	

LEACH, JIM (continued)
129. Bar purchase of Sergeant York guns N
130. El Salvador military/economic aid N
131. Bar mining of Nicaraguan waters Y
132. Physician fee freeze for Medicare Y
133. $49b in "sin"/phone/insurance taxes Y
134. Allow sale of Conrail Y
135. Equal Rights Amendment Y
136. Authorize Marines in Lebanon Y

137. Eminent domain for coal companies N
138. Prohibit EPA clean air sanctions ?
139. SS retirement age increase/reforms Y
140. Auto domestic content requirement Y
141. Delete jobs program funding Y
142. Highway-gas tax bill N
143. Cut $5b from defense for Medicare Y
144. Emergency housing aid of $1b Y

Presidential Support Score: 1991 - 59%   1990 - 38%

NUSSLE, JIM -- Iowa 2nd District [Republican]. Counties of Allamakee, Buchanan, Cedar, Clayton, Clinton, Delaware, Dubuque, Fayette, Jackson, Jones and Linn. Prior Terms: 1991-92. Born: June 27, 1960; Des Moines, IA. Education: Luther College (B.A.); Drake University (J.D.). Occupation: Lawyer; staff assistant to Rep. Tauke; Delaware County attorney (1986-90).

1. Protection to Haitian refugees N
2. Raise tax on wealthy; lower others N
3. Investigate Reagan hostage delay N
4. Campaign finance revisions N
5. Unpaid leave to care for children N
6. Restrict NEA use of funds Y
7. Bar race-bias claim/habeas corpus Y
8. Ban race as death sentence factor Y
9. Exceptions to exclusionary rule Y
10. Allow sale of assault weapons Y
11. Life in prison/abolish death penalty N
12. Req conspiracy-price fixing cases Y

13. Unemployment benefits extension N
14. Tissue use of aborted fetuses N
15. Bar replacement of union strikers N
16. Hold foreign aid at $15b for '92 N
17. Restore space station funding N
18. Civil Rights Act of 1991 N
19. Unlimited damages-discrimination N
20. Eliminate funds for supercollider N
21. Terminate SDI except for research N
22. Req 7-day handgun waiting period N
23. Provide $30b for failed S&Ls N
24. Allow use of force against Iraq Y

Presidential Support Score: 1991 - 80%

NAGLE, DAVID R. -- Iowa 3rd District [Democrat]. Counties of Benton, Black Hawk, Bremer, Butler, Chickasaw, Floyd, Grundy, Howard, Iowa, Johnson, Marshall, Mitchell, Poweshiek, Toma, Winneshiek and Worth. Prior Terms: 1987-92. Born: April 15, 1943; Grinnell, IA. Education: University of Northern Iowa; University of Iowa Law School (LL.B.). Occupation: Attorney; Assistant Black Hawk County Attorney (1969-1970); Evansdale City Attorney (1972-1974); Black Hawk County conservation board president (1975-1980); adjunct professor (1978-1981); state Democratic Party chairman (1982-1985).

1. Protection to Haitian refugees Y
2. Raise tax on wealthy; lower others N
3. Investigate Reagan hostage delay Y
4. Campaign finance revisions N
5. Unpaid leave to care for children Y
6. Restrict NEA use of funds N
7. Bar race-bias claim/habeas corpus N
8. Ban race as death sentence factor N
9. Exceptions to exclusionary rule N
10. Allow sale of assault weapons Y
11. Life in prison/abolish death penalty Y
12. Req conspiracy-price fixing cases N
13. Unemployment benefits extension Y
14. Tissue use of aborted fetuses Y
15. Bar replacement of union strikers Y
16. Hold foreign aid at $15b for '92 Y
17. Restore space station funding N
18. Civil Rights Act of 1991 Y
19. Unlimited damages-discrimination Y
20. Eliminate funds for supercollider N
21. Terminate SDI except for research ?
22. Req 7-day handgun waiting period N

23. Provide $30b for failed S&Ls N
24. Allow use of force against Iraq N
25. Allow $15b in foreign aid for '91 Y
26. Revise & extend legal immigration Y
27. Suspend aid to Angolan rebels Y
28. Democratic tax plan proposals Y
29. Cut defense 5% across the board N
30. Textile import quotas-veto override Y
31. Abortion service for military abroad Y
32. Limits on high income farmers N
33. Family medical leave-veto override N
34. Req submission of balanced budget N
35. Balanced budget amendment N
36. Amendment to ban flag desecration N
37. Reauthorize Amtrak-veto override Y
38. Retraining aid for coal miners Y
39. Suspend El Salvador military aid Y
40. Expand child care aid/tax credit Y
41. Raise House salary/omit honoraria Y
42. Toughen oil-spill liability Y
43. Restitution to Japanese interned Y
44. Protect Chinese & C.A. nationals Y

NAGLE, DAVID R. (continued)

45. Abortion $ for rape/incest cases	Y		72. Allow CIA to fund Contras	N	
46. Allow religious schools to bar gays	N		73. Revise unfair trade practices	Y	
47. Bar broadcaster fairness doctrine	Y		74. Focus SDI on accidental launch	Y	
48. Bar cap gains cut/reinstate IRA	Y		75. Bar Air Force $ for MX missile	Y	
49. Bar unions equal voice in pension	N		76. Allow "real" increase in defense	N	
50. Bar assembly of chemical weapons	Y		77. Troop reduction in Europe of 50%	N	
51. Ban plutonium/uranium production	Y		78. Ban nuclear tests above 1 kiloton	Y	
52. Cap MX missile deployment at 50	Y		79. Ban anti-satellite missile tests	Y	
53. Allow $3b for 2 stealth bombers	Y		80. Observe certain limits of SALT II	Y	
54. Publish bio-warfare experiments	Y		81. Restore four Civil Rights laws	Y	
55. Raise minimum wage-veto override	Y		82. Prohibit aliens as strikebreakers	Y	
56. Bar transfer of FS-X technology	N		83. Allow military malpractice suits	Y	
57. Cut defense and raise domestic $	N		84. Approval of $36m in Contra aid	N	
58. Uniform poll closing in 48 states	N		85. $18b deficit reduction compromise	N	
59. Req foreign investment disclosure	Y		86. Welfare reform of $5.7b for 5 years	Y	
60. Textile import quotas-veto override	Y		87. Raise taxes $12b/cut spending $3b	Y	
61. Bar abortion funding in Wash, DC	N		88. Board to assess occupational risk	Y	
62. Notify spouses of AIDS+ carriers	N		89. Balanced budget by '93-via targets	Y	
63. Seize conveyance-drug trafficking	N		90. Bar licensing of two nuclear plants	Y	
64. South Africa sanctions	Y		91. Remove victims compensation cap	N	
65. 60 days' notice of plant closings	Y		92. Catastrophic health insurance	Y	
66. Close unneeded military bases	N		93. Ban airline smoking-2 hours or less	N	
67. Keep welfare reform within $2.8b	N		94. $1b/two year aid for the homeless	Y	
68. Allow children housing exclusion	N		95. Bar non-unions in union companies	Y	
69. Shift $400m of NASA to homeless	N		96. Increase FSLIC rescue to $15b	Y	
70. Cap Medicare patients' liability	Y		97. Impose quotas to lower trade deficit	Y	
71. Prohibit employee polygraph testing	Y		98. Reduce discretionary budget 21%	N	

Presidential Support Score: 1991 - 29%   1990 - 20%

SMITH, NEAL -- Iowa 4th District [Democrat].   Counties of Boone, Dallas, Hamilton, Jasper, Polk and Story.   Prior Terms: 1959-92.   Born: March 23, 1920; Hedrick, IA.   Education: Drake University Law School; Missouri University; Syracuse University.   Military Service: W W II.   Occupation: Attorney.

1. Protection to Haitian refugees	Y		29. Cut defense 5% across the board	N	
2. Raise tax on wealthy; lower others	N		30. Textile import quotas-veto override	N	
3. Investigate Reagan hostage delay	Y		31. Abortion service for military abroad	Y	
4. Campaign finance revisions	Y		32. Limits on high income farmers	N	
5. Unpaid leave to care for children	Y		33. Family medical leave-veto override	Y	
6. Restrict NEA use of funds	N		34. Req submission of balanced budget	Y	
7. Bar race-bias claim/habeas corpus	N		35. Balanced budget amendment	N	
8. Ban race as death sentence factor	N		36. Amendment to ban flag desecration	N	
9. Exceptions to exclusionary rule	N		37. Reauthorize Amtrak-veto override	Y	
10. Allow sale of assault weapons	Y		38. Retraining aid for coal miners	Y	
11. Life in prison/abolish death penalty	Y		39. Suspend El Salvador military aid	Y	
12. Req conspiracy-price fixing cases	N		40. Expand child care aid/tax credit	Y	
13. Unemployment benefits extension	Y		41. Raise House salary/omit honoraria	Y	
14. Tissue use of aborted fetuses	Y		42. Toughen oil-spill liability	?	
15. Bar replacement of union strikers	Y		43. Restitution to Japanese interned	Y	
16. Hold foreign aid at $15b for '92	Y		44. Protect Chinese & C.A. nationals	Y	
17. Restore space station funding	N		45. Abortion $ for rape/incest cases	Y	
18. Civil Rights Act of 1991	Y		46. Allow religious schools to bar gays	N	
19. Unlimited damages-discrimination	N		47. Bar broadcaster fairness doctrine	N	
20. Eliminate funds for supercollider	N		48. Bar cap gains cut/reinstate IRA	N	
21. Terminate SDI except for research	N		49. Bar unions equal voice in pension	N	
22. Req 7-day handgun waiting period	N		50. Bar assembly of chemical weapons	Y	
23. Provide $30b for failed S&Ls	Y		51. Ban plutonium/uranium production	Y	
24. Allow use of force against Iraq	N		52. Cap MX missile deployment at 50	Y	
25. Allow $15b in foreign aid for '91	Y		53. Allow $3b for 2 stealth bombers	N	
26. Revise & extend legal immigration	Y		54. Publish bio-warfare experiments	Y	
27. Suspend aid to Angolan rebels	Y		55. Raise minimum wage-veto override	Y	
28. Democratic tax plan proposals	Y		56. Bar transfer of FS-X technology	N	

SMITH, NEAL (continued)

57. Cut defense and raise domestic $	N	
58. Uniform poll closing in 48 states	Y	
59. Req foreign investment disclosure	N	
60. Textile import quotas-veto override	N	
61. Bar abortion funding in Wash, DC	N	
62. Notify spouses of AIDS+ carriers	N	
63. Seize conveyance-drug trafficking	N	
64. South Africa sanctions	Y	
65. 60 days' notice of plant closings	Y	
66. Close unneeded military bases	Y	
67. Keep welfare reform within $2.8b	N	
68. Allow children housing exclusion	N	
69. Shift $400m of NASA to homeless	N	
70. Cap Medicare patients' liability	Y	
71. Prohibit employee polygraph testing	Y	
72. Allow CIA to fund Contras	N	
73. Revise unfair trade practices	Y	
74. Focus SDI on accidental launch	Y	
75. Bar Air Force $ for MX missile	Y	
76. Allow "real" increase in defense	N	
77. Troop reduction in Europe of 50%	N	
78. Ban nuclear tests above 1 kiloton	Y	
79. Ban anti-satellite missile tests	Y	
80. Observe certain limits of SALT II	Y	
81. Restore four Civil Rights laws	Y	
82. Prohibit aliens as strikebreakers	Y	
83. Allow military malpractice suits	?	
84. Approval of $36m in Contra aid	N	
85. $18b deficit reduction compromise	Y	
86. Welfare reform of $5.7b for 5 years	Y	
87. Raise taxes $12b/cut spending $3b	Y	
88. Board to assess occupational risk	Y	
89. Balanced budget by '93-via targets	N	
90. Bar licensing of two nuclear plants	N	
91. Remove victims compensation cap	N	
92. Catastrophic health insurance	Y	
93. Ban airline smoking-2 hours or less	Y	
94. $1b/two year aid for the homeless	Y	
95. Bar non-unions in union companies	Y	
96. Increase FSLIC rescue to $15b	Y	
97. Impose quotas to lower trade deficit	N	
98. Reduce discretionary budget 21%	N	
99. Immigration reform/alien amnesty	Y	
100. South Africa sanctions-veto override	Y	

101. Tax overhaul to revise income tax	Y	
102. Use of military in drug war	Y	
103. Delete 12 MX/add conventional wpn	?	
104. Raise speed limit to 65 mph	Y	
105. Require Pentagon to buy US goods	Y	
106. AIDS insurance non-discrimination	Y	
107. Prohibit Saudi arms sales	Y	
108. Ease Gun Control Act of 1968	Y	
109. Bar interstate handgun transport	N	
110. Make company emissions known	Y	
111. Allow toxic victims to sue in fed ct	Y	
112. Superfund waste cleanup of $10b	Y	
113. 90 days notice of plant closings	?	
114. $20b in Medicare cuts/tax increases	Y	
115. Spending cuts and tax increases	N	
116. Set school lunch lmt-250% poverty	N	
117. $75m for youth work projects	Y	
118. Allow Angolan military assistance	N	
119. Suspend defense payments for abuse	N	
120. Drop SS COLAs/$12b tax increase	N	
121. Approve $1.5b for 21 MX missiles	N	
122. Emergency farm credit/revisions	Y	
123. Duty on Taiwan/Hong Kong/S Korea	Y	
124. Limit steel imports to 17%	N	
125. Cut $ to schools that bar prayer	N	
126. $50b-taxes; cut Medicare/spending	Y	
127. Limit Pershing II/cruise in Europe	N	
128. Delete $7.1b for 34 B-1 bombers	Y	
129. Bar purchase of Sergeant York guns	?	
130. El Salvador military/economic aid	N	
131. Bar mining of Nicaraguan waters	Y	
132. Physician fee freeze for Medicare	N	
133. $49b in "sin"/phone/insurance taxes	Y	
134. Allow sale of Conrail	N	
135. Equal Rights Amendment	Y	
136. Authorize Marines in Lebanon	N	
137. Eminent domain for coal companies	Y	
138. Prohibit EPA clean air sanctions	N	
139. SS retirement age increase/reforms	N	
140. Auto domestic content requirement	N	
141. Delete jobs program funding	N	
142. Highway-gas tax bill	Y	
143. Cut $5b from defense for Medicare	Y	
144. Emergency housing aid of $1b	Y	

Presidential Support Score: 1991 - 37% 1990 - 27%

LIGHTFOOT, JAMES ROSS -- Iowa 5th District [Republican]. Counties of Adair, Adams, Audubon, Calhoun, Carroll, Cass, Clarke, Crawford, Decatur, Fremont, Greene, Guthrie, Harrison, Madison, Marion, Mills, Montgomery, Page, Pottawattomie, Ringgold, Sac, Shelby, Taylor, Union, Warren, Wayne and Webster. Prior Terms: 1985-92. Born: September 27, 1938; Sioux City, IA. Military Service: U.S. Army and Army Reserve, 1956-1964. Occupation: Farm equipment plant manager (1970-1976); Corsicana city commissioner (1974-1976); businessman; radio broadcaster; farm editor.

1. Protection to Haitian refugees	N	
2. Raise tax on wealthy; lower others	N	
3. Investigate Reagan hostage delay	?	
4. Campaign finance revisions	N	
5. Unpaid leave to care for children	N	
6. Restrict NEA use of funds	N	
7. Bar race-bias claim/habeas corpus	Y	
8. Ban race as death sentence factor	Y	

9. Exceptions to exclusionary rule	Y	
10. Allow sale of assault weapons	Y	
11. Life in prison/abolish death penalty	N	
12. Req conspiracy-price fixing cases	Y	
13. Unemployment benefits extension	N	
14. Tissue use of aborted fetuses	N	
15. Bar replacement of union strikers	N	
16. Hold foreign aid at $15b for '92	Y	

LIGHTFOOT, JAMES ROSS (continued)

17. Restore space station funding	Y
18. Civil Rights Act of 1991	N
19. Unlimited damages-discrimination	N
20. Eliminate funds for supercollider	N
21. Terminate SDI except for research	N
22. Req 7-day handgun waiting period	N
23. Provide $30b for failed S&Ls	Y
24. Allow use of force against Iraq	Y
25. Allow $15b in foreign aid for '91	Y
26. Revise & extend legal immigration	Y
27. Suspend aid to Angolan rebels	N
28. Democratic tax plan proposals	N
29. Cut defense 5% across the board	N
30. Textile import quotas-veto override	N
31. Abortion service for military abroad	N
32. Limits on high income farmers	N
33. Family medical leave-veto override	N
34. Req submission of balanced budget	N
35. Balanced budget amendment	Y
36. Amendment to ban flag desecration	Y
37. Reauthorize Amtrak-veto override	Y
38. Retraining aid for coal miners	N
39. Suspend El Salvador military aid	N
40. Expand child care aid/tax credit	N
41. Raise House salary/omit honoraria	N
42. Toughen oil-spill liability	N
43. Restitution to Japanese interned	N
44. Protect Chinese & C.A. nationals	N
45. Abortion $ for rape/incest cases	N
46. Allow religious schools to bar gays	Y
47. Bar broadcaster fairness doctrine	Y
48. Bar cap gains cut/reinstate IRA	N
49. Bar unions equal voice in pension	Y
50. Bar assembly of chemical weapons	N
51. Ban plutonium/uranium production	N
52. Cap MX missile deployment at 50	N
53. Allow $3b for 2 stealth bombers	Y
54. Publish bio-warfare experiments	N
55. Raise minimum wage-veto override	N
56. Bar transfer of FS-X technology	N
57. Cut defense and raise domestic $	N
58. Uniform poll closing in 48 states	N
59. Req foreign investment disclosure	N
60. Textile import quotas-veto override	N
61. Bar abortion funding in Wash, DC	Y
62. Notify spouses of AIDS+ carriers	N
63. Seize conveyance-drug trafficking	Y
64. South Africa sanctions	N
65. 60 days' notice of plant closings	N
66. Close unneeded military bases	Y
67. Keep welfare reform within $2.8b	Y
68. Allow children housing exclusion	Y
69. Shift $400m of NASA to homeless	N

70. Cap Medicare patients' liability	Y
71. Prohibit employee polygraph testing	N
72. Allow CIA to fund Contras	N
73. Revise unfair trade practices	N
74. Focus SDI on accidental launch	Y
75. Bar Air Force $ for MX missile	N
76. Allow "real" increase in defense	N
77. Troop reduction in Europe of 50%	N
78. Ban nuclear tests above 1 kiloton	N
79. Ban anti-satellite missile tests	N
80. Observe certain limits of SALT II	N
81. Restore four Civil Rights laws	?
82. Prohibit aliens as strikebreakers	?
83. Allow military malpractice suits	?
84. Approval of $36m in Contra aid	?
85. $18b deficit reduction compromise	N
86. Welfare reform of $5.7b for 5 years	N
87. Raise taxes $12b/cut spending $3b	N
88. Board to assess occupational risk	N
89. Balanced budget by '93-via targets	N
90. Bar licensing of two nuclear plants	N
91. Remove victims compensation cap	N
92. Catastrophic health insurance	N
93. Ban airline smoking-2 hours or less	N
94. $1b/two year aid for the homeless	N
95. Bar non-unions in union companies	N
96. Increase FSLIC rescue to $15b	Y
97. Impose quotas to lower trade deficit	N
98. Reduce discretionary budget 21%	N
99. Immigration reform/alien amnesty	Y
100. South Africa sanctions-veto override	Y
101. Tax overhaul to revise income tax	Y
102. Use of military in drug war	Y
103. Delete 12 MX/add conventional wpn	Y
104. Raise speed limit to 65 mph	Y
105. Require Pentagon to buy US goods	Y
106. AIDS insurance non-discrimination	N
107. Prohibit Saudi arms sales	Y
108. Ease Gun Control Act of 1968	Y
109. Bar interstate handgun transport	N
110. Make company emissions known	N
111. Allow toxic victims to sue in fed ct	N
112. Superfund waste cleanup of $10b	Y
113. 90 days notice of plant closings	N
114. $20b in Medicare cuts/tax increases	N
115. Spending cuts and tax increases	N
116. Set school lunch lmt-250% poverty	N
117. $75m for youth work projects	N
118. Allow Angolan military assistance	Y
119. Suspend defense payments for abuse	N
120. Drop SS COLAs/$12b tax increase	N
121. Approve $1.5b for 21 MX missiles	Y
122. Emergency farm credit/revisions	Y

Presidential Support Score: 1991 - 81%   1990 - 68%

GRANDY, FRED -- Iowa 6th District [Republican]. Counties of Buena Vista, Cerro Gordo, Cherokee, Clay, Dickinson, Emmet, Franklin, Hancock, Hardin, Humboldt, Ida, Kossuth, Lyon, Monona, O'Brien, Osceola, Palo Alto, Plymouth, Pocahontas, Sioux, Winnebago, Woodbury and Wright. Prior Terms: 1987-92. Born: June 29, 1948; Sioux City, IA. Education: Harvard College. Occupation: Congressional aide (1970-1971); professional actor (1971-1985); college trustee.

GRANDY, FRED (continued)

1. Protection to Haitian refugees	N	
2. Raise tax on wealthy; lower others	N	
3. Investigate Reagan hostage delay	N	
4. Campaign finance revisions	N	
5. Unpaid leave to care for children	N	
6. Restrict NEA use of funds	N	
7. Bar race-bias claim/habeas corpus	Y	
8. Ban race as death sentence factor	Y	
9. Exceptions to exclusionary rule	Y	
10. Allow sale of assault weapons	Y	
11. Life in prison/abolish death penalty	N	
12. Req conspiracy-price fixing cases	Y	
13. Unemployment benefits extension	N	
14. Tissue use of aborted fetuses	N	
15. Bar replacement of union strikers	N	
16. Hold foreign aid at $15b for '92	Y	
17. Restore space station funding	N	
18. Civil Rights Act of 1991	N	
19. Unlimited damages-discrimination	N	
20. Eliminate funds for supercollider	Y	
21. Terminate SDI except for research	N	
22. Req 7-day handgun waiting period	N	
23. Provide $30b for failed S&Ls	Y	
24. Allow use of force against Iraq	Y	
25. Allow $15b in foreign aid for '91	Y	
26. Revise & extend legal immigration	Y	
27. Suspend aid to Angolan rebels	Y	
28. Democratic tax plan proposals	N	
29. Cut defense 5% across the board	Y	
30. Textile import quotas-veto override	N	
31. Abortion service for military abroad	N	
32. Limits on high income farmers	N	
33. Family medical leave-veto override	N	
34. Req submission of balanced budget	N	
35. Balanced budget amendment	Y	
36. Amendment to ban flag desecration	N	
37. Reauthorize Amtrak-veto override	Y	
38. Retraining aid for coal miners	N	
39. Suspend El Salvador military aid	Y	
40. Expand child care aid/tax credit	N	
41. Raise House salary/omit honoraria	N	
42. Toughen oil-spill liability	N	
43. Restitution to Japanese interned	N	
44. Protect Chinese & C.A. nationals	N	
45. Abortion $ for rape/incest cases	N	
46. Allow religious schools to bar gays	Y	
47. Bar broadcaster fairness doctrine	Y	
48. Bar cap gains cut/reinstate IRA	N	
49. Bar unions equal voice in pension	Y	
50. Bar assembly of chemical weapons	Y
51. Ban plutonium/uranium production	Y
52. Cap MX missile deployment at 50	Y
53. Allow $3b for 2 stealth bombers	N
54. Publish bio-warfare experiments	Y
55. Raise minimum wage-veto override	N
56. Bar transfer of FS-X technology	N
57. Cut defense and raise domestic $	N
58. Uniform poll closing in 48 states	N
59. Req foreign investment disclosure	Y
60. Textile import quotas-veto override	N
61. Bar abortion funding in Wash, DC	Y
62. Notify spouses of AIDS+ carriers	Y
63. Seize conveyance-drug trafficking	Y
64. South Africa sanctions	N
65. 60 days' notice of plant closings	Y
66. Close unneeded military bases	Y
67. Keep welfare reform within $2.8b	Y
68. Allow children housing exclusion	N
69. Shift $400m of NASA to homeless	N
70. Cap Medicare patients' liability	Y
71. Prohibit employee polygraph testing	Y
72. Allow CIA to fund Contras	Y
73. Revise unfair trade practices	Y
74. Focus SDI on accidental launch	Y
75. Bar Air Force $ for MX missile	N
76. Allow "real" increase in defense	N
77. Troop reduction in Europe of 50%	N
78. Ban nuclear tests above 1 kiloton	Y
79. Ban anti-satellite missile tests	N
80. Observe certain limits of SALT II	Y
81. Restore four Civil Rights laws	N
82. Prohibit aliens as strikebreakers	Y
83. Allow military malpractice suits	Y
84. Approval of $36m in Contra aid	Y
85. $18b deficit reduction compromise	N
86. Welfare reform of $5.7b for 5 years	N
87. Raise taxes $12b/cut spending $3b	N
88. Board to assess occupational risk	N
89. Balanced budget by '93-via targets	N
90. Bar licensing of two nuclear plants	N
91. Remove victims compensation cap	N
92. Catastrophic health insurance	N
93. Ban airline smoking-2 hours or less	N
94. $1b/two year aid for the homeless	Y
95. Bar non-unions in union companies	N
96. Increase FSLIC rescue to $15b	Y
97. Impose quotas to lower trade deficit	N
98. Reduce discretionary budget 21%	N

Presidential Support Score: 1991 - 83%   1990 - 63%

KANSAS

ROBERTS, PAT -- Kansas 1st District [Republican]. Counties of Barber, Barton, Cheyenne, Clark, Cloud, Comanche, Decatur, Dickinson, Edwards, Ellis, Ellsworth, Finney, Ford, Gove, Graham, Grant, Gray, Greeley, Hamilton, Haskell, Hodgeman, Jewell, Kearny, Kiowa, Lane, Lincoln, Logan, Marshall, Meade, Mitchell, Morton, Ness, Norton, Osborne,

ROBERTS, PAT (continued)
Ottawa, Pawnee, Phillips, Pratt, Rawlins, Republic, Rice, Rooks, Rush, Russell, Saline, Scott, Seward, Sheridan, Sherman, Smith, Stafford, Stanton, Stevens, Thomas, Trego, Wallace, Washington and Wichita. Prior Terms: 1981-92. Born: April 23, 1936; Topeka, KS. Education: Kansas State University (B.A.). Military Service: U.S. Marine Corps, 1958-62. Occupation: Newspaper owner and editor; congressional press secretary; congressional administrative assistant.

1. Protection to Haitian refugees	N	58. Uniform poll closing in 48 states	N
2. Raise tax on wealthy; lower others	N	59. Req foreign investment disclosure	N
3. Investigate Reagan hostage delay	N	60. Textile import quotas-veto override	N
4. Campaign finance revisions	N	61. Bar abortion funding in Wash, DC	Y
5. Unpaid leave to care for children	N	62. Notify spouses of AIDS+ carriers	?
6. Restrict NEA use of funds	Y	63. Seize conveyance-drug trafficking	Y
7. Bar race-bias claim/habeas corpus	Y	64. South Africa sanctions	N
8. Ban race as death sentence factor	Y	65. 60 days' notice of plant closings	Y
9. Exceptions to exclusionary rule	Y	66. Close unneeded military bases	Y
10. Allow sale of assault weapons	Y	67. Keep welfare reform within $2.8b	Y
11. Life in prison/abolish death penalty	N	68. Allow children housing exclusion	Y
12. Req conspiracy-price fixing cases	Y	69. Shift $400m of NASA to homeless	N
13. Unemployment benefits extension	N	70. Cap Medicare patients' liability	?
14. Tissue use of aborted fetuses	N	71. Prohibit employee polygraph testing	?
15. Bar replacement of union strikers	N	72. Allow CIA to fund Contras	Y
16. Hold foreign aid at $15b for '92	N	73. Revise unfair trade practices	Y
17. Restore space station funding	Y	74. Focus SDI on accidental launch	N
18. Civil Rights Act of 1991	N	75. Bar Air Force $ for MX missile	N
19. Unlimited damages-discrimination	N	76. Allow "real" increase in defense	N
20. Eliminate funds for supercollider	N	77. Troop reduction in Europe of 50%	N
21. Terminate SDI except for research	N	78. Ban nuclear tests above 1 kiloton	N
22. Req 7-day handgun waiting period	N	79. Ban anti-satellite missile tests	N
23. Provide $30b for failed S&Ls	Y	80. Observe certain limits of SALT II	N
24. Allow use of force against Iraq	Y	81. Restore four Civil Rights laws	N
25. Allow $15b in foreign aid for '91	N	82. Prohibit aliens as strikebreakers	N
26. Revise & extend legal immigration	N	83. Allow military malpractice suits	N
27. Suspend aid to Angolan rebels	N	84. Approval of $36m in Contra aid	Y
28. Democratic tax plan proposals	N	85. $18b deficit reduction compromise	N
29. Cut defense 5% across the board	N	86. Welfare reform of $5.7b for 5 years	N
30. Textile import quotas-veto override	N	87. Raise taxes $12b/cut spending $3b	N
31. Abortion service for military abroad	N	88. Board to assess occupational risk	N
32. Limits on high income farmers	N	89. Balanced budget by '93-via targets	Y
33. Family medical leave-veto override	N	90. Bar licensing of two nuclear plants	N
34. Req submission of balanced budget	N	91. Remove victims compensation cap	N
35. Balanced budget amendment	Y	92. Catastrophic health insurance	N
36. Amendment to ban flag desecration	Y	93. Ban airline smoking-2 hours or less	N
37. Reauthorize Amtrak-veto override	Y	94. $1b/two year aid for the homeless	N
38. Retraining aid for coal miners	N	95. Bar non-unions in union companies	N
39. Suspend El Salvador military aid	N	96. Increase FSLIC rescue to $15b	N
40. Expand child care aid/tax credit	N	97. Impose quotas to lower trade deficit	N
41. Raise House salary/omit honoraria	Y	98. Reduce discretionary budget 21%	Y
42. Toughen oil-spill liability	N	99. Immigration reform/alien amnesty	N
43. Restitution to Japanese interned	N	100. South Africa sanctions-veto override	Y
44. Protect Chinese & C.A. nationals	N	101. Tax overhaul to revise income tax	N
45. Abortion $ for rape/incest cases	N	102. Use of military in drug war	Y
46. Allow religious schools to bar gays	Y	103. Delete 12 MX/add conventional wpn	N
47. Bar broadcaster fairness doctrine	Y	104. Raise speed limit to 65 mph	Y
48. Bar cap gains cut/reinstate IRA	N	105. Require Pentagon to buy US goods	N
49. Bar unions equal voice in pension	Y	106. AIDS insurance non-discrimination	N
50. Bar assembly of chemical weapons	N	107. Prohibit Saudi arms sales	Y
51. Ban plutonium/uranium production	N	108. Ease Gun Control Act of 1968	Y
52. Cap MX missile deployment at 50	Y	109. Bar interstate handgun transport	N
53. Allow $3b for 2 stealth bombers	Y	110. Make company emissions known	N
54. Publish bio-warfare experiments	N	111. Allow toxic victims to sue in fed ct	N
55. Raise minimum wage-veto override	N	112. Superfund waste cleanup of $10b	N
56. Bar transfer of FS-X technology	N	113. 90 days notice of plant closings	N
57. Cut defense and raise domestic $	N	114. $20b in Medicare cuts/tax increases	N

ROBERTS, PAT (continued)

115.	Spending cuts and tax increases	N	130.	El Salvador military/economic aid	Y
116.	Set school lunch lmt-250% poverty	Y	131.	Bar mining of Nicaraguan waters	N
117.	$75m for youth work projects	N	132.	Physician fee freeze for Medicare	Y
118.	Allow Angolan military assistance	Y	133.	$49b in "sin"/phone/insurance taxes	N
119.	Suspend defense payments for abuse	N	134.	Allow sale of Conrail	Y
120.	Drop SS COLAs/$12b tax increase	N	135.	Equal Rights Amendment	N
121.	Approve $1.5b for 21 MX missiles	N	136.	Authorize Marines in Lebanon	Y
122.	Emergency farm credit/revisions	Y	137.	Eminent domain for coal companies	N
123.	Duty on Taiwan/Hong Kong/S Korea	N	138.	Prohibit EPA clean air sanctions	N
124.	Limit steel imports to 17%	N	139.	SS retirement age increase/reforms	Y
125.	Cut $ to schools that bar prayer	Y	140.	Auto domestic content requirement	N
126.	$50b-taxes; cut Medicare/spending	N	141.	Delete jobs program funding	Y
127.	Limit Pershing II/cruise in Europe	N	142.	Highway-gas tax bill	N
128.	Delete $7.1b for 34 B-1 bombers	N	143.	Cut $5b from defense for Medicare	N
129.	Bar purchase of Sergeant York guns	N	144.	Emergency housing aid of $1b	N

Presidential Support Score: 1991 - 82%   1990 - 71%

SLATTERY, JIM -- Kansas 2nd District [Democrat]. Counties of Atchison, Brown, Clay, Doniphan, Douglas, Geary, Jackson, Jefferson, Leavenworth, Nemaha, Pottawatomie, Riley and Shawnee. Prior Terms: 1983-92. Born:August 4, 1948; Good Intent, KS. Education: Washburn University (B.S., J.D.).Occupation: Realtor; Kansas representative (1972-78); acting secretary of revenue (1979); member, Board of Directors, Highland Park Bank & Trust; member, Board of Regents, Washburn University.

1.	Protection to Haitian refugees	Y	39.	Suspend El Salvador military aid	Y
2.	Raise tax on wealthy; lower others	N	40.	Expand child care aid/tax credit	N
3.	Investigate Reagan hostage delay	Y	41.	Raise House salary/omit honoraria	N
4.	Campaign finance revisions	Y	42.	Toughen oil-spill liability	Y
5.	Unpaid leave to care for children	N	43.	Restitution to Japanese interned	Y
6.	Restrict NEA use of funds	N	44.	Protect Chinese & C.A. nationals	Y
7.	Bar race-bias claim/habeas corpus	N	45.	Abortion $ for rape/incest cases	N
8.	Ban race as death sentence factor	N	46.	Allow religious schools to bar gays	Y
9.	Exceptions to exclusionary rule	N	47.	Bar broadcaster fairness doctrine	N
10.	Allow sale of assault weapons	Y	48.	Bar cap gains cut/reinstate IRA	Y
11.	Life in prison/abolish death penalty	N	49.	Bar unions equal voice in pension	Y
12.	Req conspiracy-price fixing cases	N	50.	Bar assembly of chemical weapons	Y
13.	Unemployment benefits extension	Y	51.	Ban plutonium/uranium production	Y
14.	Tissue use of aborted fetuses	Y	52.	Cap MX missile deployment at 50	Y
15.	Bar replacement of union strikers	Y	53.	Allow $3b for 2 stealth bombers	N
16.	Hold foreign aid at $15b for '92	N	54.	Publish bio-warfare experiments	Y
17.	Restore space station funding	Y	55.	Raise minimum wage-veto override	Y
18.	Civil Rights Act of 1991	Y	56.	Bar transfer of FS-X technology	Y
19.	Unlimited damages-discrimination	N	57.	Cut defense and raise domestic $	N
20.	Eliminate funds for supercollider	Y	58.	Uniform poll closing in 48 states	N
21.	Terminate SDI except for research	N	59.	Req foreign investment disclosure	Y
22.	Req 7-day handgun waiting period	N	60.	Textile import quotas-veto override	N
23.	Provide $30b for failed S&Ls	Y	61.	Bar abortion funding in Wash, DC	Y
24.	Allow use of force against Iraq	Y	62.	Notify spouses of AIDS+ carriers	N
25.	Allow $15b in foreign aid for '91	N	63.	Seize conveyance-drug trafficking	N
26.	Revise & extend legal immigration	Y	64.	South Africa sanctions	Y
27.	Suspend aid to Angolan rebels	Y	65.	60 days' notice of plant closings	+
28.	Democratic tax plan proposals	Y	66.	Close unneeded military bases	N
29.	Cut defense 5% across the board	N	67.	Keep welfare reform within $2.8b	Y
30.	Textile import quotas-veto override	N	68.	Allow children housing exclusion	N
31.	Abortion service for military abroad	Y	69.	Shift $400m of NASA to homeless	N
32.	Limits on high income farmers	N	70.	Cap Medicare patients' liability	Y
33.	Family medical leave-veto override	N	71.	Prohibit employee polygraph testing	Y
34.	Req submission of balanced budget	Y	72.	Allow CIA to fund Contras	N
35.	Balanced budget amendment	N	73.	Revise unfair trade practices	Y
36.	Amendment to ban flag desecration	N	74.	Focus SDI on accidental launch	Y
37.	Reauthorize Amtrak-veto override	Y	75.	Bar Air Force $ for MX missile	N
38.	Retraining aid for coal miners	Y	76.	Allow "real" increase in defense	X

SLATTERY, JIM (continued)

77. Troop reduction in Europe of 50%	N	
78. Ban nuclear tests above 1 kiloton	N	
79. Ban anti-satellite missile tests	N	
80. Observe certain limits of SALT II	Y	
81. Restore four Civil Rights laws	Y	
82. Prohibit aliens as strikebreakers	Y	
83. Allow military malpractice suits	Y	
84. Approval of $36m in Contra aid	N	
85. $18b deficit reduction compromise	Y	
86. Welfare reform of $5.7b for 5 years	Y	
87. Raise taxes $12b/cut spending $3b	Y	
88. Board to assess occupational risk	N	
89. Balanced budget by '93-via targets	Y	
90. Bar licensing of two nuclear plants	Y	
91. Remove victims compensation cap	N	
92. Catastrophic health insurance	N	
93. Ban airline smoking-2 hours or less	Y	
94. $1b/two year aid for the homeless	Y	
95. Bar non-unions in union companies	Y	
96. Increase FSLIC rescue to $15b	N	
97. Impose quotas to lower trade deficit	Y	
98. Reduce discretionary budget 21%	Y	
99. Immigration reform/alien amnesty	Y	
100. South Africa sanctions-veto override	Y	
101. Tax overhaul to revise income tax	Y	
102. Use of military in drug war	Y	
103. Delete 12 MX/add conventional wpn	Y	
104. Raise speed limit to 65 mph	Y	
105. Require Pentagon to buy US goods	N	
106. AIDS insurance non-discrimination	N	
107. Prohibit Saudi arms sales	Y	
108. Ease Gun Control Act of 1968	Y	

109. Bar interstate handgun transport	N
110. Make company emissions known	N
111. Allow toxic victims to sue in fed ct	N
112. Superfund waste cleanup of $10b	N
113. 90 days notice of plant closings	Y
114. $20b in Medicare cuts/tax increases	Y
115. Spending cuts and tax increases	N
116. Set school lunch lmt-250% poverty	N
117. $75m for youth work projects	N
118. Allow Angolan military assistance	Y
119. Suspend defense payments for abuse	N
120. Drop SS COLAs/$12b tax increase	Y
121. Approve $1.5b for 21 MX missiles	N
122. Emergency farm credit/revisions	Y
123. Duty on Taiwan/Hong Kong/S Korea	Y
124. Limit steel imports to 17%	N
125. Cut $ to schools that bar prayer	N
126. $50b-taxes; cut Medicare/spending	N
127. Limit Pershing II/cruise in Europe	N
128. Delete $7.1b for 34 B-1 bombers	N
129. Bar purchase of Sergeant York guns	N
130. El Salvador military/economic aid	N
131. Bar mining of Nicaraguan waters	Y
132. Physician fee freeze for Medicare	N
133. $49b in "sin"/phone/insurance taxes	Y
134. Allow sale of Conrail	N
135. Equal Rights Amendment	Y
136. Authorize Marines in Lebanon	Y
137. Eminent domain for coal companies	N
138. Prohibit EPA clean air sanctions	N
139. SS retirement age increase/reforms	Y

Presidential Support Score: 1991 - 38%   1990 - 32%

MEYERS, JAN -- Kansas 3rd District [Republican]. Counties of Johnson, Linn, Miami and Wyandotte. Prior Terms: 1985-92. Born: July 20, 1928; Lincoln, NE. Education: William Woods College (A.F.A.); University of Nebraska (B.A.). Occupation: State senator (1972-1984); Overland Park city councilwoman and president (1967-1972); assistant, advertising and public relations, KFAB Radio, and retail sales, Lincoln, NE.

1. Protection to Haitian refugees	N	
2. Raise tax on wealthy; lower others	N	
3. Investigate Reagan hostage delay	N	
4. Campaign finance revisions	N	
5. Unpaid leave to care for children	N	
6. Restrict NEA use of funds	Y	
7. Bar race-bias claim/habeas corpus	Y	
8. Ban race as death sentence factor	Y	
9. Exceptions to exclusionary rule	Y	
10. Allow sale of assault weapons	N	
11. Life in prison/abolish death penalty	N	
12. Req conspiracy-price fixing cases	N	
13. Unemployment benefits extension	N	
14. Tissue use of aborted fetuses	Y	
15. Bar replacement of union strikers	N	
16. Hold foreign aid at $15b for '92	Y	
17. Restore space station funding	Y	
18. Civil Rights Act of 1991	N	
19. Unlimited damages-discrimination	N	
20. Eliminate funds for supercollider	Y	
21. Terminate SDI except for research	N	
22. Req 7-day handgun waiting period	Y	

23. Provide $30b for failed S&Ls	Y
24. Allow use of force against Iraq	Y
25. Allow $15b in foreign aid for '91	Y
26. Revise & extend legal immigration	N
27. Suspend aid to Angolan rebels	N
28. Democratic tax plan proposals	N
29. Cut defense 5% across the board	N
30. Textile import quotas-veto override	N
31. Abortion service for military abroad	Y
32. Limits on high income farmers	N
33. Family medical leave-veto override	N
34. Req submission of balanced budget	Y
35. Balanced budget amendment	Y
36. Amendment to ban flag desecration	Y
37. Reauthorize Amtrak-veto override	Y
38. Retraining aid for coal miners	N
39. Suspend El Salvador military aid	N
40. Expand child care aid/tax credit	N
41. Raise House salary/omit honoraria	N
42. Toughen oil-spill liability	Y
43. Restitution to Japanese interned	N
44. Protect Chinese & C.A. nationals	N

MEYERS, JAN (continued)

45. Abortion $ for rape/incest cases	Y	
46. Allow religious schools to bar gays	Y	
47. Bar broadcaster fairness doctrine	Y	
48. Bar cap gains cut/reinstate IRA	N	
49. Bar unions equal voice in pension	Y	
50. Bar assembly of chemical weapons	N	
51. Ban plutonium/uranium production	Y	
52. Cap MX missile deployment at 50	Y	
53. Allow $3b for 2 stealth bombers	N	
54. Publish bio-warfare experiments	Y	
55. Raise minimum wage-veto override	N	
56. Bar transfer of FS-X technology	N	
57. Cut defense and raise domestic $	N	
58. Uniform poll closing in 48 states	N	
59. Req foreign investment disclosure	N	
60. Textile import quotas-veto override	N	
61. Bar abortion funding in Wash, DC	N	
62. Notify spouses of AIDS+ carriers	Y	
63. Seize conveyance-drug trafficking	Y	
64. South Africa sanctions	?	
65. 60 days' notice of plant closings	N	
66. Close unneeded military bases	Y	
67. Keep welfare reform within $2.8b	Y	
68. Allow children housing exclusion	Y	
69. Shift $400m of NASA to homeless	N	
70. Cap Medicare patients' liability	Y	
71. Prohibit employee polygraph testing	N	
72. Allow CIA to fund Contras	Y	
73. Revise unfair trade practices	N	
74. Focus SDI on accidental launch	Y	
75. Bar Air Force $ for MX missile	N	
76. Allow "real" increase in defense	N	
77. Troop reduction in Europe of 50%	N	
78. Ban nuclear tests above 1 kiloton	Y	
79. Ban anti-satellite missile tests	N	
80. Observe certain limits of SALT II	N	
81. Restore four Civil Rights laws	Y	
82. Prohibit aliens as strikebreakers	Y	
83. Allow military malpractice suits	Y	

84. Approval of $36m in Contra aid	Y	
85. $18b deficit reduction compromise	N	
86. Welfare reform of $5.7b for 5 years	N	
87. Raise taxes $12b/cut spending $3b	N	
88. Board to assess occupational risk	N	
89. Balanced budget by '93-via targets	Y	
90. Bar licensing of two nuclear plants	N	
91. Remove victims compensation cap	N	
92. Catastrophic health insurance	N	
93. Ban airline smoking-2 hours or less	Y	
94. $1b/two year aid for the homeless	Y	
95. Bar non-unions in union companies	N	
96. Increase FSLIC rescue to $15b	Y	
97. Impose quotas to lower trade deficit	N	
98. Reduce discretionary budget 21%	Y	
99. Immigration reform/alien amnesty	N	
100. South Africa sanctions-veto override	Y	
101. Tax overhaul to revise income tax	Y	
102. Use of military in drug war	Y	
103. Delete 12 MX/add conventional wpn	N	
104. Raise speed limit to 65 mph	N	
105. Require Pentagon to buy US goods	N	
106. AIDS insurance non-discrimination	N	
107. Prohibit Saudi arms sales	Y	
108. Ease Gun Control Act of 1968	Y	
109. Bar interstate handgun transport	Y	
110. Make company emissions known	N	
111. Allow toxic victims to sue in fed ct	N	
112. Superfund waste cleanup of $10b	Y	
113. 90 days notice of plant closings	N	
114. $20b in Medicare cuts/tax increases	N	
115. Spending cuts and tax increases	N	
116. Set school lunch lmt-250% poverty	Y	
117. $75m for youth work projects	?	
118. Allow Angolan military assistance	Y	
119. Suspend defense payments for abuse	Y	
120. Drop SS COLAs/$12b tax increase	N	
121. Approve $1.5b for 21 MX missiles	Y	
122. Emergency farm credit/revisions	Y	

Presidential Support Score: 1991 - 68%   1990 - 65%

GLICKMAN, DAN -- Kansas 4th District [Democrat]. Counties of Harper, Kingman, Reno, Sedgwick and Sumner. Prior Terms: 1977-92. Born: November 24, 1944; Wichita, KS. Education: University of Michigan (B.A.); George Washington University (J.D.). Occupation: Attorney; businessman; trial attorney for U.S. Securities and Exchange Commission (1969-70); member, Wichita Board of Education.

1. Protection to Haitian refugees	Y	
2. Raise tax on wealthy; lower others	N	
3. Investigate Reagan hostage delay	Y	
4. Campaign finance revisions	Y	
5. Unpaid leave to care for children	N	
6. Restrict NEA use of funds	Y	
7. Bar race-bias claim/habeas corpus	Y	
8. Ban race as death sentence factor	N	
9. Exceptions to exclusionary rule	N	
10. Allow sale of assault weapons	N	
11. Life in prison/abolish death penalty	N	
12. Req conspiracy-price fixing cases	N	
13. Unemployment benefits extension	Y	
14. Tissue use of aborted fetuses	Y	
15. Bar replacement of union strikers	Y	

16. Hold foreign aid at $15b for '92	Y	
17. Restore space station funding	Y	
18. Civil Rights Act of 1991	Y	
19. Unlimited damages-discrimination	N	
20. Eliminate funds for supercollider	Y	
21. Terminate SDI except for research	N	
22. Req 7-day handgun waiting period	Y	
23. Provide $30b for failed S&Ls	N	
24. Allow use of force against Iraq	N	
25. Allow $15b in foreign aid for '91	?	
26. Revise & extend legal immigration	?	
27. Suspend aid to Angolan rebels	Y	
28. Democratic tax plan proposals	Y	
29. Cut defense 5% across the board	N	
30. Textile import quotas-veto override	N	

GLICKMAN, DAN (continued)

31. Abortion service for military abroad	Y	88. Board to assess occupational risk	N
32. Limits on high income farmers	N	89. Balanced budget by '93-via targets	Y
33. Family medical leave-veto override	N	90. Bar licensing of two nuclear plants	Y
34. Req submission of balanced budget	Y	91. Remove victims compensation cap	Y
35. Balanced budget amendment	N	92. Catastrophic health insurance	Y
36. Amendment to ban flag desecration	N	93. Ban airline smoking-2 hours or less	Y
37. Reauthorize Amtrak-veto override	Y	94. $1b/two year aid for the homeless	Y
38. Retraining aid for coal miners	Y	95. Bar non-unions in union companies	Y
39. Suspend El Salvador military aid	Y	96. Increase FSLIC rescue to $15b	Y
40. Expand child care aid/tax credit	Y	97. Impose quotas to lower trade deficit	N
41. Raise House salary/omit honoraria	Y	98. Reduce discretionary budget 21%	Y
42. Toughen oil-spill liability	Y	99. Immigration reform/alien amnesty	Y
43. Restitution to Japanese interned	Y	100. South Africa sanctions-veto override	Y
44. Protect Chinese & C.A. nationals	Y	101. Tax overhaul to revise income tax	Y
45. Abortion $ for rape/incest cases	Y	102. Use of military in drug war	N
46. Allow religious schools to bar gays	Y	103. Delete 12 MX/add conventional wpn	Y
47. Bar broadcaster fairness doctrine	N	104. Raise speed limit to 65 mph	Y
48. Bar cap gains cut/reinstate IRA	Y	105. Require Pentagon to buy US goods	N
49. Bar unions equal voice in pension	Y	106. AIDS insurance non-discrimination	N
50. Bar assembly of chemical weapons	Y	107. Prohibit Saudi arms sales	Y
51. Ban plutonium/uranium production	Y	108. Ease Gun Control Act of 1968	Y
52. Cap MX missile deployment at 50	Y	109. Bar interstate handgun transport	N
53. Allow $3b for 2 stealth bombers	N	110. Make company emissions known	Y
54. Publish bio-warfare experiments	Y	111. Allow toxic victims to sue in fed ct	N
55. Raise minimum wage-veto override	Y	112. Superfund waste cleanup of $10b	N
56. Bar transfer of FS-X technology	Y	113. 90 days notice of plant closings	N
57. Cut defense and raise domestic $	N	114. $20b in Medicare cuts/tax increases	Y
58. Uniform poll closing in 48 states	N	115. Spending cuts and tax increases	Y
59. Req foreign investment disclosure	Y	116. Set school lunch lmt-250% poverty	N
60. Textile import quotas-veto override	N	117. $75m for youth work projects	N
61. Bar abortion funding in Wash, DC	N	118. Allow Angolan military assistance	Y
62. Notify spouses of AIDS+ carriers	N	119. Suspend defense payments for abuse	N
63. Seize conveyance-drug trafficking	Y	120. Drop SS COLAs/$12b tax increase	N
64. South Africa sanctions	Y	121. Approve $1.5b for 21 MX missiles	N
65. 60 days' notice of plant closings	Y	122. Emergency farm credit/revisions	Y
66. Close unneeded military bases	N	123. Duty on Taiwan/Hong Kong/S Korea	Y
67. Keep welfare reform within $2.8b	Y	124. Limit steel imports to 17%	N
68. Allow children housing exclusion	N	125. Cut $ to schools that bar prayer	N
69. Shift $400m of NASA to homeless	N	126. $50b-taxes; cut Medicare/spending	Y
70. Cap Medicare patients' liability	Y	127. Limit Pershing II/cruise in Europe	N
71. Prohibit employee polygraph testing	Y	128. Delete $7.1b for 34 B-1 bombers	N
72. Allow CIA to fund Contras	N	129. Bar purchase of Sergeant York guns	N
73. Revise unfair trade practices	Y	130. El Salvador military/economic aid	N
74. Focus SDI on accidental launch	Y	131. Bar mining of Nicaraguan waters	Y
75. Bar Air Force $ for MX missile	N	132. Physician fee freeze for Medicare	N
76. Allow "real" increase in defense	Y	133. $49b in "sin"/phone/insurance taxes	Y
77. Troop reduction in Europe of 50%	Y	134. Allow sale of Conrail	Y
78. Ban nuclear tests above 1 kiloton	Y	135. Equal Rights Amendment	Y
79. Ban anti-satellite missile tests	Y	136. Authorize Marines in Lebanon	Y
80. Observe certain limits of SALT II	Y	137. Eminent domain for coal companies	N
81. Restore four Civil Rights laws	Y	138. Prohibit EPA clean air sanctions	N
82. Prohibit aliens as strikebreakers	Y	139. SS retirement age increase/reforms	Y
83. Allow military malpractice suits	Y	140. Auto domestic content requirement	N
84. Approval of $36m in Contra aid	N	141. Delete jobs program funding	N
85. $18b deficit reduction compromise	Y	142. Highway-gas tax bill	N
86. Welfare reform of $5.7b for 5 years	Y	143. Cut $5b from defense for Medicare	N
87. Raise taxes $12b/cut spending $3b	Y	144. Emergency housing aid of $1b	Y

Presidential Support Score: 1991 - 35% 1990 - 27%

NICHOLS, DICK -- Kansas 5th District [Republican]. Counties of Allen, Anderson, Bourbon, Butler, Chase, Chautauqua, Cherokee, Coffey, Cowley, Crawford, Elk, Franklin, Greenwood, Harvey, Labette, Lyon, McPherson, Marion, Montgomery, Morris, Neosho,

NICHOLS, DICK (continued)
Osage, Wabaunsee, Wilson and Woodson. Prior Terms: 1991-92. Born: April 29, 1926; Fort Scott, KS. Education: Kansas State University (dual B.S.); University of Wisconsin; Northwestern University. Military Service: U.S. Navy. Occupation: State agriculture board informational counsel; farm broadcaster; banker; Home State Bank & Trust president (1969-79) and chairman (1979-90); president, Home State Bancshares, Inc. (1979-90).

1. Protection to Haitian refugees	N	13. Unemployment benefits extension	N
2. Raise tax on wealthy; lower others	N	14. Tissue use of aborted fetuses	N
3. Investigate Reagan hostage delay	N	15. Bar replacement of union strikers	N
4. Campaign finance revisions	N	16. Hold foreign aid at $15b for '92	Y
5. Unpaid leave to care for children	N	17. Restore space station funding	Y
6. Restrict NEA use of funds	Y	18. Civil Rights Act of 1991	N
7. Bar race-bias claim/habeas corpus	Y	19. Unlimited damages-discrimination	N
8. Ban race as death sentence factor	Y	20. Eliminate funds for supercollider	N
9. Exceptions to exclusionary rule	Y	21. Terminate SDI except for research	N
10. Allow sale of assault weapons	Y	22. Req 7-day handgun waiting period	N
11. Life in prison/abolish death penalty	N	23. Provide $30b for failed S&Ls	Y
12. Req conspiracy-price fixing cases	Y	24. Allow use of force against Iraq	Y

Presidential Support Score: 1991 - 77%

KENTUCKY

HUBBARD, CARROLL, Jr. -- Kentucky 1st District [Democrat]. Counties of Ballard, Butler, Caldwell, Calloway, Carlisle, Christian, Crittenden, Fulton, Graves, Henderson, Hickman, Hopkins, Livingston, Logan, Lyon, McCracken, McLean, Marshall, Muhlenberg, Ohio, Todd, Trigg, Union and Webster. Prior Terms: 1975-92. Born: July 7, 1937; Murray, KY. Education: Georgetown College (B.A.); University of Louisville (J.D.). Occupation: Attorney; Kentucky senator (1967-74).

1. Protection to Haitian refugees	Y	31. Abortion service for military abroad	Y
2. Raise tax on wealthy; lower others	N	32. Limits on high income farmers	N
3. Investigate Reagan hostage delay	Y	33. Family medical leave-veto override	N
4. Campaign finance revisions	Y	34. Req submission of balanced budget	Y
5. Unpaid leave to care for children	Y	35. Balanced budget amendment	Y
6. Restrict NEA use of funds	Y	36. Amendment to ban flag desecration	Y
7. Bar race-bias claim/habeas corpus	Y	37. Reauthorize Amtrak-veto override	N
8. Ban race as death sentence factor	Y	38. Retraining aid for coal miners	Y
9. Exceptions to exclusionary rule	Y	39. Suspend El Salvador military aid	Y
10. Allow sale of assault weapons	Y	40. Expand child care aid/tax credit	Y
11. Life in prison/abolish death penalty	N	41. Raise House salary/omit honoraria	Y
12. Req conspiracy-price fixing cases	Y	42. Toughen oil-spill liability	N
13. Unemployment benefits extension	Y	43. Restitution to Japanese interned	N
14. Tissue use of aborted fetuses	Y	44. Protect Chinese & C.A. nationals	Y
15. Bar replacement of union strikers	Y	45. Abortion $ for rape/incest cases	Y
16. Hold foreign aid at $15b for '92	N	46. Allow religious schools to bar gays	Y
17. Restore space station funding	Y	47. Bar broadcaster fairness doctrine	Y
18. Civil Rights Act of 1991	Y	48. Bar cap gains cut/reinstate IRA	N
19. Unlimited damages-discrimination	N	49. Bar unions equal voice in pension	Y
20. Eliminate funds for supercollider	N	50. Bar assembly of chemical weapons	N
21. Terminate SDI except for research	?	51. Ban plutonium/uranium production	Y
22. Req 7-day handgun waiting period	Y	52. Cap MX missile deployment at 50	Y
23. Provide $30b for failed S&Ls	N	53. Allow $3b for 2 stealth bombers	Y
24. Allow use of force against Iraq	Y	54. Publish bio-warfare experiments	Y
25. Allow $15b in foreign aid for '91	N	55. Raise minimum wage-veto override	?
26. Revise & extend legal immigration	N	56. Bar transfer of FS-X technology	Y
27. Suspend aid to Angolan rebels	N	57. Cut defense and raise domestic $	N
28. Democratic tax plan proposals	N	58. Uniform poll closing in 48 states	Y
29. Cut defense 5% across the board	Y	59. Req foreign investment disclosure	N
30. Textile import quotas-veto override	Y	60. Textile import quotas-veto override	Y

HUBBARD, CARROLL, Jr. (continued)

61. Bar abortion funding in Wash, DC	Y	
62. Notify spouses of AIDS+ carriers	Y	
63. Seize conveyance-drug trafficking	N	
64. South Africa sanctions	Y	
65. 60 days' notice of plant closings	Y	
66. Close unneeded military bases	Y	
67. Keep welfare reform within $2.8b	Y	
68. Allow children housing exclusion	N	
69. Shift $400m of NASA to homeless	Y	
70. Cap Medicare patients' liability	Y	
71. Prohibit employee polygraph testing	Y	
72. Allow CIA to fund Contras	Y	
73. Revise unfair trade practices	#	
74. Focus SDI on accidental launch	N	
75. Bar Air Force $ for MX missile	N	
76. Allow "real" increase in defense	Y	
77. Troop reduction in Europe of 50%	Y	
78. Ban nuclear tests above 1 kiloton	N	
79. Ban anti-satellite missile tests	Y	
80. Observe certain limits of SALT II	N	
81. Restore four Civil Rights laws	N	
82. Prohibit aliens as strikebreakers	Y	
83. Allow military malpractice suits	Y	
84. Approval of $36m in Contra aid	Y	
85. $18b deficit reduction compromise	N	
86. Welfare reform of $5.7b for 5 years	Y	
87. Raise taxes $12b/cut spending $3b	N	
88. Board to assess occupational risk	Y	
89. Balanced budget by '93-via targets	N	
90. Bar licensing of two nuclear plants	N	
91. Remove victims compensation cap	?	
92. Catastrophic health insurance	Y	
93. Ban airline smoking-2 hours or less	N	
94. $1b/two year aid for the homeless	Y	
95. Bar non-unions in union companies	N	
96. Increase FSLIC rescue to $15b	Y	
97. Impose quotas to lower trade deficit	Y	
98. Reduce discretionary budget 21%	Y	
99. Immigration reform/alien amnesty	N	
100. South Africa sanctions-veto override	Y	
101. Tax overhaul to revise income tax	N	
102. Use of military in drug war	Y	

103. Delete 12 MX/add conventional wpn	N
104. Raise speed limit to 65 mph	Y
105. Require Pentagon to buy US goods	Y
106. AIDS insurance non-discrimination	N
107. Prohibit Saudi arms sales	Y
108. Ease Gun Control Act of 1968	Y
109. Bar interstate handgun transport	N
110. Make company emissions known	N
111. Allow toxic victims to sue in fed ct	N
112. Superfund waste cleanup of $10b	N
113. 90 days notice of plant closings	?
114. $20b in Medicare cuts/tax increases	N
115. Spending cuts and tax increases	N
116. Set school lunch lmt-250% poverty	N
117. $75m for youth work projects	N
118. Allow Angolan military assistance	Y
119. Suspend defense payments for abuse	N
120. Drop SS COLAs/$12b tax increase	N
121. Approve $1.5b for 21 MX missiles	Y
122. Emergency farm credit/revisions	Y
123. Duty on Taiwan/Hong Kong/S Korea	N
124. Limit steel imports to 17%	Y
125. Cut $ to schools that bar prayer	?
126. $50b-taxes; cut Medicare/spending	N
127. Limit Pershing II/cruise in Europe	N
128. Delete $7.1b for 34 B-1 bombers	N
129. Bar purchase of Sergeant York guns	N
130. El Salvador military/economic aid	Y
131. Bar mining of Nicaraguan waters	Y
132. Physician fee freeze for Medicare	Y
133. $49b in "sin"/phone/insurance taxes	N
134. Allow sale of Conrail	N
135. Equal Rights Amendment	N
136. Authorize Marines in Lebanon	N
137. Eminent domain for coal companies	N
138. Prohibit EPA clean air sanctions	Y
139. SS retirement age increase/reforms	N
140. Auto domestic content requirement	Y
141. Delete jobs program funding	Y
142. Highway-gas tax bill	N
143. Cut $5b from defense for Medicare	N
144. Emergency housing aid of $1b	Y

Presidential Support Score: 1991 - 37% 1990 - 42%

NATCHER, WILLIAM H. -- Kentucky 2nd District [Democrat]. Counties of Allen, Barren, Breckenridge, Bullitt, Daviess, Edmonson, Grayson, Hancock, Hardin, Hart, Larus, Marion, Meade, Nelson, Simpson, Spencer, Warren and Washington. Prior Terms: 1953 (Special Election)-1992. Born: September 11, 1909; Bowling Green, KY. Education: Western Kentucky State College (A.B.); Ohio State University (LL.B.). Military Service: U.S. Navy, 1942-45. Occupation: Attorney; federal conciliation commissioner (1936-37); Warren County attorney (1937-49); commonwealth attorney (1951-53).

1. Protection to Haitian refugees	Y	
2. Raise tax on wealthy; lower others	N	
3. Investigate Reagan hostage delay	Y	
4. Campaign finance revisions	Y	
5. Unpaid leave to care for children	Y	
6. Restrict NEA use of funds	N	
7. Bar race-bias claim/habeas corpus	N	
8. Ban race as death sentence factor	Y	
9. Exceptions to exclusionary rule	N	
10. Allow sale of assault weapons	Y	

11. Life in prison/abolish death penalty	N
12. Req conspiracy-price fixing cases	Y
13. Unemployment benefits extension	Y
14. Tissue use of aborted fetuses	Y
15. Bar replacement of union strikers	Y
16. Hold foreign aid at $15b for '92	Y
17. Restore space station funding	N
18. Civil Rights Act of 1991	Y
19. Unlimited damages-discrimination	N
20. Eliminate funds for supercollider	N

NATCHER, WILLIAM H. (continued)

21. Terminate SDI except for research	N	
22. Req 7-day handgun waiting period	N	
23. Provide $30b for failed S&Ls	Y	
24. Allow use of force against Iraq	N	
25. Allow $15b in foreign aid for '91	Y	
26. Revise & extend legal immigration	N	
27. Suspend aid to Angolan rebels	Y	
28. Democratic tax plan proposals	Y	
29. Cut defense 5% across the board	N	
30. Textile import quotas-veto override	Y	
31. Abortion service for military abroad	N	
32. Limits on high income farmers	N	
33. Family medical leave-veto override	Y	
34. Req submission of balanced budget	Y	
35. Balanced budget amendment	Y	
36. Amendment to ban flag desecration	Y	
37. Reauthorize Amtrak-veto override	Y	
38. Retraining aid for coal miners	Y	
39. Suspend El Salvador military aid	Y	
40. Expand child care aid/tax credit	Y	
41. Raise House salary/omit honoraria	Y	
42. Toughen oil-spill liability	Y	
43. Restitution to Japanese interned	Y	
44. Protect Chinese & C.A. nationals	Y	
45. Abortion $ for rape/incest cases	N	
46. Allow religious schools to bar gays	Y	
47. Bar broadcaster fairness doctrine	Y	
48. Bar cap gains cut/reinstate IRA	N	
49. Bar unions equal voice in pension	Y	
50. Bar assembly of chemical weapons	Y	
51. Ban plutonium/uranium production	Y	
52. Cap MX missile deployment at 50	Y	
53. Allow $3b for 2 stealth bombers	N	
54. Publish bio-warfare experiments	Y	
55. Raise minimum wage-veto override	Y	
56. Bar transfer of FS-X technology	Y	
57. Cut defense and raise domestic $	N	
58. Uniform poll closing in 48 states	N	
59. Req foreign investment disclosure	Y	
60. Textile import quotas-veto override	N	
61. Bar abortion funding in Wash, DC	N	
62. Notify spouses of AIDS+ carriers	N	
63. Seize conveyance-drug trafficking	N	
64. South Africa sanctions	Y	
65. 60 days' notice of plant closings	Y	
66. Close unneeded military bases	N	
67. Keep welfare reform within $2.8b	N	
68. Allow children housing exclusion	N	
69. Shift $400m of NASA to homeless	N	
70. Cap Medicare patients' liability	Y	
71. Prohibit employee polygraph testing	Y	
72. Allow CIA to fund Contras	N	
73. Revise unfair trade practices	Y	
74. Focus SDI on accidental launch	Y	
75. Bar Air Force $ for MX missile	N	
76. Allow "real" increase in defense	N	
77. Troop reduction in Europe of 50%	N	
78. Ban nuclear tests above 1 kiloton	Y	
79. Ban anti-satellite missile tests	N	
80. Observe certain limits of SALT II	Y	
81. Restore four Civil Rights laws	Y	
82. Prohibit aliens as strikebreakers	Y	

83. Allow military malpractice suits	Y	
84. Approval of $36m in Contra aid	N	
85. $18b deficit reduction compromise	Y	
86. Welfare reform of $5.7b for 5 years	Y	
87. Raise taxes $12b/cut spending $3b	Y	
88. Board to assess occupational risk	Y	
89. Balanced budget by '93-via targets	N	
90. Bar licensing of two nuclear plants	N	
91. Remove victims compensation cap	N	
92. Catastrophic health insurance	Y	
93. Ban airline smoking-2 hours or less	N	
94. $1b/two year aid for the homeless	Y	
95. Bar non-unions in union companies	Y	
96. Increase FSLIC rescue to $15b	N	
97. Impose quotas to lower trade deficit	Y	
98. Reduce discretionary budget 21%	N	
99. Immigration reform/alien amnesty	Y	
100. South Africa sanctions-veto override	Y	
101. Tax overhaul to revise income tax	Y	
102. Use of military in drug war	Y	
103. Delete 12 MX/add conventional wpn	N	
104. Raise speed limit to 65 mph	N	
105. Require Pentagon to buy US goods	Y	
106. AIDS insurance non-discrimination	Y	
107. Prohibit Saudi arms sales	Y	
108. Ease Gun Control Act of 1968	Y	
109. Bar interstate handgun transport	N	
110. Make company emissions known	N	
111. Allow toxic victims to sue in fed ct	Y	
112. Superfund waste cleanup of $10b	N	
113. 90 days notice of plant closings	Y	
114. $20b in Medicare cuts/tax increases	Y	
115. Spending cuts and tax increases	Y	
116. Set school lunch lmt-250% poverty	N	
117. $75m for youth work projects	Y	
118. Allow Angolan military assistance	N	
119. Suspend defense payments for abuse	N	
120. Drop SS COLAs/$12b tax increase	N	
121. Approve $1.5b for 21 MX missiles	N	
122. Emergency farm credit/revisions	Y	
123. Duty on Taiwan/Hong Kong/S Korea	Y	
124. Limit steel imports to 17%	Y	
125. Cut $ to schools that bar prayer	Y	
126. $50b-taxes; cut Medicare/spending	N	
127. Limit Pershing II/cruise in Europe	N	
128. Delete $7.1b for 34 B-1 bombers	N	
129. Bar purchase of Sergeant York guns	N	
130. El Salvador military/economic aid	N	
131. Bar mining of Nicaraguan waters	Y	
132. Physician fee freeze for Medicare	N	
133. $49b in "sin"/phone/insurance taxes	N	
134. Allow sale of Conrail	N	
135. Equal Rights Amendment	Y	
136. Authorize Marines in Lebanon	N	
137. Eminent domain for coal companies	N	
138. Prohibit EPA clean air sanctions	N	
139. SS retirement age increase/reforms	N	
140. Auto domestic content requirement	Y	
141. Delete jobs program funding	N	
142. Highway-gas tax bill	Y	
143. Cut $5b from defense for Medicare	Y	
144. Emergency housing aid of $1b	Y	

Presidential Support Score: 1991 - 35%   1990 - 29%

MAZZOLI, ROMANO L. -- Kentucky 3rd District [Democrat]. County of Jefferson (pt.). Prior Terms: 1971-92. Born: November 2, 1932; Louisville, KY. Education: University of Notre Dame (B.S.); University of Louisville (J.D.). Military Service: U.S. Army, 1954-56. Occupation: Attorney, Louisville & Nashville Railroad Co. (1960-62); attorney (1962-70); lecturer (1963-67); Kentucky senator (1967-70).

1.	Protection to Haitian refugees	Y	60.	Textile import quotas-veto override	N
2.	Raise tax on wealthy; lower others	N	61.	Bar abortion funding in Wash, DC	Y
3.	Investigate Reagan hostage delay	Y	62.	Notify spouses of AIDS+ carriers	N
4.	Campaign finance revisions	Y	63.	Seize conveyance-drug trafficking	N
5.	Unpaid leave to care for children	Y	64.	South Africa sanctions	+
6.	Restrict NEA use of funds	N	65.	60 days' notice of plant closings	Y
7.	Bar race-bias claim/habeas corpus	N	66.	Close unneeded military bases	Y
8.	Ban race as death sentence factor	N	67.	Keep welfare reform within $2.8b	N
9.	Exceptions to exclusionary rule	Y	68.	Allow children housing exclusion	N
10.	Allow sale of assault weapons	N	69.	Shift $400m of NASA to homeless	Y
11.	Life in prison/abolish death penalty	N	70.	Cap Medicare patients' liability	Y
12.	Req conspiracy-price fixing cases	N	71.	Prohibit employee polygraph testing	Y
13.	Unemployment benefits extension	Y	72.	Allow CIA to fund Contras	N
14.	Tissue use of aborted fetuses	Y	73.	Revise unfair trade practices	N
15.	Bar replacement of union strikers	Y	74.	Focus SDI on accidental launch	Y
16.	Hold foreign aid at $15b for '92	N	75.	Bar Air Force $ for MX missile	N
17.	Restore space station funding	N	76.	Allow "real" increase in defense	N
18.	Civil Rights Act of 1991	Y	77.	Troop reduction in Europe of 50%	--
19.	Unlimited damages-discrimination	N	78.	Ban nuclear tests above 1 kiloton	Y
20.	Eliminate funds for supercollider	N	79.	Ban anti-satellite missile tests	Y
21.	Terminate SDI except for research	N	80.	Observe certain limits of SALT II	Y
22.	Req 7-day handgun waiting period	Y	81.	Restore four Civil Rights laws	Y
23.	Provide $30b for failed S&Ls	N	82.	Prohibit aliens as strikebreakers	Y
24.	Allow use of force against Iraq	N	83.	Allow military malpractice suits	Y
25.	Allow $15b in foreign aid for '91	N	84.	Approval of $36m in Contra aid	N
26.	Revise & extend legal immigration	Y	85.	$18b deficit reduction compromise	Y
27.	Suspend aid to Angolan rebels	Y	86.	Welfare reform of $5.7b for 5 years	Y
28.	Democratic tax plan proposals	Y	87.	Raise taxes $12b/cut spending $3b	N
29.	Cut defense 5% across the board	Y	88.	Board to assess occupational risk	Y
30.	Textile import quotas-veto override	N	89.	Balanced budget by '93-via targets	Y
31.	Abortion service for military abroad	N	90.	Bar licensing of two nuclear plants	N
32.	Limits on high income farmers	Y	91.	Remove victims compensation cap	N
33.	Family medical leave-veto override	Y	92.	Catastrophic health insurance	Y
34.	Req submission of balanced budget	Y	93.	Ban airline smoking-2 hours or less	Y
35.	Balanced budget amendment	N	94.	$1b/two year aid for the homeless	Y
36.	Amendment to ban flag desecration	Y	95.	Bar non-unions in union companies	N
37.	Reauthorize Amtrak-veto override	Y	96.	Increase FSLIC rescue to $15b	Y
38.	Retraining aid for coal miners	Y	97.	Impose quotas to lower trade deficit	N
39.	Suspend El Salvador military aid	Y	98.	Reduce discretionary budget 21%	Y
40.	Expand child care aid/tax credit	Y	99.	Immigration reform/alien amnesty	Y
41.	Raise House salary/omit honoraria	Y	100.	South Africa sanctions-veto override	Y
42.	Toughen oil-spill liability	Y	101.	Tax overhaul to revise income tax	Y
43.	Restitution to Japanese interned	Y	102.	Use of military in drug war	N
44.	Protect Chinese & C.A. nationals	Y	103.	Delete 12 MX/add conventional wpn	Y
45.	Abortion $ for rape/incest cases	N	104.	Raise speed limit to 65 mph	N
46.	Allow religious schools to bar gays	N	105.	Require Pentagon to buy US goods	Y
47.	Bar broadcaster fairness doctrine	Y	106.	AIDS insurance non-discrimination	N
48.	Bar cap gains cut/reinstate IRA	N	107.	Prohibit Saudi arms sales	N
49.	Bar unions equal voice in pension	Y	108.	Ease Gun Control Act of 1968	Y
50.	Bar assembly of chemical weapons	Y	109.	Bar interstate handgun transport	Y
51.	Ban plutonium/uranium production	Y	110.	Make company emissions known	N
52.	Cap MX missile deployment at 50	Y	111.	Allow toxic victims to sue in fed ct	N
53.	Allow $3b for 2 stealth bombers	N	112.	Superfund waste cleanup of $10b	N
54.	Publish bio-warfare experiments	Y	113.	90 days notice of plant closings	Y
55.	Raise minimum wage-veto override	N	114.	$20b in Medicare cuts/tax increases	Y
56.	Bar transfer of FS-X technology	N	115.	Spending cuts and tax increases	Y
57.	Cut defense and raise domestic $	N	116.	Set school lunch lmt-250% poverty	Y
58.	Uniform poll closing in 48 states	Y	117.	$75m for youth work projects	N
59.	Req foreign investment disclosure	N	118.	Allow Angolan military assistance	N

MAZZOLI, ROMANO L. (continued)

119. Suspend defense payments for abuse	Y	132. Physician fee freeze for Medicare	N
120. Drop SS COLAs/$12b tax increase	N	133. $49b in "sin"/phone/insurance taxes	N
121. Approve $1.5b for 21 MX missiles	N	134. Allow sale of Conrail	+
122. Emergency farm credit/revisions	N	135. Equal Rights Amendment	N
123. Duty on Taiwan/Hong Kong/S Korea	N	136. Authorize Marines in Lebanon	N
124. Limit steel imports to 17%	N	137. Eminent domain for coal companies	N
125. Cut $ to schools that bar prayer	N	138. Prohibit EPA clean air sanctions	N
126. $50b-taxes; cut Medicare/spending	Y	139. SS retirement age increase/reforms	Y
127. Limit Pershing II/cruise in Europe	N	140. Auto domestic content requirement	Y
128. Delete $7.1b for 34 B-1 bombers	Y	141. Delete jobs program funding	N
129. Bar purchase of Sergeant York guns	N	142. Highway-gas tax bill	Y
130. El Salvador military/economic aid	N	143. Cut $5b from defense for Medicare	N
131. Bar mining of Nicaraguan waters	Y	144. Emergency housing aid of $1b	Y

Presidential Support Score: 1991 - 38% 1990 - 31%

BUNNING, JIM -- Kentucky 4th District [Republican]. Counties of Boone, Campbell, Carroll, Gallatin, Grant, Henry, Jefferson (pt.), Kenton, Oldham, Owen, Pendleton and Trimble. Prior Terms: 1991-92. Born: Marhc 14, 1947; Lake Providence, LA. Education: Southern University and AGM College (B.A.); Harvard University Law School (J.D.). Military Service: U.S. Army, Judge Advocate General Corps. Occupation: U.S. Court of Appeals law clerk; lawyer; legislative assistant to Sen. Johnston; state senator (1981-90).

1. Protection to Haitian refugees	N	41. Raise House salary/omit honoraria	N
2. Raise tax on wealthy; lower others	N	42. Toughen oil-spill liability	?
3. Investigate Reagan hostage delay	N	43. Restitution to Japanese interned	N
4. Campaign finance revisions	N	44. Protect Chinese & C.A. nationals	N
5. Unpaid leave to care for children	N	45. Abortion $ for rape/incest cases	N
6. Restrict NEA use of funds	Y	46. Allow religious schools to bar gays	Y
7. Bar race-bias claim/habeas corpus	Y	47. Bar broadcaster fairness doctrine	Y
8. Ban race as death sentence factor	Y	48. Bar cap gains cut/reinstate IRA	N
9. Exceptions to exclusionary rule	Y	49. Bar unions equal voice in pension	Y
10. Allow sale of assault weapons	Y	50. Bar assembly of chemical weapons	N
11. Life in prison/abolish death penalty	N	51. Ban plutonium/uranium production	N
12. Req conspiracy-price fixing cases	Y	52. Cap MX missile deployment at 50	N
13. Unemployment benefits extension	N	53. Allow $3b for 2 stealth bombers	Y
14. Tissue use of aborted fetuses	N	54. Publish bio-warfare experiments	N
15. Bar replacement of union strikers	N	55. Raise minimum wage-veto override	N
16. Hold foreign aid at $15b for '92	N	56. Bar transfer of FS-X technology	N
17. Restore space station funding	N	57. Cut defense and raise domestic $	N
18. Civil Rights Act of 1991	N	58. Uniform poll closing in 48 states	N
19. Unlimited damages-discrimination	N	59. Req foreign investment disclosure	N
20. Eliminate funds for supercollider	Y	60. Textile import quotas-veto override	N
21. Terminate SDI except for research	N	61. Bar abortion funding in Wash, DC	Y
22. Req 7-day handgun waiting period	N	62. Notify spouses of AIDS+ carriers	Y
23. Provide $30b for failed S&Ls	Y	63. Seize conveyance-drug trafficking	N
24. Allow use of force against Iraq	Y	64. South Africa sanctions	?
25. Allow $15b in foreign aid for '91	N	65. 60 days' notice of plant closings	N
26. Revise & extend legal immigration	N	66. Close unneeded military bases	?
27. Suspend aid to Angolan rebels	N	67. Keep welfare reform within $2.8b	Y
28. Democratic tax plan proposals	N	68. Allow children housing exclusion	N
29. Cut defense 5% across the board	N	69. Shift $400m of NASA to homeless	N
30. Textile import quotas-veto override	N	70. Cap Medicare patients' liability	N
31. Abortion service for military abroad	N	71. Prohibit employee polygraph testing	N
32. Limits on high income farmers	N	72. Allow CIA to fund Contras	Y
33. Family medical leave-veto override	N	73. Revise unfair trade practices	N
34. Req submission of balanced budget	N	74. Focus SDI on accidental launch	N
35. Balanced budget amendment	Y	75. Bar Air Force $ for MX missile	N
36. Amendment to ban flag desecration	Y	76. Allow "real" increase in defense	Y
37. Reauthorize Amtrak-veto override	N	77. Troop reduction in Europe of 50%	N
38. Retraining aid for coal miners	Y	78. Ban nuclear tests above 1 kiloton	N
39. Suspend El Salvador military aid	N	79. Ban anti-satellite missile tests	N
40. Expand child care aid/tax credit	N	80. Observe certain limits of SALT II	N

BUNNING, JIM (continued)

81. Restore four Civil Rights laws	N	90. Bar licensing of two nuclear plants	N
82. Prohibit aliens as strikebreakers	N	91. Remove victims compensation cap	N
83. Allow military malpractice suits	Y	92. Catastrophic health insurance	N
84. Approval of $36m in Contra aid	Y	93. Ban airline smoking-2 hours or less	N
85. $18b deficit reduction compromise	N	94. $1b/two year aid for the homeless	N
86. Welfare reform of $5.7b for 5 years	N	95. Bar non-unions in union companies	N
87. Raise taxes $12b/cut spending $3b	N	96. Increase FSLIC rescue to $15b	Y
88. Board to assess occupational risk	N	97. Impose quotas to lower trade deficit	N
89. Balanced budget by '93-via targets	N	98. Reduce discretionary budget 21%	Y

Presidential Support Score: 1991 - 76% 1990 - 71%

ROGERS, HAROLD -- Kentucky 5th District [Republican]. Counties of Adair, Bell, Casey, Clay, Clinton, Cumberland, Estill, Garrard, Green, Harlan, Jackson Jessamine, Knox. Laurel, Lee, Leslie, Letcher (pt.), Lincoln, McCreary, Metcalfe, Monroe, Owsley, Pulaski, Rockcastle, Russell, Taylor, Wayne and Whitley. Prior Terms: 1981-92. Born: December 31, 1937; Barrier, KY. Education: University of Kentucky (A.B., LL.B.); Western Kentucky University. Military Service: U.S. National Gaurd, 1957-64. Occupation: Radio newsman and announcer; attorney; commonwealth attorney, Pulaskie and Rockcastle Counties (1969-80).

1. Protection to Haitian refugees	N	42. Toughen oil-spill liability	N
2. Raise tax on wealthy; lower others	N	43. Restitution to Japanese interned	N
3. Investigate Reagan hostage delay	N	44. Protect Chinese & C.A. nationals	N
4. Campaign finance revisions	N	45. Abortion $ for rape/incest cases	N
5. Unpaid leave to care for children	N	46. Allow religious schools to bar gays	Y
6. Restrict NEA use of funds	Y	47. Bar broadcaster fairness doctrine	Y
7. Bar race-bias claim/habeas corpus	Y	48. Bar cap gains cut/reinstate IRA	N
8. Ban race as death sentence factor	Y	49. Bar unions equal voice in pension	Y
9. Exceptions to exclusionary rule	Y	50. Bar assembly of chemical weapons	N
10. Allow sale of assault weapons	Y	51. Ban plutonium/uranium production	N
11. Life in prison/abolish death penalty	N	52. Cap MX missile deployment at 50	N
12. Req conspiracy-price fixing cases	Y	53. Allow $3b for 2 stealth bombers	N
13. Unemployment benefits extension	Y	54. Publish bio-warfare experiments	N
14. Tissue use of aborted fetuses	N	55. Raise minimum wage-veto override	N
15. Bar replacement of union strikers	N	56. Bar transfer of FS-X technology	N
16. Hold foreign aid at $15b for '92	N	57. Cut defense and raise domestic $	N
17. Restore space station funding	Y	58. Uniform poll closing in 48 states	N
18. Civil Rights Act of 1991	N	59. Req foreign investment disclosure	N
19. Unlimited damages-discrimination	N	60. Textile import quotas-veto override	Y
20. Eliminate funds for supercollider	N	61. Bar abortion funding in Wash, DC	Y
21. Terminate SDI except for research	--	62. Notify spouses of AIDS+ carriers	Y
22. Req 7-day handgun waiting period	N	63. Seize conveyance-drug trafficking	Y
23. Provide $30b for failed S&Ls	N	64. South Africa sanctions	N
24. Allow use of force against Iraq	Y	65. 60 days' notice of plant closings	N
25. Allow $15b in foreign aid for '91	N	66. Close unneeded military bases	Y
26. Revise & extend legal immigration	N	67. Keep welfare reform within $2.8b	Y
27. Suspend aid to Angolan rebels	N	68. Allow children housing exclusion	N
28. Democratic tax plan proposals	N	69. Shift $400m of NASA to homeless	?
29. Cut defense 5% across the board	N	70. Cap Medicare patients' liability	Y
30. Textile import quotas-veto override	Y	71. Prohibit employee polygraph testing	N
31. Abortion service for military abroad	N	72. Allow CIA to fund Contras	Y
32. Limits on high income farmers	N	73. Revise unfair trade practices	N
33. Family medical leave-veto override	N	74. Focus SDI on accidental launch	N
34. Req submission of balanced budget	N	75. Bar Air Force $ for MX missile	N
35. Balanced budget amendment	Y	76. Allow "real" increase in defense	Y
36. Amendment to ban flag desecration	Y	77. Troop reduction in Europe of 50%	Y
37. Reauthorize Amtrak-veto override	N	78. Ban nuclear tests above 1 kiloton	N
38. Retraining aid for coal miners	Y	79. Ban anti-satellite missile tests	N
39. Suspend El Salvador military aid	N	80. Observe certain limits of SALT II	N
40. Expand child care aid/tax credit	N	81. Restore four Civil Rights laws	N
41. Raise House salary/omit honoraria	N	82. Prohibit aliens as strikebreakers	N

ROGERS, HAROLD (continued)

83. Allow military malpractice suits	Y
84. Approval of $36m in Contra aid	Y
85. $18b deficit reduction compromise	Y
86. Welfare reform of $5.7b for 5 years	N
87. Raise taxes $12b/cut spending $3b	N
88. Board to assess occupational risk	N
89. Balanced budget by '93-via targets	Y
90. Bar licensing of two nuclear plants	N
91. Remove victims compensation cap	N
92. Catastrophic health insurance	N
93. Ban airline smoking-2 hours or less	N
94. $1b/two year aid for the homeless	Y
95. Bar non-unions in union companies	N
96. Increase FSLIC rescue to $15b	N
97. Impose quotas to lower trade deficit	N
98. Reduce discretionary budget 21%	Y
99. Immigration reform/alien amnesty	Y
100. South Africa sanctions-veto override	N
101. Tax overhaul to revise income tax	Y
102. Use of military in drug war	Y
103. Delete 12 MX/add conventional wpn	N
104. Raise speed limit to 65 mph	N
105. Require Pentagon to buy US goods	Y
106. AIDS insurance non-discrimination	N
107. Prohibit Saudi arms sales	N
108. Ease Gun Control Act of 1968	Y
109. Bar interstate handgun transport	N
110. Make company emissions known	N
111. Allow toxic victims to sue in fed ct	N
112. Superfund waste cleanup of $10b	N
113. 90 days notice of plant closings	N

114. $20b in Medicare cuts/tax increases	Y
115. Spending cuts and tax increases	N
116. Set school lunch lmt-250% poverty	Y
117. $75m for youth work projects	N
118. Allow Angolan military assistance	Y
119. Suspend defense payments for abuse	N
120. Drop SS COLAs/$12b tax increase	N
121. Approve $1.5b for 21 MX missiles	Y
122. Emergency farm credit/revisions	Y
123. Duty on Taiwan/Hong Kong/S Korea	N
124. Limit steel imports to 17%	Y
125. Cut $ to schools that bar prayer	Y
126. $50b-taxes; cut Medicare/spending	N
127. Limit Pershing II/cruise in Europe	N
128. Delete $7.1b for 34 B-1 bombers	N
129. Bar purchase of Sergeant York guns	N
130. El Salvador military/economic aid	Y
131. Bar mining of Nicaraguan waters	N
132. Physician fee freeze for Medicare	Y
133. $49b in "sin"/phone/insurance taxes	N
134. Allow sale of Conrail	Y
135. Equal Rights Amendment	N
136. Authorize Marines in Lebanon	Y
137. Eminent domain for coal companies	N
138. Prohibit EPA clean air sanctions	Y
139. SS retirement age increase/reforms	Y
140. Auto domestic content requirement	Y
141. Delete jobs program funding	Y
142. Highway-gas tax bill	N
143. Cut $5b from defense for Medicare	N
144. Emergency housing aid of $1b	Y

Presidential Support Score: 1991 - 70%   1990 - 69%

HOPKINS, LARRY J. -- Kentucky 6th District [Republican]. Counties of Anderson, Bourbon, Boyle, Bracken, Clark, Fayette, Franklin, Harrison, Madison, Mercer, Montgomery, Nicholas, Robertson, Scott, Shelby and Woodford. Prior Terms: 1979-92. Born: October 25, 1933; Detroit, MI. Education: Murray State University; Southern Methodist University; Purdue University. Military Service: U.S. Marine Corps, 1954-56. Occupation: Broker; county clerk (1969); Kentucky representative (1972-77); Kentucky senator (1978).

1. Protection to Haitian refugees	N
2. Raise tax on wealthy; lower others	N
3. Investigate Reagan hostage delay	N
4. Campaign finance revisions	N
5. Unpaid leave to care for children	N
6. Restrict NEA use of funds	?
7. Bar race-bias claim/habeas corpus	?
8. Ban race as death sentence factor	?
9. Exceptions to exclusionary rule	?
10. Allow sale of assault weapons	?
11. Life in prison/abolish death penalty	?
12. Req conspiracy-price fixing cases	?
13. Unemployment benefits extension	?
14. Tissue use of aborted fetuses	?
15. Bar replacement of union strikers	?
16. Hold foreign aid at $15b for '92	?
17. Restore space station funding	Y
18. Civil Rights Act of 1991	N
19. Unlimited damages-discrimination	N
20. Eliminate funds for supercollider	?
21. Terminate SDI except for research	?

22. Req 7-day handgun waiting period	N
23. Provide $30b for failed S&Ls	N
24. Allow use of force against Iraq	Y
25. Allow $15b in foreign aid for '91	N
26. Revise & extend legal immigration	N
27. Suspend aid to Angolan rebels	N
28. Democratic tax plan proposals	N
29. Cut defense 5% across the board	N
30. Textile import quotas-veto override	Y
31. Abortion service for military abroad	N
32. Limits on high income farmers	N
33. Family medical leave-veto override	N
34. Req submission of balanced budget	N
35. Balanced budget amendment	Y
36. Amendment to ban flag desecration	Y
37. Reauthorize Amtrak-veto override	Y
38. Retraining aid for coal miners	Y
39. Suspend El Salvador military aid	N
40. Expand child care aid/tax credit	N
41. Raise House salary/omit honoraria	N
42. Toughen oil-spill liability	N

HOPKINS, LARRY J. (continued)

43. Restitution to Japanese interned	N	94. $1b/two year aid for the homeless	N
44. Protect Chinese & C.A. nationals	N	95. Bar non-unions in union companies	N
45. Abortion $ for rape/incest cases	N	96. Increase FSLIC rescue to $15b	N
46. Allow religious schools to bar gays	Y	97. Impose quotas to lower trade deficit	N
47. Bar broadcaster fairness doctrine	Y	98. Reduce discretionary budget 21%	Y
48. Bar cap gains cut/reinstate IRA	N	99. Immigration reform/alien amnesty	N
49. Bar unions equal voice in pension	Y	100. South Africa sanctions-veto override	Y
50. Bar assembly of chemical weapons	N	101. Tax overhaul to revise income tax	Y
51. Ban plutonium/uranium production	N	102. Use of military in drug war	Y
52. Cap MX missile deployment at 50	Y	103. Delete 12 MX/add conventional wpn	N
53. Allow $3b for 2 stealth bombers	N	104. Raise speed limit to 65 mph	Y
54. Publish bio-warfare experiments	N	105. Require Pentagon to buy US goods	Y
55. Raise minimum wage-veto override	N	106. AIDS insurance non-discrimination	N
56. Bar transfer of FS-X technology	Y	107. Prohibit Saudi arms sales	N
57. Cut defense and raise domestic $	N	108. Ease Gun Control Act of 1968	Y
58. Uniform poll closing in 48 states	N	109. Bar interstate handgun transport	N
59. Req foreign investment disclosure	N	110. Make company emissions known	N
60. Textile import quotas-veto override	Y	111. Allow toxic victims to sue in fed ct	N
61. Bar abortion funding in Wash, DC	Y	112. Superfund waste cleanup of $10b	Y
62. Notify spouses of AIDS+ carriers	Y	113. 90 days notice of plant closings	N
63. Seize conveyance-drug trafficking	Y	114. $20b in Medicare cuts/tax increases	N
64. South Africa sanctions	N	115. Spending cuts and tax increases	N
65. 60 days' notice of plant closings	N	116. Set school lunch lmt-250% poverty	Y
66. Close unneeded military bases	Y	117. $75m for youth work projects	N
67. Keep welfare reform within $2.8b	Y	118. Allow Angolan military assistance	Y
68. Allow children housing exclusion	Y	119. Suspend defense payments for abuse	N
69. Shift $400m of NASA to homeless	N	120. Drop SS COLAs/$12b tax increase	N
70. Cap Medicare patients' liability	N	121. Approve $1.5b for 21 MX missiles	Y
71. Prohibit employee polygraph testing	N	122. Emergency farm credit/revisions	Y
72. Allow CIA to fund Contras	Y	123. Duty on Taiwan/Hong Kong/S Korea	N
73. Revise unfair trade practices	N	124. Limit steel imports to 17%	N
74. Focus SDI on accidental launch	Y	125. Cut $ to schools that bar prayer	Y
75. Bar Air Force $ for MX missile	Y	126. $50b-taxes; cut Medicare/spending	N
76. Allow "real" increase in defense	Y	127. Limit Pershing II/cruise in Europe	N
77. Troop reduction in Europe of 50%	N	128. Delete $7.1b for 34 B-1 bombers	N
78. Ban nuclear tests above 1 kiloton	N	129. Bar purchase of Sergeant York guns	Y
79. Ban anti-satellite missile tests	N	130. El Salvador military/economic aid	Y
80. Observe certain limits of SALT II	N	131. Bar mining of Nicaraguan waters	N
81. Restore four Civil Rights laws	Y	132. Physician fee freeze for Medicare	Y
82. Prohibit aliens as strikebreakers	Y	133. $49b in "sin"/phone/insurance taxes	N
83. Allow military malpractice suits	Y	134. Allow sale of Conrail	Y
84. Approval of $36m in Contra aid	Y	135. Equal Rights Amendment	Y
85. $18b deficit reduction compromise	N	136. Authorize Marines in Lebanon	N
86. Welfare reform of $5.7b for 5 years	N	137. Eminent domain for coal companies	#
87. Raise taxes $12b/cut spending $3b	N	138. Prohibit EPA clean air sanctions	N
88. Board to assess occupational risk	N	139. SS retirement age increase/reforms	Y
89. Balanced budget by '93-via targets	Y	140. Auto domestic content requirement	Y
90. Bar licensing of two nuclear plants	N	141. Delete jobs program funding	Y
91. Remove victims compensation cap	N	142. Highway-gas tax bill	N
92. Catastrophic health insurance	N	143. Cut $5b from defense for Medicare	Y
93. Ban airline smoking-2 hours or less	N	144. Emergency housing aid of $1b	Y

Presidential Support Score: 1991 - 35% 1990 - 66%

PERKINS, CARL C. -- Kentucky 7th District [Democrat]. Counties of Bath, Boyd, Breathitt, Carter, Elliott, Fleming, Floyd, Greenup, Johnson, Knott, Lawrence, Letcher (pt.), Lewis, Magoffin, Martin, Mason, Menifee, Morgan, Perry, Pike, Powell, Rowan and Wolfe. Prior Terms: 1985-92. Born: August 6, 1954. Education: Davidson College; University of Louisville (J.D.). Occupation: Law clerk; assistant attorney; partner and practicing attorney, Weinberg, Perkins & Campbell; hosted weekly television talk-show since 1980; farmer.

1. Protection to Haitian refugees	Y	2. Raise tax on wealthy; lower others	N

PERKINS, CARL C. (continued)

3. Investigate Reagan hostage delay	N
4. Campaign finance revisions	N
5. Unpaid leave to care for children	Y
6. Restrict NEA use of funds	N
7. Bar race-bias claim/habeas corpus	N
8. Ban race as death sentence factor	N
9. Exceptions to exclusionary rule	N
10. Allow sale of assault weapons	Y
11. Life in prison/abolish death penalty	N
12. Req conspiracy-price fixing cases	N
13. Unemployment benefits extension	Y
14. Tissue use of aborted fetuses	Y
15. Bar replacement of union strikers	Y
16. Hold foreign aid at $15b for '92	N
17. Restore space station funding	Y
18. Civil Rights Act of 1991	Y
19. Unlimited damages-discrimination	Y
20. Eliminate funds for supercollider	N
21. Terminate SDI except for research	Y
22. Req 7-day handgun waiting period	N
23. Provide $30b for failed S&Ls	N
24. Allow use of force against Iraq	N
25. Allow $15b in foreign aid for '91	N
26. Revise & extend legal immigration	N
27. Suspend aid to Angolan rebels	Y
28. Democratic tax plan proposals	Y
29. Cut defense 5% across the board	N
30. Textile import quotas-veto override	Y
31. Abortion service for military abroad	N
32. Limits on high income farmers	N
33. Family medical leave-veto override	Y
34. Req submission of balanced budget	Y
35. Balanced budget amendment	N
36. Amendment to ban flag desecration	Y
37. Reauthorize Amtrak-veto override	Y
38. Retraining aid for coal miners	Y
39. Suspend El Salvador military aid	Y
40. Expand child care aid/tax credit	Y
41. Raise House salary/omit honoraria	Y
42. Toughen oil-spill liability	Y
43. Restitution to Japanese interned	Y
44. Protect Chinese & C.A. nationals	Y
45. Abortion $ for rape/incest cases	N
46. Allow religious schools to bar gays	Y
47. Bar broadcaster fairness doctrine	Y
48. Bar cap gains cut/reinstate IRA	N
49. Bar unions equal voice in pension	N
50. Bar assembly of chemical weapons	Y
51. Ban plutonium/uranium production	Y
52. Cap MX missile deployment at 50	Y
53. Allow $3b for 2 stealth bombers	N
54. Publish bio-warfare experiments	Y
55. Raise minimum wage-veto override	Y
56. Bar transfer of FS-X technology	Y
57. Cut defense and raise domestic $	Y
58. Uniform poll closing in 48 states	N
59. Req foreign investment disclosure	Y
60. Textile import quotas-veto override	Y
61. Bar abortion funding in Wash, DC	Y
62. Notify spouses of AIDS+ carriers	N
63. Seize conveyance-drug trafficking	N
64. South Africa sanctions	Y
65. 60 days' notice of plant closings	Y
66. Close unneeded military bases	N
67. Keep welfare reform within $2.8b	N
68. Allow children housing exclusion	N
69. Shift $400m of NASA to homeless	N
70. Cap Medicare patients' liability	Y
71. Prohibit employee polygraph testing	Y
72. Allow CIA to fund Contras	N
73. Revise unfair trade practices	Y
74. Focus SDI on accidental launch	Y
75. Bar Air Force $ for MX missile	Y
76. Allow "real" increase in defense	N
77. Troop reduction in Europe of 50%	N
78. Ban nuclear tests above 1 kiloton	Y
79. Ban anti-satellite missile tests	Y
80. Observe certain limits of SALT II	Y
81. Restore four Civil Rights laws	Y
82. Prohibit aliens as strikebreakers	Y
83. Allow military malpractice suits	Y
84. Approval of $36m in Contra aid	N
85. $18b deficit reduction compromise	Y
86. Welfare reform of $5.7b for 5 years	Y
87. Raise taxes $12b/cut spending $3b	Y
88. Board to assess occupational risk	Y
89. Balanced budget by '93-via targets	Y
90. Bar licensing of two nuclear plants	Y
91. Remove victims compensation cap	N
92. Catastrophic health insurance	Y
93. Ban airline smoking-2 hours or less	N
94. $1b/two year aid for the homeless	Y
95. Bar non-unions in union companies	Y
96. Increase FSLIC rescue to $15b	Y
97. Impose quotas to lower trade deficit	Y
98. Reduce discretionary budget 21%	N
99. Immigration reform/alien amnesty	Y
100. South Africa sanctions-veto override	Y
101. Tax overhaul to revise income tax	N
102. Use of military in drug war	Y
103. Delete 12 MX/add conventional wpn	Y
104. Raise speed limit to 65 mph	N
105. Require Pentagon to buy US goods	Y
106. AIDS insurance non-discrimination	Y
107. Prohibit Saudi arms sales	Y
108. Ease Gun Control Act of 1968	Y
109. Bar interstate handgun transport	N
110. Make company emissions known	N
111. Allow toxic victims to sue in fed ct	N
112. Superfund waste cleanup of $10b	N
113. 90 days notice of plant closings	Y
114. $20b in Medicare cuts/tax increases	Y
115. Spending cuts and tax increases	Y
116. Set school lunch lmt-250% poverty	N
117. $75m for youth work projects	Y
118. Allow Angolan military assistance	N
119. Suspend defense payments for abuse	N
120. Drop SS COLAs/$12b tax increase	N
121. Approve $1.5b for 21 MX missiles	N
122. Emergency farm credit/revisions	Y

Presidential Support Score: 1991 - 28% 1990 - 24%

LOUISIANA

LIVINGSTON, BOB -- Louisiana 1st District [Republican]. Counties of Orleans (pt.), Plaquemines, St. Bernard and St. Tammany. Prior Terms: 1977 (Special Election)-1992. Born: April 30, 1943; Colorado Springs, CO. Education: Tulane University (B.A., LL.B.); Loyola University. Military Service: U.S. Navy, 1961-63; U.S. Navy Reserve, 1967. Occupation: Attorney; assistant U.S. attorney (1970-73); chief special prosecutor and chief of the Armed Robbery Division, District Attorney's Office (1974-75); chief prosecutor, Attorney General's Office (1975-76).

1.	Protection to Haitian refugees	N	50.	Bar assembly of chemical weapons	N
2.	Raise tax on wealthy; lower others	N	51.	Ban plutonium/uranium production	N
3.	Investigate Reagan hostage delay	N	52.	Cap MX missile deployment at 50	N
4.	Campaign finance revisions	N	53.	Allow $3b for 2 stealth bombers	Y
5.	Unpaid leave to care for children	N	54.	Publish bio-warfare experiments	N
6.	Restrict NEA use of funds	Y	55.	Raise minimum wage-veto override	N
7.	Bar race-bias claim/habeas corpus	Y	56.	Bar transfer of FS-X technology	N
8.	Ban race as death sentence factor	Y	57.	Cut defense and raise domestic $	N
9.	Exceptions to exclusionary rule	Y	58.	Uniform poll closing in 48 states	N
10.	Allow sale of assault weapons	Y	59.	Req foreign investment disclosure	N
11.	Life in prison/abolish death penalty	N	60.	Textile import quotas-veto override	N
12.	Req conspiracy-price fixing cases	Y	61.	Bar abortion funding in Wash, DC	Y
13.	Unemployment benefits extension	N	62.	Notify spouses of AIDS+ carriers	?
14.	Tissue use of aborted fetuses	N	63.	Seize conveyance-drug trafficking	Y
15.	Bar replacement of union strikers	N	64.	South Africa sanctions	?
16.	Hold foreign aid at $15b for '92	Y	65.	60 days' notice of plant closings	?
17.	Restore space station funding	Y	66.	Close unneeded military bases	Y
18.	Civil Rights Act of 1991	N	67.	Keep welfare reform within $2.8b	Y
19.	Unlimited damages-discrimination	N	68.	Allow children housing exclusion	Y
20.	Eliminate funds for supercollider	N	69.	Shift $400m of NASA to homeless	N
21.	Terminate SDI except for research	N	70.	Cap Medicare patients' liability	Y
22.	Req 7-day handgun waiting period	N	71.	Prohibit employee polygraph testing	N
23.	Provide $30b for failed S&Ls	Y	72.	Allow CIA to fund Contras	Y
24.	Allow use of force against Iraq	Y	73.	Revise unfair trade practices	N
25.	Allow $15b in foreign aid for '91	Y	74.	Focus SDI on accidental launch	N
26.	Revise & extend legal immigration	Y	75.	Bar Air Force $ for MX missile	N
27.	Suspend aid to Angolan rebels	N	76.	Allow "real" increase in defense	Y
28.	Democratic tax plan proposals	N	77.	Troop reduction in Europe of 50%	N
29.	Cut defense 5% across the board	N	78.	Ban nuclear tests above 1 kiloton	N
30.	Textile import quotas-veto override	N	79.	Ban anti-satellite missile tests	N
31.	Abortion service for military abroad	N	80.	Observe certain limits of SALT II	N
32.	Limits on high income farmers	Y	81.	Restore four Civil Rights laws	N
33.	Family medical leave-veto override	N	82.	Prohibit aliens as strikebreakers	N
34.	Req submission of balanced budget	N	83.	Allow military malpractice suits	Y
35.	Balanced budget amendment	Y	84.	Approval of $36m in Contra aid	Y
36.	Amendment to ban flag desecration	Y	85.	$18b deficit reduction compromise	N
37.	Reauthorize Amtrak-veto override	N	86.	Welfare reform of $5.7b for 5 years	N
38.	Retraining aid for coal miners	N	87.	Raise taxes $12b/cut spending $3b	N
39.	Suspend El Salvador military aid	N	88.	Board to assess occupational risk	?
40.	Expand child care aid/tax credit	N	89.	Balanced budget by '93-via targets	#
41.	Raise House salary/omit honoraria	Y	90.	Bar licensing of two nuclear plants	N
42.	Toughen oil-spill liability	N	91.	Remove victims compensation cap	N
43.	Restitution to Japanese interned	N	92.	Catastrophic health insurance	Y
44.	Protect Chinese & C.A. nationals	N	93.	Ban airline smoking-2 hours or less	?
45.	Abortion $ for rape/incest cases	N	94.	$1b/two year aid for the homeless	?
46.	Allow religious schools to bar gays	Y	95.	Bar non-unions in union companies	N
47.	Bar broadcaster fairness doctrine	Y	96.	Increase FSLIC rescue to $15b	N
48.	Bar cap gains cut/reinstate IRA	N	97.	Impose quotas to lower trade deficit	N
49.	Bar unions equal voice in pension	Y	98.	Reduce discretionary budget 21%	?

LIVINGSTON, BOB (continued)

99.	Immigration reform/alien amnesty	Y	122. Emergency farm credit/revisions	N
100.	South Africa sanctions-veto override	N	123. Duty on Taiwan/Hong Kong/S Korea	N
101.	Tax overhaul to revise income tax	Y	124. Limit steel imports to 17%	N
102.	Use of military in drug war	Y	125. Cut $ to schools that bar prayer	Y
103.	Delete 12 MX/add conventional wpn	N	126. $50b-taxes; cut Medicare/spending	N
104.	Raise speed limit to 65 mph	Y	127. Limit Pershing II/cruise in Europe	N
105.	Require Pentagon to buy US goods	N	128. Delete $7.1b for 34 B-1 bombers	N
106.	AIDS insurance non-discrimination	N	129. Bar purchase of Sergeant York guns	N
107.	Prohibit Saudi arms sales	N	130. El Salvador military/economic aid	Y
108.	Ease Gun Control Act of 1968	Y	131. Bar mining of Nicaraguan waters	N
109.	Bar interstate handgun transport	N	132. Physician fee freeze for Medicare	Y
110.	Make company emissions known	N	133. $49b in "sin"/phone/insurance taxes	N
111.	Allow toxic victims to sue in fed ct	N	134. Allow sale of Conrail	?
112.	Superfund waste cleanup of $10b	N	135. Equal Rights Amendment	N
113.	90 days notice of plant closings	N	136. Authorize Marines in Lebanon	Y
114.	$20b in Medicare cuts/tax increases	N	137. Eminent domain for coal companies	Y
115.	Spending cuts and tax increases	Y	138. Prohibit EPA clean air sanctions	N
116.	Set school lunch lmt-250% poverty	Y	139. SS retirement age increase/reforms	Y
117.	$75m for youth work projects	N	140. Auto domestic content requirement	N
118.	Allow Angolan military assistance	Y	141. Delete jobs program funding	Y
119.	Suspend defense payments for abuse	N	142. Highway-gas tax bill	N
120.	Drop SS COLAs/$12b tax increase	N	143. Cut $5b from defense for Medicare	N
121.	Approve $1.5b for 21 MX missiles	Y	144. Emergency housing aid of $1b	?

Presidential Support Score: 1991 - 86% 1990 - 75%

JEFFERSON, WILLIAM J. -- Louisiana 2nd District [Democrat]. Counties of Jefferson (pt.) and Orleans (pt.). Prior Term: 1991-92. Born: March 14, 1947; Lake Providence, LA. Education: Southern Univ. and AGM College (B.A.); Harvard University Law School (J.D.). Military Service: U.S. Army, Judge Advocate General Corps. Occupation: U.S. Court of Appeals law clerk; lawyer, legislative assistant to Sen. Johnston; state senator (1981-90).

1.	Protection to Haitian refugees	Y	13. Unemployment benefits extension	Y
2.	Raise tax on wealthy; lower others	N	14. Tissue use of aborted fetuses	Y
3.	Investigate Reagan hostage delay	Y	15. Bar replacement of union strikers	Y
4.	Campaign finance revisions	Y	16. Hold foreign aid at $15b for '92	Y
5.	Unpaid leave to care for children	Y	17. Restore space station funding	Y
6.	Restrict NEA use of funds	N	18. Civil Rights Act of 1991	Y
7.	Bar race-bias claim/habeas corpus	N	19. Unlimited damages-discrimination	Y
8.	Ban race as death sentence factor	N	20. Eliminate funds for supercollider	N
9.	Exceptions to exclusionary rule	N	21. Terminate SDI except for research	Y
10.	Allow sale of assault weapons	N	22. Req 7-day handgun waiting period	Y
11.	Life in prison/abolish death penalty	Y	23. Provide $30b for failed S&Ls	?
12.	Req conspiracy-price fixing cases	N	24. Allow use of force against Iraq	N

Presidential Support Score: 1991 - 26%

TAUZIN, W. J. (BILLY) -- Louisiana 3rd District [Democrat]. Counties of Assumption, Iberia, Jefferson (pt.), Lafourche, St. Charles, St. Martin (pt.), St. Mary and Terrebonne. Prior Terms: 1980 (Special Election)-1992. Born: June 14, 1943; Chackbay, LA. Education: Nicholls State University (B.A.); Louisiana State University Law School (J.D.). Occupation: Attorney, Marcel, Marcel, Fanquy & Tauzin; Lousiana representative (1971-80).

1.	Protection to Haitian refugees	N	11. Life in prison/abolish death penalty	N
2.	Raise tax on wealthy; lower others	N	12. Req conspiracy-price fixing cases	Y
3.	Investigate Reagan hostage delay	N	13. Unemployment benefits extension	Y
4.	Campaign finance revisions	Y	14. Tissue use of aborted fetuses	N
5.	Unpaid leave to care for children	N	15. Bar replacement of union strikers	N
6.	Restrict NEA use of funds	Y	16. Hold foreign aid at $15b for '92	N
7.	Bar race-bias claim/habeas corpus	Y	17. Restore space station funding	Y
8.	Ban race as death sentence factor	Y	18. Civil Rights Act of 1991	Y
9.	Exceptions to exclusionary rule	Y	19. Unlimited damages-discrimination	N
10.	Allow sale of assault weapons	Y	20. Eliminate funds for supercollider	N

TAUZIN, W. J. (continued)

21. Terminate SDI except for research	N	
22. Req 7-day handgun waiting period	N	
23. Provide $30b for failed S&Ls	N	
24. Allow use of force against Iraq	Y	
25. Allow $15b in foreign aid for '91	N	
26. Revise & extend legal immigration	N	
27. Suspend aid to Angolan rebels	N	
28. Democratic tax plan proposals	N	
29. Cut defense 5% across the board	N	
30. Textile import quotas-veto override	Y	
31. Abortion service for military abroad	N	
32. Limits on high income farmers	N	
33. Family medical leave-veto override	N	
34. Req submission of balanced budget	Y	
35. Balanced budget amendment	Y	
36. Amendment to ban flag desecration	Y	
37. Reauthorize Amtrak-veto override	Y	
38. Retraining aid for coal miners	N	
39. Suspend El Salvador military aid	N	
40. Expand child care aid/tax credit	Y	
41. Raise House salary/omit honoraria	N	
42. Toughen oil-spill liability	N	
43. Restitution to Japanese interned	N	
44. Protect Chinese & C.A. nationals	N	
45. Abortion $ for rape/incest cases	N	
46. Allow religious schools to bar gays	Y	
47. Bar broadcaster fairness doctrine	Y	
48. Bar cap gains cut/reinstate IRA	N	
49. Bar unions equal voice in pension	Y	
50. Bar assembly of chemical weapons	N	
51. Ban plutonium/uranium production	Y	
52. Cap MX missile deployment at 50	N	
53. Allow $3b for 2 stealth bombers	Y	
54. Publish bio-warfare experiments	N	
55. Raise minimum wage-veto override	N	
56. Bar transfer of FS-X technology	N	
57. Cut defense and raise domestic $	N	
58. Uniform poll closing in 48 states	Y	
59. Req foreign investment disclosure	Y	
60. Textile import quotas-veto override	Y	
61. Bar abortion funding in Wash, DC	Y	
62. Notify spouses of AIDS+ carriers	N	
63. Seize conveyance-drug trafficking	Y	
64. South Africa sanctions	Y	
65. 60 days' notice of plant closings	Y	
66. Close unneeded military bases	Y	
67. Keep welfare reform within $2.8b	Y	
68. Allow children housing exclusion	Y	
69. Shift $400m of NASA to homeless	N	
70. Cap Medicare patients' liability	Y	
71. Prohibit employee polygraph testing	Y	
72. Allow CIA to fund Contras	Y	
73. Revise unfair trade practices	Y	
74. Focus SDI on accidental launch	Y	
75. Bar Air Force $ for MX missile	N	
76. Allow "real" increase in defense	Y	
77. Troop reduction in Europe of 50%	Y	
78. Ban nuclear tests above 1 kiloton	N	
79. Ban anti-satellite missile tests	N	
80. Observe certain limits of SALT II	N	
81. Restore four Civil Rights laws	Y	
82. Prohibit aliens as strikebreakers	N	

83. Allow military malpractice suits	Y	
84. Approval of $36m in Contra aid	Y	
85. $18b deficit reduction compromise	N	
86. Welfare reform of $5.7b for 5 years	Y	
87. Raise taxes $12b/cut spending $3b	N	
88. Board to assess occupational risk	?	
89. Balanced budget by '93-via targets	?	
90. Bar licensing of two nuclear plants	?	
91. Remove victims compensation cap	N	
92. Catastrophic health insurance	Y	
93. Ban airline smoking-2 hours or less	?	
94. $1b/two year aid for the homeless	?	
95. Bar non-unions in union companies	N	
96. Increase FSLIC rescue to $15b	?	
97. Impose quotas to lower trade deficit	Y	
98. Reduce discretionary budget 21%	Y	
99. Immigration reform/alien amnesty	N	
100. South Africa sanctions-veto override	Y	
101. Tax overhaul to revise income tax	Y	
102. Use of military in drug war	Y	
103. Delete 12 MX/add conventional wpn	N	
104. Raise speed limit to 65 mph	Y	
105. Require Pentagon to buy US goods	Y	
106. AIDS insurance non-discrimination	Y	
107. Prohibit Saudi arms sales	Y	
108. Ease Gun Control Act of 1968	Y	
109. Bar interstate handgun transport	N	
110. Make company emissions known	N	
111. Allow toxic victims to sue in fed ct	N	
112. Superfund waste cleanup of $10b	N	
113. 90 days notice of plant closings	N	
114. $20b in Medicare cuts/tax increases	#	
115. Spending cuts and tax increases	Y	
116. Set school lunch lmt-250% poverty	Y	
117. $75m for youth work projects	?	
118. Allow Angolan military assistance	Y	
119. Suspend defense payments for abuse	N	
120. Drop SS COLAs/$12b tax increase	N	
121. Approve $1.5b for 21 MX missiles	Y	
122. Emergency farm credit/revisions	Y	
123. Duty on Taiwan/Hong Kong/S Korea	Y	
124. Limit steel imports to 17%	Y	
125. Cut $ to schools that bar prayer	Y	
126. $50b-taxes; cut Medicare/spending	N	
127. Limit Pershing II/cruise in Europe	N	
128. Delete $7.1b for 34 B-1 bombers	N	
129. Bar purchase of Sergeant York guns	Y	
130. El Salvador military/economic aid	Y	
131. Bar mining of Nicaraguan waters	?	
132. Physician fee freeze for Medicare	X	
133. $49b in "sin"/phone/insurance taxes	Y	
134. Allow sale of Conrail	Y	
135. Equal Rights Amendment	Y	
136. Authorize Marines in Lebanon	Y	
137. Eminent domain for coal companies	Y	
138. Prohibit EPA clean air sanctions	Y	
139. SS retirement age increase/reforms	Y	
140. Auto domestic content requirement	Y	
141. Delete jobs program funding	Y	
142. Highway-gas tax bill	N	
143. Cut $5b from defense for Medicare	N	
144. Emergency housing aid of $1b	Y	

Presidential Support Score: 1991 - 53%   1990 - 46%

McCRERY, JIM -- Louisiana 4th District [Republican]. Counties of Beauregard (pt.), Bossier, Caddo, Claiborne, De Soto, Red River, Sabine, Vernon and Webster. Prior Terms: 1988 (Special Election)-1992. Born: September 18, 1949; Shreveport, LA. Education: Louisiana Tech University (B.A.); Louisiana State University (J.D.). Occupation: Shreveport assistant city attorney (1975-81); congressional aide (1981-84); regional government affairs manager, Georgia-Pacific Corp. (1984-88); chairman, Louisiana Business Task Force on Unemployment Compensation (1986).

1. Protection to Haitian refugees	N	41. Raise House salary/omit honoraria	Y
2. Raise tax on wealthy; lower others	N	42. Toughen oil-spill liability	N
3. Investigate Reagan hostage delay	N	43. Restitution to Japanese interned	N
4. Campaign finance revisions	N	44. Protect Chinese & C.A. nationals	N
5. Unpaid leave to care for children	N	45. Abortion $ for rape/incest cases	N
6. Restrict NEA use of funds	Y	46. Allow religious schools to bar gays	Y
7. Bar race-bias claim/habeas corpus	Y	47. Bar broadcaster fairness doctrine	Y
8. Ban race as death sentence factor	Y	48. Bar cap gains cut/reinstate IRA	N
9. Exceptions to exclusionary rule	Y	49. Bar unions equal voice in pension	Y
10. Allow sale of assault weapons	Y	50. Bar assembly of chemical weapons	N
11. Life in prison/abolish death penalty	N	51. Ban plutonium/uranium production	N
12. Req conspiracy-price fixing cases	Y	52. Cap MX missile deployment at 50	N
13. Unemployment benefits extension	N	53. Allow $3b for 2 stealth bombers	Y
14. Tissue use of aborted fetuses	?	54. Publish bio-warfare experiments	N
15. Bar replacement of union strikers	N	55. Raise minimum wage-veto override	N
16. Hold foreign aid at $15b for '92	Y	56. Bar transfer of FS-X technology	N
17. Restore space station funding	Y	57. Cut defense and raise domestic $	N
18. Civil Rights Act of 1991	N	58. Uniform poll closing in 48 states	N
19. Unlimited damages-discrimination	N	59. Req foreign investment disclosure	N
20. Eliminate funds for supercollider	N	60. Textile import quotas-veto override	Y
21. Terminate SDI except for research	N	61. Bar abortion funding in Wash, DC	Y
22. Req 7-day handgun waiting period	N	62. Notify spouses of AIDS+ carriers	N
23. Provide $30b for failed S&Ls	Y	63. Seize conveyance-drug trafficking	N
24. Allow use of force against Iraq	Y	64. South Africa sanctions	N
25. Allow $15b in foreign aid for '91	Y	65. 60 days' notice of plant closings	N
26. Revise & extend legal immigration	Y	66. Close unneeded military bases	Y
27. Suspend aid to Angolan rebels	N	67. Keep welfare reform within $2.8b	Y
28. Democratic tax plan proposals	N	68. Allow children housing exclusion	Y
29. Cut defense 5% across the board	N	69. Shift $400m of NASA to homeless	N
30. Textile import quotas-veto override	Y	70. Cap Medicare patients' liability	N
31. Abortion service for military abroad	N	71. Prohibit employee polygraph testing	N
32. Limits on high income farmers	N	72. Allow CIA to fund Contras	Y
33. Family medical leave-veto override	N	73. Revise unfair trade practices	N
34. Req submission of balanced budget	Y	74. Focus SDI on accidental launch	N
35. Balanced budget amendment	Y	75. Bar Air Force $ for MX missile	N
36. Amendment to ban flag desecration	Y	76. Allow "real" increase in defense	Y
37. Reauthorize Amtrak-veto override	N	77. Troop reduction in Europe of 50%	N
38. Retraining aid for coal miners	N	78. Ban nuclear tests above 1 kiloton	N
39. Suspend El Salvador military aid	N	79. Ban anti-satellite missile tests	?
40. Expand child care aid/tax credit	N	80. Observe certain limits of SALT II	N

Presidential Support Score: 1991 - 84%   1990 - 68%

HUCKABY, JERRY -- Louisiana 5th District [Democrat]. Counties of Bienville, Caldwell, Catahoula, Concordia, East Carroll, Franklin, Grant Jackson, La Salle, Lincoln, Madison, Morehouse, Natchitoches, Ouachita, Rapides (pt.), Richland, Tensas, Union, West Carroll and Winn. Prior Terms: 1977-1992. Born: July 19, 1941; Hodge, Jackson Parish, LA. Education: Louisiana State University (B.S.); Georgia State University (M.B.A.). Occupation: Dairyman; farmer; businessman, Western Electric (1963-73).

1. Protection to Haitian refugees	Y	7. Bar race-bias claim/habeas corpus	Y
2. Raise tax on wealthy; lower others	N	8. Ban race as death sentence factor	Y
3. Investigate Reagan hostage delay	N	9. Exceptions to exclusionary rule	?
4. Campaign finance revisions	Y	10. Allow sale of assault weapons	#
5. Unpaid leave to care for children	N	11. Life in prison/abolish death penalty	N
6. Restrict NEA use of funds	Y	12. Req conspiracy-price fixing cases	?

HUCKABY, JERRY (continued)

13. Unemployment benefits extension	Y	
14. Tissue use of aborted fetuses	Y	
15. Bar replacement of union strikers	N	
16. Hold foreign aid at $15b for '92	?	
17. Restore space station funding	?	
18. Civil Rights Act of 1991	N	
19. Unlimited damages-discrimination	N	
20. Eliminate funds for supercollider	N	
21. Terminate SDI except for research	N	
22. Req 7-day handgun waiting period	N	
23. Provide $30b for failed S&Ls	Y	
24. Allow use of force against Iraq	Y	
25. Allow $15b in foreign aid for '91	?	
26. Revise & extend legal immigration	N	
27. Suspend aid to Angolan rebels	N	
28. Democratic tax plan proposals	Y	
29. Cut defense 5% across the board	N	
30. Textile import quotas-veto override	Y	
31. Abortion service for military abroad	N	
32. Limits on high income farmers	N	
33. Family medical leave-veto override	N	
34. Req submission of balanced budget	Y	
35. Balanced budget amendment	Y	
36. Amendment to ban flag desecration	Y	
37. Reauthorize Amtrak-veto override	Y	
38. Retraining aid for coal miners	N	
39. Suspend El Salvador military aid	N	
40. Expand child care aid/tax credit	N	
41. Raise House salary/omit honoraria	N	
42. Toughen oil-spill liability	N	
43. Restitution to Japanese interned	N	
44. Protect Chinese & C.A. nationals	N	
45. Abortion $ for rape/incest cases	N	
46. Allow religious schools to bar gays	Y	
47. Bar broadcaster fairness doctrine	Y	
48. Bar cap gains cut/reinstate IRA	N	
49. Bar unions equal voice in pension	Y	
50. Bar assembly of chemical weapons	Y	
51. Ban plutonium/uranium production	Y	
52. Cap MX missile deployment at 50	N	
53. Allow $3b for 2 stealth bombers	Y	
54. Publish bio-warfare experiments	N	
55. Raise minimum wage-veto override	N	
56. Bar transfer of FS-X technology	N	
57. Cut defense and raise domestic $	N	
58. Uniform poll closing in 48 states	?	
59. Req foreign investment disclosure	N	
60. Textile import quotas-veto override	Y	
61. Bar abortion funding in Wash, DC	Y	
62. Notify spouses of AIDS+ carriers	?	
63. Seize conveyance-drug trafficking	N	
64. South Africa sanctions	N	
65. 60 days' notice of plant closings	Y	
66. Close unneeded military bases	Y	
67. Keep welfare reform within $2.8b	Y	
68. Allow children housing exclusion	Y	
69. Shift $400m of NASA to homeless	N	
70. Cap Medicare patients' liability	Y	
71. Prohibit employee polygraph testing	N	
72. Allow CIA to fund Contras	Y	
73. Revise unfair trade practices	Y	
74. Focus SDI on accidental launch	Y	
75. Bar Air Force $ for MX missile	N	
76. Allow "real" increase in defense	N	

77. Troop reduction in Europe of 50%	?	
78. Ban nuclear tests above 1 kiloton	?	
79. Ban anti-satellite missile tests	N	
80. Observe certain limits of SALT II	Y	
81. Restore four Civil Rights laws	Y	
82. Prohibit aliens as strikebreakers	N	
83. Allow military malpractice suits	N	
84. Approval of $36m in Contra aid	Y	
85. $18b deficit reduction compromise	Y	
86. Welfare reform of $5.7b for 5 years	Y	
87. Raise taxes $12b/cut spending $3b	N	
88. Board to assess occupational risk	N	
89. Balanced budget by '93-via targets	Y	
90. Bar licensing of two nuclear plants	N	
91. Remove victims compensation cap	N	
92. Catastrophic health insurance	Y	
93. Ban airline smoking-2 hours or less	N	
94. $1b/two year aid for the homeless	Y	
95. Bar non-unions in companies	N	
96. Increase FSLIC rescue to $15b	Y	
97. Impose quotas to lower trade deficit	Y	
98. Reduce discretionary budget 21%	Y	
99. Immigration reform/alien amnesty	Y	
100. South Africa sanctions-veto override	?	
101. Tax overhaul to revise income tax	Y	
102. Use of military in drug war	?	
103. Delete 12 MX/add conventional wpn	N	
104. Raise speed limit to 65 mph	Y	
105. Require Pentagon to buy US goods	Y	
106. AIDS insurance non-discrimination	?	
107. Prohibit Saudi arms sales	Y	
108. Ease Gun Control Act of 1968	Y	
109. Bar interstate handgun transport	N	
110. Make company emissions known	Y	
111. Allow toxic victims to sue in fed ct	N	
112. Superfund waste cleanup of $10b	N	
113. 90 days notice of plant closings	N	
114. $20b in Medicare cuts/tax increases	Y	
115. Spending cuts and tax increases	Y	
116. Set school lunch lmt-250% poverty	N	
117. $75m for youth work projects	Y	
118. Allow Angolan military assistance	Y	
119. Suspend defense payments for abuse	N	
120. Drop SS COLAs/$12b tax increase	N	
121. Approve $1.5b for 21 MX missiles	Y	
122. Emergency farm credit/revisions	Y	
123. Duty on Taiwan/Hong Kong/S Korea	N	
124. Limit steel imports to 17%	N	
125. Cut $ to schools that bar prayer	Y	
126. $50b-taxes; cut Medicare/spending	Y	
127. Limit Pershing II/cruise in Europe	N	
128. Delete $7.1b for 34 B-1 bombers	N	
129. Bar purchase of Sergeant York guns	N	
130. El Salvador military/economic aid	Y	
131. Bar mining of Nicaraguan waters	Y	
132. Physician fee freeze for Medicare	N	
133. $49b in "sin"/phone/insurance taxes	Y	
134. Allow sale of Conrail	N	
135. Equal Rights Amendment	Y	
136. Authorize Marines in Lebanon	Y	
137. Eminent domain for coal companies	Y	
138. Prohibit EPA clean air sanctions	N	
139. SS retirement age increase/reforms	N	
140. Auto domestic content requirement	N	

HUCKABY, JERRY (continued)

141. Delete jobs program funding	Y	143. Cut $5b from defense for Medicare	N
142. Highway-gas tax bill	N	144. Emergency housing aid of $1b	Y

Presidential Support Score: 1991 - 57%   1990 - 50%

BAKER, RICHARD HUGH -- Louisiana 6th District [Republican]. Counties of East Baton Rouge (pt.), Livingston, Tangipahoa and Washington. Prior Terms: 1987-92. Born: May 22, 1948; New Orleans, LA. Education: Louisiana State University. Occupation: Real estate broker; state representative (1972-1986).

1. Protection to Haitian refugees	N	50. Bar assembly of chemical weapons	N
2. Raise tax on wealthy; lower others	N	51. Ban plutonium/uranium production	N
3. Investigate Reagan hostage delay	N	52. Cap MX missile deployment at 50	N
4. Campaign finance revisions	N	53. Allow $3b for 2 stealth bombers	N
5. Unpaid leave to care for children	N	54. Publish bio-warfare experiments	Y
6. Restrict NEA use of funds	Y	55. Raise minimum wage-veto override	N
7. Bar race-bias claim/habeas corpus	#	56. Bar transfer of FS-X technology	N
8. Ban race as death sentence factor	#	57. Cut defense and raise domestic $	N
9. Exceptions to exclusionary rule	Y	58. Uniform poll closing in 48 states	N
10. Allow sale of assault weapons	Y	59. Req foreign investment disclosure	N
11. Life in prison/abolish death penalty	N	60. Textile import quotas-veto override	Y
12. Req conspiracy-price fixing cases	Y	61. Bar abortion funding in Wash, DC	Y
13. Unemployment benefits extension	N	62. Notify spouses of AIDS+ carriers	Y
14. Tissue use of aborted fetuses	N	63. Seize conveyance-drug trafficking	Y
15. Bar replacement of union strikers	N	64. South Africa sanctions	?
16. Hold foreign aid at $15b for '92	Y	65. 60 days' notice of plant closings	N
17. Restore space station funding	Y	66. Close unneeded military bases	Y
18. Civil Rights Act of 1991	N	67. Keep welfare reform within $2.8b	Y
19. Unlimited damages-discrimination	N	68. Allow children housing exclusion	Y
20. Eliminate funds for supercollider	N	69. Shift $400m of NASA to homeless	N
21. Terminate SDI except for research	N	70. Cap Medicare patients' liability	N
22. Req 7-day handgun waiting period	N	71. Prohibit employee polygraph testing	N
23. Provide $30b for failed S&Ls	Y	72. Allow CIA to fund Contras	Y
24. Allow use of force against Iraq	Y	73. Revise unfair trade practices	N
25. Allow $15b in foreign aid for '91	N	74. Focus SDI on accidental launch	N
26. Revise & extend legal immigration	Y	75. Bar Air Force $ for MX missile	N
27. Suspend aid to Angolan rebels	N	76. Allow "real" increase in defense	Y
28. Democratic tax plan proposals	N	77. Troop reduction in Europe of 50%	N
29. Cut defense 5% across the board	N	78. Ban nuclear tests above 1 kiloton	N
30. Textile import quotas-veto override	Y	79. Ban anti-satellite missile tests	N
31. Abortion service for military abroad	N	80. Observe certain limits of SALT II	N
32. Limits on high income farmers	N	81. Restore four Civil Rights laws	N
33. Family medical leave-veto override	N	82. Prohibit aliens as strikebreakers	N
34. Req submission of balanced budget	?	83. Allow military malpractice suits	Y
35. Balanced budget amendment	?	84. Approval of $36m in Contra aid	Y
36. Amendment to ban flag desecration	Y	85. $18b deficit reduction compromise	N
37. Reauthorize Amtrak-veto override	N	86. Welfare reform of $5.7b for 5 years	N
38. Retraining aid for coal miners	N	87. Raise taxes $12b/cut spending $3b	?
39. Suspend El Salvador military aid	N	88. Board to assess occupational risk	N
40. Expand child care aid/tax credit	?	89. Balanced budget by '93-via targets	Y
41. Raise House salary/omit honoraria	Y	90. Bar licensing of two nuclear plants	N
42. Toughen oil-spill liability	N	91. Remove victims compensation cap	N
43. Restitution to Japanese interned	N	92. Catastrophic health insurance	N
44. Protect Chinese & C.A. nationals	N	93. Ban airline smoking-2 hours or less	Y
45. Abortion $ for rape/incest cases	Y	94. $1b/two year aid for the homeless	N
46. Allow religious schools to bar gays	Y	95. Bar non-unions in union companies	N
47. Bar broadcaster fairness doctrine	Y	96. Increase FSLIC rescue to $15b	Y
48. Bar cap gains cut/reinstate IRA	N	97. Impose quotas to lower trade deficit	N
49. Bar unions equal voice in pension	Y	98. Reduce discretionary budget 21%	Y

Presidential Support Score: 1991 - 79%   1990 - 69%

HAYES, JAMES A. -- Louisiana 7th District [Democrat]. Counties of Acadia, Allen (pt.), Beauregard (pt.), Calcasieu, Cameron, Jefferson Davis, Lafayette, St. Martin (pt.) and Vermilion. Prior Terms: 1987-92. Born: December 21, 1946; Lafayette, IN. Education: University of Southwestern Louisiana (B.A.); Tulane University (J.D.). Military Service: Air National Guard, 1968-1974. Occupation: Assistant city attorney (1971-1972); assistant district attorney (1974-1983); state Financial Institutions commissioner (1984-1985); partner, Hayes, Durio, and McGoffin; real estate developer.

1. Protection to Haitian refugees	Y	50. Bar assembly of chemical weapons	N
2. Raise tax on wealthy; lower others	N	51. Ban plutonium/uranium production	Y
3. Investigate Reagan hostage delay	N	52. Cap MX missile deployment at 50	Y
4. Campaign finance revisions	Y	53. Allow $3b for 2 stealth bombers	N
5. Unpaid leave to care for children	N	54. Publish bio-warfare experiments	Y
6. Restrict NEA use of funds	Y	55. Raise minimum wage-veto override	Y
7. Bar race-bias claim/habeas corpus	Y	56. Bar transfer of FS-X technology	N
8. Ban race as death sentence factor	Y	57. Cut defense and raise domestic $	N
9. Exceptions to exclusionary rule	Y	58. Uniform poll closing in 48 states	N
10. Allow sale of assault weapons	Y	59. Req foreign investment disclosure	Y
11. Life in prison/abolish death penalty	N	60. Textile import quotas-veto override	Y
12. Req conspiracy-price fixing cases	?	61. Bar abortion funding in Wash, DC	Y
13. Unemployment benefits extension	N	62. Notify spouses of AIDS+ carriers	N
14. Tissue use of aborted fetuses	N	63. Seize conveyance-drug trafficking	N
15. Bar replacement of union strikers	Y	64. South Africa sanctions	Y
16. Hold foreign aid at $15b for '92	N	65. 60 days' notice of plant closings	?
17. Restore space station funding	Y	66. Close unneeded military bases	Y
18. Civil Rights Act of 1991	N	67. Keep welfare reform within $2.8b	Y
19. Unlimited damages-discrimination	Y	68. Allow children housing exclusion	N
20. Eliminate funds for supercollider	N	69. Shift $400m of NASA to homeless	N
21. Terminate SDI except for research	N	70. Cap Medicare patients' liability	Y
22. Req 7-day handgun waiting period	N	71. Prohibit employee polygraph testing	Y
23. Provide $30b for failed S&Ls	N	72. Allow CIA to fund Contras	Y
24. Allow use of force against Iraq	Y	73. Revise unfair trade practices	Y
25. Allow $15b in foreign aid for '91	N	74. Focus SDI on accidental launch	Y
26. Revise & extend legal immigration	N	75. Bar Air Force $ for MX missile	N
27. Suspend aid to Angolan rebels	?	76. Allow "real" increase in defense	N
28. Democratic tax plan proposals	N	77. Troop reduction in Europe of 50%	Y
29. Cut defense 5% across the board	N	78. Ban nuclear tests above 1 kiloton	Y
30. Textile import quotas-veto override	Y	79. Ban anti-satellite missile tests	Y
31. Abortion service for military abroad	N	80. Observe certain limits of SALT II	?
32. Limits on high income farmers	N	81. Restore four Civil Rights laws	Y
33. Family medical leave-veto override	N	82. Prohibit aliens as strikebreakers	?
34. Req submission of balanced budget	Y	83. Allow military malpractice suits	Y
35. Balanced budget amendment	Y	84. Approval of $36m in Contra aid	Y
36. Amendment to ban flag desecration	Y	85. $18b deficit reduction compromise	Y
37. Reauthorize Amtrak-veto override	Y	86. Welfare reform of $5.7b for 5 years	Y
38. Retraining aid for coal miners	Y	87. Raise taxes $12b/cut spending $3b	N
39. Suspend El Salvador military aid	Y	88. Board to assess occupational risk	Y
40. Expand child care aid/tax credit	Y	89. Balanced budget by '93-via targets	Y
41. Raise House salary/omit honoraria	Y	90. Bar licensing of two nuclear plants	N
42. Toughen oil-spill liability	X	91. Remove victims compensation cap	N
43. Restitution to Japanese interned	N	92. Catastrophic health insurance	N
44. Protect Chinese & C.A. nationals	N	93. Ban airline smoking-2 hours or less	N
45. Abortion $ for rape/incest cases	N	94. $1b/two year aid for the homeless	Y
46. Allow religious schools to bar gays	Y	95. Bar non-unions in union companies	N
47. Bar broadcaster fairness doctrine	Y	96. Increase FSLIC rescue to $15b	N
48. Bar cap gains cut/reinstate IRA	N	97. Impose quotas to lower trade deficit	Y
49. Bar unions equal voice in pension	Y	98. Reduce discretionary budget 21%	Y

Presidential Support Score: 1991 - 54%   1990 - 38%

HOLLOWAY, CLYDE C. -- Louisiana 8th District [Republican]. Counties of Allen (pt.), Ascension, Avoyelles, East Baton Rouge (pt.), East Feliciana, Evangeline, Iberville, Pointe Coupee, Rapides (pt.), St. Helena, St. James, St. John the Baptist, St. Landry, West Baton Rouge and West Feliciana. Prior Terms: 1987-92. Born: November 28, 1943; Lecompte,

HOLLOWAY, CLYDE C. (continued)
LA. Education: National School of Aeronautics. Occupation: Sales and promotion, Pan American Airways; owner and operator, commercial nursery.

1.	Protection to Haitian refugees	N	50.	Bar assembly of chemical weapons	N
2.	Raise tax on wealthy; lower others	N	51.	Ban plutonium/uranium production	N
3.	Investigate Reagan hostage delay	N	52.	Cap MX missile deployment at 50	N
4.	Campaign finance revisions	N	53.	Allow $3b for 2 stealth bombers	Y
5.	Unpaid leave to care for children	N	54.	Publish bio-warfare experiments	N
6.	Restrict NEA use of funds	Y	55.	Raise minimum wage-veto override	N
7.	Bar race-bias claim/habeas corpus	Y	56.	Bar transfer of FS-X technology	N
8.	Ban race as death sentence factor	Y	57.	Cut defense and raise domestic $	N
9.	Exceptions to exclusionary rule	?	58.	Uniform poll closing in 48 states	N
10.	Allow sale of assault weapons	#	59.	Req foreign investment disclosure	Y
11.	Life in prison/abolish death penalty	?	60.	Textile import quotas-veto override	Y
12.	Req conspiracy-price fixing cases	?	61.	Bar abortion funding in Wash, DC	Y
13.	Unemployment benefits extension	?	62.	Notify spouses of AIDS+ carriers	Y
14.	Tissue use of aborted fetuses	?	63.	Seize conveyance-drug trafficking	Y
15.	Bar replacement of union strikers	N	64.	South Africa sanctions	N
16.	Hold foreign aid at $15b for '92	Y	65.	60 days' notice of plant closings	N
17.	Restore space station funding	Y	66.	Close unneeded military bases	Y
18.	Civil Rights Act of 1991	N	67.	Keep welfare reform within $2.8b	Y
19.	Unlimited damages-discrimination	N	68.	Allow children housing exclusion	Y
20.	Eliminate funds for supercollider	N	69.	Shift $400m of NASA to homeless	N
21.	Terminate SDI except for research	N	70.	Cap Medicare patients' liability	N
22.	Req 7-day handgun waiting period	N	71.	Prohibit employee polygraph testing	N
23.	Provide $30b for failed S&Ls	Y	72.	Allow CIA to fund Contras	Y
24.	Allow use of force against Iraq	Y	73.	Revise unfair trade practices	Y
25.	Allow $15b in foreign aid for '91	?	74.	Focus SDI on accidental launch	N
26.	Revise & extend legal immigration	?	75.	Bar Air Force $ for MX missile	N
27.	Suspend aid to Angolan rebels	N	76.	Allow "real" increase in defense	Y
28.	Democratic tax plan proposals	N	77.	Troop reduction in Europe of 50%	Y
29.	Cut defense 5% across the board	N	78.	Ban nuclear tests above 1 kiloton	N
30.	Textile import quotas-veto override	Y	79.	Ban anti-satellite missile tests	N
31.	Abortion service for military abroad	N	80.	Observe certain limits of SALT II	N
32.	Limits on high income farmers	N	81.	Restore four Civil Rights laws	N
33.	Family medical leave-veto override	N	82.	Prohibit aliens as strikebreakers	N
34.	Req submission of balanced budget	Y	83.	Allow military malpractice suits	N
35.	Balanced budget amendment	Y	84.	Approval of $36m in Contra aid	Y
36.	Amendment to ban flag desecration	Y	85.	$18b deficit reduction compromise	N
37.	Reauthorize Amtrak-veto override	N	86.	Welfare reform of $5.7b for 5 years	N
38.	Retraining aid for coal miners	?	87.	Raise taxes $12b/cut spending $3b	N
39.	Suspend El Salvador military aid	N	88.	Board to assess occupational risk	N
40.	Expand child care aid/tax credit	N	89.	Balanced budget by '93-via targets	Y
41.	Raise House salary/omit honoraria	N	90.	Bar licensing of two nuclear plants	N
42.	Toughen oil-spill liability	N	91.	Remove victims compensation cap	N
43.	Restitution to Japanese interned	N	92.	Catastrophic health insurance	N
44.	Protect Chinese & C.A. nationals	N	93.	Ban airline smoking-2 hours or less	N
45.	Abortion $ for rape/incest cases	N	94.	$1b/two year aid for the homeless	N
46.	Allow religious schools to bar gays	Y	95.	Bar non-unions in union companies	N
47.	Bar broadcaster fairness doctrine	Y	96.	Increase FSLIC rescue to $15b	N
48.	Bar cap gains cut/reinstate IRA	N	97.	Impose quotas to lower trade deficit	N
49.	Bar unions equal voice in pension	Y	98.	Reduce discretionary budget 21%	Y

Presidential Support Score: 1991 - 60%   1990 - 67%

MAINE

ANDREWS, THOMAS H. -- Maine 1st District [Democrat]. Counties of Cumberland, Kennebec, Knox, Lincoln, Sagadahoc, Waldo (pt.) and York. Prior Term: 1991-92. Born: March 23, 1953; North Easton, MA. Education: Bowdoin College (B.A.). Occupation: Maine Health

ANDREWS, THOMAS H. (continued)
and Hazardous Waste Task Force organizer; executive director, Maine Association of Handicapped Persons; founder-executive director, Maine Studies Center; state representative (1983-84) and senator (1985-90).

1. Protection to Haitian refugees	Y	13. Unemployment benefits extension	Y
2. Raise tax on wealthy; lower others	N	14. Tissue use of aborted fetuses	Y
3. Investigate Reagan hostage delay	Y	15. Bar replacement of union strikers	Y
4. Campaign finance revisions	Y	16. Hold foreign aid at $15b for '92	Y
5. Unpaid leave to care for children	Y	17. Restore space station funding	N
6. Restrict NEA use of funds	N	18. Civil Rights Act of 1991	Y
7. Bar race-bias claim/habeas corpus	N	19. Unlimited damages-discrimination	Y
8. Ban race as death sentence factor	N	20. Eliminate funds for supercollider	Y
9. Exceptions to exclusionary rule	N	21. Terminate SDI except for research	Y
10. Allow sale of assault weapons	N	22. Req 7-day handgun waiting period	Y
11. Life in prison/abolish death penalty	Y	23. Provide $30b for failed S&Ls	N
12. Req conspiracy-price fixing cases	N	24. Allow use of force against Iraq	N

Presidential Support Score: 1991 - 23%

SNOWE, OLYMPIA J. -- Maine 2nd District [Republican]. Counties of Androscoggin, Aroostook, Franklin, Hancock, Oxford, Penobscott, Piscataquis, Somerset and Washington, Prior Terms: 1979-92. Born: February 21, 1947; Augusta, ME. Education: University of Maine (B.A.). Occupation: Maine representative (1973-76); Maine senator (1976-78).

1. Protection to Haitian refugees	N	40. Expand child care aid/tax credit	Y
2. Raise tax on wealthy; lower others	N	41. Raise House salary/omit honoraria	N
3. Investigate Reagan hostage delay	N	42. Toughen oil-spill liability	?
4. Campaign finance revisions	Y	43. Restitution to Japanese interned	Y
5. Unpaid leave to care for children	Y	44. Protect Chinese & C.A. nationals	Y
6. Restrict NEA use of funds	Y	45. Abortion $ for rape/incest cases	Y
7. Bar race-bias claim/habeas corpus	Y	46. Allow religious schools to bar gays	Y
8. Ban race as death sentence factor	Y	47. Bar broadcaster fairness doctrine	N
9. Exceptions to exclusionary rule	Y	48. Bar cap gains cut/reinstate IRA	N
10. Allow sale of assault weapons	Y	49. Bar unions equal voice in pension	Y
11. Life in prison/abolish death penalty	N	50. Bar assembly of chemical weapons	Y
12. Req conspiracy-price fixing cases	Y	51. Ban plutonium/uranium production	N
13. Unemployment benefits extension	Y	52. Cap MX missile deployment at 50	Y
14. Tissue use of aborted fetuses	Y	53. Allow $3b for 2 stealth bombers	N
15. Bar replacement of union strikers	N	54. Publish bio-warfare experiments	Y
16. Hold foreign aid at $15b for '92	Y	55. Raise minimum wage-veto override	N
17. Restore space station funding	Y	56. Bar transfer of FS-X technology	Y
18. Civil Rights Act of 1991	Y	57. Cut defense and raise domestic $	N
19. Unlimited damages-discrimination	N	58. Uniform poll closing in 48 states	N
20. Eliminate funds for supercollider	Y	59. Req foreign investment disclosure	Y
21. Terminate SDI except for research	N	60. Textile import quotas-veto override	Y
22. Req 7-day handgun waiting period	N	61. Bar abortion funding in Wash, DC	N
23. Provide $30b for failed S&Ls	Y	62. Notify spouses of AIDS+ carriers	N
24. Allow use of force against Iraq	Y	63. Seize conveyance-drug trafficking	N
25. Allow $15b in foreign aid for '91	N	64. South Africa sanctions	N
26. Revise & extend legal immigration	Y	65. 60 days' notice of plant closings	N
27. Suspend aid to Angolan rebels	N	66. Close unneeded military bases	N
28. Democratic tax plan proposals	N	67. Keep welfare reform within $2.8b	Y
29. Cut defense 5% across the board	N	68. Allow children housing exclusion	Y
30. Textile import quotas-veto override	Y	69. Shift $400m of NASA to homeless	Y
31. Abortion service for military abroad	Y	70. Cap Medicare patients' liability	N
32. Limits on high income farmers	Y	71. Prohibit employee polygraph testing	Y
33. Family medical leave-veto override	Y	72. Allow CIA to fund Contras	N
34. Req submission of balanced budget	Y	73. Revise unfair trade practices	Y
35. Balanced budget amendment	Y	74. Focus SDI on accidental launch	Y
36. Amendment to ban flag desecration	Y	75. Bar Air Force $ for MX missile	N
37. Reauthorize Amtrak-veto override	Y	76. Allow "real" increase in defense	Y
38. Retraining aid for coal miners	N	77. Troop reduction in Europe of 50%	N
39. Suspend El Salvador military aid	N	78. Ban nuclear tests above 1 kiloton	Y

SNOWE, OLYMPIA J. (continued)

79. Ban anti-satellite missile tests	N	112. Superfund waste cleanup of $10b	Y
80. Observe certain limits of SALT II	Y	113. 90 days notice of plant closings	N
81. Restore four Civil Rights laws	Y	114. $20b in Medicare cuts/tax increases	Y
82. Prohibit aliens as strikebreakers	Y	115. Spending cuts and tax increases	N
83. Allow military malpractice suits	Y	116. Set school lunch lmt-250% poverty	N
84. Approval of $36m in Contra aid	Y	117. $75m for youth work projects	Y
85. $18b deficit reduction compromise	Y	118. Allow Angolan military assistance	Y
86. Welfare reform of $5.7b for 5 years	N	119. Suspend defense payments for abuse	N
87. Raise taxes $12b/cut spending $3b	N	120. Drop SS COLAs/$12b tax increase	N
88. Board to assess occupational risk	N	121. Approve $1.5b for 21 MX missiles	Y
89. Balanced budget by '93-via targets	Y	122. Emergency farm credit/revisions	Y
90. Bar licensing of two nuclear plants	Y	123. Duty on Taiwan/Hong Kong/S Korea	Y
91. Remove victims compensation cap	Y	124. Limit steel imports to 17%	Y
92. Catastrophic health insurance	Y	125. Cut $ to schools that bar prayer	N
93. Ban airline smoking-2 hours or less	N	126. $50b-taxes; cut Medicare/spending	Y
94. $1b/two year aid for the homeless	Y	127. Limit Pershing II/cruise in Europe	N
95. Bar non-unions in union companies	N	128. Delete $7.1b for 34 B-1 bombers	N
96. Increase FSLIC rescue to $15b	Y	129. Bar purchase of Sergeant York guns	Y
97. Impose quotas to lower trade deficit	Y	130. El Salvador military/economic aid	Y
98. Reduce discretionary budget 21%	Y	131. Bar mining of Nicaraguan waters	Y
99. Immigration reform/alien amnesty	Y	132. Physician fee freeze for Medicare	Y
100. South Africa sanctions-veto override	Y	133. $49b in "sin"/phone/insurance taxes	Y
101. Tax overhaul to revise income tax	Y	134. Allow sale of Conrail	Y
102. Use of military in drug war	Y	135. Equal Rights Amendment	Y
103. Delete 12 MX/add conventional wpn	N	136. Authorize Marines in Lebanon	Y
104. Raise speed limit to 65 mph	N	137. Eminent domain for coal companies	Y
105. Require Pentagon to buy US goods	Y	138. Prohibit EPA clean air sanctions	N
106. AIDS insurance non-discrimination	N	139. SS retirement age increase/reforms	Y
107. Prohibit Saudi arms sales	Y	140. Auto domestic content requirement	N
108. Ease Gun Control Act of 1968	Y	141. Delete jobs program funding	Y
109. Bar interstate handgun transport	N	142. Highway-gas tax bill	N
110. Make company emissions known	Y	143. Cut $5b from defense for Medicare	Y
111. Allow toxic victims to sue in fed ct	Y	144. Emergency housing aid of $1b	Y

Presidential Support Score: 1991 - 47%   1990 - 48%

MARYLAND

GILCHREST, WAYNE T. -- Maryland 1st District [Republican]. Counties of Calvert, Caroline, Cecil, Charles, Dorchester, Harford (pt.), Kent, Queen Anne's, St. Mary's, Somerset, Talbot, Wicomico and Worcester. Prior Term: 1991-92. Born: April 15, 1946; Rahway, NJ. Education: Wesley College (A.A.); Delaware State College (B.A.); Loyola College, Baltimore (M.A. candidate). Military Service: U.S. Marine Corps. Occupation: High school teacher.

1. Protection to Haitian refugees	N	13. Unemployment benefits extension	Y
2. Raise tax on wealthy; lower others	N	14. Tissue use of aborted fetuses	Y
3. Investigate Reagan hostage delay	N	15. Bar replacement of union strikers	N
4. Campaign finance revisions	N	16. Hold foreign aid at $15b for '92	Y
5. Unpaid leave to care for children	N	17. Restore space station funding	Y
6. Restrict NEA use of funds	Y	18. Civil Rights Act of 1991	N
7. Bar race-bias claim/habeas corpus	Y	19. Unlimited damages-discrimination	N
8. Ban race as death sentence factor	Y	20. Eliminate funds for supercollider	N
9. Exceptions to exclusionary rule	Y	21. Terminate SDI except for research	N
10. Allow sale of assault weapons	Y	22. Req 7-day handgun waiting period	Y
11. Life in prison/abolish death penalty	N	23. Provide $30b for failed S&Ls	Y
12. Req conspiracy-price fixing cases	Y	24. Allow use of force against Iraq	Y

Presidential Support Score: 1991 - 70%

BENTLEY, H. DELICH -- Maryland 2nd District [Republican]. Counties of Baltimore (pt.) and Harford (pt.). Prior Terms: 1985-92. Education: University of Missouri. Occupation: Business consultant; founder, HDB International; reporter; editor, Baltimore Sun.

1. Protection to Haitian refugees	N	
2. Raise tax on wealthy; lower others	N	
3. Investigate Reagan hostage delay	N	
4. Campaign finance revisions	N	
5. Unpaid leave to care for children	N	
6. Restrict NEA use of funds	Y	
7. Bar race-bias claim/habeas corpus	Y	
8. Ban race as death sentence factor	Y	
9. Exceptions to exclusionary rule	Y	
10. Allow sale of assault weapons	Y	
11. Life in prison/abolish death penalty	N	
12. Req conspiracy-price fixing cases	N	
13. Unemployment benefits extension	Y	
14. Tissue use of aborted fetuses	Y	
15. Bar replacement of union strikers	Y	
16. Hold foreign aid at $15b for '92	Y	
17. Restore space station funding	Y	
18. Civil Rights Act of 1991	N	
19. Unlimited damages-discrimination	N	
20. Eliminate funds for supercollider	N	
21. Terminate SDI except for research	N	
22. Req 7-day handgun waiting period	Y	
23. Provide $30b for failed S&Ls	?	
24. Allow use of force against Iraq	Y	
25. Allow $15b in foreign aid for '91	Y	
26. Revise & extend legal immigration	N	
27. Suspend aid to Angolan rebels	N	
28. Democratic tax plan proposals	N	
29. Cut defense 5% across the board	N	
30. Textile import quotas-veto override	Y	
31. Abortion service for military abroad	N	
32. Limits on high income farmers	N	
33. Family medical leave-veto override	N	
34. Req submission of balanced budget	N	
35. Balanced budget amendment	Y	
36. Amendment to ban flag desecration	Y	
37. Reauthorize Amtrak-veto override	Y	
38. Retraining aid for coal miners	Y	
39. Suspend El Salvador military aid	N	
40. Expand child care aid/tax credit	N	
41. Raise House salary/omit honoraria	N	
42. Toughen oil-spill liability	N	
43. Restitution to Japanese interned	N	
44. Protect Chinese & C.A. nationals	N	
45. Abortion $ for rape/incest cases	Y	
46. Allow religious schools to bar gays	Y	
47. Bar broadcaster fairness doctrine	N	
48. Bar cap gains cut/reinstate IRA	N	
49. Bar unions equal voice in pension	Y	
50. Bar assembly of chemical weapons	N	
51. Ban plutonium/uranium production	N	
52. Cap MX missile deployment at 50	N	
53. Allow $3b for 2 stealth bombers	Y	
54. Publish bio-warfare experiments	N	
55. Raise minimum wage-veto override	N	
56. Bar transfer of FS-X technology	Y	
57. Cut defense and raise domestic $	N	
58. Uniform poll closing in 48 states	Y	
59. Req foreign investment disclosure	Y	
60. Textile import quotas-veto override	Y	
61. Bar abortion funding in Wash, DC	Y
62. Notify spouses of AIDS+ carriers	N
63. Seize conveyance-drug trafficking	N
64. South Africa sanctions	N
65. 60 days' notice of plant closings	Y
66. Close unneeded military bases	Y
67. Keep welfare reform within $2.8b	Y
68. Allow children housing exclusion	Y
69. Shift $400m of NASA to homeless	N
70. Cap Medicare patients' liability	Y
71. Prohibit employee polygraph testing	Y
72. Allow CIA to fund Contras	Y
73. Revise unfair trade practices	Y
74. Focus SDI on accidental launch	N
75. Bar Air Force $ for MX missile	N
76. Allow "real" increase in defense	Y
77. Troop reduction in Europe of 50%	Y
78. Ban nuclear tests above 1 kiloton	N
79. Ban anti-satellite missile tests	N
80. Observe certain limits of SALT II	?
81. Restore four Civil Rights laws	N
82. Prohibit aliens as strikebreakers	Y
83. Allow military malpractice suits	N
84. Approval of $36m in Contra aid	Y
85. $18b deficit reduction compromise	N
86. Welfare reform of $5.7b for 5 years	N
87. Raise taxes $12b/cut spending $3b	N
88. Board to assess occupational risk	N
89. Balanced budget by '93-via targets	N
90. Bar licensing of two nuclear plants	N
91. Remove victims compensation cap	N
92. Catastrophic health insurance	Y
93. Ban airline smoking-2 hours or less	N
94. $1b/two year aid for the homeless	N
95. Bar non-unions in union companies	Y
96. Increase FSLIC rescue to $15b	Y
97. Impose quotas to lower trade deficit	Y
98. Reduce discretionary budget 21%	Y
99. Immigration reform/alien amnesty	N
100. South Africa sanctions-veto override	Y
101. Tax overhaul to revise income tax	N
102. Use of military in drug war	Y
103. Delete 12 MX/add conventional wpn	N
104. Raise speed limit to 65 mph	N
105. Require Pentagon to buy US goods	Y
106. AIDS insurance non-discrimination	Y
107. Prohibit Saudi arms sales	Y
108. Ease Gun Control Act of 1968	Y
109. Bar interstate handgun transport	N
110. Make company emissions known	N
111. Allow toxic victims to sue in fed ct	N
112. Superfund waste cleanup of $10b	N
113. 90 days notice of plant closings	N
114. $20b in Medicare cuts/tax increases	N
115. Spending cuts and tax increases	N
116. Set school lunch lmt-250% poverty	Y
117. $75m for youth work projects	N
118. Allow Angolan military assistance	Y
119. Suspend defense payments for abuse	N
120. Drop SS COLAs/$12b tax increase	N

BENTLEY, H. DELICH (continued)
121. Approve $1.5b for 21 MX missiles Y   122. Emergency farm credit/revisions Y

Presidential Support Score: 1991 - 60%   1990 - 61%

CARDIN, BENJAMIN L. -- Maryland 3rd District [Democrat]. Counties of Baltimore (pt.), Howard (pt.) and City of Baltimore (pt.). Prior Terms: 1987-92. Born: October 5, 1943; Baltimore, MD. Education: University of Pittsburgh (B.A.); University of Maryland (LL.B.). Occupation: Attorney; state delegate (1966-86).

1. Protection to Haitian refugees	Y	50. Bar assembly of chemical weapons	Y
2. Raise tax on wealthy; lower others	N	51. Ban plutonium/uranium production	Y
3. Investigate Reagan hostage delay	Y	52. Cap MX missile deployment at 50	Y
4. Campaign finance revisions	Y	53. Allow $3b for 2 stealth bombers	N
5. Unpaid leave to care for children	Y	54. Publish bio-warfare experiments	Y
6. Restrict NEA use of funds	N	55. Raise minimum wage-veto override	Y
7. Bar race-bias claim/habeas corpus	N	56. Bar transfer of FS-X technology	Y
8. Ban race as death sentence factor	N	57. Cut defense and raise domestic $	Y
9. Exceptions to exclusionary rule	N	58. Uniform poll closing in 48 states	Y
10. Allow sale of assault weapons	N	59. Req foreign investment disclosure	Y
11. Life in prison/abolish death penalty	N	60. Textile import quotas-veto override	Y
12. Req conspiracy-price fixing cases	N	61. Bar abortion funding in Wash, DC	N
13. Unemployment benefits extension	Y	62. Notify spouses of AIDS+ carriers	N
14. Tissue use of aborted fetuses	Y	63. Seize conveyance-drug trafficking	N
15. Bar replacement of union strikers	Y	64. South Africa sanctions	Y
16. Hold foreign aid at $15b for '92	Y	65. 60 days' notice of plant closings	Y
17. Restore space station funding	Y	66. Close unneeded military bases	N
18. Civil Rights Act of 1991	Y	67. Keep welfare reform within $2.8b	N
19. Unlimited damages-discrimination	Y	68. Allow children housing exclusion	N
20. Eliminate funds for supercollider	N	69. Shift $400m of NASA to homeless	Y
21. Terminate SDI except for research	N	70. Cap Medicare patients' liability	Y
22. Req 7-day handgun waiting period	Y	71. Prohibit employee polygraph testing	Y
23. Provide $30b for failed S&Ls	Y	72. Allow CIA to fund Contras	N
24. Allow use of force against Iraq	N	73. Revise unfair trade practices	Y
25. Allow $15b in foreign aid for '91	Y	74. Focus SDI on accidental launch	Y
26. Revise & extend legal immigration	Y	75. Bar Air Force $ for MX missile	Y
27. Suspend aid to Angolan rebels	Y	76. Allow "real" increase in defense	N
28. Democratic tax plan proposals	Y	77. Troop reduction in Europe of 50%	N
29. Cut defense 5% across the board	N	78. Ban nuclear tests above 1 kiloton	Y
30. Textile import quotas-veto override	Y	79. Ban anti-satellite missile tests	Y
31. Abortion service for military abroad	Y	80. Observe certain limits of SALT II	Y
32. Limits on high income farmers	Y	81. Restore four Civil Rights laws	Y
33. Family medical leave-veto override	Y	82. Prohibit aliens as strikebreakers	Y
34. Req submission of balanced budget	N	83. Allow military malpractice suits	Y
35. Balanced budget amendment	N	84. Approval of $36m in Contra aid	N
36. Amendment to ban flag desecration	N	85. $18b deficit reduction compromise	Y
37. Reauthorize Amtrak-veto override	Y	86. Welfare reform of $5.7b for 5 years	Y
38. Retraining aid for coal miners	Y	87. Raise taxes $12b/cut spending $3b	Y
39. Suspend El Salvador military aid	Y	88. Board to assess occupational risk	Y
40. Expand child care aid/tax credit	Y	89. Balanced budget by '93-via targets	N
41. Raise House salary/omit honoraria	Y	90. Bar licensing of two nuclear plants	N
42. Toughen oil-spill liability	N	91. Remove victims compensation cap	N
43. Restitution to Japanese interned	Y	92. Catastrophic health insurance	Y
44. Protect Chinese & C.A. nationals	Y	93. Ban airline smoking-2 hours or less	Y
45. Abortion $ for rape/incest cases	Y	94. $1b/two year aid for the homeless	Y
46. Allow religious schools to bar gays	?	95. Bar non-unions in union companies	Y
47. Bar broadcaster fairness doctrine	Y	96. Increase FSLIC rescue to $15b	Y
48. Bar cap gains cut/reinstate IRA	Y	97. Impose quotas to lower trade deficit	Y
49. Bar unions equal voice in pension	N	98. Reduce discretionary budget 21%	N

Presidential Support Score: 1991 - 32%   1990 - 21%

McMILLEN, C. THOMAS -- Maryland 4th District [Democrat]. Counties of Anne Arundel, Howard (pt.) and Prince George's (pt.). Prior Terms: 1987-92. Born: May 26, 1952; Elmira, NY. Education: University of Maryland (B.S.); Oxford University (B.A., M.A.). Occupation: Professional athlete; founder, McMillen Communications Corp.; chairman of the board, Summit Capital Corp.; director, Second National Building & Loan.

1. Protection to Haitian refugees	Y	
2. Raise tax on wealthy; lower others	N	
3. Investigate Reagan hostage delay	Y	
4. Campaign finance revisions	Y	
5. Unpaid leave to care for children	Y	
6. Restrict NEA use of funds	Y	
7. Bar race-bias claim/habeas corpus	N	
8. Ban race as death sentence factor	N	
9. Exceptions to exclusionary rule	N	
10. Allow sale of assault weapons	Y	
11. Life in prison/abolish death penalty	N	
12. Req conspiracy-price fixing cases	N	
13. Unemployment benefits extension	Y	
14. Tissue use of aborted fetuses	Y	
15. Bar replacement of union strikers	Y	
16. Hold foreign aid at $15b for '92	Y	
17. Restore space station funding	Y	
18. Civil Rights Act of 1991	Y	
19. Unlimited damages-discrimination	N	
20. Eliminate funds for supercollider	N	
21. Terminate SDI except for research	N	
22. Req 7-day handgun waiting period	Y	
23. Provide $30b for failed S&Ls	Y	
24. Allow use of force against Iraq	Y	
25. Allow $15b in foreign aid for '91	Y	
26. Revise & extend legal immigration	Y	
27. Suspend aid to Angolan rebels	Y	
28. Democratic tax plan proposals	Y	
29. Cut defense 5% across the board	N	
30. Textile import quotas-veto override	Y	
31. Abortion service for military abroad	Y	
32. Limits on high income farmers	Y	
33. Family medical leave-veto override	Y	
34. Req submission of balanced budget	Y	
35. Balanced budget amendment	Y	
36. Amendment to ban flag desecration	Y	
37. Reauthorize Amtrak-veto override	Y	
38. Retraining aid for coal miners	Y	
39. Suspend El Salvador military aid	Y	
40. Expand child care aid/tax credit	Y	
41. Raise House salary/omit honoraria	Y	
42. Toughen oil-spill liability	N	
43. Restitution to Japanese interned	Y	
44. Protect Chinese & C.A. nationals	Y	
45. Abortion $ for rape/incest cases	Y	
46. Allow religious schools to bar gays	Y	
47. Bar broadcaster fairness doctrine	N	
48. Bar cap gains cut/reinstate IRA	N	
49. Bar unions equal voice in pension	N	
50. Bar assembly of chemical weapons	Y
51. Ban plutonium/uranium production	Y
52. Cap MX missile deployment at 50	Y
53. Allow $3b for 2 stealth bombers	N
54. Publish bio-warfare experiments	Y
55. Raise minimum wage-veto override	Y
56. Bar transfer of FS-X technology	Y
57. Cut defense and raise domestic $	N
58. Uniform poll closing in 48 states	Y
59. Req foreign investment disclosure	Y
60. Textile import quotas-veto override	Y
61. Bar abortion funding in Wash, DC	N
62. Notify spouses of AIDS+ carriers	N
63. Seize conveyance-drug trafficking	N
64. South Africa sanctions	Y
65. 60 days' notice of plant closings	Y
66. Close unneeded military bases	N
67. Keep welfare reform within $2.8b	Y
68. Allow children housing exclusion	N
69. Shift $400m of NASA to homeless	N
70. Cap Medicare patients' liability	Y
71. Prohibit employee polygraph testing	Y
72. Allow CIA to fund Contras	N
73. Revise unfair trade practices	Y
74. Focus SDI on accidental launch	Y
75. Bar Air Force $ for MX missile	N
76. Allow "real" increase in defense	Y
77. Troop reduction in Europe of 50%	N
78. Ban nuclear tests above 1 kiloton	Y
79. Ban anti-satellite missile tests	Y
80. Observe certain limits of SALT II	Y
81. Restore four Civil Rights laws	Y
82. Prohibit aliens as strikebreakers	Y
83. Allow military malpractice suits	Y
84. Approval of $36m in Contra aid	N
85. $18b deficit reduction compromise	Y
86. Welfare reform of $5.7b for 5 years	Y
87. Raise taxes $12b/cut spending $3b	N
88. Board to assess occupational risk	Y
89. Balanced budget by '93-via targets	Y
90. Bar licensing of two nuclear plants	N
91. Remove victims compensation cap	N
92. Catastrophic health insurance	Y
93. Ban airline smoking-2 hours or less	N
94. $1b/two year aid for the homeless	Y
95. Bar non-unions in union companies	Y
96. Increase FSLIC rescue to $15b	N
97. Impose quotas to lower trade deficit	Y
98. Reduce discretionary budget 21%	Y

Presidential Support Score: 1991 - 40%   1990 - 27%

HOYER, STENY H. -- Maryland 5th District [Democrat]. County of Prince George's (pt.). Prior Terms: 1981 (Special Election)-1992. Born: June 14, 1939; New York City, NY. Education: University of Maryland (B.S.); Georgetown University Law Center (J.D.). Occupation: Federal employee; executive assistant to a U.S. senator; Maryland senator; attorney; chairman, Joint Commission on Intergovernmental Cooperation; member, State Board for Higher Education.

HOYER, STENY H. (continued)

1. Protection to Haitian refugees	#	
2. Raise tax on wealthy; lower others	N	
3. Investigate Reagan hostage delay	Y	
4. Campaign finance revisions	Y	
5. Unpaid leave to care for children	Y	
6. Restrict NEA use of funds	N	
7. Bar race-bias claim/habeas corpus	N	
8. Ban race as death sentence factor	N	
9. Exceptions to exclusionary rule	N	
10. Allow sale of assault weapons	N	
11. Life in prison/abolish death penalty	Y	
12. Req conspiracy-price fixing cases	X	
13. Unemployment benefits extension	Y	
14. Tissue use of aborted fetuses	Y	
15. Bar replacement of union strikers	Y	
16. Hold foreign aid at $15b for '92	Y	
17. Restore space station funding	N	
18. Civil Rights Act of 1991	Y	
19. Unlimited damages-discrimination	Y	
20. Eliminate funds for supercollider	N	
21. Terminate SDI except for research	N	
22. Req 7-day handgun waiting period	Y	
23. Provide $30b for failed S&Ls	Y	
24. Allow use of force against Iraq	N	
25. Allow $15b in foreign aid for '91	Y	
26. Revise & extend legal immigration	Y	
27. Suspend aid to Angolan rebels	Y	
28. Democratic tax plan proposals	Y	
29. Cut defense 5% across the board	N	
30. Textile import quotas-veto override	Y	
31. Abortion service for military abroad	Y	
32. Limits on high income farmers	N	
33. Family medical leave-veto override	Y	
34. Req submission of balanced budget	Y	
35. Balanced budget amendment	N	
36. Amendment to ban flag desecration	N	
37. Reauthorize Amtrak-veto override	Y	
38. Retraining aid for coal miners	Y	
39. Suspend El Salvador military aid	Y	
40. Expand child care aid/tax credit	Y	
41. Raise House salary/omit honoraria	Y	
42. Toughen oil-spill liability	Y	
43. Restitution to Japanese interned	Y	
44. Protect Chinese & C.A. nationals	Y	
45. Abortion $ for rape/incest cases	Y	
46. Allow religious schools to bar gays	N	
47. Bar broadcaster fairness doctrine	N	
48. Bar cap gains cut/reinstate IRA	Y	
49. Bar unions equal voice in pension	N	
50. Bar assembly of chemical weapons	Y	
51. Ban plutonium/uranium production	Y	
52. Cap MX missile deployment at 50	Y	
53. Allow $3b for 2 stealth bombers	N	
54. Publish bio-warfare experiments	Y	
55. Raise minimum wage-veto override	Y	
56. Bar transfer of FS-X technology	Y	
57. Cut defense and raise domestic $	Y	
58. Uniform poll closing in 48 states	Y	
59. Req foreign investment disclosure	Y	
60. Textile import quotas-veto override	Y	
61. Bar abortion funding in Wash, DC	N	
62. Notify spouses of AIDS+ carriers	N	
63. Seize conveyance-drug trafficking	N	
64. South Africa sanctions	Y	

65. 60 days' notice of plant closings	Y	
66. Close unneeded military bases	N	
67. Keep welfare reform within $2.8b	N	
68. Allow children housing exclusion	N	
69. Shift $400m of NASA to homeless	Y	
70. Cap Medicare patients' liability	Y	
71. Prohibit employee polygraph testing	Y	
72. Allow CIA to fund Contras	N	
73. Revise unfair trade practices	Y	
74. Focus SDI on accidental launch	Y	
75. Bar Air Force $ for MX missile	Y	
76. Allow "real" increase in defense	N	
77. Troop reduction in Europe of 50%	N	
78. Ban nuclear tests above 1 kiloton	Y	
79. Ban anti-satellite missile tests	Y	
80. Observe certain limits of SALT II	Y	
81. Restore four Civil Rights laws	Y	
82. Prohibit aliens as strikebreakers	Y	
83. Allow military malpractice suits	Y	
84. Approval of $36m in Contra aid	N	
85. $18b deficit reduction compromise	Y	
86. Welfare reform of $5.7b for 5 years	Y	
87. Raise taxes $12b/cut spending $3b	Y	
88. Board to assess occupational risk	Y	
89. Balanced budget by '93-via targets	N	
90. Bar licensing of two nuclear plants	Y	
91. Remove victims compensation cap	N	
92. Catastrophic health insurance	Y	
93. Ban airline smoking-2 hours or less	Y	
94. $1b/two year aid for the homeless	Y	
95. Bar non-unions in union companies	Y	
96. Increase FSLIC rescue to $15b	Y	
97. Impose quotas to lower trade deficit	Y	
98. Reduce discretionary budget 21%	N	
99. Immigration reform/alien amnesty	Y	
100. South Africa sanctions-veto override	Y	
101. Tax overhaul to revise income tax	N	
102. Use of military in drug war	N	
103. Delete 12 MX/add conventional wpn	N	
104. Raise speed limit to 65 mph	N	
105. Require Pentagon to buy US goods	N	
106. AIDS insurance non-discrimination	Y	
107. Prohibit Saudi arms sales	Y	
108. Ease Gun Control Act of 1968	N	
109. Bar interstate handgun transport	?	
110. Make company emissions known	Y	
111. Allow toxic victims to sue in fed ct	N	
112. Superfund waste cleanup of $10b	Y	
113. 90 days notice of plant closings	Y	
114. $20b in Medicare cuts/tax increases	Y	
115. Spending cuts and tax increases	Y	
116. Set school lunch lmt-250% poverty	N	
117. $75m for youth work projects	Y	
118. Allow Angolan military assistance	N	
119. Suspend defense payments for abuse	Y	
120. Drop SS COLAs/$12b tax increase	N	
121. Approve $1.5b for 21 MX missiles	Y	
122. Emergency farm credit/revisions	Y	
123. Duty on Taiwan/Hong Kong/S Korea	Y	
124. Limit steel imports to 17%	Y	
125. Cut $ to schools that bar prayer	N	
126. $50b-taxes; cut Medicare/spending	Y	
127. Limit Pershing II/cruise in Europe	N	
128. Delete $7.1b for 34 B-1 bombers	N	

HOYER, STENY H. (continued)

129. Bar purchase of Sergeant York guns	N
130. El Salvador military/economic aid	N
131. Bar mining of Nicaraguan waters	Y
132. Physician fee freeze for Medicare	N
133. $49b in "sin"/phone/insurance taxes	Y
134. Allow sale of Conrail	N
135. Equal Rights Amendment	Y
136. Authorize Marines in Lebanon	Y
137. Eminent domain for coal companies	N
138. Prohibit EPA clean air sanctions	N
139. SS retirement age increase/reforms	N
140. Auto domestic content requirement	Y
141. Delete jobs program funding	N
142. Highway-gas tax bill	Y
143. Cut $5b from defense for Medicare	Y
144. Emergency housing aid of $1b	Y

Presidential Support Score: 1991 - 33%   1990 - 19%

BYRON, BEVERLY B. -- Maryland 6th District [Democrat].   Counties of Allegany, Carroll, Frederick Garrett, Howard (pt.), Montgomery (pt.) and Washington. Prior Terms: 1979-92. Born: July 27, 1932; Baltimore, MD.   Education: Hood College.   Occupation: Boardmember, American Red Cross; secretary, Frederick Heart Association.

1. Protection to Haitian refugees	N
2. Raise tax on wealthy; lower others	N
3. Investigate Reagan hostage delay	N
4. Campaign finance revisions	Y
5. Unpaid leave to care for children	N
6. Restrict NEA use of funds	Y
7. Bar race-bias claim/habeas corpus	Y
8. Ban race as death sentence factor	Y
9. Exceptions to exclusionary rule	Y
10. Allow sale of assault weapons	Y
11. Life in prison/abolish death penalty	N
12. Req conspiracy-price fixing cases	Y
13. Unemployment benefits extension	Y
14. Tissue use of aborted fetuses	Y
15. Bar replacement of union strikers	Y
16. Hold foreign aid at $15b for '92	Y
17. Restore space station funding	Y
18. Civil Rights Act of 1991	Y
19. Unlimited damages-discrimination	N
20. Eliminate funds for supercollider	N
21. Terminate SDI except for research	N
22. Req 7-day handgun waiting period	N
23. Provide $30b for failed S&Ls	N
24. Allow use of force against Iraq	Y
25. Allow $15b in foreign aid for '91	N
26. Revise & extend legal immigration	N
27. Suspend aid to Angolan rebels	N
28. Democratic tax plan proposals	Y
29. Cut defense 5% across the board	N
30. Textile import quotas-veto override	Y
31. Abortion service for military abroad	N
32. Limits on high income farmers	N
33. Family medical leave-veto override	N
34. Req submission of balanced budget	Y
35. Balanced budget amendment	Y
36. Amendment to ban flag desecration	Y
37. Reauthorize Amtrak-veto override	Y
38. Retraining aid for coal miners	Y
39. Suspend El Salvador military aid	N
40. Expand child care aid/tax credit	Y
41. Raise House salary/omit honoraria	Y
42. Toughen oil-spill liability	N
43. Restitution to Japanese interned	N
44. Protect Chinese & C.A. nationals	Y
45. Abortion $ for rape/incest cases	N
46. Allow religious schools to bar gays	Y
47. Bar broadcaster fairness doctrine	N
48. Bar cap gains cut/reinstate IRA	N
49. Bar unions equal voice in pension	Y
50. Bar assembly of chemical weapons	N
51. Ban plutonium/uranium production	N
52. Cap MX missile deployment at 50	Y
53. Allow $3b for 2 stealth bombers	Y
54. Publish bio-warfare experiments	N
55. Raise minimum wage-veto override	N
56. Bar transfer of FS-X technology	N
57. Cut defense and raise domestic $	N
58. Uniform poll closing in 48 states	?
59. Req foreign investment disclosure	Y
60. Textile import quotas-veto override	Y
61. Bar abortion funding in Wash, DC	Y
62. Notify spouses of AIDS+ carriers	N
63. Seize conveyance-drug trafficking	N
64. South Africa sanctions	N
65. 60 days' notice of plant closings	Y
66. Close unneeded military bases	Y
67. Keep welfare reform within $2.8b	Y
68. Allow children housing exclusion	Y
69. Shift $400m of NASA to homeless	N
70. Cap Medicare patients' liability	Y
71. Prohibit employee polygraph testing	Y
72. Allow CIA to fund Contras	Y
73. Revise unfair trade practices	?
74. Focus SDI on accidental launch	Y
75. Bar Air Force $ for MX missile	N
76. Allow "real" increase in defense	Y
77. Troop reduction in Europe of 50%	N
78. Ban nuclear tests above 1 kiloton	?
79. Ban anti-satellite missile tests	N
80. Observe certain limits of SALT II	N
81. Restore four Civil Rights laws	Y
82. Prohibit aliens as strikebreakers	Y
83. Allow military malpractice suits	N
84. Approval of $36m in Contra aid	Y
85. $18b deficit reduction compromise	Y
86. Welfare reform of $5.7b for 5 years	N
87. Raise taxes $12b/cut spending $3b	N
88. Board to assess occupational risk	Y
89. Balanced budget by '93-via targets	N
90. Bar licensing of two nuclear plants	N
91. Remove victims compensation cap	N
92. Catastrophic health insurance	Y
93. Ban airline smoking-2 hours or less	Y
94. $1b/two year aid for the homeless	N

BYRON, BEVERLY B. (continued)

95.	Bar non-unions in union companies	N
96.	Increase FSLIC rescue to $15b	N
97.	Impose quotas to lower trade deficit	Y
98.	Reduce discretionary budget 21%	Y
99.	Immigration reform/alien amnesty	Y
100.	South Africa sanctions-veto override	Y
101.	Tax overhaul to revise income tax	Y
102.	Use of military in drug war	N
103.	Delete 12 MX/add conventional wpn	N
104.	Raise speed limit to 65 mph	N
105.	Require Pentagon to buy US goods	N
106.	AIDS insurance non-discrimination	Y
107.	Prohibit Saudi arms sales	Y
108.	Ease Gun Control Act of 1968	Y
109.	Bar interstate handgun transport	N
110.	Make company emissions known	N
111.	Allow toxic victims to sue in fed ct	N
112.	Superfund waste cleanup of $10b	Y
113.	90 days notice of plant closings	N
114.	$20b in Medicare cuts/tax increases	Y
115.	Spending cuts and tax increases	Y
116.	Set school lunch lmt-250% poverty	Y
117.	$75m for youth work projects	Y
118.	Allow Angolan military assistance	Y
119.	Suspend defense payments for abuse	N
120.	Drop SS COLAs/$12b tax increase	N
121.	Approve $1.5b for 21 MX missiles	Y
122.	Emergency farm credit/revisions	Y
123.	Duty on Taiwan/Hong Kong/S Korea	N
124.	Limit steel imports to 17%	Y
125.	Cut $ to schools that bar prayer	Y
126.	$50b-taxes; cut Medicare/spending	N
127.	Limit Pershing II/cruise in Europe	N
128.	Delete $7.1b for 34 B-1 bombers	N
129.	Bar purchase of Sergeant York guns	N
130.	El Salvador military/economic aid	Y
131.	Bar mining of Nicaraguan waters	N
132.	Physician fee freeze for Medicare	N
133.	$49b in "sin"/phone/insurance taxes	N
134.	Allow sale of Conrail	N
135.	Equal Rights Amendment	Y
136.	Authorize Marines in Lebanon	N
137.	Eminent domain for coal companies	N
138.	Prohibit EPA clean air sanctions	Y
139.	SS retirement age increase/reforms	Y
140.	Auto domestic content requirement	N
141.	Delete jobs program funding	N
142.	Highway-gas tax bill	?
143.	Cut $5b from defense for Medicare	Y
144.	Emergency housing aid of $1b	Y

Presidential Support Score: 1991 - 51%   1990 - 48%

MFUME, KWEISI -- Maryland 7th District [Democrat].   County of Baltimore (pt.) and City of Baltimore (pt.).   Prior Terms: 1987-92.   Born: October 24, 1948; Baltimore, MD. Education: Morgan State University (B.S.); Johns Hopkins University (M.A.).   Occupation: Baltimore city councilman (1970-1986); assistant professor of political science and campus radio station program director, Morgan State University.

1.	Protection to Haitian refugees	Y
2.	Raise tax on wealthy; lower others	N
3.	Investigate Reagan hostage delay	Y
4.	Campaign finance revisions	Y
5.	Unpaid leave to care for children	Y
6.	Restrict NEA use of funds	N
7.	Bar race-bias claim/habeas corpus	N
8.	Ban race as death sentence factor	N
9.	Exceptions to exclusionary rule	N
10.	Allow sale of assault weapons	N
11.	Life in prison/abolish death penalty	Y
12.	Req conspiracy-price fixing cases	N
13.	Unemployment benefits extension	Y
14.	Tissue use of aborted fetuses	Y
15.	Bar replacement of union strikers	Y
16.	Hold foreign aid at $15b for '92	+
17.	Restore space station funding	N
18.	Civil Rights Act of 1991	Y
19.	Unlimited damages-discrimination	Y
20.	Eliminate funds for supercollider	Y
21.	Terminate SDI except for research	Y
22.	Req 7-day handgun waiting period	Y
23.	Provide $30b for failed S&Ls	N
24.	Allow use of force against Iraq	N
25.	Allow $15b in foreign aid for '91	N
26.	Revise & extend legal immigration	Y
27.	Suspend aid to Angolan rebels	Y
28.	Democratic tax plan proposals	Y
29.	Cut defense 5% across the board	Y
30.	Textile import quotas-veto override	Y
31.	Abortion service for military abroad	Y
32.	Limits on high income farmers	Y
33.	Family medical leave-veto override	Y
34.	Req submission of balanced budget	Y
35.	Balanced budget amendment	Y
36.	Amendment to ban flag desecration	N
37.	Reauthorize Amtrak-veto override	?
38.	Retraining aid for coal miners	Y
39.	Suspend El Salvador military aid	Y
40.	Expand child care aid/tax credit	Y
41.	Raise House salary/omit honoraria	Y
42.	Toughen oil-spill liability	N
43.	Restitution to Japanese interned	Y
44.	Protect Chinese & C.A. nationals	Y
45.	Abortion $ for rape/incest cases	Y
46.	Allow religious schools to bar gays	N
47.	Bar broadcaster fairness doctrine	N
48.	Bar cap gains cut/reinstate IRA	Y
49.	Bar unions equal voice in pension	N
50.	Bar assembly of chemical weapons	Y
51.	Ban plutonium/uranium production	Y
52.	Cap MX missile deployment at 50	Y
53.	Allow $3b for 2 stealth bombers	N
54.	Publish bio-warfare experiments	Y
55.	Raise minimum wage-veto override	Y
56.	Bar transfer of FS-X technology	Y
57.	Cut defense and raise domestic $	Y
58.	Uniform poll closing in 48 states	Y

MFUME, KWEISI (continued)

59. Req foreign investment disclosure	Y	79. Ban anti-satellite missile tests	Y
60. Textile import quotas-veto override	Y	80. Observe certain limits of SALT II	Y
61. Bar abortion funding in Wash, DC	N	81. Restore four Civil Rights laws	Y
62. Notify spouses of AIDS+ carriers	N	82. Prohibit aliens as strikebreakers	Y
63. Seize conveyance-drug trafficking	N	83. Allow military malpractice suits	Y
64. South Africa sanctions	Y	84. Approval of $36m in Contra aid	N
65. 60 days' notice of plant closings	Y	85. $18b deficit reduction compromise	N
66. Close unneeded military bases	N	86. Welfare reform of $5.7b for 5 years	Y
67. Keep welfare reform within $2.8b	N	87. Raise taxes $12b/cut spending $3b	Y
68. Allow children housing exclusion	N	88. Board to assess occupational risk	Y
69. Shift $400m of NASA to homeless	Y	89. Balanced budget by '93-via targets	N
70. Cap Medicare patients' liability	Y	90. Bar licensing of two nuclear plants	Y
71. Prohibit employee polygraph testing	Y	91. Remove victims compensation cap	Y
72. Allow CIA to fund Contras	N	92. Catastrophic health insurance	Y
73. Revise unfair trade practices	Y	93. Ban airline smoking-2 hours or less	Y
74. Focus SDI on accidental launch	Y	94. $1b/two year aid for the homeless	Y
75. Bar Air Force $ for MX missile	Y	95. Bar non-unions in union companies	Y
76. Allow "real" increase in defense	N	96. Increase FSLIC rescue to $15b	N
77. Troop reduction in Europe of 50%	Y	97. Impose quotas to lower trade deficit	Y
78. Ban nuclear tests above 1 kiloton	Y	98. Reduce discretionary budget 21%	N

Presidential Support Score: 1991 - 23% 1990 - 15%

MORELLA, CONSTANCE A. -- Maryland 8th District [Republican]. County of Montgomery (pt.). Prior Terms: 1987-92. Born: February 12, 1931; Somerville, MA. Education: Boston University (A.B.); American University (M.A.). Occupation: Public school teacher; college professor and instructor; college trustee; state assemblywoman (1979-1986).

1. Protection to Haitian refugees	Y	36. Amendment to ban flag desecration	N
2. Raise tax on wealthy; lower others	N	37. Reauthorize Amtrak-veto override	Y
3. Investigate Reagan hostage delay	N	38. Retraining aid for coal miners	Y
4. Campaign finance revisions	Y	39. Suspend El Salvador military aid	Y
5. Unpaid leave to care for children	Y	40. Expand child care aid/tax credit	Y
6. Restrict NEA use of funds	N	41. Raise House salary/omit honoraria	Y
7. Bar race-bias claim/habeas corpus	N	42. Toughen oil-spill liability	Y
8. Ban race as death sentence factor	N	43. Restitution to Japanese interned	Y
9. Exceptions to exclusionary rule	N	44. Protect Chinese & C.A. nationals	Y
10. Allow sale of assault weapons	N	45. Abortion $ for rape/incest cases	Y
11. Life in prison/abolish death penalty	N	46. Allow religious schools to bar gays	N
12. Req conspiracy-price fixing cases	Y	47. Bar broadcaster fairness doctrine	N
13. Unemployment benefits extension	Y	48. Bar cap gains cut/reinstate IRA	N
14. Tissue use of aborted fetuses	Y	49. Bar unions equal voice in pension	N
15. Bar replacement of union strikers	N	50. Bar assembly of chemical weapons	Y
16. Hold foreign aid at $15b for '92	Y	51. Ban plutonium/uranium production	Y
17. Restore space station funding	Y	52. Cap MX missile deployment at 50	Y
18. Civil Rights Act of 1991	Y	53. Allow $3b for 2 stealth bombers	N
19. Unlimited damages-discrimination	Y	54. Publish bio-warfare experiments	Y
20. Eliminate funds for supercollider	Y	55. Raise minimum wage-veto override	Y
21. Terminate SDI except for research	N	56. Bar transfer of FS-X technology	Y
22. Req 7-day handgun waiting period	Y	57. Cut defense and raise domestic $	Y
23. Provide $30b for failed S&Ls	Y	58. Uniform poll closing in 48 states	Y
24. Allow use of force against Iraq	N	59. Req foreign investment disclosure	N
25. Allow $15b in foreign aid for '91	N	60. Textile import quotas-veto override	N
26. Revise & extend legal immigration	Y	61. Bar abortion funding in Wash, DC	N
27. Suspend aid to Angolan rebels	Y	62. Notify spouses of AIDS+ carriers	N
28. Democratic tax plan proposals	Y	63. Seize conveyance-drug trafficking	N
29. Cut defense 5% across the board	N	64. South Africa sanctions	Y
30. Textile import quotas-veto override	N	65. 60 days' notice of plant closings	Y
31. Abortion service for military abroad	Y	66. Close unneeded military bases	N
32. Limits on high income farmers	Y	67. Keep welfare reform within $2.8b	N
33. Family medical leave-veto override	Y	68. Allow children housing exclusion	N
34. Req submission of balanced budget	N	69. Shift $400m of NASA to homeless	Y
35. Balanced budget amendment	Y	70. Cap Medicare patients' liability	Y

MORELLA, CONSTANCE A. (continued)

71.	Prohibit employee polygraph testing	Y	85.	$18b deficit reduction compromise	Y
72.	Allow CIA to fund Contras	N	86.	Welfare reform of $5.7b for 5 years	Y
73.	Revise unfair trade practices	Y	87.	Raise taxes $12b/cut spending $3b	N
74.	Focus SDI on accidental launch	Y	88.	Board to assess occupational risk	N
75.	Bar Air Force $ for MX missile	+	89.	Balanced budget by '93-via targets	N
76.	Allow "real" increase in defense	N	90.	Bar licensing of two nuclear plants	Y
77.	Troop reduction in Europe of 50%	N	91.	Remove victims compensation cap	N
78.	Ban nuclear tests above 1 kiloton	Y	92.	Catastrophic health insurance	Y
79.	Ban anti-satellite missile tests	Y	93.	Ban airline smoking-2 hours or less	Y
80.	Observe certain limits of SALT II	Y	94.	$1b/two year aid for the homeless	Y
81.	Restore four Civil Rights laws	Y	95.	Bar non-unions in union companies	N
82.	Prohibit aliens as strikebreakers	Y	96.	Increase FSLIC rescue to $15b	Y
83.	Allow military malpractice suits	Y	97.	Impose quotas to lower trade deficit	N
84.	Approval of $36m in Contra aid	N	98.	Reduce discretionary budget 21%	N

Presidential Support Score: 1991 - 43%   1990 - 26%

MASSACHUSETTS

OLVER, JOHN W. -- Massachusetts 1st District [Democrat]. Counties of Berkshire, Franklin, Hampden (pt.), Hampshire and Worcester (pt.). Prior Term: 1991 (Special Election)-1992. Born: September 3, 1936. Education: Rensselaer Polytechnic Institute (B.S.); Tufts University (M.S.); Massachusetts Institute of Technology (Ph.D.). Occupation: College instructor; university professor (1961-69); state representative (1969-72) and senator (1973-91).

1.	Protection to Haitian refugees	Y	9.	Exceptions to exclusionary rule	N
2.	Raise tax on wealthy; lower others	N	10.	Allow sale of assault weapons	N
3.	Investigate Reagan hostage delay	Y	11.	Life in prison/abolish death penalty	Y
4.	Campaign finance revisions	Y	12.	Req conspiracy-price fixing cases	N
5.	Unpaid leave to care for children	Y	13.	Unemployment benefits extension	Y
6.	Restrict NEA use of funds	N	14.	Tissue use of aborted fetuses	Y
7.	Bar race-bias claim/habeas corpus	N	15.	Bar replacement of union strikers	Y
8.	Ban race as death sentence factor	N	16.	Hold foreign aid at $15b for '92	Y

Rep. Olver was sworn in June 18, 1991, to succeed Silvio O. Conte.

Presidential Support Score: 1991 - 20%

NEAL, RICHARD E. -- Massachusetts 2nd District [Democrat]. Counties of Hampden (pt.) and Worcester (pt.). Prior Terms: 1989-92. Born: February 14, 1949; Springfield, MA. Education: American International College (B.A.); University of Hartford (M.P.A.). Occupation: Assistant to Springfield mayor (1973); Springfield city councilman (1978-82) and mayor (1983-88); high school instructor and college lecturer.

1.	Protection to Haitian refugees	Y	13.	Unemployment benefits extension	Y
2.	Raise tax on wealthy; lower others	N	14.	Tissue use of aborted fetuses	Y
3.	Investigate Reagan hostage delay	Y	15.	Bar replacement of union strikers	Y
4.	Campaign finance revisions	Y	16.	Hold foreign aid at $15b for '92	Y
5.	Unpaid leave to care for children	Y	17.	Restore space station funding	N
6.	Restrict NEA use of funds	N	18.	Civil Rights Act of 1991	Y
7.	Bar race-bias claim/habeas corpus	N	19.	Unlimited damages-discrimination	Y
8.	Ban race as death sentence factor	N	20.	Eliminate funds for supercollider	Y
9.	Exceptions to exclusionary rule	N	21.	Terminate SDI except for research	Y
10.	Allow sale of assault weapons	N	22.	Req 7-day handgun waiting period	Y
11.	Life in prison/abolish death penalty	Y	23.	Provide $30b for failed S&Ls	N
12.	Req conspiracy-price fixing cases	N	24.	Allow use of force against Iraq	N

NEAL, RICHARD E. (continued)

25.	Allow $15b in foreign aid for '91	?	42.	Toughen oil-spill liability	Y
26.	Revise & extend legal immigration	Y	43.	Restitution to Japanese interned	Y
27.	Suspend aid to Angolan rebels	Y	44.	Protect Chinese & C.A. nationals	?
28.	Democratic tax plan proposals	Y	45.	Abortion $ for rape/incest cases	N
29.	Cut defense 5% across the board	Y	46.	Allow religious schools to bar gays	N
30.	Textile import quotas-veto override	#	47.	Bar broadcaster fairness doctrine	N
31.	Abortion service for military abroad	+	48.	Bar cap gains cut/reinstate IRA	Y
32.	Limits on high income farmers	Y	49.	Bar unions equal voice in pension	N
33.	Family medical leave-veto override	Y	50.	Bar assembly of chemical weapons	Y
34.	Req submission of balanced budget	Y	51.	Ban plutonium/uranium production	Y
35.	Balanced budget amendment	Y	52.	Cap MX missile deployment at 50	Y
36.	Amendment to ban flag desecration	Y	53.	Allow $3b for 2 stealth bombers	N
37.	Reauthorize Amtrak-veto override	Y	54.	Publish bio-warfare experiments	Y
38.	Retraining aid for coal miners	Y	55.	Raise minimum wage-veto override	Y
39.	Suspend El Salvador military aid	Y	56.	Bar transfer of FS-X technology	Y
40.	Expand child care aid/tax credit	Y	57.	Cut defense and raise domestic $	Y
41.	Raise House salary/omit honoraria	N	58.	Uniform poll closing in 48 states	?

Presidential Support Score: 1991 - 26% 1990 - 19%

EARLY, JOSEPH D. -- Massachusetts 3rd District [Democrat]. Counties of Middlesex (pt.), Norfolk (pt.) and Worcester (pt.). Prior Terms: 1975-92. Born:January 31, 1933; Worcester, MA. Education: College of the Holy Cross (B.S.). Military Service: U.S. Navy, 1955-57. Occupation: Prep-school teacher (1959-63); Massachusetts representative (1963-74).

1.	Protection to Haitian refugees	Y	39.	Suspend El Salvador military aid	Y
2.	Raise tax on wealthy; lower others	N	40.	Expand child care aid/tax credit	Y
3.	Investigate Reagan hostage delay	Y	41.	Raise House salary/omit honoraria	N
4.	Campaign finance revisions	Y	42.	Toughen oil-spill liability	?
5.	Unpaid leave to care for children	Y	43.	Restitution to Japanese interned	Y
6.	Restrict NEA use of funds	Y	44.	Protect Chinese & C.A. nationals	?
7.	Bar race-bias claim/habeas corpus	N	45.	Abortion $ for rape/incest cases	N
8.	Ban race as death sentence factor	Y	46.	Allow religious schools to bar gays	N
9.	Exceptions to exclusionary rule	N	47.	Bar broadcaster fairness doctrine	N
10.	Allow sale of assault weapons	N	48.	Bar cap gains cut/reinstate IRA	N
11.	Life in prison/abolish death penalty	N	49.	Bar unions equal voice in pension	Y
12.	Req conspiracy-price fixing cases	N	50.	Bar assembly of chemical weapons	Y
13.	Unemployment benefits extension	Y	51.	Ban plutonium/uranium production	Y
14.	Tissue use of aborted fetuses	Y	52.	Cap MX missile deployment at 50	Y
15.	Bar replacement of union strikers	Y	53.	Allow $3b for 2 stealth bombers	N
16.	Hold foreign aid at $15b for '92	N	54.	Publish bio-warfare experiments	Y
17.	Restore space station funding	N	55.	Raise minimum wage-veto override	Y
18.	Civil Rights Act of 1991	Y	56.	Bar transfer of FS-X technology	Y
19.	Unlimited damages-discrimination	Y	57.	Cut defense and raise domestic $	Y
20.	Eliminate funds for supercollider	Y	58.	Uniform poll closing in 48 states	Y
21.	Terminate SDI except for research	Y	59.	Req foreign investment disclosure	Y
22.	Req 7-day handgun waiting period	Y	60.	Textile import quotas-veto override	Y
23.	Provide $30b for failed S&Ls	N	61.	Bar abortion funding in Wash, DC	N
24.	Allow use of force against Iraq	N	62.	Notify spouses of AIDS+ carriers	Y
25.	Allow $15b in foreign aid for '91	?	63.	Seize conveyance-drug trafficking	Y
26.	Revise & extend legal immigration	Y	64.	South Africa sanctions	Y
27.	Suspend aid to Angolan rebels	Y	65.	60 days' notice of plant closings	Y
28.	Democratic tax plan proposals	Y	66.	Close unneeded military bases	N
29.	Cut defense 5% across the board	N	67.	Keep welfare reform within $2.8b	N
30.	Textile import quotas-veto override	Y	68.	Allow children housing exclusion	N
31.	Abortion service for military abroad	N	69.	Shift $400m of NASA to homeless	N
32.	Limits on high income farmers	?	70.	Cap Medicare patients' liability	Y
33.	Family medical leave-veto override	Y	71.	Prohibit employee polygraph testing	Y
34.	Req submission of balanced budget	Y	72.	Allow CIA to fund Contras	N
35.	Balanced budget amendment	Y	73.	Revise unfair trade practices	Y
36.	Amendment to ban flag desecration	N	74.	Focus SDI on accidental launch	Y
37.	Reauthorize Amtrak-veto override	Y	75.	Bar Air Force $ for MX missile	Y
38.	Retraining aid for coal miners	N	76.	Allow "real" increase in defense	?

EARLY, JOSEPH D. (continued)

77. Troop reduction in Europe of 50%	?	111. Allow toxic victims to sue in fed ct	Y
78. Ban nuclear tests above 1 kiloton	Y	112. Superfund waste cleanup of $10b	Y
79. Ban anti-satellite missile tests	Y	113. 90 days notice of plant closings	Y
80. Observe certain limits of SALT II	Y	114. $20b in Medicare cuts/tax increases	Y
81. Restore four Civil Rights laws	Y	115. Spending cuts and tax increases	Y
82. Prohibit aliens as strikebreakers	Y	116. Set school lunch lmt-250% poverty	N
83. Allow military malpractice suits	Y	117. $75m for youth work projects	N
84. Approval of $36m in Contra aid	N	118. Allow Angolan military assistance	N
85. $18b deficit reduction compromise	Y	119. Suspend defense payments for abuse	N
86. Welfare reform of $5.7b for 5 years	Y	120. Drop SS COLAs/$12b tax increase	N
87. Raise taxes $12b/cut spending $3b	Y	121. Approve $1.5b for 21 MX missiles	N
88. Board to assess occupational risk	Y	122. Emergency farm credit/revisions	Y
89. Balanced budget by '93-via targets	N	123. Duty on Taiwan/Hong Kong/S Korea	Y
90. Bar licensing of two nuclear plants	N	124. Limit steel imports to 17%	Y
91. Remove victims compensation cap	N	125. Cut $ to schools that bar prayer	?
92. Catastrophic health insurance	?	126. $50b-taxes; cut Medicare/spending	N
93. Ban airline smoking-2 hours or less	N	127. Limit Pershing II/cruise in Europe	Y
94. $1b/two year aid for the homeless	Y	128. Delete $7.1b for 34 B-1 bombers	Y
95. Bar non-unions in union companies	Y	129. Bar purchase of Sergeant York guns	?
96. Increase FSLIC rescue to $15b	Y	130. El Salvador military/economic aid	N
97. Impose quotas to lower trade deficit	Y	131. Bar mining of Nicaraguan waters	Y
98. Reduce discretionary budget 21%	?	132. Physician fee freeze for Medicare	N
99. Immigration reform/alien amnesty	Y	133. $49b in "sin"/phone/insurance taxes	N
100. South Africa sanctions-veto override	Y	134. Allow sale of Conrail	N
101. Tax overhaul to revise income tax	Y	135. Equal Rights Amendment	Y
102. Use of military in drug war	Y	136. Authorize Marines in Lebanon	N
103. Delete 12 MX/add conventional wpn	Y	137. Eminent domain for coal companies	Y
104. Raise speed limit to 65 mph	N	138. Prohibit EPA clean air sanctions	N
105. Require Pentagon to buy US goods	N	139. SS retirement age increase/reforms	N
106. AIDS insurance non-discrimination	Y	140. Auto domestic content requirement	Y
107. Prohibit Saudi arms sales	Y	141. Delete jobs program funding	N
108. Ease Gun Control Act of 1968	N	142. Highway-gas tax bill	Y
109. Bar interstate handgun transport	Y	143. Cut $5b from defense for Medicare	Y
110. Make company emissions known	Y	144. Emergency housing aid of $1b	N

Presidential Support Score: 1991 - 27% 1990 - 28%

FRANK, BARNEY -- Massachusetts 4th District [Democrat]. Counties of Bristol (pt.), Middlesex (pt.) and Norfolk (pt.). Prior Terms: 1981-92. Born: March 31, 1940; Bayonne, NJ. Education: Harvard College (B.A.); Harvard University. Occupation: Teaching fellow, Harvard College (1963-67); assistant to the director, Kennedy Institute of Politics (1966-67); executive assistant to mayor (1968-71); administative assistant to congressman (1971-72); Massachusetts representative (1973-80); lecturer, Kennedy School of Government(1978-80); attorney.

1. Protection to Haitian refugees	Y	19. Unlimited damages-discrimination	Y
2. Raise tax on wealthy; lower others	N	20. Eliminate funds for supercollider	Y
3. Investigate Reagan hostage delay	Y	21. Terminate SDI except for research	Y
4. Campaign finance revisions	Y	22. Req 7-day handgun waiting period	Y
5. Unpaid leave to care for children	Y	23. Provide $30b for failed S&Ls	Y
6. Restrict NEA use of funds	N	24. Allow use of force against Iraq	N
7. Bar race-bias claim/habeas corpus	N	25. Allow $15b in foreign aid for '91	Y
8. Ban race as death sentence factor	Y	26. Revise & extend legal immigration	Y
9. Exceptions to exclusionary rule	Y	27. Suspend aid to Angolan rebels	Y
10. Allow sale of assault weapons	N	28. Democratic tax plan proposals	Y
11. Life in prison/abolish death penalty	Y	29. Cut defense 5% across the board	Y
12. Req conspiracy-price fixing cases	N	30. Textile import quotas-veto override	Y
13. Unemployment benefits extension	Y	31. Abortion service for military abroad	Y
14. Tissue use of aborted fetuses	Y	32. Limits on high income farmers	Y
15. Bar replacement of union strikers	Y	33. Family medical leave-veto override	Y
16. Hold foreign aid at $15b for '92	Y	34. Req submission of balanced budget	Y
17. Restore space station funding	N	35. Balanced budget amendment	N
18. Civil Rights Act of 1991	Y	36. Amendment to ban flag desecration	N

FRANK, BARNEY (continued)

37. Reauthorize Amtrak-veto override	Y	
38. Retraining aid for coal miners	Y	
39. Suspend El Salvador military aid	Y	
40. Expand child care aid/tax credit	Y	
41. Raise House salary/omit honoraria	N	
42. Toughen oil-spill liability	Y	
43. Restitution to Japanese interned	Y	
44. Protect Chinese & C.A. nationals	Y	
45. Abortion $ for rape/incest cases	Y	
46. Allow religious schools to bar gays	N	
47. Bar broadcaster fairness doctrine	N	
48. Bar cap gains cut/reinstate IRA	Y	
49. Bar unions equal voice in pension	N	
50. Bar assembly of chemical weapons	Y	
51. Ban plutonium/uranium production	Y	
52. Cap MX missile deployment at 50	Y	
53. Allow $3b for 2 stealth bombers	N	
54. Publish bio-warfare experiments	Y	
55. Raise minimum wage-veto override	Y	
56. Bar transfer of FS-X technology	Y	
57. Cut defense and raise domestic $	Y	
58. Uniform poll closing in 48 states	Y	
59. Req foreign investment disclosure	N	
60. Textile import quotas-veto override	Y	
61. Bar abortion funding in Wash, DC	?	
62. Notify spouses of AIDS+ carriers	N	
63. Seize conveyance-drug trafficking	N	
64. South Africa sanctions	Y	
65. 60 days' notice of plant closings	Y	
66. Close unneeded military bases	N	
67. Keep welfare reform within $2.8b	N	
68. Allow children housing exclusion	N	
69. Shift $400m of NASA to homeless	Y	
70. Cap Medicare patients' liability	Y	
71. Prohibit employee polygraph testing	Y	
72. Allow CIA to fund Contras	N	
73. Revise unfair trade practices	Y	
74. Focus SDI on accidental launch	Y	
75. Bar Air Force $ for MX missile	Y	
76. Allow "real" increase in defense	N	
77. Troop reduction in Europe of 50%	Y	
78. Ban nuclear tests above 1 kiloton	Y	
79. Ban anti-satellite missile tests	Y	
80. Observe certain limits of SALT II	Y	
81. Restore four Civil Rights laws	Y	
82. Prohibit aliens as strikebreakers	Y	
83. Allow military malpractice suits	Y	
84. Approval of $36m in Contra aid	N	
85. $18b deficit reduction compromise	Y	
86. Welfare reform of $5.7b for 5 years	Y	
87. Raise taxes $12b/cut spending $3b	Y	
88. Board to assess occupational risk	Y	
89. Balanced budget by '93-via targets	N	
90. Bar licensing of two nuclear plants	Y	

91. Remove victims compensation cap	Y	
92. Catastrophic health insurance	Y	
93. Ban airline smoking-2 hours or less	Y	
94. $1b/two year aid for the homeless	Y	
95. Bar non-unions in union companies	Y	
96. Increase FSLIC rescue to $15b	Y	
97. Impose quotas to lower trade deficit	Y	
98. Reduce discretionary budget 21%	Y	
99. Immigration reform/alien amnesty	Y	
100. South Africa sanctions-veto override	Y	
101. Tax overhaul to revise income tax	Y	
102. Use of military in drug war	N	
103. Delete 12 MX/add conventional wpn	Y	
104. Raise speed limit to 65 mph	N	
105. Require Pentagon to buy US goods	N	
106. AIDS insurance non-discrimination	Y	
107. Prohibit Saudi arms sales	Y	
108. Ease Gun Control Act of 1968	N	
109. Bar interstate handgun transport	Y	
110. Make company emissions known	Y	
111. Allow toxic victims to sue in fed ct	Y	
112. Superfund waste cleanup of $10b	Y	
113. 90 days notice of plant closings	Y	
114. $20b in Medicare cuts/tax increases	Y	
115. Spending cuts and tax increases	Y	
116. Set school lunch lmt-250% poverty	N	
117. $75m for youth work projects	Y	
118. Allow Angolan military assistance	N	
119. Suspend defense payments for abuse	Y	
120. Drop SS COLAs/$12b tax increase	N	
121. Approve $1.5b for 21 MX missiles	N	
122. Emergency farm credit/revisions	Y	
123. Duty on Taiwan/Hong Kong/S Korea	Y	
124. Limit steel imports to 17%	Y	
125. Cut $ to schools that bar prayer	N	
126. $50b-taxes; cut Medicare/spending	?	
127. Limit Pershing II/cruise in Europe	Y	
128. Delete $7.1b for 34 B-1 bombers	Y	
129. Bar purchase of Sergeant York guns	Y	
130. El Salvador military/economic aid	N	
131. Bar mining of Nicaraguan waters	Y	
132. Physician fee freeze for Medicare	N	
133. $49b in "sin"/phone/insurance taxes	Y	
134. Allow sale of Conrail	N	
135. Equal Rights Amendment	Y	
136. Authorize Marines in Lebanon	N	
137. Eminent domain for coal companies	Y	
138. Prohibit EPA clean air sanctions	Y	
139. SS retirement age increase/reforms	N	
140. Auto domestic content requirement	Y	
141. Delete jobs program funding	N	
142. Highway-gas tax bill	Y	
143. Cut $5b from defense for Medicare	Y	
144. Emergency housing aid of $1b	Y	

Presidential Support Score: 1991 - 29% 1990 - 19%

ATKINS, CHESTER G. -- Massachusetts 5th District [Democrat]. Counties of Essex (pt.), Middlesex (pt.) and Worcester (pt.). Prior Terms: 1985-92. Born: April 15, 1948. Education: Antioch College (B.A.). Occupation: State representative; state senator.

1. Protection to Haitian refugees	Y	
2. Raise tax on wealthy; lower others	N	

3. Investigate Reagan hostage delay	Y	
4. Campaign finance revisions	Y	

ATKINS, CHESTER G. (continued)

5. Unpaid leave to care for children	Y	
6. Restrict NEA use of funds	N	
7. Bar race-bias claim/habeas corpus	N	
8. Ban race as death sentence factor	N	
9. Exceptions to exclusionary rule	N	
10. Allow sale of assault weapons	N	
11. Life in prison/abolish death penalty	N	
12. Req conspiracy-price fixing cases	N	
13. Unemployment benefits extension	Y	
14. Tissue use of aborted fetuses	Y	
15. Bar replacement of union strikers	Y	
16. Hold foreign aid at $15b for '92	Y	
17. Restore space station funding	N	
18. Civil Rights Act of 1991	Y	
19. Unlimited damages-discrimination	Y	
20. Eliminate funds for supercollider	Y	
21. Terminate SDI except for research	Y	
22. Req 7-day handgun waiting period	Y	
23. Provide $30b for failed S&Ls	Y	
24. Allow use of force against Iraq	N	
25. Allow $15b in foreign aid for '91	Y	
26. Revise & extend legal immigration	Y	
27. Suspend aid to Angolan rebels	Y	
28. Democratic tax plan proposals	Y	
29. Cut defense 5% across the board	N	
30. Textile import quotas-veto override	Y	
31. Abortion service for military abroad	Y	
32. Limits on high income farmers	Y	
33. Family medical leave-veto override	Y	
34. Req submission of balanced budget	Y	
35. Balanced budget amendment	N	
36. Amendment to ban flag desecration	N	
37. Reauthorize Amtrak-veto override	Y	
38. Retraining aid for coal miners	Y	
39. Suspend El Salvador military aid	Y	
40. Expand child care aid/tax credit	Y	
41. Raise House salary/omit honoraria	Y	
42. Toughen oil-spill liability	Y	
43. Restitution to Japanese interned	Y	
44. Protect Chinese & C.A. nationals	Y	
45. Abortion $ for rape/incest cases	Y	
46. Allow religious schools to bar gays	N	
47. Bar broadcaster fairness doctrine	N	
48. Bar cap gains cut/reinstate IRA	Y	
49. Bar unions equal voice in pension	N	
50. Bar assembly of chemical weapons	Y	
51. Ban plutonium/uranium production	Y	
52. Cap MX missile deployment at 50	Y	
53. Allow $3b for 2 stealth bombers	N	
54. Publish bio-warfare experiments	Y	
55. Raise minimum wage-veto override	Y	
56. Bar transfer of FS-X technology	Y	
57. Cut defense and raise domestic $	Y	
58. Uniform poll closing in 48 states	Y	
59. Req foreign investment disclosure	Y	
60. Textile import quotas-veto override	Y	
61. Bar abortion funding in Wash, DC	N	
62. Notify spouses of AIDS+ carriers	N	
63. Seize conveyance-drug trafficking	N	

64. South Africa sanctions	Y	
65. 60 days' notice of plant closings	Y	
66. Close unneeded military bases	--	
67. Keep welfare reform within $2.8b	N	
68. Allow children housing exclusion	N	
69. Shift $400m of NASA to homeless	Y	
70. Cap Medicare patients' liability	Y	
71. Prohibit employee polygraph testing	Y	
72. Allow CIA to fund Contras	N	
73. Revise unfair trade practices	Y	
74. Focus SDI on accidental launch	Y	
75. Bar Air Force $ for MX missile	Y	
76. Allow "real" increase in defense	N	
77. Troop reduction in Europe of 50%	Y	
78. Ban nuclear tests above 1 kiloton	Y	
79. Ban anti-satellite missile tests	Y	
80. Observe certain limits of SALT II	Y	
81. Restore four Civil Rights laws	Y	
82. Prohibit aliens as strikebreakers	Y	
83. Allow military malpractice suits	Y	
84. Approval of $36m in Contra aid	N	
85. $18b deficit reduction compromise	Y	
86. Welfare reform of $5.7b for 5 years	Y	
87. Raise taxes $12b/cut spending $3b	Y	
88. Board to assess occupational risk	Y	
89. Balanced budget by '93-via targets	Y	
90. Bar licensing of two nuclear plants	Y	
91. Remove victims compensation cap	Y	
92. Catastrophic health insurance	Y	
93. Ban airline smoking-2 hours or less	Y	
94. $1b/two year aid for the homeless	Y	
95. Bar non-unions in union companies	Y	
96. Increase FSLIC rescue to $15b	Y	
97. Impose quotas to lower trade deficit	Y	
98. Reduce discretionary budget 21%	N	
99. Immigration reform/alien amnesty	Y	
100. South Africa sanctions-veto override	Y	
101. Tax overhaul to revise income tax	Y	
102. Use of military in drug war	N	
103. Delete 12 MX/add conventional wpn	Y	
104. Raise speed limit to 65 mph	N	
105. Require Pentagon to buy US goods	N	
106. AIDS insurance non-discrimination	Y	
107. Prohibit Saudi arms sales	Y	
108. Ease Gun Control Act of 1968	N	
109. Bar interstate handgun transport	Y	
110. Make company emissions known	Y	
111. Allow toxic victims to sue in fed ct	Y	
112. Superfund waste cleanup of $10b	Y	
113. 90 days notice of plant closings	?	
114. $20b in Medicare cuts/tax increases	Y	
115. Spending cuts and tax increases	Y	
116. Set school lunch lmt-250% poverty	N	
117. $75m for youth work projects	Y	
118. Allow Angolan military assistance	N	
119. Suspend defense payments for abuse	Y	
120. Drop SS COLAs/$12b tax increase	N	
121. Approve $1.5b for 21 MX missiles	N	
122. Emergency farm credit/revisions	Y	

Presidential Support Score: 1991 - 25%   1990 - 20%

MAVROULES, NICHOLAS -- Massachusetts 6th District [Democrat]. Counties of Essex (pt.) and Middlesex (pt.). Prior Terms: 1979-92. Born: November 1, 1929; Peabody, MA. Education: Massachusetts Institute of Technology. Occupation: Employee, Sylvania Corp. (1949-67); mayor (1967-79).

1. Protection to Haitian refugees	Y	61. Bar abortion funding in Wash, DC	Y
2. Raise tax on wealthy; lower others	N	62. Notify spouses of AIDS+ carriers	N
3. Investigate Reagan hostage delay	Y	63. Seize conveyance-drug trafficking	N
4. Campaign finance revisions	Y	64. South Africa sanctions	Y
5. Unpaid leave to care for children	Y	65. 60 days' notice of plant closings	Y
6. Restrict NEA use of funds	N	66. Close unneeded military bases	N
7. Bar race-bias claim/habeas corpus	N	67. Keep welfare reform within $2.8b	N
8. Ban race as death sentence factor	N	68. Allow children housing exclusion	N
9. Exceptions to exclusionary rule	N	69. Shift $400m of NASA to homeless	Y
10. Allow sale of assault weapons	N	70. Cap Medicare patients' liability	Y
11. Life in prison/abolish death penalty	N	71. Prohibit employee polygraph testing	Y
12. Req conspiracy-price fixing cases	N	72. Allow CIA to fund Contras	N
13. Unemployment benefits extension	Y	73. Revise unfair trade practices	Y
14. Tissue use of aborted fetuses	Y	74. Focus SDI on accidental launch	Y
15. Bar replacement of union strikers	Y	75. Bar Air Force $ for MX missile	Y
16. Hold foreign aid at $15b for '92	Y	76. Allow "real" increase in defense	Y
17. Restore space station funding	N	77. Troop reduction in Europe of 50%	N
18. Civil Rights Act of 1991	Y	78. Ban nuclear tests above 1 kiloton	Y
19. Unlimited damages-discrimination	Y	79. Ban anti-satellite missile tests	Y
20. Eliminate funds for supercollider	N	80. Observe certain limits of SALT II	Y
21. Terminate SDI except for research	Y	81. Restore four Civil Rights laws	Y
22. Req 7-day handgun waiting period	Y	82. Prohibit aliens as strikebreakers	Y
23. Provide $30b for failed S&Ls	Y	83. Allow military malpractice suits	Y
24. Allow use of force against Iraq	N	84. Approval of $36m in Contra aid	N
25. Allow $15b in foreign aid for '91	Y	85. $18b deficit reduction compromise	Y
26. Revise & extend legal immigration	Y	86. Welfare reform of $5.7b for 5 years	Y
27. Suspend aid to Angolan rebels	Y	87. Raise taxes $12b/cut spending $3b	Y
28. Democratic tax plan proposals	Y	88. Board to assess occupational risk	Y
29. Cut defense 5% across the board	N	89. Balanced budget by '93-via targets	Y
30. Textile import quotas-veto override	Y	90. Bar licensing of two nuclear plants	Y
31. Abortion service for military abroad	N	91. Remove victims compensation cap	Y
32. Limits on high income farmers	Y	92. Catastrophic health insurance	Y
33. Family medical leave-veto override	Y	93. Ban airline smoking-2 hours or less	Y
34. Req submission of balanced budget	Y	94. $1b/two year aid for the homeless	Y
35. Balanced budget amendment	N	95. Bar non-unions in union companies	Y
36. Amendment to ban flag desecration	N	96. Increase FSLIC rescue to $15b	Y
37. Reauthorize Amtrak-veto override	Y	97. Impose quotas to lower trade deficit	Y
38. Retraining aid for coal miners	Y	98. Reduce discretionary budget 21%	N
39. Suspend El Salvador military aid	Y	99. Immigration reform/alien amnesty	Y
40. Expand child care aid/tax credit	Y	100. South Africa sanctions-veto override	Y
41. Raise House salary/omit honoraria	Y	101. Tax overhaul to revise income tax	Y
42. Toughen oil-spill liability	Y	102. Use of military in drug war	N
43. Restitution to Japanese interned	Y	103. Delete 12 MX/add conventional wpn	Y
44. Protect Chinese & C.A. nationals	Y	104. Raise speed limit to 65 mph	N
45. Abortion $ for rape/incest cases	N	105. Require Pentagon to buy US goods	N
46. Allow religious schools to bar gays	N	106. AIDS insurance non-discrimination	Y
47. Bar broadcaster fairness doctrine	N	107. Prohibit Saudi arms sales	Y
48. Bar cap gains cut/reinstate IRA	Y	108. Ease Gun Control Act of 1968	N
49. Bar unions equal voice in pension	N	109. Bar interstate handgun transport	Y
50. Bar assembly of chemical weapons	Y	110. Make company emissions known	Y
51. Ban plutonium/uranium production	Y	111. Allow toxic victims to sue in fed ct	Y
52. Cap MX missile deployment at 50	Y	112. Superfund waste cleanup of $10b	Y
53. Allow $3b for 2 stealth bombers	N	113. 90 days notice of plant closings	Y
54. Publish bio-warfare experiments	Y	114. $20b in Medicare cuts/tax increases	Y
55. Raise minimum wage-veto override	Y	115. Spending cuts and tax increases	Y
56. Bar transfer of FS-X technology	Y	116. Set school lunch lmt-250% poverty	N
57. Cut defense and raise domestic $	N	117. $75m for youth work projects	Y
58. Uniform poll closing in 48 states	Y	118. Allow Angolan military assistance	N
59. Req foreign investment disclosure	Y	119. Suspend defense payments for abuse	Y
60. Textile import quotas-veto override	Y	120. Drop SS COLAs/$12b tax increase	N

MAVROULES, NICHOLAS (continued)

121. Approve $1.5b for 21 MX missiles	N	
122. Emergency farm credit/revisions	Y	
123. Duty on Taiwan/Hong Kong/S Korea	Y	
124. Limit steel imports to 17%	Y	
125. Cut $ to schools that bar prayer	N	
126. $50b-taxes; cut Medicare/spending	Y	
127. Limit Pershing II/cruise in Europe	Y	
128. Delete $7.1b for 34 B-1 bombers	Y	
129. Bar purchase of Sergeant York guns	N	
130. El Salvador military/economic aid	N	
131. Bar mining of Nicaraguan waters	Y	
132. Physician fee freeze for Medicare	N	
133. $49b in "sin"/phone/insurance taxes	Y
134. Allow sale of Conrail	N
135. Equal Rights Amendment	Y
136. Authorize Marines in Lebanon	Y
137. Eminent domain for coal companies	Y
138. Prohibit EPA clean air sanctions	N
139. SS retirement age increase/reforms	N
140. Auto domestic content requirement	Y
141. Delete jobs program funding	N
142. Highway-gas tax bill	Y
143. Cut $5b from defense for Medicare	Y
144. Emergency housing aid of $1b	Y

Presidential Support Score: 1991 - 34% 1990 - 23%

MARKEY, EDWARD J. -- Massachusetts 7th District [Democrat]. Counties of Middlesex (pt.) and Suffolk (pt.). Prior Terms: 1976 (Special Election)-1992. Born: July 11, 1946; Malden, MA. Education: Boston College (B.A., J.D.). Military Service: U.S. Army Reserve, 1968-73. Occupation: Massachusetts representative (1972).

1. Protection to Haitian refugees	Y		44. Protect Chinese & C.A. nationals	Y
2. Raise tax on wealthy; lower others	N		45. Abortion $ for rape/incest cases	Y
3. Investigate Reagan hostage delay	Y		46. Allow religious schools to bar gays	N
4. Campaign finance revisions	Y		47. Bar broadcaster fairness doctrine	N
5. Unpaid leave to care for children	Y		48. Bar cap gains cut/reinstate IRA	Y
6. Restrict NEA use of funds	N		49. Bar unions equal voice in pension	N
7. Bar race-bias claim/habeas corpus	N		50. Bar assembly of chemical weapons	Y
8. Ban race as death sentence factor	N		51. Ban plutonium/uranium production	Y
9. Exceptions to exclusionary rule	N		52. Cap MX missile deployment at 50	Y
10. Allow sale of assault weapons	N		53. Allow $3b for 2 stealth bombers	N
11. Life in prison/abolish death penalty	Y		54. Publish bio-warfare experiments	Y
12. Req conspiracy-price fixing cases	N		55. Raise minimum wage-veto override	Y
13. Unemployment benefits extension	Y		56. Bar transfer of FS-X technology	Y
14. Tissue use of aborted fetuses	Y		57. Cut defense and raise domestic $	Y
15. Bar replacement of union strikers	Y		58. Uniform poll closing in 48 states	Y
16. Hold foreign aid at $15b for '92	Y		59. Req foreign investment disclosure	Y
17. Restore space station funding	N		60. Textile import quotas-veto override	Y
18. Civil Rights Act of 1991	Y		61. Bar abortion funding in Wash, DC	N
19. Unlimited damages-discrimination	Y		62. Notify spouses of AIDS+ carriers	N
20. Eliminate funds for supercollider	Y		63. Seize conveyance-drug trafficking	N
21. Terminate SDI except for research	Y		64. South Africa sanctions	Y
22. Req 7-day handgun waiting period	Y		65. 60 days' notice of plant closings	Y
23. Provide $30b for failed S&Ls	Y		66. Close unneeded military bases	N
24. Allow use of force against Iraq	N		67. Keep welfare reform within $2.8b	N
25. Allow $15b in foreign aid for '91	Y		68. Allow children housing exclusion	N
26. Revise & extend legal immigration	Y		69. Shift $400m of NASA to homeless	Y
27. Suspend aid to Angolan rebels	Y		70. Cap Medicare patients' liability	Y
28. Democratic tax plan proposals	Y		71. Prohibit employee polygraph testing	#
29. Cut defense 5% across the board	Y		72. Allow CIA to fund Contras	N
30. Textile import quotas-veto override	Y		73. Revise unfair trade practices	Y
31. Abortion service for military abroad	Y		74. Focus SDI on accidental launch	Y
32. Limits on high income farmers	Y		75. Bar Air Force $ for MX missile	Y
33. Family medical leave-veto override	Y		76. Allow "real" increase in defense	N
34. Req submission of balanced budget	Y		77. Troop reduction in Europe of 50%	Y
35. Balanced budget amendment	N		78. Ban nuclear tests above 1 kiloton	Y
36. Amendment to ban flag desecration	N		79. Ban anti-satellite missile tests	Y
37. Reauthorize Amtrak-veto override	Y		80. Observe certain limits of SALT II	Y
38. Retraining aid for coal miners	Y		81. Restore four Civil Rights laws	Y
39. Suspend El Salvador military aid	Y		82. Prohibit aliens as strikebreakers	Y
40. Expand child care aid/tax credit	Y		83. Allow military malpractice suits	Y
41. Raise House salary/omit honoraria	Y		84. Approval of $36m in Contra aid	N
42. Toughen oil-spill liability	Y		85. $18b deficit reduction compromise	Y
43. Restitution to Japanese interned	Y		86. Welfare reform of $5.7b for 5 years	Y

MARKEY, EDWARD J. (continued)

87. Raise taxes $12b/cut spending $3b	Y	
88. Board to assess occupational risk	Y	
89. Balanced budget by '93-via targets	Y	
90. Bar licensing of two nuclear plants	Y	
91. Remove victims compensation cap	Y	
92. Catastrophic health insurance	Y	
93. Ban airline smoking-2 hours or less	Y	
94. $1b/two year aid for the homeless	Y	
95. Bar non-unions in union companies	Y	
96. Increase FSLIC rescue to $15b	Y	
97. Impose quotas to lower trade deficit	Y	
98. Reduce discretionary budget 21%	N	
99. Immigration reform/alien amnesty	Y	
100. South Africa sanctions-veto override	Y	
101. Tax overhaul to revise income tax	Y	
102. Use of military in drug war	?	
103. Delete 12 MX/add conventional wpn	Y	
104. Raise speed limit to 65 mph	N	
105. Require Pentagon to buy US goods	N	
106. AIDS insurance non-discrimination	Y	
107. Prohibit Saudi arms sales	Y	
108. Ease Gun Control Act of 1968	N	
109. Bar interstate handgun transport	Y	
110. Make company emissions known	Y	
111. Allow toxic victims to sue in fed ct	Y	
112. Superfund waste cleanup of $10b	Y	
113. 90 days notice of plant closings	Y	
114. $20b in Medicare cuts/tax increases	Y	
115. Spending cuts and tax increases	Y	

116. Set school lunch lmt-250% poverty	N	
117. $75m for youth work projects	Y	
118. Allow Angolan military assistance	N	
119. Suspend defense payments for abuse	Y	
120. Drop SS COLAs/$12b tax increase	N	
121. Approve $1.5b for 21 MX missiles	N	
122. Emergency farm credit/revisions	Y	
123. Duty on Taiwan/Hong Kong/S Korea	Y	
124. Limit steel imports to 17%	Y	
125. Cut $ to schools that bar prayer	N	
126. $50b-taxes; cut Medicare/spending	N	
127. Limit Pershing II/cruise in Europe	Y	
128. Delete $7.1b for 34 B-1 bombers	Y	
129. Bar purchase of Sergeant York guns	Y	
130. El Salvador military/economic aid	N	
131. Bar mining of Nicaraguan waters	Y	
132. Physician fee freeze for Medicare	N	
133. $49b in "sin"/phone/insurance taxes	Y	
134. Allow sale of Conrail	?	
135. Equal Rights Amendment	Y	
136. Authorize Marines in Lebanon	Y	
137. Eminent domain for coal companies	N	
138. Prohibit EPA clean air sanctions	Y	
139. SS retirement age increase/reforms	N	
140. Auto domestic content requirement	Y	
141. Delete jobs program funding	N	
142. Highway-gas tax bill	Y	
143. Cut $5b from defense for Medicare	Y	
144. Emergency housing aid of $1b	Y	

Presidential Support Score: 1991 - 23%   1990 - 15%

KENNEDY, JOSEPH P., II -- Massachusetts 8th District [Democrat].   Counties of Middlesex (pt.) and Suffolk (pt.).   Prior Terms: 1987-92. Born: September 24, 1952; Brighton, MA. Education: University of Massachusetts. Occupation: Peace Corps and Community Services Administration worker; president, Citizens Energy Corporation.

1. Protection to Haitian refugees	Y	
2. Raise tax on wealthy; lower others	N	
3. Investigate Reagan hostage delay	Y	
4. Campaign finance revisions	Y	
5. Unpaid leave to care for children	Y	
6. Restrict NEA use of funds	N	
7. Bar race-bias claim/habeas corpus	N	
8. Ban race as death sentence factor	N	
9. Exceptions to exclusionary rule	N	
10. Allow sale of assault weapons	N	
11. Life in prison/abolish death penalty	N	
12. Req conspiracy-price fixing cases	N	
13. Unemployment benefits extension	Y	
14. Tissue use of aborted fetuses	Y	
15. Bar replacement of union strikers	Y	
16. Hold foreign aid at $15b for '92	Y	
17. Restore space station funding	N	
18. Civil Rights Act of 1991	Y	
19. Unlimited damages-discrimination	Y	
20. Eliminate funds for supercollider	N	
21. Terminate SDI except for research	Y	
22. Req 7-day handgun waiting period	Y	
23. Provide $30b for failed S&Ls	N	
24. Allow use of force against Iraq	N	
25. Allow $15b in foreign aid for '91	Y	

26. Revise & extend legal immigration	Y	
27. Suspend aid to Angolan rebels	Y	
28. Democratic tax plan proposals	Y	
29. Cut defense 5% across the board	?	
30. Textile import quotas-veto override	Y	
31. Abortion service for military abroad	Y	
32. Limits on high income farmers	Y	
33. Family medical leave-veto override	Y	
34. Req submission of balanced budget	Y	
35. Balanced budget amendment	N	
36. Amendment to ban flag desecration	N	
37. Reauthorize Amtrak-veto override	Y	
38. Retraining aid for coal miners	Y	
39. Suspend El Salvador military aid	Y	
40. Expand child care aid/tax credit	Y	
41. Raise House salary/omit honoraria	Y	
42. Toughen oil-spill liability	Y	
43. Restitution to Japanese interned	Y	
44. Protect Chinese & C.A. nationals	Y	
45. Abortion $ for rape/incest cases	Y	
46. Allow religious schools to bar gays	N	
47. Bar broadcaster fairness doctrine	N	
48. Bar cap gains cut/reinstate IRA	Y	
49. Bar unions equal voice in pension	N	
50. Bar assembly of chemical weapons	Y	

KENNEDY, JOSEPH P., II (continued)

51. Ban plutonium/uranium production	Y	
52. Cap MX missile deployment at 50	Y	
53. Allow $3b for 2 stealth bombers	N	
54. Publish bio-warfare experiments	Y	
55. Raise minimum wage-veto override	Y	
56. Bar transfer of FS-X technology	Y	
57. Cut defense and raise domestic $	Y	
58. Uniform poll closing in 48 states	Y	
59. Req foreign investment disclosure	Y	
60. Textile import quotas-veto override	Y	
61. Bar abortion funding in Wash, DC	N	
62. Notify spouses of AIDS+ carriers	N	
63. Seize conveyance-drug trafficking	N	
64. South Africa sanctions	Y	
65. 60 days' notice of plant closings	Y	
66. Close unneeded military bases	N	
67. Keep welfare reform within $2.8b	N	
68. Allow children housing exclusion	N	
69. Shift $400m of NASA to homeless	Y	
70. Cap Medicare patients' liability	Y	
71. Prohibit employee polygraph testing	Y	
72. Allow CIA to fund Contras	N	
73. Revise unfair trade practices	Y	
74. Focus SDI on accidental launch	Y	
75. Bar Air Force $ for MX missile	Y
76. Allow "real" increase in defense	N
77. Troop reduction in Europe of 50%	Y
78. Ban nuclear tests above 1 kiloton	Y
79. Ban anti-satellite missile tests	Y
80. Observe certain limits of SALT II	Y
81. Restore four Civil Rights laws	Y
82. Prohibit aliens as strikebreakers	Y
83. Allow military malpractice suits	?
84. Approval of $36m in Contra aid	N
85. $18b deficit reduction compromise	Y
86. Welfare reform of $5.7b for 5 years	Y
87. Raise taxes $12b/cut spending $3b	Y
88. Board to assess occupational risk	Y
89. Balanced budget by '93-via targets	N
90. Bar licensing of two nuclear plants	Y
91. Remove victims compensation cap	Y
92. Catastrophic health insurance	Y
93. Ban airline smoking-2 hours or less	Y
94. $1b/two year aid for the homeless	Y
95. Bar non-unions in union companies	Y
96. Increase FSLIC rescue to $15b	Y
97. Impose quotas to lower trade deficit	N
98. Reduce discretionary budget 21%	N

Presidential Support Score: 1991 - 24%   1990 - 21%

MOAKLEY, JOE -- Massachusetts 9th District [Democrat]. Counties of Bristol (pt.), Norfolk (pt.), Plymouth (pt.) and Suffolk (pt.). Prior Terms: 1973-92. Born: April 27, 1927. Education: University of Miami; Suffolk University Law School (LL.B.). Military Service: U.S. Navy, 1943-46. Occupation: Massachusetts representative (1952-64); Massachusetts senator (1964-71); city councilor (1971-72).

1. Protection to Haitian refugees	?	
2. Raise tax on wealthy; lower others	N	
3. Investigate Reagan hostage delay	Y	
4. Campaign finance revisions	Y	
5. Unpaid leave to care for children	Y	
6. Restrict NEA use of funds	N	
7. Bar race-bias claim/habeas corpus	N	
8. Ban race as death sentence factor	N	
9. Exceptions to exclusionary rule	N	
10. Allow sale of assault weapons	N	
11. Life in prison/abolish death penalty	N	
12. Req conspiracy-price fixing cases	N	
13. Unemployment benefits extension	Y	
14. Tissue use of aborted fetuses	Y	
15. Bar replacement of union strikers	Y	
16. Hold foreign aid at $15b for '92	Y	
17. Restore space station funding	N	
18. Civil Rights Act of 1991	Y	
19. Unlimited damages-discrimination	Y	
20. Eliminate funds for supercollider	N	
21. Terminate SDI except for research	Y	
22. Req 7-day handgun waiting period	Y	
23. Provide $30b for failed S&Ls	Y	
24. Allow use of force against Iraq	N	
25. Allow $15b in foreign aid for '91	Y	
26. Revise & extend legal immigration	Y	
27. Suspend aid to Angolan rebels	Y	
28. Democratic tax plan proposals	Y	
29. Cut defense 5% across the board	N	
30. Textile import quotas-veto override	Y	
31. Abortion service for military abroad	N
32. Limits on high income farmers	N
33. Family medical leave-veto override	Y
34. Req submission of balanced budget	Y
35. Balanced budget amendment	N
36. Amendment to ban flag desecration	N
37. Reauthorize Amtrak-veto override	Y
38. Retraining aid for coal miners	Y
39. Suspend El Salvador military aid	Y
40. Expand child care aid/tax credit	Y
41. Raise House salary/omit honoraria	Y
42. Toughen oil-spill liability	Y
43. Restitution to Japanese interned	Y
44. Protect Chinese & C.A. nationals	Y
45. Abortion $ for rape/incest cases	N
46. Allow religious schools to bar gays	N
47. Bar broadcaster fairness doctrine	N
48. Bar cap gains cut/reinstate IRA	Y
49. Bar unions equal voice in pension	?
50. Bar assembly of chemical weapons	Y
51. Ban plutonium/uranium production	Y
52. Cap MX missile deployment at 50	Y
53. Allow $3b for 2 stealth bombers	N
54. Publish bio-warfare experiments	Y
55. Raise minimum wage-veto override	Y
56. Bar transfer of FS-X technology	Y
57. Cut defense and raise domestic $	Y
58. Uniform poll closing in 48 states	Y
59. Req foreign investment disclosure	Y
60. Textile import quotas-veto override	Y

MOAKLEY, JOE (continued)

61. Bar abortion funding in Wash, DC	Y	103. Delete 12 MX/add conventional wpn	Y
62. Notify spouses of AIDS+ carriers	N	104. Raise speed limit to 65 mph	N
63. Seize conveyance-drug trafficking	N	105. Require Pentagon to buy US goods	Y
64. South Africa sanctions	Y	106. AIDS insurance non-discrimination	Y
65. 60 days' notice of plant closings	Y	107. Prohibit Saudi arms sales	Y
66. Close unneeded military bases	N	108. Ease Gun Control Act of 1968	N
67. Keep welfare reform within $2.8b	N	109. Bar interstate handgun transport	Y
68. Allow children housing exclusion	N	110. Make company emissions known	Y
69. Shift $400m of NASA to homeless	Y	111. Allow toxic victims to sue in fed ct	Y
70. Cap Medicare patients' liability	Y	112. Superfund waste cleanup of $10b	Y
71. Prohibit employee polygraph testing	Y	113. 90 days notice of plant closings	Y
72. Allow CIA to fund Contras	N	114. $20b in Medicare cuts/tax increases	Y
73. Revise unfair trade practices	Y	115. Spending cuts and tax increases	Y
74. Focus SDI on accidental launch	Y	116. Set school lunch lmt-250% poverty	N
75. Bar Air Force $ for MX missile	Y	117. $75m for youth work projects	Y
76. Allow "real" increase in defense	N	118. Allow Angolan military assistance	N
77. Troop reduction in Europe of 50%	Y	119. Suspend defense payments for abuse	Y
78. Ban nuclear tests above 1 kiloton	Y	120. Drop SS COLAs/$12b tax increase	N
79. Ban anti-satellite missile tests	Y	121. Approve $1.5b for 21 MX missiles	N
80. Observe certain limits of SALT II	Y	122. Emergency farm credit/revisions	Y
81. Restore four Civil Rights laws	Y	123. Duty on Taiwan/Hong Kong/S Korea	Y
82. Prohibit aliens as strikebreakers	Y	124. Limit steel imports to 17%	Y
83. Allow military malpractice suits	Y	125. Cut $ to schools that bar prayer	N
84. Approval of $36m in Contra aid	N	126. $50b-taxes; cut Medicare/spending	Y
85. $18b deficit reduction compromise	Y	127. Limit Pershing II/cruise in Europe	Y
86. Welfare reform of $5.7b for 5 years	Y	128. Delete $7.1b for 34 B-1 bombers	Y
87. Raise taxes $12b/cut spending $3b	Y	129. Bar purchase of Sergeant York guns	?
88. Board to assess occupational risk	Y	130. El Salvador military/economic aid	N
89. Balanced budget by '93-via targets	N	131. Bar mining of Nicaraguan waters	Y
90. Bar licensing of two nuclear plants	Y	132. Physician fee freeze for Medicare	N
91. Remove victims compensation cap	Y	133. $49b in "sin"/phone/insurance taxes	Y
92. Catastrophic health insurance	Y	134. Allow sale of Conrail	N
93. Ban airline smoking-2 hours or less	Y	135. Equal Rights Amendment	Y
94. $1b/two year aid for the homeless	Y	136. Authorize Marines in Lebanon	N
95. Bar non-unions in union companies	Y	137. Eminent domain for coal companies	N
96. Increase FSLIC rescue to $15b	Y	138. Prohibit EPA clean air sanctions	N
97. Impose quotas to lower trade deficit	Y	139. SS retirement age increase/reforms	N
98. Reduce discretionary budget 21%	N	140. Auto domestic content requirement	Y
99. Immigration reform/alien amnesty	Y	141. Delete jobs program funding	N
100. South Africa sanctions-veto override	Y	142. Highway-gas tax bill	Y
101. Tax overhaul to revise income tax	Y	143. Cut $5b from defense for Medicare	Y
102. Use of military in drug war	N	144. Emergency housing aid of $1b	Y

Presidential Support Score: 1991 - 32% 1990 - 24%

STUDDS, GERRY E. -- Massachusetts 10th District [Democrat]. Counties of Barnstable, Bristol (pt.), Dukes, Nantucket, Norfolk (pt.) and Plymouth (pt.). Prior Terms: 1973-92. Born: May 12, 1937; Mineola, NY. Education: Yale University (B.A., M.A.T.). Occupation: Foreign service officer, State Department (1961-62); executive director, Domestic Peace Corps; legislative assistant (1964); teacher (1965-69).

1. Protection to Haitian refugees	Y	12. Req conspiracy-price fixing cases	N
2. Raise tax on wealthy; lower others	N	13. Unemployment benefits extension	Y
3. Investigate Reagan hostage delay	Y	14. Tissue use of aborted fetuses	Y
4. Campaign finance revisions	Y	15. Bar replacement of union strikers	Y
5. Unpaid leave to care for children	Y	16. Hold foreign aid at $15b for '92	Y
6. Restrict NEA use of funds	N	17. Restore space station funding	N
7. Bar race-bias claim/habeas corpus	N	18. Civil Rights Act of 1991	Y
8. Ban race as death sentence factor	N	19. Unlimited damages-discrimination	Y
9. Exceptions to exclusionary rule	N	20. Eliminate funds for supercollider	Y
10. Allow sale of assault weapons	N	21. Terminate SDI except for research	?
11. Life in prison/abolish death penalty	Y	22. Req 7-day handgun waiting period	Y

STUDDS, GERRY E. (continued)

23. Provide $30b for failed S&Ls	N	
24. Allow use of force against Iraq	N	
25. Allow $15b in foreign aid for '91	Y	
26. Revise & extend legal immigration	Y	
27. Suspend aid to Angolan rebels	Y	
28. Democratic tax plan proposals	Y	
29. Cut defense 5% across the board	N	
30. Textile import quotas-veto override	Y	
31. Abortion service for military abroad	Y	
32. Limits on high income farmers	Y	
33. Family medical leave-veto override	Y	
34. Req submission of balanced budget	N	
35. Balanced budget amendment	N	
36. Amendment to ban flag desecration	N	
37. Reauthorize Amtrak-veto override	Y	
38. Retraining aid for coal miners	Y	
39. Suspend El Salvador military aid	Y	
40. Expand child care aid/tax credit	Y	
41. Raise House salary/omit honoraria	Y	
42. Toughen oil-spill liability	Y	
43. Restitution to Japanese interned	Y	
44. Protect Chinese & C.A. nationals	Y	
45. Abortion $ for rape/incest cases	Y	
46. Allow religious schools to bar gays	N	
47. Bar broadcaster fairness doctrine	N	
48. Bar cap gains cut/reinstate IRA	Y	
49. Bar unions equal voice in pension	N	
50. Bar assembly of chemical weapons	Y	
51. Ban plutonium/uranium production	Y	
52. Cap MX missile deployment at 50	Y	
53. Allow $3b for 2 stealth bombers	N	
54. Publish bio-warfare experiments	Y	
55. Raise minimum wage-veto override	Y	
56. Bar transfer of FS-X technology	Y	
57. Cut defense and raise domestic $	Y	
58. Uniform poll closing in 48 states	Y	
59. Req foreign investment disclosure	Y	
60. Textile import quotas-veto override	Y	
61. Bar abortion funding in Wash, DC	N	
62. Notify spouses of AIDS+ carriers	N	
63. Seize conveyance-drug trafficking	N	
64. South Africa sanctions	Y	
65. 60 days' notice of plant closings	Y	
66. Close unneeded military bases	N	
67. Keep welfare reform within $2.8b	N	
68. Allow children housing exclusion	N	
69. Shift $400m of NASA to homeless	Y	
70. Cap Medicare patients' liability	Y	
71. Prohibit employee polygraph testing	Y	
72. Allow CIA to fund Contras	N	
73. Revise unfair trade practices	Y	
74. Focus SDI on accidental launch	Y	
75. Bar Air Force $ for MX missile	Y	
76. Allow "real" increase in defense	N	
77. Troop reduction in Europe of 50%	Y	
78. Ban nuclear tests above 1 kiloton	Y	
79. Ban anti-satellite missile tests	Y	
80. Observe certain limits of SALT II	Y	
81. Restore four Civil Rights laws	Y	
82. Prohibit aliens as strikebreakers	Y	
83. Allow military malpractice suits	Y	
84. Approval of $36m in Contra aid	N
85. $18b deficit reduction compromise	Y
86. Welfare reform of $5.7b for 5 years	Y
87. Raise taxes $12b/cut spending $3b	Y
88. Board to assess occupational risk	Y
89. Balanced budget by '93-via targets	N
90. Bar licensing of two nuclear plants	Y
91. Remove victims compensation cap	Y
92. Catastrophic health insurance	Y
93. Ban airline smoking-2 hours or less	Y
94. $1b/two year aid for the homeless	Y
95. Bar non-unions in union companies	Y
96. Increase FSLIC rescue to $15b	?
97. Impose quotas to lower trade deficit	Y
98. Reduce discretionary budget 21%	N
99. Immigration reform/alien amnesty	Y
100. South Africa sanctions-veto override	Y
101. Tax overhaul to revise income tax	Y
102. Use of military in drug war	N
103. Delete 12 MX/add conventional wpn	Y
104. Raise speed limit to 65 mph	N
105. Require Pentagon to buy US goods	N
106. AIDS insurance non-discrimination	Y
107. Prohibit Saudi arms sales	N
108. Ease Gun Control Act of 1968	N
109. Bar interstate handgun transport	Y
110. Make company emissions known	Y
111. Allow toxic victims to sue in fed ct	Y
112. Superfund waste cleanup of $10b	Y
113. 90 days notice of plant closings	Y
114. $20b in Medicare cuts/tax increases	Y
115. Spending cuts and tax increases	Y
116. Set school lunch lmt-250% poverty	N
117. $75m for youth work projects	Y
118. Allow Angolan military assistance	N
119. Suspend defense payments for abuse	Y
120. Drop SS COLAs/$12b tax increase	N
121. Approve $1.5b for 21 MX missiles	N
122. Emergency farm credit/revisions	Y
123. Duty on Taiwan/Hong Kong/S Korea	Y
124. Limit steel imports to 17%	Y
125. Cut $ to schools that bar prayer	N
126. $50b-taxes; cut Medicare/spending	Y
127. Limit Pershing II/cruise in Europe	Y
128. Delete $7.1b for 34 B-1 bombers	Y
129. Bar purchase of Sergeant York guns	Y
130. El Salvador military/economic aid	N
131. Bar mining of Nicaraguan waters	Y
132. Physician fee freeze for Medicare	N
133. $49b in "sin"/phone/insurance taxes	Y
134. Allow sale of Conrail	N
135. Equal Rights Amendment	Y
136. Authorize Marines in Lebanon	N
137. Eminent domain for coal companies	N
138. Prohibit EPA clean air sanctions	N
139. SS retirement age increase/reforms	Y
140. Auto domestic content requirement	Y
141. Delete jobs program funding	N
142. Highway-gas tax bill	N
143. Cut $5b from defense for Medicare	Y
144. Emergency housing aid of $1b	Y

Presidential Support Score: 1991 - 20%   1990 - 18%

DONNELLY, BRIAN J. -- Massachusetts 11th District [Democrat]. Counties of Norfolk (pt.), Plymouth (pt.) and Suffolk (pt.). Prior Terms: 1979-92. Born: March 2, 1946; Dorchester, MA. Education: Boston University (B.S.). Occupation: Director of Youth Activities, YMCA (1968-70); coach (1969-72); Massachusetts representative (1973-78).

1. Protection to Haitian refugees	Y	
2. Raise tax on wealthy; lower others	N	
3. Investigate Reagan hostage delay	Y	
4. Campaign finance revisions	Y	
5. Unpaid leave to care for children	Y	
6. Restrict NEA use of funds	Y	
7. Bar race-bias claim/habeas corpus	N	
8. Ban race as death sentence factor	N	
9. Exceptions to exclusionary rule	N	
10. Allow sale of assault weapons	N	
11. Life in prison/abolish death penalty	N	
12. Req conspiracy-price fixing cases	N	
13. Unemployment benefits extension	Y	
14. Tissue use of aborted fetuses	Y	
15. Bar replacement of union strikers	Y	
16. Hold foreign aid at $15b for '92	N	
17. Restore space station funding	N	
18. Civil Rights Act of 1991	Y	
19. Unlimited damages-discrimination	Y	
20. Eliminate funds for supercollider	Y	
21. Terminate SDI except for research	Y	
22. Req 7-day handgun waiting period	Y	
23. Provide $30b for failed S&Ls	N	
24. Allow use of force against Iraq	N	
25. Allow $15b in foreign aid for '91	N	
26. Revise & extend legal immigration	Y	
27. Suspend aid to Angolan rebels	N	
28. Democratic tax plan proposals	Y	
29. Cut defense 5% across the board	Y	
30. Textile import quotas-veto override	Y	
31. Abortion service for military abroad	N	
32. Limits on high income farmers	Y	
33. Family medical leave-veto override	N	
34. Req submission of balanced budget	Y	
35. Balanced budget amendment	N	
36. Amendment to ban flag desecration	Y	
37. Reauthorize Amtrak-veto override	Y	
38. Retraining aid for coal miners	Y	
39. Suspend El Salvador military aid	Y	
40. Expand child care aid/tax credit	Y	
41. Raise House salary/omit honoraria	Y	
42. Toughen oil-spill liability	Y	
43. Restitution to Japanese interned	Y	
44. Protect Chinese & C.A. nationals	Y	
45. Abortion $ for rape/incest cases	N	
46. Allow religious schools to bar gays	N	
47. Bar broadcaster fairness doctrine	N	
48. Bar cap gains cut/reinstate IRA	Y	
49. Bar unions equal voice in pension	N	
50. Bar assembly of chemical weapons	Y	
51. Ban plutonium/uranium production	Y	
52. Cap MX missile deployment at 50	Y	
53. Allow $3b for 2 stealth bombers	N	
54. Publish bio-warfare experiments	Y	
55. Raise minimum wage-veto override	Y	
56. Bar transfer of FS-X technology	Y	
57. Cut defense and raise domestic $	N	
58. Uniform poll closing in 48 states	Y	
59. Req foreign investment disclosure	Y	
60. Textile import quotas-veto override	?	
61. Bar abortion funding in Wash, DC	Y
62. Notify spouses of AIDS+ carriers	N
63. Seize conveyance-drug trafficking	N
64. South Africa sanctions	Y
65. 60 days' notice of plant closings	Y
66. Close unneeded military bases	N
67. Keep welfare reform within $2.8b	N
68. Allow children housing exclusion	N
69. Shift $400m of NASA to homeless	N
70. Cap Medicare patients' liability	Y
71. Prohibit employee polygraph testing	Y
72. Allow CIA to fund Contras	N
73. Revise unfair trade practices	Y
74. Focus SDI on accidental launch	Y
75. Bar Air Force $ for MX missile	Y
76. Allow "real" increase in defense	?
77. Troop reduction in Europe of 50%	Y
78. Ban nuclear tests above 1 kiloton	Y
79. Ban anti-satellite missile tests	Y
80. Observe certain limits of SALT II	Y
81. Restore four Civil Rights laws	Y
82. Prohibit aliens as strikebreakers	Y
83. Allow military malpractice suits	Y
84. Approval of $36m in Contra aid	N
85. $18b deficit reduction compromise	Y
86. Welfare reform of $5.7b for 5 years	Y
87. Raise taxes $12b/cut spending $3b	Y
88. Board to assess occupational risk	Y
89. Balanced budget by '93-via targets	Y
90. Bar licensing of two nuclear plants	N
91. Remove victims compensation cap	Y
92. Catastrophic health insurance	Y
93. Ban airline smoking-2 hours or less	Y
94. $1b/two year aid for the homeless	Y
95. Bar non-unions in union companies	Y
96. Increase FSLIC rescue to $15b	Y
97. Impose quotas to lower trade deficit	Y
98. Reduce discretionary budget 21%	Y
99. Immigration reform/alien amnesty	Y
100. South Africa sanctions-veto override	Y
101. Tax overhaul to revise income tax	Y
102. Use of military in drug war	Y
103. Delete 12 MX/add conventional wpn	Y
104. Raise speed limit to 65 mph	N
105. Require Pentagon to buy US goods	Y
106. AIDS insurance non-discrimination	Y
107. Prohibit Saudi arms sales	+
108. Ease Gun Control Act of 1968	N
109. Bar interstate handgun transport	Y
110. Make company emissions known	Y
111. Allow toxic victims to sue in fed ct	Y
112. Superfund waste cleanup of $10b	Y
113. 90 days notice of plant closings	Y
114. $20b in Medicare cuts/tax increases	Y
115. Spending cuts and tax increases	Y
116. Set school lunch lmt-250% poverty	N
117. $75m for youth work projects	Y
118. Allow Angolan military assistance	N
119. Suspend defense payments for abuse	Y
120. Drop SS COLAs/$12b tax increase	N

DONNELLY, BRIAN J. (continued)

121. Approve $1.5b for 21 MX missiles	N	
122. Emergency farm credit/revisions	Y	
123. Duty on Taiwan/Hong Kong/S Korea	Y	
124. Limit steel imports to 17%	Y	
125. Cut $ to schools that bar prayer	N	
126. $50b-taxes; cut Medicare/spending	Y	
127. Limit Pershing II/cruise in Europe	N	
128. Delete $7.1b for 34 B-1 bombers	Y	
129. Bar purchase of Sergeant York guns	Y	
130. El Salvador military/economic aid	N	
131. Bar mining of Nicaraguan waters	Y	
132. Physician fee freeze for Medicare	N	
133. $49b in "sin"/phone/insurance taxes	Y
134. Allow sale of Conrail	N
135. Equal Rights Amendment	Y
136. Authorize Marines in Lebanon	N
137. Eminent domain for coal companies	Y
138. Prohibit EPA clean air sanctions	N
139. SS retirement age increase/reforms	N
140. Auto domestic content requirement	N
141. Delete jobs program funding	N
142. Highway-gas tax bill	Y
143. Cut $5b from defense for Medicare	N
144. Emergency housing aid of $1b	N

Presidential Support Score: 1991 - 25%   1990 - 26%

MICHIGAN

CONYERS, JOHN Jr. -- Michigan 1st District [Democrat]. County of Wayne (pt.). Prior Terms: 1965-92. Born: May 16, 1929; Detroit, MI. Education: Wayne State University (B.A., LL.B.). Military Service: U.S. Army. Occupation: Congressional legislative assistant (1958-61).

1. Protection to Haitian refugees	Y	37. Reauthorize Amtrak-veto override	Y
2. Raise tax on wealthy; lower others	N	38. Retraining aid for coal miners	Y
3. Investigate Reagan hostage delay	Y	39. Suspend El Salvador military aid	Y
4. Campaign finance revisions	Y	40. Expand child care aid/tax credit	Y
5. Unpaid leave to care for children	Y	41. Raise House salary/omit honoraria	N
6. Restrict NEA use of funds	N	42. Toughen oil-spill liability	Y
7. Bar race-bias claim/habeas corpus	N	43. Restitution to Japanese interned	Y
8. Bar race as death sentence factor	N	44. Protect Chinese & C.A. nationals	Y
9. Exceptions to exclusionary rule	N	45. Abortion $ for rape/incest cases	Y
10. Allow sale of assault weapons	N	46. Allow religious schools to bar gays	N
11. Life in prison/abolish death penalty	Y	47. Bar broadcaster fairness doctrine	N
12. Req conspiracy-price fixing cases	N	48. Bar cap gains cut/reinstate IRA	Y
13. Unemployment benefits extension	Y	49. Bar unions equal voice in pension	N
14. Tissue use of aborted fetuses	Y	50. Bar assembly of chemical weapons	Y
15. Bar replacement of union strikers	Y	51. Ban plutonium/uranium production	Y
16. Hold foreign aid at $15b for '92	Y	52. Cap MX missile deployment at 50	Y
17. Restore space station funding	N	53. Allow $3b for 2 stealth bombers	?
18. Civil Rights Act of 1991	Y	54. Publish bio-warfare experiments	Y
19. Unlimited damages-discrimination	Y	55. Raise minimum wage-veto override	Y
20. Eliminate funds for supercollider	Y	56. Bar transfer of FS-X technology	Y
21. Terminate SDI except for research	?	57. Cut defense and raise domestic $	Y
22. Req 7-day handgun waiting period	Y	58. Uniform poll closing in 48 states	Y
23. Provide $30b for failed S&Ls	N	59. Req foreign investment disclosure	Y
24. Allow use of force against Iraq	N	60. Textile import quotas-veto override	Y
25. Allow $15b in foreign aid for '91	Y	61. Bar abortion funding in Wash, DC	N
26. Revise & extend legal immigration	Y	62. Notify spouses of AIDS+ carriers	N
27. Suspend aid to Angolan rebels	Y	63. Seize conveyance-drug trafficking	N
28. Democratic tax plan proposals	Y	64. South Africa sanctions	Y
29. Cut defense 5% across the board	Y	65. 60 days' notice of plant closings	Y
30. Textile import quotas-veto override	Y	66. Close unneeded military bases	N
31. Abortion service for military abroad	Y	67. Keep welfare reform within $2.8b	N
32. Limits on high income farmers	N	68. Allow children housing exclusion	N
33. Family medical leave-veto override	Y	69. Shift $400m of NASA to homeless	Y
34. Req submission of balanced budget	N	70. Cap Medicare patients' liability	Y
35. Balanced budget amendment	N	71. Prohibit employee polygraph testing	Y
36. Amendment to ban flag desecration	N	72. Allow CIA to fund Contras	N

CONYERS, JOHN Jr. (continued)

73.	Revise unfair trade practices	Y	109.	Bar interstate handgun transport	Y
74.	Focus SDI on accidental launch	?	110.	Make company emissions known	Y
75.	Bar Air Force $ for MX missile	Y	111.	Allow toxic victims to sue in fed ct	Y
76.	Allow "real" increase in defense	N	112.	Superfund waste cleanup of $10b	Y
77.	Troop reduction in Europe of 50%	N	113.	90 days notice of plant closings	?
78.	Ban nuclear tests above 1 kiloton	Y	114.	$20b in Medicare cuts/tax increases	Y
79.	Ban anti-satellite missile tests	Y	115.	Spending cuts and tax increases	?
80.	Observe certain limits of SALT II	Y	116.	Set school lunch lmt-250% poverty	N
81.	Restore four Civil Rights laws	Y	117.	$75m for youth work projects	Y
82.	Prohibit aliens as strikebreakers	Y	118.	Allow Angolan military assistance	N
83.	Allow military malpractice suits	Y	119.	Suspend defense payments for abuse	?
84.	Approval of $36m in Contra aid	N	120.	Drop SS COLAs/$12b tax increase	N
85.	$18b deficit reduction compromise	Y	121.	Approve $1.5b for 21 MX missiles	N
86.	Welfare reform of $5.7b for 5 years	Y	122.	Emergency farm credit/revisions	Y
87.	Raise taxes $12b/cut spending $3b	Y	123.	Duty on Taiwan/Hong Kong/S Korea	Y
88.	Board to assess occupational risk	Y	124.	Limit steel imports to 17%	Y
89.	Balanced budget by '93-via targets	?	125.	Cut $ to schools that bar prayer	N
90.	Bar licensing of two nuclear plants	Y	126.	$50b-taxes; cut Medicare/spending	N
91.	Remove victims compensation cap	Y	127.	Limit Pershing II/cruise in Europe	Y
92.	Catastrophic health insurance	Y	128.	Delete $7.1b for 34 B-1 bombers	Y
93.	Ban airline smoking-2 hours or less	?	129.	Bar purchase of Sergeant York guns	Y
94.	$1b/two year aid for the homeless	Y	130.	El Salvador military/economic aid	N
95.	Bar non-unions in union companies	Y	131.	Bar mining of Nicaraguan waters	Y
96.	Increase FSLIC rescue to $15b	N	132.	Physician fee freeze for Medicare	N
97.	Impose quotas to lower trade deficit	Y	133.	$49b in "sin"/phone/insurance taxes	Y
98.	Reduce discretionary budget 21%	?	134.	Allow sale of Conrail	N
99.	Immigration reform/alien amnesty	X	135.	Equal Rights Amendment	Y
100.	South Africa sanctions-veto override	Y	136.	Authorize Marines in Lebanon	N
101.	Tax overhaul to revise income tax	N	137.	Eminent domain for coal companies	Y
102.	Use of military in drug war	N	138.	Prohibit EPA clean air sanctions	?
103.	Delete 12 MX/add conventional wpn	Y	139.	SS retirement age increase/reforms	N
104.	Raise speed limit to 65 mph	N	140.	Auto domestic content requirement	Y
105.	Require Pentagon to buy US goods	?	141.	Delete jobs program funding	N
106.	AIDS insurance non-discrimination	Y	142.	Highway-gas tax bill	N
107.	Prohibit Saudi arms sales	N	143.	Cut $5b from defense for Medicare	Y
108.	Ease Gun Control Act of 1968	N	144.	Emergency housing aid of $1b	Y

Presidential Support Score: 1991 - 23% 1990 - 16%

PURSELL, CARL D. -- Michigan 2nd District [Republican]. Counties of Branch (pt.), Hillsdale, Jackson (pt.), Lenawee (pt.), Washtenaw (pt.) and Wayne (pt.). Prior Terms: 1977-92. Born: December 19, 1932; Imlay City, MI. Education: Eastern Michigan University (B.A., M.A.). Military Service: U.S. Army, 1957-59. Occupation: Wayne County commissioner (1969-70); Michigan senator (1971-76).

1.	Protection to Haitian refugees	N	19.	Unlimited damages-discrimination	N
2.	Raise tax on wealthy; lower others	N	20.	Eliminate funds for supercollider	N
3.	Investigate Reagan hostage delay	N	21.	Terminate SDI except for research	N
4.	Campaign finance revisions	N	22.	Req 7-day handgun waiting period	Y
5.	Unpaid leave to care for children	N	23.	Provide $30b for failed S&Ls	N
6.	Restrict NEA use of funds	Y	24.	Allow use of force against Iraq	Y
7.	Bar race-bias claim/habeas corpus	Y	25.	Allow $15b in foreign aid for '91	?
8.	Ban race as death sentence factor	?	26.	Revise & extend legal immigration	?
9.	Exceptions to exclusionary rule	Y	27.	Suspend aid to Angolan rebels	N
10.	Allow sale of assault weapons	N	28.	Democratic tax plan proposals	N
11.	Life in prison/abolish death penalty	N	29.	Cut defense 5% across the board	?
12.	Req conspiracy-price fixing cases	Y	30.	Textile import quotas-veto override	N
13.	Unemployment benefits extension	Y	31.	Abortion service for military abroad	N
14.	Tissue use of aborted fetuses	Y	32.	Limits on high income farmers	N
15.	Bar replacement of union strikers	N	33.	Family medical leave-veto override	N
16.	Hold foreign aid at $15b for '92	N	34.	Req submission of balanced budget	Y
17.	Restore space station funding	N	35.	Balanced budget amendment	Y
18.	Civil Rights Act of 1991	N	36.	Amendment to ban flag desecration	Y

PURSELL, CARL D. (continued)

37. Reauthorize Amtrak-veto override	?	
38. Retraining aid for coal miners	Y	
39. Suspend El Salvador military aid	Y	
40. Expand child care aid/tax credit	N	
41. Raise House salary/omit honoraria	Y	
42. Toughen oil-spill liability	N	
43. Restitution to Japanese interned	N	
44. Protect Chinese & C.A. nationals	N	
45. Abortion $ for rape/incest cases	Y	
46. Allow religious schools to bar gays	Y	
47. Bar broadcaster fairness doctrine	N	
48. Bar cap gains cut/reinstate IRA	N	
49. Bar unions equal voice in pension	Y	
50. Bar assembly of chemical weapons	Y	
51. Ban plutonium/uranium production	Y	
52. Cap MX missile deployment at 50	Y	
53. Allow $3b for 2 stealth bombers	N	
54. Publish bio-warfare experiments	Y	
55. Raise minimum wage-veto override	N	
56. Bar transfer of FS-X technology	N	
57. Cut defense and raise domestic $	N	
58. Uniform poll closing in 48 states	N	
59. Req foreign investment disclosure	N	
60. Textile import quotas-veto override	N	
61. Bar abortion funding in Wash, DC	N	
62. Notify spouses of AIDS+ carriers	Y	
63. Seize conveyance-drug trafficking	N	
64. South Africa sanctions	N	
65. 60 days' notice of plant closings	Y	
66. Close unneeded military bases	Y	
67. Keep welfare reform within $2.8b	Y	
68. Allow children housing exclusion	N	
69. Shift $400m of NASA to homeless	Y	
70. Cap Medicare patients' liability	N	
71. Prohibit employee polygraph testing	?	
72. Allow CIA to fund Contras	Y	
73. Revise unfair trade practices	Y	
74. Focus SDI on accidental launch	Y	
75. Bar Air Force $ for MX missile	N	
76. Allow "real" increase in defense	N	
77. Troop reduction in Europe of 50%	N	
78. Ban nuclear tests above 1 kiloton	Y	
79. Ban anti-satellite missile tests	N	
80. Observe certain limits of SALT II	Y	
81. Restore four Civil Rights laws	N	
82. Prohibit aliens as strikebreakers	Y	
83. Allow military malpractice suits	?	
84. Approval of $36m in Contra aid	Y	
85. $18b deficit reduction compromise	Y	
86. Welfare reform of $5.7b for 5 years	N	
87. Raise taxes $12b/cut spending $3b	N	
88. Board to assess occupational risk	N	
89. Balanced budget by '93-via targets	Y	
90. Bar licensing of two nuclear plants	N	

91. Remove victims compensation cap	N	
92. Catastrophic health insurance	N	
93. Ban airline smoking-2 hours or less	Y	
94. $1b/two year aid for the homeless	Y	
95. Bar non-unions in union companies	N	
96. Increase FSLIC rescue to $15b	N	
97. Impose quotas to lower trade deficit	N	
98. Reduce discretionary budget 21%	N	
99. Immigration reform/alien amnesty	N	
100. South Africa sanctions-veto override	Y	
101. Tax overhaul to revise income tax	Y	
102. Use of military in drug war	N	
103. Delete 12 MX/add conventional wpn	N	
104. Raise speed limit to 65 mph	N	
105. Require Pentagon to buy US goods	Y	
106. AIDS insurance non-discrimination	N	
107. Prohibit Saudi arms sales	Y	
108. Ease Gun Control Act of 1968	N	
109. Bar interstate handgun transport	Y	
110. Make company emissions known	N	
111. Allow toxic victims to sue in fed ct	N	
112. Superfund waste cleanup of $10b	Y	
113. 90 days notice of plant closings	N	
114. $20b in Medicare cuts/tax increases	N	
115. Spending cuts and tax increases	N	
116. Set school lunch lmt-250% poverty	N	
117. $75m for youth work projects	X	
118. Allow Angolan military assistance	Y	
119. Suspend defense payments for abuse	N	
120. Drop SS COLAs/$12b tax increase	N	
121. Approve $1.5b for 21 MX missiles	Y	
122. Emergency farm credit/revisions	Y	
123. Duty on Taiwan/Hong Kong/S Korea	?	
124. Limit steel imports to 17%	Y	
125. Cut $ to schools that bar prayer	N	
126. $50b-taxes; cut Medicare/spending	N	
127. Limit Pershing II/cruise in Europe	N	
128. Delete $7.1b for 34 B-1 bombers	Y	
129. Bar purchase of Sergeant York guns	N	
130. El Salvador military/economic aid	Y	
131. Bar mining of Nicaraguan waters	Y	
132. Physician fee freeze for Medicare	Y	
133. $49b in "sin"/phone/insurance taxes	N	
134. Allow sale of Conrail	Y	
135. Equal Rights Amendment	Y	
136. Authorize Marines in Lebanon	Y	
137. Eminent domain for coal companies	Y	
138. Prohibit EPA clean air sanctions	?	
139. SS retirement age increase/reforms	Y	
140. Auto domestic content requirement	?	
141. Delete jobs program funding	Y	
142. Highway-gas tax bill	N	
143. Cut $5b from defense for Medicare	Y	
144. Emergency housing aid of $1b	Y	

Presidential Support Score: 1991 - 65%   1990 - 53%

WOLPE, HOWARD -- Michigan 3rd District [Democrat]. Counties of Barry (pt.), Calhoun, Eaton, Ingham (pt.) and Kalamazoo (pt.). Prior Terms: 1979-92. Born: November 2, 1939; Los Angeles, CA. Education: Reed College (B.A.); Massachusetts Institute of Technology (Ph.D.). Occupation: Consultant, Peace Corps (1966-67); consultant, Foreign Service Institute (1967-72); professor (1967-72); city commissioner (1969-72); Michigan representative (1972-76); senator's regional representative and state liaison (1976-78).

WOLPE, HOWARD (continued)

1. Protection to Haitian refugees	Y
2. Raise tax on wealthy; lower others	N
3. Investigate Reagan hostage delay	Y
4. Campaign finance revisions	Y
5. Unpaid leave to care for children	Y
6. Restrict NEA use of funds	N
7. Bar race-bias claim/habeas corpus	N
8. Ban race as death sentence factor	N
9. Exceptions to exclusionary rule	N
10. Allow sale of assault weapons	N
11. Life in prison/abolish death penalty	Y
12. Req conspiracy-price fixing cases	N
13. Unemployment benefits extension	Y
14. Tissue use of aborted fetuses	Y
15. Bar replacement of union strikers	Y
16. Hold foreign aid at $15b for '92	Y
17. Restore space station funding	N
18. Civil Rights Act of 1991	Y
19. Unlimited damages-discrimination	Y
20. Eliminate funds for supercollider	Y
21. Terminate SDI except for research	Y
22. Req 7-day handgun waiting period	Y
23. Provide $30b for failed S&Ls	N
24. Allow use of force against Iraq	N
25. Allow $15b in foreign aid for '91	Y
26. Revise & extend legal immigration	Y
27. Suspend aid to Angolan rebels	Y
28. Democratic tax plan proposals	Y
29. Cut defense 5% across the board	Y
30. Textile import quotas-veto override	Y
31. Abortion service for military abroad	Y
32. Limits on high income farmers	N
33. Family medical leave-veto override	Y
34. Req submission of balanced budget	Y
35. Balanced budget amendment	N
36. Amendment to ban flag desecration	N
37. Reauthorize Amtrak-veto override	Y
38. Retraining aid for coal miners	Y
39. Suspend El Salvador military aid	Y
40. Expand child care aid/tax credit	Y
41. Raise House salary/omit honoraria	Y
42. Toughen oil-spill liability	Y
43. Restitution to Japanese interned	Y
44. Protect Chinese & C.A. nationals	Y
45. Abortion $ for rape/incest cases	Y
46. Allow religious schools to bar gays	N
47. Bar broadcaster fairness doctrine	N
48. Bar cap gains cut/reinstate IRA	Y
49. Bar unions equal voice in pension	N
50. Bar assembly of chemical weapons	Y
51. Ban plutonium/uranium production	Y
52. Cap MX missile deployment at 50	Y
53. Allow $3b for 2 stealth bombers	N
54. Publish bio-warfare experiments	Y
55. Raise minimum wage-veto override	Y
56. Bar transfer of FS-X technology	Y
57. Cut defense and raise domestic $	N
58. Uniform poll closing in 48 states	Y
59. Req foreign investment disclosure	Y
60. Textile import quotas-veto override	Y
61. Bar abortion funding in Wash, DC	N
62. Notify spouses of AIDS+ carriers	N
63. Seize conveyance-drug trafficking	N
64. South Africa sanctions	Y

65. 60 days' notice of plant closings	Y
66. Close unneeded military bases	N
67. Keep welfare reform within $2.8b	N
68. Allow children housing exclusion	N
69. Shift $400m of NASA to homeless	Y
70. Cap Medicare patients' liability	?
71. Prohibit employee polygraph testing	Y
72. Allow CIA to fund Contras	X
73. Revise unfair trade practices	Y
74. Focus SDI on accidental launch	Y
75. Bar Air Force $ for MX missile	Y
76. Allow "real" increase in defense	N
77. Troop reduction in Europe of 50%	N
78. Ban nuclear tests above 1 kiloton	Y
79. Ban anti-satellite missile tests	Y
80. Observe certain limits of SALT II	Y
81. Restore four Civil Rights laws	Y
82. Prohibit aliens as strikebreakers	Y
83. Allow military malpractice suits	Y
84. Approval of $36m in Contra aid	N
85. $18b deficit reduction compromise	Y
86. Welfare reform of $5.7b for 5 years	Y
87. Raise taxes $12b/cut spending $3b	Y
88. Board to assess occupational risk	Y
89. Balanced budget by '93-via targets	Y
90. Bar licensing of two nuclear plants	Y
91. Remove victims compensation cap	Y
92. Catastrophic health insurance	Y
93. Ban airline smoking-2 hours or less	Y
94. $1b/two year aid for the homeless	Y
95. Bar non-unions in union companies	Y
96. Increase FSLIC rescue to $15b	N
97. Impose quotas to lower trade deficit	Y
98. Reduce discretionary budget 21%	Y
99. Immigration reform/alien amnesty	Y
100. South Africa sanctions-veto override	Y
101. Tax overhaul to revise income tax	Y
102. Use of military in drug war	N
103. Delete 12 MX/add conventional wpn	Y
104. Raise speed limit to 65 mph	N
105. Require Pentagon to buy US goods	Y
106. AIDS insurance non-discrimination	Y
107. Prohibit Saudi arms sales	Y
108. Ease Gun Control Act of 1968	--
109. Bar interstate handgun transport	Y
110. Make company emissions known	Y
111. Allow toxic victims to sue in fed ct	Y
112. Superfund waste cleanup of $10b	Y
113. 90 days notice of plant closings	Y
114. $20b in Medicare cuts/tax increases	Y
115. Spending cuts and tax increases	Y
116. Set school lunch lmt-250% poverty	N
117. $75m for youth work projects	Y
118. Allow Angolan military assistance	N
119. Suspend defense payments for abuse	Y
120. Drop SS COLAs/$12b tax increase	N
121. Approve $1.5b for 21 MX missiles	N
122. Emergency farm credit/revisions	Y
123. Duty on Taiwan/Hong Kong/S Korea	Y
124. Limit steel imports to 17%	Y
125. Cut $ to schools that bar prayer	N
126. $50b-taxes; cut Medicare/spending	N
127. Limit Pershing II/cruise in Europe	Y
128. Delete $7.1b for 34 B-1 bombers	Y

WOLPE, HOWARD (continued)

129. Bar purchase of Sergeant York guns	Y	
130. El Salvador military/economic aid	N	
131. Bar mining of Nicaraguan waters	Y	
132. Physician fee freeze for Medicare	N	
133. $49b in "sin"/phone/insurance taxes	Y	
134. Allow sale of Conrail	N	
135. Equal Rights Amendment	Y	
136. Authorize Marines in Lebanon	N	

137. Eminent domain for coal companies	?
138. Prohibit EPA clean air sanctions	Y
139. SS retirement age increase/reforms	N
140. Auto domestic content requirement	Y
141. Delete jobs program funding	N
142. Highway-gas tax bill	Y
143. Cut $5b from defense for Medicare	Y
144. Emergency housing aid of $1b	Y

Presidential Support Score: 1991 - 23%   1990 - 15%

UPTON, FRED -- Michigan 4th District [Republican]. Counties of Allegan (pt.), Berrien, Branch (pt.), Cass, Kalamazoo (pt.), Ottawa (pt.), St. Joseph and Van Buren. Prior Terms: 1987-92. Born: April 23, 1953; St. Joseph, MI. Education: University of Michigan (B.A.). Occupation: Congressional campaign field manager and staff member; legislative assistant, Assistant Director for Legislative Affairs, and Director of Congressional Affairs Office, Office of Management and Budget (1981-1985).

1. Protection to Haitian refugees	N	
2. Raise tax on wealthy; lower others	N	
3. Investigate Reagan hostage delay	N	
4. Campaign finance revisions	N	
5. Unpaid leave to care for children	N	
6. Restrict NEA use of funds	Y	
7. Bar race-bias claim/habeas corpus	Y	
8. Ban race as death sentence factor	Y	
9. Exceptions to exclusionary rule	Y	
10. Allow sale of assault weapons	Y	
11. Life in prison/abolish death penalty	N	
12. Req conspiracy-price fixing cases	Y	
13. Unemployment benefits extension	Y	
14. Tissue use of aborted fetuses	Y	
15. Bar replacement of union strikers	N	
16. Hold foreign aid at $15b for '92	Y	
17. Restore space station funding	Y	
18. Civil Rights Act of 1991	N	
19. Unlimited damages-discrimination	N	
20. Eliminate funds for supercollider	Y	
21. Terminate SDI except for research	N	
22. Req 7-day handgun waiting period	Y	
23. Provide $30b for failed S&Ls	N	
24. Allow use of force against Iraq	Y	
25. Allow $15b in foreign aid for '91	N	
26. Revise & extend legal immigration	Y	
27. Suspend aid to Angolan rebels	N	
28. Democratic tax plan proposals	N	
29. Cut defense 5% across the board	Y	
30. Textile import quotas-veto override	N	
31. Abortion service for military abroad	N	
32. Limits on high income farmers	N	
33. Family medical leave-veto override	N	
34. Req submission of balanced budget	Y	
35. Balanced budget amendment	Y	
36. Amendment to ban flag desecration	Y	
37. Reauthorize Amtrak-veto override	N	
38. Retraining aid for coal miners	Y	
39. Suspend El Salvador military aid	Y	
40. Expand child care aid/tax credit	N	
41. Raise House salary/omit honoraria	Y	
42. Toughen oil-spill liability	N	
43. Restitution to Japanese interned	Y	
44. Protect Chinese & C.A. nationals	N	
45. Abortion $ for rape/incest cases	Y	
46. Allow religious schools to bar gays	Y	

47. Bar broadcaster fairness doctrine	Y
48. Bar cap gains cut/reinstate IRA	N
49. Bar unions equal voice in pension	Y
50. Bar assembly of chemical weapons	Y
51. Ban plutonium/uranium production	Y
52. Cap MX missile deployment at 50	Y
53. Allow $3b for 2 stealth bombers	N
54. Publish bio-warfare experiments	N
55. Raise minimum wage-veto override	N
56. Bar transfer of FS-X technology	N
57. Cut defense and raise domestic $	N
58. Uniform poll closing in 48 states	N
59. Req foreign investment disclosure	N
60. Textile import quotas-veto override	N
61. Bar abortion funding in Wash, DC	N
62. Notify spouses of AIDS+ carriers	Y
63. Seize conveyance-drug trafficking	N
64. South Africa sanctions	N
65. 60 days' notice of plant closings	Y
66. Close unneeded military bases	Y
67. Keep welfare reform within $2.8b	Y
68. Allow children housing exclusion	Y
69. Shift $400m of NASA to homeless	Y
70. Cap Medicare patients' liability	Y
71. Prohibit employee polygraph testing	Y
72. Allow CIA to fund Contras	Y
73. Revise unfair trade practices	Y
74. Focus SDI on accidental launch	N
75. Bar Air Force $ for MX missile	N
76. Allow "real" increase in defense	N
77. Troop reduction in Europe of 50%	N
78. Ban nuclear tests above 1 kiloton	N
79. Ban anti-satellite missile tests	N
80. Observe certain limits of SALT II	N
81. Restore four Civil Rights laws	N
82. Prohibit aliens as strikebreakers	N
83. Allow military malpractice suits	Y
84. Approval of $36m in Contra aid	Y
85. $18b deficit reduction compromise	N
86. Welfare reform of $5.7b for 5 years	N
87. Raise taxes $12b/cut spending $3b	N
88. Board to assess occupational risk	N
89. Balanced budget by '93-via targets	Y
90. Bar licensing of two nuclear plants	N
91. Remove victims compensation cap	N
92. Catastrophic health insurance	N

UPTON, FRED (continued)

93.	Ban airline smoking-2 hours or less	N	96.	Increase FSLIC rescue to $15b	N
94.	$1b/two year aid for the homeless	Y	97.	Impose quotas to lower trade deficit	N
95.	Bar non-unions in union companies	N	98.	Reduce discretionary budget 21%	Y

Presidential Support Score: 1991 - 60% 1990 - 61%

HENRY, PAUL B. -- Michigan 5th District [Republican]. Counties of Allegan (pt.), Barry (pt.), Ionia (pt.), Kent (pt.) and Newaygo (pt.). Prior Terms: 1985-92. Born: July 9, 1942; Chicago, IL. Education: Wheaton College; Duke University (M.A., Ph.D.). Occupation: Educator; Michigan representative; Michigan senator; professor, Calvin College and Duke University; congressional assistant.

1.	Protection to Haitian refugees	N	52.	Cap MX missile deployment at 50	N
2.	Raise tax on wealthy; lower others	N	53.	Allow $3b for 2 stealth bombers	Y
3.	Investigate Reagan hostage delay	N	54.	Publish bio-warfare experiments	N
4.	Campaign finance revisions	N	55.	Raise minimum wage-veto override	N
5.	Unpaid leave to care for children	N	56.	Bar transfer of FS-X technology	Y
6.	Restrict NEA use of funds	Y	57.	Cut defense and raise domestic $	N
7.	Bar race-bias claim/habeas corpus	Y	58.	Uniform poll closing in 48 states	N
8.	Ban race as death sentence factor	Y	59.	Req foreign investment disclosure	N
9.	Exceptions to exclusionary rule	Y	60.	Textile import quotas-veto override	Y
10.	Allow sale of assault weapons	N	61.	Bar abortion funding in Wash, DC	Y
11.	Life in prison/abolish death penalty	N	62.	Notify spouses of AIDS+ carriers	Y
12.	Req conspiracy-price fixing cases	Y	63.	Seize conveyance-drug trafficking	N
13.	Unemployment benefits extension	Y	64.	South Africa sanctions	N
14.	Tissue use of aborted fetuses	N	65.	60 days' notice of plant closings	Y
15.	Bar replacement of union strikers	N	66.	Close unneeded military bases	Y
16.	Hold foreign aid at $15b for '92	N	67.	Keep welfare reform within $2.8b	Y
17.	Restore space station funding	N	68.	Allow children housing exclusion	N
18.	Civil Rights Act of 1991	Y	69.	Shift $400m of NASA to homeless	N
19.	Unlimited damages-discrimination	N	70.	Cap Medicare patients' liability	Y
20.	Eliminate funds for supercollider	Y	71.	Prohibit employee polygraph testing	Y
21.	Terminate SDI except for research	N	72.	Allow CIA to fund Contras	N
22.	Req 7-day handgun waiting period	Y	73.	Revise unfair trade practices	Y
23.	Provide $30b for failed S&Ls	N	74.	Focus SDI on accidental launch	N
24.	Allow use of force against Iraq	Y	75.	Bar Air Force $ for MX missile	N
25.	Allow $15b in foreign aid for '91	N	76.	Allow "real" increase in defense	N
26.	Revise & extend legal immigration	Y	77.	Troop reduction in Europe of 50%	?
27.	Suspend aid to Angolan rebels	N	78.	Ban nuclear tests above 1 kiloton	N
28.	Democratic tax plan proposals	N	79.	Ban anti-satellite missile tests	N
29.	Cut defense 5% across the board	Y	80.	Observe certain limits of SALT II	Y
30.	Textile import quotas-veto override	?	81.	Restore four Civil Rights laws	N
31.	Abortion service for military abroad	N	82.	Prohibit aliens as strikebreakers	N
32.	Limits on high income farmers	N	83.	Allow military malpractice suits	N
33.	Family medical leave-veto override	N	84.	Approval of $36m in Contra aid	N
34.	Req submission of balanced budget	Y	85.	$18b deficit reduction compromise	N
35.	Balanced budget amendment	Y	86.	Welfare reform of $5.7b for 5 years	N
36.	Amendment to ban flag desecration	N	87.	Raise taxes $12b/cut spending $3b	N
37.	Reauthorize Amtrak-veto override	N	88.	Board to assess occupational risk	N
38.	Retraining aid for coal miners	Y	89.	Balanced budget by '93-via targets	Y
39.	Suspend El Salvador military aid	Y	90.	Bar licensing of two nuclear plants	N
40.	Expand child care aid/tax credit	N	91.	Remove victims compensation cap	N
41.	Raise House salary/omit honoraria	Y	92.	Catastrophic health insurance	N
42.	Toughen oil-spill liability	Y	93.	Ban airline smoking-2 hours or less	N
43.	Restitution to Japanese interned	N	94.	$1b/two year aid for the homeless	Y
44.	Protect Chinese & C.A. nationals	N	95.	Bar non-unions in union companies	N
45.	Abortion $ for rape/incest cases	N	96.	Increase FSLIC rescue to $15b	N
46.	Allow religious schools to bar gays	Y	97.	Impose quotas to lower trade deficit	Y
47.	Bar broadcaster fairness doctrine	Y	98.	Reduce discretionary budget 21%	Y
48.	Bar cap gains cut/reinstate IRA	N	99.	Immigration reform/alien amnesty	N
49.	Bar unions equal voice in pension	Y	100.	South Africa sanctions-veto override	Y
50.	Bar assembly of chemical weapons	Y	101.	Tax overhaul to revise income tax	Y
51.	Ban plutonium/uranium production	Y	102.	Use of military in drug war	Y

HENRY, PAUL B. (continued)

103.	Delete 12 MX/add conventional wpn	Y	113.	90 days notice of plant closings	N
104.	Raise speed limit to 65 mph	Y	114.	$20b in Medicare cuts/tax increases	N
105.	Require Pentagon to buy US goods	Y	115.	Spending cuts and tax increases	N
106.	AIDS insurance non-discrimination	N	116.	Set school lunch lmt-250% poverty	N
107.	Prohibit Saudi arms sales	Y	117.	$75m for youth work projects	N
108.	Ease Gun Control Act of 1968	N	118.	Allow Angolan military assistance	Y
109.	Bar interstate handgun transport	N	119.	Suspend defense payments for abuse	Y
110.	Make company emissions known	N	120.	Drop SS COLAs/$12b tax increase	N
111.	Allow toxic victims to sue in fed ct	N	121.	Approve $1.5b for 21 MX missiles	N
112.	Superfund waste cleanup of $10b	Y	122.	Emergency farm credit/revisions	Y

Presidential Support Score: 1991 - 64%   1990 - 58%

CARR, BOB -- Michigan 6th District [Democrat]. Counties of Clinton (pt.), Genesee (pt.), Ingham (pt.), Jackson (pt.), Livingston (pt.), Oakland (pt.) and Shiawassee (pt.). Prior Terms: 1975-80; 1983-92. Born: March 27, 1944. Education: University of Wisconsin Law School. Occupation: Senate staff member (1968-69); assistant attorney general, Michigan (1970-72); counsel, Joint Committee on Legal Education (1971-72).

1.	Protection to Haitian refugees	N	45.	Abortion $ for rape/incest cases	Y
2.	Raise tax on wealthy; lower others	N	46.	Allow religious schools to bar gays	Y
3.	Investigate Reagan hostage delay	Y	47.	Bar broadcaster fairness doctrine	N
4.	Campaign finance revisions	N	48.	Bar cap gains cut/reinstate IRA	N
5.	Unpaid leave to care for children	N	49.	Bar unions equal voice in pension	N
6.	Restrict NEA use of funds	N	50.	Bar assembly of chemical weapons	Y
7.	Bar race-bias claim/habeas corpus	N	51.	Ban plutonium/uranium production	Y
8.	Ban race as death sentence factor	N	52.	Cap MX missile deployment at 50	Y
9.	Exceptions to exclusionary rule	?	53.	Allow $3b for 2 stealth bombers	N
10.	Allow sale of assault weapons	Y	54.	Publish bio-warfare experiments	Y
11.	Life in prison/abolish death penalty	?	55.	Raise minimum wage-veto override	Y
12.	Req conspiracy-price fixing cases	N	56.	Bar transfer of FS-X technology	Y
13.	Unemployment benefits extension	Y	57.	Cut defense and raise domestic $	N
14.	Tissue use of aborted fetuses	Y	58.	Uniform poll closing in 48 states	Y
15.	Bar replacement of union strikers	Y	59.	Req foreign investment disclosure	Y
16.	Hold foreign aid at $15b for '92	?	60.	Textile import quotas-veto override	N
17.	Restore space station funding	N	61.	Bar abortion funding in Wash, DC	N
18.	Civil Rights Act of 1991	Y	62.	Notify spouses of AIDS+ carriers	N
19.	Unlimited damages-discrimination	N	63.	Seize conveyance-drug trafficking	Y
20.	Eliminate funds for supercollider	N	64.	South Africa sanctions	#
21.	Terminate SDI except for research	N	65.	60 days' notice of plant closings	Y
22.	Req 7-day handgun waiting period	N	66.	Close unneeded military bases	Y
23.	Provide $30b for failed S&Ls	N	67.	Keep welfare reform within $2.8b	N
24.	Allow use of force against Iraq	N	68.	Allow children housing exclusion	N
25.	Allow $15b in foreign aid for '91	Y	69.	Shift $400m of NASA to homeless	N
26.	Revise & extend legal immigration	Y	70.	Cap Medicare patients' liability	Y
27.	Suspend aid to Angolan rebels	Y	71.	Prohibit employee polygraph testing	Y
28.	Democratic tax plan proposals	Y	72.	Allow CIA to fund Contras	N
29.	Cut defense 5% across the board	N	73.	Revise unfair trade practices	Y
30.	Textile import quotas-veto override	Y	74.	Focus SDI on accidental launch	Y
31.	Abortion service for military abroad	Y	75.	Bar Air Force $ for MX missile	Y
32.	Limits on high income farmers	Y	76.	Allow "real" increase in defense	N
33.	Family medical leave-veto override	N	77.	Troop reduction in Europe of 50%	Y
34.	Req submission of balanced budget	Y	78.	Ban nuclear tests above 1 kiloton	Y
35.	Balanced budget amendment	Y	79.	Ban anti-satellite missile tests	Y
36.	Amendment to ban flag desecration	N	80.	Observe certain limits of SALT II	Y
37.	Reauthorize Amtrak-veto override	Y	81.	Restore four Civil Rights laws	Y
38.	Retraining aid for coal miners	Y	82.	Prohibit aliens as strikebreakers	Y
39.	Suspend El Salvador military aid	Y	83.	Allow military malpractice suits	Y
40.	Expand child care aid/tax credit	Y	84.	Approval of $36m in Contra aid	N
41.	Raise House salary/omit honoraria	N	85.	$18b deficit reduction compromise	N
42.	Toughen oil-spill liability	Y	86.	Welfare reform of $5.7b for 5 years	N
43.	Restitution to Japanese interned	Y	87.	Raise taxes $12b/cut spending $3b	N
44.	Protect Chinese & C.A. nationals	Y	88.	Board to assess occupational risk	Y

CARR, BOB (continued)

89. Balanced budget by '93-via targets	N
90. Bar licensing of two nuclear plants	N
91. Remove victims compensation cap	N
92. Catastrophic health insurance	Y
93. Ban airline smoking-2 hours or less	N
94. $1b/two year aid for the homeless	Y
95. Bar non-unions in union companies	Y
96. Increase FSLIC rescue to $15b	N
97. Impose quotas to lower trade deficit	Y
98. Reduce discretionary budget 21%	N
99. Immigration reform/alien amnesty	N
100. South Africa sanctions-veto override	Y
101. Tax overhaul to revise income tax	N
102. Use of military in drug war	Y
103. Delete 12 MX/add conventional wpn	Y
104. Raise speed limit to 65 mph	Y
105. Require Pentagon to buy US goods	Y
106. AIDS insurance non-discrimination	Y
107. Prohibit Saudi arms sales	Y
108. Ease Gun Control Act of 1968	Y
109. Bar interstate handgun transport	N
110. Make company emissions known	N
111. Allow toxic victims to sue in fed ct	N
112. Superfund waste cleanup of $10b	Y
113. 90 days notice of plant closings	Y
114. $20b in Medicare cuts/tax increases	Y

115. Spending cuts and tax increases	N
116. Set school lunch lmt-250% poverty	N
117. $75m for youth work projects	Y
118. Allow Angolan military assistance	N
119. Suspend defense payments for abuse	Y
120. Drop SS COLAs/$12b tax increase	N
121. Approve $1.5b for 21 MX missiles	N
122. Emergency farm credit/revisions	Y
123. Duty on Taiwan/Hong Kong/S Korea	Y
124. Limit steel imports to 17%	Y
125. Cut $ to schools that bar prayer	Y
126. $50b-taxes; cut Medicare/spending	N
127. Limit Pershing II/cruise in Europe	N
128. Delete $7.1b for 34 B-1 bombers	N
129. Bar purchase of Sergeant York guns	N
130. El Salvador military/economic aid	N
131. Bar mining of Nicaraguan waters	Y
132. Physician fee freeze for Medicare	N
133. $49b in "sin"/phone/insurance taxes	N
134. Allow sale of Conrail	Y
135. Equal Rights Amendment	Y
136. Authorize Marines in Lebanon	Y
137. Eminent domain for coal companies	N
138. Prohibit EPA clean air sanctions	N
139. SS retirement age increase/reforms	N

Presidential Support Score: 1991 - 34%   1990 - 29%

KILDEE, DALE E. -- Michigan 7th District [Democrat]. Counties of Genesee (pt.), Lapeer (pt.), Oakland (pt.), Sanilac (pt.) and Shiawassee (pt.). Prior Terms: 1977-92. Born: September 16, 1929; Flint, MI. Education: Sacred Heart Seminary (B.A.); University of Michigan (M.A.). Occupation: Teacher; Michigan representative (1965-74); Michigan senator (1975-77).

1. Protection to Haitian refugees	Y
2. Raise tax on wealthy; lower others	N
3. Investigate Reagan hostage delay	Y
4. Campaign finance revisions	Y
5. Unpaid leave to care for children	Y
6. Restrict NEA use of funds	N
7. Bar race-bias claim/habeas corpus	N
8. Ban race as death sentence factor	N
9. Exceptions to exclusionary rule	N
10. Allow sale of assault weapons	N
11. Life in prison/abolish death penalty	Y
12. Req conspiracy-price fixing cases	N
13. Unemployment benefits extension	Y
14. Tissue use of aborted fetuses	Y
15. Bar replacement of union strikers	Y
16. Hold foreign aid at $15b for '92	Y
17. Restore space station funding	N
18. Civil Rights Act of 1991	Y
19. Unlimited damages-discrimination	Y
20. Eliminate funds for supercollider	N
21. Terminate SDI except for research	Y
22. Req 7-day handgun waiting period	Y
23. Provide $30b for failed S&Ls	N
24. Allow use of force against Iraq	N
25. Allow $15b in foreign aid for '91	Y
26. Revise & extend legal immigration	Y
27. Suspend aid to Angolan rebels	Y
28. Democratic tax plan proposals	Y

29. Cut defense 5% across the board	N
30. Textile import quotas-veto override	Y
31. Abortion service for military abroad	N
32. Limits on high income farmers	N
33. Family medical leave-veto override	Y
34. Req submission of balanced budget	Y
35. Balanced budget amendment	N
36. Amendment to ban flag desecration	N
37. Reauthorize Amtrak-veto override	Y
38. Retraining aid for coal miners	Y
39. Suspend El Salvador military aid	Y
40. Expand child care aid/tax credit	Y
41. Raise House salary/omit honoraria	N
42. Toughen oil-spill liability	Y
43. Restitution to Japanese interned	Y
44. Protect Chinese & C.A. nationals	Y
45. Abortion $ for rape/incest cases	N
46. Allow religious schools to bar gays	N
47. Bar broadcaster fairness doctrine	N
48. Bar cap gains cut/reinstate IRA	Y
49. Bar unions equal voice in pension	N
50. Bar assembly of chemical weapons	Y
51. Ban plutonium/uranium production	Y
52. Cap MX missile deployment at 50	Y
53. Allow $3b for 2 stealth bombers	N
54. Publish bio-warfare experiments	Y
55. Raise minimum wage-veto override	Y
56. Bar transfer of FS-X technology	Y

KILDEE, DALE E. (continued)

57. Cut defense and raise domestic $	Y
58. Uniform poll closing in 48 states	Y
59. Req foreign investment disclosure	Y
60. Textile import quotas-veto override	Y
61. Bar abortion funding in Wash, DC	Y
62. Notify spouses of AIDS+ carriers	N
63. Seize conveyance-drug trafficking	N
64. South Africa sanctions	Y
65. 60 days' notice of plant closings	Y
66. Close unneeded military bases	N
67. Keep welfare reform within $2.8b	N
68. Allow children housing exclusion	N
69. Shift $400m of NASA to homeless	Y
70. Cap Medicare patients' liability	Y
71. Prohibit employee polygraph testing	Y
72. Allow CIA to fund Contras	N
73. Revise unfair trade practices	Y
74. Focus SDI on accidental launch	Y
75. Bar Air Force $ for MX missile	Y
76. Allow "real" increase in defense	N
77. Troop reduction in Europe of 50%	Y
78. Ban nuclear tests above 1 kiloton	Y
79. Ban anti-satellite missile tests	Y
80. Observe certain limits of SALT II	Y
81. Restore four Civil Rights laws	Y
82. Prohibit aliens as strikebreakers	Y
83. Allow military malpractice suits	Y
84. Approval of $36m in Contra aid	N
85. $18b deficit reduction compromise	Y
86. Welfare reform of $5.7b for 5 years	Y
87. Raise taxes $12b/cut spending $3b	Y
88. Board to assess occupational risk	Y
89. Balanced budget by '93-via targets	N
90. Bar licensing of two nuclear plants	Y
91. Remove victims compensation cap	Y
92. Catastrophic health insurance	Y
93. Ban airline smoking-2 hours or less	Y
94. $1b/two year aid for the homeless	Y
95. Bar non-unions in union companies	Y
96. Increase FSLIC rescue to $15b	Y
97. Impose quotas to lower trade deficit	Y
98. Reduce discretionary budget 21%	N
99. Immigration reform/alien amnesty	Y
100. South Africa sanctions-veto override	Y

101. Tax overhaul to revise income tax	Y
102. Use of military in drug war	N
103. Delete 12 MX/add conventional wpn	Y
104. Raise speed limit to 65 mph	N
105. Require Pentagon to buy US goods	Y
106. AIDS insurance non-discrimination	Y
107. Prohibit Saudi arms sales	Y
108. Ease Gun Control Act of 1968	N
109. Bar interstate handgun transport	Y
110. Make company emissions known	Y
111. Allow toxic victims to sue in fed ct	Y
112. Superfund waste cleanup of $10b	Y
113. 90 days notice of plant closings	Y
114. $20b in Medicare cuts/tax increases	Y
115. Spending cuts and tax increases	Y
116. Set school lunch lmt-250% poverty	N
117. $75m for youth work projects	Y
118. Allow Angolan military assistance	N
119. Suspend defense payments for abuse	Y
120. Drop SS COLAs/$12b tax increase	N
121. Approve $1.5b for 21 MX missiles	N
122. Emergency farm credit/revisions	Y
123. Duty on Taiwan/Hong Kong/S Korea	Y
124. Limit steel imports to 17%	Y
125. Cut $ to schools that bar prayer	N
126. $50b-taxes; cut Medicare/spending	N
127. Limit Pershing II/cruise in Europe	Y
128. Delete $7.1b for 34 B-1 bombers	Y
129. Bar purchase of Sergeant York guns	Y
130. El Salvador military/economic aid	N
131. Bar mining of Nicaraguan waters	Y
132. Physician fee freeze for Medicare	N
133. $49b in "sin"/phone/insurance taxes	Y
134. Allow sale of Conrail	N
135. Equal Rights Amendment	Y
136. Authorize Marines in Lebanon	N
137. Eminent domain for coal companies	N
138. Prohibit EPA clean air sanctions	N
139. SS retirement age increase/reforms	N
140. Auto domestic content requirement	Y
141. Delete jobs program funding	N
142. Highway-gas tax bill	Y
143. Cut $5b from defense for Medicare	Y
144. Emergency housing aid of $1b	Y

Presidential Support Score: 1991 - 29%   1990 - 19%

TRAXLER, BOB -- Michigan 8th District [Democrat]. Counties of Arenac, Bay, Genesee (pt.), Huron, Lapeer (pt.), Midland (pt.), Saginaw (pt.), St. Clair (pt.), Sanilac (pt.) and Tuscola. Prior Terms: 1974 (Special Election)-1992. Born: July 21, 1931; Kawakawlin, MI. Education: Michigan State University (B.A.); Detroit College of Law (LL.B.). Occupation: Assistant prosecutor (1960-62); Michigan representative (1962-74).

1. Protection to Haitian refugees	Y
2. Raise tax on wealthy; lower others	N
3. Investigate Reagan hostage delay	Y
4. Campaign finance revisions	Y
5. Unpaid leave to care for children	Y
6. Restrict NEA use of funds	N
7. Bar race-bias claim/habeas corpus	N
8. Ban race as death sentence factor	N
9. Exceptions to exclusionary rule	?
10. Allow sale of assault weapons	Y

11. Life in prison/abolish death penalty	N
12. Req conspiracy-price fixing cases	N
13. Unemployment benefits extension	Y
14. Tissue use of aborted fetuses	Y
15. Bar replacement of union strikers	Y
16. Hold foreign aid at $15b for '92	Y
17. Restore space station funding	Y
18. Civil Rights Act of 1991	Y
19. Unlimited damages-discrimination	Y
20. Eliminate funds for supercollider	Y

TRAXLER, BOB (continued)

21. Terminate SDI except for research	Y	
22. Req 7-day handgun waiting period	N	
23. Provide $30b for failed S&Ls	Y	
24. Allow use of force against Iraq	N	
25. Allow $15b in foreign aid for '91	?	
26. Revise & extend legal immigration	?	
27. Suspend aid to Angolan rebels	Y	
28. Democratic tax plan proposals	Y	
29. Cut defense 5% across the board	Y	
30. Textile import quotas-veto override	Y	
31. Abortion service for military abroad	N	
32. Limits on high income farmers	N	
33. Family medical leave-veto override	Y	
34. Req submission of balanced budget	Y	
35. Balanced budget amendment	N	
36. Amendment to ban flag desecration	Y	
37. Reauthorize Amtrak-veto override	Y	
38. Retraining aid for coal miners	Y	
39. Suspend El Salvador military aid	Y	
40. Expand child care aid/tax credit	#	
41. Raise House salary/omit honoraria	Y	
42. Toughen oil-spill liability	?	
43. Restitution to Japanese interned	Y	
44. Protect Chinese & C.A. nationals	Y	
45. Abortion $ for rape/incest cases	N	
46. Allow religious schools to bar gays	Y	
47. Bar broadcaster fairness doctrine	N	
48. Bar cap gains cut/reinstate IRA	Y	
49. Bar unions equal voice in pension	N	
50. Bar assembly of chemical weapons	Y	
51. Ban plutonium/uranium production	Y	
52. Cap MX missile deployment at 50	Y	
53. Allow $3b for 2 stealth bombers	N	
54. Publish bio-warfare experiments	Y	
55. Raise minimum wage-veto override	Y	
56. Bar transfer of FS-X technology	Y	
57. Cut defense and raise domestic $	N	
58. Uniform poll closing in 48 states	Y	
59. Req foreign investment disclosure	Y	
60. Textile import quotas-veto override	Y	
61. Bar abortion funding in Wash, DC	Y	
62. Notify spouses of AIDS+ carriers	N	
63. Seize conveyance-drug trafficking	N	
64. South Africa sanctions	Y	
65. 60 days' notice of plant closings	Y	
66. Close unneeded military bases	Y	
67. Keep welfare reform within $2.8b	N	
68. Allow children housing exclusion	N	
69. Shift $400m of NASA to homeless	N	
70. Cap Medicare patients' liability	Y	
71. Prohibit employee polygraph testing	Y	
72. Allow CIA to fund Contras	N	
73. Revise unfair trade practices	Y	
74. Focus SDI on accidental launch	?	
75. Bar Air Force $ for MX missile	Y	
76. Allow "real" increase in defense	N	
77. Troop reduction in Europe of 50%	Y	
78. Ban nuclear tests above 1 kiloton	Y	
79. Ban anti-satellite missile tests	Y	
80. Observe certain limits of SALT II	Y	
81. Restore four Civil Rights laws	Y	
82. Prohibit aliens as strikebreakers	Y	

83. Allow military malpractice suits	Y	
84. Approval of $36m in Contra aid	N	
85. $18b deficit reduction compromise	Y	
86. Welfare reform of $5.7b for 5 years	Y	
87. Raise taxes $12b/cut spending $3b	Y	
88. Board to assess occupational risk	?	
89. Balanced budget by '93-via targets	Y	
90. Bar licensing of two nuclear plants	N	
91. Remove victims compensation cap	N	
92. Catastrophic health insurance	Y	
93. Ban airline smoking-2 hours or less	N	
94. $1b/two year aid for the homeless	Y	
95. Bar non-unions in union companies	Y	
96. Increase FSLIC rescue to $15b	Y	
97. Impose quotas to lower trade deficit	Y	
98. Reduce discretionary budget 21%	N	
99. Immigration reform/alien amnesty	?	
100. South Africa sanctions-veto override	Y	
101. Tax overhaul to revise income tax	Y	
102. Use of military in drug war	N	
103. Delete 12 MX/add conventional wpn	Y	
104. Raise speed limit to 65 mph	Y	
105. Require Pentagon to buy US goods	Y	
106. AIDS insurance non-discrimination	Y	
107. Prohibit Saudi arms sales	Y	
108. Ease Gun Control Act of 1968	Y	
109. Bar interstate handgun transport	N	
110. Make company emissions known	Y	
111. Allow toxic victims to sue in fed ct	N	
112. Superfund waste cleanup of $10b	Y	
113. 90 days notice of plant closings	Y	
114. $20b in Medicare cuts/tax increases	Y	
115. Spending cuts and tax increases	N	
116. Set school lunch lmt-250% poverty	N	
117. $75m for youth work projects	Y	
118. Allow Angolan military assistance	N	
119. Suspend defense payments for abuse	Y	
120. Drop SS COLAs/$12b tax increase	N	
121. Approve $1.5b for 21 MX missiles	N	
122. Emergency farm credit/revisions	Y	
123. Duty on Taiwan/Hong Kong/S Korea	Y	
124. Limit steel imports to 17%	Y	
125. Cut $ to schools that bar prayer	N	
126. $50b-taxes; cut Medicare/spending	N	
127. Limit Pershing II/cruise in Europe	Y	
128. Delete $7.1b for 34 B-1 bombers	Y	
129. Bar purchase of Sergeant York guns	?	
130. El Salvador military/economic aid	N	
131. Bar mining of Nicaraguan waters	Y	
132. Physician fee freeze for Medicare	N	
133. $49b in "sin"/phone/insurance taxes	N	
134. Allow sale of Conrail	N	
135. Equal Rights Amendment	Y	
136. Authorize Marines in Lebanon	N	
137. Eminent domain for coal companies	N	
138. Prohibit EPA clean air sanctions	?	
139. SS retirement age increase/reforms	N	
140. Auto domestic content requirement	Y	
141. Delete jobs program funding	N	
142. Highway-gas tax bill	Y	
143. Cut $5b from defense for Medicare	Y	
144. Emergency housing aid of $1b	Y	

Presidential Support Score: 1991 - 28%   1990 - 25%

VANDER JAGT, GUY -- Michigan 9th District [Republican]. Counties of Benzie, Grand Traverse (pt.), Ionia (pt.), Kent (pt.), Lake Leelanau, Manistee, Mason, Montcalm, Muskegon, Newaygo (pt.), Oceana and Ottawa (pt.). Prior Terms: 1966 (Special Election)-1992. Born: August 26, 1931; Cadillac, MI. Education: Hope College (B.A.); Yale University (B.D.); Bonn University, Rotary Fellowship (1956); University of Michigan (LL.B.). Occupation: Attorney, Warner, Norcross & Judd (1960-64); Michigan senator (1965-66).

1. Protection to Haitian refugees	N	
2. Raise tax on wealthy; lower others	N	
3. Investigate Reagan hostage delay	N	
4. Campaign finance revisions	N	
5. Unpaid leave to care for children	N	
6. Restrict NEA use of funds	Y	
7. Bar race-bias claim/habeas corpus	Y	
8. Ban race as death sentence factor	Y	
9. Exceptions to exclusionary rule	?	
10. Allow sale of assault weapons	Y	
11. Life in prison/abolish death penalty	N	
12. Req conspiracy-price fixing cases	Y	
13. Unemployment benefits extension	N	
14. Tissue use of aborted fetuses	N	
15. Bar replacement of union strikers	N	
16. Hold foreign aid at $15b for '92	Y	
17. Restore space station funding	Y	
18. Civil Rights Act of 1991	N	
19. Unlimited damages-discrimination	N	
20. Eliminate funds for supercollider	Y	
21. Terminate SDI except for research	N	
22. Req 7-day handgun waiting period	N	
23. Provide $30b for failed S&Ls	Y	
24. Allow use of force against Iraq	Y	
25. Allow $15b in foreign aid for '91	Y	
26. Revise & extend legal immigration	N	
27. Suspend aid to Angolan rebels	N	
28. Democratic tax plan proposals	N	
29. Cut defense 5% across the board	N	
30. Textile import quotas-veto override	N	
31. Abortion service for military abroad	N	
32. Limits on high income farmers	N	
33. Family medical leave-veto override	N	
34. Req submission of balanced budget	Y	
35. Balanced budget amendment	Y	
36. Amendment to ban flag desecration	Y	
37. Reauthorize Amtrak-veto override	Y	
38. Retraining aid for coal miners	N	
39. Suspend El Salvador military aid	N	
40. Expand child care aid/tax credit	N	
41. Raise House salary/omit honoraria	Y	
42. Toughen oil-spill liability	N	
43. Restitution to Japanese interned	Y	
44. Protect Chinese & C.A. nationals	N	
45. Abortion $ for rape/incest cases	N	
46. Allow religious schools to bar gays	?	
47. Bar broadcaster fairness doctrine	?	
48. Bar cap gains cut/reinstate IRA	N	
49. Bar unions equal voice in pension	Y	
50. Bar assembly of chemical weapons	N	
51. Ban plutonium/uranium production	N	
52. Cap MX missile deployment at 50	N	
53. Allow $3b for 2 stealth bombers	Y	
54. Publish bio-warfare experiments	N	
55. Raise minimum wage-veto override	N	
56. Bar transfer of FS-X technology	N	
57. Cut defense and raise domestic $	N	
58. Uniform poll closing in 48 states	N
59. Req foreign investment disclosure	N
60. Textile import quotas-veto override	N
61. Bar abortion funding in Wash, DC	Y
62. Notify spouses of AIDS+ carriers	Y
63. Seize conveyance-drug trafficking	Y
64. South Africa sanctions	N
65. 60 days' notice of plant closings	N
66. Close unneeded military bases	Y
67. Keep welfare reform within $2.8b	Y
68. Allow children housing exclusion	Y
69. Shift $400m of NASA to homeless	N
70. Cap Medicare patients' liability	Y
71. Prohibit employee polygraph testing	N
72. Allow CIA to fund Contras	Y
73. Revise unfair trade practices	N
74. Focus SDI on accidental launch	N
75. Bar Air Force $ for MX missile	N
76. Allow "real" increase in defense	Y
77. Troop reduction in Europe of 50%	N
78. Ban nuclear tests above 1 kiloton	N
79. Ban anti-satellite missile tests	N
80. Observe certain limits of SALT II	N
81. Restore four Civil Rights laws	N
82. Prohibit aliens as strikebreakers	N
83. Allow military malpractice suits	Y
84. Approval of $36m in Contra aid	Y
85. $18b deficit reduction compromise	N
86. Welfare reform of $5.7b for 5 years	N
87. Raise taxes $12b/cut spending $3b	N
88. Board to assess occupational risk	N
89. Balanced budget by '93-via targets	Y
90. Bar licensing of two nuclear plants	N
91. Remove victims compensation cap	N
92. Catastrophic health insurance	?
93. Ban airline smoking-2 hours or less	N
94. $1b/two year aid for the homeless	N
95. Bar non-unions in union companies	N
96. Increase FSLIC rescue to $15b	N
97. Impose quotas to lower trade deficit	N
98. Reduce discretionary budget 21%	?
99. Immigration reform/alien amnesty	N
100. South Africa sanctions-veto override	?
101. Tax overhaul to revise income tax	N
102. Use of military in drug war	Y
103. Delete 12 MX/add conventional wpn	?
104. Raise speed limit to 65 mph	Y
105. Require Pentagon to buy US goods	Y
106. AIDS insurance non-discrimination	N
107. Prohibit Saudi arms sales	Y
108. Ease Gun Control Act of 1968	Y
109. Bar interstate handgun transport	N
110. Make company emissions known	N
111. Allow toxic victims to sue in fed ct	N
112. Superfund waste cleanup of $10b	N
113. 90 days notice of plant closings	N
114. $20b in Medicare cuts/tax increases	N

VANDER JAGT, GUY (continued)

115.	Spending cuts and tax increases	N	130.	El Salvador military/economic aid	Y
116.	Set school lunch lmt-250% poverty	Y	131.	Bar mining of Nicaraguan waters	X
117.	$75m for youth work projects	N	132.	Physician fee freeze for Medicare	#
118.	Allow Angolan military assistance	Y	133.	$49b in "sin"/phone/insurance taxes	Y
119.	Suspend defense payments for abuse	N	134.	Allow sale of Conrail	Y
120.	Drop SS COLAs/$12b tax increase	N	135.	Equal Rights Amendment	N
121.	Approve $1.5b for 21 MX missiles	Y	136.	Authorize Marines in Lebanon	Y
122.	Emergency farm credit/revisions	N	137.	Eminent domain for coal companies	Y
123.	Duty on Taiwan/Hong Kong/S Korea	N	138.	Prohibit EPA clean air sanctions	N
124.	Limit steel imports to 17%	Y	139.	SS retirement age increase/reforms	Y
125.	Cut $ to schools that bar prayer	Y	140.	Auto domestic content requirement	N
126.	$50b-taxes; cut Medicare/spending	N	141.	Delete jobs program funding	Y
127.	Limit Pershing II/cruise in Europe	?	142.	Highway-gas tax bill	N
128.	Delete $7.1b for 34 B-1 bombers	N	143.	Cut $5b from defense for Medicare	N
129.	Bar purchase of Sergeant York guns	N	144.	Emergency housing aid of $1b	Y

Presidential Support Score: 1991 - 78%   1990 - 66%

CAMP, DAVE -- Michigan 10th District [Republican]. Counties of Antrim (pt.), Clare, Clinton (pt.), Crawford (pt.), Gladwin, Grand Traverse (pt.), Gratiot,Iosco (pt.), Isabella, Kalkaska, Mecosta, Midland (pt.), Missaukee, Ogemaw, Osceola, Oscoda (pt.), Rosscommon, Saginaw (pt.), Shiawassee (pt.) and Wexford. Prior Term: 1991-92. Born: July 9, 1953; Midland, MI. Education: Albion College (B.A.); University of California-San Diego (J.D.). Occupation: Lawyer; real estate broker; special state assistant attorney general (1980-84); administrative assistant to Rep. Schuette (1985-87); state representative (1989-90).

1.	Protection to Haitian refugees	N	13.	Unemployment benefits extension	Y
2.	Raise tax on wealthy; lower others	N	14.	Tissue use of aborted fetuses	N
3.	Investigate Reagan hostage delay	N	15.	Bar replacement of union strikers	N
4.	Campaign finance revisions	N	16.	Hold foreign aid at $15b for '92	Y
5.	Unpaid leave to care for children	N	17.	Restore space station funding	N
6.	Restrict NEA use of funds	Y	18.	Civil Rights Act of 1991	N
7.	Bar race-bias claim/habeas corpus	Y	19.	Unlimited damages-discrimination	N
8.	Ban race as death sentence factor	Y	20.	Eliminate funds for supercollider	Y
9.	Exceptions to exclusionary rule	Y	21.	Terminate SDI except for research	N
10.	Allow sale of assault weapons	Y	22.	Req 7-day handgun waiting period	N
11.	Life in prison/abolish death penalty	N	23.	Provide $30b for failed S&Ls	N
12.	Req conspiracy-price fixing cases	Y	24.	Allow use of force against Iraq	Y

Presidential Support Score: 1991 - 71%

DAVIS, ROBERT W. -- Michigan 11th District [Republican]. Counties of Alcona, Alger, Alpena, Antrim (pt.), Baraga, Charlevoix, Cheboygan, Chippewa, Crawford (pt.), Delta, Dickinson, Emmet, Gogebic, Grand Traverse (pt.), Houghton, Iosco (pt.), Iron, Keweenaw, Luce, Machinac, Marquette, Menominee, Montmorency, Ontonagon, Oscoda (pt.), Otsego, Presque Isle and Schoolcraft. Prior Terms: 1979-92. Born: July 31, 1932; Marquette, MI. Education: Northern Michigan University; Hillsdale College; Wayne State University (B.S.). Occupation: Funeral director (1954-66); city councilman (1964-66); Michigan representative (1966-70); Michigan senator (1970-78).

1.	Protection to Haitian refugees	?	13.	Unemployment benefits extension	Y
2.	Raise tax on wealthy; lower others	N	14.	Tissue use of aborted fetuses	N
3.	Investigate Reagan hostage delay	N	15.	Bar replacement of union strikers	Y
4.	Campaign finance revisions	N	16.	Hold foreign aid at $15b for '92	Y
5.	Unpaid leave to care for children	Y	17.	Restore space station funding	Y
6.	Restrict NEA use of funds	N	18.	Civil Rights Act of 1991	Y
7.	Bar race-bias claim/habeas corpus	Y	19.	Unlimited damages-discrimination	N
8.	Ban race as death sentence factor	Y	20.	Eliminate funds for supercollider	Y
9.	Exceptions to exclusionary rule	Y	21.	Terminate SDI except for research	N
10.	Allow sale of assault weapons	Y	22.	Req 7-day handgun waiting period	N
11.	Life in prison/abolish death penalty	N	23.	Provide $30b for failed S&Ls	Y
12.	Req conspiracy-price fixing cases	Y	24.	Allow use of force against Iraq	Y

DAVIS, ROBERT W. (continued)

25.	Allow $15b in foreign aid for '91	Y		85.	$18b deficit reduction compromise	Y
26.	Revise & extend legal immigration	N		86.	Welfare reform of $5.7b for 5 years	Y
27.	Suspend aid to Angolan rebels	N		87.	Raise taxes $12b/cut spending $3b	N
28.	Democratic tax plan proposals	Y		88.	Board to assess occupational risk	Y
29.	Cut defense 5% across the board	N		89.	Balanced budget by '93-via targets	Y
30.	Textile import quotas-veto override	Y		90.	Bar licensing of two nuclear plants	N
31.	Abortion service for military abroad	N		91.	Remove victims compensation cap	N
32.	Limits on high income farmers	N		92.	Catastrophic health insurance	Y
33.	Family medical leave-veto override	Y		93.	Ban airline smoking-2 hours or less	Y
34.	Req submission of balanced budget	N		94.	$1b/two year aid for the homeless	Y
35.	Balanced budget amendment	Y		95.	Bar non-unions in union companies	Y
36.	Amendment to ban flag desecration	Y		96.	Increase FSLIC rescue to $15b	Y
37.	Reauthorize Amtrak-veto override	Y		97.	Impose quotas to lower trade deficit	Y
38.	Retraining aid for coal miners	Y		98.	Reduce discretionary budget 21%	Y
39.	Suspend El Salvador military aid	N		99.	Immigration reform/alien amnesty	Y
40.	Expand child care aid/tax credit	Y		100.	South Africa sanctions-veto override	Y
41.	Raise House salary/omit honoraria	Y		101.	Tax overhaul to revise income tax	Y
42.	Toughen oil-spill liability	N		102.	Use of military in drug war	Y
43.	Restitution to Japanese interned	Y		103.	Delete 12 MX/add conventional wpn	N
44.	Protect Chinese & C.A. nationals	N		104.	Raise speed limit to 65 mph	Y
45.	Abortion $ for rape/incest cases	N		105.	Require Pentagon to buy US goods	Y
46.	Allow religious schools to bar gays	Y		106.	AIDS insurance non-discrimination	N
47.	Bar broadcaster fairness doctrine	N		107.	Prohibit Saudi arms sales	Y
48.	Bar cap gains cut/reinstate IRA	N		108.	Ease Gun Control Act of 1968	Y
49.	Bar unions equal voice in pension	N		109.	Bar interstate handgun transport	N
50.	Bar assembly of chemical weapons	N		110.	Make company emissions known	N
51.	Ban plutonium/uranium production	N		111.	Allow toxic victims to sue in fed ct	N
52.	Cap MX missile deployment at 50	N		112.	Superfund waste cleanup of $10b	Y
53.	Allow $3b for 2 stealth bombers	Y		113.	90 days notice of plant closings	Y
54.	Publish bio-warfare experiments	Y		114.	$20b in Medicare cuts/tax increases	Y
55.	Raise minimum wage-veto override	Y		115.	Spending cuts and tax increases	N
56.	Bar transfer of FS-X technology	N		116.	Set school lunch lmt-250% poverty	N
57.	Cut defense and raise domestic $	N		117.	$75m for youth work projects	Y
58.	Uniform poll closing in 48 states	?		118.	Allow Angolan military assistance	Y
59.	Req foreign investment disclosure	Y		119.	Suspend defense payments for abuse	N
60.	Textile import quotas-veto override	Y		120.	Drop SS COLAs/$12b tax increase	N
61.	Bar abortion funding in Wash, DC	Y		121.	Approve $1.5b for 21 MX missiles	Y
62.	Notify spouses of AIDS+ carriers	N		122.	Emergency farm credit/revisions	Y
63.	Seize conveyance-drug trafficking	N		123.	Duty on Taiwan/Hong Kong/S Korea	N
64.	South Africa sanctions	Y		124.	Limit steel imports to 17%	?
65.	60 days' notice of plant closings	Y		125.	Cut $ to schools that bar prayer	N
66.	Close unneeded military bases	Y		126.	$50b-taxes; cut Medicare/spending	N
67.	Keep welfare reform within $2.8b	N		127.	Limit Pershing II/cruise in Europe	N
68.	Allow children housing exclusion	N		128.	Delete $7.1b for 34 B-1 bombers	N
69.	Shift $400m of NASA to homeless	Y		129.	Bar purchase of Sergeant York guns	N
70.	Cap Medicare patients' liability	Y		130.	El Salvador military/economic aid	Y
71.	Prohibit employee polygraph testing	Y		131.	Bar mining of Nicaraguan waters	N
72.	Allow CIA to fund Contras	Y		132.	Physician fee freeze for Medicare	Y
73.	Revise unfair trade practices	Y		133.	$49b in "sin"/phone/insurance taxes	Y
74.	Focus SDI on accidental launch	N		134.	Allow sale of Conrail	Y
75.	Bar Air Force $ for MX missile	N		135.	Equal Rights Amendment	N
76.	Allow "real" increase in defense	N		136.	Authorize Marines in Lebanon	Y
77.	Troop reduction in Europe of 50%	N		137.	Eminent domain for coal companies	Y
78.	Ban nuclear tests above 1 kiloton	N		138.	Prohibit EPA clean air sanctions	N
79.	Ban anti-satellite missile tests	N		139.	SS retirement age increase/reforms	N
80.	Observe certain limits of SALT II	Y		140.	Auto domestic content requirement	Y
81.	Restore four Civil Rights laws	Y		141.	Delete jobs program funding	N
82.	Prohibit aliens as strikebreakers	Y		142.	Highway-gas tax bill	N
83.	Allow military malpractice suits	Y		143.	Cut $5b from defense for Medicare	Y
84.	Approval of $36m in Contra aid	Y		144.	Emergency housing aid of $1b	Y

Presidential Support Score: 1991 - 62%   1990 - 44%

BONIOR, DAVID E. -- Michigan 12th District [Democrat]. Counties of Macomb (pt.) and St. Clair (pt.). Prior Terms: 1977-92. Born: June 6, 1945; Detroit, MI. Education: University of Iowa (B.A.); Chapman College (M.A.). Military Service: U.S. Air Force, 1968-72. Occupation: Michigan representative (1973-77).

1. Protection to Haitian refugees	Y	
2. Raise tax on wealthy; lower others	N	
3. Investigate Reagan hostage delay	Y	
4. Campaign finance revisions	Y	
5. Unpaid leave to care for children	Y	
6. Restrict NEA use of funds	N	
7. Bar race-bias claim/habeas corpus	N	
8. Ban race as death sentence factor	N	
9. Exceptions to exclusionary rule	N	
10. Allow sale of assault weapons	N	
11. Life in prison/abolish death penalty	Y	
12. Req conspiracy-price fixing cases	N	
13. Unemployment benefits extension	Y	
14. Tissue use of aborted fetuses	Y	
15. Bar replacement of union strikers	Y	
16. Hold foreign aid at $15b for '92	Y	
17. Restore space station funding	N	
18. Civil Rights Act of 1991	Y	
19. Unlimited damages-discrimination	Y	
20. Eliminate funds for supercollider	?	
21. Terminate SDI except for research	Y	
22. Req 7-day handgun waiting period	Y	
23. Provide $30b for failed S&Ls	Y	
24. Allow use of force against Iraq	N	
25. Allow $15b in foreign aid for '91	Y	
26. Revise & extend legal immigration	Y	
27. Suspend aid to Angolan rebels	Y	
28. Democratic tax plan proposals	Y	
29. Cut defense 5% across the board	N	
30. Textile import quotas-veto override	Y	
31. Abortion service for military abroad	N	
32. Limits on high income farmers	Y	
33. Family medical leave-veto override	Y	
34. Req submission of balanced budget	Y	
35. Balanced budget amendment	N	
36. Amendment to ban flag desecration	N	
37. Reauthorize Amtrak-veto override	Y	
38. Retraining aid for coal miners	Y	
39. Suspend El Salvador military aid	Y	
40. Expand child care aid/tax credit	Y	
41. Raise House salary/omit honoraria	Y	
42. Toughen oil-spill liability	Y	
43. Restitution to Japanese interned	Y	
44. Protect Chinese & C.A. nationals	Y	
45. Abortion $ for rape/incest cases	N	
46. Allow religious schools to bar gays	N	
47. Bar broadcaster fairness doctrine	N	
48. Bar cap gains cut/reinstate IRA	Y	
49. Bar unions equal voice in pension	N	
50. Bar assembly of chemical weapons	Y	
51. Ban plutonium/uranium production	Y	
52. Cap MX missile deployment at 50	Y	
53. Allow $3b for 2 stealth bombers	N	
54. Publish bio-warfare experiments	Y	
55. Raise minimum wage-veto override	Y	
56. Bar transfer of FS-X technology	Y	
57. Cut defense and raise domestic $	Y	
58. Uniform poll closing in 48 states	Y	
59. Req foreign investment disclosure	Y	
60. Textile import quotas-veto override	Y	

61. Bar abortion funding in Wash, DC	?	
62. Notify spouses of AIDS+ carriers	N	
63. Seize conveyance-drug trafficking	N	
64. South Africa sanctions	Y	
65. 60 days' notice of plant closings	Y	
66. Close unneeded military bases	N	
67. Keep welfare reform within $2.8b	N	
68. Allow children housing exclusion	N	
69. Shift $400m of NASA to homeless	Y	
70. Cap Medicare patients' liability	Y	
71. Prohibit employee polygraph testing	Y	
72. Allow CIA to fund Contras	N	
73. Revise unfair trade practices	Y	
74. Focus SDI on accidental launch	Y	
75. Bar Air Force $ for MX missile	Y	
76. Allow "real" increase in defense	N	
77. Troop reduction in Europe of 50%	Y	
78. Ban nuclear tests above 1 kiloton	Y	
79. Ban anti-satellite missile tests	Y	
80. Observe certain limits of SALT II	Y	
81. Restore four Civil Rights laws	Y	
82. Prohibit aliens as strikebreakers	Y	
83. Allow military malpractice suits	Y	
84. Approval of $36m in Contra aid	N	
85. $18b deficit reduction compromise	Y	
86. Welfare reform of $5.7b for 5 years	Y	
87. Raise taxes $12b/cut spending $3b	Y	
88. Board to assess occupational risk	Y	
89. Balanced budget by '93-via targets	N	
90. Bar licensing of two nuclear plants	Y	
91. Remove victims compensation cap	Y	
92. Catastrophic health insurance	Y	
93. Ban airline smoking-2 hours or less	N	
94. $1b/two year aid for the homeless	Y	
95. Bar non-unions in union companies	#	
96. Increase FSLIC rescue to $15b	Y	
97. Impose quotas to lower trade deficit	Y	
98. Reduce discretionary budget 21%	Y	
99. Immigration reform/alien amnesty	Y	
100. South Africa sanctions-veto override	Y	
101. Tax overhaul to revise income tax	Y	
102. Use of military in drug war	N	
103. Delete 12 MX/add conventional wpn	Y	
104. Raise speed limit to 65 mph	?	
105. Require Pentagon to buy US goods	Y	
106. AIDS insurance non-discrimination	Y	
107. Prohibit Saudi arms sales	N	
108. Ease Gun Control Act of 1968	N	
109. Bar interstate handgun transport	Y	
110. Make company emissions known	Y	
111. Allow toxic victims to sue in fed ct	Y	
112. Superfund waste cleanup of $10b	Y	
113. 90 days notice of plant closings	#	
114. $20b in Medicare cuts/tax increases	Y	
115. Spending cuts and tax increases	Y	
116. Set school lunch lmt-250% poverty	N	
117. $75m for youth work projects	Y	
118. Allow Angolan military assistance	N	
119. Suspend defense payments for abuse	?	
120. Drop SS COLAs/$12b tax increase	N	

BONIOR, DAVID E. (continued)

121.	Approve $1.5b for 21 MX missiles	N		133.	$49b in "sin"/phone/insurance taxes	Y
122.	Emergency farm credit/revisions	Y		134.	Allow sale of Conrail	N
123.	Duty on Taiwan/Hong Kong/S Korea	Y		135.	Equal Rights Amendment	Y
124.	Limit steel imports to 17%	Y		136.	Authorize Marines in Lebanon	Y
125.	Cut $ to schools that bar prayer	N		137.	Eminent domain for coal companies	N
126.	$50b-taxes; cut Medicare/spending	Y		138.	Prohibit EPA clean air sanctions	N
127.	Limit Pershing II/cruise in Europe	Y		139.	SS retirement age increase/reforms	N
128.	Delete $7.1b for 34 B-1 bombers	Y		140.	Auto domestic content requirement	Y
129.	Bar purchase of Sergeant York guns	Y		141.	Delete jobs program funding	N
130.	El Salvador military/economic aid	N		142.	Highway-gas tax bill	Y
131.	Bar mining of Nicaraguan waters	Y		143.	Cut $5b from defense for Medicare	Y
132.	Physician fee freeze for Medicare	N		144.	Emergency housing aid of $1b	Y

Presidential Support Score: 1991 - 30%   1990 - 18%

COLLINS, BARBARA-ROSE -- Michigan 13th District [Democrat]. County of Wayne (pt.).
Prior Term: 1991-92. Born: April 13, 1939; Detroit, MI. Education: Wayne State
University. Occupation: State representative (1975-82); Detroit public school board member
(1971-73) and city councilwoman (1982-90).

1.	Protection to Haitian refugees	Y		13.	Unemployment benefits extension	Y
2.	Raise tax on wealthy; lower others	N		14.	Tissue use of aborted fetuses	Y
3.	Investigate Reagan hostage delay	Y		15.	Bar replacement of union strikers	Y
4.	Campaign finance revisions	Y		16.	Hold foreign aid at $15b for '92	Y
5.	Unpaid leave to care for children	Y		17.	Restore space station funding	N
6.	Restrict NEA use of funds	N		18.	Civil Rights Act of 1991	Y
7.	Bar race-bias claim/habeas corpus	N		19.	Unlimited damages-discrimination	Y
8.	Ban race as death sentence factor	N		20.	Eliminate funds for supercollider	Y
9.	Exceptions to exclusionary rule	N		21.	Terminate SDI except for research	Y
10.	Allow sale of assault weapons	N		22.	Req 7-day handgun waiting period	Y
11.	Life in prison/abolish death penalty	Y		23.	Provide $30b for failed S&Ls	N
12.	Req conspiracy-price fixing cases	N		24.	Allow use of force against Iraq	N

Presidential Support Score: 1991 - 23%

HERTEL, DENNIS M. -- Michigan 14th District [Democrat]. Counties of Macoma (pt.),
Oakland (pt.) and Wayne (pt.). Prior Terms: 1981-92. Born: December 7, 1948; Detroit,
MI. Education: Eastern Michigan University (B.A.); Wayne State University (J.D.).
Occupation: Attorney; law school teaching assistant; intern, State Attorney General's Office;
staff member, Governor's Corrections and Reform Committee; teacher; Michigan
representative (1975-80).

1.	Protection to Haitian refugees	Y		21.	Terminate SDI except for research	Y
2.	Raise tax on wealthy; lower others	N		22.	Req 7-day handgun waiting period	Y
3.	Investigate Reagan hostage delay	Y		23.	Provide $30b for failed S&Ls	N
4.	Campaign finance revisions	Y		24.	Allow use of force against Iraq	N
5.	Unpaid leave to care for children	Y		25.	Allow $15b in foreign aid for '91	Y
6.	Restrict NEA use of funds	N		26.	Revise & extend legal immigration	N
7.	Bar race-bias claim/habeas corpus	N		27.	Suspend aid to Angolan rebels	Y
8.	Ban race as death sentence factor	N		28.	Democratic tax plan proposals	Y
9.	Exceptions to exclusionary rule	N		29.	Cut defense 5% across the board	N
10.	Allow sale of assault weapons	N		30.	Textile import quotas-veto override	Y
11.	Life in prison/abolish death penalty	Y		31.	Abortion service for military abroad	N
12.	Req conspiracy-price fixing cases	N		32.	Limits on high income farmers	Y
13.	Unemployment benefits extension	Y		33.	Family medical leave-veto override	Y
14.	Tissue use of aborted fetuses	Y		34.	Req submission of balanced budget	Y
15.	Bar replacement of union strikers	Y		35.	Balanced budget amendment	Y
16.	Hold foreign aid at $15b for '92	Y		36.	Amendment to ban flag desecration	N
17.	Restore space station funding	N		37.	Reauthorize Amtrak-veto override	Y
18.	Civil Rights Act of 1991	Y		38.	Retraining aid for coal miners	Y
19.	Unlimited damages-discrimination	Y		39.	Suspend El Salvador military aid	Y
20.	Eliminate funds for supercollider	Y		40.	Expand child care aid/tax credit	Y

HERTEL, DENNIS M. (continued)

41. Raise House salary/omit honoraria	N
42. Toughen oil-spill liability	Y
43. Restitution to Japanese interned	Y
44. Protect Chinese & C.A. nationals	Y
45. Abortion $ for rape/incest cases	N
46. Allow religious schools to bar gays	N
47. Bar broadcaster fairness doctrine	N
48. Bar cap gains cut/reinstate IRA	Y
49. Bar unions equal voice in pension	N
50. Bar assembly of chemical weapons	Y
51. Ban plutonium/uranium production	Y
52. Cap MX missile deployment at 50	Y
53. Allow $3b for 2 stealth bombers	N
54. Publish bio-warfare experiments	Y
55. Raise minimum wage-veto override	Y
56. Bar transfer of FS-X technology	Y
57. Cut defense and raise domestic $	N
58. Uniform poll closing in 48 states	Y
59. Req foreign investment disclosure	Y
60. Textile import quotas-veto override	Y
61. Bar abortion funding in Wash, DC	N
62. Notify spouses of AIDS+ carriers	N
63. Seize conveyance-drug trafficking	N
64. South Africa sanctions	Y
65. 60 days' notice of plant closings	Y
66. Close unneeded military bases	N
67. Keep welfare reform within $2.8b	N
68. Allow children housing exclusion	N
69. Shift $400m of NASA to homeless	Y
70. Cap Medicare patients' liability	Y
71. Prohibit employee polygraph testing	Y
72. Allow CIA to fund Contras	N
73. Revise unfair trade practices	Y
74. Focus SDI on accidental launch	Y
75. Bar Air Force $ for MX missile	Y
76. Allow "real" increase in defense	N
77. Troop reduction in Europe of 50%	N
78. Ban nuclear tests above 1 kiloton	Y
79. Ban anti-satellite missile tests	Y
80. Observe certain limits of SALT II	Y
81. Restore four Civil Rights laws	Y
82. Prohibit aliens as strikebreakers	Y
83. Allow military malpractice suits	Y
84. Approval of $36m in Contra aid	N
85. $18b deficit reduction compromise	N
86. Welfare reform of $5.7b for 5 years	Y
87. Raise taxes $12b/cut spending $3b	Y
88. Board to assess occupational risk	Y
89. Balanced budget by '93-via targets	N
90. Bar licensing of two nuclear plants	Y
91. Remove victims compensation cap	Y
92. Catastrophic health insurance	Y

93. Ban airline smoking-2 hours or less	Y
94. $1b/two year aid for the homeless	Y
95. Bar non-unions in union companies	Y
96. Increase FSLIC rescue to $15b	Y
97. Impose quotas to lower trade deficit	Y
98. Reduce discretionary budget 21%	Y
99. Immigration reform/alien amnesty	Y
100. South Africa sanctions-veto override	Y
101. Tax overhaul to revise income tax	N
102. Use of military in drug war	Y
103. Delete 12 MX/add conventional wpn	Y
104. Raise speed limit to 65 mph	N
105. Require Pentagon to buy US goods	Y
106. AIDS insurance non-discrimination	Y
107. Prohibit Saudi arms sales	Y
108. Ease Gun Control Act of 1968	N
109. Bar interstate handgun transport	Y
110. Make company emissions known	Y
111. Allow toxic victims to sue in fed ct	Y
112. Superfund waste cleanup of $10b	Y
113. 90 days notice of plant closings	Y
114. $20b in Medicare cuts/tax increases	N
115. Spending cuts and tax increases	N
116. Set school lunch lmt-250% poverty	N
117. $75m for youth work projects	Y
118. Allow Angolan military assistance	N
119. Suspend defense payments for abuse	Y
120. Drop SS COLAs/$12b tax increase	N
121. Approve $1.5b for 21 MX missiles	N
122. Emergency farm credit/revisions	Y
123. Duty on Taiwan/Hong Kong/S Korea	Y
124. Limit steel imports to 17%	Y
125. Cut $ to schools that bar prayer	N
126. $50b-taxes; cut Medicare/spending	N
127. Limit Pershing II/cruise in Europe	N
128. Delete $7.1b for 34 B-1 bombers	Y
129. Bar purchase of Sergeant York guns	?
130. El Salvador military/economic aid	N
131. Bar mining of Nicaraguan waters	Y
132. Physician fee freeze for Medicare	N
133. $49b in "sin"/phone/insurance taxes	N
134. Allow sale of Conrail	?
135. Equal Rights Amendment	Y
136. Authorize Marines in Lebanon	N
137. Eminent domain for coal companies	N
138. Prohibit EPA clean air sanctions	N
139. SS retirement age increase/reforms	N
140. Auto domestic content requirement	Y
141. Delete jobs program funding	N
142. Highway-gas tax bill	Y
143. Cut $5b from defense for Medicare	Y
144. Emergency housing aid of $1b	Y

Presidential Support Score: 1991 - 24%   1990 - 18%

FORD, WILLIAM D. -- Michigan 15th District [Democrat]. Counties of Washtenaw (pt.) and Wayne (pt.). Prior Terms: 1965-92. Born: August 6, 1927; Detroit, MI. Education: Wayne University; University of Denver (B.S., LL.B.). Military Service: U.S. Navy, 1944-46; U.S. Air Force Reserve, 1950-58. Occupation: Attorney; justice of the peace (1955-57); Melvindale city attorney (1957-59); Michigan senator (1962-64).

1. Protection to Haitian refugees	#
2. Raise tax on wealthy; lower others	N

3. Investigate Reagan hostage delay	Y
4. Campaign finance revisions	Y

FORD, WILLIAM D. (continued)

5. Unpaid leave to care for children	Y	
6. Restrict NEA use of funds	N	
7. Bar race-bias claim/habeas corpus	N	
8. Ban race as death sentence factor	N	
9. Exceptions to exclusionary rule	?	
10. Allow sale of assault weapons	Y	
11. Life in prison/abolish death penalty	Y	
12. Req conspiracy-price fixing cases	?	
13. Unemployment benefits extension	Y	
14. Tissue use of aborted fetuses	Y	
15. Bar replacement of union strikers	Y	
16. Hold foreign aid at $15b for '92	Y	
17. Restore space station funding	N	
18. Civil Rights Act of 1991	Y	
19. Unlimited damages-discrimination	Y	
20. Eliminate funds for supercollider	Y	
21. Terminate SDI except for research	Y	
22. Req 7-day handgun waiting period	Y	
23. Provide $30b for failed S&Ls	N	
24. Allow use of force against Iraq	N	
25. Allow $15b in foreign aid for '91	Y	
26. Revise & extend legal immigration	Y	
27. Suspend aid to Angolan rebels	?	
28. Democratic tax plan proposals	Y	
29. Cut defense 5% across the board	?	
30. Textile import quotas-veto override	Y	
31. Abortion service for military abroad	?	
32. Limits on high income farmers	N	
33. Family medical leave-veto override	Y	
34. Req submission of balanced budget	Y	
35. Balanced budget amendment	N	
36. Amendment to ban flag desecration	N	
37. Reauthorize Amtrak-veto override	Y	
38. Retraining aid for coal miners	Y	
39. Suspend El Salvador military aid	Y	
40. Expand child care aid/tax credit	Y	
41. Raise House salary/omit honoraria	Y	
42. Toughen oil-spill liability	Y	
43. Restitution to Japanese interned	Y	
44. Protect Chinese & C.A. nationals	Y	
45. Abortion $ for rape/incest cases	Y	
46. Allow religious schools to bar gays	N	
47. Bar broadcaster fairness doctrine	N	
48. Bar cap gains cut/reinstate IRA	Y	
49. Bar unions equal voice in pension	N	
50. Bar assembly of chemical weapons	Y	
51. Ban plutonium/uranium production	?	
52. Cap MX missile deployment at 50	Y	
53. Allow $3b for 2 stealth bombers	?	
54. Publish bio-warfare experiments	Y	
55. Raise minimum wage-veto override	Y	
56. Bar transfer of FS-X technology	Y	
57. Cut defense and raise domestic $	Y	
58. Uniform poll closing in 48 states	?	
59. Req foreign investment disclosure	#	
60. Textile import quotas-veto override	Y	
61. Bar abortion funding in Wash, DC	N	
62. Notify spouses of AIDS+ carriers	N	
63. Seize conveyance-drug trafficking	N	
64. South Africa sanctions	Y	
65. 60 days' notice of plant closings	Y	
66. Close unneeded military bases	N	
67. Keep welfare reform within $2.8b	N	
68. Allow children housing exclusion	N	

69. Shift $400m of NASA to homeless	Y	
70. Cap Medicare patients' liability	Y	
71. Prohibit employee polygraph testing	Y	
72. Allow CIA to fund Contras	N	
73. Revise unfair trade practices	Y	
74. Focus SDI on accidental launch	?	
75. Bar Air Force $ for MX missile	Y	
76. Allow "real" increase in defense	N	
77. Troop reduction in Europe of 50%	Y	
78. Ban nuclear tests above 1 kiloton	Y	
79. Ban anti-satellite missile tests	Y	
80. Observe certain limits of SALT II	Y	
81. Restore four Civil Rights laws	Y	
82. Prohibit aliens as strikebreakers	Y	
83. Allow military malpractice suits	Y	
84. Approval of $36m in Contra aid	N	
85. $18b deficit reduction compromise	Y	
86. Welfare reform of $5.7b for 5 years	Y	
87. Raise taxes $12b/cut spending $3b	Y	
88. Board to assess occupational risk	Y	
89. Balanced budget by '93-via targets	N	
90. Bar licensing of two nuclear plants	?	
91. Remove victims compensation cap	N	
92. Catastrophic health insurance	Y	
93. Ban airline smoking-2 hours or less	N	
94. $1b/two year aid for the homeless	Y	
95. Bar non-unions in union companies	Y	
96. Increase FSLIC rescue to $15b	N	
97. Impose quotas to lower trade deficit	Y	
98. Reduce discretionary budget 21%	N	
99. Immigration reform/alien amnesty	Y	
100. South Africa sanctions-veto override	Y	
101. Tax overhaul to revise income tax	N	
102. Use of military in drug war	N	
103. Delete 12 MX/add conventional wpn	Y	
104. Raise speed limit to 65 mph	?	
105. Require Pentagon to buy US goods	Y	
106. AIDS insurance non-discrimination	Y	
107. Prohibit Saudi arms sales	Y	
108. Ease Gun Control Act of 1968	Y	
109. Bar interstate handgun transport	Y	
110. Make company emissions known	N	
111. Allow toxic victims to sue in fed ct	Y	
112. Superfund waste cleanup of $10b	Y	
113. 90 days notice of plant closings	Y	
114. $20b in Medicare cuts/tax increases	Y	
115. Spending cuts and tax increases	Y	
116. Set school lunch lmt-250% poverty	N	
117. $75m for youth work projects	#	
118. Allow Angolan military assistance	N	
119. Suspend defense payments for abuse	Y	
120. Drop SS COLAs/$12b tax increase	N	
121. Approve $1.5b for 21 MX missiles	N	
122. Emergency farm credit/revisions	Y	
123. Duty on Taiwan/Hong Kong/S Korea	Y	
124. Limit steel imports to 17%	Y	
125. Cut $ to schools that bar prayer	N	
126. $50b-taxes; cut Medicare/spending	Y	
127. Limit Pershing II/cruise in Europe	Y	
128. Delete $7.1b for 34 B-1 bombers	Y	
129. Bar purchase of Sergeant York guns	Y	
130. El Salvador military/economic aid	N	
131. Bar mining of Nicaraguan waters	Y	
132. Physician fee freeze for Medicare	N	

FORD, WILLIAM D. (continued)

133. $49b in "sin"/phone/insurance taxes	Y	
134. Allow sale of Conrail	N	
135. Equal Rights Amendment	Y	
136. Authorize Marines in Lebanon	N	
137. Eminent domain for coal companies	N	
138. Prohibit EPA clean air sanctions	N	

139. SS retirement age increase/reforms	N	
140. Auto domestic content requirement	Y	
141. Delete jobs program funding	N	
142. Highway-gas tax bill	Y	
143. Cut $5b from defense for Medicare	Y	
144. Emergency housing aid of $1b	Y	

Presidential Support Score: 1991 - 22%   1990 - 12%

DINGELL, JOHN D. -- Michigan 16th District [Democrat]. Counties of Lenawee (pt.), Monroe and Wayne (pt.). Prior Terms: 1955 (Special Election)-1992. Born: July 8, 1926; Colorado Springs, CO. Education: Georgetown University (B.S., J.D.). Military Service: WW II. Occupation: Attorney; research assistant to U.S. district judge; prosecuting attorney (1953-55).

1. Protection to Haitian refugees	Y	
2. Raise tax on wealthy; lower others	N	
3. Investigate Reagan hostage delay	Y	
4. Campaign finance revisions	Y	
5. Unpaid leave to care for children	Y	
6. Restrict NEA use of funds	N	
7. Bar race-bias claim/habeas corpus	N	
8. Ban race as death sentence factor	N	
9. Exceptions to exclusionary rule	N	
10. Allow sale of assault weapons	Y	
11. Life in prison/abolish death penalty	N	
12. Req conspiracy-price fixing cases	N	
13. Unemployment benefits extension	Y	
14. Tissue use of aborted fetuses	Y	
15. Bar replacement of union strikers	Y	
16. Hold foreign aid at $15b for '92	Y	
17. Restore space station funding	N	
18. Civil Rights Act of 1991	Y	
19. Unlimited damages-discrimination	N	
20. Eliminate funds for supercollider	Y	
21. Terminate SDI except for research	N	
22. Req 7-day handgun waiting period	N	
23. Provide $30b for failed S&Ls	Y	
24. Allow use of force against Iraq	Y	
25. Allow $15b in foreign aid for '91	?	
26. Revise & extend legal immigration	?	
27. Suspend aid to Angolan rebels	Y	
28. Democratic tax plan proposals	Y	
29. Cut defense 5% across the board	N	
30. Textile import quotas-veto override	Y	
31. Abortion service for military abroad	Y	
32. Limits on high income farmers	N	
33. Family medical leave-veto override	Y	
34. Req submission of balanced budget	Y	
35. Balanced budget amendment	N	
36. Amendment to ban flag desecration	N	
37. Reauthorize Amtrak-veto override	Y	
38. Retraining aid for coal miners	Y	
39. Suspend El Salvador military aid	Y	
40. Expand child care aid/tax credit	Y	
41. Raise House salary/omit honoraria	Y	
42. Toughen oil-spill liability	N	
43. Restitution to Japanese interned	?	
44. Protect Chinese & C.A. nationals	Y	
45. Abortion $ for rape/incest cases	Y	
46. Allow religious schools to bar gays	Y	
47. Bar broadcaster fairness doctrine	N	
48. Bar cap gains cut/reinstate IRA	Y	

49. Bar unions equal voice in pension	N	
50. Bar assembly of chemical weapons	N	
51. Ban plutonium/uranium production	Y	
52. Cap MX missile deployment at 50	Y	
53. Allow $3b for 2 stealth bombers	N	
54. Publish bio-warfare experiments	Y	
55. Raise minimum wage-veto override	Y	
56. Bar transfer of FS-X technology	Y	
57. Cut defense and raise domestic $	?	
58. Uniform poll closing in 48 states	Y	
59. Req foreign investment disclosure	Y	
60. Textile import quotas-veto override	Y	
61. Bar abortion funding in Wash, DC	N	
62. Notify spouses of AIDS+ carriers	N	
63. Seize conveyance-drug trafficking	Y	
64. South Africa sanctions	Y	
65. 60 days' notice of plant closings	Y	
66. Close unneeded military bases	N	
67. Keep welfare reform within $2.8b	N	
68. Allow children housing exclusion	N	
69. Shift $400m of NASA to homeless	N	
70. Cap Medicare patients' liability	Y	
71. Prohibit employee polygraph testing	Y	
72. Allow CIA to fund Contras	N	
73. Revise unfair trade practices	Y	
74. Focus SDI on accidental launch	Y	
75. Bar Air Force $ for MX missile	Y	
76. Allow "real" increase in defense	N	
77. Troop reduction in Europe of 50%	N	
78. Ban nuclear tests above 1 kiloton	Y	
79. Ban anti-satellite missile tests	?	
80. Observe certain limits of SALT II	Y	
81. Restore four Civil Rights laws	Y	
82. Prohibit aliens as strikebreakers	Y	
83. Allow military malpractice suits	Y	
84. Approval of $36m in Contra aid	N	
85. $18b deficit reduction compromise	Y	
86. Welfare reform of $5.7b for 5 years	Y	
87. Raise taxes $12b/cut spending $3b	Y	
88. Board to assess occupational risk	Y	
89. Balanced budget by '93-via targets	N	
90. Bar licensing of two nuclear plants	Y	
91. Remove victims compensation cap	Y	
92. Catastrophic health insurance	Y	
93. Ban airline smoking-2 hours or less	N	
94. $1b/two year aid for the homeless	Y	
95. Bar non-unions in union companies	Y	
96. Increase FSLIC rescue to $15b	?	

DINGELL, JOHN D. (continued)

97. Impose quotas to lower trade deficit	Y	
98. Reduce discretionary budget 21%	Y	
99. Immigration reform/alien amnesty	Y	
100. South Africa sanctions-veto override	Y	
101. Tax overhaul to revise income tax	N	
102. Use of military in drug war	N	
103. Delete 12 MX/add conventional wpn	Y	
104. Raise speed limit to 65 mph	N	
105. Require Pentagon to buy US goods	Y	
106. AIDS insurance non-discrimination	Y	
107. Prohibit Saudi arms sales	N	
108. Ease Gun Control Act of 1968	Y	
109. Bar interstate handgun transport	N	
110. Make company emissions known	N	
111. Allow toxic victims to sue in fed ct	N	
112. Superfund waste cleanup of $10b	N	
113. 90 days notice of plant closings	Y	
114. $20b in Medicare cuts/tax increases	Y	
115. Spending cuts and tax increases	Y	
116. Set school lunch lmt-250% poverty	N	
117. $75m for youth work projects	#	
118. Allow Angolan military assistance	N	
119. Suspend defense payments for abuse	Y	
120. Drop SS COLAs/$12b tax increase	N	

121. Approve $1.5b for 21 MX missiles	N	
122. Emergency farm credit/revisions	Y	
123. Duty on Taiwan/Hong Kong/S Korea	Y	
124. Limit steel imports to 17%	Y	
125. Cut $ to schools that bar prayer	N	
126. $50b-taxes; cut Medicare/spending	Y	
127. Limit Pershing II/cruise in Europe	N	
128. Delete $7.1b for 34 B-1 bombers	Y	
129. Bar purchase of Sergeant York guns	Y	
130. El Salvador military/economic aid	N	
131. Bar mining of Nicaraguan waters	Y	
132. Physician fee freeze for Medicare	N	
133. $49b in "sin"/phone/insurance taxes	Y	
134. Allow sale of Conrail	N	
135. Equal Rights Amendment	Y	
136. Authorize Marines in Lebanon	N	
137. Eminent domain for coal companies	Y	
138. Prohibit EPA clean air sanctions	N	
139. SS retirement age increase/reforms	N	
140. Auto domestic content requirement	Y	
141. Delete jobs program funding	N	
142. Highway-gas tax bill	Y	
143. Cut $5b from defense for Medicare	Y	
144. Emergency housing aid of $1b	Y	

Presidential Support Score: 1991 - 28% 1990 - 20%

LEVIN, SANDER M. -- Michigan 17th District [Democrat]. Counties of Oakland (pt.) and Wayne (pt.). Prior Terms: 1983-92. Born: September 6, 1931; Detroit, MI. Education: University of Chicago (B.A.); Columbia University (M.A.); Harvard University (LL.B.). Occupation: Partner, Schwartz, O'Hare and Levin (1957-64); Oakland County Board of Supervisors (1961-64); Michigan senator (1965-70); adjunct professor of law (1971-74); private law practice (1971-74); fellow, Kennedy School of Government, Institute of Politics, Harvard University (1975); assistant administrator, Agency for International Development (1977-81); counsel for Jaffe, Snider, Raitt, Garrett & Heuer (1981-82).

1. Protection to Haitian refugees	Y	
2. Raise tax on wealthy; lower others	N	
3. Investigate Reagan hostage delay	Y	
4. Campaign finance revisions	Y	
5. Unpaid leave to care for children	Y	
6. Restrict NEA use of funds	N	
7. Bar race-bias claim/habeas corpus	N	
8. Ban race as death sentence factor	N	
9. Exceptions to exclusionary rule	N	
10. Allow sale of assault weapons	N	
11. Life in prison/abolish death penalty	Y	
12. Req conspiracy-price fixing cases	N	
13. Unemployment benefits extension	Y	
14. Tissue use of aborted fetuses	Y	
15. Bar replacement of union strikers	Y	
16. Hold foreign aid at $15b for '92	Y	
17. Restore space station funding	N	
18. Civil Rights Act of 1991	Y	
19. Unlimited damages-discrimination	Y	
20. Eliminate funds for supercollider	Y	
21. Terminate SDI except for research	Y	
22. Req 7-day handgun waiting period	Y	
23. Provide $30b for failed S&Ls	Y	
24. Allow use of force against Iraq	N	
25. Allow $15b in foreign aid for '91	Y	
26. Revise & extend legal immigration	Y	
27. Suspend aid to Angolan rebels	Y	

28. Democratic tax plan proposals	Y	
29. Cut defense 5% across the board	N	
30. Textile import quotas-veto override	Y	
31. Abortion service for military abroad	Y	
32. Limits on high income farmers	Y	
33. Family medical leave-veto override	Y	
34. Req submission of balanced budget	Y	
35. Balanced budget amendment	N	
36. Amendment to ban flag desecration	N	
37. Reauthorize Amtrak-veto override	Y	
38. Retraining aid for coal miners	Y	
39. Suspend El Salvador military aid	Y	
40. Expand child care aid/tax credit	Y	
41. Raise House salary/omit honoraria	Y	
42. Toughen oil-spill liability	Y	
43. Restitution to Japanese interned	Y	
44. Protect Chinese & C.A. nationals	Y	
45. Abortion $ for rape/incest cases	Y	
46. Allow religious schools to bar gays	N	
47. Bar broadcaster fairness doctrine	N	
48. Bar cap gains cut/reinstate IRA	Y	
49. Bar unions equal voice in pension	N	
50. Bar assembly of chemical weapons	Y	
51. Ban plutonium/uranium production	Y	
52. Cap MX missile deployment at 50	Y	
53. Allow $3b for 2 stealth bombers	N	
54. Publish bio-warfare experiments	Y	

LEVIN, SANDER M. (continued)

55. Raise minimum wage-veto override	Y	
56. Bar transfer of FS-X technology	Y	
57. Cut defense and raise domestic $	N	
58. Uniform poll closing in 48 states	Y	
59. Req foreign investment disclosure	Y	
60. Textile import quotas-veto override	Y	
61. Bar abortion funding in Wash, DC	N	
62. Notify spouses of AIDS+ carriers	N	
63. Seize conveyance-drug trafficking	N	
64. South Africa sanctions	Y	
65. 60 days' notice of plant closings	Y	
66. Close unneeded military bases	?	
67. Keep welfare reform within $2.8b	N	
68. Allow children housing exclusion	N	
69. Shift $400m of NASA to homeless	Y	
70. Cap Medicare patients' liability	Y	
71. Prohibit employee polygraph testing	Y	
72. Allow CIA to fund Contras	N	
73. Revise unfair trade practices	Y	
74. Focus SDI on accidental launch	?	
75. Bar Air Force $ for MX missile	Y	
76. Allow "real" increase in defense	N	
77. Troop reduction in Europe of 50%	N	
78. Ban nuclear tests above 1 kiloton	Y	
79. Ban anti-satellite missile tests	Y	
80. Observe certain limits of SALT II	Y	
81. Restore four Civil Rights laws	Y	
82. Prohibit aliens as strikebreakers	Y	
83. Allow military malpractice suits	Y	
84. Approval of $36m in Contra aid	N	
85. $18b deficit reduction compromise	Y	
86. Welfare reform of $5.7b for 5 years	Y	
87. Raise taxes $12b/cut spending $3b	Y	
88. Board to assess occupational risk	Y	
89. Balanced budget by '93-via targets	Y	
90. Bar licensing of two nuclear plants	Y	
91. Remove victims compensation cap	Y	
92. Catastrophic health insurance	Y	
93. Ban airline smoking-2 hours or less	Y	
94. $1b/two year aid for the homeless	Y	
95. Bar non-unions in union companies	Y	
96. Increase FSLIC rescue to $15b	Y	
97. Impose quotas to lower trade deficit	Y	
98. Reduce discretionary budget 21%	Y
99. Immigration reform/alien amnesty	Y
100. South Africa sanctions-veto override	Y
101. Tax overhaul to revise income tax	Y
102. Use of military in drug war	N
103. Delete 12 MX/add conventional wpn	?
104. Raise speed limit to 65 mph	N
105. Require Pentagon to buy US goods	Y
106. AIDS insurance non-discrimination	Y
107. Prohibit Saudi arms sales	Y
108. Ease Gun Control Act of 1968	N
109. Bar interstate handgun transport	Y
110. Make company emissions known	Y
111. Allow toxic victims to sue in fed ct	N
112. Superfund waste cleanup of $10b	Y
113. 90 days notice of plant closings	Y
114. $20b in Medicare cuts/tax increases	Y
115. Spending cuts and tax increases	Y
116. Set school lunch lmt-250% poverty	N
117. $75m for youth work projects	Y
118. Allow Angolan military assistance	N
119. Suspend defense payments for abuse	Y
120. Drop SS COLAs/$12b tax increase	N
121. Approve $1.5b for 21 MX missiles	N
122. Emergency farm credit/revisions	Y
123. Duty on Taiwan/Hong Kong/S Korea	Y
124. Limit steel imports to 17%	Y
125. Cut $ to schools that bar prayer	N
126. $50b-taxes; cut Medicare/spending	C
127. Limit Pershing II/cruise in Europe	N
128. Delete $7.1b for 34 B-1 bombers	Y
129. Bar purchase of Sergeant York guns	Y
130. El Salvador military/economic aid	N
131. Bar mining of Nicaraguan waters	Y
132. Physician fee freeze for Medicare	N
133. $49b in "sin"/phone/insurance taxes	C
134. Allow sale of Conrail	N
135. Equal Rights Amendment	Y
136. Authorize Marines in Lebanon	N
137. Eminent domain for coal companies	N
138. Prohibit EPA clean air sanctions	Y
139. SS retirement age increase/reforms	N

Presidential Support Score: 1991 - 28%   1990 - 19%

BROOMFIELD, WILLIAM S. -- Michigan 18th District [Republican]. Counties of Livingston (pt.), Macomb (pt.) and Oakland (pt.). Prior Terms: 1957-92. Born: April 28, 1922; Royal Oak, MI. Education: Michigan State University. Occupation: Michigan representative (1948-54); Michigan senator (1954).

1. Protection to Haitian refugees	N	
2. Raise tax on wealthy; lower others	N	
3. Investigate Reagan hostage delay	N	
4. Campaign finance revisions	N	
5. Unpaid leave to care for children	N	
6. Restrict NEA use of funds	Y	
7. Bar race-bias claim/habeas corpus	Y	
8. Ban race as death sentence factor	Y	
9. Exceptions to exclusionary rule	Y	
10. Allow sale of assault weapons	N	
11. Life in prison/abolish death penalty	N	
12. Req conspiracy-price fixing cases	#	
13. Unemployment benefits extension	N
14. Tissue use of aborted fetuses	N
15. Bar replacement of union strikers	N
16. Hold foreign aid at $15b for '92	Y
17. Restore space station funding	Y
18. Civil Rights Act of 1991	N
19. Unlimited damages-discrimination	N
20. Eliminate funds for supercollider	Y
21. Terminate SDI except for research	N
22. Req 7-day handgun waiting period	Y
23. Provide $30b for failed S&Ls	Y
24. Allow use of force against Iraq	Y

BROOMFIELD, WILLIAM S. (continued)

25. Allow $15b in foreign aid for '91	Y	85. $18b deficit reduction compromise	N
26. Revise & extend legal immigration	Y	86. Welfare reform of $5.7b for 5 years	N
27. Suspend aid to Angolan rebels	N	87. Raise taxes $12b/cut spending $3b	N
28. Democratic tax plan proposals	N	88. Board to assess occupational risk	N
29. Cut defense 5% across the board	N	89. Balanced budget by '93-via targets	Y
30. Textile import quotas-veto override	N	90. Bar licensing of two nuclear plants	N
31. Abortion service for military abroad	N	91. Remove victims compensation cap	N
32. Limits on high income farmers	Y	92. Catastrophic health insurance	N
33. Family medical leave-veto override	N	93. Ban airline smoking-2 hours or less	Y
34. Req submission of balanced budget	Y	94. $1b/two year aid for the homeless	Y
35. Balanced budget amendment	Y	95. Bar non-unions in union companies	N
36. Amendment to ban flag desecration	Y	96. Increase FSLIC rescue to $15b	N
37. Reauthorize Amtrak-veto override	N	97. Impose quotas to lower trade deficit	N
38. Retraining aid for coal miners	Y	98. Reduce discretionary budget 21%	N
39. Suspend El Salvador military aid	N	99. Immigration reform/alien amnesty	N
40. Expand child care aid/tax credit	N	100. South Africa sanctions-veto override	N
41. Raise House salary/omit honoraria	Y	101. Tax overhaul to revise income tax	Y
42. Toughen oil-spill liability	?	102. Use of military in drug war	Y
43. Restitution to Japanese interned	Y	103. Delete 12 MX/add conventional wpn	N
44. Protect Chinese & C.A. nationals	Y	104. Raise speed limit to 65 mph	Y
45. Abortion $ for rape/incest cases	N	105. Require Pentagon to buy US goods	N
46. Allow religious schools to bar gays	Y	106. AIDS insurance non-discrimination	N
47. Bar broadcaster fairness doctrine	Y	107. Prohibit Saudi arms sales	Y
48. Bar cap gains cut/reinstate IRA	N	108. Ease Gun Control Act of 1968	N
49. Bar unions equal voice in pension	Y	109. Bar interstate handgun transport	Y
50. Bar assembly of chemical weapons	N	110. Make company emissions known	N
51. Ban plutonium/uranium production	N	111. Allow toxic victims to sue in fed ct	N
52. Cap MX missile deployment at 50	N	112. Superfund waste cleanup of $10b	Y
53. Allow $3b for 2 stealth bombers	Y	113. 90 days notice of plant closings	N
54. Publish bio-warfare experiments	N	114. $20b in Medicare cuts/tax increases	N
55. Raise minimum wage-veto override	N	115. Spending cuts and tax increases	N
56. Bar transfer of FS-X technology	?	116. Set school lunch lmt-250% poverty	Y
57. Cut defense and raise domestic $	N	117. $75m for youth work projects	?
58. Uniform poll closing in 48 states	N	118. Allow Angolan military assistance	Y
59. Req foreign investment disclosure	N	119. Suspend defense payments for abuse	Y
60. Textile import quotas-veto override	N	120. Drop SS COLAs/$12b tax increase	N
61. Bar abortion funding in Wash, DC	Y	121. Approve $1.5b for 21 MX missiles	Y
62. Notify spouses of AIDS+ carriers	Y	122. Emergency farm credit/revisions	N
63. Seize conveyance-drug trafficking	Y	123. Duty on Taiwan/Hong Kong/S Korea	N
64. South Africa sanctions	N	124. Limit steel imports to 17%	Y
65. 60 days' notice of plant closings	N	125. Cut $ to schools that bar prayer	Y
66. Close unneeded military bases	Y	126. $50b-taxes; cut Medicare/spending	N
67. Keep welfare reform within $2.8b	Y	127. Limit Pershing II/cruise in Europe	N
68. Allow children housing exclusion	N	128. Delete $7.1b for 34 B-1 bombers	N
69. Shift $400m of NASA to homeless	N	129. Bar purchase of Sergeant York guns	N
70. Cap Medicare patients' liability	Y	130. El Salvador military/economic aid	Y
71. Prohibit employee polygraph testing	Y	131. Bar mining of Nicaraguan waters	Y
72. Allow CIA to fund Contras	Y	132. Physician fee freeze for Medicare	Y
73. Revise unfair trade practices	N	133. $49b in "sin"/phone/insurance taxes	Y
74. Focus SDI on accidental launch	N	134. Allow sale of Conrail	Y
75. Bar Air Force $ for MX missile	N	135. Equal Rights Amendment	N
76. Allow "real" increase in defense	Y	136. Authorize Marines in Lebanon	Y
77. Troop reduction in Europe of 50%	N	137. Eminent domain for coal companies	N
78. Ban nuclear tests above 1 kiloton	N	138. Prohibit EPA clean air sanctions	N
79. Ban anti-satellite missile tests	N	139. SS retirement age increase/reforms	Y
80. Observe certain limits of SALT II	N	140. Auto domestic content requirement	Y
81. Restore four Civil Rights laws	N	141. Delete jobs program funding	Y
82. Prohibit aliens as strikebreakers	Y	142. Highway-gas tax bill	N
83. Allow military malpractice suits	N	143. Cut $5b from defense for Medicare	N
84. Approval of $36m in Contra aid	Y	144. Emergency housing aid of $1b	Y

Presidential Support Score: 1991 - 83%   1990 - 72%

MINNESOTA

PENNY, TIMOTHY J. -- Minnesota 1st District [Democrat]. Counties of Blue Earth, Dakota (pt.), Dodge, Filmore, Freeborn, Goodhue (pt.), Houston, Le Sueur (pt.), Mower, Olmsted, Rice, Scott (pt.), Steele, Wabasha, Waseca and Winona. Prior Terms: 1983-92. **Born:** November 19, 1951; Freeborn County, MN. Education: Winona State University. Occupation: Minnesota senator (1976, re-elected 1980).

1.	Protection to Haitian refugees	Y	52.	Cap MX missile deployment at 50	Y
2.	Raise tax on wealthy; lower others	N	53.	Allow $3b for 2 stealth bombers	N
3.	Investigate Reagan hostage delay	N	54.	Publish bio-warfare experiments	Y
4.	Campaign finance revisions	Y	55.	Raise minimum wage-veto override	N
5.	Unpaid leave to care for children	Y	56.	Bar transfer of FS-X technology	Y
6.	Restrict NEA use of funds	Y	57.	Cut defense and raise domestic $	N
7.	Bar race-bias claim/habeas corpus	N	58.	Uniform poll closing in 48 states	Y
8.	Ban race as death sentence factor	N	59.	Req foreign investment disclosure	Y
9.	Exceptions to exclusionary rule	Y	60.	Textile import quotas-veto override	N
10.	Allow sale of assault weapons	Y	61.	Bar abortion funding in Wash, DC	Y
11.	Life in prison/abolish death penalty	Y	62.	Notify spouses of AIDS+ carriers	N
12.	Req conspiracy-price fixing cases	Y	63.	Seize conveyance-drug trafficking	Y
13.	Unemployment benefits extension	N	64.	South Africa sanctions	N
14.	Tissue use of aborted fetuses	N	65.	60 days' notice of plant closings	Y
15.	Bar replacement of union strikers	Y	66.	Close unneeded military bases	Y
16.	Hold foreign aid at $15b for '92	Y	67.	Keep welfare reform within $2.8b	Y
17.	Restore space station funding	N	68.	Allow children housing exclusion	N
18.	Civil Rights Act of 1991	Y	69.	Shift $400m of NASA to homeless	N
19.	Unlimited damages-discrimination	N	70.	Cap Medicare patients' liability	N
20.	Eliminate funds for supercollider	Y	71.	Prohibit employee polygraph testing	Y
21.	Terminate SDI except for research	N	72.	Allow CIA to fund Contras	N
22.	Req 7-day handgun waiting period	N	73.	Revise unfair trade practices	Y
23.	Provide $30b for failed S&Ls	N	74.	Focus SDI on accidental launch	Y
24.	Allow use of force against Iraq	N	75.	Bar Air Force $ for MX missile	N
25.	Allow $15b in foreign aid for '91	Y	76.	Allow "real" increase in defense	N
26.	Revise & extend legal immigration	Y	77.	Troop reduction in Europe of 50%	N
27.	Suspend aid to Angolan rebels	Y	78.	Ban nuclear tests above 1 kiloton	Y
28.	Democratic tax plan proposals	Y	79.	Ban anti-satellite missile tests	Y
29.	Cut defense 5% across the board	N	80.	Observe certain limits of SALT II	Y
30.	Textile import quotas-veto override	N	81.	Restore four Civil Rights laws	Y
31.	Abortion service for military abroad	N	82.	Prohibit aliens as strikebreakers	Y
32.	Limits on high income farmers	N	83.	Allow military malpractice suits	Y
33.	Family medical leave-veto override	N	84.	Approval of $36m in Contra aid	N
34.	Req submission of balanced budget	Y	85.	$18b deficit reduction compromise	Y
35.	Balanced budget amendment	Y	86.	Welfare reform of $5.7b for 5 years	N
36.	Amendment to ban flag desecration	N	87.	Raise taxes $12b/cut spending $3b	N
37.	Reauthorize Amtrak-veto override	Y	88.	Board to assess occupational risk	Y
38.	Retraining aid for coal miners	Y	89.	Balanced budget by '93-via targets	Y
39.	Suspend El Salvador military aid	Y	90.	Bar licensing of two nuclear plants	Y
40.	Expand child care aid/tax credit	Y	91.	Remove victims compensation cap	N
41.	Raise House salary/omit honoraria	N	92.	Catastrophic health insurance	Y
42.	Toughen oil-spill liability	N	93.	Ban airline smoking-2 hours or less	Y
43.	Restitution to Japanese interned	N	94.	$1b/two year aid for the homeless	N
44.	Protect Chinese & C.A. nationals	Y	95.	Bar non-unions in union companies	N
45.	Abortion $ for rape/incest cases	N	96.	Increase FSLIC rescue to $15b	N
46.	Allow religious schools to bar gays	Y	97.	Impose quotas to lower trade deficit	N
47.	Bar broadcaster fairness doctrine	Y	98.	Reduce discretionary budget 21%	Y
48.	Bar cap gains cut/reinstate IRA	Y	99.	Immigration reform/alien amnesty	Y
49.	Bar unions equal voice in pension	N	100.	South Africa sanctions-veto override	N
50.	Bar assembly of chemical weapons	Y	101.	Tax overhaul to revise income tax	Y
51.	Ban plutonium/uranium production	Y	102.	Use of military in drug war	Y

PENNY, TIMOTHY J. (continued)

103. Delete 12 MX/add conventional wpn	Y
104. Raise speed limit to 65 mph	N
105. Require Pentagon to buy US goods	Y
106. AIDS insurance non-discrimination	Y
107. Prohibit Saudi arms sales	Y
108. Ease Gun Control Act of 1968	Y
109. Bar interstate handgun transport	N
110. Make company emissions known	Y
111. Allow toxic victims to sue in fed ct	Y
112. Superfund waste cleanup of $10b	Y
113. 90 days notice of plant closings	Y
114. $20b in Medicare cuts/tax increases	Y
115. Spending cuts and tax increases	Y
116. Set school lunch lmt-250% poverty	N
117. $75m for youth work projects	N
118. Allow Angolan military assistance	N
119. Suspend defense payments for abuse	Y
120. Drop SS COLAs/$12b tax increase	Y
121. Approve $1.5b for 21 MX missiles	N
122. Emergency farm credit/revisions	Y
123. Duty on Taiwan/Hong Kong/S Korea	N
124. Limit steel imports to 17%	N
125. Cut $ to schools that bar prayer	N
126. $50b-taxes; cut Medicare/spending	Y
127. Limit Pershing II/cruise in Europe	Y
128. Delete $7.1b for 34 B-1 bombers	Y
129. Bar purchase of Sergeant York guns	Y
130. El Salvador military/economic aid	N
131. Bar mining of Nicaraguan waters	Y
132. Physician fee freeze for Medicare	N
133. $49b in "sin"/phone/insurance taxes	Y
134. Allow sale of Conrail	N
135. Equal Rights Amendment	Y
136. Authorize Marines in Lebanon	N
137. Eminent domain for coal companies	N
138. Prohibit EPA clean air sanctions	Y
139. SS retirement age increase/reforms	Y

Presidential Support Score: 1991 - 50%   1990 - 34%

WEBER, VIN -- Minnesota 2nd District [Republican]. Counties of Big Stone, Brown, Chippewa, Cottonwood, Douglas, Faribault, Grant (pt.), Jackson, Kandiyohi, Lac qui Parle, Le Sueur (pt.), Lincoln, Lyon, McLeod, Martin, Meeker, Murray, Nicollet, Nobles, Pipestone, Pope, Redwood, Renville, Rock, Sibley, Stevens, Swift, Traverse, Watonwen, Wright (pt.) and Yellow Medicine. Prior Terms: 1981-92. Born: July 24, 1952; Slayton, MN. Education: University of Minnesota. Occupation: President, Weber Publishing Co.; publisher; congressional press secretary (1974-75); senator's aide (1979-80).

1. Protection to Haitian refugees	Y
2. Raise tax on wealthy; lower others	N
3. Investigate Reagan hostage delay	N
4. Campaign finance revisions	N
5. Unpaid leave to care for children	N
6. Restrict NEA use of funds	Y
7. Bar race-bias claim/habeas corpus	Y
8. Ban race as death sentence factor	Y
9. Exceptions to exclusionary rule	Y
10. Allow sale of assault weapons	Y
11. Life in prison/abolish death penalty	Y
12. Req conspiracy-price fixing cases	Y
13. Unemployment benefits extension	N
14. Tissue use of aborted fetuses	N
15. Bar replacement of union strikers	Y
16. Hold foreign aid at $15b for '92	Y
17. Restore space station funding	Y
18. Civil Rights Act of 1991	N
19. Unlimited damages-discrimination	N
20. Eliminate funds for supercollider	N
21. Terminate SDI except for research	N
22. Req 7-day handgun waiting period	N
23. Provide $30b for failed S&Ls	Y
24. Allow use of force against Iraq	Y
25. Allow $15b in foreign aid for '91	?
26. Revise & extend legal immigration	?
27. Suspend aid to Angolan rebels	N
28. Democratic tax plan proposals	N
29. Cut defense 5% across the board	?
30. Textile import quotas-veto override	N
31. Abortion service for military abroad	N
32. Limits on high income farmers	N
33. Family medical leave-veto override	N
34. Req submission of balanced budget	N
35. Balanced budget amendment	Y
36. Amendment to ban flag desecration	Y
37. Reauthorize Amtrak-veto override	N
38. Retraining aid for coal miners	N
39. Suspend El Salvador military aid	N
40. Expand child care aid/tax credit	N
41. Raise House salary/omit honoraria	N
42. Toughen oil-spill liability	N
43. Restitution to Japanese interned	Y
44. Protect Chinese & C.A. nationals	N
45. Abortion $ for rape/incest cases	N
46. Allow religious schools to bar gays	Y
47. Bar broadcaster fairness doctrine	Y
48. Bar cap gains cut/reinstate IRA	N
49. Bar unions equal voice in pension	Y
50. Bar assembly of chemical weapons	Y
51. Ban plutonium/uranium production	N
52. Cap MX missile deployment at 50	N
53. Allow $3b for 2 stealth bombers	Y
54. Publish bio-warfare experiments	N
55. Raise minimum wage-veto override	N
56. Bar transfer of FS-X technology	N
57. Cut defense and raise domestic $	N
58. Uniform poll closing in 48 states	N
59. Req foreign investment disclosure	N
60. Textile import quotas-veto override	N
61. Bar abortion funding in Wash, DC	Y
62. Notify spouses of AIDS+ carriers	N
63. Seize conveyance-drug trafficking	Y
64. South Africa sanctions	N
65. 60 days' notice of plant closings	N
66. Close unneeded military bases	Y

WEBER, VIN (continued)

67. Keep welfare reform within $2.8b	Y	
68. Allow children housing exclusion	N	
69. Shift $400m of NASA to homeless	N	
70. Cap Medicare patients' liability	N	
71. Prohibit employee polygraph testing	Y	
72. Allow CIA to fund Contras	Y	
73. Revise unfair trade practices	N	
74. Focus SDI on accidental launch	N	
75. Bar Air Force $ for MX missile	N	
76. Allow "real" increase in defense	Y	
77. Troop reduction in Europe of 50%	N	
78. Ban nuclear tests above 1 kiloton	N	
79. Ban anti-satellite missile tests	N	
80. Observe certain limits of SALT II	N	
81. Restore four Civil Rights laws	N	
82. Prohibit aliens as strikebreakers	N	
83. Allow military malpractice suits	Y	
84. Approval of $36m in Contra aid	Y	
85. $18b deficit reduction compromise	N	
86. Welfare reform of $5.7b for 5 years	N	
87. Raise taxes $12b/cut spending $3b	N	
88. Board to assess occupational risk	N	
89. Balanced budget by '93-via targets	N	
90. Bar licensing of two nuclear plants	N	
91. Remove victims compensation cap	Y	
92. Catastrophic health insurance	N	
93. Ban airline smoking-2 hours or less	Y	
94. $1b/two year aid for the homeless	N	
95. Bar non-unions in union companies	N	
96. Increase FSLIC rescue to $15b	N	
97. Impose quotas to lower trade deficit	N	
98. Reduce discretionary budget 21%	N	
99. Immigration reform/alien amnesty	Y	
100. South Africa sanctions-veto override	Y	
101. Tax overhaul to revise income tax	Y	
102. Use of military in drug war	Y	
103. Delete 12 MX/add conventional wpn	N	
104. Raise speed limit to 65 mph	Y	
105. Require Pentagon to buy US goods	N	

106. AIDS insurance non-discrimination	N	
107. Prohibit Saudi arms sales	Y	
108. Ease Gun Control Act of 1968	Y	
109. Bar interstate handgun transport	N	
110. Make company emissions known	?	
111. Allow toxic victims to sue in fed ct	?	
112. Superfund waste cleanup of $10b	#	
113. 90 days notice of plant closings	N	
114. $20b in Medicare cuts/tax increases	N	
115. Spending cuts and tax increases	N	
116. Set school lunch lmt-250% poverty	N	
117. $75m for youth work projects	?	
118. Allow Angolan military assistance	Y	
119. Suspend defense payments for abuse	Y	
120. Drop SS COLAs/$12b tax increase	N	
121. Approve $1.5b for 21 MX missiles	Y	
122. Emergency farm credit/revisions	Y	
123. Duty on Taiwan/Hong Kong/S Korea	N	
124. Limit steel imports to 17%	N	
125. Cut $ to schools that bar prayer	Y	
126. $50b-taxes; cut Medicare/spending	N	
127. Limit Pershing II/cruise in Europe	N	
128. Delete $7.1b for 34 B-1 bombers	Y	
129. Bar purchase of Sergeant York guns	Y	
130. El Salvador military/economic aid	Y	
131. Bar mining of Nicaraguan waters	N	
132. Physician fee freeze for Medicare	Y	
133. $49b in "sin"/phone/insurance taxes	N	
134. Allow sale of Conrail	Y	
135. Equal Rights Amendment	N	
136. Authorize Marines in Lebanon	Y	
137. Eminent domain for coal companies	N	
138. Prohibit EPA clean air sanctions	N	
139. SS retirement age increase/reforms	Y	
140. Auto domestic content requirement	N	
141. Delete jobs program funding	Y	
142. Highway-gas tax bill	N	
143. Cut $5b from defense for Medicare	N	
144. Emergency housing aid of $1b	N	

Presidential Support Score: 1991 - 73%   1990 - 63%

RAMSTAD, JIM -- Minnesota 3rd District [Republican]. Counties of Carver, Dakota (pt.), Goodhue (pt.), Hennepin (pt.) and Scott (pt.). Prior Term: 1991-92. Born: May 6, 1946; Jamestown, ND. Education: University of Minnesota (B.A.); George Washington University Law School (J.D.). Military Service: U.S. Army Reserve. Occupation: State senator (1981-90).

1. Protection to Haitian refugees	N	
2. Raise tax on wealthy; lower others	N	
3. Investigate Reagan hostage delay	N	
4. Campaign finance revisions	N	
5. Unpaid leave to care for children	Y	
6. Restrict NEA use of funds	Y	
7. Bar race-bias claim/habeas corpus	Y	
8. Ban race as death sentence factor	Y	
9. Exceptions to exclusionary rule	Y	
10. Allow sale of assault weapons	Y	
11. Life in prison/abolish death penalty	N	
12. Req conspiracy-price fixing cases	Y	

13. Unemployment benefits extension	N	
14. Tissue use of aborted fetuses	N	
15. Bar replacement of union strikers	N	
16. Hold foreign aid at $15b for '92	Y	
17. Restore space station funding	N	
18. Civil Rights Act of 1991	N	
19. Unlimited damages-discrimination	N	
20. Eliminate funds for supercollider	#	
21. Terminate SDI except for research	N	
22. Req 7-day handgun waiting period	N	
23. Provide $30b for failed S&Ls	N	
24. Allow use of force against Iraq	Y	

Presidential Support Score: 1991 - 65%

VENTO, BRUCE F. -- Minnesota 4th District [Democrat]. Counties of Dakota (pt.), Ramsey (pt.), and Washington (pt.). Prior Terms: 1977-92. Born: October 7, 1940; St. Paul, MN. Education: University of Minnesota (A.A.); Wisconsin State University (B.S.). Occupation: Teacher; Minnesota representative (1970).

1. Protection to Haitian refugees	Y	
2. Raise tax on wealthy; lower others	N	
3. Investigate Reagan hostage delay	Y	
4. Campaign finance revisions	Y	
5. Unpaid leave to care for children	Y	
6. Restrict NEA use of funds	N	
7. Bar race-bias claim/habeas corpus	N	
8. Ban race as death sentence factor	N	
9. Exceptions to exclusionary rule	N	
10. Allow sale of assault weapons	N	
11. Life in prison/abolish death penalty	Y	
12. Req conspiracy-price fixing cases	N	
13. Unemployment benefits extension	Y	
14. Tissue use of aborted fetuses	Y	
15. Bar replacement of union strikers	Y	
16. Hold foreign aid at $15b for '92	Y	
17. Restore space station funding	X	
18. Civil Rights Act of 1991	Y	
19. Unlimited damages-discrimination	Y	
20. Eliminate funds for supercollider	Y	
21. Terminate SDI except for research	Y	
22. Req 7-day handgun waiting period	Y	
23. Provide $30b for failed S&Ls	Y	
24. Allow use of force against Iraq	N	
25. Allow $15b in foreign aid for '91	Y	
26. Revise & extend legal immigration	Y	
27. Suspend aid to Angolan rebels	Y	
28. Democratic tax plan proposals	Y	
29. Cut defense 5% across the board	Y	
30. Textile import quotas-veto override	Y	
31. Abortion service for military abroad	Y	
32. Limits on high income farmers	Y	
33. Family medical leave-veto override	Y	
34. Req submission of balanced budget	Y	
35. Balanced budget amendment	N	
36. Amendment to ban flag desecration	N	
37. Reauthorize Amtrak-veto override	Y	
38. Retraining aid for coal miners	Y	
39. Suspend El Salvador military aid	Y	
40. Expand child care aid/tax credit	Y	
41. Raise House salary/omit honoraria	Y	
42. Toughen oil-spill liability	?	
43. Restitution to Japanese interned	Y	
44. Protect Chinese & C.A. nationals	Y	
45. Abortion $ for rape/incest cases	N	
46. Allow religious schools to bar gays	N	
47. Bar broadcaster fairness doctrine	N	
48. Bar cap gains cut/reinstate IRA	Y	
49. Bar unions equal voice in pension	N	
50. Bar assembly of chemical weapons	Y	
51. Ban plutonium/uranium production	Y	
52. Cap MX missile deployment at 50	Y	
53. Allow $3b for 2 stealth bombers	N	
54. Publish bio-warfare experiments	Y	
55. Raise minimum wage-veto override	Y	
56. Bar transfer of FS-X technology	Y	
57. Cut defense and raise domestic $	Y	
58. Uniform poll closing in 48 states	Y	
59. Req foreign investment disclosure	Y	
60. Textile import quotas-veto override	Y	

61. Bar abortion funding in Wash, DC	N	
62. Notify spouses of AIDS+ carriers	N	
63. Seize conveyance-drug trafficking	N	
64. South Africa sanctions	Y	
65. 60 days' notice of plant closings	Y	
66. Close unneeded military bases	Y	
67. Keep welfare reform within $2.8b	N	
68. Allow children housing exclusion	N	
69. Shift $400m of NASA to homeless	Y	
70. Cap Medicare patients' liability	Y	
71. Prohibit employee polygraph testing	?	
72. Allow CIA to fund Contras	N	
73. Revise unfair trade practices	Y	
74. Focus SDI on accidental launch	Y	
75. Bar Air Force $ for MX missile	Y	
76. Allow "real" increase in defense	N	
77. Troop reduction in Europe of 50%	Y	
78. Ban nuclear tests above 1 kiloton	Y	
79. Ban anti-satellite missile tests	Y	
80. Observe certain limits of SALT II	Y	
81. Restore four Civil Rights laws	Y	
82. Prohibit aliens as strikebreakers	Y	
83. Allow military malpractice suits	Y	
84. Approval of $36m in Contra aid	N	
85. $18b deficit reduction compromise	Y	
86. Welfare reform of $5.7b for 5 years	Y	
87. Raise taxes $12b/cut spending $3b	Y	
88. Board to assess occupational risk	+	
89. Balanced budget by '93-via targets	N	
90. Bar licensing of two nuclear plants	Y	
91. Remove victims compensation cap	Y	
92. Catastrophic health insurance	Y	
93. Ban airline smoking-2 hours or less	#	
94. $1b/two year aid for the homeless	Y	
95. Bar non-unions in union companies	Y	
96. Increase FSLIC rescue to $15b	N	
97. Impose quotas to lower trade deficit	Y	
98. Reduce discretionary budget 21%	Y	
99. Immigration reform/alien amnesty	Y	
100. South Africa sanctions-veto override	Y	
101. Tax overhaul to revise income tax	Y	
102. Use of military in drug war	N	
103. Delete 12 MX/add conventional wpn	Y	
104. Raise speed limit to 65 mph	N	
105. Require Pentagon to buy US goods	Y	
106. AIDS insurance non-discrimination	Y	
107. Prohibit Saudi arms sales	Y	
108. Ease Gun Control Act of 1968	N	
109. Bar interstate handgun transport	Y	
110. Make company emissions known	Y	
111. Allow toxic victims to sue in fed ct	Y	
112. Superfund waste cleanup of $10b	Y	
113. 90 days notice of plant closings	Y	
114. $20b in Medicare cuts/tax increases	Y	
115. Spending cuts and tax increases	Y	
116. Set school lunch lmt-250% poverty	N	
117. $75m for youth work projects	Y	
118. Allow Angolan military assistance	N	
119. Suspend defense payments for abuse	Y	
120. Drop SS COLAs/$12b tax increase	N	

VENTO, BRUCE F. (continued)

121. Approve $1.5b for 21 MX missiles	N	
122. Emergency farm credit/revisions	Y	
123. Duty on Taiwan/Hong Kong/S Korea	Y	
124. Limit steel imports to 17%	Y	
125. Cut $ to schools that bar prayer	N	
126. $50b-taxes; cut Medicare/spending	Y	
127. Limit Pershing II/cruise in Europe	Y	
128. Delete $7.1b for 34 B-1 bombers	Y	
129. Bar purchase of Sergeant York guns	#	
130. El Salvador military/economic aid	N	
131. Bar mining of Nicaraguan waters	Y	
132. Physician fee freeze for Medicare	N	
133. $49b in "sin"/phone/insurance taxes	Y
134. Allow sale of Conrail	N
135. Equal Rights Amendment	Y
136. Authorize Marines in Lebanon	N
137. Eminent domain for coal companies	N
138. Prohibit EPA clean air sanctions	Y
139. SS retirement age increase/reforms	N
140. Auto domestic content requirement	Y
141. Delete jobs program funding	N
142. Highway-gas tax bill	Y
143. Cut $5b from defense for Medicare	Y
144. Emergency housing aid of $1b	Y

Presidential Support Score: 1991 - 26%   1990 - 13%

SABO, MARTIN OLAV -- Minnesota 5th District [Democrat]. County of Hennepin (pt.). Prior Terms: 1979-92. Born: February 28, 1938; Crosby, ND. Education: Augsburg College (B.A.); University of Minnesota. Occupation: Minnesota representative (1960-78).

1. Protection to Haitian refugees	Y	
2. Raise tax on wealthy; lower others	N	
3. Investigate Reagan hostage delay	Y	
4. Campaign finance revisions	Y	
5. Unpaid leave to care for children	Y	
6. Restrict NEA use of funds	N	
7. Bar race-bias claim/habeas corpus	N	
8. Ban race as death sentence factor	N	
9. Exceptions to exclusionary rule	N	
10. Allow sale of assault weapons	N	
11. Life in prison/abolish death penalty	Y	
12. Req conspiracy-price fixing cases	N	
13. Unemployment benefits extension	Y	
14. Tissue use of aborted fetuses	Y	
15. Bar replacement of union strikers	Y	
16. Hold foreign aid at $15b for '92	Y	
17. Restore space station funding	N	
18. Civil Rights Act of 1991	Y	
19. Unlimited damages-discrimination	Y	
20. Eliminate funds for supercollider	Y	
21. Terminate SDI except for research	Y	
22. Req 7-day handgun waiting period	Y	
23. Provide $30b for failed S&Ls	Y	
24. Allow use of force against Iraq	N	
25. Allow $15b in foreign aid for '91	Y	
26. Revise & extend legal immigration	Y	
27. Suspend aid to Angolan rebels	Y	
28. Democratic tax plan proposals	Y	
29. Cut defense 5% across the board	N	
30. Textile import quotas-veto override	Y	
31. Abortion service for military abroad	Y	
32. Limits on high income farmers	Y	
33. Family medical leave-veto override	Y	
34. Req submission of balanced budget	N	
35. Balanced budget amendment	N	
36. Amendment to ban flag desecration	N	
37. Reauthorize Amtrak-veto override	Y	
38. Retraining aid for coal miners	Y	
39. Suspend El Salvador military aid	Y	
40. Expand child care aid/tax credit	Y	
41. Raise House salary/omit honoraria	Y	
42. Toughen oil-spill liability	Y	
43. Restitution to Japanese interned	Y	
44. Protect Chinese & C.A. nationals	Y	
45. Abortion $ for rape/incest cases	Y
46. Allow religious schools to bar gays	N
47. Bar broadcaster fairness doctrine	N
48. Bar cap gains cut/reinstate IRA	Y
49. Bar unions equal voice in pension	N
50. Bar assembly of chemical weapons	Y
51. Ban plutonium/uranium production	Y
52. Cap MX missile deployment at 50	Y
53. Allow $3b for 2 stealth bombers	N
54. Publish bio-warfare experiments	Y
55. Raise minimum wage-veto override	Y
56. Bar transfer of FS-X technology	Y
57. Cut defense and raise domestic $	Y
58. Uniform poll closing in 48 states	Y
59. Req foreign investment disclosure	Y
60. Textile import quotas-veto override	Y
61. Bar abortion funding in Wash, DC	N
62. Notify spouses of AIDS+ carriers	N
63. Seize conveyance-drug trafficking	N
64. South Africa sanctions	Y
65. 60 days' notice of plant closings	Y
66. Close unneeded military bases	N
67. Keep welfare reform within $2.8b	N
68. Allow children housing exclusion	N
69. Shift $400m of NASA to homeless	N
70. Cap Medicare patients' liability	Y
71. Prohibit employee polygraph testing	Y
72. Allow CIA to fund Contras	N
73. Revise unfair trade practices	Y
74. Focus SDI on accidental launch	Y
75. Bar Air Force $ for MX missile	Y
76. Allow "real" increase in defense	N
77. Troop reduction in Europe of 50%	N
78. Ban nuclear tests above 1 kiloton	Y
79. Ban anti-satellite missile tests	Y
80. Observe certain limits of SALT II	Y
81. Restore four Civil Rights laws	Y
82. Prohibit aliens as strikebreakers	Y
83. Allow military malpractice suits	Y
84. Approval of $36m in Contra aid	N
85. $18b deficit reduction compromise	Y
86. Welfare reform of $5.7b for 5 years	Y
87. Raise taxes $12b/cut spending $3b	Y
88. Board to assess occupational risk	Y

SABO, MARTIN OLAV (continued)

89. Balanced budget by '93-via targets	N	
90. Bar licensing of two nuclear plants	Y	
91. Remove victims compensation cap	Y	
92. Catastrophic health insurance	Y	
93. Ban airline smoking-2 hours or less	N	
94. $1b/two year aid for the homeless	Y	
95. Bar non-unions in union companies	Y	
96. Increase FSLIC rescue to $15b	N	
97. Impose quotas to lower trade deficit	Y	
98. Reduce discretionary budget 21%	N	
99. Immigration reform/alien amnesty	Y	
100. South Africa sanctions-veto override	Y	
101. Tax overhaul to revise income tax	Y	
102. Use of military in drug war	N	
103. Delete 12 MX/add conventional wpn	Y	
104. Raise speed limit to 65 mph	N	
105. Require Pentagon to buy US goods	Y	
106. AIDS insurance non-discrimination	Y	
107. Prohibit Saudi arms sales	Y	
108. Ease Gun Control Act of 1968	N	
109. Bar interstate handgun transport	Y	
110. Make company emissions known	Y	
111. Allow toxic victims to sue in fed ct	Y	
112. Superfund waste cleanup of $10b	Y	
113. 90 days notice of plant closings	Y	
114. $20b in Medicare cuts/tax increases	Y	
115. Spending cuts and tax increases	Y	
116. Set school lunch lmt-250% poverty	N	

117. $75m for youth work projects	Y
118. Allow Angolan military assistance	N
119. Suspend defense payments for abuse	Y
120. Drop SS COLAs/$12b tax increase	N
121. Approve $1.5b for 21 MX missiles	N
122. Emergency farm credit/revisions	Y
123. Duty on Taiwan/Hong Kong/S Korea	N
124. Limit steel imports to 17%	Y
125. Cut $ to schools that bar prayer	N
126. $50b-taxes; cut Medicare/spending	Y
127. Limit Pershing II/cruise in Europe	?
128. Delete $7.1b for 34 B-1 bombers	Y
129. Bar purchase of Sergeant York guns	Y
130. El Salvador military/economic aid	N
131. Bar mining of Nicaraguan waters	Y
132. Physician fee freeze for Medicare	N
133. $49b in "sin"/phone/insurance taxes	Y
134. Allow sale of Conrail	N
135. Equal Rights Amendment	Y
136. Authorize Marines in Lebanon	N
137. Eminent domain for coal companies	N
138. Prohibit EPA clean air sanctions	?
139. SS retirement age increase/reforms	N
140. Auto domestic content requirement	Y
141. Delete jobs program funding	N
142. Highway-gas tax bill	Y
143. Cut $5b from defense for Medicare	Y
144. Emergency housing aid of $1b	Y

Presidential Support Score: 1991 - 30%   1990 - 19%

SIKORSKI, GERRY -- Minnesota 6th District [Democrat]. Counties of Anoka, Hennepin (pt.), Ramsey (pt.), Sherburne (pt.), Washington (pt.) and Wright (pt.). Prior Terms: 1983-92. Born: April 26, 1948; Breckenridge, MN. Education: University of Minnesota (B.A., J.D.). Occupation: Attorney; township and city attorney; treasurer, Legal Assistance of Minnesota; president, Washington County Legal Assistance; Minnesota senator (1976-82).

1. Protection to Haitian refugees	Y	
2. Raise tax on wealthy; lower others	N	
3. Investigate Reagan hostage delay	Y	
4. Campaign finance revisions	Y	
5. Unpaid leave to care for children	Y	
6. Restrict NEA use of funds	N	
7. Bar race-bias claim/habeas corpus	N	
8. Ban race as death sentence factor	N	
9. Exceptions to exclusionary rule	N	
10. Allow sale of assault weapons	N	
11. Life in prison/abolish death penalty	N	
12. Req conspiracy-price fixing cases	N	
13. Unemployment benefits extension	Y	
14. Tissue use of aborted fetuses	Y	
15. Bar replacement of union strikers	Y	
16. Hold foreign aid at $15b for '92	Y	
17. Restore space station funding	N	
18. Civil Rights Act of 1991	Y	
19. Unlimited damages-discrimination	Y	
20. Eliminate funds for supercollider	Y	
21. Terminate SDI except for research	Y	
22. Req 7-day handgun waiting period	Y	
23. Provide $30b for failed S&Ls	N	
24. Allow use of force against Iraq	N	
25. Allow $15b in foreign aid for '91	?	
26. Revise & extend legal immigration	?	

27. Suspend aid to Angolan rebels	Y
28. Democratic tax plan proposals	Y
29. Cut defense 5% across the board	Y
30. Textile import quotas-veto override	Y
31. Abortion service for military abroad	N
32. Limits on high income farmers	Y
33. Family medical leave-veto override	Y
34. Req submission of balanced budget	Y
35. Balanced budget amendment	N
36. Amendment to ban flag desecration	N
37. Reauthorize Amtrak-veto override	Y
38. Retraining aid for coal miners	Y
39. Suspend El Salvador military aid	Y
40. Expand child care aid/tax credit	Y
41. Raise House salary/omit honoraria	Y
42. Toughen oil-spill liability	Y
43. Restitution to Japanese interned	Y
44. Protect Chinese & C.A. nationals	Y
45. Abortion $ for rape/incest cases	Y
46. Allow religious schools to bar gays	N
47. Bar broadcaster fairness doctrine	N
48. Bar cap gains cut/reinstate IRA	Y
49. Bar unions equal voice in pension	N
50. Bar assembly of chemical weapons	Y
51. Ban plutonium/uranium production	Y
52. Cap MX missile deployment at 50	Y

SIKORSKI, GERRY (continued)

53. Allow $3b for 2 stealth bombers	N
54. Publish bio-warfare experiments	Y
55. Raise minimum wage-veto override	Y
56. Bar transfer of FS-X technology	Y
57. Cut defense and raise domestic $	N
58. Uniform poll closing in 48 states	Y
59. Req foreign investment disclosure	Y
60. Textile import quotas-veto override	Y
61. Bar abortion funding in Wash, DC	Y
62. Notify spouses of AIDS+ carriers	N
63. Seize conveyance-drug trafficking	N
64. South Africa sanctions	Y
65. 60 days' notice of plant closings	Y
66. Close unneeded military bases	Y
67. Keep welfare reform within $2.8b	N
68. Allow children housing exclusion	N
69. Shift $400m of NASA to homeless	Y
70. Cap Medicare patients' liability	Y
71. Prohibit employee polygraph testing	Y
72. Allow CIA to fund Contras	N
73. Revise unfair trade practices	Y
74. Focus SDI on accidental launch	Y
75. Bar Air Force $ for MX missile	Y
76. Allow "real" increase in defense	N
77. Troop reduction in Europe of 50%	Y
78. Ban nuclear tests above 1 kiloton	Y
79. Ban anti-satellite missile tests	Y
80. Observe certain limits of SALT II	Y
81. Restore four Civil Rights laws	Y
82. Prohibit aliens as strikebreakers	Y
83. Allow military malpractice suits	Y
84. Approval of $36m in Contra aid	N
85. $18b deficit reduction compromise	Y
86. Welfare reform of $5.7b for 5 years	Y
87. Raise taxes $12b/cut spending $3b	Y
88. Board to assess occupational risk	Y
89. Balanced budget by '93-via targets	Y
90. Bar licensing of two nuclear plants	Y
91. Remove victims compensation cap	Y
92. Catastrophic health insurance	Y
93. Ban airline smoking-2 hours or less	Y
94. $1b/two year aid for the homeless	Y
95. Bar non-unions in union companies	Y
96. Increase FSLIC rescue to $15b	N

97. Impose quotas to lower trade deficit	Y
98. Reduce discretionary budget 21%	Y
99. Immigration reform/alien amnesty	N
100. South Africa sanctions-veto override	Y
101. Tax overhaul to revise income tax	Y
102. Use of military in drug war	?
103. Delete 12 MX/add conventional wpn	Y
104. Raise speed limit to 65 mph	N
105. Require Pentagon to buy US goods	Y
106. AIDS insurance non-discrimination	Y
107. Prohibit Saudi arms sales	Y
108. Ease Gun Control Act of 1968	Y
109. Bar interstate handgun transport	N
110. Make company emissions known	Y
111. Allow toxic victims to sue in fed ct	Y
112. Superfund waste cleanup of $10b	Y
113. 90 days notice of plant closings	Y
114. $20b in Medicare cuts/tax increases	Y
115. Spending cuts and tax increases	Y
116. Set school lunch lmt-250% poverty	N
117. $75m for youth work projects	Y
118. Allow Angolan military assistance	N
119. Suspend defense payments for abuse	Y
120. Drop SS COLAs/$12b tax increase	N
121. Approve $1.5b for 21 MX missiles	N
122. Emergency farm credit/revisions	Y
123. Duty on Taiwan/Hong Kong/S Korea	Y
124. Limit steel imports to 17%	Y
125. Cut $ to schools that bar prayer	N
126. $50b-taxes; cut Medicare/spending	N
127. Limit Pershing II/cruise in Europe	Y
128. Delete $7.1b for 34 B-1 bombers	Y
129. Bar purchase of Sergeant York guns	Y
130. El Salvador military/economic aid	N
131. Bar mining of Nicaraguan waters	Y
132. Physician fee freeze for Medicare	N
133. $49b in "sin"/phone/insurance taxes	Y
134. Allow sale of Conrail	N
135. Equal Rights Amendment	Y
136. Authorize Marines in Lebanon	N
137. Eminent domain for coal companies	N
138. Prohibit EPA clean air sanctions	Y
139. SS retirement age increase/reforms	N

Presidential Support Score: 1991 - 22%   1990 - 15%

PETERSON, COLLIN C. -- Minnesota 7th District [Democrat]. Counties of Becker, Beltrami (pt.), Benton, Clay, Clearwater, Grant (pt.), Hubbard (pt.), Kittson, Lake of the Woods, Mahnomen, Marshall, Morrison, Norman, Otter Tail, Pennington, Polk, Red Lake, Roseau, Sherburne (pt.), Sterns, Todd, Wadena and Wilkin. Prior Term: 1991-92. Born: June 29, 1944; Fargo, N.D. Education: Moorhead State University (dual B.A.). Military Service: U.S. Army National Guard. Occupation: Accountant; state senator (1976-86).

1. Protection to Haitian refugees	?
2. Raise tax on wealthy; lower others	N
3. Investigate Reagan hostage delay	Y
4. Campaign finance revisions	Y
5. Unpaid leave to care for children	Y
6. Restrict NEA use of funds	Y
7. Bar race-bias claim/habeas corpus	N
8. Ban race as death sentence factor	N
9. Exceptions to exclusionary rule	Y

10. Allow sale of assault weapons	Y
11. Life in prison/abolish death penalty	Y
12. Req conspiracy-price fixing cases	N
13. Unemployment benefits extension	Y
14. Tissue use of aborted fetuses	Y
15. Bar replacement of union strikers	Y
16. Hold foreign aid at $15b for '92	Y
17. Restore space station funding	N
18. Civil Rights Act of 1991	Y

PETERSON, COLLIN C. (continued)

19.	Unlimited damages-discrimination	N	22. Req 7-day handgun waiting period	N
20.	Eliminate funds for supercollider	Y	23. Provide $30b for failed S&Ls	N
21.	Terminate SDI except for research	Y	24. Allow use of force against Iraq	N

Presidential Support Score: 1991 - 39%

OBERSTAR, JAMES L. -- Minnesota 8th District [Democrat]. Counties of Aitkin, Beltrami (pt.), Carlton, Cass, Chisago, Cook, Crow Wing, Hubbard (pt.), Isanti, Itasca, Kanabec, Koochiching, Lake, Mille Locs, Pine, St. Louis and Sherburne (pt.). Prior Terms: 1975-92. Born: September 10, 1934; Chisholm, MN. Education: St. Thomas College (B.A.); College of Europe, Bruges, Belgium (M.A.); Georgetown University. Occupation: Administrative assistant to congressman (1963-74).

1.	Protection to Haitian refugees	Y	51. Ban plutonium/uranium production	Y
2.	Raise tax on wealthy; lower others	N	52. Cap MX missile deployment at 50	Y
3.	Investigate Reagan hostage delay	Y	53. Allow $3b for 2 stealth bombers	N
4.	Campaign finance revisions	Y	54. Publish bio-warfare experiments	Y
5.	Unpaid leave to care for children	Y	55. Raise minimum wage-veto override	Y
6.	Restrict NEA use of funds	N	56. Bar transfer of FS-X technology	Y
7.	Bar race-bias claim/habeas corpus	N	57. Cut defense and raise domestic $	Y
8.	Ban race as death sentence factor	N	58. Uniform poll closing in 48 states	Y
9.	Exceptions to exclusionary rule	N	59. Req foreign investment disclosure	Y
10.	Allow sale of assault weapons	Y	60. Textile import quotas-veto override	Y
11.	Life in prison/abolish death penalty	Y	61. Bar abortion funding in Wash, DC	Y
12.	Req conspiracy-price fixing cases	N	62. Notify spouses of AIDS+ carriers	N
13.	Unemployment benefits extension	Y	63. Seize conveyance-drug trafficking	N
14.	Tissue use of aborted fetuses	Y	64. South Africa sanctions	Y
15.	Bar replacement of union strikers	Y	65. 60 days' notice of plant closings	Y
16.	Hold foreign aid at $15b for '92	?	66. Close unneeded military bases	Y
17.	Restore space station funding	N	67. Keep welfare reform within $2.8b	N
18.	Civil Rights Act of 1991	Y	68. Allow children housing exclusion	?
19.	Unlimited damages-discrimination	Y	69. Shift $400m of NASA to homeless	N
20.	Eliminate funds for supercollider	Y	70. Cap Medicare patients' liability	Y
21.	Terminate SDI except for research	Y	71. Prohibit employee polygraph testing	Y
22.	Req 7-day handgun waiting period	N	72. Allow CIA to fund Contras	N
23.	Provide $30b for failed S&Ls	Y	73. Revise unfair trade practices	Y
24.	Allow use of force against Iraq	N	74. Focus SDI on accidental launch	Y
25.	Allow $15b in foreign aid for '91	Y	75. Bar Air Force $ for MX missile	Y
26.	Revise & extend legal immigration	Y	76. Allow "real" increase in defense	N
27.	Suspend aid to Angolan rebels	Y	77. Troop reduction in Europe of 50%	Y
28.	Democratic tax plan proposals	Y	78. Ban nuclear tests above 1 kiloton	Y
29.	Cut defense 5% across the board	Y	79. Ban anti-satellite missile tests	Y
30.	Textile import quotas-veto override	Y	80. Observe certain limits of SALT II	Y
31.	Abortion service for military abroad	N	81. Restore four Civil Rights laws	Y
32.	Limits on high income farmers	N	82. Prohibit aliens as strikebreakers	Y
33.	Family medical leave-veto override	Y	83. Allow military malpractice suits	Y
34.	Req submission of balanced budget	Y	84. Approval of $36m in Contra aid	N
35.	Balanced budget amendment	N	85. $18b deficit reduction compromise	Y
36.	Amendment to ban flag desecration	N	86. Welfare reform of $5.7b for 5 years	Y
37.	Reauthorize Amtrak-veto override	Y	87. Raise taxes $12b/cut spending $3b	Y
38.	Retraining aid for coal miners	Y	88. Board to assess occupational risk	Y
39.	Suspend El Salvador military aid	Y	89. Balanced budget by '93-via targets	N
40.	Expand child care aid/tax credit	Y	90. Bar licensing of two nuclear plants	Y
41.	Raise House salary/omit honoraria	Y	91. Remove victims compensation cap	Y
42.	Toughen oil-spill liability	Y	92. Catastrophic health insurance	Y
43.	Restitution to Japanese interned	Y	93. Ban airline smoking-2 hours or less	Y
44.	Protect Chinese & C.A. nationals	Y	94. $1b/two year aid for the homeless	Y
45.	Abortion $ for rape/incest cases	N	95. Bar non-unions in union companies	Y
46.	Allow religious schools to bar gays	N	96. Increase FSLIC rescue to $15b	N
47.	Bar broadcaster fairness doctrine	N	97. Impose quotas to lower trade deficit	Y
48.	Bar cap gains cut/reinstate IRA	Y	98. Reduce discretionary budget 21%	N
49.	Bar unions equal voice in pension	N	99. Immigration reform/alien amnesty	Y
50.	Bar assembly of chemical weapons	Y	100. South Africa sanctions-veto override	Y

OBERSTAR, JAMES L. (continued)

101.	Tax overhaul to revise income tax	Y	123. Duty on Taiwan/Hong Kong/S Korea	Y
102.	Use of military in drug war	N	124. Limit steel imports to 17%	Y
103.	Delete 12 MX/add conventional wpn	Y	125. Cut $ to schools that bar prayer	N
104.	Raise speed limit to 65 mph	N	126. $50b-taxes; cut Medicare/spending	Y
105.	Require Pentagon to buy US goods	Y	127. Limit Pershing II/cruise in Europe	Y
106.	AIDS insurance non-discrimination	Y	128. Delete $7.1b for 34 B-1 bombers	Y
107.	Prohibit Saudi arms sales	Y	129. Bar purchase of Sergeant York guns	Y
108.	Ease Gun Control Act of 1968	Y	130. El Salvador military/economic aid	N
109.	Bar interstate handgun transport	N	131. Bar mining of Nicaraguan waters	Y
110.	Make company emissions known	Y	132. Physician fee freeze for Medicare	N
111.	Allow toxic victims to sue in fed ct	Y	133. $49b in "sin"/phone/insurance taxes	Y
112.	Superfund waste cleanup of $10b	Y	134. Allow sale of Conrail	N
113.	90 days notice of plant closings	Y	135. Equal Rights Amendment	Y
114.	$20b in Medicare cuts/tax increases	Y	136. Authorize Marines in Lebanon	N
115.	Spending cuts and tax increases	Y	137. Eminent domain for coal companies	N
116.	Set school lunch lmt-250% poverty	N	138. Prohibit EPA clean air sanctions	Y
117.	$75m for youth work projects	Y	139. SS retirement age increase/reforms	N
118.	Allow Angolan military assistance	N	140. Auto domestic content requirement	Y
119.	Suspend defense payments for abuse	Y	141. Delete jobs program funding	N
120.	Drop SS COLAs/$12b tax increase	N	142. Highway-gas tax bill	N
121.	Approve $1.5b for 21 MX missiles	N	143. Cut $5b from defense for Medicare	Y
122.	Emergency farm credit/revisions	Y	144. Emergency housing aid of $1b	Y

Presidential Support Score: 1991 - 30%   1990 - 17%

MISSISSIPPI

WHITTEN, JAMIE L. -- Mississippi 1st District [Democrat]. Counties of Alcorn, Benton, Calhoun, Chickasaw, DeSoto, Grenada, Itawamba, Lafayette, Lee, Marshall, Monroe, Panola, Pontotoc, Prentiss, Tallahatchie (pt.), Tate, Tippah, Tishomingo, Union and Yalobusha. Prior Terms: 1941 (Special Election)-1992. Born: April 18, 1910; Cascilla, MS. Education: University of Mississippi. Occupation: Attorney; school principal (1930-31); district attorney; Mississippi representative.

1.	Protection to Haitian refugees	?	25. Allow $15b in foreign aid for '91	N
2.	Raise tax on wealthy; lower others	N	26. Revise & extend legal immigration	Y
3.	Investigate Reagan hostage delay	?	27. Suspend aid to Angolan rebels	N
4.	Campaign finance revisions	Y	28. Democratic tax plan proposals	Y
5.	Unpaid leave to care for children	N	29. Cut defense 5% across the board	N
6.	Restrict NEA use of funds	Y	30. Textile import quotas-veto override	Y
7.	Bar race-bias claim/habeas corpus	P	31. Abortion service for military abroad	N
8.	Ban race as death sentence factor	Y	32. Limits on high income farmers	N
9.	Exceptions to exclusionary rule	?	33. Family medical leave-veto override	Y
10.	Allow sale of assault weapons	Y	34. Req submission of balanced budget	Y
11.	Life in prison/abolish death penalty	N	35. Balanced budget amendment	Y
12.	Req conspiracy-price fixing cases	N	36. Amendment to ban flag desecration	Y
13.	Unemployment benefits extension	Y	37. Reauthorize Amtrak-veto override	Y
14.	Tissue use of aborted fetuses	Y	38. Retraining aid for coal miners	Y
15.	Bar replacement of union strikers	N	39. Suspend El Salvador military aid	Y
16.	Hold foreign aid at $15b for '92	Y	40. Expand child care aid/tax credit	Y
17.	Restore space station funding	N	41. Raise House salary/omit honoraria	Y
18.	Civil Rights Act of 1991	Y	42. Toughen oil-spill liability	N
19.	Unlimited damages-discrimination	N	43. Restitution to Japanese interned	Y
20.	Eliminate funds for supercollider	N	44. Protect Chinese & C.A. nationals	Y
21.	Terminate SDI except for research	?	45. Abortion $ for rape/incest cases	N
22.	Req 7-day handgun waiting period	?	46. Allow religious schools to bar gays	Y
23.	Provide $30b for failed S&Ls	N	47. Bar broadcaster fairness doctrine	Y
24.	Allow use of force against Iraq	Y	48. Bar cap gains cut/reinstate IRA	N

WHITTEN, JAMIE L. (continued)

49.	Bar unions equal voice in pension	Y	97.	Impose quotas to lower trade deficit	Y
50.	Bar assembly of chemical weapons	Y	98.	Reduce discretionary budget 21%	N
51.	Ban plutonium/uranium production	Y	99.	Immigration reform/alien amnesty	N
52.	Cap MX missile deployment at 50	Y	100.	South Africa sanctions-veto override	Y
53.	Allow $3b for 2 stealth bombers	N	101.	Tax overhaul to revise income tax	Y
54.	Publish bio-warfare experiments	Y	102.	Use of military in drug war	?
55.	Raise minimum wage-veto override	N	103.	Delete 12 MX/add conventional wpn	N
56.	Bar transfer of FS-X technology	Y	104.	Raise speed limit to 65 mph	N
57.	Cut defense and raise domestic $	N	105.	Require Pentagon to buy US goods	Y
58.	Uniform poll closing in 48 states	Y	106.	AIDS insurance non-discrimination	Y
59.	Req foreign investment disclosure	Y	107.	Prohibit Saudi arms sales	Y
60.	Textile import quotas-veto override	Y	108.	Ease Gun Control Act of 1968	Y
61.	Bar abortion funding in Wash, DC	N	109.	Bar interstate handgun transport	N
62.	Notify spouses of AIDS+ carriers	N	110.	Make company emissions known	?
63.	Seize conveyance-drug trafficking	N	111.	Allow toxic victims to sue in fed ct	?
64.	South Africa sanctions	Y	112.	Superfund waste cleanup of $10b	Y
65.	60 days' notice of plant closings	Y	113.	90 days notice of plant closings	Y
66.	Close unneeded military bases	N	114.	$20b in Medicare cuts/tax increases	Y
67.	Keep welfare reform within $2.8b	N	115.	Spending cuts and tax increases	N
68.	Allow children housing exclusion	?	116.	Set school lunch lmt-250% poverty	N
69.	Shift $400m of NASA to homeless	N	117.	$75m for youth work projects	Y
70.	Cap Medicare patients' liability	Y	118.	Allow Angolan military assistance	Y
71.	Prohibit employee polygraph testing	Y	119.	Suspend defense payments for abuse	N
72.	Allow CIA to fund Contras	N	120.	Drop SS COLAs/$12b tax increase	N
73.	Revise unfair trade practices	Y	121.	Approve $1.5b for 21 MX missiles	N
74.	Focus SDI on accidental launch	?	122.	Emergency farm credit/revisions	Y
75.	Bar Air Force $ for MX missile	N	123.	Duty on Taiwan/Hong Kong/S Korea	Y
76.	Allow "real" increase in defense	N	124.	Limit steel imports to 17%	Y
77.	Troop reduction in Europe of 50%	N	125.	Cut $ to schools that bar prayer	Y
78.	Ban nuclear tests above 1 kiloton	Y	126.	$50b-taxes; cut Medicare/spending	N
79.	Ban anti-satellite missile tests	Y	127.	Limit Pershing II/cruise in Europe	N
80.	Observe certain limits of SALT II	N	128.	Delete $7.1b for 34 B-1 bombers	N
81.	Restore four Civil Rights laws	Y	129.	Bar purchase of Sergeant York guns	N
82.	Prohibit aliens as strikebreakers	Y	130.	El Salvador military/economic aid	N
83.	Allow military malpractice suits	Y	131.	Bar mining of Nicaraguan waters	Y
84.	Approval of $36m in Contra aid	N	132.	Physician fee freeze for Medicare	N
85.	$18b deficit reduction compromise	Y	133.	$49b in "sin"/phone/insurance taxes	N
86.	Welfare reform of $5.7b for 5 years	Y	134.	Allow sale of Conrail	Y
87.	Raise taxes $12b/cut spending $3b	Y	135.	Equal Rights Amendment	Y
88.	Board to assess occupational risk	Y	136.	Authorize Marines in Lebanon	Y
89.	Balanced budget by '93-via targets	Y	137.	Eminent domain for coal companies	N
90.	Bar licensing of two nuclear plants	N	138.	Prohibit EPA clean air sanctions	N
91.	Remove victims compensation cap	N	139.	SS retirement age increase/reforms	N
92.	Catastrophic health insurance	Y	140.	Auto domestic content requirement	Y
93.	Ban airline smoking-2 hours or less	N	141.	Delete jobs program funding	N
94.	$1b/two year aid for the homeless	?	142.	Highway-gas tax bill	Y
95.	Bar non-unions in union companies	N	143.	Cut $5b from defense for Medicare	Y
96.	Increase FSLIC rescue to $15b	N	144.	Emergency housing aid of $1b	Y

Presidential Support Score: 1991 - 39%   1990 - 34%

ESPY, MIKE -- Mississippi 2nd District [Democrat]. Counties of Attala (pt.), Bolivar, Carroll, Claiborne, Coahoma, Grenada, Hinds (pt.), Holmes, Humphreys, Issaquena, Jefferson, Leflore, Madison (pt.), Panola (pt.), Quitman, Sharkey, Sunflower, Tallahatchie, Warren, Washington, and Yazoo. Prior Terms: 1987-92. Born: November 30, 1953; Yazoo City, MS. Education: Howard University (B.A.); University of Santa Clara Law School. Occupation: Managing attorney, Central Mississippi Legal Services, Yazoo City branch office (1978-1980); state Public Lands Division director (1980-1984); assistant state attorney general, Consumer Protection Division (1984-1985).

1.	Protection to Haitian refugees	Y	4.	Campaign finance revisions	Y
2.	Raise tax on wealthy; lower others	N	5.	Unpaid leave to care for children	Y
3.	Investigate Reagan hostage delay	Y	6.	Restrict NEA use of funds	N

ESPY, MIKE (continued)

7. Bar race-bias claim/habeas corpus	N	
8. Ban race as death sentence factor	?	
9. Exceptions to exclusionary rule	N	
10. Allow sale of assault weapons	Y	
11. Life in prison/abolish death penalty	N	
12. Req conspiracy-price fixing cases	Y	
13. Unemployment benefits extension	Y	
14. Tissue use of aborted fetuses	Y	
15. Bar replacement of union strikers	Y	
16. Hold foreign aid at $15b for '92	Y	
17. Restore space station funding	N	
18. Civil Rights Act of 1991	Y	
19. Unlimited damages-discrimination	Y	
20. Eliminate funds for supercollider	Y	
21. Terminate SDI except for research	Y	
22. Req 7-day handgun waiting period	N	
23. Provide $30b for failed S&Ls	N	
24. Allow use of force against Iraq	N	
25. Allow $15b in foreign aid for '91	Y	
26. Revise & extend legal immigration	Y	
27. Suspend aid to Angolan rebels	Y	
28. Democratic tax plan proposals	Y	
29. Cut defense 5% across the board	Y	
30. Textile import quotas-veto override	Y	
31. Abortion service for military abroad	Y	
32. Limits on high income farmers	N	
33. Family medical leave-veto override	Y	
34. Req submission of balanced budget	Y	
35. Balanced budget amendment	Y	
36. Amendment to ban flag desecration	N	
37. Reauthorize Amtrak-veto override	Y	
38. Retraining aid for coal miners	Y	
39. Suspend El Salvador military aid	Y	
40. Expand child care aid/tax credit	Y	
41. Raise House salary/omit honoraria	N	
42. Toughen oil-spill liability	N	
43. Restitution to Japanese interned	Y	
44. Protect Chinese & C.A. nationals	Y	
45. Abortion $ for rape/incest cases	Y	
46. Allow religious schools to bar gays	Y	
47. Bar broadcaster fairness doctrine	N	
48. Bar cap gains cut/reinstate IRA	Y	
49. Bar unions equal voice in pension	N	
50. Bar assembly of chemical weapons	Y	
51. Ban plutonium/uranium production	Y	
52. Cap MX missile deployment at 50	Y	

53. Allow $3b for 2 stealth bombers	N	
54. Publish bio-warfare experiments	Y	
55. Raise minimum wage-veto override	Y	
56. Bar transfer of FS-X technology	Y	
57. Cut defense and raise domestic $	P	
58. Uniform poll closing in 48 states	Y	
59. Req foreign investment disclosure	Y	
60. Textile import quotas-veto override	Y	
61. Bar abortion funding in Wash, DC	N	
62. Notify spouses of AIDS+ carriers	N	
63. Seize conveyance-drug trafficking	N	
64. South Africa sanctions	Y	
65. 60 days' notice of plant closings	Y	
66. Close unneeded military bases	Y	
67. Keep welfare reform within $2.8b	N	
68. Allow children housing exclusion	N	
69. Shift $400m of NASA to homeless	Y	
70. Cap Medicare patients' liability	Y	
71. Prohibit employee polygraph testing	Y	
72. Allow CIA to fund Contras	?	
73. Revise unfair trade practices	Y	
74. Focus SDI on accidental launch	Y	
75. Bar Air Force $ for MX missile	Y	
76. Allow "real" increase in defense	N	
77. Troop reduction in Europe of 50%	Y	
78. Ban nuclear tests above 1 kiloton	Y	
79. Ban anti-satellite missile tests	Y	
80. Observe certain limits of SALT II	Y	
81. Restore four Civil Rights laws	Y	
82. Prohibit aliens as strikebreakers	Y	
83. Allow military malpractice suits	Y	
84. Approval of $36m in Contra aid	N	
85. $18b deficit reduction compromise	Y	
86. Welfare reform of $5.7b for 5 years	Y	
87. Raise taxes $12b/cut spending $3b	Y	
88. Board to assess occupational risk	Y	
89. Balanced budget by '93-via targets	Y	
90. Bar licensing of two nuclear plants	N	
91. Remove victims compensation cap	N	
92. Catastrophic health insurance	Y	
93. Ban airline smoking-2 hours or less	N	
94. $1b/two year aid for the homeless	Y	
95. Bar non-unions in union companies	Y	
96. Increase FSLIC rescue to $15b	N	
97. Impose quotas to lower trade deficit	Y	
98. Reduce discretionary budget 21%	N	

Presidential Support Score: 1991 - 32%   1990 - 20%

MONTGOMERY, G. V. (Sonny) -- Mississippi 3rd District [Democrat]. Counties of Clarke, Clay, Jasper, Jones, Kemper, Lauderdale, Leake, Lownces, Nesnoba, Newton, Noxubee, Oktibbeha, Rankin, Scott, Simpson (pt.), Smith and Winston. Prior Terms: 1967-92. Born: Meridian, MS. Education: Mississippi State University (B.S.). Military Service: U.S. Army. Occupation: Mississippi senator (1956-66).

1. Protection to Haitian refugees	N	
2. Raise tax on wealthy; lower others	N	
3. Investigate Reagan hostage delay	N	
4. Campaign finance revisions	Y	
5. Unpaid leave to care for children	N	
6. Restrict NEA use of funds	Y	
7. Bar race-bias claim/habeas corpus	Y	
8. Ban race as death sentence factor	Y	

9. Exceptions to exclusionary rule	Y	
10. Allow sale of assault weapons	Y	
11. Life in prison/abolish death penalty	N	
12. Req conspiracy-price fixing cases	Y	
13. Unemployment benefits extension	N	
14. Tissue use of aborted fetuses	N	
15. Bar replacement of union strikers	N	
16. Hold foreign aid at $15b for '92	N	

MONTGOMERY, G. V. (Sonny) (continued)

17. Restore space station funding	N
18. Civil Rights Act of 1991	N
19. Unlimited damages-discrimination	N
20. Eliminate funds for supercollider	N
21. Terminate SDI except for research	N
22. Req 7-day handgun waiting period	N
23. Provide $30b for failed S&Ls	Y
24. Allow use of force against Iraq	Y
25. Allow $15b in foreign aid for '91	Y
26. Revise & extend legal immigration	N
27. Suspend aid to Angolan rebels	N
28. Democratic tax plan proposals	Y
29. Cut defense 5% across the board	N
30. Textile import quotas-veto override	Y
31. Abortion service for military abroad	N
32. Limits on high income farmers	N
33. Family medical leave-veto override	N
34. Req submission of balanced budget	Y
35. Balanced budget amendment	Y
36. Amendment to ban flag desecration	Y
37. Reauthorize Amtrak-veto override	Y
38. Retraining aid for coal miners	N
39. Suspend El Salvador military aid	N
40. Expand child care aid/tax credit	N
41. Raise House salary/omit honoraria	Y
42. Toughen oil-spill liability	N
43. Restitution to Japanese interned	N
44. Protect Chinese & C.A. nationals	N
45. Abortion $ for rape/incest cases	N
46. Allow religious schools to bar gays	Y
47. Bar broadcaster fairness doctrine	Y
48. Bar cap gains cut/reinstate IRA	N
49. Bar unions equal voice in pension	Y
50. Bar assembly of chemical weapons	N
51. Ban plutonium/uranium production	Y
52. Cap MX missile deployment at 50	?
53. Allow $3b for 2 stealth bombers	N
54. Publish bio-warfare experiments	Y
55. Raise minimum wage-veto override	N
56. Bar transfer of FS-X technology	N
57. Cut defense and raise domestic $	N
58. Uniform poll closing in 48 states	N
59. Req foreign investment disclosure	Y
60. Textile import quotas-veto override	Y
61. Bar abortion funding in Wash, DC	Y
62. Notify spouses of AIDS+ carriers	N
63. Seize conveyance-drug trafficking	Y
64. South Africa sanctions	N
65. 60 days' notice of plant closings	N
66. Close unneeded military bases	N
67. Keep welfare reform within $2.8b	Y
68. Allow children housing assistance	N
69. Shift $400m of NASA to homeless	N
70. Cap Medicare patients' liability	Y
71. Prohibit employee polygraph testing	N
72. Allow CIA to fund Contras	Y
73. Revise unfair trade practices	Y
74. Focus SDI on accidental launch	N
75. Bar Air Force $ for MX missile	N
76. Allow "real" increase in defense	Y
77. Troop reduction in Europe of 50%	N
78. Ban nuclear tests above 1 kiloton	N

79. Ban anti-satellite missile tests	N
80. Observe certain limits of SALT II	N
81. Restore four Civil Rights laws	Y
82. Prohibit aliens as strikebreakers	N
83. Allow military malpractice suits	N
84. Approval of $36m in Contra aid	Y
85. $18b deficit reduction compromise	Y
86. Welfare reform of $5.7b for 5 years	N
87. Raise taxes $12b/cut spending $3b	Y
88. Board to assess occupational risk	N
89. Balanced budget by '93-via targets	Y
90. Bar licensing of two nuclear plants	N
91. Remove victims compensation cap	N
92. Catastrophic health insurance	N
93. Ban airline smoking-2 hours or less	Y
94. $1b/two year aid for the homeless	Y
95. Bar non-unions in union companies	N
96. Increase FSLIC rescue to $15b	N
97. Impose quotas to lower trade deficit	N
98. Reduce discretionary budget 21%	Y
99. Immigration reform/alien amnesty	N
100. South Africa sanctions-veto override	N
101. Tax overhaul to revise income tax	N
102. Use of military in drug war	N
103. Delete 12 MX/add conventional wpn	N
104. Raise speed limit to 65 mph	Y
105. Require Pentagon to buy US goods	N
106. AIDS insurance non-discrimination	N
107. Prohibit Saudi arms sales	N
108. Ease Gun Control Act of 1968	Y
109. Bar interstate handgun transport	N
110. Make company emissions known	N
111. Allow toxic victims to sue in fed ct	N
112. Superfund waste cleanup of $10b	N
113. 90 days notice of plant closings	N
114. $20b in Medicare cuts/tax increases	Y
115. Spending cuts and tax increases	Y
116. Set school lunch lmt-250% poverty	Y
117. $75m for youth work projects	N
118. Allow Angolan military assistance	Y
119. Suspend defense payments for abuse	Y
120. Drop SS COLAs/$12b tax increase	Y
121. Approve $1.5b for 21 MX missiles	Y
122. Emergency farm credit/revisions	Y
123. Duty on Taiwan/Hong Kong/S Korea	Y
124. Limit steel imports to 17%	Y
125. Cut $ to schools that bar prayer	Y
126. $50b-taxes; cut Medicare/spending	Y
127. Limit Pershing II/cruise in Europe	N
128. Delete $7.1b for 34 B-1 bombers	N
129. Bar purchase of Sergeant York guns	N
130. El Salvador military/economic aid	Y
131. Bar mining of Nicaraguan waters	N
132. Physician fee freeze for Medicare	Y
133. $49b in "sin"/phone/insurance taxes	Y
134. Allow sale of Conrail	Y
135. Equal Rights Amendment	N
136. Authorize Marines in Lebanon	Y
137. Eminent domain for coal companies	Y
138. Prohibit EPA clean air sanctions	Y
139. SS retirement age increase/reforms	Y
140. Auto domestic content requirement	N

MONTGOMERY, G. V. (Sonny) (continued)

141. Delete jobs program funding	Y	143. Cut $5b from defense for Medicare N
142. Highway-gas tax bill	Y	144. Emergency housing aid of $1b Y

Presidential Support Score: 1991 - 66%   1990 - 56%

PARKER, MIKE -- Mississippi 4th District [Democrat]. Counties of Adams, Amite, Claiborne, Copiah, Franklin, Hinds (pt.), Jefferson Davis, Lawrence, Lincoln, Marion, Pike, Rankin (pt.), Simpson, Walthall and Wilkinson. Prior Terms: 1989-92. Born: October 31, 1949; Laurel, MS. Education: William Carey College (B.A.). Occupation: Funeral home, insurance company and livestock farm operator.

1. Protection to Haitian refugees	N	30. Textile import quotas-veto override	Y
2. Raise tax on wealthy; lower others	N	31. Abortion service for military abroad	N
3. Investigate Reagan hostage delay	N	32. Limits on high income farmers	N
4. Campaign finance revisions	Y	33. Family medical leave-veto override	N
5. Unpaid leave to care for children	N	34. Req submission of balanced budget	Y
6. Restrict NEA use of funds	Y	35. Balanced budget amendment	Y
7. Bar race-bias claim/habeas corpus	Y	36. Amendment to ban flag desecration	Y
8. Ban race as death sentence factor	Y	37. Reauthorize Amtrak-veto override	Y
9. Exceptions to exclusionary rule	Y	38. Retraining aid for coal miners	N
10. Allow sale of assault weapons	Y	39. Suspend El Salvador military aid	N
11. Life in prison/abolish death penalty	N	40. Expand child care aid/tax credit	N
12. Req conspiracy-price fixing cases	Y	41. Raise House salary/omit honoraria	N
13. Unemployment benefits extension	N	42. Toughen oil-spill liability	N
14. Tissue use of aborted fetuses	N	43. Restitution to Japanese interned	N
15. Bar replacement of union strikers	Y	44. Protect Chinese & C.A. nationals	N
16. Hold foreign aid at $15b for '92	N	45. Abortion $ for rape/incest cases	N
17. Restore space station funding	N	46. Allow religious schools to bar gays	Y
18. Civil Rights Act of 1991	N	47. Bar broadcaster fairness doctrine	Y
19. Unlimited damages-discrimination	N	48. Bar cap gains cut/reinstate IRA	N
20. Eliminate funds for supercollider	Y	49. Bar unions equal voice in pension	Y
21. Terminate SDI except for research	?	50. Bar assembly of chemical weapons	N
22. Req 7-day handgun waiting period	N	51. Ban plutonium/uranium production	Y
23. Provide $30b for failed S&Ls	Y	52. Cap MX missile deployment at 50	N
24. Allow use of force against Iraq	Y	53. Allow $3b for 2 stealth bombers	Y
25. Allow $15b in foreign aid for '91	Y	54. Publish bio-warfare experiments	Y
26. Revise & extend legal immigration	N	55. Raise minimum wage-veto override	N
27. Suspend aid to Angolan rebels	N	56. Bar transfer of FS-X technology	N
28. Democratic tax plan proposals	Y	57. Cut defense and raise domestic $	X
29. Cut defense 5% across the board	N	58. Uniform poll closing in 48 states	?

Presidential Support Score: 1991 - 58%   1990 - 56%

TAYLOR, GENE -- Mississippi 5th District [Democrat]. Counties of Covington, Forrest, George, Greene, Hancock, Harrison, Jackson, Jones (pt.), Lamar, Pearl River, Perry, Stone and Wayne. Prior Terms: 1989 (Special Election)-1992. Education: Tulane University; University of Southern Mississippi. Occupation: Container company sales; state senator.

1. Protection to Haitian refugees	N	15. Bar replacement of union strikers	N
2. Raise tax on wealthy; lower others	N	16. Hold foreign aid at $15b for '92	N
3. Investigate Reagan hostage delay	N	17. Restore space station funding	Y
4. Campaign finance revisions	Y	18. Civil Rights Act of 1991	N
5. Unpaid leave to care for children	N	19. Unlimited damages-discrimination	N
6. Restrict NEA use of funds	Y	20. Eliminate funds for supercollider	N
7. Bar race-bias claim/habeas corpus	Y	21. Terminate SDI except for research	N
8. Ban race as death sentence factor	Y	22. Req 7-day handgun waiting period	N
9. Exceptions to exclusionary rule	Y	23. Provide $30b for failed S&Ls	N
10. Allow sale of assault weapons	Y	24. Allow use of force against Iraq	N
11. Life in prison/abolish death penalty	N	25. Allow $15b in foreign aid for '91	N
12. Req conspiracy-price fixing cases	Y	26. Revise & extend legal immigration	N
13. Unemployment benefits extension	N	27. Suspend aid to Angolan rebels	N
14. Tissue use of aborted fetuses	N	28. Democratic tax plan proposals	N

TAYLOR, GENE (continued)

29. Cut defense 5% across the board	N	37. Reauthorize Amtrak-veto override	Y
30. Textile import quotas-veto override	Y	38. Retraining aid for coal miners	Y
31. Abortion service for military abroad	N	39. Suspend El Salvador military aid	Y
32. Limits on high income farmers	N	40. Expand child care aid/tax credit	N
33. Family medical leave-veto override	N	41. Raise House salary/omit honoraria	N
34. Req submission of balanced budget	Y	42. Toughen oil-spill liability	Y
35. Balanced budget amendment	Y	43. Restitution to Japanese interned	N
36. Amendment to ban flag desecration	Y	44. Protect Chinese & C.A. nationals	N

Presidential Support Score: 1991 - 55%   1990 - 49%

MISSOURI

CLAY, WILLIAM (Bill) -- Missouri 1st District [Democrat]. County of St. Louis (pt.), St. Louis City (pt.). Prior Terms: 1969-92. Born: April 30, 1931; St. Louis, MO. Education: St. Louis University (B.S.). Occupation: Real estate broker; manager, life insurance co. (1959-61); alderman (1959-64).

1. Protection to Haitian refugees	Y	40. Expand child care aid/tax credit	N
2. Raise tax on wealthy; lower others	N	41. Raise House salary/omit honoraria	Y
3. Investigate Reagan hostage delay	?	42. Toughen oil-spill liability	Y
4. Campaign finance revisions	Y	43. Restitution to Japanese interned	Y
5. Unpaid leave to care for children	Y	44. Protect Chinese & C.A. nationals	Y
6. Restrict NEA use of funds	N	45. Abortion $ for rape/incest cases	Y
7. Bar race-bias claim/habeas corpus	N	46. Allow religious schools to bar gays	N
8. Ban race as death sentence factor	N	47. Bar broadcaster fairness doctrine	N
9. Exceptions to exclusionary rule	N	48. Bar cap gains cut/reinstate IRA	Y
10. Allow sale of assault weapons	--	49. Bar unions equal voice in pension	N
11. Life in prison/abolish death penalty	Y	50. Bar assembly of chemical weapons	Y
12. Req conspiracy-price fixing cases	N	51. Ban plutonium/uranium production	Y
13. Unemployment benefits extension	Y	52. Cap MX missile deployment at 50	Y
14. Tissue use of aborted fetuses	Y	53. Allow $3b for 2 stealth bombers	?
15. Bar replacement of union strikers	Y	54. Publish bio-warfare experiments	Y
16. Hold foreign aid at $15b for '92	Y	55. Raise minimum wage-veto override	Y
17. Restore space station funding	N	56. Bar transfer of FS-X technology	Y
18. Civil Rights Act of 1991	Y	57. Cut defense and raise domestic $	Y
19. Unlimited damages-discrimination	Y	58. Uniform poll closing in 48 states	Y
20. Eliminate funds for supercollider	N	59. Req foreign investment disclosure	Y
21. Terminate SDI except for research	Y	60. Textile import quotas-veto override	Y
22. Req 7-day handgun waiting period	Y	61. Bar abortion funding in Wash, DC	N
23. Provide $30b for failed S&Ls	N	62. Notify spouses of AIDS+ carriers	N
24. Allow use of force against Iraq	N	63. Seize conveyance-drug trafficking	?
25. Allow $15b in foreign aid for '91	?	64. South Africa sanctions	Y
26. Revise & extend legal immigration	Y	65. 60 days' notice of plant closings	Y
27. Suspend aid to Angolan rebels	Y	66. Close unneeded military bases	N
28. Democratic tax plan proposals	Y	67. Keep welfare reform within $2.8b	N
29. Cut defense 5% across the board	Y	68. Allow children housing exclusion	N
30. Textile import quotas-veto override	Y	69. Shift $400m of NASA to homeless	Y
31. Abortion service for military abroad	Y	70. Cap Medicare patients' liability	Y
32. Limits on high income farmers	N	71. Prohibit employee polygraph testing	Y
33. Family medical leave-veto override	Y	72. Allow CIA to fund Contras	N
34. Req submission of balanced budget	Y	73. Revise unfair trade practices	Y
35. Balanced budget amendment	N	74. Focus SDI on accidental launch	Y
36. Amendment to ban flag desecration	N	75. Bar Air Force $ for MX missile	Y
37. Reauthorize Amtrak-veto override	Y	76. Allow "real" increase in defense	N
38. Retraining aid for coal miners	Y	77. Troop reduction in Europe of 50%	Y
39. Suspend El Salvador military aid	Y	78. Ban nuclear tests above 1 kiloton	Y

CLAY, WILLIAM (Bill) (continued)

79.	Ban anti-satellite missile tests	Y	112. Superfund waste cleanup of $10b	Y
80.	Observe certain limits of SALT II	Y	113. 90 days notice of plant closings	Y
81.	Restore four Civil Rights laws	Y	114. $20b in Medicare cuts/tax increases	Y
82.	Prohibit aliens as strikebreakers	Y	115. Spending cuts and tax increases	Y
83.	Allow military malpractice suits	?	116. Set school lunch lmt-250% poverty	N
84.	Approval of $36m in Contra aid	N	117. $75m for youth work projects	Y
85.	$18b deficit reduction compromise	N	118. Allow Angolan military assistance	N
86.	Welfare reform of $5.7b for 5 years	Y	119. Suspend defense payments for abuse	Y
87.	Raise taxes $12b/cut spending $3b	Y	120. Drop SS COLAs/$12b tax increase	N
88.	Board to assess occupational risk	Y	121. Approve $1.5b for 21 MX missiles	N
89.	Balanced budget by '93-via targets	Y	122. Emergency farm credit/revisions	Y
90.	Bar licensing of two nuclear plants	Y	123. Duty on Taiwan/Hong Kong/S Korea	Y
91.	Remove victims compensation cap	Y	124. Limit steel imports to 17%	Y
92.	Catastrophic health insurance	Y	125. Cut $ to schools that bar prayer	N
93.	Ban airline smoking-2 hours or less	?	126. $50b-taxes; cut Medicare/spending	N
94.	$1b/two year aid for the homeless	Y	127. Limit Pershing II/cruise in Europe	Y
95.	Bar non-unions in union companies	Y	128. Delete $7.1b for 34 B-1 bombers	Y
96.	Increase FSLIC rescue to $15b	Y	129. Bar purchase of Sergeant York guns	Y
97.	Impose quotas to lower trade deficit	Y	130. El Salvador military/economic aid	N
98.	Reduce discretionary budget 21%	N	131. Bar mining of Nicaraguan waters	Y
99.	Immigration reform/alien amnesty	Y	132. Physician fee freeze for Medicare	N
100.	South Africa sanctions-veto override	Y	133. $49b in "sin"/phone/insurance taxes	Y
101.	Tax overhaul to revise income tax	N	134. Allow sale of Conrail	N
102.	Use of military in drug war	N	135. Equal Rights Amendment	Y
103.	Delete 12 MX/add conventional wpn	?	136. Authorize Marines in Lebanon	N
104.	Raise speed limit to 65 mph	N	137. Eminent domain for coal companies	N
105.	Require Pentagon to buy US goods	?	138. Prohibit EPA clean air sanctions	?
106.	AIDS insurance non-discrimination	Y	139. SS retirement age increase/reforms	N
107.	Prohibit Saudi arms sales	Y	140. Auto domestic content requirement	Y
108.	Ease Gun Control Act of 1968	N	141. Delete jobs program funding	N
109.	Bar interstate handgun transport	Y	142. Highway-gas tax bill	Y
110.	Make company emissions known	Y	143. Cut $5b from defense for Medicare	Y
111.	Allow toxic victims to sue in fed ct	Y	144. Emergency housing aid of $1b	Y

Presidential Support Score: 1991 - 24%   1990 - 16%

HORN, JOAN KELLY -- Missouri 2nd District [Democrat]. Counties of St. Charles (pt.) and St. Louis (pt.). Prior Term: 1991-92. Born: October 18, 1936; St. Louis, MO. Education: St. Louis University; University of Missouri-St. Louis (B.A., M.A.). Occupation: Pre-school and elementary school teacher; pre-school founder; graduate research and teaching assistant; university adjunct professor; member, St. Louis County Office of Community Development (1977-80); St. Louis city housing authority contract officer and executive director staff member (1980-82); founder and co-principal, research and planning firm (1975-90).

1.	Protection to Haitian refugees	Y	13. Unemployment benefits extension	Y
2.	Raise tax on wealthy; lower others	N	14. Tissue use of aborted fetuses	Y
3.	Investigate Reagan hostage delay	Y	15. Bar replacement of union strikers	Y
4.	Campaign finance revisions	Y	16. Hold foreign aid at $15b for '92	Y
5.	Unpaid leave to care for children	Y	17. Restore space station funding	Y
6.	Restrict NEA use of funds	N	18. Civil Rights Act of 1991	Y
7.	Bar race-bias claim/habeas corpus	N	19. Unlimited damages-discrimination	Y
8.	Ban race as death sentence factor	N	20. Eliminate funds for supercollider	Y
9.	Exceptions to exclusionary rule	N	21. Terminate SDI except for research	N
10.	Allow sale of assault weapons	N	22. Req 7-day handgun waiting period	Y
11.	Life in prison/abolish death penalty	N	23. Provide $30b for failed S&Ls	Y
12.	Req conspiracy-price fixing cases	Y	24. Allow use of force against Iraq	N

Presidential Support Score: 1991 - 30%

GEPHARDT, RICHARD A. -- Missouri 3rd District [Democrat]. Counties of Jefferson and St. Louis (pt.), St. Louis City (pt.). Prior Terms: 1977-92. Born: January 31, 1941; St. Louis,

GEPHARDT, RICHARD A. (continued)

MO. Education: Northwestern University (B.S.);Michigan Law School (J.D.). Military Service: Missouri Air National Guard, 1965-1971. Occupation: Attorney; alderman (1971-77).

1.	Protection to Haitian refugees	Y	61.	Bar abortion funding in Wash, DC	Y
2.	Raise tax on wealthy; lower others	N	62.	Notify spouses of AIDS+ carriers	X
3.	Investigate Reagan hostage delay	Y	63.	Seize conveyance-drug trafficking	N
4.	Campaign finance revisions	Y	64.	South Africa sanctions	#
5.	Unpaid leave to care for children	Y	65.	60 days' notice of plant closings	Y
6.	Restrict NEA use of funds	N	66.	Close unneeded military bases	N
7.	Bar race-bias claim/habeas corpus	N	67.	Keep welfare reform within $2.8b	N
8.	Ban race as death sentence factor	N	68.	Allow children housing exclusion	N
9.	Exceptions to exclusionary rule	N	69.	Shift $400m of NASA to homeless	Y
10.	Allow sale of assault weapons	Y	70.	Cap Medicare patients' liability	?
11.	Life in prison/abolish death penalty	N	71.	Prohibit employee polygraph testing	Y
12.	Req conspiracy-price fixing cases	N	72.	Allow CIA to fund Contras	N
13.	Unemployment benefits extension	Y	73.	Revise unfair trade practices	Y
14.	Tissue use of aborted fetuses	Y	74.	Focus SDI on accidental launch	Y
15.	Bar replacement of union strikers	Y	75.	Bar Air Force $ for MX missile	Y
16.	Hold foreign aid at $15b for '92	Y	76.	Allow "real" increase in defense	N
17.	Restore space station funding	Y	77.	Troop reduction in Europe of 50%	N
18.	Civil Rights Act of 1991	Y	78.	Ban nuclear tests above 1 kiloton	Y
19.	Unlimited damages-discrimination	Y	79.	Ban anti-satellite missile tests	Y
20.	Eliminate funds for supercollider	N	80.	Observe certain limits of SALT II	Y
21.	Terminate SDI except for research	Y	81.	Restore four Civil Rights laws	?
22.	Req 7-day handgun waiting period	Y	82.	Prohibit aliens as strikebreakers	?
23.	Provide $30b for failed S&Ls	Y	83.	Allow military malpractice suits	?
24.	Allow use of force against Iraq	N	84.	Approval of $36m in Contra aid	N
25.	Allow $15b in foreign aid for '91	Y	85.	$18b deficit reduction compromise	?
26.	Revise & extend legal immigration	Y	86.	Welfare reform of $5.7b for 5 years	#
27.	Suspend aid to Angolan rebels	Y	87.	Raise taxes $12b/cut spending $3b	#
28.	Democratic tax plan proposals	Y	88.	Board to assess occupational risk	#
29.	Cut defense 5% across the board	N	89.	Balanced budget by '93-via targets	?
30.	Textile import quotas-veto override	Y	90.	Bar licensing of two nuclear plants	Y
31.	Abortion service for military abroad	?	91.	Remove victims compensation cap	#
32.	Limits on high income farmers	N	92.	Catastrophic health insurance	?
33.	Family medical leave-veto override	Y	93.	Ban airline smoking-2 hours or less	?
34.	Req submission of balanced budget	Y	94.	$1b/two year aid for the homeless	?
35.	Balanced budget amendment	N	95.	Bar non-unions in union companies	Y
36.	Amendment to ban flag desecration	N	96.	Increase FSLIC rescue to $15b	?
37.	Reauthorize Amtrak-veto override	Y	97.	Impose quotas to lower trade deficit	Y
38.	Retraining aid for coal miners	Y	98.	Reduce discretionary budget 21%	N
39.	Suspend El Salvador military aid	Y	99.	Immigration reform/alien amnesty	#
40.	Expand child care aid/tax credit	Y	100.	South Africa sanctions-veto override	Y
41.	Raise House salary/omit honoraria	Y	101.	Tax overhaul to revise income tax	Y
42.	Toughen oil-spill liability	Y	102.	Use of military in drug war	N
43.	Restitution to Japanese interned	Y	103.	Delete 12 MX/add conventional wpn	Y
44.	Protect Chinese & C.A. nationals	Y	104.	Raise speed limit to 65 mph	N
45.	Abortion $ for rape/incest cases	Y	105.	Require Pentagon to buy US goods	Y
46.	Allow religious schools to bar gays	N	106.	AIDS insurance non-discrimination	Y
47.	Bar broadcaster fairness doctrine	N	107.	Prohibit Saudi arms sales	Y
48.	Bar cap gains cut/reinstate IRA	Y	108.	Ease Gun Control Act of 1968	X
49.	Bar unions equal voice in pension	N	109.	Bar interstate handgun transport	?
50.	Bar assembly of chemical weapons	Y	110.	Make company emissions known	Y
51.	Ban plutonium/uranium production	Y	111.	Allow toxic victims to sue in fed ct	Y
52.	Cap MX missile deployment at 50	Y	112.	Superfund waste cleanup of $10b	N
53.	Allow $3b for 2 stealth bombers	N	113.	90 days notice of plant closings	Y
54.	Publish bio-warfare experiments	Y	114.	$20b in Medicare cuts/tax increases	Y
55.	Raise minimum wage-veto override	Y	115.	Spending cuts and tax increases	Y
56.	Bar transfer of FS-X technology	Y	116.	Set school lunch lmt-250% poverty	N
57.	Cut defense and raise domestic $	Y	117.	$75m for youth work projects	Y
58.	Uniform poll closing in 48 states	N	118.	Allow Angolan military assistance	N
59.	Req foreign investment disclosure	Y	119.	Suspend defense payments for abuse	Y
60.	Textile import quotas-veto override	Y	120.	Drop SS COLAs/$12b tax increase	Y

GEPHARDT, RICHARD A. (continued)

121. Approve $1.5b for 21 MX missiles	N	133. $49b in "sin"/phone/insurance taxes	Y
122. Emergency farm credit/revisions	Y	134. Allow sale of Conrail	N
123. Duty on Taiwan/Hong Kong/S Korea	Y	135. Equal Rights Amendment	Y
124. Limit steel imports to 17%	Y	136. Authorize Marines in Lebanon	Y
125. Cut $ to schools that bar prayer	N	137. Eminent domain for coal companies	N
126. $50b-taxes; cut Medicare/spending	Y	138. Prohibit EPA clean air sanctions	Y
127. Limit Pershing II/cruise in Europe	N	139. SS retirement age increase/reforms	N
128. Delete $7.1b for 34 B-1 bombers	Y	140. Auto domestic content requirement	Y
129. Bar purchase of Sergeant York guns	N	141. Delete jobs program funding	N
130. El Salvador military/economic aid	N	142. Highway-gas tax bill	Y
131. Bar mining of Nicaraguan waters	Y	143. Cut $5b from defense for Medicare	N
132. Physician fee freeze for Medicare	N	144. Emergency housing aid of $1b	N

Presidential Support Score: 1991 - 30% 1990 - 14%

SKELTON, IKE -- Missouri 4th District [Democrat]. Counties of Barton, Bates, Benton, Camden, Cass, Cole, Henry, Hickory, Jackson (pt.), Johnson, Laclede, Lafayette, Maries, Miller, Moniteau, Morgan, Pettis, Pulaski, St. Clair, Texas and Vernon. Prior Terms: 1977-92. Born: December 20, 1931; Lexington, MO. Education: University of Missouri (A.B., LL.B.); University of Edinburgh. Occupation: Prosecuting attorney (1957-60); special assistant, Missouri attorney general (1961-63); Missouri senator (1970-76).

1. Protection to Haitian refugees	N	42. Toughen oil-spill liability	?
2. Raise tax on wealthy; lower others	N	43. Restitution to Japanese interned	N
3. Investigate Reagan hostage delay	N	44. Protect Chinese & C.A. nationals	Y
4. Campaign finance revisions	Y	45. Abortion $ for rape/incest cases	N
5. Unpaid leave to care for children	N	46. Allow religious schools to bar gays	Y
6. Restrict NEA use of funds	Y	47. Bar broadcaster fairness doctrine	N
7. Bar race-bias claim/habeas corpus	Y	48. Bar cap gains cut/reinstate IRA	N
8. Ban race as death sentence factor	Y	49. Bar unions equal voice in pension	Y
9. Exceptions to exclusionary rule	Y	50. Bar assembly of chemical weapons	N
10. Allow sale of assault weapons	Y	51. Ban plutonium/uranium production	N
11. Life in prison/abolish death penalty	N	52. Cap MX missile deployment at 50	Y
12. Req conspiracy-price fixing cases	N	53. Allow $3b for 2 stealth bombers	Y
13. Unemployment benefits extension	Y	54. Publish bio-warfare experiments	N
14. Tissue use of aborted fetuses	N	55. Raise minimum wage-veto override	Y
15. Bar replacement of union strikers	Y	56. Bar transfer of FS-X technology	N
16. Hold foreign aid at $15b for '92	Y	57. Cut defense and raise domestic $	N
17. Restore space station funding	N	58. Uniform poll closing in 48 states	?
18. Civil Rights Act of 1991	Y	59. Req foreign investment disclosure	N
19. Unlimited damages-discrimination	N	60. Textile import quotas-veto override	Y
20. Eliminate funds for supercollider	N	61. Bar abortion funding in Wash, DC	Y
21. Terminate SDI except for research	N	62. Notify spouses of AIDS+ carriers	N
22. Req 7-day handgun waiting period	N	63. Seize conveyance-drug trafficking	Y
23. Provide $30b for failed S&Ls	Y	64. South Africa sanctions	?
24. Allow use of force against Iraq	Y	65. 60 days' notice of plant closings	N
25. Allow $15b in foreign aid for '91	?	66. Close unneeded military bases	N
26. Revise & extend legal immigration	?	67. Keep welfare reform within $2.8b	N
27. Suspend aid to Angolan rebels	N	68. Allow children housing exclusion	N
28. Democratic tax plan proposals	Y	69. Shift $400m of NASA to homeless	N
29. Cut defense 5% across the board	N	70. Cap Medicare patients' liability	Y
30. Textile import quotas-veto override	Y	71. Prohibit employee polygraph testing	?
31. Abortion service for military abroad	N	72. Allow CIA to fund Contras	Y
32. Limits on high income farmers	N	73. Revise unfair trade practices	Y
33. Family medical leave-veto override	N	74. Focus SDI on accidental launch	Y
34. Req submission of balanced budget	Y	75. Bar Air Force $ for MX missile	N
35. Balanced budget amendment	Y	76. Allow "real" increase in defense	Y
36. Amendment to ban flag desecration	Y	77. Troop reduction in Europe of 50%	N
37. Reauthorize Amtrak-veto override	Y	78. Ban nuclear tests above 1 kiloton	N
38. Retraining aid for coal miners	Y	79. Ban anti-satellite missile tests	N
39. Suspend El Salvador military aid	N	80. Observe certain limits of SALT II	N
40. Expand child care aid/tax credit	N	81. Restore four Civil Rights laws	Y
41. Raise House salary/omit honoraria	Y	82. Prohibit aliens as strikebreakers	Y

SKELTON, IKE (continued)

83. Allow military malpractice suits	Y	
84. Approval of $36m in Contra aid	Y	
85. $18b deficit reduction compromise	Y	
86. Welfare reform of $5.7b for 5 years	N	
87. Raise taxes $12b/cut spending $3b	N	
88. Board to assess occupational risk	N	
89. Balanced budget by '93-via targets	Y	
90. Bar licensing of two nuclear plants	Y	
91. Remove victims compensation cap	N	
92. Catastrophic health insurance	Y	
93. Ban airline smoking-2 hours or less	N	
94. $1b/two year aid for the homeless	Y	
95. Bar non-unions in union companies	Y	
96. Increase FSLIC rescue to $15b	N	
97. Impose quotas to lower trade deficit	Y	
98. Reduce discretionary budget 21%	Y	
99. Immigration reform/alien amnesty	N	
100. South Africa sanctions-veto override	?	
101. Tax overhaul to revise income tax	Y	
102. Use of military in drug war	N	
103. Delete 12 MX/add conventional wpn	N	
104. Raise speed limit to 65 mph	Y	
105. Require Pentagon to buy US goods	N	
106. AIDS insurance non-discrimination	Y	
107. Prohibit Saudi arms sales	Y	
108. Ease Gun Control Act of 1968	Y	
109. Bar interstate handgun transport	N	
110. Make company emissions known	N	
111. Allow toxic victims to sue in fed ct	N	
112. Superfund waste cleanup of $10b	Y	
113. 90 days notice of plant closings	Y	
114. $20b in Medicare cuts/tax increases	Y	
115. Spending cuts and tax increases	?	
116. Set school lunch lmt-250% poverty	N	
117. $75m for youth work projects	?	
118. Allow Angolan military assistance	Y	
119. Suspend defense payments for abuse	N	
120. Drop SS COLAs/$12b tax increase	N	
121. Approve $1.5b for 21 MX missiles	Y	
122. Emergency farm credit/revisions	Y	
123. Duty on Taiwan/Hong Kong/S Korea	Y	
124. Limit steel imports to 17%	Y	
125. Cut $ to schools that bar prayer	Y	
126. $50b-taxes; cut Medicare/spending	Y	
127. Limit Pershing II/cruise in Europe	N	
128. Delete $7.1b for 34 B-1 bombers	N	
129. Bar purchase of Sergeant York guns	N	
130. El Salvador military/economic aid	Y	
131. Bar mining of Nicaraguan waters	Y	
132. Physician fee freeze for Medicare	N	
133. $49b in "sin"/phone/insurance taxes	N	
134. Allow sale of Conrail	N	
135. Equal Rights Amendment	N	
136. Authorize Marines in Lebanon	N	
137. Eminent domain for coal companies	N	
138. Prohibit EPA clean air sanctions	?	
139. SS retirement age increase/reforms	N	
140. Auto domestic content requirement	Y	
141. Delete jobs program funding	N	
142. Highway-gas tax bill	?	
143. Cut $5b from defense for Medicare	N	
144. Emergency housing aid of $1b	Y	

Presidential Support Score: 1991 - 52%   1990 - 50%

WHEAT, ALAN -- Missouri 5th District [Democrat]. County of Jackson (pt.). Prior Terms: 1983-92. Born: October 16, 1951; San Antonio, TX. Education: Grinnell College (B.A.). Occupation: Economist; county executive aide; Missouri representative (1976-82).

1. Protection to Haitian refugees	Y	26. Revise & extend legal immigration	Y
2. Raise tax on wealthy; lower others	Y	27. Suspend aid to Angolan rebels	Y
3. Investigate Reagan hostage delay	Y	28. Democratic tax plan proposals	Y
4. Campaign finance revisions	Y	29. Cut defense 5% across the board	Y
5. Unpaid leave to care for children	Y	30. Textile import quotas-veto override	Y
6. Restrict NEA use of funds	N	31. Abortion service for military abroad	Y
7. Bar race-bias claim/habeas corpus	N	32. Limits on high income farmers	N
8. Ban race as death sentence factor	N	33. Family medical leave-veto override	Y
9. Exceptions to exclusionary rule	N	34. Req submission of balanced budget	N
10. Allow sale of assault weapons	N	35. Balanced budget amendment	N
11. Life in prison/abolish death penalty	Y	36. Amendment to ban flag desecration	N
12. Req conspiracy-price fixing cases	N	37. Reauthorize Amtrak-veto override	Y
13. Unemployment benefits extension	Y	38. Retraining aid for coal miners	Y
14. Tissue use of aborted fetuses	Y	39. Suspend El Salvador military aid	Y
15. Bar replacement of union strikers	Y	40. Expand child care aid/tax credit	Y
16. Hold foreign aid at $15b for '92	Y	41. Raise House salary/omit honoraria	Y
17. Restore space station funding	N	42. Toughen oil-spill liability	Y
18. Civil Rights Act of 1991	Y	43. Restitution to Japanese interned	Y
19. Unlimited damages-discrimination	Y	44. Protect Chinese & C.A. nationals	Y
20. Eliminate funds for supercollider	N	45. Abortion $ for rape/incest cases	Y
21. Terminate SDI except for research	Y	46. Allow religious schools to bar gays	N
22. Req 7-day handgun waiting period	Y	47. Bar broadcaster fairness doctrine	N
23. Provide $30b for failed S&Ls	N	48. Bar cap gains cut/reinstate IRA	Y
24. Allow use of force against Iraq	N	49. Bar unions equal voice in pension	N
25. Allow $15b in foreign aid for '91	N	50. Bar assembly of chemical weapons	Y

WHEAT, ALAN (continued)

51. Ban plutonium/uranium production	Y	
52. Cap MX missile deployment at 50	Y	
53. Allow $3b for 2 stealth bombers	N	
54. Publish bio-warfare experiments	Y	
55. Raise minimum wage-veto override	Y	
56. Bar transfer of FS-X technology	Y	
57. Cut defense and raise domestic $	Y	
58. Uniform poll closing in 48 states	Y	
59. Req foreign investment disclosure	Y	
60. Textile import quotas-veto override	Y	
61. Bar abortion funding in Wash, DC	N	
62. Notify spouses of AIDS+ carriers	N	
63. Seize conveyance-drug trafficking	N	
64. South Africa sanctions	Y	
65. 60 days' notice of plant closings	Y	
66. Close unneeded military bases	N	
67. Keep welfare reform within $2.8b	N	
68. Allow children housing exclusion	N	
69. Shift $400m of NASA to homeless	Y	
70. Cap Medicare patients' liability	N	
71. Prohibit employee polygraph testing	Y	
72. Allow CIA to fund Contras	N	
73. Revise unfair trade practices	Y	
74. Focus SDI on accidental launch	Y	
75. Bar Air Force $ for MX missile	Y	
76. Allow "real" increase in defense	N	
77. Troop reduction in Europe of 50%	Y	
78. Ban nuclear tests above 1 kiloton	Y	
79. Ban anti-satellite missile tests	Y	
80. Observe certain limits of SALT II	Y	
81. Restore four Civil Rights laws	Y	
82. Prohibit aliens as strikebreakers	Y	
83. Allow military malpractice suits	Y	
84. Approval of $36m in Contra aid	N	
85. $18b deficit reduction compromise	Y	
86. Welfare reform of $5.7b for 5 years	Y	
87. Raise taxes $12b/cut spending $3b	Y	
88. Board to assess occupational risk	Y	
89. Balanced budget by '93-via targets	N	
90. Bar licensing of two nuclear plants	Y	
91. Remove victims compensation cap	Y	
92. Catastrophic health insurance	Y	
93. Ban airline smoking-2 hours or less	Y	
94. $1b/two year aid for the homeless	Y	
95. Bar non-unions in union companies	Y	

96. Increase FSLIC rescue to $15b	N	
97. Impose quotas to lower trade deficit	Y	
98. Reduce discretionary budget 21%	N	
99. Immigration reform/alien amnesty	Y	
100. South Africa sanctions-veto override	Y	
101. Tax overhaul to revise income tax	Y	
102. Use of military in drug war	N	
103. Delete 12 MX/add conventional wpn	Y	
104. Raise speed limit to 65 mph	N	
105. Require Pentagon to buy US goods	Y	
106. AIDS insurance non-discrimination	Y	
107. Prohibit Saudi arms sales	Y	
108. Ease Gun Control Act of 1968	N	
109. Bar interstate handgun transport	Y	
110. Make company emissions known	Y	
111. Allow toxic victims to sue in fed ct	Y	
112. Superfund waste cleanup of $10b	Y	
113. 90 days notice of plant closings	Y	
114. $20b in Medicare cuts/tax increases	#	
115. Spending cuts and tax increases	Y	
116. Set school lunch lmt-250% poverty	N	
117. $75m for youth work projects	Y	
118. Allow Angolan military assistance	N	
119. Suspend defense payments for abuse	Y	
120. Drop SS COLAs/$12b tax increase	N	
121. Approve $1.5b for 21 MX missiles	N	
122. Emergency farm credit/revisions	Y	
123. Duty on Taiwan/Hong Kong/S Korea	Y	
124. Limit steel imports to 17%	Y	
125. Cut $ to schools that bar prayer	N	
126. $50b-taxes; cut Medicare/spending	Y	
127. Limit Pershing II/cruise in Europe	Y	
128. Delete $7.1b for 34 B-1 bombers	Y	
129. Bar purchase of Sergeant York guns	Y	
130. El Salvador military/economic aid	N	
131. Bar mining of Nicaraguan waters	Y	
132. Physician fee freeze for Medicare	N	
133. $49b in "sin"/phone/insurance taxes	Y	
134. Allow sale of Conrail	N	
135. Equal Rights Amendment	Y	
136. Authorize Marines in Lebanon	N	
137. Eminent domain for coal companies	N	
138. Prohibit EPA clean air sanctions	Y	
139. SS retirement age increase/reforms	N	

Presidential Support Score: 1991 - 23% 1990 - 13%

COLEMAN, E. THOMAS -- Missouri 6th District [Republican]. Counties of Andrew, Atchison, Buchanan, Caldwell, Carroll, Chariton, Clay, Clinton, Cooper, Daviess, De Kalb, Gentry, Grundy, Harrison, Holt, Howard, Jackson (pt.), Linn, Livingston, Mercer, Nodaway, Platte, Putnam, Ray, Saline, Schuyler, Sullivan and Worth. Prior Terms: 1976 (Special Election)-1992. Born: May 29, 1943; Kansas City, MO. Education: William Jewell College (B.A.); New York University (M.A.); Washington University (J.D.). Occupation: Attorney; assistant attorney general (1969-72); Missouri representative (1972-76).

1. Protection to Haitian refugees	N	
2. Raise tax on wealthy; lower others	N	
3. Investigate Reagan hostage delay	N	
4. Campaign finance revisions	N	
5. Unpaid leave to care for children	N	
6. Restrict NEA use of funds	N	

7. Bar race-bias claim/habeas corpus	Y	
8. Ban race as death sentence factor	Y	
9. Exceptions to exclusionary rule	Y	
10. Allow sale of assault weapons	Y	
11. Life in prison/abolish death penalty	N	
12. Req conspiracy-price fixing cases	Y	

COLEMAN, E. THOMAS (continued)

13. Unemployment benefits extension	N
14. Tissue use of aborted fetuses	N
15. Bar replacement of union strikers	N
16. Hold foreign aid at $15b for '92	Y
17. Restore space station funding	Y
18. Civil Rights Act of 1991	N
19. Unlimited damages-discrimination	N
20. Eliminate funds for supercollider	N
21. Terminate SDI except for research	?
22. Req 7-day handgun waiting period	Y
23. Provide $30b for failed S&Ls	?
24. Allow use of force against Iraq	Y
25. Allow $15b in foreign aid for '91	N
26. Revise & extend legal immigration	Y
27. Suspend aid to Angolan rebels	?
28. Democratic tax plan proposals	Y
29. Cut defense 5% across the board	N
30. Textile import quotas-veto override	Y
31. Abortion service for military abroad	N
32. Limits on high income farmers	N
33. Family medical leave-veto override	N
34. Req submission of balanced budget	N
35. Balanced budget amendment	Y
36. Amendment to ban flag desecration	N
37. Reauthorize Amtrak-veto override	N
38. Retraining aid for coal miners	N
39. Suspend El Salvador military aid	N
40. Expand child care aid/tax credit	N
41. Raise House salary/omit honoraria	Y
42. Toughen oil-spill liability	Y
43. Restitution to Japanese interned	Y
44. Protect Chinese & C.A. nationals	N
45. Abortion $ for rape/incest cases	N
46. Allow religious schools to bar gays	Y
47. Bar broadcaster fairness doctrine	N
48. Bar cap gains cut/reinstate IRA	N
49. Bar unions equal voice in pension	Y
50. Bar assembly of chemical weapons	N
51. Ban plutonium/uranium production	N
52. Cap MX missile deployment at 50	N
53. Allow $3b for 2 stealth bombers	Y
54. Publish bio-warfare experiments	Y
55. Raise minimum wage-veto override	N
56. Bar transfer of FS-X technology	Y
57. Cut defense and raise domestic $	N
58. Uniform poll closing in 48 states	Y
59. Req foreign investment disclosure	Y
60. Textile import quotas-veto override	Y
61. Bar abortion funding in Wash, DC	Y
62. Notify spouses of AIDS+ carriers	Y
63. Seize conveyance-drug trafficking	N
64. South Africa sanctions	N
65. 60 days' notice of plant closings	Y
66. Close unneeded military bases	Y
67. Keep welfare reform within $2.8b	Y
68. Allow children housing exclusion	N
69. Shift $400m of NASA to homeless	N
70. Cap Medicare patients' liability	Y
71. Prohibit employee polygraph testing	Y
72. Allow CIA to fund Contras	Y
73. Revise unfair trade practices	Y
74. Focus SDI on accidental launch	N
75. Bar Air Force $ for MX missile	N
76. Allow "real" increase in defense	Y

77. Troop reduction in Europe of 50%	N
78. Ban nuclear tests above 1 kiloton	N
79. Ban anti-satellite missile tests	N
80. Observe certain limits of SALT II	N
81. Restore four Civil Rights laws	N
82. Prohibit aliens as strikebreakers	Y
83. Allow military malpractice suits	Y
84. Approval of $36m in Contra aid	Y
85. $18b deficit reduction compromise	N
86. Welfare reform of $5.7b for 5 years	N
87. Raise taxes $12b/cut spending $3b	N
88. Board to assess occupational risk	N
89. Balanced budget by '93-via targets	Y
90. Bar licensing of two nuclear plants	N
91. Remove victims compensation cap	N
92. Catastrophic health insurance	Y
93. Ban airline smoking-2 hours or less	Y
94. $1b/two year aid for the homeless	Y
95. Bar non-unions in union companies	N
96. Increase FSLIC rescue to $15b	Y
97. Impose quotas to lower trade deficit	N
98. Reduce discretionary budget 21%	N
99. Immigration reform/alien amnesty	Y
100. South Africa sanctions-veto override	?
101. Tax overhaul to revise income tax	N
102. Use of military in drug war	Y
103. Delete 12 MX/add conventional wpn	N
104. Raise speed limit to 65 mph	Y
105. Require Pentagon to buy US goods	N
106. AIDS insurance non-discrimination	N
107. Prohibit Saudi arms sales	Y
108. Ease Gun Control Act of 1968	Y
109. Bar interstate handgun transport	Y
110. Make company emissions known	N
111. Allow toxic victims to sue in fed ct	N
112. Superfund waste cleanup of $10b	Y
113. 90 days notice of plant closings	N
114. $20b in Medicare cuts/tax increases	N
115. Spending cuts and tax increases	N
116. Set school lunch lmt-250% poverty	N
117. $75m for youth work projects	N
118. Allow Angolan military assistance	Y
119. Suspend defense payments for abuse	N
120. Drop SS COLAs/$12b tax increase	N
121. Approve $1.5b for 21 MX missiles	Y
122. Emergency farm credit/revisions	Y
123. Duty on Taiwan/Hong Kong/S Korea	N
124. Limit steel imports to 17%	N
125. Cut $ to schools that bar prayer	N
126. $50b-taxes; cut Medicare/spending	N
127. Limit Pershing II/cruise in Europe	N
128. Delete $7.1b for 34 B-1 bombers	N
129. Bar purchase of Sergeant York guns	?
130. El Salvador military/economic aid	Y
131. Bar mining of Nicaraguan waters	N
132. Physician fee freeze for Medicare	Y
133. $49b in "sin"/phone/insurance taxes	?
134. Allow sale of Conrail	Y
135. Equal Rights Amendment	N
136. Authorize Marines in Lebanon	Y
137. Eminent domain for coal companies	N
138. Prohibit EPA clean air sanctions	N
139. SS retirement age increase/reforms	Y
140. Auto domestic content requirement	Y

COLEMAN, E. THOMAS (continued)

141. Delete jobs program funding	Y	143. Cut $5b from defense for Medicare	Y
142. Highway-gas tax bill	N	144. Emergency housing aid of $1b	Y

Presidential Support Score: 1991 - 77%   1990 - 64%

HANCOCK, MEL -- Missouri 7th District [Republican]. Counties of Barry, Cedar, Christian, Dade, Dallas, Douglas, Greene, Jasper, Lawrence, McDonald, Newton, Ozark, Polk, Stone, Taney, Webster and Wright. Prior Terms: 1989-92. Born: September 14, 1929; Cape Fair, MO. Education: Southwest Missouri State College (B.S.). Military Service: U.S. Air Force and Air Force Reserves. Occupation: International Harvester Co. employee; insurance executive; security equipment leasing company founder; state tax and spending limitation activist.

1. Protection to Haitian refugees	N	30. Textile import quotas-veto override	N
2. Raise tax on wealthy; lower others	N	31. Abortion service for military abroad	N
3. Investigate Reagan hostage delay	N	32. Limits on high income farmers	Y
4. Campaign finance revisions	N	33. Family medical leave-veto override	N
5. Unpaid leave to care for children	N	34. Req submission of balanced budget	N
6. Restrict NEA use of funds	Y	35. Balanced budget amendment	Y
7. Bar race-bias claim/habeas corpus	Y	36. Amendment to ban flag desecration	Y
8. Ban race as death sentence factor	Y	37. Reauthorize Amtrak-veto override	N
9. Exceptions to exclusionary rule	Y	38. Retraining aid for coal miners	N
10. Allow sale of assault weapons	Y	39. Suspend El Salvador military aid	N
11. Life in prison/abolish death penalty	N	40. Expand child care aid/tax credit	N
12. Req conspiracy-price fixing cases	Y	41. Raise House salary/omit honoraria	N
13. Unemployment benefits extension	N	42. Toughen oil-spill liability	N
14. Tissue use of aborted fetuses	N	43. Restitution to Japanese interned	N
15. Bar replacement of union strikers	N	44. Protect Chinese & C.A. nationals	N
16. Hold foreign aid at $15b for '92	N	45. Abortion $ for rape/incest cases	N
17. Restore space station funding	Y	46. Allow religious schools to bar gays	Y
18. Civil Rights Act of 1991	N	47. Bar broadcaster fairness doctrine	Y
19. Unlimited damages-discrimination	N	48. Bar cap gains cut/reinstate IRA	N
20. Eliminate funds for supercollider	Y	49. Bar unions equal voice in pension	Y
21. Terminate SDI except for research	N	50. Bar assembly of chemical weapons	N
22. Req 7-day handgun waiting period	N	51. Ban plutonium/uranium production	N
23. Provide $30b for failed S&Ls	Y	52. Cap MX missile deployment at 50	N
24. Allow use of force against Iraq	Y	53. Allow $3b for 2 stealth bombers	Y
25. Allow $15b in foreign aid for '91	N	54. Publish bio-warfare experiments	N
26. Revise & extend legal immigration	N	55. Raise minimum wage-veto override	N
27. Suspend aid to Angolan rebels	N	56. Bar transfer of FS-X technology	N
28. Democratic tax plan proposals	N	57. Cut defense and raise domestic $	N
29. Cut defense 5% across the board	N	58. Uniform poll closing in 48 states	N

Presidential Support Score: 1991 - 79%   1990 - 80%

EMERSON, BILL -- Missouri 8th District [Republican]. Counties of Bollinger, Butler, Cape Girardeau, Carter, Crawford, Dent, Dunklin, Franklin (pt.), Howell, Iron, Madison, Mississippi, New Madrid, Oregon, Pemiscot, Perry, Phelps, Reynolds, Ripley, Ste. Genevieve, St. Francois, Scott, Shannon, Stoddard, Washington and Wayne. Prior Terms: 1981-92. Born: January 1, 1938; St. Louis, MO. Education: Westminster College (B.A.); University of Baltimore (LL.B.). Military Service: U.S. Air Force Reserve. Occupation: Page, U.S. House of Representatives; congressional administrative assistant; director, government relations, Fairchild Industries; director, public affairs, Interstate Natural Gas Assn.; director, federal relations, TRW, Inc.; executive assistant to the chairman of the Federal Election Commission.

1. Protection to Haitian refugees	N	7. Bar race-bias claim/habeas corpus	Y
2. Raise tax on wealthy; lower others	N	8. Ban race as death sentence factor	Y
3. Investigate Reagan hostage delay	N	9. Exceptions to exclusionary rule	Y
4. Campaign finance revisions	N	10. Allow sale of assault weapons	Y
5. Unpaid leave to care for children	N	11. Life in prison/abolish death penalty	N
6. Restrict NEA use of funds	Y	12. Req conspiracy-price fixing cases	Y

EMERSON, BILL (continued)

13. Unemployment benefits extension	Y	
14. Tissue use of aborted fetuses	N	
15. Bar replacement of union strikers	N	
16. Hold foreign aid at $15b for '92	Y	
17. Restore space station funding	Y	
18. Civil Rights Act of 1991	N	
19. Unlimited damages-discrimination	N	
20. Eliminate funds for supercollider	N	
21. Terminate SDI except for research	N	
22. Req 7-day handgun waiting period	N	
23. Provide $30b for failed S&Ls	Y	
24. Allow use of force against Iraq	Y	
25. Allow $15b in foreign aid for '91	N	
26. Revise & extend legal immigration	N	
27. Suspend aid to Angolan rebels	N	
28. Democratic tax plan proposals	N	
29. Cut defense 5% across the board	N	
30. Textile import quotas-veto override	Y	
31. Abortion service for military abroad	N	
32. Limits on high income farmers	N	
33. Family medical leave-veto override	N	
34. Req submission of balanced budget	Y	
35. Balanced budget amendment	Y	
36. Amendment to ban flag desecration	Y	
37. Reauthorize Amtrak-veto override	Y	
38. Retraining aid for coal miners	Y	
39. Suspend El Salvador military aid	N	
40. Expand child care aid/tax credit	N	
41. Raise House salary/omit honoraria	N	
42. Toughen oil-spill liability	N	
43. Restitution to Japanese interned	N	
44. Protect Chinese & C.A. nationals	--	
45. Abortion $ for rape/incest cases	N	
46. Allow religious schools to bar gays	Y	
47. Bar broadcaster fairness doctrine	Y	
48. Bar cap gains cut/reinstate IRA	N	
49. Bar unions equal voice in pension	Y	
50. Bar assembly of chemical weapons	N	
51. Ban plutonium/uranium production	N	
52. Cap MX missile deployment at 50	N	
53. Allow $3b for 2 stealth bombers	Y	
54. Publish bio-warfare experiments	Y	
55. Raise minimum wage-veto override	N	
56. Bar transfer of FS-X technology	Y	
57. Cut defense and raise domestic $	N	
58. Uniform poll closing in 48 states	?	
59. Req foreign investment disclosure	Y	
60. Textile import quotas-veto override	Y	
61. Bar abortion funding in Wash, DC	Y	
62. Notify spouses of AIDS+ carriers	Y	
63. Seize conveyance-drug trafficking	Y	
64. South Africa sanctions	N	
65. 60 days' notice of plant closings	Y	
66. Close unneeded military bases	Y	
67. Keep welfare reform within $2.8b	Y	
68. Allow children housing exclusion	N	
69. Shift $400m of NASA to homeless	N	
70. Cap Medicare patients' liability	Y	
71. Prohibit employee polygraph testing	N	
72. Allow CIA to fund Contras	Y	
73. Revise unfair trade practices	Y	
74. Focus SDI on accidental launch	N	
75. Bar Air Force $ for MX missile	N	
76. Allow "real" increase in defense	Y	

77. Troop reduction in Europe of 50%	N	
78. Ban nuclear tests above 1 kiloton	?	
79. Ban anti-satellite missile tests	?	
80. Observe certain limits of SALT II	?	
81. Restore four Civil Rights laws	N	
82. Prohibit aliens as strikebreakers	Y	
83. Allow military malpractice suits	Y	
84. Approval of $36m in Contra aid	Y	
85. $18b deficit reduction compromise	N	
86. Welfare reform of $5.7b for 5 years	N	
87. Raise taxes $12b/cut spending $3b	N	
88. Board to assess occupational risk	N	
89. Balanced budget by '93-via targets	Y	
90. Bar licensing of two nuclear plants	N	
91. Remove victims compensation cap	N	
92. Catastrophic health insurance	Y	
93. Ban airline smoking-2 hours or less	N	
94. $1b/two year aid for the homeless	Y	
95. Bar non-unions in union companies	N	
96. Increase FSLIC rescue to $15b	N	
97. Impose quotas to lower trade deficit	N	
98. Reduce discretionary budget 21%	Y	
99. Immigration reform/alien amnesty	N	
100. South Africa sanctions-veto override	N	
101. Tax overhaul to revise income tax	Y	
102. Use of military in drug war	Y	
103. Delete 12 MX/add conventional wpn	N	
104. Raise speed limit to 65 mph	Y	
105. Require Pentagon to buy US goods	Y	
106. AIDS insurance non-discrimination	N	
107. Prohibit Saudi arms sales	Y	
108. Ease Gun Control Act of 1968	Y	
109. Bar interstate handgun transport	N	
110. Make company emissions known	N	
111. Allow toxic victims to sue in fed ct	N	
112. Superfund waste cleanup of $10b	N	
113. 90 days notice of plant closings	N	
114. $20b in Medicare cuts/tax increases	N	
115. Spending cuts and tax increases	N	
116. Set school lunch lmt-250% poverty	Y	
117. $75m for youth work projects	N	
118. Allow Angolan military assistance	Y	
119. Suspend defense payments for abuse	N	
120. Drop SS COLAs/$12b tax increase	N	
121. Approve $1.5b for 21 MX missiles	Y	
122. Emergency farm credit/revisions	Y	
123. Duty on Taiwan/Hong Kong/S Korea	N	
124. Limit steel imports to 17%	N	
125. Cut $ to schools that bar prayer	Y	
126. $50b-taxes; cut Medicare/spending	N	
127. Limit Pershing II/cruise in Europe	N	
128. Delete $7.1b for 34 B-1 bombers	N	
129. Bar purchase of Sergeant York guns	N	
130. El Salvador military/economic aid	Y	
131. Bar mining of Nicaraguan waters	N	
132. Physician fee freeze for Medicare	N	
133. $49b in "sin"/phone/insurance taxes	N	
134. Allow sale of Conrail	Y	
135. Equal Rights Amendment	N	
136. Authorize Marines in Lebanon	Y	
137. Eminent domain for coal companies	N	
138. Prohibit EPA clean air sanctions	Y	
139. SS retirement age increase/reforms	Y	
140. Auto domestic content requirement	N	

EMERSON, BILL (continued)

141. Delete jobs program funding	Y	143. Cut $5b from defense for Medicare	N
142. Highway-gas tax bill	N	144. Emergency housing aid of $1b	Y

Presidential Support Score: 1991 - 71%   1990 - 57%

VOLKMER, HAROLD L. -- Missouri 9th District [Democrat]. Counties of Adair, Audrain, Boone, Callaway, Clark, Franklin (pt.), Gasconade, Knox, Lewis, Lincoln, Macon, Marion, Monroe, Montgomery, Osage, Pike, Ralls, Randolph, St. Charles (pt.), Scotland, Shelby and Warren. Prior Terms: 1977-92. Born: April 4, 1931; Jefferson City, MO. Education: St. Louis University; University of Missouri (LL.B.). Military Service: U.S. Army, 1955-57. Occupation: Assistant attorney general; prosecuting attorney (1960-66); Missouri representative.

1. Protection to Haitian refugees	N	51. Ban plutonium/uranium production	Y
2. Raise tax on wealthy; lower others	Y	52. Cap MX missile deployment at 50	Y
3. Investigate Reagan hostage delay	N	53. Allow $3b for 2 stealth bombers	Y
4. Campaign finance revisions	Y	54. Publish bio-warfare experiments	Y
5. Unpaid leave to care for children	Y	55. Raise minimum wage-veto override	Y
6. Restrict NEA use of funds	N	56. Bar transfer of FS-X technology	Y
7. Bar race-bias claim/habeas corpus	Y	57. Cut defense and raise domestic $	N
8. Ban race as death sentence factor	Y	58. Uniform poll closing in 48 states	N
9. Exceptions to exclusionary rule	Y	59. Req foreign investment disclosure	Y
10. Allow sale of assault weapons	Y	60. Textile import quotas-veto override	Y
11. Life in prison/abolish death penalty	N	61. Bar abortion funding in Wash, DC	Y
12. Req conspiracy-price fixing cases	N	62. Notify spouses of AIDS+ carriers	N
13. Unemployment benefits extension	Y	63. Seize conveyance-drug trafficking	Y
14. Tissue use of aborted fetuses	N	64. South Africa sanctions	Y
15. Bar replacement of union strikers	Y	65. 60 days' notice of plant closings	Y
16. Hold foreign aid at $15b for '92	N	66. Close unneeded military bases	Y
17. Restore space station funding	Y	67. Keep welfare reform within $2.8b	Y
18. Civil Rights Act of 1991	Y	68. Allow children housing exclusion	N
19. Unlimited damages-discrimination	N	69. Shift $400m of NASA to homeless	N
20. Eliminate funds for supercollider	N	70. Cap Medicare patients' liability	Y
21. Terminate SDI except for research	N	71. Prohibit employee polygraph testing	Y
22. Req 7-day handgun waiting period	N	72. Allow CIA to fund Contras	N
23. Provide $30b for failed S&Ls	Y	73. Revise unfair trade practices	Y
24. Allow use of force against Iraq	Y	74. Focus SDI on accidental launch	Y
25. Allow $15b in foreign aid for '91	N	75. Bar Air Force $ for MX missile	N
26. Revise & extend legal immigration	N	76. Allow "real" increase in defense	N
27. Suspend aid to Angolan rebels	Y	77. Troop reduction in Europe of 50%	#
28. Democratic tax plan proposals	Y	78. Ban nuclear tests above 1 kiloton	#
29. Cut defense 5% across the board	Y	79. Ban anti-satellite missile tests	?
30. Textile import quotas-veto override	Y	80. Observe certain limits of SALT II	Y
31. Abortion service for military abroad	N	81. Restore four Civil Rights laws	Y
32. Limits on high income farmers	N	82. Prohibit aliens as strikebreakers	Y
33. Family medical leave-veto override	Y	83. Allow military malpractice suits	Y
34. Req submission of balanced budget	Y	84. Approval of $36m in Contra aid	N
35. Balanced budget amendment	Y	85. $18b deficit reduction compromise	Y
36. Amendment to ban flag desecration	Y	86. Welfare reform of $5.7b for 5 years	Y
37. Reauthorize Amtrak-veto override	Y	87. Raise taxes $12b/cut spending $3b	Y
38. Retraining aid for coal miners	Y	88. Board to assess occupational risk	Y
39. Suspend El Salvador military aid	Y	89. Balanced budget by '93-via targets	Y
40. Expand child care aid/tax credit	Y	90. Bar licensing of two nuclear plants	N
41. Raise House salary/omit honoraria	Y	91. Remove victims compensation cap	N
42. Toughen oil-spill liability	N	92. Catastrophic health insurance	Y
43. Restitution to Japanese interned	N	93. Ban airline smoking-2 hours or less	N
44. Protect Chinese & C.A. nationals	Y	94. $1b/two year aid for the homeless	Y
45. Abortion $ for rape/incest cases	N	95. Bar non-unions in union companies	Y
46. Allow religious schools to bar gays	Y	96. Increase FSLIC rescue to $15b	N
47. Bar broadcaster fairness doctrine	N	97. Impose quotas to lower trade deficit	Y
48. Bar cap gains cut/reinstate IRA	Y	98. Reduce discretionary budget 21%	Y
49. Bar unions equal voice in pension	N	99. Immigration reform/alien amnesty	N
50. Bar assembly of chemical weapons	N	100. South Africa sanctions-veto override	Y

VOLKMER, HAROLD L. (continued)

101. Tax overhaul to revise income tax	Y	123. Duty on Taiwan/Hong Kong/S Korea	Y
102. Use of military in drug war	Y	124. Limit steel imports to 17%	Y
103. Delete 12 MX/add conventional wpn	Y	125. Cut $ to schools that bar prayer	Y
104. Raise speed limit to 65 mph	N	126. $50b-taxes; cut Medicare/spending	N
105. Require Pentagon to buy US goods	Y	127. Limit Pershing II/cruise in Europe	N
106. AIDS insurance non-discrimination	Y	128. Delete $7.1b for 34 B-1 bombers	N
107. Prohibit Saudi arms sales	Y	129. Bar purchase of Sergeant York guns	N
108. Ease Gun Control Act of 1968	Y	130. El Salvador military/economic aid	N
109. Bar interstate handgun transport	N	131. Bar mining of Nicaraguan waters	Y
110. Make company emissions known	Y	132. Physician fee freeze for Medicare	N
111. Allow toxic victims to sue in fed ct	N	133. $49b in "sin"/phone/insurance taxes	Y
112. Superfund waste cleanup of $10b	N	134. Allow sale of Conrail	N
113. 90 days notice of plant closings	Y	135. Equal Rights Amendment	Y
114. $20b in Medicare cuts/tax increases	N	136. Authorize Marines in Lebanon	N
115. Spending cuts and tax increases	N	137. Eminent domain for coal companies	N
116. Set school lunch lmt-250% poverty	N	138. Prohibit EPA clean air sanctions	Y
117. $75m for youth work projects	Y	139. SS retirement age increase/reforms	N
118. Allow Angolan military assistance	Y	140. Auto domestic content requirement	Y
119. Suspend defense payments for abuse	N	141. Delete jobs program funding	N
120. Drop SS COLAs/$12b tax increase	N	142. Highway-gas tax bill	N
121. Approve $1.5b for 21 MX missiles	N	143. Cut $5b from defense for Medicare	Y
122. Emergency farm credit/revisions	Y	144. Emergency housing aid of $1b	Y

Presidential Support Score: 1991 - 49%   1990 - 35%

MONTANA

WILLIAMS, PAT -- Montana 1st District [Democrat]. Counties of Beaverhead, Broadwater, Deer Lodge, Flathead, Gallatin, Glacier, Granite, Jefferson, Lake, Lewis and Clark, Liberty, Lincoln, Madison, Meagher, Mineral, Missoula, Park, Pondera, Powell, Ravalli, Sanders, Silver Bow, Toole and Yellowstone National Park. Prior Terms: 1979-92. Born: October 30, 1937; Helena, MT. Education: University of Montana; University of Denver (B.A.); Western Montana College. Military Service: U.S. Army, 1960-61. Occupation: Teacher (1960-66); Montana representative (1966-68); congressional executive assistant (1969-71); Montana state coordinator, Family Education Program (1971-78); member, State Legislative Reapportionment Commission (1973); member, Montana Employment and Training Council (1972-78).

1. Protection to Haitian refugees	#	21. Terminate SDI except for research	Y
2. Raise tax on wealthy; lower others	Y	22. Req 7-day handgun waiting period	N
3. Investigate Reagan hostage delay	Y	23. Provide $30b for failed S&Ls	N
4. Campaign finance revisions	Y	24. Allow use of force against Iraq	N
5. Unpaid leave to care for children	Y	25. Allow $15b in foreign aid for '91	N
6. Restrict NEA use of funds	N	26. Revise & extend legal immigration	Y
7. Bar race-bias claim/habeas corpus	N	27. Suspend aid to Angolan rebels	?
8. Ban race as death sentence factor	N	28. Democratic tax plan proposals	Y
9. Exceptions to exclusionary rule	N	29. Cut defense 5% across the board	N
10. Allow sale of assault weapons	Y	30. Textile import quotas-veto override	Y
11. Life in prison/abolish death penalty	N	31. Abortion service for military abroad	Y
12. Req conspiracy-price fixing cases	N	32. Limits on high income farmers	N
13. Unemployment benefits extension	Y	33. Family medical leave-veto override	Y
14. Tissue use of aborted fetuses	Y	34. Req submission of balanced budget	Y
15. Bar replacement of union strikers	Y	35. Balanced budget amendment	N
16. Hold foreign aid at $15b for '92	N	36. Amendment to ban flag desecration	N
17. Restore space station funding	?	37. Reauthorize Amtrak-veto override	Y
18. Civil Rights Act of 1991	Y	38. Retraining aid for coal miners	#
19. Unlimited damages-discrimination	Y	39. Suspend El Salvador military aid	Y
20. Eliminate funds for supercollider	Y	40. Expand child care aid/tax credit	N

WILLIAMS, PAT (continued)

41.	Raise House salary/omit honoraria	N	93.	Ban airline smoking-2 hours or less	N
42.	Toughen oil-spill liability	Y	94.	$1b/two year aid for the homeless	Y
43.	Restitution to Japanese interned	Y	95.	Bar non-unions in union companies	Y
44.	Protect Chinese & C.A. nationals	Y	96.	Increase FSLIC rescue to $15b	N
45.	Abortion $ for rape/incest cases	Y	97.	Impose quotas to lower trade deficit	Y
46.	Allow religious schools to bar gays	?	98.	Reduce discretionary budget 21%	N
47.	Bar broadcaster fairness doctrine	N	99.	Immigration reform/alien amnesty	Y
48.	Bar cap gains cut/reinstate IRA	Y	100.	South Africa sanctions-veto override	Y
49.	Bar unions equal voice in pension	N	101.	Tax overhaul to revise income tax	N
50.	Bar assembly of chemical weapons	Y	102.	Use of military in drug war	N
51.	Ban plutonium/uranium production	Y	103.	Delete 12 MX/add conventional wpn	Y
52.	Cap MX missile deployment at 50	Y	104.	Raise speed limit to 65 mph	Y
53.	Allow $3b for 2 stealth bombers	N	105.	Require Pentagon to buy US goods	Y
54.	Publish bio-warfare experiments	Y	106.	AIDS insurance non-discrimination	Y
55.	Raise minimum wage-veto override	Y	107.	Prohibit Saudi arms sales	Y
56.	Bar transfer of FS-X technology	?	108.	Ease Gun Control Act of 1968	Y
57.	Cut defense and raise domestic $	N	109.	Bar interstate handgun transport	N
58.	Uniform poll closing in 48 states	N	110.	Make company emissions known	Y
59.	Req foreign investment disclosure	Y	111.	Allow toxic victims to sue in fed ct	Y
60.	Textile import quotas-veto override	Y	112.	Superfund waste cleanup of $10b	Y
61.	Bar abortion funding in Wash, DC	N	113.	90 days notice of plant closings	Y
62.	Notify spouses of AIDS+ carriers	Y	114.	$20b in Medicare cuts/tax increases	Y
63.	Seize conveyance-drug trafficking	?	115.	Spending cuts and tax increases	Y
64.	South Africa sanctions	Y	116.	Set school lunch lmt-250% poverty	N
65.	60 days' notice of plant closings	Y	117.	$75m for youth work projects	Y
66.	Close unneeded military bases	N	118.	Allow Angolan military assistance	N
67.	Keep welfare reform within $2.8b	N	119.	Suspend defense payments for abuse	Y
68.	Allow children housing exclusion	N	120.	Drop SS COLAs/$12b tax increase	N
69.	Shift $400m of NASA to homeless	Y	121.	Approve $1.5b for 21 MX missiles	N
70.	Cap Medicare patients' liability	Y	122.	Emergency farm credit/revisions	Y
71.	Prohibit employee polygraph testing	Y	123.	Duty on Taiwan/Hong Kong/S Korea	?
72.	Allow CIA to fund Contras	N	124.	Limit steel imports to 17%	Y
73.	Revise unfair trade practices	Y	125.	Cut $ to schools that bar prayer	N
74.	Focus SDI on accidental launch	N	126.	$50b-taxes; cut Medicare/spending	N
75.	Bar Air Force $ for MX missile	Y	127.	Limit Pershing II/cruise in Europe	Y
76.	Allow "real" increase in defense	N	128.	Delete $7.1b for 34 B-1 bombers	Y
77.	Troop reduction in Europe of 50%	Y	129.	Bar purchase of Sergeant York guns	Y
78.	Ban nuclear tests above 1 kiloton	Y	130.	El Salvador military/economic aid	N
79.	Ban anti-satellite missile tests	Y	131.	Bar mining of Nicaraguan waters	Y
80.	Observe certain limits of SALT II	Y	132.	Physician fee freeze for Medicare	N
81.	Restore four Civil Rights laws	Y	133.	$49b in "sin"/phone/insurance taxes	Y
82.	Prohibit aliens as strikebreakers	Y	134.	Allow sale of Conrail	N
83.	Allow military malpractice suits	Y	135.	Equal Rights Amendment	Y
84.	Approval of $36m in Contra aid	N	136.	Authorize Marines in Lebanon	N
85.	$18b deficit reduction compromise	?	137.	Eminent domain for coal companies	N
86.	Welfare reform of $5.7b for 5 years	Y	138.	Prohibit EPA clean air sanctions	Y
87.	Raise taxes $12b/cut spending $3b	Y	139.	SS retirement age increase/reforms	N
88.	Board to assess occupational risk	Y	140.	Auto domestic content requirement	Y
89.	Balanced budget by '93-via targets	N	141.	Delete jobs program funding	N
90.	Bar licensing of two nuclear plants	Y	142.	Highway-gas tax bill	Y
91.	Remove victims compensation cap	N	143.	Cut $5b from defense for Medicare	Y
92.	Catastrophic health insurance	Y	144.	Emergency housing aid of $1b	Y

Presidential Support Score: 1991 - 31% 1990 - 24%

MARLENEE, RON -- Montana 2nd District [Republican]. Counties of Big Horn, Blaine, Carbon, Carter, Cascade, Chouteau, Custer, Daniels, Dawson, Fallon, Fergus, Garfield, Golden Valley, Hill, Judith Basin, McCone, Musselshell, Petroleum, Phillips, Powder River, Prairie, Richland, Roosevelt, Rosebud, Sheridan, Stillwater, Sweet Grass, Teton, Treasure, Valley, Wheatland, Wibaux and Yellowstone. Prior Terms: 1977-92. Born: August 8, 1935; Scobey, MT. Education: University of Montana; Montana State University. Occupation: Rancher, congressional committeeman (1975-76).

MARLENEE, RON (continued)

1. Protection to Haitian refugees	X
2. Raise tax on wealthy; lower others	N
3. Investigate Reagan hostage delay	N
4. Campaign finance revisions	Y
5. Unpaid leave to care for children	N
6. Restrict NEA use of funds	Y
7. Bar race-bias claim/habeas corpus	Y
8. Ban race as death sentence factor	Y
9. Exceptions to exclusionary rule	Y
10. Allow sale of assault weapons	Y
11. Life in prison/abolish death penalty	N
12. Req conspiracy-price fixing cases	Y
13. Unemployment benefits extension	?
14. Tissue use of aborted fetuses	N
15. Bar replacement of union strikers	N
16. Hold foreign aid at $15b for '92	N
17. Restore space station funding	Y
18. Civil Rights Act of 1991	N
19. Unlimited damages-discrimination	N
20. Eliminate funds for supercollider	?
21. Terminate SDI except for research	N
22. Req 7-day handgun waiting period	N
23. Provide $30b for failed S&Ls	N
24. Allow use of force against Iraq	Y
25. Allow $15b in foreign aid for '91	N
26. Revise & extend legal immigration	N
27. Suspend aid to Angolan rebels	N
28. Democratic tax plan proposals	N
29. Cut defense 5% across the board	N
30. Textile import quotas-veto override	N
31. Abortion service for military abroad	N
32. Limits on high income farmers	N
33. Family medical leave-veto override	N
34. Req submission of balanced budget	Y
35. Balanced budget amendment	Y
36. Amendment to ban flag desecration	Y
37. Reauthorize Amtrak-veto override	Y
38. Retraining aid for coal miners	N
39. Suspend El Salvador military aid	X
40. Expand child care aid/tax credit	N
41. Raise House salary/omit honoraria	N
42. Toughen oil-spill liability	N
43. Restitution to Japanese interned	N
44. Protect Chinese & C.A. nationals	N
45. Abortion $ for rape/incest cases	N
46. Allow religious schools to bar gays	Y
47. Bar broadcaster fairness doctrine	Y
48. Bar cap gains cut/reinstate IRA	N
49. Bar unions equal voice in pension	Y
50. Bar assembly of chemical weapons	N
51. Ban plutonium/uranium production	N
52. Cap MX missile deployment at 50	N
53. Allow $3b for 2 stealth bombers	Y
54. Publish bio-warfare experiments	N
55. Raise minimum wage-veto override	N
56. Bar transfer of FS-X technology	N
57. Cut defense and raise domestic $	N
58. Uniform poll closing in 48 states	N
59. Req foreign investment disclosure	N
60. Textile import quotas-veto override	N
61. Bar abortion funding in Wash, DC	Y
62. Notify spouses of AIDS+ carriers	Y
63. Seize conveyance-drug trafficking	N
64. South Africa sanctions	N

65. 60 days' notice of plant closings	N
66. Close unneeded military bases	Y
67. Keep welfare reform within $2.8b	Y
68. Allow children housing exclusion	Y
69. Shift $400m of NASA to homeless	N
70. Cap Medicare patients' liability	N
71. Prohibit employee polygraph testing	N
72. Allow CIA to fund Contras	Y
73. Revise unfair trade practices	X
74. Focus SDI on accidental launch	N
75. Bar Air Force $ for MX missile	N
76. Allow "real" increase in defense	Y
77. Troop reduction in Europe of 50%	N
78. Ban nuclear tests above 1 kiloton	N
79. Ban anti-satellite missile tests	N
80. Observe certain limits of SALT II	N
81. Restore four Civil Rights laws	N
82. Prohibit aliens as strikebreakers	N
83. Allow military malpractice suits	N
84. Approval of $36m in Contra aid	Y
85. $18b deficit reduction compromise	N
86. Welfare reform of $5.7b for 5 years	N
87. Raise taxes $12b/cut spending $3b	N
88. Board to assess occupational risk	N
89. Balanced budget by '93-via targets	N
90. Bar licensing of two nuclear plants	N
91. Remove victims compensation cap	N
92. Catastrophic health insurance	N
93. Ban airline smoking-2 hours or less	Y
94. $1b/two year aid for the homeless	N
95. Bar non-unions in union companies	N
96. Increase FSLIC rescue to $15b	N
97. Impose quotas to lower trade deficit	N
98. Reduce discretionary budget 21%	Y
99. Immigration reform/alien amnesty	N
100. South Africa sanctions-veto override	N
101. Tax overhaul to revise income tax	N
102. Use of military in drug war	Y
103. Delete 12 MX/add conventional wpn	N
104. Raise speed limit to 65 mph	Y
105. Require Pentagon to buy US goods	N
106. AIDS insurance non-discrimination	N
107. Prohibit Saudi arms sales	N
108. Ease Gun Control Act of 1968	Y
109. Bar interstate handgun transport	N
110. Make company emissions known	N
111. Allow toxic victims to sue in fed ct	N
112. Superfund waste cleanup of $10b	N
113. 90 days notice of plant closings	N
114. $20b in Medicare cuts/tax increases	?
115. Spending cuts and tax increases	N
116. Set school lunch lmt-250% poverty	N
117. $75m for youth work projects	N
118. Allow Angolan military assistance	Y
119. Suspend defense payments for abuse	N
120. Drop SS COLAs/$12b tax increase	N
121. Approve $1.5b for 21 MX missiles	Y
122. Emergency farm credit/revisions	Y
123. Duty on Taiwan/Hong Kong/S Korea	N
124. Limit steel imports to 17%	N
125. Cut $ to schools that bar prayer	Y
126. $50b-taxes; cut Medicare/spending	N
127. Limit Pershing II/cruise in Europe	N
128. Delete $7.1b for 34 B-1 bombers	N

MARLENEE, RON (continued)

129.	Bar purchase of Sergeant York guns	N	137.	Eminent domain for coal companies	N
130.	El Salvador military/economic aid	Y	138.	Prohibit EPA clean air sanctions	?
131.	Bar mining of Nicaraguan waters	N	139.	SS retirement age increase/reforms	Y
132.	Physician fee freeze for Medicare	Y	140.	Auto domestic content requirement	N
133.	$49b in "sin"/phone/insurance taxes	N	141.	Delete jobs program funding	Y
134.	Allow sale of Conrail	N	142.	Highway-gas tax bill	?
135.	Equal Rights Amendment	N	143.	Cut $5b from defense for Medicare	Y
136.	Authorize Marines in Lebanon	Y	144.	Emergency housing aid of $1b	Y

Presidential Support Score: 1991 - 65%   1990 - 69%

NEBRASKA

BEREUTER, DOUGLAS K. -- Nebraska 1st District [Republican]. Counties of Butler, Cass (pt.), Cedar, Colfax, Cuming, Dakota, Dixon, Dodge, Fillmore, Gage, Jefferson, Johnson, Knox, Lancaster, Madison, Nemaha, Otoe, Pawnee, Pierce, Richardson, Saline, Saunders, Seward, Stanton, Thurston, Wayne and York. Prior Terms: 1979-92. Born: October 6, 1939; York, NE. Education: University of Nebraska (B.A.); Harvard University (M.C.P., M.P.A.); Eagleton Institute of Politics. Military Service: U.S. Army, 1963-65. Occupation: Residential and commercial development consultant; part owner, automobile and hardware dealership; division director, Nebraska Department of Economic Development (1967-68); director, state office of Planning and Programming (1968-71); federal-state relations coordinator, Nebraska (1967-71); Nebraska senator (1975-78).

1.	Protection to Haitian refugees	N	35.	Balanced budget amendment	Y
2.	Raise tax on wealthy; lower others	N	36.	Amendment to ban flag desecration	Y
3.	Investigate Reagan hostage delay	N	37.	Reauthorize Amtrak-veto override	N
4.	Campaign finance revisions	N	38.	Retraining aid for coal miners	N
5.	Unpaid leave to care for children	N	39.	Suspend El Salvador military aid	Y
6.	Restrict NEA use of funds	N	40.	Expand child care aid/tax credit	Y
7.	Bar race-bias claim/habeas corpus	Y	41.	Raise House salary/omit honoraria	N
8.	Ban race as death sentence factor	Y	42.	Toughen oil-spill liability	N
9.	Exceptions to exclusionary rule	Y	43.	Restitution to Japanese interned	Y
10.	Allow sale of assault weapons	N	44.	Protect Chinese & C.A. nationals	N
11.	Life in prison/abolish death penalty	N	45.	Abortion $ for rape/incest cases	N
12.	Req conspiracy-price fixing cases	Y	46.	Allow religious schools to bar gays	Y
13.	Unemployment benefits extension	N	47.	Bar broadcaster fairness doctrine	N
14.	Tissue use of aborted fetuses	N	48.	Bar cap gains cut/reinstate IRA	Y
15.	Bar replacement of union strikers	N	49.	Bar unions equal voice in pension	Y
16.	Hold foreign aid at $15b for '92	Y	50.	Bar assembly of chemical weapons	N
17.	Restore space station funding	N	51.	Ban plutonium/uranium production	N
18.	Civil Rights Act of 1991	N	52.	Cap MX missile deployment at 50	Y
19.	Unlimited damages-discrimination	N	53.	Allow $3b for 2 stealth bombers	N
20.	Eliminate funds for supercollider	Y	54.	Publish bio-warfare experiments	N
21.	Terminate SDI except for research	N	55.	Raise minimum wage-veto override	N
22.	Req 7-day handgun waiting period	N	56.	Bar transfer of FS-X technology	N
23.	Provide $30b for failed S&Ls	Y	57.	Cut defense and raise domestic $	N
24.	Allow use of force against Iraq	Y	58.	Uniform poll closing in 48 states	N
25.	Allow $15b in foreign aid for '91	N	59.	Req foreign investment disclosure	Y
26.	Revise & extend legal immigration	Y	60.	Textile import quotas-veto override	N
27.	Suspend aid to Angolan rebels	N	61.	Bar abortion funding in Wash, DC	Y
28.	Democratic tax plan proposals	N	62.	Notify spouses of AIDS+ carriers	N
29.	Cut defense 5% across the board	N	63.	Seize conveyance-drug trafficking	N
30.	Textile import quotas-veto override	N	64.	South Africa sanctions	N
31.	Abortion service for military abroad	N	65.	60 days' notice of plant closings	Y
32.	Limits on high income farmers	N	66.	Close unneeded military bases	Y
33.	Family medical leave-veto override	N	67.	Keep welfare reform within $2.8b	Y
34.	Req submission of balanced budget	Y	68.	Allow children housing exclusion	N

BEREUTER, DOUGLAS K. (continued)

69. Shift $400m of NASA to homeless	Y	107. Prohibit Saudi arms sales	Y
70. Cap Medicare patients' liability	Y	108. Ease Gun Control Act of 1968	Y
71. Prohibit employee polygraph testing	Y	109. Bar interstate handgun transport	Y
72. Allow CIA to fund Contras	Y	110. Make company emissions known	N
73. Revise unfair trade practices	Y	111. Allow toxic victims to sue in fed ct	N
74. Focus SDI on accidental launch	N	112. Superfund waste cleanup of $10b	N
75. Bar Air Force $ for MX missile	N	113. 90 days notice of plant closings	N
76. Allow "real" increase in defense	N	114. $20b in Medicare cuts/tax increases	Y
77. Troop reduction in Europe of 50%	N	115. Spending cuts and tax increases	N
78. Ban nuclear tests above 1 kiloton	N	116. Set school lunch lmt-250% poverty	Y
79. Ban anti-satellite missile tests	N	117. $75m for youth work projects	Y
80. Observe certain limits of SALT II	N	118. Allow Angolan military assistance	Y
81. Restore four Civil Rights laws	Y	119. Suspend defense payments for abuse	Y
82. Prohibit aliens as strikebreakers	N	120. Drop SS COLAs/$12b tax increase	N
83. Allow military malpractice suits	Y	121. Approve $1.5b for 21 MX missiles	N
84. Approval of $36m in Contra aid	Y	122. Emergency farm credit/revisions	Y
85. $18b deficit reduction compromise	N	123. Duty on Taiwan/Hong Kong/S Korea	N
86. Welfare reform of $5.7b for 5 years	N	124. Limit steel imports to 17%	N
87. Raise taxes $12b/cut spending $3b	N	125. Cut $ to schools that bar prayer	N
88. Board to assess occupational risk	N	126. $50b-taxes; cut Medicare/spending	Y
89. Balanced budget by '93-via targets	Y	127. Limit Pershing II/cruise in Europe	N
90. Bar licensing of two nuclear plants	N	128. Delete $7.1b for 34 B-1 bombers	N
91. Remove victims compensation cap	N	129. Bar purchase of Sergeant York guns	N
92. Catastrophic health insurance	N	130. El Salvador military/economic aid	Y
93. Ban airline smoking-2 hours or less	Y	131. Bar mining of Nicaraguan waters	Y
94. $1b/two year aid for the homeless	N	132. Physician fee freeze for Medicare	Y
95. Bar non-unions in union companies	N	133. $49b in "sin"/phone/insurance taxes	Y
96. Increase FSLIC rescue to $15b	Y	134. Allow sale of Conrail	Y
97. Impose quotas to lower trade deficit	N	135. Equal Rights Amendment	Y
98. Reduce discretionary budget 21%	Y	136. Authorize Marines in Lebanon	Y
99. Immigration reform/alien amnesty	N	137. Eminent domain for coal companies	N
100. South Africa sanctions-veto override	Y	138. Prohibit EPA clean air sanctions	N
101. Tax overhaul to revise income tax	Y	139. SS retirement age increase/reforms	Y
102. Use of military in drug war	N	140. Auto domestic content requirement	N
103. Delete 12 MX/add conventional wpn	N	141. Delete jobs program funding	Y
104. Raise speed limit to 65 mph	Y	142. Highway-gas tax bill	N
105. Require Pentagon to buy US goods	N	143. Cut $5b from defense for Medicare	Y
106. AIDS insurance non-discrimination	N	144. Emergency housing aid of $1b	Y

Presidential Support Score: 1991 - 79%   1990 - 62%

HOAGLAND, PETER J. -- Nebraska 2nd District [Democrat]. Counties of Burt, Cass (pt.), Douglas, Sarpy and Washington. Prior Terms: 1989-92. Born: November 17, 1941; Omaha, NE. Education: Stanford University; Yale University Law School. Military Service: U.S. Army. Occupation: Law clerk; lawyer; state senator (1978-86).

1. Protection to Haitian refugees	Y	18. Civil Rights Act of 1991	Y
2. Raise tax on wealthy; lower others	Y	19. Unlimited damages-discrimination	N
3. Investigate Reagan hostage delay	Y	20. Eliminate funds for supercollider	Y
4. Campaign finance revisions	Y	21. Terminate SDI except for research	N
5. Unpaid leave to care for children	Y	22. Req 7-day handgun waiting period	Y
6. Restrict NEA use of funds	Y	23. Provide $30b for failed S&Ls	Y
7. Bar race-bias claim/habeas corpus	N	24. Allow use of force against Iraq	Y
8. Ban race as death sentence factor	Y	25. Allow $15b in foreign aid for '91	Y
9. Exceptions to exclusionary rule	N	26. Revise & extend legal immigration	N
10. Allow sale of assault weapons	N	27. Suspend aid to Angolan rebels	Y
11. Life in prison/abolish death penalty	N	28. Democratic tax plan proposals	Y
12. Req conspiracy-price fixing cases	N	29. Cut defense 5% across the board	N
13. Unemployment benefits extension	Y	30. Textile import quotas-veto override	Y
14. Tissue use of aborted fetuses	Y	31. Abortion service for military abroad	Y
15. Bar replacement of union strikers	Y	32. Limits on high income farmers	N
16. Hold foreign aid at $15b for '92	Y	33. Family medical leave-veto override	N
17. Restore space station funding	N	34. Req submission of balanced budget	Y

HOAGLAND, PETER J. (continued)

35. Balanced budget amendment	Y	47. Bar broadcaster fairness doctrine	N
36. Amendment to ban flag desecration	N	48. Bar cap gains cut/reinstate IRA	Y
37. Reauthorize Amtrak-veto override	Y	49. Bar unions equal voice in pension	N
38. Retraining aid for coal miners	Y	50. Bar assembly of chemical weapons	Y
39. Suspend El Salvador military aid	N	51. Ban plutonium/uranium production	Y
40. Expand child care aid/tax credit	Y	52. Cap MX missile deployment at 50	Y
41. Raise House salary/omit honoraria	N	53. Allow $3b for 2 stealth bombers	N
42. Toughen oil-spill liability	Y	54. Publish bio-warfare experiments	Y
43. Restitution to Japanese interned	Y	55. Raise minimum wage-veto override	Y
44. Protect Chinese & C.A. nationals	Y	56. Bar transfer of FS-X technology	Y
45. Abortion $ for rape/incest cases	Y	57. Cut defense and raise domestic $	N
46. Allow religious schools to bar gays	Y	58. Uniform poll closing in 48 states	Y

Presidential Support Score: 1991 - 42%   1990 - 27%

BARRETT, BILL -- Nebraska 3rd District [Republican]. Counties of Adams, Antelope, Arthur, Banner, Blaine, Boone, Box Butte, Boyd, Brown, Buffalo, Chase, Cherry, Cheyenne, Clay, Custer, Dawes, Dawson, Deuel, Dundy, Franklin, Frontier, Furnas, Garden, Garfield, Gosper, Grant, Greeley, Hall, Hamilton, Harlan, Hayes, Hitchcock, Hocker, Holt, Howard, Kearney, Keith, Keya Paha, Kimball, Lincoln, Logan, Loup, McPherson, Merrick, Morrill, Nance, Nuckolls, Perkins, Phelps, Platte, Polk, Red Willow, Rock, Scotts Bluff, Sheridan, Shermon, Sioux, Thayer, Thomas, Valley, Webster and Wheeler. Prior Term: 1991-92. Born: February 9, 1929; Lexington, NE. Education: Hastings College (B.A.). Military Service: U.S. Navy. Occupation: President, general insurance-real estate brokerage-appraisal firm; bank director; state legislator (1979-1988).

1. Protection to Haitian refugees	N	13. Unemployment benefits extension	N
2. Raise tax on wealthy; lower others	N	14. Tissue use of aborted fetuses	N
3. Investigate Reagan hostage delay	N	15. Bar replacement of union strikers	N
4. Campaign finance revisions	N	16. Hold foreign aid at $15b for '92	N
5. Unpaid leave to care for children	N	17. Restore space station funding	Y
6. Restrict NEA use of funds	Y	18. Civil Rights Act of 1991	N
7. Bar race-bias claim/habeas corpus	Y	19. Unlimited damages-discrimination	N
8. Ban race as death sentence factor	Y	20. Eliminate funds for supercollider	N
9. Exceptions to exclusionary rule	Y	21. Terminate SDI except for research	N
10. Allow sale of assault weapons	Y	22. Req 7-day handgun waiting period	N
11. Life in prison/abolish death penalty	N	23. Provide $30b for failed S&Ls	Y
12. Req conspiracy-price fixing cases	Y	24. Allow use of force against Iraq	Y

Presidential Support Score: 1991 - 84%

NEVADA

BILBRAY, JAMES H. -- Nevada 1st District [Democrat]. County of Clark (pt.). Prior Terms: 1987-92. Born: 1938; Las Vegas, NV. Education: University of Nevada at Las Vegas; American University, Washington College of Law. Military Service: Nevada National Guard, 1955-1963; Reserve. Occupation: Attorney; congressional aide (1960-1964); deputy district attorney (1964-1967); Las Vegas alternate municipal judge (1978-1980); state senator.

1. Protection to Haitian refugees	Y	7. Bar race-bias claim/habeas corpus	Y
2. Raise tax on wealthy; lower others	Y	8. Ban race as death sentence factor	Y
3. Investigate Reagan hostage delay	Y	9. Exceptions to exclusionary rule	Y
4. Campaign finance revisions	Y	10. Allow sale of assault weapons	Y
5. Unpaid leave to care for children	Y	11. Life in prison/abolish death penalty	N
6. Restrict NEA use of funds	N	12. Req conspiracy-price fixing cases	N

BILBRAY, JAMES H. (continued)

13. Unemployment benefits extension	Y	56. Bar transfer of FS-X technology	Y
14. Tissue use of aborted fetuses	Y	57. Cut defense and raise domestic $	N
15. Bar replacement of union strikers	Y	58. Uniform poll closing in 48 states	Y
16. Hold foreign aid at $15b for '92	Y	59. Req foreign investment disclosure	Y
17. Restore space station funding	?	60. Textile import quotas-veto override	Y
18. Civil Rights Act of 1991	Y	61. Bar abortion funding in Wash, DC	Y
19. Unlimited damages-discrimination	N	62. Notify spouses of AIDS+ carriers	N
20. Eliminate funds for supercollider	Y	63. Seize conveyance-drug trafficking	N
21. Terminate SDI except for research	N	64. South Africa sanctions	Y
22. Req 7-day handgun waiting period	N	65. 60 days' notice of plant closings	Y
23. Provide $30b for failed S&Ls	N	66. Close unneeded military bases	N
24. Allow use of force against Iraq	Y	67. Keep welfare reform within $2.8b	Y
25. Allow $15b in foreign aid for '91	Y	68. Allow children housing exclusion	N
26. Revise & extend legal immigration	Y	69. Shift $400m of NASA to homeless	N
27. Suspend aid to Angolan rebels	Y	70. Cap Medicare patients' liability	Y
28. Democratic tax plan proposals	N	71. Prohibit employee polygraph testing	Y
29. Cut defense 5% across the board	N	72. Allow CIA to fund Contras	N
30. Textile import quotas-veto override	Y	73. Revise unfair trade practices	Y
31. Abortion service for military abroad	N	74. Focus SDI on accidental launch	Y
32. Limits on high income farmers	Y	75. Bar Air Force $ for MX missile	?
33. Family medical leave-veto override	Y	76. Allow "real" increase in defense	Y
34. Req submission of balanced budget	Y	77. Troop reduction in Europe of 50%	Y
35. Balanced budget amendment	Y	78. Ban nuclear tests above 1 kiloton	N
36. Amendment to ban flag desecration	Y	79. Ban anti-satellite missile tests	N
37. Reauthorize Amtrak-veto override	Y	80. Observe certain limits of SALT II	Y
38. Retraining aid for coal miners	Y	81. Restore four Civil Rights laws	Y
39. Suspend El Salvador military aid	Y	82. Prohibit aliens as strikebreakers	Y
40. Expand child care aid/tax credit	Y	83. Allow military malpractice suits	Y
41. Raise House salary/omit honoraria	Y	84. Approval of $36m in Contra aid	N
42. Toughen oil-spill liability	N	85. $18b deficit reduction compromise	N
43. Restitution to Japanese interned	Y	86. Welfare reform of $5.7b for 5 years	N
44. Protect Chinese & C.A. nationals	Y	87. Raise taxes $12b/cut spending $3b	N
45. Abortion $ for rape/incest cases	Y	88. Board to assess occupational risk	Y
46. Allow religious schools to bar gays	Y	89. Balanced budget by '93-via targets	Y
47. Bar broadcaster fairness doctrine	N	90. Bar licensing of two nuclear plants	Y
48. Bar cap gains cut/reinstate IRA	Y	91. Remove victims compensation cap	N
49. Bar unions equal voice in pension	Y	92. Catastrophic health insurance	Y
50. Bar assembly of chemical weapons	Y	93. Ban airline smoking-2 hours or less	N
51. Ban plutonium/uranium production	Y	94. $1b/two year aid for the homeless	Y
52. Cap MX missile deployment at 50	Y	95. Bar non-unions in union companies	Y
53. Allow $3b for 2 stealth bombers	N	96. Increase FSLIC rescue to $15b	N
54. Publish bio-warfare experiments	Y	97. Impose quotas to lower trade deficit	Y
55. Raise minimum wage-veto override	Y	98. Reduce discretionary budget 21%	Y

Presidential Support Score: 1991 - 41% 1990 - 33%

VUCANOVICH, BARBARA F. -- Nevada 2nd District [Republican]. Counties of Carson City, Churchill, Clark (pt.), Douglas, Elko, Esmeralda, Eureka, Humboldt, Lander, Lincoln, Lyon, Mineral, Nye, Pershing, Storey, Washoe and White Pine. Prior Terms: 1983-92. Born: June 22, 1921; Camp Dix, NJ. Education: Manhattanville College of the Sacred Heart. Occupation: Operated speed reading school (1965-68); travel agent (1968-74); senator's aide.

1. Protection to Haitian refugees	N	10. Allow sale of assault weapons	Y
2. Raise tax on wealthy; lower others	N	11. Life in prison/abolish death penalty	N
3. Investigate Reagan hostage delay	N	12. Req conspiracy-price fixing cases	Y
4. Campaign finance revisions	N	13. Unemployment benefits extension	N
5. Unpaid leave to care for children	N	14. Tissue use of aborted fetuses	N
6. Restrict NEA use of funds	N	15. Bar replacement of union strikers	N
7. Bar race-bias claim/habeas corpus	Y	16. Hold foreign aid at $15b for '92	?
8. Ban race as death sentence factor	Y	17. Restore space station funding	Y
9. Exceptions to exclusionary rule	Y	18. Civil Rights Act of 1991	N

VUCANOVICH, BARBARA F. (continued)

19. Unlimited damages-discrimination	N
20. Eliminate funds for supercollider	N
21. Terminate SDI except for research	N
22. Req 7-day handgun waiting period	N
23. Provide $30b for failed S&Ls	Y
24. Allow use of force against Iraq	Y
25. Allow $15b in foreign aid for '91	N
26. Revise & extend legal immigration	Y
27. Suspend aid to Angolan rebels	N
28. Democratic tax plan proposals	N
29. Cut defense 5% across the board	N
30. Textile import quotas-veto override	Y
31. Abortion service for military abroad	N
32. Limits on high income farmers	N
33. Family medical leave-veto override	N
34. Req submission of balanced budget	N
35. Balanced budget amendment	Y
36. Amendment to ban flag desecration	Y
37. Reauthorize Amtrak-veto override	N
38. Retraining aid for coal miners	N
39. Suspend El Salvador military aid	N
40. Expand child care aid/tax credit	N
41. Raise House salary/omit honoraria	Y
42. Toughen oil-spill liability	N
43. Restitution to Japanese interned	Y
44. Protect Chinese & C.A. nationals	N
45. Abortion $ for rape/incest cases	N
46. Allow religious schools to bar gays	Y
47. Bar broadcaster fairness doctrine	N
48. Bar cap gains cut/reinstate IRA	N
49. Bar unions equal voice in pension	Y
50. Bar assembly of chemical weapons	N
51. Ban plutonium/uranium production	N
52. Cap MX missile deployment at 50	N
53. Allow $3b for 2 stealth bombers	Y
54. Publish bio-warfare experiments	N
55. Raise minimum wage-veto override	N
56. Bar transfer of FS-X technology	N
57. Cut defense and raise domestic $	N
58. Uniform poll closing in 48 states	Y
59. Req foreign investment disclosure	N
60. Textile import quotas-veto override	N
61. Bar abortion funding in Wash, DC	Y
62. Notify spouses of AIDS+ carriers	Y
63. Seize conveyance-drug trafficking	Y
64. South Africa sanctions	N
65. 60 days' notice of plant closings	N
66. Close unneeded military bases	N
67. Keep welfare reform within $2.8b	Y
68. Allow children housing exclusion	Y
69. Shift $400m of NASA to homeless	N
70. Cap Medicare patients' liability	Y
71. Prohibit employee polygraph testing	N
72. Allow CIA to fund Contras	Y
73. Revise unfair trade practices	N
74. Focus SDI on accidental launch	N
75. Bar Air Force $ for MX missile	N
76. Allow "real" increase in defense	Y
77. Troop reduction in Europe of 50%	N
78. Ban nuclear tests above 1 kiloton	N
79. Ban anti-satellite missile tests	N

80. Observe certain limits of SALT II	N
81. Restore four Civil Rights laws	N
82. Prohibit aliens as strikebreakers	N
83. Allow military malpractice suits	Y
84. Approval of $36m in Contra aid	Y
85. $18b deficit reduction compromise	N
86. Welfare reform of $5.7b for 5 years	N
87. Raise taxes $12b/cut spending $3b	N
88. Board to assess occupational risk	N
89. Balanced budget by '93-via targets	N
90. Bar licensing of two nuclear plants	N
91. Remove victims compensation cap	N
92. Catastrophic health insurance	Y
93. Ban airline smoking-2 hours or less	N
94. $1b/two year aid for the homeless	N
95. Bar non-unions in union companies	N
96. Increase FSLIC rescue to $15b	N
97. Impose quotas to lower trade deficit	N
98. Reduce discretionary budget 21%	Y
99. Immigration reform/alien amnesty	Y
100. South Africa sanctions-veto override	N
101. Tax overhaul to revise income tax	N
102. Use of military in drug war	Y
103. Delete 12 MX/add conventional wpn	N
104. Raise speed limit to 65 mph	Y
105. Require Pentagon to buy US goods	N
106. AIDS insurance non-discrimination	N
107. Prohibit Saudi arms sales	Y
108. Ease Gun Control Act of 1968	Y
109. Bar interstate handgun transport	N
110. Make company emissions known	N
111. Allow toxic victims to sue in fed ct	N
112. Superfund waste cleanup of $10b	Y
113. 90 days notice of plant closings	N
114. $20b in Medicare cuts/tax increases	N
115. Spending cuts and tax increases	N
116. Set school lunch lmt-250% poverty	N
117. $75m for youth work projects	?
118. Allow Angolan military assistance	Y
119. Suspend defense payments for abuse	N
120. Drop SS COLAs/$12b tax increase	N
121. Approve $1.5b for 21 MX missiles	Y
122. Emergency farm credit/revisions	N
123. Duty on Taiwan/Hong Kong/S Korea	N
124. Limit steel imports to 17%	N
125. Cut $ to schools that bar prayer	Y
126. $50b-taxes; cut Medicare/spending	N
127. Limit Pershing II/cruise in Europe	N
128. Delete $7.1b for 34 B-1 bombers	N
129. Bar purchase of Sergeant York guns	N
130. El Salvador military/economic aid	Y
131. Bar mining of Nicaraguan waters	N
132. Physician fee freeze for Medicare	N
133. $49b in "sin"/phone/insurance taxes	N
134. Allow sale of Conrail	Y
135. Equal Rights Amendment	N
136. Authorize Marines in Lebanon	Y
137. Eminent domain for coal companies	Y
138. Prohibit EPA clean air sanctions	+
139. SS retirement age increase/reforms	Y

Presidential Support Score: 1991 - 84%   1990 - 72%

NEW HAMPSHIRE

ZELIFF, BILL -- New Hampshire 1st District [Republican]. Counties of Belknap, Carroll, Hillsborough (pt.), Merrimack (pt.), Rockingham (pt.) and Strafford. Prior Term: 1991-92. Born: June 12, 1936; East Orange, NJ. Education: University of Connecticut (B.S.). Military Service: U.S. Army National Guard. Occupation: DuPont Co. sales and marketing manager; farm inn, restaurant and store owner.

1. Protection to Haitian refugees	N	13. Unemployment benefits extension	N
2. Raise tax on wealthy; lower others	N	14. Tissue use of aborted fetuses	N
3. Investigate Reagan hostage delay	N	15. Bar replacement of union strikers	N
4. Campaign finance revisions	N	16. Hold foreign aid at $15b for '92	Y
5. Unpaid leave to care for children	N	17. Restore space station funding	Y
6. Restrict NEA use of funds	Y	18. Civil Rights Act of 1991	N
7. Bar race-bias claim/habeas corpus	Y	19. Unlimited damages-discrimination	N
8. Ban race as death sentence factor	Y	20. Eliminate funds for supercollider	Y
9. Exceptions to exclusionary rule	Y	21. Terminate SDI except for research	N
10. Allow sale of assault weapons	Y	22. Req 7-day handgun waiting period	N
11. Life in prison/abolish death penalty	N	23. Provide $30b for failed S&Ls	Y
12. Req conspiracy-price fixing cases	Y	24. Allow use of force against Iraq	Y

Presidential Support Score: 1991 - 80%

SWETT, RICHARD NELSON -- New Hampshire 2nd District [Democrat]. Counties of Cheshire, Coos, Grafton, Hillsborough (pt.), Merrimack (pt.), Rockingham (pt.) and Sullivan. Prior Term: 1991-92. Born: May 1, 1957; Bryn Mawr, PA. Education: Yale University (B.A.). Occupation: Architect-builder; housing developer; alternative fuel-cogeneration development company president.

1. Protection to Haitian refugees	Y	13. Unemployment benefits extension	Y
2. Raise tax on wealthy; lower others	N	14. Tissue use of aborted fetuses	Y
3. Investigate Reagan hostage delay	Y	15. Bar replacement of union strikers	Y
4. Campaign finance revisions	Y	16. Hold foreign aid at $15b for '92	Y
5. Unpaid leave to care for children	Y	17. Restore space station funding	Y
6. Restrict NEA use of funds	Y	18. Civil Rights Act of 1991	Y
7. Bar race-bias claim/habeas corpus	Y	19. Unlimited damages-discrimination	N
8. Ban race as death sentence factor	Y	20. Eliminate funds for supercollider	Y
9. Exceptions to exclusionary rule	Y	21. Terminate SDI except for research	N
10. Allow sale of assault weapons	Y	22. Req 7-day handgun waiting period	Y
11. Life in prison/abolish death penalty	N	23. Provide $30b for failed S&Ls	Y
12. Req conspiracy-price fixing cases	N	24. Allow use of force against Iraq	Y

Presidential Support Score: 1991 - 46%

NEW JERSEY

ANDREWS, ROBERT E. -- New Jersey 1st District [Democrat]. Counties of Burlington (pt.), Camden (pt.) and Gloucester (pt.). Prior Term: 1991-92. Born: August 4, 1957; Camden, NJ. Education: Bucknell University (B.S.); Cornell Law School (J.D.). Occupation: Lawyer; adjunct law professor; Camden County chosen freeholder (1987-88) and board director (1988-90).

ANDREWS, ROBERT E. (continued)

1. Protection to Haitian refugees	Y	
2. Raise tax on wealthy; lower others	N	
3. Investigate Reagan hostage delay	Y	
4. Campaign finance revisions	Y	
5. Unpaid leave to care for children	Y	
6. Restrict NEA use of funds	N	
7. Bar race-bias claim/habeas corpus	N	
8. Ban race as death sentence factor	N	
9. Exceptions to exclusionary rule	Y	
10. Allow sale of assault weapons	N	
11. Life in prison/abolish death penalty	N	
12. Req conspiracy-price fixing cases	N	
13. Unemployment benefits extension	Y	
14. Tissue use of aborted fetuses	Y	
15. Bar replacement of union strikers	Y	
16. Hold foreign aid at $15b for '92	Y	
17. Restore space station funding	Y	
18. Civil Rights Act of 1991	Y	
19. Unlimited damages-discrimination	Y	
20. Eliminate funds for supercollider	N	
21. Terminate SDI except for research	N	
22. Req 7-day handgun waiting period	Y	
23. Provide $30b for failed S&Ls	N	
24. Allow use of force against Iraq	N	

Presidential Support Score: 1991 - 35%

HUGHES, WILLIAM J. -- New Jersey 2nd District [Democrat]. Counties of Atlantic, Burlington (pt.), Cape May, Cumberland, Ocean (pt.) and Salem. Prior Terms: 1975-92. Born: October 17, 1932; Salem NJ. Education: Rutgers University (A.B., J.D.). Occupation: Attorney; Cape May County assistant prosecutor (1960-70).

1. Protection to Haitian refugees	Y	44. Protect Chinese & C.A. nationals	Y
2. Raise tax on wealthy; lower others	N	45. Abortion $ for rape/incest cases	Y
3. Investigate Reagan hostage delay	Y	46. Allow religious schools to bar gays	N
4. Campaign finance revisions	Y	47. Bar broadcaster fairness doctrine	N
5. Unpaid leave to care for children	Y	48. Bar cap gains cut/reinstate IRA	Y
6. Restrict NEA use of funds	N	49. Bar unions equal voice in pension	Y
7. Bar race-bias claim/habeas corpus	N	50. Bar assembly of chemical weapons	Y
8. Ban race as death sentence factor	N	51. Ban plutonium/uranium production	Y
9. Exceptions to exclusionary rule	N	52. Cap MX missile deployment at 50	Y
10. Allow sale of assault weapons	N	53. Allow $3b for 2 stealth bombers	N
11. Life in prison/abolish death penalty	N	54. Publish bio-warfare experiments	Y
12. Req conspiracy-price fixing cases	N	55. Raise minimum wage-veto override	Y
13. Unemployment benefits extension	Y	56. Bar transfer of FS-X technology	Y
14. Tissue use of aborted fetuses	Y	57. Cut defense and raise domestic $	N
15. Bar replacement of union strikers	Y	58. Uniform poll closing in 48 states	Y
16. Hold foreign aid at $15b for '92	N	59. Req foreign investment disclosure	Y
17. Restore space station funding	N	60. Textile import quotas-veto override	Y
18. Civil Rights Act of 1991	Y	61. Bar abortion funding in Wash, DC	N
19. Unlimited damages-discrimination	N	62. Notify spouses of AIDS+ carriers	N
20. Eliminate funds for supercollider	N	63. Seize conveyance-drug trafficking	N
21. Terminate SDI except for research	N	64. South Africa sanctions	Y
22. Req 7-day handgun waiting period	Y	65. 60 days' notice of plant closings	Y
23. Provide $30b for failed S&Ls	N	66. Close unneeded military bases	N
24. Allow use of force against Iraq	Y	67. Keep welfare reform within $2.8b	Y
25. Allow $15b in foreign aid for '91	N	68. Allow children housing exclusion	N
26. Revise & extend legal immigration	Y	69. Shift $400m of NASA to homeless	Y
27. Suspend aid to Angolan rebels	N	70. Cap Medicare patients' liability	Y
28. Democratic tax plan proposals	Y	71. Prohibit employee polygraph testing	Y
29. Cut defense 5% across the board	N	72. Allow CIA to fund Contras	N
30. Textile import quotas-veto override	Y	73. Revise unfair trade practices	Y
31. Abortion service for military abroad	Y	74. Focus SDI on accidental launch	Y
32. Limits on high income farmers	Y	75. Bar Air Force $ for MX missile	N
33. Family medical leave-veto override	?	76. Allow "real" increase in defense	N
34. Req submission of balanced budget	Y	77. Troop reduction in Europe of 50%	Y
35. Balanced budget amendment	N	78. Ban nuclear tests above 1 kiloton	Y
36. Amendment to ban flag desecration	N	79. Ban anti-satellite missile tests	Y
37. Reauthorize Amtrak-veto override	Y	80. Observe certain limits of SALT II	Y
38. Retraining aid for coal miners	Y	81. Restore four Civil Rights laws	Y
39. Suspend El Salvador military aid	Y	82. Prohibit aliens as strikebreakers	Y
40. Expand child care aid/tax credit	Y	83. Allow military malpractice suits	Y
41. Raise House salary/omit honoraria	Y	84. Approval of $36m in Contra aid	N
42. Toughen oil-spill liability	Y	85. $18b deficit reduction compromise	Y
43. Restitution to Japanese interned	Y	86. Welfare reform of $5.7b for 5 years	Y

HUGHES, WILLIAM J. (continued)

87. Raise taxes $12b/cut spending $3b	Y	
88. Board to assess occupational risk	Y	
89. Balanced budget by '93-via targets	N	
90. Bar licensing of two nuclear plants	Y	
91. Remove victims compensation cap	N	
92. Catastrophic health insurance	Y	
93. Ban airline smoking-2 hours or less	N	
94. $1b/two year aid for the homeless	Y	
95. Bar non-unions in union companies	Y	
96. Increase FSLIC rescue to $15b	Y	
97. Impose quotas to lower trade deficit	N	
98. Reduce discretionary budget 21%	Y	
99. Immigration reform/alien amnesty	N	
100. South Africa sanctions-veto override	Y	
101. Tax overhaul to revise income tax	N	
102. Use of military in drug war	N	
103. Delete 12 MX/add conventional wpn	Y	
104. Raise speed limit to 65 mph	N	
105. Require Pentagon to buy US goods	Y	
106. AIDS insurance non-discrimination	Y	
107. Prohibit Saudi arms sales	Y	
108. Ease Gun Control Act of 1968	N	
109. Bar interstate handgun transport	Y	
110. Make company emissions known	Y	
111. Allow toxic victims to sue in fed ct	N	
112. Superfund waste cleanup of $10b	Y	
113. 90 days notice of plant closings	Y	
114. $20b in Medicare cuts/tax increases	Y	
115. Spending cuts and tax increases	N	

116. Set school lunch lmt-250% poverty	N
117. $75m for youth work projects	N
118. Allow Angolan military assistance	N
119. Suspend defense payments for abuse	N
120. Drop SS COLAs/$12b tax increase	N
121. Approve $1.5b for 21 MX missiles	N
122. Emergency farm credit/revisions	Y
123. Duty on Taiwan/Hong Kong/S Korea	N
124. Limit steel imports to 17%	Y
125. Cut $ to schools that bar prayer	N
126. $50b-taxes; cut Medicare/spending	N
127. Limit Pershing II/cruise in Europe	N
128. Delete $7.1b for 34 B-1 bombers	Y
129. Bar purchase of Sergeant York guns	?
130. El Salvador military/economic aid	N
131. Bar mining of Nicaraguan waters	Y
132. Physician fee freeze for Medicare	N
133. $49b in "sin"/phone/insurance taxes	Y
134. Allow sale of Conrail	N
135. Equal Rights Amendment	Y
136. Authorize Marines in Lebanon	N
137. Eminent domain for coal companies	N
138. Prohibit EPA clean air sanctions	N
139. SS retirement age increase/reforms	N
140. Auto domestic content requirement	Y
141. Delete jobs program funding	N
142. Highway-gas tax bill	N
143. Cut $5b from defense for Medicare	Y
144. Emergency housing aid of $1b	Y

Presidential Support Score: 1991 - 29% 1990 - 26%

PALLONE, FRANK Jr. -- New Jersey 3rd District [Democrat]. Counties of Middlesex (pt.), Monmouth (pt.) and Ocean (pt.). Prior Terms: 1989-92. Born: October 30, 1951; Long Branch, NJ. Education: Middlebury College; Tufts University; Rutgers University. Occupation: Lawyer; Long Branch city councilman (1982-88) and state senator (1984-88).

1. Protection to Haitian refugees	Y	
2. Raise tax on wealthy; lower others	N	
3. Investigate Reagan hostage delay	Y	
4. Campaign finance revisions	Y	
5. Unpaid leave to care for children	Y	
6. Restrict NEA use of funds	Y	
7. Bar race-bias claim/habeas corpus	N	
8. Ban race as death sentence factor	N	
9. Exceptions to exclusionary rule	Y	
10. Allow sale of assault weapons	Y	
11. Life in prison/abolish death penalty	N	
12. Req conspiracy-price fixing cases	N	
13. Unemployment benefits extension	Y	
14. Tissue use of aborted fetuses	Y	
15. Bar replacement of union strikers	Y	
16. Hold foreign aid at $15b for '92	Y	
17. Restore space station funding	Y	
18. Civil Rights Act of 1991	Y	
19. Unlimited damages-discrimination	Y	
20. Eliminate funds for supercollider	Y	
21. Terminate SDI except for research	N	
22. Req 7-day handgun waiting period	Y	
23. Provide $30b for failed S&Ls	N	
24. Allow use of force against Iraq	Y	
25. Allow $15b in foreign aid for '91	Y	
26. Revise & extend legal immigration	Y	

27. Suspend aid to Angolan rebels	Y
28. Democratic tax plan proposals	N
29. Cut defense 5% across the board	N
30. Textile import quotas-veto override	Y
31. Abortion service for military abroad	Y
32. Limits on high income farmers	Y
33. Family medical leave-veto override	Y
34. Req submission of balanced budget	Y
35. Balanced budget amendment	Y
36. Amendment to ban flag desecration	Y
37. Reauthorize Amtrak-veto override	Y
38. Retraining aid for coal miners	Y
39. Suspend El Salvador military aid	Y
40. Expand child care aid/tax credit	Y
41. Raise House salary/omit honoraria	N
42. Toughen oil-spill liability	Y
43. Restitution to Japanese interned	Y
44. Protect Chinese & C.A. nationals	Y
45. Abortion $ for rape/incest cases	N
46. Allow religious schools to bar gays	Y
47. Bar broadcaster fairness doctrine	N
48. Bar cap gains cut/reinstate IRA	Y
49. Bar unions equal voice in pension	N
50. Bar assembly of chemical weapons	Y
51. Ban plutonium/uranium production	Y
52. Cap MX missile deployment at 50	Y

PALLONE, FRANK Jr. (continued)

53. Allow $3b for 2 stealth bombers	N
54. Publish bio-warfare experiments	Y
55. Raise minimum wage-veto override	Y
56. Bar transfer of FS-X technology	Y
57. Cut defense and raise domestic $	N
58. Uniform poll closing in 48 states	Y

Presidential Support Score: 1991 - 33%   1990 - 29%

SMITH, CHRISTOPHER H. -- New Jersey 4th District [Republican]. Counties of Burlington (pt.), Camden (pt.), Mercer (pt.), Middlesex (pt.) and Monmouth (pt.). Prior Terms: 1981-92. Born: March 4, 1953; Rahway, NJ. Education: Trenton State College (B.A.); Worcester College. Occupation: Businessman; executive director, New Jersey Right to Life Committee, Inc. (1976-78); legislative agent, New Jersey state legislature (1979).

1. Protection to Haitian refugees	Y	52. Cap MX missile deployment at 50	Y
2. Raise tax on wealthy; lower others	N	53. Allow $3b for 2 stealth bombers	N
3. Investigate Reagan hostage delay	N	54. Publish bio-warfare experiments	Y
4. Campaign finance revisions	Y	55. Raise minimum wage-veto override	Y
5. Unpaid leave to care for children	Y	56. Bar transfer of FS-X technology	N
6. Restrict NEA use of funds	Y	57. Cut defense and raise domestic $	N
7. Bar race-bias claim/habeas corpus	Y	58. Uniform poll closing in 48 states	Y
8. Ban race as death sentence factor	Y	59. Req foreign investment disclosure	Y
9. Exceptions to exclusionary rule	Y	60. Textile import quotas-veto override	Y
10. Allow sale of assault weapons	N	61. Bar abortion funding in Wash, DC	Y
11. Life in prison/abolish death penalty	Y	62. Notify spouses of AIDS+ carriers	N
12. Req conspiracy-price fixing cases	Y	63. Seize conveyance-drug trafficking	N
13. Unemployment benefits extension	Y	64. South Africa sanctions	Y
14. Tissue use of aborted fetuses	N	65. 60 days' notice of plant closings	Y
15. Bar replacement of union strikers	Y	66. Close unneeded military bases	Y
16. Hold foreign aid at $15b for '92	N	67. Keep welfare reform within $2.8b	Y
17. Restore space station funding	Y	68. Allow children housing exclusion	N
18. Civil Rights Act of 1991	N	69. Shift $400m of NASA to homeless	Y
19. Unlimited damages-discrimination	N	70. Cap Medicare patients' liability	Y
20. Eliminate funds for supercollider	N	71. Prohibit employee polygraph testing	Y
21. Terminate SDI except for research	N	72. Allow CIA to fund Contras	Y
22. Req 7-day handgun waiting period	Y	73. Revise unfair trade practices	Y
23. Provide $30b for failed S&Ls	Y	74. Focus SDI on accidental launch	N
24. Allow use of force against Iraq	Y	75. Bar Air Force $ for MX missile	Y
25. Allow $15b in foreign aid for '91	Y	76. Allow "real" increase in defense	N
26. Revise & extend legal immigration	Y	77. Troop reduction in Europe of 50%	N
27. Suspend aid to Angolan rebels	N	78. Ban nuclear tests above 1 kiloton	N
28. Democratic tax plan proposals	N	79. Ban anti-satellite missile tests	N
29. Cut defense 5% across the board	N	80. Observe certain limits of SALT II	N
30. Textile import quotas-veto override	Y	81. Restore four Civil Rights laws	Y
31. Abortion service for military abroad	N	82. Prohibit aliens as strikebreakers	Y
32. Limits on high income farmers	Y	83. Allow military malpractice suits	Y
33. Family medical leave-veto override	Y	84. Approval of $36m in Contra aid	Y
34. Req submission of balanced budget	Y	85. $18b deficit reduction compromise	Y
35. Balanced budget amendment	Y	86. Welfare reform of $5.7b for 5 years	Y
36. Amendment to ban flag desecration	Y	87. Raise taxes $12b/cut spending $3b	N
37. Reauthorize Amtrak-veto override	Y	88. Board to assess occupational risk	Y
38. Retraining aid for coal miners	Y	89. Balanced budget by '93-via targets	Y
39. Suspend El Salvador military aid	N	90. Bar licensing of two nuclear plants	N
40. Expand child care aid/tax credit	Y	91. Remove victims compensation cap	N
41. Raise House salary/omit honoraria	Y	92. Catastrophic health insurance	Y
42. Toughen oil-spill liability	N	93. Ban airline smoking-2 hours or less	Y
43. Restitution to Japanese interned	Y	94. $1b/two year aid for the homeless	Y
44. Protect Chinese & C.A. nationals	Y	95. Bar non-unions in union companies	Y
45. Abortion $ for rape/incest cases	N	96. Increase FSLIC rescue to $15b	N
46. Allow religious schools to bar gays	Y	97. Impose quotas to lower trade deficit	Y
47. Bar broadcaster fairness doctrine	N	98. Reduce discretionary budget 21%	Y
48. Bar cap gains cut/reinstate IRA	N	99. Immigration reform/alien amnesty	Y
49. Bar unions equal voice in pension	N	100. South Africa sanctions-veto override	Y
50. Bar assembly of chemical weapons	Y	101. Tax overhaul to revise income tax	Y
51. Ban plutonium/uranium production	Y	102. Use of military in drug war	Y

SMITH, CHRISTOPHER H. (continued)

103. Delete 12 MX/add conventional wpn	Y	124. Limit steel imports to 17%	Y
104. Raise speed limit to 65 mph	N	125. Cut $ to schools that bar prayer	Y
105. Require Pentagon to buy US goods	Y	126. $50b-taxes; cut Medicare/spending	Y
106. AIDS insurance non-discrimination	N	127. Limit Pershing II/cruise in Europe	N
107. Prohibit Saudi arms sales	Y	128. Delete $7.1b for 34 B-1 bombers	N
108. Ease Gun Control Act of 1968	Y	129. Bar purchase of Sergeant York guns	N
109. Bar interstate handgun transport	Y	130. El Salvador military/economic aid	Y
110. Make company emissions known	Y	131. Bar mining of Nicaraguan waters	Y
111. Allow toxic victims to sue in fed ct	Y	132. Physician fee freeze for Medicare	Y
112. Superfund waste cleanup of $10b	Y	133. $49b in "sin"/phone/insurance taxes	Y
113. 90 days notice of plant closings	Y	134. Allow sale of Conrail	Y
114. $20b in Medicare cuts/tax increases	N	135. Equal Rights Amendment	N
115. Spending cuts and tax increases	N	136. Authorize Marines in Lebanon	Y
116. Set school lunch lmt-250% poverty	N	137. Eminent domain for coal companies	N
117. $75m for youth work projects	Y	138. Prohibit EPA clean air sanctions	N
118. Allow Angolan military assistance	Y	139. SS retirement age increase/reforms	Y
119. Suspend defense payments for abuse	N	140. Auto domestic content requirement	Y
120. Drop SS COLAs/$12b tax increase	N	141. Delete jobs program funding	N
121. Approve $1.5b for 21 MX missiles	N	142. Highway-gas tax bill	Y
122. Emergency farm credit/revisions	Y	143. Cut $5b from defense for Medicare	Y
123. Duty on Taiwan/Hong Kong/S Korea	Y	144. Emergency housing aid of $1b	Y

Presidential Support Score: 1991 - 62%   1990 - 43%

ROUKEMA, MARGE -- New Jersey 5th District [Republican]. Counties of Bergen (pt.), Hunterdon (pt.), Mercer (pt.), Morris (pt.), Passaic (pt.), Sussex (pt.) and Warren (pt.). Prior Terms: 1981-92. Born: September 19, 1929; Newark, NJ. Education: Montclair State College (B.A.); Rutgers University. Occupation: Teacher (1970-73); chairman, State Legislation Committee; co-founder, Ridgewood Senior Citizens Housing Corp.; member, Mayor's Advisory Charter Study Committee.

1. Protection to Haitian refugees	N	33. Family medical leave-veto override	Y
2. Raise tax on wealthy; lower others	N	34. Req submission of balanced budget	Y
3. Investigate Reagan hostage delay	N	35. Balanced budget amendment	Y
4. Campaign finance revisions	N	36. Amendment to ban flag desecration	Y
5. Unpaid leave to care for children	Y	37. Reauthorize Amtrak-veto override	Y
6. Restrict NEA use of funds	Y	38. Retraining aid for coal miners	N
7. Bar race-bias claim/habeas corpus	Y	39. Suspend El Salvador military aid	Y
8. Ban race as death sentence factor	Y	40. Expand child care aid/tax credit	?
9. Exceptions to exclusionary rule	Y	41. Raise House salary/omit honoraria	Y
10. Allow sale of assault weapons	N	42. Toughen oil-spill liability	#
11. Life in prison/abolish death penalty	N	43. Restitution to Japanese interned	Y
12. Req conspiracy-price fixing cases	Y	44. Protect Chinese & C.A. nationals	Y
13. Unemployment benefits extension	Y	45. Abortion $ for rape/incest cases	Y
14. Tissue use of aborted fetuses	Y	46. Allow religious schools to bar gays	Y
15. Bar replacement of union strikers	N	47. Bar broadcaster fairness doctrine	N
16. Hold foreign aid at $15b for '92	Y	48. Bar cap gains cut/reinstate IRA	N
17. Restore space station funding	N	49. Bar unions equal voice in pension	N
18. Civil Rights Act of 1991	N	50. Bar assembly of chemical weapons	Y
19. Unlimited damages-discrimination	N	51. Ban plutonium/uranium production	Y
20. Eliminate funds for supercollider	Y	52. Cap MX missile deployment at 50	Y
21. Terminate SDI except for research	N	53. Allow $3b for 2 stealth bombers	N
22. Req 7-day handgun waiting period	Y	54. Publish bio-warfare experiments	Y
23. Provide $30b for failed S&Ls	Y	55. Raise minimum wage-veto override	Y
24. Allow use of force against Iraq	Y	56. Bar transfer of FS-X technology	Y
25. Allow $15b in foreign aid for '91	X	57. Cut defense and raise domestic $	N
26. Revise & extend legal immigration	X	58. Uniform poll closing in 48 states	N
27. Suspend aid to Angolan rebels	N	59. Req foreign investment disclosure	N
28. Democratic tax plan proposals	N	60. Textile import quotas-veto override	Y
29. Cut defense 5% across the board	N	61. Bar abortion funding in Wash, DC	N
30. Textile import quotas-veto override	Y	62. Notify spouses of AIDS+ carriers	Y
31. Abortion service for military abroad	Y	63. Seize conveyance-drug trafficking	N
32. Limits on high income farmers	Y	64. South Africa sanctions	Y

ROUKEMA, MARGE (continued)

65. 60 days' notice of plant closings	Y	
66. Close unneeded military bases	Y	
67. Keep welfare reform within $2.8b	Y	
68. Allow children housing exclusion	N	
69. Shift $400m of NASA to homeless	Y	
70. Cap Medicare patients' liability	Y	
71. Prohibit employee polygraph testing	Y	
72. Allow CIA to fund Contras	?	
73. Revise unfair trade practices	Y	
74. Focus SDI on accidental launch	Y	
75. Bar Air Force $ for MX missile	N	
76. Allow "real" increase in defense	N	
77. Troop reduction in Europe of 50%	N	
78. Ban nuclear tests above 1 kiloton	N	
79. Ban anti-satellite missile tests	N	
80. Observe certain limits of SALT II	N	
81. Restore four Civil Rights laws	Y	
82. Prohibit aliens as strikebreakers	Y	
83. Allow military malpractice suits	?	
84. Approval of $36m in Contra aid	Y	
85. $18b deficit reduction compromise	Y	
86. Welfare reform of $5.7b for 5 years	N	
87. Raise taxes $12b/cut spending $3b	N	
88. Board to assess occupational risk	Y	
89. Balanced budget by '93-via targets	Y	
90. Bar licensing of two nuclear plants	N	
91. Remove victims compensation cap	N	
92. Catastrophic health insurance	Y	
93. Ban airline smoking-2 hours or less	Y	
94. $1b/two year aid for the homeless	Y	
95. Bar non-unions in union companies	N	
96. Increase FSLIC rescue to $15b	Y	
97. Impose quotas to lower trade deficit	N	
98. Reduce discretionary budget 21%	Y	
99. Immigration reform/alien amnesty	N	
100. South Africa sanctions-veto override	Y	
101. Tax overhaul to revise income tax	Y	
102. Use of military in drug war	Y	
103. Delete 12 MX/add conventional wpn	Y	
104. Raise speed limit to 65 mph	N	

105. Require Pentagon to buy US goods	Y	
106. AIDS insurance non-discrimination	N	
107. Prohibit Saudi arms sales	Y	
108. Ease Gun Control Act of 1968	N	
109. Bar interstate handgun transport	Y	
110. Make company emissions known	Y	
111. Allow toxic victims to sue in fed ct	N	
112. Superfund cleanup of $10b	N	
113. 90 days notice of plant closings	N	
114. $20b in Medicare cuts/tax increases	N	
115. Spending cuts and tax increases	N	
116. Set school lunch lmt-250% poverty	N	
117. $75m for youth work projects	N	
118. Allow Angolan military assistance	Y	
119. Suspend defense payments for abuse	N	
120. Drop SS COLAs/$12b tax increase	N	
121. Approve $1.5b for 21 MX missiles	N	
122. Emergency farm credit/revisions	N	
123. Duty on Taiwan/Hong Kong/S Korea	N	
124. Limit steel imports to 17%	N	
125. Cut $ to schools that bar prayer	N	
126. $50b-taxes; cut Medicare/spending	Y	
127. Limit Pershing II/cruise in Europe	N	
128. Delete $7.1b for 34 B-1 bombers	N	
129. Bar purchase of Sergeant York guns	Y	
130. El Salvador military/economic aid	N	
131. Bar mining of Nicaraguan waters	Y	
132. Physician fee freeze for Medicare	Y	
133. $49b in "sin"/phone/insurance taxes	Y	
134. Allow sale of Conrail	Y	
135. Equal Rights Amendment	Y	
136. Authorize Marines in Lebanon	Y	
137. Eminent domain for coal companies	Y	
138. Prohibit EPA clean air sanctions	N	
139. SS retirement age increase/reforms	Y	
140. Auto domestic content requirement	N	
141. Delete jobs program funding	Y	
142. Highway-gas tax bill	N	
143. Cut $5b from defense for Medicare	Y	
144. Emergency housing aid of $1b	N	

Presidential Support Score: 1991 - 54%   1990 - 45%

DWYER, BERNARD J. -- New Jersey 6th District [Democrat]. Counties of Middlesex (pt.) and Union (pt.). Prior Terms: 1981-92. Born: January 24, 1921; Perth Amboy, NJ. Education: Rutgers University. Military Service: U.S. Navy, 1940-45. Occupation: Insurance broker-owner, Fraser Bros.; township councilman (1958-70); mayor (1969-73); New Jersey senator (1974-80); trustee, John F. Kennedy Medical Center; member, Chamber of Commerce.

1. Protection to Haitian refugees	Y	
2. Raise tax on wealthy; lower others	N	
3. Investigate Reagan hostage delay	Y	
4. Campaign finance revisions	Y	
5. Unpaid leave to care for children	Y	
6. Restrict NEA use of funds	N	
7. Bar race-bias claim/habeas corpus	N	
8. Ban race as death sentence factor	N	
9. Exceptions to exclusionary rule	Y	
10. Allow sale of assault weapons	N	
11. Life in prison/abolish death penalty	N	
12. Req conspiracy-price fixing cases	N	
13. Unemployment benefits extension	Y	

14. Tissue use of aborted fetuses	Y	
15. Bar replacement of union strikers	Y	
16. Hold foreign aid at $15b for '92	Y	
17. Restore space station funding	N	
18. Civil Rights Act of 1991	Y	
19. Unlimited damages-discrimination	Y	
20. Eliminate funds for supercollider	N	
21. Terminate SDI except for research	N	
22. Req 7-day handgun waiting period	Y	
23. Provide $30b for failed S&Ls	Y	
24. Allow use of force against Iraq	N	
25. Allow $15b in foreign aid for '91	Y	
26. Revise & extend legal immigration	Y	

DWYER, BERNARD J. (continued)

27. Suspend aid to Angolan rebels	Y	
28. Democratic tax plan proposals	Y	
29. Cut defense 5% across the board	N	
30. Textile import quotas-veto override	Y	
31. Abortion service for military abroad	Y	
32. Limits on high income farmers	Y	
33. Family medical leave-veto override	Y	
34. Req submission of balanced budget	Y	
35. Balanced budget amendment	N	
36. Amendment to ban flag desecration	N	
37. Reauthorize Amtrak-veto override	Y	
38. Retraining aid for coal miners	Y	
39. Suspend El Salvador military aid	Y	
40. Expand child care aid/tax credit	#	
41. Raise House salary/omit honoraria	Y	
42. Toughen oil-spill liability	Y	
43. Restitution to Japanese interned	Y	
44. Protect Chinese & C.A. nationals	Y	
45. Abortion $ for rape/incest cases	Y	
46. Allow religious schools to bar gays	N	
47. Bar broadcaster fairness doctrine	N	
48. Bar cap gains cut/reinstate IRA	Y	
49. Bar unions equal voice in pension	N	
50. Bar assembly of chemical weapons	Y	
51. Ban plutonium/uranium production	Y	
52. Cap MX missile deployment at 50	Y	
53. Allow $3b for 2 stealth bombers	N	
54. Publish bio-warfare experiments	Y	
55. Raise minimum wage-veto override	Y	
56. Bar transfer of FS-X technology	?	
57. Cut defense and raise domestic $	N	
58. Uniform poll closing in 48 states	Y	
59. Req foreign investment disclosure	Y	
60. Textile import quotas-veto override	Y	
61. Bar abortion funding in Wash, DC	N	
62. Notify spouses of AIDS+ carriers	N	
63. Seize conveyance-drug trafficking	N	
64. South Africa sanctions	Y	
65. 60 days' notice of plant closings	Y	
66. Close unneeded military bases	N	
67. Keep welfare reform within $2.8b	?	
68. Allow children housing exclusion	N	
69. Shift $400m of NASA to homeless	N	
70. Cap Medicare patients' liability	Y	
71. Prohibit employee polygraph testing	Y	
72. Allow CIA to fund Contras	N	
73. Revise unfair trade practices	Y	
74. Focus SDI on accidental launch	Y	
75. Bar Air Force $ for MX missile	Y	
76. Allow "real" increase in defense	N	
77. Troop reduction in Europe of 50%	N	
78. Ban nuclear tests above 1 kiloton	Y	
79. Ban anti-satellite missile tests	Y	
80. Observe certain limits of SALT II	Y	
81. Restore four Civil Rights laws	Y	
82. Prohibit aliens as strikebreakers	Y	
83. Allow military malpractice suits	Y	
84. Approval of $36m in Contra aid	N	
85. $18b deficit reduction compromise	Y	

86. Welfare reform of $5.7b for 5 years	Y	
87. Raise taxes $12b/cut spending $3b	Y	
88. Board to assess occupational risk	Y	
89. Balanced budget by '93-via targets	Y	
90. Bar licensing of two nuclear plants	N	
91. Remove victims compensation cap	N	
92. Catastrophic health insurance	Y	
93. Ban airline smoking-2 hours or less	N	
94. $1b/two year aid for the homeless	Y	
95. Bar non-unions in union companies	Y	
96. Increase FSLIC rescue to $15b	N	
97. Impose quotas to lower trade deficit	Y	
98. Reduce discretionary budget 21%	N	
99. Immigration reform/alien amnesty	Y	
100. South Africa sanctions-veto override	Y	
101. Tax overhaul to revise income tax	Y	
102. Use of military in drug war	Y	
103. Delete 12 MX/add conventional wpn	Y	
104. Raise speed limit to 65 mph	N	
105. Require Pentagon to buy US goods	?	
106. AIDS insurance non-discrimination	Y	
107. Prohibit Saudi arms sales	Y	
108. Ease Gun Control Act of 1968	N	
109. Bar interstate handgun transport	Y	
110. Make company emissions known	Y	
111. Allow toxic victims to sue in fed ct	Y	
112. Superfund waste cleanup of $10b	Y	
113. 90 days notice of plant closings	Y	
114. $20b in Medicare cuts/tax increases	Y	
115. Spending cuts and tax increases	Y	
116. Set school lunch lmt-250% poverty	N	
117. $75m for youth work projects	Y	
118. Allow Angolan military assistance	N	
119. Suspend defense payments for abuse	Y	
120. Drop SS COLAs/$12b tax increase	N	
121. Approve $1.5b for 21 MX missiles	N	
122. Emergency farm credit/revisions	Y	
123. Duty on Taiwan/Hong Kong/S Korea	Y	
124. Limit steel imports to 17%	Y	
125. Cut $ to schools that bar prayer	N	
126. $50b-taxes; cut Medicare/spending	Y	
127. Limit Pershing II/cruise in Europe	N	
128. Delete $7.1b for 34 B-1 bombers	Y	
129. Bar purchase of Sergeant York guns	Y	
130. El Salvador military/economic aid	N	
131. Bar mining of Nicaraguan waters	Y	
132. Physician fee freeze for Medicare	N	
133. $49b in "sin"/phone/insurance taxes	Y	
134. Allow sale of Conrail	N	
135. Equal Rights Amendment	Y	
136. Authorize Marines in Lebanon	Y	
137. Eminent domain for coal companies	Y	
138. Prohibit EPA clean air sanctions	N	
139. SS retirement age increase/reforms	N	
140. Auto domestic content requirement	Y	
141. Delete jobs program funding	N	
142. Highway-gas tax bill	Y	
143. Cut $5b from defense for Medicare	Y	
144. Emergency housing aid of $1b	Y	

Presidential Support Score: 1991 - 30% 1990 - 19%

RINALDO, MATTHEW J. -- New Jersey 7th District [Republican]. Counties of Mercer (pt.), Middlesex (pt.), Monmouth (pt.), Somerset (pt.) and Union (pt.). Prior Terms: 1973-92. Born: September 1, 1931; Elizabeth, NJ. Education: Rutgers University (B.S.); Seton Hall University (M.B.A.); New York University. Occupation: Faculty member, Rutgers University; boardmember, Union Center National Bank (1970-72); boardmember, Union County Board of Freeholders (1963-64); president, Township of Union Zoning Board of Adjustment (1962-63); New Jersey senator (1967-72).

1. Protection to Haitian refugees	Y	
2. Raise tax on wealthy; lower others	N	
3. Investigate Reagan hostage delay	N	
4. Campaign finance revisions	Y	
5. Unpaid leave to care for children	Y	
6. Restrict NEA use of funds	Y	
7. Bar race-bias claim/habeas corpus	Y	
8. Ban race as death sentence factor	Y	
9. Exceptions to exclusionary rule	Y	
10. Allow sale of assault weapons	N	
11. Life in prison/abolish death penalty	N	
12. Req conspiracy-price fixing cases	N	
13. Unemployment benefits extension	Y	
14. Tissue use of aborted fetuses	N	
15. Bar replacement of union strikers	Y	
16. Hold foreign aid at $15b for '92	Y	
17. Restore space station funding	Y	
18. Civil Rights Act of 1991	Y	
19. Unlimited damages-discrimination	N	
20. Eliminate funds for supercollider	N	
21. Terminate SDI except for research	N	
22. Req 7-day handgun waiting period	Y	
23. Provide $30b for failed S&Ls	N	
24. Allow use of force against Iraq	Y	
25. Allow $15b in foreign aid for '91	Y	
26. Revise & extend legal immigration	Y	
27. Suspend aid to Angolan rebels	N	
28. Democratic tax plan proposals	N	
29. Cut defense 5% across the board	N	
30. Textile import quotas-veto override	Y	
31. Abortion service for military abroad	N	
32. Limits on high income farmers	Y	
33. Family medical leave-veto override	Y	
34. Req submission of balanced budget	Y	
35. Balanced budget amendment	Y	
36. Amendment to ban flag desecration	Y	
37. Reauthorize Amtrak-veto override	Y	
38. Retraining aid for coal miners	Y	
39. Suspend El Salvador military aid	Y	
40. Expand child care aid/tax credit	Y	
41. Raise House salary/omit honoraria	Y	
42. Toughen oil-spill liability	Y	
43. Restitution to Japanese interned	N	
44. Protect Chinese & C.A. nationals	Y	
45. Abortion $ for rape/incest cases	N	
46. Allow religious schools to bar gays	Y	
47. Bar broadcaster fairness doctrine	N	
48. Bar cap gains cut/reinstate IRA	N	
49. Bar unions equal voice in pension	N	
50. Bar assembly of chemical weapons	Y	
51. Ban plutonium/uranium production	Y	
52. Cap MX missile deployment at 50	N	
53. Allow $3b for 2 stealth bombers	Y	
54. Publish bio-warfare experiments	Y	
55. Raise minimum wage-veto override	Y	
56. Bar transfer of FS-X technology	Y	
57. Cut defense and raise domestic $	N	

58. Uniform poll closing in 48 states	N	
59. Req foreign investment disclosure	Y	
60. Textile import quotas-veto override	Y	
61. Bar abortion funding in Wash, DC	Y	
62. Notify spouses of AIDS+ carriers	N	
63. Seize conveyance-drug trafficking	Y	
64. South Africa sanctions	Y	
65. 60 days' notice of plant closings	Y	
66. Close unneeded military bases	Y	
67. Keep welfare reform within $2.8b	Y	
68. Allow children housing exclusion	N	
69. Shift $400m of NASA to homeless	N	
70. Cap Medicare patients' liability	Y	
71. Prohibit employee polygraph testing	Y	
72. Allow CIA to fund Contras	N	
73. Revise unfair trade practices	Y	
74. Focus SDI on accidental launch	N	
75. Bar Air Force $ for MX missile	N	
76. Allow "real" increase in defense	N	
77. Troop reduction in Europe of 50%	N	
78. Ban nuclear tests above 1 kiloton	N	
79. Ban anti-satellite missile tests	N	
80. Observe certain limits of SALT II	N	
81. Restore four Civil Rights laws	Y	
82. Prohibit aliens as strikebreakers	Y	
83. Allow military malpractice suits	Y	
84. Approval of $36m in Contra aid	Y	
85. $18b deficit reduction compromise	N	
86. Welfare reform of $5.7b for 5 years	Y	
87. Raise taxes $12b/cut spending $3b	N	
88. Board to assess occupational risk	Y	
89. Balanced budget by '93-via targets	N	
90. Bar licensing of two nuclear plants	N	
91. Remove victims compensation cap	N	
92. Catastrophic health insurance	Y	
93. Ban airline smoking-2 hours or less	Y	
94. $1b/two year aid for the homeless	Y	
95. Bar non-unions in union companies	Y	
96. Increase FSLIC rescue to $15b	N	
97. Impose quotas to lower trade deficit	Y	
98. Reduce discretionary budget 21%	Y	
99. Immigration reform/alien amnesty	N	
100. South Africa sanctions-veto override	Y	
101. Tax overhaul to revise income tax	?	
102. Use of military in drug war	Y	
103. Delete 12 MX/add conventional wpn	N	
104. Raise speed limit to 65 mph	N	
105. Require Pentagon to buy US goods	Y	
106. AIDS insurance non-discrimination	N	
107. Prohibit Saudi arms sales	Y	
108. Ease Gun Control Act of 1968	Y	
109. Bar interstate handgun transport	Y	
110. Make company emissions known	Y	
111. Allow toxic victims to sue in fed ct	Y	
112. Superfund waste cleanup of $10b	N	
113. 90 days notice of plant closings	Y	
114. $20b in Medicare cuts/tax increases	Y	

RINALDO, MATTHEW J. (continued)

115. Spending cuts and tax increases	N
116. Set school lunch lmt-250% poverty	N
117. $75m for youth work projects	Y
118. Allow Angolan military assistance	Y
119. Suspend defense payments for abuse	N
120. Drop SS COLAs/$12b tax increase	N
121. Approve $1.5b for 21 MX missiles	Y
122. Emergency farm credit/revisions	N
123. Duty on Taiwan/Hong Kong/S Korea	Y
124. Limit steel imports to 17%	Y
125. Cut $ to schools that bar prayer	?
126. $50b-taxes; cut Medicare/spending	N
127. Limit Pershing II/cruise in Europe	N
128. Delete $7.1b for 34 B-1 bombers	N
129. Bar purchase of Sergeant York guns	N
130. El Salvador military/economic aid	Y
131. Bar mining of Nicaraguan waters	Y
132. Physician fee freeze for Medicare	N
133. $49b in "sin"/phone/insurance taxes	Y
134. Allow sale of Conrail	N
135. Equal Rights Amendment	Y
136. Authorize Marines in Lebanon	Y
137. Eminent domain for coal companies	N
138. Prohibit EPA clean air sanctions	N
139. SS retirement age increase/reforms	N
140. Auto domestic content requirement	Y
141. Delete jobs program funding	N
142. Highway-gas tax bill	Y
143. Cut $5b from defense for Medicare	Y
144. Emergency housing aid of $1b	Y

Presidential Support Score: 1991 - 62%   1990 - 47%

ROE, ROBERT A. -- New Jersey 8th District [Democrat]. Counties of Bergen (pt.), Morris (pt.) and Passaic (pt.). Prior Terms: 1969 (Special Election)-1992. Born: February 28, 1924; Wayne, NJ. Education: Oregon State University; Washington State University. Military Service: U.S. Army, WW II. Occupation: Committeeman, Wayne Township (1955-56); mayor, Wayne Township (1956-61); Passaic County Freeholder (1959-63); director of board, Chosen Freeholders (1962-63); commissioner, Conservation and Economic Development New Jersey (1963-69).

1. Protection to Haitian refugees	Y
2. Raise tax on wealthy; lower others	N
3. Investigate Reagan hostage delay	Y
4. Campaign finance revisions	Y
5. Unpaid leave to care for children	Y
6. Restrict NEA use of funds	N
7. Bar race-bias claim/habeas corpus	N
8. Ban race as death sentence factor	N
9. Exceptions to exclusionary rule	N
10. Allow sale of assault weapons	N
11. Life in prison/abolish death penalty	N
12. Req conspiracy-price fixing cases	N
13. Unemployment benefits extension	Y
14. Tissue use of aborted fetuses	N
15. Bar replacement of union strikers	Y
16. Hold foreign aid at $15b for '92	Y
17. Restore space station funding	Y
18. Civil Rights Act of 1991	Y
19. Unlimited damages-discrimination	Y
20. Eliminate funds for supercollider	N
21. Terminate SDI except for research	N
22. Req 7-day handgun waiting period	Y
23. Provide $30b for failed S&Ls	--
24. Allow use of force against Iraq	N
25. Allow $15b in foreign aid for '91	Y
26. Revise & extend legal immigration	N
27. Suspend aid to Angolan rebels	N
28. Democratic tax plan proposals	Y
29. Cut defense 5% across the board	N
30. Textile import quotas-veto override	Y
31. Abortion service for military abroad	N
32. Limits on high income farmers	?
33. Family medical leave-veto override	Y
34. Req submission of balanced budget	Y
35. Balanced budget amendment	N
36. Amendment to ban flag desecration	Y
37. Reauthorize Amtrak-veto override	Y
38. Retraining aid for coal miners	Y
39. Suspend El Salvador military aid	N
40. Expand child care aid/tax credit	Y
41. Raise House salary/omit honoraria	Y
42. Toughen oil-spill liability	?
43. Restitution to Japanese interned	Y
44. Protect Chinese & C.A. nationals	Y
45. Abortion $ for rape/incest cases	?
46. Allow religious schools to bar gays	N
47. Bar broadcaster fairness doctrine	N
48. Bar cap gains cut/reinstate IRA	N
49. Bar unions equal voice in pension	N
50. Bar assembly of chemical weapons	N
51. Ban plutonium/uranium production	Y
52. Cap MX missile deployment at 50	?
53. Allow $3b for 2 stealth bombers	N
54. Publish bio-warfare experiments	Y
55. Raise minimum wage-veto override	Y
56. Bar transfer of FS-X technology	Y
57. Cut defense and raise domestic $	N
58. Uniform poll closing in 48 states	Y
59. Req foreign investment disclosure	Y
60. Textile import quotas-veto override	Y
61. Bar abortion funding in Wash, DC	Y
62. Notify spouses of AIDS+ carriers	N
63. Seize conveyance-drug trafficking	Y
64. South Africa sanctions	Y
65. 60 days' notice of plant closings	Y
66. Close unneeded military bases	N
67. Keep welfare reform within $2.8b	N
68. Allow children housing exclusion	N
69. Shift $400m of NASA to homeless	N
70. Cap Medicare patients' liability	Y
71. Prohibit employee polygraph testing	Y
72. Allow CIA to fund Contras	N
73. Revise unfair trade practices	Y
74. Focus SDI on accidental launch	Y

ROE, ROBERT A. (continued)

75. Bar Air Force $ for MX missile	N	110. Make company emissions known	Y
76. Allow "real" increase in defense	N	111. Allow toxic victims to sue in fed ct	Y
77. Troop reduction in Europe of 50%	N	112. Superfund waste cleanup of $10b	N
78. Ban nuclear tests above 1 kiloton	Y	113. 90 days notice of plant closings	Y
79. Ban anti-satellite missile tests	Y	114. $20b in Medicare cuts/tax increases	Y
80. Observe certain limits of SALT II	Y	115. Spending cuts and tax increases	Y
81. Restore four Civil Rights laws	Y	116. Set school lunch lmt-250% poverty	N
82. Prohibit aliens as strikebreakers	Y	117. $75m for youth work projects	Y
83. Allow military malpractice suits	Y	118. Allow Angolan military assistance	?
84. Approval of $36m in Contra aid	N	119. Suspend defense payments for abuse	Y
85. $18b deficit reduction compromise	Y	120. Drop SS COLAs/$12b tax increase	N
86. Welfare reform of $5.7b for 5 years	Y	121. Approve $1.5b for 21 MX missiles	N
87. Raise taxes $12b/cut spending $3b	Y	122. Emergency farm credit/revisions	Y
88. Board to assess occupational risk	Y	123. Duty on Taiwan/Hong Kong/S Korea	Y
89. Balanced budget by '93-via targets	Y	124. Limit steel imports to 17%	N
90. Bar licensing of two nuclear plants	N	125. Cut $ to schools that bar prayer	N
91. Remove victims compensation cap	N	126. $50b-taxes; cut Medicare/spending	Y
92. Catastrophic health insurance	Y	127. Limit Pershing II/cruise in Europe	?
93. Ban airline smoking-2 hours or less	?	128. Delete $7.1b for 34 B-1 bombers	Y
94. $1b/two year aid for the homeless	Y	129. Bar purchase of Sergeant York guns	?
95. Bar non-unions in union companies	Y	130. El Salvador military/economic aid	N
96. Increase FSLIC rescue to $15b	?	131. Bar mining of Nicaraguan waters	Y
97. Impose quotas to lower trade deficit	Y	132. Physician fee freeze for Medicare	N
98. Reduce discretionary budget 21%	Y	133. $49b in "sin"/phone/insurance taxes	Y
99. Immigration reform/alien amnesty	Y	134. Allow sale of Conrail	N
100. South Africa sanctions-veto override	Y	135. Equal Rights Amendment	Y
101. Tax overhaul to revise income tax	Y	136. Authorize Marines in Lebanon	Y
102. Use of military in drug war	Y	137. Eminent domain for coal companies	Y
103. Delete 12 MX/add conventional wpn	Y	138. Prohibit EPA clean air sanctions	N
104. Raise speed limit to 65 mph	N	139. SS retirement age increase/reforms	N
105. Require Pentagon to buy US goods	Y	140. Auto domestic content requirement	Y
106. AIDS insurance non-discrimination	Y	141. Delete jobs program funding	N
107. Prohibit Saudi arms sales	Y	142. Highway-gas tax bill	N
108. Ease Gun Control Act of 1968	N	143. Cut $5b from defense for Medicare	Y
109. Bar interstate handgun transport	Y	144. Emergency housing aid of $1b	Y

Presidential Support Score: 1991 - 37%   1990 - 27%

TORRICELLI, ROBERT G. -- New Jersey 9th District [Democrat].   County of Bergen (pt.). Prior Terms: 1983-92.   Born: August 26, 1951; Paterson, NJ.   Education: Rutgers University; Rutgers University School of Law (J.D.); Harvard University (M.P.A.). Occupation: Attorney; governor's assistant (1975-78); Vice president's counsel (1978-80).

1. Protection to Haitian refugees	Y	21. Terminate SDI except for research	N
2. Raise tax on wealthy; lower others	N	22. Req 7-day handgun waiting period	Y
3. Investigate Reagan hostage delay	Y	23. Provide $30b for failed S&Ls	N
4. Campaign finance revisions	Y	24. Allow use of force against Iraq	Y
5. Unpaid leave to care for children	Y	25. Allow $15b in foreign aid for '91	Y
6. Restrict NEA use of funds	N	26. Revise & extend legal immigration	Y
7. Bar race-bias claim/habeas corpus	Y	27. Suspend aid to Angolan rebels	Y
8. Ban race as death sentence factor	N	28. Democratic tax plan proposals	Y
9. Exceptions to exclusionary rule	N	29. Cut defense 5% across the board	N
10. Allow sale of assault weapons	N	30. Textile import quotas-veto override	Y
11. Life in prison/abolish death penalty	N	31. Abortion service for military abroad	?
12. Req conspiracy-price fixing cases	N	32. Limits on high income farmers	Y
13. Unemployment benefits extension	Y	33. Family medical leave-veto override	Y
14. Tissue use of aborted fetuses	Y	34. Req submission of balanced budget	Y
15. Bar replacement of union strikers	Y	35. Balanced budget amendment	N
16. Hold foreign aid at $15b for '92	?	36. Amendment to ban flag desecration	N
17. Restore space station funding	Y	37. Reauthorize Amtrak-veto override	Y
18. Civil Rights Act of 1991	Y	38. Retraining aid for coal miners	Y
19. Unlimited damages-discrimination	Y	39. Suspend El Salvador military aid	Y
20. Eliminate funds for supercollider	N	40. Expand child care aid/tax credit	#

TORRICELLI, ROBERT G. (continued)

41.	Raise House salary/omit honoraria	Y		91.	Remove victims compensation cap	N
42.	Toughen oil-spill liability	?		92.	Catastrophic health insurance	Y
43.	Restitution to Japanese interned	Y		93.	Ban airline smoking-2 hours or less	Y
44.	Protect Chinese & C.A. nationals	N		94.	$1b/two year aid for the homeless	Y
45.	Abortion $ for rape/incest cases	Y		95.	Bar non-unions in union companies	?
46.	Allow religious schools to bar gays	N		96.	Increase FSLIC rescue to $15b	N
47.	Bar broadcaster fairness doctrine	N		97.	Impose quotas to lower trade deficit	Y
48.	Bar cap gains cut/reinstate IRA	Y		98.	Reduce discretionary budget 21%	?
49.	Bar unions equal voice in pension	N		99.	Immigration reform/alien amnesty	Y
50.	Bar assembly of chemical weapons	Y		100.	South Africa sanctions-veto override	Y
51.	Ban plutonium/uranium production	Y		101.	Tax overhaul to revise income tax	Y
52.	Cap MX missile deployment at 50	Y		102.	Use of military in drug war	N
53.	Allow $3b for 2 stealth bombers	N		103.	Delete 12 MX/add conventional wpn	Y
54.	Publish bio-warfare experiments	Y		104.	Raise speed limit to 65 mph	N
55.	Raise minimum wage-veto override	Y		105.	Require Pentagon to buy US goods	Y
56.	Bar transfer of FS-X technology	Y		106.	AIDS insurance non-discrimination	Y
57.	Cut defense and raise domestic $	N		107.	Prohibit Saudi arms sales	Y
58.	Uniform poll closing in 48 states	Y		108.	Ease Gun Control Act of 1968	N
59.	Req foreign investment disclosure	Y		109.	Bar interstate handgun transport	Y
60.	Textile import quotas-veto override	Y		110.	Make company emissions known	Y
61.	Bar abortion funding in Wash, DC	N		111.	Allow toxic victims to sue in fed ct	Y
62.	Notify spouses of AIDS+ carriers	N		112.	Superfund waste cleanup of $10b	Y
63.	Seize conveyance-drug trafficking	N		113.	90 days notice of plant closings	Y
64.	South Africa sanctions	Y		114.	$20b in Medicare cuts/tax increases	Y
65.	60 days' notice of plant closings	Y		115.	Spending cuts and tax increases	Y
66.	Close unneeded military bases	N		116.	Set school lunch lmt-250% poverty	Y
67.	Keep welfare reform within $2.8b	N		117.	$75m for youth work projects	Y
68.	Allow children housing exclusion	N		118.	Allow Angolan military assistance	N
69.	Shift $400m of NASA to homeless	N		119.	Suspend defense payments for abuse	Y
70.	Cap Medicare patients' liability	Y		120.	Drop SS COLAs/$12b tax increase	N
71.	Prohibit employee polygraph testing	Y		121.	Approve $1.5b for 21 MX missiles	N
72.	Allow CIA to fund Contras	N		122.	Emergency farm credit/revisions	?
73.	Revise unfair trade practices	Y		123.	Duty on Taiwan/Hong Kong/S Korea	Y
74.	Focus SDI on accidental launch	Y		124.	Limit steel imports to 17%	Y
75.	Bar Air Force $ for MX missile	Y		125.	Cut $ to schools that bar prayer	N
76.	Allow "real" increase in defense	N		126.	$50b-taxes; cut Medicare/spending	N
77.	Troop reduction in Europe of 50%	N		127.	Limit Pershing II/cruise in Europe	Y
78.	Ban nuclear tests above 1 kiloton	Y		128.	Delete $7.1b for 34 B-1 bombers	Y
79.	Ban anti-satellite missile tests	Y		129.	Bar purchase of Sergeant York guns	Y
80.	Observe certain limits of SALT II	Y		130.	El Salvador military/economic aid	N
81.	Restore four Civil Rights laws	Y		131.	Bar mining of Nicaraguan waters	Y
82.	Prohibit aliens as strikebreakers	Y		132.	Physician fee freeze for Medicare	Y
83.	Allow military malpractice suits	Y		133.	$49b in "sin"/phone/insurance taxes	Y
84.	Approval of $36m in Contra aid	N		134.	Allow sale of Conrail	N
85.	$18b deficit reduction compromise	Y		135.	Equal Rights Amendment	Y
86.	Welfare reform of $5.7b for 5 years	Y		136.	Authorize Marines in Lebanon	Y
87.	Raise taxes $12b/cut spending $3b	Y		137.	Eminent domain for coal companies	N
88.	Board to assess occupational risk	Y		138.	Prohibit EPA clean air sanctions	Y
89.	Balanced budget by '93-via targets	N		139.	SS retirement age increase/reforms	N
90.	Bar licensing of two nuclear plants	N				

Presidential Support Score: 1991 - 33%   1990 - 20%

PAYNE, DONALD -- New Jersey 10th District [Democrat]. Counties of Essex (pt.) and Union (pt.). Prior Terms: 1989-92. Born: July 16, 1934; Newark, NJ. Education: Seton Hall University (B.A.). Occupation: Essex County freeholder (1973-78); Newark municipal council member (1982-89); insurance company executive; computer forms manufacturer vice president; president, YMCAs of the USA; chairman, World YMCA Refugee and Rehabilitation Committee (1973-81).

1.	Protection to Haitian refugees	Y		4.	Campaign finance revisions	Y
2.	Raise tax on wealthy; lower others	Y		5.	Unpaid leave to care for children	Y
3.	Investigate Reagan hostage delay	Y		6.	Restrict NEA use of funds	N

PAYNE, DONALD (continued)

7. Bar race-bias claim/habeas corpus	N	33. Family medical leave-veto override	Y
8. Ban race as death sentence factor	N	34. Req submission of balanced budget	N
9. Exceptions to exclusionary rule	N	35. Balanced budget amendment	N
10. Allow sale of assault weapons	N	36. Amendment to ban flag desecration	N
11. Life in prison/abolish death penalty	Y	37. Reauthorize Amtrak-veto override	Y
12. Req conspiracy-price fixing cases	N	38. Retraining aid for coal miners	Y
13. Unemployment benefits extension	Y	39. Suspend El Salvador military aid	Y
14. Tissue use of aborted fetuses	Y	40. Expand child care aid/tax credit	Y
15. Bar replacement of union strikers	Y	41. Raise House salary/omit honoraria	Y
16. Hold foreign aid at $15b for '92	Y	42. Toughen oil-spill liability	#
17. Restore space station funding	N	43. Restitution to Japanese interned	Y
18. Civil Rights Act of 1991	Y	44. Protect Chinese & C.A. nationals	Y
19. Unlimited damages-discrimination	Y	45. Abortion $ for rape/incest cases	Y
20. Eliminate funds for supercollider	Y	46. Allow religious schools to bar gays	N
21. Terminate SDI except for research	?	47. Bar broadcaster fairness doctrine	N
22. Req 7-day handgun waiting period	Y	48. Bar cap gains cut/reinstate IRA	Y
23. Provide $30b for failed S&Ls	N	49. Bar unions equal voice in pension	N
24. Allow use of force against Iraq	N	50. Bar assembly of chemical weapons	Y
25. Allow $15b in foreign aid for '91	Y	51. Ban plutonium/uranium production	Y
26. Revise & extend legal immigration	Y	52. Cap MX missile deployment at 50	Y
27. Suspend aid to Angolan rebels	Y	53. Allow $3b for 2 stealth bombers	N
28. Democratic tax plan proposals	Y	54. Publish bio-warfare experiments	Y
29. Cut defense 5% across the board	Y	55. Raise minimum wage-veto override	Y
30. Textile import quotas-veto override	Y	56. Bar transfer of FS-X technology	Y
31. Abortion service for military abroad	Y	57. Cut defense and raise domestic $	Y
32. Limits on high income farmers	Y	58. Uniform poll closing in 48 states	?

Presidential Support Score: 1991 - 24% 1990 - 16%

GALLO, DEAN A. -- New Jersey 11th District [Republican]. Counties of Bergen (pt.), Essex (pt.), Hudson (pt.), Morris (pt.) and Possaic (pt.). Prior Terms: 1985-92. Born: November 23, 1935. Occupation: Businessman; New Jersey assemblyman.

1. Protection to Haitian refugees	X	31. Abortion service for military abroad	Y
2. Raise tax on wealthy; lower others	N	32. Limits on high income farmers	Y
3. Investigate Reagan hostage delay	N	33. Family medical leave-veto override	N
4. Campaign finance revisions	N	34. Req submission of balanced budget	N
5. Unpaid leave to care for children	N	35. Balanced budget amendment	Y
6. Restrict NEA use of funds	Y	36. Amendment to ban flag desecration	Y
7. Bar race-bias claim/habeas corpus	Y	37. Reauthorize Amtrak-veto override	Y
8. Ban race as death sentence factor	Y	38. Retraining aid for coal miners	N
9. Exceptions to exclusionary rule	Y	39. Suspend El Salvador military aid	N
10. Allow sale of assault weapons	Y	40. Expand child care aid/tax credit	?
11. Life in prison/abolish death penalty	N	41. Raise House salary/omit honoraria	Y
12. Req conspiracy-price fixing cases	Y	42. Toughen oil-spill liability	Y
13. Unemployment benefits extension	Y	43. Restitution to Japanese interned	N
14. Tissue use of aborted fetuses	Y	44. Protect Chinese & C.A. nationals	N
15. Bar replacement of union strikers	N	45. Abortion $ for rape/incest cases	Y
16. Hold foreign aid at $15b for '92	Y	46. Allow religious schools to bar gays	Y
17. Restore space station funding	?	47. Bar broadcaster fairness doctrine	N
18. Civil Rights Act of 1991	N	48. Bar cap gains cut/reinstate IRA	N
19. Unlimited damages-discrimination	N	49. Bar unions equal voice in pension	Y
20. Eliminate funds for supercollider	N	50. Bar assembly of chemical weapons	N
21. Terminate SDI except for research	N	51. Ban plutonium/uranium production	N
22. Req 7-day handgun waiting period	Y	52. Cap MX missile deployment at 50	N
23. Provide $30b for failed S&Ls	Y	53. Allow $3b for 2 stealth bombers	Y
24. Allow use of force against Iraq	Y	54. Publish bio-warfare experiments	N
25. Allow $15b in foreign aid for '91	Y	55. Raise minimum wage-veto override	N
26. Revise & extend legal immigration	Y	56. Bar transfer of FS-X technology	N
27. Suspend aid to Angolan rebels	N	57. Cut defense and raise domestic $	N
28. Democratic tax plan proposals	N	58. Uniform poll closing in 48 states	N
29. Cut defense 5% across the board	N	59. Req foreign investment disclosure	N
30. Textile import quotas-veto override	N	60. Textile import quotas-veto override	N

GALLO, DEAN A. (continued)

61. Bar abortion funding in Wash, DC	N	
62. Notify spouses of AIDS+ carriers	N	
63. Seize conveyance-drug trafficking	Y	
64. South Africa sanctions	Y	
65. 60 days' notice of plant closings	N	
66. Close unneeded military bases	Y	
67. Keep welfare reform within $2.8b	Y	
68. Allow children housing exclusion	N	
69. Shift $400m of NASA to homeless	Y	
70. Cap Medicare patients' liability	Y	
71. Prohibit employee polygraph testing	?	
72. Allow CIA to fund Contras	#	
73. Revise unfair trade practices	N	
74. Focus SDI on accidental launch	N	
75. Bar Air Force $ for MX missile	N	
76. Allow "real" increase in defense	Y	
77. Troop reduction in Europe of 50%	N	
78. Ban nuclear tests above 1 kiloton	N	
79. Ban anti-satellite missile tests	N	
80. Observe certain limits of SALT II	N	
81. Restore four Civil Rights laws	Y	
82. Prohibit aliens as strikebreakers	Y	
83. Allow military malpractice suits	Y	
84. Approval of $36m in Contra aid	Y	
85. $18b deficit reduction compromise	Y	
86. Welfare reform of $5.7b for 5 years	N	
87. Raise taxes $12b/cut spending $3b	N	
88. Board to assess occupational risk	Y	
89. Balanced budget by '93-via targets	Y	
90. Bar licensing of two nuclear plants	N	
91. Remove victims compensation cap	N	

92. Catastrophic health insurance	Y	
93. Ban airline smoking-2 hours or less	N	
94. $1b/two year aid for the homeless	Y	
95. Bar non-unions in union companies	Y	
96. Increase FSLIC rescue to $15b	Y	
97. Impose quotas to lower trade deficit	N	
98. Reduce discretionary budget 21%	Y	
99. Immigration reform/alien amnesty	N	
100. South Africa sanctions-veto override	Y	
101. Tax overhaul to revise income tax	Y	
102. Use of military in drug war	Y	
103. Delete 12 MX/add conventional wpn	N	
104. Raise speed limit to 65 mph	Y	
105. Require Pentagon to buy US goods	N	
106. AIDS insurance non-discrimination	Y	
107. Prohibit Saudi arms sales	Y	
108. Ease Gun Control Act of 1968	Y	
109. Bar interstate handgun transport	N	
110. Make company emissions known	Y	
111. Allow toxic victims to sue in fed ct	Y	
112. Superfund waste cleanup of $10b	N	
113. 90 days notice of plant closings	N	
114. $20b in Medicare cuts/tax increases	N	
115. Spending cuts and tax increases	N	
116. Set school lunch lmt-250% poverty	Y	
117. $75m for youth work projects	N	
118. Allow Angolan military assistance	Y	
119. Suspend defense payments for abuse	N	
120. Drop SS COLAs/$12b tax increase	N	
121. Approve $1.5b for 21 MX missiles	Y	
122. Emergency farm credit/revisions	N	

Presidential Support Score: 1991 - 67%   1990 - 60%

ZIMMER, RICHARD -- New Jersey 12th District [Republican].   Counties of Essex (pt.), Hunterdon (pt.), Morris (pt.), Somerset (pt.), Sussex (pt.), Union (pt.) and Warren (pt.). Prior Term: 1991-92. Born: August 16, 1944; Newark, NJ.   Education: Yale University (B.A.); Yale Law School (LL.B.).   Occupation: Lawyer; general attorney, Johnson and Johnson; state assemblyman (1981-87) and senator (1987-90).

1. Protection to Haitian refugees	N	
2. Raise tax on wealthy; lower others	N	
3. Investigate Reagan hostage delay	N	
4. Campaign finance revisions	N	
5. Unpaid leave to care for children	Y	
6. Restrict NEA use of funds	Y	
7. Bar race-bias claim/habeas corpus	Y	
8. Ban race as death sentence factor	Y	
9. Exceptions to exclusionary rule	Y	
10. Allow sale of assault weapons	Y	
11. Life in prison/abolish death penalty	N	
12. Req conspiracy-price fixing cases	Y	

13. Unemployment benefits extension	Y	
14. Tissue use of aborted fetuses	Y	
15. Bar replacement of union strikers	N	
16. Hold foreign aid at $15b for '92	Y	
17. Restore space station funding	N	
18. Civil Rights Act of 1991	Y	
19. Unlimited damages-discrimination	N	
20. Eliminate funds for supercollider	Y	
21. Terminate SDI except for research	N	
22. Req 7-day handgun waiting period	N	
23. Provide $30b for failed S&Ls	Y	
24. Allow use of force against Iraq	Y	

Presidential Support Score: 1991 - 60%

SAXTON, H. JAMES -- New Jersey 13th District [Republican]. Counties of Burlington (pt.), Camden (pt.), Monmouth (pt.) and Ocean (pt.). Prior Terms: 1985-92. Born: January 22, 1943; Nicholson, PA.   Occupation: Realtor; New Jersey assemblyman, New Jersey senator; teacher.

1. Protection to Haitian refugees	N	
2. Raise tax on wealthy; lower others	N	

3. Investigate Reagan hostage delay	N	
4. Campaign finance revisions	N	

SAXTON, H. JAMES (continued)

5. Unpaid leave to care for children	N
6. Restrict NEA use of funds	Y
7. Bar race-bias claim/habeas corpus	Y
8. Ban race as death sentence factor	Y
9. Exceptions to exclusionary rule	Y
10. Allow sale of assault weapons	Y
11. Life in prison/abolish death penalty	N
12. Req conspiracy-price fixing cases	Y
13. Unemployment benefits extension	?
14. Tissue use of aborted fetuses	N
15. Bar replacement of union strikers	N
16. Hold foreign aid at $15b for '92	Y
17. Restore space station funding	Y
18. Civil Rights Act of 1991	N
19. Unlimited damages-discrimination	N
20. Eliminate funds for supercollider	N
21. Terminate SDI except for research	N
22. Req 7-day handgun waiting period	Y
23. Provide $30b for failed S&Ls	Y
24. Allow use of force against Iraq	Y
25. Allow $15b in foreign aid for '91	Y
26. Revise & extend legal immigration	Y
27. Suspend aid to Angolan rebels	N
28. Democratic tax plan proposals	N
29. Cut defense 5% across the board	N
30. Textile import quotas-veto override	N
31. Abortion service for military abroad	N
32. Limits on high income farmers	Y
33. Family medical leave-veto override	N
34. Req submission of balanced budget	N
35. Balanced budget amendment	Y
36. Amendment to ban flag desecration	Y
37. Reauthorize Amtrak-veto override	?
38. Retraining aid for coal miners	N
39. Suspend El Salvador military aid	N
40. Expand child care aid/tax credit	Y
41. Raise House salary/omit honoraria	Y
42. Toughen oil-spill liability	Y
43. Restitution to Japanese interned	Y
44. Protect Chinese & C.A. nationals	N
45. Abortion $ for rape/incest cases	N
46. Allow religious schools to bar gays	Y
47. Bar broadcaster fairness doctrine	N
48. Bar cap gains cut/reinstate IRA	N
49. Bar unions equal voice in pension	Y
50. Bar assembly of chemical weapons	N
51. Ban plutonium/uranium production	N
52. Cap MX missile deployment at 50	N
53. Allow $3b for 2 stealth bombers	Y
54. Publish bio-warfare experiments	Y
55. Raise minimum wage-veto override	N
56. Bar transfer of FS-X technology	Y
57. Cut defense and raise domestic $	N
58. Uniform poll closing in 48 states	N
59. Req foreign investment disclosure	N
60. Textile import quotas-veto override	N
61. Bar abortion funding in Wash, DC	Y
62. Notify spouses of AIDS+ carriers	N
63. Seize conveyance-drug trafficking	N

64. South Africa sanctions	N
65. 60 days' notice of plant closings	N
66. Close unneeded military bases	Y
67. Keep welfare reform within $2.8b	Y
68. Allow children housing exclusion	Y
69. Shift $400m of NASA to homeless	Y
70. Cap Medicare patients' liability	Y
71. Prohibit employee polygraph testing	Y
72. Allow CIA to fund Contras	Y
73. Revise unfair trade practices	Y
74. Focus SDI on accidental launch	N
75. Bar Air Force $ for MX missile	N
76. Allow "real" increase in defense	N
77. Troop reduction in Europe of 50%	N
78. Ban nuclear tests above 1 kiloton	N
79. Ban anti-satellite missile tests	N
80. Observe certain limits of SALT II	N
81. Restore four Civil Rights laws	Y
82. Prohibit aliens as strikebreakers	Y
83. Allow military malpractice suits	Y
84. Approval of $36m in Contra aid	Y
85. $18b deficit reduction compromise	N
86. Welfare reform of $5.7b for 5 years	N
87. Raise taxes $12b/cut spending $3b	N
88. Board to assess occupational risk	Y
89. Balanced budget by '93-via targets	Y
90. Bar licensing of two nuclear plants	N
91. Remove victims compensation cap	N
92. Catastrophic health insurance	Y
93. Ban airline smoking-2 hours or less	N
94. $1b/two year aid for the homeless	Y
95. Bar non-unions in union companies	N
96. Increase FSLIC rescue to $15b	Y
97. Impose quotas to lower trade deficit	N
98. Reduce discretionary budget 21%	Y
99. Immigration reform/alien amnesty	N
100. South Africa sanctions-veto override	Y
101. Tax overhaul to revise income tax	Y
102. Use of military in drug war	Y
103. Delete 12 MX/add conventional wpn	N
104. Raise speed limit to 65 mph	N
105. Require Pentagon to buy US goods	N
106. AIDS insurance non-discrimination	N
107. Prohibit Saudi arms sales	Y
108. Ease Gun Control Act of 1968	Y
109. Bar interstate handgun transport	Y
110. Make company emissions known	N
111. Allow toxic victims to sue in fed ct	N
112. Superfund waste cleanup of $10b	N
113. 90 days notice of plant closings	N
114. $20b in Medicare cuts/tax increases	N
115. Spending cuts and tax increases	N
116. Set school lunch lmt-250% poverty	Y
117. $75m for youth work projects	N
118. Allow Angolan military assistance	Y
119. Suspend defense payments for abuse	Y
120. Drop SS COLAs/$12b tax increase	N
121. Approve $1.5b for 21 MX missiles	Y
122. Emergency farm credit/revisions	Y

Presidential Support Score: 1991 - 69% 1990 - 57%

GUARINI, FRANK J. -- New Jersey 14th District [Democrat]. Counties of Bergen (pt.) and Hudson (pt.). Prior Terms: 1979-92. Born: August 20, 1924; Jersey City, NJ. Education: Dartmouth College; Columbia University; New York University (J.D.); Hague Academy of International Law. Military Service: U.S. Navy, WW II. Occupation: Attorney; New Jersey senator (1965-76).

1. Protection to Haitian refugees	Y		60. Textile import quotas-veto override	Y
2. Raise tax on wealthy; lower others	Y		61. Bar abortion funding in Wash, DC	N
3. Investigate Reagan hostage delay	Y		62. Notify spouses of AIDS+ carriers	N
4. Campaign finance revisions	Y		63. Seize conveyance-drug trafficking	N
5. Unpaid leave to care for children	Y		64. South Africa sanctions	Y
6. Restrict NEA use of funds	Y		65. 60 days' notice of plant closings	Y
7. Bar race-bias claim/habeas corpus	N		66. Close unneeded military bases	Y
8. Ban race as death sentence factor	N		67. Keep welfare reform within $2.8b	N
9. Exceptions to exclusionary rule	Y		68. Allow children housing exclusion	N
10. Allow sale of assault weapons	N		69. Shift $400m of NASA to homeless	Y
11. Life in prison/abolish death penalty	N		70. Cap Medicare patients' liability	Y
12. Req conspiracy-price fixing cases	N		71. Prohibit employee polygraph testing	Y
13. Unemployment benefits extension	Y		72. Allow CIA to fund Contras	N
14. Tissue use of aborted fetuses	Y		73. Revise unfair trade practices	N
15. Bar replacement of union strikers	Y		74. Focus SDI on accidental launch	Y
16. Hold foreign aid at $15b for '92	Y		75. Bar Air Force $ for MX missile	N
17. Restore space station funding	N		76. Allow "real" increase in defense	N
18. Civil Rights Act of 1991	Y		77. Troop reduction in Europe of 50%	N
19. Unlimited damages-discrimination	N		78. Ban nuclear tests above 1 kiloton	#
20. Eliminate funds for supercollider	N		79. Ban anti-satellite missile tests	Y
21. Terminate SDI except for research	N		80. Observe certain limits of SALT II	?
22. Req 7-day handgun waiting period	Y		81. Restore four Civil Rights laws	Y
23. Provide $30b for failed S&Ls	N		82. Prohibit aliens as strikebreakers	Y
24. Allow use of force against Iraq	N		83. Allow military malpractice suits	Y
25. Allow $15b in foreign aid for '91	?		84. Approval of $36m in Contra aid	N
26. Revise & extend legal immigration	Y		85. $18b deficit reduction compromise	Y
27. Suspend aid to Angolan rebels	Y		86. Welfare reform of $5.7b for 5 years	Y
28. Democratic tax plan proposals	Y		87. Raise taxes $12b/cut spending $3b	Y
29. Cut defense 5% across the board	N		88. Board to assess occupational risk	Y
30. Textile import quotas-veto override	Y		89. Balanced budget by '93-via targets	N
31. Abortion service for military abroad	Y		90. Bar licensing of two nuclear plants	N
32. Limits on high income farmers	Y		91. Remove victims compensation cap	Y
33. Family medical leave-veto override	Y		92. Catastrophic health insurance	Y
34. Req submission of balanced budget	Y		93. Ban airline smoking-2 hours or less	Y
35. Balanced budget amendment	N		94. $1b/two year aid for the homeless	Y
36. Amendment to ban flag desecration	Y		95. Bar non-unions in union companies	Y
37. Reauthorize Amtrak-veto override	Y		96. Increase FSLIC rescue to $15b	Y
38. Retraining aid for coal miners	Y		97. Impose quotas to lower trade deficit	Y
39. Suspend El Salvador military aid	Y		98. Reduce discretionary budget 21%	Y
40. Expand child care aid/tax credit	Y		99. Immigration reform/alien amnesty	N
41. Raise House salary/omit honoraria	Y		100. South Africa sanctions-veto override	Y
42. Toughen oil-spill liability	Y		101. Tax overhaul to revise income tax	Y
43. Restitution to Japanese interned	N		102. Use of military in drug war	Y
44. Protect Chinese & C.A. nationals	Y		103. Delete 12 MX/add conventional wpn	N
45. Abortion $ for rape/incest cases	Y		104. Raise speed limit to 65 mph	N
46. Allow religious schools to bar gays	N		105. Require Pentagon to buy US goods	N
47. Bar broadcaster fairness doctrine	N		106. AIDS insurance non-discrimination	Y
48. Bar cap gains cut/reinstate IRA	Y		107. Prohibit Saudi arms sales	Y
49. Bar unions equal voice in pension	Y		108. Ease Gun Control Act of 1968	N
50. Bar assembly of chemical weapons	Y		109. Bar interstate handgun transport	Y
51. Ban plutonium/uranium production	Y		110. Make company emissions known	Y
52. Cap MX missile deployment at 50	Y		111. Allow toxic victims to sue in fed ct	N
53. Allow $3b for 2 stealth bombers	N		112. Superfund waste cleanup of $10b	Y
54. Publish bio-warfare experiments	Y		113. 90 days notice of plant closings	Y
55. Raise minimum wage-veto override	Y		114. $20b in Medicare cuts/tax increases	Y
56. Bar transfer of FS-X technology	Y		115. Spending cuts and tax increases	Y
57. Cut defense and raise domestic $	N		116. Set school lunch lmt-250% poverty	N
58. Uniform poll closing in 48 states	Y		117. $75m for youth work projects	Y
59. Req foreign investment disclosure	Y		118. Allow Angolan military assistance	N

GUARINI, FRANK J. (continued)

119. Suspend defense payments for abuse	Y	
120. Drop SS COLAs/$12b tax increase	N	
121. Approve $1.5b for 21 MX missiles	N	
122. Emergency farm credit/revisions	Y	
123. Duty on Taiwan/Hong Kong/S Korea	Y	
124. Limit steel imports to 17%	Y	
125. Cut $ to schools that bar prayer	N	
126. $50b-taxes; cut Medicare/spending	N	
127. Limit Pershing II/cruise in Europe	?	
128. Delete $7.1b for 34 B-1 bombers	Y	
129. Bar purchase of Sergeant York guns	Y	
130. El Salvador military/economic aid	N	
131. Bar mining of Nicaraguan waters	Y	

132. Physician fee freeze for Medicare	N	
133. $49b in "sin"/phone/insurance taxes	Y	
134. Allow sale of Conrail	N	
135. Equal Rights Amendment	Y	
136. Authorize Marines in Lebanon	N	
137. Eminent domain for coal companies	Y	
138. Prohibit EPA clean air sanctions	N	
139. SS retirement age increase/reforms	N	
140. Auto domestic content requirement	Y	
141. Delete jobs program funding	N	
142. Highway-gas tax bill	Y	
143. Cut $5b from defense for Medicare	Y	
144. Emergency housing aid of $1b	Y	

Presidential Support Score: 1991 - 33%   1990 - 33%

NEW MEXICO

SCHIFF, STEVEN H. -- New Mexico 1st District [Republican]. Counties of Bernalillo, De Baca, Guadalupe and Torrance. Prior Terms: 1989-92. Born: March 18, 1947; Chicago, IL. Education: University of Illinois, Chicago (B.A.); University of New Mexico Law School. Military Service: New Mexico Air National Guard. Occupation: Bernalillo County assistant district attorney (1972-77); private attorney; Albuquerque assistant attorney (1979-80); district attorney (1980-88).

1. Protection to Haitian refugees	N	
2. Raise tax on wealthy; lower others	N	
3. Investigate Reagan hostage delay	N	
4. Campaign finance revisions	N	
5. Unpaid leave to care for children	N	
6. Restrict NEA use of funds	N	
7. Bar race-bias claim/habeas corpus	Y	
8. Ban race as death sentence factor	Y	
9. Exceptions to exclusionary rule	Y	
10. Allow sale of assault weapons	Y	
11. Life in prison/abolish death penalty	N	
12. Req conspiracy-price fixing cases	Y	
13. Unemployment benefits extension	N	
14. Tissue use of aborted fetuses	Y	
15. Bar replacement of union strikers	N	
16. Hold foreign aid at $15b for '92	Y	
17. Restore space station funding	Y	
18. Civil Rights Act of 1991	Y	
19. Unlimited damages-discrimination	Y	
20. Eliminate funds for supercollider	N	
21. Terminate SDI except for research	N	
22. Req 7-day handgun waiting period	N	
23. Provide $30b for failed S&Ls	Y	
24. Allow use of force against Iraq	Y	
25. Allow $15b in foreign aid for '91	Y	
26. Revise & extend legal immigration	Y	
27. Suspend aid to Angolan rebels	N	
28. Democratic tax plan proposals	N	
29. Cut defense 5% across the board	N	

30. Textile import quotas-veto override	Y	
31. Abortion service for military abroad	Y	
32. Limits on high income farmers	N	
33. Family medical leave-veto override	N	
34. Req submission of balanced budget	N	
35. Balanced budget amendment	Y	
36. Amendment to ban flag desecration	Y	
37. Reauthorize Amtrak-veto override	N	
38. Retraining aid for coal miners	Y	
39. Suspend El Salvador military aid	N	
40. Expand child care aid/tax credit	Y	
41. Raise House salary/omit honoraria	N	
42. Toughen oil-spill liability	N	
43. Restitution to Japanese interned	Y	
44. Protect Chinese & C.A. nationals	Y	
45. Abortion $ for rape/incest cases	N	
46. Allow religious schools to bar gays	N	
47. Bar broadcaster fairness doctrine	N	
48. Bar cap gains cut/reinstate IRA	N	
49. Bar unions equal voice in pension	Y	
50. Bar assembly of chemical weapons	N	
51. Ban plutonium/uranium production	N	
52. Cap MX missile deployment at 50	N	
53. Allow $3b for 2 stealth bombers	Y	
54. Publish bio-warfare experiments	N	
55. Raise minimum wage-veto override	N	
56. Bar transfer of FS-X technology	N	
57. Cut defense and raise domestic $	N	
58. Uniform poll closing in 48 states	Y	

Presidential Support Score: 1991 - 67%   1990 - 55%

SKEEN, JOE -- New Mexico 2nd District [Republican]. Counties of Chaves, Curry, Dona Ana, Eddy, Grant, Hidalgo, Lea, Lincoln, Luna, Otero, Quay, Roosevelt, Sierra and Union. Prior Terms: 1981-92. Born: June 30, 1927; Roswell, NM. Education: Texas A&M. Military Service: U.S. Navy. Occupation: Rancher; New Mexico senator.

1. Protection to Haitian refugees	N	61. Bar abortion funding in Wash, DC	Y
2. Raise tax on wealthy; lower others	N	62. Notify spouses of AIDS+ carriers	N
3. Investigate Reagan hostage delay	N	63. Seize conveyance-drug trafficking	Y
4. Campaign finance revisions	N	64. South Africa sanctions	N
5. Unpaid leave to care for children	N	65. 60 days' notice of plant closings	N
6. Restrict NEA use of funds	N	66. Close unneeded military bases	Y
7. Bar race-bias claim/habeas corpus	Y	67. Keep welfare reform within $2.8b	Y
8. Ban race as death sentence factor	Y	68. Allow children housing exclusion	Y
9. Exceptions to exclusionary rule	Y	69. Shift $400m of NASA to homeless	N
10. Allow sale of assault weapons	Y	70. Cap Medicare patients' liability	Y
11. Life in prison/abolish death penalty	N	71. Prohibit employee polygraph testing	N
12. Req conspiracy-price fixing cases	Y	72. Allow CIA to fund Contras	Y
13. Unemployment benefits extension	N	73. Revise unfair trade practices	N
14. Tissue use of aborted fetuses	Y	74. Focus SDI on accidental launch	N
15. Bar replacement of union strikers	N	75. Bar Air Force $ for MX missile	N
16. Hold foreign aid at $15b for '92	Y	76. Allow "real" increase in defense	Y
17. Restore space station funding	Y	77. Troop reduction in Europe of 50%	N
18. Civil Rights Act of 1991	N	78. Ban nuclear tests above 1 kiloton	N
19. Unlimited damages-discrimination	N	79. Ban anti-satellite missile tests	N
20. Eliminate funds for supercollider	N	80. Observe certain limits of SALT II	N
21. Terminate SDI except for research	N	81. Restore four Civil Rights laws	N
22. Req 7-day handgun waiting period	N	82. Prohibit aliens as strikebreakers	N
23. Provide $30b for failed S&Ls	Y	83. Allow military malpractice suits	Y
24. Allow use of force against Iraq	Y	84. Approval of $36m in Contra aid	Y
25. Allow $15b in foreign aid for '91	Y	85. $18b deficit reduction compromise	Y
26. Revise & extend legal immigration	Y	86. Welfare reform of $5.7b for 5 years	N
27. Suspend aid to Angolan rebels	N	87. Raise taxes $12b/cut spending $3b	N
28. Democratic tax plan proposals	N	88. Board to assess occupational risk	N
29. Cut defense 5% across the board	N	89. Balanced budget by '93-via targets	N
30. Textile import quotas-veto override	Y	90. Bar licensing of two nuclear plants	N
31. Abortion service for military abroad	N	91. Remove victims compensation cap	N
32. Limits on high income farmers	N	92. Catastrophic health insurance	Y
33. Family medical leave-veto override	N	93. Ban airline smoking-2 hours or less	N
34. Req submission of balanced budget	N	94. $1b/two year aid for the homeless	Y
35. Balanced budget amendment	Y	95. Bar non-unions in union companies	N
36. Amendment to ban flag desecration	Y	96. Increase FSLIC rescue to $15b	N
37. Reauthorize Amtrak-veto override	N	97. Impose quotas to lower trade deficit	N
38. Retraining aid for coal miners	N	98. Reduce discretionary budget 21%	Y
39. Suspend El Salvador military aid	N	99. Immigration reform/alien amnesty	N
40. Expand child care aid/tax credit	N	100. South Africa sanctions-veto override	N
41. Raise House salary/omit honoraria	N	101. Tax overhaul to revise income tax	Y
42. Toughen oil-spill liability	N	102. Use of military in drug war	Y
43. Restitution to Japanese interned	N	103. Delete 12 MX/add conventional wpn	N
44. Protect Chinese & C.A. nationals	N	104. Raise speed limit to 65 mph	Y
45. Abortion $ for rape/incest cases	N	105. Require Pentagon to buy US goods	N
46. Allow religious schools to bar gays	Y	106. AIDS insurance non-discrimination	N
47. Bar broadcaster fairness doctrine	Y	107. Prohibit Saudi arms sales	Y
48. Bar cap gains cut/reinstate IRA	N	108. Ease Gun Control Act of 1968	Y
49. Bar unions equal voice in pension	Y	109. Bar interstate handgun transport	N
50. Bar assembly of chemical weapons	N	110. Make company emissions known	N
51. Ban plutonium/uranium production	N	111. Allow toxic victims to sue in fed ct	N
52. Cap MX missile deployment at 50	N	112. Superfund waste cleanup of $10b	N
53. Allow $3b for 2 stealth bombers	Y	113. 90 days notice of plant closings	N
54. Publish bio-warfare experiments	N	114. $20b in Medicare cuts/tax increases	N
55. Raise minimum wage-veto override	N	115. Spending cuts and tax increases	N
56. Bar transfer of FS-X technology	N	116. Set school lunch lmt-250% poverty	Y
57. Cut defense and raise domestic $	N	117. $75m for youth work projects	N
58. Uniform poll closing in 48 states	Y	118. Allow Angolan military assistance	Y
59. Req foreign investment disclosure	N	119. Suspend defense payments for abuse	N
60. Textile import quotas-veto override	Y	120. Drop SS COLAs/$12b tax increase	N

SKEEN, JOE (continued)

121. Approve $1.5b for 21 MX missiles	Y	133. $49b in "sin"/phone/insurance taxes	N
122. Emergency farm credit/revisions	Y	134. Allow sale of Conrail	Y
123. Duty on Taiwan/Hong Kong/S Korea	N	135. Equal Rights Amendment	N
124. Limit steel imports to 17%	N	136. Authorize Marines in Lebanon	Y
125. Cut $ to schools that bar prayer	Y	137. Eminent domain for coal companies	N
126. $50b-taxes; cut Medicare/spending	N	138. Prohibit EPA clean air sanctions	Y
127. Limit Pershing II/cruise in Europe	N	139. SS retirement age increase/reforms	Y
128. Delete $7.1b for 34 B-1 bombers	N	140. Auto domestic content requirement	N
129. Bar purchase of Sergeant York guns	N	141. Delete jobs program funding	Y
130. El Salvador military/economic aid	Y	142. Highway-gas tax bill	N
131. Bar mining of Nicaraguan waters	N	143. Cut $5b from defense for Medicare	N
132. Physician fee freeze for Medicare	Y	144. Emergency housing aid of $1b	N

Presidential Support Score: 1991 - 75%   1990 - 68%

RICHARDSON, BILL -- New Mexico 3rd District [Democrat]. Counties of Catron, Cibola, Colfax, Harding, Los Alamos, McKinley, Mora, Rio Arriba, Sandoval, San Juan, San Miguel, Sante Fe, Socorro, Taos and Valencia. Prior Terms: 1983-92. Born: November 15, 1947; Pasadena, CA. Education: Tufts University (B.A.); Fletcher School of Law & Diplomacy (M.A.). Occupation: Office of Congressional Relations, Dept. of State (1973-75); professional staff member and investigator, Senate subcommittee on Foreign Relations assistance (1975-78).

1. Protection to Haitian refugees	?	41. Raise House salary/omit honoraria	N
2. Raise tax on wealthy; lower others	Y	42. Toughen oil-spill liability	Y
3. Investigate Reagan hostage delay	Y	43. Restitution to Japanese interned	Y
4. Campaign finance revisions	Y	44. Protect Chinese & C.A. nationals	Y
5. Unpaid leave to care for children	Y	45. Abortion $ for rape/incest cases	Y
6. Restrict NEA use of funds	N	46. Allow religious schools to bar gays	N
7. Bar race-bias claim/habeas corpus	Y	47. Bar broadcaster fairness doctrine	Y
8. Ban race as death sentence factor	Y	48. Bar cap gains cut/reinstate IRA	Y
9. Exceptions to exclusionary rule	Y	49. Bar unions equal voice in pension	Y
10. Allow sale of assault weapons	Y	50. Bar assembly of chemical weapons	Y
11. Life in prison/abolish death penalty	N	51. Ban plutonium/uranium production	Y
12. Req conspiracy-price fixing cases	N	52. Cap MX missile deployment at 50	Y
13. Unemployment benefits extension	Y	53. Allow $3b for 2 stealth bombers	Y
14. Tissue use of aborted fetuses	Y	54. Publish bio-warfare experiments	Y
15. Bar replacement of union strikers	Y	55. Raise minimum wage-veto override	Y
16. Hold foreign aid at $15b for '92	Y	56. Bar transfer of FS-X technology	Y
17. Restore space station funding	Y	57. Cut defense and raise domestic $	N
18. Civil Rights Act of 1991	Y	58. Uniform poll closing in 48 states	Y
19. Unlimited damages-discrimination	Y	59. Req foreign investment disclosure	N
20. Eliminate funds for supercollider	N	60. Textile import quotas-veto override	N
21. Terminate SDI except for research	N	61. Bar abortion funding in Wash, DC	N
22. Req 7-day handgun waiting period	N	62. Notify spouses of AIDS+ carriers	N
23. Provide $30b for failed S&Ls	N	63. Seize conveyance-drug trafficking	N
24. Allow use of force against Iraq	N	64. South Africa sanctions	Y
25. Allow $15b in foreign aid for '91	Y	65. 60 days' notice of plant closings	Y
26. Revise & extend legal immigration	Y	66. Close unneeded military bases	Y
27. Suspend aid to Angolan rebels	Y	67. Keep welfare reform within $2.8b	?
28. Democratic tax plan proposals	Y	68. Allow children housing exclusion	N
29. Cut defense 5% across the board	N	69. Shift $400m of NASA to homeless	N
30. Textile import quotas-veto override	Y	70. Cap Medicare patients' liability	Y
31. Abortion service for military abroad	?	71. Prohibit employee polygraph testing	Y
32. Limits on high income farmers	N	72. Allow CIA to fund Contras	N
33. Family medical leave-veto override	Y	73. Revise unfair trade practices	Y
34. Req submission of balanced budget	Y	74. Focus SDI on accidental launch	Y
35. Balanced budget amendment	Y	75. Bar Air Force $ for MX missile	N
36. Amendment to ban flag desecration	Y	76. Allow "real" increase in defense	Y
37. Reauthorize Amtrak-veto override	Y	77. Troop reduction in Europe of 50%	?
38. Retraining aid for coal miners	Y	78. Ban nuclear tests above 1 kiloton	Y
39. Suspend El Salvador military aid	Y	79. Ban anti-satellite missile tests	Y
40. Expand child care aid/tax credit	Y	80. Observe certain limits of SALT II	Y

RICHARDSON, BILL (continued)

81. Restore four Civil Rights laws	Y	
82. Prohibit aliens as strikebreakers	Y	
83. Allow military malpractice suits	Y	
84. Approval of $36m in Contra aid	N	
85. $18b deficit reduction compromise	Y	
86. Welfare reform of $5.7b for 5 years	Y	
87. Raise taxes $12b/cut spending $3b	N	
88. Board to assess occupational risk	Y	
89. Balanced budget by '93-via targets	Y	
90. Bar licensing of two nuclear plants	N	
91. Remove victims compensation cap	N	
92. Catastrophic health insurance	Y	
93. Ban airline smoking-2 hours or less	Y	
94. $1b/two year aid for the homeless	Y	
95. Bar non-unions in union companies	Y	
96. Increase FSLIC rescue to $15b	N	
97. Impose quotas to lower trade deficit	Y	
98. Reduce discretionary budget 21%	Y	
99. Immigration reform/alien amnesty	Y	
100. South Africa sanctions-veto override	Y	
101. Tax overhaul to revise income tax	Y	
102. Use of military in drug war	Y	
103. Delete 12 MX/add conventional wpn	Y	
104. Raise speed limit to 65 mph	Y	
105. Require Pentagon to buy US goods	Y	
106. AIDS insurance non-discrimination	Y	
107. Prohibit Saudi arms sales	Y	
108. Ease Gun Control Act of 1968	Y	
109. Bar interstate handgun transport	N	
110. Make company emissions known	Y	

111. Allow toxic victims to sue in fed ct	N
112. Superfund waste cleanup of $10b	N
113. 90 days notice of plant closings	Y
114. $20b in Medicare cuts/tax increases	Y
115. Spending cuts and tax increases	Y
116. Set school lunch lmt-250% poverty	N
117. $75m for youth work projects	Y
118. Allow Angolan military assistance	N
119. Suspend defense payments for abuse	Y
120. Drop SS COLAs/$12b tax increase	N
121. Approve $1.5b for 21 MX missiles	N
122. Emergency farm credit/revisions	Y
123. Duty on Taiwan/Hong Kong/S Korea	Y
124. Limit steel imports to 17%	Y
125. Cut $ to schools that bar prayer	N
126. $50b-taxes; cut Medicare/spending	Y
127. Limit Pershing II/cruise in Europe	N
128. Delete $7.1b for 34 B-1 bombers	Y
129. Bar purchase of Sergeant York guns	?
130. El Salvador military/economic aid	N
131. Bar mining of Nicaraguan waters	Y
132. Physician fee freeze for Medicare	N
133. $49b in "sin"/phone/insurance taxes	Y
134. Allow sale of Conrail	N
135. Equal Rights Amendment	Y
136. Authorize Marines in Lebanon	N
137. Eminent domain for coal companies	N
138. Prohibit EPA clean air sanctions	Y
139. SS retirement age increase/reforms	N

Presidential Support Score: 1991 - 33%   1990 - 29%

NEW YORK

HOCHBRUECKNER, GEORGE J. -- New York 1st District [Democrat]. County of Suffolk (pt.). Prior Terms: 1987-92. Born: September 20, 1938; Long Island, NY. Education: State University of New York-Stony Brook; Hofstra University. Military Service: U.S. Navy. Occupation: Aerospace design engineer; state assemblyman (1974-84).

1. Protection to Haitian refugees	Y	
2. Raise tax on wealthy; lower others	Y	
3. Investigate Reagan hostage delay	Y	
4. Campaign finance revisions	Y	
5. Unpaid leave to care for children	Y	
6. Restrict NEA use of funds	Y	
7. Bar race-bias claim/habeas corpus	N	
8. Ban race as death sentence factor	N	
9. Exceptions to exclusionary rule	N	
10. Allow sale of assault weapons	N	
11. Life in prison/abolish death penalty	Y	
12. Req conspiracy-price fixing cases	N	
13. Unemployment benefits extension	Y	
14. Tissue use of aborted fetuses	Y	
15. Bar replacement of union strikers	Y	
16. Hold foreign aid at $15b for '92	Y	
17. Restore space station funding	Y	
18. Civil Rights Act of 1991	Y	

19. Unlimited damages-discrimination	N
20. Eliminate funds for supercollider	N
21. Terminate SDI except for research	N
22. Req 7-day handgun waiting period	Y
23. Provide $30b for failed S&Ls	N
24. Allow use of force against Iraq	N
25. Allow $15b in foreign aid for '91	Y
26. Revise & extend legal immigration	N
27. Suspend aid to Angolan rebels	Y
28. Democratic tax plan proposals	Y
29. Cut defense 5% across the board	N
30. Textile import quotas-veto override	Y
31. Abortion service for military abroad	N
32. Limits on high income farmers	Y
33. Family medical leave-veto override	Y
34. Req submission of balanced budget	Y
35. Balanced budget amendment	N
36. Amendment to ban flag desecration	Y

HOCHBRUECKNER, GEORGE (continued)

37. Reauthorize Amtrak-veto override	Y	
38. Retraining aid for coal miners	Y	
39. Suspend El Salvador military aid	Y	
40. Expand child care aid/tax credit	Y	
41. Raise House salary/omit honoraria	N	
42. Toughen oil-spill liability	Y	
43. Restitution to Japanese interned	Y	
44. Protect Chinese & C.A. nationals	Y	
45. Abortion $ for rape/incest cases	Y	
46. Allow religious schools to bar gays	Y	
47. Bar broadcaster fairness doctrine	N	
48. Bar cap gains cut/reinstate IRA	Y	
49. Bar unions equal voice in pension	N	
50. Bar assembly of chemical weapons	Y	
51. Ban plutonium/uranium production	Y	
52. Cap MX missile deployment at 50	Y	
53. Allow $3b for 2 stealth bombers	N	
54. Publish bio-warfare experiments	Y	
55. Raise minimum wage-veto override	Y	
56. Bar transfer of FS-X technology	Y	
57. Cut defense and raise domestic $	N	
58. Uniform poll closing in 48 states	Y	
59. Req foreign investment disclosure	N	
60. Textile import quotas-veto override	Y	
61. Bar abortion funding in Wash, DC	Y	
62. Notify spouses of AIDS+ carriers	N	
63. Seize conveyance-drug trafficking	N	
64. South Africa sanctions	Y	
65. 60 days' notice of plant closings	Y	
66. Close unneeded military bases	N	
67. Keep welfare reform within $2.8b	N	

68. Allow children housing exclusion	N	
69. Shift $400m of NASA to homeless	Y	
70. Cap Medicare patients' liability	Y	
71. Prohibit employee polygraph testing	Y	
72. Allow CIA to fund Contras	N	
73. Revise unfair trade practices	Y	
74. Focus SDI on accidental launch	Y	
75. Bar Air Force $ for MX missile	N	
76. Allow "real" increase in defense	N	
77. Troop reduction in Europe of 50%	Y	
78. Ban nuclear tests above 1 kiloton	Y	
79. Ban anti-satellite missile tests	Y	
80. Observe certain limits of SALT II	Y	
81. Restore four Civil Rights laws	Y	
82. Prohibit aliens as strikebreakers	Y	
83. Allow military malpractice suits	Y	
84. Approval of $36m in Contra aid	N	
85. $18b deficit reduction compromise	Y	
86. Welfare reform of $5.7b for 5 years	Y	
87. Raise taxes $12b/cut spending $3b	Y	
88. Board to assess occupational risk	Y	
89. Balanced budget by '93-via targets	N	
90. Bar licensing of two nuclear plants	Y	
91. Remove victims compensation cap	Y	
92. Catastrophic health insurance	Y	
93. Ban airline smoking-2 hours or less	Y	
94. $1b/two year aid for the homeless	Y	
95. Bar non-unions in union companies	Y	
96. Increase FSLIC rescue to $15b	Y	
97. Impose quotas to lower trade deficit	Y	
98. Reduce discretionary budget 21%	Y	

Presidential Support Score: 1991 - 29% 1990 - 23%

DOWNEY, THOMAS J. -- New York 2nd District [Democrat]. County of Suffolk (pt.). Prior Terms: 1975-92. Born: January 28, 1949; Ozone Park, NY. Education: Cornell University; St. John's University Law School. Occupation: Suffolk County legislator (1971-75).

1. Protection to Haitian refugees	Y	
2. Raise tax on wealthy; lower others	Y	
3. Investigate Reagan hostage delay	Y	
4. Campaign finance revisions	Y	
5. Unpaid leave to care for children	Y	
6. Restrict NEA use of funds	N	
7. Bar race-bias claim/habeas corpus	N	
8. Ban race as death sentence factor	N	
9. Exceptions to exclusionary rule	N	
10. Allow sale of assault weapons	N	
11. Life in prison/abolish death penalty	Y	
12. Req conspiracy-price fixing cases	N	
13. Unemployment benefits extension	Y	
14. Tissue use of aborted fetuses	Y	
15. Bar replacement of union strikers	Y	
16. Hold foreign aid at $15b for '92	Y	
17. Restore space station funding	Y	
18. Civil Rights Act of 1991	Y	
19. Unlimited damages-discrimination	N	
20. Eliminate funds for supercollider	Y	
21. Terminate SDI except for research	Y	
22. Req 7-day handgun waiting period	Y	
23. Provide $30b for failed S&Ls	N	
24. Allow use of force against Iraq	N	
25. Allow $15b in foreign aid for '91	Y	

26. Revise & extend legal immigration	Y	
27. Suspend aid to Angolan rebels	Y	
28. Democratic tax plan proposals	Y	
29. Cut defense 5% across the board	N	
30. Textile import quotas-veto override	N	
31. Abortion service for military abroad	N	
32. Limits on high income farmers	Y	
33. Family medical leave-veto override	Y	
34. Req submission of balanced budget	Y	
35. Balanced budget amendment	N	
36. Amendment to ban flag desecration	N	
37. Reauthorize Amtrak-veto override	Y	
38. Retraining aid for coal miners	Y	
39. Suspend El Salvador military aid	Y	
40. Expand child care aid/tax credit	Y	
41. Raise House salary/omit honoraria	Y	
42. Toughen oil-spill liability	Y	
43. Restitution to Japanese interned	Y	
44. Protect Chinese & C.A. nationals	Y	
45. Abortion $ for rape/incest cases	Y	
46. Allow religious schools to bar gays	N	
47. Bar broadcaster fairness doctrine	N	
48. Bar cap gains cut/reinstate IRA	Y	
49. Bar unions equal voice in pension	N	
50. Bar assembly of chemical weapons	Y	

DOWNEY, THOMAS J. (continued)

51.	Ban plutonium/uranium production	Y	98.	Reduce discretionary budget 21%	Y
52.	Cap MX missile deployment at 50	Y	99.	Immigration reform/alien amnesty	Y
53.	Allow $3b for 2 stealth bombers	N	100.	South Africa sanctions-veto override	Y
54.	Publish bio-warfare experiments	Y	101.	Tax overhaul to revise income tax	Y
55.	Raise minimum wage-veto override	Y	102.	Use of military in drug war	N
56.	Bar transfer of FS-X technology	Y	103.	Delete 12 MX/add conventional wpn	Y
57.	Cut defense and raise domestic $	N	104.	Raise speed limit to 65 mph	N
58.	Uniform poll closing in 48 states	Y	105.	Require Pentagon to buy US goods	N
59.	Req foreign investment disclosure	N	106.	AIDS insurance non-discrimination	Y
60.	Textile import quotas-veto override	N	107.	Prohibit Saudi arms sales	Y
61.	Bar abortion funding in Wash, DC	N	108.	Ease Gun Control Act of 1968	N
62.	Notify spouses of AIDS+ carriers	N	109.	Bar interstate handgun transport	Y
63.	Seize conveyance-drug trafficking	N	110.	Make company emissions known	Y
64.	South Africa sanctions	Y	111.	Allow toxic victims to sue in fed ct	Y
65.	60 days' notice of plant closings	Y	112.	Superfund waste cleanup of $10b	Y
66.	Close unneeded military bases	N	113.	90 days notice of plant closings	Y
67.	Keep welfare reform within $2.8b	N	114.	$20b in Medicare cuts/tax increases	Y
68.	Allow children housing exclusion	N	115.	Spending cuts and tax increases	Y
69.	Shift $400m of NASA to homeless	Y	116.	Set school lunch lmt-250% poverty	N
70.	Cap Medicare patients' liability	Y	117.	$75m for youth work projects	Y
71.	Prohibit employee polygraph testing	Y	118.	Allow Angolan military assistance	N
72.	Allow CIA to fund Contras	N	119.	Suspend defense payments for abuse	Y
73.	Revise unfair trade practices	Y	120.	Drop SS COLAs/$12b tax increase	N
74.	Focus SDI on accidental launch	Y	121.	Approve $1.5b for 21 MX missiles	N
75.	Bar Air Force $ for MX missile	Y	122.	Emergency farm credit/revisions	Y
76.	Allow "real" increase in defense	N	123.	Duty on Taiwan/Hong Kong/S Korea	N
77.	Troop reduction in Europe of 50%	Y	124.	Limit steel imports to 17%	Y
78.	Ban nuclear tests above 1 kiloton	Y	125.	Cut $ to schools that bar prayer	N
79.	Ban anti-satellite missile tests	Y	126.	$50b-taxes; cut Medicare/spending	Y
80.	Observe certain limits of SALT II	Y	127.	Limit Pershing II/cruise in Europe	Y
81.	Restore four Civil Rights laws	Y	128.	Delete $7.1b for 34 B-1 bombers	Y
82.	Prohibit aliens as strikebreakers	Y	129.	Bar purchase of Sergeant York guns	Y
83.	Allow military malpractice suits	Y	130.	El Salvador military/economic aid	N
84.	Approval of $36m in Contra aid	N	131.	Bar mining of Nicaraguan waters	Y
85.	$18b deficit reduction compromise	Y	132.	Physician fee freeze for Medicare	N
86.	Welfare reform of $5.7b for 5 years	Y	133.	$49b in "sin"/phone/insurance taxes	Y
87.	Raise taxes $12b/cut spending $3b	Y	134.	Allow sale of Conrail	N
88.	Board to assess occupational risk	Y	135.	Equal Rights Amendment	Y
89.	Balanced budget by '93-via targets	N	136.	Authorize Marines in Lebanon	N
90.	Bar licensing of two nuclear plants	Y	137.	Eminent domain for coal companies	N
91.	Remove victims compensation cap	Y	138.	Prohibit EPA clean air sanctions	N
92.	Catastrophic health insurance	Y	139.	SS retirement age increase/reforms	Y
93.	Ban airline smoking-2 hours or less	Y	140.	Auto domestic content requirement	Y
94.	$1b/two year aid for the homeless	Y	141.	Delete jobs program funding	N
95.	Bar non-unions in union companies	Y	142.	Highway-gas tax bill	Y
96.	Increase FSLIC rescue to $15b	Y	143.	Cut $5b from defense for Medicare	C
97.	Impose quotas to lower trade deficit	N	144.	Emergency housing aid of $1b	Y

Presidential Support Score: 1991 - 25%   1990 - 19%

MRAZEK, ROBERT J. -- New York 3rd District [Democrat]. Counties of Nassau (pt.) and Suffolk (pt.). Prior Terms: 1983-92. Born: November 6, 1945; Newport, RI. Education: Cornell University. Military Service: U.S. Navy. Occupation: Writer, small businessman; U.S. senate staff member; county legislator (1975-82).

1.	Protection to Haitian refugees	Y	9.	Exceptions to exclusionary rule	?
2.	Raise tax on wealthy; lower others	N	10.	Allow sale of assault weapons	N
3.	Investigate Reagan hostage delay	?	11.	Life in prison/abolish death penalty	Y
4.	Campaign finance revisions	?	12.	Req conspiracy-price fixing cases	?
5.	Unpaid leave to care for children	Y	13.	Unemployment benefits extension	Y
6.	Restrict NEA use of funds	N	14.	Tissue use of aborted fetuses	#
7.	Bar race-bias claim/habeas corpus	?	15.	Bar replacement of union strikers	Y
8.	Ban race as death sentence factor	?	16.	Hold foreign aid at $15b for '92	Y

MRAZEK, ROBERT J. (continued)

17. Restore space station funding	?	79. Ban anti-satellite missile tests	Y
18. Civil Rights Act of 1991	Y	80. Observe certain limits of SALT II	Y
19. Unlimited damages-discrimination	Y	81. Restore four Civil Rights laws	Y
20. Eliminate funds for supercollider	?	82. Prohibit aliens as strikebreakers	Y
21. Terminate SDI except for research	Y	83. Allow military malpractice suits	N
22. Req 7-day handgun waiting period	Y	84. Approval of $36m in Contra aid	N
23. Provide $30b for failed S&Ls	N	85. $18b deficit reduction compromise	Y
24. Allow use of force against Iraq	N	86. Welfare reform of $5.7b for 5 years	Y
25. Allow $15b in foreign aid for '91	?	87. Raise taxes $12b/cut spending $3b	Y
26. Revise & extend legal immigration	Y	88. Board to assess occupational risk	Y
27. Suspend aid to Angolan rebels	Y	89. Balanced budget by '93-via targets	N
28. Democratic tax plan proposals	Y	90. Bar licensing of two nuclear plants	Y
29. Cut defense 5% across the board	N	91. Remove victims compensation cap	Y
30. Textile import quotas-veto override	Y	92. Catastrophic health insurance	Y
31. Abortion service for military abroad	Y	93. Ban airline smoking-2 hours or less	Y
32. Limits on high income farmers	Y	94. $1b/two year aid for the homeless	Y
33. Family medical leave-veto override	Y	95. Bar non-unions in union companies	Y
34. Req submission of balanced budget	Y	96. Increase FSLIC rescue to $15b	Y
35. Balanced budget amendment	N	97. Impose quotas to lower trade deficit	N
36. Amendment to ban flag desecration	N	98. Reduce discretionary budget 21%	N
37. Reauthorize Amtrak-veto override	Y	99. Immigration reform/alien amnesty	Y
38. Retraining aid for coal miners	Y	100. South Africa sanctions-veto override	Y
39. Suspend El Salvador military aid	Y	101. Tax overhaul to revise income tax	N
40. Expand child care aid/tax credit	Y	102. Use of military in drug war	N
41. Raise House salary/omit honoraria	Y	103. Delete 12 MX/add conventional wpn	Y
42. Toughen oil-spill liability	Y	104. Raise speed limit to 65 mph	Y
43. Restitution to Japanese interned	?	105. Require Pentagon to buy US goods	Y
44. Protect Chinese & C.A. nationals	Y	106. AIDS insurance non-discrimination	Y
45. Abortion $ for rape/incest cases	Y	107. Prohibit Saudi arms sales	Y
46. Allow religious schools to bar gays	N	108. Ease Gun Control Act of 1968	N
47. Bar broadcaster fairness doctrine	N	109. Bar interstate handgun transport	Y
48. Bar cap gains cut/reinstate IRA	N	110. Make company emissions known	Y
49. Bar unions equal voice in pension	N	111. Allow toxic victims to sue in fed ct	N
50. Bar assembly of chemical weapons	Y	112. Superfund waste cleanup of $10b	Y
51. Ban plutonium/uranium production	Y	113. 90 days notice of plant closings	Y
52. Cap MX missile deployment at 50	Y	114. $20b in Medicare cuts/tax increases	Y
53. Allow $3b for 2 stealth bombers	N	115. Spending cuts and tax increases	Y
54. Publish bio-warfare experiments	Y	116. Set school lunch lmt-250% poverty	N
55. Raise minimum wage-veto override	Y	117. $75m for youth work projects	Y
56. Bar transfer of FS-X technology	N	118. Allow Angolan military assistance	N
57. Cut defense and raise domestic $	Y	119. Suspend defense payments for abuse	Y
58. Uniform poll closing in 48 states	Y	120. Drop SS COLAs/$12b tax increase	N
59. Req foreign investment disclosure	N	121. Approve $1.5b for 21 MX missiles	N
60. Textile import quotas-veto override	Y	122. Emergency farm credit/revisions	Y
61. Bar abortion funding in Wash, DC	N	123. Duty on Taiwan/Hong Kong/S Korea	Y
62. Notify spouses of AIDS+ carriers	N	124. Limit steel imports to 17%	Y
63. Seize conveyance-drug trafficking	N	125. Cut $ to schools that bar prayer	N
64. South Africa sanctions	Y	126. $50b-taxes; cut Medicare/spending	Y
65. 60 days' notice of plant closings	Y	127. Limit Pershing II/cruise in Europe	Y
66. Close unneeded military bases	N	128. Delete $7.1b for 34 B-1 bombers	Y
67. Keep welfare reform within $2.8b	?	129. Bar purchase of Sergeant York guns	N
68. Allow children housing exclusion	N	130. El Salvador military/economic aid	N
69. Shift $400m of NASA to homeless	N	131. Bar mining of Nicaraguan waters	Y
70. Cap Medicare patients' liability	Y	132. Physician fee freeze for Medicare	N
71. Prohibit employee polygraph testing	Y	133. $49b in "sin"/phone/insurance taxes	Y
72. Allow CIA to fund Contras	N	134. Allow sale of Conrail	N
73. Revise unfair trade practices	N	135. Equal Rights Amendment	Y
74. Focus SDI on accidental launch	Y	136. Authorize Marines in Lebanon	Y
75. Bar Air Force $ for MX missile	Y	137. Eminent domain for coal companies	N
76. Allow "real" increase in defense	N	138. Prohibit EPA clean air sanctions	N
77. Troop reduction in Europe of 50%	Y	139. SS retirement age increase/reforms	N
78. Ban nuclear tests above 1 kiloton	Y		

Presidential Support Score: 1991 - 13%   1990 - 16%

LENT, NORMAN F. -- New York 4th District [Republican]. County of Nassau (pt.). Prior Terms: 1971-92. Born: March 23, 1931; Oceanside, NY. Education: Hofstra University (B.A.); Cornell Law School (LL.B.). Military Service: U.S. Navy. Occupation: Associate police justice (1960-62); New York senator (1962-70); attorney, Hill, Lent and Troescher.

1. Protection to Haitian refugees	N	61. Bar abortion funding in Wash, DC	Y
2. Raise tax on wealthy; lower others	N	62. Notify spouses of AIDS+ carriers	N
3. Investigate Reagan hostage delay	N	63. Seize conveyance-drug trafficking	Y
4. Campaign finance revisions	N	64. South Africa sanctions	Y
5. Unpaid leave to care for children	N	65. 60 days' notice of plant closings	Y
6. Restrict NEA use of funds	Y	66. Close unneeded military bases	Y
7. Bar race-bias claim/habeas corpus	Y	67. Keep welfare reform within $2.8b	Y
8. Ban race as death sentence factor	Y	68. Allow children housing exclusion	N
9. Exceptions to exclusionary rule	Y	69. Shift $400m of NASA to homeless	N
10. Allow sale of assault weapons	N	70. Cap Medicare patients' liability	Y
11. Life in prison/abolish death penalty	N	71. Prohibit employee polygraph testing	?
12. Req conspiracy-price fixing cases	N	72. Allow CIA to fund Contras	Y
13. Unemployment benefits extension	N	73. Revise unfair trade practices	N
14. Tissue use of aborted fetuses	N	74. Focus SDI on accidental launch	N
15. Bar replacement of union strikers	N	75. Bar Air Force $ for MX missile	N
16. Hold foreign aid at $15b for '92	Y	76. Allow "real" increase in defense	Y
17. Restore space station funding	Y	77. Troop reduction in Europe of 50%	?
18. Civil Rights Act of 1991	N	78. Ban nuclear tests above 1 kiloton	N
19. Unlimited damages-discrimination	N	79. Ban anti-satellite missile tests	N
20. Eliminate funds for supercollider	N	80. Observe certain limits of SALT II	N
21. Terminate SDI except for research	?	81. Restore four Civil Rights laws	Y
22. Req 7-day handgun waiting period	Y	82. Prohibit aliens as strikebreakers	Y
23. Provide $30b for failed S&Ls	Y	83. Allow military malpractice suits	?
24. Allow use of force against Iraq	Y	84. Approval of $36m in Contra aid	Y
25. Allow $15b in foreign aid for '91	Y	85. $18b deficit reduction compromise	Y
26. Revise & extend legal immigration	Y	86. Welfare reform of $5.7b for 5 years	N
27. Suspend aid to Angolan rebels	N	87. Raise taxes $12b/cut spending $3b	N
28. Democratic tax plan proposals	N	88. Board to assess occupational risk	?
29. Cut defense 5% across the board	N	89. Balanced budget by '93-via targets	Y
30. Textile import quotas-veto override	N	90. Bar licensing of two nuclear plants	N
31. Abortion service for military abroad	N	91. Remove victims compensation cap	N
32. Limits on high income farmers	Y	92. Catastrophic health insurance	N
33. Family medical leave-veto override	N	93. Ban airline smoking-2 hours or less	Y
34. Req submission of balanced budget	N	94. $1b/two year aid for the homeless	Y
35. Balanced budget amendment	Y	95. Bar non-unions in union companies	Y
36. Amendment to ban flag desecration	Y	96. Increase FSLIC rescue to $15b	Y
37. Reauthorize Amtrak-veto override	Y	97. Impose quotas to lower trade deficit	N
38. Retraining aid for coal miners	N	98. Reduce discretionary budget 21%	Y
39. Suspend El Salvador military aid	N	99. Immigration reform/alien amnesty	N
40. Expand child care aid/tax credit	N	100. South Africa sanctions-veto override	Y
41. Raise House salary/omit honoraria	Y	101. Tax overhaul to revise income tax	Y
42. Toughen oil-spill liability	N	102. Use of military in drug war	Y
43. Restitution to Japanese interned	Y	103. Delete 12 MX/add conventional wpn	N
44. Protect Chinese & C.A. nationals	Y	104. Raise speed limit to 65 mph	Y
45. Abortion $ for rape/incest cases	N	105. Require Pentagon to buy US goods	Y
46. Allow religious schools to bar gays	Y	106. AIDS insurance non-discrimination	N
47. Bar broadcaster fairness doctrine	N	107. Prohibit Saudi arms sales	Y
48. Bar cap gains cut/reinstate IRA	N	108. Ease Gun Control Act of 1968	Y
49. Bar unions equal voice in pension	Y	109. Bar interstate handgun transport	Y
50. Bar assembly of chemical weapons	N	110. Make company emissions known	N
51. Ban plutonium/uranium production	N	111. Allow toxic victims to sue in fed ct	N
52. Cap MX missile deployment at 50	N	112. Superfund waste cleanup of $10b	N
53. Allow $3b for 2 stealth bombers	Y	113. 90 days notice of plant closings	N
54. Publish bio-warfare experiments	Y	114. $20b in Medicare cuts/tax increases	N
55. Raise minimum wage-veto override	N	115. Spending cuts and tax increases	N
56. Bar transfer of FS-X technology	N	116. Set school lunch lmt-250% poverty	N
57. Cut defense and raise domestic $	N	117. $75m for youth work projects	N
58. Uniform poll closing in 48 states	Y	118. Allow Angolan military assistance	Y
59. Req foreign investment disclosure	N	119. Suspend defense payments for abuse	N
60. Textile import quotas-veto override	N	120. Drop SS COLAs/$12b tax increase	N

LENT, NORMAN F. (continued)

121. Approve $1.5b for 21 MX missiles	Y	133. $49b in "sin"/phone/insurance taxes	Y
122. Emergency farm credit/revisions	N	134. Allow sale of Conrail	Y
123. Duty on Taiwan/Hong Kong/S Korea	N	135. Equal Rights Amendment	?
124. Limit steel imports to 17%	Y	136. Authorize Marines in Lebanon	Y
125. Cut $ to schools that bar prayer	Y	137. Eminent domain for coal companies	N
126. $50b-taxes; cut Medicare/spending	Y	138. Prohibit EPA clean air sanctions	N
127. Limit Pershing II/cruise in Europe	N	139. SS retirement age increase/reforms	Y
128. Delete $7.1b for 34 B-1 bombers	N	140. Auto domestic content requirement	N
129. Bar purchase of Sergeant York guns	N	141. Delete jobs program funding	Y
130. El Salvador military/economic aid	Y	142. Highway-gas tax bill	Y
131. Bar mining of Nicaraguan waters	Y	143. Cut $5b from defense for Medicare	Y
132. Physician fee freeze for Medicare	Y	144. Emergency housing aid of $1b	Y

Presidential Support Score: 1991 - 77% 1990 - 67%

McGRATH, RAYMOND J. -- New York 5th District [Republican]. County of Nassau (pt.). Prior Terms: 1981-92. Born: March 27, 1942; Valley Stream, NY. Education: State University, Brockport (B.S.); New York University (M.A.). Occupation: Teacher; lecturer (1969); author; New York assemblyman.

1. Protection to Haitian refugees	N	44. Protect Chinese & C.A. nationals	Y
2. Raise tax on wealthy; lower others	N	45. Abortion $ for rape/incest cases	Y
3. Investigate Reagan hostage delay	N	46. Allow religious schools to bar gays	Y
4. Campaign finance revisions	N	47. Bar broadcaster fairness doctrine	N
5. Unpaid leave to care for children	Y	48. Bar cap gains cut/reinstate IRA	N
6. Restrict NEA use of funds	Y	49. Bar unions equal voice in pension	Y
7. Bar race-bias claim/habeas corpus	Y	50. Bar assembly of chemical weapons	N
8. Ban race as death sentence factor	Y	51. Ban plutonium/uranium production	N
9. Exceptions to exclusionary rule	Y	52. Cap MX missile deployment at 50	N
10. Allow sale of assault weapons	N	53. Allow $3b for 2 stealth bombers	Y
11. Life in prison/abolish death penalty	N	54. Publish bio-warfare experiments	N
12. Req conspiracy-price fixing cases	N	55. Raise minimum wage-veto override	N
13. Unemployment benefits extension	Y	56. Bar transfer of FS-X technology	N
14. Tissue use of aborted fetuses	N	57. Cut defense and raise domestic $	N
15. Bar replacement of union strikers	Y	58. Uniform poll closing in 48 states	N
16. Hold foreign aid at $15b for '92	Y	59. Req foreign investment disclosure	N
17. Restore space station funding	Y	60. Textile import quotas-veto override	Y
18. Civil Rights Act of 1991	N	61. Bar abortion funding in Wash, DC	Y
19. Unlimited damages-discrimination	N	62. Notify spouses of AIDS+ carriers	Y
20. Eliminate funds for supercollider	N	63. Seize conveyance-drug trafficking	N
21. Terminate SDI except for research	N	64. South Africa sanctions	?
22. Req 7-day handgun waiting period	Y	65. 60 days' notice of plant closings	Y
23. Provide $30b for failed S&Ls	N	66. Close unneeded military bases	Y
24. Allow use of force against Iraq	Y	67. Keep welfare reform within $2.8b	Y
25. Allow $15b in foreign aid for '91	#	68. Allow children housing exclusion	N
26. Revise & extend legal immigration	?	69. Shift $400m of NASA to homeless	N
27. Suspend aid to Angolan rebels	N	70. Cap Medicare patients' liability	?
28. Democratic tax plan proposals	Y	71. Prohibit employee polygraph testing	#
29. Cut defense 5% across the board	N	72. Allow CIA to fund Contras	Y
30. Textile import quotas-veto override	Y	73. Revise unfair trade practices	Y
31. Abortion service for military abroad	N	74. Focus SDI on accidental launch	?
32. Limits on high income farmers	Y	75. Bar Air Force $ for MX missile	N
33. Family medical leave-veto override	Y	76. Allow "real" increase in defense	Y
34. Req submission of balanced budget	N	77. Troop reduction in Europe of 50%	N
35. Balanced budget amendment	Y	78. Ban nuclear tests above 1 kiloton	N
36. Amendment to ban flag desecration	Y	79. Ban anti-satellite missile tests	N
37. Reauthorize Amtrak-veto override	Y	80. Observe certain limits of SALT II	N
38. Retraining aid for coal miners	Y	81. Restore four Civil Rights laws	Y
39. Suspend El Salvador military aid	Y	82. Prohibit aliens as strikebreakers	Y
40. Expand child care aid/tax credit	Y	83. Allow military malpractice suits	Y
41. Raise House salary/omit honoraria	Y	84. Approval of $36m in Contra aid	Y
42. Toughen oil-spill liability	Y	85. $18b deficit reduction compromise	Y
43. Restitution to Japanese interned	Y	86. Welfare reform of $5.7b for 5 years	N

McGRATH, RAYMOND J. (continued)

87. Raise taxes $12b/cut spending $3b	N	
88. Board to assess occupational risk	N	
89. Balanced budget by '93-via targets	Y	
90. Bar licensing of two nuclear plants	Y	
91. Remove victims compensation cap	N	
92. Catastrophic health insurance	N	
93. Ban airline smoking-2 hours or less	N	
94. $1b/two year aid for the homeless	Y	
95. Bar non-unions in union companies	Y	
96. Increase FSLIC rescue to $15b	Y	
97. Impose quotas to lower trade deficit	N	
98. Reduce discretionary budget 21%	Y	
99. Immigration reform/alien amnesty	N	
100. South Africa sanctions-veto override	Y	
101. Tax overhaul to revise income tax	Y	
102. Use of military in drug war	Y	
103. Delete 12 MX/add conventional wpn	N	
104. Raise speed limit to 65 mph	N	
105. Require Pentagon to buy US goods	N	
106. AIDS insurance non-discrimination	N	
107. Prohibit Saudi arms sales	Y	
108. Ease Gun Control Act of 1968	Y	
109. Bar interstate handgun transport	Y	
110. Make company emissions known	Y	
111. Allow toxic victims to sue in fed ct	N	
112. Superfund waste cleanup of $10b	Y	
113. 90 days notice of plant closings	N	
114. $20b in Medicare cuts/tax increases	?	
115. Spending cuts and tax increases	N	
116. Set school lunch lmt-250% poverty	N	
117. $75m for youth work projects	N	
118. Allow Angolan military assistance	Y	
119. Suspend defense payments for abuse	N	
120. Drop SS COLAs/$12b tax increase	N	
121. Approve $1.5b for 21 MX missiles	Y	
122. Emergency farm credit/revisions	?	
123. Duty on Taiwan/Hong Kong/S Korea	?	
124. Limit steel imports to 17%	?	
125. Cut $ to schools that bar prayer	Y	
126. $50b-taxes; cut Medicare/spending	Y	
127. Limit Pershing II/cruise in Europe	N	
128. Delete $7.1b for 34 B-1 bombers	N	
129. Bar purchase of Sergeant York guns	N	
130. El Salvador military/economic aid	Y	
131. Bar mining of Nicaraguan waters	Y	
132. Physician fee freeze for Medicare	Y	
133. $49b in "sin"/phone/insurance taxes	Y	
134. Allow sale of Conrail	?	
135. Equal Rights Amendment	N	
136. Authorize Marines in Lebanon	Y	
137. Eminent domain for coal companies	Y	
138. Prohibit EPA clean air sanctions	N	
139. SS retirement age increase/reforms	Y	
140. Auto domestic content requirement	N	
141. Delete jobs program funding	Y	
142. Highway-gas tax bill	Y	
143. Cut $5b from defense for Medicare	Y	
144. Emergency housing aid of $1b	Y	

Presidential Support Score: 1991 - 57%   1990 - 49%

FLAKE, FLOYD H. -- New York 6th District [Democrat]. County of Queens (pt.). Prior Terms: 1987-92. Born: January 30, 1945; Los Angeles, CA. Education: Wilberforce University (B.A.); Payne Theological Seminary; Northeastern University; St. John's University. Occupation: Minister and church pastor (1976-86); community center sponsor and manager; Associate Dean of Students and Director of Student Activities, Lincoln University (1970-73); Dean of Students, Chaplain, and Afro-American Center director, Boston University (1973-76); chairman and CEO, community development corporations.

1. Protection to Haitian refugees	Y	
2. Raise tax on wealthy; lower others	Y	
3. Investigate Reagan hostage delay	?	
4. Campaign finance revisions	Y	
5. Unpaid leave to care for children	Y	
6. Restrict NEA use of funds	N	
7. Bar race-bias claim/habeas corpus	N	
8. Ban race as death sentence factor	N	
9. Exceptions to exclusionary rule	N	
10. Allow sale of assault weapons	N	
11. Life in prison/abolish death penalty	Y	
12. Req conspiracy-price fixing cases	N	
13. Unemployment benefits extension	Y	
14. Tissue use of aborted fetuses	Y	
15. Bar replacement of union strikers	Y	
16. Hold foreign aid at $15b for '92	Y	
17. Restore space station funding	N	
18. Civil Rights Act of 1991	Y	
19. Unlimited damages-discrimination	Y	
20. Eliminate funds for supercollider	Y	
21. Terminate SDI except for research	Y	
22. Req 7-day handgun waiting period	Y	
23. Provide $30b for failed S&Ls	?	
24. Allow use of force against Iraq	N	
25. Allow $15b in foreign aid for '91	?	
26. Revise & extend legal immigration	Y	
27. Suspend aid to Angolan rebels	Y	
28. Democratic tax plan proposals	Y	
29. Cut defense 5% across the board	Y	
30. Textile import quotas-veto override	Y	
31. Abortion service for military abroad	Y	
32. Limits on high income farmers	?	
33. Family medical leave-veto override	?	
34. Req submission of balanced budget	Y	
35. Balanced budget amendment	N	
36. Amendment to ban flag desecration	N	
37. Reauthorize Amtrak-veto override	Y	
38. Retraining aid for coal miners	Y	
39. Suspend El Salvador military aid	Y	
40. Expand child care aid/tax credit	Y	
41. Raise House salary/omit honoraria	Y	
42. Toughen oil-spill liability	N	
43. Restitution to Japanese interned	Y	
44. Protect Chinese & C.A. nationals	Y	
45. Abortion $ for rape/incest cases	Y	
46. Allow religious schools to bar gays	N	

FLAKE, FLOYD H. (continued)

47. Bar broadcaster fairness doctrine	N
48. Bar cap gains cut/reinstate IRA	Y
49. Bar unions equal voice in pension	N
50. Bar assembly of chemical weapons	Y
51. Ban plutonium/uranium production	Y
52. Cap MX missile deployment at 50	Y
53. Allow $3b for 2 stealth bombers	N
54. Publish bio-warfare experiments	Y
55. Raise minimum wage-veto override	Y
56. Bar transfer of FS-X technology	Y
57. Cut defense and raise domestic $	Y
58. Uniform poll closing in 48 states	Y
59. Req foreign investment disclosure	Y
60. Textile import quotas-veto override	Y
61. Bar abortion funding in Wash, DC	Y
62. Notify spouses of AIDS+ carriers	N
63. Seize conveyance-drug trafficking	N
64. South Africa sanctions	Y
65. 60 days' notice of plant closings	Y
66. Close unneeded military bases	?
67. Keep welfare reform within $2.8b	?
68. Allow children housing exclusion	N
69. Shift $400m of NASA to homeless	Y
70. Cap Medicare patients' liability	Y
71. Prohibit employee polygraph testing	Y
72. Allow CIA to fund Contras	X

73. Revise unfair trade practices	Y
74. Focus SDI on accidental launch	?
75. Bar Air Force $ for MX missile	Y
76. Allow "real" increase in defense	N
77. Troop reduction in Europe of 50%	Y
78. Ban nuclear tests above 1 kiloton	Y
79. Ban anti-satellite missile tests	Y
80. Observe certain limits of SALT II	Y
81. Restore four Civil Rights laws	Y
82. Prohibit aliens as strikebreakers	Y
83. Allow military malpractice suits	Y
84. Approval of $36m in Contra aid	N
85. $18b deficit reduction compromise	Y
86. Welfare reform of $5.7b for 5 years	Y
87. Raise taxes $12b/cut spending $3b	Y
88. Board to assess occupational risk	Y
89. Balanced budget by '93-via targets	Y
90. Bar licensing of two nuclear plants	Y
91. Remove victims compensation cap	Y
92. Catastrophic health insurance	Y
93. Ban airline smoking-2 hours or less	?
94. $1b/two year aid for the homeless	Y
95. Bar non-unions in union companies	Y
96. Increase FSLIC rescue to $15b	N
97. Impose quotas to lower trade deficit	Y
98. Reduce discretionary budget 21%	N

Presidential Support Score: 1991 - 23%   1990 - 14%

ACKERMAN, GARY L. -- New York 7th District [Democrat]. County of Queens (pt.). Prior Terms: 1983-92. Born: November 19, 1942; Brooklyn, NY. Education: Queens College; St. John's University. Occupation: Public school teacher; newspaper editor; businessman; New York senator (1979-83).

1. Protection to Haitian refugees	Y
2. Raise tax on wealthy; lower others	Y
3. Investigate Reagan hostage delay	Y
4. Campaign finance revisions	Y
5. Unpaid leave to care for children	Y
6. Restrict NEA use of funds	N
7. Bar race-bias claim/habeas corpus	N
8. Ban race as death sentence factor	N
9. Exceptions to exclusionary rule	N
10. Allow sale of assault weapons	N
11. Life in prison/abolish death penalty	Y
12. Req conspiracy-price fixing cases	N
13. Unemployment benefits extension	Y
14. Tissue use of aborted fetuses	Y
15. Bar replacement of union strikers	Y
16. Hold foreign aid at $15b for '92	Y
17. Restore space station funding	X
18. Civil Rights Act of 1991	Y
19. Unlimited damages-discrimination	Y
20. Eliminate funds for supercollider	?
21. Terminate SDI except for research	Y
22. Req 7-day handgun waiting period	Y
23. Provide $30b for failed S&Ls	?
24. Allow use of force against Iraq	Y
25. Allow $15b in foreign aid for '91	#
26. Revise & extend legal immigration	Y
27. Suspend aid to Angolan rebels	?
28. Democratic tax plan proposals	Y
29. Cut defense 5% across the board	Y

30. Textile import quotas-veto override	Y
31. Abortion service for military abroad	Y
32. Limits on high income farmers	N
33. Family medical leave-veto override	Y
34. Req submission of balanced budget	Y
35. Balanced budget amendment	N
36. Amendment to ban flag desecration	N
37. Reauthorize Amtrak-veto override	Y
38. Retraining aid for coal miners	Y
39. Suspend El Salvador military aid	Y
40. Expand child care aid/tax credit	N
41. Raise House salary/omit honoraria	Y
42. Toughen oil-spill liability	Y
43. Restitution to Japanese interned	Y
44. Protect Chinese & C.A. nationals	Y
45. Abortion $ for rape/incest cases	Y
46. Allow religious schools to bar gays	N
47. Bar broadcaster fairness doctrine	N
48. Bar cap gains cut/reinstate IRA	Y
49. Bar unions equal voice in pension	N
50. Bar assembly of chemical weapons	Y
51. Ban plutonium/uranium production	Y
52. Cap MX missile deployment at 50	Y
53. Allow $3b for 2 stealth bombers	N
54. Publish bio-warfare experiments	Y
55. Raise minimum wage-veto override	Y
56. Bar transfer of FS-X technology	?
57. Cut defense and raise domestic $	Y
58. Uniform poll closing in 48 states	Y

ACKERMAN, GARY L. (continued)

59. Req foreign investment disclosure	Y		100. South Africa sanctions-veto override	Y
60. Textile import quotas-veto override	Y		101. Tax overhaul to revise income tax	N
61. Bar abortion funding in Wash, DC	N		102. Use of military in drug war	N
62. Notify spouses of AIDS+ carriers	N		103. Delete 12 MX/add conventional wpn	Y
63. Seize conveyance-drug trafficking	N		104. Raise speed limit to 65 mph	N
64. South Africa sanctions	Y		105. Require Pentagon to buy US goods	Y
65. 60 days' notice of plant closings	Y		106. AIDS insurance non-discrimination	Y
66. Close unneeded military bases	N		107. Prohibit Saudi arms sales	Y
67. Keep welfare reform within $2.8b	?		108. Ease Gun Control Act of 1968	N
68. Allow children housing exclusion	N		109. Bar interstate handgun transport	Y
69. Shift $400m of NASA to homeless	?		110. Make company emissions known	Y
70. Cap Medicare patients' liability	Y		111. Allow toxic victims to sue in fed ct	Y
71. Prohibit employee polygraph testing	Y		112. Superfund waste cleanup of $10b	Y
72. Allow CIA to fund Contras	N		113. 90 days notice of plant closings	Y
73. Revise unfair trade practices	Y		114. $20b in Medicare cuts/tax increases	Y
74. Focus SDI on accidental launch	Y		115. Spending cuts and tax increases	Y
75. Bar Air Force $ for MX missile	Y		116. Set school lunch lmt-250% poverty	N
76. Allow "real" increase in defense	N		117. $75m for youth work projects	Y
77. Troop reduction in Europe of 50%	Y		118. Allow Angolan military assistance	N
78. Ban nuclear tests above 1 kiloton	Y		119. Suspend defense payments for abuse	Y
79. Ban anti-satellite missile tests	Y		120. Drop SS COLAs/$12b tax increase	N
80. Observe certain limits of SALT II	Y		121. Approve $1.5b for 21 MX missiles	N
81. Restore four Civil Rights laws	Y		122. Emergency farm credit/revisions	?
82. Prohibit aliens as strikebreakers	Y		123. Duty on Taiwan/Hong Kong/S Korea	N
83. Allow military malpractice suits	Y		124. Limit steel imports to 17%	Y
84. Approval of $36m in Contra aid	N		125. Cut $ to schools that bar prayer	N
85. $18b deficit reduction compromise	N		126. $50b-taxes; cut Medicare/spending	N
86. Welfare reform of $5.7b for 5 years	Y		127. Limit Pershing II/cruise in Europe	Y
87. Raise taxes $12b/cut spending $3b	Y		128. Delete $7.1b for 34 B-1 bombers	Y
88. Board to assess occupational risk	Y		129. Bar purchase of Sergeant York guns	Y
89. Balanced budget by '93-via targets	N		130. El Salvador military/economic aid	N
90. Bar licensing of two nuclear plants	Y		131. Bar mining of Nicaraguan waters	Y
91. Remove victims compensation cap	Y		132. Physician fee freeze for Medicare	N
92. Catastrophic health insurance	Y		133. $49b in "sin"/phone/insurance taxes	Y
93. Ban airline smoking-2 hours or less	?		134. Allow sale of Conrail	--
94. $1b/two year aid for the homeless	Y		135. Equal Rights Amendment	Y
95. Bar non-unions in union companies	Y		136. Authorize Marines in Lebanon	Y
96. Increase FSLIC rescue to $15b	Y		137. Eminent domain for coal companies	Y
97. Impose quotas to lower trade deficit	Y		138. Prohibit EPA clean air sanctions	N
98. Reduce discretionary budget 21%	Y		139. SS retirement age increase/reforms	N
99. Immigration reform/alien amnesty	Y			

Presidential Support Score: 1991 - 25%   1990 - 14%

SCHEUER, JAMES H. -- New York 8th District [Democrat]. Counties of Bronx (pt.), Nassau (pt.) and Queens (pt.). Prior Terms: 1964-72; 1974-92. Born: February 6, 1920; New York City, NY. Education: Swarthmore College (A.B.); Columbia Law School (LL.B.); Howard Graduate School. Military Service: U.S. Army, 1943-45. Occupation: Economist, U.S. Foreign Economic Administration (1945-46); staff member, Office of Price Stabilization (1951-52); member, Citizens' Housing and Planning Council of New York City.

1. Protection to Haitian refugees	Y		13. Unemployment benefits extension	Y
2. Raise tax on wealthy; lower others	Y		14. Tissue use of aborted fetuses	Y
3. Investigate Reagan hostage delay	Y		15. Bar replacement of union strikers	Y
4. Campaign finance revisions	Y		16. Hold foreign aid at $15b for '92	Y
5. Unpaid leave to care for children	Y		17. Restore space station funding	N
6. Restrict NEA use of funds	N		18. Civil Rights Act of 1991	Y
7. Bar race-bias claim/habeas corpus	N		19. Unlimited damages-discrimination	Y
8. Ban race as death sentence factor	N		20. Eliminate funds for supercollider	Y
9. Exceptions to exclusionary rule	N		21. Terminate SDI except for research	Y
10. Allow sale of assault weapons	N		22. Req 7-day handgun waiting period	Y
11. Life in prison/abolish death penalty	Y		23. Provide $30b for failed S&Ls	N
12. Req conspiracy-price fixing cases	N		24. Allow use of force against Iraq	N

SCHEUER, JAMES H. (continued)

25. Allow $15b in foreign aid for '91	Y
26. Revise & extend legal immigration	Y
27. Suspend aid to Angolan rebels	Y
28. Democratic tax plan proposals	Y
29. Cut defense 5% across the board	Y
30. Textile import quotas-veto override	Y
31. Abortion service for military abroad	Y
32. Limits on high income farmers	Y
33. Family medical leave-veto override	Y
34. Req submission of balanced budget	Y
35. Balanced budget amendment	N
36. Amendment to ban flag desecration	N
37. Reauthorize Amtrak-veto override	Y
38. Retraining aid for coal miners	Y
39. Suspend El Salvador military aid	Y
40. Expand child care aid/tax credit	Y
41. Raise House salary/omit honoraria	Y
42. Toughen oil-spill liability	Y
43. Restitution to Japanese interned	Y
44. Protect Chinese & C.A. nationals	Y
45. Abortion $ for rape/incest cases	Y
46. Allow religious schools to bar gays	N
47. Bar broadcaster fairness doctrine	N
48. Bar cap gains cut/reinstate IRA	Y
49. Bar unions equal voice in pension	N
50. Bar assembly of chemical weapons	Y
51. Ban plutonium/uranium production	Y
52. Cap MX missile deployment at 50	Y
53. Allow $3b for 2 stealth bombers	?
54. Publish bio-warfare experiments	Y
55. Raise minimum wage-veto override	Y
56. Bar transfer of FS-X technology	?
57. Cut defense and raise domestic $	Y
58. Uniform poll closing in 48 states	Y
59. Req foreign investment disclosure	N
60. Textile import quotas-veto override	N
61. Bar abortion funding in Wash, DC	N
62. Notify spouses of AIDS+ carriers	?
63. Seize conveyance-drug trafficking	?
64. South Africa sanctions	Y
65. 60 days' notice of plant closings	Y
66. Close unneeded military bases	Y
67. Keep welfare reform within $2.8b	?
68. Allow children housing exclusion	N
69. Shift $400m of NASA to homeless	N
70. Cap Medicare patients' liability	Y
71. Prohibit employee polygraph testing	Y
72. Allow CIA to fund Contras	N
73. Revise unfair trade practices	Y
74. Focus SDI on accidental launch	Y
75. Bar Air Force $ for MX missile	Y
76. Allow "real" increase in defense	N
77. Troop reduction in Europe of 50%	N
78. Ban nuclear tests above 1 kiloton	Y
79. Ban anti-satellite missile tests	Y
80. Observe certain limits of SALT II	Y
81. Restore four Civil Rights laws	Y
82. Prohibit aliens as strikebreakers	Y
83. Allow military malpractice suits	?
84. Approval of $36m in Contra aid	N

85. $18b deficit reduction compromise	Y
86. Welfare reform of $5.7b for 5 years	Y
87. Raise taxes $12b/cut spending $3b	Y
88. Board to assess occupational risk	#
89. Balanced budget by '93-via targets	N
90. Bar licensing of two nuclear plants	Y
91. Remove victims compensation cap	Y
92. Catastrophic health insurance	Y
93. Ban airline smoking-2 hours or less	#
94. $1b/two year aid for the homeless	Y
95. Bar non-unions in union companies	Y
96. Increase FSLIC rescue to $15b	Y
97. Impose quotas to lower trade deficit	N
98. Reduce discretionary budget 21%	?
99. Immigration reform/alien amnesty	Y
100. South Africa sanctions-veto override	Y
101. Tax overhaul to revise income tax	Y
102. Use of military in drug war	N
103. Delete 12 MX/add conventional wpn	Y
104. Raise speed limit to 65 mph	N
105. Require Pentagon to buy US goods	Y
106. AIDS insurance non-discrimination	Y
107. Prohibit Saudi arms sales	Y
108. Ease Gun Control Act of 1968	N
109. Bar interstate handgun transport	Y
110. Make company emissions known	Y
111. Allow toxic victims to sue in fed ct	Y
112. Superfund waste cleanup of $10b	Y
113. 90 days notice of plant closings	Y
114. $20b in Medicare cuts/tax increases	Y
115. Spending cuts and tax increases	Y
116. Set school lunch lmt-250% poverty	N
117. $75m for youth work projects	Y
118. Allow Angolan military assistance	N
119. Suspend defense payments for abuse	N
120. Drop SS COLAs/$12b tax increase	N
121. Approve $1.5b for 21 MX missiles	N
122. Emergency farm credit/revisions	Y
123. Duty on Taiwan/Hong Kong/S Korea	N
124. Limit steel imports to 17%	Y
125. Cut $ to schools that bar prayer	N
126. $50b-taxes; cut Medicare/spending	Y
127. Limit Pershing II/cruise in Europe	Y
128. Delete $7.1b for 34 B-1 bombers	Y
129. Bar purchase of Sergeant York guns	Y
130. El Salvador military/economic aid	N
131. Bar mining of Nicaraguan waters	Y
132. Physician fee freeze for Medicare	N
133. $49b in "sin"/phone/insurance taxes	Y
134. Allow sale of Conrail	N
135. Equal Rights Amendment	Y
136. Authorize Marines in Lebanon	N
137. Eminent domain for coal companies	N
138. Prohibit EPA clean air sanctions	Y
139. SS retirement age increase/reforms	N
140. Auto domestic content requirement	Y
141. Delete jobs program funding	N
142. Highway-gas tax bill	Y
143. Cut $5b from defense for Medicare	Y
144. Emergency housing aid of $1b	Y

Presidential Support Score: 1991 - 19%   1990 - 16%

MANTON, THOMAS J. -- New York 9th District [Democrat]. County of Queens (pt.). Prior Terms: 1985-92. Born: November 3, 1932; New York, NY. Education: St. Johns University (B.B.A., J.D.). Military Service: U.S. Marine Corps, 1951-1953. Occupation: New York City councilman (1970-1984), New York City policeman (1955-1960); IBM Corp. marketing representative (1960-1964); private attorney (1964-1984).

1. Protection to Haitian refugees	Y	
2. Raise tax on wealthy; lower others	Y	
3. Investigate Reagan hostage delay	Y	
4. Campaign finance revisions	Y	
5. Unpaid leave to care for children	Y	
6. Restrict NEA use of funds	N	
7. Bar race-bias claim/habeas corpus	N	
8. Ban race as death sentence factor	N	
9. Exceptions to exclusionary rule	N	
10. Allow sale of assault weapons	N	
11. Life in prison/abolish death penalty	N	
12. Req conspiracy-price fixing cases	N	
13. Unemployment benefits extension	Y	
14. Tissue use of aborted fetuses	Y	
15. Bar replacement of union strikers	Y	
16. Hold foreign aid at $15b for '92	Y	
17. Restore space station funding	N	
18. Civil Rights Act of 1991	Y	
19. Unlimited damages-discrimination	Y	
20. Eliminate funds for supercollider	N	
21. Terminate SDI except for research	N	
22. Req 7-day handgun waiting period	Y	
23. Provide $30b for failed S&Ls	?	
24. Allow use of force against Iraq	N	
25. Allow $15b in foreign aid for '91	Y	
26. Revise & extend legal immigration	Y	
27. Suspend aid to Angolan rebels	Y	
28. Democratic tax plan proposals	Y	
29. Cut defense 5% across the board	N	
30. Textile import quotas-veto override	Y	
31. Abortion service for military abroad	N	
32. Limits on high income farmers	Y	
33. Family medical leave-veto override	Y	
34. Req submission of balanced budget	Y	
35. Balanced budget amendment	N	
36. Amendment to ban flag desecration	Y	
37. Reauthorize Amtrak-veto override	Y	
38. Retraining aid for coal miners	Y	
39. Suspend El Salvador military aid	Y	
40. Expand child care aid/tax credit	Y	
41. Raise House salary/omit honoraria	Y	
42. Toughen oil-spill liability	Y	
43. Restitution to Japanese interned	Y	
44. Protect Chinese & C.A. nationals	Y	
45. Abortion $ for rape/incest cases	N	
46. Allow religious schools to bar gays	N	
47. Bar broadcaster fairness doctrine	N	
48. Bar cap gains cut/reinstate IRA	Y	
49. Bar unions equal voice in pension	N	
50. Bar assembly of chemical weapons	Y	
51. Ban plutonium/uranium production	Y	
52. Cap MX missile deployment at 50	Y	
53. Allow $3b for 2 stealth bombers	N	
54. Publish bio-warfare experiments	Y	
55. Raise minimum wage-veto override	Y	
56. Bar transfer of FS-X technology	Y	
57. Cut defense and raise domestic $	N	
58. Uniform poll closing in 48 states	Y	
59. Req foreign investment disclosure	Y	

60. Textile import quotas-veto override	Y	
61. Bar abortion funding in Wash, DC	Y	
62. Notify spouses of AIDS+ carriers	N	
63. Seize conveyance-drug trafficking	N	
64. South Africa sanctions	Y	
65. 60 days' notice of plant closings	Y	
66. Close unneeded military bases	N	
67. Keep welfare reform within $2.8b	N	
68. Allow children housing exclusion	N	
69. Shift $400m of NASA to homeless	Y	
70. Cap Medicare patients' liability	?	
71. Prohibit employee polygraph testing	Y	
72. Allow CIA to fund Contras	N	
73. Revise unfair trade practices	Y	
74. Focus SDI on accidental launch	Y	
75. Bar Air Force $ for MX missile	N	
76. Allow "real" increase in defense	N	
77. Troop reduction in Europe of 50%	Y	
78. Ban nuclear tests above 1 kiloton	?	
79. Ban anti-satellite missile tests	?	
80. Observe certain limits of SALT II	Y	
81. Restore four Civil Rights laws	Y	
82. Prohibit aliens as strikebreakers	Y	
83. Allow military malpractice suits	Y	
84. Approval of $36m in Contra aid	N	
85. $18b deficit reduction compromise	Y	
86. Welfare reform of $5.7b for 5 years	Y	
87. Raise taxes $12b/cut spending $3b	Y	
88. Board to assess occupational risk	Y	
89. Balanced budget by '93-via targets	Y	
90. Bar licensing of two nuclear plants	Y	
91. Remove victims compensation cap	Y	
92. Catastrophic health insurance	Y	
93. Ban airline smoking-2 hours or less	N	
94. $1b/two year aid for the homeless	Y	
95. Bar non-unions in union companies	Y	
96. Increase FSLIC rescue to $15b	N	
97. Impose quotas to lower trade deficit	Y	
98. Reduce discretionary budget 21%	N	
99. Immigration reform/alien amnesty	Y	
100. South Africa sanctions-veto override	Y	
101. Tax overhaul to revise income tax	N	
102. Use of military in drug war	Y	
103. Delete 12 MX/add conventional wpn	Y	
104. Raise speed limit to 65 mph	N	
105. Require Pentagon to buy US goods	?	
106. AIDS insurance non-discrimination	Y	
107. Prohibit Saudi arms sales	Y	
108. Ease Gun Control Act of 1968	N	
109. Bar interstate handgun transport	Y	
110. Make company emissions known	Y	
111. Allow toxic victims to sue in fed ct	N	
112. Superfund waste cleanup of $10b	N	
113. 90 days notice of plant closings	Y	
114. $20b in Medicare cuts/tax increases	Y	
115. Spending cuts and tax increases	Y	
116. Set school lunch lmt-250% poverty	N	
117. $75m for youth work projects	Y	
118. Allow Angolan military assistance	N	

MANTON, THOMAS J. (continued)

119. Suspend defense payments for abuse Y
120. Drop SS COLAs/$12b tax increase N
121. Approve $1.5b for 21 MX missiles N
122. Emergency farm credit/revisions ?

Presidential Support Score: 1991 - 28% 1990 - 19%

SCHUMER, CHARLES E. -- New York 10th District [Democrat]. County of Kings (pt.). Prior Terms: 1981-92. Born: November 23, 1950; Brooklyn, NY. Education: Harvard College (J.D.). Occupation: New York assemblyman (1974-80).

1. Protection to Haitian refugees	Y	55. Raise minimum wage-veto override	Y
2. Raise tax on wealthy; lower others	Y	56. Bar transfer of FS-X technology	Y
3. Investigate Reagan hostage delay	Y	57. Cut defense and raise domestic $	Y
4. Campaign finance revisions	Y	58. Uniform poll closing in 48 states	Y
5. Unpaid leave to care for children	Y	59. Req foreign investment disclosure	N
6. Restrict NEA use of funds	N	60. Textile import quotas-veto override	N
7. Bar race-bias claim/habeas corpus	N	61. Bar abortion funding in Wash, DC	N
8. Ban race as death sentence factor	N	62. Notify spouses of AIDS+ carriers	N
9. Exceptions to exclusionary rule	N	63. Seize conveyance-drug trafficking	N
10. Allow sale of assault weapons	N	64. South Africa sanctions	Y
11. Life in prison/abolish death penalty	N	65. 60 days' notice of plant closings	Y
12. Req conspiracy-price fixing cases	N	66. Close unneeded military bases	Y
13. Unemployment benefits extension	Y	67. Keep welfare reform within $2.8b	N
14. Tissue use of aborted fetuses	Y	68. Allow children housing exclusion	?
15. Bar replacement of union strikers	Y	69. Shift $400m of NASA to homeless	Y
16. Hold foreign aid at $15b for '92	Y	70. Cap Medicare patients' liability	Y
17. Restore space station funding	N	71. Prohibit employee polygraph testing	Y
18. Civil Rights Act of 1991	Y	72. Allow CIA to fund Contras	N
19. Unlimited damages-discrimination	N	73. Revise unfair trade practices	Y
20. Eliminate funds for supercollider	N	74. Focus SDI on accidental launch	Y
21. Terminate SDI except for research	Y	75. Bar Air Force $ for MX missile	Y
22. Req 7-day handgun waiting period	Y	76. Allow "real" increase in defense	N
23. Provide $30b for failed S&Ls	Y	77. Troop reduction in Europe of 50%	Y
24. Allow use of force against Iraq	N	78. Ban nuclear tests above 1 kiloton	Y
25. Allow $15b in foreign aid for '91	Y	79. Ban anti-satellite missile tests	Y
26. Revise & extend legal immigration	Y	80. Observe certain limits of SALT II	Y
27. Suspend aid to Angolan rebels	Y	81. Restore four Civil Rights laws	Y
28. Democratic tax plan proposals	Y	82. Prohibit aliens as strikebreakers	Y
29. Cut defense 5% across the board	Y	83. Allow military malpractice suits	Y
30. Textile import quotas-veto override	N	84. Approval of $36m in Contra aid	N
31. Abortion service for military abroad	Y	85. $18b deficit reduction compromise	Y
32. Limits on high income farmers	Y	86. Welfare reform of $5.7b for 5 years	Y
33. Family medical leave-veto override	Y	87. Raise taxes $12b/cut spending $3b	Y
34. Req submission of balanced budget	Y	88. Board to assess occupational risk	Y
35. Balanced budget amendment	N	89. Balanced budget by '93-via targets	N
36. Amendment to ban flag desecration	N	90. Bar licensing of two nuclear plants	Y
37. Reauthorize Amtrak-veto override	Y	91. Remove victims compensation cap	Y
38. Retraining aid for coal miners	Y	92. Catastrophic health insurance	Y
39. Suspend El Salvador military aid	Y	93. Ban airline smoking-2 hours or less	?
40. Expand child care aid/tax credit	Y	94. $1b/two year aid for the homeless	Y
41. Raise House salary/omit honoraria	Y	95. Bar non-unions in union companies	Y
42. Toughen oil-spill liability	Y	96. Increase FSLIC rescue to $15b	Y
43. Restitution to Japanese interned	Y	97. Impose quotas to lower trade deficit	N
44. Protect Chinese & C.A. nationals	Y	98. Reduce discretionary budget 21%	Y
45. Abortion $ for rape/incest cases	Y	99. Immigration reform/alien amnesty	Y
46. Allow religious schools to bar gays	N	100. South Africa sanctions-veto override	Y
47. Bar broadcaster fairness doctrine	N	101. Tax overhaul to revise income tax	Y
48. Bar cap gains cut/reinstate IRA	Y	102. Use of military in drug war	Y
49. Bar unions equal voice in pension	N	103. Delete 12 MX/add conventional wpn	Y
50. Bar assembly of chemical weapons	Y	104. Raise speed limit to 65 mph	N
51. Ban plutonium/uranium production	Y	105. Require Pentagon to buy US goods	N
52. Cap MX missile deployment at 50	Y	106. AIDS insurance non-discrimination	?
53. Allow $3b for 2 stealth bombers	N	107. Prohibit Saudi arms sales	Y
54. Publish bio-warfare experiments	Y	108. Ease Gun Control Act of 1968	N

SCHUMER, CHARLES E. (continued)

109. Bar interstate handgun transport	Y	
110. Make company emissions known	Y	
111. Allow toxic victims to sue in fed ct	Y	
112. Superfund waste cleanup of $10b	Y	
113. 90 days notice of plant closings	Y	
114. $20b in Medicare cuts/tax increases	Y	
115. Spending cuts and tax increases	Y	
116. Set school lunch lmt-250% poverty	N	
117. $75m for youth work projects	?	
118. Allow Angolan military assistance	N	
119. Suspend defense payments for abuse	Y	
120. Drop SS COLAs/$12b tax increase	N	
121. Approve $1.5b for 21 MX missiles	N	
122. Emergency farm credit/revisions	Y	
123. Duty on Taiwan/Hong Kong/S Korea	Y	
124. Limit steel imports to 17%	Y	
125. Cut $ to schools that bar prayer	N	
126. $50b-taxes; cut Medicare/spending	N	
127. Limit Pershing II/cruise in Europe	Y
128. Delete $7.1b for 34 B-1 bombers	Y
129. Bar purchase of Sergeant York guns	Y
130. El Salvador military/economic aid	N
131. Bar mining of Nicaraguan waters	Y
132. Physician fee freeze for Medicare	N
133. $49b in "sin"/phone/insurance taxes	Y
134. Allow sale of Conrail	N
135. Equal Rights Amendment	Y
136. Authorize Marines in Lebanon	Y
137. Eminent domain for coal companies	Y
138. Prohibit EPA clean air sanctions	Y
139. SS retirement age increase/reforms	N
140. Auto domestic content requirement	Y
141. Delete jobs program funding	N
142. Highway-gas tax bill	Y
143. Cut $5b from defense for Medicare	Y
144. Emergency housing aid of $1b	Y

Presidential Support Score: 1991 - 28%   1990 - 19%

TOWNS, EDOLPHUS -- New York 11th District [Democrat]. County of Kings (pt.). Prior Terms: 1983-92. Born: July 21, 1934; Chadbourn, NC. Education: North Carolina A&T State University (B.S.); Adelphi University. Military Service: U.S. Army, 1956-58. Occupation: Teacher; deputy hospital administrator (1965-71); deputy president, Borough of Brooklyn (1976-82).

1. Protection to Haitian refugees	Y	
2. Raise tax on wealthy; lower others	Y	
3. Investigate Reagan hostage delay	Y	
4. Campaign finance revisions	Y	
5. Unpaid leave to care for children	Y	
6. Restrict NEA use of funds	N	
7. Bar race-bias claim/habeas corpus	N	
8. Ban race as death sentence factor	X	
9. Exceptions to exclusionary rule	N	
10. Allow sale of assault weapons	N	
11. Life in prison/abolish death penalty	Y	
12. Req conspiracy-price fixing cases	N	
13. Unemployment benefits extension	Y	
14. Tissue use of aborted fetuses	Y	
15. Bar replacement of union strikers	Y	
16. Hold foreign aid at $15b for '92	Y	
17. Restore space station funding	N	
18. Civil Rights Act of 1991	Y	
19. Unlimited damages-discrimination	Y	
20. Eliminate funds for supercollider	N	
21. Terminate SDI except for research	Y	
22. Req 7-day handgun waiting period	Y	
23. Provide $30b for failed S&Ls	N	
24. Allow use of force against Iraq	N	
25. Allow $15b in foreign aid for '91	?	
26. Revise & extend legal immigration	Y	
27. Suspend aid to Angolan rebels	Y	
28. Democratic tax plan proposals	Y	
29. Cut defense 5% across the board	Y	
30. Textile import quotas-veto override	Y	
31. Abortion service for military abroad	Y	
32. Limits on high income farmers	N	
33. Family medical leave-veto override	Y	
34. Req submission of balanced budget	Y	
35. Balanced budget amendment	N	
36. Amendment to ban flag desecration	N	
37. Reauthorize Amtrak-veto override	Y
38. Retraining aid for coal miners	Y
39. Suspend El Salvador military aid	Y
40. Expand child care aid/tax credit	Y
41. Raise House salary/omit honoraria	Y
42. Toughen oil-spill liability	Y
43. Restitution to Japanese interned	Y
44. Protect Chinese & C.A. nationals	?
45. Abortion $ for rape/incest cases	Y
46. Allow religious schools to bar gays	N
47. Bar broadcaster fairness doctrine	N
48. Bar cap gains cut/reinstate IRA	Y
49. Bar unions equal voice in pension	N
50. Bar assembly of chemical weapons	Y
51. Ban plutonium/uranium production	Y
52. Cap MX missile deployment at 50	Y
53. Allow $3b for 2 stealth bombers	N
54. Publish bio-warfare experiments	Y
55. Raise minimum wage-veto override	Y
56. Bar transfer of FS-X technology	Y
57. Cut defense and raise domestic $	Y
58. Uniform poll closing in 48 states	Y
59. Req foreign investment disclosure	Y
60. Textile import quotas-veto override	Y
61. Bar abortion funding in Wash, DC	N
62. Notify spouses of AIDS+ carriers	N
63. Seize conveyance-drug trafficking	?
64. South Africa sanctions	Y
65. 60 days' notice of plant closings	Y
66. Close unneeded military bases	?
67. Keep welfare reform within $2.8b	N
68. Allow children housing exclusion	N
69. Shift $400m of NASA to homeless	Y
70. Cap Medicare patients' liability	Y
71. Prohibit employee polygraph testing	Y
72. Allow CIA to fund Contras	N

TOWNS, EDOLPHUS (continued)

73.	Revise unfair trade practices	Y		107.	Prohibit Saudi arms sales	Y
74.	Focus SDI on accidental launch	Y		108.	Ease Gun Control Act of 1968	N
75.	Bar Air Force $ for MX missile	Y		109.	Bar interstate handgun transport	Y
76.	Allow "real" increase in defense	N		110.	Make company emissions known	Y
77.	Troop reduction in Europe of 50%	?		111.	Allow toxic victims to sue in fed ct	N
78.	Ban nuclear tests above 1 kiloton	Y		112.	Superfund waste cleanup of $10b	Y
79.	Ban anti-satellite missile tests	Y		113.	90 days notice of plant closings	Y
80.	Observe certain limits of SALT II	Y		114.	$20b in Medicare cuts/tax increases	Y
81.	Restore four Civil Rights laws	Y		115.	Spending cuts and tax increases	Y
82.	Prohibit aliens as strikebreakers	Y		116.	Set school lunch lmt-250% poverty	N
83.	Allow malpractice suits	Y		117.	$75m for youth work projects	?
84.	Approval of $36m in Contra aid	N		118.	Allow Angolan military assistance	N
85.	$18b deficit reduction compromise	Y		119.	Suspend defense payments for abuse	?
86.	Welfare reform of $5.7b for 5 years	Y		120.	Drop SS COLAs/$12b tax increase	N
87.	Raise taxes $12b/cut spending $3b	Y		121.	Approve $1.5b for 21 MX missiles	N
88.	Board to assess occupational risk	Y		122.	Emergency farm credit/revisions	Y
89.	Balanced budget by '93-via targets	N		123.	Duty on Taiwan/Hong Kong/S Korea	Y
90.	Bar licensing of two nuclear plants	Y		124.	Limit steel imports to 17%	Y
91.	Remove victims compensation cap	Y		125.	Cut $ to schools that bar prayer	N
92.	Catastrophic health insurance	Y		126.	$50b-taxes; cut Medicare/spending	N
93.	Ban airline smoking-2 hours or less	?		127.	Limit Pershing II/cruise in Europe	Y
94.	$1b/two year aid for the homeless	Y		128.	Delete $7.1b for 34 B-1 bombers	Y
95.	Bar non-unions in union companies	Y		129.	Bar purchase of Sergeant York guns	?
96.	Increase FSLIC rescue to $15b	Y		130.	El Salvador military/economic aid	N
97.	Impose quotas to lower trade deficit	Y		131.	Bar mining of Nicaraguan waters	Y
98.	Reduce discretionary budget 21%	?		132.	Physician fee freeze for Medicare	N
99.	Immigration reform/alien amnesty	N		133.	$49b in "sin"/phone/insurance taxes	Y
100.	South Africa sanctions-veto override	Y		134.	Allow sale of Conrail	N
101.	Tax overhaul to revise income tax	Y		135.	Equal Rights Amendment	Y
102.	Use of military in drug war	N		136.	Authorize Marines in Lebanon	N
103.	Delete 12 MX/add conventional wpn	Y		137.	Eminent domain for coal companies	Y
104.	Raise speed limit to 65 mph	N		138.	Prohibit EPA clean air sanctions	N
105.	Require Pentagon to buy US goods	?		139.	SS retirement age increase/reforms	N
106.	AIDS insurance non-discrimination	Y				

Presidential Support Score: 1991 - 21% 1990 - 11%

OWENS, MAJOR R. -- New York 12th District [Democrat]. County of Kings (pt.). Prior Terms: 1983-92. Born: June, 1936; Memphis, TN. Education: Morehouse College; Atlanta University (M.S.). Occupation: Vice president, Metropolitan Council on Housing; community coordinator, Brooklyn Public Library; executive director, Brownsville Community Council; commissioner New York City Community Development Agency (1968-73); director, Community Media Library Program (1974); author; lecturer; New York state senator (1974-82).

1.	Protection to Haitian refugees	Y		19.	Unlimited damages-discrimination	Y
2.	Raise tax on wealthy; lower others	Y		20.	Eliminate funds for supercollider	Y
3.	Investigate Reagan hostage delay	Y		21.	Terminate SDI except for research	Y
4.	Campaign finance revisions	Y		22.	Req 7-day handgun waiting period	Y
5.	Unpaid leave to care for children	Y		23.	Provide $30b for failed S&Ls	N
6.	Restrict NEA use of funds	N		24.	Allow use of force against Iraq	N
7.	Bar race-bias claim/habeas corpus	N		25.	Allow $15b in foreign aid for '91	Y
8.	Ban race as death sentence factor	N		26.	Revise & extend legal immigration	Y
9.	Exceptions to exclusionary rule	N		27.	Suspend aid to Angolan rebels	Y
10.	Allow sale of assault weapons	N		28.	Democratic tax plan proposals	Y
11.	Life in prison/abolish death penalty	Y		29.	Cut defense 5% across the board	Y
12.	Req conspiracy-price fixing cases	N		30.	Textile import quotas-veto override	#
13.	Unemployment benefits extension	Y		31.	Abortion service for military abroad	Y
14.	Tissue use of aborted fetuses	Y		32.	Limits on high income farmers	Y
15.	Bar replacement of union strikers	Y		33.	Family medical leave-veto override	Y
16.	Hold foreign aid at $15b for '92	Y		34.	Req submission of balanced budget	Y
17.	Restore space station funding	N		35.	Balanced budget amendment	N
18.	Civil Rights Act of 1991	Y		36.	Amendment to ban flag desecration	N

OWENS, MAJOR R. (continued)

37.	Reauthorize Amtrak-veto override	Y	89.	Balanced budget by '93-via targets	N
38.	Retraining aid for coal miners	Y	90.	Bar licensing of two nuclear plants	Y
39.	Suspend El Salvador military aid	Y	91.	Remove victims compensation cap	Y
40.	Expand child care aid/tax credit	Y	92.	Catastrophic health insurance	Y
41.	Raise House salary/omit honoraria	Y	93.	Ban airline smoking-2 hours or less	?
42.	Toughen oil-spill liability	Y	94.	$1b/two year aid for the homeless	Y
43.	Restitution to Japanese interned	Y	95.	Bar non-unions in union companies	Y
44.	Protect Chinese & C.A. nationals	Y	96.	Increase FSLIC rescue to $15b	N
45.	Abortion $ for rape/incest cases	Y	97.	Impose quotas to lower trade deficit	Y
46.	Allow religious schools to bar gays	N	98.	Reduce discretionary budget 21%	N
47.	Bar broadcaster fairness doctrine	N	99.	Immigration reform/alien amnesty	Y
48.	Bar cap gains cut/reinstate IRA	Y	100.	South Africa sanctions-veto override	Y
49.	Bar unions equal voice in pension	N	101.	Tax overhaul to revise income tax	Y
50.	Bar assembly of chemical weapons	Y	102.	Use of military in drug war	N
51.	Ban plutonium/uranium production	Y	103.	Delete 12 MX/add conventional wpn	Y
52.	Cap MX missile deployment at 50	Y	104.	Raise speed limit to 65 mph	N
53.	Allow $3b for 2 stealth bombers	N	105.	Require Pentagon to buy US goods	Y
54.	Publish bio-warfare experiments	Y	106.	AIDS insurance non-discrimination	Y
55.	Raise minimum wage-veto override	Y	107.	Prohibit Saudi arms sales	Y
56.	Bar transfer of FS-X technology	Y	108.	Ease Gun Control Act of 1968	N
57.	Cut defense and raise domestic $	Y	109.	Bar interstate handgun transport	Y
58.	Uniform poll closing in 48 states	Y	110.	Make company emissions known	Y
59.	Req foreign investment disclosure	Y	111.	Allow toxic victims to sue in fed ct	Y
60.	Textile import quotas-veto override	Y	112.	Superfund waste cleanup of $10b	Y
61.	Bar abortion funding in Wash, DC	N	113.	90 days notice of plant closings	Y
62.	Notify spouses of AIDS+ carriers	N	114.	$20b in Medicare cuts/tax increases	Y
63.	Seize conveyance-drug trafficking	?	115.	Spending cuts and tax increases	Y
64.	South Africa sanctions	Y	116.	Set school lunch lmt-250% poverty	N
65.	60 days' notice of plant closings	Y	117.	$75m for youth work projects	Y
66.	Close unneeded military bases	N	118.	Allow Angolan military assistance	N
67.	Keep welfare reform within $2.8b	N	119.	Suspend defense payments for abuse	+
68.	Allow children housing exclusion	N	120.	Drop SS COLAs/$12b tax increase	N
69.	Shift $400m of NASA to homeless	Y	121.	Approve $1.5b for 21 MX missiles	N
70.	Cap Medicare patients' liability	Y	122.	Emergency farm credit/revisions	Y
71.	Prohibit employee polygraph testing	Y	123.	Duty on Taiwan/Hong Kong/S Korea	Y
72.	Allow CIA to fund Contras	N	124.	Limit steel imports to 17%	Y
73.	Revise unfair trade practices	Y	125.	Cut $ to schools that bar prayer	N
74.	Focus SDI on accidental launch	Y	126.	$50b-taxes; cut Medicare/spending	N
75.	Bar Air Force $ for MX missile	?	127.	Limit Pershing II/cruise in Europe	Y
76.	Allow "real" increase in defense	N	128.	Delete $7.1b for 34 B-1 bombers	Y
77.	Troop reduction in Europe of 50%	?	129.	Bar purchase of Sergeant York guns	Y
78.	Ban nuclear tests above 1 kiloton	Y	130.	El Salvador military/economic aid	N
79.	Ban anti-satellite missile tests	Y	131.	Bar mining of Nicaraguan waters	Y
80.	Observe certain limits of SALT II	Y	132.	Physician fee freeze for Medicare	N
81.	Restore four Civil Rights laws	Y	133.	$49b in "sin"/phone/insurance taxes	Y
82.	Prohibit aliens as strikebreakers	Y	134.	Allow sale of Conrail	N
83.	Allow military malpractice suits	Y	135.	Equal Rights Amendment	Y
84.	Approval of $36m in Contra aid	N	136.	Authorize Marines in Lebanon	N
85.	$18b deficit reduction compromise	N	137.	Eminent domain for coal companies	N
86.	Welfare reform of $5.7b for 5 years	Y	138.	Prohibit EPA clean air sanctions	N
87.	Raise taxes $12b/cut spending $3b	Y	139.	SS retirement age increase/reforms	N
88.	Board to assess occupational risk	Y			

Presidential Support Score: 1991 - 21%   1990 - 12%

SOLARZ, STEPHEN J. -- New York 13th District [Democrat].   County of Kings (pt.).   Prior Terms: 1975-92.   Born: September 12, 1940; New York City, NY.   Education: Brandeis University (A.B.); Columbia University (M.A.).   Occupation: Attorney; New York assemblyman (1968-72); trustee, Brandeis University.

1.	Protection to Haitian refugees	Y	4.	Campaign finance revisions	Y
2.	Raise tax on wealthy; lower others	Y	5.	Unpaid leave to care for children	Y
3.	Investigate Reagan hostage delay	Y	6.	Restrict NEA use of funds	N

SOLARZ, STEPHEN J. (continued)

7. Bar race-bias claim/habeas corpus	N	
8. Ban race as death sentence factor	N	
9. Exceptions to exclusionary rule	N	
10. Allow sale of assault weapons	N	
11. Life in prison/abolish death penalty	N	
12. Req conspiracy-price fixing cases	?	
13. Unemployment benefits extension	Y	
14. Tissue use of aborted fetuses	Y	
15. Bar replacement of union strikers	Y	
16. Hold foreign aid at $15b for '92	Y	
17. Restore space station funding	N	
18. Civil Rights Act of 1991	Y	
19. Unlimited damages-discrimination	N	
20. Eliminate funds for supercollider	Y	
21. Terminate SDI except for research	Y	
22. Req 7-day handgun waiting period	Y	
23. Provide $30b for failed S&Ls	Y	
24. Allow use of force against Iraq	Y	
25. Allow $15b in foreign aid for '91	Y	
26. Revise & extend legal immigration	Y	
27. Suspend aid to Angolan rebels	Y	
28. Democratic tax plan proposals	Y	
29. Cut defense 5% across the board	N	
30. Textile import quotas-veto override	N	
31. Abortion service for military abroad	Y	
32. Limits on high income farmers	Y	
33. Family medical leave-veto override	Y	
34. Req submission of balanced budget	Y	
35. Balanced budget amendment	N	
36. Amendment to ban flag desecration	N	
37. Reauthorize Amtrak-veto override	Y	
38. Retraining aid for coal miners	Y	
39. Suspend El Salvador military aid	Y	
40. Expand child care aid/tax credit	Y	
41. Raise House salary/omit honoraria	Y	
42. Toughen oil-spill liability	Y	
43. Restitution to Japanese interned	Y	
44. Protect Chinese & C.A. nationals	Y	
45. Abortion $ for rape/incest cases	Y	
46. Allow religious schools to bar gays	N	
47. Bar broadcaster fairness doctrine	N	
48. Bar cap gains cut/reinstate IRA	Y	
49. Bar unions equal voice in pension	N	
50. Bar assembly of chemical weapons	N	
51. Ban plutonium/uranium production	Y	
52. Cap MX missile deployment at 50	Y	
53. Allow $3b for 2 stealth bombers	N	
54. Publish bio-warfare experiments	Y	
55. Raise minimum wage-veto override	Y	
56. Bar transfer of FS-X technology	N	
57. Cut defense and raise domestic $	Y	
58. Uniform poll closing in 48 states	Y	
59. Req foreign investment disclosure	Y	
60. Textile import quotas-veto override	N	
61. Bar abortion funding in Wash, DC	N	
62. Notify spouses of AIDS+ carriers	N	
63. Seize conveyance-drug trafficking	N	
64. South Africa sanctions	Y	
65. 60 days' notice of plant closings	Y	
66. Close unneeded military bases	Y	
67. Keep welfare reform within $2.8b	X	
68. Allow children housing exclusion	N	
69. Shift $400m of NASA to homeless	Y	
70. Cap Medicare patients' liability	Y	

71. Prohibit employee polygraph testing	Y	
72. Allow CIA to fund Contras	N	
73. Revise unfair trade practices	Y	
74. Focus SDI on accidental launch	N	
75. Bar Air Force $ for MX missile	Y	
76. Allow "real" increase in defense	N	
77. Troop reduction in Europe of 50%	N	
78. Ban nuclear tests above 1 kiloton	Y	
79. Ban anti-satellite missile tests	Y	
80. Observe certain limits of SALT II	Y	
81. Restore four Civil Rights laws	Y	
82. Prohibit aliens as strikebreakers	Y	
83. Allow military malpractice suits	Y	
84. Approval of $36m in Contra aid	N	
85. $18b deficit reduction compromise	Y	
86. Welfare reform of $5.7b for 5 years	Y	
87. Raise taxes $12b/cut spending $3b	Y	
88. Board to assess occupational risk	Y	
89. Balanced budget by '93-via targets	N	
90. Bar licensing of two nuclear plants	Y	
91. Remove victims compensation cap	Y	
92. Catastrophic health insurance	Y	
93. Ban airline smoking-2 hours or less	Y	
94. $1b/two year aid for the homeless	Y	
95. Bar non-unions in union companies	Y	
96. Increase FSLIC rescue to $15b	Y	
97. Impose quotas to lower trade deficit	Y	
98. Reduce discretionary budget 21%	N	
99. Immigration reform/alien amnesty	#	
100. South Africa sanctions-veto override	Y	
101. Tax overhaul to revise income tax	Y	
102. Use of military in drug war	N	
103. Delete 12 MX/add conventional wpn	Y	
104. Raise speed limit to 65 mph	N	
105. Require Pentagon to buy US goods	N	
106. AIDS insurance non-discrimination	Y	
107. Prohibit Saudi arms sales	Y	
108. Ease Gun Control Act of 1968	N	
109. Bar interstate handgun transport	Y	
110. Make company emissions known	Y	
111. Allow toxic victims to sue in fed ct	Y	
112. Superfund waste cleanup of $10b	Y	
113. 90 days notice of plant closings	Y	
114. $20b in Medicare cuts/tax increases	Y	
115. Spending cuts and tax increases	Y	
116. Set school lunch lmt-250% poverty	N	
117. $75m for youth work projects	Y	
118. Allow Angolan military assistance	N	
119. Suspend defense payments for abuse	Y	
120. Drop SS COLAs/$12b tax increase	N	
121. Approve $1.5b for 21 MX missiles	N	
122. Emergency farm credit/revisions	Y	
123. Duty on Taiwan/Hong Kong/S Korea	N	
124. Limit steel imports to 17%	Y	
125. Cut $ to schools that bar prayer	N	
126. $50b-taxes; cut Medicare/spending	Y	
127. Limit Pershing II/cruise in Europe	Y	
128. Delete $7.1b for 34 B-1 bombers	Y	
129. Bar purchase of Sergeant York guns	Y	
130. El Salvador military/economic aid	N	
131. Bar mining of Nicaraguan waters	?	
132. Physician fee freeze for Medicare	N	
133. $49b in "sin"/phone/insurance taxes	Y	
134. Allow sale of Conrail	N	

SOLARZ, STEPHEN J. (continued)

135. Equal Rights Amendment	Y	140. Auto domestic content requirement	Y
136. Authorize Marines in Lebanon	Y	141. Delete jobs program funding	N
137. Eminent domain for coal companies	Y	142. Highway-gas tax bill	Y
138. Prohibit EPA clean air sanctions	Y	143. Cut $5b from defense for Medicare	Y
139. SS retirement age increase/reforms	N	144. Emergency housing aid of $1b	Y

Presidential Support Score: 1991 - 31%   1990 - 22%

MOLINARI, SUSAN -- New York 14th District [Republican].   Counties of Kings (pt.) and Richmond.   Prior Terms: 1990 (Special Election)-1992. Born: March 27, 1958;   Staten Island, NY.   Education: SUNY-Albany (B.A., M.A.).   Occupation: State Senate staff member & research analyst; university graduate teacher assistant; Finance Assistant, National Republican Governor's Association; Ethnic Community Liaison, RNC Political Division; New York City councilwoman (1985-90).

1. Protection to Haitian refugees	N	21. Terminate SDI except for research	N
2. Raise tax on wealthy; lower others	N	22. Req 7-day handgun waiting period	Y
3. Investigate Reagan hostage delay	N	23. Provide $30b for failed S&Ls	Y
4. Campaign finance revisions	N	24. Allow use of force against Iraq	Y
5. Unpaid leave to care for children	Y	25. Allow $15b in foreign aid for '91	Y
6. Restrict NEA use of funds	Y	26. Revise & extend legal immigration	Y
7. Bar race-bias claim/habeas corpus	Y	27. Suspend aid to Angolan rebels	N
8. Ban race as death sentence factor	Y	28. Democratic tax plan proposals	Y
9. Exceptions to exclusionary rule	Y	29. Cut defense 5% across the board	N
10. Allow sale of assault weapons	Y	30. Textile import quotas-veto override	N
11. Life in prison/abolish death penalty	N	31. Abortion service for military abroad	Y
12. Req conspiracy-price fixing cases	N	32. Limits on high income farmers	Y
13. Unemployment benefits extension	Y	33. Family medical leave-veto override	Y
14. Tissue use of aborted fetuses	Y	34. Req submission of balanced budget	N
15. Bar replacement of union strikers	N	35. Balanced budget amendment	Y
16. Hold foreign aid at $15b for '92	Y	36. Amendment to ban flag desecration	Y
17. Restore space station funding	N	37. Reauthorize Amtrak-veto override	N
18. Civil Rights Act of 1991	N	38. Retraining aid for coal miners	N
19. Unlimited damages-discrimination	N	39. Suspend El Salvador military aid	N
20. Eliminate funds for supercollider	N	40. Expand child care aid/tax credit	Y

Presidential Support Score: 1991 - 62%   1990 - 56%

GREEN, BILL -- New York 15th District [Republican].   County of New York (pt.).   Prior Terms: 1978 (Special Election)-1992.   Born: October 16, 1929; New York City, NY. Education: Harvard College (B.A.); Harvard Law School (J.D.).   Military Service: U.S. Army, 1953-55. Occupation: Attorney; law secretary to judge (1955-56); chief counsel, New York legislative committee (1961-64).

1. Protection to Haitian refugees	Y	19. Unlimited damages-discrimination	Y
2. Raise tax on wealthy; lower others	N	20. Eliminate funds for supercollider	N
3. Investigate Reagan hostage delay	N	21. Terminate SDI except for research	N
4. Campaign finance revisions	Y	22. Req 7-day handgun waiting period	Y
5. Unpaid leave to care for children	Y	23. Provide $30b for failed S&Ls	Y
6. Restrict NEA use of funds	N	24. Allow use of force against Iraq	Y
7. Bar race-bias claim/habeas corpus	N	25. Allow $15b in foreign aid for '91	Y
8. Ban race as death sentence factor	N	26. Revise & extend legal immigration	Y
9. Exceptions to exclusionary rule	Y	27. Suspend aid to Angolan rebels	Y
10. Allow sale of assault weapons	N	28. Democratic tax plan proposals	N
11. Life in prison/abolish death penalty	N	29. Cut defense 5% across the board	N
12. Req conspiracy-price fixing cases	Y	30. Textile import quotas-veto override	N
13. Unemployment benefits extension	N	31. Abortion service for military abroad	Y
14. Tissue use of aborted fetuses	Y	32. Limits on high income farmers	Y
15. Bar replacement of union strikers	Y	33. Family medical leave-veto override	Y
16. Hold foreign aid at $15b for '92	Y	34. Req submission of balanced budget	N
17. Restore space station funding	N	35. Balanced budget amendment	N
18. Civil Rights Act of 1991	Y	36. Amendment to ban flag desecration	N

GREEN, BILL (continued)

37.	Reauthorize Amtrak-veto override	Y	91.	Remove victims compensation cap	N
38.	Retraining aid for coal miners	N	92.	Catastrophic health insurance	Y
39.	Suspend El Salvador military aid	Y	93.	Ban airline smoking-2 hours or less	N
40.	Expand child care aid/tax credit	Y	94.	$1b/two year aid for the homeless	Y
41.	Raise House salary/omit honoraria	Y	95.	Bar non-unions in union companies	Y
42.	Toughen oil-spill liability	N	96.	Increase FSLIC rescue to $15b	Y
43.	Restitution to Japanese interned	N	97.	Impose quotas to lower trade deficit	N
44.	Protect Chinese & C.A. nationals	Y	98.	Reduce discretionary budget 21%	N
45.	Abortion $ for rape/incest cases	Y	99.	Immigration reform/alien amnesty	Y
46.	Allow religious schools to bar gays	N	100.	South Africa sanctions-veto override	Y
47.	Bar broadcaster fairness doctrine	N	101.	Tax overhaul to revise income tax	N
48.	Bar cap gains cut/reinstate IRA	N	102.	Use of military in drug war	N
49.	Bar unions equal voice in pension	Y	103.	Delete 12 MX/add conventional wpn	Y
50.	Bar assembly of chemical weapons	Y	104.	Raise speed limit to 65 mph	N
51.	Ban plutonium/uranium production	Y	105.	Require Pentagon to buy US goods	N
52.	Cap MX missile deployment at 50	Y	106.	AIDS insurance non-discrimination	Y
53.	Allow $3b for 2 stealth bombers	N	107.	Prohibit Saudi arms sales	Y
54.	Publish bio-warfare experiments	Y	108.	Ease Gun Control Act of 1968	N
55.	Raise minimum wage-veto override	N	109.	Bar interstate handgun transport	Y
56.	Bar transfer of FS-X technology	?	110.	Make company emissions known	Y
57.	Cut defense and raise domestic $	N	111.	Allow toxic victims to sue in fed ct	Y
58.	Uniform poll closing in 48 states	X	112.	Superfund waste cleanup of $10b	Y
59.	Req foreign investment disclosure	N	113.	90 days notice of plant closings	N
60.	Textile import quotas-veto override	N	114.	$20b in Medicare cuts/tax increases	Y
61.	Bar abortion funding in Wash, DC	N	115.	Spending cuts and tax increases	Y
62.	Notify spouses of AIDS+ carriers	N	116.	Set school lunch lmt-250% poverty	Y
63.	Seize conveyance-drug trafficking	Y	117.	$75m for youth work projects	N
64.	South Africa sanctions	Y	118.	Allow Angolan military assistance	Y
65.	60 days' notice of plant closings	N	119.	Suspend defense payments for abuse	N
66.	Close unneeded military bases	Y	120.	Drop SS COLAs/$12b tax increase	N
67.	Keep welfare reform within $2.8b	Y	121.	Approve $1.5b for 21 MX missiles	N
68.	Allow children housing exclusion	N	122.	Emergency farm credit/revisions	N
69.	Shift $400m of NASA to homeless	N	123.	Duty on Taiwan/Hong Kong/S Korea	N
70.	Cap Medicare patients' liability	Y	124.	Limit steel imports to 17%	N
71.	Prohibit employee polygraph testing	Y	125.	Cut $ to schools that bar prayer	N
72.	Allow CIA to fund Contras	N	126.	$50b-taxes; cut Medicare/spending	Y
73.	Revise unfair trade practices	N	127.	Limit Pershing II/cruise in Europe	N
74.	Focus SDI on accidental launch	Y	128.	Delete $7.1b for 34 B-1 bombers	Y
75.	Bar Air Force $ for MX missile	N	129.	Bar purchase of Sergeant York guns	N
76.	Allow "real" increase in defense	N	130.	El Salvador military/economic aid	N
77.	Troop reduction in Europe of 50%	Y	131.	Bar mining of Nicaraguan waters	Y
78.	Ban nuclear tests above 1 kiloton	Y	132.	Physician fee freeze for Medicare	N
79.	Ban anti-satellite missile tests	Y	133.	$49b in "sin"/phone/insurance taxes	Y
80.	Observe certain limits of SALT II	Y	134.	Allow sale of Conrail	Y
81.	Restore four Civil Rights laws	Y	135.	Equal Rights Amendment	Y
82.	Prohibit aliens as strikebreakers	Y	136.	Authorize Marines in Lebanon	Y
83.	Allow military malpractice suits	Y	137.	Eminent domain for coal companies	Y
84.	Approval of $36m in Contra aid	N	138.	Prohibit EPA clean air sanctions	N
85.	$18b deficit reduction compromise	Y	139.	SS retirement age increase/reforms	Y
86.	Welfare reform of $5.7b for 5 years	Y	140.	Auto domestic content requirement	N
87.	Raise taxes $12b/cut spending $3b	N	141.	Delete jobs program funding	Y
88.	Board to assess occupational risk	Y	142.	Highway-gas tax bill	Y
89.	Balanced budget by '93-via targets	Y	143.	Cut $5b from defense for Medicare	Y
90.	Bar licensing of two nuclear plants	N	144.	Emergency housing aid of $1b	N

Presidential Support Score: 1991 - 39% 1990 - 41%

RANGEL, CHARLES B. -- New York 16th District [Democrat]. County of New York (pt.). Prior Terms: 1971-92. Born: June 11, 1930; New York, NY. Education: New York University; St. John's University Law School. Military Service: U.S. Army, 1948-52. Occupation: Assistant U.S. attorney; counsel to speaker, state Assembly; counsel, New York Housing Authority; counsel, presidential Draft Revision Committee; state assemblyman (1966-70).

RANGEL, CHARLES B. (continued)

1. Protection to Haitian refugees	Y	
2. Raise tax on wealthy; lower others	Y	
3. Investigate Reagan hostage delay	Y	
4. Campaign finance revisions	Y	
5. Unpaid leave to care for children	Y	
6. Restrict NEA use of funds	N	
7. Bar race-bias claim/habeas corpus	N	
8. Ban race as death sentence factor	N	
9. Exceptions to exclusionary rule	N	
10. Allow sale of assault weapons	N	
11. Life in prison/abolish death penalty	Y	
12. Req conspiracy-price fixing cases	N	
13. Unemployment benefits extension	Y	
14. Tissue use of aborted fetuses	Y	
15. Bar replacement of union strikers	Y	
16. Hold foreign aid at $15b for '92	Y	
17. Restore space station funding	N	
18. Civil Rights Act of 1991	Y	
19. Unlimited damages-discrimination	Y	
20. Eliminate funds for supercollider	N	
21. Terminate SDI except for research	#	
22. Req 7-day handgun waiting period	Y	
23. Provide $30b for failed S&Ls	N	
24. Allow use of force against Iraq	N	
25. Allow $15b in foreign aid for '91	Y	
26. Revise & extend legal immigration	Y	
27. Suspend aid to Angolan rebels	Y	
28. Democratic tax plan proposals	Y	
29. Cut defense 5% across the board	Y	
30. Textile import quotas-veto override	Y	
31. Abortion service for military abroad	Y	
32. Limits on high income farmers	Y	
33. Family medical leave-veto override	Y	
34. Req submission of balanced budget	Y	
35. Balanced budget amendment	N	
36. Amendment to ban flag desecration	?	
37. Reauthorize Amtrak-veto override	Y	
38. Retraining aid for coal miners	Y	
39. Suspend El Salvador military aid	Y	
40. Expand child care aid/tax credit	Y	
41. Raise House salary/omit honoraria	Y	
42. Toughen oil-spill liability	?	
43. Restitution to Japanese interned	Y	
44. Protect Chinese & C.A. nationals	Y	
45. Abortion $ for rape/incest cases	Y	
46. Allow religious schools to bar gays	N	
47. Bar broadcaster fairness doctrine	N	
48. Bar cap gains cut/reinstate IRA	Y	
49. Bar unions equal voice in pension	N	
50. Bar assembly of chemical weapons	Y	
51. Ban plutonium/uranium production	Y	
52. Cap MX missile deployment at 50	Y	
53. Allow $3b for 2 stealth bombers	N	
54. Publish bio-warfare experiments	Y	
55. Raise minimum wage-veto override	Y	
56. Bar transfer of FS-X technology	N	
57. Cut defense and raise domestic $	Y	
58. Uniform poll closing in 48 states	Y	
59. Req foreign investment disclosure	Y	
60. Textile import quotas-veto override	Y	
61. Bar abortion funding in Wash, DC	N	
62. Notify spouses of AIDS+ carriers	N	
63. Seize conveyance-drug trafficking	N	
64. South Africa sanctions	Y	

65. 60 days' notice of plant closings	Y	
66. Close unneeded military bases	?	
67. Keep welfare reform within $2.8b	N	
68. Allow children housing exclusion	N	
69. Shift $400m of NASA to homeless	Y	
70. Cap Medicare patients' liability	Y	
71. Prohibit employee polygraph testing	?	
72. Allow CIA to fund Contras	X	
73. Revise unfair trade practices	Y	
74. Focus SDI on accidental launch	Y	
75. Bar Air Force $ for MX missile	Y	
76. Allow "real" increase in defense	N	
77. Troop reduction in Europe of 50%	Y	
78. Ban nuclear tests above 1 kiloton	Y	
79. Ban anti-satellite missile tests	Y	
80. Observe certain limits of SALT II	Y	
81. Restore four Civil Rights laws	Y	
82. Prohibit aliens as strikebreakers	Y	
83. Allow military malpractice suits	Y	
84. Approval of $36m in Contra aid	N	
85. $18b deficit reduction compromise	Y	
86. Welfare reform of $5.7b for 5 years	Y	
87. Raise taxes $12b/cut spending $3b	Y	
88. Board to assess occupational risk	Y	
89. Balanced budget by '93-via targets	N	
90. Bar licensing of two nuclear plants	Y	
91. Remove victims compensation cap	Y	
92. Catastrophic health insurance	Y	
93. Ban airline smoking-2 hours or less	Y	
94. $1b/two year aid for the homeless	Y	
95. Bar non-unions in union companies	?	
96. Increase FSLIC rescue to $15b	Y	
97. Impose quotas to lower trade deficit	Y	
98. Reduce discretionary budget 21%	N	
99. Immigration reform/alien amnesty	Y	
100. South Africa sanctions-veto override	Y	
101. Tax overhaul to revise income tax	Y	
102. Use of military in drug war	N	
103. Delete 12 MX/add conventional wpn	Y	
104. Raise speed limit to 65 mph	N	
105. Require Pentagon to buy US goods	Y	
106. AIDS insurance non-discrimination	Y	
107. Prohibit Saudi arms sales	Y	
108. Ease Gun Control Act of 1968	N	
109. Bar interstate handgun transport	Y	
110. Make company emissions known	Y	
111. Allow toxic victims to sue in fed ct	Y	
112. Superfund waste cleanup of $10b	Y	
113. 90 days notice of plant closings	Y	
114. $20b in Medicare cuts/tax increases	Y	
115. Spending cuts and tax increases	Y	
116. Set school lunch lmt-250% poverty	?	
117. $75m for youth work projects	Y	
118. Allow Angolan military assistance	N	
119. Suspend defense payments for abuse	Y	
120. Drop SS COLAs/$12b tax increase	N	
121. Approve $1.5b for 21 MX missiles	N	
122. Emergency farm credit/revisions	Y	
123. Duty on Taiwan/Hong Kong/S Korea	Y	
124. Limit steel imports to 17%	Y	
125. Cut $ to schools that bar prayer	N	
126. $50b-taxes; cut Medicare/spending	Y	
127. Limit Pershing II/cruise in Europe	Y	
128. Delete $7.1b for 34 B-1 bombers	Y	

RANGEL, CHARLES B. (continued)

129. Bar purchase of Sergeant York guns	Y	
130. El Salvador military/economic aid	N	
131. Bar mining of Nicaraguan waters	Y	
132. Physician fee freeze for Medicare	N	
133. $49b in "sin"/phone/insurance taxes	Y	
134. Allow sale of Conrail	N	
135. Equal Rights Amendment	Y	
136. Authorize Marines in Lebanon	N	
137. Eminent domain for coal companies	Y
138. Prohibit EPA clean air sanctions	Y
139. SS retirement age increase/reforms	N
140. Auto domestic content requirement	Y
141. Delete jobs program funding	N
142. Highway-gas tax bill	Y
143. Cut $5b from defense for Medicare	Y
144. Emergency housing aid of $1b	Y

Presidential Support Score: 1991 - 25%   1990 - 13%

WEISS, TED -- New York 17th District [Democrat]. Counties of Bronx (pt.) and New York (pt.). Prior Terms: 1977-92. Born: September 17, 1927; Hungary. Education: Syracuse University (B.A., LL.B.). Military Service: U.S. Army, 1946-47. Occupation: Assistant district attorney (1955-59); member, city council (1962-77).

1. Protection to Haitian refugees	Y	
2. Raise tax on wealthy; lower others	Y	
3. Investigate Reagan hostage delay	Y	
4. Campaign finance revisions	Y	
5. Unpaid leave to care for children	Y	
6. Restrict NEA use of funds	N	
7. Bar race-bias claim/habeas corpus	N	
8. Ban race as death sentence factor	--	
9. Exceptions to exclusionary rule	N	
10. Allow sale of assault weapons	N	
11. Life in prison/abolish death penalty	Y	
12. Req conspiracy-price fixing cases	N	
13. Unemployment benefits extension	Y	
14. Tissue use of aborted fetuses	+	
15. Bar replacement of union strikers	+	
16. Hold foreign aid at $15b for '92	Y	
17. Restore space station funding	N	
18. Civil Rights Act of 1991	Y	
19. Unlimited damages-discrimination	Y	
20. Eliminate funds for supercollider	Y	
21. Terminate SDI except for research	Y	
22. Req 7-day handgun waiting period	Y	
23. Provide $30b for failed S&Ls	N	
24. Allow use of force against Iraq	N	
25. Allow $15b in foreign aid for '91	Y	
26. Revise & extend legal immigration	Y	
27. Suspend aid to Angolan rebels	Y	
28. Democratic tax plan proposals	Y	
29. Cut defense 5% across the board	Y	
30. Textile import quotas-veto override	Y	
31. Abortion service for military abroad	Y	
32. Limits on high income farmers	Y	
33. Family medical leave-veto override	Y	
34. Req submission of balanced budget	Y	
35. Balanced budget amendment	N	
36. Amendment to ban flag desecration	N	
37. Reauthorize Amtrak-veto override	Y	
38. Retraining aid for coal miners	Y	
39. Suspend El Salvador military aid	Y	
40. Expand child care aid/tax credit	N	
41. Raise House salary/omit honoraria	Y	
42. Toughen oil-spill liability	Y	
43. Restitution to Japanese interned	Y	
44. Protect Chinese & C.A. nationals	Y	
45. Abortion $ for rape/incest cases	Y	
46. Allow religious schools to bar gays	N	
47. Bar broadcaster fairness doctrine	N	
48. Bar cap gains cut/reinstate IRA	Y
49. Bar unions equal voice in pension	N
50. Bar assembly of chemical weapons	Y
51. Ban plutonium/uranium production	Y
52. Cap MX missile deployment at 50	Y
53. Allow $3b for 2 stealth bombers	N
54. Publish bio-warfare experiments	Y
55. Raise minimum wage-veto override	Y
56. Bar transfer of FS-X technology	N
57. Cut defense and raise domestic $	Y
58. Uniform poll closing in 48 states	Y
59. Req foreign investment disclosure	Y
60. Textile import quotas-veto override	Y
61. Bar abortion funding in Wash, DC	N
62. Notify spouses of AIDS+ carriers	N
63. Seize conveyance-drug trafficking	?
64. South Africa sanctions	Y
65. 60 days' notice of plant closings	Y
66. Close unneeded military bases	N
67. Keep welfare reform within $2.8b	N
68. Allow children housing exclusion	N
69. Shift $400m of NASA to homeless	Y
70. Cap Medicare patients' liability	+
71. Prohibit employee polygraph testing	+
72. Allow CIA to fund Contras	--
73. Revise unfair trade practices	#
74. Focus SDI on accidental launch	Y
75. Bar Air Force $ for MX missile	Y
76. Allow "real" increase in defense	N
77. Troop reduction in Europe of 50%	N
78. Ban nuclear tests above 1 kiloton	Y
79. Ban anti-satellite missile tests	Y
80. Observe certain limits of SALT II	Y
81. Restore four Civil Rights laws	Y
82. Prohibit aliens as strikebreakers	Y
83. Allow military malpractice suits	Y
84. Approval of $36m in Contra aid	N
85. $18b deficit reduction compromise	N
86. Welfare reform of $5.7b for 5 years	Y
87. Raise taxes $12b/cut spending $3b	Y
88. Board to assess occupational risk	Y
89. Balanced budget by '93-via targets	N
90. Bar licensing of two nuclear plants	Y
91. Remove victims compensation cap	Y
92. Catastrophic health insurance	Y
93. Ban airline smoking-2 hours or less	Y
94. $1b/two year aid for the homeless	Y

WEISS, TED (continued)

95. Bar non-unions in union companies	Y
96. Increase FSLIC rescue to $15b	Y
97. Impose quotas to lower trade deficit	Y
98. Reduce discretionary budget 21%	Y
99. Immigration reform/alien amnesty	+
100. South Africa sanctions-veto override	Y
101. Tax overhaul to revise income tax	N
102. Use of military in drug war	N
103. Delete 12 MX/add conventional wpn	+
104. Raise speed limit to 65 mph	N
105. Require Pentagon to buy US goods	N
106. AIDS insurance non-discrimination	Y
107. Prohibit Saudi arms sales	Y
108. Ease Gun Control Act of 1968	N
109. Bar interstate handgun transport	Y
110. Make company emissions known	Y
111. Allow toxic victims to sue in fed ct	Y
112. Superfund waste cleanup of $10b	Y
113. 90 days notice of plant closings	Y
114. $20b in Medicare cuts/tax increases	Y
115. Spending cuts and tax increases	Y
116. Set school lunch lmt-250% poverty	N
117. $75m for youth work projects	Y
118. Allow Angolan military assistance	N
119. Suspend defense payments for abuse	Y
120. Drop SS COLAs/$12b tax increase	N
121. Approve $1.5b for 21 MX missiles	N
122. Emergency farm credit/revisions	Y
123. Duty on Taiwan/Hong Kong/S Korea	N
124. Limit steel imports to 17%	Y
125. Cut $ to schools that bar prayer	N
126. $50b-taxes; cut Medicare/spending	N
127. Limit Pershing II/cruise in Europe	Y
128. Delete $7.1b for 34 B-1 bombers	Y
129. Bar purchase of Sergeant York guns	Y
130. El Salvador military/economic aid	N
131. Bar mining of Nicaraguan waters	Y
132. Physician fee freeze for Medicare	N
133. $49b in "sin"/phone/insurance taxes	Y
134. Allow sale of Conrail	N
135. Equal Rights Amendment	Y
136. Authorize Marines in Lebanon	N
137. Eminent domain for coal companies	Y
138. Prohibit EPA clean air sanctions	+
139. SS retirement age increase/reforms	N
140. Auto domestic content requirement	Y
141. Delete jobs program funding	N
142. Highway-gas tax bill	N
143. Cut $5b from defense for Medicare	Y
144. Emergency housing aid of $1b	Y

Presidential Support Score: 1991 - 20%   1990 - 14%

SERRANO, JOSE E. -- New York 18th District [Democrat]. County of Bronx (pt.). Prior Terms: 1990 (Special Election)-1992. Born: October 24, 1943; Mayaguez, PR. Military Service: U.S. Army Medical Corps. Occupation: South Bronx Community Corporation chairman; community school board employee; state assemblyman (1975-90).

1. Protection to Haitian refugees	Y
2. Raise tax on wealthy; lower others	Y
3. Investigate Reagan hostage delay	Y
4. Campaign finance revisions	Y
5. Unpaid leave to care for children	Y
6. Restrict NEA use of funds	N
7. Bar race-bias claim/habeas corpus	N
8. Ban race as death sentence factor	N
9. Exceptions to exclusionary rule	N
10. Allow sale of assault weapons	N
11. Life in prison/abolish death penalty	Y
12. Req conspiracy-price fixing cases	N
13. Unemployment benefits extension	Y
14. Tissue use of aborted fetuses	Y
15. Bar replacement of union strikers	Y
16. Hold foreign aid at $15b for '92	#
17. Restore space station funding	N
18. Civil Rights Act of 1991	Y
19. Unlimited damages-discrimination	Y
20. Eliminate funds for supercollider	N
21. Terminate SDI except for research	Y
22. Req 7-day handgun waiting period	Y
23. Provide $30b for failed S&Ls	N
24. Allow use of force against Iraq	N
25. Allow $15b in foreign aid for '91	Y
26. Revise & extend legal immigration	Y
27. Suspend aid to Angolan rebels	Y
28. Democratic tax plan proposals	Y
29. Cut defense 5% across the board	Y
30. Textile import quotas-veto override	Y
31. Abortion service for military abroad	Y
32. Limits on high income farmers	Y
33. Family medical leave-veto override	Y
34. Req submission of balanced budget	Y
35. Balanced budget amendment	N
36. Amendment to ban flag desecration	N
37. Reauthorize Amtrak-veto override	Y
38. Retraining aid for coal miners	Y
39. Suspend El Salvador military aid	Y
40. Expand child care aid/tax credit	Y

Presidential Support Score: 1991 - 19%   1990 - 17%

ENGEL, ELLIOT L. -- New York 19th District [Democrat]. Counties of Bronx (pt.) and Westchester (pt.). Prior Terms: 1989-92. Born: February 18, 1947; Bronx, NY. Education: Hunter-Lehman College (B.A.); CUNY-Lehman College (M.A.); New York Law School (J.D.). Occupation: Public school teacher and guidance counselor (1969-77); state assemblyman (1977-78).

ENGEL, ELLIOT L. (continued)

1. Protection to Haitian refugees	Y	
2. Raise tax on wealthy; lower others	Y	
3. Investigate Reagan hostage delay	Y	
4. Campaign finance revisions	Y	
5. Unpaid leave to care for children	Y	
6. Restrict NEA use of funds	N	
7. Bar race-bias claim/habeas corpus	N	
8. Ban race as death sentence factor	N	
9. Exceptions to exclusionary rule	N	
10. Allow sale of assault weapons	N	
11. Life in prison/abolish death penalty	Y	
12. Req conspiracy-price fixing cases	N	
13. Unemployment benefits extension	Y	
14. Tissue use of aborted fetuses	Y	
15. Bar replacement of union strikers	Y	
16. Hold foreign aid at $15b for '92	Y	
17. Restore space station funding	N	
18. Civil Rights Act of 1991	Y	
19. Unlimited damages-discrimination	N	
20. Eliminate funds for supercollider	?	
21. Terminate SDI except for research	Y	
22. Req 7-day handgun waiting period	Y	
23. Provide $30b for failed S&Ls	N	
24. Allow use of force against Iraq	Y	
25. Allow $15b in foreign aid for '91	Y	
26. Revise & extend legal immigration	Y	
27. Suspend aid to Angolan rebels	Y	
28. Democratic tax plan proposals	Y	
29. Cut defense 5% across the board	N	
30. Textile import quotas-veto override	Y
31. Abortion service for military abroad	Y
32. Limits on high income farmers	Y
33. Family medical leave-veto override	Y
34. Req submission of balanced budget	Y
35. Balanced budget amendment	N
36. Amendment to ban flag desecration	N
37. Reauthorize Amtrak-veto override	Y
38. Retraining aid for coal miners	Y
39. Suspend El Salvador military aid	Y
40. Expand child care aid/tax credit	Y
41. Raise House salary/omit honoraria	N
42. Toughen oil-spill liability	Y
43. Restitution to Japanese interned	Y
44. Protect Chinese & C.A. nationals	Y
45. Abortion $ for rape/incest cases	Y
46. Allow religious schools to bar gays	N
47. Bar broadcaster fairness doctrine	N
48. Bar cap gains cut/reinstate IRA	Y
49. Bar unions equal voice in pension	N
50. Bar assembly of chemical weapons	Y
51. Ban plutonium/uranium production	Y
52. Cap MX missile deployment at 50	Y
53. Allow $3b for 2 stealth bombers	N
54. Publish bio-warfare experiments	Y
55. Raise minimum wage-veto override	Y
56. Bar transfer of FS-X technology	Y
57. Cut defense and raise domestic $	N
58. Uniform poll closing in 48 states	Y

Presidential Support Score: 1991 - 27%   1990 - 18%

LOWEY, NITA M. -- New York 20th District [Democrat]. County of Westchester (pt.). Prior Terms: 1989-92. Born: July 5, 1937; New York, NY. Education: Mt. Holyoke College (B.S.). Occupation: Community activist; New York assistant secretary of state (1985-87).

1. Protection to Haitian refugees	Y	
2. Raise tax on wealthy; lower others	Y	
3. Investigate Reagan hostage delay	Y	
4. Campaign finance revisions	Y	
5. Unpaid leave to care for children	Y	
6. Restrict NEA use of funds	N	
7. Bar race-bias claim/habeas corpus	N	
8. Ban race as death sentence factor	N	
9. Exceptions to exclusionary rule	N	
10. Allow sale of assault weapons	N	
11. Life in prison/abolish death penalty	Y	
12. Req conspiracy-price fixing cases	Y	
13. Unemployment benefits extension	Y	
14. Tissue use of aborted fetuses	Y	
15. Bar replacement of union strikers	Y	
16. Hold foreign aid at $15b for '92	Y	
17. Restore space station funding	N	
18. Civil Rights Act of 1991	Y	
19. Unlimited damages-discrimination	Y	
20. Eliminate funds for supercollider	Y	
21. Terminate SDI except for research	Y	
22. Req 7-day handgun waiting period	Y	
23. Provide $30b for failed S&Ls	N	
24. Allow use of force against Iraq	N	
25. Allow $15b in foreign aid for '91	Y	
26. Revise & extend legal immigration	Y	
27. Suspend aid to Angolan rebels	Y	
28. Democratic tax plan proposals	Y
29. Cut defense 5% across the board	Y
30. Textile import quotas-veto override	Y
31. Abortion service for military abroad	Y
32. Limits on high income farmers	Y
33. Family medical leave-veto override	Y
34. Req submission of balanced budget	Y
35. Balanced budget amendment	N
36. Amendment to ban flag desecration	N
37. Reauthorize Amtrak-veto override	Y
38. Retraining aid for coal miners	Y
39. Suspend El Salvador military aid	Y
40. Expand child care aid/tax credit	Y
41. Raise House salary/omit honoraria	N
42. Toughen oil-spill liability	Y
43. Restitution to Japanese interned	Y
44. Protect Chinese & C.A. nationals	Y
45. Abortion $ for rape/incest cases	Y
46. Allow religious schools to bar gays	N
47. Bar broadcaster fairness doctrine	N
48. Bar cap gains cut/reinstate IRA	Y
49. Bar unions equal voice in pension	N
50. Bar assembly of chemical weapons	Y
51. Ban plutonium/uranium production	Y
52. Cap MX missile deployment at 50	Y
53. Allow $3b for 2 stealth bombers	N
54. Publish bio-warfare experiments	Y

LOWEY, NITA M. (continued)

55. Raise minimum wage-veto override	Y	
56. Bar transfer of FS-X technology	Y	

57. Cut defense and raise domestic $	N
58. Uniform poll closing in 48 states	Y

Presidential Support Score: 1991 - 24%   1990 - 14%

FISH, HAMILTON Jr. -- New York 21st District [Republican]. Counties of Dutchess (pt.), Orange (pt.), Putnam and Westchester (pt.). Prior Terms: 1969-92. Born: June 3, 1926; Washington, DC. Education: Harvard (A.B.); New York University (LL.B.); John F. Kennedy School of Public Administration. Military Service: U.S. Naval Reserve, 1944-46. Occupation: Vice consul, Foreign Service; assistant counsel, New York State Assembly Judiciary Committee.

1. Protection to Haitian refugees	Y	52. Cap MX missile deployment at 50	N
2. Raise tax on wealthy; lower others	N	53. Allow $3b for 2 stealth bombers	N
3. Investigate Reagan hostage delay	N	54. Publish bio-warfare experiments	Y
4. Campaign finance revisions	Y	55. Raise minimum wage-veto override	N
5. Unpaid leave to care for children	Y	56. Bar transfer of FS-X technology	N
6. Restrict NEA use of funds	N	57. Cut defense and raise domestic $	N
7. Bar race-bias claim/habeas corpus	N	58. Uniform poll closing in 48 states	Y
8. Ban race as death sentence factor	N	59. Req foreign investment disclosure	N
9. Exceptions to exclusionary rule	Y	60. Textile import quotas-veto override	Y
10. Allow sale of assault weapons	Y	61. Bar abortion funding in Wash, DC	Y
11. Life in prison/abolish death penalty	N	62. Notify spouses of AIDS+ carriers	N
12. Req conspiracy-price fixing cases	Y	63. Seize conveyance-drug trafficking	N
13. Unemployment benefits extension	Y	64. South Africa sanctions	Y
14. Tissue use of aborted fetuses	N	65. 60 days' notice of plant closings	Y
15. Bar replacement of union strikers	Y	66. Close unneeded military bases	Y
16. Hold foreign aid at $15b for '92	Y	67. Keep welfare reform within $2.8b	Y
17. Restore space station funding	N	68. Allow children housing exclusion	N
18. Civil Rights Act of 1991	Y	69. Shift $400m of NASA to homeless	Y
19. Unlimited damages-discrimination	N	70. Cap Medicare patients' liability	Y
20. Eliminate funds for supercollider	Y	71. Prohibit employee polygraph testing	Y
21. Terminate SDI except for research	N	72. Allow CIA to fund Contras	Y
22. Req 7-day handgun waiting period	Y	73. Revise unfair trade practices	Y
23. Provide $30b for failed S&Ls	Y	74. Focus SDI on accidental launch	N
24. Allow use of force against Iraq	Y	75. Bar Air Force $ for MX missile	N
25. Allow $15b in foreign aid for '91	Y	76. Allow "real" increase in defense	Y
26. Revise & extend legal immigration	Y	77. Troop reduction in Europe of 50%	N
27. Suspend aid to Angolan rebels	?	78. Ban nuclear tests above 1 kiloton	Y
28. Democratic tax plan proposals	Y	79. Ban anti-satellite missile tests	Y
29. Cut defense 5% across the board	N	80. Observe certain limits of SALT II	Y
30. Textile import quotas-veto override	Y	81. Restore four Civil Rights laws	Y
31. Abortion service for military abroad	N	82. Prohibit aliens as strikebreakers	Y
32. Limits on high income farmers	N	83. Allow military malpractice suits	Y
33. Family medical leave-veto override	Y	84. Approval of $36m in Contra aid	Y
34. Req submission of balanced budget	N	85. $18b deficit reduction compromise	Y
35. Balanced budget amendment	Y	86. Welfare reform of $5.7b for 5 years	N
36. Amendment to ban flag desecration	Y	87. Raise taxes $12b/cut spending $3b	N
37. Reauthorize Amtrak-veto override	N	88. Board to assess occupational risk	N
38. Retraining aid for coal miners	Y	89. Balanced budget by '93-via targets	Y
39. Suspend El Salvador military aid	?	90. Bar licensing of two nuclear plants	Y
40. Expand child care aid/tax credit	Y	91. Remove victims compensation cap	N
41. Raise House salary/omit honoraria	Y	92. Catastrophic health insurance	Y
42. Toughen oil-spill liability	N	93. Ban airline smoking-2 hours or less	Y
43. Restitution to Japanese interned	?	94. $1b/two year aid for the homeless	Y
44. Protect Chinese & C.A. nationals	Y	95. Bar non-unions in union companies	Y
45. Abortion $ for rape/incest cases	N	96. Increase FSLIC rescue to $15b	Y
46. Allow religious schools to bar gays	N	97. Impose quotas to lower trade deficit	N
47. Bar broadcaster fairness doctrine	Y	98. Reduce discretionary budget 21%	N
48. Bar cap gains cut/reinstate IRA	N	99. Immigration reform/alien amnesty	Y
49. Bar unions equal voice in pension	Y	100. South Africa sanctions-veto override	Y
50. Bar assembly of chemical weapons	Y	101. Tax overhaul to revise income tax	Y
51. Ban plutonium/uranium production	Y	102. Use of military in drug war	N

FISH, HAMILTON Jr. (continued)

103. Delete 12 MX/add conventional wpn	N	
104. Raise speed limit to 65 mph	N	
105. Require Pentagon to buy US goods	Y	
106. AIDS insurance non-discrimination	N	
107. Prohibit Saudi arms sales	Y	
108. Ease Gun Control Act of 1968	Y	
109. Bar interstate handgun transport	N	
110. Make company emissions known	Y	
111. Allow toxic victims to sue in fed ct	N	
112. Superfund waste cleanup of $10b	Y	
113. 90 days notice of plant closings	Y	
114. $20b in Medicare cuts/tax increases	?	
115. Spending cuts and tax increases	Y	
116. Set school lunch lmt-250% poverty	N	
117. $75m for youth work projects	N	
118. Allow Angolan military assistance	Y	
119. Suspend defense payments for abuse	?	
120. Drop SS COLAs/$12b tax increase	--	
121. Approve $1.5b for 21 MX missiles	Y	
122. Emergency farm credit/revisions	Y	
123. Duty on Taiwan/Hong Kong/S Korea	?	

124. Limit steel imports to 17%	Y
125. Cut $ to schools that bar prayer	N
126. $50b-taxes; cut Medicare/spending	Y
127. Limit Pershing II/cruise in Europe	N
128. Delete $7.1b for 34 B-1 bombers	Y
129. Bar purchase of Sergeant York guns	Y
130. El Salvador military/economic aid	Y
131. Bar mining of Nicaraguan waters	N
132. Physician fee freeze for Medicare	Y
133. $49b in "sin"/phone/insurance taxes	Y
134. Allow sale of Conrail	N
135. Equal Rights Amendment	N
136. Authorize Marines in Lebanon	Y
137. Eminent domain for coal companies	Y
138. Prohibit EPA clean air sanctions	Y
139. SS retirement age increase/reforms	Y
140. Auto domestic content requirement	Y
141. Delete jobs program funding	Y
142. Highway-gas tax bill	Y
143. Cut $5b from defense for Medicare	Y
144. Emergency housing aid of $1b	Y

Presidential Support Score: 1991 - 52% 1990 - 42%

GILMAN, BENJAMIN A. -- New York 22nd District [Republican]. Counties of Orange (pt.), Rockland, Sullivan (pt.) and Westchester (pt.). Prior Terms: 1973-92. Born: December 6, 1922; Poughkeepsie, NY. Education: Wharton School of Business and Finance; University of Pennsylvania (B.S.); New York Law School(LL.B.). Military Service: U.S. Army Air Corps, WW II. Occupation: New York deputy assistant attorney general; assistant attorney general; attorney; New York representative (1967-72).

1. Protection to Haitian refugees	Y	
2. Raise tax on wealthy; lower others	N	
3. Investigate Reagan hostage delay	N	
4. Campaign finance revisions	Y	
5. Unpaid leave to care for children	Y	
6. Restrict NEA use of funds	N	
7. Bar race-bias claim/habeas corpus	N	
8. Ban race as death sentence factor	N	
9. Exceptions to exclusionary rule	Y	
10. Allow sale of assault weapons	N	
11. Life in prison/abolish death penalty	N	
12. Req conspiracy-price fixing cases	N	
13. Unemployment benefits extension	Y	
14. Tissue use of aborted fetuses	Y	
15. Bar replacement of union strikers	Y	
16. Hold foreign aid at $15b for '92	Y	
17. Restore space station funding	N	
18. Civil Rights Act of 1991	Y	
19. Unlimited damages-discrimination	N	
20. Eliminate funds for supercollider	Y	
21. Terminate SDI except for research	N	
22. Req 7-day handgun waiting period	Y	
23. Provide $30b for failed S&Ls	Y	
24. Allow use of force against Iraq	Y	
25. Allow $15b in foreign aid for '91	Y	
26. Revise & extend legal immigration	Y	
27. Suspend aid to Angolan rebels	Y	
28. Democratic tax plan proposals	N	
29. Cut defense 5% across the board	N	
30. Textile import quotas-veto override	Y	
31. Abortion service for military abroad	Y	
32. Limits on high income farmers	N	

33. Family medical leave-veto override	Y
34. Req submission of balanced budget	N
35. Balanced budget amendment	N
36. Amendment to ban flag desecration	Y
37. Reauthorize Amtrak-veto override	Y
38. Retraining aid for coal miners	Y
39. Suspend El Salvador military aid	Y
40. Expand child care aid/tax credit	Y
41. Raise House salary/omit honoraria	Y
42. Toughen oil-spill liability	Y
43. Restitution to Japanese interned	Y
44. Protect Chinese & C.A. nationals	Y
45. Abortion $ for rape/incest cases	Y
46. Allow religious schools to bar gays	N
47. Bar broadcaster fairness doctrine	N
48. Bar cap gains cut/reinstate IRA	N
49. Bar unions equal voice in pension	N
50. Bar assembly of chemical weapons	Y
51. Ban plutonium/uranium production	Y
52. Cap MX missile deployment at 50	N
53. Allow $3b for 2 stealth bombers	Y
54. Publish bio-warfare experiments	Y
55. Raise minimum wage-veto override	Y
56. Bar transfer of FS-X technology	Y
57. Cut defense and raise domestic $	N
58. Uniform poll closing in 48 states	Y
59. Req foreign investment disclosure	N
60. Textile import quotas-veto override	Y
61. Bar abortion funding in Wash, DC	N
62. Notify spouses of AIDS+ carriers	N
63. Seize conveyance-drug trafficking	Y
64. South Africa sanctions	Y

GILMAN, BENJAMIN A. (continued)

65. 60 days' notice of plant closings	Y
66. Close unneeded military bases	N
67. Keep welfare reform within $2.8b	Y
68. Allow children housing exclusion	N
69. Shift $400m of NASA to homeless	Y
70. Cap Medicare patients' liability	Y
71. Prohibit employee polygraph testing	Y
72. Allow CIA to fund Contras	Y
73. Revise unfair trade practices	Y
74. Focus SDI on accidental launch	N
75. Bar Air Force $ for MX missile	N
76. Allow "real" increase in defense	Y
77. Troop reduction in Europe of 50%	N
78. Ban nuclear tests above 1 kiloton	N
79. Ban anti-satellite missile tests	N
80. Observe certain limits of SALT II	N
81. Restore four Civil Rights laws	Y
82. Prohibit aliens as strikebreakers	Y
83. Allow military malpractice suits	Y
84. Approval of $36m in Contra aid	Y
85. $18b deficit reduction compromise	N
86. Welfare reform of $5.7b for 5 years	Y
87. Raise taxes $12b/cut spending $3b	N
88. Board to assess occupational risk	Y
89. Balanced budget by '93-via targets	N
90. Bar licensing of two nuclear plants	Y
91. Remove victims compensation cap	Y
92. Catastrophic health insurance	Y
93. Ban airline smoking-2 hours or less	Y
94. $1b/two year aid for the homeless	Y
95. Bar non-unions in union companies	Y
96. Increase FSLIC rescue to $15b	N
97. Impose quotas to lower trade deficit	Y
98. Reduce discretionary budget 21%	N
99. Immigration reform/alien amnesty	Y
100. South Africa sanctions-veto override	Y
101. Tax overhaul to revise income tax	N
102. Use of military in drug war	N
103. Delete 12 MX/add conventional wpn	N
104. Raise speed limit to 65 mph	N

105. Require Pentagon to buy US goods	Y
106. AIDS insurance non-discrimination	N
107. Prohibit Saudi arms sales	Y
108. Ease Gun Control Act of 1968	Y
109. Bar interstate handgun transport	N
110. Make company emissions known	Y
111. Allow toxic victims to sue in fed ct	Y
112. Superfund waste cleanup of $10b	N
113. 90 days notice of plant closings	Y
114. $20b in Medicare cuts/tax increases	Y
115. Spending cuts and tax increases	Y
116. Set school lunch lmt-250% poverty	N
117. $75m for youth work projects	Y
118. Allow Angolan military assistance	Y
119. Suspend defense payments for abuse	Y
120. Drop SS COLAs/$12b tax increase	N
121. Approve $1.5b for 21 MX missiles	Y
122. Emergency farm credit/revisions	Y
123. Duty on Taiwan/Hong Kong/S Korea	Y
124. Limit steel imports to 17%	Y
125. Cut $ to schools that bar prayer	N
126. $50b-taxes; cut Medicare/spending	N
127. Limit Pershing II/cruise in Europe	N
128. Delete $7.1b for 34 B-1 bombers	N
129. Bar purchase of Sergeant York guns	N
130. El Salvador military/economic aid	Y
131. Bar mining of Nicaraguan waters	Y
132. Physician fee freeze for Medicare	Y
133. $49b in "sin"/phone/insurance taxes	Y
134. Allow sale of Conrail	N
135. Equal Rights Amendment	Y
136. Authorize Marines in Lebanon	Y
137. Eminent domain for coal companies	N
138. Prohibit EPA clean air sanctions	Y
139. SS retirement age increase/reforms	N
140. Auto domestic content requirement	Y
141. Delete jobs program funding	Y
142. Highway-gas tax bill	N
143. Cut $5b from defense for Medicare	Y
144. Emergency housing aid of $1b	Y

Presidential Support Score: 1991 - 50%   1990 - 33%

McNULTY, MICHAEL R. -- New York 23rd District [Democrat]. Counties of Albany, Montgomery (pt.), Rensselaer (pt.) and Schenectady (pt.). Prior Terms: 1989-92. Born: September 16, 1947; Troy, NY. Education: St. Joseph's Institute; Loyola University (Rome Center); Holy Cross College (B.A.); Hill School of Insurance. Occupation: Green Island town supervisor (1970-78) and mayor (1979-82); state assemblyman (1983-88).

1. Protection to Haitian refugees	Y
2. Raise tax on wealthy; lower others	Y
3. Investigate Reagan hostage delay	N
4. Campaign finance revisions	Y
5. Unpaid leave to care for children	Y
6. Restrict NEA use of funds	Y
7. Bar race-bias claim/habeas corpus	N
8. Ban race as death sentence factor	N
9. Exceptions to exclusionary rule	N
10. Allow sale of assault weapons	N
11. Life in prison/abolish death penalty	Y
12. Req conspiracy-price fixing cases	N
13. Unemployment benefits extension	Y
14. Tissue use of aborted fetuses	Y

15. Bar replacement of union strikers	Y
16. Hold foreign aid at $15b for '92	Y
17. Restore space station funding	N
18. Civil Rights Act of 1991	Y
19. Unlimited damages-discrimination	N
20. Eliminate funds for supercollider	N
21. Terminate SDI except for research	N
22. Req 7-day handgun waiting period	Y
23. Provide $30b for failed S&Ls	N
24. Allow use of force against Iraq	Y
25. Allow $15b in foreign aid for '91	Y
26. Revise & extend legal immigration	Y
27. Suspend aid to Angolan rebels	Y
28. Democratic tax plan proposals	Y

McNULTY, MICHAEL R. (continued)

29. Cut defense 5% across the board	N	44. Protect Chinese & C.A. nationals	Y
30. Textile import quotas-veto override	Y	45. Abortion $ for rape/incest cases	Y
31. Abortion service for military abroad	N	46. Allow religious schools to bar gays	Y
32. Limits on high income farmers	Y	47. Bar broadcaster fairness doctrine	N
33. Family medical leave-veto override	Y	48. Bar cap gains cut/reinstate IRA	Y
34. Req submission of balanced budget	Y	49. Bar unions equal voice in pension	N
35. Balanced budget amendment	Y	50. Bar assembly of chemical weapons	Y
36. Amendment to ban flag desecration	Y	51. Ban plutonium/uranium production	Y
37. Reauthorize Amtrak-veto override	Y	52. Cap MX missile deployment at 50	Y
38. Retraining aid for coal miners	Y	53. Allow $3b for 2 stealth bombers	Y
39. Suspend El Salvador military aid	Y	54. Publish bio-warfare experiments	Y
40. Expand child care aid/tax credit	Y	55. Raise minimum wage-veto override	Y
41. Raise House salary/omit honoraria	Y	56. Bar transfer of FS-X technology	N
42. Toughen oil-spill liability	Y	57. Cut defense and raise domestic $	N
43. Restitution to Japanese interned	Y	58. Uniform poll closing in 48 states	?

Presidential Support Score: 1991 - 31%   1990 - 27%

SOLOMON, GERALD B. H. -- New York 24th District [Republican]. Counties of Columbia, Dutchess (pt.), Greene, Rensselaer (pt.), Saratoga, Warren and Washington. Prior Terms: 1979-92. Born: August 14, 1930; Okeechobee, FL. Education: Siene College; St. Lawrence University. Military Service: U.S. Marines, 1951-52. Occupation: New York assemblyman (1972-78); founding partner, insurance and investments firm.

1. Protection to Haitian refugees	N	40. Expand child care aid/tax credit	N
2. Raise tax on wealthy; lower others	N	41. Raise House salary/omit honoraria	Y
3. Investigate Reagan hostage delay	N	42. Toughen oil-spill liability	N
4. Campaign finance revisions	N	43. Restitution to Japanese interned	N
5. Unpaid leave to care for children	Y	44. Protect Chinese & C.A. nationals	N
6. Restrict NEA use of funds	Y	45. Abortion $ for rape/incest cases	N
7. Bar race-bias claim/habeas corpus	Y	46. Allow religious schools to bar gays	Y
8. Ban race as death sentence factor	Y	47. Bar broadcaster fairness doctrine	Y
9. Exceptions to exclusionary rule	Y	48. Bar cap gains cut/reinstate IRA	N
10. Allow sale of assault weapons	Y	49. Bar unions equal voice in pension	Y
11. Life in prison/abolish death penalty	N	50. Bar assembly of chemical weapons	N
12. Req conspiracy-price fixing cases	Y	51. Ban plutonium/uranium production	N
13. Unemployment benefits extension	N	52. Cap MX missile deployment at 50	N
14. Tissue use of aborted fetuses	N	53. Allow $3b for 2 stealth bombers	Y
15. Bar replacement of union strikers	Y	54. Publish bio-warfare experiments	N
16. Hold foreign aid at $15b for '92	N	55. Raise minimum wage-veto override	Y
17. Restore space station funding	#	56. Bar transfer of FS-X technology	N
18. Civil Rights Act of 1991	N	57. Cut defense and raise domestic $	N
19. Unlimited damages-discrimination	N	58. Uniform poll closing in 48 states	N
20. Eliminate funds for supercollider	Y	59. Req foreign investment disclosure	Y
21. Terminate SDI except for research	N	60. Textile import quotas-veto override	Y
22. Req 7-day handgun waiting period	N	61. Bar abortion funding in Wash, DC	Y
23. Provide $30b for failed S&Ls	N	62. Notify spouses of AIDS+ carriers	Y
24. Allow use of force against Iraq	Y	63. Seize conveyance-drug trafficking	Y
25. Allow $15b in foreign aid for '91	N	64. South Africa sanctions	N
26. Revise & extend legal immigration	Y	65. 60 days' notice of plant closings	N
27. Suspend aid to Angolan rebels	N	66. Close unneeded military bases	Y
28. Democratic tax plan proposals	N	67. Keep welfare reform within $2.8b	Y
29. Cut defense 5% across the board	N	68. Allow children housing exclusion	Y
30. Textile import quotas-veto override	Y	69. Shift $400m of NASA to homeless	N
31. Abortion service for military abroad	N	70. Cap Medicare patients' liability	Y
32. Limits on high income farmers	N	71. Prohibit employee polygraph testing	N
33. Family medical leave-veto override	Y	72. Allow CIA to fund Contras	Y
34. Req submission of balanced budget	N	73. Revise unfair trade practices	Y
35. Balanced budget amendment	Y	74. Focus SDI on accidental launch	N
36. Amendment to ban flag desecration	Y	75. Bar Air Force $ for MX missile	N
37. Reauthorize Amtrak-veto override	Y	76. Allow "real" increase in defense	N
38. Retraining aid for coal miners	Y	77. Troop reduction in Europe of 50%	N
39. Suspend El Salvador military aid	N	78. Ban nuclear tests above 1 kiloton	N

SOLOMON, GERALD B. H. (continued)

79. Ban anti-satellite missile tests	N		112. Superfund waste cleanup of $10b	Y
80. Observe certain limits of SALT II	N		113. 90 days notice of plant closings	N
81. Restore four Civil Rights laws	N		114. $20b in Medicare cuts/tax increases	N
82. Prohibit aliens as strikebreakers	N		115. Spending cuts and tax increases	N
83. Allow military malpractice suits	N		116. Set school lunch lmt-250% poverty	Y
84. Approval of $36m in Contra aid	Y		117. $75m for youth work projects	N
85. $18b deficit reduction compromise	N		118. Allow Angolan military assistance	Y
86. Welfare reform of $5.7b for 5 years	N		119. Suspend defense payments for abuse	N
87. Raise taxes $12b/cut spending $3b	N		120. Drop SS COLAs/$12b tax increase	N
88. Board to assess occupational risk	Y		121. Approve $1.5b for 21 MX missiles	Y
89. Balanced budget by '93-via targets	?		122. Emergency farm credit/revisions	N
90. Bar licensing of two nuclear plants	N		123. Duty on Taiwan/Hong Kong/S Korea	Y
91. Remove victims compensation cap	N		124. Limit steel imports to 17%	Y
92. Catastrophic health insurance	Y		125. Cut $ to schools that bar prayer	Y
93. Ban airline smoking-2 hours or less	N		126. $50b-taxes; cut Medicare/spending	N
94. $1b/two year aid for the homeless	N		127. Limit Pershing II/cruise in Europe	N
95. Bar non-unions in union companies	N		128. Delete $7.1b for 34 B-1 bombers	N
96. Increase FSLIC rescue to $15b	N		129. Bar purchase of Sergeant York guns	N
97. Impose quotas to lower trade deficit	N		130. El Salvador military/economic aid	Y
98. Reduce discretionary budget 21%	?		131. Bar mining of Nicaraguan waters	N
99. Immigration reform/alien amnesty	--		132. Physician fee freeze for Medicare	Y
100. South Africa sanctions-veto override	N		133. $49b in "sin"/phone/insurance taxes	N
101. Tax overhaul to revise income tax	Y		134. Allow sale of Conrail	Y
102. Use of military in drug war	Y		135. Equal Rights Amendment	N
103. Delete 12 MX/add conventional wpn	N		136. Authorize Marines in Lebanon	Y
104. Raise speed limit to 65 mph	Y		137. Eminent domain for coal companies	N
105. Require Pentagon to buy US goods	Y		138. Prohibit EPA clean air sanctions	N
106. AIDS insurance non-discrimination	N		139. SS retirement age increase/reforms	Y
107. Prohibit Saudi arms sales	N		140. Auto domestic content requirement	Y
108. Ease Gun Control Act of 1968	Y		141. Delete jobs program funding	N
109. Bar interstate handgun transport	N		142. Highway-gas tax bill	N
110. Make company emissions known	N		143. Cut $5b from defense for Medicare	N
111. Allow toxic victims to sue in fed ct	N		144. Emergency housing aid of $1b	Y

Presidential Support Score: 1991 - 71%   1990 - 67%

BOEHLERT, SHERWOOD L. -- New York 25th District [Republican]. Counties of Chenango, Cortland, Delaware (pt.), Madison (pt.), Montgomery (pt.), Oneida (pt.), Otsego, Schoharie and Tompkins (pt.).   Prior Terms: 1983-92.   Born: September 28, 1936; Utica, NY. Education: Utica College (A.B.). Military Service: U.S. Army, 1956-58. Occupation: Chief of Staff (1964-79); Oneida county executive (1979); Board of Directors, Utica College Foundation.

1. Protection to Haitian refugees	N		21. Terminate SDI except for research	N
2. Raise tax on wealthy; lower others	N		22. Req 7-day handgun waiting period	Y
3. Investigate Reagan hostage delay	N		23. Provide $30b for failed S&Ls	Y
4. Campaign finance revisions	Y		24. Allow use of force against Iraq	Y
5. Unpaid leave to care for children	Y		25. Allow $15b in foreign aid for '91	Y
6. Restrict NEA use of funds	N		26. Revise & extend legal immigration	Y
7. Bar race-bias claim/habeas corpus	Y		27. Suspend aid to Angolan rebels	N
8. Ban race as death sentence factor	Y		28. Democratic tax plan proposals	Y
9. Exceptions to exclusionary rule	Y		29. Cut defense 5% across the board	N
10. Allow sale of assault weapons	Y		30. Textile import quotas-veto override	Y
11. Life in prison/abolish death penalty	N		31. Abortion service for military abroad	Y
12. Req conspiracy-price fixing cases	Y		32. Limits on high income farmers	N
13. Unemployment benefits extension	Y		33. Family medical leave-veto override	Y
14. Tissue use of aborted fetuses	Y		34. Req submission of balanced budget	N
15. Bar replacement of union strikers	Y		35. Balanced budget amendment	Y
16. Hold foreign aid at $15b for '92	Y		36. Amendment to ban flag desecration	Y
17. Restore space station funding	Y		37. Reauthorize Amtrak-veto override	Y
18. Civil Rights Act of 1991	Y		38. Retraining aid for coal miners	N
19. Unlimited damages-discrimination	N		39. Suspend El Salvador military aid	Y
20. Eliminate funds for supercollider	Y		40. Expand child care aid/tax credit	Y

BOEHLERT, SHERWOOD L. (continued)

41.	Raise House salary/omit honoraria	Y	91.	Remove victims compensation cap	N
42.	Toughen oil-spill liability	Y	92.	Catastrophic health insurance	Y
43.	Restitution to Japanese interned	Y	93.	Ban airline smoking-2 hours or less	N
44.	Protect Chinese & C.A. nationals	Y	94.	$1b/two year aid for the homeless	Y
45.	Abortion $ for rape/incest cases	Y	95.	Bar non-unions in union companies	N
46.	Allow religious schools to bar gays	N	96.	Increase FSLIC rescue to $15b	?
47.	Bar broadcaster fairness doctrine	N	97.	Impose quotas to lower trade deficit	Y
48.	Bar cap gains cut/reinstate IRA	N	98.	Reduce discretionary budget 21%	N
49.	Bar unions equal voice in pension	Y	99.	Immigration reform/alien amnesty	Y
50.	Bar assembly of chemical weapons	N	100.	South Africa sanctions-veto override	Y
51.	Ban plutonium/uranium production	Y	101.	Tax overhaul to revise income tax	Y
52.	Cap MX missile deployment at 50	Y	102.	Use of military in drug war	Y
53.	Allow $3b for 2 stealth bombers	Y	103.	Delete 12 MX/add conventional wpn	Y
54.	Publish bio-warfare experiments	Y	104.	Raise speed limit to 65 mph	N
55.	Raise minimum wage-veto override	Y	105.	Require Pentagon to buy US goods	Y
56.	Bar transfer of FS-X technology	N	106.	AIDS insurance non-discrimination	N
57.	Cut defense and raise domestic $	N	107.	Prohibit Saudi arms sales	Y
58.	Uniform poll closing in 48 states	Y	108.	Ease Gun Control Act of 1968	Y
59.	Req foreign investment disclosure	N	109.	Bar interstate handgun transport	N
60.	Textile import quotas-veto override	Y	110.	Make company emissions known	Y
61.	Bar abortion funding in Wash, DC	N	111.	Allow toxic victims to sue in fed ct	Y
62.	Notify spouses of AIDS+ carriers	N	112.	Superfund waste cleanup of $10b	Y
63.	Seize conveyance-drug trafficking	N	113.	90 days notice of plant closings	Y
64.	South Africa sanctions	N	114.	$20b in Medicare cuts/tax increases	Y
65.	60 days' notice of plant closings	Y	115.	Spending cuts and tax increases	N
66.	Close unneeded military bases	Y	116.	Set school lunch lmt-250% poverty	N
67.	Keep welfare reform within $2.8b	Y	117.	$75m for youth work projects	Y
68.	Allow children housing exclusion	N	118.	Allow Angolan military assistance	Y
69.	Shift $400m of NASA to homeless	N	119.	Suspend defense payments for abuse	N
70.	Cap Medicare patients' liability	Y	120.	Drop SS COLAs/$12b tax increase	N
71.	Prohibit employee polygraph testing	Y	121.	Approve $1.5b for 21 MX missiles	Y
72.	Allow CIA to fund Contras	N	122.	Emergency farm credit/revisions	Y
73.	Revise unfair trade practices	Y	123.	Duty on Taiwan/Hong Kong/S Korea	N
74.	Focus SDI on accidental launch	Y	124.	Limit steel imports to 17%	Y
75.	Bar Air Force $ for MX missile	N	125.	Cut $ to schools that bar prayer	N
76.	Allow "real" increase in defense	N	126.	$50b-taxes; cut Medicare/spending	Y
77.	Troop reduction in Europe of 50%	N	127.	Limit Pershing II/cruise in Europe	N
78.	Ban nuclear tests above 1 kiloton	N	128.	Delete $7.1b for 34 B-1 bombers	N
79.	Ban anti-satellite missile tests	Y	129.	Bar purchase of Sergeant York guns	Y
80.	Observe certain limits of SALT II	Y	130.	El Salvador military/economic aid	Y
81.	Restore four Civil Rights laws	Y	131.	Bar mining of Nicaraguan waters	Y
82.	Prohibit aliens as strikebreakers	Y	132.	Physician fee freeze for Medicare	Y
83.	Allow military malpractice suits	?	133.	$49b in "sin"/phone/insurance taxes	Y
84.	Approval of $36m in Contra aid	N	134.	Allow sale of Conrail	Y
85.	$18b deficit reduction compromise	Y	135.	Equal Rights Amendment	Y
86.	Welfare reform of $5.7b for 5 years	Y	136.	Authorize Marines in Lebanon	Y
87.	Raise taxes $12b/cut spending $3b	N	137.	Eminent domain for coal companies	N
88.	Board to assess occupational risk	N	138.	Prohibit EPA clean air sanctions	N
89.	Balanced budget by '93-via targets	N	139.	SS retirement age increase/reforms	Y
90.	Bar licensing of two nuclear plants	N			

Presidential Support Score: 1991 - 58%   1990 - 40%

MARTIN, DAVID O'B. -- New York 26th District [Republican]. Counties of Clinton, Jefferson, Lewis and St. Lawrence. Prior Terms: 1981-92. Born: April 26, 1944; Ogdensburg, NY. Education: University of Notre Dame (B.B.A.); Albany Law School. Military Service: U.S. Marine Corps. Occupation: County legislator (1973, 1975); New York state assemblyman (1976, 1978).

1.	Protection to Haitian refugees	N	5.	Unpaid leave to care for children	Y
2.	Raise tax on wealthy; lower others	N	6.	Restrict NEA use of funds	Y
3.	Investigate Reagan hostage delay	N	7.	Bar race-bias claim/habeas corpus	Y
4.	Campaign finance revisions	N	8.	Ban race as death sentence factor	Y

MARTIN, DAVID O'B. (continued)

9.	Exceptions to exclusionary rule	Y
10.	Allow sale of assault weapons	Y
11.	Life in prison/abolish death penalty	N
12.	Req conspiracy-price fixing cases	Y
13.	Unemployment benefits extension	Y
14.	Tissue use of aborted fetuses	Y
15.	Bar replacement of union strikers	N
16.	Hold foreign aid at $15b for '92	?
17.	Restore space station funding	?
18.	Civil Rights Act of 1991	N
19.	Unlimited damages-discrimination	N
20.	Eliminate funds for supercollider	Y
21.	Terminate SDI except for research	N
22.	Req 7-day handgun waiting period	?
23.	Provide $30b for failed S&Ls	Y
24.	Allow use of force against Iraq	Y
25.	Allow $15b in foreign aid for '91	N
26.	Revise & extend legal immigration	Y
27.	Suspend aid to Angolan rebels	N
28.	Democratic tax plan proposals	N
29.	Cut defense 5% across the board	N
30.	Textile import quotas-veto override	Y
31.	Abortion service for military abroad	N
32.	Limits on high income farmers	N
33.	Family medical leave-veto override	Y
34.	Req submission of balanced budget	N
35.	Balanced budget amendment	Y
36.	Amendment to ban flag desecration	Y
37.	Reauthorize Amtrak-veto override	Y
38.	Retraining aid for coal miners	Y
39.	Suspend El Salvador military aid	N
40.	Expand child care aid/tax credit	N
41.	Raise House salary/omit honoraria	Y
42.	Toughen oil-spill liability	N
43.	Restitution to Japanese interned	N
44.	Protect Chinese & C.A. nationals	N
45.	Abortion $ for rape/incest cases	N
46.	Allow religious schools to bar gays	Y
47.	Bar broadcaster fairness doctrine	Y
48.	Bar cap gains cut/reinstate IRA	N
49.	Bar unions equal voice in pension	Y
50.	Bar assembly of chemical weapons	N
51.	Ban plutonium/uranium production	N
52.	Cap MX missile deployment at 50	Y
53.	Allow $3b for 2 stealth bombers	Y
54.	Publish bio-warfare experiments	N
55.	Raise minimum wage-veto override	N
56.	Bar transfer of FS-X technology	N
57.	Cut defense and raise domestic $	N
58.	Uniform poll closing in 48 states	N
59.	Req foreign investment disclosure	N
60.	Textile import quotas-veto override	Y
61.	Bar abortion funding in Wash, DC	Y
62.	Notify spouses of AIDS+ carriers	?
63.	Seize conveyance-drug trafficking	Y
64.	South Africa sanctions	N
65.	60 days' notice of plant closings	Y
66.	Close unneeded military bases	N
67.	Keep welfare reform within $2.8b	Y
68.	Allow children housing exclusion	N
69.	Shift $400m of NASA to homeless	Y
70.	Cap Medicare patients' liability	Y
71.	Prohibit employee polygraph testing	N
72.	Allow CIA to fund Contras	Y
73.	Revise unfair trade practices	Y
74.	Focus SDI on accidental launch	N
75.	Bar Air Force $ for MX missile	N
76.	Allow "real" increase in defense	Y
77.	Troop reduction in Europe of 50%	?
78.	Ban nuclear tests above 1 kiloton	N
79.	Ban anti-satellite missile tests	N
80.	Observe certain limits of SALT II	N
81.	Restore four Civil Rights laws	Y
82.	Prohibit aliens as strikebreakers	Y
83.	Allow military malpractice suits	Y
84.	Approval of $36m in Contra aid	Y
85.	$18b deficit reduction compromise	Y
86.	Welfare reform of $5.7b for 5 years	N
87.	Raise taxes $12b/cut spending $3b	N
88.	Board to assess occupational risk	?
89.	Balanced budget by '93-via targets	N
90.	Bar licensing of two nuclear plants	N
91.	Remove victims compensation cap	N
92.	Catastrophic health insurance	Y
93.	Ban airline smoking-2 hours or less	N
94.	$1b/two year aid for the homeless	Y
95.	Bar non-unions in union companies	Y
96.	Increase FSLIC rescue to $15b	N
97.	Impose quotas to lower trade deficit	N
98.	Reduce discretionary budget 21%	N
99.	Immigration reform/alien amnesty	N
100.	South Africa sanctions-veto override	?
101.	Tax overhaul to revise income tax	N
102.	Use of military in drug war	Y
103.	Delete 12 MX/add conventional wpn	N
104.	Raise speed limit to 65 mph	Y
105.	Require Pentagon to buy US goods	N
106.	AIDS insurance non-discrimination	N
107.	Prohibit Saudi arms sales	Y
108.	Ease Gun Control Act of 1968	Y
109.	Bar interstate handgun transport	?
110.	Make company emissions known	N
111.	Allow toxic victims to sue in fed ct	N
112.	Superfund waste cleanup of $10b	Y
113.	90 days notice of plant closings	N
114.	$20b in Medicare cuts/tax increases	N
115.	Spending cuts and tax increases	N
116.	Set school lunch lmt-250% poverty	N
117.	$75m for youth work projects	N
118.	Allow Angolan military assistance	Y
119.	Suspend defense payments for abuse	N
120.	Drop SS COLAs/$12b tax increase	N
121.	Approve $1.5b for 21 MX missiles	Y
122.	Emergency farm credit/revisions	Y
123.	Duty on Taiwan/Hong Kong/S Korea	N
124.	Limit steel imports to 17%	N
125.	Cut $ to schools that bar prayer	Y
126.	$50b-taxes; cut Medicare/spending	N
127.	Limit Pershing II/cruise in Europe	N
128.	Delete $7.1b for 34 B-1 bombers	N
129.	Bar purchase of Sergeant York guns	N
130.	El Salvador military/economic aid	Y
131.	Bar mining of Nicaraguan waters	N
132.	Physician fee freeze for Medicare	Y
133.	$49b in "sin"/phone/insurance taxes	Y
134.	Allow sale of Conrail	Y
135.	Equal Rights Amendment	N
136.	Authorize Marines in Lebanon	Y

MARTIN, DAVID O'B. (continued)

137. Eminent domain for coal companies	Y	
138. Prohibit EPA clean air sanctions	N	
139. SS retirement age increase/reforms	Y	
140. Auto domestic content requirement	N	

141. Delete jobs program funding	Y	
142. Highway-gas tax bill	N	
143. Cut $5b from defense for Medicare	N	
144. Emergency housing aid of $1b	Y	

Presidential Support Score: 1991 - 70%   1990 - 60%

WALSH, JAMES T. -- New York 27th District [Republican]. Counties of Madison (pt.) and Onondaga (pt.). Prior Terms: 1989-92. Born: June 19, 1947; Syracuse, NY. Education: St. Bonaventure University (B.A.). Occupation: Peace Corps agriculture exension agent (1970-72); telecommunications company marketing executive (1974-88); Syracuse common councilor (1977-84) and common council president (1985-88).

1. Protection to Haitian refugees	N	30. Textile import quotas-veto override	N
2. Raise tax on wealthy; lower others	N	31. Abortion service for military abroad	N
3. Investigate Reagan hostage delay	N	32. Limits on high income farmers	N
4. Campaign finance revisions	N	33. Family medical leave-veto override	N
5. Unpaid leave to care for children	N	34. Req submission of balanced budget	N
6. Restrict NEA use of funds	Y	35. Balanced budget amendment	Y
7. Bar race-bias claim/habeas corpus	Y	36. Amendment to ban flag desecration	Y
8. Ban race as death sentence factor	Y	37. Reauthorize Amtrak-veto override	Y
9. Exceptions to exclusionary rule	Y	38. Retraining aid for coal miners	Y
10. Allow sale of assault weapons	Y	39. Suspend El Salvador military aid	Y
11. Life in prison/abolish death penalty	N	40. Expand child care aid/tax credit	Y
12. Req conspiracy-price fixing cases	Y	41. Raise House salary/omit honoraria	Y
13. Unemployment benefits extension	Y	42. Toughen oil-spill liability	Y
14. Tissue use of aborted fetuses	N	43. Restitution to Japanese interned	N
15. Bar replacement of union strikers	N	44. Protect Chinese & C.A. nationals	Y
16. Hold foreign aid at $15b for '92	N	45. Abortion $ for rape/incest cases	N
17. Restore space station funding	Y	46. Allow religious schools to bar gays	Y
18. Civil Rights Act of 1991	Y	47. Bar broadcaster fairness doctrine	Y
19. Unlimited damages-discrimination	N	48. Bar cap gains cut/reinstate IRA	N
20. Eliminate funds for supercollider	N	49. Bar unions equal voice in pension	Y
21. Terminate SDI except for research	N	50. Bar assembly of chemical weapons	Y
22. Req 7-day handgun waiting period	Y	51. Ban plutonium/uranium production	Y
23. Provide $30b for failed S&Ls	Y	52. Cap MX missile deployment at 50	Y
24. Allow use of force against Iraq	Y	53. Allow $3b for 2 stealth bombers	Y
25. Allow $15b in foreign aid for '91	?	54. Publish bio-warfare experiments	Y
26. Revise & extend legal immigration	?	55. Raise minimum wage-veto override	Y
27. Suspend aid to Angolan rebels	N	56. Bar transfer of FS-X technology	N
28. Democratic tax plan proposals	N	57. Cut defense and raise domestic $	N
29. Cut defense 5% across the board	N	58. Uniform poll closing in 48 states	Y

Presidential Support Score: 1991 - 70%   1990 - 44%

McHUGH, MATTHEW F. -- New York 28th District [Democrat]. Counties of Broome, Delaware, (pt.), Sullivan (pt.), Tioga, Tompkins (pt.) and Ulster. Prior Terms: 1975-92. Born: December 6, 1938; Philadelphia, PA. Education: Mount St. Mary's College (B.A.); Villanova Law School (J.D.). Occupation: Attorney; district attorney (1969-72); vice president, Chamber of Commerce.

1. Protection to Haitian refugees	Y	12. Req conspiracy-price fixing cases	Y
2. Raise tax on wealthy; lower others	Y	13. Unemployment benefits extension	Y
3. Investigate Reagan hostage delay	Y	14. Tissue use of aborted fetuses	Y
4. Campaign finance revisions	Y	15. Bar replacement of union strikers	Y
5. Unpaid leave to care for children	Y	16. Hold foreign aid at $15b for '92	Y
6. Restrict NEA use of funds	N	17. Restore space station funding	N
7. Bar race-bias claim/habeas corpus	N	18. Civil Rights Act of 1991	Y
8. Ban race as death sentence factor	N	19. Unlimited damages-discrimination	Y
9. Exceptions to exclusionary rule	N	20. Eliminate funds for supercollider	N
10. Allow sale of assault weapons	N	21. Terminate SDI except for research	Y
11. Life in prison/abolish death penalty	Y	22. Req 7-day handgun waiting period	Y

McHUGH, MATTHEW F. (continued)

23. Provide $30b for failed S&Ls	Y	84. Approval of $36m in Contra aid	N
24. Allow use of force against Iraq	N	85. $18b deficit reduction compromise	Y
25. Allow $15b in foreign aid for '91	Y	86. Welfare reform of $5.7b for 5 years	Y
26. Revise & extend legal immigration	Y	87. Raise taxes $12b/cut spending $3b	Y
27. Suspend aid to Angolan rebels	Y	88. Board to assess occupational risk	Y
28. Democratic tax plan proposals	Y	89. Balanced budget by '93-via targets	N
29. Cut defense 5% across the board	N	90. Bar licensing of two nuclear plants	Y
30. Textile import quotas-veto override	N	91. Remove victims compensation cap	Y
31. Abortion service for military abroad	Y	92. Catastrophic health insurance	Y
32. Limits on high income farmers	N	93. Ban airline smoking-2 hours or less	Y
33. Family medical leave-veto override	Y	94. $1b/two year aid for the homeless	Y
34. Req submission of balanced budget	Y	95. Bar non-unions in union companies	Y
35. Balanced budget amendment	N	96. Increase FSLIC rescue to $15b	Y
36. Amendment to ban flag desecration	N	97. Impose quotas to lower trade deficit	N
37. Reauthorize Amtrak-veto override	Y	98. Reduce discretionary budget 21%	N
38. Retraining aid for coal miners	Y	99. Immigration reform/alien amnesty	Y
39. Suspend El Salvador military aid	Y	100. South Africa sanctions-veto override	Y
40. Expand child care aid/tax credit	Y	101. Tax overhaul to revise income tax	Y
41. Raise House salary/omit honoraria	Y	102. Use of military in drug war	Y
42. Toughen oil-spill liability	Y	103. Delete 12 MX/add conventional wpn	Y
43. Restitution to Japanese interned	Y	104. Raise speed limit to 65 mph	N
44. Protect Chinese & C.A. nationals	Y	105. Require Pentagon to buy US goods	N
45. Abortion $ for rape/incest cases	N	106. AIDS insurance non-discrimination	Y
46. Allow religious schools to bar gays	N	107. Prohibit Saudi arms sales	Y
47. Bar broadcaster fairness doctrine	N	108. Ease Gun Control Act of 1968	N
48. Bar cap gains cut/reinstate IRA	Y	109. Bar interstate handgun transport	Y
49. Bar unions equal voice in pension	N	110. Make company emissions known	Y
50. Bar assembly of chemical weapons	Y	111. Allow toxic victims to sue in fed ct	Y
51. Ban plutonium/uranium production	Y	112. Superfund waste cleanup of $10b	Y
52. Cap MX missile deployment at 50	Y	113. 90 days notice of plant closings	Y
53. Allow $3b for 2 stealth bombers	N	114. $20b in Medicare cuts/tax increases	Y
54. Publish bio-warfare experiments	Y	115. Spending cuts and tax increases	Y
55. Raise minimum wage-veto override	Y	116. Set school lunch lmt-250% poverty	N
56. Bar transfer of FS-X technology	Y	117. $75m for youth work projects	Y
57. Cut defense and raise domestic $	N	118. Allow Angolan military assistance	N
58. Uniform poll closing in 48 states	Y	119. Suspend defense payments for abuse	--
59. Req foreign investment disclosure	Y	120. Drop SS COLAs/$12b tax increase	N
60. Textile import quotas-veto override	N	121. Approve $1.5b for 21 MX missiles	N
61. Bar abortion funding in Wash, DC	N	122. Emergency farm credit/revisions	Y
62. Notify spouses of AIDS+ carriers	N	123. Duty on Taiwan/Hong Kong/S Korea	N
63. Seize conveyance-drug trafficking	N	124. Limit steel imports to 17%	N
64. South Africa sanctions	Y	125. Cut $ to schools that bar prayer	N
65. 60 days' notice of plant closings	Y	126. $50b-taxes; cut Medicare/spending	Y
66. Close unneeded military bases	Y	127. Limit Pershing II/cruise in Europe	Y
67. Keep welfare reform within $2.8b	N	128. Delete $7.1b for 34 B-1 bombers	Y
68. Allow children housing exclusion	N	129. Bar purchase of Sergeant York guns	Y
69. Shift $400m of NASA to homeless	N	130. El Salvador military/economic aid	N
70. Cap Medicare patients' liability	Y	131. Bar mining of Nicaraguan waters	Y
71. Prohibit employee polygraph testing	Y	132. Physician fee freeze for Medicare	N
72. Allow CIA to fund Contras	N	133. $49b in "sin"/phone/insurance taxes	Y
73. Revise unfair trade practices	Y	134. Allow sale of Conrail	N
74. Focus SDI on accidental launch	Y	135. Equal Rights Amendment	Y
75. Bar Air Force $ for MX missile	Y	136. Authorize Marines in Lebanon	N
76. Allow "real" increase in defense	N	137. Eminent domain for coal companies	N
77. Troop reduction in Europe of 50%	N	138. Prohibit EPA clean air sanctions	N
78. Ban nuclear tests above 1 kiloton	Y	139. SS retirement age increase/reforms	N
79. Ban anti-satellite missile tests	Y	140. Auto domestic content requirement	N
80. Observe certain limits of SALT II	Y	141. Delete jobs program funding	N
81. Restore four Civil Rights laws	Y	142. Highway-gas tax bill	Y
82. Prohibit aliens as strikebreakers	Y	143. Cut $5b from defense for Medicare	Y
83. Allow military malpractice suits	Y	144. Emergency housing aid of $1b	Y

Presidential Support Score: 1991 - 32%   1990 - 23%

HORTON, FRANK -- New York 29th District [Republican]. Counties of Cayuga, Monroe (pt.), Oneida (pt.), Oswego, Seneca and Wayne. Prior Terms: 1963-92. Born: December 12, 1919; Cuero, TX. Education: Louisiana State University (B.A.); Cornell Law School (LL.B.). Military Service: U.S. Army, 1941-45. Occupation: Attorney; Rochester city councilman (1955-61).

1. Protection to Haitian refugees	N	
2. Raise tax on wealthy; lower others	N	
3. Investigate Reagan hostage delay	N	
4. Campaign finance revisions	N	
5. Unpaid leave to care for children	Y	
6. Restrict NEA use of funds	N	
7. Bar race-bias claim/habeas corpus	N	
8. Ban race as death sentence factor	N	
9. Exceptions to exclusionary rule	N	
10. Allow sale of assault weapons	Y	
11. Life in prison/abolish death penalty	N	
12. Req conspiracy-price fixing cases	Y	
13. Unemployment benefits extension	Y	
14. Tissue use of aborted fetuses	Y	
15. Bar replacement of union strikers	Y	
16. Hold foreign aid at $15b for '92	Y	
17. Restore space station funding	Y	
18. Civil Rights Act of 1991	Y	
19. Unlimited damages-discrimination	N	
20. Eliminate funds for supercollider	?	
21. Terminate SDI except for research	N	
22. Req 7-day handgun waiting period	N	
23. Provide $30b for failed S&Ls	Y	
24. Allow use of force against Iraq	Y	
25. Allow $15b in foreign aid for '91	?	
26. Revise & extend legal immigration	Y	
27. Suspend aid to Angolan rebels	N	
28. Democratic tax plan proposals	Y	
29. Cut defense 5% across the board	N	
30. Textile import quotas-veto override	Y	
31. Abortion service for military abroad	Y	
32. Limits on high income farmers	N	
33. Family medical leave-veto override	Y	
34. Req submission of balanced budget	N	
35. Balanced budget amendment	Y	
36. Amendment to ban flag desecration	Y	
37. Reauthorize Amtrak-veto override	Y	
38. Retraining aid for coal miners	Y	
39. Suspend El Salvador military aid	Y	
40. Expand child care aid/tax credit	Y	
41. Raise House salary/omit honoraria	Y	
42. Toughen oil-spill liability	N	
43. Restitution to Japanese interned	Y	
44. Protect Chinese & C.A. nationals	Y	
45. Abortion $ for rape/incest cases	Y	
46. Allow religious schools to bar gays	N	
47. Bar broadcaster fairness doctrine	N	
48. Bar cap gains cut/reinstate IRA	N	
49. Bar unions equal voice in pension	N	
50. Bar assembly of chemical weapons	Y	
51. Ban plutonium/uranium production	Y	
52. Cap MX missile deployment at 50	Y	
53. Allow $3b for 2 stealth bombers	N	
54. Publish bio-warfare experiments	Y	
55. Raise minimum wage-veto override	Y	
56. Bar transfer of FS-X technology	Y	
57. Cut defense and raise domestic $	N	
58. Uniform poll closing in 48 states	Y	
59. Req foreign investment disclosure	N	

60. Textile import quotas-veto override	Y	
61. Bar abortion funding in Wash, DC	N	
62. Notify spouses of AIDS+ carriers	N	
63. Seize conveyance-drug trafficking	Y	
64. South Africa sanctions	?	
65. 60 days' notice of plant closings	Y	
66. Close unneeded military bases	N	
67. Keep welfare reform within $2.8b	Y	
68. Allow children housing exclusion	N	
69. Shift $400m of NASA to homeless	Y	
70. Cap Medicare patients' liability	Y	
71. Prohibit employee polygraph testing	Y	
72. Allow CIA to fund Contras	N	
73. Revise unfair trade practices	Y	
74. Focus SDI on accidental launch	Y	
75. Bar Air Force $ for MX missile	Y	
76. Allow "real" increase in defense	N	
77. Troop reduction in Europe of 50%	N	
78. Ban nuclear tests above 1 kiloton	N	
79. Ban anti-satellite missile tests	N	
80. Observe certain limits of SALT II	Y	
81. Restore four Civil Rights laws	Y	
82. Prohibit aliens as strikebreakers	Y	
83. Allow military malpractice suits	?	
84. Approval of $36m in Contra aid	N	
85. $18b deficit reduction compromise	Y	
86. Welfare reform of $5.7b for 5 years	Y	
87. Raise taxes $12b/cut spending $3b	N	
88. Board to assess occupational risk	N	
89. Balanced budget by '93-via targets	Y	
90. Bar licensing of two nuclear plants	N	
91. Remove victims compensation cap	N	
92. Catastrophic health insurance	Y	
93. Ban airline smoking-2 hours or less	N	
94. $1b/two year aid for the homeless	Y	
95. Bar non-unions in union companies	Y	
96. Increase FSLIC rescue to $15b	?	
97. Impose quotas to lower trade deficit	Y	
98. Reduce discretionary budget 21%	N	
99. Immigration reform/alien amnesty	N	
100. South Africa sanctions-veto override	Y	
101. Tax overhaul to revise income tax	N	
102. Use of military in drug war	N	
103. Delete 12 MX/add conventional wpn	?	
104. Raise speed limit to 65 mph	Y	
105. Require Pentagon to buy US goods	Y	
106. AIDS insurance non-discrimination	Y	
107. Prohibit Saudi arms sales	Y	
108. Ease Gun Control Act of 1968	Y	
109. Bar interstate handgun transport	N	
110. Make company emissions known	Y	
111. Allow toxic victims to sue in fed ct	Y	
112. Superfund waste cleanup of $10b	Y	
113. 90 days notice of plant closings	#	
114. $20b in Medicare cuts/tax increases	Y·	
115. Spending cuts and tax increases	Y	
116. Set school lunch lmt-250% poverty	N	
117. $75m for youth work projects	#	
118. Allow Angolan military assistance	N	

HORTON, FRANK (continued)

119.	Suspend defense payments for abuse	N	132.	Physician fee freeze for Medicare	Y
120.	Drop SS COLAs/$12b tax increase	N	133.	$49b in "sin"/phone/insurance taxes	Y
121.	Approve $1.5b for 21 MX missiles	Y	134.	Allow sale of Conrail	N
122.	Emergency farm credit/revisions	Y	135.	Equal Rights Amendment	Y
123.	Duty on Taiwan/Hong Kong/S Korea	N	136.	Authorize Marines in Lebanon	N
124.	Limit steel imports to 17%	Y	137.	Eminent domain for coal companies	N
125.	Cut $ to schools that bar prayer	N	138.	Prohibit EPA clean air sanctions	Y
126.	$50b-taxes; cut Medicare/spending	Y	139.	SS retirement age increase/reforms	Y
127.	Limit Pershing II/cruise in Europe	N	140.	Auto domestic content requirement	Y
128.	Delete $7.1b for 34 B-1 bombers	Y	141.	Delete jobs program funding	Y
129.	Bar purchase of Sergeant York guns	N	142.	Highway-gas tax bill	N
130.	El Salvador military/economic aid	Y	143.	Cut $5b from defense for Medicare	Y
131.	Bar mining of Nicaraguan waters	Y	144.	Emergency housing aid of $1b	Y

Presidential Support Score: 1991 - 52% 1990 - 32%

SLAUGHTER, LOUISE M. -- New York 30th District [Democrat]. Counties of Genesee, Livingston (pt.), Monroe (pt.) and Ontario (pt.). Prior Terms: 1987-92. Born: August 14, 1929; Harlan County, KY. Education: University of Kentucky (B.S., M.S.). Occupation: Democratic State committeewoman (1972-1982); Monroe County Legislature member (1976-1979); regional coordinator for Lieutenant Governor Cuomo (1979-1982); state assemblywoman (1982-1986).

1.	Protection to Haitian refugees	Y	41.	Raise House salary/omit honoraria	Y
2.	Raise tax on wealthy; lower others	Y	42.	Toughen oil-spill liability	Y
3.	Investigate Reagan hostage delay	Y	43.	Restitution to Japanese interned	Y
4.	Campaign finance revisions	Y	44.	Protect Chinese & C.A. nationals	Y
5.	Unpaid leave to care for children	Y	45.	Abortion $ for rape/incest cases	Y
6.	Restrict NEA use of funds	N	46.	Allow religious schools to bar gays	N
7.	Bar race-bias claim/habeas corpus	N	47.	Bar broadcaster fairness doctrine	N
8.	Ban race as death sentence factor	N	48.	Bar cap gains cut/reinstate IRA	Y
9.	Exceptions to exclusionary rule	N	49.	Bar unions equal voice in pension	N
10.	Allow sale of assault weapons	N	50.	Bar assembly of chemical weapons	Y
11.	Life in prison/abolish death penalty	Y	51.	Ban plutonium/uranium production	Y
12.	Req conspiracy-price fixing cases	Y	52.	Cap MX missile deployment at 50	Y
13.	Unemployment benefits extension	Y	53.	Allow $3b for 2 stealth bombers	N
14.	Tissue use of aborted fetuses	Y	54.	Publish bio-warfare experiments	Y
15.	Bar replacement of union strikers	Y	55.	Raise minimum wage-veto override	Y
16.	Hold foreign aid at $15b for '92	Y	56.	Bar transfer of FS-X technology	Y
17.	Restore space station funding	--	57.	Cut defense and raise domestic $	Y
18.	Civil Rights Act of 1991	Y	58.	Uniform poll closing in 48 states	Y
19.	Unlimited damages-discrimination	Y	59.	Req foreign investment disclosure	Y
20.	Eliminate funds for supercollider	Y	60.	Textile import quotas-veto override	Y
21.	Terminate SDI except for research	Y	61.	Bar abortion funding in Wash, DC	N
22.	Req 7-day handgun waiting period	Y	62.	Notify spouses of AIDS+ carriers	N
23.	Provide $30b for failed S&Ls	N	63.	Seize conveyance-drug trafficking	N
24.	Allow use of force against Iraq	N	64.	South Africa sanctions	Y
25.	Allow $15b in foreign aid for '91	Y	65.	60 days' notice of plant closings	Y
26.	Revise & extend legal immigration	Y	66.	Close unneeded military bases	Y
27.	Suspend aid to Angolan rebels	Y	67.	Keep welfare reform within $2.8b	Y
28.	Democratic tax plan proposals	Y	68.	Allow children housing exclusion	N
29.	Cut defense 5% across the board	Y	69.	Shift $400m of NASA to homeless	Y
30.	Textile import quotas-veto override	Y	70.	Cap Medicare patients' liability	Y
31.	Abortion service for military abroad	Y	71.	Prohibit employee polygraph testing	Y
32.	Limits on high income farmers	N	72.	Allow CIA to fund Contras	N
33.	Family medical leave-veto override	Y	73.	Revise unfair trade practices	Y
34.	Req submission of balanced budget	Y	74.	Focus SDI on accidental launch	Y
35.	Balanced budget amendment	Y	75.	Bar Air Force $ for MX missile	Y
36.	Amendment to ban flag desecration	N	76.	Allow "real" increase in defense	N
37.	Reauthorize Amtrak-veto override	Y	77.	Troop reduction in Europe of 50%	Y
38.	Retraining aid for coal miners	Y	78.	Ban nuclear tests above 1 kiloton	Y
39.	Suspend El Salvador military aid	Y	79.	Ban anti-satellite missile tests	Y
40.	Expand child care aid/tax credit	Y	80.	Observe certain limits of SALT II	Y

SLAUGHTER, LOUISE M. (continued)

81.	Restore four Civil Rights laws	Y	90.	Bar licensing of two nuclear plants	Y
82.	Prohibit aliens as strikebreakers	Y	91.	Remove victims compensation cap	Y
83.	Allow military malpractice suits	Y	92.	Catastrophic health insurance	Y
84.	Approval of $36m in Contra aid	N	93.	Ban airline smoking-2 hours or less	Y
85.	$18b deficit reduction compromise	N	94.	$1b/two year aid for the homeless	Y
86.	Welfare reform of $5.7b for 5 years	Y	95.	Bar non-unions in union companies	+
87.	Raise taxes $12b/cut spending $3b	N	96.	Increase FSLIC rescue to $15b	N
88.	Board to assess occupational risk	Y	97.	Impose quotas to lower trade deficit	Y
89.	Balanced budget by '93-via targets	Y	98.	Reduce discretionary budget 21%	Y

Presidential Support Score: 1991 - 25%   1990 - 16%

PAXON, WILLIAM -- New York 31st District [Republican]. Counties of Cattaraugus (pt.), Erie (pt.), Livingston (pt.), Ontario (pt.) and Wyoming (pt.). Prior Terms: 1989-92. Born: April 29, 1954; Buffalo, NY. Education: Canisius College (B.A.). Occupation: Erie County legislator; state assemblyman; campaign co-chairman for Representative Kemp.

1.	Protection to Haitian refugees	N	30.	Textile import quotas-veto override	N
2.	Raise tax on wealthy; lower others	N	31.	Abortion service for military abroad	N
3.	Investigate Reagan hostage delay	N	32.	Limits on high income farmers	N
4.	Campaign finance revisions	N	33.	Family medical leave-veto override	N
5.	Unpaid leave to care for children	N	34.	Req submission of balanced budget	N
6.	Restrict NEA use of funds	Y	35.	Balanced budget amendment	Y
7.	Bar race-bias claim/habeas corpus	Y	36.	Amendment to ban flag desecration	Y
8.	Ban race as death sentence factor	Y	37.	Reauthorize Amtrak-veto override	N
9.	Exceptions to exclusionary rule	Y	38.	Retraining aid for coal miners	N
10.	Allow sale of assault weapons	Y	39.	Suspend El Salvador military aid	N
11.	Life in prison/abolish death penalty	N	40.	Expand child care aid/tax credit	N
12.	Req conspiracy-price fixing cases	Y	41.	Raise House salary/omit honoraria	N
13.	Unemployment benefits extension	Y	42.	Toughen oil-spill liability	N
14.	Tissue use of aborted fetuses	N	43.	Restitution to Japanese interned	N
15.	Bar replacement of union strikers	N	44.	Protect Chinese & C.A. nationals	N
16.	Hold foreign aid at $15b for '92	Y	45.	Abortion $ for rape/incest cases	N
17.	Restore space station funding	N	46.	Allow religious schools to bar gays	Y
18.	Civil Rights Act of 1991	N	47.	Bar broadcaster fairness doctrine	Y
19.	Unlimited damages-discrimination	N	48.	Bar cap gains cut/reinstate IRA	N
20.	Eliminate funds for supercollider	Y	49.	Bar unions equal voice in pension	Y
21.	Terminate SDI except for research	N	50.	Bar assembly of chemical weapons	N
22.	Req 7-day handgun waiting period	N	51.	Ban plutonium/uranium production	N
23.	Provide $30b for failed S&Ls	Y	52.	Cap MX missile deployment at 50	N
24.	Allow use of force against Iraq	Y	53.	Allow $3b for 2 stealth bombers	Y
25.	Allow $15b in foreign aid for '91	Y	54.	Publish bio-warfare experiments	N
26.	Revise & extend legal immigration	Y	55.	Raise minimum wage-veto override	N
27.	Suspend aid to Angolan rebels	N	56.	Bar transfer of FS-X technology	N
28.	Democratic tax plan proposals	N	57.	Cut defense and raise domestic $	N
29.	Cut defense 5% across the board	N	58.	Uniform poll closing in 48 states	N

Presidential Support Score: 1991 - 75%   1990 - 69%

LaFALCE, JOHN J. -- New York 32nd District [Democrat]. Counties of Erie (pt.), Monroe (pt.), Niagara and Orleans. Prior Terms: 1975-92. Born: October 6, 1939; Buffalo, NY. Education: Canisuis College (B.S.); Villanova Law School (J.D.). Military Service: U.S. Army, 1965-67. Occupation: New York senator (1971-72); New York assemblyman (1973-74).

1.	Protection to Haitian refugees	Y	8.	Ban race as death sentence factor	N
2.	Raise tax on wealthy; lower others	Y	9.	Exceptions to exclusionary rule	N
3.	Investigate Reagan hostage delay	Y	10.	Allow sale of assault weapons	N
4.	Campaign finance revisions	Y	11.	Life in prison/abolish death penalty	Y
5.	Unpaid leave to care for children	Y	12.	Req conspiracy-price fixing cases	N
6.	Restrict NEA use of funds	N	13.	Unemployment benefits extension	Y
7.	Bar race-bias claim/habeas corpus	N	14.	Tissue use of aborted fetuses	Y

LaFALCE, JOHN J. (continued)

15. Bar replacement of union strikers	Y	
16. Hold foreign aid at $15b for '92	Y	
17. Restore space station funding	N	
18. Civil Rights Act of 1991	Y	
19. Unlimited damages-discrimination	N	
20. Eliminate funds for supercollider	Y	
21. Terminate SDI except for research	Y	
22. Req 7-day handgun waiting period	Y	
23. Provide $30b for failed S&Ls	N	
24. Allow use of force against Iraq	N	
25. Allow $15b in foreign aid for '91	?	
26. Revise & extend legal immigration	?	
27. Suspend aid to Angolan rebels	Y	
28. Democratic tax plan proposals	Y	
29. Cut defense 5% across the board	Y	
30. Textile import quotas-veto override	N	
31. Abortion service for military abroad	N	
32. Limits on high income farmers	Y	
33. Family medical leave-veto override	N	
34. Req submission of balanced budget	Y	
35. Balanced budget amendment	N	
36. Amendment to ban flag desecration	N	
37. Reauthorize Amtrak-veto override	Y	
38. Retraining aid for coal miners	Y	
39. Suspend El Salvador military aid	Y	
40. Expand child care aid/tax credit	Y	
41. Raise House salary/omit honoraria	Y	
42. Toughen oil-spill liability	N	
43. Restitution to Japanese interned	?	
44. Protect Chinese & C.A. nationals	Y	
45. Abortion $ for rape/incest cases	N	
46. Allow religious schools to bar gays	Y	
47. Bar broadcaster fairness doctrine	N	
48. Bar cap gains cut/reinstate IRA	Y	
49. Bar unions equal voice in pension	Y	
50. Bar assembly of chemical weapons	Y	
51. Ban plutonium/uranium production	Y	
52. Cap MX missile deployment at 50	Y	
53. Allow $3b for 2 stealth bombers	N	
54. Publish bio-warfare experiments	Y	
55. Raise minimum wage-veto override	Y	
56. Bar transfer of FS-X technology	Y	
57. Cut defense and raise domestic $	N	
58. Uniform poll closing in 48 states	Y	
59. Req foreign investment disclosure	Y	
60. Textile import quotas-veto override	N	
61. Bar abortion funding in Wash, DC	Y	
62. Notify spouses of AIDS+ carriers	N	
63. Seize conveyance-drug trafficking	N	
64. South Africa sanctions	Y	
65. 60 days' notice of plant closings	Y	
66. Close unneeded military bases	N	
67. Keep welfare reform within $2.8b	N	
68. Allow children housing exclusion	?	
69. Shift $400m of NASA to homeless	Y	
70. Cap Medicare patients' liability	Y	
71. Prohibit employee polygraph testing	Y	
72. Allow CIA to fund Contras	N	
73. Revise unfair trade practices	Y	
74. Focus SDI on accidental launch	Y	
75. Bar Air Force $ for MX missile	N	
76. Allow "real" increase in defense	?	
77. Troop reduction in Europe of 50%	N	
78. Ban nuclear tests above 1 kiloton	Y	

79. Ban anti-satellite missile tests	Y	
80. Observe certain limits of SALT II	Y	
81. Restore four Civil Rights laws	Y	
82. Prohibit aliens as strikebreakers	Y	
83. Allow military malpractice suits	Y	
84. Approval of $36m in Contra aid	N	
85. $18b deficit reduction compromise	Y	
86. Welfare reform of $5.7b for 5 years	Y	
87. Raise taxes $12b/cut spending $3b	N	
88. Board to assess occupational risk	Y	
89. Balanced budget by '93-via targets	N	
90. Bar licensing of two nuclear plants	Y	
91. Remove victims compensation cap	Y	
92. Catastrophic health insurance	Y	
93. Ban airline smoking-2 hours or less	Y	
94. $1b/two year aid for the homeless	Y	
95. Bar non-unions in union companies	Y	
96. Increase FSLIC rescue to $15b	Y	
97. Impose quotas to lower trade deficit	Y	
98. Reduce discretionary budget 21%	?	
99. Immigration reform/alien amnesty	Y	
100. South Africa sanctions-veto override	Y	
101. Tax overhaul to revise income tax	Y	
102. Use of military in drug war	Y	
103. Delete 12 MX/add conventional wpn	#	
104. Raise speed limit to 65 mph	N	
105. Require Pentagon to buy US goods	N	
106. AIDS insurance non-discrimination	N	
107. Prohibit Saudi arms sales	Y	
108. Ease Gun Control Act of 1968	N	
109. Bar interstate handgun transport	Y	
110. Make company emissions known	Y	
111. Allow toxic victims to sue in fed ct	Y	
112. Superfund waste cleanup of $10b	Y	
113. 90 days notice of plant closings	Y	
114. $20b in Medicare cuts/tax increases	#	
115. Spending cuts and tax increases	Y	
116. Set school lunch lmt-250% poverty	N	
117. $75m for youth work projects	Y	
118. Allow Angolan military assistance	N	
119. Suspend defense payments for abuse	N	
120. Drop SS COLAs/$12b tax increase	N	
121. Approve $1.5b for 21 MX missiles	N	
122. Emergency farm credit/revisions	Y	
123. Duty on Taiwan/Hong Kong/S Korea	?	
124. Limit steel imports to 17%	Y	
125. Cut $ to schools that bar prayer	N	
126. $50b-taxes; cut Medicare/spending	Y	
127. Limit Pershing II/cruise in Europe	Y	
128. Delete $7.1b for 34 B-1 bombers	Y	
129. Bar purchase of Sergeant York guns	Y	
130. El Salvador military/economic aid	N	
131. Bar mining of Nicaraguan waters	Y	
132. Physician fee freeze for Medicare	N	
133. $49b in "sin"/phone/insurance taxes	Y	
134. Allow sale of Conrail	N	
135. Equal Rights Amendment	Y	
136. Authorize Marines in Lebanon	N	
137. Eminent domain for coal companies	N	
138. Prohibit EPA clean air sanctions	N	
139. SS retirement age increase/reforms	N	
140. Auto domestic content requirement	Y	
141. Delete jobs program funding	N	
142. Highway-gas tax bill	N	

LaFALCE, JOHN J. (continued)
143. Cut $5b from defense for Medicare Y   144. Emergency housing aid of $1b   Y

Presidential Support Score: 1991 - 32%   1990 - 30%

NOWAK, HENRY J. -- New York 33rd District [Democrat]. County of Erie (pt.). Prior Terms: 1975-92. Born: February 21, 1935; Buffalo, NY. Education: Canisius College (B.B.A.); University of Buffalo (J.D.). Military Service: U.S. Army, 1957-58. Occupation: Attorney; confidential secretary to Supreme Court justice; county comptroller (1966-74).

1. Protection to Haitian refugees	Y	55. Raise minimum wage-veto override	Y
2. Raise tax on wealthy; lower others	Y	56. Bar transfer of FS-X technology	Y
3. Investigate Reagan hostage delay	Y	57. Cut defense and raise domestic $	Y
4. Campaign finance revisions	Y	58. Uniform poll closing in 48 states	Y
5. Unpaid leave to care for children	Y	59. Req foreign investment disclosure	Y
6. Restrict NEA use of funds	N	60. Textile import quotas-veto override	Y
7. Bar race-bias claim/habeas corpus	N	61. Bar abortion funding in Wash, DC	Y
8. Ban race as death sentence factor	N	62. Notify spouses of AIDS+ carriers	?
9. Exceptions to exclusionary rule	N	63. Seize conveyance-drug trafficking	N
10. Allow sale of assault weapons	N	64. South Africa sanctions	Y
11. Life in prison/abolish death penalty	N	65. 60 days' notice of plant closings	Y
12. Req conspiracy-price fixing cases	N	66. Close unneeded military bases	Y
13. Unemployment benefits extension	Y	67. Keep welfare reform within $2.8b	N
14. Tissue use of aborted fetuses	Y	68. Allow children housing exclusion	N
15. Bar replacement of union strikers	Y	69. Shift $400m of NASA to homeless	Y
16. Hold foreign aid at $15b for '92	Y	70. Cap Medicare patients' liability	Y
17. Restore space station funding	N	71. Prohibit employee polygraph testing	Y
18. Civil Rights Act of 1991	Y	72. Allow CIA to fund Contras	N
19. Unlimited damages-discrimination	Y	73. Revise unfair trade practices	Y
20. Eliminate funds for supercollider	Y	74. Focus SDI on accidental launch	Y
21. Terminate SDI except for research	N	75. Bar Air Force $ for MX missile	Y
22. Req 7-day handgun waiting period	Y	76. Allow "real" increase in defense	?
23. Provide $30b for failed S&Ls	N	77. Troop reduction in Europe of 50%	N
24. Allow use of force against Iraq	N	78. Ban nuclear tests above 1 kiloton	Y
25. Allow $15b in foreign aid for '91	?	79. Ban anti-satellite missile tests	Y
26. Revise & extend legal immigration	?	80. Observe certain limits of SALT II	Y
27. Suspend aid to Angolan rebels	Y	81. Restore four Civil Rights laws	Y
28. Democratic tax plan proposals	Y	82. Prohibit aliens as strikebreakers	Y
29. Cut defense 5% across the board	Y	83. Allow military malpractice suits	Y
30. Textile import quotas-veto override	Y	84. Approval of $36m in Contra aid	N
31. Abortion service for military abroad	N	85. $18b deficit reduction compromise	Y
32. Limits on high income farmers	Y	86. Welfare reform of $5.7b for 5 years	Y
33. Family medical leave-veto override	Y	87. Raise taxes $12b/cut spending $3b	Y
34. Req submission of balanced budget	Y	88. Board to assess occupational risk	Y
35. Balanced budget amendment	N	89. Balanced budget by '93-via targets	Y
36. Amendment to ban flag desecration	N	90. Bar licensing of two nuclear plants	Y
37. Reauthorize Amtrak-veto override	Y	91. Remove victims compensation cap	Y
38. Retraining aid for coal miners	Y	92. Catastrophic health insurance	Y
39. Suspend El Salvador military aid	Y	93. Ban airline smoking-2 hours or less	Y
40. Expand child care aid/tax credit	Y	94. $1b/two year aid for the homeless	Y
41. Raise House salary/omit honoraria	Y	95. Bar non-unions in union companies	Y
42. Toughen oil-spill liability	Y	96. Increase FSLIC rescue to $15b	Y
43. Restitution to Japanese interned	Y	97. Impose quotas to lower trade deficit	Y
44. Protect Chinese & C.A. nationals	Y	98. Reduce discretionary budget 21%	N
45. Abortion $ for rape/incest cases	N	99. Immigration reform/alien amnesty	Y
46. Allow religious schools to bar gays	Y	100. South Africa sanctions-veto override	Y
47. Bar broadcaster fairness doctrine	N	101. Tax overhaul to revise income tax	Y
48. Bar cap gains cut/reinstate IRA	Y	102. Use of military in drug war	Y
49. Bar unions equal voice in pension	N	103. Delete 12 MX/add conventional wpn	Y
50. Bar assembly of chemical weapons	Y	104. Raise speed limit to 65 mph	N
51. Ban plutonium/uranium production	Y	105. Require Pentagon to buy US goods	Y
52. Cap MX missile deployment at 50	Y	106. AIDS insurance non-discrimination	Y
53. Allow $3b for 2 stealth bombers	N	107. Prohibit Saudi arms sales	Y
54. Publish bio-warfare experiments	Y	108. Ease Gun Control Act of 1968	N

NOWAK, HENRY J. (continued)

109. Bar interstate handgun transport	Y	
110. Make company emissions known	Y	
111. Allow toxic victims to sue in fed ct	Y	
112. Superfund waste cleanup of $10b	Y	
113. 90 days notice of plant closings	Y	
114. $20b in Medicare cuts/tax increases	Y	
115. Spending cuts and tax increases	Y	
116. Set school lunch lmt-250% poverty	N	
117. $75m for youth work projects	Y	
118. Allow Angola military assistance	N	
119. Suspend defense payments for abuse	Y	
120. Drop SS COLAs/$12b tax increase	N	
121. Approve $1.5b for 21 MX missiles	N	
122. Emergency farm credit/revisions	Y	
123. Duty on Taiwan/Hong Kong/S Korea	Y	
124. Limit steel imports to 17%	Y	
125. Cut $ to schools that bar prayer	N	
126. $50b-taxes; cut Medicare/spending	Y	
127. Limit Pershing II/cruise in Europe	Y
128. Delete $7.1b for 34 B-1 bombers	Y
129. Bar purchase of Sergeant York guns	Y
130. El Salvador military/economic aid	N
131. Bar mining of Nicaraguan waters	Y
132. Physician fee freeze for Medicare	N
133. $49b in "sin"/phone/insurance taxes	Y
134. Allow sale of Conrail	N
135. Equal Rights Amendment	N
136. Authorize Marines in Lebanon	N
137. Eminent domain for coal companies	N
138. Prohibit EPA clean air sanctions	Y
139. SS retirement age increase/reforms	N
140. Auto domestic content requirement	Y
141. Delete jobs program funding	N
142. Highway-gas tax bill	N
143. Cut $5b from defense for Medicare	Y
144. Emergency housing aid of $1b	Y

Presidential Support Score: 1991 - 32%   1990 - 17%

HOUGHTON, AMORY, Jr. -- New York 34th District [Republican]. Counties of Allegany, Cattaraugus (pt.), Chautauqua, Chemung, Schuyler, Steuben, Tompkins (pt.) and Yates. Prior Terms: 1987-92. Born: August 7, 1926; Corning, NY. Education: Harvard University (B.A.) and Harvard Business School (M.A.). Military Service: U.S. Marine Corps, 1945-1946. Occupation: Chief Executive Officer and Executive Committee chairman, Corning Glass Works; founder, Corning Enterprises.

1. Protection to Haitian refugees	N	
2. Raise tax on wealthy; lower others	N	
3. Investigate Reagan hostage delay	N	
4. Campaign finance revisions	N	
5. Unpaid leave to care for children	N	
6. Restrict NEA use of funds	N	
7. Bar race-bias claim/habeas corpus	Y	
8. Ban race as death sentence factor	Y	
9. Exceptions to exclusionary rule	Y	
10. Allow sale of assault weapons	Y	
11. Life in prison/abolish death penalty	N	
12. Req conspiracy-price fixing cases	Y	
13. Unemployment benefits extension	Y	
14. Tissue use of aborted fetuses	Y	
15. Bar replacement of union strikers	N	
16. Hold foreign aid at $15b for '92	Y	
17. Restore space station funding	Y	
18. Civil Rights Act of 1991	Y	
19. Unlimited damages-discrimination	N	
20. Eliminate funds for supercollider	N	
21. Terminate SDI except for research	N	
22. Req 7-day handgun waiting period	N	
23. Provide $30b for failed S&Ls	Y	
24. Allow use of force against Iraq	Y	
25. Allow $15b in foreign aid for '91	Y	
26. Revise & extend legal immigration	Y	
27. Suspend aid to Angolan rebels	Y	
28. Democratic tax plan proposals	N	
29. Cut defense 5% across the board	N	
30. Textile import quotas-veto override	Y	
31. Abortion service for military abroad	Y	
32. Limits on high income farmers	N	
33. Family medical leave-veto override	N	
34. Req submission of balanced budget	N	
35. Balanced budget amendment	N	
36. Amendment to ban flag desecration	N
37. Reauthorize Amtrak-veto override	N
38. Retraining aid for coal miners	Y
39. Suspend El Salvador military aid	N
40. Expand child care aid/tax credit	N
41. Raise House salary/omit honoraria	N
42. Toughen oil-spill liability	N
43. Restitution to Japanese interned	N
44. Protect Chinese & C.A. nationals	N
45. Abortion $ for rape/incest cases	Y
46. Allow religious schools to bar gays	?
47. Bar broadcaster fairness doctrine	?
48. Bar cap gains cut/reinstate IRA	N
49. Bar unions equal voice in pension	Y
50. Bar assembly of chemical weapons	N
51. Ban plutonium/uranium production	N
52. Cap MX missile deployment at 50	N
53. Allow $3b for 2 stealth bombers	Y
54. Publish bio-warfare experiments	N
55. Raise minimum wage-veto override	N
56. Bar transfer of FS-X technology	?
57. Cut defense and raise domestic $	N
58. Uniform poll closing in 48 states	N
59. Req foreign investment disclosure	N
60. Textile import quotas-veto override	Y
61. Bar abortion funding in Wash, DC	N
62. Notify spouses of AIDS+ carriers	N
63. Seize conveyance-drug trafficking	Y
64. South Africa sanctions	N
65. 60 days' notice of plant closings	Y
66. Close unneeded military bases	Y
67. Keep welfare reform within $2.8b	Y
68. Allow children housing exclusion	N
69. Shift $400m of NASA to homeless	Y
70. Cap Medicare patients' liability	Y

HOUGHTON, AMORY, Jr. (continued)

71. Prohibit employee polygraph testing	Y
72. Allow CIA to fund Contras	Y
73. Revise unfair trade practices	Y
74. Focus SDI on accidental launch	N
75. Bar Air Force $ for MX missile	N
76. Allow "real" increase in defense	Y
77. Troop reduction in Europe of 50%	N
78. Ban nuclear tests above 1 kiloton	N
79. Ban anti-satellite missile tests	N
80. Observe certain limits of SALT II	N
81. Restore four Civil Rights laws	Y
82. Prohibit aliens as strikebreakers	Y
83. Allow military malpractice suits	Y
84. Approval of $36m in Contra aid	N

85. $18b deficit reduction compromise	Y
86. Welfare reform of $5.7b for 5 years	N
87. Raise taxes $12b/cut spending $3b	N
88. Board to assess occupational risk	N
89. Balanced budget by '93-via targets	Y
90. Bar licensing of two nuclear plants	N
91. Remove victims compensation cap	N
92. Catastrophic health insurance	Y
93. Ban airline smoking-2 hours or less	N
94. $1b/two year aid for the homeless	N
95. Bar non-unions in union companies	Y
96. Increase FSLIC rescue to $15b	Y
97. Impose quotas to lower trade deficit	N
98. Reduce discretionary budget 21%	Y

Presidential Support Score: 1991 - 71%   1990 - 57%

NORTH CAROLINA

JONES, WALTER B. -- North Carolina 1st District [Democrat]. Counties of Beaufort, Bertie, Camden, Carteret, Chowan, Craven, Currituck, Dare, Gates, Greene, Hartford, Hyde, Lenoir, Martin, Northhampton, Pamlico, Pasquotank, Perquimans, Pitt, Tyrrell and Washington. Prior Terms: 1966 (Special Election)-1992. Born: August 19, 1913; Fayetteville, NC. Education: North Carolina State University (B.S.). Occupation: Office supply businessman (1934-49); mayor of Farmville (1949-53); North Carolina representative (1955, 1957, 1959); North Carolina senator (1965).

1. Protection to Haitian refugees	Y
2. Raise tax on wealthy; lower others	Y
3. Investigate Reagan hostage delay	Y
4. Campaign finance revisions	Y
5. Unpaid leave to care for children	Y
6. Restrict NEA use of funds	N
7. Bar race-bias claim/habeas corpus	Y
8. Ban race as death sentence factor	Y
9. Exceptions to exclusionary rule	Y
10. Allow sale of assault weapons	Y
11. Life in prison/abolish death penalty	N
12. Req conspiracy-price fixing cases	N
13. Unemployment benefits extension	?
14. Tissue use of aborted fetuses	Y
15. Bar replacement of union strikers	Y
16. Hold foreign aid at $15b for '92	Y
17. Restore space station funding	Y
18. Civil Rights Act of 1991	Y
19. Unlimited damages-discrimination	N
20. Eliminate funds for supercollider	N
21. Terminate SDI except for research	N
22. Req 7-day handgun waiting period	Y
23. Provide $30b for failed S&Ls	Y
24. Allow use of force against Iraq	Y
25. Allow $15b in foreign aid for '91	N
26. Revise & extend legal immigration	Y
27. Suspend aid to Angolan rebels	N
28. Democratic tax plan proposals	Y
29. Cut defense 5% across the board	Y
30. Textile import quotas-veto override	Y
31. Abortion service for military abroad	Y

32. Limits on high income farmers	N
33. Family medical leave-veto override	N
34. Req submission of balanced budget	Y
35. Balanced budget amendment	Y
36. Amendment to ban flag desecration	Y
37. Reauthorize Amtrak-veto override	Y
38. Retraining aid for coal miners	Y
39. Suspend El Salvador military aid	Y
40. Expand child care aid/tax credit	#
41. Raise House salary/omit honoraria	Y
42. Toughen oil-spill liability	Y
43. Restitution to Japanese interned	N
44. Protect Chinese & C.A. nationals	Y
45. Abortion $ for rape/incest cases	?
46. Allow religious schools to bar gays	Y
47. Bar broadcaster fairness doctrine	N
48. Bar cap gains cut/reinstate IRA	Y
49. Bar unions equal voice in pension	Y
50. Bar assembly of chemical weapons	Y
51. Ban plutonium/uranium production	Y
52. Cap MX missile deployment at 50	Y
53. Allow $3b for 2 stealth bombers	N
54. Publish bio-warfare experiments	Y
55. Raise minimum wage-veto override	Y
56. Bar transfer of FS-X technology	Y
57. Cut defense and raise domestic $	N
58. Uniform poll closing in 48 states	Y
59. Req foreign investment disclosure	Y
60. Textile import quotas-veto override	Y
61. Bar abortion funding in Wash, DC	N
62. Notify spouses of AIDS+ carriers	N

JONES, WALTER B. (continued)

63. Seize conveyance-drug trafficking	N	
64. South Africa sanctions	Y	
65. 60 days' notice of plant closings	Y	
66. Close unneeded military bases	N	
67. Keep welfare reform within $2.8b	N	
68. Allow children housing exclusion	N	
69. Shift $400m of NASA to homeless	N	
70. Cap Medicare patients' liability	Y	
71. Prohibit employee polygraph testing	N	
72. Allow CIA to fund Contras	N	
73. Revise unfair trade practices	Y	
74. Focus SDI on accidental launch	Y	
75. Bar Air Force $ for MX missile	Y	
76. Allow "real" increase in defense	Y	
77. Troop reduction in Europe of 50%	?	
78. Ban nuclear tests above 1 kiloton	Y	
79. Ban anti-satellite missile tests	Y	
80. Observe certain limits of SALT II	Y	
81. Restore four Civil Rights laws	Y	
82. Prohibit aliens as strikebreakers	Y	
83. Allow military malpractice suits	Y	
84. Approval of $36m in Contra aid	N	
85. $18b deficit reduction compromise	#	
86. Welfare reform of $5.7b for 5 years	Y	
87. Raise taxes $12b/cut spending $3b	Y	
88. Board to assess occupational risk	N	
89. Balanced budget by '93-via targets	Y	
90. Bar licensing of two nuclear plants	N	
91. Remove victims compensation cap	N	
92. Catastrophic health insurance	Y	
93. Ban airline smoking-2 hours or less	N	
94. $1b/two year aid for the homeless	Y	
95. Bar non-unions in union companies	Y	
96. Increase FSLIC rescue to $15b	N	
97. Impose quotas to lower trade deficit	Y	
98. Reduce discretionary budget 21%	N	
99. Immigration reform/alien amnesty	N	
100. South Africa sanctions-veto override	?	
101. Tax overhaul to revise income tax	Y	
102. Use of military in drug war	N	
103. Delete 12 MX/add conventional wpn	Y	

104. Raise speed limit to 65 mph	N	
105. Require Pentagon to buy US goods	Y	
106. AIDS insurance non-discrimination	Y	
107. Prohibit Saudi arms sales	?	
108. Ease Gun Control Act of 1968	Y	
109. Bar interstate handgun transport	Y	
110. Make company emissions known	N	
111. Allow toxic victims to sue in fed ct	N	
112. Superfund waste cleanup of $10b	N	
113. 90 days notice of plant closings	N	
114. $20b in Medicare cuts/tax increases	Y	
115. Spending cuts and tax increases	Y	
116. Set school lunch lmt-250% poverty	N	
117. $75m for youth work projects	N	
118. Allow Angolan military assistance	N	
119. Suspend defense payments for abuse	?	
120. Drop SS COLAs/$12b tax increase	N	
121. Approve $1.5b for 21 MX missiles	N	
122. Emergency farm credit/revisions	Y	
123. Duty on Taiwan/Hong Kong/S Korea	?	
124. Limit steel imports to 17%	Y	
125. Cut $ to schools that bar prayer	N	
126. $50b-taxes; cut Medicare/spending	Y	
127. Limit Pershing II/cruise in Europe	N	
128. Delete $7.1b for 34 B-1 bombers	N	
129. Bar purchase of Sergeant York guns	N	
130. El Salvador military/economic aid	N	
131. Bar mining of Nicaraguan waters	?	
132. Physician fee freeze for Medicare	?	
133. $49b in "sin"/phone/insurance taxes	?	
134. Allow sale of Conrail	N	
135. Equal Rights Amendment	Y	
136. Authorize Marines in Lebanon	Y	
137. Eminent domain for coal companies	Y	
138. Prohibit EPA clean air sanctions	N	
139. SS retirement age increase/reforms	Y	
140. Auto domestic content requirement	Y	
141. Delete jobs program funding	N	
142. Highway-gas tax bill	Y	
143. Cut $5b from defense for Medicare	Y	
144. Emergency housing aid of $1b	Y	

Presidential Support Score: 1991 - 40%   1990 - 28%

VALENTINE, TIM -- North Carolina 2nd District [Democrat]. Counties of Caswell, Durham, Edgecombe, Granville, Halifax, Johnston (pt.), Nash, Person, Vance, Warren and Wilson. Prior Terms: 1983-92. Born: March 15, 1926; Nashville, TN. Education: The Citadel (A.B.); University of North Carolina, Chapel Hill (LL.B.). Military Service: U.S. Air Force, 1944-46. Occupation: Attorney; North Carolina representative (1955-60); legal advisor to Governor (1965); legislative counsel to Governor (1967).

1. Protection to Haitian refugees	N	
2. Raise tax on wealthy; lower others	Y	
3. Investigate Reagan hostage delay	N	
4. Campaign finance revisions	Y	
5. Unpaid leave to care for children	N	
6. Restrict NEA use of funds	Y	
7. Bar race-bias claim/habeas corpus	Y	
8. Ban race as death sentence factor	Y	
9. Exceptions to exclusionary rule	Y	
10. Allow sale of assault weapons	Y	
11. Life in prison/abolish death penalty	N	
12. Req conspiracy-price fixing cases	Y	

13. Unemployment benefits extension	N	
14. Tissue use of aborted fetuses	N	
15. Bar replacement of union strikers	N	
16. Hold foreign aid at $15b for '92	N	
17. Restore space station funding	Y	
18. Civil Rights Act of 1991	Y	
19. Unlimited damages-discrimination	N	
20. Eliminate funds for supercollider	Y	
21. Terminate SDI except for research	N	
22. Req 7-day handgun waiting period	Y	
23. Provide $30b for failed S&Ls	N	
24. Allow use of force against Iraq	Y	

VALENTINE, TIM (continued)

25. Allow $15b in foreign aid for '91	N	
26. Revise & extend legal immigration	N	
27. Suspend aid to Angolan rebels	N	
28. Democratic tax plan proposals	Y	
29. Cut defense 5% across the board	N	
30. Textile import quotas-veto override	Y	
31. Abortion service for military abroad	Y	
32. Limits on high income farmers	N	
33. Family medical leave-veto override	N	
34. Req submission of balanced budget	Y	
35. Balanced budget amendment	Y	
36. Amendment to ban flag desecration	N	
37. Reauthorize Amtrak-veto override	Y	
38. Retraining aid for coal miners	N	
39. Suspend El Salvador military aid	Y	
40. Expand child care aid/tax credit	Y	
41. Raise House salary/omit honoraria	Y	
42. Toughen oil-spill liability	Y	
43. Restitution to Japanese interned	Y	
44. Protect Chinese & C.A. nationals	N	
45. Abortion $ for rape/incest cases	Y	
46. Allow religious schools to bar gays	Y	
47. Bar broadcaster fairness doctrine	N	
48. Bar cap gains cut/reinstate IRA	Y	
49. Bar unions equal voice in pension	Y	
50. Bar assembly of chemical weapons	Y	
51. Ban plutonium/uranium production	Y	
52. Cap MX missile deployment at 50	Y	
53. Allow $3b for 2 stealth bombers	N	
54. Publish bio-warfare experiments	Y	
55. Raise minimum wage-veto override	N	
56. Bar transfer of FS-X technology	Y	
57. Cut defense and raise domestic $	N	
58. Uniform poll closing in 48 states	N	
59. Req foreign investment disclosure	Y	
60. Textile import quotas-veto override	Y	
61. Bar abortion funding in Wash, DC	N	
62. Notify spouses of AIDS+ carriers	N	
63. Seize conveyance-drug trafficking	N	
64. South Africa sanctions	Y	
65. 60 days' notice of plant closings	Y	
66. Close unneeded military bases	N	
67. Keep welfare reform within $2.8b	Y	
68. Allow children housing exclusion	N	
69. Shift $400m of NASA to homeless	Y	
70. Cap Medicare patients' liability	Y	
71. Prohibit employee polygraph testing	N	
72. Allow CIA to fund Contras	N	
73. Revise unfair trade practices	Y	
74. Focus SDI on accidental launch	Y	
75. Bar Air Force $ for MX missile	N	
76. Allow "real" increase in defense	Y	
77. Troop reduction in Europe of 50%	Y	
78. Ban nuclear tests above 1 kiloton	N	
79. Ban anti-satellite missile tests	N	
80. Observe certain limits of SALT II	N	
81. Restore four Civil Rights laws	Y	
82. Prohibit aliens as strikebreakers	N	

83. Allow military malpractice suits	Y	
84. Approval of $36m in Contra aid	N	
85. $18b deficit reduction compromise	Y	
86. Welfare reform of $5.7b for 5 years	Y	
87. Raise taxes $12b/cut spending $3b	Y	
88. Board to assess occupational risk	N	
89. Balanced budget by '93-via targets	Y	
90. Bar licensing of two nuclear plants	N	
91. Remove victims compensation cap	N	
92. Catastrophic health insurance	Y	
93. Ban airline smoking-2 hours or less	N	
94. $1b/two year aid for the homeless	Y	
95. Bar non-unions in union companies	N	
96. Increase FSLIC rescue to $15b	N	
97. Impose quotas to lower trade deficit	Y	
98. Reduce discretionary budget 21%	Y	
99. Immigration reform/alien amnesty	N	
100. South Africa sanctions-veto override	Y	
101. Tax overhaul to revise income tax	Y	
102. Use of military in drug war	N	
103. Delete 12 MX/add conventional wpn	N	
104. Raise speed limit to 65 mph	N	
105. Require Pentagon to buy US goods	Y	
106. AIDS insurance non-discrimination	Y	
107. Prohibit Saudi arms sales	Y	
108. Ease Gun Control Act of 1968	Y	
109. Bar interstate handgun transport	N	
110. Make company emissions known	N	
111. Allow toxic victims to sue in fed ct	N	
112. Superfund waste cleanup of $10b	Y	
113. 90 days notice of plant closings	N	
114. $20b in Medicare cuts/tax increases	Y	
115. Spending cuts and tax increases	Y	
116. Set school lunch lmt-250% poverty	N	
117. $75m for youth work projects	Y	
118. Allow Angolan military assistance	Y	
119. Suspend defense payments for abuse	N	
120. Drop SS COLAs/$12b tax increase	N	
121. Approve $1.5b for 21 MX missiles	Y	
122. Emergency farm credit/revisions	Y	
123. Duty on Taiwan/Hong Kong/S Korea	Y	
124. Limit steel imports to 17%	N	
125. Cut $ to schools that bar prayer	Y	
126. $50b-taxes; cut Medicare/spending	Y	
127. Limit Pershing II/cruise in Europe	N	
128. Delete $7.1b for 34 B-1 bombers	N	
129. Bar purchase of Sergeant York guns	N	
130. El Salvador military/economic aid	Y	
131. Bar mining of Nicaraguan waters	Y	
132. Physician fee freeze for Medicare	N	
133. $49b in "sin"/phone/insurance taxes	Y	
134. Allow sale of Conrail	N	
135. Equal Rights Amendment	N	
136. Authorize Marines in Lebanon	Y	
137. Eminent domain for coal companies	Y	
138. Prohibit EPA clean air sanctions	Y	
139. SS retirement age increase/reforms	Y	

Presidential Support Score: 1991 - 45% 1990 - 42%

LANCASTER, H. MARTIN, III -- North Carolina 3rd District [Democrat]. Counties of Bladen, Duplin, Harnett, Johnston (pt.), Jones, Lee, Moore (pt.), Onslow, Pender, Sampson and

LANCASTER, H. MARTIN, III (continued)
Wayne. Prior Terms: 1987-92. Born: March 24, 1943; Patetown Community, NC. Education: University of North Carolina (A.B., J.D.). Military Service: U.S. Navy, 1967-70; Naval Reserves, 1970-87. Occupation: Attorney; partner, Baddour, Lancaster, Parker, Hine & Keller; Senate Constitutional Rights Subcommittee research assistant (1966); state representative (1978-86).

1. Protection to Haitian refugees	Y	50. Bar assembly of chemical weapons	Y
2. Raise tax on wealthy; lower others	N	51. Ban plutonium/uranium production	Y
3. Investigate Reagan hostage delay	Y	52. Cap MX missile deployment at 50	Y
4. Campaign finance revisions	Y	53. Allow $3b for 2 stealth bombers	Y
5. Unpaid leave to care for children	N	54. Publish bio-warfare experiments	Y
6. Restrict NEA use of funds	Y	55. Raise minimum wage-veto override	N
7. Bar race-bias claim/habeas corpus	Y	56. Bar transfer of FS-X technology	Y
8. Ban race as death sentence factor	Y	57. Cut defense and raise domestic $	N
9. Exceptions to exclusionary rule	Y	58. Uniform poll closing in 48 states	N
10. Allow sale of assault weapons	Y	59. Req foreign investment disclosure	Y
11. Life in prison/abolish death penalty	N	60. Textile import quotas-veto override	N
12. Req conspiracy-price fixing cases	N	61. Bar abortion funding in Wash, DC	N
13. Unemployment benefits extension	Y	62. Notify spouses of AIDS+ carriers	N
14. Tissue use of aborted fetuses	Y	63. Seize conveyance-drug trafficking	N
15. Bar replacement of union strikers	N	64. South Africa sanctions	Y
16. Hold foreign aid at $15b for '92	Y	65. 60 days' notice of plant closings	N
17. Restore space station funding	N	66. Close unneeded military bases	N
18. Civil Rights Act of 1991	Y	67. Keep welfare reform within $2.8b	Y
19. Unlimited damages-discrimination	N	68. Allow children housing exclusion	N
20. Eliminate funds for supercollider	Y	69. Shift $400m of NASA to homeless	Y
21. Terminate SDI except for research	N	70. Cap Medicare patients' liability	Y
22. Req 7-day handgun waiting period	Y	71. Prohibit employee polygraph testing	Y
23. Provide $30b for failed S&Ls	N	72. Allow CIA to fund Contras	N
24. Allow use of force against Iraq	Y	73. Revise unfair trade practices	Y
25. Allow $15b in foreign aid for '91	Y	74. Focus SDI on accidental launch	Y
26. Revise & extend legal immigration	N	75. Bar Air Force $ for MX missile	Y
27. Suspend aid to Angolan rebels	N	76. Allow "real" increase in defense	Y
28. Democratic tax plan proposals	Y	77. Troop reduction in Europe of 50%	N
29. Cut defense 5% across the board	N	78. Ban nuclear tests above 1 kiloton	N
30. Textile import quotas-veto override	Y	79. Ban anti-satellite missile tests	N
31. Abortion service for military abroad	Y	80. Observe certain limits of SALT II	Y
32. Limits on high income farmers	N	81. Restore four Civil Rights laws	Y
33. Family medical leave-veto override	N	82. Prohibit aliens as strikebreakers	Y
34. Req submission of balanced budget	Y	83. Allow military malpractice suits	Y
35. Balanced budget amendment	Y	84. Approval of $36m in Contra aid	N
36. Amendment to ban flag desecration	Y	85. $18b deficit reduction compromise	Y
37. Reauthorize Amtrak-veto override	Y	86. Welfare reform of $5.7b for 5 years	Y
38. Retraining aid for coal miners	Y	87. Raise taxes $12b/cut spending $3b	N
39. Suspend El Salvador military aid	N	88. Board to assess occupational risk	N
40. Expand child care aid/tax credit	Y	89. Balanced budget by '93-via targets	Y
41. Raise House salary/omit honoraria	Y	90. Bar licensing of two nuclear plants	N
42. Toughen oil-spill liability	Y	91. Remove victims compensation cap	N
43. Restitution to Japanese interned	Y	92. Catastrophic health insurance	Y
44. Protect Chinese & C.A. nationals	Y	93. Ban airline smoking-2 hours or less	N
45. Abortion $ for rape/incest cases	Y	94. $1b/two year aid for the homeless	Y
46. Allow religious schools to bar gays	N	95. Bar non-unions in union companies	N
47. Bar broadcaster fairness doctrine	N	96. Increase FSLIC rescue to $15b	N
48. Bar cap gains cut/reinstate IRA	Y	97. Impose quotas to lower trade deficit	Y
49. Bar unions equal voice in pension	Y	98. Reduce discretionary budget 21%	Y

Presidential Support Score: 1991 - 40% 1990 - 38%

PRICE, DAVID E. -- North Carolina 4th District [Democrat]. Counties of Chatham, Franklin, Orange, Randolph and Wake. Prior Terms: 1987-92. Born: August 17, 1940; Johnson City, TN. Education: University of North Carolina, Chapel Hill (B.A.); Yale University (B. Div.). Occupation: University professor; senatorial aide; employee, Office of Management and Budget, Department of Housing and Urban Development; state Democratic

PRICE, DAVID E. (continued)
Party executive director (1979-80) and chairman and executive director (1983-1984); Hunt
Commission on Presidential Nomination staff director (1981-82).

1. Protection to Haitian refugees	Y	50. Bar assembly of chemical weapons	Y
2. Raise tax on wealthy; lower others	Y	51. Ban plutonium/uranium production	Y
3. Investigate Reagan hostage delay	Y	52. Cap MX missile deployment at 50	Y
4. Campaign finance revisions	Y	53. Allow $3b for 2 stealth bombers	N
5. Unpaid leave to care for children	Y	54. Publish bio-warfare experiments	Y
6. Restrict NEA use of funds	Y	55. Raise minimum wage-veto override	Y
7. Bar race-bias claim/habeas corpus	Y	56. Bar transfer of FS-X technology	Y
8. Ban race as death sentence factor	Y	57. Cut defense and raise domestic $	N
9. Exceptions to exclusionary rule	Y	58. Uniform poll closing in 48 states	N
10. Allow sale of assault weapons	N	59. Req foreign investment disclosure	Y
11. Life in prison/abolish death penalty	N	60. Textile import quotas-veto override	Y
12. Req conspiracy-price fixing cases	N	61. Bar abortion funding in Wash, DC	N
13. Unemployment benefits extension	Y	62. Notify spouses of AIDS+ carriers	N
14. Tissue use of aborted fetuses	Y	63. Seize conveyance-drug trafficking	N
15. Bar replacement of union strikers	Y	64. South Africa sanctions	Y
16. Hold foreign aid at $15b for '92	Y	65. 60 days' notice of plant closings	Y
17. Restore space station funding	N	66. Close unneeded military bases	Y
18. Civil Rights Act of 1991	Y	67. Keep welfare reform within $2.8b	Y
19. Unlimited damages-discrimination	N	68. Allow children housing exclusion	N
20. Eliminate funds for supercollider	N	69. Shift $400m of NASA to homeless	N
21. Terminate SDI except for research	N	70. Cap Medicare patients' liability	Y
22. Req 7-day handgun waiting period	Y	71. Prohibit employee polygraph testing	Y
23. Provide $30b for failed S&Ls	Y	72. Allow CIA to fund Contras	N
24. Allow use of force against Iraq	N	73. Revise unfair trade practices	Y
25. Allow $15b in foreign aid for '91	Y	74. Focus SDI on accidental launch	Y
26. Revise & extend legal immigration	Y	75. Bar Air Force $ for MX missile	Y
27. Suspend aid to Angolan rebels	Y	76. Allow "real" increase in defense	N
28. Democratic tax plan proposals	Y	77. Troop reduction in Europe of 50%	Y
29. Cut defense 5% across the board	N	78. Ban nuclear tests above 1 kiloton	Y
30. Textile import quotas-veto override	Y	79. Ban anti-satellite missile tests	Y
31. Abortion service for military abroad	Y	80. Observe certain limits of SALT II	Y
32. Limits on high income farmers	Y	81. Restore four Civil Rights laws	Y
33. Family medical leave-veto override	Y	82. Prohibit aliens as strikebreakers	Y
34. Req submission of balanced budget	Y	83. Allow military malpractice suits	Y
35. Balanced budget amendment	Y	84. Approval of $36m in Contra aid	N
36. Amendment to ban flag desecration	N	85. $18b deficit reduction compromise	Y
37. Reauthorize Amtrak-veto override	Y	86. Welfare reform of $5.7b for 5 years	Y
38. Retraining aid for coal miners	Y	87. Raise taxes $12b/cut spending $3b	Y
39. Suspend El Salvador military aid	Y	88. Board to assess occupational risk	Y
40. Expand child care aid/tax credit	Y	89. Balanced budget by '93-via targets	Y
41. Raise House salary/omit honoraria	Y	90. Bar licensing of two nuclear plants	N
42. Toughen oil-spill liability	Y	91. Remove victims compensation cap	N
43. Restitution to Japanese interned	Y	92. Catastrophic health insurance	Y
44. Protect Chinese & C.A. nationals	Y	93. Ban airline smoking-2 hours or less	N
45. Abortion $ for rape/incest cases	Y	94. $1b/two year aid for the homeless	Y
46. Allow religious schools to bar gays	N	95. Bar non-unions in union companies	N
47. Bar broadcaster fairness doctrine	N	96. Increase FSLIC rescue to $15b	N
48. Bar cap gains cut/reinstate IRA	Y	97. Impose quotas to lower trade deficit	Y
49. Bar unions equal voice in pension	Y	98. Reduce discretionary budget 21%	Y

Presidential Support Score: 1991 - 40% 1990 - 24%

NEAL, STEPHEN L. -- North Carolina 5th District [Democrat]. Counties of Alexander,
Alleghany, Ashe, Forsyth, Rockingham, Stokes, Surry and Wilkes. Prior Terms: 1975-92.
Born: November 7, 1934; Winston-Salem, NC. Education: University of Hawaii.
Occupation: Resort businessman; mortgage banker; newspaper publisher.

1. Protection to Haitian refugees	Y	4. Campaign finance revisions	Y
2. Raise tax on wealthy; lower others	Y	5. Unpaid leave to care for children	N
3. Investigate Reagan hostage delay	Y	6. Restrict NEA use of funds	?

NEAL, STEPHEN L. (continued)

7. Bar race-bias claim/habeas corpus	Y
8. Ban race as death sentence factor	Y
9. Exceptions to exclusionary rule	N
10. Allow sale of assault weapons	Y
11. Life in prison/abolish death penalty	?
12. Req conspiracy-price fixing cases	Y
13. Unemployment benefits extension	Y
14. Tissue use of aborted fetuses	Y
15. Bar replacement of union strikers	N
16. Hold foreign aid at $15b for '92	N
17. Restore space station funding	N
18. Civil Rights Act of 1991	Y
19. Unlimited damages-discrimination	N
20. Eliminate funds for supercollider	Y
21. Terminate SDI except for research	?
22. Req 7-day handgun waiting period	Y
23. Provide $30b for failed S&Ls	N
24. Allow use of force against Iraq	N
25. Allow $15b in foreign aid for '91	N
26. Revise & extend legal immigration	N
27. Suspend aid to Angolan rebels	?
28. Democratic tax plan proposals	Y
29. Cut defense 5% across the board	N
30. Textile import quotas-veto override	Y
31. Abortion service for military abroad	Y
32. Limits on high income farmers	N
33. Family medical leave-veto override	N
34. Req submission of balanced budget	Y
35. Balanced budget amendment	Y
36. Amendment to ban flag desecration	N
37. Reauthorize Amtrak-veto override	N
38. Retraining aid for coal miners	N
39. Suspend El Salvador military aid	Y
40. Expand child care aid/tax credit	Y
41. Raise House salary/omit honoraria	N
42. Toughen oil-spill liability	N
43. Restitution to Japanese interned	N
44. Protect Chinese & C.A. nationals	Y
45. Abortion $ for rape/incest cases	Y
46. Allow religious schools to bar gays	N
47. Bar broadcaster fairness doctrine	N
48. Bar cap gains cut/reinstate IRA	Y
49. Bar unions equal voice in pension	Y
50. Bar assembly of chemical weapons	Y
51. Ban plutonium/uranium production	Y
52. Cap MX missile deployment at 50	Y
53. Allow $3b for 2 stealth bombers	N
54. Publish bio-warfare experiments	Y
55. Raise minimum wage-veto override	Y
56. Bar transfer of FS-X technology	Y
57. Cut defense and raise domestic $	N
58. Uniform poll closing in 48 states	Y
59. Req foreign investment disclosure	?
60. Textile import quotas-veto override	Y
61. Bar abortion funding in Wash, DC	N
62. Notify spouses of AIDS+ carriers	N
63. Seize conveyance-drug trafficking	N
64. South Africa sanctions	Y
65. 60 days' notice of plant closings	Y
66. Close unneeded military bases	Y
67. Keep welfare reform within $2.8b	Y
68. Allow children housing exclusion	N
69. Shift $400m of NASA to homeless	N
70. Cap Medicare patients' liability	Y

71. Prohibit employee polygraph testing	Y
72. Allow CIA to fund Contras	N
73. Revise unfair trade practices	Y
74. Focus SDI on accidental launch	Y
75. Bar Air Force $ for MX missile	?
76. Allow "real" increase in defense	?
77. Troop reduction in Europe of 50%	N
78. Ban nuclear tests above 1 kiloton	Y
79. Ban anti-satellite missile tests	Y
80. Observe certain limits of SALT II	Y
81. Restore four Civil Rights laws	Y
82. Prohibit aliens as strikebreakers	Y
83. Allow military malpractice suits	Y
84. Approval of $36m in Contra aid	N
85. $18b deficit reduction compromise	Y
86. Welfare reform of $5.7b for 5 years	Y
87. Raise taxes $12b/cut spending $3b	Y
88. Board to assess occupational risk	N
89. Balanced budget by '93-via targets	N
90. Bar licensing of two nuclear plants	N
91. Remove victims compensation cap	N
92. Catastrophic health insurance	Y
93. Ban airline smoking-2 hours or less	N
94. $1b/two year aid for the homeless	Y
95. Bar non-unions in union companies	N
96. Increase FSLIC rescue to $15b	N
97. Impose quotas to lower trade deficit	Y
98. Reduce discretionary budget 21%	Y
99. Immigration reform/alien amnesty	Y
100. South Africa sanctions-veto override	Y
101. Tax overhaul to revise income tax	Y
102. Use of military in drug war	N
103. Delete 12 MX/add conventional wpn	N
104. Raise speed limit to 65 mph	Y
105. Require Pentagon to buy US goods	Y
106. AIDS insurance non-discrimination	Y
107. Prohibit Saudi arms sales	Y
108. Ease Gun Control Act of 1968	Y
109. Bar interstate handgun transport	N
110. Make company emissions known	Y
111. Allow toxic victims to sue in fed ct	N
112. Superfund waste cleanup of $10b	Y
113. 90 days notice of plant closings	N
114. $20b in Medicare cuts/tax increases	Y
115. Spending cuts and tax increases	Y
116. Set school lunch lmt-250% poverty	N
117. $75m for youth work projects	Y
118. Allow Angolan military assistance	N
119. Suspend defense payments for abuse	N
120. Drop SS COLAs/$12b tax increase	N
121. Approve $1.5b for 21 MX missiles	Y
122. Emergency farm credit/revisions	Y
123. Duty on Taiwan/Hong Kong/S Korea	N
124. Limit steel imports to 17%	N
125. Cut $ to schools that bar prayer	?
126. $50b-taxes; cut Medicare/spending	Y
127. Limit Pershing II/cruise in Europe	N
128. Delete $7.1b for 34 B-1 bombers	N
129. Bar purchase of Sergeant York guns	N
130. El Salvador military/economic aid	N
131. Bar mining of Nicaraguan waters	Y
132. Physician fee freeze for Medicare	Y
133. $49b in "sin"/phone/insurance taxes	Y
134. Allow sale of Conrail	N

NEAL, STEPHEN L. (continued)

135. Equal Rights Amendment	Y	140. Auto domestic content requirement	N
136. Authorize Marines in Lebanon	N	141. Delete jobs program funding	N
137. Eminent domain for coal companies	Y	142. Highway-gas tax bill	N
138. Prohibit EPA clean air sanctions	Y	143. Cut $5b from defense for Medicare	N
139. SS retirement age increase/reforms	?	144. Emergency housing aid of $1b	?

Presidential Support Score: 1991 - 38% 1990 - 36%

COBLE, HOWARD -- North Carolina 6th District [Republican]. Counties of Alamance, Davidson and Guilford. Prior Terms: 1985-92. Born: March 18, 1931; Greensboro, NC. Education: Appalachian State University; Guilford College (A.B.); University of North Carolina, Chapel Hill (J.D.). Military Service: U.S. Coast Guard, 1952-56, 1977-78; Reserves, 1960-82. Occupation: Attorney; auto insurer field claim representative and superintendent (1961-67); state representative (1969, 1979-83); assistant U.S. attorney (1969-73); commissioner (secretary), state revenue department (1973-77).

1. Protection to Haitian refugees	N	48. Bar cap gains cut/reinstate IRA	N
2. Raise tax on wealthy; lower others	N	49. Bar unions equal voice in pension	Y
3. Investigate Reagan hostage delay	N	50. Bar assembly of chemical weapons	Y
4. Campaign finance revisions	N	51. Ban plutonium/uranium production	N
5. Unpaid leave to care for children	N	52. Cap MX missile deployment at 50	Y
6. Restrict NEA use of funds	Y	53. Allow $3b for 2 stealth bombers	Y
7. Bar race-bias claim/habeas corpus	Y	54. Publish bio-warfare experiments	N
8. Ban race as death sentence factor	Y	55. Raise minimum wage-veto override	N
9. Exceptions to exclusionary rule	Y	56. Bar transfer of FS-X technology	N
10. Allow sale of assault weapons	Y	57. Cut defense and raise domestic $	N
11. Life in prison/abolish death penalty	N	58. Uniform poll closing in 48 states	N
12. Req conspiracy-price fixing cases	Y	59. Req foreign investment disclosure	N
13. Unemployment benefits extension	N	60. Textile import quotas-veto override	Y
14. Tissue use of aborted fetuses	N	61. Bar abortion funding in Wash, DC	Y
15. Bar replacement of union strikers	N	62. Notify spouses of AIDS+ carriers	Y
16. Hold foreign aid at $15b for '92	Y	63. Seize conveyance-drug trafficking	Y
17. Restore space station funding	N	64. South Africa sanctions	N
18. Civil Rights Act of 1991	N	65. 60 days' notice of plant closings	N
19. Unlimited damages-discrimination	N	66. Close unneeded military bases	Y
20. Eliminate funds for supercollider	Y	67. Keep welfare reform within $2.8b	Y
21. Terminate SDI except for research	N	68. Allow children housing exclusion	Y
22. Req 7-day handgun waiting period	N	69. Shift $400m of NASA to homeless	Y
23. Provide $30b for failed S&Ls	N	70. Cap Medicare patients' liability	Y
24. Allow use of force against Iraq	Y	71. Prohibit employee polygraph testing	N
25. Allow $15b in foreign aid for '91	N	72. Allow CIA to fund Contras	Y
26. Revise & extend legal immigration	Y	73. Revise unfair trade practices	N
27. Suspend aid to Angolan rebels	N	74. Focus SDI on accidental launch	N
28. Democratic tax plan proposals	N	75. Bar Air Force $ for MX missile	N
29. Cut defense 5% across the board	N	76. Allow "real" increase in defense	N
30. Textile import quotas-veto override	Y	77. Troop reduction in Europe of 50%	N
31. Abortion service for military abroad	N	78. Ban nuclear tests above 1 kiloton	N
32. Limits on high income farmers	Y	79. Ban anti-satellite missile tests	N
33. Family medical leave-veto override	N	80. Observe certain limits of SALT II	N
34. Req submission of balanced budget	N	81. Restore four Civil Rights laws	N
35. Balanced budget amendment	Y	82. Prohibit aliens as strikebreakers	Y
36. Amendment to ban flag desecration	Y	83. Allow military malpractice suits	Y
37. Reauthorize Amtrak-veto override	N	84. Approval of $36m in Contra aid	Y
38. Retraining aid for coal miners	N	85. $18b deficit reduction compromise	N
39. Suspend El Salvador military aid	N	86. Welfare reform of $5.7b for 5 years	N
40. Expand child care aid/tax credit	N	87. Raise taxes $12b/cut spending $3b	N
41. Raise House salary/omit honoraria	N	88. Board to assess occupational risk	N
42. Toughen oil-spill liability	N	89. Balanced budget by '93-via targets	Y
43. Restitution to Japanese interned	N	90. Bar licensing of two nuclear plants	N
44. Protect Chinese & C.A. nationals	N	91. Remove victims compensation cap	N
45. Abortion $ for rape/incest cases	N	92. Catastrophic health insurance	N
46. Allow religious schools to bar gays	Y	93. Ban airline smoking-2 hours or less	N
47. Bar broadcaster fairness doctrine	Y	94. $1b/two year aid for the homeless	N

COBLE, HOWARD (continued)

95. Bar non-unions in union companies	N	
96. Increase FSLIC rescue to $15b	N	
97. Impose quotas to lower trade deficit	N	
98. Reduce discretionary budget 21%	Y	
99. Immigration reform/alien amnesty	N	
100. South Africa sanctions-veto override	N	
101. Tax overhaul to revise income tax	Y	
102. Use of military in drug war	Y	
103. Delete 12 MX/add conventional wpn	N	
104. Raise speed limit to 65 mph	Y	
105. Require Pentagon to buy US goods	Y	
106. AIDS insurance non-discrimination	N	
107. Prohibit Saudi arms sales	Y	
108. Ease Gun Control Act of 1968	Y	
109. Bar interstate handgun transport	N	
110. Make company emissions known	N	
111. Allow toxic victims to sue in fed ct	N	
112. Superfund waste cleanup of $10b	N	
113. 90 days notice of plant closings	N	
114. $20b in Medicare cuts/tax increases	N	
115. Spending cuts and tax increases	N	
116. Set school lunch lmt-250% poverty	Y	
117. $75m for youth work projects	N	
118. Allow Angolan military assistance	Y	
119. Suspend defense payments for abuse	Y	
120. Drop SS COLAs/$12b tax increase	N	
121. Approve $1.5b for 21 MX missiles	Y	
122. Emergency farm credit/revisions	N	

Presidential Support Score: 1991 - 70%   1990 - 68%

ROSE, CHARLES -- North Carolina 7th District [Democrat]. Counties of Brunswick, Columbus, Cumberland, New Hanover and Robeson. Prior Terms: 1973-92. Born: August 10, 1939; Fayetteville, NC. Education: Davidson College (A.B.); University of North Carolina (LL.B.). Occupation: Chief district prosecutor, Cumberland and Hoke Counties (1967-70); board member, Lumbee Bank.

1. Protection to Haitian refugees	Y	
2. Raise tax on wealthy; lower others	Y	
3. Investigate Reagan hostage delay	Y	
4. Campaign finance revisions	Y	
5. Unpaid leave to care for children	Y	
6. Restrict NEA use of funds	Y	
7. Bar race-bias claim/habeas corpus	N	
8. Ban race as death sentence factor	N	
9. Exceptions to exclusionary rule	N	
10. Allow sale of assault weapons	Y	
11. Life in prison/abolish death penalty	N	
12. Req conspiracy-price fixing cases	N	
13. Unemployment benefits extension	Y	
14. Tissue use of aborted fetuses	Y	
15. Bar replacement of union strikers	Y	
16. Hold foreign aid at $15b for '92	Y	
17. Restore space station funding	N	
18. Civil Rights Act of 1991	Y	
19. Unlimited damages-discrimination	Y	
20. Eliminate funds for supercollider	N	
21. Terminate SDI except for research	Y	
22. Req 7-day handgun waiting period	Y	
23. Provide $30b for failed S&Ls	N	
24. Allow use of force against Iraq	N	
25. Allow $15b in foreign aid for '91	?	
26. Revise & extend legal immigration	?	
27. Suspend aid to Angolan rebels	Y	
28. Democratic tax plan proposals	Y	
29. Cut defense 5% across the board	N	
30. Textile import quotas-veto override	Y	
31. Abortion service for military abroad	Y	
32. Limits on high income farmers	N	
33. Family medical leave-veto override	Y	
34. Req submission of balanced budget	Y	
35. Balanced budget amendment	Y	
36. Amendment to ban flag desecration	N	
37. Reauthorize Amtrak-veto override	Y	
38. Retraining aid for coal miners	Y	
39. Suspend El Salvador military aid	Y	
40. Expand child care aid/tax credit	Y	
41. Raise House salary/omit honoraria	N	
42. Toughen oil-spill liability	Y	
43. Restitution to Japanese interned	Y	
44. Protect Chinese & C.A. nationals	Y	
45. Abortion $ for rape/incest cases	Y	
46. Allow religious schools to bar gays	Y	
47. Bar broadcaster fairness doctrine	N	
48. Bar cap gains cut/reinstate IRA	Y	
49. Bar unions equal voice in pension	Y	
50. Bar assembly of chemical weapons	N	
51. Ban plutonium/uranium production	Y	
52. Cap MX missile deployment at 50	Y	
53. Allow $3b for 2 stealth bombers	N	
54. Publish bio-warfare experiments	Y	
55. Raise minimum wage-veto override	Y	
56. Bar transfer of FS-X technology	N	
57. Cut defense and raise domestic $	N	
58. Uniform poll closing in 48 states	Y	
59. Req foreign investment disclosure	Y	
60. Textile import quotas-veto override	Y	
61. Bar abortion funding in Wash, DC	N	
62. Notify spouses of AIDS+ carriers	N	
63. Seize conveyance-drug trafficking	N	
64. South Africa sanctions	Y	
65. 60 days' notice of plant closings	Y	
66. Close unneeded military bases	N	
67. Keep welfare reform within $2.8b	N	
68. Allow children housing exclusion	N	
69. Shift $400m of NASA to homeless	N	
70. Cap Medicare patients' liability	Y	
71. Prohibit employee polygraph testing	?	
72. Allow CIA to fund Contras	N	
73. Revise unfair trade practices	Y	
74. Focus SDI on accidental launch	Y	
75. Bar Air Force $ for MX missile	N	
76. Allow "real" increase in defense	?	
77. Troop reduction in Europe of 50%	N	
78. Ban nuclear tests above 1 kiloton	?	
79. Ban anti-satellite missile tests	?	
80. Observe certain limits of SALT II	Y	

ROSE, CHARLES (continued)

81.	Restore four Civil Rights laws	Y	113.	90 days notice of plant closings	?
82.	Prohibit aliens as strikebreakers	Y	114.	$20b in Medicare cuts/tax increases	Y
83.	Allow military malpractice suits	Y	115.	Spending cuts and tax increases	Y
84.	Approval of $36m in Contra aid	N	116.	Set school lunch lmt-250% poverty	N
85.	$18b deficit reduction compromise	?	117.	$75m for youth work projects	N
86.	Welfare reform of $5.7b for 5 years	Y	118.	Allow Angolan military assistance	?
87.	Raise taxes $12b/cut spending $3b	?	119.	Suspend defense payments for abuse	N
88.	Board to assess occupational risk	N	120.	Drop SS COLAs/$12b tax increase	N
89.	Balanced budget by '93-via targets	Y	121.	Approve $1.5b for 21 MX missiles	N
90.	Bar licensing of two nuclear plants	N	122.	Emergency farm credit/revisions	Y
91.	Remove victims compensation cap	N	123.	Duty on Taiwan/Hong Kong/S Korea	Y
92.	Catastrophic health insurance	Y	124.	Limit steel imports to 17%	Y
93.	Ban airline smoking-2 hours or less	N	125.	Cut $ to schools that bar prayer	Y
94.	$1b/two year aid for the homeless	Y	126.	$50b-taxes; cut Medicare/spending	Y
95.	Bar non-unions in union companies	N	127.	Limit Pershing II/cruise in Europe	?
96.	Increase FSLIC rescue to $15b	N	128.	Delete $7.1b for 34 B-1 bombers	N
97.	Impose quotas to lower trade deficit	Y	129.	Bar purchase of Sergeant York guns	Y
98.	Reduce discretionary budget 21%	Y	130.	El Salvador military/economic aid	N
99.	Immigration reform/alien amnesty	Y	131.	Bar mining of Nicaraguan waters	Y
100.	South Africa sanctions-veto override	?	132.	Physician fee freeze for Medicare	N
101.	Tax overhaul to revise income tax	Y	133.	$49b in "sin"/phone/insurance taxes	Y
102.	Use of military in drug war	N	134.	Delete $7.1b for Conrail	N
103.	Delete 12 MX/add conventional wpn	N	135.	Equal Rights Amendment	Y
104.	Raise speed limit to 65 mph	Y	136.	Authorize Marines in Lebanon	Y
105.	Require Pentagon to buy US goods	Y	137.	Eminent domain for coal companies	Y
106.	AIDS insurance non-discrimination	Y	138.	Prohibit EPA clean air sanctions	Y
107.	Prohibit Saudi arms sales	N	139.	SS retirement age increase/reforms	N
108.	Ease Gun Control Act of 1968	Y	140.	Auto domestic content requirement	Y
109.	Bar interstate handgun transport	Y	141.	Delete jobs program funding	N
110.	Make company emissions known	N	142.	Highway-gas tax bill	Y
111.	Allow toxic victims to sue in fed ct	N	143.	Cut $5b from defense for Medicare	N
112.	Superfund waste cleanup of $10b	N	144.	Emergency housing aid of $1b	Y

Presidential Support Score: 1991 - 29%   1990 - 19%

HEFNER, W. G. (Bill) -- North Carolina 8th District [Democrat]. Counties of Anson, Cabarrus, Davie, Hoke, Montgomery, Moore (pt.), Richmond, Rowan, Scotland, Stanly, Union and Yadkin (pt.). Prior Terms: 1975-92. Born: April 11, 1930; Elora, TN. Occupation: Entertainer and gospel music broadcaster; president, WRKB radio station.

1.	Protection to Haitian refugees	Y	24.	Allow use of force against Iraq	N
2.	Raise tax on wealthy; lower others	Y	25.	Allow $15b in foreign aid for '91	N
3.	Investigate Reagan hostage delay	Y	26.	Revise & extend legal immigration	Y
4.	Campaign finance revisions	Y	27.	Suspend aid to Angolan rebels	Y
5.	Unpaid leave to care for children	Y	28.	Democratic tax plan proposals	Y
6.	Restrict NEA use of funds	Y	29.	Cut defense 5% across the board	N
7.	Bar race-bias claim/habeas corpus	Y	30.	Textile import quotas-veto override	Y
8.	Ban race as death sentence factor	Y	31.	Abortion service for military abroad	Y
9.	Exceptions to exclusionary rule	Y	32.	Limits on high income farmers	N
10.	Allow sale of assault weapons	Y	33.	Family medical leave-veto override	N
11.	Life in prison/abolish death penalty	N	34.	Req submission of balanced budget	Y
12.	Req conspiracy-price fixing cases	N	35.	Balanced budget amendment	Y
13.	Unemployment benefits extension	Y	36.	Amendment to ban flag desecration	Y
14.	Tissue use of aborted fetuses	?	37.	Reauthorize Amtrak-veto override	Y
15.	Bar replacement of union strikers	Y	38.	Retraining aid for coal miners	Y
16.	Hold foreign aid at $15b for '92	N	39.	Suspend El Salvador military aid	Y
17.	Restore space station funding	N	40.	Expand child care aid/tax credit	Y
18.	Civil Rights Act of 1991	Y	41.	Raise House salary/omit honoraria	Y
19.	Unlimited damages-discrimination	N	42.	Toughen oil-spill liability	Y
20.	Eliminate funds for supercollider	N	43.	Restitution to Japanese interned	Y
21.	Terminate SDI except for research	N	44.	Protect Chinese & C.A. nationals	Y
22.	Req 7-day handgun waiting period	Y	45.	Abortion $ for rape/incest cases	Y
23.	Provide $30b for failed S&Ls	N	46.	Allow religious schools to bar gays	Y

HEFNER, W. G. (continued)

47.	Bar broadcaster fairness doctrine	N	96.	Increase FSLIC rescue to $15b	N
48.	Bar cap gains cut/reinstate IRA	Y	97.	Impose quotas to lower trade deficit	Y
49.	Bar unions equal voice in pension	Y	98.	Reduce discretionary budget 21%	Y
50.	Bar assembly of chemical weapons	Y	99.	Immigration reform/alien amnesty	?
51.	Ban plutonium/uranium production	Y	100.	South Africa sanctions-veto override	Y
52.	Cap MX missile deployment at 50	Y	101.	Tax overhaul to revise income tax	Y
53.	Allow $3b for 2 stealth bombers	N	102.	Use of military in drug war	N
54.	Publish bio-warfare experiments	Y	103.	Delete 12 MX/add conventional wpn	N
55.	Raise minimum wage-veto override	Y	104.	Raise speed limit to 65 mph	N
56.	Bar transfer of FS-X technology	Y	105.	Require Pentagon to buy US goods	Y
57.	Cut defense and raise domestic $	N	106.	AIDS insurance non-discrimination	Y
58.	Uniform poll closing in 48 states	Y	107.	Prohibit Saudi arms sales	Y
59.	Req foreign investment disclosure	Y	108.	Ease Gun Control Act of 1968	Y
60.	Textile import quotas-veto override	Y	109.	Bar interstate handgun transport	N
61.	Bar abortion funding in Wash, DC	Y	110.	Make company emissions known	N
62.	Notify spouses of AIDS+ carriers	N	111.	Allow toxic victims to sue in fed ct	N
63.	Seize conveyance-drug trafficking	N	112.	Superfund waste cleanup of $10b	N
64.	South Africa sanctions	Y	113.	90 days notice of plant closings	N
65.	60 days' notice of plant closings	Y	114.	$20b in Medicare cuts/tax increases	Y
66.	Close unneeded military bases	N	115.	Spending cuts and tax increases	Y
67.	Keep welfare reform within $2.8b	Y	116.	Set school lunch lmt-250% poverty	N
68.	Allow children housing exclusion	N	117.	$75m for youth work projects	?
69.	Shift $400m of NASA to homeless	N	118.	Allow Angolan military assistance	?
70.	Cap Medicare patients' liability	Y	119.	Suspend defense payments for abuse	N
71.	Prohibit employee polygraph testing	?	120.	Drop SS COLAs/$12b tax increase	N
72.	Allow CIA to fund Contras	N	121.	Approve $1.5b for 21 MX missiles	Y
73.	Revise unfair trade practices	Y	122.	Emergency farm credit/revisions	Y
74.	Focus SDI on accidental launch	Y	123.	Duty on Taiwan/Hong Kong/S Korea	N
75.	Bar Air Force $ for MX missile	N	124.	Limit steel imports to 17%	Y
76.	Allow "real" increase in defense	?	125.	Cut $ to schools that bar prayer	Y
77.	Troop reduction in Europe of 50%	Y	126.	$50b-taxes; cut Medicare/spending	Y
78.	Ban nuclear tests above 1 kiloton	Y	127.	Limit Pershing II/cruise in Europe	N
79.	Ban anti-satellite missile tests	Y	128.	Delete $7.1b for 34 B-1 bombers	N
80.	Observe certain limits of SALT II	Y	129.	Bar purchase of Sergeant York guns	N
81.	Restore four Civil Rights laws	Y	130.	El Salvador military/economic aid	N
82.	Prohibit aliens as strikebreakers	Y	131.	Bar mining of Nicaraguan waters	Y
83.	Allow military malpractice suits	Y	132.	Physician fee freeze for Medicare	N
84.	Approval of $36m in Contra aid	N	133.	$49b in "sin"/phone/insurance taxes	Y
85.	$18b deficit reduction compromise	Y	134.	Allow sale of Conrail	N
86.	Welfare reform of $5.7b for 5 years	Y	135.	Equal Rights Amendment	Y
87.	Raise taxes $12b/cut spending $3b	Y	136.	Authorize Marines in Lebanon	Y
88.	Board to assess occupational risk	N	137.	Eminent domain for coal companies	N
89.	Balanced budget by '93-via targets	Y	138.	Prohibit EPA clean air sanctions	Y
90.	Bar licensing of two nuclear plants	N	139.	SS retirement age increase/reforms	Y
91.	Remove victims compensation cap	N	140.	Auto domestic content requirement	N
92.	Catastrophic health insurance	Y	141.	Delete jobs program funding	N
93.	Ban airline smoking-2 hours or less	N	142.	Highway-gas tax bill	N
94.	$1b/two year aid for the homeless	Y	143.	Cut $5b from defense for Medicare	N
95.	Bar non-unions in union companies	N	144.	Emergency housing aid of $1b	Y

Presidential Support Score: 1991 - 34%   1990 - 33%

McMILLAN, ALEX -- North Carolina 9th District [Republican]. Counties of Iredell, Lincoln, Mecklenburg and Yadkin (pt.). Prior Terms: 1985-92. Born: May 9, 1932; Charlotte, NC. Education: University of North Carolina, Chapel Hill (B.A.); University of Virginia (M.B.A.). Military Service: U.S. Army Intelligence Corps, 1954-56. Occupation: Mecklenburg County commissioner (1972-74); officer, Ruddick Corp. (1976-77); president, Harris-Teeter Super Markets (1977-83); university trustee.

1.	Protection to Haitian refugees	N	5.	Unpaid leave to care for children	N
2.	Raise tax on wealthy; lower others	N	6.	Restrict NEA use of funds	Y
3.	Investigate Reagan hostage delay	N	7.	Bar race-bias claim/habeas corpus	Y
4.	Campaign finance revisions	N	8.	Ban race as death sentence factor	Y

McMILLAN, ALEX (continued)

9. Exceptions to exclusionary rule	Y	
10. Allow sale of assault weapons	Y	
11. Life in prison/abolish death penalty	N	
12. Req conspiracy-price fixing cases	Y	
13. Unemployment benefits extension	N	
14. Tissue use of aborted fetuses	N	
15. Bar replacement of union strikers	N	
16. Hold foreign aid at $15b for '92	Y	
17. Restore space station funding	N	
18. Civil Rights Act of 1991	N	
19. Unlimited damages-discrimination	N	
20. Eliminate funds for supercollider	N	
21. Terminate SDI except for research	N	
22. Req 7-day handgun waiting period	Y	
23. Provide $30b for failed S&Ls	Y	
24. Allow use of force against Iraq	Y	
25. Allow $15b in foreign aid for '91	Y	
26. Revise & extend legal immigration	Y	
27. Suspend aid to Angolan rebels	N	
28. Democratic tax plan proposals	N	
29. Cut defense 5% across the board	N	
30. Textile import quotas-veto override	Y	
31. Abortion service for military abroad	N	
32. Limits on high income farmers	Y	
33. Family medical leave-veto override	N	
34. Req submission of balanced budget	N	
35. Balanced budget amendment	Y	
36. Amendment to ban flag desecration	Y	
37. Reauthorize Amtrak-veto override	Y	
38. Retraining aid for coal miners	N	
39. Suspend El Salvador military aid	N	
40. Expand child care aid/tax credit	N	
41. Raise House salary/omit honoraria	Y	
42. Toughen oil-spill liability	N	
43. Restitution to Japanese interned	N	
44. Protect Chinese & C.A. nationals	N	
45. Abortion $ for rape/incest cases	N	
46. Allow religious schools to bar gays	Y	
47. Bar broadcaster fairness doctrine	N	
48. Bar cap gains cut/reinstate IRA	N	
49. Bar unions equal voice in pension	Y	
50. Bar assembly of chemical weapons	N	
51. Ban plutonium/uranium production	N	
52. Cap MX missile deployment at 50	N	
53. Allow $3b for 2 stealth bombers	Y	
54. Publish bio-warfare experiments	Y	
55. Raise minimum wage-veto override	N	
56. Bar transfer of FS-X technology	N	
57. Cut defense and raise domestic $	N	
58. Uniform poll closing in 48 states	N	
59. Req foreign investment disclosure	N	
60. Textile import quotas-veto override	Y	
61. Bar abortion funding in Wash, DC	Y	
62. Notify spouses of AIDS+ carriers	N	
63. Seize conveyance-drug trafficking	Y	
64. South Africa sanctions	N	
65. 60 days' notice of plant closings	N	

66. Close unneeded military bases	Y	
67. Keep welfare reform within $2.8b	Y	
68. Allow children housing exclusion	Y	
69. Shift $400m of NASA to homeless	N	
70. Cap Medicare patients' liability	N	
71. Prohibit employee polygraph testing	N	
72. Allow CIA to fund Contras	Y	
73. Revise unfair trade practices	N	
74. Focus SDI on accidental launch	N	
75. Bar Air Force $ for MX missile	N	
76. Allow "real" increase in defense	N	
77. Troop reduction in Europe of 50%	N	
78. Ban nuclear tests above 1 kiloton	N	
79. Ban anti-satellite missile tests	N	
80. Observe certain limits of SALT II	N	
81. Restore four Civil Rights laws	N	
82. Prohibit aliens as strikebreakers	Y	
83. Allow military malpractice suits	Y	
84. Approval of $36m in Contra aid	Y	
85. $18b deficit reduction compromise	N	
86. Welfare reform of $5.7b for 5 years	N	
87. Raise taxes $12b/cut spending $3b	N	
88. Board to assess occupational risk	N	
89. Balanced budget by '93-via targets	Y	
90. Bar licensing of two nuclear plants	N	
91. Remove victims compensation cap	N	
92. Catastrophic health insurance	N	
93. Ban airline smoking-2 hours or less	N	
94. $1b/two year aid for the homeless	Y	
95. Bar non-unions in union companies	N	
96. Increase FSLIC rescue to $15b	N	
97. Impose quotas to lower trade deficit	N	
98. Reduce discretionary budget 21%	Y	
99. Immigration reform/alien amnesty	Y	
100. South Africa sanctions-veto override	N	
101. Tax overhaul to revise income tax	Y	
102. Use of military in drug war	Y	
103. Delete 12 MX/add conventional wpn	N	
104. Raise speed limit to 65 mph	Y	
105. Require Pentagon to buy US goods	Y	
106. AIDS insurance non-discrimination	?	
107. Prohibit Saudi arms sales	Y	
108. Ease Gun Control Act of 1968	Y	
109. Bar interstate handgun transport	N	
110. Make company emissions known	N	
111. Allow toxic victims to sue in fed ct	N	
112. Superfund waste cleanup of $10b	N	
113. 90 days notice of plant closings	N	
114. $20b in Medicare cuts/tax increases	N	
115. Spending cuts and tax increases	N	
116. Set school lunch lmt-250% poverty	Y	
117. $75m for youth work projects	N	
118. Allow Angolan military assistance	Y	
119. Suspend defense payments for abuse	N	
120. Drop SS COLAs/$12b tax increase	N	
121. Approve $1.5b for 21 MX missiles	Y	
122. Emergency farm credit/revisions	N	

Presidential Support Score: 1991 - 78%   1990 - 66%

BALLENGER, CASS -- North Carolina 10th District [Republican]. Counties of Avery (pt.), Burke, Caldwell, Catawba, Cleveland, Gaston and Watauga. Prior Terms: 1987-92. Born: December 6, 1926; Hickory, NC. Education: University of North Carolina, Chapel Hill;

BALLENGER, CASS (continued)

Amherst College (B.A.). Military Service: U.S. Navy Air Corps, 1944-45. Occupation: President, Hickory Paper Box Company (1960-75); founder and president, Plastic Packaging, Inc.; Catawba County commissioner (1966-74); state representative (1974-76) and senator (1976-86).

1. Protection to Haitian refugees	?	50. Bar assembly of chemical weapons	N
2. Raise tax on wealthy; lower others	N	51. Ban plutonium/uranium production	N
3. Investigate Reagan hostage delay	N	52. Cap MX missile deployment at 50	N
4. Campaign finance revisions	N	53. Allow $3b for 2 stealth bombers	Y
5. Unpaid leave to care for children	N	54. Publish bio-warfare experiments	N
6. Restrict NEA use of funds	Y	55. Raise minimum wage-veto override	N
7. Bar race-bias claim/habeas corpus	Y	56. Bar transfer of FS-X technology	N
8. Ban race as death sentence factor	Y	57. Cut defense and raise domestic $	N
9. Exceptions to exclusionary rule	Y	58. Uniform poll closing in 48 states	N
10. Allow sale of assault weapons	Y	59. Req foreign investment disclosure	N
11. Life in prison/abolish death penalty	N	60. Textile import quotas-veto override	Y
12. Req conspiracy-price fixing cases	Y	61. Bar abortion funding in Wash, DC	Y
13. Unemployment benefits extension	N	62. Notify spouses of AIDS+ carriers	Y
14. Tissue use of aborted fetuses	N	63. Seize conveyance-drug trafficking	Y
15. Bar replacement of union strikers	N	64. South Africa sanctions	N
16. Hold foreign aid at $15b for '92	+	65. 60 days' notice of plant closings	N
17. Restore space station funding	Y	66. Close unneeded military bases	Y
18. Civil Rights Act of 1991	N	67. Keep welfare reform within $2.8b	Y
19. Unlimited damages-discrimination	N	68. Allow children housing exclusion	Y
20. Eliminate funds for supercollider	N	69. Shift $400m of NASA to homeless	N
21. Terminate SDI except for research	N	70. Cap Medicare patients' liability	N
22. Req 7-day handgun waiting period	N	71. Prohibit employee polygraph testing	N
23. Provide $30b for failed S&Ls	Y	72. Allow CIA to fund Contras	Y
24. Allow use of force against Iraq	Y	73. Revise unfair trade practices	N
25. Allow $15b in foreign aid for '91	Y	74. Focus SDI on accidental launch	N
26. Revise & extend legal immigration	Y	75. Bar Air Force $ for MX missile	N
27. Suspend aid to Angolan rebels	N	76. Allow "real" increase in defense	N
28. Democratic tax plan proposals	N	77. Troop reduction in Europe of 50%	N
29. Cut defense 5% across the board	N	78. Ban nuclear tests above 1 kiloton	N
30. Textile import quotas-veto override	Y	79. Ban anti-satellite missile tests	N
31. Abortion service for military abroad	N	80. Observe certain limits of SALT II	N
32. Limits on high income farmers	Y	81. Restore four Civil Rights laws	N
33. Family medical leave-veto override	N	82. Prohibit aliens as strikebreakers	N
34. Req submission of balanced budget	Y	83. Allow military malpractice suits	?
35. Balanced budget amendment	Y	84. Approval of $36m in Contra aid	Y
36. Amendment to ban flag desecration	Y	85. $18b deficit reduction compromise	N
37. Reauthorize Amtrak-veto override	N	86. Welfare reform of $5.7b for 5 years	N
38. Retraining aid for coal miners	N	87. Raise taxes $12b/cut spending $3b	N
39. Suspend El Salvador military aid	N	88. Board to assess occupational risk	N
40. Expand child care aid/tax credit	N	89. Balanced budget by '93-via targets	N
41. Raise House salary/omit honoraria	Y	90. Bar licensing of two nuclear plants	N
42. Toughen oil-spill liability	N	91. Remove victims compensation cap	N
43. Restitution to Japanese interned	N	92. Catastrophic health insurance	--
44. Protect Chinese & C.A. nationals	N	93. Ban airline smoking-2 hours or less	N
45. Abortion $ for rape/incest cases	Y	94. $1b/two year aid for the homeless	N
46. Allow religious schools to bar gays	Y	95. Bar non-unions in union companies	N
47. Bar broadcaster fairness doctrine	Y	96. Increase FSLIC rescue to $15b	Y
48. Bar cap gains cut/reinstate IRA	N	97. Impose quotas to lower trade deficit	Y
49. Bar unions equal voice in pension	Y	98. Reduce discretionary budget 21%	Y

Presidential Support Score: 1991 - 79%   1990 - 73%

TAYLOR, CHARLES H. -- North Carolina 11th District [Republican]. Counties of Avery (pt.), Buncombe, Cherokee, Clay, Graham, Haywood, Henderson, Jackson, McDowell, Macon, Madison, Mitchell, Polk, Rutherford, Swain, Transylvania and Yancey. Prior Term: 1991-92. Born: September 17, 1953; New Orleans, LA. Education: Wake Forest University (B.A., J.D.). Occupation: Tree farmer; state representative (1967-73) and senator (1973-75).

TAYLOR, CHARLES H. (continued)

1. Protection to Haitian refugees	X		13. Unemployment benefits extension	N
2. Raise tax on wealthy; lower others	N		14. Tissue use of aborted fetuses	N
3. Investigate Reagan hostage delay	N		15. Bar replacement of union strikers	N
4. Campaign finance revisions	N		16. Hold foreign aid at $15b for '92	Y
5. Unpaid leave to care for children	N		17. Restore space station funding	Y
6. Restrict NEA use of funds	Y		18. Civil Rights Act of 1991	N
7. Bar race-bias claim/habeas corpus	Y		19. Unlimited damages-discrimination	N
8. Ban race as death sentence factor	Y		20. Eliminate funds for supercollider	N
9. Exceptions to exclusionary rule	N		21. Terminate SDI except for research	N
10. Allow sale of assault weapons	Y		22. Req 7-day handgun waiting period	N
11. Life in prison/abolish death penalty	N		23. Provide $30b for failed S&Ls	Y
12. Req conspiracy-price fixing cases	Y		24. Allow use of force against Iraq	Y

Presidential Support Score: 1991 - 84%

NORTH DAKOTA

DORGAN, BYRON L. -- Representative at Large [Democrat]. Prior Terms: 1981-92. Born: May 14, 1942; Dickinson, ND. Education: University of North Dakota (B.S.); University of Denver (M.B.A.). Occupation: Employee, executive development program, Martin-Marietta Corp. (1966-67); deputy tax commissioner (1966-69); tax commissioner (1969-76); chairman, multi-state tax commission (1972-74); president, Midwest Association of Tax Administrators (1970).

1. Protection to Haitian refugees	Y	35. Balanced budget amendment	Y
2. Raise tax on wealthy; lower others	Y	36. Amendment to ban flag desecration	N
3. Investigate Reagan hostage delay	Y	37. Reauthorize Amtrak-veto override	Y
4. Campaign finance revisions	Y	38. Retraining aid for coal miners	Y
5. Unpaid leave to care for children	Y	39. Suspend El Salvador military aid	Y
6. Restrict NEA use of funds	N	40. Expand child care aid/tax credit	Y
7. Bar race-bias claim/habeas corpus	N	41. Raise House salary/omit honoraria	N
8. Ban race as death sentence factor	N	42. Toughen oil-spill liability	Y
9. Exceptions to exclusionary rule	N	43. Restitution to Japanese interned	N
10. Allow sale of assault weapons	Y	44. Protect Chinese & C.A. nationals	Y
11. Life in prison/abolish death penalty	Y	45. Abortion $ for rape/incest cases	Y
12. Req conspiracy-price fixing cases	N	46. Allow religious schools to bar gays	Y
13. Unemployment benefits extension	Y	47. Bar broadcaster fairness doctrine	N
14. Tissue use of aborted fetuses	Y	48. Bar cap gains cut/reinstate IRA	Y
15. Bar replacement of union strikers	Y	49. Bar unions equal voice in pension	Y
16. Hold foreign aid at $15b for '92	Y	50. Bar assembly of chemical weapons	Y
17. Restore space station funding	N	51. Ban plutonium/uranium production	Y
18. Civil Rights Act of 1991	Y	52. Cap MX missile deployment at 50	Y
19. Unlimited damages-discrimination	N	53. Allow $3b for 2 stealth bombers	N
20. Eliminate funds for supercollider	Y	54. Publish bio-warfare experiments	Y
21. Terminate SDI except for research	Y	55. Raise minimum wage-veto override	Y
22. Req 7-day handgun waiting period	N	56. Bar transfer of FS-X technology	Y
23. Provide $30b for failed S&Ls	N	57. Cut defense and raise domestic $	N
24. Allow use of force against Iraq	N	58. Uniform poll closing in 48 states	Y
25. Allow $15b in foreign aid for '91	N	59. Req foreign investment disclosure	Y
26. Revise & extend legal immigration	Y	60. Textile import quotas-veto override	N
27. Suspend aid to Angolan rebels	Y	61. Bar abortion funding in Wash, DC	Y
28. Democratic tax plan proposals	Y	62. Notify spouses of AIDS+ carriers	N
29. Cut defense 5% across the board	Y	63. Seize conveyance-drug trafficking	N
30. Textile import quotas-veto override	N	64. South Africa sanctions	#
31. Abortion service for military abroad	N	65. 60 days' notice of plant closings	Y
32. Limits on high income farmers	N	66. Close unneeded military bases	Y
33. Family medical leave-veto override	Y	67. Keep welfare reform within $2.8b	N
34. Req submission of balanced budget	Y	68. Allow children housing exclusion	N

DORGAN, BYRON L. (continued)

69.	Shift $400m of NASA to homeless	Y
70.	Cap Medicare patients' liability	Y
71.	Prohibit employee polygraph testing	Y
72.	Allow CIA to fund Contras	N
73.	Revise unfair trade practices	Y
74.	Focus SDI on accidental launch	Y
75.	Bar Air Force $ for MX missile	N
76.	Allow "real" increase in defense	N
77.	Troop reduction in Europe of 50%	Y
78.	Ban nuclear tests above 1 kiloton	Y
79.	Ban anti-satellite missile tests	Y
80.	Observe certain limits of SALT II	Y
81.	Restore four Civil Rights laws	Y
82.	Prohibit aliens as strikebreakers	Y
83.	Allow military malpractice suits	Y
84.	Approval of $36m in Contra aid	N
85.	$18b deficit reduction compromise	Y
86.	Welfare reform of $5.7b for 5 years	Y
87.	Raise taxes $12b/cut spending $3b	Y
88.	Board to assess occupational risk	Y
89.	Balanced budget by '93-via targets	N
90.	Bar licensing of two nuclear plants	Y
91.	Remove victims compensation cap	Y
92.	Catastrophic health insurance	Y
93.	Ban airline smoking-2 hours or less	Y
94.	$1b/two year aid for the homeless	Y
95.	Bar non-unions in union companies	Y
96.	Increase FSLIC rescue to $15b	N
97.	Impose quotas to lower trade deficit	Y
98.	Reduce discretionary budget 21%	?
99.	Immigration reform/alien amnesty	Y
100.	South Africa sanctions-veto override	Y
101.	Tax overhaul to revise income tax	Y
102.	Use of military in drug war	N
103.	Delete 12 MX/add conventional wpn	Y
104.	Raise speed limit to 65 mph	Y
105.	Require Pentagon to buy US goods	Y
106.	AIDS insurance non-discrimination	Y
107.	Prohibit Saudi arms sales	Y
108.	Ease Gun Control Act of 1968	Y
109.	Bar interstate handgun transport	N
110.	Make company emissions known	Y
111.	Allow toxic victims to sue in fed ct	N
112.	Superfund waste cleanup of $10b	Y
113.	90 days notice of plant closings	Y
114.	$20b in Medicare cuts/tax increases	Y
115.	Spending cuts and tax increases	N
116.	Set school lunch lmt-250% poverty	N
117.	$75m for youth work projects	Y
118.	Allow Angolan military assistance	N
119.	Suspend defense payments for abuse	Y
120.	Drop SS COLAs/$12b tax increase	N
121.	Approve $1.5b for 21 MX missiles	N
122.	Emergency farm credit/revisions	Y
123.	Duty on Taiwan/Hong Kong/S Korea	Y
124.	Limit steel imports to 17%	N
125.	Cut $ to schools that bar prayer	N
126.	$50b-taxes; cut Medicare/spending	Y
127.	Limit Pershing II/cruise in Europe	Y
128.	Delete $7.1b for 34 B-1 bombers	N
129.	Bar purchase of Sergeant York guns	Y
130.	El Salvador military/economic aid	N
131.	Bar mining of Nicaraguan waters	Y
132.	Physician fee freeze for Medicare	N
133.	$49b in "sin"/phone/insurance taxes	Y
134.	Allow sale of Conrail	N
135.	Equal Rights Amendment	Y
136.	Authorize Marines in Lebanon	N
137.	Eminent domain for coal companies	N
138.	Prohibit EPA clean air sanctions	Y
139.	SS retirement age increase/reforms	N
140.	Auto domestic content requirement	Y
141.	Delete jobs program funding	N
142.	Highway-gas tax bill	Y
143.	Cut $5b from defense for Medicare	Y
144.	Emergency housing aid of $1b	Y

Presidential Support Score: 1991 - 30%   1990 - 17%

OHIO

LUKEN, CHARLES -- Ohio 1st District [Democrat]. County of Hamilton (pt.). Prior Term: 1991-92. Born: July 16, 1951; Cincinnati, OH. Education: Notre Dame University (B.A.); University of Cincinnati College of Law (LL.B.). Occupation: Lawyer; Cincinnati city councilman (1981-84) and mayor (1984-90).

1.	Protection to Haitian refugees	Y
2.	Raise tax on wealthy; lower others	Y
3.	Investigate Reagan hostage delay	?
4.	Campaign finance revisions	Y
5.	Unpaid leave to care for children	N
6.	Restrict NEA use of funds	Y
7.	Bar race-bias claim/habeas corpus	Y
8.	Ban race as death sentence factor	Y
9.	Exceptions to exclusionary rule	Y
10.	Allow sale of assault weapons	N
11.	Life in prison/abolish death penalty	N
12.	Req conspiracy-price fixing cases	N
13.	Unemployment benefits extension	Y
14.	Tissue use of aborted fetuses	N
15.	Bar replacement of union strikers	Y
16.	Hold foreign aid at $15b for '92	+
17.	Restore space station funding	N
18.	Civil Rights Act of 1991	Y
19.	Unlimited damages-discrimination	N
20.	Eliminate funds for supercollider	N

LUKEN, CHARLES (continued)

21. Terminate SDI except for research	N	23. Provide $30b for failed S&Ls	N
22. Req 7-day handgun waiting period	Y	24. Allow use of force against Iraq	Y

Presidential Support Score: 1991 - 50%

GRADISON, WILLIS D., Jr. -- Ohio 2nd District [Republican]. Counties of Brown, Clermont (pt.) and Hamilton (pt.). Prior Terms: 1975-92. Born: December 28, 1928; Cincinnati, OH. Education: Yale University (B.A.); Harvard (M.B.A., D.C.S). Occupation: Investment broker; assistant to under secretary of the Treasury (1953-55); assistant to Secretary of Health, Education and Welfare (1955-57); Cincinnati city councilman (1961-74); member, National Advisory Council on Economic Opportunity (1971-74); member, Tax Policy Advisory Committee, Council on Environmental Quality (1970-72); Cincinnati mayor (1971); board chairman, Federal Home Loan Bank of Cincinnati (1970-74).

1. Protection to Haitian refugees	N	50. Bar assembly of chemical weapons	N
2. Raise tax on wealthy; lower others	N	51. Ban plutonium/uranium production	Y
3. Investigate Reagan hostage delay	N	52. Cap MX missile deployment at 50	Y
4. Campaign finance revisions	N	53. Allow $3b for 2 stealth bombers	Y
5. Unpaid leave to care for children	N	54. Publish bio-warfare experiments	Y
6. Restrict NEA use of funds	Y	55. Raise minimum wage-veto override	N
7. Bar race-bias claim/habeas corpus	Y	56. Bar transfer of FS-X technology	N
8. Ban race as death sentence factor	Y	57. Cut defense and raise domestic $	N
9. Exceptions to exclusionary rule	Y	58. Uniform poll closing in 48 states	N
10. Allow sale of assault weapons	N	59. Req foreign investment disclosure	N
11. Life in prison/abolish death penalty	N	60. Textile import quotas-veto override	N
12. Req conspiracy-price fixing cases	Y	61. Bar abortion funding in Wash, DC	N
13. Unemployment benefits extension	N	62. Notify spouses of AIDS+ carriers	Y
14. Tissue use of aborted fetuses	N	63. Seize conveyance-drug trafficking	Y
15. Bar replacement of union strikers	N	64. South Africa sanctions	N
16. Hold foreign aid at $15b for '92	Y	65. 60 days' notice of plant closings	N
17. Restore space station funding	Y	66. Close unneeded military bases	?
18. Civil Rights Act of 1991	N	67. Keep welfare reform within $2.8b	Y
19. Unlimited damages-discrimination	N	68. Allow children housing exclusion	N
20. Eliminate funds for supercollider	Y	69. Shift $400m of NASA to homeless	Y
21. Terminate SDI except for research	N	70. Cap Medicare patients' liability	Y
22. Req 7-day handgun waiting period	Y	71. Prohibit employee polygraph testing	N
23. Provide $30b for failed S&Ls	Y	72. Allow CIA to fund Contras	Y
24. Allow use of force against Iraq	Y	73. Revise unfair trade practices	N
25. Allow $15b in foreign aid for '91	?	74. Focus SDI on accidental launch	N
26. Revise & extend legal immigration	Y	75. Bar Air Force $ for MX missile	N
27. Suspend aid to Angolan rebels	N	76. Allow "real" increase in defense	N
28. Democratic tax plan proposals	N	77. Troop reduction in Europe of 50%	N
29. Cut defense 5% across the board	N	78. Ban nuclear tests above 1 kiloton	?
30. Textile import quotas-veto override	N	79. Ban anti-satellite missile tests	?
31. Abortion service for military abroad	N	80. Observe certain limits of SALT II	N
32. Limits on high income farmers	Y	81. Restore four Civil Rights laws	Y
33. Family medical leave-veto override	N	82. Prohibit aliens as strikebreakers	N
34. Req submission of balanced budget	N	83. Allow military malpractice suits	Y
35. Balanced budget amendment	Y	84. Approval of $36m in Contra aid	Y
36. Amendment to ban flag desecration	Y	85. $18b deficit reduction compromise	N
37. Reauthorize Amtrak-veto override	N	86. Welfare reform of $5.7b for 5 years	N
38. Retraining aid for coal miners	N	87. Raise taxes $12b/cut spending $3b	N
39. Suspend El Salvador military aid	N	88. Board to assess occupational risk	N
40. Expand child care aid/tax credit	N	89. Balanced budget by '93-via targets	Y
41. Raise House salary/omit honoraria	Y	90. Bar licensing of two nuclear plants	N
42. Toughen oil-spill liability	?	91. Remove victims compensation cap	N
43. Restitution to Japanese interned	Y	92. Catastrophic health insurance	Y
44. Protect Chinese & C.A. nationals	N	93. Ban airline smoking-2 hours or less	Y
45. Abortion $ for rape/incest cases	N	94. $1b/two year aid for the homeless	Y
46. Allow religious schools to bar gays	N	95. Bar non-unions in union companies	N
47. Bar broadcaster fairness doctrine	Y	96. Increase FSLIC rescue to $15b	Y
48. Bar cap gains cut/reinstate IRA	N	97. Impose quotas to lower trade deficit	N
49. Bar unions equal voice in pension	Y	98. Reduce discretionary budget 21%	Y

GRADISON, WILLIS D., Jr. (continued)

99. Immigration reform/alien amnesty	N	122. Emergency farm credit/revisions	N
100. South Africa sanctions-veto override	Y	123. Duty on Taiwan/Hong Kong/S Korea	N
101. Tax overhaul to revise income tax	Y	124. Limit steel imports to 17%	N
102. Use of military in drug war	Y	125. Cut $ to schools that bar prayer	N
103. Delete 12 MX/add conventional wpn	Y	126. $50b-taxes; cut Medicare/spending	Y
104. Raise speed limit to 65 mph	Y	127. Limit Pershing II/cruise in Europe	N
105. Require Pentagon to buy US goods	N	128. Delete $7.1b for 34 B-1 bombers	N
106. AIDS insurance non-discrimination	Y	129. Bar purchase of Sergeant York guns	N
107. Prohibit Saudi arms sales	Y	130. El Salvador military/economic aid	Y
108. Ease Gun Control Act of 1968	N	131. Bar mining of Nicaraguan waters	Y
109. Bar interstate handgun transport	Y	132. Physician fee freeze for Medicare	Y
110. Make company emissions known	N	133. $49b in "sin"/phone/insurance taxes	Y
111. Allow toxic victims to sue in fed ct	N	134. Allow sale of Conrail	Y
112. Superfund waste cleanup of $10b	N	135. Equal Rights Amendment	Y
113. 90 days notice of plant closings	N	136. Authorize Marines in Lebanon	N
114. $20b in Medicare cuts/tax increases	N	137. Eminent domain for coal companies	Y
115. Spending cuts and tax increases	N	138. Prohibit EPA clean air sanctions	?
116. Set school lunch lmt-250% poverty	Y	139. SS retirement age increase/reforms	Y
117. $75m for youth work projects	N	140. Auto domestic content requirement	N
118. Allow Angolan military assistance	Y	141. Delete jobs program funding	Y
119. Suspend defense payments for abuse	N	142. Highway-gas tax bill	Y
120. Drop SS COLAs/$12b tax increase	?	143. Cut $5b from defense for Medicare	N
121. Approve $1.5b for 21 MX missiles	N	144. Emergency housing aid of $1b	N

Presidential Support Score: 1991 - 77% 1990 - 76%

HALL, TONY P. -- Ohio 3rd District [Democrat]. County of Montgomery (pt.). Prior Terms: 1979-92. Born: January 16, 1942; Dayton, OH. Education: Denison University (A.B.). Occupation: Peace Corps teacher; small businessman; real estate investor; Ohio representative (1969-73); Ohio senator (1973-79).

1. Protection to Haitian refugees	Y	33. Family medical leave-veto override	Y
2. Raise tax on wealthy; lower others	Y	34. Req submission of balanced budget	Y
3. Investigate Reagan hostage delay	Y	35. Balanced budget amendment	N
4. Campaign finance revisions	Y	36. Amendment to ban flag desecration	N
5. Unpaid leave to care for children	Y	37. Reauthorize Amtrak-veto override	Y
6. Restrict NEA use of funds	Y	38. Retraining aid for coal miners	Y
7. Bar race-bias claim/habeas corpus	N	39. Suspend El Salvador military aid	Y
8. Ban race as death sentence factor	N	40. Expand child care aid/tax credit	Y
9. Exceptions to exclusionary rule	N	41. Raise House salary/omit honoraria	Y
10. Allow sale of assault weapons	N	42. Toughen oil-spill liability	Y
11. Life in prison/abolish death penalty	N	43. Restitution to Japanese interned	Y
12. Req conspiracy-price fixing cases	N	44. Protect Chinese & C.A. nationals	Y
13. Unemployment benefits extension	Y	45. Abortion $ for rape/incest cases	N
14. Tissue use of aborted fetuses	N	46. Allow religious schools to bar gays	?
15. Bar replacement of union strikers	Y	47. Bar broadcaster fairness doctrine	?
16. Hold foreign aid at $15b for '92	Y	48. Bar cap gains cut/reinstate IRA	Y
17. Restore space station funding	Y	49. Bar unions equal voice in pension	Y
18. Civil Rights Act of 1991	Y	50. Bar assembly of chemical weapons	Y
19. Unlimited damages-discrimination	N	51. Ban plutonium/uranium production	Y
20. Eliminate funds for supercollider	Y	52. Cap MX missile deployment at 50	Y
21. Terminate SDI except for research	Y	53. Allow $3b for 2 stealth bombers	N
22. Req 7-day handgun waiting period	Y	54. Publish bio-warfare experiments	Y
23. Provide $30b for failed S&Ls	N	55. Raise minimum wage-veto override	Y
24. Allow use of force against Iraq	N	56. Bar transfer of FS-X technology	Y
25. Allow $15b in foreign aid for '91	?	57. Cut defense and raise domestic $	N
26. Revise & extend legal immigration	Y	58. Uniform poll closing in 48 states	N
27. Suspend aid to Angolan rebels	Y	59. Req foreign investment disclosure	Y
28. Democratic tax plan proposals	Y	60. Textile import quotas-veto override	Y
29. Cut defense 5% across the board	?	61. Bar abortion funding in Wash, DC	Y
30. Textile import quotas-veto override	Y	62. Notify spouses of AIDS+ carriers	?
31. Abortion service for military abroad	N	63. Seize conveyance-drug trafficking	N
32. Limits on high income farmers	N	64. South Africa sanctions	Y

HALL, TONY P. (continued)

65. 60 days' notice of plant closings	Y	
66. Close unneeded military bases	N	
67. Keep welfare reform within $2.8b	N	
68. Allow children housing exclusion	N	
69. Shift $400m of NASA to homeless	N	
70. Cap Medicare patients' liability	Y	
71. Prohibit employee polygraph testing	N	
72. Allow CIA to fund Contras	N	
73. Revise unfair trade practices	Y	
74. Focus SDI on accidental launch	Y	
75. Bar Air Force $ for MX missile	Y	
76. Allow "real" increase in defense	?	
77. Troop reduction in Europe of 50%	N	
78. Ban nuclear tests above 1 kiloton	Y	
79. Ban anti-satellite missile tests	Y	
80. Observe certain limits of SALT II	Y	
81. Restore four Civil Rights laws	Y	
82. Prohibit aliens as strikebreakers	Y	
83. Allow military malpractice suits	Y	
84. Approval of $36m in Contra aid	N	
85. $18b deficit reduction compromise	Y	
86. Welfare reform of $5.7b for 5 years	?	
87. Raise taxes $12b/cut spending $3b	Y	
88. Board to assess occupational risk	Y	
89. Balanced budget by '93-via targets	Y	
90. Bar licensing of two nuclear plants	Y	
91. Remove victims compensation cap	Y	
92. Catastrophic health insurance	Y	
93. Ban airline smoking-2 hours or less	Y	
94. $1b/two year aid for the homeless	Y	
95. Bar non-unions in union companies	Y	
96. Increase FSLIC rescue to $15b	N	
97. Impose quotas to lower trade deficit	Y	
98. Reduce discretionary budget 21%	Y	
99. Immigration reform/alien amnesty	?	
100. South Africa sanctions-veto override	Y	
101. Tax overhaul to revise income tax	N	
102. Use of military in drug war	Y	
103. Delete 12 MX/add conventional wpn	Y	
104. Raise speed limit to 65 mph	Y	

105. Require Pentagon to buy US goods	Y	
106. AIDS insurance non-discrimination	N	
107. Prohibit Saudi arms sales	Y	
108. Ease Gun Control Act of 1968	N	
109. Bar interstate handgun transport	Y	
110. Make company emissions known	Y	
111. Allow toxic victims to sue in fed ct	Y	
112. Superfund waste cleanup of $10b	Y	
113. 90 days notice of plant closings	Y	
114. $20b in Medicare cuts/tax increases	Y	
115. Spending cuts and tax increases	Y	
116. Set school lunch lmt-250% poverty	N	
117. $75m for youth work projects	Y	
118. Allow Angolan military assistance	?	
119. Suspend defense payments for abuse	Y	
120. Drop SS COLAs/$12b tax increase	N	
121. Approve $1.5b for 21 MX missiles	N	
122. Emergency farm credit/revisions	Y	
123. Duty on Taiwan/Hong Kong/S Korea	Y	
124. Limit steel imports to 17%	Y	
125. Cut $ to schools that bar prayer	Y	
126. $50b-taxes; cut Medicare/spending	N	
127. Limit Pershing II/cruise in Europe	N	
128. Delete $7.1b for 34 B-1 bombers	N	
129. Bar purchase of Sergeant York guns	N	
130. El Salvador military/economic aid	N	
131. Bar mining of Nicaraguan waters	Y	
132. Physician fee freeze for Medicare	N	
133. $49b in "sin"/phone/insurance taxes	Y	
134. Allow sale of Conrail	N	
135. Equal Rights Amendment	Y	
136. Authorize Marines in Lebanon	Y	
137. Eminent domain for coal companies	N	
138. Prohibit EPA clean air sanctions	Y	
139. SS retirement age increase/reforms	N	
140. Auto domestic content requirement	Y	
141. Delete jobs program funding	N	
142. Highway-gas tax bill	Y	
143. Cut $5b from defense for Medicare	Y	
144. Emergency housing aid of $1b	Y	

Presidential Support Score: 1991 - 35%   1990 - 22%

OXLEY, MICHAEL G. -- Ohio 4th District [Republican]. Counties of Allen, Auglaize, Crawford, Hancock, Hardin, Knox, Richland (pt.), Shelby and Wyandot. Prior Terms: 1981 (Special Election)-1992. Born: February 11, 1944; Findlay, OH. Education: Miami University (B.A.); Ohio State University (J.D.). Occupation: Attorney; Ohio representative (1972-79); congressional staff member; staff member, lieutenant governor; staff member, attorney general; special agent, FBI.

1. Protection to Haitian refugees	N	
2. Raise tax on wealthy; lower others	N	
3. Investigate Reagan hostage delay	N	
4. Campaign finance revisions	N	
5. Unpaid leave to care for children	N	
6. Restrict NEA use of funds	Y	
7. Bar race-bias claim/habeas corpus	Y	
8. Ban race as death sentence factor	Y	
9. Exceptions to exclusionary rule	Y	
10. Allow sale of assault weapons	Y	
11. Life in prison/abolish death penalty	N	
12. Req conspiracy-price fixing cases	Y	
13. Unemployment benefits extension	N	

14. Tissue use of aborted fetuses	N	
15. Bar replacement of union strikers	N	
16. Hold foreign aid at $15b for '92	Y	
17. Restore space station funding	Y	
18. Civil Rights Act of 1991	N	
19. Unlimited damages-discrimination	N	
20. Eliminate funds for supercollider	N	
21. Terminate SDI except for research	N	
22. Req 7-day handgun waiting period	Y	
23. Provide $30b for failed S&Ls	Y	
24. Allow use of force against Iraq	Y	
25. Allow $15b in foreign aid for '91	N	
26. Revise & extend legal immigration	Y	

OXLEY, MICHAEL G. (continued)

27. Suspend aid to Angolan rebels	N
28. Democratic tax plan proposals	N
29. Cut defense 5% across the board	N
30. Textile import quotas-veto override	N
31. Abortion service for military abroad	N
32. Limits on high income farmers	N
33. Family medical leave-veto override	N
34. Req submission of balanced budget	N
35. Balanced budget amendment	Y
36. Amendment to ban flag desecration	Y
37. Reauthorize Amtrak-veto override	N
38. Retraining aid for coal miners	Y
39. Suspend El Salvador military aid	N
40. Expand child care aid/tax credit	N
41. Raise House salary/omit honoraria	Y
42. Toughen oil-spill liability	N
43. Restitution to Japanese interned	N
44. Protect Chinese & C.A. nationals	N
45. Abortion $ for rape/incest cases	N
46. Allow religious schools to bar gays	Y
47. Bar broadcaster fairness doctrine	Y
48. Bar cap gains cut/reinstate IRA	N
49. Bar unions equal voice in pension	Y
50. Bar assembly of chemical weapons	N
51. Ban plutonium/uranium production	N
52. Cap MX missile deployment at 50	N
53. Allow $3b for 2 stealth bombers	Y
54. Publish bio-warfare experiments	N
55. Raise minimum wage-veto override	N
56. Bar transfer of FS-X technology	N
57. Cut defense and raise domestic $	N
58. Uniform poll closing in 48 states	N
59. Req foreign investment disclosure	N
60. Textile import quotas-veto override	N
61. Bar abortion funding in Wash, DC	Y
62. Notify spouses of AIDS+ carriers	N
63. Seize conveyance-drug trafficking	Y
64. South Africa sanctions	N
65. 60 days' notice of plant closings	N
66. Close unneeded military bases	Y
67. Keep welfare reform within $2.8b	Y
68. Allow children housing exclusion	N
69. Shift $400m of NASA to homeless	N
70. Cap Medicare patients' liability	N
71. Prohibit employee polygraph testing	N
72. Allow CIA to fund Contras	Y
73. Revise unfair trade practices	N
74. Focus SDI on accidental launch	N
75. Bar Air Force $ for MX missile	N
76. Allow "real" increase in defense	Y
77. Troop reduction in Europe of 50%	N
78. Ban nuclear tests above 1 kiloton	N
79. Ban anti-satellite missile tests	N
80. Observe certain limits of SALT II	N
81. Restore four Civil Rights laws	N
82. Prohibit aliens as strikebreakers	N
83. Allow military malpractice suits	Y
84. Approval of $36m in Contra aid	Y
85. $18b deficit reduction compromise	N
86. Welfare reform of $5.7b for 5 years	N
87. Raise taxes $12b/cut spending $3b	N
88. Board to assess occupational risk	N
89. Balanced budget by '93-via targets	Y
90. Bar licensing of two nuclear plants	N
91. Remove victims compensation cap	N
92. Catastrophic health insurance	N
93. Ban airline smoking-2 hours or less	N
94. $1b/two year aid for the homeless	N
95. Bar non-unions in union companies	N
96. Increase FSLIC rescue to $15b	N
97. Impose quotas to lower trade deficit	N
98. Reduce discretionary budget 21%	Y
99. Immigration reform/alien amnesty	N
100. South Africa sanctions-veto override	X
101. Tax overhaul to revise income tax	Y
102. Use of military in drug war	N
103. Delete 12 MX/add conventional wpn	N
104. Raise speed limit to 65 mph	Y
105. Require Pentagon to buy US goods	N
106. AIDS insurance non-discrimination	N
107. Prohibit Saudi arms sales	N
108. Ease Gun Control Act of 1968	Y
109. Bar interstate handgun transport	Y
110. Make company emissions known	N
111. Allow toxic victims to sue in fed ct	N
112. Superfund waste cleanup of $10b	N
113. 90 days notice of plant closings	N
114. $20b in Medicare cuts/tax increases	N
115. Spending cuts and tax increases	N
116. Set school lunch lmt-250% poverty	Y
117. $75m for youth work projects	N
118. Allow Angolan military assistance	Y
119. Suspend defense payments for abuse	N
120. Drop SS COLAs/$12b tax increase	N
121. Approve $1.5b for 21 MX missiles	Y
122. Emergency farm credit/revisions	Y
123. Duty on Taiwan/Hong Kong/S Korea	N
124. Limit steel imports to 17%	N
125. Cut $ to schools that bar prayer	+
126. $50b-taxes; cut Medicare/spending	Y
127. Limit Pershing II/cruise in Europe	N
128. Delete $7.1b for 34 B-1 bombers	N
129. Bar purchase of Sergeant York guns	N
130. El Salvador military/economic aid	Y
131. Bar mining of Nicaraguan waters	N
132. Physician fee freeze for Medicare	Y
133. $49b in "sin"/phone/insurance taxes	Y
134. Allow sale of Conrail	Y
135. Equal Rights Amendment	N
136. Authorize Marines in Lebanon	Y
137. Eminent domain for coal companies	N
138. Prohibit EPA clean air sanctions	Y
139. SS retirement age increase/reforms	Y
140. Auto domestic content requirement	N
141. Delete jobs program funding	Y
142. Highway-gas tax bill	N
143. Cut $5b from defense for Medicare	N
144. Emergency housing aid of $1b	Y

Presidential Support Score: 1991 - 79%   1990 - 73%

GILLMOR, PAUL E. -- Ohio 5th District [Republican]. Counties of Defiance, Erie, Fulton (pt.), Henry, Huron (pt.), Ottawa, Paulding, Putnam, Sandusky, Seneca, Williams and Wood (pt.). Prior Terms: 1989-92. Born: February 1, 1939; Tiffin, OH. Education: Ohio Wesleyan University (B.A.); University of Michigan Law School. Military Service: U.S. Air Force; Judge Advocate General's Office. Occupation: Private attorney; state senator (1967-88).

1. Protection to Haitian refugees	N		30. Textile import quotas-veto override	N
2. Raise tax on wealthy; lower others	N		31. Abortion service for military abroad	N
3. Investigate Reagan hostage delay	N		32. Limits on high income farmers	N
4. Campaign finance revisions	N		33. Family medical leave-veto override	Y
5. Unpaid leave to care for children	Y		34. Req submission of balanced budget	N
6. Restrict NEA use of funds	Y		35. Balanced budget amendment	Y
7. Bar race-bias claim/habeas corpus	Y		36. Amendment to ban flag desecration	Y
8. Ban race as death sentence factor	Y		37. Reauthorize Amtrak-veto override	N
9. Exceptions to exclusionary rule	Y		38. Retraining aid for coal miners	N
10. Allow sale of assault weapons	Y		39. Suspend El Salvador military aid	N
11. Life in prison/abolish death penalty	N		40. Expand child care aid/tax credit	Y
12. Req conspiracy-price fixing cases	Y		41. Raise House salary/omit honoraria	N
13. Unemployment benefits extension	Y		42. Toughen oil-spill liability	N
14. Tissue use of aborted fetuses	N		43. Restitution to Japanese interned	Y
15. Bar replacement of union strikers	N		44. Protect Chinese & C.A. nationals	N
16. Hold foreign aid at $15b for '92	Y		45. Abortion $ for rape/incest cases	N
17. Restore space station funding	Y		46. Allow religious schools to bar gays	Y
18. Civil Rights Act of 1991	N		47. Bar broadcaster fairness doctrine	N
19. Unlimited damages-discrimination	N		48. Bar cap gains cut/reinstate IRA	N
20. Eliminate funds for supercollider	Y		49. Bar unions equal voice in pension	Y
21. Terminate SDI except for research	N		50. Bar assembly of chemical weapons	N
22. Req 7-day handgun waiting period	N		51. Ban plutonium/uranium production	Y
23. Provide $30b for failed S&Ls	Y		52. Cap MX missile deployment at 50	N
24. Allow use of force against Iraq	Y		53. Allow $3b for 2 stealth bombers	Y
25. Allow $15b in foreign aid for '91	Y		54. Publish bio-warfare experiments	N
26. Revise & extend legal immigration	Y		55. Raise minimum wage-veto override	N
27. Suspend aid to Angolan rebels	N		56. Bar transfer of FS-X technology	N
28. Democratic tax plan proposals	N		57. Cut defense and raise domestic $	N
29. Cut defense 5% across the board	N		58. Uniform poll closing in 48 states	N

Presidential Support Score: 1991 - 73%   1990 - 69%

McEWEN, BOB -- Ohio 6th District [Republican]. Counties of Adams, Athens (pt.), Clermont (pt.), Clinton, Fayette (pt.), Highland, Hocking, Jackson, Montgomery (pt.), Pike, Ross, Scioto, Vinton and Warren. Prior Terms: 1981-92. Born: January 12, 1950; Hillsboro, OH. Education: University of Miami (B.B.A.). Occupation: Ohio representative (1974-80); congressional assistant; vice president, Boebinger, Inc.

1. Protection to Haitian refugees	N		20. Eliminate funds for supercollider	N
2. Raise tax on wealthy; lower others	N		21. Terminate SDI except for research	N
3. Investigate Reagan hostage delay	N		22. Req 7-day handgun waiting period	N
4. Campaign finance revisions	N		23. Provide $30b for failed S&Ls	Y
5. Unpaid leave to care for children	N		24. Allow use of force against Iraq	Y
6. Restrict NEA use of funds	Y		25. Allow $15b in foreign aid for '91	N
7. Bar race-bias claim/habeas corpus	Y		26. Revise & extend legal immigration	Y
8. Ban race as death sentence factor	Y		27. Suspend aid to Angolan rebels	N
9. Exceptions to exclusionary rule	Y		28. Democratic tax plan proposals	N
10. Allow sale of assault weapons	Y		29. Cut defense 5% across the board	N
11. Life in prison/abolish death penalty	N		30. Textile import quotas-veto override	N
12. Req conspiracy-price fixing cases	Y		31. Abortion service for military abroad	N
13. Unemployment benefits extension	N		32. Limits on high income farmers	N
14. Tissue use of aborted fetuses	N		33. Family medical leave-veto override	N
15. Bar replacement of union strikers	N		34. Req submission of balanced budget	N
16. Hold foreign aid at $15b for '92	N		35. Balanced budget amendment	Y
17. Restore space station funding	Y		36. Amendment to ban flag desecration	Y
18. Civil Rights Act of 1991	N		37. Reauthorize Amtrak-veto override	N
19. Unlimited damages-discrimination	N		38. Retraining aid for coal miners	Y

McEWEN, BOB (continued)

39. Suspend El Salvador military aid	N		92. Catastrophic health insurance	N
40. Expand child care aid/tax credit	N		93. Ban airline smoking-2 hours or less	?
41. Raise House salary/omit honoraria	Y		94. $1b/two year aid for the homeless	Y
42. Toughen oil-spill liability	N		95. Bar non-unions in union companies	?
43. Restitution to Japanese interned	N		96. Increase FSLIC rescue to $15b	N
44. Protect Chinese & C.A. nationals	Y		97. Impose quotas to lower trade deficit	N
45. Abortion $ for rape/incest cases	N		98. Reduce discretionary budget 21%	Y
46. Allow religious schools to bar gays	Y		99. Immigration reform/alien amnesty	#
47. Bar broadcaster fairness doctrine	Y		100. South Africa sanctions-veto override	N
48. Bar cap gains cut/reinstate IRA	N		101. Tax overhaul to revise income tax	Y
49. Bar unions equal voice in pension	Y		102. Use of military in drug war	N
50. Bar assembly of chemical weapons	N		103. Delete 12 MX/add conventional wpn	N
51. Ban plutonium/uranium production	N		104. Raise speed limit to 65 mph	Y
52. Cap MX missile deployment at 50	N		105. Require Pentagon to buy US goods	Y
53. Allow $3b for 2 stealth bombers	Y		106. AIDS insurance non-discrimination	N
54. Publish bio-warfare experiments	N		107. Prohibit Saudi arms sales	Y
55. Raise minimum wage-veto override	N		108. Ease Gun Control Act of 1968	Y
56. Bar transfer of FS-X technology	Y		109. Bar interstate handgun transport	N
57. Cut defense and raise domestic $	N		110. Make company emissions known	N
58. Uniform poll closing in 48 states	N		111. Allow toxic victims to sue in fed ct	N
59. Req foreign investment disclosure	N		112. Superfund waste cleanup of $10b	Y
60. Textile import quotas-veto override	N		113. 90 days notice of plant closings	N
61. Bar abortion funding in Wash, DC	Y		114. $20b in Medicare cuts/tax increases	N
62. Notify spouses of AIDS+ carriers	N		115. Spending cuts and tax increases	N
63. Seize conveyance-drug trafficking	Y		116. Set school lunch lmt-250% poverty	N
64. South Africa sanctions	N		117. $75m for youth work projects	N
65. 60 days' notice of plant closings	N		118. Allow Angolan military assistance	Y
66. Close unneeded military bases	Y		119. Suspend defense payments for abuse	Y
67. Keep welfare reform within $2.8b	Y		120. Drop SS COLAs/$12b tax increase	N
68. Allow children housing exclusion	N		121. Approve $1.5b for 21 MX missiles	Y
69. Shift $400m of NASA to homeless	N		122. Emergency farm credit/revisions	N
70. Cap Medicare patients' liability	Y		123. Duty on Taiwan/Hong Kong/S Korea	N
71. Prohibit employee polygraph testing	N		124. Limit steel imports to 17%	Y
72. Allow CIA to fund Contras	Y		125. Cut $ to schools that bar prayer	Y
73. Revise unfair trade practices	N		126. $50b-taxes; cut Medicare/spending	N
74. Focus SDI on accidental launch	N		127. Limit Pershing II/cruise in Europe	N
75. Bar Air Force $ for MX missile	N		128. Delete $7.1b for 34 B-1 bombers	N
76. Allow "real" increase in defense	Y		129. Bar purchase of Sergeant York guns	N
77. Troop reduction in Europe of 50%	N		130. El Salvador military/economic aid	Y
78. Ban nuclear tests above 1 kiloton	N		131. Bar mining of Nicaraguan waters	N
79. Ban anti-satellite missile tests	N		132. Physician fee freeze for Medicare	Y
80. Observe certain limits of SALT II	N		133. $49b in "sin"/phone/insurance taxes	N
81. Restore four Civil Rights laws	N		134. Allow sale of Conrail	Y
82. Prohibit aliens as strikebreakers	N		135. Equal Rights Amendment	N
83. Allow military malpractice suits	Y		136. Authorize Marines in Lebanon	Y
84. Approval of $36m in Contra aid	Y		137. Eminent domain for coal companies	N
85. $18b deficit reduction compromise	N		138. Prohibit EPA clean air sanctions	Y
86. Welfare reform of $5.7b for 5 years	N		139. SS retirement age increase/reforms	Y
87. Raise taxes $12b/cut spending $3b	N		140. Auto domestic content requirement	Y
88. Board to assess occupational risk	N		141. Delete jobs program funding	Y
89. Balanced budget by '93-via targets	N		142. Highway-gas tax bill	N
90. Bar licensing of two nuclear plants	N		143. Cut $5b from defense for Medicare	N
91. Remove victims compensation cap	N		144. Emergency housing aid of $1b	Y

Presidential Support Score: 1991 - 78%   1990 - 69%

HOBSON, DAVID L. -- Ohio 7th District [Republican]. Counties of Champaign (pt.), Clark, Fayette (pt.), Greene, Logan, Madison (pt.), Marion, Pickaway and Union. Prior Term: 1991-92. Born: October 17, 1936; Cincinnati, OH. Education: Ohio Wesleyan University (B.A.); Ohio State College of Law (J.D.). Military Service: Ohio Air National Guard. Occupation: Real estate financing, oil company, bank and restaurant-chain director; state senator (1982-90).

HOBSON, DAVID L. (continued)

1. Protection to Haitian refugees	N	13. Unemployment benefits extension	N
2. Raise tax on wealthy; lower others	N	14. Tissue use of aborted fetuses	Y
3. Investigate Reagan hostage delay	N	15. Bar replacement of union strikers	N
4. Campaign finance revisions	N	16. Hold foreign aid at $15b for '92	Y
5. Unpaid leave to care for children	N	17. Restore space station funding	Y
6. Restrict NEA use of funds	Y	18. Civil Rights Act of 1991	Y
7. Bar race-bias claim/habeas corpus	Y	19. Unlimited damages-discrimination	N
8. Ban race as death sentence factor	Y	20. Eliminate funds for supercollider	N
9. Exceptions to exclusionary rule	Y	21. Terminate SDI except for research	N
10. Allow sale of assault weapons	Y	22. Req 7-day handgun waiting period	N
11. Life in prison/abolish death penalty	N	23. Provide $30b for failed S&Ls	Y
12. Req conspiracy-price fixing cases	Y	24. Allow use of force against Iraq	Y

Presidential Support Score: 1991 - 77%

BOEHNER, JOHN A. -- Ohio 8th District [Republican]. Counties of Butler, Champaign (pt.), Darke, Mercer, Miami, Preble and Van Wert. Prior Term: 1991-92. Born: November 17, 1949; Reading, OH. Education: Xavier University (B.S.). Occupation: President, Nucite Sales, Inc.; state representative (1985-90).

1. Protection to Haitian refugees	X	13. Unemployment benefits extension	N
2. Raise tax on wealthy; lower others	N	14. Tissue use of aborted fetuses	N
3. Investigate Reagan hostage delay	N	15. Bar replacement of union strikers	N
4. Campaign finance revisions	N	16. Hold foreign aid at $15b for '92	Y
5. Unpaid leave to care for children	N	17. Restore space station funding	Y
6. Restrict NEA use of funds	Y	18. Civil Rights Act of 1991	N
7. Bar race-bias claim/habeas corpus	Y	19. Unlimited damages-discrimination	N
8. Ban race as death sentence factor	Y	20. Eliminate funds for supercollider	N
9. Exceptions to exclusionary rule	Y	21. Terminate SDI except for research	N
10. Allow sale of assault weapons	Y	22. Req 7-day handgun waiting period	N
11. Life in prison/abolish death penalty	N	23. Provide $30b for failed S&Ls	Y
12. Req conspiracy-price fixing cases	Y	24. Allow use of force against Iraq	Y

Presidential Support Score: 1991 - 84%

KAPTUR, MARCY -- Ohio 9th District [Democrat]. Counties of Fulton (pt.), Lucas and Wood (pt.). Prior Terms: 1983-92. Born: June 17, 1946; Toledo, OH. Education: University of Wisconsin (B.A.); University of Michigan (M.A.). Occupation: Urban planner; county commissioner (1969-73); self-employed consultant; Director of Planning and Urban Development, National Center for Urban Ethnic Affairs (1975-76); White House aide (1977-79); deputy secretary for Policy, Research, and Operations, National Consumer Cooperative Bank (1979-81).

1. Protection to Haitian refugees	Y	20. Eliminate funds for supercollider	N
2. Raise tax on wealthy; lower others	Y	21. Terminate SDI except for research	N
3. Investigate Reagan hostage delay	Y	22. Req 7-day handgun waiting period	Y
4. Campaign finance revisions	Y	23. Provide $30b for failed S&Ls	N
5. Unpaid leave to care for children	Y	24. Allow use of force against Iraq	N
6. Restrict NEA use of funds	N	25. Allow $15b in foreign aid for '91	N
7. Bar race-bias claim/habeas corpus	N	26. Revise & extend legal immigration	Y
8. Ban race as death sentence factor	N	27. Suspend aid to Angolan rebels	Y
9. Exceptions to exclusionary rule	Y	28. Democratic tax plan proposals	Y
10. Allow sale of assault weapons	N	29. Cut defense 5% across the board	N
11. Life in prison/abolish death penalty	N	30. Textile import quotas-veto override	Y
12. Req conspiracy-price fixing cases	N	31. Abortion service for military abroad	N
13. Unemployment benefits extension	Y	32. Limits on high income farmers	N
14. Tissue use of aborted fetuses	Y	33. Family medical leave-veto override	?
15. Bar replacement of union strikers	Y	34. Req submission of balanced budget	Y
16. Hold foreign aid at $15b for '92	Y	35. Balanced budget amendment	N
17. Restore space station funding	N	36. Amendment to ban flag desecration	N
18. Civil Rights Act of 1991	Y	37. Reauthorize Amtrak-veto override	Y
19. Unlimited damages-discrimination	Y	38. Retraining aid for coal miners	Y

KAPTUR, MARCY (continued)

39. Suspend El Salvador military aid	Y	
40. Expand child care aid/tax credit	Y	
41. Raise House salary/omit honoraria	N	
42. Toughen oil-spill liability	Y	
43. Restitution to Japanese interned	Y	
44. Protect Chinese & C.A. nationals	?	
45. Abortion $ for rape/incest cases	N	
46. Allow religious schools to bar gays	Y	
47. Bar broadcaster fairness doctrine	N	
48. Bar cap gains cut/reinstate IRA	Y	
49. Bar unions equal voice in pension	N	
50. Bar assembly of chemical weapons	Y	
51. Ban plutonium/uranium production	Y	
52. Cap MX missile deployment at 50	Y	
53. Allow $3b for 2 stealth bombers	N	
54. Publish bio-warfare experiments	Y	
55. Raise minimum wage-veto override	Y	
56. Bar transfer of FS-X technology	Y	
57. Cut defense and raise domestic $	N	
58. Uniform poll closing in 48 states	+	
59. Req foreign investment disclosure	Y	
60. Textile import quotas-veto override	Y	
61. Bar abortion funding in Wash, DC	Y	
62. Notify spouses of AIDS+ carriers	N	
63. Seize conveyance-drug trafficking	N	
64. South Africa sanctions	Y	
65. 60 days' notice of plant closings	Y	
66. Close unneeded military bases	N	
67. Keep welfare reform within $2.8b	Y	
68. Allow children housing exclusion	N	
69. Shift $400m of NASA to homeless	Y	
70. Cap Medicare patients' liability	Y	
71. Prohibit employee polygraph testing	Y	
72. Allow CIA to fund Contras	N	
73. Revise unfair trade practices	Y	
74. Focus SDI on accidental launch	Y	
75. Bar Air Force $ for MX missile	Y	
76. Allow "real" increase in defense	N	
77. Troop reduction in Europe of 50%	Y	
78. Ban nuclear tests above 1 kiloton	Y	
79. Ban anti-satellite missile tests	Y	
80. Observe certain limits of SALT II	Y	
81. Restore four Civil Rights laws	Y	
82. Prohibit aliens as strikebreakers	Y	
83. Allow military malpractice suits	Y	
84. Approval of $36m in Contra aid	N	
85. $18b deficit reduction compromise	N	
86. Welfare reform of $5.7b for 5 years	Y	
87. Raise taxes $12b/cut spending $3b	Y	
88. Board to assess occupational risk	Y	
89. Balanced budget by '93-via targets	Y	

90. Bar licensing of two nuclear plants	Y
91. Remove victims compensation cap	Y
92. Catastrophic health insurance	Y
93. Ban airline smoking-2 hours or less	Y
94. $1b/two year aid for the homeless	Y
95. Bar non-unions in union companies	Y
96. Increase FSLIC rescue to $15b	N
97. Impose quotas to lower trade deficit	Y
98. Reduce discretionary budget 21%	Y
99. Immigration reform/alien amnesty	?
100. South Africa sanctions-veto override	Y
101. Tax overhaul to revise income tax	N
102. Use of military in drug war	Y
103. Delete 12 MX/add conventional wpn	Y
104. Raise speed limit to 65 mph	N
105. Require Pentagon to buy US goods	Y
106. AIDS insurance non-discrimination	Y
107. Prohibit Saudi arms sales	Y
108. Ease Gun Control Act of 1968	N
109. Bar interstate handgun transport	Y
110. Make company emissions known	Y
111. Allow toxic victims to sue in fed ct	Y
112. Superfund waste cleanup of $10b	Y
113. 90 days notice of plant closings	Y
114. $20b in Medicare cuts/tax increases	Y
115. Spending cuts and tax increases	Y
116. Set school lunch lmt-250% poverty	N
117. $75m for youth work projects	Y
118. Allow Angolan military assistance	N
119. Suspend defense payments for abuse	Y
120. Drop SS COLAs/$12b tax increase	N
121. Approve $1.5b for 21 MX missiles	N
122. Emergency farm credit/revisions	Y
123. Duty on Taiwan/Hong Kong/S Korea	N
124. Limit steel imports to 17%	Y
125. Cut $ to schools that bar prayer	N
126. $50b-taxes; cut Medicare/spending	N
127. Limit Pershing II/cruise in Europe	Y
128. Delete $7.1b for 34 B-1 bombers	Y
129. Bar purchase of Sergeant York guns	Y
130. El Salvador military/economic aid	N
131. Bar mining of Nicaraguan waters	Y
132. Physician fee freeze for Medicare	N
133. $49b in "sin"/phone/insurance taxes	Y
134. Allow sale of Conrail	N
135. Equal Rights Amendment	Y
136. Authorize Marines in Lebanon	N
137. Eminent domain for coal companies	N
138. Prohibit EPA clean air sanctions	N
139. SS retirement age increase/reforms	N

Presidential Support Score: 1991 - 29% 1990 - 23%

MILLER, CLARENCE E. -- Ohio 10th District [Republican]. Counties of Athens (pt.), Fairfield, Gallia, Guernsey (pt.), Lawrence, Licking (pt.), Meigs, Morgan, Muskingum, Perry and Washington (pt.). Prior Terms: 1967-92. Born: November 1, 1917; Lancaster, OH. Education: International Correspondence Schools. Occupation: City councilman (1957-63); mayor (1963-65).

1. Protection to Haitian refugees	N	4. Campaign finance revisions	N
2. Raise tax on wealthy; lower others	N	5. Unpaid leave to care for children	N
3. Investigate Reagan hostage delay	N	6. Restrict NEA use of funds	Y

MILLER, CLARENCE E. (continued)

7. Bar race-bias claim/habeas corpus	Y	
8. Ban race as death sentence factor	Y	
9. Exceptions to exclusionary rule	Y	
10. Allow sale of assault weapons	Y	
11. Life in prison/abolish death penalty	N	
12. Req conspiracy-price fixing cases	Y	
13. Unemployment benefits extension	N	
14. Tissue use of aborted fetuses	N	
15. Bar replacement of union strikers	N	
16. Hold foreign aid at $15b for '92	N	
17. Restore space station funding	Y	
18. Civil Rights Act of 1991	N	
19. Unlimited damages-discrimination	N	
20. Eliminate funds for supercollider	N	
21. Terminate SDI except for research	N	
22. Req 7-day handgun waiting period	N	
23. Provide $30b for failed S&Ls	?	
24. Allow use of force against Iraq	Y	
25. Allow $15b in foreign aid for '91	N	
26. Revise & extend legal immigration	N	
27. Suspend aid to Angolan rebels	N	
28. Democratic tax plan proposals	N	
29. Cut defense 5% across the board	N	
30. Textile import quotas-veto override	Y	
31. Abortion service for military abroad	N	
32. Limits on high income farmers	Y	
33. Family medical leave-veto override	N	
34. Req submission of balanced budget	Y	
35. Balanced budget amendment	Y	
36. Amendment to ban flag desecration	Y	
37. Reauthorize Amtrak-veto override	N	
38. Retraining aid for coal miners	Y	
39. Suspend El Salvador military aid	N	
40. Expand child care aid/tax credit	N	
41. Raise House salary/omit honoraria	N	
42. Toughen oil-spill liability	N	
43. Restitution to Japanese interned	N	
44. Protect Chinese & C.A. nationals	N	
45. Abortion $ for rape/incest cases	N	
46. Allow religious schools to bar gays	Y	
47. Bar broadcaster fairness doctrine	N	
48. Bar cap gains cut/reinstate IRA	N	
49. Bar unions equal voice in pension	Y	
50. Bar assembly of chemical weapons	N	
51. Ban plutonium/uranium production	N	
52. Cap MX missile deployment at 50	Y	
53. Allow $3b for 2 stealth bombers	Y	
54. Publish bio-warfare experiments	Y	
55. Raise minimum wage-veto override	N	
56. Bar transfer of FS-X technology	N	
57. Cut defense and raise domestic $	N	
58. Uniform poll closing in 48 states	N	
59. Req foreign investment disclosure	Y	
60. Textile import quotas-veto override	Y	
61. Bar abortion funding in Wash, DC	Y	
62. Notify spouses of AIDS+ carriers	Y	
63. Seize conveyance-drug trafficking	Y	
64. South Africa sanctions	N	
65. 60 days' notice of plant closings	N	
66. Close unneeded military bases	Y	
67. Keep welfare reform within $2.8b	Y	
68. Allow children housing exclusion	Y	
69. Shift $400m of NASA to homeless	N	
70. Cap Medicare patients' liability	Y	

71. Prohibit employee polygraph testing	N	
72. Allow CIA to fund Contras	Y	
73. Revise unfair trade practices	Y	
74. Focus SDI on accidental launch	N	
75. Bar Air Force $ for MX missile	N	
76. Allow "real" increase in defense	Y	
77. Troop reduction in Europe of 50%	N	
78. Ban nuclear tests above 1 kiloton	N	
79. Ban anti-satellite missile tests	N	
80. Observe certain limits of SALT II	N	
81. Restore four Civil Rights laws	N	
82. Prohibit aliens as strikebreakers	Y	
83. Allow military malpractice suits	Y	
84. Approval of $36m in Contra aid	Y	
85. $18b deficit reduction compromise	N	
86. Welfare reform of $5.7b for 5 years	N	
87. Raise taxes $12b/cut spending $3b	N	
88. Board to assess occupational risk	N	
89. Balanced budget by '93-via targets	Y	
90. Bar licensing of two nuclear plants	N	
91. Remove victims compensation cap	N	
92. Catastrophic health insurance	N	
93. Ban airline smoking-2 hours or less	?	
94. $1b/two year aid for the homeless	?	
95. Bar non-unions in union companies	N	
96. Increase FSLIC rescue to $15b	N	
97. Impose quotas to lower trade deficit	N	
98. Reduce discretionary budget 21%	N	
99. Immigration reform/alien amnesty	N	
100. South Africa sanctions-veto override	N	
101. Tax overhaul to revise income tax	N	
102. Use of military in drug war	Y	
103. Delete 12 MX/add conventional wpn	N	
104. Raise speed limit to 65 mph	Y	
105. Require Pentagon to buy US goods	N	
106. AIDS insurance non-discrimination	N	
107. Prohibit Saudi arms sales	N	
108. Ease Gun Control Act of 1968	Y	
109. Bar interstate handgun transport	N	
110. Make company emissions known	?	
111. Allow toxic victims to sue in fed ct	?	
112. Superfund waste cleanup of $10b	?	
113. 90 days notice of plant closings	N	
114. $20b in Medicare cuts/tax increases	N	
115. Spending cuts and tax increases	N	
116. Set school lunch lmt-250% poverty	Y	
117. $75m for youth work projects	N	
118. Allow Angolan military assistance	Y	
119. Suspend defense payments for abuse	Y	
120. Drop SS COLAs/$12b tax increase	N	
121. Approve $1.5b for 21 MX missiles	Y	
122. Emergency farm credit/revisions	Y	
123. Duty on Taiwan/Hong Kong/S Korea	N	
124. Limit steel imports to 17%	Y	
125. Cut $ to schools that bar prayer	Y	
126. $50b-taxes; cut Medicare/spending	Y	
127. Limit Pershing II/cruise in Europe	N	
128. Delete $7.1b for 34 B-1 bombers	N	
129. Bar purchase of Sergeant York guns	Y	
130. El Salvador military/economic aid	Y	
131. Bar mining of Nicaraguan waters	Y	
132. Physician fee freeze for Medicare	Y	
133. $49b in "sin"/phone/insurance taxes	Y	
134. Allow sale of Conrail	Y	

MILLER, CLARENCE E. (continued)

135. Equal Rights Amendment	N
136. Authorize Marines in Lebanon	N
137. Eminent domain for coal companies	N
138. Prohibit EPA clean air sanctions	Y
139. SS retirement age increase/reforms	N

140. Auto domestic content requirement	Y
141. Delete jobs program funding	Y
142. Highway-gas tax bill	N
143. Cut $5b from defense for Medicare	N
144. Emergency housing aid of $1b	N

Presidential Support Score: 1991 - 66%   1990 - 68%

ECKART, DENNIS E. -- Ohio 11th District [Democrat]. Counties of Ashtabula, Geauga, Lake (pt.), Portage and Trumbull (pt.). Prior Terms: 1981-92. Born: April 6, 1950; Cleveland OH. Education: Xavier University; Cleveland Marshall Law School. Occupation: Ohio legislator (1975-80).

1. Protection to Haitian refugees	Y		51. Ban plutonium/uranium production	Y
2. Raise tax on wealthy; lower others	Y		52. Cap MX missile deployment at 50	Y
3. Investigate Reagan hostage delay	?		53. Allow $3b for 2 stealth bombers	N
4. Campaign finance revisions	Y		54. Publish bio-warfare experiments	Y
5. Unpaid leave to care for children	Y		55. Raise minimum wage-veto override	Y
6. Restrict NEA use of funds	N		56. Bar transfer of FS-X technology	Y
7. Bar race-bias claim/habeas corpus	N		57. Cut defense and raise domestic $	N
8. Ban race as death sentence factor	N		58. Uniform poll closing in 48 states	Y
9. Exceptions to exclusionary rule	N		59. Req foreign investment disclosure	Y
10. Allow sale of assault weapons	N		60. Textile import quotas-veto override	Y
11. Life in prison/abolish death penalty	N		61. Bar abortion funding in Wash, DC	N
12. Req conspiracy-price fixing cases	N		62. Notify spouses of AIDS+ carriers	N
13. Unemployment benefits extension	Y		63. Seize conveyance-drug trafficking	N
14. Tissue use of aborted fetuses	Y		64. South Africa sanctions	Y
15. Bar replacement of union strikers	Y		65. 60 days' notice of plant closings	Y
16. Hold foreign aid at $15b for '92	Y		66. Close unneeded military bases	N
17. Restore space station funding	Y		67. Keep welfare reform within $2.8b	N
18. Civil Rights Act of 1991	Y		68. Allow children housing exclusion	N
19. Unlimited damages-discrimination	N		69. Shift $400m of NASA to homeless	Y
20. Eliminate funds for supercollider	Y		70. Cap Medicare patients' liability	Y
21. Terminate SDI except for research	Y		71. Prohibit employee polygraph testing	Y
22. Req 7-day handgun waiting period	Y		72. Allow CIA to fund Contras	N
23. Provide $30b for failed S&Ls	N		73. Revise unfair trade practices	Y
24. Allow use of force against Iraq	N		74. Focus SDI on accidental launch	Y
25. Allow $15b in foreign aid for '91	N		75. Bar Air Force $ for MX missile	Y
26. Revise & extend legal immigration	N		76. Allow "real" increase in defense	N
27. Suspend aid to Angolan rebels	Y		77. Troop reduction in Europe of 50%	Y
28. Democratic tax plan proposals	Y		78. Ban nuclear tests above 1 kiloton	Y
29. Cut defense 5% across the board	Y		79. Ban anti-satellite missile tests	Y
30. Textile import quotas-veto override	Y		80. Observe certain limits of SALT II	Y
31. Abortion service for military abroad	Y		81. Restore four Civil Rights laws	Y
32. Limits on high income farmers	Y		82. Prohibit aliens as strikebreakers	Y
33. Family medical leave-veto override	Y		83. Allow military malpractice suits	Y
34. Req submission of balanced budget	Y		84. Approval of $36m in Contra aid	N
35. Balanced budget amendment	Y		85. $18b deficit reduction compromise	Y
36. Amendment to ban flag desecration	Y		86. Welfare reform of $5.7b for 5 years	Y
37. Reauthorize Amtrak-veto override	Y		87. Raise taxes $12b/cut spending $3b	N
38. Retraining aid for coal miners	Y		88. Board to assess occupational risk	Y
39. Suspend El Salvador military aid	Y		89. Balanced budget by '93-via targets	Y
40. Expand child care aid/tax credit	Y		90. Bar licensing of two nuclear plants	Y
41. Raise House salary/omit honoraria	N		91. Remove victims compensation cap	Y
42. Toughen oil-spill liability	N		92. Catastrophic health insurance	Y
43. Restitution to Japanese interned	Y		93. Ban airline smoking-2 hours or less	Y
44. Protect Chinese & C.A. nationals	Y		94. $1b/two year aid for the homeless	Y
45. Abortion $ for rape/incest cases	Y		95. Bar non-unions in union companies	Y
46. Allow religious schools to bar gays	Y		96. Increase FSLIC rescue to $15b	N
47. Bar broadcaster fairness doctrine	N		97. Impose quotas to lower trade deficit	Y
48. Bar cap gains cut/reinstate IRA	Y		98. Reduce discretionary budget 21%	Y
49. Bar unions equal voice in pension	N		99. Immigration reform/alien amnesty	Y
50. Bar assembly of chemical weapons	Y		100. South Africa sanctions-veto override	Y

ECKART, DENNIS E. (continued)

101.	Tax overhaul to revise income tax	Y	123.	Duty on Taiwan/Hong Kong/S Korea	Y
102.	Use of military in drug war	Y	124.	Limit steel imports to 17%	Y
103.	Delete 12 MX/add conventional wpn	Y	125.	Cut $ to schools that bar prayer	N
104.	Raise speed limit to 65 mph	N	126.	$50b-taxes; cut Medicare/spending	N
105.	Require Pentagon to buy US goods	Y	127.	Limit Pershing II/cruise in Europe	Y
106.	AIDS insurance non-discrimination	Y	128.	Delete $7.1b for 34 B-1 bombers	N
107.	Prohibit Saudi arms sales	--	129.	Bar purchase of Sergeant York guns	Y
108.	Ease Gun Control Act of 1968	Y	130.	El Salvador military/economic aid	N
109.	Bar interstate handgun transport	N	131.	Bar mining of Nicaraguan waters	Y
110.	Make company emissions known	N	132.	Physician fee freeze for Medicare	N
111.	Allow toxic victims to sue in fed ct	N	133.	$49b in "sin"/phone/insurance taxes	Y
112.	Superfund waste cleanup of $10b	Y	134.	Allow sale of Conrail	N
113.	90 days notice of plant closings	Y	135.	Equal Rights Amendment	Y
114.	$20b in Medicare cuts/tax increases	Y	136.	Authorize Marines in Lebanon	N
115.	Spending cuts and tax increases	Y	137.	Eminent domain for coal companies	N
116.	Set school lunch lmt-250% poverty	N	138.	Prohibit EPA clean air sanctions	Y
117.	$75m for youth work projects	Y	139.	SS retirement age increase/reforms	N
118.	Allow Angolan military assistance	N	140.	Auto domestic content requirement	Y
119.	Suspend defense payments for abuse	Y	141.	Delete jobs program funding	N
120.	Drop SS COLAs/$12b tax increase	N	142.	Highway-gas tax bill	Y
121.	Approve $1.5b for 21 MX missiles	N	143.	Cut $5b from defense for Medicare	Y
122.	Emergency farm credit/revisions	Y	144.	Emergency housing aid of $1b	Y

Presidential Support Score: 1991 - 22%   1990 - 20%

KASICH, JOHN R. -- Ohio 12th District [Republican]. Counties of Delaware, Franklin (pt.), Licking (pt.) and Morrow. Prior Terms: 1983-92. Born: May 13, 1952; McKees Rocks, PA. Education: Ohio State University (B.A.). Occupation: Administrative assistant (1975-77); Ohio senator (1979-82).

1.	Protection to Haitian refugees	N	34.	Req submission of balanced budget	N
2.	Raise tax on wealthy; lower others	N	35.	Balanced budget amendment	Y
3.	Investigate Reagan hostage delay	N	36.	Amendment to ban flag desecration	Y
4.	Campaign finance revisions	N	37.	Reauthorize Amtrak-veto override	N
5.	Unpaid leave to care for children	N	38.	Retraining aid for coal miners	Y
6.	Restrict NEA use of funds	Y	39.	Suspend El Salvador military aid	N
7.	Bar race-bias claim/habeas corpus	Y	40.	Expand child care aid/tax credit	N
8.	Ban race as death sentence factor	Y	41.	Raise House salary/omit honoraria	N
9.	Exceptions to exclusionary rule	Y	42.	Toughen oil-spill liability	N
10.	Allow sale of assault weapons	Y	43.	Restitution to Japanese interned	N
11.	Life in prison/abolish death penalty	N	44.	Protect Chinese & C.A. nationals	N
12.	Req conspiracy-price fixing cases	Y	45.	Abortion $ for rape/incest cases	N
13.	Unemployment benefits extension	N	46.	Allow religious schools to bar gays	Y
14.	Tissue use of aborted fetuses	N	47.	Bar broadcaster fairness doctrine	Y
15.	Bar replacement of union strikers	N	48.	Bar cap gains cut/reinstate IRA	N
16.	Hold foreign aid at $15b for '92	Y	49.	Bar unions equal voice in pension	Y
17.	Restore space station funding	Y	50.	Bar assembly of chemical weapons	N
18.	Civil Rights Act of 1991	N	51.	Ban plutonium/uranium production	N
19.	Unlimited damages-discrimination	N	52.	Cap MX missile deployment at 50	N
20.	Eliminate funds for supercollider	N	53.	Allow $3b for 2 stealth bombers	N
21.	Terminate SDI except for research	N	54.	Publish bio-warfare experiments	N
22.	Req 7-day handgun waiting period	N	55.	Raise minimum wage-veto override	N
23.	Provide $30b for failed S&Ls	Y	56.	Bar transfer of FS-X technology	Y
24.	Allow use of force against Iraq	Y	57.	Cut defense and raise domestic $	N
25.	Allow $15b in foreign aid for '91	N	58.	Uniform poll closing in 48 states	N
26.	Revise & extend legal immigration	Y	59.	Req foreign investment disclosure	Y
27.	Suspend aid to Angolan rebels	N	60.	Textile import quotas-veto override	N
28.	Democratic tax plan proposals	N	61.	Bar abortion funding in Wash, DC	Y
29.	Cut defense 5% across the board	N	62.	Notify spouses of AIDS+ carriers	N
30.	Textile import quotas-veto override	N	63.	Seize conveyance-drug trafficking	Y
31.	Abortion service for military abroad	N	64.	South Africa sanctions	N
32.	Limits on high income farmers	N	65.	60 days' notice of plant closings	N
33.	Family medical leave-veto override	N	66.	Close unneeded military bases	Y

KASICH, JOHN R. (continued)

67. Keep welfare reform within $2.8b	Y	
68. Allow children housing exclusion	N	
69. Shift $400m of NASA to homeless	N	
70. Cap Medicare patients' liability	Y	
71. Prohibit employee polygraph testing	N	
72. Allow CIA to fund Contras	Y	
73. Revise unfair trade practices	N	
74. Focus SDI on accidental launch	N	
75. Bar Air Force $ for MX missile	N	
76. Allow "real" increase in defense	Y	
77. Troop reduction in Europe of 50%	N	
78. Ban nuclear tests above 1 kiloton	N	
79. Ban anti-satellite missile tests	N	
80. Observe certain limits of SALT II	N	
81. Restore four Civil Rights laws	N	
82. Prohibit aliens as strikebreakers	N	
83. Allow military malpractice suits	Y	
84. Approval of $36m in Contra aid	Y	
85. $18b deficit reduction compromise	N	
86. Welfare reform of $5.7b for 5 years	N	
87. Raise taxes $12b/cut spending $3b	N	
88. Board to assess occupational risk	N	
89. Balanced budget by '93-via targets	Y	
90. Bar licensing of two nuclear plants	N	
91. Remove victims compensation cap	N	
92. Catastrophic health insurance	Y	
93. Ban airline smoking-2 hours or less	Y	
94. $1b/two year aid for the homeless	Y	
95. Bar non-unions in union companies	N	
96. Increase FSLIC rescue to $15b	N	
97. Impose quotas to lower trade deficit	N	
98. Reduce discretionary budget 21%	N	
99. Immigration reform/alien amnesty	N	
100. South Africa sanctions-veto override	Y	
101. Tax overhaul to revise income tax	Y	
102. Use of military in drug war	Y	
103. Delete 12 MX/add conventional wpn	N	

104. Raise speed limit to 65 mph	Y	
105. Require Pentagon to buy US goods	Y	
106. AIDS insurance non-discrimination	N	
107. Prohibit Saudi arms sales	Y	
108. Ease Gun Control Act of 1968	Y	
109. Bar interstate handgun transport	N	
110. Make company emissions known	N	
111. Allow toxic victims to sue in fed ct	N	
112. Superfund waste cleanup of $10b	N	
113. 90 days notice of plant closings	N	
114. $20b in Medicare cuts/tax increases	N	
115. Spending cuts and tax increases	N	
116. Set school lunch lmt-250% poverty	Y	
117. $75m for youth work projects	N	
118. Allow Angolan military assistance	Y	
119. Suspend defense payments for abuse	N	
120. Drop SS COLAs/$12b tax increase	N	
121. Approve $1.5b for 21 MX missiles	Y	
122. Emergency farm credit/revisions	N	
123. Duty on Taiwan/Hong Kong/S Korea	Y	
124. Limit steel imports to 17%	Y	
125. Cut $ to schools that bar prayer	Y	
126. $50b-taxes; cut Medicare/spending	N	
127. Limit Pershing II/cruise in Europe	N	
128. Delete $7.1b for 34 B-1 bombers	N	
129. Bar purchase of Sergeant York guns	N	
130. El Salvador military/economic aid	Y	
131. Bar mining of Nicaraguan waters	N	
132. Physician fee freeze for Medicare	Y	
133. $49b in "sin"/phone/insurance taxes	Y	
134. Allow sale of Conrail	Y	
135. Equal Rights Amendment	N	
136. Authorize Marines in Lebanon	N	
137. Eminent domain for coal companies	N	
138. Prohibit EPA clean air sanctions	Y	
139. SS retirement age increase/reforms	Y	

Presidential Support Score: 1991 - 77%   1990 - 69%

PEASE, DONALD J. -- Ohio 13th District [Democrat]. Counties of Ashland, Huron (pt.), Loran (pt.), Medina, Richland (pt.) and Summit (pt.). Prior Terms: 1977-92. Born: September 26, 1931; Toledo, OH. Education: Ohio University (B.S., M.A.); King's College, University of Durham. Military Service: U.S. Army, 1955-57. Occupation: Newspaper editor; Oberlin city councilman (1962-64); Ohio senator (1965-66, 1975-76); Ohio representative (1969-74).

1. Protection to Haitian refugees	N	
2. Raise tax on wealthy; lower others	Y	
3. Investigate Reagan hostage delay	Y	
4. Campaign finance revisions	Y	
5. Unpaid leave to care for children	Y	
6. Restrict NEA use of funds	N	
7. Bar race-bias claim/habeas corpus	N	
8. Ban race as death sentence factor	N	
9. Exceptions to exclusionary rule	N	
10. Allow sale of assault weapons	N	
11. Life in prison/abolish death penalty	N	
12. Req conspiracy-price fixing cases	N	
13. Unemployment benefits extension	Y	
14. Tissue use of aborted fetuses	Y	
15. Bar replacement of union strikers	Y	
16. Hold foreign aid at $15b for '92	N	
17. Restore space station funding	Y	

18. Civil Rights Act of 1991	Y	
19. Unlimited damages-discrimination	N	
20. Eliminate funds for supercollider	N	
21. Terminate SDI except for research	Y	
22. Req 7-day handgun waiting period	Y	
23. Provide $30b for failed S&Ls	N	
24. Allow use of force against Iraq	N	
25. Allow $15b in foreign aid for '91	N	
26. Revise & extend legal immigration	Y	
27. Suspend aid to Angolan rebels	Y	
28. Democratic tax plan proposals	Y	
29. Cut defense 5% across the board	N	
30. Textile import quotas-veto override	N	
31. Abortion service for military abroad	Y	
32. Limits on high income farmers	Y	
33. Family medical leave-veto override	Y	
34. Req submission of balanced budget	Y	

PEASE, DONALD J. (continued)

35. Balanced budget amendment	N	
36. Amendment to ban flag desecration	N	
37. Reauthorize Amtrak-veto override	Y	
38. Retraining aid for coal miners	Y	
39. Suspend El Salvador military aid	Y	
40. Expand child care aid/tax credit	Y	
41. Raise House salary/omit honoraria	Y	
42. Toughen oil-spill liability	N	
43. Restitution to Japanese interned	Y	
44. Protect Chinese & C.A. nationals	Y	
45. Abortion $ for rape/incest cases	Y	
46. Allow religious schools to bar gays	N	
47. Bar broadcaster fairness doctrine	Y	
48. Bar cap gains cut/reinstate IRA	Y	
49. Bar unions equal voice in pension	N	
50. Bar assembly of chemical weapons	Y	
51. Ban plutonium/uranium production	Y	
52. Cap MX missile deployment at 50	Y	
53. Allow $3b for 2 stealth bombers	N	
54. Publish bio-warfare experiments	Y	
55. Raise minimum wage-veto override	Y	
56. Bar transfer of FS-X technology	Y	
57. Cut defense and raise domestic $	N	
58. Uniform poll closing in 48 states	N	
59. Req foreign investment disclosure	N	
60. Textile import quotas-veto override	N	
61. Bar abortion funding in Wash, DC	N	
62. Notify spouses of AIDS+ carriers	N	
63. Seize conveyance-drug trafficking	N	
64. South Africa sanctions	Y	
65. 60 days' notice of plant closings	Y	
66. Close unneeded military bases	Y	
67. Keep welfare reform within $2.8b	N	
68. Allow children housing exclusion	Y	
69. Shift $400m of NASA to homeless	Y	
70. Cap Medicare patients' liability	Y	
71. Prohibit employee polygraph testing	Y	
72. Allow CIA to fund Contras	N	
73. Revise unfair trade practices	Y	
74. Focus SDI on accidental launch	N	
75. Bar Air Force $ for MX missile	Y	
76. Allow "real" increase in defense	N	
77. Troop reduction in Europe of 50%	N	
78. Ban nuclear tests above 1 kiloton	#	
79. Ban anti-satellite missile tests	Y	
80. Observe certain limits of SALT II	Y	
81. Restore four Civil Rights laws	Y	
82. Prohibit aliens as strikebreakers	Y	
83. Allow military malpractice suits	Y	
84. Approval of $36m in Contra aid	N	
85. $18b deficit reduction compromise	Y	
86. Welfare reform of $5.7b for 5 years	Y	
87. Raise taxes $12b/cut spending $3b	Y	
88. Board to assess occupational risk	Y	
89. Balanced budget by '93-via targets	Y	

90. Bar licensing of two nuclear plants	Y	
91. Remove victims compensation cap	N	
92. Catastrophic health insurance	Y	
93. Ban airline smoking-2 hours or less	Y	
94. $1b/two year aid for the homeless	Y	
95. Bar non-unions in union companies	Y	
96. Increase FSLIC rescue to $15b	Y	
97. Impose quotas to lower trade deficit	Y	
98. Reduce discretionary budget 21%	Y	
99. Immigration reform/alien amnesty	Y	
100. South Africa sanctions-veto override	Y	
101. Tax overhaul to revise income tax	Y	
102. Use of military in drug war	N	
103. Delete 12 MX/add conventional wpn	Y	
104. Raise speed limit to 65 mph	N	
105. Require Pentagon to buy US goods	Y	
106. AIDS insurance non-discrimination	Y	
107. Prohibit Saudi arms sales	Y	
108. Ease Gun Control Act of 1968	Y	
109. Bar interstate handgun transport	Y	
110. Make company emissions known	Y	
111. Allow toxic victims to sue in fed ct	N	
112. Superfund waste cleanup of $10b	Y	
113. 90 days notice of plant closings	Y	
114. $20b in Medicare cuts/tax increases	Y	
115. Spending cuts and tax increases	Y	
116. Set school lunch lmt-250% poverty	N	
117. $75m for youth work projects	Y	
118. Allow Angolan military assistance	N	
119. Suspend defense payments for abuse	N	
120. Drop SS COLAs/$12b tax increase	Y	
121. Approve $1.5b for 21 MX missiles	N	
122. Emergency farm credit/revisions	Y	
123. Duty on Taiwan/Hong Kong/S Korea	N	
124. Limit steel imports to 17%	Y	
125. Cut $ to schools that bar prayer	N	
126. $50b-taxes; cut Medicare/spending	Y	
127. Limit Pershing II/cruise in Europe	Y	
128. Delete $7.1b for 34 B-1 bombers	Y	
129. Bar purchase of Sergeant York guns	Y	
130. El Salvador military/economic aid	N	
131. Bar mining of Nicaraguan waters	Y	
132. Physician fee freeze for Medicare	N	
133. $49b in "sin"/phone/insurance taxes	Y	
134. Allow sale of Conrail	Y	
135. Equal Rights Amendment	Y	
136. Authorize Marines in Lebanon	N	
137. Eminent domain for coal companies	N	
138. Prohibit EPA clean air sanctions	Y	
139. SS retirement age increase/reforms	N	
140. Auto domestic content requirement	Y	
141. Delete jobs program funding	N	
142. Highway-gas tax bill	Y	
143. Cut $5b from defense for Medicare	Y	
144. Emergency housing aid of $1b	Y	

Presidential Support Score: 1991 - 39%   1990 - 30%

SAWYER, THOMAS C. -- Ohio 14th District [Democrat]. County of Summit (pt.). **Prior Terms:** 1987-92. **Born:** August 15, 1945; Akron, OH. **Education:** University of Akron (B.A., M.A.). **Occupation:** Public school teacher; administrator, state school for delinquent boys; legislative agent, Public Utilities Commission; state representative (1977-83); Akron mayor (1984-86).

SAWYER, THOMAS C. (continued)

1. Protection to Haitian refugees	Y	50. Bar assembly of chemical weapons	Y
2. Raise tax on wealthy; lower others	Y	51. Ban plutonium/uranium production	Y
3. Investigate Reagan hostage delay	Y	52. Cap MX missile deployment at 50	Y
4. Campaign finance revisions	Y	53. Allow $3b for 2 stealth bombers	N
5. Unpaid leave to care for children	Y	54. Publish bio-warfare experiments	Y
6. Restrict NEA use of funds	N	55. Raise minimum wage-veto override	Y
7. Bar race-bias claim/habeas corpus	N	56. Bar transfer of FS-X technology	Y
8. Ban race as death sentence factor	N	57. Cut defense and raise domestic $	N
9. Exceptions to exclusionary rule	N	58. Uniform poll closing in 48 states	N
10. Allow sale of assault weapons	N	59. Req foreign investment disclosure	Y
11. Life in prison/abolish death penalty	Y	60. Textile import quotas-veto override	N
12. Req conspiracy-price fixing cases	N	61. Bar abortion funding in Wash, DC	N
13. Unemployment benefits extension	Y	62. Notify spouses of AIDS+ carriers	N
14. Tissue use of aborted fetuses	Y	63. Seize conveyance-drug trafficking	N
15. Bar replacement of union strikers	Y	64. South Africa sanctions	Y
16. Hold foreign aid at $15b for '92	Y	65. 60 days' notice of plant closings	Y
17. Restore space station funding	Y	66. Close unneeded military bases	N
18. Civil Rights Act of 1991	Y	67. Keep welfare reform within $2.8b	N
19. Unlimited damages-discrimination	Y	68. Allow children housing exclusion	N
20. Eliminate funds for supercollider	Y	69. Shift $400m of NASA to homeless	Y
21. Terminate SDI except for research	Y	70. Cap Medicare patients' liability	Y
22. Req 7-day handgun waiting period	Y	71. Prohibit employee polygraph testing	Y
23. Provide $30b for failed S&Ls	Y	72. Allow CIA to fund Contras	N
24. Allow use of force against Iraq	N	73. Revise unfair trade practices	Y
25. Allow $15b in foreign aid for '91	Y	74. Focus SDI on accidental launch	Y
26. Revise & extend legal immigration	Y	75. Bar Air Force $ for MX missile	Y
27. Suspend aid to Angolan rebels	Y	76. Allow "real" increase in defense	N
28. Democratic tax plan proposals	Y	77. Troop reduction in Europe of 50%	N
29. Cut defense 5% across the board	Y	78. Ban nuclear tests above 1 kiloton	Y
30. Textile import quotas-veto override	N	79. Ban anti-satellite missile tests	Y
31. Abortion service for military abroad	Y	80. Observe certain limits of SALT II	Y
32. Limits on high income farmers	N	81. Restore four Civil Rights laws	Y
33. Family medical leave-veto override	Y	82. Prohibit aliens as strikebreakers	Y
34. Req submission of balanced budget	Y	83. Allow military malpractice suits	Y
35. Balanced budget amendment	N	84. Approval of $36m in Contra aid	N
36. Amendment to ban flag desecration	N	85. $18b deficit reduction compromise	Y
37. Reauthorize Amtrak-veto override	Y	86. Welfare reform of $5.7b for 5 years	Y
38. Retraining aid for coal miners	Y	87. Raise taxes $12b/cut spending $3b	Y
39. Suspend El Salvador military aid	Y	88. Board to assess occupational risk	Y
40. Expand child care aid/tax credit	Y	89. Balanced budget by '93-via targets	Y
41. Raise House salary/omit honoraria	Y	90. Bar licensing of two nuclear plants	Y
42. Toughen oil-spill liability	N	91. Remove victims compensation cap	N
43. Restitution to Japanese interned	Y	92. Catastrophic health insurance	Y
44. Protect Chinese & C.A. nationals	Y	93. Ban airline smoking-2 hours or less	Y
45. Abortion $ for rape/incest cases	Y	94. $1b/two year aid for the homeless	Y
46. Allow religious schools to bar gays	N	95. Bar non-unions in union companies	Y
47. Bar broadcaster fairness doctrine	N	96. Increase FSLIC rescue to $15b	N
48. Bar cap gains cut/reinstate IRA	Y	97. Impose quotas to lower trade deficit	Y
49. Bar unions equal voice in pension	N	98. Reduce discretionary budget 21%	Y

Presidential Support Score: 1991 - 31%   1990 - 21%

WYLIE, CHALMERS P. -- Ohio 15th District [Republican]. Counties of Franklin (pt.) and Madison (pt.).   Prior Terms: 1967-92.   Born: November 23, 1920; Norwich, OH. Education: Otterbein College; Ohio State University; Harvard Law School. Military Service: U.S. Army. Occupation: Assistant attorney general (1948, 1951-53); assistant city attorney (1949-50); city attorney (1953); administrator, Bureau of Workmen's Compensation (1957); partner, Gingher & Christensen (1959); Ohio legislator (1961-66).

1. Protection to Haitian refugees	N	5. Unpaid leave to care for children	N
2. Raise tax on wealthy; lower others	N	6. Restrict NEA use of funds	Y
3. Investigate Reagan hostage delay	N	7. Bar race-bias claim/habeas corpus	Y
4. Campaign finance revisions	N	8. Ban race as death sentence factor	Y

WYLIE, CHALMERS P. (continued)

9. Exceptions to exclusionary rule	Y
10. Allow sale of assault weapons	N
11. Life in prison/abolish death penalty	N
12. Req conspiracy-price fixing cases	Y
13. Unemployment benefits extension	N
14. Tissue use of aborted fetuses	N
15. Bar replacement of union strikers	N
16. Hold foreign aid at $15b for '92	N
17. Restore space station funding	Y
18. Civil Rights Act of 1991	N
19. Unlimited damages-discrimination	N
20. Eliminate funds for supercollider	N
21. Terminate SDI except for research	N
22. Req 7-day handgun waiting period	Y
23. Provide $30b for failed S&Ls	Y
24. Allow use of force against Iraq	Y
25. Allow $15b in foreign aid for '91	N
26. Revise & extend legal immigration	Y
27. Suspend aid to Angolan rebels	N
28. Democratic tax plan proposals	N
29. Cut defense 5% across the board	N
30. Textile import quotas-veto override	N
31. Abortion service for military abroad	N
32. Limits on high income farmers	Y
33. Family medical leave-veto override	N
34. Req submission of balanced budget	N
35. Balanced budget amendment	Y
36. Amendment to ban flag desecration	Y
37. Reauthorize Amtrak-veto override	N
38. Retraining aid for coal miners	N
39. Suspend El Salvador military aid	N
40. Expand child care aid/tax credit	Y
41. Raise House salary/omit honoraria	N
42. Toughen oil-spill liability	N
43. Restitution to Japanese interned	N
44. Protect Chinese & C.A. nationals	N
45. Abortion $ for rape/incest cases	N
46. Allow religious schools to bar gays	Y
47. Bar broadcaster fairness doctrine	Y
48. Bar cap gains cut/reinstate IRA	N
49. Bar unions equal voice in pension	Y
50. Bar assembly of chemical weapons	N
51. Ban plutonium/uranium production	Y
52. Cap MX missile deployment at 50	N
53. Allow $3b for 2 stealth bombers	Y
54. Publish bio-warfare experiments	N
55. Raise minimum wage-veto override	N
56. Bar transfer of FS-X technology	N
57. Cut defense and raise domestic $	N
58. Uniform poll closing in 48 states	?
59. Req foreign investment disclosure	N
60. Textile import quotas-veto override	N
61. Bar abortion funding in Wash, DC	Y
62. Notify spouses of AIDS+ carriers	Y
63. Seize conveyance-drug trafficking	Y
64. South Africa sanctions	Y
65. 60 days' notice of plant closings	N
66. Close unneeded military bases	N
67. Keep welfare reform within $2.8b	Y
68. Allow children housing exclusion	N
69. Shift $400m of NASA to homeless	N
70. Cap Medicare patients' liability	Y
71. Prohibit employee polygraph testing	Y
72. Allow CIA to fund Contras	Y

73. Revise unfair trade practices	N
74. Focus SDI on accidental launch	N
75. Bar Air Force $ for MX missile	N
76. Allow "real" increase in defense	?
77. Troop reduction in Europe of 50%	N
78. Ban nuclear tests above 1 kiloton	N
79. Ban anti-satellite missile tests	N
80. Observe certain limits of SALT II	N
81. Restore four Civil Rights laws	N
82. Prohibit aliens as strikebreakers	Y
83. Allow military malpractice suits	Y
84. Approval of $36m in Contra aid	Y
85. $18b deficit reduction compromise	Y
86. Welfare reform of $5.7b for 5 years	N
87. Raise taxes $12b/cut spending $3b	?
88. Board to assess occupational risk	N
89. Balanced budget by '93-via targets	Y
90. Bar licensing of two nuclear plants	N
91. Remove victims compensation cap	N
92. Catastrophic health insurance	Y
93. Ban airline smoking-2 hours or less	?
94. $1b/two year aid for the homeless	Y
95. Bar non-unions in union companies	N
96. Increase FSLIC rescue to $15b	Y
97. Impose quotas to lower trade deficit	N
98. Reduce discretionary budget 21%	Y
99. Immigration reform/alien amnesty	N
100. South Africa sanctions-veto override	Y
101. Tax overhaul to revise income tax	Y
102. Use of military in drug war	Y
103. Delete 12 MX/add conventional wpn	N
104. Raise speed limit to 65 mph	N
105. Require Pentagon to buy US goods	Y
106. AIDS insurance non-discrimination	N
107. Prohibit Saudi arms sales	Y
108. Ease Gun Control Act of 1968	N
109. Bar interstate handgun transport	N
110. Make company emissions known	N
111. Allow toxic victims to sue in fed ct	N
112. Superfund waste cleanup of $10b	Y
113. 90 days notice of plant closings	N
114. $20b in Medicare cuts/tax increases	N
115. Spending cuts and tax increases	N
116. Set school lunch lmt-250% poverty	Y
117. $75m for youth work projects	N
118. Allow Angolan military assistance	Y
119. Suspend defense payments for abuse	N
120. Drop SS COLAs/$12b tax increase	N
121. Approve $1.5b for 21 MX missiles	Y
122. Emergency farm credit/revisions	N
123. Duty on Taiwan/Hong Kong/S Korea	N
124. Limit steel imports to 17%	Y
125. Cut $ to schools that bar prayer	Y
126. $50b-taxes; cut Medicare/spending	N
127. Limit Pershing II/cruise in Europe	N
128. Delete $7.1b for 34 B-1 bombers	N
129. Bar purchase of Sergeant York guns	N
130. El Salvador military/economic aid	Y
131. Bar mining of Nicaraguan waters	N
132. Physician fee freeze for Medicare	Y
133. $49b in "sin"/phone/insurance taxes	Y
134. Allow sale of Conrail	?
135. Equal Rights Amendment	N
136. Authorize Marines in Lebanon	Y

WYLIE, CHALMERS P. (continued)

137. Eminent domain for coal companies	N	141. Delete jobs program funding	Y
138. Prohibit EPA clean air sanctions	N	142. Highway-gas tax bill	Y
139. SS retirement age increase/reforms	Y	143. Cut $5b from defense for Medicare	Y
140. Auto domestic content requirement	Y	144. Emergency housing aid of $1b	Y

Presidential Support Score: 1991 - 83% 1990 - 69%

REGULA, RALPH -- Ohio 16th District [Republican]. Counties of Carroll (pt.), Holmes, Stark and Wayne. Prior Terms: 1973-92. Born: December 3, 1924; Beach City, OH. Education: Mount Union College (B.A.); William McKinley School of Law (LL.B.). Military Service: U.S. Navy, WW II. Occupation: Attorney; director, Stark County Bar Assn.; member, Ohio Board of Education (1960-64); Ohio representative (1965 66); Ohio senator (1967-72).

1. Protection to Haitian refugees	N	51. Ban plutonium/uranium production	Y
2. Raise tax on wealthy; lower others	N	52. Cap MX missile deployment at 50	N
3. Investigate Reagan hostage delay	N	53. Allow $3b for 2 stealth bombers	N
4. Campaign finance revisions	N	54. Publish bio-warfare experiments	Y
5. Unpaid leave to care for children	Y	55. Raise minimum wage-veto override	N
6. Restrict NEA use of funds	Y	56. Bar transfer of FS-X technology	Y
7. Bar race-bias claim/habeas corpus	Y	57. Cut defense and raise domestic $	N
8. Ban race as death sentence factor	Y	58. Uniform poll closing in 48 states	N
9. Exceptions to exclusionary rule	Y	59. Req foreign investment disclosure	Y
10. Allow sale of assault weapons	Y	60. Textile import quotas-veto override	Y
11. Life in prison/abolish death penalty	N	61. Bar abortion funding in Wash, DC	Y
12. Req conspiracy-price fixing cases	Y	62. Notify spouses of AIDS+ carriers	Y
13. Unemployment benefits extension	Y	63. Seize conveyance-drug trafficking	Y
14. Tissue use of aborted fetuses	N	64. South Africa sanctions	N
15. Bar replacement of union strikers	Y	65. 60 days' notice of plant closings	Y
16. Hold foreign aid at $15b for '92	Y	66. Close unneeded military bases	Y
17. Restore space station funding	Y	67. Keep welfare reform within $2.8b	Y
18. Civil Rights Act of 1991	N	68. Allow children housing exclusion	N
19. Unlimited damages-discrimination	N	69. Shift $400m of NASA to homeless	N
20. Eliminate funds for supercollider	Y	70. Cap Medicare patients' liability	Y
21. Terminate SDI except for research	N	71. Prohibit employee polygraph testing	Y
22. Req 7-day handgun waiting period	Y	72. Allow CIA to fund Contras	N
23. Provide $30b for failed S&Ls	Y	73. Revise unfair trade practices	Y
24. Allow use of force against Iraq	Y	74. Focus SDI on accidental launch	N
25. Allow $15b in foreign aid for '91	N	75. Bar Air Force $ for MX missile	N
26. Revise & extend legal immigration	N	76. Allow "real" increase in defense	N
27. Suspend aid to Angolan rebels	N	77. Troop reduction in Europe of 50%	N
28. Democratic tax plan proposals	N	78. Ban nuclear tests above 1 kiloton	N
29. Cut defense 5% across the board	N	79. Ban anti-satellite missile tests	N
30. Textile import quotas-veto override	Y	80. Observe certain limits of SALT II	N
31. Abortion service for military abroad	N	81. Restore four Civil Rights laws	N
32. Limits on high income farmers	Y	82. Prohibit aliens as strikebreakers	Y
33. Family medical leave-veto override	Y	83. Allow military malpractice suits	Y
34. Req submission of balanced budget	Y	84. Approval of $36m in Contra aid	Y
35. Balanced budget amendment	Y	85. $18b deficit reduction compromise	N
36. Amendment to ban flag desecration	Y	86. Welfare reform of $5.7b for 5 years	N
37. Reauthorize Amtrak-veto override	Y	87. Raise taxes $12b/cut spending $3b	N
38. Retraining aid for coal miners	Y	88. Board to assess occupational risk	N
39. Suspend El Salvador military aid	Y	89. Balanced budget by '93-via targets	Y
40. Expand child care aid/tax credit	N	90. Bar licensing of two nuclear plants	N
41. Raise House salary/omit honoraria	Y	91. Remove victims compensation cap	N
42. Toughen oil-spill liability	N	92. Catastrophic health insurance	Y
43. Restitution to Japanese interned	N	93. Ban airline smoking-2 hours or less	Y
44. Protect Chinese & C.A. nationals	Y	94. $1b/two year aid for the homeless	Y
45. Abortion $ for rape/incest cases	N	95. Bar non-unions in union companies	N
46. Allow religious schools to bar gays	Y	96. Increase FSLIC rescue to $15b	Y
47. Bar broadcaster fairness doctrine	Y	97. Impose quotas to lower trade deficit	Y
48. Bar cap gains cut/reinstate IRA	N	98. Reduce discretionary budget 21%	Y
49. Bar unions equal voice in pension	Y	99. Immigration reform/alien amnesty	N
50. Bar assembly of chemical weapons	Y	100. South Africa sanctions-veto override	Y

REGULA, RALPH (continued)

101. Tax overhaul to revise income tax	N	
102. Use of military in drug war	Y	
103. Delete 12 MX/add conventional wpn	N	
104. Raise speed limit to 65 mph	N	
105. Require Pentagon to buy US goods	Y	
106. AIDS insurance non-discrimination	N	
107. Prohibit Saudi arms sales	Y	
108. Ease Gun Control Act of 1968	Y	
109. Bar interstate handgun transport	N	
110. Make company emissions known	N	
111. Allow toxic victims to sue in fed ct	N	
112. Superfund waste cleanup of $10b	Y	
113. 90 days notice of plant closings	N	
114. $20b in Medicare cuts/tax increases	N	
115. Spending cuts and tax increases	N	
116. Set school lunch lmt-250% poverty	Y	
117. $75m for youth work projects	Y	
118. Allow Angolan military assistance	Y	
119. Suspend defense payments for abuse	N	
120. Drop SS COLAs/$12b tax increase	N	
121. Approve $1.5b for 21 MX missiles	Y	
122. Emergency farm credit/revisions	Y	
123. Duty on Taiwan/Hong Kong/S Korea	Y	
124. Limit steel imports to 17%	Y	
125. Cut $ to schools that bar prayer	Y	
126. $50b-taxes; cut Medicare/spending	Y	
127. Limit Pershing II/cruise in Europe	N	
128. Delete $7.1b for 34 B-1 bombers	N	
129. Bar purchase of Sergeant York guns	N	
130. El Salvador military/economic aid	Y	
131. Bar mining of Nicaraguan waters	Y	
132. Physician fee freeze for Medicare	Y	
133. $49b in "sin"/phone/insurance taxes	Y	
134. Allow sale of Conrail	N	
135. Equal Rights Amendment	Y	
136. Authorize Marines in Lebanon	Y	
137. Eminent domain for coal companies	N	
138. Prohibit EPA clean air sanctions	N	
139. SS retirement age increase/reforms	N	
140. Auto domestic content requirement	Y	
141. Delete jobs program funding	Y	
142. Highway-gas tax bill	N	
143. Cut $5b from defense for Medicare	N	
144. Emergency housing aid of $1b	Y	

Presidential Support Score: 1991 - 69%   1990 - 56%

TRAFICANT, JAMES A., Jr. -- Ohio 17th District [Democrat]. Counties of Columbiana (pt.), Mahoning and Trumbull (pt.). Prior Terms: 1985-92. Born: May 8, 1941; Youngstown, OH. Education: University of Pittsburgh (B.S.); Youngstown State (M.S.). Occupation: Sheriff; director, county drug program; consumer finance director.

1. Protection to Haitian refugees	Y	
2. Raise tax on wealthy; lower others	N	
3. Investigate Reagan hostage delay	Y	
4. Campaign finance revisions	Y	
5. Unpaid leave to care for children	Y	
6. Restrict NEA use of funds	Y	
7. Bar race-bias claim/habeas corpus	N	
8. Ban race as death sentence factor	N	
9. Exceptions to exclusionary rule	Y	
10. Allow sale of assault weapons	N	
11. Life in prison/abolish death penalty	N	
12. Req conspiracy-price fixing cases	N	
13. Unemployment benefits extension	Y	
14. Tissue use of aborted fetuses	Y	
15. Bar replacement of union strikers	Y	
16. Hold foreign aid at $15b for '92	N	
17. Restore space station funding	Y	
18. Civil Rights Act of 1991	Y	
19. Unlimited damages-discrimination	Y	
20. Eliminate funds for supercollider	N	
21. Terminate SDI except for research	Y	
22. Req 7-day handgun waiting period	Y	
23. Provide $30b for failed S&Ls	N	
24. Allow use of force against Iraq	N	
25. Allow $15b in foreign aid for '91	N	
26. Revise & extend legal immigration	N	
27. Suspend aid to Angolan rebels	Y	
28. Democratic tax plan proposals	N	
29. Cut defense 5% across the board	N	
30. Textile import quotas-veto override	Y	
31. Abortion service for military abroad	Y	
32. Limits on high income farmers	N	
33. Family medical leave-veto override	Y	
34. Req submission of balanced budget	Y	
35. Balanced budget amendment	N	
36. Amendment to ban flag desecration	Y	
37. Reauthorize Amtrak-veto override	Y	
38. Retraining aid for coal miners	Y	
39. Suspend El Salvador military aid	Y	
40. Expand child care aid/tax credit	Y	
41. Raise House salary/omit honoraria	N	
42. Toughen oil-spill liability	N	
43. Restitution to Japanese interned	Y	
44. Protect Chinese & C.A. nationals	N	
45. Abortion $ for rape/incest cases	Y	
46. Allow religious schools to bar gays	Y	
47. Bar broadcaster fairness doctrine	N	
48. Bar cap gains cut/reinstate IRA	Y	
49. Bar unions equal voice in pension	N	
50. Bar assembly of chemical weapons	Y	
51. Ban plutonium/uranium production	Y	
52. Cap MX missile deployment at 50	Y	
53. Allow $3b for 2 stealth bombers	N	
54. Publish bio-warfare experiments	Y	
55. Raise minimum wage-veto override	Y	
56. Bar transfer of FS-X technology	Y	
57. Cut defense and raise domestic $	N	
58. Uniform poll closing in 48 states	Y	
59. Req foreign investment disclosure	Y	
60. Textile import quotas-veto override	Y	
61. Bar abortion funding in Wash, DC	N	
62. Notify spouses of AIDS+ carriers	N	
63. Seize conveyance-drug trafficking	Y	
64. South Africa sanctions	Y	
65. 60 days' notice of plant closings	Y	
66. Close unneeded military bases	N	

TRAFICANT, JAMES A., Jr. (continued)

67. Keep welfare reform within $2.8b	N
68. Allow children housing exclusion	N
69. Shift $400m of NASA to homeless	Y
70. Cap Medicare patients' liability	Y
71. Prohibit employee polygraph testing	Y
72. Allow CIA to fund Contras	N
73. Revise unfair trade practices	Y
74. Focus SDI on accidental launch	Y
75. Bar Air Force $ for MX missile	Y
76. Allow "real" increase in defense	N
77. Troop reduction in Europe of 50%	Y
78. Ban nuclear tests above 1 kiloton	Y
79. Ban anti-satellite missile tests	Y
80. Observe certain limits of SALT II	Y
81. Restore four Civil Rights laws	Y
82. Prohibit aliens as strikebreakers	Y
83. Allow military malpractice suits	Y
84. Approval of $36m in Contra aid	N
85. $18b deficit reduction compromise	N
86. Welfare reform of $5.7b for 5 years	Y
87. Raise taxes $12b/cut spending $3b	#
88. Board to assess occupational risk	Y
89. Balanced budget by '93-via targets	N
90. Bar licensing of two nuclear plants	Y
91. Remove victims compensation cap	N
92. Catastrophic health insurance	Y
93. Ban airline smoking-2 hours or less	N
94. $1b/two year aid for the homeless	Y

95. Bar non-unions in union companies	Y
96. Increase FSLIC rescue to $15b	N
97. Impose quotas to lower trade deficit	Y
98. Reduce discretionary budget 21%	N
99. Immigration reform/alien amnesty	N
100. South Africa sanctions-veto override	Y
101. Tax overhaul to revise income tax	Y
102. Use of military in drug war	Y
103. Delete 12 MX/add conventional wpn	Y
104. Raise speed limit to 65 mph	N
105. Require Pentagon to buy US goods	Y
106. AIDS insurance non-discrimination	Y
107. Prohibit Saudi arms sales	Y
108. Ease Gun Control Act of 1968	N
109. Bar interstate handgun transport	Y
110. Make company emissions known	Y
111. Allow toxic victims to sue in fed ct	Y
112. Superfund waste cleanup of $10b	Y
113. 90 days notice of plant closings	Y
114. $20b in Medicare cuts/tax increases	Y
115. Spending cuts and tax increases	N
116. Set school lunch lmt-250% poverty	N
117. $75m for youth work projects	Y
118. Allow Angolan military assistance	N
119. Suspend defense payments for abuse	Y
120. Drop SS COLAs/$12b tax increase	N
121. Approve $1.5b for 21 MX missiles	N
122. Emergency farm credit/revisions	Y

Presidential Support Score: 1991 - 26% 1990 - 19%

APPLEGATE, DOUGLAS -- Ohio 18th District [Democrat]. Counties of Belmont, Carroll (pt.), Columbiana (pt.), Coshocton, Guernsey (pt.), Harrison, Jefferson, Monroe, Noble and Tuscarawas (pt.). Prior Terms: 1977-92. Born: March 27, 1928; Steubenville, OH. Occupation: Ohio representative (1961-69) Ohio senator (1969-77); Ohio Constitutional Revision commissioner.

1. Protection to Haitian refugees	N
2. Raise tax on wealthy; lower others	Y
3. Investigate Reagan hostage delay	Y
4. Campaign finance revisions	Y
5. Unpaid leave to care for children	Y
6. Restrict NEA use of funds	Y
7. Bar race-bias claim/habeas corpus	N
8. Ban race as death sentence factor	Y
9. Exceptions to exclusionary rule	Y
10. Allow sale of assault weapons	Y
11. Life in prison/abolish death penalty	N
12. Req conspiracy-price fixing cases	N
13. Unemployment benefits extension	Y
14. Tissue use of aborted fetuses	N
15. Bar replacement of union strikers	Y
16. Hold foreign aid at $15b for '92	N
17. Restore space station funding	Y
18. Civil Rights Act of 1991	Y
19. Unlimited damages-discrimination	N
20. Eliminate funds for supercollider	N
21. Terminate SDI except for research	?
22. Req 7-day handgun waiting period	N
23. Provide $30b for failed S&Ls	N
24. Allow use of force against Iraq	N
25. Allow $15b in foreign aid for '91	N
26. Revise & extend legal immigration	N

27. Suspend aid to Angolan rebels	Y
28. Democratic tax plan proposals	N
29. Cut defense 5% across the board	Y
30. Textile import quotas-veto override	Y
31. Abortion service for military abroad	N
32. Limits on high income farmers	N
33. Family medical leave-veto override	Y
34. Req submission of balanced budget	Y
35. Balanced budget amendment	N
36. Amendment to ban flag desecration	Y
37. Reauthorize Amtrak-veto override	Y
38. Retraining aid for coal miners	Y
39. Suspend El Salvador military aid	Y
40. Expand child care aid/tax credit	Y
41. Raise House salary/omit honoraria	N
42. Toughen oil-spill liability	N
43. Restitution to Japanese interned	?
44. Protect Chinese & C.A. nationals	N
45. Abortion $ for rape/incest cases	N
46. Allow religious schools to bar gays	Y
47. Bar broadcaster fairness doctrine	Y
48. Bar cap gains cut/reinstate IRA	Y
49. Bar unions equal voice in pension	Y
50. Bar assembly of chemical weapons	Y
51. Ban plutonium/uranium production	Y
52. Cap MX missile deployment at 50	Y

APPLEGATE, DOUGLAS (continued)

53. Allow $3b for 2 stealth bombers	N	99. Immigration reform/alien amnesty	N
54. Publish bio-warfare experiments	Y	100. South Africa sanctions-veto override	Y
55. Raise minimum wage-veto override	Y	101. Tax overhaul to revise income tax	N
56. Bar transfer of FS-X technology	Y	102. Use of military in drug war	Y
57. Cut defense and raise domestic $	N	103. Delete 12 MX/add conventional wpn	Y
58. Uniform poll closing in 48 states	Y	104. Raise speed limit to 65 mph	N
59. Req foreign investment disclosure	Y	105. Require Pentagon to buy US goods	Y
60. Textile import quotas-veto override	Y	106. AIDS insurance non-discrimination	Y
61. Bar abortion funding in Wash, DC	Y	107. Prohibit Saudi arms sales	Y
62. Notify spouses of AIDS+ carriers	Y	108. Ease Gun Control Act of 1968	Y
63. Seize conveyance-drug trafficking	Y	109. Bar interstate handgun transport	Y
64. South Africa sanctions	Y	110. Make company emissions known	Y
65. 60 days' notice of plant closings	Y	111. Allow toxic victims to sue in fed ct	N
66. Close unneeded military bases	N	112. Superfund waste cleanup of $10b	N
67. Keep welfare reform within $2.8b	N	113. 90 days notice of plant closings	Y
68. Allow children housing exclusion	Y	114. $20b in Medicare cuts/tax increases	N
69. Shift $400m of NASA to homeless	Y	115. Spending cuts and tax increases	N
70. Cap Medicare patients' liability	Y	116. Set school lunch lmt-250% poverty	N
71. Prohibit employee polygraph testing	Y	117. $75m for youth work projects	Y
72. Allow CIA to fund Contras	N	118. Allow Angolan military assistance	N
73. Revise unfair trade practices	Y	119. Suspend defense payments for abuse	Y
74. Focus SDI on accidental launch	N	120. Drop SS COLAs/$12b tax increase	N
75. Bar Air Force $ for MX missile	N	121. Approve $1.5b for 21 MX missiles	N
76. Allow "real" increase in defense	N	122. Emergency farm credit/revisions	Y
77. Troop reduction in Europe of 50%	?	123. Duty on Taiwan/Hong Kong/S Korea	Y
78. Ban nuclear tests above 1 kiloton	Y	124. Limit steel imports to 17%	Y
79. Ban anti-satellite missile tests	N	125. Cut $ to schools that bar prayer	Y
80. Observe certain limits of SALT II	Y	126. $50b-taxes; cut Medicare/spending	N
81. Restore four Civil Rights laws	Y	127. Limit Pershing II/cruise in Europe	N
82. Prohibit aliens as strikebreakers	Y	128. Delete $7.1b for 34 B-1 bombers	N
83. Allow military malpractice suits	?	129. Bar purchase of Sergeant York guns	N
84. Approval of $36m in Contra aid	N	130. El Salvador military/economic aid	N
85. $18b deficit reduction compromise	N	131. Bar mining of Nicaraguan waters	Y
86. Welfare reform of $5.7b for 5 years	Y	132. Physician fee freeze for Medicare	N
87. Raise taxes $12b/cut spending $3b	N	133. $49b in "sin"/phone/insurance taxes	Y
88. Board to assess occupational risk	Y	134. Allow sale of Conrail	N
89. Balanced budget by '93-via targets	N	135. Equal Rights Amendment	Y
90. Bar licensing of two nuclear plants	N	136. Authorize Marines in Lebanon	N
91. Remove victims compensation cap	N	137. Eminent domain for coal companies	N
92. Catastrophic health insurance	Y	138. Prohibit EPA clean air sanctions	Y
93. Ban airline smoking-2 hours or less	N	139. SS retirement age increase/reforms	N
94. $1b/two year aid for the homeless	Y	140. Auto domestic content requirement	Y
95. Bar non-unions in union companies	Y	141. Delete jobs program funding	N
96. Increase FSLIC rescue to $15b	N	142. Highway-gas tax bill	Y
97. Impose quotas to lower trade deficit	Y	143. Cut $5b from defense for Medicare	Y
98. Reduce discretionary budget 21%	Y	144. Emergency housing aid of $1b	Y

Presidential Support Score: 1991 - 41%   1990 - 30%

FEIGHAN, EDWARD F. -- Ohio 19th District [Democrat]. Counties of Cuyahoga (pt.), Lake (pt.) and Lorain (pt.) Prior Terms: 1983-92. Born: October 22, 1947; Lakewood, OH. Education: Loyola University; Cleveland State University (J.D.). Occupation: Ohio representative(1973-78); county commissioner (1979-82); former member, National Advisory Council on Economic Opportunity.

1. Protection to Haitian refugees	Y	9. Exceptions to exclusionary rule	N
2. Raise tax on wealthy; lower others	Y	10. Allow sale of assault weapons	N
3. Investigate Reagan hostage delay	Y	11. Life in prison/abolish death penalty	Y
4. Campaign finance revisions	Y	12. Req conspiracy-price fixing cases	N
5. Unpaid leave to care for children	Y	13. Unemployment benefits extension	Y
6. Restrict NEA use of funds	N	14. Tissue use of aborted fetuses	Y
7. Bar race-bias claim/habeas corpus	N	15. Bar replacement of union strikers	Y
8. Ban race as death sentence factor	N	16. Hold foreign aid at $15b for '92	Y

FEIGHAN, EDWARD F. (continued)

17. Restore space station funding	Y	79. Ban anti-satellite missile tests	Y
18. Civil Rights Act of 1991	Y	80. Observe certain limits of SALT II	Y
19. Unlimited damages-discrimination	Y	81. Restore four Civil Rights laws	Y
20. Eliminate funds for supercollider	Y	82. Prohibit aliens as strikebreakers	Y
21. Terminate SDI except for research	Y	83. Allow military malpractice suits	Y
22. Req 7-day handgun waiting period	Y	84. Approval of $36m in Contra aid	N
23. Provide $30b for failed S&Ls	N	85. $18b deficit reduction compromise	Y
24. Allow use of force against Iraq	N	86. Welfare reform of $5.7b for 5 years	Y
25. Allow $15b in foreign aid for '91	Y	87. Raise taxes $12b/cut spending $3b	Y
26. Revise & extend legal immigration	Y	88. Board to assess occupational risk	Y
27. Suspend aid to Angolan rebels	Y	89. Balanced budget by '93-via targets	Y
28. Democratic tax plan proposals	Y	90. Bar licensing of two nuclear plants	Y
29. Cut defense 5% across the board	Y	91. Remove victims compensation cap	Y
30. Textile import quotas-veto override	Y	92. Catastrophic health insurance	Y
31. Abortion service for military abroad	?	93. Ban airline smoking-2 hours or less	Y
32. Limits on high income farmers	Y	94. $1b/two year aid for the homeless	Y
33. Family medical leave-veto override	Y	95. Bar non-unions in union companies	Y
34. Req submission of balanced budget	Y	96. Increase FSLIC rescue to $15b	N
35. Balanced budget amendment	N	97. Impose quotas to lower trade deficit	Y
36. Amendment to ban flag desecration	N	98. Reduce discretionary budget 21%	Y
37. Reauthorize Amtrak-veto override	Y	99. Immigration reform/alien amnesty	Y
38. Retraining aid for coal miners	Y	100. South Africa sanctions-veto override	Y
39. Suspend El Salvador military aid	Y	101. Tax overhaul to revise income tax	Y
40. Expand child care aid/tax credit	Y	102. Use of military in drug war	N
41. Raise House salary/omit honoraria	N	103. Delete 12 MX/add conventional wpn	Y
42. Toughen oil-spill liability	N	104. Raise speed limit to 65 mph	N
43. Restitution to Japanese interned	Y	105. Require Pentagon to buy US goods	Y
44. Protect Chinese & C.A. nationals	Y	106. AIDS insurance non-discrimination	Y
45. Abortion $ for rape/incest cases	Y	107. Prohibit Saudi arms sales	Y
46. Allow religious schools to bar gays	?	108. Ease Gun Control Act of 1968	N
47. Bar broadcaster fairness doctrine	N	109. Bar interstate handgun transport	Y
48. Bar cap gains cut/reinstate IRA	Y	110. Make company emissions known	N
49. Bar unions equal voice in pension	N	111. Allow toxic victims to sue in fed ct	Y
50. Bar assembly of chemical weapons	Y	112. Superfund waste cleanup of $10b	N
51. Ban plutonium/uranium production	Y	113. 90 days notice of plant closings	Y
52. Cap MX missile deployment at 50	Y	114. $20b in Medicare cuts/tax increases	Y
53. Allow $3b for 2 stealth bombers	N	115. Spending cuts and tax increases	Y
54. Publish bio-warfare experiments	Y	116. Set school lunch lmt-250% poverty	N
55. Raise minimum wage-veto override	Y	117. $75m for youth work projects	Y
56. Bar transfer of FS-X technology	Y	118. Allow Angolan military assistance	N
57. Cut defense and raise domestic $	N	119. Suspend defense payments for abuse	Y
58. Uniform poll closing in 48 states	Y	120. Drop SS COLAs/$12b tax increase	N
59. Req foreign investment disclosure	Y	121. Approve $1.5b for 21 MX missiles	N
60. Textile import quotas-veto override	Y	122. Emergency farm credit/revisions	Y
61. Bar abortion funding in Wash, DC	N	123. Duty on Taiwan/Hong Kong/S Korea	Y
62. Notify spouses of AIDS+ carriers	N	124. Limit steel imports to 17%	Y
63. Seize conveyance-drug trafficking	N	125. Cut $ to schools that bar prayer	N
64. South Africa sanctions	Y	126. $50b-taxes; cut Medicare/spending	N
65. 60 days' notice of plant closings	Y	127. Limit Pershing II/cruise in Europe	Y
66. Close unneeded military bases	N	128. Delete $7.1b for 34 B-1 bombers	Y
67. Keep welfare reform within $2.8b	N	129. Bar purchase of Sergeant York guns	Y
68. Allow children housing exclusion	N	130. El Salvador military/economic aid	N
69. Shift $400m of NASA to homeless	N	131. Bar mining of Nicaraguan waters	Y
70. Cap Medicare patients' liability	Y	132. Physician fee freeze for Medicare	N
71. Prohibit employee polygraph testing	?	133. $49b in "sin"/phone/insurance taxes	Y
72. Allow CIA to fund Contras	N	134. Allow sale of Conrail	N
73. Revise unfair trade practices	Y	135. Equal Rights Amendment	Y
74. Focus SDI on accidental launch	Y	136. Authorize Marines in Lebanon	Y
75. Bar Air Force $ for MX missile	Y	137. Eminent domain for coal companies	N
76. Allow "real" increase in defense	N	138. Prohibit EPA clean air sanctions	Y
77. Troop reduction in Europe of 50%	Y	139. SS retirement age increase/reforms	N
78. Ban nuclear tests above 1 kiloton	Y		

Presidential Support Score: 1991 - 28% 1990 - 18%

OAKAR, MARY ROSE -- Ohio 20th District [Democrat]. County of Cuyahoga (pt.). Prior Terms: 1977-92. Born: March 5, 1940; Cleveland, OH. Education: Ursuline College (B.A.); John Carrol University (M.A.). Occupation: Clerk, Higbee Co. (1956-58); telephone operator (1957-62); instructor, Lourdes Academy (1963-70); assistant professor, English, Cuyahoga Community College (1968-75); Cleveland city councilman (1973-77).

1.	Protection to Haitian refugees	Y	60.	Textile import quotas-veto override	Y
2.	Raise tax on wealthy; lower others	Y	61.	Bar abortion funding in Wash, DC	Y
3.	Investigate Reagan hostage delay	Y	62.	Notify spouses of AIDS+ carriers	N
4.	Campaign finance revisions	Y	63.	Seize conveyance-drug trafficking	N
5.	Unpaid leave to care for children	Y	64.	South Africa sanctions	Y
6.	Restrict NEA use of funds	N	65.	60 days' notice of plant closings	Y
7.	Bar race-bias claim/habeas corpus	N	66.	Close unneeded military bases	N
8.	Ban race as death sentence factor	N	67.	Keep welfare reform within $2.8b	N
9.	Exceptions to exclusionary rule	N	68.	Allow children housing exclusion	N
10.	Allow sale of assault weapons	N	69.	Shift $400m of NASA to homeless	N
11.	Life in prison/abolish death penalty	N	70.	Cap Medicare patients' liability	Y
12.	Req conspiracy-price fixing cases	N	71.	Prohibit employee polygraph testing	Y
13.	Unemployment benefits extension	Y	72.	Allow CIA to fund Contras	N
14.	Tissue use of aborted fetuses	Y	73.	Revise unfair trade practices	Y
15.	Bar replacement of union strikers	Y	74.	Focus SDI on accidental launch	N
16.	Hold foreign aid at $15b for '92	Y	75.	Bar Air Force $ for MX missile	Y
17.	Restore space station funding	Y	76.	Allow "real" increase in defense	--
18.	Civil Rights Act of 1991	Y	77.	Troop reduction in Europe of 50%	?
19.	Unlimited damages-discrimination	Y	78.	Ban nuclear tests above 1 kiloton	Y
20.	Eliminate funds for supercollider	N	79.	Ban anti-satellite missile tests	Y
21.	Terminate SDI except for research	Y	80.	Observe certain limits of SALT II	Y
22.	Req 7-day handgun waiting period	Y	81.	Restore four Civil Rights laws	Y
23.	Provide $30b for failed S&Ls	Y	82.	Prohibit aliens as strikebreakers	Y
24.	Allow use of force against Iraq	N	83.	Allow military malpractice suits	Y
25.	Allow $15b in foreign aid for '91	Y	84.	Approval of $36m in Contra aid	N
26.	Revise & extend legal immigration	Y	85.	$18b deficit reduction compromise	Y
27.	Suspend aid to Angolan rebels	Y	86.	Welfare reform of $5.7b for 5 years	Y
28.	Democratic tax plan proposals	Y	87.	Raise taxes $12b/cut spending $3b	Y
29.	Cut defense 5% across the board	Y	88.	Board to assess occupational risk	Y
30.	Textile import quotas-veto override	Y	89.	Balanced budget by '93-via targets	N
31.	Abortion service for military abroad	N	90.	Bar licensing of two nuclear plants	Y
32.	Limits on high income farmers	Y	91.	Remove victims compensation cap	Y
33.	Family medical leave-veto override	Y	92.	Catastrophic health insurance	Y
34.	Req submission of balanced budget	Y	93.	Ban airline smoking-2 hours or less	N
35.	Balanced budget amendment	N	94.	$1b/two year aid for the homeless	Y
36.	Amendment to ban flag desecration	N	95.	Bar non-unions in union companies	Y
37.	Reauthorize Amtrak-veto override	?	96.	Increase FSLIC rescue to $15b	N
38.	Retraining aid for coal miners	Y	97.	Impose quotas to lower trade deficit	Y
39.	Suspend El Salvador military aid	Y	98.	Reduce discretionary budget 21%	?
40.	Expand child care aid/tax credit	Y	99.	Immigration reform/alien amnesty	Y
41.	Raise House salary/omit honoraria	Y	100.	South Africa sanctions-veto override	Y
42.	Toughen oil-spill liability	Y	101.	Tax overhaul to revise income tax	Y
43.	Restitution to Japanese interned	Y	102.	Use of military in drug war	N
44.	Protect Chinese & C.A. nationals	Y	103.	Delete 12 MX/add conventional wpn	Y
45.	Abortion $ for rape/incest cases	N	104.	Raise speed limit to 65 mph	N
46.	Allow religious schools to bar gays	?	105.	Require Pentagon to buy US goods	Y
47.	Bar broadcaster fairness doctrine	N	106.	AIDS insurance non-discrimination	Y
48.	Bar cap gains cut/reinstate IRA	Y	107.	Prohibit Saudi arms sales	Y
49.	Bar unions equal voice in pension	N	108.	Ease Gun Control Act of 1968	N
50.	Bar assembly of chemical weapons	Y	109.	Bar interstate handgun transport	Y
51.	Ban plutonium/uranium production	Y	110.	Make company emissions known	Y
52.	Cap MX missile deployment at 50	Y	111.	Allow toxic victims to sue in fed ct	Y
53.	Allow $3b for 2 stealth bombers	N	112.	Superfund waste cleanup of $10b	N
54.	Publish bio-warfare experiments	Y	113.	90 days notice of plant closings	Y
55.	Raise minimum wage-veto override	Y	114.	$20b in Medicare cuts/tax increases	Y
56.	Bar transfer of FS-X technology	Y	115.	Spending cuts and tax increases	Y
57.	Cut defense and raise domestic $	Y	116.	Set school lunch lmt-250% poverty	N
58.	Uniform poll closing in 48 states	Y	117.	$75m for youth work projects	Y
59.	Req foreign investment disclosure	Y	118.	Allow Angolan military assistance	N

OAKAR, MARY ROSE (continued)

119. Suspend defense payments for abuse	Y	
120. Drop SS COLAs/$12b tax increase	N	
121. Approve $1.5b for 21 MX missiles	N	
122. Emergency farm credit/revisions	Y	
123. Duty on Taiwan/Hong Kong/S Korea	Y	
124. Limit steel imports to 17%	Y	
125. Cut $ to schools that bar prayer	N	
126. $50b-taxes; cut Medicare/spending	Y	
127. Limit Pershing II/cruise in Europe	Y	
128. Delete $7.1b for 34 B-1 bombers	Y	
129. Bar purchase of Sergeant York guns	N	
130. El Salvador military/economic aid	N	
131. Bar mining of Nicaraguan waters	Y	

132. Physician fee freeze for Medicare	N	
133. $49b in "sin"/phone/insurance taxes	Y	
134. Allow sale of Conrail	N	
135. Equal Rights Amendment	Y	
136. Authorize Marines in Lebanon	Y	
137. Eminent domain for coal companies	N	
138. Prohibit EPA clean air sanctions	Y	
139. SS retirement age increase/reforms	N	
140. Auto domestic content requirement	Y	
141. Delete jobs program funding	N	
142. Highway-gas tax bill	Y	
143. Cut $5b from defense for Medicare	Y	
144. Emergency housing aid of $1b	Y	

Presidential Support Score: 1991 - 30%   1990 - 17%

STOKES, LOUIS -- Ohio 21st District [Democrat].   County of Cuyahoga (pt.).   Prior Terms: 1969-92.   Born: February 23, 1925; Cleveland, OH.   Education: Cleveland College of Western Reserve University (B.S.); Cleveland Marshall Law College (J.D.).   Military Service: U.S. Army, 1943-46.   Occupation: Attorney, Stokes, Character, Terry and Perry.

1. Protection to Haitian refugees	Y	
2. Raise tax on wealthy; lower others	Y	
3. Investigate Reagan hostage delay	Y	
4. Campaign finance revisions	Y	
5. Unpaid leave to care for children	Y	
6. Restrict NEA use of funds	N	
7. Bar race-bias claim/habeas corpus	N	
8. Ban race as death sentence factor	N	
9. Exceptions to exclusionary rule	N	
10. Allow sale of assault weapons	N	
11. Life in prison/abolish death penalty	Y	
12. Req conspiracy-price fixing cases	N	
13. Unemployment benefits extension	Y	
14. Tissue use of aborted fetuses	Y	
15. Bar replacement of union strikers	Y	
16. Hold foreign aid at $15b for '92	Y	
17. Restore space station funding	N	
18. Civil Rights Act of 1991	Y	
19. Unlimited damages-discrimination	Y	
20. Eliminate funds for supercollider	N	
21. Terminate SDI except for research	Y	
22. Req 7-day handgun waiting period	Y	
23. Provide $30b for failed S&Ls	N	
24. Allow use of force against Iraq	N	
25. Allow $15b in foreign aid for '91	Y	
26. Revise & extend legal immigration	Y	
27. Suspend aid to Angolan rebels	Y	
28. Democratic tax plan proposals	Y	
29. Cut defense 5% across the board	Y	
30. Textile import quotas-veto override	Y	
31. Abortion service for military abroad	Y	
32. Limits on high income farmers	N	
33. Family medical leave-veto override	Y	
34. Req submission of balanced budget	Y	
35. Balanced budget amendment	N	
36. Amendment to ban flag desecration	N	
37. Reauthorize Amtrak-veto override	Y	
38. Retraining aid for coal miners	Y	
39. Suspend El Salvador military aid	#	
40. Expand child care aid/tax credit	N	
41. Raise House salary/omit honoraria	Y	
42. Toughen oil-spill liability	Y	

43. Restitution to Japanese interned	Y	
44. Protect Chinese & C.A. nationals	Y	
45. Abortion $ for rape/incest cases	Y	
46. Allow religious schools to bar gays	?	
47. Bar broadcaster fairness doctrine	N	
48. Bar cap gains cut/reinstate IRA	Y	
49. Bar unions equal voice in pension	N	
50. Bar assembly of chemical weapons	#	
51. Ban plutonium/uranium production	?	
52. Cap MX missile deployment at 50	Y	
53. Allow $3b for 2 stealth bombers	N	
54. Publish bio-warfare experiments	Y	
55. Raise minimum wage-veto override	Y	
56. Bar transfer of FS-X technology	Y	
57. Cut defense and raise domestic $	Y	
58. Uniform poll closing in 48 states	Y	
59. Req foreign investment disclosure	Y	
60. Textile import quotas-veto override	Y	
61. Bar abortion funding in Wash, DC	N	
62. Notify spouses of AIDS+ carriers	N	
63. Seize conveyance-drug trafficking	N	
64. South Africa sanctions	Y	
65. 60 days' notice of plant closings	Y	
66. Close unneeded military bases	N	
67. Keep welfare reform within $2.8b	N	
68. Allow children housing exclusion	N	
69. Shift $400m of NASA to homeless	Y	
70. Cap Medicare patients' liability	Y	
71. Prohibit employee polygraph testing	Y	
72. Allow CIA to fund Contras	N	
73. Revise unfair trade practices	Y	
74. Focus SDI on accidental launch	Y	
75. Bar Air Force $ for MX missile	?	
76. Allow "real" increase in defense	?	
77. Troop reduction in Europe of 50%	#	
78. Ban nuclear tests above 1 kiloton	#	
79. Ban anti-satellite missile tests	#	
80. Observe certain limits of SALT II	#	
81. Restore four Civil Rights laws	Y	
82. Prohibit aliens as strikebreakers	Y	
83. Allow military malpractice suits	Y	
84. Approval of $36m in Contra aid	N	

STOKES, LOUIS (continued)

85. $18b deficit reduction compromise	Y
86. Welfare reform of $5.7b for 5 years	Y
87. Raise taxes $12b/cut spending $3b	Y
88. Board to assess occupational risk	Y
89. Balanced budget by '93-via targets	Y
90. Bar licensing of two nuclear plants	Y
91. Remove victims compensation cap	Y
92. Catastrophic health insurance	Y
93. Ban airline smoking-2 hours or less	N
94. $1b/two year aid for the homeless	Y
95. Bar non-unions in union companies	Y
96. Increase FSLIC rescue to $15b	Y
97. Impose quotas to lower trade deficit	Y
98. Reduce discretionary budget 21%	N
99. Immigration reform/alien amnesty	Y
100. South Africa sanctions-veto override	Y
101. Tax overhaul to revise income tax	?
102. Use of military in drug war	N
103. Delete 12 MX/add conventional wpn	Y
104. Raise speed limit to 65 mph	N
105. Require Pentagon to buy US goods	Y
106. AIDS insurance non-discrimination	Y
107. Prohibit Saudi arms sales	Y
108. Ease Gun Control Act of 1968	X
109. Bar interstate handgun transport	?
110. Make company emissions known	Y
111. Allow toxic victims to sue in fed ct	Y
112. Superfund waste cleanup of $10b	Y
113. 90 days notice of plant closings	Y
114. $20b in Medicare cuts/tax increases	Y

115. Spending cuts and tax increases	Y
116. Set school lunch lmt-250% poverty	N
117. $75m for youth work projects	Y
118. Allow Angolan military assistance	N
119. Suspend defense payments for abuse	Y
120. Drop SS COLAs/$12b tax increase	N
121. Approve $1.5b for 21 MX missiles	N
122. Emergency farm credit/revisions	Y
123. Duty on Taiwan/Hong Kong/S Korea	Y
124. Limit steel imports to 17%	Y
125. Cut $ to schools that bar prayer	N
126. $50b-taxes; cut Medicare/spending	Y
127. Limit Pershing II/cruise in Europe	Y
128. Delete $7.1b for 34 B-1 bombers	#
129. Bar purchase of Sergeant York guns	Y
130. El Salvador military/economic aid	N
131. Bar mining of Nicaraguan waters	Y
132. Physician fee freeze for Medicare	N
133. $49b in "sin"/phone/insurance taxes	Y
134. Allow sale of Conrail	N
135. Equal Rights Amendment	Y
136. Authorize Marines in Lebanon	N
137. Eminent domain for coal companies	N
138. Prohibit EPA clean air sanctions	N
139. SS retirement age increase/reforms	N
140. Auto domestic content requirement	#
141. Delete jobs program funding	N
142. Highway-gas tax bill	Y
143. Cut $5b from defense for Medicare	Y
144. Emergency housing aid of $1b	Y

Presidential Support Score: 1991 - 24%   1990 - 14%

OKLAHOMA

INHOFE, JAMES M. -- Oklahoma 1st District [Republican].   Counties of Creek (pt.), Osage (pt.), Tulsa (pt.) and Washington (pt.).   Prior Terms: 1987-92.   Born: November 17, 1934; Des Moines, IA.   Education: University of Tulsa (B.A.).   Military Service: U.S. Army, 1955-56.   Occupation: President, Quaker Life Insurance Company; state representative (1967-69) and senator (1969-77); Tulsa mayor (1978-84).

1. Protection to Haitian refugees	N
2. Raise tax on wealthy; lower others	N
3. Investigate Reagan hostage delay	N
4. Campaign finance revisions	N
5. Unpaid leave to care for children	N
6. Restrict NEA use of funds	Y
7. Bar race-bias claim/habeas corpus	Y
8. Ban race as death sentence factor	Y
9. Exceptions to exclusionary rule	Y
10. Allow sale of assault weapons	Y
11. Life in prison/abolish death penalty	N
12. Req conspiracy-price fixing cases	Y
13. Unemployment benefits extension	N
14. Tissue use of aborted fetuses	N
15. Bar replacement of union strikers	N
16. Hold foreign aid at $15b for '92	Y
17. Restore space station funding	Y

18. Civil Rights Act of 1991	N
19. Unlimited damages-discrimination	N
20. Eliminate funds for supercollider	N
21. Terminate SDI except for research	N
22. Req 7-day handgun waiting period	N
23. Provide $30b for failed S&Ls	N
24. Allow use of force against Iraq	Y
25. Allow $15b in foreign aid for '91	Y
26. Revise & extend legal immigration	N
27. Suspend aid to Angolan rebels	N
28. Democratic tax plan proposals	N
29. Cut defense 5% across the board	N
30. Textile import quotas-veto override	N
31. Abortion service for military abroad	N
32. Limits on high income farmers	N
33. Family medical leave-veto override	N
34. Req submission of balanced budget	N

INHOFE, JAMES M. (continued)

35. Balanced budget amendment	Y	
36. Amendment to ban flag desecration	Y	
37. Reauthorize Amtrak-veto override	N	
38. Retraining aid for coal miners	N	
39. Suspend El Salvador military aid	N	
40. Expand child care aid/tax credit	N	
41. Raise House salary/omit honoraria	N	
42. Toughen oil-spill liability	N	
43. Restitution to Japanese interned	N	
44. Protect Chinese & C.A. nationals	N	
45. Abortion $ for rape/incest cases	N	
46. Allow religious schools to bar gays	Y	
47. Bar broadcaster fairness doctrine	Y	
48. Bar cap gains cut/reinstate IRA	N	
49. Bar unions equal voice in pension	Y	
50. Bar assembly of chemical weapons	N	
51. Ban plutonium/uranium production	N	
52. Cap MX missile deployment at 50	N	
53. Allow $3b for 2 stealth bombers	Y	
54. Publish bio-warfare experiments	N	
55. Raise minimum wage-veto override	N	
56. Bar transfer of FS-X technology	N	
57. Cut defense and raise domestic $	N	
58. Uniform poll closing in 48 states	N	
59. Req foreign investment disclosure	Y	
60. Textile import quotas-veto override	N	
61. Bar abortion funding in Wash, DC	Y	
62. Notify spouses of AIDS+ carriers	Y	
63. Seize conveyance-drug trafficking	Y	
64. South Africa sanctions	N	
65. 60 days' notice of plant closings	N	
66. Close unneeded military bases	Y	

67. Keep welfare reform within $2.8b	Y	
68. Allow children housing exclusion	Y	
69. Shift $400m of NASA to homeless	N	
70. Cap Medicare patients' liability	Y	
71. Prohibit employee polygraph testing	--	
72. Allow CIA to fund Contras	Y	
73. Revise unfair trade practices	Y	
74. Focus SDI on accidental launch	N	
75. Bar Air Force $ for MX missile	N	
76. Allow "real" increase in defense	Y	
77. Troop reduction in Europe of 50%	N	
78. Ban nuclear tests above 1 kiloton	N	
79. Ban anti-satellite missile tests	N	
80. Observe certain limits of SALT II	N	
81. Restore four Civil Rights laws	N	
82. Prohibit aliens as strikebreakers	N	
83. Allow military malpractice suits	N	
84. Approval of $36m in Contra aid	Y	
85. $18b deficit reduction compromise	N	
86. Welfare reform of $5.7b for 5 years	N	
87. Raise taxes $12b/cut spending $3b	N	
88. Board to assess occupational risk	N	
89. Balanced budget by '93-via targets	N	
90. Bar licensing of two nuclear plants	N	
91. Remove victims compensation cap	N	
92. Catastrophic health insurance	N	
93. Ban airline smoking-2 hours or less	N	
94. $1b/two year aid for the homeless	N	
95. Bar non-unions in union companies	N	
96. Increase FSLIC rescue to $15b	N	
97. Impose quotas to lower trade deficit	N	
98. Reduce discretionary budget 21%	Y	

Presidential Support Score: 1991 - 68%   1990 - 69%

SYNAR, MIKE -- Oklahoma 2nd District [Democrat]. Counties of Adair, Cherokee, Craig, Creek (pt.), Delaware, Haskell, McIntosh, Mayes, Muskogee, Nowata, Okfuskee, Okmulgee, Ottawa, Pawnee, Rogers, Sequoyah, Tulsa (pt.) and Wagoner. Prior Terms: 1979-92. Born: October 17, 1950; Vinita, OK. Education: University of Oklahoma (B.B.A., LL.B.); Northwestern University (M.S.). Occupation: Real estate broker; employee, U.S. forestry service; employee, Oklahoma attorney general's office.

1. Protection to Haitian refugees	Y	
2. Raise tax on wealthy; lower others	Y	
3. Investigate Reagan hostage delay	Y	
4. Campaign finance revisions	Y	
5. Unpaid leave to care for children	Y	
6. Restrict NEA use of funds	Y	
7. Bar race-bias claim/habeas corpus	N	
8. Ban race as death sentence factor	N	
9. Exceptions to exclusionary rule	N	
10. Allow sale of assault weapons	N	
11. Life in prison/abolish death penalty	N	
12. Req conspiracy-price fixing cases	N	
13. Unemployment benefits extension	Y	
14. Tissue use of aborted fetuses	Y	
15. Bar replacement of union strikers	Y	
16. Hold foreign aid at $15b for '92	Y	
17. Restore space station funding	N	
18. Civil Rights Act of 1991	Y	
19. Unlimited damages-discrimination	Y	
20. Eliminate funds for supercollider	Y	
21. Terminate SDI except for research	Y	

22. Req 7-day handgun waiting period	Y	
23. Provide $30b for failed S&Ls	N	
24. Allow use of force against Iraq	N	
25. Allow $15b in foreign aid for '91	Y	
26. Revise & extend legal immigration	Y	
27. Suspend aid to Angolan rebels	Y	
28. Democratic tax plan proposals	Y	
29. Cut defense 5% across the board	Y	
30. Textile import quotas-veto override	N	
31. Abortion service for military abroad	Y	
32. Limits on high income farmers	N	
33. Family medical leave-veto override	Y	
34. Req submission of balanced budget	Y	
35. Balanced budget amendment	N	
36. Amendment to ban flag desecration	N	
37. Reauthorize Amtrak-veto override	Y	
38. Retraining aid for coal miners	Y	
39. Suspend El Salvador military aid	Y	
40. Expand child care aid/tax credit	Y	
41. Raise House salary/omit honoraria	Y	
42. Toughen oil-spill liability	Y	

SYNAR, MIKE (continued)

43. Restitution to Japanese interned	Y	
44. Protect Chinese & C.A. nationals	Y	
45. Abortion $ for rape/incest cases	Y	
46. Allow religious schools to bar gays	N	
47. Bar broadcaster fairness doctrine	N	
48. Bar cap gains cut/reinstate IRA	Y	
49. Bar unions equal voice in pension	N	
50. Bar assembly of chemical weapons	Y	
51. Ban plutonium/uranium production	Y	
52. Cap MX missile deployment at 50	Y	
53. Allow $3b for 2 stealth bombers	N	
54. Publish bio-warfare experiments	Y	
55. Raise minimum wage-veto override	Y	
56. Bar transfer of FS-X technology	Y	
57. Cut defense and raise domestic $	N	
58. Uniform poll closing in 48 states	Y	
59. Req foreign investment disclosure	N	
60. Textile import quotas-veto override	N	
61. Bar abortion funding in Wash, DC	N	
62. Notify spouses of AIDS+ carriers	N	
63. Seize conveyance-drug trafficking	N	
64. South Africa sanctions	Y	
65. 60 days' notice of plant closings	Y	
66. Close unneeded military bases	N	
67. Keep welfare reform within $2.8b	N	
68. Allow children housing exclusion	N	
69. Shift $400m of NASA to homeless	Y	
70. Cap Medicare patients' liability	Y	
71. Prohibit employee polygraph testing	Y	
72. Allow CIA to fund Contras	N	
73. Revise unfair trade practices	Y	
74. Focus SDI on accidental launch	Y	
75. Bar Air Force $ for MX missile	Y	
76. Allow "real" increase in defense	N	
77. Troop reduction in Europe of 50%	N	
78. Ban nuclear tests above 1 kiloton	Y	
79. Ban anti-satellite missile tests	Y	
80. Observe certain limits of SALT II	Y	
81. Restore four Civil Rights laws	Y	
82. Prohibit aliens as strikebreakers	Y	
83. Allow military malpractice suits	Y	
84. Approval of $36m in Contra aid	N	
85. $18b deficit reduction compromise	Y	
86. Welfare reform of $5.7b for 5 years	Y	
87. Raise taxes $12b/cut spending $3b	Y	
88. Board to assess occupational risk	Y	
89. Balanced budget by '93-via targets	N	
90. Bar licensing of two nuclear plants	Y	
91. Remove victims compensation cap	N	
92. Catastrophic health insurance	Y	
93. Ban airline smoking-2 hours or less	Y	

94. $1b/two year aid for the homeless	Y	
95. Bar non-unions in union companies	N	
96. Increase FSLIC rescue to $15b	Y	
97. Impose quotas to lower trade deficit	N	
98. Reduce discretionary budget 21%	N	
99. Immigration reform/alien amnesty	Y	
100. South Africa sanctions-veto override	Y	
101. Tax overhaul to revise income tax	N	
102. Use of military in drug war	N	
103. Delete 12 MX/add conventional wpn	Y	
104. Raise speed limit to 65 mph	N	
105. Require Pentagon to buy US goods	N	
106. AIDS insurance non-discrimination	Y	
107. Prohibit Saudi arms sales	Y	
108. Ease Gun Control Act of 1968	Y	
109. Bar interstate handgun transport	N	
110. Make company emissions known	N	
111. Allow toxic victims to sue in fed ct	Y	
112. Superfund waste cleanup of $10b	N	
113. 90 days notice of plant closings	N	
114. $20b in Medicare cuts/tax increases	Y	
115. Spending cuts and tax increases	Y	
116. Set school lunch lmt-250% poverty	N	
117. $75m for youth work projects	N	
118. Allow Angolan military assistance	N	
119. Suspend defense payments for abuse	N	
120. Drop SS COLAs/$12b tax increase	N	
121. Approve $1.5b for 21 MX missiles	N	
122. Emergency farm credit/revisions	Y	
123. Duty on Taiwan/Hong Kong/S Korea	N	
124. Limit steel imports to 17%	Y	
125. Cut $ to schools that bar prayer	Y	
126. $50b-taxes; cut Medicare/spending	Y	
127. Limit Pershing II/cruise in Europe	N	
128. Delete $7.1b for 34 B-1 bombers	N	
129. Bar purchase of Sergeant York guns	N	
130. El Salvador military/economic aid	N	
131. Bar mining of Nicaraguan waters	Y	
132. Physician fee freeze for Medicare	N	
133. $49b in "sin"/phone/insurance taxes	Y	
134. Allow sale of Conrail	N	
135. Equal Rights Amendment	Y	
136. Authorize Marines in Lebanon	Y	
137. Eminent domain for coal companies	Y	
138. Prohibit EPA clean air sanctions	Y	
139. SS retirement age increase/reforms	Y	
140. Auto domestic content requirement	N	
141. Delete jobs program funding	Y	
142. Highway-gas tax bill	N	
143. Cut $5b from defense for Medicare	N	
144. Emergency housing aid of $1b	Y	

Presidential Support Score: 1991 - 28%   1990 - 17%

BREWSTER, BILL K. -- Oklahoma 3rd District [Democrat]. Counties of Atoka, Bryan, Carter, Choctaw, Coal, Hughes, Johnston, Latimer, Le Flore, Lincoln, Love, McCurtain, Marshall, Murray, Payne, Pittsburg, Pontotoc, Pottawatomie (pt.), Pushmataha and Seminole. Prior Term: 1990-91. Born: November 8, 1941; Ardmore, OK. Education: Southwestern Oklahoma State University (B.S.). Military Service: U.S. Army Reserve. Occupation: Cattleman and farm co-owner; real estate firm co-owner; retail pharmacist; bank director; state representative (1983-90); South/West Energy Council member (1982-90); National Conference of State Legislatures delegate (1983-90).

BREWSTER, BILL K. (continued)

1. Protection to Haitian refugees	N	13. Unemployment benefits extension	N
2. Raise tax on wealthy; lower others	Y	14. Tissue use of aborted fetuses	Y
3. Investigate Reagan hostage delay	Y	15. Bar replacement of union strikers	N
4. Campaign finance revisions	Y	16. Hold foreign aid at $15b for '92	Y
5. Unpaid leave to care for children	N	17. Restore space station funding	Y
6. Restrict NEA use of funds	Y	18. Civil Rights Act of 1991	Y
7. Bar race-bias claim/habeas corpus	Y	19. Unlimited damages-discrimination	N
8. Ban race as death sentence factor	Y	20. Eliminate funds for supercollider	N
9. Exceptions to exclusionary rule	Y	21. Terminate SDI except for research	?
10. Allow sale of assault weapons	Y	22. Req 7-day handgun waiting period	N
11. Life in prison/abolish death penalty	N	23. Provide $30b for failed S&Ls	N
12. Req conspiracy-price fixing cases	Y	24. Allow use of force against Iraq	Y

Presidential Support Score: 1991 - 45%

McCURDY, DAVE -- Oklahoma 4th District [Democrat].   Counties of Cleveland, Comanche, Cotton, Garvin, Grady, Jackson, Jefferson, McClain, Oklahoma (pt.), Pottawatomie (pt.), Stephens and Tillman.   Prior Terms: 1981-92.   Born: March 30, 1950; Canadian, TX. Education: University of Oklahoma (B.A., J.D.).   Military Service: U.S. Air Force Reserve, 1969-72.   Occupation: Attorney; assistant attorney general, Oklahoma (1975-77); member, Luttrell, Pendarvis & Rawlinson (1978-79).

1. Protection to Haitian refugees	Y	42. Toughen oil-spill liability	Y
2. Raise tax on wealthy; lower others	N	43. Restitution to Japanese interned	N
3. Investigate Reagan hostage delay	Y	44. Protect Chinese & C.A. nationals	Y
4. Campaign finance revisions	Y	45. Abortion $ for rape/incest cases	Y
5. Unpaid leave to care for children	Y	46. Allow religious schools to bar gays	Y
6. Restrict NEA use of funds	Y	47. Bar broadcaster fairness doctrine	N
7. Bar race-bias claim/habeas corpus	Y	48. Bar cap gains cut/reinstate IRA	Y
8. Ban race as death sentence factor	Y	49. Bar unions equal voice in pension	N
9. Exceptions to exclusionary rule	Y	50. Bar assembly of chemical weapons	N
10. Allow sale of assault weapons	Y	51. Ban plutonium/uranium production	Y
11. Life in prison/abolish death penalty	N	52. Cap MX missile deployment at 50	Y
12. Req conspiracy-price fixing cases	N	53. Allow $3b for 2 stealth bombers	Y
13. Unemployment benefits extension	Y	54. Publish bio-warfare experiments	N
14. Tissue use of aborted fetuses	Y	55. Raise minimum wage-veto override	N
15. Bar replacement of union strikers	N	56. Bar transfer of FS-X technology	N
16. Hold foreign aid at $15b for '92	Y	57. Cut defense and raise domestic $	?
17. Restore space station funding	Y	58. Uniform poll closing in 48 states	Y
18. Civil Rights Act of 1991	Y	59. Req foreign investment disclosure	Y
19. Unlimited damages-discrimination	N	60. Textile import quotas-veto override	N
20. Eliminate funds for supercollider	Y	61. Bar abortion funding in Wash, DC	N
21. Terminate SDI except for research	N	62. Notify spouses of AIDS+ carriers	N
22. Req 7-day handgun waiting period	Y	63. Seize conveyance-drug trafficking	N
23. Provide $30b for failed S&Ls	N	64. South Africa sanctions	Y
24. Allow use of force against Iraq	Y	65. 60 days' notice of plant closings	Y
25. Allow $15b in foreign aid for '91	N	66. Close unneeded military bases	Y
26. Revise & extend legal immigration	N	67. Keep welfare reform within $2.8b	Y
27. Suspend aid to Angolan rebels	N	68. Allow children housing exclusion	N
28. Democratic tax plan proposals	Y	69. Shift $400m of NASA to homeless	N
29. Cut defense 5% across the board	N	70. Cap Medicare patients' liability	Y
30. Textile import quotas-veto override	N	71. Prohibit employee polygraph testing	Y
31. Abortion service for military abroad	Y	72. Allow CIA to fund Contras	N
32. Limits on high income farmers	N	73. Revise unfair trade practices	Y
33. Family medical leave-veto override	Y	74. Focus SDI on accidental launch	Y
34. Req submission of balanced budget	Y	75. Bar Air Force $ for MX missile	N
35. Balanced budget amendment	Y	76. Allow "real" increase in defense	Y
36. Amendment to ban flag desecration	N	77. Troop reduction in Europe of 50%	N
37. Reauthorize Amtrak-veto override	N	78. Ban nuclear tests above 1 kiloton	N
38. Retraining aid for coal miners	N	79. Ban anti-satellite missile tests	N
39. Suspend El Salvador military aid	N	80. Observe certain limits of SALT II	Y
40. Expand child care aid/tax credit	Y	81. Restore four Civil Rights laws	Y
41. Raise House salary/omit honoraria	Y	82. Prohibit aliens as strikebreakers	N

McCURDY, DAVE (continued)

83.	Allow military malpractice suits	Y	114.	$20b in Medicare cuts/tax increases	Y
84.	Approval of $36m in Contra aid	N	115.	Spending cuts and tax increases	Y
85.	$18b deficit reduction compromise	Y	116.	Set school lunch lmt-250% poverty	N
86.	Welfare reform of $5.7b for 5 years	N	117.	$75m for youth work projects	N
87.	Raise taxes $12b/cut spending $3b	Y	118.	Allow Angolan military assistance	Y
88.	Board to assess occupational risk	Y	119.	Suspend defense payments for abuse	N
89.	Balanced budget by '93-via targets	?	120.	Drop SS COLAs/$12b tax increase	Y
90.	Bar licensing of two nuclear plants	N	121.	Approve $1.5b for 21 MX missiles	Y
91.	Remove victims compensation cap	N	122.	Emergency farm credit/revisions	Y
92.	Catastrophic health insurance	N	123.	Duty on Taiwan/Hong Kong/S Korea	N
93.	Ban airline smoking-2 hours or less	Y	124.	Limit steel imports to 17%	N
94.	$1b/two year aid for the homeless	Y	125.	Cut $ to schools that bar prayer	Y
95.	Bar non-unions in union companies	N	126.	$50b-taxes; cut Medicare/spending	Y
96.	Increase FSLIC rescue to $15b	N	127.	Limit Pershing II/cruise in Europe	?
97.	Impose quotas to lower trade deficit	N	128.	Delete $7.1b for 34 B-1 bombers	N
98.	Reduce discretionary budget 21%	Y	129.	Bar purchase of Sergeant York guns	N
99.	Immigration reform/alien amnesty	?	130.	El Salvador military/economic aid	Y
100.	South Africa sanctions-veto override	Y	131.	Bar mining of Nicaraguan waters	Y
101.	Tax overhaul to revise income tax	N	132.	Physician fee freeze for Medicare	N
102.	Use of military in drug war	Y	133.	$49b in "sin"/phone/insurance taxes	Y
103.	Delete 12 MX/add conventional wpn	N	134.	Allow sale of Conrail	N
104.	Raise speed limit to 65 mph	Y	135.	Equal Rights Amendment	Y
105.	Require Pentagon to buy US goods	N	136.	Authorize Marines in Lebanon	N
106.	AIDS insurance non-discrimination	Y	137.	Eminent domain for coal companies	Y
107.	Prohibit Saudi arms sales	Y	138.	Prohibit EPA clean air sanctions	Y
108.	Ease Gun Control Act of 1968	Y	139.	SS retirement age increase/reforms	Y
109.	Bar interstate handgun transport	N	140.	Auto domestic content requirement	Y
110.	Make company emissions known	Y	141.	Delete jobs program funding	Y
111.	Allow toxic victims to sue in fed ct	N	142.	Highway-gas tax bill	N
112.	Superfund waste cleanup of $10b	N	143.	Cut $5b from defense for Medicare	N
113.	90 days notice of plant closings	N	144.	Emergency housing aid of $1b	Y

Presidential Support Score: 1991 - 41%   1990 - 44%

EDWARDS, MICKEY -- Oklahoma 5th District [Republican]. Counties of Canadian (pt.), Kay, Logan, Noble, Oklahoma (pt.), Osage (pt.) and Washington (pt.). Prior Terms: 1977-92. Born: July 12, 1937. Education: University of Oklahoma (B.A.); Oklahoma City University (J.D.). Occupation: Journalist; assistant city editor; editor; journalism teacher; legislative consultant (1973-76).

1.	Protection to Haitian refugees	N	24.	Allow use of force against Iraq	Y
2.	Raise tax on wealthy; lower others	N	25.	Allow $15b in foreign aid for '91	N
3.	Investigate Reagan hostage delay	N	26.	Revise & extend legal immigration	N
4.	Campaign finance revisions	N	27.	Suspend aid to Angolan rebels	N
5.	Unpaid leave to care for children	N	28.	Democratic tax plan proposals	N
6.	Restrict NEA use of funds	N	29.	Cut defense 5% across the board	N
7.	Bar race-bias claim/habeas corpus	Y	30.	Textile import quotas-veto override	N
8.	Ban race as death sentence factor	Y	31.	Abortion service for military abroad	N
9.	Exceptions to exclusionary rule	Y	32.	Limits on high income farmers	N
10.	Allow sale of assault weapons	Y	33.	Family medical leave-veto override	N
11.	Life in prison/abolish death penalty	N	34.	Req submission of balanced budget	N
12.	Req conspiracy-price fixing cases	Y	35.	Balanced budget amendment	Y
13.	Unemployment benefits extension	?	36.	Amendment to ban flag desecration	Y
14.	Tissue use of aborted fetuses	N	37.	Reauthorize Amtrak-veto override	N
15.	Bar replacement of union strikers	N	38.	Retraining aid for coal miners	N
16.	Hold foreign aid at $15b for '92	Y	39.	Suspend El Salvador military aid	N
17.	Restore space station funding	Y	40.	Expand child care aid/tax credit	N
18.	Civil Rights Act of 1991	N	41.	Raise House salary/omit honoraria	Y
19.	Unlimited damages-discrimination	N	42.	Toughen oil-spill liability	Y
20.	Eliminate funds for supercollider	N	43.	Restitution to Japanese interned	Y
21.	Terminate SDI except for research	N	44.	Protect Chinese & C.A. nationals	N
22.	Req 7-day handgun waiting period	N	45.	Abortion $ for rape/incest cases	N
23.	Provide $30b for failed S&Ls	Y	46.	Allow religious schools to bar gays	Y

EDWARDS, MICKEY (continued)

47. Bar broadcaster fairness doctrine	Y	
48. Bar cap gains cut/reinstate IRA	N	
49. Bar unions equal voice in pension	Y	
50. Bar assembly of chemical weapons	N	
51. Ban plutonium/uranium production	N	
52. Cap MX missile deployment at 50	N	
53. Allow $3b for 2 stealth bombers	Y	
54. Publish bio-warfare experiments	N	
55. Raise minimum wage-veto override	N	
56. Bar transfer of FS-X technology	N	
57. Cut defense and raise domestic $	N	
58. Uniform poll closing in 48 states	N	
59. Req foreign investment disclosure	Y	
60. Textile import quotas-veto override	N	
61. Bar abortion funding in Wash, DC	Y	
62. Notify spouses of AIDS+ carriers	N	
63. Seize conveyance-drug trafficking	Y	
64. South Africa sanctions	N	
65. 60 days' notice of plant closings	N	
66. Close unneeded military bases	Y	
67. Keep welfare reform within $2.8b	Y	
68. Allow children housing exclusion	N	
69. Shift $400m of NASA to homeless	N	
70. Cap Medicare patients' liability	Y	
71. Prohibit employee polygraph testing	N	
72. Allow CIA to fund Contras	Y	
73. Revise unfair trade practices	Y	
74. Focus SDI on accidental launch	N	
75. Bar Air Force $ for MX missile	N	
76. Allow "real" increase in defense	Y	
77. Troop reduction in Europe of 50%	Y	
78. Ban nuclear tests above 1 kiloton	N	
79. Ban anti-satellite missile tests	N	
80. Observe certain limits of SALT II	N	
81. Restore four Civil Rights laws	N	
82. Prohibit aliens as strikebreakers	N	
83. Allow military malpractice suits	Y	
84. Approval of $36m in Contra aid	Y	
85. $18b deficit reduction compromise	N	
86. Welfare reform of $5.7b for 5 years	N	
87. Raise taxes $12b/cut spending $3b	N	
88. Board to assess occupational risk	N	
89. Balanced budget by '93-via targets	Y	
90. Bar licensing of two nuclear plants	N	
91. Remove victims compensation cap	Y	
92. Catastrophic health insurance	N	
93. Ban airline smoking-2 hours or less	?	
94. $1b/two year aid for the homeless	N	
95. Bar non-unions in union companies	N	

96. Increase FSLIC rescue to $15b	N	
97. Impose quotas to lower trade deficit	N	
98. Reduce discretionary budget 21%	Y	
99. Immigration reform/alien amnesty	?	
100. South Africa sanctions-veto override	?	
101. Tax overhaul to revise income tax	N	
102. Use of military in drug war	Y	
103. Delete 12 MX/add conventional wpn	N	
104. Raise speed limit to 65 mph	Y	
105. Require Pentagon to buy US goods	N	
106. AIDS insurance non-discrimination	N	
107. Prohibit Saudi arms sales	Y	
108. Ease Gun Control Act of 1968	Y	
109. Bar interstate handgun transport	?	
110. Make company emissions known	N	
111. Allow toxic victims to sue in fed ct	N	
112. Superfund waste cleanup of $10b	N	
113. 90 days notice of plant closings	N	
114. $20b in Medicare cuts/tax increases	N	
115. Spending cuts and tax increases	N	
116. Set school lunch lmt-250% poverty	Y	
117. $75m for youth work projects	N	
118. Allow Angolan military assistance	Y	
119. Suspend defense payments for abuse	N	
120. Drop SS COLAs/$12b tax increase	N	
121. Approve $1.5b for 21 MX missiles	Y	
122. Emergency farm credit/revisions	Y	
123. Duty on Taiwan/Hong Kong/S Korea	N	
124. Limit steel imports to 17%	N	
125. Cut $ to schools that bar prayer	Y	
126. $50b-taxes; cut Medicare/spending	N	
127. Limit Pershing II/cruise in Europe	?	
128. Delete $7.1b for 34 B-1 bombers	N	
129. Bar purchase of Sergeant York guns	N	
130. El Salvador military/economic aid	Y	
131. Bar mining of Nicaraguan waters	N	
132. Physician fee freeze for Medicare	N	
133. $49b in "sin"/phone/insurance taxes	N	
134. Allow sale of Conrail	N	
135. Equal Rights Amendment	N	
136. Authorize Marines in Lebanon	Y	
137. Eminent domain for coal companies	Y	
138. Prohibit EPA clean air sanctions	Y	
139. SS retirement age increase/reforms	Y	
140. Auto domestic content requirement	N	
141. Delete jobs program funding	Y	
142. Highway-gas tax bill	N	
143. Cut $5b from defense for Medicare	N	
144. Emergency housing aid of $1b	Y	

Presidential Support Score: 1991 - 74%   1990 - 69%

ENGLISH, GLENN -- Oklahoma 6th District [Democrat]. Counties of Alfalfa, Beaver, Beckhorn, Blaine, Caddo, Canadian (pt.), Cimarron, Custer, Dewey, Ellis, Garfield, Grant, Greer, Harmon, Harper, Kingfisher, Kiowa, Major, Oklahoma (pt.), Roger Mills, Texas, Washita, Woods and Woodward. Prior Terms: 1975-92. Born: November 30, 1940; Cordell, OK. Education: Southwestern State College. Military Service: U.S. Army Reserves, 1965-71. Occupation: Petroleum landman; congressional staff member.

1. Protection to Haitian refugees	N	
2. Raise tax on wealthy; lower others	N	
3. Investigate Reagan hostage delay	N	
4. Campaign finance revisions	Y	

5. Unpaid leave to care for children	Y	
6. Restrict NEA use of funds	Y	
7. Bar race-bias claim/habeas corpus	Y	
8. Ban race as death sentence factor	N	

ENGLISH, GLENN (continued)

9. Exceptions to exclusionary rule	Y	
10. Allow sale of assault weapons	Y	
11. Life in prison/abolish death penalty	N	
12. Req conspiracy-price fixing cases	Y	
13. Unemployment benefits extension	Y	
14. Tissue use of aborted fetuses	Y	
15. Bar replacement of union strikers	N	
16. Hold foreign aid at $15b for '92	N	
17. Restore space station funding	Y	
18. Civil Rights Act of 1991	Y	
19. Unlimited damages-discrimination	N	
20. Eliminate funds for supercollider	N	
21. Terminate SDI except for research	N	
22. Req 7-day handgun waiting period	N	
23. Provide $30b for failed S&Ls	N	
24. Allow use of force against Iraq	N	
25. Allow $15b in foreign aid for '91	N	
26. Revise & extend legal immigration	N	
27. Suspend aid to Angolan rebels	N	
28. Democratic tax plan proposals	Y	
29. Cut defense 5% across the board	N	
30. Textile import quotas-veto override	N	
31. Abortion service for military abroad	N	
32. Limits on high income farmers	N	
33. Family medical leave-veto override	Y	
34. Req submission of balanced budget	Y	
35. Balanced budget amendment	Y	
36. Amendment to ban flag desecration	Y	
37. Reauthorize Amtrak-veto override	N	
38. Retraining aid for coal miners	Y	
39. Suspend El Salvador military aid	N	
40. Expand child care aid/tax credit	Y	
41. Raise House salary/omit honoraria	N	
42. Toughen oil-spill liability	N	
43. Restitution to Japanese interned	N	
44. Protect Chinese & C.A. nationals	N	
45. Abortion $ for rape/incest cases	N	
46. Allow religious schools to bar gays	Y	
47. Bar broadcaster fairness doctrine	Y	
48. Bar cap gains cut/reinstate IRA	N	
49. Bar unions equal voice in pension	Y	
50. Bar assembly of chemical weapons	N	
51. Ban plutonium/uranium production	Y	
52. Cap MX missile deployment at 50	N	
53. Allow $3b for 2 stealth bombers	Y	
54. Publish bio-warfare experiments	Y	
55. Raise minimum wage-veto override	N	
56. Bar transfer of FS-X technology	Y	
57. Cut defense and raise domestic $	N	
58. Uniform poll closing in 48 states	Y	
59. Req foreign investment disclosure	Y	
60. Textile import quotas-veto override	N	
61. Bar abortion funding in Wash, DC	Y	
62. Notify spouses of AIDS+ carriers	N	
63. Seize conveyance-drug trafficking	Y	
64. South Africa sanctions	Y	
65. 60 days' notice of plant closings	Y	
66. Close unneeded military bases	N	
67. Keep welfare reform within $2.8b	Y	
68. Allow children housing exclusion	Y	
69. Shift $400m of NASA to homeless	N	
70. Cap Medicare patients' liability	Y	
71. Prohibit employee polygraph testing	Y	
72. Allow CIA to fund Contras	N	

73. Revise unfair trade practices	Y	
74. Focus SDI on accidental launch	Y	
75. Bar Air Force $ for MX missile	N	
76. Allow "real" increase in defense	Y	
77. Troop reduction in Europe of 50%	Y	
78. Ban nuclear tests above 1 kiloton	N	
79. Ban anti-satellite missile tests	N	
80. Observe certain limits of SALT II	N	
81. Restore four Civil Rights laws	N	
82. Prohibit aliens as strikebreakers	N	
83. Allow military malpractice suits	Y	
84. Approval of $36m in Contra aid	Y	
85. $18b deficit reduction compromise	N	
86. Welfare reform of $5.7b for 5 years	N	
87. Raise taxes $12b/cut spending $3b	N	
88. Board to assess occupational risk	N	
89. Balanced budget by '93-via targets	N	
90. Bar licensing of two nuclear plants	N	
91. Remove victims compensation cap	N	
92. Catastrophic health insurance	Y	
93. Ban airline smoking-2 hours or less	Y	
94. $1b/two year aid for the homeless	Y	
95. Bar non-unions in union companies	N	
96. Increase FSLIC rescue to $15b	N	
97. Impose quotas to lower trade deficit	N	
98. Reduce discretionary budget 21%	Y	
99. Immigration reform/alien amnesty	N	
100. South Africa sanctions-veto override	Y	
101. Tax overhaul to revise income tax	N	
102. Use of military in drug war	N	
103. Delete 12 MX/add conventional wpn	N	
104. Raise speed limit to 65 mph	Y	
105. Require Pentagon to buy US goods	N	
106. AIDS insurance non-discrimination	Y	
107. Prohibit Saudi arms sales	Y	
108. Ease Gun Control Act of 1968	Y	
109. Bar interstate handgun transport	N	
110. Make company emissions known	N	
111. Allow toxic victims to sue in fed ct	N	
112. Superfund waste cleanup of $10b	N	
113. 90 days notice of plant closings	N	
114. $20b in Medicare cuts/tax increases	N	
115. Spending cuts and tax increases	N	
116. Set school lunch lmt-250% poverty	N	
117. $75m for youth work projects	N	
118. Allow Angolan military assistance	Y	
119. Suspend defense payments for abuse	N	
120. Drop SS COLAs/$12b tax increase	N	
121. Approve $1.5b for 21 MX missiles	Y	
122. Emergency farm credit/revisions	N	
123. Duty on Taiwan/Hong Kong/S Korea	N	
124. Limit steel imports to 17%	N	
125. Cut $ to schools that bar prayer	Y	
126. $50b-taxes; cut Medicare/spending	N	
127. Limit Pershing II/cruise in Europe	?	
128. Delete $7.1b for 34 B-1 bombers	N	
129. Bar purchase of Sergeant York guns	N	
130. El Salvador military/economic aid	Y	
131. Bar mining of Nicaraguan waters	Y	
132. Physician fee freeze for Medicare	N	
133. $49b in "sin"/phone/insurance taxes	N	
134. Allow sale of Conrail	N	
135. Equal Rights Amendment	Y	
136. Authorize Marines in Lebanon	N	

ENGLISH, GLENN (continued)

137. Eminent domain for coal companies	Y	
138. Prohibit EPA clean air sanctions	Y	
139. SS retirement age increase/reforms	Y	
140. Auto domestic content requirement	Y	
141. Delete jobs program funding	Y
142. Highway-gas tax bill	N
143. Cut $5b from defense for Medicare	N
144. Emergency housing aid of $1b	Y

Presidential Support Score: 1991 - 43% 1990 - 47%

OREGON

AuCOIN, LES -- Oregon 1st District [Democrat]. Counties of Clatsop, Columbia, Lincoln, Multnomah (pt.), Polk (pt.), Tillamook, Washington and Yamhill. Prior Terms: 1975-92. Born: October 21, 1942; Redmond, OR. Education: University of the Pacific (B.A.). Military Service: U.S. Army, 1961-64. Occupation: Newsman, *Redmond Spokesman* (1960, 1964); *Portland Oregonian* (1965-66); director, public information, Pacific University (1966-73); administrator, Skidmore, Owings and Merrill (1973-74); Oregon representative (1973-75).

1. Protection to Haitian refugees	#	42. Toughen oil-spill liability	Y
2. Raise tax on wealthy; lower others	Y	43. Restitution to Japanese interned	Y
3. Investigate Reagan hostage delay	Y	44. Protect Chinese & C.A. nationals	Y
4. Campaign finance revisions	Y	45. Abortion $ for rape/incest cases	Y
5. Unpaid leave to care for children	Y	46. Allow religious schools to bar gays	N
6. Restrict NEA use of funds	N	47. Bar broadcaster fairness doctrine	N
7. Bar race-bias claim/habeas corpus	N	48. Bar cap gains cut/reinstate IRA	Y
8. Ban race as death sentence factor	N	49. Bar unions equal voice in pension	N
9. Exceptions to exclusionary rule	N	50. Bar assembly of chemical weapons	Y
10. Allow sale of assault weapons	N	51. Ban plutonium/uranium production	Y
11. Life in prison/abolish death penalty	Y	52. Cap MX missile deployment at 50	Y
12. Req conspiracy-price fixing cases	N	53. Allow $3b for 2 stealth bombers	Y
13. Unemployment benefits extension	Y	54. Publish bio-warfare experiments	Y
14. Tissue use of aborted fetuses	Y	55. Raise minimum wage-veto override	Y
15. Bar replacement of union strikers	Y	56. Bar transfer of FS-X technology	Y
16. Hold foreign aid at $15b for '92	Y	57. Cut defense and raise domestic $	N
17. Restore space station funding	N	58. Uniform poll closing in 48 states	?
18. Civil Rights Act of 1991	Y	59. Req foreign investment disclosure	N
19. Unlimited damages-discrimination	Y	60. Textile import quotas-veto override	N
20. Eliminate funds for supercollider	?	61. Bar abortion funding in Wash, DC	N
21. Terminate SDI except for research	Y	62. Notify spouses of AIDS+ carriers	N
22. Req 7-day handgun waiting period	Y	63. Seize conveyance-drug trafficking	N
23. Provide $30b for failed S&Ls	N	64. South Africa sanctions	Y
24. Allow use of force against Iraq	N	65. 60 days' notice of plant closings	Y
25. Allow $15b in foreign aid for '91	Y	66. Close unneeded military bases	Y
26. Revise & extend legal immigration	Y	67. Keep welfare reform within $2.8b	N
27. Suspend aid to Angolan rebels	Y	68. Allow children housing exclusion	N
28. Democratic tax plan proposals	Y	69. Shift $400m of NASA to homeless	Y
29. Cut defense 5% across the board	N	70. Cap Medicare patients' liability	Y
30. Textile import quotas-veto override	N	71. Prohibit employee polygraph testing	Y
31. Abortion service for military abroad	?	72. Allow CIA to fund Contras	N
32. Limits on high income farmers	N	73. Revise unfair trade practices	Y
33. Family medical leave-veto override	Y	74. Focus SDI on accidental launch	Y
34. Req submission of balanced budget	Y	75. Bar Air Force $ for MX missile	Y
35. Balanced budget amendment	N	76. Allow "real" increase in defense	N
36. Amendment to ban flag desecration	N	77. Troop reduction in Europe of 50%	N
37. Reauthorize Amtrak-veto override	Y	78. Ban nuclear tests above 1 kiloton	Y
38. Retraining aid for coal miners	Y	79. Ban anti-satellite missile tests	Y
39. Suspend El Salvador military aid	Y	80. Observe certain limits of SALT II	Y
40. Expand child care aid/tax credit	Y	81. Restore four Civil Rights laws	Y
41. Raise House salary/omit honoraria	Y	82. Prohibit aliens as strikebreakers	Y

AuCOIN, LES (continued)

83. Allow military malpractice suits	Y
84. Approval of $36m in Contra aid	N
85. $18b deficit reduction compromise	Y
86. Welfare reform of $5.7b for 5 years	N
87. Raise taxes $12b/cut spending $3b	Y
88. Board to assess occupational risk	Y
89. Balanced budget by '93-via targets	Y
90. Bar licensing of two nuclear plants	Y
91. Remove victims compensation cap	Y
92. Catastrophic health insurance	Y
93. Ban airline smoking-2 hours or less	Y
94. $1b/two year aid for the homeless	Y
95. Bar non-unions in union companies	Y
96. Increase FSLIC rescue to $15b	N
97. Impose quotas to lower trade deficit	N
98. Reduce discretionary budget 21%	N
99. Immigration reform/alien amnesty	Y
100. South Africa sanctions-veto override	Y
101. Tax overhaul to revise income tax	Y
102. Use of military in drug war	N
103. Delete 12 MX/add conventional wpn	Y
104. Raise speed limit to 65 mph	N
105. Require Pentagon to buy US goods	N
106. AIDS insurance non-discrimination	Y
107. Prohibit Saudi arms sales	Y
108. Ease Gun Control Act of 1968	Y
109. Bar interstate handgun transport	N
110. Make company emissions known	Y
111. Allow toxic victims to sue in fed ct	Y
112. Superfund waste cleanup of $10b	Y
113. 90 days notice of plant closings	N

114. $20b in Medicare cuts/tax increases	Y
115. Spending cuts and tax increases	Y
116. Set school lunch lmt-250% poverty	N
117. $75m for youth work projects	Y
118. Allow Angolan military assistance	N
119. Suspend defense payments for abuse	Y
120. Drop SS COLAs/$12b tax increase	N
121. Approve $1.5b for 21 MX missiles	N
122. Emergency farm credit/revisions	Y
123. Duty on Taiwan/Hong Kong/S Korea	N
124. Limit steel imports to 17%	Y
125. Cut $ to schools that bar prayer	N
126. $50b-taxes; cut Medicare/spending	Y
127. Limit Pershing II/cruise in Europe	Y
128. Delete $7.1b for 34 B-1 bombers	Y
129. Bar purchase of Sergeant York guns	Y
130. El Salvador military/economic aid	N
131. Bar mining of Nicaraguan waters	Y
132. Physician fee freeze for Medicare	Y
133. $49b in "sin"/phone/insurance taxes	Y
134. Allow sale of Conrail	N
135. Equal Rights Amendment	Y
136. Authorize Marines in Lebanon	N
137. Eminent domain for coal companies	N
138. Prohibit EPA clean air sanctions	?
139. SS retirement age increase/reforms	Y
140. Auto domestic content requirement	N
141. Delete jobs program funding	N
142. Highway-gas tax bill	Y
143. Cut $5b from defense for Medicare	Y
144. Emergency housing aid of $1b	Y

Presidential Support Score: 1991 - 26%   1990 - 20%

SMITH, ROBERT F. (Bob) -- Oregon 2nd District [Republican]. Counties of Baker, Crook, Deschutes, Gilliam, Grant, Harney, Hood River, Jackson (pt.), Jefferson, Josephine (pt.), Klamath, Lake, Malheur, Morrow, Sherman, Umatilla, Union, Wallowa, Wasco and Wheeler. Prior Terms: 1983-92. Born: June 16, 1931; Portland, OR. Education: Willamette University (B.A.). Occupation: Oregon legislator (1960-72); Oregon senator (1972-82); member, Harney County Chamber of Commerce; trustee, Willamette University.

1. Protection to Haitian refugees	?
2. Raise tax on wealthy; lower others	N
3. Investigate Reagan hostage delay	N
4. Campaign finance revisions	N
5. Unpaid leave to care for children	N
6. Restrict NEA use of funds	Y
7. Bar race-bias claim/habeas corpus	Y
8. Ban race as death sentence factor	Y
9. Exceptions to exclusionary rule	Y
10. Allow sale of assault weapons	Y
11. Life in prison/abolish death penalty	N
12. Req conspiracy-price fixing cases	Y
13. Unemployment benefits extension	N
14. Tissue use of aborted fetuses	N
15. Bar replacement of union strikers	N
16. Hold foreign aid at $15b for '92	N
17. Restore space station funding	Y
18. Civil Rights Act of 1991	N
19. Unlimited damages-discrimination	N
20. Eliminate funds for supercollider	N
21. Terminate SDI except for research	N
22. Req 7-day handgun waiting period	N

23. Provide $30b for failed S&Ls	N
24. Allow use of force against Iraq	Y
25. Allow $15b in foreign aid for '91	N
26. Revise & extend legal immigration	N
27. Suspend aid to Angolan rebels	N
28. Democratic tax plan proposals	N
29. Cut defense 5% across the board	N
30. Textile import quotas-veto override	N
31. Abortion service for military abroad	N
32. Limits on high income farmers	N
33. Family medical leave-veto override	N
34. Req submission of balanced budget	N
35. Balanced budget amendment	Y
36. Amendment to ban flag desecration	Y
37. Reauthorize Amtrak-veto override	Y
38. Retraining aid for coal miners	Y
39. Suspend El Salvador military aid	N
40. Expand child care aid/tax credit	N
41. Raise House salary/omit honoraria	N
42. Toughen oil-spill liability	N
43. Restitution to Japanese interned	Y
44. Protect Chinese & C.A. nationals	N

SMITH, ROBERT F. (continued)

45. Abortion $ for rape/incest cases	N	93. Ban airline smoking-2 hours or less	N
46. Allow religious schools to bar gays	Y	94. $1b/two year aid for the homeless	Y
47. Bar broadcaster fairness doctrine	Y	95. Bar non-unions in union companies	N
48. Bar cap gains cut/reinstate IRA	N	96. Increase FSLIC rescue to $15b	N
49. Bar unions equal voice in pension	Y	97. Impose quotas to lower trade deficit	N
50. Bar assembly of chemical weapons	Y	98. Reduce discretionary budget 21%	Y
51. Ban plutonium/uranium production	Y	99. Immigration reform/alien amnesty	N
52. Cap MX missile deployment at 50	N	100. South Africa sanctions-veto override	N
53. Allow $3b for 2 stealth bombers	Y	101. Tax overhaul to revise income tax	Y
54. Publish bio-warfare experiments	N	102. Use of military in drug war	Y
55. Raise minimum wage-veto override	N	103. Delete 12 MX/add conventional wpn	N
56. Bar transfer of FS-X technology	N	104. Raise speed limit to 65 mph	Y
57. Cut defense and raise domestic $	N	105. Require Pentagon to buy US goods	Y
58. Uniform poll closing in 48 states	#	106. AIDS insurance non-discrimination	N
59. Req foreign investment disclosure	Y	107. Prohibit Saudi arms sales	Y
60. Textile import quotas-veto override	N	108. Ease Gun Control Act of 1968	Y
61. Bar abortion funding in Wash, DC	Y	109. Bar interstate handgun transport	N
62. Notify spouses of AIDS+ carriers	N	110. Make company emissions known	N
63. Seize conveyance-drug trafficking	Y	111. Allow toxic victims to sue in fed ct	N
64. South Africa sanctions	N	112. Superfund waste cleanup of $10b	N
65. 60 days' notice of plant closings	N	113. 90 days notice of plant closings	X
66. Close unneeded military bases	Y	114. $20b in Medicare cuts/tax increases	N
67. Keep welfare reform within $2.8b	Y	115. Spending cuts and tax increases	N
68. Allow children housing exclusion	Y	116. Set school lunch lmt-250% poverty	N
69. Shift $400m of NASA to homeless	Y	117. $75m for youth work projects	N
70. Cap Medicare patients' liability	Y	118. Allow Angolan military assistance	Y
71. Prohibit employee polygraph testing	N	119. Suspend defense payments for abuse	N
72. Allow CIA to fund Contras	Y	120. Drop SS COLAs/$12b tax increase	N
73. Revise unfair trade practices	N	121. Approve $1.5b for 21 MX missiles	Y
74. Focus SDI on accidental launch	N	122. Emergency farm credit/revisions	N
75. Bar Air Force $ for MX missile	N	123. Duty on Taiwan/Hong Kong/S Korea	N
76. Allow "real" increase in defense	Y	124. Limit steel imports to 17%	N
77. Troop reduction in Europe of 50%	N	125. Cut $ to schools that bar prayer	Y
78. Ban nuclear tests above 1 kiloton	N	126. $50b-taxes; cut Medicare/spending	N
79. Ban anti-satellite missile tests	N	127. Limit Pershing II/cruise in Europe	N
80. Observe certain limits of SALT II	N	128. Delete $7.1b for 34 B-1 bombers	N
81. Restore four Civil Rights laws	N	129. Bar purchase of Sergeant York guns	N
82. Prohibit aliens as strikebreakers	N	130. El Salvador military/economic aid	Y
83. Allow military malpractice suits	Y	131. Bar mining of Nicaraguan waters	Y
84. Approval of $36m in Contra aid	Y	132. Physician fee freeze for Medicare	Y
85. $18b deficit reduction compromise	N	133. $49b in "sin"/phone/insurance taxes	N
86. Welfare reform of $5.7b for 5 years	N	134. Allow sale of Conrail	Y
87. Raise taxes $12b/cut spending $3b	?	135. Equal Rights Amendment	N
88. Board to assess occupational risk	N	136. Authorize Marines in Lebanon	Y
89. Balanced budget by '93-via targets	N	137. Eminent domain for coal companies	Y
90. Bar licensing of two nuclear plants	N	138. Prohibit EPA clean air sanctions	Y
91. Remove victims compensation cap	N	139. SS retirement age increase/reforms	Y
92. Catastrophic health insurance	N		

Presidential Support Score: 1991 - 78% 1990 - 66%

WYDEN, RON -- Oregon 3rd District [Democrat]. Counties of Clackamas (pt.) and Multnomah (pt.). Prior Terms: 1981-92. Born: May 3, 1949; Wichita, KS. Education: University of California; Stanford University (A.B.); University of Oregon School of Law (J.D.). Occupation: Attorney; co-founder, co-director, Gray Panthers; director, Oregon Legal Services for the Elderly; instructor.

1. Protection to Haitian refugees	Y	7. Bar race-bias claim/habeas corpus	N
2. Raise tax on wealthy; lower others	Y	8. Ban race as death sentence factor	N
3. Investigate Reagan hostage delay	Y	9. Exceptions to exclusionary rule	Y
4. Campaign finance revisions	Y	10. Allow sale of assault weapons	N
5. Unpaid leave to care for children	Y	11. Life in prison/abolish death penalty	N
6. Restrict NEA use of funds	N	12. Req conspiracy-price fixing cases	N

WYDEN, RON (continued)

13. Unemployment benefits extension	Y	
14. Tissue use of aborted fetuses	Y	
15. Bar replacement of union strikers	Y	
16. Hold foreign aid at $15b for '92	Y	
17. Restore space station funding	N	
18. Civil Rights Act of 1991	Y	
19. Unlimited damages-discrimination	Y	
20. Eliminate funds for supercollider	Y	
21. Terminate SDI except for research	Y	
22. Req 7-day handgun waiting period	Y	
23. Provide $30b for failed S&Ls	N	
24. Allow use of force against Iraq	N	
25. Allow $15b in foreign aid for '91	Y	
26. Revise & extend legal immigration	Y	
27. Suspend aid to Angolan rebels	Y	
28. Democratic tax plan proposals	Y	
29. Cut defense 5% across the board	Y	
30. Textile import quotas-veto override	N	
31. Abortion service for military abroad	Y	
32. Limits on high income farmers	Y	
33. Family medical leave-veto override	Y	
34. Req submission of balanced budget	Y	
35. Balanced budget amendment	N	
36. Amendment to ban flag desecration	N	
37. Reauthorize Amtrak-veto override	Y	
38. Retraining aid for coal miners	Y	
39. Suspend El Salvador military aid	Y	
40. Expand child care aid/tax credit	Y	
41. Raise House salary/omit honoraria	N	
42. Toughen oil-spill liability	Y	
43. Restitution to Japanese interned	Y	
44. Protect Chinese & C.A. nationals	Y	
45. Abortion $ for rape/incest cases	Y	
46. Allow religious schools to bar gays	N	
47. Bar broadcaster fairness doctrine	N	
48. Bar cap gains cut/reinstate IRA	N	
49. Bar unions equal voice in pension	N	
50. Bar assembly of chemical weapons	Y	
51. Ban plutonium/uranium production	Y	
52. Cap MX missile deployment at 50	Y	
53. Allow $3b for 2 stealth bombers	N	
54. Publish bio-warfare experiments	Y	
55. Raise minimum wage-veto override	Y	
56. Bar transfer of FS-X technology	?	
57. Cut defense and raise domestic $	N	
58. Uniform poll closing in 48 states	Y	
59. Req foreign investment disclosure	N	
60. Textile import quotas-veto override	N	
61. Bar abortion funding in Wash, DC	N	
62. Notify spouses of AIDS+ carriers	N	
63. Seize conveyance-drug trafficking	N	
64. South Africa sanctions	Y	
65. 60 days' notice of plant closings	Y	
66. Close unneeded military bases	Y	
67. Keep welfare reform within $2.8b	N	
68. Allow children housing exclusion	N	
69. Shift $400m of NASA to homeless	Y	
70. Cap Medicare patients' liability	Y	
71. Prohibit employee polygraph testing	Y	
72. Allow CIA to fund Contras	N	
73. Revise unfair trade practices	Y	
74. Focus SDI on accidental launch	Y	
75. Bar Air Force $ for MX missile	Y	
76. Allow "real" increase in defense	N	

77. Troop reduction in Europe of 50%	N	
78. Ban nuclear tests above 1 kiloton	Y	
79. Ban anti-satellite missile tests	Y	
80. Observe certain limits of SALT II	Y	
81. Restore four Civil Rights laws	Y	
82. Prohibit aliens as strikebreakers	Y	
83. Allow military malpractice suits	Y	
84. Approval of $36m in Contra aid	N	
85. $18b deficit reduction compromise	Y	
86. Welfare reform of $5.7b for 5 years	Y	
87. Raise taxes $12b/cut spending $3b	Y	
88. Board to assess occupational risk	Y	
89. Balanced budget by '93-via targets	Y	
90. Bar licensing of two nuclear plants	Y	
91. Remove victims compensation cap	Y	
92. Catastrophic health insurance	Y	
93. Ban airline smoking-2 hours or less	Y	
94. $1b/two year aid for the homeless	Y	
95. Bar non-unions in union companies	Y	
96. Increase FSLIC rescue to $15b	N	
97. Impose quotas to lower trade deficit	N	
98. Reduce discretionary budget 21%	N	
99. Immigration reform/alien amnesty	Y	
100. South Africa sanctions-veto override	Y	
101. Tax overhaul to revise income tax	Y	
102. Use of military in drug war	Y	
103. Delete 12 MX/add conventional wpn	Y	
104. Raise speed limit to 65 mph	Y	
105. Require Pentagon to buy US goods	N	
106. AIDS insurance non-discrimination	Y	
107. Prohibit Saudi arms sales	Y	
108. Ease Gun Control Act of 1968	Y	
109. Bar interstate handgun transport	N	
110. Make company emissions known	Y	
111. Allow toxic victims to sue in fed ct	Y	
112. Superfund waste cleanup of $10b	Y	
113. 90 days notice of plant closings	N	
114. $20b in Medicare cuts/tax increases	Y	
115. Spending cuts and tax increases	Y	
116. Set school lunch lmt-250% poverty	N	
117. $75m for youth work projects	Y	
118. Allow Angolan military assistance	N	
119. Suspend defense payments for abuse	N	
120. Drop SS COLAs/$12b tax increase	N	
121. Approve $1.5b for 21 MX missiles	N	
122. Emergency farm credit/revisions	Y	
123. Duty on Taiwan/Hong Kong/S Korea	N	
124. Limit steel imports to 17%	N	
125. Cut $ to schools that bar prayer	N	
126. $50b-taxes; cut Medicare/spending	Y	
127. Limit Pershing II/cruise in Europe	Y	
128. Delete $7.1b for 34 B-1 bombers	Y	
129. Bar purchase of Sergeant York guns	Y	
130. El Salvador military/economic aid	N	
131. Bar mining of Nicaraguan waters	Y	
132. Physician fee freeze for Medicare	N	
133. $49b in "sin"/phone/insurance taxes	Y	
134. Allow sale of Conrail	N	
135. Equal Rights Amendment	Y	
136. Authorize Marines in Lebanon	N	
137. Eminent domain for coal companies	N	
138. Prohibit EPA clean air sanctions	Y	
139. SS retirement age increase/reforms	N	
140. Auto domestic content requirement	N	

WYDEN, RON (continued)

141. Delete jobs program funding	N	143. Cut $5b from defense for Medicare	Y
142. Highway-gas tax bill	Y	144. Emergency housing aid of $1b	Y

Presidential Support Score: 1991 - 31% 1990 - 24%

DeFAZIO, PETER A. -- Oregon 4th District [Democrat]. Counties of Benton (pt.), Coos, Curry, Douglas, Jackson (pt.), Josephine (pt.), Lane, Linn (pt.) and Marion (pt.). Prior Terms: 1987-92. Born: May 27, 1947; Needham, MA. Education: Tufts University (B.A.); University of Oregon (M.S.). Occupation: Assistant to Representative Weaver (1977-82); member (1983-86) and chairman (1984-86), Lane County Board of Commissioners.

1. Protection to Haitian refugees	Y	50. Bar assembly of chemical weapons	Y
2. Raise tax on wealthy; lower others	Y	51. Ban plutonium/uranium production	Y
3. Investigate Reagan hostage delay	?	52. Cap MX missile deployment at 50	Y
4. Campaign finance revisions	Y	53. Allow $3b for 2 stealth bombers	N
5. Unpaid leave to care for children	Y	54. Publish bio-warfare experiments	Y
6. Restrict NEA use of funds	N	55. Raise minimum wage-veto override	Y
7. Bar race-bias claim/habeas corpus	N	56. Bar transfer of FS-X technology	N
8. Ban race as death sentence factor	N	57. Cut defense and raise domestic $	Y
9. Exceptions to exclusionary rule	N	58. Uniform poll closing in 48 states	Y
10. Allow sale of assault weapons	Y	59. Req foreign investment disclosure	Y
11. Life in prison/abolish death penalty	Y	60. Textile import quotas-veto override	N
12. Req conspiracy-price fixing cases	N	61. Bar abortion funding in Wash, DC	N
13. Unemployment benefits extension	Y	62. Notify spouses of AIDS+ carriers	N
14. Tissue use of aborted fetuses	Y	63. Seize conveyance-drug trafficking	N
15. Bar replacement of union strikers	Y	64. South Africa sanctions	Y
16. Hold foreign aid at $15b for '92	N	65. 60 days' notice of plant closings	Y
17. Restore space station funding	Y	66. Close unneeded military bases	Y
18. Civil Rights Act of 1991	Y	67. Keep welfare reform within $2.8b	?
19. Unlimited damages-discrimination	Y	68. Allow children housing exclusion	N
20. Eliminate funds for supercollider	Y	69. Shift $400m of NASA to homeless	Y
21. Terminate SDI except for research	Y	70. Cap Medicare patients' liability	N
22. Req 7-day handgun waiting period	Y	71. Prohibit employee polygraph testing	Y
23. Provide $30b for failed S&Ls	N	72. Allow CIA to fund Contras	N
24. Allow use of force against Iraq	N	73. Revise unfair trade practices	Y
25. Allow $15b in foreign aid for '91	N	74. Focus SDI on accidental launch	Y
26. Revise & extend legal immigration	Y	75. Bar Air Force $ for MX missile	Y
27. Suspend aid to Angolan rebels	Y	76. Allow "real" increase in defense	N
28. Democratic tax plan proposals	Y	77. Troop reduction in Europe of 50%	Y
29. Cut defense 5% across the board	Y	78. Ban nuclear tests above 1 kiloton	Y
30. Textile import quotas-veto override	N	79. Ban anti-satellite missile tests	Y
31. Abortion service for military abroad	Y	80. Observe certain limits of SALT II	Y
32. Limits on high income farmers	N	81. Restore four Civil Rights laws	Y
33. Family medical leave-veto override	Y	82. Prohibit aliens as strikebreakers	Y
34. Req submission of balanced budget	N	83. Allow military malpractice suits	Y
35. Balanced budget amendment	Y	84. Approval of $36m in Contra aid	N
36. Amendment to ban flag desecration	N	85. $18b deficit reduction compromise	N
37. Reauthorize Amtrak-veto override	Y	86. Welfare reform of $5.7b for 5 years	Y
38. Retraining aid for coal miners	Y	87. Raise taxes $12b/cut spending $3b	N
39. Suspend El Salvador military aid	Y	88. Board to assess occupational risk	Y
40. Expand child care aid/tax credit	Y	89. Balanced budget by '93-via targets	N
41. Raise House salary/omit honoraria	N	90. Bar licensing of two nuclear plants	Y
42. Toughen oil-spill liability	Y	91. Remove victims compensation cap	Y
43. Restitution to Japanese interned	Y	92. Catastrophic health insurance	Y
44. Protect Chinese & C.A. nationals	Y	93. Ban airline smoking-2 hours or less	N
45. Abortion $ for rape/incest cases	Y	94. $1b/two year aid for the homeless	Y
46. Allow religious schools to bar gays	N	95. Bar non-unions in union companies	Y
47. Bar broadcaster fairness doctrine	Y	96. Increase FSLIC rescue to $15b	N
48. Bar cap gains cut/reinstate IRA	Y	97. Impose quotas to lower trade deficit	Y
49. Bar unions equal voice in pension	N	98. Reduce discretionary budget 21%	Y

Presidential Support Score: 1991 - 26% 1990 - 19%

KOPETSKI, MIKE -- Oregon 5th District [Democrat]. Counties of Benton (pt.), Clackamas (pt.), Linn (pt.), Marion (pt.) and Polk (pt.). Prior Term: 1991-92. Born: October 27, 1949; Pendleton, OR. Education: American University (B.A.); Northwestern School of Law (J.D.). Occupation: U.S. Senate Watergate Committee investigator; state legislative committee administrator; labor-management consultant to state governor and education department; state representative (1985-88); Currier/McCormick Communications vice president.

1. Protection to Haitian refugees	Y		13. Unemployment benefits extension	Y
2. Raise tax on wealthy; lower others	Y		14. Tissue use of aborted fetuses	Y
3. Investigate Reagan hostage delay	Y		15. Bar replacement of union strikers	Y
4. Campaign finance revisions	Y		16. Hold foreign aid at $15b for '92	Y
5. Unpaid leave to care for children	Y		17. Restore space station funding	Y
6. Restrict NEA use of funds	N		18. Civil Rights Act of 1991	Y
7. Bar race-bias claim/habeas corpus	N		19. Unlimited damages-discrimination	Y
8. Ban race as death sentence factor	N		20. Eliminate funds for supercollider	N
9. Exceptions to exclusionary rule	N		21. Terminate SDI except for research	Y
10. Allow sale of assault weapons	Y		22. Req 7-day handgun waiting period	N
11. Life in prison/abolish death penalty	Y		23. Provide $30b for failed S&Ls	Y
12. Req conspiracy-price fixing cases	N		24. Allow use of force against Iraq	N

Presidential Support Score: 1991 - 37%

PENNSYLVANIA

FOGLIETTA, THOMAS M. -- Pennsylvania 1st District [Democrat]. County of Philadelphia (pt.). Prior Terms: 1981-92. Born: December 3, 1928; Philadelphia, PA. Education: St. Joseph's College (B.A.); Temple University (J.D.). Occupation: Philadelphia city councilman; attorney; boardmember, St. Luke's Hospital; boardmember, Guiffre Medical Center; Labor Department regional director.

1. Protection to Haitian refugees	?		29. Cut defense 5% across the board	N
2. Raise tax on wealthy; lower others	Y		30. Textile import quotas-veto override	Y
3. Investigate Reagan hostage delay	Y		31. Abortion service for military abroad	N
4. Campaign finance revisions	Y		32. Limits on high income farmers	Y
5. Unpaid leave to care for children	Y		33. Family medical leave-veto override	Y
6. Restrict NEA use of funds	N		34. Req submission of balanced budget	Y
7. Bar race-bias claim/habeas corpus	N		35. Balanced budget amendment	N
8. Ban race as death sentence factor	N		36. Amendment to ban flag desecration	N
9. Exceptions to exclusionary rule	N		37. Reauthorize Amtrak-veto override	Y
10. Allow sale of assault weapons	N		38. Retraining aid for coal miners	Y
11. Life in prison/abolish death penalty	Y		39. Suspend El Salvador military aid	Y
12. Req conspiracy-price fixing cases	N		40. Expand child care aid/tax credit	Y
13. Unemployment benefits extension	Y		41. Raise House salary/omit honoraria	Y
14. Tissue use of aborted fetuses	Y		42. Toughen oil-spill liability	Y
15. Bar replacement of union strikers	Y		43. Restitution to Japanese interned	Y
16. Hold foreign aid at $15b for '92	Y		44. Protect Chinese & C.A. nationals	Y
17. Restore space station funding	N		45. Abortion $ for rape/incest cases	?
18. Civil Rights Act of 1991	Y		46. Allow religious schools to bar gays	N
19. Unlimited damages-discrimination	Y		47. Bar broadcaster fairness doctrine	N
20. Eliminate funds for supercollider	N		48. Bar cap gains cut/reinstate IRA	Y
21. Terminate SDI except for research	Y		49. Bar unions equal voice in pension	N
22. Req 7-day handgun waiting period	Y		50. Bar assembly of chemical weapons	Y
23. Provide $30b for failed S&Ls	N		51. Ban plutonium/uranium production	Y
24. Allow use of force against Iraq	N		52. Cap MX missile deployment at 50	Y
25. Allow $15b in foreign aid for '91	Y		53. Allow $3b for 2 stealth bombers	N
26. Revise & extend legal immigration	Y		54. Publish bio-warfare experiments	Y
27. Suspend aid to Angolan rebels	Y		55. Raise minimum wage-veto override	Y
28. Democratic tax plan proposals	Y		56. Bar transfer of FS-X technology	Y

FOGLIETTA, THOMAS M. (continued)

57.	Cut defense and raise domestic $	Y	101. Tax overhaul to revise income tax	Y
58.	Uniform poll closing in 48 states	Y	102. Use of military in drug war	N
59.	Req foreign investment disclosure	N	103. Delete 12 MX/add conventional wpn	Y
60.	Textile import quotas-veto override	Y	104. Raise speed limit to 65 mph	N
61.	Bar abortion funding in Wash, DC	N	105. Require Pentagon to buy US goods	Y
62.	Notify spouses of AIDS+ carriers	N	106. AIDS insurance non-discrimination	Y
63.	Seize conveyance-drug trafficking	N	107. Prohibit Saudi arms sales	Y
64.	South Africa sanctions	Y	108. Ease Gun Control Act of 1968	N
65.	60 days' notice of plant closings	+	109. Bar interstate handgun transport	Y
66.	Close unneeded military bases	N	110. Make company emissions known	Y
67.	Keep welfare reform within $2.8b	N	111. Allow toxic victims to sue in fed ct	Y
68.	Allow children housing exclusion	N	112. Superfund waste cleanup of $10b	N
69.	Shift $400m of NASA to homeless	Y	113. 90 days notice of plant closings	Y
70.	Cap Medicare patients' liability	Y	114. $20b in Medicare cuts/tax increases	Y
71.	Prohibit employee polygraph testing	?	115. Spending cuts and tax increases	Y
72.	Allow CIA to fund Contras	N	116. Set school lunch lmt-250% poverty	N
73.	Revise unfair trade practices	Y	117. $75m for youth work projects	Y
74.	Focus SDI on accidental launch	Y	118. Allow Angolan military assistance	N
75.	Bar Air Force $ for MX missile	Y	119. Suspend defense payments for abuse	Y
76.	Allow "real" increase in defense	N	120. Drop SS COLAs/$12b tax increase	N
77.	Troop reduction in Europe of 50%	N	121. Approve $1.5b for 21 MX missiles	N
78.	Ban nuclear tests above 1 kiloton	Y	122. Emergency farm credit/revisions	Y
79.	Ban anti-satellite missile tests	Y	123. Duty on Taiwan/Hong Kong/S Korea	Y
80.	Observe certain limits of SALT II	Y	124. Limit steel imports to 17%	Y
81.	Restore four Civil Rights laws	Y	125. Cut $ to schools that bar prayer	N
82.	Prohibit aliens as strikebreakers	Y	126. $50b-taxes; cut Medicare/spending	Y
83.	Allow military malpractice suits	Y	127. Limit Pershing II/cruise in Europe	Y
84.	Approval of $36m in Contra aid	N	128. Delete $7.1b for 34 B-1 bombers	Y
85.	$18b deficit reduction compromise	Y	129. Bar purchase of Sergeant York guns	N
86.	Welfare reform of $5.7b for 5 years	Y	130. El Salvador military/economic aid	N
87.	Raise taxes $12b/cut spending $3b	Y	131. Bar mining of Nicaraguan waters	Y
88.	Board to assess occupational risk	Y	132. Physician fee freeze for Medicare	N
89.	Balanced budget by '93-via targets	N	133. $49b in "sin"/phone/insurance taxes	?
90.	Bar licensing of two nuclear plants	Y	134. Allow sale of Conrail	?
91.	Remove victims compensation cap	N	135. Equal Rights Amendment	Y
92.	Catastrophic health insurance	Y	136. Authorize Marines in Lebanon	Y
93.	Ban airline smoking-2 hours or less	?	137. Eminent domain for coal companies	Y
94.	$1b/two year aid for the homeless	Y	138. Prohibit EPA clean air sanctions	?
95.	Bar non-unions in union companies	Y	139. SS retirement age increase/reforms	N
96.	Increase FSLIC rescue to $15b	N	140. Auto domestic content requirement	Y
97.	Impose quotas to lower trade deficit	Y	141. Delete jobs program funding	N
98.	Reduce discretionary budget 21%	?	142. Highway-gas tax bill	Y
99.	Immigration reform/alien amnesty	Y	143. Cut $5b from defense for Medicare	Y
100.	South Africa sanctions-veto override	Y	144. Emergency housing aid of $1b	?

Presidential Support Score: 1991 - 23%   1990 - 24%

BLACKWELL, LUCIEN E. -- Pennsylvania 2nd District [Democrat]. County of Philadelphia (pt.). Prior Term: 1991 (Special Election)-1992. Born: August 1, 1931. Military Service: U.S. Army. Occupation: Longshoreman and city union local president; Philadelphia Gas Commission chairman; state representative; Philadelphia city councilman (1975-91).

1.	Protection to Haitian refugees	Y	4. Campaign finance revisions	Y
2.	Raise tax on wealthy; lower others	Y	5. Unpaid leave to care for children	Y
3.	Investigate Reagan hostage delay	Y		

Rep. Blackwell was sworn in Nov. 13, 1991, to succeed William H. Gray.

Presidential Support Score: 1991 - 31%

BORSKI, ROBERT A. -- Pennsylvania 3rd District [Democrat]. County of Philadelphia (pt.). Prior Terms: 1983-92. Born: October 20, 1948; Philadelphia, PA. Education: University

BORSKI, ROBERT A. (continued)
of Baltimore (B.A.). Occupation: Assistant basketball coach; stockbroker; Pennsylvania legislator (1976-82).

1. Protection to Haitian refugees	Y	62. Notify spouses of AIDS+ carriers	N
2. Raise tax on wealthy; lower others	Y	63. Seize conveyance-drug trafficking	N
3. Investigate Reagan hostage delay	Y	64. South Africa sanctions	Y
4. Campaign finance revisions	Y	65. 60 days' notice of plant closings	Y
5. Unpaid leave to care for children	Y	66. Close unneeded military bases	N
6. Restrict NEA use of funds	N	67. Keep welfare reform within $2.8b	N
7. Bar race-bias claim/habeas corpus	Y	68. Allow children housing exclusion	N
8. Ban race as death sentence factor	Y	69. Shift $400m of NASA to homeless	Y
9. Exceptions to exclusionary rule	Y	70. Cap Medicare patients' liability	Y
10. Allow sale of assault weapons	N	71. Prohibit employee polygraph testing	Y
11. Life in prison/abolish death penalty	N	72. Allow CIA to fund Contras	N
12. Req conspiracy-price fixing cases	N	73. Revise unfair trade practices	Y
13. Unemployment benefits extension	Y	74. Focus SDI on accidental launch	Y
14. Tissue use of aborted fetuses	Y	75. Bar Air Force $ for MX missile	N
15. Bar replacement of union strikers	Y	76. Allow "real" increase in defense	N
16. Hold foreign aid at $15b for '92	Y	77. Troop reduction in Europe of 50%	Y
17. Restore space station funding	?	78. Ban nuclear tests above 1 kiloton	Y
18. Civil Rights Act of 1991	Y	79. Ban anti-satellite missile tests	Y
19. Unlimited damages-discrimination	N	80. Observe certain limits of SALT II	Y
20. Eliminate funds for supercollider	N	81. Restore four Civil Rights laws	Y
21. Terminate SDI except for research	N	82. Prohibit aliens as strikebreakers	Y
22. Req 7-day handgun waiting period	Y	83. Allow military malpractice suits	Y
23. Provide $30b for failed S&Ls	Y	84. Approval of $36m in Contra aid	N
24. Allow use of force against Iraq	Y	85. $18b deficit reduction compromise	Y
25. Allow $15b in foreign aid for '91	Y	86. Welfare reform of $5.7b for 5 years	Y
26. Revise & extend legal immigration	Y	87. Raise taxes $12b/cut spending $3b	Y
27. Suspend aid to Angolan rebels	Y	88. Board to assess occupational risk	Y
28. Democratic tax plan proposals	Y	89. Balanced budget by '93-via targets	N
29. Cut defense 5% across the board	N	90. Bar licensing of two nuclear plants	Y
30. Textile import quotas-veto override	Y	91. Remove victims compensation cap	N
31. Abortion service for military abroad	N	92. Catastrophic health insurance	Y
32. Limits on high income farmers	Y	93. Ban airline smoking-2 hours or less	N
33. Family medical leave-veto override	Y	94. $1b/two year aid for the homeless	Y
34. Req submission of balanced budget	Y	95. Bar non-unions in union companies	Y
35. Balanced budget amendment	N	96. Increase FSLIC rescue to $15b	N
36. Amendment to ban flag desecration	N	97. Impose quotas to lower trade deficit	Y
37. Reauthorize Amtrak-veto override	Y	98. Reduce discretionary budget 21%	Y
38. Retraining aid for coal miners	Y	99. Immigration reform/alien amnesty	Y
39. Suspend El Salvador military aid	Y	100. South Africa sanctions-veto override	Y
40. Expand child care aid/tax credit	Y	101. Tax overhaul to revise income tax	Y
41. Raise House salary/omit honoraria	Y	102. Use of military in drug war	N
42. Toughen oil-spill liability	N	103. Delete 12 MX/add conventional wpn	Y
43. Restitution to Japanese interned	Y	104. Raise speed limit to 65 mph	N
44. Protect Chinese & C.A. nationals	Y	105. Require Pentagon to buy US goods	Y
45. Abortion $ for rape/incest cases	N	106. AIDS insurance non-discrimination	Y
46. Allow religious schools to bar gays	N	107. Prohibit Saudi arms sales	Y
47. Bar broadcaster fairness doctrine	N	108. Ease Gun Control Act of 1968	N
48. Bar cap gains cut/reinstate IRA	Y	109. Bar interstate handgun transport	Y
49. Bar unions equal voice in pension	Y	110. Make company emissions known	Y
50. Bar assembly of chemical weapons	Y	111. Allow toxic victims to sue in fed ct	N
51. Ban plutonium/uranium production	Y	112. Superfund waste cleanup of $10b	N
52. Cap MX missile deployment at 50	Y	113. 90 days notice of plant closings	Y
53. Allow $3b for 2 stealth bombers	N	114. $20b in Medicare cuts/tax increases	Y
54. Publish bio-warfare experiments	Y	115. Spending cuts and tax increases	Y
55. Raise minimum wage-veto override	Y	116. Set school lunch lmt-250% poverty	N
56. Bar transfer of FS-X technology	Y	117. $75m for youth work projects	Y
57. Cut defense and raise domestic $	N	118. Allow Angolan military assistance	N
58. Uniform poll closing in 48 states	N	119. Suspend defense payments for abuse	Y
59. Req foreign investment disclosure	Y	120. Drop SS COLAs/$12b tax increase	N
60. Textile import quotas-veto override	Y	121. Approve $1.5b for 21 MX missiles	N
61. Bar abortion funding in Wash, DC	Y	122. Emergency farm credit/revisions	Y

BORSKI, ROBERT A. (continued)

123. Duty on Taiwan/Hong Kong/S Korea	Y	132. Physician fee freeze for Medicare	N
124. Limit steel imports to 17%	Y	133. $49b in "sin"/phone/insurance taxes	Y
125. Cut $ to schools that bar prayer	N	134. Allow sale of Conrail	N
126. $50b-taxes; cut Medicare/spending	Y	135. Equal Rights Amendment	Y
127. Limit Pershing II/cruise in Europe	N	136. Authorize Marines in Lebanon	Y
128. Delete $7.1b for 34 B-1 bombers	Y	137. Eminent domain for coal companies	Y
129. Bar purchase of Sergeant York guns	Y	138. Prohibit EPA clean air sanctions	Y
130. El Salvador military/economic aid	N	139. SS retirement age increase/reforms	N
131. Bar mining of Nicaraguan waters	Y		

Presidential Support Score: 1991 - 36%   1990 - 27%

KOLTER, JOE -- Pennsylvania 4th District [Democrat]. Counties of Armstrong (pt.), Beaver (pt.), Butler, Indiana, Lawrence (pt.) and Westmoreland (pt.). Prior Terms: 1983-92. Born: September 3, 1946; McDonald, OH. Education: Geneva College. Military Service: U.S. Army. Occupation: Accountant; teacher; councilman; Pennsylvania legislator (1968-82).

1. Protection to Haitian refugees	?	47. Bar broadcaster fairness doctrine	N
2. Raise tax on wealthy; lower others	Y	48. Bar cap gains cut/reinstate IRA	Y
3. Investigate Reagan hostage delay	?	49. Bar unions equal voice in pension	N
4. Campaign finance revisions	Y	50. Bar assembly of chemical weapons	Y
5. Unpaid leave to care for children	Y	51. Ban plutonium/uranium production	Y
6. Restrict NEA use of funds	N	52. Cap MX missile deployment at 50	Y
7. Bar race-bias claim/habeas corpus	Y	53. Allow $3b for 2 stealth bombers	N
8. Ban race as death sentence factor	Y	54. Publish bio-warfare experiments	Y
9. Exceptions to exclusionary rule	Y	55. Raise minimum wage-veto override	Y
10. Allow sale of assault weapons	Y	56. Bar transfer of FS-X technology	Y
11. Life in prison/abolish death penalty	N	57. Cut defense and raise domestic $	N
12. Req conspiracy-price fixing cases	N	58. Uniform poll closing in 48 states	Y
13. Unemployment benefits extension	Y	59. Req foreign investment disclosure	Y
14. Tissue use of aborted fetuses	N	60. Textile import quotas-veto override	Y
15. Bar replacement of union strikers	Y	61. Bar abortion funding in Wash, DC	Y
16. Hold foreign aid at $15b for '92	?	62. Notify spouses of AIDS+ carriers	N
17. Restore space station funding	Y	63. Seize conveyance-drug trafficking	N
18. Civil Rights Act of 1991	Y	64. South Africa sanctions	?
19. Unlimited damages-discrimination	Y	65. 60 days' notice of plant closings	Y
20. Eliminate funds for supercollider	N	66. Close unneeded military bases	N
21. Terminate SDI except for research	?	67. Keep welfare reform within $2.8b	?
22. Req 7-day handgun waiting period	N	68. Allow children housing exclusion	N
23. Provide $30b for failed S&Ls	N	69. Shift $400m of NASA to homeless	Y
24. Allow use of force against Iraq	N	70. Cap Medicare patients' liability	Y
25. Allow $15b in foreign aid for '91	N	71. Prohibit employee polygraph testing	Y
26. Revise & extend legal immigration	Y	72. Allow CIA to fund Contras	N
27. Suspend aid to Angolan rebels	Y	73. Revise unfair trade practices	N
28. Democratic tax plan proposals	N	74. Focus SDI on accidental launch	N
29. Cut defense 5% across the board	Y	75. Bar Air Force $ for MX missile	N
30. Textile import quotas-veto override	Y	76. Allow "real" increase in defense	N
31. Abortion service for military abroad	N	77. Troop reduction in Europe of 50%	Y
32. Limits on high income farmers	?	78. Ban nuclear tests above 1 kiloton	Y
33. Family medical leave-veto override	Y	79. Ban anti-satellite missile tests	Y
34. Req submission of balanced budget	Y	80. Observe certain limits of SALT II	Y
35. Balanced budget amendment	N	81. Restore four Civil Rights laws	Y
36. Amendment to ban flag desecration	Y	82. Prohibit aliens as strikebreakers	Y
37. Reauthorize Amtrak-veto override	Y	83. Allow military malpractice suits	?
38. Retraining aid for coal miners	Y	84. Approval of $36m in Contra aid	N
39. Suspend El Salvador military aid	Y	85. $18b deficit reduction compromise	N
40. Expand child care aid/tax credit	Y	86. Welfare reform of $5.7b for 5 years	Y
41. Raise House salary/omit honoraria	N	87. Raise taxes $12b/cut spending $3b	?
42. Toughen oil-spill liability	Y	88. Board to assess occupational risk	Y
43. Restitution to Japanese interned	Y	89. Balanced budget by '93-via targets	N
44. Protect Chinese & C.A. nationals	Y	90. Bar licensing of two nuclear plants	N
45. Abortion $ for rape/incest cases	N	91. Remove victims compensation cap	N
46. Allow religious schools to bar gays	Y	92. Catastrophic health insurance	Y

KOLTER, JOE (continued)

93. Ban airline smoking-2 hours or less	N
94. $1b/two year aid for the homeless	Y
95. Bar non-unions in union companies	Y
96. Increase FSLIC rescue to $15b	?
97. Impose quotas to lower trade deficit	Y
98. Reduce discretionary budget 21%	Y
99. Immigration reform/alien amnesty	N
100. South Africa sanctions-veto override	Y
101. Tax overhaul to revise income tax	N
102. Use of military in drug war	Y
103. Delete 12 MX/add conventional wpn	Y
104. Raise speed limit to 65 mph	N
105. Require Pentagon to buy US goods	Y
106. AIDS insurance non-discrimination	Y
107. Prohibit Saudi arms sales	Y
108. Ease Gun Control Act of 1968	Y
109. Bar interstate handgun transport	N
110. Make company emissions known	Y
111. Allow toxic victims to sue in fed ct	N
112. Superfund waste cleanup of $10b	N
113. 90 days notice of plant closings	Y
114. $20b in Medicare cuts/tax increases	N
115. Spending cuts and tax increases	N
116. Set school lunch lmt-250% poverty	N

117. $75m for youth work projects	?
118. Allow Angolan military assistance	N
119. Suspend defense payments for abuse	Y
120. Drop SS COLAs/$12b tax increase	N
121. Approve $1.5b for 21 MX missiles	N
122. Emergency farm credit/revisions	Y
123. Duty on Taiwan/Hong Kong/S Korea	Y
124. Limit steel imports to 17%	Y
125. Cut $ to schools that bar prayer	Y
126. $50b-taxes; cut Medicare/spending	N
127. Limit Pershing II/cruise in Europe	?
128. Delete $7.1b for 34 B-1 bombers	Y
129. Bar purchase of Sergeant York guns	Y
130. El Salvador military/economic aid	N
131. Bar mining of Nicaraguan waters	Y
132. Physician fee freeze for Medicare	N
133. $49b in "sin"/phone/insurance taxes	Y
134. Allow sale of Conrail	N
135. Equal Rights Amendment	Y
136. Authorize Marines in Lebanon	Y
137. Eminent domain for coal companies	N
138. Prohibit EPA clean air sanctions	?
139. SS retirement age increase/reforms	N

Presidential Support Score: 1991 - 36%   1990 - 24%

SCHULZE, RICHARD T. -- Pennsylvania 5th District [Republican]. Counties of Chester (pt.), Delaware (pt.) and Montgomery (pt.). Prior Terms: 1975-92. Born: August 7, 1929; Philadelphia, PA. Education: Houston University; Villanova University; Temple University Extension. Military Service: U.S.Army, 1951-53. Occupation: Retail electrical appliance businessman; Registrar, wills and clerk, Orphans Court (1967-69); Pennsylvania representative (1969-74).

1. Protection to Haitian refugees	N
2. Raise tax on wealthy; lower others	N
3. Investigate Reagan hostage delay	N
4. Campaign finance revisions	N
5. Unpaid leave to care for children	?
6. Restrict NEA use of funds	?
7. Bar race-bias claim/habeas corpus	Y
8. Ban race as death sentence factor	Y
9. Exceptions to exclusionary rule	Y
10. Allow sale of assault weapons	Y
11. Life in prison/abolish death penalty	N
12. Req conspiracy-price fixing cases	Y
13. Unemployment benefits extension	N
14. Tissue use of aborted fetuses	Y
15. Bar replacement of union strikers	N
16. Hold foreign aid at $15b for '92	Y
17. Restore space station funding	Y
18. Civil Rights Act of 1991	Y
19. Unlimited damages-discrimination	N
20. Eliminate funds for supercollider	Y
21. Terminate SDI except for research	N
22. Req 7-day handgun waiting period	N
23. Provide $30b for failed S&Ls	N
24. Allow use of force against Iraq	Y
25. Allow $15b in foreign aid for '91	?
26. Revise & extend legal immigration	Y
27. Suspend aid to Angolan rebels	N
28. Democratic tax plan proposals	N
29. Cut defense 5% across the board	N

30. Textile import quotas-veto override	Y
31. Abortion service for military abroad	N
32. Limits on high income farmers	Y
33. Family medical leave-veto override	N
34. Req submission of balanced budget	N
35. Balanced budget amendment	Y
36. Amendment to ban flag desecration	Y
37. Reauthorize Amtrak-veto override	Y
38. Retraining aid for coal miners	Y
39. Suspend El Salvador military aid	N
40. Expand child care aid/tax credit	N
41. Raise House salary/omit honoraria	Y
42. Toughen oil-spill liability	N
43. Restitution to Japanese interned	N
44. Protect Chinese & C.A. nationals	N
45. Abortion $ for rape/incest cases	N
46. Allow religious schools to bar gays	Y
47. Bar broadcaster fairness doctrine	Y
48. Bar cap gains cut/reinstate IRA	N
49. Bar unions equal voice in pension	Y
50. Bar assembly of chemical weapons	N
51. Ban plutonium/uranium production	Y
52. Cap MX missile deployment at 50	Y
53. Allow $3b for 2 stealth bombers	Y
54. Publish bio-warfare experiments	Y
55. Raise minimum wage-veto override	N
56. Bar transfer of FS-X technology	N
57. Cut defense and raise domestic $	N
58. Uniform poll closing in 48 states	N

SCHULZE, RICHARD T. (continued)

59. Req foreign investment disclosure	N	102. Use of military in drug war	Y
60. Textile import quotas-veto override	Y	103. Delete 12 MX/add conventional wpn	N
61. Bar abortion funding in Wash, DC	Y	104. Raise speed limit to 65 mph	N
62. Notify spouses of AIDS+ carriers	Y	105. Require Pentagon to buy US goods	Y
63. Seize conveyance-drug trafficking	?	106. AIDS insurance non-discrimination	N
64. South Africa sanctions	Y	107. Prohibit Saudi arms sales	Y
65. 60 days' notice of plant closings	N	108. Ease Gun Control Act of 1968	#
66. Close unneeded military bases	Y	109. Bar interstate handgun transport	N
67. Keep welfare reform within $2.8b	Y	110. Make company emissions known	N
68. Allow children housing exclusion	Y	111. Allow toxic victims to sue in fed ct	N
69. Shift $400m of NASA to homeless	Y	112. Superfund waste cleanup of $10b	N
70. Cap Medicare patients' liability	?	113. 90 days notice of plant closings	N
71. Prohibit employee polygraph testing	Y	114. $20b in Medicare cuts/tax increases	N
72. Allow CIA to fund Contras	Y	115. Spending cuts and tax increases	N
73. Revise unfair trade practices	N	116. Set school lunch lmt-250% poverty	Y
74. Focus SDI on accidental launch	N	117. $75m for youth work projects	N
75. Bar Air Force $ for MX missile	N	118. Allow Angolan military assistance	Y
76. Allow "real" increase in defense	Y	119. Suspend defense payments for abuse	Y
77. Troop reduction in Europe of 50%	N	120. Drop SS COLAs/$12b tax increase	Y
78. Ban nuclear tests above 1 kiloton	N	121. Approve $1.5b for 21 MX missiles	Y
79. Ban anti-satellite missile tests	N	122. Emergency farm credit/revisions	N
80. Observe certain limits of SALT II	N	123. Duty on Taiwan/Hong Kong/S Korea	N
81. Restore four Civil Rights laws	Y	124. Limit steel imports to 17%	Y
82. Prohibit aliens as strikebreakers	N	125. Cut $ to schools that bar prayer	Y
83. Allow military malpractice suits	?	126. $50b-taxes; cut Medicare/spending	Y
84. Approval of $36m in Contra aid	Y	127. Limit Pershing II/cruise in Europe	N
85. $18b deficit reduction compromise	N	128. Delete $7.1b for 34 B-1 bombers	N
86. Welfare reform of $5.7b for 5 years	N	129. Bar purchase of Sergeant York guns	N
87. Raise taxes $12b/cut spending $3b	?	130. El Salvador military/economic aid	Y
88. Board to assess occupational risk	N	131. Bar mining of Nicaraguan waters	Y
89. Balanced budget by '93-via targets	Y	132. Physician fee freeze for Medicare	Y
90. Bar licensing of two nuclear plants	N	133. $49b in "sin"/phone/insurance taxes	Y
91. Remove victims compensation cap	N	134. Allow sale of Conrail	Y
92. Catastrophic health insurance	Y	135. Equal Rights Amendment	N
93. Ban airline smoking-2 hours or less	N	136. Authorize Marines in Lebanon	N
94. $1b/two year aid for the homeless	N	137. Eminent domain for coal companies	N
95. Bar non-unions in union companies	N	138. Prohibit EPA clean air sanctions	?
96. Increase FSLIC rescue to $15b	N	139. SS retirement age increase/reforms	Y
97. Impose quotas to lower trade deficit	N	140. Auto domestic content requirement	?
98. Reduce discretionary budget 21%	N	141. Delete jobs program funding	?
99. Immigration reform/alien amnesty	?	142. Highway-gas tax bill	Y
100. South Africa sanctions-veto override	Y	143. Cut $5b from defense for Medicare	N
101. Tax overhaul to revise income tax	Y	144. Emergency housing aid of $1b	Y

Presidential Support Score: 1991 - 73%   1990 - 61%

YATRON, GUS -- Pennsylvania 6th District [Democrat]. Counties of Berks, Carbon (pt.), Lancaster (pt.) and Schuylkill. Prior Terms: 1969-92. Born: October 16, 1927; Reading, PA. Education: Kutztown State Teachers College. Occupation: Ice cream businessman; school board member (1955); Pennsylvania representative (1956-59); Pennsylvania senator (1960-68).

1. Protection to Haitian refugees	Y	12. Req conspiracy-price fixing cases	N
2. Raise tax on wealthy; lower others	Y	13. Unemployment benefits extension	?
3. Investigate Reagan hostage delay	Y	14. Tissue use of aborted fetuses	?
4. Campaign finance revisions	Y	15. Bar replacement of union strikers	?
5. Unpaid leave to care for children	Y	16. Hold foreign aid at $15b for '92	Y
6. Restrict NEA use of funds	N	17. Restore space station funding	Y
7. Bar race-bias claim/habeas corpus	Y	18. Civil Rights Act of 1991	Y
8. Ban race as death sentence factor	N	19. Unlimited damages-discrimination	N
9. Exceptions to exclusionary rule	Y	20. Eliminate funds for supercollider	N
10. Allow sale of assault weapons	Y	21. Terminate SDI except for research	?
11. Life in prison/abolish death penalty	N	22. Req 7-day handgun waiting period	N

YATRON, GUS (continued)

23. Provide $30b for failed S&Ls	N	
24. Allow use of force against Iraq	N	
25. Allow $15b in foreign aid for '91	N	
26. Revise & extend legal immigration	N	
27. Suspend aid to Angolan rebels	Y	
28. Democratic tax plan proposals	N	
29. Cut defense 5% across the board	Y	
30. Textile import quotas-veto override	Y	
31. Abortion service for military abroad	N	
32. Limits on high income farmers	N	
33. Family medical leave-veto override	Y	
34. Req submission of balanced budget	Y	
35. Balanced budget amendment	N	
36. Amendment to ban flag desecration	Y	
37. Reauthorize Amtrak-veto override	Y	
38. Retraining aid for coal miners	Y	
39. Suspend El Salvador military aid	Y	
40. Expand child care aid/tax credit	Y	
41. Raise House salary/omit honoraria	N	
42. Toughen oil-spill liability	Y	
43. Restitution to Japanese interned	?	
44. Protect Chinese & C.A. nationals	?	
45. Abortion $ for rape/incest cases	?	
46. Allow religious schools to bar gays	?	
47. Bar broadcaster fairness doctrine	?	
48. Bar cap gains cut/reinstate IRA	?	
49. Bar unions equal voice in pension	?	
50. Bar assembly of chemical weapons	Y	
51. Ban plutonium/uranium production	Y	
52. Cap MX missile deployment at 50	Y	
53. Allow $3b for 2 stealth bombers	N	
54. Publish bio-warfare experiments	Y	
55. Raise minimum wage-veto override	Y	
56. Bar transfer of FS-X technology	N	
57. Cut defense and raise domestic $	N	
58. Uniform poll closing in 48 states	Y	
59. Req foreign investment disclosure	N	
60. Textile import quotas-veto override	Y	
61. Bar abortion funding in Wash, DC	Y	
62. Notify spouses of AIDS+ carriers	N	
63. Seize conveyance-drug trafficking	Y	
64. South Africa sanctions	Y	
65. 60 days' notice of plant closings	Y	
66. Close unneeded military bases	N	
67. Keep welfare reform within $2.8b	Y	
68. Allow children housing exclusion	Y	
69. Shift $400m of NASA to homeless	Y	
70. Cap Medicare patients' liability	Y	
71. Prohibit employee polygraph testing	Y	
72. Allow CIA to fund Contras	N	
73. Revise unfair trade practices	Y	
74. Focus SDI on accidental launch	N	
75. Bar Air Force $ for MX missile	N	
76. Allow "real" increase in defense	N	
77. Troop reduction in Europe of 50%	N	
78. Ban nuclear tests above 1 kiloton	Y	
79. Ban anti-satellite missile tests	Y	
80. Observe certain limits of SALT II	Y	
81. Restore four Civil Rights laws	Y	
82. Prohibit aliens as strikebreakers	Y	
83. Allow military malpractice suits	Y	

84. Approval of $36m in Contra aid	N	
85. $18b deficit reduction compromise	Y	
86. Welfare reform of $5.7b for 5 years	Y	
87. Raise taxes $12b/cut spending $3b	N	
88. Board to assess occupational risk	Y	
89. Balanced budget by '93-via targets	N	
90. Bar licensing of two nuclear plants	N	
91. Remove victims compensation cap	N	
92. Catastrophic health insurance	Y	
93. Ban airline smoking-2 hours or less	Y	
94. $1b/two year aid for the homeless	Y	
95. Bar non-unions in union companies	Y	
96. Increase FSLIC rescue to $15b	?	
97. Impose quotas to lower trade deficit	Y	
98. Reduce discretionary budget 21%	N	
99. Immigration reform/alien amnesty	N	
100. South Africa sanctions-veto override	Y	
101. Tax overhaul to revise income tax	Y	
102. Use of military in drug war	Y	
103. Delete 12 MX/add conventional wpn	N	
104. Raise speed limit to 65 mph	N	
105. Require Pentagon to buy US goods	Y	
106. AIDS insurance non-discrimination	Y	
107. Prohibit Saudi arms sales	Y	
108. Ease Gun Control Act of 1968	Y	
109. Bar interstate handgun transport	N	
110. Make company emissions known	Y	
111. Allow toxic victims to sue in fed ct	N	
112. Superfund waste cleanup of $10b	Y	
113. 90 days notice of plant closings	Y	
114. $20b in Medicare cuts/tax increases	N	
115. Spending cuts and tax increases	N	
116. Set school lunch lmt-250% poverty	N	
117. $75m for youth work projects	?	
118. Allow Angolan military assistance	N	
119. Suspend defense payments for abuse	Y	
120. Drop SS COLAs/$12b tax increase	N	
121. Approve $1.5b for 21 MX missiles	Y	
122. Emergency farm credit/revisions	Y	
123. Duty on Taiwan/Hong Kong/S Korea	?	
124. Limit steel imports to 17%	Y	
125. Cut $ to schools that bar prayer	Y	
126. $50b-taxes; cut Medicare/spending	N	
127. Limit Pershing II/cruise in Europe	N	
128. Delete $7.1b for 34 B-1 bombers	N	
129. Bar purchase of Sergeant York guns	Y	
130. El Salvador military/economic aid	N	
131. Bar mining of Nicaraguan waters	Y	
132. Physician fee freeze for Medicare	N	
133. $49b in "sin"/phone/insurance taxes	N	
134. Allow sale of Conrail	N	
135. Equal Rights Amendment	N	
136. Authorize Marines in Lebanon	Y	
137. Eminent domain for coal companies	N	
138. Prohibit EPA clean air sanctions	Y	
139. SS retirement age increase/reforms	N	
140. Auto domestic content requirement	Y	
141. Delete jobs program funding	N	
142. Highway-gas tax bill	N	
143. Cut $5b from defense for Medicare	Y	
144. Emergency housing aid of $1b	Y	

Presidential Support Score: 1991 - 36%   1990 - 34%

WELDON, CURT -- Pennsylvania 7th District [Republican]. Counties of Delaware (pt.) and Philadelphia (pt.). Prior Terms: 1987-92. Born: July 22, 1947; Marcus Hook, PA. Education: West Chester State College (B.A.); Cabrini College; Temple University; St. Joseph's University. Occupation: Volunteer firefighter; public school teacher and administrator; Marcus Hook Borough mayor (1977-82); Delaware County Council member (1981-86) and chairman; CIGNA Corporation employee.

1. Protection to Haitian refugees	N	50. Bar assembly of chemical weapons	Y
2. Raise tax on wealthy; lower others	N	51. Ban plutonium/uranium production	N
3. Investigate Reagan hostage delay	N	52. Cap MX missile deployment at 50	N
4. Campaign finance revisions	Y	53. Allow $3b for 2 stealth bombers	N
5. Unpaid leave to care for children	Y	54. Publish bio-warfare experiments	N
6. Restrict NEA use of funds	Y	55. Raise minimum wage-veto override	?
7. Bar race-bias claim/habeas corpus	Y	56. Bar transfer of FS-X technology	Y
8. Ban race as death sentence factor	Y	57. Cut defense and raise domestic $	N
9. Exceptions to exclusionary rule	Y	58. Uniform poll closing in 48 states	?
10. Allow sale of assault weapons	Y	59. Req foreign investment disclosure	N
11. Life in prison/abolish death penalty	N	60. Textile import quotas-veto override	Y
12. Req conspiracy-price fixing cases	Y	61. Bar abortion funding in Wash, DC	Y
13. Unemployment benefits extension	Y	62. Notify spouses of AIDS+ carriers	?
14. Tissue use of aborted fetuses	N	63. Seize conveyance-drug trafficking	N
15. Bar replacement of union strikers	Y	64. South Africa sanctions	N
16. Hold foreign aid at $15b for '92	Y	65. 60 days' notice of plant closings	Y
17. Restore space station funding	N	66. Close unneeded military bases	Y
18. Civil Rights Act of 1991	N	67. Keep welfare reform within $2.8b	Y
19. Unlimited damages-discrimination	N	68. Allow children housing exclusion	N
20. Eliminate funds for supercollider	Y	69. Shift $400m of NASA to homeless	Y
21. Terminate SDI except for research	N	70. Cap Medicare patients' liability	Y
22. Req 7-day handgun waiting period	Y	71. Prohibit employee polygraph testing	Y
23. Provide $30b for failed S&Ls	N	72. Allow CIA to fund Contras	Y
24. Allow use of force against Iraq	Y	73. Revise unfair trade practices	Y
25. Allow $15b in foreign aid for '91	N	74. Focus SDI on accidental launch	N
26. Revise & extend legal immigration	Y	75. Bar Air Force $ for MX missile	N
27. Suspend aid to Angolan rebels	N	76. Allow "real" increase in defense	Y
28. Democratic tax plan proposals	N	77. Troop reduction in Europe of 50%	N
29. Cut defense 5% across the board	N	78. Ban nuclear tests above 1 kiloton	X
30. Textile import quotas-veto override	Y	79. Ban anti-satellite missile tests	N
31. Abortion service for military abroad	N	80. Observe certain limits of SALT II	N
32. Limits on high income farmers	Y	81. Restore four Civil Rights laws	Y
33. Family medical leave-veto override	Y	82. Prohibit aliens as strikebreakers	Y
34. Req submission of balanced budget	N	83. Allow military malpractice suits	Y
35. Balanced budget amendment	Y	84. Approval of $36m in Contra aid	Y
36. Amendment to ban flag desecration	Y	85. $18b deficit reduction compromise	Y
37. Reauthorize Amtrak-veto override	Y	86. Welfare reform of $5.7b for 5 years	N
38. Retraining aid for coal miners	Y	87. Raise taxes $12b/cut spending $3b	N
39. Suspend El Salvador military aid	Y	88. Board to assess occupational risk	N
40. Expand child care aid/tax credit	Y	89. Balanced budget by '93-via targets	N
41. Raise House salary/omit honoraria	Y	90. Bar licensing of two nuclear plants	N
42. Toughen oil-spill liability	N	91. Remove victims compensation cap	N
43. Restitution to Japanese interned	N	92. Catastrophic health insurance	Y
44. Protect Chinese & C.A. nationals	Y	93. Ban airline smoking-2 hours or less	N
45. Abortion $ for rape/incest cases	N	94. $1b/two year aid for the homeless	Y
46. Allow religious schools to bar gays	Y	95. Bar non-unions in union companies	Y
47. Bar broadcaster fairness doctrine	Y	96. Increase FSLIC rescue to $15b	N
48. Bar cap gains cut/reinstate IRA	N	97. Impose quotas to lower trade deficit	N
49. Bar unions equal voice in pension	Y	98. Reduce discretionary budget 21%	Y

Presidential Support Score: 1991 - 54% 1990 - 50%

KOSTMAYER, PETER H. -- Pennsylvania 8th District [Democrat]. Counties of Bucks and Montgomery (pt.). Prior Terms: 1977-80; 1983-92. Born: September 27, 1946; New York City, NY. Education: Columbia University. Occupation: Journalist, *The Trentonian*; press secretary to the attorney general (1972-73); deputy press secretary to the governor (1973-76).

KOSTMAYER, PETER H. (continued)

1.	Protection to Haitian refugees	Y
2.	Raise tax on wealthy; lower others	Y
3.	Investigate Reagan hostage delay	Y
4.	Campaign finance revisions	Y
5.	Unpaid leave to care for children	Y
6.	Restrict NEA use of funds	N
7.	Bar race-bias claim/habeas corpus	N
8.	Ban race as death sentence factor	N
9.	Exceptions to exclusionary rule	N
10.	Allow sale of assault weapons	Y
11.	Life in prison/abolish death penalty	Y
12.	Req conspiracy-price fixing cases	N
13.	Unemployment benefits extension	Y
14.	Tissue use of aborted fetuses	Y
15.	Bar replacement of union strikers	Y
16.	Hold foreign aid at $15b for '92	Y
17.	Restore space station funding	?
18.	Civil Rights Act of 1991	Y
19.	Unlimited damages-discrimination	Y
20.	Eliminate funds for supercollider	Y
21.	Terminate SDI except for research	Y
22.	Req 7-day handgun waiting period	Y
23.	Provide $30b for failed S&Ls	Y
24.	Allow use of force against Iraq	N
25.	Allow $15b in foreign aid for '91	Y
26.	Revise & extend legal immigration	Y
27.	Suspend aid to Angolan rebels	Y
28.	Democratic tax plan proposals	Y
29.	Cut defense 5% across the board	N
30.	Textile import quotas-veto override	Y
31.	Abortion service for military abroad	Y
32.	Limits on high income farmers	Y
33.	Family medical leave-veto override	Y
34.	Req submission of balanced budget	Y
35.	Balanced budget amendment	N
36.	Amendment to ban flag desecration	N
37.	Reauthorize Amtrak-veto override	Y
38.	Retraining aid for coal miners	Y
39.	Suspend El Salvador military aid	Y
40.	Expand child care aid/tax credit	Y
41.	Raise House salary/omit honoraria	N
42.	Toughen oil-spill liability	Y
43.	Restitution to Japanese interned	Y
44.	Protect Chinese & C.A. nationals	Y
45.	Abortion $ for rape/incest cases	Y
46.	Allow religious schools to bar gays	N
47.	Bar broadcaster fairness doctrine	N
48.	Bar cap gains cut/reinstate IRA	Y
49.	Bar unions equal voice in pension	Y
50.	Bar assembly of chemical weapons	Y
51.	Ban plutonium/uranium production	Y
52.	Cap MX missile deployment at 50	Y
53.	Allow $3b for 2 stealth bombers	N
54.	Publish bio-warfare experiments	Y
55.	Raise minimum wage-veto override	Y
56.	Bar transfer of FS-X technology	Y
57.	Cut defense and raise domestic $	Y
58.	Uniform poll closing in 48 states	Y
59.	Req foreign investment disclosure	Y
60.	Textile import quotas-veto override	Y
61.	Bar abortion funding in Wash, DC	N
62.	Notify spouses of AIDS+ carriers	N
63.	Seize conveyance-drug trafficking	N
64.	South Africa sanctions	Y

65.	60 days' notice of plant closings	Y
66.	Close unneeded military bases	N
67.	Keep welfare reform within $2.8b	Y
68.	Allow children housing exclusion	N
69.	Shift $400m of NASA to homeless	Y
70.	Cap Medicare patients' liability	Y
71.	Prohibit employee polygraph testing	Y
72.	Allow CIA to fund Contras	N
73.	Revise unfair trade practices	Y
74.	Focus SDI on accidental launch	Y
75.	Bar Air Force $ for MX missile	N
76.	Allow "real" increase in defense	N
77.	Troop reduction in Europe of 50%	Y
78.	Ban nuclear tests above 1 kiloton	Y
79.	Ban anti-satellite missile tests	Y
80.	Observe certain limits of SALT II	Y
81.	Restore four Civil Rights laws	Y
82.	Prohibit aliens as strikebreakers	Y
83.	Allow military malpractice suits	Y
84.	Approval of $36m in Contra aid	N
85.	$18b deficit reduction compromise	Y
86.	Welfare reform of $5.7b for 5 years	Y
87.	Raise taxes $12b/cut spending $3b	Y
88.	Board to assess occupational risk	Y
89.	Balanced budget by '93-via targets	Y
90.	Bar licensing of two nuclear plants	Y
91.	Remove victims compensation cap	Y
92.	Catastrophic health insurance	Y
93.	Ban airline smoking-2 hours or less	Y
94.	$1b/two year aid for the homeless	Y
95.	Bar non-unions in union companies	Y
96.	Increase FSLIC rescue to $15b	N
97.	Impose quotas to lower trade deficit	Y
98.	Reduce discretionary budget 21%	Y
99.	Immigration reform/alien amnesty	Y
100.	South Africa sanctions-veto override	Y
101.	Tax overhaul to revise income tax	Y
102.	Use of military in drug war	N
103.	Delete 12 MX/add conventional wpn	Y
104.	Raise speed limit to 65 mph	N
105.	Require Pentagon to buy US goods	Y
106.	AIDS insurance non-discrimination	Y
107.	Prohibit Saudi arms sales	Y
108.	Ease Gun Control Act of 1968	N
109.	Bar interstate handgun transport	N
110.	Make company emissions known	Y
111.	Allow toxic victims to sue in fed ct	N
112.	Superfund waste cleanup of $10b	N
113.	90 days notice of plant closings	Y
114.	$20b in Medicare cuts/tax increases	Y
115.	Spending cuts and tax increases	Y
116.	Set school lunch 1mt-250% poverty	N
117.	$75m for youth work projects	Y
118.	Allow Angolan military assistance	N
119.	Suspend defense payments for abuse	Y
120.	Drop SS COLAs/$12b tax increase	N
121.	Approve $1.5b for 21 MX missiles	N
122.	Emergency farm credit/revisions	Y
123.	Duty on Taiwan/Hong Kong/S Korea	Y
124.	Limit steel imports to 17%	Y
125.	Cut $ to schools that bar prayer	N
126.	$50b-taxes; cut Medicare/spending	Y
127.	Limit Pershing II/cruise in Europe	Y
128.	Delete $7.1b for 34 B-1 bombers	Y

KOSTMAYER, PETER H. (continued)

129. Bar purchase of Sergeant York guns	Y
130. El Salvador military/economic aid	N
131. Bar mining of Nicaraguan waters	Y
132. Physician fee freeze for Medicare	N
133. $49b in "sin"/phone/insurance taxes	Y
134. Allow sale of Conrail	N
135. Equal Rights Amendment	Y
136. Authorize Marines in Lebanon	Y
137. Eminent domain for coal companies	Y
138. Prohibit EPA clean air sanctions	?
139. SS retirement age increase/reforms	N

Presidential Support Score: 1991 - 26%   1990 - 20%

SHUSTER, BUD -- Pennsylvania 9th District [Republican]. Counties of Bedford, Blair, Cambria (pt.), Clearfield (pt.), Cumberland (pt.), Franklin, Fulton, Huntingdon, Juniata and Mifflin. Prior Terms: 1973-92. Born: January 23, 1932; Glassport, PA. Education: University of Pittsburgh; Duquesne University (M.B.A.); American University (Ph.D.). Military Service: U.S. Army. Occupation: Vice president, Radio Corp.

1. Protection to Haitian refugees	N	49. Bar unions equal voice in pension	Y
2. Raise tax on wealthy; lower others	N	50. Bar assembly of chemical weapons	N
3. Investigate Reagan hostage delay	N	51. Ban plutonium/uranium production	N
4. Campaign finance revisions	?	52. Cap MX missile deployment at 50	N
5. Unpaid leave to care for children	N	53. Allow $3b for 2 stealth bombers	Y
6. Restrict NEA use of funds	Y	54. Publish bio-warfare experiments	N
7. Bar race-bias claim/habeas corpus	Y	55. Raise minimum wage-veto override	N
8. Ban race as death sentence factor	Y	56. Bar transfer of FS-X technology	Y
9. Exceptions to exclusionary rule	Y	57. Cut defense and raise domestic $	N
10. Allow sale of assault weapons	Y	58. Uniform poll closing in 48 states	N
11. Life in prison/abolish death penalty	N	59. Req foreign investment disclosure	N
12. Req conspiracy-price fixing cases	Y	60. Textile import quotas-veto override	Y
13. Unemployment benefits extension	Y	61. Bar abortion funding in Wash, DC	Y
14. Tissue use of aborted fetuses	N	62. Notify spouses of AIDS+ carriers	Y
15. Bar replacement of union strikers	N	63. Seize conveyance-drug trafficking	Y
16. Hold foreign aid at $15b for '92	N	64. South Africa sanctions	N
17. Restore space station funding	?	65. 60 days' notice of plant closings	N
18. Civil Rights Act of 1991	N	66. Close unneeded military bases	N
19. Unlimited damages-discrimination	N	67. Keep welfare reform within $2.8b	Y
20. Eliminate funds for supercollider	Y	68. Allow children housing exclusion	Y
21. Terminate SDI except for research	N	69. Shift $400m of NASA to homeless	Y
22. Req 7-day handgun waiting period	N	70. Cap Medicare patients' liability	N
23. Provide $30b for failed S&Ls	N	71. Prohibit employee polygraph testing	N
24. Allow use of force against Iraq	Y	72. Allow CIA to fund Contras	Y
25. Allow $15b in foreign aid for '91	N	73. Revise unfair trade practices	N
26. Revise & extend legal immigration	N	74. Focus SDI on accidental launch	N
27. Suspend aid to Angolan rebels	N	75. Bar Air Force $ for MX missile	N
28. Democratic tax plan proposals	N	76. Allow "real" increase in defense	Y
29. Cut defense 5% across the board	N	77. Troop reduction in Europe of 50%	N
30. Textile import quotas-veto override	Y	78. Ban nuclear tests above 1 kiloton	N
31. Abortion service for military abroad	N	79. Ban anti-satellite missile tests	N
32. Limits on high income farmers	Y	80. Observe certain limits of SALT II	N
33. Family medical leave-veto override	N	81. Restore four Civil Rights laws	N
34. Req submission of balanced budget	N	82. Prohibit aliens as strikebreakers	N
35. Balanced budget amendment	Y	83. Allow military malpractice suits	N
36. Amendment to ban flag desecration	Y	84. Approval of $36m in Contra aid	Y
37. Reauthorize Amtrak-veto override	Y	85. $18b deficit reduction compromise	N
38. Retraining aid for coal miners	N	86. Welfare reform of $5.7b for 5 years	N
39. Suspend El Salvador military aid	N	87. Raise taxes $12b/cut spending $3b	N
40. Expand child care aid/tax credit	N	88. Board to assess occupational risk	N
41. Raise House salary/omit honoraria	N	89. Balanced budget by '93-via targets	N
42. Toughen oil-spill liability	N	90. Bar licensing of two nuclear plants	N
43. Restitution to Japanese interned	N	91. Remove victims compensation cap	N
44. Protect Chinese & C.A. nationals	N	92. Catastrophic health insurance	N
45. Abortion $ for rape/incest cases	N	93. Ban airline smoking-2 hours or less	N
46. Allow religious schools to bar gays	Y	94. $1b/two year aid for the homeless	N
47. Bar broadcaster fairness doctrine	Y	95. Bar non-unions in union companies	N
48. Bar cap gains cut/reinstate IRA	N	96. Increase FSLIC rescue to $15b	N

SHUSTER, BUD (continued)

97. Impose quotas to lower trade deficit	Y	
98. Reduce discretionary budget 21%	Y	
99. Immigration reform/alien amnesty	N	
100. South Africa sanctions-veto override	N	
101. Tax overhaul to revise income tax	N	
102. Use of military in drug war	Y	
103. Delete 12 MX/add conventional wpn	N	
104. Raise speed limit to 65 mph	N	
105. Require Pentagon to buy US goods	Y	
106. AIDS insurance non-discrimination	N	
107. Prohibit Saudi arms sales	Y	
108. Ease Gun Control Act of 1968	Y	
109. Bar interstate handgun transport	N	
110. Make company emissions known	N	
111. Allow toxic victims to sue in fed ct	N	
112. Superfund waste cleanup of $10b	Y	
113. 90 days notice of plant closings	N	
114. $20b in Medicare cuts/tax increases	N	
115. Spending cuts and tax increases	N	
116. Set school lunch lmt-250% poverty	Y	
117. $75m for youth work projects	N	
118. Allow Angolan military assistance	Y	
119. Suspend defense payments for abuse	N	
120. Drop SS COLAs/$12b tax increase	N	
121. Approve $1.5b for 21 MX missiles	Y
122. Emergency farm credit/revisions	Y
123. Duty on Taiwan/Hong Kong/S Korea	N
124. Limit steel imports to 17%	Y
125. Cut $ to schools that bar prayer	Y
126. $50b-taxes; cut Medicare/spending	N
127. Limit Pershing II/cruise in Europe	N
128. Delete $7.1b for 34 B-1 bombers	N
129. Bar purchase of Sergeant York guns	N
130. El Salvador military/economic aid	Y
131. Bar mining of Nicaraguan waters	N
132. Physician fee freeze for Medicare	Y
133. $49b in "sin"/phone/insurance taxes	N
134. Allow sale of Conrail	N
135. Equal Rights Amendment	N
136. Authorize Marines in Lebanon	Y
137. Eminent domain for coal companies	N
138. Prohibit EPA clean air sanctions	?
139. SS retirement age increase/reforms	Y
140. Auto domestic content requirement	?
141. Delete jobs program funding	?
142. Highway-gas tax bill	Y
143. Cut $5b from defense for Medicare	Y
144. Emergency housing aid of $1b	Y

Presidential Support Score: 1991 - 68% 1990 - 63%

McDADE, JOSEPH M. -- Pennsylvania 10th District [Republican]. Counties of Bradford, Clinton (pt.), Lackawanna, Monroe (pt.), Pike, Potter, Susquehanna, Tioga, Wayne and Wyoming. Prior Terms: 1963-92. Born: September 29, 1931; Scranton, PA. Education: University of Notre Dame (B.A.); University of Pennsylvania (LL.B.). Occupation: Clerk, office of chief federal judge; attorney; city solicitor, City of Scranton (1962).

1. Protection to Haitian refugees	?	31. Abortion service for military abroad	?
2. Raise tax on wealthy; lower others	N	32. Limits on high income farmers	N
3. Investigate Reagan hostage delay	?	33. Family medical leave-veto override	Y
4. Campaign finance revisions	N	34. Req submission of balanced budget	N
5. Unpaid leave to care for children	Y	35. Balanced budget amendment	Y
6. Restrict NEA use of funds	N	36. Amendment to ban flag desecration	Y
7. Bar race-bias claim/habeas corpus	Y	37. Reauthorize Amtrak-veto override	N
8. Ban race as death sentence factor	Y	38. Retraining aid for coal miners	Y
9. Exceptions to exclusionary rule	Y	39. Suspend El Salvador military aid	N
10. Allow sale of assault weapons	N	40. Expand child care aid/tax credit	Y
11. Life in prison/abolish death penalty	N	41. Raise House salary/omit honoraria	Y
12. Req conspiracy-price fixing cases	N	42. Toughen oil-spill liability	N
13. Unemployment benefits extension	Y	43. Restitution to Japanese interned	N
14. Tissue use of aborted fetuses	N	44. Protect Chinese & C.A. nationals	Y
15. Bar replacement of union strikers	Y	45. Abortion $ for rape/incest cases	N
16. Hold foreign aid at $15b for '92	Y	46. Allow religious schools to bar gays	Y
17. Restore space station funding	Y	47. Bar broadcaster fairness doctrine	N
18. Civil Rights Act of 1991	N	48. Bar cap gains cut/reinstate IRA	N
19. Unlimited damages-discrimination	N	49. Bar unions equal voice in pension	Y
20. Eliminate funds for supercollider	N	50. Bar assembly of chemical weapons	Y
21. Terminate SDI except for research	N	51. Ban plutonium/uranium production	Y
22. Req 7-day handgun waiting period	Y	52. Cap MX missile deployment at 50	N
23. Provide $30b for failed S&Ls	Y	53. Allow $3b for 2 stealth bombers	N
24. Allow use of force against Iraq	Y	54. Publish bio-warfare experiments	N
25. Allow $15b in foreign aid for '91	?	55. Raise minimum wage-veto override	Y
26. Revise & extend legal immigration	Y	56. Bar transfer of FS-X technology	N
27. Suspend aid to Angolan rebels	N	57. Cut defense and raise domestic $	N
28. Democratic tax plan proposals	N	58. Uniform poll closing in 48 states	Y
29. Cut defense 5% across the board	N	59. Req foreign investment disclosure	N
30. Textile import quotas-veto override	Y	60. Textile import quotas-veto override	Y

McDADE, JOSEPH M. (continued)

61. Bar abortion funding in Wash, DC	Y	
62. Notify spouses of AIDS+ carriers	N	
63. Seize conveyance-drug trafficking	Y	
64. South Africa sanctions	Y	
65. 60 days' notice of plant closings	Y	
66. Close unneeded military bases	Y	
67. Keep welfare reform within $2.8b	Y	
68. Allow children housing exclusion	N	
69. Shift $400m of NASA to homeless	Y	
70. Cap Medicare patients' liability	Y	
71. Prohibit employee polygraph testing	Y	
72. Allow CIA to fund Contras	Y	
73. Revise unfair trade practices	Y	
74. Focus SDI on accidental launch	N	
75. Bar Air Force $ for MX missile	N	
76. Allow "real" increase in defense	Y	
77. Troop reduction in Europe of 50%	N	
78. Ban nuclear tests above 1 kiloton	N	
79. Ban anti-satellite missile tests	N	
80. Observe certain limits of SALT II	N	
81. Restore four Civil Rights laws	N	
82. Prohibit aliens as strikebreakers	Y	
83. Allow military malpractice suits	Y	
84. Approval of $36m in Contra aid	Y	
85. $18b deficit reduction compromise	Y	
86. Welfare reform of $5.7b for 5 years	N	
87. Raise taxes $12b/cut spending $3b	N	
88. Board to assess occupational risk	Y	
89. Balanced budget by '93-via targets	N	
90. Bar licensing of two nuclear plants	N	
91. Remove victims compensation cap	N	
92. Catastrophic health insurance	Y	
93. Ban airline smoking-2 hours or less	N	
94. $1b/two year aid for the homeless	Y	
95. Bar non-unions in union companies	Y	
96. Increase FSLIC rescue to $15b	Y	
97. Impose quotas to lower trade deficit	Y	
98. Reduce discretionary budget 21%	?	
99. Immigration reform/alien amnesty	Y	
100. South Africa sanctions-veto override	?	
101. Tax overhaul to revise income tax	Y	
102. Use of military in drug war	N	
103. Delete 12 MX/add conventional wpn	N	
104. Raise speed limit to 65 mph	N	
105. Require Pentagon to buy US goods	Y	
106. AIDS insurance non-discrimination	Y	
107. Prohibit Saudi arms sales	Y	
108. Ease Gun Control Act of 1968	Y	
109. Bar interstate handgun transport	N	
110. Make company emissions known	Y	
111. Allow toxic victims to sue in fed ct	Y	
112. Superfund waste cleanup of $10b	Y	
113. 90 days notice of plant closings	Y	
114. $20b in Medicare cuts/tax increases	Y	
115. Spending cuts and tax increases	N	
116. Set school lunch lmt-250% poverty	N	
117. $75m for youth work projects	N	
118. Allow Angolan military assistance	Y	
119. Suspend defense payments for abuse	Y	
120. Drop SS COLAs/$12b tax increase	N	
121. Approve $1.5b for 21 MX missiles	Y	
122. Emergency farm credit/revisions	N	
123. Duty on Taiwan/Hong Kong/S Korea	N	
124. Limit steel imports to 17%	Y	
125. Cut $ to schools that bar prayer	Y	
126. $50b-taxes; cut Medicare/spending	Y	
127. Limit Pershing II/cruise in Europe	N	
128. Delete $7.1b for 34 B-1 bombers	X	
129. Bar purchase of Sergeant York guns	N	
130. El Salvador military/economic aid	Y	
131. Bar mining of Nicaraguan waters	Y	
132. Physician fee freeze for Medicare	Y	
133. $49b in "sin"/phone/insurance taxes	Y	
134. Allow sale of Conrail	N	
135. Equal Rights Amendment	Y	
136. Authorize Marines in Lebanon	Y	
137. Eminent domain for coal companies	N	
138. Prohibit EPA clean air sanctions	N	
139. SS retirement age increase/reforms	N	
140. Auto domestic content requirement	Y	
141. Delete jobs program funding	N	
142. Highway-gas tax bill	Y	
143. Cut $5b from defense for Medicare	Y	
144. Emergency housing aid of $1b	Y	

Presidential Support Score: 1991 - 68%   1990 - 47%

KANJORSKI, PAUL E. -- Pennsylvania 11th District [Democrat]. Counties of Carbon (pt.), Columbia, Luzerne, Monroe (pt.), Montour, Northumberland (pt.) and Sullivan. Prior Terms: 1985-92. Born: April 2, 1937; Nanticoke, PA. Education: Wyoming Seminary; Temple University (B.S.); Dickinson School of Law (J.D.). Military Service: U.S. Army, 1960-61. Occupation: Attorney; sanitary authority commissioner.

1. Protection to Haitian refugees	N	
2. Raise tax on wealthy; lower others	Y	
3. Investigate Reagan hostage delay	Y	
4. Campaign finance revisions	Y	
5. Unpaid leave to care for children	Y	
6. Restrict NEA use of funds	N	
7. Bar race-bias claim/habeas corpus	Y	
8. Ban race as death sentence factor	Y	
9. Exceptions to exclusionary rule	Y	
10. Allow sale of assault weapons	Y	
11. Life in prison/abolish death penalty	N	
12. Req conspiracy-price fixing cases	N	
13. Unemployment benefits extension	Y	
14. Tissue use of aborted fetuses	N	
15. Bar replacement of union strikers	Y	
16. Hold foreign aid at $15b for '92	Y	
17. Restore space station funding	N	
18. Civil Rights Act of 1991	Y	
19. Unlimited damages-discrimination	N	
20. Eliminate funds for supercollider	Y	
21. Terminate SDI except for research	N	
22. Req 7-day handgun waiting period	N	
23. Provide $30b for failed S&Ls	N	
24. Allow use of force against Iraq	N	

KANJORSKI, PAUL E. (continued)

25. Allow $15b in foreign aid for '91	N	
26. Revise & extend legal immigration	Y	
27. Suspend aid to Angolan rebels	Y	
28. Democratic tax plan proposals	Y	
29. Cut defense 5% across the board	N	
30. Textile import quotas-veto override	Y	
31. Abortion service for military abroad	N	
32. Limits on high income farmers	Y	
33. Family medical leave-veto override	Y	
34. Req submission of balanced budget	Y	
35. Balanced budget amendment	N	
36. Amendment to ban flag desecration	Y	
37. Reauthorize Amtrak-veto override	Y	
38. Retraining aid for coal miners	Y	
39. Suspend El Salvador military aid	Y	
40. Expand child care aid/tax credit	Y	
41. Raise House salary/omit honoraria	Y	
42. Toughen oil-spill liability	Y	
43. Restitution to Japanese interned	N	
44. Protect Chinese & C.A. nationals	Y	
45. Abortion $ for rape/incest cases	N	
46. Allow religious schools to bar gays	Y	
47. Bar broadcaster fairness doctrine	N	
48. Bar cap gains cut/reinstate IRA	Y	
49. Bar unions equal voice in pension	N	
50. Bar assembly of chemical weapons	Y	
51. Ban plutonium/uranium production	Y	
52. Cap MX missile deployment at 50	Y	
53. Allow $3b for 2 stealth bombers	N	
54. Publish bio-warfare experiments	Y	
55. Raise minimum wage-veto override	Y	
56. Bar transfer of FS-X technology	Y	
57. Cut defense and raise domestic $	N	
58. Uniform poll closing in 48 states	Y	
59. Req foreign investment disclosure	Y	
60. Textile import quotas-veto override	Y	
61. Bar abortion funding in Wash, DC	Y	
62. Notify spouses of AIDS+ carriers	N	
63. Seize conveyance-drug trafficking	Y	
64. South Africa sanctions	Y	
65. 60 days' notice of plant closings	Y	
66. Close unneeded military bases	N	
67. Keep welfare reform within $2.8b	N	
68. Allow children housing exclusion	Y	
69. Shift $400m of NASA to homeless	Y	
70. Cap Medicare patients' liability	Y	
71. Prohibit employee polygraph testing	Y	
72. Allow CIA to fund Contras	N	
73. Revise unfair trade practices	Y	

74. Focus SDI on accidental launch	Y	
75. Bar Air Force $ for MX missile	N	
76. Allow "real" increase in defense	N	
77. Troop reduction in Europe of 50%	N	
78. Ban nuclear tests above 1 kiloton	Y	
79. Ban anti-satellite missile tests	Y	
80. Observe certain limits of SALT II	Y	
81. Restore four Civil Rights laws	Y	
82. Prohibit aliens as strikebreakers	Y	
83. Allow military malpractice suits	Y	
84. Approval of $36m in Contra aid	N	
85. $18b deficit reduction compromise	Y	
86. Welfare reform of $5.7b for 5 years	Y	
87. Raise taxes $12b/cut spending $3b	Y	
88. Board to assess occupational risk	Y	
89. Balanced budget by '93-via targets	N	
90. Bar licensing of two nuclear plants	N	
91. Remove victims compensation cap	N	
92. Catastrophic health insurance	Y	
93. Ban airline smoking-2 hours or less	Y	
94. $1b/two year aid for the homeless	Y	
95. Bar non-unions in union companies	Y	
96. Increase FSLIC rescue to $15b	N	
97. Impose quotas to lower trade deficit	Y	
98. Reduce discretionary budget 21%	Y	
99. Immigration reform/alien amnesty	Y	
100. South Africa sanctions-veto override	Y	
101. Tax overhaul to revise income tax	Y	
102. Use of military in drug war	Y	
103. Delete 12 MX/add conventional wpn	Y	
104. Raise speed limit to 65 mph	N	
105. Require Pentagon to buy US goods	Y	
106. AIDS insurance non-discrimination	Y	
107. Prohibit Saudi arms sales	Y	
108. Ease Gun Control Act of 1968	Y	
109. Bar interstate handgun transport	N	
110. Make company emissions known	Y	
111. Allow toxic victims to sue in fed ct	N	
112. Superfund waste cleanup of $10b	Y	
113. 90 days notice of plant closings	Y	
114. $20b in Medicare cuts/tax increases	Y	
115. Spending cuts and tax increases	N	
116. Set school lunch lmt-250% poverty	N	
117. $75m for youth work projects	Y	
118. Allow Angolan military assistance	N	
119. Suspend defense payments for abuse	Y	
120. Drop SS COLAs/$12b tax increase	N	
121. Approve $1.5b for 21 MX missiles	N	
122. Emergency farm credit/revisions	Y	

Presidential Support Score: 1991 - 37%   1990 - 25%

MURTHA, JOHN P. -- Pennsylvania 12th District [Democrat].

Counties of Armstrong (pt.), Cambria (pt.), Somerset and Westmoreland (pt.). Prior Terms: 1974 (Special Election)-1992. Born: June 17, 1932; New Martinsville, WV. Education: University of Pittsburgh (B.A.); University of Indiana. Military Service: U.S. Marine Corps. Occupation: Pennsylvania representative (1969-74).

1. Protection to Haitian refugees	Y	
2. Raise tax on wealthy; lower others	Y	
3. Investigate Reagan hostage delay	Y	
4. Campaign finance revisions	Y	
5. Unpaid leave to care for children	Y	

6. Restrict NEA use of funds	N	
7. Bar race-bias claim/habeas corpus	Y	
8. Ban race as death sentence factor	N	
9. Exceptions to exclusionary rule	Y	
10. Allow sale of assault weapons	Y	

MURTHA, JOHN P. (continued)

11. Life in prison/abolish death penalty	N	
12. Req conspiracy-price fixing cases	N	
13. Unemployment benefits extension	Y	
14. Tissue use of aborted fetuses	N	
15. Bar replacement of union strikers	Y	
16. Hold foreign aid at $15b for '92	Y	
17. Restore space station funding	N	
18. Civil Rights Act of 1991	Y	
19. Unlimited damages-discrimination	Y	
20. Eliminate funds for supercollider	N	
21. Terminate SDI except for research	N	
22. Req 7-day handgun waiting period	N	
23. Provide $30b for failed S&Ls	Y	
24. Allow use of force against Iraq	Y	
25. Allow $15b in foreign aid for '91	Y	
26. Revise & extend legal immigration	Y	
27. Suspend aid to Angolan rebels	N	
28. Democratic tax plan proposals	Y	
29. Cut defense 5% across the board	N	
30. Textile import quotas-veto override	Y	
31. Abortion service for military abroad	N	
32. Limits on high income farmers	N	
33. Family medical leave-veto override	Y	
34. Req submission of balanced budget	N	
35. Balanced budget amendment	N	
36. Amendment to ban flag desecration	Y	
37. Reauthorize Amtrak-veto override	Y	
38. Retraining aid for coal miners	Y	
39. Suspend El Salvador military aid	Y	
40. Expand child care aid/tax credit	Y	
41. Raise House salary/omit honoraria	Y	
42. Toughen oil-spill liability	N	
43. Restitution to Japanese interned	Y	
44. Protect Chinese & C.A. nationals	N	
45. Abortion $ for rape/incest cases	N	
46. Allow religious schools to bar gays	Y	
47. Bar broadcaster fairness doctrine	N	
48. Bar cap gains cut/reinstate IRA	Y	
49. Bar unions equal voice in pension	N	
50. Bar assembly of chemical weapons	N	
51. Ban plutonium/uranium production	Y	
52. Cap MX missile deployment at 50	N	
53. Allow $3b for 2 stealth bombers	Y	
54. Publish bio-warfare experiments	N	
55. Raise minimum wage-veto override	Y	
56. Bar transfer of FS-X technology	Y	
57. Cut defense and raise domestic $	N	
58. Uniform poll closing in 48 states	Y	
59. Req foreign investment disclosure	Y	
60. Textile import quotas-veto override	Y	
61. Bar abortion funding in Wash, DC	Y	
62. Notify spouses of AIDS+ carriers	N	
63. Seize conveyance-drug trafficking	N	
64. South Africa sanctions	Y	
65. 60 days' notice of plant closings	Y	
66. Close unneeded military bases	Y	
67. Keep welfare reform within $2.8b	N	
68. Allow children housing exclusion	?	
69. Shift $400m of NASA to homeless	N	
70. Cap Medicare patients' liability	Y	
71. Prohibit employee polygraph testing	Y	
72. Allow CIA to fund Contras	Y	
73. Revise unfair trade practices	Y	
74. Focus SDI on accidental launch	N	

75. Bar Air Force $ for MX missile	N	
76. Allow "real" increase in defense	N	
77. Troop reduction in Europe of 50%	N	
78. Ban nuclear tests above 1 kiloton	N	
79. Ban anti-satellite missile tests	N	
80. Observe certain limits of SALT II	N	
81. Restore four Civil Rights laws	Y	
82. Prohibit aliens as strikebreakers	Y	
83. Allow military malpractice suits	Y	
84. Approval of $36m in Contra aid	Y	
85. $18b deficit reduction compromise	Y	
86. Welfare reform of $5.7b for 5 years	Y	
87. Raise taxes $12b/cut spending $3b	Y	
88. Board to assess occupational risk	Y	
89. Balanced budget by '93-via targets	Y	
90. Bar licensing of two nuclear plants	N	
91. Remove victims compensation cap	N	
92. Catastrophic health insurance	Y	
93. Ban airline smoking-2 hours or less	N	
94. $1b/two year aid for the homeless	?	
95. Bar non-unions in union companies	Y	
96. Increase FSLIC rescue to $15b	N	
97. Impose quotas to lower trade deficit	Y	
98. Reduce discretionary budget 21%	N	
99. Immigration reform/alien amnesty	Y	
100. South Africa sanctions-veto override	Y	
101. Tax overhaul to revise income tax	Y	
102. Use of military in drug war	N	
103. Delete 12 MX/add conventional wpn	N	
104. Raise speed limit to 65 mph	Y	
105. Require Pentagon to buy US goods	Y	
106. AIDS insurance non-discrimination	Y	
107. Prohibit Saudi arms sales	Y	
108. Ease Gun Control Act of 1968	Y	
109. Bar interstate handgun transport	N	
110. Make company emissions known	N	
111. Allow toxic victims to sue in fed ct	N	
112. Superfund waste cleanup of $10b	N	
113. 90 days notice of plant closings	Y	
114. $20b in Medicare cuts/tax increases	N	
115. Spending cuts and tax increases	Y	
116. Set school lunch lmt-250% poverty	N	
117. $75m for youth work projects	Y	
118. Allow Angolan military assistance	Y	
119. Suspend defense payments for abuse	N	
120. Drop SS COLAs/$12b tax increase	N	
121. Approve $1.5b for 21 MX missiles	Y	
122. Emergency farm credit/revisions	Y	
123. Duty on Taiwan/Hong Kong/S Korea	Y	
124. Limit steel imports to 17%	Y	
125. Cut $ to schools that bar prayer	Y	
126. $50b-taxes; cut Medicare/spending	Y	
127. Limit Pershing II/cruise in Europe	N	
128. Delete $7.1b for 34 B-1 bombers	N	
129. Bar purchase of Sergeant York guns	N	
130. El Salvador military/economic aid	Y	
131. Bar mining of Nicaraguan waters	Y	
132. Physician fee freeze for Medicare	N	
133. $49b in "sin"/phone/insurance taxes	Y	
134. Allow sale of Conrail	N	
135. Equal Rights Amendment	N	
136. Authorize Marines in Lebanon	Y	
137. Eminent domain for coal companies	N	
138. Prohibit EPA clean air sanctions	Y	

MURTHA, JOHN P. (continued)

139. SS retirement age increase/reforms	N	142. Highway-gas tax bill	Y
140. Auto domestic content requirement	Y	143. Cut $5b from defense for Medicare	N
141. Delete jobs program funding	N	144. Emergency housing aid of $1b	Y

Presidential Support Score: 1991 - 44%   1990 - 33%

COUGHLIN, LAWRENCE -- Pennsylvania 13th District [Republican]. Counties of Montgomery (pt.) and Philadelphia (pt.). Prior Terms: 1969-92. Born: April 11, 1929; Wilkes-Barre, PA. Education: Yale (A.B.); Harvard (M.B.A.); Temple University Evening Law School (LL.B.). Military Service: U.S. Marine Corps. Occupation: Attorney, Saul, Ewing, Remick and Saul; Pennsylvania representative (1964); Pennsylvania senator (1966).

1. Protection to Haitian refugees	N	52. Cap MX missile deployment at 50	Y
2. Raise tax on wealthy; lower others	N	53. Allow $3b for 2 stealth bombers	Y
3. Investigate Reagan hostage delay	N	54. Publish bio-warfare experiments	N
4. Campaign finance revisions	N	55. Raise minimum wage-veto override	N
5. Unpaid leave to care for children	Y	56. Bar transfer of FS-X technology	N
6. Restrict NEA use of funds	N	57. Cut defense and raise domestic $	N
7. Bar race-bias claim/habeas corpus	Y	58. Uniform poll closing in 48 states	Y
8. Ban race as death sentence factor	Y	59. Req foreign investment disclosure	N
9. Exceptions to exclusionary rule	Y	60. Textile import quotas-veto override	N
10. Allow sale of assault weapons	N	61. Bar abortion funding in Wash, DC	N
11. Life in prison/abolish death penalty	N	62. Notify spouses of AIDS+ carriers	Y
12. Req conspiracy-price fixing cases	Y	63. Seize conveyance-drug trafficking	Y
13. Unemployment benefits extension	Y	64. South Africa sanctions	N
14. Tissue use of aborted fetuses	N	65. 60 days' notice of plant closings	Y
15. Bar replacement of union strikers	N	66. Close unneeded military bases	Y
16. Hold foreign aid at $15b for '92	Y	67. Keep welfare reform within $2.8b	Y
17. Restore space station funding	Y	68. Allow children housing exclusion	N
18. Civil Rights Act of 1991	N	69. Shift $400m of NASA to homeless	N
19. Unlimited damages-discrimination	N	70. Cap Medicare patients' liability	Y
20. Eliminate funds for supercollider	Y	71. Prohibit employee polygraph testing	Y
21. Terminate SDI except for research	N	72. Allow CIA to fund Contras	Y
22. Req 7-day handgun waiting period	Y	73. Revise unfair trade practices	Y
23. Provide $30b for failed S&Ls	Y	74. Focus SDI on accidental launch	Y
24. Allow use of force against Iraq	Y	75. Bar Air Force $ for MX missile	N
25. Allow $15b in foreign aid for '91	Y	76. Allow "real" increase in defense	Y
26. Revise & extend legal immigration	Y	77. Troop reduction in Europe of 50%	N
27. Suspend aid to Angolan rebels	N	78. Ban nuclear tests above 1 kiloton	Y
28. Democratic tax plan proposals	N	79. Ban anti-satellite missile tests	Y
29. Cut defense 5% across the board	N	80. Observe certain limits of SALT II	N
30. Textile import quotas-veto override	N	81. Restore four Civil Rights laws	Y
31. Abortion service for military abroad	Y	82. Prohibit aliens as strikebreakers	Y
32. Limits on high income farmers	Y	83. Allow military malpractice suits	Y
33. Family medical leave-veto override	Y	84. Approval of $36m in Contra aid	Y
34. Req submission of balanced budget	N	85. $18b deficit reduction compromise	Y
35. Balanced budget amendment	Y	86. Welfare reform of $5.7b for 5 years	N
36. Amendment to ban flag desecration	Y	87. Raise taxes $12b/cut spending $3b	N
37. Reauthorize Amtrak-veto override	N	88. Board to assess occupational risk	Y
38. Retraining aid for coal miners	N	89. Balanced budget by '93-via targets	N
39. Suspend El Salvador military aid	Y	90. Bar licensing of two nuclear plants	N
40. Expand child care aid/tax credit	Y	91. Remove victims compensation cap	N
41. Raise House salary/omit honoraria	Y	92. Catastrophic health insurance	N
42. Toughen oil-spill liability	Y	93. Ban airline smoking-2 hours or less	N
43. Restitution to Japanese interned	N	94. $1b/two year aid for the homeless	Y
44. Protect Chinese & C.A. nationals	Y	95. Bar non-unions in union companies	N
45. Abortion $ for rape/incest cases	Y	96. Increase FSLIC rescue to $15b	Y
46. Allow religious schools to bar gays	Y	97. Impose quotas to lower trade deficit	N
47. Bar broadcaster fairness doctrine	Y	98. Reduce discretionary budget 21%	Y
48. Bar cap gains cut/reinstate IRA	N	99. Immigration reform/alien amnesty	Y
49. Bar unions equal voice in pension	Y	100. South Africa sanctions-veto override	Y
50. Bar assembly of chemical weapons	N	101. Tax overhaul to revise income tax	N
51. Ban plutonium/uranium production	N	102. Use of military in drug war	N

COUGHLIN, LAWRENCE (continued)

103. Delete 12 MX/add conventional wpn	N	
104. Raise speed limit to 65 mph	N	
105. Require Pentagon to buy US goods	Y	
106. AIDS insurance non-discrimination	Y	
107. Prohibit Saudi arms sales	Y	
108. Ease Gun Control Act of 1968	N	
109. Bar interstate handgun transport	N	
110. Make company emissions known	Y	
111. Allow toxic victims to sue in fed ct	Y	
112. Superfund waste cleanup of $10b	N	
113. 90 days notice of plant closings	Y	
114. $20b in Medicare cuts/tax increases	N	
115. Spending cuts and tax increases	N	
116. Set school lunch lmt-250% poverty	Y	
117. $75m for youth work projects	N	
118. Allow Angolan military assistance	Y	
119. Suspend defense payments for abuse	N	
120. Drop SS COLAs/$12b tax increase	N	
121. Approve $1.5b for 21 MX missiles	N	
122. Emergency farm credit/revisions	N	
123. Duty on Taiwan/Hong Kong/S Korea	N	
124. Limit steel imports to 17%	Y	
125. Cut $ to schools that bar prayer	N	
126. $50b-taxes; cut Medicare/spending	Y	
127. Limit Pershing II/cruise in Europe	N	
128. Delete $7.1b for 34 B-1 bombers	Y	
129. Bar purchase of Sergeant York guns	N	
130. El Salvador military/economic aid	Y	
131. Bar mining of Nicaraguan waters	Y	
132. Physician fee freeze for Medicare	Y	
133. $49b in "sin"/phone/insurance taxes	Y	
134. Allow sale of Conrail	Y	
135. Equal Rights Amendment	Y	
136. Authorize Marines in Lebanon	Y	
137. Eminent domain for coal companies	N	
138. Prohibit EPA clean air sanctions	N	
139. SS retirement age increase/reforms	Y	
140. Auto domestic content requirement	Y	
141. Delete jobs program funding	Y	
142. Highway-gas tax bill	Y	
143. Cut $5b from defense for Medicare	N	
144. Emergency housing aid of $1b	Y	

Presidential Support Score: 1991 - 66% 1990 - 58%

COYNE, WILLIAM J. -- Pennsylvania 14th District [Democrat]. County of Allegheny (pt.). Prior Terms: 1981-92. Born: August 24, 1936; Pittsburgh, PA. Education: Robert Morris College. Military Service: U.S. Army, 1955-57. Occupation: Pennsylvania legislator (1970-72); Pittsburgh city councilman (1974); member, Pittsburgh Housing Authority; member, Governor's Justice Commission; chairman, Public Works Commission; board member, OIC.

1. Protection to Haitian refugees	Y	
2. Raise tax on wealthy; lower others	Y	
3. Investigate Reagan hostage delay	Y	
4. Campaign finance revisions	Y	
5. Unpaid leave to care for children	Y	
6. Restrict NEA use of funds	N	
7. Bar race-bias claim/habeas corpus	N	
8. Ban race as death sentence factor	N	
9. Exceptions to exclusionary rule	N	
10. Allow sale of assault weapons	N	
11. Life in prison/abolish death penalty	N	
12. Req conspiracy-price fixing cases	N	
13. Unemployment benefits extension	Y	
14. Tissue use of aborted fetuses	Y	
15. Bar replacement of union strikers	Y	
16. Hold foreign aid at $15b for '92	Y	
17. Restore space station funding	N	
18. Civil Rights Act of 1991	Y	
19. Unlimited damages-discrimination	Y	
20. Eliminate funds for supercollider	N	
21. Terminate SDI except for research	?	
22. Req 7-day handgun waiting period	Y	
23. Provide $30b for failed S&Ls	Y	
24. Allow use of force against Iraq	N	
25. Allow $15b in foreign aid for '91	Y	
26. Revise & extend legal immigration	Y	
27. Suspend aid to Angolan rebels	Y	
28. Democratic tax plan proposals	Y	
29. Cut defense 5% across the board	Y	
30. Textile import quotas-veto override	Y	
31. Abortion service for military abroad	Y	
32. Limits on high income farmers	Y	
33. Family medical leave-veto override	Y	
34. Req submission of balanced budget	Y	
35. Balanced budget amendment	N	
36. Amendment to ban flag desecration	N	
37. Reauthorize Amtrak-veto override	Y	
38. Retraining aid for coal miners	Y	
39. Suspend El Salvador military aid	Y	
40. Expand child care aid/tax credit	Y	
41. Raise House salary/omit honoraria	Y	
42. Toughen oil-spill liability	Y	
43. Restitution to Japanese interned	Y	
44. Protect Chinese & C.A. nationals	Y	
45. Abortion $ for rape/incest cases	Y	
46. Allow religious schools to bar gays	N	
47. Bar broadcaster fairness doctrine	N	
48. Bar cap gains cut/reinstate IRA	Y	
49. Bar unions equal voice in pension	N	
50. Bar assembly of chemical weapons	Y	
51. Ban plutonium/uranium production	Y	
52. Cap MX missile deployment at 50	Y	
53. Allow $3b for 2 stealth bombers	N	
54. Publish bio-warfare experiments	Y	
55. Raise minimum wage-veto override	Y	
56. Bar transfer of FS-X technology	Y	
57. Cut defense and raise domestic $	Y	
58. Uniform poll closing in 48 states	Y	
59. Req foreign investment disclosure	Y	
60. Textile import quotas-veto override	Y	
61. Bar abortion funding in Wash, DC	N	
62. Notify spouses of AIDS+ carriers	N	
63. Seize conveyance-drug trafficking	N	
64. South Africa sanctions	Y	
65. 60 days' notice of plant closings	Y	
66. Close unneeded military bases	N	

COYNE, WILLIAM J. (continued)

67. Keep welfare reform within $2.8b	N	106. AIDS insurance non-discrimination	Y
68. Allow children housing exclusion	N	107. Prohibit Saudi arms sales	Y
69. Shift $400m of NASA to homeless	Y	108. Ease Gun Control Act of 1968	N
70. Cap Medicare patients' liability	Y	109. Bar interstate handgun transport	Y
71. Prohibit employee polygraph testing	Y	110. Make company emissions known	Y
72. Allow CIA to fund Contras	N	111. Allow toxic victims to sue in fed ct	Y
73. Revise unfair trade practices	Y	112. Superfund waste cleanup of $10b	Y
74. Focus SDI on accidental launch	Y	113. 90 days notice of plant closings	Y
75. Bar Air Force $ for MX missile	Y	114. $20b in Medicare cuts/tax increases	Y
76. Allow "real" increase in defense	N	115. Spending cuts and tax increases	Y
77. Troop reduction in Europe of 50%	N	116. Set school lunch lmt-250% poverty	N
78. Ban nuclear tests above 1 kiloton	Y	117. $75m for youth work projects	Y
79. Ban anti-satellite missile tests	Y	118. Allow Angolan military assistance	N
80. Observe certain limits of SALT II	Y	119. Suspend defense payments for abuse	Y
81. Restore four Civil Rights laws	Y	120. Drop SS COLAs/$12b tax increase	N
82. Prohibit aliens as strikebreakers	Y	121. Approve $1.5b for 21 MX missiles	N
83. Allow military malpractice suits	Y	122. Emergency farm credit/revisions	Y
84. Approval of $36m in Contra aid	N	123. Duty on Taiwan/Hong Kong/S Korea	Y
85. $18b deficit reduction compromise	Y	124. Limit steel imports to 17%	Y
86. Welfare reform of $5.7b for 5 years	Y	125. Cut $ to schools that bar prayer	N
87. Raise taxes $12b/cut spending $3b	Y	126. $50b-taxes; cut Medicare/spending	Y
88. Board to assess occupational risk	Y	127. Limit Pershing II/cruise in Europe	Y
89. Balanced budget by '93-via targets	Y	128. Delete $7.1b for 34 B-1 bombers	Y
90. Bar licensing of two nuclear plants	Y	129. Bar purchase of Sergeant York guns	Y
91. Remove victims compensation cap	Y	130. El Salvador military/economic aid	N
92. Catastrophic health insurance	Y	131. Bar mining of Nicaraguan waters	Y
93. Ban airline smoking-2 hours or less	N	132. Physician fee freeze for Medicare	N
94. $1b/two year aid for the homeless	Y	133. $49b in "sin"/phone/insurance taxes	Y
95. Bar non-unions in union companies	Y	134. Allow sale of Conrail	N
96. Increase FSLIC rescue to $15b	Y	135. Equal Rights Amendment	Y
97. Impose quotas to lower trade deficit	Y	136. Authorize Marines in Lebanon	Y
98. Reduce discretionary budget 21%	N	137. Eminent domain for coal companies	N
99. Immigration reform/alien amnesty	Y	138. Prohibit EPA clean air sanctions	N
100. South Africa sanctions-veto override	Y	139. SS retirement age increase/reforms	N
101. Tax overhaul to revise income tax	Y	140. Auto domestic content requirement	Y
102. Use of military in drug war	N	141. Delete jobs program funding	N
103. Delete 12 MX/add conventional wpn	Y	142. Highway-gas tax bill	Y
104. Raise speed limit to 65 mph	N	143. Cut $5b from defense for Medicare	Y
105. Require Pentagon to buy US goods	Y	144. Emergency housing aid of $1b	Y

Presidential Support Score: 1991 - 28%   1990 - 17%

RITTER, DON -- Pennsylvania 15th District [Republican]. Counties of Lehigh, Monroe (pt.) and Northampton. Prior Terms: 1979-92. Born: October 21, 1940; New York City, NY. Education: Lehigh University (B.S.); Massachusetts Institute of Technology (M.S., SC.D.); scientific exchange fellow, U.S. National Academy of Science/Soviet Academy of Science. Occupation: Research assistant, M.I.T. (1961-66); assistant professor, California State Polytechnic University (1968-69); contract consultant, General Dynamics Pamona Division (1968-69); assistant professor, researcher, Lehigh University (1969-78).

1. Protection to Haitian refugees	N	14. Tissue use of aborted fetuses	N
2. Raise tax on wealthy; lower others	N	15. Bar replacement of union strikers	N
3. Investigate Reagan hostage delay	N	16. Hold foreign aid at $15b for '92	Y
4. Campaign finance revisions	N	17. Restore space station funding	Y
5. Unpaid leave to care for children	N	18. Civil Rights Act of 1991	N
6. Restrict NEA use of funds	Y	19. Unlimited damages-discrimination	N
7. Bar race-bias claim/habeas corpus	Y	20. Eliminate funds for supercollider	Y
8. Ban race as death sentence factor	Y	21. Terminate SDI except for research	N
9. Exceptions to exclusionary rule	Y	22. Req 7-day handgun waiting period	N
10. Allow sale of assault weapons	Y	23. Provide $30b for failed S&Ls	Y
11. Life in prison/abolish death penalty	N	24. Allow use of force against Iraq	Y
12. Req conspiracy-price fixing cases	Y	25. Allow $15b in foreign aid for '91	N
13. Unemployment benefits extension	Y	26. Revise & extend legal immigration	Y

RITTER, DON (continued)

27. Suspend aid to Angolan rebels	N	
28. Democratic tax plan proposals	N	
29. Cut defense 5% across the board	N	
30. Textile import quotas-veto override	Y	
31. Abortion service for military abroad	N	
32. Limits on high income farmers	N	
33. Family medical leave-veto override	N	
34. Req submission of balanced budget	N	
35. Balanced budget amendment	Y	
36. Amendment to ban flag desecration	Y	
37. Reauthorize Amtrak-veto override	N	
38. Retraining aid for coal miners	Y	
39. Suspend El Salvador military aid	N	
40. Expand child care aid/tax credit	N	
41. Raise House salary/omit honoraria	N	
42. Toughen oil-spill liability	N	
43. Restitution to Japanese interned	N	
44. Protect Chinese & C.A. nationals	N	
45. Abortion $ for rape/incest cases	N	
46. Allow religious schools to bar gays	Y	
47. Bar broadcaster fairness doctrine	N	
48. Bar cap gains cut/reinstate IRA	N	
49. Bar unions equal voice in pension	Y	
50. Bar assembly of chemical weapons	N	
51. Ban plutonium/uranium production	N	
52. Cap MX missile deployment at 50	N	
53. Allow $3b for 2 stealth bombers	Y	
54. Publish bio-warfare experiments	N	
55. Raise minimum wage-veto override	N	
56. Bar transfer of FS-X technology	N	
57. Cut defense and raise domestic $	N	
58. Uniform poll closing in 48 states	N	
59. Req foreign investment disclosure	Y	
60. Textile import quotas-veto override	Y	
61. Bar abortion funding in Wash, DC	Y	
62. Notify spouses of AIDS+ carriers	N	
63. Seize conveyance-drug trafficking	Y	
64. South Africa sanctions	N	
65. 60 days' notice of plant closings	Y	
66. Close unneeded military bases	Y	
67. Keep welfare reform within $2.8b	Y	
68. Allow children housing exclusion	N	
69. Shift $400m of NASA to homeless	N	
70. Cap Medicare patients' liability	N	
71. Prohibit employee polygraph testing	?	
72. Allow CIA to fund Contras	Y	
73. Revise unfair trade practices	Y	
74. Focus SDI on accidental launch	N	
75. Bar Air Force $ for MX missile	N	
76. Allow "real" increase in defense	N	
77. Troop reduction in Europe of 50%	Y	
78. Ban nuclear tests above 1 kiloton	N	
79. Ban anti-satellite missile tests	N	
80. Observe certain limits of SALT II	N	
81. Restore four Civil Rights laws	N	
82. Prohibit aliens as strikebreakers	Y	
83. Allow military malpractice suits	N	
84. Approval of $36m in Contra aid	Y	
85. $18b deficit reduction compromise	N	

86. Welfare reform of $5.7b for 5 years	N	
87. Raise taxes $12b/cut spending $3b	N	
88. Board to assess occupational risk	N	
89. Balanced budget by '93-via targets	N	
90. Bar licensing of two nuclear plants	N	
91. Remove victims compensation cap	N	
92. Catastrophic health insurance	N	
93. Ban airline smoking-2 hours or less	Y	
94. $1b/two year aid for the homeless	N	
95. Bar non-unions in union companies	N	
96. Increase FSLIC rescue to $15b	Y	
97. Impose quotas to lower trade deficit	Y	
98. Reduce discretionary budget 21%	Y	
99. Immigration reform/alien amnesty	N	
100. South Africa sanctions-veto override	N	
101. Tax overhaul to revise income tax	Y	
102. Use of military in drug war	Y	
103. Delete 12 MX/add conventional wpn	?	
104. Raise speed limit to 65 mph	Y	
105. Require Pentagon to buy US goods	Y	
106. AIDS insurance non-discrimination	N	
107. Prohibit Saudi arms sales	Y	
108. Ease Gun Control Act of 1968	Y	
109. Bar interstate handgun transport	N	
110. Make company emissions known	N	
111. Allow toxic victims to sue in fed ct	N	
112. Superfund waste cleanup of $10b	N	
113. 90 days notice of plant closings	Y	
114. $20b in Medicare cuts/tax increases	N	
115. Spending cuts and tax increases	N	
116. Set school lunch lmt-250% poverty	Y	
117. $75m for youth work projects	?	
118. Allow Angolan military assistance	Y	
119. Suspend defense payments for abuse	Y	
120. Drop SS COLAs/$12b tax increase	N	
121. Approve $1.5b for 21 MX missiles	Y	
122. Emergency farm credit/revisions	N	
123. Duty on Taiwan/Hong Kong/S Korea	Y	
124. Limit steel imports to 17%	Y	
125. Cut $ to schools that bar prayer	Y	
126. $50b-taxes; cut Medicare/spending	N	
127. Limit Pershing II/cruise in Europe	N	
128. Delete $7.1b for 34 B-1 bombers	N	
129. Bar purchase of Sergeant York guns	Y	
130. El Salvador military/economic aid	Y	
131. Bar mining of Nicaraguan waters	N	
132. Physician fee freeze for Medicare	Y	
133. $49b in "sin"/phone/insurance taxes	Y	
134. Allow sale of Conrail	N	
135. Equal Rights Amendment	N	
136. Authorize Marines in Lebanon	Y	
137. Eminent domain for coal companies	Y	
138. Prohibit EPA clean air sanctions	N	
139. SS retirement age increase/reforms	Y	
140. Auto domestic content requirement	Y	
141. Delete jobs program funding	Y	
142. Highway-gas tax bill	N	
143. Cut $5b from defense for Medicare	Y	
144. Emergency housing aid of $1b	Y	

Presidential Support Score: 1991 - 70% 1990 - 66%

WALKER, ROBERT S. -- Pennsylvania 16th District [Republican]. Counties of Chester (pt.), Lancaster (pt.) and Lebanon. Prior Terms: 1977-92. Born: December 23, 1942; Bradford, PA. Education: Millersville State College (B.S.); University of Delaware (M.A.). Military Service: National Guard, 1967-73. Occupation: Administrative assistant (1967-77).

1. Protection to Haitian refugees	N	
2. Raise tax on wealthy; lower others	N	
3. Investigate Reagan hostage delay	N	
4. Campaign finance revisions	N	
5. Unpaid leave to care for children	N	
6. Restrict NEA use of funds	Y	
7. Bar race-bias claim/habeas corpus	Y	
8. Ban race as death sentence factor	Y	
9. Exceptions to exclusionary rule	Y	
10. Allow sale of assault weapons	Y	
11. Life in prison/abolish death penalty	N	
12. Req conspiracy-price fixing cases	Y	
13. Unemployment benefits extension	N	
14. Tissue use of aborted fetuses	N	
15. Bar replacement of union strikers	N	
16. Hold foreign aid at $15b for '92	N	
17. Restore space station funding	Y	
18. Civil Rights Act of 1991	N	
19. Unlimited damages-discrimination	N	
20. Eliminate funds for supercollider	N	
21. Terminate SDI except for research	N	
22. Req 7-day handgun waiting period	N	
23. Provide $30b for failed S&Ls	Y	
24. Allow use of force against Iraq	Y	
25. Allow $15b in foreign aid for '91	N	
26. Revise & extend legal immigration	Y	
27. Suspend aid to Angolan rebels	N	
28. Democratic tax plan proposals	N	
29. Cut defense 5% across the board	N	
30. Textile import quotas-veto override	N	
31. Abortion service for military abroad	N	
32. Limits on high income farmers	Y	
33. Family medical leave-veto override	N	
34. Req submission of balanced budget	N	
35. Balanced budget amendment	Y	
36. Amendment to ban flag desecration	Y	
37. Reauthorize Amtrak-veto override	N	
38. Retraining aid for coal miners	N	
39. Suspend El Salvador military aid	N	
40. Expand child care aid/tax credit	N	
41. Raise House salary/omit honoraria	N	
42. Toughen oil-spill liability	N	
43. Restitution to Japanese interned	N	
44. Protect Chinese & C.A. nationals	N	
45. Abortion $ for rape/incest cases	N	
46. Allow religious schools to bar gays	Y	
47. Bar broadcaster fairness doctrine	Y	
48. Bar cap gains cut/reinstate IRA	N	
49. Bar unions equal voice in pension	Y	
50. Bar assembly of chemical weapons	N	
51. Ban plutonium/uranium production	N	
52. Cap MX missile deployment at 50	N	
53. Allow $3b for 2 stealth bombers	Y	
54. Publish bio-warfare experiments	N	
55. Raise minimum wage-veto override	N	
56. Bar transfer of FS-X technology	N	
57. Cut defense and raise domestic $	N	
58. Uniform poll closing in 48 states	N	
59. Req foreign investment disclosure	N	
60. Textile import quotas-veto override	N	

61. Bar abortion funding in Wash, DC	Y	
62. Notify spouses of AIDS+ carriers	Y	
63. Seize conveyance-drug trafficking	Y	
64. South Africa sanctions	N	
65. 60 days' notice of plant closings	N	
66. Close unneeded military bases	Y	
67. Keep welfare reform within $2.8b	Y	
68. Allow children housing exclusion	N	
69. Shift $400m of NASA to homeless	N	
70. Cap Medicare patients' liability	N	
71. Prohibit employee polygraph testing	N	
72. Allow CIA to fund Contras	Y	
73. Revise unfair trade practices	N	
74. Focus SDI on accidental launch	N	
75. Bar Air Force $ for MX missile	N	
76. Allow "real" increase in defense	Y	
77. Troop reduction in Europe of 50%	N	
78. Ban nuclear tests above 1 kiloton	N	
79. Ban anti-satellite missile tests	N	
80. Observe certain limits of SALT II	N	
81. Restore four Civil Rights laws	N	
82. Prohibit aliens as strikebreakers	N	
83. Allow military malpractice suits	N	
84. Approval of $36m in Contra aid	Y	
85. $18b deficit reduction compromise	N	
86. Welfare reform of $5.7b for 5 years	N	
87. Raise taxes $12b/cut spending $3b	N	
88. Board to assess occupational risk	N	
89. Balanced budget by '93-via targets	N	
90. Bar licensing of two nuclear plants	Y	
91. Remove victims compensation cap	N	
92. Catastrophic health insurance	N	
93. Ban airline smoking-2 hours or less	N	
94. $1b/two year aid for the homeless	N	
95. Bar non-unions in union companies	N	
96. Increase FSLIC rescue to $15b	Y	
97. Impose quotas to lower trade deficit	N	
98. Reduce discretionary budget 21%	N	
99. Immigration reform/alien amnesty	N	
100. South Africa sanctions-veto override	Y	
101. Tax overhaul to revise income tax	Y	
102. Use of military in drug war	Y	
103. Delete 12 MX/add conventional wpn	N	
104. Raise speed limit to 65 mph	Y	
105. Require Pentagon to buy US goods	N	
106. AIDS insurance non-discrimination	N	
107. Prohibit Saudi arms sales	Y	
108. Ease Gun Control Act of 1968	Y	
109. Bar interstate handgun transport	N	
110. Make company emissions known	N	
111. Allow toxic victims to sue in fed ct	N	
112. Superfund waste cleanup of $10b	Y	
113. 90 days notice of plant closings	N	
114. $20b in Medicare cuts/tax increases	N	
115. Spending cuts and tax increases	N	
116. Set school lunch lmt-250% poverty	Y	
117. $75m for youth work projects	N	
118. Allow Angolan military assistance	Y	
119. Suspend defense payments for abuse	N	
120. Drop SS COLAs/$12b tax increase	N	

WALKER, ROBERT S. (continued)

121. Approve $1.5b for 21 MX missiles	Y
122. Emergency farm credit/revisions	N
123. Duty on Taiwan/Hong Kong/S Korea	N
124. Limit steel imports to 17%	Y
125. Cut $ to schools that bar prayer	Y
126. $50b-taxes; cut Medicare/spending	N
127. Limit Pershing II/cruise in Europe	N
128. Delete $7.1b for 34 B-1 bombers	N
129. Bar purchase of Sergeant York guns	N
130. El Salvador military/economic aid	Y
131. Bar mining of Nicaraguan waters	N
132. Physician fee freeze for Medicare	Y

133. $49b in "sin"/phone/insurance taxes	?
134. Allow sale of Conrail	Y
135. Equal Rights Amendment	N
136. Authorize Marines in Lebanon	N
137. Eminent domain for coal companies	N
138. Prohibit EPA clean air sanctions	Y
139. SS retirement age increase/reforms	Y
140. Auto domestic content requirement	N
141. Delete jobs program funding	Y
142. Highway-gas tax bill	N
143. Cut $5b from defense for Medicare	N
144. Emergency housing aid of $1b	N

Presidential Support Score: 1991 - 81% 1990 - 85%

GEKAS, GEORGE W. -- Pennsylvania 17th District [Republican]. Counties of Dauphin, Lycoming, Northumberland (pt.), Perry, Snyder and Union. Prior Terms: 1983-92. Born: April 14, 1930; Harrisburg, PA. Education: Dickinson College; Dickinson Law School. Military Service: U.S. Army, 1953-56. Occupation: Attorney; assistant district attorney (1960-66); Pennsylvania representative (1967-74); Pennsylvania senator (1976-82).

1. Protection to Haitian refugees	N
2. Raise tax on wealthy; lower others	N
3. Investigate Reagan hostage delay	N
4. Campaign finance revisions	N
5. Unpaid leave to care for children	N
6. Restrict NEA use of funds	Y
7. Bar race-bias claim/habeas corpus	Y
8. Ban race as death sentence factor	Y
9. Exceptions to exclusionary rule	Y
10. Allow sale of assault weapons	Y
11. Life in prison/abolish death penalty	N
12. Req conspiracy-price fixing cases	Y
13. Unemployment benefits extension	Y
14. Tissue use of aborted fetuses	Y
15. Bar replacement of union strikers	N
16. Hold foreign aid at $15b for '92	Y
17. Restore space station funding	Y
18. Civil Rights Act of 1991	N
19. Unlimited damages-discrimination	N
20. Eliminate funds for supercollider	N
21. Terminate SDI except for research	N
22. Req 7-day handgun waiting period	N
23. Provide $30b for failed S&Ls	Y
24. Allow use of force against Iraq	Y
25. Allow $15b in foreign aid for '91	Y
26. Revise & extend legal immigration	Y
27. Suspend aid to Angolan rebels	N
28. Democratic tax plan proposals	N
29. Cut defense 5% across the board	N
30. Textile import quotas-veto override	Y
31. Abortion service for military abroad	N
32. Limits on high income farmers	N
33. Family medical leave-veto override	N
34. Req submission of balanced budget	N
35. Balanced budget amendment	Y
36. Amendment to ban flag desecration	Y
37. Reauthorize Amtrak-veto override	N
38. Retraining aid for coal miners	N
39. Suspend El Salvador military aid	N
40. Expand child care aid/tax credit	N
41. Raise House salary/omit honoraria	N
42. Toughen oil-spill liability	N

43. Restitution to Japanese interned	N
44. Protect Chinese & C.A. nationals	N
45. Abortion $ for rape/incest cases	N
46. Allow religious schools to bar gays	Y
47. Bar broadcaster fairness doctrine	Y
48. Bar cap gains cut/reinstate IRA	N
49. Bar unions equal voice in pension	Y
50. Bar assembly of chemical weapons	N
51. Ban plutonium/uranium production	N
52. Cap MX missile deployment at 50	N
53. Allow $3b for 2 stealth bombers	Y
54. Publish bio-warfare experiments	N
55. Raise minimum wage-veto override	N
56. Bar transfer of FS-X technology	Y
57. Cut defense and raise domestic $	N
58. Uniform poll closing in 48 states	?
59. Req foreign investment disclosure	N
60. Textile import quotas-veto override	N
61. Bar abortion funding in Wash, DC	N
62. Notify spouses of AIDS+ carriers	Y
63. Seize conveyance-drug trafficking	Y
64. South Africa sanctions	Y
65. 60 days' notice of plant closings	N
66. Close unneeded military bases	Y
67. Keep welfare reform within $2.8b	Y
68. Allow children housing exclusion	Y
69. Shift $400m of NASA to homeless	N
70. Cap Medicare patients' liability	N
71. Prohibit employee polygraph testing	N
72. Allow CIA to fund Contras	Y
73. Revise unfair trade practices	N
74. Focus SDI on accidental launch	N
75. Bar Air Force $ for MX missile	N
76. Allow "real" increase in defense	N
77. Troop reduction in Europe of 50%	N
78. Ban nuclear tests above 1 kiloton	N
79. Ban anti-satellite missile tests	N
80. Observe certain limits of SALT II	N
81. Restore four Civil Rights laws	N
82. Prohibit aliens as strikebreakers	N
83. Allow military malpractice suits	N
84. Approval of $36m in Contra aid	Y

GEKAS, GEORGE W. (continued)

85.	$18b deficit reduction compromise	N	113.	90 days notice of plant closings	N
86.	Welfare reform of $5.7b for 5 years	N	114.	$20b in Medicare cuts/tax increases	N
87.	Raise taxes $12b/cut spending $3b	N	115.	Spending cuts and tax increases	N
88.	Board to assess occupational risk	N	116.	Set school lunch lmt-250% poverty	N
89.	Balanced budget by '93-via targets	Y	117.	$75m for youth work projects	N
90.	Bar licensing of two nuclear plants	Y	118.	Allow Angolan military assistance	Y
91.	Remove victims compensation cap	N	119.	Suspend defense payments for abuse	N
92.	Catastrophic health insurance	N	120.	Drop SS COLAs/$12b tax increase	N
93.	Ban airline smoking-2 hours or less	Y	121.	Approve $1.5b for 21 MX missiles	Y
94.	$1b/two year aid for the homeless	N	122.	Emergency farm credit/revisions	N
95.	Bar non-unions in union companies	N	123.	Duty on Taiwan/Hong Kong/S Korea	N
96.	Increase FSLIC rescue to $15b	N	124.	Limit steel imports to 17%	Y
97.	Impose quotas to lower trade deficit	N	125.	Cut $ to schools that bar prayer	Y
98.	Reduce discretionary budget 21%	Y	126.	$50b-taxes; cut Medicare/spending	Y
99.	Immigration reform/alien amnesty	N	127.	Limit Pershing II/cruise in Europe	N
100.	South Africa sanctions-veto override	Y	128.	Delete $7.1b for 34 B-1 bombers	N
101.	Tax overhaul to revise income tax	N	129.	Bar purchase of Sergeant York guns	Y
102.	Use of military in drug war	Y	130.	El Salvador military/economic aid	Y
103.	Delete 12 MX/add conventional wpn	N	131.	Bar mining of Nicaraguan waters	N
104.	Raise speed limit to 65 mph	N	132.	Physician fee freeze for Medicare	Y
105.	Require Pentagon to buy US goods	Y	133.	$49b in "sin"/phone/insurance taxes	Y
106.	AIDS insurance non-discrimination	N	134.	Allow sale of Conrail	N
107.	Prohibit Saudi arms sales	Y	135.	Equal Rights Amendment	Y
108.	Ease Gun Control Act of 1968	Y	136.	Authorize Marines in Lebanon	Y
109.	Bar interstate handgun transport	N	137.	Eminent domain for coal companies	N
110.	Make company emissions known	N	138.	Prohibit EPA clean air sanctions	Y
111.	Allow toxic victims to sue in fed ct	N	139.	SS retirement age increase/reforms	Y
112.	Superfund waste cleanup of $10b	Y			

Presidential Support Score: 1991 - 74%   1990 - 81%

SANTORUM, RICK -- Pennsylvania 18th District [Republican].   County of Allegheny (pt.). Prior Term: 1991-92. Born: May 10, 1958; Winchester, VA.   Education: Penn State University (B.A.); University of Pittsburgh (M.B.A.); Dickinson School of Law (J.D.). Occupation: Lawyer; administrative assistant to state senator.

1.	Protection to Haitian refugees	N	13.	Unemployment benefits extension	N
2.	Raise tax on wealthy; lower others	N	14.	Tissue use of aborted fetuses	N
3.	Investigate Reagan hostage delay	?	15.	Bar replacement of union strikers	Y
4.	Campaign finance revisions	N	16.	Hold foreign aid at $15b for '92	Y
5.	Unpaid leave to care for children	N	17.	Restore space station funding	Y
6.	Restrict NEA use of funds	Y	18.	Civil Rights Act of 1991	N
7.	Bar race-bias claim/habeas corpus	Y	19.	Unlimited damages-discrimination	N
8.	Ban race as death sentence factor	Y	20.	Eliminate funds for supercollider	Y
9.	Exceptions to exclusionary rule	Y	21.	Terminate SDI except for research	N
10.	Allow sale of assault weapons	Y	22.	Req 7-day handgun waiting period	N
11.	Life in prison/abolish death penalty	N	23.	Provide $30b for failed S&Ls	Y
12.	Req conspiracy-price fixing cases	Y	24.	Allow use of force against Iraq	Y

Presidential Support Score: 1991 - 72%

GOODLING, WILLIAM F. -- Pennsylvania 19th District [Republican].   Counties of Adams, Cumberland (pt.) and York.   Prior Terms: 1975-92.   Born: 1928; Loganville, PA. Education: University of Maryland (B.S.); Western Maryland College (M.A.); Pennsylvania State University. Military Service: 1946-48. Occupation: High school teacher; guidance counselor; principal; school superintendent.

1.	Protection to Haitian refugees	N	6.	Restrict NEA use of funds	Y
2.	Raise tax on wealthy; lower others	N	7.	Bar race-bias claim/habeas corpus	P
3.	Investigate Reagan hostage delay	N	8.	Ban race as death sentence factor	P
4.	Campaign finance revisions	N	9.	Exceptions to exclusionary rule	P
5.	Unpaid leave to care for children	N	10.	Allow sale of assault weapons	Y

GOODLING, WILLIAM F. (continued)

11. Life in prison/abolish death penalty	Y	
12. Req conspiracy-price fixing cases	Y	
13. Unemployment benefits extension	N	
14. Tissue use of aborted fetuses	N	
15. Bar replacement of union strikers	N	
16. Hold foreign aid at $15b for '92	--	
17. Restore space station funding	Y	
18. Civil Rights Act of 1991	N	
19. Unlimited damages-discrimination	N	
20. Eliminate funds for supercollider	Y	
21. Terminate SDI except for research	N	
22. Req 7-day handgun waiting period	Y	
23. Provide $30b for failed S&Ls	Y	
24. Allow use of force against Iraq	Y	
25. Allow $15b in foreign aid for '91	N	
26. Revise & extend legal immigration	N	
27. Suspend aid to Angolan rebels	N	
28. Democratic tax plan proposals	N	
29. Cut defense 5% across the board	N	
30. Textile import quotas-veto override	Y	
31. Abortion service for military abroad	N	
32. Limits on high income farmers	Y	
33. Family medical leave-veto override	N	
34. Req submission of balanced budget	N	
35. Balanced budget amendment	Y	
36. Amendment to ban flag desecration	Y	
37. Reauthorize Amtrak-veto override	N	
38. Retraining aid for coal miners	Y	
39. Suspend El Salvador military aid	N	
40. Expand child care aid/tax credit	N	
41. Raise House salary/omit honoraria	N	
42. Toughen oil-spill liability	N	
43. Restitution to Japanese interned	N	
44. Protect Chinese & C.A. nationals	N	
45. Abortion $ for rape/incest cases	N	
46. Allow religious schools to bar gays	Y	
47. Bar broadcaster fairness doctrine	N	
48. Bar cap gains cut/reinstate IRA	N	
49. Bar unions equal voice in pension	Y	
50. Bar assembly of chemical weapons	N	
51. Ban plutonium/uranium production	Y	
52. Cap MX missile deployment at 50	N	
53. Allow $3b for 2 stealth bombers	N	
54. Publish bio-warfare experiments	N	
55. Raise minimum wage-veto override	N	
56. Bar transfer of FS-X technology	Y	
57. Cut defense and raise domestic $	N	
58. Uniform poll closing in 48 states	N	
59. Req foreign investment disclosure	N	
60. Textile import quotas-veto override	Y	
61. Bar abortion funding in Wash, DC	Y	
62. Notify spouses of AIDS+ carriers	Y	
63. Seize conveyance-drug trafficking	Y	
64. South Africa sanctions	N	
65. 60 days' notice of plant closings	Y	
66. Close unneeded military bases	Y	
67. Keep welfare reform within $2.8b	Y	
68. Allow children housing exclusion	Y	
69. Shift $400m of NASA to homeless	Y	
70. Cap Medicare patients' liability	N	
71. Prohibit employee polygraph testing	Y	
72. Allow CIA to fund Contras	Y	
73. Revise unfair trade practices	N	
74. Focus SDI on accidental launch	N	

75. Bar Air Force $ for MX missile	N	
76. Allow "real" increase in defense	Y	
77. Troop reduction in Europe of 50%	N	
78. Ban nuclear tests above 1 kiloton	N	
79. Ban anti-satellite missile tests	N	
80. Observe certain limits of SALT II	N	
81. Restore four Civil Rights laws	Y	
82. Prohibit aliens as strikebreakers	Y	
83. Allow military malpractice suits	Y	
84. Approval of $36m in Contra aid	Y	
85. $18b deficit reduction compromise	Y	
86. Welfare reform of $5.7b for 5 years	N	
87. Raise taxes $12b/cut spending $3b	N	
88. Board to assess occupational risk	N	
89. Balanced budget by '93-via targets	Y	
90. Bar licensing of two nuclear plants	Y	
91. Remove victims compensation cap	N	
92. Catastrophic health insurance	N	
93. Ban airline smoking-2 hours or less	Y	
94. $1b/two year aid for the homeless	N	
95. Bar non-unions in union companies	N	
96. Increase FSLIC rescue to $15b	N	
97. Impose quotas to lower trade deficit	N	
98. Reduce discretionary budget 21%	Y	
99. Immigration reform/alien amnesty	Y	
100. South Africa sanctions-veto override	Y	
101. Tax overhaul to revise income tax	Y	
102. Use of military in drug war	Y	
103. Delete 12 MX/add conventional wpn	Y	
104. Raise speed limit to 65 mph	N	
105. Require Pentagon to buy US goods	Y	
106. AIDS insurance non-discrimination	N	
107. Prohibit Saudi arms sales	Y	
108. Ease Gun Control Act of 1968	Y	
109. Bar interstate handgun transport	Y	
110. Make company emissions known	Y	
111. Allow toxic victims to sue in fed ct	N	
112. Superfund waste cleanup of $10b	Y	
113. 90 days notice of plant closings	N	
114. $20b in Medicare cuts/tax increases	N	
115. Spending cuts and tax increases	N	
116. Set school lunch lmt-250% poverty	N	
117. $75m for youth work projects	N	
118. Allow Angolan military assistance	Y	
119. Suspend defense payments for abuse	N	
120. Drop SS COLAs/$12b tax increase	Y	
121. Approve $1.5b for 21 MX missiles	N	
122. Emergency farm credit/revisions	N	
123. Duty on Taiwan/Hong Kong/S Korea	N	
124. Limit steel imports to 17%	Y	
125. Cut $ to schools that bar prayer	Y	
126. $50b-taxes; cut Medicare/spending	N	
127. Limit Pershing II/cruise in Europe	N	
128. Delete $7.1b for 34 B-1 bombers	N	
129. Bar purchase of Sergeant York guns	Y	
130. El Salvador military/economic aid	Y	
131. Bar mining of Nicaraguan waters	Y	
132. Physician fee freeze for Medicare	Y	
133. $49b in "sin"/phone/insurance taxes	Y	
134. Allow sale of Conrail	N	
135. Equal Rights Amendment	Y	
136. Authorize Marines in Lebanon	Y	
137. Eminent domain for coal companies	N	
138. Prohibit EPA clean air sanctions	Y	

GOODLING, WILLIAM F. (continued)

139. SS retirement age increase/reforms	N	142. Highway-gas tax bill	N
140. Auto domestic content requirement	Y	143. Cut $5b from defense for Medicare	N
141. Delete jobs program funding	Y	144. Emergency housing aid of $1b	N

Presidential Support Score: 1991 - 68%   1990 - 54%

GAYDOS, JOSEPH M. -- Pennsylvania 20th District [Democrat]. Counties of Allegheny (pt.) and Westmoreland (pt.). Prior Terms: 1968 (Special Election)-1992. Born: July 3, 1926; Braddock, PA. Education: Duquesne University; University of Notre Dame Law School (LL.B.). Military Service: U.S. Naval Reserve, WW II. Occupation: Pennsylvania senator; Pennsylvania deputy attorney general; Allegheny County assistant solicitor; general counsel, United Mine Workers of America.

1. Protection to Haitian refugees	N	51. Ban plutonium/uranium production	Y
2. Raise tax on wealthy; lower others	Y	52. Cap MX missile deployment at 50	Y
3. Investigate Reagan hostage delay	?	53. Allow $3b for 2 stealth bombers	N
4. Campaign finance revisions	N	54. Publish bio-warfare experiments	N
5. Unpaid leave to care for children	Y	55. Raise minimum wage-veto override	Y
6. Restrict NEA use of funds	N	56. Bar transfer of FS-X technology	N
7. Bar race-bias claim/habeas corpus	Y	57. Cut defense and raise domestic $	N
8. Ban race as death sentence factor	N	58. Uniform poll closing in 48 states	Y
9. Exceptions to exclusionary rule	?	59. Req foreign investment disclosure	Y
10. Allow sale of assault weapons	Y	60. Textile import quotas-veto override	Y
11. Life in prison/abolish death penalty	N	61. Bar abortion funding in Wash, DC	Y
12. Req conspiracy-price fixing cases	N	62. Notify spouses of AIDS+ carriers	N
13. Unemployment benefits extension	Y	63. Seize conveyance-drug trafficking	N
14. Tissue use of aborted fetuses	?	64. South Africa sanctions	Y
15. Bar replacement of union strikers	Y	65. 60 days' notice of plant closings	Y
16. Hold foreign aid at $15b for '92	N	66. Close unneeded military bases	N
17. Restore space station funding	Y	67. Keep welfare reform within $2.8b	Y
18. Civil Rights Act of 1991	Y	68. Allow children housing exclusion	Y
19. Unlimited damages-discrimination	Y	69. Shift $400m of NASA to homeless	Y
20. Eliminate funds for supercollider	N	70. Cap Medicare patients' liability	Y
21. Terminate SDI except for research	N	71. Prohibit employee polygraph testing	Y
22. Req 7-day handgun waiting period	Y	72. Allow CIA to fund Contras	N
23. Provide $30b for failed S&Ls	N	73. Revise unfair trade practices	Y
24. Allow use of force against Iraq	N	74. Focus SDI on accidental launch	N
25. Allow $15b in foreign aid for '91	N	75. Bar Air Force $ for MX missile	N
26. Revise & extend legal immigration	Y	76. Allow "real" increase in defense	N
27. Suspend aid to Angolan rebels	Y	77. Troop reduction in Europe of 50%	?
28. Democratic tax plan proposals	N	78. Ban nuclear tests above 1 kiloton	Y
29. Cut defense 5% across the board	N	79. Ban anti-satellite missile tests	Y
30. Textile import quotas-veto override	Y	80. Observe certain limits of SALT II	Y
31. Abortion service for military abroad	N	81. Restore four Civil Rights laws	Y
32. Limits on high income farmers	Y	82. Prohibit aliens as strikebreakers	Y
33. Family medical leave-veto override	Y	83. Allow military malpractice suits	Y
34. Req submission of balanced budget	Y	84. Approval of $36m in Contra aid	N
35. Balanced budget amendment	Y	85. $18b deficit reduction compromise	N
36. Amendment to ban flag desecration	Y	86. Welfare reform of $5.7b for 5 years	Y
37. Reauthorize Amtrak-veto override	Y	87. Raise taxes $12b/cut spending $3b	Y
38. Retraining aid for coal miners	Y	88. Board to assess occupational risk	Y
39. Suspend El Salvador military aid	Y	89. Balanced budget by '93-via targets	Y
40. Expand child care aid/tax credit	Y	90. Bar licensing of two nuclear plants	N
41. Raise House salary/omit honoraria	Y	91. Remove victims compensation cap	N
42. Toughen oil-spill liability	?	92. Catastrophic health insurance	Y
43. Restitution to Japanese interned	Y	93. Ban airline smoking-2 hours or less	N
44. Protect Chinese & C.A. nationals	Y	94. $1b/two year aid for the homeless	Y
45. Abortion $ for rape/incest cases	N	95. Bar non-unions in union companies	Y
46. Allow religious schools to bar gays	Y	96. Increase FSLIC rescue to $15b	N
47. Bar broadcaster fairness doctrine	N	97. Impose quotas to lower trade deficit	Y
48. Bar cap gains cut/reinstate IRA	Y	98. Reduce discretionary budget 21%	Y
49. Bar unions equal voice in pension	N	99. Immigration reform/alien amnesty	N
50. Bar assembly of chemical weapons	Y	100. South Africa sanctions-veto override	?

GAYDOS, JOSEPH M. (continued)

101. Tax overhaul to revise income tax	Y	123. Duty on Taiwan/Hong Kong/S Korea	Y
102. Use of military in drug war	Y	124. Limit steel imports to 17%	Y
103. Delete 12 MX/add conventional wpn	N	125. Cut $ to schools that bar prayer	Y
104. Raise speed limit to 65 mph	N	126. $50b-taxes; cut Medicare/spending	N
105. Require Pentagon to buy US goods	Y	127. Limit Pershing II/cruise in Europe	N
106. AIDS insurance non-discrimination	Y	128. Delete $7.1b for 34 B-1 bombers	N
107. Prohibit Saudi arms sales	Y	129. Bar purchase of Sergeant York guns	N
108. Ease Gun Control Act of 1968	Y	130. El Salvador military/economic aid	N
109. Bar interstate handgun transport	N	131. Bar mining of Nicaraguan waters	Y
110. Make company emissions known	Y	132. Physician fee freeze for Medicare	N
111. Allow toxic victims to sue in fed ct	N	133. $49b in "sin"/phone/insurance taxes	Y
112. Superfund waste cleanup of $10b	N	134. Allow sale of Conrail	N
113. 90 days notice of plant closings	Y	135. Equal Rights Amendment	N
114. $20b in Medicare cuts/tax increases	N	136. Authorize Marines in Lebanon	N
115. Spending cuts and tax increases	N	137. Eminent domain for coal companies	N
116. Set school lunch lmt-250% poverty	N	138. Prohibit EPA clean air sanctions	Y
117. $75m for youth work projects	Y	139. SS retirement age increase/reforms	N
118. Allow Angolan military assistance	N	140. Auto domestic content requirement	Y
119. Suspend defense payments for abuse	N	141. Delete jobs program funding	N
120. Drop SS COLAs/$12b tax increase	N	142. Highway-gas tax bill	Y
121. Approve $1.5b for 21 MX missiles	N	143. Cut $5b from defense for Medicare	Y
122. Emergency farm credit/revisions	Y	144. Emergency housing aid of $1b	Y

Presidential Support Score: 1991 - 36% 1990 - 32%

RIDGE, THOMAS J. -- Pennsylvania 21st District [Republican]. Counties of Crawford, Erie, Lawrence (pt.) and Mercer. Prior Terms: 1983-92. Born: August 26, 1945; Munhall, PA. Education: Harvard University (B.A.); Dickinson School of Law (J.D.). Military Service: U.S. Army. Occupation: Congressional aide; legal instructor; law clerk; attorney; assistant district attorney.

1. Protection to Haitian refugees	N	33. Family medical leave-veto override	N
2. Raise tax on wealthy; lower others	N	34. Req submission of balanced budget	N
3. Investigate Reagan hostage delay	N	35. Balanced budget amendment	Y
4. Campaign finance revisions	N	36. Amendment to ban flag desecration	Y
5. Unpaid leave to care for children	N	37. Reauthorize Amtrak-veto override	Y
6. Restrict NEA use of funds	Y	38. Retraining aid for coal miners	Y
7. Bar race-bias claim/habeas corpus	Y	39. Suspend El Salvador military aid	Y
8. Ban race as death sentence factor	Y	40. Expand child care aid/tax credit	Y
9. Exceptions to exclusionary rule	Y	41. Raise House salary/omit honoraria	N
10. Allow sale of assault weapons	Y	42. Toughen oil-spill liability	N
11. Life in prison/abolish death penalty	N	43. Restitution to Japanese interned	N
12. Req conspiracy-price fixing cases	N	44. Protect Chinese & C.A. nationals	N
13. Unemployment benefits extension	Y	45. Abortion $ for rape/incest cases	Y
14. Tissue use of aborted fetuses	Y	46. Allow religious schools to bar gays	Y
15. Bar replacement of union strikers	N	47. Bar broadcaster fairness doctrine	N
16. Hold foreign aid at $15b for '92	Y	48. Bar cap gains cut/reinstate IRA	N
17. Restore space station funding	Y	49. Bar unions equal voice in pension	Y
18. Civil Rights Act of 1991	N	50. Bar assembly of chemical weapons	N
19. Unlimited damages-discrimination	N	51. Ban plutonium/uranium production	N
20. Eliminate funds for supercollider	Y	52. Cap MX missile deployment at 50	Y
21. Terminate SDI except for research	?	53. Allow $3b for 2 stealth bombers	N
22. Req 7-day handgun waiting period	N	54. Publish bio-warfare experiments	N
23. Provide $30b for failed S&Ls	Y	55. Raise minimum wage-veto override	Y
24. Allow use of force against Iraq	Y	56. Bar transfer of FS-X technology	N
25. Allow $15b in foreign aid for '91	Y	57. Cut defense and raise domestic $	N
26. Revise & extend legal immigration	N	58. Uniform poll closing in 48 states	Y
27. Suspend aid to Angolan rebels	N	59. Req foreign investment disclosure	N
28. Democratic tax plan proposals	N	60. Textile import quotas-veto override	Y
29. Cut defense 5% across the board	N	61. Bar abortion funding in Wash, DC	N
30. Textile import quotas-veto override	Y	62. Notify spouses of AIDS+ carriers	Y
31. Abortion service for military abroad	Y	63. Seize conveyance-drug trafficking	Y
32. Limits on high income farmers	N	64. South Africa sanctions	N

RIDGE, THOMAS J. (continued)

65.	60 days' notice of plant closings	Y	103. Delete 12 MX/add conventional wpn	Y
66.	Close unneeded military bases	N	104. Raise speed limit to 65 mph	N
67.	Keep welfare reform within $2.8b	Y	105. Require Pentagon to buy US goods	Y
68.	Allow children housing exclusion	Y	106. AIDS insurance non-discrimination	N
69.	Shift $400m of NASA to homeless	Y	107. Prohibit Saudi arms sales	N
70.	Cap Medicare patients' liability	Y	108. Ease Gun Control Act of 1968	Y
71.	Prohibit employee polygraph testing	Y	109. Bar interstate handgun transport	Y
72.	Allow CIA to fund Contras	Y	110. Make company emissions known	Y
73.	Revise unfair trade practices	Y	111. Allow toxic victims to sue in fed ct	N
74.	Focus SDI on accidental launch	N	112. Superfund waste cleanup of $10b	N
75.	Bar Air Force $ for MX missile	N	113. 90 days notice of plant closings	Y
76.	Allow "real" increase in defense	N	114. $20b in Medicare cuts/tax increases	Y
77.	Troop reduction in Europe of 50%	N	115. Spending cuts and tax increases	N
78.	Ban nuclear tests above 1 kiloton	N	116. Set school lunch lmt-250% poverty	N
79.	Ban anti-satellite missile tests	Y	117. $75m for youth work projects	Y
80.	Observe certain limits of SALT II	Y	118. Allow Angolan military assistance	Y
81.	Restore four Civil Rights laws	Y	119. Suspend defense payments for abuse	N
82.	Prohibit aliens as strikebreakers	Y	120. Drop SS COLAs/$12b tax increase	N
83.	Allow military malpractice suits	Y	121. Approve $1.5b for 21 MX missiles	N
84.	Approval of $36m in Contra aid	Y	122. Emergency farm credit/revisions	Y
85.	$18b deficit reduction compromise	Y	123. Duty on Taiwan/Hong Kong/S Korea	Y
86.	Welfare reform of $5.7b for 5 years	N	124. Limit steel imports to 17%	Y
87.	Raise taxes $12b/cut spending $3b	N	125. Cut $ to schools that bar prayer	N
88.	Board to assess occupational risk	N	126. $50b-taxes; cut Medicare/spending	N
89.	Balanced budget by '93-via targets	Y	127. Limit Pershing II/cruise in Europe	?
90.	Bar licensing of two nuclear plants	Y	128. Delete $7.1b for 34 B-1 bombers	N
91.	Remove victims compensation cap	N	129. Bar purchase of Sergeant York guns	Y
92.	Catastrophic health insurance	Y	130. El Salvador military/economic aid	Y
93.	Ban airline smoking-2 hours or less	Y	131. Bar mining of Nicaraguan waters	Y
94.	$1b/two year aid for the homeless	Y	132. Physician fee freeze for Medicare	Y
95.	Bar non-unions in union companies	Y	133. $49b in "sin"/phone/insurance taxes	Y
96.	Increase FSLIC rescue to $15b	Y	134. Allow sale of Conrail	Y
97.	Impose quotas to lower trade deficit	Y	135. Equal Rights Amendment	Y
98.	Reduce discretionary budget 21%	Y	136. Authorize Marines in Lebanon	Y
99.	Immigration reform/alien amnesty	Y	137. Eminent domain for coal companies	N
100.	South Africa sanctions-veto override	Y	138. Prohibit EPA clean air sanctions	Y
101.	Tax overhaul to revise income tax	Y	139. SS retirement age increase/reforms	Y
102.	Use of military in drug war	Y		

Presidential Support Score: 1991 - 58%   1990 - 49%

MURPHY, AUSTIN J. -- Pennsylvania 22nd District [Democrat]. Counties of Allegheny (pt.), Beaver (pt.), Fayette, Greene and Washington. Prior Terms: 1977-92. Born: June 17, 1927; North Charleroi, PA. Education: Duquesne University (B.A.); University of Pittsburgh (LL.B.). Occupation: Pennsylvania representative (1959-71); Pennsylvania senator (1971); assistant district attorney.

1.	Protection to Haitian refugees	?	17. Restore space station funding	N
2.	Raise tax on wealthy; lower others	Y	18. Civil Rights Act of 1991	Y
3.	Investigate Reagan hostage delay	Y	19. Unlimited damages-discrimination	N
4.	Campaign finance revisions	Y	20. Eliminate funds for supercollider	Y
5.	Unpaid leave to care for children	Y	21. Terminate SDI except for research	?
6.	Restrict NEA use of funds	N	22. Req 7-day handgun waiting period	N
7.	Bar race-bias claim/habeas corpus	Y	23. Provide $30b for failed S&Ls	N
8.	Ban race as death sentence factor	Y	24. Allow use of force against Iraq	N
9.	Exceptions to exclusionary rule	N	25. Allow $15b in foreign aid for '91	?
10.	Allow sale of assault weapons	Y	26. Revise & extend legal immigration	?
11.	Life in prison/abolish death penalty	N	27. Suspend aid to Angolan rebels	Y
12.	Req conspiracy-price fixing cases	N	28. Democratic tax plan proposals	Y
13.	Unemployment benefits extension	Y	29. Cut defense 5% across the board	Y
14.	Tissue use of aborted fetuses	N	30. Textile import quotas-veto override	Y
15.	Bar replacement of union strikers	Y	31. Abortion service for military abroad	N
16.	Hold foreign aid at $15b for '92	N	32. Limits on high income farmers	Y

MURPHY, AUSTIN J. (continued)

33. Family medical leave-veto override	Y	
34. Req submission of balanced budget	Y	
35. Balanced budget amendment	Y	
36. Amendment to ban flag desecration	Y	
37. Reauthorize Amtrak-veto override	Y	
38. Retraining aid for coal miners	Y	
39. Suspend El Salvador military aid	Y	
40. Expand child care aid/tax credit	?	
41. Raise House salary/omit honoraria	N	
42. Toughen oil-spill liability	Y	
43. Restitution to Japanese interned	N	
44. Protect Chinese & C.A. nationals	N	
45. Abortion $ for rape/incest cases	N	
46. Allow religious schools to bar gays	Y	
47. Bar broadcaster fairness doctrine	N	
48. Bar cap gains cut/reinstate IRA	Y	
49. Bar unions equal voice in pension	N	
50. Bar assembly of chemical weapons	Y	
51. Ban plutonium/uranium production	Y	
52. Cap MX missile deployment at 50	Y	
53. Allow $3b for 2 stealth bombers	N	
54. Publish bio-warfare experiments	Y	
55. Raise minimum wage-veto override	Y	
56. Bar transfer of FS-X technology	Y	
57. Cut defense and raise domestic $	N	
58. Uniform poll closing in 48 states	Y	
59. Req foreign investment disclosure	Y	
60. Textile import quotas-veto override	Y	
61. Bar abortion funding in Wash, DC	Y	
62. Notify spouses of AIDS+ carriers	N	
63. Seize conveyance-drug trafficking	Y	
64. South Africa sanctions	?	
65. 60 days' notice of plant closings	Y	
66. Close unneeded military bases	Y	
67. Keep welfare reform within $2.8b	N	
68. Allow children housing exclusion	N	
69. Shift $400m of NASA to homeless	Y	
70. Cap Medicare patients' liability	Y	
71. Prohibit employee polygraph testing	Y	
72. Allow CIA to fund Contras	N	
73. Revise unfair trade practices	Y	
74. Focus SDI on accidental launch	Y	
75. Bar Air Force $ for MX missile	N	
76. Allow "real" increase in defense	N	
77. Troop reduction in Europe of 50%	Y	
78. Ban nuclear tests above 1 kiloton	N	
79. Ban anti-satellite missile tests	Y	
80. Observe certain limits of SALT II	Y	
81. Restore four Civil Rights laws	Y	
82. Prohibit aliens as strikebreakers	Y	
83. Allow military malpractice suits	Y	
84. Approval of $36m in Contra aid	N	
85. $18b deficit reduction compromise	?	
86. Welfare reform of $5.7b for 5 years	Y	
87. Raise taxes $12b/cut spending $3b	?	
88. Board to assess occupational risk	Y	

89. Balanced budget by '93-via targets	N	
90. Bar licensing of two nuclear plants	N	
91. Remove victims compensation cap	N	
92. Catastrophic health insurance	Y	
93. Ban airline smoking-2 hours or less	Y	
94. $1b/two year aid for the homeless	Y	
95. Bar non-unions in union companies	Y	
96. Increase FSLIC rescue to $15b	N	
97. Impose quotas to lower trade deficit	Y	
98. Reduce discretionary budget 21%	?	
99. Immigration reform/alien amnesty	N	
100. South Africa sanctions-veto override	Y	
101. Tax overhaul to revise income tax	N	
102. Use of military in drug war	Y	
103. Delete 12 MX/add conventional wpn	?	
104. Raise speed limit to 65 mph	N	
105. Require Pentagon to buy US goods	Y	
106. AIDS insurance non-discrimination	Y	
107. Prohibit Saudi arms sales	?	
108. Ease Gun Control Act of 1968	Y	
109. Bar interstate handgun transport	Y	
110. Make company emissions known	Y	
111. Allow toxic victims to sue in fed ct	N	
112. Superfund waste cleanup of $10b	N	
113. 90 days notice of plant closings	Y	
114. $20b in Medicare cuts/tax increases	N	
115. Spending cuts and tax increases	N	
116. Set school lunch lmt-250% poverty	N	
117. $75m for youth work projects	Y	
118. Allow Angolan military assistance	N	
119. Suspend defense payments for abuse	Y	
120. Drop SS COLAs/$12b tax increase	N	
121. Approve $1.5b for 21 MX missiles	N	
122. Emergency farm credit/revisions	Y	
123. Duty on Taiwan/Hong Kong/S Korea	Y	
124. Limit steel imports to 17%	Y	
125. Cut $ to schools that bar prayer	Y	
126. $50b-taxes; cut Medicare/spending	N	
127. Limit Pershing II/cruise in Europe	N	
128. Delete $7.1b for 34 B-1 bombers	N	
129. Bar purchase of Sergeant York guns	N	
130. El Salvador military/economic aid	N	
131. Bar mining of Nicaraguan waters	?	
132. Physician fee freeze for Medicare	Y	
133. $49b in "sin"/phone/insurance taxes	N	
134. Allow sale of Conrail	N	
135. Equal Rights Amendment	Y	
136. Authorize Marines in Lebanon	N	
137. Eminent domain for coal companies	N	
138. Prohibit EPA clean air sanctions	Y	
139. SS retirement age increase/reforms	N	
140. Auto domestic content requirement	Y	
141. Delete jobs program funding	N	
142. Highway-gas tax bill	N	
143. Cut $5b from defense for Medicare	Y	
144. Emergency housing aid of $1b	Y	

Presidential Support Score: 1991 - 34%   1990 - 29%

CLINGER, WILLIAM F., Jr. -- Pennsylvania 23rd District [Republican]. Counties of Armstrong (pt.), Cameron, Centre, Clarion, Clearfield (pt.), Clinton (pt.), Elk, Forest, Jefferson, McKean, Venango and Warren. Prior Terms: 1979-92. Born: April 4, 1929; Warren, PA. Education: Johns Hopkins University (B.A.); University of Virginia Law School (LL.B.).

CLINGER, WILLIAM F., Jr. (continued)

Military Service: U.S. Navy, 1951-55. Occupation: Advertiser, New Process (1954-62); attorney, Harper, Clinger and Eberly (1965-75); Pennsylvania committeeman (1968-75); chief counsel, Economic Development Administration (1975-77).

1. Protection to Haitian refugees	N	61. Bar abortion funding in Wash, DC	Y
2. Raise tax on wealthy; lower others	N	62. Notify spouses of AIDS+ carriers	N
3. Investigate Reagan hostage delay	N	63. Seize conveyance-drug trafficking	N
4. Campaign finance revisions	N	64. South Africa sanctions	N
5. Unpaid leave to care for children	N	65. 60 days' notice of plant closings	Y
6. Restrict NEA use of funds	N	66. Close unneeded military bases	Y
7. Bar race-bias claim/habeas corpus	Y	67. Keep welfare reform within $2.8b	Y
8. Ban race as death sentence factor	Y	68. Allow children housing exclusion	Y
9. Exceptions to exclusionary rule	Y	69. Shift $400m of NASA to homeless	Y
10. Allow sale of assault weapons	Y	70. Cap Medicare patients' liability	Y
11. Life in prison/abolish death penalty	N	71. Prohibit employee polygraph testing	Y
12. Req conspiracy-price fixing cases	Y	72. Allow CIA to fund Contras	Y
13. Unemployment benefits extension	Y	73. Revise unfair trade practices	Y
14. Tissue use of aborted fetuses	N	74. Focus SDI on accidental launch	Y
15. Bar replacement of union strikers	N	75. Bar Air Force $ for MX missile	N
16. Hold foreign aid at $15b for '92	N	76. Allow "real" increase in defense	N
17. Restore space station funding	Y	77. Troop reduction in Europe of 50%	N
18. Civil Rights Act of 1991	N	78. Ban nuclear tests above 1 kiloton	N
19. Unlimited damages-discrimination	N	79. Ban anti-satellite missile tests	N
20. Eliminate funds for supercollider	N	80. Observe certain limits of SALT II	Y
21. Terminate SDI except for research	N	81. Restore four Civil Rights laws	N
22. Req 7-day handgun waiting period	N	82. Prohibit aliens as strikebreakers	Y
23. Provide $30b for failed S&Ls	Y	83. Allow military malpractice suits	Y
24. Allow use of force against Iraq	Y	84. Approval of $36m in Contra aid	Y
25. Allow $15b in foreign aid for '91	N	85. $18b deficit reduction compromise	Y
26. Revise & extend legal immigration	Y	86. Welfare reform of $5.7b for 5 years	N
27. Suspend aid to Angolan rebels	N	87. Raise taxes $12b/cut spending $3b	N
28. Democratic tax plan proposals	N	88. Board to assess occupational risk	N
29. Cut defense 5% across the board	N	89. Balanced budget by '93-via targets	Y
30. Textile import quotas-veto override	Y	90. Bar licensing of two nuclear plants	N
31. Abortion service for military abroad	N	91. Remove victims compensation cap	N
32. Limits on high income farmers	N	92. Catastrophic health insurance	Y
33. Family medical leave-veto override	N	93. Ban airline smoking-2 hours or less	N
34. Req submission of balanced budget	N	94. $1b/two year aid for the homeless	Y
35. Balanced budget amendment	Y	95. Bar non-unions in union companies	N
36. Amendment to ban flag desecration	N	96. Increase FSLIC rescue to $15b	N
37. Reauthorize Amtrak-veto override	N	97. Impose quotas to lower trade deficit	N
38. Retraining aid for coal miners	+	98. Reduce discretionary budget 21%	Y
39. Suspend El Salvador military aid	N	99. Immigration reform/alien amnesty	Y
40. Expand child care aid/tax credit	N	100. South Africa sanctions-veto override	Y
41. Raise House salary/omit honoraria	N	101. Tax overhaul to revise income tax	Y
42. Toughen oil-spill liability	N	102. Use of military in drug war	Y
43. Restitution to Japanese interned	Y	103. Delete 12 MX/add conventional wpn	N
44. Protect Chinese & C.A. nationals	Y	104. Raise speed limit to 65 mph	N
45. Abortion $ for rape/incest cases	N	105. Require Pentagon to buy US goods	Y
46. Allow religious schools to bar gays	Y	106. AIDS insurance non-discrimination	Y
47. Bar broadcaster fairness doctrine	Y	107. Prohibit Saudi arms sales	Y
48. Bar cap gains cut/reinstate IRA	N	108. Ease Gun Control Act of 1968	Y
49. Bar unions equal voice in pension	Y	109. Bar interstate handgun transport	N
50. Bar assembly of chemical weapons	Y	110. Make company emissions known	Y
51. Ban plutonium/uranium production	Y	111. Allow toxic victims to sue in fed ct	N
52. Cap MX missile deployment at 50	N	112. Superfund waste cleanup of $10b	N
53. Allow $3b for 2 stealth bombers	Y	113. 90 days notice of plant closings	Y
54. Publish bio-warfare experiments	N	114. $20b in Medicare cuts/tax increases	Y
55. Raise minimum wage-veto override	N	115. Spending cuts and tax increases	N
56. Bar transfer of FS-X technology	N	116. Set school lunch lmt-250% poverty	N
57. Cut defense and raise domestic $	N	117. $75m for youth work projects	Y
58. Uniform poll closing in 48 states	N	118. Allow Angolan military assistance	Y
59. Req foreign investment disclosure	N	119. Suspend defense payments for abuse	N
60. Textile import quotas-veto override	Y	120. Drop SS COLAs/$12b tax increase	N

CLINGER, WILLIAM F., Jr. (continued)

121. Approve $1.5b for 21 MX missiles	Y	
122. Emergency farm credit/revisions	Y	
123. Duty on Taiwan/Hong Kong/S Korea	N	
124. Limit steel imports to 17%	Y	
125. Cut $ to schools that bar prayer	Y	
126. $50b-taxes; cut Medicare/spending	N	
127. Limit Pershing II/cruise in Europe	N	
128. Delete $7.1b for 34 B-1 bombers	Y	
129. Bar purchase of Sergeant York guns	N	
130. El Salvador military/economic aid	Y	
131. Bar mining of Nicaraguan waters	Y	
132. Physician fee freeze for Medicare	Y	
133. $49b in "sin"/phone/insurance taxes	Y
134. Allow sale of Conrail	N
135. Equal Rights Amendment	Y
136. Authorize Marines in Lebanon	Y
137. Eminent domain for coal companies	Y
138. Prohibit EPA clean air sanctions	N
139. SS retirement age increase/reforms	Y
140. Auto domestic content requirement	N
141. Delete jobs program funding	Y
142. Highway-gas tax bill	Y
143. Cut $5b from defense for Medicare	N
144. Emergency housing aid of $1b	N

Presidential Support Score: 1991 - 76%   1990 - 66%

RHODE ISLAND

MACHTLEY, RONALD K. -- Rhode Island 1st District [Republican]. Counties of Bristol, Newport and Providence (pt.). Prior Terms: 1989-92. Born: July 13, 1948; Johnstown, PA. Education: U.S. Naval Academy (B.S.); Suffolk University Law School (J.D.). Military Service: U.S. Navy and Naval Reserves. Occupation: Lawyer; hospital trustee.

1. Protection to Haitian refugees	Y	30. Textile import quotas-veto override	Y
2. Raise tax on wealthy; lower others	N	31. Abortion service for military abroad	Y
3. Investigate Reagan hostage delay	N	32. Limits on high income farmers	Y
4. Campaign finance revisions	N	33. Family medical leave-veto override	Y
5. Unpaid leave to care for children	Y	34. Req submission of balanced budget	Y
6. Restrict NEA use of funds	N	35. Balanced budget amendment	Y
7. Bar race-bias claim/habeas corpus	Y	36. Amendment to ban flag desecration	Y
8. Ban race as death sentence factor	Y	37. Reauthorize Amtrak-veto override	Y
9. Exceptions to exclusionary rule	Y	38. Retraining aid for coal miners	N
10. Allow sale of assault weapons	N	39. Suspend El Salvador military aid	Y
11. Life in prison/abolish death penalty	N	40. Expand child care aid/tax credit	Y
12. Req conspiracy-price fixing cases	N	41. Raise House salary/omit honoraria	N
13. Unemployment benefits extension	Y	42. Toughen oil-spill liability	Y
14. Tissue use of aborted fetuses	?	43. Restitution to Japanese interned	Y
15. Bar replacement of union strikers	N	44. Protect Chinese & C.A. nationals	Y
16. Hold foreign aid at $15b for '92	Y	45. Abortion $ for rape/incest cases	Y
17. Restore space station funding	Y	46. Allow religious schools to bar gays	N
18. Civil Rights Act of 1991	Y	47. Bar broadcaster fairness doctrine	Y
19. Unlimited damages-discrimination	N	48. Bar cap gains cut/reinstate IRA	N
20. Eliminate funds for supercollider	Y	49. Bar unions equal voice in pension	N
21. Terminate SDI except for research	N	50. Bar assembly of chemical weapons	Y
22. Req 7-day handgun waiting period	Y	51. Ban plutonium/uranium production	Y
23. Provide $30b for failed S&Ls	N	52. Cap MX missile deployment at 50	N
24. Allow use of force against Iraq	Y	53. Allow $3b for 2 stealth bombers	N
25. Allow $15b in foreign aid for '91	?	54. Publish bio-warfare experiments	Y
26. Revise & extend legal immigration	Y	55. Raise minimum wage-veto override	Y
27. Suspend aid to Angolan rebels	Y	56. Bar transfer of FS-X technology	N
28. Democratic tax plan proposals	N	57. Cut defense and raise domestic $	N
29. Cut defense 5% across the board	N	58. Uniform poll closing in 48 states	N

Presidential Support Score: 1991 - 52%   1990 - 38%

REED, JOHN F. (JACK) -- Rhode Island 2nd District [Democrat]. Counties of Kent, Providence (pt.) and Washington. Prior Term: 1991-92. Born: November 12, 1949; Providence, RI. Education: U.S. Military Academy (B.S.); Harvard University (M.P.P.);

REED, JOHN F. (continued)
Harvard Law School (J.D.). Military Service: U.S. Army. Occupation: Associate social sciences professor; lawyer; state senator (1985-90).

1. Protection to Haitian refugees	Y	13. Unemployment benefits extension	Y
2. Raise tax on wealthy; lower others	Y	14. Tissue use of aborted fetuses	Y
3. Investigate Reagan hostage delay	Y	15. Bar replacement of union strikers	Y
4. Campaign finance revisions	Y	16. Hold foreign aid at $15b for '92	Y
5. Unpaid leave to care for children	Y	17. Restore space station funding	N
6. Restrict NEA use of funds	N	18. Civil Rights Act of 1991	Y
7. Bar race-bias claim/habeas corpus	N	19. Unlimited damages-discrimination	Y
8. Ban race as death sentence factor	N	20. Eliminate funds for supercollider	Y
9. Exceptions to exclusionary rule	Y	21. Terminate SDI except for research	Y
10. Allow sale of assault weapons	N	22. Req 7-day handgun waiting period	Y
11. Life in prison/abolish death penalty	N	23. Provide $30b for failed S&Ls	N
12. Req conspiracy-price fixing cases	N	24. Allow use of force against Iraq	N

Presidential Support Score: 1991 - 29%

SOUTH CAROLINA

RAVENEL, ARTHUR, Jr. -- South Carolina 1st District [Republican]. Counties of Beaufort, Berkley (pt.), Charleston, Colleton, Dorchester, Hampton and Jasper. Prior Terms: 1987-92. Born: March 29, 1927; Charleston, SC. Education: College of Charleston (B.S.). Military Service: U.S. Marine Corps, 1945-46. Occupation: Real estate, general contracting, and agriculture businessman; cattleman; state representative (1953-58) and senator (1980-86).

1. Protection to Haitian refugees	N	33. Family medical leave-veto override	Y
2. Raise tax on wealthy; lower others	N	34. Req submission of balanced budget	N
3. Investigate Reagan hostage delay	N	35. Balanced budget amendment	Y
4. Campaign finance revisions	Y	36. Amendment to ban flag desecration	Y
5. Unpaid leave to care for children	Y	37. Reauthorize Amtrak-veto override	Y
6. Restrict NEA use of funds	Y	38. Retraining aid for coal miners	N
7. Bar race-bias claim/habeas corpus	Y	39. Suspend El Salvador military aid	N
8. Ban race as death sentence factor	Y	40. Expand child care aid/tax credit	Y
9. Exceptions to exclusionary rule	Y	41. Raise House salary/omit honoraria	N
10. Allow sale of assault weapons	Y	42. Toughen oil-spill liability	Y
11. Life in prison/abolish death penalty	N	43. Restitution to Japanese interned	Y
12. Req conspiracy-price fixing cases	Y	44. Protect Chinese & C.A. nationals	Y
13. Unemployment benefits extension	Y	45. Abortion $ for rape/incest cases	Y
14. Tissue use of aborted fetuses	Y	46. Allow religious schools to bar gays	Y
15. Bar replacement of union strikers	N	47. Bar broadcaster fairness doctrine	N
16. Hold foreign aid at $15b for '92	Y	48. Bar cap gains cut/reinstate IRA	N
17. Restore space station funding	N	49. Bar unions equal voice in pension	Y
18. Civil Rights Act of 1991	N	50. Bar assembly of chemical weapons	Y
19. Unlimited damages-discrimination	N	51. Ban plutonium/uranium production	N
20. Eliminate funds for supercollider	Y	52. Cap MX missile deployment at 50	N
21. Terminate SDI except for research	N	53. Allow $3b for 2 stealth bombers	Y
22. Req 7-day handgun waiting period	N	54. Publish bio-warfare experiments	N
23. Provide $30b for failed S&Ls	N	55. Raise minimum wage-veto override	N
24. Allow use of force against Iraq	Y	56. Bar transfer of FS-X technology	N
25. Allow $15b in foreign aid for '91	N	57. Cut defense and raise domestic $	N
26. Revise & extend legal immigration	Y	58. Uniform poll closing in 48 states	N
27. Suspend aid to Angolan rebels	N	59. Req foreign investment disclosure	Y
28. Democratic tax plan proposals	N	60. Textile import quotas-veto override	Y
29. Cut defense 5% across the board	N	61. Bar abortion funding in Wash, DC	Y
30. Textile import quotas-veto override	Y	62. Notify spouses of AIDS+ carriers	?
31. Abortion service for military abroad	N	63. Seize conveyance-drug trafficking	N
32. Limits on high income farmers	N	64. South Africa sanctions	N

RAVENEL, ARTHUR, Jr. (continued)

65.	60 days' notice of plant closings	Y
66.	Close unneeded military bases	Y
67.	Keep welfare reform within $2.8b	Y
68.	Allow children housing exclusion	N
69.	Shift $400m of NASA to homeless	Y
70.	Cap Medicare patients' liability	Y
71.	Prohibit employee polygraph testing	Y
72.	Allow CIA to fund Contras	Y
73.	Revise unfair trade practices	Y
74.	Focus SDI on accidental launch	N
75.	Bar Air Force $ for MX missile	N
76.	Allow "real" increase in defense	Y
77.	Troop reduction in Europe of 50%	N
78.	Ban nuclear tests above 1 kiloton	N
79.	Ban anti-satellite missile tests	N
80.	Observe certain limits of SALT II	N
81.	Restore four Civil Rights laws	N

82.	Prohibit aliens as strikebreakers	Y
83.	Allow military malpractice suits	N
84.	Approval of $36m in Contra aid	Y
85.	$18b deficit reduction compromise	Y
86.	Welfare reform of $5.7b for 5 years	N
87.	Raise taxes $12b/cut spending $3b	N
88.	Board to assess occupational risk	N
89.	Balanced budget by '93-via targets	N
90.	Bar licensing of two nuclear plants	N
91.	Remove victims compensation cap	N
92.	Catastrophic health insurance	Y
93.	Ban airline smoking-2 hours or less	Y
94.	$1b/two year aid for the homeless	Y
95.	Bar non-unions in union companies	N
96.	Increase FSLIC rescue to $15b	Y
97.	Impose quotas to lower trade deficit	N
98.	Reduce discretionary budget 21%	Y

Presidential Support Score: 1991 - 57%   1990 - 54%

SPENCE, FLOYD -- South Carolina 2nd District [Republican]. Counties of Bamberg, Calhoun, Lexington, Orangeburg and Richland. Prior Terms: 1971-92. Born: April 9, 1928; Columbia, SC. Education: University of South Carolina (B.A., LL.B.); National Defense War College. Military Service: U.S. Navy. Occupation: South Carolina representative and senator; attorney, Callison and Spence.

1.	Protection to Haitian refugees	N
2.	Raise tax on wealthy; lower others	N
3.	Investigate Reagan hostage delay	N
4.	Campaign finance revisions	N
5.	Unpaid leave to care for children	N
6.	Restrict NEA use of funds	Y
7.	Bar race-bias claim/habeas corpus	Y
8.	Ban race as death sentence factor	Y
9.	Exceptions to exclusionary rule	Y
10.	Allow sale of assault weapons	Y
11.	Life in prison/abolish death penalty	N
12.	Req conspiracy-price fixing cases	Y
13.	Unemployment benefits extension	N
14.	Tissue use of aborted fetuses	Y
15.	Bar replacement of union strikers	N
16.	Hold foreign aid at $15b for '92	X
17.	Restore space station funding	Y
18.	Civil Rights Act of 1991	N
19.	Unlimited damages-discrimination	N
20.	Eliminate funds for supercollider	N
21.	Terminate SDI except for research	N
22.	Req 7-day handgun waiting period	N
23.	Provide $30b for failed S&Ls	N
24.	Allow use of force against Iraq	Y
25.	Allow $15b in foreign aid for '91	N
26.	Revise & extend legal immigration	N
27.	Suspend aid to Angolan rebels	N
28.	Democratic tax plan proposals	N
29.	Cut defense 5% across the board	N
30.	Textile import quotas-veto override	Y
31.	Abortion service for military abroad	N
32.	Limits on high income farmers	N
33.	Family medical leave-veto override	N
34.	Req submission of balanced budget	Y
35.	Balanced budget amendment	Y
36.	Amendment to ban flag desecration	Y
37.	Reauthorize Amtrak-veto override	N

38.	Retraining aid for coal miners	N
39.	Suspend El Salvador military aid	N
40.	Expand child care aid/tax credit	?
41.	Raise House salary/omit honoraria	N
42.	Toughen oil-spill liability	N
43.	Restitution to Japanese interned	N
44.	Protect Chinese & C.A. nationals	Y
45.	Abortion $ for rape/incest cases	N
46.	Allow religious schools to bar gays	Y
47.	Bar broadcaster fairness doctrine	Y
48.	Bar cap gains cut/reinstate IRA	N
49.	Bar unions equal voice in pension	Y
50.	Bar assembly of chemical weapons	N
51.	Ban plutonium/uranium production	N
52.	Cap MX missile deployment at 50	N
53.	Allow $3b for 2 stealth bombers	Y
54.	Publish bio-warfare experiments	N
55.	Raise minimum wage-veto override	N
56.	Bar transfer of FS-X technology	N
57.	Cut defense and raise domestic $	N
58.	Uniform poll closing in 48 states	N
59.	Req foreign investment disclosure	Y
60.	Textile import quotas-veto override	Y
61.	Bar abortion funding in Wash, DC	Y
62.	Notify spouses of AIDS+ carriers	N
63.	Seize conveyance-drug trafficking	Y
64.	South Africa sanctions	?
65.	60 days' notice of plant closings	?
66.	Close unneeded military bases	?
67.	Keep welfare reform within $2.8b	?
68.	Allow children housing exclusion	?
69.	Shift $400m of NASA to homeless	N
70.	Cap Medicare patients' liability	?
71.	Prohibit employee polygraph testing	?
72.	Allow CIA to fund Contras	?
73.	Revise unfair trade practices	?
74.	Focus SDI on accidental launch	?

SPENCE, FLOYD (continued)

75. Bar Air Force $ for MX missile	N	110. Make company emissions known	N
76. Allow "real" increase in defense	Y	111. Allow toxic victims to sue in fed ct	N
77. Troop reduction in Europe of 50%	N	112. Superfund waste cleanup of $10b	N
78. Ban nuclear tests above 1 kiloton	N	113. 90 days notice of plant closings	N
79. Ban anti-satellite missile tests	N	114. $20b in Medicare cuts/tax increases	N
80. Observe certain limits of SALT II	N	115. Spending cuts and tax increases	N
81. Restore four Civil Rights laws	N	116. Set school lunch lmt-250% poverty	Y
82. Prohibit aliens as strikebreakers	Y	117. $75m for youth work projects	N
83. Allow military malpractice suits	N	118. Allow Angolan military assistance	Y
84. Approval of $36m in Contra aid	Y	119. Suspend defense payments for abuse	N
85. $18b deficit reduction compromise	N	120. Drop SS COLAs/$12b tax increase	N
86. Welfare reform of $5.7b for 5 years	N	121. Approve $1.5b for 21 MX missiles	Y
87. Raise taxes $12b/cut spending $3b	X	122. Emergency farm credit/revisions	Y
88. Board to assess occupational risk	N	123. Duty on Taiwan/Hong Kong/S Korea	N
89. Balanced budget by '93-via targets	?	124. Limit steel imports to 17%	N
90. Bar licensing of two nuclear plants	N	125. Cut $ to schools that bar prayer	Y
91. Remove victims compensation cap	N	126. $50b-taxes; cut Medicare/spending	Y
92. Catastrophic health insurance	Y	127. Limit Pershing II/cruise in Europe	N
93. Ban airline smoking-2 hours or less	N	128. Delete $7.1b for 34 B-1 bombers	N
94. $1b/two year aid for the homeless	Y	129. Bar purchase of Sergeant York guns	N
95. Bar non-unions in union companies	N	130. El Salvador military/economic aid	Y
96. Increase FSLIC rescue to $15b	N	131. Bar mining of Nicaraguan waters	N
97. Impose quotas to lower trade deficit	N	132. Physician fee freeze for Medicare	Y
98. Reduce discretionary budget 21%	Y	133. $49b in "sin"/phone/insurance taxes	Y
99. Immigration reform/alien amnesty	N	134. Allow sale of Conrail	Y
100. South Africa sanctions-veto override	N	135. Equal Rights Amendment	N
101. Tax overhaul to revise income tax	N	136. Authorize Marines in Lebanon	Y
102. Use of military in drug war	Y	137. Eminent domain for coal companies	N
103. Delete 12 MX/add conventional wpn	N	138. Prohibit EPA clean air sanctions	Y
104. Raise speed limit to 65 mph	Y	139. SS retirement age increase/reforms	Y
105. Require Pentagon to buy US goods	Y	140. Auto domestic content requirement	N
106. AIDS insurance non-discrimination	N	141. Delete jobs program funding	Y
107. Prohibit Saudi arms sales	Y	142. Highway-gas tax bill	N
108. Ease Gun Control Act of 1968	Y	143. Cut $5b from defense for Medicare	N
109. Bar interstate handgun transport	N	144. Emergency housing aid of $1b	Y

Presidential Support Score: 1991 - 74% 1990 - 62%

DERRICK, BUTLER -- South Carolina 3rd District [Democrat]. Counties of Abbeville, Aiken, Allendale, Anderson, Barnwell, Edgefield, Greenwood, McCormick, Oconee, Pickens and Saluda. Prior Terms: 1975-92. Born: September 30, 1936. Education: University of South Carolina; University of Georgia Law School (LL.B.). Occupation: Attorney; South Carolina legislator (1969-74).

1. Protection to Haitian refugees	Y	20. Eliminate funds for supercollider	Y
2. Raise tax on wealthy; lower others	Y	21. Terminate SDI except for research	N
3. Investigate Reagan hostage delay	Y	22. Req 7-day handgun waiting period	Y
4. Campaign finance revisions	Y	23. Provide $30b for failed S&Ls	Y
5. Unpaid leave to care for children	N	24. Allow use of force against Iraq	Y
6. Restrict NEA use of funds	N	25. Allow $15b in foreign aid for '91	?
7. Bar race-bias claim/habeas corpus	N	26. Revise & extend legal immigration	?
8. Ban race as death sentence factor	N	27. Suspend aid to Angolan rebels	Y
9. Exceptions to exclusionary rule	N	28. Democratic tax plan proposals	Y
10. Allow sale of assault weapons	N	29. Cut defense 5% across the board	N
11. Life in prison/abolish death penalty	N	30. Textile import quotas-veto override	Y
12. Req conspiracy-price fixing cases	Y	31. Abortion service for military abroad	Y
13. Unemployment benefits extension	Y	32. Limits on high income farmers	N
14. Tissue use of aborted fetuses	Y	33. Family medical leave-veto override	N
15. Bar replacement of union strikers	N	34. Req submission of balanced budget	Y
16. Hold foreign aid at $15b for '92	Y	35. Balanced budget amendment	Y
17. Restore space station funding	N	36. Amendment to ban flag desecration	Y
18. Civil Rights Act of 1991	Y	37. Reauthorize Amtrak-veto override	Y
19. Unlimited damages-discrimination	N	38. Retraining aid for coal miners	Y

DERRICK, BUTLER (continued)

39.	Suspend El Salvador military aid	Y	92.	Catastrophic health insurance	N
40.	Expand child care aid/tax credit	Y	93.	Ban airline smoking-2 hours or less	N
41.	Raise House salary/omit honoraria	N	94.	$1b/two year aid for the homeless	Y
42.	Toughen oil-spill liability	N	95.	Bar non-unions in union companies	N
43.	Restitution to Japanese interned	Y	96.	Increase FSLIC rescue to $15b	N
44.	Protect Chinese & C.A. nationals	Y	97.	Impose quotas to lower trade deficit	Y
45.	Abortion $ for rape/incest cases	Y	98.	Reduce discretionary budget 21%	Y
46.	Allow religious schools to bar gays	Y	99.	Immigration reform/alien amnesty	Y
47.	Bar broadcaster fairness doctrine	N	100.	South Africa sanctions-veto override	?
48.	Bar cap gains cut/reinstate IRA	N	101.	Tax overhaul to revise income tax	Y
49.	Bar unions equal voice in pension	Y	102.	Use of military in drug war	N
50.	Bar assembly of chemical weapons	Y	103.	Delete 12 MX/add conventional wpn	Y
51.	Ban plutonium/uranium production	Y	104.	Raise speed limit to 65 mph	N
52.	Cap MX missile deployment at 50	Y	105.	Require Pentagon to buy US goods	Y
53.	Allow $3b for 2 stealth bombers	N	106.	AIDS insurance non-discrimination	Y
54.	Publish bio-warfare experiments	Y	107.	Prohibit Saudi arms sales	Y
55.	Raise minimum wage-veto override	N	108.	Ease Gun Control Act of 1968	Y
56.	Bar transfer of FS-X technology	Y	109.	Bar interstate handgun transport	N
57.	Cut defense and raise domestic $	N	110.	Make company emissions known	N
58.	Uniform poll closing in 48 states	Y	111.	Allow toxic victims to sue in fed ct	N
59.	Req foreign investment disclosure	Y	112.	Superfund waste cleanup of $10b	N
60.	Textile import quotas-veto override	Y	113.	90 days notice of plant closings	N
61.	Bar abortion funding in Wash, DC	N	114.	$20b in Medicare cuts/tax increases	Y
62.	Notify spouses of AIDS+ carriers	N	115.	Spending cuts and tax increases	Y
63.	Seize conveyance-drug trafficking	Y	116.	Set school lunch lmt-250% poverty	N
64.	South Africa sanctions	Y	117.	$75m for youth work projects	Y
65.	60 days' notice of plant closings	N	118.	Allow Angolan military assistance	N
66.	Close unneeded military bases	Y	119.	Suspend defense payments for abuse	Y
67.	Keep welfare reform within $2.8b	N	120.	Drop SS COLAs/$12b tax increase	N
68.	Allow children housing exclusion	N	121.	Approve $1.5b for 21 MX missiles	N
69.	Shift $400m of NASA to homeless	Y	122.	Emergency farm credit/revisions	Y
70.	Cap Medicare patients' liability	Y	123.	Duty on Taiwan/Hong Kong/S Korea	N
71.	Prohibit employee polygraph testing	N	124.	Limit steel imports to 17%	N
72.	Allow CIA to fund Contras	N	125.	Cut $ to schools that bar prayer	Y
73.	Revise unfair trade practices	Y	126.	$50b-taxes; cut Medicare/spending	Y
74.	Focus SDI on accidental launch	Y	127.	Limit Pershing II/cruise in Europe	N
75.	Bar Air Force $ for MX missile	N	128.	Delete $7.1b for 34 B-1 bombers	Y
76.	Allow "real" increase in defense	X	129.	Bar purchase of Sergeant York guns	N
77.	Troop reduction in Europe of 50%	N	130.	El Salvador military/economic aid	N
78.	Ban nuclear tests above 1 kiloton	Y	131.	Bar mining of Nicaraguan waters	Y
79.	Ban anti-satellite missile tests	N	132.	Physician fee freeze for Medicare	N
80.	Observe certain limits of SALT II	Y	133.	$49b in "sin"/phone/insurance taxes	Y
81.	Restore four Civil Rights laws	Y	134.	Allow sale of Conrail	N
82.	Prohibit aliens as strikebreakers	Y	135.	Equal Rights Amendment	Y
83.	Allow military malpractice suits	Y	136.	Authorize Marines in Lebanon	N
84.	Approval of $36m in Contra aid	N	137.	Eminent domain for coal companies	N
85.	$18b deficit reduction compromise	Y	138.	Prohibit EPA clean air sanctions	?
86.	Welfare reform of $5.7b for 5 years	Y	139.	SS retirement age increase/reforms	N
87.	Raise taxes $12b/cut spending $3b	Y	140.	Auto domestic content requirement	N
88.	Board to assess occupational risk	Y	141.	Delete jobs program funding	N
89.	Balanced budget by '93-via targets	Y	142.	Highway-gas tax bill	Y
90.	Bar licensing of two nuclear plants	Y	143.	Cut $5b from defense for Medicare	Y
91.	Remove victims compensation cap	N	144.	Emergency housing aid of $1b	Y

Presidential Support Score: 1991 - 41%   1990 - 31%

PATTERSON, LIZ J. -- South Carolina 4th District [Democrat].   Counties of Greenville, Spartanburg and Union. Prior Terms: 1987-92. Born: November 18,1939; Columbia, SC. Education: Columbia College (B.A.); University of South Carolina. Occupation: Peace Corps and VISTA recruiter; state Office of Economic Opportunity recruitment director and Head Start coordinator; congressional aide (1960-70); Spartanburg County Council member (1975-76); state senator (1979-86).

PATTERSON, LIZ J. (continued)

1.	Protection to Haitian refugees	N	50.	Bar assembly of chemical weapons	N
2.	Raise tax on wealthy; lower others	N	51.	Ban plutonium/uranium production	Y
3.	Investigate Reagan hostage delay	N	52.	Cap MX missile deployment at 50	N
4.	Campaign finance revisions	Y	53.	Allow $3b for 2 stealth bombers	N
5.	Unpaid leave to care for children	N	54.	Publish bio-warfare experiments	N
6.	Restrict NEA use of funds	Y	55.	Raise minimum wage-veto override	N
7.	Bar race-bias claim/habeas corpus	Y	56.	Bar transfer of FS-X technology	Y
8.	Ban race as death sentence factor	N	57.	Cut defense and raise domestic $	N
9.	Exceptions to exclusionary rule	Y	58.	Uniform poll closing in 48 states	N
10.	Allow sale of assault weapons	N	59.	Req foreign investment disclosure	Y
11.	Life in prison/abolish death penalty	N	60.	Textile import quotas-veto override	Y
12.	Req conspiracy-price fixing cases	Y	61.	Bar abortion funding in Wash, DC	Y
13.	Unemployment benefits extension	Y	62.	Notify spouses of AIDS+ carriers	N
14.	Tissue use of aborted fetuses	Y	63.	Seize conveyance-drug trafficking	Y
15.	Bar replacement of union strikers	N	64.	South Africa sanctions	Y
16.	Hold foreign aid at $15b for '92	N	65.	60 days' notice of plant closings	Y
17.	Restore space station funding	N	66.	Close unneeded military bases	N
18.	Civil Rights Act of 1991	Y	67.	Keep welfare reform within $2.8b	Y
19.	Unlimited damages-discrimination	N	68.	Allow children housing exclusion	N
20.	Eliminate funds for supercollider	Y	69.	Shift $400m of NASA to homeless	Y
21.	Terminate SDI except for research	N	70.	Cap Medicare patients' liability	Y
22.	Req 7-day handgun waiting period	N	71.	Prohibit employee polygraph testing	N
23.	Provide $30b for failed S&Ls	N	72.	Allow CIA to fund Contras	Y
24.	Allow use of force against Iraq	Y	73.	Revise unfair trade practices	Y
25.	Allow $15b in foreign aid for '91	N	74.	Focus SDI on accidental launch	Y
26.	Revise & extend legal immigration	N	75.	Bar Air Force $ for MX missile	N
27.	Suspend aid to Angolan rebels	Y	76.	Allow "real" increase in defense	N
28.	Democratic tax plan proposals	N	77.	Troop reduction in Europe of 50%	Y
29.	Cut defense 5% across the board	N	78.	Ban nuclear tests above 1 kiloton	N
30.	Textile import quotas-veto override	Y	79.	Ban anti-satellite missile tests	N
31.	Abortion service for military abroad	Y	80.	Observe certain limits of SALT II	N
32.	Limits on high income farmers	N	81.	Restore four Civil Rights laws	Y
33.	Family medical leave-veto override	N	82.	Prohibit aliens as strikebreakers	Y
34.	Req submission of balanced budget	Y	83.	Allow military malpractice suits	Y
35.	Balanced budget amendment	Y	84.	Approval of $36m in Contra aid	Y
36.	Amendment to ban flag desecration	Y	85.	$18b deficit reduction compromise	N
37.	Reauthorize Amtrak-veto override	Y	86.	Welfare reform of $5.7b for 5 years	Y
38.	Retraining aid for coal miners	Y	87.	Raise taxes $12b/cut spending $3b	N
39.	Suspend El Salvador military aid	Y	88.	Board to assess occupational risk	N
40.	Expand child care aid/tax credit	Y	89.	Balanced budget by '93-via targets	Y
41.	Raise House salary/omit honoraria	N	90.	Bar licensing of two nuclear plants	N
42.	Toughen oil-spill liability	N	91.	Remove victims compensation cap	N
43.	Restitution to Japanese interned	N	92.	Catastrophic health insurance	Y
44.	Protect Chinese & C.A. nationals	Y	93.	Ban airline smoking-2 hours or less	N
45.	Abortion $ for rape/incest cases	Y	94.	$1b/two year aid for the homeless	Y
46.	Allow religious schools to bar gays	Y	95.	Bar non-unions in union companies	N
47.	Bar broadcaster fairness doctrine	Y	96.	Increase FSLIC rescue to $15b	N
48.	Bar cap gains cut/reinstate IRA	N	97.	Impose quotas to lower trade deficit	Y
49.	Bar unions equal voice in pension	Y	98.	Reduce discretionary budget 21%	Y

Presidential Support Score: 1991 - 39%   1990 - 37%

SPRATT, JOHN M., Jr. -- South Carolina 5th District [Democrat]. Counties of Cherokee, Chester, Chesterfield, Fairfield, Kershaw, Lancaster, Laurens, Lee, Newberry, Sumter and York. Prior Terms: 1983-92. Born: November 1, 1942; Charlotte, NC. Education: Davidson College (A.B.); Oxford University, Corpus Christi College (M.A.); Yale Law School (LL.B.). Military Service: U.S. Army, 1969-71. Occupation: Private law practice (1971-82); county attorney (1973-82); banker (1973-82); president, insurance agency; chairman, hospital board.

1.	Protection to Haitian refugees	Y	4.	Campaign finance revisions	Y
2.	Raise tax on wealthy; lower others	Y	5.	Unpaid leave to care for children	Y
3.	Investigate Reagan hostage delay	Y	6.	Restrict NEA use of funds	Y

SPRATT, JOHN M., Jr. (continued)

7. Bar race-bias claim/habeas corpus	N	
8. Ban race as death sentence factor	N	
9. Exceptions to exclusionary rule	N	
10. Allow sale of assault weapons	Y	
11. Life in prison/abolish death penalty	N	
12. Req conspiracy-price fixing cases	Y	
13. Unemployment benefits extension	Y	
14. Tissue use of aborted fetuses	Y	
15. Bar replacement of union strikers	N	
16. Hold foreign aid at $15b for '92	Y	
17. Restore space station funding	Y	
18. Civil Rights Act of 1991	Y	
19. Unlimited damages-discrimination	N	
20. Eliminate funds for supercollider	Y	
21. Terminate SDI except for research	N	
22. Req 7-day handgun waiting period	Y	
23. Provide $30b for failed S&Ls	Y	
24. Allow use of force against Iraq	Y	
25. Allow $15b in foreign aid for '91	Y	
26. Revise & extend legal immigration	Y	
27. Suspend aid to Angolan rebels	Y	
28. Democratic tax plan proposals	Y	
29. Cut defense 5% across the board	N	
30. Textile import quotas-veto override	Y	
31. Abortion service for military abroad	Y	
32. Limits on high income farmers	N	
33. Family medical leave-veto override	N	
34. Req submission of balanced budget	Y	
35. Balanced budget amendment	Y	
36. Amendment to ban flag desecration	N	
37. Reauthorize Amtrak-veto override	Y	
38. Retraining aid for coal miners	Y	
39. Suspend El Salvador military aid	Y	
40. Expand child care aid/tax credit	Y	
41. Raise House salary/omit honoraria	N	
42. Toughen oil-spill liability	Y	
43. Restitution to Japanese interned	Y	
44. Protect Chinese & C.A. nationals	Y	
45. Abortion $ for rape/incest cases	Y	
46. Allow religious schools to bar gays	Y	
47. Bar broadcaster fairness doctrine	N	
48. Bar cap gains cut/reinstate IRA	Y	
49. Bar unions equal voice in pension	Y	
50. Bar assembly of chemical weapons	Y	
51. Ban plutonium/uranium production	Y	
52. Cap MX missile deployment at 50	Y	
53. Allow $3b for 2 stealth bombers	Y	
54. Publish bio-warfare experiments	Y	
55. Raise minimum wage-veto override	N	
56. Bar transfer of FS-X technology	Y	
57. Cut defense and raise domestic $	N	
58. Uniform poll closing in 48 states	Y	
59. Req foreign investment disclosure	Y	
60. Textile import quotas-veto override	Y	
61. Bar abortion funding in Wash, DC	Y	
62. Notify spouses of AIDS+ carriers	N	
63. Seize conveyance-drug trafficking	Y	
64. South Africa sanctions	Y	
65. 60 days' notice of plant closings	Y	
66. Close unneeded military bases	N	
67. Keep welfare reform within $2.8b	Y	
68. Allow children housing exclusion	N	
69. Shift $400m of NASA to homeless	N	
70. Cap Medicare patients' liability	Y	

71. Prohibit employee polygraph testing	Y	
72. Allow CIA to fund Contras	N	
73. Revise unfair trade practices	Y	
74. Focus SDI on accidental launch	Y	
75. Bar Air Force $ for MX missile	N	
76. Allow "real" increase in defense	Y	
77. Troop reduction in Europe of 50%	N	
78. Ban nuclear tests above 1 kiloton	N	
79. Ban anti-satellite missile tests	Y	
80. Observe certain limits of SALT II	Y	
81. Restore four Civil Rights laws	Y	
82. Prohibit aliens as strikebreakers	Y	
83. Allow military malpractice suits	Y	
84. Approval of $36m in Contra aid	N	
85. $18b deficit reduction compromise	Y	
86. Welfare reform of $5.7b for 5 years	Y	
87. Raise taxes $12b/cut spending $3b	Y	
88. Board to assess occupational risk	Y	
89. Balanced budget by '93-via targets	Y	
90. Bar licensing of two nuclear plants	N	
91. Remove victims compensation cap	N	
92. Catastrophic health insurance	Y	
93. Ban airline smoking-2 hours or less	Y	
94. $1b/two year aid for the homeless	Y	
95. Bar non-unions in union companies	N	
96. Increase FSLIC rescue to $15b	N	
97. Impose quotas to lower trade deficit	Y	
98. Reduce discretionary budget 21%	Y	
99. Immigration reform/alien amnesty	Y	
100. South Africa sanctions-veto override	Y	
101. Tax overhaul to revise income tax	Y	
102. Use of military in drug war	N	
103. Delete 12 MX/add conventional wpn	N	
104. Raise speed limit to 65 mph	Y	
105. Require Pentagon to buy US goods	Y	
106. AIDS insurance non-discrimination	Y	
107. Prohibit Saudi arms sales	N	
108. Ease Gun Control Act of 1968	Y	
109. Bar interstate handgun transport	Y	
110. Make company emissions known	Y	
111. Allow toxic victims to sue in fed ct	N	
112. Superfund waste cleanup of $10b	N	
113. 90 days notice of plant closings	N	
114. $20b in Medicare cuts/tax increases	Y	
115. Spending cuts and tax increases	Y	
116. Set school lunch lmt-250% poverty	N	
117. $75m for youth work projects	Y	
118. Allow Angolan military assistance	Y	
119. Suspend defense payments for abuse	Y	
120. Drop SS COLAs/$12b tax increase	Y	
121. Approve $1.5b for 21 MX missiles	N	
122. Emergency farm credit/revisions	Y	
123. Duty on Taiwan/Hong Kong/S Korea	N	
124. Limit steel imports to 17%	Y	
125. Cut $ to schools that bar prayer	N	
126. $50b-taxes; cut Medicare/spending	Y	
127. Limit Pershing II/cruise in Europe	N	
128. Delete $7.1b for 34 B-1 bombers	N	
129. Bar purchase of Sergeant York guns	N	
130. El Salvador military/economic aid	N	
131. Bar mining of Nicaragua waters	Y	
132. Physician fee freeze for Medicare	N	
133. $49b in "sin"/phone/insurance taxes	Y	
134. Allow sale of Conrail	N	

SPRATT, JOHN M., Jr. (continued)

135. Equal Rights Amendment	Y	
136. Authorize Marines in Lebanon	Y	
137. Eminent domain for coal companies	N	
138. Prohibit EPA clean air sanctions	Y	
139. SS retirement age increase/reforms	N	

Presidential Support Score: 1991 - 40%   1990 - 29%

TALLON, ROBIN -- South Carolina 6th District [Democrat]. Counties of Berkeley (pt.), Clarendon, Darlington, Dillon, Florence, Georgetown, Horry, Marlon, Marlboro and Williamsburg. Prior Terms: 1983-92. Born: August 8, 1946; Hemingway, SC. Education: University of South Carolina. Occupation: Owner, Robin's Men's Stores; South Carolina representative (1980-82).

1. Protection to Haitian refugees	?		52. Cap MX missile deployment at 50	Y
2. Raise tax on wealthy; lower others	Y		53. Allow $3b for 2 stealth bombers	N
3. Investigate Reagan hostage delay	Y		54. Publish bio-warfare experiments	Y
4. Campaign finance revisions	Y		55. Raise minimum wage-veto override	Y
5. Unpaid leave to care for children	Y		56. Bar transfer of FS-X technology	Y
6. Restrict NEA use of funds	Y		57. Cut defense and raise domestic $	N
7. Bar race-bias claim/habeas corpus	N		58. Uniform poll closing in 48 states	Y
8. Ban race as death sentence factor	N		59. Req foreign investment disclosure	Y
9. Exceptions to exclusionary rule	Y		60. Textile import quotas-veto override	Y
10. Allow sale of assault weapons	Y		61. Bar abortion funding in Wash, DC	Y
11. Life in prison/abolish death penalty	N		62. Notify spouses of AIDS+ carriers	N
12. Req conspiracy-price fixing cases	Y		63. Seize conveyance-drug trafficking	N
13. Unemployment benefits extension	Y		64. South Africa sanctions	Y
14. Tissue use of aborted fetuses	N		65. 60 days' notice of plant closings	Y
15. Bar replacement of union strikers	N		66. Close unneeded military bases	N
16. Hold foreign aid at $15b for '92	Y		67. Keep welfare reform within $2.8b	Y
17. Restore space station funding	Y		68. Allow children housing exclusion	N
18. Civil Rights Act of 1991	Y		69. Shift $400m of NASA to homeless	Y
19. Unlimited damages-discrimination	Y		70. Cap Medicare patients' liability	Y
20. Eliminate funds for supercollider	Y		71. Prohibit employee polygraph testing	N
21. Terminate SDI except for research	N		72. Allow CIA to fund Contras	Y
22. Req 7-day handgun waiting period	N		73. Revise unfair trade practices	Y
23. Provide $30b for failed S&Ls	N		74. Focus SDI on accidental launch	Y
24. Allow use of force against Iraq	Y		75. Bar Air Force $ for MX missile	N
25. Allow $15b in foreign aid for '91	?		76. Allow "real" increase in defense	?
26. Revise & extend legal immigration	Y		77. Troop reduction in Europe of 50%	Y
27. Suspend aid to Angolan rebels	N		78. Ban nuclear tests above 1 kiloton	N
28. Democratic tax plan proposals	Y		79. Ban anti-satellite missile tests	N
29. Cut defense 5% across the board	N		80. Observe certain limits of SALT II	N
30. Textile import quotas-veto override	Y		81. Restore four Civil Rights laws	Y
31. Abortion service for military abroad	N		82. Prohibit aliens as strikebreakers	Y
32. Limits on high income farmers	N		83. Allow military malpractice suits	Y
33. Family medical leave-veto override	N		84. Approval of $36m in Contra aid	Y
34. Req submission of balanced budget	Y		85. $18b deficit reduction compromise	N
35. Balanced budget amendment	Y		86. Welfare reform of $5.7b for 5 years	Y
36. Amendment to ban flag desecration	N		87. Raise taxes $12b/cut spending $3b	N
37. Reauthorize Amtrak-veto override	Y		88. Board to assess occupational risk	Y
38. Retraining aid for coal miners	Y		89. Balanced budget by '93-via targets	N
39. Suspend El Salvador military aid	N		90. Bar licensing of two nuclear plants	N
40. Expand child care aid/tax credit	Y		91. Remove victims compensation cap	N
41. Raise House salary/omit honoraria	N		92. Catastrophic health insurance	Y
42. Toughen oil-spill liability	N		93. Ban airline smoking-2 hours or less	N
43. Restitution to Japanese interned	N		94. $1b/two year aid for the homeless	Y
44. Protect Chinese & C.A. nationals	N		95. Bar non-unions in union companies	N
45. Abortion $ for rape/incest cases	N		96. Increase FSLIC rescue to $15b	N
46. Allow religious schools to bar gays	Y		97. Impose quotas to lower trade deficit	Y
47. Bar broadcaster fairness doctrine	Y		98. Reduce discretionary budget 21%	Y
48. Bar cap gains cut/reinstate IRA	N		99. Immigration reform/alien amnesty	Y
49. Bar unions equal voice in pension	Y		100. South Africa sanctions-veto override	Y
50. Bar assembly of chemical weapons	N		101. Tax overhaul to revise income tax	N
51. Ban plutonium/uranium production	Y		102. Use of military in drug war	Y

TALLON, ROBIN (continued)

103. Delete 12 MX/add conventional wpn	N
104. Raise speed limit to 65 mph	Y
105. Require Pentagon to buy US goods	Y
106. AIDS insurance non-discrimination	Y
107. Prohibit Saudi arms sales	Y
108. Ease Gun Control Act of 1968	Y
109. Bar interstate handgun transport	N
110. Make company emissions known	N
111. Allow toxic victims to sue in fed ct	N
112. Superfund waste cleanup of $10b	N
113. 90 days notice of plant closings	N
114. $20b in Medicare cuts/tax increases	Y
115. Spending cuts and tax increases	Y
116. Set school lunch lmt-250% poverty	N
117. $75m for youth work projects	N
118. Allow Angolan military assistance	Y
119. Suspend defense payments for abuse	N
120. Drop SS COLAs/$12b tax increase	N
121. Approve $1.5b for 21 MX missiles	N

122. Emergency farm credit/revisions	Y
123. Duty on Taiwan/Hong Kong/S Korea	N
124. Limit steel imports to 17%	Y
125. Cut $ to schools that bar prayer	Y
126. $50b-taxes; cut Medicare/spending	Y
127. Limit Pershing II/cruise in Europe	N
128. Delete $7.1b for 34 B-1 bombers	N
129. Bar purchase of Sergeant York guns	N
130. El Salvador military/economic aid	Y
131. Bar mining of Nicaraguan waters	Y
132. Physician fee freeze for Medicare	N
133. $49b in "sin"/phone/insurance taxes	Y
134. Allow sale of Conrail	N
135. Equal Rights Amendment	Y
136. Authorize Marines in Lebanon	Y
137. Eminent domain for coal companies	N
138. Prohibit EPA clean air sanctions	Y
139. SS retirement age increase/reforms	N

Presidential Support Score: 1991 - 47%   1990 - 43%

SOUTH DAKOTA

JOHNSON, TIM -- Representative at Large [Democrat]. Prior Terms: 1987-92. Born: December 28, 1946; Canton, SD. Education: University of South Dakota (B.A., M.A., J.D.). Occupation: Attorney; state committee budget advisor (19711972); state representative (1978-82) and senator (1982-86); Clay County deputy state's attorney (1985).

1. Protection to Haitian refugees	Y	30. Textile import quotas-veto override	Y
2. Raise tax on wealthy; lower others	Y	31. Abortion service for military abroad	Y
3. Investigate Reagan hostage delay	Y	32. Limits on high income farmers	N
4. Campaign finance revisions	Y	33. Family medical leave-veto override	Y
5. Unpaid leave to care for children	Y	34. Req submission of balanced budget	Y
6. Restrict NEA use of funds	Y	35. Balanced budget amendment	Y
7. Bar race-bias claim/habeas corpus	N	36. Amendment to ban flag desecration	Y
8. Ban race as death sentence factor	Y	37. Reauthorize Amtrak-veto override	Y
9. Exceptions to exclusionary rule	Y	38. Retraining aid for coal miners	Y
10. Allow sale of assault weapons	Y	39. Suspend El Salvador military aid	Y
11. Life in prison/abolish death penalty	N	40. Expand child care aid/tax credit	Y
12. Req conspiracy-price fixing cases	N	41. Raise House salary/omit honoraria	N
13. Unemployment benefits extension	Y	42. Toughen oil-spill liability	Y
14. Tissue use of aborted fetuses	Y	43. Restitution to Japanese interned	N
15. Bar replacement of union strikers	Y	44. Protect Chinese & C.A. nationals	N
16. Hold foreign aid at $15b for '92	Y	45. Abortion $ for rape/incest cases	Y
17. Restore space station funding	N	46. Allow religious schools to bar gays	Y
18. Civil Rights Act of 1991	Y	47. Bar broadcaster fairness doctrine	N
19. Unlimited damages-discrimination	Y	48. Bar cap gains cut/reinstate IRA	Y
20. Eliminate funds for supercollider	Y	49. Bar unions equal voice in pension	N
21. Terminate SDI except for research	N	50. Bar assembly of chemical weapons	Y
22. Req 7-day handgun waiting period	N	51. Ban plutonium/uranium production	Y
23. Provide $30b for failed S&Ls	N	52. Cap MX missile deployment at 50	Y
24. Allow use of force against Iraq	N	53. Allow $3b for 2 stealth bombers	N
25. Allow $15b in foreign aid for '91	N	54. Publish bio-warfare experiments	Y
26. Revise & extend legal immigration	Y	55. Raise minimum wage-veto override	Y
27. Suspend aid to Angolan rebels	Y	56. Bar transfer of FS-X technology	Y
28. Democratic tax plan proposals	Y	57. Cut defense and raise domestic $	N
29. Cut defense 5% across the board	Y	58. Uniform poll closing in 48 states	Y

JOHNSON, TIM (continued)

59. Req foreign investment disclosure	Y	79. Ban anti-satellite missile tests	Y
60. Textile import quotas-veto override	Y	80. Observe certain limits of SALT II	Y
61. Bar abortion funding in Wash, DC	Y	81. Restore four Civil Rights laws	Y
62. Notify spouses of AIDS+ carriers	N	82. Prohibit aliens as strikebreakers	Y
63. Seize conveyance-drug trafficking	N	83. Allow military malpractice suits	Y
64. South Africa sanctions	Y	84. Approval of $36m in Contra aid	N
65. 60 days' notice of plant closings	Y	85. $18b deficit reduction compromise	N
66. Close unneeded military bases	N	86. Welfare reform of $5.7b for 5 years	N
67. Keep welfare reform within $2.8b	Y	87. Raise taxes $12b/cut spending $3b	N
68. Allow children housing exclusion	Y	88. Board to assess occupational risk	N
69. Shift $400m of NASA to homeless	Y	89. Balanced budget by '93-via targets	Y
70. Cap Medicare patients' liability	Y	90. Bar licensing of two nuclear plants	Y
71. Prohibit employee polygraph testing	Y	91. Remove victims compensation cap	Y
72. Allow CIA to fund Contras	N	92. Catastrophic health insurance	Y
73. Revise unfair trade practices	Y	93. Ban airline smoking-2 hours or less	Y
74. Focus SDI on accidental launch	Y	94. $1b/two year aid for the homeless	Y
75. Bar Air Force $ for MX missile	Y	95. Bar non-unions in union companies	Y
76. Allow "real" increase in defense	N	96. Increase FSLIC rescue to $15b	N
77. Troop reduction in Europe of 50%	Y	97. Impose quotas to lower trade deficit	Y
78. Ban nuclear tests above 1 kiloton	Y	98. Reduce discretionary budget 21%	N

Presidential Support Score: 1991 - 34%   1990 - 25%

TENNESSEE

QUILLEN, JAMES H. (Jimmy) -- Tennessee 1st District [Republican]. Counties of Carter, Cocke, Greene, Hawkins, Jefferson, Johnson, Sevier, Sullivan, Unicoi and Washington. Prior Terms: 1963-92. Born: January 11, 1916; Gate City, VA. Military Service: U.S. Navy, WW II. Occupation: Newspaper publisher; real estate businessman; mortgage banker; insurance businessman; Tennessee representative (1955-62).

1. Protection to Haitian refugees	X	28. Democratic tax plan proposals	N
2. Raise tax on wealthy; lower others	N	29. Cut defense 5% across the board	N
3. Investigate Reagan hostage delay	N	30. Textile import quotas-veto override	Y
4. Campaign finance revisions	N	31. Abortion service for military abroad	N
5. Unpaid leave to care for children	N	32. Limits on high income farmers	N
6. Restrict NEA use of funds	Y	33. Family medical leave-veto override	N
7. Bar race-bias claim/habeas corpus	Y	34. Req submission of balanced budget	N
8. Ban race as death sentence factor	Y	35. Balanced budget amendment	Y
9. Exceptions to exclusionary rule	Y	36. Amendment to ban flag desecration	Y
10. Allow sale of assault weapons	Y	37. Reauthorize Amtrak-veto override	N
11. Life in prison/abolish death penalty	N	38. Retraining aid for coal miners	Y
12. Req conspiracy-price fixing cases	Y	39. Suspend El Salvador military aid	N
13. Unemployment benefits extension	N	40. Expand child care aid/tax credit	N
14. Tissue use of aborted fetuses	X	41. Raise House salary/omit honoraria	Y
15. Bar replacement of union strikers	N	42. Toughen oil-spill liability	X
16. Hold foreign aid at $15b for '92	N	43. Restitution to Japanese interned	N
17. Restore space station funding	Y	44. Protect Chinese & C.A. nationals	Y
18. Civil Rights Act of 1991	N	45. Abortion $ for rape/incest cases	N
19. Unlimited damages-discrimination	N	46. Allow religious schools to bar gays	Y
20. Eliminate funds for supercollider	N	47. Bar broadcaster fairness doctrine	Y
21. Terminate SDI except for research	N	48. Bar cap gains cut/reinstate IRA	N
22. Req 7-day handgun waiting period	N	49. Bar unions equal voice in pension	Y
23. Provide $30b for failed S&Ls	N	50. Bar assembly of chemical weapons	N
24. Allow use of force against Iraq	Y	51. Ban plutonium/uranium production	N
25. Allow $15b in foreign aid for '91	#	52. Cap MX missile deployment at 50	N
26. Revise & extend legal immigration	?	53. Allow $3b for 2 stealth bombers	Y
27. Suspend aid to Angolan rebels	N	54. Publish bio-warfare experiments	N

QUILLEN, JAMES H. (continued)

55. Raise minimum wage-veto override	N
56. Bar transfer of FS-X technology	N
57. Cut defense and raise domestic $	N
58. Uniform poll closing in 48 states	Y
59. Req foreign investment disclosure	N
60. Textile import quotas-veto override	Y
61. Bar abortion funding in Wash, DC	Y
62. Notify spouses of AIDS+ carriers	?
63. Seize conveyance-drug trafficking	Y
64. South Africa sanctions	X
65. 60 days' notice of plant closings	N
66. Close unneeded military bases	Y
67. Keep welfare reform within $2.8b	Y
68. Allow children housing exclusion	Y
69. Shift $400m of NASA to homeless	N
70. Cap Medicare patients' liability	Y
71. Prohibit employee polygraph testing	N
72. Allow CIA to fund Contras	#
73. Revise unfair trade practices	Y
74. Focus SDI on accidental launch	N
75. Bar Air Force $ for MX missile	?
76. Allow "real" increase in defense	Y
77. Troop reduction in Europe of 50%	?
78. Ban nuclear tests above 1 kiloton	N
79. Ban anti-satellite missile tests	N
80. Observe certain limits of SALT II	N
81. Restore four Civil Rights laws	N
82. Prohibit aliens as strikebreakers	Y
83. Allow military malpractice suits	Y
84. Approval of $36m in Contra aid	Y
85. $18b deficit reduction compromise	Y
86. Welfare reform of $5.7b for 5 years	N
87. Raise taxes $12b/cut spending $3b	N
88. Board to assess occupational risk	X
89. Balanced budget by '93-via targets	Y
90. Bar licensing of two nuclear plants	N
91. Remove victims compensation cap	N
92. Catastrophic health insurance	N
93. Ban airline smoking-2 hours or less	N
94. $1b/two year aid for the homeless	N
95. Bar non-unions in union companies	N
96. Increase FSLIC rescue to $15b	N
97. Impose quotas to lower trade deficit	N
98. Reduce discretionary budget 21%	N
99. Immigration reform/alien amnesty	Y

100. South Africa sanctions-veto override	N
101. Tax overhaul to revise income tax	Y
102. Use of military in drug war	Y
103. Delete 12 MX/add conventional wpn	N
104. Raise speed limit to 65 mph	N
105. Require Pentagon to buy US goods	Y
106. AIDS insurance non-discrimination	N
107. Prohibit Saudi arms sales	?
108. Ease Gun Control Act of 1968	Y
109. Bar interstate handgun transport	N
110. Make company emissions known	N
111. Allow toxic victims to sue in fed ct	N
112. Superfund waste cleanup of $10b	N
113. 90 days notice of plant closings	N
114. $20b in Medicare cuts/tax increases	?
115. Spending cuts and tax increases	N
116. Set school lunch lmt-250% poverty	N
117. $75m for youth work projects	N
118. Allow Angolan military assistance	Y
119. Suspend defense payments for abuse	N
120. Drop SS COLAs/$12b tax increase	N
121. Approve $1.5b for 21 MX missiles	Y
122. Emergency farm credit/revisions	N
123. Duty on Taiwan/Hong Kong/S Korea	N
124. Limit steel imports to 17%	Y
125. Cut $ to schools that bar prayer	Y
126. $50b-taxes; cut Medicare/spending	Y
127. Limit Pershing II/cruise in Europe	N
128. Delete $7.1b for 34 B-1 bombers	N
129. Bar purchase of Sergeant York guns	N
130. El Salvador military/economic aid	Y
131. Bar mining of Nicaraguan waters	X
132. Physician fee freeze for Medicare	Y
133. $49b in "sin"/phone/insurance taxes	Y
134. Allow sale of Conrail	Y
135. Equal Rights Amendment	N
136. Authorize Marines in Lebanon	Y
137. Eminent domain for coal companies	N
138. Prohibit EPA clean air sanctions	Y
139. SS retirement age increase/reforms	Y
140. Auto domestic content requirement	N
141. Delete jobs program funding	Y
142. Highway-gas tax bill	N
143. Cut $5b from defense for Medicare	Y
144. Emergency housing aid of $1b	Y

Presidential Support Score: 1991 - 68% 1990 - 65%

DUNCAN, JOHN J., Jr. -- Tennessee 2nd District [Republican]. Counties of Blount, Knox, Loudon, McMinn, Monroe and Polk. Prior Terms: 1989-92. Born: July 21, 1947; Lebanon, TN. Education: University of Tennessee (B.S.); George Washington University (J.D.). Military Service: Army National Guard and U.S. Army Reserve. Occupation: Private law practice (1973-81); state trial judge (1981-88).

1. Protection to Haitian refugees	N
2. Raise tax on wealthy; lower others	N
3. Investigate Reagan hostage delay	N
4. Campaign finance revisions	Y
5. Unpaid leave to care for children	N
6. Restrict NEA use of funds	Y
7. Bar race-bias claim/habeas corpus	Y
8. Ban race as death sentence factor	Y
9. Exceptions to exclusionary rule	Y

10. Allow sale of assault weapons	Y
11. Life in prison/abolish death penalty	N
12. Req conspiracy-price fixing cases	Y
13. Unemployment benefits extension	N
14. Tissue use of aborted fetuses	N
15. Bar replacement of union strikers	N
16. Hold foreign aid at $15b for '92	N
17. Restore space station funding	N
18. Civil Rights Act of 1991	N

DUNCAN, JOHN J., Jr. (continued)

19. Unlimited damages-discrimination	N	
20. Eliminate funds for supercollider	Y	
21. Terminate SDI except for research	?	
22. Req 7-day handgun waiting period	N	
23. Provide $30b for failed S&Ls	N	
24. Allow use of force against Iraq	Y	
25. Allow $15b in foreign aid for '91	N	
26. Revise & extend legal immigration	N	
27. Suspend aid to Angolan rebels	N	
28. Democratic tax plan proposals	N	
29. Cut defense 5% across the board	N	
30. Textile import quotas-veto override	Y	
31. Abortion service for military abroad	N	
32. Limits on high income farmers	Y	
33. Family medical leave-veto override	N	
34. Req submission of balanced budget	Y	
35. Balanced budget amendment	Y	
36. Amendment to ban flag desecration	Y	
37. Reauthorize Amtrak-veto override	N	
38. Retraining aid for coal miners	Y	

39. Suspend El Salvador military aid	N
40. Expand child care aid/tax credit	N
41. Raise House salary/omit honoraria	N
42. Toughen oil-spill liability	N
43. Restitution to Japanese interned	N
44. Protect Chinese & C.A. nationals	N
45. Abortion $ for rape/incest cases	N
46. Allow religious schools to bar gays	Y
47. Bar broadcaster fairness doctrine	Y
48. Bar cap gains cut/reinstate IRA	N
49. Bar unions equal voice in pension	Y
50. Bar assembly of chemical weapons	Y
51. Ban plutonium/uranium production	N
52. Cap MX missile deployment at 50	N
53. Allow $3b for 2 stealth bombers	N
54. Publish bio-warfare experiments	Y
55. Raise minimum wage-veto override	N
56. Bar transfer of FS-X technology	Y
57. Cut defense and raise domestic $	N
58. Uniform poll closing in 48 states	N

Presidential Support Score: 1991 - 65% 1990 - 74%

LLOYD, MARILYN -- Tennessee 3rd District [Democrat]. Counties of Anderson, Bradley, Grundy, Hamilton, Marion, Meigs, and Roane. Prior Terms: 1975-78, 1983-92. Born: January 3, 1929; Fort Smith, AR. Education: Shorter College. Occupation: Manager, radio station WTTI.

1. Protection to Haitian refugees	?	
2. Raise tax on wealthy; lower others	N	
3. Investigate Reagan hostage delay	N	
4. Campaign finance revisions	Y	
5. Unpaid leave to care for children	N	
6. Restrict NEA use of funds	Y	
7. Bar race-bias claim/habeas corpus	Y	
8. Ban race as death sentence factor	Y	
9. Exceptions to exclusionary rule	Y	
10. Allow sale of assault weapons	Y	
11. Life in prison/abolish death penalty	N	
12. Req conspiracy-price fixing cases	Y	
13. Unemployment benefits extension	?	
14. Tissue use of aborted fetuses	Y	
15. Bar replacement of union strikers	Y	
16. Hold foreign aid at $15b for '92	?	
17. Restore space station funding	Y	
18. Civil Rights Act of 1991	Y	
19. Unlimited damages-discrimination	N	
20. Eliminate funds for supercollider	N	
21. Terminate SDI except for research	N	
22. Req 7-day handgun waiting period	Y	
23. Provide $30b for failed S&Ls	X	
24. Allow use of force against Iraq	Y	
25. Allow $15b in foreign aid for '91	N	
26. Revise & extend legal immigration	N	
27. Suspend aid to Angolan rebels	N	
28. Democratic tax plan proposals	Y	
29. Cut defense 5% across the board	N	
30. Textile import quotas-veto override	Y	
31. Abortion service for military abroad	N	
32. Limits on high income farmers	N	
33. Family medical leave-veto override	N	
34. Req submission of balanced budget	Y	
35. Balanced budget amendment	Y	

36. Amendment to ban flag desecration	Y
37. Reauthorize Amtrak-veto override	Y
38. Retraining aid for coal miners	Y
39. Suspend El Salvador military aid	N
40. Expand child care aid/tax credit	N
41. Raise House salary/omit honoraria	Y
42. Toughen oil-spill liability	?
43. Restitution to Japanese interned	N
44. Protect Chinese & C.A. nationals	Y
45. Abortion $ for rape/incest cases	N
46. Allow religious schools to bar gays	Y
47. Bar broadcaster fairness doctrine	Y
48. Bar cap gains cut/reinstate IRA	N
49. Bar unions equal voice in pension	?
50. Bar assembly of chemical weapons	N
51. Ban plutonium/uranium production	N
52. Cap MX missile deployment at 50	Y
53. Allow $3b for 2 stealth bombers	N
54. Publish bio-warfare experiments	Y
55. Raise minimum wage-veto override	Y
56. Bar transfer of FS-X technology	Y
57. Cut defense and raise domestic $	N
58. Uniform poll closing in 48 states	Y
59. Req foreign investment disclosure	Y
60. Textile import quotas-veto override	Y
61. Bar abortion funding in Wash, DC	Y
62. Notify spouses of AIDS+ carriers	Y
63. Seize conveyance-drug trafficking	Y
64. South Africa sanctions	Y
65. 60 days' notice of plant closings	N
66. Close unneeded military bases	N
67. Keep welfare reform within $2.8b	Y
68. Allow children housing exclusion	N
69. Shift $400m of NASA to homeless	N
70. Cap Medicare patients' liability	Y

LLOYD, MARILYN (continued)

71. Prohibit employee polygraph testing	Y	
72. Allow CIA to fund Contras	Y	
73. Revise unfair trade practices	Y	
74. Focus SDI on accidental launch	Y	
75. Bar Air Force $ for MX missile	N	
76. Allow "real" increase in defense	Y	
77. Troop reduction in Europe of 50%	N	
78. Ban nuclear tests above 1 kiloton	N	
79. Ban anti-satellite missile tests	N	
80. Observe certain limits of SALT II	N	
81. Restore four Civil Rights laws	Y	
82. Prohibit aliens as strikebreakers	Y	
83. Allow military malpractice suits	Y	
84. Approval of $36m in Contra aid	Y	
85. $18b deficit reduction compromise	Y	
86. Welfare reform of $5.7b for 5 years	N	
87. Raise taxes $12b/cut spending $3b	Y	
88. Board to assess occupational risk	Y	
89. Balanced budget by '93-via targets	Y	
90. Bar licensing of two nuclear plants	N	
91. Remove victims compensation cap	N	
92. Catastrophic health insurance	Y	
93. Ban airline smoking-2 hours or less	N	
94. $1b/two year aid for the homeless	Y	
95. Bar non-unions in union companies	N	
96. Increase FSLIC rescue to $15b	N	
97. Impose quotas to lower trade deficit	Y	
98. Reduce discretionary budget 21%	Y	
99. Immigration reform/alien amnesty	Y	
100. South Africa sanctions-veto override	Y	
101. Tax overhaul to revise income tax	Y	
102. Use of military in drug war	Y	
103. Delete 12 MX/add conventional wpn	N	
104. Raise speed limit to 65 mph	Y	
105. Require Pentagon to buy US goods	Y	

106. AIDS insurance non-discrimination	N
107. Prohibit Saudi arms sales	Y
108. Ease Gun Control Act of 1968	Y
109. Bar interstate handgun transport	N
110. Make company emissions known	N
111. Allow toxic victims to sue in fed ct	N
112. Superfund waste cleanup of $10b	Y
113. 90 days notice of plant closings	Y
114. $20b in Medicare cuts/tax increases	N
115. Spending cuts and tax increases	Y
116. Set school lunch lmt-250% poverty	?
117. $75m for youth work projects	?
118. Allow Angolan military assistance	Y
119. Suspend defense payments for abuse	N
120. Drop SS COLAs/$12b tax increase	N
121. Approve $1.5b for 21 MX missiles	Y
122. Emergency farm credit/revisions	+
123. Duty on Taiwan/Hong Kong/S Korea	N
124. Limit steel imports to 17%	Y
125. Cut $ to schools that bar prayer	Y
126. $50b-taxes; cut Medicare/spending	Y
127. Limit Pershing II/cruise in Europe	N
128. Delete $7.1b for 34 B-1 bombers	N
129. Bar purchase of Sergeant York guns	N
130. El Salvador military/economic aid	Y
131. Bar mining of Nicaraguan waters	N
132. Physician fee freeze for Medicare	N
133. $49b in "sin"/phone/insurance taxes	Y
134. Allow sale of Conrail	N
135. Equal Rights Amendment	N
136. Authorize Marines in Lebanon	Y
137. Eminent domain for coal companies	N
138. Prohibit EPA clean air sanctions	?
139. SS retirement age increase/reforms	Y

Presidential Support Score: 1991 - 37%   1990 - 43%

COOPER, JIM -- Tennessee 4th District [Democrat]. Counties of Bedford, Bledsoe, Campbell, Claiborne, Coffee, Cumberland, Fentress, Franklin, Giles, Grainger, Hamblen, Hancock, Lawrence, Lincoln, Moore, Morgan, Rhea, Scott, Sequatchie, Union, Van Buren, Warren and White. Prior Terms: 1983-92. Born: June 19, 1954. Education: University of North Carolina, Chapel Hill (B.S.); Harvard Law School (J.D.).   Occupation: Attorney; businessman, congressional page and assistant.

1. Protection to Haitian refugees	Y	
2. Raise tax on wealthy; lower others	N	
3. Investigate Reagan hostage delay	Y	
4. Campaign finance revisions	Y	
5. Unpaid leave to care for children	N	
6. Restrict NEA use of funds	Y	
7. Bar race-bias claim/habeas corpus	Y	
8. Ban race as death sentence factor	N	
9. Exceptions to exclusionary rule	Y	
10. Allow sale of assault weapons	Y	
11. Life in prison/abolish death penalty	N	
12. Req conspiracy-price fixing cases	N	
13. Unemployment benefits extension	N	
14. Tissue use of aborted fetuses	Y	
15. Bar replacement of union strikers	N	
16. Hold foreign aid at $15b for '92	Y	
17. Restore space station funding	Y	
18. Civil Rights Act of 1991	Y	

19. Unlimited damages-discrimination	N
20. Eliminate funds for supercollider	N
21. Terminate SDI except for research	N
22. Req 7-day handgun waiting period	Y
23. Provide $30b for failed S&Ls	Y
24. Allow use of force against Iraq	Y
25. Allow $15b in foreign aid for '91	Y
26. Revise & extend legal immigration	N
27. Suspend aid to Angolan rebels	N
28. Democratic tax plan proposals	Y
29. Cut defense 5% across the board	N
30. Textile import quotas-veto override	Y
31. Abortion service for military abroad	Y
32. Limits on high income farmers	C
33. Family medical leave-veto override	N
34. Req submission of balanced budget	Y
35. Balanced budget amendment	Y
36. Amendment to ban flag desecration	N

COOPER, JIM (continued)

37.	Reauthorize Amtrak-veto override	Y	89.	Balanced budget by '93-via targets	Y
38.	Retraining aid for coal miners	N	90.	Bar licensing of two nuclear plants	Y
39.	Suspend El Salvador military aid	N	91.	Remove victims compensation cap	N
40.	Expand child care aid/tax credit	N	92.	Catastrophic health insurance	Y
41.	Raise House salary/omit honoraria	Y	93.	Ban airline smoking-2 hours or less	?
42.	Toughen oil-spill liability	?	94.	$1b/two year aid for the homeless	Y
43.	Restitution to Japanese interned	N	95.	Bar non-unions in union companies	N
44.	Protect Chinese & C.A. nationals	Y	96.	Increase FSLIC rescue to $15b	?
45.	Abortion $ for rape/incest cases	Y	97.	Impose quotas to lower trade deficit	Y
46.	Allow religious schools to bar gays	Y	98.	Reduce discretionary budget 21%	Y
47.	Bar broadcaster fairness doctrine	N	99.	Immigration reform/alien amnesty	Y
48.	Bar cap gains cut/reinstate IRA	Y	100.	South Africa sanctions-veto override	Y
49.	Bar unions equal voice in pension	Y	101.	Tax overhaul to revise income tax	Y
50.	Bar assembly of chemical weapons	Y	102.	Use of military in drug war	Y
51.	Ban plutonium/uranium production	Y	103.	Delete 12 MX/add conventional wpn	Y
52.	Cap MX missile deployment at 50	Y	104.	Raise speed limit to 65 mph	Y
53.	Allow $3b for 2 stealth bombers	N	105.	Require Pentagon to buy US goods	N
54.	Publish bio-warfare experiments	Y	106.	AIDS insurance non-discrimination	Y
55.	Raise minimum wage-veto override	N	107.	Prohibit Saudi arms sales	N
56.	Bar transfer of FS-X technology	Y	108.	Ease Gun Control Act of 1968	Y
57.	Cut defense and raise domestic $	N	109.	Bar interstate handgun transport	N
58.	Uniform poll closing in 48 states	Y	110.	Make company emissions known	N
59.	Req foreign investment disclosure	N	111.	Allow toxic victims to sue in fed ct	Y
60.	Textile import quotas-veto override	Y	112.	Superfund waste cleanup of $10b	Y
61.	Bar abortion funding in Wash, DC	N	113.	90 days notice of plant closings	Y
62.	Notify spouses of AIDS+ carriers	N	114.	$20b in Medicare cuts/tax increases	Y
63.	Seize conveyance-drug trafficking	N	115.	Spending cuts and tax increases	Y
64.	South Africa sanctions	Y	116.	Set school lunch lmt-250% poverty	N
65.	60 days' notice of plant closings	Y	117.	$75m for youth work projects	Y
66.	Close unneeded military bases	Y	118.	Allow Angolan military assistance	N
67.	Keep welfare reform within $2.8b	N	119.	Suspend defense payments for abuse	Y
68.	Allow children housing exclusion	N	120.	Drop SS COLAs/$12b tax increase	Y
69.	Shift $400m of NASA to homeless	N	121.	Approve $1.5b for 21 MX missiles	Y
70.	Cap Medicare patients' liability	Y	122.	Emergency farm credit/revisions	Y
71.	Prohibit employee polygraph testing	Y	123.	Duty on Taiwan/Hong Kong/S Korea	N
72.	Allow CIA to fund Contras	N	124.	Limit steel imports to 17%	Y
73.	Revise unfair trade practices	Y	125.	Cut $ to schools that bar prayer	N
74.	Focus SDI on accidental launch	Y	126.	$50b-taxes; cut Medicare/spending	Y
75.	Bar Air Force $ for MX missile	Y	127.	Limit Pershing II/cruise in Europe	N
76.	Allow "real" increase in defense	N	128.	Delete $7.1b for 34 B-1 bombers	Y
77.	Troop reduction in Europe of 50%	Y	129.	Bar purchase of Sergeant York guns	Y
78.	Ban nuclear tests above 1 kiloton	N	130.	El Salvador military/economic aid	N
79.	Ban anti-satellite missile tests	N	131.	Bar mining of Nicaraguan waters	Y
80.	Observe certain limits of SALT II	Y	132.	Physician fee freeze for Medicare	N
81.	Restore four Civil Rights laws	Y	133.	$49b in "sin"/phone/insurance taxes	Y
82.	Prohibit aliens as strikebreakers	Y	134.	Allow sale of Conrail	N
83.	Allow military malpractice suits	Y	135.	Equal Rights Amendment	N
84.	Approval of $36m in Contra aid	N	136.	Authorize Marines in Lebanon	Y
85.	$18b deficit reduction compromise	Y	137.	Eminent domain for coal companies	N
86.	Welfare reform of $5.7b for 5 years	Y	138.	Prohibit EPA clean air sanctions	N
87.	Raise taxes $12b/cut spending $3b	Y	139.	SS retirement age increase/reforms	Y
88.	Board to assess occupational risk	Y			

Presidential Support Score: 1991 - 49% 1990 - 37%

CLEMENT, BOB -- Tennessee 5th District [Democrat]. Counties of Davidson and Robertson. Prior Terms: 1988 (Special Election)-1992. Born: September 23, 1943; Nashville, TN. Education: Memphis State University (B.A.); Center for Government Training, University of Tennessee. Military Service: Tennessee Army National Guard. Occupation: State public service commissioner (1973-79); founder, marketing and management firm; partner and owner, real estate investment firm (1981-83); Cumberland University president (1983-87).

CLEMENT, BOB (continued)

1. Protection to Haitian refugees	Y		43. Restitution to Japanese interned	N	
2. Raise tax on wealthy; lower others	Y		44. Protect Chinese & C.A. nationals	N	
3. Investigate Reagan hostage delay	Y		45. Abortion $ for rape/incest cases	N	
4. Campaign finance revisions	Y		46. Allow religious schools to bar gays	Y	
5. Unpaid leave to care for children	Y		47. Bar broadcaster fairness doctrine	N	
6. Restrict NEA use of funds	Y		48. Bar cap gains cut/reinstate IRA	Y	
7. Bar race-bias claim/habeas corpus	Y		49. Bar unions equal voice in pension	Y	
8. Ban race as death sentence factor	Y		50. Bar assembly of chemical weapons	Y	
9. Exceptions to exclusionary rule	Y		51. Ban plutonium/uranium production	Y	
10. Allow sale of assault weapons	Y		52. Cap MX missile deployment at 50	Y	
11. Life in prison/abolish death penalty	N		53. Allow $3b for 2 stealth bombers	N	
12. Req conspiracy-price fixing cases	N		54. Publish bio-warfare experiments	Y	
13. Unemployment benefits extension	Y		55. Raise minimum wage-veto override	Y	
14. Tissue use of aborted fetuses	Y		56. Bar transfer of FS-X technology	N	
15. Bar replacement of union strikers	Y		57. Cut defense and raise domestic $	N	
16. Hold foreign aid at $15b for '92	Y		58. Uniform poll closing in 48 states	Y	
17. Restore space station funding	N		59. Req foreign investment disclosure	N	
18. Civil Rights Act of 1991	Y		60. Textile import quotas-veto override	Y	
19. Unlimited damages-discrimination	N		61. Bar abortion funding in Wash, DC	?	
20. Eliminate funds for supercollider	Y		62. Notify spouses of AIDS+ carriers	N	
21. Terminate SDI except for research	N		63. Seize conveyance-drug trafficking	Y	
22. Req 7-day handgun waiting period	Y		64. South Africa sanctions	Y	
23. Provide $30b for failed S&Ls	N		65. 60 days' notice of plant closings	Y	
24. Allow use of force against Iraq	Y		66. Close unneeded military bases	N	
25. Allow $15b in foreign aid for '91	N		67. Keep welfare reform within $2.8b	N	
26. Revise & extend legal immigration	N		68. Allow children housing exclusion	N	
27. Suspend aid to Angolan rebels	Y		69. Shift $400m of NASA to homeless	N	
28. Democratic tax plan proposals	Y		70. Cap Medicare patients' liability	Y	
29. Cut defense 5% across the board	N		71. Prohibit employee polygraph testing	Y	
30. Textile import quotas-veto override	Y		72. Allow CIA to fund Contras	N	
31. Abortion service for military abroad	Y		73. Revise unfair trade practices	Y	
32. Limits on high income farmers	N		74. Focus SDI on accidental launch	Y	
33. Family medical leave-veto override	Y		75. Bar Air Force $ for MX missile	N	
34. Req submission of balanced budget	Y		76. Allow "real" increase in defense	Y	
35. Balanced budget amendment	Y		77. Troop reduction in Europe of 50%	Y	
36. Amendment to ban flag desecration	Y		78. Ban nuclear tests above 1 kiloton	Y	
37. Reauthorize Amtrak-veto override	Y		79. Ban anti-satellite missile tests	N	
38. Retraining aid for coal miners	Y		80. Observe certain limits of SALT II	Y	
39. Suspend El Salvador military aid	Y		81. Restore four Civil Rights laws	Y	
40. Expand child care aid/tax credit	Y		82. Prohibit aliens as strikebreakers	Y	
41. Raise House salary/omit honoraria	N		83. Allow military malpractice suits	Y	
42. Toughen oil-spill liability	N		84. Approval of $36m in Contra aid	N	

Presidential Support Score: 1991 - 43% 1990 - 25%

GORDON, BART -- Tennessee 6th District [Democrat]. Counties of Cannon, Clay, De Kalb, Jackson, Lewis, Macon, Marshall, Maury, Overton, Pickett, Putman, Rutherford, Smith, Sumner, Trousdale, Williamson, and Wilson. Prior Terms: 1985-92. Born: January 24, 1949; Murfreesboro, TN. Education: Middle Tennessee State University (B.S.); University of Tennessee Law School (J.D.). Occupation: Attorney.

1. Protection to Haitian refugees	Y		13. Unemployment benefits extension	Y	
2. Raise tax on wealthy; lower others	Y		14. Tissue use of aborted fetuses	Y	
3. Investigate Reagan hostage delay	Y		15. Bar replacement of union strikers	Y	
4. Campaign finance revisions	Y		16. Hold foreign aid at $15b for '92	Y	
5. Unpaid leave to care for children	Y		17. Restore space station funding	Y	
6. Restrict NEA use of funds	N		18. Civil Rights Act of 1991	Y	
7. Bar race-bias claim/habeas corpus	Y		19. Unlimited damages-discrimination	N	
8. Ban race as death sentence factor	N		20. Eliminate funds for supercollider	N	
9. Exceptions to exclusionary rule	Y		21. Terminate SDI except for research	N	
10. Allow sale of assault weapons	Y		22. Req 7-day handgun waiting period	Y	
11. Life in prison/abolish death penalty	N		23. Provide $30b for failed S&Ls	Y	
12. Req conspiracy-price fixing cases	N		24. Allow use of force against Iraq	Y	

GORDON, BART (continued)

25. Allow $15b in foreign aid for '91	?	74. Focus SDI on accidental launch	Y
26. Revise & extend legal immigration	N	75. Bar Air Force $ for MX missile	N
27. Suspend aid to Angolan rebels	Y	76. Allow "real" increase in defense	N
28. Democratic tax plan proposals	Y	77. Troop reduction in Europe of 50%	Y
29. Cut defense 5% across the board	N	78. Ban nuclear tests above 1 kiloton	Y
30. Textile import quotas-veto override	Y	79. Ban anti-satellite missile tests	Y
31. Abortion service for military abroad	Y	80. Observe certain limits of SALT II	Y
32. Limits on high income farmers	N	81. Restore four Civil Rights laws	Y
33. Family medical leave-veto override	Y	82. Prohibit aliens as strikebreakers	Y
34. Req submission of balanced budget	Y	83. Allow military malpractice suits	Y
35. Balanced budget amendment	Y	84. Approval of $36m in Contra aid	N
36. Amendment to ban flag desecration	N	85. $18b deficit reduction compromise	Y
37. Reauthorize Amtrak-veto override	Y	86. Welfare reform of $5.7b for 5 years	Y
38. Retraining aid for coal miners	Y	87. Raise taxes $12b/cut spending $3b	Y
39. Suspend El Salvador military aid	Y	88. Board to assess occupational risk	N
40. Expand child care aid/tax credit	Y	89. Balanced budget by '93-via targets	Y
41. Raise House salary/omit honoraria	Y	90. Bar licensing of two nuclear plants	Y
42. Toughen oil-spill liability	Y	91. Remove victims compensation cap	N
43. Restitution to Japanese interned	N	92. Catastrophic health insurance	Y
44. Protect Chinese & C.A. nationals	Y	93. Ban airline smoking-2 hours or less	N
45. Abortion $ for rape/incest cases	Y	94. $1b/two year aid for the homeless	Y
46. Allow religious schools to bar gays	Y	95. Bar non-unions in union companies	Y
47. Bar broadcaster fairness doctrine	Y	96. Increase FSLIC rescue to $15b	N
48. Bar cap gains cut/reinstate IRA	Y	97. Impose quotas to lower trade deficit	Y
49. Bar unions equal voice in pension	Y	98. Reduce discretionary budget 21%	Y
50. Bar assembly of chemical weapons	Y	99. Immigration reform/alien amnesty	N
51. Ban plutonium/uranium production	Y	100. South Africa sanctions-veto override	Y
52. Cap MX missile deployment at 50	Y	101. Tax overhaul to revise income tax	N
53. Allow $3b for 2 stealth bombers	N	102. Use of military in drug war	N
54. Publish bio-warfare experiments	Y	103. Delete 12 MX/add conventional wpn	Y
55. Raise minimum wage-veto override	Y	104. Raise speed limit to 65 mph	Y
56. Bar transfer of FS-X technology	Y	105. Require Pentagon to buy US goods	Y
57. Cut defense and raise domestic $	N	106. AIDS insurance non-discrimination	Y
58. Uniform poll closing in 48 states	Y	107. Prohibit Saudi arms sales	Y
59. Req foreign investment disclosure	N	108. Ease Gun Control Act of 1968	Y
60. Textile import quotas-veto override	Y	109. Bar interstate handgun transport	N
61. Bar abortion funding in Wash, DC	?	110. Make company emissions known	Y
62. Notify spouses of AIDS+ carriers	N	111. Allow toxic victims to sue in fed ct	N
63. Seize conveyance-drug trafficking	?	112. Superfund waste cleanup of $10b	Y
64. South Africa sanctions	Y	113. 90 days notice of plant closings	Y
65. 60 days' notice of plant closings	Y	114. $20b in Medicare cuts/tax increases	Y
66. Close unneeded military bases	N	115. Spending cuts and tax increases	Y
67. Keep welfare reform within $2.8b	N	116. Set school lunch lmt-250% poverty	N
68. Allow children housing exclusion	N	117. $75m for youth work projects	N
69. Shift $400m of NASA to homeless	N	118. Allow Angolan military assistance	N
70. Cap Medicare patients' liability	Y	119. Suspend defense payments for abuse	N
71. Prohibit employee polygraph testing	Y	120. Drop SS COLAs/$12b tax increase	Y
72. Allow CIA to fund Contras	N	121. Approve $1.5b for 21 MX missiles	N
73. Revise unfair trade practices	Y	122. Emergency farm credit/revisions	Y

Presidential Support Score: 1991 - 37%   1990 - 25%

SUNDQUIST, DON -- Tennessee 7th District [Republican]. Counties of Cheatham, Chester, Decatur, Dickson, Fayette, Hardeman, Hardin, Henderson, Hickman, Houston, Humphreys, McNairy, Montgomery, Perry, Shelby (pt.) and Wayne. Prior Terms: 1983-92. Born: March 15, 1936; Moline, IL. Education: Augustana College (B.A.). Military Service: U.S. Navy, 1957-59; Navy Reserve, 1959-63. Occupation: Advertising executive; boardmember, Mid-South Coliseum; banker.

1. Protection to Haitian refugees	N	5. Unpaid leave to care for children	N
2. Raise tax on wealthy; lower others	N	6. Restrict NEA use of funds	Y
3. Investigate Reagan hostage delay	N	7. Bar race-bias claim/habeas corpus	Y
4. Campaign finance revisions	N	8. Ban race as death sentence factor	Y

SUNDQUIST, DON (continued)

9. Exceptions to exclusionary rule	Y
10. Allow sale of assault weapons	Y
11. Life in prison/abolish death penalty	N
12. Req conspiracy-price fixing cases	Y
13. Unemployment benefits extension	N
14. Tissue use of aborted fetuses	?
15. Bar replacement of union strikers	N
16. Hold foreign aid at $15b for '92	Y
17. Restore space station funding	Y
18. Civil Rights Act of 1991	N
19. Unlimited damages-discrimination	N
20. Eliminate funds for supercollider	Y
21. Terminate SDI except for research	?
22. Req 7-day handgun waiting period	N
23. Provide $30b for failed S&Ls	Y
24. Allow use of force against Iraq	Y
25. Allow $15b in foreign aid for '91	Y
26. Revise & extend legal immigration	N
27. Suspend aid to Angolan rebels	N
28. Democratic tax plan proposals	N
29. Cut defense 5% across the board	N
30. Textile import quotas-veto override	N
31. Abortion service for military abroad	N
32. Limits on high income farmers	N
33. Family medical leave-veto override	N
34. Req submission of balanced budget	N
35. Balanced budget amendment	Y
36. Amendment to ban flag desecration	Y
37. Reauthorize Amtrak-veto override	N
38. Retraining aid for coal miners	N
39. Suspend El Salvador military aid	N
40. Expand child care aid/tax credit	N
41. Raise House salary/omit honoraria	Y
42. Toughen oil-spill liability	N
43. Restitution to Japanese interned	N
44. Protect Chinese & C.A. nationals	N
45. Abortion $ for rape/incest cases	N
46. Allow religious schools to bar gays	Y
47. Bar broadcaster fairness doctrine	N
48. Bar cap gains cut/reinstate IRA	N
49. Bar unions equal voice in pension	Y
50. Bar assembly of chemical weapons	N
51. Ban plutonium/uranium production	N
52. Cap MX missile deployment at 50	N
53. Allow $3b for 2 stealth bombers	Y
54. Publish bio-warfare experiments	N
55. Raise minimum wage-veto override	N
56. Bar transfer of FS-X technology	N
57. Cut defense and raise domestic $	N
58. Uniform poll closing in 48 states	Y
59. Req foreign investment disclosure	N
60. Textile import quotas-veto override	N
61. Bar abortion funding in Wash, DC	Y
62. Notify spouses of AIDS+ carriers	?
63. Seize conveyance-drug trafficking	Y
64. South Africa sanctions	X
65. 60 days' notice of plant closings	N
66. Close unneeded military bases	Y
67. Keep welfare reform within $2.8b	Y
68. Allow children housing exclusion	?
69. Shift $400m of NASA to homeless	N
70. Cap Medicare patients' liability	Y
71. Prohibit employee polygraph testing	?
72. Allow CIA to fund Contras	Y

73. Revise unfair trade practices	N
74. Focus SDI on accidental launch	N
75. Bar Air Force $ for MX missile	N
76. Allow "real" increase in defense	Y
77. Troop reduction in Europe of 50%	N
78. Ban nuclear tests above 1 kiloton	N
79. Ban anti-satellite missile tests	N
80. Observe certain limits of SALT II	N
81. Restore four Civil Rights laws	N
82. Prohibit aliens as strikebreakers	N
83. Allow military malpractice suits	N
84. Approval of $36m in Contra aid	Y
85. $18b deficit reduction compromise	N
86. Welfare reform of $5.7b for 5 years	N
87. Raise taxes $12b/cut spending $3b	N
88. Board to assess occupational risk	N
89. Balanced budget by '93-via targets	Y
90. Bar licensing of two nuclear plants	N
91. Remove victims compensation cap	N
92. Catastrophic health insurance	N
93. Ban airline smoking-2 hours or less	N
94. $1b/two year aid for the homeless	N
95. Bar non-unions in union companies	N
96. Increase FSLIC rescue to $15b	N
97. Impose quotas to lower trade deficit	N
98. Reduce discretionary budget 21%	Y
99. Immigration reform/alien amnesty	N
100. South Africa sanctions-veto override	N
101. Tax overhaul to revise income tax	N
102. Use of military in drug war	Y
103. Delete 12 MX/add conventional wpn	N
104. Raise speed limit to 65 mph	N
105. Require Pentagon to buy US goods	N
106. AIDS insurance non-discrimination	N
107. Prohibit Saudi arms sales	Y
108. Ease Gun Control Act of 1968	Y
109. Bar interstate handgun transport	N
110. Make company emissions known	N
111. Allow toxic victims to sue in fed ct	N
112. Superfund waste cleanup of $10b	N
113. 90 days notice of plant closings	N
114. $20b in Medicare cuts/tax increases	N
115. Spending cuts and tax increases	N
116. Set school lunch lmt-250% poverty	Y
117. $75m for youth work projects	N
118. Allow Angolan military assistance	Y
119. Suspend defense payments for abuse	N
120. Drop SS COLAs/$12b tax increase	N
121. Approve $1.5b for 21 MX missiles	Y
122. Emergency farm credit/revisions	Y
123. Duty on Taiwan/Hong Kong/S Korea	N
124. Limit steel imports to 17%	N
125. Cut $ to schools that bar prayer	Y
126. $50b-taxes; cut Medicare/spending	Y
127. Limit Pershing II/cruise in Europe	N
128. Delete $7.1b for 34 B-1 bombers	N
129. Bar purchase of Sergeant York guns	N
130. El Salvador military/economic aid	Y
131. Bar mining of Nicaraguan waters	N
132. Physician fee freeze for Medicare	Y
133. $49b in "sin"/phone/insurance taxes	Y
134. Allow sale of Conrail	Y
135. Equal Rights Amendment	N
136. Authorize Marines in Lebanon	Y

SUNDQUIST, DON (continued)

137. Eminent domain for coal companies	Y	139. SS retirement age increase/reforms	Y
138. Prohibit EPA clean air sanctions	Y		

Presidential Support Score: 1991 - 74% 1990 - 74%

TANNER, JOHN S. -- Tennessee 8th District [Democrat]. Counties of Benton, Carroll, Crockett, Dyer, Gibson, Haywood, Henry, Lake, Lauderdale, Madison, Obion, Shelby (pt.), Stewart, Tipton and Weakley. Prior Terms: 1989-92. Born: September 22, 1944; Halls, TN. Education: University of Tennessee (B.A., J.D.). Military Service: U.S. Navy and Judge Advocate General's Corps.; Tennessee National Guard. Occupation: Lawyer; savings and loan executive vice-president; state representative (1977-88).

1. Protection to Haitian refugees	N	30. Textile import quotas-veto override	Y
2. Raise tax on wealthy; lower others	Y	31. Abortion service for military abroad	Y
3. Investigate Reagan hostage delay	Y	32. Limits on high income farmers	N
4. Campaign finance revisions	Y	33. Family medical leave-veto override	N
5. Unpaid leave to care for children	N	34. Req submission of balanced budget	Y
6. Restrict NEA use of funds	Y	35. Balanced budget amendment	Y
7. Bar race-bias claim/habeas corpus	Y	36. Amendment to ban flag desecration	N
8. Ban race as death sentence factor	Y	37. Reauthorize Amtrak-veto override	Y
9. Exceptions to exclusionary rule	N	38. Retraining aid for coal miners	Y
10. Allow sale of assault weapons	Y	39. Suspend El Salvador military aid	Y
11. Life in prison/abolish death penalty	N	40. Expand child care aid/tax credit	Y
12. Req conspiracy-price fixing cases	Y	41. Raise House salary/omit honoraria	N
13. Unemployment benefits extension	N	42. Toughen oil-spill liability	N
14. Tissue use of aborted fetuses	Y	43. Restitution to Japanese interned	N
15. Bar replacement of union strikers	Y	44. Protect Chinese & C.A. nationals	N
16. Hold foreign aid at $15b for '92	N	45. Abortion $ for rape/incest cases	Y
17. Restore space station funding	Y	46. Allow religious schools to bar gays	Y
18. Civil Rights Act of 1991	Y	47. Bar broadcaster fairness doctrine	N
19. Unlimited damages-discrimination	N	48. Bar cap gains cut/reinstate IRA	N
20. Eliminate funds for supercollider	N	49. Bar unions equal voice in pension	Y
21. Terminate SDI except for research	N	50. Bar assembly of chemical weapons	Y
22. Req 7-day handgun waiting period	N	51. Ban plutonium/uranium production	Y
23. Provide $30b for failed S&Ls	?	52. Cap MX missile deployment at 50	Y
24. Allow use of force against Iraq	Y	53. Allow $3b for 2 stealth bombers	N
25. Allow $15b in foreign aid for '91	N	54. Publish bio-warfare experiments	Y
26. Revise & extend legal immigration	N	55. Raise minimum wage-veto override	Y
27. Suspend aid to Angolan rebels	N	56. Bar transfer of FS-X technology	N
28. Democratic tax plan proposals	Y	57. Cut defense and raise domestic $	N
29. Cut defense 5% across the board	N	58. Uniform poll closing in 48 states	?

Presidential Support Score: 1991 - 41% 1990 - 31%

FORD, HAROLD E. -- Tennessee 9th District [Democrat]. County of Shelby (pt.). Prior Terms: 1975-92. Born: May 20, 1945; Memphis, TN. Education: Tennessee State University (B.S.); John Gupton College of Mortuary Science. Occupation: Tennessee representative; trustee, Rust College.

1. Protection to Haitian refugees	Y	14. Tissue use of aborted fetuses	Y
2. Raise tax on wealthy; lower others	Y	15. Bar replacement of union strikers	Y
3. Investigate Reagan hostage delay	Y	16. Hold foreign aid at $15b for '92	?
4. Campaign finance revisions	?	17. Restore space station funding	N
5. Unpaid leave to care for children	Y	18. Civil Rights Act of 1991	Y
6. Restrict NEA use of funds	N	19. Unlimited damages-discrimination	Y
7. Bar race-bias claim/habeas corpus	?	20. Eliminate funds for supercollider	N
8. Ban race as death sentence factor	?	21. Terminate SDI except for research	Y
9. Exceptions to exclusionary rule	N	22. Req 7-day handgun waiting period	Y
10. Allow sale of assault weapons	N	23. Provide $30b for failed S&Ls	N
11. Life in prison/abolish death penalty	Y	24. Allow use of force against Iraq	N
12. Req conspiracy-price fixing cases	N	25. Allow $15b in foreign aid for '91	?
13. Unemployment benefits extension	Y	26. Revise & extend legal immigration	Y

FORD, HAROLD E. (continued)

27. Suspend aid to Angolan rebels	?
28. Democratic tax plan proposals	Y
29. Cut defense 5% across the board	Y
30. Textile import quotas-veto override	Y
31. Abortion service for military abroad	Y
32. Limits on high income farmers	?
33. Family medical leave-veto override	Y
34. Req submission of balanced budget	Y
35. Balanced budget amendment	N
36. Amendment to ban flag desecration	N
37. Reauthorize Amtrak-veto override	Y
38. Retraining aid for coal miners	Y
39. Suspend El Salvador military aid	Y
40. Expand child care aid/tax credit	Y
41. Raise House salary/omit honoraria	Y
42. Toughen oil-spill liability	?
43. Restitution for Japanese interned	Y
44. Protect Chinese & C.A. nationals	Y
45. Abortion $ for rape/incest cases	Y
46. Allow religious schools to bar gays	N
47. Bar broadcaster fairness doctrine	N
48. Bar cap gains cut/reinstate IRA	Y
49. Bar unions equal voice in pension	N
50. Bar assembly of chemical weapons	Y
51. Ban plutonium/uranium production	Y
52. Cap MX missile deployment at 50	?
53. Allow $3b for 2 stealth bombers	N
54. Publish bio-warfare experiments	Y
55. Raise minimum wage-veto override	Y
56. Bar transfer of FS-X technology	Y
57. Cut defense and raise domestic $	Y
58. Uniform poll closing in 48 states	Y
59. Req foreign investment disclosure	Y
60. Textile import quotas-veto override	Y
61. Bar abortion funding in Wash, DC	N
62. Notify spouses of AIDS+ carriers	N
63. Seize conveyance-drug trafficking	N
64. South Africa sanctions	Y
65. 60 days' notice of plant closings	Y
66. Close unneeded military bases	N
67. Keep welfare reform within $2.8b	X
68. Allow children housing exclusion	?
69. Shift $400m of NASA to homeless	N
70. Cap Medicare patients' liability	Y
71. Prohibit employee polygraph testing	Y
72. Allow CIA to fund Contras	N
73. Revise unfair trade practices	Y
74. Focus SDI on accidental launch	Y
75. Bar Air Force $ for MX missile	Y
76. Allow "real" increase in defense	N
77. Troop reduction in Europe of 50%	?
78. Ban nuclear tests above 1 kiloton	Y
79. Ban anti-satellite missile tests	Y
80. Observe certain limits of SALT II	Y
81. Restore four Civil Rights laws	Y
82. Prohibit aliens as strikebreakers	Y
83. Allow military malpractice suits	?
84. Approval of $36m in Contra aid	N
85. $18b deficit reduction compromise	?

86. Welfare reform of $5.7b for 5 years	Y
87. Raise taxes $12b/cut spending $3b	Y
88. Board to assess occupational risk	Y
89. Balanced budget by '93-via targets	?
90. Bar licensing of two nuclear plants	Y
91. Remove victims compensation cap	N
92. Catastrophic health insurance	Y
93. Ban airline smoking-2 hours or less	Y
94. $1b/two year aid for the homeless	?
95. Bar non-unions in union companies	Y
96. Increase FSLIC rescue to $15b	N
97. Impose quotas to lower trade deficit	Y
98. Reduce discretionary budget 21%	?
99. Immigration reform/alien amnesty	Y
100. South Africa sanctions-veto override	Y
101. Tax overhaul to revise income tax	Y
102. Use of military in drug war	N
103. Delete 12 MX/add conventional wpn	Y
104. Raise speed limit to 65 mph	?
105. Require Pentagon to buy US goods	?
106. AIDS insurance non-discrimination	Y
107. Prohibit Saudi arms sales	Y
108. Ease Gun Control Act of 1968	N
109. Bar interstate handgun transport	Y
110. Make company emissions known	N
111. Allow toxic victims to sue in fed ct	Y
112. Superfund waste cleanup of $10b	N
113. 90 days notice of plant closings	Y
114. $20b in Medicare cuts/tax increases	Y
115. Spending cuts and tax increases	Y
116. Set school lunch lmt-250% poverty	N
117. $75m for youth work projects	Y
118. Allow Angolan military assistance	N
119. Suspend defense payments for abuse	Y
120. Drop SS COLAs/$12b tax increase	?
121. Approve $1.5b for 21 MX missiles	N
122. Emergency farm credit/revisions	Y
123. Duty on Taiwan/Hong Kong/S Korea	Y
124. Limit steel imports to 17%	Y
125. Cut $ to schools that bar prayer	N
126. $50b-taxes; cut Medicare/spending	Y
127. Limit Pershing II/cruise in Europe	Y
128. Delete $7.1b for 34 B-1 bombers	Y
129. Bar purchase of Sergeant York guns	Y
130. El Salvador military/economic aid	?
131. Bar mining of Nicaraguan waters	Y
132. Physician fee freeze for Medicare	N
133. $49b in "sin"/phone/insurance taxes	Y
134. Allow sale of Conrail	N
135. Equal Rights Amendment	Y
136. Authorize Marines in Lebanon	Y
137. Eminent domain for coal companies	?
138. Prohibit EPA clean air sanctions	Y
139. SS retirement age increase/reforms	N
140. Auto domestic content requirement	Y
141. Delete jobs program funding	N
142. Highway-gas tax bill	N
143. Cut $5b from defense for Medicare	Y
144. Emergency housing aid of $1b	?

Presidential Support Score: 1991 - 20%   1990 - 8%

TEXAS

CHAPMAN, JIM -- Texas 1st District [Democrat]. Counties of Bowie, Camp, Cass, Cherokee, Delta, Franklin, Harrison, Henderson, Hopkins, Hunt (pt.), Lamar, Marion, Morris, Panola, Red River, Rusk, San Augustine, Shelby, Titus and Upshur. Prior Terms: 1985 (Special Election)-1992. Born: March 8, 1945; Washington, DC. Education: University of Texas (B.B.A.); Southern Methodist University Law School (J.D.). Occupation: District Attorney, Texas (1977-85).

1. Protection to Haitian refugees	N	53. Allow $3b for 2 stealth bombers	Y
2. Raise tax on wealthy; lower others	Y	54. Publish bio-warfare experiments	Y
3. Investigate Reagan hostage delay	Y	55. Raise minimum wage-veto override	N
4. Campaign finance revisions	Y	56. Bar transfer of FS-X technology	Y
5. Unpaid leave to care for children	Y	57. Cut defense and raise domestic $	N
6. Restrict NEA use of funds	Y	58. Uniform poll closing in 48 states	Y
7. Bar race-bias claim/habeas corpus	Y	59. Req foreign investment disclosure	Y
8. Ban race as death sentence factor	?	60. Textile import quotas-veto override	Y
9. Exceptions to exclusionary rule	Y	61. Bar abortion funding in Wash, DC	Y
10. Allow sale of assault weapons	Y	62. Notify spouses of AIDS+ carriers	N
11. Life in prison/abolish death penalty	N	63. Seize conveyance-drug trafficking	N
12. Req conspiracy-price fixing cases	?	64. South Africa sanctions	N
13. Unemployment benefits extension	Y	65. 60 days' notice of plant closings	Y
14. Tissue use of aborted fetuses	Y	66. Close unneeded military bases	Y
15. Bar replacement of union strikers	Y	67. Keep welfare reform within $2.8b	Y
16. Hold foreign aid at $15b for '92	Y	68. Allow children housing exclusion	N
17. Restore space station funding	Y	69. Shift $400m of NASA to homeless	N
18. Civil Rights Act of 1991	Y	70. Cap Medicare patients' liability	Y
19. Unlimited damages-discrimination	N	71. Prohibit employee polygraph testing	N
20. Eliminate funds for supercollider	N	72. Allow CIA to fund Contras	Y
21. Terminate SDI except for research	?	73. Revise unfair trade practices	Y
22. Req 7-day handgun waiting period	Y	74. Focus SDI on accidental launch	Y
23. Provide $30b for failed S&Ls	N	75. Bar Air Force $ for MX missile	N
24. Allow use of force against Iraq	Y	76. Allow "real" increase in defense	?
25. Allow $15b in foreign aid for '91	N	77. Troop reduction in Europe of 50%	N
26. Revise & extend legal immigration	N	78. Ban nuclear tests above 1 kiloton	Y
27. Suspend aid to Angolan rebels	Y	79. Ban anti-satellite missile tests	N
28. Democratic tax plan proposals	Y	80. Observe certain limits of SALT II	Y
29. Cut defense 5% across the board	N	81. Restore four Civil Rights laws	Y
30. Textile import quotas-veto override	Y	82. Prohibit aliens as strikebreakers	N
31. Abortion service for military abroad	Y	83. Allow military malpractice suits	Y
32. Limits on high income farmers	N	84. Approval of $36m in Contra aid	Y
33. Family medical leave-veto override	Y	85. $18b deficit reduction compromise	Y
34. Req submission of balanced budget	Y	86. Welfare reform of $5.7b for 5 years	N
35. Balanced budget amendment	Y	87. Raise taxes $12b/cut spending $3b	Y
36. Amendment to ban flag desecration	Y	88. Board to assess occupational risk	Y
37. Reauthorize Amtrak-veto override	Y	89. Balanced budget by '93-via targets	N
38. Retraining aid for coal miners	Y	90. Bar licensing of two nuclear plants	N
39. Suspend El Salvador military aid	Y	91. Remove victims compensation cap	N
40. Expand child care aid/tax credit	Y	92. Catastrophic health insurance	Y
41. Raise House salary/omit honoraria	N	93. Ban airline smoking-2 hours or less	N
42. Toughen oil-spill liability	N	94. $1b/two year aid for the homeless	Y
43. Restitution to Japanese interned	N	95. Bar non-unions in union companies	Y
44. Protect Chinese & C.A. nationals	N	96. Increase FSLIC rescue to $15b	Y
45. Abortion $ for rape/incest cases	N	97. Impose quotas to lower trade deficit	Y
46. Allow religious schools to bar gays	Y	98. Reduce discretionary budget 21%	Y
47. Bar broadcaster fairness doctrine	N	99. Immigration reform/alien amnesty	N
48. Bar cap gains cut/reinstate IRA	Y	100. South Africa sanctions-veto override	Y
49. Bar unions equal voice in pension	Y	101. Tax overhaul to revise income tax	N
50. Bar assembly of chemical weapons	N	102. Use of military in drug war	Y
51. Ban plutonium/uranium production	Y	103. Delete 12 MX/add conventional wpn	N
52. Cap MX missile deployment at 50	Y	104. Raise speed limit to 65 mph	N

CHAPMAN, JIM (continued)

105.	Require Pentagon to buy US goods	Y	111.	Allow toxic victims to sue in fed ct	N
106.	AIDS insurance non-discrimination	Y	112.	Superfund waste cleanup of $10b	N
107.	Prohibit Saudi arms sales	Y	113.	90 days notice of plant closings	N
108.	Ease Gun Control Act of 1968	Y	114.	$20b in Medicare cuts/tax increases	?
109.	Bar interstate handgun transport	N	115.	Spending cuts and tax increases	Y
110.	Make company emissions known	N	116.	Set school lunch lmt-250% poverty	N

Presidential Support Score: 1991 - 40%   1990 - 34%

WILSON, CHARLES -- Texas 2nd District [Democrat].   Counties of Anderson, Angelina, Hardin, Houston, Jasper, Liberty, Montgomery (pt.), Nacogdoches, Newton,Orange, Polk, Sabine, San Jacinto, Trinity, Tyler and Walker. Prior Terms: 1973-92. Born: June 1, 1933; Trinity, TX. Education: U.S. Naval Academy (B.S.). Military Service: U.S. Navy, 1956-60. Occupation: Lumber yard manager; Texas representative (1960-66); Texas senator (1966-72).

1.	Protection to Haitian refugees	Y	48.	Bar cap gains cut/reinstate IRA	N
2.	Raise tax on wealthy; lower others	Y	49.	Bar unions equal voice in pension	N
3.	Investigate Reagan hostage delay	N	50.	Bar assembly of chemical weapons	N
4.	Campaign finance revisions	Y	51.	Ban plutonium/uranium production	N
5.	Unpaid leave to care for children	Y	52.	Cap MX missile deployment at 50	N
6.	Restrict NEA use of funds	Y	53.	Allow $3b for 2 stealth bombers	Y
7.	Bar race-bias claim/habeas corpus	Y	54.	Publish bio-warfare experiments	Y
8.	Ban race as death sentence factor	Y	55.	Raise minimum wage-veto override	Y
9.	Exceptions to exclusionary rule	N	56.	Bar transfer of FS-X technology	?
10.	Allow sale of assault weapons	Y	57.	Cut defense and raise domestic $	N
11.	Life in prison/abolish death penalty	N	58.	Uniform poll closing in 48 states	Y
12.	Req conspiracy-price fixing cases	?	59.	Req foreign investment disclosure	Y
13.	Unemployment benefits extension	Y	60.	Textile import quotas-veto override	Y
14.	Tissue use of aborted fetuses	?	61.	Bar abortion funding in Wash, DC	N
15.	Bar replacement of union strikers	Y	62.	Notify spouses of AIDS+ carriers	N
16.	Hold foreign aid at $15b for '92	N	63.	Seize conveyance-drug trafficking	N
17.	Restore space station funding	Y	64.	South Africa sanctions	N
18.	Civil Rights Act of 1991	Y	65.	60 days' notice of plant closings	Y
19.	Unlimited damages-discrimination	N	66.	Close unneeded military bases	Y
20.	Eliminate funds for supercollider	N	67.	Keep welfare reform within $2.8b	N
21.	Terminate SDI except for research	?	68.	Allow children housing exclusion	N
22.	Req 7-day handgun waiting period	N	69.	Shift $400m of NASA to homeless	N
23.	Provide $30b for failed S&Ls	Y	70.	Cap Medicare patients' liability	?
24.	Allow use of force against Iraq	Y	71.	Prohibit employee polygraph testing	?
25.	Allow $15b in foreign aid for '91	Y	72.	Allow CIA to fund Contras	Y
26.	Revise & extend legal immigration	Y	73.	Revise unfair trade practices	Y
27.	Suspend aid to Angolan rebels	?	74.	Focus SDI on accidental launch	N
28.	Democratic tax plan proposals	Y	75.	Bar Air Force $ for MX missile	N
29.	Cut defense 5% across the board	?	76.	Allow "real" increase in defense	Y
30.	Textile import quotas-veto override	Y	77.	Troop reduction in Europe of 50%	?
31.	Abortion service for military abroad	Y	78.	Ban nuclear tests above 1 kiloton	N
32.	Limits on high income farmers	N	79.	Ban anti-satellite missile tests	N
33.	Family medical leave-veto override	Y	80.	Observe certain limits of SALT II	?
34.	Req submission of balanced budget	Y	81.	Restore four Civil Rights laws	Y
35.	Balanced budget amendment	Y	82.	Prohibit aliens as strikebreakers	Y
36.	Amendment to ban flag desecration	Y	83.	Allow military malpractice suits	?
37.	Reauthorize Amtrak-veto override	Y	84.	Approval of $36m in Contra aid	Y
38.	Retraining aid for coal miners	Y	85.	$18b deficit reduction compromise	Y
39.	Suspend El Salvador military aid	N	86.	Welfare reform of $5.7b for 5 years	?
40.	Expand child care aid/tax credit	Y	87.	Raise taxes $12b/cut spending $3b	Y
41.	Raise House salary/omit honoraria	Y	88.	Board to assess occupational risk	Y
42.	Toughen oil-spill liability	N	89.	Balanced budget by '93-via targets	?
43.	Restitution to Japanese interned	Y	90.	Bar licensing of two nuclear plants	Y
44.	Protect Chinese & C.A. nationals	Y	91.	Remove victims compensation cap	N
45.	Abortion $ for rape/incest cases	Y	92.	Catastrophic health insurance	Y
46.	Allow religious schools to bar gays	N	93.	Ban airline smoking-2 hours or less	?
47.	Bar broadcaster fairness doctrine	N	94.	$1b/two year aid for the homeless	Y

WILSON, CHARLES (continued)

95. Bar non-unions in union companies	Y
96. Increase FSLIC rescue to $15b	Y
97. Impose quotas to lower trade deficit	Y
98. Reduce discretionary budget 21%	?
99. Immigration reform/alien amnesty	Y
100. South Africa sanctions-veto override	Y
101. Tax overhaul to revise income tax	Y
102. Use of military in drug war	Y
103. Delete 12 MX/add conventional wpn	N
104. Raise speed limit to 65 mph	N
105. Require Pentagon to buy US goods	N
106. AIDS insurance non-discrimination	Y
107. Prohibit Saudi arms sales	N
108. Ease Gun Control Act of 1968	Y
109. Bar interstate handgun transport	N
110. Make company emissions known	N
111. Allow toxic victims to sue in fed ct	N
112. Superfund waste cleanup of $10b	N
113. 90 days notice of plant closings	Y
114. $20b in Medicare cuts/tax increases	Y
115. Spending cuts and tax increases	Y
116. Set school lunch lmt-250% poverty	N
117. $75m for youth work projects	Y
118. Allow Angolan military assistance	Y
119. Suspend defense payments for abuse	?
120. Drop SS COLAs/$12b tax increase	Y
121. Approve $1.5b for 21 MX missiles	Y
122. Emergency farm credit/revisions	Y
123. Duty on Taiwan/Hong Kong/S Korea	?
124. Limit steel imports to 17%	Y
125. Cut $ to schools that bar prayer	Y
126. $50b-taxes; cut Medicare/spending	Y
127. Limit Pershing II/cruise in Europe	?
128. Delete $7.1b for 34 B-1 bombers	?
129. Bar purchase of Sergeant York guns	N
130. El Salvador military/economic aid	Y
131. Bar mining of Nicaraguan waters	?
132. Physician fee freeze for Medicare	?
133. $49b in "sin"/phone/insurance taxes	?
134. Allow sale of Conrail	N
135. Equal Rights Amendment	Y
136. Authorize Marines in Lebanon	Y
137. Eminent domain for coal companies	Y
138. Prohibit EPA clean air sanctions	?
139. SS retirement age increase/reforms	Y
140. Auto domestic content requirement	Y
141. Delete jobs program funding	?
142. Highway-gas tax bill	N
143. Cut $5b from defense for Medicare	N
144. Emergency housing aid of $1b	Y

Presidential Support Score: 1991 - 32%   1990 - 35%

JOHNSON, SAM -- Texas 3rd District [Republican]. Counties of Collin (pt.) and Dallas (pt.). Prior Term: 1991 (Special Election)-1992. Born: October 11, 1930; San Antonio, TX. Education: Southern Methodist University (B.A.); George Washington University (M.A.). Military Service: U.S. Air Force (ret Col.). Occupation: State representative (1984-91).

1. Protection to Haitian refugees	N
2. Raise tax on wealthy; lower others	N
3. Investigate Reagan hostage delay	?
4. Campaign finance revisions	N
5. Unpaid leave to care for children	N
6. Restrict NEA use of funds	Y
7. Bar race-bias claim/habeas corpus	Y
8. Ban race as death sentence factor	Y
9. Exceptions to exclusionary rule	Y
10. Allow sale of assault weapons	Y
11. Life in prison/abolish death penalty	N
12. Req conspiracy-price fixing cases	Y
13. Unemployment benefits extension	N
14. Tissue use of aborted fetuses	N
15. Bar replacement of union strikers	N
16. Hold foreign aid at $15b for '92	N
17. Restore space station funding	Y
18. Civil Rights Act of 1991	N
19. Unlimited damages-discrimination	N
20. Eliminate funds for supercollider	N

Rep. Johnson was sworn in May 22, 1991, to succeed Steve Bartlett.

Presidential Support Score: 1991 - 84%

HALL, RALPH M. -- Texas 4th District [Democrat]. Counties of Collin (pt.), Fannin, Grayson, Gregg, Hunt (pt.), Kaufman, Rains, Rockwall, Smith, Van Zandt and Wood. Prior Terms: 1981-92. Born: May 3, 1923; Fate, TX. Education: University of Texas; Texas Christian University; Southern Methodist University (LL.B.). Military Service: U.S. Navy, 1942-45. Occupation: Attorney; Rockwall County judge (1950-62); Texas senator (1962-72); president and chief executive officer, Texas Aluminum Corp.; general counsel, Texas Extrusion Co., Inc.; banker; board chairman, Lakeside News, Inc.

1. Protection to Haitian refugees	N
2. Raise tax on wealthy; lower others	N
3. Investigate Reagan hostage delay	N
4. Campaign finance revisions	N
5. Unpaid leave to care for children	N
6. Restrict NEA use of funds	Y
7. Bar race-bias claim/habeas corpus	Y
8. Ban race as death sentence factor	Y
9. Exceptions to exclusionary rule	Y
10. Allow sale of assault weapons	Y
11. Life in prison/abolish death penalty	N
12. Req conspiracy-price fixing cases	N

HALL, RALPH M. (continued)

13. Unemployment benefits extension	N	77. Troop reduction in Europe of 50%	Y
14. Tissue use of aborted fetuses	N	78. Ban nuclear tests above 1 kiloton	N
15. Bar replacement of union strikers	N	79. Ban anti-satellite missile tests	N
16. Hold foreign aid at $15b for '92	N	80. Observe certain limits of SALT II	N
17. Restore space station funding	Y	81. Restore four Civil Rights laws	N
18. Civil Rights Act of 1991	N	82. Prohibit aliens as strikebreakers	N
19. Unlimited damages-discrimination	N	83. Allow military malpractice suits	Y
20. Eliminate funds for supercollider	N	84. Approval of $36m in Contra aid	Y
21. Terminate SDI except for research	N	85. $18b deficit reduction compromise	N
22. Req 7-day handgun waiting period	N	86. Welfare reform of $5.7b for 5 years	N
23. Provide $30b for failed S&Ls	N	87. Raise taxes $12b/cut spending $3b	N
24. Allow use of force against Iraq	Y	88. Board to assess occupational risk	N
25. Allow $15b in foreign aid for '91	N	89. Balanced budget by '93-via targets	N
26. Revise & extend legal immigration	N	90. Bar licensing of two nuclear plants	N
27. Suspend aid to Angolan rebels	Y	91. Remove victims compensation cap	N
28. Democratic tax plan proposals	N	92. Catastrophic health insurance	Y
29. Cut defense 5% across the board	N	93. Ban airline smoking-2 hours or less	N
30. Textile import quotas-veto override	Y	94. $1b/two year aid for the homeless	Y
31. Abortion service for military abroad	N	95. Bar non-unions in union companies	N
32. Limits on high income farmers	N	96. Increase FSLIC rescue to $15b	N
33. Family medical leave-veto override	N	97. Impose quotas to lower trade deficit	Y
34. Req submission of balanced budget	Y	98. Reduce discretionary budget 21%	Y
35. Balanced budget amendment	Y	99. Immigration reform/alien amnesty	N
36. Amendment to ban flag desecration	?	100. South Africa sanctions-veto override	?
37. Reauthorize Amtrak-veto override	N	101. Tax overhaul to revise income tax	N
38. Retraining aid for coal miners	N	102. Use of military in drug war	Y
39. Suspend El Salvador military aid	N	103. Delete 12 MX/add conventional wpn	N
40. Expand child care aid/tax credit	Y	104. Raise speed limit to 65 mph	Y
41. Raise House salary/omit honoraria	N	105. Require Pentagon to buy US goods	Y
42. Toughen oil-spill liability	N	106. AIDS insurance non-discrimination	N
43. Restitution to Japanese interned	N	107. Prohibit Saudi arms sales	Y
44. Protect Chinese & C.A. nationals	N	108. Ease Gun Control Act of 1968	Y
45. Abortion $ for rape/incest cases	N	109. Bar interstate handgun transport	N
46. Allow religious schools to bar gays	Y	110. Make company emissions known	N
47. Bar broadcaster fairness doctrine	Y	111. Allow toxic victims to sue in fed ct	N
48. Bar cap gains cut/reinstate IRA	N	112. Superfund waste cleanup of $10b	N
49. Bar unions equal voice in pension	Y	113. 90 days notice of plant closings	N
50. Bar assembly of chemical weapons	N	114. $20b in Medicare cuts/tax increases	N
51. Ban plutonium/uranium production	N	115. Spending cuts and tax increases	Y
52. Cap MX missile deployment at 50	N	116. Set school lunch lmt-250% poverty	Y
53. Allow $3b for 2 stealth bombers	Y	117. $75m for youth work projects	?
54. Publish bio-warfare experiments	N	118. Allow Angolan military assistance	Y
55. Raise minimum wage-veto override	N	119. Suspend defense payments for abuse	N
56. Bar transfer of FS-X technology	N	120. Drop SS COLAs/$12b tax increase	N
57. Cut defense and raise domestic $	N	121. Approve $1.5b for 21 MX missiles	Y
58. Uniform poll closing in 48 states	Y	122. Emergency farm credit/revisions	Y
59. Req foreign investment disclosure	N	123. Duty on Taiwan/Hong Kong/S Korea	N
60. Textile import quotas-veto override	Y	124. Limit steel imports to 17%	Y
61. Bar abortion funding in Wash, DC	Y	125. Cut $ to schools that bar prayer	Y
62. Notify spouses of AIDS+ carriers	Y	126. $50b-taxes; cut Medicare/spending	N
63. Seize conveyance-drug trafficking	Y	127. Limit Pershing II/cruise in Europe	N
64. South Africa sanctions	N	128. Delete $7.1b for 34 B-1 bombers	N
65. 60 days' notice of plant closings	N	129. Bar purchase of Sergeant York guns	N
66. Close unneeded military bases	Y	130. El Salvador military/economic aid	Y
67. Keep welfare reform within $2.8b	Y	131. Bar mining of Nicaraguan waters	N
68. Allow children housing exclusion	Y	132. Physician fee freeze for Medicare	Y
69. Shift $400m of NASA to homeless	N	133. $49b in "sin"/phone/insurance taxes	N
70. Cap Medicare patients' liability	Y	134. Allow sale of Conrail	Y
71. Prohibit employee polygraph testing	N	135. Equal Rights Amendment	Y
72. Allow CIA to fund Contras	Y	136. Authorize Marines in Lebanon	N
73. Revise unfair trade practices	Y	137. Eminent domain for coal companies	N
74. Focus SDI on accidental launch	N	138. Prohibit EPA clean air sanctions	Y
75. Bar Air Force $ for MX missile	N	139. SS retirement age increase/reforms	Y
76. Allow "real" increase in defense	Y	140. Auto domestic content requirement	Y

HALL, RALPH M. (continued)

141. Delete jobs program funding	N		143. Cut $5b from defense for Medicare	N
142. Highway-gas tax bill	N		144. Emergency housing aid of $1b	Y

Presidential Support Score: 1991 - 66%   1990 - 51%

BRYANT, JOHN -- Texas 5th District [Democrat]. County of Dallas (pt.). Prior Terms: 1983-92. Born: February 22, 1947; Lake Jackson, TX. Education: Southern Methodist University (B.A., J.D.). Occupation: Attorney; chief counsel, Texas Senate subcommittee on Consumer Affairs; administrative assistant, Texas Senate; Texas representative.

1. Protection to Haitian refugees	Y		54. Publish bio-warfare experiments	Y
2. Raise tax on wealthy; lower others	Y		55. Raise minimum wage-veto override	Y
3. Investigate Reagan hostage delay	Y		56. Bar transfer of FS-X technology	Y
4. Campaign finance revisions	Y		57. Cut defense and raise domestic $	N
5. Unpaid leave to care for children	Y		58. Uniform poll closing in 48 states	Y
6. Restrict NEA use of funds	N		59. Req foreign investment disclosure	Y
7. Bar race-bias claim/habeas corpus	N		60. Textile import quotas-veto override	Y
8. Ban race as death sentence factor	N		61. Bar abortion funding in Wash, DC	N
9. Exceptions to exclusionary rule	N		62. Notify spouses of AIDS+ carriers	N
10. Allow sale of assault weapons	N		63. Seize conveyance-drug trafficking	N
11. Life in prison/abolish death penalty	N		64. South Africa sanctions	Y
12. Req conspiracy-price fixing cases	N		65. 60 days' notice of plant closings	Y
13. Unemployment benefits extension	Y		66. Close unneeded military bases	N
14. Tissue use of aborted fetuses	Y		67. Keep welfare reform within $2.8b	?
15. Bar replacement of union strikers	Y		68. Allow children housing exclusion	N
16. Hold foreign aid at $15b for '92	N		69. Shift $400m of NASA to homeless	N
17. Restore space station funding	Y		70. Cap Medicare patients' liability	Y
18. Civil Rights Act of 1991	Y		71. Prohibit employee polygraph testing	Y
19. Unlimited damages-discrimination	Y		72. Allow CIA to fund Contras	?
20. Eliminate funds for supercollider	N		73. Revise unfair trade practices	Y
21. Terminate SDI except for research	Y		74. Focus SDI on accidental launch	Y
22. Req 7-day handgun waiting period	Y		75. Bar Air Force $ for MX missile	Y
23. Provide $30b for failed S&Ls	N		76. Allow "real" increase in defense	N
24. Allow use of force against Iraq	N		77. Troop reduction in Europe of 50%	Y
25. Allow $15b in foreign aid for '91	N		78. Ban nuclear tests above 1 kiloton	Y
26. Revise & extend legal immigration	N		79. Ban anti-satellite missile tests	Y
27. Suspend aid to Angolan rebels	Y		80. Observe certain limits of SALT II	Y
28. Democratic tax plan proposals	Y		81. Restore four Civil Rights laws	Y
29. Cut defense 5% across the board	Y		82. Prohibit aliens as strikebreakers	Y
30. Textile import quotas-veto override	Y		83. Allow military malpractice suits	Y
31. Abortion service for military abroad	Y		84. Approval of $36m in Contra aid	N
32. Limits on high income farmers	N		85. $18b deficit reduction compromise	Y
33. Family medical leave-veto override	Y		86. Welfare reform of $5.7b for 5 years	Y
34. Req submission of balanced budget	Y		87. Raise taxes $12b/cut spending $3b	Y
35. Balanced budget amendment	Y		88. Board to assess occupational risk	Y
36. Amendment to ban flag desecration	N		89. Balanced budget by '93-via targets	N
37. Reauthorize Amtrak-veto override	Y		90. Bar licensing of two nuclear plants	Y
38. Retraining aid for coal miners	Y		91. Remove victims compensation cap	N
39. Suspend El Salvador military aid	Y		92. Catastrophic health insurance	Y
40. Expand child care aid/tax credit	?		93. Ban airline smoking-2 hours or less	?
41. Raise House salary/omit honoraria	Y		94. $1b/two year aid for the homeless	Y
42. Toughen oil-spill liability	?		95. Bar non-unions in union companies	Y
43. Restitution to Japanese interned	Y		96. Increase FSLIC rescue to $15b	Y
44. Protect Chinese & C.A. nationals	Y		97. Impose quotas to lower trade deficit	Y
45. Abortion $ for rape/incest cases	?		98. Reduce discretionary budget 21%	Y
46. Allow religious schools to bar gays	N		99. Immigration reform/alien amnesty	Y
47. Bar broadcaster fairness doctrine	N		100. South Africa sanctions-veto override	Y
48. Bar cap gains cut/reinstate IRA	Y		101. Tax overhaul to revise income tax	N
49. Bar unions equal voice in pension	N		102. Use of military in drug war	Y
50. Bar assembly of chemical weapons	Y		103. Delete 12 MX/add conventional wpn	Y
51. Ban plutonium/uranium production	Y		104. Raise speed limit to 65 mph	N
52. Cap MX missile deployment at 50	Y		105. Require Pentagon to buy US goods	Y
53. Allow $3b for 2 stealth bombers	Y		106. AIDS insurance non-discrimination	Y

BRYANT, JOHN (continued)

107.	Prohibit Saudi arms sales	Y	124. Limit steel imports to 17%	Y
108.	Ease Gun Control Act of 1968	Y	125. Cut $ to schools that bar prayer	N
109.	Bar interstate handgun transport	N	126. $50b-taxes; cut Medicare/spending	Y
110.	Make company emissions known	Y	127. Limit Pershing II/cruise in Europe	?
111.	Allow toxic victims to sue in fed ct	Y	128. Delete $7.1b for 34 B-1 bombers	N
112.	Superfund waste cleanup of $10b	N	129. Bar purchase of Sergeant York guns	N
113.	90 days notice of plant closings	Y	130. El Salvador military/economic aid	N
114.	$20b in Medicare cuts/tax increases	Y	131. Bar mining of Nicaraguan waters	Y
115.	Spending cuts and tax increases	Y	132. Physician fee freeze for Medicare	N
116.	Set school lunch lmt-250% poverty	N	133. $49b in "sin"/phone/insurance taxes	Y
117.	$75m for youth work projects	Y	134. Allow sale of Conrail	N
118.	Allow Angolan military assistance	N	135. Equal Rights Amendment	Y
119.	Suspend defense payments for abuse	Y	136. Authorize Marines in Lebanon	N
120.	Drop SS COLAs/$12b tax increase	N	137. Eminent domain for coal companies	N
121.	Approve $1.5b for 21 MX missiles	N	138. Prohibit EPA clean air sanctions	Y
122.	Emergency farm credit/revisions	Y	139. SS retirement age increase/reforms	N
123.	Duty on Taiwan/Hong Kong/S Korea	Y		

Presidential Support Score: 1991 - 21%   1990 - 13%

BARTON, JOE -- Texas 6th District [Republican]. Counties of Brazos, Dallas (pt.), Ellis, Freestone, Grimes, Hill, Hood, Johnston, Leon, Limestone, Madison, Montgomery (pt.), Navarro, Robertson. Prior Terms: 1985-92. Born: September 15, 1949; Waco, TX. Education: Texas A&M (B.S.); Purdue University (M.S.). Occupation: Engineer and consultant, major oil corp.

1. Protection to Haitian refugees	N	38. Retraining aid for coal miners	?
2. Raise tax on wealthy; lower others	N	39. Suspend El Salvador military aid	?
3. Investigate Reagan hostage delay	N	40. Expand child care aid/tax credit	N
4. Campaign finance revisions	N	41. Raise House salary/omit honoraria	Y
5. Unpaid leave to care for children	N	42. Toughen oil-spill liability	N
6. Restrict NEA use of funds	Y	43. Restitution to Japanese interned	N
7. Bar race-bias claim/habeas corpus	Y	44. Protect Chinese & C.A. nationals	Y
8. Ban race as death sentence factor	Y	45. Abortion $ for rape/incest cases	N
9. Exceptions to exclusionary rule	Y	46. Allow religious schools to bar gays	Y
10. Allow sale of assault weapons	Y	47. Bar broadcaster fairness doctrine	Y
11. Life in prison/abolish death penalty	N	48. Bar cap gains cut/reinstate IRA	N
12. Req conspiracy-price fixing cases	Y	49. Bar unions equal voice in pension	Y
13. Unemployment benefits extension	N	50. Bar assembly of chemical weapons	N
14. Tissue use of aborted fetuses	N	51. Ban plutonium/uranium production	N
15. Bar replacement of union strikers	N	52. Cap MX missile deployment at 50	N
16. Hold foreign aid at $15b for '92	N	53. Allow $3b for 2 stealth bombers	N
17. Restore space station funding	Y	54. Publish bio-warfare experiments	N
18. Civil Rights Act of 1991	N	55. Raise minimum wage-veto override	N
19. Unlimited damages-discrimination	Y	56. Bar transfer of FS-X technology	N
20. Eliminate funds for supercollider	N	57. Cut defense and raise domestic $	N
21. Terminate SDI except for research	X	58. Uniform poll closing in 48 states	N
22. Req 7-day handgun waiting period	N	59. Req foreign investment disclosure	N
23. Provide $30b for failed S&Ls	Y	60. Textile import quotas-veto override	N
24. Allow use of force against Iraq	Y	61. Bar abortion funding in Wash, DC	Y
25. Allow $15b in foreign aid for '91	?	62. Notify spouses of AIDS+ carriers	Y
26. Revise & extend legal immigration	Y	63. Seize conveyance-drug trafficking	Y
27. Suspend aid to Angolan rebels	N	64. South Africa sanctions	X
28. Democratic tax plan proposals	N	65. 60 days' notice of plant closings	N
29. Cut defense 5% across the board	N	66. Close unneeded military bases	Y
30. Textile import quotas-veto override	N	67. Keep welfare reform within $2.8b	Y
31. Abortion service for military abroad	N	68. Allow children housing exclusion	Y
32. Limits on high income farmers	N	69. Shift $400m of NASA to homeless	N
33. Family medical leave-veto override	N	70. Cap Medicare patients' liability	N
34. Req submission of balanced budget	N	71. Prohibit employee polygraph testing	N
35. Balanced budget amendment	Y	72. Allow CIA to fund Contras	Y
36. Amendment to ban flag desecration	Y	73. Revise unfair trade practices	N
37. Reauthorize Amtrak-veto override	N	74. Focus SDI on accidental launch	N

BARTON, JOE (continued)

75. Bar Air Force $ for MX missile	N	
76. Allow "real" increase in defense	?	
77. Troop reduction in Europe of 50%	?	
78. Ban nuclear tests above 1 kiloton	N	
79. Ban anti-satellite missile tests	N	
80. Observe certain limits of SALT II	N	
81. Restore four Civil Rights laws	N	
82. Prohibit aliens as strikebreakers	N	
83. Allow military malpractice suits	?	
84. Approval of $36m in Contra aid	Y	
85. $18b deficit reduction compromise	N	
86. Welfare reform of $5.7b for 5 years	N	
87. Raise taxes $12b/cut spending $3b	N	
88. Board to assess occupational risk	N	
89. Balanced budget by '93-via targets	Y	
90. Bar licensing of two nuclear plants	N	
91. Remove victims compensation cap	N	
92. Catastrophic health insurance	N	
93. Ban airline smoking-2 hours or less	N	
94. $1b/two year aid for the homeless	N	
95. Bar non-unions in union companies	N	
96. Increase FSLIC rescue to $15b	Y	
97. Impose quotas to lower trade deficit	N	
98. Reduce discretionary budget 21%	Y	

99. Immigration reform/alien amnesty	N
100. South Africa sanctions-veto override	N
101. Tax overhaul to revise income tax	Y
102. Use of military in drug war	Y
103. Delete 12 MX/add conventional wpn	N
104. Raise speed limit to 65 mph	Y
105. Require Pentagon to buy US goods	N
106. AIDS insurance non-discrimination	N
107. Prohibit Saudi arms sales	Y
108. Ease Gun Control Act of 1968	Y
109. Bar interstate handgun transport	N
110. Make company emissions known	N
111. Allow toxic victims to sue in fed ct	N
112. Superfund waste cleanup of $10b	N
113. 90 days notice of plant closings	N
114. $20b in Medicare cuts/tax increases	N
115. Spending cuts and tax increases	N
116. Set school lunch lmt-250% poverty	Y
117. $75m for youth work projects	N
118. Allow Angolan military assistance	Y
119. Suspend defense payments for abuse	N
120. Drop SS COLAs/$12b tax increase	N
121. Approve $1.5b for 21 MX missiles	Y
122. Emergency farm credit/revisions	N

Presidential Support Score: 1991 - 70%   1990 - 68%

ARCHER, BILL -- Texas 7th District [Republican]. County of Harris (pt.). Prior Terms: 1971-92. Born: March 22, 1928; Houston, TX. Education: Rice University; University of Texas (B.B.A., LL.B.). Military Service: U.S. Air Force. Occupation: President, Uncle Johnny Mills, Inc. (1953-61); attorney, Harris, Archer, Parks and Graul; Texas representative (1966-70).

1. Protection to Haitian refugees	N
2. Raise tax on wealthy; lower others	N
3. Investigate Reagan hostage delay	N
4. Campaign finance revisions	N
5. Unpaid leave to care for children	N
6. Restrict NEA use of funds	Y
7. Bar race-bias claim/habeas corpus	Y
8. Ban race as death sentence factor	Y
9. Exceptions to exclusionary rule	Y
10. Allow sale of assault weapons	Y
11. Life in prison/abolish death penalty	N
12. Req conspiracy-price fixing cases	Y
13. Unemployment benefits extension	N
14. Tissue use of aborted fetuses	N
15. Bar replacement of union strikers	N
16. Hold foreign aid at $15b for '92	N
17. Restore space station funding	Y
18. Civil Rights Act of 1991	N
19. Unlimited damages-discrimination	N
20. Eliminate funds for supercollider	N
21. Terminate SDI except for research	N
22. Req 7-day handgun waiting period	N
23. Provide $30b for failed S&Ls	Y
24. Allow use of force against Iraq	Y
25. Allow $15b in foreign aid for '91	N
26. Revise & extend legal immigration	N
27. Suspend aid to Angolan rebels	N
28. Democratic tax plan proposals	N
29. Cut defense 5% across the board	N
30. Textile import quotas-veto override	N

31. Abortion service for military abroad	N
32. Limits on high income farmers	Y
33. Family medical leave-veto override	N
34. Req submission of balanced budget	N
35. Balanced budget amendment	Y
36. Amendment to ban flag desecration	Y
37. Reauthorize Amtrak-veto override	N
38. Retraining aid for coal miners	N
39. Suspend El Salvador military aid	N
40. Expand child care aid/tax credit	N
41. Raise House salary/omit honoraria	Y
42. Toughen oil-spill liability	N
43. Restitution to Japanese interned	N
44. Protect Chinese & C.A. nationals	N
45. Abortion $ for rape/incest cases	N
46. Allow religious schools to bar gays	Y
47. Bar broadcaster fairness doctrine	Y
48. Bar cap gains cut/reinstate IRA	N
49. Bar unions equal voice in pension	Y
50. Bar assembly of chemical weapons	N
51. Ban plutonium/uranium production	N
52. Cap MX missile deployment at 50	N
53. Allow $3b for 2 stealth bombers	Y
54. Publish bio-warfare experiments	N
55. Raise minimum wage-veto override	N
56. Bar transfer of FS-X technology	N
57. Cut defense and raise domestic $	N
58. Uniform poll closing in 48 states	N
59. Req foreign investment disclosure	N
60. Textile import quotas-veto override	N

ARCHER, BILL (continued)

61.	Bar abortion funding in Wash, DC	Y	103.	Delete 12 MX/add conventional wpn	N
62.	Notify spouses of AIDS+ carriers	Y	104.	Raise speed limit to 65 mph	Y
63.	Seize conveyance-drug trafficking	Y	105.	Require Pentagon to buy US goods	N
64.	South Africa sanctions	N	106.	AIDS insurance non-discrimination	N
65.	60 days' notice of plant closings	N	107.	Prohibit Saudi arms sales	Y
66.	Close unneeded military bases	Y	108.	Ease Gun Control Act of 1968	Y
67.	Keep welfare reform within $2.8b	Y	109.	Bar interstate handgun transport	N
68.	Allow children housing exclusion	Y	110.	Make company emissions known	N
69.	Shift $400m of NASA to homeless	N	111.	Allow toxic victims to sue in fed ct	N
70.	Cap Medicare patients' liability	N	112.	Superfund waste cleanup of $10b	N
71.	Prohibit employee polygraph testing	N	113.	90 days notice of plant closings	X
72.	Allow CIA to fund Contras	Y	114.	$20b in Medicare cuts/tax increases	N
73.	Revise unfair trade practices	N	115.	Spending cuts and tax increases	N
74.	Focus SDI on accidental launch	?	116.	Set school lunch lmt-250% poverty	Y
75.	Bar Air Force $ for MX missile	N	117.	$75m for youth work projects	N
76.	Allow "real" increase in defense	Y	118.	Allow Angolan military assistance	Y
77.	Troop reduction in Europe of 50%	N	119.	Suspend defense payments for abuse	N
78.	Ban nuclear tests above 1 kiloton	N	120.	Drop SS COLAs/$12b tax increase	N
79.	Ban anti-satellite missile tests	N	121.	Approve $1.5b for 21 MX missiles	Y
80.	Observe certain limits of SALT II	N	122.	Emergency farm credit/revisions	N
81.	Restore four Civil Rights laws	N	123.	Duty on Taiwan/Hong Kong/S Korea	N
82.	Prohibit aliens as strikebreakers	N	124.	Limit steel imports to 17%	N
83.	Allow military malpractice suits	N	125.	Cut $ to schools that bar prayer	Y
84.	Approval of $36m in Contra aid	Y	126.	$50b-taxes; cut Medicare/spending	N
85.	$18b deficit reduction compromise	N	127.	Limit Pershing II/cruise in Europe	N
86.	Welfare reform of $5.7b for 5 years	N	128.	Delete $7.1b for 34 B-1 bombers	N
87.	Raise taxes $12b/cut spending $3b	N	129.	Bar purchase of Sergeant York guns	N
88.	Board to assess occupational risk	N	130.	El Salvador military/economic aid	Y
89.	Balanced budget by '93-via targets	Y	131.	Bar mining of Nicaraguan waters	N
90.	Bar licensing of two nuclear plants	N	132.	Physician fee freeze for Medicare	Y
91.	Remove victims compensation cap	N	133.	$49b in "sin"/phone/insurance taxes	N
92.	Catastrophic health insurance	N	134.	Allow sale of Conrail	Y
93.	Ban airline smoking-2 hours or less	Y	135.	Equal Rights Amendment	N
94.	$1b/two year aid for the homeless	N	136.	Authorize Marines in Lebanon	N
95.	Bar non-unions in union companies	N	137.	Eminent domain for coal companies	Y
96.	Increase FSLIC rescue to $15b	Y	138.	Prohibit EPA clean air sanctions	Y
97.	Impose quotas to lower trade deficit	N	139.	SS retirement age increase/reforms	Y
98.	Reduce discretionary budget 21%	Y	140.	Auto domestic content requirement	N
99.	Immigration reform/alien amnesty	N	141.	Delete jobs program funding	Y
100.	South Africa sanctions-veto override	N	142.	Highway-gas tax bill	Y
101.	Tax overhaul to revise income tax	N	143.	Cut $5b from defense for Medicare	N
102.	Use of military in drug war	Y	144.	Emergency housing aid of $1b	Y

Presidential Support Score: 1991 - 84%   1990 - 84%

FIELDS, JACK -- Texas 8th District [Republican]. Counties of Harris (pt.) and Montgomery (pt.). Prior Terms: 1981-92. Born: February 3, 1952; Humble, TX. Education: Baylor University (B.A., J.D.). Occupation: Attorney; executive vice president, Rosewood Memorial Park; executive board member, Humble-Northeast Medical Center; executive board member, Small Business Advisory Assistance Council; Humble Chamber of Commerce chairman.

1.	Protection to Haitian refugees	N	13.	Unemployment benefits extension	N
2.	Raise tax on wealthy; lower others	N	14.	Tissue use of aborted fetuses	N
3.	Investigate Reagan hostage delay	N	15.	Bar replacement of union strikers	N
4.	Campaign finance revisions	N	16.	Hold foreign aid at $15b for '92	N
5.	Unpaid leave to care for children	N	17.	Restore space station funding	Y
6.	Restrict NEA use of funds	Y	18.	Civil Rights Act of 1991	N
7.	Bar race-bias claim/habeas corpus	Y	19.	Unlimited damages-discrimination	N
8.	Ban race as death sentence factor	?	20.	Eliminate funds for supercollider	N
9.	Exceptions to exclusionary rule	Y	21.	Terminate SDI except for research	N
10.	Allow sale of assault weapons	Y	22.	Req 7-day handgun waiting period	N
11.	Life in prison/abolish death penalty	N	23.	Provide $30b for failed S&Ls	Y
12.	Req conspiracy-price fixing cases	Y	24.	Allow use of force against Iraq	Y

FIELDS, JACK (continued)

25.	Allow $15b in foreign aid for '91	N
26.	Revise & extend legal immigration	N
27.	Suspend aid to Angolan rebels	N
28.	Democratic tax plan proposals	N
29.	Cut defense 5% across the board	N
30.	Textile import quotas-veto override	N
31.	Abortion service for military abroad	N
32.	Limits on high income farmers	N
33.	Family medical leave-veto override	N
34.	Req submission of balanced budget	N
35.	Balanced budget amendment	Y
36.	Amendment to ban flag desecration	Y
37.	Reauthorize Amtrak-veto override	N
38.	Retraining aid for coal miners	N
39.	Suspend El Salvador military aid	N
40.	Expand child care aid/tax credit	N
41.	Raise House salary/omit honoraria	N
42.	Toughen oil-spill liability	N
43.	Restitution to Japanese interned	N
44.	Protect Chinese & C.A. nationals	N
45.	Abortion $ for rape/incest cases	N
46.	Allow religious schools to bar gays	Y
47.	Bar broadcaster fairness doctrine	N
48.	Bar cap gains cut/reinstate IRA	N
49.	Bar unions equal voice in pension	Y
50.	Bar assembly of chemical weapons	N
51.	Ban plutonium/uranium production	N
52.	Cap MX missile deployment at 50	N
53.	Allow $3b for 2 stealth bombers	Y
54.	Publish bio-warfare experiments	N
55.	Raise minimum wage-veto override	N
56.	Bar transfer of FS-X technology	N
57.	Cut defense and raise domestic $	N
58.	Uniform poll closing in 48 states	N
59.	Req foreign investment disclosure	N
60.	Textile import quotas-veto override	N
61.	Bar abortion funding in Wash, DC	Y
62.	Notify spouses of AIDS+ carriers	Y
63.	Seize conveyance-drug trafficking	Y
64.	South Africa sanctions	N
65.	60 days' notice of plant closings	N
66.	Close unneeded military bases	Y
67.	Keep welfare reform within $2.8b	?
68.	Allow children housing exclusion	Y
69.	Shift $400m of NASA to homeless	N
70.	Cap Medicare patients' liability	N
71.	Prohibit employee polygraph testing	N
72.	Allow CIA to fund Contras	Y
73.	Revise unfair trade practices	N
74.	Focus SDI on accidental launch	N
75.	Bar Air Force $ for MX missile	N
76.	Allow "real" increase in defense	+
77.	Troop reduction in Europe of 50%	N
78.	Ban nuclear tests above 1 kiloton	N
79.	Ban anti-satellite missile tests	N
80.	Observe certain limits of SALT II	N
81.	Restore four Civil Rights laws	N
82.	Prohibit aliens as strikebreakers	N
83.	Allow military malpractice suits	--
84.	Approval of $36m in Contra aid	Y

85.	$18b deficit reduction compromise	N
86.	Welfare reform of $5.7b for 5 years	N
87.	Raise taxes $12b/cut spending $3b	N
88.	Board to assess occupational risk	N
89.	Balanced budget by '93-via targets	Y
90.	Bar licensing of two nuclear plants	N
91.	Remove victims compensation cap	N
92.	Catastrophic health insurance	N
93.	Ban airline smoking-2 hours or less	N
94.	$1b/two year aid for the homeless	N
95.	Bar non-unions in union companies	N
96.	Increase FSLIC rescue to $15b	Y
97.	Impose quotas to lower trade deficit	N
98.	Reduce discretionary budget 21%	Y
99.	Immigration reform/alien amnesty	N
100.	South Africa sanctions-veto override	N
101.	Tax overhaul to revise income tax	N
102.	Use of military in drug war	Y
103.	Delete 12 MX/add conventional wpn	N
104.	Raise speed limit to 65 mph	Y
105.	Require Pentagon to buy US goods	N
106.	AIDS insurance non-discrimination	N
107.	Prohibit Saudi arms sales	Y
108.	Ease Gun Control Act of 1968	Y
109.	Bar interstate handgun transport	N
110.	Make company emissions known	N
111.	Allow toxic victims to sue in fed ct	N
112.	Superfund waste cleanup of $10b	N
113.	90 days notice of plant closings	N
114.	$20b in Medicare cuts/tax increases	N
115.	Spending cuts and tax increases	N
116.	Set school lunch lmt-250% poverty	Y
117.	$75m for youth work projects	N
118.	Allow Angolan military assistance	Y
119.	Suspend defense payments for abuse	N
120.	Drop SS COLAs/$12b tax increase	N
121.	Approve $1.5b for 21 MX missiles	Y
122.	Emergency farm credit/revisions	N
123.	Duty on Taiwan/Hong Kong/S Korea	N
124.	Limit steel imports to 17%	Y
125.	Cut $ to schools that bar prayer	Y
126.	$50b-taxes; cut Medicare/spending	N
127.	Limit Pershing II/cruise in Europe	N
128.	Delete $7.1b for 34 B-1 bombers	N
129.	Bar purchase of Sergeant York guns	N
130.	El Salvador military/economic aid	Y
131.	Bar mining of Nicaraguan waters	N
132.	Physician fee freeze for Medicare	Y
133.	$49b in "sin"/phone/insurance taxes	N
134.	Allow sale of Conrail	Y
135.	Equal Rights Amendment	N
136.	Authorize Marines in Lebanon	N
137.	Eminent domain for coal companies	Y
138.	Prohibit EPA clean air sanctions	Y
139.	SS retirement age increase/reforms	Y
140.	Auto domestic content requirement	N
141.	Delete jobs program funding	Y
142.	Highway-gas tax bill	Y
143.	Cut $5b from defense for Medicare	N
144.	Emergency housing aid of $1b	Y

Presidential Support Score: 1991 - 79%   1990 - 79%

BROOKS, JACK -- Texas 9th District [Democrat]. Counties of Chambers, Galveston, Harris (pt.) and Jefferson. Prior Terms: 1953-92. Born: December 18, 1922; Crowley, LA. Education: University of Texas (B.J., J.D.). Military Service: U.S. Marine Corps, WW II. Occupation: Texas legislator (1946-50).

1.	Protection to Haitian refugees	Y	61.	Bar abortion funding in Wash, DC	?
2.	Raise tax on wealthy; lower others	Y	62.	Notify spouses of AIDS+ carriers	N
3.	Investigate Reagan hostage delay	N	63.	Seize conveyance-drug trafficking	N
4.	Campaign finance revisions	Y	64.	South Africa sanctions	Y
5.	Unpaid leave to care for children	Y	65.	60 days' notice of plant closings	Y
6.	Restrict NEA use of funds	N	66.	Close unneeded military bases	N
7.	Bar race-bias claim/habeas corpus	?	67.	Keep welfare reform within $2.8b	N
8.	Ban race as death sentence factor	N	68.	Allow children housing exclusion	N
9.	Exceptions to exclusionary rule	N	69.	Shift $400m of NASA to homeless	N
10.	Allow sale of assault weapons	Y	70.	Cap Medicare patients' liability	Y
11.	Life in prison/abolish death penalty	N	71.	Prohibit employee polygraph testing	Y
12.	Req conspiracy-price fixing cases	N	72.	Allow CIA to fund Contras	N
13.	Unemployment benefits extension	Y	73.	Revise unfair trade practices	Y
14.	Tissue use of aborted fetuses	Y	74.	Focus SDI on accidental launch	Y
15.	Bar replacement of union strikers	Y	75.	Bar Air Force $ for MX missile	N
16.	Hold foreign aid at $15b for '92	Y	76.	Allow "real" increase in defense	N
17.	Restore space station funding	Y	77.	Troop reduction in Europe of 50%	N
18.	Civil Rights Act of 1991	Y	78.	Ban nuclear tests above 1 kiloton	?
19.	Unlimited damages-discrimination	Y	79.	Ban anti-satellite missile tests	?
20.	Eliminate funds for supercollider	N	80.	Observe certain limits of SALT II	Y
21.	Terminate SDI except for research	N	81.	Restore four Civil Rights laws	Y
22.	Req 7-day handgun waiting period	N	82.	Prohibit aliens as strikebreakers	Y
23.	Provide $30b for failed S&Ls	Y	83.	Allow military malpractice suits	Y
24.	Allow use of force against Iraq	Y	84.	Approval of $36m in Contra aid	N
25.	Allow $15b in foreign aid for '91	Y	85.	$18b deficit reduction compromise	Y
26.	Revise & extend legal immigration	Y	86.	Welfare reform of $5.7b for 5 years	Y
27.	Suspend aid to Angolan rebels	?	87.	Raise taxes $12b/cut spending $3b	Y
28.	Democratic tax plan proposals	Y	88.	Board to assess occupational risk	Y
29.	Cut defense 5% across the board	?	89.	Balanced budget by '93-via targets	N
30.	Textile import quotas-veto override	Y	90.	Bar licensing of two nuclear plants	N
31.	Abortion service for military abroad	Y	91.	Remove victims compensation cap	N
32.	Limits on high income farmers	N	92.	Catastrophic health insurance	Y
33.	Family medical leave-veto override	Y	93.	Ban airline smoking-2 hours or less	N
34.	Req submission of balanced budget	Y	94.	$1b/two year aid for the homeless	Y
35.	Balanced budget amendment	N	95.	Bar non-unions in union companies	Y
36.	Amendment to ban flag desecration	Y	96.	Increase FSLIC rescue to $15b	N
37.	Reauthorize Amtrak-veto override	Y	97.	Impose quotas to lower trade deficit	Y
38.	Retraining aid for coal miners	Y	98.	Reduce discretionary budget 21%	N
39.	Suspend El Salvador military aid	Y	99.	Immigration reform/alien amnesty	?
40.	Expand child care aid/tax credit	Y	100.	South Africa sanctions-veto override	Y
41.	Raise House salary/omit honoraria	?	101.	Tax overhaul to revise income tax	N
42.	Toughen oil-spill liability	?	102.	Use of military in drug war	N
43.	Restitution to Japanese interned	?	103.	Delete 12 MX/add conventional wpn	Y
44.	Protect Chinese & C.A. nationals	?	104.	Raise speed limit to 65 mph	N
45.	Abortion $ for rape/incest cases	Y	105.	Require Pentagon to buy US goods	Y
46.	Allow religious schools to bar gays	Y	106.	AIDS insurance non-discrimination	Y
47.	Bar broadcaster fairness doctrine	N	107.	Prohibit Saudi arms sales	Y
48.	Bar cap gains cut/reinstate IRA	N	108.	Ease Gun Control Act of 1968	Y
49.	Bar unions equal voice in pension	Y	109.	Bar interstate handgun transport	N
50.	Bar assembly of chemical weapons	N	110.	Make company emissions known	?
51.	Ban plutonium/uranium production	Y	111.	Allow toxic victims to sue in fed ct	?
52.	Cap MX missile deployment at 50	Y	112.	Superfund waste cleanup of $10b	X
53.	Allow $3b for 2 stealth bombers	N	113.	90 days notice of plant closings	Y
54.	Publish bio-warfare experiments	Y	114.	$20b in Medicare cuts/tax increases	Y
55.	Raise minimum wage-veto override	Y	115.	Spending cuts and tax increases	Y
56.	Bar transfer of FS-X technology	Y	116.	Set school lunch lmt-250% poverty	N
57.	Cut defense and raise domestic $	Y	117.	$75m for youth work projects	Y
58.	Uniform poll closing in 48 states	Y	118.	Allow Angolan military assistance	N
59.	Req foreign investment disclosure	Y	119.	Suspend defense payments for abuse	N
60.	Textile import quotas-veto override	Y	120.	Drop SS COLAs/$12b tax increase	N

BROOKS, JACK (continued)

121. Approve $1.5b for 21 MX missiles	N	133. $49b in "sin"/phone/insurance taxes	Y
122. Emergency farm credit/revisions	Y	134. Allow sale of Conrail	N
123. Duty on Taiwan/Hong Kong/S Korea	Y	135. Equal Rights Amendment	Y
124. Limit steel imports to 17%	Y	136. Authorize Marines in Lebanon	N
125. Cut $ to schools that bar prayer	N	137. Eminent domain for coal companies	#
126. $50b-taxes; cut Medicare/spending	+	138. Prohibit EPA clean air sanctions	Y
127. Limit Pershing II/cruise in Europe	N	139. SS retirement age increase/reforms	Y
128. Delete $7.1b for 34 B-1 bombers	Y	140. Auto domestic content requirement	Y
129. Bar purchase of Sergeant York guns	N	141. Delete jobs program funding	N
130. El Salvador military/economic aid	N	142. Highway-gas tax bill	Y
131. Bar mining of Nicaraguan waters	Y	143. Cut $5b from defense for Medicare	N
132. Physician fee freeze for Medicare	N	144. Emergency housing aid of $1b	Y

Presidential Support Score: 1991 - 31%   1990 - 18%

PICKLE, J. J. -- Texas 10th District [Democrat]. Counties of Bastrop, Blanco, Burnet (pt.), Caldwell, Hays and Travis. Prior Terms: 1963 (Special Election)-1992. Born: October 11, 1913; Roscoe, TX. Education: University of Texas (B.A.). Military Service: U.S. Navy, WW II. Occupation: Area director, National Youth Administration (1938-41); radio station organizer; public relations businessman; advertising businessman; member, Texas Employment Commission (1961-63).

1. Protection to Haitian refugees	Y	42. Toughen oil-spill liability	N
2. Raise tax on wealthy; lower others	Y	43. Restitution to Japanese interned	Y
3. Investigate Reagan hostage delay	Y	44. Protect Chinese & C.A. nationals	Y
4. Campaign finance revisions	Y	45. Abortion $ for rape/incest cases	Y
5. Unpaid leave to care for children	Y	46. Allow religious schools to bar gays	Y
6. Restrict NEA use of funds	N	47. Bar broadcaster fairness doctrine	N
7. Bar race-bias claim/habeas corpus	N	48. Bar cap gains cut/reinstate IRA	N
8. Ban race as death sentence factor	Y	49. Bar unions equal voice in pension	Y
9. Exceptions to exclusionary rule	Y	50. Bar assembly of chemical weapons	Y
10. Allow sale of assault weapons	N	51. Ban plutonium/uranium production	Y
11. Life in prison/abolish death penalty	N	52. Cap MX missile deployment at 50	Y
12. Req conspiracy-price fixing cases	N	53. Allow $3b for 2 stealth bombers	Y
13. Unemployment benefits extension	?	54. Publish bio-warfare experiments	Y
14. Tissue use of aborted fetuses	Y	55. Raise minimum wage-veto override	Y
15. Bar replacement of union strikers	N	56. Bar transfer of FS-X technology	Y
16. Hold foreign aid at $15b for '92	Y	57. Cut defense and raise domestic $	N
17. Restore space station funding	Y	58. Uniform poll closing in 48 states	Y
18. Civil Rights Act of 1991	Y	59. Req foreign investment disclosure	Y
19. Unlimited damages-discrimination	N	60. Textile import quotas-veto override	?
20. Eliminate funds for supercollider	N	61. Bar abortion funding in Wash, DC	N
21. Terminate SDI except for research	N	62. Notify spouses of AIDS+ carriers	N
22. Req 7-day handgun waiting period	Y	63. Seize conveyance-drug trafficking	N
23. Provide $30b for failed S&Ls	Y	64. South Africa sanctions	Y
24. Allow use of force against Iraq	N	65. 60 days' notice of plant closings	Y
25. Allow $15b in foreign aid for '91	Y	66. Close unneeded military bases	Y
26. Revise & extend legal immigration	Y	67. Keep welfare reform within $2.8b	N
27. Suspend aid to Angolan rebels	N	68. Allow children housing vouchers	N
28. Democratic tax plan proposals	Y	69. Shift $400m of NASA to homeless	N
29. Cut defense 5% across the board	N	70. Cap Medicare patients' liability	Y
30. Textile import quotas-veto override	N	71. Prohibit employee polygraph testing	Y
31. Abortion service for military abroad	Y	72. Allow CIA to fund Contras	N
32. Limits on high income farmers	N	73. Revise unfair trade practices	Y
33. Family medical leave-veto override	N	74. Focus SDI on accidental launch	N
34. Req submission of balanced budget	Y	75. Bar Air Force $ for MX missile	N
35. Balanced budget amendment	Y	76. Allow "real" increase in defense	Y
36. Amendment to ban flag desecration	N	77. Troop reduction in Europe of 50%	Y
37. Reauthorize Amtrak-veto override	Y	78. Ban nuclear tests above 1 kiloton	Y
38. Retraining aid for coal miners	N	79. Ban anti-satellite missile tests	Y
39. Suspend El Salvador military aid	Y	80. Observe certain limits of SALT II	Y
40. Expand child care aid/tax credit	Y	81. Restore four Civil Rights laws	Y
41. Raise House salary/omit honoraria	Y	82. Prohibit aliens as strikebreakers	Y

PICKLE, J. J. (continued)

83. Allow military malpractice suits	N	114. $20b in Medicare cuts/tax increases	Y
84. Approval of $36m in Contra aid	N	115. Spending cuts and tax increases	Y
85. $18b deficit reduction compromise	Y	116. Set school lunch lmt-250% poverty	N
86. Welfare reform of $5.7b for 5 years	Y	117. $75m for youth work projects	Y
87. Raise taxes $12b/cut spending $3b	Y	118. Allow Angolan military assistance	Y
88. Board to assess occupational risk	N	119. Suspend defense payments for abuse	N
89. Balanced budget by '93-via targets	Y	120. Drop SS COLAs/$12b tax increase	Y
90. Bar licensing of two nuclear plants	N	121. Approve $1.5b for 21 MX missiles	N
91. Remove victims compensation cap	N	122. Emergency farm credit/revisions	Y
92. Catastrophic health insurance	Y	123. Duty on Taiwan/Hong Kong/S Korea	N
93. Ban airline smoking-2 hours or less	N	124. Limit steel imports to 17%	Y
94. $1b/two year aid for the homeless	Y	125. Cut $ to schools that bar prayer	N
95. Bar non-unions in union companies	Y	126. $50b-taxes; cut Medicare/spending	Y
96. Increase FSLIC rescue to $15b	N	127. Limit Pershing II/cruise in Europe	N
97. Impose quotas to lower trade deficit	N	128. Delete $7.1b for 34 B-1 bombers	N
98. Reduce discretionary budget 21%	Y	129. Bar purchase of Sergeant York guns	N
99. Immigration reform/alien amnesty	Y	130. El Salvador military/economic aid	Y
100. South Africa sanctions-veto override	Y	131. Bar mining of Nicaraguan waters	Y
101. Tax overhaul to revise income tax	Y	132. Physician fee freeze for Medicare	N
102. Use of military in drug war	Y	133. $49b in "sin"/phone/insurance taxes	Y
103. Delete 12 MX/add conventional wpn	N	134. Allow sale of Conrail	?
104. Raise speed limit to 65 mph	Y	135. Equal Rights Amendment	Y
105. Require Pentagon to buy US goods	Y	136. Authorize Marines in Lebanon	Y
106. AIDS insurance non-discrimination	Y	137. Eminent domain for coal companies	Y
107. Prohibit Saudi arms sales	Y	138. Prohibit EPA clean air sanctions	N
108. Ease Gun Control Act of 1968	Y	139. SS retirement age increase/reforms	Y
109. Bar interstate handgun transport	Y	140. Auto domestic content requirement	N
110. Make company emissions known	Y	141. Delete jobs program funding	N
111. Allow toxic victims to sue in fed ct	Y	142. Highway-gas tax bill	Y
112. Superfund waste cleanup of $10b	N	143. Cut $5b from defense for Medicare	Y
113. 90 days notice of plant closings	N	144. Emergency housing aid of $1b	Y

Presidential Support Score: 1991 - 41%   1990 - 33%

EDWARDS, CHET -- Texas 11th District [Democrat]. Counties of Bell, Bosque, Brown, Burnet (pt.), Coryell, Falls, Hamilton, Lampasas, McLennon, Milam, Mills, San Saba and Williamson (pt.). Prior Term: 1991-92. Born: November 24, 1951; Corpus Christi, TX. Education: Texas A&M University (B.A.); Harvard Business School (M.B.A.). Occupation: Legislative and district aide to Rep. Teague (1974-77); Trammell Crow Co. marketing representative; president, Edwards Communications Corp.; state senator (1983-90); Texas Sunset Commission chairman.

1. Protection to Haitian refugees	Y	13. Unemployment benefits extension	Y
2. Raise tax on wealthy; lower others	Y	14. Tissue use of aborted fetuses	Y
3. Investigate Reagan hostage delay	Y	15. Bar replacement of union strikers	Y
4. Campaign finance revisions	Y	16. Hold foreign aid at $15b for '92	Y
5. Unpaid leave to care for children	N	17. Restore space station funding	Y
6. Restrict NEA use of funds	Y	18. Civil Rights Act of 1991	Y
7. Bar race-bias claim/habeas corpus	Y	19. Unlimited damages-discrimination	N
8. Ban race as death sentence factor	Y	20. Eliminate funds for supercollider	N
9. Exceptions to exclusionary rule	Y	21. Terminate SDI except for research	N
10. Allow sale of assault weapons	N	22. Req 7-day handgun waiting period	N
11. Life in prison/abolish death penalty	N	23. Provide $30b for failed S&Ls	Y
12. Req conspiracy-price fixing cases	N	24. Allow use of force against Iraq	Y

Presidential Support Score: 1991 - 41%

GEREN, PRESTON (Pete) -- Texas 12th District [Democrat]. County of Tarrant (pt.). Prior Terms: 1989 (Special Election)-1992. Born: 1952; Fort Worth, TX. Education: University of Texas (B.A., J.D.). Occupation: Attorney; executive assistant to Senator Bentsen.

1. Protection to Haitian refugees	?	2. Raise tax on wealthy; lower others	N

GEREN, PRESTON (continued)

3. Investigate Reagan hostage delay	N	27. Suspend aid to Angolan rebels	N
4. Campaign finance revisions	Y	28. Democratic tax plan proposals	N
5. Unpaid leave to care for children	N	29. Cut defense 5% across the board	N
6. Restrict NEA use of funds	Y	30. Textile import quotas-veto override	N
7. Bar race-bias claim/habeas corpus	Y	31. Abortion service for military abroad	Y
8. Ban race as death sentence factor	Y	32. Limits on high income farmers	N
9. Exceptions to exclusionary rule	Y	33. Family medical leave-veto override	N
10. Allow sale of assault weapons	Y	34. Req submission of balanced budget	Y
11. Life in prison/abolish death penalty	N	35. Balanced budget amendment	Y
12. Req conspiracy-price fixing cases	N	36. Amendment to ban flag desecration	Y
13. Unemployment benefits extension	Y	37. Reauthorize Amtrak-veto override	N
14. Tissue use of aborted fetuses	Y	38. Retraining aid for coal miners	Y
15. Bar replacement of union strikers	N	39. Suspend El Salvador military aid	N
16. Hold foreign aid at $15b for '92	Y	40. Expand child care aid/tax credit	Y
17. Restore space station funding	Y	41. Raise House salary/omit honoraria	N
18. Civil Rights Act of 1991	Y	42. Toughen oil-spill liability	N
19. Unlimited damages-discrimination	N	43. Restitution to Japanese interned	Y
20. Eliminate funds for supercollider	N	44. Protect Chinese & C.A. nationals	Y
21. Terminate SDI except for research	N	45. Abortion $ for rape/incest cases	Y
22. Req 7-day handgun waiting period	N	46. Allow religious schools to bar gays	Y
23. Provide $30b for failed S&Ls	Y	47. Bar broadcaster fairness doctrine	N
24. Allow use of force against Iraq	Y	48. Bar cap gains cut/reinstate IRA	N
25. Allow $15b in foreign aid for '91	N	49. Bar unions equal voice in pension	Y
26. Revise & extend legal immigration	N		

Presidential Support Score: 1991 - 49%   1990 - 44%

SARPALIUS, BILL -- Texas 13th District [Democrat]. Counties of Archer, Armstrong, Baylor, Briscoe, Carson, Childress, Clay, Collingsworth, Cottle, Dallam, Dickens, Donley, Floyd, Foard, Gray, Hall, Hansford, Hardeman, Hartley, Hemphill, Hutchinson, Kent, King, Knox, Lipscomb, Moore, Motley, Ochiltree, Oldham, Potter, Randall, Roberts, Sherman, Swisher, Wheeler, Wichita and Wilbarger. Prior Terms: 1989-92. Born: January 10, 1948; Los Angeles, CA. Education: Clarendon College (A.B.); Texas Tech University (M.A.). Occupation: Boys ranch staff member and agriculture teacher; state House Speaker district office manager; agribusiness executive; staff legislator (1981-88).

1. Protection to Haitian refugees	?	28. Democratic tax plan proposals	N
2. Raise tax on wealthy; lower others	N	29. Cut defense 5% across the board	N
3. Investigate Reagan hostage delay	Y	30. Textile import quotas-veto override	Y
4. Campaign finance revisions	N	31. Abortion service for military abroad	N
5. Unpaid leave to care for children	N	32. Limits on high income farmers	N
6. Restrict NEA use of funds	Y	33. Family medical leave-veto override	N
7. Bar race-bias claim/habeas corpus	Y	34. Req submission of balanced budget	Y
8. Ban race as death sentence factor	Y	35. Balanced budget amendment	Y
9. Exceptions to exclusionary rule	Y	36. Amendment to ban flag desecration	Y
10. Allow sale of assault weapons	Y	37. Reauthorize Amtrak-veto override	Y
11. Life in prison/abolish death penalty	N	38. Retraining aid for coal miners	Y
12. Req conspiracy-price fixing cases	Y	39. Suspend El Salvador military aid	N
13. Unemployment benefits extension	N	40. Expand child care aid/tax credit	?
14. Tissue use of aborted fetuses	Y	41. Raise House salary/omit honoraria	N
15. Bar replacement of union strikers	Y	42. Toughen oil-spill liability	N
16. Hold foreign aid at $15b for '92	N	43. Restitution to Japanese interned	N
17. Restore space station funding	Y	44. Protect Chinese & C.A. nationals	Y
18. Civil Rights Act of 1991	Y	45. Abortion $ for rape/incest cases	N
19. Unlimited damages-discrimination	N	46. Allow religious schools to bar gays	Y
20. Eliminate funds for supercollider	N	47. Bar broadcaster fairness doctrine	Y
21. Terminate SDI except for research	N	48. Bar cap gains cut/reinstate IRA	Y
22. Req 7-day handgun waiting period	N	49. Bar unions equal voice in pension	Y
23. Provide $30b for failed S&Ls	Y	50. Bar assembly of chemical weapons	N
24. Allow use of force against Iraq	Y	51. Ban plutonium/uranium production	N
25. Allow $15b in foreign aid for '91	N	52. Cap MX missile deployment at 50	Y
26. Revise & extend legal immigration	N	53. Allow $3b for 2 stealth bombers	Y
27. Suspend aid to Angolan rebels	N	54. Publish bio-warfare experiments	N

SARPALIUS, BILL (continued)

55. Raise minimum wage-veto override	N	57. Cut defense and raise domestic $	N
56. Bar transfer of FS-X technology	N	58. Uniform poll closing in 48 states	Y

Presidential Support Score: 1991 - 58%   1990 - 48%

LAUGHLIN, GREG -- Texas 14th District [Democrat]. Counties of Aransas, Austin, Bee, Brazoria (pt.), Burleson, Calhoun, Colorado, DeWitt, Fayette, Goliad, Gonzales (pt.), Guadalupe, Jackson, Lavaca, Lee, Matagorda, Refugio, Victoria, Waller, Washington, Wharton and Williamson (pt.). Prior Terms: 1989-92. Born: January 21, 1942; Bay City, TX. Education: Texas A&M University (B.A.); University of Texas (LL.B.). Military Service: U.S. Army and Army Reserves. Occupation: Harris County assistant district attorney (1970-74); lawyer; real estate, oil and gas investment.

1. Protection to Haitian refugees	?	30. Textile import quotas-veto override	Y
2. Raise tax on wealthy; lower others	Y	31. Abortion service for military abroad	N
3. Investigate Reagan hostage delay	Y	32. Limits on high income farmers	N
4. Campaign finance revisions	Y	33. Family medical leave-veto override	N
5. Unpaid leave to care for children	N	34. Req submission of balanced budget	Y
6. Restrict NEA use of funds	Y	35. Balanced budget amendment	Y
7. Bar race-bias claim/habeas corpus	Y	36. Amendment to ban flag desecration	Y
8. Ban race as death sentence factor	Y	37. Reauthorize Amtrak-veto override	Y
9. Exceptions to exclusionary rule	Y	38. Retraining aid for coal miners	Y
10. Allow sale of assault weapons	Y	39. Suspend El Salvador military aid	N
11. Life in prison/abolish death penalty	N	40. Expand child care aid/tax credit	?
12. Req conspiracy-price fixing cases	N	41. Raise House salary/omit honoraria	N
13. Unemployment benefits extension	N	42. Toughen oil-spill liability	N
14. Tissue use of aborted fetuses	Y	43. Restitution to Japanese interned	N
15. Bar replacement of union strikers	Y	44. Protect Chinese & C.A. nationals	N
16. Hold foreign aid at $15b for '92	Y	45. Abortion $ for rape/incest cases	N
17. Restore space station funding	Y	46. Allow religious schools to bar gays	Y
18. Civil Rights Act of 1991	Y	47. Bar broadcaster fairness doctrine	N
19. Unlimited damages-discrimination	N	48. Bar cap gains cut/reinstate IRA	N
20. Eliminate funds for supercollider	N	49. Bar unions equal voice in pension	Y
21. Terminate SDI except for research	N	50. Bar assembly of chemical weapons	N
22. Req 7-day handgun waiting period	N	51. Ban plutonium/uranium production	Y
23. Provide $30b for failed S&Ls	Y	52. Cap MX missile deployment at 50	Y
24. Allow use of force against Iraq	Y	53. Allow $3b for 2 stealth bombers	Y
25. Allow $15b in foreign aid for '91	?	54. Publish bio-warfare experiments	N
26. Revise & extend legal immigration	N	55. Raise minimum wage-veto override	?
27. Suspend aid to Angolan rebels	N	56. Bar transfer of FS-X technology	N
28. Democratic tax plan proposals	N	57. Cut defense and raise domestic $	N
29. Cut defense 5% across the board	N	58. Uniform poll closing in 48 states	N

Presidential Support Score: 1991 - 49%   1990 - 47%

de la GARZA, E. (Kika) -- Texas 15th District [Democrat]. Counties of Atascosa, Brooks, Duval, Frio, Gonzales (pt.), Hidalgo, Jim Hogg, Jim Wells, Karnes, LaSalle, Live Oak, McMullen, Nueces (pt.), San Patricio, Starr, Wilson and Zapata. Prior Terms: 1963-92. Born: September 22, 1927; Mercedes, TX. Education: Edinburg Junior College; St. Mary's University (LL.B., J.D.). Military Service: U.S. Navy, WW II; U.S. Army, 1950-52. Occupation: Attorney; Texas representative.

1. Protection to Haitian refugees	?	11. Life in prison/abolish death penalty	N
2. Raise tax on wealthy; lower others	#	12. Req conspiracy-price fixing cases	N
3. Investigate Reagan hostage delay	Y	13. Unemployment benefits extension	Y
4. Campaign finance revisions	Y	14. Tissue use of aborted fetuses	Y
5. Unpaid leave to care for children	Y	15. Bar replacement of union strikers	Y
6. Restrict NEA use of funds	N	16. Hold foreign aid at $15b for '92	Y
7. Bar race-bias claim/habeas corpus	Y	17. Restore space station funding	Y
8. Ban race as death sentence factor	N	18. Civil Rights Act of 1991	Y
9. Exceptions to exclusionary rule	N	19. Unlimited damages-discrimination	Y
10. Allow sale of assault weapons	Y	20. Eliminate funds for supercollider	?

de la GARZA, E. (continued)

21. Terminate SDI except for research	N	
22. Req 7-day handgun waiting period	N	
23. Provide $30b for failed S&Ls	Y	
24. Allow use of force against Iraq	Y	
25. Allow $15b in foreign aid for '91	Y	
26. Revise & extend legal immigration	Y	
27. Suspend aid to Angolan rebels	?	
28. Democratic tax plan proposals	Y	
29. Cut defense 5% across the board	N	
30. Textile import quotas-veto override	Y	
31. Abortion service for military abroad	N	
32. Limits on high income farmers	N	
33. Family medical leave-veto override	Y	
34. Req submission of balanced budget	Y	
35. Balanced budget amendment	Y	
36. Amendment to ban flag desecration	Y	
37. Reauthorize Amtrak-veto override	Y	
38. Retraining aid for coal miners	Y	
39. Suspend El Salvador military aid	Y	
40. Expand child care aid/tax credit	Y	
41. Raise House salary/omit honoraria	Y	
42. Toughen oil-spill liability	N	
43. Restitution to Japanese interned	Y	
44. Protect Chinese & C.A. nationals	?	
45. Abortion $ for rape/incest cases	N	
46. Allow religious schools to bar gays	?	
47. Bar broadcaster fairness doctrine	?	
48. Bar cap gains cut/reinstate IRA	Y	
49. Bar unions equal voice in pension	?	
50. Bar assembly of chemical weapons	N	
51. Ban plutonium/uranium production	?	
52. Cap MX missile deployment at 50	Y	
53. Allow $3b for 2 stealth bombers	Y	
54. Publish bio-warfare experiments	N	
55. Raise minimum wage-veto override	Y	
56. Bar transfer of FS-X technology	Y	
57. Cut defense and raise domestic $	N	
58. Uniform poll closing in 48 states	?	
59. Req foreign investment disclosure	Y	
60. Textile import quotas-veto override	Y	
61. Bar abortion funding in Wash, DC	N	
62. Notify spouses of AIDS+ carriers	N	
63. Seize conveyance-drug trafficking	?	
64. South Africa sanctions	Y	
65. 60 days' notice of plant closings	Y	
66. Close unneeded military bases	N	
67. Keep welfare reform within $2.8b	N	
68. Allow children housing exclusion	N	
69. Shift $400m of NASA to homeless	Y	
70. Cap Medicare patients' liability	Y	
71. Prohibit employee polygraph testing	N	
72. Allow CIA to fund Contras	N	
73. Revise unfair trade practices	Y	
74. Focus SDI on accidental launch	N	
75. Bar Air Force $ for MX missile	N	
76. Allow "real" increase in defense	?	
77. Troop reduction in Europe of 50%	?	
78. Ban nuclear tests above 1 kiloton	?	
79. Ban anti-satellite missile tests	?	
80. Observe certain limits of SALT II	Y	
81. Restore four Civil Rights laws	Y	
82. Prohibit aliens as strikebreakers	N	

83. Allow military malpractice suits	?	
84. Approval of $36m in Contra aid	N	
85. $18b deficit reduction compromise	Y	
86. Welfare reform of $5.7b for 5 years	Y	
87. Raise taxes $12b/cut spending $3b	Y	
88. Board to assess occupational risk	Y	
89. Balanced budget by '93-via targets	?	
90. Bar licensing of two nuclear plants	N	
91. Remove victims compensation cap	Y	
92. Catastrophic health insurance	Y	
93. Ban airline smoking-2 hours or less	N	
94. $1b/two year aid for the homeless	Y	
95. Bar non-unions in union companies	Y	
96. Increase FSLIC rescue to $15b	N	
97. Impose quotas to lower trade deficit	Y	
98. Reduce discretionary budget 21%	N	
99. Immigration reform/alien amnesty	N	
100. South Africa sanctions-veto override	Y	
101. Tax overhaul to revise income tax	N	
102. Use of military in drug war	Y	
103. Delete 12 MX/add conventional wpn	N	
104. Raise speed limit to 65 mph	Y	
105. Require Pentagon to buy US goods	Y	
106. AIDS insurance non-discrimination	Y	
107. Prohibit Saudi arms sales	Y	
108. Ease Gun Control Act of 1968	Y	
109. Bar interstate handgun transport	N	
110. Make company emissions known	Y	
111. Allow toxic victims to sue in fed ct	N	
112. Superfund waste cleanup of $10b	N	
113. 90 days notice of plant closings	Y	
114. $20b in Medicare cuts/tax increases	Y	
115. Spending cuts and tax increases	Y	
116. Set school lunch lmt-250% poverty	N	
117. $75m for youth work projects	Y	
118. Allow Angolan military assistance	N	
119. Suspend defense payments for abuse	N	
120. Drop SS COLAs/$12b tax increase	N	
121. Approve $1.5b for 21 MX missiles	Y	
122. Emergency farm credit/revisions	Y	
123. Duty on Taiwan/Hong Kong/S Korea	N	
124. Limit steel imports to 17%	Y	
125. Cut $ to schools that bar prayer	N	
126. $50b-taxes; cut Medicare/spending	N	
127. Limit Pershing II/cruise in Europe	N	
128. Delete $7.1b for 34 B-1 bombers	N	
129. Bar purchase of Sergeant York guns	N	
130. El Salvador military/economic aid	Y	
131. Bar mining of Nicaraguan waters	Y	
132. Physician fee freeze for Medicare	N	
133. $49b in "sin"/phone/insurance taxes	Y	
134. Allow sale of Conrail	N	
135. Equal Rights Amendment	Y	
136. Authorize Marines in Lebanon	Y	
137. Eminent domain for coal companies	Y	
138. Prohibit EPA clean air sanctions	N	
139. SS retirement age increase/reforms	N	
140. Auto domestic content requirement	N	
141. Delete jobs program funding	N	
142. Highway-gas tax bill	Y	
143. Cut $5b from defense for Medicare	Y	
144. Emergency housing aid of $1b	Y	

Presidential Support Score: 1991 - 38%   1990 - 24%

COLEMAN, RONALD D. -- Texas 16th District [Democrat]. Counties of Culberson, El Paso, Hudspeth, Jeff Davis, Loving, Reeves, Ward and Winkler. Prior Terms: 1983-92. Born: November 29, 1941; El Paso, TX. Education: University of Texas (B.A., J.D.). Military Service: U.S. Army, 1967-69. Occupation: Attorney; teacher (1967); first assistant county attorney (1971); Texas legislator (1973-82).

1.	Protection to Haitian refugees	?	60.	Textile import quotas-veto override	Y
2.	Raise tax on wealthy; lower others	Y	61.	Bar abortion funding in Wash, DC	N
3.	Investigate Reagan hostage delay	?	62.	Notify spouses of AIDS+ carriers	N
4.	Campaign finance revisions	Y	63.	Seize conveyance-drug trafficking	?
5.	Unpaid leave to care for children	Y	64.	South Africa sanctions	Y
6.	Restrict NEA use of funds	N	65.	60 days' notice of plant closings	Y
7.	Bar race-bias claim/habeas corpus	N	66.	Close unneeded military bases	N
8.	Ban race as death sentence factor	N	67.	Keep welfare reform within $2.8b	N
9.	Exceptions to exclusionary rule	N	68.	Allow children housing exclusion	N
10.	Allow sale of assault weapons	Y	69.	Shift $400m of NASA to homeless	N
11.	Life in prison/abolish death penalty	N	70.	Cap Medicare patients' liability	Y
12.	Req conspiracy-price fixing cases	N	71.	Prohibit employee polygraph testing	Y
13.	Unemployment benefits extension	Y	72.	Allow CIA to fund Contras	X
14.	Tissue use of aborted fetuses	Y	73.	Revise unfair trade practices	Y
15.	Bar replacement of union strikers	Y	74.	Focus SDI on accidental launch	Y
16.	Hold foreign aid at $15b for '92	Y	75.	Bar Air Force $ for MX missile	N
17.	Restore space station funding	Y	76.	Allow "real" increase in defense	Y
18.	Civil Rights Act of 1991	Y	77.	Troop reduction in Europe of 50%	N
19.	Unlimited damages-discrimination	Y	78.	Ban nuclear tests above 1 kiloton	Y
20.	Eliminate funds for supercollider	N	79.	Ban anti-satellite missile tests	N
21.	Terminate SDI except for research	N	80.	Observe certain limits of SALT II	Y
22.	Req 7-day handgun waiting period	N	81.	Restore four Civil Rights laws	Y
23.	Provide $30b for failed S&Ls	Y	82.	Prohibit aliens as strikebreakers	Y
24.	Allow use of force against Iraq	N	83.	Allow military malpractice suits	Y
25.	Allow $15b in foreign aid for '91	Y	84.	Approval of $36m in Contra aid	N
26.	Revise & extend legal immigration	Y	85.	$18b deficit reduction compromise	N
27.	Suspend aid to Angolan rebels	Y	86.	Welfare reform of $5.7b for 5 years	Y
28.	Democratic tax plan proposals	Y	87.	Raise taxes $12b/cut spending $3b	Y
29.	Cut defense 5% across the board	N	88.	Board to assess occupational risk	Y
30.	Textile import quotas-veto override	Y	89.	Balanced budget by '93-via targets	N
31.	Abortion service for military abroad	Y	90.	Bar licensing of two nuclear plants	N
32.	Limits on high income farmers	N	91.	Remove victims compensation cap	N
33.	Family medical leave-veto override	Y	92.	Catastrophic health insurance	Y
34.	Req submission of balanced budget	Y	93.	Ban airline smoking-2 hours or less	Y
35.	Balanced budget amendment	Y	94.	$1b/two year aid for the homeless	Y
36.	Amendment to ban flag desecration	N	95.	Bar non-unions in union companies	Y
37.	Reauthorize Amtrak-veto override	?	96.	Increase FSLIC rescue to $15b	Y
38.	Retraining aid for coal miners	Y	97.	Impose quotas to lower trade deficit	Y
39.	Suspend El Salvador military aid	Y	98.	Reduce discretionary budget 21%	N
40.	Expand child care aid/tax credit	Y	99.	Immigration reform/alien amnesty	N
41.	Raise House salary/omit honoraria	N	100.	South Africa sanctions-veto override	Y
42.	Toughen oil-spill liability	Y	101.	Tax overhaul to revise income tax	N
43.	Restitution to Japanese interned	Y	102.	Use of military in drug war	Y
44.	Protect Chinese & C.A. nationals	Y	103.	Delete 12 MX/add conventional wpn	Y
45.	Abortion $ for rape/incest cases	Y	104.	Raise speed limit to 65 mph	Y
46.	Allow religious schools to bar gays	N	105.	Require Pentagon to buy US goods	Y
47.	Bar broadcaster fairness doctrine	N	106.	AIDS insurance non-discrimination	Y
48.	Bar cap gains cut/reinstate IRA	Y	107.	Prohibit Saudi arms sales	Y
49.	Bar unions equal voice in pension	Y	108.	Ease Gun Control Act of 1968	Y
50.	Bar assembly of chemical weapons	Y	109.	Bar interstate handgun transport	N
51.	Ban plutonium/uranium production	Y	110.	Make company emissions known	Y
52.	Cap MX missile deployment at 50	Y	111.	Allow toxic victims to sue in fed ct	Y
53.	Allow $3b for 2 stealth bombers	N	112.	Superfund waste cleanup of $10b	N
54.	Publish bio-warfare experiments	Y	113.	90 days notice of plant closings	Y
55.	Raise minimum wage-veto override	Y	114.	$20b in Medicare cuts/tax increases	Y
56.	Bar transfer of FS-X technology	Y	115.	Spending cuts and tax increases	Y
57.	Cut defense and raise domestic $	N	116.	Set school lunch lmt-250% poverty	N
58.	Uniform poll closing in 48 states	Y	117.	$75m for youth work projects	Y
59.	Req foreign investment disclosure	Y	118.	Allow Angolan military assistance	N

COLEMAN, RONALD D. (continued)

119. Suspend defense payments for abuse	Y	
120. Drop SS COLAs/$12b tax increase	N	
121. Approve $1.5b for 21 MX missiles	N	
122. Emergency farm credit/revisions	Y	
123. Duty on Taiwan/Hong Kong/S Korea	N	
124. Limit steel imports to 17%	?	
125. Cut $ to schools that bar prayer	N	
126. $50b-taxes; cut Medicare/spending	N	
127. Limit Pershing II/cruise in Europe	N	
128. Delete $7.1b for 34 B-1 bombers	N	
129. Bar purchase of Sergeant York guns	N	
130. El Salvador military/economic aid	Y	
131. Bar mining of Nicaraguan waters	Y	
132. Physician fee freeze for Medicare	N	
133. $49b in "sin"/phone/insurance taxes	N	
134. Allow sale of Conrail	N	
135. Equal Rights Amendment	Y	
136. Authorize Marines in Lebanon	Y	
137. Eminent domain for coal companies	N	
138. Prohibit EPA clean air sanctions	Y	
139. SS retirement age increase/reforms	Y	

Presidential Support Score: 1991 - 34%   1990 - 20%

STENHOLM, CHARLES W. -- Texas 17th District [Democrat].

Counties of Borden, Callahan, Coke, Coleman, Comanche, Concho, Cooks (pt.), Crosby, Eastland, Erath, Fisher, Garza, Glasscock, Haskell, Howard, Jack, Jones, Lynn, Martin, Mitchell, Montague, Nolan, Palo Pinto, Parker, Runnels, Scurry, Shackleford, Somervell, Stephens, Sterling, Stonewall, Taylor, Throckmorton, Wise and Young. Prior Terms: 1979-92. Born: October 26, 1938; Stamford, TX. Education: Tarleton Junior College; Texas Tech University (B.S., M.S.). Occupation: Teacher (1962-65); partner, L. W. Stenholm & Son Farms (1961-69); executive vice president, Rolling Plains Cotton Growers; general manager, Stamford Electric Cooperative; owner-manager, Stenholm Farms (1969-76); manager, Watson Farms (1976-78); president, Double S. Farms, Inc. (1976-78); director, First National Bank of Stamford (1975-78).

1. Protection to Haitian refugees	N	
2. Raise tax on wealthy; lower others	Y	
3. Investigate Reagan hostage delay	N	
4. Campaign finance revisions	Y	
5. Unpaid leave to care for children	N	
6. Restrict NEA use of funds	Y	
7. Bar race-bias claim/habeas corpus	Y	
8. Ban race as death sentence factor	Y	
9. Exceptions to exclusionary rule	Y	
10. Allow sale of assault weapons	Y	
11. Life in prison/abolish death penalty	N	
12. Req conspiracy-price fixing cases	Y	
13. Unemployment benefits extension	N	
14. Tissue use of aborted fetuses	Y	
15. Bar replacement of union strikers	N	
16. Hold foreign aid at $15b for '92	Y	
17. Restore space station funding	Y	
18. Civil Rights Act of 1991	N	
19. Unlimited damages-discrimination	N	
20. Eliminate funds for supercollider	N	
21. Terminate SDI except for research	N	
22. Req 7-day handgun waiting period	Y	
23. Provide $30b for failed S&Ls	Y	
24. Allow use of force against Iraq	Y	
25. Allow $15b in foreign aid for '91	Y	
26. Revise & extend legal immigration	N	
27. Suspend aid to Angolan rebels	N	
28. Democratic tax plan proposals	Y	
29. Cut defense 5% across the board	N	
30. Textile import quotas-veto override	Y	
31. Abortion service for military abroad	N	
32. Limits on high income farmers	N	
33. Family medical leave-veto override	N	
34. Req submission of balanced budget	Y	
35. Balanced budget amendment	Y	
36. Amendment to ban flag desecration	N	
37. Reauthorize Amtrak-veto override	Y	
38. Retraining aid for coal miners	N	
39. Suspend El Salvador military aid	N	
40. Expand child care aid/tax credit	N	
41. Raise House salary/omit honoraria	Y	
42. Toughen oil-spill liability	?	
43. Restitution to Japanese interned	N	
44. Protect Chinese & C.A. nationals	N	
45. Abortion $ for rape/incest cases	N	
46. Allow religious schools to bar gays	Y	
47. Bar broadcaster fairness doctrine	Y	
48. Bar cap gains cut/reinstate IRA	Y	
49. Bar unions equal voice in pension	Y	
50. Bar assembly of chemical weapons	N	
51. Ban plutonium/uranium production	Y	
52. Cap MX missile deployment at 50	N	
53. Allow $3b for 2 stealth bombers	Y	
54. Publish bio-warfare experiments	N	
55. Raise minimum wage-veto override	N	
56. Bar transfer of FS-X technology	N	
57. Cut defense and raise domestic $	N	
58. Uniform poll closing in 48 states	?	
59. Req foreign investment disclosure	Y	
60. Textile import quotas-veto override	Y	
61. Bar abortion funding in Wash, DC	Y	
62. Notify spouses of AIDS+ carriers	Y	
63. Seize conveyance-drug trafficking	Y	
64. South Africa sanctions	?	
65. 60 days' notice of plant closings	N	
66. Close unneeded military bases	N	
67. Keep welfare reform within $2.8b	Y	
68. Allow children housing exclusion	N	
69. Shift $400m of NASA to homeless	N	
70. Cap Medicare patients' liability	N	
71. Prohibit employee polygraph testing	N	
72. Allow CIA to fund Contras	Y	
73. Revise unfair trade practices	N	
74. Focus SDI on accidental launch	N	

STENHOLM, CHARLES W. (continued)

75. Bar Air Force $ for MX missile	N	110. Make company emissions known	N
76. Allow "real" increase in defense	Y	111. Allow toxic victims to sue in fed ct	N
77. Troop reduction in Europe of 50%	N	112. Superfund waste cleanup of $10b	N
78. Ban nuclear tests above 1 kiloton	N	113. 90 days notice of plant closings	N
79. Ban anti-satellite missile tests	N	114. $20b in Medicare cuts/tax increases	Y
80. Observe certain limits of SALT II	N	115. Spending cuts and tax increases	Y
81. Restore four Civil Rights laws	N	116. Set school lunch lmt-250% poverty	Y
82. Prohibit aliens as strikebreakers	N	117. $75m for youth work projects	N
83. Allow military malpractice suits	N	118. Allow Angolan military assistance	Y
84. Approval of $36m in Contra aid	Y	119. Suspend defense payments for abuse	N
85. $18b deficit reduction compromise	Y	120. Drop SS COLAs/$12b tax increase	Y
86. Welfare reform of $5.7b for 5 years	N	121. Approve $1.5b for 21 MX missiles	Y
87. Raise taxes $12b/cut spending $3b	N	122. Emergency farm credit/revisions	Y
88. Board to assess occupational risk	N	123. Duty on Taiwan/Hong Kong/S Korea	N
89. Balanced budget by '93-via targets	Y	124. Limit steel imports to 17%	N
90. Bar licensing of two nuclear plants	N	125. Cut $ to schools that bar prayer	Y
91. Remove victims compensation cap	N	126. $50b-taxes; cut Medicare/spending	Y
92. Catastrophic health insurance	N	127. Limit Pershing II/cruise in Europe	N
93. Ban airline smoking-2 hours or less	Y	128. Delete $7.1b for 34 B-1 bombers	N
94. $1b/two year aid for the homeless	N	129. Bar purchase of Sergeant York guns	N
95. Bar non-unions in union companies	N	130. El Salvador military/economic aid	Y
96. Increase FSLIC rescue to $15b	Y	131. Bar mining of Nicaraguan waters	N
97. Impose quotas to lower trade deficit	N	132. Physician fee freeze for Medicare	Y
98. Reduce discretionary budget 21%	Y	133. $49b in "sin"/phone/insurance taxes	Y
99. Immigration reform/alien amnesty	N	134. Allow sale of Conrail	Y
100. South Africa sanctions-veto override	N	135. Equal Rights Amendment	N
101. Tax overhaul to revise income tax	N	136. Authorize Marines in Lebanon	N
102. Use of military in drug war	Y	137. Eminent domain for coal companies	Y
103. Delete 12 MX/add conventional wpn	N	138. Prohibit EPA clean air sanctions	Y
104. Raise speed limit to 65 mph	Y	139. SS retirement age increase/reforms	Y
105. Require Pentagon to buy US goods	N	140. Auto domestic content requirement	N
106. AIDS insurance non-discrimination	N	141. Delete jobs program funding	Y
107. Prohibit Saudi arms sales	Y	142. Highway-gas tax bill	N
108. Ease Gun Control Act of 1968	Y	143. Cut $5b from defense for Medicare	N
109. Bar interstate handgun transport	N	144. Emergency housing aid of $1b	N

Presidential Support Score: 1991 - 66%   1990 - 56%

WASHINGTON, CRAIG A. -- Texas 18th District [Democrat]. County of Harris (pt.). Prior Terms: 1990 (Special Election)-1992. Born: October 12, 1941; Longview, TX. Education: Prairie View A&M University; Texas Southern University. Occupation: Criminal defense lawyer; state representative (1973-82) and senator (1983-90).

1. Protection to Haitian refugees	Y	20. Eliminate funds for supercollider	N
2. Raise tax on wealthy; lower others	Y	21. Terminate SDI except for research	?
3. Investigate Reagan hostage delay	Y	22. Req 7-day handgun waiting period	Y
4. Campaign finance revisions	Y	23. Provide $30b for failed S&Ls	N
5. Unpaid leave to care for children	Y	24. Allow use of force against Iraq	N
6. Restrict NEA use of funds	N	25. Allow $15b in foreign aid for '91	Y
7. Bar race-bias claim/habeas corpus	N	26. Revise & extend legal immigration	Y
8. Ban race as death sentence factor	N	27. Suspend aid to Angolan rebels	Y
9. Exceptions to exclusionary rule	N	28. Democratic tax plan proposals	Y
10. Allow sale of assault weapons	N	29. Cut defense 5% across the board	Y
11. Life in prison/abolish death penalty	Y	30. Textile import quotas-veto override	Y
12. Req conspiracy-price fixing cases	?	31. Abortion service for military abroad	Y
13. Unemployment benefits extension	Y	32. Limits on high income farmers	N
14. Tissue use of aborted fetuses	Y	33. Family medical leave-veto override	?
15. Bar replacement of union strikers	Y	34. Req submission of balanced budget	Y
16. Hold foreign aid at $15b for '92	Y	35. Balanced budget amendment	N
17. Restore space station funding	N	36. Amendment to ban flag desecration	N
18. Civil Rights Act of 1991	Y	37. Reauthorize Amtrak-veto override	Y
19. Unlimited damages-discrimination	Y	38. Retraining aid for coal miners	Y

WASHINGTON, CRAIG A. (continued)

39. Suspend El Salvador military aid	Y	40. Expand child care aid/tax credit	Y

Presidential Support Score: 1991 - 23% 1990 - 12%

COMBEST, LARRY -- Texas 19th District [Republican]. Counties of Andrews, Bailey, Castro, Cochran, Dawson, Deaf Smith, Ector, Gaines, Hale, Hockley, Lamb, Lubbock, Parmer, Terry and Yoakum. Prior Terms: 1985-92. Born: March 20, 1945; Memphis, TX. Education: West Texas State University. Occupation: Owner and operator wholesale electrical distributing company; legislative assistant (1971-78); rancher; wholesale oil business.

1. Protection to Haitian refugees	N	53. Allow $3b for 2 stealth bombers	Y
2. Raise tax on wealthy; lower others	N	54. Publish bio-warfare experiments	N
3. Investigate Reagan hostage delay	N	55. Raise minimum wage-veto override	N
4. Campaign finance revisions	N	56. Bar transfer of FS-X technology	N
5. Unpaid leave to care for children	N	57. Cut defense and raise domestic $	N
6. Restrict NEA use of funds	Y	58. Uniform poll closing in 48 states	N
7. Bar race-bias claim/habeas corpus	Y	59. Req foreign investment disclosure	N
8. Ban race as death sentence factor	Y	60. Textile import quotas-veto override	Y
9. Exceptions to exclusionary rule	Y	61. Bar abortion funding in Wash, DC	Y
10. Allow sale of assault weapons	Y	62. Notify spouses of AIDS+ carriers	Y
11. Life in prison/abolish death penalty	N	63. Seize conveyance-drug trafficking	Y
12. Req conspiracy-price fixing cases	Y	64. South Africa sanctions	N
13. Unemployment benefits extension	N	65. 60 days' notice of plant closings	N
14. Tissue use of aborted fetuses	N	66. Close unneeded military bases	N
15. Bar replacement of union strikers	N	67. Keep welfare reform within $2.8b	Y
16. Hold foreign aid at $15b for '92	N	68. Allow children housing exclusion	Y
17. Restore space station funding	Y	69. Shift $400m of NASA to homeless	N
18. Civil Rights Act of 1991	N	70. Cap Medicare patients' liability	N
19. Unlimited damages-discrimination	N	71. Prohibit employee polygraph testing	N
20. Eliminate funds for supercollider	N	72. Allow CIA to fund Contras	Y
21. Terminate SDI except for research	N	73. Revise unfair trade practices	Y
22. Req 7-day handgun waiting period	N	74. Focus SDI on accidental launch	N
23. Provide $30b for failed S&Ls	Y	75. Bar Air Force $ for MX missile	N
24. Allow use of force against Iraq	Y	76. Allow "real" increase in defense	Y
25. Allow $15b in foreign aid for '91	N	77. Troop reduction in Europe of 50%	N
26. Revise & extend legal immigration	N	78. Ban nuclear tests above 1 kiloton	N
27. Suspend aid to Angolan rebels	N	79. Ban anti-satellite missile tests	N
28. Democratic tax plan proposals	N	80. Observe certain limits of SALT II	N
29. Cut defense 5% across the board	N	81. Restore four Civil Rights laws	N
30. Textile import quotas-veto override	Y	82. Prohibit aliens as strikebreakers	Y
31. Abortion service for military abroad	N	83. Allow military malpractice suits	N
32. Limits on high income farmers	N	84. Approval of $36m in Contra aid	Y
33. Family medical leave-veto override	N	85. $18b deficit reduction compromise	N
34. Req submission of balanced budget	N	86. Welfare reform of $5.7b for 5 years	N
35. Balanced budget amendment	Y	87. Raise taxes $12b/cut spending $3b	N
36. Amendment to ban flag desecration	Y	88. Board to assess occupational risk	N
37. Reauthorize Amtrak-veto override	N	89. Balanced budget by '93-via targets	Y
38. Retraining aid for coal miners	N	90. Bar licensing of two nuclear plants	N
39. Suspend El Salvador military aid	N	91. Remove victims compensation cap	N
40. Expand child care aid/tax credit	N	92. Catastrophic health insurance	N
41. Raise House salary/omit honoraria	N	93. Ban airline smoking-2 hours or less	N
42. Toughen oil-spill liability	N	94. $1b/two year aid for the homeless	N
43. Restitution to Japanese interned	N	95. Bar non-unions in union companies	N
44. Protect Chinese & C.A. nationals	N	96. Increase FSLIC rescue to $15b	+
45. Abortion $ for rape/incest cases	N	97. Impose quotas to lower trade deficit	N
46. Allow religious schools to bar gays	Y	98. Reduce discretionary budget 21%	Y
47. Bar broadcaster fairness doctrine	Y	99. Immigration reform/alien amnesty	N
48. Bar cap gains cut/reinstate IRA	N	100. South Africa sanctions-veto override	N
49. Bar unions equal voice in pension	Y	101. Tax overhaul to revise income tax	N
50. Bar assembly of chemical weapons	N	102. Use of military in drug war	Y
51. Ban plutonium/uranium production	N	103. Delete 12 MX/add conventional wpn	N
52. Cap MX missile deployment at 50	N	104. Raise speed limit to 65 mph	Y

COMBEST, LARRY (continued)

105. Require Pentagon to buy US goods	N	114. $20b in Medicare cuts/tax increases	N
106. AIDS insurance non-discrimination	N	115. Spending cuts and tax increases	N
107. Prohibit Saudi arms sales	N	116. Set school lunch lmt-250% poverty	Y
108. Ease Gun Control Act of 1968	Y	117. $75m for youth work projects	N
109. Bar interstate handgun transport	N	118. Allow Angolan military assistance	Y
110. Make company emissions known	N	119. Suspend defense payments for abuse	N
111. Allow toxic victims to sue in fed ct	N	120. Drop SS COLAs/$12b tax increase	N
112. Superfund waste cleanup of $10b	N	121. Approve $1.5b for 21 MX missiles	Y
113. 90 days notice of plant closings	N	122. Emergency farm credit/revisions	Y

Presidential Support Score: 1991 - 77%   1990 - 78%

GONZALEZ, HENRY B. -- Texas 20th District [Democrat].   County of Bexar (pt.).   Prior Terms: 1961 (Special Election)-1992. Born: May 3, 1916; San Antonio, TX.   Education: San Antonio College; University of Texas; St. Mary's University Law School (LL.B.). Occupation: San Antonio city councilman; mayor pro tem; Bexar County chief probation officer; Texas senator (1956-61).

1. Protection to Haitian refugees	Y	46. Allow religious schools to bar gays	N
2. Raise tax on wealthy; lower others	Y	47. Bar broadcaster fairness doctrine	N
3. Investigate Reagan hostage delay	Y	48. Bar cap gains cut/reinstate IRA	Y
4. Campaign finance revisions	Y	49. Bar unions equal voice in pension	N
5. Unpaid leave to care for children	Y	50. Bar assembly of chemical weapons	Y
6. Restrict NEA use of funds	N	51. Ban plutonium/uranium production	Y
7. Bar race-bias claim/habeas corpus	Y	52. Cap MX missile deployment at 50	Y
8. Ban race as death sentence factor	N	53. Allow $3b for 2 stealth bombers	?
9. Exceptions to exclusionary rule	N	54. Publish bio-warfare experiments	Y
10. Allow sale of assault weapons	N	55. Raise minimum wage-veto override	Y
11. Life in prison/abolish death penalty	N	56. Bar transfer of FS-X technology	Y
12. Req conspiracy-price fixing cases	N	57. Cut defense and raise domestic $	Y
13. Unemployment benefits extension	Y	58. Uniform poll closing in 48 states	Y
14. Tissue use of aborted fetuses	Y	59. Req foreign investment disclosure	Y
15. Bar replacement of union strikers	Y	60. Textile import quotas-veto override	Y
16. Hold foreign aid at $15b for '92	N	61. Bar abortion funding in Wash, DC	N
17. Restore space station funding	N	62. Notify spouses of AIDS+ carriers	N
18. Civil Rights Act of 1991	Y	63. Seize conveyance-drug trafficking	N
19. Unlimited damages-discrimination	Y	64. South Africa sanctions	Y
20. Eliminate funds for supercollider	N	65. 60 days' notice of plant closings	Y
21. Terminate SDI except for research	Y	66. Close unneeded military bases	N
22. Req 7-day handgun waiting period	Y	67. Keep welfare reform within $2.8b	N
23. Provide $30b for failed S&Ls	Y	68. Allow children housing exclusion	N
24. Allow use of force against Iraq	N	69. Shift $400m of NASA to homeless	Y
25. Allow $15b in foreign aid for '91	Y	70. Cap Medicare patients' liability	Y
26. Revise & extend legal immigration	Y	71. Prohibit employee polygraph testing	Y
27. Suspend aid to Angolan rebels	Y	72. Allow CIA to fund Contras	N
28. Democratic tax plan proposals	Y	73. Revise unfair trade practices	Y
29. Cut defense 5% across the board	N	74. Focus SDI on accidental launch	Y
30. Textile import quotas-veto override	Y	75. Bar Air Force $ for MX missile	Y
31. Abortion service for military abroad	Y	76. Allow "real" increase in defense	N
32. Limits on high income farmers	N	77. Troop reduction in Europe of 50%	Y
33. Family medical leave-veto override	Y	78. Ban nuclear tests above 1 kiloton	Y
34. Req submission of balanced budget	N	79. Ban anti-satellite missile tests	Y
35. Balanced budget amendment	N	80. Observe certain limits of SALT II	Y
36. Amendment to ban flag desecration	N	81. Restore four Civil Rights laws	Y
37. Reauthorize Amtrak-veto override	Y	82. Prohibit aliens as strikebreakers	Y
38. Retraining aid for coal miners	Y	83. Allow military malpractice suits	Y
39. Suspend El Salvador military aid	Y	84. Approval of $36m in Contra aid	N
40. Expand child care aid/tax credit	Y	85. $18b deficit reduction compromise	N
41. Raise House salary/omit honoraria	Y	86. Welfare reform of $5.7b for 5 years	Y
42. Toughen oil-spill liability	Y	87. Raise taxes $12b/cut spending $3b	Y
43. Restitution to Japanese interned	Y	88. Board to assess occupational risk	Y
44. Protect Chinese & C.A. nationals	Y	89. Balanced budget by '93-via targets	N
45. Abortion $ for rape/incest cases	Y	90. Bar licensing of two nuclear plants	Y

GONZALEZ, HENRY B. (continued)

91. Remove victims compensation cap	Y	118. Allow Angolan military assistance	N
92. Catastrophic health insurance	Y	119. Suspend defense payments for abuse	N
93. Ban airline smoking-2 hours or less	N	120. Drop SS COLAs/$12b tax increase	N
94. $1b/two year aid for the homeless	Y	121. Approve $1.5b for 21 MX missiles	N
95. Bar non-unions in union companies	Y	122. Emergency farm credit/revisions	Y
96. Increase FSLIC rescue to $15b	Y	123. Duty on Taiwan/Hong Kong/S Korea	Y
97. Impose quotas to lower trade deficit	N	124. Limit steel imports to 17%	Y
98. Reduce discretionary budget 21%	N	125. Cut $ to schools that bar prayer	N
99. Immigration reform/alien amnesty	N	126. $50b-taxes; cut Medicare/spending	N
100. South Africa sanctions-veto override	Y	127. Limit Pershing II/cruise in Europe	Y
101. Tax overhaul to revise income tax	N	128. Delete $7.1b for 34 B-1 bombers	N
102. Use of military in drug war	N	129. Bar purchase of Sergeant York guns	N
103. Delete 12 MX/add conventional wpn	Y	130. El Salvador military/economic aid	N
104. Raise speed limit to 65 mph	N	131. Bar mining of Nicaraguan waters	Y
105. Require Pentagon to buy US goods	Y	132. Physician fee freeze for Medicare	N
106. AIDS insurance non-discrimination	Y	133. $49b in "sin"/phone/insurance taxes	N
107. Prohibit Saudi arms sales	Y	134. Allow sale of Conrail	N
108. Ease Gun Control Act of 1968	N	135. Equal Rights Amendment	Y
109. Bar interstate handgun transport	Y	136. Authorize Marines in Lebanon	N
110. Make company emissions known	Y	137. Eminent domain for coal companies	Y
111. Allow toxic victims to sue in fed ct	Y	138. Prohibit EPA clean air sanctions	Y
112. Superfund waste cleanup of $10b	Y	139. SS retirement age increase/reforms	N
113. 90 days notice of plant closings	Y	140. Auto domestic content requirement	Y
114. $20b in Medicare cuts/tax increases	N	141. Delete jobs program funding	N
115. Spending cuts and tax increases	Y	142. Highway-gas tax bill	N
116. Set school lunch lmt-250% poverty	N	143. Cut $5b from defense for Medicare	Y
117. $75m for youth work projects	Y	144. Emergency housing aid of $1b	Y

Presidential Support Score: 1991 - 32%   1990 - 15%

SMITH, LAMAR -- Texas 21st District [Republican]. Counties of Bandera, Bexar (pt.), Brewster, Comal, Crane, Crockett, Edwards, Gillespie, Irion, Kendall, Kerr, Kimble, Llano, McCulloch, Mason, Menard, Midland, Pecos, Presidio, Reagan, Real, Schneider, Sutton, Terrell, Tom Green, Upton and Val Verde. Prior Terms: 1987-92. Born: November 19, 1947; San Antonio, TX. Education: Yale University (B.A.); Southern Methodist University (J.D.). Occupation: Attorney; rancher; Bexar County Commissioner (1982-86) and Republican Party chairman; Small Business Administration employee; business and financial writer; state representative (1981-82).

1. Protection to Haitian refugees	N	25. Allow $15b in foreign aid for '91	N
2. Raise tax on wealthy; lower others	N	26. Revise & extend legal immigration	Y
3. Investigate Reagan hostage delay	N	27. Suspend aid to Angolan rebels	N
4. Campaign finance revisions	N	28. Democratic tax plan proposals	N
5. Unpaid leave to care for children	Y	29. Cut defense 5% across the board	N
6. Restrict NEA use of funds	Y	30. Textile import quotas-veto override	Y
7. Bar race-bias claim/habeas corpus	Y	31. Abortion service for military abroad	N
8. Ban race as death sentence factor	Y	32. Limits on high income farmers	N
9. Exceptions to exclusionary rule	Y	33. Family medical leave-veto override	Y
10. Allow sale of assault weapons	Y	34. Req submission of balanced budget	N
11. Life in prison/abolish death penalty	N	35. Balanced budget amendment	Y
12. Req conspiracy-price fixing cases	Y	36. Amendment to ban flag desecration	Y
13. Unemployment benefits extension	N	37. Reauthorize Amtrak-veto override	Y
14. Tissue use of aborted fetuses	Y	38. Retraining aid for coal miners	N
15. Bar replacement of union strikers	N	39. Suspend El Salvador military aid	N
16. Hold foreign aid at $15b for '92	Y	40. Expand child care aid/tax credit	N
17. Restore space station funding	Y	41. Raise House salary/omit honoraria	Y
18. Civil Rights Act of 1991	N	42. Toughen oil-spill liability	N
19. Unlimited damages-discrimination	N	43. Restitution to Japanese interned	?
20. Eliminate funds for supercollider	N	44. Protect Chinese & C.A. nationals	?
21. Terminate SDI except for research	N	45. Abortion $ for rape/incest cases	N
22. Req 7-day handgun waiting period	N	46. Allow religious schools to bar gays	Y
23. Provide $30b for failed S&Ls	Y	47. Bar broadcaster fairness doctrine	Y
24. Allow use of force against Iraq	Y	48. Bar cap gains cut/reinstate IRA	N

SMITH, LAMAR (continued)

49. Bar unions equal voice in pension	Y	
50. Bar assembly of chemical weapons	N	
51. Ban plutonium/uranium production	N	
52. Cap MX missile deployment at 50	N	
53. Allow $3b for 2 stealth bombers	Y	
54. Publish bio-warfare experiments	Y	
55. Raise minimum wage-veto override	N	
56. Bar transfer of FS-X technology	N	
57. Cut defense and raise domestic $	N	
58. Uniform poll closing in 48 states	N	
59. Req foreign investment disclosure	Y	
60. Textile import quotas-veto override	Y	
61. Bar abortion funding in Wash, DC	Y	
62. Notify spouses of AIDS+ carriers	Y	
63. Seize conveyance-drug trafficking	Y	
64. South Africa sanctions	N	
65. 60 days' notice of plant closings	N	
66. Close unneeded military bases	Y	
67. Keep welfare reform within $2.8b	Y	
68. Allow children housing exclusion	Y	
69. Shift $400m of NASA to homeless	N	
70. Cap Medicare patients' liability	N	
71. Prohibit employee polygraph testing	N	
72. Allow CIA to fund Contras	Y	
73. Revise unfair trade practices	N	

74. Focus SDI on accidental launch	N
75. Bar Air Force $ for MX missile	N
76. Allow "real" increase in defense	Y
77. Troop reduction in Europe of 50%	N
78. Ban nuclear tests above 1 kiloton	N
79. Ban anti-satellite missile tests	N
80. Observe certain limits of SALT II	N
81. Restore four Civil Rights laws	N
82. Prohibit aliens as strikebreakers	N
83. Allow military malpractice suits	Y
84. Approval of $36m in Contra aid	Y
85. $18b deficit reduction compromise	N
86. Welfare reform of $5.7b for 5 years	N
87. Raise taxes $12b/cut spending $3b	N
88. Board to assess occupational risk	N
89. Balanced budget by '93-via targets	Y
90. Bar licensing of two nuclear plants	N
91. Remove victims compensation cap	N
92. Catastrophic health insurance	N
93. Ban airline smoking-2 hours or less	Y
94. $1b/two year aid for the homeless	N
95. Bar non-unions in union companies	N
96. Increase FSLIC rescue to $15b	Y
97. Impose quotas to lower trade deficit	N
98. Reduce discretionary budget 21%	Y

Presidential Support Score: 1991 - 75%   1990 - 68%

DeLAY, TOM -- Texas 22nd District [Republican]. Counties of Brazoria (pt.), Fort Bend and Harris (pt.). Prior Terms: 1985-92. Born: April 8, 1947; Laredo, TX. Education: University of Houston. Occupation: Businessman; Texas representative.

1. Protection to Haitian refugees	N
2. Raise tax on wealthy; lower others	N
3. Investigate Reagan hostage delay	N
4. Campaign finance revisions	N
5. Unpaid leave to care for children	N
6. Restrict NEA use of funds	Y
7. Bar race-bias claim/habeas corpus	Y
8. Ban race as death sentence factor	Y
9. Exceptions to exclusionary rule	Y
10. Allow sale of assault weapons	Y
11. Life in prison/abolish death penalty	N
12. Req conspiracy-price fixing cases	Y
13. Unemployment benefits extension	N
14. Tissue use of aborted fetuses	N
15. Bar replacement of union strikers	N
16. Hold foreign aid at $15b for '92	X
17. Restore space station funding	Y
18. Civil Rights Act of 1991	N
19. Unlimited damages-discrimination	N
20. Eliminate funds for supercollider	N
21. Terminate SDI except for research	N
22. Req 7-day handgun waiting period	N
23. Provide $30b for failed S&Ls	Y
24. Allow use of force against Iraq	Y
25. Allow $15b in foreign aid for '91	N
26. Revise & extend legal immigration	Y
27. Suspend aid to Angolan rebels	N
28. Democratic tax plan proposals	N
29. Cut defense 5% across the board	?
30. Textile import quotas-veto override	N
31. Abortion service for military abroad	N

32. Limits on high income farmers	N
33. Family medical leave-veto override	N
34. Req submission of balanced budget	N
35. Balanced budget amendment	Y
36. Amendment to ban flag desecration	Y
37. Reauthorize Amtrak-veto override	N
38. Retraining aid for coal miners	N
39. Suspend El Salvador military aid	N
40. Expand child care aid/tax credit	N
41. Raise House salary/omit honoraria	Y
42. Toughen oil-spill liability	N
43. Restitution to Japanese interned	N
44. Protect Chinese & C.A. nationals	N
45. Abortion $ for rape/incest cases	N
46. Allow religious schools to bar gays	Y
47. Bar broadcaster fairness doctrine	Y
48. Bar cap gains cut/reinstate IRA	N
49. Bar unions equal voice in pension	Y
50. Bar assembly of chemical weapons	N
51. Ban plutonium/uranium production	N
52. Cap MX missile deployment at 50	N
53. Allow $3b for 2 stealth bombers	Y
54. Publish bio-warfare experiments	N
55. Raise minimum wage-veto override	N
56. Bar transfer of FS-X technology	N
57. Cut defense and raise domestic $	N
58. Uniform poll closing in 48 states	N
59. Req foreign investment disclosure	N
60. Textile import quotas-veto override	N
61. Bar abortion funding in Wash, DC	Y
62. Notify spouses of AIDS+ carriers	Y

DeLAY, TOM (continued)

63.	Seize conveyance-drug trafficking	Y
64.	South Africa sanctions	X
65.	60 days' notice of plant closings	N
66.	Close unneeded military bases	Y
67.	Keep welfare reform within $2.8b	Y
68.	Allow children housing exclusion	Y
69.	Shift $400m of NASA to homeless	N
70.	Cap Medicare patients' liability	N
71.	Prohibit employee polygraph testing	?
72.	Allow CIA to fund Contras	Y
73.	Revise unfair trade practices	N
74.	Focus SDI on accidental launch	N
75.	Bar Air Force $ for MX missile	N
76.	Allow "real" increase in defense	Y
77.	Troop reduction in Europe of 50%	N
78.	Ban nuclear tests above 1 kiloton	N
79.	Ban anti-satellite missile tests	?
80.	Observe certain limits of SALT II	N
81.	Restore four Civil Rights laws	N
82.	Prohibit aliens as strikebreakers	N
83.	Allow military malpractice suits	N
84.	Approval of $36m in Contra aid	Y
85.	$18b deficit reduction compromise	N
86.	Welfare reform of $5.7b for 5 years	N
87.	Raise taxes $12b/cut spending $3b	N
88.	Board to assess occupational risk	N
89.	Balanced budget by '93-via targets	Y
90.	Bar licensing of two nuclear plants	N
91.	Remove victims compensation cap	N
92.	Catastrophic health insurance	N

93.	Ban airline smoking-2 hours or less	N
94.	$1b/two year aid for the homeless	N
95.	Bar non-unions in union companies	N
96.	Increase FSLIC rescue to $15b	Y
97.	Impose quotas to lower trade deficit	N
98.	Reduce discretionary budget 21%	Y
99.	Immigration reform/alien amnesty	N
100.	South Africa sanctions-veto override	N
101.	Tax overhaul to revise income tax	N
102.	Use of military in drug war	Y
103.	Delete 12 MX/add conventional wpn	N
104.	Raise speed limit to 65 mph	Y
105.	Require Pentagon to buy US goods	N
106.	AIDS insurance non-discrimination	N
107.	Prohibit Saudi arms sales	Y
108.	Ease Gun Control Act of 1968	Y
109.	Bar interstate handgun transport	N
110.	Make company emissions known	N
111.	Allow toxic victims to sue in fed ct	N
112.	Superfund waste cleanup of $10b	N
113.	90 days notice of plant closings	N
114.	$20b in Medicare cuts/tax increases	N
115.	Spending cuts and tax increases	N
116.	Set school lunch lmt-250% poverty	Y
117.	$75m for youth work projects	N
118.	Allow Angolan military assistance	Y
119.	Suspend defense payments for abuse	N
120.	Drop SS COLAs/$12b tax increase	N
121.	Approve $1.5b for 21 MX missiles	Y
122.	Emergency farm credit/revisions	N

Presidential Support Score: 1991 - 75%   1990 - 83%

BUSTAMANTE, A. G. -- Texas 23rd District [Democrat]. Counties of Bexar (pt.), Dimmit, Kinney, Maverick, Medina, Uvalde, Webb and Zavala. Prior Terms: 1985-92. Born: April 8, 1935; Asherton, TX. Education: Sul Ross University (B.A.). Military Service: U.S. Army, 1954-56. Occupation: County judge; county commissioner.

1.	Protection to Haitian refugees	Y
2.	Raise tax on wealthy; lower others	Y
3.	Investigate Reagan hostage delay	Y
4.	Campaign finance revisions	Y
5.	Unpaid leave to care for children	Y
6.	Restrict NEA use of funds	N
7.	Bar race-bias claim/habeas corpus	N
8.	Ban race as death sentence factor	N
9.	Exceptions to exclusionary rule	?
10.	Allow use of assault weapons	Y
11.	Life in prison/abolish death penalty	N
12.	Req conspiracy-price fixing cases	N
13.	Unemployment benefits extension	Y
14.	Tissue use of aborted fetuses	Y
15.	Bar replacement of union strikers	Y
16.	Hold foreign aid at $15b for '92	Y
17.	Restore space station funding	Y
18.	Civil Rights Act of 1991	Y
19.	Unlimited damages-discrimination	Y
20.	Eliminate funds for supercollider	N
21.	Terminate SDI except for research	N
22.	Req 7-day handgun waiting period	N
23.	Provide $30b for failed S&Ls	?
24.	Allow use of force against Iraq	N
25.	Allow $15b in foreign aid for '91	Y

26.	Revise & extend legal immigration	Y
27.	Suspend aid to Angolan rebels	Y
28.	Democratic tax plan proposals	Y
29.	Cut defense 5% across the board	N
30.	Textile import quotas-veto override	Y
31.	Abortion service for military abroad	?
32.	Limits on high income farmers	N
33.	Family medical leave-veto override	Y
34.	Req submission of balanced budget	Y
35.	Balanced budget amendment	Y
36.	Amendment to ban flag desecration	Y
37.	Reauthorize Amtrak-veto override	Y
38.	Retraining aid for coal miners	Y
39.	Suspend El Salvador military aid	Y
40.	Expand child care aid/tax credit	Y
41.	Raise House salary/omit honoraria	Y
42.	Toughen oil-spill liability	N
43.	Restitution to Japanese interned	Y
44.	Protect Chinese & C.A. nationals	Y
45.	Abortion $ for rape/incest cases	Y
46.	Allow religious schools to bar gays	N
47.	Bar broadcaster fairness doctrine	N
48.	Bar cap gains cut/reinstate IRA	Y
49.	Bar unions equal voice in pension	N
50.	Bar assembly of chemical weapons	N

BUSTAMANTE, A. G. (continued)

51. Ban plutonium/uranium production	Y		87. Raise taxes $12b/cut spending $3b	Y
52. Cap MX missile deployment at 50	Y		88. Board to assess occupational risk	?
53. Allow $3b for 2 stealth bombers	Y		89. Balanced budget by '93-via targets	Y
54. Publish bio-warfare experiments	N		90. Bar licensing of two nuclear plants	Y
55. Raise minimum wage-veto override	Y		91. Remove victims compensation cap	N
56. Bar transfer of FS-X technology	Y		92. Catastrophic health insurance	Y
57. Cut defense and raise domestic $	N		93. Ban airline smoking-2 hours or less	N
58. Uniform poll closing in 48 states	Y		94. $1b/two year aid for the homeless	Y
59. Req foreign investment disclosure	Y		95. Bar non-unions in union companies	Y
60. Textile import quotas-veto override	Y		96. Increase FSLIC rescue to $15b	N
61. Bar abortion funding in Wash, DC	N		97. Impose quotas to lower trade deficit	Y
62. Notify spouses of AIDS+ carriers	?		98. Reduce discretionary budget 21%	Y
63. Seize conveyance-drug trafficking	N		99. Immigration reform/alien amnesty	Y
64. South Africa sanctions	Y		100. South Africa sanctions-veto override	Y
65. 60 days' notice of plant closings	Y		101. Tax overhaul to revise income tax	N
66. Close unneeded military bases	N		102. Use of military in drug war	N
67. Keep welfare reform within $2.8b	N		103. Delete 12 MX/add conventional wpn	N
68. Allow children housing exclusion	N		104. Raise speed limit to 65 mph	Y
69. Shift $400m of NASA to homeless	N		105. Require Pentagon to buy US goods	Y
70. Cap Medicare patients' liability	#		106. AIDS insurance non-discrimination	Y
71. Prohibit employee polygraph testing	?		107. Prohibit Saudi arms sales	Y
72. Allow CIA to fund Contras	N		108. Ease Gun Control Act of 1968	Y
73. Revise unfair trade practices	Y		109. Bar interstate handgun transport	?
74. Focus SDI on accidental launch	Y		110. Make company emissions known	Y
75. Bar Air Force $ for MX missile	N		111. Allow toxic victims to sue in fed ct	N
76. Allow "real" increase in defense	N		112. Superfund waste cleanup of $10b	N
77. Troop reduction in Europe of 50%	N		113. 90 days notice of plant closings	Y
78. Ban nuclear tests above 1 kiloton	Y		114. $20b in Medicare cuts/tax increases	Y
79. Ban anti-satellite missile tests	Y		115. Spending cuts and tax increases	Y
80. Observe certain limits of SALT II	Y		116. Set school lunch lmt-250% poverty	N
81. Restore four Civil Rights laws	Y		117. $75m for youth work projects	Y
82. Prohibit aliens as strikebreakers	Y		118. Allow Angolan military assistance	N
83. Allow military malpractice suits	Y		119. Suspend defense payments for abuse	N
84. Approval of $36m in Contra aid	N		120. Drop SS COLAs/$12b tax increase	Y
85. $18b deficit reduction compromise	Y		121. Approve $1.5b for 21 MX missiles	Y
86. Welfare reform of $5.7b for 5 years	Y		122. Emergency farm credit/revisions	Y

Presidential Support Score: 1991 - 32%   1990 - 25%

FROST, MARTIN -- Texas 24th District [Democrat]. Counties of Dallas (pt.) and Tarrant (pt.). Prior Terms: 1979-92. Born: January 1, 1942; Glendale, CA. Education: University of Missouri (B.A., B.J.); Georgetown Law Center (J.D.). Military Service: U.S. Army Reserve, 1966-72. Occupation: Staff writer, *Congressional Quarterly Weekly Report*; attorney; law clerk for federal judge.

1. Protection to Haitian refugees	Y		19. Unlimited damages-discrimination	Y
2. Raise tax on wealthy; lower others	Y		20. Eliminate funds for supercollider	N
3. Investigate Reagan hostage delay	Y		21. Terminate SDI except for research	N
4. Campaign finance revisions	Y		22. Req 7-day handgun waiting period	Y
5. Unpaid leave to care for children	Y		23. Provide $30b for failed S&Ls	Y
6. Restrict NEA use of funds	N		24. Allow use of force against Iraq	Y
7. Bar race-bias claim/habeas corpus	N		25. Allow $15b in foreign aid for '91	Y
8. Ban race as death sentence factor	N		26. Revise & extend legal immigration	Y
9. Exceptions to exclusionary rule	N		27. Suspend aid to Angolan rebels	Y
10. Allow sale of assault weapons	N		28. Democratic tax plan proposals	Y
11. Life in prison/abolish death penalty	N		29. Cut defense 5% across the board	N
12. Req conspiracy-price fixing cases	N		30. Textile import quotas-veto override	Y
13. Unemployment benefits extension	Y		31. Abortion service for military abroad	Y
14. Tissue use of aborted fetuses	Y		32. Limits on high income farmers	N
15. Bar replacement of union strikers	Y		33. Family medical leave-veto override	Y
16. Hold foreign aid at $15b for '92	Y		34. Req submission of balanced budget	Y
17. Restore space station funding	Y		35. Balanced budget amendment	N
18. Civil Rights Act of 1991	Y		36. Amendment to ban flag desecration	N

FROST, MARTIN (continued)

37. Reauthorize Amtrak-veto override	Y	
38. Retraining aid for coal miners	Y	
39. Suspend El Salvador military aid	Y	
40. Expand child care aid/tax credit	Y	
41. Raise House salary/omit honoraria	Y	
42. Toughen oil-spill liability	N	
43. Restitution to Japanese interned	Y	
44. Protect Chinese & C.A. nationals	Y	
45. Abortion $ for rape/incest cases	Y	
46. Allow religious schools to bar gays	N	
47. Bar broadcaster fairness doctrine	N	
48. Bar cap gains cut/reinstate IRA	Y	
49. Bar unions equal voice in pension	Y	
50. Bar assembly of chemical weapons	Y	
51. Ban plutonium/uranium production	Y	
52. Cap MX missile deployment at 50	Y	
53. Allow $3b for 2 stealth bombers	Y	
54. Publish bio-warfare experiments	Y	
55. Raise minimum wage-veto override	Y	
56. Bar transfer of FS-X technology	Y	
57. Cut defense and raise domestic $	N	
58. Uniform poll closing in 48 states	Y	
59. Req foreign investment disclosure	Y	
60. Textile import quotas-veto override	Y	
61. Bar abortion funding in Wash, DC	N	
62. Notify spouses of AIDS+ carriers	?	
63. Seize conveyance-drug trafficking	?	
64. South Africa sanctions	Y	
65. 60 days' notice of plant closings	Y	
66. Close unneeded military bases	N	
67. Keep welfare reform within $2.8b	N	
68. Allow children housing exclusion	N	
69. Shift $400m of NASA to homeless	N	
70. Cap Medicare patients' liability	Y	
71. Prohibit employee polygraph testing	N	
72. Allow CIA to fund Contras	N	
73. Revise unfair trade practices	Y	
74. Focus SDI on accidental launch	Y	
75. Bar Air Force $ for MX missile	N	
76. Allow "real" increase in defense	?	
77. Troop reduction in Europe of 50%	Y	
78. Ban nuclear tests above 1 kiloton	Y	
79. Ban anti-satellite missile tests	N	
80. Observe certain limits of SALT II	Y	
81. Restore four Civil Rights laws	Y	
82. Prohibit aliens as strikebreakers	Y	
83. Allow military malpractice suits	?	
84. Approval of $36m in Contra aid	N	
85. $18b deficit reduction compromise	Y	
86. Welfare reform of $5.7b for 5 years	Y	
87. Raise taxes $12b/cut spending $3b	Y	
88. Board to assess occupational risk	Y	
89. Balanced budget by '93-via targets	N	
90. Bar licensing of two nuclear plants	N	

91. Remove victims compensation cap	N	
92. Catastrophic health insurance	Y	
93. Ban airline smoking-2 hours or less	?	
94. $1b/two year aid for the homeless	Y	
95. Bar non-unions in union companies	Y	
96. Increase FSLIC rescue to $15b	N	
97. Impose quotas to lower trade deficit	Y	
98. Reduce discretionary budget 21%	Y	
99. Immigration reform/alien amnesty	Y	
100. South Africa sanctions-veto override	Y	
101. Tax overhaul to revise income tax	N	
102. Use of military in drug war	Y	
103. Delete 12 MX/add conventional wpn	N	
104. Raise speed limit to 65 mph	N	
105. Require Pentagon to buy US goods	Y	
106. AIDS insurance non-discrimination	Y	
107. Prohibit Saudi arms sales	Y	
108. Ease Gun Control Act of 1968	N	
109. Bar interstate handgun transport	N	
110. Make company emissions known	N	
111. Allow toxic victims to sue in fed ct	N	
112. Superfund waste cleanup of $10b	N	
113. 90 days notice of plant closings	Y	
114. $20b in Medicare cuts/tax increases	Y	
115. Spending cuts and tax increases	Y	
116. Set school lunch lmt-250% poverty	N	
117. $75m for youth work projects	Y	
118. Allow Angolan military assistance	N	
119. Suspend defense payments for abuse	N	
120. Drop SS COLAs/$12b tax increase	N	
121. Approve $1.5b for 21 MX missiles	Y	
122. Emergency farm credit/revisions	Y	
123. Duty on Taiwan/Hong Kong/S Korea	Y	
124. Limit steel imports to 17%	Y	
125. Cut $ to schools that bar prayer	N	
126. $50b-taxes; cut Medicare/spending	Y	
127. Limit Pershing II/cruise in Europe	N	
128. Delete $7.1b for 34 B-1 bombers	N	
129. Bar purchase of Sergeant York guns	N	
130. El Salvador military/economic aid	N	
131. Bar mining of Nicaraguan waters	?	
132. Physician fee freeze for Medicare	?	
133. $49b in "sin"/phone/insurance taxes	N	
134. Allow sale of Conrail	N	
135. Equal Rights Amendment	Y	
136. Authorize Marines in Lebanon	N	
137. Eminent domain for coal companies	N	
138. Prohibit EPA clean air sanctions	?	
139. SS retirement age increase/reforms	Y	
140. Auto domestic content requirement	Y	
141. Delete jobs program funding	N	
142. Highway-gas tax bill	Y	
143. Cut $5b from defense for Medicare	Y	
144. Emergency housing aid of $1b	Y	

Presidential Support Score: 1991 - 35%   1990 - 22%

ANDREWS, MICHAEL A. -- Texas 25th District [Democrat]. County of Harris (pt.). Prior Terms: 1983-92. Born: February 7, 1944; Houston, TX. Education: University of Texas (B.A.); Southern Methodist University School of Law (J.D.). Occupation: Law clerk, U.S. district judge (1971-72); assistant district attorney (1972-76); attorney (1976).

1. Protection to Haitian refugees	Y	2. Raise tax on wealthy; lower others	Y

ANDREWS, MICHAEL A. (continued)

3. Investigate Reagan hostage delay	Y
4. Campaign finance revisions	Y
5. Unpaid leave to care for children	Y
6. Restrict NEA use of funds	Y
7. Bar race-bias claim/habeas corpus	Y
8. Ban race as death sentence factor	Y
9. Exceptions to exclusionary rule	Y
10. Allow sale of assault weapons	Y
11. Life in prison/abolish death penalty	N
12. Req conspiracy-price fixing cases	N
13. Unemployment benefits extension	Y
14. Tissue use of aborted fetuses	Y
15. Bar replacement of union strikers	Y
16. Hold foreign aid at $15b for '92	Y
17. Restore space station funding	Y
18. Civil Rights Act of 1991	Y
19. Unlimited damages-discrimination	N
20. Eliminate funds for supercollider	N
21. Terminate SDI except for research	N
22. Req 7-day handgun waiting period	Y
23. Provide $30b for failed S&Ls	Y
24. Allow use of force against Iraq	Y
25. Allow $15b in foreign aid for '91	Y
26. Revise & extend legal immigration	N
27. Suspend aid to Angolan rebels	Y
28. Democratic tax plan proposals	Y
29. Cut defense 5% across the board	N
30. Textile import quotas-veto override	Y
31. Abortion service for military abroad	Y
32. Limits on high income farmers	Y
33. Family medical leave-veto override	Y
34. Req submission of balanced budget	Y
35. Balanced budget amendment	Y
36. Amendment to ban flag desecration	Y
37. Reauthorize Amtrak-veto override	Y
38. Retraining aid for coal miners	N
39. Suspend El Salvador military aid	Y
40. Expand child care aid/tax credit	Y
41. Raise House salary/omit honoraria	Y
42. Toughen oil-spill liability	Y
43. Restitution to Japanese interned	Y
44. Protect Chinese & C.A. nationals	Y
45. Abortion $ for rape/incest cases	Y
46. Allow religious schools to bar gays	Y
47. Bar broadcaster fairness doctrine	N
48. Bar cap gains cut/reinstate IRA	N
49. Bar unions equal voice in pension	Y
50. Bar assembly of chemical weapons	N
51. Ban plutonium/uranium production	Y
52. Cap MX missile deployment at 50	Y
53. Allow $3b for 2 stealth bombers	N
54. Publish bio-warfare experiments	Y
55. Raise minimum wage-veto override	Y
56. Bar transfer of FS-X technology	Y
57. Cut defense and raise domestic $	N
58. Uniform poll closing in 48 states	Y
59. Req foreign investment disclosure	Y
60. Textile import quotas-veto override	Y
61. Bar abortion funding in Wash, DC	N
62. Notify spouses of AIDS+ carriers	N
63. Seize conveyance-drug trafficking	N
64. South Africa sanctions	Y
65. 60 days' notice of plant closings	Y
66. Close unneeded military bases	Y

67. Keep welfare reform within $2.8b	N
68. Allow children housing exclusion	N
69. Shift $400m of NASA to homeless	N
70. Cap Medicare patients' liability	Y
71. Prohibit employee polygraph testing	Y
72. Allow CIA to fund Contras	N
73. Revise unfair trade practices	Y
74. Focus SDI on accidental launch	Y
75. Bar Air Force $ for MX missile	N
76. Allow "real" increase in defense	Y
77. Troop reduction in Europe of 50%	N
78. Ban nuclear tests above 1 kiloton	Y
79. Ban anti-satellite missile tests	N
80. Observe certain limits of SALT II	Y
81. Restore four Civil Rights laws	Y
82. Prohibit aliens as strikebreakers	N
83. Allow military malpractice suits	Y
84. Approval of $36m in Contra aid	N
85. $18b deficit reduction compromise	Y
86. Welfare reform of $5.7b for 5 years	Y
87. Raise taxes $12b/cut spending $3b	Y
88. Board to assess occupational risk	Y
89. Balanced budget by '93-via targets	Y
90. Bar licensing of two nuclear plants	N
91. Remove victims compensation cap	N
92. Catastrophic health insurance	Y
93. Ban airline smoking-2 hours or less	Y
94. $1b/two year aid for the homeless	Y
95. Bar non-unions in union companies	Y
96. Increase FSLIC rescue to $15b	Y
97. Impose quotas to lower trade deficit	Y
98. Reduce discretionary budget 21%	Y
99. Immigration reform/alien amnesty	Y
100. South Africa sanctions-veto override	Y
101. Tax overhaul to revise income tax	Y
102. Use of military in drug war	Y
103. Delete 12 MX/add conventional wpn	N
104. Raise speed limit to 65 mph	N
105. Require Pentagon to buy US goods	Y
106. AIDS insurance non-discrimination	Y
107. Prohibit Saudi arms sales	Y
108. Ease Gun Control Act of 1968	Y
109. Bar interstate handgun transport	N
110. Make company emissions known	N
111. Allow toxic victims to sue in fed ct	N
112. Superfund waste cleanup of $10b	N
113. 90 days notice of plant closings	N
114. $20b in Medicare cuts/tax increases	Y
115. Spending cuts and tax increases	Y
116. Set school lunch lmt-250% poverty	N
117. $75m for youth work projects	?
118. Allow Angolan military assistance	Y
119. Suspend defense payments for abuse	N
120. Drop SS COLAs/$12b tax increase	Y
121. Approve $1.5b for 21 MX missiles	Y
122. Emergency farm credit/revisions	Y
123. Duty on Taiwan/Hong Kong/S Korea	Y
124. Limit steel imports to 17%	Y
125. Cut $ to schools that bar prayer	Y
126. $50b-taxes; cut Medicare/spending	Y
127. Limit Pershing II/cruise in Europe	N
128. Delete $7.1b for 34 B-1 bombers	N
129. Bar purchase of Sergeant York guns	N
130. El Salvador military/economic aid	Y

ANDREWS, MICHAEL A. (continued)

131. Bar mining of Nicaraguan waters	Y		136. Authorize Marines in Lebanon	Y
132. Physician fee freeze for Medicare	N		137. Eminent domain for coal companies	Y
133. $49b in "sin"/phone/insurance taxes	Y		138. Prohibit EPA clean air sanctions	Y
134. Allow sale of Conrail	Y		139. SS retirement age increase/reforms	Y
135. Equal Rights Amendment	Y			

Presidential Support Score: 1991 - 47%   1990 - 32%

ARMEY, DICK -- Texas 26th District [Republican]. Counties of Collin (pt.), Cooke (pt.), Denton and Tarrant (pt.). Prior Terms: 1985-92. Born: July 7, 1940; Cando, ND. Education: Jamestown College (B.A.); University of North Dakota (M.A.); University of Oklahoma (Ph.D.). Occupation: Economist; educator; chairman, Economics Dept., North Texas State University.

1. Protection to Haitian refugees	N		50. Bar assembly of chemical weapons	N
2. Raise tax on wealthy; lower others	N		51. Ban plutonium/uranium production	N
3. Investigate Reagan hostage delay	N		52. Cap MX missile deployment at 50	N
4. Campaign finance revisions	N		53. Allow $3b for 2 stealth bombers	Y
5. Unpaid leave to care for children	N		54. Publish bio-warfare experiments	N
6. Restrict NEA use of funds	Y		55. Raise minimum wage-veto override	N
7. Bar race-bias claim/habeas corpus	Y		56. Bar transfer of FS-X technology	N
8. Ban race as death sentence factor	Y		57. Cut defense and raise domestic $	N
9. Exceptions to exclusionary rule	Y		58. Uniform poll closing in 48 states	N
10. Allow sale of assault weapons	Y		59. Req foreign investment disclosure	N
11. Life in prison/abolish death penalty	N		60. Textile import quotas-veto override	N
12. Req conspiracy-price fixing cases	Y		61. Bar abortion funding in Wash, DC	Y
13. Unemployment benefits extension	N		62. Notify spouses of AIDS+ carriers	Y
14. Tissue use of aborted fetuses	N		63. Seize conveyance-drug trafficking	Y
15. Bar replacement of union strikers	N		64. South Africa sanctions	X
16. Hold foreign aid at $15b for '92	N		65. 60 days' notice of plant closings	N
17. Restore space station funding	Y		66. Close unneeded military bases	Y
18. Civil Rights Act of 1991	N		67. Keep welfare reform within $2.8b	Y
19. Unlimited damages-discrimination	N		68. Allow children housing exclusion	Y
20. Eliminate funds for supercollider	N		69. Shift $400m of NASA to homeless	N
21. Terminate SDI except for research	N		70. Cap Medicare patients' liability	N
22. Req 7-day handgun waiting period	N		71. Prohibit employee polygraph testing	N
23. Provide $30b for failed S&Ls	Y		72. Allow CIA to fund Contras	Y
24. Allow use of force against Iraq	Y		73. Revise unfair trade practices	N
25. Allow $15b in foreign aid for '91	N		74. Focus SDI on accidental launch	N
26. Revise & extend legal immigration	Y		75. Bar Air Force $ for MX missile	N
27. Suspend aid to Angolan rebels	N		76. Allow "real" increase in defense	Y
28. Democratic tax plan proposals	N		77. Troop reduction in Europe of 50%	N
29. Cut defense 5% across the board	N		78. Ban nuclear tests above 1 kiloton	N
30. Textile import quotas-veto override	N		79. Ban anti-satellite missile tests	N
31. Abortion service for military abroad	N		80. Observe certain limits of SALT II	N
32. Limits on high income farmers	Y		81. Restore four Civil Rights laws	N
33. Family medical leave-veto override	N		82. Prohibit aliens as strikebreakers	N
34. Req submission of balanced budget	N		83. Allow military malpractice suits	N
35. Balanced budget amendment	Y		84. Approval of $36m in Contra aid	Y
36. Amendment to ban flag desecration	Y		85. $18b deficit reduction compromise	N
37. Reauthorize Amtrak-veto override	N		86. Welfare reform of $5.7b for 5 years	N
38. Retraining aid for coal miners	N		87. Raise taxes $12b/cut spending $3b	N
39. Suspend El Salvador military aid	N		88. Board to assess occupational risk	N
40. Expand child care aid/tax credit	N		89. Balanced budget by '93-via targets	Y
41. Raise House salary/omit honoraria	N		90. Bar licensing of two nuclear plants	N
42. Toughen oil-spill liability	N		91. Remove victims compensation cap	N
43. Restitution to Japanese interned	?		92. Catastrophic health insurance	N
44. Protect Chinese & C.A. nationals	N		93. Ban airline smoking-2 hours or less	N
45. Abortion $ for rape/incest cases	N		94. $1b/two year aid for the homeless	N
46. Allow religious schools to bar gays	Y		95. Bar non-unions in union companies	N
47. Bar broadcaster fairness doctrine	Y		96. Increase FSLIC rescue to $15b	Y
48. Bar cap gains cut/reinstate IRA	N		97. Impose quotas to lower trade deficit	N
49. Bar unions equal voice in pension	Y		98. Reduce discretionary budget 21%	Y

ARMEY, DICK (continued)

99. Immigration reform/alien amnesty	N	111. Allow toxic victims to sue in fed ct	N
100. South Africa sanctions-veto override	N	112. Superfund waste cleanup of $10b	N
101. Tax overhaul to revise income tax	Y	113. 90 days notice of plant closings	N
102. Use of military in drug war	Y	114. $20b in Medicare cuts/tax increases	N
103. Delete 12 MX/add conventional wpn	N	115. Spending cuts and tax increases	N
104. Raise speed limit to 65 mph	Y	116. Set school lunch lmt-250% poverty	Y
105. Require Pentagon to buy US goods	N	117. $75m for youth work projects	N
106. AIDS insurance non-discrimination	N	118. Allow Angolan military assistance	Y
107. Prohibit Saudi arms sales	Y	119. Suspend defense payments for abuse	N
108. Ease Gun Control Act of 1968	Y	120. Drop SS COLAs/$12b tax increase	N
109. Bar interstate handgun transport	N	121. Approve $1.5b for 21 MX missiles	Y
110. Make company emissions known	N	122. Emergency farm credit/revisions	N

Presidential Support Score: 1991 - 86% 1990 - 81%

ORTIZ, SOLOMON P. -- Texas 27th District [Democrat]. Counties of Cameron, Kenedy, Kleberg, Nueces (pt.) and Willacy. Prior Terms: 1983-92. Born: June 3, 1937; Robstown, TX. Education: Del Mar College. Military Service: U.S. Army, 1960-62. Occupation: Law enforcement official; constable (1964); county commissioner (1969); county sheriff (1977).

1. Protection to Haitian refugees	#	43. Restitution to Japanese interned	Y
2. Raise tax on wealthy; lower others	Y	44. Protect Chinese & C.A. nationals	N
3. Investigate Reagan hostage delay	Y	45. Abortion $ for rape/incest cases	Y
4. Campaign finance revisions	Y	46. Allow religious schools to bar gays	Y
5. Unpaid leave to care for children	Y	47. Bar broadcaster fairness doctrine	N
6. Restrict NEA use of funds	Y	48. Bar cap gains cut/reinstate IRA	N
7. Bar race-bias claim/habeas corpus	N	49. Bar unions equal voice in pension	Y
8. Ban race as death sentence factor	N	50. Bar assembly of chemical weapons	N
9. Exceptions to exclusionary rule	N	51. Ban plutonium/uranium production	Y
10. Allow sale of assault weapons	Y	52. Cap MX missile deployment at 50	Y
11. Life in prison/abolish death penalty	N	53. Allow $3b for 2 stealth bombers	Y
12. Req conspiracy-price fixing cases	N	54. Publish bio-warfare experiments	N
13. Unemployment benefits extension	Y	55. Raise minimum wage-veto override	Y
14. Tissue use of aborted fetuses	Y	56. Bar transfer of FS-X technology	Y
15. Bar replacement of union strikers	N	57. Cut defense and raise domestic $	N
16. Hold foreign aid at $15b for '92	Y	58. Uniform poll closing in 48 states	Y
17. Restore space station funding	Y	59. Req foreign investment disclosure	Y
18. Civil Rights Act of 1991	Y	60. Textile import quotas-veto override	Y
19. Unlimited damages-discrimination	N	61. Bar abortion funding in Wash, DC	Y
20. Eliminate funds for supercollider	N	62. Notify spouses of AIDS+ carriers	N
21. Terminate SDI except for research	N	63. Seize conveyance-drug trafficking	?
22. Req 7-day handgun waiting period	N	64. South Africa sanctions	Y
23. Provide $30b for failed S&Ls	Y	65. 60 days' notice of plant closings	Y
24. Allow use of force against Iraq	Y	66. Close unneeded military bases	N
25. Allow $15b in foreign aid for '91	Y	67. Keep welfare reform within $2.8b	N
26. Revise & extend legal immigration	Y	68. Allow children housing exclusion	?
27. Suspend aid to Angolan rebels	Y	69. Shift $400m of NASA to homeless	N
28. Democratic tax plan proposals	Y	70. Cap Medicare patients' liability	?
29. Cut defense 5% across the board	N	71. Prohibit employee polygraph testing	?
30. Textile import quotas-veto override	Y	72. Allow CIA to fund Contras	N
31. Abortion service for military abroad	N	73. Revise unfair trade practices	Y
32. Limits on high income farmers	N	74. Focus SDI on accidental launch	Y
33. Family medical leave-veto override	Y	75. Bar Air Force $ for MX missile	N
34. Req submission of balanced budget	Y	76. Allow "real" increase in defense	N
35. Balanced budget amendment	Y	77. Troop reduction in Europe of 50%	N
36. Amendment to ban flag desecration	Y	78. Ban nuclear tests above 1 kiloton	Y
37. Reauthorize Amtrak-veto override	Y	79. Ban anti-satellite missile tests	N
38. Retraining aid for coal miners	Y	80. Observe certain limits of SALT II	Y
39. Suspend El Salvador military aid	Y	81. Restore four Civil Rights laws	Y
40. Expand child care aid/tax credit	Y	82. Prohibit aliens as strikebreakers	Y
41. Raise House salary/omit honoraria	Y	83. Allow military malpractice suits	Y
42. Toughen oil-spill liability	N	84. Approval of $36m in Contra aid	Y

ORTIZ, SOLOMON P. (continued)

85. $18b deficit reduction compromise	Y	
86. Welfare reform of $5.7b for 5 years	Y	
87. Raise taxes $12b/cut spending $3b	Y	
88. Board to assess occupational risk	N	
89. Balanced budget by '93-via targets	Y	
90. Bar licensing of two nuclear plants	Y	
91. Remove victims compensation cap	N	
92. Catastrophic health insurance	Y	
93. Ban airline smoking-2 hours or less	N	
94. $1b/two year aid for the homeless	Y	
95. Bar non-unions in union companies	N	
96. Increase FSLIC rescue to $15b	Y	
97. Impose quotas to lower trade deficit	Y	
98. Reduce discretionary budget 21%	Y	
99. Immigration reform/alien amnesty	Y	
100. South Africa sanctions-veto override	Y	
101. Tax overhaul to revise income tax	N	
102. Use of military in drug war	Y	
103. Delete 12 MX/add conventional wpn	N	
104. Raise speed limit to 65 mph	Y	
105. Require Pentagon to buy US goods	Y	
106. AIDS insurance non-discrimination	Y	
107. Prohibit Saudi arms sales	Y	
108. Ease Gun Control Act of 1968	Y	
109. Bar interstate handgun transport	N	
110. Make company emissions known	Y	
111. Allow toxic victims to sue in fed ct	Y	
112. Superfund waste cleanup of $10b	N	
113. 90 days notice of plant closings	Y	
114. $20b in Medicare cuts/tax increases	Y	
115. Spending cuts and tax increases	Y	
116. Set school lunch lmt-250% poverty	N	
117. $75m for youth work projects	Y	
118. Allow Angolan military assistance	N	
119. Suspend defense payments for abuse	N	
120. Drop SS COLAs/$12b tax increase	N	
121. Approve $1.5b for 21 MX missiles	Y	
122. Emergency farm credit/revisions	Y	
123. Duty on Taiwan/Hong Kong/S Korea	N	
124. Limit steel imports to 17%	Y	
125. Cut $ to schools that bar prayer	N	
126. $50b-taxes; cut Medicare/spending	Y	
127. Limit Pershing II/cruise in Europe	N	
128. Delete $7.1b for 34 B-1 bombers	N	
129. Bar purchase of Sergeant York guns	?	
130. El Salvador military/economic aid	Y	
131. Bar mining of Nicaraguan waters	Y	
132. Physician fee freeze for Medicare	N	
133. $49b in "sin"/phone/insurance taxes	Y	
134. Allow sale of Conrail	N	
135. Equal Rights Amendment	Y	
136. Authorize Marines in Lebanon	Y	
137. Eminent domain for coal companies	Y	
138. Prohibit EPA clean air sanctions	Y	
139. SS retirement age increase/reforms	Y	

Presidential Support Score: 1991 - 41%   1990 - 30%

UTAH

HANSEN, JAMES V. -- Utah 1st District [Republican]. Counties of Beaver, Box Elder, Cache, Davis, Garfield, Iron, Juab, Kane, Millard, Morgan, Piute, Rich, Tooele, Washington, Wayne and Weber. Prior Terms: 1981-92. Born: August 14, 1932; Salt Lake City, UT. Education: University of Utah (B.S.). Military Service: U.S. Navy, 1951-55. Occupation: Utah representative (1973-80); Farmington City councilman; acting mayor; insurance company executive.

1. Protection to Haitian refugees	N	
2. Raise tax on wealthy; lower others	N	
3. Investigate Reagan hostage delay	N	
4. Campaign finance revisions	N	
5. Unpaid leave to care for children	N	
6. Restrict NEA use of funds	N	
7. Bar race-bias claim/habeas corpus	Y	
8. Ban race as death sentence factor	Y	
9. Exceptions to exclusionary rule	Y	
10. Allow sale of assault weapons	Y	
11. Life in prison/abolish death penalty	N	
12. Req conspiracy-price fixing cases	Y	
13. Unemployment benefits extension	N	
14. Tissue use of aborted fetuses	N	
15. Bar replacement of union strikers	N	
16. Hold foreign aid at $15b for '92	N	
17. Restore space station funding	Y	
18. Civil Rights Act of 1991	N	
19. Unlimited damages-discrimination	N	
20. Eliminate funds for supercollider	N	
21. Terminate SDI except for research	N	
22. Req 7-day handgun waiting period	N	
23. Provide $30b for failed S&Ls	Y	
24. Allow use of force against Iraq	Y	
25. Allow $15b in foreign aid for '91	N	
26. Revise & extend legal immigration	N	
27. Suspend aid to Angolan rebels	N	
28. Democratic tax plan proposals	N	
29. Cut defense 5% across the board	N	
30. Textile import quotas-veto override	N	
31. Abortion service for military abroad	N	
32. Limits on high income farmers	Y	
33. Family medical leave-veto override	N	
34. Req submission of balanced budget	N	
35. Balanced budget amendment	Y	
36. Amendment to ban flag desecration	Y	

HANSEN, JAMES V. (continued)

37. Reauthorize Amtrak-veto override	N
38. Retraining aid for coal miners	N
39. Suspend El Salvador military aid	N
40. Expand child care aid/tax credit	N
41. Raise House salary/omit honoraria	N
42. Toughen oil-spill liability	N
43. Restitution to Japanese interned	N
44. Protect Chinese & C.A. nationals	N
45. Abortion $ for rape/incest cases	N
46. Allow religious schools to bar gays	Y
47. Bar broadcaster fairness doctrine	Y
48. Bar cap gains cut/reinstate IRA	N
49. Bar unions equal voice in pension	Y
50. Bar assembly of chemical weapons	N
51. Ban plutonium/uranium production	N
52. Cap MX missile deployment at 50	N
53. Allow $3b for 2 stealth bombers	Y
54. Publish bio-warfare experiments	N
55. Raise minimum wage-veto override	N
56. Bar transfer of FS-X technology	N
57. Cut defense and raise domestic $	N
58. Uniform poll closing in 48 states	Y
59. Req foreign investment disclosure	N
60. Textile import quotas-veto override	N
61. Bar abortion funding in Wash, DC	Y
62. Notify spouses of AIDS+ carriers	Y
63. Seize conveyance-drug trafficking	Y
64. South Africa sanctions	N
65. 60 days' notice of plant closings	N
66. Close unneeded military bases	Y
67. Keep welfare reform within $2.8b	Y
68. Allow children housing exclusion	Y
69. Shift $400m of NASA to homeless	N
70. Cap Medicare patients' liability	?
71. Prohibit employee polygraph testing	X
72. Allow CIA to fund Contras	#
73. Revise unfair trade practices	N
74. Focus SDI on accidental launch	N
75. Bar Air Force $ for MX missile	N
76. Allow "real" increase in defense	Y
77. Troop reduction in Europe of 50%	?
78. Ban nuclear tests above 1 kiloton	N
79. Ban anti-satellite missile tests	N
80. Observe certain limits of SALT II	N
81. Restore four Civil Rights laws	N
82. Prohibit aliens as strikebreakers	N
83. Allow military malpractice suits	?
84. Approval of $36m in Contra aid	Y
85. $18b deficit reduction compromise	N
86. Welfare reform of $5.7b for 5 years	N
87. Raise taxes $12b/cut spending $3b	N
88. Board to assess occupational risk	N
89. Balanced budget by '93-via targets	N
90. Bar licensing of two nuclear plants	N

91. Remove victims compensation cap	N
92. Catastrophic health insurance	N
93. Ban airline smoking-2 hours or less	Y
94. $1b/two year aid for the homeless	N
95. Bar non-unions in union companies	N
96. Increase FSLIC rescue to $15b	N
97. Impose quotas to lower trade deficit	N
98. Reduce discretionary budget 21%	Y
99. Immigration reform/alien amnesty	N
100. South Africa sanctions-veto override	N
101. Tax overhaul to revise income tax	N
102. Use of military in drug war	N
103. Delete 12 MX/add conventional wpn	N
104. Raise speed limit to 65 mph	Y
105. Require Pentagon to buy US goods	N
106. AIDS insurance non-discrimination	N
107. Prohibit Saudi arms sales	N
108. Ease Gun Control Act of 1968	Y
109. Bar interstate handgun transport	N
110. Make company emissions known	N
111. Allow toxic victims to sue in fed ct	N
112. Superfund waste cleanup of $10b	N
113. 90 days notice of plant closings	N
114. $20b in Medicare cuts/tax increases	N
115. Spending cuts and tax increases	N
116. Set school lunch lmt-250% poverty	Y
117. $75m for youth work projects	N
118. Allow Angolan military assistance	Y
119. Suspend defense payments for abuse	N
120. Drop SS COLAs/$12b tax increase	N
121. Approve $1.5b for 21 MX missiles	Y
122. Emergency farm credit/revisions	N
123. Duty on Taiwan/Hong Kong/S Korea	N
124. Limit steel imports to 17%	Y
125. Cut $ to schools that bar prayer	Y
126. $50b-taxes; cut Medicare/spending	Y
127. Limit Pershing II/cruise in Europe	N
128. Delete $7.1b for 34 B-1 bombers	N
129. Bar purchase of Sergeant York guns	N
130. El Salvador military/economic aid	?
131. Bar mining of Nicaraguan waters	N
132. Physician fee freeze for Medicare	Y
133. $49b in "sin"/phone/insurance taxes	Y
134. Allow sale of Conrail	Y
135. Equal Rights Amendment	N
136. Authorize Marines in Lebanon	Y
137. Eminent domain for coal companies	Y
138. Prohibit EPA clean air sanctions	?
139. SS retirement age increase/reforms	Y
140. Auto domestic content requirement	N
141. Delete jobs program funding	Y
142. Highway-gas tax bill	N
143. Cut $5b from defense for Medicare	N
144. Emergency housing aid of $1b	?

Presidential Support Score: 1991 - 82%   1990 - 83%

OWENS, WAYNE -- Utah 2nd District [Democrat]. County of Salt Lake (pt.). Prior Terms: 1972-74; 1987-92. Born: May 2, 1932; Panguitch, UT. Education: University of Utah (J.D.). Occupation: Attorney; state Board of Regents vice chairman; senatorial aide and administrative assistant; presidential campaign regional coordinator, church mission president.

1. Protection to Haitian refugees	Y	2. Raise tax on wealthy; lower others	Y

OWENS, WAYNE (continued)

3. Investigate Reagan hostage delay	Y	
4. Campaign finance revisions	Y	
5. Unpaid leave to care for children	Y	
6. Restrict NEA use of funds	N	
7. Bar race-bias claim/habeas corpus	Y	
8. Ban race as death sentence factor	N	
9. Exceptions to exclusionary rule	N	
10. Allow sale of assault weapons	Y	
11. Life in prison/abolish death penalty	N	
12. Req conspiracy-price fixing cases	N	
13. Unemployment benefits extension	Y	
14. Tissue use of aborted fetuses	Y	
15. Bar replacement of union strikers	Y	
16. Hold foreign aid at $15b for '92	Y	
17. Restore space station funding	N	
18. Civil Rights Act of 1991	Y	
19. Unlimited damages-discrimination	N	
20. Eliminate funds for supercollider	N	
21. Terminate SDI except for research	?	
22. Req 7-day handgun waiting period	Y	
23. Provide $30b for failed S&Ls	Y	
24. Allow use of force against Iraq	N	
25. Allow $15b in foreign aid for '91	Y	
26. Revise & extend legal immigration	Y	
27. Suspend aid to Angolan rebels	Y	
28. Democratic tax plan proposals	Y	
29. Cut defense 5% across the board	Y	
30. Textile import quotas-veto override	N	
31. Abortion service for military abroad	Y	
32. Limits on high income farmers	Y	
33. Family medical leave-veto override	Y	
34. Req submission of balanced budget	Y	
35. Balanced budget amendment	Y	
36. Amendment to ban flag desecration	N	
37. Reauthorize Amtrak-veto override	?	
38. Retraining aid for coal miners	Y	
39. Suspend El Salvador military aid	Y	
40. Expand child care aid/tax credit	?	
41. Raise House salary/omit honoraria	Y	
42. Toughen oil-spill liability	Y	
43. Restitution to Japanese interned	Y	
44. Protect Chinese & C.A. nationals	?	
45. Abortion $ for rape/incest cases	Y	
46. Allow religious schools to bar gays	N	
47. Bar broadcaster fairness doctrine	N	
48. Bar cap gains cut/reinstate IRA	N	
49. Bar unions equal voice in pension	N	
50. Bar assembly of chemical weapons	Y	

51. Ban plutonium/uranium production	Y
52. Cap MX missile deployment at 50	Y
53. Allow $3b for 2 stealth bombers	N
54. Publish bio-warfare experiments	Y
55. Raise minimum wage-veto override	Y
56. Bar transfer of FS-X technology	?
57. Cut defense and raise domestic $	N
58. Uniform poll closing in 48 states	Y
59. Req foreign investment disclosure	Y
60. Textile import quotas-veto override	N
61. Bar abortion funding in Wash, DC	Y
62. Notify spouses of AIDS+ carriers	N
63. Seize conveyance-drug trafficking	N
64. South Africa sanctions	Y
65. 60 days' notice of plant closings	Y
66. Close unneeded military bases	Y
67. Keep welfare reform within $2.8b	N
68. Allow children housing exclusion	N
69. Shift $400m of NASA to homeless	Y
70. Cap Medicare patients' liability	Y
71. Prohibit employee polygraph testing	Y
72. Allow CIA to fund Contras	N
73. Revise unfair trade practices	Y
74. Focus SDI on accidental launch	Y
75. Bar Air Force $ for MX missile	?
76. Allow "real" increase in defense	N
77. Troop reduction in Europe of 50%	N
78. Ban nuclear tests above 1 kiloton	Y
79. Ban anti-satellite missile tests	Y
80. Observe certain limits of SALT II	Y
81. Restore four Civil Rights laws	Y
82. Prohibit aliens as strikebreakers	Y
83. Allow military malpractice suits	Y
84. Approval of $36m in Contra aid	N
85. $18b deficit reduction compromise	Y
86. Welfare reform of $5.7b for 5 years	Y
87. Raise taxes $12b/cut spending $3b	Y
88. Board to assess occupational risk	Y
89. Balanced budget by '93-via targets	Y
90. Bar licensing of two nuclear plants	Y
91. Remove victims compensation cap	N
92. Catastrophic health insurance	Y
93. Ban airline smoking-2 hours or less	Y
94. $1b/two year aid for the homeless	Y
95. Bar non-unions in union companies	Y
96. Increase FSLIC rescue to $15b	N
97. Impose quotas to lower trade deficit	Y
98. Reduce discretionary budget 21%	Y

Presidential Support Score: 1991 - 38%   1990 - 21%

ORTON, BILL -- Utah 3rd District [Democrat].   Counties of Carbon, Daggett, Duchesne, Emery, Grand, Salt Lake (pt.), San Juan, Sanpete, Sevier, Summit, Uintah, Utah and Wasatch. Prior Term: 1991-92. Born: September 22, 1949; Ogden, UT. Education: Brigham Young University (B.S., J.D.).   Occupation: IRS and private tax attorney; accounting and tax instructor; corporate director; Real Estate Tax Institute Advisory Board chairman.

1. Protection to Haitian refugees	#	6. Restrict NEA use of funds	N
2. Raise tax on wealthy; lower others	Y	7. Bar race-bias claim/habeas corpus	Y
3. Investigate Reagan hostage delay	Y	8. Ban race as death sentence factor	Y
4. Campaign finance revisions	Y	9. Exceptions to exclusionary rule	N
5. Unpaid leave to care for children	N	10. Allow sale of assault weapons	Y

ORTON, BILL (continued)

11. Life in prison/abolish death penalty	N	18. Civil Rights Act of 1991	N
12. Req conspiracy-price fixing cases	Y	19. Unlimited damages-discrimination	N
13. Unemployment benefits extension	N	20. Eliminate funds for supercollider	N
14. Tissue use of aborted fetuses	X	21. Terminate SDI except for research	N
15. Bar replacement of union strikers	Y	22. Req 7-day handgun waiting period	N
16. Hold foreign aid at $15b for '92	Y	23. Provide $30b for failed S&Ls	Y
17. Restore space station funding	N	24. Allow use of force against Iraq	Y

Presidential Support Score: 1991 - 58%

VERMONT

SANDERS, BERNARD -- Representative at Large [Independent]. Prior Term: 1991-92. Born: September 8, 1941; Brooklyn, NY. Education: University of Chicago (B.S.). Occupation: Freelance writer; youth counselor; carpenter; American People's History Society director; Burlington mayor (1981-89); college lecturer and professor.

1. Protection to Haitian refugees	Y	13. Unemployment benefits extension	Y
2. Raise tax on wealthy; lower others	Y	14. Tissue use of aborted fetuses	Y
3. Investigate Reagan hostage delay	Y	15. Bar replacement of union strikers	Y
4. Campaign finance revisions	Y	16. Hold foreign aid at $15b for '92	Y
5. Unpaid leave to care for children	Y	17. Restore space station funding	N
6. Restrict NEA use of funds	N	18. Civil Rights Act of 1991	Y
7. Bar race-bias claim/habeas corpus	N	19. Unlimited damages-discrimination	Y
8. Ban race as death sentence factor	N	20. Eliminate funds for supercollider	Y
9. Exceptions to exclusionary rule	N	21. Terminate SDI except for research	Y
10. Allow sale of assault weapons	N	22. Req 7-day handgun waiting period	N
11. Life in prison/abolish death penalty	Y	23. Provide $30b for failed S&Ls	N
12. Req conspiracy-price fixing cases	N	24. Allow use of force against Iraq	N

Presidential Support Score: 1991 - 22%

VIRGINIA

BATEMAN, HERBERT H. -- Virginia 1st District [Republican]. Counties of Accomack, Caroline, Charles City, Essex, Gloucester, James City, King and Queen, King George, King William, Lancaster, Mathews, Middlesex, New Kent, Northampton, Northumberland, Richmond, Westmoreland and York. Cities of Hampton, Newport News, Poquoson and Williamsburg. Prior Terms: 1983-92. Born: August 7, 1928; Elizabeth City, NC. Education: College of William and Mary (B.A.); Georgetown University (LL.B.). Military Service: U.S. Air Force, 1951-53. Occupation: High school teacher; law clerk (1956-57); attorney; associate legal counsel, U.S. Junior Chamber of Commerce (1962-63); general legal counsel, U.S. Junior Chamber of Commerce (1964-65); Virginia senator (1968-72).

1. Protection to Haitian refugees	N	9. Exceptions to exclusionary rule	Y
2. Raise tax on wealthy; lower others	N	10. Allow sale of assault weapons	N
3. Investigate Reagan hostage delay	N	11. Life in prison/abolish death penalty	N
4. Campaign finance revisions	N	12. Req conspiracy-price fixing cases	Y
5. Unpaid leave to care for children	N	13. Unemployment benefits extension	N
6. Restrict NEA use of funds	Y	14. Tissue use of aborted fetuses	N
7. Bar race-bias claim/habeas corpus	Y	15. Bar replacement of union strikers	N
8. Ban race as death sentence factor	Y	16. Hold foreign aid at $15b for '92	Y

BATEMAN, HERBERT H. (continued)

17. Restore space station funding	Y
18. Civil Rights Act of 1991	N
19. Unlimited damages-discrimination	N
20. Eliminate funds for supercollider	N
21. Terminate SDI except for research	N
22. Req 7-day handgun waiting period	Y
23. Provide $30b for failed S&Ls	Y
24. Allow use of force against Iraq	Y
25. Allow $15b in foreign aid for '91	Y
26. Revise & extend legal immigration	Y
27. Suspend aid to Angolan rebels	N
28. Democratic tax plan proposals	N
29. Cut defense 5% across the board	N
30. Textile import quotas-veto override	N
31. Abortion service for military abroad	N
32. Limits on high income farmers	N
33. Family medical leave-veto override	N
34. Req submission of balanced budget	N
35. Balanced budget amendment	Y
36. Amendment to ban flag desecration	Y
37. Reauthorize Amtrak-veto override	Y
38. Retraining aid for coal miners	N
39. Suspend El Salvador military aid	N
40. Expand child care aid/tax credit	N
41. Raise House salary/omit honoraria	Y
42. Toughen oil-spill liability	N
43. Restitution to Japanese interned	Y
44. Protect Chinese & C.A. nationals	N
45. Abortion $ for rape/incest cases	N
46. Allow religious schools to bar gays	Y
47. Bar broadcaster fairness doctrine	Y
48. Bar cap gains cut/reinstate IRA	N
49. Bar unions equal voice in pension	Y
50. Bar assembly of chemical weapons	N
51. Ban plutonium/uranium production	N
52. Cap MX missile deployment at 50	N
53. Allow $3b for 2 stealth bombers	Y
54. Publish bio-warfare experiments	N
55. Raise minimum wage-veto override	N
56. Bar transfer of FS-X technology	N
57. Cut defense and raise domestic $	?
58. Uniform poll closing in 48 states	N
59. Req foreign investment disclosure	N
60. Textile import quotas-veto override	Y
61. Bar abortion funding in Wash, DC	Y
62. Notify spouses of AIDS+ carriers	N
63. Seize conveyance-drug trafficking	Y
64. South Africa sanctions	N
65. 60 days' notice of plant closings	N
66. Close unneeded military bases	N
67. Keep welfare reform within $2.8b	Y
68. Allow children housing exclusion	Y
69. Shift $400m of NASA to homeless	N
70. Cap Medicare patients' liability	N
71. Prohibit employee polygraph testing	N
72. Allow CIA to fund Contras	Y
73. Revise unfair trade practices	N
74. Focus SDI on accidental launch	N
75. Bar Air Force $ for MX missile	N
76. Allow "real" increase in defense	Y
77. Troop reduction in Europe of 50%	N
78. Ban nuclear tests above 1 kiloton	N

79. Ban anti-satellite missile tests	N
80. Observe certain limits of SALT II	N
81. Restore four Civil Rights laws	N
82. Prohibit aliens as strikebreakers	N
83. Allow military malpractice suits	N
84. Approval of $36m in Contra aid	Y
85. $18b deficit reduction compromise	N
86. Welfare reform of $5.7b for 5 years	N
87. Raise taxes $12b/cut spending $3b	N
88. Board to assess occupational risk	N
89. Balanced budget by '93-via targets	N
90. Bar licensing of two nuclear plants	N
91. Remove victims compensation cap	N
92. Catastrophic health insurance	N
93. Ban airline smoking-2 hours or less	N
94. $1b/two year aid for the homeless	N
95. Bar non-unions in union companies	C
96. Increase FSLIC rescue to $15b	C
97. Impose quotas to lower trade deficit	N
98. Reduce discretionary budget 21%	N
99. Immigration reform/alien amnesty	N
100. South Africa sanctions-veto override	Y
101. Tax overhaul to revise income tax	N
102. Use of military in drug war	N
103. Delete 12 MX/add conventional wpn	N
104. Raise speed limit to 65 mph	Y
105. Require Pentagon to buy US goods	N
106. AIDS insurance non-discrimination	N
107. Prohibit Saudi arms sales	Y
108. Ease Gun Control Act of 1968	Y
109. Bar interstate handgun transport	Y
110. Make company emissions known	N
111. Allow toxic victims to sue in fed ct	N
112. Superfund waste cleanup of $10b	N
113. 90 days notice of plant closings	N
114. $20b in Medicare cuts/tax increases	N
115. Spending cuts and tax increases	N
116. Set school lunch lmt-250% poverty	Y
117. $75m for youth work projects	N
118. Allow Angolan military assistance	Y
119. Suspend defense payments for abuse	N
120. Drop SS COLAs/$12b tax increase	Y
121. Approve $1.5b for 21 MX missiles	Y
122. Emergency farm credit/revisions	N
123. Duty on Taiwan/Hong Kong/S Korea	N
124. Limit steel imports to 17%	N
125. Cut $ to schools that bar prayer	Y
126. $50b-taxes; cut Medicare/spending	Y
127. Limit Pershing II/cruise in Europe	N
128. Delete $7.1b for 34 B-1 bombers	N
129. Bar purchase of Sergeant York guns	N
130. El Salvador military/economic aid	Y
131. Bar mining of Nicaraguan waters	N
132. Physician fee freeze for Medicare	Y
133. $49b in "sin"/phone/insurance taxes	Y
134. Allow sale of Conrail	Y
135. Equal Rights Amendment	N
136. Authorize Marines in Lebanon	Y
137. Eminent domain for coal companies	N
138. Prohibit EPA clean air sanctions	Y
139. SS retirement age increase/reforms	Y

Presidential Support Score: 1991 - 82%   1990 - 69%

PICKETT, OWEN B. -- Virginia 2nd District [Democrat]. Cities of Norfolk and Virginia Beach. Prior Terms: 1987-92. Born: August 31, 1930; Richmond, VA. Education: Virginia Polytechnic Institute (B.S.); Virginia State University; University of Richmond (LL.B.). Occupation: Attorney; senior partner, Pickett, Lyle, Siegel, Drescher & Croshaw; state delegate (1972-86); Democratic State Central Committee chairman (1980-82).

1.	Protection to Haitian refugees	N	50.	Bar assembly of chemical weapons	N
2.	Raise tax on wealthy; lower others	N	51.	Ban plutonium/uranium production	N
3.	Investigate Reagan hostage delay	Y	52.	Cap MX missile deployment at 50	Y
4.	Campaign finance revisions	N	53.	Allow $3b for 2 stealth bombers	Y
5.	Unpaid leave to care for children	N	54.	Publish bio-warfare experiments	N
6.	Restrict NEA use of funds	Y	55.	Raise minimum wage-veto override	Y
7.	Bar race-bias claim/habeas corpus	Y	56.	Bar transfer of FS-X technology	N
8.	Ban race as death sentence factor	N	57.	Cut defense and raise domestic $	N
9.	Exceptions to exclusionary rule	N	58.	Uniform poll closing in 48 states	N
10.	Allow sale of assault weapons	Y	59.	Req foreign investment disclosure	Y
11.	Life in prison/abolish death penalty	N	60.	Textile import quotas-veto override	Y
12.	Req conspiracy-price fixing cases	N	61.	Bar abortion funding in Wash, DC	N
13.	Unemployment benefits extension	Y	62.	Notify spouses of AIDS+ carriers	N
14.	Tissue use of aborted fetuses	Y	63.	Seize conveyance-drug trafficking	N
15.	Bar replacement of union strikers	N	64.	South Africa sanctions	Y
16.	Hold foreign aid at $15b for '92	Y	65.	60 days' notice of plant closings	Y
17.	Restore space station funding	Y	66.	Close unneeded military bases	N
18.	Civil Rights Act of 1991	Y	67.	Keep welfare reform within $2.8b	N
19.	Unlimited damages-discrimination	N	68.	Allow children housing exclusion	N
20.	Eliminate funds for supercollider	N	69.	Shift $400m of NASA to homeless	N
21.	Terminate SDI except for research	N	70.	Cap Medicare patients' liability	Y
22.	Req 7-day handgun waiting period	N	71.	Prohibit employee polygraph testing	N
23.	Provide $30b for failed S&Ls	Y	72.	Allow CIA to fund Contras	Y
24.	Allow use of force against Iraq	Y	73.	Revise unfair trade practices	Y
25.	Allow $15b in foreign aid for '91	N	74.	Focus SDI on accidental launch	Y
26.	Revise & extend legal immigration	Y	75.	Bar Air Force $ for MX missile	N
27.	Suspend aid to Angolan rebels	Y	76.	Allow "real" increase in defense	N
28.	Democratic tax plan proposals	Y	77.	Troop reduction in Europe of 50%	N
29.	Cut defense 5% across the board	N	78.	Ban nuclear tests above 1 kiloton	N
30.	Textile import quotas-veto override	Y	79.	Ban anti-satellite missile tests	N
31.	Abortion service for military abroad	Y	80.	Observe certain limits of SALT II	N
32.	Limits on high income farmers	N	81.	Restore four Civil Rights laws	Y
33.	Family medical leave-veto override	N	82.	Prohibit aliens as strikebreakers	Y
34.	Req submission of balanced budget	N	83.	Allow military malpractice suits	Y
35.	Balanced budget amendment	N	84.	Approval of $36m in Contra aid	Y
36.	Amendment to ban flag desecration	Y	85.	$18b deficit reduction compromise	Y
37.	Reauthorize Amtrak-veto override	Y	86.	Welfare reform of $5.7b for 5 years	N
38.	Retraining aid for coal miners	N	87.	Raise taxes $12b/cut spending $3b	Y
39.	Suspend El Salvador military aid	N	88.	Board to assess occupational risk	N
40.	Expand child care aid/tax credit	N	89.	Balanced budget by '93-via targets	N
41.	Raise House salary/omit honoraria	N	90.	Bar licensing of two nuclear plants	N
42.	Toughen oil-spill liability	N	91.	Remove victims compensation cap	N
43.	Restitution to Japanese interned	N	92.	Catastrophic health insurance	Y
44.	Protect Chinese & C.A. nationals	Y	93.	Ban airline smoking-2 hours or less	Y
45.	Abortion $ for rape/incest cases	Y	94.	$1b/two year aid for the homeless	Y
46.	Allow religious schools to bar gays	Y	95.	Bar non-unions in union companies	Y
47.	Bar broadcaster fairness doctrine	N	96.	Increase FSLIC rescue to $15b	N
48.	Bar cap gains cut/reinstate IRA	N	97.	Impose quotas to lower trade deficit	N
49.	Bar unions equal voice in pension	Y	98.	Reduce discretionary budget 21%	Y

Presidential Support Score: 1991 - 52%   1990 - 47%

BLILEY, THOMAS J., Jr. -- Virginia 3rd District [Republican]. Counties of Chesterfield (pt.) and Henrico. City of Richmond. Prior Terms: 1981-92. Born: January 28, 1932; Chesterfield County, VA. Education: Georgetown University (B.A.). Military Service: U.S. Navy. Occupation: Richmond city councilman (1968); vice-mayor (1968); mayor (1970-77); president, Virginia Municipal League; board member, National League of Cities; board member, Metropolitan Richmond Chamber of Commerce; board member, Crippled

BLILEY, THOMAS J., Jr. (continued)
Children's Hospital; board member, St. Mary's Hospital; board member, Board of Visitors, Virginia Commonwealth University; board member, Southern Bank and Trust Co.

1. Protection to Haitian refugees	N	62. Notify spouses of AIDS+ carriers	Y
2. Raise tax on wealthy; lower others	N	63. Seize conveyance-drug trafficking	Y
3. Investigate Reagan hostage delay	N	64. South Africa sanctions	Y
4. Campaign finance revisions	N	65. 60 days' notice of plant closings	N
5. Unpaid leave to care for children	N	66. Close unneeded military bases	Y
6. Restrict NEA use of funds	Y	67. Keep welfare reform within $2.8b	Y
7. Bar race-bias claim/habeas corpus	Y	68. Allow children housing exclusion	N
8. Ban race as death sentence factor	Y	69. Shift $400m of NASA to homeless	N
9. Exceptions to exclusionary rule	Y	70. Cap Medicare patients' liability	N
10. Allow sale of assault weapons	Y	71. Prohibit employee polygraph testing	N
11. Life in prison/abolish death penalty	N	72. Allow CIA to fund Contras	Y
12. Req conspiracy-price fixing cases	Y	73. Revise unfair trade practices	N
13. Unemployment benefits extension	N	74. Focus SDI on accidental launch	N
14. Tissue use of aborted fetuses	N	75. Bar Air Force $ for MX missile	N
15. Bar replacement of union strikers	N	76. Allow "real" increase in defense	Y
16. Hold foreign aid at $15b for '92	Y	77. Troop reduction in Europe of 50%	N
17. Restore space station funding	Y	78. Ban nuclear tests above 1 kiloton	N
18. Civil Rights Act of 1991	N	79. Ban anti-satellite missile tests	N
19. Unlimited damages-discrimination	N	80. Observe certain limits of SALT II	N
20. Eliminate funds for supercollider	N	81. Restore four Civil Rights laws	N
21. Terminate SDI except for research	N	82. Prohibit aliens as strikebreakers	N
22. Req 7-day handgun waiting period	N	83. Allow military malpractice suits	Y
23. Provide $30b for failed S&Ls	Y	84. Approval of $36m in Contra aid	Y
24. Allow use of force against Iraq	Y	85. $18b deficit reduction compromise	Y
25. Allow $15b in foreign aid for '91	Y	86. Welfare reform of $5.7b for 5 years	N
26. Revise & extend legal immigration	Y	87. Raise taxes $12b/cut spending $3b	N
27. Suspend aid to Angolan rebels	N	88. Board to assess occupational risk	X
28. Democratic tax plan proposals	N	89. Balanced budget by '93-via targets	Y
29. Cut defense 5% across the board	N	90. Bar licensing of two nuclear plants	N
30. Textile import quotas-veto override	Y	91. Remove victims compensation cap	N
31. Abortion service for military abroad	N	92. Catastrophic health insurance	N
32. Limits on high income farmers	Y	93. Ban airline smoking-2 hours or less	N
33. Family medical leave-veto override	N	94. $1b/two year aid for the homeless	N
34. Req submission of balanced budget	N	95. Bar non-unions in union companies	N
35. Balanced budget amendment	Y	96. Increase FSLIC rescue to $15b	N
36. Amendment to ban flag desecration	Y	97. Impose quotas to lower trade deficit	N
37. Reauthorize Amtrak-veto override	Y	98. Reduce discretionary budget 21%	Y
38. Retraining aid for coal miners	N	99. Immigration reform/alien amnesty	N
39. Suspend El Salvador military aid	N	100. South Africa sanctions-veto override	Y
40. Expand child care aid/tax credit	N	101. Tax overhaul to revise income tax	Y
41. Raise House salary/omit honoraria	N	102. Use of military in drug war	Y
42. Toughen oil-spill liability	N	103. Delete 12 MX/add conventional wpn	N
43. Restitution to Japanese interned	N	104. Raise speed limit to 65 mph	Y
44. Protect Chinese & C.A. nationals	N	105. Require Pentagon to buy US goods	N
45. Abortion $ for rape/incest cases	N	106. AIDS insurance non-discrimination	N
46. Allow religious schools to bar gays	Y	107. Prohibit Saudi arms sales	N
47. Bar broadcaster fairness doctrine	N	108. Ease Gun Control Act of 1968	Y
48. Bar cap gains cut/reinstate IRA	N	109. Bar interstate handgun transport	N
49. Bar unions equal voice in pension	Y	110. Make company emissions known	N
50. Bar assembly of chemical weapons	N	111. Allow toxic victims to sue in fed ct	N
51. Ban plutonium/uranium production	N	112. Superfund waste cleanup of $10b	N
52. Cap MX missile deployment at 50	N	113. 90 days notice of plant closings	N
53. Allow $3b for 2 stealth bombers	Y	114. $20b in Medicare cuts/tax increases	N
54. Publish bio-warfare experiments	N	115. Spending cuts and tax increases	N
55. Raise minimum wage-veto override	N	116. Set school lunch lmt-250% poverty	Y
56. Bar transfer of FS-X technology	N	117. $75m for youth work projects	N
57. Cut defense and raise domestic $	N	118. Allow Angolan military assistance	Y
58. Uniform poll closing in 48 states	N	119. Suspend defense payments for abuse	N
59. Req foreign investment disclosure	N	120. Drop SS COLAs/$12b tax increase	N
60. Textile import quotas-veto override	Y	121. Approve $1.5b for 21 MX missiles	Y
61. Bar abortion funding in Wash, DC	Y	122. Emergency farm credit/revisions	Y

BLILEY, THOMAS J., Jr. (continued)

123. Duty on Taiwan/Hong Kong/S Korea	N	
124. Limit steel imports to 17%	N	
125. Cut $ to schools that bar prayer	Y	
126. $50b-taxes; cut Medicare/spending	Y	
127. Limit Pershing II/cruise in Europe	N	
128. Delete $7.1b for 34 B-1 bombers	N	
129. Bar purchase of Sergeant York guns	N	
130. El Salvador military/economic aid	Y	
131. Bar mining of Nicaraguan waters	N	
132. Physician fee freeze for Medicare	Y	
133. $49b in "sin"/phone/insurance taxes	Y	
134. Allow sale of Conrail	Y	
135. Equal Rights Amendment	N	
136. Authorize Marines in Lebanon	Y	
137. Eminent domain for coal companies	N	
138. Prohibit EPA clean air sanctions	Y	
139. SS retirement age increase/reforms	Y	
140. Auto domestic content requirement	N	
141. Delete jobs program funding	Y	
142. Highway-gas tax bill	N	
143. Cut $5b from defense for Medicare	N	
144. Emergency housing aid of $1b	Y	

Presidential Support Score: 1991 - 81%   1990 - 66%

SISISKY, NORMAN -- Virginia 4th District [Democrat]. Counties of Amelia, Brunswick, Chesterfield (pt.), Dinwiddie, Greensville, Isle of Wight, Nottoway, Powhatan, Prince George, Southampton, Surry and Sussex. Cities of Chesapeake, Colonial Heights, Emporia, Franklin, Hopewell, Petersburg, Portsmouth and Suffolk. Prior Terms: 1983-92. Born: June 9, 1927; Baltimore, MD. Education: Virginia Commonwealth University (B.S.). Military Service: U.S. Navy, 1945-46. Occupation: Operated Pepsi-Cola bottling company; Virginia representative (1973-82); served on Board of Visitors for Virginia State University; commissioner, Petersburg Hospital Authority; trustee, Virginia State College Foundation.

1. Protection to Haitian refugees	Y	41. Raise House salary/omit honoraria	Y
2. Raise tax on wealthy; lower others	Y	42. Toughen oil-spill liability	N
3. Investigate Reagan hostage delay	Y	43. Restitution to Japanese interned	N
4. Campaign finance revisions	N	44. Protect Chinese & C.A. nationals	N
5. Unpaid leave to care for children	N	45. Abortion $ for rape/incest cases	Y
6. Restrict NEA use of funds	Y	46. Allow religious schools to bar gays	N
7. Bar race-bias claim/habeas corpus	Y	47. Bar broadcaster fairness doctrine	N
8. Ban race as death sentence factor	N	48. Bar cap gains cut/reinstate IRA	Y
9. Exceptions to exclusionary rule	Y	49. Bar unions equal voice in pension	Y
10. Allow sale of assault weapons	Y	50. Bar assembly of chemical weapons	N
11. Life in prison/abolish death penalty	N	51. Ban plutonium/uranium production	N
12. Req conspiracy-price fixing cases	Y	52. Cap MX missile deployment at 50	Y
13. Unemployment benefits extension	Y	53. Allow $3b for 2 stealth bombers	N
14. Tissue use of aborted fetuses	Y	54. Publish bio-warfare experiments	Y
15. Bar replacement of union strikers	N	55. Raise minimum wage-veto override	Y
16. Hold foreign aid at $15b for '92	Y	56. Bar transfer of FS-X technology	Y
17. Restore space station funding	?	57. Cut defense and raise domestic $	N
18. Civil Rights Act of 1991	?	58. Uniform poll closing in 48 states	N
19. Unlimited damages-discrimination	?	59. Req foreign investment disclosure	Y
20. Eliminate funds for supercollider	Y	60. Textile import quotas-veto override	Y
21. Terminate SDI except for research	N	61. Bar abortion funding in Wash, DC	N
22. Req 7-day handgun waiting period	N	62. Notify spouses of AIDS+ carriers	N
23. Provide $30b for failed S&Ls	Y	63. Seize conveyance-drug trafficking	N
24. Allow use of force against Iraq	Y	64. South Africa sanctions	Y
25. Allow $15b in foreign aid for '91	Y	65. 60 days' notice of plant closings	Y
26. Revise & extend legal immigration	Y	66. Close unneeded military bases	N
27. Suspend aid to Angolan rebels	N	67. Keep welfare reform within $2.8b	Y
28. Democratic tax plan proposals	Y	68. Allow children housing exclusion	N
29. Cut defense 5% across the board	N	69. Shift $400m of NASA to homeless	N
30. Textile import quotas-veto override	Y	70. Cap Medicare patients' liability	Y
31. Abortion service for military abroad	Y	71. Prohibit employee polygraph testing	N
32. Limits on high income farmers	N	72. Allow CIA to fund Contras	Y
33. Family medical leave-veto override	N	73. Revise unfair trade practices	Y
34. Req submission of balanced budget	Y	74. Focus SDI on accidental launch	Y
35. Balanced budget amendment	Y	75. Bar Air Force $ for MX missile	N
36. Amendment to ban flag desecration	Y	76. Allow "real" increase in defense	Y
37. Reauthorize Amtrak-veto override	N	77. Troop reduction in Europe of 50%	N
38. Retraining aid for coal miners	N	78. Ban nuclear tests above 1 kiloton	N
39. Suspend El Salvador military aid	N	79. Ban anti-satellite missile tests	N
40. Expand child care aid/tax credit	Y	80. Observe certain limits of SALT II	N

SISISKY, NORMAN (continued)

81. Restore four Civil Rights laws	Y
82. Prohibit aliens as strikebreakers	Y
83. Allow military malpractice suits	Y
84. Approval of $36m in Contra aid	Y
85. $18b deficit reduction compromise	Y
86. Welfare reform of $5.7b for 5 years	Y
87. Raise taxes $12b/cut spending $3b	Y
88. Board to assess occupational risk	Y
89. Balanced budget by '93-via targets	Y
90. Bar licensing of two nuclear plants	N
91. Remove victims compensation cap	N
92. Catastrophic health insurance	Y
93. Ban airline smoking-2 hours or less	N
94. $1b/two year aid for the homeless	Y
95. Bar non-unions in union companies	N
96. Increase FSLIC rescue to $15b	N
97. Impose quotas to lower trade deficit	N
98. Reduce discretionary budget 21%	Y
99. Immigration reform/alien amnesty	Y
100. South Africa sanctions-veto override	Y
101. Tax overhaul to revise income tax	N
102. Use of military in drug war	N
103. Delete 12 MX/add conventional wpn	N
104. Raise speed limit to 65 mph	Y
105. Require Pentagon to buy US goods	N
106. AIDS insurance non-discrimination	Y
107. Prohibit Saudi arms sales	Y
108. Ease Gun Control Act of 1968	Y
109. Bar interstate handgun transport	N
110. Make company emissions known	N

111. Allow toxic victims to sue in fed ct	N
112. Superfund waste cleanup of $10b	N
113. 90 days notice of plant closings	N
114. $20b in Medicare cuts/tax increases	Y
115. Spending cuts and tax increases	Y
116. Set school lunch lmt-250% poverty	N
117. $75m for youth work projects	N
118. Allow Angolan military assistance	N
119. Suspend defense payments for abuse	N
120. Drop SS COLAs/$12b tax increase	N
121. Approve $1.5b for 21 MX missiles	N
122. Emergency farm credit/revisions	Y
123. Duty on Taiwan/Hong Kong/S Korea	N
124. Limit steel imports to 17%	Y
125. Cut $ to schools that bar prayer	N
126. $50b-taxes; cut Medicare/spending	Y
127. Limit Pershing II/cruise in Europe	N
128. Delete $7.1b for 34 B-1 bombers	N
129. Bar purchase of Sergeant York guns	N
130. El Salvador military/economic aid	Y
131. Bar mining of Nicaraguan waters	Y
132. Physician fee freeze for Medicare	N
133. $49b in "sin"/phone/insurance taxes	Y
134. Allow sale of Conrail	?
135. Equal Rights Amendment	Y
136. Authorize Marines in Lebanon	Y
137. Eminent domain for coal companies	N
138. Prohibit EPA clean air sanctions	?
139. SS retirement age increase/reforms	N

Presidential Support Score: 1991 - 45%   1990 - 43%

PAYNE, LEWIS F., Jr. -- Virginia 5th District [Democrat]. Counties of Appomattox, Bedford, Buckingham, Campbell, Carroll, Charlotte, Cumberland, Fluvanna, Franklin, Halifax, Henry, Lunenburg, Mecklenburg, Nelson, Patrick, Pittsylvania, Prince Edward. Cities of Bedford, Danville, Lynchburg (pt.), Martinsville and South Boston. Prior Terms: 1988 (Special Election)-1992. Born: July 9, 1945. Education: Virginia Military Institute (B.S.), University of Virginia (M.B.A.). Military Service: U.S. Army & Army Reserves. Occupation: Construction engineer; staff engineering associate, C&P Telephone Co. of Virginia (1970-71); planning and development manager (1973-75), president (1976-85) and CEO (1985-88), Wintergreen Development, Inc.

1. Protection to Haitian refugees	Y
2. Raise tax on wealthy; lower others	Y
3. Investigate Reagan hostage delay	Y
4. Campaign finance revisions	Y
5. Unpaid leave to care for children	N
6. Restrict NEA use of funds	Y
7. Bar race-bias claim/habeas corpus	Y
8. Ban race as death sentence factor	Y
9. Exceptions to exclusionary rule	Y
10. Allow sale of assault weapons	Y
11. Life in prison/abolish death penalty	N
12. Req conspiracy-price fixing cases	Y
13. Unemployment benefits extension	Y
14. Tissue use of aborted fetuses	Y
15. Bar replacement of union strikers	N
16. Hold foreign aid at $15b for '92	Y
17. Restore space station funding	N
18. Civil Rights Act of 1991	Y
19. Unlimited damages-discrimination	N
20. Eliminate funds for supercollider	N

21. Terminate SDI except for research	N
22. Req 7-day handgun waiting period	N
23. Provide $30b for failed S&Ls	Y
24. Allow use of force against Iraq	Y
25. Allow $15b in foreign aid for '91	Y
26. Revise & extend legal immigration	N
27. Suspend aid to Angolan rebels	Y
28. Democratic tax plan proposals	Y
29. Cut defense 5% across the board	N
30. Textile import quotas-veto override	Y
31. Abortion service for military abroad	Y
32. Limits on high income farmers	N
33. Family medical leave-veto override	N
34. Req submission of balanced budget	Y
35. Balanced budget amendment	Y
36. Amendment to ban flag desecration	Y
37. Reauthorize Amtrak-veto override	Y
38. Retraining aid for coal miners	Y
39. Suspend El Salvador military aid	Y
40. Expand child care aid/tax credit	Y

PAYNE, LEWIS F., Jr. (continued)

41. Raise House salary/omit honoraria	N	56. Bar transfer of FS-X technology	Y
42. Toughen oil-spill liability	N	57. Cut defense and raise domestic $	N
43. Restitution to Japanese interned	N	58. Uniform poll closing in 48 states	N
44. Protect Chinese & C.A. nationals	N	59. Req foreign investment disclosure	Y
45. Abortion $ for rape/incest cases	Y	60. Textile import quotas-veto override	Y
46. Allow religious schools to bar gays	Y	61. Bar abortion funding in Wash, DC	N
47. Bar broadcaster fairness doctrine	Y	62. Notify spouses of AIDS+ carriers	N
48. Bar cap gains cut/reinstate IRA	N	63. Seize conveyance-drug trafficking	Y
49. Bar unions equal voice in pension	Y	64. South Africa sanctions	Y
50. Bar assembly of chemical weapons	N	65. 60 days' notice of plant closings	Y
51. Ban plutonium/uranium production	Y	66. Close unneeded military bases	N
52. Cap MX missile deployment at 50	Y	67. Keep welfare reform within $2.8b	Y
53. Allow $3b for 2 stealth bombers	N	68. Allow children housing exclusion	N
54. Publish bio-warfare experiments	Y	69. Shift $400m of NASA to homeless	N
55. Raise minimum wage-veto override	N		

Presidential Support Score: 1991 - 47%   1990 - 42%

OLIN, JAMES R. (Jim) -- Virginia 6th District [Democrat].   Counties of Alleghany, Amherst, Augusta, Bath, Botetourt, Highland, Roanoke, Rockbridge and Rockingham.   Cities of Buena Vista, Clifton Forge, Covington, Harrisburg, Lexington, Lynchburg (pt.), Roanoke, Salem, Staunton and Waynesboro.   Prior Terms: 1983-92.   Born: February 28, 1920; Chicago. IL.   Education: Cornell University (B.S.).   Military Service: U.S. Army, 1943-46.   Occupation: General Electric executive; county board of supervisors; board member, Burrell Memorial Hospital.

1. Protection to Haitian refugees	Y	38. Retraining aid for coal miners	Y
2. Raise tax on wealthy; lower others	Y	39. Suspend El Salvador military aid	Y
3. Investigate Reagan hostage delay	Y	40. Expand child care aid/tax credit	N
4. Campaign finance revisions	Y	41. Raise House salary/omit honoraria	N
5. Unpaid leave to care for children	N	42. Toughen oil-spill liability	?
6. Restrict NEA use of funds	Y	43. Restitution to Japanese interned	N
7. Bar race-bias claim/habeas corpus	Y	44. Protect Chinese & C.A. nationals	Y
8. Ban race as death sentence factor	Y	45. Abortion $ for rape/incest cases	Y
9. Exceptions to exclusionary rule	N	46. Allow religious schools to bar gays	N
10. Allow sale of assault weapons	Y	47. Bar broadcaster fairness doctrine	N
11. Life in prison/abolish death penalty	Y	48. Bar cap gains cut/reinstate IRA	Y
12. Req conspiracy-price fixing cases	Y	49. Bar unions equal voice in pension	Y
13. Unemployment benefits extension	N	50. Bar assembly of chemical weapons	Y
14. Tissue use of aborted fetuses	Y	51. Ban plutonium/uranium production	Y
15. Bar replacement of union strikers	Y	52. Cap MX missile deployment at 50	Y
16. Hold foreign aid at $15b for '92	Y	53. Allow $3b for 2 stealth bombers	N
17. Restore space station funding	N	54. Publish bio-warfare experiments	Y
18. Civil Rights Act of 1991	Y	55. Raise minimum wage-veto override	Y
19. Unlimited damages-discrimination	N	56. Bar transfer of FS-X technology	Y
20. Eliminate funds for supercollider	N	57. Cut defense and raise domestic $	N
21. Terminate SDI except for research	N	58. Uniform poll closing in 48 states	N
22. Req 7-day handgun waiting period	N	59. Req foreign investment disclosure	Y
23. Provide $30b for failed S&Ls	Y	60. Textile import quotas-veto override	Y
24. Allow use of force against Iraq	N	61. Bar abortion funding in Wash, DC	N
25. Allow $15b in foreign aid for '91	?	62. Notify spouses of AIDS+ carriers	N
26. Revise & extend legal immigration	N	63. Seize conveyance-drug trafficking	N
27. Suspend aid to Angolan rebels	N	64. South Africa sanctions	Y
28. Democratic tax plan proposals	Y	65. 60 days' notice of plant closings	Y
29. Cut defense 5% across the board	N	66. Close unneeded military bases	Y
30. Textile import quotas-veto override	Y	67. Keep welfare reform within $2.8b	Y
31. Abortion service for military abroad	Y	68. Allow children housing exclusion	N
32. Limits on high income farmers	N	69. Shift $400m of NASA to homeless	N
33. Family medical leave-veto override	N	70. Cap Medicare patients' liability	N
34. Req submission of balanced budget	Y	71. Prohibit employee polygraph testing	Y
35. Balanced budget amendment	Y	72. Allow CIA to fund Contras	N
36. Amendment to ban flag desecration	Y	73. Revise unfair trade practices	Y
37. Reauthorize Amtrak-veto override	Y	74. Focus SDI on accidental launch	Y

OLIN, JAMES R. (continued)

75.	Bar Air Force $ for MX missile	Y	108.	Ease Gun Control Act of 1968	Y
76.	Allow "real" increase in defense	N	109.	Bar interstate handgun transport	N
77.	Troop reduction in Europe of 50%	N	110.	Make company emissions known	N
78.	Ban nuclear tests above 1 kiloton	Y	111.	Allow toxic victims to sue in fed ct	N
79.	Ban anti-satellite missile tests	Y	112.	Superfund waste cleanup of $10b	N
80.	Observe certain limits of SALT II	Y	113.	90 days notice of plant closings	N
81.	Restore four Civil Rights laws	Y	114.	$20b in Medicare cuts/tax increases	Y
82.	Prohibit aliens as strikebreakers	Y	115.	Spending cuts and tax increases	N
83.	Allow military malpractice suits	Y	116.	Set school lunch lmt-250% poverty	Y
84.	Approval of $36m in Contra aid	N	117.	$75m for youth work projects	N
85.	$18b deficit reduction compromise	N	118.	Allow Angolan military assistance	N
86.	Welfare reform of $5.7b for 5 years	N	119.	Suspend defense payments for abuse	N
87.	Raise taxes $12b/cut spending $3b	Y	120.	Drop SS COLAs/$12b tax increase	Y
88.	Board to assess occupational risk	Y	121.	Approve $1.5b for 21 MX missiles	N
89.	Balanced budget by '93-via targets	Y	122.	Emergency farm credit/revisions	Y
90.	Bar licensing of two nuclear plants	N	123.	Duty on Taiwan/Hong Kong/S Korea	Y
91.	Remove victims compensation cap	N	124.	Limit steel imports to 17%	N
92.	Catastrophic health insurance	N	125.	Cut $ to schools that bar prayer	N
93.	Ban airline smoking-2 hours or less	N	126.	$50b-taxes; cut Medicare/spending	Y
94.	$1b/two year aid for the homeless	N	127.	Limit Pershing II/cruise in Europe	N
95.	Bar non-unions in union companies	N	128.	Delete $7.1b for 34 B-1 bombers	N
96.	Increase FSLIC rescue to $15b	N	129.	Bar purchase of Sergeant York guns	Y
97.	Impose quotas to lower trade deficit	N	130.	El Salvador military/economic aid	N
98.	Reduce discretionary budget 21%	Y	131.	Bar mining of Nicaraguan waters	Y
99.	Immigration reform/alien amnesty	N	132.	Physician fee freeze for Medicare	Y
100.	South Africa sanctions-veto override	Y	133.	$49b in "sin"/phone/insurance taxes	Y
101.	Tax overhaul to revise income tax	N	134.	Allow sale of Conrail	N
102.	Use of military in drug war	N	135.	Equal Rights Amendment	Y
103.	Delete 12 MX/add conventional wpn	Y	136.	Authorize Marines in Lebanon	Y
104.	Raise speed limit to 65 mph	N	137.	Eminent domain for coal companies	N
105.	Require Pentagon to buy US goods	Y	138.	Prohibit EPA clean air sanctions	N
106.	AIDS insurance non-discrimination	Y	139.	SS retirement age increase/reforms	Y
107.	Prohibit Saudi arms sales	Y			

Presidential Support Score: 1991 - 45%   1990 - 35%

ALLEN, GEORGE F. -- Virginia 7th District [Republican]. Counties of Albemarle, Clark, Culpeper, Fauquier, Frederick, Goochland, Greene, Hanover, Louisa, Madison, Orange, Page, Prince William (pt.), Rappahannock, Shenandoah, Spotsylvania, Stafford (pt.) and Warren.   Cities of Charlottesville, Fredericksburg, Manassas, Manassas Park and Winchester. Prior Term: 1991 (Special Election)-1992. Born: March 8, 1952. Education: University of Virginia (B.A., J.D.). Occupation: Lawyer; state delegate (1983-89).

1.	Protection to Haitian refugees	N	4.	Campaign finance revisions	N
2.	Raise tax on wealthy; lower others	N	5.	Unpaid leave to care for children	N
3.	Investigate Reagan hostage delay	N			

Rep. Allen was sworn in Nov. 12, 1991, to succeed D. French Slaughter.

Presidential Support Score: 1991 - 69%

MORAN, JAMES P., Jr. -- Virginia 8th District [Democrat]. Counties of Fairfax (pt.), Prince William (pt.) and Stafford (pt.). City of Alexandria. Prior Term: 1991-92. Born: May 16, 1945; Buffalo, NY. Education: Holy Cross College (B.A.); University of Pittsburgh (M.P.A.); University of Southern California. Occupation: Special assistant to defense research and analysis contractor; investment broker; Senate committee staff member; Library of Congress policy specialist, HEW auditor, accountant, senior budget analyst and comptroller; Alexandria city councilman (1979-82), vice-mayor (1982-84) and mayor (1985-90).

1.	Protection to Haitian refugees	Y	3.	Investigate Reagan hostage delay	Y
2.	Raise tax on wealthy; lower others	Y	4.	Campaign finance revisions	Y

MORAN, JAMES P., Jr. (continued)

5.	Unpaid leave to care for children	Y	15.	Bar replacement of union strikers	Y
6.	Restrict NEA use of funds	?	16.	Hold foreign aid at $15b for '92	Y
7.	Bar race-bias claim/habeas corpus	Y	17.	Restore space station funding	Y
8.	Ban race as death sentence factor	N	18.	Civil Rights Act of 1991	Y
9.	Exceptions to exclusionary rule	Y	19.	Unlimited damages-discrimination	Y
10.	Allow sale of assault weapons	N	20.	Eliminate funds for supercollider	Y
11.	Life in prison/abolish death penalty	N	21.	Terminate SDI except for research	N
12.	Req conspiracy-price fixing cases	Y	22.	Req 7-day handgun waiting period	Y
13.	Unemployment benefits extension	Y	23.	Provide $30b for failed S&Ls	Y
14.	Tissue use of aborted fetuses	Y	24.	Allow use of force against Iraq	N

Presidential Support Score: 1991 - 40%

BOUCHER, FREDERICK C. (Rick) -- Virginia 9th District [Democrat]. Counties of Bland, Buchanan, Craig, Dickenson, Floyd, Giles, Grayson, Lee, Montgomery, Pulaski, Russell, Scott, Smyth, Tazewell, Washington, Wise and Wythe. Cities of Bristol, Galax, Norton and Radford. Prior Terms: 1983-92. Born: August 1, 1946; Washington County, VA. Education: Roanoke College (B.A.); University of Virginia. Occupation: Virginia senator (1975-82).

1.	Protection to Haitian refugees	N	44.	Protect Chinese & C.A. nationals	Y
2.	Raise tax on wealthy; lower others	Y	45.	Abortion $ for rape/incest cases	Y
3.	Investigate Reagan hostage delay	Y	46.	Allow religious schools to bar gays	Y
4.	Campaign finance revisions	Y	47.	Bar broadcaster fairness doctrine	N
5.	Unpaid leave to care for children	Y	48.	Bar cap gains cut/reinstate IRA	Y
6.	Restrict NEA use of funds	?	49.	Bar unions equal voice in pension	N
7.	Bar race-bias claim/habeas corpus	N	50.	Bar assembly of chemical weapons	Y
8.	Ban race as death sentence factor	N	51.	Ban plutonium/uranium production	Y
9.	Exceptions to exclusionary rule	N	52.	Cap MX missile deployment at 50	Y
10.	Allow sale of assault weapons	Y	53.	Allow $3b for 2 stealth bombers	N
11.	Life in prison/abolish death penalty	N	54.	Publish bio-warfare experiments	Y
12.	Req conspiracy-price fixing cases	N	55.	Raise minimum wage-veto override	Y
13.	Unemployment benefits extension	Y	56.	Bar transfer of FS-X technology	Y
14.	Tissue use of aborted fetuses	Y	57.	Cut defense and raise domestic $	N
15.	Bar replacement of union strikers	Y	58.	Uniform poll closing in 48 states	N
16.	Hold foreign aid at $15b for '92	Y	59.	Req foreign investment disclosure	Y
17.	Restore space station funding	Y	60.	Textile import quotas-veto override	Y
18.	Civil Rights Act of 1991	Y	61.	Bar abortion funding in Wash, DC	N
19.	Unlimited damages-discrimination	N	62.	Notify spouses of AIDS+ carriers	?
20.	Eliminate funds for supercollider	N	63.	Seize conveyance-drug trafficking	N
21.	Terminate SDI except for research	Y	64.	South Africa sanctions	Y
22.	Req 7-day handgun waiting period	N	65.	60 days' notice of plant closings	Y
23.	Provide $30b for failed S&Ls	Y	66.	Close unneeded military bases	N
24.	Allow use of force against Iraq	N	67.	Keep welfare reform within $2.8b	Y
25.	Allow $15b in foreign aid for '91	?	68.	Allow children housing exclusion	N
26.	Revise & extend legal immigration	?	69.	Shift $400m of NASA to homeless	N
27.	Suspend aid to Angolan rebels	Y	70.	Cap Medicare patients' liability	Y
28.	Democratic tax plan proposals	Y	71.	Prohibit employee polygraph testing	Y
29.	Cut defense 5% across the board	N	72.	Allow CIA to fund Contras	N
30.	Textile import quotas-veto override	Y	73.	Revise unfair trade practices	Y
31.	Abortion service for military abroad	Y	74.	Focus SDI on accidental launch	Y
32.	Limits on high income farmers	Y	75.	Bar Air Force $ for MX missile	Y
33.	Family medical leave-veto override	Y	76.	Allow "real" increase in defense	N
34.	Req submission of balanced budget	Y	77.	Troop reduction in Europe of 50%	Y
35.	Balanced budget amendment	N	78.	Ban nuclear tests above 1 kiloton	Y
36.	Amendment to ban flag desecration	N	79.	Ban anti-satellite missile tests	Y
37.	Reauthorize Amtrak-veto override	Y	80.	Observe certain limits of SALT II	Y
38.	Retraining aid for coal miners	Y	81.	Restore four Civil Rights laws	Y
39.	Suspend El Salvador military aid	Y	82.	Prohibit aliens as strikebreakers	Y
40.	Expand child care aid/tax credit	Y	83.	Allow military malpractice suits	Y
41.	Raise House salary/omit honoraria	Y	84.	Approval of $36m in Contra aid	N
42.	Toughen oil-spill liability	Y	85.	$18b deficit reduction compromise	N
43.	Restitution to Japanese interned	Y	86.	Welfare reform of $5.7b for 5 years	Y

BOUCHER, FREDERICK C. (continued)

87. Raise taxes $12b/cut spending $3b	Y	
88. Board to assess occupational risk	Y	
89. Balanced budget by '93-via targets	Y	
90. Bar licensing of two nuclear plants	Y	
91. Remove victims compensation cap	N	
92. Catastrophic health insurance	Y	
93. Ban airline smoking-2 hours or less	N	
94. $1b/two year aid for the homeless	Y	
95. Bar non-unions in union companies	Y	
96. Increase FSLIC rescue to $15b	?	
97. Impose quotas to lower trade deficit	Y	
98. Reduce discretionary budget 21%	Y	
99. Immigration reform/alien amnesty	Y	
100. South Africa sanctions-veto override	Y	
101. Tax overhaul to revise income tax	N	
102. Use of military in drug war	N	
103. Delete 12 MX/add conventional wpn	Y	
104. Raise speed limit to 65 mph	Y	
105. Require Pentagon to buy US goods	Y	
106. AIDS insurance non-discrimination	?	
107. Prohibit Saudi arms sales	Y	
108. Ease Gun Control Act of 1968	Y	
109. Bar interstate handgun transport	N	
110. Make company emissions known	Y	
111. Allow toxic victims to sue in fed ct	Y	
112. Superfund waste cleanup of $10b	Y	
113. 90 days notice of plant closings	N	
114. $20b in Medicare cuts/tax increases	N
115. Spending cuts and tax increases	Y
116. Set school lunch lmt-250% poverty	N
117. $75m for youth work projects	Y
118. Allow Angolan military assistance	N
119. Suspend defense payments for abuse	Y
120. Drop SS COLAs/$12b tax increase	N
121. Approve $1.5b for 21 MX missiles	N
122. Emergency farm credit/revisions	Y
123. Duty on Taiwan/Hong Kong/S Korea	N
124. Limit steel imports to 17%	Y
125. Cut $ to schools that bar prayer	Y
126. $50b-taxes; cut Medicare/spending	N
127. Limit Pershing II/cruise in Europe	N
128. Delete $7.1b for 34 B-1 bombers	N
129. Bar purchase of Sergeant York guns	N
130. El Salvador military/economic aid	N
131. Bar mining of Nicaraguan waters	?
132. Physician fee freeze for Medicare	N
133. $49b in "sin"/phone/insurance taxes	Y
134. Allow sale of Conrail	N
135. Equal Rights Amendment	Y
136. Authorize Marines in Lebanon	Y
137. Eminent domain for coal companies	N
138. Prohibit EPA clean air sanctions	Y
139. SS retirement age increase/reforms	N

Presidential Support Score: 1991 - 34%   1990 - 20%

WOLF, FRANK R. -- Virginia 10th District [Republican]. Counties of Arlington, Fairfax (pt.) and Loudoun. Cities of Fairfax and Falls Church. Prior Terms: 1981-92. Born: January 30, 1939; Philadelphia, PA. Education: Pennsylvania State University (B.A.); Georgetown University Law School. Military Service: U.S. Army Signal Corps (Reserves). Occupation: Congressional legislative assistant (1968-71); assistant, Secretary of Interior (1971-74); deputy assistant secretary, Congressional and Legislative Affairs, Department of Interior (1974-75).

1. Protection to Haitian refugees	N	
2. Raise tax on wealthy; lower others	N	
3. Investigate Reagan hostage delay	N	
4. Campaign finance revisions	N	
5. Unpaid leave to care for children	N	
6. Restrict NEA use of funds	Y	
7. Bar race-bias claim/habeas corpus	Y	
8. Ban race as death sentence factor	Y	
9. Exceptions to exclusionary rule	Y	
10. Allow sale of assault weapons	N	
11. Life in prison/abolish death penalty	N	
12. Req conspiracy-price fixing cases	Y	
13. Unemployment benefits extension	N	
14. Tissue use of aborted fetuses	N	
15. Bar replacement of union strikers	N	
16. Hold foreign aid at $15b for '92	Y	
17. Restore space station funding	Y	
18. Civil Rights Act of 1991	N	
19. Unlimited damages-discrimination	N	
20. Eliminate funds for supercollider	N	
21. Terminate SDI except for research	N	
22. Req 7-day handgun waiting period	Y	
23. Provide $30b for failed S&Ls	Y	
24. Allow use of force against Iraq	Y	
25. Allow $15b in foreign aid for '91	Y	
26. Revise & extend legal immigration	Y
27. Suspend aid to Angolan rebels	N
28. Democratic tax plan proposals	N
29. Cut defense 5% across the board	N
30. Textile import quotas-veto override	N
31. Abortion service for military abroad	N
32. Limits on high income farmers	Y
33. Family medical leave-veto override	N
34. Req submission of balanced budget	N
35. Balanced budget amendment	Y
36. Amendment to ban flag desecration	Y
37. Reauthorize Amtrak-veto override	Y
38. Retraining aid for coal miners	N
39. Suspend El Salvador military aid	N
40. Expand child care aid/tax credit	N
41. Raise House salary/omit honoraria	Y
42. Toughen oil-spill liability	N
43. Restitution to Japanese interned	N
44. Protect Chinese & C.A. nationals	N
45. Abortion $ for rape/incest cases	N
46. Allow religious schools to bar gays	Y
47. Bar broadcaster fairness doctrine	N
48. Bar cap gains cut/reinstate IRA	N
49. Bar unions equal voice in pension	Y
50. Bar assembly of chemical weapons	N

WOLF, FRANK R. (continued)

51. Ban plutonium/uranium production	N	98. Reduce discretionary budget 21%	N
52. Cap MX missile deployment at 50	N	99. Immigration reform/alien amnesty	N
53. Allow $3b for 2 stealth bombers	Y	100. South Africa sanctions-veto override	Y
54. Publish bio-warfare experiments	Y	101. Tax overhaul to revise income tax	N
55. Raise minimum wage-veto override	N	102. Use of military in drug war	Y
56. Bar transfer of FS-X technology	N	103. Delete 12 MX/add conventional wpn	N
57. Cut defense and raise domestic $	N	104. Raise speed limit to 65 mph	N
58. Uniform poll closing in 48 states	N	105. Require Pentagon to buy US goods	N
59. Req foreign investment disclosure	Y	106. AIDS insurance non-discrimination	N
60. Textile import quotas-veto override	N	107. Prohibit Saudi arms sales	Y
61. Bar abortion funding in Wash, DC	Y	108. Ease Gun Control Act of 1968	Y
62. Notify spouses of AIDS+ carriers	Y	109. Bar interstate handgun transport	Y
63. Seize conveyance-drug trafficking	Y	110. Make company emissions known	Y
64. South Africa sanctions	N	111. Allow toxic victims to sue in fed ct	N
65. 60 days' notice of plant closings	N	112. Superfund waste cleanup of $10b	Y
66. Close unneeded military bases	Y	113. 90 days notice of plant closings	N
67. Keep welfare reform within $2.8b	Y	114. $20b in Medicare cuts/tax increases	N
68. Allow children housing exclusion	N	115. Spending cuts and tax increases	Y
69. Shift $400m of NASA to homeless	N	116. Set school lunch lmt-250% poverty	N
70. Cap Medicare patients' liability	Y	117. $75m for youth work projects	N
71. Prohibit employee polygraph testing	Y	118. Allow Angolan military assistance	Y
72. Allow CIA to fund Contras	Y	119. Suspend defense payments for abuse	N
73. Revise unfair trade practices	N	120. Drop SS COLAs/$12b tax increase	N
74. Focus SDI on accidental launch	N	121. Approve $1.5b for 21 MX missiles	Y
75. Bar Air Force $ for MX missile	N	122. Emergency farm credit/revisions	Y
76. Allow "real" increase in defense	Y	123. Duty on Taiwan/Hong Kong/S Korea	N
77. Troop reduction in Europe of 50%	N	124. Limit steel imports to 17%	N
78. Ban nuclear tests above 1 kiloton	N	125. Cut $ to schools that bar prayer	Y
79. Ban anti-satellite missile tests	N	126. $50b-taxes; cut Medicare/spending	Y
80. Observe certain limits of SALT II	N	127. Limit Pershing II/cruise in Europe	N
81. Restore four Civil Rights laws	N	128. Delete $7.1b for 34 B-1 bombers	N
82. Prohibit aliens as strikebreakers	Y	129. Bar purchase of Sergeant York guns	N
83. Allow military malpractice suits	Y	130. El Salvador military/economic aid	Y
84. Approval of $36m in Contra aid	Y	131. Bar mining of Nicaraguan waters	N
85. $18b deficit reduction compromise	Y	132. Physician fee freeze for Medicare	Y
86. Welfare reform of $5.7b for 5 years	N	133. $49b in "sin"/phone/insurance taxes	Y
87. Raise taxes $12b/cut spending $3b	N	134. Allow sale of Conrail	Y
88. Board to assess occupational risk	N	135. Equal Rights Amendment	N
89. Balanced budget by '93-via targets	N	136. Authorize Marines in Lebanon	Y
90. Bar licensing of two nuclear plants	N	137. Eminent domain for coal companies	Y
91. Remove victims compensation cap	N	138. Prohibit EPA clean air sanctions	N
92. Catastrophic health insurance	N	139. SS retirement age increase/reforms	Y
93. Ban airline smoking-2 hours or less	Y	140. Auto domestic content requirement	N
94. $1b/two year aid for the homeless	Y	141. Delete jobs program funding	Y
95. Bar non-unions in union companies	N	142. Highway-gas tax bill	N
96. Increase FSLIC rescue to $15b	Y	143. Cut $5b from defense for Medicare	Y
97. Impose quotas to lower trade deficit	N	144. Emergency housing aid of $1b	Y

Presidential Support Score: 1991 - 81% 1990 - 71%

WASHINGTON

MILLER, JOHN -- Washington 1st District [Republican]. Counties of King (pt.), Kitsap (pt.) and Snohomish (pt.). Prior Terms: 1985-92. Born: May 23, 1938; New York, NY. Occupation: Attorney; city councilman; commentator; assistant attorney general (1965-70).

1. Protection to Haitian refugees	Y	3. Investigate Reagan hostage delay	N
2. Raise tax on wealthy; lower others	N	4. Campaign finance revisions	Y

MILLER, JOHN (continued)

5. Unpaid leave to care for children	Y	
6. Restrict NEA use of funds	N	
7. Bar race-bias claim/habeas corpus	Y	
8. Ban race as death sentence factor	Y	
9. Exceptions to exclusionary rule	Y	
10. Allow sale of assault weapons	N	
11. Life in prison/abolish death penalty	N	
12. Req conspiracy-price fixing cases	Y	
13. Unemployment benefits extension	N	
14. Tissue use of aborted fetuses	Y	
15. Bar replacement of union strikers	N	
16. Hold foreign aid at $15b for '92	Y	
17. Restore space station funding	+	
18. Civil Rights Act of 1991	N	
19. Unlimited damages-discrimination	N	
20. Eliminate funds for supercollider	N	
21. Terminate SDI except for research	N	
22. Req 7-day handgun waiting period	Y	
23. Provide $30b for failed S&Ls	Y	
24. Allow use of force against Iraq	Y	
25. Allow $15b in foreign aid for '91	Y	
26. Revise & extend legal immigration	Y	
27. Suspend aid to Angolan rebels	Y	
28. Democratic tax plan proposals	N	
29. Cut defense 5% across the board	N	
30. Textile import quotas-veto override	N	
31. Abortion service for military abroad	Y	
32. Limits on high income farmers	Y	
33. Family medical leave-veto override	Y	
34. Req submission of balanced budget	N	
35. Balanced budget amendment	Y	
36. Amendment to ban flag desecration	Y	
37. Reauthorize Amtrak-veto override	Y	
38. Retraining aid for coal miners	N	
39. Suspend El Salvador military aid	Y	
40. Expand child care aid/tax credit	Y	
41. Raise House salary/omit honoraria	N	
42. Toughen oil-spill liability	Y	
43. Restitution to Japanese interned	Y	
44. Protect Chinese & C.A. nationals	Y	
45. Abortion $ for rape/incest cases	Y	
46. Allow religious schools to bar gays	N	
47. Bar broadcaster fairness doctrine	N	
48. Bar cap gains cut/reinstate IRA	N	
49. Bar unions equal voice in pension	Y	
50. Bar assembly of chemical weapons	N	
51. Ban plutonium/uranium production	Y	
52. Cap MX missile deployment at 50	Y	
53. Allow $3b for 2 stealth bombers	N	
54. Publish bio-warfare experiments	N	
55. Raise minimum wage-veto override	N	
56. Bar transfer of FS-X technology	N	
57. Cut defense and raise domestic $	N	
58. Uniform poll closing in 48 states	Y	
59. Req foreign investment disclosure	N	
60. Textile import quotas-veto override	N	
61. Bar abortion funding in Wash, DC	N	
62. Notify spouses of AIDS+ carriers	N	
63. Seize conveyance-drug trafficking	N	

64. South Africa sanctions	Y	
65. 60 days' notice of plant closings	Y	
66. Close unneeded military bases	Y	
67. Keep welfare reform within $2.8b	Y	
68. Allow children housing exclusion	N	
69. Shift $400m of NASA to homeless	Y	
70. Cap Medicare patients' liability	Y	
71. Prohibit employee polygraph testing	Y	
72. Allow CIA to fund Contras	Y	
73. Revise unfair trade practices	Y	
74. Focus SDI on accidental launch	N	
75. Bar Air Force $ for MX missile	N	
76. Allow "real" increase in defense	N	
77. Troop reduction in Europe of 50%	+	
78. Ban nuclear tests above 1 kiloton	N	
79. Ban anti-satellite missile tests	N	
80. Observe certain limits of SALT II	N	
81. Restore four Civil Rights laws	Y	
82. Prohibit aliens as strikebreakers	Y	
83. Allow military malpractice suits	Y	
84. Approval of $36m in Contra aid	Y	
85. $18b deficit reduction compromise	N	
86. Welfare reform of $5.7b for 5 years	N	
87. Raise taxes $12b/cut spending $3b	N	
88. Board to assess occupational risk	N	
89. Balanced budget by '93-via targets	Y	
90. Bar licensing of two nuclear plants	N	
91. Remove victims compensation cap	Y	
92. Catastrophic health insurance	Y	
93. Ban airline smoking-2 hours or less	Y	
94. $1b/two year aid for the homeless	Y	
95. Bar non-unions in union companies	Y	
96. Increase FSLIC rescue to $15b	N	
97. Impose quotas to lower trade deficit	N	
98. Reduce discretionary budget 21%	Y	
99. Immigration reform/alien amnesty	Y	
100. South Africa sanctions-veto override	Y	
101. Tax overhaul to revise income tax	Y	
102. Use of military in drug war	Y	
103. Delete 12 MX/add conventional wpn	Y	
104. Raise speed limit to 65 mph	N	
105. Require Pentagon to buy US goods	N	
106. AIDS insurance non-discrimination	Y	
107. Prohibit Saudi arms sales	Y	
108. Ease Gun Control Act of 1968	N	
109. Bar interstate handgun transport	Y	
110. Make company emissions known	Y	
111. Allow toxic victims to sue in fed ct	N	
112. Superfund waste cleanup of $10b	Y	
113. 90 days notice of plant closings	N	
114. $20b in Medicare cuts/tax increases	N	
115. Spending cuts and tax increases	N	
116. Set school lunch lmt-250% poverty	Y	
117. $75m for youth work projects	N	
118. Allow Angolan military assistance	Y	
119. Suspend defense payments for abuse	N	
120. Drop SS COLAs/$12b tax increase	Y	
121. Approve $1.5b for 21 MX missiles	N	
122. Emergency farm credit/revisions	N	

Presidential Support Score: 1991 - 63%   1990 - 55%

SWIFT, AL -- Washington 2nd District [Democrat]. Counties of Clallam, Grays Harbor (pt.), Island, Jefferson, Kitsap (pt.), Mason (pt.), San Juan, Skagit, Snohomish (pt.) and Whatcom. Prior Terms: 1979-92. Born: September 12, 1935; Tacoma, WA. Education: Whitman College; Central Washington University. Occupation: Public affairs director, KVOS-TV (1962); administrative assistant (1965-69).

1.	Protection to Haitian refugees	Y	60.	Textile import quotas-veto override	N
2.	Raise tax on wealthy; lower others	Y	61.	Bar abortion funding in Wash, DC	N
3.	Investigate Reagan hostage delay	Y	62.	Notify spouses of AIDS+ carriers	N
4.	Campaign finance revisions	Y	63.	Seize conveyance-drug trafficking	N
5.	Unpaid leave to care for children	Y	64.	South Africa sanctions	Y
6.	Restrict NEA use of funds	N	65.	60 days' notice of plant closings	Y
7.	Bar race-bias claim/habeas corpus	N	66.	Close unneeded military bases	N
8.	Ban race as death sentence factor	N	67.	Keep welfare reform within $2.8b	N
9.	Exceptions to exclusionary rule	N	68.	Allow children housing exclusion	N
10.	Allow sale of assault weapons	N	69.	Shift $400m of NASA to homeless	N
11.	Life in prison/abolish death penalty	Y	70.	Cap Medicare patients' liability	Y
12.	Req conspiracy-price fixing cases	N	71.	Prohibit employee polygraph testing	Y
13.	Unemployment benefits extension	Y	72.	Allow CIA to fund Contras	N
14.	Tissue use of aborted fetuses	Y	73.	Revise unfair trade practices	Y
15.	Bar replacement of union strikers	Y	74.	Focus SDI on accidental launch	Y
16.	Hold foreign aid at $15b for '92	?	75.	Bar Air Force $ for MX missile	Y
17.	Restore space station funding	Y	76.	Allow "real" increase in defense	N
18.	Civil Rights Act of 1991	Y	77.	Troop reduction in Europe of 50%	N
19.	Unlimited damages-discrimination	Y	78.	Ban nuclear tests above 1 kiloton	Y
20.	Eliminate funds for supercollider	Y	79.	Ban anti-satellite missile tests	Y
21.	Terminate SDI except for research	Y	80.	Observe certain limits of SALT II	Y
22.	Req 7-day handgun waiting period	Y	81.	Restore four Civil Rights laws	Y
23.	Provide $30b for failed S&Ls	Y	82.	Prohibit aliens as strikebreakers	Y
24.	Allow use of force against Iraq	N	83.	Allow military malpractice suits	Y
25.	Allow $15b in foreign aid for '91	Y	84.	Approval of $36m in Contra aid	N
26.	Revise & extend legal immigration	Y	85.	$18b deficit reduction compromise	Y
27.	Suspend aid to Angolan rebels	Y	86.	Welfare reform of $5.7b for 5 years	Y
28.	Democratic tax plan proposals	Y	87.	Raise taxes $12b/cut spending $3b	Y
29.	Cut defense 5% across the board	N	88.	Board to assess occupational risk	Y
30.	Textile import quotas-veto override	N	89.	Balanced budget by '93-via targets	Y
31.	Abortion service for military abroad	Y	90.	Bar licensing of two nuclear plants	?
32.	Limits on high income farmers	N	91.	Remove victims compensation cap	Y
33.	Family medical leave-veto override	Y	92.	Catastrophic health insurance	Y
34.	Req submission of balanced budget	Y	93.	Ban airline smoking-2 hours or less	N
35.	Balanced budget amendment	N	94.	$1b/two year aid for the homeless	Y
36.	Amendment to ban flag desecration	N	95.	Bar non-unions in union companies	Y
37.	Reauthorize Amtrak-veto override	Y	96.	Increase FSLIC rescue to $15b	N
38.	Retraining aid for coal miners	Y	97.	Impose quotas to lower trade deficit	N
39.	Suspend El Salvador military aid	Y	98.	Reduce discretionary budget 21%	Y
40.	Expand child care aid/tax credit	N	99.	Immigration reform/alien amnesty	Y
41.	Raise House salary/omit honoraria	Y	100.	South Africa sanctions-veto override	Y
42.	Toughen oil-spill liability	Y	101.	Tax overhaul to revise income tax	N
43.	Restitution to Japanese interned	Y	102.	Use of military in drug war	N
44.	Protect Chinese & C.A. nationals	Y	103.	Delete 12 MX/add conventional wpn	Y
45.	Abortion $ for rape/incest cases	Y	104.	Raise speed limit to 65 mph	N
46.	Allow religious schools to bar gays	N	105.	Require Pentagon to buy US goods	N
47.	Bar broadcaster fairness doctrine	N	106.	AIDS insurance non-discrimination	Y
48.	Bar cap gains cut/reinstate IRA	Y	107.	Prohibit Saudi arms sales	Y
49.	Bar unions equal voice in pension	N	108.	Ease Gun Control Act of 1968	Y
50.	Bar assembly of chemical weapons	Y	109.	Bar interstate handgun transport	N
51.	Ban plutonium/uranium production	Y	110.	Make company emissions known	N
52.	Cap MX missile deployment at 50	Y	111.	Allow toxic victims to sue in fed ct	N
53.	Allow $3b for 2 stealth bombers	N	112.	Superfund waste cleanup of $10b	Y
54.	Publish bio-warfare experiments	Y	113.	90 days notice of plant closings	Y
55.	Raise minimum wage-veto override	Y	114.	$20b in Medicare cuts/tax increases	Y
56.	Bar transfer of FS-X technology	Y	115.	Spending cuts and tax increases	Y
57.	Cut defense and raise domestic $	N	116.	Set school lunch lmt-250% poverty	N
58.	Uniform poll closing in 48 states	Y	117.	$75m for youth work projects	Y
59.	Req foreign investment disclosure	N	118.	Allow Angolan military assistance	N

SWIFT, AL (continued)

119. Suspend defense payments for abuse	?	
120. Drop SS COLAs/$12b tax increase	Y	
121. Approve $1.5b for 21 MX missiles	N	
122. Emergency farm credit/revisions	Y	
123. Duty on Taiwan/Hong Kong/S Korea	N	
124. Limit steel imports to 17%	Y	
125. Cut $ to schools that bar prayer	N	
126. $50b-taxes; cut Medicare/spending	Y	
127. Limit Pershing II/cruise in Europe	Y	
128. Delete $7.1b for 34 B-1 bombers	Y	
129. Bar purchase of Sergeant York guns	Y	
130. El Salvador military/economic aid	N	
131. Bar mining of Nicaraguan waters	Y	
132. Physician fee freeze for Medicare	N	
133. $49b in "sin"/phone/insurance taxes	Y	
134. Allow sale of Conrail	N	
135. Equal Rights Amendment	Y	
136. Authorize Marines in Lebanon	N	
137. Eminent domain for coal companies	N	
138. Prohibit EPA clean air sanctions	Y	
139. SS retirement age increase/reforms	N	
140. Auto domestic content requirement	Y	
141. Delete jobs program funding	N	
142. Highway-gas tax bill	N	
143. Cut $5b from defense for Medicare	N	
144. Emergency housing aid of $1b	Y	

Presidential Support Score: 1991 - 31% 1990 - 19%

UNSOELD, JOLENE -- Washington 3rd District [Democrat]. Counties of Clark, Cowlitz, Grays Harbor (pt.), Lewis, Pacific, Pierce (pt.), Thurston and Wahkiakum. Prior Terms: 1989-92. Born: December 3, 1931; Corvallis, OR. Occupation: Director, U.S. Information Service English Language Institute, Kathmandu, Nepal (1965-67); independent citizen lobbyist, consultant and lecturer; author; state representative (1985-88).

1. Protection to Haitian refugees	Y	
2. Raise tax on wealthy; lower others	Y	
3. Investigate Reagan hostage delay	Y	
4. Campaign finance revisions	Y	
5. Unpaid leave to care for children	Y	
6. Restrict NEA use of funds	N	
7. Bar race-bias claim/habeas corpus	N	
8. Ban race as death sentence factor	N	
9. Exceptions to exclusionary rule	N	
10. Allow sale of assault weapons	Y	
11. Life in prison/abolish death penalty	Y	
12. Req conspiracy-price fixing cases	N	
13. Unemployment benefits extension	Y	
14. Tissue use of aborted fetuses	Y	
15. Bar replacement of union strikers	Y	
16. Hold foreign aid at $15b for '92	Y	
17. Restore space station funding	N	
18. Civil Rights Act of 1991	Y	
19. Unlimited damages-discrimination	Y	
20. Eliminate funds for supercollider	Y	
21. Terminate SDI except for research	Y	
22. Req 7-day handgun waiting period	N	
23. Provide $30b for failed S&Ls	Y	
24. Allow use of force against Iraq	N	
25. Allow $15b in foreign aid for '91	Y	
26. Revise & extend legal immigration	Y	
27. Suspend aid to Angolan rebels	Y	
28. Democratic tax plan proposals	Y	
29. Cut defense 5% across the board	Y	
30. Textile import quotas-veto override	N	
31. Abortion service for military abroad	+	
32. Limits on high income farmers	N	
33. Family medical leave-veto override	Y	
34. Req submission of balanced budget	Y	
35. Balanced budget amendment	N	
36. Amendment to ban flag desecration	N	
37. Reauthorize Amtrak-veto override	Y	
38. Retraining aid for coal miners	Y	
39. Suspend El Salvador military aid	Y	
40. Expand child care aid/tax credit	Y	
41. Raise House salary/omit honoraria	N	
42. Toughen oil-spill liability	Y	
43. Restitution to Japanese interned	Y	
44. Protect Chinese & C.A. nationals	Y	
45. Abortion $ for rape/incest cases	Y	
46. Allow religious schools to bar gays	N	
47. Bar broadcaster fairness doctrine	N	
48. Bar cap gains cut/reinstate IRA	Y	
49. Bar unions equal voice in pension	N	
50. Bar assembly of chemical weapons	Y	
51. Ban plutonium/uranium production	Y	
52. Cap MX missile deployment at 50	Y	
53. Allow $3b for 2 stealth bombers	N	
54. Publish bio-warfare experiments	Y	
55. Raise minimum wage-veto override	Y	
56. Bar transfer of FS-X technology	N	
57. Cut defense and raise domestic $	Y	
58. Uniform poll closing in 48 states	Y	

Presidential Support Score: 1991 - 25% 1990 - 15%

MORRISON, SID -- Washington 4th District [Republican]. Counties of Benton, Chelan, Douglas, Franklin, Grant, Kittitas, Klickitat, Okanogan, Skamania and Yakima. Prior Terms: 1981-92. Born: May 13, 1933; Yakima, WA. Education: Yakima Valley College; Washington State University (B.S.). Military Service: U.S. Army, 1954-56. Occupation: Orchardist; Washington representative (1966-74); Washington senator (1974-80); chairman, Washington State Apple Commission; member, Board of Directors, Washington State Horticultural Association; board member, United Way.

MORRISON, SID (continued)

1. Protection to Haitian refugees	Y	
2. Raise tax on wealthy; lower others	N	
3. Investigate Reagan hostage delay	?	
4. Campaign finance revisions	Y	
5. Unpaid leave to care for children	Y	
6. Restrict NEA use of funds	Y	
7. Bar race-bias claim/habeas corpus	Y	
8. Ban race as death sentence factor	Y	
9. Exceptions to exclusionary rule	Y	
10. Allow sale of assault weapons	N	
11. Life in prison/abolish death penalty	N	
12. Req conspiracy-price fixing cases	Y	
13. Unemployment benefits extension	N	
14. Tissue use of aborted fetuses	Y	
15. Bar replacement of union strikers	N	
16. Hold foreign aid at $15b for '92	Y	
17. Restore space station funding	Y	
18. Civil Rights Act of 1991	N	
19. Unlimited damages-discrimination	N	
20. Eliminate funds for supercollider	N	
21. Terminate SDI except for research	N	
22. Req 7-day handgun waiting period	Y	
23. Provide $30b for failed S&Ls	Y	
24. Allow use of force against Iraq	Y	
25. Allow $15b in foreign aid for '91	Y	
26. Revise & extend legal immigration	Y	
27. Suspend aid to Angolan rebels	Y	
28. Democratic tax plan proposals	N	
29. Cut defense 5% across the board	N	
30. Textile import quotas-veto override	N	
31. Abortion service for military abroad	Y	
32. Limits on high income farmers	N	
33. Family medical leave-veto override	Y	
34. Req submission of balanced budget	Y	
35. Balanced budget amendment	Y	
36. Amendment to ban flag desecration	Y	
37. Reauthorize Amtrak-veto override	N	
38. Retraining aid for coal miners	N	
39. Suspend El Salvador military aid	Y	
40. Expand child care aid/tax credit	Y	
41. Raise House salary/omit honoraria	Y	
42. Toughen oil-spill liability	Y	
43. Restitution to Japanese interned	Y	
44. Protect Chinese & C.A. nationals	Y	
45. Abortion $ for rape/incest cases	Y	
46. Allow religious schools to bar gays	N	
47. Bar broadcaster fairness doctrine	N	
48. Bar cap gains cut/reinstate IRA	N	
49. Bar unions equal voice in pension	Y	
50. Bar assembly of chemical weapons	N	
51. Ban plutonium/uranium production	N	
52. Cap MX missile deployment at 50	N	
53. Allow $3b for 2 stealth bombers	Y	
54. Publish bio-warfare experiments	N	
55. Raise minimum wage-veto override	N	
56. Bar transfer of FS-X technology	N	
57. Cut defense and raise domestic $	N	
58. Uniform poll closing in 48 states	Y	
59. Req foreign investment disclosure	N	
60. Textile import quotas-veto override	N	
61. Bar abortion funding in Wash, DC	N	
62. Notify spouses of AIDS+ carriers	N	
63. Seize conveyance-drug trafficking	Y	
64. South Africa sanctions	N	

65. 60 days' notice of plant closings	N	
66. Close unneeded military bases	Y	
67. Keep welfare reform within $2.8b	Y	
68. Allow children housing exclusion	N	
69. Shift $400m of NASA to homeless	N	
70. Cap Medicare patients' liability	Y	
71. Prohibit employee polygraph testing	Y	
72. Allow CIA to fund Contras	N	
73. Revise unfair trade practices	N	
74. Focus SDI on accidental launch	N	
75. Bar Air Force $ for MX missile	N	
76. Allow "real" increase in defense	Y	
77. Troop reduction in Europe of 50%	N	
78. Ban nuclear tests above 1 kiloton	N	
79. Ban anti-satellite missile tests	N	
80. Observe certain limits of SALT II	Y	
81. Restore four Civil Rights laws	Y	
82. Prohibit aliens as strikebreakers	N	
83. Allow military malpractice suits	N	
84. Approval of $36m in Contra aid	Y	
85. $18b deficit reduction compromise	Y	
86. Welfare reform of $5.7b for 5 years	Y	
87. Raise taxes $12b/cut spending $3b	N	
88. Board to assess occupational risk	N	
89. Balanced budget by '93-via targets	Y	
90. Bar licensing of two nuclear plants	N	
91. Remove victims compensation cap	N	
92. Catastrophic health insurance	Y	
93. Ban airline smoking-2 hours or less	Y	
94. $1b/two year aid for the homeless	Y	
95. Bar non-unions in union companies	Y	
96. Increase FSLIC rescue to $15b	N	
97. Impose quotas to lower trade deficit	N	
98. Reduce discretionary budget 21%	Y	
99. Immigration reform/alien amnesty	Y	
100. South Africa sanctions-veto override	Y	
101. Tax overhaul to revise income tax	Y	
102. Use of military in drug war	Y	
103. Delete 12 MX/add conventional wpn	N	
104. Raise speed limit to 65 mph	Y	
105. Require Pentagon to buy US goods	Y	
106. AIDS insurance non-discrimination	N	
107. Prohibit Saudi arms sales	N	
108. Ease Gun Control Act of 1968	Y	
109. Bar interstate handgun transport	N	
110. Make company emissions known	N	
111. Allow toxic victims to sue in fed ct	N	
112. Superfund waste cleanup of $10b	Y	
113. 90 days notice of plant closings	N	
114. $20b in Medicare cuts/tax increases	N	
115. Spending cuts and tax increases	N	
116. Set school lunch lmt-250% poverty	N	
117. $75m for youth work projects	N	
118. Allow Angolan military assistance	Y	
119. Suspend defense payments for abuse	N	
120. Drop SS COLAs/$12b tax increase	Y	
121. Approve $1.5b for 21 MX missiles	Y	
122. Emergency farm credit/revisions	Y	
123. Duty on Taiwan/Hong Kong/S Korea	N	
124. Limit steel imports to 17%	N	
125. Cut $ to schools that bar prayer	N	
126. $50b-taxes; cut Medicare/spending	Y	
127. Limit Pershing II/cruise in Europe	N	
128. Delete $7.1b for 34 B-1 bombers	N	

MORRISON, SID (continued)

129. Bar purchase of Sergeant York guns	?	
130. El Salvador military/economic aid	Y	
131. Bar mining of Nicaraguan waters	Y	
132. Physician fee freeze for Medicare	Y	
133. $49b in "sin"/phone/insurance taxes	Y	
134. Allow sale of Conrail	Y	
135. Equal Rights Amendment	Y	
136. Authorize Marines in Lebanon	Y	
137. Eminent domain for coal companies	N	
138. Prohibit EPA clean air sanctions	+	
139. SS retirement age increase/reforms	Y	
140. Auto domestic content requirement	N	
141. Delete jobs program funding	Y	
142. Highway-gas tax bill	N	
143. Cut $5b from defense for Medicare	N	
144. Emergency housing aid of $1b	Y	

Presidential Support Score: 1991 - 68% 1990 - 51%

FOLEY, THOMAS S. -- Washington 5th District [Democrat]. Counties of Adams, Asatin, Columbia, Ferry, Garfield, Lincoln, Pend Oreille, Spokane, Stevens, Walla Walla and Whitman. Prior Terms: 1965-92. Born: March 6, 1929; Spokane, WA. Education: University of Washington (B.A., LL.B.). Occupation: Spokane County deputy prosecuting attorney; instructor, Gonzaga University Law School; Washington assistant attorney general.

2. Raise tax on wealthy; lower others	Y	96. Increase FSLIC rescue to $15b	Y
15. Bar replacement of union strikers	Y	97. Impose quotas to lower trade deficit	N
18. Civil Rights Act of 1991	Y	98. Reduce discretionary budget 21%	N
24. Allow use of force against Iraq	N	99. Immigration reform/alien amnesty	Y
27. Suspend aid to Angolan rebels	Y	100. South Africa sanctions-veto override	Y
36. Amendment to ban flag desecration	N	101. Tax overhaul to revise income tax	Y
41. Raise House salary/omit honoraria	Y	102. Use of military in drug war	N
57. Cut defense and raise domestic $	N	103. Delete 12 MX/add conventional wpn	N
58. Uniform poll closing in 48 states	Y	104. Raise speed limit to 65 mph	N
59. Req foreign investment disclosure	N	105. Require Pentagon to buy US goods	N
60. Textile import quotas-veto override	N	106. AIDS insurance non-discrimination	Y
61. Bar abortion funding in Wash, DC	N	107. Prohibit Saudi arms sales	Y
62. Notify spouses of AIDS+ carriers	N	108. Ease Gun Control Act of 1968	Y
63. Seize conveyance-drug trafficking	N	109. Bar interstate handgun transport	N
64. South Africa sanctions	Y	110. Make company emissions known	N
65. 60 days' notice of plant closings	Y	111. Allow toxic victims to sue in fed ct	N
66. Close unneeded military bases	N	112. Superfund waste cleanup of $10b	Y
67. Keep welfare reform within $2.8b	N	113. 90 days notice of plant closings	Y
68. Allow children housing exclusion	N	114. $20b in Medicare cuts/tax increases	Y
69. Shift $400m of NASA to homeless	N	115. Spending cuts and tax increases	Y
70. Cap Medicare patients' liability	Y	116. Set school lunch lmt-250% poverty	N
71. Prohibit employee polygraph testing	Y	117. $75m for youth work projects	Y
72. Allow CIA to fund Contras	N	118. Allow Angolan military assistance	N
73. Revise unfair trade practices	Y	119. Suspend defense payments for abuse	Y
74. Focus SDI on accidental launch	Y	120. Drop SS COLAs/$12b tax increase	N
75. Bar Air Force $ for MX missile	?	121. Approve $1.5b for 21 MX missiles	N
76. Allow "real" increase in defense	N	122. Emergency farm credit/revisions	Y
77. Troop reduction in Europe of 50%	N	123. Duty on Taiwan/Hong Kong/S Korea	N
78. Ban nuclear tests above 1 kiloton	Y	124. Limit steel imports to 17%	N
79. Ban anti-satellite missile tests	Y	125. Cut $ to schools that bar prayer	N
80. Observe certain limits of SALT II	Y	126. $50b-taxes; cut Medicare/spending	Y
81. Restore four Civil Rights laws	Y	127. Limit Pershing II/cruise in Europe	N
82. Prohibit aliens as strikebreakers	Y	128. Delete $7.1b for 34 B-1 bombers	N
83. Allow military malpractice suits	Y	129. Bar purchase of Sergeant York guns	Y
84. Approval of $36m in Contra aid	N	130. El Salvador military/economic aid	N
85. $18b deficit reduction compromise	Y	131. Bar mining of Nicaraguan waters	Y
86. Welfare reform of $5.7b for 5 years	Y	132. Physician fee freeze for Medicare	N
87. Raise taxes $12b/cut spending $3b	Y	133. $49b in "sin"/phone/insurance taxes	Y
88. Board to assess occupational risk	Y	134. Allow sale of Conrail	N
89. Balanced budget by '93-via targets	Y	135. Equal Rights Amendment	Y
90. Bar licensing of two nuclear plants	N	136. Authorize Marines in Lebanon	Y
91. Remove victims compensation cap	N	137. Eminent domain for coal companies	N
92. Catastrophic health insurance	Y	138. Prohibit EPA clean air sanctions	Y
93. Ban airline smoking-2 hours or less	Y	139. SS retirement age increase/reforms	N
94. $1b/two year aid for the homeless	Y	140. Auto domestic content requirement	N
95. Bar non-unions in union companies	Y	141. Delete jobs program funding	N

FOLEY, THOMAS S. (continued)

142. Highway-gas tax bill	Y	144. Emergency housing aid of $1b	Y
143. Cut $5b from defense for Medicare	N		

Speaker of the House votes at his discretion and to break ties.

Presidential Support Score: 1990 - 40%

DICKS, NORMAN D. -- Washington 6th District [Democrat]. Counties of Kitsap (pt.), Mason (pt.) and Pierce (pt.). Prior Terms: 1977-92. Born: December 16, 1940; Bremerton, WA. Education: University of Washington (B.A., J.D.). Occupation: Congressional assistant (1968-76).

1. Protection to Haitian refugees	?	52. Cap MX missile deployment at 50	Y
2. Raise tax on wealthy; lower others	Y	53. Allow $3b for 2 stealth bombers	Y
3. Investigate Reagan hostage delay	Y	54. Publish bio-warfare experiments	Y
4. Campaign finance revisions	Y	55. Raise minimum wage-veto override	Y
5. Unpaid leave to care for children	?	56. Bar transfer of FS-X technology	Y
6. Restrict NEA use of funds	N	57. Cut defense and raise domestic $	N
7. Bar race-bias claim/habeas corpus	N	58. Uniform poll closing in 48 states	Y
8. Ban race as death sentence factor	N	59. Req foreign investment disclosure	N
9. Exceptions to exclusionary rule	N	60. Textile import quotas-veto override	N
10. Allow sale of assault weapons	N	61. Bar abortion funding in Wash, DC	N
11. Life in prison/abolish death penalty	N	62. Notify spouses of AIDS+ carriers	N
12. Req conspiracy-price fixing cases	N	63. Seize conveyance-drug trafficking	N
13. Unemployment benefits extension	Y	64. South Africa sanctions	Y
14. Tissue use of aborted fetuses	Y	65. 60 days' notice of plant closings	Y
15. Bar replacement of union strikers	Y	66. Close unneeded military bases	N
16. Hold foreign aid at $15b for '92	Y	67. Keep welfare reform within $2.8b	N
17. Restore space station funding	Y	68. Allow children housing exclusion	N
18. Civil Rights Act of 1991	Y	69. Shift $400m of NASA to homeless	N
19. Unlimited damages-discrimination	Y	70. Cap Medicare patients' liability	Y
20. Eliminate funds for supercollider	N	71. Prohibit employee polygraph testing	Y
21. Terminate SDI except for research	N	72. Allow CIA to fund Contras	?
22. Req 7-day handgun waiting period	Y	73. Revise unfair trade practices	Y
23. Provide $30b for failed S&Ls	Y	74. Focus SDI on accidental launch	Y
24. Allow use of force against Iraq	N	75. Bar Air Force $ for MX missile	N
25. Allow $15b in foreign aid for '91	Y	76. Allow "real" increase in defense	Y
26. Revise & extend legal immigration	Y	77. Troop reduction in Europe of 50%	N
27. Suspend aid to Angolan rebels	Y	78. Ban nuclear tests above 1 kiloton	Y
28. Democratic tax plan proposals	Y	79. Ban anti-satellite missile tests	Y
29. Cut defense 5% across the board	N	80. Observe certain limits of SALT II	Y
30. Textile import quotas-veto override	N	81. Restore four Civil Rights laws	Y
31. Abortion service for military abroad	Y	82. Prohibit aliens as strikebreakers	?
32. Limits on high income farmers	N	83. Allow military malpractice suits	Y
33. Family medical leave-veto override	Y	84. Approval of $36m in Contra aid	N
34. Req submission of balanced budget	Y	85. $18b deficit reduction compromise	Y
35. Balanced budget amendment	N	86. Welfare reform of $5.7b for 5 years	Y
36. Amendment to ban flag desecration	N	87. Raise taxes $12b/cut spending $3b	Y
37. Reauthorize Amtrak-veto override	Y	88. Board to assess occupational risk	Y
38. Retraining aid for coal miners	Y	89. Balanced budget by '93-via targets	Y
39. Suspend El Salvador military aid	Y	90. Bar licensing of two nuclear plants	Y
40. Expand child care aid/tax credit	Y	91. Remove victims compensation cap	N
41. Raise House salary/omit honoraria	Y	92. Catastrophic health insurance	Y
42. Toughen oil-spill liability	Y	93. Ban airline smoking-2 hours or less	Y
43. Restitution to Japanese interned	Y	94. $1b/two year aid for the homeless	Y
44. Protect Chinese & C.A. nationals	Y	95. Bar non-unions in union companies	Y
45. Abortion $ for rape/incest cases	Y	96. Increase FSLIC rescue to $15b	N
46. Allow religious schools to bar gays	N	97. Impose quotas to lower trade deficit	N
47. Bar broadcaster fairness doctrine	N	98. Reduce discretionary budget 21%	N
48. Bar cap gains cut/reinstate IRA	Y	99. Immigration reform/alien amnesty	Y
49. Bar unions equal voice in pension	N	100. South Africa sanctions-veto override	Y
50. Bar assembly of chemical weapons	Y	101. Tax overhaul to revise income tax	Y
51. Ban plutonium/uranium production	Y	102. Use of military in drug war	N

DICKS, NORMAN D. (continued)

103. Delete 12 MX/add conventional wpn	N		124. Limit steel imports to 17%	Y
104. Raise speed limit to 65 mph	Y		125. Cut $ to schools that bar prayer	N
105. Require Pentagon to buy US goods	N		126. $50b-taxes; cut Medicare/spending	Y
106. AIDS insurance non-discrimination	Y		127. Limit Pershing II/cruise in Europe	N
107. Prohibit Saudi arms sales	Y		128. Delete $7.1b for 34 B-1 bombers	N
108. Ease Gun Control Act of 1968	Y		129. Bar purchase of Sergeant York guns	Y
109. Bar interstate handgun transport	Y		130. El Salvador military/economic aid	N
110. Make company emissions known	Y		131. Bar mining of Nicaraguan waters	Y
111. Allow toxic victims to sue in fed ct	N		132. Physician fee freeze for Medicare	N
112. Superfund waste cleanup of $10b	Y		133. $49b in "sin"/phone/insurance taxes	Y
113. 90 days notice of plant closings	Y		134. Allow sale of Conrail	N
114. $20b in Medicare cuts/tax increases	Y		135. Equal Rights Amendment	Y
115. Spending cuts and tax increases	Y		136. Authorize Marines in Lebanon	Y
116. Set school lunch lmt-250% poverty	N		137. Eminent domain for coal companies	N
117. $75m for youth work projects	Y		138. Prohibit EPA clean air sanctions	Y
118. Allow Angolan military assistance	N		139. SS retirement age increase/reforms	N
119. Suspend defense payments for abuse	Y		140. Auto domestic content requirement	Y
120. Drop SS COLAs/$12b tax increase	N		141. Delete jobs program funding	N
121. Approve $1.5b for 21 MX missiles	Y		142. Highway-gas tax bill	Y
122. Emergency farm credit/revisions	Y		143. Cut $5b from defense for Medicare	N
123. Duty on Taiwan/Hong Kong/S Korea	N		144. Emergency housing aid of $1b	Y

Presidential Support Score: 1991 - 36%   1990 - 28%

McDERMOTT, JAMES A. -- Washington 7th District [Democrat]. County of King (pt.). Prior Terms: 1989-92. Born: December 28, 1936; Chicago, IL. Education: Wheaton College (B.S.); University of Illinois Medical School (M.D.). Military Service: U.S. Navy Medical Corps. Occupation: Psychiatrist; college professor; state representative (1970-73) and senator (1974-87); U.S. Foreign Service regional medical officer (1987-88).

1. Protection to Haitian refugees	Y		30. Textile import quotas-veto override	N
2. Raise tax on wealthy; lower others	Y		31. Abortion service for military abroad	Y
3. Investigate Reagan hostage delay	Y		32. Limits on high income farmers	N
4. Campaign finance revisions	Y		33. Family medical leave-veto override	Y
5. Unpaid leave to care for children	Y		34. Req submission of balanced budget	Y
6. Restrict NEA use of funds	N		35. Balanced budget amendment	N
7. Bar race-bias claim/habeas corpus	N		36. Amendment to ban flag desecration	N
8. Ban race as death sentence factor	N		37. Reauthorize Amtrak-veto override	Y
9. Exceptions to exclusionary rule	N		38. Retraining aid for coal miners	Y
10. Allow sale of assault weapons	N		39. Suspend El Salvador military aid	Y
11. Life in prison/abolish death penalty	Y		40. Expand child care aid/tax credit	N
12. Req conspiracy-price fixing cases	N		41. Raise House salary/omit honoraria	Y
13. Unemployment benefits extension	Y		42. Toughen oil-spill liability	#
14. Tissue use of aborted fetuses	Y		43. Restitution to Japanese interned	Y
15. Bar replacement of union strikers	Y		44. Protect Chinese & C.A. nationals	Y
16. Hold foreign aid at $15b for '92	Y		45. Abortion $ for rape/incest cases	Y
17. Restore space station funding	N		46. Allow religious schools to bar gays	N
18. Civil Rights Act of 1991	Y		47. Bar broadcaster fairness doctrine	N
19. Unlimited damages-discrimination	Y		48. Bar cap gains cut/reinstate IRA	Y
20. Eliminate funds for supercollider	Y		49. Bar unions equal voice in pension	N
21. Terminate SDI except for research	Y		50. Bar assembly of chemical weapons	Y
22. Req 7-day handgun waiting period	Y		51. Ban plutonium/uranium production	Y
23. Provide $30b for failed S&Ls	Y		52. Cap MX missile deployment at 50	Y
24. Allow use of force against Iraq	N		53. Allow $3b for 2 stealth bombers	N
25. Allow $15b in foreign aid for '91	Y		54. Publish bio-warfare experiments	Y
26. Revise & extend legal immigration	Y		55. Raise minimum wage-veto override	Y
27. Suspend aid to Angolan rebels	Y		56. Bar transfer of FS-X technology	Y
28. Democratic tax plan proposals	Y		57. Cut defense and raise domestic $	Y
29. Cut defense 5% across the board	Y		58. Uniform poll closing in 48 states	Y

Presidential Support Score: 1991 - 27%   1990 - 20%

CHANDLER, ROD -- Washington 8th District [Republican]. Counties of King (pt.) and Pierce (pt.). Prior Terms: 1983-92. Born: July 13, 1942; LaGrande, OR. Education: Oregon State University (B.S.). Occupation: Political correspondent, TV news anchorman; assistant vice president, Washington Mutual Savings Bank; partner, public relations firm; Washington State representative.

1.	Protection to Haitian refugees	?	60.	Textile import quotas-veto override	N
2.	Raise tax on wealthy; lower others	N	61.	Bar abortion funding in Wash, DC	N
3.	Investigate Reagan hostage delay	N	62.	Notify spouses of AIDS+ carriers	N
4.	Campaign finance revisions	N	63.	Seize conveyance-drug trafficking	Y
5.	Unpaid leave to care for children	N	64.	South Africa sanctions	N
6.	Restrict NEA use of funds	Y	65.	60 days' notice of plant closings	N
7.	Bar race-bias claim/habeas corpus	Y	66.	Close unneeded military bases	Y
8.	Ban race as death sentence factor	#	67.	Keep welfare reform within $2.8b	Y
9.	Exceptions to exclusionary rule	Y	68.	Allow children housing exclusion	N
10.	Allow sale of assault weapons	Y	69.	Shift $400m of NASA to homeless	N
11.	Life in prison/abolish death penalty	N	70.	Cap Medicare patients' liability	N
12.	Req conspiracy-price fixing cases	Y	71.	Prohibit employee polygraph testing	Y
13.	Unemployment benefits extension	N	72.	Allow CIA to fund Contras	Y
14.	Tissue use of aborted fetuses	Y	73.	Revise unfair trade practices	N
15.	Bar replacement of union strikers	N	74.	Focus SDI on accidental launch	Y
16.	Hold foreign aid at $15b for '92	Y	75.	Bar Air Force $ for MX missile	N
17.	Restore space station funding	Y	76.	Allow "real" increase in defense	Y
18.	Civil Rights Act of 1991	N	77.	Troop reduction in Europe of 50%	N
19.	Unlimited damages-discrimination	N	78.	Ban nuclear tests above 1 kiloton	N
20.	Eliminate funds for supercollider	X	79.	Ban anti-satellite missile tests	N
21.	Terminate SDI except for research	N	80.	Observe certain limits of SALT II	N
22.	Req 7-day handgun waiting period	Y	81.	Restore four Civil Rights laws	Y
23.	Provide $30b for failed S&Ls	Y	82.	Prohibit aliens as strikebreakers	Y
24.	Allow use of force against Iraq	Y	83.	Allow military malpractice suits	Y
25.	Allow $15b in foreign aid for '91	Y	84.	Approval of $36m in Contra aid	Y
26.	Revise & extend legal immigration	Y	85.	$18b deficit reduction compromise	N
27.	Suspend aid to Angolan rebels	N	86.	Welfare reform of $5.7b for 5 years	N
28.	Democratic tax plan proposals	N	87.	Raise taxes $12b/cut spending $3b	N
29.	Cut defense 5% across the board	N	88.	Board to assess occupational risk	N
30.	Textile import quotas-veto override	N	89.	Balanced budget by '93-via targets	Y
31.	Abortion service for military abroad	Y	90.	Bar licensing of two nuclear plants	N
32.	Limits on high income farmers	N	91.	Remove victims compensation cap	N
33.	Family medical leave-veto override	N	92.	Catastrophic health insurance	N
34.	Req submission of balanced budget	N	93.	Ban airline smoking-2 hours or less	Y
35.	Balanced budget amendment	Y	94.	$1b/two year aid for the homeless	Y
36.	Amendment to ban flag desecration	N	95.	Bar non-unions in union companies	N
37.	Reauthorize Amtrak-veto override	N	96.	Increase FSLIC rescue to $15b	N
38.	Retraining aid for coal miners	N	97.	Impose quotas to lower trade deficit	N
39.	Suspend El Salvador military aid	Y	98.	Reduce discretionary budget 21%	Y
40.	Expand child care aid/tax credit	N	99.	Immigration reform/alien amnesty	Y
41.	Raise House salary/omit honoraria	Y	100.	South Africa sanctions-veto override	Y
42.	Toughen oil-spill liability	?	101.	Tax overhaul to revise income tax	N
43.	Restitution to Japanese interned	Y	102.	Use of military in drug war	N
44.	Protect Chinese & C.A. nationals	N	103.	Delete 12 MX/add conventional wpn	N
45.	Abortion $ for rape/incest cases	Y	104.	Raise speed limit to 65 mph	Y
46.	Allow religious schools to bar gays	N	105.	Require Pentagon to buy US goods	N
47.	Bar broadcaster fairness doctrine	N	106.	AIDS insurance non-discrimination	Y
48.	Bar cap gains cut/reinstate IRA	N	107.	Prohibit Saudi arms sales	N
49.	Bar unions equal voice in pension	Y	108.	Ease Gun Control Act of 1968	Y
50.	Bar assembly of chemical weapons	N	109.	Bar interstate handgun transport	Y
51.	Ban plutonium/uranium production	Y	110.	Make company emissions known	N
52.	Cap MX missile deployment at 50	N	111.	Allow toxic victims to sue in fed ct	N
53.	Allow $3b for 2 stealth bombers	N	112.	Superfund waste cleanup of $10b	Y
54.	Publish bio-warfare experiments	N	113.	90 days notice of plant closings	N
55.	Raise minimum wage-veto override	N	114.	$20b in Medicare cuts/tax increases	N
56.	Bar transfer of FS-X technology	N	115.	Spending cuts and tax increases	N
57.	Cut defense and raise domestic $	N	116.	Set school lunch lmt-250% poverty	Y
58.	Uniform poll closing in 48 states	Y	117.	$75m for youth work projects	N
59.	Req foreign investment disclosure	N	118.	Allow Angolan military assistance	Y

CHANDLER, ROD (continued)

119. Suspend defense payments for abuse	Y	
120. Drop SS COLAs/$12b tax increase	Y	
121. Approve $1.5b for 21 MX missiles	Y	
122. Emergency farm credit/revisions	N	
123. Duty on Taiwan/Hong Kong/S Korea	N	
124. Limit steel imports to 17%	N	
125. Cut $ to schools that bar prayer	N	
126. $50b-taxes; cut Medicare/spending	Y	
127. Limit Pershing II/cruise in Europe	N	
128. Delete $7.1b for 34 B-1 bombers	N	
129. Bar purchase of Sergeant York guns	N	
130. El Salvador military/economic aid	Y	
131. Bar mining of Nicaraguan waters	Y	
132. Physician fee freeze for Medicare	Y	
133. $49b in "sin"/phone/insurance taxes	Y	
134. Allow sale of Conrail	Y	
135. Equal Rights Amendment	Y	
136. Authorize Marines in Lebanon	Y	
137. Eminent domain for coal companies	Y	
138. Prohibit EPA clean air sanctions	Y	
139. SS retirement age increase/reforms	Y	

Presidential Support Score: 1991 - 73%   1990 - 59%

WEST VIRGINIA

MOLLOHAN, ALAN B. -- West Virginia 1st District [Democrat]. Counties of Brooke, Doddridge, Hancock, Harrison, Marion, Marshall, Ohio, Pleasants, Ritchie, Taylor, Tyler, Wetzel and Wood. Prior Terms: 1983-92. Born: May 14, 1943; Fairmont, WV. Education: William and Mary (A.B.); West Virginia University College of Law (J.D.). Military Service: U.S. Army, U.S. Army Reserve. Occupation: Attorney.

1. Protection to Haitian refugees	Y	
2. Raise tax on wealthy; lower others	Y	
3. Investigate Reagan hostage delay	Y	
4. Campaign finance revisions	Y	
5. Unpaid leave to care for children	Y	
6. Restrict NEA use of funds	N	
7. Bar race-bias claim/habeas corpus	N	
8. Ban race as death sentence factor	N	
9. Exceptions to exclusionary rule	N	
10. Allow sale of assault weapons	Y	
11. Life in prison/abolish death penalty	Y	
12. Req conspiracy-price fixing cases	Y	
13. Unemployment benefits extension	Y	
14. Tissue use of aborted fetuses	N	
15. Bar replacement of union strikers	Y	
16. Hold foreign aid at $15b for '92	N	
17. Restore space station funding	Y	
18. Civil Rights Act of 1991	Y	
19. Unlimited damages-discrimination	N	
20. Eliminate funds for supercollider	N	
21. Terminate SDI except for research	N	
22. Req 7-day handgun waiting period	N	
23. Provide $30b for failed S&Ls	N	
24. Allow use of force against Iraq	Y	
25. Allow $15b in foreign aid for '91	N	
26. Revise & extend legal immigration	Y	
27. Suspend aid to Angolan rebels	N	
28. Democratic tax plan proposals	Y	
29. Cut defense 5% across the board	N	
30. Textile import quotas-veto override	Y	
31. Abortion service for military abroad	N	
32. Limits on high income farmers	N	
33. Family medical leave-veto override	Y	
34. Req submission of balanced budget	Y	
35. Balanced budget amendment	N	
36. Amendment to ban flag desecration	Y	
37. Reauthorize Amtrak-veto override	Y	
38. Retraining aid for coal miners	Y	
39. Suspend El Salvador military aid	Y	
40. Expand child care aid/tax credit	Y	
41. Raise House salary/omit honoraria	Y	
42. Toughen oil-spill liability	N	
43. Restitution to Japanese interned	Y	
44. Protect Chinese & C.A. nationals	N	
45. Abortion $ for rape/incest cases	N	
46. Allow religious schools to bar gays	Y	
47. Bar broadcaster fairness doctrine	N	
48. Bar cap gains cut/reinstate IRA	Y	
49. Bar unions equal voice in pension	Y	
50. Bar assembly of chemical weapons	N	
51. Ban plutonium/uranium production	Y	
52. Cap MX missile deployment at 50	N	
53. Allow $3b for 2 stealth bombers	Y	
54. Publish bio-warfare experiments	N	
55. Raise minimum wage-veto override	Y	
56. Bar transfer of FS-X technology	Y	
57. Cut defense and raise domestic $	N	
58. Uniform poll closing in 48 states	N	
59. Req foreign investment disclosure	Y	
60. Textile import quotas-veto override	Y	
61. Bar abortion funding in Wash, DC	Y	
62. Notify spouses of AIDS+ carriers	N	
63. Seize conveyance-drug trafficking	Y	
64. South Africa sanctions	Y	
65. 60 days' notice of plant closings	Y	
66. Close unneeded military bases	N	
67. Keep welfare reform within $2.8b	Y	
68. Allow children housing exclusion	Y	
69. Shift $400m of NASA to homeless	N	
70. Cap Medicare patients' liability	N	
71. Prohibit employee polygraph testing	Y	
72. Allow CIA to fund Contras	Y	

MOLLOHAN, ALAN B. (continued)

73.	Revise unfair trade practices	Y	107.	Prohibit Saudi arms sales	Y
74.	Focus SDI on accidental launch	N	108.	Ease Gun Control Act of 1968	Y
75.	Bar Air Force $ for MX missile	N	109.	Bar interstate handgun transport	N
76.	Allow "real" increase in defense	?	110.	Make company emissions known	N
77.	Troop reduction in Europe of 50%	Y	111.	Allow toxic victims to sue in fed ct	N
78.	Ban nuclear tests above 1 kiloton	N	112.	Superfund waste cleanup of $10b	N
79.	Ban anti-satellite missile tests	N	113.	90 days notice of plant closings	Y
80.	Observe certain limits of SALT II	N	114.	$20b in Medicare cuts/tax increases	N
81.	Restore four Civil Rights laws	Y	115.	Spending cuts and tax increases	Y
82.	Prohibit aliens as strikebreakers	Y	116.	Set school lunch lmt-250% poverty	N
83.	Allow military malpractice suits	?	117.	$75m for youth work projects	Y
84.	Approval of $36m in Contra aid	Y	118.	Allow Angolan military assistance	Y
85.	$18b deficit reduction compromise	Y	119.	Suspend defense payments for abuse	N
86.	Welfare reform of $5.7b for 5 years	Y	120.	Drop SS COLAs/$12b tax increase	N
87.	Raise taxes $12b/cut spending $3b	Y	121.	Approve $1.5b for 21 MX missiles	Y
88.	Board to assess occupational risk	Y	122.	Emergency farm credit/revisions	Y
89.	Balanced budget by '93-via targets	N	123.	Duty on Taiwan/Hong Kong/S Korea	Y
90.	Bar licensing of two nuclear plants	N	124.	Limit steel imports to 17%	Y
91.	Remove victims compensation cap	N	125.	Cut $ to schools that bar prayer	Y
92.	Catastrophic health insurance	Y	126.	$50b-taxes; cut Medicare/spending	Y
93.	Ban airline smoking-2 hours or less	N	127.	Limit Pershing II/cruise in Europe	N
94.	$1b/two year aid for the homeless	Y	128.	Delete $7.1b for 34 B-1 bombers	N
95.	Bar non-unions in union companies	Y	129.	Bar purchase of Sergeant York guns	N
96.	Increase FSLIC rescue to $15b	N	130.	El Salvador military/economic aid	Y
97.	Impose quotas to lower trade deficit	Y	131.	Bar mining of Nicaraguan waters	Y
98.	Reduce discretionary budget 21%	N	132.	Physician fee freeze for Medicare	N
99.	Immigration reform/alien amnesty	Y	133.	$49b in "sin"/phone/insurance taxes	Y
100.	South Africa sanctions-veto override	Y	134.	Allow sale of Conrail	N
101.	Tax overhaul to revise income tax	Y	135.	Equal Rights Amendment	N
102.	Use of military in drug war	Y	136.	Authorize Marines in Lebanon	Y
103.	Delete 12 MX/add conventional wpn	N	137.	Eminent domain for coal companies	N
104.	Raise speed limit to 65 mph	N	138.	Prohibit EPA clean air sanctions	Y
105.	Require Pentagon to buy US goods	Y	139.	SS retirement age increase/reforms	N
106.	AIDS insurance non-discrimination	Y			

Presidential Support Score: 1991 - 41%   1990 - 31%

STAGGERS, HARLEY O., Jr. -- West Virginia 2nd District [Democrat]. Counties of Barbour, Berkely, Fayette, Grant, Greenbrier, Hampshire, Hardy, Jefferson, Mineral, Monongalia, Monroe, Morgan, Pendleton, Pocahontas, Preston, Randolph, Summers, Tucker, Upshur and Webster. Prior Terms: 1983-92. Born: February 22, 1951; Washington, DC. Education: Harvard University (B.A.); West Virginia University School of Law (J.D.). Occupation: Attorney; assistant attorney general; West Virginia senator (1980-82).

1.	Protection to Haitian refugees	Y	20.	Eliminate funds for supercollider	?
2.	Raise tax on wealthy; lower others	Y	21.	Terminate SDI except for research	N
3.	Investigate Reagan hostage delay	Y	22.	Req 7-day handgun waiting period	N
4.	Campaign finance revisions	Y	23.	Provide $30b for failed S&Ls	N
5.	Unpaid leave to care for children	Y	24.	Allow use of force against Iraq	N
6.	Restrict NEA use of funds	Y	25.	Allow $15b in foreign aid for '91	N
7.	Bar race-bias claim/habeas corpus	N	26.	Revise & extend legal immigration	N
8.	Ban race as death sentence factor	N	27.	Suspend aid to Angolan rebels	Y
9.	Exceptions to exclusionary rule	N	28.	Democratic tax plan proposals	Y
10.	Allow sale of assault weapons	Y	29.	Cut defense 5% across the board	N
11.	Life in prison/abolish death penalty	Y	30.	Textile import quotas-veto override	Y
12.	Req conspiracy-price fixing cases	N	31.	Abortion service for military abroad	N
13.	Unemployment benefits extension	Y	32.	Limits on high income farmers	N
14.	Tissue use of aborted fetuses	N	33.	Family medical leave-veto override	Y
15.	Bar replacement of union strikers	Y	34.	Req submission of balanced budget	Y
16.	Hold foreign aid at $15b for '92	N	35.	Balanced budget amendment	N
17.	Restore space station funding	N	36.	Amendment to ban flag desecration	Y
18.	Civil Rights Act of 1991	Y	37.	Reauthorize Amtrak-veto override	Y
19.	Unlimited damages-discrimination	Y	38.	Retraining aid for coal miners	Y

STAGGERS, HARLEY O., Jr. (continued)

39.	Suspend El Salvador military aid	Y	90.	Bar licensing of two nuclear plants	Y
40.	Expand child care aid/tax credit	Y	91.	Remove victims compensation cap	Y
41.	Raise House salary/omit honoraria	N	92.	Catastrophic health insurance	Y
42.	Toughen oil-spill liability	Y	93.	Ban airline smoking-2 hours or less	N
43.	Restitution to Japanese interned	Y	94.	$1b/two year aid for the homeless	Y
44.	Protect Chinese & C.A. nationals	Y	95.	Bar non-unions in union companies	Y
45.	Abortion $ for rape/incest cases	N	96.	Increase FSLIC rescue to $15b	N
46.	Allow religious schools to bar gays	Y	97.	Impose quotas to lower trade deficit	Y
47.	Bar broadcaster fairness doctrine	N	98.	Reduce discretionary budget 21%	Y
48.	Bar cap gains cut/reinstate IRA	Y	99.	Immigration reform/alien amnesty	Y
49.	Bar unions equal voice in pension	Y	100.	South Africa sanctions-veto override	Y
50.	Bar assembly of chemical weapons	Y	101.	Tax overhaul to revise income tax	Y
51.	Ban plutonium/uranium production	Y	102.	Use of military in drug war	Y
52.	Cap MX missile deployment at 50	Y	103.	Delete 12 MX/add conventional wpn	Y
53.	Allow $3b for 2 stealth bombers	N	104.	Raise speed limit to 65 mph	N
54.	Publish bio-warfare experiments	Y	105.	Require Pentagon to buy US goods	Y
55.	Raise minimum wage-veto override	Y	106.	AIDS insurance non-discrimination	Y
56.	Bar transfer of FS-X technology	Y	107.	Prohibit Saudi arms sales	Y
57.	Cut defense and raise domestic $	N	108.	Ease Gun Control Act of 1968	Y
58.	Uniform poll closing in 48 states	N	109.	Bar interstate handgun transport	Y
59.	Req foreign investment disclosure	Y	110.	Make company emissions known	Y
60.	Textile import quotas-veto override	Y	111.	Allow toxic victims to sue in fed ct	Y
61.	Bar abortion funding in Wash, DC	Y	112.	Superfund waste cleanup of $10b	N
62.	Notify spouses of AIDS+ carriers	N	113.	90 days notice of plant closings	Y
63.	Seize conveyance-drug trafficking	Y	114.	$20b in Medicare cuts/tax increases	N
64.	South Africa sanctions	Y	115.	Spending cuts and tax increases	Y
65.	60 days' notice of plant closings	Y	116.	Set school lunch lmt-250% poverty	N
66.	Close unneeded military bases	N	117.	$75m for youth work projects	Y
67.	Keep welfare reform within $2.8b	N	118.	Allow Angolan military assistance	N
68.	Allow children housing exclusion	N	119.	Suspend defense payments for abuse	Y
69.	Shift $400m of NASA to homeless	N	120.	Drop SS COLAs/$12b tax increase	N
70.	Cap Medicare patients' liability	Y	121.	Approve $1.5b for 21 MX missiles	N
71.	Prohibit employee polygraph testing	Y	122.	Emergency farm credit/revisions	Y
72.	Allow CIA to fund Contras	N	123.	Duty on Taiwan/Hong Kong/S Korea	Y
73.	Revise unfair trade practices	Y	124.	Limit steel imports to 17%	Y
74.	Focus SDI on accidental launch	Y	125.	Cut $ to schools that bar prayer	N
75.	Bar Air Force $ for MX missile	Y	126.	$50b-taxes; cut Medicare/spending	Y
76.	Allow "real" increase in defense	N	127.	Limit Pershing II/cruise in Europe	Y
77.	Troop reduction in Europe of 50%	N	128.	Delete $7.1b for 34 B-1 bombers	Y
78.	Ban nuclear tests above 1 kiloton	Y	129.	Bar purchase of Sergeant York guns	Y
79.	Ban anti-satellite missile tests	Y	130.	El Salvador military/economic aid	N
80.	Observe certain limits of SALT II	Y	131.	Bar mining of Nicaraguan waters	Y
81.	Restore four Civil Rights laws	Y	132.	Physician fee freeze for Medicare	N
82.	Prohibit aliens as strikebreakers	Y	133.	$49b in "sin"/phone/insurance taxes	Y
83.	Allow military malpractice suits	Y	134.	Allow sale of Conrail	N
84.	Approval of $36m in Contra aid	N	135.	Equal Rights Amendment	Y
85.	$18b deficit reduction compromise	Y	136.	Authorize Marines in Lebanon	Y
86.	Welfare reform of $5.7b for 5 years	Y	137.	Eminent domain for coal companies	N
87.	Raise taxes $12b/cut spending $3b	Y	138.	Prohibit EPA clean air sanctions	Y
88.	Board to assess occupational risk	Y	139.	SS retirement age increase/reforms	N
89.	Balanced budget by '93-via targets	N			

Presidential Support Score: 1991 - 32%   1990 - 17%

WISE, ROBERT E., Jr. -- West Virginia 3rd District [Democrat]. Counties of Boone, Braxton, Calhoun, Clay, Gilmer, Jackson, Kanawha, Lewis, Lincoln, Mason, Nicholas, Putnam, Roane and Wirt.   Prior Terms: 1983-92.   Born: January 6, 1948; Washington, DC. Education: Duke University (B.A.); Tulane University College of Law (J.D.).   Occupation: Attorney; consultant (1977-80); West Virginia senator (1980-82).

1.	Protection to Haitian refugees	Y	4.	Campaign finance revisions	Y
2.	Raise tax on wealthy; lower others	Y	5.	Unpaid leave to care for children	Y
3.	Investigate Reagan hostage delay	Y	6.	Restrict NEA use of funds	N

WISE, ROBERT E., Jr. (continued)

7.	Bar race-bias claim/habeas corpus	N
8.	Ban race as death sentence factor	N
9.	Exceptions to exclusionary rule	N
10.	Allow sale of assault weapons	Y
11.	Life in prison/abolish death penalty	Y
12.	Req conspiracy-price fixing cases	N
13.	Unemployment benefits extension	Y
14.	Tissue use of aborted fetuses	Y
15.	Bar replacement of union strikers	Y
16.	Hold foreign aid at $15b for '92	Y
17.	Restore space station funding	Y
18.	Civil Rights Act of 1991	Y
19.	Unlimited damages-discrimination	N
20.	Eliminate funds for supercollider	Y
21.	Terminate SDI except for research	N
22.	Req 7-day handgun waiting period	N
23.	Provide $30b for failed S&Ls	N
24.	Allow use of force against Iraq	N
25.	Allow $15b in foreign aid for '91	Y
26.	Revise & extend legal immigration	N
27.	Suspend aid to Angolan rebels	Y
28.	Democratic tax plan proposals	Y
29.	Cut defense 5% across the board	N
30.	Textile import quotas-veto override	Y
31.	Abortion service for military abroad	Y
32.	Limits on high income farmers	Y
33.	Family medical leave-veto override	Y
34.	Req submission of balanced budget	Y
35.	Balanced budget amendment	N
36.	Amendment to ban flag desecration	Y
37.	Reauthorize Amtrak-veto override	Y
38.	Retraining aid for coal miners	Y
39.	Suspend El Salvador military aid	Y
40.	Expand child care aid/tax credit	Y
41.	Raise House salary/omit honoraria	N
42.	Toughen oil-spill liability	Y
43.	Restitution to Japanese interned	Y
44.	Protect Chinese & C.A. nationals	Y
45.	Abortion $ for rape/incest cases	Y
46.	Allow religious schools to bar gays	Y
47.	Bar broadcaster fairness doctrine	N
48.	Bar cap gains cut/reinstate IRA	Y
49.	Bar unions equal voice in pension	N
50.	Bar assembly of chemical weapons	Y
51.	Ban plutonium/uranium production	Y
52.	Cap MX missile deployment at 50	Y
53.	Allow $3b for 2 stealth bombers	N
54.	Publish bio-warfare experiments	Y
55.	Raise minimum wage-veto override	Y
56.	Bar transfer of FS-X technology	Y
57.	Cut defense and raise domestic $	N
58.	Uniform poll closing in 48 states	N
59.	Req foreign investment disclosure	Y
60.	Textile import quotas-veto override	Y
61.	Bar abortion funding in Wash, DC	N
62.	Notify spouses of AIDS+ carriers	N
63.	Seize conveyance-drug trafficking	N
64.	South Africa sanctions	Y
65.	60 days' notice of plant closings	Y
66.	Close unneeded military bases	Y
67.	Keep welfare reform within $2.8b	Y
68.	Allow children housing exclusion	N
69.	Shift $400m of NASA to homeless	N
70.	Cap Medicare patients' liability	Y

71.	Prohibit employee polygraph testing	Y
72.	Allow CIA to fund Contras	N
73.	Revise unfair trade practices	Y
74.	Focus SDI on accidental launch	Y
75.	Bar Air Force $ for MX missile	N
76.	Allow "real" increase in defense	N
77.	Troop reduction in Europe of 50%	N
78.	Ban nuclear tests above 1 kiloton	Y
79.	Ban anti-satellite missile tests	Y
80.	Observe certain limits of SALT II	Y
81.	Restore four Civil Rights laws	Y
82.	Prohibit aliens as strikebreakers	Y
83.	Allow military malpractice suits	Y
84.	Approval of $36m in Contra aid	N
85.	$18b deficit reduction compromise	Y
86.	Welfare reform of $5.7b for 5 years	Y
87.	Raise taxes $12b/cut spending $3b	Y
88.	Board to assess occupational risk	Y
89.	Balanced budget by '93-via targets	Y
90.	Bar licensing of two nuclear plants	Y
91.	Remove victims compensation cap	Y
92.	Catastrophic health insurance	Y
93.	Ban airline smoking-2 hours or less	N
94.	$1b/two year aid for the homeless	Y
95.	Bar non-unions in union companies	Y
96.	Increase FSLIC rescue to $15b	Y
97.	Impose quotas to lower trade deficit	Y
98.	Reduce discretionary budget 21%	Y
99.	Immigration reform/alien amnesty	Y
100.	South Africa sanctions-veto override	Y
101.	Tax overhaul to revise income tax	Y
102.	Use of military in drug war	Y
103.	Delete 12 MX/add conventional wpn	Y
104.	Raise speed limit to 65 mph	N
105.	Require Pentagon to buy US goods	Y
106.	AIDS insurance non-discrimination	Y
107.	Prohibit Saudi arms sales	Y
108.	Ease Gun Control Act of 1968	Y
109.	Bar interstate handgun transport	Y
110.	Make company emissions known	Y
111.	Allow toxic victims to sue in fed ct	N
112.	Superfund waste cleanup of $10b	N
113.	90 days notice of plant closings	Y
114.	$20b in Medicare cuts/tax increases	N
115.	Spending cuts and tax increases	Y
116.	Set school lunch lmt-250% poverty	N
117.	$75m for youth work projects	Y
118.	Allow Angolan military assistance	N
119.	Suspend defense payments for abuse	Y
120.	Drop SS COLAs/$12b tax increase	N
121.	Approve $1.5b for 21 MX missiles	N
122.	Emergency farm credit/revisions	Y
123.	Duty on Taiwan/Hong Kong/S Korea	Y
124.	Limit steel imports to 17%	Y
125.	Cut $ to schools that bar prayer	Y
126.	$50b-taxes; cut Medicare/spending	Y
127.	Limit Pershing II/cruise in Europe	N
128.	Delete $7.1b for 34 B-1 bombers	Y
129.	Bar purchase of Sergeant York guns	N
130.	El Salvador military/economic aid	N
131.	Bar mining of Nicaraguan waters	N
132.	Physician fee freeze for Medicare	N
133.	$49b in "sin"/phone/insurance taxes	Y
134.	Allow sale of Conrail	N

WISE, ROBERT E., Jr. (continued)

135. Equal Rights Amendment	Y		138. Prohibit EPA clean air sanctions	Y
136. Authorize Marines in Lebanon	N		139. SS retirement age increase/reforms	N
137. Eminent domain for coal companies	N			

Presidential Support Score: 1991 - 26% 1990 - 19%

RAHALL, NICK JOE, II -- West Virginia 4th District [Democrat]. Counties of Cabell, Logan, McDowell, Mercer, Mingo, Raleigh, Wayne and Wyoming. Prior Terms: 1977-92. Born: May 20, 1949; Beckley, WV. Education: Duke University (A.B.); George Washington University. Occupation: Congressional staff member; president, Mountaineer Tour and Travel, Inc.; board member, Rahall Communications Corp.; sales representative, WWNR radio station.

1. Protection to Haitian refugees	Y		51. Ban plutonium/uranium production	Y
2. Raise tax on wealthy; lower others	Y		52. Cap MX missile deployment at 50	Y
3. Investigate Reagan hostage delay	N		53. Allow $3b for 2 stealth bombers	N
4. Campaign finance revisions	Y		54. Publish bio-warfare experiments	Y
5. Unpaid leave to care for children	Y		55. Raise minimum wage-veto override	Y
6. Restrict NEA use of funds	N		56. Bar transfer of FS-X technology	Y
7. Bar race-bias claim/habeas corpus	N		57. Cut defense and raise domestic $	Y
8. Ban race as death sentence factor	N		58. Uniform poll closing in 48 states	N
9. Exceptions to exclusionary rule	Y		59. Req foreign investment disclosure	Y
10. Allow sale of assault weapons	Y		60. Textile import quotas-veto override	Y
11. Life in prison/abolish death penalty	Y		61. Bar abortion funding in Wash, DC	Y
12. Req conspiracy-price fixing cases	N		62. Notify spouses of AIDS+ carriers	N
13. Unemployment benefits extension	#		63. Seize conveyance-drug trafficking	Y
14. Tissue use of aborted fetuses	N		64. South Africa sanctions	Y
15. Bar replacement of union strikers	Y		65. 60 days' notice of plant closings	Y
16. Hold foreign aid at $15b for '92	N		66. Close unneeded military bases	Y
17. Restore space station funding	Y		67. Keep welfare reform within $2.8b	N
18. Civil Rights Act of 1991	Y		68. Allow children housing exclusion	N
19. Unlimited damages-discrimination	Y		69. Shift $400m of NASA to homeless	Y
20. Eliminate funds for supercollider	N		70. Cap Medicare patients' liability	Y
21. Terminate SDI except for research	Y		71. Prohibit employee polygraph testing	Y
22. Req 7-day handgun waiting period	N		72. Allow CIA to fund Contras	N
23. Provide $30b for failed S&Ls	N		73. Revise unfair trade practices	Y
24. Allow use of force against Iraq	Y		74. Focus SDI on accidental launch	Y
25. Allow $15b in foreign aid for '91	N		75. Bar Air Force $ for MX missile	Y
26. Revise & extend legal immigration	Y		76. Allow "real" increase in defense	N
27. Suspend aid to Angolan rebels	Y		77. Troop reduction in Europe of 50%	+
28. Democratic tax plan proposals	Y		78. Ban nuclear tests above 1 kiloton	Y
29. Cut defense 5% across the board	Y		79. Ban anti-satellite missile tests	#
30. Textile import quotas-veto override	Y		80. Observe certain limits of SALT II	+
31. Abortion service for military abroad	N		81. Restore four Civil Rights laws	Y
32. Limits on high income farmers	N		82. Prohibit aliens as strikebreakers	Y
33. Family medical leave-veto override	Y		83. Allow military malpractice suits	Y
34. Req submission of balanced budget	Y		84. Approval of $36m in Contra aid	N
35. Balanced budget amendment	N		85. $18b deficit reduction compromise	N
36. Amendment to ban flag desecration	Y		86. Welfare reform of $5.7b for 5 years	Y
37. Reauthorize Amtrak-veto override	Y		87. Raise taxes $12b/cut spending $3b	Y
38. Retraining aid for coal miners	Y		88. Board to assess occupational risk	Y
39. Suspend El Salvador military aid	Y		89. Balanced budget by '93-via targets	N
40. Expand child care aid/tax credit	Y		90. Bar licensing of two nuclear plants	N
41. Raise House salary/omit honoraria	Y		91. Remove victims compensation cap	N
42. Toughen oil-spill liability	Y		92. Catastrophic health insurance	Y
43. Restitution to Japanese interned	Y		93. Ban airline smoking-2 hours or less	N
44. Protect Chinese & C.A. nationals	Y		94. $1b/two year aid for the homeless	Y
45. Abortion $ for rape/incest cases	N		95. Bar non-unions in union companies	Y
46. Allow religious schools to bar gays	Y		96. Increase FSLIC rescue to $15b	N
47. Bar broadcaster fairness doctrine	Y		97. Impose quotas to lower trade deficit	Y
48. Bar cap gains cut/reinstate IRA	Y		98. Reduce discretionary budget 21%	N
49. Bar unions equal voice in pension	N		99. Immigration reform/alien amnesty	Y
50. Bar assembly of chemical weapons	Y		100. South Africa sanctions-veto override	Y

RAHALL, NICK JOE, II (continued)

101. Tax overhaul to revise income tax	Y
102. Use of military in drug war	Y
103. Delete 12 MX/add conventional wpn	Y
104. Raise speed limit to 65 mph	N
105. Require Pentagon to buy US goods	Y
106. AIDS insurance non-discrimination	Y
107. Prohibit Saudi arms sales	N
108. Ease Gun Control Act of 1968	Y
109. Bar interstate handgun transport	N
110. Make company emissions known	Y
111. Allow toxic victims to sue in fed ct	Y
112. Superfund waste cleanup of $10b	N
113. 90 days notice of plant closings	Y
114. $20b in Medicare cuts/tax increases	N
115. Spending cuts and tax increases	Y
116. Set school lunch lmt-250% poverty	--
117. $75m for youth work projects	Y
118. Allow Angolan military assistance	N
119. Suspend defense payments for abuse	Y
120. Drop SS COLAs/$12b tax increase	N
121. Approve $1.5b for 21 MX missiles	N
122. Emergency farm credit/revisions	Y

123. Duty on Taiwan/Hong Kong/S Korea	Y
124. Limit steel imports to 17%	Y
125. Cut $ to schools that bar prayer	N
126. $50b-taxes; cut Medicare/spending	Y
127. Limit Pershing II/cruise in Europe	Y
128. Delete $7.1b for 34 B-1 bombers	?
129. Bar purchase of Sergeant York guns	?
130. El Salvador military/economic aid	N
131. Bar mining of Nicaraguan waters	Y
132. Physician fee freeze for Medicare	N
133. $49b in "sin"/phone/insurance taxes	Y
134. Allow sale of Conrail	N
135. Equal Rights Amendment	Y
136. Authorize Marines in Lebanon	Y
137. Eminent domain for coal companies	N
138. Prohibit EPA clean air sanctions	?
139. SS retirement age increase/reforms	N
140. Auto domestic content requirement	Y
141. Delete jobs program funding	N
142. Highway-gas tax bill	N
143. Cut $5b from defense for Medicare	Y
144. Emergency housing aid of $1b	Y

Presidential Support Score: 1991 - 36% 1990 - 14%

WISCONSIN

ASPIN, LES -- Wisconsin 1st District [Democrat]. Counties of Green (pt.), Jefferson (pt.), Kenosha, Racine, Rock and Walworth. Prior Terms: 1971-92. Born: July 21, 1938; Milwaukee, WI. Education: Yale University (B.S.); Oxford University (M.A.); Massachusetts Institute of Technology (Ph.D.). Military Service: U.S. Army, 1966-68. Occupation: Assistant professor (1969-70); assistant, President Kennedy's Council of Economic Advisors; senate staff member (1964).

1. Protection to Haitian refugees	?
2. Raise tax on wealthy; lower others	Y
3. Investigate Reagan hostage delay	Y
4. Campaign finance revisions	Y
5. Unpaid leave to care for children	N
6. Restrict NEA use of funds	N
7. Bar race-bias claim/habeas corpus	Y
8. Ban race as death sentence factor	Y
9. Exceptions to exclusionary rule	Y
10. Allow sale of assault weapons	N
11. Life in prison/abolish death penalty	N
12. Req conspiracy-price fixing cases	N
13. Unemployment benefits extension	Y
14. Tissue use of aborted fetuses	Y
15. Bar replacement of union strikers	Y
16. Hold foreign aid at $15b for '92	Y
17. Restore space station funding	Y
18. Civil Rights Act of 1991	Y
19. Unlimited damages-discrimination	Y
20. Eliminate funds for supercollider	?
21. Terminate SDI except for research	N
22. Req 7-day handgun waiting period	Y
23. Provide $30b for failed S&Ls	Y
24. Allow use of force against Iraq	Y

25. Allow $15b in foreign aid for '91	?
26. Revise & extend legal immigration	?
27. Suspend aid to Angolan rebels	Y
28. Democratic tax plan proposals	Y
29. Cut defense 5% across the board	N
30. Textile import quotas-veto override	Y
31. Abortion service for military abroad	Y
32. Limits on high income farmers	Y
33. Family medical leave-veto override	N
34. Req submission of balanced budget	Y
35. Balanced budget amendment	N
36. Amendment to ban flag desecration	N
37. Reauthorize Amtrak-veto override	Y
38. Retraining aid for coal miners	Y
39. Suspend El Salvador military aid	Y
40. Expand child care aid/tax credit	Y
41. Raise House salary/omit honoraria	Y
42. Toughen oil-spill liability	Y
43. Restitution to Japanese interned	Y
44. Protect Chinese & C.A. nationals	Y
45. Abortion $ for rape/incest cases	?
46. Allow religious schools to bar gays	Y
47. Bar broadcaster fairness doctrine	N
48. Bar cap gains cut/reinstate IRA	Y

ASPIN, LES (continued)

49.	Bar unions equal voice in pension	N	97.	Impose quotas to lower trade deficit	Y
50.	Bar assembly of chemical weapons	Y	98.	Reduce discretionary budget 21%	?
51.	Ban plutonium/uranium production	N	99.	Immigration reform/alien amnesty	Y
52.	Cap MX missile deployment at 50	Y	100.	South Africa sanctions-veto override	Y
53.	Allow $3b for 2 stealth bombers	N	101.	Tax overhaul to revise income tax	Y
54.	Publish bio-warfare experiments	Y	102.	Use of military in drug war	N
55.	Raise minimum wage-veto override	Y	103.	Delete 12 MX/add conventional wpn	N
56.	Bar transfer of FS-X technology	N	104.	Raise speed limit to 65 mph	Y
57.	Cut defense and raise domestic $	N	105.	Require Pentagon to buy US goods	N
58.	Uniform poll closing in 48 states	?	106.	AIDS insurance non-discrimination	Y
59.	Req foreign investment disclosure	Y	107.	Prohibit Saudi arms sales	Y
60.	Textile import quotas-veto override	Y	108.	Ease Gun Control Act of 1968	Y
61.	Bar abortion funding in Wash, DC	N	109.	Bar interstate handgun transport	Y
62.	Notify spouses of AIDS+ carriers	N	110.	Make company emissions known	Y
63.	Seize conveyance-drug trafficking	N	111.	Allow toxic victims to sue in fed ct	Y
64.	South Africa sanctions	Y	112.	Superfund waste cleanup of $10b	Y
65.	60 days' notice of plant closings	Y	113.	90 days notice of plant closings	Y
66.	Close unneeded military bases	N	114.	$20b in Medicare cuts/tax increases	Y
67.	Keep welfare reform within $2.8b	?	115.	Spending cuts and tax increases	Y
68.	Allow children housing exclusion	N	116.	Set school lunch lmt-250% poverty	N
69.	Shift $400m of NASA to homeless	N	117.	$75m for youth work projects	Y
70.	Cap Medicare patients' liability	Y	118.	Allow Angolan military assistance	N
71.	Prohibit employee polygraph testing	?	119.	Suspend defense payments for abuse	N
72.	Allow CIA to fund Contras	?	120.	Drop SS COLAs/$12b tax increase	N
73.	Revise unfair trade practices	Y	121.	Approve $1.5b for 21 MX missiles	Y
74.	Focus SDI on accidental launch	Y	122.	Emergency farm credit/revisions	Y
75.	Bar Air Force $ for MX missile	N	123.	Duty on Taiwan/Hong Kong/S Korea	Y
76.	Allow "real" increase in defense	Y	124.	Limit steel imports to 17%	Y
77.	Troop reduction in Europe of 50%	N	125.	Cut $ to schools that bar prayer	N
78.	Ban nuclear tests above 1 kiloton	Y	126.	$50b-taxes; cut Medicare/spending	Y
79.	Ban anti-satellite missile tests	Y	127.	Limit Pershing II/cruise in Europe	N
80.	Observe certain limits of SALT II	Y	128.	Delete $7.1b for 34 B-1 bombers	Y
81.	Restore four Civil Rights laws	Y	129.	Bar purchase of Sergeant York guns	Y
82.	Prohibit aliens as strikebreakers	?	130.	El Salvador military/economic aid	N
83.	Allow military malpractice suits	Y	131.	Bar mining of Nicaraguan waters	Y
84.	Approval of $36m in Contra aid	N	132.	Physician fee freeze for Medicare	N
85.	$18b deficit reduction compromise	Y	133.	$49b in "sin"/phone/insurance taxes	Y
86.	Welfare reform of $5.7b for 5 years	Y	134.	Allow sale of Conrail	N
87.	Raise taxes $12b/cut spending $3b	Y	135.	Equal Rights Amendment	Y
88.	Board to assess occupational risk	Y	136.	Authorize Marines in Lebanon	Y
89.	Balanced budget by '93-via targets	Y	137.	Eminent domain for coal companies	N
90.	Bar licensing of two nuclear plants	Y	138.	Prohibit EPA clean air sanctions	Y
91.	Remove victims compensation cap	N	139.	SS retirement age increase/reforms	N
92.	Catastrophic health insurance	Y	140.	Auto domestic content requirement	Y
93.	Ban airline smoking-2 hours or less	?	141.	Delete jobs program funding	N
94.	$1b/two year aid for the homeless	?	142.	Highway-gas tax bill	N
95.	Bar non-unions in union companies	Y	143.	Cut $5b from defense for Medicare	N
96.	Increase FSLIC rescue to $15b	Y	144.	Emergency housing aid of $1b	Y

Presidential Support Score: 1991 - 38%   1990 - 24%

KLUG, SCOTT -- Wisconsin 2nd District [Republican]. Counties of Adams (pt.), Columbia, Dane, Dodge (pt.), Grant (pt.), Green (pt.), Iowa, Juneau (pt.), Lafayette, Richland (pt.) and Sauk. Prior Term: 1991-92. Born: January 16, 1953; Milwaukee, WI. Education: Lawrence University (B.A.); Northwestern University (M.A.); University of Wisconsin (M.B.A.). Occupation: Investigative reporter; television anchorman; college journalism professor.

1.	Protection to Haitian refugees	N	6.	Restrict NEA use of funds	N
2.	Raise tax on wealthy; lower others	N	7.	Bar race-bias claim/habeas corpus	Y
3.	Investigate Reagan hostage delay	N	8.	Ban race as death sentence factor	Y
4.	Campaign finance revisions	Y	9.	Exceptions to exclusionary rule	Y
5.	Unpaid leave to care for children	Y	10.	Allow sale of assault weapons	Y

KLUG, SCOTT (continued)

11. Life in prison/abolish death penalty	Y	18. Civil Rights Act of 1991	Y
12. Req conspiracy-price fixing cases	Y	19. Unlimited damages-discrimination	N
13. Unemployment benefits extension	N	20. Eliminate funds for supercollider	N
14. Tissue use of aborted fetuses	Y	21. Terminate SDI except for research	?
15. Bar replacement of union strikers	N	22. Req 7-day handgun waiting period	Y
16. Hold foreign aid at $15b for '92	Y	23. Provide $30b for failed S&Ls	Y
17. Restore space station funding	Y	24. Allow use of force against Iraq	Y

Presidential Support Score: 1991 - 68%

GUNDERSON, STEVE -- Wisconsin 3rd District [Republican]. Counties of Barron, Buffalo, Clark (pt.), Crawford, Dunn, Eau Claire, Grant (pt.), Jackson, La Crosse, Pepin, Pierce, Polk (pt.), Richland (pt.), St. Croix, Trempealeau and Vernon. Prior Terms: 1981-92. Born: May 10, 1951; Eau Claire, WI. Education: University of Wisconsin (B.A.); Brown School of Broadcasting. Occupation: Wisconsin legislator (1975-79); legislative director for congressman.

1. Protection to Haitian refugees	N	47. Bar broadcaster fairness doctrine	Y
2. Raise tax on wealthy; lower others	N	48. Bar cap gains cut/reinstate IRA	N
3. Investigate Reagan hostage delay	N	49. Bar unions equal voice in pension	Y
4. Campaign finance revisions	N	50. Bar assembly of chemical weapons	N
5. Unpaid leave to care for children	N	51. Ban plutonium/uranium production	Y
6. Restrict NEA use of funds	Y	52. Cap MX missile deployment at 50	N
7. Bar race-bias claim/habeas corpus	Y	53. Allow $3b for 2 stealth bombers	Y
8. Ban race as death sentence factor	Y	54. Publish bio-warfare experiments	N
9. Exceptions to exclusionary rule	Y	55. Raise minimum wage-veto override	N
10. Allow sale of assault weapons	Y	56. Bar transfer of FS-X technology	Y
11. Life in prison/abolish death penalty	N	57. Cut defense and raise domestic $	N
12. Req conspiracy-price fixing cases	Y	58. Uniform poll closing in 48 states	N
13. Unemployment benefits extension	Y	59. Req foreign investment disclosure	N
14. Tissue use of aborted fetuses	N	60. Textile import quotas-veto override	Y
15. Bar replacement of union strikers	N	61. Bar abortion funding in Wash, DC	Y
16. Hold foreign aid at $15b for '92	Y	62. Notify spouses of AIDS+ carriers	N
17. Restore space station funding	Y	63. Seize conveyance-drug trafficking	N
18. Civil Rights Act of 1991	N	64. South Africa sanctions	N
19. Unlimited damages-discrimination	N	65. 60 days' notice of plant closings	Y
20. Eliminate funds for supercollider	N	66. Close unneeded military bases	Y
21. Terminate SDI except for research	N	67. Keep welfare reform within $2.8b	Y
22. Req 7-day handgun waiting period	N	68. Allow children housing exclusion	Y
23. Provide $30b for failed S&Ls	Y	69. Shift $400m of NASA to homeless	N
24. Allow use of force against Iraq	Y	70. Cap Medicare patients' liability	Y
25. Allow $15b in foreign aid for '91	?	71. Prohibit employee polygraph testing	Y
26. Revise & extend legal immigration	Y	72. Allow CIA to fund Contras	N
27. Suspend aid to Angolan rebels	N	73. Revise unfair trade practices	Y
28. Democratic tax plan proposals	N	74. Focus SDI on accidental launch	Y
29. Cut defense 5% across the board	N	75. Bar Air Force $ for MX missile	N
30. Textile import quotas-veto override	Y	76. Allow "real" increase in defense	N
31. Abortion service for military abroad	N	77. Troop reduction in Europe of 50%	N
32. Limits on high income farmers	N	78. Ban nuclear tests above 1 kiloton	N
33. Family medical leave-veto override	N	79. Ban anti-satellite missile tests	N
34. Req submission of balanced budget	N	80. Observe certain limits of SALT II	N
35. Balanced budget amendment	Y	81. Restore four Civil Rights laws	Y
36. Amendment to ban flag desecration	Y	82. Prohibit aliens as strikebreakers	Y
37. Reauthorize Amtrak-veto override	N	83. Allow military malpractice suits	N
38. Retraining aid for coal miners	N	84. Approval of $36m in Contra aid	Y
39. Suspend El Salvador military aid	N	85. $18b deficit reduction compromise	N
40. Expand child care aid/tax credit	N	86. Welfare reform of $5.7b for 5 years	N
41. Raise House salary/omit honoraria	Y	87. Raise taxes $12b/cut spending $3b	N
42. Toughen oil-spill liability	N	88. Board to assess occupational risk	N
43. Restitution to Japanese interned	N	89. Balanced budget by '93-via targets	N
44. Protect Chinese & C.A. nationals	Y	90. Bar licensing of two nuclear plants	N
45. Abortion $ for rape/incest cases	N	91. Remove victims compensation cap	N
46. Allow religious schools to bar gays	N	92. Catastrophic health insurance	Y

GUNDERSON, STEVE (continued)

93. Ban airline smoking-2 hours or less	X
94. $1b/two year aid for the homeless	Y
95. Bar non-unions in union companies	N
96. Increase FSLIC rescue to $15b	Y
97. Impose quotas to lower trade deficit	N
98. Reduce discretionary budget 21%	N
99. Immigration reform/alien amnesty	Y
100. South Africa sanctions-veto override	Y
101. Tax overhaul to revise income tax	Y
102. Use of military in drug war	Y
103. Delete 12 MX/add conventional wpn	N
104. Raise speed limit to 65 mph	Y
105. Require Pentagon to buy US goods	Y
106. AIDS insurance non-discrimination	Y
107. Prohibit Saudi arms sales	Y
108. Ease Gun Control Act of 1968	Y
109. Bar interstate handgun transport	N
110. Make company emissions known	N
111. Allow toxic victims to sue in fed ct	N
112. Superfund waste cleanup of $10b	Y
113. 90 days notice of plant closings	Y
114. $20b in Medicare cuts/tax increases	N
115. Spending cuts and tax increases	N
116. Set school lunch lmt-250% poverty	N
117. $75m for youth work projects	N
118. Allow Angolan military assistance	Y

119. Suspend defense payments for abuse	N
120. Drop SS COLAs/$12b tax increase	N
121. Approve $1.5b for 21 MX missiles	Y
122. Emergency farm credit/revisions	Y
123. Duty on Taiwan/Hong Kong/S Korea	N
124. Limit steel imports to 17%	Y
125. Cut $ to schools that bar prayer	N
126. $50b-taxes; cut Medicare/spending	Y
127. Limit Pershing II/cruise in Europe	N
128. Delete $7.1b for 34 B-1 bombers	Y
129. Bar purchase of Sergeant York guns	N
130. El Salvador military/economic aid	Y
131. Bar mining of Nicaraguan waters	Y
132. Physician fee freeze for Medicare	Y
133. $49b in "sin"/phone/insurance taxes	Y
134. Allow sale of Conrail	Y
135. Equal Rights Amendment	Y
136. Authorize Marines in Lebanon	N
137. Eminent domain for coal companies	N
138. Prohibit EPA clean air sanctions	N
139. SS retirement age increase/reforms	Y
140. Auto domestic content requirement	N
141. Delete jobs program funding	Y
142. Highway-gas tax bill	N
143. Cut $5b from defense for Medicare	Y
144. Emergency housing aid of $1b	Y

Presidential Support Score: 1991 - 68%   1990 - 60%

KLECZKA, GERALD D. -- Wisconsin 4th District [Democrat]. Counties of Milwaukee (pt.) and Waukesha (pt.). Prior Terms: 1984 (Special Election)-1992. Born: November 26, 1943; Milwaukee, WI. Education: University of Wisconsin. Military Service: National Guard, 1963-69. Occupation: Wisconsin assemblyman (1968-72); Wisconsin senator (1974-84).

1. Protection to Haitian refugees	#
2. Raise tax on wealthy; lower others	Y
3. Investigate Reagan hostage delay	Y
4. Campaign finance revisions	Y
5. Unpaid leave to care for children	Y
6. Restrict NEA use of funds	N
7. Bar race-bias claim/habeas corpus	N
8. Ban race as death sentence factor	N
9. Exceptions to exclusionary rule	N
10. Allow sale of assault weapons	N
11. Life in prison/abolish death penalty	Y
12. Req conspiracy-price fixing cases	N
13. Unemployment benefits extension	Y
14. Tissue use of aborted fetuses	Y
15. Bar replacement of union strikers	+
16. Hold foreign aid at $15b for '92	Y
17. Restore space station funding	N
18. Civil Rights Act of 1991	Y
19. Unlimited damages-discrimination	Y
20. Eliminate funds for supercollider	Y
21. Terminate SDI except for research	Y
22. Req 7-day handgun waiting period	Y
23. Provide $30b for failed S&Ls	N
24. Allow use of force against Iraq	N
25. Allow $15b in foreign aid for '91	X
26. Revise & extend legal immigration	?
27. Suspend aid to Angolan rebels	Y
28. Democratic tax plan proposals	Y
29. Cut defense 5% across the board	Y

30. Textile import quotas-veto override	N
31. Abortion service for military abroad	N
32. Limits on high income farmers	Y
33. Family medical leave-veto override	Y
34. Req submission of balanced budget	Y
35. Balanced budget amendment	Y
36. Amendment to ban flag desecration	N
37. Reauthorize Amtrak-veto override	Y
38. Retraining aid for coal miners	Y
39. Suspend El Salvador military aid	Y
40. Expand child care aid/tax credit	Y
41. Raise House salary/omit honoraria	Y
42. Toughen oil-spill liability	#
43. Restitution to Japanese interned	Y
44. Protect Chinese & C.A. nationals	Y
45. Abortion $ for rape/incest cases	Y
46. Allow religious schools to bar gays	N
47. Bar broadcaster fairness doctrine	N
48. Bar cap gains cut/reinstate IRA	Y
49. Bar unions equal voice in pension	N
50. Bar assembly of chemical weapons	Y
51. Ban plutonium/uranium production	Y
52. Cap MX missile deployment at 50	Y
53. Allow $3b for 2 stealth bombers	N
54. Publish bio-warfare experiments	Y
55. Raise minimum wage-veto override	Y
56. Bar transfer of FS-X technology	Y
57. Cut defense and raise domestic $	N
58. Uniform poll closing in 48 states	Y

KLECZKA, GERALD D. (continued)

59. Req foreign investment disclosure	Y	97. Impose quotas to lower trade deficit	Y
60. Textile import quotas-veto override	N	98. Reduce discretionary budget 21%	Y
61. Bar abortion funding in Wash, DC	Y	99. Immigration reform/alien amnesty	N
62. Notify spouses of AIDS+ carriers	N	100. South Africa sanctions-veto override	Y
63. Seize conveyance-drug trafficking	N	101. Tax overhaul to revise income tax	Y
64. South Africa sanctions	Y	102. Use of military in drug war	N
65. 60 days' notice of plant closings	Y	103. Delete 12 MX/add conventional wpn	Y
66. Close unneeded military bases	N	104. Raise speed limit to 65 mph	N
67. Keep welfare reform within $2.8b	N	105. Require Pentagon to buy US goods	Y
68. Allow children housing exclusion	N	106. AIDS insurance non-discrimination	Y
69. Shift $400m of NASA to homeless	Y	107. Prohibit Saudi arms sales	Y
70. Cap Medicare patients' liability	Y	108. Ease Gun Control Act of 1968	Y
71. Prohibit employee polygraph testing	Y	109. Bar interstate handgun transport	Y
72. Allow CIA to fund Contras	N	110. Make company emissions known	Y
73. Revise unfair trade practices	Y	111. Allow toxic victims to sue in fed ct	Y
74. Focus SDI on accidental launch	Y	112. Superfund waste cleanup of $10b	Y
75. Bar Air Force $ for MX missile	Y	113. 90 days notice of plant closings	Y
76. Allow "real" increase in defense	N	114. $20b in Medicare cuts/tax increases	Y
77. Troop reduction in Europe of 50%	Y	115. Spending cuts and tax increases	Y
78. Ban nuclear tests above 1 kiloton	Y	116. Set school lunch lmt-250% poverty	N
79. Ban anti-satellite missile tests	Y	117. $75m for youth work projects	N
80. Observe certain limits of SALT II	Y	118. Allow Angolan military assistance	N
81. Restore four Civil Rights laws	Y	119. Suspend defense payments for abuse	Y
82. Prohibit aliens as strikebreakers	Y	120. Drop SS COLAs/$12b tax increase	N
83. Allow military malpractice suits	Y	121. Approve $1.5b for 21 MX missiles	N
84. Approval of $36m in Contra aid	N	122. Emergency farm credit/revisions	Y
85. $18b deficit reduction compromise	Y	123. Duty on Taiwan/Hong Kong/S Korea	Y
86. Welfare reform of $5.7b for 5 years	Y	124. Limit steel imports to 17%	Y
87. Raise taxes $12b/cut spending $3b	Y	125. Cut $ to schools that bar prayer	N
88. Board to assess occupational risk	Y	126. $50b-taxes; cut Medicare/spending	Y
89. Balanced budget by '93-via targets	Y	127. Limit Pershing II/cruise in Europe	N
90. Bar licensing of two nuclear plants	Y	128. Delete $7.1b for 34 B-1 bombers	N
91. Remove victims compensation cap	Y	129. Bar purchase of Sergeant York guns	Y
92. Catastrophic health insurance	Y	130. El Salvador military/economic aid	N
93. Ban airline smoking-2 hours or less	Y	131. Bar mining of Nicaraguan waters	Y
94. $1b/two year aid for the homeless	Y	132. Physician fee freeze for Medicare	N
95. Bar non-unions in union companies	Y	133. $49b in "sin"/phone/insurance taxes	Y
96. Increase FSLIC rescue to $15b	Y		

Presidential Support Score: 1991 - 23%   1990 - 21%

MOODY, JIM -- Wisconsin 5th District [Democrat].   Counties of Milwaukee (pt.) and Washington (pt.).   Prior Terms: 1983-92.   Born: September 2, 1935; Richlands, VA. Education: Haverford College (B.A.); Harvard University (M.B.A.); University of California (Ph.D.). Occupation: Field representative, CARE (1958-60); Country Director, Peace Corps (1961); economist, U.S. Department of Transportation (1967-69); assistant professor of Economics (1973-82); Wisconsin assemblyman (1977-78); Wisconsin senator (1979-82).

1. Protection to Haitian refugees	Y	16. Hold foreign aid at $15b for '92	Y
2. Raise tax on wealthy; lower others	Y	17. Restore space station funding	N
3. Investigate Reagan hostage delay	Y	18. Civil Rights Act of 1991	Y
4. Campaign finance revisions	+	19. Unlimited damages-discrimination	Y
5. Unpaid leave to care for children	Y	20. Eliminate funds for supercollider	Y
6. Restrict NEA use of funds	N	21. Terminate SDI except for research	Y
7. Bar race-bias claim/habeas corpus	N	22. Req 7-day handgun waiting period	Y
8. Ban race as death sentence factor	N	23. Provide $30b for failed S&Ls	N
9. Exceptions to exclusionary rule	N	24. Allow use of force against Iraq	N
10. Allow sale of assault weapons	N	25. Allow $15b in foreign aid for '91	N
11. Life in prison/abolish death penalty	Y	26. Revise & extend legal immigration	Y
12. Req conspiracy-price fixing cases	N	27. Suspend aid to Angolan rebels	Y
13. Unemployment benefits extension	Y	28. Democratic tax plan proposals	Y
14. Tissue use of aborted fetuses	#	29. Cut defense 5% across the board	Y
15. Bar replacement of union strikers	Y	30. Textile import quotas-veto override	Y

MOODY, JIM (continued)

31.	Abortion service for military abroad	Y	86.	Welfare reform of $5.7b for 5 years	Y
32.	Limits on high income farmers	Y	87.	Raise taxes $12b/cut spending $3b	Y
33.	Family medical leave-veto override	Y	88.	Board to assess occupational risk	Y
34.	Req submission of balanced budget	Y	89.	Balanced budget by '93-via targets	N
35.	Balanced budget amendment	Y	90.	Bar licensing of two nuclear plants	N
36.	Amendment to ban flag desecration	N	91.	Remove victims compensation cap	?
37.	Reauthorize Amtrak-veto override	?	92.	Catastrophic health insurance	Y
38.	Retraining aid for coal miners	Y	93.	Ban airline smoking-2 hours or less	Y
39.	Suspend El Salvador military aid	Y	94.	$1b/two year aid for the homeless	Y
40.	Expand child care aid/tax credit	Y	95.	Bar non-unions in union companies	Y
41.	Raise House salary/omit honoraria	Y	96.	Increase FSLIC rescue to $15b	N
42.	Toughen oil-spill liability	Y	97.	Impose quotas to lower trade deficit	Y
43.	Restitution to Japanese interned	Y	98.	Reduce discretionary budget 21%	Y
44.	Protect Chinese & C.A. nationals	Y	99.	Immigration reform/alien amnesty	Y
45.	Abortion $ for rape/incest cases	Y	100.	South Africa sanctions-veto override	Y
46.	Allow religious schools to bar gays	N	101.	Tax overhaul to revise income tax	Y
47.	Bar broadcaster fairness doctrine	Y	102.	Use of military in drug war	N
48.	Bar cap gains cut/reinstate IRA	Y	103.	Delete 12 MX/add conventional wpn	Y
49.	Bar unions equal voice in pension	N	104.	Raise speed limit to 65 mph	N
50.	Bar assembly of chemical weapons	?	105.	Require Pentagon to buy US goods	N
51.	Ban plutonium/uranium production	Y	106.	AIDS insurance non-discrimination	Y
52.	Cap MX missile deployment at 50	Y	107.	Prohibit Saudi arms sales	Y
53.	Allow $3b for 2 stealth bombers	N	108.	Ease Gun Control Act of 1968	Y
54.	Publish bio-warfare experiments	Y	109.	Bar interstate handgun transport	Y
55.	Raise minimum wage-veto override	Y	110.	Make company emissions known	Y
56.	Bar transfer of FS-X technology	Y	111.	Allow toxic victims to sue in fed ct	Y
57.	Cut defense and raise domestic $	Y	112.	Superfund waste cleanup of $10b	Y
58.	Uniform poll closing in 48 states	?	113.	90 days notice of plant closings	Y
59.	Req foreign investment disclosure	Y	114.	$20b in Medicare cuts/tax increases	Y
60.	Textile import quotas-veto override	Y	115.	Spending cuts and tax increases	Y
61.	Bar abortion funding in Wash, DC	N	116.	Set school lunch lmt-250% poverty	N
62.	Notify spouses of AIDS+ carriers	N	117.	$75m for youth work projects	Y
63.	Seize conveyance-drug trafficking	N	118.	Allow Angolan military assistance	N
64.	South Africa sanctions	Y	119.	Suspend defense payments for abuse	Y
65.	60 days' notice of plant closings	Y	120.	Drop SS COLAs/$12b tax increase	Y
66.	Close unneeded military bases	N	121.	Approve $1.5b for 21 MX missiles	N
67.	Keep welfare reform within $2.8b	N	122.	Emergency farm credit/revisions	Y
68.	Allow children housing exclusion	?	123.	Duty on Taiwan/Hong Kong/S Korea	Y
69.	Shift $400m of NASA to homeless	Y	124.	Limit steel imports to 17%	Y
70.	Cap Medicare patients' liability	Y	125.	Cut $ to schools that bar prayer	N
71.	Prohibit employee polygraph testing	#	126.	$50b-taxes; cut Medicare/spending	Y
72.	Allow CIA to fund Contras	N	127.	Limit Pershing II/cruise in Europe	Y
73.	Revise unfair trade practices	Y	128.	Delete $7.1b for 34 B-1 bombers	Y
74.	Focus SDI on accidental launch	Y	129.	Bar purchase of Sergeant York guns	Y
75.	Bar Air Force $ for MX missile	Y	130.	El Salvador military/economic aid	?
76.	Allow "real" increase in defense	X	131.	Bar mining of Nicaraguan waters	Y
77.	Troop reduction in Europe of 50%	+	132.	Physician fee freeze for Medicare	N
78.	Ban nuclear tests above 1 kiloton	#	133.	$49b in "sin"/phone/insurance taxes	Y
79.	Ban anti-satellite missile tests	+	134.	Allow sale of Conrail	N
80.	Observe certain limits of SALT II	Y	135.	Equal Rights Amendment	Y
81.	Restore four Civil Rights laws	Y	136.	Authorize Marines in Lebanon	N
82.	Prohibit aliens as strikebreakers	Y	137.	Eminent domain for coal companies	Y
83.	Allow military malpractice suits	Y	138.	Prohibit EPA clean air sanctions	Y
84.	Approval of $36m in Contra aid	N	139.	SS retirement age increase/reforms	N
85.	$18b deficit reduction compromise	Y			

Presidential Support Score: 1991 - 19%   1990 - 17%

PETRI, THOMAS E. -- Wisconsin 6th District [Republican]. Counties of Adams (pt.), Calumet, Fond du Lac (pt.), Green Lake, Juneau (pt.), Manitowoc, Marquette, Monroe, Sheboygan (pt.), Waupaca, Waushara, Winnebago and Wood (pt.).   Prior Terms: 1979 (Special Election)-1992. Born: May 28, 1940; Marinette, WI.   Education: Harvard College (B.A., J.D.). Occupation: Law clerk, federal district judge; Peace Corps volunteer; director, crime

PETRI, THOMAS E. (continued)
and drug studies, President's National Advisory Council on Executive Organization (1969); Wisconsin senator (1972-79).

1. Protection to Haitian refugees	N	
2. Raise tax on wealthy; lower others	N	
3. Investigate Reagan hostage delay	N	
4. Campaign finance revisions	Y	
5. Unpaid leave to care for children	N	
6. Restrict NEA use of funds	Y	
7. Bar race-bias claim/habeas corpus	Y	
8. Ban race as death sentence factor	Y	
9. Exceptions to exclusionary rule	Y	
10. Allow sale of assault weapons	Y	
11. Life in prison/abolish death penalty	N	
12. Req conspiracy-price fixing cases	Y	
13. Unemployment benefits extension	N	
14. Tissue use of aborted fetuses	N	
15. Bar replacement of union strikers	N	
16. Hold foreign aid at $15b for '92	N	
17. Restore space station funding	Y	
18. Civil Rights Act of 1991	N	
19. Unlimited damages-discrimination	N	
20. Eliminate funds for supercollider	Y	
21. Terminate SDI except for research	N	
22. Req 7-day handgun waiting period	N	
23. Provide $30b for failed S&Ls	N	
24. Allow use of force against Iraq	Y	
25. Allow $15b in foreign aid for '91	N	
26. Revise & extend legal immigration	N	
27. Suspend aid to Angolan rebels	N	
28. Democratic tax plan proposals	N	
29. Cut defense 5% across the board	Y	
30. Textile import quotas-veto override	N	
31. Abortion service for military abroad	N	
32. Limits on high income farmers	Y	
33. Family medical leave-veto override	N	
34. Req submission of balanced budget	Y	
35. Balanced budget amendment	Y	
36. Amendment to ban flag desecration	N	
37. Reauthorize Amtrak-veto override	Y	
38. Retraining aid for coal miners	N	
39. Suspend El Salvador military aid	N	
40. Expand child care aid/tax credit	Y	
41. Raise House salary/omit honoraria	N	
42. Toughen oil-spill liability	Y	
43. Restitution to Japanese interned	N	
44. Protect Chinese & C.A. nationals	N	
45. Abortion $ for rape/incest cases	N	
46. Allow religious schools to bar gays	Y	
47. Bar broadcaster fairness doctrine	Y	
48. Bar cap gains cut/reinstate IRA	N	
49. Bar unions equal voice in pension	Y	
50. Bar assembly of chemical weapons	N	
51. Ban plutonium/uranium production	N	
52. Cap MX missile deployment at 50	Y	
53. Allow $3b for 2 stealth bombers	N	
54. Publish bio-warfare experiments	Y	
55. Raise minimum wage-veto override	N	
56. Bar transfer of FS-X technology	N	
57. Cut defense and raise domestic $	N	
58. Uniform poll closing in 48 states	N	
59. Req foreign investment disclosure	N	
60. Textile import quotas-veto override	N	
61. Bar abortion funding in Wash, DC	Y	
62. Notify spouses of AIDS+ carriers	N
63. Seize conveyance-drug trafficking	Y
64. South Africa sanctions	N
65. 60 days' notice of plant closings	Y
66. Close unneeded military bases	Y
67. Keep welfare reform within $2.8b	Y
68. Allow children housing exclusion	Y
69. Shift $400m of NASA to homeless	N
70. Cap Medicare patients' liability	Y
71. Prohibit employee polygraph testing	Y
72. Allow CIA to fund Contras	Y
73. Revise unfair trade practices	N
74. Focus SDI on accidental launch	N
75. Bar Air Force $ for MX missile	Y
76. Allow "real" increase in defense	Y
77. Troop reduction in Europe of 50%	N
78. Ban nuclear tests above 1 kiloton	N
79. Ban anti-satellite missile tests	X
80. Observe certain limits of SALT II	N
81. Restore four Civil Rights laws	Y
82. Prohibit aliens as strikebreakers	N
83. Allow military malpractice suits	Y
84. Approval of $36m in Contra aid	Y
85. $18b deficit reduction compromise	Y
86. Welfare reform of $5.7b for 5 years	N
87. Raise taxes $12b/cut spending $3b	N
88. Board to assess occupational risk	Y
89. Balanced budget by '93-via targets	N
90. Bar licensing of two nuclear plants	N
91. Remove victims compensation cap	Y
92. Catastrophic health insurance	Y
93. Ban airline smoking-2 hours or less	Y
94. $1b/two year aid for the homeless	N
95. Bar non-unions in union companies	N
96. Increase FSLIC rescue to $15b	N
97. Impose quotas to lower trade deficit	N
98. Reduce discretionary budget 21%	Y
99. Immigration reform/alien amnesty	N
100. South Africa sanctions-veto override	Y
101. Tax overhaul to revise income tax	Y
102. Use of military in drug war	Y
103. Delete 12 MX/add conventional wpn	Y
104. Raise speed limit to 65 mph	Y
105. Require Pentagon to buy US goods	N
106. AIDS insurance non-discrimination	N
107. Prohibit Saudi arms sales	N
108. Ease Gun Control Act of 1968	Y
109. Bar interstate handgun transport	N
110. Make company emissions known	Y
111. Allow toxic victims to sue in fed ct	Y
112. Superfund waste cleanup of $10b	Y
113. 90 days notice of plant closings	Y
114. $20b in Medicare cuts/tax increases	N
115. Spending cuts and tax increases	N
116. Set school lunch lmt-250% poverty	N
117. $75m for youth work projects	Y
118. Allow Angolan military assistance	Y
119. Suspend defense payments for abuse	Y
120. Drop SS COLAs/$12b tax increase	N
121. Approve $1.5b for 21 MX missiles	N
122. Emergency farm credit/revisions	Y

PETRI, THOMAS E. (continued)

123. Duty on Taiwan/Hong Kong/S Korea	N
124. Limit steel imports to 17%	N
125. Cut $ to schools that bar prayer	Y
126. $50b-taxes; cut Medicare/spending	N
127. Limit Pershing II/cruise in Europe	N
128. Delete $7.1b for 34 B-1 bombers	Y
129. Bar purchase of Sergeant York guns	N
130. El Salvador military/economic aid	Y
131. Bar mining of Nicaraguan waters	Y
132. Physician fee freeze for Medicare	Y
133. $49b in "sin"/phone/insurance taxes	Y
134. Allow sale of Conrail	Y
135. Equal Rights Amendment	Y
136. Authorize Marines in Lebanon	N
137. Eminent domain for coal companies	Y
138. Prohibit EPA clean air sanctions	N
139. SS retirement age increase/reforms	Y
140. Auto domestic content requirement	N
141. Delete jobs program funding	Y
142. Highway-gas tax bill	N
143. Cut $5b from defense for Medicare	Y
144. Emergency housing aid of $1b	N

Presidential Support Score: 1991 - 68%   1990 - 69%

OBEY, DAVID R. -- Wisconsin 7th District [Democrat]. Counties of Ashland, Bayfield, Burnett, Chippewa, Clark (pt.), Douglas, Iron, Lincoln, Marathon, Oneida (pt.), Polk (pt.), Portage, Price, Rusk, Sawyer, Taylor, Washburn and Wood (pt.). Prior Terms: 1969 (Special Election)-1992. Born: October 3, 1938; Okmulgee, OK. Education: University of Wisconsin (M.A.). Occupation: Wisconsin assemblyman.

1. Protection to Haitian refugees	Y	44. Protect Chinese & C.A. nationals	Y
2. Raise tax on wealthy; lower others	N	45. Abortion $ for rape/incest cases	Y
3. Investigate Reagan hostage delay	Y	46. Allow religious schools to bar gays	N
4. Campaign finance revisions	Y	47. Bar broadcaster fairness doctrine	N
5. Unpaid leave to care for children	Y	48. Bar cap gains cut/reinstate IRA	Y
6. Restrict NEA use of funds	N	49. Bar unions equal voice in pension	N
7. Bar race-bias claim/habeas corpus	N	50. Bar assembly of chemical weapons	Y
8. Ban race as death sentence factor	N	51. Ban plutonium/uranium production	Y
9. Exceptions to exclusionary rule	N	52. Cap MX missile deployment at 50	Y
10. Allow sale of assault weapons	Y	53. Allow $3b for 2 stealth bombers	N
11. Life in prison/abolish death penalty	Y	54. Publish bio-warfare experiments	Y
12. Req conspiracy-price fixing cases	N	55. Raise minimum wage-veto override	Y
13. Unemployment benefits extension	Y	56. Bar transfer of FS-X technology	Y
14. Tissue use of aborted fetuses	Y	57. Cut defense and raise domestic $	Y
15. Bar replacement of union strikers	Y	58. Uniform poll closing in 48 states	N
16. Hold foreign aid at $15b for '92	Y	59. Req foreign investment disclosure	Y
17. Restore space station funding	N	60. Textile import quotas-veto override	Y
18. Civil Rights Act of 1991	Y	61. Bar abortion funding in Wash, DC	N
19. Unlimited damages-discrimination	N	62. Notify spouses of AIDS+ carriers	N
20. Eliminate funds for supercollider	Y	63. Seize conveyance-drug trafficking	N
21. Terminate SDI except for research	Y	64. South Africa sanctions	Y
22. Req 7-day handgun waiting period	N	65. 60 days' notice of plant closings	Y
23. Provide $30b for failed S&Ls	N	66. Close unneeded military bases	N
24. Allow use of force against Iraq	N	67. Keep welfare reform within $2.8b	N
25. Allow $15b in foreign aid for '91	Y	68. Allow children housing exclusion	N
26. Revise & extend legal immigration	Y	69. Shift $400m of NASA to homeless	Y
27. Suspend aid to Angolan rebels	Y	70. Cap Medicare patients' liability	Y
28. Democratic tax plan proposals	Y	71. Prohibit employee polygraph testing	Y
29. Cut defense 5% across the board	N	72. Allow CIA to fund Contras	N
30. Textile import quotas-veto override	Y	73. Revise unfair trade practices	Y
31. Abortion service for military abroad	Y	74. Focus SDI on accidental launch	Y
32. Limits on high income farmers	Y	75. Bar Air Force $ for MX missile	Y
33. Family medical leave-veto override	Y	76. Allow "real" increase in defense	N
34. Req submission of balanced budget	Y	77. Troop reduction in Europe of 50%	Y
35. Balanced budget amendment	N	78. Ban nuclear tests above 1 kiloton	Y
36. Amendment to ban flag desecration	N	79. Ban anti-satellite missile tests	Y
37. Reauthorize Amtrak-veto override	Y	80. Observe certain limits of SALT II	Y
38. Retraining aid for coal miners	Y	81. Restore four Civil Rights laws	Y
39. Suspend El Salvador military aid	Y	82. Prohibit aliens as strikebreakers	Y
40. Expand child care aid/tax credit	Y	83. Allow military malpractice suits	Y
41. Raise House salary/omit honoraria	Y	84. Approval of $36m in Contra aid	N
42. Toughen oil-spill liability	Y	85. $18b deficit reduction compromise	Y
43. Restitution to Japanese interned	Y	86. Welfare reform of $5.7b for 5 years	Y

OBEY, DAVID R. (continued)

87. Raise taxes $12b/cut spending $3b	Y	
88. Board to assess occupational risk	Y	
89. Balanced budget by '93-via targets	N	
90. Bar licensing of two nuclear plants	Y	
91. Remove victims compensation cap	Y	
92. Catastrophic health insurance	Y	
93. Ban airline smoking-2 hours or less	N	
94. $1b/two year aid for the homeless	Y	
95. Bar non-unions in union companies	Y	
96. Increase FSLIC rescue to $15b	N	
97. Impose quotas to lower trade deficit	Y	
98. Reduce discretionary budget 21%	N	
99. Immigration reform/alien amnesty	Y	
100. South Africa sanctions-veto override	Y	
101. Tax overhaul to revise income tax	Y	
102. Use of military in drug war	N	
103. Delete 12 MX/add conventional wpn	Y	
104. Raise speed limit to 65 mph	N	
105. Require Pentagon to buy US goods	Y	
106. AIDS insurance non-discrimination	Y	
107. Prohibit Saudi arms sales	Y	
108. Ease Gun Control Act of 1968	Y	
109. Bar interstate handgun transport	N	
110. Make company emissions known	Y	
111. Allow toxic victims to sue in fed ct	Y	
112. Superfund waste cleanup of $10b	Y	
113. 90 days notice of plant closings	Y	
114. $20b in Medicare cuts/tax increases	Y	
115. Spending cuts and tax increases	Y	

116. Set school lunch lmt-250% poverty	N	
117. $75m for youth work projects	Y	
118. Allow Angolan military assistance	N	
119. Suspend defense payments for abuse	Y	
120. Drop SS COLAs/$12b tax increase	N	
121. Approve $1.5b for 21 MX missiles	N	
122. Emergency farm credit/revisions	Y	
123. Duty on Taiwan/Hong Kong/S Korea	N	
124. Limit steel imports to 17%	Y	
125. Cut $ to schools that bar prayer	?	
126. $50b-taxes; cut Medicare/spending	Y	
127. Limit Pershing II/cruise in Europe	N	
128. Delete $7.1b for 34 B-1 bombers	Y	
129. Bar purchase of Sergeant York guns	Y	
130. El Salvador military/economic aid	N	
131. Bar mining of Nicaraguan waters	Y	
132. Physician fee freeze for Medicare	N	
133. $49b in "sin"/phone/insurance taxes	Y	
134. Allow sale of Conrail	N	
135. Equal Rights Amendment	Y	
136. Authorize Marines in Lebanon	N	
137. Eminent domain for coal companies	N	
138. Prohibit EPA clean air sanctions	Y	
139. SS retirement age increase/reforms	N	
140. Auto domestic content requirement	Y	
141. Delete jobs program funding	N	
142. Highway-gas tax bill	N	
143. Cut $5b from defense for Medicare	Y	
144. Emergency housing aid of $1b	Y	

Presidential Support Score: 1991 - 29%   1990 - 15%

ROTH, TOBY -- Wisconsin 8th District [Republican]. Counties of Brown, Door, Florence, Forest, Kewaunee, Langlade, Mannette, Menominee, Oconto, Oneida (pt.), Outagamie, Shawano and Vilas. Prior Terms: 1979-92. Born: October 10, 1938; Appleton, WI. Education: Marquette University (B.A.). Military Service: U.S. Army Reserve, 1962-69. Occupation: Realtor; Wisconsin legislator (1972-78).

1. Protection to Haitian refugees	N	
2. Raise tax on wealthy; lower others	N	
3. Investigate Reagan hostage delay	N	
4. Campaign finance revisions	N	
5. Unpaid leave to care for children	N	
6. Restrict NEA use of funds	Y	
7. Bar race-bias claim/habeas corpus	Y	
8. Ban race as death sentence factor	Y	
9. Exceptions to exclusionary rule	Y	
10. Allow sale of assault weapons	Y	
11. Life in prison/abolish death penalty	N	
12. Req conspiracy-price fixing cases	Y	
13. Unemployment benefits extension	N	
14. Tissue use of aborted fetuses	N	
15. Bar replacement of union strikers	N	
16. Hold foreign aid at $15b for '92	N	
17. Restore space station funding	N	
18. Civil Rights Act of 1991	N	
19. Unlimited damages-discrimination	N	
20. Eliminate funds for supercollider	Y	
21. Terminate SDI except for research	N	
22. Req 7-day handgun waiting period	N	
23. Provide $30b for failed S&Ls	N	
24. Allow use of force against Iraq	Y	
25. Allow $15b in foreign aid for '91	N	

26. Revise & extend legal immigration	N	
27. Suspend aid to Angolan rebels	N	
28. Democratic tax plan proposals	N	
29. Cut defense 5% across the board	Y	
30. Textile import quotas-veto override	Y	
31. Abortion service for military abroad	N	
32. Limits on high income farmers	Y	
33. Family medical leave-veto override	N	
34. Req submission of balanced budget	Y	
35. Balanced budget amendment	Y	
36. Amendment to ban flag desecration	Y	
37. Reauthorize Amtrak-veto override	N	
38. Retraining aid for coal miners	N	
39. Suspend El Salvador military aid	N	
40. Expand child care aid/tax credit	N	
41. Raise House salary/omit honoraria	N	
42. Toughen oil-spill liability	N	
43. Restitution to Japanese interned	N	
44. Protect Chinese & C.A. nationals	N	
45. Abortion $ for rape/incest cases	N	
46. Allow religious schools to bar gays	Y	
47. Bar broadcaster fairness doctrine	Y	
48. Bar cap gains cut/reinstate IRA	N	
49. Bar unions equal voice in pension	Y	
50. Bar assembly of chemical weapons	Y	

ROTH, TOBY (continued)

51. Ban plutonium/uranium production	N	98. Reduce discretionary budget 21%	Y
52. Cap MX missile deployment at 50	Y	99. Immigration reform/alien amnesty	N
53. Allow $3b for 2 stealth bombers	N	100. South Africa sanctions-veto override	N
54. Publish bio-warfare experiments	N	101. Tax overhaul to revise income tax	Y
55. Raise minimum wage-veto override	N	102. Use of military in drug war	Y
56. Bar transfer of FS-X technology	N	103. Delete 12 MX/add conventional wpn	Y
57. Cut defense and raise domestic $	N	104. Raise speed limit to 65 mph	Y
58. Uniform poll closing in 48 states	N	105. Require Pentagon to buy US goods	Y
59. Req foreign investment disclosure	Y	106. AIDS insurance non-discrimination	N
60. Textile import quotas-veto override	N	107. Prohibit Saudi arms sales	Y
61. Bar abortion funding in Wash, DC	Y	108. Ease Gun Control Act of 1968	Y
62. Notify spouses of AIDS+ carriers	Y	109. Bar interstate handgun transport	N
63. Seize conveyance-drug trafficking	Y	110. Make company emissions known	N
64. South Africa sanctions	N	111. Allow toxic victims to sue in fed ct	N
65. 60 days' notice of plant closings	Y	112. Superfund waste cleanup of $10b	Y
66. Close unneeded military bases	Y	113. 90 days notice of plant closings	N
67. Keep welfare reform within $2.8b	Y	114. $20b in Medicare cuts/tax increases	N
68. Allow children housing exclusion	Y	115. Spending cuts and tax increases	N
69. Shift $400m of NASA to homeless	N	116. Set school lunch lmt-250% poverty	Y
70. Cap Medicare patients' liability	N	117. $75m for youth work projects	Y
71. Prohibit employee polygraph testing	N	118. Allow Angolan military assistance	Y
72. Allow CIA to fund Contras	Y	119. Suspend defense payments for abuse	Y
73. Revise unfair trade practices	Y	120. Drop SS COLAs/$12b tax increase	N
74. Focus SDI on accidental launch	?	121. Approve $1.5b for 21 MX missiles	Y
75. Bar Air Force $ for MX missile	N	122. Emergency farm credit/revisions	Y
76. Allow "real" increase in defense	Y	123. Duty on Taiwan/Hong Kong/S Korea	N
77. Troop reduction in Europe of 50%	X	124. Limit steel imports to 17%	Y
78. Ban nuclear tests above 1 kiloton	N	125. Cut $ to schools that bar prayer	Y
79. Ban anti-satellite missile tests	N	126. $50b-taxes; cut Medicare/spending	N
80. Observe certain limits of SALT II	N	127. Limit Pershing II/cruise in Europe	N
81. Restore four Civil Rights laws	N	128. Delete $7.1b for 34 B-1 bombers	Y
82. Prohibit aliens as strikebreakers	N	129. Bar purchase of Sergeant York guns	Y
83. Allow military malpractice suits	Y	130. El Salvador military/economic aid	Y
84. Approval of $36m in Contra aid	Y	131. Bar mining of Nicaraguan waters	Y
85. $18b deficit reduction compromise	N	132. Physician fee freeze for Medicare	Y
86. Welfare reform of $5.7b for 5 years	N	133. $49b in "sin"/phone/insurance taxes	Y
87. Raise taxes $12b/cut spending $3b	N	134. Allow sale of Conrail	Y
88. Board to assess occupational risk	N	135. Equal Rights Amendment	N
89. Balanced budget by '93-via targets	N	136. Authorize Marines in Lebanon	N
90. Bar licensing of two nuclear plants	N	137. Eminent domain for coal companies	Y
91. Remove victims compensation cap	N	138. Prohibit EPA clean air sanctions	Y
92. Catastrophic health insurance	N	139. SS retirement age increase/reforms	Y
93. Ban airline smoking-2 hours or less	N	140. Auto domestic content requirement	Y
94. $1b/two year aid for the homeless	Y	141. Delete jobs program funding	Y
95. Bar non-unions in union companies	N	142. Highway-gas tax bill	N
96. Increase FSLIC rescue to $15b	Y	143. Cut $5b from defense for Medicare	N
97. Impose quotas to lower trade deficit	N	144. Emergency housing aid of $1b	Y

Presidential Support Score: 1991 - 69% 1990 - 63%

SENSENBRENNER, F. JAMES, Jr. -- Wisconsin 9th District [Republican]. Counties of Dodge(pt.), Fond du Lac (pt.), Jefferson (pt.), Milwaukee (pt.), Ozaukee, Sheboygan (pt.), Washington (pt.) and Waukesha (pt.). Prior Terms: 1979-92. Born: June 14, 1943; Chicago, IL. Education: Stanford University (A.B.); Wisconsin Law School (J.D.). Occupation: Wisconsin assemblyman (1968-75); Wisconsin senator (1975-78).

1. Protection to Haitian refugees	N	8. Ban race as death sentence factor	Y
2. Raise tax on wealthy; lower others	N	9. Exceptions to exclusionary rule	Y
3. Investigate Reagan hostage delay	N	10. Allow sale of assault weapons	Y
4. Campaign finance revisions	N	11. Life in prison/abolish death penalty	N
5. Unpaid leave to care for children	N	12. Req conspiracy-price fixing cases	Y
6. Restrict NEA use of funds	Y	13. Unemployment benefits extension	N
7. Bar race-bias claim/habeas corpus	Y	14. Tissue use of aborted fetuses	N

SENSENBRENNER, F. JAMES, (continued)

15. Bar replacement of union strikers	N
16. Hold foreign aid at $15b for '92	N
17. Restore space station funding	Y
18. Civil Rights Act of 1991	N
19. Unlimited damages-discrimination	N
20. Eliminate funds for supercollider	Y
21. Terminate SDI except for research	N
22. Req 7-day handgun waiting period	Y
23. Provide $30b for failed S&Ls	N
24. Allow use of force against Iraq	Y
25. Allow $15b in foreign aid for '91	N
26. Revise & extend legal immigration	N
27. Suspend aid to Angolan rebels	N
28. Democratic tax plan proposals	N
29. Cut defense 5% across the board	Y
30. Textile import quotas-veto override	N
31. Abortion service for military abroad	N
32. Limits on high income farmers	Y
33. Family medical leave-veto override	N
34. Req submission of balanced budget	N
35. Balanced budget amendment	Y
36. Amendment to ban flag desecration	Y
37. Reauthorize Amtrak-veto override	N
38. Retraining aid for coal miners	N
39. Suspend El Salvador military aid	N
40. Expand child care aid/tax credit	N
41. Raise House salary/omit honoraria	N
42. Toughen oil-spill liability	N
43. Restitution to Japanese interned	N
44. Protect Chinese & C.A. nationals	N
45. Abortion $ for rape/incest cases	N
46. Allow religious schools to bar gays	Y
47. Bar broadcaster fairness doctrine	Y
48. Bar cap gains cut/reinstate IRA	N
49. Bar unions equal voice in pension	Y
50. Bar assembly of chemical weapons	Y
51. Ban plutonium/uranium production	N
52. Cap MX missile deployment at 50	Y
53. Allow $3b for 2 stealth bombers	N
54. Publish bio-warfare experiments	Y
55. Raise minimum wage-veto override	N
56. Bar transfer of FS-X technology	N
57. Cut defense and raise domestic $	N
58. Uniform poll closing in 48 states	N
59. Req foreign investment disclosure	N
60. Textile import quotas-veto override	N
61. Bar abortion funding in Wash, DC	Y
62. Notify spouses of AIDS+ carriers	Y
63. Seize conveyance-drug trafficking	N
64. South Africa sanctions	N
65. 60 days' notice of plant closings	N
66. Close unneeded military bases	Y
67. Keep welfare reform within $2.8b	Y
68. Allow children housing exclusion	Y
69. Shift $400m of NASA to homeless	N
70. Cap Medicare patients' liability	N
71. Prohibit employee polygraph testing	N
72. Allow CIA to fund Contras	Y
73. Revise unfair trade practices	Y
74. Focus SDI on accidental launch	N
75. Bar Air Force $ for MX missile	Y
76. Allow "real" increase in defense	Y
77. Troop reduction in Europe of 50%	Y
78. Ban nuclear tests above 1 kiloton	N

79. Ban anti-satellite missile tests	N
80. Observe certain limits of SALT II	N
81. Restore four Civil Rights laws	N
82. Prohibit aliens as strikebreakers	N
83. Allow military malpractice suits	Y
84. Approval of $36m in Contra aid	Y
85. $18b deficit reduction compromise	N
86. Welfare reform of $5.7b for 5 years	N
87. Raise taxes $12b/cut spending $3b	?
88. Board to assess occupational risk	N
89. Balanced budget by '93-via targets	N
90. Bar licensing of two nuclear plants	N
91. Remove victims compensation cap	N
92. Catastrophic health insurance	N
93. Ban airline smoking-2 hours or less	Y
94. $1b/two year aid for the homeless	N
95. Bar non-unions in union companies	N
96. Increase FSLIC rescue to $15b	N
97. Impose quotas to lower trade deficit	N
98. Reduce discretionary budget 21%	Y
99. Immigration reform/alien amnesty	N
100. South Africa sanctions-veto override	Y
101. Tax overhaul to revise income tax	N
102. Use of military in drug war	Y
103. Delete 12 MX/add conventional wpn	Y
104. Raise speed limit to 65 mph	Y
105. Require Pentagon to buy US goods	Y
106. AIDS insurance non-discrimination	N
107. Prohibit Saudi arms sales	Y
108. Ease Gun Control Act of 1968	Y
109. Bar interstate handgun transport	N
110. Make company emissions known	Y
111. Allow toxic victims to sue in fed ct	N
112. Superfund waste cleanup of $10b	Y
113. 90 days notice of plant closings	N
114. $20b in Medicare cuts/tax increases	N
115. Spending cuts and tax increases	N
116. Set school lunch lmt-250% poverty	Y
117. $75m for youth work projects	N
118. Allow Angolan military assistance	Y
119. Suspend defense payments for abuse	Y
120. Drop SS COLAs/$12b tax increase	N
121. Approve $1.5b for 21 MX missiles	N
122. Emergency farm credit/revisions	Y
123. Duty on Taiwan/Hong Kong/S Korea	N
124. Limit steel imports to 17%	N
125. Cut $ to schools that bar prayer	Y
126. $50b-taxes; cut Medicare/spending	?
127. Limit Pershing II/cruise in Europe	?
128. Delete $7.1b for 34 B-1 bombers	?
129. Bar purchase of Sergeant York guns	N
130. El Salvador military/economic aid	Y
131. Bar mining of Nicaraguan waters	Y
132. Physician fee freeze for Medicare	Y
133. $49b in "sin"/phone/insurance taxes	N
134. Allow sale of Conrail	?
135. Equal Rights Amendment	N
136. Authorize Marines in Lebanon	N
137. Eminent domain for coal companies	N
138. Prohibit EPA clean air sanctions	Y
139. SS retirement age increase/reforms	Y
140. Auto domestic content requirement	N
141. Delete jobs program funding	Y
142. Highway-gas tax bill	N

SENSENBRENNER, F. JAMES, (continued)
143. Cut $5b from defense for Medicare N   144. Emergency housing aid of $1b   Y

Presidential Support Score: 1991 - 66%   1990 - 75%

WYOMING

THOMAS, CRAIG -- Representative at Large [Republican].   Prior Terms: 1989 (Special Election)-1992. Born: February 17,1933; Cody, WY.   Education: University of Wyoming (B.A.).   Military Service: U.S. Marine Corps.   Occupation: Small businessman; state farm bureau vice president; rural electric association general manager; state representative.

1. Protection to Haitian refugees	N	
2. Raise tax on wealthy; lower others	N	
3. Investigate Reagan hostage delay	N	
4. Campaign finance revisions	N	
5. Unpaid leave to care for children	N	
6. Restrict NEA use of funds	N	
7. Bar race-bias claim/habeas corpus	Y	
8. Ban race as death sentence factor	Y	
9. Exceptions to exclusionary rule	Y	
10. Allow sale of assault weapons	Y	
11. Life in prison/abolish death penalty	N	
12. Req conspiracy-price fixing cases	Y	
13. Unemployment benefits extension	N	
14. Tissue use of aborted fetuses	N	
15. Bar replacement of union strikers	N	
16. Hold foreign aid at $15b for '92	Y	
17. Restore space station funding	Y	
18. Civil Rights Act of 1991	N	
19. Unlimited damages-discrimination	N	
20. Eliminate funds for supercollider	Y	
21. Terminate SDI except for research	?	
22. Req 7-day handgun waiting period	N	
23. Provide $30b for failed S&Ls	Y	
24. Allow use of force against Iraq	Y	
25. Allow $15b in foreign aid for '91	N	
26. Revise & extend legal immigration	Y	
27. Suspend aid to Angolan rebels	N	
28. Democratic tax plan proposals	N	
29. Cut defense 5% across the board	N	

30. Textile import quotas-veto override	N
31. Abortion service for military abroad	N
32. Limits on high income farmers	N
33. Family medical leave-veto override	N
34. Req submission of balanced budget	Y
35. Balanced budget amendment	Y
36. Amendment to ban flag desecration	Y
37. Reauthorize Amtrak-veto override	N
38. Retraining aid for coal miners	N
39. Suspend El Salvador military aid	N
40. Expand child care aid/tax credit	N
41. Raise House salary/omit honoraria	N
42. Toughen oil-spill liability	N
43. Restitution to Japanese interned	Y
44. Protect Chinese & C.A. nationals	N
45. Abortion $ for rape/incest cases	Y
46. Allow religious schools to bar gays	Y
47. Bar broadcaster fairness doctrine	Y
48. Bar cap gains cut/reinstate IRA	N
49. Bar unions equal voice in pension	Y
50. Bar assembly of chemical weapons	N
51. Ban plutonium/uranium production	N
52. Cap MX missile deployment at 50	N
53. Allow $3b for 2 stealth bombers	Y
54. Publish bio-warfare experiments	N
55. Raise minimum wage-veto override	N
56. Bar transfer of FS-X technology	N
57. Cut defense and raise domestic $	N

Presidential Support Score: 1991 - 77%   1990 - 70%

Senate Measures

In this section Senate Measures are listed in reverse chronological order, i.e., starting with the most recent. The number in the lefthand margin of each entry is a locator from the Subject Index.

1. **HR 2212. Conditional MFN for China in 1992/Conference Report.** Adoption of the conference report to prohibit the president from granting most-favored-nation (MFN) status to China for the 12-month period beginning July 3, 1992, unless he reports that China has accounted for and released prisoners detained because of 1989 pro-democracy protests ending in the June 3 crackdown in Tiananmen Square, and he reports that China has made significant progress in preventing human rights abuses, remedying unfair trade practices and limiting weapons proliferation. Adopted 59-39: R 9-34; D 50-5 [ND 35-3, SD 15-2] Feb. 25, 1992. A "nay" was a vote supporting the president's position.

2. **S 2. Elementary and Secondary Education/Withholding Benefits.** Bentsen, D-Texas, motion to table (kill) the Nickles, R-Okla., amendment to allow states the option of withholding welfare benefits from parents of children who do not regularly attend school. Motion agreed to 55-43: R 6-37; D 49-6 [ND 36-2, SD 13-4], Jan. 28, 1992.

3. **S 543. Banking Reform/Limit Credit Card Interest Rates.** D'Amato, R-N.Y., amendment to limit the annual interest rate on credit cards to 4 percentage points above the rate charged by the Internal Revenue Service for interest on the underpayment of taxes, which adjusts quarterly based on average short-term Treasury rates (currently 10 percent). Adopted 74-19: R 26-14; D 48-5 [ND 33-3, SD 15-2], Nov. 13, 1991.

4. **Gates Nomination/Confirmation.** Confirmation of President Bush's nomination of Robert M. Gates of Virginia to be director of central intelligence. Confirmed 64-31: R 42-0; D 22-31 [ND 11-25, SD 11-6], Nov. 5, 1991. A "yea" was a vote supporting the president's position.

5. **S 1220. National Energy Policy/Cloture.** Mitchell, D-Maine, motion to invoke cloture (thus limiting debate) on the motion to proceed to the bill to allow drilling in the Arctic National Wildlife Refuge, mandate that federal and private vehicle fleets use alternative fuels and direct the secretary of Transportation to adopt new corporate average fuel economy (CAFE) standards, and enact other programs related to energy production and consumption. Motion rejected 50-44: R 32-9; D 18-35 [ND 9-28, SD 9-7], Nov. 1, 1991. A three-fifths majority (60) of the total Senate is required to invoke cloture.

6. **HR 2686. Fiscal 1992 Interior Appropriations/National Endowment for the Arts.** Byrd, D-W.Va., motion to table (kill) Helms, R-N.C., motion to concur in the House amendment to the Senate amendment with an amendment to prohibit the National Endowment for the Arts from using funds to promote, disseminate or produce materials that depict or describe, in a patently offensive way, sexual or excretory activities or organs. Motion agreed to 73-25: R 23-19; D 50-6 [ND 37-2, SD 13-4], Oct. 31, 1991.

7. **S 1722. Unemployment Benefits Extension/Passage**. Passage, over President Bush's Oct. 11 veto, of the bill to provide an estimated $6.4 billion in unemployment benefits for up to 20 additional weeks, based on a state's average total unemployment rate. The benefits would temporarily be extended from Oct. 6, 1991, through July 4, 1992. The bill designates the spending as an emergency and would not require a presidential declaration to be exempt from the spending limits of last year's budget agreement. Rejected 65-35: R 8-35; D 57-0 [ND 40-0, SD 17-0], Oct 16, 1991. A two-thirds majority of those present and voting (67 in this case) of both houses is required to override a veto. A "nay" was a vote supporting the president's position. (An unemployment benefits extension bill was later passed by both houses with the president's approval.)

8. **Thomas Nomination/Confirmation**. Confirmation of President Bush's nomination of Clarence Thomas of Georgia to be an associate justice of the U.S. Supreme Court. Confirmed 52-48: R 41-2; D 11-46 [ND 3-37, SD 8-9], Oct. 15, 1991. A "yea" was a vote supporting the president's position.

9. **S 5. Family and Medical Leave Act/Substitute**. Bond, R-Mo., substitute amendment to raise the number of hours an employee must work in order to be eligible for up to 12 weeks of unpaid leave for the birth or adoption of a child or for the serious illness of the worker or an immediate family member. Adopted 65-32: R 15-28; D 50-4 [ND 38-0, SD 12-4], Oct. 2, 1991. A "nay" was a vote supporting the president's position.

10. **HR 2707. Fiscal 1992 Labor, HHS and Education Appropriations/Parental Consent for Abortions**. Nickles, R-Okla., amendment to require organizations that receive funding under Title X of the Public Health Service Act to notify at least one parent or legal guardian 48 hours before performing an abortion on a minor unless the life of the minor is endangered, the pregnancy is the result of parental incest, or the minor has been subjected to sexual abuse, child abuse or child neglect. Rejected 45-55: R 31-12; D 14-43 [ND 6-34, SD 8-9], Sept. 11, 1991. A "yea" was a vote supporting the president's position.

11. **HR 2707. Fiscal 1992 Labor, HHS, and Education Appropriations/Budget Waiver**. Harkin, D-Iowa, motion to waive the Budget Act with respect to the Harkin amendment to the committee amendment, to rescind $3.148 billion in budget authority from unobligated balances in Defense Department accounts from fiscal 1988-91, and transfer the $3.148 billion in budget authority to domestic programs. Motion rejected 28-69: R 3-39; D 25-30 [ND 24-14, SD 1-16], Sept. 10, 1991. A "nay" was a vote supporting the president's position.

12. **S 1507. Fiscal 1992-93 Defense Authorization/B-2 Bomber**. Leahy, D-Vt., amendment to eliminate bill provision allowing for producing four B-2 bombers, stopping production at the 15 planes already funded. The amendment would change the scope of the B-2 program to end production of the bomber but allow for research and development, testing, and evaluation. Rejected 42-57: R 7-36; D 35-21 [ND 31-9, SD 4-12], Aug. 1, 1991. A "nay" was a vote supporting the president's position.

13. **S 1507. Fiscal 1992-93 Defense Authorization/Strategic Defense Initiative**. Bumpers, D-Ark., amendment to cut $1 billion of the $4.6 billion authorized for the Strategic Defense Initiative and transfer the savings to reducing the deficit. Rejected 46-52: R 5-38; D 41-14 [ND 32-7, SD 9-7], Aug. 1, 1991. A "nay" was a vote supporting the president's position.

14. **S 1507. Fiscal 1992-93 Defense Authorization/Strategic Stability**. Bingaman, D-N.M., amendment to state that it is the goal of the United States to maintain strategic stability with the Soviet Union while deploying an anti-ballistic missile system with one or more ground-based sites and space-based sensors. The amendment would clarify that current actions by the U.S. are treaty compliant, and the U.S. would deploy at only one site and additional sites as the result of a mutual agreement. Rejected 43-56: R 2-41; D 41-15 [ND 33-7, SD 8-8], July 31, 1991. A "nay" was a vote supporting the president's position.

15. **S 1507. Fiscal 1992-93 Defense Authorization/Women in Combat Pilot Positions**. Glenn, D-Ohio, motion to table (kill) the Roth, R-Del., amendment to repeal the 1948 law that prohibits women from flying in combat pilot positions. Motion rejected 30-69: R 14-29; D 16-40 [ND 6-34, SD 10-6], July 31, 1991. (The Roth amendment was subsequently adopted by voice vote.)

16. **HR 2608. Fiscal 1992 Commerce, Justice, State Appropriations/HIV Testing.** Kennedy, D-Mass., motion to table (kill) the Helms, R-N.C., amendment to allow health-care professionals to test patients for human immunodeficiency virus (HIV) before invasive medical procedures except in emergencies. The test results would be confidential, and a person violating the confidentiality would be fined $10,000 or face a prison term of not more than one year. States without regulations to protect health-care workers from HIV after one year would be ineligible to receive federal funds under the Public Health Service Act. Motion rejected 44-55: R 9-34; D 35-21 [ND 31-9, SD 4-12], July 30, 1991. (The Helms amendment was subsequently adopted by voice vote.)

17. **S 1435. Fiscal 1992-93 Foreign Aid Authorization/International Monetary Fund.** Brown, R-Colo., amendment to strike from the bill U.S. contributions to the International Monetary Fund of $12 billion. Rejected 31-65: R 18-24; D 13-41 [ND 10-29, SD 3-12], July 25, 1991. A "nay" was a vote supporting the president's position.

18. **HR 2506. Fiscal 1992 Legislative Branch Appropriations/Pay Raise.** Byrd, D-W.Va., amendment to raise senators' pay from $101,900 to $125,100, ban senators' honoraria and limit outside earned income to 15 percent of a senator's base pay. Adopted 53-45: R 25-18; D 28-27 [ND 22-18, SD 6-9], July 17, 1991.

19. **HR 2519. Fiscal 1992 VA-HUD Appropriations/Space Station.** Bumpers, D-Ark., amendment to reduce funding for the space station from $2 billion to $100 million and transfer $182 million to other federal science programs, $431 million to veterans' programs, and about $1.3 billion to deficit reduction. Rejected 35-64: R 3-40; D 32-24 [ND 24-16, SD 8-8], July 17, 1991.

20. **HR 2427. Fiscal 1992 Energy and Water Appropriations/Superconducting Super Collider.** Johnston, D-La., motion to table (kill) the Bumpers, D-Ark., amendment to eliminate all funding for the superconducting super collider by reducing the bill's funding level for the General Science and Research Activities account by $508,700,000. Motion agreed to 62-37: R 33-10; D 29-27 [ND 19-21, SD 10-6], July 10, 1991. A "yea" was a vote supporting the president's position.

21. **S 1241. Crime Bill/Handgun Waiting Period.** Dole, R-Kan., amendment to require a waiting period of five business days before handgun purchases, during which time a mandatory background check of the prospective handgun buyers would be conducted, and to require the attorney general within six months of enactment to select a system and computer software for a National Instant Check system that within five years would be able to provide a record of criminal activity. Adopted 67-32: R 19-24: D 48-8 [ND 37-3, SD 11-5], June 28, 1991.

22. **S 1241. Crime Bill/Replace Death Penalty.** Simon, D-Ill., amendment to substitute where the bill would impose the death penalty a mandatory life imprisonment term without the possibility of release. Rejected 25-73: R 5-37; D 20-36 [ND 19-21, SD 1-15], June 25, 1991. A "nay" was a vote supporting the president's position.

23. **S 1241. Crime Bill/Search and Seizure.** Thurmond, R-S.C., amendment to codify the "good faith" exception to the exclusionary rule that allows evidence seized without a warrant but under an objectively reasonable belief that the search was in conformity with the Fourth Amendment to be used against a defendant. Rejected 43-54: R 32-9; D 11-45 [ND 5-35, SD 6-10], June 25, 1991. A "yea" was a vote supporting the president's position.

24. **S 1241. Crime Bill/Minority Discrimination.** Mitchell, D-Maine, for Graham, D-Fla., amendment to strike the Racial Justice Act provisions that allow minorities to challenge a death sentence as discriminatory if statistics show a disproportionate number of their race being condemned to die. Adopted 55-41: R 35-7; D 20-34 [ND 8-30, SD 12-4], June 20, 1991.

25. **S 3. Campaign Finance/Passage.** Passage of the bill to revise federal laws governing the financing of federal campaigns by providing for a voluntary system of spending limits for elections that gives candidates public subsidies as an incentive to participate. Motion agreed to 56-42: R 5-37; D 51-5 [ND 39-1, SD 12-4], May 23, 1991. A "nay" was a vote supporting the president's position.

26. **S 3. Campaign Finance/Limit Terms.** Boren, D-Okla., motion to table (kill) the Brown, R-Colo., amendment to the McConnell, R-Ky., amendment, to limit terms of successful Senate candidates to two consecutive terms if they received public financing. Motion agreed to 68-30: R 12-30; D 56-0 [ND 40-0, SD 16-0], May 22, 1991.

27. **S 3. Campaign Finance/Presidential Debates.** Graham, D-Fla., amendment to the Boren, D-Okla., substitute amendment, to require presidential candidates to participate in four debates and vice presidential candidates to participate in one debate to be eligible for public campaign financing during the general election. Adopted 44-43: R 2-34; D 42-9 [ND 30-7, SD 12-2], May 17, 1991.

28. **S 429. Vertical Price Fixing.** Mitchell, D-Maine, motion to invoke cloture (thus limiting debate) on the bill to amend the Sherman Antitrust Act of 1890 to tighten the ban on vertical price fixing, which occurs when a manufacturer conspires with a retailer to force a competing merchant to charge at least a certain price for goods or face a cutoff of supplies. The bill would lower the standard for evidence needed to get a resale price maintenance case to a jury. Motion agreed to 63-35: R 13-30; D 50-5 [ND 37-2, SD 13-3], May 8, 1991. A three-fifths majority vote (60) of the total Senate is required to invoke cloture.

29. **S Con Res 29. Fiscal 1992 Budget Resolution/Freeze.** Sasser, D-Tenn., motion to table (kill) the Grassley, R-Iowa, substitute amendment to freeze budget authority and outlays for all fiscal 1992 discretionary spending at fiscal 1991 levels, reducing outlays by $8.2 billion in fiscal 1992 and $22.4 billion in fiscal 1992-96. Motion agreed to 60-37: R 18-24; D 42-13 [ND 32-7, SD 10-6], April 24, 1991.

30. **S 419. RTC Funding/Passage.** Passage of the bill to provide the Resolution Trust Corporation (RTC) with $30 billion in financing to cover losses in failed thrifts through fiscal 1991; require the RTC to provide Congress with financial operating plans and schedules of projected insolvencies; require the RTC to provide audit and financial statements within six months of the end of the fiscal year; and clarify the personal civil liability of the RTC's officers and directors. Passed 69-30: R 36-7, D 33-23 [ND 21-18, SD 12-5], March 7, 1991. A "yea" was a vote supporting the president's position.

31. **S J Res 2. Use of Force Against Iraq/Passage.** Passage of the joint resolution to authorize military force if Iraq has not withdrawn from Kuwait and complied with U.N. Security Council resolutions by Jan 15. The resolution authorizes using force and expending funds under the War Powers Act. Passed 52-47: R 42-2; D 10-45 [ND 3-35, SD 7-10], Jan. 12, 1991. A "yea" was a vote supporting the president's position.

32. **HR 5114. Fiscal 1991 Foreign Operations Appropriations/Passage.** Passage of the bill to appropriate $15,533,040,543 for foreign military and economic assistance and export financing in fiscal 1991. The president requested $15,518,826,537. Passed 76-23: R 35-9; D 41-14 [ND 30-8, SD 11-6], Oct. 24, 1990.

33. **S 2104. Civil Rights Act of 1990/Veto Override.** Passage, over President Bush's Oct. 22 veto, of the bill to reverse or modify six recent Supreme Court decisions that narrowed the reach and remedies of job discrimination law and to authorize monetary damages under Title VII of the 1964 Civil Rights Act. Rejected 66-34: R 11-34; D 55-0 [ND 38-0, SD 17-0], Oct. 24, 1990. A two-thirds majority of those present and voting (67 in this case) of both houses is required to override a veto. A "nay" was a vote supporting the president's position.

34. **HR 5114. Fiscal 1991 Foreign Operations Appropriations/Egyptian Debt.** Harkin, D-Iowa, amendment to the committee amendment, to strike provisions canceling Egypt's debt to the United States and to require the president to develop in cooperation with Congress a proposal to restructure that debt and convene and international conference to develop a comprehensive and multilateral solution to Egypt's international debt problem. Rejected 42-55: R 10-34; D 32-21 [ND 20-16, SD 12-5], Oct. 19, 1990. A "nay" was a vote supporting the president's position.

35. **HR 5114. Fiscal 1991 Foreign Operations Appropriations/El Salvador.** Leahy, D-Vt., amendmenet to the committee amendment, to reduce military aid to the government of El Salvador by 50 percent and link future military aid to improvements in human rights and

progress toward a negotiated peace settlement. Adopted 74-25: R 19-25; D 55-0 [ND 38-0, SD 17-0], Oct. 19, 1990. A "nay" was a vote supporting the president's position.

36. **S 3189. Fiscal 1991 Defense Appropriations/Troop Cuts.** Conrad, D-N.D., amendment to reduce U.S. forces in NATO by 30,000 troops below the Senate-passed authorization level and reduce the Department of Defense military personnel level by a corresponding 30,000 below the authorized level. Rejected 46-50: R 8-34; D 38-16 [ND 31-6, SD 7-10], Oct. 15, 1990. A "nay" was a vote supporting the president's position.

37. **S 1224. Motor Vehicle Fuel Efficiency Act/Cloture.** Motion to invoke cloture (thus limiting debate) on the bill to require manufacturers of passenger vehicles and light trucks to increase their 1988 corporate average fuel economy standards by 20 percent by 1995 model year and by 40 percent by the 2001 model year. Motion rejected 57-42: R 15-29; D 42-13 [ND 33-5, SD 9-8], Sept. 25, 1990. A three-fifths majority vote (60) of the total Senate is required to invoke cloture.

38. **S 137. Campaign Finance Overhaul/Taxpayer Funding.** McConnell, R-Ky., amendment to the Boren, D-Okla., substitute amendment to eliminate all taxpayer funding of Senate campaigns. Rejected 46-49; R 44-0; D 2-49 [ND 1-34, SD 1-15], July 30, 1990.

39. **HR 4328. Textile Trade Act/Passage.** Passage of the bill to limit growth in imports of textiles, textile products and non-rubber footwear to 1 percent annually. Passed 68-32: R 22-23; D 46-9 [ND 30-8, SD 16-1], July 17, 1990. A "nay" was a vote supporting the president's position.

40. **S J Res 332. Constitutional Amendment on the Flag/Passage.** Passage of the joint resolution to propose an amendment to the Constitution to prohibit the physical desecration of the U.S. flag. Rejected 58-42: R 38-7; D 20-35 [ND 10-28, SD 10-7], June 26, 1990. A two-thirds majority of those present and voting (67 in this case) of both houses is required for passage of a joint resolution proposing an amendment to the Constitution. A "yea" was a vote supporting the president's position.

41. **HR 20. Hatch Act Revisions/Veto Override.** Passage, over President Bush's June 15 veto, of the bill to allow greater political activity by federal employees and to protect them from political pressure. Rejected 65-35: R 10-35; D 55-0 [ND 38-0, SD 17-0], June 21, 1990. A two-thirds majority of those present and voting of both houses (67 in this case) is required to override a veto. A "nay" was a vote supporting the president's position.

42. **HR 2364. Amtrak Reauthorization/Veto Override.** Passage, over President Bush's May 24 veto, of the bill to reauthorize the National Railroad Passenger Corporation (Amtrak) for fiscal years 1989-92. Rejected 64-36: R 10-35; D 54-1 [ND 37-1, SD 17-0], June 12, 1990. A two-thirds majority of those present and voting (67 in this case) of both houses is required to override a veto. A "nay" was a vote supporting the president's position.

43. **S 1970. Omnibus Crime Package/Assault-Style Weapons.** Hatch, R-Utah, amendment to strike provisions that would prohibit for three years making, selling and possessing nine types of semiautomatic assault-style weapons. Rejected 48-52: R 36-9; D 12-43 [ND 5-33, SD 7-10], May 23, 1990. A "yea" was a vote supporting the president's position.

44. **S 1630. Clean Air Act Reauthorization/Coal Miner Benefits.** Byrd, D-W.Va., amendment to provide severance pay and retraining benefits to coal miners who lose their jobs as a result of provisions to control acid rain. Rejected 49-50: R 11-34; D 38-16 [ND 29-9, SD 9-7], March 29, 1990. A "nay" was a vote supporting the president's position.

45. **S 1630. Clean Air Act Reauthorization/Motor Vehicles.** Mitchell, D-Maine, motion to table (kill) the Wirth, D-Colo., amendment to provide for a second round of tailpipe emissions reductions in the year 2003; to require cleaner-burning reformulated gasoline in all ozone non-attainment areas; to require light-duty vehicles to meet new-car emission standards for 100,000 miles; and to provide for use of clean fuels and clean-fuel vehicles by the government and commercial and general passenger-car fleets in the nation's smoggiest cities. Motion agreed to 52-46: R 25-19; D 27-27 [ND 14-23, SD 13-4], March 20, 1990. A "yea" was a vote supporting the president's position.

46. **S 1630. Clean Air Act Reauthorization/NRC Authority.** Breaux, D-La., motion to table the Glenn, D-Ohio, amendment to strike a provision that would remove the authority of the Environmental Protection Agency and the states to regulate radioactive emissions at facilities regulated by the Nuclear Regulatory Commission (NRC), such as nuclear power plants, making the NRC the sole regulator under the Atomic Energy Act. Motion rejected 36-61: R 24-20; D 12-41 [ND 5-31, SD 7-10], March 7, 1990. A "yea" was a vote supporting the president's position. (The Glenn amendment was subsequently adopted by voice vote.)

47. **HR 2712. Chinese Students/Veto Override.** Passage, over President Bush's Nov. 30 veto, of the bill to defer indefinitely the deportation of Chinese students whose visas expire and to waive for students on "J" visas a requirement that they return to their home country for two years before applying for permanent residence in the United States. Rejected 62-37: R 8-37; D 54-0 [ND 38-0, SD 16-0], Jan. 25, 1990. A two-thirds majority of those present and voting (66) in this case of both houses is required to override a veto. A "nay" was a vote supporting the president's position.

48. **HR 3628. Capital Gains Tax Cut/Cloture.** Motion to invoke cloture (thus limiting debate) on the Packwood, R-Ore., substitute amendment to exclude capital gains from taxable income in the amount of 5 percent for each full year an asset is held (to a maximum of 35 percent) and to make Individual Retirement Accounts available to all taxpayers with varying tax benefits. Motion rejected 51-47: R 45-0; D 6-47 [ND 2-34, SD 4-13], Nov. 15, 1989. A three-fifths majority vote (60) of the total Senate is required to invoke cloture. A "yea" was a vote supporting the president's position.

49. **HR 2748. Fiscal 1990-91 Intelligence Authorizations/CIA Inspector General.** Boren, D-Okla., motion to table (kill) the Hollings, D-S.C., amendment to strike from the bill a provision to establish at the CIA an independent inspector general appointed by the president and confirmed by the Senate. Motion agreed to 64-34: R 20-24; D 44-10 [ND 31-6, SD 13-4], Nov. 7, 1989. A "nay" was a vote supporting the president's position.

50. **HR 2991. Fiscal 1990 Commerce, Justice, State Appropriations/China Sanctions.** Hollings, D-S.C., motion to table (kill) the Helms, R-N.C., amendment to impose sanctions against China for its suppression of pro-democracy forces. Motion agreed to 53-45: R 14-30; D 39-15 [ND 28-9, SD 11-6], Nov. 1, 1989.

51. **S 1711. Omnibus Anti-Drug Package/Drug Testing.** Biden, D-Del., motion to table (kill) the Wallop, R-Wyo., amendment to require drug testing of those applying for and receiving assistance under Aid to Families with Dependent Children. Motion agreed to 75-24: R 21-23; D 54-1 [ND 37-1, SD 17-0], Oct. 5, 1989.

52. **S 1711. Omnibus Anti-Drug Package/Drug Interdiction.** Glenn, D-Ohio, motion to table (kill) the McConnell, R-Ky., amendment to allow federal drug-enforcement officials, under certain conditions, to use weapons to force airborne drug traffickers to land their aircraft. Motion agreed to 52-48: R 13-32; D 39-16 [ND 26-12, SD 13-4], Oct. 5, 1989.

53. **HR 2991. Fiscal 1990 Commerce, Justice, State Appropriations/Census Count.** Bingaman, D-N.M., motion to table (kill) the Shelby, D-Ala., amendment to prohibit the Census Bureau from including illegal aliens in the 1990 census count for reapportionment of the House of Representatives. Motion rejected 41-50: R 7-33; D 34-17 [ND 27-8, SD 7-9], Sept. 9, 1989.

54. **HR 2991. Fiscal 1990 Commerce, Justice, State Appropriations/Budget Act Waiver.** Hollings, D-S.C., motion to waive section 303 of the Congressional Budget Act of 1974 to permit consideration of the committee amendment to set up an entitlement program for fiscal 1991 to pay $1.25 billion over 10 years in reparations to Japanese-Americans who were forced into U.S. camps during World War II. Motion agreed to 74-22: R 24-18; D 50-4 [ND 35-2, SD 15-2], Sept. 29, 1989. A three-fifths majority vote (60) of the total Senate is required to waive the Budget Act.

55. **HR 3072. Fiscal 1990 Defense Appropriations/European Forces.** Metzenbaum, D-Ohio, amendment to reduce by 30,000 the number of U.S. military personnel stationed in Europe. Rejected 25-75: R 4-41; D 21-34 [ND 16-22, SD 5-12], Sept. 28, 1989. A "nay" was a vote supporting the president's position.

56. **HR 3072. Fiscal 1990 Defense Appropriations/SDI Funding.** Stevens, R-Alaska, amendment to the committee amendment, to increase to $4.3 billion the amount authorized for the Defense Department share of the strategic defense initiative (SDI). Adopted 53-47: R 39-6; D 14-41 [ND 5-33, SD 9-8], Sept. 28, 1989. A "yea" was a vote supporting the president's position.

57. **HR 2916. Fiscal 1990 VA, HUD Appropriations/Housing.** Mikulski, D-Md., motion to table (kill) the Nickles, R-Okla., amendment to allow contractors building or repairing federal subsidized homes or shelters to hire tenants and homeless people, and to pay them less than required by prevailing-wage laws and regulations, including the Davis-Bacon Act. Motion agreed to 58-42: R 7-38; D 51-4 [ND 37-1, SD 14-3], Sept. 19, 1989.

58. **HR 3015. Fiscal 1990 Transportation Appropriations/Cloture.** Mitchell, D.-Maine, motion to invoke cloture (thus limiting debate) on the Lautenberg, D.-N.J. amendment to ban permanently smoking on all airline flights within the United States. Motion agreed to 77-21: R 33-11; D 44-10 [ND 35-2, SD 9-8], Sept. 14, 1989.

59. **S J Res 113. FS-X Plane Development/Veto Override.** Passage, over President Bush's July 31 veto, of the joint resolution to require that a subsequent U.S.-Japan agreement governing joint production of the FS-X bar transfer to Japanese firms of certain jet-engine technologies and prohibit the sale or transfer by Japan to any other country of the FS-X or any technologies developed in the FS-X project. Rejected 66-34: R 12-33; D 54-1 [ND 37-1, SD 17-0], Sept. 13, 1989. A two-thirds majority of those present and voting (67 in this case) of both houses is required to override a veto. A "nay" was a vote supporting the president's position.

60. **S 686. Oil-Spill Liability/Liability Limit.** Mitchell, D-Maine, motion to table (kill) the Wilson, R-Calif., amendment to strike the $100 million liability limit for oil spills from outer continental shelf facilities, and replace it with unlimited cleanup costs plus $75 million. Motion rejected 34-66: R 9-36; D 25-30 [ND 14-24, SD 11-6], Aug. 3, 1989. (The Wilson amendment was subsequently adopted by voice vote.)

61. **HR 1278. Savings and Loan Restructuring/Budget Act Waiver.** Riegle, D-Mich., motion to waive Titles III and IV (which, among other things, prohibit breaching deficit ceilings established by the current budget resolution) of the Congressional Budget Act of 1974 with respect to the conference report on the bill to salvage the nation's savings and loan industry and overhaul federal thrift regulation. Motion rejected 54-46: R 1-44; D 53-2 [ND 36-2, SD 17-0], Aug. 3, 1989. A three-fifths majority vote (60) of the total Senate is required to waive the Budget Act. A "nay" was a vote supporting the president's position.

62. **S 1160. Fiscal 1990 State Department Authorization/Prohibited Activities.** Moynihan, D-N.Y., amendment to prohibit the solicitation or diversion of funds to carry out activities for which U.S. foreign assistance is prohibited. Adopted 57-42: R 4-41; D 53-1 [ND 37-0, SD 16-1], July 18, 1989.

63. **S 358. Visa Quota Restrictions/English Language Points.** Simpson, R-Wyo., amendment to add to the qualifications for a new category of "independent" immigrants fluency in the English language. Rejected 43-56: R 29-16; D 14-40 [ND 7-30, SD 7-10], July 13, 1989.

64. **S 358. Visa Quota Restrictions/Deportation Stay.** Chafee, R-R.I., amendment to grant a stay of deportation and work authorization to the spouses and minor children of aliens whose status was legalized under the 1986 Immigration Reform and Control Act (PL 99-603), provided those relatives were in the United States at the time of that law's enactment. Adopted 61-38: R 16-29; D 45-9 [ND 34-3, SD 11-6], July 12, 1989.

65. **S 5. Child Care/Mitchell Substitute.** Mitchell, D-Maine, substitute to authorize $1.75 billion in child-care subsidies to parents and day-care providers; to require states to set standards for child care; to increase the dependent-care tax credit and make it refundable to create a new tax credit for health-insurance premiums paid to cover a worker's children; to make permanent the 3 percent telephone excise tax; and to revamp Section 89 of the Internal Revenue Code, which prohibits discrimination in employee benefits. Adopted 63-37: R 9-36; D 54-1 [ND 38-0, SD 16-1], June 22, 1989.

66. **HR 2. Minimum-Wage Increase/Conference Report.** Adoption of the conference report (thus clearing the measure for the president) on the bill to raise the minimum wage from $3.35 an hour to $4.55 over three years, and to provide for a 60-day training wage -- equal to 85 percent of the minimum -- for workers who have not worked a total of 60 days. Adopted 63-37: R 10-35; D 53-2 [ND 38-0, SD 15-2], May 17, 1989. A "nay" was a vote supporting the president's position. (A bill was later passed by both houses, with the president's approval, that raised the minimum wage to $4.25 an hour.)

67. **S Con Res 30. Fiscal 1990 Budget Resolution/Budget Freeze.** Hollings, D-S.C., substitute amendment to freeze outlays at the fiscal 1989 level, except for cost-of-living adjustments and growth in beneficiaries for Social Security, Medicare and Medicaid, to increase outlays for unspecified program priorities, and to maintain revenue assumptions of the bipartisan budget agreement between the president and leaders of Congress. Rejected 18-82: R 5-40; D 13-42 [ND 7-31, SD 6-11], May 4, 1989.

68. **S Con Res 30. Fiscal 1990 Budget Resolution/Increased Domestic Spending.** Mitchell, D-Maine, motion to table (kill) the Simon, D-Ill., amendment to reallocate $3 billion in budget authority and $2 billion in outlays from national defense to education, training and social services, and to express the sense of the Congress that this increased funding should be provided for Head Start, drug education, programs for disabled and handicapped students, drug-free schools, teacher training, historically black colleges and universities, Smart Start, literacy and child care. Motion agreed to 64-31: R 38-5; D 26-26 [ND 14-22, SD 12-4], May 3, 1989.

69. **Tower Nomination.** Confirmation of President Bush's nomination of John Tower of Texas to be secretary of defense. Rejected 47-53: R 44-1; D 3-52 [ND 1-37, SD 2-15], March 9, 1989.

70. **HR 4776. Fiscal 1989 District of Columbia Appropriations/Abortion Funding.** Nickles, R-Okla., motion to table (kill) the Bradley, D-N.J., motion to disagree with the House amendment that no funds in the bill, federal or District, be used to perform abortions except where the life of the mother would be endangered. Motion agreed to 45-44: R 31-10; D 14-34 [ND 8-24, SD 6-10], Sept. 30, 1988. A "yea" was a vote supporting the president's position.

71. **HR 4783. Fiscal 1989 Labor, Health and Human Services, Education Appropriations/Spousal Notification.** Chiles, D-Fla., motion to table (kill) the Helms, R-N.C., amendment to an Appropriations Committee amendment. The Helms amendment would have prohibited any state from receiving AIDS education funds unless that state adopted a policy requiring a "good-faith" effort to tell spouses of AIDS carriers of their risk of contracting AIDS. Motion agreed to 49-48: R 9-37; D 40-11 [ND 28-6, SD 12-5], July 27, 1988.

72. **HR 4776. Fiscal 1989 District of Columbia Appropriations/Discrimination Against Homosexual Groups.** Armstrong, R-Colo., amendment to exempt religious institutions in the District from a local law prohibiting bias against homosexuals. The amendment would overturn a recent District court decision, which held that Georgetown University must provide homosexual groups with facilities and funding comparable to that provided other student groups. Adopted 58-33: R 36-7; D 22-26 [ND 12-21, SD 10-5], July 11, 1988.

73. **S 2527. Plant Closings/Passage.** Passage of the bill to require 60 days' advance notice of plant closings or mass layoffs. Passed 72-23: R 19-23; D 53-0 [ND 35-0, SD 18-0], July 6, 1988.

74. **S 1323. Corporate Takeovers/Poison Pills.** Proxmire, D-Wis., motion to table (kill) division 1-B of the Armstrong, R-Colo., amendment to ban the adoption of so-called poison pills, unless approved by a majority of stockholders. Poison pills are devices used by corporations to ward off takeovers by guaranteeing existing shareholders certain rights that would make takeovers less attractive. Motion rejected 40-57: R 7-38; D 33-19 [ND 24-11, SD 9-8], June 21, 1988.

75. **S 1511. Welfare Reform/"Workfare" Amendment.** Moynihan, D-N.Y., motion to table (kill) the Dole, R-Kan., amendment to require that by 1994, states require at least one parent in two-parent families receiving welfare to work a minimum of 16 hours per week in either

unpaid community work experience or subsidized jobs. Motion rejected 41-54: R 3-40; D 38-14 [ND 27-7, SD 11-7], June 16, 1988. (The Dole amendment subsequently was adopted by voice vote.) A "nay" was a vote supporting the president's position.

76. **HR 1212. Polygraph Protection/Conference Report.** Adoption of the conference report on the bill (thus clearing the measure for the president) to ban use of lie-detector tests for job applicants or workers. Exempted would be all federal, state and local governments; contractors or consultants to government agencies engaged in intelligence or national-security activities; companies providing security services for specified purposes; companies engaged in the manufacture and distribution of controlled drugs; and employers with reasonable cause to suspect a worker of involvement in criminal wrongdoing that resulted in economic loss to the company. Adopted 68-24: R 20-23; D 48-1 [ND 33-0, SD 15-1], June 9, 1988.

77. **HR 2470. Catastrophic Health Insurance/Conference Report.** Adoption of the conference report on the bill (thus clearing the measure for the president) to cap the amounts for which Medicare beneficiaries will be financially liable for Medicare-covered services and to make other changes in the program. Adopted 86-11: R 34-11; D 52-0 [ND 35-0, SD 17-0], June 8, 1988.

78. **HR 3. Omnibus Trade Bill/Veto Override.** Passage, over President Reagan's May 24 veto, of the bill to revise statutory procedures for dealing with unfair foreign trade practices and import damage to U.S. industries, to clarify the law against business-related bribes abroad by U.S. businesses, to streamline controls on militarily sensitive exports, to revise agriculture and education programs, to repeal the windfall-profits tax on oil and to require certain employers to provide workers with 60 days' notice of plant closings or layoffs. Rejected 61-37: R 10-35; D 51-2 [ND 33-2, SD 18-0], June 8, 1988. A two-thirds majority of those present and voting (66 in this case) of both houses is required to override a veto. A "nay" was a vote supporting the president's position.

79. **S 2355. Fiscal 1989 Defense Authorization/SDI Funding.** Exon, D-Neb., motion to table (kill) the Levin, D-Mich., amendment to reduce by $600 million the amount authorized for the strategic defense initiative (SDI) and to increase the authorization for various conventional defense programs by the same amount. Motion agreed to 51-43: R 38-5; D 13-38 [ND 5-28, SD 8-10], May 13, 1988. A "yea" was a vote supporting the president's position.

80. **S 2355. Fiscal 1989 Defense Authorization/Accidental Launch Protection System.** Exon, D-Neb., motion to table (kill) the Wallop, R-Wyo., amendment to earmark $100 million of the funds authorized for the strategic defense initiative (SDI) to provide for the rapid deployment of an accidental launch protection system as the first step of a phased deployment of SDI. Motion agreed to 56-37: R 9-34; D 47-3 [ND 31-2, SD 16-1], May 13, 1988.

81. **S 2355. Fiscal 1989 Defense Authorization/MX and Other Fundings.** Exon, D-Neb., motion to table (kill) the Simon, D-Ill., amendment to reduce the amount authorized for the MX intercontinental ballistic missile (ICBM) to $200 million, from $700 million, and to increase the amounts authorized for Army supply operations by $100 million, for Army procurement of Hellfire missiles by $70 million, for Navy procurement of aircraft electronic countermeasures by $30 million and for Air Force war reserve spare parts by $300 million. Motion agreed to 61-36: R 39-5; D 22-31 [ND 11-24, SD 11-7], May 12, 1988. A "yea" was a vote supporting the president's position.

82. **S 2355. Fiscal 1989 Defense Authorization/Purchase of American-Made Products.** Gramm, R-Texas, motion to table (kill) the Heinz, R-Pa., amendment to restore "Buy America" provisions, dropped by the committee, to ensure that domestic suppliers are given preference by the Department of Defense (DOD) when it purchases clothing, food and critical materials. Motion rejected 32-64: R 19-25; D 13-39 [ND 10-25, SD 3-14], May 12, 1988.

83. **S 2355. Fiscal 1989 Defense Authorization/Underground Nuclear Testing.** Reid, D-Nev., motion to table (kill) the Hatfield, R-Ore., and Kennedy, D-Mass., amendment, as modified to prohibit underground nuclear tests with a yield greater than five kilotons, to provide for seismic monitoring and to require the designation of a single test site, provided the Soviet Union observes the same ban. Motion agreed to 57-39: R 37-6; D 20-33 [ND 7-28, SD 13-5], May 12, 1988. A "yea" was a vote supporting the president's position.

84. **S 2355. Fiscal 1989 Defense Authorization/SALT II Limits.** Nunn, D-Ga., motion to table (kill) the Bumpers, D-Ark., amendment to bar the deployment of multiple-warhead (MIRVed) intercontinental ballistic missiles (ICBMs), MIRVed ballistic missiles of any type, and MIRVed ballistic missiles plus bombers armed with long-range cruise missiles in excess of the number of each of those weapons categories that were deployed on Jan. 25, 1988. Motion agreed to 51-45: R 39-5; D 12-40 [ND 3-32, SD 9-8], May 11, 1988. A "yea" was a vote supporting the president's position.

85. **HR 1811. Atomic Veterans' Compensation/Passage.** Passage of the bill to provide compensation to veterans and survivors of veterans who participated in U.S. atmospheric nuclear tests or in the occupation of Hiroshima or Nagasaki and who suffer from diseases that may be attributable to ionizing radiation exposure. Passed 48-30: R 10-28; D 38-2 [ND 25-1, SD 13-1], April 25, 1988. A "nay" was a vote supporting the president's position.

86. **S 79. High-Risk Occupational Disease Notification/Cloture.** Byrd, D-W.Va., motion to invoke cloture (thus limiting debate) on the Labor and Human Resources Committee substitute to the bill. The substitute calls for notification of workers who are at risk of contracting a life-threatening disease due to past or current exposure to toxic substances on the job. Motion rejected 42-52: R 8-37; D 34-15 [ND 29-3, SD 5-12], March 29, 1988. A three-fifths majority (60) of the total Senate is required to invoke cloture.

87. **S 557. Civil Rights Restoration Act/Passage.** Passage over President Reagan's March 16 veto, of the bill to provide broad coverage of four civil rights laws -- Title IX of the 1972 Education Act Amendments; Title VI of the 1964 Civil Rights Act; Section 504 of the 1973 Rehabilitation Act; and the 1975 Age Discrimination Act -- by making clear that, if one entity of an institution receives federal funds, the entire institution must abide by the anti-discrimination laws. Passed (thus cleared for House action) 73-24: R 21-24; D 52-0 [ND 35-0, SD 17-0], March 22, 1988. A two-thirds majority of those present and voting (65 in this case) of both houses is required to override a veto. A "nay" was a vote supporting the president's position.

88. **S J Res 241. U.S.-Japan Nuclear Energy Agreement.** Passage of the joint resolution to disapprove the proposed agreement on U.S.-Japan uranium sales. Rejected 30-53: R 8-33; D 22-20 [ND 19-10, SD 3-10], March 21, 1988. A "nay" was a vote supporting the president's position.

89. **S 1721. Intelligence Oversight/Passage.** Passage of the bill to require the president to notify Congress of all covert activities. The bill gives the president sole responsibility to notify Congress and puts into law a definition of covert operations or "special activities." Under "ordinary circumstances," the president must tell Intelligence committees in both chambers in advance of a covert operation. But in "rare occasions when time is of the essence," the president may wait up to 48 hours after a covert activity begins. The president also has the option of informing only the House and Senate majority and minority leaders, or to also include the chairmen and ranking members of the Intelligence committees if he determines an operation is so sensitive that avoiding the full committees "is essential to meet extraordinary circumstances affecting vital interests of the United States." Passed 71-19: R 26-17; D 45-2 [ND 31-2, SD 14-0], March 15, 1988.

90. **S J Res 243. Contra Aid/Passage.** Passage of the joint resolution to approve President Reagan's request for $36.25 million in continued military and non-military aid for the Nicaraguan contra guerrillas. Passed 51-48: R 39-7; D 12-41 [ND 1-34, SD 11-7], Feb. 4, 1988. A "yea" was a vote supporting the president's position. The House previously had rejected the president's contra-aid request.

91. **HR 3545. Fiscal 1988 Budget Reconciliation/Conference Report.** Adoption of the conference report on the bill to meet deficit-reduction targets set by the fiscal 1988 budget resolution (H Con Res 93) and the November "budget summit" agreement between the White House and Congress. The bill provided for $9.1 billion in new taxes in fiscal 1988 and $14.1 billion in 1989, plus sales of government assets, user fees, savings from the Medicare and health program for the elderly, savings from farm subsidy and other programs, and savings from reduced interest payments on the federal debt to yield $17.6 billion in deficit reduction in fiscal 1988 and $22 billion in fiscal 1989. Adopted (thus cleared for the president) 61-28: R 18-23; D 43-5 [ND 31-2, SD 12-3], in the session that began Dec. 21, 1987.

92. **S 9. Omnibus Veterans' Benefits/Ban on Hard-to-Detect Firearms.** McClure, R-Idaho, motion to table (kill) the Thurmond, R-S.C. amendment to add to the bill provisions that would ban the manufacture, sale and possession of guns not readily detectable by standard airport equipment. Motion agreed to 47-42; R 35-8; D 12-34 [ND 5-25, SD 7-9], Dec. 4, 1987. A "yea" was a vote supporting the president's position.

93. **HR 2470. Catastrophic Health Insurance Passage.** Passage of the bill to expand the Medicare program to protect beneficiaries from catastrophic health-care costs and to otherwise expand the Medicare and federal-state Medicaid programs. Passed 86-11: R 36-10; D 50-1 [ND 34-0, SD 16-1], Oct. 27, 1987. A "yea" was a vote supporting the president's position. (The Senate previously moved to strike all language after the enacting clause of HR 2470, the House-passed bill, and insert instead the text of S 1127.) This bill was repealed unanimously in 1989.

94. **Bork Nomination.** Confirmation of President Reagan's nomination of Robert H. Bork of the District of Columbia to be an associate justice of the Supreme Court. Rejected 42-58: R 40-6; D 2-52 [ND 0-36, SD 2-16], Oct. 23, 1987. A "yea" was a vote supporting the president's position.

95. **S 1394. State Department Authorization, Fiscal 1988/Panama Canal Treaties.** Pell, D-R.I., motion to table (kill) the Symms, R-Idaho, amendment to state that the Senate should not have approved ratification of the Panama Canal treaties in 1978 and that the treaties should be voided unless Panama accepts within six months the DeConcini, D-Ariz., reservation to the treaties, which gives the United States the right to defend the canal after the year 2000. Motion agreed to 59-39: R 15-30; D 44-9 [ND 32-3, SD 12-6], Oct. 7, 1987.

96. **HR 2713. District of Columbia Appropriations, Fiscal 1988/AIDS.** Harkin, D-Iowa, motion to table (kill) the Helms R-N.C., amendment to cut off funds in the bill after Dec. 31, 1987 if by then the District has not repealed a local law that prohibits insurance companies from denying coverage to people because they tested positive for exposure to the AIDS virus. Motion rejected 44-55: R 10-36; D 34-19 [ND 27-8, SD 7-11], Sept. 30, 1987. The Helms amendment subsequently was adopted by voice vote.

97. **S 1174. Defense Authorization, Fiscal 1988-89/Diplomatic Immunity.** Dixon, D-Ill., motion to table (kill) the Helms, R-N.C., amendment to deny diplomatic immunity to certain members of foreign missions who are not diplomatic agents. Motion agreed to 48-46: R 9-33; D 39-13 [ND 28-7, SD 11-6], Sept. 25, 1987.

98. **S 1174. Defense Authorization, Fiscal 1988-89/Bigeye Bomb.** Shelby, D-Ala., motion to table (kill) the Pryor, D-Ark., amendment to eliminate funds for production of the Bigeye nerve gas bomb. Motion agreed to 49-48: R 34-12; D 15-36 [ND 5-29, SD 10-7], Sept. 24, 1987. A "yea" was a vote supporting the president's position.

99. **H J Res 324. Permanent Debt-Limit Extension -- Gramm-Rudman Revision/ Conference Agreement.** Adoption of the conference report on the resolution to raise the permanent ceiling on the federal debt to $2.8 trillion, from $2.1 trillion; to establish an automatic spending-cut procedure; to set maximum allowable budget deficit targets: for fiscal 1988, $144 billion (or another, undetermined figure because the legislation limited 1988 mandatory spending cuts under the automatic procedure to $23 billion, regardless of the difference between the estimated deficit and the target); for fiscal 1989, $136 billion (or another, undetermined figure because of a $36 billion limit on the mandated spending cuts); for fiscal 1990, $100 billion; for fiscal 1991, $64 billion; for fiscal 1992, $28 billion; for fiscal 1993, zero; to provide that the automatic spending-cut procedure would be triggered in most years if the estimated deficit exceeded the target by more than $10 billion; and to revise certain other budget rules. Adopted 64-34: R 33-13; D 31-21 [ND 19-16; SD 12-5], Sept. 23, 1987. (The conference report, previously adopted by the House, therefore was cleared for the president.)

100. **S 1174. Defense Authorization, Fiscal 1988-89/ASAT Testing.** Quayle, R-Ind., motion to table (kill) the Kerry, D-Mass., amendment to bar tests against a target in space of the anti-satellite (ASAT) missile. Motion agreed to 51-47: R 38-8; D 13-39 [ND 5-30, SD 8-9], Sept. 22, 1987. A "yea" was a vote supporting the president's position.

101. **S 1174. Defense Authorization, Fiscal 1988-89/Missile Testing.** Nunn, D-Ga., motion to table (kill) the Warner, R-Va., amendment to strike a provision limiting the development or testing of space-based and other mobile anti-ballistic missile systems. Motion agreed to 58-38: R 8-37; D 50-1 [ND 34-0, SD 16-1], Sept. 17, 1987. A "nay" was a vote supporting the president's position.

102. **HR 3. Omnibus Trade Bill/Passage.** Passage of the bill (which was amended by substituting the text of S 1420, as amended) to authorize presidential negotiations to reduce international tariffs and non-tariff barriers to trade; to mandate retaliation against countries that maintain a consistent pattern of unfair trade practices against the United States, unless negotiated agreements lead to the elimination of such practices; to enhance worker and company benefits for industries injured by imports; to relax controls on exports of certain high-technology products to Western countries; to expand programs for worker retraining; and to improve math, science and foreign language education. Passed 71-27: R 19-27; D 52-0 [ND 35-0, SD 17-0], July 21, 1987. A "nay" was a vote supporting the president's position.

103. **S 1420. Omnibus Trade Bill/Windfall Profits Tax Repeal.** Boren, D-Okla., amendment to repeal the windfall profits tax on domestic crude oil. Adopted 58-40: R 35-11; D 23-29 [ND 11-24, SD 12-5], in the session that began July 15, 1987. A "yea" was a vote supporting the president's position.

104. **HR 558. Urgent Relief for the Homeless.** Adoption of the conference report on the bill to authorize $443 million in fiscal 1987 and $616 million in fiscal 1988 to provide housing, health, food, job training and other assistance for the nation's homeless, and to set up an interagency homeless council to oversee federal homeless-aid programs. Adopted 65-8: R 26-7; D 39-1 [ND 26-1, SD 13-0], June 27, 1987. A "nay" was a vote supporting the president's position.

105. **HR 1827. Fiscal 1987 Supplemental Appropriations/AIDS Treatment.** Danforth, R-Mo., motion to table (kill) the Appropriations Committee amendment to authorize $30 million to provide AZT (or retrovir), a life-prolonging drug, for victims of acquired immune deficiency syndrome who could not otherwise afford it. Motion rejected 21-74: R 17-29; D 4-45 [ND 3-29, SD 1-16], May 21, 1987.

106. **HR 1827. Fiscal 1987 Supplemental Appropriations/AIDS Testing.** Danforth, R-Mo., motion to table (kill) the Helms, R-N.C., amendment to provide for mandatory testing for acquired immune deficiency syndrome (AIDS) for all immigrants and to require states to have mandatory AIDS testing for marriage license applicants, if state residents are to qualify for new AIDS assistance provided under the bill. Motion agreed to 63-32: R 23-23, D 40-9 [ND 28-4, SD 12-5], May 21, 1987.

107. **S Con Res 49. Fiscal 1988 Budget Resolution/Biennial Budget.** Chiles, D-Fla., motion to table (kill) the Roth, R-Del., perfecting amendment to express the sense of the Senate that a biennial budget and appropriations process should be approved this year. Motion agreed to 53-45: R 4-40; D 49-5 [ND 35-1, SD 14-4], May 6, 1987.

108. **S 742. Fairness in Broadcasting/Final Passage.** Passage of the bill to write into law the fairness doctrine, which requires broadcasters to air matters of public importance and to present contrasting viewpoints on such matters. Passed 59-31: R 18-25; D 41-6 [ND 26-4, SD 15-2], April 21, 1987. A "nay" was a vote supporting the president's position.

109. **S 387. Omnibus Highway Reauthorization Speed Limit.** Symms, R-Idaho, amendment to allow states to raise the speed limit to 65 mph on rural Interstates outside urban areas with populations of 50,000 or more. Adopted 65-33: R 30-13; D 35-20 [ND 19-18, SD 16-2], Feb. 3, 1987. A "yea" was a vote supporting the president's position.

110. **S 1200. Immigration Reform.** Adoption of the conference report on the bill to overhaul the nation's immigration laws by creating new penalties against employers who knowingly hire illegal aliens; granting amnesty to illegal aliens who can prove they were in the country prior to Jan. 1, 1982; and creating a special farm worker program for Western agricultural growers. Adopted 63-24: R 29-16; D 34-8 [ND 25-5; SD 9-3], Oct. 17, 1986.

111. **HR 4868. South Africa Sanctions.** Passage, over President Reagan's Sept. 26 veto, of the bill to impose sanctions against South Africa. Among the sanctions imposed by the bill were bans on imports of South African iron, steel, sugar and other agricultural products. The bill also prohibited exports to South Africa of petroleum products, banned new U.S. investments there, and banned imports of South African uranium, coal and textiles. Passed (thus enacted into law) 78-21: R 31-21; D 47-0 [ND 33-0; SD 14-0], October 2, 1986. A two-thirds majority of those present and voting (66 in this case) of both houses is required to override a veto. A "nay" was a vote supporting the president's position.

112. **HR 5484. Omnibus Drug Bill.** Goldwater, R-Ariz., motion to table (kill) the Dixon, D-Ill., amendment to the Dole, R-Kan.-Byrd, D-W.Va., substitute, to require the president, within 30 days of enactment, to deploy military personnel and equipment "to the extent possible" to combat drug smuggling, and within 45 days of enactment to "substantially halt" drug smuggling across U.S. borders "to the extent possible." Motion agreed to 72-14: R 37-9; D 35-5 [ND 25-4; SD 10-1], Sept. 27, 1986. (The Dole-Byrd substitute later was adopted by voice vote.) A "yea" was a vote supporting the president's position.

113. **HR 3838. Tax Overhaul.** Adoption of the conference report on the bill to revise the federal income tax system by reducing individual and corporate tax rates, eliminating or curtailing many deductions, credits and exclusions, repealing the investment tax credit, taxing capital gains as ordinary income and making other changes. Adopted 74-23: R 41-11; D 33-12 [ND 25-7; SD 8-5], Sept. 27, 1986. A "yea" was a vote supporting the president's position.

114. **S 2638. Department of Defense Authorization, Fiscal 1987.** Mathias, R-Md., perfecting amendment to the Kennedy, D-Mass., amendment, to call on President Reagan to submit to the Senate two nuclear test ban treaties -- the Peaceful Nuclear Explosions Treaty and the Threshold Test Ban Treaty -- and to propose an immediate resumption of negotiations with the Soviet Union toward a comprehensive nuclear test ban treaty. Adopted 64-35: R 21-32; D 43-3 [ND 32-1; SD 11-2], Aug. 7, 1986. (The Kennedy amendment subsequently was adopted by voice vote.) A "nay" was a vote supporting the president's position.

115. **S 2638. Department of Defense Authorization, Fiscal 1987.** DeConcini, D-Ariz., amendment to prohibit the sale or transfer of "Stinger" portable anti-aircraft missiles to U.S.-backed guerilla movements in foreign countries unless strict security measures were taken to guard the missiles. Rejected 37-63: R 8-45; D 29-18 [ND 23-10; SD 6-8], Aug. 7, 1986.

116. **S 2638. Department of Defense Authorization, Fiscal 1987.** Hatfield, R-Ore., amendment to prohibit procurement or assembly of "binary" chemical munitions until Congress gives its approval. Rejected 43-57: R 14-39; D 29-18 [ND 26-7; SD 3-11], Aug. 7, 1986. A "nay" was a vote supporting the president's position.

117. **H J Res 668. Public Debt Limit/Oil Import Tariff.** Heinz, R-Pa., motion to table (kill) the Hart, D-Colo., amendment to the Finance Committee amendment, to increase the existing tariff on crude oil and refined petroleum products by $10 a barrel. Motion agreed to 82-15: R 47-4; D 35-11 [ND 27-6; SD 8-5], July 31, 1986.

118. **HR 3838. Tax Overhaul.** Baucus, D-Mont., substitute for the Bumpers, D-Ark., amendment to reinstate provisions granting immunity from criminal prosecution, but not civil penalties, to those who confess to unpaid taxes; to make the provisions contingent on a $200 million appropriation to the Internal Revenue Service for enforcement; to make the provisions inapplicable to income from illegal sources; and to limit the immunity from criminal prosecution to two years. Rejected 40-43: R 21-21; D 19-22 [ND 12-17; SD 7-5], June 20, 1986. (The Bumpers amendment subsequently was adopted by voice vote.)

119. **S J Res 316. Saudi Arms Sale.** Passage, over President Reagan's May 21 veto, of a resolution blocking the sale of weapons to Saudi Arabia. Rejected (thus sustaining the president's veto) 66-34: R 24-29; D 42-5 [ND 31-2; SD 11-3], June 5, 1986. A two-thirds majority of those present and voting (67 in this case) is required to override a veto. A "nay" was a vote supporting the president's position.

120. **S J Res 225. Balanced Budget Constitutional Amendment.** Passage of the joint resolution to propose a constitutional amendment to require a balanced federal budget every year unless a three-fifths majority of the total membership of both houses of Congress votes for a specific amount of deficit spending; to require that the public debt of the United States may be

increased only by a law enacted by a three-fifths majority of the total membership of both houses of Congress; to require that a bill to increase revenue shall become law only if passed by a majority of the total membership of both houses of Congress; to require the president to submit annually a proposed balanced budget to Congress; and to allow Congress to waive the requirement for a balanced budget during a declared war. Rejected 66-34: R 43-10; D 23-24 [ND 10-23; SD 13-1], March 25, 1986. A two-thirds majority of those present and voting (67 in this case) is required for passage of a constitutional amendment. A "yea" was a vote supporting the president's position.

121. **H J Res 372. Public Debt Limit.** Packwood, R-Ore., motion to table (kill) the Riegle, D-Mich., amendment to the Packwood amendment to the House amendment to the Senate amendment, to exempt veterans' compensation and medical programs from any automatic spending reductions. Motion agreed to 52-44: R 46-5; D 6-39 [ND 3-28; SD 3-11], Nov. 5, 1985.

122. **S 51. Superfund Reauthorization, Fiscal 1986-90.** Roth, R-Del., amendment to strike from the bill a section establishing a new demonstration program to pay for medical expenses of victims of hazardous substance releases, and to authorize appropriations of $30 million annually during fiscal 1986-90 for that purpose. Adopted 49-45: R 40-11; D 9-34 [ND 3-28; SD 6-6], Sept. 24, 1985. A "yea" was a vote supporting the president's position.

123. **S 1200. Immigration Reform and Control Act.** Wilson, R-Calif., amendment to create a "seasonal worker" program to allow foreign workers into the country for up to nine months each year for agricultural work, with a cap allowing no more than 350,000 of these workers in the United States at any one time. Adopted 51-44: R 36-15; D 15-29 [ND 6-25; SD 9-4], Sept. 17, 1985.

124. **S 47. School Prayer.** Weicker, R-Conn., motion to table (kill) the bill to bar the federal courts, including the Supreme Court, from considering cases involving prayer in public schools. Motion agreed to 62-36: R 24-28; D 38-8 [ND 31-1; SD 7-7], Sept. 10, 1985. (The effect of the bill would have been to restore the right of states or local communities to permit prayer in public schools without being subject to challenges in the federal courts.)

125. **S 43. Line-Item Veto.** Dole, R-Kan., motion to invoke cloture (thus limiting debate) on the Dole motion to proceed to the consideration of the bill to give the president power to veto individual spending items by requiring that appropriations bills be split by paragraph or section into separate bills before being sent to the White House. Motion rejected 58-40: R 46-7; D 12-33 [ND 8-24; SD 4-9], July 24, 1985. A three-fifths majority vote (60) of the total Senate is required to invoke cloture. A "yea" was a vote supporting the president's position.

126. **S 49. Firearm Owners' Protection.** Passage of the bill to revise the Gun Control Act of 1968 to exempt many gun collectors from licensing requirements, remove the ban on interstate sales of rifles, shotguns and handguns, require advance notice for routine compliance inspections, and impose a mandatory five-year sentence on anyone convicted of using a firearm in a violent federal crime. Passed 79-15: R 49-2; D 30-13 [ND 18-13; SD 12-0], July 9, 1985. A "yea" was a vote supporting the president's position.

127. **S 49. Firearm Owners' Protection.** McClure, R-Idaho, motion to table (kill) the Inouye, D-Hawaii, amendment to require a 14-day waiting period between the purchase of a handgun and its delivery to the buyer. Motion agreed to 71-23: R 46-5; D 25-18 [ND 14-17; SD 11-1], July 9, 1985. A "yea" was a vote supporting the president's position.

128. **S Con Res 32. First Budget Resolution, Fiscal 1986.** Dole, R-Kan., motion to table (kill) the Metzenbaum, D-Ohio, perfecting amendment to the Dole-Domenici, R-N.M., amendment to the instructions of the Dole motion to recommit the concurrent resolution to the Budget Committee, to impose a 15 percent minimum tax on corporate earnings in excess of $50,000 and to use the revenues to reduce the federal deficit. Motion agreed to 61-37: R 49-3; D 12-34 [ND 8-24; SD 4-10], in the session that began May 9, 1985.

129. **S Con Res 32. First Budget Resolution Fiscal 1986.** Dole, R-Kan., motion to table (kill) the Moynihan, D-N.Y., perfecting amendment to the Dole-Domenici, R-N.M., amendment to the instructions of the Dole motion to recommit the concurrent resolution to the Budget Committee, to restore the full Social Security cost-of-living adjustment (COLA) for fiscal

1986. Motion agreed to 51-47: R 49-3; D 2-44 [ND 1-31; SD 1-13], in the session that began May 9, 1985. A "yea" was a vote supporting the president's position.

130. **S Con Res 32. First Budget Resolution, Fiscal 1986.** Grassley, R-Iowa, perfecting amendment to the Dole, R-Kan.,-Domenici, R-N.M., amendment to the instructions of the Dole motion to recommit the concurrent resolution to the Budget Committee, to freeze funding for all federal programs in fiscal 1986 at fiscal 1985 levels, with no allowances for inflation. Rejected 27-70: R 9-42; D 18-28 [ND 13-19; SD 5-9], May 9, 1985. The amendment would save an estimated $40 billion for fiscal year 1986.

131. **H J Res 654. Debt Limit Increase.** Baker, R-Tenn., motion to table (kill) the Kennedy, D-Mass., amendment to call for a mutual and verifiable freeze on the production, testing and deployment of nuclear weapons and a reduction in nuclear weapons stockpiles worldwide. Motion agreed to 55-42: R 46-8; D 9-34 [ND 2-29; SD 7-5], Oct. 5, 1984. A "yea" was a vote supporting the president's position.

132. **H J Res 648. Continuing Appropriations, Fiscal 1985.** Packwood, R-Ore., motion to table (kill) the Byrd, D-W.Va., amendment to overturn the Feb. 28, 1984, Supreme Court decision in Grove City College v. Bell narrowing the reach of Title IX of the 1972 Education Amendments, a law designed to bar sex discrimination in educational institutions receiving federal aid. Motion agreed to 53-45: R 51-4; D 2-41 [ND 2-28; SD 0-13], Oct. 2, 1984. A "yea" was a vote supporting the president's position.

133. **HR 4616. Motor Vehicle Safety/Minimum Drinking Age.** Lautenberg, D-N.J., amendment to withhold a percentage of highway funds from states whose minimum drinking ages are under 21 and to provide incentives for other actions aimed at reducing drunk driving. Adopted 81-16: R 45-10; D 36-6 [ND 25-3; SD 11-3], June 26, 1984. A "yea" was a vote supporting the president's position.

134. **S 2723. Omnibus Defense Authorization.** Tower, R-Texas, motion to table (kill) the Moynihan, D-N.Y., amendment to produce no additional MX missiles in fiscal 1985 but to keep the MX production line ready for production pending completion of a new study of the mobile, single-warhead "Midgetman" missile. Motion agreed to 49-48: R 43-10; D 5-38 [ND 2-28; SD 3-10], June 14, 1984, with Vice President Bush casting a "yea" vote to break the 48-48 tie. A "yea" was a vote supporting the president's position.

135. **HR 2163. Deficit Reduction.** Baker, R-Tenn., amendment to reduce federal deficits by $140 billion through fiscal 1987 by increasing taxes, limiting the increases in military spending, cutting federal benefit and other non-defense programs. Adopted 65-32: R 53-0; D 12-32 [ND 6-24; SD 6-8], May 17, 1984. A "yea" was a vote supporting the president's position.

136. **S J Res 73. Constitutional Amendment on School Prayer.** Passage of the joint resolution to propose an amendment to the Constitution to permit organized, recited prayer in public schools and other public places. Rejected 56-44: R 37-18; D 19-26 [ND 6-25; SD 13-1], March 20, 1984. A two-thirds majority of those present and voting (67 in this case) of both houses is required for passage of a joint resolution proposing an amendment to the Constitution. A "yea" was a vote supporting the president's position.

137. **S 1765. Capital Punishment.** Passage of the bill to reinstitute the death penalty for certain federal crimes, including assassination or attempted assassination of a president, treason, espionage and specified other federal crimes resulting in the death of another person. The bill requires a separate hearing on the issue of punishment after the defendant is convicted of an offense carrying the death penalty. Passed 63-32: R 43-11; D 20-21 [ND 9-19; SD 11-2], Feb. 22, 1984. A "yea" was a vote supporting the president's position.

138. **S 1762. Comprehensive Crime Control Act.** Metzenbaum, D-Ohio, amendment to prohibit government officials from tape recording their telephone conversations without consent of the other party, with exceptions permitted for law enforcement and intelligence officers. Rejected 41-51: R 10-43; D 31-8 [ND 23-4; SD 8-4], Feb. 2, 1984. A "nay" was a vote supporting the president's position.

139. **HR 3706. Martin Luther King Jr. Holiday.** Passage of the bill to declare the third Monday in January a legal public holiday honoring Martin Luther King Jr. Passed 78-22; R 37-18; D 41-4 [ND 28-3; SD 13-1], Oct. 19, 1983.

140. **S J Res 159. Multinational Force in Lebanon.** Passage of the joint resolution to provide statutory authorization under the War Powers Resolution for continued U.S. participation in the multinational peacekeeping force in Lebanon for up to 18 months after the enactment of the resolution. Passed 54-46: R 52-3; D 2-43 [ND 2-29; SD 0-14], Sept. 29, 1983. A "yea" was a vote supporting the president's position.

141. **S J Res 3. Human Life Federalism Amendment.** Passage of the joint resolution to propose an amendment to the Constitution that would overturn the 1973 Supreme Court decision, Roe v. Wade, which made abortion legal. Rejected 49-50: R 34-19; D 15-31 [ND 7-25; SD 8-6], June 28, 1983. A two-thirds majority of those present and voting (67 in this case) of both houses is required for passage of a joint resolution proposing an amendment to the Constitution. A "yea" was a vote supporting the president's position.

142. **H J Res 631. Continuing Appropriations, Fiscal 1983.** Domenici, R-N.M., amendment to delete the section of the joint resolution providing $1.2 billion for public works jobs. Rejected 46-50: R 39-12; D 7-38 [ND 3-27; SD 4-11], in the session which began Dec. 16, 1982. A "yea" was a vote supporting the president's position.

143. **HR 6590. Tobacco Program Revisions.** Baker, R-Tenn., motion to table (kill) the Eagleton, D-Mo., amendment to authorize tobacco price support loans through 1985 (thus ending permanent authorization for these loans). Motion agreed to 49-47: R 29-23; D 20-24 [ND 7-23; SD 13-1], July 14, 1982.

144. **HR 5922. Urgent Supplemental Appropriations, Fiscal 1982.** Lugar, R-Ind., amendment to establish a new subsidy program to provide mortgages at below-market interest rates for buyers of new homes. The amendment contained a fiscal 1982 appropriation of $5.1 billion. Adopted 69-23: R 29-20; D 40-3 [ND 27-1; SD 13-2], May 27, 1982. A "nay" was a vote supporting the president's position.

Senate Voting Records

ALABAMA

HEFLIN, HOWELL -- Alabama [Democrat]. Term Began/Expires: 1991/1996. Prior Terms: Senate: 1979-90. Born: June 19, 1921; Tuscumbia, AL. Education: Birmingham-Southern College (B.A.); University of Alabama Law School (J.D.). Military Service: U.S. Marine Corps, 1942-46. Occupation: Attorney; chief justice of the Alabama Supreme Court (1971-77).

1. Prohibit MFN status for China	Y	
2. Kill-Tie welfare to school attendance	Y	
3. Limit credit card interest rates	N	
4. Confirm Gates as head of CIA	Y	
5. Adoption of national energy policies	Y	
6. Kill-Restrict NEA use of funds	N	
7. Unemployment benefits extension	Y	
8. Confirm Thomas to Supreme Court	N	
9. Raise eligibility for unpaid leave	N	
10. Notify parents of minors' abortions	Y	
11. Move $3b from defense to domestic	N	
12. End production of B-2 bomber	N	
13. Cut SDI $1b to reduce deficit	N	
14. Maintain strategic stability-Soviets	N	
15. Kill-Allow women as combat pilots	Y	
16. Kill-Allow HIV tests before surgery	N	
17. Strike $12b aid to Int'l Mon Fund	N	
18. Raise Senate salary/omit honoraria	N	
19. Reduce space station funding $1.9b	N	
20. Kill-Eliminate supercollider funds	Y	
21. Req 5-day handgun waiting period	N	
22. Life in prison instead of death	N	
23. Exceptions to exclusionary rule	Y	
24. Ban race as death sentence factor	Y	
25. Campaign finance revisions	Y	
26. Kill-Term limits for senators	Y	
27. Require four presidential debates	N	
28. Tighten ban on vertical price fixing	N	
29. Kill-Freeze discretionary budget	Y	
30. Provide $30b for failed S&Ls	Y	
31. Allow use of force against Iraq	Y	
32. Allow $15b in foreign aid for 1991	N	
33. Civil Rights Act of 1990	Y	
34. Block cancellation of Egypt's debt	Y	
35. Cut El Salvador military aid 50%	Y	
36. Reduce troops in NATO by 30,000	N	
37. Req increases in auto fuel efficiency	N	
38. Bar taxpayer funding of campaigns	?	
39. Limit textile import growth to 1%	Y	
40. Amendment to ban flag desecration	Y	
41. Let fed emp be politically active	Y	
42. Reauthorize Amtrak-veto override	Y	
43. Allow sale of assault weapons	Y	
44. Retraining aid for coal miners	Y	
45. Kill-Raise car emission standards	Y	
46. Pull EPA nuclear plant authority	Y	
47. Defer Chinese students' deportation	Y	
48. Cut in capital gains tax	Y	
49. Establish CIA inspector general	N	
50. Kill-Sanctions against China	N	
51. Bar drug testing to receive AFDC	Y	
52. Kill-Allow force against drug planes	N	
53. Include illegal aliens in census	N	
54. Restitution to Japanese interned	N	
55. Troop reduction in Europe of 50%	N	
56. Increase SDI research to $4.3b	Y	
57. Kill-Pay homeless below min wage	Y	
58. Ban airline smoking within US	N	
59. Bar transfer of FS-X technology	Y	
60. Limit liability for oil spills	N	
61. Restructure S&L industry	Y	
62. Ban $ to illegal foreign activities	N	
63. Req immigrant fluency in English	Y	
64. Allow aliens' families to stay in US	Y	

HEFLIN, HOWELL (continued)

65. Expand child care aid/tax credit	Y	
66. Raise minimum wage w/subminimum	Y	
67. Freeze outlays except SS/Medicare	N	
68. Kill-Shift $5b of DOD to domestic	Y	
69. Confirm Tower as sec of defense	Y	
70. Bar abortion $ except to save mother	Y	
71. Kill-Warn AIDS carriers' spouses	N	
72. Allow religious schools to bar gays	Y	
73. 60 days' notice of plant closings	Y	
74. Allow poison pills in corp takeovers	Y	
75. Kill-Workfare program	N	
76. Prohibit employee polygraph testing	Y	
77. Cap Medicare patients' liability	Y	
78. Revise unfair trade practices	Y	
79. Kill-Shift SDI $ to conv weapons	Y	
80. Kill-Shift SDI $ to accidental launch	Y	
81. Kill-Shift MX $ to supplies/parts	Y	
82. Kill-Buy America provision at DOD	N	
83. Allow nuclear testing-5+ kilotons	Y	
84. Allow SALT II to be exceeded	Y	
85. $ to vets exposed to nuclear bomb	Y	
86. Warn workers of disease exposure	N	
87. Restore four civil rights laws	Y	
88. Disapprove uranium sales to Japan	N	
89. Notify Congress of covert operations	?	
90. Approval of $36m in Contra aid	Y	
91. $18b deficit reduction compromise	N	
92. Allow sale of hard-to-detect guns	Y	
93. Catastrophic health insurance	Y	
94. Bork nomination to Supreme Court	N	
95. Kill-Void Panama Canal treaties	N	
96. Kill-Insurance denial to AIDS+	N	
97. Keep diplomatic immunity intact	N	
98. Produce Bigeye nerve gas bomb	Y	
99. Balanced budget by '93-via targets	N	
100. Allow ASAT missile tests in space	Y	
101. Limit space-based/ABM system tests	Y	
102. Force reduction in trade barriers	Y	
103. Repeal windfall profit tax on oil	Y	
104. $1b/two year aid for the homeless	Y	

105. Disallow $30m for AZT to poor	N
106. Bar AIDS test-immigrants/marriage	Y
107. Kill-Biennial budget approval	N
108. Fairness doctrine in broadcasting	N
109. Raise speed limit to 65 mph	Y
110. Immigration reform/alien amnesty	N
111. South Africa sanctions-veto override	Y
112. Kill-Use of military in drug war	Y
113. Tax overhaul to revise income tax	N
114. Submit nuclear test ban treaties	N
115. Prohibit sale of Stinger missiles	N
116. Prohibit binary chemical weapons	N
117. Kill-$10/barrel oil tariff increase	Y
118. Grant tax amnesty provisions	Y
119. Block Saudi arms sale-veto override	Y
120. Balanced budget amendment	Y
121. Include veterans in spending cuts	N
122. Bar $ to hazardous substance victims	Y
123. Allow seasonal workers in the US	Y
124. Let fed courts rule on school prayer	N
125. Presidential line-item veto	Y
126. Ease Gun Control Act of 1968	Y
127. Kill-Req 14-day wait for handguns	Y
128. Kill-15% min tax on corporations	Y
129. Drop Social Security COLA	N
130. Freeze funding for all programs	N
131. Kill-Nuclear weapon freeze	Y
132. Keep decision narrowing Title IX	N
133. Raise drinking age to 21	Y
134. Allow production of MX missile	Y
135. Raise taxes/cut spending by $140b	Y
136. School prayer amendment	Y
137. Capital punishment-federal crimes	Y
138. Ban government officials from taping	N
139. Martin Luther King holiday	Y
140. Authorize Marines in Lebanon	N
141. Amendment making abortion illegal	Y
142. Delete $1.2b for jobs creation	N
143. Keep tobacco price supports	Y
144. Emergency housing aid of $5.1b	Y

Presidential Support Score: 1991 - 73% 1990 - 60%

SHELBY, RICHARD C. -- Alabama [Democrat]. Term Began/Expires: 1987/1992. Prior Terms: House: 1979-86. Born: May 6, 1934; Birmingham, AL. Education: University of Alabama (A.B., LL.B.). Occupation: Tuscaloosa city prosecutor (1963-71); U.S. commissioner (1966-70); special assistant state attorney general (1968-70); state senator (1970-78).

1. Prohibit MFN status for China	N
2. Kill-Tie welfare to school attendance	Y
3. Limit credit card interest rates	Y
4. Confirm Gates as head of CIA	Y
5. Adoption of national energy policies	Y
6. Kill-Restrict NEA use of funds	N
7. Unemployment benefits extension	Y
8. Confirm Thomas to Supreme Court	Y
9. Raise eligibility for unpaid leave	N
10. Notify parents of minors' abortions	Y
11. Move $3b from defense to domestic	N
12. End production of B-2 bomber	N
13. Cut SDI $1b to reduce deficit	N
14. Maintain strategic stability-Soviets	N

15. Kill-Allow women as combat pilots	Y
16. Kill-Allow HIV tests before surgery	N
17. Strike $12b aid to Int'l Mon Fund	N
18. Raise Senate salary/omit honoraria	N
19. Reduce space station funding $1.9b	N
20. Kill-Eliminate supercollider funds	Y
21. Req 5-day handgun waiting period	N
22. Life in prison instead of death	N
23. Exceptions to exclusionary rule	N
24. Ban race as death sentence factor	Y
25. Campaign finance revisions	N
26. Kill-Term limits for senators	Y
27. Require four presidential debates	Y
28. Tighten ban on vertical price fixing	Y

SHELBY, RICHARD C. (continued)

29.	Kill-Freeze discretionary budget	Y
30.	Provide $30b for failed S&Ls	N
31.	Allow use of force against Iraq	Y
32.	Allow $15b in foreign aid for 1991	Y
33.	Civil Rights Act of 1990	Y
34.	Block cancellation of Egypt's debt	Y
35.	Cut El Salvador military aid 50%	Y
36.	Reduce troops in NATO by 30,000	Y
37.	Req increases in auto fuel efficiency	N
38.	Bar taxpayer funding of campaigns	N
39.	Limit textile import growth to 1%	Y
40.	Amendment to ban flag desecration	Y
41.	Let fed emp be politically active	Y
42.	Reauthorize Amtrak-veto override	Y
43.	Allow sale of assault weapons	Y
44.	Retraining aid for coal miners	Y
45.	Kill-Raise car emission standards	Y
46.	Pull EPA nuclear plant authority	Y
47.	Defer Chinese students' deportation	Y
48.	Cut in capital gains tax	Y
49.	Establish CIA inspector general	N
50.	Kill-Sanctions against China	N
51.	Bar drug testing to receive AFDC	Y
52.	Kill-Allow force against drug planes	N
53.	Include illegal aliens in census	N
54.	Restitution to Japanese interned	N
55.	Troop reduction in Europe of 50%	N
56.	Increase SDI research to $4.3b	Y
57.	Kill-Pay homeless below min wage	Y
58.	Ban airline smoking within US	Y
59.	Bar transfer of FS-X technology	Y
60.	Limit liability for oil spills	Y
61.	Restructure S&L industry	Y
62.	Ban $ to illegal foreign activities	Y
63.	Req immigrant fluency in English	Y
64.	Allow aliens' families to stay in US	N
65.	Expand child care aid/tax credit	Y
66.	Raise minimum wage w/subminimum	Y
67.	Freeze outlays except SS/Medicare	N
68.	Kill-Shift $5b of DOD to domestic	Y
69.	Confirm Tower as sec of defense	N
70.	Bar abortion $ except to save mother	Y
71.	Kill-Warn AIDS carriers' spouses	N
72.	Allow religious schools to bar gays	Y
73.	60 days' notice of plant closings	Y
74.	Allow poison pills in corp takeovers	N
75.	Kill-Workfare program	N
76.	Prohibit employee polygraph testing	Y
77.	Cap Medicare patients' liability	Y
78.	Revise unfair trade practices	Y
79.	Kill-Shift SDI $ to conv weapons	Y
80.	Kill-Shift SDI $ to accidental launch	Y
81.	Kill-Shift MX $ to supplies/parts	Y
82.	Kill-Buy America provision at DOD	N
83.	Allow nuclear testing-5+ kilotons	Y
84.	Allow SALT II to be exceeded	Y
85.	$ to vets exposed to nuclear bomb	Y
86.	Warn workers of disease exposure	N
87.	Restore four civil rights laws	Y
88.	Disapprove uranium sales to Japan	N
89.	Notify Congress of covert operations	Y
90.	Approval of $36m in Contra aid	Y
91.	$18b deficit reduction compromise	N
92.	Allow sale of hard-to-detect guns	Y
93.	Catastrophic health insurance	Y
94.	Bork nomination to Supreme Court	N
95.	Kill-Void Panama Canal treaties	N
96.	Kill-Insurance denial to AIDS+	N
97.	Keep diplomatic immunity intact	N
98.	Produce Bigeye nerve gas bomb	Y
99.	Balanced budget by '93-via targets	N
100.	Allow ASAT missile tests in space	Y
101.	Limit space-based/ABM system tests	Y
102.	Force reduction in trade barriers	Y
103.	Repeal windfall profit tax on oil	Y
104.	$1b/two year aid for the homeless	Y
105.	Disallow $30m for AZT to poor	Y
106.	Bar AIDS test-immigrants/marriage	N
107.	Kill-Biennial budget approval	N
108.	Fairness doctrine in broadcasting	Y
109.	Raise speed limit to 65 mph	Y

The following are House measures voted on between 1982-1986:

99.	Immigration reform/alien amnesty	N
100.	South Africa sanctions-veto override	Y
101.	Tax overhaul to revise income tax	Y
102.	Use of military in drug war	Y
103.	Delete 12 MX/add conventional wpn	N
104.	Raise speed limit to 65 mph	?
105.	Require Pentagon to buy US goods	Y
106.	AIDS insurance non-discrimination	N
107.	Prohibit Saudi arms sales	Y
108.	Ease Gun Control Act of 1968	Y
109.	Bar interstate handgun transport	N
110.	Make company emissions known	N
111.	Allow toxic victims to sue in fed ct	N
112.	Superfund waste cleanup of $10b	N
113.	90 days notice of plant closings	N
114.	$20b in Medicare cuts/tax increases	Y
115.	Spending cuts and tax increases	N
116.	Set school lunch lmt-250% poverty	N
117.	$75m for youth work projects	Y
118.	Allow Angolan military assistance	Y
119.	Suspend defense payments for abuse	N
120.	Drop SS COLAs/$12b tax increase	N
121.	Approve $1.5b for 21 MX missiles	Y
122.	Emergency farm credit/revisions	Y
123.	Duty on Taiwan/Hong Kong/S Korea	Y
124.	Limit steel imports to 17%	Y
125.	Cut $ to schools that bar prayer	Y
126.	$50b-taxes; cut Medicare/spending	N
127.	Limit Pershing II/cruise in Europe	N
128.	Delete $7.1b for 34 B-1 bombers	N
129.	Bar purchase of Sergeant York guns	N
130.	El Salvador military/economic aid	Y
131.	Bar mining of Nicaraguan waters	?
132.	Physician fee freeze for Medicare	Y
133.	$49b in "sin"/phone/insurance taxes	N
134.	Allow sale of Conrail	Y
135.	Equal Rights Amendment	N
136.	Authorize Marines in Lebanon	N
137.	Eminent domain for coal companies	N
138.	Prohibit EPA clean air sanctions	N

SHELBY, RICHARD C. (continued)

139.	SS retirement age increase/reforms	Y	142.	Highway-gas tax bill	N
140.	Auto domestic content requirement	Y	143.	Cut $5b from defense for Medicare	N
141.	Delete jobs program funding	N	144.	Emergency housing aid of $1b	Y

Presidential Support Score: 1991 - 69% 1990 - 55%

ALASKA

STEVENS, TED -- Alaska [Republican]. Term Began/Expires: 1991/1996. Prior Terms: House: 1965-68; Senate: 1968 (Special Appointment)-1990. Born: November 18, 1923; Indianapolis, IN. Education: Oregon State College; University of California; Harvard Law School (LL.B.). Military Service: U.S. Air Force, 1943-46. Occupation: Attorney, Northcutt Ely (1950-52), Collins & Clasby (1953); U.S. states attorney (1953-56); legislative counselman, Department of Interior (1956-58); assistant to the secretary of Interior (1958-60); solicitor, Department of Interior (1960-61); attorney (1961-68).

1. Prohibit MFN status for China	N	43. Allow sale of assault weapons	Y
2. Kill-Tie welfare to school attendance	N	44. Retraining aid for coal miners	Y
3. Limit credit card interest rates	Y	45. Kill-Raise car emission standards	?
4. Confirm Gates as head of CIA	Y	46. Pull EPA nuclear plant authority	Y
5. Adoption of national energy policies	Y	47. Defer Chinese students' deportation	N
6. Kill-Restrict NEA use of funds	Y	48. Cut in capital gains tax	Y
7. Unemployment benefits extension	N	49. Establish CIA inspector general	N
8. Confirm Thomas to Supreme Court	Y	50. Kill-Sanctions against China	Y
9. Raise eligibility for unpaid leave	Y	51. Bar drug testing to receive AFDC	Y
10. Notify parents of minors' abortions	N	52. Kill-Allow force against drug planes	N
11. Move $3b from defense to domestic	N	53. Include illegal aliens in census	N
12. End production of B-2 bomber	N	54. Restitution to Japanese interned	Y
13. Cut SDI $1b to reduce deficit	N	55. Troop reduction in Europe of 50%	N
14. Maintain strategic stability-Soviets	N	56. Increase SDI research to $4.3b	Y
15. Kill-Allow women as combat pilots	N	57. Kill-Pay homeless below min wage	Y
16. Kill-Allow HIV tests before surgery	N	58. Ban airline smoking within US	Y
17. Strike $12b aid to Int'l Mon Fund	N	59. Bar transfer of FS-X technology	N
18. Raise Senate salary/omit honoraria	Y	60. Limit liability for oil spills	N
19. Reduce space station funding $1.9b	N	61. Restructure S&L industry	N
20. Kill-Eliminate supercollider funds	Y	62. Ban $ to illegal foreign activities	N
21. Req 5-day handgun waiting period	N	63. Req immigrant fluency in English	Y
22. Life in prison instead of death	N	64. Allow aliens' families to stay in US	N
23. Exceptions to exclusionary rule	Y	65. Expand child care aid/tax credit	N
24. Ban race as death sentence factor	Y	66. Raise minimum wage w/subminimum	N
25. Campaign finance revisions	N	67. Freeze outlays except SS/Medicare	N
26. Kill-Term limits for senators	N	68. Kill-Shift $5b of DOD to domestic	Y
27. Require four presidential debates	?	69. Confirm Tower as sec of defense	Y
28. Tighten ban on vertical price fixing	N	70. Bar abortion $ except to save mother	N
29. Kill-Freeze discretionary budget	Y	71. Kill-Warn AIDS carriers' spouses	N
30. Provide $30b for failed S&Ls	Y	72. Allow religious schools to bar gays	Y
31. Allow use of force against Iraq	Y	73. 60 days' notice of plant closings	N
32. Allow $15b in foreign aid for 1991	Y	74. Allow poison pills in corp takeovers	N
33. Civil Rights Act of 1990	N	75. Kill-Workfare program	N
34. Block cancellation of Egypt's debt	N	76. Prohibit employee polygraph testing	Y
35. Cut El Salvador military aid 50%	Y	77. Cap Medicare patients' liability	Y
36. Reduce troops in NATO by 30,000	N	78. Revise unfair trade practices	N
37. Req increases in auto fuel efficiency	N	79. Kill-Shift SDI $ to conv weapons	Y
38. Bar taxpayer funding of campaigns	Y	80. Kill-Shift SDI $ to accidental launch	N
39. Limit textile import growth to 1%	Y	81. Kill-Shift MX $ to supplies/parts	Y
40. Amendment to ban flag desecration	Y	82. Kill-Buy America provision at DOD	N
41. Let fed emp be politically active	Y	83. Allow nuclear testing-5 + kilotons	Y
42. Reauthorize Amtrak-veto override	N	84. Allow SALT II to be exceeded	Y

STEVENS, TED (continued)

85. $ to vets exposed to nuclear bomb	N	
86. Warn workers of disease exposure	N	
87. Restore four civil rights laws	Y	
88. Disapprove uranium sales to Japan	N	
89. Notify Congress of covert operations	Y	
90. Approval of $36m in Contra aid	Y	
91. $18b deficit reduction compromise	Y	
92. Allow sale of hard-to-detect guns	Y	
93. Catastrophic health insurance	Y	
94. Bork nomination to Supreme Court	Y	
95. Kill-Void Panama Canal treaties	Y	
96. Kill-Insurance denial to AIDS+	N	
97. Keep diplomatic immunity intact	Y	
98. Produce Bigeye nerve gas bomb	Y	
99. Balanced budget by '93-via targets	Y	
100. Allow ASAT missile tests in space	Y	
101. Limit space-based/ABM system tests	N	
102. Force reduction in trade barriers	N	
103. Repeal windfall profit tax on oil	Y	
104. $1b/two year aid for the homeless	?	
105. Disallow $30m for AZT to poor	N	
106. Bar AIDS test-immigrants/marriage	N	
107. Kill-Biennial budget approval	N	
108. Fairness doctrine in broadcasting	N	
109. Raise speed limit to 65 mph	Y	
110. Immigration reform/alien amnesty	Y	
111. South Africa sanctions-veto override	N	
112. Kill-Use of military in drug war	Y	
113. Tax overhaul to revise income tax	Y	
114. Submit nuclear test ban treaties	N	
115. Prohibit sale of Stinger missiles	N
116. Prohibit binary chemical weapons	N
117. Kill-$10/barrel oil tariff increase	Y
118. Grant tax amnesty provisions	Y
119. Block Saudi arms sale-veto override	N
120. Balanced budget amendment	Y
121. Include veterans in spending cuts	Y
122. Bar $ to hazardous substance victims	Y
123. Allow seasonal workers in the US	Y
124. Let fed courts rule on school prayer	Y
125. Presidential line-item veto	Y
126. Ease Gun Control Act of 1968	Y
127. Kill-Req 14-day wait for handguns	Y
128. Kill-15% min tax on corporations	Y
129. Drop Social Security COLA	Y
130. Freeze funding for all programs	N
131. Kill-Nuclear weapon freeze	Y
132. Keep decision narrowing Title IX	Y
133. Raise drinking age to 21	Y
134. Allow production of MX missile	Y
135. Raise taxes/cut spending by $140b	Y
136. School prayer amendment	Y
137. Capital punishment-federal crimes	Y
138. Ban government officials from taping	N
139. Martin Luther King holiday	Y
140. Authorize Marines in Lebanon	Y
141. Amendment making abortion illegal	N
142. Delete $1.2b for jobs creation	Y
143. Keep tobacco price supports	Y
144. Emergency housing aid of $5.1b	Y

Presidential Support Score: 1991 - 83%   1990 - 72%

MURKOWSKI, FRANK H. -- Alaska [Republican]. Term Began/Expires: 1987/1992. Prior Terms: Senate: 1981-86. Born: March 28, 1933, Seattle, WA. Education: University of Santa Clara; Seattle University (B.A.). Military Service: U.S. Coast Guard, 1955-56. Occupation: Banker; Alaska commissioner of economic development (1966-70); president, Alaska Bankers Assn. (1972); president, Alaska Chamber of Commerce (1977); president, Alaska National Bank of the North (1971-80).

1. Prohibit MFN status for China	N	
2. Kill-Tie welfare to school attendance	N	
3. Limit credit card interest rates	Y	
4. Confirm Gates as head of CIA	Y	
5. Adoption of national energy policies	Y	
6. Kill-Restrict NEA use of funds	Y	
7. Unemployment benefits extension	N	
8. Confirm Thomas to Supreme Court	Y	
9. Raise eligibility for unpaid leave	N	
10. Notify parents of minors' abortions	Y	
11. Move $3b from defense to domestic	N	
12. End production of B-2 bomber	N	
13. Cut SDI $1b to reduce deficit	N	
14. Maintain strategic stability-Soviets	N	
15. Kill-Allow women as combat pilots	N	
16. Kill-Allow HIV tests before surgery	N	
17. Strike $12b aid to Int'l Mon Fund	N	
18. Raise Senate salary/omit honoraria	Y	
19. Reduce space station funding $1.9b	N	
20. Kill-Eliminate supercollider funds	Y	
21. Req 5-day handgun waiting period	N	
22. Life in prison instead of death	N	
23. Exceptions to exclusionary rule	Y	
24. Ban race as death sentence factor	Y
25. Campaign finance revisions	N
26. Kill-Term limits for senators	N
27. Require four presidential debates	N
28. Tighten ban on vertical price fixing	Y
29. Kill-Freeze discretionary budget	N
30. Provide $30b for failed S&Ls	Y
31. Allow use of force against Iraq	Y
32. Allow $15b in foreign aid for 1991	Y
33. Civil Rights Act of 1990	N
34. Block cancellation of Egypt's debt	N
35. Cut El Salvador military aid 50%	Y
36. Reduce troops in NATO by 30,000	N
37. Req increases in auto fuel efficiency	N
38. Bar taxpayer funding of campaigns	Y
39. Limit textile import growth to 1%	Y
40. Amendment to ban flag desecration	Y
41. Let fed emp be politically active	N
42. Reauthorize Amtrak-veto override	N
43. Allow sale of assault weapons	Y
44. Retraining aid for coal miners	N
45. Kill-Raise car emission standards	Y
46. Pull EPA nuclear plant authority	Y

MURKOWSKI, FRANK H. (continued)

47. Defer Chinese students' deportation	N	
48. Cut in capital gains tax	Y	
49. Establish CIA inspector general	N	
50. Kill-Sanctions against China	N	
51. Bar drug testing to receive AFDC	N	
52. Kill-Allow force against drug planes	Y	
53. Include illegal aliens in census	N	
54. Restitution to Japanese interned	Y	
55. Troop reduction in Europe of 50%	N	
56. Increase SDI research to $4.3b	Y	
57. Kill-Pay homeless below min wage	N	
58. Ban airline smoking within US	Y	
59. Bar transfer of FS-X technology	N	
60. Limit liability for oil spills	N	
61. Restructure S&L industry	N	
62. Ban $ to illegal foreign activities	N	
63. Req immigrant fluency in English	Y	
64. Allow aliens' families to stay in US	N	
65. Expand child care aid/tax credit	N	
66. Raise minimum wage w/subminimum	N	
67. Freeze outlays except SS/Medicare	N	
68. Kill-Shift $5b of DOD to domestic	Y	
69. Confirm Tower as sec of defense	Y	
70. Bar abortion $ except to save mother	Y	
71. Kill-Warn AIDS carriers' spouses	N	
72. Allow religious schools to bar gays	Y	
73. 60 days' notice of plant closings	?	
74. Allow poison pills in corp takeovers	N	
75. Kill-Workfare program	N	
76. Prohibit employee polygraph testing	Y	
77. Cap Medicare patients' liability	Y	
78. Revise unfair trade practices	N	
79. Kill-Shift SDI $ to conv weapons	Y	
80. Kill-Shift SDI $ to accidental launch	N	
81. Kill-Shift MX $ to supplies/parts	Y	
82. Kill-Buy America provision at DOD	Y	
83. Allow nuclear testing-5+ kilotons	N	
84. Allow SALT II to be exceeded	Y	
85. $ to vets exposed to nuclear bomb	N	
86. Warn workers of disease exposure	N	
87. Restore four civil rights laws	Y	
88. Disapprove uranium sales to Japan	N	
89. Notify Congress of covert operations	Y	
90. Approval of $36m in Contra aid	Y	
91. $18b deficit reduction compromise	?	
92. Allow sale of hard-to-detect guns	Y	
93. Catastrophic health insurance	Y	
94. Bork nomination to Supreme Court	Y	
95. Kill-Void Panama Canal treaties	N	

96. Kill-Insurance denial to AIDS+	N	
97. Keep diplomatic immunity intact	N	
98. Produce Bigeye nerve gas bomb	Y	
99. Balanced budget by '93-via targets	Y	
100. Allow ASAT missile tests in space	Y	
101. Limit space-based/ABM system tests	N	
102. Force reduction in trade barriers	Y	
103. Repeal windfall profit tax on oil	Y	
104. $1b/two year aid for the homeless	Y	
105. Disallow $30m for AZT to poor	Y	
106. Bar AIDS test-immigrants/marriage	N	
107. Kill-Biennial budget approval	N	
108. Fairness doctrine in broadcasting	N	
109. Raise speed limit to 65 mph	Y	
110. Immigration reform/alien amnesty	#	
111. South Africa sanctions-veto override	Y	
112. Kill-Use of military in drug war	N	
113. Tax overhaul to revise income tax	Y	
114. Submit nuclear test ban treaties	Y	
115. Prohibit sale of Stinger missiles	N	
116. Prohibit binary chemical weapons	N	
117. Kill-$10/barrel oil tariff increase	Y	
118. Grant tax amnesty provisions	?	
119. Block Saudi arms sale-veto override	Y	
120. Balanced budget amendment	Y	
121. Include veterans in spending cuts	Y	
122. Bar $ to hazardous substance victims	Y	
123. Allow seasonal workers in the US	Y	
124. Let fed courts rule on school prayer	N	
125. Presidential line-item veto	Y	
126. Ease Gun Control Act of 1968	Y	
127. Kill-Req 14-day wait for handguns	Y	
128. Kill-15% min tax on corporations	Y	
129. Drop Social Security COLA	Y	
130. Freeze funding for all programs	N	
131. Kill-Nuclear weapon freeze	Y	
132. Keep decision narrowing Title IX	Y	
133. Raise drinking age to 21	Y	
134. Allow production of MX missile	Y	
135. Raise taxes/cut spending by $140b	Y	
136. School prayer amendment	Y	
137. Capital punishment-federal crimes	?	
138. Ban government officials from taping	N	
139. Martin Luther King holiday	N	
140. Authorize Marines in Lebanon	Y	
141. Amendment making abortion illegal	Y	
142. Delete $1.2b for jobs creation	Y	
143. Keep tobacco price supports	?	
144. Emergency housing aid of $5.1b	N	

Presidential Support Score: 1991 - 89%   1990 - 75%

ARIZONA

DeCONCINI, DENNIS -- Arizona [Democrat]. Term Began/Expires: 1989/1994. Prior Terms: Senate: 1976-88. Born: May 8, 1937; Tucson, AZ. Education: University of Arizona (B.A., LL.B.). Military Service: U.S. Army, 1959-60; Army Reserves, 1960-67. Occupation: Attorney; Pima county attorney.

DeCONCINI, DENNIS (continued)

1.	Prohibit MFN status for China	Y
2.	Kill-Tie welfare to school attendance	Y
3.	Limit credit card interest rates	Y
4.	Confirm Gates as head of CIA	N
5.	Adoption of national energy policies	Y
6.	Kill-Restrict NEA use of funds	Y
7.	Unemployment benefits extension	Y
8.	Confirm Thomas to Supreme Court	Y
9.	Raise eligibility for unpaid leave	Y
10.	Notify parents of minors' abortions	Y
11.	Move $3b from defense to domestic	?
12.	End production of B-2 bomber	Y
13.	Cut SDI $1b to reduce deficit	Y
14.	Maintain strategic stability-Soviets	Y
15.	Kill-Allow women as combat pilots	N
16.	Kill-Allow HIV tests before surgery	N
17.	Strike $12b aid to Int'l Mon Fund	Y
18.	Raise Senate salary/omit honoraria	N
19.	Reduce space station funding $1.9b	Y
20.	Kill-Eliminate supercollider funds	N
21.	Req 5-day handgun waiting period	N
22.	Life in prison instead of death	N
23.	Exceptions to exclusionary rule	Y
24.	Ban race as death sentence factor	+
25.	Campaign finance revisions	Y
26.	Kill-Term limits for senators	Y
27.	Require four presidential debates	N
28.	Tighten ban on vertical price fixing	Y
29.	Kill-Freeze discretionary budget	N
30.	Provide $30b for failed S&Ls	N
31.	Allow use of force against Iraq	N
32.	Allow $15b in foreign aid for 1991	Y
33.	Civil Rights Act of 1990	Y
34.	Block cancellation of Egypt's debt	N
35.	Cut El Salvador military aid 50%	Y
36.	Reduce troops in NATO by 30,000	Y
37.	Req increases in auto fuel efficiency	Y
38.	Bar taxpayer funding of campaigns	--
39.	Limit textile import growth to 1%	Y
40.	Amendment to ban flag desecration	Y
41.	Let fed emp be politically active	Y
42.	Reauthorize Amtrak-veto override	Y
43.	Allow sale of assault weapons	N
44.	Retraining aid for coal miners	Y
45.	Kill-Raise car emission standards	N
46.	Pull EPA nuclear plant authority	Y
47.	Defer Chinese students' deportation	Y
48.	Cut in capital gains tax	Y
49.	Establish CIA inspector general	Y
50.	Kill-Sanctions against China	N
51.	Bar drug testing to receive AFDC	Y
52.	Kill-Allow force against drug planes	N
53.	Include illegal aliens in census	Y
54.	Restitution to Japanese interned	Y
55.	Troop reduction in Europe of 50%	Y
56.	Increase SDI research to $4.3b	N
57.	Kill-Pay homeless below min wage	Y
58.	Ban airline smoking within US	Y
59.	Bar transfer of FS-X technology	Y
60.	Limit liability for oil spills	N
61.	Restructure S&L industry	Y
62.	Ban $ to illegal foreign activities	Y
63.	Req immigrant fluency in English	N
64.	Allow aliens' families to stay in US	Y
65.	Expand child care aid/tax credit	Y
66.	Raise minimum wage w/subminimum	Y
67.	Freeze outlays except SS/Medicare	N
68.	Kill-Shift $5b of DOD to domestic	N
69.	Confirm Tower as sec of defense	N
70.	Bar abortion $ except to save mother	Y
71.	Kill-Warn AIDS carriers' spouses	N
72.	Allow religious schools to bar gays	Y
73.	60 days' notice of plant closings	Y
74.	Allow poison pills in corp takeovers	Y
75.	Kill-Workfare program	N
76.	Prohibit employee polygraph testing	Y
77.	Cap Medicare patients' liability	Y
78.	Revise unfair trade practices	Y
79.	Kill-Shift SDI $ to conv weapons	N
80.	Kill-Shift SDI $ to accidental launch	Y
81.	Kill-Shift MX $ to supplies/parts	Y
82.	Kill-Buy America provision at DOD	N
83.	Allow nuclear testing-5+ kilotons	N
84.	Allow SALT II to be exceeded	Y
85.	$ to vets exposed to nuclear bomb	+
86.	Warn workers of disease exposure	Y
87.	Restore four civil rights laws	Y
88.	Disapprove uranium sales to Japan	N
89.	Notify Congress of covert operations	Y
90.	Approval of $36m in Contra aid	N
91.	$18b deficit reduction compromise	Y
92.	Allow sale of hard-to-detect guns	Y
93.	Catastrophic health insurance	Y
94.	Bork nomination to Supreme Court	N
95.	Kill-Void Panama Canal treaties	Y
96.	Kill-Insurance denial to AIDS+	N
97.	Keep diplomatic immunity intact	N
98.	Produce Bigeye nerve gas bomb	N
99.	Balanced budget by '93-via targets	N
100.	Allow ASAT missile tests in space	Y
101.	Limit space-based/ABM system tests	Y
102.	Force reduction in trade barriers	Y
103.	Repeal windfall profit tax on oil	N
104.	$1b/two year aid for the homeless	Y
105.	Disallow $30m for AZT to poor	N
106.	Bar AIDS test-immigrants/marriage	Y
107.	Kill-Biennial budget approval	Y
108.	Fairness doctrine in broadcasting	Y
109.	Raise speed limit to 65 mph	Y
110.	Immigration reform/alien amnesty	--
111.	South Africa sanctions-veto override	Y
112.	Kill-Use of military in drug war	N
113.	Tax overhaul to revise income tax	N
114.	Submit nuclear test ban treaties	Y
115.	Prohibit sale of Stinger missiles	Y
116.	Prohibit binary chemical weapons	N
117.	Kill-$10/barrel oil tariff increase	Y
118.	Grant tax amnesty provisions	N
119.	Block Saudi arms sale-veto override	Y
120.	Balanced budget amendment	N
121.	Include veterans in spending cuts	N
122.	Bar $ to hazardous substance victims	N
123.	Allow seasonal workers in the US	Y
124.	Let fed courts rule on school prayer	Y
125.	Presidential line-item veto	#
126.	Ease Gun Control Act of 1968	Y
127.	Kill-Req 14-day wait for handguns	Y
128.	Kill-15% min tax on corporations	Y

DeCONCINI, DENNIS (continued)

129. Drop Social Security COLA	N	137. Capital punishment-federal crimes	Y
130. Freeze funding for all programs	Y	138. Ban government officials from taping	N
131. Kill-Nuclear weapon freeze	N	139. Martin Luther King holiday	Y
132. Keep decision narrowing Title IX	N	140. Authorize Marines in Lebanon	N
133. Raise drinking age to 21	Y	141. Amendment making abortion illegal	Y
134. Allow production of MX missile	#	142. Delete $1.2b for jobs creation	N
135. Raise taxes/cut spending by $140b	N	143. Keep tobacco price supports	N
136. School prayer amendment	N	144. Emergency housing aid of $5.1b	Y

Presidential Support Score: 1991 - 41% 1990 - 40%

McCAIN, JOHN -- Arizona [Republican]. Term Began/Expires: 1987/1992. Prior Terms: House: 1983-86. Born: August 29, 1936, Panama Canal Zone. Education: U.S. Naval Academy; National War College. Military Service: U.S. Navy, 1958-81. Occupation: Director, Navy Liaison Office.

1. Prohibit MFN status for China	N	48. Cut in capital gains tax	Y
2. Kill-Tie welfare to school attendance	N	49. Establish CIA inspector general	Y
3. Limit credit card interest rates	Y	50. Kill-Sanctions against China	N
4. Confirm Gates as head of CIA	Y	51. Bar drug testing to receive AFDC	N
5. Adoption of national energy policies	Y	52. Kill-Allow force against drug planes	Y
6. Kill-Restrict NEA use of funds	N	53. Include illegal aliens in census	Y
7. Unemployment benefits extension	N	54. Restitution to Japanese interned	N
8. Confirm Thomas to Supreme Court	Y	55. Troop reduction in Europe of 50%	N
9. Raise eligibility for unpaid leave	Y	56. Increase SDI research to $4.3b	Y
10. Notify parents of minors' abortions	Y	57. Kill-Pay homeless below min wage	N
11. Move $3b from defense to domestic	N	58. Ban airline smoking within US	Y
12. End production of B-2 bomber	Y	59. Bar transfer of FS-X technology	N
13. Cut SDI $1b to reduce deficit	N	60. Limit liability for oil spills	N
14. Maintain strategic stability-Soviets	N	61. Restructure S&L industry	N
15. Kill-Allow women as combat pilots	Y	62. Ban $ to illegal foreign activities	N
16. Kill-Allow HIV tests before surgery	N	63. Req immigrant fluency in English	N
17. Strike $12b aid to Int'l Mon Fund	N	64. Allow aliens' families to stay in US	Y
18. Raise Senate salary/omit honoraria	Y	65. Expand child care aid/tax credit	N
19. Reduce space station funding $1.9b	N	66. Raise minimum wage w/subminimum	N
20. Kill-Eliminate supercollider funds	Y	67. Freeze outlays except SS/Medicare	N
21. Req 5-day handgun waiting period	N	68. Kill-Shift $5b of DOD to domestic	Y
22. Life in prison instead of death	N	69. Confirm Tower as sec of defense	Y
23. Exceptions to exclusionary rule	Y	70. Bar abortion $ except to save mother	Y
24. Ban race as death sentence factor	Y	71. Kill-Warn AIDS carriers' spouses	N
25. Campaign finance revisions	Y	72. Allow religious schools to bar gays	Y
26. Kill-Term limits for senators	N	73. 60 days' notice of plant closings	Y
27. Require four presidential debates	N	74. Allow poison pills in corp takeovers	N
28. Tighten ban on vertical price fixing	N	75. Kill-Workfare program	N
29. Kill-Freeze discretionary budget	N	76. Prohibit employee polygraph testing	N
30. Provide $30b for failed S&Ls	Y	77. Cap Medicare patients' liability	N
31. Allow use of force against Iraq	Y	78. Revise unfair trade practices	N
32. Allow $15b in foreign aid for 1991	Y	79. Kill-Shift SDI $ to conv weapons	Y
33. Civil Rights Act of 1990	N	80. Kill-Shift SDI $ to accidental launch	N
34. Block cancellation of Egypt's debt	N	81. Kill-Shift MX $ to supplies/parts	N
35. Cut El Salvador military aid 50%	N	82. Kill-Buy America provision at DOD	Y
36. Reduce troops in NATO by 30,000	N	83. Allow nuclear testing-5+ kilotons	Y
37. Req increases in auto fuel efficiency	Y	84. Allow SALT II to be exceeded	Y
38. Bar taxpayer funding of campaigns	Y	85. $ to vets exposed to nuclear bomb	N
39. Limit textile import growth to 1%	N	86. Warn workers of disease exposure	N
40. Amendment to ban flag desecration	Y	87. Restore four civil rights laws	N
41. Let fed emp be politically active	Y	88. Disapprove uranium sales to Japan	N
42. Reauthorize Amtrak-veto override	N	89. Notify Congress of covert operations	N
43. Allow sale of assault weapons	Y	90. Approval of $36m in Contra aid	Y
44. Retraining aid for coal miners	N	91. $18b deficit reduction compromise	N
45. Kill-Raise car emission standards	N	92. Allow sale of hard-to-detect guns	Y
46. Pull EPA nuclear plant authority	Y	93. Catastrophic health insurance	Y
47. Defer Chinese students' deportation	N	94. Bork nomination to Supreme Court	Y

McCAIN, JOHN (continued)

95. Kill-Void Panama Canal treaties	N	
96. Kill-Insurance denial to AIDS+	N	
97. Keep diplomatic immunity intact	?	
98. Produce Bigeye nerve gas bomb	Y	
99. Balanced budget by '93-via targets	Y	
100. Allow ASAT missile tests in space	Y	
101. Limit space-based/ABM system tests	N	
102. Force reduction in trade barriers	N	

103. Repeal windfall profit tax on oil	Y	
104. $1b/two year aid for the homeless	?	
105. Disallow $30m for AZT to poor	N	
106. Bar AIDS test-immigrants/marriage	N	
107. Kill-Biennial budget approval	N	
108. Fairness doctrine in broadcasting	N	
109. Raise speed limit to 65 mph	Y	

The following are House measures voted on between 1983-1986:

99. Immigration reform/alien amnesty	N	
100. South Africa sanctions-veto override	Y	
101. Tax overhaul to revise income tax	Y	
102. Use of military in drug war	Y	
103. Delete 12 MX/add conventional wpn	N	
104. Raise speed limit to 65 mph	+	
105. Require Pentagon to buy US goods	N	
106. AIDS insurance non-discrimination	N	
107. Prohibit Saudi arms sales	Y	
108. Ease Gun Control Act of 1968	Y	
109. Bar interstate handgun transport	N	
110. Make company emissions known	N	
111. Allow toxic victims to sue in fed ct	N	
112. Superfund waste cleanup of $10b	Y	
113. 90 days notice of plant closings	N	
114. $20b in Medicare cuts/tax increases	N	
115. Spending cuts and tax increases	N	
116. Set school lunch lmt-250% poverty	Y	
117. $75m for youth work projects	N	
118. Allow Angolan military assistance	Y	
119. Suspend defense payments for abuse	N	

120. Drop SS COLAs/$12b tax increase	N	
121. Approve $1.5b for 21 MX missiles	Y	
122. Emergency farm credit/revisions	Y	
123. Duty on Taiwan/Hong Kong/S Korea	N	
124. Limit steel imports to 17%	Y	
125. Cut $ to schools that bar prayer	Y	
126. $50b-taxes; cut Medicare/spending	N	
127. Limit Pershing II/cruise in Europe	N	
128. Delete $7.1b for 34 B-1 bombers	N	
129. Bar purchase of Sergeant York guns	N	
130. El Salvador military/economic aid	Y	
131. Bar mining of Nicaraguan waters	N	
132. Physician fee freeze for Medicare	Y	
133. $49b in "sin"/phone/insurance taxes	N	
134. Allow sale of Conrail	Y	
135. Equal Rights Amendment	N	
136. Authorize Marines in Lebanon	N	
137. Eminent domain for coal companies	Y	
138. Prohibit EPA clean air sanctions	?	
139. SS retirement age increase/reforms	Y	

Presidential Support Score: 1991 - 86%   1990 - 74%

ARKANSAS

BUMPERS, DALE -- Arkansas [Democrat]. Term Began/Expires: 1987/1992. Prior Terms: Senate: 1975-86. Born: August 12, 1925; Charleston, AR. Education: University of Arkansas; Northwestern University Law School (LL.B.). Military Service: Marine Corps, 1943-46. Occupation: Owner, Charleston Hardware and Furniture Co. (1951-66); owner, Angus Breeding Farm (1966-70); special justice, Arkansas Supreme Court; governor of Arkansas (1970-74).

1. Prohibit MFN status for China	Y	
2. Kill-Tie welfare to school attendance	N	
3. Limit credit card interest rates	Y	
4. Confirm Gates as head of CIA	N	
5. Adoption of national energy policies	Y	
6. Kill-Restrict NEA use of funds	Y	
7. Unemployment benefits extension	Y	
8. Confirm Thomas to Supreme Court	N	
9. Raise eligibility for unpaid leave	Y	
10. Notify parents of minors' abortions	N	
11. Move $3b from defense to domestic	N	
12. End production of B-2 bomber	Y	
13. Cut SDI $1b to reduce deficit	Y	
14. Maintain strategic stability-Soviets	Y	

15. Kill-Allow women as combat pilots	Y	
16. Kill-Allow HIV tests before surgery	N	
17. Strike $12b aid to Int'l Mon Fund	Y	
18. Raise Senate salary/omit honoraria	N	
19. Reduce space station funding $1.9b	Y	
20. Kill-Eliminate supercollider funds	N	
21. Req 5-day handgun waiting period	Y	
22. Life in prison instead of death	N	
23. Exceptions to exclusionary rule	N	
24. Ban race as death sentence factor	Y	
25. Campaign finance revisions	Y	
26. Kill-Term limits for senators	Y	
27. Require four presidential debates	?	
28. Tighten ban on vertical price fixing	Y	

BUMPERS, DALE (continued)

29. Kill-Freeze discretionary budget	Y	
30. Provide $30b for failed S&Ls	Y	
31. Allow use of force against Iraq	N	
32. Allow $15b in foreign aid for 1991	Y	
33. Civil Rights Act of 1990	Y	
34. Block cancellation of Egypt's debt	Y	
35. Cut El Salvador military aid 50%	Y	
36. Reduce troops in NATO by 30,000	Y	
37. Req increases in auto fuel efficiency	Y	
38. Bar taxpayer funding of campaigns	N	
39. Limit textile import growth to 1%	Y	
40. Amendment to ban flag desecration	N	
41. Let fed emp be politically active	Y	
42. Reauthorize Amtrak-veto override	Y	
43. Allow sale of assault weapons	N	
44. Retraining aid for coal miners	Y	
45. Kill-Raise car emission standards	Y	
46. Pull EPA nuclear plant authority	N	
47. Defer Chinese students' deportation	Y	
48. Cut in capital gains tax	N	
49. Establish CIA inspector general	Y	
50. Kill-Sanctions against China	Y	
51. Bar drug testing to receive AFDC	Y	
52. Kill-Allow force against drug planes	Y	
53. Include illegal aliens in census	?	
54. Restitution to Japanese interned	Y	
55. Troop reduction in Europe of 50%	Y	
56. Increase SDI research to $4.3b	N	
57. Kill-Pay homeless below min wage	N	
58. Ban airline smoking within US	Y	
59. Bar transfer of FS-X technology	Y	
60. Limit liability for oil spills	N	
61. Restructure S&L industry	Y	
62. Ban $ to illegal foreign activities	Y	
63. Req immigrant fluency in English	N	
64. Allow aliens' families to stay in US	Y	
65. Expand child care aid/tax credit	Y	
66. Raise minimum wage w/subminimum	Y	
67. Freeze outlays except SS/Medicare	N	
68. Kill-Shift $5b of DOD to domestic	N	
69. Confirm Tower as sec of defense	N	
70. Bar abortion $ except to save mother	N	
71. Kill-Warn AIDS carriers' spouses	Y	
72. Allow religious schools to bar gays	N	
73. 60 days' notice of plant closings	Y	
74. Allow poison pills in corp takeovers	N	
75. Kill-Workfare program	N	
76. Prohibit employee polygraph testing	Y	
77. Cap Medicare patients' liability	Y	
78. Revise unfair trade practices	Y	
79. Kill-Shift SDI $ to conv weapons	N	
80. Kill-Shift SDI $ to accidental launch	Y	
81. Kill-Shift MX $ to supplies/parts	N	
82. Kill-Buy America provision at DOD	N	
83. Allow nuclear testing-5+ kilotons	N	
84. Allow SALT II to be exceeded	N	
85. $ to vets exposed to nuclear bomb	Y	
86. Warn workers of disease exposure	N	

87. Restore four civil rights laws	Y	
88. Disapprove uranium sales to Japan	?	
89. Notify Congress of covert operations	Y	
90. Approval of $36m in Contra aid	N	
91. $18b deficit reduction compromise	Y	
92. Allow sale of hard-to-detect guns	N	
93. Catastrophic health insurance	Y	
94. Bork nomination to Supreme Court	N	
95. Kill-Void Panama Canal treaties	Y	
96. Kill-Insurance denial to AIDS+	Y	
97. Keep diplomatic immunity intact	N	
98. Produce Bigeye nerve gas bomb	N	
99. Balanced budget by '93-via targets	Y	
100. Allow ASAT missile tests in space	N	
101. Limit space-based/ABM system tests	Y	
102. Force reduction in trade barriers	Y	
103. Repeal windfall profit tax on oil	Y	
104. $1b/two year aid for the homeless	Y	
105. Disallow $30m for AZT to poor	N	
106. Bar AIDS test-immigrants/marriage	Y	
107. Kill-Biennial budget approval	Y	
108. Fairness doctrine in broadcasting	Y	
109. Raise speed limit to 65 mph	Y	
110. Immigration reform/alien amnesty	N	
111. South Africa sanctions-veto override	Y	
112. Kill-Use of military in drug war	Y	
113. Tax overhaul to revise income tax	Y	
114. Submit nuclear test ban treaties	Y	
115. Prohibit sale of Stinger missiles	N	
116. Prohibit binary chemical weapons	N	
117. Kill-$10/barrel oil tariff increase	Y	
118. Grant tax amnesty provisions	N	
119. Block Saudi arms sale-veto override	Y	
120. Balanced budget amendment	N	
121. Include veterans in spending cuts	N	
122. Bar $ to hazardous substance victims	N	
123. Allow seasonal workers in the US	Y	
124. Let fed courts rule on school prayer	Y	
125. Presidential line-item veto	N	
126. Ease Gun Control Act of 1968	Y	
127. Kill-Req 14-day wait for handguns	Y	
128. Kill-15% min tax on corporations	N	
129. Drop Social Security COLA	N	
130. Freeze funding for all programs	Y	
131. Kill-Nuclear weapon freeze	N	
132. Keep decision narrowing Title IX	N	
133. Raise drinking age to 21	Y	
134. Allow production of MX missile	N	
135. Raise taxes/cut spending by $140b	N	
136. School prayer amendment	N	
137. Capital punishment-federal crimes	Y	
138. Ban government officials from taping	Y	
139. Martin Luther King holiday	Y	
140. Authorize Marines in Lebanon	N	
141. Amendment making abortion illegal	N	
142. Delete $1.2b for jobs creation	N	
143. Keep tobacco price supports	N	
144. Emergency housing aid of $5.1b	Y	

Presidential Support Score: 1991 - 40%   1990 - 35%

PRYOR, DAVID -- Arkansas [Democrat]. Term Began/Expires: 1991/1996. **Prior Terms:** House: 1965-72; Senate: 1979-90. Born: August 29, 1934; Camden, AR. Education:

PRYOR, DAVID (continued)
University of Arkansas (B.A., LL.B.). Occupation: Attorney, Pryor and Barnes; publisher; Arkansas representative.

1. Prohibit MFN status for China	Y	
2. Kill-Tie welfare to school attendance	Y	
3. Limit credit card interest rates	Y	
4. Confirm Gates as head of CIA	N	
5. Adoption of national energy policies	Y	
6. Kill-Restrict NEA use of funds	Y	
7. Unemployment benefits extension	Y	
8. Confirm Thomas to Supreme Court	N	
9. Raise eligibility for unpaid leave	?	
10. Notify parents of minors' abortions	N	
11. Move $3b from defense to domestic	N	
12. End production of B-2 bomber	?	
13. Cut SDI $1b to reduce deficit	#	
14. Maintain strategic stability-Soviets	?	
15. Kill-Allow women as combat pilots	?	
16. Kill-Allow HIV tests before surgery	?	
17. Strike $12b aid to Int'l Mon Fund	?	
18. Raise Senate salary/omit honoraria	#	
19. Reduce space station funding $1.9b	?	
20. Kill-Eliminate supercollider funds	?	
21. Req 5-day handgun waiting period	?	
22. Life in prison instead of death	?	
23. Exceptions to exclusionary rule	?	
24. Ban race as death sentence factor	?	
25. Campaign finance revisions	?	
26. Kill-Term limits for senators	?	
27. Require four presidential debates	?	
28. Tighten ban on vertical price fixing	?	
29. Kill-Freeze discretionary budget	?	
30. Provide $30b for failed S&Ls	N	
31. Allow use of force against Iraq	N	
32. Allow $15b in foreign aid for 1991	N	
33. Civil Rights Act of 1990	Y	
34. Block cancellation of Egypt's debt	Y	
35. Cut El Salvador military aid 50%	Y	
36. Reduce troops in NATO by 30,000	Y	
37. Req increases in auto fuel efficiency	Y	
38. Bar taxpayer funding of campaigns	N	
39. Limit textile import growth to 1%	Y	
40. Amendment to ban flag desecration	N	
41. Let fed emp be politically active	Y	
42. Reauthorize Amtrak-veto override	Y	
43. Allow sale of assault weapons	N	
44. Retraining aid for coal miners	N	
45. Kill-Raise car emission standards	Y	
46. Pull EPA nuclear plant authority	N	
47. Defer Chinese students' deportation	Y	
48. Cut in capital gains tax	N	
49. Establish CIA inspector general	Y	
50. Kill-Sanctions against China	N	
51. Bar drug testing to receive AFDC	Y	
52. Kill-Allow force against drug planes	N	
53. Include illegal aliens in census	Y	
54. Restitution to Japanese interned	Y	
55. Troop reduction in Europe of 50%	Y	
56. Increase SDI research to $4.3b	N	
57. Kill-Pay homeless below min wage	N	
58. Ban airline smoking within US	Y	
59. Bar transfer of FS-X technology	Y	
60. Limit liability for oil spills	N	
61. Restructure S&L industry	Y	

62. Ban $ to illegal foreign activities	Y	
63. Req immigrant fluency in English	N	
64. Allow aliens' families to stay in US	N	
65. Expand child care aid/tax credit	Y	
66. Raise minimum wage w/subminimum	Y	
67. Freeze outlays except SS/Medicare	N	
68. Kill-Shift $5b of DOD to domestic	?	
69. Confirm Tower as sec of defense	N	
70. Bar abortion $ except to save mother	N	
71. Kill-Warn AIDS carriers' spouses	Y	
72. Allow religious schools to bar gays	Y	
73. 60 days' notice of plant closings	Y	
74. Allow poison pills in corp takeovers	Y	
75. Kill-Workfare program	Y	
76. Prohibit employee polygraph testing	Y	
77. Cap Medicare patients' liability	Y	
78. Revise unfair trade practices	Y	
79. Kill-Shift SDI $ to conv weapons	N	
80. Kill-Shift SDI $ to accidental launch	Y	
81. Kill-Shift MX $ to supplies/parts	N	
82. Kill-Buy America provision at DOD	N	
83. Allow nuclear testing-5+ kilotons	Y	
84. Allow SALT II to be exceeded	N	
85. $ to vets exposed to nuclear bomb	Y	
86. Warn workers of disease exposure	N	
87. Restore four civil rights laws	Y	
88. Disapprove uranium sales to Japan	Y	
89. Notify Congress of covert operations	Y	
90. Approval of $36m in Contra aid	N	
91. $18b deficit reduction compromise	Y	
92. Allow sale of hard-to-detect guns	N	
93. Catastrophic health insurance	Y	
94. Bork nomination to Supreme Court	N	
95. Kill-Void Panama Canal treaties	Y	
96. Kill-Insurance denial to AIDS+	N	
97. Keep diplomatic immunity intact	Y	
98. Produce Bigeye nerve gas bomb	N	
99. Balanced budget by '93-via targets	Y	
100. Allow ASAT missile tests in space	N	
101. Limit space-based/ABM system tests	Y	
102. Force reduction in trade barriers	Y	
103. Repeal windfall profit tax on oil	#	
104. $1b/two year aid for the homeless	Y	
105. Disallow $30m for AZT to poor	N	
106. Bar AIDS test-immigrants/marriage	Y	
107. Kill-Biennial budget approval	Y	
108. Fairness doctrine in broadcasting	Y	
109. Raise speed limit to 65 mph	Y	
110. Immigration reform/alien amnesty	Y	
111. South Africa sanctions-veto override	Y	
112. Kill-Use of military in drug war	?	
113. Tax overhaul to revise income tax	?	
114. Submit nuclear test ban treaties	Y	
115. Prohibit sale of Stinger missiles	Y	
116. Prohibit binary chemical weapons	Y	
117. Kill-$10/barrel oil tariff increase	Y	
118. Grant tax amnesty provisions	N	
119. Block Saudi arms sale-veto override	Y	
120. Balanced budget amendment	Y	
121. Include veterans in spending cuts	N	
122. Bar $ to hazardous substance victims	N	

PRYOR, DAVID (continued)

123. Allow seasonal workers in the US	Y	
124. Let fed courts rule on school prayer	Y	
125. Presidential line-item veto	N	
126. Ease Gun Control Act of 1968	Y	
127. Kill-Req 14-day wait for handguns	Y	
128. Kill-15% min tax on corporations	N	
129. Drop Social Security COLA	N	
130. Freeze funding for all programs	Y	
131. Kill-Nuclear weapon freeze	?	
132. Keep decision narrowing Title IX	N	
133. Raise drinking age to 21	Y	
134. Allow production of MX missile	N	
135. Raise taxes/cut spending by $140b	Y	
136. School prayer amendment	Y	
137. Capital punishment-federal crimes	Y	
138. Ban government officials from taping	Y	
139. Martin Luther King holiday	Y	
140. Authorize Marines in Lebanon	N	
141. Amendment making abortion illegal	N	
142. Delete $1.2b for jobs creation	N	
143. Keep tobacco price supports	?	
144. Emergency housing aid of $5.1b	Y	

Presidential Support Score: 1991 - 19%   1990 - 34%

CALIFORNIA

CRANSTON, ALAN -- California [Democrat]. Term Began/Expires: 1987/1992. Prior Terms: Senate: 1969-86. Born: June 19, 1914; Palo Alto, CA. Education: Stanford University (B.A.). Military Service: U.S. Army, 1944-45. Occupation: Foreign correspondent, International News Service, Europe and Africa (1937-38); foreign language division, Office of War Information (1940-44); author; realtor property manager; state controller, California (1958-66).

1. Prohibit MFN status for China	Y	
2. Kill-Tie welfare to school attendance	Y	
3. Limit credit card interest rates	?	
4. Confirm Gates as head of CIA	?	
5. Adoption of national energy policies	N	
6. Kill-Restrict NEA use of funds	Y	
7. Unemployment benefits extension	Y	
8. Confirm Thomas to Supreme Court	N	
9. Raise eligibility for unpaid leave	Y	
10. Notify parents of minors' abortions	N	
11. Move $3b from defense to domestic	N	
12. End production of B-2 bomber	Y	
13. Cut SDI $1b to reduce deficit	Y	
14. Maintain strategic stability-Soviets	Y	
15. Kill-Allow women as combat pilots	N	
16. Kill-Allow HIV tests before surgery	Y	
17. Strike $12b aid to Int'l Mon Fund	N	
18. Raise Senate salary/omit honoraria	Y	
19. Reduce space station funding $1.9b	N	
20. Kill-Eliminate supercollider funds	N	
21. Req 5-day handgun waiting period	Y	
22. Life in prison instead of death	Y	
23. Exceptions to exclusionary rule	N	
24. Ban race as death sentence factor	N	
25. Campaign finance revisions	Y	
26. Kill-Term limits for senators	Y	
27. Require four presidential debates	N	
28. Tighten ban on vertical price fixing	Y	
29. Kill-Freeze discretionary budget	Y	
30. Provide $30b for failed S&Ls	Y	
31. Allow use of force against Iraq	--	
32. Allow $15b in foreign aid for 1991	Y	
33. Civil Rights Act of 1990	Y	
34. Block cancellation of Egypt's debt	N	
35. Cut El Salvador military aid 50%	Y	
36. Reduce troops in NATO by 30,000	Y	
37. Req increases in auto fuel efficiency	Y	
38. Bar taxpayer funding of campaigns	N	
39. Limit textile import growth to 1%	N	
40. Amendment to ban flag desecration	N	
41. Let fed emp be politically active	Y	
42. Reauthorize Amtrak-veto override	Y	
43. Allow sale of assault weapons	N	
44. Retraining aid for coal miners	Y	
45. Kill-Raise car emission standards	N	
46. Pull EPA nuclear plant authority	N	
47. Defer Chinese students' deportation	Y	
48. Cut in capital gains tax	N	
49. Establish CIA inspector general	Y	
50. Kill-Sanctions against China	N	
51. Bar drug testing to receive AFDC	Y	
52. Kill-Allow force against drug planes	Y	
53. Include illegal aliens in census	Y	
54. Restitution to Japanese interned	Y	
55. Troop reduction in Europe of 50%	N	
56. Increase SDI research to $4.3b	N	
57. Kill-Pay homeless below min wage	Y	
58. Ban airline smoking within US	Y	
59. Bar transfer of FS-X technology	N	
60. Limit liability for oil spills	N	
61. Restructure S&L industry	Y	
62. Ban $ to illegal foreign activities	Y	
63. Req immigrant fluency in English	N	
64. Allow aliens' families to stay in US	Y	
65. Expand child care aid/tax credit	Y	
66. Raise minimum wage w/subminimum	Y	
67. Freeze outlays except SS/Medicare	N	
68. Kill-Shift $5b of DOD to domestic	Y	
69. Confirm Tower as sec of defense	N	
70. Bar abortion $ except to save mother	?	
71. Kill-Warn AIDS carriers' spouses	Y	
72. Allow religious schools to bar gays	N	

CRANSTON, ALAN (continued)

73.	60 days' notice of plant closings	Y	109.	Raise speed limit to 65 mph	Y
74.	Allow poison pills in corp takeovers	Y	110.	Immigration reform/alien amnesty	Y
75.	Kill-Workfare program	Y	111.	South Africa sanctions-veto override	Y
76.	Prohibit employee polygraph testing	Y	112.	Kill-Use of military in drug war	Y
77.	Cap Medicare patients' liability	Y	113.	Tax overhaul to revise income tax	Y
78.	Revise unfair trade practices	Y	114.	Submit nuclear test ban treaties	Y
79.	Kill-Shift SDI $ to conv weapons	N	115.	Prohibit sale of Stinger missiles	Y
80.	Kill-Shift SDI $ to accidental launch	Y	116.	Prohibit binary chemical weapons	Y
81.	Kill-Shift MX $ to supplies/parts	N	117.	Kill-$10/barrel oil tariff increase	Y
82.	Kill-Buy America provision at DOD	Y	118.	Grant tax amnesty provisions	?
83.	Allow nuclear testing-5+ kilotons	N	119.	Block Saudi arms sale-veto override	Y
84.	Allow SALT II to be exceeded	N	120.	Balanced budget amendment	N
85.	$ to vets exposed to nuclear bomb	Y	121.	Include veterans in spending cuts	N
86.	Warn workers of disease exposure	Y	122.	Bar $ to hazardous substance victims	N
87.	Restore four civil rights laws	Y	123.	Allow seasonal workers in the US	N
88.	Disapprove uranium sales to Japan	Y	124.	Let fed courts rule on school prayer	Y
89.	Notify Congress of covert operations	Y	125.	Presidential line-item veto	N
90.	Approval of $36m in Contra aid	N	126.	Ease Gun Control Act of 1968	N
91.	$18b deficit reduction compromise	Y	127.	Kill-Req 14-day wait for handguns	N
92.	Allow sale of hard-to-detect guns	N	128.	Kill-15% min tax on corporations	N
93.	Catastrophic health insurance	Y	129.	Drop Social Security COLA	N
94.	Bork nomination to Supreme Court	N	130.	Freeze funding for all programs	N
95.	Kill-Void Panama Canal treaties	Y	131.	Kill-Nuclear weapon freeze	N
96.	Kill-Insurance denial to AIDS+	Y	132.	Keep decision narrowing Title IX	N
97.	Keep diplomatic immunity intact	Y	133.	Raise drinking age to 21	Y
98.	Produce Bigeye nerve gas bomb	N	134.	Allow production of MX missile	N
99.	Balanced budget by '93-via targets	Y	135.	Raise taxes/cut spending by $140b	N
100.	Allow ASAT missile tests in space	N	136.	School prayer amendment	N
101.	Limit space-based/ABM system tests	Y	137.	Capital punishment-federal crimes	?
102.	Force reduction in trade barriers	Y	138.	Ban government officials from taping	?
103.	Repeal windfall profit tax on oil	N	139.	Martin Luther King holiday	N
104.	$1b/two year aid for the homeless	Y	140.	Authorize Marines in Lebanon	N
105.	Disallow $30m for AZT to poor	N	141.	Amendment making abortion illegal	N
106.	Bar AIDS test-immigrants/marriage	Y	142.	Delete $1.2b for jobs creation	N
107.	Kill-Biennial budget approval	Y	143.	Keep tobacco price supports	Y
108.	Fairness doctrine in broadcasting	?	144.	Emergency housing aid of $5.1b	Y

Presidential Support Score: 1991 - 23%   1990 - 27%

SEYMOUR, JOHN -- California [Republican]. Term Began/Expires: 1991 (Special Appointment)-1994. Born: December 3, 1937; Chicago, IL. Education: University of California, Los Angeles (B.A.). Military Service: U.S. Marine Corps. Occupation: Real estate brokerage, property management and escrow business founder; Anaheim city councilman and mayor; state senator (1983-88).

1.	Prohibit MFN status for China	N	17.	Strike $12b aid to Int'l Mon Fund	N
2.	Kill-Tie welfare to school attendance	N	18.	Raise Senate salary/omit honoraria	N
3.	Limit credit card interest rates	Y	19.	Reduce space station funding $1.9b	N
4.	Confirm Gates as head of CIA	Y	20.	Kill-Eliminate supercollider funds	Y
5.	Adoption of national energy policies	Y	21.	Req 5-day handgun waiting period	Y
6.	Kill-Restrict NEA use of funds	N	22.	Life in prison instead of death	N
7.	Unemployment benefits extension	N	23.	Exceptions to exclusionary rule	Y
8.	Confirm Thomas to Supreme Court	Y	24.	Ban race as death sentence factor	Y
9.	Raise eligibility for unpaid leave	N	25.	Campaign finance revisions	N
10.	Notify parents of minors' abortions	N	26.	Kill-Term limits for senators	N
11.	Move $3b from defense to domestic	N	27.	Require four presidential debates	?
12.	End production of B-2 bomber	N	28.	Tighten ban on vertical price fixing	N
13.	Cut SDI $1b to reduce deficit	N	29.	Kill-Freeze discretionary budget	Y
14.	Maintain strategic stability-Soviets	N	30.	Provide $30b for failed S&Ls	Y
15.	Kill-Allow women as combat pilots	N	31.	Allow use of force against Iraq	Y
16.	Kill-Allow HIV tests before surgery	N			

Presidential Support Score: 1991 - 84%

COLORADO

WIRTH, TIMOTHY E. -- Colorado [Democrat]. Term Began/Expires: 1987/1992. Prior Terms: House: 1975-86. Born: September 22, 1939; Santa Fe, NM. Education: Harvard College (A.B., M.Ed.); Stanford University (Ph.D.). Military Service: U.S. Army Reserve, 1961-67. Occupation: Special assistant to secretary of HEW; deputy assistant secretary of education, HEW (1969-70); employee, Great Western United Corp. and Arthur D. Little, Inc.; member, governor's task force on returned Vietnam veterans.

1. Prohibit MFN status for China	Y	
2. Kill-Tie welfare to school attendance	Y	
3. Limit credit card interest rates	Y	
4. Confirm Gates as head of CIA	+	
5. Adoption of national energy policies	N	
6. Kill-Restrict NEA use of funds	Y	
7. Unemployment benefits extension	Y	
8. Confirm Thomas to Supreme Court	N	
9. Raise eligibility for unpaid leave	Y	
10. Notify parents of minors' abortions	N	
11. Move $3b from defense to domestic	Y	
12. End production of B-2 bomber	Y	
13. Cut SDI $1b to reduce deficit	Y	
14. Maintain strategic stability-Soviets	Y	
15. Kill-Allow women as combat pilots	N	
16. Kill-Allow HIV tests before surgery	Y	
17. Strike $12b aid to Int'l Mon Fund	Y	
18. Raise Senate salary/omit honoraria	Y	
19. Reduce space station funding $1.9b	N	
20. Kill-Eliminate supercollider funds	N	
21. Req 5-day handgun waiting period	Y	
22. Life in prison instead of death	N	
23. Exceptions to exclusionary rule	N	
24. Ban race as death sentence factor	N	
25. Campaign finance revisions	Y	
26. Kill-Term limits for senators	Y	
27. Require four presidential debates	?	
28. Tighten ban on vertical price fixing	Y	
29. Kill-Freeze discretionary budget	Y	
30. Provide $30b for failed S&Ls	N	
31. Allow use of force against Iraq	N	
32. Allow $15b in foreign aid for 1991	Y	
33. Civil Rights Act of 1990	Y	
34. Block cancellation of Egypt's debt	N	
35. Cut El Salvador military aid 50%	Y	
36. Reduce troops in NATO by 30,000	Y	
37. Req increases in auto fuel efficiency	Y	
38. Bar taxpayer funding of campaigns	N	
39. Limit textile import growth to 1%	N	
40. Amendment to ban flag desecration	N	
41. Let fed emp be politically active	Y	
42. Reauthorize Amtrak-veto override	Y	
43. Allow sale of assault weapons	N	
44. Retraining aid for coal miners	Y	
45. Kill-Raise car emission standards	N	
46. Pull EPA nuclear plant authority	N	
47. Defer Chinese students' deportation	Y	
48. Cut in capital gains tax	N	
49. Establish CIA inspector general	N	
50. Kill-Sanctions against China	Y
51. Bar drug testing to receive AFDC	Y
52. Kill-Allow force against drug planes	Y
53. Include illegal aliens in census	Y
54. Restitution to Japanese interned	Y
55. Troop reduction in Europe of 50%	N
56. Increase SDI research to $4.3b	N
57. Kill-Pay homeless below min wage	Y
58. Ban airline smoking within US	Y
59. Bar transfer of FS-X technology	Y
60. Limit liability for oil spills	N
61. Restructure S&L industry	Y
62. Ban $ to illegal foreign activities	Y
63. Req immigrant fluency in English	N
64. Allow aliens' families to stay in US	Y
65. Expand child care aid/tax credit	Y
66. Raise minimum wage w/subminimum	Y
67. Freeze outlays except SS/Medicare	N
68. Kill-Shift $5b of DOD to domestic	N
69. Confirm Tower as sec of defense	N
70. Bar abortion $ except to save mother	N
71. Kill-Warn AIDS carriers' spouses	Y
72. Allow religious schools to bar gays	N
73. 60 days' notice of plant closings	Y
74. Allow poison pills in corp takeovers	Y
75. Kill-Workfare program	Y
76. Prohibit employee polygraph testing	Y
77. Cap Medicare patients' liability	Y
78. Revise unfair trade practices	Y
79. Kill-Shift SDI $ to conv weapons	N
80. Kill-Shift SDI $ to accidental launch	Y
81. Kill-Shift MX $ to supplies/parts	N
82. Kill-Buy America provision at DOD	Y
83. Allow nuclear testing-5+ kilotons	N
84. Allow SALT II to be exceeded	N
85. $ to vets exposed to nuclear bomb	Y
86. Warn workers of disease exposure	Y
87. Restore four civil rights laws	Y
88. Disapprove uranium sales to Japan	Y
89. Notify Congress of covert operations	Y
90. Approval of $36m in Contra aid	N
91. $18b deficit reduction compromise	Y
92. Allow sale of hard-to-detect guns	?
93. Catastrophic health insurance	Y
94. Bork nomination to Supreme Court	N
95. Kill-Void Panama Canal treaties	Y
96. Kill-Insurance denial to AIDS+	Y
97. Keep diplomatic immunity intact	Y
98. Produce Bigeye nerve gas bomb	N

WIRTH, TIMOTHY E. (continued)

99. Balanced budget by '93-via targets	N	105. Disallow $30m for AZT to poor	Y
100. Allow ASAT missile tests in space	N	106. Bar AIDS test-immigrants/marriage	Y
101. Limit space-based/ABM system tests	Y	107. Kill-Biennial budget approval	Y
102. Force reduction in trade barriers	Y	108. Fairness doctrine in broadcasting	Y
103. Repeal windfall profit tax on oil	Y	109. Raise speed limit to 65 mph	Y
104. $1b/two year aid for the homeless	?		

The following are House measures voted on between 1982-1986:

99. Immigration reform/alien amnesty	N	122. Emergency farm credit/revisions	Y
100. South Africa sanctions-veto override	Y	123. Duty on Taiwan/Hong Kong/S Korea	N
101. Tax overhaul to revise income tax	Y	124. Limit steel imports to 17%	Y
102. Use of military in drug war	N	125. Cut $ to schools that bar prayer	N
103. Delete 12 MX/add conventional wpn	Y	126. $50b-taxes; cut Medicare/spending	Y
104. Raise speed limit to 65 mph	Y	127. Limit Pershing II/cruise in Europe	Y
105. Require Pentagon to buy US goods	Y	128. Delete $7.1b for 34 B-1 bombers	Y
106. AIDS insurance non-discrimination	Y	129. Bar purchase of Sergeant York guns	?
107. Prohibit Saudi arms sales	Y	130. El Salvador military/economic aid	N
108. Ease Gun Control Act of 1968	Y	131. Bar mining of Nicaraguan waters	Y
109. Bar interstate handgun transport	Y	132. Physician fee freeze for Medicare	N
110. Make company emissions known	Y	133. $49b in "sin"/phone/insurance taxes	Y
111. Allow toxic victims to sue in fed ct	N	134. Allow sale of Conrail	N
112. Superfund waste cleanup of $10b	N	135. Equal Rights Amendment	Y
113. 90 days notice of plant closings	Y	136. Authorize Marines in Lebanon	N
114. $20b in Medicare cuts/tax increases	Y	137. Eminent domain for coal companies	N
115. Spending cuts and tax increases	Y	138. Prohibit EPA clean air sanctions	Y
116. Set school lunch lmt-250% poverty	N	139. SS retirement age increase/reforms	N
117. $75m for youth work projects	Y	140. Auto domestic content requirement	Y
118. Allow Angolan military assistance	N	141. Delete jobs program funding	N
119. Suspend defense payments for abuse	Y	142. Highway-gas tax bill	Y
120. Drop SS COLAs/$12b tax increase	N	143. Cut $5b from defense for Medicare	N
121. Approve $1.5b for 21 MX missiles	N	144. Emergency housing aid of $1b	Y

Presidential Support Score: 1991 - 36%   1990 - 37%

BROWN, HANK -- Colorado [Republican]. Term Began/Expires: 1991/1996. Prior Terms: House: 1981-90. Born: February 12, 1940; Denver, CO. Education: University of Colorado (B.S., J.D.). Military Service: U.S. Navy (1962-66). Occupation: Vice-president, Monfort of Colorado, Inc. (1969-80); Colorado senator (1972-76).

1. Prohibit MFN status for China	N	17. Strike $12b aid to Int'l Mon Fund	Y
2. Kill-Tie welfare to school attendance	N	18. Raise Senate salary/omit honoraria	N
3. Limit credit card interest rates	N	19. Reduce space station funding $1.9b	N
4. Confirm Gates as head of CIA	Y	20. Kill-Eliminate supercollider funds	Y
5. Adoption of national energy policies	Y	21. Req 5-day handgun waiting period	N
6. Kill-Restrict NEA use of funds	N	22. Life in prison instead of death	N
7. Unemployment benefits extension	N	23. Exceptions to exclusionary rule	Y
8. Confirm Thomas to Supreme Court	Y	24. Ban race as death sentence factor	Y
9. Raise eligibility for unpaid leave	N	25. Campaign finance revisions	N
10. Notify parents of minors' abortions	Y	26. Kill-Term limits for senators	N
11. Move $3b from defense to domestic	N	27. Require four presidential debates	Y
12. End production of B-2 bomber	N	28. Tighten ban on vertical price fixing	Y
13. Cut SDI $1b to reduce deficit	N	29. Kill-Freeze discretionary budget	N
14. Maintain strategic stability-Soviets	N	30. Provide $30b for failed S&Ls	N
15. Kill-Allow women as combat pilots	N	31. Allow use of force against Iraq	Y
16. Kill-Allow HIV tests before surgery	N		

The following are House measures voted on between 1982-1990:

36. Amendment to ban flag desecration	Y	40. Expand child care aid/tax credit	N
37. Reauthorize Amtrak-veto override	N	41. Raise House salary/omit honoraria	N
38. Retraining aid for coal miners	N	42. Toughen oil-spill liability	Y
39. Suspend El Salvador military aid	N	43. Restitution to Japanese interned	Y

BROWN, HANK (continued)

44. Protect Chinese & C.A. nationals	N	
45. Abortion $ for rape/incest cases	Y	
46. Allow religious schools to bar gays	Y	
47. Bar broadcaster fairness doctrine	Y	
48. Bar cap gains cut/reinstate IRA	N	
49. Bar unions equal voice in pension	Y	
50. Bar assembly of chemical weapons	N	
51. Ban plutonium/uranium production	Y	
52. Cap MX missile deployment at 50	N	
53. Allow $3b for 2 stealth bombers	N	
54. Publish bio-warfare experiments	Y	
55. Raise minimum wage-veto override	N	
56. Bar transfer of FS-X technology	Y	
57. Cut defense and raise domestic $	N	
58. Uniform poll closing in 48 states	N	
59. Req foreign investment disclosure	N	
60. Textile import quotas-veto override	N	
61. Bar abortion funding in Wash, DC	N	
62. Notify spouses of AIDS+ carriers	Y	
63. Seize conveyance-drug trafficking	Y	
64. South Africa sanctions	N	
65. 60 days' notice of plant closings	N	
66. Close unneeded military bases	Y	
67. Keep welfare reform within $2.8b	Y	
68. Allow children housing exclusion	Y	
69. Shift $400m of NASA to homeless	N	
70. Cap Medicare patients' liability	N	
71. Prohibit employee polygraph testing	N	
72. Allow CIA to fund Contras	Y	
73. Revise unfair trade practices	N	
74. Focus SDI on accidental launch	N	
75. Bar Air Force $ for MX missile	N	
76. Allow "real" increase in defense	N	
77. Troop reduction in Europe of 50%	Y	
78. Ban nuclear tests above 1 kiloton	Y	
79. Ban anti-satellite missile tests	N	
80. Observe certain limits of SALT II	Y	
81. Restore four Civil Rights laws	Y	
82. Prohibit aliens as strikebreakers	N	
83. Allow military malpractice suits	Y	
84. Approval of $36m in Contra aid	Y	
85. $18b deficit reduction compromise	N	
86. Welfare reform of $5.7b for 5 years	N	
87. Raise taxes $12b/cut spending $3b	N	
88. Board to assess occupational risk	N	
89. Balanced budget by '93-via targets	Y	
90. Bar licensing of two nuclear plants	N	
91. Remove victims compensation cap	N	
92. Catastrophic health insurance	N	
93. Ban airline smoking-2 hours or less	N	
94. $1b/two year aid for the homeless	N	

95. Bar non-unions in union companies	N	
96. Increase FSLIC rescue to $15b	N	
97. Impose quotas to lower trade deficit	Y	
98. Reduce discretionary budget 21%	?	
99. Immigration reform/alien amnesty	N	
100. South Africa sanctions-veto override	Y	
101. Tax overhaul to revise income tax	Y	
102. Use of military in drug war	Y	
103. Delete 12 MX/add conventional wpn	N	
104. Raise speed limit to 65 mph	Y	
105. Require Pentagon to buy US goods	N	
106. AIDS insurance non-discrimination	N	
107. Prohibit Saudi arms sales	Y	
108. Ease Gun Control Act of 1968	Y	
109. Bar interstate handgun transport	N	
110. Make company emissions known	N	
111. Allow toxic victims to sue in fed ct	N	
112. Superfund waste cleanup of $10b	N	
113. 90 days notice of plant closings	N	
114. $20b in Medicare cuts/tax increases	N	
115. Spending cuts and tax increases	N	
116. Set school lunch lmt-250% poverty	Y	
117. $75m for youth work projects	N	
118. Allow Angolan military assistance	Y	
119. Suspend defense payments for abuse	N	
120. Drop SS COLAs/$12b tax increase	Y	
121. Approve $1.5b for 21 MX missiles	Y	
122. Emergency farm credit/revisions	N	
123. Duty on Taiwan/Hong Kong/S Korea	N	
124. Limit steel imports to 17%	N	
125. Cut $ to schools that bar prayer	Y	
126. $50b-taxes; cut Medicare/spending	N	
127. Limit Pershing II/cruise in Europe	N	
128. Delete $7.1b for 34 B-1 bombers	Y	
129. Bar purchase of Sergeant York guns	Y	
130. El Salvador military/economic aid	Y	
131. Bar mining of Nicaraguan waters	Y	
132. Physician fee freeze for Medicare	Y	
133. $49b in "sin"/phone/insurance taxes	N	
134. Allow sale of Conrail	Y	
135. Equal Rights Amendment	Y	
136. Authorize Marines in Lebanon	N	
137. Eminent domain for coal companies	Y	
138. Prohibit EPA clean air sanctions	N	
139. SS retirement age increase/reforms	Y	
140. Auto domestic content requirement	N	
141. Delete jobs program funding	Y	
142. Highway-gas tax bill	N	
143. Cut $5b from defense for Medicare	Y	
144. Emergency housing aid of $1b	N	

Presidential Support Score: 1991 - 75%   1990 - 70%

CONNECTICUT

DODD, CHRISTOPHER J. -- Connecticut [Democrat]. Term Began/Expires: 1987/1992. Prior Terms: House: 1975-80; Senate: 1981-86. May 27, 1944; Williamantic, CT. Education: Providence College (B.A.); University of Louisville School of Law (J.D.). Military Service: U.S. Army, 1969-75. Occupation: Attorney; peace corps volunteer (1966-68).

DODD, CHRISTOPHER J. (continued)

1. Prohibit MFN status for China	Y
2. Kill-Tie welfare to school attendance	Y
3. Limit credit card interest rates	Y
4. Confirm Gates as head of CIA	N
5. Adoption of national energy policies	Y
6. Kill-Restrict NEA use of funds	Y
7. Unemployment benefits extension	Y
8. Confirm Thomas to Supreme Court	N
9. Raise eligibility for unpaid leave	Y
10. Notify parents of minors' abortions	N
11. Move $3b from defense to domestic	N
12. End production of B-2 bomber	N
13. Cut SDI $1b to reduce deficit	N
14. Maintain strategic stability-Soviets	Y
15. Kill-Allow women as combat pilots	N
16. Kill-Allow HIV tests before surgery	Y
17. Strike $12b aid to Int'l Mon Fund	N
18. Raise Senate salary/omit honoraria	N
19. Reduce space station funding $1.9b	N
20. Kill-Eliminate supercollider funds	Y
21. Req 5-day handgun waiting period	Y
22. Life in prison instead of death	N
23. Exceptions to exclusionary rule	N
24. Ban race as death sentence factor	N
25. Campaign finance revisions	Y
26. Kill-Term limits for senators	Y
27. Require four presidential debates	Y
28. Tighten ban on vertical price fixing	Y
29. Kill-Freeze discretionary budget	Y
30. Provide $30b for failed S&Ls	Y
31. Allow use of force against Iraq	N
32. Allow $15b in foreign aid for 1991	Y
33. Civil Rights Act of 1990	Y
34. Block cancellation of Egypt's debt	Y
35. Cut El Salvador military aid 50%	Y
36. Reduce troops in NATO by 30,000	Y
37. Req increases in auto fuel efficiency	Y
38. Bar taxpayer funding of campaigns	N
39. Limit textile import growth to 1%	Y
40. Amendment to ban flag desecration	N
41. Let fed emp be politically active	Y
42. Reauthorize Amtrak-veto override	Y
43. Allow sale of assault weapons	N
44. Retraining aid for coal miners	N
45. Kill-Raise car emission standards	Y
46. Pull EPA nuclear plant authority	N
47. Defer Chinese students' deportation	Y
48. Cut in capital gains tax	N
49. Establish CIA inspector general	Y
50. Kill-Sanctions against China	Y
51. Bar drug testing to receive AFDC	Y
52. Kill-Allow force against drug planes	Y
53. Include illegal aliens in census	?
54. Restitution to Japanese interned	Y
55. Troop reduction in Europe of 50%	Y
56. Increase SDI research to $4.3b	N
57. Kill-Pay homeless below min wage	Y
58. Ban airline smoking within US	Y
59. Bar transfer of FS-X technology	Y
60. Limit liability for oil spills	N
61. Restructure S&L industry	Y
62. Ban $ to illegal foreign activities	Y
63. Req immigrant fluency in English	N
64. Allow aliens' families to stay in US	Y

65. Expand child care aid/tax credit	Y
66. Raise minimum wage w/subminimum	Y
67. Freeze outlays except SS/Medicare	N
68. Kill-Shift $5b of DOD to domestic	Y
69. Confirm Tower as sec of defense	Y
70. Bar abortion $ except to save mother	?
71. Kill-Warn AIDS carriers' spouses	Y
72. Allow religious schools to bar gays	N
73. 60 days' notice of plant closings	Y
74. Allow poison pills in corp takeovers	Y
75. Kill-Workfare program	Y
76. Prohibit employee polygraph testing	Y
77. Cap Medicare patients' liability	Y
78. Revise unfair trade practices	Y
79. Kill-Shift SDI $ to conv weapons	N
80. Kill-Shift SDI $ to accidental launch	Y
81. Kill-Shift MX $ to supplies/parts	Y
82. Kill-Buy America provision at DOD	Y
83. Allow nuclear testing-5+ kilotons	N
84. Allow SALT II to be exceeded	N
85. $ to vets exposed to nuclear bomb	?
86. Warn workers of disease exposure	Y
87. Restore four civil rights laws	Y
88. Disapprove uranium sales to Japan	?
89. Notify Congress of covert operations	Y
90. Approval of $36m in Contra aid	N
91. $18b deficit reduction compromise	Y
92. Allow sale of hard-to-detect guns	?
93. Catastrophic health insurance	?
94. Bork nomination to Supreme Court	N
95. Kill-Void Panama Canal treaties	Y
96. Kill-Insurance denial to AIDS+	N
97. Keep diplomatic immunity intact	Y
98. Produce Bigeye nerve gas bomb	N
99. Balanced budget by '93-via targets	Y
100. Allow ASAT missile tests in space	N
101. Limit space-based/ABM system tests	Y
102. Force reduction in trade barriers	Y
103. Repeal windfall profit tax on oil	N
104. $1b/two year aid for the homeless	?
105. Disallow $30m for AZT to poor	N
106. Bar AIDS test-immigrants/marriage	Y
107. Kill-Biennial budget approval	Y
108. Fairness doctrine in broadcasting	Y
109. Raise speed limit to 65 mph	Y
110. Immigration reform/alien amnesty	Y
111. South Africa sanctions-veto override	Y
112. Kill-Use of military in drug war	Y
113. Tax overhaul to revise income tax	N
114. Submit nuclear test ban treaties	Y
115. Prohibit sale of Stinger missiles	N
116. Prohibit binary chemical weapons	Y
117. Kill-$10/barrel oil tariff increase	Y
118. Grant tax amnesty provisions	N
119. Block Saudi arms sale-veto override	Y
120. Balanced budget amendment	N
121. Include veterans in spending cuts	N
122. Bar $ to hazardous substance victims	N
123. Allow seasonal workers in the US	N
124. Let fed courts rule on school prayer	Y
125. Presidential line-item veto	N
126. Ease Gun Control Act of 1968	N
127. Kill-Req 14-day wait for handguns	N
128. Kill-15% min tax on corporations	N

DODD, CHRISTOPHER J. (continued)

129. Drop Social Security COLA	N	137. Capital punishment-federal crimes	N
130. Freeze funding for all programs	Y	138. Ban government officials from taping	Y
131. Kill-Nuclear weapon freeze	N	139. Martin Luther King holiday	Y
132. Keep decision narrowing Title IX	N	140. Authorize Marines in Lebanon	N
133. Raise drinking age to 21	Y	141. Amendment making abortion illegal	N
134. Allow production of MX missile	N	142. Delete $1.2b for jobs creation	N
135. Raise taxes/cut spending by $140b	Y	143. Keep tobacco price supports	N
136. School prayer amendment	N	144. Emergency housing aid of $5.1b	Y

Presidential Support Score: 1991 - 49% 1990 - 39%

LIEBERMAN, JOSEPH J. -- Connecticut [Democrat]. Term Began/Expires: 1989/1994. Born: February 24, 1942; Stamford, CT. Education: Yale College and Law School. Occupation: Author; state senator (1971-80) and attorney general (1983-88).

1. Prohibit MFN status for China	Y	36. Reduce troops in NATO by 30,000	N
2. Kill-Tie welfare to school attendance	N	37. Req increases in auto fuel efficiency	Y
3. Limit credit card interest rates	Y	38. Bar taxpayer funding of campaigns	N
4. Confirm Gates as head of CIA	Y	39. Limit textile import growth to 1%	Y
5. Adoption of national energy policies	N	40. Amendment to ban flag desecration	N
6. Kill-Restrict NEA use of funds	Y	41. Let fed emp be politically active	Y
7. Unemployment benefits extension	Y	42. Reauthorize Amtrak-veto override	Y
8. Confirm Thomas to Supreme Court	N	43. Allow sale of assault weapons	N
9. Raise eligibility for unpaid leave	Y	44. Retraining aid for coal miners	Y
10. Notify parents of minors' abortions	N	45. Kill-Raise car emission standards	N
11. Move $3b from defense to domestic	N	46. Pull EPA nuclear plant authority	N
12. End production of B-2 bomber	Y	47. Defer Chinese students' deportation	Y
13. Cut SDI $1b to reduce deficit	Y	48. Cut in capital gains tax	Y
14. Maintain strategic stability-Soviets	Y	49. Establish CIA inspector general	Y
15. Kill-Allow women as combat pilots	N	50. Kill-Sanctions against China	N
16. Kill-Allow HIV tests before surgery	Y	51. Bar drug testing to receive AFDC	Y
17. Strike $12b aid to Int'l Mon Fund	N	52. Kill-Allow force against drug planes	N
18. Raise Senate salary/omit honoraria	Y	53. Include illegal aliens in census	Y
19. Reduce space station funding $1.9b	N	54. Restitution to Japanese interned	Y
20. Kill-Eliminate supercollider funds	Y	55. Troop reduction in Europe of 50%	N
21. Req 5-day handgun waiting period	Y	56. Increase SDI research to $4.3b	N
22. Life in prison instead of death	N	57. Kill-Pay homeless below min wage	Y
23. Exceptions to exclusionary rule	Y	58. Ban airline smoking within US	Y
24. Ban race as death sentence factor	Y	59. Bar transfer of FS-X technology	Y
25. Campaign finance revisions	Y	60. Limit liability for oil spills	N
26. Kill-Term limits for senators	Y	61. Restructure S&L industry	Y
27. Require four presidential debates	Y	62. Ban $ to illegal foreign activities	Y
28. Tighten ban on vertical price fixing	Y	63. Req immigrant fluency in English	Y
29. Kill-Freeze discretionary budget	Y	64. Allow aliens' families to stay in US	Y
30. Provide $30b for failed S&Ls	Y	65. Expand child care aid/tax credit	Y
31. Allow use of force against Iraq	Y	66. Raise minimum wage w/subminimum	Y
32. Allow $15b in foreign aid for 1991	Y	67. Freeze outlays except SS/Medicare	N
33. Civil Rights Act of 1990	Y	68. Kill-Shift $5b of DOD to domestic	Y
34. Block cancellation of Egypt's debt	N	69. Confirm Tower as sec of defense	N
35. Cut El Salvador military aid 50%	Y		

Presidential Support Score: 1991 - 49% 1990 - 37%

DELAWARE

ROTH, WILLIAM V., Jr. -- Delaware [Republican]. Term Began/Expires: 1989/1994. Prior Terms: House: 1967-70; Senate: 1971-88. Born: July 22, 1921; Great Falls, MT. Education: University of Oregon (B.A.); Harvard University (M.B.A., LL.B.). Military Service: U.S. Army, 1943-46. Occupation: Attorney.

ROTH, WILLIAM V., Jr. (continued)

1. Prohibit MFN status for China	N
2. Kill-Tie welfare to school attendance	N
3. Limit credit card interest rates	?
4. Confirm Gates as head of CIA	Y
5. Adoption of national energy policies	N
6. Kill-Restrict NEA use of funds	N
7. Unemployment benefits extension	N
8. Confirm Thomas to Supreme Court	Y
9. Raise eligibility for unpaid leave	Y
10. Notify parents of minors' abortions	Y
11. Move $3b from defense to domestic	?
12. End production of B-2 bomber	Y
13. Cut SDI $1b to reduce deficit	N
14. Maintain strategic stability-Soviets	N
15. Kill-Allow women as combat pilots	N
16. Kill-Allow HIV tests before surgery	N
17. Strike $12b aid to Int'l Mon Fund	N
18. Raise Senate salary/omit honoraria	Y
19. Reduce space station funding $1.9b	N
20. Kill-Eliminate supercollider funds	Y
21. Req 5-day handgun waiting period	Y
22. Life in prison instead of death	N
23. Exceptions to exclusionary rule	Y
24. Ban race as death sentence factor	Y
25. Campaign finance revisions	N
26. Kill-Term limits for senators	Y
27. Require four presidential debates	N
28. Tighten ban on vertical price fixing	N
29. Kill-Freeze discretionary budget	N
30. Provide $30b for failed S&Ls	Y
31. Allow use of force against Iraq	Y
32. Allow $15b in foreign aid for 1991	N
33. Civil Rights Act of 1990	N
34. Block cancellation of Egypt's debt	N
35. Cut El Salvador military aid 50%	Y
36. Reduce troops in NATO by 30,000	N
37. Req increases in auto fuel efficiency	Y
38. Bar taxpayer funding of campaigns	Y
39. Limit textile import growth to 1%	Y
40. Amendment to ban flag desecration	Y
41. Let fed emp be politically active	N
42. Reauthorize Amtrak-veto override	Y
43. Allow sale of assault weapons	Y
44. Retraining aid for coal miners	N
45. Kill-Raise car emission standards	N
46. Pull EPA nuclear plant authority	N
47. Defer Chinese students' deportation	N
48. Cut in capital gains tax	Y
49. Establish CIA inspector general	Y
50. Kill-Sanctions against China	N
51. Bar drug testing to receive AFDC	Y
52. Kill-Allow force against drug planes	N
53. Include illegal aliens in census	N
54. Restitution to Japanese interned	N
55. Troop reduction in Europe of 50%	N
56. Increase SDI research to $4.3b	Y
57. Kill-Pay homeless below min wage	N
58. Ban airline smoking within US	Y
59. Bar transfer of FS-X technology	N
60. Limit liability for oil spills	N
61. Restructure S&L industry	N
62. Ban $ to illegal foreign activities	N
63. Req immigrant fluency in English	Y
64. Allow aliens' families to stay in US	N

65. Expand child care aid/tax credit	N
66. Raise minimum wage w/subminimum	N
67. Freeze outlays except SS/Medicare	Y
68. Kill-Shift $5b of DOD to domestic	Y
69. Confirm Tower as sec of defense	Y
70. Bar abortion $ except to save mother	N
71. Kill-Warn AIDS carriers' spouses	N
72. Allow religious schools to bar gays	Y
73. 60 days' notice of plant closings	Y
74. Allow poison pills in corp takeovers	Y
75. Kill-Workfare program	N
76. Prohibit employee polygraph testing	N
77. Cap Medicare patients' liability	N
78. Revise unfair trade practices	Y
79. Kill-Shift SDI $ to conv weapons	Y
80. Kill-Shift SDI $ to accidental launch	N
81. Kill-Shift MX $ to supplies/parts	Y
82. Kill-Buy America provision at DOD	Y
83. Allow nuclear testing-5+ kilotons	Y
84. Allow SALT II to be exceeded	Y
85. $ to vets exposed to nuclear bomb	N
86. Warn workers of disease exposure	N
87. Restore four civil rights laws	Y
88. Disapprove uranium sales to Japan	N
89. Notify Congress of covert operations	Y
90. Approval of $36m in Contra aid	Y
91. $18b deficit reduction compromise	N
92. Allow sale of hard-to-detect guns	Y
93. Catastrophic health insurance	N
94. Bork nomination to Supreme Court	Y
95. Kill-Void Panama Canal treaties	N
96. Kill-Insurance denial to AIDS+	N
97. Keep diplomatic immunity intact	Y
98. Produce Bigeye nerve gas bomb	Y
99. Balanced budget by '93-via targets	N
100. Allow ASAT missile tests in space	Y
101. Limit space-based/ABM system tests	N
102. Force reduction in trade barriers	Y
103. Repeal windfall profit tax on oil	Y
104. $1b/two year aid for the homeless	N
105. Disallow $30m for AZT to poor	N
106. Bar AIDS test-immigrants/marriage	Y
107. Kill-Biennial budget approval	N
108. Fairness doctrine in broadcasting	Y
109. Raise speed limit to 65 mph	Y
110. Immigration reform/alien amnesty	Y
111. South Africa sanctions-veto override	Y
112. Kill-Use of military in drug war	Y
113. Tax overhaul to revise income tax	N
114. Submit nuclear test ban treaties	Y
115. Prohibit sale of Stinger missiles	N
116. Prohibit binary chemical weapons	N
117. Kill-$10/barrel oil tariff increase	Y
118. Grant tax amnesty provisions	Y
119. Block Saudi arms sale-veto override	N
120. Balanced budget amendment	Y
121. Include veterans in spending cuts	Y
122. Bar $ to hazardous substance victims	Y
123. Allow seasonal workers in the US	N
124. Let fed courts rule on school prayer	N
125. Presidential line-item veto	Y
126. Ease Gun Control Act of 1968	Y
127. Kill-Req 14-day wait for handguns	Y
128. Kill-15% min tax on corporations	Y

ROTH, WILLIAM V., Jr. (continued)

129. Drop Social Security COLA	Y	137. Capital punishment-federal crimes	Y
130. Freeze funding for all programs	N	138. Ban government officials from taping	N
131. Kill-Nuclear weapon freeze	Y	139. Martin Luther King holiday	Y
132. Keep decision narrowing Title IX	Y	140. Authorize Marines in Lebanon	N
133. Raise drinking age to 21	Y	141. Amendment making abortion illegal	N
134. Allow production of MX missile	Y	142. Delete $1.2b for jobs creation	Y
135. Raise taxes/cut spending by $140b	Y	143. Keep tobacco price supports	N
136. School prayer amendment	Y	144. Emergency housing aid of $5.1b	N

Presidential Support Score: 1991 - 83%   1990 - 72%

BIDEN, JOSEPH R., Jr. -- Delaware [Democrat]. Term Began/Expires: 1991/1996. Prior Terms: Senate: 1973-90. Born: November 20, 1942; Scranton, PA. Education: University of Delaware (A.B.); Syracuse University College of Law (J.D.). Occupation: New Castle County councilman, Delaware (1970-72).

1. Prohibit MFN status for China	Y	48. Cut in capital gains tax	N
2. Kill-Tie welfare to school attendance	Y	49. Establish CIA inspector general	Y
3. Limit credit card interest rates	Y	50. Kill-Sanctions against China	Y
4. Confirm Gates as head of CIA	N	51. Bar drug testing to receive AFDC	Y
5. Adoption of national energy policies	N	52. Kill-Allow force against drug planes	N
6. Kill-Restrict NEA use of funds	Y	53. Include illegal aliens in census	Y
7. Unemployment benefits extension	Y	54. Restitution to Japanese interned	Y
8. Confirm Thomas to Supreme Court	N	55. Troop reduction in Europe of 50%	N
9. Raise eligibility for unpaid leave	Y	56. Increase SDI research to $4.3b	N
10. Notify parents of minors' abortions	N	57. Kill-Pay homeless below min wage	Y
11. Move $3b from defense to domestic	Y	58. Ban airline smoking within US	Y
12. End production of B-2 bomber	Y	59. Bar transfer of FS-X technology	Y
13. Cut SDI $1b to reduce deficit	Y	60. Limit liability for oil spills	N
14. Maintain strategic stability-Soviets	Y	61. Restructure S&L industry	Y
15. Kill-Allow women as combat pilots	N	62. Ban $ to illegal foreign activities	Y
16. Kill-Allow HIV tests before surgery	Y	63. Req immigrant fluency in English	N
17. Strike $12b aid to Int'l Mon Fund	N	64. Allow aliens' families to stay in US	Y
18. Raise Senate salary/omit honoraria	Y	65. Expand child care aid/tax credit	Y
19. Reduce space station funding $1.9b	Y	66. Raise minimum wage w/subminimum	Y
20. Kill-Eliminate supercollider funds	N	67. Freeze outlays except SS/Medicare	Y
21. Req 5-day handgun waiting period	Y	68. Kill-Shift $5b of DOD to domestic	?
22. Life in prison instead of death	N	69. Confirm Tower as sec of defense	N
23. Exceptions to exclusionary rule	N	70. Bar abortion $ except to save mother	--
24. Ban race as death sentence factor	N	71. Kill-Warn AIDS carriers' spouses	?
25. Campaign finance revisions	Y	72. Allow religious schools to bar gays	?
26. Kill-Term limits for senators	Y	73. 60 days' notice of plant closings	?
27. Require four presidential debates	?	74. Allow poison pills in corp takeovers	?
28. Tighten ban on vertical price fixing	Y	75. Kill-Workfare program	?
29. Kill-Freeze discretionary budget	N	76. Prohibit employee polygraph testing	?
30. Provide $30b for failed S&Ls	Y	77. Cap Medicare patients' liability	?
31. Allow use of force against Iraq	N	78. Revise unfair trade practices	?
32. Allow $15b in foreign aid for 1991	N	79. Kill-Shift SDI $ to conv weapons	?
33. Civil Rights Act of 1990	Y	80. Kill-Shift SDI $ to accidental launch	?
34. Block cancellation of Egypt's debt	Y	81. Kill-Shift MX $ to supplies/parts	?
35. Cut El Salvador military aid 50%	Y	82. Kill-Buy America provision at DOD	?
36. Reduce troops in NATO by 30,000	Y	83. Allow nuclear testing-5+ kilotons	?
37. Req increases in auto fuel efficiency	Y	84. Allow SALT II to be exceeded	?
38. Bar taxpayer funding of campaigns	N	85. $ to vets exposed to nuclear bomb	?
39. Limit textile import growth to 1%	Y	86. Warn workers of disease exposure	?
40. Amendment to ban flag desecration	N	87. Restore four civil rights laws	?
41. Let fed emp be politically active	Y	88. Disapprove uranium sales to Japan	?
42. Reauthorize Amtrak-veto override	Y	89. Notify Congress of covert operations	?
43. Allow sale of assault weapons	N	90. Approval of $36m in Contra aid	?
44. Retraining aid for coal miners	N	91. $18b deficit reduction compromise	Y
45. Kill-Raise car emission standards	Y	92. Allow sale of hard-to-detect guns	N
46. Pull EPA nuclear plant authority	N	93. Catastrophic health insurance	Y
47. Defer Chinese students' deportation	Y	94. Bork nomination to Supreme Court	N

BIDEN, JOSEPH R., Jr. (continued)

95.	Kill-Void Panama Canal treaties	Y		
96.	Kill-Insurance denial to AIDS+	Y		
97.	Keep diplomatic immunity intact	Y		
98.	Produce Bigeye nerve gas bomb	?		
99.	Balanced budget by '93-via targets	Y		
100.	Allow ASAT missile tests in space	N		
101.	Limit space-based/ABM system tests	Y		
102.	Force reduction in trade barriers	Y		
103.	Repeal windfall profit tax on oil	N		
104.	$1b/two year aid for the homeless	?		
105.	Disallow $30m for AZT to poor	?		
106.	Bar AIDS test-immigrants/marriage	?		
107.	Kill-Biennial budget approval	N		
108.	Fairness doctrine in broadcasting	?		
109.	Raise speed limit to 65 mph	Y		
110.	Immigration reform/alien amnesty	Y		
111.	South Africa sanctions-veto override	Y		
112.	Kill-Use of military in drug war	Y		
113.	Tax overhaul to revise income tax	Y		
114.	Submit nuclear test ban treaties	Y		
115.	Prohibit sale of Stinger missiles	Y		
116.	Prohibit binary chemical weapons	Y		
117.	Kill-$10/barrel oil tariff increase	Y		
118.	Grant tax amnesty provisions	Y		
119.	Block Saudi arms sale-veto override	Y		

120.	Balanced budget amendment	N
121.	Include veterans in spending cuts	?
122.	Bar $ to hazardous substance victims	N
123.	Allow seasonal workers in the US	N
124.	Let fed courts rule on school prayer	Y
125.	Presidential line-item veto	Y
126.	Ease Gun Control Act of 1968	Y
127.	Kill-Req 14-day wait for handguns	Y
128.	Kill-15% min tax on corporations	Y
129.	Drop Social Security COLA	N
130.	Freeze funding for all programs	Y
131.	Kill-Nuclear weapon freeze	N
132.	Keep decision narrowing Title IX	N
133.	Raise drinking age to 21	Y
134.	Allow production of MX missile	N
135.	Raise taxes/cut spending by $140b	Y
136.	School prayer amendment	N
137.	Capital punishment-federal crimes	N
138.	Ban government officials from taping	N
139.	Martin Luther King holiday	Y
140.	Authorize Marines in Lebanon	N
141.	Amendment making abortion illegal	N
142.	Delete $1.2b for jobs creation	N
143.	Keep tobacco price supports	N
144.	Emergency housing aid of $5.1b	Y

Presidential Support Score: 1991 - 33%   1990 - 33%

FLORIDA

GRAHAM, BOB -- Florida [Democrat]. Term Began/Expires: 1987/1992. Born: November 9, 1936; Coral Gables, FL. Education: University of Florida (B.S.); Harvard Law School (LL.B.). Occupation: Attorney; builder; cattleman; executive, Sengra Corporation and The Graham Company; state representative, senator (1970-78), and governor (1979-86).

1.	Prohibit MFN status for China	Y
2.	Kill-Tie welfare to school attendance	Y
3.	Limit credit card interest rates	Y
4.	Confirm Gates as head of CIA	Y
5.	Adoption of national energy policies	N
6.	Kill-Restrict NEA use of funds	N
7.	Unemployment benefits extension	Y
8.	Confirm Thomas to Supreme Court	N
9.	Raise eligibility for unpaid leave	Y
10.	Notify parents of minors' abortions	Y
11.	Move $3b from defense to domestic	N
12.	End production of B-2 bomber	Y
13.	Cut SDI $1b to reduce deficit	Y
14.	Maintain strategic stability-Soviets	Y
15.	Kill-Allow women as combat pilots	N
16.	Kill-Allow HIV tests before surgery	N
17.	Strike $12b aid to Int'l Mon Fund	N
18.	Raise Senate salary/omit honoraria	N
19.	Reduce space station funding $1.9b	N
20.	Kill-Eliminate supercollider funds	Y
21.	Req 5-day handgun waiting period	Y
22.	Life in prison instead of death	N
23.	Exceptions to exclusionary rule	N

24.	Ban race as death sentence factor	Y
25.	Campaign finance revisions	Y
26.	Kill-Term limits for senators	Y
27.	Require four presidential debates	Y
28.	Tighten ban on vertical price fixing	Y
29.	Kill-Freeze discretionary budget	Y
30.	Provide $30b for failed S&Ls	N
31.	Allow use of force against Iraq	Y
32.	Allow $15b in foreign aid for 1991	Y
33.	Civil Rights Act of 1990	Y
34.	Block cancellation of Egypt's debt	N
35.	Cut El Salvador military aid 50%	Y
36.	Reduce troops in NATO by 30,000	N
37.	Req increases in auto fuel efficiency	Y
38.	Bar taxpayer funding of campaigns	N
39.	Limit textile import growth to 1%	N
40.	Amendment to ban flag desecration	Y
41.	Let fed emp be politically active	Y
42.	Reauthorize Amtrak-veto override	Y
43.	Allow sale of assault weapons	N
44.	Retraining aid for coal miners	N
45.	Kill-Raise car emission standards	N
46.	Pull EPA nuclear plant authority	N

GRAHAM, BOB (continued)

47. Defer Chinese students' deportation	Y	
48. Cut in capital gains tax	N	
49. Establish CIA inspector general	Y	
50. Kill-Sanctions against China	N	
51. Bar drug testing to receive AFDC	Y	
52. Kill-Allow force against drug planes	N	
53. Include illegal aliens in census	Y	
54. Restitution to Japanese interned	Y	
55. Troop reduction in Europe of 50%	N	
56. Increase SDI research to $4.3b	Y	
57. Kill-Pay homeless below min wage	Y	
58. Ban airline smoking within US	Y	
59. Bar transfer of FS-X technology	Y	
60. Limit liability for oil spills	N	
61. Restructure S&L industry	Y	
62. Ban $ to illegal foreign activities	Y	
63. Req immigrant fluency in English	N	
64. Allow aliens' families to stay in US	Y	
65. Expand child care aid/tax credit	Y	
66. Raise minimum wage w/subminimum	Y	
67. Freeze outlays except SS/Medicare	N	
68. Kill-Shift $5b of DOD to domestic	Y	
69. Confirm Tower as sec of defense	N	
70. Bar abortion $ except to save mother	N	
71. Kill-Warn AIDS carriers' spouses	Y	
72. Kill religious schools to bar gays	N	
73. 60 days' notice of plant closings	Y	
74. Allow poison pills in corp takeovers	Y	
75. Kill-Workfare program	Y	
76. Prohibit employee polygraph testing	N	
77. Cap Medicare patients' liability	Y	
78. Revise unfair trade practices	Y	

79. Kill-Shift SDI $ to conv weapons	Y
80. Kill-Shift SDI $ to accidental launch	Y
81. Kill-Shift MX $ to supplies/parts	Y
82. Kill-Buy America provision at DOD	Y
83. Allow nuclear testing-5+ kilotons	Y
84. Allow SALT II to be exceeded	Y
85. $ to vets exposed to nuclear bomb	Y
86. Warn workers of disease exposure	Y
87. Restore four civil rights laws	Y
88. Disapprove uranium sales to Japan	N
89. Notify Congress of covert operations	Y
90. Approval of $36m in Contra aid	Y
91. $18b deficit reduction compromise	Y
92. Allow sale of hard-to-detect guns	N
93. Catastrophic health insurance	Y
94. Bork nomination to Supreme Court	N
95. Kill-Void Panama Canal treaties	Y
96. Kill-Insurance denial to AIDS+	Y
97. Keep diplomatic immunity intact	Y
98. Produce Bigeye nerve gas bomb	Y
99. Balanced budget by '93-via targets	Y
100. Allow ASAT missile tests in space	Y
101. Limit space-based/ABM system tests	Y
102. Force reduction in trade barriers	Y
103. Repeal windfall profit tax on oil	N
104. $1b/two year aid for the homeless	Y
105. Disallow $30m for AZT to poor	N
106. Bar AIDS test-immigrants/marriage	Y
107. Kill-Biennial budget approval	Y
108. Fairness doctrine in broadcasting	Y
109. Raise speed limit to 65 mph	Y

Presidential Support Score: 1991 - 47% 1990 - 53%

MACK, CONNIE, III -- Florida [Republican]. Term Began/Expires: 1989/1994. Prior Terms: House: 1983-88. Born: October 29, 1940; Philadelphia, PA. Education; University of Florida (B.A.). Occupation: Vice-president, First National Bank of Ft. Myers; senior vice-president, Sun Bank (1971); president and director, Florida National Bank (1975); appointed to Miami Branch of Federal Reserve Board (1981).

1. Prohibit MFN status for China	Y
2. Kill-Tie welfare to school attendance	N
3. Limit credit card interest rates	N
4. Confirm Gates as head of CIA	Y
5. Adoption of national energy policies	N
6. Kill-Restrict NEA use of funds	N
7. Unemployment benefits extension	N
8. Confirm Thomas to Supreme Court	Y
9. Raise eligibility for unpaid leave	N
10. Notify parents of minors' abortions	Y
11. Move $3b from defense to domestic	N
12. End production of B-2 bomber	N
13. Cut SDI $1b to reduce deficit	N
14. Maintain strategic stability-Soviets	N
15. Kill-Allow women as combat pilots	N
16. Kill-Allow HIV tests before surgery	N
17. Strike $12b aid to Int'l Mon Fund	Y
18. Raise Senate salary/omit honoraria	N
19. Reduce space station funding $1.9b	N
20. Kill-Eliminate supercollider funds	Y
21. Req 5-day handgun waiting period	N
22. Life in prison instead of death	N

23. Exceptions to exclusionary rule	Y
24. Ban race as death sentence factor	Y
25. Campaign finance revisions	N
26. Kill-Term limits for senators	N
27. Require four presidential debates	?
28. Tighten ban on vertical price fixing	N
29. Kill-Freeze discretionary budget	N
30. Provide $30b for failed S&Ls	Y
31. Allow use of force against Iraq	Y
32. Allow $15b in foreign aid for 1991	Y
33. Civil Rights Act of 1990	N
34. Block cancellation of Egypt's debt	N
35. Cut El Salvador military aid 50%	N
36. Reduce troops in NATO by 30,000	N
37. Req increases in auto fuel efficiency	N
38. Bar taxpayer funding of campaigns	Y
39. Limit textile import growth to 1%	N
40. Amendment to ban flag desecration	Y
41. Let fed emp be politically active	N
42. Reauthorize Amtrak-veto override	N
43. Allow sale of assault weapons	Y
44. Retraining aid for coal miners	N

MACK, CONNIE, III (continued)

45. Kill-Raise car emission standards	Y	
46. Pull EPA nuclear plant authority	N	
47. Defer Chinese students' deportation	N	
48. Cut in capital gains tax	Y	
49. Establish CIA inspector general	N	
50. Kill-Sanctions against China	N	
51. Bar drug testing to receive AFDC	N	
52. Kill-Allow force against drug planes	N	
53. Include illegal aliens in census	Y	
54. Restitution to Japanese interned	N	
55. Troop reduction in Europe of 50%	N	
56. Increase SDI research to $4.3b	Y	
57. Kill-Pay homeless below min wage	N	

58. Ban airline smoking within US	Y
59. Bar transfer of FS-X technology	N
60. Limit liability for oil spills	N
61. Restructure S&L industry	N
62. Ban $ to illegal foreign activities	N
63. Req immigrant fluency in English	N
64. Allow aliens' families to stay in US	Y
65. Expand child care aid/tax credit	N
66. Raise minimum wage w/subminimum	N
67. Freeze outlays except SS/Medicare	N
68. Kill-Shift $5b of DOD to domestic	Y
69. Confirm Tower as sec of defense	Y

The following are House measures voted on between 1983-1988:

59. Req foreign investment disclosure	?
60. Textile import quotas-veto override	?
61. Bar abortion funding in Wash, DC	?
62. Notify spouses of AIDS+ carriers	?
63. Seize conveyance-drug trafficking	?
64. South Africa sanctions	?
65. 60 days' notice of plant closings	N
66. Close unneeded military bases	Y
67. Keep welfare reform within $2.8b	Y
68. Allow children housing exclusion	Y
69. Shift $400m of NASA to homeless	N
70. Cap Medicare patients' liability	?
71. Prohibit employee polygraph testing	X
72. Allow CIA to fund Contras	#
73. Revise unfair trade practices	N
74. Focus SDI on accidental launch	N
75. Bar Air Force $ for MX missile	X
76. Allow "real" increase in defense	?
77. Troop reduction in Europe of 50%	?
78. Ban nuclear tests above 1 kiloton	X
79. Ban anti-satellite missile tests	?
80. Observe certain limits of SALT II	X
81. Restore four Civil Rights laws	N
82. Prohibit aliens as strikebreakers	N
83. Allow military malpractice suits	?
84. Approval of $36m in Contra aid	Y
85. $18b deficit reduction compromise	N
86. Welfare reform of $5.7b for 5 years	N
87. Raise taxes $12b/cut spending $3b	N
88. Board to assess occupational risk	N
89. Balanced budget by '93-via targets	Y
90. Bar licensing of two nuclear plants	N
91. Remove victims compensation cap	N
92. Catastrophic health insurance	N
93. Ban airline smoking-2 hours or less	N
94. $1b/two year aid for the homeless	N
95. Bar non-unions in union companies	N
96. Increase FSLIC rescue to $15b	N
97. Impose quotas to lower trade deficit	N
98. Reduce discretionary budget 21%	N
99. Immigration reform/alien amnesty	N

100. South Africa sanctions-veto override	N
101. Tax overhaul to revise income tax	Y
102. Use of military in drug war	Y
103. Delete 12 MX/add conventional wpn	N
104. Raise speed limit to 65 mph	Y
105. Require Pentagon to buy US goods	N
106. AIDS insurance non-discrimination	N
107. Prohibit Saudi arms sales	Y
108. Ease Gun Control Act of 1968	Y
109. Bar interstate handgun transport	N
110. Make company emissions known	N
111. Allow toxic victims to sue in fed ct	N
112. Superfund waste cleanup of $10b	Y
113. 90 days notice of plant closings	N
114. $20b in Medicare cuts/tax increases	N
115. Spending cuts and tax increases	N
116. Set school lunch lmt-250% poverty	Y
117. $75m for youth work projects	N
118. Allow Angolan military assistance	Y
119. Suspend defense payments for abuse	N
120. Drop SS COLAs/$12b tax increase	N
121. Approve $1.5b for 21 MX missiles	Y
122. Emergency farm credit/revisions	N
123. Duty on Taiwan/Hong Kong/S Korea	N
124. Limit steel imports to 17%	N
125. Cut $ to schools that bar prayer	Y
126. $50b-taxes; cut Medicare/spending	N
127. Limit Pershing II/cruise in Europe	N
128. Delete $7.1b for 34 B-1 bombers	N
129. Bar purchase of Sergeant York guns	N
130. El Salvador military/economic aid	Y
131. Bar mining of Nicaraguan waters	N
132. Physician fee freeze for Medicare	Y
133. $49b in "sin"/phone/insurance taxes	N
134. Allow sale of Conrail	Y
135. Equal Rights Amendment	Y
136. Authorize Marines in Lebanon	Y
137. Eminent domain for coal companies	Y
138. Prohibit EPA clean air sanctions	N
139. SS retirement age increase/reforms	Y

Presidential Support Score: 1991 - 86%   1990 - 88%

GEORGIA

NUNN, SAM -- Georgia [Democrat]. Term Began/Expires: 1991/1996. Prior Terms: Senate: 1972-90. Born: September 8, 1938; Perry, GA. Education: Georgia Institute of Technology; Emory University (A.B., LL.B.). Military Service: U.S. Coast Guard, 1959-60; Reserve, 1960-68. Occupation: Attorney; farmer; Georgia representative (1968-72); president, Perry Chamber of Commerce (1964).

1. Prohibit MFN status for China	Y	
2. Kill-Tie welfare to school attendance	N	
3. Limit credit card interest rates	N	
4. Confirm Gates as head of CIA	Y	
5. Adoption of national energy policies	Y	
6. Kill-Restrict NEA use of funds	Y	
7. Unemployment benefits extension	Y	
8. Confirm Thomas to Supreme Court	Y	
9. Raise eligibility for unpaid leave	Y	
10. Notify parents of minors' abortions	N	
11. Move $3b from defense to domestic	N	
12. End production of B-2 bomber	N	
13. Cut SDI $1b to reduce deficit	N	
14. Maintain strategic stability-Soviets	N	
15. Kill-Allow women as combat pilots	Y	
16. Kill-Allow HIV tests before surgery	N	
17. Strike $12b aid to Int'l Mon Fund	Y	
18. Raise Senate salary/omit honoraria	Y	
19. Reduce space station funding $1.9b	Y	
20. Kill-Eliminate supercollider funds	Y	
21. Req 5-day handgun waiting period	Y	
22. Life in prison instead of death	N	
23. Exceptions to exclusionary rule	N	
24. Ban race as death sentence factor	Y	
25. Campaign finance revisions	Y	
26. Kill-Term limits for senators	Y	
27. Require four presidential debates	Y	
28. Tighten ban on vertical price fixing	Y	
29. Kill-Freeze discretionary budget	N	
30. Provide $30b for failed S&Ls	Y	
31. Allow use of force against Iraq	N	
32. Allow $15b in foreign aid for 1991	Y	
33. Civil Rights Act of 1990	Y	
34. Block cancellation of Egypt's debt	Y	
35. Cut El Salvador military aid 50%	Y	
36. Reduce troops in NATO by 30,000	N	
37. Req increases in auto fuel efficiency	N	
38. Bar taxpayer funding of campaigns	N	
39. Limit textile import growth to 1%	Y	
40. Amendment to ban flag desecration	Y	
41. Let fed emp be politically active	Y	
42. Reauthorize Amtrak-veto override	Y	
43. Allow sale of assault weapons	N	
44. Retraining aid for coal miners	N	
45. Kill-Raise car emission standards	N	
46. Pull EPA nuclear plant authority	N	
47. Defer Chinese students' deportation	Y	
48. Cut in capital gains tax	N	
49. Establish CIA inspector general	Y	
50. Kill-Sanctions against China	Y	
51. Bar drug testing to receive AFDC	Y	
52. Kill-Allow force against drug planes	Y
53. Include illegal aliens in census	N
54. Restitution to Japanese interned	Y
55. Troop reduction in Europe of 50%	N
56. Increase SDI research to $4.3b	Y
57. Kill-Pay homeless below min wage	Y
58. Ban airline smoking within US	Y
59. Bar transfer of FS-X technology	Y
60. Limit liability for oil spills	N
61. Restructure S&L industry	Y
62. Ban $ to illegal foreign activities	Y
63. Req immigrant fluency in English	Y
64. Allow aliens' families to stay in US	N
65. Expand child care aid/tax credit	N
66. Raise minimum wage w/subminimum	Y
67. Freeze outlays except SS/Medicare	Y
68. Kill-Shift $5b of DOD to domestic	Y
69. Confirm Tower as sec of defense	N
70. Bar abortion $ except to save mother	N
71. Kill-Warn AIDS carriers' spouses	Y
72. Allow religious schools to bar gays	Y
73. 60 days' notice of plant closings	Y
74. Allow poison pills in corp takeovers	N
75. Kill-Workfare program	N
76. Prohibit employee polygraph testing	Y
77. Cap Medicare patients' liability	Y
78. Revise unfair trade practices	Y
79. Kill-Shift SDI $ to conv weapons	Y
80. Kill-Shift SDI $ to accidental launch	Y
81. Kill-Shift MX $ to supplies/parts	Y
82. Kill-Buy America provision at DOD	Y
83. Allow nuclear testing-5+ kilotons	Y
84. Allow SALT II to be exceeded	Y
85. $ to vets exposed to nuclear bomb	?
86. Warn workers of disease exposure	N
87. Restore four civil rights laws	Y
88. Disapprove uranium sales to Japan	N
89. Notify Congress of covert operations	?
90. Approval of $36m in Contra aid	Y
91. $18b deficit reduction compromise	Y
92. Allow sale of hard-to-detect guns	N
93. Catastrophic health insurance	Y
94. Bork nomination to Supreme Court	N
95. Kill-Void Panama Canal treaties	Y
96. Kill-Insurance denial to AIDS+	Y
97. Keep diplomatic immunity intact	Y
98. Produce Bigeye nerve gas bomb	Y
99. Balanced budget by '93-via targets	N
100. Allow ASAT missile tests in space	Y
101. Limit space-based/ABM system tests	Y
102. Force reduction in trade barriers	Y

NUNN, SAM (continued)

103.	Repeal windfall profit tax on oil	Y	124.	Let fed courts rule on school prayer	Y
104.	$1b/two year aid for the homeless	Y	125.	Presidential line-item veto	Y
105.	Disallow $30m for AZT to poor	N	126.	Ease Gun Control Act of 1968	Y
106.	Bar AIDS test-immigrants/marriage	Y	127.	Kill-Req 14-day wait for handguns	Y
107.	Kill-Biennial budget approval	N	128.	Kill-15% min tax on corporations	N
108.	Fairness doctrine in broadcasting	Y	129.	Drop Social Security COLA	N
109.	Raise speed limit to 65 mph	Y	130.	Freeze funding for all programs	N
110.	Immigration reform/alien amnesty	Y	131.	Kill-Nuclear weapon freeze	Y
111.	South Africa sanctions-veto override	Y	132.	Keep decision narrowing Title IX	N
112.	Kill-Use of military in drug war	Y	133.	Raise drinking age to 21	Y
113.	Tax overhaul to revise income tax	N	134.	Allow production of MX missile	Y
114.	Submit nuclear test ban treaties	Y	135.	Raise taxes/cut spending by $140b	Y
115.	Prohibit sale of Stinger missiles	N	136.	School prayer amendment	Y
116.	Prohibit binary chemical weapons	N	137.	Capital punishment-federal crimes	Y
117.	Kill-$10/barrel oil tariff increase	Y	138.	Ban government officials from taping	N
118.	Grant tax amnesty provisions	Y	139.	Martin Luther King holiday	Y
119.	Block Saudi arms sale-veto override	Y	140.	Authorize Marines in Lebanon	N
120.	Balanced budget amendment	Y	141.	Amendment making abortion illegal	Y
121.	Include veterans in spending cuts	Y	142.	Delete $1.2b for jobs creation	Y
122.	Bar $ to hazardous substance victims	Y	143.	Keep tobacco price supports	Y
123.	Allow seasonal workers in the US	Y	144.	Emergency housing aid of $5.1b	Y

Presidential Support Score: 1991 - 57%   1990 - 57%

FOWLER, WYCHE, Jr.

FOWLER, WYCHE, Jr. -- Georgia [Democrat]. Term Began/Expires: 1987/1992. Prior Terms: House: 1977 (Special Election)-1986. Born: October 6, 1940; Atlanta, GA. Education: Davidson College (A.B.); Emory University School of Law (J.D.). Military Service: U.S. Army Intelligence, 1963-64. Occupation: Attorney; Atlanta alderman (1970-73); president, Atlanta City Council (1974-77).

1.	Prohibit MFN status for China	Y	34.	Block cancellation of Egypt's debt	N
2.	Kill-Tie welfare to school attendance	N	35.	Cut El Salvador military aid 50%	Y
3.	Limit credit card interest rates	Y	36.	Reduce troops in NATO by 30,000	Y
4.	Confirm Gates as head of CIA	N	37.	Req increases in auto fuel efficiency	Y
5.	Adoption of national energy policies	N	38.	Bar taxpayer funding of campaigns	N
6.	Kill-Restrict NEA use of funds	Y	39.	Limit textile import growth to 1%	Y
7.	Unemployment benefits extension	Y	40.	Amendment to ban flag desecration	Y
8.	Confirm Thomas to Supreme Court	Y	41.	Let fed emp be politically active	Y
9.	Raise eligibility for unpaid leave	Y	42.	Reauthorize Amtrak-veto override	Y
10.	Notify parents of minors' abortions	N	43.	Allow sale of assault weapons	N
11.	Move $3b from defense to domestic	N	44.	Retraining aid for coal miners	N
12.	End production of B-2 bomber	N	45.	Kill-Raise car emission standards	N
13.	Cut SDI $1b to reduce deficit	Y	46.	Pull EPA nuclear plant authority	N
14.	Maintain strategic stability-Soviets	Y	47.	Defer Chinese students' deportation	Y
15.	Kill-Allow women as combat pilots	Y	48.	Cut in capital gains tax	N
16.	Kill-Allow HIV tests before surgery	N	49.	Establish CIA inspector general	Y
17.	Strike $12b aid to Int'l Mon Fund	Y	50.	Kill-Sanctions against China	Y
18.	Raise Senate salary/omit honoraria	N	51.	Bar drug testing to receive AFDC	Y
19.	Reduce space station funding $1.9b	Y	52.	Kill-Allow force against drug planes	Y
20.	Kill-Eliminate supercollider funds	N	53.	Include illegal aliens in census	N
21.	Req 5-day handgun waiting period	Y	54.	Restitution to Japanese interned	Y
22.	Life in prison instead of death	Y	55.	Troop reduction in Europe of 50%	Y
23.	Exceptions to exclusionary rule	N	56.	Increase SDI research to $4.3b	N
24.	Ban race as death sentence factor	Y	57.	Kill-Pay homeless below min wage	Y
25.	Campaign finance revisions	Y	58.	Ban airline smoking within US	N
26.	Kill-Term limits for senators	Y	59.	Bar transfer of FS-X technology	Y
27.	Require four presidential debates	Y	60.	Limit liability for oil spills	Y
28.	Tighten ban on vertical price fixing	Y	61.	Restructure S&L industry	Y
29.	Kill-Freeze discretionary budget	N	62.	Ban $ to illegal foreign activities	Y
30.	Provide $30b for failed S&Ls	Y	63.	Req immigrant fluency in English	Y
31.	Allow use of force against Iraq	N	64.	Allow aliens' families to stay in US	N
32.	Allow $15b in foreign aid for 1991	Y	65.	Expand child care aid/tax credit	Y
33.	Civil Rights Act of 1990	Y	66.	Raise minimum wage w/subminimum	Y

FOWLER, WYCHE, Jr. (continued)

67. Freeze outlays except SS/Medicare	Y	89. Notify Congress of covert operations	Y
68. Kill-Shift $5b of DOD to domestic	Y	90. Approval of $36m in Contra aid	N
69. Confirm Tower as sec of defense	N	91. $18b deficit reduction compromise	Y
70. Bar abortion $ except to save mother	N	92. Allow sale of hard-to-detect guns	N
71. Kill-Warn AIDS carriers' spouses	Y	93. Catastrophic health insurance	Y
72. Allow religious schools to bar gays	Y	94. Bork nomination to Supreme Court	N
73. 60 days' notice of plant closings	Y	95. Kill-Void Panama Canal treaties	Y
74. Allow poison pills in corp takeovers	N	96. Kill-Insurance denial to AIDS+	Y
75. Kill-Workfare program	Y	97. Keep diplomatic immunity intact	Y
76. Prohibit employee polygraph testing	Y	98. Produce Bigeye nerve gas bomb	N
77. Cap Medicare patients' liability	Y	99. Balanced budget by '93-via targets	Y
78. Revise unfair trade practices	Y	100. Allow ASAT missile tests in space	Y
79. Kill-Shift SDI $ to conv weapons	N	101. Limit space-based/ABM system tests	Y
80. Kill-Shift SDI $ to accidental launch	Y	102. Force reduction in trade barriers	Y
81. Kill-Shift MX $ to supplies/parts	N	103. Repeal windfall profit tax on oil	N
82. Kill-Buy America provision at DOD	N	104. $1b/two year aid for the homeless	?
83. Allow nuclear testing-5+ kilotons	N	105. Disallow $30m for AZT to poor	N
84. Allow SALT II to be exceeded	N	106. Bar AIDS test-immigrants/marriage	Y
85. $ to vets exposed to nuclear bomb	Y	107. Kill-Biennial budget approval	Y
86. Warn workers of disease exposure	N	108. Fairness doctrine in broadcasting	Y
87. Restore four civil rights laws	Y	109. Raise speed limit to 65 mph	Y
88. Disapprove uranium sales to Japan	N		

The following are House measures voted on between 1982-1986:

99. Immigration reform/alien amnesty	?	122. Emergency farm credit/revisions	Y
100. South Africa sanctions-veto override	?	123. Duty on Taiwan/Hong Kong/S Korea	N
101. Tax overhaul to revise income tax	Y	124. Limit steel imports to 17%	Y
102. Use of military in drug war	?	125. Cut $ to schools that bar prayer	Y
103. Delete 12 MX/add conventional wpn	?	126. $50b-taxes; cut Medicare/spending	Y
104. Raise speed limit to 65 mph	?	127. Limit Pershing II/cruise in Europe	N
105. Require Pentagon to buy US goods	?	128. Delete $7.1b for 34 B-1 bombers	Y
106. AIDS insurance non-discrimination	?	129. Bar purchase of Sergeant York guns	N
107. Prohibit Saudi arms sales	Y	130. El Salvador military/economic aid	N
108. Ease Gun Control Act of 1968	Y	131. Bar mining of Nicaraguan waters	Y
109. Bar interstate handgun transport	Y	132. Physician fee freeze for Medicare	N
110. Make company emissions known	Y	133. $49b in "sin"/phone/insurance taxes	Y
111. Allow toxic victims to sue in fed ct	N	134. Allow sale of Conrail	N
112. Superfund waste cleanup of $10b	N	135. Equal Rights Amendment	Y
113. 90 days notice of plant closings	N	136. Authorize Marines in Lebanon	Y
114. $20b in Medicare cuts/tax increases	Y	137. Eminent domain for coal companies	N
115. Spending cuts and tax increases	Y	138. Prohibit EPA clean air sanctions	N
116. Set school lunch lmt-250% poverty	N	139. SS retirement age increase/reforms	N
117. $75m for youth work projects	Y	140. Auto domestic content requirement	Y
118. Allow Angolan military assistance	Y	141. Delete jobs program funding	Y
119. Suspend defense payments for abuse	N	142. Highway-gas tax bill	Y
120. Drop SS COLAs/$12b tax increase	N	143. Cut $5b from defense for Medicare	Y
121. Approve $1.5b for 21 MX missiles	N	144. Emergency housing aid of $1b	Y

Presidential Support Score: 1991 - 44% 1990 - 43%

HAWAII

INOUYE, DANIEL K. -- Hawaii [Democrat]. Term Began/Expires: 1987/1992. **Prior Terms:** House: 1959 (Special Election)-1962; Senate: 1963-86. Born: September 7, 1924; Honolulu, HI. Education: University of Hawaii (A.B.); George Washington University Law School (J.D.). Military Service: U.S. Army, WWII. Occupation: Hawaii territory representative (1954-58); Hawaii territory senator (1958-59).

INOUYE, DANIEL K. (continued)

1. Prohibit MFN status for China	Y
2. Kill-Tie welfare to school attendance	Y
3. Limit credit card interest rates	Y
4. Confirm Gates as head of CIA	Y
5. Adoption of national energy policies	Y
6. Kill-Restrict NEA use of funds	Y
7. Unemployment benefits extension	Y
8. Confirm Thomas to Supreme Court	N
9. Raise eligibility for unpaid leave	Y
10. Notify parents of minors' abortions	N
11. Move $3b from defense to domestic	N
12. End production of B-2 bomber	N
13. Cut SDI $1b to reduce deficit	N
14. Maintain strategic stability-Soviets	N
15. Kill-Allow women as combat pilots	Y
16. Kill-Allow HIV tests before surgery	Y
17. Strike $12b aid to Int'l Mon Fund	N
18. Raise Senate salary/omit honoraria	Y
19. Reduce space station funding $1.9b	N
20. Kill-Eliminate supercollider funds	Y
21. Req 5-day handgun waiting period	Y
22. Life in prison instead of death	Y
23. Exceptions to exclusionary rule	N
24. Ban race as death sentence factor	N
25. Campaign finance revisions	Y
26. Kill-Term limits for senators	Y
27. Require four presidential debates	Y
28. Tighten ban on vertical price fixing	Y
29. Kill-Freeze discretionary budget	Y
30. Provide $30b for failed S&Ls	Y
31. Allow use of force against Iraq	N
32. Allow $15b in foreign aid for 1991	Y
33. Civil Rights Act of 1990	Y
34. Block cancellation of Egypt's debt	N
35. Cut El Salvador military aid 50%	Y
36. Reduce troops in NATO by 30,000	N
37. Req increases in auto fuel efficiency	Y
38. Bar taxpayer funding of campaigns	N
39. Limit textile import growth to 1%	Y
40. Amendment to ban flag desecration	N
41. Let fed emp be politically active	Y
42. Reauthorize Amtrak-veto override	Y
43. Allow sale of assault weapons	N
44. Retraining aid for coal miners	Y
45. Kill-Raise car emission standards	Y
46. Pull EPA nuclear plant authority	Y
47. Defer Chinese students' deportation	Y
48. Cut in capital gains tax	N
49. Establish CIA inspector general	Y
50. Kill-Sanctions against China	Y
51. Bar drug testing to receive AFDC	Y
52. Kill-Allow force against drug planes	Y
53. Include illegal aliens in census	Y
54. Restitution to Japanese interned	Y
55. Troop reduction in Europe of 50%	N
56. Increase SDI research to $4.3b	Y
57. Kill-Pay homeless below min wage	Y
58. Ban airline smoking within US	N
59. Bar transfer of FS-X technology	Y
60. Limit liability for oil spills	Y
61. Restructure S&L industry	Y
62. Ban $ to illegal foreign activities	Y
63. Req immigrant fluency in English	N
64. Allow aliens' families to stay in US	Y
65. Expand child care aid/tax credit	Y
66. Raise minimum wage w/subminimum	Y
67. Freeze outlays except SS/Medicare	N
68. Kill-Shift $5b of DOD to domestic	Y
69. Confirm Tower as sec of defense	N
70. Bar abortion $ except to save mother	N
71. Kill-Warn AIDS carriers' spouses	Y
72. Allow religious schools to bar gays	N
73. 60 days' notice of plant closings	Y
74. Allow poison pills in corp takeovers	N
75. Kill-Workfare program	Y
76. Prohibit employee polygraph testing	Y
77. Cap Medicare patients' liability	Y
78. Revise unfair trade practices	Y
79. Kill-Shift SDI $ to conv weapons	Y
80. Kill-Shift SDI $ to accidental launch	Y
81. Kill-Shift MX $ to supplies/parts	Y
82. Kill-Buy America provision at DOD	N
83. Allow nuclear testing-5+ kilotons	N
84. Allow SALT II to be exceeded	N
85. $ to vets exposed to nuclear bomb	Y
86. Warn workers of disease exposure	Y
87. Restore four civil rights laws	Y
88. Disapprove uranium sales to Japan	?
89. Notify Congress of covert operations	Y
90. Approval of $36m in Contra aid	N
91. $18b deficit reduction compromise	Y
92. Allow sale of hard-to-detect guns	N
93. Catastrophic health insurance	Y
94. Bork nomination to Supreme Court	N
95. Kill-Void Panama Canal treaties	Y
96. Kill-Insurance denial to AIDS+	Y
97. Keep diplomatic immunity intact	Y
98. Produce Bigeye nerve gas bomb	N
99. Balanced budget by '93-via targets	Y
100. Allow ASAT missile tests in space	N
101. Limit space-based/ABM system tests	Y
102. Force reduction in trade barriers	Y
103. Repeal windfall profit tax on oil	Y
104. $1b/two year aid for the homeless	?
105. Disallow $30m for AZT to poor	N
106. Bar AIDS test-immigrants/marriage	Y
107. Kill-Biennial budget approval	Y
108. Fairness doctrine in broadcasting	Y
109. Raise speed limit to 65 mph	N
110. Immigration reform/alien amnesty	N
111. South Africa sanctions-veto override	Y
112. Kill-Use of military in drug war	Y
113. Tax overhaul to revise income tax	N
114. Submit nuclear test ban treaties	Y
115. Prohibit sale of Stinger missiles	Y
116. Prohibit binary chemical weapons	Y
117. Kill-$10/barrel oil tariff increase	Y
118. Grant tax amnesty provisions	N
119. Block Saudi arms sale-veto override	Y
120. Balanced budget amendment	N
121. Include veterans in spending cuts	N
122. Bar $ to hazardous substance victims	N
123. Allow seasonal workers in the US	?
124. Let fed courts rule on school prayer	Y
125. Presidential line-item veto	N
126. Ease Gun Control Act of 1968	N
127. Kill-Req 14-day wait for handguns	N
128. Kill-15% min tax on corporations	N

INOUYE, DANIEL K. (continued)

129. Drop Social Security COLA	N	137. Capital punishment-federal crimes	N
130. Freeze funding for all programs	N	138. Ban government officials from taping	Y
131. Kill-Nuclear weapon freeze	N	139. Martin Luther King holiday	Y
132. Keep decision narrowing Title IX	N	140. Authorize Marines in Lebanon	N
133. Raise drinking age to 21	Y	141. Amendment making abortion illegal	N
134. Allow production of MX missile	N	142. Delete $1.2b for jobs creation	N
135. Raise taxes/cut spending by $140b	N	143. Keep tobacco price supports	Y
136. School prayer amendment	N	144. Emergency housing aid of $5.1b	?

Presidential Support Score: 1991 - 51% 1990 - 45%

AKAKA, DANIEL K. -- Hawaii [Democrat]. Term Began: 1990 (Special Appointment)/1994. Prior Terms: House: 1977-90. Born: September 11, 1924; Honolulu, HI. Education: University of Hawaii. Military Service: U.S. Army, 1945-47. Occupation: Teacher (1953-60); vice-principal (1960); principal (1963-71); program specialist (1968-71); director (1971-74); director, Hawaii Office of Economic Opportunity; special assistant, Human Resources, and director, Progressive Neighborhoods Program (1975-76).

1. Prohibit MFN status for China	Y	23. Exceptions to exclusionary rule	N
2. Kill-Tie welfare to school attendance	Y	24. Ban race as death sentence factor	N
3. Limit credit card interest rates	Y	25. Campaign finance revisions	Y
4. Confirm Gates as head of CIA	Y	26. Kill-Term limits for senators	Y
5. Adoption of national energy policies	Y	27. Require four presidential debates	Y
6. Kill-Restrict NEA use of funds	Y	28. Tighten ban on vertical price fixing	Y
7. Unemployment benefits extension	Y	29. Kill-Freeze discretionary budget	Y
8. Confirm Thomas to Supreme Court	N	30. Provide $30b for failed S&Ls	N
9. Raise eligibility for unpaid leave	Y	31. Allow use of force against Iraq	N
10. Notify parents of minors' abortions	N	32. Allow $15b in foreign aid for 1991	Y
11. Move $3b from defense to domestic	Y	33. Civil Rights Act of 1990	Y
12. End production of B-2 bomber	N	34. Block cancellation of Egypt's debt	N
13. Cut SDI $1b to reduce deficit	Y	35. Cut El Salvador military aid 50%	Y
14. Maintain strategic stability-Soviets	N	36. Reduce troops in NATO by 30,000	N
15. Kill-Allow women as combat pilots	N	37. Req increases in auto fuel efficiency	Y
16. Kill-Allow HIV tests before surgery	Y	38. Bar taxpayer funding of campaigns	N
17. Strike $12b aid to Int'l Mon Fund	N	39. Limit textile import growth to 1%	Y
18. Raise Senate salary/omit honoraria	Y	40. Amendment to ban flag desecration	N
19. Reduce space station funding $1.9b	N	41. Let fed emp be politically active	Y
20. Kill-Eliminate supercollider funds	Y	42. Reauthorize Amtrak-veto override	Y
21. Req 5-day handgun waiting period	Y	43. Allow sale of assault weapons	N
22. Life in prison instead of death	Y		

The following are House measures voted on between 1982-1990:

40. Expand child care aid/tax credit	Y	60. Textile import quotas-veto override	N
41. Raise House salary/omit honoraria	Y	61. Bar abortion funding in Wash, DC	N
42. Toughen oil-spill liability	Y	62. Notify spouses of AIDS+ carriers	N
43. Restitution to Japanese interned	Y	63. Seize conveyance-drug trafficking	N
44. Protect Chinese & C.A. nationals	Y	64. South Africa sanctions	#
45. Abortion $ for rape/incest cases	Y	65. 60 days' notice of plant closings	Y
46. Allow religious schools to bar gays	N	66. Close unneeded military bases	N
47. Bar broadcaster fairness doctrine	N	67. Keep welfare reform within $2.8b	N
48. Bar cap gains cut/reinstate IRA	Y	68. Allow children housing exclusion	N
49. Bar unions equal voice in pension	N	69. Shift $400m of NASA to homeless	N
50. Bar assembly of chemical weapons	Y	70. Cap Medicare patients' liability	Y
51. Ban plutonium/uranium production	Y	71. Prohibit employee polygraph testing	Y
52. Cap MX missile deployment at 50	Y	72. Allow CIA to fund Contras	N
53. Allow $3b for 2 stealth bombers	N	73. Revise unfair trade practices	Y
54. Publish bio-warfare experiments	Y	74. Focus SDI on accidental launch	Y
55. Raise minimum wage-veto override	Y	75. Bar Air Force $ for MX missile	Y
56. Bar transfer of FS-X technology	N	76. Allow "real" increase in defense	N
57. Cut defense and raise domestic $	Y	77. Troop reduction in Europe of 50%	N
58. Uniform poll closing in 48 states	Y	78. Ban nuclear tests above 1 kiloton	Y
59. Req foreign investment disclosure	Y	79. Ban anti-satellite missile tests	Y

AKAKA, DANIEL K. (continued)

80. Observe certain limits of SALT II	Y	
81. Restore four Civil Rights laws	Y	
82. Prohibit aliens as strikebreakers	Y	
83. Allow military malpractice suits	Y	
84. Approval of $36m in Contra aid	N	
85. $18b deficit reduction compromise	Y	
86. Welfare reform of $5.7b for 5 years	Y	
87. Raise taxes $12b/cut spending $3b	Y	
88. Board to assess occupational risk	Y	
89. Balanced budget by '93-via targets	Y	
90. Bar licensing of two nuclear plants	Y	
91. Remove victims compensation cap	N	
92. Catastrophic health insurance	Y	
93. Ban airline smoking-2 hours or less	N	
94. $1b/two year aid for the homeless	Y	
95. Bar non-unions in union companies	Y	
96. Increase FSLIC rescue to $15b	N	
97. Impose quotas to lower trade deficit	Y	
98. Reduce discretionary budget 21%	N	
99. Immigration reform/alien amnesty	N	
100. South Africa sanctions-veto override	Y	
101. Tax overhaul to revise income tax	N	
102. Use of military in drug war	N	
103. Delete 12 MX/add conventional wpn	Y	
104. Raise speed limit to 65 mph	N	
105. Require Pentagon to buy US goods	Y	
106. AIDS insurance non-discrimination	Y	
107. Prohibit Saudi arms sales	Y	
108. Ease Gun Control Act of 1968	N	
109. Bar interstate handgun transport	Y	
110. Make company emissions known	Y	
111. Allow toxic victims to sue in fed ct	Y	
112. Superfund waste cleanup of $10b	Y	

113. 90 days notice of plant closings	Y	
114. $20b in Medicare cuts/tax increases	Y	
115. Spending cuts and tax increases	Y	
116. Set school lunch lmt-250% poverty	N	
117. $75m for youth work projects	Y	
118. Allow Angolan military assistance	N	
119. Suspend defense payments for abuse	N	
120. Drop SS COLAs/$12b tax increase	N	
121. Approve $1.5b for 21 MX missiles	N	
122. Emergency farm credit/revisions	Y	
123. Duty on Taiwan/Hong Kong/S Korea	Y	
124. Limit steel imports to 17%	Y	
125. Cut $ to schools that bar prayer	N	
126. $50b-taxes; cut Medicare/spending	#	
127. Limit Pershing II/cruise in Europe	N	
128. Delete $7.1b for 34 B-1 bombers	N	
129. Bar purchase of Sergeant York guns	Y	
130. El Salvador military/economic aid	N	
131. Bar mining of Nicaraguan waters	?	
132. Physician fee freeze for Medicare	N	
133. $49b in "sin"/phone/insurance taxes	Y	
134. Allow sale of Conrail	N	
135. Equal Rights Amendment	Y	
136. Authorize Marines in Lebanon	Y	
137. Eminent domain for coal companies	Y	
138. Prohibit EPA clean air sanctions	N	
139. SS retirement age increase/reforms	N	
140. Auto domestic content requirement	Y	
141. Delete jobs program funding	N	
142. Highway-gas tax bill	Y	
143. Cut $5b from defense for Medicare	Y	
144. Emergency housing aid of $1b	Y	

Presidential Support Score: 1991 - 35%   1990 - 23%

IDAHO

SYMMS, STEVEN D. -- Idaho [Republican]. Term Began/Expires: 1987/1992. Prior Terms: House: 1972-80; Senate: 1981-86. Born: August 23, 1938; Nampa, ID. Education: University of Idaho (B.S.). Military Service: U.S. Marines, 1960-63. Occupation: Vice president, personnel and production manager, Symms Fruit Ranch; treasurer, American Conservative Union.

1. Prohibit MFN status for China	N	
2. Kill-Tie welfare to school attendance	N	
3. Limit credit card interest rates	N	
4. Confirm Gates as head of CIA	Y	
5. Adoption of national energy policies	Y	
6. Kill-Restrict NEA use of funds	Y	
7. Unemployment benefits extension	N	
8. Confirm Thomas to Supreme Court	Y	
9. Raise eligibility for unpaid leave	N	
10. Notify parents of minors' abortions	Y	
11. Move $3b from defense to domestic	N	
12. End production of B-2 bomber	N	
13. Cut SDI $1b to reduce deficit	N	
14. Maintain strategic stability-Soviets	N	
15. Kill-Allow women as combat pilots	Y	

16. Kill-Allow HIV tests before surgery	N	
17. Strike $12b aid to Int'l Mon Fund	Y	
18. Raise Senate salary/omit honoraria	Y	
19. Reduce space station funding $1.9b	N	
20. Kill-Eliminate supercollider funds	Y	
21. Req 5-day handgun waiting period	N	
22. Life in prison instead of death	N	
23. Exceptions to exclusionary rule	Y	
24. Ban race as death sentence factor	Y	
25. Campaign finance revisions	N	
26. Kill-Term limits for senators	N	
27. Require four presidential debates	?	
28. Tighten ban on vertical price fixing	N	
29. Kill-Freeze discretionary budget	N	
30. Provide $30b for failed S&Ls	Y	

SYMMS, STEVEN D. (continued)

31. Allow use of force against Iraq	Y	
32. Allow $15b in foreign aid for 1991	N	
33. Civil Rights Act of 1990	N	
34. Block cancellation of Egypt's debt	N	
35. Cut El Salvador military aid 50%	N	
36. Reduce troops in NATO by 30,000	N	
37. Req increases in auto fuel efficiency	N	
38. Bar taxpayer funding of campaigns	Y	
39. Limit textile import growth to 1%	N	
40. Amendment to ban flag desecration	Y	
41. Let fed emp be politically active	N	
42. Reauthorize Amtrak-veto override	N	
43. Allow sale of assault weapons	Y	
44. Retraining aid for coal miners	N	
45. Kill-Raise car emission standards	N	
46. Pull EPA nuclear plant authority	Y	
47. Defer Chinese students' deportation	N	
48. Cut in capital gains tax	Y	
49. Establish CIA inspector general	N	
50. Kill-Sanctions against China	N	
51. Bar drug testing to receive AFDC	N	
52. Kill-Allow force against drug planes	N	
53. Include illegal aliens in census	N	
54. Restitution to Japanese interned	N	
55. Troop reduction in Europe of 50%	N	
56. Increase SDI research to $4.3b	Y	
57. Kill-Pay homeless below min wage	N	
58. Ban airline smoking within US	N	
59. Bar transfer of FS-X technology	N	
60. Limit liability for oil spills	Y	
61. Restructure S&L industry	N	
62. Ban $ to illegal foreign activities	N	
63. Req immigrant fluency in English	Y	
64. Allow aliens' families to stay in US	N	
65. Expand child care aid/tax credit	N	
66. Raise minimum wage w/subminimum	N	
67. Freeze outlays except SS/Medicare	N	
68. Kill-Shift $5b of DOD to domestic	Y	
69. Confirm Tower as sec of defense	Y	
70. Bar abortion $ except to save mother	Y	
71. Kill-Warn AIDS carriers' spouses	N	
72. Allow religious schools to bar gays	Y	
73. 60 days' notice of plant closings	N	
74. Allow poison pills in corp takeovers	N	
75. Kill-Workfare program	N	
76. Prohibit employee polygraph testing	N	
77. Cap Medicare patients' liability	N	
78. Revise unfair trade practices	N	
79. Kill-Shift SDI $ to conv weapons	Y	
80. Kill-Shift SDI $ to accidental launch	N	
81. Kill-Shift MX $ to supplies/parts	Y	
82. Kill-Buy America provision at DOD	Y	
83. Allow nuclear testing-5+ kilotons	Y	
84. Allow SALT II to be exceeded	Y	
85. $ to vets exposed to nuclear bomb	N	
86. Warn workers of disease exposure	N	
87. Restore four civil rights laws	N	

88. Disapprove uranium sales to Japan	N
89. Notify Congress of covert operations	N
90. Approval of $36m in Contra aid	Y
91. $18b deficit reduction compromise	N
92. Allow sale of hard-to-detect guns	Y
93. Catastrophic health insurance	N
94. Bork nomination to Supreme Court	Y
95. Kill-Void Panama Canal treaties	N
96. Kill-Insurance denial to AIDS+	N
97. Keep diplomatic immunity intact	?
98. Produce Bigeye nerve gas bomb	Y
99. Balanced budget by '93-via targets	Y
100. Allow ASAT missile tests in space	Y
101. Limit space-based/ABM system tests	N
102. Force reduction in trade barriers	N
103. Repeal windfall profit tax on oil	Y
104. $1b/two year aid for the homeless	N
105. Disallow $30m for AZT to poor	N
106. Bar AIDS test-immigrants/marriage	N
107. Kill-Biennial budget approval	N
108. Fairness doctrine in broadcasting	N
109. Raise speed limit to 65 mph	Y
110. Immigration reform/alien amnesty	X
111. South Africa sanctions-veto override	N
112. Kill-Use of military in drug war	Y
113. Tax overhaul to revise income tax	Y
114. Submit nuclear test ban treaties	N
115. Prohibit sale of Stinger missiles	N
116. Prohibit binary chemical weapons	N
117. Kill-$10/barrel oil tariff increase	Y
118. Grant tax amnesty provisions	?
119. Block Saudi arms sale-veto override	Y
120. Balanced budget amendment	Y
121. Include veterans in spending cuts	Y
122. Bar $ to hazardous substance victims	Y
123. Allow seasonal workers in the US	Y
124. Let fed courts rule on school prayer	N
125. Presidential line-item veto	Y
126. Ease Gun Control Act of 1968	Y
127. Kill-Req 14-day wait for handguns	Y
128. Kill-15% min tax on corporations	Y
129. Drop Social Security COLA	Y
130. Freeze funding for all programs	N
131. Kill-Nuclear weapon freeze	Y
132. Keep decision narrowing Title IX	Y
133. Raise drinking age to 21	N
134. Allow production of MX missile	Y
135. Raise taxes/cut spending by $140b	Y
136. School prayer amendment	Y
137. Capital punishment-federal crimes	Y
138. Ban government officials from taping	N
139. Martin Luther King holiday	N
140. Authorize Marines in Lebanon	Y
141. Amendment making abortion illegal	Y
142. Delete $1.2b for jobs creation	Y
143. Keep tobacco price supports	Y
144. Emergency housing aid of $5.1b	N

Presidential Support Score: 1991 - 91%   1990 - 74%

CRAIG, LARRY E. -- Idaho [Republican]. Term Began/Expires: 1991/1996. Prior Terms: House: 1981-90. Born: July 20, 1945; Council, ID. Education: University of Idaho (B.A.). Occupation: Farmer-rancher; Idaho senator.

CRAIG, LARRY E. (continued)

1. Prohibit MFN status for China	N	
2. Kill-Tie welfare to school attendance	N	
3. Limit credit card interest rates	Y	
4. Confirm Gates as head of CIA	Y	
5. Adoption of national energy policies	Y	
6. Kill-Restrict NEA use of funds	Y	
7. Unemployment benefits extension	N	
8. Confirm Thomas to Supreme Court	Y	
9. Raise eligibility for unpaid leave	N	
10. Notify parents of minors' abortions	Y	
11. Move $3b from defense to domestic	N	
12. End production of B-2 bomber	N	
13. Cut SDI $1b to reduce deficit	N	
14. Maintain strategic stability-Soviets	N	
15. Kill-Allow women as combat pilots	Y	
16. Kill-Allow HIV tests before surgery	N	
17. Strike $12b aid to Int'l Mon Fund	Y	
18. Raise Senate salary/omit honoraria	Y	
19. Reduce space station funding $1.9b	N	
20. Kill-Eliminate supercollider funds	N	
21. Req 5-day handgun waiting period	N	
22. Life in prison instead of death	N	
23. Exceptions to exclusionary rule	Y	
24. Ban race as death sentence factor	Y	
25. Campaign finance revisions	N	
26. Kill-Term limits for senators	N	
27. Require four presidential debates	N	
28. Tighten ban on vertical price fixing	N	
29. Kill-Freeze discretionary budget	N	
30. Provide $30b for failed S&Ls	N	
31. Allow use of force against Iraq	Y	

The following are House measures voted on between 1982-1990:

36. Amendment to ban flag desecration	Y	
37. Reauthorize Amtrak-veto override	N	
38. Retraining aid for coal miners	X	
39. Suspend El Salvador military aid	X	
40. Expand child care aid/tax credit	N	
41. Raise House salary/omit honoraria	N	
42. Toughen oil-spill liability	N	
43. Restitution to Japanese interned	Y	
44. Protect Chinese & C.A. nationals	N	
45. Abortion $ for rape/incest cases	N	
46. Allow religious schools to bar gays	Y	
47. Bar broadcaster fairness doctrine	N	
48. Bar cap gains cut/reinstate IRA	N	
49. Bar unions equal voice in pension	Y	
50. Bar assembly of chemical weapons	N	
51. Ban plutonium/uranium production	N	
52. Cap MX missile deployment at 50	N	
53. Allow $3b for 2 stealth bombers	Y	
54. Publish bio-warfare experiments	N	
55. Raise minimum wage-veto override	N	
56. Bar transfer of FS-X technology	N	
57. Cut defense and raise domestic $	N	
58. Uniform poll closing in 48 states	Y	
59. Req foreign investment disclosure	N	
60. Textile import quotas-veto override	N	
61. Bar abortion funding in Wash, DC	Y	
62. Notify spouses of AIDS+ carriers	Y	
63. Seize conveyance-drug trafficking	N	
64. South Africa sanctions	X	
65. 60 days' notice of plant closings	N	
66. Close unneeded military bases	Y	
67. Keep welfare reform within $2.8b	Y	
68. Allow children housing exclusion	Y	
69. Shift $400m of NASA to homeless	N	
70. Cap Medicare patients' liability	N	
71. Prohibit employee polygraph testing	N	
72. Allow CIA to fund Contras	#	
73. Revise unfair trade practices	N	
74. Focus SDI on accidental launch	N	
75. Bar Air Force $ for MX missile	N	
76. Allow "real" increase in defense	#	
77. Troop reduction in Europe of 50%	X	
78. Ban nuclear tests above 1 kiloton	X	
79. Ban anti-satellite missile tests	X	
80. Observe certain limits of SALT II	N	
81. Restore four Civil Rights laws	N	
82. Prohibit aliens as strikebreakers	N	
83. Allow military malpractice suits	?	
84. Approval of $36m in Contra aid	Y	
85. $18b deficit reduction compromise	N	
86. Welfare reform of $5.7b for 5 years	N	
87. Raise taxes $12b/cut spending $3b	N	
88. Board to assess occupational risk	N	
89. Balanced budget by '93-via targets	X	
90. Bar licensing of two nuclear plants	N	
91. Remove victims compensation cap	N	
92. Catastrophic health insurance	N	
93. Ban airline smoking-2 hours or less	N	
94. $1b/two year aid for the homeless	N	
95. Bar non-unions in union companies	N	
96. Increase FSLIC rescue to $15b	N	
97. Impose quotas to lower trade deficit	N	
98. Reduce discretionary budget 21%	Y	
99. Immigration reform/alien amnesty	N	
100. South Africa sanctions-veto override	N	
101. Tax overhaul to revise income tax	N	
102. Use of military in drug war	Y	
103. Delete 12 MX/add conventional wpn	N	
104. Raise speed limit to 65 mph	Y	
105. Require Pentagon to buy US goods	Y	
106. AIDS insurance non-discrimination	N	
107. Prohibit Saudi arms sales	Y	
108. Ease Gun Control Act of 1968	Y	
109. Bar interstate handgun transport	N	
110. Make company emissions known	N	
111. Allow toxic victims to sue in fed ct	N	
112. Superfund waste cleanup of $10b	N	
113. 90 days notice of plant closings	N	
114. $20b in Medicare cuts/tax increases	N	
115. Spending cuts and tax increases	N	
116. Set school lunch lmt-250% poverty	Y	
117. $75m for youth work projects	N	
118. Allow Angolan military assistance	Y	
119. Suspend defense payments for abuse	N	
120. Drop SS COLAs/$12b tax increase	N	
121. Approve $1.5b for 21 MX missiles	Y	
122. Emergency farm credit/revisions	N	
123. Duty on Taiwan/Hong Kong/S Korea	N	
124. Limit steel imports to 17%	N	
125. Cut $ to schools that bar prayer	Y	

CRAIG, LARRY E. (continued)

126. $50b-taxes; cut Medicare/spending	N
127. Limit Pershing II/cruise in Europe	N
128. Delete $7.1b for 34 B-1 bombers	N
129. Bar purchase of Sergeant York guns	N
130. El Salvador military/economic aid	Y
131. Bar mining of Nicaraguan waters	X
132. Physician fee freeze for Medicare	#
133. $49b in "sin"/phone/insurance taxes	N
134. Allow sale of Conrail	Y
135. Equal Rights Amendment	N
136. Authorize Marines in Lebanon	Y
137. Eminent domain for coal companies	N
138. Prohibit EPA clean air sanctions	?
139. SS retirement age increase/reforms	Y
140. Auto domestic content requirement	N
141. Delete jobs program funding	Y
142. Highway-gas tax bill	N
143. Cut $5b from defense for Medicare	N
144. Emergency housing aid of $1b	Y

Presidential Support Score: 1991 - 91%   1990 - 91%

ILLINOIS

DIXON, ALAN J. -- Illinois [Democrat]. Term Began/Expires: 1987/1992. Prior Terms: Senate: 1981-86. Born: July 7, 1927; Belleville, IL. Education: University of Illinois; Washington (St. Louis) University Law School. Military Service: U.S. Navy. Occupation: Police magistrate (1949); Illinois representative (1951-63); Illinois senator (1963-71); Illinois treasurer (1971-77); Illinois secretary of state (1977-81).

1. Prohibit MFN status for China	Y	38. Bar taxpayer funding of campaigns	N
2. Kill-Tie welfare to school attendance	Y	39. Limit textile import growth to 1%	Y
3. Limit credit card interest rates	Y	40. Amendment to ban flag desecration	Y
4. Confirm Gates as head of CIA	N	41. Let fed emp be politically active	Y
5. Adoption of national energy policies	N	42. Reauthorize Amtrak-veto override	Y
6. Kill-Restrict NEA use of funds	N	43. Allow sale of assault weapons	N
7. Unemployment benefits extension	Y	44. Retraining aid for coal miners	Y
8. Confirm Thomas to Supreme Court	Y	45. Kill-Raise car emission standards	Y
9. Raise eligibility for unpaid leave	Y	46. Pull EPA nuclear plant authority	N
10. Notify parents of minors' abortions	Y	47. Defer Chinese students' deportation	Y
11. Move $3b from defense to domestic	N	48. Cut in capital gains tax	N
12. End production of B-2 bomber	N	49. Establish CIA inspector general	Y
13. Cut SDI $1b to reduce deficit	N	50. Kill-Sanctions against China	N
14. Maintain strategic stability-Soviets	N	51. Bar drug testing to receive AFDC	Y
15. Kill-Allow women as combat pilots	N	52. Kill-Allow force against drug planes	N
16. Kill-Allow HIV tests before surgery	N	53. Include illegal aliens in census	Y
17. Strike $12b aid to Int'l Mon Fund	Y	54. Restitution to Japanese interned	Y
18. Raise Senate salary/omit honoraria	N	55. Troop reduction in Europe of 50%	N
19. Reduce space station funding $1.9b	Y	56. Increase SDI research to $4.3b	N
20. Kill-Eliminate supercollider funds	Y	57. Kill-Pay homeless below min wage	Y
21. Req 5-day handgun waiting period	Y	58. Ban airline smoking within US	Y
22. Life in prison instead of death	N	59. Bar transfer of FS-X technology	Y
23. Exceptions to exclusionary rule	Y	60. Limit liability for oil spills	N
24. Ban race as death sentence factor	Y	61. Restructure S&L industry	N
25. Campaign finance revisions	Y	62. Ban $ to illegal foreign activities	Y
26. Kill-Term limits for senators	Y	63. Req immigrant fluency in English	N
27. Require four presidential debates	N	64. Allow aliens' families to stay in US	Y
28. Tighten ban on vertical price fixing	N	65. Expand child care aid/tax credit	Y
29. Kill-Freeze discretionary budget	N	66. Raise minimum wage w/subminimum	Y
30. Provide $30b for failed S&Ls	Y	67. Freeze outlays except SS/Medicare	N
31. Allow use of force against Iraq	N	68. Kill-Shift $5b of DOD to domestic	N
32. Allow $15b in foreign aid for 1991	Y	69. Confirm Tower as sec of defense	N
33. Civil Rights Act of 1990	Y	70. Bar abortion $ except to save mother	Y
34. Block cancellation of Egypt's debt	Y	71. Kill-Warn AIDS carriers' spouses	N
35. Cut El Salvador military aid 50%	Y	72. Allow religious schools to bar gays	Y
36. Reduce troops in NATO by 30,000	Y	73. 60 days' notice of plant closings	Y
37. Req increases in auto fuel efficiency	N	74. Allow poison pills in corp takeovers	Y

DIXON, ALAN J. (continued)

75. Kill-Workfare program	N	
76. Prohibit employee polygraph testing	Y	
77. Cap Medicare patients' liability	Y	
78. Revise unfair trade practices	Y	
79. Kill-Shift SDI $ to conv weapons	N	
80. Kill-Shift SDI $ to accidental launch	Y	
81. Kill-Shift MX $ to supplies/parts	Y	
82. Kill-Buy America provision at DOD	N	
83. Allow nuclear testing-5+ kilotons	Y	
84. Allow SALT II to be exceeded	N	
85. $ to vets exposed to nuclear bomb	?	
86. Warn workers of disease exposure	N	
87. Restore four civil rights laws	Y	
88. Disapprove uranium sales to Japan	N	
89. Notify Congress of covert operations	N	
90. Approval of $36m in Contra aid	N	
91. $18b deficit reduction compromise	Y	
92. Allow sale of hard-to-detect guns	Y	
93. Catastrophic health insurance	Y	
94. Bork nomination to Supreme Court	N	
95. Kill-Void Panama Canal treaties	Y	
96. Kill-Insurance denial to AIDS+	N	
97. Keep diplomatic immunity intact	Y	
98. Produce Bigeye nerve gas bomb	Y	
99. Balanced budget by '93-via targets	Y	
100. Allow ASAT missile tests in space	Y	
101. Limit space-based/ABM system tests	Y	
102. Force reduction in trade barriers	Y	
103. Repeal windfall profit tax on oil	Y	
104. $1b/two year aid for the homeless	Y	
105. Disallow $30m for AZT to poor	N	
106. Bar AIDS test-immigrants/marriage	Y	
107. Kill-Biennial budget approval	Y	
108. Fairness doctrine in broadcasting	N	
109. Raise speed limit to 65 mph	N	

110. Immigration reform/alien amnesty	Y
111. South Africa sanctions-veto override	Y
112. Kill-Use of military in drug war	N
113. Tax overhaul to revise income tax	Y
114. Submit nuclear test ban treaties	Y
115. Prohibit sale of Stinger missiles	N
116. Prohibit binary chemical weapons	N
117. Kill-$10/barrel oil tariff increase	Y
118. Grant tax amnesty provisions	+
119. Block Saudi arms sale-veto override	Y
120. Balanced budget amendment	Y
121. Include veterans in spending cuts	N
122. Bar $ to hazardous substance victims	N
123. Allow seasonal workers in the US	N
124. Let fed courts rule on school prayer	Y
125. Presidential line-item veto	Y
126. Ease Gun Control Act of 1968	Y
127. Kill-Req 14-day wait for handguns	Y
128. Kill-15% min tax on corporations	Y
129. Drop Social Security COLA	N
130. Freeze funding for all programs	Y
131. Kill-Nuclear weapon freeze	N
132. Keep decision narrowing Title IX	N
133. Raise drinking age to 21	+
134. Allow production of MX missile	N
135. Raise taxes/cut spending by $140b	N
136. School prayer amendment	N
137. Capital punishment-federal crimes	Y
138. Ban government officials from taping	Y
139. Martin Luther King holiday	Y
140. Authorize Marines in Lebanon	N
141. Amendment making abortion illegal	N
142. Delete $1.2b for jobs creation	N
143. Keep tobacco price supports	N
144. Emergency housing aid of $5.1b	Y

Presidential Support Score: 1991 - 57%   1990 - 53%

SIMON, PAUL -- Illinois [Democrat]. Term Began/Expires: 1991/1996. Prior Terms: House: 1975-84; Senate: 1985-90. Born: November 29, 1928; Eugene, OR. Education: University of Oregon; Dana College. Occupation: Teacher; newspaper editor; (1947-66); Illinois lieutenant governor (1969-73); Illinois representative (1954-62); Illinois senator (1962-69).

1. Prohibit MFN status for China	Y	
2. Kill-Tie welfare to school attendance	Y	
3. Limit credit card interest rates	Y	
4. Confirm Gates as head of CIA	N	
5. Adoption of national energy policies	N	
6. Kill-Restrict NEA use of funds	Y	
7. Unemployment benefits extension	Y	
8. Confirm Thomas to Supreme Court	N	
9. Raise eligibility for unpaid leave	Y	
10. Notify parents of minors' abortions	N	
11. Move $3b from defense to domestic	Y	
12. End production of B-2 bomber	Y	
13. Cut SDI $1b to reduce deficit	Y	
14. Maintain strategic stability-Soviets	Y	
15. Kill-Allow women as combat pilots	N	
16. Kill-Allow HIV tests before surgery	Y	
17. Strike $12b aid to Int'l Mon Fund	N	
18. Raise Senate salary/omit honoraria	Y	
19. Reduce space station funding $1.9b	Y	
20. Kill-Eliminate supercollider funds	Y	

21. Req 5-day handgun waiting period	Y
22. Life in prison instead of death	Y
23. Exceptions to exclusionary rule	N
24. Ban race as death sentence factor	N
25. Campaign finance revisions	Y
26. Kill-Term limits for senators	Y
27. Require four presidential debates	Y
28. Tighten ban on vertical price fixing	Y
29. Kill-Freeze discretionary budget	Y
30. Provide $30b for failed S&Ls	Y
31. Allow use of force against Iraq	N
32. Allow $15b in foreign aid for 1991	Y
33. Civil Rights Act of 1990	Y
34. Block cancellation of Egypt's debt	Y
35. Cut El Salvador military aid 50%	Y
36. Reduce troops in NATO by 30,000	Y
37. Req increases in auto fuel efficiency	Y
38. Bar taxpayer funding of campaigns	N
39. Limit textile import growth to 1%	Y
40. Amendment to ban flag desecration	N

SIMON, PAUL (continued)

41. Let fed emp be politically active	Y	86. Warn workers of disease exposure	?
42. Reauthorize Amtrak-veto override	Y	87. Restore four civil rights laws	Y
43. Allow sale of assault weapons	N	88. Disapprove uranium sales to Japan	Y
44. Retraining aid for coal miners	Y	89. Notify Congress of covert operations	?
45. Kill-Raise car emission standards	N	90. Approval of $36m in Contra aid	N
46. Pull EPA nuclear plant authority	N	91. $18b deficit reduction compromise	?
47. Defer Chinese students' deportation	Y	92. Allow sale of hard-to-detect guns	?
48. Cut in capital gains tax	N	93. Catastrophic health insurance	?
49. Establish CIA inspector general	Y	94. Bork nomination to Supreme Court	N
50. Kill-Sanctions against China	N	95. Kill-Void Panama Canal treaties	?
51. Bar drug testing to receive AFDC	Y	96. Kill-Insurance denial to AIDS+	?
52. Kill-Allow force against drug planes	Y	97. Keep diplomatic immunity intact	?
53. Include illegal aliens in census	Y	98. Produce Bigeye nerve gas bomb	?
54. Restitution to Japanese interned	Y	99. Balanced budget by '93-via targets	?
55. Troop reduction in Europe of 50%	Y	100. Allow ASAT missile tests in space	--
56. Increase SDI research to $4.3b	N	101. Limit space-based/ABM system tests	?
57. Kill-Pay homeless below min wage	Y	102. Force reduction in trade barriers	+
58. Ban airline smoking within US	Y	103. Repeal windfall profit tax on oil	X
59. Bar transfer of FS-X technology	Y	104. $1b/two year aid for the homeless	?
60. Limit liability for oil spills	N	105. Disallow $30m for AZT to poor	?
61. Restructure S&L industry	Y	106. Bar AIDS test-immigrants/marriage	?
62. Ban $ to illegal foreign activities	Y	107. Kill-Biennial budget approval	Y
63. Req immigrant fluency in English	N	108. Fairness doctrine in broadcasting	?
64. Allow aliens' families to stay in US	Y	109. Raise speed limit to 65 mph	N
65. Expand child care aid/tax credit	Y	110. Immigration reform/alien amnesty	Y
66. Raise minimum wage w/subminimum	Y	111. South Africa sanctions-veto override	Y
67. Freeze outlays except SS/Medicare	N	112. Kill-Use of military in drug war	?
68. Kill-Shift $5b of DOD to domestic	N	113. Tax overhaul to revise income tax	--
69. Confirm Tower as sec of defense	N	114. Submit nuclear test ban treaties	Y
70. Bar abortion $ except to save mother	N	115. Prohibit sale of Stinger missiles	Y
71. Kill-Warn AIDS carriers' spouses	Y	116. Prohibit binary chemical weapons	Y
72. Allow religious schools to bar gays	--	117. Kill-$10/barrel oil tariff increase	N
73. 60 days' notice of plant closings	Y	118. Grant tax amnesty provisions	N
74. Allow poison pills in corp takeovers	Y	119. Block Saudi arms sale-veto override	Y
75. Kill-Workfare program	Y	120. Balanced budget amendment	Y
76. Prohibit employee polygraph testing	Y	121. Include veterans in spending cuts	N
77. Cap Medicare patients' liability	Y	122. Bar $ to hazardous substance victims	N
78. Revise unfair trade practices	Y	123. Allow seasonal workers in the US	Y
79. Kill-Shift SDI $ to conv weapons	?	124. Let fed courts rule on school prayer	Y
80. Kill-Shift SDI $ to accidental launch	?	125. Presidential line-item veto	N
81. Kill-Shift MX $ to supplies/parts	N	126. Ease Gun Control Act of 1968	?
82. Kill-Buy America provision at DOD	N	127. Kill-Req 14-day wait for handguns	?
83. Allow nuclear testing-5+ kilotons	N	128. Kill-15% min tax on corporations	N
84. Allow SALT II to be exceeded	N	129. Drop Social Security COLA	N
85. $ to vets exposed to nuclear bomb	Y	130. Freeze funding for all programs	Y

The following are House measures voted on between 1982-1984:

123. Duty on Taiwan/Hong Kong/S Korea	?	134. Allow sale of Conrail	N
124. Limit steel imports to 17%	?	135. Equal Rights Amendment	Y
125. Cut $ to schools that bar prayer	?	136. Authorize Marines in Lebanon	Y
126. $50b-taxes; cut Medicare/spending	Y	137. Eminent domain for coal companies	N
127. Limit Pershing II/cruise in Europe	?	138. Prohibit EPA clean air sanctions	?
128. Delete $7.1b for 34 B-1 bombers	Y	139. SS retirement age increase/reforms	N
129. Bar purchase of Sergeant York guns	Y	140. Auto domestic content requirement	Y
130. El Salvador military/economic aid	N	141. Delete jobs program funding	N
131. Bar mining of Nicaraguan waters	?	142. Highway-gas tax bill	Y
132. Physician fee freeze for Medicare	X	143. Cut $5b from defense for Medicare	Y
133. $49b in "sin"/phone/insurance taxes	?	144. Emergency housing aid of $1b	Y

Presidential Support Score: 1991 - 32%   1990 - 20%

INDIANA

LUGAR, RICHARD G. -- Indiana [Republican]. Term Began/Expires: 1989/1994. Prior Terms: Senate: 1977-88. Born: April 4, 1932; Indianapolis, IN. Education: Denison University. Occupation: Businessman; Indianapolis mayor (1968-74); visiting professor, Indiana Central University.

1. Prohibit MFN status for China	N	
2. Kill-Tie welfare to school attendance	N	
3. Limit credit card interest rates	N	
4. Confirm Gates as head of CIA	Y	
5. Adoption of national energy policies	Y	
6. Kill-Restrict NEA use of funds	Y	
7. Unemployment benefits extension	N	
8. Confirm Thomas to Supreme Court	Y	
9. Raise eligibility for unpaid leave	N	
10. Notify parents of minors' abortions	Y	
11. Move $3b from defense to domestic	N	
12. End production of B-2 bomber	N	
13. Cut SDI $1b to reduce deficit	N	
14. Maintain strategic stability-Soviets	N	
15. Kill-Allow women as combat pilots	N	
16. Kill-Allow HIV tests before surgery	N	
17. Strike $12b aid to Int'l Mon Fund	N	
18. Raise Senate salary/omit honoraria	Y	
19. Reduce space station funding $1.9b	N	
20. Kill-Eliminate supercollider funds	N	
21. Req 5-day handgun waiting period	Y	
22. Life in prison instead of death	N	
23. Exceptions to exclusionary rule	Y	
24. Ban race as death sentence factor	Y	
25. Campaign finance revisions	N	
26. Kill-Term limits for senators	Y	
27. Require four presidential debates	N	
28. Tighten ban on vertical price fixing	N	
29. Kill-Freeze discretionary budget	N	
30. Provide $30b for failed S&Ls	Y	
31. Allow use of force against Iraq	Y	
32. Allow $15b in foreign aid for 1991	Y	
33. Civil Rights Act of 1990	N	
34. Block cancellation of Egypt's debt	N	
35. Cut El Salvador military aid 50%	N	
36. Reduce troops in NATO by 30,000	N	
37. Req increases in auto fuel efficiency	N	
38. Bar taxpayer funding of campaigns	Y	
39. Limit textile import growth to 1%	N	
40. Amendment to ban flag desecration	Y	
41. Let fed emp be politically active	N	
42. Reauthorize Amtrak-veto override	N	
43. Allow sale of assault weapons	Y	
44. Retraining aid for coal miners	N	
45. Kill-Raise car emission standards	Y	
46. Pull EPA nuclear plant authority	Y	
47. Defer Chinese students' deportation	N	
48. Cut in capital gains tax	Y	
49. Establish CIA inspector general	N	
50. Kill-Sanctions against China	Y	
51. Bar drug testing to receive AFDC	Y	
52. Kill-Allow force against drug planes	N
53. Include illegal aliens in census	N
54. Restitution to Japanese interned	Y
55. Troop reduction in Europe of 50%	N
56. Increase SDI research to $4.3b	Y
57. Kill-Pay homeless below min wage	N
58. Ban airline smoking within US	Y
59. Bar transfer of FS-X technology	N
60. Limit liability for oil spills	N
61. Restructure S&L industry	N
62. Ban $ to illegal foreign activities	N
63. Req immigrant fluency in English	Y
64. Allow aliens' families to stay in US	N
65. Expand child care aid/tax credit	N
66. Raise minimum wage w/subminimum	N
67. Freeze outlays except SS/Medicare	N
68. Kill-Shift $5b of DOD to domestic	Y
69. Confirm Tower as sec of defense	Y
70. Bar abortion $ except to save mother	Y
71. Kill-Warn AIDS carriers' spouses	N
72. Allow religious schools to bar gays	Y
73. 60 days' notice of plant closings	N
74. Allow poison pills in corp takeovers	N
75. Kill-Workfare program	N
76. Prohibit employee polygraph testing	Y
77. Cap Medicare patients' liability	Y
78. Revise unfair trade practices	N
79. Kill-Shift SDI $ to conv weapons	Y
80. Kill-Shift SDI $ to accidental launch	N
81. Kill-Shift MX $ to supplies/parts	Y
82. Kill-Buy America provision at DOD	N
83. Allow nuclear testing-5+ kilotons	Y
84. Allow SALT II to be exceeded	Y
85. $ to vets exposed to nuclear bomb	N
86. Warn workers of disease exposure	N
87. Restore four civil rights laws	N
88. Disapprove uranium sales to Japan	N
89. Notify Congress of covert operations	Y
90. Approval of $36m in Contra aid	Y
91. $18b deficit reduction compromise	Y
92. Allow sale of hard-to-detect guns	Y
93. Catastrophic health insurance	Y
94. Bork nomination to Supreme Court	Y
95. Kill-Void Panama Canal treaties	Y
96. Kill-Insurance denial to AIDS+	N
97. Keep diplomatic immunity intact	Y
98. Produce Bigeye nerve gas bomb	Y
99. Balanced budget by '93-via targets	Y
100. Allow ASAT missile tests in space	Y
101. Limit space-based/ABM system tests	N
102. Force reduction in trade barriers	N

LUGAR, RICHARD G. (continued)

103. Repeal windfall profit tax on oil	Y	124. Let fed courts rule on school prayer	Y
104. $1b/two year aid for the homeless	?	125. Presidential line-item veto	Y
105. Disallow $30m for AZT to poor	Y	126. Ease Gun Control Act of 1968	Y
106. Bar AIDS test-immigrants/marriage	Y	127. Kill-Req 14-day wait for handguns	Y
107. Kill-Biennial budget approval	N	128. Kill-15% min tax on corporations	Y
108. Fairness doctrine in broadcasting	N	129. Drop Social Security COLA	Y
109. Raise speed limit to 65 mph	Y	130. Freeze funding for all programs	N
110. Immigration reform/alien amnesty	Y	131. Kill-Nuclear weapon freeze	Y
111. South Africa sanctions-veto override	Y	132. Keep decision narrowing Title IX	Y
112. Kill-Use of military in drug war	Y	133. Raise drinking age to 21	Y
113. Tax overhaul to revise income tax	Y	134. Allow production of MX missile	Y
114. Submit nuclear test ban treaties	N	135. Raise taxes/cut spending by $140b	Y
115. Prohibit sale of Stinger missiles	N	136. School prayer amendment	Y
116. Prohibit binary chemical weapons	N	137. Capital punishment-federal crimes	Y
117. Kill-$10/barrel oil tariff increase	Y	138. Ban government officials from taping	N
118. Grant tax amnesty provisions	N	139. Martin Luther King holiday	Y
119. Block Saudi arms sale-veto override	N	140. Authorize Marines in Lebanon	Y
120. Balanced budget amendment	Y	141. Amendment making abortion illegal	Y
121. Include veterans in spending cuts	Y	142. Delete $1.2b for jobs creation	Y
122. Bar $ to hazardous substance victims	Y	143. Keep tobacco price supports	N
123. Allow seasonal workers in the US	Y	144. Emergency housing aid of $5.1b	Y

Presidential Support Score: 1991 - 93%   1990 - 86%

COATS, DAN -- Indiana [Republican]. Term Began/Expires: 1991/1996. Prior Terms: House: 1981-89; Senate: 1989 (Special Appointment)-1990. Born: May 16, 1943; Jackson, MI. Education: Wheaton College (B.A.); Indiana University Law School (J.D.). Military Service: U.S. Army, 1966-68. Occupation: Private attorney; assistant vice-president and counsel, Mutual Security Life Insurance Co.; congressional district representative (1976-80); board member, Anthony Wayne Rehabilitation Center and Historic River Cruises of Fort Wayne.

1. Prohibit MFN status for China	N	32. Allow $15b in foreign aid for 1991	Y
2. Kill-Tie welfare to school attendance	N	33. Civil Rights Act of 1990	N
3. Limit credit card interest rates	N	34. Block cancellation of Egypt's debt	Y
4. Confirm Gates as head of CIA	Y	35. Cut El Salvador military aid 50%	N
5. Adoption of national energy policies	Y	36. Reduce troops in NATO by 30,000	N
6. Kill-Restrict NEA use of funds	N	37. Req increases in auto fuel efficiency	N
7. Unemployment benefits extension	N	38. Bar taxpayer funding of campaigns	Y
8. Confirm Thomas to Supreme Court	Y	39. Limit textile import growth to 1%	N
9. Raise eligibility for unpaid leave	Y	40. Amendment to ban flag desecration	Y
10. Notify parents of minors' abortions	Y	41. Let fed emp be politically active	N
11. Move $3b from defense to domestic	N	42. Reauthorize Amtrak-veto override	N
12. End production of B-2 bomber	N	43. Allow sale of assault weapons	Y
13. Cut SDI $1b to reduce deficit	N	44. Retraining aid for coal miners	Y
14. Maintain strategic stability-Soviets	N	45. Kill-Raise car emission standards	Y
15. Kill-Allow women as combat pilots	N	46. Pull EPA nuclear plant authority	N
16. Kill-Allow HIV tests before surgery	N	47. Defer Chinese students' deportation	N
17. Strike $12b aid to Int'l Mon Fund	Y	48. Cut in capital gains tax	Y
18. Raise Senate salary/omit honoraria	N	49. Establish CIA inspector general	N
19. Reduce space station funding $1.9b	N	50. Kill-Sanctions against China	N
20. Kill-Eliminate supercollider funds	N	51. Bar drug testing to receive AFDC	Y
21. Req 5-day handgun waiting period	Y	52. Kill-Allow force against drug planes	N
22. Life in prison instead of death	N	53. Include illegal aliens in census	N
23. Exceptions to exclusionary rule	Y	54. Restitution to Japanese interned	N
24. Ban race as death sentence factor	Y	55. Troop reduction in Europe of 50%	N
25. Campaign finance revisions	N	56. Increase SDI research to $4.3b	Y
26. Kill-Term limits for senators	N	57. Kill-Pay homeless below min wage	N
27. Require four presidential debates	N	58. Ban airline smoking within US	Y
28. Tighten ban on vertical price fixing	N	59. Bar transfer of FS-X technology	Y
29. Kill-Freeze discretionary budget	N	60. Limit liability for oil spills	N
30. Provide $30b for failed S&Ls	Y	61. Restructure S&L industry	N
31. Allow use of force against Iraq	Y	62. Ban $ to illegal foreign activities	N

COATS, DAN (continued)

63. Req immigrant fluency in English	Y	67. Freeze outlays except SS/Medicare	N
64. Allow aliens' families to stay in US	N	68. Kill-Shift $5b of DOD to domestic	Y
65. Expand child care aid/tax credit	N	69. Confirm Tower as sec of defense	Y
66. Raise minimum wage w/subminimum	N		

The following are House measures voted on between 1982-1989:

59. Req foreign investment disclosure	N	102. Use of military in drug war	Y
60. Textile import quotas-veto override	N	103. Delete 12 MX/add conventional wpn	N
61. Bar abortion funding in Wash, DC	Y	104. Raise speed limit to 65 mph	Y
62. Notify spouses of AIDS+ carriers	Y	105. Require Pentagon to buy US goods	Y
63. Seize conveyance-drug trafficking	Y	106. AIDS insurance non-discrimination	N
64. South Africa sanctions	N	107. Prohibit Saudi arms sales	Y
65. 60 days' notice of plant closings	Y	108. Ease Gun Control Act of 1968	Y
66. Close unneeded military bases	Y	109. Bar interstate handgun transport	N
67. Keep welfare reform within $2.8b	Y	110. Make company emissions known	N
68. Allow children housing exclusion	N	111. Allow toxic victims to sue in fed ct	N
69. Shift $400m of NASA to homeless	N	112. Superfund waste cleanup of $10b	Y
70. Cap Medicare patients' liability	Y	113. 90 days notice of plant closings	N
71. Prohibit employee polygraph testing	N	114. $20b in Medicare cuts/tax increases	N
72. Allow CIA to fund Contras	Y	115. Spending cuts and tax increases	N
73. Revise unfair trade practices	N	116. Set school lunch lmt-250% poverty	Y
74. Focus SDI on accidental launch	N	117. $75m for youth work projects	N
75. Bar Air Force $ for MX missile	N	118. Allow Angolan military assistance	Y
76. Allow "real" increase in defense	N	119. Suspend defense payments for abuse	N
77. Troop reduction in Europe of 50%	N	120. Drop SS COLAs/$12b tax increase	N
78. Ban nuclear tests above 1 kiloton	N	121. Approve $1.5b for 21 MX missiles	Y
79. Ban anti-satellite missile tests	N	122. Emergency farm credit/revisions	Y
80. Observe certain limits of SALT II	N	123. Duty on Taiwan/Hong Kong/S Korea	N
81. Restore four Civil Rights laws	N	124. Limit steel imports to 17%	N
82. Prohibit aliens as strikebreakers	N	125. Cut $ to schools that bar prayer	Y
83. Allow military malpractice suits	Y	126. $50b-taxes; cut Medicare/spending	N
84. Approval of $36m in Contra aid	Y	127. Limit Pershing II/cruise in Europe	N
85. $18b deficit reduction compromise	N	128. Delete $7.1b for 34 B-1 bombers	N
86. Welfare reform of $5.7b for 5 years	N	129. Bar purchase of Sergeant York guns	N
87. Raise taxes $12b/cut spending $3b	N	130. El Salvador military/economic aid	Y
88. Board to assess occupational risk	N	131. Bar mining of Nicaraguan waters	N
89. Balanced budget by '93-via targets	N	132. Physician fee freeze for Medicare	Y
90. Bar licensing of two nuclear plants	N	133. $49b in "sin"/phone/insurance taxes	N
91. Remove victims compensation cap	N	134. Allow sale of Conrail	Y
92. Catastrophic health insurance	N	135. Equal Rights Amendment	N
93. Ban airline smoking-2 hours or less	N	136. Authorize Marines in Lebanon	Y
94. $1b/two year aid for the homeless	Y	137. Eminent domain for coal companies	Y
95. Bar non-unions in union companies	N	138. Prohibit EPA clean air sanctions	N
96. Increase FSLIC rescue to $15b	N	139. SS retirement age increase/reforms	Y
97. Impose quotas to lower trade deficit	N	140. Auto domestic content requirement	N
98. Reduce discretionary budget 21%	Y	141. Delete jobs program funding	Y
99. Immigration reform/alien amnesty	N	142. Highway-gas tax bill	N
100. South Africa sanctions-veto override	Y	143. Cut $5b from defense for Medicare	N
101. Tax overhaul to revise income tax	Y	144. Emergency housing aid of $1b	Y

Presidential Support Score: 1991 - 85%   1990 - 77%

IOWA

GRASSLEY, CHARLES E. -- Iowa [Republican]. Term Began/Expires: 1987/1992. Prior Terms: House: 1975-80; Senate: 1981-86. Born: September 17, 1933; New Hartford, IA. Education: University of Northern Iowa (B.A., M.A.). Occupation: Iowa legislator (1959-74); farmer.

GRASSLEY, CHARLES E. (continued)

1. Prohibit MFN status for China	N	
2. Kill-Tie welfare to school attendance	N	
3. Limit credit card interest rates	Y	
4. Confirm Gates as head of CIA	Y	
5. Adoption of national energy policies	N	
6. Kill-Restrict NEA use of funds	N	
7. Unemployment benefits extension	N	
8. Confirm Thomas to Supreme Court	Y	
9. Raise eligibility for unpaid leave	N	
10. Notify parents of minors' abortions	Y	
11. Move $3b from defense to domestic	N	
12. End production of B-2 bomber	Y	
13. Cut SDI $1b to reduce deficit	Y	
14. Maintain strategic stability-Soviets	Y	
15. Kill-Allow women as combat pilots	N	
16. Kill-Allow HIV tests before surgery	N	
17. Strike $12b aid to Int'l Mon Fund	Y	
18. Raise Senate salary/omit honoraria	N	
19. Reduce space station funding $1.9b	N	
20. Kill-Eliminate supercollider funds	Y	
21. Req 5-day handgun waiting period	N	
22. Life in prison instead of death	N	
23. Exceptions to exclusionary rule	Y	
24. Ban race as death sentence factor	Y	
25. Campaign finance revisions	N	
26. Kill-Term limits for senators	N	
27. Require four presidential debates	N	
28. Tighten ban on vertical price fixing	N	
29. Kill-Freeze discretionary budget	N	
30. Provide $30b for failed S&Ls	Y	
31. Allow use of force against Iraq	N	
32. Allow $15b in foreign aid for 1991	Y	
33. Civil Rights Act of 1990	N	
34. Block cancellation of Egypt's debt	Y	
35. Cut El Salvador military aid 50%	Y	
36. Reduce troops in NATO by 30,000	N	
37. Req increases in auto fuel efficiency	N	
38. Bar taxpayer funding of campaigns	Y	
39. Limit textile import growth to 1%	N	
40. Amendment to ban flag desecration	Y	
41. Let fed emp be politically active	N	
42. Reauthorize Amtrak-veto override	Y	
43. Allow sale of assault weapons	Y	
44. Retraining aid for coal miners	Y	
45. Kill-Raise car emission standards	Y	
46. Pull EPA nuclear plant authority	Y	
47. Defer Chinese students' deportation	N	
48. Cut in capital gains tax	Y	
49. Establish CIA inspector general	Y	
50. Kill-Sanctions against China	N	
51. Bar drug testing to receive AFDC	N	
52. Kill-Allow force against drug planes	N	
53. Include illegal aliens in census	N	
54. Restitution to Japanese interned	N	
55. Troop reduction in Europe of 50%	N	
56. Increase SDI research to $4.3b	N	
57. Kill-Pay homeless below min wage	N	
58. Ban airline smoking within US	N	
59. Bar transfer of FS-X technology	N	
60. Limit liability for oil spills	N	
61. Restructure S&L industry	N	
62. Ban $ to illegal foreign activities	N	
63. Req immigrant fluency in English	N	
64. Allow aliens' families to stay in US	N	

65. Expand child care aid/tax credit	N	
66. Raise minimum wage w/subminimum	N	
67. Freeze outlays except SS/Medicare	N	
68. Kill-Shift $5b of DOD to domestic	N	
69. Confirm Tower as sec of defense	Y	
70. Bar abortion $ except to save mother	Y	
71. Kill-Warn AIDS carriers' spouses	N	
72. Allow religious schools to bar gays	Y	
73. 60 days' notice of plant closings	N	
74. Allow poison pills in corp takeovers	N	
75. Kill-Workfare program	N	
76. Prohibit employee polygraph testing	N	
77. Cap Medicare patients' liability	Y	
78. Revise unfair trade practices	N	
79. Kill-Shift SDI $ to conv weapons	N	
80. Kill-Shift SDI $ to accidental launch	N	
81. Kill-Shift MX $ to supplies/parts	Y	
82. Kill-Buy America provision at DOD	N	
83. Allow nuclear testing-5+ kilotons	Y	
84. Allow SALT II to be exceeded	Y	
85. $ to vets exposed to nuclear bomb	N	
86. Warn workers of disease exposure	N	
87. Restore four civil rights laws	N	
88. Disapprove uranium sales to Japan	N	
89. Notify Congress of covert operations	Y	
90. Approval of $36m in Contra aid	Y	
91. $18b deficit reduction compromise	?	
92. Allow sale of hard-to-detect guns	Y	
93. Catastrophic health insurance	Y	
94. Bork nomination to Supreme Court	Y	
95. Kill-Void Panama Canal treaties	N	
96. Kill-Insurance denial to AIDS+	N	
97. Keep diplomatic immunity intact	N	
98. Produce Bigeye nerve gas bomb	N	
99. Balanced budget by '93-via targets	Y	
100. Allow ASAT missile tests in space	Y	
101. Limit space-based/ABM system tests	N	
102. Force reduction in trade barriers	Y	
103. Repeal windfall profit tax on oil	N	
104. $1b/two year aid for the homeless	Y	
105. Disallow $30m for AZT to poor	N	
106. Bar AIDS test-immigrants/marriage	N	
107. Kill-Biennial budget approval	N	
108. Fairness doctrine in broadcasting	Y	
109. Raise speed limit to 65 mph	Y	
110. Immigration reform/alien amnesty	Y	
111. South Africa sanctions-veto override	Y	
112. Kill-Use of military in drug war	N	
113. Tax overhaul to revise income tax	Y	
114. Submit nuclear test ban treaties	Y	
115. Prohibit sale of Stinger missiles	N	
116. Prohibit binary chemical weapons	Y	
117. Kill-$10/barrel oil tariff increase	Y	
118. Grant tax amnesty provisions	Y	
119. Block Saudi arms sale-veto override	Y	
120. Balanced budget amendment	Y	
121. Include veterans in spending cuts	Y	
122. Bar $ to hazardous substance victims	Y	
123. Allow seasonal workers in the US	N	
124. Let fed courts rule on school prayer	N	
125. Presidential line-item veto	Y	
126. Ease Gun Control Act of 1968	Y	
127. Kill-Req 14-day wait for handguns	Y	
128. Kill-15% min tax on corporations	Y	

GRASSLEY, CHARLES E. (continued)

129. Drop Social Security COLA	Y	137. Capital punishment-federal crimes	Y
130. Freeze funding for all programs	Y	138. Ban government officials from taping	N
131. Kill-Nuclear weapon freeze	Y	139. Martin Luther King holiday	N
132. Keep decision narrowing Title IX	Y	140. Authorize Marines in Lebanon	Y
133. Raise drinking age to 21	N	141. Amendment making abortion illegal	Y
134. Allow production of MX missile	N	142. Delete $1.2b for jobs creation	Y
135. Raise taxes/cut spending by $140b	Y	143. Keep tobacco price supports	Y
136. School prayer amendment	Y	144. Emergency housing aid of $5.1b	Y

Presidential Support Score: 1991 - 75%   1990 - 70%

HARKIN, TOM -- Iowa [Democrat]. Term Began/Expires: 1991/1996. Prior Terms: House: 1975-84; Senate: 1985-90. Born: November 19, 1939; Cumming, IA. Education: Iowa State University (B.S.); Catholic University of America Law School. Military Service: U.S. Navy, 1962-67. Occupation: Legislative assistant; attorney.

1. Prohibit MFN status for China	+	48. Cut in capital gains tax	N
2. Kill-Tie welfare to school attendance	?	49. Establish CIA inspector general	Y
3. Limit credit card interest rates	?	50. Kill-Sanctions against China	N
4. Confirm Gates as head of CIA	N	51. Bar drug testing to receive AFDC	Y
5. Adoption of national energy policies	N	52. Kill-Allow force against drug planes	Y
6. Kill-Restrict NEA use of funds	Y	53. Include illegal aliens in census	N
7. Unemployment benefits extension	Y	54. Restitution to Japanese interned	Y
8. Confirm Thomas to Supreme Court	N	55. Troop reduction in Europe of 50%	Y
9. Raise eligibility for unpaid leave	?	56. Increase SDI research to $4.3b	N
10. Notify parents of minors' abortions	N	57. Kill-Pay homeless below min wage	Y
11. Move $3b from defense to domestic	Y	58. Ban airline smoking within US	Y
12. End production of B-2 bomber	Y	59. Bar transfer of FS-X technology	Y
13. Cut SDI $1b to reduce deficit	Y	60. Limit liability for oil spills	Y
14. Maintain strategic stability-Soviets	Y	61. Restructure S&L industry	Y
15. Kill-Allow women as combat pilots	N	62. Ban $ to illegal foreign activities	Y
16. Kill-Allow HIV tests before surgery	Y	63. Req immigrant fluency in English	N
17. Strike $12b aid to Int'l Mon Fund	?	64. Allow aliens' families to stay in US	Y
18. Raise Senate salary/omit honoraria	Y	65. Expand child care aid/tax credit	Y
19. Reduce space station funding $1.9b	Y	66. Raise minimum wage w/subminimum	Y
20. Kill-Eliminate supercollider funds	N	67. Freeze outlays except SS/Medicare	Y
21. Req 5-day handgun waiting period	Y	68. Kill-Shift $5b of DOD to domestic	N
22. Life in prison instead of death	Y	69. Confirm Tower as sec of defense	N
23. Exceptions to exclusionary rule	N	70. Bar abortion $ except to save mother	N
24. Ban race as death sentence factor	N	71. Kill-Warn AIDS carriers' spouses	Y
25. Campaign finance revisions	Y	72. Allow religious schools to bar gays	N
26. Kill-Term limits for senators	Y	73. 60 days' notice of plant closings	Y
27. Require four presidential debates	Y	74. Allow poison pills in corp takeovers	N
28. Tighten ban on vertical price fixing	Y	75. Kill-Workfare program	Y
29. Kill-Freeze discretionary budget	Y	76. Prohibit employee polygraph testing	Y
30. Provide $30b for failed S&Ls	N	77. Cap Medicare patients' liability	Y
31. Allow use of force against Iraq	N	78. Revise unfair trade practices	Y
32. Allow $15b in foreign aid for 1991	Y	79. Kill-Shift SDI $ to conv weapons	N
33. Civil Rights Act of 1990	Y	80. Kill-Shift SDI $ to accidental launch	Y
34. Block cancellation of Egypt's debt	Y	81. Kill-Shift MX $ to supplies/parts	N
35. Cut El Salvador military aid 50%	Y	82. Kill-Buy America provision at DOD	N
36. Reduce troops in NATO by 30,000	Y	83. Allow nuclear testing-5+ kilotons	N
37. Req increases in auto fuel efficiency	Y	84. Allow SALT II to be exceeded	N
38. Bar taxpayer funding of campaigns	N	85. $ to vets exposed to nuclear bomb	Y
39. Limit textile import growth to 1%	Y	86. Warn workers of disease exposure	Y
40. Amendment to ban flag desecration	N	87. Restore four civil rights laws	Y
41. Let fed emp be politically active	Y	88. Disapprove uranium sales to Japan	Y
42. Reauthorize Amtrak-veto override	Y	89. Notify Congress of covert operations	Y
43. Allow sale of assault weapons	N	90. Approval of $36m in Contra aid	N
44. Retraining aid for coal miners	Y	91. $18b deficit reduction compromise	?
45. Kill-Raise car emission standards	N	92. Allow sale of hard-to-detect guns	N
46. Pull EPA nuclear plant authority	N	93. Catastrophic health insurance	Y
47. Defer Chinese students' deportation	Y	94. Bork nomination to Supreme Court	N

HARKIN, TOM (continued)

95. Kill-Void Panama Canal treaties	Y
96. Kill-Insurance denial to AIDS+	Y
97. Keep diplomatic immunity intact	Y
98. Produce Bigeye nerve gas bomb	N
99. Balanced budget by '93-via targets	N
100. Allow ASAT missile tests in space	N
101. Limit space-based/ABM system tests	Y
102. Force reduction in trade barriers	Y
103. Repeal windfall profit tax on oil	N
104. $1b/two year aid for the homeless	Y
105. Disallow $30m for AZT to poor	N
106. Bar AIDS test-immigrants/marriage	Y
107. Kill-Biennial budget approval	Y
108. Fairness doctrine in broadcasting	Y
109. Raise speed limit to 65 mph	Y
110. Immigration reform/alien amnesty	Y
111. South Africa sanctions-veto override	Y
112. Kill-Use of military in drug war	Y

113. Tax overhaul to revise income tax	Y
114. Submit nuclear test ban treaties	Y
115. Prohibit sale of Stinger missiles	Y
116. Prohibit binary chemical weapons	Y
117. Kill-$10/barrel oil tariff increase	Y
118. Grant tax amnesty provisions	N
119. Block Saudi arms sale-veto override	Y
120. Balanced budget amendment	Y
121. Include veterans in spending cuts	N
122. Bar $ to hazardous substance victims	N
123. Allow seasonal workers in the US	N
124. Let fed courts rule on school prayer	Y
125. Presidential line-item veto	N
126. Ease Gun Control Act of 1968	Y
127. Kill-Req 14-day wait for handguns	N
128. Kill-15% min tax on corporations	N
129. Drop Social Security COLA	N
130. Freeze funding for all programs	Y

The following are House measures voted on between 1982-1984:

123. Duty on Taiwan/Hong Kong/S Korea	N
124. Limit steel imports to 17%	N
125. Cut $ to schools that bar prayer	N
126. $50b-taxes; cut Medicare/spending	Y
127. Limit Pershing II/cruise in Europe	Y
128. Delete $7.1b for 34 B-1 bombers	Y
129. Bar purchase of Sergeant York guns	Y
130. El Salvador military/economic aid	N
131. Bar mining of Nicaraguan waters	Y
132. Physician fee freeze for Medicare	N
133. $49b in "sin"/phone/insurance taxes	Y

134. Allow sale of Conrail	N
135. Equal Rights Amendment	Y
136. Authorize Marines in Lebanon	N
137. Eminent domain for coal companies	N
138. Prohibit EPA clean air sanctions	?
139. SS retirement age increase/reforms	N
140. Auto domestic content requirement	Y
141. Delete jobs program funding	N
142. Highway-gas tax bill	N
143. Cut $5b from defense for Medicare	Y
144. Emergency housing aid of $1b	Y

Presidential Support Score: 1991 - 19%   1990 - 22%

KANSAS

DOLE, ROBERT -- Kansas [Republican]. Term Began/Expires: 1987/1992. Prior Terms: House: 1961-68; Senate: 1969-86. Born: July 22, 1923; Russell, KS. Education: Washburn Municipal University (A.B., LL.B.); University of Kansas. Military Service: U.S. Army, WW II. Occupation: Kansas representative (1951-53); Russell county attorney (1953-61); attorney.

1. Prohibit MFN status for China	N
2. Kill-Tie welfare to school attendance	N
3. Limit credit card interest rates	Y
4. Confirm Gates as head of CIA	Y
5. Adoption of national energy policies	Y
6. Kill-Restrict NEA use of funds	N
7. Unemployment benefits extension	N
8. Confirm Thomas to Supreme Court	Y
9. Raise eligibility for unpaid leave	N
10. Notify parents of minors' abortions	Y
11. Move $3b from defense to domestic	N
12. End production of B-2 bomber	N
13. Cut SDI $1b to reduce deficit	N
14. Maintain strategic stability-Soviets	N
15. Kill-Allow women as combat pilots	N
16. Kill-Allow HIV tests before surgery	N

17. Strike $12b aid to Int'l Mon Fund	N
18. Raise Senate salary/omit honoraria	Y
19. Reduce space station funding $1.9b	N
20. Kill-Eliminate supercollider funds	Y
21. Req 5-day handgun waiting period	Y
22. Life in prison instead of death	N
23. Exceptions to exclusionary rule	Y
24. Ban race as death sentence factor	Y
25. Campaign finance revisions	N
26. Kill-Term limits for senators	N
27. Require four presidential debates	N
28. Tighten ban on vertical price fixing	N
29. Kill-Freeze discretionary budget	Y
30. Provide $30b for failed S&Ls	Y
31. Allow use of force against Iraq	Y
32. Allow $15b in foreign aid for 1991	Y

DOLE, ROBERT (continued)

33. Civil Rights Act of 1990	N	89. Notify Congress of covert operations	?
34. Block cancellation of Egypt's debt	N	90. Approval of $36m in Contra aid	Y
35. Cut El Salvador military aid 50%	N	91. $18b deficit reduction compromise	Y
36. Reduce troops in NATO by 30,000	N	92. Allow sale of hard-to-detect guns	Y
37. Req increases in auto fuel efficiency	N	93. Catastrophic health insurance	Y
38. Bar taxpayer funding of campaigns	Y	94. Bork nomination to Supreme Court	Y
39. Limit textile import growth to 1%	Y	95. Kill-Void Panama Canal treaties	N
40. Amendment to ban flag desecration	Y	96. Kill-Insurance denial to AIDS+	N
41. Let fed emp be politically active	N	97. Keep diplomatic immunity intact	N
42. Reauthorize Amtrak-veto override	N	98. Produce Bigeye nerve gas bomb	Y
43. Allow sale of assault weapons	N	99. Balanced budget by '93-via targets	Y
44. Retraining aid for coal miners	N	100. Allow ASAT missile tests in space	Y
45. Kill-Raise car emission standards	Y	101. Limit space-based/ABM system tests	N
46. Pull EPA nuclear plant authority	Y	102. Force reduction in trade barriers	N
47. Defer Chinese students' deportation	N	103. Repeal windfall profit tax on oil	Y
48. Cut in capital gains tax	Y	104. $1b/two year aid for the homeless	Y
49. Establish CIA inspector general	N	105. Disallow $30m for AZT to poor	Y
50. Kill-Sanctions against China	Y	106. Bar AIDS test-immigrants/marriage	Y
51. Bar drug testing to receive AFDC	N	107. Kill-Biennial budget approval	N
52. Kill-Allow force against drug planes	N	108. Fairness doctrine in broadcasting	N
53. Include illegal aliens in census	N	109. Raise speed limit to 65 mph	Y
54. Restitution to Japanese interned	Y	110. Immigration reform/alien amnesty	Y
55. Troop reduction in Europe of 50%	N	111. South Africa sanctions-veto override	N
56. Increase SDI research to $4.3b	Y	112. Kill-Use of military in drug war	Y
57. Kill-Pay homeless below min wage	N	113. Tax overhaul to revise income tax	Y
58. Ban airline smoking within US	Y	114. Submit nuclear test ban treaties	N
59. Bar transfer of FS-X technology	N	115. Prohibit sale of Stinger missiles	N
60. Limit liability for oil spills	N	116. Prohibit binary chemical weapons	N
61. Restructure S&L industry	N	117. Kill-$10/barrel oil tariff increase	Y
62. Ban $ to illegal foreign activities	N	118. Grant tax amnesty provisions	N
63. Req immigrant fluency in English	Y	119. Block Saudi arms sale-veto override	N
64. Allow aliens' families to stay in US	N	120. Balanced budget amendment	Y
65. Expand child care aid/tax credit	N	121. Include veterans in spending cuts	Y
66. Raise minimum wage w/subminimum	N	122. Bar $ to hazardous substance victims	Y
67. Freeze outlays except SS/Medicare	N	123. Allow seasonal workers in the US	Y
68. Kill-Shift $5b of DOD to domestic	Y	124. Let fed courts rule on school prayer	N
69. Confirm Tower as sec of defense	Y	125. Presidential line-item veto	Y
70. Bar abortion $ except to save mother	Y	126. Ease Gun Control Act of 1968	Y
71. Kill-Warn AIDS carriers' spouses	N	127. Kill-Req 14-day wait for handguns	Y
72. Allow religious schools to bar gays	Y	128. Kill-15% min tax on corporations	Y
73. 60 days' notice of plant closings	N	129. Drop Social Security COLA	Y
74. Allow poison pills in corp takeovers	N	130. Freeze funding for all programs	N
75. Kill-Workfare program	N	131. Kill-Nuclear weapon freeze	Y
76. Prohibit employee polygraph testing	Y	132. Keep decision narrowing Title IX	Y
77. Cap Medicare patients' liability	Y	133. Raise drinking age to 21	Y
78. Revise unfair trade practices	N	134. Allow production of MX missile	Y
79. Kill-Shift SDI $ to conv weapons	Y	135. Raise taxes/cut spending by $140b	Y
80. Kill-Shift SDI $ to accidental launch	N	136. School prayer amendment	Y
81. Kill-Shift MX $ to supplies/parts	Y	137. Capital punishment-federal crimes	Y
82. Kill-Buy America provision at DOD	N	138. Ban government officials from taping	N
83. Allow nuclear testing-5+ kilotons	Y	139. Martin Luther King holiday	Y
84. Allow SALT II to be exceeded	Y	140. Authorize Marines in Lebanon	Y
85. $ to vets exposed to nuclear bomb	N	141. Amendment making abortion illegal	Y
86. Warn workers of disease exposure	N	142. Delete $1.2b for jobs creation	Y
87. Restore four civil rights laws	?	143. Keep tobacco price supports	Y
88. Disapprove uranium sales to Japan	?	144. Emergency housing aid of $5.1b	N

Presidential Support Score: 1991 - 96%   1990 - 80%

KASSEBAUM, NANCY LANDON -- Kansas [Republican]. Term Began/Expires: 1991/1996. Prior Terms: Senate: 1979-90. Born: July 29, 1932, Topeka, KS. Education: University of Kansas (B.A.); University of Michigan (M.A.). Occupation: Vice president, KFH, KBRA-FM radio stations.

KASSEBAUM, NANCY LANDON (continued)

1.	Prohibit MFN status for China	N	65.	Expand child care aid/tax credit	Y
2.	Kill-Tie welfare to school attendance	N	66.	Raise minimum wage w/subminimum	N
3.	Limit credit card interest rates	Y	67.	Freeze outlays except SS/Medicare	N
4.	Confirm Gates as head of CIA	Y	68.	Kill-Shift $5b of DOD to domestic	Y
5.	Adoption of national energy policies	Y	69.	Confirm Tower as sec of defense	Y
6.	Kill-Restrict NEA use of funds	Y	70.	Bar abortion $ except to save mother	Y
7.	Unemployment benefits extension	N	71.	Kill-Warn AIDS carriers' spouses	N
8.	Confirm Thomas to Supreme Court	Y	72.	Allow religious schools to bar gays	Y
9.	Raise eligibility for unpaid leave	N	73.	60 days' notice of plant closings	Y
10.	Notify parents of minors' abortions	N	74.	Allow poison pills in corp takeovers	Y
11.	Move $3b from defense to domestic	N	75.	Kill-Workfare program	N
12.	End production of B-2 bomber	N	76.	Prohibit employee polygraph testing	N
13.	Cut SDI $1b to reduce deficit	Y	77.	Cap Medicare patients' liability	N
14.	Maintain strategic stability-Soviets	N	78.	Revise unfair trade practices	N
15.	Kill-Allow women as combat pilots	N	79.	Kill-Shift SDI $ to conv weapons	Y
16.	Kill-Allow HIV tests before surgery	Y	80.	Kill-Shift SDI $ to accidental launch	Y
17.	Strike $12b aid to Int'l Mon Fund	N	81.	Kill-Shift MX $ to supplies/parts	Y
18.	Raise Senate salary/omit honoraria	Y	82.	Kill-Buy America provision at DOD	Y
19.	Reduce space station funding $1.9b	N	83.	Allow nuclear testing-5+ kilotons	Y
20.	Kill-Eliminate supercollider funds	N	84.	Allow SALT II to be exceeded	Y
21.	Req 5-day handgun waiting period	Y	85.	$ to vets exposed to nuclear bomb	N
22.	Life in prison instead of death	N	86.	Warn workers of disease exposure	N
23.	Exceptions to exclusionary rule	Y	87.	Restore four civil rights laws	Y
24.	Ban race as death sentence factor	Y	88.	Disapprove uranium sales to Japan	N
25.	Campaign finance revisions	N	89.	Notify Congress of covert operations	Y
26.	Kill-Term limits for senators	Y	90.	Approval of $36m in Contra aid	Y
27.	Require four presidential debates	Y	91.	$18b deficit reduction compromise	Y
28.	Tighten ban on vertical price fixing	Y	92.	Allow sale of hard-to-detect guns	--
29.	Kill-Freeze discretionary budget	N	93.	Catastrophic health insurance	N
30.	Provide $30b for failed S&Ls	Y	94.	Bork nomination to Supreme Court	Y
31.	Allow use of force against Iraq	Y	95.	Kill-Void Panama Canal treaties	Y
32.	Allow $15b in foreign aid for 1991	Y	96.	Kill-Insurance denial to AIDS+	N
33.	Civil Rights Act of 1990	N	97.	Keep diplomatic immunity intact	N
34.	Block cancellation of Egypt's debt	Y	98.	Produce Bigeye nerve gas bomb	N
35.	Cut El Salvador military aid 50%	Y	99.	Balanced budget by '93-via targets	N
36.	Reduce troops in NATO by 30,000	?	100.	Allow ASAT missile tests in space	Y
37.	Req increases in auto fuel efficiency	N	101.	Limit space-based/ABM system tests	Y
38.	Bar taxpayer funding of campaigns	Y	102.	Force reduction in trade barriers	N
39.	Limit textile import growth to 1%	N	103.	Repeal windfall profit tax on oil	Y
40.	Amendment to ban flag desecration	Y	104.	$1b/two year aid for the homeless	Y
41.	Let fed emp be politically active	N	105.	Disallow $30m for AZT to poor	N
42.	Reauthorize Amtrak-veto override	Y	106.	Bar AIDS test-immigrants/marriage	Y
43.	Allow sale of assault weapons	N	107.	Kill-Biennial budget approval	N
44.	Retraining aid for coal miners	N	108.	Fairness doctrine in broadcasting	N
45.	Kill-Raise car emission standards	N	109.	Raise speed limit to 65 mph	Y
46.	Pull EPA nuclear plant authority	N	110.	Immigration reform/alien amnesty	Y
47.	Defer Chinese students' deportation	N	111.	South Africa sanctions-veto override	Y
48.	Cut in capital gains tax	Y	112.	Kill-Use of military in drug war	Y
49.	Establish CIA inspector general	N	113.	Tax overhaul to revise income tax	Y
50.	Kill-Sanctions against China	N	114.	Submit nuclear test ban treaties	Y
51.	Bar drug testing to receive AFDC	Y	115.	Prohibit sale of Stinger missiles	Y
52.	Kill-Allow force against drug planes	Y	116.	Prohibit binary chemical weapons	Y
53.	Include illegal aliens in census	N	117.	Kill-$10/barrel oil tariff increase	Y
54.	Restitution to Japanese interned	N	118.	Grant tax amnesty provisions	Y
55.	Troop reduction in Europe of 50%	N	119.	Block Saudi arms sale-veto override	N
56.	Increase SDI research to $4.3b	Y	120.	Balanced budget amendment	N
57.	Kill-Pay homeless below min wage	N	121.	Include veterans in spending cuts	Y
58.	Ban airline smoking within US	Y	122.	Bar $ to hazardous substance victims	Y
59.	Bar transfer of FS-X technology	N	123.	Allow seasonal workers in the US	Y
60.	Limit liability for oil spills	N	124.	Let fed courts rule on school prayer	Y
61.	Restructure S&L industry	N	125.	Presidential line-item veto	Y
62.	Ban $ to illegal foreign activities	N	126.	Ease Gun Control Act of 1968	Y
63.	Req immigrant fluency in English	N	127.	Kill-Req 14-day wait for handguns	N
64.	Allow aliens' families to stay in US	N	128.	Kill-15% min tax on corporations	Y

KASSEBAUM, NANCY L. (continued)

129. Drop Social Security COLA	Y	137. Capital punishment-federal crimes	Y
130. Freeze funding for all programs	Y	138. Ban government officials from taping	N
131. Kill-Nuclear weapon freeze	Y	139. Martin Luther King holiday	Y
132. Keep decision narrowing Title IX	Y	140. Authorize Marines in Lebanon	Y
133. Raise drinking age to 21	Y	141. Amendment making abortion illegal	N
134. Allow production of MX missile	Y	142. Delete $1.2b for jobs creation	Y
135. Raise taxes/cut spending by $140b	Y	143. Keep tobacco price supports	Y
136. School prayer amendment	N	144. Emergency housing aid of $5.1b	N

Presidential Support Score: 1991 - 79%   1990 - 68%

KENTUCKY

FORD, WENDELL H. -- Kentucky [Democrat]. Term Began/Expires: 1987/1992. Prior Terms: Senate: 1975-86. Born: September 8, 1924; Daviess County, KY. Education: University of Kentucky; Maryland School of Insurance. Military Service: U.S. Army, WW II. Occupation: Chief administrative assistant to governor (1959); Kentucky senator (1965-67); lieutenant governor (1967-71); governor (1971-74).

1. Prohibit MFN status for China	Y	40. Amendment to ban flag desecration	Y
2. Kill-Tie welfare to school attendance	Y	41. Let fed emp be politically active	Y
3. Limit credit card interest rates	Y	42. Reauthorize Amtrak-veto override	Y
4. Confirm Gates as head of CIA	Y	43. Allow sale of assault weapons	Y
5. Adoption of national energy policies	Y	44. Retraining aid for coal miners	Y
6. Kill-Restrict NEA use of funds	Y	45. Kill-Raise car emission standards	Y
7. Unemployment benefits extension	Y	46. Pull EPA nuclear plant authority	Y
8. Confirm Thomas to Supreme Court	N	47. Defer Chinese students' deportation	Y
9. Raise eligibility for unpaid leave	Y	48. Cut in capital gains tax	N
10. Notify parents of minors' abortions	Y	49. Establish CIA inspector general	N
11. Move $3b from defense to domestic	N	50. Kill-Sanctions against China	N
12. End production of B-2 bomber	N	51. Bar drug testing to receive AFDC	Y
13. Cut SDI $1b to reduce deficit	Y	52. Kill-Allow force against drug planes	Y
14. Maintain strategic stability-Soviets	N	53. Include illegal aliens in census	N
15. Kill-Allow women as combat pilots	N	54. Restitution to Japanese interned	Y
16. Kill-Allow HIV tests before surgery	N	55. Troop reduction in Europe of 50%	Y
17. Strike $12b aid to Int'l Mon Fund	N	56. Increase SDI research to $4.3b	Y
18. Raise Senate salary/omit honoraria	X	57. Kill-Pay homeless below min wage	Y
19. Reduce space station funding $1.9b	N	58. Ban airline smoking within US	N
20. Kill-Eliminate supercollider funds	Y	59. Bar transfer of FS-X technology	Y
21. Req 5-day handgun waiting period	Y	60. Limit liability for oil spills	Y
22. Life in prison instead of death	N	61. Restructure S&L industry	Y
23. Exceptions to exclusionary rule	Y	62. Ban $ to illegal foreign activities	Y
24. Ban race as death sentence factor	Y	63. Req immigrant fluency in English	Y
25. Campaign finance revisions	Y	64. Allow aliens' families to stay in US	N
26. Kill-Term limits for senators	Y	65. Expand child care aid/tax credit	Y
27. Require four presidential debates	Y	66. Raise minimum wage w/subminimum	Y
28. Tighten ban on vertical price fixing	Y	67. Freeze outlays except SS/Medicare	N
29. Kill-Freeze discretionary budget	N	68. Kill-Shift $5b of DOD to domestic	Y
30. Provide $30b for failed S&Ls	Y	69. Confirm Tower as sec of defense	N
31. Allow use of force against Iraq	N	70. Bar abortion $ except to save mother	Y
32. Allow $15b in foreign aid for 1991	Y	71. Kill-Warn AIDS carriers' spouses	N
33. Civil Rights Act of 1990	Y	72. Allow religious schools to bar gays	Y
34. Block cancellation of Egypt's debt	Y	73. 60 days' notice of plant closings	Y
35. Cut El Salvador military aid 50%	Y	74. Allow poison pills in corp takeovers	Y
36. Reduce troops in NATO by 30,000	N	75. Kill-Workfare program	Y
37. Req increases in auto fuel efficiency	N	76. Prohibit employee polygraph testing	Y
38. Bar taxpayer funding of campaigns	N	77. Cap Medicare patients' liability	Y
39. Limit textile import growth to 1%	Y	78. Revise unfair trade practices	Y

FORD, WENDELL H. (continued)

79. Kill-Shift SDI $ to conv weapons	N	
80. Kill-Shift SDI $ to accidental launch	Y	
81. Kill-Shift MX $ to supplies/parts	N	
82. Kill-Buy America provision at DOD	N	
83. Allow nuclear testing-5+ kilotons	Y	
84. Allow SALT II to be exceeded	N	
85. $ to vets exposed to nuclear bomb	?	
86. Warn workers of disease exposure	Y	
87. Restore four civil rights laws	Y	
88. Disapprove uranium sales to Japan	N	
89. Notify Congress of covert operations	Y	
90. Approval of $36m in Contra aid	N	
91. $18b deficit reduction compromise	Y	
92. Allow sale of hard-to-detect guns	Y	
93. Catastrophic health insurance	Y	
94. Bork nomination to Supreme Court	N	
95. Kill-Void Panama Canal treaties	N	
96. Kill-Insurance denial to AIDS+	N	
97. Keep diplomatic immunity intact	N	
98. Produce Bigeye nerve gas bomb	N	
99. Balanced budget by '93-via targets	N	
100. Allow ASAT missile tests in space	N	
101. Limit space-based/ABM system tests	Y	
102. Force reduction in trade barriers	Y	
103. Repeal windfall profit tax on oil	N	
104. $1b/two year aid for the homeless	Y	
105. Disallow $30m for AZT to poor	Y	
106. Bar AIDS test-immigrants/marriage	N	
107. Kill-Biennial budget approval	Y	
108. Fairness doctrine in broadcasting	Y	
109. Raise speed limit to 65 mph	Y	
110. Immigration reform/alien amnesty	N	
111. South Africa sanctions-veto override	Y	

112. Kill-Use of military in drug war	Y
113. Tax overhaul to revise income tax	Y
114. Submit nuclear test ban treaties	Y
115. Prohibit sale of Stinger missiles	Y
116. Prohibit binary chemical weapons	Y
117. Kill-$10/barrel oil tariff increase	Y
118. Grant tax amnesty provisions	N
119. Block Saudi arms sale-veto override	Y
120. Balanced budget amendment	Y
121. Include veterans in spending cuts	N
122. Bar $ to hazardous substance victims	N
123. Allow seasonal workers in the US	N
124. Let fed courts rule on school prayer	N
125. Presidential line-item veto	N
126. Ease Gun Control Act of 1968	Y
127. Kill-Req 14-day wait for handguns	Y
128. Kill-15% min tax on corporations	Y
129. Drop Social Security COLA	N
130. Freeze funding for all programs	N
131. Kill-Nuclear weapon freeze	N
132. Keep decision narrowing Title IX	N
133. Raise drinking age to 21	Y
134. Allow production of MX missile	N
135. Raise taxes/cut spending by $140b	N
136. School prayer amendment	Y
137. Capital punishment-federal crimes	Y
138. Ban government officials from taping	Y
139. Martin Luther King holiday	Y
140. Authorize Marines in Lebanon	N
141. Amendment making abortion illegal	Y
142. Delete $1.2b for jobs creation	N
143. Keep tobacco price supports	Y
144. Emergency housing aid of $5.1b	Y

Presidential Support Score: 1991 - 57%   1990 - 55%

McCONNELL, MITCH -- Kentucky [Republican]. Term Began/Expires: 1991/1996. Prior Term: Senate: 1985-90. Born: February 20, 1942; Colbert County, AL. Education: University of Louisville (B.A.); University of Kentucky Law School (J.D.). Occupation: Attorney; chief legislative assistant (1968-70); deputy assistant U.S. attorney (1974-75); county judge/executive.

1. Prohibit MFN status for China	N	
2. Kill-Tie welfare to school attendance	N	
3. Limit credit card interest rates	N	
4. Confirm Gates as head of CIA	Y	
5. Adoption of national energy policies	Y	
6. Kill-Restrict NEA use of funds	N	
7. Unemployment benefits extension	N	
8. Confirm Thomas to Supreme Court	Y	
9. Raise eligibility for unpaid leave	N	
10. Notify parents of minors' abortions	Y	
11. Move $3b from defense to domestic	N	
12. End production of B-2 bomber	N	
13. Cut SDI $1b to reduce deficit	N	
14. Maintain strategic stability-Soviets	N	
15. Kill-Allow women as combat pilots	N	
16. Kill-Allow HIV tests before surgery	N	
17. Strike $12b aid to Int'l Mon Fund	N	
18. Raise Senate salary/omit honoraria	N	
19. Reduce space station funding $1.9b	N	
20. Kill-Eliminate supercollider funds	Y	
21. Req 5-day handgun waiting period	N	

22. Life in prison instead of death	N
23. Exceptions to exclusionary rule	Y
24. Ban race as death sentence factor	Y
25. Campaign finance revisions	N
26. Kill-Term limits for senators	N
27. Require four presidential debates	N
28. Tighten ban on vertical price fixing	N
29. Kill-Freeze discretionary budget	N
30. Provide $30b for failed S&Ls	Y
31. Allow use of force against Iraq	Y
32. Allow $15b in foreign aid for 1991	Y
33. Civil Rights Act of 1990	N
34. Block cancellation of Egypt's debt	N
35. Cut El Salvador military aid 50%	N
36. Reduce troops in NATO by 30,000	N
37. Req increases in auto fuel efficiency	N
38. Bar taxpayer funding of campaigns	Y
39. Limit textile import growth to 1%	Y
40. Amendment to ban flag desecration	Y
41. Let fed emp be politically active	N
42. Reauthorize Amtrak-veto override	N

McCONNELL, MITCH (continued)

43. Allow sale of assault weapons	Y	
44. Retraining aid for coal miners	Y	
45. Kill-Raise car emission standards	Y	
46. Pull EPA nuclear plant authority	Y	
47. Defer Chinese students' deportation	N	
48. Cut in capital gains tax	Y	
49. Establish CIA inspector general	N	
50. Kill-Sanctions against China	N	
51. Bar drug testing to receive AFDC	N	
52. Kill-Allow force against drug planes	N	
53. Include illegal aliens in census	N	
54. Restitution to Japanese interned	N	
55. Troop reduction in Europe of 50%	N	
56. Increase SDI research to $4.3b	Y	
57. Kill-Pay homeless below min wage	N	
58. Ban airline smoking within US	N	
59. Bar transfer of FS-X technology	Y	
60. Limit liability for oil spills	N	
61. Restructure S&L industry	N	
62. Ban $ to illegal foreign activities	N	
63. Req immigrant fluency in English	Y	
64. Allow aliens' families to stay in US	N	
65. Expand child care aid/tax credit	N	
66. Raise minimum wage w/subminimum	N	
67. Freeze outlays except SS/Medicare	N	
68. Kill-Shift $5b of DOD to domestic	Y	
69. Confirm Tower as sec of defense	Y	
70. Bar abortion $ except to save mother	Y	
71. Kill-Warn AIDS carriers' spouses	N	
72. Allow religious schools to bar gays	Y	
73. 60 days' notice of plant closings	N	
74. Allow poison pills in corp takeovers	N	
75. Kill-Workfare program	N	
76. Prohibit employee polygraph testing	N	
77. Cap Medicare patients' liability	Y	
78. Revise unfair trade practices	N	
79. Kill-Shift SDI $ to conv weapons	Y	
80. Kill-Shift SDI $ to accidental launch	N	
81. Kill-Shift MX $ to supplies/parts	Y	
82. Kill-Buy America provision at DOD	N	
83. Allow nuclear testing-5+ kilotons	Y	
84. Allow SALT II to be exceeded	Y	
85. $ to vets exposed to nuclear bomb	N	
86. Warn workers of disease exposure	N	

87. Restore four civil rights laws	N	
88. Disapprove uranium sales to Japan	N	
89. Notify Congress of covert operations	Y	
90. Approval of $36m in Contra aid	Y	
91. $18b deficit reduction compromise	N	
92. Allow sale of hard-to-detect guns	Y	
93. Catastrophic health insurance	Y	
94. Bork nomination to Supreme Court	Y	
95. Kill-Void Panama Canal treaties	N	
96. Kill-Insurance denial to AIDS+	N	
97. Keep diplomatic immunity intact	N	
98. Produce Bigeye nerve gas bomb	Y	
99. Balanced budget by '93-via targets	Y	
100. Allow ASAT missile tests in space	Y	
101. Limit space-based/ABM system tests	N	
102. Force reduction in trade barriers	N	
103. Repeal windfall profit tax on oil	Y	
104. $1b/two year aid for the homeless	Y	
105. Disallow $30m for AZT to poor	N	
106. Bar AIDS test-immigrants/marriage	Y	
107. Kill-Biennial budget approval	N	
108. Fairness doctrine in broadcasting	?	
109. Raise speed limit to 65 mph	Y	
110. Immigration reform/alien amnesty	Y	
111. South Africa sanctions-veto override	Y	
112. Kill-Use of military in drug war	N	
113. Tax overhaul to revise income tax	Y	
114. Submit nuclear test ban treaties	N	
115. Prohibit sale of Stinger missiles	N	
116. Prohibit binary chemical weapons	N	
117. Kill-$10/barrel oil tariff increase	Y	
118. Grant tax amnesty provisions	N	
119. Block Saudi arms sale-veto override	N	
120. Balanced budget amendment	Y	
121. Include veterans in spending cuts	Y	
122. Bar $ to hazardous substance victims	Y	
123. Allow seasonal workers in the US	Y	
124. Let fed courts rule on school prayer	N	
125. Presidential line-item veto	Y	
126. Ease Gun Control Act of 1968	Y	
127. Kill-Req 14-day wait for handguns	Y	
128. Kill-15% min tax on corporations	Y	
129. Drop Social Security COLA	Y	
130. Freeze funding for all programs	N	

Presidential Support Score: 1991 - 93%   1990 - 78%

LOUISIANA

JOHNSTON, J. BENNETT -- Louisiana [Democrat]. Term Began/Expires: 1991/1996. Prior Terms: Senate: 1973-90. Born: June 10, 1932; Shreveport, LA. Education: Washington and Lee University; United States Military Academy; Louisiana State University Law School (LL.B.). Military Service: U.S. Army, 1956-59. Occupation: Louisiana representative (1964-68); Louisiana senator (1968-72).

1. Prohibit MFN status for China	N	
2. Kill-Tie welfare to school attendance	Y	
3. Limit credit card interest rates	Y	

4. Confirm Gates as head of CIA	Y	
5. Adoption of national energy policies	Y	
6. Kill-Restrict NEA use of funds	Y	

JOHNSTON, J. BENNETT (continued)

7. Unemployment benefits extension	Y
8. Confirm Thomas to Supreme Court	Y
9. Raise eligibility for unpaid leave	Y
10. Notify parents of minors' abortions	Y
11. Move $3b from defense to domestic	N
12. End production of B-2 bomber	N
13. Cut SDI $1b to reduce deficit	Y
14. Maintain strategic stability-Soviets	Y
15. Kill-Allow women as combat pilots	Y
16. Kill-Allow HIV tests before surgery	N
17. Strike $12b aid to Int'l Mon Fund	N
18. Raise Senate salary/omit honoraria	Y
19. Reduce space station funding $1.9b	Y
20. Kill-Eliminate supercollider funds	Y
21. Req 5-day handgun waiting period	N
22. Life in prison instead of death	N
23. Exceptions to exclusionary rule	Y
24. Ban race as death sentence factor	Y
25. Campaign finance revisions	N
26. Kill-Term limits for senators	Y
27. Require four presidential debates	Y
28. Tighten ban on vertical price fixing	N
29. Kill-Freeze discretionary budget	Y
30. Provide $30b for failed S&Ls	Y
31. Allow use of force against Iraq	Y
32. Allow $15b in foreign aid for 1991	N
33. Civil Rights Act of 1990	Y
34. Block cancellation of Egypt's debt	N
35. Cut El Salvador military aid 50%	Y
36. Reduce troops in NATO by 30,000	N
37. Req increases in auto fuel efficiency	N
38. Bar taxpayer funding of campaigns	N
39. Limit textile import growth to 1%	Y
40. Amendment to ban flag desecration	Y
41. Let fed emp be politically active	Y
42. Reauthorize Amtrak-veto override	Y
43. Allow sale of assault weapons	Y
44. Retraining aid for coal miners	+
45. Kill-Raise car emission standards	Y
46. Pull EPA nuclear plant authority	Y
47. Defer Chinese students' deportation	Y
48. Cut in capital gains tax	Y
49. Establish CIA inspector general	Y
50. Kill-Sanctions against China	Y
51. Bar drug testing to receive AFDC	Y
52. Kill-Allow force against drug planes	Y
53. Include illegal aliens in census	Y
54. Restitution to Japanese interned	Y
55. Troop reduction in Europe of 50%	N
56. Increase SDI research to $4.3b	N
57. Kill-Pay homeless below min wage	Y
58. Ban airline smoking within US	N
59. Bar transfer of FS-X technology	Y
60. Limit liability for oil spills	Y
61. Restructure S&L industry	Y
62. Ban $ to illegal foreign activities	Y
63. Req immigrant fluency in English	N
64. Allow aliens' families to stay in US	Y
65. Expand child care aid/tax credit	Y
66. Raise minimum wage w/subminimum	Y
67. Freeze outlays except SS/Medicare	Y
68. Kill-Shift $5b of DOD to domestic	Y
69. Confirm Tower as sec of defense	N
70. Bar abortion $ except to save mother	Y

71. Kill-Warn AIDS carriers' spouses	Y
72. Allow religious schools to bar gays	Y
73. 60 days' notice of plant closings	Y
74. Allow poison pills in corp takeovers	N
75. Kill-Workfare program	Y
76. Prohibit employee polygraph testing	Y
77. Cap Medicare patients' liability	Y
78. Revise unfair trade practices	Y
79. Kill-Shift SDI $ to conv weapons	N
80. Kill-Shift SDI $ to accidental launch	Y
81. Kill-Shift MX $ to supplies/parts	Y
82. Kill-Buy America provision at DOD	N
83. Allow nuclear testing-5+ kilotons	Y
84. Allow SALT II to be exceeded	N
85. $ to vets exposed to nuclear bomb	Y
86. Warn workers of disease exposure	N
87. Restore four civil rights laws	Y
88. Disapprove uranium sales to Japan	N
89. Notify Congress of covert operations	Y
90. Approval of $36m in Contra aid	Y
91. $18b deficit reduction compromise	Y
92. Allow sale of hard-to-detect guns	Y
93. Catastrophic health insurance	Y
94. Bork nomination to Supreme Court	N
95. Kill-Void Panama Canal treaties	N
96. Kill-Insurance denial to AIDS+	Y
97. Keep diplomatic immunity intact	Y
98. Produce Bigeye nerve gas bomb	Y
99. Balanced budget by '93-via targets	N
100. Allow ASAT missile tests in space	N
101. Limit space-based/ABM system tests	Y
102. Force reduction in trade barriers	Y
103. Repeal windfall profit tax on oil	Y
104. $1b/two year aid for the homeless	?
105. Disallow $30m for AZT to poor	N
106. Bar AIDS test-immigrants/marriage	Y
107. Kill-Biennial budget approval	Y
108. Fairness doctrine in broadcasting	Y
109. Raise speed limit to 65 mph	Y
110. Immigration reform/alien amnesty	Y
111. South Africa sanctions-veto override	Y
112. Kill-Use of military in drug war	Y
113. Tax overhaul to revise income tax	Y
114. Submit nuclear test ban treaties	Y
115. Prohibit sale of Stinger missiles	Y
116. Prohibit binary chemical weapons	N
117. Kill-$10/barrel oil tariff increase	N
118. Grant tax amnesty provisions	N
119. Block Saudi arms sale-veto override	Y
120. Balanced budget amendment	Y
121. Include veterans in spending cuts	N
122. Bar $ to hazardous substance victims	Y
123. Allow seasonal workers in the US	N
124. Let fed courts rule on school prayer	N
125. Presidential line-item veto	N
126. Ease Gun Control Act of 1968	Y
127. Kill-Req 14-day wait for handguns	Y
128. Kill-15% min tax on corporations	N
129. Drop Social Security COLA	N
130. Freeze funding for all programs	N
131. Kill-Nuclear weapon freeze	Y
132. Keep decision narrowing Title IX	N
133. Raise drinking age to 21	N
134. Allow production of MX missile	N

JOHNSTON, J. BENNETT (continued)

135. Raise taxes/cut spending by $140b	N	140. Authorize Marines in Lebanon	N
136. School prayer amendment	Y	141. Amendment making abortion illegal	Y
137. Capital punishment-federal crimes	Y	142. Delete $1.2b for jobs creation	N
138. Ban government officials from taping	N	143. Keep tobacco price supports	Y
139. Martin Luther King holiday	Y	144. Emergency housing aid of $5.1b	N

Presidential Support Score: 1991 - 56%   1990 - 53%

BREAUX, JOHN B. -- Louisiana [Democrat]. Term Began/Expires: 1987/1992. Prior Terms: House: 1972 (Special Election)-1986. Born: March 1, 1944; Crowley, LA. Education: University of Southwestern Louisiana (B.A.); Louisiana State University (J.D.). Occupation: Attorney, Brown, McKernan, Ingram & Breaux (1967-68); congressional assistant (1968-72).

1. Prohibit MFN status for China	Y	51. Bar drug testing to receive AFDC	Y
2. Kill-Tie welfare to school attendance	Y	52. Kill-Allow force against drug planes	Y
3. Limit credit card interest rates	Y	53. Include illegal aliens in census	Y
4. Confirm Gates as head of CIA	Y	54. Restitution to Japanese interned	Y
5. Adoption of national energy policies	Y	55. Troop reduction in Europe of 50%	N
6. Kill-Restrict NEA use of funds	Y	56. Increase SDI research to $4.3b	N
7. Unemployment benefits extension	Y	57. Kill-Pay homeless below min wage	Y
8. Confirm Thomas to Supreme Court	Y	58. Ban airline smoking within US	N
9. Raise eligibility for unpaid leave	Y	59. Bar transfer of FS-X technology	Y
10. Notify parents of minors' abortions	Y	60. Limit liability for oil spills	Y
11. Move $3b from defense to domestic	N	61. Restructure S&L industry	Y
12. End production of B-2 bomber	N	62. Ban $ to illegal foreign activities	Y
13. Cut SDI $1b to reduce deficit	N	63. Req immigrant fluency in English	N
14. Maintain strategic stability-Soviets	Y	64. Allow aliens' families to stay in US	Y
15. Kill-Allow women as combat pilots	Y	65. Expand child care aid/tax credit	Y
16. Kill-Allow HIV tests before surgery	N	66. Raise minimum wage w/subminimum	Y
17. Strike $12b aid to Int'l Mon Fund	N	67. Freeze outlays except SS/Medicare	N
18. Raise Senate salary/omit honoraria	Y	68. Kill-Shift $5b of DOD to domestic	Y
19. Reduce space station funding $1.9b	Y	69. Confirm Tower as sec of defense	N
20. Kill-Eliminate supercollider funds	Y	70. Bar abortion $ except to save mother	Y
21. Req 5-day handgun waiting period	N	71. Kill-Warn AIDS carriers' spouses	Y
22. Life in prison instead of death	N	72. Allow religious schools to bar gays	Y
23. Exceptions to exclusionary rule	Y	73. 60 days' notice of plant closings	Y
24. Ban race as death sentence factor	Y	74. Allow poison pills in corp takeovers	N
25. Campaign finance revisions	N	75. Kill-Workfare program	Y
26. Kill-Term limits for senators	Y	76. Prohibit employee polygraph testing	Y
27. Require four presidential debates	?	77. Cap Medicare patients' liability	Y
28. Tighten ban on vertical price fixing	Y	78. Revise unfair trade practices	Y
29. Kill-Freeze discretionary budget	Y	79. Kill-Shift SDI $ to conv weapons	N
30. Provide $30b for failed S&Ls	Y	80. Kill-Shift SDI $ to accidental launch	Y
31. Allow use of force against Iraq	Y	81. Kill-Shift MX $ to supplies/parts	N
32. Allow $15b in foreign aid for 1991	N	82. Kill-Buy America provision at DOD	?
33. Civil Rights Act of 1990	Y	83. Allow nuclear testing-5+ kilotons	Y
34. Block cancellation of Egypt's debt	Y	84. Allow SALT II to be exceeded	Y
35. Cut El Salvador military aid 50%	Y	85. $ to vets exposed to nuclear bomb	Y
36. Reduce troops in NATO by 30,000	N	86. Warn workers of disease exposure	Y
37. Req increases in auto fuel efficiency	Y	87. Restore four civil rights laws	Y
38. Bar taxpayer funding of campaigns	N	88. Disapprove uranium sales to Japan	N
39. Limit textile import growth to 1%	Y	89. Notify Congress of covert operations	Y
40. Amendment to ban flag desecration	Y	90. Approval of $36m in Contra aid	Y
41. Let fed emp be politically active	Y	91. $18b deficit reduction compromise	Y
42. Reauthorize Amtrak-veto override	Y	92. Allow sale of hard-to-detect guns	N
43. Allow sale of assault weapons	Y	93. Catastrophic health insurance	Y
44. Retraining aid for coal miners	N	94. Bork nomination to Supreme Court	N
45. Kill-Raise car emission standards	Y	95. Kill-Void Panama Canal treaties	N
46. Pull EPA nuclear plant authority	Y	96. Kill-Insurance denial to AIDS+	Y
47. Defer Chinese students' deportation	?	97. Keep diplomatic immunity intact	Y
48. Cut in capital gains tax	N	98. Produce Bigeye nerve gas bomb	Y
49. Establish CIA inspector general	Y	99. Balanced budget by '93-via targets	Y
50. Kill-Sanctions against China	Y	100. Allow ASAT missile tests in space	N

BREAUX, JOHN B. (continued)

101. Limit space-based/ABM system tests	Y	
102. Force reduction in trade barriers	Y	
103. Repeal windfall profit tax on oil	Y	
104. $1b/two year aid for the homeless	Y	
105. Disallow $30m for AZT to poor	N	

106. Bar AIDS test-immigrants/marriage	Y
107. Kill-Biennial budget approval	Y
108. Fairness doctrine in broadcasting	Y
109. Raise speed limit to 65 mph	Y

The following are House measures voted on between 1982-1986:

99. Immigration reform/alien amnesty	?
100. South Africa sanctions-veto override	?
101. Tax overhaul to revise income tax	Y
102. Use of military in drug war	?
103. Delete 12 MX/add conventional wpn	?
104. Raise speed limit to 65 mph	?
105. Require Pentagon to buy US goods	?
106. AIDS insurance non-discrimination	Y
107. Prohibit Saudi arms sales	#
108. Ease Gun Control Act of 1968	Y
109. Bar interstate handgun transport	N
110. Make company emissions known	N
111. Allow toxic victims to sue in fed ct	N
112. Superfund waste cleanup of $10b	N
113. 90 days notice of plant closings	Y
114. $20b in Medicare cuts/tax increases	Y
115. Spending cuts and tax increases	Y
116. Set school lunch lmt-250% poverty	N
117. $75m for youth work projects	N
118. Allow Angolan military assistance	Y
119. Suspend defense payments for abuse	?
120. Drop SS COLAs/$12b tax increase	N
121. Approve $1.5b for 21 MX missiles	Y

122. Emergency farm credit/revisions	Y
123. Duty on Taiwan/Hong Kong/S Korea	N
124. Limit steel imports to 17%	Y
125. Cut $ to schools that bar prayer	Y
126. $50b-taxes; cut Medicare/spending	Y
127. Limit Pershing II/cruise in Europe	N
128. Delete $7.1b for 34 B-1 bombers	N
129. Bar purchase of Sergeant York guns	Y
130. El Salvador military/economic aid	Y
131. Bar mining of Nicaraguan waters	Y
132. Physician fee freeze for Medicare	N
133. $49b in "sin"/phone/insurance taxes	Y
134. Allow sale of Conrail	Y
135. Equal Rights Amendment	Y
136. Authorize Marines in Lebanon	Y
137. Eminent domain for coal companies	Y
138. Prohibit EPA clean air sanctions	N
139. SS retirement age increase/reforms	Y
140. Auto domestic content requirement	N
141. Delete jobs program funding	N
142. Highway-gas tax bill	Y
143. Cut $5b from defense for Medicare	N
144. Emergency housing aid of $1b	Y

Presidential Support Score: 1991 - 65%   1990 - 57%

MAINE

COHEN, WILLIAM S. -- Maine [Republican]. Term Began/Expires: 1991/1996. Prior Terms: House: 1973-78; Senate: 1979-90. Born: August 28, 1940; Bangor, ME. Education: Bowdoin College (B.A.); Boston University Law School (LL.B.). Occupation: Instructor, University of Maine; partner, Paine, Cohen, Lynch, Weatherbee and Kobritz (1965-73); assistant editor, *Journal of American Trial Lawyers Association* (1965-66); assistant county attorney (1968-70); mayor (1971-72).

1. Prohibit MFN status for China	N
2. Kill-Tie welfare to school attendance	N
3. Limit credit card interest rates	Y
4. Confirm Gates as head of CIA	Y
5. Adoption of national energy policies	N
6. Kill-Restrict NEA use of funds	Y
7. Unemployment benefits extension	Y
8. Confirm Thomas to Supreme Court	Y
9. Raise eligibility for unpaid leave	Y
10. Notify parents of minors' abortions	N
11. Move $3b from defense to domestic	N
12. End production of B-2 bomber	Y
13. Cut SDI $1b to reduce deficit	N
14. Maintain strategic stability-Soviets	N
15. Kill-Allow women as combat pilots	N
16. Kill-Allow HIV tests before surgery	Y
17. Strike $12b aid to Int'l Mon Fund	N
18. Raise Senate salary/omit honoraria	N

19. Reduce space station funding $1.9b	Y
20. Kill-Eliminate supercollider funds	N
21. Req 5-day handgun waiting period	Y
22. Life in prison instead of death	Y
23. Exceptions to exclusionary rule	N
24. Ban race as death sentence factor	N
25. Campaign finance revisions	Y
26. Kill-Term limits for senators	Y
27. Require four presidential debates	N
28. Tighten ban on vertical price fixing	Y
29. Kill-Freeze discretionary budget	Y
30. Provide $30b for failed S&Ls	Y
31. Allow use of force against Iraq	Y
32. Allow $15b in foreign aid for 1991	Y
33. Civil Rights Act of 1990	Y
34. Block cancellation of Egypt's debt	Y
35. Cut El Salvador military aid 50%	Y
36. Reduce troops in NATO by 30,000	Y

COHEN, WILLIAM S. (continued)

37. Req increases in auto fuel efficiency	Y	
38. Bar taxpayer funding of campaigns	Y	
39. Limit textile import growth to 1%	Y	
40. Amendment to ban flag desecration	Y	
41. Let fed emp be politically active	N	
42. Reauthorize Amtrak-veto override	Y	
43. Allow sale of assault weapons	Y	
44. Retraining aid for coal miners	N	
45. Kill-Raise car emission standards	N	
46. Pull EPA nuclear plant authority	N	
47. Defer Chinese students' deportation	Y	
48. Cut in capital gains tax	Y	
49. Establish CIA inspector general	Y	
50. Kill-Sanctions against China	Y	
51. Bar drug testing to receive AFDC	Y	
52. Kill-Allow force against drug planes	Y	
53. Include illegal aliens in census	N	
54. Restitution to Japanese interned	Y	
55. Troop reduction in Europe of 50%	N	
56. Increase SDI research to $4.3b	Y	
57. Kill-Pay homeless below min wage	N	
58. Ban airline smoking within US	Y	
59. Bar transfer of FS-X technology	Y	
60. Limit liability for oil spills	N	
61. Restructure S&L industry	N	
62. Ban $ to illegal foreign activities	Y	
63. Req immigrant fluency in English	Y	
64. Allow aliens' families to stay in US	N	
65. Expand child care aid/tax credit	Y	
66. Raise minimum wage w/subminimum	Y	
67. Freeze outlays except SS/Medicare	N	
68. Kill-Shift $5b of DOD to domestic	Y	
69. Confirm Tower as sec of defense	Y	
70. Bar abortion $ except to save mother	N	
71. Kill-Warn AIDS carriers' spouses	N	
72. Allow religious schools to bar gays	N	
73. 60 days' notice of plant closings	Y	
74. Allow poison pills in corp takeovers	N	
75. Kill-Workfare program	N	
76. Prohibit employee polygraph testing	?	
77. Cap Medicare patients' liability	Y	
78. Revise unfair trade practices	Y	
79. Kill-Shift SDI $ to conv weapons	Y	
80. Kill-Shift SDI $ to accidental launch	Y	
81. Kill-Shift MX $ to supplies/parts	Y	
82. Kill-Buy America provision at DOD	N	
83. Allow nuclear testing-5+ kilotons	Y	
84. Allow SALT II to be exceeded	Y	
85. $ to vets exposed to nuclear bomb	?	
86. Warn workers of disease exposure	N	
87. Restore four civil rights laws	Y	
88. Disapprove uranium sales to Japan	Y	
89. Notify Congress of covert operations	Y	
90. Approval of $36m in Contra aid	Y	

91. $18b deficit reduction compromise	Y	
92. Allow sale of hard-to-detect guns	Y	
93. Catastrophic health insurance	Y	
94. Bork nomination to Supreme Court	Y	
95. Kill-Void Panama Canal treaties	N	
96. Kill-Insurance denial to AIDS+	Y	
97. Keep diplomatic immunity intact	?	
98. Produce Bigeye nerve gas bomb	Y	
99. Balanced budget by '93-via targets	Y	
100. Allow ASAT missile tests in space	Y	
101. Limit space-based/ABM system tests	Y	
102. Force reduction in trade barriers	Y	
103. Repeal windfall profit tax on oil	N	
104. $1b/two year aid for the homeless	Y	
105. Disallow $30m for AZT to poor	N	
106. Bar AIDS test-immigrants/marriage	N	
107. Kill-Biennial budget approval	N	
108. Fairness doctrine in broadcasting	Y	
109. Raise speed limit to 65 mph	N	
110. Immigration reform/alien amnesty	N	
111. South Africa sanctions-veto override	Y	
112. Kill-Use of military in drug war	Y	
113. Tax overhaul to revise income tax	Y	
114. Submit nuclear test ban treaties	Y	
115. Prohibit sale of Stinger missiles	N	
116. Prohibit binary chemical weapons	N	
117. Kill-$10/barrel oil tariff increase	Y	
118. Grant tax amnesty provisions	N	
119. Block Saudi arms sale-veto override	Y	
120. Balanced budget amendment	N	
121. Include veterans in spending cuts	Y	
122. Bar $ to hazardous substance victims	N	
123. Allow seasonal workers in the US	N	
124. Let fed courts rule on school prayer	Y	
125. Presidential line-item veto	Y	
126. Ease Gun Control Act of 1968	Y	
127. Kill-Req 14-day wait for handguns	Y	
128. Kill-15% min tax on corporations	N	
129. Drop Social Security COLA	Y	
130. Freeze funding for all programs	N	
131. Kill-Nuclear weapon freeze	Y	
132. Keep decision narrowing Title IX	N	
133. Raise drinking age to 21	Y	
134. Allow production of MX missile	Y	
135. Raise taxes/cut spending by $140b	Y	
136. School prayer amendment	N	
137. Capital punishment-federal crimes	N	
138. Ban government officials from taping	Y	
139. Martin Luther King holiday	Y	
140. Authorize Marines in Lebanon	Y	
141. Amendment making abortion illegal	N	
142. Delete $1.2b for jobs creation	N	
143. Keep tobacco price supports	N	
144. Emergency housing aid of $5.1b	N	

Presidential Support Score: 1991 - 67%   1990 - 44%

MITCHELL, GEORGE J. -- Maine [Democrat]. Term Began/Expires: 1989/1994. Prior Terms: Senate: 1980 (Special Election)-1988. Born: August 20, 1933; Waterville, ME. Education: Bowdoin College; Georgetown University Law Center. Military Service: U.S. Army, 1954-56. Occupation: Justice Department attorney (1960-62); Senate staff member (1962-65); partner, Jensen, Baird, Gardner, Donovan and Henry (1965-77); assistant county attorney, Cumberland County, Maine (1971); U.S. attorney, Maine (1977-79).

MITCHELL, GEORGE J. (continued)

1. Prohibit MFN status for China	Y	
2. Kill-Tie welfare to school attendance	Y	
3. Limit credit card interest rates	Y	
4. Confirm Gates as head of CIA	N	
5. Adoption of national energy policies	Y	
6. Kill-Restrict NEA use of funds	Y	
7. Unemployment benefits extension	Y	
8. Confirm Thomas to Supreme Court	N	
9. Raise eligibility for unpaid leave	Y	
10. Notify parents of minors' abortions	N	
11. Move $3b from defense to domestic	Y	
12. End production of B-2 bomber	Y	
13. Cut SDI $1b to reduce deficit	Y	
14. Maintain strategic stability-Soviets	Y	
15. Kill-Allow women as combat pilots	N	
16. Kill-Allow HIV tests before surgery	Y	
17. Strike $12b aid to Int'l Mon Fund	N	
18. Raise Senate salary/omit honoraria	Y	
19. Reduce space station funding $1.9b	Y	
20. Kill-Eliminate supercollider funds	N	
21. Req 5-day handgun waiting period	Y	
22. Life in prison instead of death	Y	
23. Exceptions to exclusionary rule	N	
24. Ban race as death sentence factor	N	
25. Campaign finance revisions	Y	
26. Kill-Term limits for senators	Y	
27. Require four presidential debates	Y	
28. Tighten ban on vertical price fixing	Y	
29. Kill-Freeze discretionary budget	Y	
30. Provide $30b for failed S&Ls	Y	
31. Allow use of force against Iraq	N	
32. Allow $15b in foreign aid for 1991	Y	
33. Civil Rights Act of 1990	Y	
34. Block cancellation of Egypt's debt	N	
35. Cut El Salvador military aid 50%	Y	
36. Reduce troops in NATO by 30,000	Y	
37. Req increases in auto fuel efficiency	Y	
38. Bar taxpayer funding of campaigns	N	
39. Limit textile import growth to 1%	Y	
40. Amendment to ban flag desecration	N	
41. Let fed emp be politically active	Y	
42. Reauthorize Amtrak-veto override	N	
43. Allow sale of assault weapons	N	
44. Retraining aid for coal miners	N	
45. Kill-Raise car emission standards	Y	
46. Pull EPA nuclear plant authority	N	
47. Defer Chinese students' deportation	Y	
48. Cut in capital gains tax	N	
49. Establish CIA inspector general	Y	
50. Kill-Sanctions against China	Y	
51. Bar drug testing to receive AFDC	Y	
52. Kill-Allow force against drug planes	Y	
53. Include illegal aliens in census	Y	
54. Restitution to Japanese interned	Y	
55. Troop reduction in Europe of 50%	N	
56. Increase SDI research to $4.3b	N	
57. Kill-Pay homeless below min wage	Y	
58. Ban airline smoking within US	Y	
59. Bar transfer of FS-X technology	Y	
60. Limit liability for oil spills	Y	
61. Restructure S&L industry	Y	
62. Ban $ to illegal foreign activities	Y	
63. Req immigrant fluency in English	N	
64. Allow aliens' families to stay in US	N	
65. Expand child care aid/tax credit	Y
66. Raise minimum wage w/subminimum	Y
67. Freeze outlays except SS/Medicare	N
68. Kill-Shift $5b of DOD to domestic	Y
69. Confirm Tower as sec of defense	N
70. Bar abortion $ except to save mother	N
71. Kill-Warn AIDS carriers' spouses	Y
72. Allow religious schools to bar gays	N
73. 60 days' notice of plant closings	Y
74. Allow poison pills in corp takeovers	Y
75. Kill-Workfare program	Y
76. Prohibit employee polygraph testing	Y
77. Cap Medicare patients' liability	Y
78. Revise unfair trade practices	Y
79. Kill-Shift SDI $ to conv weapons	N
80. Kill-Shift SDI $ to accidental launch	Y
81. Kill-Shift MX $ to supplies/parts	Y
82. Kill-Buy America provision at DOD	N
83. Allow nuclear testing-5+ kilotons	N
84. Allow SALT II to be exceeded	N
85. $ to vets exposed to nuclear bomb	Y
86. Warn workers of disease exposure	Y
87. Restore four civil rights laws	Y
88. Disapprove uranium sales to Japan	Y
89. Notify Congress of covert operations	Y
90. Approval of $36m in Contra aid	N
91. $18b deficit reduction compromise	Y
92. Allow sale of hard-to-detect guns	N
93. Catastrophic health insurance	Y
94. Bork nomination to Supreme Court	N
95. Kill-Void Panama Canal treaties	Y
96. Kill-Insurance denial to AIDS+	Y
97. Keep diplomatic immunity intact	Y
98. Produce Bigeye nerve gas bomb	N
99. Balanced budget by '93-via targets	Y
100. Allow ASAT missile tests in space	N
101. Limit space-based/ABM system tests	Y
102. Force reduction in trade barriers	Y
103. Repeal windfall profit tax on oil	N
104. $1b/two year aid for the homeless	Y
105. Disallow $30m for AZT to poor	N
106. Bar AIDS test-immigrants/marriage	Y
107. Kill-Biennial budget approval	Y
108. Fairness doctrine in broadcasting	Y
109. Raise speed limit to 65 mph	N
110. Immigration reform/alien amnesty	N
111. South Africa sanctions-veto override	Y
112. Kill-Use of military in drug war	Y
113. Tax overhaul to revise income tax	Y
114. Submit nuclear test ban treaties	Y
115. Prohibit sale of Stinger missiles	Y
116. Prohibit binary chemical weapons	Y
117. Kill-$10/barrel oil tariff increase	Y
118. Grant tax amnesty provisions	Y
119. Block Saudi arms sale-veto override	Y
120. Balanced budget amendment	N
121. Include veterans in spending cuts	N
122. Bar $ to hazardous substance victims	N
123. Allow seasonal workers in the US	Y
124. Let fed courts rule on school prayer	Y
125. Presidential line-item veto	N
126. Ease Gun Control Act of 1968	N
127. Kill-Req 14-day wait for handguns	Y
128. Kill-15% min tax on corporations	N

MITCHELL, GEORGE J. (continued)

129. Drop Social Security COLA	N	
130. Freeze funding for all programs	N	
131. Kill-Nuclear weapon freeze	N	
132. Keep decision narrowing Title IX	N	
133. Raise drinking age to 21	Y	
134. Allow production of MX missile	N	
135. Raise taxes/cut spending by $140b	N	
136. School prayer amendment	N	
137. Capital punishment-federal crimes	N	
138. Ban government officials from taping	Y	
139. Martin Luther King holiday	Y	
140. Authorize Marines in Lebanon	Y	
141. Amendment making abortion illegal	N	
142. Delete $1.2b for jobs creation	N	
143. Keep tobacco price supports	N	
144. Emergency housing aid of $5.1b	Y	

Presidential Support Score: 1991 - 35% 1990 - 34%

MARYLAND

SARBANES, PAUL S. -- Maryland [Democrat]. Term Began/Expires: 1989/1994. Prior Terms: House: 1971-76; Senate: 1977-88. Born: Feb. 3, 1933; Salisbury, MD. Education: Princeton University (A.B.); Oxford University (B.A.); Harvard Law School (LL.B.). Occupation: Attorney, Venable, Baetjer and Howard; assistant to the chairman, Council on Economic Advisers (1962-63); executive director, Baltimore City Charter Revision Committee (1963-64); Maryland Delegate (1967-71).

1. Prohibit MFN status for China	Y	39. Limit textile import growth to 1%	Y
2. Kill-Tie welfare to school attendance	Y	40. Amendment to ban flag desecration	N
3. Limit credit card interest rates	Y	41. Let fed emp be politically active	Y
4. Confirm Gates as head of CIA	N	42. Reauthorize Amtrak-veto override	Y
5. Adoption of national energy policies	N	43. Allow sale of assault weapons	N
6. Kill-Restrict NEA use of funds	Y	44. Retraining aid for coal miners	N
7. Unemployment benefits extension	Y	45. Kill-Raise car emission standards	N
8. Confirm Thomas to Supreme Court	N	46. Pull EPA nuclear plant authority	N
9. Raise eligibility for unpaid leave	Y	47. Defer Chinese students' deportation	Y
10. Notify parents of minors' abortions	N	48. Cut in capital gains tax	N
11. Move $3b from defense to domestic	Y	49. Establish CIA inspector general	Y
12. End production of B-2 bomber	Y	50. Kill-Sanctions against China	Y
13. Cut SDI $1b to reduce deficit	Y	51. Bar drug testing to receive AFDC	Y
14. Maintain strategic stability-Soviets	Y	52. Kill-Allow force against drug planes	Y
15. Kill-Allow women as combat pilots	N	53. Include illegal aliens in census	Y
16. Kill-Allow HIV tests before surgery	Y	54. Restitution to Japanese interned	Y
17. Strike $12b aid to Int'l Mon Fund	N	55. Troop reduction in Europe of 50%	N
18. Raise Senate salary/omit honoraria	Y	56. Increase SDI research to $4.3b	N
19. Reduce space station funding $1.9b	N	57. Kill-Pay homeless below min wage	Y
20. Kill-Eliminate supercollider funds	Y	58. Ban airline smoking within US	Y
21. Req 5-day handgun waiting period	Y	59. Bar transfer of FS-X technology	Y
22. Life in prison instead of death	Y	60. Limit liability for oil spills	Y
23. Exceptions to exclusionary rule	N	61. Restructure S&L industry	Y
24. Ban race as death sentence factor	N	62. Ban $ to illegal foreign activities	Y
25. Campaign finance revisions	Y	63. Req immigrant fluency in English	N
26. Kill-Term limits for senators	Y	64. Allow aliens' families to stay in US	Y
27. Require four presidential debates	Y	65. Expand child care aid/tax credit	Y
28. Tighten ban on vertical price fixing	Y	66. Raise minimum wage w/subminimum	Y
29. Kill-Freeze discretionary budget	Y	67. Freeze outlays except SS/Medicare	N
30. Provide $30b for failed S&Ls	Y	68. Kill-Shift $5b of DOD to domestic	Y
31. Allow use of force against Iraq	N	69. Confirm Tower as sec of defense	N
32. Allow $15b in foreign aid for 1991	Y	70. Bar abortion $ except to save mother	N
33. Civil Rights Act of 1990	Y	71. Kill-Warn AIDS carriers' spouses	Y
34. Block cancellation of Egypt's debt	N	72. Allow religious schools to bar gays	N
35. Cut El Salvador military aid 50%	Y	73. 60 days' notice of plant closings	Y
36. Reduce troops in NATO by 30,000	Y	74. Allow poison pills in corp takeovers	Y
37. Req increases in auto fuel efficiency	Y	75. Kill-Workfare program	Y
38. Bar taxpayer funding of campaigns	N	76. Prohibit employee polygraph testing	Y

SARBANES, PAUL S. (continued)

77. Cap Medicare patients' liability	Y	
78. Revise unfair trade practices	Y	
79. Kill-Shift SDI $ to conv weapons	N	
80. Kill-Shift SDI $ to accidental launch	Y	
81. Kill-Shift MX $ to supplies/parts	N	
82. Kill-Buy America provision at DOD	N	
83. Allow nuclear testing-5+ kilotons	N	
84. Allow SALT II to be exceeded	N	
85. $ to vets exposed to nuclear bomb	Y	
86. Warn workers of disease exposure	Y	
87. Restore four civil rights laws	Y	
88. Disapprove uranium sales to Japan	Y	
89. Notify Congress of covert operations	Y	
90. Approval of $36m in Contra aid	N	
91. $18b deficit reduction compromise	Y	
92. Allow sale of hard-to-detect guns	N	
93. Catastrophic health insurance	Y	
94. Bork nomination to Supreme Court	N	
95. Kill-Void Panama Canal treaties	Y	
96. Kill-Insurance denial to AIDS+	Y	
97. Keep diplomatic immunity intact	N	
98. Produce Bigeye nerve gas bomb	N	
99. Balanced budget by '93-via targets	N	
100. Allow ASAT missile tests in space	N	
101. Limit space-based/ABM system tests	Y	
102. Force reduction in trade barriers	Y	
103. Repeal windfall profit tax on oil	N	
104. $1b/two year aid for the homeless	Y	
105. Disallow $30m for AZT to poor	N	
106. Bar AIDS test-immigrants/marriage	Y	
107. Kill-Biennial budget approval	Y	
108. Fairness doctrine in broadcasting	Y	
109. Raise speed limit to 65 mph	N	
110. Immigration reform/alien amnesty	Y	

111. South Africa sanctions-veto override	Y
112. Kill-Use of military in drug war	Y
113. Tax overhaul to revise income tax	Y
114. Submit nuclear test ban treaties	Y
115. Prohibit sale of Stinger missiles	Y
116. Prohibit binary chemical weapons	Y
117. Kill-$10/barrel oil tariff increase	Y
118. Grant tax amnesty provisions	N
119. Block Saudi arms sale-veto override	Y
120. Balanced budget amendment	N
121. Include veterans in spending cuts	N
122. Bar $ to hazardous substance victims	N
123. Allow seasonal workers in the US	N
124. Let fed courts rule on school prayer	N
125. Presidential line-item veto	N
126. Ease Gun Control Act of 1968	N
127. Kill-Req 14-day wait for handguns	N
128. Kill-15% min tax on corporations	N
129. Drop Social Security COLA	N
130. Freeze funding for all programs	N
131. Kill-Nuclear weapon freeze	N
132. Keep decision narrowing Title IX	N
133. Raise drinking age to 21	Y
134. Allow production of MX missile	N
135. Raise taxes/cut spending by $140b	N
136. School prayer amendment	N
137. Capital punishment-federal crimes	N
138. Ban government officials from taping	Y
139. Martin Luther King holiday	Y
140. Authorize Marines in Lebanon	N
141. Amendment making abortion illegal	N
142. Delete $1.2b for jobs creation	N
143. Keep tobacco price supports	Y
144. Emergency housing aid of $5.1b	Y

Presidential Support Score: 1991 - 30% 1990 - 31%

MIKULSKI, BARBARA A. -- Maryland [Democrat]. Term Began/Expires: 1987/1992. Prior Terms: House: 1977-86. Born: July 20, 1936; Baltimore, MD. Education: Mount Saint Agnes College (B.A.); University of Maryland (M.S.W.). Occupation: City councilwoman (1971-76); adjunct professor of sociology; author; lecturer; teacher; social worker.

1. Prohibit MFN status for China	Y	
2. Kill-Tie welfare to school attendance	Y	
3. Limit credit card interest rates	Y	
4. Confirm Gates as head of CIA	Y	
5. Adoption of national energy policies	N	
6. Kill-Restrict NEA use of funds	Y	
7. Unemployment benefits extension	Y	
8. Confirm Thomas to Supreme Court	N	
9. Raise eligibility for unpaid leave	Y	
10. Notify parents of minors' abortions	N	
11. Move $3b from defense to domestic	N	
12. End production of B-2 bomber	Y	
13. Cut SDI $1b to reduce deficit	Y	
14. Maintain strategic stability-Soviets	Y	
15. Kill-Allow women as combat pilots	N	
16. Kill-Allow HIV tests before surgery	Y	
17. Strike $12b aid to Int'l Mon Fund	N	
18. Raise Senate salary/omit honoraria	N	
19. Reduce space station funding $1.9b	N	
20. Kill-Eliminate supercollider funds	Y	
21. Req 5-day handgun waiting period	Y	

22. Life in prison instead of death	N
23. Exceptions to exclusionary rule	N
24. Ban race as death sentence factor	N
25. Campaign finance revisions	Y
26. Kill-Term limits for senators	Y
27. Require four presidential debates	Y
28. Tighten ban on vertical price fixing	N
29. Kill-Freeze discretionary budget	Y
30. Provide $30b for failed S&Ls	Y
31. Allow use of force against Iraq	N
32. Allow $15b in foreign aid for 1991	Y
33. Civil Rights Act of 1990	Y
34. Block cancellation of Egypt's debt	Y
35. Cut El Salvador military aid 50%	Y
36. Reduce troops in NATO by 30,000	Y
37. Req increases in auto fuel efficiency	Y
38. Bar taxpayer funding of campaigns	?
39. Limit textile import growth to 1%	Y
40. Amendment to ban flag desecration	N
41. Let fed emp be politically active	Y
42. Reauthorize Amtrak-veto override	Y

MIKULSKI, BARBARA A. (continued)

43. Allow sale of assault weapons	N	77. Cap Medicare patients' liability	Y
44. Retraining aid for coal miners	Y	78. Revise unfair trade practices	Y
45. Kill-Raise car emission standards	N	79. Kill-Shift SDI $ to conv weapons	N
46. Pull EPA nuclear plant authority	N	80. Kill-Shift SDI $ to accidental launch	Y
47. Defer Chinese students' deportation	Y	81. Kill-Shift MX $ to supplies/parts	N
48. Cut in capital gains tax	N	82. Kill-Buy America provision at DOD	N
49. Establish CIA inspector general	Y	83. Allow nuclear testing-5+ kilotons	N
50. Kill-Sanctions against China	Y	84. Allow SALT II to be exceeded	N
51. Bar drug testing to receive AFDC	Y	85. $ to vets exposed to nuclear bomb	+
52. Kill-Allow force against drug planes	Y	86. Warn workers of disease exposure	Y
53. Include illegal aliens in census	Y	87. Restore four civil rights laws	Y
54. Restitution to Japanese interned	Y	88. Disapprove uranium sales to Japan	Y
55. Troop reduction in Europe of 50%	Y	89. Notify Congress of covert operations	Y
56. Increase SDI research to $4.3b	N	90. Approval of $36m in Contra aid	N
57. Kill-Pay homeless below min wage	Y	91. $18b deficit reduction compromise	Y
58. Ban airline smoking within US	Y	92. Allow sale of hard-to-detect guns	N
59. Bar transfer of FS-X technology	Y	93. Catastrophic health insurance	Y
60. Limit liability for oil spills	N	94. Bork nomination to Supreme Court	N
61. Restructure S&L industry	Y	95. Kill-Void Panama Canal treaties	Y
62. Ban $ to illegal foreign activities	Y	96. Kill-Insurance denial to AIDS+	Y
63. Req immigrant fluency in English	N	97. Keep diplomatic immunity intact	N
64. Allow aliens' families to stay in US	Y	98. Produce Bigeye nerve gas bomb	N
65. Expand child care aid/tax credit	Y	99. Balanced budget by '93-via targets	N
66. Raise minimum wage w/subminimum	Y	100. Allow ASAT missile tests in space	N
67. Freeze outlays except SS/Medicare	N	101. Limit space-based/ABM system tests	Y
68. Kill-Shift $5b of DOD to domestic	N	102. Force reduction in trade barriers	Y
69. Confirm Tower as sec of defense	N	103. Repeal windfall profit tax on oil	N
70. Bar abortion $ except to save mother	N	104. $1b/two year aid for the homeless	?
71. Kill-Warn AIDS carriers' spouses	Y	105. Disallow $30m for AZT to poor	?
72. Allow religious schools to bar gays	N	106. Bar AIDS test-immigrants/marriage	?
73. 60 days' notice of plant closings	Y	107. Kill-Biennial budget approval	Y
74. Allow poison pills in corp takeovers	Y	108. Fairness doctrine in broadcasting	Y
75. Kill-Workfare program	Y	109. Raise speed limit to 65 mph	N
76. Prohibit employee polygraph testing	Y		

The following are House measures voted on between 1982-1986:

99. Immigration reform/alien amnesty	Y	122. Emergency farm credit/revisions	Y
100. South Africa sanctions-veto override	Y	123. Duty on Taiwan/Hong Kong/S Korea	Y
101. Tax overhaul to revise income tax	Y	124. Limit steel imports to 17%	Y
102. Use of military in drug war	N	125. Cut $ to schools that bar prayer	N
103. Delete 12 MX/add conventional wpn	#	126. $50b-taxes; cut Medicare/spending	Y
104. Raise speed limit to 65 mph	N	127. Limit Pershing II/cruise in Europe	Y
105. Require Pentagon to buy US goods	Y	128. Delete $7.1b for 34 B-1 bombers	Y
106. AIDS insurance non-discrimination	?	129. Bar purchase of Sergeant York guns	N
107. Prohibit Saudi arms sales	Y	130. El Salvador military/economic aid	N
108. Ease Gun Control Act of 1968	N	131. Bar mining of Nicaraguan waters	Y
109. Bar interstate handgun transport	Y	132. Physician fee freeze for Medicare	N
110. Make company emissions known	Y	133. $49b in "sin"/phone/insurance taxes	#
111. Allow toxic victims to sue in fed ct	Y	134. Allow sale of Conrail	?
112. Superfund waste cleanup of $10b	Y	135. Equal Rights Amendment	Y
113. 90 days notice of plant closings	Y	136. Authorize Marines in Lebanon	Y
114. $20b in Medicare cuts/tax increases	Y	137. Eminent domain for coal companies	N
115. Spending cuts and tax increases	Y	138. Prohibit EPA clean air sanctions	Y
116. Set school lunch lmt-250% poverty	N	139. SS retirement age increase/reforms	N
117. $75m for youth work projects	Y	140. Auto domestic content requirement	Y
118. Allow Angolan military assistance	N	141. Delete jobs program funding	N
119. Suspend defense payments for abuse	Y	142. Highway-gas tax bill	Y
120. Drop SS COLAs/$12b tax increase	N	143. Cut $5b from defense for Medicare	Y
121. Approve $1.5b for 21 MX missiles	N	144. Emergency housing aid of $1b	?

Presidential Support Score: 1991 - 33%   1990 - 26%

MASSACHUSETTS

KENNEDY, EDWARD M. -- Massachusetts [Democrat]. Term Began/Expires: 1989/1994. Prior Terms: Senate: 1962 (Special Election)-1988. Born: February 22, 1932; Boston, MA. Education: Milton Academy; Harvard College (A.B.); International Law School, the Hague, Holland; University of Virginia Law School (LL.B.). Military Service: U.S. Army, 1951-53. Occupation: Suffolk County assistant district attorney (1961-62).

1. Prohibit MFN status for China	Y	
2. Kill-Tie welfare to school attendance	Y	
3. Limit credit card interest rates	Y	
4. Confirm Gates as head of CIA	N	
5. Adoption of national energy policies	N	
6. Kill-Restrict NEA use of funds	Y	
7. Unemployment benefits extension	Y	
8. Confirm Thomas to Supreme Court	N	
9. Raise eligibility for unpaid leave	Y	
10. Notify parents of minors' abortions	N	
11. Move $3b from defense to domestic	Y	
12. End production of B-2 bomber	Y	
13. Cut SDI $1b to reduce deficit	Y	
14. Maintain strategic stability-Soviets	Y	
15. Kill-Allow women as combat pilots	N	
16. Kill-Allow HIV tests before surgery	Y	
17. Strike $12b aid to Int'l Mon Fund	N	
18. Raise Senate salary/omit honoraria	Y	
19. Reduce space station funding $1.9b	Y	
20. Kill-Eliminate supercollider funds	N	
21. Req 5-day handgun waiting period	Y	
22. Life in prison instead of death	Y	
23. Exceptions to exclusionary rule	N	
24. Ban race as death sentence factor	N	
25. Campaign finance revisions	Y	
26. Kill-Term limits for senators	Y	
27. Require four presidential debates	N	
28. Tighten ban on vertical price fixing	Y	
29. Kill-Freeze discretionary budget	Y	
30. Provide $30b for failed S&Ls	Y	
31. Allow use of force against Iraq	N	
32. Allow $15b in foreign aid for 1991	Y	
33. Civil Rights Act of 1990	Y	
34. Block cancellation of Egypt's debt	N	
35. Cut El Salvador military aid 50%	Y	
36. Reduce troops in NATO by 30,000	Y	
37. Req increases in auto fuel efficiency	Y	
38. Bar taxpayer funding of campaigns	Y	
39. Limit textile import growth to 1%	Y	
40. Amendment to ban flag desecration	N	
41. Let fed emp be politically active	Y	
42. Reauthorize Amtrak-veto override	Y	
43. Allow sale of assault weapons	N	
44. Retraining aid for coal miners	Y	
45. Kill-Raise car emission standards	N	
46. Pull EPA nuclear plant authority	N	
47. Defer Chinese students' deportation	Y	
48. Cut in capital gains tax	N	
49. Establish CIA inspector general	Y	
50. Kill-Sanctions against China	Y	
51. Bar drug testing to receive AFDC	Y	

52. Kill-Allow force against drug planes	Y	
53. Include illegal aliens in census	Y	
54. Restitution to Japanese interned	Y	
55. Troop reduction in Europe of 50%	N	
56. Increase SDI research to $4.3b	N	
57. Kill-Pay homeless below min wage	Y	
58. Ban airline smoking within US	Y	
59. Bar transfer of FS-X technology	Y	
60. Limit liability for oil spills	N	
61. Restructure S&L industry	Y	
62. Ban $ to illegal foreign activities	Y	
63. Req immigrant fluency in English	N	
64. Allow aliens' families to stay in US	Y	
65. Expand child care aid/tax credit	Y	
66. Raise minimum wage w/subminimum	Y	
67. Freeze outlays except SS/Medicare	N	
68. Kill-Shift $5b of DOD to domestic	Y	
69. Confirm Tower as sec of defense	N	
70. Bar abortion $ except to save mother	?	
71. Kill-Warn AIDS carriers' spouses	Y	
72. Allow religious schools to bar gays	N	
73. 60 days' notice of plant closings	Y	
74. Allow poison pills in corp takeovers	N	
75. Kill-Workfare program	Y	
76. Prohibit employee polygraph testing	Y	
77. Cap Medicare patients' liability	Y	
78. Revise unfair trade practices	Y	
79. Kill-Shift SDI $ to conv weapons	?	
80. Kill-Shift SDI $ to accidental launch	Y	
81. Kill-Shift MX $ to supplies/parts	N	
82. Kill-Buy America provision at DOD	N	
83. Allow nuclear testing-5+ kilotons	N	
84. Allow SALT II to be exceeded	N	
85. $ to vets exposed to nuclear bomb	Y	
86. Warn workers of disease exposure	?	
87. Restore four civil rights laws	Y	
88. Disapprove uranium sales to Japan	Y	
89. Notify Congress of covert operations	Y	
90. Approval of $36m in Contra aid	N	
91. $18b deficit reduction compromise	?	
92. Allow sale of hard-to-detect guns	N	
93. Catastrophic health insurance	Y	
94. Bork nomination to Supreme Court	N	
95. Kill-Void Panama Canal treaties	Y	
96. Kill-Insurance denial to AIDS+	Y	
97. Keep diplomatic immunity intact	Y	
98. Produce Bigeye nerve gas bomb	N	
99. Balanced budget by '93-via targets	Y	
100. Allow ASAT missile tests in space	N	
101. Limit space-based/ABM system tests	Y	
102. Force reduction in trade barriers	Y	

KENNEDY, EDWARD M. (continued)

103. Repeal windfall profit tax on oil	N	
104. $1b/two year aid for the homeless	Y	
105. Disallow $30m for AZT to poor	N	
106. Bar AIDS test-immigrants/marriage	Y	
107. Kill-Biennial budget approval	Y	
108. Fairness doctrine in broadcasting	Y	
109. Raise speed limit to 65 mph	Y	
110. Immigration reform/alien amnesty	N	
111. South Africa sanctions-veto override	Y	
112. Kill-Use of military in drug war	?	
113. Tax overhaul to revise income tax	Y	
114. Submit nuclear test ban treaties	Y	
115. Prohibit sale of Stinger missiles	Y	
116. Prohibit binary chemical weapons	Y	
117. Kill-$10/barrel oil tariff increase	Y	
118. Grant tax amnesty provisions	Y	
119. Block Saudi arms sale-veto override	Y	
120. Balanced budget amendment	N	
121. Include veterans in spending cuts	N	
122. Bar $ to hazardous substance victims	N	
123. Allow seasonal workers in the US	N	
124. Let fed courts rule on school prayer	Y	
125. Presidential line-item veto	Y	
126. Ease Gun Control Act of 1968	N	
127. Kill-Req 14-day wait for handguns	N	
128. Kill-15% min tax on corporations	N	
129. Drop Social Security COLA	N	
130. Freeze funding for all programs	N	
131. Kill-Nuclear weapon freeze	N	
132. Keep decision narrowing Title IX	N	
133. Raise drinking age to 21	Y	
134. Allow production of MX missile	N	
135. Raise taxes/cut spending by $140b	N	
136. School prayer amendment	N	
137. Capital punishment-federal crimes	N	
138. Ban government officials from taping	N	
139. Martin Luther King holiday	Y	
140. Authorize Marines in Lebanon	N	
141. Amendment making abortion illegal	N	
142. Delete $1.2b for jobs creation	N	
143. Keep tobacco price supports	N	
144. Emergency housing aid of $5.1b	Y	

Presidential Support Score: 1991 - 31%   1990 - 25%

KERRY, JOHN F. -- Massachusetts [Democrat]. Term Began/Expires: 1991/1996. Prior Term: Senate: 1985-90. Born: December 11, 1943; Denver, CO. Education: Yale University (B.A.); Boston College Law School (J.D.). Military Service: U.S. Navy. Occupation: Attorney; assistant district attorney; lieutenant governor (1982).

1. Prohibit MFN status for China	Y	
2. Kill-Tie welfare to school attendance	Y	
3. Limit credit card interest rates	Y	
4. Confirm Gates as head of CIA	N	
5. Adoption of national energy policies	N	
6. Kill-Restrict NEA use of funds	Y	
7. Unemployment benefits extension	Y	
8. Confirm Thomas to Supreme Court	N	
9. Raise eligibility for unpaid leave	Y	
10. Notify parents of minors' abortions	N	
11. Move $3b from defense to domestic	Y	
12. End production of B-2 bomber	Y	
13. Cut SDI $1b to reduce deficit	Y	
14. Maintain strategic stability-Soviets	Y	
15. Kill-Allow women as combat pilots	N	
16. Kill-Allow HIV tests before surgery	Y	
17. Strike $12b aid to Int'l Mon Fund	N	
18. Raise Senate salary/omit honoraria	N	
19. Reduce space station funding $1.9b	Y	
20. Kill-Eliminate supercollider funds	Y	
21. Req 5-day handgun waiting period	Y	
22. Life in prison instead of death	Y	
23. Exceptions to exclusionary rule	N	
24. Ban race as death sentence factor	N	
25. Campaign finance revisions	Y	
26. Kill-Term limits for senators	Y	
27. Require four presidential debates	Y	
28. Tighten ban on vertical price fixing	Y	
29. Kill-Freeze discretionary budget	Y	
30. Provide $30b for failed S&Ls	N	
31. Allow use of force against Iraq	N	
32. Allow $15b in foreign aid for 1991	Y	
33. Civil Rights Act of 1990	Y	
34. Block cancellation of Egypt's debt	Y	
35. Cut El Salvador military aid 50%	Y	
36. Reduce troops in NATO by 30,000	+	
37. Req increases in auto fuel efficiency	Y	
38. Bar taxpayer funding of campaigns	N	
39. Limit textile import growth to 1%	Y	
40. Amendment to ban flag desecration	N	
41. Let fed emp be politically active	Y	
42. Reauthorize Amtrak-veto override	Y	
43. Allow sale of assault weapons	N	
44. Retraining aid for coal miners	Y	
45. Kill-Raise car emission standards	N	
46. Pull EPA nuclear plant authority	N	
47. Defer Chinese students' deportation	Y	
48. Cut in capital gains tax	N	
49. Establish CIA inspector general	Y	
50. Kill-Sanctions against China	Y	
51. Bar drug testing to receive AFDC	Y	
52. Kill-Allow force against drug planes	N	
53. Include illegal aliens in census	Y	
54. Restitution to Japanese interned	Y	
55. Troop reduction in Europe of 50%	N	
56. Increase SDI research to $4.3b	N	
57. Kill-Pay homeless below min wage	Y	
58. Ban airline smoking within US	Y	
59. Bar transfer of FS-X technology	Y	
60. Limit liability for oil spills	N	
61. Restructure S&L industry	Y	
62. Ban $ to illegal foreign activities	Y	
63. Req immigrant fluency in English	N	
64. Allow aliens' families to stay in US	Y	
65. Expand child care aid/tax credit	Y	
66. Raise minimum wage w/subminimum	Y	
67. Freeze outlays except SS/Medicare	N	
68. Kill-Shift $5b of DOD to domestic	N	

KERRY, JOHN F. (continued)

69. Confirm Tower as sec of defense	N	
70. Bar abortion $ except to save mother	N	
71. Kill-Warn AIDS carriers' spouses	Y	
72. Allow religious schools to bar gays	N	
73. 60 days' notice of plant closings	Y	
74. Allow poison pills in corp takeovers	N	
75. Kill-Workfare program	Y	
76. Prohibit employee polygraph testing	+	
77. Cap Medicare patients' liability	Y	
78. Revise unfair trade practices	Y	
79. Kill-Shift SDI $ to conv weapons	N	
80. Kill-Shift SDI $ to accidental launch	Y	
81. Kill-Shift MX $ to supplies/parts	N	
82. Kill-Buy America provision at DOD	N	
83. Allow nuclear testing-5+ kilotons	N	
84. Allow SALT II to be exceeded	N	
85. $ to vets exposed to nuclear bomb	Y	
86. Warn workers of disease exposure	Y	
87. Restore four civil rights laws	Y	
88. Disapprove uranium sales to Japan	+	
89. Notify Congress of covert operations	Y	
90. Approval of $36m in Contra aid	N	
91. $18b deficit reduction compromise	Y	
92. Allow sale of hard-to-detect guns	N	
93. Catastrophic health insurance	Y	
94. Bork nomination to Supreme Court	N	
95. Kill-Void Panama Canal treaties	Y	
96. Kill-Insurance denial to AIDS+	Y	
97. Keep diplomatic immunity intact	Y	
98. Produce Bigeye nerve gas bomb	N	
99. Balanced budget by '93-via targets	Y	

100. Allow ASAT missile tests in space	N	
101. Limit space-based/ABM system tests	Y	
102. Force reduction in trade barriers	Y	
103. Repeal windfall profit tax on oil	N	
104. $1b/two year aid for the homeless	Y	
105. Disallow $30m for AZT to poor	N	
106. Bar AIDS test-immigrants/marriage	Y	
107. Kill-Biennial budget approval	Y	
108. Fairness doctrine in broadcasting	Y	
109. Raise speed limit to 65 mph	Y	
110. Immigration reform/alien amnesty	Y	
111. South Africa sanctions-veto override	Y	
112. Kill-Use of military in drug war	?	
113. Tax overhaul to revise income tax	Y	
114. Submit nuclear test ban treaties	Y	
115. Prohibit sale of Stinger missiles	Y	
116. Prohibit binary chemical weapons	Y	
117. Kill-$10/barrel oil tariff increase	Y	
118. Grant tax amnesty provisions	Y	
119. Block Saudi arms sale-veto override	Y	
120. Balanced budget amendment	N	
121. Include veterans in spending cuts	N	
122. Bar $ to hazardous substance victims	N	
123. Allow seasonal workers in the US	N	
124. Let fed courts rule on school prayer	Y	
125. Presidential line-item veto	N	
126. Ease Gun Control Act of 1968	N	
127. Kill-Req 14-day wait for handguns	N	
128. Kill-15% min tax on corporations	N	
129. Drop Social Security COLA	N	
130. Freeze funding for all programs	N	

Presidential Support Score: 1991 - 28%   1990 - 25%

MICHIGAN

RIEGLE, DONALD W., Jr. -- Michigan [Democrat]. Term Began/Expires: 1989/1994. Prior Terms: House: 1965-76; Senate: 1976 (Special Election)-1988. Born: February 4, 1938; Flint, MI. Education: University of Michigan (B.A.); Michigan State University (M.B.A.); Harvard Business School. Occupation: Employee, International Business Machines Corp. (1961-64); consultant, Harvard/MIT Joint Center on Urban Studies; faculty member, Michigan State University, Boston University, Harvard; author.

1. Prohibit MFN status for China	Y	
2. Kill-Tie welfare to school attendance	Y	
3. Limit credit card interest rates	Y	
4. Confirm Gates as head of CIA	N	
5. Adoption of national energy policies	N	
6. Kill-Restrict NEA use of funds	Y	
7. Unemployment benefits extension	Y	
8. Confirm Thomas to Supreme Court	N	
9. Raise eligibility for unpaid leave	Y	
10. Notify parents of minors' abortions	N	
11. Move $3b from defense to domestic	Y	
12. End production of B-2 bomber	Y	
13. Cut SDI $1b to reduce deficit	Y	
14. Maintain strategic stability-Soviets	Y	

15. Kill-Allow women as combat pilots	N	
16. Kill-Allow HIV tests before surgery	N	
17. Strike $12b aid to Int'l Mon Fund	N	
18. Raise Senate salary/omit honoraria	N	
19. Reduce space station funding $1.9b	N	
20. Kill-Eliminate supercollider funds	N	
21. Req 5-day handgun waiting period	Y	
22. Life in prison instead of death	N	
23. Exceptions to exclusionary rule	N	
24. Ban race as death sentence factor	N	
25. Campaign finance revisions	Y	
26. Kill-Term limits for senators	Y	
27. Require four presidential debates	Y	
28. Tighten ban on vertical price fixing	Y	

RIEGLE, DONALD W., Jr. (continued)

29.	Kill-Freeze discretionary budget	Y	87.	Restore four civil rights laws	Y
30.	Provide $30b for failed S&Ls	Y	88.	Disapprove uranium sales to Japan	?
31.	Allow use of force against Iraq	N	89.	Notify Congress of covert operations	Y
32.	Allow $15b in foreign aid for 1991	Y	90.	Approval of $36m in Contra aid	N
33.	Civil Rights Act of 1990	Y	91.	$18b deficit reduction compromise	Y
34.	Block cancellation of Egypt's debt	?	92.	Allow sale of hard-to-detect guns	N
35.	Cut El Salvador military aid 50%	Y	93.	Catastrophic health insurance	Y
36.	Reduce troops in NATO by 30,000	Y	94.	Bork nomination to Supreme Court	N
37.	Req increases in auto fuel efficiency	N	95.	Kill-Void Panama Canal treaties	Y
38.	Bar taxpayer funding of campaigns	N	96.	Kill-Insurance denial to AIDS+	Y
39.	Limit textile import growth to 1%	Y	97.	Keep diplomatic immunity intact	N
40.	Amendment to ban flag desecration	N	98.	Produce Bigeye nerve gas bomb	N
41.	Let fed emp be politically active	Y	99.	Balanced budget by '93-via targets	N
42.	Reauthorize Amtrak-veto override	Y	100.	Allow ASAT missile tests in space	N
43.	Allow sale of assault weapons	N	101.	Limit space-based/ABM system tests	Y
44.	Retraining aid for coal miners	N	102.	Force reduction in trade barriers	Y
45.	Kill-Raise car emission standards	Y	103.	Repeal windfall profit tax on oil	N
46.	Pull EPA nuclear plant authority	N	104.	$1b/two year aid for the homeless	Y
47.	Defer Chinese students' deportation	Y	105.	Disallow $30m for AZT to poor	N
48.	Cut in capital gains tax	N	106.	Bar AIDS test-immigrants/marriage	Y
49.	Establish CIA inspector general	Y	107.	Kill-Biennial budget approval	Y
50.	Kill-Sanctions against China	Y	108.	Fairness doctrine in broadcasting	Y
51.	Bar drug testing to receive AFDC	Y	109.	Raise speed limit to 65 mph	Y
52.	Kill-Allow force against drug planes	Y	110.	Immigration reform/alien amnesty	N
53.	Include illegal aliens in census	Y	111.	South Africa sanctions-veto override	Y
54.	Restitution to Japanese interned	Y	112.	Kill-Use of military in drug war	N
55.	Troop reduction in Europe of 50%	Y	113.	Tax overhaul to revise income tax	Y
56.	Increase SDI research to $4.3b	N	114.	Submit nuclear test ban treaties	Y
57.	Kill-Pay homeless below min wage	Y	115.	Prohibit sale of Stinger missiles	Y
58.	Ban airline smoking within US	Y	116.	Prohibit binary chemical weapons	Y
59.	Bar transfer of FS-X technology	Y	117.	Kill-$10/barrel oil tariff increase	Y
60.	Limit liability for oil spills	Y	118.	Grant tax amnesty provisions	N
61.	Restructure S&L industry	Y	119.	Block Saudi arms sale-veto override	Y
62.	Ban $ to illegal foreign activities	Y	120.	Balanced budget amendment	N
63.	Req immigrant fluency in English	N	121.	Include veterans in spending cuts	N
64.	Allow aliens' families to stay in US	Y	122.	Bar $ to hazardous substance victims	N
65.	Expand child care aid/tax credit	Y	123.	Allow seasonal workers in the US	Y
66.	Raise minimum wage w/subminimum	Y	124.	Let fed courts rule on school prayer	Y
67.	Freeze outlays except SS/Medicare	N	125.	Presidential line-item veto	N
68.	Kill-Shift $5b of DOD to domestic	?	126.	Ease Gun Control Act of 1968	Y
69.	Confirm Tower as sec of defense	N	127.	Kill-Req 14-day wait for handguns	Y
70.	Bar abortion $ except to save mother	N	128.	Kill-15% min tax on corporations	N
71.	Kill-Warn AIDS carriers' spouses	Y	129.	Drop Social Security COLA	N
72.	Allow religious schools to bar gays	N	130.	Freeze funding for all programs	N
73.	60 days' notice of plant closings	Y	131.	Kill-Nuclear weapon freeze	N
74.	Allow poison pills in corp takeovers	Y	132.	Keep decision narrowing Title IX	N
75.	Kill-Workfare program	Y	133.	Raise drinking age to 21	Y
76.	Prohibit employee polygraph testing	Y	134.	Allow production of MX missile	N
77.	Cap Medicare patients' liability	Y	135.	Raise taxes/cut spending by $140b	N
78.	Revise unfair trade practices	Y	136.	School prayer amendment	N
79.	Kill-Shift SDI $ to conv weapons	N	137.	Capital punishment-federal crimes	N
80.	Kill-Shift SDI $ to accidental launch	Y	138.	Ban government officials from taping	Y
81.	Kill-Shift MX $ to supplies/parts	N	139.	Martin Luther King holiday	Y
82.	Kill-Buy America provision at DOD	N	140.	Authorize Marines in Lebanon	N
83.	Allow nuclear testing-5+ kilotons	N	141.	Amendment making abortion illegal	N
84.	Allow SALT II to be exceeded	N	142.	Delete $1.2b for jobs creation	N
85.	$ to vets exposed to nuclear bomb	Y	143.	Keep tobacco price supports	N
86.	Warn workers of disease exposure	Y	144.	Emergency housing aid of $5.1b	Y

Presidential Support Score: 1991 - 33% 1990 - 30%

LEVIN, CARL -- Michigan [Democrat]. Term Began/Expires: 1991/1996. Prior Terms: Senate: 1979-90. Born: June 28, 1934; Detroit, MI. Education: Swarthmore College; Harvard Law School. Occupation: Assistant attorney general and general counsel, Michigan Civil Rights Commission (1964-67); special assistant attorney general, Michigan, and chief appellate defender, Detroit (1968-69); Detroit city councilman (1970-73); instructor, University of Detroit and Wayne State University Law School.

1. Prohibit MFN status for China	Y	
2. Kill-Tie welfare to school attendance	Y	
3. Limit credit card interest rates	Y	
4. Confirm Gates as head of CIA	N	
5. Adoption of national energy policies	N	
6. Kill-Restrict NEA use of funds	Y	
7. Unemployment benefits extension	Y	
8. Confirm Thomas to Supreme Court	N	
9. Raise eligibility for unpaid leave	Y	
10. Notify parents of minors' abortions	N	
11. Move $3b from defense to domestic	N	
12. End production of B-2 bomber	N	
13. Cut SDI $1b to reduce deficit	Y	
14. Maintain strategic stability-Soviets	Y	
15. Kill-Allow women as combat pilots	N	
16. Kill-Allow HIV tests before surgery	Y	
17. Strike $12b aid to Int'l Mon Fund	N	
18. Raise Senate salary/omit honoraria	N	
19. Reduce space station funding $1.9b	Y	
20. Kill-Eliminate supercollider funds	N	
21. Req 5-day handgun waiting period	Y	
22. Life in prison instead of death	Y	
23. Exceptions to exclusionary rule	N	
24. Ban race as death sentence factor	N	
25. Campaign finance revisions	Y	
26. Kill-Term limits for senators	Y	
27. Require four presidential debates	Y	
28. Tighten ban on vertical price fixing	Y	
29. Kill-Freeze discretionary budget	Y	
30. Provide $30b for failed S&Ls	Y	
31. Allow use of force against Iraq	N	
32. Allow $15b in foreign aid for 1991	Y	
33. Civil Rights Act of 1990	Y	
34. Block cancellation of Egypt's debt	Y	
35. Cut El Salvador military aid 50%	Y	
36. Reduce troops in NATO by 30,000	Y	
37. Req increases in auto fuel efficiency	N	
38. Bar taxpayer funding of campaigns	N	
39. Limit textile import growth to 1%	Y	
40. Amendment to ban flag desecration	N	
41. Let fed emp be politically active	Y	
42. Reauthorize Amtrak-veto override	Y	
43. Allow sale of assault weapons	N	
44. Retraining aid for coal miners	N	
45. Kill-Raise car emission standards	Y	
46. Pull EPA nuclear plant authority	N	
47. Defer Chinese students' deportation	Y	
48. Cut in capital gains tax	N	
49. Establish CIA inspector general	Y	
50. Kill-Sanctions against China	Y	
51. Bar drug testing to receive AFDC	Y	
52. Kill-Allow force against drug planes	N	
53. Include illegal aliens in census	N	
54. Restitution to Japanese interned	Y	
55. Troop reduction in Europe of 50%	N	
56. Increase SDI research to $4.3b	N	
57. Kill-Pay homeless below min wage	Y	
58. Ban airline smoking within US	Y	
59. Bar transfer of FS-X technology	Y
60. Limit liability for oil spills	N
61. Restructure S&L industry	Y
62. Ban $ to illegal foreign activities	Y
63. Req immigrant fluency in English	N
64. Allow aliens' families to stay in US	Y
65. Expand child care aid/tax credit	Y
66. Raise minimum wage w/subminimum	Y
67. Freeze outlays except SS/Medicare	N
68. Kill-Shift $5b of DOD to domestic	N
69. Confirm Tower as sec of defense	N
70. Bar abortion $ except to save mother	N
71. Kill-Warn AIDS carriers' spouses	Y
72. Allow religious schools to bar gays	N
73. 60 days' notice of plant closings	Y
74. Allow poison pills in corp takeovers	Y
75. Kill-Workfare program	?
76. Prohibit employee polygraph testing	Y
77. Cap Medicare patients' liability	Y
78. Revise unfair trade practices	Y
79. Kill-Shift SDI $ to conv weapons	N
80. Kill-Shift SDI $ to accidental launch	Y
81. Kill-Shift MX $ to supplies/parts	N
82. Kill-Buy America provision at DOD	Y
83. Allow nuclear testing-5+ kilotons	N
84. Allow SALT II to be exceeded	N
85. $ to vets exposed to nuclear bomb	Y
86. Warn workers of disease exposure	Y
87. Restore four civil rights laws	Y
88. Disapprove uranium sales to Japan	Y
89. Notify Congress of covert operations	Y
90. Approval of $36m in Contra aid	N
91. $18b deficit reduction compromise	Y
92. Allow sale of hard-to-detect guns	N
93. Catastrophic health insurance	Y
94. Bork nomination to Supreme Court	N
95. Kill-Void Panama Canal treaties	Y
96. Kill-Insurance denial to AIDS+	Y
97. Keep diplomatic immunity intact	Y
98. Produce Bigeye nerve gas bomb	N
99. Balanced budget by '93-via targets	Y
100. Allow ASAT missile tests in space	N
101. Limit space-based/ABM system tests	Y
102. Force reduction in trade barriers	N
103. Repeal windfall profit tax on oil	N
104. $1b/two year aid for the homeless	Y
105. Disallow $30m for AZT to poor	N
106. Bar AIDS test-immigrants/marriage	Y
107. Kill-Biennial budget approval	Y
108. Fairness doctrine in broadcasting	Y
109. Raise speed limit to 65 mph	N
110. Immigration reform/alien amnesty	Y
111. South Africa sanctions-veto override	Y
112. Kill-Use of military in drug war	Y
113. Tax overhaul to revise income tax	N
114. Submit nuclear test ban treaties	Y
115. Prohibit sale of Stinger missiles	N
116. Prohibit binary chemical weapons	Y

LEVIN, CARL (continued)

117.	Kill-$10/barrel oil tariff increase	N	131.	Kill-Nuclear weapon freeze	N
118.	Grant tax amnesty provisions	N	132.	Keep decision narrowing Title IX	N
119.	Block Saudi arms sale-veto override	Y	133.	Raise drinking age to 21	Y
120.	Balanced budget amendment	N	134.	Allow production of MX missile	N
121.	Include veterans in spending cuts	N	135.	Raise taxes/cut spending by $140b	N
122.	Bar $ to hazardous substance victims	N	136.	School prayer amendment	N
123.	Allow seasonal workers in the US	N	137.	Capital punishment-federal crimes	N
124.	Let fed courts rule on school prayer	Y	138.	Ban government officials from taping	Y
125.	Presidential line-item veto	N	139.	Martin Luther King holiday	Y
126.	Ease Gun Control Act of 1968	N	140.	Authorize Marines in Lebanon	N
127.	Kill-Req 14-day wait for handguns	N	141.	Amendment making abortion illegal	N
128.	Kill-15% min tax on corporations	N	142.	Delete $1.2b for jobs creation	N
129.	Drop Social Security COLA	N	143.	Keep tobacco price supports	N
130.	Freeze funding for all programs	N	144.	Emergency housing aid of $5.1b	Y

Presidential Support Score: 1991 - 37%   1990 - 33%

MINNESOTA

DURENBERGER, DAVID -- Minnesota [Republican]. Term Began/Expires: 1989/1994. Prior Terms: Senate: 1978 (Special Election)-1988. Born: August 19, 1934; St. Cloud, MN. Education: St. John's University (B.A.); University of Minnesota Law School (J.D.). Military Service: U.S. Army. Occupation: Attorney; executive secretaty to governor (1967-71).

1.	Prohibit MFN status for China	N	36.	Reduce troops in NATO by 30,000	N
2.	Kill-Tie welfare to school attendance	Y	37.	Req increases in auto fuel efficiency	Y
3.	Limit credit card interest rates	Y	38.	Bar taxpayer funding of campaigns	Y
4.	Confirm Gates as head of CIA	Y	39.	Limit textile import growth to 1%	N
5.	Adoption of national energy policies	N	40.	Amendment to ban flag desecration	N
6.	Kill-Restrict NEA use of funds	Y	41.	Let fed emp be politically active	Y
7.	Unemployment benefits extension	N	42.	Reauthorize Amtrak-veto override	Y
8.	Confirm Thomas to Supreme Court	Y	43.	Allow sale of assault weapons	Y
9.	Raise eligibility for unpaid leave	Y	44.	Retraining aid for coal miners	N
10.	Notify parents of minors' abortions	Y	45.	Kill-Raise car emission standards	Y
11.	Move $3b from defense to domestic	N	46.	Pull EPA nuclear plant authority	N
12.	End production of B-2 bomber	N	47.	Defer Chinese students' deportation	N
13.	Cut SDI $1b to reduce deficit	N	48.	Cut in capital gains tax	Y
14.	Maintain strategic stability-Soviets	N	49.	Establish CIA inspector general	Y
15.	Kill-Allow women as combat pilots	N	50.	Kill-Sanctions against China	Y
16.	Kill-Allow HIV tests before surgery	Y	51.	Bar drug testing to receive AFDC	Y
17.	Strike $12b aid to Int'l Mon Fund	N	52.	Kill-Allow force against drug planes	Y
18.	Raise Senate salary/omit honoraria	Y	53.	Include illegal aliens in census	N
19.	Reduce space station funding $1.9b	N	54.	Restitution to Japanese interned	Y
20.	Kill-Eliminate supercollider funds	Y	55.	Troop reduction in Europe of 50%	N
21.	Req 5-day handgun waiting period	Y	56.	Increase SDI research to $4.3b	N
22.	Life in prison instead of death	Y	57.	Kill-Pay homeless below min wage	Y
23.	Exceptions to exclusionary rule	N	58.	Ban airline smoking within US	Y
24.	Ban race as death sentence factor	N	59.	Bar transfer of FS-X technology	N
25.	Campaign finance revisions	Y	60.	Limit liability for oil spills	N
26.	Kill-Term limits for senators	Y	61.	Restructure S&L industry	N
27.	Require four presidential debates	?	62.	Ban $ to illegal foreign activities	Y
28.	Tighten ban on vertical price fixing	N	63.	Req immigrant fluency in English	N
29.	Kill-Freeze discretionary budget	Y	64.	Allow aliens' families to stay in US	Y
30.	Provide $30b for failed S&Ls	Y	65.	Expand child care aid/tax credit	N
31.	Allow use of force against Iraq	Y	66.	Raise minimum wage w/subminimum	Y
32.	Allow $15b in foreign aid for 1991	Y	67.	Freeze outlays except SS/Medicare	N
33.	Civil Rights Act of 1990	Y	68.	Kill-Shift $5b of DOD to domestic	Y
34.	Block cancellation of Egypt's debt	N	69.	Confirm Tower as sec of defense	Y
35.	Cut El Salvador military aid 50%	Y	70.	Bar abortion $ except to save mother	Y

DURENBERGER, DAVID (continued)

71. Kill-Warn AIDS carriers' spouses	Y	
72. Allow religious schools to bar gays	Y	
73. 60 days' notice of plant closings	Y	
74. Allow poison pills in corp takeovers	?	
75. Kill-Workfare program	?	
76. Prohibit employee polygraph testing	Y	
77. Cap Medicare patients' liability	Y	
78. Revise unfair trade practices	Y	
79. Kill-Shift SDI $ to conv weapons	N	
80. Kill-Shift SDI $ to accidental launch	Y	
81. Kill-Shift MX $ to supplies/parts	N	
82. Kill-Buy America provision at DOD	N	
83. Allow nuclear testing-5 + kilotons	Y	
84. Allow SALT II to be exceeded	Y	
85. $ to vets exposed to nuclear bomb	?	
86. Warn workers of disease exposure	Y	
87. Restore four civil rights laws	Y	
88. Disapprove uranium sales to Japan	Y	
89. Notify Congress of covert operations	Y	
90. Approval of $36m in Contra aid	N	
91. $18b deficit reduction compromise	N	
92. Allow sale of hard-to-detect guns	Y	
93. Catastrophic health insurance	Y	
94. Bork nomination to Supreme Court	Y	
95. Kill-Void Panama Canal treaties	Y	
96. Kill-Insurance denial to AIDS +	Y	
97. Keep diplomatic immunity intact	Y	
98. Produce Bigeye nerve gas bomb	N	
99. Balanced budget by '93-via targets	Y	
100. Allow ASAT missile tests in space	N	
101. Limit space-based/ABM system tests	N	
102. Force reduction in trade barriers	N	
103. Repeal windfall profit tax on oil	N	
104. $1b/two year aid for the homeless	?	
105. Disallow $30m for AZT to poor	N	
106. Bar AIDS test-immigrants/marriage	Y	
107. Kill-Biennial budget approval	N	

108. Fairness doctrine in broadcasting	Y	
109. Raise speed limit to 65 mph	Y	
110. Immigration reform/alien amnesty	Y	
111. South Africa sanctions-veto override	Y	
112. Kill-Use of military in drug war	Y	
113. Tax overhaul to revise income tax	Y	
114. Submit nuclear test ban treaties	Y	
115. Prohibit sale of Stinger missiles	N	
116. Prohibit binary chemical weapons	Y	
117. Kill-$10/barrel oil tariff increase	Y	
118. Grant tax amnesty provisions	N	
119. Block Saudi arms sale-veto override	Y	
120. Balanced budget amendment	Y	
121. Include veterans in spending cuts	Y	
122. Bar $ to hazardous substance victims	N	
123. Allow seasonal workers in the US	N	
124. Let fed courts rule on school prayer	Y	
125. Presidential line-item veto	N	
126. Ease Gun Control Act of 1968	Y	
127. Kill-Req 14-day wait for handguns	Y	
128. Kill-15% min tax on corporations	Y	
129. Drop Social Security COLA	Y	
130. Freeze funding for all programs	N	
131. Kill-Nuclear weapon freeze	Y	
132. Keep decision narrowing Title IX	Y	
133. Raise drinking age to 21	Y	
134. Allow production of MX missile	N	
135. Raise taxes/cut spending by $140b	Y	
136. School prayer amendment	N	
137. Capital punishment-federal crimes	N	
138. Ban government officials from taping	N	
139. Martin Luther King holiday	Y	
140. Authorize Marines in Lebanon	Y	
141. Amendment making abortion illegal	Y	
142. Delete $1.2b for jobs creation	Y	
143. Keep tobacco price supports	N	
144. Emergency housing aid of $5.1b	+	

Presidential Support Score: 1991 - 83% 1990 - 62%

WELLSTONE, PAUL -- Minnesota [Democrat]. Term Began/Expires: 1991/1996. Born: July 21, 1944; Washington, DC. Education: University of North Carolina-Chapel Hill (B.A., Ph.D.). Occupation: Political science professor, Carleton College; national and state voter registration organizer.

1. Prohibit MFN status for China	Y	
2. Kill-Tie welfare to school attendance	Y	
3. Limit credit card interest rates	Y	
4. Confirm Gates as head of CIA	N	
5. Adoption of national energy policies	N	
6. Kill-Restrict NEA use of funds	Y	
7. Unemployment benefits extension	Y	
8. Confirm Thomas to Supreme Court	N	
9. Raise eligibility for unpaid leave	Y	
10. Notify parents of minors' abortions	N	
11. Move $3b from defense to domestic	Y	
12. End production of B-2 bomber	Y	
13. Cut SDI $1b to reduce deficit	Y	
14. Maintain strategic stability-Soviets	Y	
15. Kill-Allow women as combat pilots	N	
16. Kill-Allow HIV tests before surgery	Y	

17. Strike $12b aid to Int'l Mon Fund	N	
18. Raise Senate salary/omit honoraria	N	
19. Reduce space station funding $1.9b	Y	
20. Kill-Eliminate supercollider funds	N	
21. Req 5-day handgun waiting period	Y	
22. Life in prison instead of death	Y	
23. Exceptions to exclusionary rule	N	
24. Ban race as death sentence factor	?	
25. Campaign finance revisions	Y	
26. Kill-Term limits for senators	Y	
27. Require four presidential debates	Y	
28. Tighten ban on vertical price fixing	Y	
29. Kill-Freeze discretionary budget	Y	
30. Provide $30b for failed S&Ls	N	
31. Allow use of force against Iraq	N	

Presidential Support Score: 1991 - 22%

MISSISSIPPI

COCHRAN, THAD -- Mississippi [Republican]. Term Began/Expires: 1991/1996. Prior Terms: House: 1973-78; Senate: 1978 (Special Appointment)-1990. Born: December 7, 1937; Pontotoc, MS. Education: University of Mississippi (B.A., J.D.); Trinity College, Dublin. Military Service: U.S. Navy, 1959-61. Occupation: Attorney, Watkins and Eager (1965).

1. Prohibit MFN status for China	N	52. Kill-Allow force against drug planes	Y
2. Kill-Tie welfare to school attendance	N	53. Include illegal aliens in census	N
3. Limit credit card interest rates	Y	54. Restitution to Japanese interned	Y
4. Confirm Gates as head of CIA	Y	55. Troop reduction in Europe of 50%	N
5. Adoption of national energy policies	Y	56. Increase SDI research to $4.3b	Y
6. Kill-Restrict NEA use of funds	Y	57. Kill-Pay homeless below min wage	N
7. Unemployment benefits extension	N	58. Ban airline smoking within US	Y
8. Confirm Thomas to Supreme Court	Y	59. Bar transfer of FS-X technology	N
9. Raise eligibility for unpaid leave	N	60. Limit liability for oil spills	Y
10. Notify parents of minors' abortions	Y	61. Restructure S&L industry	N
11. Move $3b from defense to domestic	N	62. Ban $ to illegal foreign activities	N
12. End production of B-2 bomber	N	63. Req immigrant fluency in English	Y
13. Cut SDI $1b to reduce deficit	N	64. Allow aliens' families to stay in US	N
14. Maintain strategic stability-Soviets	N	65. Expand child care aid/tax credit	N
15. Kill-Allow women as combat pilots	N	66. Raise minimum wage w/subminimum	N
16. Kill-Allow HIV tests before surgery	N	67. Freeze outlays except SS/Medicare	N
17. Strike $12b aid to Int'l Mon Fund	?	68. Kill-Shift $5b of DOD to domestic	Y
18. Raise Senate salary/omit honoraria	Y	69. Confirm Tower as sec of defense	Y
19. Reduce space station funding $1.9b	N	70. Bar abortion $ except to save mother	Y
20. Kill-Eliminate supercollider funds	Y	71. Kill-Warn AIDS carriers' spouses	Y
21. Req 5-day handgun waiting period	N	72. Allow religious schools to bar gays	Y
22. Life in prison instead of death	N	73. 60 days' notice of plant closings	N
23. Exceptions to exclusionary rule	Y	74. Allow poison pills in corp takeovers	N
24. Ban race as death sentence factor	Y	75. Kill-Workfare program	N
25. Campaign finance revisions	N	76. Prohibit employee polygraph testing	N
26. Kill-Term limits for senators	N	77. Cap Medicare patients' liability	Y
27. Require four presidential debates	N	78. Revise unfair trade practices	N
28. Tighten ban on vertical price fixing	N	79. Kill-Shift SDI $ to conv weapons	Y
29. Kill-Freeze discretionary budget	Y	80. Kill-Shift SDI $ to accidental launch	N
30. Provide $30b for failed S&Ls	Y	81. Kill-Shift MX $ to supplies/parts	Y
31. Allow use of force against Iraq	Y	82. Kill-Buy America provision at DOD	Y
32. Allow $15b in foreign aid for 1991	Y	83. Allow nuclear testing-5+ kilotons	Y
33. Civil Rights Act of 1990	N	84. Allow SALT II to be exceeded	Y
34. Block cancellation of Egypt's debt	N	85. $ to vets exposed to nuclear bomb	N
35. Cut El Salvador military aid 50%	N	86. Warn workers of disease exposure	N
36. Reduce troops in NATO by 30,000	N	87. Restore four civil rights laws	N
37. Req increases in auto fuel efficiency	N	88. Disapprove uranium sales to Japan	N
38. Bar taxpayer funding of campaigns	Y	89. Notify Congress of covert operations	N
39. Limit textile import growth to 1%	Y	90. Approval of $36m in Contra aid	Y
40. Amendment to ban flag desecration	Y	91. $18b deficit reduction compromise	Y
41. Let fed emp be politically active	N	92. Allow sale of hard-to-detect guns	Y
42. Reauthorize Amtrak-veto override	N	93. Catastrophic health insurance	Y
43. Allow sale of assault weapons	Y	94. Bork nomination to Supreme Court	Y
44. Retraining aid for coal miners	Y	95. Kill-Void Panama Canal treaties	N
45. Kill-Raise car emission standards	Y	96. Kill-Insurance denial to AIDS+	N
46. Pull EPA nuclear plant authority	Y	97. Keep diplomatic immunity intact	N
47. Defer Chinese students' deportation	N	98. Produce Bigeye nerve gas bomb	Y
48. Cut in capital gains tax	Y	99. Balanced budget by '93-via targets	Y
49. Establish CIA inspector general	N	100. Allow ASAT missile tests in space	Y
50. Kill-Sanctions against China	Y	101. Limit space-based/ABM system tests	N
51. Bar drug testing to receive AFDC	Y	102. Force reduction in trade barriers	N

COCHRAN, THAD (continued)

103. Repeal windfall profit tax on oil	Y
104. $1b/two year aid for the homeless	Y
105. Disallow $30m for AZT to poor	N
106. Bar AIDS test-immigrants/marriage	N
107. Kill-Biennial budget approval	N
108. Fairness doctrine in broadcasting	Y
109. Raise speed limit to 65 mph	Y
110. Immigration reform/alien amnesty	N
111. South Africa sanctions-veto override	N
112. Kill-Use of military in drug war	?
113. Tax overhaul to revise income tax	Y
114. Submit nuclear test ban treaties	N
115. Prohibit sale of Stinger missiles	N
116. Prohibit binary chemical weapons	N
117. Kill-$10/barrel oil tariff increase	Y
118. Grant tax amnesty provisions	N
119. Block Saudi arms sale-veto override	N
120. Balanced budget amendment	Y
121. Include veterans in spending cuts	Y
122. Bar $ to hazardous substance victims	Y
123. Allow seasonal workers in the US	Y

124. Let fed courts rule on school prayer	N
125. Presidential line-item veto	Y
126. Ease Gun Control Act of 1968	Y
127. Kill-Req 14-day wait for handguns	Y
128. Kill-15% min tax on corporations	Y
129. Drop Social Security COLA	Y
130. Freeze funding for all programs	N
131. Kill-Nuclear weapon freeze	Y
132. Keep decision narrowing Title IX	Y
133. Raise drinking age to 21	Y
134. Allow production of MX missile	Y
135. Raise taxes/cut spending by $140b	Y
136. School prayer amendment	Y
137. Capital punishment-federal crimes	Y
138. Ban government officials from taping	N
139. Martin Luther King holiday	Y
140. Authorize Marines in Lebanon	Y
141. Amendment making abortion illegal	Y
142. Delete $1.2b for jobs creation	N
143. Keep tobacco price supports	Y
144. Emergency housing aid of $5.1b	Y

Presidential Support Score: 1991 - 90%   1990 - 85%

LOTT, TRENT -- Mississippi [Republican]. Term Began/Expires: 1989/1994. Prior Terms: House: 1973-88. Born: October 9, 1941; Grenada, MS. Education: University of Mississippi(B.P.A., J.D.). Occupation: Attorney, Bryan & Gordon (1967-68), congressional administrative assistant (1968-72).

1. Prohibit MFN status for China	Y
2. Kill-Tie welfare to school attendance	N
3. Limit credit card interest rates	Y
4. Confirm Gates as head of CIA	Y
5. Adoption of national energy policies	N
6. Kill-Restrict NEA use of funds	N
7. Unemployment benefits extension	N
8. Confirm Thomas to Supreme Court	Y
9. Raise eligibility for unpaid leave	N
10. Notify parents of minors' abortions	Y
11. Move $3b from defense to domestic	N
12. End production of B-2 bomber	N
13. Cut SDI $1b to reduce deficit	N
14. Maintain strategic stability-Soviets	N
15. Kill-Allow women as combat pilots	Y
16. Kill-Allow HIV tests before surgery	N
17. Strike $12b aid to Int'l Mon Fund	Y
18. Raise Senate salary/omit honoraria	Y
19. Reduce space station funding $1.9b	N
20. Kill-Eliminate supercollider funds	Y
21. Req 5-day handgun waiting period	N
22. Life in prison instead of death	N
23. Exceptions to exclusionary rule	Y
24. Ban race as death sentence factor	Y
25. Campaign finance revisions	N
26. Kill-Term limits for senators	N
27. Require four presidential debates	N
28. Tighten ban on vertical price fixing	N
29. Kill-Freeze discretionary budget	N
30. Provide $30b for failed S&Ls	Y
31. Allow use of force against Iraq	Y
32. Allow $15b in foreign aid for 1991	Y
33. Civil Rights Act of 1990	N
34. Block cancellation of Egypt's debt	Y

35. Cut El Salvador military aid 50%	N
36. Reduce troops in NATO by 30,000	N
37. Req increases in auto fuel efficiency	N
38. Bar taxpayer funding of campaigns	Y
39. Limit textile import growth to 1%	Y
40. Amendment to ban flag desecration	Y
41. Let fed emp be politically active	N
42. Reauthorize Amtrak-veto override	N
43. Allow sale of assault weapons	Y
44. Retraining aid for coal miners	N
45. Kill-Raise car emission standards	Y
46. Pull EPA nuclear plant authority	Y
47. Defer Chinese students' deportation	N
48. Cut in capital gains tax	Y
49. Establish CIA inspector general	N
50. Kill-Sanctions against China	N
51. Bar drug testing to receive AFDC	N
52. Kill-Allow force against drug planes	N
53. Include illegal aliens in census	N
54. Restitution to Japanese interned	N
55. Troop reduction in Europe of 50%	N
56. Increase SDI research to $4.3b	Y
57. Kill-Pay homeless below min wage	N
58. Ban airline smoking within US	?
59. Bar transfer of FS-X technology	N
60. Limit liability for oil spills	Y
61. Restructure S&L industry	Y
62. Ban $ to illegal foreign activities	N
63. Req immigrant fluency in English	Y
64. Allow aliens' families to stay in US	N
65. Expand child care aid/tax credit	N
66. Raise minimum wage w/subminimum	N
67. Freeze outlays except SS/Medicare	N
68. Kill-Shift $5b of DOD to domestic	Y

LOTT, TRENT (continued)
69. Confirm Tower as sec of defense   Y

The following are House measures voted on between 1982-1988:

85. $18b deficit reduction compromise	Y	115. Spending cuts and tax increases	N
86. Welfare reform of $5.7b for 5 years	N	116. Set school lunch lmt-250% poverty	Y
87. Raise taxes $12b/cut spending $3b	N	117. $75m for youth work projects	N
88. Board to assess occupational risk	N	118. Allow Angolan military assistance	Y
89. Balanced budget by '93-via targets	Y	119. Suspend defense payments for abuse	N
90. Bar licensing of two nuclear plants	N	120. Drop SS COLAs/$12b tax increase	N
91. Remove victims compensation cap	?	121. Approve $1.5b for 21 MX missiles	Y
92. Catastrophic health insurance	N	122. Emergency farm credit/revisions	N
93. Ban airline smoking-2 hours or less	N	123. Duty on Taiwan/Hong Kong/S Korea	N
94. $1b/two year aid for the homeless	N	124. Limit steel imports to 17%	N
95. Bar non-unions in union companies	N	125. Cut $ to schools that bar prayer	Y
96. Increase FSLIC rescue to $15b	N	126. $50b-taxes; cut Medicare/spending	N
97. Impose quotas to lower trade deficit	N	127. Limit Pershing II/cruise in Europe	N
98. Reduce discretionary budget 21%	N	128. Delete $7.1b for 34 B-1 bombers	N
99. Immigration reform/alien amnesty	Y	129. Bar purchase of Sergeant York guns	N
100. South Africa sanctions-veto override	N	130. El Salvador military/economic aid	Y
101. Tax overhaul to revise income tax	Y	131. Bar mining of Nicaraguan waters	N
102. Use of military in drug war	Y	132. Physician fee freeze for Medicare	Y
103. Delete 12 MX/add conventional wpn	N	133. $49b in "sin"/phone/insurance taxes	Y
104. Raise speed limit to 65 mph	Y	134. Allow sale of Conrail	Y
105. Require Pentagon to buy US goods	N	135. Equal Rights Amendment	N
106. AIDS insurance non-discrimination	N	136. Authorize Marines in Lebanon	Y
107. Prohibit Saudi arms sales	Y	137. Eminent domain for coal companies	Y
108. Ease Gun Control Act of 1968	Y	138. Prohibit EPA clean air sanctions	Y
109. Bar interstate handgun transport	N	139. SS retirement age increase/reforms	Y
110. Make company emissions known	N	140. Auto domestic content requirement	N
111. Allow toxic victims to sue in fed ct	N	141. Delete jobs program funding	Y
112. Superfund waste cleanup of $10b	N	142. Highway-gas tax bill	Y
113. 90 days notice of plant closings	N	143. Cut $5b from defense for Medicare	N
114. $20b in Medicare cuts/tax increases	N	144. Emergency housing aid of $1b	Y

Presidential Support Score: 1991 - 88%   1990 - 76%

MISSOURI

DANFORTH, JOHN C. -- Missouri [Republican]. Term Began/Expires: 1989/1994. Prior Terms: Senate: 1977-88. Born: September 5, 1936; St. Louis, MO. Education: Princeton University (A.B.); Yale University (B.D., LL.B.). Occupation: Attorney; Missouri attorney general (1969-76); ordained clergyman.

1. Prohibit MFN status for China	N	17. Strike $12b aid to Int'l Mon Fund	N
2. Kill-Tie welfare to school attendance	N	18. Raise Senate salary/omit honoraria	Y
3. Limit credit card interest rates	?	19. Reduce space station funding $1.9b	N
4. Confirm Gates as head of CIA	Y	20. Kill-Eliminate supercollider funds	Y
5. Adoption of national energy policies	Y	21. Req 5-day handgun waiting period	N
6. Kill-Restrict NEA use of funds	Y	22. Life in prison instead of death	Y
7. Unemployment benefits extension	N	23. Exceptions to exclusionary rule	Y
8. Confirm Thomas to Supreme Court	Y	24. Ban race as death sentence factor	N
9. Raise eligibility for unpaid leave	Y	25. Campaign finance revisions	N
10. Notify parents of minors' abortions	Y	26. Kill-Term limits for senators	Y
11. Move $3b from defense to domestic	N	27. Require four presidential debates	?
12. End production of B-2 bomber	N	28. Tighten ban on vertical price fixing	N
13. Cut SDI $1b to reduce deficit	N	29. Kill-Freeze discretionary budget	Y
14. Maintain strategic stability-Soviets	N	30. Provide $30b for failed S&Ls	Y
15. Kill-Allow women as combat pilots	N	31. Allow use of force against Iraq	Y
16. Kill-Allow HIV tests before surgery	N	32. Allow $15b in foreign aid for 1991	Y

DANFORTH, JOHN C. (continued)

33.	Civil Rights Act of 1990	Y		89.	Notify Congress of covert operations	N
34.	Block cancellation of Egypt's debt	N		90.	Approval of $36m in Contra aid	Y
35.	Cut El Salvador military aid 50%	Y		91.	$18b deficit reduction compromise	Y
36.	Reduce troops in NATO by 30,000	N		92.	Allow sale of hard-to-detect guns	Y
37.	Req increases in auto fuel efficiency	Y		93.	Catastrophic health insurance	Y
38.	Bar taxpayer funding of campaigns	Y		94.	Bork nomination to Supreme Court	Y
39.	Limit textile import growth to 1%	N		95.	Kill-Void Panama Canal treaties	Y
40.	Amendment to ban flag desecration	N		96.	Kill-Insurance denial to AIDS+	N
41.	Let fed emp be politically active	N		97.	Keep diplomatic immunity intact	Y
42.	Reauthorize Amtrak-veto override	N		98.	Produce Bigeye nerve gas bomb	N
43.	Allow sale of assault weapons	Y		99.	Balanced budget by '93-via targets	Y
44.	Retraining aid for coal miners	Y		100.	Allow ASAT missile tests in space	Y
45.	Kill-Raise car emission standards	Y		101.	Limit space-based/ABM system tests	N
46.	Pull EPA nuclear plant authority	Y		102.	Force reduction in trade barriers	Y
47.	Defer Chinese students' deportation	N		103.	Repeal windfall profit tax on oil	Y
48.	Cut in capital gains tax	Y		104.	$1b/two year aid for the homeless	Y
49.	Establish CIA inspector general	N		105.	Disallow $30m for AZT to poor	Y
50.	Kill-Sanctions against China	N		106.	Bar AIDS test-immigrants/marriage	Y
51.	Bar drug testing to receive AFDC	Y		107.	Kill-Biennial budget approval	N
52.	Kill-Allow force against drug planes	Y		108.	Fairness doctrine in broadcasting	Y
53.	Include illegal aliens in census	?		109.	Raise speed limit to 65 mph	N
54.	Restitution to Japanese interned	N		110.	Immigration reform/alien amnesty	Y
55.	Troop reduction in Europe of 50%	N		111.	South Africa sanctions-veto override	Y
56.	Increase SDI research to $4.3b	Y		112.	Kill-Use of military in drug war	Y
57.	Kill-Pay homeless below min wage	N		113.	Tax overhaul to revise income tax	N
58.	Ban airline smoking within US	Y		114.	Submit nuclear test ban treaties	Y
59.	Bar transfer of FS-X technology	Y		115.	Prohibit sale of Stinger missiles	N
60.	Limit liability for oil spills	N		116.	Prohibit binary chemical weapons	Y
61.	Restructure S&L industry	N		117.	Kill-$10/barrel oil tariff increase	Y
62.	Ban $ to illegal foreign activities	N		118.	Grant tax amnesty provisions	N
63.	Req immigrant fluency in English	N		119.	Block Saudi arms sale-veto override	Y
64.	Allow aliens' families to stay in US	N		120.	Balanced budget amendment	Y
65.	Expand child care aid/tax credit	N		121.	Include veterans in spending cuts	Y
66.	Raise minimum wage w/subminimum	N		122.	Bar $ to hazardous substance victims	Y
67.	Freeze outlays except SS/Medicare	N		123.	Allow seasonal workers in the US	N
68.	Kill-Shift $5b of DOD to domestic	Y		124.	Let fed courts rule on school prayer	Y
69.	Confirm Tower as sec of defense	Y		125.	Presidential line-item veto	Y
70.	Bar abortion $ except to save mother	Y		126.	Ease Gun Control Act of 1968	Y
71.	Kill-Warn AIDS carriers' spouses	N		127.	Kill-Req 14-day wait for handguns	Y
72.	Allow religious schools to bar gays	Y		128.	Kill-15% min tax on corporations	Y
73.	60 days' notice of plant closings	Y		129.	Drop Social Security COLA	Y
74.	Allow poison pills in corp takeovers	N		130.	Freeze funding for all programs	N
75.	Kill-Workfare program	N		131.	Kill-Nuclear weapon freeze	Y
76.	Prohibit employee polygraph testing	Y		132.	Keep decision narrowing Title IX	Y
77.	Cap Medicare patients' liability	Y		133.	Raise drinking age to 21	Y
78.	Revise unfair trade practices	Y		134.	Allow production of MX missile	Y
79.	Kill-Shift SDI $ to conv weapons	Y		135.	Raise taxes/cut spending by $140b	Y
80.	Kill-Shift SDI $ to accidental launch	N		136.	School prayer amendment	N
81.	Kill-Shift MX $ to supplies/parts	Y		137.	Capital punishment-federal crimes	N
82.	Kill-Buy America provision at DOD	N		138.	Ban government officials from taping	N
83.	Allow nuclear testing-5+ kilotons	N		139.	Martin Luther King holiday	Y
84.	Allow SALT II to be exceeded	Y		140.	Authorize Marines in Lebanon	Y
85.	$ to vets exposed to nuclear bomb	N		141.	Amendment making abortion illegal	Y
86.	Warn workers of disease exposure	N		142.	Delete $1.2b for jobs creation	Y
87.	Restore four civil rights laws	N		143.	Keep tobacco price supports	N
88.	Disapprove uranium sales to Japan	N		144.	Emergency housing aid of $5.1b	Y

Presidential Support Score: 1991 - 77%   1990 - 74%

BOND, CHRISTOPHER S. -- Missouri [Republican]. Term Began/Expires: 1987/1992. Born: March 6, 1939; St. Louis, MO. Education: Princeton University (B.A.); University of Virginia (J.D.). Occupation: Attorney; assistant state attorney general, Consumer Protection Division; state auditor; governor (1973-1977, 1981-1985).

BOND, CHRISTOPHER S. (continued)

1. Prohibit MFN status for China	N	
2. Kill-Tie welfare to school attendance	N	
3. Limit credit card interest rates	?	
4. Confirm Gates as head of CIA	Y	
5. Adoption of national energy policies	N	
6. Kill-Restrict NEA use of funds	Y	
7. Unemployment benefits extension	N	
8. Confirm Thomas to Supreme Court	Y	
9. Raise eligibility for unpaid leave	Y	
10. Notify parents of minors' abortions	Y	
11. Move $3b from defense to domestic	N	
12. End production of B-2 bomber	N	
13. Cut SDI $1b to reduce deficit	N	
14. Maintain strategic stability-Soviets	N	
15. Kill-Allow women as combat pilots	Y	
16. Kill-Allow HIV tests before surgery	N	
17. Strike $12b aid to Int'l Mon Fund	N	
18. Raise Senate salary/omit honoraria	N	
19. Reduce space station funding $1.9b	N	
20. Kill-Eliminate supercollider funds	N	
21. Req 5-day handgun waiting period	N	
22. Life in prison instead of death	N	
23. Exceptions to exclusionary rule	Y	
24. Ban race as death sentence factor	Y	
25. Campaign finance revisions	N	
26. Kill-Term limits for senators	N	
27. Require four presidential debates	N	
28. Tighten ban on vertical price fixing	N	
29. Kill-Freeze discretionary budget	Y	
30. Provide $30b for failed S&Ls	Y	
31. Allow use of force against Iraq	Y	
32. Allow $15b in foreign aid for 1991	Y	
33. Civil Rights Act of 1990	N	
34. Block cancellation of Egypt's debt	N	
35. Cut El Salvador military aid 50%	N	
36. Reduce troops in NATO by 30,000	N	
37. Req increases in auto fuel efficiency	N	
38. Bar taxpayer funding of campaigns	Y	
39. Limit textile import growth to 1%	Y	
40. Amendment to ban flag desecration	Y	
41. Let fed emp be politically active	N	
42. Reauthorize Amtrak-veto override	N	
43. Allow sale of assault weapons	Y	
44. Retraining aid for coal miners	Y	
45. Kill-Raise car emission standards	Y	
46. Pull EPA nuclear plant authority	Y	
47. Defer Chinese students' deportation	N	
48. Cut in capital gains tax	Y	
49. Establish CIA inspector general	N	
50. Kill-Sanctions against China	Y	
51. Bar drug testing to receive AFDC	Y	
52. Kill-Allow force against drug planes	N	
53. Include illegal aliens in census	?	
54. Restitution to Japanese interned	N	
55. Troop reduction in Europe of 50%	N	

56. Increase SDI research to $4.3b	Y
57. Kill-Pay homeless below min wage	N
58. Ban airline smoking within US	N
59. Bar transfer of FS-X technology	Y
60. Limit liability for oil spills	N
61. Restructure S&L industry	N
62. Ban $ to illegal foreign activities	N
63. Req immigrant fluency in English	Y
64. Allow aliens' families to stay in US	N
65. Expand child care aid/tax credit	N
66. Raise minimum wage w/subminimum	N
67. Freeze outlays except SS/Medicare	N
68. Kill-Shift $5b of DOD to domestic	Y
69. Confirm Tower as sec of defense	Y
70. Bar abortion $ except to save mother	Y
71. Kill-Warn AIDS carriers' spouses	Y
72. Allow religious schools to bar gays	Y
73. 60 days' notice of plant closings	N
74. Allow poison pills in corp takeovers	Y
75. Kill-Workfare program	N
76. Prohibit employee polygraph testing	N
77. Cap Medicare patients' liability	Y
78. Revise unfair trade practices	Y
79. Kill-Shift SDI $ to conv weapons	Y
80. Kill-Shift SDI $ to accidental launch	N
81. Kill-Shift MX $ to supplies/parts	Y
82. Kill-Buy America provision at DOD	Y
83. Allow nuclear testing-5 + kilotons	Y
84. Allow SALT II to be exceeded	Y
85. $ to vets exposed to nuclear bomb	N
86. Warn workers of disease exposure	N
87. Restore four civil rights laws	N
88. Disapprove uranium sales to Japan	N
89. Notify Congress of covert operations	?
90. Approval of $36m in Contra aid	Y
91. $18b deficit reduction compromise	N
92. Allow sale of hard-to-detect guns	Y
93. Catastrophic health insurance	Y
94. Bork nomination to Supreme Court	Y
95. Kill-Void Panama Canal treaties	N
96. Kill-Insurance denial to AIDS+	N
97. Keep diplomatic immunity intact	N
98. Produce Bigeye nerve gas bomb	Y
99. Balanced budget by '93-via targets	Y
100. Allow ASAT missile tests in space	Y
101. Limit space-based/ABM system tests	N
102. Force reduction in trade barriers	Y
103. Repeal windfall profit tax on oil	Y
104. $1b/two year aid for the homeless	Y
105. Disallow $30m for AZT to poor	Y
106. Bar AIDS test-immigrants/marriage	Y
107. Kill-Biennial budget approval	N
108. Fairness doctrine in broadcasting	N
109. Raise speed limit to 65 mph	Y

Presidential Support Score: 1991 - 85% 1990 - 82%

MONTANA

BAUCUS, MAX -- Montana [Democrat]. Term Began/Expires: 1991/1996. Prior Terms: House: 1975-78; Senate; 1978 (Special Appointment)-1990. Born December 11, 1941; Helena, MT. Education: Stanford University (B.A., LL.B.). Occupation: Attorney, Civil Aeronautics Board (1967-68); legal assistant, Securities and Exchange Commission (1968-71); private attorney (1971); Montana representative (1973).

1. Prohibit MFN status for China	N	
2. Kill-Tie welfare to school attendance	Y	
3. Limit credit card interest rates	Y	
4. Confirm Gates as head of CIA	N	
5. Adoption of national energy policies	N	
6. Kill-Restrict NEA use of funds	Y	
7. Unemployment benefits extension	Y	
8. Confirm Thomas to Supreme Court	N	
9. Raise eligibility for unpaid leave	Y	
10. Notify parents of minors' abortions	N	
11. Move $3b from defense to domestic	Y	
12. End production of B-2 bomber	Y	
13. Cut SDI $1b to reduce deficit	Y	
14. Maintain strategic stability-Soviets	Y	
15. Kill-Allow women as combat pilots	N	
16. Kill-Allow HIV tests before surgery	Y	
17. Strike $12b aid to Int'l Mon Fund	N	
18. Raise Senate salary/omit honoraria	Y	
19. Reduce space station funding $1.9b	Y	
20. Kill-Eliminate supercollider funds	Y	
21. Req 5-day handgun waiting period	N	
22. Life in prison instead of death	N	
23. Exceptions to exclusionary rule	N	
24. Ban race as death sentence factor	Y	
25. Campaign finance revisions	Y	
26. Kill-Term limits for senators	Y	
27. Require four presidential debates	Y	
28. Tighten ban on vertical price fixing	Y	
29. Kill-Freeze discretionary budget	Y	
30. Provide $30b for failed S&Ls	N	
31. Allow use of force against Iraq	N	
32. Allow $15b in foreign aid for 1991	N	
33. Civil Rights Act of 1990	Y	
34. Block cancellation of Egypt's debt	Y	
35. Cut El Salvador military aid 50%	Y	
36. Reduce troops in NATO by 30,000	Y	
37. Req increases in auto fuel efficiency	Y	
38. Bar taxpayer funding of campaigns	N	
39. Limit textile import growth to 1%	N	
40. Amendment to ban flag desecration	Y	
41. Let fed emp be politically active	Y	
42. Reauthorize Amtrak-veto override	Y	
43. Allow sale of assault weapons	Y	
44. Retraining aid for coal miners	N	
45. Kill-Raise car emission standards	Y	
46. Pull EPA nuclear plant authority	Y	
47. Defer Chinese students' deportation	Y	
48. Cut in capital gains tax	N	
49. Establish CIA inspector general	Y	
50. Kill-Sanctions against China	Y	
51. Bar drug testing to receive AFDC	Y	

52. Kill-Allow force against drug planes	N	
53. Include illegal aliens in census	N	
54. Restitution to Japanese interned	N	
55. Troop reduction in Europe of 50%	Y	
56. Increase SDI research to $4.3b	N	
57. Kill-Pay homeless below min wage	Y	
58. Ban airline smoking within US	Y	
59. Bar transfer of FS-X technology	Y	
60. Limit liability for oil spills	Y	
61. Restructure S&L industry	Y	
62. Ban $ to illegal foreign activities	Y	
63. Req immigrant fluency in English	Y	
64. Allow aliens' families to stay in US	Y	
65. Expand child care aid/tax credit	Y	
66. Raise minimum wage w/subminimum	Y	
67. Freeze outlays except SS/Medicare	Y	
68. Kill-Shift $5b of DOD to domestic	N	
69. Confirm Tower as sec of defense	N	
70. Bar abortion $ except to save mother	N	
71. Kill-Warn AIDS carriers' spouses	Y	
72. Allow religious schools to bar gays	Y	
73. 60 days' notice of plant closings	Y	
74. Allow poison pills in corp takeovers	Y	
75. Kill-Workfare program	Y	
76. Prohibit employee polygraph testing	Y	
77. Cap Medicare patients' liability	Y	
78. Revise unfair trade practices	Y	
79. Kill-Shift SDI $ to conv weapons	N	
80. Kill-Shift SDI $ to accidental launch	Y	
81. Kill-Shift MX $ to supplies/parts	N	
82. Kill-Buy America provision at DOD	N	
83. Allow nuclear testing-5+ kilotons	N	
84. Allow SALT II to be exceeded	N	
85. $ to vets exposed to nuclear bomb	Y	
86. Warn workers of disease exposure	Y	
87. Restore four civil rights laws	Y	
88. Disapprove uranium sales to Japan	N	
89. Notify Congress of covert operations	Y	
90. Approval of $36m in Contra aid	N	
91. $18b deficit reduction compromise	Y	
92. Allow sale of hard-to-detect guns	?	
93. Catastrophic health insurance	Y	
94. Bork nomination to Supreme Court	N	
95. Kill-Void Panama Canal treaties	Y	
96. Kill-Insurance denial to AIDS+	N	
97. Keep diplomatic immunity intact	Y	
98. Produce Bigeye nerve gas bomb	N	
99. Balanced budget by '93-via targets	Y	
100. Allow ASAT missile tests in space	N	
101. Limit space-based/ABM system tests	Y	
102. Force reduction in trade barriers	Y	

BAUCUS, MAX (continued)

103. Repeal windfall profit tax on oil	Y	
104. $1b/two year aid for the homeless	Y	
105. Disallow $30m for AZT to poor	N	
106. Bar AIDS test-immigrants/marriage	Y	
107. Kill-Biennial budget approval	Y	
108. Fairness doctrine in broadcasting	N	
109. Raise speed limit to 65 mph	Y	
110. Immigration reform/alien amnesty	Y	
111. South Africa sanctions-veto override	Y	
112. Kill-Use of military in drug war	Y	
113. Tax overhaul to revise income tax	Y	
114. Submit nuclear test ban treaties	Y	
115. Prohibit sale of Stinger missiles	N	
116. Prohibit binary chemical weapons	Y	
117. Kill-$10/barrel oil tariff increase	Y	
118. Grant tax amnesty provisions	Y	
119. Block Saudi arms sale-veto override	Y	
120. Balanced budget amendment	N	
121. Include veterans in spending cuts	N	
122. Bar $ to hazardous substance victims	--	
123. Allow seasonal workers in the US	Y	

124. Let fed courts rule on school prayer	Y
125. Presidential line-item veto	N
126. Ease Gun Control Act of 1968	Y
127. Kill-Req 14-day wait for handguns	Y
128. Kill-15% min tax on corporations	N
129. Drop Social Security COLA	N
130. Freeze funding for all programs	Y
131. Kill-Nuclear weapon freeze	N
132. Keep decision narrowing Title IX	N
133. Raise drinking age to 21	N
134. Allow production of MX missile	N
135. Raise taxes/cut spending by $140b	Y
136. School prayer amendment	N
137. Capital punishment-federal crimes	Y
138. Ban government officials from taping	Y
139. Martin Luther King holiday	Y
140. Authorize Marines in Lebanon	N
141. Amendment making abortion illegal	N
142. Delete $1.2b for jobs creation	N
143. Keep tobacco price supports	N
144. Emergency housing aid of $5.1b	Y

Presidential Support Score: 1991 - 40%   1990 - 51%

BURNS, CONRAD -- Montana [Republican]. Term Began/Expires: 1989/1994. Born: January 25, 1935; Gallatin, MO. Education: University of Missouri. Military Service: U.S. Marine Corps. Occupation: Employee, TWA and Ozark Airlines; Polled Hereford World field representative; livestock show manager; television farm and ranch news reporter; founder, Northern Agriculture Network; Yellowstone County commissioner.

1. Prohibit MFN status for China	N	
2. Kill-Tie welfare to school attendance	N	
3. Limit credit card interest rates	Y	
4. Confirm Gates as head of CIA	Y	
5. Adoption of national energy policies	Y	
6. Kill-Restrict NEA use of funds	Y	
7. Unemployment benefits extension	N	
8. Confirm Thomas to Supreme Court	Y	
9. Raise eligibility for unpaid leave	N	
10. Notify parents of minors' abortions	Y	
11. Move $3b from defense to domestic	N	
12. End production of B-2 bomber	N	
13. Cut SDI $1b to reduce deficit	N	
14. Maintain strategic stability-Soviets	N	
15. Kill-Allow women as combat pilots	Y	
16. Kill-Allow HIV tests before surgery	N	
17. Strike $12b aid to Int'l Mon Fund	N	
18. Raise Senate salary/omit honoraria	Y	
19. Reduce space station funding $1.9b	N	
20. Kill-Eliminate supercollider funds	N	
21. Req 5-day handgun waiting period	N	
22. Life in prison instead of death	N	
23. Exceptions to exclusionary rule	Y	
24. Ban race as death sentence factor	Y	
25. Campaign finance revisions	N	
26. Kill-Term limits for senators	N	
27. Require four presidential debates	N	
28. Tighten ban on vertical price fixing	N	
29. Kill-Freeze discretionary budget	N	
30. Provide $30b for failed S&Ls	N	
31. Allow use of force against Iraq	Y	
32. Allow $15b in foreign aid for 1991	Y	
33. Civil Rights Act of 1990	N	

34. Block cancellation of Egypt's debt	N
35. Cut El Salvador military aid 50%	N
36. Reduce troops in NATO by 30,000	N
37. Req increases in auto fuel efficiency	N
38. Bar taxpayer funding of campaigns	Y
39. Limit textile import growth to 1%	N
40. Amendment to ban flag desecration	Y
41. Let fed emp be politically active	N
42. Reauthorize Amtrak-veto override	N
43. Allow sale of assault weapons	Y
44. Retraining aid for coal miners	N
45. Kill-Raise car emission standards	Y
46. Pull EPA nuclear plant authority	N
47. Defer Chinese students' deportation	N
48. Cut in capital gains tax	Y
49. Establish CIA inspector general	N
50. Kill-Sanctions against China	N
51. Bar drug testing to receive AFDC	Y
52. Kill-Allow force against drug planes	N
53. Include illegal aliens in census	N
54. Restitution to Japanese interned	N
55. Troop reduction in Europe of 50%	N
56. Increase SDI research to $4.3b	Y
57. Kill-Pay homeless below min wage	N
58. Ban airline smoking within US	N
59. Bar transfer of FS-X technology	N
60. Limit liability for oil spills	N
61. Restructure S&L industry	N
62. Ban $ to illegal foreign activities	N
63. Req immigrant fluency in English	Y
64. Allow aliens' families to stay in US	N
65. Expand child care aid/tax credit	N
66. Raise minimum wage w/subminimum	N

BURNS, CONRAD (continued)

67. Freeze outlays except SS/Medicare	N	69. Confirm Tower as sec of defense	Y
68. Kill-Shift $5b of DOD to domestic	Y		

Presidential Support Score: 1991 - 89%   1990 - 81%

NEBRASKA

EXON, J. JAMES -- Nebraska [Democrat]. Term Began/Expires: 1991/1996. Prior Terms: Senate: 1979-90. Born: August 9, 1921; Geddes, SD. Education: University of Omaha. Military Service: U.S. Army, 1942-45; Army Reserve, 1945-49. Occupation: Branch manager, Universal Finance Corp. (1945-53); president, Exon's Inc. (1953-71); governor (1971-78).

1. Prohibit MFN status for China	Y	46. Pull EPA nuclear plant authority	N
2. Kill-Tie welfare to school attendance	Y	47. Defer Chinese students' deportation	Y
3. Limit credit card interest rates	Y	48. Cut in capital gains tax	N
4. Confirm Gates as head of CIA	N	49. Establish CIA inspector general	Y
5. Adoption of national energy policies	N	50. Kill-Sanctions against China	Y
6. Kill-Restrict NEA use of funds	Y	51. Bar drug testing to receive AFDC	N
7. Unemployment benefits extension	Y	52. Kill-Allow force against drug planes	N
8. Confirm Thomas to Supreme Court	Y	53. Include illegal aliens in census	N
9. Raise eligibility for unpaid leave	Y	54. Restitution to Japanese interned	Y
10. Notify parents of minors' abortions	Y	55. Troop reduction in Europe of 50%	N
11. Move $3b from defense to domestic	N	56. Increase SDI research to $4.3b	Y
12. End production of B-2 bomber	N	57. Kill-Pay homeless below min wage	Y
13. Cut SDI $1b to reduce deficit	N	58. Ban airline smoking within US	Y
14. Maintain strategic stability-Soviets	N	59. Bar transfer of FS-X technology	Y
15. Kill-Allow women as combat pilots	N	60. Limit liability for oil spills	N
16. Kill-Allow HIV tests before surgery	N	61. Restructure S&L industry	Y
17. Strike $12b aid to Int'l Mon Fund	Y	62. Ban $ to illegal foreign activities	Y
18. Raise Senate salary/omit honoraria	Y	63. Req immigrant fluency in English	Y
19. Reduce space station funding $1.9b	Y	64. Allow aliens' families to stay in US	N
20. Kill-Eliminate supercollider funds	N	65. Expand child care aid/tax credit	Y
21. Req 5-day handgun waiting period	Y	66. Raise minimum wage w/subminimum	Y
22. Life in prison instead of death	N	67. Freeze outlays except SS/Medicare	Y
23. Exceptions to exclusionary rule	Y	68. Kill-Shift $5b of DOD to domestic	Y
24. Ban race as death sentence factor	Y	69. Confirm Tower as sec of defense	N
25. Campaign finance revisions	Y	70. Bar abortion $ except to save mother	Y
26. Kill-Term limits for senators	Y	71. Kill-Warn AIDS carriers' spouses	Y
27. Require final presidential debates	Y	72. Allow religious schools to bar gays	Y
28. Tighten ban on vertical price fixing	Y	73. 60 days' notice of plant closings	Y
29. Kill-Freeze discretionary budget	Y	74. Allow poison pills in corp takeovers	Y
30. Provide $30b for failed S&Ls	N	75. Kill-Workfare program	N
31. Allow use of force against Iraq	N	76. Prohibit employee polygraph testing	Y
32. Allow $15b in foreign aid for 1991	N	77. Cap Medicare patients' liability	Y
33. Civil Rights Act of 1990	Y	78. Revise unfair trade practices	Y
34. Block cancellation of Egypt's debt	Y	79. Kill-Shift SDI $ to conv weapons	Y
35. Cut El Salvador military aid 50%	Y	80. Kill-Shift SDI $ to accidental launch	Y
36. Reduce troops in NATO by 30,000	Y	81. Kill-Shift MX $ to supplies/parts	Y
37. Req increases in auto fuel efficiency	Y	82. Kill-Buy America provision at DOD	N
38. Bar taxpayer funding of campaigns	Y	83. Allow nuclear testing-5+ kilotons	Y
39. Limit textile import growth to 1%	Y	84. Allow SALT II to be exceeded	Y
40. Amendment to ban flag desecration	Y	85. $ to vets exposed to nuclear bomb	?
41. Let fed emp be politically active	Y	86. Warn workers of disease exposure	N
42. Reauthorize Amtrak-veto override	Y	87. Restore four civil rights laws	Y
43. Allow sale of assault weapons	Y	88. Disapprove uranium sales to Japan	N
44. Retraining aid for coal miners	Y	89. Notify Congress of covert operations	Y
45. Kill-Raise car emission standards	Y	90. Approval of $36m in Contra aid	Y

EXON, J. JAMES (continued)

91. $18b deficit reduction compromise	Y	
92. Allow sale of hard-to-detect guns	N	
93. Catastrophic health insurance	Y	
94. Bork nomination to Supreme Court	N	
95. Kill-Void Panama Canal treaties	N	
96. Kill-Insurance denial to AIDS+	N	
97. Keep diplomatic immunity intact	N	
98. Produce Bigeye nerve gas bomb	Y	
99. Balanced budget by '93-via targets	N	
100. Allow ASAT missile tests in space	Y	
101. Limit space-based/ABM system tests	Y	
102. Force reduction in trade barriers	Y	
103. Repeal windfall profit tax on oil	Y	
104. $1b/two year aid for the homeless	N	
105. Disallow $30m for AZT to poor	Y	
106. Bar AIDS test-immigrants/marriage	N	
107. Kill-Biennial budget approval	Y	
108. Fairness doctrine in broadcasting	Y	
109. Raise speed limit to 65 mph	N	
110. Immigration reform/alien amnesty	Y	
111. South Africa sanctions-veto override	Y	
112. Kill-Use of military in drug war	Y	
113. Tax overhaul to revise income tax	N	
114. Submit nuclear test ban treaties	Y	
115. Prohibit sale of Stinger missiles	N	
116. Prohibit binary chemical weapons	N	
117. Kill-$10/barrel oil tariff increase	Y	
118. Grant tax amnesty provisions	N	
119. Block Saudi arms sale-veto override	N	
120. Balanced budget amendment	Y	
121. Include veterans in spending cuts	N	
122. Bar $ to hazardous substance victims	N	
123. Allow seasonal workers in the US	Y	
124. Let fed courts rule on school prayer	N	
125. Presidential line-item veto	Y	
126. Ease Gun Control Act of 1968	Y	
127. Kill-Req 14-day wait for handguns	Y	
128. Kill-15% min tax on corporations	?	
129. Drop Social Security COLA	?	
130. Freeze funding for all programs	?	
131. Kill-Nuclear weapon freeze	N	
132. Keep decision narrowing Title IX	Y	
133. Raise drinking age to 21	Y	
134. Allow production of MX missile	N	
135. Raise taxes/cut spending by $140b	Y	
136. School prayer amendment	Y	
137. Capital punishment-federal crimes	Y	
138. Ban government officials from taping	Y	
139. Martin Luther King holiday	N	
140. Authorize Marines in Lebanon	N	
141. Amendment making abortion illegal	Y	
142. Delete $1.2b for jobs creation	Y	
143. Keep tobacco price supports	N	
144. Emergency housing aid of $5.1b	Y	

Presidential Support Score: 1991 - 52%   1990 - 54%

KERREY, BOB -- Nebraska [Democrat]. Term Began/Expires: 1989/1994. Born: August 27, 1943; Lincoln, NE. Education: University of Nebraska (B.S.). Military Service: U.S. Navy. Occupation: Cofounder, restaurant and fitness center chain; Nebraska governor (1982-88).

1. Prohibit MFN status for China	+	
2. Kill-Tie welfare to school attendance	?	
3. Limit credit card interest rates	?	
4. Confirm Gates as head of CIA	?	
5. Adoption of national energy policies	X	
6. Kill-Restrict NEA use of funds	Y	
7. Unemployment benefits extension	Y	
8. Confirm Thomas to Supreme Court	N	
9. Raise eligibility for unpaid leave	?	
10. Notify parents of minors' abortions	N	
11. Move $3b from defense to domestic	N	
12. End production of B-2 bomber	Y	
13. Cut SDI $1b to reduce deficit	Y	
14. Maintain strategic stability-Soviets	Y	
15. Kill-Allow women as combat pilots	N	
16. Kill-Allow HIV tests before surgery	Y	
17. Strike $12b aid to Int'l Mon Fund	Y	
18. Raise Senate salary/omit honoraria	Y	
19. Reduce space station funding $1.9b	N	
20. Kill-Eliminate supercollider funds	N	
21. Req 5-day handgun waiting period	Y	
22. Life in prison instead of death	N	
23. Exceptions to exclusionary rule	N	
24. Ban race as death sentence factor	N	
25. Campaign finance revisions	Y	
26. Kill-Term limits for senators	Y	
27. Require four presidential debates	Y	
28. Tighten ban on vertical price fixing	Y	
29. Kill-Freeze discretionary budget	Y	
30. Provide $30b for failed S&Ls	N	
31. Allow use of force against Iraq	N	
32. Allow $15b in foreign aid for 1991	Y	
33. Civil Rights Act of 1990	Y	
34. Block cancellation of Egypt's debt	Y	
35. Cut El Salvador military aid 50%	Y	
36. Reduce troops in NATO by 30,000	Y	
37. Req increases in auto fuel efficiency	Y	
38. Bar taxpayer funding of campaigns	N	
39. Limit textile import growth to 1%	N	
40. Amendment to ban flag desecration	N	
41. Let fed emp be politically active	Y	
42. Reauthorize Amtrak-veto override	Y	
43. Allow sale of assault weapons	N	
44. Retraining aid for coal miners	Y	
45. Kill-Raise car emission standards	Y	
46. Pull EPA nuclear plant authority	N	
47. Defer Chinese students' deportation	Y	
48. Cut in capital gains tax	N	
49. Establish CIA inspector general	Y	
50. Kill-Sanctions against China	Y	
51. Bar drug testing to receive AFDC	Y	
52. Kill-Allow force against drug planes	Y	
53. Include illegal aliens in census	Y	
54. Restitution to Japanese interned	Y	
55. Troop reduction in Europe of 50%	N	
56. Increase SDI research to $4.3b	N	

KERREY, BOB (continued)

57. Kill-Pay homeless below min wage	Y
58. Ban airline smoking within US	Y
59. Bar transfer of FS-X technology	Y
60. Limit liability for oil spills	N
61. Restructure S&L industry	Y
62. Ban $ to illegal foreign activities	Y
63. Req immigrant fluency in English	N

64. Allow aliens' families to stay in US	Y
65. Expand child care aid/tax credit	Y
66. Raise minimum wage w/subminimum	Y
67. Freeze outlays except SS/Medicare	Y
68. Kill-Shift $5b of DOD to domestic	Y
69. Confirm Tower as sec of defense	N

Presidential Support Score: 1991 - 32%   1990 - 40%

NEVADA

REID, HARRY M. -- Nevada [Democrat]. Term Began/Expires: 1987/1992. Prior Terms: House: 1983-86. Born: December 2, 1939; Searchlight, NV. Education: Southern Utah State College (A.S.); Utah St. University (B.S.); George Washington School of Law (J.D.). Occupation: Attorney; city attorney (1964-66); member, Board of Trustees, Southern Nevada Memorial Hospital (1967-69); state assemblyman (1969-70); lt. governor (1970-74); chairman, Nevada gaming commission (1977-81).

1. Prohibit MFN status for China	Y	40. Amendment to ban flag desecration	Y
2. Kill-Tie welfare to school attendance	N	41. Let fed emp be politically active	Y
3. Limit credit card interest rates	Y	42. Reauthorize Amtrak-veto override	Y
4. Confirm Gates as head of CIA	Y	43. Allow sale of assault weapons	Y
5. Adoption of national energy policies	N	44. Retraining aid for coal miners	Y
6. Kill-Restrict NEA use of funds	Y	45. Kill-Raise car emission standards	N
7. Unemployment benefits extension	Y	46. Pull EPA nuclear plant authority	N
8. Confirm Thomas to Supreme Court	N	47. Defer Chinese students' deportation	Y
9. Raise eligibility for unpaid leave	Y	48. Cut in capital gains tax	N
10. Notify parents of minors' abortions	Y	49. Establish CIA inspector general	Y
11. Move $3b from defense to domestic	N	50. Kill-Sanctions against China	N
12. End production of B-2 bomber	Y	51. Bar drug testing to receive AFDC	Y
13. Cut SDI $1b to reduce deficit	Y	52. Kill-Allow force against drug planes	N
14. Maintain strategic stability-Soviets	Y	53. Include illegal aliens in census	Y
15. Kill-Allow women as combat pilots	N	54. Restitution to Japanese interned	Y
16. Kill-Allow HIV tests before surgery	N	55. Troop reduction in Europe of 50%	Y
17. Strike $12b aid to Int'l Mon Fund	N	56. Increase SDI research to $4.3b	N
18. Raise Senate salary/omit honoraria	N	57. Kill-Pay homeless below min wage	Y
19. Reduce space station funding $1.9b	N	58. Ban airline smoking within US	Y
20. Kill-Eliminate supercollider funds	Y	59. Bar transfer of FS-X technology	Y
21. Req 5-day handgun waiting period	Y	60. Limit liability for oil spills	N
22. Life in prison instead of death	N	61. Restructure S&L industry	Y
23. Exceptions to exclusionary rule	Y	62. Ban $ to illegal foreign activities	Y
24. Ban race as death sentence factor	N	63. Req immigrant fluency in English	N
25. Campaign finance revisions	Y	64. Allow aliens' families to stay in US	Y
26. Kill-Term limits for senators	Y	65. Expand child care aid/tax credit	Y
27. Require four presidential debates	Y	66. Raise minimum wage w/subminimum	Y
28. Tighten ban on vertical price fixing	Y	67. Freeze outlays except SS/Medicare	N
29. Kill-Freeze discretionary budget	Y	68. Kill-Shift $5b of DOD to domestic	N
30. Provide $30b for failed S&Ls	Y	69. Confirm Tower as sec of defense	N
31. Allow use of force against Iraq	Y	70. Bar abortion $ except to save mother	Y
32. Allow $15b in foreign aid for 1991	Y	71. Kill-Warn AIDS carriers' spouses	N
33. Civil Rights Act of 1990	Y	72. Allow religious schools to bar gays	Y
34. Block cancellation of Egypt's debt	Y	73. 60 days' notice of plant closings	Y
35. Cut El Salvador military aid 50%	Y	74. Allow poison pills in corp takeovers	Y
36. Reduce troops in NATO by 30,000	Y	75. Kill-Workfare program	N
37. Req increases in auto fuel efficiency	Y	76. Prohibit employee polygraph testing	Y
38. Bar taxpayer funding of campaigns	N	77. Cap Medicare patients' liability	Y
39. Limit textile import growth to 1%	Y	78. Revise unfair trade practices	Y

REID, HARRY M. (continued)

79. Kill-Shift SDI $ to conv weapons	Y	95. Kill-Void Panama Canal treaties	Y
80. Kill-Shift SDI $ to accidental launch	Y	96. Kill-Insurance denial to AIDS+	Y
81. Kill-Shift MX $ to supplies/parts	Y	97. Keep diplomatic immunity intact	Y
82. Kill-Buy America provision at DOD	N	98. Produce Bigeye nerve gas bomb	N
83. Allow nuclear testing-5+ kilotons	Y	99. Balanced budget by '93-via targets	Y
84. Allow SALT II to be exceeded	N	100. Allow ASAT missile tests in space	N
85. $ to vets exposed to nuclear bomb	Y	101. Limit space-based/ABM system tests	Y
86. Warn workers of disease exposure	Y	102. Force reduction in trade barriers	Y
87. Restore four civil rights laws	Y	103. Repeal windfall profit tax on oil	N
88. Disapprove uranium sales to Japan	Y	104. $1b/two year aid for the homeless	Y
89. Notify Congress of covert operations	Y	105. Disallow $30m for AZT to poor	N
90. Approval of $36m in Contra aid	N	106. Bar AIDS test-immigrants/marriage	N
91. $18b deficit reduction compromise	N	107. Kill-Biennial budget approval	Y
92. Allow sale of hard-to-detect guns	N	108. Fairness doctrine in broadcasting	Y
93. Catastrophic health insurance	Y	109. Raise speed limit to 65 mph	Y
94. Bork nomination to Supreme Court	N		

The following are House measures voted on between 1983-1986:

99. Immigration reform/alien amnesty	N	120. Drop SS COLAs/$12b tax increase	N
100. South Africa sanctions-veto override	Y	121. Approve $1.5b for 21 MX missiles	Y
101. Tax overhaul to revise income tax	Y	122. Emergency farm credit/revisions	Y
102. Use of military in drug war	Y	123. Duty on Taiwan/Hong Kong/S Korea	Y
103. Delete 12 MX/add conventional wpn	N	124. Limit steel imports to 17%	Y
104. Raise speed limit to 65 mph	Y	125. Cut $ to schools that bar prayer	N
105. Require Pentagon to buy US goods	Y	126. $50b-taxes; cut Medicare/spending	Y
106. AIDS insurance non-discrimination	Y	127. Limit Pershing II/cruise in Europe	N
107. Prohibit Saudi arms sales	Y	128. Delete $7.1b for 34 B-1 bombers	Y
108. Ease Gun Control Act of 1968	Y	129. Bar purchase of Sergeant York guns	Y
109. Bar interstate handgun transport	N	130. El Salvador military/economic aid	N
110. Make company emissions known	Y	131. Bar mining of Nicaraguan waters	Y
111. Allow toxic victims to sue in fed ct	Y	132. Physician fee freeze for Medicare	N
112. Superfund waste cleanup of $10b	Y	133. $49b in "sin"/phone/insurance taxes	Y
113. 90 days notice of plant closings	Y	134. Allow sale of Conrail	N
114. $20b in Medicare cuts/tax increases	N	135. Equal Rights Amendment	N
115. Spending cuts and tax increases	Y	136. Authorize Marines in Lebanon	Y
116. Set school lunch lmt-250% poverty	N	137. Eminent domain for coal companies	N
117. $75m for youth work projects	#	138. Prohibit EPA clean air sanctions	Y
118. Allow Angolan military assistance	N	139. SS retirement age increase/reforms	N
119. Suspend defense payments for abuse	Y		

Presidential Support Score: 1991 - 51%   1990 - 44%

BRYAN, RICHARD H.

-- Nevada [Democrat]. Term Began/Expires: 1989/1994. Born: July 16, 1937; Washington, DC. Education: University of Nevada-Reno; University of California, Hastings College of Law. Military Service: U.S. Army and Army Reserve. Occupation: Clark County deputy district attorney; state public defender, assemblyman, senator, attorney general and governor (1982-88).

1. Prohibit MFN status for China	Y	15. Kill-Allow women as combat pilots	Y
2. Kill-Tie welfare to school attendance	Y	16. Kill-Allow HIV tests before surgery	N
3. Limit credit card interest rates	Y	17. Strike $12b aid to Int'l Mon Fund	N
4. Confirm Gates as head of CIA	Y	18. Raise Senate salary/omit honoraria	N
5. Adoption of national energy policies	N	19. Reduce space station funding $1.9b	Y
6. Kill-Restrict NEA use of funds	Y	20. Kill-Eliminate supercollider funds	N
7. Unemployment benefits extension	Y	21. Req 5-day handgun waiting period	Y
8. Confirm Thomas to Supreme Court	N	22. Life in prison instead of death	N
9. Raise eligibility for unpaid leave	Y	23. Exceptions to exclusionary rule	N
10. Notify parents of minors' abortions	N	24. Ban race as death sentence factor	Y
11. Move $3b from defense to domestic	N	25. Campaign finance revisions	Y
12. End production of B-2 bomber	N	26. Kill-Term limits for senators	Y
13. Cut SDI $1b to reduce deficit	Y	27. Require four presidential debates	Y
14. Maintain strategic stability-Soviets	Y	28. Tighten ban on vertical price fixing	Y

BRYAN, RICHARD H. (continued)

29. Kill-Freeze discretionary budget	Y	50. Kill-Sanctions against China	N
30. Provide $30b for failed S&Ls	Y	51. Bar drug testing to receive AFDC	Y
31. Allow use of force against Iraq	Y	52. Kill-Allow force against drug planes	N
32. Allow $15b in foreign aid for 1991	Y	53. Include illegal aliens in census	Y
33. Civil Rights Act of 1990	Y	54. Restitution to Japanese interned	Y
34. Block cancellation of Egypt's debt	Y	55. Troop reduction in Europe of 50%	N
35. Cut El Salvador military aid 50%	Y	56. Increase SDI research to $4.3b	Y
36. Reduce troops in NATO by 30,000	Y	57. Kill-Pay homeless below min wage	Y
37. Req increases in auto fuel efficiency	Y	58. Ban airline smoking within US	Y
38. Bar taxpayer funding of campaigns	N	59. Bar transfer of FS-X technology	Y
39. Limit textile import growth to 1%	Y	60. Limit liability for oil spills	N
40. Amendment to ban flag desecration	Y	61. Restructure S&L industry	Y
41. Let fed emp be politically active	Y	62. Ban $ to illegal foreign activities	Y
42. Reauthorize Amtrak-veto override	Y	63. Req immigrant fluency in English	N
43. Allow sale of assault weapons	Y	64. Allow aliens' families to stay in US	Y
44. Retraining aid for coal miners	Y	65. Expand child care aid/tax credit	Y
45. Kill-Raise car emission standards	N	66. Raise minimum wage w/subminimum	Y
46. Pull EPA nuclear plant authority	N	67. Freeze outlays except SS/Medicare	N
47. Defer Chinese students' deportation	Y	68. Kill-Shift $5b of DOD to domestic	N
48. Cut in capital gains tax	N	69. Confirm Tower as sec of defense	N
49. Establish CIA inspector general	Y		

Presidential Support Score: 1991 - 47% 1990 - 44%

NEW HAMPSHIRE

RUDMAN, WARREN -- New Hampshire [Republican]. Term Began/Expires: 1987/1992. Prior Terms: Senate: 1981-86. Born: May 18, 1930; Boston, MA. Education: Boston College of Law. Military Service: U.S. Army, 1952-54. Occupation: New Hampshire attorney general (1970-76); business manager.

1. Prohibit MFN status for China	N	28. Tighten ban on vertical price fixing	Y
2. Kill-Tie welfare to school attendance	N	29. Kill-Freeze discretionary budget	Y
3. Limit credit card interest rates	N	30. Provide $30b for failed S&Ls	Y
4. Confirm Gates as head of CIA	Y	31. Allow use of force against Iraq	Y
5. Adoption of national energy policies	Y	32. Allow $15b in foreign aid for 1991	Y
6. Kill-Restrict NEA use of funds	N	33. Civil Rights Act of 1990	N
7. Unemployment benefits extension	N	34. Block cancellation of Egypt's debt	N
8. Confirm Thomas to Supreme Court	Y	35. Cut El Salvador military aid 50%	N
9. Raise eligibility for unpaid leave	N	36. Reduce troops in NATO by 30,000	N
10. Notify parents of minors' abortions	N	37. Req increases in auto fuel efficiency	Y
11. Move $3b from defense to domestic	N	38. Bar taxpayer funding of campaigns	Y
12. End production of B-2 bomber	N	39. Limit textile import growth to 1%	Y
13. Cut SDI $1b to reduce deficit	N	40. Amendment to ban flag desecration	N
14. Maintain strategic stability-Soviets	N	41. Let fed emp be politically active	N
15. Kill-Allow women as combat pilots	Y	42. Reauthorize Amtrak-veto override	N
16. Kill-Allow HIV tests before surgery	N	43. Allow sale of assault weapons	Y
17. Strike $12b aid to Int'l Mon Fund	N	44. Retraining aid for coal miners	N
18. Raise Senate salary/omit honoraria	Y	45. Kill-Raise car emission standards	Y
19. Reduce space station funding $1.9b	N	46. Pull EPA nuclear plant authority	N
20. Kill-Eliminate supercollider funds	Y	47. Defer Chinese students' deportation	N
21. Req 5-day handgun waiting period	Y	48. Cut in capital gains tax	Y
22. Life in prison instead of death	N	49. Establish CIA inspector general	Y
23. Exceptions to exclusionary rule	N	50. Kill-Sanctions against China	Y
24. Ban race as death sentence factor	Y	51. Bar drug testing to receive AFDC	Y
25. Campaign finance revisions	N	52. Kill-Allow force against drug planes	Y
26. Kill-Term limits for senators	Y	53. Include illegal aliens in census	Y
27. Require four presidential debates	N	54. Restitution to Japanese interned	Y

RUDMAN, WARREN (continued)

55. Troop reduction in Europe of 50%	N
56. Increase SDI research to $4.3b	Y
57. Kill-Pay homeless below min wage	N
58. Ban airline smoking within US	Y
59. Bar transfer of FS-X technology	N
60. Limit liability for oil spills	N
61. Restructure S&L industry	N
62. Ban $ to illegal foreign activities	Y
63. Req immigrant fluency in English	Y
64. Allow aliens' families to stay in US	N
65. Expand child care aid/tax credit	N
66. Raise minimum wage w/subminimum	N
67. Freeze outlays except SS/Medicare	N
68. Kill-Shift $5b of DOD to domestic	Y
69. Confirm Tower as sec of defense	Y
70. Bar abortion $ except to save mother	N
71. Kill-Warn AIDS carriers' spouses	N
72. Allow religious schools to bar gays	Y
73. 60 days' notice of plant closings	N
74. Allow poison pills in corp takeovers	N
75. Kill-Workfare program	N
76. Prohibit employee polygraph testing	N
77. Cap Medicare patients' liability	Y
78. Revise unfair trade practices	N
79. Kill-Shift SDI $ to conv weapons	Y
80. Kill-Shift SDI $ to accidental launch	N
81. Kill-Shift MX $ to supplies/parts	Y
82. Kill-Buy America provision at DOD	N
83. Allow nuclear testing-5+ kilotons	Y
84. Allow SALT II to be exceeded	Y
85. $ to vets exposed to nuclear bomb	N
86. Warn workers of disease exposure	N
87. Restore four civil rights laws	Y
88. Disapprove uranium sales to Japan	Y
89. Notify Congress of covert operations	Y
90. Approval of $36m in Contra aid	Y
91. $18b deficit reduction compromise	Y
92. Allow sale of hard-to-detect guns	N
93. Catastrophic health insurance	Y
94. Bork nomination to Supreme Court	Y
95. Kill-Void Panama Canal treaties	N
96. Kill-Insurance denial to AIDS+	N
97. Keep diplomatic immunity intact	N
98. Produce Bigeye nerve gas bomb	Y
99. Balanced budget by '93-via targets	Y

100. Allow ASAT missile tests in space	Y
101. Limit space-based/ABM system tests	N
102. Force reduction in trade barriers	N
103. Repeal windfall profit tax on oil	N
104. $1b/two year aid for the homeless	N
105. Disallow $30m for AZT to poor	N
106. Bar AIDS test-immigrants/marriage	Y
107. Kill-Biennial budget approval	N
108. Fairness doctrine in broadcasting	Y
109. Raise speed limit to 65 mph	Y
110. Immigration reform/alien amnesty	N
111. South Africa sanctions-veto override	N
112. Kill-Use of military in drug war	Y
113. Tax overhaul to revise income tax	Y
114. Submit nuclear test ban treaties	N
115. Prohibit sale of Stinger missiles	N
116. Prohibit binary chemical weapons	N
117. Kill-$10/barrel oil tariff increase	Y
118. Grant tax amnesty provisions	N
119. Block Saudi arms sale-veto override	Y
120. Balanced budget amendment	Y
121. Include veterans in spending cuts	Y
122. Bar $ to hazardous substance victims	Y
123. Allow seasonal workers in the US	Y
124. Let fed courts rule on school prayer	Y
125. Presidential line-item veto	Y
126. Ease Gun Control Act of 1968	Y
127. Kill-Req 14-day wait for handguns	Y
128. Kill-15% min tax on corporations	Y
129. Drop Social Security COLA	Y
130. Freeze funding for all programs	N
131. Kill-Nuclear weapon freeze	Y
132. Keep decision narrowing Title IX	Y
133. Raise drinking age to 21	Y
134. Allow production of MX missile	Y
135. Raise taxes/cut spending by $140b	Y
136. School prayer amendment	N
137. Capital punishment-federal crimes	Y
138. Ban government officials from taping	Y
139. Martin Luther King holiday	N
140. Authorize Marines in Lebanon	Y
141. Amendment making abortion illegal	N
142. Delete $1.2b for jobs creation	N
143. Keep tobacco price supports	N
144. Emergency housing aid of $5.1b	Y

Presidential Support Score: 1991 - 85%   1990 - 74%

SMITH, ROBERT C. -- New Hampshire [Republican]. Term Began/Expires: 1991/1996. Prior Terms: House: 1985-90. Born: March 30, 1941; Trenton, NJ. Education: Lafayette College (B.S.). Military Service: U.S. Navy, 1965-67; U.S. Naval Reserve. Occupation: Teacher; school board member; Carroll County probation department volunteer; realtor.

1. Prohibit MFN status for China	Y
2. Kill-Tie welfare to school attendance	N
3. Limit credit card interest rates	N
4. Confirm Gates as head of CIA	Y
5. Adoption of national energy policies	N
6. Kill-Restrict NEA use of funds	N
7. Unemployment benefits extension	N
8. Confirm Thomas to Supreme Court	Y
9. Raise eligibility for unpaid leave	N

10. Notify parents of minors' abortions	Y
11. Move $3b from defense to domestic	N
12. End production of B-2 bomber	N
13. Cut SDI $1b to reduce deficit	N
14. Maintain strategic stability-Soviets	N
15. Kill-Allow women as combat pilots	Y
16. Kill-Allow HIV tests before surgery	N
17. Strike $12b aid to Int'l Mon Fund	Y
18. Raise Senate salary/omit honoraria	Y

SMITH, ROBERT C. (continued)

19. Reduce space station funding $1.9b	N	
20. Kill-Eliminate supercollider funds	N	
21. Req 5-day handgun waiting period	N	
22. Life in prison instead of death	N	
23. Exceptions to exclusionary rule	?	
24. Ban race as death sentence factor	Y	
25. Campaign finance revisions	N	

26. Kill-Term limits for senators	N	
27. Require four presidential debates	N	
28. Tighten ban on vertical price fixing	N	
29. Kill-Freeze discretionary budget	N	
30. Provide $30b for failed S&Ls	N	
31. Allow use of force against Iraq	Y	

The following are House measures voted on between 1985-1990:

36. Amendment to ban flag desecration	Y
37. Reauthorize Amtrak-veto override	N
38. Retraining aid for coal miners	N
39. Suspend El Salvador military aid	N
40. Expand child care aid/tax credit	N
41. Raise House salary/omit honoraria	N
42. Toughen oil-spill liability	Y
43. Restitution to Japanese interned	N
44. Protect Chinese & C.A. nationals	N
45. Abortion $ for rape/incest cases	N
46. Allow religious schools to bar gays	Y
47. Bar broadcaster fairness doctrine	Y
48. Bar cap gains cut/reinstate IRA	N
49. Bar unions equal voice in pension	Y
50. Bar assembly of chemical weapons	N
51. Ban plutonium/uranium production	N
52. Cap MX missile deployment at 50	N
53. Allow $3b for 2 stealth bombers	Y
54. Publish bio-warfare experiments	N
55. Raise minimum wage-veto override	N
56. Bar transfer of FS-X technology	Y
57. Cut defense and raise domestic $	N
58. Uniform poll closing in 48 states	N
59. Req foreign investment disclosure	N
60. Textile import quotas-veto override	Y
61. Bar abortion funding in Wash, DC	Y
62. Notify spouses of AIDS+ carriers	Y
63. Seize conveyance-drug trafficking	Y
64. South Africa sanctions	N
65. 60 days' notice of plant closings	N
66. Close unneeded military bases	Y
67. Keep welfare reform within $2.8b	Y
68. Allow children housing exclusion	Y
69. Shift $400m of NASA to homeless	N
70. Cap Medicare patients' liability	N
71. Prohibit employee polygraph testing	N
72. Allow CIA to fund Contras	Y
73. Revise unfair trade practices	N
74. Focus SDI on accidental launch	N
75. Bar Air Force $ for MX missile	N
76. Allow "real" increase in defense	Y
77. Troop reduction in Europe of 50%	N
78. Ban nuclear tests above 1 kiloton	N
79. Ban anti-satellite missile tests	N

80. Observe certain limits of SALT II	N
81. Restore four Civil Rights laws	N
82. Prohibit aliens as strikebreakers	N
83. Allow military malpractice suits	Y
84. Approval of $36m in Contra aid	Y
85. $18b deficit reduction compromise	N
86. Welfare reform of $5.7b for 5 years	N
87. Raise taxes $12b/cut spending $3b	N
88. Board to assess occupational risk	N
89. Balanced budget by '93-via targets	Y
90. Bar licensing of two nuclear plants	N
91. Remove victims compensation cap	Y
92. Catastrophic health insurance	N
93. Ban airline smoking-2 hours or less	Y
94. $1b/two year aid for the homeless	N
95. Bar non-unions in union companies	N
96. Increase FSLIC rescue to $15b	Y
97. Impose quotas to lower trade deficit	N
98. Reduce discretionary budget 21%	Y
99. Immigration reform/alien amnesty	N
100. South Africa sanctions-veto override	N
101. Tax overhaul to revise income tax	Y
102. Use of military in drug war	Y
103. Delete 12 MX/add conventional wpn	N
104. Raise speed limit to 65 mph	Y
105. Require Pentagon to buy US goods	N
106. AIDS insurance non-discrimination	N
107. Prohibit Saudi arms sales	Y
108. Ease Gun Control Act of 1968	Y
109. Bar interstate handgun transport	Y
110. Make company emissions known	Y
111. Allow toxic victims to sue in fed ct	N
112. Superfund waste cleanup of $10b	Y
113. 90 days notice of plant closings	N
114. $20b in Medicare cuts/tax increases	N
115. Spending cuts and tax increases	N
116. Set school lunch lmt-250% poverty	Y
117. $75m for youth work projects	N
118. Allow Angolan military assistance	Y
119. Suspend defense payments for abuse	N
120. Drop SS COLAs/$12b tax increase	N
121. Approve $1.5b for 21 MX missiles	Y
122. Emergency farm credit/revisions	N

Presidential Support Score: 1991 - 85% 1990 - 73%

NEW JERSEY

BRADLEY, BILL -- New Jersey [Democrat]. Term Began/Expires: 1991/1996. Prior Terms: Senate: 1979-84. Born: July 28, 1943; Crystal City, MO. Education: Princeton University (Baccalaureate); Oxford University. Occupation: Professional athlete (1967-77); assistant to director, Office of Economic Opportunity.

1.	Prohibit MFN status for China	Y	53.	Include illegal aliens in census	?
2.	Kill-Tie welfare to school attendance	Y	54.	Restitution to Japanese interned	Y
3.	Limit credit card interest rates	?	55.	Troop reduction in Europe of 50%	N
4.	Confirm Gates as head of CIA	N	56.	Increase SDI research to $4.3b	N
5.	Adoption of national energy policies	N	57.	Kill-Pay homeless below min wage	Y
6.	Kill-Restrict NEA use of funds	Y	58.	Ban airline smoking within US	Y
7.	Unemployment benefits extension	Y	59.	Bar transfer of FS-X technology	N
8.	Confirm Thomas to Supreme Court	N	60.	Limit liability for oil spills	N
9.	Raise eligibility for unpaid leave	Y	61.	Restructure S&L industry	Y
10.	Notify parents of minors' abortions	N	62.	Ban $ to illegal foreign activities	Y
11.	Move $3b from defense to domestic	Y	63.	Req immigrant fluency in English	N
12.	End production of B-2 bomber	Y	64.	Allow aliens' families to stay in US	Y
13.	Cut SDI $1b to reduce deficit	Y	65.	Expand child care aid/tax credit	Y
14.	Maintain strategic stability-Soviets	Y	66.	Raise minimum wage w/subminimum	Y
15.	Kill-Allow women as combat pilots	N	67.	Freeze outlays except SS/Medicare	N
16.	Kill-Allow HIV tests before surgery	Y	68.	Kill-Shift $5b of DOD to domestic	N
17.	Strike $12b aid to Int'l Mon Fund	N	69.	Confirm Tower as sec of defense	N
18.	Raise Senate salary/omit honoraria	N	70.	Bar abortion $ except to save mother	N
19.	Reduce space station funding $1.9b	Y	71.	Kill-Warn AIDS carriers' spouses	Y
20.	Kill-Eliminate supercollider funds	N	72.	Allow religious schools to bar gays	?
21.	Req 5-day handgun waiting period	Y	73.	60 days' notice of plant closings	Y
22.	Life in prison instead of death	N	74.	Allow poison pills in corp takeovers	N
23.	Exceptions to exclusionary rule	N	75.	Kill-Workfare program	Y
24.	Ban race as death sentence factor	N	76.	Prohibit employee polygraph testing	Y
25.	Campaign finance revisions	Y	77.	Cap Medicare patients' liability	Y
26.	Kill-Term limits for senators	Y	78.	Revise unfair trade practices	Y
27.	Require four presidential debates	Y	79.	Kill-Shift SDI $ to conv weapons	N
28.	Tighten ban on vertical price fixing	Y	80.	Kill-Shift SDI $ to accidental launch	?
29.	Kill-Freeze discretionary budget	Y	81.	Kill-Shift MX $ to supplies/parts	N
30.	Provide $30b for failed S&Ls	N	82.	Kill-Buy America provision at DOD	Y
31.	Allow use of force against Iraq	N	83.	Allow nuclear testing-5+ kilotons	Y
32.	Allow $15b in foreign aid for 1991	Y	84.	Allow SALT II to be exceeded	N
33.	Civil Rights Act of 1990	Y	85.	$ to vets exposed to nuclear bomb	Y
34.	Block cancellation of Egypt's debt	N	86.	Warn workers of disease exposure	?
35.	Cut El Salvador military aid 50%	Y	87.	Restore four civil rights laws	Y
36.	Reduce troops in NATO by 30,000	Y	88.	Disapprove uranium sales to Japan	Y
37.	Req increases in auto fuel efficiency	Y	89.	Notify Congress of covert operations	Y
38.	Bar taxpayer funding of campaigns	N	90.	Approval of $36m in Contra aid	N
39.	Limit textile import growth to 1%	N	91.	$18b deficit reduction compromise	Y
40.	Amendment to ban flag desecration	N	92.	Allow sale of hard-to-detect guns	?
41.	Let fed emp be politically active	Y	93.	Catastrophic health insurance	Y
42.	Reauthorize Amtrak-veto override	Y	94.	Bork nomination to Supreme Court	N
43.	Allow sale of assault weapons	N	95.	Kill-Void Panama Canal treaties	Y
44.	Retraining aid for coal miners	Y	96.	Kill-Insurance denial to AIDS+	Y
45.	Kill-Raise car emission standards	N	97.	Keep diplomatic immunity intact	Y
46.	Pull EPA nuclear plant authority	N	98.	Produce Bigeye nerve gas bomb	N
47.	Defer Chinese students' deportation	Y	99.	Balanced budget by '93-via targets	N
48.	Cut in capital gains tax	N	100.	Allow ASAT missile tests in space	N
49.	Establish CIA inspector general	N	101.	Limit space-based/ABM system tests	Y
50.	Kill-Sanctions against China	N	102.	Force reduction in trade barriers	Y
51.	Bar drug testing to receive AFDC	Y	103.	Repeal windfall profit tax on oil	N
52.	Kill-Allow force against drug planes	Y	104.	$1b/two year aid for the homeless	?

BRADLEY, BILL (continued)

105. Disallow $30m for AZT to poor	?	
106. Bar AIDS test-immigrants/marriage	?	
107. Kill-Biennial budget approval	Y	
108. Fairness doctrine in broadcasting	?	
109. Raise speed limit to 65 mph	N	
110. Immigration reform/alien amnesty	Y	
111. South Africa sanctions-veto override	Y	
112. Kill-Use of military in drug war	Y	
113. Tax overhaul to revise income tax	Y	
114. Submit nuclear test ban treaties	Y	
115. Prohibit sale of Stinger missiles	Y	
116. Prohibit binary chemical weapons	Y	
117. Kill-$10/barrel oil tariff increase	Y	
118. Grant tax amnesty provisions	Y	
119. Block Saudi arms sale-veto override	Y	
120. Balanced budget amendment	N	
121. Include veterans in spending cuts	N	
122. Bar $ to hazardous substance victims	N	
123. Allow seasonal workers in the US	N	
124. Let fed courts rule on school prayer	Y	
125. Presidential line-item veto	N	
126. Ease Gun Control Act of 1968	?	
127. Kill-Req 14-day wait for handguns	?	
128. Kill-15% min tax on corporations	Y	
129. Drop Social Security COLA	N	
130. Freeze funding for all programs	N	
131. Kill-Nuclear weapon freeze	N	
132. Keep decision narrowing Title IX	N	
133. Raise drinking age to 21	Y	
134. Allow production of MX missile	N	
135. Raise taxes/cut spending by $140b	N	
136. School prayer amendment	N	
137. Capital punishment-federal crimes	Y	
138. Ban government officials from taping	Y	
139. Martin Luther King holiday	Y	
140. Authorize Marines in Lebanon	N	
141. Amendment making abortion illegal	N	
142. Delete $1.2b for jobs creation	N	
143. Keep tobacco price supports	N	
144. Emergency housing aid of $5.1b	Y	

Presidential Support Score: 1991 - 32%   1990 - 32%

LAUTENBERG, FRANK R. -- New Jersey [Democrat]. Term Began/Expires: 1989-1994. Prior Terms: Senate: 1983-88. Born: January 23, 1924; Paterson, NJ. Education: Columbia University (B.S.). Military Service: U.S. Army, 1942. Occupation: Chief executive officer, Automatic Data Processing, Inc.; commissioner, Port Authority of New York and New Jersey.

1. Prohibit MFN status for China	Y	
2. Kill-Tie welfare to school attendance	Y	
3. Limit credit card interest rates	Y	
4. Confirm Gates as head of CIA	N	
5. Adoption of national energy policies	N	
6. Kill-Restrict NEA use of funds	Y	
7. Unemployment benefits extension	Y	
8. Confirm Thomas to Supreme Court	N	
9. Raise eligibility for unpaid leave	Y	
10. Notify parents of minors' abortions	N	
11. Move $3b from defense to domestic	Y	
12. End production of B-2 bomber	Y	
13. Cut SDI $1b to reduce deficit	Y	
14. Maintain strategic stability-Soviets	Y	
15. Kill-Allow women as combat pilots	N	
16. Kill-Allow HIV tests before surgery	Y	
17. Strike $12b aid to Int'l Mon Fund	N	
18. Raise Senate salary/omit honoraria	N	
19. Reduce space station funding $1.9b	Y	
20. Kill-Eliminate supercollider funds	N	
21. Req 5-day handgun waiting period	Y	
22. Life in prison instead of death	Y	
23. Exceptions to exclusionary rule	N	
24. Ban race as death sentence factor	N	
25. Campaign finance revisions	Y	
26. Kill-Term limits for senators	Y	
27. Require four presidential debates	Y	
28. Tighten ban on vertical price fixing	Y	
29. Kill-Freeze discretionary budget	Y	
30. Provide $30b for failed S&Ls	N	
31. Allow use of force against Iraq	N	
32. Allow $15b in foreign aid for 1991	Y	
33. Civil Rights Act of 1990	Y	
34. Block cancellation of Egypt's debt	N	
35. Cut El Salvador military aid 50%	Y	
36. Reduce troops in NATO by 30,000	Y	
37. Req increases in auto fuel efficiency	Y	
38. Bar taxpayer funding of campaigns	N	
39. Limit textile import growth to 1%	Y	
40. Amendment to ban flag desecration	N	
41. Let fed emp be politically active	Y	
42. Reauthorize Amtrak-veto override	Y	
43. Allow sale of assault weapons	N	
44. Retraining aid for coal miners	Y	
45. Kill-Raise car emission standards	N	
46. Pull EPA nuclear plant authority	N	
47. Defer Chinese students' deportation	Y	
48. Cut in capital gains tax	N	
49. Establish CIA inspector general	Y	
50. Kill-Sanctions against China	?	
51. Bar drug testing to receive AFDC	Y	
52. Kill-Allow force against drug planes	Y	
53. Include illegal aliens in census	Y	
54. Restitution to Japanese interned	Y	
55. Troop reduction in Europe of 50%	N	
56. Increase SDI research to $4.3b	N	
57. Kill-Pay homeless below min wage	Y	
58. Ban airline smoking within US	Y	
59. Bar transfer of FS-X technology	Y	
60. Limit liability for oil spills	N	
61. Restructure S&L industry	Y	
62. Ban $ to illegal foreign activities	Y	
63. Req immigrant fluency in English	N	
64. Allow aliens' families to stay in US	Y	
65. Expand child care aid/tax credit	Y	
66. Raise minimum wage w/subminimum	Y	
67. Freeze outlays except SS/Medicare	N	
68. Kill-Shift $5b of DOD to domestic	Y	

LAUTENBERG, FRANK R. (continued)

69. Confirm Tower as sec of defense	N	
70. Bar abortion $ except to save mother	N	
71. Kill-Warn AIDS carriers' spouses	Y	
72. Allow religious schools to bar gays	N	
73. 60 days' notice of plant closings	Y	
74. Allow poison pills in corp takeovers	N	
75. Kill-Workfare program	Y	
76. Prohibit employee polygraph testing	Y	
77. Cap Medicare patients' liability	Y	
78. Revise unfair trade practices	Y	
79. Kill-Shift SDI $ to conv weapons	N	
80. Kill-Shift SDI $ to accidental launch	Y	
81. Kill-Shift MX $ to supplies/parts	N	
82. Kill-Buy America provision at DOD	N	
83. Allow nuclear testing-5+ kilotons	N	
84. Allow SALT II to be exceeded	N	
85. $ to vets exposed to nuclear bomb	?	
86. Warn workers of disease exposure	Y	
87. Restore four civil rights laws	Y	
88. Disapprove uranium sales to Japan	?	
89. Notify Congress of covert operations	Y	
90. Approval of $36m in Contra aid	N	
91. $18b deficit reduction compromise	Y	
92. Allow sale of hard-to-detect guns	N	
93. Catastrophic health insurance	Y	
94. Bork nomination to Supreme Court	N	
95. Kill-Void Panama Canal treaties	Y	
96. Kill-Insurance denial to AIDS+	Y	
97. Keep diplomatic immunity intact	Y	
98. Produce Bigeye nerve gas bomb	N	
99. Balanced budget by '93-via targets	N	
100. Allow ASAT missile tests in space	N	
101. Limit space-based/ABM system tests	?	
102. Force reduction in trade barriers	Y	
103. Repeal windfall profit tax on oil	N	
104. $1b/two year aid for the homeless	Y	
105. Disallow $30m for AZT to poor	N	
106. Bar AIDS test-immigrants/marriage	Y	
107. Kill-Biennial budget approval	Y	
108. Fairness doctrine in broadcasting	?	
109. Raise speed limit to 65 mph	N	
110. Immigration reform/alien amnesty	Y	
111. South Africa sanctions-veto override	Y	
112. Kill-Use of military in drug war	?	
113. Tax overhaul to revise income tax	Y	
114. Submit nuclear test ban treaties	Y	
115. Prohibit sale of Stinger missiles	Y	
116. Prohibit binary chemical weapons	Y	
117. Kill-$10/barrel oil tariff increase	Y	
118. Grant tax amnesty provisions	?	
119. Block Saudi arms sale-veto override	Y	
120. Balanced budget amendment	N	
121. Include veterans in spending cuts	N	
122. Bar $ to hazardous substance victims	N	
123. Allow seasonal workers in the US	N	
124. Let fed courts rule on school prayer	Y	
125. Presidential line-item veto	N	
126. Ease Gun Control Act of 1968	N	
127. Kill-Req 14-day wait for handguns	N	
128. Kill-15% min tax on corporations	Y	
129. Drop Social Security COLA	N	
130. Freeze funding for all programs	N	
131. Kill-Nuclear weapon freeze	N	
132. Keep decision narrowing Title IX	N	
133. Raise drinking age to 21	Y	
134. Allow production of MX missile	N	
135. Raise taxes/cut spending by $140b	N	
136. School prayer amendment	N	
137. Capital punishment-federal crimes	N	
138. Ban government officials from taping	Y	
139. Martin Luther King holiday	Y	
140. Authorize Marines in Lebanon	N	
141. Amendment making abortion illegal	N	

Presidential Support Score: 1991 - 31%   1990 - 25%

NEW MEXICO

DOMENICI, PETE V. -- New Mexico [Republican]. Term Began/Expires: 1991/1996. Prior Terms: Senate: 1973-84. Born: May 7, 1932; Albuquerque, NM. Education: University of Albuquerque; University of New Mexico (B.S.); Denver University (LL.D.). Occupation: Albuquerque city commissioner.

1. Prohibit MFN status for China	N	
2. Kill-Tie welfare to school attendance	N	
3. Limit credit card interest rates	Y	
4. Confirm Gates as head of CIA	Y	
5. Adoption of national energy policies	Y	
6. Kill-Restrict NEA use of funds	Y	
7. Unemployment benefits extension	N	
8. Confirm Thomas to Supreme Court	Y	
9. Raise eligibility for unpaid leave	N	
10. Notify parents of minors' abortions	Y	
11. Move $3b from defense to domestic	N	
12. End production of B-2 bomber	N	
13. Cut SDI $1b to reduce deficit	N	
14. Maintain strategic stability-Soviets	N	
15. Kill-Allow women as combat pilots	N	
16. Kill-Allow HIV tests before surgery	N	
17. Strike $12b aid to Int'l Mon Fund	N	
18. Raise Senate salary/omit honoraria	Y	
19. Reduce space station funding $1.9b	N	
20. Kill-Eliminate supercollider funds	Y	
21. Req 5-day handgun waiting period	Y	
22. Life in prison instead of death	N	

DOMENICI, PETE V. (continued)

23. Exceptions to exclusionary rule	Y
24. Ban race as death sentence factor	Y
25. Campaign finance revisions	N
26. Kill-Term limits for senators	N
27. Require four presidential debates	N
28. Tighten ban on vertical price fixing	Y
29. Kill-Freeze discretionary budget	Y
30. Provide $30b for failed S&Ls	Y
31. Allow use of force against Iraq	Y
32. Allow $15b in foreign aid for 1991	N
33. Civil Rights Act of 1990	Y
34. Block cancellation of Egypt's debt	N
35. Cut El Salvador military aid 50%	Y
36. Reduce troops in NATO by 30,000	N
37. Req increases in auto fuel efficiency	N
38. Bar taxpayer funding of campaigns	Y
39. Limit textile import growth to 1%	Y
40. Amendment to ban flag desecration	Y
41. Let fed emp be politically active	N
42. Reauthorize Amtrak-veto override	N
43. Allow sale of assault weapons	Y
44. Retraining aid for coal miners	N
45. Kill-Raise car emission standards	Y
46. Pull EPA nuclear plant authority	N
47. Defer Chinese students' deportation	N
48. Cut in capital gains tax	Y
49. Establish CIA inspector general	Y
50. Kill-Sanctions against China	N
51. Bar drug testing to receive AFDC	N
52. Kill-Allow force against drug planes	N
53. Include illegal aliens in census	Y
54. Restitution to Japanese interned	Y
55. Troop reduction in Europe of 50%	N
56. Increase SDI research to $4.3b	Y
57. Kill-Pay homeless below min wage	N
58. Ban airline smoking within US	Y
59. Bar transfer of FS-X technology	N
60. Limit liability for oil spills	Y
61. Restructure S&L industry	N
62. Ban $ to illegal foreign activities	N
63. Req immigrant fluency in English	N
64. Allow aliens' families to stay in US	Y
65. Expand child care aid/tax credit	N
66. Raise minimum wage w/subminimum	N
67. Freeze outlays except SS/Medicare	N
68. Kill-Shift $5b of DOD to domestic	Y
69. Confirm Tower as sec of defense	Y
70. Bar abortion $ except to save mother	Y
71. Kill-Warn AIDS carriers' spouses	N
72. Allow religious schools to bar gays	Y
73. 60 days' notice of plant closings	N
74. Allow poison pills in corp takeovers	N
75. Kill-Workfare program	N
76. Prohibit employee polygraph testing	?
77. Cap Medicare patients' liability	Y
78. Revise unfair trade practices	N
79. Kill-Shift SDI $ to conv weapons	Y
80. Kill-Shift SDI $ to accidental launch	Y
81. Kill-Shift MX $ to supplies/parts	Y
82. Kill-Buy America provision at DOD	N
83. Allow nuclear testing-5+ kilotons	Y

84. Allow SALT II to be exceeded	Y
85. $ to vets exposed to nuclear bomb	Y
86. Warn workers of disease exposure	N
87. Restore four civil rights laws	Y
88. Disapprove uranium sales to Japan	N
89. Notify Congress of covert operations	Y
90. Approval of $36m in Contra aid	Y
91. $18b deficit reduction compromise	Y
92. Allow sale of hard-to-detect guns	Y
93. Catastrophic health insurance	Y
94. Bork nomination to Supreme Court	Y
95. Kill-Void Panama Canal treaties	N
96. Kill-Insurance denial to AIDS+	N
97. Keep diplomatic immunity intact	N
98. Produce Bigeye nerve gas bomb	Y
99. Balanced budget by '93-via targets	N
100. Allow ASAT missile tests in space	Y
101. Limit space-based/ABM system tests	N
102. Force reduction in trade barriers	N
103. Repeal windfall profit tax on oil	Y
104. $1b/two year aid for the homeless	Y
105. Disallow $30m for AZT to poor	N
106. Bar AIDS test-immigrants/marriage	Y
107. Kill-Biennial budget approval	N
108. Fairness doctrine in broadcasting	N
109. Raise speed limit to 65 mph	Y
110. Immigration reform/alien amnesty	N
111. South Africa sanctions-veto override	Y
112. Kill-Use of military in drug war	Y
113. Tax overhaul to revise income tax	Y
114. Submit nuclear test ban treaties	N
115. Prohibit sale of Stinger missiles	N
116. Prohibit binary chemical weapons	N
117. Kill-$10/barrel oil tariff increase	N
118. Grant tax amnesty provisions	Y
119. Block Saudi arms sale-veto override	N
120. Balanced budget amendment	Y
121. Include veterans in spending cuts	Y
122. Bar $ to hazardous substance victims	Y
123. Allow seasonal workers in the US	Y
124. Let fed courts rule on school prayer	Y
125. Presidential line-item veto	Y
126. Ease Gun Control Act of 1968	Y
127. Kill-Req 14-day wait for handguns	Y
128. Kill-15% min tax on corporations	Y
129. Drop Social Security COLA	Y
130. Freeze funding for all programs	N
131. Kill-Nuclear weapon freeze	Y
132. Keep decision narrowing Title IX	Y
133. Raise drinking age to 21	Y
134. Allow production of MX missile	Y
135. Raise taxes/cut spending by $140b	Y
136. School prayer amendment	Y
137. Capital punishment-federal crimes	Y
138. Ban government officials from taping	N
139. Martin Luther King holiday	Y
140. Authorize Marines in Lebanon	Y
141. Amendment making abortion illegal	Y
142. Delete $1.2b for jobs creation	Y
143. Keep tobacco price supports	Y
144. Emergency housing aid of $5.1b	N

Presidential Support Score: 1991 - 93% 1990 - 67%

BINGAMAN, JEFF -- New Mexico [Democrat]. Term Began/Expires: 1989/1994. Prior Terms: Senate: 1983-88. Born: October 3, 1943; El Paso, TX. Education: Harvard College (B.A.); Stanford Law School. Military Service: U.S. Army Reserve, 1968-74. Occupation: New Mexico assistant attorney general (1969); private attorney (1971-73); attorney general (1979-82).

1. Prohibit MFN status for China	Y	
2. Kill-Tie welfare to school attendance	Y	
3. Limit credit card interest rates	N	
4. Confirm Gates as head of CIA	N	
5. Adoption of national energy policies	Y	
6. Kill-Restrict NEA use of funds	Y	
7. Unemployment benefits extension	Y	
8. Confirm Thomas to Supreme Court	N	
9. Raise eligibility for unpaid leave	Y	
10. Notify parents of minors' abortions	N	
11. Move $3b from defense to domestic	N	
12. End production of B-2 bomber	N	
13. Cut SDI $1b to reduce deficit	N	
14. Maintain strategic stability-Soviets	Y	
15. Kill-Allow women as combat pilots	N	
16. Kill-Allow HIV tests before surgery	Y	
17. Strike $12b aid to Int'l Mon Fund	N	
18. Raise Senate salary/omit honoraria	Y	
19. Reduce space station funding $1.9b	N	
20. Kill-Eliminate supercollider funds	Y	
21. Req 5-day handgun waiting period	Y	
22. Life in prison instead of death	N	
23. Exceptions to exclusionary rule	N	
24. Ban race as death sentence factor	Y	
25. Campaign finance revisions	Y	
26. Kill-Term limits for senators	Y	
27. Require four presidential debates	Y	
28. Tighten ban on vertical price fixing	Y	
29. Kill-Freeze discretionary budget	Y	
30. Provide $30b for failed S&Ls	Y	
31. Allow use of force against Iraq	N	
32. Allow $15b in foreign aid for 1991	Y	
33. Civil Rights Act of 1990	Y	
34. Block cancellation of Egypt's debt	N	
35. Cut El Salvador military aid 50%	Y	
36. Reduce troops in NATO by 30,000	Y	
37. Req increases in auto fuel efficiency	Y	
38. Bar taxpayer funding of campaigns	N	
39. Limit textile import growth to 1%	N	
40. Amendment to ban flag desecration	N	
41. Let fed emp be politically active	Y	
42. Reauthorize Amtrak-veto override	Y	
43. Allow sale of assault weapons	Y	
44. Retraining aid for coal miners	Y	
45. Kill-Raise car emission standards	N	
46. Pull EPA nuclear plant authority	Y	
47. Defer Chinese students' deportation	Y	
48. Cut in capital gains tax	N	
49. Establish CIA inspector general	Y	
50. Kill-Sanctions against China	Y	
51. Bar drug testing to receive AFDC	Y	
52. Kill-Allow force against drug planes	Y	
53. Include illegal aliens in census	Y	
54. Restitution to Japanese interned	Y	
55. Troop reduction in Europe of 50%	N	
56. Increase SDI research to $4.3b	Y	
57. Kill-Pay homeless below min wage	Y	
58. Ban airline smoking within US	Y	
59. Bar transfer of FS-X technology	Y	

60. Limit liability for oil spills	Y	
61. Restructure S&L industry	Y	
62. Ban $ to illegal foreign activities	Y	
63. Req immigrant fluency in English	N	
64. Allow aliens' families to stay in US	Y	
65. Expand child care aid/tax credit	Y	
66. Raise minimum wage w/subminimum	Y	
67. Freeze outlays except SS/Medicare	N	
68. Kill-Shift $5b of DOD to domestic	N	
69. Confirm Tower as sec of defense	N	
70. Bar abortion $ except to save mother	N	
71. Kill-Warn AIDS carriers' spouses	Y	
72. Allow religious schools to bar gays	Y	
73. 60 days' notice of plant closings	Y	
74. Allow poison pills in corp takeovers	Y	
75. Kill-Workfare program	Y	
76. Prohibit employee polygraph testing	Y	
77. Cap Medicare patients' liability	Y	
78. Revise unfair trade practices	Y	
79. Kill-Shift SDI $ to conv weapons	Y	
80. Kill-Shift SDI $ to accidental launch	Y	
81. Kill-Shift MX $ to supplies/parts	N	
82. Kill-Buy America provision at DOD	Y	
83. Allow nuclear testing-5+ kilotons	Y	
84. Allow SALT II to be exceeded	N	
85. $ to vets exposed to nuclear bomb	Y	
86. Warn workers of disease exposure	N	
87. Restore four civil rights laws	Y	
88. Disapprove uranium sales to Japan	N	
89. Notify Congress of covert operations	Y	
90. Approval of $36m in Contra aid	N	
91. $18b deficit reduction compromise	Y	
92. Allow sale of hard-to-detect guns	?	
93. Catastrophic health insurance	Y	
94. Bork nomination to Supreme Court	N	
95. Kill-Void Panama Canal treaties	Y	
96. Kill-Insurance denial to AIDS+	N	
97. Keep diplomatic immunity intact	Y	
98. Produce Bigeye nerve gas bomb	Y	
99. Balanced budget by '93-via targets	N	
100. Allow ASAT missile tests in space	N	
101. Limit space-based/ABM system tests	Y	
102. Force reduction in trade barriers	Y	
103. Repeal windfall profit tax on oil	Y	
104. $1b/two year aid for the homeless	Y	
105. Disallow $30m for AZT to poor	N	
106. Bar AIDS test-immigrants/marriage	Y	
107. Kill-Biennial budget approval	Y	
108. Fairness doctrine in broadcasting	Y	
109. Raise speed limit to 65 mph	Y	
110. Immigration reform/alien amnesty	Y	
111. South Africa sanctions-veto override	Y	
112. Kill-Use of military in drug war	Y	
113. Tax overhaul to revise income tax	Y	
114. Submit nuclear test ban treaties	Y	
115. Prohibit sale of Stinger missiles	Y	
116. Prohibit binary chemical weapons	N	
117. Kill-$10/barrel oil tariff increase	N	
118. Grant tax amnesty provisions	Y	

BINGAMAN, JEFF (continued)

119. Block Saudi arms sale-veto override	Y	
120. Balanced budget amendment	Y	
121. Include veterans in spending cuts	Y	
122. Bar $ to hazardous substance victims	Y	
123. Allow seasonal workers in the US	N	
124. Let fed courts rule on school prayer	Y	
125. Presidential line-item veto	N	
126. Ease Gun Control Act of 1968	Y	
127. Kill-Req 14-day wait for handguns	Y	
128. Kill-15% min tax on corporations	Y	
129. Drop Social Security COLA	N	
130. Freeze funding for all programs	Y	
131. Kill-Nuclear weapon freeze	N	
132. Keep decision narrowing Title IX	N	
133. Raise drinking age to 21	Y	
134. Allow production of MX missile	N	
135. Raise taxes/cut spending by $140b	N	
136. School prayer amendment	N	
137. Capital punishment-federal crimes	N	
138. Ban government officials from taping	Y	
139. Martin Luther King holiday	Y	
140. Authorize Marines in Lebanon	N	
141. Amendment making abortion illegal	N	

Presidential Support Score: 1991 - 51%   1990 - 35%

NEW YORK

MOYNIHAN, DANIEL PATRICK -- New York [Democrat]. Term Began/Expires: 1989/1994. Prior Terms: Senate: 1977-88. Born: March 16, 1927; Tulsa, OK. Education: City College of New York; Tufts University (B.A.); Fletcher School of Law and Diplomacy (M.A., Ph.D.); London School of Economics and Political Science. Military Service: U.S. Navy, 1944-47. Occupation: Assistant secretary and acting secretary to the governor of New York (1955-58); director, New York State Government Research Project (1959-61); special assistant secretary of Labor (1961-62); executive assistant to secretary of Labor (1962-63); assistant secretary of Labor (1963-65); director, Joint Center of Urban Studies, MIT and Harvard (1966-69); professor, education and politics, Harvard (1966-73); assistant to president for Urban Affairs; counselor to president (1969-70); presidential consultant (1971-73); U.N. representative (1971); ambassador to India (1973-75); professor of government, Harvard (1972); author; ambassador to U.N. (1975-76).

1. Prohibit MFN status for China	Y	
2. Kill-Tie welfare to school attendance	Y	
3. Limit credit card interest rates	Y	
4. Confirm Gates as head of CIA	N	
5. Adoption of national energy policies	N	
6. Kill-Restrict NEA use of funds	Y	
7. Unemployment benefits extension	Y	
8. Confirm Thomas to Supreme Court	N	
9. Raise eligibility for unpaid leave	Y	
10. Notify parents of minors' abortions	N	
11. Move $3b from defense to domestic	N	
12. End production of B-2 bomber	Y	
13. Cut SDI $1b to reduce deficit	Y	
14. Maintain strategic stability-Soviets	Y	
15. Kill-Allow women as combat pilots	Y	
16. Kill-Allow HIV tests before surgery	Y	
17. Strike $12b aid to Int'l Mon Fund	N	
18. Raise Senate salary/omit honoraria	Y	
19. Reduce space station funding $1.9b	Y	
20. Kill-Eliminate supercollider funds	Y	
21. Req 5-day handgun waiting period	Y	
22. Life in prison instead of death	Y	
23. Exceptions to exclusionary rule	N	
24. Ban race as death sentence factor	N	
25. Campaign finance revisions	Y	
26. Kill-Term limits for senators	Y	
27. Require four presidential debates	?	
28. Tighten ban on vertical price fixing	Y	
29. Kill-Freeze discretionary budget	Y	
30. Provide $30b for failed S&Ls	Y	
31. Allow use of force against Iraq	N	
32. Allow $15b in foreign aid for 1991	Y	
33. Civil Rights Act of 1990	Y	
34. Block cancellation of Egypt's debt	N	
35. Cut El Salvador military aid 50%	Y	
36. Reduce troops in NATO by 30,000	Y	
37. Req increases in auto fuel efficiency	Y	
38. Bar taxpayer funding of campaigns	N	
39. Limit textile import growth to 1%	Y	
40. Amendment to ban flag desecration	N	
41. Let fed emp be politically active	Y	
42. Reauthorize Amtrak-veto override	Y	
43. Allow sale of assault weapons	N	
44. Retraining aid for coal miners	Y	
45. Kill-Raise car emission standards	N	
46. Pull EPA nuclear plant authority	N	
47. Defer Chinese students' deportation	Y	
48. Cut in capital gains tax	N	
49. Establish CIA inspector general	Y	
50. Kill-Sanctions against China	Y	
51. Bar drug testing to receive AFDC	Y	
52. Kill-Allow force against drug planes	Y	
53. Include illegal aliens in census	Y	
54. Restitution to Japanese interned	Y	
55. Troop reduction in Europe of 50%	N	
56. Increase SDI research to $4.3b	N	

MOYNIHAN, DANIEL P. (continued)

57. Kill-Pay homeless below min wage	Y	
58. Ban airline smoking within US	Y	
59. Bar transfer of FS-X technology	Y	
60. Limit liability for oil spills	Y	
61. Restructure S&L industry	Y	
62. Ban $ to illegal foreign activities	Y	
63. Req immigrant fluency in English	N	
64. Allow aliens' families to stay in US	Y	
65. Expand child care aid/tax credit	Y	
66. Raise minimum wage w/subminimum	Y	
67. Freeze outlays except SS/Medicare	N	
68. Kill-Shift $5b of DOD to domestic	Y	
69. Confirm Tower as sec of defense	N	
70. Bar abortion $ except to save mother	N	
71. Kill-Warn AIDS carriers' spouses	Y	
72. Allow religious schools to bar gays	N	
73. 60 days' notice of plant closings	Y	
74. Allow poison pills in corp takeovers	Y	
75. Kill-Workfare program	Y	
76. Prohibit employee polygraph testing	Y	
77. Cap Medicare patients' liability	Y	
78. Revise unfair trade practices	Y	
79. Kill-Shift SDI $ to conv weapons	N	
80. Kill-Shift SDI $ to accidental launch	Y	
81. Kill-Shift MX $ to supplies/parts	Y	
82. Kill-Buy America provision at DOD	N	
83. Allow nuclear testing-5+ kilotons	N	
84. Allow SALT II to be exceeded	N	
85. $ to vets exposed to nuclear bomb	?	
86. Warn workers of disease exposure	Y	
87. Restore four civil rights laws	Y	
88. Disapprove uranium sales to Japan	Y	
89. Notify Congress of covert operations	Y	
90. Approval of $36m in Contra aid	N	
91. $18b deficit reduction compromise	Y	
92. Allow sale of hard-to-detect guns	N	
93. Catastrophic health insurance	Y	
94. Bork nomination to Supreme Court	N	
95. Kill-Void Panama Canal treaties	Y	
96. Kill-Insurance denial to AIDS+	Y	
97. Keep diplomatic immunity intact	Y	
98. Produce Bigeye nerve gas bomb	N	
99. Balanced budget by '93-via targets	Y	
100. Allow ASAT missile tests in space	N	

101. Limit space-based/ABM system tests	Y
102. Force reduction in trade barriers	Y
103. Repeal windfall profit tax on oil	N
104. $1b/two year aid for the homeless	Y
105. Disallow $30m for AZT to poor	N
106. Bar AIDS test-immigrants/marriage	Y
107. Kill-Biennial budget approval	Y
108. Fairness doctrine in broadcasting	Y
109. Raise speed limit to 65 mph	N
110. Immigration reform/alien amnesty	Y
111. South Africa sanctions-veto override	Y
112. Kill-Use of military in drug war	Y
113. Tax overhaul to revise income tax	Y
114. Submit nuclear test ban treaties	Y
115. Prohibit sale of Stinger missiles	N
116. Prohibit binary chemical weapons	Y
117. Kill-$10/barrel oil tariff increase	Y
118. Grant tax amnesty provisions	Y
119. Block Saudi arms sale-veto override	Y
120. Balanced budget amendment	N
121. Include veterans in spending cuts	N
122. Bar $ to hazardous substance victims	?
123. Allow seasonal workers in the US	N
124. Let fed courts rule on school prayer	Y
125. Presidential line-item veto	N
126. Ease Gun Control Act of 1968	N
127. Kill-Req 14-day wait for handguns	N
128. Kill-15% min tax on corporations	N
129. Drop Social Security COLA	N
130. Freeze funding for all programs	N
131. Kill-Nuclear weapon freeze	N
132. Keep decision narrowing Title IX	N
133. Raise drinking age to 21	Y
134. Allow production of MX missile	N
135. Raise taxes/cut spending by $140b	N
136. School prayer amendment	N
137. Capital punishment-federal crimes	Y
138. Ban government officials from taping	Y
139. Martin Luther King holiday	Y
140. Authorize Marines in Lebanon	N
141. Amendment making abortion illegal	N
142. Delete $1.2b for jobs creation	N
143. Keep tobacco price supports	N
144. Emergency housing aid of $5.1b	Y

Presidential Support Score: 1991 - 35%   1990 - 31%

D'AMATO, ALFONSE M. -- New York [Republican]. Term Began/Expires: 1987/1992. Prior Term: Senate: 1981-86. Born: August 1, 1937; Brooklyn, NY. Education: Syracuse University (B.S., J.D.). Occupation: Attorney; public administrator (1965-68); receiver of taxes (1969); town supervisor (1971-77); presiding supervisor and vice chairman, county board of supervisors (1977-80).

1. Prohibit MFN status for China	N	
2. Kill-Tie welfare to school attendance	N	
3. Limit credit card interest rates	Y	
4. Confirm Gates as head of CIA	Y	
5. Adoption of national energy policies	Y	
6. Kill-Restrict NEA use of funds	N	
7. Unemployment benefits extension	Y	
8. Confirm Thomas to Supreme Court	Y	
9. Raise eligibility for unpaid leave	Y	
10. Notify parents of minors' abortions	Y	

11. Move $3b from defense to domestic	N
12. End production of B-2 bomber	N
13. Cut SDI $1b to reduce deficit	N
14. Maintain strategic stability-Soviets	N
15. Kill-Allow women as combat pilots	N
16. Kill-Allow HIV tests before surgery	N
17. Strike $12b aid to Int'l Mon Fund	N
18. Raise Senate salary/omit honoraria	N
19. Reduce space station funding $1.9b	N
20. Kill-Eliminate supercollider funds	Y

D'AMATO, ALFONSE M. (continued)

21. Req 5-day handgun waiting period	Y	
22. Life in prison instead of death	N	
23. Exceptions to exclusionary rule	Y	
24. Ban race as death sentence factor	Y	
25. Campaign finance revisions	N	
26. Kill-Term limits for senators	N	
27. Require four presidential debates	N	
28. Tighten ban on vertical price fixing	Y	
29. Kill-Freeze discretionary budget	N	
30. Provide $30b for failed S&Ls	Y	
31. Allow use of force against Iraq	Y	
32. Allow $15b in foreign aid for 1991	Y	
33. Civil Rights Act of 1990	N	
34. Block cancellation of Egypt's debt	N	
35. Cut El Salvador military aid 50%	Y	
36. Reduce troops in NATO by 30,000	Y	
37. Req increases in auto fuel efficiency	Y	
38. Bar taxpayer funding of campaigns	Y	
39. Limit textile import growth to 1%	Y	
40. Amendment to ban flag desecration	Y	
41. Let fed emp be politically active	N	
42. Reauthorize Amtrak-veto override	Y	
43. Allow sale of assault weapons	N	
44. Retraining aid for coal miners	N	
45. Kill-Raise car emission standards	N	
46. Pull EPA nuclear plant authority	N	
47. Defer Chinese students' deportation	N	
48. Cut in capital gains tax	Y	
49. Establish CIA inspector general	Y	
50. Kill-Sanctions against China	Y	
51. Bar drug testing to receive AFDC	Y	
52. Kill-Allow force against drug planes	N	
53. Include illegal aliens in census	Y	
54. Restitution to Japanese interned	Y	
55. Troop reduction in Europe of 50%	N	
56. Increase SDI research to $4.3b	Y	
57. Kill-Pay homeless below min wage	Y	
58. Ban airline smoking within US	Y	
59. Bar transfer of FS-X technology	Y	
60. Limit liability for oil spills	N	
61. Restructure S&L industry	N	
62. Ban $ to illegal foreign activities	N	
63. Req immigrant fluency in English	N	
64. Allow aliens' families to stay in US	Y	
65. Expand child care aid/tax credit	Y	
66. Raise minimum wage w/subminimum	Y	
67. Freeze outlays except SS/Medicare	N	
68. Kill-Shift $5b of DOD to domestic	Y	
69. Confirm Tower as sec of defense	Y	
70. Bar abortion $ except to save mother	Y	
71. Kill-Warn AIDS carriers' spouses	N	
72. Allow religious schools to bar gays	Y	
73. 60 days' notice of plant closings	Y	
74. Allow poison pills in corp takeovers	N	
75. Kill-Workfare program	N	
76. Prohibit employee polygraph testing	Y	
77. Cap Medicare patients' liability	Y	
78. Revise unfair trade practices	N	
79. Kill-Shift SDI $ to conv weapons	Y	
80. Kill-Shift SDI $ to accidental launch	N	
81. Kill-Shift MX $ to supplies/parts	Y	
82. Kill-Buy America provision at DOD	N	

83. Allow nuclear testing-5+ kilotons	Y	
84. Allow SALT II to be exceeded	Y	
85. $ to vets exposed to nuclear bomb	Y	
86. Warn workers of disease exposure	N	
87. Restore four civil rights laws	N	
88. Disapprove uranium sales to Japan	N	
89. Notify Congress of covert operations	Y	
90. Approval of $36m in Contra aid	Y	
91. $18b deficit reduction compromise	Y	
92. Allow sale of hard-to-detect guns	N	
93. Catastrophic health insurance	Y	
94. Bork nomination to Supreme Court	Y	
95. Kill-Void Panama Canal treaties	Y	
96. Kill-Insurance denial to AIDS+	N	
97. Keep diplomatic immunity intact	N	
98. Produce Bigeye nerve gas bomb	Y	
99. Balanced budget by '93-via targets	N	
100. Allow ASAT missile tests in space	Y	
101. Limit space-based/ABM system tests	N	
102. Force reduction in trade barriers	Y	
103. Repeal windfall profit tax on oil	N	
104. $1b/two year aid for the homeless	N	
105. Disallow $30m for AZT to poor	N	
106. Bar AIDS test-immigrants/marriage	N	
107. Kill-Biennial budget approval	N	
108. Fairness doctrine in broadcasting	N	
109. Raise speed limit to 65 mph	N	
110. Immigration reform/alien amnesty	Y	
111. South Africa sanctions-veto override	Y	
112. Kill-Use of military in drug war	N	
113. Tax overhaul to revise income tax	Y	
114. Submit nuclear test ban treaties	Y	
115. Prohibit sale of Stinger missiles	Y	
116. Prohibit binary chemical weapons	N	
117. Kill-$10/barrel oil tariff increase	Y	
118. Grant tax amnesty provisions	Y	
119. Block Saudi arms sale-veto override	Y	
120. Balanced budget amendment	Y	
121. Include veterans in spending cuts	Y	
122. Bar $ to hazardous substance victims	N	
123. Allow seasonal workers in the US	Y	
124. Let fed courts rule on school prayer	Y	
125. Presidential line-item veto	Y	
126. Ease Gun Control Act of 1968	Y	
127. Kill-Req 14-day wait for handguns	Y	
128. Kill-15% min tax on corporations	Y	
129. Drop Social Security COLA	N	
130. Freeze funding for all programs	N	
131. Kill-Nuclear weapon freeze	Y	
132. Keep decision narrowing Title IX	Y	
133. Raise drinking age to 21	Y	
134. Allow production of MX missile	Y	
135. Raise taxes/cut spending by $140b	Y	
136. School prayer amendment	Y	
137. Capital punishment-federal crimes	Y	
138. Ban government officials from taping	N	
139. Martin Luther King holiday	Y	
140. Authorize Marines in Lebanon	Y	
141. Amendment making abortion illegal	Y	
142. Delete $1.2b for jobs creation	N	
143. Keep tobacco price supports	N	
144. Emergency housing aid of $5.1b	Y	

Presidential Support Score: 1991 - 79%   1990 - 68%

NORTH CAROLINA

HELMS, JESSE -- North Carolina [Republican]. Term Began/Expires: 1991/1996. Prior Terms: Senate: 1973-90. Born: October 18, 1921; Monroe, N.C. Education: Wingate Junior College; Wake Forest College. Military Service: U.S. Navy, 1942-45. Occupation: City Editor, *The Raleigh Times*; Senate staff member; executive director, North Carolina Bankers Assn. (1953-60); executive vice president, WRAL-TV and Tobacco Radio Network (1960-72).

1. Prohibit MFN status for China	Y	
2. Kill-Tie welfare to school attendance	N	
3. Limit credit card interest rates	N	
4. Confirm Gates as head of CIA	Y	
5. Adoption of national energy policies	Y	
6. Kill-Restrict NEA use of funds	N	
7. Unemployment benefits extension	N	
8. Confirm Thomas to Supreme Court	Y	
9. Raise eligibility for unpaid leave	N	
10. Notify parents of minors' abortions	Y	
11. Move $3b from defense to domestic	N	
12. End production of B-2 bomber	N	
13. Cut SDI $1b to reduce deficit	N	
14. Maintain strategic stability-Soviets	N	
15. Kill-Allow women as combat pilots	Y	
16. Kill-Allow HIV tests before surgery	N	
17. Strike $12b aid to Int'l Mon Fund	Y	
18. Raise Senate salary/omit honoraria	Y	
19. Reduce space station funding $1.9b	N	
20. Kill-Eliminate supercollider funds	Y	
21. Req 5-day handgun waiting period	N	
22. Life in prison instead of death	N	
23. Exceptions to exclusionary rule	Y	
24. Ban race as death sentence factor	Y	
25. Campaign finance revisions	?	
26. Kill-Term limits for senators	?	
27. Require four presidential debates	N	
28. Tighten ban on vertical price fixing	N	
29. Kill-Freeze discretionary budget	N	
30. Provide $30b for failed S&Ls	N	
31. Allow use of force against Iraq	Y	
32. Allow $15b in foreign aid for 1991	N	
33. Civil Rights Act of 1990	N	
34. Block cancellation of Egypt's debt	Y	
35. Cut El Salvador military aid 50%	N	
36. Reduce troops in NATO by 30,000	Y	
37. Req increases in auto fuel efficiency	N	
38. Bar taxpayer funding of campaigns	Y	
39. Limit textile import growth to 1%	Y	
40. Amendment to ban flag desecration	Y	
41. Let fed emp be politically active	N	
42. Reauthorize Amtrak-veto override	N	
43. Allow sale of assault weapons	Y	
44. Retraining aid for coal miners	N	
45. Kill-Raise car emission standards	N	
46. Pull EPA nuclear plant authority	Y	
47. Defer Chinese students' deportation	Y	
48. Cut in capital gains tax	Y	
49. Establish CIA inspector general	N	
50. Kill-Sanctions against China	N	

51. Bar drug testing to receive AFDC	N	
52. Kill-Allow force against drug planes	N	
53. Include illegal aliens in census	N	
54. Restitution to Japanese interned	N	
55. Troop reduction in Europe of 50%	Y	
56. Increase SDI research to $4.3b	Y	
57. Kill-Pay homeless below min wage	N	
58. Ban airline smoking within US	N	
59. Bar transfer of FS-X technology	Y	
60. Limit liability for oil spills	N	
61. Restructure S&L industry	N	
62. Ban $ to illegal foreign activities	N	
63. Req immigrant fluency in English	Y	
64. Allow aliens' families to stay in US	N	
65. Expand child care aid/tax credit	N	
66. Raise minimum wage w/subminimum	N	
67. Freeze outlays except SS/Medicare	Y	
68. Kill-Shift $5b of DOD to domestic	Y	
69. Confirm Tower as sec of defense	Y	
70. Bar abortion $ except to save mother	Y	
71. Kill-Warn AIDS carriers' spouses	N	
72. Allow religious schools to bar gays	?	
73. 60 days' notice of plant closings	?	
74. Allow poison pills in corp takeovers	N	
75. Kill-Workfare program	N	
76. Prohibit employee polygraph testing	N	
77. Cap Medicare patients' liability	N	
78. Revise unfair trade practices	N	
79. Kill-Shift SDI $ to conv weapons	Y	
80. Kill-Shift SDI $ to accidental launch	N	
81. Kill-Shift MX $ to supplies/parts	Y	
82. Kill-Buy America provision at DOD	N	
83. Allow nuclear testing-5+ kilotons	Y	
84. Allow SALT II to be exceeded	Y	
85. $ to vets exposed to nuclear bomb	N	
86. Warn workers of disease exposure	N	
87. Restore four civil rights laws	N	
88. Disapprove uranium sales to Japan	Y	
89. Notify Congress of covert operations	N	
90. Approval of $36m in Contra aid	Y	
91. $18b deficit reduction compromise	N	
92. Allow sale of hard-to-detect guns	Y	
93. Catastrophic health insurance	N	
94. Bork nomination to Supreme Court	Y	
95. Kill-Void Panama Canal treaties	N	
96. Kill-Insurance denial to AIDS+	N	
97. Keep diplomatic immunity intact	N	
98. Produce Bigeye nerve gas bomb	Y	
99. Balanced budget by '93-via targets	Y	
100. Allow ASAT missile tests in space	Y	

HELMS, JESSE (continued)

101. Limit space-based/ABM system tests	N	123. Allow seasonal workers in the US	Y
102. Force reduction in trade barriers	N	124. Let fed courts rule on school prayer	N
103. Repeal windfall profit tax on oil	Y	125. Presidential line-item veto	Y
104. $1b/two year aid for the homeless	?	126. Ease Gun Control Act of 1968	Y
105. Disallow $30m for AZT to poor	Y	127. Kill-Req 14-day wait for handguns	Y
106. Bar AIDS test-immigrants/marriage	N	128. Kill-15% min tax on corporations	Y
107. Kill-Biennial budget approval	N	129. Drop Social Security COLA	Y
108. Fairness doctrine in broadcasting	Y	130. Freeze funding for all programs	N
109. Raise speed limit to 65 mph	Y	131. Kill-Nuclear weapon freeze	Y
110. Immigration reform/alien amnesty	N	132. Keep decision narrowing Title IX	Y
111. South Africa sanctions-veto override	N	133. Raise drinking age to 21	Y
112. Kill-Use of military in drug war	Y	134. Allow production of MX missile	Y
113. Tax overhaul to revise income tax	N	135. Raise taxes/cut spending by $140b	Y
114. Submit nuclear test ban treaties	N	136. School prayer amendment	Y
115. Prohibit sale of Stinger missiles	N	137. Capital punishment-federal crimes	Y
116. Prohibit binary chemical weapons	N	138. Ban government officials from taping	N
117. Kill-$10/barrel oil tariff increase	Y	139. Martin Luther King holiday	N
118. Grant tax amnesty provisions	N	140. Authorize Marines in Lebanon	Y
119. Block Saudi arms sale-veto override	N	141. Amendment making abortion illegal	P
120. Balanced budget amendment	Y	142. Delete $1.2b for jobs creation	Y
121. Include veterans in spending cuts	Y	143. Keep tobacco price supports	Y
122. Bar $ to hazardous substance victims	Y	144. Emergency housing aid of $5.1b	Y

Presidential Support Score: 1991 - 84%   1990 - 68%

SANFORD, TERRY -- North Carolina [Democrat]. Term Began/Expires: 1987/1992. Born: August 20, 1917; Laurinburg, NC. Education: Presbyterian Junior College; University of North Carolina-Chapel Hill (A.B.); University of North Carolina School of Law (J.D.). Military Service: U.S. Army, 1942-45; North Carolina National Guard, 1948-60. Occupation: Special Agent, Federal Bureau of Investigation (1941-42); Assistant Director, Institute of Government, University of North Carolina (1946-48); attorney and partner, Sanford, Phillips, McCoy & Weaver (1948-60) and Sanford, Adams, McCullough & Beard (1965-86); member and Secretary-Treasurer, North Carolina State Ports Authority (1950-53); state senator (1953-55); governor (1961-65); president, Duke University (1969-85); author.

1. Prohibit MFN status for China	Y	29. Kill-Freeze discretionary budget	Y
2. Kill-Tie welfare to school attendance	Y	30. Provide $30b for failed S&Ls	N
3. Limit credit card interest rates	Y	31. Allow use of force against Iraq	N
4. Confirm Gates as head of CIA	Y	32. Allow $15b in foreign aid for 1991	Y
5. Adoption of national energy policies	N	33. Civil Rights Act of 1990	Y
6. Kill-Restrict NEA use of funds	Y	34. Block cancellation of Egypt's debt	Y
7. Unemployment benefits extension	Y	35. Cut El Salvador military aid 50%	Y
8. Confirm Thomas to Supreme Court	N	36. Reduce troops in NATO by 30,000	Y
9. Raise eligibility for unpaid leave	Y	37. Req increases in auto fuel efficiency	Y
10. Notify parents of minors' abortions	N	38. Bar taxpayer funding of campaigns	N
11. Move $3b from defense to domestic	N	39. Limit textile import growth to 1%	Y
12. End production of B-2 bomber	N	40. Amendment to ban flag desecration	N
13. Cut SDI $1b to reduce deficit	Y	41. Let fed emp be politically active	Y
14. Maintain strategic stability-Soviets	Y	42. Reauthorize Amtrak-veto override	Y
15. Kill-Allow women as combat pilots	Y	43. Allow sale of assault weapons	N
16. Kill-Allow HIV tests before surgery	Y	44. Retraining aid for coal miners	Y
17. Strike $12b aid to Int'l Mon Fund	N	45. Kill-Raise car emission standards	Y
18. Raise Senate salary/omit honoraria	N	46. Pull EPA nuclear plant authority	N
19. Reduce space station funding $1.9b	Y	47. Defer Chinese students' deportation	Y
20. Kill-Eliminate supercollider funds	N	48. Cut in capital gains tax	N
21. Req 5-day handgun waiting period	Y	49. Establish CIA inspector general	Y
22. Life in prison instead of death	N	50. Kill-Sanctions against China	N
23. Exceptions to exclusionary rule	N	51. Bar drug testing to receive AFDC	Y
24. Ban race as death sentence factor	N	52. Kill-Allow force against drug planes	Y
25. Campaign finance revisions	Y	53. Include illegal aliens in census	N
26. Kill-Term limits for senators	Y	54. Restitution to Japanese interned	Y
27. Require four presidential debates	Y	55. Troop reduction in Europe of 50%	N
28. Tighten ban on vertical price fixing	Y	56. Increase SDI research to $4.3b	N

SANFORD, TERRY (continued)

57. Kill-Pay homeless below min wage	Y	
58. Ban airline smoking within US	N	
59. Bar transfer of FS-X technology	Y	
60. Limit liability for oil spills	Y	
61. Restructure S&L industry	Y	
62. Ban $ to illegal foreign activities	Y	
63. Req immigrant fluency in English	Y	
64. Allow aliens' families to stay in US	Y	
65. Expand child care aid/tax credit	Y	
66. Raise minimum wage w/subminimum	Y	
67. Freeze outlays except SS/Medicare	N	
68. Kill-Shift $5b of DOD to domestic	Y	
69. Confirm Tower as sec of defense	N	
70. Bar abortion $ except to save mother	N	
71. Kill-Warn AIDS carriers' spouses	Y	
72. Allow religious schools to bar gays	N	
73. 60 days' notice of plant closings	Y	
74. Allow poison pills in corp takeovers	Y	
75. Kill-Workfare program	Y	
76. Prohibit employee polygraph testing	Y	
77. Cap Medicare patients' liability	Y	
78. Revise unfair trade practices	Y	
79. Kill-Shift SDI $ to conv weapons	N	
80. Kill-Shift SDI $ to accidental launch	Y	
81. Kill-Shift MX $ to supplies/parts	N	
82. Kill-Buy America provision at DOD	N	
83. Allow nuclear testing-5+ kilotons	N	

84. Allow SALT II to be exceeded	N	
85. $ to vets exposed to nuclear bomb	Y	
86. Warn workers of disease exposure	N	
87. Restore four civil rights laws	Y	
88. Disapprove uranium sales to Japan	?	
89. Notify Congress of covert operations	Y	
90. Approval of $36m in Contra aid	N	
91. $18b deficit reduction compromise	Y	
92. Allow sale of hard-to-detect guns	?	
93. Catastrophic health insurance	Y	
94. Bork nomination to Supreme Court	N	
95. Kill-Void Panama Canal treaties	Y	
96. Kill-Insurance denial to AIDS+	N	
97. Keep diplomatic immunity intact	Y	
98. Produce Bigeye nerve gas bomb	N	
99. Balanced budget by '93-via targets	Y	
100. Allow ASAT missile tests in space	N	
101. Limit space-based/ABM system tests	Y	
102. Force reduction in trade barriers	Y	
103. Repeal windfall profit tax on oil	Y	
104. $1b/two year aid for the homeless	?	
105. Disallow $30m for AZT to poor	N	
106. Bar AIDS test-immigrants/marriage	Y	
107. Kill-Biennial budget approval	Y	
108. Fairness doctrine in broadcasting	Y	
109. Raise speed limit to 65 mph	Y	

Presidential Support Score: 1991 - 33%   1990 - 41%

NORTH DAKOTA

BURDICK, QUENTIN N. -- North Dakota [Democrat]. Term Began/Expires: 1989/1994. Prior Terms: House: 1959-60; Senate: 1960 (Special Election)-1988. Born: June 19, 1908; Munich, ND. Education: University of Minnesota (B.A., LL.B.). Occupation: Attorney.

1. Prohibit MFN status for China	N	
2. Kill-Tie welfare to school attendance	Y	
3. Limit credit card interest rates	Y	
4. Confirm Gates as head of CIA	N	
5. Adoption of national energy policies	N	
6. Kill-Restrict NEA use of funds	Y	
7. Unemployment benefits extension	Y	
8. Confirm Thomas to Supreme Court	N	
9. Raise eligibility for unpaid leave	Y	
10. Notify parents of minors' abortions	N	
11. Move $3b from defense to domestic	Y	
12. End production of B-2 bomber	Y	
13. Cut SDI $1b to reduce deficit	X	
14. Maintain strategic stability-Soviets	Y	
15. Kill-Allow women as combat pilots	N	
16. Kill-Allow HIV tests before surgery	Y	
17. Strike $12b aid to Int'l Mon Fund	N	
18. Raise Senate salary/omit honoraria	Y	
19. Reduce space station funding $1.9b	Y	
20. Kill-Eliminate supercollider funds	Y	
21. Req 5-day handgun waiting period	Y	
22. Life in prison instead of death	Y	
23. Exceptions to exclusionary rule	N	
24. Ban race as death sentence factor	N	

25. Campaign finance revisions	N	
26. Kill-Term limits for senators	Y	
27. Require four presidential debates	Y	
28. Tighten ban on vertical price fixing	Y	
29. Kill-Freeze discretionary budget	Y	
30. Provide $30b for failed S&Ls	Y	
31. Allow use of force against Iraq	N	
32. Allow $15b in foreign aid for 1991	N	
33. Civil Rights Act of 1990	Y	
34. Block cancellation of Egypt's debt	Y	
35. Cut El Salvador military aid 50%	Y	
36. Reduce troops in NATO by 30,000	Y	
37. Req increases in auto fuel efficiency	Y	
38. Bar taxpayer funding of campaigns	N	
39. Limit textile import growth to 1%	Y	
40. Amendment to ban flag desecration	Y	
41. Let fed emp be politically active	Y	
42. Reauthorize Amtrak-veto override	Y	
43. Allow sale of assault weapons	N	
44. Retraining aid for coal miners	Y	
45. Kill-Raise car emission standards	Y	
46. Pull EPA nuclear plant authority	Y	
47. Defer Chinese students' deportation	Y	
48. Cut in capital gains tax	N	

BURDICK, QUENTIN N. (continued)

49. Establish CIA inspector general	Y
50. Kill-Sanctions against China	Y
51. Bar drug testing to receive AFDC	Y
52. Kill-Allow force against drug planes	Y
53. Include illegal aliens in census	N
54. Restitution to Japanese interned	Y
55. Troop reduction in Europe of 50%	Y
56. Increase SDI research to $4.3b	N
57. Kill-Pay homeless below min wage	Y
58. Ban airline smoking within US	Y
59. Bar transfer of FS-X technology	Y
60. Limit liability for oil spills	Y
61. Restructure S&L industry	Y
62. Ban $ to illegal foreign activities	Y
63. Req immigrant fluency in English	Y
64. Allow aliens' families to stay in US	Y
65. Expand child care aid/tax credit	Y
66. Raise minimum wage w/subminimum	Y
67. Freeze outlays except SS/Medicare	N
68. Kill-Shift $5b of DOD to domestic	N
69. Confirm Tower as sec of defense	N
70. Bar abortion $ except to save mother	N
71. Kill-Warn AIDS carriers' spouses	Y
72. Allow religious schools to bar gays	Y
73. 60 days' notice of plant closings	Y
74. Allow poison pills in corp takeovers	Y
75. Kill-Workfare program	Y
76. Prohibit employee polygraph testing	Y
77. Cap Medicare patients' liability	Y
78. Revise unfair trade practices	Y
79. Kill-Shift SDI $ to conv weapons	N
80. Kill-Shift SDI $ to accidental launch	N
81. Kill-Shift MX $ to supplies/parts	Y
82. Kill-Buy America provision at DOD	N
83. Allow nuclear testing-5+ kilotons	N
84. Allow SALT II to be exceeded	N
85. $ to vets exposed to nuclear bomb	?
86. Warn workers of disease exposure	Y
87. Restore four civil rights laws	Y
88. Disapprove uranium sales to Japan	N
89. Notify Congress of covert operations	Y
90. Approval of $36m in Contra aid	N
91. $18b deficit reduction compromise	Y
92. Allow sale of hard-to-detect guns	Y
93. Catastrophic health insurance	Y
94. Bork nomination to Supreme Court	N
95. Kill-Void Panama Canal treaties	N
96. Kill-Insurance denial to AIDS+	Y

97. Keep diplomatic immunity intact	Y
98. Produce Bigeye nerve gas bomb	N
99. Balanced budget by '93-via targets	N
100. Allow ASAT missile tests in space	N
101. Limit space-based/ABM system tests	Y
102. Force reduction in trade barriers	Y
103. Repeal windfall profit tax on oil	Y
104. $1b/two year aid for the homeless	Y
105. Disallow $30m for AZT to poor	N
106. Bar AIDS test-immigrants/marriage	Y
107. Kill-Biennial budget approval	Y
108. Fairness doctrine in broadcasting	Y
109. Raise speed limit to 65 mph	Y
110. Immigration reform/alien amnesty	Y
111. South Africa sanctions-veto override	Y
112. Kill-Use of military in drug war	N
113. Tax overhaul to revise income tax	Y
114. Submit nuclear test ban treaties	Y
115. Prohibit sale of Stinger missiles	Y
116. Prohibit binary chemical weapons	Y
117. Kill-$10/barrel oil tariff increase	Y
118. Grant tax amnesty provisions	Y
119. Block Saudi arms sale-veto override	Y
120. Balanced budget amendment	N
121. Include veterans in spending cuts	N
122. Bar $ to hazardous substance victims	N
123. Allow seasonal workers in the US	N
124. Let fed courts rule on school prayer	+
125. Presidential line-item veto	N
126. Ease Gun Control Act of 1968	Y
127. Kill-Req 14-day wait for handguns	Y
128. Kill-15% min tax on corporations	N
129. Drop Social Security COLA	N
130. Freeze funding for all programs	Y
131. Kill-Nuclear weapon freeze	N
132. Keep decision narrowing Title IX	N
133. Raise drinking age to 21	+
134. Allow production of MX missile	N
135. Raise taxes/cut spending by $140b	N
136. School prayer amendment	N
137. Capital punishment-federal crimes	N
138. Ban government officials from taping	Y
139. Martin Luther King holiday	Y
140. Authorize Marines in Lebanon	N
141. Amendment making abortion illegal	N
142. Delete $1.2b for jobs creation	N
143. Keep tobacco price supports	N
144. Emergency housing aid of $5.1b	Y

Presidential Support Score: 1991 - 37%   1990 - 27%

CONRAD, KENT -- North Dakota [Democrat]. Term Began/Expires: 1987/1992. Born: March 12, 1948; Bismarck, ND. Education: University of Missouri; Stanford University (B.A.); George Washington University (M.B.A.). Occupation: Assistant to the Commissioner (1974-80) and Director of Management Planning and Personnel (1980), North Dakota Tax Department; state tax commissioner (1981-86).

1. Prohibit MFN status for China	N
2. Kill-Tie welfare to school attendance	Y
3. Limit credit card interest rates	Y
4. Confirm Gates as head of CIA	N
5. Adoption of national energy policies	Y
6. Kill-Restrict NEA use of funds	Y

7. Unemployment benefits extension	Y
8. Confirm Thomas to Supreme Court	N
9. Raise eligibility for unpaid leave	Y
10. Notify parents of minors' abortions	Y
11. Move $3b from defense to domestic	Y
12. End production of B-2 bomber	Y

CONRAD, KENT (continued)

13.	Cut SDI $1b to reduce deficit	N
14.	Maintain strategic stability-Soviets	Y
15.	Kill-Allow women as combat pilots	Y
16.	Kill-Allow HIV tests before surgery	N
17.	Strike $12b aid to Int'l Mon Fund	Y
18.	Raise Senate salary/omit honoraria	N
19.	Reduce space station funding $1.9b	Y
20.	Kill-Eliminate supercollider funds	N
21.	Req 5-day handgun waiting period	Y
22.	Life in prison instead of death	N
23.	Exceptions to exclusionary rule	N
24.	Ban race as death sentence factor	N
25.	Campaign finance revisions	Y
26.	Kill-Term limits for senators	Y
27.	Require four presidential debates	Y
28.	Tighten ban on vertical price fixing	Y
29.	Kill-Freeze discretionary budget	N
30.	Provide $30b for failed S&Ls	N
31.	Allow use of force against Iraq	N
32.	Allow $15b in foreign aid for 1991	N
33.	Civil Rights Act of 1990	Y
34.	Block cancellation of Egypt's debt	Y
35.	Cut El Salvador military aid 50%	Y
36.	Reduce troops in NATO by 30,000	Y
37.	Req increases in auto fuel efficiency	Y
38.	Bar taxpayer funding of campaigns	N
39.	Limit textile import growth to 1%	N
40.	Amendment to ban flag desecration	Y
41.	Let fed emp be politically active	Y
42.	Reauthorize Amtrak-veto override	Y
43.	Allow sale of assault weapons	N
44.	Retraining aid for coal miners	Y
45.	Kill-Raise car emission standards	N
46.	Pull EPA nuclear plant authority	N
47.	Defer Chinese students' deportation	Y
48.	Cut in capital gains tax	N
49.	Establish CIA inspector general	Y
50.	Kill-Sanctions against China	Y
51.	Bar drug testing to receive AFDC	Y
52.	Kill-Allow force against drug planes	Y
53.	Include illegal aliens in census	N
54.	Restitution to Japanese interned	N
55.	Troop reduction in Europe of 50%	Y
56.	Increase SDI research to $4.3b	N
57.	Kill-Pay homeless below min wage	Y
58.	Ban airline smoking within US	Y
59.	Bar transfer of FS-X technology	Y
60.	Limit liability for oil spills	Y
61.	Restructure S&L industry	N

62.	Ban $ to illegal foreign activities	Y
63.	Req immigrant fluency in English	Y
64.	Allow aliens' families to stay in US	Y
65.	Expand child care aid/tax credit	Y
66.	Raise minimum wage w/subminimum	Y
67.	Freeze outlays except SS/Medicare	Y
68.	Kill-Shift $5b of DOD to domestic	N
69.	Confirm Tower as sec of defense	N
70.	Bar abortion $ except to save mother	Y
71.	Kill-Warn AIDS carriers' spouses	N
72.	Allow religious schools to bar gays	Y
73.	60 days' notice of plant closings	Y
74.	Allow poison pills in corp takeovers	N
75.	Kill-Workfare program	Y
76.	Prohibit employee polygraph testing	Y
77.	Cap Medicare patients' liability	Y
78.	Revise unfair trade practices	Y
79.	Kill-Shift SDI $ to conv weapons	N
80.	Kill-Shift SDI $ to accidental launch	N
81.	Kill-Shift MX $ to supplies/parts	Y
82.	Kill-Buy America provision at DOD	N
83.	Allow nuclear testing-5+ kilotons	N
84.	Allow SALT II to be exceeded	N
85.	$ to vets exposed to nuclear bomb	Y
86.	Warn workers of disease exposure	Y
87.	Restore four civil rights laws	Y
88.	Disapprove uranium sales to Japan	N
89.	Notify Congress of covert operations	Y
90.	Approval of $36m in Contra aid	N
91.	$18b deficit reduction compromise	Y
92.	Allow sale of hard-to-detect guns	Y
93.	Catastrophic health insurance	Y
94.	Bork nomination to Supreme Court	N
95.	Kill-Void Panama Canal treaties	Y
96.	Kill-Insurance denial to AIDS+	Y
97.	Keep diplomatic immunity intact	N
98.	Produce Bigeye nerve gas bomb	N
99.	Balanced budget by '93-via targets	N
100.	Allow ASAT missile tests in space	N
101.	Limit space-based/ABM system tests	Y
102.	Force reduction in trade barriers	Y
103.	Repeal windfall profit tax on oil	Y
104.	$1b/two year aid for the homeless	Y
105.	Disallow $30m for AZT to poor	N
106.	Bar AIDS test-immigrants/marriage	Y
107.	Kill-Biennial budget approval	Y
108.	Fairness doctrine in broadcasting	Y
109.	Raise speed limit to 65 mph	Y

Presidential Support Score: 1991 - 36% 1990 - 34%

OHIO

GLENN, JOHN -- Ohio [Democrat]. Term Began/Expires: 1987/1992. Prior Terms: Senate: 1975-86. Born: July 18, 1921; Cambridge, OH. Education: Muskingum College (B.S.). Military Service: U.S. Marine Corps, 1942-65; NASA, 1959-65. Occupation: Military Serviceman; astronaut; vice president, Royal Crown (1966-68); president, Royal Crown International (1967-69); board member, Questor Corp. (1970-74).

GLENN, JOHN (continued)

1. Prohibit MFN status for China	Y	65. Expand child care aid/tax credit	Y
2. Kill-Tie welfare to school attendance	Y	66. Raise minimum wage w/subminimum	Y
3. Limit credit card interest rates	N	67. Freeze outlays except SS/Medicare	N
4. Confirm Gates as head of CIA	Y	68. Kill-Shift $5b of DOD to domestic	Y
5. Adoption of national energy policies	N	69. Confirm Tower as sec of defense	N
6. Kill-Restrict NEA use of funds	Y	70. Bar abortion $ except to save mother	N
7. Unemployment benefits extension	Y	71. Kill-Warn AIDS carriers' spouses	Y
8. Confirm Thomas to Supreme Court	N	72. Allow religious schools to bar gays	N
9. Raise eligibility for unpaid leave	Y	73. 60 days' notice of plant closings	Y
10. Notify parents of minors' abortions	N	74. Allow poison pills in corp takeovers	Y
11. Move $3b from defense to domestic	N	75. Kill-Workfare program	Y
12. End production of B-2 bomber	Y	76. Prohibit employee polygraph testing	Y
13. Cut SDI $1b to reduce deficit	Y	77. Cap Medicare patients' liability	Y
14. Maintain strategic stability-Soviets	N	78. Revise unfair trade practices	Y
15. Kill-Allow women as combat pilots	Y	79. Kill-Shift SDI $ to conv weapons	Y
16. Kill-Allow HIV tests before surgery	N	80. Kill-Shift SDI $ to accidental launch	Y
17. Strike $12b aid to Int'l Mon Fund	N	81. Kill-Shift MX $ to supplies/parts	Y
18. Raise Senate salary/omit honoraria	N	82. Kill-Buy America provision at DOD	Y
19. Reduce space station funding $1.9b	N	83. Allow nuclear testing-5+ kilotons	Y
20. Kill-Eliminate supercollider funds	Y	84. Allow SALT II to be exceeded	N
21. Req 5-day handgun waiting period	Y	85. $ to vets exposed to nuclear bomb	Y
22. Life in prison instead of death	Y	86. Warn workers of disease exposure	Y
23. Exceptions to exclusionary rule	N	87. Restore four civil rights laws	Y
24. Ban race as death sentence factor	N	88. Disapprove uranium sales to Japan	Y
25. Campaign finance revisions	Y	89. Notify Congress of covert operations	Y
26. Kill-Term limits for senators	Y	90. Approval of $36m in Contra aid	N
27. Require four presidential debates	N	91. $18b deficit reduction compromise	Y
28. Tighten ban on vertical price fixing	Y	92. Allow sale of hard-to-detect guns	N
29. Kill-Freeze discretionary budget	Y	93. Catastrophic health insurance	Y
30. Provide $30b for failed S&Ls	Y	94. Bork nomination to Supreme Court	N
31. Allow use of force against Iraq	N	95. Kill-Void Panama Canal treaties	Y
32. Allow $15b in foreign aid for 1991	Y	96. Kill-Insurance denial to AIDS+	Y
33. Civil Rights Act of 1990	Y	97. Keep diplomatic immunity intact	Y
34. Block cancellation of Egypt's debt	N	98. Produce Bigeye nerve gas bomb	Y
35. Cut El Salvador military aid 50%	Y	99. Balanced budget by '93-via targets	N
36. Reduce troops in NATO by 30,000	N	100. Allow ASAT missile tests in space	Y
37. Req increases in auto fuel efficiency	N	101. Limit space-based/ABM system tests	Y
38. Bar taxpayer funding of campaigns	N	102. Force reduction in trade barriers	Y
39. Limit textile import growth to 1%	N	103. Repeal windfall profit tax on oil	N
40. Amendment to ban flag desecration	N	104. $1b/two year aid for the homeless	Y
41. Let fed emp be politically active	Y	105. Disallow $30m for AZT to poor	N
42. Reauthorize Amtrak-veto override	Y	106. Bar AIDS test-immigrants/marriage	Y
43. Allow sale of assault weapons	N	107. Kill-Biennial budget approval	Y
44. Retraining aid for coal miners	Y	108. Fairness doctrine in broadcasting	Y
45. Kill-Raise car emission standards	Y	109. Raise speed limit to 65 mph	N
46. Pull EPA nuclear plant authority	N	110. Immigration reform/alien amnesty	+
47. Defer Chinese students' deportation	Y	111. South Africa sanctions-veto override	Y
48. Cut in capital gains tax	N	112. Kill-Use of military in drug war	Y
49. Establish CIA inspector general	Y	113. Tax overhaul to revise income tax	Y
50. Kill-Sanctions against China	N	114. Submit nuclear test ban treaties	Y
51. Bar drug testing to receive AFDC	Y	115. Prohibit sale of Stinger missiles	N
52. Kill-Allow force against drug planes	Y	116. Prohibit binary chemical weapons	N
53. Include illegal aliens in census	Y	117. Kill-$10/barrel oil tariff increase	Y
54. Restitution to Japanese interned	Y	118. Grant tax amnesty provisions	N
55. Troop reduction in Europe of 50%	N	119. Block Saudi arms sale-veto override	Y
56. Increase SDI research to $4.3b	Y	120. Balanced budget amendment	N
57. Kill-Pay homeless below min wage	Y	121. Include veterans in spending cuts	N
58. Ban airline smoking within US	Y	122. Bar $ to hazardous substance victims	Y
59. Bar transfer of FS-X technology	Y	123. Allow seasonal workers in the US	N
60. Limit liability for oil spills	Y	124. Let fed courts rule on school prayer	Y
61. Restructure S&L industry	Y	125. Presidential line-item veto	N
62. Ban $ to illegal foreign activities	Y	126. Ease Gun Control Act of 1968	Y
63. Req immigrant fluency in English	N	127. Kill-Req 14-day wait for handguns	N
64. Allow aliens' families to stay in US	Y	128. Kill-15% min tax on corporations	Y

GLENN, JOHN (continued)

129. Drop Social Security COLA	N	137. Capital punishment-federal crimes	--
130. Freeze funding for all programs	N	138. Ban government officials from taping	?
131. Kill-Nuclear weapon freeze	N	139. Martin Luther King holiday	Y
132. Keep decision narrowing Title IX	?	140. Authorize Marines in Lebanon	N
133. Raise drinking age to 21	Y	141. Amendment making abortion illegal	N
134. Allow production of MX missile	N	142. Delete $1.2b for jobs creation	?
135. Raise taxes/cut spending by $140b	N	143. Keep tobacco price supports	?
136. School prayer amendment	N	144. Emergency housing aid of $5.1b	Y

Presidential Support Score: 1991 - 41% 1990 - 39%

METZENBAUM, HOWARD M. -- Ohio [Democrat]. Term Began/Expires: 1989/1994. Prior Terms: Senate: 1974 (Special Appointment); 1977-1988. Born: June 4, 1917; Cleveland, OH. Education: Ohio State University (B.A., LL.D.). Occupation: Ohio representative (1943-47); Ohio senator (1947-50); Ohio judicial councilman (1949-50); member, Ohio Bureau of Code Revision (1949-50); attorney, Metzenbaum, Gaines & Stern Co., L.P.A. (1941).

1. Prohibit MFN status for China	Y	46. Pull EPA nuclear plant authority	?
2. Kill-Tie welfare to school attendance	Y	47. Defer Chinese students' deportation	Y
3. Limit credit card interest rates	Y	48. Cut in capital gains tax	N
4. Confirm Gates as head of CIA	N	49. Establish CIA inspector general	Y
5. Adoption of national energy policies	N	50. Kill-Sanctions against China	Y
6. Kill-Restrict NEA use of funds	Y	51. Bar drug testing to receive AFDC	Y
7. Unemployment benefits extension	Y	52. Kill-Allow force against drug planes	Y
8. Confirm Thomas to Supreme Court	N	53. Include illegal aliens in census	Y
9. Raise eligibility for unpaid leave	Y	54. Restitution to Japanese interned	Y
10. Notify parents of minors' abortions	N	55. Troop reduction in Europe of 50%	Y
11. Move $3b from defense to domestic	Y	56. Increase SDI research to $4.3b	N
12. End production of B-2 bomber	Y	57. Kill-Pay homeless below min wage	Y
13. Cut SDI $1b to reduce deficit	Y	58. Ban airline smoking within US	Y
14. Maintain strategic stability-Soviets	Y	59. Bar transfer of FS-X technology	Y
15. Kill-Allow women as combat pilots	N	60. Limit liability for oil spills	N
16. Kill-Allow HIV tests before surgery	Y	61. Restructure S&L industry	Y
17. Strike $12b aid to Int'l Mon Fund	Y	62. Ban $ to illegal foreign activities	Y
18. Raise Senate salary/omit honoraria	Y	63. Req immigrant fluency in English	N
19. Reduce space station funding $1.9b	Y	64. Allow aliens' families to stay in US	Y
20. Kill-Eliminate supercollider funds	N	65. Expand child care aid/tax credit	Y
21. Req 5-day handgun waiting period	Y	66. Raise minimum wage w/subminimum	Y
22. Life in prison instead of death	Y	67. Freeze outlays except SS/Medicare	N
23. Exceptions to exclusionary rule	N	68. Kill-Shift $5b of DOD to domestic	N
24. Ban race as death sentence factor	N	69. Confirm Tower as sec of defense	N
25. Campaign finance revisions	Y	70. Bar abortion $ except to save mother	N
26. Kill-Term limits for senators	Y	71. Kill-Warn AIDS carriers' spouses	N
27. Require four presidential debates	N	72. Allow religious schools to bar gays	N
28. Tighten ban on vertical price fixing	Y	73. 60 days' notice of plant closings	Y
29. Kill-Freeze discretionary budget	Y	74. Allow poison pills in corp takeovers	N
30. Provide $30b for failed S&Ls	Y	75. Kill-Workfare program	Y
31. Allow use of force against Iraq	N	76. Prohibit employee polygraph testing	?
32. Allow $15b in foreign aid for 1991	Y	77. Cap Medicare patients' liability	Y
33. Civil Rights Act of 1990	Y	78. Revise unfair trade practices	Y
34. Block cancellation of Egypt's debt	N	79. Kill-Shift SDI $ to conv weapons	N
35. Cut El Salvador military aid 50%	Y	80. Kill-Shift SDI $ to accidental launch	Y
36. Reduce troops in NATO by 30,000	Y	81. Kill-Shift MX $ to supplies/parts	N
37. Req increases in auto fuel efficiency	Y	82. Kill-Buy America provision at DOD	N
38. Bar taxpayer funding of campaigns	N	83. Allow nuclear testing-5+ kilotons	N
39. Limit textile import growth to 1%	Y	84. Allow SALT II to be exceeded	N
40. Amendment to ban flag desecration	N	85. $ to vets exposed to nuclear bomb	Y
41. Let fed emp be politically active	Y	86. Warn workers of disease exposure	Y
42. Reauthorize Amtrak-veto override	Y	87. Restore four civil rights laws	Y
43. Allow sale of assault weapons	N	88. Disapprove uranium sales to Japan	?
44. Retraining aid for coal miners	Y	89. Notify Congress of covert operations	Y
45. Kill-Raise car emission standards	Y	90. Approval of $36m in Contra aid	N

METZENBAUM, HOWARD M. (continued)

91. $18b deficit reduction compromise	Y	
92. Allow sale of hard-to-detect guns	N	
93. Catastrophic health insurance	Y	
94. Bork nomination to Supreme Court	N	
95. Kill-Void Panama Canal treaties	Y	
96. Kill-Insurance denial to AIDS+	Y	
97. Keep diplomatic immunity intact	Y	
98. Produce Bigeye nerve gas bomb	N	
99. Balanced budget by '93-via targets	N	
100. Allow ASAT missile tests in space	N	
101. Limit space-based/ABM system tests	Y	
102. Force reduction in trade barriers	Y	
103. Repeal windfall profit tax on oil	N	
104. $1b/two year aid for the homeless	Y	
105. Disallow $30m for AZT to poor	N	
106. Bar AIDS test-immigrants/marriage	Y	
107. Kill-Biennial budget approval	Y	
108. Fairness doctrine in broadcasting	Y	
109. Raise speed limit to 65 mph	N	
110. Immigration reform/alien amnesty	Y	
111. South Africa sanctions-veto override	Y	
112. Kill-Use of military in drug war	Y	
113. Tax overhaul to revise income tax	Y	
114. Submit nuclear test ban treaties	Y	
115. Prohibit sale of Stinger missiles	Y	
116. Prohibit binary chemical weapons	Y	
117. Kill-$10/barrel oil tariff increase	Y	

118. Grant tax amnesty provisions	N
119. Block Saudi arms sale-veto override	Y
120. Balanced budget amendment	N
121. Include veterans in spending cuts	N
122. Bar $ to hazardous substance victims	N
123. Allow seasonal workers in the US	N
124. Let fed courts rule on school prayer	Y
125. Presidential line-item veto	N
126. Ease Gun Control Act of 1968	N
127. Kill-Req 14-day wait for handguns	N
128. Kill-15% min tax on corporations	N
129. Drop Social Security COLA	N
130. Freeze funding for all programs	N
131. Kill-Nuclear weapon freeze	N
132. Keep decision narrowing Title IX	N
133. Raise drinking age to 21	Y
134. Allow production of MX missile	N
135. Raise taxes/cut spending by $140b	N
136. School prayer amendment	N
137. Capital punishment-federal crimes	N
138. Ban government officials from taping	Y
139. Martin Luther King holiday	Y
140. Authorize Marines in Lebanon	N
141. Amendment making abortion illegal	N
142. Delete $1.2b for jobs creation	N
143. Keep tobacco price supports	N
144. Emergency housing aid of $5.1b	Y

Presidential Support Score: 1991 - 27%   1990 - 27%

OKLAHOMA

BOREN, DAVID L. -- Oklahoma [Democrat]. Term Began/Expires: 1991/1996. Prior Terms: Senate: 1979-90. Born: April 21, 1941; Washington, DC. Education: Yale University; Oxford; University of Oklahoma College of Law. Occupation: Oklahoma representative (1967-75); governor of Oklahoma (1975-77).

1. Prohibit MFN status for China	Y	
2. Kill-Tie welfare to school attendance	N	
3. Limit credit card interest rates	Y	
4. Confirm Gates as head of CIA	Y	
5. Adoption of national energy policies	?	
6. Kill-Restrict NEA use of funds	Y	
7. Unemployment benefits extension	Y	
8. Confirm Thomas to Supreme Court	Y	
9. Raise eligibility for unpaid leave	N	
10. Notify parents of minors' abortions	Y	
11. Move $3b from defense to domestic	N	
12. End production of B-2 bomber	N	
13. Cut SDI $1b to reduce deficit	Y	
14. Maintain strategic stability-Soviets	N	
15. Kill-Allow women as combat pilots	Y	
16. Kill-Allow HIV tests before surgery	N	
17. Strike $12b aid to Int'l Mon Fund	N	
18. Raise Senate salary/omit honoraria	Y	
19. Reduce space station funding $1.9b	N	
20. Kill-Eliminate supercollider funds	Y	
21. Req 5-day handgun waiting period	Y	

22. Life in prison instead of death	N
23. Exceptions to exclusionary rule	N
24. Ban race as death sentence factor	N
25. Campaign finance revisions	Y
26. Kill-Term limits for senators	Y
27. Require four presidential debates	N
28. Tighten ban on vertical price fixing	N
29. Kill-Freeze discretionary budget	N
30. Provide $30b for failed S&Ls	Y
31. Allow use of force against Iraq	N
32. Allow $15b in foreign aid for 1991	N
33. Civil Rights Act of 1990	Y
34. Block cancellation of Egypt's debt	N
35. Cut El Salvador military aid 50%	Y
36. Reduce troops in NATO by 30,000	Y
37. Req increases in auto fuel efficiency	N
38. Bar taxpayer funding of campaigns	N
39. Limit textile import growth to 1%	Y
40. Amendment to ban flag desecration	N
41. Let fed emp be politically active	Y
42. Reauthorize Amtrak-veto override	Y

BOREN, DAVID L. (continued)

43.	Allow sale of assault weapons	N	94.	Bork nomination to Supreme Court	Y
44.	Retraining aid for coal miners	N	95.	Kill-Void Panama Canal treaties	N
45.	Kill-Raise car emission standards	Y	96.	Kill-Insurance denial to AIDS+	N
46.	Pull EPA nuclear plant authority	Y	97.	Keep diplomatic immunity intact	N
47.	Defer Chinese students' deportation	Y	98.	Produce Bigeye nerve gas bomb	Y
48.	Cut in capital gains tax	Y	99.	Balanced budget by '93-via targets	Y
49.	Establish CIA inspector general	Y	100.	Allow ASAT missile tests in space	Y
50.	Kill-Sanctions against China	Y	101.	Limit space-based/ABM system tests	?
51.	Bar drug testing to receive AFDC	Y	102.	Force reduction in trade barriers	Y
52.	Kill-Allow force against drug planes	Y	103.	Repeal windfall profit tax on oil	Y
53.	Include illegal aliens in census	N	104.	$1b/two year aid for the homeless	Y
54.	Restitution to Japanese interned	Y	105.	Disallow $30m for AZT to poor	N
55.	Troop reduction in Europe of 50%	N	106.	Bar AIDS test-immigrants/marriage	N
56.	Increase SDI research to $4.3b	Y	107.	Kill-Biennial budget approval	Y
57.	Kill-Pay homeless below min wage	N	108.	Fairness doctrine in broadcasting	?
58.	Ban airline smoking within US	Y	109.	Raise speed limit to 65 mph	Y
59.	Bar transfer of FS-X technology	Y	110.	Immigration reform/alien amnesty	?
60.	Limit liability for oil spills	Y	111.	South Africa sanctions-veto override	Y
61.	Restructure S&L industry	Y	112.	Kill-Use of military in drug war	?
62.	Ban $ to illegal foreign activities	Y	113.	Tax overhaul to revise income tax	N
63.	Req immigrant fluency in English	N	114.	Submit nuclear test ban treaties	Y
64.	Allow aliens' families to stay in US	Y	115.	Prohibit sale of Stinger missiles	N
65.	Expand child care aid/tax credit	Y	116.	Prohibit binary chemical weapons	N
66.	Raise minimum wage w/subminimum	N	117.	Kill-$10/barrel oil tariff increase	N
67.	Freeze outlays except SS/Medicare	Y	118.	Grant tax amnesty provisions	Y
68.	Kill-Shift $5b of DOD to domestic	N	119.	Block Saudi arms sale-veto override	Y
69.	Confirm Tower as sec of defense	N	120.	Balanced budget amendment	Y
70.	Bar abortion $ except to save mother	?	121.	Include veterans in spending cuts	Y
71.	Kill-Warn AIDS carriers' spouses	N	122.	Bar $ to hazardous substance victims	?
72.	Allow religious schools to bar gays	Y	123.	Allow seasonal workers in the US	Y
73.	60 days' notice of plant closings	Y	124.	Let fed courts rule on school prayer	Y
74.	Allow poison pills in corp takeovers	?	125.	Presidential line-item veto	Y
75.	Kill-Workfare program	N	126.	Ease Gun Control Act of 1968	Y
76.	Prohibit employee polygraph testing	Y	127.	Kill-Req 14-day wait for handguns	N
77.	Cap Medicare patients' liability	Y	128.	Kill-15% min tax on corporations	N
78.	Revise unfair trade practices	Y	129.	Drop Social Security COLA	N
79.	Kill-Shift SDI $ to conv weapons	N	130.	Freeze funding for all programs	Y
80.	Kill-Shift SDI $ to accidental launch	Y	131.	Kill-Nuclear weapon freeze	?
81.	Kill-Shift MX $ to supplies/parts	Y	132.	Keep decision narrowing Title IX	N
82.	Kill-Buy America provision at DOD	N	133.	Raise drinking age to 21	Y
83.	Allow nuclear testing-5+ kilotons	Y	134.	Allow production of MX missile	N
84.	Allow SALT II to be exceeded	Y	135.	Raise taxes/cut spending by $140b	Y
85.	$ to vets exposed to nuclear bomb	Y	136.	School prayer amendment	Y
86.	Warn workers of disease exposure	N	137.	Capital punishment-federal crimes	Y
87.	Restore four civil rights laws	Y	138.	Ban government officials from taping	Y
88.	Disapprove uranium sales to Japan	N	139.	Martin Luther King holiday	Y
89.	Notify Congress of covert operations	Y	140.	Authorize Marines in Lebanon	N
90.	Approval of $36m in Contra aid	Y	141.	Amendment making abortion illegal	N
91.	$18b deficit reduction compromise	?	142.	Delete $1.2b for jobs creation	Y
92.	Allow sale of hard-to-detect guns	N	143.	Keep tobacco price supports	Y
93.	Catastrophic health insurance	Y	144.	Emergency housing aid of $5.1b	Y

Presidential Support Score: 1991 - 60%   1990 - 58%

NICKLES, DON -- Oklahoma [Republican]. Term Began/Expires: 1987/1992. Prior Terms: Senate: 1981-86. Born: December 6, 1948; Ponca City, OK. Education: Oklahoma State University (B.A.). Occupation: Oklahoma senator; vice and general manager, Nickles Machine Corp.

1.	Prohibit MFN status for China	N	5.	Adoption of national energy policies	Y
2.	Kill-Tie welfare to school attendance	N	6.	Kill-Restrict NEA use of funds	N
3.	Limit credit card interest rates	Y	7.	Unemployment benefits extension	N
4.	Confirm Gates as head of CIA	Y	8.	Confirm Thomas to Supreme Court	Y

NICKLES, DON (continued)

9. Raise eligibility for unpaid leave	N	
10. Notify parents of minors' abortions	Y	
11. Move $3b from defense to domestic	N	
12. End production of B-2 bomber	N	
13. Cut SDI $1b to reduce deficit	N	
14. Maintain strategic stability-Soviets	N	
15. Kill-Allow women as combat pilots	N	
16. Kill-Allow HIV tests before surgery	N	
17. Strike $12b aid to Int'l Mon Fund	Y	
18. Raise Senate salary/omit honoraria	N	
19. Reduce space station funding $1.9b	N	
20. Kill-Eliminate supercollider funds	Y	
21. Req 5-day handgun waiting period	N	
22. Life in prison instead of death	N	
23. Exceptions to exclusionary rule	Y	
24. Ban race as death sentence factor	Y	
25. Campaign finance revisions	N	
26. Kill-Term limits for senators	N	
27. Require four presidential debates	?	
28. Tighten ban on vertical price fixing	N	
29. Kill-Freeze discretionary budget	N	
30. Provide $30b for failed S&Ls	Y	
31. Allow use of force against Iraq	Y	
32. Allow $15b in foreign aid for 1991	Y	
33. Civil Rights Act of 1990	N	
34. Block cancellation of Egypt's debt	N	
35. Cut El Salvador military aid 50%	N	
36. Reduce troops in NATO by 30,000	Y	
37. Req increases in auto fuel efficiency	N	
38. Bar taxpayer funding of campaigns	Y	
39. Limit textile import growth to 1%	N	
40. Amendment to ban flag desecration	Y	
41. Let fed emp be politically active	N	
42. Reauthorize Amtrak-veto override	N	
43. Allow sale of assault weapons	Y	
44. Retraining aid for coal miners	N	
45. Kill-Raise car emission standards	Y	
46. Pull EPA nuclear plant authority	Y	
47. Defer Chinese students' deportation	N	
48. Cut in capital gains tax	Y	
49. Establish CIA inspector general	N	
50. Kill-Sanctions against China	N	
51. Bar drug testing to receive AFDC	N	
52. Kill-Allow force against drug planes	N	
53. Include illegal aliens in census	N	
54. Restitution to Japanese interned	N	
55. Troop reduction in Europe of 50%	N	
56. Increase SDI research to $4.3b	Y	
57. Kill-Pay homeless below min wage	N	
58. Ban airline smoking within US	Y	
59. Bar transfer of FS-X technology	N	
60. Limit liability for oil spills	Y	
61. Restructure S&L industry	N	
62. Ban $ to illegal foreign activities	N	
63. Req immigrant fluency in English	Y	
64. Allow aliens' families to stay in US	N	
65. Expand child care aid/tax credit	N	
66. Raise minimum wage w/subminimum	N	
67. Freeze outlays except SS/Medicare	Y	
68. Kill-Shift $5b of DOD to domestic	Y	
69. Confirm Tower as sec of defense	Y	
70. Bar abortion $ except to save mother	Y	
71. Kill-Warn AIDS carriers' spouses	N	
72. Allow religious schools to bar gays	Y	

73. 60 days' notice of plant closings	N	
74. Allow poison pills in corp takeovers	Y	
75. Kill-Workfare program	N	
76. Prohibit employee polygraph testing	N	
77. Cap Medicare patients' liability	N	
78. Revise unfair trade practices	Y	
79. Kill-Shift SDI $ to conv weapons	Y	
80. Kill-Shift SDI $ to accidental launch	N	
81. Kill-Shift MX $ to supplies/parts	Y	
82. Kill-Buy America provision at DOD	Y	
83. Allow nuclear testing-5+ kilotons	Y	
84. Allow SALT II to be exceeded	Y	
85. $ to vets exposed to nuclear bomb	N	
86. Warn workers of disease exposure	N	
87. Restore four civil rights laws	N	
88. Disapprove uranium sales to Japan	N	
89. Notify Congress of covert operations	N	
90. Approval of $36m in Contra aid	Y	
91. $18b deficit reduction compromise	N	
92. Allow sale of hard-to-detect guns	Y	
93. Catastrophic health insurance	N	
94. Bork nomination to Supreme Court	Y	
95. Kill-Void Panama Canal treaties	N	
96. Kill-Insurance denial to AIDS+	N	
97. Keep diplomatic immunity intact	N	
98. Produce Bigeye nerve gas bomb	Y	
99. Balanced budget by '93-via targets	Y	
100. Allow ASAT missile tests in space	Y	
101. Limit space-based/ABM system tests	N	
102. Force reduction in trade barriers	Y	
103. Repeal windfall profit tax on oil	Y	
104. $1b/two year aid for the homeless	N	
105. Disallow $30m for AZT to poor	Y	
106. Bar AIDS test-immigrants/marriage	N	
107. Kill-Biennial budget approval	N	
108. Fairness doctrine in broadcasting	N	
109. Raise speed limit to 65 mph	Y	
110. Immigration reform/alien amnesty	N	
111. South Africa sanctions-veto override	N	
112. Kill-Use of military in drug war	N	
113. Tax overhaul to revise income tax	N	
114. Submit nuclear test ban treaties	N	
115. Prohibit sale of Stinger missiles	N	
116. Prohibit binary chemical weapons	N	
117. Kill-$10/barrel oil tariff increase	N	
118. Grant tax amnesty provisions	Y	
119. Block Saudi arms sale-veto override	Y	
120. Balanced budget amendment	Y	
121. Include veterans in spending cuts	Y	
122. Bar $ to hazardous substance victims	Y	
123. Allow seasonal workers in the US	Y	
124. Let fed courts rule on school prayer	N	
125. Presidential line-item veto	Y	
126. Ease Gun Control Act of 1968	Y	
127. Kill-Req 14-day wait for handguns	Y	
128. Kill-15% min tax on corporations	Y	
129. Drop Social Security COLA	Y	
130. Freeze funding for all programs	N	
131. Kill-Nuclear weapon freeze	Y	
132. Keep decision narrowing Title IX	Y	
133. Raise drinking age to 21	Y	
134. Allow production of MX missile	Y	
135. Raise taxes/cut spending by $140b	Y	
136. School prayer amendment	Y	

NICKLES, DON (continued)

137. Capital punishment-federal crimes	Y	
138. Ban government officials from taping	N	
139. Martin Luther King holiday	N	
140. Authorize Marines in Lebanon	Y	
141. Amendment making abortion illegal	Y	
142. Delete $1.2b for jobs creation	Y	
143. Keep tobacco price supports	N	
144. Emergency housing aid of $5.1b	N	

Presidential Support Score: 1991 - 89%   1990 - 83%

OREGON

HATFIELD, MARK -- Oregon [Republican]. Term Began/Expires: 1991/1996. Prior Terms: Senate: 1967-90. Born July 12, 1922; Dallas, OR. Education: Willamette University (B.A.); Stanford University (A.M.). Military Service: U.S. Navy,WW II. Occupation: Associate professor, Willamette University (1949-56); dean of students (1950-56); Oregon representative (1950-54); Oregon senator (1954-56); secretary of state (1956-58); governor (1958-66).

1. Prohibit MFN status for China	N	43. Allow sale of assault weapons	N
2. Kill-Tie welfare to school attendance	Y	44. Retraining aid for coal miners	Y
3. Limit credit card interest rates	Y	45. Kill-Raise car emission standards	N
4. Confirm Gates as head of CIA	Y	46. Pull EPA nuclear plant authority	N
5. Adoption of national energy policies	Y	47. Defer Chinese students' deportation	N
6. Kill-Restrict NEA use of funds	Y	48. Cut in capital gains tax	Y
7. Unemployment benefits extension	Y	49. Establish CIA inspector general	Y
8. Confirm Thomas to Supreme Court	Y	50. Kill-Sanctions against China	Y
9. Raise eligibility for unpaid leave	Y	51. Bar drug testing to receive AFDC	Y
10. Notify parents of minors' abortions	Y	52. Kill-Allow force against drug planes	Y
11. Move $3b from defense to domestic	Y	53. Include illegal aliens in census	Y
12. End production of B-2 bomber	Y	54. Restitution to Japanese interned	Y
13. Cut SDI $1b to reduce deficit	Y	55. Troop reduction in Europe of 50%	N
14. Maintain strategic stability-Soviets	N	56. Increase SDI research to $4.3b	N
15. Kill-Allow women as combat pilots	N	57. Kill-Pay homeless below min wage	N
16. Kill-Allow HIV tests before surgery	Y	58. Ban airline smoking within US	Y
17. Strike $12b aid to Int'l Mon Fund	N	59. Bar transfer of FS-X technology	N
18. Raise Senate salary/omit honoraria	Y	60. Limit liability for oil spills	N
19. Reduce space station funding $1.9b	N	61. Restructure S&L industry	N
20. Kill-Eliminate supercollider funds	Y	62. Ban $ to illegal foreign activities	N
21. Req 5-day handgun waiting period	Y	63. Req immigrant fluency in English	N
22. Life in prison instead of death	Y	64. Allow aliens' families to stay in US	Y
23. Exceptions to exclusionary rule	N	65. Expand child care aid/tax credit	Y
24. Ban race as death sentence factor	N	66. Raise minimum wage w/subminimum	Y
25. Campaign finance revisions	N	67. Freeze outlays except SS/Medicare	N
26. Kill-Term limits for senators	Y	68. Kill-Shift $5b of DOD to domestic	N
27. Require four presidential debates	N	69. Confirm Tower as sec of defense	N
28. Tighten ban on vertical price fixing	Y	70. Bar abortion $ except to save mother	Y
29. Kill-Freeze discretionary budget	Y	71. Kill-Warn AIDS carriers' spouses	N
30. Provide $30b for failed S&Ls	Y	72. Allow religious schools to bar gays	Y
31. Allow use of force against Iraq	N	73. 60 days' notice of plant closings	Y
32. Allow $15b in foreign aid for 1991	--	74. Allow poison pills in corp takeovers	N
33. Civil Rights Act of 1990	Y	75. Kill-Workfare program	N
34. Block cancellation of Egypt's debt	Y	76. Prohibit employee polygraph testing	Y
35. Cut El Salvador military aid 50%	Y	77. Cap Medicare patients' liability	Y
36. Reduce troops in NATO by 30,000	+	78. Revise unfair trade practices	N
37. Req increases in auto fuel efficiency	Y	79. Kill-Shift SDI $ to conv weapons	?
38. Bar taxpayer funding of campaigns	Y	80. Kill-Shift SDI $ to accidental launch	?
39. Limit textile import growth to 1%	N	81. Kill-Shift MX $ to supplies/parts	N
40. Amendment to ban flag desecration	Y	82. Kill-Buy America provision at DOD	Y
41. Let fed emp be politically active	Y	83. Allow nuclear testing-5+ kilotons	N
42. Reauthorize Amtrak-veto override	Y	84. Allow SALT II to be exceeded	N

HATFIELD, MARK (continued)

85. $ to vets exposed to nuclear bomb	N	
86. Warn workers of disease exposure	Y	
87. Restore four civil rights laws	Y	
88. Disapprove uranium sales to Japan	Y	
89. Notify Congress of covert operations	Y	
90. Approval of $36m in Contra aid	N	
91. $18b deficit reduction compromise	#	
92. Allow sale of hard-to-detect guns	Y	
93. Catastrophic health insurance	Y	
94. Bork nomination to Supreme Court	Y	
95. Kill-Void Panama Canal treaties	Y	
96. Kill-Insurance denial to AIDS+	N	
97. Keep diplomatic immunity intact	Y	
98. Produce Bigeye nerve gas bomb	N	
99. Balanced budget by '93-via targets	N	
100. Allow ASAT missile tests in space	N	
101. Limit space-based/ABM system tests	Y	
102. Force reduction in trade barriers	N	
103. Repeal windfall profit tax on oil	Y	
104. $1b/two year aid for the homeless	Y	
105. Disallow $30m for AZT to poor	N	
106. Bar AIDS test-immigrants/marriage	Y	
107. Kill-Biennial budget approval	Y	
108. Fairness doctrine in broadcasting	Y	
109. Raise speed limit to 65 mph	?	
110. Immigration reform/alien amnesty	Y	
111. South Africa sanctions-veto override	Y	
112. Kill-Use of military in drug war	Y	
113. Tax overhaul to revise income tax	Y	
114. Submit nuclear test ban treaties	Y	
115. Prohibit sale of Stinger missiles	Y
116. Prohibit binary chemical weapons	Y
117. Kill-$10/barrel oil tariff increase	N
118. Grant tax amnesty provisions	Y
119. Block Saudi arms sale-veto override	Y
120. Balanced budget amendment	N
121. Include veterans in spending cuts	Y
122. Bar $ to hazardous substance victims	Y
123. Allow seasonal workers in the US	+
124. Let fed courts rule on school prayer	Y
125. Presidential line-item veto	N
126. Ease Gun Control Act of 1968	+
127. Kill-Req 14-day wait for handguns	?
128. Kill-15% min tax on corporations	Y
129. Drop Social Security COLA	Y
130. Freeze funding for all programs	N
131. Kill-Nuclear weapon freeze	N
132. Keep decision narrowing Title IX	Y
133. Raise drinking age to 21	Y
134. Allow production of MX missile	N
135. Raise taxes/cut spending by $140b	Y
136. School prayer amendment	N
137. Capital punishment-federal crimes	N
138. Ban government officials from taping	Y
139. Martin Luther King holiday	Y
140. Authorize Marines in Lebanon	N
141. Amendment making abortion illegal	Y
142. Delete $1.2b for jobs creation	N
143. Keep tobacco price supports	N
144. Emergency housing aid of $5.1b	Y

Presidential Support Score: 1991 - 59%   1990 - 38%

PACKWOOD, BOB -- Oregon [Republican]. Term Began/Expires: 1987/1992. **Prior Terms:** Senate: 1969-86. Born: September 11, 1932; Portland, OR. Education: Willamette University (B.A.); New York University School of Law (LL.B.). Occupation: Partner, McMurry, Packwood & Stearns; Oregon representative (1962-68).

1. Prohibit MFN status for China	N	
2. Kill-Tie welfare to school attendance	Y	
3. Limit credit card interest rates	Y	
4. Confirm Gates as head of CIA	Y	
5. Adoption of national energy policies	Y	
6. Kill-Restrict NEA use of funds	Y	
7. Unemployment benefits extension	Y	
8. Confirm Thomas to Supreme Court	N	
9. Raise eligibility for unpaid leave	Y	
10. Notify parents of minors' abortions	N	
11. Move $3b from defense to domestic	Y	
12. End production of B-2 bomber	Y	
13. Cut SDI $1b to reduce deficit	N	
14. Maintain strategic stability-Soviets	N	
15. Kill-Allow women as combat pilots	N	
16. Kill-Allow HIV tests before surgery	N	
17. Strike $12b aid to Int'l Mon Fund	N	
18. Raise Senate salary/omit honoraria	N	
19. Reduce space station funding $1.9b	N	
20. Kill-Eliminate supercollider funds	Y	
21. Req 5-day handgun waiting period	Y	
22. Life in prison instead of death	N	
23. Exceptions to exclusionary rule	N	
24. Ban race as death sentence factor	N	
25. Campaign finance revisions	N	
26. Kill-Term limits for senators	Y
27. Require four presidential debates	N
28. Tighten ban on vertical price fixing	N
29. Kill-Freeze discretionary budget	Y
30. Provide $30b for failed S&Ls	Y
31. Allow use of force against Iraq	Y
32. Allow $15b in foreign aid for 1991	Y
33. Civil Rights Act of 1990	Y
34. Block cancellation of Egypt's debt	N
35. Cut El Salvador military aid 50%	Y
36. Reduce troops in NATO by 30,000	Y
37. Req increases in auto fuel efficiency	Y
38. Bar taxpayer funding of campaigns	Y
39. Limit textile import growth to 1%	N
40. Amendment to ban flag desecration	N
41. Let fed emp be politically active	Y
42. Reauthorize Amtrak-veto override	N
43. Allow sale of assault weapons	N
44. Retraining aid for coal miners	N
45. Kill-Raise car emission standards	N
46. Pull EPA nuclear plant authority	?
47. Defer Chinese students' deportation	N
48. Cut in capital gains tax	Y
49. Establish CIA inspector general	Y
50. Kill-Sanctions against China	N

PACKWOOD, BOB (continued)

51. Bar drug testing to receive AFDC	Y	
52. Kill-Allow force against drug planes	N	
53. Include illegal aliens in census	N	
54. Restitution to Japanese interned	Y	
55. Troop reduction in Europe of 50%	Y	
56. Increase SDI research to $4.3b	Y	
57. Kill-Pay homeless below min wage	Y	
58. Ban airline smoking within US	Y	
59. Bar transfer of FS-X technology	N	
60. Limit liability for oil spills	N	
61. Restructure S&L industry	N	
62. Ban $ to illegal foreign activities	N	
63. Req immigrant fluency in English	N	
64. Allow aliens' families to stay in US	Y	
65. Expand child care aid/tax credit	N	
66. Raise minimum wage w/subminimum	Y	
67. Freeze outlays except SS/Medicare	N	
68. Kill-Shift $5b of DOD to domestic	Y	
69. Confirm Tower as sec of defense	Y	
70. Bar abortion $ except to save mother	N	
71. Kill-Warn AIDS carriers' spouses	Y	
72. Allow religious schools to bar gays	N	
73. 60 days' notice of plant closings	Y	
74. Allow poison pills in corp takeovers	N	
75. Kill-Workfare program	N	
76. Prohibit employee polygraph testing	Y	
77. Cap Medicare patients' liability	Y	
78. Revise unfair trade practices	Y	
79. Kill-Shift SDI $ to conv weapons	Y	
80. Kill-Shift SDI $ to accidental launch	Y	
81. Kill-Shift MX $ to supplies/parts	Y	
82. Kill-Buy America provision at DOD	Y	
83. Allow nuclear testing-5+ kilotons	Y	
84. Allow SALT II to be exceeded	Y	
85. $ to vets exposed to nuclear bomb	Y	
86. Warn workers of disease exposure	Y	
87. Restore four civil rights laws	Y	
88. Disapprove uranium sales to Japan	N	
89. Notify Congress of covert operations	Y	
90. Approval of $36m in Contra aid	N	
91. $18b deficit reduction compromise	N	
92. Allow sale of hard-to-detect guns	N	
93. Catastrophic health insurance	Y	
94. Bork nomination to Supreme Court	N	
95. Kill-Void Panama Canal treaties	?	
96. Kill-Insurance denial to AIDS+	Y	
97. Keep diplomatic immunity intact	N	
98. Produce Bigeye nerve gas bomb	N
99. Balanced budget by '93-via targets	Y
100. Allow ASAT missile tests in space	Y
101. Limit space-based/ABM system tests	Y
102. Force reduction in trade barriers	Y
103. Repeal windfall profit tax on oil	N
104. $1b/two year aid for the homeless	Y
105. Disallow $30m for AZT to poor	N
106. Bar AIDS test-immigrants/marriage	Y
107. Kill-Biennial budget approval	N
108. Fairness doctrine in broadcasting	N
109. Raise speed limit to 65 mph	?
110. Immigration reform/alien amnesty	Y
111. South Africa sanctions-veto override	Y
112. Kill-Use of military in drug war	Y
113. Tax overhaul to revise income tax	Y
114. Submit nuclear test ban treaties	Y
115. Prohibit sale of Stinger missiles	Y
116. Prohibit binary chemical weapons	Y
117. Kill-$10/barrel oil tariff increase	Y
118. Grant tax amnesty provisions	Y
119. Block Saudi arms sale-veto override	Y
120. Balanced budget amendment	Y
121. Include veterans in spending cuts	Y
122. Bar $ to hazardous substance victims	N
123. Allow seasonal workers in the US	N
124. Let fed courts rule on school prayer	Y
125. Presidential line-item veto	N
126. Ease Gun Control Act of 1968	Y
127. Kill-Req 14-day wait for handguns	Y
128. Kill-15% min tax on corporations	Y
129. Drop Social Security COLA	Y
130. Freeze funding for all programs	N
131. Kill-Nuclear weapon freeze	N
132. Keep decision narrowing Title IX	Y
133. Raise drinking age to 21	Y
134. Allow production of MX missile	N
135. Raise taxes/cut spending by $140b	Y
136. School prayer amendment	N
137. Capital punishment-federal crimes	Y
138. Ban government officials from taping	Y
139. Martin Luther King holiday	Y
140. Authorize Marines in Lebanon	Y
141. Amendment making abortion illegal	N
142. Delete $1.2b for jobs creation	N
143. Keep tobacco price supports	N
144. Emergency housing aid of $5.1b	Y

Presidential Support Score: 1991 - 68% 1990 - 56%

PENNSYLVANIA

SPECTER, ARLEN -- Pennsylvania [Republican]. Term Began/Expires: 1987/1992. Prior Terms: Senate: 1981-86. Born: February 12, 1930; Wichita, KS. Education: Yale Law School. Occupation: Attorney, Dechert, Price and Rhoades; Philadelphia assistant district attorney.

1. Prohibit MFN status for China	Y	2. Kill-Tie welfare to school attendance	Y

SPECTER, ARLEN (continued)

3. Limit credit card interest rates	Y	
4. Confirm Gates as head of CIA	Y	
5. Adoption of national energy policies	Y	
6. Kill-Restrict NEA use of funds	N	
7. Unemployment benefits extension	Y	
8. Confirm Thomas to Supreme Court	Y	
9. Raise eligibility for unpaid leave	Y	
10. Notify parents of minors' abortions	N	
11. Move $3b from defense to domestic	Y	
12. End production of B-2 bomber	N	
13. Cut SDI $1b to reduce deficit	N	
14. Maintain strategic stability-Soviets	N	
15. Kill-Allow women as combat pilots	N	
16. Kill-Allow HIV tests before surgery	Y	
17. Strike $12b aid to Int'l Mon Fund	N	
18. Raise Senate salary/omit honoraria	N	
19. Reduce space station funding $1.9b	Y	
20. Kill-Eliminate supercollider funds	Y	
21. Req 5-day handgun waiting period	N	
22. Life in prison instead of death	N	
23. Exceptions to exclusionary rule	N	
24. Ban race as death sentence factor	Y	
25. Campaign finance revisions	N	
26. Kill-Term limits for senators	Y	
27. Require four presidential debates	N	
28. Tighten ban on vertical price fixing	Y	
29. Kill-Freeze discretionary budget	N	
30. Provide $30b for failed S&Ls	N	
31. Allow use of force against Iraq	Y	
32. Allow $15b in foreign aid for 1991	Y	
33. Civil Rights Act of 1990	Y	
34. Block cancellation of Egypt's debt	N	
35. Cut El Salvador military aid 50%	Y	
36. Reduce troops in NATO by 30,000	N	
37. Req increases in auto fuel efficiency	N	
38. Bar taxpayer funding of campaigns	Y	
39. Limit textile import growth to 1%	Y	
40. Amendment to ban flag desecration	Y	
41. Let fed emp be politically active	Y	
42. Reauthorize Amtrak-veto override	Y	
43. Allow sale of assault weapons	Y	
44. Retraining aid for coal miners	Y	
45. Kill-Raise car emission standards	Y	
46. Pull EPA nuclear plant authority	N	
47. Defer Chinese students' deportation	N	
48. Cut in capital gains tax	Y	
49. Establish CIA inspector general	Y	
50. Kill-Sanctions against China	Y	
51. Bar drug testing to receive AFDC	Y	
52. Kill-Allow force against drug planes	N	
53. Include illegal aliens in census	N	
54. Restitution to Japanese interned	Y	
55. Troop reduction in Europe of 50%	N	
56. Increase SDI research to $4.3b	N	
57. Kill-Pay homeless below min wage	Y	
58. Ban airline smoking within US	Y	
59. Bar transfer of FS-X technology	N	
60. Limit liability for oil spills	N	
61. Restructure S&L industry	N	
62. Ban $ to illegal foreign activities	Y	
63. Req immigrant fluency in English	N	
64. Allow aliens' families to stay in US	Y	
65. Expand child care aid/tax credit	Y	
66. Raise minimum wage w/subminimum	Y	

67. Freeze outlays except SS/Medicare	N	
68. Kill-Shift $5b of DOD to domestic	N	
69. Confirm Tower as sec of defense	Y	
70. Bar abortion $ except to save mother	N	
71. Kill-Warn AIDS carriers' spouses	N	
72. Allow religious schools to bar gays	N	
73. 60 days' notice of plant closings	Y	
74. Allow poison pills in corp takeovers	N	
75. Kill-Workfare program	N	
76. Prohibit employee polygraph testing	?	
77. Cap Medicare patients' liability	?	
78. Revise unfair trade practices	?	
79. Kill-Shift SDI $ to conv weapons	Y	
80. Kill-Shift SDI $ to accidental launch	N	
81. Kill-Shift MX $ to supplies/parts	Y	
82. Kill-Buy America provision at DOD	N	
83. Allow nuclear testing-5+ kilotons	Y	
84. Allow SALT II to be exceeded	N	
85. $ to vets exposed to nuclear bomb	?	
86. Warn workers of disease exposure	Y	
87. Restore four civil rights laws	Y	
88. Disapprove uranium sales to Japan	N	
89. Notify Congress of covert operations	Y	
90. Approval of $36m in Contra aid	N	
91. $18b deficit reduction compromise	Y	
92. Allow sale of hard-to-detect guns	Y	
93. Catastrophic health insurance	Y	
94. Bork nomination to Supreme Court	N	
95. Kill-Void Panama Canal treaties	Y	
96. Kill-Insurance denial to AIDS+	Y	
97. Keep diplomatic immunity intact	N	
98. Produce Bigeye nerve gas bomb	N	
99. Balanced budget by '93-via targets	N	
100. Allow ASAT missile tests in space	N	
101. Limit space-based/ABM system tests	N	
102. Force reduction in trade barriers	Y	
103. Repeal windfall profit tax on oil	N	
104. $1b/two year aid for the homeless	Y	
105. Disallow $30m for AZT to poor	N	
106. Bar AIDS test-immigrants/marriage	Y	
107. Kill-Biennial budget approval	Y	
108. Fairness doctrine in broadcasting	N	
109. Raise speed limit to 65 mph	N	
110. Immigration reform/alien amnesty	Y	
111. South Africa sanctions-veto override	Y	
112. Kill-Use of military in drug war	Y	
113. Tax overhaul to revise income tax	Y	
114. Submit nuclear test ban treaties	Y	
115. Prohibit sale of Stinger missiles	Y	
116. Prohibit binary chemical weapons	Y	
117. Kill-$10/barrel oil tariff increase	Y	
118. Grant tax amnesty provisions	N	
119. Block Saudi arms sale-veto override	Y	
120. Balanced budget amendment	Y	
121. Include veterans in spending cuts	N	
122. Bar $ to hazardous substance victims	N	
123. Allow seasonal workers in the US	Y	
124. Let fed courts rule on school prayer	Y	
125. Presidential line-item veto	Y	
126. Ease Gun Control Act of 1968	Y	
127. Kill-Req 14-day wait for handguns	Y	
128. Kill-15% min tax on corporations	Y	
129. Drop Social Security COLA	N	
130. Freeze funding for all programs	N	

SPECTER, ARLEN (continued)

131. Kill-Nuclear weapon freeze	N		138. Ban government officials from taping	N
132. Keep decision narrowing Title IX	N		139. Martin Luther King holiday	Y
133. Raise drinking age to 21	Y		140. Authorize Marines in Lebanon	Y
134. Allow production of MX missile	N		141. Amendment making abortion illegal	N
135. Raise taxes/cut spending by $140b	Y		142. Delete $1.2b for jobs creation	N
136. School prayer amendment	N		143. Keep tobacco price supports	N
137. Capital punishment-federal crimes	Y		144. Emergency housing aid of $5.1b	Y

Presidential Support Score: 1991 - 68% 1990 - 58%

WOFFORD, HARRIS -- Pennsylvania [Democrat]. Term Began/Expires: 1991 (Special Appointment)/1994. Born: April 9, 1926; New York City, NY. Education: University of Chicago (B.A.); Howard University (J.D.); Yale University (LL.B.). Occupation: Lawyer; law professor and lecturer; author; U.S. Commission on Civil Rights counsel; special assistant to President Kennedy and Subcabinet Group on Civil Rights chairman; Peace Corps co-founder, special representative to Africa and associate director; president, SUNY-Old Westbury (1966-70) and Bryn Mawr College (1970-78); state Secretary of Labor and Industry (1987-91).

1. Prohibit MFN status for China	Y		15. Kill-Allow women as combat pilots	N
2. Kill-Tie welfare to school attendance	Y		16. Kill-Allow HIV tests before surgery	Y
3. Limit credit card interest rates	Y		17. Strike $12b aid to Int'l Mon Fund	N
4. Confirm Gates as head of CIA	?		18. Raise Senate salary/omit honoraria	N
5. Adoption of national energy policies	?		19. Reduce space station funding $1.9b	N
6. Kill-Restrict NEA use of funds	?		20. Kill-Eliminate supercollider funds	Y
7. Unemployment benefits extension	Y		21. Req 5-day handgun waiting period	Y
8. Confirm Thomas to Supreme Court	N		22. Life in prison instead of death	N
9. Raise eligibility for unpaid leave	Y		23. Exceptions to exclusionary rule	N
10. Notify parents of minors' abortions	N		24. Ban race as death sentence factor	Y
11. Move $3b from defense to domestic	Y		25. Campaign finance revisions	Y
12. End production of B-2 bomber	Y		26. Kill-Term limits for senators	Y
13. Cut SDI $1b to reduce deficit	Y		27. Require four presidential debates	Y
14. Maintain strategic stability-Soviets	Y			

Sen. Wofford was sworn in May 9, 1991, to succeed John Heinz.

Presidential Support Score: 1991 - 27%

RHODE ISLAND

PELL, CLAIBORNE -- Rhode Island [Democrat]. Term Began/Expires: 1991/1996. Prior Terms: Senate: 1961-90. Born: November 22, 1918; New York, NY. Education: Princeton University (A.B.); Columbia University (A.M.). Military Service: U.S. Coast Guard. Occupation: Business executive; special assistant, U.N. Conference.

1. Prohibit MFN status for China	Y		13. Cut SDI $1b to reduce deficit	Y
2. Kill-Tie welfare to school attendance	Y		14. Maintain strategic stability-Soviets	Y
3. Limit credit card interest rates	Y		15. Kill-Allow women as combat pilots	N
4. Confirm Gates as head of CIA	Y		16. Kill-Allow HIV tests before surgery	Y
5. Adoption of national energy policies	#		17. Strike $12b aid to Int'l Mon Fund	N
6. Kill-Restrict NEA use of funds	Y		18. Raise Senate salary/omit honoraria	Y
7. Unemployment benefits extension	Y		19. Reduce space station funding $1.9b	Y
8. Confirm Thomas to Supreme Court	N		20. Kill-Eliminate supercollider funds	Y
9. Raise eligibility for unpaid leave	Y		21. Req 5-day handgun waiting period	Y
10. Notify parents of minors' abortions	N		22. Life in prison instead of death	Y
11. Move $3b from defense to domestic	Y		23. Exceptions to exclusionary rule	N
12. End production of B-2 bomber	Y		24. Ban race as death sentence factor	N

PELL, CLAIBORNE (continued)

25. Campaign finance revisions	Y	
26. Kill-Term limits for senators	Y	
27. Require four presidential debates	Y	
28. Tighten ban on vertical price fixing	Y	
29. Kill-Freeze discretionary budget	Y	
30. Provide $30b for failed S&Ls	Y	
31. Allow use of force against Iraq	N	
32. Allow $15b in foreign aid for 1991	Y	
33. Civil Rights Act of 1990	Y	
34. Block cancellation of Egypt's debt	Y	
35. Cut El Salvador military aid 50%	Y	
36. Reduce troops in NATO by 30,000	Y	
37. Req increases in auto fuel efficiency	Y	
38. Bar taxpayer funding of campaigns	--	
39. Limit textile import growth to 1%	Y	
40. Amendment to ban flag desecration	N	
41. Let fed emp be politically active	Y	
42. Reauthorize Amtrak-veto override	Y	
43. Allow sale of assault weapons	N	
44. Retraining aid for coal miners	Y	
45. Kill-Raise car emission standards	N	
46. Pull EPA nuclear plant authority	N	
47. Defer Chinese students' deportation	Y	
48. Cut in capital gains tax	#	
49. Establish CIA inspector general	Y	
50. Kill-Sanctions against China	Y	
51. Bar drug testing to receive AFDC	Y	
52. Kill-Allow force against drug planes	Y	
53. Include illegal aliens in census	Y	
54. Restitution to Japanese interned	Y	
55. Troop reduction in Europe of 50%	Y	
56. Increase SDI research to $4.3b	N	
57. Kill-Pay homeless below min wage	Y	
58. Ban airline smoking within US	Y	
59. Bar transfer of FS-X technology	Y	
60. Limit liability for oil spills	N	
61. Restructure S&L industry	Y	
62. Ban $ to illegal foreign activities	Y	
63. Req immigrant fluency in English	Y	
64. Allow aliens' families to stay in US	Y	
65. Expand child care aid/tax credit	Y	
66. Raise minimum wage w/subminimum	Y	
67. Freeze outlays except SS/Medicare	N	
68. Kill-Shift $5b of DOD to domestic	N	
69. Confirm Tower as sec of defense	N	
70. Bar abortion $ except to save mother	N	
71. Kill-Warn AIDS carriers' spouses	Y	
72. Allow religious schools to bar gays	Y	
73. 60 days' notice of plant closings	Y	
74. Allow poison pills in corp takeovers	N	
75. Kill-Workfare program	Y	
76. Prohibit employee polygraph testing	Y	
77. Cap Medicare patients' liability	Y	
78. Revise unfair trade practices	Y	
79. Kill-Shift SDI $ to conv weapons	N	
80. Kill-Shift SDI $ to accidental launch	Y	
81. Kill-Shift MX $ to supplies/parts	N	
82. Kill-Buy America provision at DOD	N	
83. Allow nuclear testing-5+ kilotons	N	
84. Allow SALT II to be exceeded	N	

85. $ to vets exposed to nuclear bomb	+	
86. Warn workers of disease exposure	Y	
87. Restore four civil rights laws	Y	
88. Disapprove uranium sales to Japan	Y	
89. Notify Congress of covert operations	Y	
90. Approval of $36m in Contra aid	N	
91. $18b deficit reduction compromise	Y	
92. Allow sale of hard-to-detect guns	N	
93. Catastrophic health insurance	Y	
94. Bork nomination to Supreme Court	N	
95. Kill-Void Panama Canal treaties	Y	
96. Kill-Insurance denial to AIDS+	Y	
97. Keep diplomatic immunity intact	Y	
98. Produce Bigeye nerve gas bomb	N	
99. Balanced budget by '93-via targets	Y	
100. Allow ASAT missile tests in space	N	
101. Limit space-based/ABM system tests	Y	
102. Force reduction in trade barriers	Y	
103. Repeal windfall profit tax on oil	N	
104. $1b/two year aid for the homeless	Y	
105. Disallow $30m for AZT to poor	N	
106. Bar AIDS test-immigrants/marriage	Y	
107. Kill-Biennial budget approval	Y	
108. Fairness doctrine in broadcasting	Y	
109. Raise speed limit to 65 mph	N	
110. Immigration reform/alien amnesty	Y	
111. South Africa sanctions-veto override	Y	
112. Kill-Use of military in drug war	Y	
113. Tax overhaul to revise income tax	Y	
114. Submit nuclear test ban treaties	Y	
115. Prohibit sale of Stinger missiles	Y	
116. Prohibit binary chemical weapons	Y	
117. Kill-$10/barrel oil tariff increase	Y	
118. Grant tax amnesty provisions	Y	
119. Block Saudi arms sale-veto override	Y	
120. Balanced budget amendment	Y	
121. Include veterans in spending cuts	Y	
122. Bar $ to hazardous substance victims	N	
123. Allow seasonal workers in the US	N	
124. Let fed courts rule on school prayer	Y	
125. Presidential line-item veto	Y	
126. Ease Gun Control Act of 1968	N	
127. Kill-Req 14-day wait for handguns	N	
128. Kill-15% min tax on corporations	N	
129. Drop Social Security COLA	N	
130. Freeze funding for all programs	Y	
131. Kill-Nuclear weapon freeze	N	
132. Keep decision narrowing Title IX	N	
133. Raise drinking age to 21	Y	
134. Allow production of MX missile	N	
135. Raise taxes/cut spending by $140b	N	
136. School prayer amendment	N	
137. Capital punishment-federal crimes	N	
138. Ban government officials from taping	Y	
139. Martin Luther King holiday	Y	
140. Authorize Marines in Lebanon	N	
141. Amendment making abortion illegal	N	
142. Delete $1.2b for jobs creation	N	
143. Keep tobacco price supports	N	
144. Emergency housing aid of $5.1b	+	

Presidential Support Score: 1991 - 32%   1990 - 25%

CHAFEE, JOHN H. -- Rhode Island [Republican]. Term Began/Expires: 1989/1994. Prior Terms: Senate: 1977-88. Born: October 22, 1922; Providence, RI. Education: Yale University (B.A.); Harvard Law School (LL.B.). Military Service: U.S. Marines. Occupation: Rhode Island representative (1957-63); governor (1963-69); secretary of the Navy (1969-72); attorney, Edwards and Angell.

1.	Prohibit MFN status for China	N	60.	Limit liability for oil spills	N
2.	Kill-Tie welfare to school attendance	Y	61.	Restructure S&L industry	N
3.	Limit credit card interest rates	Y	62.	Ban $ to illegal foreign activities	N
4.	Confirm Gates as head of CIA	Y	63.	Req immigrant fluency in English	Y
5.	Adoption of national energy policies	N	64.	Allow aliens' families to stay in US	Y
6.	Kill-Restrict NEA use of funds	Y	65.	Expand child care aid/tax credit	Y
7.	Unemployment benefits extension	Y	66.	Raise minimum wage w/subminimum	Y
8.	Confirm Thomas to Supreme Court	Y	67.	Freeze outlays except SS/Medicare	N
9.	Raise eligibility for unpaid leave	Y	68.	Kill-Shift $5b of DOD to domestic	Y
10.	Notify parents of minors' abortions	N	69.	Confirm Tower as sec of defense	Y
11.	Move $3b from defense to domestic	N	70.	Bar abortion $ except to save mother	N
12.	End production of B-2 bomber	N	71.	Kill-Warn AIDS carriers' spouses	Y
13.	Cut SDI $1b to reduce deficit	Y	72.	Allow religious schools to bar gays	N
14.	Maintain strategic stability-Soviets	Y	73.	60 days' notice of plant closings	Y
15.	Kill-Allow women as combat pilots	N	74.	Allow poison pills in corp takeovers	Y
16.	Kill-Allow HIV tests before surgery	Y	75.	Kill-Workfare program	Y
17.	Strike $12b aid to Int'l Mon Fund	N	76.	Prohibit employee polygraph testing	Y
18.	Raise Senate salary/omit honoraria	Y	77.	Cap Medicare patients' liability	Y
19.	Reduce space station funding $1.9b	Y	78.	Revise unfair trade practices	Y
20.	Kill-Eliminate supercollider funds	N	79.	Kill-Shift SDI $ to conv weapons	Y
21.	Req 5-day handgun waiting period	Y	80.	Kill-Shift SDI $ to accidental launch	Y
22.	Life in prison instead of death	Y	81.	Kill-Shift MX $ to supplies/parts	N
23.	Exceptions to exclusionary rule	N	82.	Kill-Buy America provision at DOD	N
24.	Ban race as death sentence factor	N	83.	Allow nuclear testing-5+ kilotons	N
25.	Campaign finance revisions	N	84.	Allow SALT II to be exceeded	N
26.	Kill-Term limits for senators	Y	85.	$ to vets exposed to nuclear bomb	Y
27.	Require four presidential debates	N	86.	Warn workers of disease exposure	Y
28.	Tighten ban on vertical price fixing	Y	87.	Restore four civil rights laws	Y
29.	Kill-Freeze discretionary budget	Y	88.	Disapprove uranium sales to Japan	N
30.	Provide $30b for failed S&Ls	Y	89.	Notify Congress of covert operations	Y
31.	Allow use of force against Iraq	Y	90.	Approval of $36m in Contra aid	N
32.	Allow $15b in foreign aid for 1991	Y	91.	$18b deficit reduction compromise	Y
33.	Civil Rights Act of 1990	Y	92.	Allow sale of hard-to-detect guns	N
34.	Block cancellation of Egypt's debt	N	93.	Catastrophic health insurance	Y
35.	Cut El Salvador military aid 50%	Y	94.	Bork nomination to Supreme Court	N
36.	Reduce troops in NATO by 30,000	N	95.	Kill-Void Panama Canal treaties	Y
37.	Req increases in auto fuel efficiency	Y	96.	Kill-Insurance denial to AIDS+	Y
38.	Bar taxpayer funding of campaigns	Y	97.	Keep diplomatic immunity intact	Y
39.	Limit textile import growth to 1%	N	98.	Produce Bigeye nerve gas bomb	N
40.	Amendment to ban flag desecration	N	99.	Balanced budget by '93-via targets	Y
41.	Let fed emp be politically active	N	100.	Allow ASAT missile tests in space	N
42.	Reauthorize Amtrak-veto override	N	101.	Limit space-based/ABM system tests	Y
43.	Allow sale of assault weapons	N	102.	Force reduction in trade barriers	Y
44.	Retraining aid for coal miners	N	103.	Repeal windfall profit tax on oil	N
45.	Kill-Raise car emission standards	Y	104.	$1b/two year aid for the homeless	?
46.	Pull EPA nuclear plant authority	Y	105.	Disallow $30m for AZT to poor	N
47.	Defer Chinese students' deportation	N	106.	Bar AIDS test-immigrants/marriage	Y
48.	Cut in capital gains tax	Y	107.	Kill-Biennial budget approval	N
49.	Establish CIA inspector general	N	108.	Fairness doctrine in broadcasting	Y
50.	Kill-Sanctions against China	Y	109.	Raise speed limit to 65 mph	N
51.	Bar drug testing to receive AFDC	Y	110.	Immigration reform/alien amnesty	Y
52.	Kill-Allow force against drug planes	N	111.	South Africa sanctions-veto override	Y
53.	Include illegal aliens in census	N	112.	Kill-Use of military in drug war	Y
54.	Restitution to Japanese interned	Y	113.	Tax overhaul to revise income tax	Y
55.	Troop reduction in Europe of 50%	N	114.	Submit nuclear test ban treaties	Y
56.	Increase SDI research to $4.3b	N	115.	Prohibit sale of Stinger missiles	Y
57.	Kill-Pay homeless below min wage	N	116.	Prohibit binary chemical weapons	Y
58.	Ban airline smoking within US	Y	117.	Kill-$10/barrel oil tariff increase	Y
59.	Bar transfer of FS-X technology	N	118.	Grant tax amnesty provisions	?

CHAFEE, JOHN H. (continued)

119. Block Saudi arms sale-veto override	N	
120. Balanced budget amendment	N	
121. Include veterans in spending cuts	Y	
122. Bar $ to hazardous substance victims	N	
123. Allow seasonal workers in the US	N	
124. Let fed courts rule on school prayer	Y	
125. Presidential line-item veto	Y	
126. Ease Gun Control Act of 1968	N	
127. Kill-Req 14-day wait for handguns	N	
128. Kill-15% min tax on corporations	Y	
129. Drop Social Security COLA	Y	
130. Freeze funding for all programs	N	
131. Kill-Nuclear weapon freeze	N	
132. Keep decision narrowing Title IX	Y
133. Raise drinking age to 21	Y
134. Allow production of MX missile	Y
135. Raise taxes/cut spending by $140b	Y
136. School prayer amendment	N
137. Capital punishment-federal crimes	N
138. Ban government officials from taping	N
139. Martin Luther King holiday	Y
140. Authorize Marines in Lebanon	Y
141. Amendment making abortion illegal	N
142. Delete $1.2b for jobs creation	N
143. Keep tobacco price supports	N
144. Emergency housing aid of $5.1b	Y

Presidential Support Score: 1991 - 62% 1990 - 58%

SOUTH CAROLINA

THURMOND, STROM -- South Carolina [Republican]. Term Began/Expires: 1991/1996. Prior Terms: Senate: 1955-90. Born: December 5, 1902; Edgefield, SC. Education: Clemson College. Military Service: U.S. Army, 1942-46. Occupation: Teacher, athletic coach; county superintendent of education; city and county attorney; South Carolina senator; circuit judge; governor of South Carolina (1947-51).

1. Prohibit MFN status for China	N	33. Civil Rights Act of 1990	N
2. Kill-Tie welfare to school attendance	N	34. Block cancellation of Egypt's debt	N
3. Limit credit card interest rates	Y	35. Cut El Salvador military aid 50%	N
4. Confirm Gates as head of CIA	Y	36. Reduce troops in NATO by 30,000	N
5. Adoption of national energy policies	Y	37. Req increases in auto fuel efficiency	N
6. Kill-Restrict NEA use of funds	N	38. Bar taxpayer funding of campaigns	Y
7. Unemployment benefits extension	N	39. Limit textile import growth to 1%	Y
8. Confirm Thomas to Supreme Court	Y	40. Amendment to ban flag desecration	Y
9. Raise eligibility for unpaid leave	N	41. Let fed emp be politically active	N
10. Notify parents of minors' abortions	Y	42. Reauthorize Amtrak-veto override	N
11. Move $3b from defense to domestic	N	43. Allow sale of assault weapons	Y
12. End production of B-2 bomber	N	44. Retraining aid for coal miners	N
13. Cut SDI $1b to reduce deficit	N	45. Kill-Raise car emission standards	Y
14. Maintain strategic stability-Soviets	N	46. Pull EPA nuclear plant authority	Y
15. Kill-Allow women as combat pilots	Y	47. Defer Chinese students' deportation	N
16. Kill-Allow HIV tests before surgery	N	48. Cut in capital gains tax	Y
17. Strike $12b aid to Int'l Mon Fund	Y	49. Establish CIA inspector general	N
18. Raise Senate salary/omit honoraria	Y	50. Kill-Sanctions against China	N
19. Reduce space station funding $1.9b	N	51. Bar drug testing to receive AFDC	N
20. Kill-Eliminate supercollider funds	Y	52. Kill-Allow force against drug planes	N
21. Req 5-day handgun waiting period	Y	53. Include illegal aliens in census	N
22. Life in prison instead of death	N	54. Restitution to Japanese interned	N
23. Exceptions to exclusionary rule	Y	55. Troop reduction in Europe of 50%	N
24. Ban race as death sentence factor	Y	56. Increase SDI research to $4.3b	Y
25. Campaign finance revisions	N	57. Kill-Pay homeless below min wage	Y
26. Kill-Term limits for senators	N	58. Ban airline smoking within US	Y
27. Require four presidential debates	N	59. Bar transfer of FS-X technology	N
28. Tighten ban on vertical price fixing	N	60. Limit liability for oil spills	N
29. Kill-Freeze discretionary budget	N	61. Restructure S&L industry	N
30. Provide $30b for failed S&Ls	+	62. Ban $ to illegal foreign activities	N
31. Allow use of force against Iraq	Y	63. Req immigrant fluency in English	Y
32. Allow $15b in foreign aid for 1991	Y	64. Allow aliens' families to stay in US	N

THURMOND, STROM (continued)

65. Expand child care aid/tax credit	N
66. Raise minimum wage w/subminimum	N
67. Freeze outlays except SS/Medicare	N
68. Kill-Shift $5b of DOD to domestic	Y
69. Confirm Tower as sec of defense	Y
70. Bar abortion $ except to save mother	Y
71. Kill-Warn AIDS carriers' spouses	N
72. Allow religious schools to bar gays	N
73. 60 days' notice of plant closings	N
74. Allow poison pills in corp takeovers	N
75. Kill-Workfare program	N
76. Prohibit employee polygraph testing	N
77. Cap Medicare patients' liability	Y
78. Revise unfair trade practices	N
79. Kill-Shift SDI $ to conv weapons	Y
80. Kill-Shift SDI $ to accidental launch	N
81. Kill-Shift MX $ to supplies/parts	Y
82. Kill-Buy America provision at DOD	N
83. Allow nuclear testing-5+ kilotons	Y
84. Allow SALT II to be exceeded	Y
85. $ to vets exposed to nuclear bomb	N
86. Warn workers of disease exposure	N
87. Restore four civil rights laws	N
88. Disapprove uranium sales to Japan	--
89. Notify Congress of covert operations	Y
90. Approval of $36m in Contra aid	Y
91. $18b deficit reduction compromise	Y
92. Allow sale of hard-to-detect guns	N
93. Catastrophic health insurance	Y
94. Bork nomination to Supreme Court	Y
95. Kill-Void Panama Canal treaties	N
96. Kill-Insurance denial to AIDS+	N
97. Keep diplomatic immunity intact	N
98. Produce Bigeye nerve gas bomb	Y
99. Balanced budget by '93-via targets	Y
100. Allow ASAT missile tests in space	Y
101. Limit space-based/ABM system tests	N
102. Force reduction in trade barriers	Y
103. Repeal windfall profit tax on oil	Y
104. $1b/two year aid for the homeless	Y

105. Disallow $30m for AZT to poor	Y
106. Bar AIDS test-immigrants/marriage	N
107. Kill-Biennial budget approval	N
108. Fairness doctrine in broadcasting	Y
109. Raise speed limit to 65 mph	Y
110. Immigration reform/alien amnesty	Y
111. South Africa sanctions-veto override	N
112. Kill-Use of military in drug war	Y
113. Tax overhaul to revise income tax	Y
114. Submit nuclear test ban treaties	N
115. Prohibit sale of Stinger missiles	N
116. Prohibit binary chemical weapons	N
117. Kill-$10/barrel oil tariff increase	Y
118. Grant tax amnesty provisions	Y
119. Block Saudi arms sale-veto override	N
120. Balanced budget amendment	Y
121. Include veterans in spending cuts	Y
122. Bar $ to hazardous substance victims	Y
123. Allow seasonal workers in the US	Y
124. Let fed courts rule on school prayer	N
125. Presidential line-item veto	Y
126. Ease Gun Control Act of 1968	Y
127. Kill-Req 14-day wait for handguns	Y
128. Kill-15% min tax on corporations	Y
129. Drop Social Security COLA	Y
130. Freeze funding for all programs	N
131. Kill-Nuclear weapon freeze	Y
132. Keep decision narrowing Title IX	Y
133. Raise drinking age to 21	N
134. Allow production of MX missile	Y
135. Raise taxes/cut spending by $140b	Y
136. School prayer amendment	Y
137. Capital punishment-federal crimes	Y
138. Ban government officials from taping	N
139. Martin Luther King holiday	N
140. Authorize Marines in Lebanon	Y
141. Amendment making abortion illegal	Y
142. Delete $1.2b for jobs creation	Y
143. Keep tobacco price supports	Y
144. Emergency housing aid of $5.1b	Y

Presidential Support Score: 1991 - 88%   1990 - 78%

HOLLINGS, ERNEST F. -- South Carolina [Democrat]. Term Began/Expires: 1987/1992. Prior Terms: Senate: 1966 (Special Election)-1986. Born: January 1, 1922; Charleston, SC. Education: The Citadel (B.A.); University of South Carolina (LL.B.). Military Service: Armed Forces, 1942-45. Occupation: South Carolina representative (1948-53); lieutenant governor (1954-58); governor (1959-63).

1. Prohibit MFN status for China	Y
2. Kill-Tie welfare to school attendance	Y
3. Limit credit card interest rates	Y
4. Confirm Gates as head of CIA	N
5. Adoption of national energy policies	N
6. Kill-Restrict NEA use of funds	N
7. Unemployment benefits extension	Y
8. Confirm Thomas to Supreme Court	Y
9. Raise eligibility for unpaid leave	N
10. Notify parents of minors' abortions	N
11. Move $3b from defense to domestic	Y
12. End production of B-2 bomber	Y
13. Cut SDI $1b to reduce deficit	N

14. Maintain strategic stability-Soviets	N
15. Kill-Allow women as combat pilots	Y
16. Kill-Allow HIV tests before surgery	N
17. Strike $12b aid to Int'l Mon Fund	N
18. Raise Senate salary/omit honoraria	N
19. Reduce space station funding $1.9b	Y
20. Kill-Eliminate supercollider funds	N
21. Req 5-day handgun waiting period	N
22. Life in prison instead of death	N
23. Exceptions to exclusionary rule	Y
24. Ban race as death sentence factor	Y
25. Campaign finance revisions	N
26. Kill-Term limits for senators	Y

HOLLINGS, ERNEST F. (continued)

27.	Require four presidential debates	Y
28.	Tighten ban on vertical price fixing	Y
29.	Kill-Freeze discretionary budget	N
30.	Provide $30b for failed S&Ls	N
31.	Allow use of force against Iraq	N
32.	Allow $15b in foreign aid for 1991	N
33.	Civil Rights Act of 1990	Y
34.	Block cancellation of Egypt's debt	Y
35.	Cut El Salvador military aid 50%	Y
36.	Reduce troops in NATO by 30,000	N
37.	Req increases in auto fuel efficiency	Y
38.	Bar taxpayer funding of campaigns	Y
39.	Limit textile import growth to 1%	Y
40.	Amendment to ban flag desecration	Y
41.	Let fed emp be politically active	Y
42.	Reauthorize Amtrak-veto override	Y
43.	Allow sale of assault weapons	Y
44.	Retraining aid for coal miners	Y
45.	Kill-Raise car emission standards	Y
46.	Pull EPA nuclear plant authority	Y
47.	Defer Chinese students' deportation	Y
48.	Cut in capital gains tax	N
49.	Establish CIA inspector general	N
50.	Kill-Sanctions against China	Y
51.	Bar drug testing to receive AFDC	Y
52.	Kill-Allow force against drug planes	Y
53.	Include illegal aliens in census	N
54.	Restitution to Japanese interned	Y
55.	Troop reduction in Europe of 50%	N
56.	Increase SDI research to $4.3b	Y
57.	Kill-Pay homeless below min wage	Y
58.	Ban airline smoking within US	N
59.	Bar transfer of FS-X technology	Y
60.	Limit liability for oil spills	Y
61.	Restructure S&L industry	Y
62.	Ban $ to illegal foreign activities	Y
63.	Req immigrant fluency in English	Y
64.	Allow aliens' families to stay in US	N
65.	Expand child care aid/tax credit	Y
66.	Raise minimum wage w/subminimum	N
67.	Freeze outlays except SS/Medicare	Y
68.	Kill-Shift $5b of DOD to domestic	N
69.	Confirm Tower as sec of defense	N
70.	Bar abortion $ except to save mother	N
71.	Kill-Warn AIDS carriers' spouses	Y
72.	Allow religious schools to bar gays	N
73.	60 days' notice of plant closings	Y
74.	Allow poison pills in corp takeovers	N
75.	Kill-Workfare program	Y
76.	Prohibit employee polygraph testing	Y
77.	Cap Medicare patients' liability	Y
78.	Revise unfair trade practices	Y
79.	Kill-Shift SDI $ to conv weapons	Y
80.	Kill-Shift SDI $ to accidental launch	N
81.	Kill-Shift MX $ to supplies/parts	Y
82.	Kill-Buy America provision at DOD	N
83.	Allow nuclear testing-5+ kilotons	Y
84.	Allow SALT II to be exceeded	Y
85.	$ to vets exposed to nuclear bomb	Y

86.	Warn workers of disease exposure	N
87.	Restore four civil rights laws	Y
88.	Disapprove uranium sales to Japan	Y
89.	Notify Congress of covert operations	Y
90.	Approval of $36m in Contra aid	Y
91.	$18b deficit reduction compromise	N
92.	Allow sale of hard-to-detect guns	N
93.	Catastrophic health insurance	N
94.	Bork nomination to Supreme Court	Y
95.	Kill-Void Panama Canal treaties	Y
96.	Kill-Insurance denial to AIDS+	N
97.	Keep diplomatic immunity intact	Y
98.	Produce Bigeye nerve gas bomb	Y
99.	Balanced budget by '93-via targets	Y
100.	Allow ASAT missile tests in space	Y
101.	Limit space-based/ABM system tests	N
102.	Force reduction in trade barriers	Y
103.	Repeal windfall profit tax on oil	Y
104.	$1b/two year aid for the homeless	Y
105.	Disallow $30m for AZT to poor	N
106.	Bar AIDS test-immigrants/marriage	N
107.	Kill-Biennial budget approval	Y
108.	Fairness doctrine in broadcasting	Y
109.	Raise speed limit to 65 mph	N
110.	Immigration reform/alien amnesty	Y
111.	South Africa sanctions-veto override	Y
112.	Kill-Use of military in drug war	Y
113.	Tax overhaul to revise income tax	Y
114.	Submit nuclear test ban treaties	Y
115.	Prohibit sale of Stinger missiles	Y
116.	Prohibit binary chemical weapons	N
117.	Kill-$10/barrel oil tariff increase	N
118.	Grant tax amnesty provisions	N
119.	Block Saudi arms sale-veto override	Y
120.	Balanced budget amendment	Y
121.	Include veterans in spending cuts	N
122.	Bar $ to hazardous substance victims	Y
123.	Allow seasonal workers in the US	Y
124.	Let fed courts rule on school prayer	Y
125.	Presidential line-item veto	Y
126.	Ease Gun Control Act of 1968	Y
127.	Kill-Req 14-day wait for handguns	Y
128.	Kill-15% min tax on corporations	N
129.	Drop Social Security COLA	N
130.	Freeze funding for all programs	Y
131.	Kill-Nuclear weapon freeze	N
132.	Keep decision narrowing Title IX	N
133.	Raise drinking age to 21	Y
134.	Allow production of MX missile	N
135.	Raise taxes/cut spending by $140b	N
136.	School prayer amendment	Y
137.	Capital punishment-federal crimes	?
138.	Ban government officials from taping	?
139.	Martin Luther King holiday	Y
140.	Authorize Marines in Lebanon	N
141.	Amendment making abortion illegal	N
142.	Delete $1.2b for jobs creation	N
143.	Keep tobacco price supports	Y
144.	Emergency housing aid of $5.1b	Y

Presidential Support Score: 1991 - 56%   1990 - 52%

SOUTH DAKOTA

PRESSLER, LARRY -- South Dakota [Republican]. Term Began/Expires: 1985-1990. Prior Terms: House: 1974-78; Senate: 1979-90. Born: March 29, 1942; Humboldt, SD. Education: University of South Dakota (B.A.); Oxford University; Kennedy School of Government (M.A.); Harvard University (J.D.). Military Service: U.S. Army, 1966-68. Occupation: State Department employee; Senate staff member.

1. Prohibit MFN status for China	Y	
2. Kill-Tie welfare to school attendance	N	
3. Limit credit card interest rates	N	
4. Confirm Gates as head of CIA	Y	
5. Adoption of national energy policies	Y	
6. Kill-Restrict NEA use of funds	Y	
7. Unemployment benefits extension	N	
8. Confirm Thomas to Supreme Court	Y	
9. Raise eligibility for unpaid leave	N	
10. Notify parents of minors' abortions	Y	
11. Move $3b from defense to domestic	N	
12. End production of B-2 bomber	N	
13. Cut SDI $1b to reduce deficit	N	
14. Maintain strategic stability-Soviets	N	
15. Kill-Allow women as combat pilots	N	
16. Kill-Allow HIV tests before surgery	N	
17. Strike $12b aid to Int'l Mon Fund	Y	
18. Raise Senate salary/omit honoraria	N	
19. Reduce space station funding $1.9b	N	
20. Kill-Eliminate supercollider funds	Y	
21. Req 5-day handgun waiting period	N	
22. Life in prison instead of death	N	
23. Exceptions to exclusionary rule	Y	
24. Ban race as death sentence factor	Y	
25. Campaign finance revisions	N	
26. Kill-Term limits for senators	N	
27. Require four presidential debates	N	
28. Tighten ban on vertical price fixing	N	
29. Kill-Freeze discretionary budget	N	
30. Provide $30b for failed S&Ls	Y	
31. Allow use of force against Iraq	Y	
32. Allow $15b in foreign aid for 1991	N	
33. Civil Rights Act of 1990	N	
34. Block cancellation of Egypt's debt	Y	
35. Cut El Salvador military aid 50%	Y	
36. Reduce troops in NATO by 30,000	Y	
37. Req increases in auto fuel efficiency	Y	
38. Bar taxpayer funding of campaigns	Y	
39. Limit textile import growth to 1%	N	
40. Amendment to ban flag desecration	Y	
41. Let fed emp be politically active	N	
42. Reauthorize Amtrak-veto override	N	
43. Allow sale of assault weapons	Y	
44. Retraining aid for coal miners	N	
45. Kill-Raise car emission standards	N	
46. Pull EPA nuclear plant authority	N	
47. Defer Chinese students' deportation	Y	
48. Cut in capital gains tax	Y	
49. Establish CIA inspector general	Y	
50. Kill-Sanctions against China	N	
51. Bar drug testing to receive AFDC	N	
52. Kill-Allow force against drug planes	N
53. Include illegal aliens in census	N
54. Restitution to Japanese interned	N
55. Troop reduction in Europe of 50%	Y
56. Increase SDI research to $4.3b	N
57. Kill-Pay homeless below min wage	N
58. Ban airline smoking within US	Y
59. Bar transfer of FS-X technology	Y
60. Limit liability for oil spills	N
61. Restructure S&L industry	Y
62. Ban $ to illegal foreign activities	N
63. Req immigrant fluency in English	Y
64. Allow aliens' families to stay in US	N
65. Expand child care aid/tax credit	N
66. Raise minimum wage w/subminimum	Y
67. Freeze outlays except SS/Medicare	N
68. Kill-Shift $5b of DOD to domestic	N
69. Confirm Tower as sec of defense	Y
70. Bar abortion $ except to save mother	Y
71. Kill-Warn AIDS carriers' spouses	N
72. Allow religious schools to bar gays	Y
73. 60 days' notice of plant closings	N
74. Allow poison pills in corp takeovers	N
75. Kill-Workfare program	N
76. Prohibit employee polygraph testing	N
77. Cap Medicare patients' liability	Y
78. Revise unfair trade practices	N
79. Kill-Shift SDI $ to conv weapons	Y
80. Kill-Shift SDI $ to accidental launch	N
81. Kill-Shift MX $ to supplies/parts	Y
82. Kill-Buy America provision at DOD	N
83. Allow nuclear testing-5+ kilotons	Y
84. Allow SALT II to be exceeded	Y
85. $ to vets exposed to nuclear bomb	Y
86. Warn workers of disease exposure	N
87. Restore four civil rights laws	N
88. Disapprove uranium sales to Japan	N
89. Notify Congress of covert operations	N
90. Approval of $36m in Contra aid	Y
91. $18b deficit reduction compromise	N
92. Allow sale of hard-to-detect guns	Y
93. Catastrophic health insurance	Y
94. Bork nomination to Supreme Court	Y
95. Kill-Void Panama Canal treaties	N
96. Kill-Insurance denial to AIDS+	N
97. Keep diplomatic immunity intact	N
98. Produce Bigeye nerve gas bomb	Y
99. Balanced budget by '93-via targets	N
100. Allow ASAT missile tests in space	N
101. Limit space-based/ABM system tests	N
102. Force reduction in trade barriers	Y

PRESSLER, LARRY (continued)

103. Repeal windfall profit tax on oil	Y
104. $1b/two year aid for the homeless	Y
105. Disallow $30m for AZT to poor	N
106. Bar AIDS test-immigrants/marriage	N
107. Kill-Biennial budget approval	?
108. Fairness doctrine in broadcasting	Y
109. Raise speed limit to 65 mph	Y
110. Immigration reform/alien amnesty	N
111. South Africa sanctions-veto override	N
112. Kill-Use of military in drug war	?
113. Tax overhaul to revise income tax	N
114. Submit nuclear test ban treaties	N
115. Prohibit sale of Stinger missiles	N
116. Prohibit binary chemical weapons	N
117. Kill-$10/barrel oil tariff increase	Y
118. Grant tax amnesty provisions	N
119. Block Saudi arms sale-veto override	Y
120. Balanced budget amendment	Y
121. Include veterans in spending cuts	N
122. Bar $ to hazardous substance victims	Y
123. Allow seasonal workers in the US	N

124. Let fed courts rule on school prayer	N
125. Presidential line-item veto	Y
126. Ease Gun Control Act of 1968	Y
127. Kill-Req 14-day wait for handguns	Y
128. Kill-15% min tax on corporations	Y
129. Drop Social Security COLA	Y
130. Freeze funding for all programs	N
131. Kill-Nuclear weapon freeze	Y
132. Keep decision narrowing Title IX	Y
133. Raise drinking age to 21	Y
134. Allow production of MX missile	N
135. Raise taxes/cut spending by $140b	Y
136. School prayer amendment	Y
137. Capital punishment-federal crimes	Y
138. Ban government officials from taping	N
139. Martin Luther King holiday	N
140. Authorize Marines in Lebanon	Y
141. Amendment making abortion illegal	Y
142. Delete $1.2b for jobs creation	Y
143. Keep tobacco price supports	Y
144. Emergency housing aid of $5.1b	+

Presidential Support Score: 1991 - 88% 1990 - 58%

DASCHLE, THOMAS A. -- South Dakota [Democrat]. Term Began/Expires: 1987/1992. Prior Terms: House: 1979-86. Born: December 9, 1947; Aberdeen, SD. Education: South Dakota State University (B.A.). Military Service: U.S. Air Force, 1969-72. Occupation: Financial investment firm representative; Congressional legislative assistant (1972-77).

1. Prohibit MFN status for China	Y
2. Kill-Tie welfare to school attendance	Y
3. Limit credit card interest rates	N
4. Confirm Gates as head of CIA	N
5. Adoption of national energy policies	Y
6. Kill-Restrict NEA use of funds	N
7. Unemployment benefits extension	Y
8. Confirm Thomas to Supreme Court	N
9. Raise eligibility for unpaid leave	Y
10. Notify parents of minors' abortions	N
11. Move $3b from defense to domestic	Y
12. End production of B-2 bomber	Y
13. Cut SDI $1b to reduce deficit	Y
14. Maintain strategic stability-Soviets	N
15. Kill-Allow women as combat pilots	N
16. Kill-Allow HIV tests before surgery	Y
17. Strike $12b aid to Int'l Mon Fund	N
18. Raise Senate salary/omit honoraria	N
19. Reduce space station funding $1.9b	Y
20. Kill-Eliminate supercollider funds	Y
21. Req 5-day handgun waiting period	Y
22. Life in prison instead of death	N
23. Exceptions to exclusionary rule	N
24. Ban race as death sentence factor	N
25. Campaign finance revisions	Y
26. Kill-Term limits for senators	Y
27. Require four presidential debates	Y
28. Tighten ban on vertical price fixing	Y
29. Kill-Freeze discretionary budget	N
30. Provide $30b for failed S&Ls	N
31. Allow use of force against Iraq	N
32. Allow $15b in foreign aid for 1991	N
33. Civil Rights Act of 1990	Y
34. Block cancellation of Egypt's debt	+

35. Cut El Salvador military aid 50%	Y
36. Reduce troops in NATO by 30,000	Y
37. Req increases in auto fuel efficiency	Y
38. Bar taxpayer funding of campaigns	N
39. Limit textile import growth to 1%	Y
40. Amendment to ban flag desecration	N
41. Let fed emp be politically active	Y
42. Reauthorize Amtrak-veto override	Y
43. Allow sale of assault weapons	N
44. Retraining aid for coal miners	N
45. Kill-Raise car emission standards	N
46. Pull EPA nuclear plant authority	N
47. Defer Chinese students' deportation	Y
48. Cut in capital gains tax	N
49. Establish CIA inspector general	Y
50. Kill-Sanctions against China	N
51. Bar drug testing to receive AFDC	Y
52. Kill-Allow force against drug planes	Y
53. Include illegal aliens in census	Y
54. Restitution to Japanese interned	Y
55. Troop reduction in Europe of 50%	Y
56. Increase SDI research to $4.3b	N
57. Kill-Pay homeless below min wage	Y
58. Ban airline smoking within US	Y
59. Bar transfer of FS-X technology	Y
60. Limit liability for oil spills	Y
61. Restructure S&L industry	Y
62. Ban $ to illegal foreign activities	Y
63. Req immigrant fluency in English	N
64. Allow aliens' families to stay in US	Y
65. Expand child care aid/tax credit	Y
66. Raise minimum wage w/subminimum	Y
67. Freeze outlays except SS/Medicare	N
68. Kill-Shift $5b of DOD to domestic	Y

DASCHLE, THOMAS A. (continued)

69. Confirm Tower as sec of defense	N	
70. Bar abortion $ except to save mother	N	
71. Kill-Warn AIDS carriers' spouses	Y	
72. Allow religious schools to bar gays	Y	
73. 60 days' notice of plant closings	Y	
74. Allow poison pills in corp takeovers	Y	
75. Kill-Workfare program	Y	
76. Prohibit employee polygraph testing	Y	
77. Cap Medicare patients' liability	Y	
78. Revise unfair trade practices	Y	
79. Kill-Shift SDI $ to conv weapons	N	
80. Kill-Shift SDI $ to accidental launch	Y	
81. Kill-Shift MX $ to supplies/parts	N	
82. Kill-Buy America provision at DOD	N	
83. Allow nuclear testing-5+ kilotons	N	
84. Allow SALT II to be exceeded	N	
85. $ to vets exposed to nuclear bomb	Y	
86. Warn workers of disease exposure	Y	
87. Restore four civil rights laws	Y	
88. Disapprove uranium sales to Japan	N	
89. Notify Congress of covert operations	Y	

90. Approval of $36m in Contra aid	N
91. $18b deficit reduction compromise	N
92. Allow sale of hard-to-detect guns	N
93. Catastrophic health insurance	Y
94. Bork nomination to Supreme Court	N
95. Kill-Void Panama Canal treaties	Y
96. Kill-Insurance denial to AIDS+	N
97. Keep diplomatic immunity intact	Y
98. Produce Bigeye nerve gas bomb	N
99. Balanced budget by '93-via targets	Y
100. Allow ASAT missile tests in space	N
101. Limit space-based/ABM system tests	Y
102. Force reduction in trade barriers	Y
103. Repeal windfall profit tax on oil	Y
104. $1b/two year aid for the homeless	Y
105. Disallow $30m for AZT to poor	N
106. Bar AIDS test-immigrants/marriage	Y
107. Kill-Biennial budget approval	Y
108. Fairness doctrine in broadcasting	Y
109. Raise speed limit to 65 mph	Y

The following are House measures voted on between 1982-1986:

99. Immigration reform/alien amnesty	Y	
100. South Africa sanctions-veto override	Y	
101. Tax overhaul to revise income tax	N	
102. Use of military in drug war	Y	
103. Delete 12 MX/add conventional wpn	Y	
104. Raise speed limit to 65 mph	Y	
105. Require Pentagon to buy US goods	Y	
106. AIDS insurance non-discrimination	Y	
107. Prohibit Saudi arms sales	Y	
108. Ease Gun Control Act of 1968	Y	
109. Bar interstate handgun transport	N	
110. Make company emissions known	Y	
111. Allow toxic victims to sue in fed ct	N	
112. Superfund waste cleanup of $10b	Y	
113. 90 days notice of plant closings	?	
114. $20b in Medicare cuts/tax increases	Y	
115. Spending cuts and tax increases	Y	
116. Set school lunch lmt-250% poverty	N	
117. $75m for youth work projects	Y	
118. Allow Angolan military assistance	N	
119. Suspend defense payments for abuse	Y	
120. Drop SS COLAs/$12b tax increase	Y	
121. Approve $1.5b for 21 MX missiles	N	

122. Emergency farm credit/revisions	Y
123. Duty on Taiwan/Hong Kong/S Korea	N
124. Limit steel imports to 17%	Y
125. Cut $ to schools that bar prayer	N
126. $50b-taxes; cut Medicare/spending	Y
127. Limit Pershing II/cruise in Europe	Y
128. Delete $7.1b for 34 B-1 bombers	N
129. Bar purchase of Sergeant York guns	Y
130. El Salvador military/economic aid	N
131. Bar mining of Nicaraguan waters	Y
132. Physician fee freeze for Medicare	N
133. $49b in "sin"/phone/insurance taxes	N
134. Allow sale of Conrail	N
135. Equal Rights Amendment	Y
136. Authorize Marines in Lebanon	N
137. Eminent domain for coal companies	Y
138. Prohibit EPA clean air sanctions	Y
139. SS retirement age increase/reforms	Y
140. Auto domestic content requirement	?
141. Delete jobs program funding	Y
142. Highway-gas tax bill	N
143. Cut $5b from defense for Medicare	Y
144. Emergency housing aid of $1b	Y

Presidential Support Score: 1991 - 27%   1990 - 31%

TENNESSEE

SASSER, JIM -- Tennessee [Democrat]. Term Began/Expires: 1989/1994. Prior Terms: Senate: 1977-88. Born: September 30, 1936; Memphis, TN. Education: University of Tennessee; Vanderbilt University (B.A., LL.B.). Military Service: U.S. Marine Corps Reserve. Occupation: Attorney, Goodpasture, Carpenter, Woods & Sasser.

1. Prohibit MFN status for China	Y	2. Kill-Tie welfare to school attendance	Y

SASSER, JIM (continued)

3. Limit credit card interest rates	Y
4. Confirm Gates as head of CIA	N
5. Adoption of national energy policies	N
6. Kill-Restrict NEA use of funds	Y
7. Unemployment benefits extension	Y
8. Confirm Thomas to Supreme Court	N
9. Raise eligibility for unpaid leave	Y
10. Notify parents of minors' abortions	N
11. Move $3b from defense to domestic	N
12. End production of B-2 bomber	Y
13. Cut SDI $1b to reduce deficit	Y
14. Maintain strategic stability-Soviets	Y
15. Kill-Allow women as combat pilots	N
16. Kill-Allow HIV tests before surgery	Y
17. Strike $12b aid to Int'l Mon Fund	N
18. Raise Senate salary/omit honoraria	N
19. Reduce space station funding $1.9b	Y
20. Kill-Eliminate supercollider funds	N
21. Req 5-day handgun waiting period	Y
22. Life in prison instead of death	N
23. Exceptions to exclusionary rule	N
24. Ban race as death sentence factor	N
25. Campaign finance revisions	Y
26. Kill-Term limits for senators	Y
27. Require four presidential debates	Y
28. Tighten ban on vertical price fixing	Y
29. Kill-Freeze discretionary budget	Y
30. Provide $30b for failed S&Ls	Y
31. Allow use of force against Iraq	N
32. Allow $15b in foreign aid for 1991	Y
33. Civil Rights Act of 1990	Y
34. Block cancellation of Egypt's debt	Y
35. Cut El Salvador military aid 50%	Y
36. Reduce troops in NATO by 30,000	Y
37. Req increases in auto fuel efficiency	N
38. Bar taxpayer funding of campaigns	N
39. Limit textile import growth to 1%	Y
40. Amendment to ban flag desecration	N
41. Let fed emp be politically active	Y
42. Reauthorize Amtrak-veto override	Y
43. Allow sale of assault weapons	N
44. Retraining aid for coal miners	Y
45. Kill-Raise car emission standards	Y
46. Pull EPA nuclear plant authority	N
47. Defer Chinese students' deportation	Y
48. Cut in capital gains tax	N
49. Establish CIA inspector general	Y
50. Kill-Sanctions against China	Y
51. Bar drug testing to receive AFDC	Y
52. Kill-Allow force against drug planes	Y
53. Include illegal aliens in census	Y
54. Restitution to Japanese interned	Y
55. Troop reduction in Europe of 50%	Y
56. Increase SDI research to $4.3b	N
57. Kill-Pay homeless below min wage	Y
58. Ban airline smoking within US	N
59. Bar transfer of FS-X technology	Y
60. Limit liability for oil spills	Y
61. Restructure S&L industry	Y
62. Ban $ to illegal foreign activities	Y
63. Req immigrant fluency in English	N
64. Allow aliens' families to stay in US	Y
65. Expand child care aid/tax credit	Y
66. Raise minimum wage w/subminimum	Y

67. Freeze outlays except SS/Medicare	N
68. Kill-Shift $5b of DOD to domestic	Y
69. Confirm Tower as sec of defense	N
70. Bar abortion $ except to save mother	N
71. Kill-Warn AIDS carriers' spouses	N
72. Allow religious schools to bar gays	?
73. 60 days' notice of plant closings	Y
74. Allow poison pills in corp takeovers	Y
75. Kill-Workfare program	Y
76. Prohibit employee polygraph testing	Y
77. Cap Medicare patients' liability	Y
78. Revise unfair trade practices	Y
79. Kill-Shift SDI $ to conv weapons	N
80. Kill-Shift SDI $ to accidental launch	Y
81. Kill-Shift MX $ to supplies/parts	N
82. Kill-Buy America provision at DOD	N
83. Allow nuclear testing-5+ kilotons	N
84. Allow SALT II to be exceeded	N
85. $ to vets exposed to nuclear bomb	Y
86. Warn workers of disease exposure	N
87. Restore four civil rights laws	Y
88. Disapprove uranium sales to Japan	Y
89. Notify Congress of covert operations	Y
90. Approval of $36m in Contra aid	N
91. $18b deficit reduction compromise	Y
92. Allow sale of hard-to-detect guns	Y
93. Catastrophic health insurance	Y
94. Bork nomination to Supreme Court	N
95. Kill-Void Panama Canal treaties	Y
96. Kill-Insurance denial to AIDS+	N
97. Keep diplomatic immunity intact	Y
98. Produce Bigeye nerve gas bomb	N
99. Balanced budget by '93-via targets	Y
100. Allow ASAT missile tests in space	N
101. Limit space-based/ABM system tests	Y
102. Force reduction in trade barriers	Y
103. Repeal windfall profit tax on oil	N
104. $1b/two year aid for the homeless	Y
105. Disallow $30m for AZT to poor	N
106. Bar AIDS test-immigrants/marriage	Y
107. Kill-Biennial budget approval	Y
108. Fairness doctrine in broadcasting	Y
109. Raise speed limit to 65 mph	Y
110. Immigration reform/alien amnesty	Y
111. South Africa sanctions-veto override	Y
112. Kill-Use of military in drug war	Y
113. Tax overhaul to revise income tax	N
114. Submit nuclear test ban treaties	Y
115. Prohibit sale of Stinger missiles	Y
116. Prohibit binary chemical weapons	Y
117. Kill-$10/barrel oil tariff increase	Y
118. Grant tax amnesty provisions	N
119. Block Saudi arms sale-veto override	Y
120. Balanced budget amendment	Y
121. Include veterans in spending cuts	N
122. Bar $ to hazardous substance victims	N
123. Allow seasonal workers in the US	Y
124. Let fed courts rule on school prayer	N
125. Presidential line-item veto	N
126. Ease Gun Control Act of 1968	Y
127. Kill-Req 14-day wait for handguns	Y
128. Kill-15% min tax on corporations	N
129. Drop Social Security COLA	N
130. Freeze funding for all programs	N

SASSER, JIM (continued)

131. Kill-Nuclear weapon freeze	N	138. Ban government officials from taping	Y
132. Keep decision narrowing Title IX	N	139. Martin Luther King holiday	Y
133. Raise drinking age to 21	Y	140. Authorize Marines in Lebanon	N
134. Allow production of MX missile	N	141. Amendment making abortion illegal	N
135. Raise taxes/cut spending by $140b	N	142. Delete $1.2b for jobs creation	N
136. School prayer amendment	Y	143. Keep tobacco price supports	Y
137. Capital punishment-federal crimes	N	144. Emergency housing aid of $5.1b	Y

Presidential Support Score: 1991 - 36%   1990 - 33%

GORE, ALBERT, Jr. -- Tennessee [Democrat]. Term Began/Expires: 1991/1996. Prior Terms: House: 1977-84; Senate: 1985-90. Born: March 31, 1948. Education: Harvard University; Vanderbilt Graduate School of Religion; Vanderbilt School of Law. Military Service: U.S. Army, 1969-71. Occupation: Reporter; writer; construction business.

1. Prohibit MFN status for China	Y	49. Establish CIA inspector general	Y
2. Kill-Tie welfare to school attendance	Y	50. Kill-Sanctions against China	Y
3. Limit credit card interest rates	Y	51. Bar drug testing to receive AFDC	Y
4. Confirm Gates as head of CIA	N	52. Kill-Allow force against drug planes	Y
5. Adoption of national energy policies	N	53. Include illegal aliens in census	Y
6. Kill-Restrict NEA use of funds	Y	54. Restitution to Japanese interned	Y
7. Unemployment benefits extension	Y	55. Troop reduction in Europe of 50%	N
8. Confirm Thomas to Supreme Court	N	56. Increase SDI research to $4.3b	Y
9. Raise eligibility for unpaid leave	Y	57. Kill-Pay homeless below min wage	Y
10. Notify parents of minors' abortions	N	58. Ban airline smoking within US	Y
11. Move $3b from defense to domestic	N	59. Bar transfer of FS-X technology	Y
12. End production of B-2 bomber	Y	60. Limit liability for oil spills	N
13. Cut SDI $1b to reduce deficit	Y	61. Restructure S&L industry	Y
14. Maintain strategic stability-Soviets	Y	62. Ban $ to illegal foreign activities	Y
15. Kill-Allow women as combat pilots	N	63. Req immigrant fluency in English	N
16. Kill-Allow HIV tests before surgery	Y	64. Allow aliens' families to stay in US	Y
17. Strike $12b aid to Int'l Mon Fund	N	65. Expand child care aid/tax credit	Y
18. Raise Senate salary/omit honoraria	N	66. Raise minimum wage w/subminimum	Y
19. Reduce space station funding $1.9b	N	67. Freeze outlays except SS/Medicare	Y
20. Kill-Eliminate supercollider funds	N	68. Kill-Shift $5b of DOD to domestic	Y
21. Req 5-day handgun waiting period	Y	69. Confirm Tower as sec of defense	N
22. Life in prison instead of death	N	70. Bar abortion $ except to save mother	N
23. Exceptions to exclusionary rule	N	71. Kill-Warn AIDS carriers' spouses	Y
24. Ban race as death sentence factor	N	72. Allow religious schools to bar gays	?
25. Campaign finance revisions	Y	73. 60 days' notice of plant closings	Y
26. Kill-Term limits for senators	Y	74. Allow poison pills in corp takeovers	Y
27. Require four presidential debates	Y	75. Kill-Workfare program	N
28. Tighten ban on vertical price fixing	Y	76. Prohibit employee polygraph testing	+
29. Kill-Freeze discretionary budget	Y	77. Cap Medicare patients' liability	Y
30. Provide $30b for failed S&Ls	Y	78. Revise unfair trade practices	Y
31. Allow use of force against Iraq	Y	79. Kill-Shift SDI $ to conv weapons	Y
32. Allow $15b in foreign aid for 1991	Y	80. Kill-Shift SDI $ to accidental launch	Y
33. Civil Rights Act of 1990	Y	81. Kill-Shift MX $ to supplies/parts	Y
34. Block cancellation of Egypt's debt	N	82. Kill-Buy America provision at DOD	N
35. Cut El Salvador military aid 50%	Y	83. Allow nuclear testing-5+ kilotons	N
36. Reduce troops in NATO by 30,000	Y	84. Allow SALT II to be exceeded	N
37. Req increases in auto fuel efficiency	Y	85. $ to vets exposed to nuclear bomb	+
38. Bar taxpayer funding of campaigns	N	86. Warn workers of disease exposure	?
39. Limit textile import growth to 1%	Y	87. Restore four civil rights laws	Y
40. Amendment to ban flag desecration	N	88. Disapprove uranium sales to Japan	?
41. Let fed emp be politically active	Y	89. Notify Congress of covert operations	+
42. Reauthorize Amtrak-veto override	Y	90. Approval of $36m in Contra aid	N
43. Allow sale of assault weapons	N	91. $18b deficit reduction compromise	?
44. Retraining aid for coal miners	Y	92. Allow sale of hard-to-detect guns	--
45. Kill-Raise car emission standards	N	93. Catastrophic health insurance	+
46. Pull EPA nuclear plant authority	N	94. Bork nomination to Supreme Court	N
47. Defer Chinese students' deportation	Y	95. Kill-Void Panama Canal treaties	Y
48. Cut in capital gains tax	N	96. Kill-Insurance denial to AIDS+	Y

GORE, ALBERT, Jr. (continued)

97. Keep diplomatic immunity intact	?	
98. Produce Bigeye nerve gas bomb	--	
99. Balanced budget by '93-via targets	?	
100. Allow ASAT missile tests in space	N	
101. Limit space-based/ABM system tests	Y	
102. Force reduction in trade barriers	+	
103. Repeal windfall profit tax on oil	Y	
104. $1b/two year aid for the homeless	+	
105. Disallow $30m for AZT to poor	?	
106. Bar AIDS test-immigrants/marriage	?	
107. Kill-Biennial budget approval	Y	
108. Fairness doctrine in broadcasting	Y	
109. Raise speed limit to 65 mph	N	
110. Immigration reform/alien amnesty	Y	
111. South Africa sanctions-veto override	Y	
112. Kill-Use of military in drug war	Y	
113. Tax overhaul to revise income tax	Y	

114. Submit nuclear test ban treaties	Y
115. Prohibit sale of Stinger missiles	Y
116. Prohibit binary chemical weapons	N
117. Kill-$10/barrel oil tariff increase	Y
118. Grant tax amnesty provisions	Y
119. Block Saudi arms sale-veto override	Y
120. Balanced budget amendment	Y
121. Include veterans in spending cuts	N
122. Bar $ to hazardous substance victims	N
123. Allow seasonal workers in the US	Y
124. Let fed courts rule on school prayer	Y
125. Presidential line-item veto	N
126. Ease Gun Control Act of 1968	Y
127. Kill-Req 14-day wait for handguns	Y
128. Kill-15% min tax on corporations	N
129. Drop Social Security COLA	N
130. Freeze funding for all programs	Y

The following are House measures voted on between 1982-1984:

123. Duty on Taiwan/Hong Kong/S Korea	Y
124. Limit steel imports to 17%	Y
125. Cut $ to schools that bar prayer	N
126. $50b-taxes; cut Medicare/spending	Y
127. Limit Pershing II/cruise in Europe	N
128. Delete $7.1b for 34 B-1 bombers	N
129. Bar purchase of Sergeant York guns	Y
130. El Salvador military/economic aid	N
131. Bar mining of Nicaraguan waters	Y
132. Physician fee freeze for Medicare	N
133. $49b in "sin"/phone/insurance taxes	Y

134. Allow sale of Conrail	N
135. Equal Rights Amendment	Y
136. Authorize Marines in Lebanon	Y
137. Eminent domain for coal companies	N
138. Prohibit EPA clean air sanctions	Y
139. SS retirement age increase/reforms	N
140. Auto domestic content requirement	N
141. Delete jobs program funding	N
142. Highway-gas tax bill	N
143. Cut $5b from defense for Medicare	Y
144. Emergency housing aid of $1b	Y

Presidential Support Score: 1991 - 46% 1990 - 38%

TEXAS

BENTSEN, LLOYD -- Texas [Democrat]. Term Began/Expires: 1989/1994. Prior Terms: House: 1948 (Special Election)-1954; Senate: 1971-88. Born: February 11, 1921; Mission, TX. Education: University of Texas (LL.B.). Military Service: U.S. Army. Occupation: Chairman, Board of Lincoln Liberty Life Insurance Co.; president, Lincoln Consolidated, Inc.; director, Continental Oil Co.; Lockheed Aircraft Corp., Trunkline Gas Co., Panhandle Eastern Pipeline Co., Bank Southwest National Association.

1. Prohibit MFN status for China	Y
2. Kill-Tie welfare to school attendance	Y
3. Limit credit card interest rates	Y
4. Confirm Gates as head of CIA	Y
5. Adoption of national energy policies	Y
6. Kill-Restrict NEA use of funds	Y
7. Unemployment benefits extension	Y
8. Confirm Thomas to Supreme Court	N
9. Raise eligibility for unpaid leave	Y
10. Notify parents of minors' abortions	Y
11. Move $3b from defense to domestic	N
12. End production of B-2 bomber	N
13. Cut SDI $1b to reduce deficit	N
14. Maintain strategic stability-Soviets	N
15. Kill-Allow women as combat pilots	N
16. Kill-Allow HIV tests before surgery	N

17. Strike $12b aid to Int'l Mon Fund	?
18. Raise Senate salary/omit honoraria	Y
19. Reduce space station funding $1.9b	N
20. Kill-Eliminate supercollider funds	Y
21. Req 5-day handgun waiting period	Y
22. Life in prison instead of death	N
23. Exceptions to exclusionary rule	N
24. Ban race as death sentence factor	N
25. Campaign finance revisions	Y
26. Kill-Term limits for senators	Y
27. Require four presidential debates	Y
28. Tighten ban on vertical price fixing	Y
29. Kill-Freeze discretionary budget	Y
30. Provide $30b for failed S&Ls	Y
31. Allow use of force against Iraq	N
32. Allow $15b in foreign aid for 1991	Y

BENTSEN, LLOYD (continued)

33. Civil Rights Act of 1990	Y	
34. Block cancellation of Egypt's debt	N	
35. Cut El Salvador military aid 50%	Y	
36. Reduce troops in NATO by 30,000	N	
37. Req increases in auto fuel efficiency	Y	
38. Bar taxpayer funding of campaigns	N	
39. Limit textile import growth to 1%	Y	
40. Amendment to ban flag desecration	Y	
41. Let fed emp be politically active	Y	
42. Reauthorize Amtrak-veto override	Y	
43. Allow sale of assault weapons	N	
44. Retraining aid for coal miners	Y	
45. Kill-Raise car emission standards	Y	
46. Pull EPA nuclear plant authority	N	
47. Defer Chinese students' deportation	Y	
48. Cut in capital gains tax	N	
49. Establish CIA inspector general	Y	
50. Kill-Sanctions against China	Y	
51. Bar drug testing to receive AFDC	Y	
52. Kill-Allow force against drug planes	Y	
53. Include illegal aliens in census	Y	
54. Restitution to Japanese interned	Y	
55. Troop reduction in Europe of 50%	N	
56. Increase SDI research to $4.3b	N	
57. Kill-Pay homeless below min wage	Y	
58. Ban airline smoking within US	Y	
59. Bar transfer of FS-X technology	Y	
60. Limit liability for oil spills	Y	
61. Restructure S&L industry	Y	
62. Ban $ to illegal foreign activities	Y	
63. Req immigrant fluency in English	N	
64. Allow aliens' families to stay in US	Y	
65. Expand child care aid/tax credit	Y	
66. Raise minimum wage w/subminimum	Y	
67. Freeze outlays except SS/Medicare	N	
68. Kill-Shift $5b of DOD to domestic	Y	
69. Confirm Tower as sec of defense	Y	
70. Bar abortion $ except to save mother	?	
71. Kill-Warn AIDS carriers' spouses	?	
72. Allow religious schools to bar gays	Y	
73. 60 days' notice of plant closings	Y	
74. Allow poison pills in corp takeovers	N	
75. Kill-Workfare program	N	
76. Prohibit employee polygraph testing	Y	
77. Cap Medicare patients' liability	Y	
78. Revise unfair trade practices	Y	
79. Kill-Shift SDI $ to conv weapons	Y	
80. Kill-Shift SDI $ to accidental launch	Y	
81. Kill-Shift MX $ to supplies/parts	Y	
82. Kill-Buy America provision at DOD	N	
83. Allow nuclear testing-5+ kilotons	Y	
84. Allow SALT II to be exceeded	Y	
85. $ to vets exposed to nuclear bomb	N	
86. Warn workers of disease exposure	Y	
87. Restore four civil rights laws	Y	
88. Disapprove uranium sales to Japan	N	

89. Notify Congress of covert operations	Y	
90. Approval of $36m in Contra aid	Y	
91. $18b deficit reduction compromise	?	
92. Allow sale of hard-to-detect guns	Y	
93. Catastrophic health insurance	Y	
94. Bork nomination to Supreme Court	N	
95. Kill-Void Panama Canal treaties	Y	
96. Kill-Insurance denial to AIDS+	N	
97. Keep diplomatic immunity intact	Y	
98. Produce Bigeye nerve gas bomb	N	
99. Balanced budget by '93-via targets	Y	
100. Allow ASAT missile tests in space	N	
101. Limit space-based/ABM system tests	Y	
102. Force reduction in trade barriers	Y	
103. Repeal windfall profit tax on oil	Y	
104. $1b/two year aid for the homeless	Y	
105. Disallow $30m for AZT to poor	N	
106. Bar AIDS test-immigrants/marriage	N	
107. Kill-Biennial budget approval	N	
108. Fairness doctrine in broadcasting	Y	
109. Raise speed limit to 65 mph	Y	
110. Immigration reform/alien amnesty	Y	
111. South Africa sanctions-veto override	Y	
112. Kill-Use of military in drug war	?	
113. Tax overhaul to revise income tax	Y	
114. Submit nuclear test ban treaties	Y	
115. Prohibit sale of Stinger missiles	N	
116. Prohibit binary chemical weapons	N	
117. Kill-$10/barrel oil tariff increase	N	
118. Grant tax amnesty provisions	?	
119. Block Saudi arms sale-veto override	N	
120. Balanced budget amendment	Y	
121. Include veterans in spending cuts	N	
122. Bar $ to hazardous substance victims	Y	
123. Allow seasonal workers in the US	Y	
124. Let fed courts rule on school prayer	N	
125. Presidential line-item veto	N	
126. Ease Gun Control Act of 1968	Y	
127. Kill-Req 14-day wait for handguns	Y	
128. Kill-15% min tax on corporations	N	
129. Drop Social Security COLA	N	
130. Freeze funding for all programs	N	
131. Kill-Nuclear weapon freeze	Y	
132. Keep decision narrowing Title IX	N	
133. Raise drinking age to 21	Y	
134. Allow production of MX missile	X	
135. Raise taxes/cut spending by $140b	N	
136. School prayer amendment	Y	
137. Capital punishment-federal crimes	N	
138. Ban government officials from taping	Y	
139. Martin Luther King holiday	Y	
140. Authorize Marines in Lebanon	N	
141. Amendment making abortion illegal	N	
142. Delete $1.2b for jobs creation	N	
143. Keep tobacco price supports	Y	
144. Emergency housing aid of $5.1b	Y	

Presidential Support Score: 1991 - 56%   1990 - 52%

GRAMM, PHIL -- Texas [Republican]. Term Began/Expires: 1991/1996. Prior Terms: House: 1979-84; Senate: 1985-90. Born: July 8, 1942; Fort Benning, GA. Education: Georgia Military Academy; University of Georgia (B.B.A., Ph.D.). Occupation: Professor; partner, Gramm and Associates; consultant; author.

GRAMM, PHIL (continued)

1. Prohibit MFN status for China	N	65. Expand child care aid/tax credit	N
2. Kill-Tie welfare to school attendance	N	66. Raise minimum wage w/subminimum	N
3. Limit credit card interest rates	N	67. Freeze outlays except SS/Medicare	N
4. Confirm Gates as head of CIA	Y	68. Kill-Shift $5b of DOD to domestic	Y
5. Adoption of national energy policies	?	69. Confirm Tower as sec of defense	Y
6. Kill-Restrict NEA use of funds	?	70. Bar abortion $ except to save mother	?
7. Unemployment benefits extension	N	71. Kill-Warn AIDS carriers' spouses	N
8. Confirm Thomas to Supreme Court	Y	72. Allow religious schools to bar gays	Y
9. Raise eligibility for unpaid leave	N	73. 60 days' notice of plant closings	N
10. Notify parents of minors' abortions	Y	74. Allow poison pills in corp takeovers	N
11. Move $3b from defense to domestic	N	75. Kill-Workfare program	N
12. End production of B-2 bomber	N	76. Prohibit employee polygraph testing	N
13. Cut SDI $1b to reduce deficit	N	77. Cap Medicare patients' liability	N
14. Maintain strategic stability-Soviets	N	78. Revise unfair trade practices	N
15. Kill-Allow women as combat pilots	Y	79. Kill-Shift SDI $ to conv weapons	Y
16. Kill-Allow HIV tests before surgery	N	80. Kill-Shift SDI $ to accidental launch	N
17. Strike $12b aid to Int'l Mon Fund	Y	81. Kill-Shift MX $ to supplies/parts	Y
18. Raise Senate salary/omit honoraria	N	82. Kill-Buy America provision at DOD	Y
19. Reduce space station funding $1.9b	N	83. Allow nuclear testing-5+ kilotons	Y
20. Kill-Eliminate supercollider funds	Y	84. Allow SALT II to be exceeded	Y
21. Req 5-day handgun waiting period	N	85. $ to vets exposed to nuclear bomb	N
22. Life in prison instead of death	N	86. Warn workers of disease exposure	N
23. Exceptions to exclusionary rule	Y	87. Restore four civil rights laws	N
24. Ban race as death sentence factor	Y	88. Disapprove uranium sales to Japan	N
25. Campaign finance revisions	N	89. Notify Congress of covert operations	N
26. Kill-Term limits for senators	N	90. Approval of $36m in Contra aid	Y
27. Require four presidential debates	N	91. $18b deficit reduction compromise	N
28. Tighten ban on vertical price fixing	N	92. Allow sale of hard-to-detect guns	Y
29. Kill-Freeze discretionary budget	N	93. Catastrophic health insurance	Y
30. Provide $30b for failed S&Ls	Y	94. Bork nomination to Supreme Court	Y
31. Allow use of force against Iraq	Y	95. Kill-Void Panama Canal treaties	N
32. Allow $15b in foreign aid for 1991	Y	96. Kill-Insurance denial to AIDS+	N
33. Civil Rights Act of 1990	N	97. Keep diplomatic immunity intact	N
34. Block cancellation of Egypt's debt	?	98. Produce Bigeye nerve gas bomb	Y
35. Cut El Salvador military aid 50%	?	99. Balanced budget by '93-via targets	Y
36. Reduce troops in NATO by 30,000	N	100. Allow ASAT missile tests in space	Y
37. Req increases in auto fuel efficiency	N	101. Limit space-based/ABM system tests	N
38. Bar taxpayer funding of campaigns	Y	102. Force reduction in trade barriers	N
39. Limit textile import growth to 1%	N	103. Repeal windfall profit tax on oil	Y
40. Amendment to ban flag desecration	Y	104. $1b/two year aid for the homeless	N
41. Let fed emp be politically active	N	105. Disallow $30m for AZT to poor	Y
42. Reauthorize Amtrak-veto override	N	106. Bar AIDS test-immigrants/marriage	N
43. Allow sale of assault weapons	Y	107. Kill-Biennial budget approval	N
44. Retraining aid for coal miners	N	108. Fairness doctrine in broadcasting	N
45. Kill-Raise car emission standards	Y	109. Raise speed limit to 65 mph	Y
46. Pull EPA nuclear plant authority	N	110. Immigration reform/alien amnesty	N
47. Defer Chinese students' deportation	N	111. South Africa sanctions-veto override	N
48. Cut in capital gains tax	Y	112. Kill-Use of military in drug war	N
49. Establish CIA inspector general	N	113. Tax overhaul to revise income tax	Y
50. Kill-Sanctions against China	N	114. Submit nuclear test ban treaties	N
51. Bar drug testing to receive AFDC	N	115. Prohibit sale of Stinger missiles	N
52. Kill-Allow force against drug planes	N	116. Prohibit binary chemical weapons	N
53. Include illegal aliens in census	?	117. Kill-$10/barrel oil tariff increase	Y
54. Restitution to Japanese interned	?	118. Grant tax amnesty provisions	?
55. Troop reduction in Europe of 50%	N	119. Block Saudi arms sale-veto override	N
56. Increase SDI research to $4.3b	Y	120. Balanced budget amendment	Y
57. Kill-Pay homeless below min wage	N	121. Include veterans in spending cuts	Y
58. Ban airline smoking within US	N	122. Bar $ to hazardous substance victims	Y
59. Bar transfer of FS-X technology	N	123. Allow seasonal workers in the US	Y
60. Limit liability for oil spills	Y	124. Let fed courts rule on school prayer	N
61. Restructure S&L industry	N	125. Presidential line-item veto	Y
62. Ban $ to illegal foreign activities	N	126. Ease Gun Control Act of 1968	Y
63. Req immigrant fluency in English	Y	127. Kill-Req 14-day wait for handguns	Y
64. Allow aliens' families to stay in US	Y	128. Kill-15% min tax on corporations	Y

GRAMM, PHIL (continued)
129. Drop Social Security COLA   Y   130. Freeze funding for all programs   N

The following are House measures voted on between 1982-1984:

123.	Duty on Taiwan/Hong Kong/S Korea	?	134.	Allow sale of Conrail	Y
124.	Limit steel imports to 17%	Y	135.	Equal Rights Amendment	N
125.	Cut $ to schools that bar prayer	?	136.	Authorize Marines in Lebanon	Y
126.	$50b-taxes; cut Medicare/spending	N	137.	Eminent domain for coal companies	Y
127.	Limit Pershing II/cruise in Europe	N	138.	Prohibit EPA clean air sanctions	Y
128.	Delete $7.1b for 34 B-1 bombers	N	139.	SS retirement age increase/reforms	Y
129.	Bar purchase of Sergeant York guns	N	140.	Auto domestic content requirement	N
130.	El Salvador military/economic aid	Y	141.	Delete jobs program funding	Y
131.	Bar mining of Nicaraguan waters	N	142.	Highway-gas tax bill	N
132.	Physician fee freeze for Medicare	Y	143.	Cut $5b from defense for Medicare	N
133.	$49b in "sin"/phone/insurance taxes	N	144.	Emergency housing aid of $1b	N

Presidential Support Score: 1991 - 93%   1990 - 78%

UTAH

GARN, JAKE -- Utah [Republican]. Term Began/Expires: 1987/1992. Prior Terms: Senate: 1975-86. Born: October 12, 1932; Richfield, UT. Education: University of Utah (B.S.). Military Service: U.S. Navy, 1960; Utah Air National Guard. Occupation: Insurance agent; assistant manager, Home Life Insurance Co. (1961-66); Salt Lake City commissioner (1968-72); Salt Lake City mayor (1972-74).

1.	Prohibit MFN status for China	Y	33.	Civil Rights Act of 1990	N
2.	Kill-Tie welfare to school attendance	N	34.	Block cancellation of Egypt's debt	N
3.	Limit credit card interest rates	N	35.	Cut El Salvador military aid 50%	N
4.	Confirm Gates as head of CIA	Y	36.	Reduce troops in NATO by 30,000	N
5.	Adoption of national energy policies	Y	37.	Req increases in auto fuel efficiency	N
6.	Kill-Restrict NEA use of funds	Y	38.	Bar taxpayer funding of campaigns	Y
7.	Unemployment benefits extension	N	39.	Limit textile import growth to 1%	Y
8.	Confirm Thomas to Supreme Court	Y	40.	Amendment to ban flag desecration	Y
9.	Raise eligibility for unpaid leave	N	41.	Let fed emp be politically active	N
10.	Notify parents of minors' abortions	Y	42.	Reauthorize Amtrak-veto override	N
11.	Move $3b from defense to domestic	N	43.	Allow sale of assault weapons	Y
12.	End production of B-2 bomber	N	44.	Retraining aid for coal miners	N
13.	Cut SDI $1b to reduce deficit	N	45.	Kill-Raise car emission standards	N
14.	Maintain strategic stability-Soviets	N	46.	Pull EPA nuclear plant authority	Y
15.	Kill-Allow women as combat pilots	Y	47.	Defer Chinese students' deportation	N
16.	Kill-Allow HIV tests before surgery	N	48.	Cut in capital gains tax	Y
17.	Strike $12b aid to Int'l Mon Fund	N	49.	Establish CIA inspector general	N
18.	Raise Senate salary/omit honoraria	Y	50.	Kill-Sanctions against China	N
19.	Reduce space station funding $1.9b	N	51.	Bar drug testing to receive AFDC	N
20.	Kill-Eliminate supercollider funds	Y	52.	Kill-Allow force against drug planes	N
21.	Req 5-day handgun waiting period	N	53.	Include illegal aliens in census	N
22.	Life in prison instead of death	?	54.	Restitution to Japanese interned	N
23.	Exceptions to exclusionary rule	?	55.	Troop reduction in Europe of 50%	N
24.	Ban race as death sentence factor	Y	56.	Increase SDI research to $4.3b	Y
25.	Campaign finance revisions	N	57.	Kill-Pay homeless below min wage	N
26.	Kill-Term limits for senators	N	58.	Ban airline smoking within US	Y
27.	Require four presidential debates	N	59.	Bar transfer of FS-X technology	N
28.	Tighten ban on vertical price fixing	N	60.	Limit liability for oil spills	N
29.	Kill-Freeze discretionary budget	?	61.	Restructure S&L industry	N
30.	Provide $30b for failed S&Ls	Y	62.	Ban $ to illegal foreign activities	N
31.	Allow use of force against Iraq	Y	63.	Req immigrant fluency in English	Y
32.	Allow $15b in foreign aid for 1991	N	64.	Allow aliens' families to stay in US	N

GARN, JAKE (continued)

65. Expand child care aid/tax credit	N	
66. Raise minimum wage w/subminimum	N	
67. Freeze outlays except SS/Medicare	N	
68. Kill-Shift $5b of DOD to domestic	Y	
69. Confirm Tower as sec of defense	Y	
70. Bar abortion $ except to save mother	Y	
71. Kill-Warn AIDS carriers' spouses	N	
72. Allow religious schools to bar gays	?	
73. 60 days' notice of plant closings	N	
74. Allow poison pills in corp takeovers	N	
75. Kill-Workfare program	N	
76. Prohibit employee polygraph testing	N	
77. Cap Medicare patients' liability	N	
78. Revise unfair trade practices	N	
79. Kill-Shift SDI $ to conv weapons	Y	
80. Kill-Shift SDI $ to accidental launch	N	
81. Kill-Shift MX $ to supplies/parts	Y	
82. Kill-Buy America provision at DOD	N	
83. Allow nuclear testing-5+ kilotons	Y	
84. Allow SALT II to be exceeded	Y	
85. $ to vets exposed to nuclear bomb	?	
86. Warn workers of disease exposure	N	
87. Restore four civil rights laws	N	
88. Disapprove uranium sales to Japan	N	
89. Notify Congress of covert operations	N	
90. Approval of $36m in Contra aid	Y	
91. $18b deficit reduction compromise	X	
92. Allow sale of hard-to-detect guns	Y	
93. Catastrophic health insurance	N	
94. Bork nomination to Supreme Court	Y	
95. Kill-Void Panama Canal treaties	N	
96. Kill-Insurance denial to AIDS+	N	
97. Keep diplomatic immunity intact	N	
98. Produce Bigeye nerve gas bomb	Y	
99. Balanced budget by '93-via targets	N	
100. Allow ASAT missile tests in space	Y	
101. Limit space-based/ABM system tests	N	
102. Force reduction in trade barriers	N	
103. Repeal windfall profit tax on oil	Y	
104. $1b/two year aid for the homeless	?	
105. Disallow $30m for AZT to poor	N	
106. Bar AIDS test-immigrants/marriage	N	
107. Kill-Biennial budget approval	N	
108. Fairness doctrine in broadcasting	N	
109. Raise speed limit to 65 mph	Y	
110. Immigration reform/alien amnesty	N	
111. South Africa sanctions-veto override	?	
112. Kill-Use of military in drug war	?	
113. Tax overhaul to revise income tax	--	
114. Submit nuclear test ban treaties	N	
115. Prohibit sale of Stinger missiles	N	
116. Prohibit binary chemical weapons	N	
117. Kill-$10/barrel oil tariff increase	Y	
118. Grant tax amnesty provisions	?	
119. Block Saudi arms sale-veto override	N	
120. Balanced budget amendment	Y	
121. Include veterans in spending cuts	Y	
122. Bar $ to hazardous substance victims	Y	
123. Allow seasonal workers in the US	Y	
124. Let fed courts rule on school prayer	N	
125. Presidential line-item veto	Y	
126. Ease Gun Control Act of 1968	Y	
127. Kill-Req 14-day wait for handguns	Y	
128. Kill-15% min tax on corporations	Y	
129. Drop Social Security COLA	Y	
130. Freeze funding for all programs	N	
131. Kill-Nuclear weapon freeze	Y	
132. Keep decision narrowing Title IX	Y	
133. Raise drinking age to 21	Y	
134. Allow production of MX missile	Y	
135. Raise taxes/cut spending by $140b	Y	
136. School prayer amendment	Y	
137. Capital punishment-federal crimes	Y	
138. Ban government officials from taping	N	
139. Martin Luther King holiday	N	
140. Authorize Marines in Lebanon	Y	
141. Amendment making abortion illegal	Y	
142. Delete $1.2b for jobs creation	Y	
143. Keep tobacco price supports	N	
144. Emergency housing aid of $5.1b	Y	

Presidential Support Score: 1991 - 85%   1990 - 73%

HATCH, ORRIN G. -- Utah [Republican]. Term Began/Expires: 1989/1994. Prior Terms: Senate: 1977-88. Born: March 22, 1934; Pittsburgh, PA. Education: Brigham Young University (B.S.); University of Pittsburgh (LL.B.). Occupation: Attorney.

1. Prohibit MFN status for China	N	
2. Kill-Tie welfare to school attendance	N	
3. Limit credit card interest rates	N	
4. Confirm Gates as head of CIA	+	
5. Adoption of national energy policies	Y	
6. Kill-Restrict NEA use of funds	Y	
7. Unemployment benefits extension	N	
8. Confirm Thomas to Supreme Court	Y	
9. Raise eligibility for unpaid leave	N	
10. Notify parents of minors' abortions	Y	
11. Move $3b from defense to domestic	N	
12. End production of B-2 bomber	N	
13. Cut SDI $1b to reduce deficit	N	
14. Maintain strategic stability-Soviets	N	
15. Kill-Allow women as combat pilots	N	
16. Kill-Allow HIV tests before surgery	Y	
17. Strike $12b aid to Int'l Mon Fund	Y	
18. Raise Senate salary/omit honoraria	N	
19. Reduce space station funding $1.9b	N	
20. Kill-Eliminate supercollider funds	Y	
21. Req 5-day handgun waiting period	N	
22. Life in prison instead of death	N	
23. Exceptions to exclusionary rule	Y	
24. Ban race as death sentence factor	Y	
25. Campaign finance revisions	N	
26. Kill-Term limits for senators	N	
27. Require four presidential debates	N	
28. Tighten ban on vertical price fixing	N	
29. Kill-Freeze discretionary budget	N	
30. Provide $30b for failed S&Ls	Y	

HATCH, ORRIN G. (continued)

31. Allow use of force against Iraq	Y	
32. Allow $15b in foreign aid for 1991	Y	
33. Civil Rights Act of 1990	N	
34. Block cancellation of Egypt's debt	N	
35. Cut El Salvador military aid 50%	N	
36. Reduce troops in NATO by 30,000	N	
37. Req increases in auto fuel efficiency	N	
38. Bar taxpayer funding of campaigns	Y	
39. Limit textile import growth to 1%	Y	
40. Amendment to ban flag desecration	Y	
41. Let fed emp be politically active	N	
42. Reauthorize Amtrak-veto override	N	
43. Allow sale of assault weapons	Y	
44. Retraining aid for coal miners	N	
45. Kill-Raise car emission standards	N	
46. Pull EPA nuclear plant authority	Y	
47. Defer Chinese students' deportation	N	
48. Cut in capital gains tax	Y	
49. Establish CIA inspector general	Y	
50. Kill-Sanctions against China	N	
51. Bar drug testing to receive AFDC	N	
52. Kill-Allow force against drug planes	N	
53. Include illegal aliens in census	N	
54. Restitution to Japanese interned	Y	
55. Troop reduction in Europe of 50%	N	
56. Increase SDI research to $4.3b	Y	
57. Kill-Pay homeless below min wage	N	
58. Ban airline smoking within US	Y	
59. Bar transfer of FS-X technology	N	
60. Limit liability for oil spills	N	
61. Restructure S&L industry	N	
62. Ban $ to illegal foreign activities	N	
63. Req immigrant fluency in English	N	
64. Allow aliens' families to stay in US	N	
65. Expand child care aid/tax credit	Y	
66. Raise minimum wage w/subminimum	N	
67. Freeze outlays except SS/Medicare	N	
68. Kill-Shift $5b of DOD to domestic	Y	
69. Confirm Tower as sec of defense	Y	
70. Bar abortion $ except to save mother	Y	
71. Kill-Warn AIDS carriers' spouses	N	
72. Allow religious schools to bar gays	Y	
73. 60 days' notice of plant closings	N	
74. Allow poison pills in corp takeovers	N	
75. Kill-Workfare program	N	
76. Prohibit employee polygraph testing	Y	
77. Cap Medicare patients' liability	Y	
78. Revise unfair trade practices	N	
79. Kill-Shift SDI $ to conv weapons	Y	
80. Kill-Shift SDI $ to accidental launch	N	
81. Kill-Shift MX $ to supplies/parts	Y	
82. Kill-Buy America provision at DOD	N	
83. Allow nuclear testing-5+ kilotons	Y	
84. Allow SALT II to be exceeded	Y	
85. $ to vets exposed to nuclear bomb	Y	
86. Warn workers of disease exposure	N	
87. Restore four civil rights laws	N	
88. Disapprove uranium sales to Japan	N	
89. Notify Congress of covert operations	N	
90. Approval of $36m in Contra aid	Y	
91. $18b deficit reduction compromise	N	
92. Allow sale of hard-to-detect guns	Y	
93. Catastrophic health insurance	Y	
94. Bork nomination to Supreme Court	Y	
95. Kill-Void Panama Canal treaties	N	
96. Kill-Insurance denial to AIDS+	N	
97. Keep diplomatic immunity intact	N	
98. Produce Bigeye nerve gas bomb	Y	
99. Balanced budget by '93-via targets	Y	
100. Allow ASAT missile tests in space	Y	
101. Limit space-based/ABM system tests	N	
102. Force reduction in trade barriers	N	
103. Repeal windfall profit tax on oil	Y	
104. $1b/two year aid for the homeless	Y	
105. Disallow $30m for AZT to poor	N	
106. Bar AIDS test-immigrants/marriage	N	
107. Kill-Biennial budget approval	N	
108. Fairness doctrine in broadcasting	N	
109. Raise speed limit to 65 mph	Y	
110. Immigration reform/alien amnesty	N	
111. South Africa sanctions-veto override	N	
112. Kill-Use of military in drug war	Y	
113. Tax overhaul to revise income tax	N	
114. Submit nuclear test ban treaties	N	
115. Prohibit sale of Stinger missiles	N	
116. Prohibit binary chemical weapons	N	
117. Kill-$10/barrel oil tariff increase	N	
118. Grant tax amnesty provisions	N	
119. Block Saudi arms sale-veto override	N	
120. Balanced budget amendment	Y	
121. Include veterans in spending cuts	Y	
122. Bar $ to hazardous substance victims	N	
123. Allow seasonal workers in the US	Y	
124. Let fed courts rule on school prayer	Y	
125. Presidential line-item veto	Y	
126. Ease Gun Control Act of 1968	Y	
127. Kill-Req 14-day wait for handguns	Y	
128. Kill-15% min tax on corporations	Y	
129. Drop Social Security COLA	Y	
130. Freeze funding for all programs	N	
131. Kill-Nuclear weapon freeze	Y	
132. Keep decision narrowing Title IX	Y	
133. Raise drinking age to 21	Y	
134. Allow production of MX missile	Y	
135. Raise taxes/cut spending by $140b	Y	
136. School prayer amendment	Y	
137. Capital punishment-federal crimes	Y	
138. Ban government officials from taping	N	
139. Martin Luther King holiday	N	
140. Authorize Marines in Lebanon	Y	
141. Amendment making abortion illegal	Y	
142. Delete $1.2b for jobs creation	Y	
143. Keep tobacco price supports	N	
144. Emergency housing aid of $5.1b	Y	

Presidential Support Score: 1991 - 86%   1990 - 77%

VERMONT

LEAHY, PATRICK J. -- Vermont [Democrat]. Term Began/Expires: 1987/1992. Prior Terms: Senate: 1975-86. Born: March 31, 1940; Montpelier, VT. Education: St. Michael's College (B.A.); Georgetown University (J.D.). Occupation: Chittenden County state's attorney (1966-74).

1. Prohibit MFN status for China	Y	
2. Kill-Tie welfare to school attendance	Y	
3. Limit credit card interest rates	Y	
4. Confirm Gates as head of CIA	Y	
5. Adoption of national energy policies	N	
6. Kill-Restrict NEA use of funds	Y	
7. Unemployment benefits extension	Y	
8. Confirm Thomas to Supreme Court	N	
9. Raise eligibility for unpaid leave	Y	
10. Notify parents of minors' abortions	N	
11. Move $3b from defense to domestic	Y	
12. End production of B-2 bomber	Y	
13. Cut SDI $1b to reduce deficit	Y	
14. Maintain strategic stability-Soviets	N	
15. Kill-Allow women as combat pilots	Y	
16. Kill-Allow HIV tests before surgery	Y	
17. Strike $12b aid to Int'l Mon Fund	Y	
18. Raise Senate salary/omit honoraria	Y	
19. Reduce space station funding $1.9b	Y	
20. Kill-Eliminate supercollider funds	N	
21. Req 5-day handgun waiting period	N	
22. Life in prison instead of death	Y	
23. Exceptions to exclusionary rule	N	
24. Ban race as death sentence factor	N	
25. Campaign finance revisions	Y	
26. Kill-Term limits for senators	Y	
27. Require four presidential debates	Y	
28. Tighten ban on vertical price fixing	Y	
29. Kill-Freeze discretionary budget	N	
30. Provide $30b for failed S&Ls	N	
31. Allow use of force against Iraq	N	
32. Allow $15b in foreign aid for 1991	Y	
33. Civil Rights Act of 1990	Y	
34. Block cancellation of Egypt's debt	N	
35. Cut El Salvador military aid 50%	Y	
36. Reduce troops in NATO by 30,000	N	
37. Req increases in auto fuel efficiency	Y	
38. Bar taxpayer funding of campaigns	N	
39. Limit textile import growth to 1%	Y	
40. Amendment to ban flag desecration	N	
41. Let fed emp be politically active	Y	
42. Reauthorize Amtrak-veto override	Y	
43. Allow sale of assault weapons	N	
44. Retraining aid for coal miners	N	
45. Kill-Raise car emission standards	N	
46. Pull EPA nuclear plant authority	N	
47. Defer Chinese students' deportation	Y	
48. Cut in capital gains tax	N	
49. Establish CIA inspector general	Y	
50. Kill-Sanctions against China	Y	
51. Bar drug testing to receive AFDC	Y	
52. Kill-Allow force against drug planes	Y	
53. Include illegal aliens in census	Y
54. Restitution to Japanese interned	Y
55. Troop reduction in Europe of 50%	N
56. Increase SDI research to $4.3b	N
57. Kill-Pay homeless below min wage	Y
58. Ban airline smoking within US	?
59. Bar transfer of FS-X technology	Y
60. Limit liability for oil spills	N
61. Restructure S&L industry	Y
62. Ban $ to illegal foreign activities	Y
63. Req immigrant fluency in English	N
64. Allow aliens' families to stay in US	Y
65. Expand child care aid/tax credit	Y
66. Raise minimum wage w/subminimum	Y
67. Freeze outlays except SS/Medicare	N
68. Kill-Shift $5b of DOD to domestic	N
69. Confirm Tower as sec of defense	N
70. Bar abortion $ except to save mother	N
71. Kill-Warn AIDS carriers' spouses	Y
72. Allow religious schools to bar gays	N
73. 60 days' notice of plant closings	Y
74. Allow poison pills in corp takeovers	N
75. Kill-Workfare program	Y
76. Prohibit employee polygraph testing	Y
77. Cap Medicare patients' liability	Y
78. Revise unfair trade practices	Y
79. Kill-Shift SDI $ to conv weapons	N
80. Kill-Shift SDI $ to accidental launch	Y
81. Kill-Shift MX $ to supplies/parts	N
82. Kill-Buy America provision at DOD	Y
83. Allow nuclear testing-5+ kilotons	N
84. Allow SALT II to be exceeded	N
85. $ to vets exposed to nuclear bomb	Y
86. Warn workers of disease exposure	Y
87. Restore four civil rights laws	Y
88. Disapprove uranium sales to Japan	Y
89. Notify Congress of covert operations	Y
90. Approval of $36m in Contra aid	N
91. $18b deficit reduction compromise	Y
92. Allow sale of hard-to-detect guns	N
93. Catastrophic health insurance	Y
94. Bork nomination to Supreme Court	N
95. Kill-Void Panama Canal treaties	Y
96. Kill-Insurance denial to AIDS+	Y
97. Keep diplomatic immunity intact	Y
98. Produce Bigeye nerve gas bomb	N
99. Balanced budget by '93-via targets	Y
100. Allow ASAT missile tests in space	N
101. Limit space-based/ABM system tests	Y
102. Force reduction in trade barriers	Y
103. Repeal windfall profit tax on oil	N
104. $1b/two year aid for the homeless	Y

LEAHY, PATRICK J. (continued)

105. Disallow $30m for AZT to poor	N	
106. Bar AIDS test-immigrants/marriage	Y	
107. Kill-Biennial budget approval	Y	
108. Fairness doctrine in broadcasting	?	
109. Raise speed limit to 65 mph	Y	
110. Immigration reform/alien amnesty	+	
111. South Africa sanctions-veto override	Y	
112. Kill-Use of military in drug war	Y	
113. Tax overhaul to revise income tax	Y	
114. Submit nuclear test ban treaties	Y	
115. Prohibit sale of Stinger missiles	Y	
116. Prohibit binary chemical weapons	Y	
117. Kill-$10/barrel oil tariff increase	Y	
118. Grant tax amnesty provisions	?	
119. Block Saudi arms sale-veto override	Y	
120. Balanced budget amendment	N	
121. Include veterans in spending cuts	N	
122. Bar $ to hazardous substance victims	N	
123. Allow seasonal workers in the US	Y	
124. Let fed courts rule on school prayer	Y	
125. Presidential line-item veto	Y
126. Ease Gun Control Act of 1968	Y
127. Kill-Req 14-day wait for handguns	Y
128. Kill-15% min tax on corporations	N
129. Drop Social Security COLA	N
130. Freeze funding for all programs	N
131. Kill-Nuclear weapon freeze	N
132. Keep decision narrowing Title IX	N
133. Raise drinking age to 21	N
134. Allow production of MX missile	N
135. Raise taxes/cut spending by $140b	N
136. School prayer amendment	N
137. Capital punishment-federal crimes	N
138. Ban government officials from taping	Y
139. Martin Luther King holiday	Y
140. Authorize Marines in Lebanon	N
141. Amendment making abortion illegal	N
142. Delete $1.2b for jobs creation	N
143. Keep tobacco price supports	N
144. Emergency housing aid of $5.1b	Y

Presidential Support Score: 1991 - 28% 1990 - 32%

JEFFORDS, JAMES M. -- Vermont [Republican]. Term Began/Expires: 1989/1994. Prior Terms: House: 1975-88. Born: May 11, 1934; Rutland, VT. Education: Yale University (B.A.); Harvard Law School (LL.B.). Military Service: U.S. Navy. Occupation: Attorney; Vermont senator; attorney general; member, Governor's Commission on Crime Control and Prevention; member, Drug Abuse Council.

1. Prohibit MFN status for China	N	
2. Kill-Tie welfare to school attendance	Y	
3. Limit credit card interest rates	Y	
4. Confirm Gates as head of CIA	Y	
5. Adoption of national energy policies	?	
6. Kill-Restrict NEA use of funds	Y	
7. Unemployment benefits extension	Y	
8. Confirm Thomas to Supreme Court	N	
9. Raise eligibility for unpaid leave	Y	
10. Notify parents of minors' abortions	N	
11. Move $3b from defense to domestic	N	
12. End production of B-2 bomber	Y	
13. Cut SDI $1b to reduce deficit	Y	
14. Maintain strategic stability-Soviets	Y	
15. Kill-Allow women as combat pilots	N	
16. Kill-Allow HIV tests before surgery	Y	
17. Strike $12b aid to Int'l Mon Fund	N	
18. Raise Senate salary/omit honoraria	Y	
19. Reduce space station funding $1.9b	N	
20. Kill-Eliminate supercollider funds	N	
21. Req 5-day handgun waiting period	Y	
22. Life in prison instead of death	N	
23. Exceptions to exclusionary rule	N	
24. Ban race as death sentence factor	N	
25. Campaign finance revisions	Y	
26. Kill-Term limits for senators	Y	
27. Require four presidential debates	N	
28. Tighten ban on vertical price fixing	Y	
29. Kill-Freeze discretionary budget	Y	
30. Provide $30b for failed S&Ls	Y	
31. Allow use of force against Iraq	Y	
32. Allow $15b in foreign aid for 1991	Y	
33. Civil Rights Act of 1990	Y	
34. Block cancellation of Egypt's debt	N	
35. Cut El Salvador military aid 50%	Y
36. Reduce troops in NATO by 30,000	N
37. Req increases in auto fuel efficiency	Y
38. Bar taxpayer funding of campaigns	Y
39. Limit textile import growth to 1%	Y
40. Amendment to ban flag desecration	N
41. Let fed emp be politically active	Y
42. Reauthorize Amtrak-veto override	N
43. Allow sale of assault weapons	N
44. Retraining aid for coal miners	N
45. Kill-Raise car emission standards	Y
46. Pull EPA nuclear plant authority	N
47. Defer Chinese students' deportation	N
48. Cut in capital gains tax	Y
49. Establish CIA inspector general	Y
50. Kill-Sanctions against China	N
51. Bar drug testing to receive AFDC	Y
52. Kill-Allow force against drug planes	Y
53. Include illegal aliens in census	?
54. Restitution to Japanese interned	?
55. Troop reduction in Europe of 50%	Y
56. Increase SDI research to $4.3b	N
57. Kill-Pay homeless below min wage	Y
58. Ban airline smoking within US	Y
59. Bar transfer of FS-X technology	N
60. Limit liability for oil spills	N
61. Restructure S&L industry	N
62. Ban $ to illegal foreign activities	N
63. Req immigrant fluency in English	N
64. Allow aliens' families to stay in US	Y
65. Expand child care aid/tax credit	Y
66. Raise minimum wage w/subminimum	Y
67. Freeze outlays except SS/Medicare	N
68. Kill-Shift $5b of DOD to domestic	?

JEFFORDS, JAMES M. (continued)
69. Confirm Tower as sec of defense Y

The following are House measures voted on between 1982-1988:

59. Req foreign investment disclosure	Y	102. Use of military in drug war	N
60. Textile import quotas-veto override	Y	103. Delete 12 MX/add conventional wpn	Y
61. Bar abortion funding in Wash, DC	N	104. Raise speed limit to 65 mph	N
62. Notify spouses of AIDS+ carriers	N	105. Require Pentagon to buy US goods	Y
63. Seize conveyance-drug trafficking	N	106. AIDS insurance non-discrimination	Y
64. South Africa sanctions	Y	107. Prohibit Saudi arms sales	N
65. 60 days' notice of plant closings	Y	108. Ease Gun Control Act of 1968	Y
66. Close unneeded military bases	Y	109. Bar interstate handgun transport	N
67. Keep welfare reform within $2.8b	Y	110. Make company emissions known	Y
68. Allow children housing exclusion	N	111. Allow toxic victims to sue in fed ct	Y
69. Shift $400m of NASA to homeless	Y	112. Superfund waste cleanup of $10b	Y
70. Cap Medicare patients' liability	?	113. 90 days notice of plant closings	Y
71. Prohibit employee polygraph testing	Y	114. $20b in Medicare cuts/tax increases	N
72. Allow CIA to fund Contras	N	115. Spending cuts and tax increases	Y
73. Revise unfair trade practices	Y	116. Set school lunch lmt-250% poverty	N
74. Focus SDI on accidental launch	N	117. $75m for youth work projects	Y
75. Bar Air Force $ for MX missile	Y	118. Allow Angolan military assistance	N
76. Allow "real" increase in defense	Y	119. Suspend defense payments for abuse	Y
77. Troop reduction in Europe of 50%	Y	120. Drop SS COLAs/$12b tax increase	N
78. Ban nuclear tests above 1 kiloton	Y	121. Approve $1.5b for 21 MX missiles	N
79. Ban anti-satellite missile tests	Y	122. Emergency farm credit/revisions	Y
80. Observe certain limits of SALT II	Y	123. Duty on Taiwan/Hong Kong/S Korea	N
81. Restore four Civil Rights laws	Y	124. Limit steel imports to 17%	N
82. Prohibit aliens as strikebreakers	Y	125. Cut $ to schools that bar prayer	N
83. Allow military malpractice suits	Y	126. $50b-taxes; cut Medicare/spending	Y
84. Approval of $36m in Contra aid	N	127. Limit Pershing II/cruise in Europe	?
85. $18b deficit reduction compromise	Y	128. Delete $7.1b for 34 B-1 bombers	Y
86. Welfare reform of $5.7b for 5 years	Y	129. Bar purchase of Sergeant York guns	Y
87. Raise taxes $12b/cut spending $3b	Y	130. El Salvador military/economic aid	N
88. Board to assess occupational risk	N	131. Bar mining of Nicaraguan waters	#
89. Balanced budget by '93-via targets	N	132. Physician fee freeze for Medicare	Y
90. Bar licensing of two nuclear plants	Y	133. $49b in "sin"/phone/insurance taxes	Y
91. Remove victims compensation cap	Y	134. Allow sale of Conrail	N
92. Catastrophic health insurance	Y	135. Equal Rights Amendment	Y
93. Ban airline smoking-2 hours or less	N	136. Authorize Marines in Lebanon	Y
94. $1b/two year aid for the homeless	Y	137. Eminent domain for coal companies	N
95. Bar non-unions in union companies	N	138. Prohibit EPA clean air sanctions	N
96. Increase FSLIC rescue to $15b	Y	139. SS retirement age increase/reforms	Y
97. Impose quotas to lower trade deficit	N	140. Auto domestic content requirement	N
98. Reduce discretionary budget 21%	N	141. Delete jobs program funding	Y
99. Immigration reform/alien amnesty	Y	142. Highway-gas tax bill	N
100. South Africa sanctions-veto override	Y	143. Cut $5b from defense for Medicare	Y
101. Tax overhaul to revise income tax	Y	144. Emergency housing aid of $1b	Y

Presidential Support Score: 1991 - 54%   1990 - 51%

VIRGINIA

WARNER, JOHN W. -- Virginia [Republican]. Term Began/Expires: 1991/1996. Prior Terms: Senate: 1979-90. Born: February 18, 1927. Education: Washington and Lee University (B.S.); University of Virginia (LL.B.). Military Service: U.S. Navy, 1944-46; U.S. Marine Corps, 1950-52. Occupation: Special assistant to U.S. attorney (1956); assistant U.S. attorney (1957-60); attorney, Hogan & Hartson; under secretary of Navy (1969-72); director of Ocean Affairs (1971-72); secretary of the Navy (1972-74); administrator, American Revolution Bicentennial Administration (1974).

WARNER, JOHN W. (continued)

1. Prohibit MFN status for China	N	
2. Kill-Tie welfare to school attendance	N	
3. Limit credit card interest rates	Y	
4. Confirm Gates as head of CIA	Y	
5. Adoption of national energy policies	Y	
6. Kill-Restrict NEA use of funds	Y	
7. Unemployment benefits extension	N	
8. Confirm Thomas to Supreme Court	Y	
9. Raise eligibility for unpaid leave	N	
10. Notify parents of minors' abortions	N	
11. Move $3b from defense to domestic	N	
12. End production of B-2 bomber	N	
13. Cut SDI $1b to reduce deficit	N	
14. Maintain strategic stability-Soviets	N	
15. Kill-Allow women as combat pilots	Y	
16. Kill-Allow HIV tests before surgery	N	
17. Strike $12b aid to Int'l Mon Fund	Y	
18. Raise Senate salary/omit honoraria	Y	
19. Reduce space station funding $1.9b	N	
20. Kill-Eliminate supercollider funds	Y	
21. Req 5-day handgun waiting period	Y	
22. Life in prison instead of death	N	
23. Exceptions to exclusionary rule	Y	
24. Ban race as death sentence factor	Y	
25. Campaign finance revisions	N	
26. Kill-Term limits for senators	N	
27. Require four presidential debates	N	
28. Tighten ban on vertical price fixing	Y	
29. Kill-Freeze discretionary budget	Y	
30. Provide $30b for failed S&Ls	Y	
31. Allow use of force against Iraq	Y	
32. Allow $15b in foreign aid for 1991	Y	
33. Civil Rights Act of 1990	N	
34. Block cancellation of Egypt's debt	N	
35. Cut El Salvador military aid 50%	Y	
36. Reduce troops in NATO by 30,000	N	
37. Req increases in auto fuel efficiency	N	
38. Bar taxpayer funding of campaigns	Y	
39. Limit textile import growth to 1%	Y	
40. Amendment to ban flag desecration	Y	
41. Let fed emp be politically active	Y	
42. Reauthorize Amtrak-veto override	Y	
43. Allow sale of assault weapons	N	
44. Retraining aid for coal miners	N	
45. Kill-Raise car emission standards	Y	
46. Pull EPA nuclear plant authority	Y	
47. Defer Chinese students' deportation	N	
48. Cut in capital gains tax	Y	
49. Establish CIA inspector general	Y	
50. Kill-Sanctions against China	N	
51. Bar drug testing to receive AFDC	Y	
52. Kill-Allow force against drug planes	Y	
53. Include illegal aliens in census	N	
54. Restitution to Japanese interned	Y	
55. Troop reduction in Europe of 50%	N	
56. Increase SDI research to $4.3b	Y	
57. Kill-Pay homeless below min wage	N	
58. Ban airline smoking within US	N	
59. Bar transfer of FS-X technology	N	
60. Limit liability for oil spills	N	
61. Restructure S&L industry	N	
62. Ban $ to illegal foreign activities	N	
63. Req immigrant fluency in English	Y	
64. Allow aliens' families to stay in US	N	
65. Expand child care aid/tax credit	N
66. Raise minimum wage w/subminimum	N
67. Freeze outlays except SS/Medicare	N
68. Kill-Shift $5b of DOD to domestic	Y
69. Confirm Tower as sec of defense	Y
70. Bar abortion $ except to save mother	Y
71. Kill-Warn AIDS carriers' spouses	Y
72. Allow religious schools to bar gays	Y
73. 60 days' notice of plant closings	Y
74. Allow poison pills in corp takeovers	N
75. Kill-Workfare program	N
76. Prohibit employee polygraph testing	N
77. Cap Medicare patients' liability	Y
78. Revise unfair trade practices	N
79. Kill-Shift SDI $ to conv weapons	Y
80. Kill-Shift SDI $ to accidental launch	N
81. Kill-Shift MX $ to supplies/parts	Y
82. Kill-Buy America provision at DOD	N
83. Allow nuclear testing-5+ kilotons	Y
84. Allow SALT II to be exceeded	Y
85. $ to vets exposed to nuclear bomb	Y
86. Warn workers of disease exposure	N
87. Restore four civil rights laws	N
88. Disapprove uranium sales to Japan	N
89. Notify Congress of covert operations	Y
90. Approval of $36m in Contra aid	Y
91. $18b deficit reduction compromise	N
92. Allow sale of hard-to-detect guns	Y
93. Catastrophic health insurance	Y
94. Bork nomination to Supreme Court	N
95. Kill-Void Panama Canal treaties	Y
96. Kill-Insurance denial to AIDS+	N
97. Keep diplomatic immunity intact	N
98. Produce Bigeye nerve gas bomb	Y
99. Balanced budget by '93-via targets	N
100. Allow ASAT missile tests in space	Y
101. Limit space-based/ABM system tests	N
102. Force reduction in trade barriers	Y
103. Repeal windfall profit tax on oil	Y
104. $1b/two year aid for the homeless	Y
105. Disallow $30m for AZT to poor	Y
106. Bar AIDS test-immigrants/marriage	Y
107. Kill-Biennial budget approval	N
108. Fairness doctrine in broadcasting	Y
109. Raise speed limit to 65 mph	Y
110. Immigration reform/alien amnesty	N
111. South Africa sanctions-veto override	Y
112. Kill-Use of military in drug war	Y
113. Tax overhaul to revise income tax	N
114. Submit nuclear test ban treaties	N
115. Prohibit sale of Stinger missiles	N
116. Prohibit binary chemical weapons	N
117. Kill-$10/barrel oil tariff increase	Y
118. Grant tax amnesty provisions	Y
119. Block Saudi arms sale-veto override	N
120. Balanced budget amendment	Y
121. Include veterans in spending cuts	Y
122. Bar $ to hazardous substance victims	Y
123. Allow seasonal workers in the US	Y
124. Let fed courts rule on school prayer	N
125. Presidential line-item veto	Y
126. Ease Gun Control Act of 1968	Y
127. Kill-Req 14-day wait for handguns	N
128. Kill-15% min tax on corporations	Y

WARNER, JOHN W. (continued)

129. Drop Social Security COLA	Y	137. Capital punishment-federal crimes	Y
130. Freeze funding for all programs	N	138. Ban government officials from taping	N
131. Kill-Nuclear weapon freeze	Y	139. Martin Luther King holiday	Y
132. Keep decision narrowing Title IX	Y	140. Authorize Marines in Lebanon	Y
133. Raise drinking age to 21	Y	141. Amendment making abortion illegal	Y
134. Allow production of MX missile	Y	142. Delete $1.2b for jobs creation	Y
135. Raise taxes/cut spending by $140b	Y	143. Keep tobacco price supports	Y
136. School prayer amendment	Y	144. Emergency housing aid of $5.1b	N

Presidential Support Score: 1991 - 89%   1990 - 78%

ROBB, CHARLES S. -- Virginia [Democrat]. Term Began/Expires: 1989/1994. Born: June 26, 1939; Phoenix, AZ. Education: Cornell University; University of Wisconsin (B.B.A.); University of Virginia Law School. Military Service: U.S. Marine Corps and Marine Corps Reserve. Occupation: U.S. Court of Appeals law clerk; lawyer; financial corporation director; Virginia lieutenant governor (1978-82) and governor (1982-86).

1. Prohibit MFN status for China	Y	36. Reduce troops in NATO by 30,000	N
2. Kill-Tie welfare to school attendance	Y	37. Req increases in auto fuel efficiency	Y
3. Limit credit card interest rates	Y	38. Bar taxpayer funding of campaigns	N
4. Confirm Gates as head of CIA	Y	39. Limit textile import growth to 1%	Y
5. Adoption of national energy policies	N	40. Amendment to ban flag desecration	N
6. Kill-Restrict NEA use of funds	Y	41. Let fed emp be politically active	Y
7. Unemployment benefits extension	Y	42. Reauthorize Amtrak-veto override	Y
8. Confirm Thomas to Supreme Court	Y	43. Allow sale of assault weapons	N
9. Raise eligibility for unpaid leave	Y	44. Retraining aid for coal miners	N
10. Notify parents of minors' abortions	N	45. Kill-Raise car emission standards	Y
11. Move $3b from defense to domestic	N	46. Pull EPA nuclear plant authority	N
12. End production of B-2 bomber	N	47. Defer Chinese students' deportation	Y
13. Cut SDI $1b to reduce deficit	N	48. Cut in capital gains tax	N
14. Maintain strategic stability-Soviets	N	49. Establish CIA inspector general	Y
15. Kill-Allow women as combat pilots	N	50. Kill-Sanctions against China	Y
16. Kill-Allow HIV tests before surgery	Y	51. Bar drug testing to receive AFDC	Y
17. Strike $12b aid to Int'l Mon Fund	N	52. Kill-Allow force against drug planes	Y
18. Raise Senate salary/omit honoraria	Y	53. Include illegal aliens in census	N
19. Reduce space station funding $1.9b	N	54. Restitution to Japanese interned	Y
20. Kill-Eliminate supercollider funds	Y	55. Troop reduction in Europe of 50%	N
21. Req 5-day handgun waiting period	Y	56. Increase SDI research to $4.3b	Y
22. Life in prison instead of death	N	57. Kill-Pay homeless below min wage	Y
23. Exceptions to exclusionary rule	N	58. Ban airline smoking within US	Y
24. Ban race as death sentence factor	Y	59. Bar transfer of FS-X technology	Y
25. Campaign finance revisions	Y	60. Limit liability for oil spills	Y
26. Kill-Term limits for senators	Y	61. Restructure S&L industry	Y
27. Require four presidential debates	Y	62. Ban $ to illegal foreign activities	Y
28. Tighten ban on vertical price fixing	Y	63. Req immigrant fluency in English	N
29. Kill-Freeze discretionary budget	N	64. Allow aliens' families to stay in US	Y
30. Provide $30b for failed S&Ls	Y	65. Expand child care aid/tax credit	Y
31. Allow use of force against Iraq	Y	66. Raise minimum wage w/subminimum	Y
32. Allow $15b in foreign aid for 1991	Y	67. Freeze outlays except SS/Medicare	Y
33. Civil Rights Act of 1990	Y	68. Kill-Shift $5b of DOD to domestic	N
34. Block cancellation of Egypt's debt	N	69. Confirm Tower as sec of defense	N
35. Cut El Salvador military aid 50%	Y		

Presidential Support Score: 1991 - 59%   1990 - 55%

WASHINGTON

GORTON, SLADE -- Washington [Republican]. Term Began/Expires: 1989/1994. Prior Term: Senate: 1981-86. Born: January 8, 1928; Chicago, IL. Education: Dartmouth College

GORTON, SLADE (continued)
(B.A.); Columbia University Law School (LL.B.). Military Service: U.S. Army, 1945-46; U.S. Air Force, 1953-56; U.S Air Force Reserve, 1956-81. Occupation: State representative (1959-68) and attorney general (1969-80).

1.	Prohibit MFN status for China	Y	53.	Include illegal aliens in census	N
2.	Kill-Tie welfare to school attendance	N	54.	Restitution to Japanese interned	Y
3.	Limit credit card interest rates	Y	55.	Troop reduction in Europe of 50%	N
4.	Confirm Gates as head of CIA	Y	56.	Increase SDI research to $4.3b	Y
5.	Adoption of national energy policies	Y	57.	Kill-Pay homeless below min wage	N
6.	Kill-Restrict NEA use of funds	Y	58.	Ban airline smoking within US	Y
7.	Unemployment benefits extension	N	59.	Bar transfer of FS-X technology	Y
8.	Confirm Thomas to Supreme Court	Y	60.	Limit liability for oil spills	N
9.	Raise eligibility for unpaid leave	N	61.	Restructure S&L industry	N
10.	Notify parents of minors' abortions	N	62.	Ban $ to illegal foreign activities	N
11.	Move $3b from defense to domestic	N	63.	Req immigrant fluency in English	Y
12.	End production of B-2 bomber	N	64.	Allow aliens' families to stay in US	N
13.	Cut SDI $1b to reduce deficit	N	65.	Expand child care aid/tax credit	N
14.	Maintain strategic stability-Soviets	N	66.	Raise minimum wage w/subminimum	N
15.	Kill-Allow women as combat pilots	N	67.	Freeze outlays except SS/Medicare	N
16.	Kill-Allow HIV tests before surgery	Y	68.	Kill-Shift $5b of DOD to domestic	Y
17.	Strike $12b aid to Int'l Mon Fund	N	69.	Confirm Tower as sec of defense	Y
18.	Raise Senate salary/omit honoraria	Y	110.	Immigration reform/alien amnesty	#
19.	Reduce space station funding $1.9b	N	111.	South Africa sanctions-veto override	Y
20.	Kill-Eliminate supercollider funds	Y	112.	Kill-Use of military in drug war	?
21.	Req 5-day handgun waiting period	Y	113.	Tax overhaul to revise income tax	Y
22.	Life in prison instead of death	N	114.	Submit nuclear test ban treaties	Y
23.	Exceptions to exclusionary rule	N	115.	Prohibit sale of Stinger missiles	N
24.	Ban race as death sentence factor	Y	116.	Prohibit binary chemical weapons	N
25.	Campaign finance revisions	N	117.	Kill-$10/barrel oil tariff increase	Y
26.	Kill-Term limits for senators	N	118.	Grant tax amnesty provisions	Y
27.	Require four presidential debates	N	119.	Block Saudi arms sale-veto override	Y
28.	Tighten ban on vertical price fixing	Y	120.	Balanced budget amendment	N
29.	Kill-Freeze discretionary budget	Y	121.	Include veterans in spending cuts	Y
30.	Provide $30b for failed S&Ls	Y	122.	Bar $ to hazardous substance victims	Y
31.	Allow use of force against Iraq	Y	123.	Allow seasonal workers in the US	Y
32.	Allow $15b in foreign aid for 1991	Y	124.	Let fed courts rule on school prayer	Y
33.	Civil Rights Act of 1990	N	125.	Presidential line-item veto	Y
34.	Block cancellation of Egypt's debt	N	126.	Ease Gun Control Act of 1968	Y
35.	Cut El Salvador military aid 50%	N	127.	Kill-Req 14-day wait for handguns	Y
36.	Reduce troops in NATO by 30,000	N	128.	Kill-15% min tax on corporations	Y
37.	Req increases in auto fuel efficiency	Y	129.	Drop Social Security COLA	Y
38.	Bar taxpayer funding of campaigns	Y	130.	Freeze funding for all programs	N
39.	Limit textile import growth to 1%	N	131.	Kill-Nuclear weapon freeze	Y
40.	Amendment to ban flag desecration	Y	132.	Keep decision narrowing Title IX	Y
41.	Let fed emp be politically active	N	133.	Raise drinking age to 21	Y
42.	Reauthorize Amtrak-veto override	N	134.	Allow production of MX missile	Y
43.	Allow sale of assault weapons	Y	135.	Raise taxes/cut spending by $140b	Y
44.	Retraining aid for coal miners	N	136.	School prayer amendment	N
45.	Kill-Raise car emission standards	N	137.	Capital punishment-federal crimes	Y
46.	Pull EPA nuclear plant authority	N	138.	Ban government officials from taping	N
47.	Defer Chinese students' deportation	Y	139.	Martin Luther King holiday	Y
48.	Cut in capital gains tax	Y	140.	Authorize Marines in Lebanon	Y
49.	Establish CIA inspector general	Y	141.	Amendment making abortion illegal	N
50.	Kill-Sanctions against China	N	142.	Delete $1.2b for jobs creation	Y
51.	Bar drug testing to receive AFDC	Y	143.	Keep tobacco price supports	N
52.	Kill-Allow force against drug planes	N	144.	Emergency housing aid of $5.1b	Y

Sen. Gorton was not in office for votes 70-109.

Presidential Support Score: 1991 - 86%   1990 - 76%

ADAMS, BROCK -- Washington [Democrat]. Term Began/Expires: 1987/1992. Prior Terms: House: 1965-77. Born: January 13, 1927; Atlanta, GA. Education: University of Washington (B.A.); Harvard Law School (J.D.). Military Service: U.S. Navy, 1944-46. Occupation: U.S. District Attorney (1961-64); U.S. Secretary of Transportation (1977-79); Attorney, Garvey, Schubert, Adams and Barer.

1. Prohibit MFN status for China	Y	56. Increase SDI research to $4.3b	N
2. Kill-Tie welfare to school attendance	Y	57. Kill-Pay homeless below min wage	Y
3. Limit credit card interest rates	Y	58. Ban airline smoking within US	Y
4. Confirm Gates as head of CIA	N	59. Bar transfer of FS-X technology	Y
5. Adoption of national energy policies	N	60. Limit liability for oil spills	N
6. Kill-Restrict NEA use of funds	Y	61. Restructure S&L industry	Y
7. Unemployment benefits extension	Y	62. Ban $ to illegal foreign activities	Y
8. Confirm Thomas to Supreme Court	N	63. Req immigrant fluency in English	N
9. Raise eligibility for unpaid leave	Y	64. Allow aliens' families to stay in US	Y
10. Notify parents of minors' abortions	N	65. Expand child care aid/tax credit	Y
11. Move $3b from defense to domestic	Y	66. Raise minimum wage w/subminimum	Y
12. End production of B-2 bomber	Y	67. Freeze outlays except SS/Medicare	N
13. Cut SDI $1b to reduce deficit	Y	68. Kill-Shift $5b of DOD to domestic	N
14. Maintain strategic stability-Soviets	Y	69. Confirm Tower as sec of defense	N
15. Kill-Allow women as combat pilots	N	70. Bar abortion $ except to save mother	N
16. Kill-Allow HIV tests before surgery	Y	71. Kill-Warn AIDS carriers' spouses	?
17. Strike $12b aid to Int'l Mon Fund	N	72. Allow religious schools to bar gays	N
18. Raise Senate salary/omit honoraria	N	73. 60 days' notice of plant closings	Y
19. Reduce space station funding $1.9b	N	74. Allow poison pills in corp takeovers	N
20. Kill-Eliminate supercollider funds	N	75. Kill-Workfare program	Y
21. Req 5-day handgun waiting period	Y	76. Prohibit employee polygraph testing	Y
22. Life in prison instead of death	N	77. Cap Medicare patients' liability	Y
23. Exceptions to exclusionary rule	N	78. Revise unfair trade practices	Y
24. Ban race as death sentence factor	N	79. Kill-Shift SDI $ to conv weapons	N
25. Campaign finance revisions	Y	80. Kill-Shift SDI $ to accidental launch	Y
26. Kill-Term limits for senators	Y	81. Kill-Shift MX $ to supplies/parts	N
27. Require four presidential debates	Y	82. Kill-Buy America provision at DOD	Y
28. Tighten ban on vertical price fixing	Y	83. Allow nuclear testing-5+ kilotons	N
29. Kill-Freeze discretionary budget	Y	84. Allow SALT II to be exceeded	N
30. Provide $30b for failed S&Ls	N	85. $ to vets exposed to nuclear bomb	Y
31. Allow use of force against Iraq	N	86. Warn workers of disease exposure	Y
32. Allow $15b in foreign aid for 1991	Y	87. Restore four civil rights laws	Y
33. Civil Rights Act of 1990	Y	88. Disapprove uranium sales to Japan	Y
34. Block cancellation of Egypt's debt	N	89. Notify Congress of covert operations	Y
35. Cut El Salvador military aid 50%	Y	90. Approval of $36m in Contra aid	N
36. Reduce troops in NATO by 30,000	Y	91. $18b deficit reduction compromise	Y
37. Req increases in auto fuel efficiency	Y	92. Allow sale of hard-to-detect guns	N
38. Bar taxpayer funding of campaigns	N	93. Catastrophic health insurance	Y
39. Limit textile import growth to 1%	N	94. Bork nomination to Supreme Court	N
40. Amendment to ban flag desecration	N	95. Kill-Void Panama Canal treaties	Y
41. Let fed emp be politically active	Y	96. Kill-Insurance denial to AIDS+	Y
42. Reauthorize Amtrak-veto override	Y	97. Keep diplomatic immunity intact	Y
43. Allow sale of assault weapons	N	98. Produce Bigeye nerve gas bomb	N
44. Retraining aid for coal miners	Y	99. Balanced budget by '93-via targets	N
45. Kill-Raise car emission standards	N	100. Allow ASAT missile tests in space	N
46. Pull EPA nuclear plant authority	N	101. Limit space-based/ABM system tests	Y
47. Defer Chinese students' deportation	Y	102. Force reduction in trade barriers	Y
48. Cut in capital gains tax	N	103. Repeal windfall profit tax on oil	N
49. Establish CIA inspector general	N	104. $1b/two year aid for the homeless	Y
50. Kill-Sanctions against China	Y	105. Disallow $30m for AZT to poor	N
51. Bar drug testing to receive AFDC	Y	106. Bar AIDS test-immigrants/marriage	Y
52. Kill-Allow force against drug planes	N	107. Kill-Biennial budget approval	Y
53. Include illegal aliens in census	Y	108. Fairness doctrine in broadcasting	Y
54. Restitution to Japanese interned	Y	109. Raise speed limit to 65 mph	N
55. Troop reduction in Europe of 50%	Y		

Presidential Support Score: 1991 - 26% 1990 - 34%

WEST VIRGINIA

BYRD, ROBERT C. -- West Virginia [Democrat]. Term Began/Expires: 1989/1994. Prior Terms: House: 1953-58; Senate: 1959-88. Born: November 20, 1917; North Wilkesboro, NC. Education: American University (J.D.). Occupation: West Virginia delegate (1946-50); West Virginia senator (1950-52).

1. Prohibit MFN status for China	Y		53. Include illegal aliens in census	N
2. Kill-Tie welfare to school attendance	Y		54. Restitution to Japanese interned	Y
3. Limit credit card interest rates	Y		55. Troop reduction in Europe of 50%	Y
4. Confirm Gates as head of CIA	Y		56. Increase SDI research to $4.3b	N
5. Adoption of national energy policies	Y		57. Kill-Pay homeless below min wage	Y
6. Kill-Restrict NEA use of funds	Y		58. Ban airline smoking within US	N
7. Unemployment benefits extension	Y		59. Bar transfer of FS-X technology	Y
8. Confirm Thomas to Supreme Court	N		60. Limit liability for oil spills	Y
9. Raise eligibility for unpaid leave	Y		61. Restructure S&L industry	Y
10. Notify parents of minors' abortions	Y		62. Ban $ to illegal foreign activities	Y
11. Move $3b from defense to domestic	N		63. Req immigrant fluency in English	Y
12. End production of B-2 bomber	N		64. Allow aliens' families to stay in US	N
13. Cut SDI $1b to reduce deficit	N		65. Expand child care aid/tax credit	Y
14. Maintain strategic stability-Soviets	N		66. Raise minimum wage w/subminimum	Y
15. Kill-Allow women as combat pilots	Y		67. Freeze outlays except SS/Medicare	N
16. Kill-Allow HIV tests before surgery	N		68. Kill-Shift $5b of DOD to domestic	Y
17. Strike $12b aid to Int'l Mon Fund	Y		69. Confirm Tower as sec of defense	N
18. Raise Senate salary/omit honoraria	Y		70. Bar abortion $ except to save mother	Y
19. Reduce space station funding $1.9b	N		71. Kill-Warn AIDS carriers' spouses	Y
20. Kill-Eliminate supercollider funds	Y		72. Allow religious schools to bar gays	Y
21. Req 5-day handgun waiting period	Y		73. 60 days' notice of plant closings	Y
22. Life in prison instead of death	N		74. Allow poison pills in corp takeovers	Y
23. Exceptions to exclusionary rule	N		75. Kill-Workfare program	N
24. Ban race as death sentence factor	Y		76. Prohibit employee polygraph testing	Y
25. Campaign finance revisions	Y		77. Cap Medicare patients' liability	Y
26. Kill-Term limits for senators	Y		78. Revise unfair trade practices	N
27. Require four presidential debates	N		79. Kill-Shift SDI $ to conv weapons	Y
28. Tighten ban on vertical price fixing	Y		80. Kill-Shift SDI $ to accidental launch	Y
29. Kill-Freeze discretionary budget	Y		81. Kill-Shift MX $ to supplies/parts	Y
30. Provide $30b for failed S&Ls	N		82. Kill-Buy America provision at DOD	N
31. Allow use of force against Iraq	N		83. Allow nuclear testing-5+ kilotons	Y
32. Allow $15b in foreign aid for 1991	N		84. Allow SALT II to be exceeded	N
33. Civil Rights Act of 1990	Y		85. $ to vets exposed to nuclear bomb	Y
34. Block cancellation of Egypt's debt	Y		86. Warn workers of disease exposure	Y
35. Cut El Salvador military aid 50%	Y		87. Restore four civil rights laws	Y
36. Reduce troops in NATO by 30,000	N		88. Disapprove uranium sales to Japan	Y
37. Req increases in auto fuel efficiency	N		89. Notify Congress of covert operations	Y
38. Bar taxpayer funding of campaigns	N		90. Approval of $36m in Contra aid	N
39. Limit textile import growth to 1%	Y		91. $18b deficit reduction compromise	Y
40. Amendment to ban flag desecration	Y		92. Allow sale of hard-to-detect guns	N
41. Let fed emp be politically active	Y		93. Catastrophic health insurance	Y
42. Reauthorize Amtrak-veto override	Y		94. Bork nomination to Supreme Court	N
43. Allow sale of assault weapons	N		95. Kill-Void Panama Canal treaties	Y
44. Retraining aid for coal miners	Y		96. Kill-Insurance denial to AIDS+	N
45. Kill-Raise car emission standards	N		97. Keep diplomatic immunity intact	N
46. Pull EPA nuclear plant authority	N		98. Produce Bigeye nerve gas bomb	N
47. Defer Chinese students' deportation	Y		99. Balanced budget by '93-via targets	Y
48. Cut in capital gains tax	N		100. Allow ASAT missile tests in space	Y
49. Establish CIA inspector general	Y		101. Limit space-based/ABM system tests	Y
50. Kill-Sanctions against China	Y		102. Force reduction in trade barriers	Y
51. Bar drug testing to receive AFDC	Y		103. Repeal windfall profit tax on oil	N
52. Kill-Allow force against drug planes	Y		104. $1b/two year aid for the homeless	Y

BYRD, ROBERT C. (continued)

105. Disallow $30m for AZT to poor	N	125. Presidential line-item veto	N
106. Bar AIDS test-immigrants/marriage	N	126. Ease Gun Control Act of 1968	Y
107. Kill-Biennial budget approval	Y	127. Kill-Req 14-day wait for handguns	Y
108. Fairness doctrine in broadcasting	Y	128. Kill-15% min tax on corporations	N
109. Raise speed limit to 65 mph	N	129. Drop Social Security COLA	N
110. Immigration reform/alien amnesty	Y	130. Freeze funding for all programs	N
111. South Africa sanctions-veto override	Y	131. Kill-Nuclear weapon freeze	N
112. Kill-Use of military in drug war	Y	132. Keep decision narrowing Title IX	N
113. Tax overhaul to revise income tax	Y	133. Raise drinking age to 21	Y
114. Submit nuclear test ban treaties	Y	134. Allow production of MX missile	Y
115. Prohibit sale of Stinger missiles	N	135. Raise taxes/cut spending by $140b	N
116. Prohibit binary chemical weapons	Y	136. School prayer amendment	Y
117. Kill-$10/barrel oil tariff increase	Y	137. Capital punishment-federal crimes	Y
118. Grant tax amnesty provisions	N	138. Ban government officials from taping	Y
119. Block Saudi arms sale-veto override	Y	139. Martin Luther King holiday	Y
120. Balanced budget amendment	N	140. Authorize Marines in Lebanon	N
121. Include veterans in spending cuts	N	141. Amendment making abortion illegal	N
122. Bar $ to hazardous substance victims	N	142. Delete $1.2b for jobs creation	N
123. Allow seasonal workers in the US	N	143. Keep tobacco price supports	Y
124. Let fed courts rule on school prayer	Y	144. Emergency housing aid of $5.1b	Y

Presidential Support Score: 1991 - 49%   1990 - 42%

ROCKEFELLER, JOHN D., IV -- West Virginia [Democrat].   Term Began/Expires: 1991/1996.   Prior Term: Senate: 1985-90.   Born: June 18, 1937; New York City, N.Y. Education: Harvard University (A.B.).   Occupation: VISTA volunteer (1964); West Virginia House of Delegates (1966-68); secretary of state (1968); governor (1976-84).

1. Prohibit MFN status for China	Y	36. Reduce troops in NATO by 30,000	Y
2. Kill-Tie welfare to school attendance	Y	37. Req increases in auto fuel efficiency	Y
3. Limit credit card interest rates	Y	38. Bar taxpayer funding of campaigns	N
4. Confirm Gates as head of CIA	N	39. Limit textile import growth to 1%	Y
5. Adoption of national energy policies	N	40. Amendment to ban flag desecration	Y
6. Kill-Restrict NEA use of funds	Y	41. Let fed emp be politically active	Y
7. Unemployment benefits extension	Y	42. Reauthorize Amtrak-veto override	Y
8. Confirm Thomas to Supreme Court	N	43. Allow sale of assault weapons	N
9. Raise eligibility for unpaid leave	Y	44. Retraining aid for coal miners	Y
10. Notify parents of minors' abortions	N	45. Kill-Raise car emission standards	N
11. Move $3b from defense to domestic	Y	46. Pull EPA nuclear plant authority	N
12. End production of B-2 bomber	Y	47. Defer Chinese students' deportation	Y
13. Cut SDI $1b to reduce deficit	Y	48. Cut in capital gains tax	N
14. Maintain strategic stability-Soviets	Y	49. Establish CIA inspector general	N
15. Kill-Allow women as combat pilots	N	50. Kill-Sanctions against China	Y
16. Kill-Allow HIV tests before surgery	Y	51. Bar drug testing to receive AFDC	Y
17. Strike $12b aid to Int'l Mon Fund	N	52. Kill-Allow force against drug planes	N
18. Raise Senate salary/omit honoraria	Y	53. Include illegal aliens in census	N
19. Reduce space station funding $1.9b	Y	54. Restitution to Japanese interned	Y
20. Kill-Eliminate supercollider funds	Y	55. Troop reduction in Europe of 50%	Y
21. Req 5-day handgun waiting period	Y	56. Increase SDI research to $4.3b	N
22. Life in prison instead of death	N	57. Kill-Pay homeless below min wage	Y
23. Exceptions to exclusionary rule	N	58. Ban airline smoking within US	Y
24. Ban race as death sentence factor	N	59. Bar transfer of FS-X technology	Y
25. Campaign finance revisions	Y	60. Limit liability for oil spills	N
26. Kill-Term limits for senators	Y	61. Restructure S&L industry	Y
27. Require four presidential debates	Y	62. Ban $ to illegal foreign activities	Y
28. Tighten ban on vertical price fixing	Y	63. Req immigrant fluency in English	N
29. Kill-Freeze discretionary budget	Y	64. Allow aliens' families to stay in US	Y
30. Provide $30b for failed S&Ls	N	65. Expand child care aid/tax credit	Y
31. Allow use of force against Iraq	N	66. Raise minimum wage w/subminimum	Y
32. Allow $15b in foreign aid for 1991	N	67. Freeze outlays except SS/Medicare	N
33. Civil Rights Act of 1990	Y	68. Kill-Shift $5b of DOD to domestic	N
34. Block cancellation of Egypt's debt	Y	69. Confirm Tower as sec of defense	N
35. Cut El Salvador military aid 50%	Y	70. Bar abortion $ except to save mother	N

ROCKEFELLER, JOHN D., IV (continued)

71. Kill-Warn AIDS carriers' spouses	N
72. Allow religious schools to bar gays	Y
73. 60 days' notice of plant closings	Y
74. Allow poison pills in corp takeovers	Y
75. Kill-Workfare program	N
76. Prohibit employee polygraph testing	Y
77. Cap Medicare patients' liability	Y
78. Revise unfair trade practices	Y
79. Kill-Shift SDI $ to conv weapons	N
80. Kill-Shift SDI $ to accidental launch	Y
81. Kill-Shift MX $ to supplies/parts	N
82. Kill-Buy America provision at DOD	N
83. Allow nuclear testing-5+ kilotons	N
84. Allow SALT II to be exceeded	N
85. $ to vets exposed to nuclear bomb	Y
86. Warn workers of disease exposure	Y
87. Restore four civil rights laws	Y
88. Disapprove uranium sales to Japan	N
89. Notify Congress of covert operations	Y
90. Approval of $36m in Contra aid	N
91. $18b deficit reduction compromise	Y
92. Allow sale of hard-to-detect guns	N
93. Catastrophic health insurance	Y
94. Bork nomination to Supreme Court	N
95. Kill-Void Panama Canal treaties	Y
96. Kill-Insurance denial to AIDS+	Y
97. Keep diplomatic immunity intact	Y
98. Produce Bigeye nerve gas bomb	Y
99. Balanced budget by '93-via targets	Y
100. Allow ASAT missile tests in space	N

101. Limit space-based/ABM system tests	Y
102. Force reduction in trade barriers	Y
103. Repeal windfall profit tax on oil	N
104. $1b/two year aid for the homeless	+
105. Disallow $30m for AZT to poor	N
106. Bar AIDS test-immigrants/marriage	N
107. Kill-Biennial budget approval	Y
108. Fairness doctrine in broadcasting	Y
109. Raise speed limit to 65 mph	N
110. Immigration reform/alien amnesty	Y
111. South Africa sanctions-veto override	Y
112. Kill-Use of military in drug war	Y
113. Tax overhaul to revise income tax	Y
114. Submit nuclear test ban treaties	Y
115. Prohibit sale of Stinger missiles	N
116. Prohibit binary chemical weapons	N
117. Kill-$10/barrel oil tariff increase	Y
118. Grant tax amnesty provisions	N
119. Block Saudi arms sale-veto override	Y
120. Balanced budget amendment	N
121. Include veterans in spending cuts	N
122. Bar $ to hazardous substance victims	N
123. Allow seasonal workers in the US	N
124. Let fed courts rule on school prayer	Y
125. Presidential line-item veto	N
126. Ease Gun Control Act of 1968	Y
127. Kill-Req 14-day wait for handguns	Y
128. Kill-15% min tax on corporations	N
129. Drop Social Security COLA	N
130. Freeze funding for all programs	N

Presidential Support Score: 1991 - 36%   1990 - 26%

WISCONSIN

KASTEN, BOB -- Wisconsin [Republican]. Term Began/Expires: 1987/1992. Prior Terms: House: 1975-78; Senate: 1981-86. Born: June 19, 1942; Milwaukee, WI. Education: University of Arizona (B.A.); Columbia University (M.B.A.). Military Service: U.S. Air Force; Wisconsin Air National Guard. Occupation: Wisconsin senator (1972-74); vice president, Real Estate Resources; general partner, Oliver Plunkett & Associates.

1. Prohibit MFN status for China	N
2. Kill-Tie welfare to school attendance	N
3. Limit credit card interest rates	Y
4. Confirm Gates as head of CIA	Y
5. Adoption of national energy policies	Y
6. Kill-Restrict NEA use of funds	N
7. Unemployment benefits extension	Y
8. Confirm Thomas to Supreme Court	Y
9. Raise eligibility for unpaid leave	N
10. Notify parents of minors' abortions	Y
11. Move $3b from defense to domestic	N
12. End production of B-2 bomber	N
13. Cut SDI $1b to reduce deficit	N
14. Maintain strategic stability-Soviets	N
15. Kill-Allow women as combat pilots	N
16. Kill-Allow HIV tests before surgery	N
17. Strike $12b aid to Int'l Mon Fund	Y

18. Raise Senate salary/omit honoraria	N
19. Reduce space station funding $1.9b	N
20. Kill-Eliminate supercollider funds	Y
21. Req 5-day handgun waiting period	Y
22. Life in prison instead of death	N
23. Exceptions to exclusionary rule	Y
24. Ban race as death sentence factor	Y
25. Campaign finance revisions	N
26. Kill-Term limits for senators	N
27. Require four presidential debates	N
28. Tighten ban on vertical price fixing	N
29. Kill-Freeze discretionary budget	Y
30. Provide $30b for failed S&Ls	N
31. Allow use of force against Iraq	Y
32. Allow $15b in foreign aid for 1991	Y
33. Civil Rights Act of 1990	N
34. Block cancellation of Egypt's debt	N

KASTEN, BOB (continued)

35. Cut El Salvador military aid 50%	N	
36. Reduce troops in NATO by 30,000	Y	
37. Req increases in auto fuel efficiency	N	
38. Bar taxpayer funding of campaigns	Y	
39. Limit textile import growth to 1%	Y	
40. Amendment to ban flag desecration	Y	
41. Let fed emp be politically active	Y	
42. Reauthorize Amtrak-veto override	N	
43. Allow sale of assault weapons	Y	
44. Retraining aid for coal miners	N	
45. Kill-Raise car emission standards	Y	
46. Pull EPA nuclear plant authority	N	
47. Defer Chinese students' deportation	Y	
48. Cut in capital gains tax	Y	
49. Establish CIA inspector general	N	
50. Kill-Sanctions against China	N	
51. Bar drug testing to receive AFDC	N	
52. Kill-Allow force against drug planes	N	
53. Include illegal aliens in census	N	
54. Restitution to Japanese interned	Y	
55. Troop reduction in Europe of 50%	N	
56. Increase SDI research to $4.3b	Y	
57. Kill-Pay homeless below min wage	N	
58. Ban airline smoking within US	N	
59. Bar transfer of FS-X technology	Y	
60. Limit liability for oil spills	N	
61. Restructure S&L industry	N	
62. Ban $ to illegal foreign activities	N	
63. Req immigrant fluency in English	Y	
64. Allow aliens' families to stay in US	Y	
65. Expand child care aid/tax credit	N	
66. Raise minimum wage w/subminimum	N	
67. Freeze outlays except SS/Medicare	N	
68. Kill-Shift $5b of DOD to domestic	Y	
69. Confirm Tower as sec of defense	Y	
70. Bar abortion $ except to save mother	Y	
71. Kill-Warn AIDS carriers' spouses	N	
72. Allow religious schools to bar gays	Y	
73. 60 days' notice of plant closings	Y	
74. Allow poison pills in corp takeovers	N	
75. Kill-Workfare program	N	
76. Prohibit employee polygraph testing	Y	
77. Cap Medicare patients' liability	Y	
78. Revise unfair trade practices	N	
79. Kill-Shift SDI $ to conv weapons	Y	
80. Kill-Shift SDI $ to accidental launch	N	
81. Kill-Shift MX $ to supplies/parts	Y	
82. Kill-Buy America provision at DOD	N	
83. Allow nuclear testing-5+ kilotons	Y	
84. Allow SALT II to be exceeded	Y	
85. $ to vets exposed to nuclear bomb	N	
86. Warn workers of disease exposure	N	
87. Restore four civil rights laws	Y	
88. Disapprove uranium sales to Japan	N	
89. Notify Congress of covert operations	N	

90. Approval of $36m in Contra aid	Y	
91. $18b deficit reduction compromise	N	
92. Allow sale of hard-to-detect guns	Y	
93. Catastrophic health insurance	Y	
94. Bork nomination to Supreme Court	Y	
95. Kill-Void Panama Canal treaties	N	
96. Kill-Insurance denial to AIDS+	N	
97. Keep diplomatic immunity intact	N	
98. Produce Bigeye nerve gas bomb	Y	
99. Balanced budget by '93-via targets	Y	
100. Allow ASAT missile tests in space	Y	
101. Limit space-based/ABM system tests	N	
102. Force reduction in trade barriers	Y	
103. Repeal windfall profit tax on oil	Y	
104. $1b/two year aid for the homeless	Y	
105. Disallow $30m for AZT to poor	N	
106. Bar AIDS test-immigrants/marriage	N	
107. Kill-Biennial budget approval	N	
108. Fairness doctrine in broadcasting	N	
109. Raise speed limit to 65 mph	Y	
110. Immigration reform/alien amnesty	Y	
111. South Africa sanctions-veto override	Y	
112. Kill-Use of military in drug war	Y	
113. Tax overhaul to revise income tax	Y	
114. Submit nuclear test ban treaties	Y	
115. Prohibit sale of Stinger missiles	N	
116. Prohibit binary chemical weapons	N	
117. Kill-$10/barrel oil tariff increase	Y	
118. Grant tax amnesty provisions	Y	
119. Block Saudi arms sale-veto override	Y	
120. Balanced budget amendment	Y	
121. Include veterans in spending cuts	Y	
122. Bar $ to hazardous substance victims	Y	
123. Allow seasonal workers in the US	N	
124. Let fed courts rule on school prayer	N	
125. Presidential line-item veto	Y	
126. Ease Gun Control Act of 1968	Y	
127. Kill-Req 14-day wait for handguns	Y	
128. Kill-15% min tax on corporations	Y	
129. Drop Social Security COLA	Y	
130. Freeze funding for all programs	Y	
131. Kill-Nuclear weapon freeze	Y	
132. Keep decision narrowing Title IX	Y	
133. Raise drinking age to 21	Y	
134. Allow production of MX missile	Y	
135. Raise taxes/cut spending by $140b	Y	
136. School prayer amendment	Y	
137. Capital punishment-federal crimes	Y	
138. Ban government officials from taping	N	
139. Martin Luther King holiday	Y	
140. Authorize Marines in Lebanon	Y	
141. Amendment making abortion illegal	Y	
142. Delete $1.2b for jobs creation	Y	
143. Keep tobacco price supports	N	
144. Emergency housing aid of $5.1b	Y	

Presidential Support Score: 1991 - 84%   1990 - 71%

KOHL, HERBERT H. -- Wisconsin [Democrat]. Term Began/Expires: 1989/1994. Born: February 7, 1935; Milwaukee, WI. Education: University of Wisconsin-Madison (B.A.); Harvard Graduate School of Business Administration (M.B.A.). Occupation: Employee (1959-70), grocery and department store chain; professional sports team owner-investor; state Democratic party chairman (1975-77).

KOHL, HERBERT H. (continued)

1. Prohibit MFN status for China	Y	36. Reduce troops in NATO by 30,000	Y
2. Kill-Tie welfare to school attendance	Y	37. Req increases in auto fuel efficiency	Y
3. Limit credit card interest rates	Y	38. Bar taxpayer funding of campaigns	N
4. Confirm Gates as head of CIA	Y	39. Limit textile import growth to 1%	Y
5. Adoption of national energy policies	N	40. Amendment to ban flag desecration	N
6. Kill-Restrict NEA use of funds	Y	41. Let fed emp be politically active	Y
7. Unemployment benefits extension	Y	42. Reauthorize Amtrak-veto override	Y
8. Confirm Thomas to Supreme Court	N	43. Allow sale of assault weapons	N
9. Raise eligibility for unpaid leave	Y	44. Retraining aid for coal miners	Y
10. Notify parents of minors' abortions	N	45. Kill-Raise car emission standards	N
11. Move $3b from defense to domestic	Y	46. Pull EPA nuclear plant authority	N
12. End production of B-2 bomber	Y	47. Defer Chinese students' deportation	Y
13. Cut SDI $1b to reduce deficit	Y	48. Cut in capital gains tax	N
14. Maintain strategic stability-Soviets	Y	49. Establish CIA inspector general	N
15. Kill-Allow women as combat pilots	N	50. Kill-Sanctions against China	Y
16. Kill-Allow HIV tests before surgery	Y	51. Bar drug testing to receive AFDC	Y
17. Strike $12b aid to Int'l Mon Fund	Y	52. Kill-Allow force against drug planes	Y
18. Raise Senate salary/omit honoraria	N	53. Include illegal aliens in census	Y
19. Reduce space station funding $1.9b	Y	54. Restitution to Japanese interned	Y
20. Kill-Eliminate supercollider funds	N	55. Troop reduction in Europe of 50%	N
21. Req 5-day handgun waiting period	Y	56. Increase SDI research to $4.3b	N
22. Life in prison instead of death	Y	57. Kill-Pay homeless below min wage	N
23. Exceptions to exclusionary rule	N	58. Ban airline smoking within US	Y
24. Ban race as death sentence factor	N	59. Bar transfer of FS-X technology	Y
25. Campaign finance revisions	Y	60. Limit liability for oil spills	N
26. Kill-Term limits for senators	Y	61. Restructure S&L industry	Y
27. Require four presidential debates	Y	62. Ban $ to illegal foreign activities	Y
28. Tighten ban on vertical price fixing	Y	63. Req immigrant fluency in English	N
29. Kill-Freeze discretionary budget	N	64. Allow aliens' families to stay in US	Y
30. Provide $30b for failed S&Ls	N	65. Expand child care aid/tax credit	Y
31. Allow use of force against Iraq	N	66. Raise minimum wage w/subminimum	Y
32. Allow $15b in foreign aid for 1991	Y	67. Freeze outlays except SS/Medicare	Y
33. Civil Rights Act of 1990	Y	68. Kill-Shift $5b of DOD to domestic	N
34. Block cancellation of Egypt's debt	Y	69. Confirm Tower as sec of defense	N
35. Cut El Salvador military aid 50%	Y		

Presidential Support Score: 1991 - 41%   1990 - 25%

WYOMING

WALLOP, MALCOLM -- Wyoming [Republican]. Term Began/Expires: 1989/1994. Prior Terms: Senate: 1977-88. Born: February 27, 1933; New York, NY. Education: Yale University (B.A.). Military Service: U.S. Army. Occupation: Rancher; Wyoming representative; Wyoming senator.

1. Prohibit MFN status for China	Y	14. Maintain strategic stability-Soviets	N
2. Kill-Tie welfare to school attendance	N	15. Kill-Allow women as combat pilots	Y
3. Limit credit card interest rates	N	16. Kill-Allow HIV tests before surgery	N
4. Confirm Gates as head of CIA	Y	17. Strike $12b aid to Int'l Mon Fund	Y
5. Adoption of national energy policies	Y	18. Raise Senate salary/omit honoraria	N
6. Kill-Restrict NEA use of funds	N	19. Reduce space station funding $1.9b	N
7. Unemployment benefits extension	N	20. Kill-Eliminate supercollider funds	Y
8. Confirm Thomas to Supreme Court	Y	21. Req 5-day handgun waiting period	N
9. Raise eligibility for unpaid leave	N	22. Life in prison instead of death	N
10. Notify parents of minors' abortions	Y	23. Exceptions to exclusionary rule	Y
11. Move $3b from defense to domestic	N	24. Ban race as death sentence factor	Y
12. End production of B-2 bomber	N	25. Campaign finance revisions	N
13. Cut SDI $1b to reduce deficit	N	26. Kill-Term limits for senators	N

WALLOP, MALCOLM (continued)

27.	Require four presidential debates	N
28.	Tighten ban on vertical price fixing	N
29.	Kill-Freeze discretionary budget	N
30.	Provide $30b for failed S&Ls	Y
31.	Allow use of force against Iraq	Y
32.	Allow $15b in foreign aid for 1991	Y
33.	Civil Rights Act of 1990	N
34.	Block cancellation of Egypt's debt	N
35.	Cut El Salvador military aid 50%	N
36.	Reduce troops in NATO by 30,000	N
37.	Req increases in auto fuel efficiency	N
38.	Bar taxpayer funding of campaigns	Y
39.	Limit textile import growth to 1%	N
40.	Amendment to ban flag desecration	Y
41.	Let fed emp be politically active	N
42.	Reauthorize Amtrak-veto override	N
43.	Allow sale of assault weapons	Y
44.	Retraining aid for coal miners	N
45.	Kill-Raise car emission standards	Y
46.	Pull EPA nuclear plant authority	Y
47.	Defer Chinese students' deportation	N
48.	Cut in capital gains tax	Y
49.	Establish CIA inspector general	N
50.	Kill-Sanctions against China	-
51.	Bar drug testing to receive AFDC	N
52.	Kill-Allow force against drug planes	N
53.	Include illegal aliens in census	N
54.	Restitution to Japanese interned	N
55.	Troop reduction in Europe of 50%	N
56.	Increase SDI research to $4.3b	Y
57.	Kill-Pay homeless below min wage	N
58.	Ban airline smoking within US	N
59.	Bar transfer of FS-X technology	N
60.	Limit liability for oil spills	Y
61.	Restructure S&L industry	N
62.	Ban $ to illegal foreign activities	N
63.	Req immigrant fluency in English	Y
64.	Allow aliens' families to stay in US	N
65.	Expand child care aid/tax credit	N
66.	Raise minimum wage w/subminimum	N
67.	Freeze outlays except SS/Medicare	N
68.	Kill-Shift $5b of DOD to domestic	Y
69.	Confirm Tower as sec of defense	Y
70.	Bar abortion $ except to save mother	?
71.	Kill-Warn AIDS carriers' spouses	N
72.	Allow religious schools to bar gays	Y
73.	60 days' notice of plant closings	N
74.	Allow poison pills in corp takeovers	N
75.	Kill-Workfare program	N
76.	Prohibit employee polygraph testing	N
77.	Cap Medicare patients' liability	Y
78.	Revise unfair trade practices	N
79.	Kill-Shift SDI $ to conv weapons	Y
80.	Kill-Shift SDI $ to accidental launch	N
81.	Kill-Shift MX $ to supplies/parts	Y
82.	Kill-Buy America provision at DOD	Y
83.	Allow nuclear testing-5 + kilotons	Y
84.	Allow SALT II to be exceeded	Y
85.	$ to vets exposed to nuclear bomb	N

86.	Warn workers of disease exposure	N
87.	Restore four civil rights laws	N
88.	Disapprove uranium sales to Japan	N
89.	Notify Congress of covert operations	N
90.	Approval of $36m in Contra aid	Y
91.	$18b deficit reduction compromise	N
92.	Allow sale of hard-to-detect guns	Y
93.	Catastrophic health insurance	Y
94.	Bork nomination to Supreme Court	Y
95.	Kill-Void Panama Canal treaties	N
96.	Kill-Insurance denial to AIDS+	N
97.	Keep diplomatic immunity intact	N
98.	Produce Bigeye nerve gas bomb	Y
99.	Balanced budget by '93-via targets	Y
100.	Allow ASAT missile tests in space	Y
101.	Limit space-based/ABM system tests	N
102.	Force reduction in trade barriers	N
103.	Repeal windfall profit tax on oil	Y
104.	$1b/two year aid for the homeless	N
105.	Disallow $30m for AZT to poor	Y
106.	Bar AIDS test-immigrants/marriage	N
107.	Kill-Biennial budget approval	?
108.	Fairness doctrine in broadcasting	N
109.	Raise speed limit to 65 mph	Y
110.	Immigration reform/alien amnesty	Y
111.	South Africa sanctions-veto override	N
112.	Kill-Use of military in drug war	?
113.	Tax overhaul to revise income tax	N
114.	Submit nuclear test ban treaties	N
115.	Prohibit sale of Stinger missiles	N
116.	Prohibit binary chemical weapons	N
117.	Kill-$10/barrel oil tariff increase	Y
118.	Grant tax amnesty provisions	?
119.	Block Saudi arms sale-veto override	N
120.	Balanced budget amendment	Y
121.	Include veterans in spending cuts	Y
122.	Bar $ to hazardous substance victims	Y
123.	Allow seasonal workers in the US	Y
124.	Let fed courts rule on school prayer	N
125.	Presidential line-item veto	Y
126.	Ease Gun Control Act of 1968	Y
127.	Kill-Req 14-day wait for handguns	Y
128.	Kill-15% min tax on corporations	Y
129.	Drop Social Security COLA	Y
130.	Freeze funding for all programs	N
131.	Kill-Nuclear weapon freeze	Y
132.	Keep decision narrowing Title IX	Y
133.	Raise drinking age to 21	N
134.	Allow production of MX missile	Y
135.	Raise taxes/cut spending by $140b	Y
136.	School prayer amendment	Y
137.	Capital punishment-federal crimes	Y
138.	Ban government officials from taping	N
139.	Martin Luther King holiday	N
140.	Authorize Marines in Lebanon	Y
141.	Amendment making abortion illegal	N
142.	Delete $1.2b for jobs creation	?
143.	Keep tobacco price supports	N
144.	Emergency housing aid of $5.1b	N

Presidential Support Score: 1991 - 86%   1990 - 76%

SIMPSON, ALAN K. -- Wyoming [Republican] Term Began/Expires: 1991/1996. Prior Terms: Senate: 1979 (Special Appointment)-1990. Born: September 2, 1931; Denver, CO. Education: University of Wyoming (B.S., LL.B.). Occupation: City attorney (1959-69); assistant attorney general (1959); U.S. commissioner (1959-69); Wyoming legislator (1964-77).

1. Prohibit MFN status for China	N	
2. Kill-Tie welfare to school attendance	N	
3. Limit credit card interest rates	Y	
4. Confirm Gates as head of CIA	Y	
5. Adoption of national energy policies	Y	
6. Kill-Restrict NEA use of funds	Y	
7. Unemployment benefits extension	N	
8. Confirm Thomas to Supreme Court	Y	
9. Raise eligibility for unpaid leave	N	
10. Notify parents of minors' abortions	N	
11. Move $3b from defense to domestic	N	
12. End production of B-2 bomber	N	
13. Cut SDI $1b to reduce deficit	N	
14. Maintain strategic stability-Soviets	N	
15. Kill-Allow women as combat pilots	N	
16. Kill-Allow HIV tests before surgery	N	
17. Strike $12b aid to Int'l Mon Fund	N	
18. Raise Senate salary/omit honoraria	Y	
19. Reduce space station funding $1.9b	N	
20. Kill-Eliminate supercollider funds	N	
21. Req 5-day handgun waiting period	N	
22. Life in prison instead of death	N	
23. Exceptions to exclusionary rule	Y	
24. Ban race as death sentence factor	+	
25. Campaign finance revisions	N	
26. Kill-Term limits for senators	N	
27. Require four presidential debates	N	
28. Tighten ban on vertical price fixing	N	
29. Kill-Freeze discretionary budget	Y	
30. Provide $30b for failed S&Ls	Y	
31. Allow use of force against Iraq	Y	
32. Allow $15b in foreign aid for 1991	Y	
33. Civil Rights Act of 1990	N	
34. Block cancellation of Egypt's debt	N	
35. Cut El Salvador military aid 50%	N	
36. Reduce troops in NATO by 30,000	N	
37. Req increases in auto fuel efficiency	N	
38. Bar taxpayer funding of campaigns	Y	
39. Limit textile import growth to 1%	N	
40. Amendment to ban flag desecration	Y	
41. Let fed emp be politically active	N	
42. Reauthorize Amtrak-veto override	N	
43. Allow sale of assault weapons	Y	
44. Retraining aid for coal miners	N	
45. Kill-Raise car emission standards	Y	
46. Pull EPA nuclear plant authority	Y	
47. Defer Chinese students' deportation	N	
48. Cut in capital gains tax	Y	
49. Establish CIA inspector general	Y	
50. Kill-Sanctions against China	Y	
51. Bar drug testing to receive AFDC	Y	
52. Kill-Allow force against drug planes	Y	
53. Include illegal aliens in census	N	
54. Restitution to Japanese interned	Y	
55. Troop reduction in Europe of 50%	N	
56. Increase SDI research to $4.3b	Y	
57. Kill-Pay homeless below min wage	N	
58. Ban airline smoking within US	Y	
59. Bar transfer of FS-X technology	N	

60. Limit liability for oil spills	Y	
61. Restructure S&L industry	N	
62. Ban $ to illegal foreign activities	N	
63. Req immigrant fluency in English	Y	
64. Allow aliens' families to stay in US	N	
65. Expand child care aid/tax credit	N	
66. Raise minimum wage w/subminimum	N	
67. Freeze outlays except SS/Medicare	N	
68. Kill-Shift $5b of DOD to domestic	Y	
69. Confirm Tower as sec of defense	Y	
70. Bar abortion $ except to save mother	Y	
71. Kill-Warn AIDS carriers' spouses	Y	
72. Allow religious schools to bar gays	Y	
73. 60 days' notice of plant closings	Y	
74. Allow poison pills in corp takeovers	N	
75. Kill-Workfare program	N	
76. Prohibit employee polygraph testing	Y	
77. Cap Medicare patients' liability	Y	
78. Revise unfair trade practices	N	
79. Kill-Shift SDI $ to conv weapons	Y	
80. Kill-Shift SDI $ to accidental launch	N	
81. Kill-Shift MX $ to supplies/parts	Y	
82. Kill-Buy America provision at DOD	Y	
83. Allow nuclear testing-5+ kilotons	Y	
84. Allow SALT II to be exceeded	Y	
85. $ to vets exposed to nuclear bomb	N	
86. Warn workers of disease exposure	N	
87. Restore four civil rights laws	N	
88. Disapprove uranium sales to Japan	N	
89. Notify Congress of covert operations	N	
90. Approval of $36m in Contra aid	Y	
91. $18b deficit reduction compromise	Y	
92. Allow sale of hard-to-detect guns	Y	
93. Catastrophic health insurance	Y	
94. Bork nomination to Supreme Court	Y	
95. Kill-Void Panama Canal treaties	N	
96. Kill-Insurance denial to AIDS+	N	
97. Keep diplomatic immunity intact	N	
98. Produce Bigeye nerve gas bomb	Y	
99. Balanced budget by '93-via targets	Y	
100. Allow ASAT missile tests in space	Y	
101. Limit space-based/ABM system tests	N	
102. Force reduction in trade barriers	N	
103. Repeal windfall profit tax on oil	Y	
104. $1b/two year aid for the homeless	Y	
105. Disallow $30m for AZT to poor	N	
106. Bar AIDS test-immigrants/marriage	N	
107. Kill-Biennial budget approval	N	
108. Fairness doctrine in broadcasting	Y	
109. Raise speed limit to 65 mph	Y	
110. Immigration reform/alien amnesty	Y	
111. South Africa sanctions-veto override	N	
112. Kill-Use of military in drug war	N	
113. Tax overhaul to revise income tax	Y	
114. Submit nuclear test ban treaties	Y	
115. Prohibit sale of Stinger missiles	N	
116. Prohibit binary chemical weapons	N	
117. Kill-$10/barrel oil tariff increase	?	
118. Grant tax amnesty provisions	Y	

SIMPSON, ALAN K. (continued)

119.	Block Saudi arms sale-veto override	N	132.	Keep decision narrowing Title IX	Y
120.	Balanced budget amendment	Y	133.	Raise drinking age to 21	N
121.	Include veterans in spending cuts	Y	134.	Allow production of MX missile	Y
122.	Bar $ to hazardous substance victims	Y	135.	Raise taxes/cut spending by $140b	Y
123.	Allow seasonal workers in the US	N	136.	School prayer amendment	Y
124.	Let fed courts rule on school prayer	N	137.	Capital punishment-federal crimes	Y
125.	Presidential line-item veto	Y	138.	Ban government officials from taping	N
126.	Ease Gun Control Act of 1968	Y	139.	Martin Luther King holiday	Y
127.	Kill-Req 14-day wait for handguns	Y	140.	Authorize Marines in Lebanon	Y
128.	Kill-15% min tax on corporations	Y	141.	Amendment making abortion illegal	N
129.	Drop Social Security COLA	Y	142.	Delete $1.2b for jobs creation	Y
130.	Freeze funding for all programs	N	143.	Keep tobacco price supports	N
131.	Kill-Nuclear weapon freeze	Y	144.	Emergency housing aid of $5.1b	N

Presidential Support Score: 1991 - 86%   1990 - 80%

Presidents' Announced Positions

BUSH, GEORGE HERBERT WALKER -- [Republican]. Term Began/Expires: 1989/1992. Born: June 12, 1924; Milton, MA. Education: Yale College (B.A.). Military Service: U.S. Navy (1942-45). Occupation: Businessman, congressman, government official, U.S. vice president.

The following were President Bush's announced positions on House measures:

1.	Protection to Haitian refugees	N	30.	Textile import quotas-veto override	N
2.	Raise tax on wealthy; lower others	N	31.	Abortion service for military abroad	N
3.	Investigate Reagan hostage delay	?	32.	Limits on high income farmers	?
4.	Campaign finance revisions	N	33.	Family medical leave-veto override	N
5.	Unpaid leave to care for children	N	34.	Req submission of balanced budget	?
6.	Restrict NEA use of funds	?	35.	Balanced budget amendment	Y
7.	Bar race-bias claim/habeas corpus	Y	36.	Amendment to ban flag desecration	Y
8.	Ban race as death sentence factor	Y	37.	Reauthorize Amtrak-veto override	N
9.	Exceptions to exclusionary rule	Y	38.	Retraining aid for coal miners	N
10.	Allow sale of assault weapons	?	39.	Suspend El Salvador military aid	N
11.	Life in prison/abolish death penalty	?	40.	Expand child care aid/tax credit	N
12.	Req conspiracy-price fixing cases	?	41.	Raise House salary/omit honoraria	?
13.	Unemployment benefits extension	N	42.	Toughen oil-spill liability	N
14.	Tissue use of aborted fetuses	N	43.	Restitution to Japanese interned	?
15.	Bar replacement of union strikers	N	44.	Protect Chinese & C.A. nationals	N
16.	Hold foreign aid at $15b for '92	?	45.	Abortion $ for rape/incest cases	N
17.	Restore space station funding	Y	46.	Allow religious schools to bar gays	?
18.	Civil Rights Act of 1991	N	47.	Bar broadcaster fairness doctrine	Y
19.	Unlimited damages-discrimination	N	48.	Bar cap gains cut/reinstate IRA	N
20.	Eliminate funds for supercollider	N	49.	Bar unions equal voice in pension	?
21.	Terminate SDI except for research	N	50.	Bar assembly of chemical weapons	?
22.	Req 7-day handgun waiting period	?	51.	Ban plutonium/uranium production	?
23.	Provide $30b for failed S&Ls	Y	52.	Cap MX missile deployment at 50	?
24.	Allow use of force against Iraq	Y	53.	Allow $3b for 2 stealth bombers	?
25.	Allow $15b in foreign aid for '91	?	54.	Publish bio-warfare experiments	?
26.	Revise & extend legal immigration	Y	55.	Raise minimum wage-veto override	N
27.	Suspend aid to Angolan rebels	N	56.	Bar transfer of FS-X technology	N
28.	Democratic tax plan proposals	N	57.	Cut defense and raise domestic $	?
29.	Cut defense 5% across the board	N	58.	Uniform poll closing in 48 states	?

The following were announced positions of the Reagan administration when George Bush was vice president:

59.	Req foreign investment disclosure	N	61.	Bar abortion funding in Wash, DC	?
60.	Textile import quotas-veto override	N	62.	Notify spouses of AIDS+ carriers	?

BUSH, GEORGE (continued)

63. Seize conveyance-drug trafficking	Y	
64. South Africa sanctions	N	
65. 60 days' notice of plant closings	N	
66. Close unneeded military bases	Y	
67. Keep welfare reform within $2.8b	?	
68. Allow children housing exclusion	Y	
69. Shift $400m of NASA to homeless	?	
70. Cap Medicare patients' liability	?	
71. Prohibit employee polygraph testing	?	
72. Allow CIA to fund Contras	?	
73. Revise unfair trade practices	N	
74. Focus SDI on accidental launch	?	
75. Bar Air Force $ for MX missile	N	
76. Allow "real" increase in defense	?	
77. Troop reduction in Europe of 50%	N	
78. Ban nuclear tests above 1 kiloton	N	
79. Ban anti-satellite missile tests	N	
80. Observe certain limits of SALT II	N	
81. Restore four Civil Rights laws	N	
82. Prohibit aliens as strikebreakers	?	
83. Allow military malpractice suits	N	
84. Approval of $36m in Contra aid	Y	
85. $18b deficit reduction compromise	?	
86. Welfare reform of $5.7b for 5 years	N	
87. Raise taxes $12b/cut spending $3b	N	
88. Board to assess occupational risk	N	
89. Balanced budget by '93-via targets	?	
90. Bar licensing of two nuclear plants	?	
91. Remove victims compensation cap	N	
92. Catastrophic health insurance	N	
93. Ban airline smoking-2 hours or less	?	
94. $1b/two year aid for the homeless	N	
95. Bar non-unions in union companies	N	
96. Increase FSLIC rescue to $15b	Y	
97. Impose quotas to lower trade deficit	N	
98. Reduce discretionary budget 21%	?	
99. Immigration reform/alien amnesty	?	
100. South Africa sanctions-veto override	N	
101. Tax overhaul to revise income tax	Y	
102. Use of military in drug war	N	
103. Delete 12 MX/add conventional wpn	?	

104. Raise speed limit to 65 mph	?	
105. Require Pentagon to buy US goods	?	
106. AIDS insurance non-discrimination	?	
107. Prohibit Saudi arms sale	N	
108. Ease Gun Control Act of 1968	Y	
109. Bar interstate handgun transport	?	
110. Make company emissions known	?	
111. Allow toxic victims to sue in fed ct	?	
112. Superfund waste cleanup of $10b	?	
113. 90 days notice of plant closings	?	
114. $20b in Medicare cuts/tax increases	N	
115. Spending cuts and tax increases	N	
116. Set school lunch lmt-250% poverty	?	
117. $75m for youth work projects	N	
118. Allow Angolan military assistance	Y	
119. Suspend defense payments for abuse	N	
120. Drop SS COLAs/$12b tax increase	?	
121. Approve $1.5b for 21 MX missiles	Y	
122. Emergency farm credit/revisions	N	
123. Duty on Taiwan/Hong Kong/S Korea	N	
124. Limit steel imports to 17%	?	
125. Cut $ to schools that bar prayer	?	
126. $50b-taxes; cut Medicare/spending	Y	
127. Limit Pershing II/cruise in Europe	N	
128. Delete $7.1b for 34 B-1 bombers	N	
129. Bar purchase of Sergeant York guns	N	
130. El Salvador military/economic aid	Y	
131. Bar mining of Nicaraguan waters	?	
132. Physician fee freeze for Medicare	?	
133. $49b in "sin"/phone/insurance taxes	Y	
134. Allow sale of Conrail	Y	
135. Equal Rights Amendment	N	
136. Authorize Marines in Lebanon	Y	
137. Eminent domain for coal companies	?	
138. Prohibit EPA clean air sanctions	?	
139. SS retirement age increase/reforms	Y	
140. Auto domestic content requirement	N	
141. Delete jobs program funding	Y	
142. Highway-gas tax bill	?	
143. Cut $5b from defense for Medicare	?	
144. Emergency housing aid of $1b	?	

The following were President Bush's announced positions on Senate measures:

1. Prohibit MFN status for China	N	
2. Kill-Tie welfare to school attendance	?	
3. Limit credit card interest rates	?	
4. Confirm Gates as head of CIA	Y	
5. Adoption of national energy policies	?	
6. Kill-Restrict NEA use of funds	?	
7. Unemployment benefits extension	N	
8. Confirm Thomas to Supreme Court	Y	
9. Raise eligibility for unpaid leave	N	
10. Notify parents of minors' abortions	Y	
11. Move $3b from defense to domestic	N	
12. End production of B-2 bomber	N	
13. Cut SDI $1b to reduce deficit	N	
14. Maintain strategic stability-Soviets	N	
15. Kill-Allow women as combat pilots	?	
16. Kill-Allow HIV tests before surgery	?	
17. Strike $12b aid to Int'l Mon Fund	N	
18. Raise Senate salary/omit honoraria	?	
19. Reduce space station funding $1.9b	?	

20. Kill-Eliminate supercollider funds	Y	
21. Req 5-day handgun waiting period	?	
22. Life in prison instead of death	N	
23. Exceptions to exclusionary rule	Y	
24. Ban race as death sentence factor	?	
25. Campaign finance revisions	N	
26. Kill-Term limits for senators	?	
27. Require four presidential debates	?	
28. Tighten ban on vertical price fixing	?	
29. Kill-Freeze discretionary budget	?	
30. Provide $30b for failed S&Ls	Y	
31. Allow use of force against Iraq	Y	
32. Allow $15b in foreign aid for 1991	?	
33. Civil Rights Act of 1990	N	
34. Block cancellation of Egypt's debt	N	
35. Cut El Salvador military aid 50%	N	
36. Reduce troops in NATO by 30,000	N	
37. Req increases in auto fuel efficiency	?	
38. Bar taxpayer funding of campaigns	?	

BUSH, GEORGE (continued)

39.	Allow sale of assault weapons	N	55.	Troop reduction in Europe of 50%	N
40.	Retraining aid for coal miners	Y	56.	Increase SDI research to $4.3b	Y
41.	Defer Chinese students' deportation	N	57.	Kill-Pay homeless below min wage	?
42.	Limit textile import growth to 1%	N	58.	Ban airline smoking within US	?
43.	Amendment to ban flag desecration	Y	59.	Bar transfer of FS-X technology	N
44.	Let fed emp be politically active	N	60.	Limit liability for oil spills	?
45.	Reauthorize Amtrak-veto override	Y	61.	Restructure S&L industry	N
46.	Kill-Raise car emission standards	Y	62.	Ban $ to illegal foreign activity	?
47.	Pull EPA nuclear plant authority	N	63.	Req immigrant fluency in English	?
48.	Cut in capital gains tax	Y	64.	Allow aliens' families to stay in US	?
49.	Establish CIA inspector general	N	65.	Expand child care aid/tax credit	?
50.	Kill-Sanctions against China	?	66.	Raise minimum wage w/subminimum	N
51.	Bar drug testing to receive AFDC	?	67.	Freeze outlays except SS/Medicare	?
52.	Kill-Allow force against drug planes	?	68.	Kill-Shift $5b of DOD to domestic	?
53.	Include illegal aliens in census	?	69.	Confirm Tower as sec of defense	Y
54.	Restitution to Japanese interned	?			

The following were announced positions of the Reagan administration when George Bush was vice president:

70.	Bar abortion $ except to save mother	Y	108.	Fairness doctrine in broadcasting	N
71.	Kill-Warn AIDS carriers' spouses	?	109.	Raise speed limit to 65 mph	Y
72.	Allow religious schools to bar gays	?	110.	Immigration reform/alien amnesty	?
73.	60 days' notice of plant closings	?	111.	South Africa sanctions-veto override	N
74.	Allow poison pills in corp takeovers	?	112.	Kill-Use of military in drug war	Y
75.	Kill-Workfare program	N	113.	Tax overhaul to revise income tax	Y
76.	Prohibit employee polygraph testing	?	114.	Submit nuclear test ban treaties	N
77.	Cap Medicare patients' liability	?	115.	Prohibit sale of Stinger missiles	?
78.	Revise unfair trade practices	N	116.	Prohibit binary chemical weapons	N
79.	Kill-Shift SDI $ to conv weapons	Y	117.	Kill-$10/barrel oil tariff increrase	?
80.	Kill-Shift SDI $ to accidental launc?	N	118.	Grant tax amnesty provisions	?
81.	Kill-Shift MX $ to supplies/parts	Y	119.	Block Saudi arms sale-veto override	N
82.	Kill-Buy America provision at DOD	?	120.	Balanced budget amendment	Y
83.	Allow nuclear testing-5+ kilotons	Y	121.	Include veterans in spending cuts	?
84.	Allow SALT II to be exceeded	Y	122.	Bar $ to hazardous substance victims	Y
85.	$ to vets exposed to nuclear bomb	N	123.	Allow seasonal workers in the US	?
86.	Warn workers of disease exposure	?	124.	Let fed courts rule on school prayer	?
87.	Restore four civil rights laws	N	125.	Presidential line-item veto	Y
88.	Disapprove uranium sales to Japan	N	126.	Ease Gun Control Act of 1968	Y
89.	Notify Congress of covert operations	?	127.	Kill-Req 14-day wait for handguns	Y
90.	Approval of $36m in Contra aid	Y	128.	Kill-15% min tax on corporations	?
91.	$18b deficit reduction compromise	Y	129.	Drop Social Security COLA	Y
92.	Allow sale of hard-to-detect guns	Y	130.	Freeze funding for all programs	?
93.	Catastrophic health insurance	Y	131.	Kill-Nuclear weapon freeze	Y
94.	Bork nomination to Supreme Court	Y	132.	Keep decision narrowing Title IX	Y
95.	Kill-Void Panama Canal treaties	?	133.	Raise drinking age to 21	Y
96.	Kill-Insurance denial to AIDS+	?	134.	Allow production of MX missile	Y
97.	Keep diplomatic immunity intact	?	135.	Raise taxes/cut spending by $140b	Y
98.	Produce Bigeye nerve gas bomb	Y	136.	School prayer amendment	Y
99.	Balanced budget by '93-via targets	?	137.	Capital punishment-federal crimes	Y
100.	Allow ASAT missile tests in space	Y	138.	Ban government officials from taping	N
101.	Limit space-based/ABM system tests	N	139.	Martin Luther King holiday	?
102.	Force reduction in trade barriers	N	140.	Authorize Marines in Lebanon	Y
103.	Repeal windfall profit tax on oil	Y	141.	Amendment making abortion illegal	Y
104.	$1b/two year aid for the homeless	N	142.	Delete $1.2b for jobs creation	Y
105.	Disallow $30m for AZT to poor	?	143.	Keep tobacco price supports	?
106.	Bar AIDS test-immigrants/marriage	?	144.	Emergency housing aid of $5.1b	N
107.	Kill-Biennial budget approval	?			

Name Index

This index includes the names of all members of the 102nd Congress as well as the names of any member of an earlier Congress who sponsored a measure or amendment included in the book. The locators refer not only to individual voting records but also to the descriptions of legislation found in the **List of House Measures** and **List of Senate Measures**.

A

B

T

U-V

W

Y

Z

Subject Index

The locators in this index refer to measures listed in the House and Senate Measures sections.

H = House Measure   S = Senate Measure